ATHLETICS 2012
THE INTERNATIONAL TRACK AND FIELD ANNUAL

BY PETER MATTHEWS

ASSOCIATION OF TRACK & FIELD STATISTICIANS

Published by SportsBooks Ltd

Copyright: SportsBooks Limited and Peter Matthews 2012

SportsBooks Limited
PO Box 422
Cheltenham
GL50 2YN
United Kingdom
Tel: 01242 256755
Fax: 0560 3108126
e-mail   randall@sportsbooks.ltd.uk
Website   www.sportsbooks.ltd.uk

This publication incorporates the ATFS Annual.

Photographs supplied by Mark Shearman, 22 Grovelands Road, Purley, Surrey, CR8 4LA.
Tel: 0208 660 0156: mark@athleticsimages.com

British Library Cataloguing in Publication Data

Athletics: the international track and
field annual – 2012
1. Athletics. Track & Field events –
Serials
1. International athletics annual (London)
796.4'2'05

ISBN 9781907524233
Cover design: Kath Grimshaw

Printed by TJ International, Padstow, Cornwall

CONTENTS

INTRODUCTION

OLYMPIC YEAR! This always brings heightened excitement for athletics enthusiasts. I was first conscious of the Olympic Games when they were staged in Melbourne in 1956, and early in the morning I listened to the crackling waves of sounds on the wireless, just as I had two years earlier to the Australia v England Test cricket series, as the commentators, perhaps Rex Alston and Harold Abrahams described the events. In particular there was the epic dual between Vladimir Kuts and Gordon Pirie at 10,000m, with the Russian constantly surging eventually to destroy his doughty rival. Later there was the superb sprinting of Bobby Morrow and Betty Cuthbert, each winning treble gold.

I had started collecting reference information from the age of 7/8 – lists of kings and queens, presidents, highest mountains, most populous cities, etc. and sport very soon dominated this. My father had a collection of the greatest of all long-standing sports reference books – *Wisden's Cricketers Almanac*. I "devoured" that from the age of 8, especially as I was a keen cricketer myself. Then in November 1956 just prior to the Olympics I discovered *World Sports*, the all sports colour magazine that was especially strong on athletics and its 'scoreboard section'. As I wrote in the introduction to ATHLETICS 2006: A few months later I saw advertised therein the International Athletics Annual 1957, published by *World Sports* at 7 shillings and 6 pence. I sent off for this and the 208-page volume arrived. I was at first disappointed as it seemed so small, but that changed rapidly to delight as I devoured the statistics that packed the volume. In the next couple of years two marvellous handbooks hugely augmented my historical data: the European Track and Field Handbook (1958) and the All-Time World List (1959).

I was now more interested in world athletics than purely British and I discovered the marvellous US magazine *Track & Field News* with its superb coverage of the sport. While at school I cheekily wrote to *Track & Field News* asking if they could send me the magazine if I supplied them with statistical features. They agreed and in 1961–3 you can find many of these in back numbers of *Track Newsletter*! I am eternally grateful to Hal Bateman for this positive response, and I am very proud that my name was appeared for over 50 years in their 'International Correspondents' list.

So, 55 years after my first purchase of the International Athletics Annual, I am delighted to present this edition, and I can scarce believe that for half that time I have been the editor – but my enthusiasm for the sport remains that of the 12-year-old who first encountered the Annual, augmented by the huge privilege of watching great action over the years and of working on Radio and TV with some of the great names of the sport. I am also most grateful now to work in a happy partnership with publisher Randall Northam of SportsBooks.

This annual includes all the usual features with lists, reviews, results and profiles plus Mark Shearman's splendid colour photographs. Bernard Linley pays tribute to Roberto Quercetani and I join in saluting the great man who has just celebrated his 90th birthday. It was this marvellous polymath who was the chief compiler of the Annual and those European and World handbooks back in the 1950s. Both he and I look forward to this year's events with undiminished pleasure – and hope that new young enthusiasts will follow in our footsteps in maintaining the data so needed by our complex sport.

Peter Matthews April 2012

Information can be sent to me to 10 Madgeways Close, Great Amwell, Ware, Herts SG12 9RU, England. **Email:** p.matthews@btinternet.com

Information or requests re sales, distribution, publication etc. to the publishers, SportsBooks Ltd.

ABBREVIATIONS

The following abbreviations have been used for meetings with, in parentheses, the first year that they were held.

AAA	(GBR) Amateur Athletic Association Championships (1880)
AAU	(USA) Amateur Athletic Union Championships (1888) (now TAC)
Af-AsG	Afro-Asian Games (2003)
AfCh	African Championships (1979)
AfG	African Games (1965)
Af-J	African Junior Championships (1994)
AmCp	America's Cup (World Cup Trial) (1977)
APM	Adriaan Paulen Memorial, Hengelo
Aragón	Gran Premio Internacional de Atletismo Gobierno de Aragón, Zaragoza (2004)
AsiC	Asian Championships (1973)
AsiG	Asian Games (1951)
Asi-J	Asian Junior Championships (1990)
ASV	Weltklasse in Köln, ASV club meeting (1934)
Athl	Athletissima, Lausanne (1976)
Balk	Balkan Games (1929), C – Championships
Barr	(Cuba) Barrientos Memorial (1946)
BGP	Budapest Grand Prix (1978)
Bisl	Bislett Games, Oslo (1965) (Bergen 2004)
Bol G	Bolivar Games (1938)
BrGP	British Grand Prix
CAC	Central American and Caribbean Championships (1967)
CAG	Central American and Caribbean Games (1926)
CalR	California Relays (1942)
C.Asian	Central Asian Championships
CAU	Inter-counties, GBR (1934)
CISM	International Military Championships (1946)
CG	Commonwealth Games (1930)
C.Cup	Continental Cup (2010)
Déca	Décanation, Paris (C) (2005)
DL	Diamond League (2010)
DNG	DN Galan, Stockholm (1966)
Drake	Drake Relays (1910)
EAsG	East Asian Games (1993)
EC	European Championships (1934)
ECCp	European Clubs Cup (1975)
EChall	European Challenge (10,000m 1997, Throws 2001)
ECp	European Cup – track & field (1965), multi-events (1973)
EI	European Indoor Championships (1970, Games 1966-9)
EICp	European Indoor Cup (2003)
EJ	European Junior Championships (1970)
ET	European Team Championships (replaced European Cup, 2009)
EU23	European Under-23 Championships (1997) and European Under-23 Cup (1992-4)
FBK	Fanny Blankers-Koen Games, Hengelo (formerly APM) (1981)
FlaR	Florida Relays (1939)
FOT	(USA) Final Olympic Trials (1920)
Franc	Francophone Games (1989)
Gaz	Gaz de France meeting, FRA (was BNP) (1968)
GGala	Golden Gala, Roma (from 1980), Verona (1988), Pescara (1989), Bologna (1990)
GL	Golden League (1998-2009)
GNR	Great North Run – Newcastle to South Shields, GBR (1981)
GP	Grand Prix
GPF	IAAF Grand Prix Final (1985)
GS	Golden Spike, Ostrava (1969)
Gugl	Zipfer Gugl Grand Prix, Linz (1988)
GWG	Goodwill Games (1986)
Hanz	Hanzekovic Memorial, Zagreb
Herc	Herculis, Monte Carlo, Monaco (1987)
IAAF	International Association of Athletics Federations
IAC	IAC meeting (1968), formerly Coca-Cola
IAU	International Association of Ultrarunners
IbAm	Ibero-American Championships (1983)
ISTAF	Internationales Stadionfest, Berlin (1921)
Jenner	Bruce Jenner Classic, San Jose (1979)
Jerome	Harry Jerome Track Classic (1984)
JUCO	Junior Colleges Championships, USA
KansR	Kansas Relays, Lawrence (1923)
Kuso	Janusz Kusocinski Memorial (1954)
Kuts	Vladimir Kuts Memorial ((1978))
LGP	London Grand Prix, Crystal Palace
MAI	Malmö AI Galan, Sweden (formerly Idag) (1958)
Mal	Malinowski Memorial, Poland
Mast	Masters pole vault, Grenoble (1987)
MedG	Mediterranean Games (1951)
Mill	Millrose Games, New York indoors (1908)
ModR	Modesto Relays
MSR	Mt. San Antonio College Relays (1959)
NA	Night of Athletics, Heusden (2000) formerly Hechtel
NACAC	North American, Central American & Caribbean Ch (2003)
NC	National Championships
NC-w	National Winter Championships
NCAA	National Collegiate Athletic Association Championships, USA (1921)
NCAA-r	NCAA Regional Championships (2003)
NCp	National Cup
NG	National Games
Nik	Nikaïa, Nice (1976)
NM	Narodna Mladezhe, Sofia (1955)
N.Sch	National Schools
Nurmi	Paavo Nurmi Games (1957)
NYG	New York Games (1989)
OD	Olympischer Tag (Olympic Day)
Oda	Mikio Oda Memorial Meeting, Hiroshima
OG	Olympic Games (1896)
OT	Olympic Trials
Owens	Jesse Owens Memorial (1981)
PAm	Pan American Games (1951)
PArab	Pan Arab Championships (1977) (G-Games 1953)
Pedro	Pedro's Cup, Poland (2005)
PennR	Pennsylvania Relays (1895)
PTS	Pravda Televízia Slovnaft, Bratislava (1957) (now GPB)
Pre	Steve Prefontaine Memorial (1976)
RdVin	Route du Vin Half Marathon, Luxembourg (1962)
RomIC	Romanian International Championships (1948)
RWC	Race Walking Challenge Final (2007)

SACh	South American Championships (1919)
SAsG	South Asian Games (1984)
SEAG	South East Asia Games (1959)
SEC	Southeast Conference Championships
SGP	IAAF Super Grand Prix
Slovn	Slovnaft, Bratislava (formerly PTS) (1990)
Spark	Sparkassen Cup, Stuttgart (indoor) (1987)
Spart	(URS) Spartakiad (1956)
Stra	Stramilano Half marathon, Milan
Super	Super Meet, Japan (Tokyo, Shizuoka, Yokohama, Kawasaki)
Tsik	Athens Grand Prix Tsiklitiria (1998)
TexR	Texas Relays (1925)
USOF	US Olympic Festival
VD	Ivo Van Damme Memorial, Brussels (1977)
Veniz	Venizélia, Haniá, Crete (1936)
WAC	Western Athletic Conference Championships
WAF	World Athletics Finals (2003)
WCh	World Championships (1983)
WCM	World Challenge Meeting (2010)
WCp	World Cup – track & field (1977), marathon (1985) Walking – Lugano Trophy – men (1961), Eschborn Cup – women (1979)
WCT	World Championships Trial
WG	World Games, Helsinki (1961)
WI	World Indoor Championships (1987), World Indoor Games (1985)
WJ	World Junior Championships (1986)
WK	Weltklasse, Zürich (1962)
WMilG	World Military Games (or CISM) (1995)
WUG	World University Games (1923)
WY	World Youth Championships (1999)
Zat	Emil Zátopek Classic, Melbourne
Znam	Znamenskiy Brothers Memorial (1958)
-j, -y, -23	Junior, Youth or under-23

Dual and triangular matches are indicated by "v" (versus) followed by the name(s) of the opposition. Quadrangular and larger inter-nation matches are denoted by the number of nations and -N; viz 8-N designates an 8-nation meeting.

Events

CC	cross-country
Dec	decathlon
DT	discus
h	hurdles
Hep	heptathlon
HJ	high jump
HMar	half marathon
HT	hammer
JT	javelin
LJ	long jump
Mar	marathon
Pen	pentathlon
PV	pole vault
R	relay
SP	shot
St	steeplechase
TJ	triple jump
W	walk
Wt	weight

Miscellaneous abbreviations

+	Intermediate time in longer race
=	Tie (ex-aequo)
A	Made at an altitude of 1000m or higher
b	date of birth
D	Made in decathlon competition
dnf	did not finish
dnq	did not qualify
dns	did not start
exh	exhibition
h	heat
H	Made in heptathlon competition
hr	hour
i	indoors
kg	kilograms
km	kilometres
m	metres
M	mile
m/s	metres per second
mx	Made in mixed men's and women's race
nh	no height
O	Made in octathlon competition
P	Made in pentathlon competition
pb	personal best
Q	Made in qualifying round
qf	quarter final (or q in lists)
r	Race number in a series of races
sf	semi final (or s in lists)
w	wind assisted
WIR	world indoor record
WR	world record or best
y	yards
*	Converted time from yards to metres: For 200m: 220 yards less 0.11 second For 400m: 440 yards less 0.26 second For 110mh: 120yh plus 0.03 second

Countries

(IAAF membership reached 213 in 2008, back to 212 in 2011). IAAF and IOC abbreviations are now identical.

AFG	Afghanistan	ARM	Armenia	BLR	Belarus
AHO	Netherlands Antilles #	ARU	Aruba	BOL	Bolivia
AIA	Anguilla	ASA	American Samoa	BOT	Botswana
ALB	Albania	AUS	Australia	BRA	Brazil
ALG	Algeria	AUT	Austria	BRN	Bahrain
AND	Andorra	AZE	Azerbaijan	BRU	Brunei
ANG	Angola	BAH	Bahamas	BUL	Bulgaria
ANT	Antigua & Barbuda	BAN	Bangladash	BUR	Burkina Faso
ARG	Argentina	BAR	Barbados	CAF	Central African Republic
		BDI	Burundi	CAM	Cambodia
		BEL	Belgium	CAN	Canada
		BEN	Benin	CAY	Cayman Islands
		BER	Bermuda	CGO	Congo
		BHU	Bhutan	CHA	Chad
		BIH	Bosnia Herzegovina	CHI	Chile
		BIZ	Belize		

CHN	People's Republic of China
CIV	Côte d'Ivoire (Ivory Coast)
CMR	Cameroon
COD	Democratic Republic of Congo
COK	Cook Islands
COL	Colombia
COM	Comoros
CPV	Cape Verde Islands
CRC	Costa Rica
CRO	Croatia
CUB	Cuba
CYP	Cyprus
CZE	Czech Republic
DEN	Denmark
DJI	Djibouti
DMA	Dominica
DOM	Dominican Republic
ECU	Ecuador
EGY	Egypt
ENG	England
ERI	Eritrea
ESA	El Salvador
ESP	Spain
EST	Estonia
ETH	Ethiopia
FIJ	Fiji
FIN	Finland
FRA	France
FRG	Federal Republic of Germany (1948-90)
FSM	Micronesia
GAB	Gabon
GAM	The Gambia
GBR	United Kingdom of Great Britain & Northern Ireland
GBS	Guinea-Bissau
GDR	German Democratic Republic (1948-90)
GEO	Georgia
GEQ	Equatorial Guinea
GER	Germany (pre 1948 and from 1991)
GHA	Ghana
GIB	Gibraltar
GRE	Greece
GRN	Grenada
GUA	Guatemala
GUI	Guinea
GUM	Guam
GUY	Guyana
HAI	Haiti
HKG	Hong Kong, China
HON	Honduras
HUN	Hungary
INA	Indonesia
IND	India
IRI	Iran
IRL	Ireland
IRQ	Iraq
ISL	Iceland
ISR	Israel
ISV	US Virgin Islands
ITA	Italy
IVB	British Virgin Islands
JAM	Jamaica
JOR	Jordan
JPN	Japan
KAZ	Kazakhstan
KEN	Kenya
KGZ	Kyrgyzstan
KIR	Kiribati
KOR	Korea
KSA	Saudi Arabia
KUW	Kuwait
LAO	Laos
LAT	Latvia
LBA	Libya
LBR	Liberia
LCA	St Lucia
LES	Lesotho
LIB	Lebanon
LIE	Liechtenstein
LTU	Lithuania
LUX	Luxembourg
MAC	Macao
MAD	Madagascar
MAR	Morocco
MAS	Malaysia
MAW	Malawi
MDA	Moldova
MDV	Maldives
MEX	Mexico
MGL	Mongolia
MKD	Former Yugoslav Republic of Macedonia
MLI	Mali
MLT	Malta
MNE	Montenegro
MNT	Montserrat
MON	Monaco
MOZ	Mozambique
MRI	Mauritius
MSH	Marshall Islands
MTN	Mauritania
MYA	Myanmar
NAM	Namibia
NCA	Nicaragua
NED	Netherlands
NEP	Nepal
NFI	Norfolk Islands
NGR	Nigeria
NGU	Papua New Guinea
NI	Northern Ireland
NIG	Niger
NMA	Northern Marianas Islands
NOR	Norway
NRU	Nauru
NZL	New Zealand
OMA	Oman
PAK	Pakistan
PAN	Panama
PAR	Paraguay
PER	Peru
PHI	Philippines
PLE	Palestine
PLW	Palau
PNG	Papua New Guinea
POL	Poland
POR	Portugal
PRK	North Korea (DPR Korea)
PUR	Puerto Rico
PYF	French Polynesia
QAT	Qatar
ROU	Romania
RSA	South Africa
RUS	Russia
RWA	Rwanda
SAM	Samoa
SCG	Serbia & Montenegro (to 2006)
SCO	Scotland
SEN	Sénégal
SEY	Seychelles
SIN	Singapore
SKN	St Kitts & Nevis
SLE	Sierra Leone
SLO	Slovenia
SMR	San Marino
SOL	Solomon Islands
SOM	Somalia
SRB	Serbia
SRI	Sri Lanka
STP	São Tomé & Principé
SUD	Sudan
SUI	Switzerland
SUR	Surinam
SVK	Slovakia
SWE	Sweden
SWZ	Swaziland
SYR	Syria
TAN	Tanzania
TCH	Czechoslovakia (to 1991)
TGA	Tonga
THA	Thailand
TJK	Tadjikistan
TKM	Turkmenistan
TKS	Turks & Caicos Islands
TLS	East Timor
TOG	Togo
TPE	Taiwan (Chinese Taipei)
TRI	Trinidad & Tobago
TUN	Tunisia
TUR	Turkey
TUV	Tuvalu
UAE	United Arab Emirates
UGA	Uganda
UKR	Ukraine
URS	Soviet Union (to 1991)
URU	Uruguay
USA	United States
UZB	Uzbekistan
VAN	Vanuatu
VEN	Venezuela
VIE	Vietnam
VIN	St Vincent & the Grenadines
WAL	Wales
YEM	Republic of Yemen
YUG	Yugoslavia (to 2002)
ZAM	Zambia
ZIM	Zimbabwe

ceased to exist as a separate territory in 2010, and absorbed into the Netherlands.

ACKNOWLEDGEMENTS

ONCE AGAIN I would like to thank all those who have helped me to compile this Annual – whether in a major way or just with a few items of information – and indeed the worldwide circle of correspondents for the valuable information I receive from them throughout the year. As they have throughout the 62-year history of the ATFS Annual, the annual world lists provide the essential core of the book and I have worked up these lists from original compilations by Richard Hymans for men and Mirko Jalava for women. I refer all who want to follow the results of the sport closely to Mirko's superb web site his superb web site www.tilastopaja.net. Milan Skocovsky again provided deep lists for juniors and I am indebted to Carlos Fernández for his expertise on the road lists and to Ray Herdt for the walks. I circulate draft lists to a number of ATFS experts and thank all who responded. From the great Spanish group Miguel Villaseñor and Juan Mari Iriondo checked the biographies and obituaries with great care. Børre Lilloe provided much index data and Ken Nakamura checked distance lists. Bob Hersh reviewed the latest rules changes with his usual expertise and I am delighted that Bob Phillips has provided an article on the Olympics of 100 years ago.

Both for this annual and throughout the year with *Athletics International* Winfried Kramer helps with national records and widespread probing for results as do the area experts: *Africa* Yves Pinaud, *Asia* Heinrich Hubbeling, *Central and South America* Eduardo Biscayart and Luis Vinker, and specialists: *Records* György Csiki, *Ultrarunning* Andy Milroy, *Indoors* Ed Gordon, *Pole vault* Kenneth Lindqvist, *Multi events* Hans van Kuijen.

Australia: Paul Jenes and David Tarbotton; *Austria*: Dr Karl Graf; *Balkans*: Nikos Muatidis, *Belarus*: Dmitri Vorobyov; *Belgium*: André de Hooghe and Alain Monet; *Bulgaria*: Aleksandar Vangelov; *China*: Mirko Jalava; *Croatia*: Vladimir Mikulec; *Cuba*: Alfredo Sánchez; *Czech Republic*: Milan Skocovsky and Milan Urban; *Denmark*: Erik Laursen; *Estonia*: Erlend Teemägi and Enn Endjärv; *Finland*: Juhani Jalava, Mirko Jalava, Mikko Nieminen and Matti Hannus; *France*: Alain Bouillé, Patrice Bertignon, Patricia Doilin and José Guilloto; *Germany*: Sven Kuus and Klaus Amrhein; *Greece*: Thomas Konstas and Nikos Kriezis; *Hungary*: György Csiki; *India*: Ram. Murali Krishnan; *Ireland*: Pierce O'Callaghan, Liam Hennessy and Killian Lonergan; *Israel*: David Eiger; *Italy*: Raul Leoni; *Jamaica*: Charles Fuller; *Japan*: Yoshimasa Noguchi, Akihiro Onishi and Ken Nakamura; *Latvia*: Andris Stagis; *Lithuania*: Stepas Misiunas; *Luxembourg*: Georges Klepper; *Montenegro*: Ivan Popovic; *New Zealand*: Murray McKinnon and Tony Hunt; *Norway*: Tore Johansen and Børre Lilloe; *Poland*: Zbigniew Jonik, Janusz Rozum and Tadeusz Wolejko; *Portugal*: Manuel Arons Carvalho; *Puerto Rico*: Pedro Anibal Diaz; *Romania*: Alexandru Boriga; *Russia*: Sergey Tikhonov and Rostislav Orlov; *Serbia*: Ozren Karamata and Olga Acic; *Slovakia*: Alfons Juck; *Slovenia*: Zdravko Peternelj; *South Africa*: Danie Cornelius and Riël Hauman; *Spain*: José Luis Hernández, Carles Baronet and the AEEA team; *Sweden*: Jonas Hedman and Peter Larsson; *Switzerland*: Alberto Bordoli and Antonin Hejda; *Trinidad*: Bernard Linley, *Turkey*: Nejat Kök, *Ukraine*: Yuriy Kostritsky; *UK*: Tony Miller; *USA*: Tom Casacky, Garry Hill, Sieg Lindstrom, Marty Post, Jack Shepherd and Miek Kennedy, and *Track Newsletter*. Also various national federation lists and to those who post results or ranking lists to various web sites.

Also to Francisco Ascorbe, Marco Buccellato, Mark Butler, Ottavio Castellini (IAAF), Silvio Garaviglio, José Maria García, Stan Greenberg, Christian Lenz, Alan Lindop, Rooney Magnusson (obituaries), Bill Mallon, Pino Mappa, David Martin, Phil Minshull, Bob Phillips, Zdenek Procházka (hammer), Roberto Quercetani and Rob Whittingham.

My apologies to anybody whose name I may have missed or who have corresponded with other key ATFS personnel, but all help, however small is deeply appreciated.

Keep the results flowing

During the year Mel Watman and I publish marks to ATFS standards (150-200 deep on world lists) in *Athletics International*, of which there are over 35 issues per year by email. This serves as a base from which the lists in this book can be compiled, together with information from web sites and the major magazines such as *Track & Field News* (USA) with its email results spin-off *Track Newsletter* and *Leichtathletik* (Germany) and the newsletters with particular spheres of interest such as *Atletismo en España* by Francisco J Ascorbe and José Luis Hernández, and Luis Vinker's *South America Bulletin*.

In order to ensure that the record of 2012 is as complete as possible I urge results contribution worldwide to AI, and then in turn our lists in *Athletics 2013* will be as comprehensive as we can make them.

Peter Matthews

THE ASSOCIATION OF TRACK & FIELD STATISTICIANS

The ATFS was founded in Brussels (at the European Championships) in 1950 and ever since has built upon the work of such key founding members as Roberto Quercetani, Don Potts and Fulvio Regli to produce authoritative ranking lists in the International Athletics Annual and elsewhere.

Current Executive Committee
President: Paul Jenes AUS
Vice-President: A.Lennart Julin SWE

Secretary General and Treasurer: Tom Casacky USA
Past Presidents: Rooney Magnusson SWE, Dr Roberto Quercetani ITA
Committee: Nejat Kök TUR, Gert le Roux RSA, Bernard Linley TRI, Peter J Matthews GBR, Yves Pinaud FRA, Tatsumi Senda JPN, Luis R Vinker ARG

Website: www.afts.org

Internet – Websites

IAAF	www.iaaf.org
IAU	www.iau-ultramarathon.org
African AC	www.webcaa.org
Asian AA	www.asianathletics.org
CAC Confederation.	www.cacacathletics.org
European AA	www.european-athletics.org
NACAC	www.athleticsnacac.org
Oceania AA	www.athletics-oceania.com
S. American Fed.	www.consudatle.org
WMRA	www.wmra.info
World Masters	www.world-masters-athletics.org
Marathon Majors	www.worldmarathonmajors.com
Africa	www.africathle.com
Algeria	www.faa.dz
Andorra	www.faa.ad
Argentina	www.cada-atletismo.org
Australia	www.athletics.com.au
Austria	www.oelv.at
Bahamas	www.bahamastrack.com
Bahrain	www.bahrainathletics.org
Belarus	www.bfla.eu
Belgium	www.val.be
Bermuda	www.btfa.bm
Bosnia Hercegovina	www.asbih.org
Brazil	www.cbat.org.br
Bulgaria	www.bfla.org
Canada	www.athletics.ca
Chile	www.fedachi.cl
China	www.athletics.org.cn
Colombia	www.fecodatle.org
Croatia	www.has.hr
Cyprus	www.koeas.org.cy
Czech Republic	www.atletika.cz
Denmark	www.dansk-atletik.dk
Dominican Republic	www.fedomatle.org
England	www.englandathletics.org
Estonia	www.ekjl.ee
Finland	www.sul.fi
France	www.athle.com
Germany	www.deutscher- leichtathletik-verband.de
Great Britain	www.uka.org.uk
deep statistics	www.topsinathletics.info
	www.thepowerof10.info
Greece	www.segas.gr
Hong Kong	www.hkaaa.com
Hungary	www.masz.hu
Iceland	www.fri.is
India	www.indianathletics.org
Indonesia	www.indonesia-athletics.org
Ireland	www.athleticsireland.ie
Israel	www.iaa.co.il
unofficial (in English)	http://eigers.tripod.com
Italy	www.fidal.it
Jamaica	www.trackandfieldja.com
Japan	www.jaaf.or.jp
Kazakhstan	www.kazathletics.kz
Kenya	www.athleticskenya.org.ke
Latvia	http://lat-athletics.lv
Lithuania	www.laf.lt
Luxembourg	www.fla.lu
Macedonia	www.afm.org.mk
Mexico	www.fmaa.mex
Moldova	www.fam.com.md/
Monaco	www.fma.mc
Montenegro	www.ascg.co.me
Morocco	www.moroccanathletics.com
Netherlands	www.atletiekunie.nl
New Zealand	www.athletics.org.nz
Northern Ireland	www.niathletics.org
Norway	www.friidrett.no
Peru	www.fepeatle.com
Poland	www.pzla.pl
Portugal	www.fpatletismo.pt
Puerto Rico	www.atletismofapur.com
Qatar	www.qatarathletics.com/en/
Romania	www.fra.ro
Russia	www.rusathletics.com
Scotland	www.scottishathletics.org.uk
	www.scotstats.com
Serbia	www.serbia-athletics.org.rs
Singapore	www.singaporeathletics.org.sg
Slovakia	www.atletikasvk.sk
Slovenia	www.atletska-zveza.si
South Africa	www.athletics.org.za
Spain	www.rfea.es
Sweden	www.friidrott.se
Switzerland	www.swiss-athletics.ch
Taiwan	www.cttfa.org.tw
Trinidad & Tobago	www.ttnaaa.org
Turkey	www.taf.org.tr
Ukraine	www.uaf.org.ua
Uruguay	www.atlecau.org.uy
USA	www.usatf.org
results	www.tfrrs.org
Venezuela	www.fva.cavillo.com.ve
Wales	www.welshathletics.org

Other recommended sites for statistics and results

AIMS	www.aimsworldrunning.org
ARRS	www.arrs.net
British historical	www.gbrathletics.com
DGLD (German stats)	www.ladgld.de Marathons
French history etc.	http://cdm.athle.com
Marathons	www.marathonguide.com
Masters Track & Field	www.mastersathletics.net
Mirko Jalava	www.tilastopaja.com
News (mainly US)	www.newsnow.co.uk/
NUTS/Track Stats	www.nuts.org.uk
Rankings etc	www.all-athletics.com
Runners World	www.runnersworld.com
Tracklion (NED/BEL)	sportslion.net/tracklione.html
Track & Field News	www.trackandfieldnews.com
Track in Sun	www.trackinsun.com
World junior news	www.wjan.org
Olympic Games	www.aafla.org
	www.sports-reference.com

DIARY OF 2011
by Peter Matthews

A chronological survey of highlights in major events in the world of track and field athletics.
See Championships or National sections for more details of these events. DL = Diamond League, WCM = World Challenge Meeting.

January

8 **Edinburgh**, GBR. Mo Farah made a fine start to the year with a convincing win in the Bupa cross-country, and Linet Masai won a tough women's race.

16 **Seville**, Spain. Leonard Komon and Vivian Cheruiyot (who beat Linet Masai) were the winners at the 20th Cross International de Itálica and just as in 2010 Komon won again the next week at Elgoíbar.

22 **Dubai**, United Arab Emirates. David Barmasai ran 2:07:18 and Aselefech Mergia 2:22:45 to take the $250,000 first prizes at the Standard Chartered Dubai Marathon.

26 **Trinec**, Czech Republic. The first meeting of the Moravia High Jump Tour featured a world junior record 1.97 from Mariya Kuchina.

28 **New York** (Madison Square Garden), USA. 104th Millrose Games. Deresse Mekonnen spoiled Bernard Lagat's hopes of winning the Wanamaker Mile for a ninth time by 3:58.58 to 3:59.01.

29 **Glasgow**, GBR. The annual Aviva International: Germany 61, GBR 56, Commonwealth Select 56, USA 52, Sweden 29. As in 2010, Jessica Ennis (7.97) and David Oliver (7.51) won at 60m hurdles.

29 **Hustopece**, Czech Republic, Ivan Ukhov set a world leading mark of 2.38 on the second leg of the Moravia High Jump Tour.

30 **Osaka**, Japan. The favourite Yukiko Akaba won the 30th Osaka Women's Marathon but was slowed to 2:26:29 by a strong headwind in the second half.

February

4-5 **Tallinn**, Estonia. Ashton Eaton broke his own world indoor record for the heptathlon by 70 points at the International Combined Events Meeting with 6569 points (6.66 pb, 7.77, 14.45 pb, 2.01, 7.60 pb, 5.20, 2:34.74).

5 **Stuttgart**, Germany. 25th Sparkassen Cup. David Oliver ran world-leading times of 7.40 in his heat and 7.37 in the final of the 60m hurdles as Dayron Robles crashed out. On his indoor debut Yenew Alamirew ran 7:27.80 for third on the world indoor all-time list for 3000m to beat Augustine Choge 7:28.00 and Eliud Kipchoge 7:29.37.

5 **Tampere**, Finland. Osku Torro set a Finnish high jump record at 2.33, but the Finnish men lost to Sweden by one point, with Sweden a clear winner in the women's match; Norway were third in both.

5 **Boston (Roxbury)**, USA. New Balance GP, Reggie Lewis Track & Athletic Center. Dejene Gebremeskel lost a shoe but still ran a last 200m in 26.33 to beat Mo Farah 7:35.37 to 7:35.81 at 3000m.

6 **Moscow**, Russia. Yelena Isinbayeva returned after ten months out of competition to win with 4.81 at the "Winter" meeting. Yuliya Rusanova ran the second fastest ever indoor 600m in 1:24.02.

8 **Liévin**, France. French stars excelled at the Meeting Pas de Calais with Teddy Tamgho winning the triple jump with 17.64 and Renaud Lavillenie the pole vault at 5.90.

9 **Banská Bystrica**, Slovakia. Ivan Ukhov tied his world 2011 best of 2.38 and had three good tries at a world record 2.44 nudging the bar off slightly each time. After tying her Italian indoor record at 2.02, Antonietta Di Martino won the women's event with 2.04, increasing her record for the greatest ever height differential by a woman high jumper to 35cm.

11 **Düsseldorf**, Germany. As in 2010 the fastest 5000m times of the indoor season were run at the PSD Bank meeting. The winner was 17 year-old Isiah Koech in 12:53.29, fourth on the all-time list and the best ever by a junior, from Eliud Kipchoge 12:55.72. At the age of 35 Kim Collins took 0.01 off his 11 year-old St Kitts Nevis 60m record with 6.52, beating Michael Rodgers 6.53.

11-12 **Fayetteville**, USA. Tyson Invitational. Just nine days after his 20th birthday Erik Kynard improved his high jump best from 2.29 to 2.30 and 2.33, and Marshevet Myers had her first long jump competition for five years and improved her best of 6.71i (2006, also with 6.89w in 2005) to 6.83; Brittney Reese was 2nd with 6.64, her first loss to an American since June 2009.

12 **Donetsk**, Ukraine. The were world-leading marks of 5.93 by Renaud Lavillenie (in a jump-off after tying at 5.88 with Maksym Mazuryk) and 4.85 by Yelena Isinbayeva, who achieved her eighth win at Sergey Bubka's Pole Vault Stars meeting.

12-13 UK Indoor Championships. Joice Maduaka (aged 37) won her 18th national title and 34th medal indoors and out by winning the 200m in 23.63 while Jodie Williams, 20 years younger, won the 60m in a pb 7.24. Dwain Chambers won his fourth successive 60m title with 6.57.

13   Gent, Belgium. Isiah Koech set his second world junior best in two days as he won the 300m in 7:37.50 at the Belgacom Indoor Flanders meeting. Paul Kipsiele Koech improved his world best 5:17.04 mark of 2010 to 5:13.77 for 2000m steeplechase (no water jump). Pawel Wojciechowski added an amazing 26cm to his previous best by vaulting 5.86 to beat the 22 year-old Polish record.

13   Karlsruhe, Germany. David Oliver and Kellie Wells consolidated their position as the world's top hurdlers of the indoor season at the BW-Bank Meeting, running 7.40 and 7.82 respectively. Kim Collins improved his SKN 60m record to 6.50 in his heat but was back in 4th in the final won by Lerone Clarke 6.62.

16-18 Russian Indoor Championships, Moscow. Yelena Rusanova won the women's 800m in 1:58.14 before the Moscow team improved their world record for 4x800m relay from 8:12.41 to 8:06.24: Aleksandra Bulanova 2:01.8, Yekaterina Martynova 2:03.1, Yelena Kofanova 2:00.4, Anna Balakshina 2:00.6.

18   Ra's Al Khaymah, United Arab Emirates. In perfect conditions Mary Keitany smashed the world record for half marathon with 65:50. She followed male pacemaker Simon Tanui (to 20k) and after 5k in 15:18, 10k 30:45 and 15k 46:40, she also ran world bests/records at 10 miles in 50:05 and 20k in 62:36. For this she earned $75,000 ($25,000 first place and $50,000 world record bonus) and left second placer Dire Tune 68:52 well behind. Men's winner was Deribe Merga 59:25.

19   Arnstadt, Germany. Ivan Ukhov 2.34 and Svetlana Shkolina 1.95, won at the 35th indoor "High Jump with Music" event.

19   Birmingham, GBR. Aviva Grand Prix. Mo Farah broke the European record for 5000m with 13:10.60 and behind him Galen Rupp took the North American record with 13:11.44. Seven world-leading marks were led by Sentayehu Ejigu, 8:30.26 for 3000m, and Augustine Choge, 3:33.23 for 1500m.

19   Kenyan CC Championships, Nairobi. The immense strength in depth of Kenyan running was demonstrated to the full and senior champions were Geoffrey Mutai and Linet Masai, with Isiah Koech winning the junior men's title.

19-20 French Indoor Championships, Aubière. Teddy Tamgho added a centimetre to his world indoor triple jump record with 17.91.

22   Stockholm, Sweden. 22nd GE Globen Galen. Two days after setting a world junior

pole vault record of 4.53 at the Swedish Junior Championships Angelica Bengtsson (17) thrilled the crowd with world junior records at 4.53. 4.58 and 4.63, in second place to Svetlana Feofanova's 4.68. The 20 year-old Abeba Arigawi followed her Birmingham win in 4:03.28 with another in 4:01.47.

25   Pretoria. South Africa. Benefitting from the 1400m altitude, L.J. van Zyl for 400m hurdles ran 47.66, a national record and a time that was to remain the best of 2011.

26   Russian Winter Walks Championships, Sochi. Although Olga Ivanova, 1:24:50 in 2001, and Olga Kaniskina, 1:24:56 in 2009, had gone faster at this event, Vera Sokolova's winning time here of 1:25:08 was able to be ratified as the world record as international judges were in place for the first time. Vladimir Kanaykin won the men's 20k in 1:19:14 and Igor Yerokhin returned from a two-year drugs ban to win the 35k title in 2:26:36.

26-27 German Indoor Championships, Leipzig. Sebastian Ernst won the 200m in a world-leading 20.42.

26-27 US Indoor Championships, Albuquerque. Jenn Suhr pole vaulted 4.86 and Jillian Camarena-Williams put the shot 19.87 for new US indoor records, while there were world-leading marks also by Mike Rodgers (60m 6.48), Ryan Whiting (shot 21.35), Natasha Hastings (400m 50.83), Kellie Wells (60m hurdles 7.79) and Janay DeLoach (long jump 6.99). Suhr and Rodgers won the 2011 Indoor Visa Championship Series and $25,000 apiece with their performances.

27   Fayetteville, USA. Kirani James lowered the world junior best for 400m to 44.80 at the SEC Championships.

March

4   Melbourne, Australia. David Rudisha won the 800m in 1:43.88 in the first of the IAAF World Challenge Meetings of 2011.

4-6   European Indoor Championships, Paris (Bercy), France. Just as he had at the World Championships in 2010, Teddy Tamgho provided the highpoint of the meeting with a world indoor record in the triple jump in the last event. Indeed he jumped 17.92 twice to add 1cm to his mark of 29 February in the French Champs. Behind him Fabrizio Donato bettered his old championship best of 17.59 with Italian records of 17.70 and 17.73 and Marian Oprea jumped 17.62. Ivan Ukhov equalled his 2011 world best with 2.38 in the high jump and Renaud Lavillenie cleared a world-leading (and French record) 6.03 in the pole vault; both men went on to attempt world record heights in their events; while Lavillenie was nowhere near at 6.16, Ukhov went tantalizingly close at 2.44. Anna Rogowska added four cm to her previous best when she scaled a national pole vault record of 4.85. At 37, 3000m winner Helen Clitheroe became the second oldest ever European Indoor champion. Carolin Nytra beat Tiffany Ofili by just 0.001 in the women's 60m hurdles, 7.80 for both, and Francis Obikwelu continued a notable return from retirement by winning the 60m in a national record 6.53. Russia topped the medal table with 15 included 6 golds. *For leading results see Athletics 2011 p.90-1.*

11-12 NCAA Indoor Championships, College Station. Highlights came with three world-leading performances: Rakleem Salaam, 20.39 in his 200m heat before taking the final in 20.41, LaKya Brookins, 7.09 for 60m equalling the collegiate record, and Jessica Beard, 400m in 50.79. Both team titles were retained: Florida the men's and Oregon the women's, their sweeping victory helped by a collegiate pentathlon record of 4540 by Brianne Theisen and a 1M/3000m double by Jordan Hasay.

12 Reims, France. Yohann Diniz set a world record for 50,000m walk on the track with 3:35:27.2. After a first kilometre in 1:54, he walked each 400m to 30k between 1:43 and 1:47, He then had a 1:50 before each 400m 1:39 to 1:45 to 40.8k, then a storming finish with each 400m to 50k between 1:37 and 1:41 (splits: 10k 44:03, 20k 1:27:47, 30k 2:11:13. 40k 2:54:15).

13 Asian Walks Championships, Nomi, Japan. Winners at 20k were Kim Hyun-sub 1:19:31 and Kumi Otoshi 1:30:44.

17-19 Havana, Cuba. Yargeris Savigne provided the highlight of the Copa Cuba with a world-leading 14.95 triple jump.

19 Sydney, Australia. Mitchell Watt long jumped 8.38 at the Track Classic.

19-20 European Cup Winter Throwing, Sofia, Bulgaria. Cold and windy weather affected performances, but there was a world junior record of 84.47 in the javelin by the 18 year-old Latvian Zigismunds Sirmais. In the hammer there were wins for Krisztián Pars with 79.84 and Tatyana Lysenko 73.70 from Betty Heidler 72.71.

20 Lisbon, Portugal. Zersenay Tadese won the Half Marathon in 58:30, a time second only to his own 58:23 world record on this course in 2010.

20 Lugano. Switzerland. Chinese walkers dominated 20k races: 1-2-3 in the men headed by 19 year-old Wang Zhen 1:18:37 and the women's winner was Liu Hong 1:29:29.

20 New York, USA. Mo Farah made a successful debut at half marathon, winning in a British record 60:23.

20 World Cross-Country Championships, Punta Umbria, Spain. Kenya captured six of the eight individual and team titles and won 11 medals while rivals Ethiopia took the other two and won 7 medals. For Kenya's men it was their 24th senior title in 26 years and 23rd junior in 24 years. Imane

Merga produced great finishing speed to win the men's race for Ethiopia with Kenyans 2-3-4-5, and Vivian Cheruiyot beat Linet Masai for the women's title with American Shalane Flanagan third. The highest placed European in any of the races was 14th. *See Athletics 2011 p.92.*

26 Dudince, Slovakia. Matej Tóth won the 50km walk in a Slovakian record 3:39:46.

April

2 Pontevedra, Spain. Vivian Cheruiyot made a winning debut in a track 10,000m with 31:07.02 in the Spanish Championship race.

6-9 Austin, USA. The 84th Texas Relays produced numerous fast sprinting and hurdling marks, especially in various relays. Top marks included Marshevet Myers, 10.90w for 100m, and Ngonidzashi Makusha, 8.40w long jump.

8-10 South African Championships, Durban. L.J. van Zyl won the 400mh at 47.73, just 0.06 off his national record, but this time at sea-level.

9 Rio Maior, Portugal. Winners at the 20th Grande Premio Internacional, an IAAF Race Walking Challenge event, were Valeriy Borchin 1:18:55, with Stanislav Yemelyanov second in 1:19:33, his first ever loss at 20k, and Olga Kaniskina 1:28:35.

10 Paris, France. The 35th edition of the Paris Marathon featured a record number of 31,133 finishers and a double Kenyan triumph… Benjamin Kiptoo 2:06:31 and Priscah Jeptoo 2:22:55.

10 Fortis Rotterdam Marathon, Netherlands. Wilson Chebet won in 2:05:27, just 6 sec ahead of Vincent Kipruto. The women's winner was Philes Ongori on debut in 2:24:20 from Hilda Kibet 2:24:27.

14-16 53rd Mt SAC Relays, Walnut, California, USA. This massive meeting included Carmelita Jeter's first individual race of the year; she went straight to the top of the world rankings with a 10.99 100m.

15-17 Australian Championships, Melbourne. Mitchell Watt added a centimetre to his 2009 pb with 8.44 and Sally Pearson won a sprint treble, 100m, 200m and 100m hurdles.

16 Gainesville, USA. Kellie Wells ran the 100m hurdles in 12.35 with a following wind of +3.7 m/s at the Tom Jones Memorial Classic.

17 Virgin London Marathon, GBR. There were 35,303 starters and 34,656 finishers on the third warmest day in the race's 30-year history with the temperature for the elite runners rising from 15°C to 18°C. Emmanuel Mutai pocketed a total of $180,000 in prize money and bonuses with a brilliant victory in 2:04:40 (62:44 & 61:56) – breaking Sammy Wanjiru's 2009 course record of 2:05:10 and smashing his own pb of 2:06:15, with Martin Lel and Patrick Makau 2nd and 3rd, both 2:05:45. The overall standard in the women's race was the best ever as nine runners broke 2:25 and 21 inside 2:30 beat the previous record of 15 at the 2009 World Champs; there were best marks for place for 3rd and 8th to 24th, The winner was Mary Keitany, whose 2:19:19 took her to fourth on the world all-time list and she won $130,000, from Liliya Shobukhova 2:20:15 (Russian record) and Edna Kiplagat 2:20:46.

19   **Boston Marathon**, USA. Perfect weather, a generous tailwind and fabulous competition made the 115th edition of the world's oldest marathon the fastest ever run although not eligible for a world record. Geoffrey Mutai ran a spectacular 2:03:02, outsprinting Moses Mosop 2:03:06. Gebre Gebremariam finished third in 2:04:53, and Ryan Hall became the fastest ever American with his fourth-place 2:04:58. Caroline Kilel 2:22:36 was women's winner from Desiree Davila 2:22:38 and Sharon Cherop 2:22:42.

20-23   **Kansas Relays**, Lawrence, USA.

22-24   **Taicang**, China. Wang Zhen headed a Chinese 1-2-3 in this IAAF Race Walking Challenge meeting and set what was to remain the fastest time of the year for 20km walk with 1:18:30. Liu Hong was a clear women's winner in 1:27:17. The 50km two days later was won by Si Tianfeng in 3:38:48.

27-30   102nd **Drake Relays**, Des Moines, USA. Lolo Jones lost at 100m hurdles in her home town, 12.80w to 12.66w by Tiffany Ofili.

28-30   117th **Penn Relays**, Philadelphia, USA. A three-day attendance of 110,087 included 48,531 for the final day that featured the USA v the World relays, in which USA won three of the six races, Jamaica two and Morocco one. The US women's 4x100m team ran a meeting record time of 42.28.

May

1   **Stanford**, USA. Payton Jordan/Cardinal Invitational. Great Kim McDonald Memorial 10,000m races headed the bill. Bidan Karoki took 9.95 secs off his best to win the men's race in 27:13.67 with 13 men under 27:33 and 19 under 28:00, both just one off the best ever such figures, and 28 under 28:25 tied the all-time record. In the women's A race Sally Kipyego beat Shalane Flanagan by 1.22 secs, taking 47.1 secs off her 2008 pb with 30:38.35.

6   **Doha**, Qatar (DL). The opening Diamond League fixture was again of a very high quality and there were eleven early season world-leading marks. The first seven at 3000m were to remain the top seven outdoor times of the year, with 20 year-old Yenew Alamirew winning in 7:27.26 from Edwin Soi 7:27.55, Eliud Kipchoge 7:27.66 and Augustine Choge 7:28.76; there were best ever times for places 10 to 16 as 16 men (10 of them Kenyans) broke 7:38 (the previous record for sub-7:40 times was 13 in one

race). In a non-Diamond League event Nixon Chepseba won the 1500m in a pb 3:31.84 from Silas Kiplagat 3:32.15.

7   **Kingston**, Jamaica (WCM). Top quality sprinting was again the feature of the Jamaican Invitational. There were world-leading marks from Carmelita Jeter, 100m 10.86 from Kelly-Ann Baptiste 10.94, and Nickel Ashmeade, who improved his 200m best from 20.40 to 19.95. The wind was just over the limit for the men's 100m, won clearly by Yohan Blake in 9.80w and the women's 200m in which Shelly-Ann Fraser ran a best ever 22.10w in a surprisingly clear win over Veronica Campbell-Brown 22.37. A third world-leading outdoor mark of 2011 came from Kenia Sinclair 1:58.41 in the women's 800m.

8   **Kawasaki**, Japan. Krisztián Pars beat Koji Murofushi 79.47 to 78.10 in the first round of the IAAF Hammer Challenge.

12   **Daegu**, Korea (WCM). David Oliver won his 18th successive final at 110m hurdles in a wind-legal world-leading 13.14 in the Colorful Pre-Championships meeting.

12-15   **African Junior Championships**, Gaborone, Botswana.

15   **Manchester**. The street races in Deansgate included a world best on automatic timing for 200m hurdles on a straight track as Andy Turner beat Bershawn Jackson 22.10 to 22.26. Tyson Gay won the 1500m in 14.51, passing 100m in 9.91 and running 50m to the finish in 8.86.

15   **Shanghai**, China (DL). Liu Xiang excelled in his first race of 2011, beating David Oliver 13.07 to 13.18 at 110m hurdles. Asafa Powell won the men's 100m in 9.95, his record 66th sub-10 sec. legal time, and Veronica Campbell-Brown beat Carmelita Jeter, 10.92 to 10.95 in the women's race. Nixon Chepseba achieved another major 1500m win as he improved his pb to 3:31.42 to head Asbel Kiprop 3:31.76.

15   **Nyahururu**, Kenya. Shock news of the death of the Olympic marathon champion Samuel Wanjiru in a fall from a balcony at his home. *See Obituary.*

21   **Halle**, Germany. Betty Heidler starred at the 38th Werfertag with a world record hammer mark of 79.42 on her third throw after opening with a German record 77.19. Robert Harting won the discus with 68.99.

21   **European Cup of Race Walking**, Olhão, Portugal. Russian walkers won all three senior races at the 9th European Cup Race Walking (Stanislav Yemelyanov 1:23:27, Denis Nizhegorodov 3:45:58 and Vera Sokolova 1:30:02) and took the team wins in all these plus the junior girls (Ukraine won junior boys individual and team).

26   **Rome**, Italy. Golden Gala (DL). Usain Bolt opened his 100m account for 2011 with a victory in 9.91 over Asafa Powell 9.93.

Eight men were inside 13:01 in the 5000m won by Imane Merga 12:54.21 from Isiah Koech 12:54.59, Allyson Felix had a big win over Amantle Montsho, 49.81 to 50.47 at 400m, and Maryam Jamal ran 4:01.60 on her seasonal debut at 1500m. The crowd was 47,732, the biggest for the meeting for more than 20 years.

26   **Rio de Janeiro**, Brazil (WCM). World-leading marks were recorded by Melaine Walker, 54.09 for 400m hurdles, and Fabiana Murer, 4.65 outdoor pole vault, at the 27th Brazilian "Grande Premio".

26-28   **NCAA Qualifying**, USA. Preliminary rounds for the NCAA Championships were held in Eastern and Western sections at Bloomington and Eugene.

28   **Dakar**, Sénégal (WCM). Betty Heidler won the hammer with 75.33.

28   **Tartu**, Estonia. Vadim Vasilevskis took the lead in world javelin lists with 88.22.

28-29   **Götzis**, Austria. In his first decathlon for nearly two years, Trey Hardee scored 8689, 249 ahead of runner-up Leonel Suárez, and Jessica Ennis had a similarly clear heptathlon win with 6790 from Tatyana Chernova 6539.

28-29   **European Clubs Cup**, Vila Real de Santo António, Portugal. Luch Moskva achieved their 13th win in 15 years in the men's cup and their 15th successive win in the women's match.

29   **Hengelo**, Netherlands. 29th Fanny Blankers-Koen Games (WCM). There were world-leading marks in the shot by Reese Hoffa 21.87 and women's 1500m by Maryam Jamal 4:00.33, while Dayron Robles matched Liu Xiang's recent 110m hurdles time of 13.07. As usual there were excellent 5000m races, won by Edwin Soi 12:59.15 and Meseret Defar 14:45.48. The day before the main meeting, Reese Hoffa won a city centre shot event with 21.87.

May 30 – June 1 **Yalta**, Ukraine. The first round of the national cup competition featured a huge breakthrough by Liliya Lobanova from her previous best of 2:01.33 (2009) to a world-leading 800m of 1:58.30.

31   **Ostrava**, Czech Republic. 50th Golden Spike (WCM). Usain Bolt closed the meeting with a 9.91 100m victory, but more impressive was the 10.76 pb run by Veronica Campbell-Brown in the women's race. En route she was timed at 9.91 for 100 yards to remove the 10.10 run by Chi Cheng in 1970 from the lists as the world's best. L.J. van Zyl ran 47.66 for 400m hurdles to match the time that he had run at high altitude in February. There were fine hammer competitions the day before, won by Aleksey Zagorniy 80.02 and Betty Heidler 77.22.

June

2-5   47th **South American Championships**, Buenos Aires, Argentina. Juan Ignacio Cerra won his ninth hammer title for the single event record at these championships. There were eight new championship records, headed by women's pole vault, Fabiana Murer 4.70, and hammer, Jennifer Dahlgren 72.70.

3   **Bydgoszcz**, Poland. European Athletics Festival. Phillips Idowu maintained his strong form, after a 17.59 win in Rome, with 17.52w here.

3   **Eugene**, USA. Toshihiko Seko's 30-year reign as world record holder for 25,000m (1:13:55.8) and 30,000m (1:29:18.8) came to an end when Moses Mosop clocked 1:12:25.4 and 1:26:47.4 at the distance running festival that preceded the Prefontaine Classic. After 29:19.7 for the first 10k, Mosop, who led for the last 12k, covered the remaining two 10k segments in 28:42,5 and 28:45.2. Mo Farah ran a perfectly planned and executed race to defeat one of the greatest 10,000m fields ever assembled and smash the European record with 26:46.67, sprinting the last lap in 55.78 to finish well clear of Imane Merga 26:46.35 and Josphat Bett 26:48.99. 14 of the 20 finishers set pbs and nine of the runners (six of them Kenyans) broke 27 minutes compared to the previous record of six in Brussels 200; there were best ever place marks from 4th to 19th (27:51.92).

4   **Clermont**, USA. Tyson Gay ran the 100m in 9.79 at the NTC Sprint Series meeting.

4   **European Cup 10,000m**, Oslo, Norway. Spain won the men's and Italy the women's team competitions.

4   **Eugene**, USA. 37th Prefontaine Classic (DL). A great meeting included world leading performances in eight events with the most eye-catching exploits coming from David Oliver, 12.94 for 110mh ahead of Liu Xiang 13.00, and Carmelita Jeter, 10.70 for 100m. The eight fastest mile times of the year were run here, with five men under 3:50 headed by Haron Keitany 3:49.09, Silas Kiplagat 3:49.39 and Asbel Kiprop 3:49.55, and there were best ever times for places 5 and 7-10 in the 2 miles won by Bernard Lagat in 8:13.62. Steve Mullings, later to test positive, won the men's 100m in 9.80 (with Darvis Patton running the fastest ever 8th place time of 10.02) and world leads in the field came in the women's triple jump, Olga Saladuha 14.98, and shot, Nadezhda Ostapchuk 20.59.

4   **Varazdin**, Croatia. Sandra Perkovic, three weeks short of her 21st birthday, produced a brilliant last-round discus throw of 69.99, the world's best by a woman since Natalya Sadova threw 70.02 in 1999, but the performance was tarnished and discounted when news came that Perkovic had failed a drugs test on 16 May.

4.5   **Russian Cup**, Yerino. Aleksey Zagorniy threw the hammer a world-leading 81.73 and Lyudmila Kolchanova long jumped 7.06w.

6   **Rabat**, Morocco. Mohammed VI meeting (WCM). Vanya Stambolova ran a Bulgarian record and world-leading 53.68 for

400m hurdles and Amine Laâlou the year's fastest 1000m of 2:15.31.

7   Montreuil-sous-Bois, France. Yohan Blake beat Christophe Lemaitre 9.95 to 9.96 (French record) with Daniel Bailey third in 10.00 at 100m and there were world-leading outdoor marks from Teddy Tamgho, 17.67 in an excellent triple jump series, and Renaud Lavillenie, who added a centimetre to his 2011 pole vault best with 5.83.

8-11   NCAA Championships, Des Moines, USA. Ngonidzashe Makusha became only the fourth man (after DeHart Hubbard, Jesse Owens and Carl Lewis) to win both long jump and 100m at the NCAAs, setting Zimbabwean records of 8.49 and 9.89 respectively, and the first to add the 4x100m as he ran a leg on the winning Florida State University team. Texas A&M narrowly retained their men's title with 55 points from Florida State 54 and Florida 53, and also retained their women's crown with 49 from Oregon 45 and LSU 43.5. Jeshua Anderson won a third NCAA title at 400m hurdles, Florida teammates Christian Taylor and Will Claye excelled with 17.80w and 17.62w for a triple jump 1-2 and the top women's marks came in the 200m with Kimberlyn Duncan beating Jenebah Tarmoh 22.24 to 22.34. *See USA section for winners.*

9   Oslo, Norway (DL). On a cool, rain soaked night Usain Bolt stormed to a world-leading 19.86 in his first 200m race of 2011 at the Exxon Mobil Bislett Games. Despite the conditions there were also world-leading marks from Paul Koech, 8:01.83 for 3000m steeplechase, and Halina Hachlaf, who sprinted to a surprise 800m victory in 1:58.27 over Mariya Savinova 1:58.44 and Caster Semenya 1:58.61. The Grete Waitz Memorial 5000m was won by Meseret Defar in 14:37.32 (a career record 36th sub 15:00 time) with three more Ethiopians under 14:40, and the Dream Mile, in pouring rain, by Asbel Kiprop in 3:50.86.

10   Turin, Italy. 12th Primo Nebiolo Memorial (EA Premium). Despite rainy weather top class performances included 3:31.92 by Amine Laâlou for 1500m and 81.49 hammer by Aleksey Zagorniy.

10-12   Japanese Championships, Marugame. Koji Murofushi threw 77.01 to win his 17th successive national hammer title.

11   Istanbul, Turkey. Six weeks after becoming eligible for Turkey after switching from Azerbaijan, Ramil Guliyev set a Turkish 200m record of 20.33 at the 64th Cezmi Or Memorial (EAA Classic).

11   New York (Randall's Island), USA. adidas GP (DL). There were upsets galore on a wet and windy evening and times were slowed so much that in the 100m featuring the two fastest men of 2011 to date Steve Mullings beat Tyson Gay with both running 10.26 into a 3.4 m/s headwind.

12   Strasbourg, France. Daniel Bailey beat his training companion Yohan Blake 9.97 to 9.98 at 100m.

13   Prague, Czech Republic. Josef Odlozil Memorial. Barbara Spotáková won the javelin with 65.77.

15-16   Kladno, Czech Republic. Leonel Suárez won the decathlon with 8231 points and Tatyana Chernova recorded a pb of 6773 to win the heptathlon at the 5th annual TNT-Fortuna meeting.

18-19   European Team Championships, Stockholm, Sweden. Russia was again clear winner by 53.5 points over Germany with Ukraine third. Christophe Lemaitre ran a French and European U23 record with 9.95 for 100m and returned on a cold and wet second day to run 20.28 for 200m. Four women, led by Christina Obergföll 66.22 exceeded 64m in the javelin, Dmytro Demyanyuk improved his high jump best from 2.32 to 2.33 and 2.35 (thus exceeding the family record – his father Aleksey's 2.33), and Anna Rogowska beat Silke Spiegelburg on count-back as both cleared a season's outdoor best of 4.75.

19-20   European Team Championships. The First League at Izmir, Turkey was won by Turkey with Greece and Norway promoted to retake their places in the Super League next year in place of the Czech Republic, Portugal and Sweden. Relegated in 2010, Estonia bounced straight back by winning the Second League at Novi Sad, Serbia, and the Third League at Reykjavik, Iceland was won by Israel.

22-25   Canadian Championships, Calgary. Dylan Armstrong opened with national records at 21.75 and 21.89 before a Commonwealth shot record of 22.21 in the final round; this was to remain the world's best mark of the year.

23-26   Jamaican Championships, Kingston. Veronica Campbell-Brown won her first 100m/200m double since 2007 with 10.84 and 22.44.

23-26   US Championships, Eugene. After running 10.01w in his heat, Tyson Gay's hip injury flared up and he had to withdraw from his 100m semi, costing him any chance of running the event at the World Championships. With favourable wind there was plenty of fast sprinting with Walter Dix winning at 100m and 200m in 9.94 and 19.95w and Carmelita Jeter winning the women's 100m in 10.74w, although beaten by Sholanda Solomon, 22.15 to 22.23 at 200m, pbs for both. A close race in the 400m hurdles was won by Jeshua Anderson 47.93 from Bershawn Jackson 47.93 and Angelo Taylor 47.94, and Kellie Wells ran a pb 12.50 to win the 100m hurdles. The only men's meeting record was set by Jesse Williams, who raised his high jump pb to 2.37, 53cm above his head, but there were three in the women's events: Brittney Reese, the 2011 world's best long jump

7.19, Michelle Carter, shot 19.86. and Shalane Flanagan, 10,000m 30:59.97. Adam Nelson scored an upset with his first shot title since 2006, as his 22.09 bested Christian Cantwell 21.87 and Reese Hoffa 21.86, and Ashton Eaton moved to fifth on the US all-time decathlon list with 8729 points. David Oliver, 110mh winner in 13.04, and Carmelita Jeter won $25,000 apiece as overall winners of the Visa Championship Series.

24   **Tomblaine**, France. David Rudisha ran 1:43.46 for 800m in his first race of the summer.

25   **Cottbus**, Germany. Top mark at the 22nd Internationales Lausitzer Meeting was Robert Harting's 68.51 discus throw.

25   **Szczecin**, Poland. 57th Kusocinski Memorial. Piotr Malachowski won the discus with 68.49.

28   **Velenje**, Slovenia. Mariya Abakumova improved the year's best at women's javelin to 67.98.

30   **Lausanne**, Switzerland. Athletissima (DL). Asafa Powell looked magnificent in clocking the year's fastest 100m of 9.78. It was his 68th time under 10.00, his 33rd sub-9.90 and eighth sub-9.80 – all records. Behind him 2-3 were Michael Frater 9.88 and Christophe Lemaitre to tie his French record. Teddy Tamgho triple jumped 17.91, well clear of Phillips Idowu 17.52 and another Frenchman to excel was Renaud Lavillenie with 5.83. In her first European outing of the season Sally Pearson clocked 12.47w as compared to her Oceania 100m hurdles record of 12.50. Andreas Thorkildsen returned to top form with 88.19 in the javelin, winning from Sergey Makarov, whose 87.12 was his best for four years.

July

2-3   60th **Balkan Championships**, Sliven, Bulgaria. Team winners were Greece (men) and Romania (women), and Ivet Lalova continued her return to form after recovering from serious injury by winning the 100m in 10.96.

2-3   **European Cup of Combined Events**. Andre Raja won the decathlon with 8114 on home ground in the Super League at Torun, Estonia, but Russia beat Estonia for the men's team title as well as winning the women's team and individual through Anna Bogdanova 6225. There was also a first-time winner of the women's team event as Poland beat Russia by 58 points. Higher heptathlon scores were recorded by Karolina Tyminska, 6297 in the First League at Bressanone, Italy, and by Austra Skujyte, 6338 in the Second League at Ribiera Brava, Poland.

2-3   **Zhukovskiy**, Russia. 53rd Znamenskiy Memorial (WCM). Nadezhda Ostapchuk added 35cm to her world leading shot mark with 20.94 and Yuriy Borzakovskiy impressed with a strong run for 1:43.99 at 800m.

5   **Reims**, France. Tesfaye Cheru of Ethiopia ran a world junior record 4:56.25 for 2000m.

6-10   **World Youth Championships**, Villeneuve d'Ascq, France. Phenomenal performances by two 16 year-olds topped the performances – Leonard Kosencha ran 800m in 1:44.08, with Mohamed Aman second in an Ethiopian record 1:44.68 and Timothy Kitum third in 1:44.98 (for 1-1-3 on the world youth all-time list), and Jacko Gill broke his own world 5kg shot best of 23.86 with 24.35 in the second round and was also over 24m with his third and sixth throws despite a minor finger injury. Three more world youth records came from Jake Stein 6491 for octathlon and the American boys' (1:49.47) and Jamaican girls' (2:03.42) 1000m medley relay teams. A total of 173 nations were represented, 18 of them winning gold medals, led by USA 6, Kenya 5, Jamaica 4 and Bahamas 3. Africans swept all the medals in the men's and women's 1500m, 3000m and steeplechase, plus the men's 800m.

7-10   **Asian Championships**, Kobe, Japan. Liu Xiang gave priority to this, his continental championship, rather than competing in the big-money meets, and was rewarded with his fourth Asian Championships title to go with his three Asian Games wins as he took the 110m hurdles in a championship record 13.22. But top mark came from high jumper Mutaz Essa Barshim, with championship records at 2.33 and 2.35. There were also fourth titles for Ehsan Hadadi at discus and Mohammed Al-Zankawi at hammer. China easily topped the medal table.

8   **Saint-Denis**, France. Areva meeting (DL). There was a crowd of 49,174 in the Stade de France, many no doubt attracted by the 200m won by Usain Bolt in 20.03 from Christophe Lemaitre 20.31. Better marks however, came from world-leading performances in the women's 400m hurdles, 5000m, triple jump and javelin. Winners respectively were Zuzana Hejnová 53.29, from her previous Czech record of 53.87, Meseret Defar 14:29.52 (her 8th sub 14:30 time), Yargeris Savigne 14.99 and Christina Obergföll, 68.01 ahead of Barbora Spotáková 67.57. Amine Laâlou won the 1500m in 3:32.15 from Asbel Kiprop 3:33.04 and Bernard Lagat 3:33.11 and the three top US runners from their Trials who had not previously reached the World's A standard, all achieved this with sub-3:35 times. Valerie Adams beat Nadezhda Ostapchuk 20.78 to 20.49 with Jill Camerena-Williams equalling the North American record of 20.18 at the shot, but much closer was the men's 110m hurdles in which Dayron Robles beat David Oliver 13.087 to 13.090, and there was an upset in the women's 100m as Kelly-Ann Baptiste beat Veronica Campbell-Brown 10.91 to 10.96. The crowd loved a splendid steeplechase win by Mahiedine Mekhissi, whose 8:02.09 was just 0.912 short of Bob Tahri's French record.

9   **London (Hendon)**. Having thrown 63.25 in his first ever competition with the 2kg implement on 14 May). Lawrence Okoye set a British record with 67.63 at the Throws Fest.

9   **Madrid**, Spain (WCM). Performances at the 39th Meeting de Madrid suffered from adverse winds, but there was a fine 400m win by Kevin Borlée in 44.74.

9-10   **Moscow Championships**, Russia. Four women, headed by Yekaterina Kostetskaya 1:58.25, broke 2 minutes for 800m.

10   **Birmingham**, GBR. Aviva Grand Prix (DL). Sally Pearson zipped to an Oceania record of 12.48 for 100m hurdles and another world-leading mark was the 88.30 javelin throw by Andreas Thorkildsen. The packed crowd in the Alexander Stadium thrilled to a 5000m victory by Mo Farah in 13:06.14 from his training partner Glen Rupp 13:06.96 pb and to the triple jump win of Phillips Idowu, maintaining his consistent form with 17.54 while Teddy Tamgho managed only 16.74 for fifth.

10   **European Mountain Running Championships**, Bursa, Turkey. Ahmet Aslan won the men's race for the fifth successive year while Italy achieved their 16th men's team win in the 17 years of the event and their tenth women's win.

14-16   **Kenyan Championships**, Nairobi. Despite the 1675m high altitude remarkable times were posted at distance events. Silas Kiplagat won the 1500m in 3:31.39 for the fastest ever altitude time, and nine men under 28 minutes at 10,000m were headed by Peter Kirui 27:32.1, Wilson Kiprop 27:32.9 and Martin Mathathi 27:38.6, while Vivian Cheruiyot won the women's 10,000m in 31:55.8. David Rudisha easily won the 800m in 1:43.76.

14-17   **European Under-23 Championships**, Ostrava, Czech Republic. Sheryf El-Sheryf made a magnificent improvement at triple jump. From a pb of 16.92 he opened with 16.99 and 17.04 in the final before a sensational 17.72 on his last effort. Another big improvement was made in the women's high jump by Esthera Petre from 1.92 to new pbs at 1.94, 1.96 and 1.98. Darya Klishina won the long jump with 7.05 and Bianca Perie added to her collection of championship gold medals by winning the hammer with 71.59. Russia headed the medal table with 11 gold, 5 silver and 5 bronze from Britain 6-5-9 and Germany 4-4-7.

15-17   23rd **Central American & Caribbean Championships**, Mayagüez, Puerto Rico. Cuba did not compete, leaving Jamaica as much the most successful nation with 10 gold, 6 silver and 10 bronze. Top performance was a championship record equalling women's long jump of 6.81 by Bianca Stuart.

16   **Heusden-Zolder**, Belgium. KBC Night of Athletics. Despite heavy rain and strong winds Yelena Isinbayeva started her summer season by winning the pole vault with a first-time clearance at 4.60.

16-17   **Eberstadt**, Germany. After Svetlana Shkolina had won the women's event on the first day with 1.99, rain ruined the men's competition on day 2 of the annual high jump meeting so that Ivan Ukhov won with just 2.24.

16-17   **Nanchang**, China The Chinese Grand Prix Final featured 14.62w for triple jump by Xie Limei and 20.11 for shot by Gong Lijiao.

16-17   **Ratingen**, Germany. Jennifer Oeser, with 6663, won the heptathlon for the third successive year and Larbi Bouraada added 181 points to his African record to win the decathlon with 8302.

19   **Lignano**, Italy. Morgan Uceny won the women's 800m in a pb 1:58.37 and the "blade runner" Oscar Pistorius achieved his aim of getting the Daegu A standard with a pb 45.07 for 400m.

19-23   **World Military (CISM) Championships**, Rio de Janeiro, Brazil. Championship records included 100m 10.07 and 200m 20.46 by Femi Ogunode, 5000m 13:06.17 by Mark Kiptoo, pole vault 5.81 by Pawel Wojciechowski, and women's hammer 74.29 by Zhang Wenxiu.

21   **Luzern**, Switzerland. The 25th Spitzenleichtathletik meeting included 20.02 for 200m by Walter Dix.

21-24   **European Under-20 Championships**, Tallinn, Estonia. World junior records were set by Yelena Lashmanova, 10,000m walk in 42:59.48, and Angelica Bengtsson, pole vault 4.57. The German 4x100m team set a European junior record of 43.42, 17 year-old Jodie Williams took the sprint double in 11.18 (a UK junior and championship record) and 22.94, and Jimmy Vicaut was just 0.03 outside the European Junior 100m record with 10.07. Russia just headed the medal table with 8 gold, 4 silver and 6 bronze from Germany 7-4-12, Britain 6-5-4 and France 6-3-4.

21-24   **Russian Championships**, Cheboksary. Anna Chicherova cleared a national record 2.07 from a previous season's best of 1.99 and pb of 2.04 and the men's high jump was also of top quality with Aleksey Dmitrik clearing 2.36 on his first attempt and Aleksandr Shustov on his second, followed by Ivan Ukhov and Andrey Silnov, both 2.34.

There were world-leading (and pb) performances from Anastasiya Kapachinskaya, 400m 49.35 with Antonina Krivoshapka 2nd in 491.92, and from Mariya Savinova who led five women under 1:58.3 with 1:56.94 in the 800m (after a world-leading 1:58.03 in her heat). Sergey Makarov won his 12th javelin title from 1996.

22   **Barcelona**, Spain. Zersenay Tadese won the 5000m in 12:59.32, but Dayron Robles hit the seventh hurdle and came in last after winning all his previous nine races in 2011 at 110m hurdles.

22   **Herculis, Monaco** (DL). A meeting of very high quality, ranked on All-Athletics.com as the top one-day meeting of 2011, was held in glorious weather. Brimin Kipruto missed the world record for 3000m steeplechase by just 0.01 with his 7:53.64 ahead of Ezekiel Kemboi 7:55.76 (fifth world all-time) and Paul Koech 7:57.32. Times for 2nd, 3rd and 10th (8:12.27) were the best ever. World-leading marks also came from David Rudisha, 800m 1:42.61, Silas Kiplagat, 1500m 3:30.47, Mo Farah, 5000m 12:53.11 UK record with a last lap in 53.73, Renaud Lavillenie, pole vault 5.90, and Barbora Spotáková, javelin 69.45. Second and third in the 1500m were Nick Willis in a New Zealand record 3:32.17 and Abubaker Kaki in a Sudanese record 3:31.75 from a previous best of 3:39.71, and Bernard Lagat improved his North American record to 12:53.60 behind Farah with Isiah Koech third in 12:54.18. Usain Bolt received a rapturous welcome and won the 100m in 9.88 but only just ahead of Nesta Carter 9.90, and Carmelita Jeter beat Allyson Felix 22.20 to 22.32 in the 200m.

22-24 **Pan-American** **Junior Championships**, Miramar, Florida, USA. The USA won 59 medals including 17 gold, but Cuba did not take part.

23-24 **German** **Championships**, Braunschweig. Betty Heidler won her seventh successive hammer title with 76.04 and Christina Obergföll achieved a javelin championship best with her season's best of 68.86. Sabine Mockenhaupt won a tenth 5000m title.

28-30 **French** **Championships**, Albi. Christophe Lemaitre continued his progress with a French record 9.92 for 100m and completed the sprint double with 20.03w for 200m. Romain Mesnil won his seventh pole vault title with 5.73, but Renaud Lavillenie failed to clear that, his opening height.

29   **Stockholm**, Sweden. 45th DN Galan (DL). Second to Jermaine Gonzales 44.69, LaShawn Merritt ran 44.74 in his first race for nearly two years following the end of his doping ban. Usain Bolt won the 200m in a moderate 20.03, and further Jamaican success came from Kenia Sinclair, 800m 1:58.21, and Kaliese Spencer, 400m hurdles 53.74. Mitchell Watt set an Australian and Oceania long jump record of 8.54 and Vivian Cheruiyot ran a Commonwealth record 14:20.87 with kilometres of 2:55.35, 2:51.84, 2:51.48 (8:38.67 at 3000m), 2:52.55 and 2:49.65. Jason Richardson impressed with a 13.17 110m hurdles win into a headwind of 2.3m/s from David Oliver 13.28.

29-30 **Greek** **Championships**, Athens. There were 14th national titles for hammer thrower Aléxandros Papadimitríou and for Periklís Iakovákis at 400m hurdles.

29-30 **UK Championships**, Birmingham. Goldie Sayers won her ninth consecutive javelin title and Perri Shakes-Drayton won at both 400m and 400m hurdles.

30   **Budapest**, Hungary. Asafa Powell ran his seventh and eighth sub-10 second 100m times of the year (9.90 and 9.86) at the inaugural István Gyulai Memorial Meeting In Budapest – to take his career total to 73 such times with 'legal' wind. With favourable wind conditions Zoltán Kövágó threw a world-leading 69.50 to win the discus.

August

4-7   **Finnish** **Championships**, Turku. Ola-Pekka Karjalainen won his 14th successive hammer title with 75.20 and Ari Mannio won the javelin with 85.12.

5-6   **London (Crystal Palace)**, GBR. Aviva London Grand Prix (DL). David Rudisha broke Steve Cram's 25 year-old UK all-comers record with 1:42.91 for 800m ahead of Abubaker Kaki 1:43.12. Yohan Blake ran an outstanding 9.95 for 100m into a 1.6m/s headwind and world-leading performances were run by Kirani James, 44.61 for 400m, and Kaliese Spencer. 52.79 for 400m hurdles, with Jenn Suhr pole vaulting an outdoor best of 4.79. Christian Taylor had a clear win in the triple jump with a pb 17.68 and Sanya Richards-Ross had her fastest 400m for two years, winning in 49.66. The Emsley Carr Mile was won by Leonel Manzano who beat Bernard Lagat 3:51.24 to 3:51.38.

6   **Moscow**, Russia. Top mark at the Kuts Memorial was a 75.70 hammer throw by Tatyana Lysenko.

6-7   **Hungarian Championships**, Szekszárd. Krisztián Pars won his 8th successive hammer title with 80.63.

6-7   **Serbian Championships**, Kragujevac. Dragutin Topic won the high jump with a world M40 record of 2.24, 21 years after he had set a world junior record of 2.37.

6-7   **Spanish Championships**, Málaga. Mario Pestano won his 11th successive Spanish discus title with 67.97 and Berta Castells set her 13th Spanish hammer record from 2001 with 69.53 in winning her ninth successive title. Others to retain their national dominance were Mercedes Chilla with her ninth successive javelin title, Jesús España his eighth at 5000m, and Concepción Montaner her seventh at long jump.

11-13 **Polish Championships**, Bydgoszcz. Tomasz Majewski won his ninth shot title in ten years with 20.94 and Szymon Ziólkowski took his 13th hammer title (his first was in 1996) with 78.79.

11-14 **Swedish Championships**, Gävle. Top marks came from Christian Olsson, 17.19 triple jump, and Carolina Klüft, 6.74w in the long jump. Anna Söderberg won her 19th successive Swedish title at the discus, improving her own record for any event, and Robert Kronberg won a 13th at 110m hurdles to add to 12 successive 1997-2008.

12-14 Norwegian   Championships, Brykjelo. Andreas Thorkildsen produced the only 90m javelin throw of 2011 with 90.61, the third best of his career.

13   Bogotá, Colombia. Caterine Ibargüen set a world-leading and South American record with a 14.99 triple jump at the 23rd Colombian Grand Prix.

13-14 Chula Vista, USA. The US women beat Germany 17,611 to 17,115 in the women's heptathlon but Germany won the men's decathlon 38,870 to 38,006. Competing only in selected events Ashton Eaton reduced his 100m pb from 10.33 to 10.26 and added nearly 2m to his discus best with 47.36.

13-14 Trinidad & Tobago Championships, Port of Spain. Richard Thompson improved his 100m best from 9.89 (2nd at Beijing Olympics) to 9.85 for 9th on the world all-time list.

16-21 World University Games, Shenzhen, China. Top performances came from Nelson Évora who won the triple jump 17.31, his first mark over 17m for two years, and Sunette Viljoen, who improved her own African javelin record to 66.47, winning by over six metres. Jamaican women sprinters starred with Carrie Russell winning the 100m in 11.05 and Anneisha McLaughlin the 200m in 22.54. The Touil twins from Algeria, Imad (the 2008 World Junior champion) and Abdelmajed, uniquely finished 1-2 in the 1500m and there was a fine women's high jump duel with Brigetta Barrett winning on countback at 1.96 over the junior Airine Palsyte, who set a Lithuanian senior record. Zalina Marghieva threw 72.93 ahead of Éva Orbán 71.33, both national records in the women's hammer. Russia led the medal table with 11 gold, 11 silver and 9 bronze.

21   IAU 50km World Trophy Final, Assen, Netherlands.

27-Sep 4   IAAF World Championships, Daegu, Kenya. Usain Bolt was sensationally disqualified for a false-start in the 100m final on the second day but on the eighth he won the 200m in 19.40, a time beaten only by the last three world records, and then ended the championships by anchoring the Jamaican team to a world record 37.04 at 4x100m. That was one of just four championship records. The first, equalling Natalya Lisovskaya in 1987, was by Valerie Adams in the women's shot and the others came from Mariya Abakumova as she beat Barbora Spotáková 71.99 to 71.58 in one of the great javelin duels of all-time, and from stellar sprint hurdling by Sally Pearson, 12.28 in the final after setting an Oceania and Commonwealth record 12.36 in her semi-final. Abakumova moved to second on the world all-time list and Pearson, like Yuliya Zaripova 9:07.03 steeplechase and Lashinda Demus 52.47 for 400m hurdles, to third. There were in all 14 area records and 6 Commonwealth records and 18 world leading marks in 15 events. The super powers of USA and Russia headed the medal table but Kenya excelled with their best ever showing in third place with seven golds. Their successes started with medal sweeps in the two events determined on the first day – women's 10,000m and marathon, heralding a switch in power in women's distance running from Ethiopia. Vivian Cheruiyot went on to complete the 5000/10,000m double and, as well as the usual Kenyan men's steeplechase success, a command performance from Daniel Rudisha and 1-2 in the 1500m showed men's middle distance supremacy. Allyson Felix was beaten by Amantle Montsho in a great women's 400m despite running a pb and had to yield to her great rival Veronica Campbell-Brown and 100m winner Carmelita Jeter in the 200m, but took her World Champs gold medal haul to eight (to tie Carl Lewis and Michael Johnson) by helping the US to wins in both relays. Her four medals at one Championships equalled the record. Susana Feitor (6th at 20k walk) competed in a record 11th World Championships and Jesús Ángel García (50k walk) competed for a men's record tenth time. *See Championships section for reports and results.*

September

8   Zürich, Switzerland. Weltklasse (DL). The meeting featured half the Diamond League finals, but came far too soon after the Worlds in Daegu for maximum performance levels for many athletes, as did the cold and rainy conditions, and eight world champions were beaten. One of those, however, Jason Richardson improved his 110mh pb to 13.10 behind the 13.01 of Dayron Robles. Christina Obergföll, 4th with 65.24 in Daegu, threw a season's best of 69.57 to beat all three medallists, and Kaliese Spencer improved from 4th in the World 400m hurdles (54.01) to victory in 53.36, again ahead of the three medal winners. Yohan Blake reduced his 100m best from 9.89 to 9.82 in finishing well clear of Asafa Powell 9.95 and Walter Dix 10.00, and Kirani James, a week after his 19th birthday, excelled again to break Alleyne Francique's Grenadian 400m record with 44.36. The shot competitions were again held the day before the main meeting at Zürich's main railway station.

8-11   Chinese Championships, Hefei.

9   Elstal, Germany, Top mark in the DKB duels came from Betty Heidler 77.53 in the hammer.

9-10   Finland v Sweden, Helsinki. In a near repeat of the 2010 result Finland were men's winners 206-194 and Sweden women's 225-182 in the annual Finnkampen.

10   Rieti, Italy (WCM). David Rudisha missed his own world 800m record by 0.32 sec. with 1:41.33 on his favourite track to highlight a memorable 41st edition of this meeting.

Second was Adam Kszczot 1:43.30 and third Mohammed Aman, who smashed the world youth best with 1:43.37; Sammy Tangui led to 400m in 48.30 and Rudisha went through 600m in 1:14.28 as against 1:14.54 when he set his first world record of 1:41.09 in Berlin and 1:14.59 en route to his 1:41.01 in Rieti in 2010. Asbel Kiprop improved the world best for the year at 1500m to 3:30.46 and Bernard Lagat led three men under 7:33 with 7:32.13 for 3000m.

10   IAU 100 Kilometres World Championships, Winschoten, Netherlands. Giorgio Calcaterra and Marina Bychkova took the individual titles by large margins, while the USA won the men's team title for the first time and Russia won the women's.

11   Berlin, Germany. 70th ISTAF (WCM). Yohan Blake matched his Zürich pb of 9.82 for 100m, well clear of Kim Collins 10.01. Maintaining top form in the field were Jesse Williams, HJ 2.33, Robert Harting, DT 67.22 and Betty Heidler, HT 77.40, while Barbora Spotáková 67.14 Christina Obergföll 64.94 and Mariya Abakumova 64.34 continued their javelin rivalry. Behind Paul Koech 8:04.48, Bernard Nganga improved his steeplechase best from 8:16.22 to 8:05.88, and Augustine Choge led seven men under 3:33 in the 1500m with his 3:31.14.

11   27th World Mountain Running Championships, Tirana, Albania. Italy returned to winning ways in taking both men's and women's team titles.

11-15   10th All-Africa Games, Maputo, Mozambique. Two world champions, Ibrahim Jeylan (10,000m) and Amantle Montsho (400m) won here.

13   Rovereto, Italy. Highlight of the 47th Palio Citta della Quercia meeting was the hammer win by Tatyana Lysenko with 74.13.

13   Zagreb, Croatia. 61st Boris Hanzekovic Memorial (WCM). Despite a poor start Usain Bolt ran his fastest 100m of the year at 9.85 before a capacity crowd of more than 12,000. Dayron Robles just held on to clock a season's best of 13.00 for 110m hurdles but Jason Richardson was close behind with a pb 13.04. Local idol Blanka Vlasic lost on count-back at 2.00 to Anna Chicherova and in the IAAF Hammer Challenge Dilshod Nazarov threw a pb 80.30 to beat Primoz Kozmus by 2 cm. The 1500m featured pbs by five of the top seven finishers, including Diamond League winner Nixon Chepseba, winner in 3:30.94, and runner-up Kenyan-turned-Turk Ilham Özbilen who set a national record of 3:31.37.

15   Dubnica nad Váhom, Slovakia. 9th Athletics Bridge meeting. Jason Richardson beat a good field by a huge margin when running 13.08 for 110m hurdles, one of 8 meeting records set in the 13 events. Betty Heidler had just 3cm to spare over Tatyana Lysenko in the hammer, 75.83 to 75.80.

16   Brussels, Belgium. 35th Van Damme Memorial (DL). Usain Bolt ran the world's quickest 100m of the year with 9.76, but just a few minutes later was totally upstaged by training partner Yohan Blake, who had a very slow reaction time of 0.269 but overcame that to run the 200m is 19.26, the second quickest ever. Walter Dix entered the straight just ahead of Blake but finished 3m behind in 19.53 to become no. 4 on the all-time list; behind them Nickel Ashmeade reduced his pb to 19.91 and Jaysuma Saidy Ndure ran 19.97. This, the second half of the Diamond League finals, was a terrific meeting and threw up other shocks, including Sally Pearson's first 100m hurdles defeat of the year. She was going well, heading for a comfortable win in the 12.5 region, when she clipped the sixth hurdle and tripped over the seventh, falling heavily, and the win by Danielle Carruthers in 12.65 deprived her of the event's $40,000 overall DL prize. It was very good to see the 10,000m restored to the programme at this meeting after its omission in 2009 and 2010 and Kenenisa Bekele returned to winning ways in 26:43.16 after his failure to finish at the Worlds. This was a world best time for 2011, as was Morgan Uceny's 4:00.06 in the women's 1500m, a race in which there were best ever times for 12th to 14th, including 13th in 4:03.68 by world champion Jennifer Simpson. Carmelita Jeter, 100m winner in 10.78, matched Christina Obergföll (javelin) as the only athletes to score maximum points (28) in the Diamond League in 2011. Anna Chicherova, after high jumping 2.05, attempted the world record height of 2.10, and looked good in doing so, only dragging the bar off with her calves on her second attempt and two men were over 22m in the shot, Reese Hoffa beating Christian Cantwell 22.09 to 22.07.

17   IAAF Race Walking Challenge Final, La Coruña, Spain. World champions Valeriy Borchin and Olga Kaniskina maintained their walking supremacy by winning the 10km races and each collected $30,000 first-place prize money. Borchin won in 38:43 from Wang Zhen 38:50 and Chu Yafei 39:07, and Kaniskina in 42:39 from Liu Hong 42:57 and Melanie Seeger 43:09.

17-18   Talence, France. Decastar Multis. With a 6679 total Tatyana Chernova won for the second successive year and sealed her overall success in the IAAF Combined Events Challenge Series for 2011. Hans Van Alphen added 59 points to the Belgian record in winning the decathlon with 8200, but Leonel Suárez, only 7th here with 7889, won the IAAF Challenge ahead of Eelco Sintnicolaas and Mikk Pahapill, respectively 3rd and 2nd here.

18   Amsterdam to Zaandam, Netherlands. Leonard Patrick Komon won the 27th annual Dam tot Damloop 10 miles race in 44:27, just 3 secs outside Haile Gebrselassie's unratified 44:24 world best (at Tilburg 2005) and 18 secs inside Paul Koech's record set on this course in 1997. Komon ran at a sensational pace with 27:17 for the first 10k and his 15k time of 41:26 was just 13 secs outside his world record for the distance, but he was slowed by cold and rain between 11k and 15k.

18   31st **Great North Run, Newcastle to South Shields**, GBR. Winners of Britain's largest race with over 54,000 entrants in the point-to-point and slightly downhill half marathon were Martin Mathathi 58:56 and Lucy Wangui Kabuu 67:06.

18   **Milan**, Italy. Mohamed Aman won the 800m in 1:43.50, overtaking Daniel Rudisha coming off the final bend to end the Kenyan's win streak that stretched back over 3 years and 26 finals (34 races including preliminary rounds). Also at the Notturna meeting Olga Saladuha beat Olga Rypakova 14.94w to 14.69w in the women's triple jump.

18   **Nice,** France. 7th DécaNation (10-event international). 1. USA 133.5, 2. RUS 129, 3. GER 115, 4. FRA 109, 5. CHN 68, 6. ESP 66.5, 7. RSA 66, 8. ENG 33. Top mark was 6.91 by Eloyse Lesueur at long jump.

18   **Tangier**, Morocco. The top mark at 4th edition of this international meeting, for which Hicham El Guerrouj is the meeting director, came in the shot, 21.75 by Dylan Armstrong.

23-25 **South American Junior Championships**, Medellín, Colombia.

23-24 **Commonwealth 24 Hour Championships**, Llandudno, UK. Lizzie Hawker set a women's world road best of 247.076.

24   **5th Avenue Mile, New York**, USA. Winners were Bernard Lagat 3:50.5 and Jennifer Simpson 4:22.3.

25   **Berlin Marathon**, Germany. Patrick Makau set a world record of 2:03:38 in the 38th edition of this race. His 10k splits were 29:17, 58:30, 1:28:38 and 1:57:15, with his 30k time a world record although Peter Kirui 1:28:37 was actually a second ahead at this point, but as a non-finishing pacemaker his time was not eligible for official ratification. Losing his world record was Haile Gebrselassie who was dropped by Makau after 26k and stopped soon afterwards stricken with an asthma attack. One of the pacemakers for the second group, Stephen Chemlany, hung in and finished second in 2:07:55. Also winning by a big margin was Florence Kiplagat in 2:19:44 from Irina Mikitenko 2:22:18, with Paula Radcliffe, returning from childbirth and a barren two years competitively, third in a creditable 2:23:46.

October

9   **Eindhoven**, Netherlands. On a new two loop course for the 28th edition of the race, Jafred Kipchumba took 1:13 off the race record with 2:05:48.

9   Bank of America **Chicago Marathon**, USA. Already assured of winning, for the second successive year, the World Marathon Majors jackpot of $500,000, Liliya Shobukhova improved her Russian record to 2:18:20 for second on the world all-time list. She went hard from the start, through the half in 69:25 and 30k in 1:38:23, better than the official world record, to win by nearly four minutes from Ejegayehu Dibaba, who ran 2:22:09 on her marathon debut. Moses Mosop broke the late Sammy Wanjiru's 2009 course record of 2:05:41 by 4 seconds with Wesley Korir 2:06:15 and Bernard Kipyego 2:06:29 following, There were 35,671 finishers (20,256 men and 15,414 (women), the second largest field in the 34th running of his race. The start time temperature at 7.30 am was 20°C with low humidity; at the finish in sunny Grant Park for the elite runners it was 22°.

16   **Toronto**, Canada. Kenneth Mungara had a fourth successive Scotiabank Waterfront Marathon win with 2:09:51, but the top marks came in the women's race as Korene Jelila took 1:50 off the pb she had set when 4th in this race in 2010 by running 2:22:43. Her Ethiopian compatriot Mare Dibaba was 2nd in 2:23:25. Ed Whitlock ran a world best for an 80 year-old with 3:15:54.

17   **Amsterdam**, Netherlands. Wilson Chebet completed a 2011 double by following his 2:05:27 Rotterdam win with 2:05:53 on the course on which he had made his marathon debut in 2010 with 2:06:12. In second and third places were the third and fourth fastest ever marathon debuts: 2:06:05 by Laban Korir and 2:06:07, also a world junior best, by Eric Ndiema 2:06:07. Six men under 2:07 equalled the all-time record (London 2008 and Boston 2011) and, with the fastest ever 7th and 8th place times, eight under 2:08 added one to the record. Women's winner Tiki Gelana took 6:20 off her pb with a brilliant course record 2:22:08.

17-19 1st **Gulf Countries Games**, Madinat Isa, Bahrain.

23-30 **Pan-American Games**, Guadalajara, Mexico. With a very poor US team, Cuba was by far the most successful nation. Most of their top stars were in action, with Dayron Robles (110mh 13.10), Guillermo Martínez (JT 87.20 CAC record), Yarelys Barrios (DT 55.40), Yipsi Moreno (HT 75.62 for her third successive title) and Misleydis González (SP 18.57) all retaining their titles (from 2007). The first four of the above also set new meeting records – of 14 events in all, many helped by the 1567 metres altitude. Other included 47.99 Cuban record at 400m hurdles by Omar Cisneros, and, completing their brilliant breakthrough seasons, 5.80 Lázaro Borges and 4.75 Yarisley Silva pole vault wins, and 14.92 at triple jump by Caterine Ibargüen. Maurren Maggi long jumped 6.94 for her third Pan-American title, after 1999 and 2007.

26-29   Pan-Arabic Championships, Al Ain, United Arab Emirates.

30   Frankfurt-am-Main, Germany. After winning with 2:04:57 in 2010, Wilson Kipsang won the 30th BMW Frankfurt Marathon with 2:03:42, just four seconds outside the world record. In perfect conditions he was accompanied by five others at halfway in 61:40 and, after 30k in 1:27:49, left pacemaker Peter Kirui at 35k. Levi Matebo was 2nd in 2:05:16 and Albert Matebor 3rd in 2:05:25 with Kirui holding on to 6th in 2:06:31, Kenyans filling the first seven places. Eight of the top ten finishers set pbs and records were 14 men under 2:10 (previous best 12 at Paris 2009), 19 under 2:11 (16 at Paris 2009), 22 under 2:12 (18 at Worlds 2003), 25 under 2:13 (24 at London 1991), and there were best ever place times from 13th to 25th. Kipsang's winnings of 95,000 euros was matched by women's winner Mamitu Daska who ran 2:21:59 after 69:46 at halfway, taking almost a minute and half off the course record.

November

6   New York City Marathon, USA. Geoffrey Mutai became the first man to win the Boston and New York City races in the same year since Rodgers Rop in 2002 and took 2:37 off the course record with his 2:05:05 as 2-3 Emmanuel Mutai 2:06:28 and Tsegaye Kebede 2:07:14 were also inside the old mark. In the women's race Mary Keitany set off on world record pace through halfway in 67:56, but over-reached herself as her second half took 75:42

and she struggled in third in 2:23:38 behind Firehiwot Dado 2:23:15 and Buzunesh Deba 2:23:19. Mutai won $200,000 and Dado $170,000 in prize and bonus money. There were a world marathon record 46,795 finishers (29,867 men & 16,928 women).

12-15   South East Asia Games, Palembang, Malaysia. Troung Thanh Hang achieved a third successive 800m and 1500m double at these biennial Games (and fourth win at 1500m).

13   Atapuerca, Spain. The first IAAF CC Permit meetings of the winter season were won by Imane Merga and Linet Masai.

23   Chiba, Japan. The annual International Ekiden in which men and women run alternate legs of the 42.195k course was won by Kenya in 2:04:40.

27   New Delhi, India. Three men beat the hour, all in pbs, headed by Lelisa Desisa 59:30, in the 7th Airtel Delhi Half marathon, an IAAF Gold Label race. There were also pbs for the first four in the women's race, won by Lucy Wangui Kabuu in 67:04.

December

4   Fukuoka, Japan. Josphat Muchiri Ndambiri, long based in Japan, made his marathon debut in the 65th Fukuoka International race, and won by over a minute in 2:07:36.

11   European Cross-Country Championships, Velenje, Slovenia. Impressive senior champions were Atelaw Bekele of Belgium and Fionnuala Britton of Ireland, but the British contingent were dominant with 12 medals (six gold, five silver and one bronze), the next best being four by France (two of them gold), Russia (one gold), Portugal and Germany. Sergiy Lebid maintained his amazing record of running in all 18 editions of this race, but did not finish.

Combination Women 100m-100mh

	100m	100mh	Points
Gall Devers	10.82	12.33	2467
Glory Alozie	10.90	12.44	2439
Lyudmila Narozhilenko ¶	11.04	12.26	2437
Sally Pearson	11.14	12.28	2416
Yordanka Donkova	11.27	12.21	2404
Virginia Powell/Crawford	11.10	12.45	2402
Olga Shishigina ¶	11.13	12.44	2398
Brigitte Foster-Hylton	11.17	12.45	2390
Michelle Freeman	11.16	12.52	2383
Patricia Girard ¶	11.11	12.59	2383
Vera Komisova	11.26	12.39	2381
Lolo Jones	11.24	12.43	2380
Ginka Zagorcheva	11.38	12.25	2380
Cornelia Oschkenat	11.31	12.45	2366
Michelle Perry	11.34	12.43	2363
Susanna Kallur	11.30	12.49	2361

Recent Marriages

Female	Male	
Lisa Koll USA	Kiel Uhl USA	10.9.11
Irina Litvinenko KAZ	Yevgeniy Ektov KAZ	
Yekaterina Martynova RUS	Yevgeniy Sharmin RUS	
Irina Naumenko KAZ	Dmitriy Karpov KAZ	
Tiffany Ofili GBR	Jeff Porter USA	7.5.11
Joanna Schulz USA	Adam Currie CAN	29.10.11
Aurora Veniero ITA	Emanuele Di Gregorio ITA	19.10.11
Kelli White USA	Robert Wagner	.12.11

ATHLETES OF 2011
By Peter Matthews

Male Athlete of the Year

WHILE THE MOST sensational incident of 2011 was Usain Bolt's false start and thus disqualification in the 100 metres at the World Championships, perhaps the most startling performance came later with Yohan Blake's 200 metres at the Brussels Diamond League final. In 2010 Blake had made a dramatic improvement of his best at the distance from 20.60 to 19.78 in Monaco, but he had run the distance only rarely, recording 20.33, 20.38 and 20.39 in his previous races in 2011. He took advice from training partner Bolt on how to run the event, and despite a sluggish 0.269 reaction time, stormed home well ahead of World silver medallist Walter Dix, 19.26 to 19.53. Blake had also had a stellar year at 100m, winning 7 of 9 finals with ten sub-10 times in all (including two with wind assistance), and ending with five successive victories including taking the World title, in Bolt's absence by a huge margin of 0.16, running 9.92 to Dix's 10.08 into a 1.4 headwind and going on to run 9.82 in Zürich and Berlin. The Jamaicans had also sealed the World Championships with a world record in the 4x100m, their 37.04 taking 0.06 off the time that they had run at the Berlin Olympics. After Nesta Carter and Michael Frater had led the way as they had in Beijing, Blake ran the

third leg and Bolt the anchor (compared to Bolt and Powell in Beijing). So Blake was a major candidate for Male Athlete of the Year.

But so too was Bolt, for apart from his World 100m debacle he was undefeated at 100m; his winning times being successively 9.91, 9.91, 9.88, 9.85 and 9.76, and he was undefeated at 200m winning in 19.86, 20.03 and 20.03 on the Diamond League circuit before showing great resolution by bouncing back from the 100m shock to win the 200m in Daegu in 19.40, three metres clear of Dix.

Other world champions to have undefeated seasons were four with few competitions at their event – Abel Kirui (one marathon), Trey Hardee (two decathlons), Sergey Bakulin (two 50k walks) and Valeriy Borchin (one 10k and three 20k walks) – and Robert Harting in 16 discus competitions. Kirani James won all his seven outdoor competitions at 400m, but had fallen in the NCAA indoor 400m; he thus won 2/3 at 400m indoors (he also won all three 200 races). Mo Farah won all his four 5000m races as well as two of three at 3000m and ran a European record at 10,000m in Eugene, but his near perfect season was just slightly marred by his defeat by Ibrahim Jeylan in the World 10,000m.

Last year's Male Athlete of the Year Daniel Rudisha was again strongly in contention as he was perhaps more dominant at his event than any other male athlete. He lost his last race of the year to the young Ethiopian Mohamed Aman, but by then had won all his ten finals at 800m, by an average margin of 0.97 secs.

Another top athlete to have close to an unbeaten season was Dayron Robles, 12/14 at 110m hurdles and those two losses were stumbling in last in Barcelona and his disqualification after crossing the line first at the Worlds.

Above all 2011 was the year of the marathon but so many (Kenyans) contributed that there was not just one standout performer at the event. Patrick Makau set the world record of 2:03:38 in Berlin, but had been third in London, where the winner was Emmanuel Mutai, who was later well beaten in New York by Geoffrey Mutai, who had run the fastest ever time of 2:03:02 on the aided course in Boston. Also Wilson Kipsang won both his marathons, missing the world record by only four seconds

Selections for World Top Ten

My selection of the top 10 athletes of 2010 together with the lists compiled by international experts polled by *Track & Field News* and those of *Athletics International* readers:

	PJM	TFN	AI
David Rudisha	1	1	2
Usain Bolt	2	2	1
Yohan Blake	3	4	3
Mo Farah	4	6	4
Robert Harting	5	3	6
Kirani James	6	7	5
Geoffrey Mutai	7	5	8
Valeriy Borchin	8	11	-
Dayron Robles	9	9	-
Christian Taylor	10	10	9
Trey Hardee		8	-
Patrick Makau		17	7
Jesse Williams		–	10

Note *Track & Field News* (TFN) does not consider road races, other than the marathon, or cross-country action.

in Frankfurt, and Abel Kirui gave a superb display to win in Daegu.

Apart from the 4x100m and marathon, world records set by men in 2011 were all at distance events: Moses Mosop ran 25,000m in 1:12:25.4 en route to 1:26:47.4 at 30,000m and Yohan Diniz walked 50,000m on the track in 3:35:27.2. Pacemaker Peter Kirui led in 1:27:37 at 30k during the Berlin Marathon, but as he did not finish the race, world record credit will go to Patrick Makau 1:27:38 behind him.

100 Metres

JAMAICANS TAKE THE top three rankings at 100m. Usain Bolt was unbeaten until his shock disqualification for a false start in the World final and ended the year with the world's fastest time, 9.76 in Brussels, but he never met his young training companion Yohan Blake, and Blake's clear World win followed by 9.82 runs in Zürich and Berlin afterwards gives him the top spot on honours won in an exceptionally close call. Blake lost twice, each time by just 0.01 sec, in 9.98 to Daniel Bailey in Strasbourg and in 10.07 to Asafa Powell at the Jamaican Champs. Powell had to miss the Worlds through a groin injury but was well beaten with 9.95 by Blake at Zürich; he completed his eighth successive year in the world top three. Tyson Gay was the fourth fastest at 9.79 but persistent problems with his right hip meant that he was restricted to just three 100m races. A record seven men had beaten 9.90 in 2010, but in 2011 that record increased to 10, and 20 beat 10.00 compared to the previous record 14 in 2008. The 100th best was also a new record at 10.21. In all there were 61 wind-legal sub-10.00 times plus 20 with excess wind assistance. Leaders were Blake 8+2w, Powell 8+1w, Steve Mullings 7+1w, Nesta Carter 6, Mike Rodgers 5+1w, Bolt 5, Christophe Lemaitre 4, Michael Frater 3+2w. Walter Dix only had one sub-10 time, but did that 9.94 to win the US title and took World silver and was third in Zürich in the Diamond League final. Third and fourth in Daegu were Kim Collins, who made a marvellous comeback to the top, and Lemaitre. Collins started the year slowly but was in great form at the end, beating Carter 2-1, although beaten by Lerone Clarke at the Pan-American Games in October. Michael Frater was 4th with Collins 5th and Carter 6th in Zürich, but Carter beat Frater 5-2 overall and was 2-1 v Rodgers. Rodgers, 3rd in the US Champs was 4-0 v Richard Thompson and 2-0 v Frater but a stimulant suspension may cost him his last four races. Bailey was 5th in the Worlds to Carter's 7th, but did not have as good depth of marks. There are no newcomers to the top ten and just outside was Justin Gatlin, 2nd at the US Champs and up on win-loss against fellow World semi-finalists Thompson and Keston Bledman. Mullings failed a drugs test for the second time (when 3rd at the Jamaican Champs) and thus faces a life ban – and he is not ranked.

Rodgers had run the fastest indoor 60m time with 6.48A to win the US title with 6.50 at low altitude, a time matched by Collins and Lemaitre.

Most times at 10.05 or faster: Carter 9, Blake 8+2w, Powell 8+1w, Rodgers 7+1w (&2dq), Dix 6+1w, Bolt, Lemaitre 6; Frater 5+2w, Thompson 5+1w, Collins 5, D Bailey 3+1w, Gay, Dwain Chambers 3; Travis Padgett, Jeff Demps, Clarke 2+2w, Keston Bledman 2+1w (Mullings 7+1w).

> 1. Blake, 2. Bolt, 3. Powell, 4. Dix, 5. Lemaitre, 6. Collins, 7. Carter, 8. D Bailey, 9, Rodgers, 10. Frater, 11. Gatlin

200 Metres

USAIN BOLT, RANKED top for the fourth successive year, shook off his 100m disappointment to win the 200m in brilliant style at the Worlds with 19.40 from Walter Dix 19.70 and had won his other three 200m races earlier. Dix, who had won all his five 200m competitions prior to Daegu, then improved to 19.53 in the Diamond League final in Brussels, but that was behind the sensational 19.26 of Yohan Blake. Blake had run just three 200m races before then in 2011, beaten in Ostrava by Marvin Anderson. As usual most of the top men ran the distance infrequently, but the World 3-4-5 Christophe Lemaitre, Jaysuma Saidy Ndure and Nickel Ashmeade were the other three men to beat 20 secs. Next fastest was Rakieem Salaam, but after his 20.05 he was only 6th at the NCAAs and 7th at the US Champs, whereas Maurice Mitchell was 1st and 4th in those, behind the US 1-2-3 Dix, Darvis Patton and Jeremy Dodson. Patton did not make the World final where 6-7 were Brazilian champion Bruno de Barros and Trinidad champion Rondel Sorrillo with Alonso Edward a non-finisher. Ashmeade, Saidy Ndure and Sorrillo were 3-4-5 in Brussels. Placing third in World semis were Jamaican third placer Mario Forsythe, 2-0 v Sorrillo and 1-1 v Anderson and Patton, and Femi Ogunode, who was Asian, World Military and Arab champion, but with a best of 20.41 without as good a set of times. There were five newcomers to the rankings as as for the 100m, 100th best was a new record, at 20.62 (previous best 20.66)

Most times at 20.30 or better: Dix 7+1w, Bolt 5, Lemaitre 4+1w, Ashmeade, Saidy Ndure, Salaam 3, (Mullings 5)

> 1. Bolt, 2. Blake, 3. Dix, 4. Lemaitre, 5. Saidy Ndure, 6. Ashmeade, 7. Barros, 8. Sorrillo, 9. Edward, 10. Forsythe

400 Metres

KIRANI JAMES, THE 2009 World Youth and 2010 World Junior champion, had an unbeaten season outdoors, including a most impressive

World Championships win and a fastest time of 44.36 in the Diamond League final at Zürich. LaShawn Merritt returned from his drugs bans with second to Jermaine Gonzales in Stockholm and to James at the Worlds after running the world's fastest time of the year, 44.35, in his heat in Daegu. Rondell Bartholomew and Nery Brenes were joint third fastest at 44.65, but Brenes had a best of just 45.29 before his 44.65A to win the Pan-American title and Bartholomew was 6th at the Worlds and beaten 5-0 by Gonzales, who was 4th at the Worlds between the Borlée twins; Kevin, beaten in their three other clashes by Gonzales, was 3rd and Jonathan 5th in Daegu. Jonathan beat Kevin 44.78 to 44.97 in their only other meeting in their last race of the year, in Brussels. Selection of 7-10 was difficult. Tony McQuay, 2nd to James in the NCAAs, won the US title from Jeremy Wariner and Greg Nixon, but after that had just one race (46.76 in his Daegu heat) and Wariner, a shadow of his old self after seven years in the top two, called a halt to his season in July, while Nixon, 5th in his World semi, had a best thereafter of 45.16. Tabarie Henry and Femi Ogunode made the World final, but the ever-dependable Chris Brown, 3rd semi in Daegu and 5th Zürich, did better. Although only 3rd at the Bahamas Champs behind Demetrius Pinder (4th NCAA, 7sf Worlds, 1st NCAA indoors) and Ramon Miller, Brown beat Angelo Taylor 3-0.

Most sub-45.00 times: Merritt 5, James 4+1i, Gonzales, K Borlée 4, McQuay 3

1. James, 2. Merritt, 3. Gonzales, 4. K Borlée,
5. J Borlée, 6. Bartholomew, 7. Brown,
8. McQuay, 9. Wariner, 10. Henry

800 Metres

DAVID RUDISHA RAN the three fastest times, 1:41.33, 1:42.61 and 1:42.91, and had another hugely impressive year, top for the fourth time in five years. He won all his eleven 800m races with the exception of the last when the 17 year-old Mohamed Aman edged him in Milan. Before then, Abubaker Kaki, as in 2010, got closest, 0.22 behind in London with 1:43.13 for second on the world list. Kaki and Yuriy Borzakovskiy (ranked for the 11th time) took World silver and bronze and were followed in Daegu by Marcin Lewandowski, Nick Symmonds, Adam Kszczot, Alfred Kirwa Yego and Aman. Kszczot was, however, clearly the top Pole, beating Lewandowski 4-1. Asbel Kiprop competed at 1500m at the Worlds, but ran the year's third fastest time of 1:43.16 behind Rudisha and ahead of Symmonds in Monaco, and also won in Doha and was third in the DL final in Brussels behind Rudisha and Aman (2nd in the World Youths to Leonard Kosencha, who had no other top races), with Lewandowski 4th and Kirwa Yego 5th. Khadevis Robinson, 2nd USA, was next best on times and was 2-1 v Kirwa Yego,

7th Worlds, who edges other Kenyans David Mutua, Boaz Lalang and Jackson Kivuva and Pan-American champion Kléberson Davide. The 100th best man at 1:46.50 improved the record (1:46.54 in 1999).

Most times sub-1:45: Rudisha 11, Kaki 7, Aman, Lewandowski, Kirwa Yego 5; Kszczot, Symonds, Robinson, Lalang 3

1. Rudisha, 2. Kaki, 3. Borzakovskiy, 4. Kszczot,
5. Aman, 6. Kiprop, 7. Lewandowski,
8. Symmonds, 9. Robinson, 10. Kirwa Yego

1500 Metres

NO ATHLETE BROKE 3:30 for 1500m this year, but the standard in depth was unprecedented as the 100th best of 3:37.77 compared to the previous best of 3:38.42 in 1997. No athlete achieved complete superiority, although a talented Kenyan quartet headed the world lists and rankings. Asbel Kiprop retained the top ranking from Silas Kiplagat as these men went 1-2 at the World Championships and ran the two fastest times of the year – Kiprop 3:30.46 at Rieti and Kiplagat 3:30.47 at Monaco. It was close, however, as overall Kiplagat beat Kiprop 3-2 but was 4-3 down to a newcomer to the top ten, Nixon Chepseba, who won the Diamond League final at Zürich with Kiplagat 2nd and Kiprop only 7th behind Haron Keitany, Mohamed Moustaoui, Augustine Choge and Mekonnen Gebremedhin. Crucially Chepseba was only 5th at the Kenyan Champs (won by Kiplagat from Kiprop and Daniel Komen) so was not in the Kenyan World team, and nor was Choge who was 7th, but who had a big win at the end of the year, with 3:31.14 at Berlin from Abdelaati Iguider and Chepseba, or Keitany (Achilles injury). Third and fourth at the Worlds were Matt Centrowitz and Manuel Olmedo, but neither had the credentials for a top ten ranking; Olmedo ran his best time of 3:34.44 when 10th at Saint-Denis, a place ahead of Centrowitz, who was slightly quicker with his best 3:34.46 for 10th at Monaco. Better were the Moroccans Iguider and Moustaoui, 5th and 6th at the Worlds, and 2-2 in their clashes. The eight fastest mile times of the year came at the Prefontaine Classic in Eugene, won by Keitany in 3:49.09, with Kiplagat, Kiprop, Gebremedhin and Caleb Ndiku also under 3:50. Keitany was 4-2 against World 7th placer Gebremedhin, who was 3-2 v Iguider and 2-1 v Ilhan Tabul Özbilen of Turkey (the former William Biwott of Kenya). Amine Laâlou faded to 7th in the World semi, but had fast wins in Turin and Saint-Denis and was 4th at Rieti in his only other 1500m races. Leonel Manzano won the celebrated Emsley Carr Mile in London from Bernard Lagat and Choge but had a hamstring injury at the Worlds.

The year's fastest indoor times were run in the Birmingham GP won in 3:33.23 by Choge from Derese Mekonnen.

Most times sub-3:34 or 3:51M: Kiplagat 8, Chepseba 7, Kiprop, Gebremedhin, Komen 5; Moustaoui 4, Özbilen, Iguider, Keitany, C Ndiku, Collins Cheboi 3, Choge 2+1i
> 1. Kiprop, 2. Kiplagat, 3. Chepseba, 4. Keitany,
> 5. Choge, 6. Iguider, 7. Moustaoui,
> 8. Gebremedhin, 9. Özbilen, 10. Laâlou

3000 Metres/2 Miles

YENEW ALAMIREW RAN the year's fastest times both indoors, 7:27.80 at Stuttgart followed under 7:30 by Augustine Choge and Eliud Kipchoge, and outdoors, 7:27.26 at Doha. The seven fastest times of the year outdoors came at Doha with Edwin Soi, Kipchoge and Choge 2-4 under 7:30 then Vincent Chepkok, Daniel Komen and Moses Kipsiro and a record 16 men under 7:38. The next three fastest times came at Rieti from Bernard Lagat, Chepkok and Thomas Longosiwa (9th Doha). Tariku Bekele was 8th in Doha and 4th in Rieti and also 4th in the Prefontaine 2 Miles, won by Lagat in 8:13.62 from Soi and Isiah Koech with Kipchoge 6th. Lagat ran the year's fastest 2 miles with 8:10.07 indoors in New York.

5000 Metres

MO FARAH MOVED from the edge of the world top ten to distance supremacy in 2011, as he won all his five races at 5000m, indoors at Birmingham, and then convincing wins outdoors in Birmingham and Monaco, adding the UK title, before using his trademark long sprint to victory in the World Champs, even outkicking the redoubtable Bernard Lagat. The year's three fastest times were run at Monaco: Farah's British record 12:53.11 followed by Lagat, a North American record 12:53.60, and Isiah Koech 12:54.18 with Imane Merga, Thomas Longosiwa and Eliud Kipchoge also under 13 minutes, a time bettered in 2011 by 13 men with 22 times outdoors and 2 indoors. Merga led the way with four sub-13 times, but was disqualified for obstruction after finishing third at the Worlds. Dejene Gebremeskel thus took the bronze with Koech 4th, Abera Kuma 5th, Longosiwa 6th and Kipchoge 7th. Other fast races were in Rome, won by Merga from Koech, Vincent Chepkok and eight men to 13:00.15, and the Diamond League final in Brussels with 1-2-3 under 13 minutes: Merga, Longosiwa and Chepkok, and Tariku Bekele 4th. Chepkok was only 8th at the Kenyan Champs (won by Koech), but beat Gebremeskel 2-0. With malaria and typhoid Moses Kipsiro was held to just one 5000m (10th in Rome) before winning the African Games title in October from Yenew Alamirew, who beat his compatriot Kuma 2-0 in their clashes, but who was just behind T Bekele in the one race in which they met, 7th and 8th at Monaco.

Most times sub 13:06: Merga, Chepkok 4; Gebremeskel, Kipchoge 3.

> 1. Farah, 2, Lagat, 3. Merga, 4. Koech,
> 5. Chepkok, 6. Gebremeskel, 7. Longosiwa,
> 8. Kipchoge, 9. T Bekele. 10. Alamirew

10,000 Metres

KENENISA BEKELE RAN the year's fastest time, 26:43.16, as he made a fine return from two years out with a calf injury to win the 10,000m at the Van Damme Memorial meeting in Brussels – and it was good to see the return of this race after two years off the programme at this great meeting. But three weeks earlier Bekele had dropped out of the World Championship race in which Ibrahim Jeylan had produced a fantastic finish to beat Mo Farah, who had looked all over a winner on the first half of the last lap. Jeylan was only 5th in his opening 10k track race of the year in Kobe, but went on to three wins – Kitami, Worlds and African Games. Farah had set a European record 26:46.57 to win in Eugene. The 17 best times of the year were set in these races in Brussels and Eugene and 16 men under 27 minutes easily beat the previous best for any year, 9 in 2007. World bronze medallist Imane Merga was 2nd in Eugene, where 3rd place went to Joseph Bett, later 7th in the Kenyan Champs and 11th in Brussels. The other man to combine those two fast races was Lucas Rotich, 2nd in 26:43.98 in Brussels, after 12th in Eugene and 10th in the Kenyan Champs. That last race was won in 27:32.1 (worth much faster at low altitude) by Peter Kirui, who went on to 6th at the Worlds. Kenyan 2nd placer Wilson Kiprop could not run in Daegu due to injury and the 3rd man Martin Mathathi had won at Kobe and was 5th at the Worlds, a place behind Zersenay Tadese, who had been 5th in Eugene. Galen Rupp was 3rd in Brussels in a North American record 26:48.00, having earlier won the US title and been 7th in Daegu and the man with the deepest collection of marks was Paul Tanui, who had six races under 27:55. He had two wins and a third (at Kobe) in Japan, with 4th in Eugene and 5th at the Kenyan Champs as well as 9th at the Worlds. Sileshi Sihine returned for 6th in Eugene and 8th at the Worlds. Tanui (also 9th in 2010) was the only one of the 2010 top ten to rank again.

> 1. Jeylan, 2. Farah, 3. Merga, 4. K Bekele,
> 5. Tadese, 6. Mathathi, 7. Kirui, 8. Rupp,
> 9. Tanui, 10. Bett

Half Marathon

ZERSENAY TADESE MISSED his world record by just seven seconds with 58:30 at Lisbon in March and also won at Porto in 59:30, in a year in which 21 men beat the 1 hour barrier but there was no World Championship. The best depth of times came, as in 2010, with five men under 1 hour in Den Haag, a race won in 59:37 by Lelisa Desisa, who also won in Delhi in 59:30. Other major winners were Mathew Kisorio, 58:46 at Philadelphia from Sammy

Kitwara 58:48, Martin Mathathi, 58:56 in the Great North Run, and Deribe Merga, 59:24 at Ra's Al Khaymah. Kisorio also won the Stramilano in 60:03. Geoffrey Kipsang had wins in 60:38 and 60:02 before 2nd in Delhi in 59:31. Haile Gebrselassie won his two half marathons of the year in 60:18 and 61:29.

Marathon

WHAT A YEAR it was for the marathon, with the fastest ever times run by Geoffrey Mutai 2:03:02 and Moses Mosop 2:03:06 on the overall downhill point-to-point course in Boston, this year strongly wind assisted, and the world record by Patrick Makau 2:03:38 in Berlin. Then Wilson Kipsang just missed that new world record with 2:03:42 in Frankfurt. Records were smashed for depth of marks with 7 men under 2:05, 13 under 2:06, 29 under 2:07 and 52 under 2:08 on all courses and individual race records being set with 8 men under 2:07:30 in Amsterdam and best ever for places 13 to 26 at Frankfurt as well as 1-5 and 9 at Boston if one includes that course. All the top men had two top class marathons, and of the above men: Geoffrey Mutai added a second American win with a consummate victory in New York, 1:22 clear of Emmanuel Mutai (London winner in 2:04:40), Makau was third in London after falling earlier in the race, Kipsang won at Lake Biwa and Mosop won at Chicago. Special mention must be made of Abel Kirui, whose World gold came in his only marathon but whose 2:07:38 came with a wonderful second half and in tough conditions. Silver went, 2:28 behind, to Vincent Kipruto, who was 2nd in Rotterdam in 2:05:33, 6 secs behind Wilson Chebet, who also ran 2:05:53 to win in Amsterdam, and bronze to Feyisa Lelisa, who had been 7th in Rotterdam. Levi Matebo Omari won in Barcelona and was 2nd in Frankfurt where Albert Matebor (1st Verona, 2nd Gold Coast) was 3rd. Others who had two top results included: Bernard Kipyego 2nd Paris and 3rd Chicago; Tsegay Kebede 5th London and 3rd New York; Gebreziabger Gebremariam 3rd Boston and 4th New York; Robert Kiprono Cheruiyot 6th Boston and 5th Boston. London second placer Martin Lel had no other races.

10th and 100th bests (including Boston) of 2:05:33 and 2:09:13 compared to 2:05:52 and 2:09:31 in 2010, 2:06:14 and 2:09:53 in 2009, and 2:06:25 and 2:10:22 in 2008. In the world top 100 there were 60 Kenyans and 27 Ethiopians.

    1. G Mutai, 2. E Mutai, 3. Makau, 4. Kipsang,
    5. Kirui, 6. Mosop, 7. Chebet, 8. Kipruto,
    9. Omari, 10. Lel

3000 Metres Steeplechase

BRIMIN KIPRUTO MISSED the world record by just 0.01 with 7:53.64 at Monaco, where he was followed home by Ezekiel Kemboi in a pb 7:55.76 and Paul Kipsiele Koech 7:57.32, the three fastest times of the year. Kemboi, however, is top for the third successive year as he retained his world title clearly from Kipruto. Koech had the best depth of times with five of the nine sub-8:05 times run in the year, but paid once again for his inability to run to form at the high-altitude Kenyan Championships, in which he was 7th (1-2-3 as Kipruto, Richard Matelong and Abraham Chirchir) and thus not selected for the World team. Mahiedine Mekhissi contested the event only three times but after 4th at Oslo behind Koech, Kipruto and Roba Gari won at Saint-Denis in 8:02.09 for fourth on the world list and was the bronze medallist in Daegu where he was followed by Bouabdellah Tahri, Gari, Jacob Araptany, Matelong, Ion Luchianov, Hamid Ezzine and Benjamin Kiplagat. Of those men Gari had the best depth of times, but he was matched by junior Hillary Yego, both having five under 8:13, and Yego had a 2-1 advantage plus 4-1 over Matelong. Matelong was 2-2 v Kiplagat, who was third to Kemboi and Koech in the Diamond League final in Zürich. Three more Kenyans broke 8:10: Bernard Nganga, Jonathan Ndiku and Patrick Langat (now Tarik Langat Akdag of Turkey).

Most times under 8:15: Koech 8, Kemboi 6, Yego, Gari 5; Matelong, Kiplagat, Ruben Ramolefi 4; Kipruto, Jairus Kipchoge 3.

    1. Kemboi, 2. Kipruto, 3. Koech, 4. Mekhissi,
    5. Tahri, 6. Yego, 7. Gari, 8. Matelong,
    9. Kiplagat, 10. Nganga

110 Metres Hurdles

DAYRON ROBLES WAS clearly back as the world number one in 2011 with 12 wins in 14 races. He came in last in Barcelona in 14.93 and was rightly disqualified at the Worlds for impeding Liu Xiang but nonetheless he crossed the line first. Gaining on Robles, Liu could have won that race but had to settle for the silver medal behind the new star Jason Richardson. David Oliver ran the one sub-13 sec. time of the year, 12.94 in Eugene, but after six wins in seven races up to winning the US title began to lose his top form with a lead leg injury and did not win another race, easily his slowest time of the year coming with 13.44 at the Worlds where he lost the bronze medal to Andy Turner. Overall Robles beat Richardson 6-2 and Richardson had that same win-loss record against Oliver, making a breakthrough in Europe and sustaining it to the end of the year after 3rd in the US Champs. Liu only had four competitions, but was 2-1 v Oliver (winning in Shanghai and 2nd in Eugene) as well as winning the Asian title. Next after the big four was US 2nd placer Aries Merritt who beat Dwight Thomas 4-3; they were 5= and dnf in the World final. Thomas had a 6-3 record against Turner, who had a very solid season and was 3-1 v Terrence Trammell (US 4th). Joel Brown was third in his semi at the US Champs but had a long season of sustained quality and was 3-2 v Turner although 0-2 v Trammell. Other highly prolific competitors were Jeff Porter (the only ranking newcomer) and Ty Akins, 6-6 in their clashes and 5th and 8th at the US Champs (6th Ronnie Ash, 7th Dominic Berger). 100th best of 13.67 ties the record.

Indoors Oliver had the three fastest 60m times, 7.37 and 7.40 at Stuttgart. and 7.40 at Karlsruhe.

Most times under 13.30: Oliver 14+2w, Richardson 14+1w, Robles 11+1dq, Thomas 8+1w, Merritt 7+2w, Liu 5, Brown 4, Ash 2+1w, Omo Osaghae 1+5w.

    1. Robles, 2. Richardson, 3. Liu, 4. Oliver,
    5. Merritt, 6. Thomas, 7. Turner, 8. Trammell,
    9. Brown, 10. Porter

400 Metres Hurdles

L.J. VAN ZYL ran the four fastest times of the year, yet ranks third. He won his first five races, starting with 47.66A at Pretoria and matching that time at Ostrava. Then he was 4th at New York and Monaco, 3rd at the Worlds and 8th in Berlin. The seventh and eighth fastest men, David Greene and Javier Culson took World gold and silver and Greene was top on win-loss, 4-2 v Culson, 3-2 v van Zyl and 2-2 v Bershawn Jackson, with Culson 2-1 v van Zyl and Jackson. Jackson slipped a little to 6th at the Worlds behind Félix Sánchez and Cornel Fredericks, but had two 2nds and a 3rd in Diamond League races. Joining van Zyl and Jackson in running sub-48 times were Jeshua Anderson and Angelo Taylor, when 1st and 3rd at the US Champs (Jackson 2nd) and Taylor also ran 47.97 at Monaco, with Omar Cisneros winning the Pan-American title in 47.99A, well clear of Isa Phillips and Sánchez. Anderson also won NCAA and World Universities titles but went out in a semi at the Worlds, where Taylor was 7th. Cisneros was last in his semi at the Worlds but had earlier won all his four 400mh races, without meeting the world élite. Fredericks had a very solid season, ending with 3rd in the Diamond League final in Brussels behind Culson and Greene and ahead of Jehue Gordon (3rd semi Worlds) and Sánchez; he was 2-0 v Anderson. US 4th placer Michael Tinsley was 2-0 v Sánchez and Gordon and 3-0 v US 5th placer Johnny Dutch, and Gordon was 5-2 v Sánchez, who just misses a ranking. The 2007 and 2009 world champion Kerron Clement was unable to regain full fitness; he started with 48.74 behind Justin Gaymon in Kingston, but his only other sub-49 time was 48.91 in his heat at the Worlds before 52.11 in his semi.

Most times under 48.60: Jackson 10, Culson 8, Greene 5, Clement, Taylor 3

    1. Greene, 2. Culson, 3. van Zyl, 4. Jackson,
    5. Fredericks, 6. Anderson, 7. Taylor, 8. Cisneros,
    9. Tinsley, 10. Gordon

High Jump

THIS YEAR ACTION in the intense indoor season was less dominant than in recent years as there were 17 performances by 11 men at 2.32 or higher indoors compared to 36 by 13 men outdoors. Ivan Ukhov cleared 2.38 three times indoors and Jesse Williams was best outdoors, with 2.37 to win the US title. Although not perfect, as he won 5 of 11 competitions outdoors and 2 of 5 indoors, Williams was the world number one, He won the World title with 2.35 and had six competitions outdoors and one indoors over 2.33. Aleksey Dmitrik also jumped 2.35 at the Worlds, but lost on count-back and he won the Russian title with 2.36. This was a top competition as Aleksandr Shustov was 2nd with 2.36 and 3-4 went to Ukhov and Andrey Silnov on 2.34. Dmitrik was 2-1 outdoors (0-1 indoors) against Silnov, who was 5-2 v Shustov outdoors (0-3 in) but whose fourth place meant that he was not on the Russian team in Daegu. Ukhov and Shustov were 5= and 8th at the Worlds, having been much better indoors, where Ukhov won all seven competitions and Shustov was 3-0 v Silnov and 3-2 v Dmitrik. Ukhov won the European Indoor title with 2.38 with 2nd Jaroslav Bába and 3rd Shustov, both 2.34. Trevor Barry came through to take the World bronze medal and, although without the depth of top marks of some others, was 3-1 against Donald Thomas (11 Worlds), 3-0 v Bába and 4-0 v Ukhov. Barry was one of five men who cleared 2.32 at the Worlds, but although last of those in 7th place, the highly promising Mutaz Essa Barshim, Asian champion with 2.35, had a good overall record, 3-1 v Shustov and Bába (4th Worlds), and 2-1 v Dmytro Demyanyuk (12=), but he was 2-3 down to Ukhov, who while inconsistent was also third at the Diamond League final in Zürich. This was won by Dimítrios Hondrokoúkis, who had only five outdoor competitions but was 5= at the Worlds, from Barry, Ukhov, Williams, Demyanyuk and Barshim. Raúl Spank was 9th Worlds and 7th Zürich; 4-4 v Bába, but 2-3 to Demyanyuk, whose top mark came with 2.35 to win the European Team event. Ranking the top men was very difficult this year!

Most competitions over 2.30m (outdoors/in): Williams 9/2, Barshim 8, Ukhov 6/8, Dmitrik 6/1, Bába 5/2, Silnov & Thomas 5/1, Hondrokoúkis 5, Shustov 4/6, Demyanyuk 4/2, Spank 3/2, Barry 3, Sergey Mudrov 1/3, Konstadínos Baniótis 0/3.

    1. Williams, 2. Dmitrik (3), 3. Ukhov (2), 4. Silnov,
    5, Barshim, 6. Barry (7), 7. Shustov (6), 8. Bába,
    9. Hondrokoúkis, 10. Demyanyuk (-); Spank –
    (10). (Including indoors).

Pole Vault

PAWEL WOJCIECHOWSKI MADE a huge breakthrough from a 2010 best of 5.60 to a Polish indoor record of 5.86 (and 4th wth 5.71 at the European Indoors), but he had a slow start to the outdoor season with no higher than 5.52 at his first eight meetings. Then he cleared 5.70 to win the European U23 title, 5.81 to win the World Military title, and a national record 5.91 at Szczecin before winning the Worlds with 5.90. Extraordinary stuff but is just six wins in 15 outdoor meetings (and 5 in 7 indoors) enough for top ranking against Renaud Lavillenie, who won 9 of 15 outdoors and 7 of 9 indoors with a best of 6.03 to win the European Indoor title and 5.90 outdoors? Another to step up a class was Lázaro Borges who went from 5.70 (2008) to 5.75 before 5.85 and 5.90 for World silver ahead of Lavillenie, against whom he was 2-1. Borges went on to clear 5.81 in Rieti and 5.80 to win the Pan-American title. Lavillenie had 7 outdoor and 7 indoor competitions over 5 80m to 3 and 1 by Wojciechowski and 3 by Borges. World fourth placer and World Universities champion Lukasz Michalski was 7-2 v Wojciechowski, but 1-2 against Konstadínos Filippídis (6th Worlds). Filippídis, who won the Diamond League final on count-back from Lavillenie with Malte Mohr 3rd, was 4-2 (0-2 indoors) v Mohr, who was 5th at the Worlds and 3rd at the European Indoors. Mateusz Didenkow, who cleared 5.75 for World Universities 2nd and Worlds 7th, made it three Poles in the top rankings. Maksym Mazuryk, who had cleared 5.86 and 5.82 indoors, was over 5.70 in three of his four outdoor competitions, but did not compete after winning the European Team event (held indoors) at 5.72 in early June. Derek Miles, and Jeremy Scott were 1st and 2nd at the US Champs, and 3-3 outdoors, but Scott was ahead at the Worlds, 9= to 13th, both at 5.65. Scott was 2nd at the Pan-American Games, where World 8th placer Fábio da Silva was only 5th. Dmitriy Starodubtsev (12th Worlds) cleared 5.90 twice indoors in December. The former number one Steve Hooker was unable to overcome a knee injury and had a best of 5.60, no heighting at the Worlds.

Most competitions over 5.70m (outdoors/in): Lavillenie 11/7, Mohr 8/6, Borges 7, Michalski 6, Wojciechowski 4/3, Filippídis 4/2, Didenkow 4, Mazuryk 3/5, Scott 3/2, Otto 3, Romain Mesnil 2/2, Miles 2/1, Starodubtsev 1/3.

> 1. Lavillenie, 2. Wojciechowski, 3. Borges,
> 4. Michalski, 5. Filippídis (6), 6. Mohr (5),
> 7. Didenkow (8), 8. Mazuryk (7), 9. Scott,
> 10. Starodubtsev. (Including indoors).

Long Jump

DWIGHT PHILLIPS PRODUCED one of the great come through performances to take his fourth World title. He jumped 8.23 in qualifying and then 8.31 and 8.45 in the final. Yet his record prior to Daegu, for which as defending champion he had a wild card entry, was 4th Shanghai 8.07, 6th Hengelo 7.97 and 10th US Champs 7.89w. He did not fare well afterwards either with 4th Zürich 7.87 and 2nd Berlin 8.05, so there is little doubt that top ranking goes to Mitchell Watt, 2nd in Daegu with 8.33 and with four of the top five jumps of the year, 8.54, 8.45 and 8.44 twice, who won 9/13 in 2011. Ngonidzashe Makusha took the World bronze and was otherwise undefeated outdoors and won 2/4 indoors; he was NCAA champion indoors and out and also won at the DL final in Zürich. With many of the world's best showing inconsistency, next best were World 4th and 6th placers, Pan-Arab champion Yahya Berrabah and European Team and U23 champion Aleksandr Menkov. Chris Tomlinson was injured when 11th at the Worlds but beat his compatriot Greg Rutherford (dnq 15 Worlds) 3-1; he improved the British record to 8.35 when 2nd at Saint-Denis and was 2nd in London with 8.30. Irving Saladino was 1st with 8.40 and 4th with 8.14 in those two competitions and also won at Hengelo with 8.38w, but failed at the Worlds with just 7.84 in qualifying. Luva Maniyonga was 2-2 v compatriot Khotso Mokoena but well ahead 5th to 15th at the Worlds and he also won at the African Games. Marquise Goodwin and Will Claye were 1-2 at the US Champs after 4th and 3rd at the NCAAs (behind Makusha and Damar Forbes) and went on to 13th and 9th at the Worlds. Su Xionfeng beat Goodwin for the World Universities title but jumped only 7.03 in the World qualifying round. Rutherford had a 3-1 advantage over World 7th placer Christian Reif, who had mixed form, and Sebastian Bayer did not have much outdoors to back up his World 8th place apart from easily beating Reif to win the German title, but indoors he won European and German titles.

Most competitions over 8.15m (outdoors/in): Watt 9+1w, Menkov 6+1i, Berrabah 4+2w, Su 4. Tomlinson & Rutherford 3+2w, Louís Tsátoumas 3+1i, Mokoena 3+1w, Saladino & Reif 3; Makusha 2+1i+2w, Claye 2+1w, Bayer 2+1i

> 1. Watt, 2. Makusha, 3. Phillips, 4. Berrabah,
> 5. Menkov, 6. Tomlinson, 7. Saladino,
> 8. Rutherford, 9. Maniyonga, 10. Reif.

Triple Jump

TWO SUPERB YOUNG talents headed the world lists. Teddy Tamgho set world indoor records at 17.91 for the French title and 17.92 (twice) at the European Indoors. He also jumped 17.91 outdoors (in Lausanne) but his summer season was restricted to four wins in seven competitions and he had three no jumps in failing to qualify at the European U23s and was unable to compete again through injury. Then Christian Taylor, a year younger than Tamgho at 21, leaped to the best distance of the year with his fifth round 17.96 at the World Championships. This followed other big jumps, 17.80w to win the NCAA title and 17.68 to win at the London GP and an overall record of five wins in eight competitions outdoors and two in four indoors. He had close rivalry with his University of Florida teammate Will Claye, and indeed they were 3-3 outdoors and 1-1 indoors. Phillips Idowu was a model of consistency apart from fading to 5th in the Diamond League final in Brussels and was at his best with 17.77 for the World silver; his six competitions (including one indoors) over 17.50 compared to seven by Tamgho (four indoors) and three by Taylor. Alexis Copello was fourth, 3cm behind Claye at the Worlds, but had much greater depth of competition; he was 3rd in both Doha and Lausanne, Tamgho's two DL wins. Sheryf El-Sheryf produced an extraordinary 17.72 to win the European U23 title, but this was a one-off as his next best was 16.93 for 2nd in Brussels and he was 12th at the Worlds. Nelson Évora made an encouraging return to form from only 6th at the European Teams to win the World Universities title and place 5th at the Worlds a place ahead of Christian Olsson, who was 1-1 v Arnie David Girat (dnq 13 Worlds). Girat was 2-1 against Leevan Sands and Benjamin Compaoré, 7th and 8th at the Worlds, but Compaoré had a big win in Brussels. Indoors Fabrizio Donato produced Italian records of 17.70 and 17.73 at the European Indoors to take silver and Marian Oprea 17.62 for bronze behind Tamgho, but their outdoor bests were Donato 17.17 and Oprea 17.00 and they were 10th and dnq 15th at the Worlds.

Most competitions over 17.15 (outdoors/in): Copello 8/1, Idowu 7/2, Taylor 4+1w/1, Tamgho 4/5, Olsson 4/2, Claye 3/2, Évora, Compaoré 3, Girat 2+1w, Oprea 1/4

> 1. Taylor, 2. Idowu (3), 3. Tamgho (2), 4. Copello,
> 5. Claye, 6. Évora (7), 7. Olsson (6), 8. Sands
> (10), 9. Compaoré (-), 10. Girat (-). – Donato (8), –
> Oprea (9) (Including indoors).

Shot

DAVID STORL, WHO had set world junior records in 2009, confirmed his exceptional talent by improving from 20.77 in 2010 to 20.78 and 21.03 in June, 21.05 in August and then to 21.50 in qualifying and 21.60 and 21.75 in the final of the World Championships. That gave him the gold medal by 14 cm over the favourite Dylan Armstrong. Storl had two more meetings over 21m after that, but did not approach the depth of quality performances of the top North Americans. Compared to Storl's 3, Armstrong had 17 meetings over 21.30, Reese Hoffa 10 and Christian Cantwell 8, Ryan Whiting 4 + 2 indoors, with Tomasz Majewski on 6 and Andrey Mikhnevich 5. Armstrong was the top man overall, improving his Canadian record four times to 22.21 and winning 14 of 24 meetings, including four Diamond League meetings. He was 4-2 v Storl but only 7-6 against Hoffa, who was 5th at the Worlds but returned to win the DL final in Brussels. At that meeting there were season's bests for both Hoffa 22.09 and Christian Cantwell 22.07 with Mikhnevich 3rd and Armstrong 4th. Hoffa was 7-5 (0-2 indoors) v Cantwell, who did well to get back to close to his best after major shoulder surger and was 4th at the Worlds where the bronze medal went to Mikhnevich, who was beaten 3-1 by both Hoffa and Cantwell and who was 3-3 v Majewski but 0-2 to Storl. Adam Nelson won the US title with 22.09 from Cantwell and Hoffa with Ryan Whiting 4th and Dan Taylor 5th, but his next best was 21.45 and he was 8th at the Worlds, a place behind Whiting who beat him 3-2 outdoors and twice indoors including 1st to 3rd (with Taylor 2nd) at the US Indoor Champs. Whiting beat Majewski (9th Worlds) 6-5, including when they were 5th and 6th in Brussels. The top eight were way ahead of the rest, of whom Russian champion Maksim Sidorov (dnq 15 Worlds) was the only man to exceed 21m, but Marco Fortes (6th Worlds, 7th Brussels) had a very solid record. Ralf Bartels, 10th at the Worlds, was consistent but only in the low 20s outdoors, having been at his best in the indoor season, beating Storl and Sidorov to take the European Indoor title with Fortes 8th.

Most competitions over 20.80 (outdoors/in): Armstrong 25, Hoffa 21, Majewski 17, Cantwell 12, Storl, Whiting 9, Mikhnevich 8, Nelson 6

> 1. Armstrong, 2. Hoffa (3), 3. Cantwell (2),
> 4. Storl, 5. Mikhnevich, 6. Whiting, 7. Majewski,
> 8. Nelson, 9. Fortes (-), 10. Sidorov. – Bartels (9).
> (including indoors).

Discus

ROBERT HARTING IS top for the third successive year; he had a superb season despite pain in his left knee for which he had surgery in October. He was unbeaten in 16 competitions, five of them over 68m, compared to one each by Zoltán Kövágó, Jarred Rome and Piotr Malachowski. Kövágó topped the world list with 69.50 but did not qualify for the World final, although he came back for third in the DL final in Zürich behind Harting and Virgilijus Alekna. Gerd Kanter was fourth in that event, and he had taken the World silver and was 5-4 v Alekna. World bronze went to Asian champion Ehsan Hadadi, who, although with lesser marks, was 3-2 v Kövágó and Malachowski. Although they fared less well at the Worlds, Malachowski (9th) and Kövágó had good depth of performance with the former having a 5-4 advantage. Märt Israel and Benn Harradine were 4th and 5th at the Worlds, with Harradine 4-3 ahead overall, and Jorge Fernández, who went on to win at the Pan-American Games, 8th as well as 2-2 v Mario Pestano, whose 11th at the Worlds was his only competition outside Spain, where he won his 11th successive national title. Martin Wierig (dnq 19 Worlds) had good marks, but was beaten 4-0 by Fernández and 4-3 by Harradine. He was 5th in Zürich and 3-3 v Frank Casañas who was 2-2 v Pestano and 2-1 v Fernández. Erik Cadée was 2-1 v Fernandez.

Most competitions over 65m: Kanter 14+1i, Harting 14, Alekna 11, Wierig 7, Kövágó, Malachowski 6; Israel, Cadée 5, Rutger Smith, Casañas 4; Pestano, Hadadi, Fernández, Martín Maric 3, Harradine 2+1i.

1. Harting, 2. Kanter, 3. Alekna, 4. Hadadi,
5. Malachowski, 6. Kövágó, 7. Israel,
8. Harradine, 9. Casañas, 10. Cadee

Hammer

THE 2004 OLYMPIC champion Koji Murofushi (top ranked in 2001, 2004 and 2006) won his first world title at his seventh attempt. But Krisztián Pars, the world silver medallist, is ranked top for the first time after seven years in the top six. His sequence of marks with 15 of the top 32 performances to 79.29 and 20 wins in 24 competitions was just too good to ignore. Murofushi won the world title with 81.24 to Pars 81.18 but his other competitions were 78.56, 78.10 and 77.01. Aleksey Zagornyi was 2nd, 3rd and 4th on the performance list with throws over 81m, but fell away and was only 4th at the Russian Championships with 75.22 and did not compete after July. Kibwé Johnson was twice over 80m and just below that to win at the Pan-American Games, but fared poorly in European meets and did not qualify for the World final. The other 80m men were Primoz Kozmus (back after a year's break), Pavel Krivitskiy, Nicola Vizzoni and Dilshod Nazarov, respectively 3rd, 5th, 8th and 10th at the Worlds. World 4th placer Markus Esser had four 79m plus competitions and was 3-3 v Kozmus, 5-1 v Nazarov and 4-1 v Vizzoni; he also won the European Team event from Pawel Fajdek, Oleksiy Sokryskyy, Krivitskiy and Vizzoni. Vizzoni was 4-0 v Johnson and 3-0 v Sergey Litvinov, who returned from Germany to Russia, and Nazarov 4-4 v Johnson. Also over 79m were Russian champion Kirill Ikonnikov (2-1 v Johnson and 2-0 v Nazarov and Vizzoni), Szymon Ziólkowski (3-1 v Johnson) and Mohamed Al-Zankawi, respectively 6th, 7th and 13th at the Worlds. Fajdek won European U23 and WUG titles before 11th at the Worlds.

Most competitions over 80m/78.50m: 80m/78.50m: Pars 6/18, Zagornyi 5/8, Esser 0/5, Krivitskiy, Litvinov 0/4; Johnson, Ikonnikov 0/3

1. Pars, 2. Murofushi, 3. Zagornyi, 4. Esser,
5. Kozmus, 6. Krivitskiy, 7. Ikonnikov, 8. Nazarov,
9. Vizzoni, 10. Johnson

Javelin

ANDREAS THORKILDSEN HELD on to his top ranking (sixth time in eigth years) but was closely challenged by Matthias de Zordo, who beat him at the World Championships. Thorkildsen struggled for full fitness, but had four of the six 88m plus performances of the year, including the top two, 90.61 at Byrkjelo and 88.43 at Stockholm, and beat de Zordo, whose best was 88.36, 4-3. Vadims Vasilevskis was the third 88m thrower, but he was a dismal dnq 25th at the Worlds. Guillermo Martínez competed only six times, but won five including CAC, Cuban and Pan-American titles and was 3rd at the Worlds. Fourth and fifth in the Worlds were Vitezslav Vesely and Fatih Avan, and they reversed that order in the Diamond League final in Brussels for 3rd and 4th behind de Zordo and Vasilevskis. Avan also won the World Universities title and was 2nd to Till Wöschler in the European U23s with Dmitriy Tarabin 3rd. 38 year-old Sergey Makarov (12th Worlds) had a 3-1 advantage over his compatriot Tarabin and was 3-0 v Vasilevskis; after a two-year absence he is ranked for the 14th year. Roman Avramenko, World Universities silver medallist, was 2-2 v Tarabin, but ahead at both Worlds, 6th to 10th, and Brussels, 6th to 8th, although with slight lesser marks overall. Jarrod Bannister (who had just five competitions), Mark Frank and Antti Ruuskanen were 7th to 9th at the Worlds. Ari Mannio had the best set of marks of the Finns and was national champion but was beaten 3-2 by Ruuskanen, including dnq 14 Worlds. Asian champion Yukifumi Murakami was undefeated in Japan, but in his only venture out of the country, was dnq 15th at the Worlds. Zigismunds Sirmais set world junior records of 84.47 and 84.60 and won the European Junior title but was well below such form at the Worlds. The 100th best of 77.38 was a new record.

Most competitions over 84m/82.50m: Thorkildsen 6/9, Vasilevskis 6/7, de Zordo 4/7, Makarov 4/5. Avan 3/9, Martínez 3/4, Zigismunds Sirmais 2/2, Tarabin 1/5, Vesely 1/4, Robert Oosthuizen 1/3, Murakami 0/5

1. Thorkildsen, 2. de Zordo, 3. Martínez, 4. Avan,
5, Vesely, 6. Makarov, 7. Vasilevskis,
8. Avramenko, 9. Tarabin, 10. Frank

Decathlon

ASHTON EATON HAD the year's top score, 8729 to win the US title, but he was 102 points behind defending champion Trey Hardee at the Worlds (8607 to 8505) and Hardee also won at Götzis, so returns to top ranking. Both Americans only contested two decathlons so did not qualify for the IAAF Challenge for which three scores were needed. The Challenge went to Leonel Suárez, 3rd Worlds, 2nd Götzis and 1st Kladno and Pan-American Games, from Eelco Sintnicolaas and Mikk Pahapill, who were 4-5-3 and 3-9-2 at Götzis, Worlds and Talence. Pahapill 8398 and Yordani García 8397 were next on the world list, but slipped to 9th and dnf at the Worlds, where Russian champion Aleksey Drozdov was 4th, Sintnicolaas 5th, Mihail Dudas 6th and Pascal Behrenbruch 7th. Drozdov however, did not finish at Talence where Hans Van Alphen was the surprise winner. Jan-Felix Knobel was 5th at Götzis and 8th at the Worlds. Larbi Bouradaa (10th Worlds) set an African record when he won at Ratingen from Rico Freimuth (7th Götzis, dnf Worlds with injured left knee) and Behrenbruch (10th Götzis, 8th Talence). The 2005 world champion Bryan Clay was a non-finisher at the US Champs suffering from knee tendinitis. 100th best of 7678 was the best since 1996.

Indoors Eaton improved his world record for the heptathlon to 6568 points at Tallinn, well ahead of the year's second highest score, 6282 by Andrey Kravchenko in winning the European title.

    1. Hardee, 2. Eaton, 3. Suárez, 4. Drozdov,
    5. Pahapill, 6. Sintnicolaas, 7. Knobel, 8. García,
    9. Bouradaa, 10. Freimuth

20 Kilometres Walk

VALERIY BORCHIN WON all his three races of 2011, including giving a consummate display to take World gold from Vladimir Kanaykin and Luis Fernando López. Wang Zhen was 4th in Daegu, but won four other races, including at the year's fastest races at Lugano and Taicang, where his compatriots Chu Yafei (11th Worlds) and Chen Ding were 2nd and 3rd and Jared Tallent (27th Worlds) 4th in both. Next in the Worlds were Stanislav Yemelyanov (5th), who won the European Cup and was 2nd to Borchin at Rio Maior, and Kim Hyun-sub (6th), who won the Asian title and was 5th at Taicang. Chen Ding had three race wins, but López had a mixed collection of results, winning the Pan-Am Cup and 2nd to Eder Sánchez (15th Worlds) at Chihuahua, but 8th at Dublin (a race won by Wang Zhen) and dnf Sesto SG (won by Borchin) before 3rd at the Pan-American Games. As usual the Russian Winter Championships provided good depth of times and this was won by Kanaykin from Sergey Morozov (12th Worlds) and Andrey Krivov, who later won the World Universities title. These three Russians did not, however, fare so well at the European Cup, as they were 6th, 13th and 8th respectively. Morozov won the later Russian title from Krivov, and Sánchez had good results with 3rd at Rio Maior and 6th at Taicang.

The IAAF Race Walking Challenge was determined over 10k in La Coruña. With ten men under 40 minutes, the winner was Borchin from Wang Zhen, Chu Yafei, João Vieira and Sánchez.

    1. Borchin, 2. Wang Zhen, 3. Kanaykin, 4.
    Yemelyanov, 5. Chu Yafei, 6. Chen Ding, 7. Kim
    Hyun-sub, 8. López, 9. Morozov, 10. Sánchez

50 Kilometres Walk

YOHANN DINIZ SET a world track record with 3:35:27.1 but set off at a ridiculous pace in the Worlds, seemingly oblivious to the judges. He was pulled out all too soon, but Sergey Bakulin, who had earlier won the Russian title, went on to a brilliant win in 3:38:46. The other sub-3:40 times of the year came from wins in Taicang by Si Tiangfeng and in Dudince by Matej Tóth (dnf Worlds). Si, with 4th at the Worlds was the only man other than Bakulin to have two sub-3:45 times, but Denis Nizhegorodov only just missed out with 2nd in the Worlds in 3:42:45 and 1st in the European Cup 3:45:58. Luke Adams was 5th in the Worlds in his only 50k of 2011, while two good results were produced by Jared Tallent 3rd Worlds and Australian champion, Koichiro Morioka, 6th Worlds and Japanese champion, and by Xu Faguang and Park Chil-sung, 2nd and 4th at Taicang and 8th and 7th Worlds. Horacio Nava was the one top man with three good results: 2nd (to José Ojeda) at Chihuahua, 3rd as a guest at the Russian Champs behind Bakulin and Yuriy Andronov, and 1st at the Pan-American Games.

    1. Bakulin, 2. Nizhegorodov, 3. Si, 4. Diniz,
    5. Tallent, 6. Tóth, 7. Morioka, 8. Xu, 9. Nava,
    10. Adams

Woman Athlete of the Year

THE OUTSTANDING PERFORMANCES by a woman in 2011 were surely the brilliant sprint hurdling by Sally Pearson in semi-final and final of the World Championships and she was voted Women Athlete of the Year by the IAAF. She was unbeaten to that point but fell in her final race, the Diamond League final in Brussels. Also in Daegu we had the finest competition, with Mariya Abakumova and Barbora Spotáková swapping the lead in the javelin. And yet, I prefer for my Athlete of the Year the claims of Vivian Cheruiyot, who won three world titles.

Cheruiyot started the year with third behind Linet Masai and Genzebe Dibaba in the Edinburgh cross-country and also lost to Masai in the Kenyan CC Championships, but beat her at Seville and in the World Championships. She was then undefeated on the track in one race at 3000m, five at 5000m, including a Commonwealth record of 14:20.87 at Stockholm, and in three at 10,000m from 31:07.02 in her debut at the distance, then the Kenyan title and finally 30:48.98 in winning the world title. She won that race with a 61.7 last lap and a mightily impressive last 100m in 14.9. Six days later she produced an even more devastating last lap of 58.68 to complete the distance double at 5000m. At the end of 2011 she was named as the Kenyan Sports Personality of the Year.

Cheruiyot had been a hugely promising junior, placing successively 5-2-1-4-3 in the World Junior Cross-country from the ages of 14 to 18 in 1998-2002, winning the African Games 5000m bronze medal in 1999 and placing 14th in the Olympic 5000m in 2000. She also won bronze medals in the World Youth 3000m in 1999 and World Junior 5000m in 2002. She ran a 5000m best of 15:11.11 in the heats of the Olympics at 17, but did not improve that time until 2006. Then she broke through to late season times of 14:52.10 and 14:47.43. In 2007 she made further dramatic improvement as she ran 14:22.51 at the Bislett Games in Oslo behind Meseret Defar's world record of 14:16.51. She followed that with the World 5000m silver behind Defar, but was 5th in the 2008 Olympics. From then, however, there has been a catalogue of success at 5000m as she won the World title in 2009 and in 2010 won at African Championships, Continental Cup and Commonwealth Games, also collecting the Diamond League crown, having earlier won World Indoor silver at 3000m.

Also unbeaten, in 15 competitions, in 2011 was shot putter Valerie Adams and she had a massive winning margin of 1.19m at the Worlds. Other top athletes unbeaten at a standard event but in limited competition were Olga Kaniskina at walks (the IAAF Challenge race at 10k and three at 20k) and Yuliya Zaripova in three steeplechases.

World champions also having outstanding seasons included Carmelita Jeter, winning 9 of 10 finals at 100m (plus taking World silver at 200m), Veronica Campbell-Brown, with World gold at 200m and silver at 100m, Mariya Savinova, winner of 7 of her 8 finals at 800m/1000m, Anna Chicherova, 6 of 8 at high jump and Tatyana Chernova, 3 of 4 at heptathlon.

World records were set by Mary Keitany, 65:50 for half marathon, and Betty Heidler, 79.42m for hammer. During the Chicago marathon Liliya Shobukhova beat the record for 30k with 1:38:23 (although it should be noted that Paula Radcliffe reached that point in 1:36:36 in her London Marathon triumph in 2003, but the course was slightly downhill to that point). Also Vera Sokolova set a ratified world record with 1:25:08 for the 20km walk although two faster times had been recorded in the past that did not satisfy stringent record conditions.

Selections for World Top Ten

	PJM	TFN	AI
Vivian Cheryuiyot	1	1	2
Sally Pearson	2	2	1
Valerie Adams	3	3	3
Carmelita Jeter	4	4	4
Tatyana Chernova	5	8	-
Anna Chicherova	6	5	7
Lashinda Demus	7	7	8
Amantle Montsho	8	11	5
Veronica Campbell-Brown	9	10	-
Mariya Abakumova	10	–	9
Mariya Savinova		9	
Yuliya Zaripova		13	10

Note *Athletics International* (AI) readers actually only voted for 1-2-3-4-5 and *Track & Field News* (TFN) does not consider road races other than the marathon.

100 Metres

CARMELITA JETER JUST headed Veronica Campbell-Brown for top ranking in 2010, but in 2011 there was little doubt of her supremacy as she won ten of eleven 100m finals including the World title in 10.90 to her rival's 10.97 and with 10.78 to 10.85 in the Diamond League final in Brussels; VCB beat her 10.92 to 10.95 in Shanghai. Jeter, top for thethird successive year, produced the fastest time with 10.70 at Eugene and VCB's best was 10.76 at Ostrava. Kelly-Ann Baptiste was third in both Worlds and Brussels and beat VCB at Saint-Denis. Shelly-Ann Fraser had only four 100m competitions, but although behind them at Eugene was ahead at the Worlds of the two women who had posted faster times, as she was 4th to 6th of Kerron Stewart and 8th Marshevet Myers, who were 2-2 in their clashes. Myers was 2nd to Jeter at the US Champs and Stewart 2nd to Campbell-Brown at the Jamaican Champs. Two other women broke 11 seconds: Ivet Lalova (7th Worlds), and Damola Osayomi (last in her World semi). Osayomi did not contest any Diamond League races but won the African Games title, a metre ahead of Blessing Okagbare, who had been 5th in the World final. Schillonie Calvert was 6th at the Jamaican Champs but had a strong series of races in Europe, beat Lalova 4-0 and was ahead of Okagbare in their only clash, 4th and 5th at the London GP, behind Jeter, Baptiste and Fraser-Pryce. Alex Anderson, 5th in the US Champs, just misses the final ranking spot with better times than Carrie Russell, the World Universities champion and Jamaican 7th, whom she did not meet, and the perennial Debbie Ferguson McKenzie. The 100th best of 11.36 tied the record.

Most times under 11.00/11.10: Jeter 8+1w/13+1w, Campbell-Brown 7/8, Baptiste 5/6, Myers 3/4, Stewart 2/5, Fraser-Pryce 2/3, Anderson 0+1w/4+2w.

1. Jeter, 2. Campbell-Brown, 3. Baptiste,
4. Fraser-Price, 5. Stewart, 6. Myers, 7. Calvert,
8. Okagbare, 9. Lalova, 10. Osayomi

200 Metres

VERONICA CAMPBELL-BROWN is top for the fourth time. She reversed the 100m results as she took the World title from Carmelita Jeter with three-time champion Allyson Felix third and Shalonda Solomon fourth. VCB's only loss in her five finals was to Shelly-Ann Fraser in May at Kingston, but Fraser's other big races were 7th in New York and then 3rd in the DL final in Zürich, behind Jeter and Felix and ahead of Solomon. Kerron Stewart was 5th and Debbie Ferguson McKenzie 6th at the Worlds and then 8th and 5th respectively in Zürich, with Bianca Knight 6th and Sherone Simpson (8th Worlds) 7th. Knight had a fine series of races on either side of the Atlantic and was 5-2 v Ferguson McKenzie (first ranked in 1998). There were plenty of fast times in the USA, notably at the NCAAs, won by Kimberlyn Duncan 22.24 from Jeneba Tarmoh 22.34, and at the US Champs won in the year's fastest time of 22.15 by Solomon from Jeter, who was followed under 22.6 by Tarmoh, Knight, Duncan and LaShauntea Moore. Duncan did not run outside the USA and Tarmoh went out in her heat at the Worlds after a respectable 6th in Monaco. Ana Cláudia Silva won South American and Pan-American titles and set a Continental record of 22.48; she was 4th in her semi at the Worlds.

Most times under 22.70: Jeter 9+1w, Solomon 7+1w, Knight 6+1w, Campbell-Brown, Felix 5+1w; Duncan 4+2w, Tarmoh 4+1w, Fraser-Pryce 2+1w.

1. Campbell-Brown, 2. Jeter, 3. Felix, 4. Solomon,
5. Knight, 6. Fraser-Pryce, 7. Stewart, 8. Tarmoh,
9. Duncan, 10. Ferguson McKenzie.

400 Metres

AMANTLE MONTSHO WAS second in her first two 400m races of the year, to Allyson Felix in Doha and Rome, but then won her remaining eight finals, six in the Diamond League and taking World and African Games gold. Felix went on to win the US title and take World silver, plus 3rd in Eugene and 5th in Lausanne, and World bronze was won by Anastasiya Kapachinskaya, who ran the year's fastest time of 49.35 to win the Russian title. The runners-up in the US and Russian Championships Francena McCorory and Antonina Krivoshapka were 4th and 5th at the Worlds, followed by Shericka Williams, Sanya Richards-Ross and Novlene Williams-Mills, but the last was 4-1 v S Williams. Richards-Ross had looked to be back at her best with a London GP win in 49.66 over the Jamaicans Rosemarie Whyte and Novlene and Shericka Williams, but managed only 51.32 in the Daegu final. Whyte, 3rd in her World semi, was 2nd at the Jamaican Champs won by Novlene with Shericka 3rd. Although well below her 2010 form, Debbie Dunn was 3rd in the US Champs and 3-0 v S Williams; but was beaten by World semi-finalist and European Team winner Antonina Yefremova in their one clash. Tatyana Firova, 3rd in Brussels, was 2-0 v Yefremova in late season meetings. Standards were depressed at the top as 10th best of 50.67 was the second lowest of the last 30 years and there were no newcomers to the top ten.

Most times under 50.50: Montsho 9, Kapachinskaya, Felix, Williams-Mills 5, Krivoshapka 4, S Williams 3.

1. Montsho, 2. Felix, 3. Kapachinskaya, 4.
McCorory, 5. Krivoshapka, 6. Richards-Ross, 7.
Williams-Wills, 8. Whyte, 9. Dunn, 10. S Williams.

800 Metres

MARIYA SAVINOVA WON the World title in the year's fastest time of 1:55.87 and went on to win the Diamond League final in Zürich; her only loss in six races was to Halima Hachlaf in Oslo, but this was the one sub-2-minute time by the Moroccan who did not finish in her semi-final at the World Championships. Caster Semenya, who started the year with seven successive wins in lowish key races, was 2nd in the Worlds (in 1:56.35) and 5th in Zürich, and the World 3rd and 4th placers Janeth Jepkosgei and Alysia Montano (née Johnson), both national champions, were 4th and 2nd in Zürich, but the year's third fastest Yuliya Rusanova (1:56.99 for 2nd to Savinova at the Russian Champs) slipped to 8th Worlds and 10th Zürich and Kenia Sinclair was 7th and 9th in those races after five earlier big race wins and 2nd to Jennifer Meadows in London. Better was Yekaterina Kostetskaya, 5th Worlds and 6th Zürich. On win-loss Semenya was 3-2 v Jepkosgei and Montano, Montano was 3-2 v Sinclair, and Meadows (3rd Zürich) 3-0 v Sinclair and 3-1 v Rusanova and Kostetskaya. US second placer Maggie Vessey was 6th at the Worlds, backed by a solid set of performances and the last ranking place is taken by Svetlana Klyuka, 4th at the Russian Champs, a place ahead of World Universities silver medallist Yelena Kofanova, whom she beat 2-1.

Indoors the fastest times came at the Russian Champs, won by Rusanova in 1:58.14 from Yevgeniya Zinurova, and Zinurova won the European Indoor title from Meadows and Rusanova. The 100th best of 2:01.86 is second only to 2:01.50 way back in 1984.

Most times under 1:59.5 (outdoors/in): Savinova 8, Jepkosgei 7, Sinclair & Vessey 6, Meadows 5/1, Semenya & Montano 5, Kostetskaya, Klyuka 4, Kofanova, Liliya Lobanova, Yusneysi Santiusti 3, Rusanova 2/2.

1. Savinova, 2. Semenya, 3. Jepkosgei,
4. Montano. 5. Meadows, 6. Kostetskaya,
7. Sinclair, 8. Vessey (9), 9. Rusanova (8),
10. Klyuka. (including indoors)

1500 Metres

THIS WAS A strange year for the event with many of the top women showing alarming variations in form. Indeed just about the only athlete to have no blemish on their record was Mariem Selsouli, who returned from her two-year drugs ban to two races in September: 1st in Rieti in 4:01.04 and 2nd in Brussels in 4:00.77. Fine for the fast-finishing medallists Jennifer Simpson, Hannah England and Natalia Rodríguez, but the World final was in many ways a most unsatisfactory race. Morgan Uceny, the favourite off fine wins at the US Champs, Lausanne and Birmingham, was brought down by Hellen Obiri with 550m to run, and also with over a lap to go world-leader Maryam Jamal clipped the heel of Tugba Karakaya when attempting to get out of a box and lost her momentum; she drifted back to finish last. Uceny came back to run the year's fastest time when winning the DL final In Brussels in 4:00.06, and really that race provided the best guide to the form of the athletes. Simpson was 13th yet ran 4:03.68, just 0.14 off her season's best (when 5th in Monaco). Jamal had clearly the best set of times in 2011, from major wins in Rome (4:01.60), Hengelo (4:00.33) and Monaco (4:00.59) and she was 3rd in Brussels, followed by Anna Mishchenko, England, Janeth Jepkosgei, Obiri, Rodríguez, Mimi Belete, Kalkedan Gezahegn, Yekaterina Martynova and Renata Plis. The Worlds 4th placer Btissam Lakhouad did not finish in Brussels, but had also been 2nd in Monaco. Simpson was obviously the hardest to rank; her other major races were 2nd to Uceny at the US Champs, 4th in Madrid, and 10th Rieti. England's results were better, including swapping wins with Lisa Dobriskey (heat Worlds) at UK Champs and London GP, and 3rd in Barcelona in her best time of 4:01.89 behind Yekaterina Gorbunova and Rodríguez. Mishchenko won the first two major races, in Doha and Daegu in May, and had a good set of results, also including 4th in Rome, 2nd Lausanne and 3rd Rieti; she was 3-0 v Lakhouad, 4-1 v Gezahegn (5th Worlds) and 2-2 v Simpson, but she went out in her semi at the Worlds. So too did Russian champion Martynova, who came back with 2nd in Rieti. Rodríguez (9th in 2010) is the only one of the 2010 top ten to reappear. The number one Nancy Langat started 2011 with 5th at Rome in 4:03.66, but could not get near that afterwards and was 11th in her Worlds semi. 103 women under 4:10 was a new record (previous best 96 in 1984).

Most times under 4:04 (or 4:23.6 mile): Mishchenko 6, Jamal 4, Uceny, Rodríguez, Martynova 3, Gezahegn 2+1i

1. Uceny, 2. Jamal, 3. Selsouli, 4. England,
5. Mishchenko, 6. Rodríguez, 7. Simpson,
8. Gezahegn, 9. Lakhouad, 10. Martynova.

3000 Metres/2 Miles

THERE WAS MUCH less activity at this distance than usual, with only one sub-8:40 time outdoors: 8:38.67 by Vivian Cheruiyot in Stockholm although six women did so indoors, headed by Sentayehu Ejigu 8:30.36 in Birmingham and Meseret Defar 8:36.91 in Stockholm.

5000 Metres

VIVIAN CHERUIYOT FOLLOWED her 10,000m success by completing the distance double in Daegu and excelled by winning all five of her 5000m races including a Kenyan record 14:20.87 in Stockholm and the Diamond League final in Zürich. Sylvia Kibet took the World silver and also won the Kenyan title but had been 6th in Hengelo, 3rd Stockholm and 4th Zürich, so ranks behind World bronze medallist Meseret Defar, who won her three other races, Hengelo, Oslo and Saint-Denis, and Sally Kipyego, 4th in Eugene and 2nd in Stockholm and Zürich. Sentayehu Ejigu had four second places in Diamond League races before 4th Worlds and 7th Zürich and was 2-1 v Linet Masai, 6th Worlds and 3rd Zürich. Masai, in turn was 3-1 v World 5th placer Mercy Cherono. Priscah Cherono had three times under 14:45 and was 5th in Zürich, a place ahead of Meselech Melkamu against whom she was 2-1, and Genzebe Dibaba, 8th Worlds, was 3rd, a place ahead of Melkamu in Oslo. The African Games medallists in a slow race were Sule Utura (2-1 v Dibaba), Emebet Anteneh and Pauline Korikwiang, but all had bests in the 14:40s.

Most times under 14:50: 6 Ejigu, 5 Cheruiyot, 4 Defar, Korikwiang, M Cherono, P Cherono; 3 Kipyego, Masai, Kibet, Melkamu, Shalane Flanagan, Sule Utura

1. Cheruiyot, 2. Defar, 3. Kipyego, 4. Kibet,
5. Ejigu, 6. Masai, 7. M Cherono, 8. P Cherono,
9. Utura, 10. G Dibaba

10,000 Metres

VIVIAN CHERUIYOT MADE her track 10,000m debut with a win at Pontevedra in April and went on to further wins at the Kenyan and World Championships. Runner-up to her in both these races was Sally Kipyego, who had earlier run the year's fastest time of 30:36.35 at Stanford. Linet Masai took the World bronze in her only 10,000m of the year. She was followed in Daegu by Priscah Cherono, Meselech Melkamu and Shitaye Eshete. Melkamu had beaten Cherono in Ostrava and Eshete had won the Asian title, but the World 7th placer Shalane Flanagan deserves to rank higher due to her sub-31 runs for 2nd at Stanford and in winning the US title. Difficult to rank because they ran just one race in fast times were Kayoko Fukushi

(3rd Stanford), Meseret Defar and Worknesh Kidane but they were all much faster than the rest of the top placers at the Worlds, headed by Dulce Félix 8th and Jen Rhines 9th.

1. Cheruiyot. 2. Kipyego, 3. Masai, 4. P Cherono, 5. Melkamu, 6. Flanagan, 7. Eshete, 8. Fukushi, 9. Defar, 10. Kidane

Half Marathon

MARY KEITANY BROKE the world record with 65:50 at Ra's Al Khaymah, and this was much the fastest time of the year, the next being from wins by Lucy Wangui, 67:06 in the Great North Run and then 67:04 in Delhi, and Kim Smith, 67:11 in Philadelphia, with Sharon Cherop, 67:08, pushing Wangui hard in Delhi. Keitany also won at Lisbon in 67:54 and clocked an extraordinary 67:56 in the New York Marathon, and Smith won in New Orleans in 67:36, both her times being Oceania records. The most prolific set of times came from Filomena Chepchirchir, under 69:30 in four races: wins at Den Haag, Zwolle and Glasgow and 3rd in Rabat.

Marathon

THERE WAS A great field in London where the best ever times were recorded for places 3 and 8 to 24, with 9 women running under 2:25 and 21 under 2:30. In the second marathon of her life Mary Keitany was the winner in 2:19:19 from Liliya Shobukhova's Russian record 2:20:15 and Edna Kiplagat 2:20:46. Kiplagat went on to win the World title and Shobukhova to beat her record with 2:18:20 in Chicago, a time ever beaten only by Paula Radcliffe (three times), but Keitany set off too fast in New York and to had to settle for third in 2:23:38 behind Firehiwot Dado and Bizunesh Deba. Dado had previously won in Rome and Deba at both Los Angeles and San Diego. Florence Kiplagat did not finish in Boston, but became the third woman to break 2:20 in 2011, with 2:19:44 in Berlin. Next fastest was Mamitu Daska, who won at Frankfurt in 2:21:59, having earlier also won at Houston. Six more women had wins in 2:22 times: Tiki Gelana in Amsterdam, Lydia Cheromei in Prague (also 2nd in Dubai). Caroline Kilel in Boston, Korine Jelila in Toronto (also won in Mumbai) Aselefech Mergia in Dubai and Priscah Jeptoo in Paris (also 2nd Worlds). Third and fourth at the Worlds were Sharon Cherop, also 3rd Boston, and Bezunesh Bekele, also 4th London. Irina Mikitenko was 7th in London and 2nd in Berlin, and it was good to see the return of Radcliffe, 3rd in Berlin. As with the men, standards reached unprecedented levels including 128 women (and a further 9 in Boston) under 2:30

1. Shobukhova, 2. Keitany, 3. E Kiplagat, 4. F Kiplagat, 5. P Jeptoo, 6. Dado, 7. Deba, 8. Daska, 9. Cherop, 10. Bekele

3000 Metres Steeplechase

IN 2010 Milcah Chemos Cheywa and Yuliya Zarudneva had vied for supremacy. The latter, now married as Zaripova, took over top ranking in 2011. She won her three steeplechases: Russian Championships and then the Worlds (in the year's best of 9:07.03) and the Diamond League final at Brussels. Chemos had five Diamond League wins but was 3rd at the Worlds and 5th in Brussels, whereas Habiba Ghribi was second in both those races. Ghribi had earlier been 3rd in Rome and 4th in Lausanne in races won by Chemos. Chemos had also won the Kenyan title from Lydia Rotich and Mercy Njoroge. Rotich was 5th in the Worlds and 8th in Brussels and had an inferior record to the other two of the six women under 9:20 in 2011: Njoroge 4th and 3rd and Sofia Assefa, 6th and 4th in the big races. Hyvin Jepkemoi won the African Games from Hiwot Ayalew (6th Brussels) and Birtukan Adama but did not have the fast times of that pair. Binnaz Uslu and Hanane Ouhaddou were 7th and 8th at the Worlds, and the latter had a 2-1 advantage over Adamu (15th Worlds), who was 1-1 v Birtukan Fente (10th Worlds) but with better times. However the Ethiopian Champs runner-up Abera Ayana beat Ouhaddou 2-0.

Most times under 9:30: Chemos, Assefa 7; Njoroge 6, Zaripova 5, Rotich 3.

1. Zaripova, 2. Ghribi, 3. Chemos, 4. Njoroge, 5. Assefa, 6. Rotich, 7. Ayalew, 8. Uslu, 9. Ouhaddou, 10. Adamu

100 Metres Hurdles

SALLY PEARSON GAVE faultless displays of top-class sprint hurdling at the World Championships and her final time of 12.28 was the world's fastest for 19 years. She was IAAF Woman Athlete of the Year and a very worthy candidate for that honour; she won all her ten finals until falling at the Diamond League final in Brussels and ran 6 of the 11 fastest times of the year. Last year's top ranker Priscilla Lopes-Schliep was missing (daughter born in September). Danielle Carruthers and Dawn Harper ran pbs of 12.47 or silver and bronze in Daegu, where Kellie Wells, who had beaten those two into 2nd and 3rd at the US Champs, did not finish. Overall Carruthers beat Harper 4-3 and Wells 6-5, and Harper was 6-3 v Wells. The former Tiffany Ofili, who married hurdler Jeff Porter in May, having earlier switched to represent Britain, had a consistent season topped by 4th at the Worlds, where 5-6-7 were Tatyana Dektyareva (who lacked the depth of performances of others), Nikita Holder and Phylicia George, while Lisa Urech just missed a place in the final. Lolo Jones, the 2008 number one, called a halt to her campaign through injury in June needing back surgery, but had done enough before then for a ranking place; she was 4-1 v Virginia Crawford and 2-1 v Perdita Felicien, who both had solid depth of times. Nia Ali won NCAA and World Universities titles and was 5th, a place behind Crawford at the US Champs, and 5-4 against another prolific competitor, Pan-American champion Yvette Lewis. Felicien was 2-1 against her compatriot George. Although 10th best of 12.73 was the worst since 2002 the 100th best of 13.16 was easily a record (previously 13.22 in 2000).

Most times at 12.70 or faster: Pearson 10+1w, Carruthers 9+3w, Harper 5, Porter 3+2w

1. Pearson, 2. Carruthers, 3. Harper, 4. Wells, 5. Porter, 6. Jones, 7. Crawford, 8. Ali, 9. Felicien, 10. Lewis

400 Metres Hurdles

LASHINDA DEMUS MAINTAINED her top ranking, reaching her peak with the third fastest ever time, 52.47 to win the World title, just 0.13 off the world record. This was her fifth win in seven finals, her only losses being to Kaliese Spencer in Shanghai and to Spencer and Melaine Walker in the Diamond League final in Zürich. Spencer was below par with 4th place at the Worlds but was overall 2-2 v Demus and 6-1 v Walker, who was 3rd in Shanghai and was 2nd in three DL races and at the Worlds. Natalya Antyukh was beaten 4-2 by Zuzana Hejnová, but crucially was ahead at the Worlds, 4th to 7th, and Zürich, 4th to 5th. Between them in Daegu were Anastasiya Rabchenyuk and Vania Stambolova with Yelena Churakova 8th. Stambolova, with 7 wins in 9 competitions, had a far superior set of times to Rabchenyuk, who was 6th in Zürich and made the world final by just 0.01 from Perri Shakes-Drayton, who was 3rd in the European Team race behind Hejnová and Antyukh, with 4th Hanna Titimets, who had a 3-2 advantage over compatriot Anna Yaroshchuk. Yaroshchuk, however, beat Titimets to take the European U23 title and also won gold at the World University Games. The two Ukrainians were World semi-finalists as was US 2nd placer Queen Harrison, who was 7th to Churakova 8th in Zürich.

Most times under 54.0/55.0: Spencer 6/10, Walker 4/9, Demus 3/9, Hejnová, Stambolova 2/9; Antyukh 2/8, Shakes-Drayton 0/3.

1. Demus, 2. Spencer, 3. Walker, 4. Antyukh, 5. Hejnová, 6. Stambolova, 7. Rabchenyuk, 8. Shakes-Drayton, 9. Yaroshchuk, 10. Titimets

High Jump

WOMEN'S HIGH JUMPING standards in 2011 were well down as there were just 12 (3 indoors) performances at 2 metres or higher compared to 45 in 2009 and 40 in 2010. Missed were 2010's 2/3 Chaunté Lowe (second daughter born in April) and Ariane Friedrich (ruptured Achilles), and Blanka Vlasic was below her best with injury problems, although she jumped a season's best of 2.03 for the World silver medal, losing on count-back to Anna Chicherova, back from the birth of her daughter in September 2010. Chicherova took her best up to 2.07 to win the Russian title and also won the Diamond League final in Brussels with 2.05; in all she won 6 of her 8 competitions and was 4-2 v Vlasic. Antonietta Di Martino was third at the Worlds, with one of her two 2.00 clearances, but was better indoors, where she topped the world list with 2.04 and won the European Indoor title with 2.01, making a late start to the outdoor season due to a foot injury. Yelena Slesarenko took 4th at the Worlds on count-back from Svetlana Shkolina, having been the other way round for 2-3 at the Russian Champs, on each occasion at 1.97. Slesarenko was also 2nd with Shkolina 4th at Brussels, but Shkolina had a top win with 1.99 at Eberstadt and was much better indoors. Brigetta Barrett improved from 1.91 to 1.96 and won the NCAA, US and World Universities titles before 10th at the Worlds, where Venelina Veneva-Mateeva, who had three outdoor competitions at 1.95 (and 1.97 indoors), disappointed with a non-qualifying 1.89. Esthera Petre cleared 1.98 for the European U23 title, but her next best was 1.92 twice, including for 14th at the Worlds. Zheng Xingjuan competed only in Asia, but had 9 wins in 11 competitions including at the Asian Champs and was 6= at the Worlds. Anna Iljustsenko had a consistent series of marks including World Universities silver and 12th Worlds and was 2-0 v Veneva. Doreen Amata, African champion, 8= Worlds and 2-0 v Barrett, completes the rankings on outdoor form, with Emma Green-Tregaro (11th Worlds) just missing out. Ruth Beitia and Ebba Jungmark, 2nd and 3rd at the European Indoors with 1.96, come into consideration including indoor form; they were dnq 16 and 17 at the Worlds but Jungmark was 3rd in Brussels.

Most competitions over 2.00/1.97m outdoors (indoors): Chicherova 4/6, Vlasic 3/7, Di Martino 2/3 (2/2), Shkolina 0/4 (1/1), Slesarenko 0/3

1. Chicherova, 2. Vlasic, 3. Di Martino, 4. Slesarenko (5), 5. Shkolina (4), 6. Barrett, 7. Zheng, 8. Iljustsenko (10), 9. Veneva-Mateeva (-), 10. Amata (-). – Beitia (8), – Jungmark (9). (Including indoors)

Pole Vault

YELENA ISINBAYEVA RETURNED 11 months after taking a break from competition and had a promising start with indoor wins at 4.81 and 4.85 in February, but she was unable to match that outdoors with a best of 4.76, and she was 6th in the Worlds with 4.65. Jenn Suhr topped the world list with 4.91, backed with 4.79 and four competitions over 4.70 outdoors and two indoors. Fabiana Murer tied her South American record in winning the World title with 4.85 from Martina Strutz 4.80, Svetlana Feofanova 4.75, Suhr 4.70 and Yarisley Silva 4.70, but had just four wins in her ten outdoor competitions. Suhr had only six outdoor competitions, winning three but was 3-1 against Murer, Strutz, Feofanova and Silke Spiegelburg; she was beaten by Kylie Hutson 4.65 to 4.60 on her outdoor debut at the US Champs, but had taken the US Indoor title with 4.86A. Suhr beat Spiegelburg on count-back at 4.72 in the Diamond League final in Zürich, with Isinbayeva and Murer tying for third at 4.62, Silva 5th and Feofanova 6th. Strutz no-heighted on that occasion, but, although beaten 4-0 by Murer, had the best depth of marks (eight times over 4.70) and had started the outdoor season with ten successive wins. Spiegelburg, although only 9th at the Worlds, had positive win-loss records against all her top rivals except Suhr, including 3-2 v Murer, 4-3 v Strutz and 4-2 v Feofanova outdoors. Silva excelled with seven CAC records from 4.55 to the 4.75A with which she won the Pan-American title. Anna Rogowska was best indoors, winning the European Indoor title with 4.85 from Spiegelburg 4.75 and Kristina Gadschiew 4.65; she beat Spiegelburg as both cleared 4.75 at the European Teams, but suffered from a badly gashed hand in the summer and was 10= at the Worlds. Jirina Ptácníková and Nikoléta Kiriakopoúlou were 7th and 8th at the Worlds, with the latter having better marks, and they edged Gadschiew (10= Worlds) on outdoor form. 10th best of 4.71 was a new high as was 105 women over 4.30 compared to 86, 73 and 96 in the three years 2008-10.

Most competitions over 4.60m (outdoors/in): Strutz 11, Spiegelburg 9/4, Murer 7/3, Silva 7, Suhr & Rogowska 6/4, Feofanova 5/3, Isinbayeva 4/2, Kiriakopoúlou 4, Gadschiew 3/5, Ptácníková 3/3, Hutson 2/1.

    1. Suhr, 2. Murer, 3. Strutz (4), 4. Spiegelburg (3),
    5. Feofanova (6), 6. Silva (7), 7. Isinbayeva (5),
    8. Rogowska, 9. Ptácníková, 10. Kiriakopoúlou.
    (Including indoors)

Long Jump

BRITTNEY REESE HAD the longest jump of the year, 7.19 to win the US title, and retained her world title although with only one valid jump in the final. Darya Klishina had the next best, 7.05 to win at the European U23s, and despite only 7th at the Worlds after breaking a foot bone in warm-up did just enough to rank second in a year when few women had consistent depth of performance and essaying a ranking was very tricky. Olga Zaytseva switched from 200/400m running back to long jump, at which she had a previous best of 6.36 (2003), and won the Russian title with a startling 7.05; she had four other competitions over 6.70 but did not qualify for the World final (6.50 for 13th). Olga Kucherenko

had only four competitions but took World silver. She was 2nd in the Russian Champs with Yuliya Pidluzhnaya 3rd, Lyudmila Kolchanova, who did 7.06 at the Russian Cup, 4th, and Anna Nazarova, later World Universities champion, 5th. Another to disappoint at the Worlds was Maurren Maggi; she led the qualifiers with 6.86 but then managed only 6.17 for 11th in the final; already South American champion, she went on to win the Pan-American title with 6.94 and had seven wins in ten competitions. Janay DeLoach improved from 6.61 in 2010 to win the US indoor title with 6.99A and was 2nd to Reese with 6.97 in the US Champs outdoors, but was usually some way down on such a level. She was 6th at the Worlds when Ineta Radevica again showed her championships ability to take the bronze medal with 6.76 but had a next best in the year of 6.61, and Anastasiya Mironchik-Ivanova was 4th. The last had a good series of marks, including second in the DL final behind Reese. It was disappointing that it took as little as 6.56 to gain 5th (Carolina Klüft) in the World final. Eloyse Lesueur jumped 6.60 or more in all her ten outdoor events except for just 6.22 in the World qualifying. She was 3-3 v Funmi Jimoh, who had three no jumps in the world final; but was 5-1 v another top American Brianna Glenn and 2-0 v Nazarova.

Klishina won the European Indoor title from Naide Gomes, Pidluzhnaya and Lesueur.

Most competitions over 6.70m (outdoors/in): Reese 9+1w/1i, Mironchik-Ivanova 8, Maggi 6+1w, Klishina 6/3, Nazarova 5/4, Glenn 5/1, Lesueur 5, Jimoh 4+1w, Zaytseva 4, Kolchanova 3+1w, DeLoach & Irène Pusterla 3/1, Rybalko, Balayeva, L Griva, Tigau 3, Pidluzhnaya 2+1w/3, Gomes 2+1w/1, Kappler 2+1w, Shutkova 2/1.

    1. Reese, 2. Klishina, 3. Maggi, 4. Zaytseva,
    5. Kolchanova, 6. Mironchik-Ivanova,
    7. Kucherenko, 8. Lesueur, 9. DeLoach,
    10. Jimoh (-). – Pidluzhnaya (10).

Triple Jump

THE ONLY JUMP over 15m in 2011 was a wind-assisted 15.06 by Olga Saladuha in Stockholm. She also jumped 14.98 outdoors as Yargeris Savigne and Caterine Ibargüen led the world list with 14.99. After jumping over 14.80 in five of her competitions leading up to the World Champs, Savigne, with a hamstring injury, could only manage 14.43 for 6th in Daegu, where the medallists, Saladuha, Olga Rypakova and Ibargüen were separated by just 10cm 14.94 to 14.84. Sorting them on win-loss, Saladuha was 2-0 v Ibargüen and 3-2 v Savigne, Ibargüen 2-1 v Savigne, and Savigne 3-1 v Rypakova and also 7-2 against her compatriot Mabel Gay, who was 4th at the Worlds. Saladuha also won in Brussels, the Diamond League final from Gay and Rypakova. Ibargüen was the big improver, setting ten Colombian records from 14.30 to 14.99 and also winning South American and Pan-American (from Savigne and Gay) titles. After a decade living in Britain, Yamilé Aldama at last gained British citizenship, just in time for the Worlds, at which, on her 39th birthday, she was fourth with 14.50 and she was also 4th in Brussels. She had competed for Cuba to 2000 and for Sudan 2004-09. Anna Kuropatkina was 7th at Worlds and in Brussels behind Simona La Mantia and Dana Veldáková, respectively dnq 15 and 11th at the Worlds, and 2-2 in their clashes outdoors. La Mantia had been best indoors winning the European Indoor title from Olesya Zabara and Veldáková. Paraskeví Papahrístou and Natalya Kutyakova were fifth and sixth on the world list with 14.72 and 14.67; the former won the European U23 title but was dnq 16 at the Worlds, while the latter did not compete after 5th in the Russian Champs in July. Baha Rahouli won African and Arab titles after 8th at the Worlds.

Most competitions over 14.40m (outdoors/in): Ibargüen 12, Saladuha 9+1w/1, Savigne 8, Gay 6, Rypakova 5+1w, Papahrístou, Martínez 3

    1. Saladuha, 2. Ibargüen, 3. Savigne,
    4. Rypakova, 5. Gay, 6. Aldama, 7. Veldáková
    (8), 8. Papahrístou (10), 9. La Mantia (7),
    10. Kuropatkina (9). (Including indoors).

Shot

VALERIE ADAMS WAS the dominant force at this event, winning all her 13 meetings, and is top for the fifth time in six years. She produced the top mark of 21.24 to take the World title by a massive 1.19m from Nadezhda Ostapchuk, who was a clear-cut second, in that place six times to Adams and winning her other two meetings. These two had the top 16 marks of the year but two other woman went over 20m: Jill Camarena-Williams with a North American record 20.18 and Gong Lijiao, and this pair were 3rd and 4th at the Worlds., 5cm apart. Gong was ahead in their other two clashes. Fifth to ninth at the Worlds were Yevgeniya Kolodko (improving her pb by 45cm to do so), Li Ling, Anna Avdeyeva, Nadine Kleinert and Michelle Carter, while below par were Natalya Mikhnevich 11th and Cleopatra Borel-Brown 13th, but the last was 6-2 v Carter. The Diamond League final (held indoors under outdoor conditions at Zürich's main railway station) was won by Adams from Ostapchuk, Camarena-W, Mikhnevich, Borel-Brown, Carter, Kolodko and Kleinert. Misleydis González (dnq 16 Worlds) won at the Pan-American Games from Borel-Brown but just misses a ranking.

Most competitions over 19m (outdoors/in): Camarena-Williams 13/2, Adams 13, Gong 11/1, Ostapchuk 9, Ling Li, Kleinert 6, Borel-Brown 4, Avdeyeva, Anna Omarova 3

    1. Adams, 2. Ostapchuk, 3. Gong, 4. Camarena-Williams, 5. Li, 6. Kolodko, 7. Borel-Brown, 8, Carter, 9. Avdeyeva, 10. Kleinert.

Discus

THE LONGEST THROW of the year was recorded by Sandra Perkovic, who, having opened with a Croatian record 67.96 in February, threw 69.99 at Varazdin in June but she lost that with a positive drugs test. So top of the world list with 67.98 was Li Yanfeng who won 9 of her 11 competitions including the World title and the Diamond League final in Brussels. Liu was beaten by Yarelys Barrios and Nadine Müller in Rome and by Müller and Ma Xueyan in Dessau. Müller, 6th in Brussels, lost 3-4 to Barrios and these two took World silver and bronze medals. Next with 4th at the Worlds and 3rd in Brussels was Zaneta Glanc ahead of Stephanie Brown Trafton who showed her best form since winning the 2008 Olympic title, was 5th at Worlds and Brussels and beat her compatriot Aretha Thurmond 6-4. Although beaten 6-5 by Ma (dnq 14th Worlds), Tan Jian came through for 6th Worlds and 4th Brussels against 13th and 7th for Thurmond. The World final was completed by Dragana Tomasevic, Nicoleta Grasu, Denia Caballero, Dani Samuels, Darya Pishchalnikova and Zinaida Sendriute as 7th to 12th. Russian champion Pishchalnikova had eight competitions prior to Daegu, winning six and 2nd twice, over 61m in all of them; these were mostly away from her main rivals but she was 2-0 v Thurmond, who was 2-0 v Ma and 4-1 v Grasu, who completed her 18th year in the top 10.

Most competitions over 63m: Müller 11, Li, Barrios 10, Brown Trafton, Glanc, Thurmond. Karsak 3.

    1. Li, 2. Müller 3. Barrios, 4. Glanc, 5. Brown Trafton, 6. Tan, 7. Pishchalnikova, 8. Thurmond, 9. Grasu, 10. Samuels

Hammer

BETTY HEIDLER SET a world record of 79.42m at Halle and had the top five and seventh to ninth best marks of the year, thus well ahead of her conqueror at the Worlds, Tatyana Lysenko, who had the 6th, 10th and 11th best marks. Heidler won 12 of her 15 competitions, and was 5-2 v Lysenko, who won 12 of 19 competitions. Zhang Wenxiu and Yipsi Moreno were next on the world list, each with five competitions over 74m and they were 3rd and 4th at the Worlds, Moreno ending her season by winning the Pan-American Games with her best mark of 75.62. Former world record holder Anita Wlodarczyk was 5th at the Worlds but 7th placer Kathrin Klaas had much better depth of marks than any of the rest. Klaas was third behind Lysenko and Moreno at the final World Challenge event at Rieti and was followed there by Zalina Marghieva, Jennifer Dahlgren,

Marina Marghieva, Bianca Perie and Amber Campbell, who had respectively been 8th, 10th, 17th, 6th and 14th at the Worlds. Zalina Marghieva was 2-1 against South American champion Dahlgren. Jessica Cosby was 2-1 against Campbell, beating her for the US title and ahead with 10th at the Worlds. There is little change in rankings from 2010 with nine returning and their 2010 positions being respectively 1-2-4-5-6-3-9-8-7-x. The 100th best of 64.79 was a record.

Most competitions over 72m: Heidler 16, Moreno 14, Lysenko 13, Klaas 10, Zhang 8, Dahlgren 7, Wlodarczyk, Z Marghieva, Cosby 3.

    1. Heidler, 2. Lysenko, 3. Zhang, 4. Moreno,
    5. Klaas, 6. Wlodarczyk, 7. Z Marghieva,
    8. Dahlgren, 9. Perie, 10. Cosby.

Javelin

THE CLASH BETWEEN Mariya Abakumova and Barbora Spotáková at the Worlds in Daegu was one of the greatest in the history of athletics with Abakumova throwing a Russian record 71.25 only for the Czech to throw 71.58 and Abakumova to respond with 71.99. Sunette Viljoen set an African and Commonwealth record of 68.39 so Christina Obergföll had to settle for 4th, having come into the Championships with the best record and throwing 68.76 in qualifying. Over the season Obergföll, who threw a year's best 69.57 to win the Diamond League final in Zürich, beat Spotáková 6-3 and Abakumova 6-2 and those two went 5-3 to Abakumova in their clashes, but the sheer quality of their Daegu efforts meant that the top two rankings went to the 71m plus women. Viljoen was a clear fourth, also beating the top two in Zürich. while the next on depth of marks was Katharina Molitor, 5th in the Worlds, followed by Goldie Sayers, who beat Worlds 6th placer Kim Mickle 2-1 and was 5th in Zürich, although only 10th in Daegu. Martina Ratej and Madara Palameika were 7th and 11th at the Worlds and 7th and 8th at Zürich with Linda Stahl taking the last ranking spot ahead of Mercedes Chilla and Jarmila Klimesová (8th Worlds, 9th Zürich). There were no newcomers to the top ten.

Most competitions over 62m: Spotáková, Obergföll 14, Abakumova 13, Molitor 9, Sayers 6, Viljoen 4.

    1. Abakumova, 2. Spotáková, 3. Obergföll,
    4. Viljoen, 5. Molitor, 6. Sayers, 7. Mickle,
    8. Ratej, 9. Palameika, 10. Stahl

Heptathlon

TATYANA CHERNOVA HAD not quite fulfilled her potential at previous major events, but excelled through the seven events at the 2011 World Championships. Further victories at Kladno and Talence earned her the IAAF World Combined Events Challenge from Jennifer Oeser, Nataliya Dobrynska and Karolina Tyminska, who had been 3rd, 5th and 4th at the Worlds. The World silver medallist was the 2009-10 world number one Jessica Ennis, who had beaten Chernova easily 6790 to 6539 at Götzis, but whose poor javelin throwing contributed to being well behind, 6751 to 6880 at the Worlds. Ennis again only contested two heptathlons and thus did not qualify for the Challenge. Dobrynska was only 5 points behind Tyminska at the Worlds but was well ahead, 6537 to 6301, when they were 2nd and 3rd behind Chernova at Talence. My top 5 were 4-1-3-2-6 in 2010, as last year's no. 5 Hyleas Fountain did not finish at the Worlds. Oeser won at Ratingen from Aiga Grabuste (12th Worlds) and Lili Schwarzkopf (6th Worlds, 8th Talence, dnf Götzis), and 7th to 10th at the Worlds were Antoinette Nana Djimou, Austra Skujyte, Jessica Zelinka (4th Talence) and Lyudmyla Yosypenko (5th Talence), respectively 3rd (6409), 7th, 5th and 9th at Götzis.

The best indoor pentathlon scores were achieved at the European Indoors won by Nana Djimou 4723 from Skujyte 4706, Ramona Fransen 4665 and Tyminska 4612.

    1. Chernova, 2. Ennis, 3. Oeser, 4. Dobrynska,
    5. Tyminska, 6. Nana Djimou, 7. Schwarzkopf,
    8, Zelinka, 9. Skujyte, 10. Grabuste

20 Kilometres Walk

ALTHOUGH SIX WOMEN produced faster times, Olga Kaniskina was again supreme and took her fourth successive top ranking. She won at Rio Maior and Sesto SG before winning the World title from Liu Hong, who had major wins in Lugano, Taicang and Dublin, and Anisya Kirdyapkina. Vera Sokolova had beaten Kiryapkina to win both Russian Winter (by a second in 1:25:08 for a ratified world record) and European Cup races, but was only 12th at the Worlds. Liu with four times and Kaniskina with three were the only women to better 1:30:00 more than once. Although only 30th on the world list, Elisa Rigaudo earns a high ranking from 3rd in the European Cup and 4th at the Worlds, a place ahead of Qieyang Shenjie, who was 2nd at Taicang, but the form of the rest is very mixed. Of them Beatriz Pascual (2nd Rio Maior and Sesto SG) and Gao Ni (3rd Lugano, 4th Taicang), 9th and 14th at the Worlds, had the best collection of times, but Susana Feitor was 6th in her record 11th appearance at the World Championships and was 3-2 v her compatriot Inês Henriques although 1-2 v Vera Santos.

Again the IAAF World Race Walking Challenge was decided in a one-off race at 10 kilometres after the women had qualified from 20k races. Kaniskina won in 42:39 from Liu, Seeger, Ana Cabecinha (7th Worlds). Feitor and Pascual.

    1. Kaniskina, 2. Liu Hong, 3. Kirdyapkina,
    4. Sokolova, 5. Rigaudo, 6. Qieyang, 7. Pascual,
    8. Gao, 9. Feitor, 10. Santos

CROSS-COUNTRY – NATIONAL CHAMPIONS 2011

	Men (long distance)	Women (long distance)
Algeria	Ahmed Naili	Abla Bendebah
Argentina	Juan José Roht	Rosa Godoy
Australia (Aug)	Liam Adams	Emily Brichacek
Austria	Günther Weidlinger	Anita Baierl
Belarus (Oct)	Sergey Platonov	Olga Kravtsova
Belgium	Atelaw Bekele	Veerle Dejaeghere
Brazil	Damião de Souza	Simone da Silva
Bulgaria	Yolo Nikolov	Silvia Danekova
Canada (Nov)	Cameron Levins	Kendra Schaaf
Colombia	Iván González	Angela Figueroa
Croatia (Nov)	Goran Grdenic	Matea Matosevic
Cuba	Henry Jaens	Dailín Belmonte
Czech Republic	Milan Kocourek	Lucie Sekanová
Denmark	Morten Munkholm	Maria Sig Møller
England	Steve Vernon	Louise Damen
Estonia	Taivo Püi	Julia Bulina
Ethiopia – World Trials	Hunegnaw Mesfin	Meselech Melkamu
Finland	Jussi Utriainen	Johana Lehtinen
France	Morhad Amdouni	Christelle Daunay
Germany	Steffen Uliczka	Sabrina Mockenhaupt
Greece	Dímos Maggínas	Konstadína Kefalá
Hungary (Nov)	Tamás Kovács	Mónika Nagy
India	Mohammad Younus	Priyanka Singh Patel
Ireland (Nov)	Joseph Sweeney	Sara Treacy
Israel	Tasama Moogas	Meigal Attias
Italy	Daniele Meucci	Nadia Ejjafini
Kenya	Gilbert Mutai	Lineth Masai
Lithuania	Vitaliy Shafar UKR	Aleksandra Duliba UKR
Luxembourg	Vincent Nothum	Tania Ley-Fransissi
Morocco	Najim El Qady	Rkia El Moukim
Netherlands	Khalid Choukoud	Miranda Boonstra
New Zealand	Matt Smith	Danielle Trevis
Northern Ireland	Paul Pollock IRL	Gladys Ganiel IRL
Norway (Sep)	Sindre Buraas	Kirsten Melkevik
Poland	Marcin Chabowski	Katarzyna Kowalska
Portugal	Yousef Kalai	Dulce Félix
Romania	Marius Ionescu	Cristiana Frumuz
Russia	Andrey Leyman	Irina Sergeyeva
(Oct)	Yuriy Chechun	Yekaterina Shlakhova
Scotland	Derek Hawkins	Freya Murray
Serbia	Goran Milicic	Amela Terzic
Slovakia (Nov)	Jaroslav Szabo	Katarina Beresová
Slovenia	Mitja Kosovelj	Lucija Krkoc
South Africa (Sep)	Tshamano Setone	Lebo Phalula
Spain	Ayad Lamdassem	Nuria Fernández
Sweden	Adil Baoufif	Charlotta Fougberg
Switzerland	Philipp Bandi	Christina Carruzzo
Turkey	Sabri Kara	Nilay Esen
Uganda	Moses Kipsiro	Annet Negesa
UK	Andy Vernon	Charlotte Purdue
Ukraine (Mar)	Oleksandr Matviychuk	Viktoriya Pogorelskaya
(Oct)	Igor Heletyi	Svitlana Svitko
USA	Brent Vaughan	Shalane Flanagan
Wales	Afan Humphries	Non Stanford
Balkan	Mirko Petrovic SRB	Olivera Jevtic SRB
European Clubs	Ayad Lamdassem ESP	Alemitu Bekele TUR
Teams	Conformlimpa ITA	Spor Kulubu TUR
Gulf	Bilisuma Shugi BRN	men only
NACAC	Robert Cheseret USA	Kathryn Harrison CAN
NCAA (Nov)	Lawi Lalang KEN	Sheila Lalang CAN
South America	Solonei da Silva BRA	Simone da Silva BRA

Short course winners

	Men	Women
Austria	Martin Pröll	
Belarus	Sergey Cheberyak	Natalya Koreyvo
Czech Republic	Lukas Kourek	
Denmark	Morten Munkholm	Maja Alm
Estonia	Roman Fosti	Jekaterina Patjuk
Finland	Janne Ukonmaanaho	
France	Nouredine Smaïl	Claire Navez
Lithuania	Justinas Berzanskis	Gintare Zenkeviciute
Norway	Sindre Buraas	Kirsten Melkevik
Poland	Tomasz Szymkowiak	Katarzyna Borniatowska
Portugal	Rui Silva	Sara Moreira
Russia	Aleksandr Krivchonkov	Yelena Zadorozhnaya
Scotland	Daniel Mulhare	Elspeth Curran
Slovenia	Mitka Krevs	
Sweden	Adil Bouafif	Charlotte Schönbeck
Ukraine	Roman Pasichnyk	Viktoriya Pogorelskaya

Winners of EAA and IAAF Permit Cross-Country Races 2011

8 Jan	Edinburgh (IAAF)	Mo Farah GBR	Linet Masai KEN
16 Jan	Rovereto (EA)	Thomas Longosiwa KEN	Birtukan Alemu ETH
16 Jan	Sevilla (IAAF)	Leonard Komon KEN	Vivian Cheruiyot KEN
22 Jan	Antrim (IAAF)	Mike Kigen KEN	Charlotte Purdue GBR
30 Jan	Belgrade (EA)	Darko Zivanovic SRB	Amela Terzic SRB
6 Feb	San Vittore Olana (IAAF)	Ayad Lamdassem ESP	Usküdar Belediyesi TUR
12 Feb	Nairobi (IAAF)	Levis Nyariki KEN	Emily Samoei KEN
13 Feb	Chiba (IAAF)	Bidan Karoki KEN	Hitomi Niiya JPN
27 Feb	Fukuoka (IAAF)	Bidan Karoki KEN	Hitomi Niiya JPN
27 Feb	Diekirch (IAAF)	Elabbassi El Hassan MAR	Maryam Jamal BRN
6 Mar	Albufeira (IAAF)	Kiprono Menjo KEN	Anikó Kálovics HUN
13 Nov	Atapuerca (IAAF)	Imane Merga ETH	Linet Masai KEN
20 Nov	Soria (EA)	Vincent Chepkok KEN	Priscah Jeptoo KEN
26 Nov	Szentendre (EA)	Tamás Kovács HUN	Mónika Nagy HUN
27 Nov	Leffinckroucke (EA)	Joseph Ebuya KEN	Feysa Tadesse ETH
27 Nov	Llodio (EA)	Leonard Komon KEN	Nadia Ejjafini ITA
27 Nov	Roeselare (EA)	Atelaw Bekele BEL	Yuliya Ruban UKR
27 Nov	Tilburg (EA)	Vitaly Shafar UKR	Adrienne Herzog NED
18 Dec	Brussels (IAAF)	Isiah Koech KEN	Caroline Chepkwony KEN

See ATHLETICS 2011 page 92 for results of the 2011 World Cross-Country Championships.

European Cross-Country Championships 2011

At Velenje, Slovenia 11 December

Senior Men (10k)
1. Atelaw Bekele BEL 29:15
2. Ayad Lamdassem ESP 29:20
3. José Rocha POR 29:21
4. Hassan Chahdi FRA 29:22
5. Joseph Sweeney IRL 29:23
6. Javier Guerra ESP 29:24
7. Mourad Amdouni FRA 29:26
8. Khalid Choukoud NED 29:27
9. Andrew Vernon GBR 29:39
10. Morten Toft Munkholm DEN 29:42
11. Mokhtar Benhari FRA 29:43
12. Benjamin Malaty FRA 29:44
13. Ryan McLeod GBR 29:45
14. Stefano La Rosa ITA 29:45
15. James Walsh GBR 29:46;
73 of 76 finished
Teams: 1. FRA 34, 2. GBR 59, 3. ESP 67, 4. POR 76, 5. ITA 84, 6. IRL 116, 7. DEN 135, 8. GER 160, 9. SLO 232, 10. SRB 250.

Under-23 Men (8k)
1. Florian Carvalho FRA 23:44
2. James Wilkinson GBR 23:47
3. Sondre Nordstad Moen NOR 23:48
4. Richard Ringer GER 23:48
5. Sergey Platonov BLR 23:51
6. Abdi Nageeye NED 23:54
7. Simon Denissel FRA 23:56
8. Mitch Goose GBR 23:57
97 of 98 finished
Teams: 1. NOR 59, 2. GBR 76, 3. FRA 94, 4. ESP 97, 5. RUS 107; 15 completed.

Junior Men (6k)
1. Ilgizar Safiulin RUS 17:49
2. Richard Goodman GBR 17:51
3. Vladimir Nikitin RUS 17:51
4. Romain Collenot-Spiret FRA 17:53
5. Pieter-Jan Hannes BEL 17:58
109 of 112 finished.
Teams: 1. GBR 30, 2. RUS 60, 3. FRA 103, 4. UKR 109, 5. BEL 118; 19 completed.

Senior Women (8k)
1. Fionnuala Britton IRL 25:55
2. Dulce Félix POR 26:02
3. Gemma Steel GBR 26:04
4. Nadia Ejjafini ITA 26:13
5. Adriënne Herzog NED 26:34
6. Sophie Duarte FRA 26:36
7. Roxana Bârca ROU 26:39
8. Leonor Carneiro POR 26:39
9. Simret Restle GER 26:40
10. Valeria Straneo ITA 26:42
11. Christine Bardelle FRA 26:50
12. Freya Murray GBR 26:51
13. Julia Bleasdale GBR 26:58
14. Elie Baker GBR 26:59
15. Cristiana Frumuz ROU 27:01
49 of 54 finished
Teams: 1. GBR 42, 2. POR 51, 3. GER 83, 4. FRA 83, 5. ROU 88, 6. ITA 101, 7. ESP 116, 8. IRL 133.

Under-23 Women (6k)
1. Emma Pallant GBR 19:57
2. Naomi Taschimowitz GBR 20:02
3. Corinna Harrer GER 20:03
4. Stephanie Twell GBR 20:03
5. Anna Hahner GER 20:05
6. Viktoriya Pogoryelska UKR 20:08
7. Hannah Walker GBR 20:12
8. Clémence Calvin FRA 20:16
42 of 43 finished
Teams: 1. GBR 14, 2. GER 41, 3. POR 77, 4. FRA 99, 5. TUR 101, 6. ESP 102.

Junior Women (4k)
1. Emelia Gorecka GBR 13:13
2. Ioana Doaga ROU 13:14
3. Amela Terzic SRB 13:22
4. Gulshat Fazlitdinova RUS 13:24
5. Zenobie Vangansbeke BEL 13:32
92 of 93 finished
Teams: 1. GBR 40, 2. RUS 43, 3. GER 50, 4. ROU 75, 5. NED 117; 16 completed

2011 WORLD ROAD RACE REVIEW
By Marty Post

MARY KEITANY CONTINUED to add to her collection of road running world records in 2011. The 29-year-old Kenyan, who set a WR of 1:19:53 for 25 kilometres in 2010, became the first woman to break 66 minutes on a record-quality half-marathon course at Ra's Al-Khaymah, UAE on February 18. She did so in remarkable style, setting personal bests through each 5km interval, speeding through the first in 15:18 and barely slowed down to pass 10km in 30:45.

Two more sub-16s gave her splits of 46:40 (15 km) and 62:36 (20km) before crossing the finish line in 65:50. Those times for the half-marathon and 20km were both ratified as world records and her split for 10 miles – not an official WR distance – was an all-time world best of 50:05. Her 15km split stood as the world leader for 2011.

Keitany also achieved the dubious distinction of becoming the first woman to finish a marathon after breaking 68 minutes for the first half. Her split at the New York City marathon was 67:56, seven seconds better than Paula Radcliffe's in her 2:15:25 WR at London 2003.

However, Keitany paid the price for her blazing start, running nearly nine minutes slower for the second half.

The half-marathon continued to produce tremendous depth of performance. There were 77 sub-70s, including eight during the first half of full marathons, by 59 different women. The Air-Delhi Half Marathon set a new standard of four finishers under 67:30. New Zealand's Kim Smith twice broke the North American all-comer's record and set Oceania records (67:36 at New Orleans and 67:11 at Philadelphia), adding a 69:51 at New Bedford. Kenyan Filomena Chepchirchir also had three winning sub-70s (Den Haag, Glasgow and Zwolle) and was third at Rabat in 68:51.

Initial reports from the Bank of America Marathon at Chicago on October 9, had Liliya Shobukhova reaching 30 kilometres in 1:38:23; however this pending world record was still awaiting ratification at year's end. (Radcliffe had a 1:37:40 at Chicago in 2002 that was unratifiable, as well as 1:37:27 at London 2005; her 1:36:36 at London in 2003 came when the net elevation drop was greater than 30 metres.)

The men's world record for that distance also had an intriguing twist. En route to his 2:03:38 marathon at Berlin, Patrick Makau passed 30 kilometres in 1:27:38. This time was ratified as a new world record, 11 seconds faster than the previous mark. Yet the fastest time in history was actually run by pacemaker, Peter Kirui, who was just enough ahead of Makau to clock a 1:27:37. However, his time could not be submitted for world record consideration since Kirui did not complete the full race distance.

Haile Gebrselassie continued to add to his collection of road race victories at the Vienna City Half Marathon (1:00:18), the Bupa Great Manchester Run 10km (28:10), the Bupa Great Birmingham Run Half Marathon (1:01:29) and the ABN AMRO Zevenheuvelenloop 15km (42:44).

The current and former 10km world record holders, Leonard Patrick Komon and Micah Kogo, shared the world lead of 27:15 at that distance in 2011 at European races. They also both picked up fast victories in the US, Komon over New York City's challenging Central Park course in 27:35 and Kogo at the Beach to Beacon 10km (27:47). Geoffrey Mutai returned to Boston in June, two months after running the fastest marathon in history there, to run the fastest 10km ever on US soil (27:19).

Zersenay Tadese (58:30) came within seven seconds of his half-marathon world record at Lisbon and broke the hour mark again at Porto.

A total of 21 men bettered the one hour for half marathon in 2011, but the only other multiple sub-60 minute men were Ethiopians Tujuba Mergesa who first surprised with a 59:58 at Rome-Ostia in February and five weeks later improved to 59:43 at Vitry-sur-Seine, and Lelisa Desisa who won in 59:37 at Den Haag in March and in 59:30 at New Delhi in November.

Matthew Kisorio (58:46) and Sammy Kitwara (58:48) both broke the previous North American all-comers record at the Philadelphia Rock 'n' Roll Half-Marathon. Kitwara also topped the Professional Road Running Organization circuit of high calibre North American road races, spearheaded by wins at the World's Best 10km and Peachtree Road Race 10km.

Leading Road Races 2011

See also Major Championships and National Championships sections

Date	Race	Men	Women
9 Jan	Egmond aan Zee HMar	Ayele Abshero ETH 62:23	Abebech Afework ETH 72:53
16 Jan	Tempe HMar	Shawn Forrest AUS 63:07	Madai Pérez MEX 71:49
16 Jan	Naples FL HMar	Nicholas Kurgat KEN 63:26	Belaynesh Gebre ETH 69:58
23 Jan	Carlsbad CA HMar	Wesley Korir KEN 62:46	Jane Kibii KEN 72:33
23 Jan	Santa Pola HMar	Asmeraw Bekele ETH 60:32	Rkia El Moukim MAR 71:49
29 Jan	Houston HMar US Ch	Mo Trafeh USA 62:17	Jen Rhines USA 71:14
30 Jan	Eldoret HMar	Abraham Chebii KEN 62:59	*men only*
30 Jan	Marrakech HMar	Muluget Wendimu ETH 62:00	Asmae Leghzaoui MAR 70:47
5 Feb	Edinburg TX 10km	Isaac Kimaiyo KEN 28:49	Shewarge Alene ETH 32:32
6 Feb	Coamo HMar	James Kwambai KEN 63:09	Yolanda Caballero COL 74:48
6 Feb	Granollers HMar	Eric Kibet KEN 63:25	Ruth Matebo KEN 74:26
6 Feb	Marugame HMar	Samuel Ndungu KEN 60:55	Kayoko Fukushi JPN 69:00
13 Feb	Bahir Dar 15km (A)	Deriba Merga ETH 41:55	Dire Tune ETH 48:32
13 Feb	Karatsu 10M/10km	Yuki Iwamoto JPN 47:20	Fumiko Hashimoto JPN 33:18
13 Feb	New Orleans HMar	Josphat Boit KEN 63:56	Kim Smith NZL 67:36
18 Feb	Ra's al Khaymah HMar	Deriba Merga ETH 59:25	Mary Keitany KEN 65:50 WR
20 Feb	Ribarroja HMar	Edwin Kipyego KEN 61:23	Hellen Mugo KEN 73:16
20 Feb	Oume 30km	Jason Lehmkuhle USA 1:32:08	Hiromi Ominami JPN 1:46:27
27 Feb	Rome to Ostia HMar	Tujuba Mergesa ETH 59:58	Anna Incerti ITA 69:06
27 Feb	San Juan 10km	Sammy Kitwara KEN 27:35	Sentayehu Ejigu ETH 31:50
6 Mar	Alphen aan den Rijn 20km	Bernard Chepkok KEN 59:26	Shitaye Bedaso ETH 67:37
6 Mar	Paris HMar	Stephen Kibet KEN 61:36	Peninah Arusei KEN 68:30
6 Mar	Verbania HMar	Dereje Deme ETH 60:00	Joyce Chepkirui KEN 71:18
12 Mar	Jacksonville 15km US Ch	Mo Trafeh USA 42:58	Jen Rhines USA 49:31
12 Mar	Laredo ESP 10km	José Manuel Martínez ESP 28:35	Paula González ESP 33:26
13 Mar	Den Haag HMar	Lelisa Desisa ETH 59:37	Flomena Chepchirchir KEN 69:06
19 Mar	Virginia Beach 8km	Josphat Boit KEN 23:10	Alemtsehay Misganaw ETH 26:59
20 Mar	Lisboa HMar	Zersenay Tadese ERI 58:30	Aberu Kebede ETH 68:28
20 Mar	New York HMar	Mo Farah GBR 60:23	Caroline Rotich KEN 68:52
20 Mar	Reading HMar	Simon Kasimili KEN 63:08	Edith Chelimo KEN 71:22
26 Mar	Azkoitia HMar	Stanley Biwott KEN 60:23	Fridah Domongole KEN 71:32
26 Mar	Mobile 10km	Richard Kandie KEN 29:15	Janet Cherobon-Bawcom USA 33:22
27 Mar	Milano HMar	Mathew Kisorio KEN 60:03	Birhane Ababel ETH 69:54
27 Mar	Venlo HMar	Stephen Chelimo KEN 62:26	Elizabeth Cherono KEN 71:26
27 Mar	Warszawa HMar	Sammy Kigen Korir KEN 61:18	Katarzyna Kowalska POL 71:27
2 Apr	Charleston 10km	Lelisa Desisa ETH 28:59	Shewarge Alene ETH 33:06
2 Apr	Praha HMar	Philemon Limo KEN 59:30	Lydia Cheromei KEN 67:33
3 Apr	Berlin HMar	Geoffrey Kipsang KEN 60:38	Valentine Kipketer KEN 70:12
3 Apr	Brunssum 10km	Micah Kogo KEN 27:15	Irina Mikitenko GER 32:06
3 Apr	Carlsbad 5km	Dejene Gebremeskel ETH 13:11	Aheza Kiros ETH 15:13
3 Apr	Madrid HMar	Enock Mitei KEN 62:42	Firehiwat Goshu ETH 73:25
3 Apr	Rabat HMar	John Mwangangi KEN 61:08	Feysa Tadesse ETH 68:44
3 Apr	Vitry-sur-Seine HMar	Dino Sefir ETH 59:42	Sarah Chepchirchir KEN 68:07
3 Apr	Washington DC 10M	Lelisa Desisa ETH 45:36	Jelliah Kerubo Tinega KEN 54:02
10 Apr	Chicago 8km	Simon Bairu CAN 23:38	Amy Begley USA 26:50
10 Apr	Dublin 10km	Jesús España ESP 29:26	Charlotte Purdue GBR 32:42
10 Apr	Korschenbroich 10km/5km	Daniel Chebii KEN 28:18	Karolina Jarzynska POL 15:58
17 Apr	Hilversum 10km	Wilfred Murgor KEN 28:07	Rkia El Moukim MAR 32:55
17 Apr	Nice HMar	Levi Matebo Omari KEN 60:06	Feysa Tadesse ETH 71:08
17 Apr	Würzburg 10km	Leonard P Komon KEN 27:33	Doris Changeiywo KEN 31:26
23 Apr	New Orleans 10km	Belete Assefa ETH 28:14	Wude Ayelew ETH 31:36
23 Apr	Paderborn 10km	Titus Mbishei KEN 28:05	Doris Changeiywo KEN 32:03
23 Apr	Paderborn HMar	Sammy Korir KEN 63:16	Abebech Afework ETH 72:45
24 Apr	Yangzhou HMar	Deriba Merga ETH 61:10	Mare Dibaba ETH 69:41
25 Apr	Dongio 10km	Imane Merga ETH 28:18	*men only*
1 May	Marseille 10km	Titus Mbishei KEN 27:32	Doris Changeiywo KEN 33:03
1 May	Puy-en-Velay 15km	Dino Sefir ETH 43:57	Sarah Chepchirchir KEN 50:28

Date	Event	Men	Women
1 May	Spokane 12km	Simon Ndirangu KEN 33:58	Misiker Mekonnin ETH 40:25
1 May	Toronto 10km dh	Reid Coolsaet CAN 28:08	Dayna Pidhoresky CAN 33:02
7 May	Indianapolis HMar	Ridouane Harroufi MAR 62:46	Everlyne Lagat KEN 71:29
8 May	Albacete HMar	Sium Kiflom ERI 62:11	Pauline Njeri Kahenya KEN 71:11
8 May	Berlin 25km	Mathew Kisorio KEN 72:13	Flomena Chepchirchir KEN 1:23:22
8 May	Glasgow 10km	women only	Linet Masai KEN 32:11
14 May	Grand Rapids 25km-US Ch	Fernando Cabada USA 75:41	Molly Pritz USA 1:25:38
14 May	Msssamagrell 15km	José Manuel Martínez ESP 44:42	Winnie Jepkemoi KEN 49:14
14 May	New York (C.Pk) 10km	Leonard P Komon KEN 27:35	Buzunesh Deba ETH 33:39
15 May	Bristol GBR 10km	Edwin Kiptoo KEN 28:39	Edinah Kwambai KEN 32:29
15 May	Manchester 10km	Haile Gebrselassie ETH 28:10	Helen Clitheroe GBR 31:45
15 May	San Francisco 12km	Ridouane Harroufi MAR 34:26	Lineth Chepkurui KEN 39:12
15 May	San Sebastián HMar	Abdellah Taghrafet MAR 62:05	Beatrice Jepchumba KEN 75:21
15 May	Santos 10km	Marílson dos Santos BRA 27:59	Eunice Jepkirui Kirwa KEN 32:07
21 May	Göteborg HMar	Albert Matebor KEN 60:52	Joyce Chepkirui KEN 69:04
22 May	Den Haag 10km	Timothy Kiptoo KEN 28:13	Nadia Ejjafini ITA 32:17
22 May	Wien, AUT 5km	women only	Ann Dulce Félix POR 15:28
28 May	Ottawa 10km	Deriba Merga ETH 28:31	Dire Tune ETH 31:44
29 May	Toa Baja 10km	Sammy Kitwara KEN 28:47	Maria del Pilar Diaz PUR 36:50
30 May	Boulder 10km (A)	Beleta Assefa ETH 29:23	Lineth Chepkurui KEN 32:30
30 May	London 10km	Mo Farah GBR 29:15	Jo Pavey GBR 32:22
4 Jun	Albany 5km	women only	Mamitu Daska ETH 15:19
5 Jun	Bangalore 10km	Philemon Limo KEN 28:01	Dire Tune ETH 33:19
5 Jun	Groesbeek 10km	Philip Langat KEN 27:54	Rkia El Moukim, MAR 33:02
5 Jun	Jakarta 10km	Henry Chirchir KEN 29:00	Aberu Kebede ETH 32:31
10 Jun	Oelde 10km	Philip Langat KEN 27:49	Tola Fate ETH 32:19
11 Jun	New York 10km	women only	Linet Masai KEN 31:40
18 Jun	Zwolle HMar	Wilson Kipsang KEN 60:49	Flomena Chepchirchir KEN 68:22
19 Jun	Olomouc HMar	Abdullah Dawit ETH 60:44	Netsanet Achamo ETH 70:40
25 Jun	Appingdem 10km	Boniface Kirui KEN 28:02	Joyce Chepkirui KEN 30:43
25 Jun	Langueux 10km	Atsedu Tsegay ETH 27:46	Miriam Wangari KEN 32:31
26 Jun	Boston 10km	Geoffrey Mutai KEN 27:19	Caroline Kilel KEN 31:58
26 Jun	Porto 15km	Peter Kimeli KEN 43:57	Hellen Mugo KEN 53:03
2 Jul	Port Elizabeth HMar	Stephen Mokoka RSA 62:07	René Kalmer RSA 72:59
3 Jul	Hamburg HMar	Joseph Kiprono Kiptum 63:15	Monica Jepkoech KEN 76:08
3 Jul	Sapporo HMar	Cyrus Njuji KEN 61:47	Florence Kiplagat KEN 70:29
4 Jul	Atlanta 10km	Sammy Kitwara KEN 28:05	Werknesh Kidane ETH 31:23
10 Jul	Utica 15km	Ridouane Harroufi MAR 43:30	Alice Timbilili KEN 48:41
13 Jul	Voorthuizen 10km	Stephen Chelimo KEN 28:48	Susan Chepkemei KEN 32:59
16 Jul	Kingsport 8km	Shadrack Kosgei KEN 22:22	Alexa Hinton USA 29:27
24 Jul	Capitola 6M	Silas Kipruto KEN 26:56	Magdalena Lewy Boulet USA 30:49
26 Jul	Castelbuono 10km	Geoffrey Mutai KEN 29:05	men only
30 Jul	Davenport 7M US Ch	Silas Kipruto KEN 32:36	Caroline Rotich KEN 36:42
31 Jul	Bogotá HMar (A)	Geoffrey Mutai KEN 62:20	Joyce Chepkirui KEN 73:34
6 Aug	Cape Elizabeth 10km	Micah Kogo KEN 27:47	Aheza Kiros ETH 32:09
7 Aug	Providence HMar	Kumsa Adugna ETH 67:32	Kim Smith NZL 71:54
14 Aug	Falmouth 7M	Lucas Rotich KEN 31:37	Magdalena Lewy Boulet USA 36:58
20 Aug	Amatrice 8.5km	Stephen Kibet KEN 24:10	Asmerawork Bekele ETH 29:28
20 Aug	Parkersburg HMar	Julius Kogo KEN 61:47	Malika Mejdoub MAR 74:45
21 Aug	Klagenfurt HMar	Wilson Kipsang KEN 62:25	Florence Kiplagat KEN 68:02
21 Aug	Rio de Janeiro HMar	Mark Korir KEN 61:33	Eunice Jepkirui Kirwa KEN 70:29
27 Aug	Flint 10M	Julius Kogo KEN 47:15	Everlyne Lagat KEN 55:15
3 Sep	Lille HMar	Geoffrey Kipsang KEN 60:02	Valentine Kipketer KEN 68:21
4 Sep	Bologna HMar	Peter Kirui KEN 61:50	Valeria Straneo ITA 70:32
4 Sep	Glasgow HMar	Joseph Birech KEN 61:26	Flomena Chepchirchir KEN 69:26
4 Sep	Düsseldorf 10km	Shadrack Kemboi KEN 28:45	Zeineba Hayato ETH 33:18
4 Sep	Tilburg 10M/10km	Philemon Rono KEN 47:21	Joyce Chepkirui KEN 30:38
4 Sep	Virginia Beach HMar	Benson Barus KEN 62:22	Yoko Miyauchi JPN 71:49
5 Sep	New Haven 20km US Ch	Abdi Abdirahman USA 60:12	Janet Cherobon-Bawcom USA 68:31
10 Sep	Praha 10km/5km	Philemon Limo KEN 27:34	Priscah Jepleting Cherono KEN 15:32
11 Sep	Bristol HMar	Edwin Kipyego KEN 63:20	Gemma Steel GBR 73:32

Date	Event	Men	Women
11 Sep	Buenos Aires HMar	Marílson dos Santos BRA 61:13	Adriana da Silva BRA 73:16
11 Sep	Hamburg 10km	Daniel Chebii KEN 28:32	Caroline Chepkwony KEN 32:49
11 Sep	Vannes HMar	Evans Kosgei KEN 62:21	Rose Chelimo KEN 71:27
18 Sep	Philadelphia HMar	Mathew Kisorio KEN 58:46	Kim Smith NZL 67:11
18 Sep	Porto HMar	Zersenay Tadese ERI 59:30	Doris Changeywo KEN 70:36
18 Sep	South Shields HMar	Martin Mathathi KEN 58:56	Lucy Wangui Kabuu KEN 67:06
18 Sep	Ústi nad Labem HMar	Philemon Limo KEN 60:57	Agnes Kiprop KEN 69:12
18 Sep	Zaandam 10M	Leonard P Komon KEN 44:27	Priscah Jepleting Cherono KEN 51:57
24 Sep	New York 5th Ave 1M	Bernard Lagat USA 3:50.5	Jenny Simpson USA 4:22.3
24 Sep	Scicili 10km/c. 7km	Imane Merga ETH 28:38	Sylvia Kibet KEN 24:36
25 Sep	Lisboa HMar	Silas Sang KEN 61:12	Mary Keitany KEN 67:53
25 Sep	Montbéliard HMar	Luka Kanda KEN 62:50	Eshetu Biruktayit ETH 73:45
25 Sep	Paris-Versailles 16km	Atsedu Tsegay ETH 47:39	Goitetom Haftu ETH 563:41
25 Sep	Remich HMar	Leonard Langat KEN 61:07	Abebech Afework ETH 70:30
25 Sep	Udine HMar	Stephen Kibet KEN 60:20	Pauline Njeri Kahanya KEN 70:44
25 Sep	Utrecht 10km	Philip Langat KEN 27:28	Winnie Jepkemoi KEN 31:32
1 Oct	Potomac HMar	Moses Kigen KEN 62:37	Bekelech Bedada ETH 72:44
2 Oct	Breda HMar	Philip Langat KEN 61:58	Elizabeth Cherono KEN 71:42
2 Oct	Edinburgh 10km	Martin Mathathi KEN 28:03	Lucy Wangui Kabuu KEN 32:28
2 Oct	Marrakech 10km	Hicham Bellani MAR 28:04	Nadia Ejjafini ITA 32:25
2 Oct	Nancy HMar	Alfred Cherop KEN 61:48	Sarah Chepchirchir KEN 70:10
2 Oct	San Jose HMar	Meb Keflezighi USA 62:17	Deena Kastor USA 72:23
2 Oct	St. Paul 10M US Champ	Mo Trafeh USA 46:46	Janet Cherobon Bawcom USA 54:15
8 Oct	Trento 10km	Edwin Soi KEN 29:17	*men only*
9 Oct	Berlin 10km	Leonard P Komon KEN 27:15	Mara Yamauchi GBR 32:19
9 Oct	Boston HMar	Ali Abdosh ETH 63:36	Janet Cherobon Bawcom USA 71:58
9 Oct	Groningen 4M	Vincent Yator KEN 17:06	Sylvia Kibet KEN 19:40
9 Oct	Paris 20km	John Mwangangi KEN 58:11	Sarah Chepchirchir KEN 66:04
9 Oct	Rennes 10km/6.25km	Philemon Limo KEN 27:42	Margaret Muriuki KEN 15:29
9 Oct	Sheffield 10km	Micah Kogo KEN 28:45	Gemma Steel GBR 32:52
10 Oct	Boston 10km	*US women champs*	Janet Cherobon Bawcom USA 32:47
16 Oct	Cardiff HMar	Edwin Kiptoo KEN 63:27	Alice Mogire KEN 71:26
16 Oct	Cremona HMar	Eric Chirchir KEN 62:17	Nadia Ejjafini ITA 68:27
16 Oct	Reims HMar	Philemon Yator KEN 61:47	Atsede Baysa ETH 69:58
16 Oct	Saint Denis HMar	Robert Kwambai KEN 62:50	Mirriam Wangari KEN 71:10
23 Oct	Birmingham HMar	Haile Gebrselassie ETH 61:29	Gemma Steel GBR 72:21
23 Oct	Montereau 10km	Alfred Cherop KEN 28:59	Rose Chelimo KEN 32:04
23 Oct	Valencia HMar	John Mwangangi KEN 59:45	Malika Asahasah MAR 70:26
29 Oct	Tulsa 15km	Josphat Boit KEN 44:10	Mulu Seboka ETH 51:54
30 Oct	Almerim Eur Clubs HMar	Hermano Ferreira POR 62:55	15km: Dulce Félix POR 51:01
30 Oct	Cassis 20.308 km	Atsedu Tsegay ETH 58:10	Lydia Cheromei KEN 68:17
30 Oct	Morlaix 10km (dh)	Abraham Niyonkuru BDI 28:18	Catherine Webombesa UGA 33:23
30 Oct	Portsmouth 10M	Leonard P Komon KEN 46:18	Aselefech Mergia ETH 52:55
5 Nov	New York 5km	Chris Thompson GBR 13:53	Sara Hall USA 15:56
13 Nov	San Antonio HMar	Augustus Maiyo KEN 64:24	Shalane Flanagan USA 70:49
20 Nov	Ageo HMar	Cosmas Ndiba KEN 62:27	Miya Nishio JPN 73:32
20 Nov	Boulogne-Billancourt HMar	Sentayehu Merga ETH 61:38	Goitetom Haftu ETH 70:57
20 Nov	Monterey Bay HMar	Ezkyas Sisay ETH 63:48	Magdalena Lewy Boulet USA 74:16
20 Nov	Nijmegen 15km	Haile Gebrselassie ETH 42:44	Waganesh Mekasha ETH 48:33
24 Nov	Manchester CT 4.8M	Brian Olinger USA 21:33	Sally Kipyego KEN 24:22
27 Nov	Addis Ababa 10km	Musnet Geremew ETH 28:37	Abebech Afework ETH 32:59
27 Nov	New Delhi HMar	Lelisa Desisa ETH 59:30	Lucy Wangui Kabuu KEN 67:04
4 Dec	Belo Horizonte 17.8km	Barnabas Kosgei KEN 53:09	Nancy Jepkosgei Kiprono KEN 62:41
4 Dec	Kosa 10M	Martin Mathathi KEN 46:20	*men only*
4 Dec	Las Vegas HMar	Sean Houseworth USA 63:12	Benita Willis AUS 70:40
4 Dec	's-Heerenberg 15km	Philip Langat KEN 42:34	Abebech Afework ETH 49:19
10 Dec	Sion 7.35km/5.25km	Titus Mbishei KEN 19:25	Caroline Chepkwony KEN 15:52
11 Dec	Miami HMar	Simon Bairu KEN 65:38	Shalane Flanagan USA 69:58
11 Dec	Zurich 8.8km/6.3km	Paul Kipkorir KEN 25:23	Caroline Chepkwony KEN 20:23
18 Dec	Houilles 10km	Edwin Soi KEN 28:17	Margaret Muriuki KEN 31:29
18 Dec	Porto 10km	Rui Pedro Silva POR 28:34	Carla Salomé Rocha POR 32:24

Date	Event	Men	Women
18 Dec	Zhuhai HMar	El Hassan Elabassi MAR 61:13	Gladys Cherono KEN 70:43
23 Dec	Okayama HMar	*women only*	Yukiko Akaba JPN 69:16
31 Dec	Bolzano 10.05km/5.05km	Edwin Soi KEN 28:17	Vivian Cheruiyot KEN 16:03
31 Dec	Luanda 10km	Zersenay Tadese ERI 27:44	Embet Mengistu ETH 32:23
31 Dec	Madrid 10km	Hagos Gebrhiwet ETH 27:57	Tirunesh Dibaba ETH 31:30
31 Dec	Peuerbach 6.8km/5.1km	Leonard P Komon KEN 18:51	Asmere Work Bekele ETH 16:24
31 Dec	São Paulo 15km	Tariku Bekele ETH 43:35	Priscah Jeptoo KEN 48:48
31 Dec	Trier 8km/5km	Mosinet Girmet ETH 22:37	Almensch Belete ETH 15:56

2011 WORLD MARATHON REVIEW
By Marty Post

IN THE HISTORY of athletics, there have been nations that have dominated a certain discipline. In the early days of the sport, milers from Great Britain were unchallenged, Americans ruled the sprints and hurdles for long periods of time and hammer throwers from the former Soviet Union reigned over the world. However, the supremacy of Kenya's marathoners in 2011 was unprecedented, especially given modern global participation.

Nothing illustrates this better than a glance at the fastest times on record-quality courses for the year, where Kenyans swept a surrealistic top 24 performances turned in by 20 different runners. At the very top of this pyramid were a new world record of 2:03:38 at Berlin by Patrick Makau and the fastest time in history of 2:03:02 at Boston by Geoffrey Mutai. Another record, the world junior mark, passed to Kenyan Eric Ndiema with his 2:06:07 at Amsterdam. Mutai also ran 2:05:06 at New York City, for the fastest ever one-year two race total of 4:08:08. Chicago Marathon winner, Moses Mosop (2:05:37), four seconds behind Mutai at Boston, with a 4:08:43 sum also beat the 4:08:52 by Haile Gebrselassie on two standard courses in 2008.

The World Marathon Majors competition, which formally began in 2006 although the races that comprise the series date back more than 30 years, never had one nation account for all winners within a year – until 2011 when Kenyans produced not just six victories, but both first *and* second places across the sextet. And for good measure they set course records at all five of the annual city races: Boston, London, Berlin, Chicago and New York City.

With the largest victory margin ever (2:28), Abel Kirui became the third man to defend his World Championship and there were also victories at Frankfurt, Rotterdam, Amsterdam, Eindhoven, Paris, Prague, Dubai and Rome, among the 137 Kenyan winning times under two hours twenty minutes. In October they ran 218 sub-2:20s, the first month one nation topped 200, and 76 men broke 2:20 at the Nairobi marathon – at high altitude, no less – the most in one race since April 1991 and the fifth best total in history. All told there were 743 sub-2:20s during the year, smashing the former record by almost 90.

The stunning statistics in 2011 were not, however, just limited to Kenyan marathoners. In 2007 leading to the Beijing Olympics, the world's elite male marathoners produced depth of performances near the highest achieved in one year: 6 times under 2:07, 25 under 2:08, 45 under 2:09 and 79 under 2:10. Flash forward four years later, the next pre-Olympic year, to a quantum leap in these performances across the board: 36 under 2:07, 63 under 2:08, 109 under 2:09 and 179 under 2:10. In addition to these single year records, there were more at sub-2:06 (17), sub-2:05 (7) and sub-2:04 (4). In terms of depth, the Frankfurt Marathon generated the most ever sub-2:10s (14), sub-2:11s (19) and best times for places 13 through 27. A few weeks earlier, Amsterdam had a record seven men under 2:07:30.

Women made sensational strides as well. Again take a look at 2007: sub-2:25s (15), sub-2:26s (19), sub-2:27s (28), sub-2:28s (36), sub-2:29s (53) and sub-2:30s (79). Four years later the corresponding numbers were 49, 69, 104, 134, 161 and 199. Russian Liliya Shubokova topped the 2011 list at 2:18:20, the fastest non-Paula Radcliffe time ever, and Kenyan Mary Keitany (2:19:19) led a record 20 sub-2:30 women at London.

Surprisingly, though, it wasn't the Kenyans who dominated the women's performance lists, but the Ethiopians with 71 of the sub-2:30s, almost twice as many (36) as their East African compatriots. And while Kenyans won a number of high prestige marathons such as the World Championships, Boston, London, Berlin,

Rotterdam and Paris, Ethiopians struck victory at New York City, Amsterdam, Dubai, Frankfurt and Rome.

There were also a couple of notable age-group world records at the Toronto Waterfront Marathon, Ed Whitlock (3:15:54, 80-84 AG) and Fauja Singh (8:11:06, 100+ AG). For the third year in a row, the New York City Marathon became the world's biggest marathon as 46,795 reached the finish and the new Osaka Marathon set first-time event records for starters (27,161) and finishers (26,175).

WINNERS OF 2011 INTERNATIONAL MARATHONS

Date	City	Men's winner	Time	Women's winner	Time
2 Jan	Xiamen, CHN	Robert Kipchumba KEN	2:08:07	Amane Gobena ETH	2:31:49
6 Jan	Tiberias, ISR	Stephen Chemlany KEN	2:10:02	Abanynesh Sisay ETH	2:44:31
16 Jan	Mumbai, IND	Girma Assefa ETH	2:09:54	Koren Jelela ETH	2:26:56
21 Jan	Dubai, UAE	David Barmasai KEN	2:07:18	Aselefech Mergia ETH	2:22:45
30 Jan	Houston, USA	Bekana Daba ETH	2:07:04	Mamitu Daska ETH	2:26:33
30 Jan	Marrakech, MAR	Gezahagn Girma ETH	2:10:22	Wudnesh Nega ETH	2:37:00
30 Jan	Miami, USA	Tesfaye Alemayehu ETH	2:12:57	Yelena Vinitskaya BLR	2:44:39
30 Jan	Osaka, JPN	*women only*		Yukiko Akaba JPN	2:26:29
6 Feb	Beppu-Oita, JPN	Ahmed Baday MAR	2:10:14	Chiyuki Mochizuki JPN	2:39:57
13 Feb	Sevilla, ESP	Daniel Abera ETH	2:09:53	Alemnesh Eshetu ETH	2:33:26
20 Feb	Hong Kong, CHN	Nelson Rotich KEN	2:16:00	Janet Rono KEN	2:33:42
20 Feb	Verona, ITA	Albert Matebor KEN	2:09:16	Rebecca Jerotich KEN	2:35:56
20 Feb	Yokohama, JPN	*women only*		Yoshimi Ozaki JPN	2:23:56
27 Feb	Tokyo, JPN	Hailu Mekonnen ETH	2:07:35	Tatyana Aryasova RUS	2:27:29
6 Mar	Barcelona, ESP	Levi Matebo KEN	2:07:31	Josephine Ambjornsson SWE	2:45:31
6 Mar	Lake Biwa, Otsu, JPN	Wilson Kipsang KEN	2:06:13	*men only*	
6 Mar	Torreón, MEX	Hillary Kimaiyo KEN	2:08:17	Paula Apolonio MEX	2:34:27
20 Mar	Los Angeles, USA	Markos Geneti ETH	2:06:35	Bizunesh Deba ETH	2:26:34
20 Mar	Roma, ITA	Dixon Chumba KEN	2:08:45	Firehiwot Dado ETH	2:24:13
20 Mar	Seoul, KOR	Abderrahim Goumri MAR	2:09:11	Robe Guta ETH	2:26:51
27 Mar	Zhengzhou, CHN	Eliud Kipchanga Cheptei KEN	2:10:21	Wei Jie CHN	2:26:41
3 Apr	Santiago, CHI	Julius Keter KEN	2:13:22	Hyvon Ngetich KEN	2:34:42
10 Apr	Brighton, GBR	Philemon Boit KEN	2:16:07	Alyson Dixon GBR	2:34:51
10 Apr	Daegu, KOR	Yusuf Songoka KEN	2:08:08	Atsede Habtamu ETH	2:25:52
10 Apr	Linz, AUT	Nixon Machichim KEN	2:09:37	Lisa Stublic CRO	2:30:46
10 Apr	Milano, ITA	Solomon Busendich KEN	2:10:38	Marcella Mancini ITA	2:41:24
10 Apr	Paris, FRA	Benjamin Kiptoo Kolum KEN	2:06:31	Priscah Jeptoo KEN	2:22:55
10 Apr	Rotterdam, NED	Wilson Chebet KEN	2:05:27	Philes Ongari KEN	2:24:20
10 Apr	Thessaloníki, GRE	Peter Biwott KEN	2:13:12	Sisay Measso ETH	2:40:39
17 Apr	Antwerp BEL	Elijah Kemboi KEN	2:11:15	Anne Marie Dupont BEL	3:08:06
17 Apr	Beograd, SRB	Tsegay Gebreselassie ETH	2:14:41	Fresiah Waithaka KEN	2:34:31
17 Apr	Enschede, NED	Stephen Kiprotich KEN	2:07:20	Ingrid Prigge NED	2:45:10
17 Apr	Kraków, POL	Cosmas Kyeva KEN	2:12:20	Tetyana Hamera-Shmyrko UKR	2:28:14
17 Apr	London, GBR	Emmanuel Mutai KEN	2:04:40	Mary Keitany KEN	2:19:19
17 Apr	Madrid, ESP	Moses Arusei Kimeli KEN	2:10:58	Girma Tadesse ETH	2:35:28
17 Apr	Padova, ITA	Tadesse Tolesa ETH	2:09:02	Florence Chepsoi KEN	2:29:25
17 Apr	Wien, AUT	John Kiprotich KEN	2:08:29	Fate Tola ETH	2:26:21
17 Apr	Zürich, SUI	John Kyui KEN	2:10:00	Svitlana Stanko UKR	2:33:25
18 Apr	Boston, USA	Geoffrey Mutai KEN	2:03:02	Caroline Kilel KEN	2:22:36
30 Apr	Dalian CHN	Stephen Chemlany KEN	2:14:15	Wang Jiali CHN	2:26:12
2 May	Belfast, NIR	Jacob Chesire KEN	2:14:56	Vera Ovcharuk UKR	2:46:04
8 May	Düsseldorf, GER	Nashon Kimaiyo KEN	2:10:54	Merima Mohammed ETH	2:28:15
8 May	Hannover, GER	Lusapho April RSA	2:09:25	Georgina Rono KEN	2:31:19
8 May	Mainz, GER	Tola Bane ETH	2:13:32	Asha Gigi ETH	2:31:10
8 May	Praha, CZE	Benson Barus KEN	2:07:07	Lydia Cheromei KEN	2:22:34
14 May	Moskva, RUS (NC)	Yuriy Abramov RUS	2:14:53	Lyubov Morgunova RUS	2:30:27
15 May	Dongying ,CHN	Luka Chelimo KEN	2:13:37	Emmah Muthoni KEN	2:31:43
15 May	Mombasa, KEN	Wilson Loyanai KEN	2:13:00	Rose Nyangacha KEN	2:39:01
22 May	Hamburg, GER	Gudisa Shentema ETH	2:11:03	Fatuma Sado ETH	2:28:30
28 May	Stockholm, SWE	Shumi Gerbaba ETH	2:14:07	Isabellah Andersson SWE	2:37:28
29 May	Mt. St Michael, FRA	Jacob Kitur FRA	2:11:00	Svetlana Prétot FRA	2:35:28

Date	Location	Men		Women	
29 May	Ottawa, CAN	Laban Moiben KEN	2:10:18	Haile Kebebush ETH	2:32:14
5 Jun	San Diego, USA	Terfa Negari ETH	2:11:18	Bizunesh Deba ETH	2:23:31
11 Jun	Luxembourg, LUX	Teferi Bacha ETH	2:15:43	Rael Kiyara KEN	2:34:30
18 Jun	Duluth, USA	Christopher Kipyego KEN	2:12:17	Delelecha Yihunlish ETH	2:30:39
19 Jun	São Paolo, BRA	David Kemboi Kiyeng KEN	2:11:53	Samira Raïf MAR	2:36:01
26 Jun	Kuala Lumpur, MAS	Lilian Kiprop KEN	2:20:09	Rose Nyangacha KEN	2:34:38
3 Jul	Gold Coast, AUS	Nicholas Manza Kamakya KEN	2:10:01	Goitetom Haftu ETH	2:30:08
6 Aug	Omsk, RUS	Keyo Kiplimo KEN	2:14:25	Nina Podnebosova RUS	2:37:22
28 Aug	C de México, MEX	Isaac Kimaiyo Kemboi KEN	2:14:23	Rose Jebet KEN	2:39:07
28 Aug	Sapporo, JPN	Harun Nijoroge KEN	2:14:10	Tomo Morimoto JPN	2:33:45
4 Sep	Taiyuan, CHN	Michael Kimani KEN	2:10:08	Haile Kebebush ETH	2:31:11
11 Sep	Tallinn, EST	Julius Muriuki KEN	2:12:56	Almaz Alemu Balcha ETH	2:34:14
25 Sep	Berlin, GER	Patrick Makau KEN	2:03:38	Florence Kiplagat KEN	2:19:44
25 Sep	Cape Town, RSA	Amus Maiyo KEN	2:14:55	Chiyedza Chokore ZIM	2:46:31
25 Sep	Montreal, CAN	Luka Chelimo KEN	2:13:45	Serkalem Biset Abrha ETH	2:33:21
25 Sep	Warszawa, POL	Sammy Kibet KEN	2:08:17	Svietlana Stanko UKR	2:31:28
2 Oct	Belaya Tserkov, UKR	Aleksandr Sitovskyy UKR	2:09:26	Mariya Kiseleva RUS	2:38:43
2 Oct	Bregenz, AUT	Mariko Kiplagat Kipchumba KEN	2:11:21	Susanne Pumper AUT	2:38:24
2 Oct	Bruxelles, BEL	Paul Kiprop Kirui KEN	2:14:51	Mariska Dute NED	3:00:01
2 Oct	Köln, GER	Samson Barmao KEN	2:08:56	Mekuna Aberume ETH	2:32:24
2 Oct	Kosice, SVK	Elijah Kemboi KEN	2:11:15	Maryna Damantsevich BLR	2:33:53
2 Oct	St. Paul, USA	Sammy Malakwen KEN	2:13:11	Yeshimebet Tadesse ETH	2:28:24
9 Oct	Bucuresti, ROU	Getu Tekla ETH	2:17:21	Marina Kovalyeva RUS	2:33:20
9 Oct	Buenos Aires, ARG	Simon Njoroge KEN	2:10:24	Andrea Graciano ARG	2:46:34
9 Oct	Carpi, ITA	Nicholas Kurgat KEN	2:08:36	Denbe Godana ETH	2:32:22
9 Oct	Chicago, USA	Moses Mosop KEN	2:05:37	Liliya Shibukhova RUS	2:18:20
9 Oct	Eindhoven, NED	Jafred Kipchumba KEN	2:05:48	Georgina Rono KEN	2:24:33
9 Oct	Graz, AUT	Edwin Kemboi KEN	2:14:58	Esther Wanjiru Macharia KEN	2:32:12
9 Oct	Melbourne, AUS	Japhet Kipkorir KEN	2:11:11	Irene Mogaka KEN	2:35:12
9 Oct	Zagreb, CRO	Yared Admasu ETH	2:17:42	Lucia Kimani BIH	2:34:57
15 Oct	Baltimore, USA	Stephen Muange KEN	2:15:16	Olena Shurhno UKR	2:29:11
16 Oct	Amsterdam, NED	Wilson Chebet KEN	2:05:53	Tiki Gelana ETH	2:22:08
16 Oct	Beijing, CHN	Francis Kiprop KEN	2:99:00	Wei Xiaojie CHN	2:28:05
16 Oct	Gyongju, KOR	Wilson Loyanai KEN	2:09:23	Lim Kyung-hee KOR	2:38:21
16 Oct	Istanbul, TUR	Vincent Kiplagat KEN	2:10:58	Alemitu Abera ETH	2:27:56
16 Oct	Poznan, POL	Cosmas Kyewa KEN	2:11:53	Arleta Meloch POL	2:39:12
16 Oct	Reims, FRA	Demessew Tsega ETH	2:09:44	Julia Mombi KEN	2:29:36
16 Oct	Toronto, CAN	Kenneth Mungara KEN	2:09:51	Koren Jelela ETH	2:22:43
22 Oct	Bilbao, ESP	Abdellah Taghrafet MAR	2:08:21	Meseret Terefe ETH	2:53:36
23 Oct	Casablanca, MAR	Ennaji El Idrissi MAR	2:12:56	Debele Wudnesh Nega ETH	2:50:05
23 Oct	Chunchon, KOR	Stanley Biwott KEN	2:07:03	Oh Jung-hee KOR	2:41:23
23 Oct	Juárez, MEX	Erik Monyenke KEN	2:15:12	Rose Chebet KEN	2:34:03
23 Oct	Ljubljana, SLO	Daniel Too KEN	2:08:25	Lydia Kurgat KEN	2:33:01
23 Oct	Toulouse, FRA	Patrick Korir KEN	2:11:36	Alice Serser KEN	2:37:06
23 Oct	Venezia, ITA	Tadese Aredo ETH	2:09:13	Helena Kirop KEN	2:23:37
30 Oct	Frankfurt, GER	Wilson Kipsang KEN	2:03:42	Mamitu Daska ETH	2:21:59
30 Oct	Nairobi, KEN (A)	Ernest Kebenei KEN	2:10:55	Margaret Toroitich KEN	2:30:18
30 Oct	Osaka, JPN	Elijah Sang KEN	2:12:43	Lidia Simon ROU	2:32:48
31 Oct	Dublin, IRL	Geoffrey Ndungu KEN	2:08:35	Helalia Johannes NAM	2:30:37
6 Nov	New York City, USA	Geoffrey Mutai KEN	2:05:06	Firehiwot Dado ETH	2:23:15
6 Nov	Porto, POR	Philemon Baaru KEN	2:09:51	Pauline Chepchumba KEN	2:41:25
6 Nov	Seoul, KOR	James Kwambai KEN	2:08:50	Choi Kyung-hee KOR	2:40:49
13 Nov	Athína, GRE	Abdelkrim Boubker MAR	2:11:40	Elfneshe Melkamu ETH	2:35:25
13 Nov	Torino, ITA	Ennaji El Idrissi MAR	2:08:13	Yuliya Ruban UKR	2:27:10
20 Nov	Cannes, FRA	Luke Kanda KEN	2:08:40	Woldegebriel Teamo ETH	2:30:53
20 Nov	Yokohama, JPN	*women only*		Ryoko Kizaki JPN	2:26:32
27 Nov	Beirut, LIB	Tariku Jifar ETH	2:11:14	Seada Kedir ETH	2:31:38
27 Nov	Firenze, ITA	Berga Bekele ETH	2:09:52	Asha Gigi ETH	2:31:36
27 Nov	La Rochelle, FRA	John Komen KEN	2:07:13	Ture Chatumoha ETH	2:36:07

Date	Location	Men's Winner	Time	Women's Winner	Time
27 Nov	Valencia, ESP	Isaiah Kosgei KEN	2:07:59	Marshet Jimma ETH	2:38:05
4 Dec	Fukuoka, JPN	Josphat Ndambiri KEN	2:07:36	*men only*	
4 Dec	Macau, MAC	Stephen Chemlany KEN	2:12:49	Tsega Gelaw ETH	2:31:48
4 Dec	Mazatlán, MEX	Simon Njoroge KEN	2:11:07	Karina Pérez MEX	2:36:15
4 Dec	Sacramento USA	Erick Monyenye Mose KEN	2:11:50	Serkalem Abrha ETH	2:33:40
4 Dec	Shanghai, CHN	Willy Kibor KEN	2:10:21	Haile Kebebush ETH	2:24:08
4 Dec	Singapore, SIN	Charles Kanyao KEN	2:14:34	Irene Jerotich KEN	2:36:43
11 Dec	Castellón, ESP	Carlos Castillejo ESP	2:10:09	Jemima Jelagat KEN	2:28:32
11 Dec	Honolulu, USA	Nicholas Chelimo KEN	2:14:55	Woynishet Girma ETH	2:31:41
17 Dec	Danzhou, CHN	Tesfaye Girma ETH	2:12:53	*men only*	
18 Dec	Hofu, JPN	Ser-od Bat Ochir MGL	2:11:56	Hisae Yoshimatsu JPN	2:44:28
18 Dec	Kisumu, KEN	Joseph Biwott KEN	2:13:41	Irene Mogaka Kemunto KEN	2:38:00
18 Dec	Taipei, TPE	Yemane Tsegaye Adhane ETH	2:10:24	Helena Kirop KEN	2:27:36

The Association of Road Racing Statisticians {ARRS} announced that the ongoing research undertaken by their network statisticians under the co-ordination of Andy Milroy into the development of the Marathon reached a significant milestone with the posting of the ranking list for 1911. This completed a unique set of historical marathon data stretching back one hundred years. Lists for the years 1911-2011 are now posted on the ARRS website www. arrs.net/YR_Mara.htm.

Review of Ultrarunning 2011
by Andy Milroy

THE YEAR WAS notable for increased interest in the 100km from African countries. South Africa contested the World 100km in which a member of its national team took third place, and Erick Wainaina ran the fastest 100km yet by a Kenyan, but only finished third in the Yubetsu race in Japan. As other fast marathon runners have discovered before, the 100km is not an easy option, easily accessible to the elite marathon runners. Just like the marathon, it takes time and patience to succeed.

The World 100km took place at Winschoten, Netherlands and Giorgio Calcaterra retained his title in 6:27:32, well clear of Americans Michael Wardian 6:42:49 and Andrew Henshaw 6:44:35. With Calcaterra running even faster to win at Faenza (6:25:47), he is indisputably the World No. 1. The team title was won by the United States, from Japan in second place and France in third. This is similar to last year's result with the US and Japanese teams swapping positions. The European 100km Championships were held in conjunction with the World event, and also won by Calcaterra with the team title going to France from Russia and Germany.

With five of the six fastest women's times of the year coming in the World 100km the World No. 1 is obviously Russia's Marina Bychkova, who ran 7:27:19, ahead of the former Pole, Joanna 'Joasia' Zakrzewski, now running for Britain, 7:41:06 with Lindsay van Aswegen RSA taking the bronze in 7:42:05. Bychkova also took the European title and Russia team gold ahead of the United States and Japan, and in the European Championships from Great Britain and Austria.

The other standard ultra is the 24 Hours and this year's event was badly hit by the cancellation of the World 24 hours in Brugg, Switzerland. However there were several major events held, including the Commonwealth 24 hours in Llandudno, North Wales and a track event in Taiwan that attracted the leading Japanese runners. The leading male performer of the year by a long way was Ryoichi Sekiya of Japan who produced yet another solid performance with 261.257 km on the track at Taipei. The next best performance in the Day run was by Frenchman Jean-Marc Bordus, with 259.496 km. Despite the absence of the World Championships there were stellar performances by women. First Britain's Elizabeth Hawker broke the long standing world 24 hour road best with 247.076 km in winning the Commonwealth title, and then the veteran Japanese Mami Kudo broke her own 24 hour track world record with 255.303km in Taipei at the age of 47. The opposition in neither event was particularly strong and thus Kudo can probably be adjudged to be the World No. 1 for 2011. Another Japanese Sumie Inagaki ran the greatest distance indoors on a non-standard layout with 240.631 km at Espoo, Finland.

It was not a vintage year for the 48-hour event with the best male marks being set by

Phil McCarthy USA with 414.148km in Augusta NJ, USA and Tiziano Marchesi ITA 413.630 km at the Balatonfüred, Hungary. As with the 24 hours the greatest distance by a woman at 48 hours was set by the indefatigable Mami Kudo with 368.687km. The most competitive women's race was probably at Kladno, Czech Republic where Cornelia Bullig GER won from Catherine Dipali Cunningham AUS/GBR with 343.302km to 332.534km.

Moving to the longer 6-day event, strong performances were set in several different races, which is good for the event. Marc Etiemble FRA was the leading performer with 838.450km at Antibes, France, William Sichel GBR won the Balatonfüred race with 834.189 km and Norway's Trond Sjavik's 6-day split of 833.000km in Athens, Greece was the third best mark. The best female mark was set by the veteran Sharon Gaytor of Britain who ran 750km in Athens, with Catherine Dipali Cunningham's 749.954km run in New York just marginally shorter. Trond Sjavik carried on to win the 1000km road race in Athens in 7 days 6 hours 28:24.

In the longest race on a certified course in the world – the 3100 miles race in New York – the Ukrainian Mikhail Ukrainsky won with 1069:38:52 with Paula Mairer SUI 1287:54:25 the only woman finisher.

In the more traditional point to point courses, which are always popular, the 86th Comrades Marathon from Durban to Pietermaritzburg at 86.96 km was won by Stephen Muzhingi ZIM for the second successive year in 5:32:46 with South Africans Fanie Matshipa 5:34:30 and Claude Moshiywa 5:42:06 second and third. The women's race was more predictable with Yelena Nurgaliyeva of Russia winning for the sixth time – in 6:24:11 from her twin sister, two time winner Olesya 6:24:35. So they have eight wins in total! American Kami Semick, the former world 100km champions, was third in 6:26:25.

The annual 245.3km Spartathlon event was won by Ivan Cudin ITA, for the second year in a row, in a time of 22:57:40 with Yuji Sakai JPN well back in 24:22:24 and Michael Vanicek GER third in 24:55:59. New faces come to the fore in the women's race as Szilvia Lubics HUN won in 29:07:45 from Ruth Podgornik SLO 32:17:19 and Marina 'Mimi' Anderson GBR 32:33:23.

There were numerous ultra stage races held around the world in 2011. The Trans-Gaule stage race 1150km/18 stages was won in 91:14:12 by Jean-Jacques Moros FRA with Carmen Hildebrand GER the first woman in 109:39:14. The longest race of the year was the 3200 miles Trans-America in 70 stages won by Rainer Koch GER with 522:55:56

With the Commonwealth 24 Hour and also the Asian 100km championships, Ultrarunning continues to extend its popularity. Japanese runners are often dominant in ultra events, and the reason for that is the sheer number and size of such races in Japan. There are currently six Japanese 100km races with a thousand or more starters each year and several others with over 500 runners. Lake Saroma is the biggest conventional 100km road race in the world with at least 2500 starters. In parallel with the road running boom across the globe, ultra events are being added to race calendars in countries new to the sport as part of the growing wider participation, particularly in the Far East.

Add to Drugs Bans 2010 (from page 108)

Men

José Alessandro Bagio BRA	10 Sep	2y
Alemayehu Bezabeh ESP		2y
Mark Edwards GBR	15 Sep	3y
Eduardo Mbengani POR	23 Dec	2y
Sammy Mutahi KEN	29 Jan	W
Marc Raquil FRA		2y
Erik Tysse NOR	1 May	2y

Women

Folashade Abugan NGR	14 Oct	2y
Geisa Arcanjo BRA	20 Jul	W
Zivile Balciunaite LTU	31 Aug	2y
Svetlana Chervan UKR	24 Sep	2y
Corina Dumbravean ROU		L
Rachel Wallader GBR		1y
Zhou Kang CHN	18 Aug	2y

Life: Jitinder Singh IND (4 Nov), **8y**: Kwa Ihuefo Sorochukwu NGR (25 Jun); **2y**: Lawal Abimbola NGR (25 Jun), Vinay Chaudhary IND (14 Sep), Steve Fikah NGR (25 Jun), Amit Kumar IND (14 Dec), Lourival Libaneo BRA (15 Aug), Rhett Medford AUS (23 Mar), Sorin Mineran ROU (4 Sep), El Mokhtar Ajjaji FRA (25 Jul), Marcio Marcos BRA (26 Sep), Prince Obus NGR (26 Jun), Ravinder Singh IND (16 Dec), Suresh Sathya IND (14 Nov), Joy Sunday NGR (26 Jun), Rani Yadav IND (7 Oct).

Add to Drugs Bans 2009

Women

Hyrsopiyi Devetzi GRE	23 May

2y: Sukanya Mishra IND (3 Nov), Than Toe Khim MYA (12 Oct)

Add to Drugs Bans 2007

Men

Frédéric Denis FRA	17 Feb	2y

IAAF WORLD CHAMPIONSHIPS 2011

August 27 – September 4, Daegu, Korea

THE 13th IAAF World Championships in Daegu were undoubtedly a success even though held in a nation not known for much interest in track and field athletics amongst the general public. Although not knowledgeable, however, the crowds gave hugely enthusiastic support to Korean athletes, who set five national records. Their top placing was Kim Hyunsub's sixth at 20km walk. There were plenty of thrills and spills associated with championship action. The major sensation came on the second day when Usain Bolt was disqualified for a false start in the final of the 200m, but he came back to win the 200m in fine style on day eight and he ended the championships by anchoring the Jamaican team to a world record 37.04 at 4x100m. That was the one new global mark and there were three other championship records with 14 area records and 6 Commonwealth records and 18 world leading marks in 15 events. In all there were 1742 competitors (931 men, 811 women) from 199 countries (compared to records of 1895 competitors in 2009 and 201 nations in 1999).

The United States clearly headed the medals table and indeed their 25 medals was just one less than their record hauls in 1991 and 2007 and two more than they won in Beijing 2008. Russia were next in the table, their successes headed by some brilliant women and winning all three walks, and Kenyan distance runners had sparkling success, with Vivian Cheruiyot (5000 and 10,000m) the one double individual winner. The table below shows medals and points for nations. Notable declines included Spain (29 points in 2009 to 11) and Finland, who did not have a single top eight place (their best was two ninth places) from a team of just 12 competitors.

Allyson Felix tied the record of four medal at one Championships and by helping the US women to win both relays she took her total of gold medals to eight (from 2005) for an all-time women's record. Also setting a record was Susana Feitor, 6th in the 20km walk, who competed in a record 11th World Championship, while Jesús Ángel Garcia set a men's record by competing in his tenth.

Eleven athletes retained their titles, including Dwight Phillips who won his fourth long jump title after poor form this year prior to Daegu, but 26 returning champions were not successful this time. Koji Murofushi, like Phillips had little form this year, but excelled in the hammer to add to the Olympic title he won back in 2004. There were, however, plenty of shocks and these, apart from Bolt's dq, included the unfortunate disqualification of Dayron Robles after winning the 110m hurdles, the collapse of Gebre Gebremariam early in the marathon, the sixth place only for Yelena Isinbayeva in the pole vault, Nancy Langat failing to make the 1500m final, and the US men being denied a place in the 4x100m final.

For the first time, preliminary rounds were held in the 100 metres for athletes who had not achieved A or B qualifying standards, but who were competing due to their nations' ability to have one

Medal and Points Table

Points: 8 for 1st to 1 for 8th place. 62 nations placed athletes in top eight, 37 won medals, and 10 won gold.

Nation	G	S	B	Points	2009	2007
USA	12	8	5	251	230	249
RUS	9	4	6	200.5	153.5	176
KEN	7	6	4	174	120	124
JAM	4	4	1	101	136	98
GER	3	3	1	83	102	84
GBR	2	4	1	70	80	61
ETH	1	0	4	66	88	44
CHN	1	2	1	60.5	50	53
CUB	0	1	3	48	51	43.5
FRA	0	1	3	45	39.5	36.6
POL	1	0	0	44	72	45
AUS	1	1	1	34	45	18
RSA	0	2	2	34	23	9
UKR	1	0	1	33	29	31.6
BLR	0	1	1	25	11	39
CZE	0	1	0	24	12.5	32.5
MAR	0	0	0	23	9	15
JPN	1	0	0	18	27	25
ITA	0	0	1	17	21	29.5
TRI	0	0	1	16	32	1
NOR	0	1	0	15	17	18
BEL	0	0	1	14	5	10
BRA	1	0	0	13	13	20
POR	0	0	0	13	19	19

EST & CAN (1S): COL & SKN (2B) 12; GRN (1G), ESP & BAH (1B) 11; SWE 9; BOT & NZL (1G), SLO (1B), TUR 8; GRE, NGR 7.5; CRO, HUN, KAZ, PUR, SUD & TUN (all 1S) 7; IRI, LAT & ZIM (1B), BRN 6; DOM, ERI, BUL, KOR, SRB, LTU 5; ANT, NED, ROU 4; UGA, QAT 3; IRL 2.5; IND, ISV, MDA 2; ALG, VEN 1; UZB 0.5.

In all 16 nations won gold medals, 41 medals and 66 placed athletes in the top eight (respectively 19, 37 and 62 in 2009).

competitor. As is now becoming an established pattern, the road events were held in the city centre.

Men

100 Metres   (prelim, h 27th, sf, F 28th -1.4)

1. Yohan Blake JAM   9.92
2. Walter Dix USA   10.08
3. Kim Collins SKN   10.09
4. Christophe Lemaitre FRA 10.19
5. Daniel Bailey ANT   10.26
6. Jimmy Vicaut FRA   10.27
7. Nesta Carter JAM   10.95
dq (fs). Usain Bolt JAM   –

BLAKE WAS A most impressive winner – by a margin of 0.16, the second widest in World Champs history, and his time of 9.92 into a 1.4m wind was highly creditable. The resurgent Collins, at his ninth Worlds and at 34 the oldest ever finalist, was fastest away from Carter, who slowed to jog in, and Vicaut, before Blake in lane 6 swept past and away. The drama had come, of course, with the disqualification of Bolt but there was no doubt at all about his early break. Bolt had been fastest in the first round with 10.10 and impressed as he eased to a smooth semi-final win in 10.05, but the first semi, won by Blake in 9.95 from Dix 10.05, was faster. Surprisingly eliminated in the semis were Richard Thompson and Justin Gatlin.

200 Metres   (h, sf 2nd, F 3rd 0.8)

1. Usain Bolt JAM   19.40
2. Walter Dix USA   19.70
3. Christophe Lemaitre FRA   19.80
4. Jaysuma Saidy Ndure NOR   19.95
5. Nickel Ashmeade JAM   20.29
6. Bruno de Barros BRA   20.31
7. Rondell Sorrillo TRI   20.34
dnf. Alonso Edward PAN   –

AFTER SAUNTERING THROUGH the rounds in 20.30 and 20.31 Bolt atoned for his 100m failure with a resounding victory in 19.40 (9.97/9.43), a time bettered only by himself (19.19 and 19.30) and Michael Johnson (19.32) – all world record marks. This despite running in lane 3 and having the slowest reaction time of 0.193. He stretched away in the home straight to beat Dix (10.11/9.59) by three metres with Lemaitre (10.24/9.56), easily the fastest in the semis with 20.17, following in a French and European U23 record time of 19.80, also tying the fastest ever third place time. The 2009 runner-up Edward pulled up injured.

400 Metres   (h 28th, sf 29th, F 30th)

1. Kirani James GRN   44.60
2. LaShawn Merritt USA   44.63
3. Kévin Borlée BEL   44.90
4. Jermaine Gonzales JAM   44.99
5. Jonathan Borlée BEL   45.07
6. Rondell Bartholomew GRN   45.45
7. Tabarie Henry ISV   45.55
8. Femi Ogunode QAT   45.55

TWO DAYS BEFORE his 19th birthday James squeezed past Merritt four strides from the finish and maintained a slim advantage on the dip to claim the title by 0.03, taking 0.01 off his pb. He went through 200m in 21.6 and 300m in 32.6, each a tenth behind Merritt with Kevin Borlée, Gonzales and Bartholomew all timed in 32.7 at 300m. Grenada had never before had any athlete in any event place better than sixth (Alleyne Francique in the 2001 and 2003 400m) but here they had first and sixth. Merritt had started with 44.35 (world lead for 2011) in the heats, when also under 45 secs were K Borlée 45.77, Bartholomew 44.82 and Renny Quow 44.84, and was also fastest in the semis with 44.76 while James ran 45.12 and 45.20. Oscar Pistorius, the "Blade Runner", qualified for the semis with his second fastest time of 45.39 in a heat in which US champion Tony McQuay was only 6th in 46.76.

800 Metres   (h 27th, sf 28th, F 30th)

1. David Rudisha KEN   1:43.91
2. Abubaker Kaki SUD   1:44.41
3. Yuriy Borzakovskiy RUS   1:44.49
4. Marcin Lewandowski POL   1:44.80
5. Nick Symmonds USA   1:45.12
6. Adam Kszczot POL   1:45.25
7. Alfred Kirwa Yego KEN   1:45.83
8. Mohammed Aman ETH   1:45.93

RUDISHA CONTROLLED THE final from the outset, going through 200m in 23.8 with Kaki a stride behind, slowing to 400m in 51.33 from Borzakovskiy 51.5 and Kaki 51.6, and then opening up through 600m in 1:17.99 and a last 200m in 24.92 to win by half a second over Kaki, who passed Borzakovskiy (2nd, 2nd, 3rd and 4th in previous World finals) 25m from the finish. Kaki had been fastest in the heats with an extravagant 1:44.83 (24.04, 50.63, 1:17.75) but he got into the final only as a fastest 3rd placer from the semis. He ran 1:44.62 behind 17 year-old Aman's Ethiopian record 1:44.57 and Lewandowski 1:44.60. Symmonds won the second semi in 1:45.73 and Rudisha front-run the third to win in 1:44.20 from Kszczot 1:44.81.

1500 Metres   (h 30th, sf 1st, F 3rd)

1. Asbel Kiprop KEN   3:35.69
2. Silas Kiplagat KEN   3:35.92
3. Matt Centrowitz USA   3:36.08
4. Manuel Olmedo ESP   3:36.33
5. Abdelaati Iguider MAR   3:36.56
6. Mohamed Moustaoui MAR   3:36.80
7. Mekonnen Gebremedhin ETH   3:36.81
8. Eduard Villanueva VEN   3:37.31

9. Mehdi Baala FRA	3:37.46
10. Ciarán O'Lionáird IRL	3:37.81
11. Tarek Boukensa ALG	3:38.05
12. Nick Willis NZL	3:38.69

KIPROP, FOURTH AT the two previous World Champs, became the first Kenyan 1500m World champion and just the third man to win both Olympic and World 1500m titles. Willis, who had collapsed at the finish of his semi and was stretchered off, led the final through 60.02 and 61.69, before Kiprop and Gebremedhin went ahead and were level at the bell in 2:44.24. Kiplagat then surged into the lead (1200m 2:57.01) before Kiprop sprinted to victory as Centrowitz passed the fading Gebremedhin. Kiprop had been quickest in the semis with 3:36.75, with Daniel Kipchirchir Komen and Amine Laâlou surprise casualties,

5000 Metres (h 1st, F 4th)

1. Mo Farah GBR	13:23.36
2. Bernard Lagat USA	13:23.64
3. Dejene Gebremeskel ETH	13:23.92
4. Isiah Koech KEN	13:24.95
5. Abera Kuma ETH	13:25.50
6. Thomas Longosiwa KEN	13:26.73
7. Eliud Kipchoge KEN	13:27.27
8. Bilisuma Shugi BRN	13:27.67
9. Galen Rupp USA	13:28.64
10. Daniele Meucci ITA	13:29.11
11. Amanuel Mesel ERI	13:33.99
12. Jesús España ESP	13:33.99
13. Hussain Al-Hamdan KSA	13:34.83
14. Alistair Cragg IRL	13:45.33
15. Jake Robertson NZL	14:03.09
dq (3). Imane Merga ETH	(13:23.78)

AFTER A BRISK start by Kuma, first lap in 63.95, the pace slowed to a dawdle with Koech leading at 1000m in 2:50.92. At 2000m (Kuma 5:35.61), Farah began to take closer order, and the race began to hot up – the final 3000m took 7:47.75. Al-Hamdan threw in laps of 62.02 and 61.81 and headed the pack through 3000m in 8:13.70 (Farah 6th in 8:15.0). The pace slowed again (65.83 tenth lap) as Kuma reached 4000m in 10:55.50 with 14 runners packed closely together. Farah and Gebremeskel were abreast with 200m to go and Merga and Lagat close behind. Farah held a narrow lead entering the final straight and, gritting his teeth, held on although Lagat, veering out into the third lane after being boxed briefly earlier, fought mightily to catch him. At the finish Farah was a stride clear, having run the last 400m in 52.61 (26.55 and 26.06) and kilometre in 2:27.86. Merga crossed the line third but was disqualified (after the medal ceremony) for stepping inside the kerb.

10,000 Metres (28th)

1. Ibrahim Jeylan ETH	27:13.81
2. Mo Farah GBR	27:14.07
3. Imane Merga ETH	27:19.14
4. Zersenay Tadese ERI	27:22.57
5. Martin Mathathi KEN	27:23.87
6. Peter Kirui KEN	27:25.63
7. Galen Rupp USA	27:26.84
8. Sileshi Sihine ETH	27:34.11
9. Paul Tanui KEN	27:54.03
10. Matt Tegenkamp USA	28:41.62
11. Rui Silva POR	28:48.62
12. Daniele Meucci ITA	28:50.28
13. Stephen Mokoka RSA	28:51.97
14. Scott Bauhs USA	29:03.92
15. Yuki Sato JPN	29:04.15

THE RACE WAS run at a dawdling early pace with Kirui leading at 1k in 2:57.08. Tadese then stepped up the pace, injecting a 61.56 lap. The second kilometre took 2:39.91, followed by 2:43.59, 2:47.22, 2:44.71 (to 5000m 13:52.43 Kirui), 2:43.32, 2:41.52 and 2:43.08. At 9000m (24:46.40) there were still eight in contention, with Mathathi in the lead. Farah, 8th at 5000m in 13:53.6, moved ahead with 600m to go and after a 60.5 lap launched his prolonged finish at the bell (26:20.71). He quickly opened a 10m advantage over Jeylan and Merga. Some 5m down with 200m remaining, Jeylan chased after Farah, gradually closed the gap and edged past some 30m out for victory. Farah ran the last lap in 53.36 (26.2 & 27.2) but Jeylan ran 52.8 (26.5 & 26.3).

Marathon (4th)

1. Abel Kirui KEN	2:07:38
2. Vincent Kipruto KEN	2:10:06
3. Feyisa Lilesa ETH	2:10:32
4. Abderrahime Bouramdane MAR	2:10:55
5. David Barmasai KEN	2:11:39
6. Eliud Kiptanui KEN	2:11:50
7. Hiroyuki Horibata KPN	2:11:52
8. Ruggero Pertile ITA	2:11:57
9. Stephen Kiprotich UGA	2:12:57
10. Kentaro Nakamoto JPN	2:13:10
11. Rachid Kisri MAR	2:13:24
12. Eshetu Wendimu ETH	2:13:37
13. Marius Ionescu ROU	2:15:32
14. Dong Guojuan CHN	2:15:45
15. David Webb GBR	2:15:48

KIRUI BECAME THE sixth man to retain a global marathon title and Kenya were clear winners in the concurrent World Cup, completing an incredible week for Kenyan runners. The race started at 24°C and 65% humidity, and after 5k splits of 15:58, 15:23, 15:07 and 15:14 halfway was reached in 1:05:07. Kirui then ran an astonishing 14:17 from 25k to 30k in 1:30:43, ahead of Kiptanui 1:30:54, Lilesa 1:30:55 and Kipruto 1:30:58. He kept up the pressure with a 14:40 split so that at 35k his lead over Kipruto and Lilesa had grown to 74 secs and widened this to 2:34 at 40k to finish 2:28 ahead for an extraordinary run in the conditions. 51 of the 67 starters finished. Sangay Wangchuk finished last (70th) in the 2009 Worlds in a national record for Bhutan of 2:47:55 and although again last (51st this time) he improved that record to 2:38:33.

World Cup: 1. KEN 6:29:23, 2. JPN 6:41:13, 3. MAR 6:42:18, 4. ESP 6:53:41, 5. CHN 6:54:32, 6. KOR 6:57:03, 7. USA 7:04:52.

3000 Metres Steeplechase

(h 29th, F 1st)

1. Ezekiel Kemboi KEN	8:14.85
2. Brimin Kipruto KEN	8:16.05
3. Mahiedine Mekhissi FRA	8:16.09
4. Bouabdellah Tahri FRA	8:17.56
5. Roba Gari ETH	8:18.37
6. Jacob Araptany UGA-J	8:18.67
7. Richard Matelong KEN	8:19.31
8. Ion Luchianov MDA	8:19.69
9. Hamid Ezzine MAR	8:21.97
10. Benjamin Kiplagat UGA	8:22.21
11. Nahom Mesfin ETH	8:25.39
12. Vincent Zouaoui Dandrieux FRA	8:30.39
13. Ruben Ramolefi RSA	8:30.47
14. Abraham Chirchir KEN	8:33.56
15. Alberto Paulo POR	8:33.84

AFTER A SLOW start (Ramolefi 2:47.63 and Araptany 5:33.42), Kemboi sprinted clear of Kipruto with 200m to go to retain his title and then celebrated with a most exuberant display. Kipruto was almost caught by Mekhissi. Faster times had been run in the second heat won by Kemboi in 8:10.93 from Ramolefi, whose front-running was rewarded with a national record 8:11.50 and Ezzine 8:11.81. The other heat winners were Araptany 8:18.57 and Kiplagat 8:19.96.

110 Metres Hurdles

(h 28th, sf, F 29th -1.1)

1. Jason Richardson USA	13.16
2. Liu Xiang CHN	13.27
3. Andy Turner GBR	13.44
4. David Oliver USA	13.44
5= Aries Merritt USA	13.67
5= William Sharman GBR	13.67
dq. Dayron Robles CUB	(13.14)
dnf. Dwight Thomas JAM	fell

SOME BIG NAMES were fast heat winners: Richardson 13.19, Liu 13.20 and Oliver 13.27, and then, after Liu had beaten Robles 13.31 to 13.32 in the first semi, Richardson excelled with a clear win in the second semi in 13.11 into a 1.6 headwind from Oliver 13.40. In the final Robles (lane 5) was out first but Liu (l6) was level with him as they rose at the ninth hurdle. At that point the Cuban's right arm made contact with Liu, throwing him off balance and causing him to smack into the last hurdle. Until then it had looked as though Liu's momentum would carry him to victory but instead he crossed the line third, well behind Robles and Richardson. There was no question that Liu had been impeded and the Chinese lodged a protest, which the jury of appeal upheld. A counter-protest by the Cubans was rejected and Robles was disqualified.

400 Metres Hurdles

(h 29th, sf 30th, F 1st)

1. David Greene GBR	48.26
2. Javier Culson PUR	48.44
3. L.J. van Zyl RSA	48.80
4. Félix Sánchez DOM	48.87
5. Cornel Fredericks RSA	49.12
6. Bershawn Jackson USA	49.24
7. Angelo Taylor USA	49.31
8. Aleksandr Derevyagin RUS	49.32

BREEZY CONDITIONS AFFECTED times and Greene's 48.26 was the slowest ever World winning time. After Greene and Fredericks had been fastest with 48.52 in the heats, the 2007 and 2009 champion Kerron Clement (injured) and US champion Jeshua Anderson failed to advance from the semis, won by Culson 48.52, Greene 48.62 and Jackson 48.80. In the final Taylor (in lane 1) led over the first five hurdles with Jackson also out hard. Van Zyl and Culson led into the home straight and Culson over the final barrier, but with a well-judged run Greene charged through.

High Jump   (Q 2.31 30th, F 1st)

1. Jesse Williams USA	2.35
2. Aleksey Dmitrik RUS	2.35
3. Trevor Barry BAH	2.32
4. Jaroslav Bába CZE	2.32
5= Dimítrios Hondrokoúkis GRE	2.32
5= Ivan Ukhov RUS	2.32
7. Mutaz Essa Barshim QAT	2.32
8. Aleksandr Shustov RUS	2.29
9. Raul Spank GER	2.29
10. Zhang Guowei CHN	2.25
11. Donald Thomas BAH	2.20
12= Dmytro Demyanyuk UKR	2.20
12= Darvin Edwards LCA	2.20

UP TO 2.32 Williams and Barry had clean cards and then, of the seven men left in, Williams won the gold medal by clearing 2.35 on his first attempt while Dmitrik (who came very close at 2.37) cleared on his second. Ten men over 2.31 in qualifying was unprecedented (to tie the best ever marks for places 8-10) and Barshim's 2.32 in the final tied the best ever 7th place mark

Pole Vault   (Q 5.75m 27th, F 29th)

1. Pawel Wojciechowski POL	5.90
2. Lázaro Borges CUB	5.90
3. Renaud Lavillenie FRA	5.85
4. Lukasz Michalski POL	5.85

5. Maite Mohr GER	5.85
6. Konstadínos Filippídis GRE	5.75
7. Mateusz Didenkow POL	5.75
8. Fabio da Silva BRA	5.65
9= Jeremy Scott USA	5.65
9= Steven Lewis GBR	5.65
9= Jan Kudlicka CZE	5.65
12. Dmitriy Starodubtsev RUS	5.65
13. Derek Miles USA	5.65
14. Daichi Sawano JPN	5.65
nh. Romain Mesnil FRA	–
nh. Igor Bychkov ESP	–

THERE WERE SHOCKS aplenty in this event, starting with qualifying when Steve Hooker failed to clear his opening height of 5.50. Although the qualifying height was set at 5.70, eleven men made 5 60 and 5.65 and were joined by five first time clearers of just 5.50, including Wojciechowski. Lavillenie cleared 5.65, 5.75 and 5.85 on his first attempts in the final and was joined by Lázaro Borges and Michalski on their first attempts and Mohr on his third at 5.85. Lavillenie surprisingly failed at 5.90 (brushing the bar with his hip when well over seemingly on his third attempt), but Wojciechowski, who had passed after one failure at 5.85, went over on his second try and Borges on his third for a CAC record (having also achieved that at 5.75 and 5.85).

Long Jump (Q 8.15m 1st, F 2nd)

1. Dwight Phillips USA	8.45/0.0
2. Mitchell Watt AUS	8.33/0.4
3. Ngonidzashe Makusha ZIM	8.29/0.3
4. Yahya Berrabah MAR	8.23/0.4
5. Luvo Maniyonga RSA	8.21/0.2
6. Aleksandr Menkov RUS	8.19/0.0
7. Christian Reif GER	8.19/0.6
8. Sebastian Bayer GER	8.17/0.3
9. Will Claye USA	8.10/0.1
10. Marcos Chuva POR	8.05/0.1
11. Chris Tomlinson GBR	7.87/0.1
dns. Kim Dyuk-hyun KOR	–

DESPITE COMING TO Daegu with a season's best of 8.09, Phillips led the qualifiers with 8.32 and maintained his supremacy in the final with 8.31 and 8.45 in the first two rounds, so taking his fourth title. Watt's best of 8.33 came in the second round and Makusha did not improve on his opening jump, but he took Zimbabwe's first ever World medal. Several top names failed to qualify, including former champion Irving Saladino, who jumped just 7.84 after two fouls.

Triple Jump (Q 17.10m 2nd, F 4th)

1. Christian Taylor USA	17.96/0.1
2. Phillips Idowu GBR	17.77/0.0
3. Will Claye USA	17.50/0.1
4. Alexis Copello CUB	17.47/0.1
5. Nelson Évora POR	17.35/0.0
6. Christian Olsson SWE	17.23/0.0
7. Leevan Sands BAH	17.21/-0.2
8. Benjamin Compaoré FRA	17.17/0.2
9. Henry Frayne AUS	16.78/-0.1
10. Fabrizio Donato ITA	16.77/0.1
11. Yoandris Betanzos CUB	16.67/-0.1
12. Sheryf El-Sheryf UKR	16.38/-0.1

COPELLO LED EIGHT men over 17m in qualifying with 17.31. Defending champion Évora opened the final with 17.35 and the 2003 champion Olsson 17.23 before Idowu jumped 17.56 (17.75 from take-off to landing). After two fouls Claye moved into second with 17.50 in the third-round, in which Idowu increased his lead to 17.70 (17.84 from take-off). Taylor improved from 17.04 to 17.40 before a sensational jump of 17.96 in the fourth round (with just 0.9cm to spare) to become, at 21, the youngest ever world champion. Idowu responded with 17.77, the second best jump of his career and went on to complete a splendid series with 17.48 and 17.49.

Shot (Q 20.60m 1st, F 2nd)

1. David Storl GER	21.78
2. Dylan Armstrong CAN	21.64
3, Andrey Mikhnevich BLR	21.40
4. Christian Cantwell USA	21.36
5. Reese Hoffa USA	20.99
6. Marco Fortes POR	20.83
7. Ryan Whiting USA	20.75
8. Adam Nelson USA	20.29
9. Tomasz Majewski POL	20.18
10. Ralf Bartels GER	20.14
11. Asmir Kolasinac SRB	19.84
12. Carlos Véliz CUB	19.70

FOR THE FIRST time in 20 years no American shot putter won a medal. Storl improved his best from 21.04 with a European U23 record 21.50 in qualifying and improved that to 21.60 (second round) and 21.78 (final round) in the final to become the youngest ever world champion in this event as well as the first German winner. Hoffa had led with 20.90 in the first round and 20.99 in the second before Storl took over. Mikhnevich moved into second with 21.40 in the third round, while in the fourth Armstrong took the lead with 21.64. Cantwell's best came in the fifth round.

Discus (Q 65.50m 29th, F 30th)

1. Robert Harting GER	68.97
2. Gerd Kanter EST	66.95
3. Ehsan Hadadi IRI	66.08
4. Märt Israel EST	65.20
5. Benn Harradine AUS	64.77
6. Virgilijus Alekna LTU	64.09
7. Vikas Gowda IND	64.05
8. Jorge Fernández CUB	63.54
9. Piotr Malachowski POL	63.37
10. Jason Young USA	63.20
11. Mario Pestano ESP	63.00
12. Brett Morse GBR	62.69

NO ONE REACHED the listed qualifying standard of 65.50 (set without regard for windless conditions), the first time in a World Champs throwing event that there were no automatic qualifiers and 62.38 or better was needed for 12 men led by Malachowski 65.48, Hadadi 65.21 and Pestano 65.13. Harting needed three pain-killing injections for his knee injury before getting through safely with 64.93 and had three more before the final, but then opened with 68.49, staying well ahead of the field with 68.10 and 68.97 in rounds three and four. Kanter had throws of 66.95 and 66.90 for silver and Hadadi was in the medals throughout from 65.29 (r1), 65.50 (r5) and a final 66.08. Alekna competed at his ninth Worlds and came sixth after seven successive top four places.

Hammer (Q 77.00m 27th, F 29th)

1. Koji Murofushi JPN		81.24
2. Krisztián Pars HUN		81.18
3. Primoz Kozmus SLO		79.39
4. Markus Esser GER		79.12
5. Pavel Krivitskiy BLR		78.53
6. Kirill Ikonnikov RUS		78.37
7. Szymon Ziólkowski POL		77.64
8. Nicola Vizzoni ITA		77.04
9. Ola-Pekka Karjalainen FIN		76.60
10. Dilshod Nazarov TJK		76.58
11. Pawel Fajdek POL		75.20
nt. Yuriy Shayunov BLR		–

Murofushi threw a season's best of 78.56 to head the qualifiers and opened the final with 79.72. He followed with 81.03, his best for three years, and 81.24, also throwing 81.24 in the fifth round to take the title as the oldest ever hammer champion at 36. Kozmus was second with 79.39 while Pars improved steadily in rounds 2-4, from third with 78.84 and 79.14 to second with 79.97 and then with the penultimate throw of the contest he went to 81.18.

Javelin (Q 82.00m 21st, F 23rd)

1. Matthias de Zordo GER		86.27
2. Andreas Thorkildsen NOR		84.78
3. Guillermo Martínez CUB		84.30
4. Vitezslav Vesely CZE		84.11
5. Fatih Avan TUR		83.34
6. Roman Avramenko UKR		82.51
7. Jarrod Bannister AUS		82.25
8. Mark Frank GER		81.81
9. Antti Ruuskanen FIN		79.46
10. Dmitriy Tarabin RUS		79.06
11. Stuart Farquhar NZL		78.99
12. Sergey Makarov RUS		78.76

ONLY FOUR MEN, led by Martínez 83.77, reached the automatic qualifying standard of 82.00 but the other finalists all went over 81m. In the first round of the final Martínez threw 84.30 and then de Zordo went out to 86.27. Surprisingly there was little change after that. Vesely took third with a third round 84.11 before a below-par Thorkildsen went into second with 84.78 in the fourth round, while de Zordo threw 85.51 in the second round before two passes after tweaking his ankle.

Decathlon (27th-28th)

1. Trey Hardee USA		8607
2. Ashton Eaton USA		8505
3. Leonel Suárez CUB		8501
4. Aleksey Drozdov RUS		8313
5. Eelco Sintnicolaas NED		8298
6. Mihail Dudas SRB		8256
7. Pascal Behrenbruch GER		8211
8. Jan Felix Knobel GER		8200
9. Mikk Pahapill EST		8164
10. Larbi Bouraada ALG		8158
11. Romain Barras FRA		8134
12. Oleksiy Kasyanov UKR		8132
13. Thomas Van Der Plaetsen BEL		8069
14. Román Sebrle CZE		8069
15. Andres Raja EST		7982

HARDEE DEFENDED HIS title successfully. His compatriot Eaton led for the first two events, with Hardee first taking the lead after the shot. Then Drozdov (with 2.14 high jump) and Eaton (46.99 for 400m) had turns leading before Hardee was back to stay from the discus onwards, including a pb 68.99 in the javelin. Suárez was only seventh after the first day, but came through strongly to second after the javelin, before Eaton excelled with a pb 4:18.94 at 1500m to pip the Cuban for the silver by just four points.

4 x 100 Metres Relay (h 21st, F 22nd)

1. JAM	37.04*	Carter, Frater, Blake, Bolt (Lee ran in heat)
2. FRA	38.20	Tinmar, Lemaitre, Lesourd, Vicaut
3. SKN	38.49	Rogers, Collins, Adams, Lawrence
4. POL	38.50	Stempel, Kuc, Kubaczyk, Krynski
5. ITA	38.96	Tumi, Collio, Di Gregorio, Cerutti
6. TRI	39.01	Bledman, Burns, Armstrong, Thompson
dnf. USA	–	Kimmons, Gatlin, Patton, Dix
dnf. GBR	–	Malcolm, Pickering, Devonish, Aikines-Aryeetey

THE FINAL EVENT of the Championships produced the one world record in Daegu– a stunning performance by the Jamaicans, who had the same team as the one that ran the previous record of 37.10 at the 2008 Olympics except with Blake and Bolt on the last two legs instead of Bolt and Powell. Their winning margin of 1.16 was easily the biggest ever. The USA (Kimmons, Gatlin, Mitchell and Padgett) won their heat in 37.79 with smooth passing, but, bringing in Patton and Dix for the last two legs in the final, had another disaster as the in-coming Patton was severely obstructed by Britain's next runner Aikines-Aryeetey, causing Britain to fail to pass the baton and Patton to fall (and dislocate his shoulder) and impede likely medallists Trinidad (impressive heat winners in 37.91).

4 x 400 Metres Relay (h 22nd, F 23rd)

1. USA	2:59.31	Nixon 44.8, Jackson 45.4, Taylor 45.00, Merritt 44.17 (Torrance and Berry ran in heat)
2. RSA	2:59.87	Victor 46.0, Mogawane 43.9, de Beer 44.88, van Zyl 45.03
3. JAM	3:00.10	Fothergill 45.5, Gonzales 44.2, Hylton 44.94, L Green 45.53
4. RUS	3:00.22	Dyldin 45,5, Svechkar 45.6, Trenikhin 44.80, Alekseyev 44.41
5. BEL	3:00.41	J Borlée 45.0, Gillet 45.6, Duerinck 45.76, K Borlée 44.11
6. KEN	3:01.15	V Kosgei 45.9, Kiilu 45.5, Mutegi 45,34, Mutai 44.48
7. GBR	3:01.16	Strachan 46.25, Levine 45.32, Clarke 45.47, Rooney 44.12
8. GER	3:01.37	Plass 45.6, Gaba 45.6, Rigau 45.61, Schneider 44.61

ALTHOUGH THE WINNING time was the slowest since the inaugural Worlds in 1983, the depth was good with the fastest ever time for 8th. The US, who surprisingly used their 400m hurdlers in the middle legs, were faster in their heat at 2:58.82 with Jamaal Torrance and Michael Berry running 43.9 and 43.95 for the middle legs before Merritt coasted in. In fact six teams ran faster in the heats than final and South Africa (Oscar Pistorius 45.58 on the first leg) set a national record of 2:59.21. In the final the US were only third at the final change, but Merritt closed in 44.17 for a comfortable win.

20 Kilometres Walk (28th)

1. Valeriy Borchin RUS	1:19:56
2. Vladimir Kanaykin RUS	1:20:27
3. Luis Fernando López COL	1:20:38
4. Wang Zhen CHN	1:20:54
5. Stanislav Yemelyanov RUS	1:21:11
6. Kim Hyun-sub KOR	1:21:17
7. Ruslan Dmytrenko UKR	1:21:31
8. Yusuke Suzuki JPN	1:21:39
9. Alex Schwazer ITA	1:21:50
10. Erick Barrondo GUA	1:22:08
11. Chu Yafei CHN	1:22:10
12. Sergey Morozov RUS	1:22:37
13. Wang Hao CHN	1:22:49
14. Matej Tóth SVK	1:22:55
15. Eder Sánchez MEX	1:23:05

BORCHIN EXHIBITED FINE judgement, taking a cautious 21:15 for the first 5k and 20:19 for the second before cutting loose with 19:08 and 19:14 for an outstanding 38:22 second half. Giorgio Rubino took an early lead, before being joined by Suzuki but was disqualified in the 13th kilometre and Borchin and Wang went past Suzuki in the 15th kilometre by the end of which Borchin was 7 sec ahead of Wang in 60:42. Wang fell back as Kanaykin covered his last 5k in 19:20 and López (winning Colombia's first World Champs medal) clocking a 19:29 split. 38 of 46 men finished (4 disqualified) on a warm and very humid day.

50 Kilometres Walk (3rd)

1. Sergey Bakulin RUS	3:41:24
2. Denis Nizhegorodov RUS	3:42:45
3. Jared Tallent AUS	3:43:36
4. Si Tianfeng CHN	3:44:40
5. Luke Adams AUS	3:45:31
6. Koichiro Morioka JPN	3:46:21
7. Park Chil-sung KOR	3:47:13
8. Xu Faguang CHN	3:47:19
9. Takayuki Tanii JPN	3:48:03
10. Hirooki Arai JPN	3:48:40
11. Andrés Chocho ECU	3:49:32
12. Marco De Luca ITA	3:49:40
13. Rafal Sikora POL	3:50:24
14. Kim Dong-young KOR	3:51:12
15. Jarkko Kinnunen FIN	3:52:32

WITH THE RACE starting at 27°C and 80% humidity, Diniz set off at a cracking pace and led at 5k in 22:17 from Bakulin 22:23 and Deakes 22:26. Deakes caught Diniz and they reached 10k in 44:31, 5 sec ahead of the eventual winner, Bakulin. Diniz increased his speed despite two warnings before 10k and was disqualified after 17k; he was seen to be protesting on several occasions to the judges. Deakes pressed on and was in the lead by 12 sec at 20k (1:28:03) and 18 sec at 30k (2:11:33) and still in a medal position at 35k, but by then Bakulin had gone well clear and Deakes was forced to quit because of persistent hamstring cramp. Tallent narrowed Bakulin's lead steadily lap by lap from 2:06 to 1:24 between 36 and 42k, but then cracked so that in the final kilometre he was overtaken by Nizhegorodov. 25 of 43 men finished (12 disqualified, including Jesús Ángel García, the 1993 champion who was contesting his tenth World Champs).

Women

100 Metres

(prelim 27th, h 28th, sf, F 29th -1.4)

1. Carmelita Jeter USA	10.90
2. Veronica Campbell-Brown JAM	10.97
3. Kelly-Ann Baptiste TRI	10.98
4. Shelly-Ann Fraser-Pryce JAM	10.99
5. Blessing Okagbare NGR	11.12
6. Kerron Stewart JAM	11.15

| 7. Ivet Lalova BUL | 11.27 |
| 8. Marshevet Myers USA | 11.33 |

OKAGBARE AND LALOVA were fastest in the heats with 11.10, and then, running into headwinds over 1m/s the semi-final winners were successively Stewart 11.26, Fraser-Pryce 11.03 (from Campbell-Brown 11.06) and Jeter 11.02 (from Baptiste 11.05). In the final the diminutive Fraser-Pryce was off quickest but couldn't match the pace of her top rivals once they got into full stride. Jeter passed her after 80m to win by a clear margin while Campbell-Brown (well away from the main action out in lane eight) edged ahead of Baptiste and Fraser-Pryce for the silver as 0.02 covered the three of them.

200 Metres   (h 1st, sf F 2nd -1.0)

1. Veronica Campbell-Brown JAM	22.22
2. Carmelita Jeter USA	22.37
3. Allyson Felix USA	22.42
4. Shalonda Solomon USA	22.61
5. Kerron Stewart JAM	22.70
6. Debbie Ferguson McKenzie BAH	22.96
7. Hrystyna Stuy UKR	23.02
8. Sherone Simpson JAM	23.17

IN QUALIFYING THE fastest time was 22.46 in the heats by Campbell-Brown and in the semis by Solomon. A surprise casualty was Jeneba Tarmoh (6th heat 23.60). In the final Campbell-Brown ran a very strong bend to lead into the straight hotly pursued by Jeter with Felix some way back and drove on to win by a metre and a half in 22.22 against the wind.

400 Metres   (h 27th, sf 28th, F 29th)

1. Amantle Montsho BOT	49.56
2. Allyson Felix USA	49.59
3. Anastasiya Kapachinskaya RUS	50.24
4. Francena McCorory USA	50.45
5. Antonina Krivoshapka RUS	50.66
6. Shericka Williams JAM	50.79
7. Sanya Richards-Ross USA	51.32
8. Novlene Williams-Mills JAM	52.89

NO ATHLETE FROM Botswana had ever placed higher than seventh in any World Champs event until Montsho, who had been last in the 2009 final, won a thrilling race against Felix. Montsho (l.4) led at 200m and 300m (23.3 and 35.7 to 23.4 and 35.9), but Felix (l.3) caught her and the two battled it out for the length of the straight. It was a test of will as well as physical resources before Montsho prevailed by the slim margin of 0.03 in a national record of 49.56, while Felix also ran a pb with 49.59. Montsho had been fastest with 50.90 in the heats and semi-final winners were Felix 50.36, McCorory 50.24 and Monstho 50.13.

800 Metres   (h 1st, sf 2nd, F 4th)

1. Mariya Savinova RUS	1:55.87
2. Caster Semenya RSA	1:56.35
3. Janeth Jepkosgei KEN	1:57.42
4. Alysia Montano USA	1:57.48
5. Yekaterina Kosketskaya RUS	1:57.82
6. Maggie Vessey USA	1:58.50
7. Kenia Sinclair JAM	1:58.66
8. Yuliya Rusanova RUS	1:59.74

THE 2007 CHAMPION Jepkosgei blazed through 200m 26.61 and 400m in 55.86 at which point 2009 champion Semenya and favourite Savinova were back in 5th and 6th at 56.9 and 57.2. Jepkosgei still led at 600m 1:26.07 from Semenya 1:26.2. Savinova 1:26.5 then raised her pace and surged past Semenya 30m from the line and came through to a magnificent victory. Jepkosgei just managed to stay ahead of Montano, both setting season's bests. Jepkosgei had been fastest in the heats with 1:59.36 and 13 women broke 2 minutes in the semis, in which winners were Rusanova 1:58.73, Savinova 1:58.45 (from Jepkosgei 1:58.50) and Semenya 1:58.07. Jennifer Meadows was fastest non-qualifier with 1:59.07.

1500 Metres   (h 28th, sf 30th, F 1st)

1. Jennifer Simpson USA	4:05.40
2. Hannah England GBR	4:05.68
3. Natalia Rodríguez ESP	4:05.87
4. Btissam Lakhouad MAR	4:06.18
5. Kalkidan Gezahegne ETH	4:06.42
6. Ingvill Måkestad Bovim NOR	4:06.85
7. Mimi Belete BRN	4:07.60
8. Tugba Karakaya TUR	4:08.14
9. Nataliya Tobias UKR	4:08.68
10. Morgan Uceny USA	4:19.71
11. Hellen Obiri KEN	4:20.23
12. Maryam Jamal BRN	4:22.67

AFTER MANY TOP names did not make it (Lisa Dobriskey out in her heat, Nancy Langat, Gelete Burka, Nuria Fernández, Siham Hilali and Yekaterina Martynova in the semis), the final was the slowest in World Champs history with a winning time of 4:05.40. Jamal, 2007 and 2009 champion, was the early leader, succeeded by her colleague, another former Ethiopian, Belete, who plodded through the first lap in 68.78 and reached 800m in 2:13.94. The race was marred with about 550m to go when Obiri fell and brought down Uceny. That was after the first major move – by Rodríguez with 600m to go. Just before the bell Jamal clipped the heel of Karakaya in trying to get out of a box and lost her momentum and chance of a medal. Rodríguez went through the bell in 3:03.47 and 1200m in 3:18.89 and led into the final straight ahead of Gezahegne and Lakhouad but then came the brilliant sprint finishes around the field from Simpson (last lap 61.4) and England to take gold and silver.

5000 Metres   (h 30th, F 2nd)

| 1. Vivian Cheruiyot KEN | 14:55.36 |

2. Sylvia Kibet KEN	14:56.21
3. Meseret Defar ETH	14:56.94
4. Sentayehu Ejigu ETH	14:59.99
5. Mercy Cherono KEN	15:00.23
6. Linet Masai KEN	15:01.01
7. Lauren Fleshman USA	15:09.25
8. Genzebe Dibaba ETH	15:09.35
9. Tejitu Daba BRN	15:14.62
10. Yelena Zadorozhnaya RUS	15:15.48
11. Zakia Mrisho TAN	15:18.81
12. Helen Clitheroe GBR	15:21.22
13. Hitomi Niiya JPN	15:41.67
14. Yelizaveta Grechishnikova RUS	15:45.61
15. Amy Hastings USA	15:56.06

THE FINAL WAS run at a very modest pace through kilometres of 3:10.87, 6:07.10 and 9:10.97. The fourth kilometre took 2:41.64 with the four Kenyans and three Ethiopians accompanied by Flanagan USA. Cheruiyot completed her distance double with a scintillating last lap of 58.68. Kibet overtook Defar, who had failed to finish in the 10,000m, for second over the last 50 metres.

10,000 Metres (15th)

1. Vivian Cheruiyot KEN	30:48.98
2. Sally Kipyego KEN	30:50.04
3. Linet Masai KEN	30:53.59
4. Priscah Cherono KEN	30:56.43
5. Meselech Melkamu ETH	30:56.55
6. Shitaye Eshete BRN	31:21.57
7. Shalane Flanagan USA	31:25.57
8. Ana Dulce Félix POR	31:37.03
9. Jennifer Rhines USA	31:47.59
10. Jéssica Augusto POR	32:06.68
11. Tigist Kiros ETH	32:11.37
12. Christelle Daunay FRA	32:22.20
13. Kara Goucher USA	32:29.58
14. Hikari Yoshimoto JPN	32:32.22
15. Kayo Sugihara JPN	32:53.89

AFTER SWEEPING THE medals in the women's marathon. the Kenyans went even better in the other event to be determined on the first day of the Championships, taking the first four places in the 10,000m. In hot and humid weather (25°C and 68%) the first lap took 79.71 before settling down to 3:13.42, 3:10.14, 3:08.88 and 3:10.18 kilometres. With Masai doing much of the pushing on, the tempo increased with 3:04.42 (15:47.04 at 5000m), 3:03.60, 3:05.08 and 2:59.55. After a penultimate kilometre in 3:03.04, Cheruiyot sped through the last in 2:50.67. With Kipyego she opened up a gap with a lap to go and held on with a last lap in 61.7 to Kipyego's 62.5 and a last 100m in 14.9.

Marathon (27th)

1. Edna Kiplagat KEN	2:28:43
2. Priscah Jeptoo KEN	2:29:00
3. Sharon Cherop KEN	2:29:14
4. Bezunesh Bekele ETH	2:29:21

5. Yukiko Akaba JPN	2:29:35
6. Zhu Xiaolin CHN	2:29:58
7. Isabellah Andersson SWE	2:30:13
8. Wang Jiali CHN	2:30:25
9. Marisa Barros POR	2:30:29
10. Remi Nakazato JPN	2:30:52
11. Chen Rong CHN	2:31:11
12. Aberu Kebede ETH	2:31:22
13. Irene Jerotich KEN	2:31:29
14. Atsede Bayisa ETH	2:31:37
15. Tetyana Hamera-Shmyrko UKR	2:31:58

KENYA COMPLETED A clean sweep of the medals, the first time this has been achieved in a marathon at either the World Championships or Olympics. The trio was led in by the favourite, Kiplagat, who – recovering well from a fall at a drinks station in the 38th kilometre – covered the second half of the race in 71:57 after a 76:46 first half. She was followed by Jeptoo and Cherop, the latter also having lost time and momentum helping Kiplagat to her feet after inadvertently being the cause of the fall by clipping her team-mate's heels while reaching for her drink. Conditions at the 9 am start (24°C with 81% humidity) were against fast times and the early pace was very slow. The Kenyans pushed on from 30k (1:48:30) with a 16:44 next 5k and Kiplagat went away after that with 16:11 to 40k. Naturally Kenya won the World Cup held in conjunction. 46 of 54 finished.

World Cup: 1. KEN 7:26:57, 2. CHN 7:31:34, 3. ETH 7:32:20, 4. JPN 7:32:58, 5. UKR 7:45:44, 6. USA 7:47:55, 7. KOR 7:59:56.

3000 Metres Steeplechase

(h 27th, F 30th)

1. Yuliya Zaripova RUS	9:07.03
2. Habiba Ghribi TUN	9:11.97
3. Milcah Chemos KEN	9:17.16
4. Mercy Njoroge KEN	9:17.88
5. Lydia Rotich KEN	9:25.74
6. Sofia Assefa ETH	9:28.24
7. Binnaz Uslu TUR	9:31.06
8. Hanana Ouhaddou MAR	9:32.36
9. Gesa Felicitas Krause GER	9:32.74
10. Birtukan Fente Alemu ETH	9:36.81
11. Lyubov Kharlamova RUS	9:44.14
12. Emma Coburn USA	9:51.40
13. Barbara Parker GBR	9:56.66
14. Birtukan Adamu ETH	10:05.10

Drugs dq (12) Sara Moreira POR 9:47.87

AFTER USLU HAD been fastest in the heats with a Turkish record 9:24.06, Zaripova led all the way in the final, charging through the opening kilometre in 3:00.70 and keeping up the pressure with a second kilometre in 3:03.66. Chemos and Njoroge stayed close, but Ghribi passed the Kenyan pair with 600m to go. At the bell (7:54.67) Zaripova was some 10m clear of Ghribi, a lead she extended to 20m by the start of the finishing straight and 30m by the end, with Ghribi setting a national record. Assefa fell heavily at the first hurdle and did very well to finish sixth. Krause set a European junior record in ninth.

100 Metres Hurdles (h 2nd, sf, F 3rd 1.1)

1. Sally Pearson AUS	12.28*
2. Danielle Carruthers USA	12.47
3. Dawn Harper USA	12.47
4. Tiffany Porter GBR	12.63
5. Tatyana Dektyareva RUS	12.82
6. Nikkita Holder CAN	12.93
7. Phylicia George CAN	17.97
dnf. Kellie Wells USA	–

PEARSON WAS EASILY the fastest on the heats with 12.53 and set ran an Oceania and Commonwealth record of 12.36 in the semis, with Tiffany Porter the next fastest at this stage with a UK record 12.56. Then, with a rocket start and an immaculate display of sprint hurdling, Pearson won the final in the world's fastest time since 1992 and by the biggest margin in World Champs history for the event. Carruthers and Harper both ran pbs of 12.47 for silver and bronze, but Wells hit the sixth hurdle hard and fell over the seventh and George crashed earlier.

400 Metres Hurdles

(h 29th, sf 30th, F 1st)

1. Lashinda Demus USA	52.47
2. Melaine Walker JAM	52.73
3. Natalya Antyukh RUS	53.85
4. Kaliese Spencer JAM	54.01
5. Anastasiya Rabchenyuk UKR	54.18
6. Vania Stambolova BUL	54.23
7. Zuzana Hejnová CZE	54.23
8. Yelena Churakova RUS	55.17

WALKER WAS JUST the fastest in the heats with 54.93 and then Demus established herself as a clear favourite with a 53.82 semi win, with Antyukh next quickest at 54.51. After being runner-up in 2005 and 2009 Demus ran brilliantly for gold in a North American record 52.47 with defending champion Walker back in top form in taking silver. Far behind Antyukh was delighted to pick off a struggling Spencer for the bronze medal and Hejnova's 54.23 was the best ever seventh place time in any race.

High Jump (Q 1.95 1st, F 3rd)

1. Anna Chicherova RUS	2.03
2. Blanka Vlasic CRO	2.03
3. Antonietta Di Martino ITA	2.00
4. Yelena Slesarenko RUS	1.97
5. Svetlana Shkolina RUS	1.97
6= Zheng Xingjuan CHN	1.93
6= Deirdre Ryan IRL	1.93
8= Doreen Amata NGR	1.93
8= Svetlana Radzivil UZB	1.93
10. Brigetta Barrett USA	1.93
11. Emma Green Tregaro SWE	1.89
12. Anna Iljustsenko EST	1.89

TWELVE WOMEN CLEARED 1.95, the most ever at that height, improving the best ever marks for places 10-12. for the highest ever in a qualifying round. Jumping in this order in the final Di Martino, Chicherova, and Vlasic kept a clean sheet at 1.89, 1.93 and 1.97. Slesarenko and Shkolina also cleared 1.97 but could not go higher. Di Martino assured bronze with a third attempt clearance at 2.00, but Chicherova (on first attempts) and Vlasic (on second attempts) went over 2.00 and 2.03. Vlasic was closest at 2.05, but the result reversed the positions in the last two World Champs when Vlasic won with Chicherova second.

Pole Vault (Q 4.60m 28th, F 30th)

1. Fabiana Murer BRA	4.85
2. Martina Strutz GER	4.80
3. Svetlana Feofanova RUS	4.75
4. Jennifer Suhr USA	4.70
5. Yarisley Silva CUB	4.70
6. Yelena Isinbayeva RUS	4.65
7. Jirina Ptácniková CZE	4.65
8. Nikoléta Kiriakopoúlou GRE	4.65
9. Silke Spiegelburg GER	4.65
10= Anna Rogowska POL	4.55
10= Kristina Gadschiew GER	4.55
10= Monika Pyrek POL	4.55

TEN WOMEN WHO cleared 4.55 were joined by two over 4.50 first-time in the final, in which the best ever marks for place were tied for 5th, 6th and 7th, set for 8th and 9th as nine women went over 4.65, and tied for 10th to 12th as three were 10= at 4.55. Also 16 women over 4.50 and 23 over 4.40 in qualifying smashed previous records. Isinbayeva was the last to enter the final with the bar at 4.65, a height she and seven others cleared, while Suhr – an uncertain starter due to injury problems – opted instead for 4.70, which she cleared as did Silva for a CAC record. Isinbayeva could go no higher (one failure at 4.75, two at 4.80) and the medals went to the three women who cleared 4.75, Murer and Feofanova on first tries and Strutz on her second. Strutz cleared first time at 4.80 to add 2cm to her recent German record and Murer made it at the second attempt, but Feofanova had to settle for the bronze medal to add to silver 2001, gold 2003 and bronze 2007, all at 4.75! Murer, equalling her South American record, went clear on her first attempt at 4.85 while Strutz failed once at 4.85 and twice at 4.90.

Long Jump (Q 6.75m 27th, F 28th)

1. Brittney Reese USA	6.82/0.1
2. Olga Kucherenko RUS	6.77/0.0
3. Ineta Radevica LAT	6.76/-0.3
4. Anastasiya Mironchk-Ivanova BLR	6.74/0.2
5. Carolina Klüft SWE	6.56/0.4

6. Janay DeLoach USA — 6.56/0.3
7. Darya Klishina RUS — 6.50/0.1
8. Karin Mey Melis TUR — 6.44/0.4
9. Mayookha Johny IND — 6.37/-0.3
10. Naide Gomes POR — 6.26/-0.2
11. Maurren Maggi BRA — 6.17/0.6
nj. Funmi Jimoh USA — –

AFTER 6.41 AND a foul, Reese was in trouble in qualifying, but then jumped 6.79 for the third longest behind Maggi 6.86 and Mironchik-Ivanova 6.80. Maggi managed only two fouls and 6.17 in the final, in which Reese took a first-round lead that was never headed as she produced five fouls after her 6.82 (the shortest winning jump in World Champs history). Shifting winds seemed to affect all, as the overall standard was low, Kucherenko jumping 6.77 in the fourth round and Radevica passing Mironchik-Ivanova (6.71 and 6.74 in second and third rounds) by improving from 6.66 to 6.76 in the last. Klishina injured her ankle warming up for the final.

Triple Jump (Q 14.45m 30th, F 1st)

1. Olga Saladuha UKR — 14.94/0.2
2. Olga Rypakova KAZ — 14.89/0.2
3. Caterine Ibargüen COL — 14.84/0.4
4. Mabel Gay CUB — 14.67/0.4
5. Yamilé Aldama GBR — 14.50/0.4
6. Yargeris Savigne CUB — 14.43/0.0
7. Anna Kuropatkina RUS — 14.23/0.2
8. Baya Rahouli ALG — 14.12/0.2
9. Nataliya Yastrebova UKR — 14.12/-0.1
10. Biljana Topic SRB — 14.03/0.0
11. Dana Veldáková SVK — 13.96/0.1
12. Keila Costa BRA — 13.72/0.0

SAVIGNE LED THE qualifiers with 14.62 (14.87 from take-off) but in the final, after an initial 14.43 followed by two fouls, had to retire with a hamstring injury. Saladuha opened with 14.94 and that was the winning mark while Ibargüen started with 14.64 twice and ended with 14.81, 14.84 (14.94 from take-off) and 14.80. That was not, however, quite enough for silver as Rypakova, after 14.72 in round two, jumped 14.89 (15.04 from take-off) in the fourth.

Shot (Q 18.65m 28th, F 29th)

1. Valerie Adams NZL — 21.24*
2. Nadezhda Ostapchuk BLR — 20.05
3. Jill Camarena-Williams USA — 20.02
4. Gong Lijiao CHN — 19.97
5. Yevgeniya Kolodko RUS — 19.78
6. Li Ling CHN — 19.71
7. Anna Avdeyeva RUS — 19.54
8. Nadine Kleinert GER — 19.26
9. Michelle Carter USA — 18.76
10. Anna Omarova RUS — 18.67
11. Natalya Mikhnevich BLR — 18.47
12. Christina Schwanitz GER — 17.96
13. Cleopatra Borel-Brown TRI — 17.62

ADAMS LED THE qualifying with 19.79 but had a slow start in the final with 19,37 and a foul before producing the first 20m throw, 20.02 in the third. In this round Kolodko moved into second with a pb 19.78, closely followed by Ostapchuk 19.87. Then Camarena-Williams threw 20.02 in the fourth before Adams moved away with 20.72 and, after Ostapchuk had gone back into second with 20.05, made a 17cm improvement on her Commonwealth and Oceania record with 21.24 on the final throw of the competition. That tied Natalya Lisovskaya's 1987 championship record and gave Adams her third successive World title.

Discus (Q 62.00m 19th, F 28th)

1. Li Yanfeng CHN — 66.52
2. Nadine Müller GER — 65.97
3. Yarelys Barrios CUB — 65.73
4. Zaneta Glanc POL — 63.91
5. Stephanie Brown Trafton USA — 63.85
6. Tan Jian CHN — 62.96
7. Dragana Tomasevic SRB — 62.48
8. Nicoleta Grasu ROU — 62.08
9. Denia Caballero CUB — 60.73
10. Dani Samuels AUS — 59.14
11. Darya Pishchalnikova RUS — 58.10
12. Zinaida Sendriute LTU — 57.30

LI LED THROUGHOUT, opening with 65.28, and hitting 66.52 in the second round. The event went to form as Müller, who had led the qualifying with 65.54, held second place from her first throw of 65.06, improving to 65.97 in the second round, while Barrios, second at the last two World Champs, settled for third place with her third round 65.73.

Hammer (Q 71.00m 2nd, F 4th)

1. Tatyana Lysenko RUS — 77.13
2. Betty Heidler GER — 76.06
3. Zhang Wenxiu CHN — 75.03
4. Yipsi Moreno CUB — 74.48
5. Anita Wlodarczyk POL — 73.56
6. Bianca Perie ROU — 72.04
7. Kathrin Klaas GER — 71.89
8. Zalina Marghieva MDA — 70.27
9. Silvia Salis ITA — 69.88
10. Jennifer Dahlgren ARG — 69.72
11. Jessica Cosby USA — 68.91
12. Stéphanie Falzon FRA — 66.57

HEIDLER, CLEARLY THE world number one in 2011, struggled for her usual form with a foul and then 73.96 and 74.70, for third place at the halfway stage. She improved to 76.06 in the fifth round, but was no match for Lysenko, who opened with 76.80, 77.09 and 77.13. Zhang, who had led the qualifiers with 74.17, took bronze with her opening 75.03. Moreno challenged with 74.48 in the third round but then had three no throws.

Javelin   (Q 61.50m 16th, F 18th)

1. Mariya Abakumova RUS	71.99*
2. Barbora Spotáková CZE	71.58
3. Sunette Viljoen RSA	68.38
4. Christina Obergföll GER	65.24
5. Kathrina Molitor GER	64.32
6. Kimberley Mickle AUS	61.96
7. Martina Ratej SLO	61.65
8. Jarmila Klimesová CZE	59.27
9. Yuki Ebihara JPN	59.08
10. Goldie Sayers GBR	58.18
11. Madara Palameika LAT	58.08
dns. Linda Stahl GER	–

OBERGFÖLL WAS CLEARLY the best in qualifying with 69.86 from Viljoen 65.34, but was unable to get within 3.5 metres of that in the final, which proved to be one of the greatest ever. Spotáková opened with 68.80 for a first-round lead over Viljoen 64.36. Then in the second round Abakumova shocked herself and everyone else by unleashing a monstrous Russian record throw of 71.25. Spotáková had three more throws over 67m and Viljoen threw a Commonwealth record 68.38 just before, in the fifth round, Spotáková showed yet again what a great champion she is – like her coach Jan Zelezny – by responding with 71.58, the third longest ever behind her own world record of 72.28 and the 71.70 by Osleidys Menéndez at the 2005 World Champs! Surely enough – but no! Abakumova delivered her reply ... 71.99. What a competition, and second and third places were the best ever.

Heptathlon   (29/30th)

1. Tatyana Chernova RUS	6880
2. Jessica Ennis GBR	6751
3. Jennifer Oeser GER	6572
4. Karolina Tyminska POL	6544
5. Natalya Dobrynska UKR	6539
6. Lilli Schwarzkopf GER	6321
7. Antoinette Nana Djimou FRA	6309
8. Austra Skujyte LTU	6297
9. Jessica Zelinka CAN	6268
10. Lyudmila Yosypenko UKR	6263
11. Anna Bogdanova RUS	6242
12. Aiga Grabuste LAT	6229
13. Ruky Abdulai CAN	6212
14. Margaret Simpson GHA	6183
15. Louise Hazel GBR	6149

THE FAVOURITE ENNIS uncharacteristically hit two hurdles in the first event although running 12.94 and was below par with 1.89 in the high jump. She recovered with pbs for shot 14.67, long jump 6.51 and 800m 2:07.81, but her 39.95 javelin was a disaster and in that event Chernova threw 52.95 for a 251-point advantage and the Russian went on to win by 129. Although Ennis scored better in 5 events to 2, Chernova, 25cm taller than Ennis, was consistently excellent with pbs at 100mh, 13.32 (equal) and 200m, 23.50, and a fine long jump of 6.61. Oeser, solid throughout, took bronze with Tyminska moving from 8th to 4th with her 2:05.21 for 800m. Hyleas Fountain was third at the end of the first day but, fourth going into the final event, pulled off the track in the 800m with a hamstring injury.

4 x 100 Metres Relay   (h & F 4th)

1. USA	41.56	B Knight, Felix, Myers, Jeter (Solomon and Anderson ran in heat)
2. JAM	41.70	Fraser-Pryce, Stewart, Simpson, Campbell-Brown (Levy ran in heat)
3. UKR	42.51	Povh, Pogrebnyak, Ryemyen, Stuy
4. TRI	42.58	Selvon, Baptiste, Hackett, Ahye
5. FRA	42.70	Soumaré, Distel, Jacques-Sebastien, Mang
6. RUS	42.93	Gushchina, Rusakova, Savlinis, Fedoriva
7. NGR	42.93	Asumnu, Osayomi, Osazuwa, Okagbare
8. BRA	43.10	Silva, Gomes, Krasucki, Santos

JAMAICA WON THEIR heat in 42.23 while the USA countered with 41.94 and these two teams dominated the final. There was little in it at halfway after Felix had run her eighth race of the meeting, but Myers ran a fine third leg against Simpson to hand Jeter a 3m lead. No one was going to catch the world's fastest woman although Campbell-Brown did marvellously to halve the gap and take Jamaica to a Commonwealth record 41.70. Trinidad & Tobago set a national record of 42.50 in their heat, but were beaten by Ukraine in a slightly slower time for the bronze.

4 x 400 Metres Relay   (h 2nd, F 3rd)

1. USA	3:18.09	Richards-Ross 49.3, Felix 49.4, Beard 49.84, McCorory 49.52 (Hastings ran in heat)
2. JAM	3:18.71	Whyte 50.0, Prendergast 49.6, N Williams-Mills 49.84, S Williams 49.22 (Lloyd and Hall ran in heat)
3. RUS	3:19.36	Krivoshapka 50.3, Antyukh 50.0, Litvinova 49.96, Kapachinskaya 49.22 (Vdovina and Zadorina ran in heat)
4. GBR	3:23.63	Shakes-Drayton 50.5, Sanders 50.7, Ohuruogu 51.98, McConnell 50.43
5. UKR	3:23.86	Pygyda 50.8, Rabchenyuk 50.5, Yaroshchuk 52.00, Yefremova 50.50
6. BLR	3:25.64	Tashpulatova 51.68, Yushchenko 51.27, I Usovich 52.56, S Usovich 50.13

7. CZE	3:26.57	Rosolová 52.3, Bergrová 51.5, Bartoníčková 52.16, Hejnová 50.67	11. Vera Sokolova RUS	1:32:13
8. NGR	3:29.82	Omotosho 52.4, Odumosu 52.5, Etim 52.40, Abogunloko 52.59	12. Olena Shumkina UKR	1:32:17

11. Vera Sokolova RUS — 1:32:13
12. Olena Shumkina UKR — 1:32:17
13. María Vasco ESP — 1:32:42
14. Gao Ni CHN — 1:32:49
15. Regan Lamble AUS — 1:33:38

RUSSIA REGISTERED THE world's fastest time of the year with 3:20.94 in their heat, with Jamaica 3:22.01 and USA 3:23.57 winning the other heats. From a splendid first leg by Sanya Richards-Ross, the USA led all the way in the final with each runner breaking 50 secs. The final leg runners Shericka Williams for Jamaica, who chased the USA all the way to clock 3:18.71 for a Commonwealth and CAC record, and Kapachinskaya for Russia, both ran 49.22. The first four placings were the same as in Berlin two years ago. Times for seventh and eighth were the best ever in any race.

20 Kilometres Walk (31st)

1. Olga Kaniskina RUS — 1:29:42
2. Liu Hong CHN — 1:30:00
3. Anisya Kirdyapkina RUS — 1:30:13
4. Elisa Rigaudo ITA — 1:30:44
5. Qieyang Shenjie CHN — 1:31:14
6. Susana Feitor POR — 1:31:26
7. Ana Cabecinha POR — 1:31:36
8. Kristina Saltanovic LTU — 1:31:40
9. Beatriz Pascual ESP — 1:31:46
10. Inês Henriques POR — 1:32:06

KANISKINA WON HER third successive world title and fifth major gold medal in five years. Wary of the hot weather and high humidity, she was content to head the lead pack through the first 5k in a steady 23:29 and 10k in 46:16 (22:47 split), at which point the group in front numbered 13. During the next few kilometres Kaniskina, Kirdyapkina and Liu Hong drew well clear of the rest, headed by Sokolova (who faded badly), and it was in the 15th kilometre that Kaniskina started to pull away. She covered the third 5k in 21:47 and the fourth in 21:39 as she built up an 18 sec margin over Liu. 40 of 50 finished. Feitor celebrated her record 11th Worlds appearance with a splendid sixth place.

Prize money
Individual Events: Winner: US $60,000, 2nd $30,000, 3rd $20,000, 4th $15,000, 5th $10,000, 6th $6000, 7th $5000, 8th $4000.
Relays: Winners $80,000, 2nd $40,000, 3rd $20,000, 4th $16,000, 5th $12,000, 6th $8000, 7th $6000, 8th $4000.
Marathon Cup (Teams): Winners: $20,000, 2nd 15,000, 3rd $12,000, 4th $10,000, 5th $8000, 6th $6000.

2011 CHAMPIONSHIPS

World Youth Championships

At Villeneuve d'Ascq, France 6-10 July

Men

100m (-0.3)
1. O'Dail Todd JAM 10.51
2. Kazuma Oseto JPN 10.52
3. Mickael-Meba Zeze FRA 10.57

200m (1.1)
1. Stephen Newbold BAH 20.89
2. O'Dail Todd JAM 21.00
3. Ronald Darby USA 21.08

400m
1. Arman Hall USA 46.01
2. Alfas Kishoyan KEN 46.58
3. Patryk Dobek POL 46.67

800m
1. Leonard Kosencha KEN 1:44.08*
2. Mohammed Aman ETH 1:44.68
3. Timothy Kitum KEN 1:44.98

1500m
1. Teshome Diressa ETH 3:39.13
2. Vincent Mutai KEN 3:39.17
3. Jonathan Sawe KEN 3:39.54

3000m
1. William Sitonik KEN 7:40.10*
2. Patrick Mutunga KEN 7:40.47
3. Abrar Osman ERI 7:40.89

2000mSt
1. Consesius Kipruto KEN 5:28.65
2. Gilbert Kirui KEN 5:30.49
3. Zacharia Kiprotich UGA 5:37.98

110mh (0.1) 91.4cm
1. Andries van der Merwe RSA 13.41
2. Joshua Hawkins NZL 13.44
3. Wilhem Belocian FRA 13.51

400mh 84cm
1. Yegor Kuznetsov RUS 50.97
2. Ibrahim Mohamed Saleh KSA 51.14
3. Takahiro Matsumoto JPN 51.26

HJ
1. Gaël Levécque FRA 2.13
2. Usman Usmanov RUS 2.13
3. Justin Fondren USA 2.13

PV
1. Robert Renner SLO 5.25
2. Melker Svärd-Jacobsson SWE 5.15
3. Jacob Blankenship USA 5.05

LJ
1. Lin Qing CHN 7.83/1.7
2. Johan Taléus SWE 7.44w/2.9
3. Stefano Braga ITA 7.42w/3.0

TJ
1. Latario Minns BAH 16.06/1.7
2. Albert Janki RSA 15.95w/2.6
3. Lathone Minns BAH 15.51/1.3

SP 5kg
1. Jacko Gill NZL 24.35*
2. Tyler Schultz USA 20.35
3. Braheme Days USA 20.14

DT 1.5kg
1. Fedrick Dacres JAM 67.05

Placing and Medal Table Leaders

Nat	G	S	B	Pts	Nat	G	S	B	Pts
USA	6	4	6	159	RSA	2	2	1	45
KEN	5	5	4	107	UKR	0	1	1	38
JAM	4	1	4	81	BAH	3	0	1	37
ETH	2	2	1	72	CUB	2	1	1	33
RUS	2	1	2	69.5	CAN	0	2	1	30
CHN	2	4	1	62	POL	0	1	1	30
GER	2	0	1	57	ITA	0	1	1	25
GBR	2	1	2	57	ROU	1	0	1	22
JPN	0	2	1	52	NZL	1	1	0	21
FRA	2	0	3	51.5	MAR	0	1	0	18
AUS	1	2	1	51	MEX	0	0	1	18
SWE	0	4	0	48	KSA	0	1	0	14

TUR (1S) 13, COL (1S), FIN 12; HUN (1G), BEL, BRA, ERI (1B) 11; medals also: IRL, SLO 1G, SUI 1S, ESP. UGA 1B. 35 nations won medals (18 gold). 60 nations scored points (athletes placing in top 8).

2. Ethan Cochran USA 61.37
3. Gerhard de Beer RSA 60.63

HT 5kg
1. Bence Pásztor HUN 82.60*
2. Özkan Baltaci TUR 78.63
3. Serhiy Reheda UKR 74.06

JT 700g
1. Reinhardt van Zyl RSA 82.96
2. Morné Moolman RSA 80.99
3. Zhang Guisheng CHN 77.62

Oct
1. Jake Stein AUS 6491*
2. Fredrick Ekholm SWE 6127
3. Felipe dos Santos BRA 5966

10,000W
1. Pavel Parshin RUS 40:51.31*
2. Kenny Pérez COL 40:59.25
3. Erwin González MEX 41:09.60

Medley R
1. USA (Ronald Darby, Aldrich Bailey, Najee Glass, Arman Hall) 1:49.47*
2. JPN (Oseto, Hashimoto, Aikyo, Fukunaga) 1:50.69
3. FRA (Belocian, Zeze, Geenen, Jordier) 1:51.81

Women

100m (-0.5)
1. Jennifer Madu USA 11.57
2. Myasia Jacobs USA 11.61
3. Christiania Williams JAM 11.63

200m (0.1)
1. Desiree Henry GBR 23.25
2. Christian Brennan CAN 23.47
3. Shericka Jackson JAM 23.62

400m
1. Shaunae Miller BAH 51.84
2. Christian Brennan CAN 52.12
3. Olivia James JAM 52.14

800m
1. Ajee' Wilson USA 2:02.64
2. Wang Chunyu CHN 2:03.23
3. Jessica Judd GBR 2:03.43

1500m
1. Faith Kipyegon KEN 4:09.48*
2. Senbera Teferi ETH 4:10.54
3. Genet Tibieso ETH 4:11.56

3000m
1. Geytetom Gebreselassie ETH 8:56.36
2. Ziporah Kingori KEN 8:56.82
3. Caroline Kipkirui KEN 8:58.63

2000mSt
1. Norah Tanui KEN 6:16.41
2. Fadwa Sidi Madane MAR 6:20.98
3. Lilian Chemweno KEN 6:21.85

100mh (-0.1) 76.2cm
1. Trinity Wilson USA 13.11
2. Noemi Zbären SUI 13.17
3. Kendell Williams USA 13.28

400mh
1. Nnenya Hailey USA 57.93
2. Sarah Carli AUS 58.05
3. Surian Hechavarría CUB 58.37

HJ
1. Ligia Damaris Grozav ROU 1.87
2. Iryna Herashchenko UKR 1.87
3. Chanice Porter JAM 1.82

PV
1. Desiree Singh GER 4.25
2. Liz Parnov AUS 4.20
3. Lucy Bryan GBR 4.10

LJ
1. Chanice Porter JAM 6.22/-0.5
2. Anastassia Angioi ITA 6.17/-0.4
3. Marina Buchelgnikova RUS 6.11/0.3

TJ
1. Sokhna Galle FRA 13.62w/2.2
2. Li Jingyu CHN 13.57/1.5
3. Ana Peleteiro ESP 12.92w/3.6

SP
1. Guo Tianqian CHN 15.24
2. Sophie McKinna GBR 14.90
3. Katinka Urbaniak GER 14.71

DT
1. Rosalía Vázquez CUB 53.51
2. Liang Yan CHN 52.89
3. Shelbi Vaughan USA 52.58

HT
1. Louisa James GBR 57.13
2. Malwina Kopron POL 57.03
3. Roxana Perie ROU 56.75

JT
1. Christin Hussong GER 59.74*
2. Sofi Flink SWE 54.62
3. Monique Cilione AUS 52.77

Hep
1. Yusleidys Mendieta CUB 5697
2. Yorgelis Rodríguez CUB 5671
3. Marjolein Lindemans BEL 5532

5000mW
1. Kate Veale IRL 21:45.59
2. Mao Yanxue CHN 22:00.15
3. Nadezhda Leontyeva RUS 22:00.84

Medley R
1. JAM (Christania Williams, Shericka Jackson, Chrisann Gordon, Olivia James) 2:03.42*
2. USA (Madu, Brown, Baisden, Reynolds) 2:03.92
3. CAN (Pless, Bingham, Brennan, Watson) 2:05.72

IAAF Hammer Throw Challenge

Final standings for 2011 (after final qualifying competition at Zagreb, best three competitions to score). Prize money from $30,000 for 1st to

IAAF World Combined Events Challenge

Based on the sum of the best scores achieved in any three of the 13 designated competitions during the year.

Men Decathlon

1	Leonel Suárez CUB	25.172	8440 Götzis	8231 Kladno	8501 World Ch
2	Eelco Sintnicolaas NED	24,772	8304 Götzis	8298 World Ch	8170 Talence
3	Mikk Pahapill EST	24,746	8398 Götzis	8164 World Ch	8184 Talence
4	Pascal Behrenbruch GER	24,507	8064 Götzis	8232 Ratingen	8211 World Ch
5	Oleksiy Kasyanov UKR	24.428	8251 Götzis	8132 World Ch	8045 Talence
6	Hans Van Alphen BEL	24.365	8045 Götzis	8120 Kladno	8200 Talence
7	Andrej Raja EST	24,025	8114 Eur Cup S	7982 World Ch	7929 Talence
8	Brent Newdick NZL	23,655	7780 Desenzano	8114 Götzis	7761 World Ch

Women Heptathlon

1	Tatyana Chernova RUS	20,332	6773 Kladno	6880 World Ch	6679 Talence
2	Jennifer Oeser GER	19,594	6359 Götzis	6663 Ratingen	6572 World Ch
3	Nataliya Dobrynska UKR	19,408	6332 Götzis	6539 World Ch	6537 Talence
4	Karolina Tyminska POL	19,361	6516 Kladno	6544 World Ch	6301 Talence
5	Aiga Grabuste LAT	18,988	6252 Kladno	6507 Ratingen	6229 World Ch
6	Jessica Zelinka CAN	18,917	6353 Götzis	6268 World Ch	6296 Talence
7	Austra Skujyte LTU	18,839	6204 Götzis	6338 Eur Cup 2	6297 World Ch
8	Lilli Schwarzkopf GER	18,794	6370 Ratingen	6321 World Ch	6103 Talence

Prize Money: 1st $30,000, 2nd $20,000, 3rd $15,000, 4th $10,000, 5th $8000, 6th $7000, 7th $6000, 8th $5000.

$500 for 12th.

Men: 1. Krisztián Pars HUN 239.03, 2. Dilshod Nazarov TJK 235.72, 3. Primoz Kozmus SLO 233.90, 4. Sergey Litvinov RUS 232.56, 5. Nicola Vizzoni ITA 232.44, 6. Markus Esser GER 231.92, 7. Aleksey Zagornyi RUS 229.59, 8. Kibwe Johnson USA 229.44, 9. Pawel Fajdek POL 226.98, 10. Igors Sokolovs LAT 223.96, 11. Anatoliy Pozdynakov RUS 221.08, 12. Szymon Ziólkowski POL 221.00. **Women**: 1. Betty Heidler GER 228.09, 2. Yipsi Moreno CUB 220.46, 3. Kathrin Klaas GER 219.77, 4. Tatyana Lysenko RUS 218.51, 5. Zalina Marghieva MDA 214.58, 6. Marina Marghieva MDA 204.75, 7. Martina Hrasnová SVK 203.53, 8. Amber Campbell USA 201.75, 9. Gulfiya Khanafeyeva RUS 191.54, 10. Zhang Wenxiu CHN 147.44, 11. Jennifer Dahlgren ARG 142.14, 12. Sultana Frizell CAN 137.86.

IAAF World Race Walking Challenge

2011 events were the A category IAAF World Walking Cup, four B category races and for category C races. Walkers needed to compete at three or more of these to qualify and pre-final positions were based on the best positions from the above races, with a sliding scale of points from the three categories. Prize money was awarded then in the finishing order of eligible walkers in the final 10k race at: 1st $30,000, 2nd $20,000, 3rd $14,000, 4th $9000, 5th $7000, 6th $6000, 7th $4500, 8th $4000, 9th $3000, 10th $2000, 11th $1000, 12th $500.

Sep 17, La Coruña, Spain. 10k: 1. Valeriy Borchin RUS 38:43, 2. Wang Zhen CHN 38:50, 3. Chu Yafei CHN 39:07, 4. João Vieira POR 39:10, 5. Eder Sánchez MEX 39:14, 6. Robert Heffernan IRL 39:15, 7. Isamu Fujisawa JPN 39:19, 8. Luke Adams AUS 39:46, 9. Ever Palma MEX 39:47, 10. Jared Tallent AUS 39:49, 11. Pedro Gómez MEX 40:02, 12. Luis Fernando López COL 41:08; **Women 10k**: 1. Olga Kaniskina 42:39, 2. Liu Hong CHN 42:57, 3. Melanie Seeger GER 43:09, 4. Ana Cabecinha POR 43:15, 5. Susana Feitor POR 43:40, 6. Beatriz Pascual ESP 43:49, 7. María José Poves ESP 44:15, 8. Gao Ni CHN 44:20, 9. Inês Henriques POR 44:28, 10. Olive Loughnane IRL 44:30, 11. Brigita Virbalyte LTU 44:33, 12. Claudia Stef ROU 45:53.

World Marathon Majors 2010-11

London, Boston, Berlin, Chicago and New York Marathons 2010 and 2011.

Final points, winners earn $500,000: **Men**: 1. Emmanuel Mutai KEN 70, 2. Geoffrey Mutai KEN 65, 3. Patrick Makau KEN 60, 4. Tsegaye Kebede ETH 51, 5= Moses Mosop KEN, Gebre Gebremariam ETH 40, 7. Abel Kirui KEN 26, 8= Robert Kiprono Cheruiyot KEN, Samuel Wanjiru KEN 25. **Women**: 1. Liliya Shobukhova RUS 90, 2. Edna Kiplagat KEN 60, 3. Mary Keitany KEN 45, 4. Bezunesh Bekele ETH 30, 5= Firehiwot Dado ETH, Teyba Erkesso ETH. Aberu Kebede ETH, Caroline Kilel KEN, Florence Kiplagat KEN 25.

World University Games

At Shenzhen, China 17-21 August

Men

100m (-0.2)	1. Jacques Harvey JAM 10 14
	2. Rytis Sakalauskas LTU 10.14
	3. Su Bingtian CHN 10.27
200m (-0.3)	1. Rasheed Dwyer JAM 20.20
	2= Thuso Mpuang RSA 20.59
	2= Jason Young JAM 20.59
400m	1. Marcell Deák Nagy HUN 45.50
	2. Peter Matthews JAM 45.62

	3. Sean Wroe AUS 45.93
800m	1. Lachlan Renshaw AUS 1:46.36
	2. Teng Haining CHN 1:46.62
	3. Fred Samoei KEN 1:46.72
1500m	1. Imad Touil ALG 3:48.13
	2. Abdelmajed Touil ALG 3:48.24
	3. Valentin Smirnov RUS 3:48.45
5000m	1. Andy Vernon GBR 14:00.06
	2. Yevgeniy Rybakov RUS 14:00.60
	3. Stefano La Rosa ITA 14:02.95
10,000m	1. Sugaru Osako JPN 28:42.83
	2. Stephen Mokoka RSA 28:53.09
	3. Ahmed Tamri MAR 29:06.20
HMar	1. Ahmed Tamri MAR 66:20
	2. Fatih Bilgic TUR 66:20
	3. Tsubasa Hayakawa JPN 66:25
3000mSt	1. Alberto Paulo POR 8:32.26
	2. Halil Akkas TUR 8:34.57
	3. Ildar Minshin RUS 8:34.86
110mh	1. Hansie Parchment JAM 13.24
(-0.3)	2. Jiang Fan CHN 13.55
	3. Ronald Brookins USA 13.56
400mh	1. Jeshua Anderson USA 49.03
	2. Takayuki Kishimoto JPN 49.52
	3. Kurt Couto MOZ 49.61
HJ	1. Bogdan Bondarenko UKR 2.28
	2. Wojciech Theiner POL 2.26
	3. Sergey Mudrov RUS 2.24
PV	1. Lukasz Michalski POL 5.75
	2. Mateusz Didenkow POL 5.75
	3. Aleksandr Gripich RUS 5.75
LJ	1. Su Xiogfeng CHN 8.17/0.2
	2. Marquise Goodwin USA 8.03/0.5
	3. Julian Reid GBR 7.96/0.2
TJ	1. Nelson Évora POR 17.31/0.0
	2. Viktor Kuznetsov UKR 16.89/0.7
	3. Yevgeniy Ektov KAZ 16.83/0.0
SP	1. O'Dayne Richards JAM 19.93
	2. Soslan Tsirikhov RUS 19.80
	3. Mason Finley USA 19.72
DT	1. Märt Israel EST 64.07
	2. Przemyslaw Czajkowski POL 63.62
	3. Ronald Julião BRA 63.30
HT	1. Pawel Fajdek POL 78.14
	2. Marcel Lomnicky SVK 73.90
	3. Lorenzo Povegliano ITA 73.39
JT	1. Fatih Avan TUR 83.79
	2. Roman Avramenko UKR 81.42
	3. Igor Janik POL 79.65
Dec	1. Valeriy Kharlamov RUS 8166
	2. Gaël Quérin FRA 7857
	3. Mikhail Logvinenko RUS 7835
4x100m	1. RSA (Dreyer, Magakwe, Sefanyetso, Mpuang) 39.25
	2. CHN 39.39
	3. HKG 39.44
4x400m	1. RUS (Sigalovskiy, Buryak, Vazhov, Kruglyakov) 3:04.51
	2. JPN 3:05.16
	3. RSA 3:05.61
20kmW	1. Andrey Krivov RUS 1:24:15
	2. Mikhail Ryzhov RUS 1:24:26
	3. Andrés Chocho ECU 1:24:44
Women	
100m	1. Carrie Russell JAM 11.05
(-0.7)	2. Hrstyna Stuy UKR 11.34

	3. Lina Grincikaite LTU 11.44
200m	1. Anneisha McLaughlin JAM 22.54
(0.7)	2. Tiffany Townsend USA 22.96
	3. Anna Kaygorodova RUS 23.16
400m	1. Olga Topilskaya RUS 51.63
	2. Yelena Migunova RUS 51.77
	3. Diamond Dixon USA 52.76
	drugs dq (3) Olga Tereshkova KAZ 52.36
800m	1. Olga Zavgorodnya UKR 1:59.94
	2. Yelena Kofanova RUS 1:59.94
	3. Liliya Lobanova RUS 2:00.42
1500m	1. Asli Çakir TUR 4:05.56
	2. Anna Mishchenko UKR 4:05.91
	3. Yekaterina Gorbunova RUS 4:06.16
5000m	1. Binnaz Uslu TUR 15:41.15
	2. Sara Moreira POR 15:45.83
	3. Natalya Popkova RUS 15:52.55
10,000m	1. Fadime Suna TUR 33:11.92
	2. Hanae Tanaka JPN 33:15.57
	3. Mai Ishibashi JPN 33:41.90
HMar	1. Ro Un-ok PRK 76:38
	2. Jin Lingling CHN 76:42
	3. Sayo Nomura JPN 76:48
3000mSt	1. Binnaz Uslu TUR 9:33.50
	2. Lyudmila Kuzmina RUS 9:44.77
	3. Jin Yuan CHN 9:45.21
100mh	1. Nia Ali USA 12.85
(-1.3)	2. Natalya Ivoninskaya KAZ 13.16
	3. Christina Manning USA 13.17
400mh	1. Anna Yaroshchuk UKR 55.15
	2. Irina Davydova RUS 55.50
	3. Nagihan Karadere TUR 55.81
HJ	1. Brigetta Barrett USA 1.96
	2. Airine Palsyte LTU 1.96
	3. Anna Iljustsenko EST 1.94
PV	1. Aleksandra Kiryashova RUS 4.65
	2. Tina Sutej SLO 4.55
	3. Ekateríni Stefanídi GRE 4.45
LJ	1. Anna Nazarova RUS 6.72/0.6
	2. Yuliya Pidluznaya RUS 6.56/-0.5
	3. Melanie Bauschke GER 6.51/-0.1
TJ	1. Yekaterina Koneva RUS 14.25/0.6
	2. Patricia Mamona POR 14.23/0.0
	3. Cristina Bujin ROU 14.21/0.1
SP	1. Irina Tarasova RUS 18.02
	2. Sophie Kleeberg GER 17.48
	3. Meng Qianqian CHN 17.21
DT	1. Zaneta Glanc POL 63.99
	2. Zinaida Sendriute LTU 62.49
	3. Svetlana Saykina RUS 60.81
HT	1. Zalina Marghieva MDA 72.93
	2. Eva Orbán HUN 71.33
	3. Bianca Perie ROU 71.18
JT	1. Sunette Viljoen RSA 66.47
	2. Marina Maksimova RUS 59.87
	3. Justine Robbeson RSA 58.78
Hep	1. Olga Kurban RUS 6151
	2. Viktorija Zemaityte LTU 5958
	3. Katerina Cachová CZE 5873
4x100m	1. UKR (Titimets, Pogrebnyak, Stuy, Bryzgina) 43.33
	2. USA 43.48
	3. JAM 43.57
4x400	1. RUS (Karnaushchenko, Migunova, Ustalova, Topilskaya) 3:27.16
	2. TUR 3:30.14

	3. GBR 3:33.09
20kW	1. Julia Takacs ESP 1:33:51
	2. Tatyana Shemyakina RUS 1:34:23
	3. Nina Okhotnikova RUS 1:35:10

10th All-Africa Games

At Maputo, Mozambique 11-15 September

100m	1. Amr Ibrahim Seoud EGY 10.20
(-0.4)	2. Ben Youssef Meité CIV 10.28
	3. Obinna Metu NGR 10.29
200m	1. Idrissa Adam CMR 20.66
(1.7)	2. Ben Youssef Meité CIV 20.76
	3. Obakeng Ngwigwa BOT 20.94
400m	1. Rabah Yousif SUD 45.27
	2. Tobi Ogunmola NGR 45.82
	3. Mark Mutai KEN 46.52
800m	1. Taoufik Makhloufi ALG 1:46.32
	2. Boaz Lalang KEN 1:46.40
	3. Job Kinyor KEN 1:46.52
1500m	1. Caleb Ndiku KEN 3:39.12
	2. Collins Cheboi KEN 3:39.72
	3. Taoufik Makhloufi ALG 3:39.99
5000m	1. Moses Kipsiro UGA 13:43.08
	2. Yenew Alamirew ETH 13:43.33
	3. Abayneh Ayele ETH 13:43.51
10,000m	1. Ibrahim Jeylan ETH 28:18.22
	2. Bedan Karoki KEN 28:19.32
	3. Azmeraw Bekele ETH 28:20.61
HMar	1. Lelisa Desisa ETH 64:31
	2. Kenneth Kipkemoi KEN 64:44
	3. Bekana Daba ETH 64:51
3000mSt	1. Getahun Shiferaw ETH 8:17.36
	2. Roba Gari ETH 8:18.41
	3. Sisay Korme ETH 8:20.72
110mh	1. Othman Hadj Lazib ALG 13.48w
(2.9)	2. Selim Nurudeen NGR 13.61
	3. Samuel Okon NGR 13.75
400mh	1. Abderahmane Hamadi ALG 50.48
	2. Kurt Couto MOZ 51.04
	3. Julius Rotich KEN 51.15
HJ	1. Mohamed Younes Idriss SUD 2.25
	2. Kabelo Kgosiemang BOT 2.20
	3. William Woodcock SEY 2.15
PV	1. Larbi Bouraada ALG 5.00
	2. Mourad Souissi ALG 4.00
LJ	1. Luvo Maniyonga RSA 8.02/-0.1
	2. Ignisious Gaisah GHA 7.86/0.2
	3. Ndiss Kaba Badji SEN 7.83/-0.6
TJ	1. Tosin Oke NGR 16.65/0.5
	2. Issam Nima ALG 16.54
	3. Hugo Mamba Schlick CMR 16.17/-0.9
SP	1. Yasser Ibrahim EGY 19.73*
	2. Jaco Engelbrecht RSA 18.89
	3. Roelie Potgieter RSA 18.68
DT	1. Yasser Ibrahim EGY 63.20*
	2. Victor Hogan RSA 62.60
	3. Rossel Tucker RSA 55.98
HT	1. Mostafa Al-Gamal EGY 74.76
	2. Chris Harmse RSA 74.66
	3. Hassan M. Mahmoud EGY 69.70
JT	1. Julius Yego KEN 78.34
	2. Bernard Crous RSA 72.68
	3. Friday Osayande NGR 71.01
Dec	1. Jangy Addy LBR 7993*
	2. Guilllaume Thierry MRI 7479

	3. Ali Kamé MAD 7436
4x100m	1. NGR 38.93 (Adukwu, Emelieze, Metu, Egweru)
	2. GHA 38.95
	3. BOT 39.09
4x400m	1. KEN 3:03.10
	2. NGR 3:05.26
	3. BOT 3:05.92
20kmW	1. Hassanine Sbaï TUN 1:24:53
	2. Hédi Teraoui TUN 1:26:44
	3. Gabriel Ngintedem CMR 1:32:08

Women

100m	1. Damola Osayomi NGR 10.90w
(2.5)	2. Blessing Okagbare NGR 11.07
	3. Gloria Asumnu NGR 11.26
200m	1. Damola Osayomi NGR 22.86
(1.9)	2. Vida Anim GHA 23.06
	3. Tjipekapora Herunga NAM 23.50
400m	1. Amantle Montsho BOT 50.87
	2. Ami Mbacké Thiam SEN 51.77
	3. Tjipekapora Herunga NAM 51.84
800m	1. Annet Negesa UGA 2:01.81
	2. Fantu Mangiso ETH 2:03.22
	3. Sylvia Chesebe KEN 2:04.16
1500m	1. Irene Jelagat KEN 4:13.67
	2. Joyce Chepkirui KEN 4:13.71
	3. Tizita Bogale ETH 4:14.41
5000	1. Sule Utura ETH 15:38.70
	2. Emebet Anteneh ETH 15:40.13
	3. Pauline Korikwiang KEN 15:40.93
10,000m	1. Sule Utura ETH 33:24.82
	2. Wude Ayalew ETH 33:24.88
	3. Pauline Korikwiang KEN 33:26.17
HMar	1. Mare Dibaba ETH 70:47*
	2. Mamitu Daska ETH 70:52
	3. Hilalia Johannes NAM 71:12
3000mSt	1. Hyvin Kiyeng Jepkemoi KEN 10:00.50
	2. Hiwot Ayalew ETH 10:00.57
	3. Birtukan Adamu ETH 10:02.22
100mh	1. Seun Adigun NGR 13.20w
(4.2)	2. Jessica Ohanaja NGR 13.36
	3. Rosa Rakotozafy MAD 13.55
400mh	1. Ajoke Odumosu NGR 56.26
	2. Wanda Theron RSA 57.13
	3. Kou Luogon LBR 57.34
HJ	1. Doreen Amata NGR 1.80
	2. Uhunoma Osazuwa NGR 1.80
	3. Lissa Labiche SEY 1.80
PV	1. Dora Mahfoudhi TUN 3.60
	2. Alima Ouattara CIV 3.20
LJ	1. Blessing Okagbare NGR 6.50w/2.3
	2. Sarah Ngo Ngoa CMR 6.46w/3.3
	3. Romaïssa Belabiod ALG 6.46/1.7
TJ	1. Baya Rahouli ALG 14.08/-2.5
	2. Kéne Ndoye SEN 13.69/-0.7
	3. Otonye Iworima NGR 13.53/-0.3
SP	1. Auriel Dogmo CMR 16.03
	2. Veronica Abrahamse RSA 15.70
	3. Sonia Smuts RSA 15.29
DT	1. Suzanne Kragbé CIV 56.56
	2. Elizna Naude RSA 53.63
	3. Alifatou Djibril TOG 46.46
HT	1. Amy Séne SEN 62.48
	2. Sarra Ben Saad TUN 59.65
	3. Rana Taha Ibrahim EGY 58.57

70

JT	1. Justine Robbeson RSA 55.33		**DT**	1. Ehsan Hadadi IRI 62.27
	2. Gerlize de Klerk RSA 52.27			2. Vikas Gowda IND 61.58
	3. Lindy Agricole SEY 51.26			3. Wu Jian CHN 56.61
Hep	1. Margaret Simpson GHA 6171		**HT**	1. Mohammed Al-Zankawi KUW 73.73
	2. Gabriella Kouassi CIV 5712			2. Hiroshi Noguchi JPN 70.89
	3. Selloane Tsoaeli LES 5588			3. Hiroaki Doi JPN 70.69
4x100m	1. NGR 43.34		**JT**	1. Yukifumi Murakami JPN 83.27*
	2. GHA 44.33			2. Park Jae-myong KOR 80.19
	3. CMR 45.00			3. Ivan Zaytsev UZB 79.22
4x400m	1. NGR 3:31.21		**Dec**	1. Hadi Sepehrzad IRI 7506
	2. SEN 3:32.21			2. Akihiko Nakamura JPN 7478
	3. KEN 3:37.37			3. Bharat Inder Singh IND 7358
20kmW	1. Chaïma Trabelsi TUN 1:40:35*		**4x100m**	1. JPN 39.18
	2. Olfa Lafi TUN 1:41.25			2. HKG 39.26
	3. Aynalem Eshitu ETH 1:42:19			3. TPE 39.30

Medal table: NGR 10G-6S-5B, ETH 6-7-7, KEN 5-5-7 22 countries won medals.

Asian Championships

At Kobe, Japan 7-10 July

100m	1. Su Bingtian CHN 10.21		**4x400m**	1. JPN 3:04.72
(1.8)	2. Masashi Eriguchi JPN 10.28			2. KSA 3:08.03
	3. Sota Kawatsura JPN 10.30			3. IRI 3:08.58
200m	1. Seun Ogunode QAT 20.41=*		**Women**	
(-0.4)	2. Hitoshi Saito JPN 20.75		**100m**	1. Guzel Khubbieva UZB 11.39
	3. Omar Al-Salfa UAE 20.97		(1.9)	2. Wei Yongli CHN 11.70
400m	1. Youssef Al-Masrahi KSA 45.79			3. Tao Yujia CHN 11.74
	2. Hideyuki Hirose JPN 46.03		**200m**	1. Chiasto Fukushima JPN 23.49
	3. Yuzo Kanemaru JPN 46.38		(-2.2)	2. Gretta Taslakian LIB 24.01
800m	1. Mohammad Al-Azimi KUW 1:46.14			3. Saori Imai JPN 24.06.
	2. Sajad Moradi IRI 1:46.35		**400m**	1. Chen Jingwen CHN 52.89
	3. Ghamanda Ram IND 1:46.46			2. Chandrika Subashini SRI 53.35
1500m	1. Mohammad Al-Azimi KUW 3:42.89			3. Chisato Tanaka JPN 54.08
	2. Sajad Moradi IRI 3:43.30			drugs dq (1) Olga Tereshkova KAZ 52.37
	3. Chaminda Wijekoon SRI 3:44.01			drugs d2 (2) Kolestane Ieso IRQ 52.80
5000m	1. Dejene Regassa BRN 13:39.71*		**800m**	1. Truong Thanh Hang VIE 2:01.41
	2. Yuki Sato JPN 13:40.78			2. Margarita Matsko KAZ 2:02.46
	3. Alemu Bekele BRN 13:41.93.			3. Tintu Luka IND 2:02.55
10,000m	1. Hasan Mahbood BRN 28:35.49		**1500m**	1. Genzeb Shumi Regasa BRN 4:15.91
	2. Bilisuma Shugi BRN 28:36.30			2. Truong Thanh Hang VIE 4:18.40
	3. Akinobu Murasawa JPN 28:40.63			3. Orchatteri P.Jaisha IND 4:21.41
3000mSt	1. Ali Abubaker Kamal QAT 8:30.23		**5000m**	1. Tejitu Daba BRN 15:22.48*
	2. Artem Kosinov KAZ 8:35.11			2. Hitoma Niiya JPN 15:34.19
	3. Tarek Mubarak Taher BRN 8:45.47			3. Yuriko Kobayashi JPN 15:42.59
110mh	1. Liu Xiang CHN 13.22*		**10,000m**	1. Shitaye Eshete BRN 32:47.80
(-0.8)	2. Shi Dongpeng CHN 13.56			2. Kareema Saleh BRN 32:50.70
	3. Park Tae-kyong KOR 13.66			3. Preeja Sreedharan IND 33:15.55
400mh	1. Takatoshi Abe JPN 49.64		**3000mSt**	1. Minoru Hayakari JPN 9:52.42*
	2. Yuta Imazeki JPN 50.22			2. Sudha Singh IND 10:08.52
	3. Chen Chieh TPE 50.39			3. Nguyen Thi Phuong VIE 10:14.94
HJ	1. Mutaz Essa Barshim QAT 2.35*		**100mh**	1. Sun Yawei CHN 13.04
	2. Majed El Dein Ghazal SYR 2.28		(-0.9)	2. Jung Hye-lim KOR 13.11
	3. Wang Chen CHN 2.26			3. Natalaya Ivoninskaya KAZ 13.15
PV	1. Daichi Sawano JPN 5.50		**400mh**	1. Satomi Kubokura JPN 56.52
	2. Hiroki Ogita JPN 5.40			2. Yang Qi CHN 56.69
	3. Yang Yansheng CHN 5.40			3. Christine Merril SRI 57.30
LJ	1. Su Xiongfeng CHN 8.19/1.0		**HJ**	1. Zheng Xingjuan CHN 1.92
	2. Suphanara Suksawat THA 8.05/1.3			2. Svetlana Radvizil UZB 1.92
	3. Rikiya Saruyama JPN 8.05/1.2			3. Marina Aitova KAZ 1.89
TJ	1. Yevgeniy Ektov KAZ 16.91/0.0		**PV**	1. Wu Sha CHN 4.35
	2. Li Yanxi CHN 16.70w/4.1			2. Li Ling CHN 4.30
	3. Roman Valiyev KAZ 16.62/0.2			3. Choi Yun-hee KOR 4.00
SP	1. Chang Ming-Huang TPE 20.14*		**LJ**	1. Mayookha Johny IND 6.56/0.5
	2. Zhang Jun CHN 19.77			2. Lu Minjia CHN 6.52/-0.2
	3. Om Prakash Singh IND 19.47			3. Saeko Okayama JPN 6.51/0.2
			TJ	1. Xie Limei CHN 14.54/1.9
				2. Valeriya Kanatova UZB 14.14w/2.3
				3. Mayookha Johny IND 14.11/0.9
			SP	1. Meng Qianqian CHN 18.31
				2. Liu Xiangrong CHN 18.30

DT
3. Leyla Rajabi IRI 16.60
1. Sun Taifeng CHN 60.89
2. Ma Xuejun CHN 59.67
3. Harwant Kaur IND 57.99

HT
1. Masumi Aya JPN 67.19
2. Liu Tingting CHN 65.42
3. Yuka Murofushi JPN 62.50

JT
1. Liu Chunhua CHN 58.05
2. Wang Ping CHN 55.80
3. Yuka Sato JPN 54.16

Hep
1. Wassana Winatho THA 5710
2. Fumie Takehara JPN 5491
3. Chie Kiroyama JPN 5442

4x100m
1. JPN 44.05
2. CHN 44.23
3. THA 44.62.

4x400m
1. JPN 3:35.00
2. IND 3:44.17
Drugs dq: (2) KAZ 3:36.61; (3) IRQ 3:41.91

Medal table leaders: JPN 11G-10S-12B, CHN 11-12-4, BRN 5-2-2, KUW 3-0-0, QAT 3-0-0, IRI 2-2-2. IND 1-2-9, KAZ 1-2-3. In all 20 nations won medals (13 won gold).

European Under-23 Championships

At Ostrava. Czech Republic 14-17 July

Men

100m (-1.5)
1. James Alaka GBR 10.45
2. Michael Tumi ITA 10.47
3. Andrew Robertson GBR 10.52

200m (-1.4)
1. Likoúrgos-Stéfanos Tsákonas GRE 20.56
2. James Alaka GBR 20.60
3. Pavel Maslák CZE 20.67

400m
1. Nigel Levine GBR 46.10
2. Brian Gregan IRL 46.12
3. Luke Lennon-Ford GBR 46.22

800m
1. Adam Kszczot POL 1:46.71
2. Kevin López ESP 1:46.93
3. Mukhtar Mohammed GBR 1:48.01

1500m
1. Florian Carvalho FRA 3:50.42
2. James Shane GBR 3:50.58
3. David Bustos ESP 3:50.59

5000m
1. Sindre Buraas NOR 14:22.69
2. Ross Millington GBR 14:22.78
3. Jesper van der Wielen NED 14:23.31

10,000m
1. Sondre Nordstad Moen NOR 28:41.66
2. Ahmed El Mazoury ITA 28:46.97
3. Musa Roba-Kinkal GER 28:57.91

3000mSt
1. Sebastián Martos ESP 8:35.35
2. Abdelaziz Merzoughi ESP 8:36.21
3. Alexandru Ghinea ROU 8:38.51

110mh (-0.4)
1. Sergey Shubenkov RUS 13.56
2. Balázs Baji HUN 13.58
3. Lawrence Clarke GBR 13.62

400mh
1. Jack Green GBR 49.13
2. Nathan Woodward GBR 49.28
3. Emir Bekric SRB 49.61

HJ
1. Bogdan Bondarenko UKR 2.30
2. Sergey Mudrov RUS 2.30
3. Miguel Angel Sancho ESP 2.21

PV
1. Pawel Wojciechowski POL 5.70
2. Karsten Dilla GER 5.60
3. Dmitriy Zhelyabin RUS 5.55

LJ
1. Aleksandr Menkov RUS 8.08/0.1
2. Marcos Chuva POR 7.94/0.6
3. Guillaume Victorin FRA 7.86/1.8

TJ
1. Sheryf El-Sheryf UKR 17.72/1.3*
2. Aleksey Fyodorov RUS 16.85/1.3
3. Yuriy Kovalyov RUS 16.82w/2.3

SP
1. David Storl GER 20.45*
2. Dmytro Savytskyy UKR 19.18
3. Marin Premeru CRO 18.83

DT
1. Lawrence Okoye GBR 60.70
2. Mykyta Nesterenko UKR 59.67
3. Fredrik Amundgård NOR 59.42

HT
1. Pawel Fajdek POL 78.54
2. Javier Cienfuegos ESP 73.03
3. Aleh Dubitski BLR 72.52

JT
1. Till Wöschler GER 84.38
2. Fatih Avan TUR 84.11
3. Dmitriy Tarabin RUS 83.18

Dec
1. Thomas Van Der Plaetsen BEL 8157
2. Eduard Mikhan BLR 8152
3. Mihail Dudas SRB 8117

4x100m
1. ITA (Tumi, Basciani, Manenti, Obou) 39.05
2. GBR 39.10
3. GER 39.19

4x400m
1. GBR (Levine, Phillips, Bowie, Lennon-Ford) 3:03.53
2. POL 3:03.62
3. RUS 3:04.01

20kW
1. Pyotr Bogatyrev RUS 1:24:20
2. Dawid Tomala POL 1:24:21
3. Denis Strelkov RUS 1:24:25

Women

100m (-1.7)
1. Andreea Ograzeanu ROU 11.65
2. Leena Günther GER 11.75
3. Anna Kielbasinska POL 11.77

200m (-1.0)
1. Anna Kielbasinska POL 23.23
2. Moa Hjelmer SWE 23.24
3. Marit Dopheide NED 23.32
drugs dq (1) Darya Pizhankova UKR 23.20

400m
1. Olga Topilskaya RUS 51.45
2. Yuliya Terekhova RUS 52.63
3. Lena Schmidt GER 52.66

800m
1. Yelena Arzhakova RUS 1:59.41
2. Merve Aydin TUR 2:00.46
3. Lynsey Sharp GBR 2:00.65

1500m
1. Yelena Arzhakova RUS 4:20.55
2. Tugba Karakaya TUR 4:20.80
3. Corinna Harrer GER 4:21.52

5000m
1. Layes Abdullayeva AZE 15:29.47
2. Yekaterina Gorbunova RUS 15:45.14
3. Stevie Stockton GBR 15:58.51

10,000m
1. Layes Abdullayeva AZE 32:18.05*
2. Lyudmyla Kovalenko UKR 33:35.36
3. Catarina Ribeiro POR 34:10.39

3000mSt
1. Gülcan Mingir TUR 9:47.83
2. Jana Sussmann GER 9:48.01
3. Mariya Shatalova UKR 9:48.22

100mh (-1.0)
1. Alina Talay BLR 12.91
2. Lisa Urech SUI 13.00
3. Cindy Roleder GER 13.10

400mh
1. Anna Yaroshchuk UKR 54.77
2. Hanna Titimets UKR 54.91
3. Meghan Beesley GBR 55.69

HJ
1. Esthera Petre ROU 1.98*

European Under-23 Placing and Medal Table Leaders

Nat	G	S	B	Pts	Nat	G	S	B	Pts
RUS	11	5	5	222	CZE	0	1	1	45
GER	4	4	7	164	NED	0	0	3	40.5
GBR	6	5	9	151	TUR	1	3	1	40
POL	4	3	2	134	NOR	2	0	1	34
UKR	3	7	1	116	GRE	2	1	0	31.5
ITA	1	2	0	86.5	SWE	0	1	0	30
FRA	1	1	2	78	POR	0	1	1	27
ESP	1	3	3	65	HUN	0	1	1	27
ROU	3	1	1	50	SRB	0	1	2	24
BLR	1	2	2	50	SUI	0	1	0	22.5

26 nations won medals (16 gold). 33 nations scored points (athletes placing in top 8).

	2. Oksana Okuneva UKR 1.94
	3. Burcu Ayhan TUR 1.94
PV	1. Holly Bleasdale GBR 4.55
	2. Ekaterini Stefanídi GRE 4.45
	3. Annika Roloff GER 4.40
LJ	1. Darya Klishina RUS 7.05/1.1*
	2. Ivana Spanovic SRB 6.74w/3.2
	3. Sosthene Moguenara GER 6.74/1.8
TJ	1. Paraskevi Papahrístou GRE 14.40/1.2
	2. Carmen Toma ROU 13.92/0.0
	3. Anna Jagaciak POL 13.86/0.0
SP	1. Yevgeniya Kolodko RUS 18.87
	2. Sophie Kleeberg GER 17.92
	3. Melissa Boekelman NED 17.88
DT	1. Julia Fischer GER 59.60
	2. Anastasiya Kashtanova BLR 56.25
	3. Anita Márton HUN 54.14
HT	1. Bianca Perie ROU 71.59*
	2. Joanna Fiodorow POL 70.06
	3. Sophie Hitchon GBR 69.59
JT	1. Sarah Mayer GER 59.29
	2. Vira Rebryk UKR 58.95
	3. Oona Sormunen FIN 58.54
Hep	1. Grit Sadeiko EST 6134
	2. Katerina Cachová CZE 6123
	3. Yana Maksimova BLR 6075
4x100m	1. RUS (Fiolatova, Tamkova, Kuzina, Argunova) 44.14
	2. FRA 44.26
	3. GBR 44.34
	drugs dq 1. UKR (Yanovska, Pizhankova ¶, Pyatachenko, Lepska ¶) 44.00
4x400m	1. RUS (Subbotina, Yefimova, Terekhova, Topilskaya) 3:27.72
	2. UKR 3:30.13
	3. FRA 3:31.73
20kW	1. Tatyana Mineyeva RUS 1:31:42
	2. Nina Ochotnikova RUS 1:31:51
	3. Julia Takács ESP 1:31:55

European Junior (U20) Championships

At Tallinn, Estonia 21-24 July

Men

100m	1. Jimmy Vicaut FRA 10.07
(0.3)	2. Adam Gemili GBR 10.41
	3. David Bolarinwa GBR 10.46
200m	1. David Bolarinwa GBR 21.07
(-2.7)	2. Pierre Vincent FRA 21.22
	3. Jeffrey John FRA 21.24
400m	1. Marcell Deák-Nagy HUN 45.42
	2. Nikita Uglov RUS 46.01
	3. Michele Tricca ITA 46.09
800m	1. Pierre-Ambroise Bosse FRA 1:47.14
	2. Zan Rudolf SLO 1:47.73
	3. Johan Rogestedt SWE 1:47.88
1500m	1. Adam Cotton GBR 3:43.98
	2. Thomas Solberg Eide NOR 3:44.70
	3. Alexander Schwab GER 3:44.8
5000m	1. Gabriel Navarro ESP 14:07.06
	2. Bartosz Kowalczyk POL 14:07.17
	3. Jonathan Hay GBR 14:07.78
10,000m	1. Gabriel Navarro ESP 30:02.18
	2. Emmanuel Lejeune BEL 31:35.19
	3. Szymon Kulka POL 31:50.13
3000mSt	1. Ilgizar Safiulin RUS 8:37.94*
	2. Muhammet Emin Tan TUR 8:46.74
	3. Martin Grau GER 8:48.79
110mh	1. Jack Meredith GBR 13.50
(-0.9)	2. Andrew Pozzi GBR 13.57
(99cm)	3. Rahib Mammadov AZE 13.78
400mh	1. Varg Königsmark GER 49.70*
	2. Stef Vanhaeren BEL 50.01
	3. José Bencosme de Leon ITA 50.30
HJ	1. Nikita Anishchenkov RUS 2.27
	2. Janick Klausen DEN 2.25
	3. Gianmarco Tamberi ITA 2.25
PV	1. Emile Denecker FRA 5.50
	2. Kévin Ménaldo FRA 5.50
	3. Didac Salas ESP 5.40
LJ	1. Sergey Morgunov RUS 8.18w/3.6
	2. Tomasz Jaszczuk POL 8.11/1.0
	3. Yevgeniy Antonov RUS 7.83w/2.9
TJ	1. Aleksandr Yurchenko RUS 16.31/-0.4
	2. Murad Ibadullayev AZE 16.25/1.3
	3. Georgi Tsonov BUL 15.90/1.4
SP 6kg	1. Krzysztof Brzozowski POL 20.92
	2. Daniele Secci ITA 20.45
	3. Christian Jagusch GER 19.80
DT 1.75kg	1. Lukas Weisshaidinger AUT 63.83
	2. Danijel Furtula MNE 63.54
	3. Benedikt Stienen GER 62.33
HT 6kg	1. Quentin Bigot FRA 78.45
	2. Sergiu Marghiev MDA 76.60
	3. Elias Håkansson SWE 74.99
JT	1. Zigismunds Sirmais LAT 81.53*
	2. Marcin Krukowski POL 79.19
	3. Pavel Myaleshko BLR 76.59
Dec Jnr	1. Kevin Mayer FRA 8124*
	2. Mathias Brugger GER 7853

European Under-20 Placing and Medal Table Leaders

Nat	G	S	B	Pts	Nat	G	S	B	Pts
GER	7	4	12	236.5	ROU	1	1	2	44
RUS	8	4	6	189	BEL	0	2	0	43
FRA	6	3	4	149	FIN	1	1	0	39
GBR	6	5	4	139	HUN	1	0	0	33
POL	1	5	2	80	LAT	1	1	1	31
ITA	1	2	3	72	CZE	0	0	0	24
TUR	1	3	0	56	BLR	0	1	1	23
UKR	1	1	2	56	SRB	2	0	0	22
ESP	2	0	2	55	SWE	1	0	2	21
NED	1	2	1	51	POR	0	0	0	21

27 nations won medals (14 gold). 34 nations scored points (athletes placing in top 8). Corrected for ties.

3. Johannes Hock GER 7806	2. Aurélie Chaboudez FRA 57.35
10000mW 1. Hagen Pohle GER 40:43.73	3. Maeva Contion FRA 58.03
2. Igor Lyashchenko UKR 41:10.43	**HJ** 1. Mariya Kuchina RUS 1.95*
3. Luís Alberto Amezcua ESP 41:34.13	2. Airine Palsyté LTU 1.91
4x100m 1. FRA (Michalet, Vicaut, John, Romain) 39.35	3. Nadja Kampschulte GER 1.88
2. GBR 39.48	**PV** 1. Angelica Bengtsson SWE 4.57*
3. POL 40.42	2. Lilli Schnitzerling GER 4.20
4x400m 1. ITA (Tricca, Danesini, Rontini, Lorenzi) 3:06.46	3. Natalya Demidenko RUS 4.20
2. RUS 3:07.47	**LJ** 1. Lena Malkus GER 6.40/0.7
3. GER 3:08.56	2. Alina Rotaru ROU 6.36/1.7

Women

100m (0.5)
1. Jodie Williams GBR 11.18*
2. Jamile Samuel NED 11.43
3. Tatjana Pinto GER 11.48

200m (-1.5)
1. Jodie Williams GBR 22.94
2. Jamile Samuel NED 23.31
3. Jennifer Galais FRA 23.55

400m
1. Bianca Razor ROU 51.96
2. Yuliya Yurenya BLR 53.03
3. Madiea Ghafoor NED 53.73

800m
1. Anastasiya Tkachuk UKR 2:02.73
2. Rowena Cole GBR 2:03.43
3. Ayvika Malanova RUS 2:03.59

1500m
1. Amela Terzic SRB 4:15.40
2. Ciara Mageean IRL 4:16.82
3. Ioana Doaga ROU 4:20.73

3000m
1. Amela Terzic SRB 9:17.61
2. Esma Aydemir TUR 9:19.61
3. Lisa Jäsert GER 9:30.23

5000m
1. Esma Aydemir TUR 16:12.16
2. Emelia Gorecka GBR 16:13.04
3. Annabel Gummow GBR 16:14.62

3000mSt
1. Gesa-Felicitas Krause GER 9:51.08
2. Gulshat Fazlitdinova RUS 9:56.98
3. Elena Panaet ROU 10:17.37

100mh (-1.0)
1. Nooralotta Neziri FIN 13.34
2. Isabelle Pedersen NOR 13.37
3. Yekaterina Bleskina RUS 13.47

400mh
1. Vera Rudakova RUS 57.24

3. Polina Yurchenko RUS 6.11/-0.1

TJ
1. Yana Borodina RUS 14.00/1.0
2. Kristina Mäkelä FIN 13.67/-0.8
3. Hanna Aleksandrova UKR 13.14/-0.7

SP
1. Lena Urbaniak GER 16.31
2. Anna Wloka POL 16.23
3. Anna Rüh GER 16.01

DT
1. Shanice Craft GER 58.65
2. Anna Rüh GER 58.10
3. Viktoriya Klochko UKR 54.03

HT
1. Barbara Spiler SLO 67.06
2. Kivilcim Kaya TUR 66.74
3. Alexia Sedykh FRA 65.02

JT
1. Liina Laasma EST 55.99
2. Lina Muze LAT 55.83
3. Laura Henkel GER 55.37

Hep
1. Dafne Schippers NED 6153
2. Sara Gambetta GER 6108
3. Laura Ikauniece LAT 6063

10000mW
1. Yelena Lashmanova RUS 42:59.48*
2. Svetlana Vasilyeva RUS 44:52.98
3. Anna Yermina RUS 46:49.00

4x100m
1. GER (Burghardt, Grompe, Pinto, Freese) 43.42*
2. ITA 44.52
3. GBR 45.00

4x400m
1. GBR (Kirk, James, Clifford, McAslan 52.42) 3:35.29
2. POL 3:35.35
3. GER 3:36.26

European Team Championships

Super League *at Stockholm, Sweden 18-19 June*
1. RUS 385, 2. GER 332.5, 3. UKR 292, 4. GBR 290, 5. FRA 285, 6. POL 265, 7. ESP 246, 8. ITA 238, 9. BLR 221, 10. CZE 218, 11. POR 177.5, 12. SWE 159.

100m (1.0)
1. Christophe Lemaitre FRA 9.95
2. Dwain Chambers GBR 10.07
3. Francis Obikwelu POR 10.22

200m
1. Christophe Lemaitre FRA 20.28/-2.8
2 (1B). Kamil Krynski POL 20.83/-1.8
3 (2B). Aleksandr Linnik BLR 20.90

400m
1. Maksim Dyldin RUS 45.82
2. Thomas Schneider GER 45.98
3. Marco Vistalli ITA 45.99

800m
1. Adam Kszczot POL 1:46.50

	2. Jeff Lastennet FRA 1:46.70
	3. Gareth Warburton GBR 1:46.95
1500m	1. Manuel Olmedo ESP 3:38.63
	2. Valentin Smirnov RUS 3:38.89
	3. James Shane GBR 3:39.21
3000m	1. Juan Carlos Higuero ESP 8:03.43
	2. Yegor Nikolayev RUS 8:03.80
	3. Rui Silva POR 8:03.88
5000m	1. Jesús España ESP 13:39.25
	2. Sergiy Lebid UKR 13:39.75
	3. Andrew Vernon GBR 13:40.15
3000mSt	1. Vincent Zouaoui-Dandrieux FRA 8:30.85
	2. Steffen Uliczka GER 8:31.01
	3. Ildar Minshin RUS 8:34.56
110mh	1. Andrew Turner GBR 13.42
(-2.4)	2. Garfield Darien FRA 13.64
	3 (1B). Jackson Quinónez ESP 13.71/-0.8
400mh	1. David Greene GBR 49.21
	2. Georg Fleischhauer GER 49.56
	3. Aleksandr Derevyagin RUS 49.70
HJ	1. Dmytro Demyanyuk UKR 2.35
	2. Aleksey Dmitrik RUS 2.31
	3= Jaroslav Bába CZE 2.28
	3= Raúl Spank GER 2.28
PV	1. Maksim Mazuryk UKR 5.72
(indoors	2. Maite Mohr GER 5.72
Sätra)	3. Aleksandr Gripich RUS 5.60
LJ	1. Aleksandr Menkov RUS 8.20/0.9
	2. Michel Tornéus SWE 8.19/1.4
	3. Chris Tomlinson GBR 8.12/1.8
TJ	1. Fabrizio Schembri ITA 16.95w/4.5
	2. Dmitriy Plotnitskiy BLR 16.81w/3.8
	3. Viktor Kuznyetsov UKR 16.79w/4.0
SP	1. David Storl GER 20.81
	2. Tomasz Majewski POL 20.51
	3. Andrey Mikhnevich BLR 20.40
DT	1. Robert Harting GER 65.63
	2. Frank Casañas ESP 62.43
	3. Piotr Malachowski POL 61.66
HT	1. Markus Esser GER 79.28
	2. Pawel Fajdek POL 76.98
	3. Oleksiy Sokyrskyy UKR 76.96
JT	1. Sergey Makarov RUS 81.20
	2. Gabriel Wallin SWE 80.88
	3. Petr Frydrych CZE 74.42
	drugs dq (1) Dmytro Kosynskyy UKR 81.29
4x100m	1. GBR (Malcolm, Pickering, Ellington, Aikines-Aryeetey) 38.60
	2. FRA (Tinmar, Lemaitre, Pessonneaux, Pognon) 38.71
	3. GER (Schaf, Broening, Unger, Menga) 38.92
4x400m	1. RUS (Dyldin, Buryak, Trenikhin, Alekseyev) 3:02.42
	2. FRA (Fillon, Venel, Hanne, Anne) 3:03.33
	3. GER (Gollnow, Plass, Jonas, Schneider) 3:04.10
Women	
100m	1 (1B). Véronique Mang FRA 11.23/-0.5
	2 (1A). Olesya Povh UKR 11.28/1.5
	3 (2A). Aleksandra Fedoriva RUS 11.34
200m	1. Mariya Ryemyen UKR 23.10/-2.2
	2. Yuliya Chermoshanskaya RUS 23.40
	3. (1B) Cathleen Tschirch GER 23.45/-2.1

400m	1. Antonina Yefremova UKR 51.02
	2. Denisa Rosolová CZE 51.37
	3. Shana Cox GBR 51.49
800m	1. Mariya Savinova RUS 1:58.75
	2. Jennifer Meadows GBR 1:59.47
	3. Liliya Lobanova UKR 2:00.18
1500m	1. Charlene Thomas GBR 4:06.85
	2. Yekaterina Martynova RUS 4:07.08
	3. Anna Mishchenko UKR 4:07.27
3000m	1. Olesya Syreva RUS 8:53.20
	2. Nataliya Tobias UKR 8:54.16
	3. Natalia Rodríguez ESP 8:55.09
5000m	1. Dolores Checa ESP 15:16.89
	2. Yelena Zadorozhnaya RUS 15:28.65
	3. Helen Clitheroe GBR 15:33.03
3000SC	1. Gulnara Galkina RUS 9:31.20
	2. Sara Moreira POR 9:35.11
	3. Jana Sussmann GER 9:43.28
100mh	1 (1B). Tatyana Dektyareva RUS 13.16/-1.0
	2 (1A). Alina Talay BLR 13.19/-0.2
	3 (2B). Marzia Caravelli ITA 13.21
400mh	1. Zuzana Hejnová CZE 53.87
	2. Natalya Antyukh RUS 54.52
	3. Perri Shakes-Drayton GBR 55.06
HJ	1. Emma Green Tregaro SWE 1.89
	2. Viktoriya Styopina UKR 1.89
	3. Ruth Beitia ESP 1.89
PV	1. Anna Rogowska POL 4.75
	2. Silke Spiegelburg GER 4.75
	3. Jirina Ptácniková CZE 4.60
LJ	1. Darya Klishina RUS 6.74/0.9
	2. Carolina Klüft SWE 6.73/0.7
	3. Éloyse Lesueur FRA 6.60w/2.2
TJ	1. Olga Saladuha UKR 14.85/1.8
	2. Simona La Mantia ITA 14.29/1.2
	3. Patricia Sarrapio ESP 14.10/1.7
SP	1. Nadina Kleinert GER 17.81
	2. Anna Avdeyeva RUS 17.33
	3. Chiara Rosa ITA 17.18
DT	1. Kateryna Karsak UKR 63.35
	2. Darya Pishchalnikova RUS 61.09
	3. Zaneta Glanc POL 59.29
HT	1. Betty Heidler GER 73.43
	2. Tatyana Lysenko RUS 71.44
	3. Katerina Safránková CZE 69.39
JT	1. Christina Obergföll GER 66.22
	2. Goldie Sayers GBR 64.46
	3. Barbora Spotáková CZE 64.40
4x100m	1. UKR (Povh, Pohrebnyak, Ryemyen, Stuy) 42.85
	2. RUS (Voronenkova, Fedoriva, Gushchina, Chermoshanskaya) 43.12
	3. GER (Kedzierski, Wagner, Tschirch, Günther) 43.37
4x400m	1. RUS (Vdovina, Zadorina, Firova, Litvinova) 3:27.17
	2. GBR (Massey, Sanders, McConnell, Shakes-Drayton) 3:27.21
	3. UKR (Karandyuk, Lohvynenko, Baraley, Yefremova) 3:28.13

First League *at Izmir, Turkey 18-19 June*
1. TUR 329, 2. GRE 307.5, 3. NOR 290, 4. ROU 282.5, 5. NED 278, 6. HUN 265, 7. SUI 251.5, 8. FIN 248, 9. BEL 245.5, 10. IRL 224.5, 11. SLO 200.5, 12. CRO 178.

Winners: **Men**: **100m/200m**: Jaysuma Saidy Ndure NOR 10.19/20.32, **400m**: Kevin Borlée BEL 45.61, **800m**: Tamás Kazi HUN 1:50.75, **1500m/3000m**: Kemal Koyuncu TUR 4:01.51/8:10.69, **5000m**: Mert Girmalegese TUR 14:00.97, **3000mSt**: Halil Akkas TUR 8:45.01, **110mh**: Gregory Sedoc NED 13.39, **400mh**: Periklís Iakovákis GRE 50.26, **HJ**: Dimítrios Hondrokoúkis GRE 2.32, **PV**: Konstadínos Filippídis GRE 5.40, **LJ**: Loúis Tsátoumas GRE 7.90, **TJ**: Marian Oprea ROU 16.83, **SP**: Lajos Kürthy HUN 19.02, **DT**: Róbert Fazekas HUN 62.31, **HT**: Krisztián Pars HUN 80.14, **JT**: Ari Mannio FIN 81.24, **4x100m**: SUI 39.20, **4x400m**: BEL 3:01.59; **Women**: **100m/200m**: Ezinne Okparaebo NOR 11.48/23.43, **400m**: Bianca Razor ROU 52.56, **800m**: Yeliz Kurt TUR 2:01.95, **1500m**: Ingvill Måkestad Bovim 4:25.92, **3000m**: Sultan Haydar TUR 9:11.60, **5000m**: Alemitu Bekele TUR 15:37.15, **3000mSt**: Binnaz Uslu TUR 9:40.29, **100mh**: Christina Vukicevic NOR 12.87, **400mh**: Élodie Ouédraogo BEL 55.74, **HJ**: Ana Simic CRO 1.92, **PV**: Nikolía Kiriakopoúlou GRE 4.30, **LJ**: Viorica Tigau ROU 6.50, **TJ**: Paraskeví Papahrístou GRE 14.09, **SP**: Melissa Boekelman NED 17.62, **DT**: Nicoleta Grasu ROU 60.85, **HT**: Bianca Perie ROU 70.37, **JT**: Martina Ratej SLO 61.53, **4x100m**: NED 43.90, **4x400m**: TUR 3:29.40.

Second League *at Novi Sad, Serbia 18-19 June*

1. EST 218, 2. BUL 215.5, 3. SRB 188.5, 4. LTU 185, 5. DEN 177.5, 6. AUT 172, 7. LAT 147, 8. SVK 134.5.
Winners: **100m**: Rytis Sakalauskas LTU 10.34, **200m**: Marek Niit EST 20.75, **400m**: Krasimir Braikov BUL 46.36, **800m**: Andreas Vojta AUT 1:50.29, **1500m**: Goran Nava SRB 3:44.49, **3000m**: Tiidrek Nurme EST 8:22.81, **5000m**: Jakob Hannibal DEN 14:25.94, **3000mSt**: Kaur Kivistik 8:56.84, **110mh**: Villam Papso SVK 14.16, **400mh**: Emir Bekric SRB 50.35, **HJ**: Viktor Ninov BUL 2.28, **PV**: Mareks Arents LAT 5.30, **LJ**: Povilas Mykolaitis LTU 8.03, **TJ**: Anders Møller DEN 16.15, **SP**: Maris Urtans LAT 20.31, **DT**: Märt Israel EST 62.91, **HT**: Libor Charfreitag SVK 77.69, **JT**: Risto Mätas EST 79.55, **4x100m**: DEN 39.71, **4x400m**: EST 3:08.16; **Women**: **100m/200m**: Ivet Lalova BUL 11.20/23.71, **400m/400mh**: Vania Stambolova BUL 50.98/53.70, **800m**: Lucia Klocová SVK 2:02.24, **1500m**: Marina Muncan 4:19.28, **3000m**: Jennifer Wenth AUT 9:31.57, **5000m**: Ana Subotic SRB 16:32.671, **3000mSt**: Jekaterina Patjuk EST 10:04.15, **100mh**: Sonata Tamosaityte LTU 13.17, **HJ**: Venelena Veneva-Mateeva BUL 1.91, **PV**: Caroline Bonde Holm DEN 4.20; **LJ**: Ivana Spanovic SRB 6.58, **TJ**: Dana Veldáková SVK 13.89, **SP**: Austra Skujyte LTU 16.39, **DT**: Dragana Tomasevic SRB 60.57, **HT**: Martina Hrasnová SVK 68.09, **JT**: Madara Palameika LAT 63.46, **4x100m/4x400m**: BUL 44.59/3:37.10.

Third League *at Reykjavik, Iceland 18-19 June*
1. ISR 490, 2. CYP 469, 3. MDA 440, 4. ISL 411, 5. BIH 390, 6. AZE 377, 7. ARM 341, 8. LUX 335, 9. MLT 270, 10. MNE 266, 11. MAC 233, 12. Small States 178, 13. AND 174, 14. GEO 144, 15. ALB 93.

European Cup Combined Events

Super League *At Torun, Estonia 2-3 July*
Men: 1. RUS 23,305, 2. EST 23,095, 3. BLR 22,956,

4. FRA 22,935, 5. POL 22,159, 6. CZE 22,113, 7. UKR 21,773, 8. FIN 21,690. **Ind Dec**: 1. Andres Raja EST 8114, 2. Vasiliy Kharlamov RUS 7935, 3. Gaël Quérin FRA 7799, 4. Aleksandr Tabala RUS 7773, 5. Sami Itani FIN 7710.
Women: 1. RUS 17,816, 2. UKR 17,600, 3. FRA 16,992, 4. NED 16,884, 5. EST 16,162, 6. GBR 16,095, 7. CZE 15,612, 8. GRE 15,508. **Ind Hep**: 1. Anna Bogdanova RUS 6225, 2. Lyudmyla Yosypenko UKR 5984, 3. Remona Fransen NED 5965, 4. Aleksandra Butvina RUS 5948, 5. Alina Fyodorova UKR 5881.

First League *At Bressanone, Italy 2-3 July*
Men: 1. GBR 22,989, 2. BEL 22,468, 3. ITA 21,838, 4. SUI 21,434, 5. SWE 21,152, 6. GRE 21,139, 7. NED 20,703, 8. ESP 20,625. **Ind**: 1. Simon Walter SUI 7973, 2. Daniel Awde GBR 7889, 3. Ashley Bryant GBR 7747.
Women: 1. POL 17,309, 2. ITA 17,050, 3. HUN 17,030, 4. BLR 16,853, 5. FIN 16,541, 6. SUI 16,123, 7. SWE 15,602. **Ind**: 1. Karolina Tyminska POL 6297, 2. Györgyi Farkas HUN 6068, 3. Yana Maksimova BLR 5998.

Second League. *At Ribeira Brava, Portugal 2-3 July*
Men: 1. HUN 20,922, 2. LAT 19,917, 3. ROU 18,724, 4. TUR 16,557. **Ind**: Edgar Erins LAT 7513; **Women**: 1. ESP 16,421, 2. ROU 16,078, 3. LTU 15,062, 4. TUR 12,218. **Ind**: Austra Skujyte LTU 6338.

European Winter Throwing Cup

At Sofia, Bulgaria 19-20 March
Men: 1. RUS 4353, 2. UKR 4343, 3. ITA 4069, 4. ESP 3995, 5. ROU 3944, 6. BUL 3610. **SP**: 1. Hamza Alic BIH 20.21, 2. Marco Fortes POR 20.18, 3. Soslan Tsirikhov RUS 19.45; **DT**: 1. Ercüment Olgundeniz TUR 63.31, 2. Erik Cadée NED 62.15, 3. Sergiu Ursu ROU 62.00; **HT**: 1. Krisztián Pars HUN 79.84, 2. Yuriy Shayunov BLR 77.41, 3. Oleksiy Sokryskyy UKR 76.84; **JT**: 1. Zigismunds Sirmais 84.47, 2. Oleksandr Pyatnytsya UKR 81.96, 3. Valeriy Iordan RUS 79.49; **U23**: 1. UKR 4201, 2. RUS 4028, 3. FIN 3881; **JT**: Fatih Avan TUR 80.19. **Women**: 1. GER 4142, 2. RUS 4079, 3. FRA 4029, 4. UKR 4027, 5. ITA 3902, 6. BLR 3861, 7. POR 3747, 8. ROU 3693; **SP**: 1. Yelena Kopets BLR 17.71, 2. Jessica Cérival FRA 17.52, 3. Chiara Cérival FRA 17.52; **DT**: 1. Olesya Korotkova RUS 60.20, 2. Nicoleta Grasu ROU 59.44, 3. Vera Ganeyeva RUS 57.45; **HT**: 1. Tatyana Lysenko RUS 73.70, 2. Betty Heidler GER 72.71, 3. Zalina Marghieva MDA 71.96; **JT**: 1. Hanna Hatsko UKR 58.35, 2. Esther Eisenlauer GER 56.99, 3. Ásdís Hjálmsdóttir ISL 56.44; **U23**: 1. HUN 3838, 2. UKR 3763, 3. RUS 3735; **SP**: 1. Anita Martón HUN 17.92, 2. Yevgenitya Kolodko RUS 17.85; **JT**: 1. Vira Rebryk UKR 57.95, 2. Liina Laasma EST 57.04.

European Cup of Race Walking

At Olhão, Portugal 21 May
Men 20km: 1. Stanislav Yemelyanov RUS 1:23:27, 2. Matej Tóth SVK 1:23:53, 3. Jakub Jelonek POL 1:23:59, 4. Benjamin Sánchez ESP 1:24:12, 5. Giorgio Rubino ITA 1:24:14, 6. Vladimir Kanaykin RUS 1:24:20, 7. Miguel Ángel López ESP 1:24:37, 8. Andrey Krivov

RUS 1:25:14, 9. Antonin Boyez FRA 1:25:21, 10. Robert Heffernan IRL 1:25:34; 36 of 50 finished. Team: 1. RUS 15, 2. ESP 30, 3. ITA 31, 4. FRA 41. 5. POL 43, 6. IRL 72, 7. UKR 75.

Men 50km: 1. Denis Nizhegorodov RUS 3:45:58, 2. Igor Yerokhin RUS 3:49:05, 3. Marco De Luca ITA 3:50:13, 4. Christopher Linke GER 3:52:56, 5. Artur Brzozowski POL 3:53:51, 6. Jean-Jacques Nkouloukidi ITA 3:54:19, 7. Rafal Augustyn POL 3;54:38, 8. Michal Stasiewicz POL 4:02:51, 9. Oleksiy Kazanin UKR 4:03:19, 10. Lorenzo Dessi ITA 4:04:00. 19 of 48 finished. Team: 1. RUS 15, 2. ITA 19, 3. POL 20, 4. ESP 42, 5, UKR 51.

U20 Men 10km: 1. Igor Lyashchenko UKR 41:26, 2. Hagen Pohle GER 41:36, 3. Dementiy Chepareva RUS 41:58; 35 of 36 finished. Team: 1. UKR 5, 2. RUS 8, 3. GER 12, 4. ESP 13, 5, ITA 22, 6, FRA 24; 12 teams scored.

Women 20 km: 1. Vera Sokolova RUS 1:30:02, 2. Anisya Kiryapkina RUS 1:30:41, 3. Elisa Rigaudo ITA 1:30:55, 4. María Vasco ESP 1:31:41, 5. Olga Yakovenko UKR 1:32:08, 6. Melanie Seeger GER 1:32:14, 7. Nadiya Borovska UKR 1:32:30, 8. María José Poves ESP 1:32:36, 9. Susana Feitor POR 1:32:43, 10. Julia Takács ESP 1:33:09; 46 of 55 finished. Team: 1. RUS 14, 2. ESP 22, 3. UKR 32, 4. POR 37, 5. ITA 50, 6. CZE 86. 7. POL 88, 8. HUN 122.

U20 Women 10km: 1. Yelena Lashmanova RUS 43:10, 2. Svetlana Vasileva RUS 44:02, 3. Kate Veale IRL 46:32; 28 of 29 finished. Team: 1. RUS 3, 2. ITA 9, 3. CZE 19, 4, TUR 20, 5. IRL 23, 6. ESP 30; 9 teams scored.

European Cup 10,000m

At Oslo, Norway 4 June

Men: 1. Youssef El Kalai POR 28:20.03. 2. José Manuel Martínez ESP 28:24.16, 3. André Pöllmacher GER 28:39.57; Team: 1. ESP 1:26:04.89, 2. FRA 1:27:51.97, 3. POR 1:28:16.51. **Women**: 1. Sara Moreira POR 31:39.11. 2. Christelle Daunay FRA 31:44.84, 3. Sabrina Mockenhaupt GER 31:57.23; Team: 1. ITA 1:37:50.55, 2. POR 1:39:17.61. 3. BLR 1:39:53.55.

Pan-American Games

At Guadalajara, Mexico 23-30 October

100m	1. Lerone Clarke JAM 10.01	
(0.2)	2. Kim Collins SKN 10.04	
	3. Emmanuel Callender TRI 10.16	
200m	1. Roberto Skyers CUB 20.37	
(-1.0)	2. Lanceford Spence JAM 20.38	
	3. Bruno de Barros BRA 20.45	
400m	1. Nery Brenes CRC 44.65	
	2. Luguelin Santos DOM 44.71	
	3. Ramon Miller BAH 45.01	
800m	1. Andy González CUB 1:45.58	
	2. Kléberson Davide BRA 1:45.75	
	3. Raidel Acea CUB 1:46.23	
1500m	1. Leandro Oliveira BRA 3:53.44	
	2. Bayron Piedra ECU 3:53.45	
	3. Eduard Villanueva VEN 3:54.06	
5000m	1. Juan Luis Barrios MEX 14:13.77	
	2. Bayron Piedra ECU 14:15.74	
	3. Joilson da Silva BRA 14:16.11	
10,000m	1. Marílson dos Santos BRA 29:00.64	
	2. Juan Carlos Romero MEX 29:41.00	
	3. Giovani dos Santos BRA 29:51.71	
Mar	1. Solonei Silva BRA 2:16:37	
	2. Diego Colorado COL 2:17:13	
	3. Juan Carlos Cardona COL 2:18:20	
3000SC	1. José Gregorio Peña VEN 8:48.19	
	2. Hudson de Souza BRA 8:48.75	
	3. José Antonio Sánchez CUB 8:49.75	
110mh	1. Dayron Robles CUB 13.10*	
(1.6)	2. Paulo Villar COL 13.27	
	3. Orlando Ortega CUB 13.30	
400mh	1. Omar Cisneros CUB 47.99*	
	2. Isa Phillips JAM 48.82	
	3. Félix Sánchez DOM 48.85	
HJ	1. Donald Thomas BAH 2.32	
	2. Diego Ferrín ECU 2.30	
	3. Víctor Moya CUB 2.26	
PV	1. Lázaro Borges CUB 5.80*	
	2. Jeremy Scott USA 5.60	
	3. Giovanni Lanaro MEX 5.50	
LJ	1. Daniel Pineda CHI 7.97/-1.0	
	2. David Registe USA 7.89/0.2	
	3. Jeremy Hicks USA 7.83/0.3	
	drugs dq (1) Victor Castillo VEN 8.05/-0.8	
TJ	1. Alexis Capello CUB 17.21/-1.3	
	2. Yoandris Betanzos CUB 16.54/0.4	
	3. Jefferson Sabino BRA 16.51/1.6	
SP	1. Dylan Armstrong CAN 21.30*	
	2. Carlos Véliz CUB 20.76	
	3. Germán Lauro ARG 20.41	
DT	1. Jorge Fernández CUB 65.58	
	2. Jarred Rome USA 61.71	
	3. Ronald Julião BRA 61.70	
HT	1. Kibwe Johnson USA 79.63*	
	2. Mike Mai USA 72.71	
	3. Noleisis Bicet CUB 72.57	
JT	1. Guillermo Martínez CUB 87.20*	
	2. Cyrus Hostetler USA 82.24	
	3. Braian Toledo ARG 79.53	
Dec	1. Leonel Suárez CUB 8373*	
	2. Maurice Smith JAM 8214	
	3. Yordani García CUB 8074	
4x100m	1. BRA (Feitosa, Viana, André, de Barros) 38.18*	
	2. SKN (Rogers, Adams, Delaney, Lawrence) 38.81	
	3. USA (C Newman, Dodson, R Williams, Edwards) 39.17	
4x400m	1. CUB (Ruíz, Acea, Cisneros, Collazo) 2:59.43	
	2. DOM (Cuesta, Peguero, Tapia, L Santos) 3:00.44	
	3. VEN (A Ramírez, Aguilar, Acevedo, Longart) 3:00.82	
20kmW	1. Erick Barrondo GUA 1:21:51	
	2. James Rendón COL 1:22:46	
	3. Luis Fernando López COL 1:22:51	
50kW	1. Horacio Nava MEX 3:48:58	
	2. José Leyver MEX 3:49:16	
	3. Jaime Quiyuch GUA 3:50:33	
Women		
100m	1. Rosángela Santos BRA 11.22	
(-0.2)	2. Barbara Pierre USA 11.25	
	3. Shakera Reece BAR 11.26	
200m	1. Ana Cláudia da Silva BRA 22.76	
(0.5)	2. Simone Facey JAM 22.86	

	3.	Mariely Sánchez DOM 23.02
400m	1.	Yenifer Padilla COL 51.53
	2.	Daysiurami Bonne CUB 51.69
	3.	Geisa Coutinho BRA 51.87
800m	1.	Adriana Muñoz CUB 2:04.08
	2.	Gabriela Medina MEX 2:04.41
	3.	Rosibel García COL 2:04.45
1500m	1.	Adriana Muñoz CUB 4:26.09
	2.	Rosibel García COL 4:26.78
	3.	Malindi Elmore CAN 4:27.57
5000m	1.	Marisol Romero MEX 16:24.08
	2.	Cruz da Silva BRA 16:29.75
	3.	Inés Melchior PER 16:41.50
10,000m	1.	Marisol Romero MEX 34:07.24
	2.	Cruz da Silva BRA 34:22.44
	3.	Yolanda Caballero COL 34:39.14
Mar	1.	Adriana da Silva BRA 2:36:37*
	2.	Madaí Pérez MEX 2:38:03
	3.	Gladys Tejeda PER 2:42:09.
3000SC	1.	Sara Hall USA 10:03.16
	2.	Ángela Figueroa COL 10:10.14
	3.	Sabine Heitling BRA 10:10.98
100mh	1.	Yvette Lewis USA 12.82
(-0.1)	2.	Angela Whyte CAN 13.09
	3.	Lina Florez COL 13.09
400mh	1.	Princesa Oliveros COL 56.26
	2.	Lucy Jaramillo ECU 56.95
	3.	Yolanda Osana DOM 57.08
HJ	1.	Lesyanís Mayor CUB 1.89
	2.	Marielys Rojas VEN 1.89
	3.	Romary Rifka MEX 1.89
PV	1.	Yarisley Silva CUB 4.75*
	2.	Fabiana Murer BRA 4.70
	3.	Becky Holliday USA 4.30
LJ	1.	Maurren Maggi BRA 6.94/1.1
	2.	Shemeka Marshall USA 6.73w/2.2
	3.	Caterine Ibargüen COL 6.63/1.6
TJ	1.	Caterine Ibargüen COL 14.92*/0.1
	2.	Yargeris Savigne CUB 14.36/-0.5
	3.	Mabel Gay CUB 14.28/0.4
SP	1.	Misleydis González CUB 18.57
	2.	Cleopatra Borel-Brown TRI 18.46
	3.	Michelle Carter USA 18.09
DT	1.	Yarelys Barrios CUB 66.40*
	2.	Aretha Thurmond USA 59.53
	3.	Denia Caballero CUB 58.63
HT	1.	Yipsi Moreno CUB 75.62*
	2.	Sultana Frizell CAN 70.11
	3.	Amber Campbell USA 69.93
JT	1.	Alice DeShasier USA 58.01
	2.	Yainelis Ribeaux CUB 56.21
	3.	Yanet Cruz CUB 56.19
Hep	1.	Lucimara da Silva BRA 6133
	2.	Yasmiany Pedroso CUB 5710
	3.	Francia Manzanillo DOM 5644
4x100m	1.	BRA (A da Silva, Gomes, Krasucki, R Santos) 42.85
	2.	USA (K Wilson, Pierre, Lewis, Riggien) 43.10
	3.	COL (Florez, Padilla, Hinestroza, González) 43.44
4x400m	1.	CUB (Martínez, Peña, Clement, Bonne) 3:28.09
	2.	BRA (Sousa, Coutinho, B de Oliveira, J de Lima) 3:29.59
	3.	COL (Oliveros, González, Aguilar, Padilla) 3:29.94
20kW	1.	Jamy Franco GUA 1:32:38*
	2.	Mirna Ortiz GUA 1:33:37
	3.	Ingrid Hernández COL 1:34:06

Medal table leaders: CUB 18G-6S-9B, BRA 10-6-7, USA 4-9-4, MEX 4-4-2, COL 3-5-9, GUA 2-1-2, JAM 1-4-0, CAN 1-2-1, VEN 1-1-2, BAH 1-0-1, CRC & CHI 1-0-0, ECU 0-4-0, DOM 0-2-4. In all 20 nations won medals (11 gold).

South American Championships

At Buenos Aires, Argentina 2-6 June

Men

100m	1.	Nilson André BRA 10.35
(0.0)	2.	Kael Becerra CHI 10.41
	3.	Sandro Viana BRA 10.44
200m	1.	Daniel Grueso COL 20.90
(1.7)	2.	Mariano Jiménez ARG 21.06
	3.	Christián Reyes CHI 21.09
400m	1.	Kléberson Davide BRA 46.74
	2.	Geiner Mosquera COL 47.19
	3.	Luis Ambrósio BRA 47.57
800m	1.	Rafith Rodríguez COL 1:51.38
	2.	Kléberson Davide BRA 1:52.41
	3.	Juan Sabastián Vega ARG 1:52.43
1500m	1.	Leandro de Oliveira BRA 3:45.55
	2.	Hudson de Souza BRA 3:46.35
	3.	Federico Bruno ARG 3:47.81
5000m	1.	Javier Carriqueo ARG 13:58.27
	2.	Víctor Aravena CHI 13:59.81
	3.	Javier Guarín COL 14:00.64
10,000m	1.	Giovanni dos Santos BRA 28:41.02
	2.	Damião de Souza BRA 28:53.94
	3.	Jhon Tello COL 28:56.46
3000mSt	1.	Hudson de Souza BRA 8:36.53
	2.	Marvin Blanco VEN 8:37.02
	3.	Mariano Mastromarino ARG 8:38.91
110mh	1.	Matheus Inocêncio BRA 13.70
(0.3)	2.	Jorge McFarlane PER 13.77
	3.	Paulo César Villar COL 13.85
400mh	1.	Andrés Silva URU 49.94
	2.	Mahau Suguimati BRA 51.11
	3.	Victor Solarte VEN 51.13
HJ	1.	Diego Ferrín ECU 2.23
	2.	Guilherme Cobbo BRA 2.20
	3.	Carlos Layoy ARG 2.20
PV	1.	Fábio Gomes da Silva BRA 5.35
	2.	Germán Chiaraviglio ARG 5.30
	3.	Rubén Benítez ARG 4.90
LJ	1.	Jorge McFarlane PER 7.95/1.2
	2.	Rafael Mello BRA 7.85/1.5
	3.	Daniel Pineda CHI 7.82/1.0
TJ	1.	Maximiliano Díaz ARG 16.51/1.2
	2.	Jonathan Silva BRA 16.45/1.0
	3.	Jefferson Sabino BRA 16.45/0.7
SP	1.	Germán Lauro ARG 19.61
	2.	Edder Moreno COL 18.93
	3.	Maximiliano Alonso CHI 17.95
DT	1.	Ronald Julião BRA 62.72
	2.	Germán Lauro ARG 59.98
	3.	Jesús Parejo VEN 57.42
HT	1.	Juan Ignacio Cerra ARG 72.12

2. Wágner Domingos BRA 70.65
3. Allan Wolski BRA 66.85
JT 1. Arley Ibargüen COL 73.61
2. Dayron Márquez COL 73.15
3. Víctor Fatecha PAR 72.51
Dec 1. Luiz Alberto de Araújo BRA 7944*
2. Román Gastaldi ARG 7545
3. Georni Jaramillo VEN 7051
4x100m 1. BRA (de Moraes Jr, Viana, André, Feitosa) 39.87
2. COL 39.88
3. CHI 40.38
4x400m 1. BRA (Ambrósio, Davide, Cardoso, Estefani) 3:08.95
2. COL 3:09.67
3. ARG 3:13.30
20000mW 1. Andrés Chocho ECU 1:20:23.8*
2. Gustavo Restrepo COL 1:20:36.6
3. Yerko Araya CHI 1:20:47.2

Women
100m 1. Ana Cláudia Silva BRA 11.46
(0.1) 2. Yomara Hinestroza COL 11.63
3. Rosemar Neto BRA 11.80
200m 1. Ana Cláudia Silva BRA 23.18
(0.4) 2. Norma González COL 23.22
3. Jailma de Lima BRA 23.54
400m 1. Norma González COL 52.14
2. Yenifer Padilla COL 52.55
3. Geisa Coutinho BRA 52.84
800m 1. Rosibel García COL 2:04.76
2. Andrea Ferris PAN 2:05.13
3. Muriel Coneo COL 2:05.25
1500m 1. Rosibel García COL 4:22.18
2. Tatiele de Carvalho BRA 4:22.94
3. Sandra Amarillo ARG 4:23.94
5000m 1. Fabiana da Silva BRA 15:39.67*
2. Rosa Godoy ARG 15:43.36
3. Cruz da Silva BRA 15:43.91
10,000m 1. Simone da Silva BRA 31:59.11*
2. Rosa Godoy ARG 32:51.10
3. Cruz da Silva BRA 32:53.72
3000mSt 1. Ángela Figueroa COL 9:58.00
2. Eliane Pereira BRA 10:22.96
3. Jovana de la Cruz PER 10:24.67
100mh 1. Briggite Merlano COL 13.07
(0.3) 2. Maíla Machado BRA 13.22
3. Lina Florez COL 13.23
400mh 1. Jaílma de Lima BRA 57.13
2. Princesa Oliveros COL 58.07
3. Déborah Rodríguez URU 58.63
HJ 1. Marielys Rojas VEN 1.80
2. Betsabé Páez ARG 1.77
3. Aline Santos BRA 1.77
PV 1. Fabiana Murer BRA 4.70*
2. Karla da Silva BRA 4.00
3. Milena Agudelo COL 3.90
LJ 1. Maurren Maggi BRA 6.52/0.0
2. Keila Costa BRA 6.45/0.0
3. Caterine Ibargüen COL 6.45/-0.5
TJ 1. Caterine Ibargüen COL 14.59w/2.2
2. Keila Costa BRA 13.96/0.0
3. Gisele de Oliveira BRA 13.43/0.9
SP 1. Natalia Ducó CHI 17.15
2. Elisângela Adriano BRA 16.55
3. Anyela Rivas COL 16.15

DT 1. Andressa de Morais BRA 57.54
2. Karen Gallardo CHI 54.91
3. Fernanda Borges BRA 54.18
HT 1. Jennifer Dahlgren ARG 72.70*
2. Eli Johana Moreno COL 68.53
3. Rosa Rodríguez VEN 67.28
JT 1. María Lucelly Murillo COL 55.85
2. Leryn Franco PAR 55.66
3. Alessandra Resende BRA 54.61
Hep 1. Vanesa Spínola BRA 5428
2. Agustina Zerboni ARG 5226
3. Melry Caldeira BRA 5208
4x100m 1. COL (Palacios, Idrobo, Hinestroza, González) 44.11
2. BRA 44.56
3. CHI 46.42
4x400m 1. BRA (Coutinho, A dos Santos, J Souza, J de Lima) 3:31.66
2. COL 3:37.66
3. CHI 3:49.51
20000mW 1. Ingrid Johana Hernández COL 1:32:09.4*
2. Milánggela Rosales VEN 1:32:17.6
3. Arabelly Orjuela COL 1:32:48.7

Medal table

	G	S	B	Total
BRA	21	16	14	51
COL	12	12	9	33
ARG	5	8	7	20
ECU	2	-	-	2
CHI	1	3	7	11
VEN	1	2	4	7
PER	1	1	1	3
URU	1	-	1	2
PAR	-	1	1	2
PAN	-	1	-	1

10th African Junior Championships

At Gaborone, Botswana 12-15 May

Men: 100m: Gideon Trotter RSA 10.49, **200m:** Siphelo Ngquboza RAA 20.94, **400m:** Sadam Koumi SUD 46.37, **800m:** Geleto Aman ETH 1:46.62, **1500m:** Hillary Maiyo KEN 3:35.43*, **5000m:** Atnafu Zerihun ETH 13:38.52*, **10,000m:** Geoffrey Kirui KEN 27:55.74*, **3000mSt:** Gilbert Kirui KEN 8:25.03, **110mh**-J: Amadou Ndiaye SEN 14.33, **400mh:** Abdelmalik Lahoulou ALG 51.69, **HJ:** Krim Hichem ALG 2.06, **PV:** Michael Cilliers RSA 4.90, **LJ/TJ:** El Mehdi Kabbachi MAR 7.69/15.84, 6k **SP:** Hisham Abdelhamid Abdelaziz 18.11, 1.75k **DT:** Atik Amine MAR 56.08, 6k **HT:** Taha Isalm Ahmad EGY 68.03, **JT:** Rocco van Rooyen RSA 75.72, **Dec:** Ahmed Saber Ahmad EGY 6776, **4x100m:** NGR 40.98, **4x400m:** SUD 3:09.87, **10000mW:** Yesref Tewfik ALG 46:04.04. **Women: 100m:** Josephine Omaka NGR 11.97, **200m:** Sonya van der Merwe RSA 23.78, **400m:** Magiso Manedo ETH 52.09, **800m/1500m:** Anette Negesa UGA 2:04.94/4:09.17, **3000m:** Azemra Gebru ETH 9:11.84, **5000m:** Caroline Kipkoech KEN 15:24.66, **3000mSt:** Birtukan Admasu 9:53.80, **100mh:** Kyla Gilbert RSA 14.25, **400mh:** Jean-Marie Senekal RSA 59.21, **HJ:** Besnet Mossad EGY 1.81, **PV:** Dorra Mahfoudhi TUN 3.40*, **LJ:** Samantha Pretorius RSA 5.90, **TJ:** Valentina da Roche RSA 12.46, **SP**: Nkechi Chime NGR 13.89, **DT**: Ischke Senekal RSA 49.90, **HT**: Rana Taha Ibrahim EGY 59.94*, **JT**: Liezl de Swaardt RSA 48.28, **Hep**: Haris Radwa Faty EGY 4839, **4x100m/4x400m**: RSA 46.11/3:38.16, **5000mW**: Eshetu Shefrawe ETH 22:59.19. **Leading Medal table**: RSA 13G-13S-8B, ETH 6-4-7, EGY 6-2-3, KEN 4-11-3, NGR 3-4-4, MAR 3-1-1, ALG 3-1-0, SUD 2-1-0, UGA 2-0-3, TUN 1-0-4; BOT 0-1-7; 17 nations won medals.

12th Arab Games 2011

At Doha, Qatar 15-20 December
Men: **100m**: Femi Ogunode QAT 10.37, **200m**: Aziz Ouhadi MAR 20.69, **400m**: Youssef Al-Masrahi KSA 45.44, **800m**: Abdulrahman Musaab Balla QAT 1:45.92, **1500m**: Ayanleh Souleiman DJI 3:34.32, **5000m**: Ali Abubaker Kamal QAT 13:45.60, **10,000m**: Hassan Mahbood Ali 28:39.88*, **3000mSt**: Ali Abubaker Kamal QAT 8:36.82, **HMar**: Rachid Kisri MAR 64:03, **110mh**: Ahmad Al-Moualed KSA 13.60, **400mh**: Bandar Yahya Sharahili KSA 50.63, **HJ**: Mutaz Esha Barshim QAT 2.30*, **PV**: Mohcine Cheaouri MAR 5.10, **LJ**: Saleh Al-Haddad KUW 7.83, **TJ**: Issam Nima ALG 16.59, **SP**: Yasser Ibrahim EGY 19.44, **DT**: Rashid Al-Dosari QAT 62.29* **HT**: Ali Mohamed Al-Zankawi KUW 73.29, **JT**: Ihab Abdelrahman Sayed EGY 78.66*, **Dec**: Mohammed Al-Qaree KSA 7677, **4x100m/4x400m**: Saudi Arabia 39.67/3:07.22, **20kW**: Hassanine Sbaï TUN 1:28:20*. **Women – 100m**: Dana Abdulrazzak IRQ 11.88. **200m**: Gretta Taslakian LIB 24.10, **400m/800m**: Malika Akkaoui MAR 53.94/2:02.42*; **1500m**: Genzabe Shumi BRN 4:20.07, **5000m**: Alia Saeed UAE 16:11.54, **10,000m**: Tejitu Daba BRN 33:09.18, **HMar**: Lishan Dula BRN 74:18*, **100mh**: Lamia Lhabz MAR 13.88, **400mh**: Hayat Lambarki MAR 56.72, **HJ**: Rhizlane Siba MAR 1.76, **PV**: Nisrine Dinar NAR 3.91*, **LJ**: Romaïssa Belablod ALG 6.07, **TJ**: Baya Rahouli ALG 14.01, **SP**: Waia Mohamed Attia EGY 14.92; **DT**: Ilham Wahba EGY 46.88, **HT**: Sarah Bensaad TUN 60.49, **JT**: Rada Ahmed Toufik EGY 45.93, **Hep**: Nadia Chéroudi TUN 4990, **4x100m/4x400m**: Morocco 46.16*/3:38.64, **10000mW**: Chaïma Trabelsi TUN 48:17.91. Medal table leaders: MAR 11G-4S-9B, QAT 6-3-4, KSA 6-0-1, EGY 5-12-5, TUN 4-5-3, BRN 4-4-6, ALG 3-3-3, KUW 2-1-2; 15 nations won medals (9 gold).

64th Balkan Championships

At Sliven, Bulgaria 2-3 July
Men: 1. GRE 159, 2. BUL 157, 3. ROU 154, 4. TUR 129, 5. MDA 119, 6. SRB 111, 7. BIH 87, 8. MKD 52, 9. MNE 30, 10. ALB 30. **100m**: Catalin Câmpeanu ROU 10.43, **200m**: Petar Kremenski 20.79, **400m**: Krasimir Braikov BUL 46.09, **800m**: Predrag Randjelovic 1:49.15, **1500m**: Andréas Dimitrákis GRE 3:54.33, **3000m/5000m**: Fatih Bilgic TUR 8:22.36/14:11.45, **3000mSt**: Hakan Duvar TUR 8:37.21, **110mh**: Konstadínos Douvalídis GRE 13.64w, **400mh**: Emir Bekric SRB 50.08, **HJ**: Viktor Ninov BUL 2.25, **PV**: Spas Buhalov BUL 5.20, **LJ**: Yeóryios Tsákonas GRE 7.86, **TJ**: Momchil Karailiev BUL 16.93w, **SP**: Asmir Kolasinac SRB 19.93, **DT**: Ercüment Olgundeniz TUR 63.05, **HT**: Stamátios Papadoníou GRE 68.67, **JT**: Yervásios Fillipídis GRE 72.72, **4x100m**: TUR 39.81, **4x400m**: GRE 3:10.07; **Women**: 1. ROU 170, 2. GRE 160.5, 3. BUL 150, 4. SRB 122, 5. MDA 86.5, 6. TUR 83.5, 7. MKD 75.5, 8. BIH 67, 9. ALB 36, 10. MNE 29. **100m**: Ivet Lalova BUL 10.96, **200m**: Grigoría-Emmanouéla Keramidá GRE 24.53, **400m/400mh**: Vania Stambolova BUL 53.34/54.23, **800m**: Eléni Filándra GRE 2:03.31, **1500m**: Luiza Gega ALB 4:14.22, **3000m**: Cristina Vasiloiu ROU 9:27.67, **5000m**: Cristina Frumuz ROU 17:18.04, **3000mSt**: María Pardaloú GRE 10:00.32, **100mh**: Kristina Damianova BUL 13.78, **HJ**: Burcu Ayhan TUR 1.86, **PV**: Anna Ivanova BUL 4.10, **LJ**: Ivana Spanovic SRB 6.56w, **TJ**: Andriana Banova BUL 14.34, **SP**: Radoslava Mavrodieva BUL 16.57, **DT**: Dragana Tomasevic SRB 61.95, **HT**: Bianca Perie ROU 66.69, **JT**: Sávva Líka GRE 57.63, **4x100m**: BUL 44.49, **4x400m**: ROU 3:42.27.
Walks: At *Bucuresti, Romania 9 April*. **Men 20km**: Recep Celik TUR 1:22:31. **Women 20km**: Claudia Stef ROU 1:33:38.

23rd Central American and Caribbean Championships

At Mayagüez, Puerto Rico 15-17 July
Men: **100m**: Keston Bledman TRI 10.05, **200m**: Michael Mathieu BAH 20.60, **400m**: Rennie Quow TRI 45.44, **800m**: Andy González CUB 1:48.15, **1500m**: Nico Herrera VEN 3:44.92, **5000m**: José Antonio Uribe MEX 14:08.10, **10,000m**: Juan Carlos Romero MEX 28:54.06*, **HMar**: Luis Collazo PUR 67:08, **3000mSt**: Luis Ibarra MEX 8:55.86, **110mh**: Eric Keddo JAM 13.49, **400mh**: Leford Green JAM 49.03, **HJ**: Trevor Barry BAH 2.28, **PV**: Cristian Sánchez MEX 5.00, **LJ**: Tyrone Smith BER 8.06, **TJ**: Samyr Laine HAI 17.09, **SP**: O'Dayne Richards JAM 19.16, **DT**: Jason Morgan JAM 60.20, **HT**: Roberto Janet CUB 71.65, **JT**: Guillermo Martínez CUB 81.55, **Dec**: Marcos Sánchez PUR 7397, **4x100m**: JAM (L Clarke, Lee, Young, Baiiey) 38.81, **4x400m**: BAH (L Williams, Moncur, Mathieu, Miller) 3:01.33, **20,000mW**: Allan Segura CRC 1:28:56.08. **Women**: **100m**: Semoy Hackett TRI 11.27, **200m**: Nivea Smith BAH 22.80, **400m**: Shereefa Lloyd JAM 51.69, **800m**: Gabriela Medina MEX 2:01.50, **1500m**: Sandra López MEX 4:22.65, **5000m**: Marisol Romero MEX 16:05.68, **HMar**: Michelle Coira PUR 1:21:07, **3000mSt**: Korine Hinds JAM 9:54.67, **100mh**: Vonette Dixon JAM 12.77, **400mh**: Andrea Sutherland JAM 56.75, **HJ**: Levern Spencer LCA 1.92, **PV**: Keisa Monterola VEN 4.00, **LJ**: Bianca Stuart BAH 6.81*, **TJ**: Ayanna Alexander TRI 13.50, **SP**: Cleopatra Borel-Brown TRI 19.00, **DT**: Denia Caballero CUB 62.06, **HT**: Johana Moreno COL 67.97, **JT**: Freisa Iris Nuñez DOM 54.29, **Hep**: Gretchen Quintana CUB 5704, **4x100m**: TRI (Howell, Ahyee, Hutchinson, Hackett) 43.47, **4x400m**: JAM (Sutherland, Lloyd, Goule, Hall) 3:29.86. **Medal Table Leaders**: JAM 10G-6S-10B, MEX 7-6-7, TRI 6-3-5, BAH 5-2-3, CUB 5-2-0, PUR 3-8-3, VEN 3-3-4, COL 1-6-7, DOM 1-4-2; in all 17 countries won medals.

Gulf Countries Championships

At Makkah, Saudi Arabia 2-4 April
Men: **100m**: Barakat Al-Harthi OMA 10.30, **200m**: Femi Ogunode QAT 20.79, **400m**: Ismail Al-Sabyani KSA 46.78, **800m**: Abdulrahman Bala QAT 1:49.0, **1500m/3000mSt**: Abubaker Ali Kamal QAT

3:39.90/8:39.00, **5000m/10,000m:** Hussein Al-Hamdan KSA 17:59.43/28:33.04, **HMar:** Abdullah Al-Joud KSA 67:20, **110mh:** Ali Hussein Al-Zaki KSA 13.84, **400mh:** Fawaz Al-Shammari KUW 50.59, **HJ:** Moataz Essa Barshim QAT 2.21, **PV:** Fahad Al-Mershad KUW 5.05, **LJ:** Mohamed Jassim Al-Qaree KSA 7.42, **TJ:** Mohamed Abdallah Darwish UAE 15.93, **SP:** Ahmad Gholoum KUW 17.42, **DT:** Essa Al-Zankawi KUW 57.60, **HT:** Mohamed Al-Zankawi KUW 76.72, **JT:** Abdullah Al-Omeiri KUW 66.99, **10000mW:** Mabrouk Saleh Nasser QAT 46:05.13, **4x100m/4x400m:** OMA 39.49/3:07.79.

1st Gulf CC Games

At Madinat Isa, Bahrain 17-19 October
Men: 100m: Barakat Al-Harthi OMA 10.17, **200m:** Femi Ogunode QAT 20.55. **400m:** Ahmed Al-Merjabi OMA 46.3h, **800m:** Mohamed Al-Azimi KUW 1:47.35, **1500m/3000mSt:** Abubaker Ali Kamal QAT 3:37.38/8:50.40, **5000m:** Hussein Al-Hamdan KSA 13:56.20, **10,000m:** Hasan Mahboob Ali BRN 28:37.91, **HMar:** Khaled Kamal Khaled BRN 66:04, **110mh:** Ahmed Al-Moualed KSA 13.81, **400mh:** Jassem Al-Mass KUW 52.15, **HJ:** Mutaz Essa Barshim QAT 2.16, **PV:** Fahad Al-Mershad KUW 5.00, **LJ:** Saleh Abdelaziz Al-Haddad KUW 7.62, **TJ:** Mohamed Abdallah Darwish UAE 15.92, **SP:** Meshari Suroor Saad KUW 18.19, **DT:** Rashid Saif Al-Makbali UAE 50.27, **HT:** Mohamed Al-Zankawi KUW 75.31, **JT:** Khamis Al-Qutaiti OMA 67.30, **Dec:** Mohamed Reza Al-Matroud KSA 7234 (drugs dq), **10kW:** Mabrouk Saleh Nasser QAT 47:38, **4x100m:** OMA 39.51, **4x400m:** KSA 3:11.46.

World Military Games (CISM)

At Rio de Janiero, Brazil 17-23 July
Men: 100m/200m: Femi Ogunode QAT 10.07*/20.46*, **400m:** Sajjad Hashemi IRI 45.81, **800m:** Marcin Lewandowski POL 1:45.77, **1500m:** Gideon Gathimba KEN 3:40.62, **5000m:** Mark Kiptoo KEN 13:06.17*, **10,000m:** Kiprono Menjo KEN 28:36.92, **Mar:** Patrick Tambwé FRA 2:18:17, **3000mSt:** Simon Ayeko UGA 8:29.39, **110mh:** Dominik Bochenek POL 13.74, **400mh:** Raphael Fernandes BRA 50.50, **HJ:** Mutaz Essa Barshim QAT 2.29*, **PV:** Pawel Wojciechowski POL 5.81*, **LJ:** Yu Zhenwei CHN 8.05, **TJ:** Jefferson Sabino BRA 16.89, **SP:** Andriy Semenov UKR 20.02, **DT:** Mahmoud Samimi IRI 61.36, **JT:** Ari Mannio FIN 82.48, **4x100m:** BRA 39.53, **4x400m:** POL 3:04.55. **Women: 100m:** Mariya Ryemyen UKR 11.34, **200m:** Ana Cláudia Silva BRA 23.01*, **400m:** Geisa Coutinho BRA 51.08*, **800m:** Marina Arzamasova BLR 2:01.39, **1500m:** Nancy Langat KEN 4:15.42, **5000m:** Shitaye Eshete BRN 15:52.84, **10,000m:** Doris Changeiywo KEN 33:38.93, **Mar:** Kim Kum-ok PRK 2:35:22, **3000mSt:** Mercy Njorege KEN 9:36.92*, **100mh:** Alina Talay BLR 12.95*, **LJ:** Keila Costa BRA 6.41, **TJ:** Simona La Mantia ITA 14.19, **HT:** Zhang Wenxiu CHN 74.29*, **4x100m:** BRA 43.73*, **4x400m:** BRA 3:32.42.

NACAC Combined Events Championships

At Kingston, Jamaica 27-28 May
Men Dec: Maurice Smith JAM 8078. **Women** Hep: Emily Pearson USA 5585.

Pan-American Race Walking Cup

At Envigado, Colombia 21-22 April
Men: 20kmW: 1. Luis Fernando López COL 1:25:26, 2. Erick Barrondo GUA 1:25:56. 3, Giovannni Torres MEX 1:26:18; **50kmW:** 1. Cristian Berdeja MEX 3:59:14, 2. Fredy Hernández COL 3:59:40, 3. Rolando Saquipay ECU 4:01:20. **Women 20kmW:** 1. Jamy Franco GUA 1:36:04, 2. Anabel Orjuela COL 1:36:12; 3. Ingrid Hernández COL 1:37:18.

16th Pan American Junior Championships

At Miramar, USA 22-24 July
Men: 100m: Marvin Bracy USA 10.09w, **200m:** Kirani James GRN 20.53w, **400m:** Josh Mance USA 45.84, **800m:** Immanuel Hutchinson USA 1:49.04, **1500m:** Omar Kaddurah USA 3:52.29, **5000m:** Jacob Hurysz USA 14:55.92, **10,000m:** Parker Stinson USA 30:37.88, **3000mSt:** Fernando Román PUR 8:59.52, **110mh**-J: Eddie Lovett USA 13.14, **400mh:** Monte Corley USA 51.21, **HJ:** Maalik Reynolds USA 2.22, **PV:** Thiago da Silva BRA 5.20, **LJ:** Devin Field USA 7.58w, **TJ:** Elton Walcott TRI 16.51w, 6k **SP/1.75k:** Ashinia Miller JAM 19.97, **DT:** Traves Smikle JAM 66.58, 6k **HT:** Alec Faldermeyer USA 72.89, **JT:** Braian Toledo ARG 76.40, **Dec**-J: Kevin Lazas USA 7979*, **10,000mW:** Eider Arevalo COL 41:29.81, **4x100m/4x400m:** USA 39.43/3:08.20. **Women: 100m:** Michelle Lee Ahyee TRI 11.25, **200m:** Antonique Strachan USA 22.70*, **400m:** Chris-Ann Gordon JAM 52.62, **800m:** Kenyetta Iyevbele USA 2:06.27, **1500m:** Cory McGee USA 4:35.46, **3000m/5000m:** Kayla Beattie USA 9:30.63/16:48.44, **3000mSt:** Alexandra Leptich USA 10:43.76, **100mh:** Trinity Wilson USA 13.14* (13.03w ht), **400mh:** Katrina Seymour BAH 57.87, **HJ:** Shanay Briscoe USA 1.83, **PV:** Morgann LeLeux USA 4.15, **LJ:** Jéssica dos Reis BRA 6.39, **TJ:** Giselly Landázuri COL 13.04w, **SP:** Alessandra Gamboa PER 15.23, **DT:** Shelbi Vaughan USA 53.12, **HT:** Shelby Ashe USA 59.25, **JT:** Avione Allgood USA 53.06*, **Hep:** Tamara Souza BRA 5477, **10,000mW:** Lorena Arenas COL 48:15.78*, **4x100m:** BAH 45.04, **4x400m:** USA 3:34.71. **Medal Table Leaders:** USA 26G-21S-12B, CAN 14 medals, JAM, BAH, BRA, COL each 3 gold.

17th Pan-Arab Championships

At Al Ain, United Arab Emirates 26-29 October
Men: 100m: Aziz Ouhadi MAR 10.24, **200m:** Femi Ogunode QAT 20.59, **400m:** Rabah Yousif SUD 45.96, **800m:** Abdulkader El Nasser SUD 1:53.24, **1500m:** Abderrrahmane Anou ALG 3:58.78, **5000m:** Ali Abubaker Kamal QAT 15:35.53, **10,000m:** Holi Ahmad Obaidullah SUD 29:57.62, **HMar:** Mansour Obaid Ahmad UAE 66:20, **3000mSt:** Hamid Ezzine MAR 8:41.98, **110mh:** Fawaz Dahesh Al-Shammari KUW 13.75*, **400mh:** Abdulrahman Hamadi ALG 51.10, **HJ:** Mutaz Essa Barshim QAT 2.25, **PV:** Fahed

Al-Mershad KUW 5.00, **LJ**: Yahya Berrabah MAR 7.85, **TJ**: Issam Nima ALG 16.41, **SP**: Meshari Suroor Saad KUW 19.15, **DT**: Haydar Shahid IRQ 57.89, **HT**: Ali Mohamed Al-Zankawi KUW 79.27*, **JT**: Ihab Abdulrahman Al-Sayed EGY 78.83*, **Dec**: Mohamed Jassem Al-Qaree KSA 7413, **4x100m**: OMA 39.53*, **4x400m**: SUD 3:06.97, **20kmW**: Hisham Medjber ALG 1:38:47. **Women: 100m/200m**: Gretta Taslakian LIB 11.97/23.68*, **400m**: Dana Hussein Abdul Razzak IRQ 55.74, **800m/1500m**: Genzeb Shumi Regasa BRN 2:03.13*/4:19.15, **5000m/10,000m**: Shitaye Eshete BRN 16:09.11/33:28.07, **HMar**: Lishan Dula Gemechu BRN 72:10, **3000mSt**: Salima El Ouali MAR 10:28.06, **100mh**: Lamia Lhabz MAR 14.23, **400mh**: Hayat Lambarki MAR 58.11, **HJ**: Ghizlane Siba MAR 1.76, **PV**: Nisrine Dinar MAR 3.60, **LJ**: Tahani R.Belabiod ALG 6.03, **TJ**: Baya Rahouli ALG 13.59, **SP**: Walaa Mohamad Attiah EGY 14.65, **DT**: Elham Sayed Wehba EGY 48.80, **HT**: Rana Ahmed Ibrahim EGY 59.40, **JT**: Reda Adel Ahmad Toufik EGY 43.73, **Hep**: Abdulhamid Wedian Mukhtar EGY 4699, **4x100m/4x400m**: MAR 46.84/3:40.58, **10kmW**: Jihad Adel Mohamad Said EGY 57:07. **Medal table**: MAR 10G-9S-8B; EGY 7-11-7, ALG 6-4-7, BRN 5-0-1, SUD 4-2-1, QAT 3-2-3, IRQ 2-3-3, LIB 2-0-0. UAE 1-6-4; OMA 1-2-2, KSA 1-1-1, SYR 0-2-6, JOR 0-0-2.

Games of the Small States of Europe

At Schaan. Liechtenstein 1-4 June
Men: 100m/200m: Panayiotis Ioannou CYP 10.60/21.46, **400m**: Kevin Moore MLT 47.68, **800**: Brice Etès MON 1:52.31, **1500m**: Amine Khadiri CYP 3:50.31, **5000m**: Pol Mellina LUX 14:42.20, **10,000m**: Antoni Bernado AND 30:57.70, **3000mSt**: Pascal Groben LEX 9:25.21, **110mh**: Alexandros Stavrides CYP 14.04, **400mh**: Aris Xoufaridis CYP 52.91, **HJ**: Emilios Xenophontos CYP 2.12, **PV**: Nikandros Stylianou CYP 5.00, **LJ**: Kristinn Torfason ISL 7.67, **TJ**: Zacharios Arnos CYP 15.98, **SP**: Odinn Thorsteinsson ISL 19.73, **DT**: Apostolos Parellis CYP 59.73, **HT**: Bergur Indi Pétursson ISL 70.60*, **JT**: Antoine Wagner LUX 69.13, **4x100m/4x400m**: CYP 41.53/3:14.02. **Women: 100m**: Anna Papaioannou CYP 11.86, **200m**: Diane Borg MLT 24.27, **400m**: Arna Gudmunsdóttir ISL 55.73, **800m/1500m**: Meropi Panagiotou CYP 2:10.52/4:36.91, **5000m/10,000m**: Sladana Perunovic MNE 17:39.70/36:00.48, **100mh**: Dimitra Arachoviti CYP 13.37, **400mh**: Kim Reuland LUX 61.47, **HJ**: Marija Vukovic MNE 1.86, **PV**: Edna Semedo Monteiro LUX 3.80, **LJ**: Nektaria Panayi CYP 6.35, **TJ**: Nina Serbezova CYP 13.63*, **SP**: Florentia Kappa CYP 14.32, **DT**: Zacharoula Georgiadou CYP 49.98. **JT**: Asdis Hjálmsdóttir ISL 58.93*, **4x100m/4x400m**: MLT 46.30/3:49.95.

39th South American Junior Championships 2009

At Medellín, Colombia 23-25 September
Men: 100m: Aldemir da Silva Jr BRA 10.36, **200m**: Diego Palomeque COL & Aldemir da Silva Jr 20.94, **400m**: Ânderson Henriques BRA 46.59, **800m**: Joseílton Cunha BRA 1:49.32, **1500m**: Frederico

Bruno ARG 3:53.04; **5000m/10,000m**: Miguel Ángel Amador COL 14:40.81/30:54.90, **3000mSt**: Mauricio Matute ECU 9:22.94, **110mh-J/400mh**: João de Oliveira BRA 13.85/52.62, **HJ**: Rebert Firmino BRA 2.07, **PV**: Heberth Gómez COL 5.00, **LJ**: Douglas Selestrino BRA 7.57, **TJ**: Adrián Sornoza ECU 15.82, 6k **SP**: Joaquín Ballivián CHI 19.31, 1.75k **DT**: Mauricio Ortega COL 58.48, 6k **HT**: Jonathan Gras ARG 67.36, **JT**: Braian Toledo ARG 74.04*, Jnr **Dec**: Víctor Santos BRA 7263, **10,000mW**: Eider Arévalo COL 39:56.01*; **4x100m/4x400m**: BRA 39.63*/3:08.35*. **Women: 100m/200m**: Tamiris de Liz BRA 11.43*/23.35*, **400m/800m**: Ana Paula da Silva BRA 53.84/2:05.76*, **1500m**: Erika Lima BRA 4:36.10, **3000m/5000m**: Charo Inga Quinto PER 9:55.01/17:13.88, **3000mSt**: Luz Mery Rojas PER 10:53.59, **100mh**: Daniela Castillo ECU 14.17, **400mh**: Déborah Rodríguez URU 60.60, **HJ**: Yulimar Rojas VEN 1.78, **PV**: Angie Hernández COL 3.70, **LJ**: Jéssica dos Reis BRA 6.38, **TJ**: Giselle Landázury COL 13.39, **SP**: Lívia Avancini BRA 14.75, **DT**: Esthefânia da Costa BRA 48.97, **HT**: Daniela Gómez ARG 54.49, **JT**: Emylyr da Conceição BRA 46.54, **Hep**: Tamara de Souza 5545, **10,000mW**: Lorena Arenas COL 47:22.68, **4x100m**: BRA 44.64, **4x400m**: COL 3:36.74*.
Medal Table: BRA 22G-16S-11B, COL 10-14-16, ARG 4-1-6, PER 3-4-0, ECU 3-0-3, VEN 1-4-0, CHI 1-2-4, URU 1-1-0, BOL 0-1-2, PAN & GUY 0-0-1.

South American Marathon Championships

At Lima, Peru 15 May.
Men: Miguel Mallqui PER 2:17:20; **Women**: Jimena Misayauri PER 2:42:40.

26th South East Asia Games

At Palembang, Indonesia 12-16 November
Men: 100m/200m: Franklin R.Burumi INA 10.37w/20.93, **400m**: Heru Astriyanto INA 47.53, **800m**: Duong Van Thai VIE 1:49.42, **1500m**: Ridwan INA 3:47.63, **5000m/10,000m**: Agus Prayogo INA 14:10.01/30:10.43, **Mar**: Yahuza INA 2:27:45, **3000mSt**: Rene Herrera PHI 8:52.23, **110mh**: Jumrus Rittidet THA 13.77*, **400mh**: Dao Xuan Cuong VIE 51.45, **HJ**: Lee Hup Wei MAS 2.15, **PV**: Kreetha Sinthawacheewa THA 5.10, **LJ**: Suphanara Ayudhaya THA 7.86, **TJ**: Theerayut Philakong THA 16.43, **SP**: Chatchawal Polyiam THA 17.59*, **DT**: James Wong Tuck Yim SIN (9th DT title) 51.32, **HT**: Tantipong Phetchaiya THA 61.46, **JT**: Nguyen Truong Giang VIE 69.07, **Dec**: Vu Van Huyen VIE 7223, **4x100m**: INA 39.91, **4x400m**: MAS 3:10.49, **20kmW**: Lo Choon Sieng MAS 1:32:34. **Women: 100m**: Serafi Anelies Unani INA 11.69, **200m**: Laphassaporn Tawoncharoen THA 23.65, **400m**: Treewadee Yongphan THA 54.13, **800m/1500m**: Truong Thanh Hang VIE 2:02.65/4:15.75, **5000m/10,000m/Mar**: Triyaningsih INA 16:06.37/34:52.74.2:45:35, **Mar**: Jho-Ann Banayag PHI 2:46:34, **3000mSt**: Rina Budiarti INA 10:00.58*, **100mh**: Wallapa Punsoongneun THA 13.51, **400mh**: Norasheela Mohd Khalid MAS 57.41, **HJ**: Duong Thi Viet Anh VIE 1.90, **PV**: Roslinda Samsu MAS 4.20*, **LJ**: Marestella Torres PHI 6.71*, **TJ**: Tran Hue Hoa VIE 13.76, **SP**: Zhang Guirong SIN 16.96, **DT**: Subenrat Insaeng THA 52.28, **HT**: Tan Song

Hwa MAS 55.15, **JT**: Natta Nacharn THA 48.80, **Hep**: Wassana Winatho THA 5488, **4x100m/4x400m**: THA 44.40/3:41.45, **20kmW**: Nguyen Thi Thanh Phuc VIE 1:43:22. **Medals**: THA 14G-8S-10B, INA 13-12-11, VIE 9-9-14, MAS 6-2-3, PHI 2-9-5, SIN 2-3-2, MYA 0-3-1.

Southern Africa Championships

At Maputo, Mozambique 2-3 July
Men: **100m/200m**: Mosito Lehate LES 9.8/21.36, **400m**: Willie de Beer RSA 47.20, **800m**: Isaac Seoke BOT 1:47.9, **1500m**: Samson Ngoepe RSA 3:50.8, **5000m**: Job Katoane LES 14:28.7, **10,000m**: Rethabile Molefi LES 30:44.4, **400mh**: Daniel Lagamang BOT 54.08, **HJ**: Hubert de Beer RSA 2.05, **LJ**: Rushwal Samaai RSA 7.08, **TJ**: Tumelo Thagane RSA 15.96, **SP**: Jaco Engelbrecht RSA 18.50, **DT**: Victor Hogan RSA 61.31, **JT**: Bernard Crous RSA 70/85, **4x100m**: RSA 40.74, **4x400m**: BOT 3:13.31. **Women**: **100m**: Cindy Stewart RSA 11.61, **200m**: Sonja van der Merwe RSA 24.37, **400m**: Tjipekapora Herunga NAM 53.9, **800m**: Elisa Cossa MOZ 2:10.7, **1500m/5000m**: Thandiwe Nyathi ZIM 4:28.9/16:55.6, **10,000m**: Portia Ngwenya RSA 36:40.1, **100mh**: Claudia Viljoen RSA 14.30, **400mh**: Wanda Theron RSA 60.09, **HJ**: Anika Smit RSA 1.75, **SP**: Sonia Smuts RSA 14.54, **DT**: Maryke Oberholzer RSA 50.78, **JT**: Justine Robbeson RSA 61.26, **4x100m**: MRI 47.47, **4x400m**: RSA 3:45.16.

25th IAU World 100km Championships

At Winschoten, Netherlands 10 September.
Incorporated European Championships.
Men: 1. Giorgio Calcaterra ITA 6:27:32, 2. Michael Wardian USA 6:42:49, 3. Andrew Henshaw USA 6:44:35, 4. Pieter Vermeesch BEL (2 EUR) 6:47:01, 5. Shinji Nakadai JPN 6:48:32, 6. Matt Wood USA 6:50:23, 7. Jonas Buud SWE (3 EUR) 6:52:19; **Team**: 1. USA 20:17:47, 2. JPN 21:05:00, 3. FRA (1 EUR) 21:36:19, 4. RUS (2 EUR) 21:57.55, 5. GER (3 EUR) 22:31:59; **Women**: 1. Marina Bychkova RUS 7:27:19, 2. Joanna Zakrzewski GBR 7:41:06, 3. Lindsay Anne van Aswegen RSA 7:42:05, 4. Irina Vishnevskaya RUS (3 EUR) 7:45:37, 5. Meghan Arbogast USA 7:51:10; **Team**: 1. RUS 23:19:40, 2. USA 23:56:20, 3. JPN 24:35.13, 4. RSA 24:40.15, 5. GBR (2 EUR) 24:42:56, 6. AUT (3 EUR) 25:55:19. Record 285 athletes from 34 countries took part.

IAU World Trophy 50km

At Assen, Netherlands 21 August
Men: Eliot Kiplagat Biwott KEN 2:55:00; **Women**: Emma Gooderham GBR 3:17:37.

Commonwealth 24 Hour Championships

At Llandudno, GBR 23/24 September
Men: John Pares WAL 244.335k; **Team**: England 668.225k; **Women**: Elizabeth Hawker ENG 247.076k; **Team**: England 643.016k.

World Mountain Running Championships

At Tirana, Albania 11 September
Men 13.07k (750m height difference): 1. Max King USA 52:06, 2. Ahmet Arslan TUR 52:41, 3. Marton De Matteis ITA 52:57; Team: 1. ITA 26, 2. TUR 65, 3. FRA 77; **Junior Men** 8.77k, 500m HD: Adem Karagoz TUR 37:91; Team: TUR 12; **Women** 8.77k, 500m HD: 1. Kasie Enman USA 40:39, 2. Yelena Rukhlyada RUS 41:47, 3. Maurie Laure Dumergues FRA 42:32; Team: 1. ITA 24, 2. CZE 30, 3. GBR 31; **Junior Women** 4.47k, 250m HD: Lea Einfalt SLO 20:23; Team: TUR 6.
13th WMRA Grand Prix: determined by best of four from six events: **Men**: 1. Ahmet Arslan TUR, 2. David Schneider SUI, 3. Martin De Matteis ITA; **Women**: 1. Lucija Krkoc SLO, 2. Antonella Confortola ITA, 3. Emma Clayton ENG.

European Mountain Racing Championships

At Bursa, Turkey 10 July
Men 12k (1245m height difference): 1. Ahmet Arslan TUR (fifth successive win) 58:08, 2. Gabriele Abate ITA 58:40, 3. José Gaspar POR 59:05; Team: 1. ITA 12, 2. TUR 34, 3. POR 36; **Junior Men** 8.5k (865m HD): Nuri Kömür TUR 43:08; Team: TUR; **Women** 8.5k (865m HD): 1. Martina Strähl SUI 48:44, 2. Antonella Confortola ITA 49:09, 3. Lucija Krkoc SLO 49:24; Team: 1. ITA 22, 2. RUS 28, 3. SUI 38; **Junior Women** 3.5k (405m HD): Denisa Dragomir ROU 21:43; Team: TUR.

Athletes to win their individual event at Youth, Junior, and Senior World Championships

Yelena Isinbayeva RUS	W PV	WY 1999, WJ 2000, EJ 2001, EU23 2003, EC 2006, WCh 2005 & 2007, OG 2004 & 2008
Jana Pittman AUS	W 400mh	WY 1999, WJ 2000, CG 2003, WCh 2003 & 2007
Jacques Freitag RSA	HJ	WY 1999, WJ 2000, WCh 2003
Veronica Campbell-Brown JAM	W 100m	WY 1999, WJ 2000, WCh 2007 (and 200m WJ 2000, OG 2004 & 2010, WCh 2011)
Valerie Adams NZL	W SP	WY 2001, WJ 2002, CG 2006 & 2010, WCh 2007, 2009 & 2011; OG 2008
Usain Bolt JAM	200m	WJ 2002, WY 2003, OG 2008, WCh 2009 & 2011
Dani Samuels AUS	W DT	WY 2005, WJ 2006, WCh 2009
Tatyana Chernova RUS	Hep	WY 2005, WJ 2006, WCh 2011
David Storl GER	SP	WY 2007, WJ 2008, EJ 2009, EU23 & WCh 2011
Kirani James GRN	400m	WY 2009, WJ 2010, WCh 2011
Note also multiple age group titles		
Bianca Perie ROU	HJ	WY 2005 & 2007, WJ 2006 & 2008, EJ 2007 & 2009, EU23 2011

IAAF DIAMOND LEAGUE

The IAAF's successor to the Golden League, the expanded and more globally widespread Diamond League, was launched in 2010 with 14 meetings spread across Asia, Europe, the Middle East and the USA. The total prize money was increased from $6.63 million (with a $50,000 bonus for any new world record) in 2010 to $8 million in 2011 and winners of each Race received a Diamond Trophy (4 carats of diamonds) and a $40,000 cash prize.

SAMSUNG DIAMOND LEAGUE – FINAL PLACINGS 2011

Men: 100m: 1. Asafa Powell 18, 2. Yohan Blake 8, 3. Nesta Carter 4; **200m**: 1. Walter Dix 18, 2. Yohan Blake 8, 3. Jaysuma Saidy Ndure 5; **400m**: 1. Kirani James 12, 2. Jermaine Gonzales 11, 3. Chris Brown 6; **800m**: 1. Daniel Rudisha 16, 2. Asbel Kiprop 8, 3. Alfred Kirwa Yego 5; **1500m**: 1. Nixon Chepseba 12, 2. Asbel Kiprop 11, 3. Silas Kiplagat 10; **5000m**: 1. Imane Merga 15, 2. Vincent Chepkok 7, 3. Dejene Gebremeskel 4; **3000mSt**: 1. Paul Kipsiele Koech 17, 2. Ezekiel Kemboi 16, 3. Benjamin Kiplagat 5; **110mh**: 1. Dayron Robles 16, 2. David Oliver 13, 3. Jason Richardson 10; **400mh**: 1. David Greene 16, 2. Javier Culson 15, 3. Cornel Fredericks 4; **HJ**: 1. Jesse Williams 9, 2. Andrey Silnov 8, 3. Dimítrios Hondrokoúkis 8; **PV**: 1. Renaud Lavillenie 20, 2. Malte Mohr 12, 3. Konstadínos Filippídis 10; **LJ**: 1. Mitchell Watt 12, 2. Ngonidzashe Makusha 8, 3. Aleksandr Menkov 4; **TJ**: 1. Phillips Idowu 18, 2. Alexis Copello 9, 3. Benjamin Compaoré 8; **SP**: 1. Dylan Armstrong 17, 2. Reese Hoffa 16, 3. Christian Cantwell 11; **DT**: 1. Virgilijus Alekna 17, 2. Robert Harting 16, 3. Gerd Kanter 9; **JT**: 1. Matthias De Zordo 17, 2. Andreas Thorkildsen 14, 3. Vadims Vasilevskis 4; **Women: 100m**: 1. Carmelita Jeter 22, 2. Veronica Campbell-Brown 10, 3. Kelly-Ann Baptiste 8; **200m**: 1. Carmelita Jeter 13, 2. Bianca Knight 10, 3. Allyson Felix 10; **400m**: 1. Amantle Montsho 28, 2. Novlene Williams-Mills 7, 3. Tatyana Firova 2; **800m**: 1. Jennifer Meadows 11, 2. Kenia Sinclair 10, 3. Marina Savinova 10; **1500m**: 1. Morgan Uceny 19, 2. Maryam Jamal 11, 3. Anna Mishchenko 6; **5000m**: 1. Vivian Cheruiyot 20, 2. Sally Kipyego 6, 3. Sentayehu Ejigu 6; **3000mSt**: 1. Milcah Chemos 20, 2. Sofia Assefa 10, 3. Yuliya Zaripova 8; **100mh**: 1. Danielle Carruthers 19, 2. Sally Pearson 12, 3. Kellie Wells 12; **400mh**: 1. Kaliese Spencer 24, 2. Melaine Walker 10, 3, Zuzana Hejnová 8; **HJ**: 1. Blanka Vlasic 18, 2. Anna Chicherenko 14, 3. Yelena Slesarenko 4; **PV**: 1. Silke Spiegelburg 14, 2. Jennifer Suhr 13, 3. Fabiana Murer 10; **LJ**: 1. Brittney Reese 23, 2. Funmi Jimoh 10, 3. Janay DeLoach 6; **TJ**: 1. Olga Saladuha 24, 2. Olga Rypakova 6, 3. Mabel Gay 5; **SP**: 1. Valerie Adams 24, 2. Nadezhda Ostapchuk 16, 3. Jllian Camarena-Williams 8; **DT**: 1. Yarelys Barrios 14, 2. Li Yanfeng 13, 3. Nadine Müller 13; **JT**: 1. Christina Obergföll 28, 2. Barbora Spotáková 10, 3. Mariya Abakumova 9.

Diamond League winners 2011

D Doha May 6, **Sh** Shanghai May 15, **R** Rome May 26, **E** Eugene Jun 4, **O** Oslo Jun 9, **NY** New York Jun 11, **L** Lausanne Jun 30, **P** Paris Saint-Denis Jul 8, **Bi** Birmingham Jul 10, **M** Monaco Jul 22, **St** Stockholm Jul 29, **CP** London (CP) Aug 5-6; Finals at: **Z** Zürich Sep 8, **Br** Brussels Sep 16.

Men:
100m: Asafa Powell Sh- 9.95, L- 9.78, Bi- 9.91; Usain Bolt R- 9.91, M- 9.88; Steve Mullings NY- 10.26; Yohan Blake Z- 9.82**; 200m**: Walter Dix D- 20.06, E- 20.19, CP- 20.16; Usain Bolt O- 19.86, P- 20.03, St- 20.03; Yohan Br 19.26**; 400m**: Calvin Smith Sh- 45.47; Angelo Taylor E- 45.16; Jeremy Wariner NY- 45.13; Chris Brown P- 44.94; Jermaine Gonzales St- 44.69; Kirani James CP- 44.61, Z- 44.36**; 800m**: Asbel Kiprop D- 1:44.74, Khadevis Robinson R- 1:45.09; Alfred Kirwa Yego NY- 1:46.57; David Rudisha L- 1:44.15, M- 1:42.61, Br- 1:43.96; Abubaker Kaki Bi- 1:44.54**; 1500m/1M**: Nixon Chepseba Sh- 3:31.42, Z- 3:32.74; Haron Keitany E- 3:49.09M; Asbel Kiprop O- 3:50.86M; Amine Laâlou P- 3:32.15; Silas Kiplagat St- 3:33.94; Leonel Manzano CP- 3:51.24M; **3/5000m**: Yenew Alamirew D- 7:27.26; Imane Merga R- 12:54.21, Br- 12:58.32; Dejene Gebremeskel NY- 13:05.22; Vincent Chepkok L- 12:59.13; Mo Farah Bi- 13:06.14, M- 12:53.11**; 3000mSt**: Brimin Kipruto Sh- 8:02.28, M- 7:53.64; Ezekiel Kemboi E- 8:08.34, Z- 8:07.72; Paul Kipsiele Koech O- 8:01.83, St- 8:05.92; Mahiedine Mekhissi P- 8:02.09; **110mh**: Liu Xiang Sh- 13.07; David Oliver E- 12.94; Aries Merritt O- 13.12; Dayron Robles P- 13.09, CP- 13.04, Z- 13.01; Jason Richardson St- 13.17**; 400mh**: L.J.van Zyl D- 48.11, R- 47.91; Javier Culson NY- 48.50, Br- 48.32; David Greene GBR L- 48.41, Bi- 48.20; Angelo Taylor M- 47.97**; HJ**: Jesse Williams D- 2.33; Raúl Spank GER 2.32; Kyriakos Ioannou O- 2.28; Jaroslav Bába & Aleksey Dmitrik P- 2.32; Ivan Ukhov St- 2.34; Andrey Silnov CP- 2.36; Dmitríos Hondrokoúkis Z- 2.32**; PV**: Malte Mohr D- 5.81; Renaud Lavillenie R- 5.82, L- 5.83, P- 5.73, M- 5.90; Romain Mesnil NY- 5.52; Konstadínos Filipídes Br- 5.72**; LJ**: Mitchell Watt Sh- 8.44, St- 8.54, CP- 8.45, ; Greg Rutherford E- 8.32w; Khotso Mokoena O- 8.08; Irving Saladino P- 8.40; Ngoni Makusha Z- 8.00**; TJ**: Teggy Tamgho D- 17.49, L- 17.91; Phillips Idowu R- 17.59, NY- 16.67, Bi- 17.54, M- 17.36; Benjamin Compaoré Br- 17.31; **SP**: Dylan Armstrong D- 21.38, R- 21.60, Bi- 21.55, Z- 21.61; Christian Cantwell L- 21.83; Reese Hoffa M- 21.25, Br- 22.09**; DT**: Gerd Kanter D- 67.49, O- 65.14; Robert Harting E- 68.40, P- 67.32, Z- 67.02; Virgilijus Alekna St- 65.05, CP- 66.21**; JT**: Peter Frydrych D- 85.32, Tero Pitkämäki Sh- 85.33; Matthias de Zordo O- 83.94, Br- 88.36; Andreas Thorkildsen L- 88.19, Bi- 88.30, St- 88.43;**; Women; 100m**: Veronica Campbell-Brown Sh- 10.92; Carmelita Jeter E- 10.70, St- 11.15, CP- 10.93, Br- 10.78; Ivet Lalova O- 11.01w; Kelly-Ann Baptiste P- 10.91**; 200m**: LaShauntea Moore D- 22.83; Bianca Knight R- 22.54, Bi- 22.59; Allyson

Felix NY- 22.92; Mariya Ryemyen L- 22.85; Carmelita Jeter M- 22.20, Z- 22.27; **400m**: Allyson Felix D- 50.33, R- 49.81; Amantle Montsho O- 50.10, L- 50.23, Bi- 50.20, M- 49.71, Br- 50.16; **800m**: Jennifer Meadows Sh- 2:00.54, CP- 1:58.60; Kenia Sinclair E- 1:58.29, St- 1:58.21; Halima Hachlaf O- 1:58.27; Caster Semenya P- 2:00.18; Mariya Savinova Z- 1:58.27; **1500m**: Anna Mishchenko D- 4:02.00; Maryam Jamal R- 4:01.60, M- 4:00.59; Kenia Sinclair NY- 4:08.06; Morgan Uceny L- 4:05.52, Bi- 4:05.64, Br- 4:00.06; **5000m**: Vivian Cheruiyot Sh- 14:31.92, E- 14:33.96, St- 14:20.87, Z- 14:30.10; Meseret Defar O- 14:37.32, P- 14:29.52; Lauren Fleshman CP- 15:00.57; **3000mSt**: Milcah Chemos D- 9:16.44, R- 9:12.89, NY- 9:27.29, L- 9:19.87, CP- 9:22.80; Sofia Assefa Bi- 9:25.87; Yuliya Zaripova Br- 9:15.43; **100mh**: Kellie Wells D- 12.58; Dawn Harper R- 12.70; Danielle Carruthers NY- 13.04, Br- 12.65; Sally Pearson L- 12.47w, Bi- 12.48, M- 12.51; **400mh**: Kaliese Spencer Sh- 54.20, St- 53.74, CP- 52.79, Z- 53.36; Lashinda Demus E- 53.31; Zuzana Hejnová O- 54.38, P- 53.29; **HJ**: Blanka Vlasic Sh- 1.94, R- 1.95, Bi- 1.99, M- 1.97; Emma Green Tregaro NY- 1.94; Anna Chicherova L- 1.95, Br- 2.05; **PV**: Silke Spiegelburg Sh- 4.55, Bi- 4.66; Anna Rogowska E- 4.68; Fabiana Murer O- 4.60; Yelena Isinbayeva St- 4.76; Jenn Suhr CP- 4.79, Z- 4.72; **LJ**: Funmi Jimoh D- 6.88, NY- 6.48; Brittney Reese R- 6.94, L- 6.85, M- 6.82, Z- 6.72; Janay DeLoach Bi- 6.78; **TJ**: Yargeris Savigne Sh- 14.68, O- 14.81, P- 14.99; Olga Saladuha E- 14.98, St- 15.06w, CP- 14.80, Br- 14.67; **SP**: Gong Lijiao Sh- 19.94; Nadezhda Ostapchuk E- 20.59; Valerie Adams O- 20.26, P- 20.78, St- 20.57, CP- 20.07, Z- 20.51; **DT**: Li Yanfeng Sh- 62.73, Br- 66.27; Yarelys Barrios R- 64.18, L- 64.29; Stephanie Brown Trafton NY- 62.94; Nadine Müller Bi- 65.75, M- 65.90. (Sandra Perkovic was original winner: D- 65.58, R- 65.56 before her drugs disqualification).; **JT**: Mariya Abakumova R- 65.40; Christina Obergföll E- 65.48, NY- 64.43, P- 68.01, CP- 66.74, Z- 69.57; Barbora Spotáková M- 69.45

The calendar for 2012 is: Doha 11 May; Shanghai 19 May; Rome 31 May; Eugene 2 Jun; Oslo 7 June; New York 9 June; Paris Saint-Denis 6 July; London 13-14 Jul; Monaco 20 July; Stockholm 17 Aug; Lausanne 23 Aug; Birmingham 16 Aug, Zürich 30 Aug; Brussels 7 Sep.

World Indoor Lists 2012 (Continued from page 608)

(Continued from page 608)

WOMEN'S PENTATHLON (continued)

4494	Marina	Goncharova	RUS	26.4.86	2	NC	Belgorod	27 Feb
	8.74	1.79	14.08		6.23		2:18.58	
4476	Aleksandra	Butvina	RUS	14.2.86	5	NC	Moskva	7 Feb
	8.80	1.80	13.38		6.27		2:17.44	
4470	Nadine	Broersen	NED	29.4.90	2	v4N	Praha Strom	29 Jan
	8.64	1.84	13.52		6.06		2:19.96	
4396	Aiga	Grabuste	LAT	24.3.88	1	NC	Riga	28 Jan
	8.60	1.74	14.10		6.20		2.22.86	
4380	Yvonne	van Langen	NED	6.6.82	3	v4N	Praha Strom	29 Jan
	8.42	1.69	13.23		6.04		2:14.65	

4373	Abbie	Norton	USA	28.4.85	4	Mar	4294	Yana	Panteleyeva	RUS	16.6.88	7	Feb
4371	Bettie	Wade	USA	11.9.86	4	Mar	4284	Christina	Kiffe	GER	2.5.92	29	Jan
4367	Ulyana	Aleksandrova	RUS	1.1.91	7	Feb	4334	Viktorija	Zemaityte	LTU	11.3.85	19	Feb
4367	Alina	Fyodorova	UKR	31.7.89	16	Feb	4325	Kamila	Chudzik	POL	12.9.86	19	Feb
4363	Györgyi	Farkas	HUN	13.2.85	19	Feb	4323	Inna	Ahkozova	UKR	16.9.84	15	Feb
4346	Laura	Ikauniece	LAT	31.5.92	4	Feb	4295	Györgyi	Farkas	HUN	13.2.85	5	Feb
4345	Stephanie	Saumweber	GER	5.3.88	12	Feb	4291	Eliska	Klucinová	CZE	14.4.88	13	Feb
4339	Blandine	Maisonnier	FRA	3.1.86	26	Feb	4289	Janay	DeLoach	USA	12.10.85	6	Mar
4322	Nafissatou	Thiam	BEL-J	19.8..94	5	Feb	4283	Ida	Marcussen	NOR	1.11.87	4	Mar
4322	Ellen	Sprunger	SUI	5.8.86	19	Feb	4282	Sara	Aerts	BEL	25.1.84	4	Mar
4318	Maren	Schwerdtner	GER	3.10.85	29	Jan	4262	Alina	Fyodorova	UKR	31.7.89	28	Jan
4316	Ida	Marcussen	NOR	1.11.87	11	Mar	4254	Dorcas	Akinniyi	USA	23.1.90	11	Mar
4310	Yekaterina	Netsvetayeva	BLR	26.6.89	20	Feb	4250	Anastasiya	Belyakova	RUS	4.12.90	5	Feb
4299	Dorcas	Akinniyi	USA	23.1.90	10	Mar	4250	Anastasiya	Mokhnyuk	UKR	1.1.91	15	Feb
4298	Helga Margrét	Thorsteinsdóttir	ISL	15.11.91	4	Feb	4241	Kasey	Hill	USA	10.10.85	6	Mar

3000 METRES WALK

11:44.10	Anisya	Kirdyapkina	RUS	23.10.89	1	Winter	Moskva		5 Feb
12:18.70	Sabine	Krantz	GER	6.2.81	1	NC	Dortmund		29 Jan
12:27.50	Claudia	Stef	ROU	25.2.78	2	Winter	Moskva		5 Feb
12:28.00	Tatyana	Korotkova	RUS	24.4.80	3	Winter	Moskva		5 Feb

5000 METRES WALK

21:39.01	Sabine	Krantz	GER	6.2.81	1		Düsseldorf		17 Dec

MAJOR MEETINGS 2011/2012

In 2010 the IAAF introduced a new series of meetings that has continued into 2012. The top tier was the IAAF Diamond League of 14 meetings at the top (all former Golden League or Super Grand Prix meetings) and the second tier the IAAF World Challenge meetings – 15 in 2012.

The Diamond League encompasses 32 individual event disciplines, with a points scoring 'Diamond Race' running throughout the 14 meeting series culminating in finals split between the last two meetings in Zürich and Brussels. Winners of each Diamond Race get a Diamond Trophy, which will include 4 carats of diamonds. The hammer, the only standard event not be part of the series, has a separate challenge with the event included at 8 World Challenge meetings.

DL – Diamond League, WC – World Challenge, EAP European Premium Meeting (EAC Classic).

Diamond League, World Challenge and European Athletics Premium Meetings

2011 date		Meeting	2012 date	
3 Mar	WC	Telstra Melbourne Track Classic, AUS	3 Mar	WC
7 May	--	Jamaica International, JAM	5 May	WC
8 May	--	Golden Grand Prix, Kawasaki, JPN	6 May	WC
6 May	DL	Qatar Super Grand Prix, Doha, QAT	11 May	DL
12 May	WC	Colorful Daegu, Korea	--	
26 May	WC	Grande Premio Brasil de Atletismo, Rio de Janeiro BRA	12 May	WC
14 May	--	Ponce Grand Prix, PUR	12 May	WC
15 May	DL	Shanghai Golden Grand Prix, CHN	19 May	DL
31 May	WC	Golden Spike, Ostrava, CZE	25 May	WC
29 May	WC	Fanny Blankers-Koen Games, Hengelo, NED	27 May	WC
26 May	DL	Golden Gala, Rome, ITA	31 May	DL
4 Jun	DL	Prefontaine Classic, Eugene, Oregon, USA	2 Jun	DL
3 Jun	EAP	European Athletics Festival, Bydgoszcz, POL	3 Jun	EAP
7 Jun		Montreuil-sous-Bois, FRA	5 Jun	EAP
9 Jun	WC	Bislett Games, Oslo, NOR	7 Jun	DL
10 Jun	EAP	Memorial Primo Nebiolo, Turin, ITA	8 Jun	EAP
11 Jun	DL	adidas Grand Prix, New York (RI), USA	9 Jun	DL
--		Meeting Lille Metropole, Villeneuve d'Ascq, FRA	9 Jun	EAP
12 Jun	EAP	Moscow Challenge, RUS	11 Jun	WC
13 Jun		Josef Odlozil Memorial, Prague, CZE	11 Jun	EAP
28 May	WC	Grand Prix, Dakar, SEN	16 Jun	WC
3 Jul	WC	Znamenskiy Memorial, Zhukovskiy RUS	17 Jun	EAC
5 Jul		Ville de Reims, FRA	4 Jul	EAP
8 Jul	DL	Meeting AREVA Paris Saint-Denis, FRA	6 Jul	DL
9 Jul	WC	Atletismo Madrid, ESP	--	
16 Jul	EAP	KBC Night of Athletics, Heusden-Zolder, BEL	7 Jul	EAP
24 Jun		Meeting Stanislas, Nancy (Tomblaine), FRA	8 Jul	EAP
2 Jul		Sotteville-lès-Rouen, FRA	10 Jul	EAP
5/6 Aug	DL	Aviva London Grand Prix, (CP), GBR	13/14 Jul	DL
22 Jul	DL	Herculis, Monaco, MON	20 Jul	DL
25 Jun	EAP	Janusz Kusocinski Memorial, Szczecin, POL	21 Jul	EAP
13 Jul	EAP	Vardinoyiannia, Réthimno, GRE	--	
23 Jul	EAP	Reunion Internacional Ciudad de Barcelona, ESP	--	
29 Jul	SGP	DN Galan, Stockholm, SWE	17 Aug	DL
30 Jun	DL	Athletissima, Lausanne, SUI	23 Aug	DL
10 Jul	DL	British Grand Prix, Birmingham, GBR	26 Aug	DL
8 Sep	GL	Weltklasse, Zürich, SUI	30 Aug	DL
11 Sep	WC	ISTAF, Berlin, GER	2 Sep	WC
13 Sep	WC	Zagreb, CRO	4 Sep	WC
13 Sep	EAP	Palio Citta della Quercia, Rovereto, ITA	4 Sep	EAP
16 Sep	DL	Van Damme Memorial, Brussels, BEL	7 Sep	DL
18 Sep	WC	Rieti, ITA	9 Sep	WC

INDOORS

2011 date		Meeting	2012 date	
IAAF and EAA – respective indoor permit meetings; Visa series in USA.				
28 Jan	IAAF	Millrose Games 2011/US Open 2012, New York, USA	28 Jan	IAAF
29 Jan		Aviva International match, Glasgow, GBR	28 Jan	EAA
5 Feb	IAAF	Sparkassen Cup, Stuttgart, GER	––	
5/6 Feb		International Combined Events, Tallinn, EST	3/4 Feb	EAA
5 Feb	Visa	New Balance Indoor GP, Boston (Roxbury), USA	4 Feb	Visa
6 Feb	IAAF	Russian Winter, Moscow, RUS	5 Feb	IAAF
12 Feb	EAA	Samsunggalan, Göteborg, SWE	––	
16 Feb	EAA	Pedro's Cup, Bydgoszcz, POL	8 Feb	EAA
9 Feb		Banská Bystrica, CZE	8 Feb	EAA
11 Feb	EAA	International PSD Bank, Düsseldorf, GER	10 Feb	EAA
13 Feb	IAAF	BW-Bank Meeting, Karlsruhe, GER	12 Feb	IAAF
6 Feb	IAAF	Meeting du Pas de Calais, Liévin, FRA	14 Feb	IAAF
19 Feb	IAAF	Aviva Indoor Grand Prix, Birmingham, GBR	18 Feb	IAAF
22 Feb	IAAF	XL-Galan, Stockholm, SWE	23 Feb	IAAF
11/12 Feb	Visa	Tyson Invitational, Fayetteville, USSR	10-11 Feb	Visa
6 Mar	EAA	Zepter Pole Vault Stars, Donetsk, UKR	12 Feb	EAA

IAAF WORLD COMBINED EVENTS CHALLENGE 2011 & 2012

7/8 May	Multistars, Desenzano del Garda, ITA	5/6 May
28/29 May	Hypo-Mehrkampf Meeting, Götzis, AUT	26/27 May
15/16 Jun	TNT-Fortuna Meeting, Kladno, CZE	9/10 Jun
16/17 Jul	Erdgas DLV Mehrkampf, Ratingen, GER	14/15 Jun
17/18 Sep	Decastars, Talence, FRA	15/16 Sep

IAAF WORLD RACE WALKING CHALLENGE 2011 & 2012

5 Mar	Chihuahua MEX	3 Mar
22 Apr	Taicang, CHN	30 Mar
9 Apr	Rio Maior, POR	15 Apr
17 Sep*	Gran Premio Cantones de La Coruña, ESP	9 Jun
1 May	Coppa Città di Sesto San Giovanni, ITA	17 Jun
	Challenge Final: Edros CHN (2012)	14 Sep

* Race Walking Challenge Final

AFRICA 2012 Golden Meetings

(with 2011 dates of these meetings first)

Brazzaville CGO 22 May/10 Jun, Abuja NGR 2 July/?, Tanger MAR 17/7 Jul

ASIAN AA Grands Prix

2011: Jiaxing 22 May, Kunchan 26 May, Wujiang 29 May (all CHN)
2012: Bangkok 6 May, Kanchanaburi 9 May, Nokomratsima 13 May (all THA)

EUROPEAN AA CLASSIC MEETINGS 2012

(with 2011 dates of these meetings first)

Dessau GER 1 Jun/25 May, Huelva ESP 4/7 Jun, Istanbul TUR (Cezmi Or Memorial) 11/9 Jun, Velenje SLO 28/14 Jun, Luzern SUI 26/17 Jul, Linz AUT (Gugl) –/20 Aug, Dubnica nad Váhom SVK (Athletic Bridge) 15 Sep/26 Aug, Terra Sarda, Ploaghe, ITA -/1 Sep, Padua ITA 17 Jul/2 Sep, Milan ITA (Notturna) 18/5 Sep.
2011 only: Kalamáta GRE 4 Jun, Kassel GER /8 Jun, Haniá (Venizelia) GRE 11 Jun, Sofia (Pavel Pavlov) 25 Jun, Biberach GER 29 Jun, Cuxhaven GER 10 Aug.

NORTH AMERICA Premium Meetings 2012

(with 2011 dates of these meetings first)

Baie Mahault, Guadeloupe 7/1 May, Fort-de-France, Martinique -/8 May, Vancouver CAN 1 July/10 Jun, Victoria CAN 3 Jul/13 Jun, Edmonton CAN 29 /15 Jun, Moncton CAN 8/5 Jul, Halifax CAN 6/8 July, Toronto 13/11 Jul

SOUTH AMERICA APM/SGP 2012
(with 2011 dates of these meetings first)
Mar del Plata ARG 30/28 Apr, Uberlândia BRA 6/18 May, São Paulo BRA 22/9 May, Fortaleza BRA 11/16 May, Belém BRA 15/20 May

MAJOR INTERNATIONAL EVENTS 2012–2018

2012

IAAF World Indoor Championships – Istanbul, Turkey (9-11 March)
European Cup Winter Throwing – Bar, Montenegro (17-18 March)
IAAF World Race Walking Cup – Saransk, Russia (12-13 May)
European Cup 10,000m – Bilbao, Spain (3 June)
Asian Junior Championships – Colombo, Sri Lanka (9-12 June)
European Championships – Helsinki, Finland (27 Jun- 1 July)
NACAC U23 Championships – Mexico City, Mexico
IAAF World Junior Championships – Barcelona, Spain (10-15 July)
African Championships – Porto Novo, Benin (27 Jul – 1 Aug)
Olympic Games – London, GBR (3-12 Aug)
IAAF World Half Marathon Championships – Kavarna, Bulgaria (6 Oct)
European Cross Country Championships – Szentendre, Hungary (9 Dec)

2013

European Indoor Championships – Göteborg, Sweden (1-3 March)
European Cup Winter Throwing – (9-10 March)
IAAF World Cross Country Championships – Bydgoszcz, Poland (24 March)
European Cup of Race Walking – Dudince, Slovakia (19 May)
Asian Championships – New Delhi, India (tbc, June)
European Team Championships – Gateshead, GBR (22-23 June)
Mediterranean Games – Mersin, Turkey (26-29 June)
European Cup Combined Events (29-30 June)
IAAF World Youth Championships – Donetsk, Ukraine (10-14 July)
World University Games – Kazan, Russia (6-17 Jul)
European U23 Championships – Tampere, Finland (11-14 July)
European Youth Games – Utrecht, Netherlands (14-19 July)
European Junior Championships – Rieti, Italy (18-21 July)
Pan-American Junior Championships – Lima, Peru (2-4 Aug)
IAAF World Championships – Moscow, Russia (10-18 Aug)
Francophone Games Nice, France (6-15 Sep)
European Cross Country Championships – Belgrade, Serbia (8 Dec)

2014

IAAF World Indoor Championships – Sopot, Poland (7-9 March)
IAAF World Half Marathon Championships – Copenhagen, Denmark (29 Mar)
IAAF World Race Walking Cup – Tiacang, China (5-6 May)
IAAF World Junior Championships – Eugene, USA (22-27 July)
Commonwealth Games – Glasgow, GBR (23 Jul – 3 Aug)
European Championships – Zürich, Switzerland (12-17 Aug)
Youth Olympic Games – Nanjing, China (16-28 August)
IAAF Continental Cup – Marrakech, Morocco (13-14 Sep)
Asian Games – Incheon, Korea (19 Sep – 4 Oct)

2015

European Indoor Championships – (6-8 Mar)
IAAF World Cross Country Championships
IAAF World Youth Championships
Pan-American Games – Toronto, CAN (10-26 July)
All-Africa Games – Brazzaville, Congo
IAAF World Championships – Beijing, China (22-30 July)

WORLD INDOOR CHAMPIONSHIPS 2012

At Istanbul, Turkey 9-11 March

WORLD RECORDS IN the combined events headed performances at the 14th IAAF World Indoor Championships. The women's pentathlon provided the best depth of excellence of any event as defending champion Jessica Ennis broke her championships record and yet was well beaten by the resurgent Nataliya Dobrynska, who added 22 points to the world record with her 5013 score. Out on his own with superb confirmation of his all-round talent was Ashton Eaton, who added 77 points to his own world heptathlon record.

Yelena Isinbayeva was back at her best to take her fourth World Indoor title. Bernard Lagat won the 3000m for the third time and Veronica Campbell-Brown at 60m and Brittney Reese at long jump retained their titles with two athletes regaining titles, Justin Gatlin, who won the 60m in 2004, and Valerie Adams, shot winner in 2008.

The 7.23 long jump by Reese headed the list of world–leading marks apart from those world records, while others by women were VCB's 7.01, 7.73 by Sally Pearson in winning the 60m hurdles by a massive margin, 1:58.83 by Pamela Jelimo at 800m, and the British 4x400m team's 3:28.76. For men there were 45.11 by Nery Brenes at 400m, 5.95 by Renaud Lavillenie in the pole vault, 17.70 by Will Claye in the triple jump, 22.00 by Ryan Whiting in the shot, and a relatively modest 8.24 long jump by Mauro da Silva (but from behind the board). There were also world low altitude bests for 2012 by Justin Gatlin 6.46 and Sanya Richards-Ross, 400m 50.79.

Mohamed Aman (800m), became the youngest ever world indoor champion at 18 years 60 days, and 39 year-old Yamilé Aldama produced a marvellous 14.82 to win the women's triple jump as well as achieving the unique feat of winning major championship medals for three different nations.

Unfortunately there were severe problems with the starting of races. Two major names were disqualified on the first day for false starts – Lerone Clarke at 60m and Kirsti Castlin at 60m hurdles – and many others were severely affected. Officials stressed that the starting equipment was functioning correctly, but the problem seems to have been with the sound systems. Athletes said that in some races they could not hear the starter clearly and not only did 400m runners, without individual lane speakers, far out in lanes 5 and 6 have particular problems but many felt that they had heard recall bangs.

MEN

60 Metres (10)

1. Justin Gatlin USA	6.46
2. Nesta Carter JAM	6.54
3. Dwain Chambers GBR	6.60
4. Trell Kimmons USA	6.60
5. Marc Burns TRI	6.62
6. Emmanuel Biron FRA	6.63
7. Justyn Warner CAN	6.65
8. Aziz Ouhadi MAR	6.72

400 Metres (10)

1. Nery Brenes CRC	45.11*
2. Demetrius Pinder BAH	45.34
3. Chris Brown BAH	45.90
4. Tabarie Henry ISV	45.96
5. Pavel Maslák CZE	46.19
6. Kirani James GRN	46.21

800 Metres (11)

1. Mohamed Aman ETH-J	1:48.36
2. Jakub Holusa CZE	1:48.62
3. Andrew Osagie GBR	1:48.92
4. Adam Kszczot POL	1:49.16
5. Jan Van Den Broeck BEL	1:50.83
6. Michael Rutt USA	1:51.47

1500 Metres (10)

1. Abdelaati Iguider MAR	3:45.21
2. Ilham Tanui Özbilen TUR	3:45.35
3. Mekonnen Gebremedhin ETH	3:45.90
4. Aman Wote ETH	3:47.02
5. Ayanleh Souleiman DJI	3:47.35
6. Silas Kiplagat KEN	3:47.42
7. Matt Centrowitz USA	3:47.42
8. Francisco J Abad ESP	3:48.14
9. Amine Laâlou MAR	3:49.14

3000 Metres (11)

1. Bernard Lagat USA	7:41.44
2. Augustine Choge KEN	7:41.77
3. Edwin Soi KEN	7:41.78
4. Mo Farah GBR	7:41.79
5. Dejen Gebremeskel ETH	7:42.60
6. Lopez Lomong USA	7:44.16
7. Moses Kipsiro UGA	7:44.59
8. Arne Gabius GER	7:45.01
9. Yenew Alamirew ETH	7:45.15
10. Yoann Kowal FRA	7:47.81
11. Craig Mottram AUS	7:48.23
12. Elroy Gelant RSA	7:48.64

60 Metres Hurdles (11)

1. Aries Merritt USA	7.44
2. Liu Xiang CHN	7.49
3. Pascal Martinot-Lagarde FRA	7.53
4. Andrew Pozzi GBR	7.58
5. Konstantin Shabanov RUS	7.60
6. Emanuele Abate ITA	7.63
7. Lehann Fourie RSA	7.69
8. Artur Noga POL	7.74

High Jump (11)

1. Dimítrios Hondrokoúkis GRE	2.33
2. Andrey Silnov RUS	2.33
3. Ivan Ukhov RUS	2.31
4= Konstadínos Baniótis GRE	2.31
4= Zhang Guowei CHN	2.31
6= Jesse Williams USA	2.31
6= Robbie Grabarz GBR	2.31
8. Trevor Barry BAH	2.31
9= Mutaz Essa Barshim QAT	2.28
9= Raúl Spank GER	2.28

Póle Vault (10)

1. Renaud Lavillenie FRA	5.95
2. Björn Otto GER	5.80
3. Brad Walker USA	5.80
4. Malte Mohr GER	5.75
5= Lázaro Borges CUB	5.70
5= Steve Lewis GBR	5.70
7. Konstadínos Filippídis GRE	5.70
8. Romain Mesnil FRA	5.50
9. Dmitriy Starodubtsev RUS	5.50

Long Jump (10)

1. Mauro da Silva BRA	8.23
2. Henry Frayne AUS	8.23
3. Aleksandr Menkov RUS	8.22

4. Will Claye USA — 8.04
5. Ndiss Kaba Badji SEN — 7.97
6. Loúis Tsátoumas GRE — 7.88
7. Ignisious Gaisah GHA — 7.86
8. Luis Felipe Méliz ESP — 7.50

Triple Jump (11)
1. Will Claye USA — 17.70
2. Christian Taylor USA — 17.63
3. Lyukman Adams RUS — 17.36
4. Fabrizio Donato ITA — 17.28
5. Daniele Greco ITA — 17.28
6. Benjamin Compaoré FRA — 17.05
7. Alexis Copello CUB — 16.92
8. Dong Bin CHN — 16.75

Shot (9)
1. Ryan Whiting USA — 22.00
2. David Storl GER — 21.88
3. Tomasz Majewski POL — 21.72
4. Reese Hoffa USA — 21.55
5. Maksim Sidorov RUS — 20.78
6. Germán Lauro ARG — 20.38
7. Rutger Smith NED — 20.30
8. Ivan Yushkov RUS — 20.10

Heptathlon (9/10)
1. Ashton Eaton USA — 6645*
2. Oleksiy Kasyanov UKR — 6071
3. Artem Lukyanenko RUS — 5969
4. Ilya Shkurenyov RUS — 5898
5. Adam Sebastian Helcelet CZE — 5878
6. Andrey Kravchenko BLR — 5746
7. Yordani García CUB — 5704
dnf. Mikk Pahapill EST — (3052)

4 x 400 Metres Relay (11)
1. USA 3:03.94 (F Wright, C Smith, Manteo Mitchell, G Roberts);
2. GBR 3:04.72 (C Williams, N Levine, M Bingham, R Buck);
3. TRI 3:06.85 (L Gordon, R Quow, J Richards, J Solomon);
4. RUS 3:07.35
5. ESP 3:10.01
6. POL 3:11.86

WOMEN

60 Metres (11)
1. V. Campbell-Brown JAM — 7.01
2. Murielle Ahouré CIV — 7.04
3. Tianna Madison USA — 7.09
4. Barbara Pierre USA — 7.14
5. Chandra Sturrup BAH — 7.19
6. Gloria Asumnu NGR — 7.22
7. Aleen Bailey JAM — 7.24
8. Ivet Lalova BUL — 7.27

400 Metres (10)
1. Sanya Richards-Ross USA — 50.79
2. Aleksandra Fedoriva RUS — 51.76
3. Natasha Hastings USA — 51.82
4. Vanya Stambolova BUL — 51.99
5. Shana Cox GBR — 52.13
6. Denisa Rosolová CZE — 52.48

800 Metres (11)
1. Pamela Jelimo KEN — 1:58.83
2. Natalia Lupu UKR — 1:59.67

3. Erica Moore USA — 1:59.97
4. Fantu Magiso ETH — 2:00.30
5. Yelena Kofanova RUS — 2:00.67
6. Yuliya Rusanova RUS — 2:01.87

1500 Metres (10)
1. Genzebe Dibaba ETH — 4:05.78
2. M. Alaoui Selsouli MAR — 4:07.78
3. Asli Cakir TUR — 4:08.74
4. Natalya Koroyvo BLR — 4:10.12
5. Hind Dehiba FRA — 4:10.30
6. Tizita Bogale ETH-J — 4:10.98
7. Yelena Arzhakova RUS — 4:13.04
8. Angelika Cichocka POL — 4:14.57
9. Isabel Macias ESP — 4:22.40

3000 Metres (11)
1. Hellen Obiri KEN — 8:37.16
2. Meseret Defar ETH — 8:38.26
3. Gelete Burka ETH — 8:40.18
4. Sylvia Kibet KEN — 8:40.50
5. Shitaye Eshete BRN — 8:51.88
6. Lidia Chojecka POL — 8:56.86
7. Helen Clitheroe GBR — 8:59.04
8. Sara Hall USA — 8:59.95
9. Nataliya Tobias UKR — 9:00.78
10. Svitlana Shmidt UKR — 9:03.99
11. Jackie Areson USA — 9:12.50
12. Alia S Mohammed UAE — 9:15.74

60 Metres Hurdles (10)
1. Sally Pearson AUS — 7.73
2. Tiffany Porter GBR — 7.94
3. Alina Talay BLR — 7.97
4. Sonata Tamosaityte LTU — 8.03
5. Eline Berings BEL — 8.08
6. Nikkita Holder CAN — 8.09
7. Beate Schrott AUT — 8.12
8. Seun Adigun NGR — 8.33

High Jump (10)
1. Chaunté Lowe USA — 1.98
2= Anna Chicherova RUS — 1.95
2= Ebba Jungmark SWE — 1.95
2= Antonietta Di Martino ITA — 1.95
5. Tia Hellebaut BEL — 1.95
6. Ruth Beitia ESP — 1.95
7. Esthera Petre ROU — 1.92
8. Svetlana Radzivil UZB — 1.92

Pole Vault (11)
1. Yelena Isinbayeva RUS — 4.80
2. Vanessa Boslak FRA — 4.70
3. Holly Bleasdale GBR — 4.70
4. Silke Spiegelburg GER — 4.65
5. Lacy Janson USA — 4.65
6. Jirína Ptácniková CZE — 4.55
7. Yarisley Silva CUB — 4.55
8. Nicole Büchler SUI — 4.55
9. Alana Boyd AUS — 4.55

Long Jump (11)
1. Brittney Reese USA — 7.23
2. Janay DeLoach USA — 6.98
3. Shara Proctor GBR — 6.89
4. Darya Klishina RUS — 6.85
5. An. Mironchik-Ivanova BLR — 6.64
6. Veronika Shutkova BLR — 6.63
7. Viorica Tigau ROU — 6.34
8. Bianca Stuart BAH — 4.71

Triple Jump (10)
1. Yamilé Aldama GBR — 14.82
2. Olga Rypakova KAZ — 14.63
3. Mabel Gay CUB — 14.29
4. Yargeris Savigne CUB — 14.28
5. Kimberly Williams JAM — 14.27
6. Anna Krylova RUS — 14.21
7. Li Yanmei CHN — 14.02
8. Dana Veldáková SVK — 13.97

Shot (11)
1. Valerie Adams NZL — 20.54
2. Nadezhda Ostapchuk BLR — 20.42
3. Michelle Carter USA — 19.58
4. J Camarena-Williams USA — 19.44
5. Nadine Kleinert GER — 19.29
6. Liu Xiangrong CHN — 18.63
7. Yevgeniya Kolodko RUS — 18.57
8. Irina Tarasova RUS — 18.54

Pentathlon (9)
1. Nataliya Dobrynska UKR — 5013*
2. Jessica Ennis GBR — 4965
3. Austra Skujyté LTU — 4802
4. Karolina Tyminska POL — 4725
5. Tatyana Chernova RUS — 4725
6. Yekaterina Bolshova RUS — 4639
7. Anna Melnychenko UKR — 4623
8. Yana Maksimova BLR — 4601

4 x 400 Metres Relay (11)
1. GBR 3:28.76 (S Cox, N Sanders, C Ohuruogu, P Shakes-Drayton)
2. USA 3:28.79 (L Cole, N Hastings, J Hayes, S Richards-Ross)
3. RUS 3:29.55 (Y Gushchina, K Ustalova, M Karnauschenko, A Fedoriva)
4. ROU 3:33.41
5. BLR 3:33.73
dq (4) UKR (3:30.62)
* = championships record

Leading Nations – Medals & Points

Nation	G	S	B	Pts
USA	10	3	5	171.5
RUS	1	3	5	104
GBR	2	3	4	83
ETH	2	1	2	52
KEN	2	1	1	37
BLR	-	1	1	33
FRA	1	1	1	32
GER	-	2	-	29
UKR	1	2	-	24
POL	-	-	1	24
JAM	1	1	-	21
CZE	-	1	-	21
CUB	-	-	1	20.5

14 nations won gold, 28 medals and 48 placed athletes in top 8.
Prize money: 1st $40,000, 2nd $20,000, 3rd $10,000, 4th $9000 ($8000 for relays), 5th $6000 and 6th $4000. Plus $50,000 for a world record.

OLYMPIC GAMES 2012

THE FIRST OLYMPIC GAMES of the modern era were staged in Athens, Greece from the 6th to 15th April 1896. Those in London 2012, the Games of the XXX Olympiad, will be the 27th to be staged, including the intercalated Games of 1906.

Just 59 athletes from ten nations contested the athletics events in 1896. In 2000 there was a record participation for a summer Games, at all sports, with 10,651 competitors from 200 nations including a record 2134 at athletics from 193 nations in Sydney. 2057 competitors (1083 men and 974 women) from 200 nations contested the athletics events at the 2008 Games in Beijing.

Olympic Games Records after 2008

Men

100m	9.69	Usain Bolt JAM 2008
200m	19.30	Usain Bolt JAM 2008
400m	43.49	Michael Johnson USA 1996
800m	1:42.58	Vebjørn Rodal NOR 1996
1500m	3:32.07	Noah Ngeny KEN 2000
5000m	12:57.82	Kenenisa Bekele ETH 2008
10,000m	27:01.17	Kenenisa Bekele ETH 2008
Mar	2:09:21	Carlos Lopes POR 1984
3000mSt	8:05.51	Julius Kariuki KEN 1988
110mh	12.91	Liu Xiang CHN 2004
400mh	46.78	Kevin Young USA 1992
HJ	2.39	Charles Austin USA 1996
PV	5.96	Steve Hooker AUS 2008
LJ	8.90A	Bob Beamon USA 1968
TJ	18.17w	Mike Conley USA 1992
	18.09	Kenny Harrison USA 1996
SP	22.47	Ulf Timmermann GDR 1988
DT	69.89	Virgilijus Alekna LTU 2004
HT	84.80	Sergey Litvinov URS 1988
JT	90.57	Andreas Thorkildsen NOR 2008
old	94.58	Miklós Németh HUN 1976
Dec	8893	Román Šebrle CZE 2004
4x100m	37.10	Jamaica 2008
4x400m	2:55.39	USA 2008
20kmW	1:18:59	Robert Korzeniowski POL 2000
50kmW	3:37:09	Alex Schwazer ITA 2008

Women

100m	10.62	Florence Griffith-Joyner USA 1988
	10.54w	Florence Griffith-Joyner USA 1988
200m	21.34	Florence Griffith-Joyner USA 1988
400m	48.25	Marie-José Pérec FRA 1996
800m	1:53.43	Nadezhda Olizarenko URS 1980
1500m	3:53.96	Paula Ivan ROM 1988
3000m	8:26.53	Tatyana Samolenko URS 1988
5000m	14:40.79	Gabriela Szabo ROM 2000
10,000m	29:54.66	Tirunesh Dibaba ETH 2008
Mar	2:23:14	Naoko Takahashi JPN 2000
3000mSt	8:58.81	Gulnara Galkina RUS 2008
100mh	12.37	Joanna Hayes USA 2004
400mh	52.64	Melaine Walker JAM 2008
HJ	2.06	Yelena Slesarenko RUS 2004
PV	5.05	Yelena Isinbayeva RUS 2008
LJ	7.40	Jackie Joyner-Kersee USA 1988
TJ	15.39	Françoise Mbango CMR 2008
SP	22.41	Ilona Slupianek GDR 1980
DT	72.30	Martina Hellmann GDR 1988
HT	76.34	Oksana Menkova BLR 2008
JT	71.53	Osleidys Menéndez CUB 2004
old	74.68	Petra Felke GDR 1988
Hep	7291	Jackie Joyner-Kersee USA 1988
4x100m	41.60	GDR 1980
4x400m	3:15.17	USSR 1988
20kmW	1:26:31	Olga Kaniskina RUS 2008

A at high altitude, Mexico City 2240m

Most gold medals – all events

Men

10 Raymond Ewry USA StHJ and StLJ 1900-04-06-08, StTJ 1900-04

9 Paavo Nurmi FIN 1500m 1924, 5000m 1924, 10000m 1920-28, 3000mSt 1924, CC 1920-24, CC team 1920-24

9 Carl Lewis USA 100m, 200m, LJ & 4x100mR 1984; 100m, LJ 1988; LJ, 4x100mR 1992; LJ 1996

5 Martin Sheridan USA DT 1904-06-08, SP 1906, DT Greek style 1908

5 Ville Ritola FIN 10000m, 3000mSt, CC team & 3000m team 1924, 5000m 1928

5 Michael Johnson USA 200m 1996, 400m 1996-2000, 4x400m 1992-2000

4 thirteen men

Women

4 Fanny Blankers-Koen NED 100m, 200m, 80mh & 4x100mR 1948

4 Betty Cuthbert AUS 100m, 200m, 4x100mR 1956, 400m 1964

4 Bärbel Eckert/Wöckel GDR 200m & 4x100mR 1976-80

4 Evelyn Ashford USA 100m 1984, 4x100mR 1984-88-92

Most medals – all events

G gold, S silver, B bronze

Men

12 Paavo Nurmi FIN 9G as above; 3S 5000m 1920-28, 3000mSt 1928

10 Raymond Ewry USA 10G as above

10 Carl Lewis USA 9G as above; 1S 200m 1988

9 Martin Sheridan USA 5G as above; 3S StHJ, StLJ & Stone 1906; 1B StLJ 1908

8 Ville Ritola FIN 5G as above; 3S 5000m & CC 1924, 10000m 1928

7 Eric Lemming SWE 4G JT 1906-08-12 freestyle 1908, 3B SP, Pen, Tug of War 1906

Women

9 Merlene Ottey JAM 3S 100m, 200m 1996; 4x100mR 2000; 6B 4x100mR 1980, 1996; 100m 1984, 2000; 200m 1984-92

7 Shirley Strickland/de la Hunty AUS 3G 80mh 1952-56, 4x100mR 1956; 1S 4x100mR 1948; 3B 100m 1948-52, 80mh 1948 (later evidence showed that she should also have been awarded the 1948 200m bronze)

7 Irena Kirszenstein/Szewinska POL 3G 200m 1968, 400m 1976, 4x100mR 1964; 2S 200m & LJ 1964, 2B 100m 1968, 200m 1972

Most gold medals at one Games: Men: 5 Paavo Nurmi FIN 1924; Women: 4 Fanny Blankers-Koen NED *as above*

<table>
<tr><td colspan="5">Medal table of leading nations
1896–2008 including 1906 Games</td></tr>
<tr><td>Nation</td><td>Gold</td><td>Silver</td><td>Bronze</td><td>Total Medals</td></tr>
<tr><td>USA</td><td>322</td><td>42</td><td>195</td><td>759</td></tr>
<tr><td>USSR/CIS</td><td>71</td><td>66</td><td>77</td><td>214</td></tr>
<tr><td>United Kingdom</td><td>52</td><td>83</td><td>62</td><td>197</td></tr>
<tr><td>Germany *</td><td>31</td><td>53</td><td>60</td><td>144</td></tr>
<tr><td>Finland</td><td>49</td><td>35</td><td>31</td><td>115</td></tr>
<tr><td>GDR</td><td>38</td><td>36</td><td>35</td><td>109</td></tr>
<tr><td>Sweden</td><td>1</td><td>25</td><td>46</td><td>92</td></tr>
<tr><td>Australia</td><td>19</td><td>24</td><td>27</td><td>70</td></tr>
<tr><td>Kenya</td><td>22</td><td>27</td><td>19</td><td>68</td></tr>
<tr><td>Russia</td><td>18</td><td>22</td><td>21</td><td>61</td></tr>
<tr><td>France</td><td>13</td><td>22</td><td>25</td><td>60</td></tr>
<tr><td>Italy</td><td>19</td><td>15</td><td>25</td><td>59</td></tr>
<tr><td>Canada</td><td>14</td><td>15</td><td>25</td><td>54</td></tr>
<tr><td>Jamaica</td><td>13</td><td>26</td><td>15</td><td>54</td></tr>
<tr><td>Poland</td><td>22</td><td>17</td><td>13</td><td>52</td></tr>
<tr><td>Hungary</td><td>10</td><td>15</td><td>18</td><td>43</td></tr>
<tr><td>Ethiopia</td><td>18</td><td>6</td><td>14</td><td>38</td></tr>
<tr><td>Cuba</td><td>10</td><td>13</td><td>14</td><td>37</td></tr>
<tr><td>Romania</td><td>11</td><td>14</td><td>10</td><td>35</td></tr>
<tr><td>Greece</td><td>7</td><td>14</td><td>14</td><td>35</td></tr>
<tr><td>Czechoslovakia</td><td>11</td><td>8</td><td>5</td><td>24</td></tr>
<tr><td>South Africa</td><td>6</td><td>11</td><td>6</td><td>23</td></tr>
<tr><td>Japan</td><td>7</td><td>7</td><td>8</td><td>22</td></tr>
<tr><td>Norway</td><td>7</td><td>5</td><td>8</td><td>20</td></tr>
<tr><td>New Zealand</td><td>9</td><td>2</td><td>8</td><td>19</td></tr>
<tr><td>Belarus</td><td>4</td><td>6</td><td>9</td><td>19</td></tr>
<tr><td>Morocco</td><td>6</td><td>5</td><td>7</td><td>18</td></tr>
<tr><td>Bulgaria</td><td>1</td><td>-</td><td>1</td><td>18</td></tr>
<tr><td>Netherlands</td><td>6</td><td>3</td><td>6</td><td>15</td></tr>
<tr><td>China</td><td>5</td><td>3</td><td>7</td><td>15</td></tr>
<tr><td>Ukraine</td><td>3</td><td>2</td><td>10</td><td>15</td></tr>
<tr><td>Brazil</td><td>4</td><td>3</td><td>7</td><td>14</td></tr>
<tr><td>Nigeria</td><td>2</td><td>3</td><td>8</td><td>13</td></tr>
<tr><td>Belgium</td><td>3</td><td>7</td><td>2</td><td>12</td></tr>
<tr><td>Spain</td><td>2</td><td>4</td><td>5</td><td>11</td></tr>
<tr><td>Portugal</td><td>4</td><td>2</td><td>4</td><td>10</td></tr>
<tr><td>Mexico</td><td>3</td><td>4</td><td>2</td><td>10</td></tr>
<tr><td>Trinidad & Tobago</td><td>1</td><td>4</td><td>5</td><td>10</td></tr>
</table>

In all 89 nations have won medals at track and field events.

**Germany 1896–1952 and from 1992, Federal Republic of Germany 1956–88. Medals won by the combined German teams of 1956, 1960 and 1964 have been allocated to FRG or GDR according to the athlete's origin.*

Jamaica also one bronze for British West Indies Federation

Most medals at one Games: Men: 6 – 4 gold, 2 silver – Ville Ritola FIN 1924; Women: 4 – 4 gold Fanny Blankers-Koen NED *as above*, 4 – 3 gold, 1 silver – Florence Griffith-Joyner USA 1988.

Note 5 – 3 gold, 2 bronze – Marion Jones 2000 lost through subsequent drugs disqualifcation.

Most Games contested

7 Merlene Ottey JAM/SLO 1980-2004 at women's 100m/200m/4x100m

6 Lia Manoliu ROM 1952-72 at women's discus

6 Tessa Sanderson GBR 1976-96 at women's javelin

6 Maria Mutola MOZ 1988-2008 at women's 800m

6 João N'Tyamba ANG 1988-2008 at 800m 1988-1992, 1500m 1992-1996, Mar 2000-2004-2008

Most finals or first eight at the same event

6 Lia Manoliu ROM W DT 1952-72: 6-9-3-3-1-9

5 Vladimir Golubnichiy URS 20kmW 1960-76: 1-3-1-2-7

5 Jan Zelezny CZE JT 1988-2004: 2-1-1-1-9

5 Maria Mutola MOZ W 800m: 1992-2008 5-3-1-4-5

Olympic Games Beijing 2008 – Medallists

100 Metres (0.0)
1. Usain Bolt JAM		WR 9.69
2. Richard Thompson TRI		9.89
3. Walter Dix USA		9.91

200 Metres (-0.9)
1. Usain Bolt JAM		WR 19.30
2. Shawn Crawford USA		19.96
3. Walter Dix USA		19.98

400 Metres
1. LaShawn Merritt USA	43.75
2. Jeremy Wariner USA	44.74
3. David Neville USA	44.80

800 Metres
1. Wilfred Bungei KEN	1:44.65
2. Ismail Ahmed Ismail SUD	1:44.70
3. Alfred Kirwa Yego KEN	1:44.82

1500 Metres
1. Asbel Kiprop KEN	3:33.11
2. Nick Willis NZL	3:34.16
3. Mehdi Baala FRA	3:34.21

5000 Metres
1. Kenenisa Bekele ETH	12:57.82
2. Eliud Kipchoge KEN	13:02.80
3. Edwin Soi KEN	13:06.22

10,000 Metres
1. Kenenisa Bekele ETH	27:01.17
2. Sileshi Sihine ETH	27:02.77
3. Micah Kogo KEN	27:04.11

Marathon
1. Samuel Wanjiru KEN	2:06:32
2. Jaoaud Gharib MAR	2:07:16
3. Tsegay Kebede ETH	2:10:00

3000 Metres Steeplechase
1. Brimin Kipruto KEN	8:10.34
2. Mahiedine Mekhissi-Benabbad FRA	8:10.49
3. Richard Matelong KEN	8:11.01

110 Metres Hurdles (+0.1)
1. Dayron Robles CUB	12.93

2. David Payne USA	13.17
3. David Oliver USA	13.18

400 Metres Hurdles

1. Angelo Taylor USA	47.25
2. Kerron Clement USA	47.98
3. Bershawn Jackson USA	48.06

High Jump

1. Andrey Silnov RUS	2.36
2. Germaine Mason GBR	2.34
3. Yaroslav Rybakov RUS	2.34

Pole Vault

1. Steve Hooker AUS	5.96
2. Yevgeniy Lukyanenko RUS	5.85
3. Denys Yurchenko UKR	5.70

Long Jump

1. Irving Saladino PAN	8.34/-0.3
2. Khotso Mokoena RSA	8.24/0.0
3. Ibrahim Camejo CUB	8.20/0.2

Triple Jump

1. Nelson Évora POR	17.67/1.1
2. Phillips Idowu GBR	17.62/0.9
3. Leevan Sands BAH	17.59/0.9

Shot

1. Tomasz Majewski POL	21.51
2. Christian Cantwell USA	21.09
3. Andrey Mikhnevich BLR	21.05

Discus

1. Gerd Kanter EST	68.82
2. Piotr Malachowski POL	67.82
3. Virgilijus Alekna LTU	67.79

Hammer

1. Primoz Kozmus SLO	82.02
2. Vadim Devyatovskiy BLR	81.61
3. Ivan Tikhon BLR	81.51

Javelin

1. Andreas Thorkildsen NOR	90.57
2. Ainars Kovals LAT	86.64
3. Tero Pitkämäki FIN	86.16

Decathlon

1. Bryan Clay USA	8791
2. Andrey Kravchenko BLR	8551
3. Leonel Suárez CUB	8527

4 x 100 Metres Relay

1. JAM	WR 37.10
2. TRI	38.06
3. JPN	38.15

4 x 400 Metres Relay

1. USA	2:55.39
2. BAH	2:58.03
3. RUS	2:58.06

20 Kilometres Walk

1. Valeriy Borchin RUS	1:19:01
2. Jefferson Pérez ECU	1:19:15
3. Jared Tallent AUS	1:19:42

50 Kilometres Walk

1. Alex Schwazer ITA	3:37:09
2. Jared Tallent AUS	3:39:27
3. Denis Nizhegorodov RUS	3:40:14

Women

100 Metres (0.0)

1. Shelly-Ann Fraser JAM	10.78
2= Kerron Stewart JAM	10.98
2= Sherone Simpson JAM	10.98

200 Metres (+0.6)

1. Veronica Campbell-Brown JAM	21.74
2. Allyson Felix USA	21.93
3. Kerron Stewart JAM	22.00

400 Metres

1. Christine Ohuruogu GBR	49.62
2. Shericka Williams JAM	49.69
3. Sanya Richards USA	49.93

800 Metres

1. Pamela Jelimo KEN	1:54.87
2. Janeth Jepkosgei KEN	1:56.07
3. Hasna Benhassi MAR	1:56.73

1500 Metres

1. Nancy Chebet Lagat KEN	4:00.23
2. Iryna Lishchynska UKR	4:01.63
3. Nataliya Tobias UKR	4:01.78

5000 Metres

1. Tirunesh Dibaba ETH	15:41.40
2. Elvan Abeylegesse TUR	15:42.74
3. Meseret Defar ETH	15:44.12

10,000 Metres

1. Tirunesh Dibaba ETH	29:54.66
2. Elvan Abeylegesse TUR	29:56.34
3. Shalane Flanagan USA	30:22.22

Marathon

1. Constantina Dita ROU	2:26:44
2. Catherine Ndereba KEN	2:27:06
3. Zhou Chunxiu CHN	2:27:07

3000 Metres Steeplechase

1. Gulnara Galkina RUS	WR 8:58.81
2. Eunice Jepkorir KEN	9:07.41
3. Yekaterina Volkova RUS	9:07.64

100 Metres Hurdles (+0.1)

1. Dawn Harper USA	12.54
2. Sally McLellan AUS	12.64
3. Priscilla Lopes-Schliep CAN	12.64

400 Metres Hurdles

1. Melaine Walker JAM	52.64
2. Sheena Tosta USA	53.70
3. Tasha Danvers GBR	53.84

High Jump

1. Tia Hellebaut BEL	2.05
2. Blanka Vlasic CRO	2.05
3. Anna Chicherova RUS	2.03

Pole Vault

1. Yelena Isinbayeva RUS	WR 5.05
2. Jenn Stuczynski USA	4.80
3. Svetlana Feofanova RUS	4.75

Long Jump

1. Maurren Maggi BRA	7.04/0.2
2. Tatyana Lebedeva RUS	7.03/0.4
3. Blessing Okagbare NGR	6.91/0.1

Triple Jump

1. Françoise Mbango CMR	15.39/0.5
2. Tatyana Lebedeva RUS	15.32/0.5
3. Hrysopiyí Devetzí GRE	15.23/1.6

Shot

1. Valerie Adams/Vili NZL	20.56
2. Natalya Mikhnevich BLR	20.28
3. Nadezhda Ostapchuk BLR	19.86

Discus

1. Stephanie Brown Trafton USA	64.74
2. Yarelys Barrios CUB	63.64
3. Olena Antonova UKR	62.59

Hammer

1. Oksana Menkova BLR	76.34
2. Yipsi Moreno CUB	75.20

3. Zhang Wenxiu CHN — 74.32

Javelin
1. Barbora Spotáková CZE — 71.42
2. Mariya Abakumova RUS — 70.78
3. Christina Obergföll GER — 66.13

Heptathlon
1. Natalya Dobrynska UKR — 6733
2. Hyleas Fountain USA — 6619
3. Tatyana Chernova RUS — 6591

4 x 100 Metres Relay
1. RUS — 42.31
2. BEL — 42.54
3. NGR — 43.04

4 x 400 Metres Relay
1. USA — 3:18.54
2. RUS — 3:18.82
3. JAM — 3:20.40

20 Kilometres Walk
1. Olga Kaniskina RUS — 1:26:31
2. Kjersti Plätzer NOR — 1:27:07
3. Elisa Rigaudo ITA — 1:27:12

OLYMPIC QUALIFICATION STANDARDS & DATES 2012

Dates are given in final columns for days in August for each round (Q – qualifying, F – final)

Event	Men A	Men B	Women A	Women B	Men's Comp	Women's Comp
100 Metres	10.18	10.24	11.29	11.38	p/h 4, s/F 5	p/h 3, s/F 4
200 Metres	20.55	20.65	23.10	23.30	h 7, s 8, F 9	h 6, s 7, F 8
400 Metres	45.30	45.90	51.55	52.35	h 4, s 5, F 6	h 3, s 4, F 5
800 Metres	1:45.60	1:46.30	1:59.90	2:01.30	h 6, s 7, F 9	h 8, s 9, F 11
1500 Metres	3:35.50	3:38.00	4:06.00	4:08.90	h 3, s 5, F 7	h 6, s 8, F 10
5000 Metres	13:20.00	13:27.00	15:20.00	15:30.00	h 8, F 11	h 7, F 10
10,000 Metres	27:45.00	28:05.00	31:45.00	32:10.00	4	3
Marathon	2:15:00	2:18:00	2:37:00	2:43.00	12	5
3000m Steeple	8:23.10	8:32.00	9:43.00	9:48.00	h 3, F 5	h 4, F 6
110/100m Hurdles	13.52	13.60	12.96	13.15	h 7, s/F 8	h 6, s/F 7
400m Hurdles	49.50	49.80	55.50	56.65	h 3, s 4, F 6	h 5, s 6, F 8
High Jump	2.31	2.28	1.95	1.92	Q 5, F 7	Q 9, F 11
Pole Vault	5.72	5.60	4.50	4.40	Q 8, F 10	Q 4, F 6
Long Jump	8.20	8.10	6.75	6.65	Q 3, F 4	Q 7, F 8
Triple Jump	17.20	16.85	14.30	14.10	Q 7, F 9	Q 3, F 5
Shot	20.50	20.00	18.30	17.20	Q & F 3	Q & F 6
Discus	65.00	63.00	62.00	59.50	Q 6, F 7	Q 3, F 4
Hammer	78.00	74.00	71.50	69.00	Q 3, F 5	Q 8, F 10
Javelin	82.00	79.50	61.00	59.00	Q 8, F 11	Q 7, F 9
Decathlon/Heptathlon	8200	7950	6150	5590	8/9	3/4
20 Km Walk	1:22:30	1:24:30	1:33:30	1:38:00	4	11
50 Km Walk	3:59:00	4:09:00			11	
4x100m Relay					h 10, F 11	h 9, F 10
4x400m Relay					h 9, F 10	h 10, F 11

Relays: There will be a maximum of 16 qualified teams in each event, based on the aggregate of the two fastest times achieved by national teams in the qualification period of 1 Jan 2011 to 2 July 2012.

A country may enter up to 3 athletes for each individual event provided they have achieved the A qualification standard, and 1 athlete per event if they have met at least the B standard. They can enter one reserve athlete per event provided he/she has also achieved the A standard. Countries without any qualified athletes may enter their best male athlete and their best female athlete for one event each, with the exception of the combined events, 10,000m and steeplechase.

Athletes must reach the qualification standards between 1 May 2011 (1 Jan 2011 for marathon, combined events and walks) and 8 July 2012 for individual events in order to be eligible to participate.

Performances must be achieved during competitions organised or authorised by the IAAF, its Area Associations or its National Member Federations in conformity with IAAF rules. Performances achieved in mixed events between male and female participants, held completely in the stadium, may be accepted under specific circumstances and conditions (See IAAF Rule 147). Wind-assisted performances or hand timed marks in 100m, 200m, 400m, 110/100mh, 400mh, and 4x100m relay will not be accepted. Indoor performances for all field events and for races of 400m or longer (except on oversized tracks) will be accepted.

For the marathon and 50k walk, senior athletes only (aged 20 and over on 31 Dec 2012) will be accepted and Junior athletes (18 or 19 on 31 Dec 2012) may compete in any other event. Youth athletes (16 or 17 on 31 Dec 2012) may compete in any event except the throws, decathlon, 10,000m, marathon and walks. Athletes younger than 16 on 31 Dec 2012 cannot be entered in any event.

WORLD JUNIOR CHAMPIONSHIPS

The 14th IAAF World Junior Championships will be staged at Barcelona, Spain on 10-15 July 2012. They were first held in Athens, Greece in 1986 and have been held every two years since then.

Championship bests after 2010

Men

100m	10.09	Darrel Brown TRI	2002
200m	20.28	Andrew Howe ITA	2004
400m	44.66	Hamdam Al-Bishi KSA	2000
800m	1:44.77	Benson Koech KEN	1992
1500m	3:35.53	Abdelati Iguider MAR	2004
5000m	13:08.57	Abreham Cherkos ETH	2008
10,000m	27:30.85	Josphat Bett KEN	2008
20km Road #	59:27	Metaferia Zeleke ETH	1988
2000mSt #	5:28.56	Juan Azkueta ESP	1986
3000mSt	8:14.00	Willy Komen KEN	2006
110mh	13.44	Colin Jackson GBR	1986
3'3" hurdles	13.23	Artur Noga POL	2006
400mh	48.51	Kerron Clement USA	2004
HJ	2.37	Dragutin Topic YUG	1990
	2.37	Steve Smith GBR	1992
PV	5.71	Germán Chiaraviglio ARG	2006
LJ	8.20	James Stallworth USAq	1990
TJ	17.04	Yoelbi Quesada CUB	1992
	17.31w	Teddy Tamgho FRA	2008
SP	19.48	Rutger Smith NED	2000
6kg	21.47	Edis Elkasevic CRO	2002
DT	60.60	Vasil Baklarov BUL	1986
1.75kg	67.32	Margus Hunt EST	2006
HT	72.40	Olli-Pekka Karjalainen FIN	1998
6kg	80.79	Conor McCullough USA	2010
JT	83.07	Robert Oosthuizen RSA	2006
Dec	7897	Dennis Leyckes GER	2000
Jnr spec	8126	Andrey Kravchenko BLR	2004
10,000mW	39:35.01	Stanislav Yemelyanov URS	2008
4x100mR	38.92	USA	2002

(Ashton Collins, Wes Felix, Ivory Williams, Willie Hordge)

4x400mR	3:01.90	USA	1986

(Clifton Campbell, Chip Rish, Percy Waddle, William Reed

Women

100m	11.12	Veronica Campbell JAM	2000
200m	22.82	Shalonda Solomon USA	2004
	22.80w	Heide Seyerling RSA	1994
400m	50.62	Fatima Yusuf NGR	1990
800m	2:00.06	Elena Mirela Lavric ROU	2008
1500m	4:05.14	Liu Dong CHN	1992
3000m	8:46.86	Zhang Linli CHN	1992
5000m	15:08.06	Genzebe Dibaba ETH	2010
10000m #	32:22.90	Wang Junxia CHN	1992
3000mSt	9:31.35	Christien Muyanga KEN	2008
100mh	12.96	Aliuska López CUB sf	1988
	12.81w	Anay Tejeda CUB	2002
400mh	54.70	Lashinda Demus USA	2002
HJ	2.00	Galina Astafei ROM	1988
PV	4.40	Floe Kühnert GER	2002
	4.40	Valeriya Volik RUS	2008
	4.40	Yekaterina Kolesova RUS	2008
LJ	6.82	Fiona May GBR	1988
	& 6.88w		
TJ	14.62	Tereza Marinova BUL	1996
SP	18.76	Cheng Xiaoyan CHN	1994
DT	68.24	Ilke Wyludda GDR	1988
HT	67.95	Bianca Perie ROM	2008
JT	68.17	Osleidys Menéndez CUB	1998
new spec	63.01	Vira Rebryk UKR	2008
Hep	6470	Carolina Klüft SWE	2002
5000mW #	21:05.41	Irina Stankina RUS	1994
10,000mW	43:24.72	Tatyana Mineyeva RUS	2008
4x100mR	43.40	Jamaica	2002

(Sherone Simpson, Kerron Stewart, Ammesisha McLaughlin, Simone Facey)

4x400mR	3:28.39	GDR	1988

(Manuela Deer, Stefanie Fabert, Anke Wöhlk, Grit Breuer

 # Events no longer contested

Most gold medals

Men: 4 Chris Nelloms USA 4x400mR 1988, 400m, 4x100mR & 4x400mR 1990

Women: 4 Gillian Russell JAM 100mh & 4x100mR 1990 & 1992

Most medals: 5 Katrin Krabbe GDR 3rd 200m, 2nd 4x100mR 1986; 1st 200m & 4x100mR, 2nd 100m 1988

Youngest champions

Men	15y 183d	Jacko Gill NZL SP 2010
	15y 332d	Usain Bolt JAM 200m 2002
Women	15y 102d	Wang Yan CHN 5000m walk 1986
	15y 169d	Ann Mwangi KEN 3000m 1988
	15y 196d	Susana Feitor POR 5000m walk 1990
	15y 245d	Diane Smith GBR 200m 1990

Youngest medalists

Men	15y 169d	Ismael Kirui KEN 2nd 10,000m 1990
	15y 183d	Jacko Gill NZL 1st SP 2010
Women	14y 182d	Sally Barsosio KEN 3rd 10,000m 1992
	14y 279d	Jackline Maranga KEN 2nd 1500m 1992

OBITUARY 2011

See ATHLETICS 2011 for obituaries of the following who died in early 2011: Kenth Andersson, Imre Babos, James Bungei, Siegfriede Dempe, Grigoriy Degtyarov, Jinas Grigas, Eduard Gushchin, Peter Hildreth, Inese Jaunzeme, Mariya Koshkaryova, Finn Larsen, Janis Lauris, George Lewis, Ollie Matson, Sally Meyerhoff, Barry McClure, Noemi Simonetto, Albert Yator, Stefka Yordanova, Robert Young.

Died in 2011

Robert Stuart 'Bob' ADAMS (GBR) (b. 27 May 1942) on 13 October. In 1969 he made four international appearances for Britain, won the AAA indoor title and was 4th in the European Indoor 800m. He was a semi-finalist at the 1969 Europeans and 1970 Commonwealth Games (for Wales). Welsh 800m champion 1967-71. Pbs: 400m 47.9 (1969), 800m 1:46.8 (1969, Welsh record), 1M 4:12.2 (1964). An enthusiastic team manager for Polytechnic Harriers, having trained as an architect, he worked in his uncle's interior design business in Herefordshire.

Eduardo Martins **ALBUQUERQUE** (Portugal) (b. 23 Jul 1928 Torres Vedras) in January. He set 14 Portuguese hammer records from 1956 to his best of 58.71 in 1961, competed at the Olympics in 1960 and was Ibero-American champion in 1962 and won 9 POR titles.

Saša ALEKSIC (Serbia) (b. 15 April 1961) in a motorcycle incident in Belgrade on 23 August. He competed twice for the Yugoslav national team. Pole vault pb 4.90 (1984).

Henk ALTMANN (RSA/GBR) (b. 2 Sep 1941 Port Elizabeth, South Africa) on 21 April in Wantage. In 1964 he won the South African 3 and 6 miles titles and set national records at 2 (8:50.2), 3 (13:31.8) and 6 (28:28.8) miles. He came to England as a Rhodes scholar to study for a masters degree in engineering at Oxford University – and stayed, setting further South African records with 2000m 5:21.4 (1966), 3000m 8:02.6 (1967), 2M 8:46.6 (1966), 3M 13:13.4 (1966), and with 13:39.0 for 5000m at Crystal Palace in June 1966, ranking 10th in the world that year. He was 2nd in the AAA 3M in 1966. Eventually gaining a British passport, he was member of Thames Hare & Hounds from 1971. Other pbs: 1500m 3:52.4 (1966), 1M 4:10.0 (1964), 6M 27:42.72 (1967), 10,000: 28:47.88 (1973).

Kenth ANDERSSON (Sweden) *add* (b. Örebro). Nine internationals, heat 800m at 1966 Europeans. Disqualified after finishing third in the 1967 European Indoor Games 1500m.

Seraphino ANTAO (Kenya) (b. 30 Oct 1937 Mombasa) on 6 September in London, where he lived from 1964. Of Asian origin (his parents came from Goa), he was Kenya's most successful sprinter, winning the Commonwealth Games 100y/220y double in 1962 (plus 5th at 4x440y), having also competed in 1958. He was eliminated in the heats of the 100m and 200m at the 1960 and 1964 Olympics and won the 100y/220y double at the 1962 AAAs. Kenyan records: 100y 9.3/9.2w (1962), 100m 10.3 (1961), 200m 20.4A* (1964) (and 20.0*Aw 1962); 120yh 14.3A (1960).

Viktor APOSTOLOV (Bulgaria) (b. 1 Oct 1962) on 30 November of a heart attack. One of four Bulgarians to have thrown the hammer over 80m, his pb was 80.62 (1990). He was Bulgarian champion in 1987 and was first at the Balkan Champs in 1990, but lost that title with a positive drugs test. He competed (dnq) at the 1988 Olympics and 1990 Europeans.

Howard ARIS (Jamaica) during a political rally at Port Antonio, Portland on 10 November at the age of 75. The president of the Jamaica AAA from 2004 and chairman of the Sports Development Foundation 1998-2007, he was an outstanding administrator and a highly regarded coach and manager of Jamaican teams at numerous international meetings.

Sunday BADA (Nigeria) (b. 22 June 1969 Kwara) suddenly in Lagos on 12 December. He was technical director of the Athletics Federation of Nigeria. He was World Indoor champion in 1997 (in a still-standing African indoor record of 45.51) after silver medals in 1993 and 1995. Running sub 45-seconds each year 1992-6, he won at 400m and 4x400m for Africa at the 1992 World Cup and was Nigerian 400m champion 1990-7 and 2002. He won an Olympic 4x400m gold medal in 2000 after the US disqualification and at 400m was a semi-finalist in 1992 and 1996 and quarter-finalist in 2000. At five World Championships 1993 to 2001, he was a 400m finalist in 1993 (5th) and 1995 (8th) with relay bronze in 1995. At African Games he won at 200m and was 2nd at 400m in 1995 and was 4th at 400m and 1st at 4x400m in 1999, and at African Champs was 3rd at 200m and 400m and 1st at 4x400m in 1990 and 2nd at 400m and 4x400m in 1991. Pbs: 100 10.27 (1997), 200m 20.28A (1995), 300m 32.66 (1992), 400m 44.63 (1993, semis World Ch).

Annual progression at 400m (position on world list): 1990- 46.19 (83=), 1991- 45.81 (56=), 1992- 44.99 (22), 1993- 44.63 (11), 1994- 44.96

(10), 1995- 44.69 (8), 1996- 44.88 (27=), 1997- 45.37 (34=)/44.89h?, 1998- 45.50 (52), 1999- 45.39 (41=), 2000- 45.74 (95=), 2001- 45.83 (91).

William **'Bill' BANGERT** (USA) (b. 14 Jan 1924 Berkeley, Mississippi) on 12 July in Marthasville, Missouri. In 1944 and 1945 he won the discus and was second in the shot for the University of Missouri at the NCAAs and 2nd in the discus in the AAUs. He won the AAU shot in 1945 and 1946 and was 3rd in 1954, in which year he set his pb of 17.40 (4th on world list). He was 2nd in the US indoors in 1952 having gone blind, but he later regained vision in his right eye. Discus best 50.04 (1946). He was an engineer, whose family owned construction firm Bangert Brothers, and served two terms as mayor of his hometown, Berkeley, a small town near St Louis. He competed as a vet into his 70s.

Mary Ethel **BARTLEET** (GBR) (b. 10 Apr 1915, née French) on 25 February in Dudley. A member of Birchfield Harriers, in 1932, aged 16, she was 3rd in the National CC championship and followed with 7th for England in an International CC against France (also 5th against Scotland in 1935). She was Midland CC champion each year 1933-6 and on the track won the 880y in 1935. In 1937 she was 2nd in the National CC.

Melvyn Richard **BATTY** (Great Britain) (b. 9 Apr 1940 Grays, Essex) on 29 August in Southend-on-Sea. A member of Thurrock Harriers, he competed in three internationals for Britain at 10,000m and set a world record for 10 miles with 47:26.8 at Hurlingham in London on 11 Apr 1964. He broke through to top class in 1962 when he was third in the International Cross Country and on the track improved at 3 miles from 13:53.6 to 13:29.8 and at 6 miles from 30:11.6 to 27:56.6; at the Commonwealth Games he was 6th in the 6 miles and 5th in the marathon. He won the National Cross Country in 1964 and in 1965, when he was controversially placed second in the International Cross Country in Ostend. The race was awarded to Jean-Claude Fayolle of France but observers felt that at worst a dead heat should have been declared. Other pbs: 1M 4:09.6 (1962), 3000m 8:10.2 (1962), 2M 8:42.2 (1962), 5000m 14:06.6 (1963), 10000m 29:01.0 (1963), Mar 2:21:30 (1964), 3000mSt 9:29.6 (1965). He became a successful coach, his star being Eamonn Martin, was associated with Brooks for many years, and worked for television and the press as a "quotes man".

Stig **Erling** Börje **BENGTSSON** (Sweden) (b. 17 Jun 1941 Falkenberg) on 30 November. Swedish champion at standing HJ 1964 and decathlon 1965 (with his pb 6754 on 1962 scoring tables, 6569 on current, 1984, tables). Represented Sweden 3 times.

Gudrun BEREND (Germany/GDR) (b. 27 Apr 1955 Eisleben) (later Wakan) on 22 August in Eisleben. At 100m hurdles she won the European Junior bronze in 1973 (plus gold at 4x100m), was 5th in 1974 and bronze medallist in her pb of 12.73 in 1978 at the Europeans, and 4th in 1976 at the Olympics. At GDR Championships she was 2nd in 1976 and 1978 and 3rd in 1974-5, 1977 and 1980. Her 13.14 in 1974 was a world junior record (on current age specification). 11 internationals 1974-80. Club: SC Chemie Halle.

Annual progression at 100mh: 1970- 15.5, 1971- 14.8, 1972- 14.0, 1973- 13.61/13.5/13.43w, 1974- 13.14/13.1/12.9w, 1975- 13.33/13.2w, 1976- 12.82/12.80w, 1977- 13.40/13.1, 1978- 12.73, 1979- 12.91, 1980- 12.80. Other pbs: 100m 11.3 (1974), 200m 24.2 (1972).

Her daughter Katja Wakan was 5th in 1973 and 7th in 2007 in the World 4x100m, pb 100m11.37 (2006).

Charles Bilanday **BODJONA** (Togo) (b. 25 May 1962). He competed at long jump in the 1983 Worlds and 1984 Olympics. Pb 7.47 (1981).

James Doyle **'Jim' BOLDING** (USA) (b. 3 Nov 1949 Tulsa) on 31 July in Stillwater, Oklahoma. A graduate of Oklahoma State University (3rd NCAA 1971), he ranked as world number one at 400m hurdles in 1974, when he ran his best ever time of 48.1 at Milan, for second on the world all-time list, and he ran the last ratified world record at 440y hurdles, 48.7 at Turin. He was also third in the world rankings in 1973, 1975 and 1976. AAU champion in 1973-4, 2nd in 1972, 1975-6; 6th at the US Olympic Trials in 1972 and 4th in 1976 when he made a very fast start and was still in second place at the final hurdle. He was later track coach at Oklahoma State.

Annual progression at 400mh (position on world list): 1970- 52.1*, 1971- 50.0* (19=), 1972- 49.5* (13=), 1973- 48.8/49.31 (1), 1974- 48.1/48.75 (1), 1975- 48.4/48.55 (1), 1976- 48.57 (4). Other pbs: 400m 45.3/45.79 (1974), 120yh 13.7 (1971).

André BRÉMEN (France) (b. 3 Jun 1923 Angers) on 21 July in Avrillé. French long jump champion and pb 7.20 in 1946.

Björn Rickard **'Ricky' BRUCH** (Sweden) (b. 3 Jul 1946 Örgryte, Gothenburg) on 30 May in Ystad of pancreatic cancer. A flamboyant and controversial character, after his athletics career he acted in films and his autobiography was published in 1990. He admitted to long-term use of steroids during his career. At the discus he won silver in 1969 (having had three no throws in the qualifying round only for one of his throws subsequently to be judged valid) and bronze in 1974 at the Europeans plus Olympic bronze in 1972, He was also 8th in 1968 and dnq 20th in 1976 at the Olympics, dnq at the

1983 Worlds, was 9th at the 1971 Europeans and won at the European Cup in 1970. At the shot he won European Indoor bronze in 1971. He first exceeded 60m and set the first of 15 Swedish discus records with 60.58 in 1968, and after moving to second on the world all-time list with a European record 68.06 in 1969, won 54 successive discus competitions in 1972-3 and during that time set a world record with 68.40 at Stockholm on 5 July 1972, which was followed by an unratified 'record' of 68.58 at Malmö on 10 Sep 1972. He continued to throw for many years, often seeking suitable windy locations on the Swedish coast, and exceeded 60m each year 1968-78 and 1981-9. In 1984 he set Swedish records of 69.10, 70.48, 71.00 and 71.26, all at Malmö, the last in November. He was Swedish champion at discus 1967, 1969-70, 1972-8 and 1983, and shot 1970 and 1972; 39 internationals. At one time he affected to wear a black bowler hat and a garish kimono and emit a 'Tarzan' yell on entering the arena for a competition.

Progression at DT: 1963- 43.57, 1964- 52.36, 1965- 53.73u/53.14, 1966- 56.26, 1967- 59.34, 1968- 61.98, 1969- 68.06, 1970- 67.14, 1971- 68.32, 1972- 68.58, 1973- 67.58, 1974- 68.16, 1975- 66.88, 1976- 63.64, 1977- 63.60, 1978- 60.78, 1979- 56.30, 1980- 56.90, 1981- 64.50, 1982- 63.44, 1983- 67.08, 1984- 71.26, 1985- 65.50, 1986- 62.02, 1987- 54.40/62.34dh. Other pbs: SP 20.28 (1973), HT 61.08 (1971), JT 51.42 (1966). 1.99m tall.

Cosimo CALIANDRO (Italy) (b. 11 Mar 1982 Francavilla Fontana, Brindisi) on 10 June when his motorcycle was in collision with a car in the Brindisi region. He won the European Junior 1500m in 2001 and the European Indoor 3000m at Birmingham in 2007, in which year he ran his pbs of 7:48.88i and 7:56.86. Italian champion at 5000m in 2006 in a pb 13:50.97. Other pbs: 1500m 3:40.57 (2004), 10,000m 28:40.94 (2010), HMar 62:41 (2010).

Jimmy CARNES (USA) (b, 29 Mar 1934 Eatonton, Georgia) on 5 March. A middle distance runner at Mercer University in the 1950s, he turned to coaching at Furman University in 1962 and then at the University of Florida 1964-76, founding the Florida Track Club. He became president of the U.S. Track & Field Federation (USTFF) in 1979 and was the first president of the newly created US governing body, The Athletics Congress (TAC), 1980-4. He was the first executive director of the United States Track Coaches Association, in office 1993-2004. He had been named as head coach of the US Olympic team in the boycott year of 1980. He co-founded the sporting goods company Athletic Attic in 1973.

Zdravko CERAJ ((Serbia) (b. 4 Oct 1920 Stara Raca) on 6 October in Zagreb. Yugoslav champion at 800m 1947, 1500m 1946-52, 5000m 1953 and cross-country 1948 and 1950, and Balkan 5000m 1953. He competed at the Europeans (1500m) in 1950 and Olympics (5000m) in 1952. 27 internationals for YUG. Yugoslav records 800m 1:53.9 (1949), 1500m (5) 1948 to 3:50.6 (1951), 2000m (2) to 5:25.2 (1951), 3000m (4) 1949 to 8:18.8 (1952), 5000m (2) to 14:26.2 (1952). He became a famous mountaineer.

Christian COLLARDOT (France) (b. 5 Jul 1933 Chartres) on 11 June in La Celle-Saint-Cloud, Yvelines. He was 6th in the Olympic long jump in 1960 and that year set French records of 7.70 and 7.73. French champion 1959, 14 internationals 1956-61.

Maxine Fay **CORCORAN** (Australia) (b. 22 Sep 1954, née Johnson) on 29 November. She was 8th at 400m and a silver medallist at 4x400m in 1978 and a 400m semi-finalist in 1982 at the Commonwealth Games. AUS champion at 400m in 1978-9 and 2nd at 400m and 800m in 1983. Pbs: 100m 12.19 (1979), 200m 23.9/24.27 (1979), 400m 52.04 (1979), 800m 2:02.48 (1983). She coached and worked for Sport Australia Hall of Fame. Her husband Danny was a former CEO of Athletics Australia.

Tommy Dan-Eric **DAHLLÖF** (Sweden) (b. 21 Aug 1944 Göteborg) on 6 January. As a race walker he had 4 internationals and two 2nd-places in the Swedish 10,000m, He became a notable international race walk judge, including officiating at the 1996 Olympic Games. Pbs: 20k 1:35:54 (1973), 50k 4:38:52 (1973).

Dolores Ann **DWYER** (USA) (née Duffy, b. 25 Dec 1934 New York) on 29 October in New York. AAU champion at 50m in 1950 and 200m in 1953 and indoors at 50y in 1949-50 and 1952 (in US record 6.2), she was 6th at 200m and helped the US team to the 4x100m gold medal at the 1951 Pan-American Games, but did not finish in her heat of the 200m at the 1952 Olympics. She then ran the second leg for the US team that set a world record of 1:40.0 for 4x220y in the match v British Empire at the White City, London. She became an actress. Pbs: 100m 12.0 (1953), 200m (straight track) 24.4 (1953).

Nils-Erik EMILSSON (Sweden) (b. 7 Apr 1950 Kristianopel) on 2 January. Swedish 800 m champion in 1971; 6 internationals. Pbs: 49.1 (1969), 1:49.3 (1970), 2:24.4 (1970), 3:48.8 (1972).

Erich-Herms **ESSMANN** (South Africa) (b. 13 Apr 1951 Lüderitz, Namibia) on 8 November in Cape Town. South African champion at 100m and 200m in 1975. Pbs: 100m 10.43 (1980), 10.1h (1976); 200m 20.96/20.5 (1979). He was an engineer.

Johan Christian EVANDT (Norway) (b. 19 Nov 1934) on 1 November. He set six unofficial world records for the standing long jump from 3.50m in 1956 to 3.65 in 1962 and five Norwegian records at standing high jump from 1.65 in 1956 to a then unofficial world record 1.77 in 1964.

Norma Beatriz FERNÁNDEZ (Argentina) (b. 8 Dec 1966) on 12 June. She set national records at 800m (2 to 2:04.67 in 1990), 1500m (3 in 1990-1 to 4:14.98), and marathon 2:54:20 (1988). Her career ended abruptly in 1992 when she received a 4-year doping ban. Third at 1500m at 1992 Ibero-Americans, and 3rd/2nd at 1988/89 South American CC Championships. Other pbs: 1000m 2:48.79i (1991), 3000m 9:18.17 (1991).

Doroteo Guamuch **'Mateo' FLORES** (Guatemala) (b. 11 Feb 1922 Cotió, Mixco) on 11 August. A mill weaver, he won the Boston Marathon in 1952 (in a national record 2:31:53) before placing 22nd at the Olympic Games. At the CAC Games he won the 10,000m and half marathon in 1946 with silver at 5000m and half marathon in 1950 and 1st 5000m and half marathon and 2nd 10,000m in 1954. At the Pan-American Games he was 5th at 10,000m in 1951 and won the marathon in 1955. He became a professor of physical education, and the national stadium in Guatemala City was named in his honour.

Nadine FOURCADE, later LEFÈVRE (France) (b. 25 Feb 1963 Reims) on 15 April in Reims. She set a French long jump record with 6.79 at Montgeron in 1985 and was 8th in the Europeans in 1986. French champion 1986-8 (and indoors 1985-6), 10 internationals 1980-8. Other pbs: 100mh 13.9 (1965), HJ 1.84 (1985), SP 13.17i (1986), 12.91 (1985); Hep 5315 (1983).

Professor Luciano FRACCHIA (Italy) in his hometown of Asti (Piedmont) on 21 May at the age of 95. A familiar figure to those who worked as journalists and film operators at major international meetings throughout the second part of the 20th century, he worked as a free-lance and/or FIDAL envoy in many parts of the world and had a marvellous film collection.

Keith FRANCIS (USA) (b. 19 Dec 1954) on 27 July in New Bedford. Massachusetts. He set his pb for 800m of 1:46.18 when 4th in the US Champs in 1974, and while at Boston College, where he became University Trustee, was 2nd in 1974 and 4th in 1975 at the NCAAs, winning the indoor 1000y title in 1975.

Stephane FRANKE (Germany) (b. 12 Feb 1964 Versailles, France) after a brief battle with cancer (diagnosed only five weeks earlier) on 23 June. He was the European bronze medallist at 10,000m in 1994 and 1998 and competed at three World Champs at this event: 1991- 12th, 1993- 4th and 1995- 7th. At the Olympic Games he went out in a heat at 10,000m in 1992 and was 9th at 10,000m and 14th at 5000m in 1996. He had two second and three third places in European Cup races and was German champion

at 10,000m in 1993 and 1995-6. He studied at Cal Poly Pomona and George Mason University in the USA and made a great breakthrough in 1993 as he reduced his 5000m best by 15 secs with 13:33.03 on 1 June and then another 20 secs to 13:13.17 for 3rd in Brussels. That year he ran 10,000m in 27:57.89 and two years later he reduced his bests to 13:03.76 (5th Zürich) and 27:48.88 (7th Worlds). In 1998 he took 4 seconds off his 13 year-old best for 1500m with 3:38.88, won European bronze at 10,000m and coached Damian Kallabis to the European steeplechase title. In 1999 he set German records at 25,000m (1:13:57.6) and 30,000m (1:33:35.6). Other pbs: 800m 1:50.81 (1988), 1000m 2:24.03 (1985), 3000m 7:39.78 (1995), Marathon 2:11:26 (1997). He worked as coach and athlete manager and joined the Eurosport commentary team in 2001, adding cross-country skiing to athletics in 2008.

Clayton Neville **GIBBS** (Trinidad/UK) (b. 20 Jun 1935 Port of Spain) on 25 April in Port of Spain. A member of Herne Hill Harriers, he had one international, for Britain against France at 220y and 4x110y in 1955 and was a finalist in the AAA 220y each year 1950-5 (3rd in 1953 and 1954); pbs 100y 9.9 (1954), 100m 10.8 (1955), 220y 21.6 (1954).

Benjamín GONZÁLEZ (Spain) (b. 12 Apr 1958 Madrid) on the weekend of 4/5 June on a walk in the mountains in the Basque Country; it seemed that he slipped and fell down a steep slope. He won the 400m bronze at the 1982 European Indoors and the 800m silver at the inaugural World Indoor Games in 1985. He also competed at 4x400m at the 1980 and 1984 Olympic Games (ht 800m in 1984) and at 400m and 4x400m at the 1982 Europeans. Spanish champion at 400m indoors and out 1980-2, he set two Spanish indoor 400m records and competed in 33 internationals. Pbs: 200m 21.46/21.2 (1981), 400m 46.48 (1981), 600m 1:16.84 (1985), 800m 1:46.53 (1985). He worked as a government advisor 1990-3, helped organise the 1999 World Student Games in Palma de Mallorca and then worked for various companies that manufactured athletics equipment.

János GÖRKÓI (GÖRK) (Hungary) (b. 10 Sep 1916 Abony) in July. He competed at 400m (4th) and 4x400m (6th) at the 1938 Europeans. Hungarian champion at 400m 1938 & 1941; 10 internationals 1937-43. Pbs: 100m 11.1 (1937), 200m 21.9 (1939); 400m 48.2 (1938).

Mirko **GRÄF** (Czech Republic) (b. 20 Sep 1928 Zbraslav) in Liberec on 11 November. Having been a footballer and tennis player, he became the first Czech athlete to defeat Emil Zátopek. He was Czechoslovak champion at 10,000m in 1959-60 and cross-country 1958-9, set a national record at 4x1 mile in 1957 and had 13 internationals 1958-61. After retirement in 1964, he worked as an organizer, coach and referee. Pbs: 1500m 3:54.0 (1954), 3000m 8:13.4 (1957), 3M 13:32.8 (1956), 5000m 14:04.2 (1957), 10,000m 29:55.4 (1959), Mar 2:40:29 (1960).

Oskar **Rune GUSTAVSSON** (Sweden) (b. 1 Dec 1919 Tutaryd) on 25 June. After 4th in 1943 and 3rd in 1944 on the world list for 1500m, he concentrated on the 800m. In 1946 he ran the world's best time of 1:50.0 and was a surprising European champion, also setting a 1000m world record with 2:21.4. In 1947 he ran on the Swedish 4x880y team that beat the world record with 7:29.0, but this was not ratified as the first runner Hans Liljekvist was barred from international competition. Swedish 800m champion 1946; two international matches. Other pbs: 400m 49.4 (1947), 1500m 3:47.4 (1944), 1M 4:04.6y (1943), 3000m 8:24.6 (1944), 5000m 14:52.0 (1952).

Geoff HARROLD (GBR) (b. 25 May 1939 on 1 April. A member of Enfield & Haringey AC (formerly Borough of Enfield H) from 1956, and a great clubman, he had a marathon best of 2:22:46 in 1973. He was a coach, team manager and a successful veteran competitor, continuing to race until 2007. He edited the magazine *Marathon & Distance Runner* in the 1980s.

George Graham **HAZLE** (South Africa) (b. 3 Oct 1924 Cape Town) in November. A top long distance walker, having developed in the sport in his 30s, he won the London to Brighton race (52 miles 758 yards) in 1964 and was 3rd in 1965. He won 22 South African titles: 3 miles 1958-65 and 1967; 5000m 1968; 20km 1961, 1963-5, 1967-8; 50km 1959-63 and 1967. At the 1960 Olympics he was 12th at 50km and 13th at 20km and he set many RSA records including bests for 20k 1:33:46.2 (1960) and 50k 4:27:55 (1961).

Kyllikki HIRVONEN (Finland) (née Naukkarinen, b. 20 Mar 1925 Enso, now part of Russia) in Pori on 12 February. At 80m hurdles she ran in the 1948 Olympics heats and won Finnish titles in 1946 and 1949; pb: 12.1 (1948).

Alf Olofsson **HOLMBERG** (Sweden) (b. 30 Jul 1928 Tullinge) on 6 November in Stockholm. While at the University of Tennessee he was 3rd in the AAU 1500m in 1950 and 2nd in the NCAA cross-country in 1951. Pbs: 800m 1:54.0, 1500m 3:49.2, 1M 4:09.1 (all 1951).

Stanislav HRNČÍŘ (Czech Republic) (b. 8 Aug 1926 Dolni Nová Ves u Jicína) on 22 October in Prague . He devoted himself to the Czech and Czechoslovak history of athletics throughout his life. Much valuable information from this rich history was saved thanks to his care and search of archives and old newspapers. A member of the ATFS and SAS (Cze), he chaired the Czechoslovak panel for records ratification 1976-81 and contributed to many publications.

Éliane JACQ (France) Later VISCART. (b. 4 Jul 1948 Brest) on 28 February in Lorient. She ran on the French teams that set world records at 4x400m with 3:34.2 at Colombes on 6 Jul 1969 (Jacq 2nd leg 53.7) and with 3:30.8 when 2nd to GBR at the European Championships in Athens on 20 Sep 1969 (Jacq 3rd leg 53.8) – actually on auto timing GBR 3:30.82, FRA 3:30.85. She was French 400m champion in 1970 and indoors in 1974. Pbs: 200m 23.9 (1973), 400m 53.9 (1970). 16 internationals 1965-74.

Ovidio DE JESÚS Vargas (Puerto Rico) (b. 7 Feb 1933) on 8 October. He set a national record for 400m hurdles with 52.1 at Mexico City in 1956 and that year competed at 400mh (heat) and 4x400m at the Olympic Games. He won a treble of 400m, 400mh and 4x400m at the CAC Games in 1959 (4th 400mh, 2nd 4x400m 1954). Pb 400m 47.8 (1956).

Albert JOHNSON (GBR) (b. 1 May 1931 Sheffield) on 20 May at his home in Tasmania, Australia. He competed at 50km walk at the Olympics of 1956 (8th) and 1960 (dq) and at two Europeans: dnf 50k 1954 and 11th 20kW 1958. He won the RWA 50k title in 1955 and was 8th at 20 miles walk at the 1966 Commonwealth Games, representing the Isle of Man, where he lived 1967-74, working as a psychiatric nurse, before emigrating to Australia, where he coached many walkers and distance runners. Walk pbs: 20k 1:36:22 (1958), 50k 4:30:00 (1960), 4:26:40 short (1958).

Donald W. **JOWETT** (New Zealand) (b. c.1931) on 21 July. He won three Empire Games medals: bronze at 220y in 1950 and gold at 220y and silver at 440y (in an NZ record 47.4) in 1954 and was NZ champion at 220y 1952-4 and at 440y 1953-5 and 1957. He moved to Australia where he became a top official, including track referee at the 1985 World Cup in Canberra and 2000 Olympic Games in Sydney and chairman of the jury at the 2006 Commonwealth Games in Melbourne. He was a rugby union winger for Otago when they won the Ranfurly Shield in 1957. He became a leading coach and treasurer of the Queensland Rugby Union and Queensland Athletics, both for 13 years. Other pbs: 100y 9.8 (1957), 220y 21.4 (1950). His daughter Susan was a quarter-finalist at 100m and 200m for New Zealand at the 1976 Olympic Games.

Péter KARÁDI (Hungary) (b. 6 Dec 1926 Budapest) in June. He competed at 200m at the 1952 Olympics, and at World University Games won silver in 1951 and bronze in 1949 and 1954 at 4x400m with 5th in 1949 and 4th in 1951 at 400m. Pbs: 100m 10.8 (1951), 200m 21.9 (1952), 400m 48.3 (1954).

John Joseph **KELLEY** (USA) (b. 24 Dec 1930 Norwich, Connecticut) on 21 August in North Stonington, Connecticut. He won 18 marathons between 1955 and 1964, including the AAU marathon for eight consecutive years 1956-63, and competed at the Olympic Games in 1956 (21st) and 1960 (19th). He won the Boston Marathon in his pb 2:20:05 in 1957 and was second five times. After 9th in 1955, he won the Pan-American title in 1959. He was also AAU road champion at 15k 1957, 20k 1956-60 and 1963, and 25k 1956-9. A graduate of Boston University, he was a high school teacher and track coach. He was not related to Johnny Kelley (1907-2004), who won the Boston Marathon in 1935 and 1945.

Tibor KERTÉSZ (Hungary) (b. 3 Apr 1927 Gyoma) on 6 November in Budapest. At decathlon he was 3rd at the 1954 World University Games with his pb 5678 (6132 on current tables) and Hungarian champion 1950-4. Later a coach, he taught at the University of Physical Education 1962-94.

Sinikka Marja-Liisa **KESKITALO** (Finland) (née Leppälä, b. 29 Jan 1951 Jalasjärvi) on 25 October in Tampere. She only started running at the age of 30, but a year later was third in the Finnish Champs on her marathon debut in 2:43:58. She was 4th at the 1986 Europeans in 2:34:31, having set her pb of 2:33:18 earlier that year when 5th at Boston. She contested two Olympic Games: 15th in 1984 and 42nd in 1988, and was 8th at the 1987 Worlds. Finnish champion at marathon 1983 & 1985, 10,000m 1986. Pbs 1500m 4:37.4 (1983), 3000m 9:20.47 (1984), 5000m 16:12.27 (1984), 10,000m 33:01.27 (1984).

Peter KIPROTICH Cherus (Kenya) (b. 1979) on 25 April as a result of injuries sustained in a car crash when driving home from Tambach to Iten, Kenya. From a marathon debut of 4th in Rotterdam in 2:11:52 in 2004, he improved to 2:10:57 in 2006 and 2:08:49 in 2007, both for fourth place in Frankfurt. He won the Great Scottish Run (half marathon) in Glasgow in 2003 and 2004 and ran his pb of 61:45 for third there in 2006. Exclusively a road racer, he had a 10k best of 28:06 (2005). He was a pacemaker in the world marathon records set in Berlin by Paul Tergat in 2003 and Haile Gebrselassie in 2007.

Kjell **Göte KJELLBERG** (Sweden) (b. 16 Aug 1926 Lund) on 2 March. He ran the first leg for Sweden's 3rd-placed 4x100m team at the 1950 Europeans. Represented Sweden six times. Pbs: 100m 10.7 (1949), 200m 22.2 (1951).

Romuald KLIM (USSR/Belarus) (b. 25 May 1933 Khvoyevo, near Minsk) on 28 May. He won the 1964 Olympic title at hammer and was 2nd in 1968, and won gold (1966) and silver (1969), followed by 4th (1971) at the European Championships. European Cup winner 1965 and 1967, he was USSR champion 1966-8 and 1971. He set a world record with 74.52 at Budapest on 15 June 1969, throwing over 70m each year 1965-73. He ranked in the world top four each year 1964-73 and number one in 1964 and 1966-7. Pb shot 17.46i (1963).

Annual progression at HT (position on world list): 1954- 43.46, 1955- 54.76, 1956- 55.68 (92=), 1957- 60.33 (38), 1958- 60.74 (39), 1959- 62.33 (30), 1960- 64.16 (21), 1961- 62.88 (31), 1962- 66.14 (11), 1963- 67.91 (6), 1964- 69.74 (2), 1965- 71.02 (3), 1966- 71.46 (2), 1967- 70.90 (2), 1968- 73.54 (2), 1969- 74.52 (2), 1970- 71.56 (6), 1971- 73.10 (8), 1972- 71.88 (20), 1973- 70.90 (26).

Hendrik Johannes 'Hentie' **KRUGER** (South Africa) (b. 30 Jul 1930 Graaff-Reinet) in March at Somerset West. He set seven South African pole vault records in 1957-9 with a best of 4.47 and was national champion in 1957-8 and 1960. An ankle injury meant that he did not qualify for the final at the 1958 Commonwealth Games. He studied at Oklahoma State University, USA and went into business in fire protection.

Franciscus Josephus Henricus 'Frans' **KÜNEN** (Netherlands) (b. 17 Apr 1930 Breda) on 23 November in Breda. In 1960 at the marathon he was Dutch champion in a pb and Dutch record 2:26:07.8 at Eindhoven and 36th at the Olympic Games. He also set Dutch records at 10,000m with 30:31.0 and 29:47,2 (1956), 1 hour 18,908m (1959), and 10M 51:36.2, 20,000m 1:03:44.6 and 25,000m 1:19:41.6 (1960). Dutch champion 10,000m 1959 and 1961, CC short 1958-9, long 1956, 1959-60 and 1962. Pb 5000m 14:26.0 (1956).

Vaclav KYNOS (Czech Republic) (b. 25 Mar 1938 Trebechovice pod Orebem) on 29 July. He ran the anchor leg for the Czechoslovak 4x100m that was 4th at the 1958 Europeans. 12 internationals 1956-60, he tied the CS record for 100m with 10.5 in 1958. Other pbs: 100m 10.4w, 200m 21.0, 400m 50.9 (all 1959).

Jan LAMMERS (Netherlands) (b. 30 Sep 1926 Drachten) on 1 September in Drachten. A former gymnast, he won the 200m bronze medal at the 1950 Europeans, having competed also in 1946 (sf 100m) and at the 1948 Olympics (qf 200m). Dutch champion at 100m 1950 and 200m 1948 and 1950. Pbs: 100m 10.6 (1948), 200m 21.6 1948), 110mh 15.6 (1948).

David Charles **LAW** (GBR) (b. 9 Sep 1930) in Broomgrove, Sheffield on 17 May. A graduate of Oxford University, he ran the second leg in 3:50.0, the fastest of the British team that set a world 4x1500m record of 15:27.2 at the White City, London on 23 Sep 1953 against Sweden. At the AAA Championships he was 3rd in the mile in 1952 and 1954. Pbs: 800m 1:51.7, 1500m 3:48.2, 1M 4:07.7 (all 1955).

Lennart LINDBERG (Finland) (b. 4 May 1927 Snappertuna) in Helsinki on 28 January. A fireman and leading 400m hurdler, his pb 52.7

against Hungary in 1954 was third-best among Finns up to then. Finnish champion in 1951 and 1956, he ran in 19 internationals, including 6th at 4x400m at the 1954 Europeans. 400m pb: 49.5 (1951).

Annie LORDET (France) (née Ségouffin b. 2 May 1938 Paris) on 19 February in St-Maur. She was the first French women to exceed 6m in the long jump with 6.02 in 1958 (holding the record for just 6 minutes!) and was French champion in 1957 and 1959. 7 internationals 1957-9.

Herbert LORENZ (USA) (b. 7 Apr 1939 Germany) on 27 February. At the marathon he won the RRCA Championship in 1970 and in 1971 ran his pb of 2:19:17 for 3rd in the AAU. He coached in New Jersey high schools for 15 years and was twice National Masters Runner of the Year.

Ragnar Torsten **LUNDBERG** (Sweden) (b. 22 Sep 1924 Madesjö) on 10 July. He ranked in the world top ten at pole vault each year 1948-55, competed at three Olympic Games, taking the bronze medal in 1952 and placing fifth in both 1948 and 1956, and at three European Championships, winning in 1950, 2nd in 1954 and 10= in 1958. He set five European records: 4.32 and 4.36 (1948), 4.38 and 4.40 (1950) and 4.44 (1952) and took the Swedish record from 4.21 in 1947 with ten improvements to 4.46 in 1956. He also won the European silver medal at 110mh in 1950. He competed for IFK Södertälje and was Swedish champion at 110mh 1949-51 and 1953, PV 1948-58. 34 internationals.

Annual progression at PV (position on world list): 1942- 3.10, 1943- 3.60, 1944- 3.60, 1945- 3.90 (c.40=), 1946- 3.80, 1947- 4.21 (14=), 1948- 4.36 (6), 1949- 4.30 (12), 1950- 4.40 (3), 1951- 4.30 (11=), 1952- 4.44 (5), 1953- 4.35 (7), 1954- 4.40 (9=), 1955- 4.45 (10), 1956- 4.46 (15), 1957- 4.30 (44=, 1958- 4.35 (52=), 1959- 4.30 (90=), 1960- 4.10, 1961- 3.90, 1962- 3.60, 1963- 3.50, 1964- 3.80. Other pbs: 110mh 14.7 (1947), 200mh 25.3 (1949), LJ 7.02 (1948).

Dr Berton Edward **LYLE** (USA) (b. 8 May 1928 Tupelo, Mississippi) on 11 May in Denton, Texas. A graduate of Duke University, he was head coach and athletic director 1965-88 at Texas Woman's University, which won three AIAW team titles and two US Track & Field Federation titles under him. He was the women's sprint and relay coach for the U.S. Olympic Team at the 1992 Barcelona Games.

Pablo S. **McNEIL** (Jamaica) (b. 12 Sep 1939) in Falmouth Hospital on 4 July. He competed at the 1964 (sf 100m, 4th 4x100m) and 1968 (ht 100m) Olympic Games and was a silver medallist at 4x110y and quarter-finalist at 100y and 220y at the 1966 Commonwealth Games. At the CAC Games he was 5th at 100m and 1st at 4x100m in 1966. He was Usain Bolt's first

coach in high school. Pbs: 100y 9.5 (1964), 100m 10.54/10.4/10.3w (1964), 220y 20.9 (1965).

Olavi MANNINEN (Finland) (b. 20 Jul 1928 Jyväskylä) in Jyväskylä on 15 February. At the marathon he was 24th in the 1960 Olympics and 4th in 1957 and 5th in 1961 at Boston. Finnish champion in 1958 and 1959, his pb was 2:21:17.8 (1956).

Davorin MARCELJA (Croatia) (b. 13 Jan 1924 Kastav) on 2 June in Zagreb. He was the Yugoslav champion at javelin 1946 and decathlon 1947-50 and won the decathlon at the 1947 Balkan and Central European Games. He set five Yugoslav decathlon records 1947-50 with a best on current scoring tables of 6269. Five internationals and participant at the Olympics in 1948 and Europeans in 1946 and 1950.

Oscar MARÍN LUZARDO (Venezuela) (b. 27 Sep 1950) on 7 September. South American champion at 110m hurdles 1974 and 1977, he held the national record from 1971 to 1979. Pb 14.56A (1977), 14.3 (1971), 13.8w (1975).

Clifton Augustus **MAYFIELD** (USA) (b. 21 Aug 1942 (1940?) New Bern, NC) in Washington, DC on 23 February. In 1963 he won the NCAA long jump for Central Ohio with 8.10w and that year had a wind-legal best of 7.87 indoors. He was injured in 1964, when his best was 7.67, and he then disappeared from the sport.

Albert MORTON (Canada) (b. 15 Oct 1914) on 17 September. He was Canadian champion at marathon in 1947 in his pb 2:45:51 and was twice 5th at Boston.

William **Harold NELSON** (New Zealand) (b. 26 Apr 1923) in Nelson on 1 July. He was the gold medallist at 6 miles and silver medallist at 3 miles at the 1950 Empire Games in Auckland. New Zealand team captain at the 1948 Olympic Games, he was 6th in his heat of the 5000m and did not finish the 10,000m. He won New Zealand titles at 1M 1947, 3M 1947-8, 6M 1948 and cross-country 1946 and 1948. In 1948 he set a NZ record for 6 miles with 29:57.4 and his 3 miles best of 14:19.6. He spent 12 years teaching physical education at Nelson College and six years at Waimea College, and taught accounting at Nelson Polytechnic until his retirement in 1983. He also coached many athletes, most notably Rod Dixon at Waimea College. He received the MBE.

Valter Erik **NYSTRÖM** (Sweden) (b. 30 Dec 1915 Högbo, Sandviken) on 10 March in Årsunda. At 10,000m he was 6th at the 1952 Olympic Games and Swedish champion in 1947, 1949 and 1951 (2nd 1950 and 1952) and at cross-country in 1947 and 1951. At 5000m he was 2nd in 1952 and 3rd in 1951 in the Swedish Champs. He set Swedish records at 1 hour with 18,699m in 1946 and with 18.810m in 1951 when he went on to 20,000m 1:03:57.4 and 25,000m 1:21:41.4. He then set Swedish records at 10,000m in 1952: 29:34.8 and 29:23.8 at Düsseldorf in an international against West Germany, then second on the world all-time list. Other pbs: 3000m 8:20.6, 5000m 14:15.8, Mar 2:38:17 (all 1952). 11 internationals.

Kennedy ONDIEK (Kenya) (b. 12 Dec 1966) on 14 July in Nairobi. He competed at the 1988 and 1992 Olympic Games (heats 100m and 200m at each), and was a 200m quarter-finalist at the 1991 Worlds. At Commonwealth Games he was 8th at 200m and a semi-finalist at 100m in 1990, also reaching the 100m quarter-final in 1994. Pbs: 100m 9.9A Kenyan record & 10.38A (1991), 200m 20.1A (1989) & 20.73 1991).

Erik Verner **ÖSTBYE** (Sweden) (b. 25 Jan 1921 Oslo, Norway) on 14 March. Swedish marathon champion 1959, 1961, 1964 and 1965; 11 internationals. Pb 2:20:20 (1960), 2:18.32 short? (1961), He continued to run remarkable times in his 50s with 2:26:35 at age 55 in 1976 and 2:27:05 at 56 in 1977.

Tapio PEKOLA (Finland) (b. 31 Mar 1940 Oulu) on 18 October. A middle distance runner and witty and controversial writer, he started the running magazine *Juoksija* in 1971, owning it until his death, and editing and publishing it until 1998.

Danuta Zdzislawa **PIECYK** (Poland) (b. 27 Sep 1950 Stargard Szczecinski) on 13 April in Olsztyn. A year before the IAAF officially recognised world records for the women's 400m hurdles, she set a world best of 56.7/56.91 auto in winning the Polish title at Warsaw on 11 Aug 1973. She improved to 56.83 when 2nd to Krystyna Kacperczyk's inaugural ratified mark of 56.51 a year later. She competed at the 1972 Olympics (heats 400m & 4x400m) and in the 4x400m at the European Championships of 1969, 1971 and 1974, reaching 400m semis in the last two. She won European Indoor 4 x 2 laps relay bronze medals in 1973 and 1975. Polish champion at 400mh 1973-5 and 400m 1975. At 400m she set three Polish records from 52.8 (1972) to 52.3 (1973); auto timed 52.62 (1972). Other pbs: 100m 11.8 (1972), 200m 23.8 (1974), 200mh 28.2 (1970).

Vera POPKOVA (Russia) (b.2 Apr 1943 Chelyabinsk) (née Kabrenyuk) on 29 September in Lvov. She ran on the USSR teams that set world records for 4x100m at high altitude with 43.9 at Leninaken and 43.6 at Mexico City in 1968 before taking bronze medals with 43.4/43.41 at the Olympic Games, when she was also a semi-finalist at 200m. At European Champs she was bronze medallist at 200m and 4x100m (plus 5th at 100m) in 1966 and at 4x400m in 1971. She won the European Indoor 400m in 1971 and World University Games medals with 3rd at 200m in 1961 and 2nd at 100m in 1963. USSR champion

at 100m 1966-7, 200m 1965-6 and 400m 1970. Pbs: 100m 11.3A (1968), 200m 23.0A (USSR record)/23.27A (1968), 400m 53.4 (1970). She lived in Lvov and worked as an engineer.

Pierre QUINON (France) (b. 20 Feb 1962 Lyon) committed suicide on 17 August in Hyères. Although he was plagued by many injuries (and rather frequently no-heighted in his later years), the peak of his pole vault career came with a world record 5.82 at Cologne in 1983, followed by winning the Olympic title a year later in Los Angeles and setting a pb of 5.90 when 2nd to Sergey Bubka at Nice on 16 July 1985; that year he was also 2nd to Bubka in the Grand Prix series. He first cleared 5m at the age of 17 in 1979 and 5.50 in 1981. He won silver medals at the 1981 European Juniors and 1984 European Indoors and was French champion each year 1982-4.

Annual progression at PV (position on world list): 1976- 3.40, 1977- 3.90, 1978- 4.50, 1979- 5.00, 1980- 5.10i, 1981- 5.50 (30=), 1982- 5.70 (7=), 1983- 5.82 (2), 1984- 5.80 (6=), 1985- 5.90 (2), 1986- 5.72i/5.70 (15=), 1987- 5.60 (43=), 1988- 5.70 (17=), 1989- 5.40i (116=), 1991- 5.70i/5.55 (26=), 1992- 5.20i, 1995- 5.00, 2003- 4.21i.

Gyuláné RÁKHELY (née **Ilona LÉDERMAYER/TOLNAI**) (Hungary) (b. 12 Mar 1921 Kaposvár) on 23 September. She competed at the 1952 Olympics (100m hts, 4x100 dq) and World University Games (1949 silver 4x100 & 4x200; 1951 silver 4x100, bronze 4x200, 5th 100). 14 internationals 1942-52. HUN record holder at 100m 12.8 (1947) & LJ (5.45, 1941 & 5.54, 1942; and champion 100m 1947-8 & 1950, LJ 1941. Pbs: 100m 12.4 (1951), 200m 25.8 (1952), LJ 5.54 (1942)

Cristian ROSALES ALONSO (Uruguay) (b. 11 Sep 1978 San José) committed suicide on 4 November. Current Uruguayan junior record holder at 1500m 3:49.9 '96, 5000m 14:20.53 '97, and 10,000m 29:59.9 '97; he won the South American Junior 1500m and 5000m in 1997. Pbs: 1500m 3:46.6 (1999), 5000m 14:04.50 (1999), 10,000m 29:59.9 (1997).

Ric SAYRE (USA) (b. 9 Aug 1953 Akron, Ohio) on 21 June. He won 12 marathons including at Houston in 2:13:54 to take the 1987 US title. His best time was 2:12:59 to win the inaugural Los Angeles Marathon in 1986.

Joe SCHATZLE (USA) (b. 10 Sep 1931 Jamaica, New York) on 4 June. He was 2nd in 21.1 at the IC4A Champs in 1951 when Andy Stanfield ran the inaugural IAAF world record for 220 yards around a turn. Pbs: 60y 6.2i (1953), 100y 9.6 (4th in the 1953 AAU Champs, when also 4th at 220y) and 9.5w (NCAA heat for Manhattan College), 220y straight 20.9 (1951). He worked as an air traffic controller before becoming a successful high school track coach.

Ágoston SCHULEK (Hungary) (b. 26 Aug 1943 Kosice (then Kassa) on 2 October. He set seven Hungarian pole vault records from 4.55 in 1965 to 4.85 in 1969 and set his pb of 4.90 in 1971; Hungarian champion 1967-9, 9th European Indoors 1970; 15 internationals 1966-71. He became a leading coach and was president of the Hungarian Athletics Federation (MASZ) 1991-2000 and 2008-09 and EAA vice-president 1995-2007.

Herbert SEMPER (USA) (b. 7 Sep 1929) on 26 June in Lawrence, Kansas. He won NCAA cross-country titles and was 3rd at 2 miles on the track for the University of Kansas in 1950 and 1951, and was 3rd in the AAU 5000m in 1951. Pbs: 1M 4:12.7, 2M 9:05.0 (both 1951).

Abdulaye SÈYE (Sénégal) (b. 30 Jul 1934 St. Louis) on 13 October in Thiès. Representing France (where he went to study in 1954), he won the 1960 Olympic 200m bronze medal and won the 100m at the 1959 Mediterranean Games. He was French champion at 100m 1959 and 200m 1956 and 1959 and set French records at 100m: 10.2 in 1959 and 1960, 200m: 20.8 in 1959 and 20.7 three times in 1960 plus 20.4 around a half turn in 1960; and 400m 46.6 in 1959 and 46.6 and 45.9/45.88 in 1960. Auto time pbs 100m 10.32 and 200m 20.82 in 1960. 17 internationals for France 1956-60. He was Sénégal's first national coach 1961-5 and was also a member of the nation's National Olympic Committee.

(Dr.) Clifford Jean SHEEHAN III (USA) (b. 3 May 1963 Orange, New Jersey) on 27 July in Missoula, Montana. A biology graduate of Harvard, he was second in the NCAA 1 mile in 1986 and had a pb of 3:59.2 (1985). After medical school at Southwestern University in Dallas, he became a cardiologist.

Takashi SHIMOKAWARA (Japan) in Kamaishi City, a victim of the tsunami in March at the age of 104. He was world record holder for the shot, discus and javelin in the age 100+ category.

Zithulele SINQE (South Africa) (b. 9 Jun 1963 Umtata) in an automobile accident in Balfour, near Johannesburg on 22 December. He was one of a brilliant group of South African distance runners who emerged in the mid-1980s. In July 1985 he was just beaten by Matthews Temane for the South African half marathon title as both ran a national record 62:19. The following year he improved at the marathon from 2:15:15 to 2:08:04, a national record on the 129m downhill Port Elizabeth course and the second fastest in the world that year. That was for the RSA title, that he retained in 1987 when he ran 2:10:51, his fastest ever on a standard course. In July 1987 Temane and Sinqe, again in that order, ran 60:11, the fastest in the world that year, at East London

on a 46.5m downhill course for the RSA half marathon title. He won four more marathons in 1994-8 and also the Two Oceans Marathon over 56k in 1996 and 1997. Other pbs: 5000m 13:51.5 (1988), 10000m 29:01.65 (1989); road: 10k 28:30 (1986), 15k 44:10 (1992), 50k 2:47:39 (1997).

Tore Ingemar **SJÖSTRAND** (Sweden) (b. 31 Jul 1921 Uppsala) on 26 January. At 3000m steeplechase he won the 1948 Olympic title and was 3rd at the 1946 Europeans (8th 1950). He won the Swedish title in 1947 and 1948 after several years as runner-up to Erik Elmsäter. 6 internationals.

Annual progression at 3000mSt (position on world list): 1940- 9:33.6 no water jump, 1941- 9:46.0/9:33.0nwj (11), 1942- 9:30.2 (11), 1943- 9:17.4 (2), 1944- 9:06.0 (2), 1945- 9:04.6 (2), 1946- 9:02.2 (3), 1947- 9:02.4 (1), 1948- 8:59.8 (1), 1949- 9:29.0 (33), 1950- 9:11.2 (6), 1951- 9:14.4 (23). Other pbs: 1500m 4:00.8 (1948), 3000m 8:26.6 (1948), 5000m 14:59.0 (1943), 10,000m 31:35.8 (1946).

Henning Elof **SJÖSTRÖM** (Sweden) (b. 13 May 1922 Burträsk) on 16 October. Two international matches for Sweden at javelin, pb: 69.48 (1944), 70.20 (intra-squad 1943).

Erik **Helge (Andersson) SKARÄNGER** (Sweden) (b. 7 Sep 1918 Tärna) on 30 August. Swedish champion at 50km walk in 1949, pb: 4:44:56.4 (1949). 2 internationals.

Ali ST LOUIS (Trinidad) (b. 13 May 1959) in a road accident in Trinidad on 25 September. He competed at the 1984 Olympics (ht 400m injured) and at the Central American & Caribbean Games won a bronze medal at 4x400m in 1982 and was 8th at 200m in 1986. Pbs: 100m 10.5 (1986), 200m 21.23 (1986), 400m 45.48 (1984). A former soldier, he became a coach. His daughter Britney St Louis has 400m best of 52.97 (2009).

Béla SZALAY (Hungary) (b. 26 Jul 1926 Budapest) in November. At the marathon he was 15th in the Europeans and Hungarian champion in 1962. He had four internationals 1961-4 and set HUN records at 25,000m 1:21:05.6 (1960), 30,000m 1:40:08.8 (1961) and marathon 2:24:58.2 (1960) and 2:23:55.4 (1961) with other pbs: 800m 1:59.2 (1947), 1500m 4:00.4 (1956), 3000m 8:26.0 (1958), 5000m 14:38.4 (1961), 10,000m 30:17.4 (1960).

Lubomir TESACEK (Czech Republic) (b. 9 Feb 1957 Slavkov u Brna) when hit by a tram on 29 June in Prague. He won the European Indoor 3000m in 1984 (4th 1983 and three other finals). He also ran at the 1986 Europeans (ht 5000m, 16th 10.000m). Pbs: 1500m 3:42.2 (1979), 3000m 7:46.99 (1983), 5000m 13:25.62 (1986), 10000m 28:09.4 (1986), HMar 72:58 (1992), Mar 2:13:48 (1990), with national indoor records 3000m 7:48.8 (1981) and 5000m 13:39.0 (1984).

Jukka TOIVOLA (Finland) (b. 7 Sep 1949 Liperi) in Pori on 27 May. A Master of Chemistry, and marathon specialist, he ran 39 of his 61 races (1973-99) abroad, winning the first Stockholm Marathon in 1979 and 2nd in 2:10:52 in New York in 1981 to Alberto Salazar´s 2:08:13 (course 150m short). His 2:11:35 for 10th in New York in 1983 remained the Finnish record for 25 years. He broke 2:20 every year from his marathon debut of 2:17:26 in 1973 to 1987 (excepting 1978). He was 27th in the 1976 Olympics and 5th in the 1982 Europeans. His total running amount of 217,400km from 1971 to 2006 is probably a Finnish record. Other pbs: 10,000m 29:52.6, 25,000m track 1:15:30.6 (1975). Only 12 days before Jukka´s death, his son Pekka won the Finnish U23 cross country title.

Carl-Gustav TOLLEMAR (Sweden) (b. 28 Jan 1924 Stockholm) on 2 November. He was a member of the IAAF Technical Committee 1981-99 (chairman 1987-99) and competitions director of the 1995 World Championships in Gothenburg.

Danny TSHINDIND KASSAP (DR of Congo/Canada) (b. 24 June 1982) on 2 May in Toronto. He came from Congo to Canada as a refugee in 2001, and set a national record for 10,000m with 28:57.28 in 2003 and won the Toronto Waterfront Marathon in a pb 2:14:50 in 2004. He received Canadian citizenship in 2008 and was 15th in the London marathon that year in 2:15:20, but he collapsed with a heart condition in the Berlin marathon. Other pbs: 5000m 13:56.76 (2003); road: 10km 28:51 (2004); HMar 64:12 (2004).

Natasa URBANCIC (Slovenia) (b. 25 Nov 1945 Celje) on 22 June in Celje. She was 6th in 1968 and 5th in 1972 when representing Yugoslavia at javelin in the Olympic Games and also competed at four European Championships: 1966 (nt), 1969 (4th), 1971 (10th) and 1974 (3rd). Balkan champion in 1969, 1971 and 1973 and Yugoslav champion in 1965, 1969 and 1971-4, she set 13 Yugoslav records from 50.68 in 1964 to 62.12 in 1973. Other pbs: 80mh 12.0 (1961), 100mh 15.1 (1969), SP 14.33 (1974), DT 47.02 (1973), Pen 3906 (1963); 42 internationals 1962-74. She was named as Slovenian Sportswoman of the Year each year 1969-74

Annual progression at JT: 1960- 31.85, 1961- 39.10, 1962- 45.40, 1963- 46.15, 1964- 50.68, 1965- 51.96, 1966- 54.06, 1967- 52.78, 1968- 55.61, 1969- 56.02, 1970- 57.16, 1971- 60.18, 1972- 59.24, 1973- 62.12, 1974- 51.66, 1980- 44.10, 1982- 48.38, 1987- 47.92. 1988- 41.78, 1989- 45.87, 1993- 47.00, 1995- 41.38.

Rocky VAITANIKI (France) (b. 7 Apr 1973 Nouméa, New Caledonia) on 30 August in Neiilly-sur-Marne. He won the South Pacific shot in 1995 and 1999 and had a best of 18.59 (2000).

Torsten VON WACHENFELDT (Sweden) (b. 24 Dec 1927 Lund) on 3 May. Represented Sweden 17 times at shot, pb: 16.58 (1961).

Grete WAITZ (Norway) (b. 1 Oct 1953 Oslo, née Andersen) on 19 April in Oslo after a six-year battle with cancer. She married Jack Waitz (né Nilsen) in 1975. Waitz was the first world champion at the women's marathon in 1983, fitting recognition of her ability and her pioneering rôle in women's distance running. She ran world bests in her first three marathons annually at New York from 1978 to 1980, her times 2:32:29.8, 2:27:32.6 and 2:25:41. She set a fourth world best with 2:25:29 in London on 17 Apr 1983 and went on to complete nine wins in the New York Marathon, adding each year 1982-6 and in 1988. In all she won 13 of her 19 marathons from 1978 to 1990, including London again in 1986 in her best ever time of 2:24:54. She was also runner-up to Joan Benoit in the first women's Olympic marathon in 1984.

She first competed in the European Championships in 1971 at 800m and 1500m, and in the Olympics at 1500m in 1972. On the track she set a European junior 1500m record in 1971 and two world records at 3000m: 8:46.6 in 1975 and 8:45.4 in 1976, with a European 5000m record of 15:08.80 in 1982; yet apart from her World Cup win at 3000m in 1977 she did not win any major titles, taking European bronze medals at 1500m in 1974 and at 3000m in 1978. Before her marathon success she was at her best in road races, where her first ever loss was to Maricica Puica in 1981, and at cross-country, where she was unbeaten for twelve years and achieved a record five wins (1978-81 and 1983) in the World Championships (also third in 1982 and 1984). She won 33 Norwegian senior titles from 1971 to 1983 and set 24 Norwegian records at track events from 800m to 5000m. World road bests for 15km: 47:53 (1984), 10M: 53:05 (1979), 20M: 1:51:23 (1980). A statue of her was erected outside the Bislett Stadium in Oslo in 1984. Other bests: 400m 57.6 (1972), 600m 1:32.4 (1973), 800m 2:03.1 (1975), 1000m 2:39.74 (1977), 1500m 4:00.55 (1978), 1 mile 4:26.90 (1979), 3000m 8:31.75 (1979), HMar 67:50 (1982), HJ 1.61 (1971).

Progress at 1500m, 3000m, marathon: 1970- 4:29.7, 1971- 4:17.0, 1972- 4:16.0, 1973- 4:12.7, 9:34.2; 1974- 4:05.21, 1975- 4:07.5, 8:46.6; 1976- 4:04.80, 8:45.4; 1977- 4:05.08, 8:36.8; 1978- 4:00.6, 8:32.1, 2:32:30; 1979- 4:00.59, 8:31.75, 2:27:33; 1980- 4:05.36, 8:40.23, 2:25:41; 1981- 4:08.34, 8:44.64; 1982- 4:12.96, 8:55.5i, 2:27:14; 1983- 8:52.86, 2:25:29; 1984- 4:12.38, 2:26:18; 1985- 4:10.54, 8:51.10, 2:28:34; 1986- 2:24:54, 1988- 2:28:06, 1990- 2:34:34.

Sammy Kamau **WANJIRU** (Kenya) (b. 10 Nov 1986 Nyahururu) in a fall from a balcony at his home in Nyahururu on 15 May. He left

Kenya in 2002 to go to school in Japan and that year ran a world age 15 record for 10000m of 28:36.08, going on to a world junior record of 26:41.75 in 2005. Just 15 days later he set the first of three world records at half marathon with 59:16 in Rotterdam. He set further world records with 58:53 and 58:33 and one at 20km, 55:31, in 2007 before making a winning marathon debut at Fukuoka (2:06:39) in December that year. He was then second in London in 2:05:24 before he became Kenya's first ever Olympic marathon champion in 2008 in 2:06:32, then easily the fastest time ever in a major championship – an amazing performance as he broke clear of the field at such a pace in the 29°C weather. Further marathon success came in London 2009 (2:05:10) and Chicago 2009 (2:05:41) and 2010 (2:06:24), and he took the World Marathon Majors Series for 2008/09 and 2009/10, but in between his Chicago successes he had to drop out of the 2010 London Marathon with a knee injury.

However, he had various problems. In December 2010 he was arrested at his home and charged with threatening his wife, striking a security guard, and possessing an illegal AK-47 rifle. He was released on bail, and his wife later withdrew her charges against him, but he still faced the weapons charge. In January, he was involved in a car accident and while he avoided serious injury, he later withdrew from the London Marathon with a knee problem.

Josephine 'Jo' **WARREN MADDEN** (USA) (b. 15 Apr 1915 Somerville) on 19 November at Stoneham, Massachusetts. She was a reserve for the 4x100m relay team which won the gold medal at the Olympics in 1936, when she ranked 7th in the world at 100m with 12.0. She was 2nd in the US 100m in 1937 and founded the Red Diamond Track and Field Club in Boston. She married Joseph Madden.

Martin WEBSTER (GBR) in London on March 28 aged 56 after battling motor neurone disease since 2005. The award-winning former executive producer of athletics coverage for the BBC joined the BBC in 1978 as a researcher, moved to BBC TV Sport in 1981 and became a producer in 1987. He covered the first of six Olympic Games in 1988 and was host director of athletics for the Sydney Games of 2000. Among his innovations were the remote home straight tracking camera. His work at the Manchester Commonwealth Games of 2002 earned him a BAFTA award, and he received another for his coverage of the 2009 World Champs. In 2007 he was presented with the Ron Pickering Memorial Award for services to athletics. His last assignment was the 2010 London Marathon.

Professor Dr. Georg WIECZISK (Germany) (b. 20 Jul 1922 Gleiwitz/Oberschlesien) on 27 October. He was president of the national federation of the GDR, the Deutschen Verband für Leichtathletik (DVfL), from 1959 to 1990, an EAA council member 1970-87 and IAAF council member 1972-91. From 1990 he was honorary president of the German federation, the DLV.

Michael Edwin '**Mike**' **WIGGS** (GBR) (b. 25 Apr 1938 Rickmansworth) on 8 December. He competed in five internationals for Britain 1960-5, making his debut at 1500m in 1960, in which year he went out in his heat at the Olympic Games. He moved up successfully to 5000m and was 11th (fell) in the 1964 Olympics, going on to set a UK record of 13:33.0 in 4th place at the Helsinki World Games behind the three men who transformed the event that year – Michel Jazy 13:27.6 (European record), Kip Keino 13:28.2 and Ron Clarke 13:29.4. Wiggs also set a UK 3 miles record of 13:08.6 en route. Other pbs: 800m 1:48.4 (1964), 1500m 3:40.7 (1964), 1M 3:57.5 (1965), 3000m 8:04.0 (1966), 2M 8:44.6 (1964), 6M 29:06.6 (1966).

Doug WOLLEN (USA) (b. 29 Jan 1960) in August. He set a discus best of 61.46 when 2nd at the Pac-10 Championships in 1962 while at the University of Washington. He worked as a project manager for Boeing.

James 'Jim' WORRALL (Canada) (b. 23 June 1914 Bury, Lancashire, England) in Toronto on 9 October. He competed (heats) in both hurdles events at the 1936 Olympics, at which he was Canada's flag bearer at the opening ceremony. He ranked 12th in the world in 1934 with a converted 400m hurdles time of 54.6. That year he was the silver medallist at 120yh and 4th at 440yh in the Empire Games. He was Canadian champion at 440yh in 1934 and high jump in 1933. Pb 120yh 15.0 (1935). A lawyer, he was President of the Canadian Olympic Committee 1964-8, was made a member of the IOC in 1967 and an honorary member in 1989. He wrote a book: "My Olympic Journey: Sixty Years with Canadian Sport and the Olympic Games."

Died in 2012

Gösta ARVIDSSON (Sweden) (b. 21 Aug 1925) on 16 February in Skövde. He had a shot best of 15.92 in 1948, in which year he was 5th at the Olympic Games. He was 9th at the Europeans in 1950 and Swedish champion 1950-1.

Márta BÁCSKAI née KRIPLI (Hungary) (b. 1 Oct 1960 Veszprém) on 3 February in Pápa . Hungarian champion at shot 1986 and discus 1983-6, and 6th at both events at the World University Games in 1985. 13 internationals 1983-8. She had a shot best of 18.16 (1986) and set Hungarian discus records with 65.35 (1985) and 65.64 and 66.48 (1986)

Margaret BISEREKO Ayo (Uganda) (b. 23 Oct 1954) on 3 January. She was 2nd in the pentathlon at the 1978 All-Africa Games and 2nd in the heptathlon in her pb of 5029 points (old tables) at the 1982 African Championships. She also represented Uganda at netball, basketball, handball and volleyball and was a leading coach.

Torgeir BRANDVOLD (Norway) (b. 17 Oct 1913) on 23 February. Norwegian champion at 100m 1936 and long jump 1937. He competed in internationals 1933-46 and later set several world veterans records. Pbs: 100m 10.8 (1934), 200m 22.5 (1939), 400m 49.8 (1939), 400mh 57.6 (1939), LJ 7.28 (1933).

John Albert **HARTFIELD** (USA) (b.1 Nov 1944) on 19 January in Houston. He went to Texas Southern University, was second in the 1966 US high jump with 2.16, and jumped 2.16 again in 1967 to rank equal sixth on that year's world list. In 1968 he just missed Olympic selection, placing fourth in the Trials with a pb 2.185. He later became an outstanding performer in masters' competition.

Francis John **'Frank' HORWILL** (b. 19 Jun 1927) on 1 January in Hackney, London. A hugely controversial coach, he made many enemies but also many athletes, perhaps most notably Tim Hutchings, benefitted immensely from his coaching and technical knowledge of distance running. He helped to set up with British Milers' Club in 1963 and in 1970 formulated his influential Five Pace Training Theory. A prolific writer, he co-authored with Denis Watts and Harry Wilson the *Complete Middle Distance Runner* (1972) and published *Obsession for Running* in 1991. He was awarded the MBE in 2011.

Laila JENSEN (Norway) (b. 9 Mar 1957) on 22 December. In 1970 she became the youngest ever Norwegian record breaker with 3000m walk in 15:59.5 at the age of 13 years 106 days. She improved this record later that year to 15:45.0 and had pbs of 3000mW 15:06.0 and 5000mW 25:31.2 (both 1973). Three internationals 1970-3

Kauko JOUPPILA (Finland) (b. 3 Mar 1921 Seinäjoki) on 10 February in Seinäjoki. A discus thrower with Finnish Champs silver in 1949 and six internationals 1949-56, 'Kaappoo' became a legendary figure due as his career spanned some 70 years. Surpassing 50m first at age 42, his best ever 54.26 came in 1973, when aged 52. He appeared in the Finnish top 100 yearly lists for over 40 years, throwing the 2kg implement to 48.22 as late as 1982. He had great success as a veteran for many decades at World and European level, closing his career with a M85 WR in 2006. His brothers were shot putters: Jaakko (1923-50) Olympics 1948 with a pb 15.93, Eero (b. 1938) 19.24 (1973) and Matti (b. 1944) 19.00 (1981). Kauko's sons, Jussi (b. 1945) put

the shot 19.10 (1972) and Antti (b. 1949) threw the discus 60.52 (1973).

Miroslav JUZA (Czech Republic) (b. 22 Jan 1943 Cebin) on 13 January. In the first European Indoor Games in 1966 he was 6th at 3000m and won a bronze at 3x1000m relay. He set a European Junior record for 1000m with 2:24.1 in 1962 and had pbs: 800m 1:49.1 (1964), 1000m 2:19.4 (1964), 1500m 3:42.9 (1965), 1M 3:59.2 (1965), 5000m 14:11.4 (1967). 8 internationals for Czechoslovakia 1963-6.

Heikki KYÖSOLA (Finland) (b. 26 Jan 1945 Turku) on 4 January in Tampere. At triple jump he had four internationals 1969-71 and was 2nd at the 1971 Finnish Champs, with pb 16.30w (15.92). He switched to decathlon, and in 1973 improved the Finnish record of his twin brother Hannu (1945-2004) from 7763 to 7831 points (present tables: Hannu 7669, Heikki 7689); also winning the Finnish title in 1973 and 1974, with 14th in the 1974 Europeans. Pbs: 100m 10.6 (1973), 400m 49.5 (1971), HJ 2.00 (1974), PV 4.40 (1974), LJ 7.50 (1971), JT 72.12 (1974).

Stevan LENERT (Serbia) (b. 6 Mar 1919 Sombor) on 10 February in Budapest. Yugoslav champion at PV 1938, 1945-6; LJ 1938, 1945-7, and TJ 1945, he set Yugoslav records at LJ 7.14 (1939), and PV 3.76 (1946) and 3.80 (1947). Eight internationals for Yugoslavia and two for Hungary (1942-3). He was Head of the Yugoslav national team 1954-62.

Pavel LITOVCHENKO (Russia) (b. 18 Jul 1952) in February. He had a best for 800m of 1:46.4 (1976) and was 2nd at the 1975 World University Games and in the Russian Championships of 1974 and 1976. He coached several top 800m runners including Viktor Kalinkin and 1991 world champion Liliya Nurutdinova. He worked in Malaysia as coach in 1996-2001.

Vernon Vorhees **McGREW** Jr (USA) (b. 7 Dec 1929 Big Spring, Texas) on 9 January in Houston. As a 6ft 3in tall 18 year-old he was 3rd in the AAU and won the US Olympic Trials with 2.04m in 1948 (joint top of the world lists that year and this remained his pb). He was, however, overawed at the Olympics and came 14th with 1.80m (1.87 in qualifying). While at Rice University he won the NCAA high jump in 1950 (after 3= in 1948 and 2= in 1949). He later worked in the oil industry for Exxon.

Albert **'Bertie' MESSITT** (Ireland) (b. 28 Sep 1930 Bray, Co. Wicklow) on 18 February in Bray. He did not finish the 1960 Olympic Games marathon, and at the Europeans was 15th at 10,000m (heat 5000m) in 1958 and 13th in the marathon in 1962. At the time he held Irish records for 3 miles 13:44.0, 5000m 14:14.8, 10,000m 30:00.0, 10M 49:35.2, 1Hr 19,442m (all 1958) and 6M 28:45.0 (1959). Marathon pb

2:25:39.4 (1963). He was Irish champion at 3M 1958, cross-country 1959-61 and marathon in 1962 and 1963, and ran seven times in the International Cross-country.

Lutz PHILIPP (Germany) (b. 14 Oct 1940 Königsberg) of leukaemia in Darmstadt on 1 February. A top distance runner for the FRG from the mid 1960s to the mid 1970s, he competed at three Olympics: ht 5000m 1964, 23rd 10,000m 1968, and 32nd marathon 1972; and two Europeans: 12th 10,000m 1966 and 7th marathon 1971 (also selected in 1969 when FRG boycotted in the Jürgen May affair). He was 2nd in the European Cup 10,000m in 1965 and won World University Games medals: silver at 5000m in 1965 and bronze at 10,000m in 1967 (with 5000m 5th 1963 and 9th 1967). FRG champion at 10,000m 1965, 1967 and 1972, marathon 1971-3, and forest run 1967, 1969-73; and indoor champion at 5000m 1963 and 1965-9, and 10,000m 1967-8 and 1970-1. German records: 10,000m (4) from 28:44.8 (1965) to 28:23.4 (1970), 20,000m 59:20.2, 1 hour 20.237m and 25,000m 1:15:31.8 (all 1973), marathon 2:12:50 (1972). Other pbs: 1500m 3:50.9 (1969), 3000m 7:59.4i/8:00.8 (1965), 5000m 13:44.0 (1965), 3000mSt 8:50.2 (1964).

Fernando ROZO (Colombia) (b. 21 Feb 1967 Huila) on 21 January in Bogotá. He was twice third (1990 and 1995) in the South American Walks Cup at 35km and set pbs in 1996 of 20k 1:25:40.3 and 50k 4:27:23. He coached leading Colombian walkers, most notably Luis Fernando López, World bronze medallist in 2011.

István RÓZSAVÖLGYI (Hungary) (né Reidl, b. 30 Mar 1929 Budapest) in Tata on 27 January. He reached his peak in the mid-1950s as one of the great trio of Hungarian middle distance runners with Sándor Iharos and László Tábori, his teammates at the Honvéd club where they were coached by Mihály Iglói. After going out in the heats of the Europeans in 1954, he burst on to the world scene in 1955 when he improved at 800m from 1:55.8 to 1:48.8 and at 1500m from 3:46.6 to 3:41.2 (having earlier set a European record at 3:42.2). He also tied the world record for 1000m with 2:19.0 on September 21 and smashed that for 2000m with 5:02.2 at Budapest on October 23 (previous mark was 5:07.0). A year later he took 0.3 off the world record for 1500m with 3:40.5 on August 3 in Tata. A month later he had a great race against Gordon Pirie in Malmö, when he was 2nd in 7:53.4 behind Pirie's 7:52.8, both well inside Pirie's previous world record of 7:55.6. The Hungarian revolution took the edge off his ability to fare well at the Olympics in December and he did not advance from the heats. He continued, however, to set quality marks over the next five years and at 1500m was 4th at the 1958 Europeans and 3rd at the 1960 Olympics, being ranked as 1st in the world in 1959. He

also ran on world record relay teams: 4x1500m 15:29.2 (1953), 15:21.2 (1954), 15:14.8 (1955), and 4x1 mile 16:25.2 (1959). 36 internationals 1953-61. Hungarian champion 800m 1955, 1500m 1956-60. 1.77m, 58kg.

Annual progression at 1500m (position on world list): 1953- 3:47.4 (12=), 1954- 3:46.6 (13=), 1955- 3:41.2 (4), 1956- 3:40.5 (1), 1957- 3:44.4 (25=, 1958- 3:40.0 (5), 1959- 3:38.9 (1), 1960- 3:38.8 (5), 1961- 3:44.6 (28), 1962- 3:45.1 (58=). Other pbs: 800m 1:48.4 (1959), 1500m 3:38.8 (1960, then 7th all-time), 1M 3:59.0 (1955), 5000m 13:59.8 (1961).

Gábor TAMÁS (Hungary) (b. 24 November 1951, Homokmégy), on 30 January in Budapest. He competed at the Europeans 1978 (10th) and at the World University Games in 1975 (4th) & 1977 (6th) at hammer. He broke Gyula Zsivótzky's national record (73.76 WR) 14 years later in 1982 with 73.86 and improved that year to 74.74. Hungarian champion 1976-81, 23 internationals 1975-82. Pb SP 14.18 (1975).

Johan Gerard 'JO' ZWAAN (Netherlands) (b. 11 Nov 1922 Amsterdam) on 5 February in Diemen. He competed at the 1948 Olympic Games, heat of the 100m and on the 6th placed 4x100m team – his brother Jan also competed at 110m hurdles. Jo was also a 100m semi-finalist at the 1946 Europeans and Dutch champion at 100m 1948. A member of Amsterdamse AC he had bests of 100m 10.6 and 200m 22.0 (both 1943).

Died in 2010

Jarl Staffan **BURMAN** (Sweden) (b. 10 Jan 1942 Burträsk) on 6 August. Swedish champion at 5000m and 10000m in 1967. 12 internationals. Pbs: 3000m 8:19.4 (1968), 5000m 14:22.0 (1967, 10000m 29:36.4 (1967).

Martin REHÁK (Czech Republic) (b. 20 Aug 1933 Hrubá Vrbka) on 25 March. At triple jump he was the European bronze medallist in 1954 and 5th at the 1956 Olympics in his pb of 15.85, his tenth Czechoslovak record (from 14.56 in 1952). He ranked in the world top ten each year 1953-6. 20 internationals 1951-60. Pbs: HJ 1.91 (1954), LJ 7.51 (1956), JT 63.14 (1953).

Died in 2008

Malcolm James William **DALRYMPLE** (GBR) (b. 2 Dec 1922 Bedford) on 17 November. He competed in four internationals for Britain at the javelin, including at the 1948 Olympic Games and his win against France in 1949 was the first ever at the event for Britain in a dual international. He set a British record with 64.24 in 1948, was AAA Junior champion in 1939 and 2nd at the AAAs in 1946 and 1948-50. He was the son of 'Jock' Dalrymple, who competed at the 1924 Olympic Games and set six British javelin records in 1923-4.

DRUG BANS

THE IAAF ANNOUNCED that 468 urine samples were collected during the World Champs in Daegu and confirmed that two athletes returned adverse analytical findings for the prohibited stimulant, methylhexaneamine: Sara Moreira (POR; 12th in women's 3000mSC) and Lim Hee-Nam (KOR; in national record 4x100m team). Both were provisionally suspended pending the outcome of their respective disciplinary hearings and later received 6-month suspensions. For the first time ever blood samples were collected from every athlete with analysis being carried out at the WADA-accredited laboratory in Lausanne.

Drugs bans in 2011

Suspension: Life - life ban, y = years, m = months, W = warning and disqualification, P = pending hearing

Men

Name	Date	Ban
Benik Abramyan GEO	?	?
Mohamed Al-Matroud KSA	26 May	6m
Alemayehu Bezabeh ESP	3 Jun	2y
Damien Broothaerts BEL	21 Aug	2y
Héctor Carrasquillo PUR	30 Apr	2y
Victor Castillo VEN	25 Oct	P
Matthew DiBuono USA	23 Jun	4y
Fouad El Kaam MAR	10 Jun	6m
Ivan Emelianov MDA	18 Jun	2y
Martin Fagan IRL	10 Dec	2y
Carl Fletcher GBR	23 Mar	4y
Jacob Freeman USA	26 Feb	1y
Vipin Kasana IND	19 Feb	2y
Josephat Kithii KEN	7 May	1y
Dmytro Kosynskyy UKR	18 Jun	2y
Kuldev Singh IND	20 Feb	2y
Lim Hee-nam KOR	4 Sep	6m
Aziz Lahbabi MAR	10 Jun	6m
Richard Mavuso RSA	22 May	2y
Steve Mullings JAM	24 Jun	L
Cédric Nabe SUI	22 Jun	1y
Mike Rodgers USA	19 Jul	9m
Gregory Sedoc NED	22 Jun	1y
Dmitriy Sorokin RUS	18 May	2y
Tian Mengzu CHN	12 Apr	2y
Xia Zhongwei CHN	3 Jun	2y

Women

Name	Date	Ban
Ashwini Akkunji IND		1y
Tatyana Aryasova RUS	27 Feb	2y
Tahesia Harrigan-Scott IVB	26 May	6m
Semoy Hackett TRI	13 Aug	6m
Koletane Ieso IRQ	8 Jul	1y
Chang Jingxue CHN	12 Mar	2y
Sini Jose IND		1y
Mandeep Kaur IND		1y
Racheal Marchand PUR	25 Jul	2y
Sara Moreira POR	30 Aug	6m
Jauma Murmu IND		1y
Josephine Onyia NGR	9 Jul	2y
Yevgeniya Pecherina RUS	25 Jun	2y
Sandra Perkovic CRO	16 May	6m
Darya Pizhankova UKR	15 Jul	2y
Lebogang Phalula RSA	27 Aug	3m
Simone da Silva BRA	3 Aug	P
Olga Tereshkova KAZ	8 Jul	2y
Bernice Wilson GBR	12 Jun	4y

2y: Mahdi Hassan Al-Qharni KSA (5 May), Ayoub Arkehy IRI (14 Apr), Bodhisatya Banerjee IND (29 May), Gaurab Bhardwaj IND (13 Jun), Artur Bigayev RUS (24 May), Nuno da Costa POR (19 Mar), Joachim De Naeyer BEL (27 Feb), Nikita Dorofeyev BLR (26 Jan), Byron Duhon USA (13 Jul), Pavel Fenck CZE (13 Jul), José Manuel Gonçalves POR (10 Jul), Alevtina Grischenko RUS (7 Aug), Adam Hricz HUN (26 Jun), Veronika Ilyina RUS (16 Sep), Kathy Jager USA (29 Jun), Jagmal IND (14 Apr), Donika Katholika BUL (20 Feb), Ali Khamani IRI (15 Apr), Katia Khristova BUL (13 Feb), Olga Kelemnicheva RUS (7 Aug), Hemant Kirulkar IND (25 Apr), Ulyana Lepska UKR (17 Jul), Yevgeniya Lyubchenko BLR (17 Nov), B Madhusudhana IND (14 Apr), Leonid Mezhenov BLR (26 Apr), Harikrishanan Muraeleedharan IND (17 Jun), Sharadha Narayana IND (16 May), Olga Ortina RUS (24 Jul), Megha Pardeshi IND (3 May), Melissa Peretti ITA (6 Mar), Zahra Raisiee IRI (14 May), Rinku Sangwan IND (20 Feb), Stephen Shumaker USA (28 Jul), Soniya IND (14 Jun), Dian Taylor DOM (13 Sep), Igor Urusov RUS (7 Aug), Anna Vlasova RUS (15 May), Mehdi Zamani IRI (17 Jun), Jacob Zorzella-Manners CAN (25 Jun); **1y**: Priyanka Panwar IND, Tiana Mary Thomas IND; **8m**: Frederick Kieser USA (28 Jul), Julien Vrielynck FRA (5 Feb); **6m**: Pavel Khvorostukhin RUS (24 Jul); **4m**: Florence Guillauma FRA (27 Aug), **3m**: Frédéric Berland FRA (12 Jun), Anna Bramley NZL (26 Mar), Estela García ESP (7 Aug), Anthony Godongwana RSA (25 Sep), Sébastien Guesdon FRA (22 Apr); **W**: Pascal Mancini SUI (8 Sep).

Zhanna Block (formerly Pintusevich), who retired from sprinting in 2006, was given a two-year ban for breaking anti-doping rules in 2002 and 2003. In 2003 she won the World Indoor 60m and was 3rd at 100m and 5th at 200m at the World Champs.

Eddy Hellebuyck tested positive for EPO in 2004 and received a two-year ban but recent information, including Hellebuyck's own public admissions, revealed that his use of performance enhancing drugs dated back to 2001 so his performances were invalidated from 1 Oct 2001 to 30 Jan 2004.

Gert Thys (RSA), who served a ban in 2006-08, was cleared by the CAS, and his 2006 Seoul Marathon win in 2:10:40 reinstated.

Continued on page 52 (bans from 2010 and earlier)

WORLD LISTS 1962

! = world record   **MEN**

100 YARDS

9.2!	Bob Hayes USA	1	Coral Gables	17 Feb
9.2!	Harry Jerome CAN	1	Vancouver	25 Aug
9.3	Stone Johnson USA	1h	Houston	11 May
9.3	Frank Budd USA	1	Villanova	12 May
9.3	Joe Thornton USA	1	Petersburg	19 May
9.3A	Seraphino Antao KEN	1	Nairobi	22 Sep
9.2w		1	Dublin	18 Jun
9.2w	R.L.Lasater USA	1	Commerce	31 Mar

9.3w eight men; 10th best 9.4, 100th 9.6

100 METRES

10.1	Bob Hayes USA	1	Hässelholm	17 Aug
10.2	Andrzej Zielinski POL	1	Praha	2 Jun
10.2	Dave James USA	1	Zürich	10 Jul
10.2	Roger Sayers USA	2	Stanford	21 Jul
10.2	Marian Foik POL	1	Olsztyn	11 Aug
10.1w		1	Lódz	1 Sep
10.2	Peter Gamper FRG	1	Praha	11 Aug
10.2	Paul Drayton USA	2	Hässelholm	17 Aug
10.2	Anatoliy Ryedko URS	1s	Alma-Ata	22 Sep
10.2	Gusman Kosanov URS	2s	Alma-Ata	22 Sep
10.2	Edvin Ozolin URS	1	Tashkent	14 Oct

10th best 10.2, 100th 10.5

10.1w	Heinz Schumann FRG	1s	Bremen	26 Aug

200 METRES (* 220y less 0.1 sec.)

20.4*!	Paul Drayton USA	1	Walnut	23 Jun
20.6*	Steve Haas USA	1	Los Angeles	14 Apr
20.6*	Homer Jones USA	1	Houston	12 May
20.6*	Harry Jerome CAN	1h	Eugene	15 Jun

20.7 ten men. 10th best 20.7, 100th 21.2

20.0*wA	Seraphino Antao KEN	1	Nairobi	22 Sep
20.4*w	Ray Knaub USA	1	Lincoln NE	12 May

220 YARDS (Straight Track)

20.0!	Frank Budd USA	1	Villanova	12 May
20.1	Henry Carr USA	1	Tempe	5 May
20.1	Paul Drayton USA	2	Villanova	12 May
20.3	Adolph Plummer USA	1	Tempe	10 Apr
20.0w		1	Abilene	14 Apr
20.3	John Moon USA	1	Fort Campbell	5 May
20.3	John Lewis USA	1	Stephenville	11 May
20.3	Dave Morris USA	1	Modesto	26 May
20.3	Ira Murchison USA	1	Chicago	24 Jun
20.0w	Anthony Watson USA	1h	Lawrence	18 May
20.0w	Odell Barry USA	1h	Findlay	19 May

400 METRES (* 440y less 0.3 sec.)

45.5*	Ulis Williams USA	1	Walnut	23 Jun
45.6*	Robbie Brightwell GBR	1	London (WC)	14 Jul
45.7*	Adolph Plummer USA	1	Abilene	14 Apr
45.7*	Ollan Cassell USA	1	Fort Hood	19 May
45.7	Peter Laeng SUI	1	Zürich	10 Jul
45.8*	Earl Young USA	2	Abilene	14 Apr
45.8*	Ted Woods USA	1	Lawrence	19 May

10th best 45.9, 100th 47.2

800 METRES (* 880y less 0.7 sec.)

1:44.3+!	Peter Snell NZL	1	Christchurch	3 Feb
1:46.3*	Jerry Siebert USA	1	Stanford	9 Jun
1:46.8	Jim Dupree USA	2	Stanford	22 Jul
1:47.0*	John Reilly USA	3	Walnut	23 Jun
1:47.1*	Ben Tucker USA	2	Stanford	9 Jun
1:47.1	Michel Jazy FRA	1	Limoux	13 Oct
1:47.1*	George Kerr JAM	2	Perth	26 Nov

10th best 1:47.4, 100th 1:49.8

1000 METRES

2:19.3	Michel Jazy FRA	1	St. Maur	6 Jun

1500 METRES

3:38.3	Michel Jazy FRA	1	St. Maur	7 Oct
3:39.3+	Peter Snell NZL	1	Wanganui	27 Jan
3:39.4	Jim Beatty USA	1	Oslo	9 Aug
3:40.2	Jim Grelle USA	2	Oslo	9 Aug
3:40.8	Witold Baran POL	1	London (WC)	4 Aug
3:41.0	Ivan Byelitskiy URS	2	Stanford	22 Jul
3:41.1	Vasiliy Savinkov URS	1	Moskva	13 Aug

10th best 3:41,7, 100th 3:47.8

1 MILE

3:54.4!	Peter Snell NZL	1	Wanganui	27 Jan
3:56.3	Jim Beatty USA	1	Helsinki	21 Aug
3:56.7	Jim Grelle USA	2	London (WC)	18 Aug
3:57.9	Dyrol Burleson USA	2	Los Angeles	18 May
3:58.0	Stanley Taylor GBR	3	London (WC)	18 Aug
3:58.1	Cary Weisiger USA	3	Walnut	23 Jun
3:58.3	Keith Forman USA	1	Modesto	26 May

10th best 3:59.1, 100th 4:08.7

2000 METRES

5:01.5!	Michel Jazy FRA	1	Paris (C)	14 Jun

3000 METRES

7:49.2	Michel Jazy FRA	1	St. Maur	27 Jun
7:54.2	Jim Beatty USA	1	Avranches	15 Aug
7:56.0	Michel Bernard FRA	2	Avranches	15 Au
7:58.2	Edward Strong GBR	1	London (WC)	11 Jun

2 Miles

8:29.8	Jim Beatty USA	1	Los Angeles	8 Jun
8:33.6	Murray Halberg NZL	1	Hamilton	24 Jan
8:33.7	Bruce Tulloh GBR	2	Hamilton	24 Jan

5000 METRES

13:38.4	Murray Halberg NZL	1	Auckland	17 Feb
13:43.8	Bruce Kidd NZL	1	Compton	2 Jun
13:45.0	Jim Beatty USA	1	Turku	24 Aug
13:48.2	Hans Grodotzki GDR	1	Turku	11 Jul
13:49.6	Max Truex USA	2	Compton	2 Jun
13:50.6	Hermann Buhl GDR	2	Turku	11 Jul
13:50.6	Pyotr Bolotnikov URS	1	Helsinki	31 Jul

10th best 13:53.4, 100th 14:17.4

3 Miles

13:12.6+	Murray Halberg NZL	1	Auckland	17 Feb
13:16.0	Bruce Tulloh GBR	1	London (WC)	14 Jul
13:17.0	Bruce Kidd NZL	2	London (WC)	14 Jul

10,000 METRES

28:18.2!	Pyotr Bolotnikov URS	1	Moskva	11 Aug
28:49.4	Hans Grodotzki GDR	1	Potsdam	30 Jun
28:55.6	Mamo Wolde ETH	1	Berlin	9 Jun
29:00.8	Abebe Bikila ETH	2	Berlin	9 Jun
29:01.4	Bruce Tulloh GBR	1	Oslo	3 Jul

10th best 29:04.8, 100th 30:02.0

6 Miles

27:49.8	Roy Fowler GBR	1	London (WC)	13 Jul
27:49.8	Mike Bullivant GBR	2	London (WC)	13 Jul
27:52.0	Martin Hyman GBRL	3	London (WC)	13 Jul
27:56.6	Mel Batty GBR	4	London (WC)	13 Jul
27:58.4	Bruce Tulloh GBR	1	London (WC)	11 Jun

MARATHON

2:16:09.6	Yu Mang-hyang PRK	1	Pyongyang	24 Oct
2:16:18.4	Toru Terasawa JPN	1	Fukuoka	2 Dec
2:16:53.4	Takayuki Nakao JPN	2	Fukuoka	2 Dec
2:18:01.8	Kenji Kimihara JPN	3	Fukuoka	2 Dec
2:18:56.8	Buddy Edelen USA	4	Fukuoka	2 Dec
2:18:57.4	Pavel Kantorek TCH	5	Fukuoka	2 Dec
2:19:09.2	Makoto Nakajima JPN	6	Fukuoka	2 Dec

10th best 2:20:16.8, 100th 2:27:28.2

3000m STEEPLECHASE

8:32.6	Gaston Roelants BEL	1	Beograd	16 Sep
8:35.4	Hermann Buhl GDR	1	Moskva	1 Jul
8:35.8	Vladimir Yevdokimova URS	1	Kyiv	17 Jun
8:36.0	Nikolay Sokolov URS	2	Kyiv	17 Jun
8:36.2	Aleksey Konov URS	1	Moskva	11 Aug
8:37.6	Zoltán Vamos ROU	2	Beograd	16 Sep
8:37.9	Zdzis. Krzyszkowiak POL	1	Chicago	1 Jul

10th best 8:39.6, 100th 9:00.8

110 METRES HURDLES (y = 120y h)

13.3y	Jerry Tarr USA	1	Eugene	19 May
13.4y	Hayes Jones USA	1	Walnut	22 Jun
13.7	Fran Washington USA	1	San Jose	7 Apr
13.8i	Anatoliy Mikhailov URS	1	Leningrad	2 Mar
13.7y	Blaine Lindgren USA	1	Compton	2 Jun
	13.6Ayw		1h Denver	25 May
13.8y	Don Styron	1	Gainesville	31 Mar
13.9	four men; 10th best 13.9, 100th 14.4			
13.7yw	Ray Cunningham	1	Odessa TX	17 Mar

220 YARDS HURDLES (Straight Track)

22.5	Don Styron USA	1	Natchitiches	1 May
22.5	John Bethea USA	1	Baltimore	3 Jun
22.1mw	Fran Washington USA	1	San Jose	7 Apr
22.5w	Blaine Lindgren USA	1h	Denver	25 May

Turn

22.8y	Jerry Tarr USA	1	Eugene	1 Jun

400 METRES HURDLES (* 440y less 0.3 sec.)

49.2!	Salvatore Morale ITA	1	Beograd	14 Sep
50.0*	Jerry Tarr USA	1	Eugene	16 Jun
50.2*	Willie Atterberry USA	1	Walnut	22 Jun
50.3*	Rex Cawley USA	2	Walnut	22 Jun
50.3	Jörg Neumann FRG	2	Beograd	14 Sep
50.4	Helmut Janz FRG	1	Prag	11 Aug
50.6	Russ Rogers USA	1	Zürich	10 Jul
50.6	Vasiliy Anisimov URS	1	Moskva	13 Aug
10th best 50.8, 100th 52.7				

HIGH JUM

2.27!	Valeriy Brumel URS	1	Moskva	29 Sep
2.17	Ni Chihchin CHN	1	Beijing	16 Sep
2.165	Jo Faust USA	1	Norwalk	19 Apr
2.16	Stig Pettersson SWE	1	Stockholm	23 Aug
2.15	Robert Shavlakadze URS	1	Yerevan	26 May
2.15	John Thomas USA	1	Göteborg	20 Aug
2.145	Colin Ridgeway AUS	1	Laredo	10 Mar
2.145	Gene Johnson USA	1	Chicago	30 Jun
10th best 2.13, 100th 2.03				

POLE VAULT

4.94!	Pentti Nikula FIN	1	Kauhava	22 Jun
4.93!	Dave Tork USA	1	Walnut	28 Apr
4.91i	Don Meyers USA	1	Chicago	20 Dec
4.90	Ron Morris USA	1	Helsinki	21 Aug
4.89i!	John Uelses USA	1	Boston	3 Feb
	4.89!	1	Santa Barbara	31 Mar
4.82	Dick Plymale USA	1	West Point	19 May
4.81	Manfred Preussger GDR	1	Jena	22 Aug
10th best 4.77, 100th 4.44				

LONG JUMP

8.31!	Igor Ter-Ovanesyan URS	1	Yerevan	10 Jun
8.07	Ralph Boston USA	1	Walnut	22 Jun
	8.15w	1	Stanford	21 Jul
7.97	Darrell Horn USA	1	Cairo	25 Oct
7.93	Anthony Watson USA	1	Eugene	15 Jun
7.92	Paul Warfield USA	2	Eugene	15 Jun
7.90	Mel Renfro USA	3	Eugene	15 Juny
7.90	Antanas Vaupshas URS	1	Yerevan	28 Oct
8.05w	Michael Ahey GHA	1	Perth	26 Nov
7.89w	Leonid Barkhovskiy URS	1	Tatabánya	18 Aug
10th best 7.86, 100th 7.47				

TRIPLE JUMP

16.65	Vladimir Goryayev URS	1	Kyiv	17 Jun
16.55	Józef Schmidt POL	1	Beograd	13 Sep
	16.57w	1	Warszawa	18 Aug
16.51	Aleksandr Zolotaryev URS	1	Mak. Kala	21 Sep
16.50	Ryszard Malcherczyk POL	1	Warszawa	9 Jun
16.48	Oleg Fyedoseyev URS	1	Moskva	1 Jul
16.38	Vitold Kreyer URS	2	Moskva	11 Aug
16.36	John Baguley AUS	*	Perth	24 Feb
	16.46w	1	Perth	24 Feb
10th best 16.25, 100th 15.46				

SHOT

20.08!	Dallas Long USA	1	Los Angeles	18 May
19.80i	Gary Gubner USA	1	New York	16 Feb
	19.78	2	Los Angeles	18 May
19.49	Arthur Rowe GBR	1	Sheffield	12 Jun
19.16	Zsigmond Nagy HUN	1	Athína	25 Jul
19.11	Vilmos Varju HUN	1	Budapest	26 May
19.03	Dave Davis USA	3	Los Angeles	18 Ma
18.93	Viktor Lipsnis URS	3	Stanford	21 Jul
18.70	Parry O'Brien USA	1	Honolulu	3 Sep
10th best 18.49, 100th 16.75				

DISCUS

62.45!	Al Oerter USA	1	Chicago	1 Jul
62.00	Bob Humphreys USA	1	Long Beach	14 Jul
61.64!	Vladimir Trusenyov URS	1	Leningrad	4 Jun
60.66	József Szecsényi HUN	1	Tatabánya	19 Aug
60.65	Jay Silvester USA	1	London (WC)	13 Ju
60.35	Rink Babka USA	1	Long Beach	25 Aug
59.52	Edmund Piatkowski POL	1	Warszawa	17 Jun
59.47	Kim Bukhantsev URS	1	Leselidze	1 May
10th best 58.76, 100th 52.15				

HAMMER

70.67!	Harold Connolly USA	1	Stanford	21 Jul
70.42	Gyulka Zsivótzky HUN	1	Budapest	23 Sep
68.90	Yuriy Bakarinov URS	1	Leningrad	20 May
68.17	Aleksey Baltovskiy URS	1	Moskva	1 Jul
67.82	Josef Matousek TCH	2	Tatabánya	19 Aug
67.80	Vasiliy Rudenkov URS	1	Moskva	12 Jul
67.14	Heinrich Thun AUT	1	Wien	23 Jul
10th best 66.66, 100th 59.12				

JAVELIN

86.04	Janis Lusis URS	1	Tashkent	14 Oct
85.64	Vladimir Kuznyetsov URS	1	Baku	23 Sep
83.65	Carlo Lievore ITA	1	Innsbruck	31 May
81.27	Marian Machowina POL	1	Lódz	2 Sep
81.01	Nick Birks AUS	1	Adelaide	24 Feb
80.98	Janusz Sidlo POL	1	Frankfurt	14 Oc
80.82	Glenn Winningham USA	1	Fort Hood	18 May
80.80	Pauli Nevala FIN	1	Turku	7 Octt
10th best 80.60, 100th 72.84				

DECATHLON (1952 tables)

8246	Yang Chuan-Kwang TPE	1	Tulare	30 Jun
8026	Werner Von Moltke FRG	2	Beograd	14 Sep
8022	Vasiliy Kuznetsov URS	1	Beograd	14 Sep
7893	Janis Lusis URS	1	Tashkent	19 Oct
7725	Paul Herman USA	2	Stanford	22 Jul
7724	Eef Kamerbeek NED	4	Beograd	14 Sep
7703	Phil Mulkey USA	1	Birmingham	29 Dec
7668	Willi Holdorf FRG	3	Hamm	24 Jun
10th best 7544, 60th 6518				

20 KILOMETRES WALK

1:27:25.2	Mikhail Lavrov RUS	1	Leningrad	20 May
1:27:25.4	Vladimir Senin RUS	2	Leningrad	20 May
1:28:15	Valentin Danilov URS	1	Kuibyshev	29 Jul
1:28:19t	Grigoriy Panichkin URS	1	Kharkov	22 Sep
1:28:40	Grigoriy Klimov URS	1	Moskva	1 Jul
1:28:40t	Pyotr Mandrakov URS	1	Leningrad	19 Aug
1:29:42.4	Hans-Joachim Pathus GDR	1	Potsdam	11 Jul

50 KILOMETRES WALK

4:04:32.8	Grigoriy Klimov URS	1	Moskva	12 Aug
4:10:55.6	Gennadiy Agapov URS	1	Tashkent	19 Oct
4:12:26.6	Grigoriy Panichkin URS	2	Moskva	12 Aug
4:13:00.0	Ivan Bakunovich URS	4	Moskva	12 Aug
4:13:11.0	Sergey Grigoryev URS	2	Tashkent	19 Oct
4:16:57.0	ILev Stepanov URS	5	Moskva	12 Aug
4:18:04.8t	István Havasi HUN	1	Budapest	3 Jun

4x100 METRES

39.5	FR Germany	1	Beograd	16 Sep
39.5	Poland	2	Beograd	16 Sep

39.6	USA	1	Stanford	21 Jul
39.8	Great Britain	1h	Beograd	14 Sep
39.9	France	1	Colombes	29 Sep
40.0	Venezuela	1	Kingston	25 Aug

4x400 METRES

3:03.7	USA	1	Chicago	1 Jul
3:05.9	FR Germany	1	Beograd	16 Sep
3:05.9	Great Britain	2	Beograd	16 Sep
3:07.0	Switzerland	3	Beograd	16 Sep
3:07.7	Sweden	4	Beograd	16 Sep

WOMEN

100 YARDS

10.5	Glenys Beasley AUS	1	Adelaide	27 Jan
10.3w	Margaret Burvill AUS	1	Perth	22 Sep
10.5w	Robin Scott, Joyce Bennett, Rhonda Bainbridge			

100 METRES

11.4	Jutta Heine FRG	1h	Praha	11 Aug
11.3w		2	Beograd	13 Sep
11.4	Wilma Rudolph USA	1	Malmö	30 Aug
11.5	Maria Itkina URS	1	Kyiv	16 Jun
11.5	Dorothy Hyman GBR	1	Blackburn	20 Jun
11.3w		1	Beograd	13 Sep
11.5	Teresa Ciepla POL	1h	Warszawa	20 Jul
11.4w		3	Beograd	13 Sep
11.5	Hannelore Raepke GDR	1	Potsdam	22 Jul
11.6 five women, 10th best 11.6, 100th 12.0				
11.4w	Joke Bijleveld NED	1	Ritswijk	13 May

200 METRES (* 220y less 0.1 sec.)

23.3	Jutta Heine FRG	1	Malmö	13 Aug
23.4	Dorothy Hyman GBR	1	London (WC)	18 Aug
23.6	Hannelore Raepke GDR	2	Malmö	13 Aug
23.6	Maria Itkina URS	1	Kyiv	23 Sep
23.7	Vivian Brown USA	1	Stanford	22 Jul
23.7*	Margaret Burvill AUS	1	Perth	8 Sep
23.6*		1	Adelaide	28 Jan
23.8 five women, 10th best 23.8, 100th 24.9				

400 METRES

51.9!	Shin Keum-dan PRK	1	Pyongyang	23 Oct
53.4	Maria Itkina URS	1	Beograd	14 Sep
53.6*	Dixie Willis AUS	1	Perth	17 Feb
53.7+	Gerda Kraan NED	1	London (WC)	29 Sep
53.7+	Tilly van der Zwaard NED	2	London (WC)	29 Sep
53.9	Joy Grieveson GBR	2	Beograd	14 Sep
54.3	Yekaterina Parlyuk URS	2s	Beograd	13 Sep
10th best 54.8, 100th 57.9, * 440y less 0.3 sec.				

800 METRES

2:01.2+!	Dixie Willis AUS	1	Perth	3 Mar
2:01.4!	Marise Chamberlain NZL	2	Perth	3 Mar
2:01.4	Shin Keum-dan PRK	1	Moskva	1 Jul
2:02.8	Gerda Kraan NED	1	Beograd	16 Sep
2:05.0	Waltraud Kaufmann GDR	2	Beograd	16 Sep
2:05.0	Olga Kazi HUN	3	Beograd	16 Sep
2:05.0	Joy Jordan GBR	4	Beograd	16 Sep
10th best 2:07.2, 100th 2:14.6, * 880y less 0.8 sec				

1500 METRES

4:19.0+!	Marise Chamberlain NZL	1	Perth	8 Dec

1 MILE

4:41.4!	Marise Chamberlain NZL	1	Perth	8 Dec
4:45.5	Joan Beretta AUS	2	Perth	8 Dec

80 METRES HURDLES

10.5!	Betty Moore AUS/GBR	1	Kassel	25 Aug
10.6	Erika Fisch FRG	1	Berlin	3 Jun
10.6	Irina Press URS	1	Moskva	1 Jul
10.6	Karin Balzer GDR	1	Rostock	15 Jul
10.6	Teresa Ciepla POL	1	Beograd	16 Sep
10.5w		1	Lódz	1 Sep
10.6	Maria Piatkowska POL	3=	Beograd	16 Sep
10.6	Pamela Kilborn AUS	1h	Melbourne	22 Sep
10th best 10.7, 100th 11.4				

HIGH JUMP

1.87	Iolanda Balas ROM	1	Praha	22 Sep
1.78	Robyn Woodhopuse AUS	1	Perth	26 Nov
1.76	Olga Gere YUG	1	Beograd	14 Sep
1.76	Galina Dolya URS	1	Baku	21 Sep
1.76	Taisia Chenchik URS	1	Tashkent	15 Oct
1.75	Helen Frith AUS	1	Auckland	17 Feb
1.75	Micheline Mason AUS	1	Melbourne	14 Oct
1.74	Galina Kostyenko URS	1	Moskva	13 Mat
10th best 1.73, 100th 1.62				

LONG JUMP

6.62!	Tatyana Shchelkanova URS	1	Bruxelles	6 Oct
6.35	Helga Hoffmann FRG	1	Hamburg	27 Jul
6.34	Hildrun Claus GDR	1	Praha	11 Aug
6.41w		1	Praha	3 Jun
6.30	Joke Bijleveld NED	1	Den Haag	29 Apr
6.30	Elzbieta Krzesinska POL	1	Lódz	2 Sep
6.29	Mary Ran GBR	Q	Beograd	14 Sep
6.26	Ingrid Becker FRG	2	Hamburg	27 Jul
6.26w	Pamela Kilborn AUS	1	Perth	1 Dec
10th best 6.21, 100th 5.82				

SHOT

18.55!	Tamara Press URS	1	Leipzig	10 Jun
& 18.55!		1	Beograd	12 Sep
17.47	Renaye Garisch GDR	1	Potsdam	22 Jul
16.95	Galina Zybina URS	3	Beograd	12 Sep
16.59	Valerie Young NZL	1	Geraldton	17 Nov
16.53	Johanna Hübner GDR	2	Potsdam	8 Sep
16.51	Wilfriede Hoffmann GDR	2	Berlin	17 Sep
16.21	Zinaida Doynikova URS	2	Vlasim	24 Jun
16.15	Mariya Kuznyetsova URS	1	Praha	3 Jun
10th best 16.10, 100th 13.72				

DISCUS

58.17	Tamara Press URS	1	Moskva	13 Aug
56.39	Doris Müller GDR	1	Leipzig	24 Jun
55.53	Jolán Kontsek HUN	1	Budapest	7 Jul
55.33	Jirina Nemcová TCH	1	Praha	12 Sep
54.99	Marie Simancová TCH	1	Praha	22 Aug
54.05	Ingrid Lotz GDR	1	Dresden	29 Sep
54.85	Nina Ponomaryeva URS	1	Moskva	13 Jul
54.03	Irene Grieser GDR	1	Rostock	15 Jul
10th best 53.77, 100th 45.60				

JAVELIN

58.33	Elvira Ozolina URS	1	Leselidze	6 May
56.33	Virve Poldsam URS	1	Pärnu	10 Jun
55.68	Aldona Stanciute URS	Q	Tashkent	14 Oct
55.66	Maraia Diaconsecu ROU	1	Bucuresti	12 Aug
55.04	Aleksandra Prasolova URS	1	Alushta	26 Apr
54.65	Anneliese Gerhards FRG	1	Itzehoe	24 Jun
54.03	Inge Schwalbe GDR	1	Praha	11 Aug
54.02	Marion Graefe GDR	1	Leipzig	29 Jul
10th best 53.48, 100th c.45m				

PENTATHLON (1954 tables)

4975	Irina Press URS	1	Leningrad	21 May
4833	Galina Bystrova URS	1	Beograd	14 Sep
4751	Jutta Heine FRG	1	Hamm	24 Jun
4735	Denise Guenard FRA	2	Beograd	14 Sep
4738	Lidiya Shmakova URS	1	Kyiv	25 Sep
4676	Helga Hoffmann FRG	3	Beograd	14 Sep
4663	Ingrid Becker FRG	4	Beograd	14 Sep
4619	Karin Balzer GDR	1	Leipzig	1 Jul
10th best 4607, 100th best 4100				

4x100 METRES

44.5	Poland	1	Beograd	16 Sep
44.6	USA	1	Stanford	22 Jul
44.6	FRG	2	Beograd	16 Sep
44.9	USSR	2	Stanford	22 Jul
44.9	Great Britain	3	Beograd	16 Sep
46.0	GDR	1	Potsdam	4 Aug
46.1*	Australia	1	Adelaide	28 Jan

Contrasting fortunes for Olympic champions

By Bob Phillips

THE OLYMPIC TRACK and field champions of 2012 will be heaped with honours and financial rewards, lionised by the media, and welcomed with open arms by monarchs and presidents. Their comfort and prosperity will, in all probability, be assured for the rest of their lives. The experiences of the title-holders at the strictly amateur Stockholm Games of 100 years ago were distinctly different. The double sprint winner promptly retired but would reappear in a different guise at the Games 36 years later. The victor in the 1500 metres, who claimed that he never trained at all, ran no other race of remotely comparable importance and preferred the golf-course to the cinder-track. The greatest all-rounder was stripped of his titles when it was discovered that he had briefly played professional baseball.

Those Stockholm Games were very much better organised than any of their predecessors, and even a capricious late change of mind by the organisers concerning the stadium's design, thus reducing the circumference of the track from the regulation 400 metres to 383, caused aggravation to no one except maybe the groundsman imported from England, Charles Perry, responsible for marking out the various starting-points. The programme of events included for the first time 5000 and 10,000 metres, 4x100 and 4x400 metres relays, though there was no 400 hurdles – impractical, as you might imagine, on the odd-sized track – and the standing high jump and standing long jump made their last appearances, as did the 'both hands' competitions in the shot, discus and javelin. It would seem that no one thought, perhaps fortunately, of providing the hammer-throwers with a second chance of gold by having them spin leftwards and rightwards in turn.

Further key technical innovations were the timing of events to one-tenth of a second and the use of electrical apparatus to assist in the judging of finishing positions. For the first time, too, there were athletes representing all five continents – 529 competitors in all from 28 countries – but no widespread share-out of the gold medals, as the USA won 16 of the 30, Finland six, Sweden three, Great Britain two, and Canada, Greece and South Africa one each. The sweeping domination of the Americans aggrieved the British, though

there was some consolation – albeit that it went unrecognised at the time – in that the Canadian 10,000 metres track walk winner, George Goulding, had been born in Yorkshire, and the South African marathon winner, Kennedy McArthur, was of Northern Ireland birth.

One member of the Japanese two-man team *did* reach the 400 metres semi-finals, but it helped that there was only a single other runner in his heat and both qualified! None of the six representatives of Chile managed to advance to a final, but then nor did any of the 28 from Czarist Russia. Sweden's tally of three gold medals (team cross-country, triple jump, javelin) from 111 athletes was maybe thought of as a low return, considering that a highly experienced US coach, Ernie Hjertberg, from New York Athletic Club, had been employed for the two previous years and the entire contingent gathered together at a training-centre for the three months leading up to the Games.

The favourite for the 100 metres had been a 22-year-old Afro-American, Howard Drew, who was still attending high school, and who in his country's various Olympic trial races had been one of three men to equal the US record of 10.8 (actually 10⁴⁄₅ on the watches then in use). Drew duly proceeded to the six-man final in Stockholm, along with four other Americans and a South African, but then failed to start after suffering a leg-muscle strain in his semi-final. There was some suggestion in later years that Drew was pressurised by his team management into withdrawing for racially-motivated reasons, but the contemporary newspaper coverage in the USA largely indicates that it was, indeed, the injury which cost him his Olympic chance. In confirmation of that evidence, he actually reported for the start of the final and ineffectually attempted to warm up.

The organisers had unwisely decided not to penalise false starts, and there were seven in the final, of which the American winner was responsible for three, but this was not Donald Lippincott, who had run a world record 10.6 in the heats. Rather it was Ralph Craig, from Detroit, and he later added the 200 metres, having previously run his own world records for 220 yards on a straight course in 1910 and

1911. Craig promptly gave up running after his successes in Stockholm to get on with earning a living as an industrial engineer, but he later found the leisure-time to develop his yachting skills and was sent to the 1948 Olympics as a reserve at the age of 59, honoured for his seniority by carrying the US flag at the opening ceremony.

Craig missed out on the opportunity for a triple sprint success in Stockholm because he was not selected for the 4 x 100 metres relay, though it did not matter that much because the Americans were disqualified in the semi-finals, anyway, and Great Britain rather suprisingly won the title. The most celebrated of the British quartet was Willie Applegarth, who was also 3rd at 200 metres and two years later would set a world record for 220 yards round a turn (a fairly gentle turn, it must be said) that would not be beaten for 18 years. Tragically, one of Applegarth's team-mates, Henry Macintosh, who was then an undergraduate at Cambridge University, was to be among the 16 British athletics Olympians who would very soon lose their lives during the First World War (or Great War as it was known at the time).

The 400 metres champion, Charles Reidpath, was another member of the US team whose athletics career came to an end immediately after the Olympics, having graduated from university with a civil engineering degree that year. His individual final was the first to be held in lanes, after the debacle in 1908 when Wyndham Halswelle (to be among the British World War I victims) won a 're-run' on his own. Reidpath's second gold medal, as anchor-man for the 4 x 400 metres relay, was also a solitary endeavour because he later cheerfully admitted that his team-mates had carried the baton so far ahead of the opposition that "by the time it came for me to take over, the race was just about over, too".

One of those relay colleagues of Reidpath's who made life so easy for him was Edward Lindberg, who also played in the 'exhibition' baseball tournament at the Games and was the longest-living of all the gold-medallists that year, dying at the age of 89 in 1978. The other two in the US quartet were among the hardest-working athletes in Stockholm. Ted Meredith, also the 800 metres champion and 4th at 400 metres, was running his eighth race in eight days, while for Melvin Sheppard, silver-medallist at 800 metres and 9th at 1500 metres, it was his seventh race in nine days – and this was an era when the quantity and quality of training by even the best of athletes was derisory compared with modern standards. 'Peerless Mel' Sheppard had also won gold medals for the 800 and 1500 metres and the medley relay at the 1908 Games and made a spectacular bid to defend his 800 title in Stockholm, running the first half in an unprecedented 52.4 but failing to shake off Meredith, who won in a world record 1:51.9 and was also timed at 880 yards (804.67 metres) in 1:52.5. Meredith was then aged 20 and in 1916 set further world records of 47.4 for 440 yards (402.34 metres) and 1:52.2 for 880 yards which lasted 12 and 10 years respectively. After the USA entered World War I, Meredith became a fighter pilot and Sheppard served as physical education director at various military training-camps.

Despite Meredith's world records in Stockholm, which would be the first at the distances to be ratified by the newly formed IAAF, plus numerous other American successes on the track, the most memorable runners at the Games were undoubtedly a Finn and an Englishman. The leader of what was to become a legion of 'Flying Finns' was Hannes Kolehmainen, who in the course of eight days achieved a feat of 'Zátopek-ian' proportions, running six races, winning three gold medals and setting world records for 3000 and 5000 metres. The Englishman was Oxford University-educated Arnold Nugent Strode Jackson, whose training was not so much derisory as non-existent but who shocked the Americans in the 1500 metres final with a withering home-straight sprint which beat all seven of them, including the soon-to-be-recognised world record-holder, Abe Kiviat.

The 5000 metres was an intensely exciting race in which Kolehmainen just managed to hold off Jean Bouin, of France, by one-tenth of a second, and both men were almost half-a-minute faster than the previous best for the distance. Kolehmainen's other victories came in the 10,000 metres and a cross-country event for which the course was kept secret from the competitors, and the Swedes – perhaps benefiting from their invention of orienteering some quarter-of-a-century before – unexpectedly won the team award. Kolehmainen added a further gold in the marathon at the 1920 Olympics, but Bouin was to die little more than two years after the Stockholm Games ended, killed in action on the battle-fields of Flanders.

Kolehmainen's 3000 metres record came in the heats of a team event at that distance, for which Finland oddly failed to qualify and the title went to a US trio in a desperately close race in which nine runners finished within 25 metres or so. The individual winner, most surely the least known in Olympic distance-running history, was Tell Berna by barely the width of his vest, and such precise judment would no doubt have come in useful in his future employment as a manager of national renown in the USA's machine-tool industry. One of Berna's team-mates was George Bonhag, who has the distinction of having also won an unusual Olympic race-walking gold, at 1500 metres in 1906, and the other was Norman Taber, who three years later was to beat all records for the mile, including Walter George's legendary 4:12¾ as a professional in 1886.

Arnold Jackson had only taken up running at Oxford the year before the Games, having previously been an oarsman, and even the British Olympic Association admitted in its post-Games report that he was something of a throwback to the 19th Century public-school ideals of effortless superiority on the playing-field. It was a radical admission to state that "natural talent, unassisted, may sometimes serve us, as it did in one brilliant instance on the track, yet on the whole it has become necessary to pay far more attention than has hitherto been our custom to the matter of training in running and, more especially, in field events". Jackson became the youngest Brigadier General in the British army and then emigrated to the USA and took citizenship there before returning to Oxford for the final years of his life. When he died in November 1972 the world record for the mile had been reduced to 3:51.1.

Ironically, two of those field events in which Britain languished so far behind the rest of the World were won by Americans, Pat McDonald (shot) and Matt McGrath (hammer), who had been born in Ireland, which was then under British rule. and had emigrated in the 1890s. McDonald beat his more favoured team-mate, Ralph Rose, who had won in 1904 and 1908 and who found some compensation in Stockholm with 1st place in the 'both hands' event (15.25m + 12.47m). Rose was another short-lived champion, dying of typhoid fever in 1913 at the age of 28, and the same year marked the death of the Greek winner of the standing long jump, Konstantinos Tsiklitiras, killed in action at 24 in the Balkan War.

McDonald was to become the one other athlete apart from Kolehmainen to win Olympic gold again eight years later, triumphing on this second occasion in the 56lb weight throw, which was being held for the one and only time at the Games. Armas Taipale, of Finland, winner of both discus events in Stockholm, was not far off emulating Kolehmainen and McDonald, losing the 1920 discus (one hand only) by less than half-a-metre. Even so, these careers were far eclipsed in terms of longevity by that of McGrath, who had won the hammer silver in 1908 and was to do so again in 1924, by then aged 45, and of the javelin champion from Sweden, Eric Lemming, who took part in every Games from 1900 to 1912 and accumulated four gold medals, including one for the tug-of-war. Though Lemming had the strongest javelin-throwing arm in Stockholm, he could only place 4th in the 'both hands' event to a Finn, Juho Saaristo, who had become the first man to exceed 60 metres, single handed, the previous May.

The high jump went to an exponent of the dramatic but restrictive 'Eastern Cut-Off' style, Alma Richards, who reckoned that his athletic skill had developed from a boyhood spent chasing rabbits across the fields and fences of the family farm in Utah. In a way, though, Richards was as representative of the old order as Arnold Jackson had been at 1500 metres because his fellow-American, George Horine, having perfected the new-fangled 'Western Roll' and taken the world record up to 6ft 7in (2.007m), was only 3rd, having apparently worn himself out beforehand demonstrating his agility to bemused coaches who probably thought, "This will never catch on". The British certainly were of that opinion because no one in that country was to attempt Horine's revolutionary technique before another 20 years or more had passed. The USA also won the 110 metres hurdles (Fred Kelly), long jump (Albert Gutterson) and pole vault (Harry Babcock), and one of the country's very few setbacks was in the triple jump (then more accurately known as the hop step and jump) in which the winner of the standing high jump, Platt Adams, was back in 5th place and all three medals went to Swedes, led by Gustaf Lindblom.

Despite those premature deaths of 1912 champions, the briefest reign of all was that of the man who was admiringly addressed by the King of Sweden at a medal ceremony, "Sir, you are the greatest athlete in the World". Jim Thorpe, the Native American winner of the pentathlon and the decathlon, is reputed to have replied, "Thanks, King", but the euphoria did not last long. In January of the following year it was revealed that Thorpe had briefly played minor-league professional baseball, and so his victories were annulled. The International Olympic Committee reinstated him posthumously in 1982, and though the names of the upgraded title-holders for the intervening 70 years still remain in the official records they are rarely recalled. You may thus care to note that Ferdinand Bie, of Norway, won the pentathlon and Hugo Wieslander, of Sweden, the decathlon. Another Norwegian, Helge Løvland, would be decathlon champion in 1920, with a Swede 3rd, but neither country has had a medal in the event since.

Sweden has, of course, much more recently produced a highly proficient muti-events exponent, Caroline Klüft, winner of the heptathlon in 2004, but the idea of women competing in any sort of track and field event at the Games of 1912 was unthinkable. This was no more no less than male chauvinistic hypocrisy because women *did* take part in swimming in Stockholm and a quartette of young ladies from Great Britain won the 4 x 100 metres freestyle relay wearing costumes that would be regared as revealing in 2012, let alone 1912. But that's a story for telling elsewhere!

World records set at the 1912 Olympic Games

100 metres 10.6 (in heats) Donald Lippincott (USA), *400 metres* 48.2 Charles Reidpath (USA), though this was actually inferior to the 440 yards record! *800 metres* 1:51.9 Ted Meredith (USA), *880 yards* 1:52.5 Meredith, *3000 metres* 8:36.8 Hannes Kolehmainen (Finland), *3 miles* 14:07.2 (intermediate time) Jean Bouin (France), *5000 metres* 14:36.6 Kolehmainen, *4 x 100 metres* 43.0 (in semi-finals) Great Britain, 42.5 (in semi-finals) Sweden, *4 x 400 metres* 3:16.6 USA, *10,000 metres walk* 46:28.4 George Goulding (Canada), *Pentathlon* 3367pts (1985 tables) Jim Thorpe (USA), *Decathlon* 6564pts (1985 tables) Thorpe.

Footnote: Bob Phillips's book about Great Britain's Olympic gold-medallists in all sports (including reference to the daring lady swimmers!), has been issued this year by Carnegie Publishing, www.carnegiepublishing. co.uk, and his biography of the 1912 and 1920 British Olympic high jumper, B. Howard Baker, has been issued by Derby Publishing, www. dbpublishing.co.uk. He is also author of The 1948 Olympics – How London Rescued the Games www.sportsbooks.ltd.uk

RLQ: NINETY AND STILL GOING STRONG
By Bernard Linley

ROBERTO LUIGI QUERCETANI (RLQ to all), one of the eleven founding members of the ATFS in 1950, its initial president and first editor of the *ATFS Annual* for almost two decades, reached the venerable age of 90 on 3 May 2012.

Born in Firenze (Florence, Italy) where he lived all his life, RLQ is a legend in world athletics although his participation in the sport never went beyond the recreational level. Running with friends in the Boboli Gardens, one of the pearls of his home town, he was outclassed as a sprinter. Had he taken time from his studies, perhaps he might have become a mediocre middle distance runner, today the 800m and 1500m still remain his favourites.

How he was first excited by track and field at the age of ten, when the Italian Luigi Beccali won the 1932 Olympic 1500m gold medal, and how he developed a passion for studying foreign languages in his teens were illustrated in his contribution to *The ATFS Golden Jubilee Book* published in 2000.

During his formative years in the thirties, following athletics news from abroad and becoming fluent (speaking, reading and writing) in English, French and German helped Roberto to see beyond the prison walls imposed by the dictatorship under which Italy was forced to live. Reading foreign newspapers and magazines, received through friends in Switzerland, helped a great deal. His outlook on the world grew wider in the immediate postwar years, when he worked as a technical interpreter with the Allied forces in Italy.

The first athletics article under the RLQ by-line appeared in *Yleisurheilu* of Finland in 1943, and was followed over the years by regular columns in *Leichtathletik* of Germany, *World Sports* of England, *Track and Field News* of the USA and others. Curiously it was only in 1951 that his first Italian byline appeared, in the Milan daily *La Gazzetta dello Sport*, which in August 2011 celebrated 60 years of his collaboration.

The first statistical publication by RLQ was done with Don Potts in 1948, and there followed a stream of others covering the European Championships, All Time lists, etc. His first non-statistical book *A World History of Track and Field Athletics 1864–1964* was published by Oxford University Press in 1964. This masterpiece has been updated on several occasions (the most recent in 2000) and translated into at least four languages. After that, while churning out articles and statistical books and reporting on track meets for the Firenze daily *La Nazione*, Roberto began working on separate histories of events.

With Cordner Nelson he co-authored in 1973 the story of the mile, and by 1999 had also published histories of the 800m and thereabouts, and the long distance track races.

No tribute to Roberto would be complete without mention of Maria Luisa, his spouse since 1964 and main support throughout his professional life as a freelance sports journalist and writer. They make a good team, despite the fact that he was from south of the Arno while she came from north bank of this river, which runs through the city of Florence and in medieval times divided it both physically and socially.

Although he never lived outside Firenze, thanks to athletics, Roberto has managed to travel a bit including a full round-the-world trip in 1956 to the Melbourne Olympics via USA and returning home via Asia and Africa.

And of course, because of his reputation and affable personality, the world came to him in Firenze. Some readers will recall seeing his famous lampshade covered with the autographs of the many ATFS members and other track and field personalities who visited. In the early fifties the RLQ homestead was visited by ATFS Secretary-General Norris McWhirter and his Oxford team mate Roger Bannister, before the world's first sub-4 minute mile ... and the lampshade!

After turning sixty Roberto began taking things easier and added walks in the Boboli gardens to his daily schedule. These walks, and the fact that there is a staircase but no lift to his second floor apartment in Via Inghirami, certainly contributed to keeping our friend in good shape.

As regards "taking things easy" we have doubts, as the RLQ byline continues appearing in the *ATFS Annual* and in articles of specialist magazines. Furthermore, since the turn of the century more titles in the history series have appeared: *The One Lap Race* (2005), *Sprint Racing* (2006), *Hurdle and Steeplechase Racing* (2009) and *Jumping Events* (2011). His work in progress includes the history of the Throwing Events, collaborating with the IAAF on its Centennial publication, and probably other projects.

Having successfully completed his four score years and ten, we join the ATFS membership and his many friends in wishing RLQ "ad multos annos", in particular spectating at the 2016 Olympics in Rio de Janeiro, Brazil.

IAAF RULE CHANGES 2011

By Bob Hersh

BY FAR THE best publicised, and most controversial, change that the IAAF made to the Rules of Competition in 2011 dealt with World Records in women's road races. At the Congress in Daegu, it was decided that women's World Records in road events are to be recognized for women–only races. Performances in mixed races, if superior, would be listed separately as World Best Performances. (Rule 261).

This decision resulted from a growing discomfort over situations in which women were paced by men in important races. Pacing is permitted under IAAF rules, but mixed road races represent the only situation in which the "rabbit" can set the pace for the entire race. This was actually being done, and many people considered that unfair assistance

The IAAF's new rule was the subject of widespread confusion and misunderstanding. It was wrongly assumed by some journalists and others that the effect of the change would necessarily be to retroactively remove the IAAF's recognition of Paula Radcliffe's World Record in the marathon, as well as other World Road Records. In fact, the IAAF never said that this would happen, and in November, the Council made it clear that it will NOT happen – the rule will affect only future records.

This should not have been at all surprising, considering that in the past, when the IAAF has changed its World Record rules to preclude other forms of possible unfair assistance, no existing records were affected. This has happened at least three times in recent years with drug-testing requirements. In any event, the new rule may be reconsidered at the next IAAF Congress in 2013. One possibility, which has been recommended by the IAAF's Road Running Commission, would be to recognize separate World Records for women-only races and mixed races (if the latter is faster).

Another significant change involving records was the recognition, for the first time, of World Junior Indoor Records. (Rule 264). After this change was adopted, Council accepted an initial list of such records, based on a consensus of statisticians as to the best legitimate performance in each event. (Several ATFS members contributed to this work).

Two important amendments that appear in the new IAAF Rulebook were actually adopted by Council on an interim basis in 2010. One was the change that made it possible to have a preliminary round in a track event limited to athletes who have not met the qualifying standard for the meet. (Rule 166.1). This new procedure was implemented at the Daegu World Championships; it will be in effect at the London Olympic Games as well.

The other 2010 amendment now made permanent enables the IAAF to regulate the participation of females who have undergone male-to-female sex reassignment as well as females with hyperandrogenism. (Rule 141.6). The application of these regulations will enable the IAAF to apply a science-based approach to this controversial subject.

A new piece of officiating equipment was introduced by a rule change relating to starts. When an athlete commits a false start and is thereby disqualified, a red and black (diagonally halved) card will be displayed to him or her, and a corresponding indication shown on the lane marker. In combined events, when the first false start in a race is committed, the card is yellow and black (again diagonally halved) and this is displayed to the offending athlete and at the same time to the entire field, warning them that the next false start will result in a disqualification.

A new rule that will be applauded by the media and spectators alike, if it is implemented, permits the IAAF and other governing bodies to require that the colour on athletes' vests be the same on the front and back. (Rule 141.1).

Several new provisions deal with relays. Close readers of Rule 170 will notice that the entire rule has been reorganized and some of it has been rewritten. However, only a few substantive changes were made. Runners are no longer permitted to wear gloves or apply substances to their hands to obtain a better grip on the baton. (Rule 170.4). If a runner drops the baton and moves sideways or forward, the runner must retrieve the baton and bring it back to the point where it was dropped before continuing in the race. (Rule 170.6). The rules now provide a procedure for the 100–200–300–400 medley relay that has been used in Youth competition. (Rule 170.14). The option of running the 4x400 relay in lanes only through the first bend was added (it had previously been possible under the rules only where not more than four teams were competing). (Rule 170.15).

A major change was made to the rules governing throws and horizontal jumps. The order of competition will no longer be adjusted after the fifth round. Only one re-ordering will be made—the one after the third round. (Rule 180.5(a)). Another amendment codifies a practice that has been seen in practice in recent years: the relevant governing body may prescribe that where there are more than eight athletes in an event, they may all have four trials. (Rule 180.5 *Note (iii))*.

The race walking rules were amended to limit the power of the Chief Judge to summarily disqualify a walker who is obviously breaking the rules. That power used to apply anywhere inside the stadium; it is now limited to the last 100 metres, as it is when the finish line of the course is outside the stadium. (Rule 230.3(a)). Presumably, in order to prevent abuse in the half lap preceding the last 100 metres, in situations where the walkers enter the stadium 300 or 350 metres from the finish line, one or two other judges will have to accompany the Chief Judge back to the stadium from the walk course.

In addition to the changes mentioned above, there were many relatively minor technical changes on such diverse subjects as:
- Establishing Chief Transponder Judge as a new official position (Rules 128 and 165.28).
- Permitting heart rate or speed distance monitors or speed sensors (Rule 144.2(g))
- Further defining who is entitled to file an appeal (Rule 146.3 and 146.6)
- Re-stating when the Referee can order a race re-run after a false start has occurred by not been recalled (Rule 146.4(b)

- Amending the width and colour of road race finish lines (Rule 164.1)
- Prescribing the uniformity of taping at the grip end of the vaulting pole (Rule 183.11)
- Adding the requirement that anything like chalk placed on a shot or discus must be easily removable (Rule 187.4(c))
- Clarifying that the touching top inside edge of the rim or stop board during a throw is prohibited (Rule 187.14)
- Limiting the number of team officials who may staff water/refreshment stations and prohibiting them from running beside the athlete who is taking water or refreshment (Rule 240.8(f))
- Adding recommended distances of 6km for Boys and 4km for Girls in Youth Cross Country races (Rule 250.6)
- Permitting a world record in an oval race to be set on a track with an outside lane that has a radius greater than 50m as long as the record is set in a lane with a radius not greater than 50m (Rule 260,18(c)), and
- Removing the requirement of a post-race measurement for record acceptance in a road race when the course was originally measured by two approved measurers and one of them is present at the race to validate that the course was run as measured (Rule 260.28(e)).

For further details about these and other technical and editorial changes, please refer to the 2012-2013 rule book, which can be purchased from the IAAF. The rules can also be downloaded from the IAAF's website. Both print and online versions show the changes from the 2010-2011 edition of the rules.

IAAF Administration

LAMINE DIACK, UNOPPOSED, was re-elected as President of the IAAF at the IAAF Congress in Daegu and The four Vice-Presidents elected for the next four years were Robert Hersh (USA) (appointed Senior Vice-President in succession to Sergey Bubka), Dahlan Al-Hamad (QAT), Sebastian Coe (GBR) and Sergey Bubka (UKR).

Two pillars of IAAF administration retired in 2011: Jean Poczobut, a former National Technical Director of the French Federation, an IAAF Council member since 1995 and Honorary Treasurer from 2003, and Pierre Weiss (64), Assistant to the General Secretary 1985–87, General Director 1991–2006 and General Secretary from 2006. The new General Secretary, appointed by the President, is another Frenchman, 43-year-old Essar Gabriel, who was the Director General of the Organising Committee for the Paris World Championships in 2003 and responsible for the organisation of the first Youth Olympic Games held in Singapore in 2010. Valentin Balakhnichev of Russia was elected as the new Honorary Treasurer.

NOTES FROM THE EDITOR

London Olympics

LONDON WILL HOST the Olympic Games for the third time in 2012. After athletics events were staged at the White City Stadium in 1908 and at Wembley in 1948 the focus switches from the west to the east of the city – to Stratford in 2012.

Some grizzled veterans will recall being taken to the Games in 1948, but there is far less easy access for youngsters this year. The requirements of the modern world mean that far more seats have to be reserved for sponsors, VIPs, media and so on than was the case 64 years ago – and demand for tickets this time inevitably far exceeded supply. That led to many complaints from people unable to get seats for the prime events, especially Londoners who felt that they had a special right to attend and that an inadequate proportion was reserved for them. And yet I would rather they had been allocated an even smaller proportion.

For the Olympic Stadium in London 2012 will be full of people who know little about athletics and the devoted followers of the sport who travel the world for major athletics events will, in the main, be absent. So too will many aspiring young athletes for whom this could have been a huge stimulus. Some, for sure, will have got tickets in the ballot, but I would have preferred that a large proportion of tickets should have gone via the clubs as is done annually in Britain for such major events as Wimbledon and the FA Cup.

There should be plenty of passion and excitement in the arena, but perhaps not as much as there could have been. However, while there may be considerable travel and security issues, I am confident that Britain will stage hugely well-managed sporting events.

Legacy?

The most vital aspect of the Games coming to London is the regeneration of the Eastern part of the city. This is proceeding nicely and the construction part of the Olympic exercise has been a great success, delivered on budget and to time.

Great stress was placed on a legacy aspect to Britain's bid for the Games, in particular in attracting more people into sport. Here there must be considerable doubts over what will happen in athletics. The number of active competitors in track and field events in Britain has fallen sharply over the past quarter century and that decline continues. Amazingly, while there are thousands of youngsters who participate in athletics, and many tens of thousands of adults of all abilities who take part, at least occasionally, in road runs, there are less than 1500 regular participants in track and field competition who are in the 20-34 age range in Britain (far, far less than is understood by UK and England Athletics). A detailed survey by Rob Whittingham (see his website for UK rankings at www.topsinathletics.info) showed that only about 1,000 men and 450 women in this senior age range competed regularly in Britain in 2011. Will the Olympic Games act as a spur to increase that number? Well, I rather doubt it, especially with the emphasis placed by our governing bodies on winning medals at major championships, and thus on the elite.

Then there is the Olympic Stadium. The original plan was for an 80,000 stadium that could be reduced to some 20,000 capacity after the Games – and built up again as and when necessary. That would have been ideal with plenty of opportunities for athletics meetings and for a wide variety of events that could make for a sustainable complex. Instead the authorities have gone for the temptation of higher rewards and we have had football clubs in contention for ongoing use of the site (with mooted plans by Tottenham Hotspur including pulling down the existing stadium and refurbishing and expanding Crystal Palace as a sop to athletics).

Given that an athletics track around the pitch is anathema for football fans there should surely never have been any discussion with football, the sport which dominates the sporting world but whose administrators care for little else. Indeed, London would surely not have been granted the 2012 Games without the plan for a permanent athletics facility. At last, after much wasted time, there has been a government promise that the athletics track will remain and UK Athletics has signed a 99-year lease for use of the Stadium.

The World Championships in athletics has been obtained for London in 2017, but apart from this and the annual Diamond League London Grand Prix meeting with the occasional major international championship (spread thin over many years) it is hard to see much use of the athletics track. Yes, the

European Championships, never held in Britain, should come some time, but that is a one off, and generally the venue will be likely to be too big and too costly for ordinary athletics meetings. West Ham United football club is the most likely tenant, and if they are successful, with football seasons extending at least from August to May, there will be a very small window for athletics, and football people do not realise the length and extent of major domestic athletics meetings. Can we really trust that the track will remain?

I just hope that the Olympic Stadium will thrive and be a centre for sport in Britain and a particular wish is that a permanent Olympic museum and library could be built into the complex at Stratford. Now that would be a real legacy. Members of the National Union of Track Statisticians, forming the Sports Archive Foundation, have set up a home for the collections of various athletics devotees at Cobham Hall in Kent, with some substantial bequests and the encouragement of the headmaster of the school there. This now houses by far the best collection of athletics books and magazines etc., in Britain, but it could grow vastly with bequests from many aging enthusiasts, and it would be marvellous if a permanent home could be found in the Olympic Park for such an athletics collection with possibilities of expansion with material from other Olympic sports.

Hard times

ONE NOTES THE cancellation of various athletics meetings this year, notably in Germany and of course in Greece (with even their Olympic participation in doubt), as the effects of the economic problems in the Euro zone in particular are inevitably reflected in sport. There seems sure to be a decline in sponsorship and government backing for athletics events in the next few years.

Olympic competition gives a boost to its sports but there could be some difficult years ahead. Interest in the sport from major media has declined, as has the number of participants in track and field events (though not road running) in the developed world, although that has been balanced by a big increase in worldwide participants and competition.

The IAAF has given a lead in taking the sport to new territories and such a trend has been seen in many sports, but while the economic resources might be there to stage a major event, all too often there is little evidence of mass appeal in these new venues – and there remains a heavy concentration of dedicated followers of athletics living in Europe and supporting the sport in the old continent. But even there only the very best meetings attract capacity crowds and much work needs to be done to retain interest and indeed to stimulate growth.

Records are scarce

IT WAS A slight surprise for me to discover that there was a definite increase in standards in depth in world indoor lists this year. Several big names passed the World Indoor Championships but quite a few of these had tested their form and fitness in competition in one or two events during the short, sharp indoor season. It was, however, a sign of the times that only three world indoor records were broken – by Yelena Isinbayeva in the women's pole vault and by the multi-eventers Nataliya Dobrynska and Ashton Eaton in wining their World Indoor titles. The shortage of world records had once again had shown in 2011 outdoors when world records went in only two standard men's events, the marathon and 4x100m relay, and only in one standard women's event – the hammer, not counting the 20km walk where a new record was set, but this was slower than previous performances in which full testing procedures had not been in place.

In *ATHLETICS 2011* I listed (on page 277) world records, indoors and out, that had lasted for 20 years or more. Not a single one of the 23 listed has been broken in the year since that list was published. The longest have now stood outdoors since 1983 for women (Jarmila Kratochvílová 800m) and since 1986 for men (Jürgen Schult) and indoors since 1977 for women (Helena Fibingerová shot) and 1984 for men (Carl Lewis (long jump). And indeed it is hard to imagine that several of these will be broken for a long time yet. All makes this a very different era from the old days of say 1955-85 when records tumbled as the world of athletics grew mightily with major technical, medical and coaching advances as well as the movement towards true worldwide participation and equality for men and women.

But standards in depth improve

I NOTED ABOVE that there had been an improvement in standards in depth indoors this year – and perhaps more significantly so there was overall in 2011. This was something of a surprise because it is usually in Olympic years that standards peak in a four-yearly cycle, but an examination of my TRENDS survey on pages 528 and 529 shows clearly the advance at many events in the past year. This was most marked for men as 10th best levels for men in 2011 were ahead of those for 2010 in 16 events to 5 (with 2 tied) and the 100th best levels in 21 events to 2 (1 tied). For women the 10th best levels were down a little: 9 events to 13 but were again well ahead for 100th bests 18 to 4.

Elsewhere in this Annual we comment on the remarkable surge in marathon running standards by the East Africans, and new records were set for both men and women for 10th and 100th bests. But also notable was that 2011 was a great year for 100m running for men, particularly at the highest levels as the 10th best man ran 9.89 compared to a previous record of 9.95 (2008 and 1010) and the 100th best of 10.21 was also a record. This was also the best ever year for depth at 1500m running, for men with the 100th best of 3:37.77 being easily better than the previous best of 3:38.42 from back in 1997 despite the fact that no man broke 3:30, and for women the best ever mark for 100th in the lists that had stood at 4:10:22 since 1984 improved in 2011 to 4:09.86 (and there were 103 women under 4:10 from a previous record of 96 in 1984). But, in similar fashion to the top men, no woman broke 4 minutes in 2011 compared to 13 doing so in 1997.

Standards for multi-events have been in decline in recent years, but there was a big improvement in the decathlon with 165 men over my list standard of 7400 points compared to 136 in 2010, and the 100th best improving from 7526 to 7678. New standards in depth were also set in women's pole vaulting, but the tenth best levels that were reached back in the 1980s remained untouched (and indeed today's marks are generally far below those) in the women's 100m to 800m, long jump, shot, discus and heptathlon and men's shot, discus and hammer. No doubt the much tougher drug-testing regime for today's athletes is a major factor in this. Slightly more surprisingly 10th best for men's high and triple jumps also date from the 1980s.

European Championships

HELSINKI WILL STAGE the European Championships in June 2012. There can hardly be a better choice as venue than this city, which hosted the 1952 Olympic Games, World Championships in 1983 and 2005, and European Championships in 1971 and 1994, with a most knowledgeable and enthusiastic crowd. And yet I was horrified when I heard that European Athletics (EA) had determined to change to a two-year cycle for their championships with an event each Olympic year. The EA has worked hard to promote the event and has issued various statements saying that it had full support from major nations who would send full teams. But I simply cannot believe that, in Olympic year, all the top European athletes will compete; indeed I expect many major absentees.

At best this will be a meeting with exciting and competitive athletics and perhaps providing an opportunity for championship development for aspiring athletes. But such opportunities are already provided with Under-20 and Under-23 Championships, and supporters like myself will judge the Helsinki event on whether it lives up to EA's 'promises'. Many continental events fail to really matter for all the athletes and African Championships, Asian Championships and Games and Pan-American Games are rarely contested by a very high proportion of their continent's top athletes. But the European Championships have always been the main focus of the season for Europe's athletes each time in their four-yearly cycle. If they are not this time, then the EA will have devalued the event and this could well affect future championships. We will see.

Retired in 2011/12

Men: Magnus Arvidsson SWE, Dmitriy Bogdanov RUS, Ivano Brugnetti ITA, Tyler Christopher CAN, Walter Henning USA, Manuel Martínez ESP. Steffan Müller SUI, Alex Nelson GBR, Toby Sandeman GBR, Jason Tunks CAN. Heber Viera URU

Women: Andrea Bunjes GER, Janina Goldfuss GER, Monique Henderson USA, Laurien Hoos NED, Chelsea Johnson USA, Jenny Kallur SWE, Kirsten Münchow GER, Eileen O'Keeffe IRL, Annike Suthe GER

Historical Dictionary of Track and Field

JUST A COUPLE of days before going to press with this annual, I received author's copies of my new book. This has been published by Scarecrow Press Inc. in the USA. Priced at $85, it is a 319 page hardback book.

After a selective chronology, covering several millennia but the past century and a half most densely, the introduction provides an overall view of the history and development of track and field. Then The Dictionary provides the detail, with entries on each track and field discipline, hundreds of top performers, and nations and organizations plus a variety of miscellaneous topics. Winners of all World and Olympic titles are listed in the Appendixes and there is an extensive bibliography initiated by Richard Hymans.

ATHLETICS BOOKS 2011-12
Reviewed by Peter Matthews

A World History of the Jumping Events (1860-2010) by Roberto L Quercetani. 240x196 mm 312pp, over 60 photos. Published by EditVallardi. Orders (credit card or bank wire) to: segreteria@editvallardi.com. Europe 48 euros, Americas €55, Rest of World €60. The author follows the format of his previous volumes on the track events as he traces the development of the high jump, pole vault, long jump and triple jump in his usual masterly manner – a mixture of narrative, results, anecdotes and off-beat items. The second half of the book is devoted to world year and all-time lists.

The Official History of the Amateur Athletic Association by Mel Watman, foreword by Sir Chris Chataway. 240 x 160mm, 388pp hardback. Published at £19.99 by SportsBooks Ltd, PO Box 422, Cheltenham GL50 2YN – www.sportsbooks.ltd.uk. Subtitled the story of the world's oldest athletic association, this book covering 130 years of British athletics is a handsome volume (with 64 pages of photographs, many in colour) and an important one, following the Official Centenary History of the AAA written by Peter Lovesey (Guinness Superlatives, 1979). A wealth of detail, based around succinct summaries of each AAA Championships, is presented in a most readable fashion, with details of British successes at major championships and extensive lists of champions.

A companion volume dealing with the WAAA and women's athletics is due to be published in 2012.

Weltrekorde und Weltrekordlerinnen – Weitsprung, Dreisprung Frauen. A4 125pp. Manfred Holzhausen continues his series of splendidly detailed surveys (text in German, but masses of statistics) of world records and world record holders with this on women's long jump and triple jump. As with previous books (12 men's and 6 women's) there are results of all WR competitions with detailed career profiles (and illustrations) of record breakers, tables of annual world bests and results of major championships. 15 euros in Europe from: Manfred Holzhausen, Dresdener Str. 4, 41516 Grevenbroich, Germany. e-mail: manfred.holzhausen@gmx.de

National Records for all Countries in the World by Winfried Kramer, Heinrich Hubbeling, Yves Pinaud and Steffen Stube. The 2012 edition of this valuable work has records for all events for each country and many territories (234 in all). New in this edition are records for Kosovo and various French overseas territories. 25 euros (cash only) from Winfried Kramer, Kohlrodweg 12, 66539 Neunkirchen-Kohlhof, Germany.

Doping's Nemesis by Arne Ljungqvist with Göran Lager. Published by SportsBooks Ltd. 240x160mm 264pp hardback. £17.99 from SportsBooks Ltd (see above). For 40 years Professor Arne Ljungqvist from Sweden (a 2.01m high jumper in 1952) has been the most influential figure in the seemingly endless battle to catch and punish the drugs cheats in our sport, and here tells the inside story in this important book. The first tests to detect anabolic steroids in athletics were at the 1974 Europeans and as a member of the IAAF medical committee since 1972 Ljungqvist was made responsible for the world governing body's anti-doping programme; for many years to come he led the campaign against the dopers.

Chris Brasher – The Man Who Made the London Marathon by John Bryant. Hardback, 310 pages, published by Aurum Press at £20. This first full biography of the redoubtable Olympic steeplechase gold medallist, mountaineer, founder of orienteering in Britain, journalist and inspiration behind the London Marathon has been written by his close friend and running colleague, John Bryant. This is the fascinating story of a most important sporting figure.

The Destiny of Ali Mimoun by Pat Butcher. A5 28pp. £4.99. A delightful monograph about the most successful athlete in French history. Algerian-born Mimoun won an Olympic gold medal (1956 marathon at the age of 35) and three silvers behind the great Emil Zátopek, was four times International Cross-country champion and won a record 32 French titles. He made a record 84 international appearances and he continued to run as a veteran, setting numerous age-group records over many years. See Pat's website www.globerunner.org for details.

Usain Bolt: The Story of the World's Fastest Man by Steven Downes. Published by SportsBooks Ltd; £7.99. In this 182-page paperback the rise and rise of the world's most famous athlete is traced, the account laced with keen insight and many quotes, and there is a compilation by Mirko Jalava of Bolt's 162 individual races from a 22.04 200m on 7 Apr 2001 to a 9.76 100m on 16 Sep 2011.

Running With Fire by Mark Ryan. 240x160mm, 380pp hardback. This is a marvellous biography of Harold Abrahams, 1924 Olympic champion and fascinating man who gave a lifetime of service to athletics as a writer, pioneering radio broadcaster, lecturer, official, team manager, announcer, statistician, rule drafter, legal adviser and high ranking administrator, Published by JR Books, 10 Greenland Street, London NW1 0ND; £20. E-mail: info@jrbooks.com. Website: www.jrbooks.com

Athletics in the United Kingdom – The rise and fall of the British Athletic Federation. 140pp, Tatham Publishing. John Lister, who was Honorary Treasurer of the AAA 1986-91 and of the BAF 1991-6, and thus at the heart of the struggle to move from 17 national federations to one governing body for athletics in Britain, tells the story of the momentous administrative changes that led to the eventual collapse of the BAF. The often agonising procedures that took place against a background of the evolution from amateurism to professionalism and great success for British athletes are detailed with great lucidity by the author, who went on to be an elected member of the Council of European Athletics. Contact the author at jlister@euro-investments.co.uk. Profits go to charity, but £10 would cover all costs.

I Also Ran by Mike Who? by Mike Fleet. 244x168mm, 272pp. Published by Speedy Publications of Purley, 2 Ridge Park, Purley, Surrey CR8 3PN, UK. £20 post free (UK customers), from the charity www.c-r-y.org.uk. Interesting and nostalgic story with plenty of anecdotes from the 1962 Commonwealth Games 880y 5th placer who has given a lifetime of service to the sport as athlete, official in many roles, administrator and coach.

490 a.C – 2010 d.C. – una Maratona lunga 2500 anni. 240x173mm, 423pp with black and white photos. By Ottavio Castellini with Carlos Fernández Canet. The IAAF statistician traces the history of the marathon (in Italian) followed by (easily the bulk of the book) detailed statistics including progressive world records and very deep all-time lists. In all 5501 marks are listed by 1728 men to 2:13:00 and 4879 by 1142 women to 2:35:00. Split times are given for the 1320 men's times to 2:10:00 and for the 1708 women's times under 2:30:00 to 2010. Inc. postage and packaging 50 euros in Europe or US $75 outside Europe from Ottavio Castellini, 14, quai Antoine 1er, 9800 Monaco.

Best of the Best of Bulgarian Athletics. 230 x 165mm, 399pp. By Aleksandar Vangelov. 100-deep men's and women's all-time lists, plus 30 best juniors, 20 best U17 and 30 best U16, with performance lists and evolution of Bulgarian records indoors and out. Cyrillic script for names. 25 euros from Vangelov at ILINDEN bl.1 ap.44, 1309 SOFIA, Bulgaria.

Dictionnaire de l'athlétisme Français. A5 305pp. Compiled by Gérard Dupuy and Gilbert Rosillo. All athletes who have competed for France or won French titles since the late 19th century are listed. Details for each include (where available): date and place of birth, height/weight, personal bests, championship and French records. 20 euros from: Fédération Française d'Athletisme, 33, Avenue Pierre de Coubertin, 75640 Paris, cedex 13, France.

Javelin Statistics – Part 6. A5 52pp. The sixth in the series by Tony Isaacs on the men's javelin, its history and statistics, is on Oceania, including progressive records, rankings 1920-2010, results of Oceania Championships and regional events and an index of record holders and champions. Each edition £5 (cheque or banknote) or 5 euros (banknote) from Tony at 43 St Georges Road, Felixstowe, Suffolk, IP11 9PN, England. email: tony.isaacs3@talktalk.net.

African Athletics 1957, 1958, 1959 and 1961 by Yves Pinaud A5 18/20pp. These four booklets continue the series reconstructing annual lists of performers from the earliest years of African athletics by Yves, who started his great work on African athletics with the 1961 lists which were never published (until now!). Each 10 euro, or US $15 including postage (banknotes if possible) from Polymédias, 46 rue des Bordeaux, 94220 Charenton-le-pont, France.

ANNUALS

Combined Events Annual 2011 by Hans van Kuijen. A5, 216pp. The 19th edition of this attractively produced annual included top 200 men's decathlon and women's heptathlon lists for 2011 and all scores over 7500 and 5600 respectively with deep all-time world lists (top 1000 for decathlon for the first time) plus indoor year and all-time lists. Also results of major events, records, profiles and complete career details for the world's top multi-eventers. In Europe: 30 euro or £30 sterling cash (no cheques). Outside Europe: US $50 cash or $70 cheques – from Hans van Kuijen, de Bergen 66, 5706 RZ Helmond, Netherlands. Email: j.kuijen4@upcmail.nl. Back numbers 2001-02, 2005-10: €15 each.

L'Athlétisme Africain/African Athletics 2011. A5, 152p. By Yves Pinaud. Published by Éditions Polymédias with support from the IAAF, the 30th edition in this splendid series has 100 deep men's and women's lists for Africa for 2010, with all-time lists, national championships and major meetings results. 20 euro, £18 or US $30 including postage from La Mémoire du Sport, 46 rue des Bordeaux, 94220 Charenton-le-pont, France. (Also available: booklist with very extensive list of athletics books and magazines for sale).

Asian Athletics 2010 Rankings. A5 92 pages. Heinrich Hubbeling continues his magnificent annual job of compiling Asian statistics despite difficulties with several nations. Top 30s for 2010 for athletes from Asian nations, with continuation lists for countries other than China and Japan, indicating new national records, and full lists of Asian records. Euro 15/US $22 in cash or by International Money Order from the author, Haydnstrasse 8, 48691 Vreden, Germany. Copies also available for 1998, 2004-08 at €10/US $15 each and for 2009 at €15/US $22.

Athlérama 2010. A5 664pp. The French Annual, edited by Patricia Doilin with a strong team of compilers, is again a superb reference book. Packed with information on French athletics – records, deep year lists for 2010, indexes, athlete profiles, results and all-time lists for all age groups. Extras include French top ten lists for 1910 and 1960. 28 euros from the FFA (see above). email Patricia.Doilin@athle.org

British Athletics 2012. A5 408 pages. The 54th NUTS Annual, edited by Rob Whittingham, Peter Matthews, and Tony Miller. Deep UK ranking lists for all age groups in 2011, top 12 merit rankings, all-time lists, results etc. £18 plus postage (£2 UK & Europe, £5 outside Europe); from Rob Whittingham, 7 Birch Green, Croft Manor, Glossop, Derbyshire SK13 8PR, UK. Cash or sterling cheques.

Israeli Athletics Annual 2011/12. 240 x 170mm, 54pp, illustrated. By David Eiger. Records, championship results, 2011 top 20s and all-time lists, with profiles of leading Israeli athletes. 7 euro or US $10 from David Eiger, 10 Ezra Hozsofer Str, Herzliya 46 371, Israel. Back numbers also available.

Latvijas Vieglatletikas Gadagramata 2012. A5 240 pp. Comprehensive coverage of Latvian athletics for 2011, including records, results, athlete profiles and year and all-time lists with some colour photos, compiled by Andris Stagis. From the Latvian Athletic Association, Augsiela 1, Riga LV-1009, Latvia.

Athletics New Zealand 2010 Almanac. A5 164pp. The first ever annual from Athletics NZ includes national ranking lists for 2010 plus all-time top 20s, records and results of championships and other major events. $NZ25 plus postage: New Zealand $NZ5, Australia & South Pacific $NZ12, Rest of World $NZ20. Purchase online at www.athletics.org.nz

Friidrott 2011. 170 x 240 mm 472pp, 299 pictures, hardback. Edited by Jonas Hedman, text in Swedish. A quality production which covers world and Scandinavian athletics, including detailed championships and major events results with narrative, world outdoor top 50 year and all-time-lists, top 25 Scandinavian and Swedish year and all-time lists plus indoor top tens and record lists for World, Europe, Scandinavia and Sweden. 395 kronor from TextoGraf Förlag, Jonas Hedman, Springarvägen 14, 142 61 Trångsund, Sweden. See www.textograf.com.

South African Athletics Annual 2011. A5. Edited by Riël Hauman. The 59th edition of this Annual included 2010 and all-time lists, records and results of important meetings. Also included were Athlete of the Year articles and a Hall of Fame of the best of the best in South African athletics history. From SA Athletics Annual, PO Box 7699, Halfway House 1685, South Africa at 80 SA Rand. Email enquiries to ckok@safcol.co.za

Southeast Asia Athletics Annual 2011/12. A5, 123 pages. This pioneer publication contains results of major meetings, annual and all-time ramking lists, national records (outdoor & indoor) for all countries and athlete's profiles for the area. Price EUR 10 (SEA), EUR 15 (outside SEA) inc. shipping and handling fees. Payment in cash or cheque, bank transfers, credit card, debit card, paypal, and western union to: Jad Adrian Washif, L7 - 12th College UPM, 43400 Serdang Selangor, Malaysia. See: www. adriansprints.com. Email: jad_adrianwashif@yahoo.com

Anuario Athlético Español Ranking 2010/2011. A5 1072pp. Once again a wonder of the athletics world, this majestic tome has immense depth of results and annual lists for Spain in 2011 as well as records, all-time lists, details of all Spanish champions, international matches, biographies of current stars and details of Spanish participation at major events. Also colour photographs. 25 euros from the Federación Española de Atletismo (RFEA), Avda. Valladolid 81 - 1° - 28.008 Madrid. SPAIN. Email: publicaciones@rfea.es.

Anuario 2010/2011 – Pista Cubierta y Campo a Través. A5 488pp. Comprehensive details for the Spanish cross country and indoor seasons with lists and results, all-time lists, lists of previous champions and photographs. 14 euros plus postage (€3.75 in Spain, €12 elsewhere) from the RFEA (see above).

Annuare FLA 2011. A4 200p. The splendid Luxembourg Annual, edited by Georges Klepper has every possible detail for this nation– reviews, results, 2011 and all-time lists, plus photographs. This year's special feature celebrates 50 years of the Route du Vin. 15 euros locally. By post €18 in Luxembourg, €27 elsewhere to account no. LU32 1111 0200 0321 0000. See www.fla.lu.

2011 USA Track & Field Media Guide & FAST Annual (general editors: Ivan P. Cropper

& Mike Hibbard). A5 776pp. With an extra 59 pages this year, the first 272 pages is the USATF Media Guide with detailed profiles of 135 top athletes plus lists of all US champions from 1990 and there follows the 33rd edition of the FAST Annual with records, 50-deep US lists for 2010 and all-time, with 12-deep junior and college all-time lists. The massive final index section includes annual progressions and championships details for top American athletes. Dedicated to the late Scott Davis who edited the US Annual from the first in 1979. $25 post paid in the USA or $42 or 30 Euros airmail from Tom Casacky, PO Box 3122, Oak Brook, IL 60523, USA. Payment is easiest by PayPal (to tom@interis.com); also cash, postal money orders and Western Union transfers.

Yleisurheilu 2011. A5 672pp. The Finnish Yearbook, published by Suomen Urheilulitto (Finnish Athletics) and compiled by Juhani and Mirko Jalava, contains every conceivable statistic for Finnish athletics (with results and deep year lists) in 2011 and also world indoor, outdoor and junior lists for the year as known at November. 17 euros plus postage and packaging. Orders by e-mail to juhani@tilastopaja.fi.

Statistical Bulletins

Hammer Throw Stats History and News Bulletin No. 9 by Zdenek Procházka. 115 pages by email. The latest in this series (January 2012) included career progressions of all 75m-plus men, all-time lists for junior 6kg and 7.26kg, youth 6kg, and Masters for each age group 35-79. Also 46 pages of a Who's Who of the world top 100 men and an index of throwers. Zdeněk Procházka, Washingtonova 9, 11000 Praha 1, Czech Republic. e-mail: atlet2003@volny.cz.

TRACK STATS. The NUTS quarterly bulletin, edited by Bob Phillips, includes a wealth of fascinating statistics and articles. A5, 68-80 pages. Annual subscription (4 issues) is £20 (UK), £25 (rest of Europe) or £28 (elsewhere); contact Liz Sissons, 9 Fairoak Lane, Chessington, Surrey KT9 2NS, UK.

2011 issues: April: Interview with former British high hurdles record holder Jack Parker, career of Albie Thomas, memories of the late Doug Wilson, career record of Carolina Klüft, and the banning and reinstatement of Foekje Dillema, the Dutch woman who was one of the world's top sprinters in 1950. **June**: Interview with 1948 Olympian Jack Braughton, British all-time mile lists 1911-71, Gunder Hägg's 1943 US tour, the early days of *Athletics Weekly*, and the career of Australian sprinter James Carlton. **September**: Career record of Kelly Holmes, Achilles tour in 1922, Harold Abrahams at long jump, British Olympic team of 1948. **December**: References in the 1920s and 1930s to Violet Piercy, women's marathon pioneer. Profiles for F.Morgan Taylor and Colin Smith. **February 2012**: Career details of Dora Ratjen and Charles Bennett. Analysis of medal winners at AAA/WAAA/UK Championships.

Don Turner (donturner@btinternet.com), 40 Rosedale Road, Stoneleigh, Epsom, Surrey KT17 2JH, UK has stocks of NUTS publications, having collected from Dave Terry, including back issues of Track Stats from 1998 to 2011.

Each £5: Event booklets (detailed statistics on UK athletes including results of championships and very detailed all-time lists, profiles etc.): UK women's hurdles (2004), Long Jump (2005), Shot Put (2006), Pole Vault (2008). Also 1930-39 UK men's ranking lists. And the two most recent publications: **Hammer** by Ian Tempest (2011), 88pp at £8 including postage.

Statistical Survey of the Decathlon (2011) 120pp by Alan Lindop on UK men's multi-events, including also pentathlon, heptathlon and octathlon. The decathlon all-time lists detail 489 performances over 6500 points by 175 performers and continuation all-time lists show all 333 men over 6000 points. Biographies are given of 54 men. £9 including postage.

The **DGLD** – the **German** statistical group, Deutsche Gesellschaft für Leichtathletik-Dokumentation produces annual national ranking lists (**Deutsche Bestenliste**) for Germany and impressive bulletins of up to 268 pages, packed with historical articles and statistical compilations. Each issue (three per year) includes statistical profiles of athletes born 70, 75, 80, 85, 90 years ago etc. Membership, with free Deutsche Bestenliste – euro 55 per year. Contact Hans Waynberg, Liebigstrasse 9, 41464 Neuss, Germany; hans.waynberg@t-online.de. Website: www.leichtathletik-dgld.de

No. 59 – 188pp included an index to the 100-deep all-time men's performer and performance lists as at 31.12.1945 compiled by Richard Hymans (published in No. 56), women's lists for Saxony 1916-26, and Germany 100y lists to 1964. **No. 60** – 226pp featured German lists, results and reprinted articles for 1922. **No. 61** – 184pp included a 46-page "development history" by Hubert Hamacher of the decathlon from earliest origins, through the all-around period to a summary of each era by the scoring tables from 1912 to current (1985), notes and documentation on Gerhard Stock and Carl Diem, and women's lists for Saxony 1927-38.

The latest in the series of books published by the DGLD dealing with the history of 100 years of athletics in Germany, event-by-event – **100 Jahre Leichtathletik in Deutschland** is **10000 m-Lauf Männer**. 25 euros from Hans Waynberg (as above). No cheques from outside Germany.

The **Spanish group, the AEEA** continues to produce magnificent publications. Membership (four bulletins per year) is 55 euros per year (€61 outside Europe) from AEEA secretary Ignacio Mansilla, C/Encinar del Rey, 18 - 28450 Collado Mediano, Madrid, Spain. email: ranking@rfea.es

AEEA Bulletin No. 88 Progresión del Récord Iberoamericano. A5 194 pp. 12 euros. This consisted primarily of lists of progressive Ibero-American records for all events by Miguel Villaseñor, with a very detailed review of the career of recently retired shot putter Manuel Martínez. **Bulletin No. 89** contained 5000 deep performance lists for both men and women at 5000m – to 13:28.12 and 15:39.16 respectively (to which one must add unofficial times in longer races and women's results in mixed races etc.). Also detailed were the top 157 men and 144 woman by the average of their top ten marks and various tables including the most prolific performers and analysis by nation. 12 euros.

IAAF Handbooks

The IAAF Statistics Handbook for the IAAF World Championships, Daegu. A5 742pp. Edited by Mark Butler with help from ATFS members. In addition to complete results from each of the previous 12 editions of the Championships, this superb book also included facts and figures from the Championships, an analysis of performance trends, superlatives, and listings of multiple medallists and placing tables. Plus results from past Olympic Games, other IAAF World Athletics Series events and Area Championships, World and Continental records , all-time world lists, national records, official World record progressions and biographical summaries of many of the stars expected to figure prominently. The book, divided into four sections, can also be downloaded from http://www.iaaf.org/wch11/index.html under the 'General Info' heading.

Progression of IAAF World Records. Edited by Imre Matrahazi. A5 604pp. The 7th edition of this work initiated by the late Ekkehard zur Megede and maintained to the 2003 edition by Richard Hymans. It was updated in house by the IAAF in 2007 and has been further updated but also incorporates corrections to previous editions from Richard Hymans and others. Comprehensive details are given for performances dating back to 1827 with such additional information as intermediate times, field event series and the complete result. World records for road events, officially recognised by the IAAF from 1 January 2003, are included as are indoor records and, for the first time, progressive world junior records as provided by Mark Butler. There is an index of all the record breakers with dates of birth and height and weight where available and there are tables of most prolific record breakers and youngests and oldests for each event. Price $32, see publications order form on the IAAF web site.

IAAF Directory and Calendar 2012. A5, 324 pages. Essential reference with contact details for officials, organisations and national federations, plus calendar and lists of records and IAAF champions. $16. Also **Outdoor Handbook** (141 pp) $12, **Winter Handbook** (38pp) $10, **Competition Rules** (282pp) $10, **Directory of Athletes' Representatives 2011** (116 pp) $8.

Contact the IAAF (or see www.iaaf.org) for their extensive list of publications and videos for sale at 17 rue Princesse Florestine, BP 359, MC 98007, Monaco. Prices include postage by airmail. Email to: headquarters@iaaf.org. Payment by credit card (Visa, Mastercard or eurocard only), quoting name on card, number of card, expiry date, name and address and signature.

Amendments to ATHLETICS 2011

p.13 **Diary**. March 14: Lugano, Switzerland (not Italy)

p.32 **World rankings**: HT: 8. Sokolovs, 9. Esser

p.59 **European Champs**. Women Marathon: Zivile Balciunaite drugs dq from 1st, rest move up a place, 8. Irina Timofeyeva RUS 2:35:53. Adjust medals, and points to RUS 265, ESP 105.5, UKR 96.5, ITA 93, POR 46, SWE 19, LTU 13, SRB 8

p.75 **World Juniors**: W HT: 2, Spiler

p.80 **CAC Games**: Women's HT: 2, Rosa Rodríguez VEN 64.16 (NOT drugs dq), 3. Grant; Medal Table: MEX 7-5-13, VEN 4-3-2, add PUR 3-6-4.

p.83 Swap headings of Asian Marathon and Walks Championships.

p.108 **Drugs Bans**: Note that Rosa Rodríguez VEN (2 year ban) was a marathon runner not the hammer record holder.

2010 World Lists

Men

100m/200m: 10.14a/10.22 & 20.23A/20.44 Magakwe

400m: 45.72 Furlough b. 27.8.89, 46.26A Lewis; hand timing: 45.6A Zaharia Kamberuka BOT 27.12.87 1 & 46.1A Pake Seribe J 7.4.91 2 Molepolole 6 Mar; Juniors: 46.32A Shaun de Jager RSA 28.6.91 1 Manzini 16 Dec

1000m: Juniors: delete 2:20.59 Aman

1500m: 3:35.00 Rassioui 8.6.85, 3:36.36 Kangogo 22.11.85, 3:40.62 Rooney b.6.8.86 and delete from Junior list; Juniors: 3:41.3 Dennis Maranta KEN .92 1 Dar es Salaam 23 Jun; **1 mile**: Indoors: 3:58.50 Hassan SOM

3000m: 7:41.18 V Rono 22.12.90 (& 5000m 13:21.96), Juniors: 7:58.73 Tom Mutie KEN .93 2 Rabat 16 Jul; delete 7:53.68 Kemboi (b. 12.12.90)

5000m: 13:18.12 Kemboi 12.12.90 (so not junior) (& 10k 28:17); 13:18.97 P Limo 2.8.85 (& 10000m 27:36.94A, 10k Rd 27:35, HMar 61:34), 13:19.07 F Assefa 18.1.89, 13:21.96 V Rono .82, 13:22.47 Yehualashet 24.1.89, 13:38.1A Kiprotich .89; Indoors: 13:36.59 Haron Lagat KEN 15.8.83 6 Feb

HMar: 60:07 Mwangi 30.4.80 (10k 28:24+, 10M 46:28+, 20k 57:58+), 60:31 Chanchaima 5.12.84 (& 10k, 15k, 10M lists)

Mar: 2:06:49 Teimet 4.6.84 (& 25k 1:14:13), 2:07:23 Nicholas Koech Kipruto 3.6.82, 2:07:36 Keny 25.12.85 (& HMar 62:00+, 25k 1:13:53+), 2:08:25 W.Girma ETH, 2:09:20 Chumba 27.10.86, 2:09:23 Kandie 7.9.86, 2:09:51 Kutton 8.1.84, 2:10:07 E Kiplagat 5.3.88

3000mSt: 8:23.23A Chirchir 1.8.80; Juniors: 8:51.6 Jaouad Chemlal MAR-Y 11.4.94 2 Rabat 3 Jul

400mh: 49.13 Bellaabouss, 50.57A Kosgeil Juniors: 51.12A Muati – also 50.9hA 2 Nairobi 17 Jun

HJ: 2.20 Maelengwe 28.4.82

TJ: Four performances (17.35, 17.32i, 17.32, 17.29) under 17.39i Donato were by Olsson; 16.74A Haitengi was wind-assisted – best legal (100th on list) 16.46A 2 Potchefstroom 17 Apr

SP: Juniors: 20.14 Ding Yongheng; **HT**: 75.50 Anatoliy Pozdynyakov, delete 68.91 Rozna (see 69.90)

JT: 74.97A Holtzhausen, delete 78.02A El Rahman (see 81.84), 100th best 76.71

10kmW: 37:44 Wang Zhen (24.8.91) (& for 20k 1:20:42)

20kmW: 1:20:36 (on probably short AfCh course at Nairobi) Sbaï next 1:21:47 7 La Coruña 19 Jun; others in this race did not have other times under 1:25. Juniors: 1:34:53 Lin Dexin 21.10.92, 1:25:41 Wang Gang 2.4.91, 1:28:01 Sun Chengang 11.3.91

Women

100m: 11.47 Morrison repeated

1500m: 4:09.24 Mary Wangari Kuria 29.11.87; 4:13.4 Janeth Kisa KEN-J 5.3.92 1 Dar es Salaam 23 Jun; Juniors: 4:16.3 Rose Maranga KEN .93 2 Dar es Salaam 23 Jun; **1M**: solo run 4:29.09 Hind Dehiba FRA 1 Carmaux 18 Sep; **Mar**: to drugs dq: 2:31:14 Balciunaite

3000mSt: 10:02.98 Nguyen 2.9.90, 10:11.70 Michel 13.10.88; **100mh**: wa: delete 13.30 Reshetkina

HJ 1.84i Schroll 24.4.88

PV: Best out: 4.35 Gergel 1 Stanford 27 May

LJ: Olga Kucherenko – add

6.91	0.7	1	Bisl Oslo			4 Jun
	6.91	6.74w	6.60	6.75	p	p
6.83	1.1	1	Békéscsaba			2 Jun
	6.83	x	p	p	6.77	p
6.80	0.9	*	Wattenscheid			26 Jun
	6.80/0.9	6.90w/2.1	6.62	p	p	x
6.84w	2.2	3	EC Barcelona			28 Jul
	6.55	6.77	x	6.84w	x	6.34

TJ: 13.34 Sandrine Mbumi CMR 22.5.86 7 Mar

SP: 15.93 James 6.1.89; **DT**: 59.47 Korotkova b. 21.12.83; **HT**: Remove ¶ from 69.10 Rose Rodríguez

JT: 57.16A Murillo, delete 54.32 Klochko in main and junior lists (was DT, as shown on p. 509).

10kmW: 44:55 Lu Xiuzhi 26.10.93

4x400m: Juniors: 3:43.69 RSA (Nice, Senekal, van der Merwe, Palframan) 1 Manzini 17 Dec

Amendments to World Indoor Lists 2011

PV: 5.63 Mark Hollis USA 1.12.84 1 Notre Dame 5 Mar

Amendments to Previous World Lists

2009: 100m: 10.12 Di Gregorio was doubtful timing, best: 10.21 0.2 2r2 ET Leiria 20 Jun; 10,000m: 28:00.97 Alex Mwangi KEN-J b.14.6.90; HT: 72.72 Anatoliy Pozdynyakov. Africa Junior Champs (p.76): 800m: Nickson Tuwei KEN 1:48.91 (as Mohamed Aman was, at 15, too young to compete).

2008: 3000mSt: 8:39.09 drugs dq Frédéric Denis; HT: 79.36 by Aleksey Korolyov (from 76.62), 76.70 Aleksandr Kozulko 1 Grodno 16 May; W 5000m: 14:44.20 mx Ongori; PV: 4.50i Kiryashova 1 Sankt-Peterburg 16 Jan (see 4.50); 4.35A Stripling on 19 Jul; 4.30i Jodi Unger USA 1 Black Springs 14 Jun (see 4.16) (4.25- 07); 4.23i Maria Eleanor Tavares 5 Dec

2007: 3000mSt: 8:36.02 drugs dq Frédéric Denis

2006: SP 6kg: 21.25 Gao Yong was with 5kg shot; 4x100m: 38.52 3rd leg W Smith, 38.72 JAM 9 Mar, 38.73 JAM 2 Forsyth, 3 Frater; 39.66 DOM 13 May, 40.05 CZE 23 May, 40.49 17 Jun; 4x400: 2:59.86 USA White, 3:00.83 JAM Ayre 44.9, 3:00.93 AUS Steffensen 45.1, 3:01.84 RSA van Zyl 44.1, 3:04.26 CHN 8 Apr, indoor 3:01.06 Clement 46.10; mixed: 3:02.12 TCU 1. Chavez; Juniors 3:05.74 BEL 3h3 19 Aug; W 400m: 49.63 Novlene Williams 1 Shanghai 23 Sep and delete 49.64 at WAF and correct to 50.36 on page 90; 4x100m: 44.38 IRL O'Rourke, Cuddihy, McSweeney, Boyle; 4x400m: 3:25.13 RUS Pospelova 51.2, 3:25.18 Sverdlovsk 1 Tula 15 Jun ?, 3:30.00 Désert 51.92, 3:33.86 KAZ 2 12 Dec. 3:42.31 TRI-J 16 Jul

2001: PV: 5.66Ai Pat Manson – Air Force Academy 25 Feb (from 5.55Ai), 5.51 Scott Hennig at San Marcos 6 May (from 5.40), 5.49 Matt Phllips 1 Tacoma 10 Mar (from 5.45); 5.40 William Inocencio FRA 7 Jul (remove from 'best out list', where 5.40 on 18 Jul is by Damien Inocencio).

1996: 2.24 Luciano may be false, if so his best (also junior lists) was 2.20 at Atlanta 26 Jul.

1984: W 4x400: 3:27.57 LTU order was Navickaite, Valiuliene, Mendzoryte, Ambraziene

With thanks to Paco Ascorbe, Winfried Kramer, Kenneth Lindqvist (PV), Keith Morbey (relays), Yves Pinaud

HALL OF FAME 2012

Each year we add five new athletes to our Hall of Fame, which has a mix of stars from the present day (minimum ten years in international competition), the recent past and long ago. This year's selection is as follows:

Kinue HITOMI (Japan) (b. 1 January 1907 Fukuhama-mura, Mitsu-gun, Okayama Prefecture. d. 2 August 1931 Osaka).
A pioneer all-rounder, Hitomi's world records included the following bests: 100m 12.2 (1928), 200m 24.7 on a straight track (1929), 400m 59.0 (1928) and long jump 5.98m (1928). She also had a wind-aided long jump of 6.075 for Japan v Germany in 1929 and took the Olympic silver medal at 800m with 2:17.6 in 1928. She set her first Japanese record in November 1924 at javelin and twice posted a world best for the triple jump, rarely contested by women, in 1925, improving again (to 11.62m) in 1926. She set Asian records at ten standard events, from 100m to 800m and 80m hurdles on the track, high and long jumps, discus and javelin. Initially a promising tennis player, she made her international début at athletics at the Women's World Games of 1926, when she won the long jump and standing long jump, was second at discus, third at 100m and fifth at 60m. In 1930 she retained her World Games long jump title, backed with a second at triathlon and third at 60m and javelin.
Her parents were wealthy rice farmers.
After school she became a physical training instructor and then in 1926 joined the sports section of the Mainichi newspaper as a journalist. She later wrote two books on athletics. She was 1.70m tall. She contracted pleurisy in April 1931 and that later developed into tyrotoxicon pneumonia of which she died in Osaka Imperial University Hospital.

Moses KIPTANUI (Kenya) (b. 1 October 1970 Elegeyo, Marakwet area).
Kiptanui, the only athlete to have held the world record for both 3000m and 3000m steeplechase, was the leader of a generation of Kenyans, and now coaches many leading runners, including Ezekiel Kemboi, at Nyahururu. He won the world title for 3000m steeplechase three times, 1991, 1993 and 1995, before taking second place in 1997. He was also second at the Olympic Games in 1996. He won the World Cup steeplechase in 1994 and the Grand Prix in 1991 and 1995, when he was overall champion, and was second in 1993 and 1997.

He made an astonishing (even by Kenyan standards) breakthrough into top-class. In 1990, with no known form the previous year he won the World Junior and African senior titles at 1500m. He was then listed with a date of birth in 1971, but he long insisted that he was a year older than this. In 1991 he threatened the world steeplechase record in his first race in Europe with 8:07.89 in Stockholm. He went on to win the world title easily, to run 8:06.46 and also win at the African Games. In 1992 he did not make the Kenyan Olympic team as he was 4th in the Kenyan Trials, slowed by injury. His first world record outdoors came in a terrific spell in August 1994 when he ran 7:28.96 for 3000m flat in Köln and three days later 8:02.08 for the steeplechase in Zürich, followed by close attempts at world records with 4:52.53 for 2000m and 13:00.93 on his début at 5000m. He set a world record for 5000m in Rome with 12:55.30 in 1995 and also set world indoor records for 3000m with 7:37.31 (1992) and 7:35.13 (1995). In 1995 he ran the first sub 8-minute 3000m steeple (7:59.18) at Zürich, unusually disdaining the use of pacemakers, and followed with another at Brussels. His dominance at the event was ended in 1997 as compatriots Wilson Boit Kipketer and Bernard Barmasai both broke his world record, but he still improved, to 7:56.16. He was a corporal in the army until 1994. Other bests: 1500m 3:34.0 (1992), 1 mile 3:52.06 (1991), 3000m 7:27.18 (1995), 2 miles 8:09.01 (1994).

Jarmila KRATOCHVÍLOVÁ (Czech Republic) (b. 26 January 1951 Golcuv Jenikov).
Kratochvílová was runner-up to Marita Koch at 400m at the 1980 Olympics and 1982 Europeans, but beat her in the 1981 World Cup 400m 48.61 to 49.27 and, while Koch concentrated on the sprints, won an unprecedented double at 400m and 800m, adding silver at 4x400m, running nine races in all, at the 1983 World Championships. There she broke Koch's world record by running 47.99 for 400m, while her 800m time of 1:54.68 was the third fastest ever and her brilliant final leg in the relay was timed at 47.75. She had run a world record for 800m with 1:53.28 in Munich just two weeks earlier.

The extremely powerful Czech followed that with an unusual double, 200m and 800m in the 1983 European Cup final. In 1985 she again won the European Cup 800m. In successive years from 1981 she was European Indoor champion three times at 400m and once at 200m.

She had broken the national junior record for 400m in 1972, but was slowed by injuries and did not set her first national record until the age of 27 in 1978. She 'retired' in 1986, but came back to run well at 800m in 1987, when she was second in the European Cup and fifth in the World Championships.

Other bests: 60m 7.30i (1981), 100m 11.09 and 200m 21.97 (both in 1981).

Tommie SMITH (USA) (b. 6 June 1944 Acworth, Texas)

Before Michael Johnson and Usain Bolt came along, Smith was the world's greatest ever 200m runner, and just as good at 400m on his rare attempts at that distance. He ran the fastest time ever recorded for 220 yards, with 19.5 on a straight course at San Jose in 1966, improving his own world record of 20.0 run there in 1965. Around a full turn he set further world records with 20.0 for 220y in 1966 and 19.8 (19.83 on auto timing) when he won the Olympic title at 200m in 1968. He beat Lee Evans by five yards to set world records at 400m 44.5 and 440y 44.8 at San Jose in 1967, and also contributed a 43.8 leg for the first ever sub 3-minute 4 x 400m relay time, run by the USA against the Commonwealth in 1966.

Smith had a phenomenal ability to change pace at high speed – his 'Tommie-Jet gear' – and many observers believe that he never reached his peak, particularly at the one lap. His career was blighted by his principled black power protest on the victory rostrum at the 1968 Olympics, following which he was expelled from the Olympic village. At 200m/220y he was AAU champion in 1967-8 and both NCAA and World Student Games champion in 1967, also winning a silver medal in the latter at 100m.

After graduation from San Jose State University in 1969, Smith played three seasons of pro football with the Cincinnati Bengals and also ran some pro track. He became professor and athletic director at Oberlin College and coached at Santa Monica College, Los Angeles for 21 years to 2000.

Other bests, all in 1966: 100y 9.3, 100m 10.1, long jump 7.90m.

Shirley STRICKLAND later **DE LA HUNTY** (Australia) (b. 18 July 1925 Guildford, Western Australia. d. 11 February 2004 Perth).

The first Australian woman athlete to win a medal at the Olympics, she went on to set an all-time record with seven. Her glittering collection would have been one more if there had been an examination of the photo-finish for the 200m in 1948, when she was actually 3rd rather than the official 4th place. In 1948 she won bronze medals at 100m and 80m hurdles with a sprint relay silver. In 1952 she won the 80m hurdles in 1952 with world records of 11.0 in a heat and 10.9 in the final and took the bronze at 100m; she also ran the opening leg on the Australian team that set a world record of 46.1 in a 4x100m heat, they dropped the baton on the final exchange in the final and came in fifth. She retained her 80mh title in 1956 and took her final gold on the 4x100m team that set world records in heat (44.9) and final (44.6). She also set a world record for 100m with 11.3 to win the World Universities title in 1955 (also gold at 80mh, bronze at 200m), and ran on three Australian teams that set world records at 4x110y. Her 80mh time of 10.89 in the Olympic semi in 1956 was then the fastest ever on auto timing. At the Empire Games she secured three golds, in the hurdles and two relays, and two silvers, 100y and 220y, in 1950, but missed the 1954 Games after the birth of her son, the first of her four children. She was Australian champion at 90yh 1948, 80mh 1950 and 1952; 440y 1950, 1952 and 1956.

Her father had been a champion professional runner. A graduate of the University of Western Australia, she became a teacher and university lecturer in mathematics and physics, and later an athletics manager and coach. She married Laurence de la Hunty in 1950.

Other bests: 100y 10.6 (1955), 200m 24.1 (1955), 440y 56.8 (1956).

For full list of athletes included in our Hall of Fame before this year see page 128 of ATHLETICS 2010.
I am very happy to receive selections from readers for five athletes to add to our list and include in the selection in ATHLETICS 2013. Send to me at p.matthews121@btinternet.com

Further recent women's name changes (see also page 23)

Original	Married name
Bianca Achilles GER	Wiecken
Adriane Blewitt USA	Wilson
Nicole Edwards CAN	Sifuentes
Lindset Gallo USA	Schnell
Viktoriya Gurova RUS	Valyukevich
Tiffany Howard USA	White
Alysia Johnson USA	Montano
Lisa Kohl USA	Uhl
Anna Kuroptakina RUS	Krylova
Natalya Kushch POL	Mazuryk
Tamsin Lewis AUS	Manou
Yekaterina Litvinova KAZ	Ektova
Yelena Priyma RUS	Rigert
Olga Salevich BLR	Dubrovskaya
Yelena Sidorchenkova RUS	Orlova
Katie Stripling USA	Tannehill
Svetlana Strukova BLR	Siarova
Yvonne Wisse NED	van Langen
Yuliya Zarudnova RUS	Zaripova

Vivian Cheruiyot, athlete of the year, won 5000m and 10,000m double in Daegu

Sally Pearson won the women's 100m hurdles in Daegu in immaculate style in fastest time at the event for 19 years

Yohan Blake – wins the 100m in Daegu, beating Walter Dix.

Christian Taylor – the 21-year-old leaped to 17.96 to win the world triple jump.

Valerie Adams – World shot win with Oceania and Commonwealth record 21.27

Mariya Abakumova – World javelin win with 71.99 after amazing duel with Barborá Spotáková

Lashinda Demus – World 400m hurdles win in 52.47

Christophe Lemaitre (third) congratulates Usain Bolt after the Jamaican overcame the disappointment of being disqualified from the 100 metres final to retain his 200m World crown

Mariya Savinova – won the World 800m in 1:55.87

Amantle Montsho just beats Allyson Felix to take World 400m title

Robert Harting was unbeaten in the discus in 2012

NATIONAL CHAMPIONS 2011
and BIOGRAPHIES OF LEADING ATHLETES
By Peter Matthews

THIS SECTION incorporates biographical profiles of 805 of the world's top athletes, 414 men and 391 women, listed by nation. Also listed are national champions at standard events in 2011 for the leading countries prominent in athletics (for which I have such details).

The athletes profiled have, as usual, changed quite considerably from the previous year , not only that all entries have been updated, but also that many newcomers have been included to replace those who have retired or faded a little from the spotlight. The choice of who to include is always invidious, but I have concentrated on those who are currently in the world's top 10-15 per event, those who have the best championship records and some up-and-coming athletes who I consider may make notable impact during the coming year.

Since this section was introduced in the 1985 Annual, biographies have been given for a total of 4124 different athletes (2351 men and 1773 women).

The ever continuing high turnover in our sport is reflected in the fact that there are as usual many newcomers to this section (117 in all, 61 men, 56 women), as well as 18 athletes (4 men, 14 women) reinstated from previous Annuals. So, as usual about 16-18% change. The athletes to have had the longest continuous stretch herein are Haile Gebrselassie 20 years, and Jesús Ángel García, Nicoleta Grasu amd Paula Radcliffe 19 years. Athletes who have retired have generally been omitted.

No doubt some of those dropped from this compilation will also again make their presence felt; the keen reader can look up their credentials in previous Annuals, and, of course, basic details may be in the athletes' index at the end of this book.

Athletes included in these biographies are identified in the index at the end of this Annual by * for those profiled in this section and by ^ for those who were included in previous Annuals.

The biographical information includes:

a)   Name, date and place of birth, height (in metres), weight (in kilograms).

b)   Previous name(s) for married women; club or university; occupation.

c)   Major championships record – all placings in such events as the Olympic Games, World Championships, European Championships, Commonwealth Games, World Cup and Continental Cup; leading placings in finals of the World Indoor Championships, European or World Junior Championships, European Under-23 Championships and other Continental Championships; and first three to six in European Indoors or World University Games. European Cup/Team Champs and IAAF Grand Prix first three at each event or overall. World Athletics Final (WAF) and Diamond League series (DL) winners

d)   National (outdoor) titles won or successes in other major events.

e)   Records set: world, continental and national; indoor world records/bests (WIR/WIB).

f)   Progression of best marks over the years at each athlete's main event(s).

g)   Personal best performances at other events.

h)   Other comments.

See Introduction to this Annual for lists of abbreviations used for events and championships.

Note that for comparison purposes decathlons and heptathlons made before the introduction of the current tables have been rescored using the 1984 IAAF Tables, except those marked *, for which event breakdowns were unavailable. Women's pentathlons (p) have not been rescored.

Information given is as known at 3 April 2012 (to include performances at the World Indoor Championships and some other early indoor and outdoor events of 2012).

I am most grateful to various ATFS members who have helped check these details. Additional information or corrections would be welcomed for next year's Annual.

Peter Matthews

ALGERIA

Governing body: Fédération Algerienne d'Athlétisme, BP n°61, Dely-Ibrahim 160410, Alger. Founded 1963.

National Champions 2011: **Men**: 100m/200m: Reda Megdoud 10.54/21.31, 400m: Fayçal Cherifi 47.44, 800m: Mahfoud Brahimi 1:47.47, 1500m: Toufik Makhloufi 3:54.26, 5000m: Lyes Belkhiri 14:37.23, 3000mSt: Hichem Bouchicha 8:36.81, 110mh: Othmane Hadj Lazib 13.50, 400mh: Abderahmane Hamadi 50.88, HJ: Hamza Labadi 2.12, PV: Rafik Mefti 4.70, LJ: Hamza Chouikh 7.65, TJ: Issam Nima 16.80, SP: Mohamed Benzaaza 15.20, DT: Abdelmoumen Bourekba 53.34, HT: Fahem Aroul 52.16, JT: Nassim Mokrani 60.09, 20kW: Hicham Medjeber 1:25.42; **Women**: 100m: Souhir Bauali 11.95, 200m: Sohier Louahla 24.82, 400m: Fassil Fnindes 56.44, 800m/1500m Amina Betiche 2:12.78/4:24.23, 5000m: Souad Aït Salem 17:30.16, 3000mSt: Nawal Yahi 10:36.32, 100mh: Amina Ferguène 13.38w, 400mh: Houria Moussa 58.14, HJ: Khadidja Amour 1.63, PV: Sonia Halliche 3.70, LJ: Romeissa Belabiod 6.04w, TJ: Baya Rahouli 14.49, SP: Souhir Dhaouadi 14.31, DT: Dalila Makhloufi 42.51, HT: Zouina Bouzebra 56.12, JT: Zahra Badrane 46.33, 10kW: Bariza Ghozlani 58:28.

Larbi BOURAADA b. 10 May 1988 1.87m 84kg.
At Dec (/PV): WCh: '09- 13, '11- 10; EC: '10- 3; WJ: '04- 1; AfG: '07- 3, '11- dnf/1; AfCh: '08- 1/2, '10- 1/2. Two African decathlon records 2009-11. Progress at Dec: 2007- 7349, 2008- 7697, 2009- 8171, 2010- 8148A, 2011- 8302. pbs: 60m 6.89i '10, 100m 10.67 '10, 10.61w '11; 400m 46.69 '09, 1000m 2:39.86i '10, 1500m 4:12.19 '06, 60mh 8.05i '10, 110mh 14.41 '09, HJ 2.10 '09, PV 5.00 '11, LJ 7.69 '09, 7.94w '11; SP 14.00i, 13.59 '10, DT 40.34 '11, JT 65.53A '10, Hep 5911i '10.

Women

Baya RAHOULI b. 27 Jul 1979 Bab el Oued 1.79m 64kg.
At TJ/(LJ): OG: '00- 5, '04- 6, '08- dnq 22; WCh: '99-03-05-11: 10/11/7/8; WJ: '96- 10, '98- 1; WI: '03- 7, '04- 10; WCp: '98- 6; AfG: '95- 4, '99- 2/6, '11- 1; AfCh: '98- 1/3, '00- 1; Af-J: '94- 1, '95- 1/2, '97- 1/2 (1 100mh); WUG: '99- 4; won MedG 2001, 2005; Arab G TJ 2011, Pan Arab 100m, 100mh, LJ & TJ 2004; TJ 2011.
Six African triple jump records 1998-9. ALG records 100m 1998-9, LJ 1997-9, TJ 1995-2005. Progress at TJ: 1993- 11.76, 1994- 12.05, 1995- 13.09, 1996- 13.48, 1997- 13.55, 1998- 14.04, 1999- 14.64A/14.30, 2000- 14.30/14.42w, 2001- 13.88/14.30w, 2002- 14.02, 2003- 14.48, 2004- 14.89, 2005- 14.98, 2006- 13.72, 2008- 14.13, 2010- 13.68, 2011- 14.49. pbs: 60m 7.45i '99, 100m 11.1/11.62/11.51w '99, 100mh 13.49 '04, LJ 6.70 '99. Brother Hamimed Rahouli set African 50km walk record of 4:19:15 in 1987.

ANTIGUA & BARBUDA

Governing body: Athletic Association of Antigua & Barbuda, P.O.Box 979, St John's, Antigua. Founded 1960.

Daniel BAILEY b. 9 Sep 1986 1.78m 77kg. Racers TC, Jamaica.
At 100m/(200m): OG: '04- h, '08- qf; WCh: '05- h, '09- 4, '11- 5; WJ: '04- 4; WY: '03- sf/4; CG: '06- qf; PAm: '03- h/sf, '07- sf; PAm-J: '05- (3); CAG: '10- 2; CCp: '10- 2/1R; won CAC-J 2004. At 60m: WI: '10- 3.
Four Antiguan 100m records 2009.
Progress at 100m: 2003- 10.53, 2004- 10.19, 2005- 10.36, 2006- 10.38, 2007- 10.25, 2008- 10.12, 2009- 9.91, 2010- 10.00/9.92w, 2011- 9.97/9.94w. pbs: 50m 5.75i '11, 60m 6.48+/6.54i '09, 100y 9.30+ '11, 200m 20.51 '11, 400m 48.73 '04.

ARGENTINA

Governing body: Confederación Argentina de Atletismo, 21 de Noviembre No. 207. 3260 Concepción del Uruguay, Entre Ríos. Founded 1954 (original governing body founded 1919).

National Championships first held in 1920 (men), 1939 (women). **2011 Champions: Men**: 100m/200m: Mariano Jiménez 10.48/21.72, 400m: Fabio Martínez 48.24, 800m: Franco Díaz 1:51.25, 1500m: Luciano Almirón 3:49.78, 5000m/10000m: Jorge Mérida 14:27.68/30:16.98, HMar: Mariano Mastromarino 66:34, Mar: Herman Cortínez 2:23:52, 3000mSt: Santiago Figueroa 8:50.90, 110mh: Federico Ruiz 14.52, 400mh: José Ignacio Pignataro 52.99, HJ: Carlos Layoy 2.15, PV: Germán Chiaraviglio 5.20, LJ/TJ: Maximiliano Díaz 7.50/16.06, SP/DT: Germán Lauro 18.99/60.41, HT: Juan Cerra 66.62, JT: Braian Toledo 74.62, Dec: Román Gastaldi 7574, 20,000W: Juan Manuel Cano 1:25:41.21. **Women**: 100m/LJ: Agustina Zerboni 12.05/5.69, 200m/400m: María Ayelén Diogo 25.12/56.08, 800m: Mariana Bortelli 2:10.63, 1500m/5000m/10000m: Rosa Godoy 4:24.69/16:25.41/34:25.81, HMar: Sandra Amarillo 74:32, Mar: Karina Neipán 2:48:00. 3000mSt: Florencia Borelli 11:11.13, 100mh: Soledad Donzino 13.70, 400mh: Belén Casetta 61.96, HJ: Jorgelina Rodríguez 1,73, PV: Alejandra García 4.30, TJ: Paula Pitzinger 12.05, SP/DT: Rocío Comba 14.47/55.82, HT: Jennifer Dalhgren 70.96, JT: Romina Maggi 51.84, Hep: Abigail Varela 3525, 20,000W: Daiana Luján 1:49:29.25.

Jennifer DAHLGREN b. 21 Apr 1984 Buenos Aires 1.80m 115kg. Studied English teaching at the University of Georgia
At HT: OG: '04-08- dnq 22/29; WCh: '05-07-09: dnq nm/24/17, '11- 10; WJ: '00- dnq 23, 02- 5; WY: '01- 4; PAm: '07- 3, '11- 6; SACh: '05-06-09-11: 1/1/3/1; CCp: '10- 5; Won SAm-J 2000, PAm-J 2003, NCAA 2006-07, IbAm 2010, ARG 2008-09, 2011. 14 S.American HT records 2004-10. Progress at HT: 1999- 46.36, 000- 56.68, 2001-

57.18, 2002- 59.48, 2003- 61.60, 2004- 66.12, 2005- 67.07, 2006- 72.01, 2007- 72.94, 2008- 66.38, 2009- 72.79, 2010- 73.74, 2011- 73.44. pbs: SP 15.54i '04, 15.03 '03; DT 44.28 '03, Wt 24.04i '06 (S.Am rec). Her mother Irene Fitzner competed at 100m at the 1972 Olympics and was 2nd in the South American 100m in 1971.

AUSTRALIA

Governing body: Athletics Australia, Suite 22, Fawkner Towers, 431 St.Kilda Rd, Melbourne, Victoria 3004. Founded 1897.

National Championships first held in 1893 (men) (Australasian until 1927), 1930 (women). **2010 Champions: Men**: 100m/200m: Aaron Rouge-Serret 10.39/20.88, 400m: Steven Solomon 45.58, 800m: James Kaan 1:47.48, 1500m: Jeff Riseley 3:39.21, 5000m/10000m: Ben St. Lawrence 13:10.08/28:01.68, HMar: Lee Trop 66:17, Mar: Peter Nowill 2:19:22, 3000mSt: Youcef Abdi 8:38.13, 110mh: Greg Eyears 14.47 (Siddhanth Thingalaya IND 14.14), 400mh: Brendan Cole 50.46, HJ: Chris Armet 2.16, PV: Joel Pocklington 5.10 (Sergey Kucheryanu RUS 5.40), LJ: Mitchell Watt 8.44, TJ: Adam Rabone 15.67, SP: Dale Stevenson 19.24, DT: Benn Harradine 63.15, HT: Timothy Driesen 68.63, JT: Jarrod Bannister 80.17, Dec: Jarrod Sims 7500, 20kW/50kW: Jared Tallent 1:20:19/3:49:33. **Women**: 100m/200m/100mh: Sally Pearson 11.38/23.20/12.83, 400m/800m: Tamsyn Lewis 52.31/2:00.80, 1500m: Zoe Buckman 4:12.85, 5000m/HMar: Belinda Martin 16:12.12/77:18, 10000m: Emily Brichacek 33:02.55, Mar: Kirsten Molloy 2:43:41, 3000mSt: Victoria Mitchell 10:10.66, 400mh: Lauren Boden 57.47, HJ: Ellen Pettitt 1.83, PV: Charmaine Lucock 4.15, LJ: Kerrie Perkins 6.42, TJ: Emma Knight 13.23, SP: Kim Mulhall 14.31 (Margaret Satupai SAM 15.86), DT: Dani Samuels 61.79, HT: Gabrielle Neighbour 64.26, JT: Kimberley Mickle 60.66, Hep: Lauren Foote 5539, 20kW: Claire Tallent 1:33:38.

Luke ADAMS b. 22 Oct 1976 Mvumi, Tanzania 1.89m 68kg. Bankstown. Studied industrial design at University of Canberra.
At 20kW(/50kW): OG: '04- 16, '08- 6/10; WCh: '03-05-07-09-11: 5/10/7/18&6/(5); CG: '02-06-10: 2/2/2; WCp: '04-06-08: 14/18/7. At 10000mW: WJ: '94- 24. Won AUS 20kW 2003, 30kW 1998, 50kW 2010.
Progress at 20kW, 50kW: 1995- 1:30:21, 1996- 1:25:27, 1999- 1:23:52, 2000- 1:24:18, 2001- 1:26:31, 2002- 1:23:56, 4:04:03; 2003- 1:19:35, 2004- 1:21:24, 2005- 1:19:19, 2006- 1:20:49, 2007- 1:20:30, 3:53:19; 2008- 1:19:15, 3:47:45; 2009- 1:21:17, 3:43:39; 2010- 1:21:35, 3:47:34; 2011- 1:21:00, 3:45:31. pbs: 3000mW 10:59.04 '10, 5000mW 18:56.67 '10, 10000mW 40:04.88 '05, 10kW 39:16 '09, 30kW 2:11:38 '09, 35kW 2:33:08 '09.

Jarrod BANNISTER b. 3 Oct 1984 Townsville 1.90m 100kg. Athletics Essendon.

At JT: OG: '08- 6; WCh: '07- dnq 22, '11- 7; CG: '06- 6, '10- 1; WJ: '02- 4; CCp: '10- 4. AUS champion 2007-08, 2010-11.
Australian javelin record 2008.
Progress at JT: 2002- 73.31, 2003- 68.34, 2005- 73.20, 2006- 78.06, 2007- 83.70, 2008- 89.02, 2010- 83.17, 2011- 82.25.

Nathan DEAKES b. 17 Aug 1977 Geelong 1.83m 66kg. Bellarine.
At 20kW(/50kW): OG: '00- 8/6, '04- 3/dq; WCh: '99- 7, '01- 4/dq, '07- (1), '11- (dnf); CG: '98- 3, '02- 1/1, '06- 1/1; WCp: '04- 3, '06- 5. At 10000mW: WJ: '96- 3. Won GWG 20000mW 2001, AUS 20kW 2000-02, 2004-06; 50kW 1999 (t), 2005-06.
Walk records: World 50k 2006, Commonwealth & Oceania 20k 2001 & 2005, 20,000m track (1:19:48.1) 2001; 30k 2006, 50k 2003, 5000m 2006.
Progress at 20kW, 50kW: 1996- 1:26:27, 1997- 1:23:58, 1998- 1:23:25, 1999- 1:20:15, 3:52:53; 2000- 1:21:03, 3:47:29; 2001- 1:18:14, 3:43:43; 2002- 1:21:07, 3:52:40; 2003- 3:39:43, 2004- 1:19:11, 2005- 1:17:33, 3:47:51; 2006- 1:19:07, 3:35:47; 2007- 1:19:34, 3:43:53; 2011- 3:48.02. pbs: 3000mW 11:17.0 '98, 5000mW 18:45.19 '06, 10000m 38:44.87 '02, 30kW 2:05:06 '06, 35kW 2:29:11e '06. Unable to compete at 2005 Worlds or 2008 Olympics due to a hamstring injuries. Achieved second Commonwealth Games double in 2006 before world record and title at 50km.

Henry FRAYNE b. 14 Apr 1990 Adelaide 1.87m 72kg. Old Melbournians. Student.
At LJ: WI: '11- 2;. At TJ: WCh: '11- 9; WJ: '08- 5, Won AUS TJ 2010.
Oceania indoor long jump record 2012.
Progress at LJ, TJ: 2006- 7.01, 2007- 7.05, 15.55; 2008- 7.39, 16.58; 2009- 7.99, 16.62; 2010- 7.50w, 16.63; 2011- 7.98, 17.04; 2012- 8.27, 17.23/17.34w
Cousin of 400m international Bruce Frayne (2nd 4x400m CG 1986).

Ryan GREGSON b. 26 Apr 1990 Bulli, NSW 1.84m 68kg. Kembla Joggers.
At 1500m: WCh: '09- h. '11- sf; WJ: '08- 5 (12 5000m); WY: '07- 5. AUS champion 2010.
Oceania 1500m record 2010.
Progress at 1500m: 2003- 4:26.00, 2004- 4:20,00, 2005- 4:06.00, 2006- 3:57.00, 2007- 3:43.84, 2008- 3:41.14, 2009- 3:37.24, 2010- 3:31.06, 2011- 3:36.64. pbs: 800m 1:46.04 '10, 1000m 2:17.69 '10, 1M 3:52.24 '10, 3000m 7:49.53 '11, 5000m 13:56.83 '09, 10km Rd 29:09 '08.

Benn HARRADINE b. 14 Oct 1982 Newcastle, NSW 1.98m 115kg. Ringwood. Personal trainer.
At DT: OG: '08- dnq 31; WCh: '09- dnq 15, '11- 5; CG: '06- 8, '10- 1; CCp: '10- 2. AUS champion 2007-08, 2010-11.
Three Oceania discus records 2008-10.
Progress at DT: 2000- 51.50, 2001- 54.76, 2002- 57.78, 2003- 55.25, 2004- 57.68, 2005- 63.65, 2006- 60.70, 2007- 62.99, 2008- 66.37, 2009- 64.97, 2010-

66.45, 2011- 66.07. pb SP 15.17 '05.

Steve HOOKER b. 16 Jul 1982 Melbourne 1.87m 85kg. Perth.
At PV: OG: '04- dnq 28=, '08- 1; WCh: '05-07-09-11: dnq 17=/9/1/dnq nh; CG: '06- 1, '10- 1; WJ: '00- 4; WI: '08- 3, '10- 1; WCp: '06- 1, '10- 1. AUS champion 2008, 2010.
Three Oceania indoor records 2007-09, two Commonwealth indoor records 2009.
Progress at PV: 1999- 5.00, 2000- 5.20, 2001- 5.30, 2002- 5.25, 2003- 5.45, 2004- 5.65, 2005- 5.87, 2006- 5.96, 2007- 5.91, 2008- 6.00, 2009- 6.06i/5.95, 2010- 6.01i/5.95, 2011- 5.60. pbs: 100m 10.82 '10, 10.6, 10.68w '05; 200m 21.1 '05, LJ 7.10 '05.
Suffering from an adductor injury, he took just one jump to qualify for the World final in 2009, amd then was able to take just two jumps in the final, but he cleared 5.90 for the gold. Played Australian Rules football before taking up pole vaulting. His father Bill was 6th CG 800m 1974, had pbs: 800m 1:45.36 '73, 400mh pb 50.6 '69, and his mother Erica (née Nixon) was 6th LJ, 4th Pen 1974 and 2nd LJ 1978 (in pb 6.58) at CG.

Fabrice LAPIERRE b. 17 Oct 1983 Réduit, Mauritius 1.79m 66kg. Westfields. Was at Texas A&M University, USA.
At LJ: OG: '08- dnq 16; WCh: '09- 4, '11- dnq 21; CG: '06- 3, '10- 1; WJ: '02- 2 (qf 100m); WI: '10- 1; WCp: '06- 8, '10- 7. Won WAF 2008-09, NCAA 2005, AUS 2006, 2009-10.
Oceania indoor long jump record 2010.
Progress at LJ: 2000- 7.39, 2001- 7.31, 2002- 7.74, 2003- 7.66i/7.57/7.85w, 2004- 7.61i/7.52/7.94Aw, 2005- 7.90i/7.83/8.15w, 2006- 8.19, 2007- 7.98, 2008- 8.15, 2009- 8.35/8.57w, 2010- 8.40/8.78w, 2011- 8.02. pbs: 60m 6.89i '06, 100m 10.56/10.48w '02, 200m 21.40 '00, TJ 15.24 '04.
Former football player.

Jared TALLENT b. 17 Oct 1984 Ballarat 1.78m 60kg. Ballarat YCW. Graduate of University of Canberra.
At 20kW(/50kW): OG: '08- 3/2; WCh: '05- 18, '07- dq, '09- 6/7, '11- 27/3; CG: '06- 3, '10- 1; WCp: '06-08-10: 14/10/(3). At 10000mW: WJ: '02- 19; WY: '01- 7. Won AUS 20kW 2008-11, 30kW 2004, 50kW 2007, 2009, 2011.
Commonwealth 5000m walk record 2009.
Progress at 20kW, 50kW: 2002- 1:40:21, 2003- 1:31:24, 2004- 1:27:02, 2005- 1:22:53, 2006- 1:21:36, 3:55:08; 2007- 1:21:25, 3:44:45, 2008- 1:19:41, 3:39:27; 2009- 1:19:42, 3:38:56; 2010- 1:19:15, 3:54:55; 2011- 1:19:57, 3:43:36; 2012- 1:20:34. pbs: 3000mW 11:15.07 '09, 5000mW 18:41.83 '09, 10000mW 40:41.5 '06, 10kW 38:29 '10, 30kW 2:11:36 '09, 35kW; 2:33:07 '09.
Won IAAF Walks Challenge 2008. Married Claire Woods on 30 Aug 2008, she has 20kW pb 1:32:12 '09.

Mitchell WATT b. 25 Mar 1988 Bendigo, Victoria 1.84m 83kg. QE2 Track Club. Studying law and commerce at University of Queensland.
At LJ: WCh: '09- 3, '11- 2; WI: '10- 3. AUS champion 2011. Oceania long jump record 2011.
Progress at LJ: 2001- 6.32, 2002- 6.98, 2008- 7.97, 2009- 8.43, 2010- 8.16, 2011- 8.54. pb 100m 10.31 '11. After playing Australian Rules football and rugby, he returned to athletics in 2008 and made rapid advance.

Women

Kimberley MICKLE b. 28 Dec 1984 Perth 1.69m 69kg. Deakin.
At JT: WCh: '09- dnq 15, '11- 6; CG: '06- 4, '10- 2; WJ: '02- 9; WY: '01- 1; WCp: '06- 5, '10- 3. AUS champion 2005-07, 2009-11.
Progress at JT: 1999- 45.13, 2000- 45.76, 2001- 51.83, 2002- 52.77, 2003- 48.03, 2004- 50.38, 2005- 58.16, 2006- 58.56, 2007- 59.36, 2008- 57.64, 2009- 63.49, 2010- 61.36, 2011- 63.82.

Sally PEARSON b. 19 Sep 1986 Sydney 1.66m 60kg. née McLellan. Gold Coast Victory. Griffith University.
At (100m)/100mh: OG: '08- 2; WCh: '03- hR, '07- sf/sf, '09- 5, '11- 1; CG: '06- fell/dq/3R, '10- dq/1; WJ: '04- 3/4; WY: '03- 1; WCp: '06- 8/4, '10- 1. At 60mh: WI: '12- 1. AUS champion 100m & 100mh 2005-7, 2009, 2011; 200m 2011.
Records: Oceania 100mh (8) 2007-11, 60m 2009 & 60mh indoors (3) 2009-12; Commonwealth 100mh (2) 2011.
Progress at 100mh: 2003- 14.01, 2004- 13.30, 2005- 13.01, 2006- 12.95, 2007- 12.71, 2008- 12.53, 2009- 12.50, 2010- 12.57, 2011- 12.28, 2012- 12.49. pbs: 60m 7.16 '11, 100m 11.14 '07, 150m 16.86 '10, 200m 23.02/22.66w '09, 300m 38.34 '09, 400m 53.86mx '11, 200mh 27.54 '06, 60mh 7.73i '12, 200mh 26.96 '09, 400mh 62.98 '07.
Married Kieran Pearson on 3 April 2010.

Dani SAMUELS b. 26 May 1988 Fairfield, NSW 1.82m 82kg. Westfields, University of Western Sydney.
At DT/(SP): OG: '08- 9; WCh: '07- dnq 13, '09- 1, '11- 10; CG: '06- 3/12; WJ: '06- 1/7; WY: '05- 1/3; WCp: '06- 6; WUG: '07- 2, '09- 1; CCp: '10- 4. AUS champion SP 2006-07, 2009; DT 2005-11.
Progress at DT: 2001- 39.17, 2002- 45.52, 2003- 47.29, 2004- 52.21, 2005- 58.52, 2006- 60.63, 2007- 60.47, 2008- 62.95, 2009- 65.44, 2010- 65.84, 2011- 62.33. pbs: SP 16.30 '08, HT 45.39 '05.

AUSTRIA

Governing body: Österreichischer Leichtath–letik Verband, 1040 Vienna, Prinz Eugenstrasse 12. Founded 1902.
National Championships first held in 1911 (men), 1918 (women). **2011 Champions: Men:** 100m: Roland Kwitt 10.64, 200m: Bernhard Chudarek 21.53, 400m: Michael Laufenböck 48.02, 800m/1500m: Andreas Vojta 1:48.80/3:45.77, 5000m/10000m: Valentin Pfeil 14:44.70/30:33.76, HMar: Günther Weidlinger 63:55, Mar: Markus

Hohenwarter 2:25:09, 3000mSt: Christian Steinhammer 9:22.91, 110mh: Manuel Prazek 14.34, 400mh: Thomas Kain 52.63, HJ: Dominik Siedlaczek & Lukas Gobold 1.94, PV: Paul Kilbertus 5.20, LJ/Dec: Dominik Distelberger 7.68/7300, TJ: Julian Kellerer 15.31, SP: Martin Gratzer 18.05, DT: Gerhard Mayer 60.71, HT: Michael Hofer 58.97, JT: Martin Strasser 67.23, 20kW/50kW: Dietmar Hirschmugl 1:53:06/5:25:31. **Women**: 100m/100mh: Beate Schrott 11.86/13.63, 200m/400m: Doris Röser 24.11/54.59, 800m/1500m: Jennifer Wenth 2:09.84/4:27.49, 5000m: Anita Baierl 17:28.36, 10000m: Andrea Mayr 34:28.58; HMar: Tanja Eberhart 78:06, Mar: Susanne Pumper 2:38:21, 3000mSt: Katharina Kreundl 10:54.90, 400mh: Sabine Kreiner 59.18, HJ: Monika Gollner 1.77, PV: Doris Auer 4.10, LJ/TJ: Michaela Egger 6.14/12.79, SP/ HT: Julia Siart 13.88/57.60, DT: Veronika Watzek 50.91, JT: Elisabeth Eberl 55.58, Hep: Stefanie Waldkircher 5172, 20kW: Viera Toporek 1:56:37.

BAHAMAS

Governing body: Bahamas Association of Athletics Associations, P.O.Box SS 5517, Nassau. Founded 1952.

National Champions 2011: **Men**: 100m: Adrian Griffith 10.41, 200m: Michael Matthieu 20.66, 400m: Demetrius Pinder 44.78, 800m: Wesley Neymour 1:52.36, 1500m/5000m: O'Neil Williams 3:59.69/15:56.14, 110mh: Dennis Bain 14.48, 400mh: Jeffery Gibson 50.82, HJ: Donald Thomas 2.32, LJ: Raymond Higgs 7.80, TJ: Leevan Sands 16.82. **Women**: 100m/200m: Debbie Ferguson McKenzie 11.34/23.09, 400m: Shaunae Miller 51.85, 800m: Itsa Smith 2:24.70, 1500m: Cosseta Hall 6:02.00, 3000m: Miriam Byfeld 13:49.07, 100mh: Ivanique Kemp 13.44, 400mh: Luo Luogon LBR 58.20, LJ: Bianca Stuart 6.24, TJ: Ayanna Alexander 13.25, SP/DT: Julianna Duncanson 12.48/36.99, JT: Laverne Eve 50.47.

Trevor BARRY b. 14 Jun 1983 1.90m 77kg. NoDak.
At HJ: WCh: '09- dnq 17, '11- 3; CG: '10- 2; PAm: '07- 7; WI: '12- 8. Won CAC 2011, BAH 2004-06, 2009.
Progress at HJ: 2002- 2.14, 2004- 2.13, 2005- 2.20, 2006- 2.19, 2007- 2.26, 2008- 2.25A, 2009- 2.28, 2010- 2.29, 2011- 2.32, 2012- 2.31i. pb LJ 7.78/7.82w '06.

Christopher BROWN b. 15 Oct 1978 Nassau 1.78m 68kg. Was at Norfolk State University.
At 400m/4x400mR: OG: '00- qf/3R, '04- sf, '08- 4/2R; WCh: '01-03-05-07-09-11: h&1R/sf&3R/4&2R/4&2R/5/sf; CG: '02- 7/3R, '06- 4; PAm: '07- 1/1R; PAm-J: '97- 2R; CAG: '98- 3R, '99-1R, '03- 2/1R; WI: '06-08-10-12: 3/3/1/3; won BAH 400m 2002, 2004, 2007-09. At 800m: CG: '98- h.
Bahamas records 400m 2007 & 2008, 800m 1998.

Progress at 400m: 1997- 47.46, 1998- 46.44, 1999-45.96, 2000- 45.08, 2001- 45.45, 2002- 45.11, 2003-44.94A/45.16, 2004- 45.09, 2005- 44.48, 2006-44.80, 2007- 44.45, 2008- 44.40, 2009- 44.81, 2010-45.05, 2011- 44.79. pbs: 200m 21.05 '03, 20.56w '06; 800m 1:49.54 '98.
Fourth at three successive global championships outdoors with two indoor bronze medals. Had fastest split (43.42 anchor leg) in 2005 World 4x400m.

Demetrius PINDER b. 13 Feb 1989 Grand Bahama 1.78m 70kg. Studied theatre at Texas A&M University, USA.
At 400m: WCh: '11- sf; WI: '12- 2; BAH champion 2010-11.
Progress at 400m: 2006- 49.03, 2007- 47.48, 2008-47.34, 2009- 48.21i, 2010- 44.93, 2011- 44.78. pb 200m 20.50Ai, 20.43i '12, 20.54 '11.

Leevan SANDS b. 16 Aug 1981 Nassau 1.90m 75kg. Was at Auburn University, USA.
At TJ (LJ): OG: '04- dnq 27, '08- 3; WCh: '03- 3, '05- 4 (dnq), '07- dnq 21, '09- 4, '11- 7; CG: '02- 3; WJ: '98- dnq, '00- 5 (dnq 19); PAm: '99- 6, '07- 6; PAm-J: '99- 2 (1); GAG: '10- 1; won CAC LJ 2005, TJ 2003, 2008; CAm-J 1998, 2000; NCAA LJ 2003 & TJ 2004, BAH LJ 2003, TJ 2008-11.
Bahamas triple jump records 2002 & 2008.
Progress at TJ: 1998- 15.70, 1999- 16.00/16.02w, 2000- 16.22, 2001- 16.39, 2002- 17.50, 2003- 17.40, 2004- 17.41, 2005- 17.30/17.39w, 2006-16.99i/17.10idq, 2007- 17.23/17.55w, 2008- 17.59, 2009- 17.32, 2010- 17.21, 2011- 17.21/17.39w. pbs: 200m 21.84 '09, LJ 8.13 '05, 8.28w '03.
6-month suspension after testing positive for a banned stimulant, methamphetamine, in Feb 2006. His cousin **Shamar** Sands (b. 30 Apr 1985) holds BAH records for 110mh 13.38 '09 (& 13.32Aw '08) (sf WCh '09, 3 WJ '02, 1 CAC '08) and 60mh 7.49i '09.

Donald THOMAS b. 1 Jul 1984 Freeport 1.90m 75kg. Lindenwood University, USA.
At HJ: OG: '08- dnq 21=; WCh: '07- 1, '09- dnq 15, '11- 11; CG: '06- 4, '10- 1; PAm: '07- 2; CAG: '06- 4=, '10- 1; CCp: '10- 2. Won WAF & NCAA indoors 2007, BAH 2007, 2010-11.
Progress at HJ: 2006- 2.24, 2007- 2.35, 2008-2.28i/2.26, 2009- 2.30, 2010- 2.32, 2011- 2.32.
A basketball player, he made a sensational start by clearing 2.22 indoors in January 2006 with no high jump training since he had jumped at school five years earlier. 19 months later he was world champion.

Women

Debbie FERGUSON McKENZIE b. 16 Jan 1976 Nassau 1.70m 57kg. Graduate of University of Georgia, USA.
At 100m/4x100mR (/200m): OG: '96- sf/res (2) R, '00- 7/4/1R, '04- 7/3/4R, '08- 7/7; WCh: '95-4R (h), '97- sf, '99- sf/5/1R, '01- 5/1, '03- sf/qf, '07- sf/sf, '09- 6/3/2R, '11- (6); CG: 94- (sf), '02-

1/1/1R; WJ: '92- qf/sf, '94- 5/4; PAm: '99- (1); PAm-J: '95- 1/1 (3 4x400m); WCp: '02- (1)/1R, '06- 1R, '10- 1R. Won GP 100m 2002 (2nd 200m 2001), CAC 100m 1997, 200m 1995, 2008; NCAA 100m & 200m 1998, CAC-J 100m 1994, GWG 200m 2001. Bahamas 200m record 1999.
Progress at 100m, 200m: 1991- 11.75, 24.26; 1992- 11.79, 23.97w; 1993- 23.82/23.32w, 1994- 11.48/11.1, 23.32/23.1; 1995- 11.19/10.9w, 22.86/22.7; 1996- 11.26/11.07Aw, 22.92; 1997- 11.20, 1998- 10.97/10.94w, 22.53; 1999- 10.98/10.91w, 22.19; 2000- 10.96, 22.37; 2001- 11.04, 22.39; 2002- 10.91, 22.20; 2003- 10.97, 22.50A/22.65; 2004- 11.04, 22.30; 2006- 11.14/11.06w, 22.56/22.4; 2007- 11.12, 22.49; 2008- 11.11, 22.49; 2009- 10.97, 22.23; 2010- 11.15, 22.62; 2011- 11.09, 22.76/22.50w. pbs: 55m 6.71i '99, 60m 7.20i '04, 100y 10.21+ '11, 400m 53.30 '01.
Won three gold medals at 2002 CG, winning both 100m and 200m in Games records. Uniquely contested both 100m and 200m finals at three successive Olympic Games (7th 100m each time). Married Andrew McKenzie on 23 Dec 2005.

BAHRAIN

Governing body: Bahrain Athletics Association, PO Box 29269, Isa Twon-Manama. Founded 1974.

Bilal Ali MANSOUR b. John Yego (KEN) 17 Oct 1983 or 17 Oct 1988 (accepted by IAAF) Kenya 1.70m 61kg.
At (800m)/1500m: OG: '08- sf/7; WCh: '05- 7/h, '07- h/11, '09- sf/9; WJ: '06- 7/3; WY: '05- 1; AsiG: '06- 2, '10- 7/3; AsiC: '11- 5; CCp: '10- (3). World CC: '05- 9J. Won Arab 800m 2009, W. Asian 800m & 1500m 2010.
Asian 1000m record 2007. World youth bests for 800m and 1500m (with 1988 birthdate).
Progress at 800m, 1500m: 2004- 1:46.8A, 2005- 1:44.34, 3:33.86; 2006- 1:45.27, 3:34.30; 2007- 1:44.02, 3:31.49; 2008- 1:45.95, 3:33.11; 2009- 1:45.26, 3:32.10; 2010- 1:44.80, 3:34.98; 2011- 1:47.22, 3:38.61. pbs: 1000m 2:15.23 '07, 1M 3:52.35 '07.

Youssef Saad KAMEL formerly Gregory Konchellah (KEN) b. 29 Mar 1983 Narok, Kenya 1.84m 70kg.
At 800m(/1500m): OG: '04- h, '08- 5; WCh: '05/07- sf, '09- 3/1, '11- (sf); ; WI: '08- 3; AsiG: '06- 1; WCp: '06- 1. Won WAF 2004, 2007; Pan Arab 2004-05, Asian indoor 2008.
Records: two Asian and four BRN 800m 2004- 08, 1000m 2008, Asian indoor 800m (1:45.26) 2008.
Progress at 800m, 1500m: 2003- 1:45.88, 2004- 1:43.11, 2005- 1:43.96, 2006- 1:43.61, 3:34.45; 2007- 1:43.87, 3:34.59; 2008- 1:42.79, 3:32.83; 2009- 1:44.83, 3:31.56; 2010- 1:46.86, 3:33.06; 2011- 1:46.89. 3:39.05. pbs: 600m 1:16.01 '03, 1000m 2:14.72 '08.
Son of Billy Konchellah (world 800m champion 1987 and 1991), he changed nationality to Bahrain in 2003.

Women

Mimi BELETE b. 9 Jun 1988 Ethiopia 1.64m 62kg.
At 1500m/(5000m): WCh: '09- sf, '11- 7; AsiG: '10- 3/1; AsiC: '09- 6; CCp: '10- 4; won W.Asian 2010.
Progress at 1500m: 2007- 4:13.55, 2008- 4:06.84, 2009- 4:04.36, 2010- 4:00.25, 2011- 4:03.13. pbs: 800m 2:04.63 '10, 3000m 8:32.18 '10, 5000m 15:15.59 '10.
From Ethiopia, now lives in Belgium; BRN from 2009. Younger sister Almensch Belete pbs 1500m 4:06.87 '10, 5000m 15:03.63 '11.

Shitaye ESHETE Habtegebrei b. 21 May 1990 Ethiopia 1.59m 46kg.
At 10000m: WCh: '11- 6; AsiG: '10- 6. At 5000m: AfC: '09- 6; CCp: '10- 6. At 3000m: WI: '12- 5. World CC: '10- 11, '11- 12. Won Arab CC 2010, Asian CC and indoor 3000m 2012.
BRN 10,000m records 2010 & 2011.
Progress at 10000m: 2010- 31:53.27, 2011- 31:21.57. pbs 3000m 8:49.27i '12, 5000m 15:15.79 '10.

Maryam Yusuf **JAMAL** b. 16 Sep 1984 Alkesa, Arsi Province, Ethiopia 1.55m 44kg. Stade Lausanne, Switzerland.
At (800m)/1500m: OG: '08- 5; WCh: '05-07-09-11: 5/1/1/12; WI: '06- 3, '08- 2; AsiG: '06- 1/1, '10- 6/1; WCp: '06- 1. World CC: '09- 9, '11- 23; Won WAF 2005-08, Swiss CC 2003, P.Arab 800m, 1500m & 5000m 2005, Arab 4k CC 2006, Asian CC 2007, 2009.
Records: Two Asian 1M 2007, 2000m 2009, Bahrain 800m (3), 1500m (3), 2000m, 3000m (3), 5000m 2005-09. Asian indoor 1500m 2006 & 2008, 1M (4:24.71) 2010.
Progress at 800m, 1500m, 5000m: 2003- 4:18.12, 2004- 2:02.18, 4:07.78, 15:19.45mx; 2005- 1:59.69, 3:56.79, 14:51.68; 2006- 1:59.04, 3:56.18, 2007- 3:58.75, 15:20.28; 2008- 1:57.80, 3:59.79i/3:59.84; 2009- 1:59.98, 3:56.55; 2010- 1:59.89, 3:58.93; 2011- 4:00.33. pbs: 1M 4:17.75 '07, 2000m 5:31.88 '09, 3000m 8:28.87 '05, HMar 71:43 '04.
Has a record 16 sub-4 min 1500m times. Formerly Ethiopian Zenebech Kotu Tola, based in Switzerland, ran series of fast times after converting to Jamal of Bahrain in 2005. Married to Mnashu Taye (now Tareq Yaqoob BRN).

BARBADOS

Governing body: Amateur Athletic Association of Barbados, P.O.Box 46, Bridgetown. Fd. 1947.
National Champions 2011: Men: 100m: Andrew Hinds 10.14, 200m: Rico Ward 21.56, 400m: Anthonio Mascoll 47.32, 800m: John Haynes 1:53.13, 1500m: Jamar Maynard 4:08.02, 5000m: Jerome Blackette 16:18.20, 110mh: Ryan Brathwaite 13.75, 400mh: Kion Joseph 52.86, HJ: Thorold Murray 2.10, LJ: Charles Greaves 7.01, TJ: Barry Batson 15.81, SP/DT: Dillon Simon DMA 14.69/45.63, JT: Juston Cummins 65.64.

Women: 100m: Shakera Reece 11.63, 200m: Jade Bailey 23.39, 400m: Kineke Alexander VIN 54.45, 800m: Sonia Gaskin 2:11.91, 1500m: Shane Adams 5:03.10, 3000m: Keisha Farrell 11:24.66, 100mh: Kierre Beckles 13.32, LJ: Akela Jones 6.16, TJ: Seidre Forde 12.13, SP/DT: Melissa Alfred DMA 12.50/44.44, JT: Shanica Yankey 36.87.

Ryan BRATHWAITE b. 6 Aug 1988 Bridgetown 1.86m 75kg. Sociology graduate of the University of Mississippi.
At 110mh: OG: '08- sf; WCh: '07- sf, '09- 1, '11- h; WY: '05- 2; WJ: '06- h; PAm: '07- 4; CAG: '10- 1; PAm-J: '07- 3; won WAF 2009, CAC-J 2006.
Seven Barbados 110mh records 2008-09
Progress at 110mh: 2005- 14.64, 2006- 14.14, 2007- 13.61, 2008- 13.38, 2009- 13.14/13.05w, 2010- 13.34/13.10w, 2011- 13.54. pbs: 60m 7.02i '08, 55mh 7.18i '09, 60mh 7.61i '10.
First world medallist for Barbados in athletics. Younger brother Shane (b. 8 Feb 1990) has 110mh pb 13.58 '11 and was world youth octathlon champion 2007.

BELARUS

Governing body: Belarus Athletic Federation, Kalinovskogo Street 111A, Minsk 220119. Founded 1991.
National Champions 2011: **Men**: 100m: Aleksandr Linnik 10.40, 200m: Yuriy Malinkov 21.86, 400m: Dmitriy Poluyan 47.74, 800m: Anis Ananenko 1:50.29, 1500m: Sergey Cheberyak 3:44.44, 5000m: Maksim Pankratov 14:15.96, 10000m: Stepan Rogovtsov 29:28.03, 3000mSt: Sergey Litovchik 8:38.76, 110mh: Maksim Lynsha 13.75, 400mh: Sergey Serkov 51.47, HJ: Andrey Churilo 2.18, PV: Stanislav Tivonchik 5.20, LJ: Artyom Bondarenko 7.54, TJ: Dmitriy Detsuk 16.37, SP: Pavel Lyzhin 20.17, DT: Sergey Roganov 57.23, HT: Pavel Krivitskiy 77.42, JT: Aleksandr Ashomko 73.23, Dec: Aleksandr Parkhomenko 7813, 20kW: Ivan Trotskiy 1:20:48, 50kW: Denis Kravchik 4:04:49. **Women**: 100m/200m: Yuliya Balykina 11.51/23.96, 400m: Yulyana Yushchenko 52.51, 800m/1500m: Natalya Koreyvo 2:02.99/4:07.43, 5000m: Anna Nosenko 15:46.08, 10000m: Anastasiya Svatovoytova 34:02.14, 3000mSt: Irina Ananenko 9:59.79, 100mh: Yekaterina Poplavskaya 13.25, 400mh: Anastasiya Buldakova 57.93, HJ: Valeriya Bog–danovich 1.80, PV: Tatyana Shakhlenkova 3.80, LJ: Olga Sidareva 6.30, TJ: Natalya Vyatkina 14.07, SP: Natalya Mikhnevich 19.05, DT: Svetlana Serova 53.48, HT: Olga Tsander 66.63, JT: Marina Novik 57.13, Hep: Yekaterina Netsv–etayeva 5662, 20kW: Anastasiya Yatsevich 1:29:30.

Andrey KRAVCHENKO b. 4 Jan 1986 Petrikov, Gomel region 1.87m 84kg.
At Dec: OG: '08- 2; WCh: '07- dq 100m, '09- 10; EC: '10- 3; WJ: '04- 1; EU23: '07- 1; EJ: 05- 1; ECp: '08-09: 1/1. At Oct: WY: '03- 2. At Hep: WI: '08-10-12: 2/4/6; EI: '07- 3, '11- 1.

World youth record for octathlon (6415) 2003.
Progress at Dec: 2005- 7833, 2006- 8013, 2007- 8617, 2008- 8585, 2009- 8336, 2010- 8370, 2011- 8023. pbs: 60m 7.03i '08, 100m 10.86 '07, 400m 47.17 '07, 1000m 2:39.80i '11, 1500m 4:24.44 '06, 60mh 7.90i '10, 110mh 13.93 '07, HJ 2.19i '05, 2.16 '04; PV 5.30i/5.20 '08, LJ 7.90 '07, SP 15.04i '11, 14.44 '10; DT 45.48 '10, JT 64.35 '07, Hep 6282i '11.
Added 604 points to pb to win with European U23 record at Götzis 2007. Won Talence decathlon and IAAF Combined Events Challenge 2008.

Pavel KRIVITSKIY b. 17 Apr 1984 Grodno 1.88m 105kg.
At HT: WCh: '09- 8, '11- 5; EC: '10- dnq 16; EU23: '05- 1; ET: '10- 1. Won BLR 2007, 2010-11.
Progress at HT: 2004- 72.05, 2005- 77.51, 2006- 78.62, 2007- 78.61, 2008- 80.02, 2009- 79.48, 2010- 80.44, 2011- 80.67.

Pavel LYZHIN b. 24 Mar 1981 Voronok, Russia 1.89m 110kg. Mogilyov. Army.
At SP(/DT): OG: '04= dnq 17, '08- 5; WCh: '03-05-07-09-11: dnq 14/nt/20/6/dnq 16; EC: '02- dnq, '06- 10, '10- 7; WJ: '00- 4/7; EU23: '01- 8, '03- 1; EJ: '99- 4/2; WI: '10- 6; EI: '02- 6, '07- 2; WUG: '03- 2, '05- 5. BLR champion 2001, 2004, 2009, 2011.
Progress at SP: 1999- 17.98, 2000- 19.12, 2001- 20.12, 2002- 20.15, 2003- 20.86, 2004- 20.92, 2005- 20.38, 2006- 20.85, 2007- 20.82i/20.02, 2008- 20.98, 2009- 20.98, 2010- 21.21, 2011- 20.85. pb DT 61.72 '07.

Andrey MIKHNEVICH b. 12 Jul 1976 Bobruysk 2.02m 140kg. Minsk.
At SP: OG: '00- 9, '04- 5, '08- 3; WCh: '01-03-05-07-09-11: dq 10/1/6/3/7/3; EC: '98- dnq 17, '06- 2, '10- 1; WUG: '97- 6, '03- 1; WI: '99-04-06-08-10: 8/6/2/4/2; EI: '07- 5; CCp: '10- 3; ET: '11- 3. BLR champion 2000, 2005-08.
BLR shot records 2010 & 2011.
Progress at SP: 1992- 13.06, 1993- 15.02, 1994- 16.74, 1995- 17.36, 1996- 19.24, 1997- 19.57i/19.27, 1998- 20.07i/19.90, 1999- 20.52i/20.30, 2000- 20.48i/20.12, 2001- 20.92, 2003- 21.69, 2004- 21.23, 2005- 21.08, 2006- 21.60, 2007- 21.27, 2008- 22.00, 2009- 21.02, 2010- 22.09, 2011- 22.10.
Two year drugs ban from positive test on 4 Aug 2001, when he lost 10th at the World Champs. Threw 21.66 four days after return from ban in August 2003, world title 2 weeks later. Married Natalya Khoroneko on 17 Mar 2007.

Yuriy SHAYUNOV b. 22 Oct 1987 Minsk 1.93m 105kg.
At HT: WCh: '09- dnq 26, '11- nt; EC: '10- dnq 20; WJ: '04- dnq 13, '06- 4; EU23: '07- 1, '09- 1; EJ: '05- 3; WUG: '09- 1. BLR champion 2009.
Progress at HT: 2007- 74.92, 2008- 77.32, 2009- 80.72, 2010- 78.73, 2011- 78.70.

Valeriy SVYATOKHO b. 20 Jul 1981 Grodno 1.86m 112kg.

At HT: OG: '08- dnq 17; WCh: '11- dnq 23; EC: '10- 4; EU23: '03- 4; WUG: '05- 3.
Progress at HT: 1999- 60.73, 2001- 68.02, 2003- 72.42, 2004- 77.25, 2005- 76.31, 2006- 81.49, 2007- 76.13, 2008- 81.37, 2009- 74.86, 2010- 78.33, 2011- 78.02.

Women

Oksana MENKOVA b. 28 Mar 1982 Krichev, Mogilev region 1.83m 91kg.
At HT: OG: '08- 1; WCh: '03/07/09- dnq 23/ nt/13; EC: '02/06: dnq 27/23; EU23: 03- 2; EJ: '01- 5; WUG: '05- 5; ECp: '07- 2, '08- 1.
Two Belarus hammer records 2006-08.
Progress at HT: 1999- 47.87, 2000- 56.50, 2001- 59.24, 2002- 66.42, 2003- 67.58, 2004- 70.23, 2005- 70.15, 2006- 76.86, 2007- 73.94, 2008- 77.32, 2009- 76.32, 2010- 67.27, 2011- 67.78.
Had a terrible record at major events and only 11th in qualifying, but took gold with Olympic record 76.34 in 2008. Gave birth to daughter on 25 Sep 2010.

Natalya MIKHNEVICH b. 25 May 1982 Nevin–nomysk, Russia 1.80m 85kg. née Khoroneko.
At SP: OG: '04- 5, '08- 2; WCh: '05- 8, '09- 4, '11- 11; EC: '06- 1, '10- 2; WJ: '00- 3; WY: '99- 2; EJ: '01- 1; EU23: '03- 1; WI: '04-06-10: dnq 9/1/3; WUG: '05- 1; WCp: '06- 4. Won WAF 2006, BLR 2001, 2004-06, 2011.
Progress at SP: 1999- 16.12, 2000- 16.58, 2001- 17.25, 2002- 17.20, 2003- 18.05, 2004- 20.04, 2005- 19.78, 2006- 20.17, 2008- 20.70, 2009- 20.03, 2010- 20.42i/19.80, 2011- 19.05.
Married Andrey Mikhnevich on 17 Mar 2007, their son Ilya was born on 11 Aug 2007.

Anastasiya MIRONCHIK-IVANOVA b. 13 Apr 1989 Slutsk 1.71m 54kg. Minsk.
At LJ: WCh: '09- 11, '11- 4; EC: '10- 6; WJ: '08- 2; WY: '05- 8; EU23: '09- 2, '11- 6; WI: '12- 5; EI: '11- 6. BLR champion 2007, 2010-11.
Progress at LJ: 2004- 5.90, 2005- 6.10/6.13w, 2007- 6.03i/5.89, 2008- 6.71, 2009- 6.65/6.76w, 2010- 6.84, 2011- 6.85/6.92w, 2012- 6.82i. pb TJ 14.29 '11.

Nadezhda OSTAPCHUK b. 12 Oct 1980 Stolin, Brest region 1.80m 90kg. Luch Moskva, RUS.
At SP: OG: '04- 4, '08- 3; WCh: '99-01-03-05-07-11: dnq 17/7/2/1/2/2; EC: '02- 5, '06- 2, '10- 1; WJ: '98- 1; EJ: '99- 1; EU23: '01- 1; WI: '01-03-04-06-08-10-12: 2/2/7/6/2/1/2, EI: '00- 6, '05- 1; CCp: '10- 2. Won DL 2010, WAF 2004, 2007; 2nd GP 2001; BLR 1999-2000, 2007-08, 2010.
Three Belarus shot records 2005.
Progress at SP: 1997- 14.23, 1998- 18.23, 1999- 18.73, 2000- 19.13i/18.83, 2001- 19.73, 2002- 19.40, 2003- 20.56i/20.12, 2004- 20.36, 2005- 21.09, 2006- 20.86i/20.56, 2007- 20.48, 2008- 20.98, 2009- 19.88, 2010- 21.70i/20.95, 2011- 20.94.

Yanina PROVALINSKAYA b. 26 Dec 1976 Grodno 1.86m 87kg. née Korolchik.
At SP: OG: '00- 1, '08- dnq 18; WCh: '97- dnq 18; '99- 4, '01- 1, '07- 10; EC: '98- 3, '10- 4; EU23: '97- 3 (3 DT); EJ: '95- 2; WI: '01- 9, '03- 7. BLR champion 2000, (2003).
BLR shot record 2000 and 2001.
Progress at SP: 1994- 16.00, 1995- 17.07, 1996- 17.48, 1997- 18.67, 1998- 19.23, 1999- 19.58, 2000- 20.56, 2001- 20.61, 2003- 19.39, 2007- 19.24, 2008- 18.86, 2010- 19.95, 2011- 18.33. pb DT 59.90 '97.
Two year drugs ban for positive test at Dortmund 15 Jun 2003.

Anastasiya SHVEDOVA b. 3 May 1979 Leningrad, RUS 1.74m 63kg. née Ivanova.
At PV: OG: '08- dnq 18=; WCh: '11- dnq 18=; EC: '10- 4; WUG: '03- 2; EI: '11- 8. RUS champion 2004, BLR 2010.
Six BLR pole vault records 2010.
Progress at PV: 1998- 3.60, 1999- 3.90. 2000- 4.10, 2001- 4.30, 2002- 4.25, 2003- 4.40, 2004- 4.55, 2006- 4.31i/4.20, 2007- 4.65, 2008- 4.65/4.72ex, 2009- 4.60, 2010- 4.65, 2011- 4.55i/4.50.
Switched from Russia to Belarus 20 July 2009.

BELGIUM

Governing bodies: Ligue Royale Belge d'Athlétisme, Stade Roi Baudouin, avenue du Marathon 199B, 1020 Bruxelles (KBAB/LRBA). Vlaamse Atletiekliga (VAL); Ligue Belge Francophone d'Athlétisme (LBFA). Original governing body founded 1889.
National Championships first held in 1889 (women 1921). **2011 Champions: Men**: 100m: Wout Verhoeven 10.74, 200m: Kevin Borlée 20.80, 400m: Jonathan Borlée 45.31, 800m: Pierre Antoine Balhan 1:50.38, 1500m: Kim Ruell 3:48.07, 5000m: Mats Lunders 14:09.66, 10000m: Koen Naert 29:15.92, HMar: Guy Fays 67:57, Mar: Gino Van Geyte 2:22:16, 3000mSt: Krijn Van Koolwyk 8:51.74, 110mh: Quentin Ruffacq 14.17, 400mh: Michaël Bultheel 50.14, HJ: Timothy Hubert 2.09, PV: Thomas Van Der Plaetsen 5.25, LJ: Nicolas Stempnick 7.49, TJ: Bjorn De Decker 15.23, SP: Wim Blondeel 17.81; DT: Philip Milanov 51.71, HT: Nicolas Pierre 65.88, JT: Tom Goyvaerts 74.46, Dec: Frédéric Xhonneux 7713. **Women**: 100m/200m: Hanna Mariën 11.64/23.09w, 400m: Wendy Den Haaze 53.72, 800m: Charlotte Debroux 2:10.63, 1500m: Barbara Maveau 4:12.75, 5000m: Sigrid Vanden Bempt 16:24.13, 10000m: Hanne Vandenbussche 35:38.73, HMar/Mar: Alemitu Bekele 78:24/2:46:16; 3000mSt: Anne Sophie Marechal 10:27.89, 100mh: Elisabeth Davin 13.28, 400mh/TJ: Jolien Van Brempt 60.50/12.17, HJ: Hanne Van Hessche 1.80, PV: Fanny Smets 4.05, LJ: Els De Wael 6.14, SP: Annelies Peetroons 14,29, DT: Anouska Hellebuyck 50.94, HT: Patricia Blondeel 53.01, JT: Melissa Dupre 56.00, Hep: Jessse Vercruysse 5104.

Jonathan BORLÉE b. 22 Feb 1988 Woluwe-Saint Lambert 1.80m 70kg. Was at Florida State University.
At 400m: OG: '08- sf/5R; WCh: '11- 5; EC: '10-

7/3R; WJ: '06- 4; WY: '05- 5; EJ: '07- h; WI: '10-2R; EI: '11- 3R. Won NCAA 2009, BEL 2006, 2011. Three Belgian 400m records 2009-10.
Progress at 400m: 2005- 47.50, 2006- 46.06, 2007-47.85, 2008- 45.11, 2009- 44.78, 2010- 44.71, 2011-44.78. pbs: 60m 6.81i '07, 100m 10.78 '07, 200m 20.42 '11, 300m 32.10 '11, 600m 1:18.60i '11.
Twin brother of Kevin Borlée, their sister Olivia (b. 10 Apr 1986) has pbs 100m 11.39 '07, 200m 22.98 '06, 3 WCh '07, 2 OG '08 at 4x100mR. Their father Jacques was an international 400m runner (45.4 '79), mother Edith Demartelaere had pbs 200m 23.89 and 400m 54.09 in 1984.

Kevin BORLÉE b. 22 Feb 1988 Woluwe-Saint Lambert 1.80m 71kg. WS. Was at Florida State University.
At 400m: OG: '08- sf/5R; WCh: '09- sf/4R, '11- 3; EC: '10- 1/3R; WJ: '06- sf; EI: '11- 3R; CCp: '10-4/2R. At 200m: WY: '05- sf. Won BEL 200m 2009, 2011; 400m 2007.
Belgian 400m record 2008.
Progress at 400m: 2005- 47.86, 2006- 46.63, 2007-46.38, 2008- 44.88, 2009- 45.28, 2010- 45.01, 2011-44.74. pbs: 60m 7.03i '07, 100m 10.62 '07, 200m 20.72 '11, 300m 32.76 '08, 600m 1:15.65i '11.

Women

Svetlana BOLSHAKOVA   b. 14 Oct 1984 Leningrad, USSR 1.74m 59kg. SPVI.
At TJ: WCh: '09- dnq 20; EC: '10- 3; WY: '01- 2; EJ: '03- 3; EU23: '05- 2; WI: '10- 8.
Four Belgian triple jump records 2009-10.
Progress at TJ: 2000- 12.93, 2001- 13.48, 2002-13.55, 2003- 13.64i/13.43, 2004- 13.75, 2005- 14.11, 2006- 14.17, 2007- 14.28i, 2009- 14.27/14.46w, 2010- 14.55, 2011- 14.31i/13.70. pb LJ 6.43i '07, 6.29 '09.
Married Stijn Stroobants (HJ 2.26 '09) on 26 Aug 2006. Belgian citizen from 13 Jul 2008.

Tia HELLEBAUT b. 16 Feb 1978 Antwerpen 1.82m 66kg. Atletica '84. Chemistry graduate.
At HJ: OG: '04- 12, '08- 1; WCh: '05- 6, '07- 14; EC: '06- 1, '10- 5; WI: '06- 6, '12- 5; EI: '07- 1; WCp: '06- 2. At Hep: WCh: '01- 14, '03- dnf; EJ: '97- 11; EU23: '99- 7. At Pen: WI: '04- 5, '08- 1.
Won BEL HJ 2000, 2002-03, 2005; LJ 2006-08, Hep 1999-2000, 2002.
Belgian records: HJ (10) 2004-08, Hep 2006, Indoor HJ (7) 2006-07, Indoor LJ 2006 & 2007, Pen 2004 & 2007.
Progress at HJ, Hep: 1992- 1.56, 1993- 1.70, 1994-1.73, 4731; 1995- 1.76, 5167; 1996- 1.78, 5104; 1997- 1.75+, 5197; 1998- 1.81, 5381; 1999-1.87i/1.82, 5629; 2000- 1.89, 5646; 2001-1.89i/1.87, 5859; 2002- 1.85, 5584; 2003- 1.91, 6019; 2004- 1.95, 5954; 2005- 1.93, 2006- 2.03, 6201; 2007- 2.05i/1.98, 2008- 2.05, 2010- 1.97, 2012- 1.97i. pbs: 200m 24.65 '06, 800m 2:14.75 '06, 50mh 7.34i '04, 60mh 8.34i '07, 100mh 13.91 '05, LJ 6.42i/6.41 '07, TJ 12.54i '01, SP 13.85i '08, 13.10 '99; JT 44.37 '01, Pen 4877i '07.

A supreme big-event competitor: Belgian records at 2.01 and 2.03 to win EC gold 2006 and at 2.03 and 2.05 to win Olympic gold (first ever by a Belgian woman) in 2008, with indoor records at 2.01, 2.03, 2.05 to win EI 2007. Partner Win Van de Ven was BEL 110mh champion in 1990; son Vince born in June 2009 and daughter Saartje in February 2011.

BOTSWANA

Governing body: Botswana Athletics Association, PO Box 2399, Gaborone. Founded 1972.

Women

Amantle MONTSHO b. 4 Jul 1983 Mabudutsa 1.73m 64kg.
At 400m: OG: '04- h, '08- 8; WCh: '05-07-09-11: h/sf/8/1; CG: '06- sf, '10- 1; AfG: '03-07-11: h/1/1; AfCh: '04-06-08-10: h/2/1/1; WI: '10- 4; CCp: '10- 1/3R.
Botswana records 100m, 200m, 400m 2001-11.
Progress at 400m: 2003- 55.03, 2004- 53.77, 2005-52.59, 2006- 52.14, 2007- 50.90, 2008-49.83A/50.54, 2009- 49.89, 2010- 49.89, 2011-49.56. pbs: 100m 11.60 '11, 200m 22.94/22.88w '11, 300m 36.33i '10 (African record).
First Botswana woman to win a major title.

BRAZIL

Governing body: Confederação Brasileira de Atletismo (CBAt), Avenida Rio Purus No. 103 - Conj. Vieiralves, Bairro N.Sra das Graças, Manaus, AM 69053-050. Founded 1914 (Confederação 1977).
National Championships first held in 1925. **2011 Champions: Men**: 100m/200m: Bruno de Barros 10.25/20.21, 400m: Ânderson Henriques 45.81, 800m: Kléberson Davide 1:44.21, 1500m: Leandro de Oliveira 3:44.3, 5000m: David de Macedo 13:58.35, 10000m: Marílson dos Santos 28:40.75, 3000mSt: André de Santana 8:49.9, 110mh: Matheus Inocêncio 13.73, 400mh: Mahau Suguimati 50.13, HJ: Rafael dos Santos 2.18, PV: Fábio da Silva 5.30, LJ: Rogério Bispo 8.04, TJ: Jefferson Dias Sabino 17.07, SP/DT: Ronald Julião 18.32/62.45, HT: Allan Wolski 67.81, JT: Júlio César de Oliveira 71.94, Dec: Luiz Alberto de Araújo 8115, 20000mW: Moacir Zimmermann 1:21:02.5. **Women**: 100m/200m: Ana Cláudia Silva 11.34/22.68, 400m: Geisa Coutinho 51.35, 800m: Christiane dos Santos 2:04.40, 1500m/5000m: Fabiana da Silva 4:29.02/15:50.67, 10000m: Cruz da Silva 33:08.97 (drugs dq Simone da Silva 15:39.37/31:16.56), 3000mSt: Sabine Heitling 9:57.59, 100mh: Maíla Machado 13.29, 400mh: Jaílma de Lima 56.38, HJ: Mônica de Freitas 1.82, PV: Karla da Silva 4.30, LJ: Maurren Maggi 6.74, TJ: Keila Costa 13.88, SP: Keely Medeiros 16.74, DT: Fernanda Borges 58.22, HT: Josiane Soares 59.21, JT: Laila e Silva 57.81, Hep: Lucimara da Silva 6074, 20000mW: Érica de Sena 1:35:29.6.

Bruno de BARROS b. 7 Jan 1987 Maceió 1.78m 70kg. AD Cruiciuma.
At 200m/4x100mR: OG: '08- h; WCh: '11- 6; PAm: '11- 3/1R. Won BRA 100m & 200m 2011. Progress at 200m: 2006- 21.15, 2007- 21.05, 2008- 20.47, 2009- 20.48, 2011- 20.16. pb 100m 10.16 '09. Two year drugs ban 2009-11.

Fábio GOMES da SILVA b. 4 Aug 1983 Campinas, São Paulo 1.78m 74kg. BM&F Atletismo.
At PV: OG: '08- dnq 21=; WCh: '07- 10, '09- dnq, '11- 8; WJ: '02- 12; PAm: '07- 1; SACh: '05-06-07-09: 1/3/1/1. Won Ib-Am 2004; and SACh-j 2002; BRA 2005-07, 2009-11.
South American pole vault records 2007 & 2011. Progress at PV: 1999- 4.75, 2000- 5.01, 2001- 5.16, 2002- 5.17, 2003- 5.25, 2004- 5.55, 2005- 5.50, 2006- 5.65, 2007- 5.77, 2008- 5.45, 2009- 5.55, 2010- 5.65, 2011- 5.80.

Mauro Vinicius da SILVA b. 26 Dec 1986 Presidemte Prudente 1.83m 69kg.
At LJ: OG: '08- dnq 26; WI: '11- 1. BRA champion 2010.
Progress at LJ: 2005- 7.35/7.73w, 2006- 7.61, 2007- 7.66, 2008- 8.10/8.20w?, 2009- 8.04i/7.94, 2010- 8.12, 2011- 8.27, 2012- 8.28i. pbs: 60m 6.76i '09, 100m 10.40 '07, 200m 21.02 '07.
Won World Indoor title with 8.23 but took off behind the board with 24cm to spare.

Women

Maurren Higa **MAGGI** b. 25 Jun 1976 São Carlos, São Paulo 1.78m 66kg. FC São Paulo.
At LJ (/100mh): OG: '00- dnq 25, '08- 1; WCh: '99- 8/qf, '01- 7/h, '07- 6, '09- 7, '11- 11; PAm: '99- 1/2, '07- 1 (4 TJ), '11- 1; SACh: '97- 1/2, '99- 1/1, '01- 1/1, '06-07-11: 1/1/1; WUG: '99- 3, '01- 1/2/2R; WI: '03- 3, '08- 2. Won GP 2002, GWG 2001, IbAm 2000, 2002; SA-J 100mh 1994, BRA 100mh 1997-2000, LJ 1999-2002, 2006, 2008, 2011; TJ 2002.
South American (BRA) records: LJ 1 (3) 1999, 100mh 4 (6) 1999-2001, TJ 2002-03 (3); S.Am indoor LJ (4) 2003-08.
Progress at 100mh, LJ, TJ: 1994- 14.13, 5.86; 1995- 14.46/14.3w, 5.75/6.02w; 1996- 13.99, 6.47; 1997- 13.67/13.53w, 6.54; 1998- 13.60, 6.42; 1999- 12.86, 7.26A/6.79/6.81w, 2000- 6.93, 2001- 12.71, 6.94/6.98w, 13.60; 2002- 7.02/7.17w, 14.32; 2003- 7.06, 14.53; 2006- 6.84/6.86Aw, 14.02; 2007- 6.95, 14.44; 2008- 7.04, 2009- 6.90, 2010- 6.45, 2011- 6.94A/6.89. pbs: 60mh 8.12i '00.
Won first Olympic medal by a Brazilian woman and first South American women's gold in 2008. Father intended to name her Maureen (after first wife of Ringo Starr), but name was misspelled on her birth certificate. Formerly a gymnast, made huge breakthrough in 1999 with her 7.26 LJ at the high altitude of Bogotá from a previous best of 6.79. Two year ban for positive drugs test 14 Jun 2003, later reversed by CBAt but not by IAAF. Daughter Sophia (with former

F1 driver Antonio Pizzonia) born December 2004.

Fabiana de Almeida **MURER** b. 16 Mar 1981 Campinas, São Paulo 1.72m 64kg. BM&F Atletismo. Degree in physiotherapy.
At PV: OG: '08- 10=; WCh: '05- dnq 15, '07- 6=, '09- 5, '11- 1; WJ: '98- dnq 14=, '00- 10; PAm: '99- 07-11: 9/1/2; WI: '08- 3=, '10- 1; SACh: '99-01-05-06-07-09-11: 3/6/2/1/1/1/1; WCp: '06- 2, '10- 3. Won DL 2010, IbAm 2006, 2010; SAm-J 1998-2000, BRA 2005-07, 2010.
13 South American pole vault records, 15 indoors 2006-11, 29 BRA records 1998-2011.
Progress at PV: 1998- 3.66, 1999- 3.81, 2000- 3.90, 2001- 3.91, 2002- 3.70, 2003- 4.06, 2004- 4.25, 2005- 4.40, 2006- 4.66, 2007- 4.66i/4.65, 2008- 4.80, 2009- 4.82, 2010- 4.85, 2011- 4.85.
Married to coach Élson de Souza (pb 5.02 '89).

BULGARIA

Governing body: Bulgarian Athletics Federation, 75 bl. Vassil Levski, Sofia 1000. Founded 1924.
National Championships first held in 1926 (men), 1938 (women). **2011 Champions: Men:** 100m/200m: Peter Kremenski 10.50/20.97, 400m: Krasimir Braikov 47.15, 800m/1500m: Sava Todorov 1:54.30/3:53.31, 5000m: Yolo Nikolov 14:59.73, HMar: Stanislav Lambev 68:53, 3000mSt: Mitko Tsenov 9:08.49, 110mh: Martin Arnaudov 14.26, 400mh: Lazar Katuchev 52.01, HJ: Viktor Ninov 2.19, PV: Spas Buhalov 5.25, LJ: Nikolay Atanasov 7.77, TJ: Momchil Karailiev 16.45, SP: Georgi Ivanov 18.68, DT: Rosen Karamfilov 58.70, HT: Anastas Papazov 60.05, JT: Kolio Neshev 70.65, 20kW: Bozhidar Vasilev 2:02:13. **Women:** 100m/200m: Inna Eftimova 11.34/23.2, 400m: Violeta Metodieva 54.27, 800m: Teodora Kolarova 2:05.57, 1500m/3000mSt: Silvia Danekova 4:37.47/01:28.0, 5000m: Daniela Yordanova 17:03.25, HMar: Silvia Danekova 81:15, 100mh: Kristina Damianova 14.02, 400mh: Iva Dimova 62.13, HJ: Mirela Demireva 1.80, PV: Anna Ivanova 3.85, LJ: Magdalena Khristova 6.23w, TJ: Andriana Bânova 13.80w, SP: Radoslava Mavrodieva 15.08, DT: Atanaska Angelova-Dimitrova 45.85, HT: Mikhaela Metodieva 46.40, JT: Denista Koleva 49.95, 20kW: Radostina Gercheva Dimitrova 2:33:44.

Women

Ivet LALOVA b. 18 May 1984 Sofia 1.68m 56kg. Levski Sofia, Panellínios GRE.
At 100m/(200m): OG: '04- 4/5, '08- sf/qf; WCh: '07/09- qf, '11- 7/sf; EC: '10- h; WJ: '02- sf; WY: '01- h/sf; EJ: '03: 1/1; EI: '05- (1). At 60m: WI: '12- 8. Won BUL 100m 2004-05, 200m 2004; Balkan 100m 2011.
Bulgarian 100m record 2004.
Progress at 100m, 200m: 1998- 13.0, 27.2; 1999- 12.71, 2000- 12.14, 25.24; 2001- 11.72, 24.03; 2002- 11.59, 24.4; 2003- 11.14, 22.87; 2004- 10.77,

22.51/22.36w; 2005- 11.03, 22.76; 2007-11.26/11.15w, 23.00; 2008- 11.31/11.28w, 23.13; 2009- 11.48/11.24w, 23.60; 2010- 11.43, 23.71; 2011- 10.96, 22.66. pb 60m 7.14i '12.
Broke her leg in a collision with another athlete on 14 Jun 2005. Her 10.77 for 100m is the best mark of the 21st century. Engaged to sprinter Simone Collio (Italy). Her father Miroslav Lalov had 100m best of 10.4 and was BUL 200m champion in 1966, her mother Liliya (née Petrunova) was a heptathlete.

Vania STAMBOLOVA b. 28 Nov 1983 Varna 1.75m 53kg. Pavel Pavlov Vratsa. Student at the Sports Academy of Sofia.
At 400m: EC: '06- 1; WI: '06-01-12: 2/3/4; EI: '11- 4; WCp: '06- 2. At 400mh: WCh: '05- h, '09- sf, '11- 6; EC: '10- 2; WUG: '09- 1; CCp: '10- 3. Won Balkan 400mh 2005, 400m & 400mh 2011; BUL 400m 2009, 400mh 2002, 2005-06.
BUL Records: 400m (5) 2006, 400mh (2) 2006-10.
Progress at 400m. 400mh: 1998- 57.91, 64.34; 1999- 57.45, 63.53; 2000- 58.82, 62.72; 2001- 57.86, 61.38; 2002- 58.30, 61.11; 2005- 52.99, 56.29; 2006- 49.53, 54.55; 2009- 51.47, 55.14; 2010- 50.88, 53.82; 2011- 50.98, 53.68. pb 200m 22.81 '06, 22.7 '10; 300m 36.81i '12, 800m 2:02.03i '12.
Former footballer. Two-year drugs ban 2007-09.

Venelina VENEVA-MATEEVA b. 13 Jun 1974 Ruse 1.79m 61kg. Pavel Pavlov Vratsa.
At HJ: OG: '96- dnq 29=, '00- 9=, '04- dnq 15; WCh: '91-5-9-09-11: dnq 21=/14/14=/15/21, '01-03-05: 4/4/10; EC: '98- 5. '06- 2, '10- dnq 22=; EJ: '91- 2; WI: '01- 3, '04- 7; EI: '00-05-07-11: 4/3/3/7=. BUL champion 1995, 2004, 2009-10; Balkan 2003.
Progress at HJ: 1987- 1.68, 1988- 1.80, 1989- 1.86, 1990- 1.93i/1.90, 1991- 1.91, 1992- 1.91, 1993- 1.89i/1.85, 1994- 1.90, 1995- 1.94, 1996- 1.94i/1.88, 1998- 2.03, 1999- 1.90, 2000- 2.01, 2001- 2.04, 2002- 2.02i, 2003- 2.01, 2004- 2.01, 2005- 1.98, 2006- 2.04, 2007- 1.96i/2.02idq, 2009- 1.95, 2010- 1.95, 2011- 1.98. pbs: LJ 6.17 '90, TJ 12.51 '95.
Daughter Neapola born in 1997. World age-15 best of 1.93i in 1990. Two year drugs ban from positive test 24 Jan 2007.

CANADA

Governing body: Athletics Canada, Suite B1-110, 2445 S-Laurent Drive, Ottawa, Ontario K1G 6C3. Formed as Canadian AAU in 1884.
National Championships first held in 1884 (men), 1925 (women). **2011 Champions: Men**: 100m: Sam Effah 10.23, 200m: Brian Barnett 20.71w, 400m: Tremaine Harris 46.24, 800m: Andrew Ellerton 1:52.12, 1500m: Nathan Brannen 3:50.33, 5000m/10000m/HMar: Reid Coolsaet 14:09.83/31:36.38/64:55, Mar: Lucas McAneney 2:19:52, 3000mSt: Alex Genest 8:44.10, 110mh: Ingvar Moseley 14.26, 400mh: Adam Kunkel 50.80, HJ: Mark Dillon 2.19, PV: Jason Wurster 5.254, LJ: Benjamin Warnock 7.61w, TJ: Jacob

Zorzella 16.11w, SP: Dylan Armstrong 22.21, DT: Brent Roubos 53.35, HT: James Steacy 76.21, JT: Scott Russell 77.46, Dec: Damian Warner 8102, 10kW: Benjamin Thorne 41:34, 20kW: Evan Dunfee 1:25:15. **Women**: 100m/200m: Crystal Emmanuel 11.45w/22.99, 400m: Jenna Martin 51.95, 800m: Helen Crofts 2:05.05, 1500m: Sheila Reid 4:16.97, 5000: Leslie Sexton 16:55.01, HMar: Megan Brown 74:09, Mar: Emily Kroshus 2:42:27, 3000mSt: Dana Buchanan 10:26.82, 100mh: Perdita Felicien 12.80w, 400mh: Sage Watson 59.72, HJ: Jillian Drouin 1.84, PV: Carly Dockendorf 4.20, LJ: Krysha Bayley 6.54w, TJ: Carolina Eberhardt 12.64, SP/DT: Julie Labonté 18.12/53.31, HT: Heather Steacy 70.86, JT: Melissa Fraser 50.25, Hep: Ruky Abdulai 6150, 10kW: Megan Wylie 53:53, 20kW: Rachel Seaman 1:37:47

Dylan ARMSTRONG b. 15 Jan 1981 Kamloop, British Columbia 1.93m 125kg. Dylan BC Athletics. Was at University of Texas.
At SP: OG: '08- 4; WCh: '07- 9, '09- dnq 17, '11- 2; CG: '10- 1; WI: '10- 4; PAm: '07- 1; PAm-J: '99- 2 (1 HT, 3 DT); CCp: '10- 5. At HT: WCh: '01- dnq 31; WJ: '00- 2 (dnq DT). Won Canadian HT 2001-02, SP 2005-10.
Seven Canadian shot records 2008-11.
Progress at SP: 1999- 16.16, 2000- 16.30, 2001- 18.07, 2004- 19.55, 2005- 19.83, 2006- 20.62, 2007- 20.72, 2008- 21.04, 2009- 20.92, 2010- 21.58, 2011- 22.21. pbs: DT 54.60 '00, HT 71.51 '03, Wt 22.78i '03.

Women

Perdita FELICIEN b. 29 Aug 1980 Oshawa, Ontario 1.65m 63kg. Phoenix TC. Studied kinesiology at University of Illinois, USA.
At 100mh: OG: '00- h, '04- dnf; WCh: '01-03-05-07-09-11: sf/1/sf/2/8/sf; PAm: '03- 2, '07- 2; CCp: '10- 3. At 60mh: WI: '04- 1, '10- 2. Won FrancG 2001, CAN 2000, 2002-07, 2009-11; NCAA 2002-03.
Canadian 100mh records 2003 & 2004.
Progress at 100mh: 1998- 13.69/13.47w, 1999- 13.69, 2000- 12.91, 2001- 12.73, 2002- 12.83/12.77w, 2003- 12.53, 2004- 12.46/12.45w, 2005- 12.58, 2006- 12.58, 2007- 12.49, 2009- 12.54, 2010- 12.58, 2011- 12.73. pbs: 60m 7.37i '02, 100m 11.62 '01, 200m 24.21 '02, 50mh 6.80i '04, 60mh 7.75i '04.
Improved her best from 12.68 to 12.53 to win World 100mh in 2003 and from 7.90 to 7.75 to win World Indoor 60mh in 2004. Fell in 2004 Olympic final.

Sultana FRIZELL b. 24 Oct 1984 Perth, Ontario 1.83m 110kg. Was at University of Georgia.
At HT: OG: '08- dnq 33; WCh: '09- 10; CG: '10- 1; PAm: '07- 7, '11- 2; PAm-J: '03- 4; Canadian champion 2007-08, 2010.
Four Commonwealth hammer records 2009-12, North American 2012, seven Canadian 2008-12.
Progress at HT: 2002- 54.75, 2003- 57.95, 2004-

63.36, 2005- 66.42, 2006- 63.39, 2007- 67.92, 2008-
70.94, 2009- 72.07, 2010- 72.24, 2011- 71.46, 2012-
75.04. pbs: SP 15.82 '06, Wt 20.37i '05, JT 46.58 '04

Priscilla LOPES-SCHLIEP b. 26 Aug 1982
Scarborough, Ontario 1.63m 67kg. née Lopes.
Elite Edge. Studied sociology and criminal justice at University of Nebraska, USA.
At 100mh: OG: '04- h, '08- 3; WCh: '05-07-09:
sf/h/2; WJ: '00- qf. Won DL 2010, NACAC 2004,
Canadian 2008. At 60mh: WI: '10- 3.
Progress at 100mh: 2000- 13.78, 2001- 14.20, 2002-
13.84, 2003- 13.12, 2004- 12.64/12.75w, 2005-
12.82/12.99w, 2006- 12.60, 2007- 12.82/12.64w,
2008- 12.61, 2009- 12.49, 2010- 12.52. pbs: 60m
7.23i '05, 100m 11.44 '03, 11.40w '04; 200m 23.50i
'06, 23.73w '04; 55mh 7.51i '08, 60mh 7.82i '10.
Five NCAA 2nds: 100mh 2004-06, 60mh indoors
2005-06. Her parents came from Guyana.
Married Bronsen Schliep in November 2007;
daughter Nataliya born in September 2011.

Jessica ZELINKA b. 3 Sep 1981 London, Ontario
1.72m 62kg. Calgary AB.
At Hep: OG: '08- 5; WCh: '05- 11, '11- 9; CG: '06-
4, '10- 2; PAm: '07- 1; WJ: '00- 5 (h 100mh). Won
CAN Hep 2001, 2004-06, 2008, 2010.
Five Canadian heptathlon records 2006-08.
Progress at Hep: 1996- 4700, 1997- 4586, 1998-
4859, 1999- 5059, 2000- 5583, 2001- 5702, 2002-
5962, 2003- 6031, 2004- 6296, 2005- 6137, 2006-
6314, 2007- 6343, 2008- 6490, 2010- 6204, 2011-
6353. pbs: 50m 6.56i '02, 60m 7.53i '04, 100m
12.10A '06, 200m 23.64 '08, 800m 2:07.95 '08,
60mh 8.19i '06, 100mh 12.97 '08, HJ 1.79 '07, LJ
6.19/6.23w '06, SP 14.97 '07, JT 44.24 '10, Pen
4386i '07.
Four pbs in Canadian heptathlon record at 2008
Olympics. Daughter Anika born 29 May 2009.

CAYMAN ISLANDS

Governing Body: Cayman Islands Amateur
Athletic Association, PO Box 527, George Town,
Grand Cayman. Founded 1980.

Women

Cydonie MOTHERSILL b. 19 Mar 1978
Kingston, Jamaica 1.70m 54kg. Was at Clemson
University, USA.
At 200m(/100m): OG: '96- (h), '00- qf/qf, '04- sf,
'08- 8; WCh: '97- (h), '01-03-05-07-09: 3/sf/8/8/
sf; WJ: '96- sf/6; CG: '02-06-10: 5/4/1; PAm: '99-
5, '03- 2; PAm-J: '97- 3/3; CAG: '10- 1; WI: '03- 4;
WCp: '06- 7/1R, '10- 3/1R; won CAC 2001,
2003, 2005. Cayman Islands records 100m 1994-
2006, 200m 1994-05, 400m 1998-2009.
Progress at 200m: 1994- 24.31, 1995- 23.83, 1996-
23.65, 1997- 23.80, 1998- 23.48, 1999- 22.81, 2000-
22.66, 2001- 22.54, 2002- 22.76, 2003-
22.45/22.41w, 2004- 22.40, 2005- 22.39/22.26w,
2006- 22.57/22.56w, 2007- 22.52, 2008- 22.61,
2009- 22.45, 2010- 22.69/22.66w, 2011- 22.85.
pbs: 60m 7.36i '03, 100m 11.08/11.02w '06, 300m
35.82 '00, 400m 52.18 '09.
Married to Ato Modibo TRI (400m 44.87 '01).

CHILE

Governing body: Federación Atlética de Chile,
Calle Santo Toribio No 660, Ñuñoa, Santiago de
Chile. Founded 1914.
National Champions 2011: **Men**: 100m: Kael
Becerra 10.50, 200m: Cristián Reyes 21.11, 400m:
Jorge Rivas 48.76, 800m: Tomás Squella 1:52.42,
1500m: Leslie Encina 3:47.40, 5000m: Víctor
Aravena 14:59.23, 10000m: Patricio Uribe 30:02.12,
3000mSt: Daniel Estrada 9:05.24, 110mh: Luis
Montenegro 14.34, 400mh: Jorge Antonio Alegría
53.28, HJ: José María Soler 2.00. PV: Jorge Naranjo
4.80, LJ: Daniel Pineda 7.67, TJ: Alejandro Horn
14.49, SP: Marco Antonio Verni 16.93, DT:
Nicolás Laso 46.95, HT: Roberto Sáez 64.17, JT:
Diego Moraga 68.65, Dec: Matías Dallaserra
5981, 20kW: Yerko Araya 1:26:15, 50kW: Edward
Araya 4:03:02. **Women**: 100m: María Carolina
Díaz 12.14, 200m/400m: María Fernanda
Mackenna 24.27/56.44, 800m: Gladys Tapia
2:14.87, 1500m: Javiera Faletto 4:43.76, 5000m:
Susana Rebolledo 17:45.86, 10000m: Natalia
Romero 36:19.94, 3000mSt: Constanza Iturraga
12:36.08, 100mh: Ljubica Milos 13.76, 400mh:
Javiera Errázuriz 63.19, HJ: Florencia Vergara
1.73, PV: Ana Dibarrat 2.90, LJ: Daniela Pávez
6.24, TJ: Camila Salas 12.10, SP/DT: Karen
Gallardo 13.04/53.99, HT: Odette Palma 63.81,
JT: María de la Paz Ríos 50.06, 20kW: Josette
Sepúlveda 1:50:57

CHINA

Governing body: Athletic Association of the
People's Republic of China, 2 Tiyuguan Road,
Beijing 100763.
National Championships first held in 1910
(men), 1959 (women). **2011 Champions**: **Men**:
100m: Su Biantiang 10.16, 200m: Zhang Peimeng
20.64, 400m: Chang Pengben 46.32, 800m: Yang
Xiaofei 1:47.63, 1500m: Zhang Haikun 3:41.56,
5000m: Yang Dinghong 14:01.56, 10,000m: Hu
Kaijun 28:59.19, Mar: Wu Shiwei 2:14:44, 3000mSt:
Yang Tao 8:40.85, 110mh: Shi Dongpeng 13.41,
400mh: Li Zhilong 49.47, HJ: Zhang Guowei
2.28, PV: Yang Yansheng 5.60, LJ: Zhang Xiaoyi
8.02, TJ: Gu Junjie 16.78, SP: Wang Like 19.61,
DT: Huang Dongyi 55.55, HT: Wan Yong 68.27,
JT: Chen Qi 80.76, Dec: Yu Bin 7845, 20kW:
Wang Zhen 1:20:54, 50kW: Zhao Jianguo 3:50:18.
Women: 100m/200m: Ha Xianping 11.48/23.76,
400m: Chen Jingwen 52.56, 800m: Zhao Jing
2:03.93, 1500m/5000m: Xue Fei 4:10.49/15:27.46,
10,000m: Wang Jiali 31:38.15, HMar: Jin Lingling
72:28, Mar: Wang Jiali 2:26:12, 3000mSt: Fu
Tinglian 9:43.71, 100mh: Sun Yawei 13.18,
400mh: Huang Xiaoxiao 56.58, HJ: Zheng
Xingjuan 1.88, PV: Li Ling 4.30, LJ: Lu Minjia
6.50, TJ: Xie Limei 13.94, SP: Gong Lijiao 19.86,

DT: Li Yanfeng 63.01, HT: Zhang Wenxiu 70.05, JT: Du Xiaowei 60.26, Hep: Mei Yiduo 5759, 20kW: Liu Hong 1:30:00.

CHU Yafei b. 5 Sep 1988 Haikou 1.72m 55kg. Inner Mongolia.
At 20kW: OG: '08- 10; WCh: '09- 13, '11- 11; WCp: '10- 2; AsiG: '10- 2; AsiC: '09- 2; WUG: '07- 1.
At 10km road walk records: Asian junior (39:00) 2006, Asian (38:40) 2010.
Progress at 20kW: 2004- 1:27:23, 2005- 1:22:18, 2006- 1:18:44, 2007- 1:24:37, 2008- 1:21:04, 2009- 1:19:51, 2010- 1:21:11, 2011- 1:18:38. Pbs: 10000mW 41:37.47 '10, 37:57R '10; 30kW 2:14:46 '06.

LI Yanxi b. 26 Jun 1984 Shijiazhuang 1.82m 72kg. Hebei province.
At TJ: OG: '04- dnq 15, '08- 10; WCh: '07- dnq 16, '09- 6, '11- dnq 20; WJ: '02- 2; AsiG '06- 1, '10- 1; AsiC: '11- 2; WCp: '06- 4. Won CHN NG 2005, 2009.
Asian triple jump record 2009.
Progress at TJ: 1999- 15.22, 2000- 15.61, 2001- 15.46i/14.96, 2002- 16.66, 2003- 16.46, 2004- 17.09, 2005- 17.15, 2006- 17.12, 2007- 16.84, 2008- 17.30, 2009- 17.59, 2010- 16.95, 2011- 16.74/16.76w.

LIU Xiang b. 13 Jul 1983 Shanghai 1.89m 74kg.
At 110mh: OG: '04- 1, '08- h; WCh: '01-03-05-07-11: sf/3/2/1/2; WJ: '00- 4; WUG: '01- 1; AsiG: '02-06-10: 1/1/1; AsiC: '02-05-09: 1/1/1; WCp: '02- dnf, '06- 2. Won WAF 2006, CHN 2002, 2004-06; CHN NG 2005, E.Asian 2001, 2005, 2009. At 60mh: WI: '03-04-08-10-12: 3/2/1/7/2. World 110mh records 2004 & 2006, five Asian & CHN records 2002-06; World junior records 110mh 2002, indoors 50mh (6.53 and 6.52) & 60mh (7.61 and 7.55). Eight Asian indoor 60mh records 2002-12.
Progress at 110mh: 1999- 14.19, 2000- 13.75, 2001- 13.32, 2002- 13.12, 2003- 13.17, 2004- 12.91, 2005- 13.05, 2006- 12.88, 2007- 12.92, 2008- 13.18, 2009- 13.15, 2010- 13.09, 2011- 13.00. pbs: 200m 21.27 '02. 50mh 6.52i '02, 60mh 7.41i '12, HJ 2.04 '98.
With his brilliant Olympic 110mh win in 2004 he tied the world record of 12.91 and become the first Chinese man to win a global athletics gold medal. Took world record to 12.88 at Lausanne 2006. Set world age records 16 (13.94)-17-18 in 2000-02. Injured at 2008 Olympics.

SI Tianfeng b. 17 Jun 1984 Xintai, Shandong 1.80m 75kg. Shandong
At 50kW: OG: '08- 17; WCh: '11- 4; AsiG '10- 1; WCp: '10- 4. CHN champion 2008.
Progress at 50kW: 2003- 3:59:23, 2004- 3:55:37, 2005- 3:42:55, 2006- 3:52:06, 2007- 3:58:27, 2008- 3:45:13, 2009- 3:44:15, 2010- 3:47:04, 2011- 3:38:48. pb 20kW 1:20:05 '05.

WANG Hao b. 16 Aug 1989 Qiqihaer, Inner Mongolia 1.80m 65kg. Heilongjiang.
At 20kW: OG: '08- 4; WCh: '09- 2, '11- 13; WCp: '10- 1; AsiG: '10- 1; won CHN 2007, CHN NG 2009.

Progress at 20kW, 50kW: 2007- 1:21:20.69t, 2008- 1:19:47, 2009- 1:18:13, 3:41:55; 2010- 1:20:50, 2011- 1:21:03. Pbs: 10000mW 41:42.08 '07, 10kW 38:00 '10, 30kW 2:20:47 '07.

WANG Zhen b. 24 Aug 1991. Heilongjiang.
At 20kW: WCh: 11- 4; CHN champion 2011. Won World Race Walking Challenge Final 10k 2010. World junior 10k walk road best 2010, Asian 20k record 2012.
Progress at 20kW: 2008- 1:28:01, 2009- 1:22:10, 2010- 1:20:42, 2011- 1:18:30, 2012- 1:17:36. Pbs: 5000mW 20:16.04 '09, 10kW 37:44 '10, 30kmW 2:08:46 '08, 50kmW 3:53:00 '09.

Women

BAI Xue b. 13 Dec 1988 Wuhan 1.61m 46kg. Hubei.
At Mar: WCh: '09- 1. At (5000m)/10000m: WCh: '08- 21; WJ: '06- (4); AsiG: '10- 8; AsiC: '05- 1/1, '09- 1. Won Chinese 5000m 2009, 10000m 2008, 2010; NG 10000m 2009.
Progress at Mar: 2003- 2:37:07, 2004- 2:42:21, 2007- 2:27:46, 2008- 2:23:27, 2009- 2:25:15, 2010- 32:39.13, 2:25:18. pbs: 1500m 4:24.51 '04, 3000m 9:16.32 '04, 5000m 15:09.84 '07, 10000m 31:17.62 '09, HMar 70:55+ '10.
Won Beijing marathon 2008 and 2009, youngest ever world marathon champion 2009.

GONG Lijiao b. 24 Jan 1989 Luquan, Hebei Prov. 1.74m 110kg. Hebei.
At SP: OG: '08- 5; WCh: '07- 7, '09- 3, '11- 4; WI: '10- 8; AsiG: '10- 2; AsiC: '09- 1; CCp: '10- 3. Chinese champion 2007-11, NG 2009; Asian indoor 2008.
Progress at SP: 2005- 15.41i, 2006- 17.92, 2007- 19.13, 2008- 19.46, 2009- 20.35, 2010- 20.13, 2011- 20.11. pb JT 53.94 '07.

LI Ling b. 7 Feb 1985 Liaoning Prov. 1.83m 84kg. Liaoning.
At SP: OG: '08- 14; WCh: '07- 4, '11- 6; AsiG: '06- 1, '10- 1; AsiC: '05- 3; AsJ: '04- 1; WCp: '06- 5. Chinese champion 2006.
Progress at SP: 2002- 15.45, 2003- 16.55, 2004- 17.34, 2005- 18.68, 2006- 19.05, 2007- 19.38, 2008- 18.86, 2009- 18.97, 2010- 19.94, 2011- 19.72.

LI Yanfeng b. 15 May 1979 Qinggang, Heilongjiang, 1.79m 90kg.
At DT: OG: '04- 9, '08- 7; WCh: '11- 1; AsiG: '10- 1; AsiC: '00-02-03-07: 3/2/1/2; WUG: '01- 2, '03- 2; WCp: '02- 4, '10- 1. Won E.Asian G & CHN NG 2009, CHN 2010-11.
Progress at DT: 1997- 56.68, 1998- 57.30, 1999- 63.67, 2000- 60.84, 2001- 61.77, 2002- 62.52, 2003- 61.87, 2004- 64.34, 2005- 61.61, 2007- 62.24, 2008- 63.79, 2009- 66.40, 2010- 66.18, 2011- 67.98.

LIU Hong b. 12 May 1987 Jiangxi Prov. 1.61m 48kg. Guangdong.
At 20kW: OG: '08- 4; WCh: '07- 19, '09- 3, '11- 2; WCp: '06- 6; AsiG: '06- 1, '10- 1; won CHN 2010-11, NG 2009. At 10000mW: WJ: '06- 1.

Asian 20k walk record 2012,
Progress at 20kW: 2004- 1:35:04, 2005- 1:29:39, 2006- 1:28:26, 2007- 1:29:41, 2008- 1:27:17, 2009- 1:28:11, 2010- 1:30:06, 2011- 1:27:17, 2012- 1:25:46. pbs: 3000mW 12:18.18 '05, 5000mW 21:30.03 '06, 10kW 42:30R '10, 45:12.84t '06.

MA Xuejun b. 26 Mar 1985 Shandong 1.85m 96kg. Shandong.
At DT: OG: '08- dnq 23; WCh: '07- 8, '09- 11, '11- dnq 14; AsiG: '06- 2; AsiCh: '09- 2, '11- 2; WJ: '02- 1, '04- 1; WY: '01- 1. Won Asi-J 2004, CHN 2006, 2009.
Progress at DT: 1999- 52.79, 2001- 58.65, 2002- 58.85, 2003- 60.20, 2004- 57.85, 2005- 61.87, 2006- 65.00, 2007- 62.57, 2008- 61.92, 2009- 63.63, 2010- 60.39, 2011- 63.93.

SONG Aimin b. 15 Mar 1978 Jizhou, Hebei Prov. 1.78m 95kg. Hebei.
At DT: OG: '04- dnq 25, '08- 4; WCh: '03-05-07-09: 7/10/dnq 13/5; AsiG: '02- 2, '06- 1, '10- 2; AsiC: '05- 1, '09- 1; WUG: '05- 2; WCp: '06- 3. Won Asi-J 1997, E.Asian 2005, CHN 2001-03, 2008.
Progress at DT: 1997- 55.84, 1998- 56.64, 1999- 60.50, 2000- 60.39, 2001- 62.34, 2002- 62.28, 2003- 65.33, 2004- 64.90, 2005- 65.23, 2006- 63.52, 2007- 62.64, 2008- 64.31, 2009- 65.44, 2010- 64.04.

TAN Jian b. 20 Jan 1988 Chengdu 1.79m 80kg. Sichuan,
At DT: WCh: '11- 6; WJ: '06- 3.
Progress at DT: 2004- 56.00, 2005- 57.01, 2007- 56.99, 2008- 55.04, 2009- 57.40, 2010- 59.65, 2011- 63.72.

XIE Limei b. 27 Jun 1986 Fujian Prov. 1.73m 57kg. Fujian.
At TJ: OG: '08- 12; WCh: '07- 8, '09- 9, '11- dnq 25; WJ: '04- 2; AsiG: '06- 1, '10- 2; AsiC: '05- 1, '11- 1; WI: '08- 8, '10- 7; CCp: '10- 4. Won CHN 2006-07, 2009-11. Asian TJ record 2007.
Progress at TJ: 2002- 13.51, 2003- 13.89, 2004- 14.08, 2005- 14.38, 2006- 14.54, 2007- 14.90, 2008- 14.39, 2009- 14.62, 2010- 14.35, 2011- 14.54/14.62w. pb LJ 6.41 '06.

ZHANG Wenxiu b. 22 Mar 1986 Dalian 1.82m 108kg. Army.
At HT: OG: '04- 7, '08- 3; WCh: '01-03-05-07-09-11: 11/dnq 14/5/3/5/3; WJ: '02- dnq 20; AsiG: '06- 1, '10- 1; AsiC: '05- 1, '09- 1; WCp: '06- 4, '10- 2. Won Asi-J 2002, CHN 2004, 2006-10; NG 2003, 2009.
Eight Asian hammer records 2001-12, world youth 2003, two world junior 2004-05.
Progress at HT: 2000- 60.30, 2001- 66.30, 2002- 67.13, 2003- 70.60, 2004- 72.42, 2005- 73.24, 2006- 74.15, 2007- 74.86, 2008- 74.32, 2009- 74.25, 2010- 73.83, 2011- 75.65, 2012- 75.72.
World age bests at 15-16-18.

ZHOU Chunxiu b. 15 Nov 1978 Suzhou, Jiangsu Prov. 1.63m 44kg. Henan.
At Mar: OG: '04- 33, '08- 3; WCh: '05- 5, '07- 2, '09- 4; AsiG: '06- 1, '10- 1. World HMar: '04- 12. Won CHN HMar 2008, Mar 2003-05
Progress at 10000m, Mar: 2000- 33:14.63, 2003- 32:13.96, 2:23:41; 2004- 33:03.04, 2:23:28; 2005- 31:09.03, 2:21:11; 2006- 32:42.46, 2:19:51; 2007- 32:44.13, 2:20:38; 2008- 32:21.13, 2:27:07; 2009- 31:59.93, 2:25:39; 2010- 2:25:00, 2011- 2:34:29, 2012- 2:23:42. pbs: 1500m 4:16.59 '98, 3000m 9:34.68 '00, 5000m 15:22.46 '03, HMar 68:59 '09, 30km 1:39:35 '08.
Seven marathon wins. Four sub 2:30 runs in 2005 (first woman to do so in one year), won Seoul in pb 2:23:24 and improved by 2:13 for 2nd in Beijing. Won Seoul 2006, London 2007.

ZHU Xiaolin b. 20 Feb 1984 Xiuyan, Liaoning Prov. 1.66m 50kg. Liaoning.
At Mar: OG: '08- 4; WCh: '07- 4, '09- 5, '11- 6; AsiG: '10- 2. Won Chinese 1500m 2006, Mar & CC 2007.
Progress at Mar: 2002- 2:23:57, 2004- 2:41:04, 2005- 2:32:27, 2006- 2:28:27, 2007- 2:26:08, 2008- 2:27:16, 2009- 2:26:08, 2010- 2:26:35, 2011- 2:26:28, 2012- 2:24:19. pbs: 800m 2:18.51 '06, 1500m 4:12.73 '05, 3000m 9:04.64i '02, 5000m 15:22.35 '05, 10000m 31:53.96 '08, HMar 70:07 '10.
Won Dalian Marathon 2002, 2005-06.

COLOMBIA

Governing body: Federación Colombiana de Atletismo, Calle 27° No. 25-18, Apartado Aéreo 6024, Santafé de Bogotá. Founded 1937.
National Champions 2011: Men: 100m: Álvaro Gómez 10.11w, 200m: Daniel Grueso 20.95, 400m: Diego Palomeque 47.3, 800m: Rafith Rodríguez 1:52.87, 1500m: Iván Darío González 3:53.44, 5000m: Mauricio González 14:38.79, 10000m: William Naranjo 30:56.31, Mar: José David Cardona 2:34:47, 3000mSt: Gabriel Giraldo 9:16.74, 110mh: Yolver Lozano 14.32, 400mh: Juan Pablo Maturana 50.99, HJ: Wanner Miller 2.15, PV: Ebert Gómez 5.00, LJ/TJ: John Freddy Murillo 7.74w/16.18, SP: Edder Moreno 18.05, DT: Julián Angulo 49.86, HT: Freiman Arias 61.91, JT: Dayron Márquez 7901, Dec: Esteban David Salvado 6608, 20kW: Gustavo Restrepo 1:24:28. **Women:** 100m: María Alejandra Idrobo 11.49, 200m/400m: Norma González 23.06/52.79, 800m/1500m: Muriel Coneo 2:07.19/4:29.74, 5000m/10000m: Yolanda Fernández 17:14.12/ 35:41.66, Mar: Ruby Riativa 3:18:01, 3000mSt: Ángela Figueroa 11:01.83, 100mh: Briggite Merlano 13.13, 400mh: Princesa Oliveros 60.36, HJ/LJ/TJ: Caterine Ibargüen 1.72/6.50/14.63w, PV: Milena Agudelo 4.00, SP: Ányela Rivas 16.38, DT: Johana Martínez 52.44, HT: Johana Moreno 67.40, JT: Flor Dennis Ruiz 54.81, Hep: Melisa Valencia 4778, 20kW: Ingrid Johana Hernández 1:38:00.

Luis Fernando LÓPEZ b. 3 Jun 1979 Pasto, Nariño 1.73m 60kg.
At 20kW: OG: '04- 24, '08- 9; WCh: '05-07-09-11:

12/22/5/3; PAm: '03-4, '07- dq; SACh: '08/09- 1; CAG: '06- 1; WCp: '10- 5. Won PAm Cup 2011. Walk records: South American 20,000m (1:20:53.6) 2009 and 10km 2010; Colombian 20km walk 2009.
Progress at 20kW: 2001- 1:26:31A, 2002- 1:26:47.6t, 2003- 1:25:09, 2004- 1:22:52, 2005- 1:20:26, 2006- 1:24:11, 2007- 1:24:22.7tA, 2008- 1:20:59, 2009- 1:20:03, 2010- 1:21:12, 2011- 1:20:38. pb 10kW Rd 38:10 '10. Won Colombia's first ever medal at the World Championships in 2011.

Women

Caterine IBARGÜEN b. 12 Feb 1984 Apartadó, Antioquia 1.81m 65kg. Studying nursing in PUR.
At HJ/TJ (LJ): WCh: '09- 28=/-, '11- -/3; WJ: '02: -/dnq 17; PAm: '07- 4/-, '11- -/1 (3); SACh: '99- 3/-, '03- -/3 (2), '05- 1/3 (3), '06- 1/2 (2), '07- 1/- (3), '09- 1/1, '11- -/1 (3); CAG: '02- 3/2, '06- 2/- (2), '10- -/2. At HJ: OG: '04- dnq 28=; PAm: '07- 4;. Won COL HJ 1999, 2001-03, 2005-11; LJ 2003-04, 2006-08, 2011; TJ 2002-05, 2007-11.
Records: South American triple jump (6) 2011, junior HJ 2004. Colombia HJ (7) 2002-05, LJ (7) 2004-11, TJ (14) 2004-11
Progress at TJ: 2001- 12.90, 2002- 13.38A, 2003- 13.23A, 2004- 13.64A, 2005- 13.66A, 2006- 13.91A/13.98Aw, 2007- 12.66A, 2008- 13.79A, 2009- 13.96A/13.93, 2010- 14.29, 2011- 14.99A/14.84. pbs: 200m 25.34 '08, 100mh 14.09 '11, HJ 1.93A '05, LJ 6.63A/6.58 '11, SP 13.79 '10, JT 44.81 '09, Hep 5742 '09.

COSTA RICA

Governing body: Federación Costarricense de Atletismo, 1032-1007 San José. Founded 1960.

Nery BRENES b. 25 Sep 1985 Limón 1.74m 62kg. Student of political science.
At 400m: OG: '08- sf; WCh: '05- h, '07/11-sf; PAm: '11- 1; CAG: '10- 1; WI: '08-10-12: 4/4/1; CCp: '10- 1R. Won IbAm 2010, C.American 2011. Six CRC 400m records 2005-11, 200m 2009.
Progress at 400m: 2004- 47.90A, 2005- 46.42, 2006- 47.57, 2007- 45.01, 2008- 44.94, 2009- 45.73A/45.92, 2010- 44.84, 2011- 44.65A/45.29, 2012- 45.11i. pb 200m 20.68A '09.
Improved pb by 0.99 to win his heat at 2007 World Champs. Won Costa Rica's first ever athletics gold medals at Pan-American Games in 2011 and World Indoors in 2012.

CROATIA

Governing body: Hrvatski Atletski Savez, Trg kralja Peetra Svacica 17, 10000 Zagreb. Founded 1912.
National Champions 2011 Men: 100m/110mh: Jurica Grabusic 10.69/14.08, 200m/400m: Zeljko Vincek 21.70/47.33, 800m/1500m: Sandy Protic 1:52.31/4:00.48, 3000m/5000m/10000m: Goran Grdenic 9:34.26/15:21.82/33:28.02, HMar: Drazen Dinjar 72:50. Mar: Drago Paripovic 2:38:09,

3000mSt: Zoran Zilic 9:39.56, 400mh: Milan Kotur 53.51, HJ: Tomislav Popek 2.00, PV: Ivan Horvat 5.30, LJ: Dino Pervan 7.59, TJ: Ivan Pucelj 14.88, SP: Marin Premeru 19.06, DT: Roland Varga 64.26, HT: Andras Haklits 74.64, JT: Marin Maric 70.26, Dec: Dec: Aleksandar Puklavec 6403, 20kmW: Zelimir Haubrih 1:50:33. **Women**: 100m: Sandra Parlov 12.03, 200m/400m: Anita Banovic 24.36/53.77, 800m: Romana Tea Kirinic 2:12.18, 1500m: Anja Simuncic 4:40.87, 3000m: Matea Matosevic 9:39.43. 5000m: Lisa Christina Stublic 16:08.33, 10000m/HMar: Matea Matosevic 35:44.99/1:22:49 Mar: Ingrid Nikolesic 3:14:41, 100mh: Ivana Loncarek 13.64, 400mh: Nikolina Horvat 58.41, HJ: Ana Simic 1.60, PV: Petra Malkoc 3.50 3.70, LJ/TJ: Mirjana Gagic 6.24/13.02, SP: Valentina Muzaric 15.74, DT: Tijana Frajtic 46.46, HT: Lucija Cvitanovic 49.00, JT: Jelena Ivancic 50.61, Hep: Marina Banovic 5297, 10kmW: Ljiljana Culibrk 60:15.

Women

Sandra PERKOVIC b. 21 Jun 1990 Zagreb 1.83m 80kg. Zagreb.
At DT(/SP): WCh: '09- 9; EC: '10- 1; WJ: '06- dnq 21, '08- 3/dnq 13; WY: '07- 2/dnq 13; EJ: '07- 2, '09- 1/5; CCp: '10- 2. Won CRO SP 2008-10, DT 2010.
FiveCroatian DT records 2009-11, SP 2010.
Progress at DT: 2006- 50.11, 2007- 55.42, 2008- 55.89, 2009- 62.79, 2010- 66.93, 2011- 67.96/69.99dq, 2012- 67.19. pb SP 16.99i/16.40 '11.
First Croatian woman to win European Champs gold. Six months drugs ban 2011.

Blanka VLASIC b. 8 Nov 1983 Split 1.92m 75kg. ASK Split.
At HJ: OG: '00- dnq 17, '04- 11, '08- 2; WCh: '01- 03-05-07-09-11: 6/7/dnq 19=/1/1/2; EC: '02- 5=, '06- 4, 10- 1; WJ: '00- 1, '02- 1; WY: '99- 8; EU23: '03- 1; EJ: '01- 7; WI: '03-04-06-08-10: 4/3/2/1/1; EI: '07- 4, '09- 5=; CCp: '10- 1. Won DL 2010, WAF 2007-09, MedG 2001, CRO 2001- 02, 2005.
Ten Croatian high jump records 2003-09.
Progress at HJ: 1998- 1.68, 1999- 1.80, 2000- 1.93, 2001- 1.95, 2002- 1.96, 2003- 2.01, 2004- 2.03, 2005- 1.95, 2006- 2.05i/2.03, 2007- 2.07, 2008- 2.06, 2009- 2.08, 2010- 2.06i/2.05, 2011- 2.03.
IAAF Woman Athlete of the Year 2010. Won 5/6 Golden League HJs in both 2007 and 2008. She has had 101 competitions at 2m or higher to the end of 2011 (and 169 jumps over 2m), including 42 successive Jul 2007- Feb 2009, but in 2008 lost on count-back both at Olympics (when she won first ever athletics medal for Croatia) and in the final Golden League meeting, thus losing her share of the Jackpot. She had 60 attempts at the world record 2007-10. Her father Josko set the Croatian decathlon record with 7659 (1983) and named his daughter after Casablanca, where he won Mediterranean Games title.

CUBA

Governing body: Federación Cubana de Atletismo, Calle 13 y C Vedado 601, Zona Postal 4, La Habana 10400. Founded 1922.

National Champions 2011: Men: 100m: Michael Herrera 10.27, 200m: Noel Ruíz 20.75w, 400m: Williams Collazo 45.97, 800m: Raidel Acea 1:51.32, 1500m: Andy González 3:51.20, 5000m: Leonardo Morales 14:38.33, 10000m: Henrry Jaén 30:35.18, Mar: Alexeis Machado 2:28:04, 3000mSt:, 110mh: Ignacio Morales 13.64, 400mh: Yasmany Copello 50.17, HJ: Víctor Moya 2.25, PV: Yordani Garcí a 4.80, LJ: Wilfredo Martínez 8.01, TJ: Alexis Copello 17.22, SP: Carlos Véliz 20.15, DT: Jorge Fernández 65.54, HT: Roberto Janet 75.60, JT: Guillermo Martínez 84.68, Dec: José Ángel Mendieta 7404, 20kW: Rubén Goliat 1:32:46. **Women**: 100m: Nelkys Casabona 11.43, 200m: Dulaimi Débora Odelín 23.42, 400m: Daysiurami Bonne 52.72, 800m: Rose Mary Almanza 2:02.83, 1500m: Adriana Muñoz 4:16.78, 5000m/10000m: Dailín Belmonte 16:14.01/35:25.15, Mar: Yadira González 3:14:40, 100mh: Rujaine Colo 13.80, 400mh: Zurian Hechavarría 60.23, HJ: Lesyaní Mayor 1.82, PV: Yarisley Silva 4.50, LJ: Suslaidy Giralt 6.56, TJ: Yargeris Savigne 14.95, SP: Misleydis González 18.72, DT: Yarelys Barrios 64.19, HT: Arasay Thondike 70.16, JT: Yanet Cruz 63.50, Hep: Gretchen Quintana 6004, 10kW: Aliuska Machado 48:12.

Yoandris BETANZOS b. 15 Feb 1982 Ciego de Ávila 1.80m 81kg
At TJ: OG: '04- 4; WCh: '03- 2, '05- 2, '07/09- dnq 20/17, '11- 11; WJ: '00- 2; WY: '99- 2; PAm: '03- 1, '07- 3, '11- 2 (1 4x400m); CAG: '06- 1; WUG: '01- 5; WI: '04-06-10: 3/3/2; Won WAF 2005-06, CAC 2005, PAm-J 2001, Cuban 2002-06.
Progress at TJ: 1998- 14.96, 1999- 15.94/16.07w, 2000- 16.82, 2001- 16.84/16.86w, 2002- 17.29, 2003- 17.28, 2004- 17.53, 2005- 17.46, 2006- 17.63/17.67w, 2007- 17.12i/16.96/17.21w, 2008- 17.11i/17.03/17.23w, 2009- 17.65, 2010- 17.69i/17.22, 2011- 17.23A/17.18. pbs: HJ 2.10, LJ 7.51i '11.

Lázaro BORGES b. 19 Jun 1986 La Habana 1.73m 70kg.
At TJ: OG: '08- dnq nh; WCh: '11- 2; WI: '12- 5=; PAm: '07- nh, '11- 1; Won IbAm 2010, CAC 2008, Cuban 2005-07, 2009-10.
Pole vault records: two CAC 2011, 7 Cuban 2011, CAC indoor 2012.
Progress at TJ: 2002- 3.60, 2003- 4.25, 2004- 4.80, 2005- 5.10, 2006- 5.30, 2007- 5.50, 2008- 5.70, 2009- 5.65, 2010- 5.60, 2011- 5.90, 2012- 5.72i.
Breakthrough season in 2011. when he improved national record by 25 centimetres from six occasions, and became first Cuban ever to medal at PV in a World Championship, and first ever PV Cuban male gold at Pan-American Games.

Omar CISNEROS b. 19 Nov 1989 Camagüey 1.87m 78kg.
At 400mh: WCh: '09/11- sf; PAmG: '11- 1/1R. Won IbAm 2010, Cuban 2009-10. At 400m: PAm: '07- sf.
Three Cuban 400mh records 2010-11.
Progress at 400mh: 2007- 49.57, 2008- 50.1, 2009- 48.87, 2010- 48.21, 2011- 47.99A/49.26. pbs: 200m 21.36 '07, 400m 45.76 '09.

Alexis COPELLO b. 12 Aug 1985 Santiago de Cuba 1.87m 78kg.
At TJ: OG: '08- dnq 13; WCh: '09- 3, '11- 4; WI: '12- 7; PAmG: '11- 1; CAG: '06- 2; CCp: '10- 2. Won IbAm 2010, CAC 2009, Cuban 2009, 2011.
Progress at TJ: 2002- 15.38, 2003- 16.34, 2004- 16.90, 2005- 16.95/17.09w, 2006- 17.38, 2007- 16.87/17.15w, 2008- 17.50, 2009- 17.65/17.69w, 2010- 17.55, 2011- 17.68A/17.47. pb LJ 7.35 '04.
Elder brother Alexander decathlon pb 7359 '02.

Junior DÍAZ b. 28 Apr 1987 Sancti Spíritus 1.93m 80kg.
At Dec: WCh: '09- 9; PAm-J: '05- 2. At 4x400m: OG: '08- hR.
Progress at Dec: 2005- 7161, 2006- 7343, 2007- 7902, 2008- 8057h, 2009- 8357, 2010- dnf, 2011- 8053. pbs: 60m 6.91i '10, 100m 10.66 '09, 10.4 '07; 400m 46.15 '09, 45.9 '07; 1000m 2:41.25i '10, 1500m 4:30.16 '07, 60mh 8.20i '09, 110mh 14.49 '09, 14.2 '07, HJ 2.05 '08, PV 4.60 '09, LJ 7.75 '07, SP 15.42 '08, DT 46.50 '11, JT 62.14 '11, Hep 5831i '10.

Jorge FERNÁNDEZ b. 2 Dec 1987 Matanzas 1.90m 100kg. MTZ.
At DT: OG: '08- dnq 27; WCh: '11- 8; PAmG: '11- 1; WJ: '06- 5. Won CAC 2008-09, Cuban 2009-12.
Progress at DT: 2005- 53.69, 2006- 54.77, 2007- 57.57, 2008- 63.31, 2009- 63.92, 2010- 66.00, 2011- 65.89, 2012- 66.05. pb SP 16.93 '12.

Yordani GARCÍA b. 21 Nov 1988 San Luis, Pinar del Río 1.94m 95kg.
At Dec: OG: '08- 15; WCh: '07- 8, '09- 8, '11- dnf; PAm: '07- 2, '11- 3; WJ: '06- 2. At Oct: WY: '05- 1. At ep: WI: '12- 7. Won Cuban Dec 2006-07, 2010; PV 2011.
Cuban & CAC junior decathlon record 2007. World youth octathlon record (6482) 2005.
Progress at Dec: 2005- 6765, 2006- 7879h, 2007- 8257, 2008- 7992, 2009- 8496, 2010- 8381h, 2011- 8397. pbs: 60m 6.89i '09, 100m 10.60 '09, 10.5dt '10, 400m 48.34 '09, 1000m 2:50.21i '12, 1500m 4:31.40 '11, 60mh 7.80i '10, 110mh 13.89 '09, HJ 2.10 '09, PV 4.90 '10, LJ 7.36 '09, SP 16.50 '09, DT 47.70 '08, JT 69.37 '09, Hep 5905i '09.

Arnie David GIRAT b. 26 Aug 1984 Santiago de Cuba 1.82m 72kg.
At TJ: OG: '04- dnq 17, '08- 4; WCh: '03-05-07-09-11: 4/8/7/5/dnq 13; WJ: '02- 1, WY: '01- 2; WI: '08- 2. '10- 3. Won PAm-J 2003 (2 LJ), Ib-Am 2004, WAF 2009, Cuban 2010.
Progress at TJ: 2000- 15.23, 2001- 16.33, 2002-

16.84, 2003- 17.31, 2004- 17.12, 2005- 17.14, 2006- 16.97/17.06w, 2007- 17.39i/17.10/17.18w, 2008- 17.52, 2009- 17.62, 2010- 17.49, 2011- 17.29/17.42w. pb LJ 7.70 '02.
Father (also David, who preferred spelling Giralt, b. 26 Jun 1955) had LJ pbs 8.22/8.32w, was 3rd in the World Cupand 2nd at Pan-American Games in 1979. Younger sister **Suslaidy** (b. 19 Aug 1987) has LJ pb 6.61 '11 despite being a deaf-mute.

Yeimer LÓPEZ b. 20 Aug 1982 Granma 1.84m 75kg.
At 800m: OG: '08- 6; WCh: '05/07- h, '09- 10; PAm: '07- 1. At 400m: OG: '04- sf; WCh: '03- sf; PAm: '03- 2; CAG: '06- 1. Won CAC 2005, 2009; IbAm 2010; Cuban 400m 2003, 2006, 800m 2002, 2005, 2007, 2009-10.
Progress at 800m: 2001- 1:50.75, 2002- 1:47.2, 2003- 1:47.94, 2005- 1:46.61, 2006- 1:48.92, 2007- 1:44.48, 2008- 1:43.07, 2009- 1:44.10, 2010- 1:44.18, 2011- 1:45.90. pb 400m 45.11 '03.
Decided to stay in Spain in 2010, so will not be representing Cuba internationally in future. Twin sister Ana María López ran at 2004 OG at 4x100m (pbs 11.1/23.50 '02).

Guillermo MARTÍNEZ b. 28 Jun 1981 Camagüey 1.87m 107kg.
At JT: WCh: '05-07-09-11: 10/9/2/3; PAm: '07- 1, '11- 1; CAG: '06- 1. Won CAC 2009, 2011; IbAm 2010, Cuban 2004-07, 2009-11.
Cuban & CAC javelin records 2006 & 2011.
Progress at JT: 1999- 64.66, 2000- 70.82, 2001- 73.50, 2002- 75.90, 2003- 75.35, 2004- 81.45, 2005- 84.06, 2006- 87.17, 2007- 85.93, 2009- 86.41, 2010- 86.38, 2011- 87.20A.

Wilfredo MARTÍNEZ b. 9 Jan 1985 La Habana 1.80m 82kg.
At LJ: OG: '08- 5; PAm: '07- 2; WI: '08- 8; PAm-J: '03- 1. Won CAC 2008, IbAm 2010, CUB 2009-12.
Progress at LJ: 2002- 7.48, 2003- 7.90, 2004- 7.77, 2005- 8.04, 2006- 8.03, 2007- 8.17, 2008- 8.31A/8.19, 2009- 8.13, 2010- 8.20, 2011- 8.11. pb TJ 15.55 '03.
Decided to stay in Spain in 2011, so will not be representing Cuba internationally in future.

Dayron ROBLES b. 19 Nov 1986 Guantánamo 1.91m 91kg.
At 110mh: OG: '08- 1; WCh: '05-07-09-11: sf/4/ sf/dq(1); WJ: '04- 2, WY: '03- 6; CAG: '06- 1; PAm: '07- 1, '11- 1; WCp: '06- 3; won PAm-J 2005, WAF 2007, CAC 2009, Cuban 2006-07. At 60mh: WI: '06- 2, '10- 1.
World 110mh record 2008, three Cuban & CAC 2006-08, CAC junior record 2005. Two CAC 60mh indoor records 2008.
Progress at 110mh: 2002- 15.01, 2003- 14.30, 2004- 13.75, 2005- 13.46/13.2/13.41w, 2006- 13.00, 2007- 12.92, 2008- 12.87, 2009- 13.04, 2010- 13.01, 2011- 13.00. pbs: 100m 10.70 '06, 200m 21.85 '06, 50mh 6.39i '08, 60mh 7.33i '08.

Season's record 7 sub-13 second times in 2008. Disqualified for obstructing Liu Xiang after finishing first at 2011 Worlds.

Leonel SUÁREZ b. 1 Sep 1987 Holguín 1.81m 76kg.
At Dec: OG: '08- 3; WCh: '09- 2, '11- 3; PAm: '07- 4, '11- 1. CAC and Cuban champion 2009. At Hep: WI: '10- 7. CAC decathlon record 2009, four Cuban records 2008-09.
Progress at Dec: 2005- 7267, 2006- 7357, 2007- 8156, 2008- 8527, 2009- 8654, 2010- 8328, 2011- 8501. pbs: 60m 7.11i '09, 100m 10.90 '08, 400m 47.65 '09, 1000m 2:36.12i '10, 1500m 4:16.70 '08, 60mh 7.90i '10, 110mh 14.12 '08, HJ 2.17 '08, PV 5.00 '09, LJ 7.42 '09, SP 15.20 '09, DT 47.32 '11, JT 77.47 '09, Hep 5964i '10.
Won at Talence 2010.

Osniel TOSCA b. 30 Jun 1984 Villa Clara 1.82m 78kg.
At TJ: WCh: '07- 4; WJ: '02- 7; WY: '01- 3; PAm: '07- 2; WI: '08- 6. NACAC champion 2006, Cuban 2007.
Progress at TJ: 2000- 15.14, 2001- 16.05, 2002- 16.45, 2003- 16.61, 2004- 17.17, 2005- 17.08, 2006- 17.01, 2007- 17.52, 2008- 17.13i/17.12/17.40w, 2009- 17.20, 2010- 17.12, 2011- 17.22. pb LJ 7.00 '03.

Women

Yarelys BARRIOS b. 12 Jul 1983 Pinar del Río 1.72m 98kg.
At DT: OG: '08- 2; WCh: '07- 2, '09- 2, '11- 3; WJ: '02- 7; PAm: '07- 1, '11- 1; CAG: '06- 2; WUG: '07- 1; CCp: '10- 3. Won DL 2010, WAF 2008-09, CAC 2005, 2008-09; Cuban 2009-12.
Progress at DT: 1999- 44.45, 2000- 50.22, 2001- 48.92, 2002- 54.10, 2003- 58.37, 2004- 59.51, 2005- 60.61, 2006- 61.01, 2007- 63.90, 2008- 66.13, 2009- 65.86, 2010- 65.96, 2011- 66.40A, 2012- 68.03.

Mabel GAY b. 5 May 1983 Santiago de Cuba 1.85m 69kg.
At TJ: OG: '08- dnq 15; WCh: '03-05-09-11: 5/ dnq 18/2/4; WJ: '02- 1; WY: '99- 1; PAm: '03-07- 11: 1/3/3; PAm-J: '01- 1; CAG: '06- 1; WI: '04-10- 12: 9/5/3; Won WAF 2009. CAC 2008, CAC-J 2002, IbAm 2002, Cuban 2003-04, 2006.
CAC junior TJ record 2002.
Progress at TJ: 1997- 13.00, 1998- 13.48, 1999- 13.82, 2000- 14.02, 2001- 14.05, 2002- 14.29, 2003- 14.52, 2004- 14.57i/14.20, 2005- 14.21/14.44w, 2006- 14.27, 2007- 14.66, 2008- 14.41A/14.39, 2009-14.64, 2010- 14.30i/14.06, 2011- 14.67. pb LJ 6.28 '09.
World age 17 record in 1999.

Misleydis GONZÁLEZ b. 19 Jun 1978 Bayamo, Granma 1.78m 85kg.
At SP: OG: '04- 7, '08- 4; WCh: '05-07-09-11: 10/11/8/dnq 16; PAm: '99-03-07-11: 1/4/1/1; CAG: '06- 2; WI: '04-08-10: 6/4/7; WUG: '05- 3; CCp: '10- 4 won CAC 2001, 2003, 2009; IbAm 2010, Cuban 2007, 2010-12.

Progress at SP: 1994- 12.41, 1995- 14.48, 1996- 15.80, 1997- 15.87, 1998- 15.76, 1999- 16.19, 2000- 17.55, 2001- 17.54, 2002- 17.79, 2003- 18.11, 2004- 18.73, 2005- 18.92, 2006- 19.10, 2007- 18.97, 2008- 19.50, 2009- 19.13, 2010- 19.22, 2011- 19.04.

Osleidys MENÉNDEZ b. 14 Nov 1979 Martí, Matanzas 1.74m 84kg.
At JT: OG: '00- 3, '04- 1, '08- 6; WCh: '97- 99-01-03-05-09: 7/4/1/5/1/7; WJ: '96- 1, '98- 1; WUG: '01- 1; PAm: '99- 1, '03- 3, '07- 1; CAG: '98- 2, '06- 2; WCp: '02- 1. Won GWG 2001, ÍbAm 2004, PAm-J 1995, 1997; Cuban 1997, 1999-2006; CAC 1997, GP 2002 (3rd 2000), WAF 2004-05.
World javelin records 2001 & 2005. Eight CAC and one world (66.45 '99) new javelin bests 1999-2001.
Progress at JT: 1994- 53.98, 1995- 54.30, 1996- 62.54, 1997- 66.92, 1998- 68.17, 1999- 67.59; new 1999- 66.49, 2000- 67.83, 2001- 71.54, 2002- 67.40, 2003- 63.96, 2004- 71.53, 2005- 71.70, 2006- 65.02, 2007- 62.34, 2008- 64.02, 2009- 63.11, 2010- 61.13. On 1 July 2001 she became the first Cuban woman to set a world record in athletics. World age 19 best in 1999.

Yipsi MORENO b. 19 Nov 1980 Camagüey 1.71m 81kg.
At HT: OG: '00- 4, '04- 2, '08- 2; WCh: '99-01-03-05-07-11: 18/1/1/2/2/4; WJ: '98- 4; PAm: '99-03-07-11: 2/1/1/1; CAG: '06- 1; WUG: '01- 2; WCp: '02-06-10: 2/3/3. Won WAF 2003, 2005, 2007-08, PAm-J 1997, IbAm 2004, Cuban 2000-04, 2007, 2012.
World junior hammer record 1999, 22 CAC records 1999-2008.
Progress at HT: 1996- 53.94, 1997- 61.96, 1998- 61.00, 1999- 66.34, 2000- 69.36, 2001- 70.65, 2002- 71.47, 2003- 75.14, 2004- 75.18, 2005- 74.95, 2006- 74.69, 2007- 76.36, 2008- 76.62, 2010- 75.19, 2011- 75.62.
Married to hammer thrower Abdel Murguía (pb 61.73 '02). Their son (Abdel Murguía Moreno) born in August 2009.

Yargeris SAVIGNE b. 13 Nov 1984 Niceto Pérez, Guantánamo 1.68m 59kg.
At (LJ)/TJ: OG: '08- dnq 17/5; WCh: '05- 4/2, '07- 1, '09- 1, '11- 6; WJ: '02- (dnq); PAm: '03- (3), '07- 3/1, '11- 2; WI: '06- 6/5, '08- 1, '10- 2, '12- 4; CCp: '10- 2/3 Won DL 2010, WAF 2007, CAC TJ 2005, 2009 (LJ 2005,); IbAm 2010, Cuban TJ 2007, 2009, 2011 (LJ 2006-07).
Records: three Cuban TJ 2005-07, two CAC indoor 2008.
Progress at LJ, TJ: 1998- 12.13, 1999- 5.60, 12.65; 2000- 5.92, 12.70; 2001- 6.24, 13.03; 2002- 6.46, 2003- 6.63, 2004- 6.60A/6.52, 2005- 6.77/6.88w, 14.82; 2006- 6.67/6.81w, 14.91; 2007- 6.79i/6.66/6.81w, 15.28; 2008- 6.77i/6.49, 15.20; 2009- 6.77, 15.00; 2010- 6.91, 15.09; 2011- 14.99.

Yarisley SILVA b. 1 Jul 1987 Pinar del Rio 1.69m 68kg.

At TJ: OG: '08- dnq 27=; WCh: '11- 5; WI: '11- 7; WJ: '06- dnq; PAm: '07- 3, '11- 1; Won CAC 2009, Cuban 2004, 2006-07, 2009, 2012.
Pole vault records: 14 Cuban & CAC 2007-11 (9 in 2011), 7 CAC indoor 2012.
Progress at TJ: 2001- 2.50, 2002- 3.10, 2003- 3.70, 2004- 4.00, 2005- 4.10, 2006- 4.20, 2007- 4.30, 2008- 4.50, 2009- 4.50, 2010- 4.40, 2011- 4.75A/4.70, 2012- 4.72i.

CYPRUS

Governing body: Amateur Athletic Association of Cyprus, Olympic House, 2025 Strovolos, Nicosia. Founded 1983. **National Champions 2011**: **Men**: 100m/200m: Panayiotis Ioannou 10.67/21.65, 800m: Stefanos Anastasiou 48.02, 800m: Christos Demetriou 1:50.86, 1500m: Andreas Misiara 4:00.18, 5000m: Charalambos Charalambous 15:34.13, 10000m: Christoforos Protopapas 34:41.0, HMar/Mar: Michael Keenan 76:17/2:46:35, 3000mSt: Georgios Tofi 9:44.56, 110mh: Charis Koutras 14.51, 400mh: Minas Alozides 50.40, HJ: Kyriakos Ioannou 2.31, PV: Nicandros Stylianou 5.30, LJ: Petros Poupas 7.44, TJ: Panayiotis Volou 15.82, SP: Georgios Arestis 18.23, DT: Apostolos Parellis 59.40, HT: Petros Sofianos 64.83, JT: Constantinos Stavrou 63.32. **Women**: 100m: Ramona Papaioannou 11.91, 200m: Nicoletta Nicolettou 25.34, 400m: Kalliopi Kountouri 58.20, 800m/1500m: Meropi Panayiotou 2:11.22/4:33.90, 5000m: Elpida Christodoulidou 17:39.72, HMar/Mar: Panayiota Andreou 1:31:16/3:41:10, 3000mSt: Chrystalla Hadjipolydorou 11:46.58, 100mh: Demetra Arachoviti 13.62, 400mh: Polyxeni Herodotou 63.69, HJ: Leontia Kallenou 1.75, PV: Anna Fitidou 3.55, TJ: Thomaida Polydorou 12.96 (Nina Serbezova BUL 6.14/13.54), SP: Florentia Kappa 14.33, DT: Zacharoula Georgiade 52.42, HT: Paraskevi Theodorou 60.83, JT: Alexandra Tsisiou 52.00.

Kyriakos IOANNOU b. 26 Jul 1984 Limassol 1.93m 66kg. GS Olympia Limassol. Student of PE at University of Athens.
At HJ: OG: '04/08- dnq 18=/18; WCh: '05- 10, '07- 3, '09- 2; CG: '06- 3; WJ: '02- dnq; WY: '01- dnq; EJ: '03- 6=; EU23: '05- 4; WI: '08- 3=, '10- 4; EI: '09- 2=; WUG: '07- 2. Won Med G 2005, 2009; Greek 2005, 2007, CYP 2004-05, 2009-11; EUR Small States 2005, 2009.
Nine Cyprus high jump records 2004-07.
Progress at HJ: 2001- 2.00, 2002- 2.15, 2003- 2.17, 2004- 2.28, 2005- 2.27, 2006- 2.30i/2.23, 2007- 2.35, 2008- 2.32i/2.27, 2009- 2.32, 2010- 2.30, 2011- 2.33.
First athlete from Cyprus to win a medal at Olympics or World Championships.

CZECH REPUBLIC

Governing body: Cesky atleticky svaz, Diskarská 100, 169 00 Praha 6 -Strahov, PO Box

40. AAU of Bohemia founded in 1897.
National Championships first held in 1907 (Bohemia), 1919 (Czechoslovakia), 1993 CZE. **2011 Champions**: **Men**: 100m: Pavel Maslák 10.22w, 200m: Vojtech Sulc 21.19, 400m: Theodor Jares 47.38, 800m: Martin Hosek 1:51.30, 1500m: Vladimír Bartunek 3:54.12, 5000m/10000m/3000mSt: Milan Kocourek 14:06.28/29:31.24/8:59.99, HMar: Jan Kreisinger 65:27, Mar: Petr Pechek 2:18:28, 110mh: Martin Mazac 13.62w, 400mh: Josef Prorok 51.26, HJ: Jaroslav Bába 2.25, PV: Jan Kudlicka 5.40, LJ/TJ: Roman Novotny 7.85/15.51, SP/DT: Jan Marcell 19.41/65.71, HT: Pavel Sedlacek 65.26, JT: Vitezslav Vesely 77.22, Dec: Adam Sebastian Helcelet 7969, 20kW: Karel Ketner 1:30:38, 50kW: Jakub Zajic 4:33:57. **Women**: 100m: Katerina Cechová 11.35w, 200m: Denisa Rosolová 23.42, 400m: Jitka Bartonicková 54.85, 800m: Tereza Capková 2:04.53, 1500m: Marcela Lustigová 4:22.24, 5000m: Kvetoslava Pecková 16:41.20, 10000m: Petra Kaminková 35:06.92, HMar: Ivana Sekyrová 75:24, Mar: Radka Churanová 2:53:11, 3000mSt: Michaela Drábková 10:38.45, 100mh: Lucie Skrobáková 13.10w, 400mh: Zuzana Bergrová 57.25, HJ: Oldriska Maresová 1.82, PV: Jirina Ptácníková 4.20, LJ: Katerina Libalová 6.15, TJ: Lucie Májková 13.16w, SP: Jana Kárníková 15.95, DT: Vera Cechlová 63.40, HT: Katerina Safránková 66.55, JT: Barbora Spotáková 64.65, Hep: Jana Koresová 5663, 20kW: Lucie Pelantová 1:37:19.

Jaroslav BÁBA b. 2 Sep 1984 Karviná 1.96m 82kg. Dukla Praha.
At HJ: OG: '04- 3, '08- 6; WCh: '03-05-07-09: 11/5=/8/5=; EC: '10- 5; WJ: '02- 8; WY: '01- 10=; EU23: '05- 1; EJ: '03- 1; WI: '03-04-08: 9/3=/9; EI: '05- 4, '11- 2; ET: '09- 2, '11- 3=. Won CZE 2003, 2005, 2009-11.
Czech high jump record 2005.
Progress at HJ: 1997- 1.72i, 1998- 1.81i/1.75, 1999- 1.93i/1.92, 2000- 1.95, 2001- 2.16i/2.15, 2002- 2.27/2.28et, 2003- 2.32i/2.30, 2004- 2.34, 2005- 2.37i/2.36, 2006- 2.28i, 2007- 2.29, 2008- 2.30i/2.29, 2009- 2.33, 2010- 2.28, 2011- 2.34i/2.32. pb TJ 15.43 '03.

Petr FRYDRYCH b. 13 Jan 1988 Klatovy 1.98m 99kg. Dukla Praha.
At JT: WCh: '09- 10, '11- dnq 24; EC: '10- 10; WJ: '06- dnq 16; WY: '05- 11; EU23: '09- 2; EJ: '07- 9; ET: '09- 6. Won CZE 2009.
Progress at JT: 2004- 57.89, 2005- 65.97, 2006- 70.91, 2007- 75.55, 2008- 74.13, 2009- 84.96, 2010- 88.23, 2011- 85.32.

Roman SEBRLE b. 26 Nov 1974 Lanskroun 1.86m 88kg. Dukla Praha. Soldier.
At Dec: OG: '00- 2, '04- 1, '08- 6; WCh: '97-99-01-03-05-07-09-11: 9/dnf/10/2/2/1/11/14; EC: '98- 6, '02- 1, '06- 1; WUG: '97- 1; ECp: '97-8-9: 1/2/2. At Hep: WI: '99-01-03-04-06-08-10: 3/1/3/1/3/dnf/5; EI: '00-02-05-07-09-11: 2/1/1/1/3/3. At 110mh: ECp: '99- 6. At LJ: ECp: '05- 7. Won Czech Dec 1996, LJ 1998.
World decathlon record 2001, European indoor heptathlon record 2004.
Progress at Dec: 1991- 5187, 1992- 6541, 1993- 7066, 1994- 7153, 1995- 7642, 1996- 8210, 1997- 8380, 1998- 8589, 1999- 8527, 2000- 8757, 2001- 9026, 2002- 8800, 2003- 8807, 2004- 8893, 2005- 8534, 2006- 8526, 2007- 8697, 2008- 8241, 2009- 8348, 2010- dnf, 2011- 8109. pbs: 60m 6.87i '02, 100m 10.64 '01, 200m 21.74 '04, 400m 47.66 '07, 1000m 2:37.86i '01, 1500m 4:21.98 '01, 60mh 7.84i '02, 110mh 13.79 '99, 13.68w '01; HJ 2.15 '00, PV 5.20 '03, LJ 8.11 '01, SP 16.47 '07, DT 49.46 '09, JT 71.18 '07, Hep 6438i '04.
Married Eva Kasalová (b. 4 Dec 1976, pb 800m 2:02.79 '98), on 14 Oct 2000. At Götzis in 2001 he became the first decathlete to exceed 9000 points with the current scoring tables, setting five personal bests. Won again at Götzis 2002-05 and at Talence in 2004-05, and he won IAAF Combined Events Challenge in 2004-05 and 2007. Has 21 decathlons over 8500 and 47 over 8000 (76 in all).

Vitezslav VESELY b. 27 Feb 1983 Hodonin 1.86m 92kg. Dukla Praha.
At JT: OG: '08- 12; WCh: '09- dnq 28, '11- 4; EC: '10- 9; WJ: '02- 9. Won CZE 2008, 2010-11.
Progress at JT: 2001- 66.18, 2002- 73.22, 2003- 66.95, 2004- 72.32, 2005- injured, 2006- 75.98, 2007- 79.45, 2008- 81.20, 2009- 80.35, 2010- 86.45, 2011- 84.11.

Women

Zuzana HEJNOVÁ b. 19 Dec 1986 Liberec 1.70m 54kg. USK Praha.
At 400mh: OG: '08- 7; WCh: '05-07-09- sf, '11- 7; EC: '06- sf, '10- 4; EU23: '07- 3; WJ: '02- 5, '04- 2; EJ: '03- 3; '05- 1; WY: '03- 1; ET: '09- 3, '11- 1. At Pen: EI: '11- 7. At 4x400m: WI: '10- 3. Won CZE 400m 2006, 2009.
Nine Czech 400mh records 2005-11.
Progress at 400mh: 2002- 58.42, 2003- 57.54, 2004- 57.44, 2005- 55.89, 2006- 55.83, 2007- 55.04, 2008- 54.96, 2009- 54.90, 2010- 54.13, 2011- 53.29. pbs: 200m 23.98 '08, 400m 52.61 '09, 800m 2:07.99i '11, 60mh 8.25i '11, 100mh 13.36 '11, 13.18w '10; 300mh 38.91 '11 (world best), HJ 1.80i '11, 1.74 '04; LJ 5.96i '11, 5.76 '07, SP 12.11i '11, JT 36.11 '10, Pen 4453i '11.
Sister of Michaela Hejnová (b. 10 Apr 1980) pb Hep 6174w/6065 '04; OG: '04- 26; EC '02- 7; EU23: '01- 5; WJ: '98- 5; EJ: '97- 6/'99- 6 (100mh); WUG: '01- 5, '03- 3.

Eliska KLUCINOVÁ b. 14 Apr 1988 Prague 1.77m 68kg. TEPO Kladno.
At Hep: WCh: '09- 23; EC: '10- 7; WJ: '06- 8; EU23: '09- 4, EJ: '07- 2. CZE champion 2008-09.
Progress at Hep: 2004- 5006, 2005- 5074, 2006- 5468, 2007- 5844, 2008- 5728, 2009- 6015, 2010- 6268. pbs: 200m 24.81 '10, 800m 2:12.82 '10,

60mh 8.71i '11, 100mh 14.17 10, HJ 1.82 '10, LJ 6.30 '10, SP 14.49i/14.48 '10, JT 50.75 '10, Pen 4291i '11.

Vera POSPÍSILOVÁ - CECHLOVÁ b. 19 Nov 1978 Litomerice 1.78m 78kg. PSK Olymp Praha.
At (SP/)DT: OG: '04- 4, '08- 5; WCh: '01-03-05: 6/5/3, '07/09/11- dnq 20/18/23; EC: '02- 4, '06- 7, '10- dnq; EU23: '99- 3; EJ: '97- 12/8; ECp: '01- 7/4, '09- 3; Won WAF 2003-04, 2nd GP 2002. Won CZE SP 2001-02, DT 2003-11.
Progress at DT: 1992- 28.24, 1993- 34.28, 1994- 39.48, 1995- 40.24, 1996- 45.72, 1997- 50.00, 1998- 54.67, 1999- 58.17, 2000- 58.28, 2001- 63.20, 2002- 64.10, 2003- 67.71, 2004- 66.42, 2005- 66.81, 2006- 65.44, 2007- 66.18, 2008- 63.10, 2009- 62.91, 2010- 63.40, 2011- 63.74. pb SP 16.92 '01.
Married wrestler Jakub Cechl on 17 Oct 2003.

Jirina PTÁCNÍKOVÁ b. 20 May 1986 Plzen 1.75m 69kg. PSK Olymp Praha.
At PV: WCh: '09- dnq 16=, '11- 7; EC: '06- dnq 27, '10- 5; WJ: '02/04- nh; EJ: '03- 6, '05- 4; WY: '03- 5; WUG: '09- 1; WI: '12- 6; EI: '11- 4=; ET: '09- 5, '10- 3. CZE champion 2009-11.
Progress at PV: 2001- 3.20, 2002- 4.00, 2003- 4.02, 2004- 4.11i/3.90, 2005- 4.15, 2006- 4.27, 2007- 4.22i/4.00, 2008- 4.28, 2009- 4.55, 2010- 4.66, 2011- 4.65, 2012- 4.70i. pb LJ 5.85 '10, 5.95i '11.

Denisa ROSOLOVÁ b. 21 Aug 1986 Karvina 1.75m 63kg. née Scerbová. USK Praha.
At 400m: WCh: '11- sf; EC: '10- 5; WI: '10- 3R, '12- 6; EI: '11- 1; ET: '11- 2. At LJ: OG: '04/08- dnq 25/20; WCh: '07- dnq 13; WJ: '04- 1; WY: '01- 10, '03- 2; EJ: '03- 4, '05- 1; EI: '07- 3. At Hep: OG: '08- dnf; EC: '06- dnf. Won CZE LJ 2004, 2007-08; 200m 2008, 2010-11.
Progress at 400m: 2001- 57.26, 2002- 55.55, 2007- 54.05i, 2008- 53.61i, 2009- 55.63i, 2010- 50.85, 2011- 50.84. pbs: 60m 7.44i '11, 100m 11.61/11.32w '10, 200m 23.03 '10, 300m 36.94i/37.09 '10, 800m 2:11.70 '08, 60mh 8.20i '08, 100mh 13.32 '08, 400mh 60.09 '04, HJ 1.80i/1.77 '06, LJ 6.68 '04, TJ 13.10 '05, SP 12.48 '08, JT 35.12 '07, Pen 4632i '06, Hep 6104 '08.
Divorced from husband tennis player Lukas Rosol.

Barbora SPOTÁKOVÁ b. 30 Jun 1981 Jablonec nad Nisou 1.82m 80kg. Dukla Praha.
At JT: OG: '04- dnq 23, '08- 1; WCh: '05-07-09-11: dnq 13/1/2/2; EC: '02- dnq 17, '06- 2, '10- 3; EU23: '03- 6; WUG: '03- 4, '05- 1; ET: '09- 2, '11- 3; won DL 2010, WAF 2006-08, Czech 2003, 2005-11. At Hep: WJ: '00- 4.
World javelin record 2008, 2 European records 2008, 11 Czech records 2006-08.
Progress at JT: 1996- 31.32, 1997- 37.28, 1998- 44.56, new: 1999- 41.69, 2000- 54.15, 2001- 51.97, 2002- 56.76, 2003- 56.65, 2004- 60.95, 2005- 65.74, 2006- 66.21, 2007- 67.12, 2008- 72.28, 2009- 68.23, 2010- 68.66, 2011- 71.58. pbs: 200m 25.33/25.11w '00, 800m 2:18.29 '00, 60mh 8.68i '07, 100mh 13.99 '00, 400mh 62.68 '98, HJ 1.78 '00, LJ 5.65 '00, SP 14.53 '07, DT 36.80 '02, Dec 6749 '04, Hep 5873 '00.

DENMARK

Governing body: Dansk Athletik Forbund, Idraettens Hus, Brøndby Stadion 20, DK-2605 Brøndby. Founded 1907.
National Championships first held in 1894. **2011 Champions**: **Men**: 100m: Andreas Trajkowski 10.64, 200m/400m: Nicklas Hyde 21.48/46.85, 800m: Andreas Bube 1:49.36, 1500m: Andreas Bueno 3:51.45, 5000m: Jakob Hannibal 14:30.56, 10000m: Michael Nielsen 30:06.24, HMar: Henrik Them 66:06, Mar: Mikkel Kleis 2:19:12, 3000mSt: Jakob Hoffmann 9:59.00, 110mh: Andreas Martinsen 14.21, 400mh: Christian Laugesen 56.30, HJ: Charles Kamau 2.00, PV: Mikkel M. Nielsen 5.25, LJ: Morten Jensen 7.73, TJ: Andreas Møller 16.88, SP: Kim Christensen 19.78, DT: Emil Mikkelsen 51.65, HT: Torben Wolf 61.73, JT: Lars Møller Laursen 67.99, 5000mW: Andreas Nielsen 22:17.64. **Women**: 100m/200m: Anna Olsson 12.13/24.83, 400m: Sara B. Svendsen 59.66, 800m: Rikke Rønholt 2:11.49, 1500m: Louise Brasen 4:43.09, 5000m/10000m: Sara Sig Møller 16:49.97/34:51.14, HMar: Maria Sig Møller 76:13, Mar: Luise Sönder 2:51:08, 3000mSt: Simone Glad 10:51.24, 100mh: Anne Møller 14.38w, 400mh: Sara Slott Petersen 59.72, HJ: Sandra B. Christensen 1.70, PV: Caroline Bonde Holm 4.25, LJ: Tine Bacj Ejlersen 5.95, TJ: Jessica Ipsen 12.87w, SP: Trine Mulbjerg 15.28, DT: Maria Sløk Hansen 47.92, HT/Hep: Meiken Greve 54.45/3556, JT: Maria L. Jensen 43.94, 3000mW/5000mW: ?

DOMINICAN REPUBLIC

Governing body: Federación Dominicana de Asociaciones de Atletismo. Avenida J.F. Kennedy, Centro Olímpico "Juan Pablo Duarte". Santo Domingo. Founded 1953.

Félix SÁNCHEZ b. 30 Aug 1977 New York, USA 1.78m 73kg. Was at University of Southern California.
At 400mh: OG: '00- sf, '04- 1, '08- h; WCh: '99- 01-03-05-07-09-11: ht/1/1/dnf/2/8/4; PAm: '99- 4, '03- 1/3R, '07- 4/3R, '11- 3; CAG: '02- 1R, '10- 4; WCp: '02- 1R. Won NCAA 2000, GWG 2001, GP 2002 (3rd overall), WAF 2003.
Three CAC 400mh records 2001-03. DOM records: 400mh (11) 1997-2003, 400m (3) 2001-02.
Progress at 400m, 400mh: 1995- 51.33, 1996- 51.19, 1997- 46.36, 50.01; 1998- 51.30, 1999- 48.60, 2000- 48.33, 2001- 44.90, 47.38; 2002- 45.14, 47.35; 2003- 45.22A/45.33, 47.25; 2004- 46.28, 47.63; 2005- 46.32, 48.24; 2006- 49.10, 2007- 48.01, 2008- 51.10, 2009- 48.34, 2010- 48.17, 2011- 48.74. pbs: 100m 10.45 '05, 200m 20.87 '01, 800m 1:49.36 '04. 200mSt 22.94 '10.
Born in New York and raised in California, he

first competed for the Dominican Republic, where his parents were born, in 1999 after placing 6th in US 400mh. He took a share of the Golden League jackpot in 2002 and won 43 successive 400mh races (including 7 heats) from loss to Dai Tamesue on 2 Jul 2001 until he pulled up in Brussels on 3 Sep 2004.

EGYPT

Governing body: Egyptian Amateur Athletic Federation, Sport Federation Building, El Estad El Bahary, Nasr City – Cairo. Founded 1910.

Omar Ahmed **EL-GHAZALY** b. 9 Feb 1984 Cairo 2.00m 130kg. Student.
At DT: OG: '04/08- dnq 33/23; WCh: '07- 6, '09- 9; AfG: '03- 1, '07- 1; AfCh: '00-02-06-10: 7/3/1/1; WJ: '00- dnq 17, '02- 10; WY: '01- 3; Af-J '01-2, '03-1; WUG: '05- 2, '07- 2; WCp: '06- 4, '10- 7. Arab champion 2000, 2003-05, 2007, 2009. Five Egyptian discus records 2006-07. World junior 1.75kg discus record (65.88) 2003.
Progress at DT: 2000- 55.35, 2001- 51.42, 2002- 52.53, 2003- 59.77, 2004- 61.46, 2005- 64.36, 2006- 65.33, 2007- 66.58, 2008- 63.08, 2009- 66.34, 2010- 64.18, 2011- 64.76.

ERITREA

Governing body: Eritream National Athletics Federation, PO Box 1117, Asmara. F'd 1992.

Teklemariam MEDHIN Weldeselassie b. 24 Jun 1989 Hazega 1.78m 57kg.
At (5000m/)10000m: OG: '08- 32; WCh: '09- 15/12; WJ: '06- (12). World CC: 2006-07-08-09- 10-11: 13J/14J/23/9/2/14. African C: '12 - 2,
Progress at 5000m, 10000m: 2006- 14:13.9, 2008- 13:48.18, 27:46.50; 2009- 13:11.01, 27:58.89; 2010- 13:04.55, 28:50.63A; 2011- 13:16.53, 27:37.21. pbs: 3000m 7:48.6+ '11, Road 10M 47:11 '09.

Zersenay TADESE b. 8 Feb 1982 Adi Bana 1.60m 56kg. C.A. Adidas. Madrid, Spain.
At (5000m)/10000m: OG: '04- 7/3, '08- 5; WCh: '03- (8), '05- 14/6, '07- 4, '09- 2, '11- 4; AfCh: '02- 6, AfG: '07- 1. World CC: 2002-03-04-05-06-07- 08-09: 30/9/6/2/4/1/3/3; 20k: '06- 1; HMar: '02-03-07-08-09-10: 21/7/1/1/1/2.
Records: World 20km and half marathon 2010. Eritrean 3000m (2), 2M, 5000m (4), 10000m (5) HMar (3) 2003-10.
Progress at 5000m, 10000m, HMar: 2002- 13:48.79, 28:47.29, 63:05; 2003- 13:05.57, 28:42.79, 61:26; 2004- 13:13.74, 27:22.57; 2005- 13:12.23, 27:04.70, 59:05; 2006- 12:59.27, 26:37.25, 59:16; 2007- 27:00.30, 58:59; 2008- 27:05.11, 59:56; 2009- 13:07.02, 26:50.12, 59:35; 2010- 58:23, 2011- 12:59.32, 26:51.09, 58:30. pbs: 3000m 7:39.93 '05, 2M 8:19.34 '07, Road: 15km 41:27 '05, 10M 45:52 '07, 20km 55:21+ '10, Mar 2:12:03 '10.
Won Eritrea's first medal at Olympics in 2004 and World CC in 2005 and first gold in the World 20k in 2006 before three more in succession at half marathon. Ran 59:05 for the fastest ever half marathon to win the Great North Run (slightly downhill overall) in 2005. Won Lisbon half marathon 2010-11 in two fastest ever times. Won a national road cycling title in 2001 before taking up athletics. His younger brother **Kidane** (b. 1987) has pbs 5000m 13:11.85 '10, 10,000m 27:06.16 '08; at 5000m/(10000m): OG: '08- 10/12, WCh: '09- h/9.

ESTONIA

Governing body: Eesti Kergejôustikuliit, Maakri 23, Tallinn 10145. Founded 1920.
National Championships first held in 1917. **2011 Champions: Men**: 100m: Mart Muru 10.91, 200m/400m: Marek Niit 21.05/47.25, 800m/1500m: Keio Kits 1:50.92/3:50.66, 5000m: Tiidrek Nurme 14:19.14, 10000m: Taivi Püi 30:32.00, HMar: Viljar Vallimäe 66:06, Mar: Kaupo Sasmon 2:28:24, 3000mSt: Sergei Tserepannikov 9:17.62, 110mh/PV: Tarmo Riitmuru 14.51/4.90, 400mh: Aarne Nirk 53.1, HJ: Karl Lumi 2.13, LJ: Tönis Sahk 7.51, TJ: Igor Syunin 16.32, SP: Raigo Toompuu 18.26, DT: Gerd Kanter 67.27, HT: Martin Lehemets 59.14, JT: Mihkel Kukk 76.76, Dec: Tarmo Riitmuru 7806, 20000mW: Lauri Lelumees 1:34:08.14, 50kW: Margus Luik 4:45:17. **Women**: 100m/100mh: Grit Sadeiko 11.8h/13.82, 200m: Maris Mägi 24.34, 400m: Ebe Reier 56.10, 800m/1500m: Liina Tsernov 2:11.25/4:25.66, 5000m: Annika Rihma 17:20.66, 10000m/HMar/Mar: Liina Luik 36:52.82/80:27/2:52:04, 3000mSt: Jekaterina Patjuk 10:03.04, 400mh: Hege Mardiste 61.54, HJ: Anna Iljustsenko 1.95, PV: Reena Koll 3.75, LJ/TJ: Veera Baranova 6.27/13.38, SP: Linda Treiel 14.04, DT: Eha Rünne 50.78 (22nd title), HT: Ellina Anissimova 57.36, JT: Raine Kuningas 49.89, Hep: Moonika Kallas 5323, 10000mW/20kW: Maarika Taukul 55:58.51/2:03:11.

Märt ISRAEL b. 23 Sep 1983 Karksi-Nuia 1.89m 118kg. Studied marketing at Washington State University.
At DT: OG: '08- dnq 14; WCh: '07/09 dnq 22, '11- 4; EC: '06- dnq 13, '10- 9; WJ: '02- 7; EU23: '03- 8; WUG: '07-09-11- 3/4/1. EST HT champion 2003-04.
Progress at DT: 2001- 52.24, 2002- 53.91, 2003- 56.57, 2004- 58.32, 2005- 63.17, 2006- 63.20, 2007- 66.56, 2008- 65.03, 2009- 66.05, 2010- 66.31, 2011- 66.98. pbs: SP 17.92 '07, HT 61.19 '05.

Gerd KANTER b. 6 May 1979 Tallinn 1.96m 126kg. Tallinna SS Kalev. Business management graduate.
At DT: OG: '04- dnq 19, '08- 1; WCh: '03-05-07- 09-11: dnq 25/2/1/3/2; EC: '02- 12, '06- 2, '10- 4; EU23: '01- 5; WUG: '05- 1. Won WAF 2007-08, Estonian 2004-09, 2011.
Five Estonian discus records 2004-06.
Progress at DT: 1998- 47.37, 1999- 49.65, 2000- 57.68, 2001- 60.47, 2002- 66.31, 2003- 67.13, 2004- 68.50, 2005- 70.10, 2006- 73.38, 2007- 72.02, 2008-

71.88, 2009- 71.64, 2010- 71.45, 2011- 67.99. pb SP 17.31i '04, 16.11 '00.
Threw over 70m in four rounds at Helsingborg on 4 Sep 2006; a feat matched only by Virgilijus Alekna. Six successive seasons over 70m.

Mikk PAHAPILL b. 18 Jul 1983 Kuresaare 1.97m 91kg. Stamina SK.
At Dec: OG: '08- 11; WCh: '05- 12, '09- dnf, '11- 9; EC: '06- dnf, '10- 4; WJ: '02- 9; ECp: '05-10: 1/2. Won EST Dec 2008, LJ 2009, 110mh 2010.
Progress at Dec: 2004- 7226, 2005- 8149, 2006- 8002, 2008- 8178, 2009- 8255, 2010- 8298, 2011- 8398. pbs: 60m 7.03i '09, 100m 11.01 '09, 10.95w '05; 400m 50.08 '09, 1000m 2:45.69i '09, 1500m 4:34.95 '10, 60mh 8.03i '09, 110mh 14.14 '09, HJ 2.15 '06, PV 5.10i '09, 5.10 '11; LJ 7.97i '09, 7.81 '08; SP 15.73i '10, 15.51 '11; DT 49.51 '09, JT 69.53 '11, Hep 6362i '09.
Set five pbs and added 393 points to heptathlon best in winning at 2009 European Indoors. His father Enri had decathlon pb of 7388 (1982).

Women

Ksenija BALTA b. 1 Nov 1986 Minsk, Belarus 1.68m 53kg. Tallinna SS Kalev.
At LJ: OG: '08- dnq 27; WCh: '09- 8; EC: '06- dnq 26 (h 100m), '10- dnq 16 (h 200m); WI: '10- 4; EI: '09- 1. At Hep: EJ: '05- 3; ECp: '06- 3. Won EST 100m 2006-08, 200m 2008, LJ 2008, 2010; Hep 2005.
EST records: 100m, 200m 2006, LJ (4) 2006-10.
Progress at TJ: 2003- 5.79, 2004- 6.01, 2005- 6.46i/6.32, 2006- 6.80, 2007- 6.55i, 2008- 6.65/6.76w, 2009- 6.87i/6.79/6.85w, 2010- 6.87, 2011- 6.73i. pbs: 50m 6.35i '08, 60m 7.34i '10, 100m 11.47 '06, 11.43w '08; 200m 23.05 '06, 400m 54.79i '05, 800m 2:09.80 '05, 60mh 8.16i '10, 100mh 13.89 '05, 13.70w '06; HJ 1.74 '06, SP 11.94 '05, JT 37.60 '05, Pen 4105i '05, Hep 6180 '06.

Anna ILJUSTSENKO b. 12 Oct 1985 Sillamäe 1.68m 49kg. Orthodontist, graduate of dental medicine from University of Tartu.
At HJ: OG: '08- dnq 21; WCh: '09 dnq 17=, '11- 12; EC: '06- dnq 20, '10- 11; WJ: '04- dnq; EU23: '05-11, '07- dnq 13; WUG: 11- 3; Estonian champion 2005-11.
Eight Estonian high jump records 2008-11.
Progress at HJ: 2002- 1.80i, 2003- 1.77, 2004- 1.82, 2005- 1.85, 2006- 1.89, 2007- 1.85, 2008- 1.91, 2009- 1.93i/1.91, 2010- 1.95, 2011- 1.96.

ETHIOPIA

Governing body: Ethiopian Athletic Federation, Addis Ababa Stadium, PO Box 3241, Addis Ababa. Founded 1961. **2011 National Champions: Men**: 100m/200m: Weter Gelcha 10.8/21.2, 400m: Bereket Desta 45.8, 800m: Esreal Awoke 1:47.3, 1500m: Tesfaye Cheru 3:38.9, 5000m: Abera Kuma 13:40.0, 10000m: Azmeraw Bekele 28:39.6, 3000mSt: Sisay Korme 8:39.0, 110mh: Zelalem Chedesa 14.9, 400mh: Degefu Debamo 51.5, HJ: Gerwich Ose 2.02, PV: Samson Beshah 3.70, LJ: Lnego Obang 7.67, TJ: Getu Gebeka 15.01, SP: Jone Obang 12.81, DT/JT: Metiku Tilahun 43.92/65.72, 20kW: Cheronet Makore 1:32:50. **Women**: 100m: Fitiya Kedir 12.1, 200m/400m: Fantu Megesso 23.6/52.2, 800m: Gelete Burka 2:06.6, 1500m: Bertukan Feysa 4:14.8, 5000m: Sule Utura 16:01.5, 10000m: Belaynesh Oljira 32:55.4, 3000mSt: Netsanet Achamo 9:54.8, 100mh: Tigest Getenet 15.5, 400mh: Wesne Belay 59.4, HJ: Konjit Herpato 1.54, LJ: Zeyba Zeyne 5.60, TJ: Marta Herpato 11.76, SP: Aynalem Negash 11.34, DT: Mersite Gegzabhar 34.77, JT: Hiwot Girma 40.15, 20kW: Bekashigne Aynalem 1:47:03.

Ayele ABSHERO b. 28 Dec 1990 Yeboda 1.67m 52kg.
At 5000m: AfCh: '09- 4. World CC: '08- 2J, '09- 1J. Progress at 10000m, Mar: 2009- 27:54.29, 2011- 27:48.94, 2012- 2:04:23. pbs: 3000m 7:40.08 '10, 5000m 13:11.38 '09; Road: 15km 42:02 '10, 10M 45:33 '10, HMar 59:42 '11.
Second fastest ever debut marathon to win at Dubai in 2012. Elder brother Tessema has marathon pb 2:08:26 '08.

Yenew ALAMIREW b. 14 Jan 1994 Tilili 1.75m 57kg.
At 5000m: AfG: '11- 2.
Progress at 5000m: 2010- 13:16.53, 2011- 13:00.46. pbs: 1500m 3:35.09+ '11, 1M 3:50.43 '11, 3000m 7:27.26 '11, 10km Rd 29:26A '10.

Mohammed AMAN Geleto b. 10 Jan 1994 Asella 1.69m 55kg.
At 800m: WCh: '11- 8; WY: '11- 2; WI: '12- 1. Won Afr-J 800m 2011, Yth OG 100m 2010.
Ethiopian (3) & world youth 800m records 2011
Progress at 800m: 2008- 1:50.29, 2009- 1:46.34, 2010- 1:48.5A, 2011- 1:43.37. pbs: 1000m 2:19.54 '10, 1500m 3:43.52 '11, 1M 3:57.14 '11.
Was disqualified from taking the African Junior 800m gold in 2009 for being under-age (at 15). Youngest ever World Indoor champion at 18 years 60 day in 2012.

Kenenisa BEKELE b. 13 Jun 1982 near Bekoji, Arsi Province 1.62m 54kg.
At 5000m(/10000m): OG: '04- 2/1, '08- 1/1; WCh: '03- 3/1, '05- (1), '07- (1), '09- 1/1; WJ: '00- 2; AfG: '03- 1; AfCh: '06- 1, '08- 1. At 3000m: WY: '99- 2; WI: '06- 1; WCp: '06- 2. World CC: '99- 9J, 4k: '01- 1J/2 4k, '02-03-04-05-06: all 1/1, '08- 1. Won WAF 3000m 2003, 2009; 5000m 2006.
World records: 5000m 2004, 10000m 2004 & 2005, indoor 5000m (12:49.60) 2004, 2000m 2007, 2M 2008; World junior record 3000m 2001.
Progress at 5000m, 10000m: 2000- 13:20.57, 2001- 13:13.33, 2002- 13:26.58, 2003- 12:52.26, 26:49.57; 2004- 12:37.35, 26:20.31; 2005- 12:40.18, 26:17.53; 2006- 12:48.09, 2007- 12:49.53, 26:46.19; 2008- 12:50.18, 26:25.97; 2009- 12:52.32, 26:46.31; 2011- 13:27e+, 26:43.16. pbs: 1000m 2:21.9+ '07, 1500m

3:32.35 '07, 1M 3:56.2+ '07, 2000m 4:49.99i '07, 4:58.40 '09, 3000m 7:25.79 '07, 2M 8:04.35i '08, 8:13.51 '07; Rd 15km 42:42 '01.
At cross-country has a record 20 (12 individual, 8 team) world gold medals from his record winning margin of 33 seconds for the World Juniors in 2001, a day after second in senior 4km. The only man to win both World senior races in the same year, he did this five times. Unbeaten in 27 races from Dec 2001 to March 2007 when he did not finish in the Worlds. After winning all his 12 10,000m track races including five major gold medals, from a brilliant debut win over Haile Gebrselassie at Hengelo in June 2003, he had two years out through injury and then dropped out of World 10,000 in 2011 before running the year's fastest time to win at Brussels. 17 successive wins at 5000m 2006-09. He has run three world indoor records/bests at Birmingham, with outdoor world records at 5000m and 10,000m, in all cases beating Gebrselassie's mark. Shared Golden League jackpot in 2009.
His fiancée Alem Techale (b. 13.12.87, the 2003 World Youth 1500m champion) died of a heart attack on 4 Jan 2005. He married film actress Danawit Gebregziabher on 18 Nov 2007.

Tariku BEKELE b. 21 Jan 1987 near Bekoji 1.65m 52kg.
At 5000m: OG: '08- 6; WCh: '05- 7, '07- 5; WJ: '04- 3, '06- 1; AfG: '07- 3; AfCh: '08- 4, '10- 6. At 3000m: WY: '03- 2; WI: '06-08-10: 6/1/4; CCp: '10- 4; won WAF 3000m 2006. World CC: '05- 6J, '06- 3J.   World junior indoor 2M best 2006.
Progress at 5000m: 2004- 13:11.97, 2005- 12:59.03, 2006- 12:53.81, 2007- 13:01.60, 2008- 12:52.45, 2010- 12:53.97, 2011- 12:59.25. pbs: 1500m 3:37.26 '08, 2000m 5:00.1 '06, 3000m 7:28.70 '10, 2M 8:04.83 '07, Road: 15km 43:35 '11, 10M 46:33 '10.
Younger brother of Kenenisa Bekele.

Abreham CHERKOS Feleke b. 23 Sep 1989 Asella, Oromia reg. 1.60m 52kg.
At 5000m: OG: '08- 5; WCh: '07- 8; WJ: '06- 2, '08- 1; AfG: '07- 4. At 3000m: WY: '05- 1; WI: '08- 3.
World youth 3000m, 2M & 5000m records 2006, world junior indoor 3000m best (7:38.03) 2008.
Progress at 5000m, Mar: 2006- 12:54.19, 2007- 13:05.83, 2008- 12:57.56, 2009- 13:07.83i, 2010- 2:07:29, 2011- 2:06:13wdh. pbs: 1500m 3:42.91 '05, 2000m 5:02.4 '06, 3000m 7:31.81 '09, 2M 8:16.07 '06, 10km 28:14 '11, HMar 61:42 '11.
4th Amsterdam on marathon debut 2010, 5th Boston 2011.

Lelisa DESISA Benti b. 14 Jan 1990 1.70m.
At 10000m: Af-J: '99- 1. World HMar: '10- 7.
Progress at HMar: 2009- 59:39, 2011- 59:30. pbs: 10000m 28:46.74 '09; Road: 10km 27:57 '10, 15km 42:25 '10, 10M 45:36 '11.

Roba GARI Chebute b. 12 Apr 1982 Wera Jarso. Oromiya region 1.81m 60kg.
At 3000mSt: OG: '08-h; WCh: '07- 10, '09- 6, '11- 5;

AfG: '07- 5, '11- 2; AfCh: '10- 3; CCp: '10- 2; ETH champion 2005, 2007, 2010.
Four Ethiopian 3000mSt records 2009-10.
Progress at 3000mSt: 2007- 8:15.05, 2008- 8:22.07, 2009- 8:11.32, 2010- 8:09.87, 2011- 8:10.03. pbs: 3000m 7:42.12i '08, 7:43.38 '10; 5000m 13:33.17 '08, 2000mSt 5:19.96 '07.

Gebre-egziabher GEBREMARIAM b. 10 Sep 1984 Shere, Tigray region 1.78m 56kg.
At 10000m (5000m): OG: '04- (4); WCh: '03- (6), '05- 15, '07- 6, '09- 10; WJ: '02- 1 (3); AfG: '03- 2, '07- 3; AfCh: '08- 1. At Mar: WCh: '11- dnf. World CC:'02-03-04-05-06-08-09-10:1J/3/2&2/9(4k)/13/17/1/10. Won ETH CC 2003 & 2009, 5000m 2005, 10000m 2005., 2009; E.Afr 2004.
Progress at 5000m, 10000m, Mar: 2001- 14:13.74A, 31:04.61A; 2002- 13:12.14, 27:25.61; 2003- 12:58.08, 28:03.03; 2004- 12:55.59, 26:53.73; 2005- 12:52.80, 27:11.57; 2006- 13:30.95, 27:03.95; 2007- 13:10.29, 26:52.33; 2008- 13:36.67, 27:20.65; 2009- 13:13.20, 27:44.04; 2010- 2:08:14, 2011- 2:04:53wdh/2:08:00. pbs: 3000m 7:39.48 '05, 2M 9:34.82i '06, HMar 60:25 '10, 3000mSt 8:57.7A '02.
Won New York 2010 on marathon debut, 3rd Boston 2011. Married Worknesh Kidane on 4 Feb 2006. She has 21 World CC medals, he has 16.

Mekonnen GEBREMEDHIN Woldegiorgis b. 11 Oct 1988 Addis Ababa 1.80m 64kg.
At 1500m: WCh: '07-09-11: sf/h/7; WI: '08-10-12: 6/4/3; AfCh: '10- 3; CCp: '10- 2. At 800m: WJ: '06- sf.
Progress at 1500m: 2004- 3:47.1A, 2006- 3:41.00, 2007- 3:36.04, 2008- 3:35.68, 2009- 3:34.49, 2010- 3:31.57, 2011- 3:31.90. pbs: 800m 1:47.8A '06, 1M 3:49.70 '11, 3000m 7:41.42 '11.

Dejen GEBREMESKEL b. 24 Nov 1989 Gulo Makeda district 1.78m 53kg.
At 5000m: WCh: '11- 3; WJ: '08- 3; Af-J: '07- 2. At 3000m: WI: '10- 10, '12- 5.
Progress at 5000m: 2007- 13:21.05, 2008- 13:08.96, 2009- 13:03.13, 2010- 12:53.56, 2011- 12:55.89. pbs: 3000m 7:34.14i '12, 7:45.9+ '10; 10km Rd 27:45 '11.

Haile GEBRSELASSIE b. 18 Apr 1973 Arsi 1.64m 53kg.
At 10000m (5000m): OG: '96- 1, '00- 1, '04- 5, '08- 6; WCh: '93- 1 (2), '95- 1, '97- 1, '99- 1, '01- 3, '03- 2; WJ: '92- 1 (1); AfG: '93- 3 (2). At 3000m: WI: '97- 1, '99- 1 (1 1500m), '03- 1. Won GP 3000m 1995, 1998. World CC: '91-2-3-4-5-6: 8J/2J/7/3/4/5; HMar: '01- 1; Rd Rly team: '94- 2.
World records 5000m (4) 1994-8, 10000m (3) 1995-8, 20000m & 1Hr 2007; 10km road (27:02) 2002, 15km & 10M road 2005, 20km, HMar & 25km 2006, Marathon 2007 & 2008, 30km road 2009; Indoors 2000m 1998, 3000m (7:30.72 '96, 7:26.15 '98), 5000m (13:10.98 '96, 12:59.04 '97, 12:50.38 '99); World best 2M 1995 (8:07.46) & 1997, indoors 8:04.69 (2003). ETH records 1993-9: 1500m (3), 1M (1), 3000m (6), 5000m (6), 10000m (3), marathon (5) 2002-08. World M35

bests 10000m & Mar 2008.

Progress at 5000m, 10000m, Mar: 1992- 13:36.06, 28:03.99; 1993- 13:03.17, 27:30.17; 1994- 12:56.96, 27:15.00; 1995- 12:44.39, 26:43.53; 1996- 12:52.70, 27:07.34; 1997- 12:41.86, 26:31.32; 1998- 12:39.36, 26:22.75; 1999- 12:49.64, 27:57.27; 2000- 12:57.95, 27:18.20; 2001- 27:54.41, 2002- 28:16.50, 2:06:35; 2003- 12:54.36, 26:29.22; 2004- 12:55.51, 26:41.58; 2005- 2:06:20, 2006- 2:05:56, 2007- 26:52.81, 2:04:26; 2008- 26:51.20, 2:03:59; 2009- 28:22.3+, 2:05:29, 2010- 2:06:09, 2011- dnf, 2012- 2:08:17. pbs: 800m 1:49.35i '97, 1000m 2:20.3+i '98, 1500m 3:31.76i '98, 3:33.73 '99; 1M 3:52.39 '99, 2000m 4:52.86i '98, 4:56.1 '97; 3000m 7:25.09 '98, 2M 8:01.08 '97, 10M 45:23.80 '07, 20000m 56:25.98 '07, 1Hr 21285m '07; Road: 15km 41:22 '05, 10M 44:24 '05, 20km 55:48 '06, HMar 58:55 '06, 25km 1:11:37 '06, 30km 1:27:49 '09.

He set the first of his 27 world records (20 officially ratified) in Hengelo in 1994 at 5000m. From 1992 to 2004 he had 13 wins in 19 races at 10,000m, 26/28 at 3000m/2M, and 28/36 at 5000 including 16 successive 1996 to 2000. He has 12/14 wins at half marathon 2001-11, including the 2010 Great North Run. He set a world 10km road record of 27:02 at Doha, Qatar in December 2002 for a reward of $1 million.

He had run c.2:48 for the marathon at the age of 15, but made his senior debut at the distance at London 2002, when he was third in 2:06:35 and won at Amsterdam in 2:06:20 in 2005. In 2006 he was 9th in London, then won the Berlin and Fukuoka marathons, but dnf London 2007. He smashed the world record with 2:04:26 to win the Berlin Marathon in 2007 and in 2008 he won in Dubai in 2:04:53 before another WR at Berlin – 2:03:59. He won again in Dubai and Berlin in 2009 and in Dubai 2010.

His brother Tekeye had marathon pb 2:11:45 '94 and was 13th in 1991 World Cup.

Markos GENETI b. 30 May 1984 Walega 1.75m 55kg.

At 5000m: WJ: '02- 2; AfG: '03- 4. At 3000m: WY: '01- 1; WI: '04- 3. At 1500m: WCh: '05- sf. World CC: '07- 15.

Progress at 5000m: 2001- 13:50.14, 2002- 13:28.83, 2003- 13:11.87, 2004- 13:17.57, 2005- 13:00.25, 2006- 13:13.98, 2007- 13:07.65, 2008- 13:08.22, 2009- 13:31.71i, 2010- 13:18.64i/13:21.99. At Mar: 2011- 2:06:35, 2012- 2:04:54. pbs: 1500m 3:33.83 '05, 1M 4:08.8 '10, 3000m 7:32.69i '07, 7:38.11 '05; 2M 8:08.39i '04, 8:19.61 '06, Road: 10km 29:38 '11, HMar 62:01 '11

Won in Los Angeles 2011 in sixth fastest ever debut marathon time. Third Dubai 2012.

Ibrahim JEYLAN Gashu b. 12 Jun 1989 1.68m 57kg. Muger Cement.

At 10000m: WCh: '11- 1; WJ: '06- 1, '08- 3; AfG: '11- 1; AfCh: '08- 2. At 3000m: WY: '05- 2. World CC: '06- 5J, '08- 1J.

Two world youth 10,000m records 2006.

Progress at 5000m, 10000m: 2006- 13:09.38, 27:02.81; 2007- 13:17.99, 27:50.53; 2008- 13:15.12, 27:13.85; 2009- 13:19.70, 27:22.19; 2010- 13:21.29, 27:12.43; 2011- 13:09.95, 27:09.02. pbs: 3000m 8:04.21 '05, 15km 43:38 '08.

Tsegaye KEBEDE Wordofa b. 15 Jan 1987 Gerar Ber 1.58m 50kg.

At Mar: OG: '08- 3; WCh: '09- 3.

Progress at Mar: 2007- 2:08:16, 2008- 2:06:10, 2009- 2:05:18, 2010- 2:05:19, 2011- 2:07:48. pbs: Road: 10km 28:10 '08, HMar 59:35 '08.

Marathon wins: Addis Ababa 2007, Paris 2008, Fukuoka 2008-09, London 2010; 2nd London 2009 and Chicago 2010; 3rd New York 2011. Won Great Ethiopian Run 2007, Great North Run 2008.

Abera KUMA Lema b. 31 Aug 1990 Ambo.

At 5000m: WCh: '11- 5; Af-J: '09- 1. At 3000m: WY: '07- 5.

Progress at 5000m, 10000m: 2009- 13:29.40, 2010- 13:07.83, 2011- 13:00.15, 27:22.54. pbs: 1500m 3:48.73 '09, 3000m 7:39.09i '12, 7:47.9+ '11; Rd 15km 42:01 '10, 1M 45:31 '10.

Feyisa LILESA b. 15 Jan 1987 Addis Ababa 1.58m 50kg.

At Mar: WCh: '11- 3, World CC: 2008-09-10-11: 14J/12/25/17.

Progress at Mar: 2009- 2:09:12, 2010- 2:05:23, 2011- 2:10:32. pbs: 5000m 13:34.80 '08, 10000m 27:46.97 '08; Road: 15km 42:31 '10, 20km 56:19+ '12, HMar 59:22 '12, 30km 1:28:58 '10.

Marathons won: Dublin 2009, Xiamen 2010. 3rd Chicago 2010, 4th Rotterdam 2010 in fastest ever by 20 year-old.

Deresse MEKONNEN Tsigu b. 20 Oct 1987 Sheno, Oromia reg. 1.75m 60kg.

At 1500m: OG: '08- sf; WCh: '07- h, '09- 2, '11- sf; WI: '08- 1, '10- 1; AfG: '07- 5, AfCh: '08- 4.

Ethiopian 1M records 2008 & 2009.

Progress at 1500m: 2007- 3:36.41, 2008- 3:33.71, 2009- 3:32.18, 2010- 3:33.10i/3:33.85, 2011- 3:32.90. pbs: 1000m 2:19.12i '11, 1M 3:48.95 '09, 3000m 7:32.93 '09, 5000m 13:07.75 '09.

Deribe MERGA Ejigu b. 26 Oct 1982 Nekemte 1.68m 52kg.

At Mar: OG: '08- 4; WCh: '09- dnf. World 20km Rd: '06- 6, HMar: '07- 4.

World 15km road record (=) 2009.

Progress at 10000m, Mar: 2007- 27:02.62, 2:06:50; 2008- 2:06:38, 2009- 2:07:52, 2010- 2:08:39, 2011- 2:09:13. pbs: Road: 10km 27:31 '11, 15km 41:29 '09, 10M 44:53 '11. 20km 56:13 '07, HMar 59:15 '08, 30km 1:28:30 '08.

Marathon career: 2006- dnf Boston, 2007- 10th Paris 2:13:33, 2nd Fukuoka, 2008- 6th London, 4th OG; 2009- 1st Houston & Boston, 2010- 3rd Boston, 2011- 2nd Lake Biwa..

Imane MERGA Jida b. 15 Oct 1988 Tulu Bolo, Oromia region 1.74m 61kg. Defence.

At 5000m/(10000m): WCh: '09- (4), '11- dq/3; AfCh: '10- 5; Af-J: '07- (3); CCp: '10- 5; won DL 2010, WAF 2009. World CC: '07- 7J, '11- 1.
Progress at 5000m, 10000m: 2007- 13:33.52, 30:12.03; 2008- 13:08.20, 27:33.53, 2009- 12:55.66, 27:15.94; 2010- 12:53.58; 2011- 12:54.21, 26:48.35. pbs: 3000m 7:45.8+ '10.

Dino SEFER Hemad b. 28 May 1988 1.71m 60kg.
At 10000m: AfG: '11- 4. World CC: '09- 15, '11- 12.
Progress at Mar: 2010- 2:20:36, 2011- 2:10:33, 2012- 2:04:50. pbs: 3000m 7:44.37 '09, 5000m 13:11.69 '08, 10000m 28:23.40 '11; Road: 15km 43:57 '11, HMar 59:42 '11.   2nd Dubai Marathon 2012.

Sileshi SIHINE b. 29 Jan 1983 Sheno 1.71m 55kg.
At (5000m)/10000m: OG: '04- 2, '08- 2; WCh: '03- 3, '05- 2/2, '07- 2, '11- 8; WJ: '02- 2; AfG: '03- 1. World CC: '02-03-04-06-07-08: 6J/7/3/2 & 12 4k/16/15. World HMar: '05- 4. Won WAF 5000m 2004-05, Ethiopian 5000m 2003, 10000m 2003-04, Af-AsG 10,000m 2003.
Progress at 5000m, 10000m: 2002- 13:21.81, 27:26.12; 2003- 13:06.53, 26:58.76; 2004- 12:47.04, 26:39.69; 2005- 13:13.04, 26:57.27; 2006- 13:06.72i, 2007- 12:50.16, 26:48.73; 2008- 12:58.41, 26:50.53; 2009- 13:06.63, 2011- 12:57.86, 26:52.84. pbs: 2000m 5:01.2i+ '04, 5:02.2 '05; 3000m 7:29.92 '05, 2M 8:27.03i '06; Road: 15km 41:38 '04, HMar 61:14 '05.   Six major silver medals. Married Tirunesh Dibaba on 26 Oct 2008.

Women

Birtukan ADAMU b. 29 Apr 1992.
At 3000mSt: WCh: '11- 15; AfG: '11- 3.
World junior 3000m steeplechase record 2011.
Progress at 3000mSt: 2010- 9:31.39, 2011- 9:20.37. pbs: 1500m 4:24.91 '11, 3000m 8:58.73i '12.

Abeba ARIGAWI b. 5 Jul 1990. 1.65m.
At 800m: Af-J: '09- 3.
Progress at 1500m: 2010- 4:01.96, 2011- 4:01.47i/4:10.30. pbs: 800m 2:01.98 '09.

Sofia ASSEFA Abebe b. 14 Nov 1987 Tenta District, south Wello 1.71m 58kg. Ethiopian Bank.
At 3000mSt: OG: '08- h; WCh: '09- 13, '11- 6; AfCh: '08- 4, '10- 2; CCp: '10- 3.
Ethiopian 3000mSt record 2011.
Progress at 3000mSt: 2006- 10:17.48, 2007- 9:48.46, 2008- 9:31.58, 2009- 9:19.91, 2010- 9:20.72, 2011- 9:15.04. pbs: 1000m 2:49.79 '07, 5000m 15:59.74 '07, 2000mSt 6:33.49 '07.

Wude AYALEW Yimer b. 4 Jul 1987 Sekela, Amhara region 1.50m 44kg.
At 10000m: WCh: '09- 3; AfG: '11- 2; AfCh: '08- 3, '10- 4. At 5000m: WJ: '06- 5. World CC: '06-07-09-11: 5/10/5/6. Won ETH CC 2009.
Progress at 5000m, 10000m: 2006- 14:57.23, 33:57.0; 2008- 15:07.65, 31:06.84; 2009- 14:38.44, 30:11.87; 2010- 15:02.47, 32:29.92A; 2011-

14:59.71, 31:24.09. pbs: 1500m 4:14.85 '07, 3000m 8:30.93 '09; Road: 10km 31:41+ '08, 15km 48:52 '11, HMar 67:58 '09. Won Great Ethiopian Run 2008.

Atsede BAYSA Tesema **(or BAYISA)** b. 16 Apr 1987.
At Mar: WCh: '09- 27, '11- 14. At HMar: WCh: '07- 11; AfG: '07- 2.
Progress at Mar: 2006- 2:37:48, 2007- 2:29:08, 2008- 2:33:07, 2009- 2:24:42, 2010- 2:22:04, 2011- 2:23:50, 2012- 2:23:13. pbs: Road: 10km 33:14 '09, HMar 68:42 '10.
Marathon wins: Istanbul 2007, Paris 2009-10, Xiamen 2010, 2nd Chicago 2010.

Bezunesh BEKELE Sertsu b. 29 Jan 1983 Addis Ababa 1.45m 38kg..
At Mar: WCh: '09- 16, '11- 4. At HMar: WCh: '07- 4. At 10000m: AfCh: '06- 5. World CC: '02- 6J; '05- 10 (12 4k)
Progress at Mar: 2008- 2:23:09, 2009- 2:24:02, 2010- 2:23:17, 2011- 2:23:42, 2012- 2:20:30. pbs: 3000m 8:52.08 '06, 5000m 15:02.48 '06, 10000m 31:10.68 '05; Road: 15km 47:36 '07, HMar 68:07 '07.
Won Dubai Marathon 2009 (2nd 2008, 4th 2010 & 2012), 2nd Berlin 2010. Married to Tessema Abshiro (Mar 2:08:26 '08).

Gelete BURKA Bati b. 15 Feb 1986 Kofele 1.65m 45kg.
At 1500m: OG: '08- h; WCh: '05- 8, '09- 10 (fell), '11- sf; WI: '08- 1, '10- 3; AfG: '07- 1; AfCh: '08- 1, '10- 2; CCp: '10- 7. At 3000m: WI: '12- 3. At 5000m: WCh: '07- 10. World CC: '03-05-06-07-08-09: 3J/1J/1 4k/4/6/8. Won ETH 800m 2011, 1500m 2004-05, 2007; 5000m 2005, 4k CC 2006. African records: 1M 2008, 200m 2009, indoor 1500m 2008, junior 1500m 2005.
Progress at 1500m, 5000m: 2003- 4:10.82, 16:23.8A, 2004- 4:06.10, 2005- 3:59.60, 14:51.47; 2006- 4:02.68, 14:40.92; 2007- 4:00.48, 14:31.20; 2008- 3:59.75i/4:00.44, 14:45.84; 2009- 3:58.79, 2010- 3:59.28, 2011- 4:03.28. pbs: 800m 2:02.89 '10, 1M 4:18.23 '08, 2000m 5:30.19 '09, 3000m 8:25.92 '06.
Married Taddele Gebrmehden in 2007.

Firehiwot DADO Tufa b. 9 Jan 1984 Arsi 1.65m.
Progress at Mar: 2008- 2:37:34, 2009- 2:27:08, 2010- 2:25:28, 2011- 2:23:15. pbs: Road: 10km 32:00+ '12, 15km 48:32+ '12, 20km 65:06+ '12, HMar 68:35 '12, 30km 1:40:45 '11.
Marathon wins: New York 2011, Rome 2009-11.

Mamitu DASKA Molisa b. 16 Oct 1983 Liteshoa 1.65m.
At HMar: AfrG: '11- 2. World CC: '09- 12, '10- 8.
Progress at Mar: 2009- 2:26:38, 2010- 2:24:19, 2011- 2:21:59, 2012- 2:24:24. pbs: 10000m 31:36.88 '09. Road: 20km 68:09 '10, HMar 68:07 '11, 30km 1:39:46 '11.
Marathon wins: Dubai 2010, Houston and Frankfurt 2011.

Bizunesh DEBA b. 8 Sep 1987.
Progress at Mar: 2009- 2:32:17, 2010- 2:27:24, 2011- 2:23:19. pbs: 5000m 15:52.33 '04, Road: 10km 32:10 '10, HMar 69:53 '11.
Lives in Bronx, New York. Marathon wins: Sacramento 2009, San Diego 2010, Los Angeles & San Diego 2011. 2nd New York 2011.

Meseret DEFAR b. 19 Nov 1983 Addis Ababa 1.55m 42kg.
At 5000m(/10000m): OG: '04- 1, '08- 3; WCh: '03- h, '05- 2, '07- 1, '09- 3/5, '11- 3/dnf; WJ: '00- 2, '02- 1; AfG: '03- 1, '07- 1; AfCh: '00-06-08-10: 2/1/2/2; WCp: '06- 1. At 3000m: WJ: '02- 1; WY: '99- 2; WI: '03-04-06-08-10-12: 3/1/1/1/1/2; CCp: '10- 1. Won WAF 3000m 2004-09, 5000m 2005, 2008-09. World CC: '02- 13J.
Records: World 5000m 2006 & 2007, 2M 2007 (2); indoor 3000m 2007, 2M 2008 (9:10.50) & 2009 (9:06.26), 5000m 2009; African 5000m 2005, Ethiopian 3000m (2) 2006-07. World 5k road best 14:46 Carlsbad 2006.
Progress at 3000m, 5000m, 10000m: 1999- 9:02.08, 33:54.9A; 2000- 8:59.90, 15:08.36; 2001- 8:52.47, 15:08.65; 2002- 8:40.28, 15:26.45; 2003- 8:38.31, 14:40.34; 2004- 8:33.44i/8:36.46, 14:44.81; 2005- 8:30.05i/8:33.57, 14:28.98; 2006- 8:24.66, 14:24.53; 2007- 8:23.72i/8:24.51, 14:16.63; 2008- 8:27.93i/8:34.53, 14:12.88; 2009- 8:26.99i/8:30.15, 14:24.37i/14:36.38, 29:59.20; 2010- 8:24.46i/8:36.09, 14:24.79i/14:38.87; 2011- 8:36.91i/8:50.36+, 14:29.52, 31:05.05. pbs: 1500m 4:02.00 '10, 1M: 4:28.5ei '06, 4:33.07+ '07; 2000m 5:34.74i/5:38.0 '06, 2M 8:58.58 '07, HMar 67:45 '10.
Married to Teodros Hailu. IAAF woman athlete of the year 2007. Record nine WAF wins.

Ejegayehu DIBABA b. 25 Jun 1982 Chefa, Arsi region 1.60m 46kg.
At (5000m/)10000m: OG: '04- 2, '08- 14; WCh: '03- 9, '05- 3/3, '07- 7; AfG: '03- 1; AfCh: '02- (3), '06- dnf, '08- 2; won Af-AsG 2003. At 5000m: AfCh: '02- 3. World CC 4k: '03-04-05: 9/10/14; 8k: '04-06: 2/14.
Progress at 5000m, 10000m, Mar: 2001- 15:32.31, 32:24.20; 2002- 15:56.02, 2003- 14:41.67, 31:01.07; 2004- 14:32.74, 30:24.98; 2005- 14:37.34, 30:18.39; 2006- 14:33.52, 2007- 14:45.22, 31:18.97; 2008- 14:36.78, 31:04.05; 2009- 14:42.06; 2011- 2:22:09. pbs: 2000m 5:39.1+i '08, 3000m 8:35.94 '06, HMar 69:25 '11.
Second Chicago on marathon debut in 2011. Older sister of Tirunesh and Genzebe Dibaba.

Genzebe DIBABA b. 8 Feb 1991 Bekoji. Muger Cement.
At 1500m: WI: '12- 1. At 5000m: WCh: '09 -8, '11- 8; WJ: '08- 2, '10- 1; Af-J: '09- 1. World CC: '07-08-09-10-11: 5J/1J/1J/11J/9. Won ETH 1500m 2010.
Progress at 1500m, 5000m: 2007- 15:53.46, 2008- 15:02.41, 2009- 14:55.52, 2010- 4:04.80i/4:06.10, 15:08.06; 2011- 4:05.90, 14:37.56; 2012- 4:00.13i. pbs: 3000m 8:47.01i/8:48.35 '10.

Mare DIBABA Hurssa b. 20 Oct 1989 Sululta 1.60m 42kg.
At Mar: WCh: '09- 16, '11- 4. At HMar: WCh: '07- 4. World CC: '02- 6J; '05- 10 (12 4k). Won AZE 3000m and 5000m 2009.
AZE records (as Mare Ibrahimova) at 3000n and 5000m 2009.
Progress at HMar, Mar: 2008- 70:28, 2009- 68:45, 2010- 67:13, 2:25:27, 2011- 68:39, 2:23:25; 2012- 2:19:52. pbs: 3000m 9:16.94 '09, 5000m 15:42.83 '09, Road: 10km 31:55+ '10, 15km 48:04+ '10, 10M 51:29+ '10, 20km 63:47+ '10.
She switched to Azerbaijan in December 2008 but back to Ethiopia as of 1 Feb 2010. Third Dubal Marathon 2012.

Tirunesh DIBABA b. 1 Oct 1985 Bekoji, Arsi region 1.60m 47kg.
At 5000m(/10000m): OG: '04- 3, '08- 1/1; WCh: '03- 1, '05- 1/1, '07- (1); WJ: '02- 2; AfG: '03- 4; AfCh: '06- 2, '08- (1), '10- (1). At 3000m: WCp: '06- 1. World CC: '01-02-03-05-06-07-08-10: 5J/2J/1J/1/1/2/1/4; 4k: '04-05: 2/1. Won WAF 5000m 2006, ETH 4k CC & 5000m 2003. 8k CC 2005.
World records: 5000m 2008, indoor 5000m 2005 (14:32.93) & 2007, junior 5000m 2003-04, indoor 3000m & 5000m 2004, world road 5k best 14:51 '05, 15k 2009. African 10000m record 2008.
Progress at 5000m: 2002- 14:49.90, 2003- 14:39.94, 2004- 14:30.88, 2005- 14:32.42, 30:15.67; 2006- 14:30.40, 2007- 14:27.42i/14:35.67, 31:55.41; 2008- 14:11.15, 29:54.66; 2009- 14:33.65, 2010- 14:34.07, 31:51.39A. pbs: 2000m 5:42.7 '05, 3000m 8:29.55 '06, 2M 9:12.23i '10, road 15k 46:28 '09.
In 2003 she became, at 17 years 333 days, the youngest ever world champion at an individual event and in 2005 the first woman to win the 5000m/10000m double (with last laps of 58.19 and 58.4) at a global event after earlier in the year winning both World CC titles. Now has women's record 21 World CC medals. Married Sileshi Sihine on 26 Oct 2008. Due to injuries, did not compete in 2011 until the final day of the year when she won a 10k road race in Madrid in 31:30.

Sentayehu EJIGU b. 21 Jun 1985 Gojjam, Amhara region 1.60m 45kg.
At 1500m: WY: '01- 3. At 3000m: WI: '06- 4, '10- 3. At 5000m: OG: '04- 10; WCh: '09- 4, '11- 4; AfG: '03- 5; AfCh: '10- 3; CCp: '10- 2. World CC: '03- 6J, '09- 14.
Progress at 5000m: 2002- 14:53.99, 2003- 15:00.53, 2004- 14:35.18, 2005- 14:51.11, 2007- 15:27.84, 2008- 15:06.37, 2009- 14:40.00, 2010- 14:28.39, 2011- 14:31.66. pbs: 1500m 4:15.89 '01, 1M 4:40.43i '03, 2000m 5:41.6+i '10, 3000m 8:25.27i/8:28.41 '10, 2M 9:12.68i '10, 10km Rd 31:50 '11.

Teyiba ERKESSO b. 30 Oct 1982 Arsi 1.60m 40kg.
At 10000m: AfG: '07- 5. World 20k: '06- 10; CC: '02-04-06: 10/3 4k & 5/12 4k.

Progress at 10000m, Mar: 2002- 33:50.6A, 2004- 31:41.26, 2006- 32:01.34, 2007- 31:13.67, 2009- 2:24:18, 2010- 2:23:53. pbs: 3000m 8:56.67 '06, 5000m 15:02.28 '04, road: 15km 47:54 '09, 20km 65:40+ '09, HMar 67:41 '10, 30k 1:41:42+ '09.
Won Houston Marathon 2009 & 2010, Boston 2010; 4th Chicago 2009.

Kalkidan GEZAHEGNE b. 8 May 1991 Addis Ababa.
At 1500m: WCh: '09- 9, '11- 5; WJ: '08- 2; WI: '10- 1; Af-J: '09- 2. At 800m: AfCh: '08- h.
World junior indoor bests 1500m & 1M 2010.
Progress at 1500m: 2008- 4:10.14, 2009- 4:02.98, 2010- 4:03.28i, 2011- 4:00.97. pbs: 800m 2:06.2 '08, 1M 4:24.10i '10, 4:37.76 '08; 3000m 8:47.37i '11, 8:38.61 '09.

Atsede HABTAMU Besuye b. 26 Oct 1987 Addis Ababa 1.62m 50kg.
World HMar: '07- 5, '08- 8.
Progress at HMar, Mar: 2007- 68:29, 2008- 69:37, 2009- 72:29, 2:24:47; 2010- 68:30, 2:25:35; 2011- 71:12+, 2:24:25l 2012- 2:25:28. pbs: Road: 10km 31:55+ '09, 15km 48:21+ '10, 20km 65:04+ '10, 30km 1:42:50 '09.
Won Berlin Marathon 2009, Eindhoven 2010, Daegu 2011, Tokyo 2012.

Koren JELELA Yal b. 18 Jan 1987 Shewa.
World HMar: '07- 5, '08- 8. World CC: '07- 08-09: 19/14/30/
Progress at Mar: 2009- 2:28:41, 2010- 2:24:33, 2011- 2:22:43. pbs: 3000m 9:11.64 '07, 5000m 15:51.81 '07, Road: 10km 32:17 '09, 15km 48:36A '11, HMar 68:39+ '11, 30km 1:38:33 '11.
Won Mumbai and Toronto Marathons 2011.

Aberu KEBEDE Shewaye b. 12 Sep 1989 Shoa 1.63m 50kg.
World HMar: '09- 3. World CC: '07- 16J. Won ETH 10000m 2009.
Progress at 10000m, Mar: 2009- 30:48.26, 2010- 32:17.74, 2:23:58; 2011- 2:24:34, 2012- 2:20:33. pbs: 5km Rd 15:13 '09, HMar 67:39 '09.
Won Rotterdam and Berlin marathons 2010 after 2nd Dubai on debut.

Werknesh KIDANE b. 21 Nov 1981 Mayshie district, Tigray region 1.58m 42kg.
At 10000m: OG: '04- 4; WCh: '03- 2, '05- 6; AfG: '03- 2; At 5000m: OG: '00- 7; WCh: '01- h; WJ: '98- 6; AfG: '99- 4. At 3000m: WI: '01- 9. World CC: '97-8-9-00-01-03-04-05-10: 13J/3J/1J/9J/1/ 3/3/9; 4k: '01-02-03-04-05: 5/2/2/4/2. Won ETH 10000m 2003, 2005; 4k CC 2001-02, E.Afr 4k & 8k CC 2004.
Progress at 5000m, 10000m: 1998- 15:50.10, 1999- 15:24.56, 2000- 14:47.40, 33:48.7A; 2001- 15:29.96, 31:43.41; 2002- 14:43.53, 2003- 14:33.04, 30:07.15; 2004- 14:38.05, 30:28.30; 2005- 15:01.6, 30:19.39; 2009- 31:19.00, 2011- 31:08.92. pbs: 1500m 4:17.0A '03, 3000m 8:36.39 '05, Road: 15km 47:37 '11, 10M 51:03 '11, HMar 67:28 '11, Mar 2:26:15dh/2:27:15 '11.

Has won women's record 21 team and individual medals at World CC. Married Gebre Gebremariam on 4 Feb 2006, sons Natnael born 2 May 2006, Mussie born 2 Aug 2007.

Meselech MELKAMU b. 27 Apr 1985 Debremarkos, Amhara region 1.58m 47kg.
At 5000m(/10000m): OG: '08- 8; WCh: '05- 4, '07- 6, '09- 5/2, '11- 5; AfG: '07- 2, '11- (dnf); AfCh: '06- 6, '08- 1, '10- (2); WJ: '04- 1. At 3000m: WI: '08- 2. World CC: '03-04-05-06-07-08-09-10-11: 4J/1J/4 & 6/3 & 3/3/9/3/3/4 (17 medals). Won ETH 5000m 2004, 4k CC 2005, CC 2006-07. African 10000m record 2009.
Progress at 5000m, 10000m: 2003- 15:27.93, 2004- 15:00.02, 2005- 14:38.97, 2006- 14:37.44, 2007- 14:33.83, 2008- 14:38.78, 31:04.93; 2009- 14:34.17, 29:53.80; 2010- 14:31.91, 31:04.52; 2011- 14:39.44, 30:56.55. pbs: 1500m 4:07.52 '07, 1M 4:33.94 '03, 2000m 5:39.2i+ '07, 5:46.3+ '07; 3000m 8:23.74i '07, 8:34.73 '05, 10km Rd 31:41 '06.

Aselefech MERGIA b. 23 Jan 1985 Woliso 1.68m 45kg.
At Mar: WCh: '09- 3, '11- dnf. HMar: WCh: '08- 2. World CC: '08- 16.
Ethiopian marathon record 2012.
Progress at HMar, Mar: 2006- 74:13, 2007- 74:50, 2008- 68:17, 2009- 67:48, 2:25:02; 2010- 67:22, 2:22:38; 2011- 67:21, 2:22:45; 2012- 2:19:31. pbs: 1500m 4:14.85 '07, 3000m 8:54.42 '08; Road: 10km 31:25+ '08, 15km 47:53 '09, 20km 64:13 '09, 30km 1:41:52 '09.
2nd Paris Marathon 2009 on debut, 3rd London 2010, won Dubai 2011-12.

Askale TAFA Magarsa b. 27 Sep 1984 Arsi Province.
At Mar: WCh: '07- 22.
Progress at Mar: 2005- 2:28:27, 2006- 2:27:57, 2007- 2:25:07, 2008- 2:21:31, 2010- 2:24:39, 2011- 2:25:24, 2012- 2:25:29. pbs: 10km 32:49 '08, 15km 49:18 '08, 20km 65:56 '08, HMar 69:37 '08, 25km 1:22:50 '08, 30km 1:39:36 '08.
Won marathons in Milan 2006, Dubai & Paris 2007; 2nd Berlin & 3rd Dubai 2008, 3rd Berlin 2005. Married to Debele Tola (Mar 2:21:31 '08).

Dire TUNE b. 19 May 1985 Bekoji 1.57m 45kg.
At Mar: OG: '08- 15; WCh: '05- 37, '07- dnf, '09- 23 (fell), '11- dq; World 20km: '06- 4; HMar: '10- 2.
World 1 hour record 2008, Ethiopian half marathon record 2009.
Progress at Mar: 2005- 2:30:48, 2006- 2:35:15, 2007- 2:26:52, 2008- 2:24:40, 2009- 2:32:17, 2010- 2:23:44, 2011- 2:25:08wdh. pbs: 3000m 9:02.08 '03, 5000m 15:47.83 '03, 10000m 32:45.6 '08, 15000m 48:54.91 '08, 10M 52:25.84 '08, 1Hr 18.517m '08, 20000m 1:05:35.3 '09; Road: 10km 31:25dh, 31:40 '10; 15km 47:53 '09, 20km 65:16 '06, HMar 67:18 '09, 30km 1:42:20 '08.
Marathon wins: Houston 2007-08, Boston 2008 (2nd 2009). Married to Kelil Aman.

FINLAND

Governing body: Suomen Urheiluliitto, Radio–katu 20, SF-00240 Helsinki. Founded 1906.
National Championships first held in 1907 (men), 1913 (women). **2011 Champions: Men**: 100m: Hannu Hämäläinen 10.72, 200m: Santeri Tukia 21.61, 400m: Matti Välimäki 47.47, 800m/1500m: Niclas Sandells 1:52.89/3:45.41, 5000m: Jukka Keskisalo 14:07.54, 10000m: Matti Räsänen 29:44.51, HMar: Jussi Utriainen 66:14, Mar: Jaakko Kero 2:34:22, 3000mSt: Janne Ukonmaan–aho 8:39.44, 110mh: Antti Korkealaakso 14.17, 400mh: Petteri Monni 51.86, HJ: Jussi Viita 2.20, PV: Jere Bergius 5.60, LJ: Tommi Evilä 8.08, TJ: Aleksi Tammentie 15.81, SP: Tomas Söderlund 18.26, DT: Mikko Kyyrö 61.11, HT: Olli-Pekka Karjalainen 75.20, JT: Tero Pitkämäki 85.19, Dec: Sami Itani 77.31, 20kW/30kW: Jarkko Kinnunen 1:23:40/2:12:06. **Women**: 100m: Ella Räsänen 12.06, 200m: Anna Hämäläinen 23.76, 400m/400mh: Anniina Laitinen 55.32/59.38, 800m/1500m: Karin Storbacka 2:03.97/4:19.35, 5000m: Heidi Eriksson 16:26.98, 10000m/HMar: Elena Lindgren 34:24.53/77:33, Mar: Leena Puotiniemi 2:38:05, 3000mSt: Sandra Eriksson 9:59.11, 100mh: Elisa Leinonen 13.79, HJ: Mari Sepänmaa 1.80, PV: Minna Nikkanen 4.12, LJ: Tiia Mäki 6.23, TJ: Kristina Mäkelä 13.47, SP: Suvi Helin 15.15, DT: Sanna Kämäräinen 54.98, HT: Merja Korpela 67.10, JT: Oona Sormunen 56.31, Hep: Nina Kelo 5752, 10kW: Karolina Kaasalainen 47:01, 20kW: Anne Halkivaha 1:42:46.

Olli-Pekka KARJALAINEN b. 7 Mar 1980 Töysä 1.94m 118kg. Töysän Veto. Political science student at University of Helsinki.
At HT: OG: '00/04- dnq 34/15, '08- 6; WCh: '99-01-03-05-07-09-11: 11/10/dnq 14/5/9/dnq 16/9; EC: '02- 8, '06- 2, '10- 10; WJ: '98- 1; EJ: '97- 3, '99- 1; EU23: '01- 2; ECp: '02- 1, '06- 3. Won WAF 2004, Finnish 1998-2011.
World junior hammer record 1999, three Finnish 2002-04.
Progress at HT: 1995- 48.26, 1996- 58.80, 1997- 69.84, 1998- 75.08, 1999- 78.33, 2000- 80.55, 2001- 80.54, 2002- 81.70, 2003- 80.20, 2004- 83.30, 2005- 79.81, 2006- 80.84, 2007- 78.35, 2008- 79.59, 2009- 78.70, 2010- 76.94, 2011- 76.60.

Ari MANNIO b. 23 Jul 1987 Lehtimäki 1.85m 104kg. Lehtimäen Jyske.
At JT: WCh: '11- dnq 14; WJ: '04- 6, '06- 2; EU23: '07- 4, '09- 1; EJ: '05- 3; ET: '10- 3. Finnish champion 2011.
Progress at JT: 2004- 70.83, 2005- 76.40, 2006- 79.68, 2007- 80.31, 2008- 81.54, 2009- 85.70, 2010- 85.12. 2011- 85.12.

Tero PITKÄMÄKI b. 19 Dec 1982 Ilmajoki 1.95m 92kg. Nurmon Urheilijat. Electrical engineer.
At JT: OG: '04- 8, '08- 3; WCh: '05-07-09-11: 4/1/5/dnq 17; EC: '06- 2, '10- 3; EU23: '03- 3; EJ: '01- 6; ECp: '06- 1. Won WAF 2005, 2007; Finnish 2004-07.
Progress at JT: 1999- 66.83, 2000- 73.75, 2001- 74.89, 2002- 77.24, 2003- 80.45, 2004- 84.64, 2005- 91.53, 2006- 91.11, 2007- 91.23, 2008- 87.70, 2009- 87.79, 2010- 86.92, 2011- 85.33.

Antti RUUSKANEN b. 21 Feb 1984 Kokkola 1.90m 85kg. Pielaveden Sampo.
At JT: WCh: '09- 6, '11- 9; E23: '05- 2; EJ: '03- 3.
Progress at JT: 2002- 66.08, 2003- 72.87, 2004- 75.84, 2005- 79.75, 2006- 84.10, 2007- 82.71/87.88dh, 2008- 87.33, 2009- 85.39, 2010- 83.45, 2011- 82.29.

Teemu WIRKKALA b. 21 Feb 1984 Pielavesi 1.87m 85kg. Toholammin Urheilijat.
At JT: OG: '08- 5; WCh: '07- 12, '09- 9; EC: '06- dnq 13, '10- 5; WJ: '02- 7; E23: '05- 6; EJ: '03- 1. Finnish champion 2009.
Progress at JT: 2001- 69.22, 2002- 74.56, 2003- 80.57, 2004- 80.87, 2005- 80.68, 2006- 82.82, 2007- 84.06, 2008- 84.10, 2009- 87.23, 2010- 86.53, 2011- 82.39.

FRANCE

Governing body: Fédération Française d'Athlétisme, 33 avenue Pierre de Coubertin, 75640 Paris cedex 13. Founded 1920.
National Championships first held in 1888 (men), 1918 (women). **2011 Champions: Men**: 100m/200m: Christophe Lemaître 9.92/20.03w, 400m: Yannick Fonsat 46.00, 800m: Jeff Lastennet 1:50.03, 1500m: Florian Carvalho 3:54.35, 5000m: Hassan Hirt 13:58.11, 10000m: Stéphane Lefrand 28:40.44; HMar: Djamel Bachiri 64:27, Mar: Alban Chorin 2:18:53, 3000mSt: Bouabdellah Tahri 8:30.46, 110mh: Dimitri Bascou 13.26w, 400mh: Adrien Clemenceau 50.15, HJ: Mickaël Hanany 2.26, PV: Romain Mesnil 5.73, LJ: Kafétien Gomis 8.22w, TJ: Karl Taillepierre 17.01w, SP: Gaëtan Bucki 19.53, DT: Jean-François Aurokiom 59.04, HT: Frédéric Pouzy 74.31, JT: Laurent Dorique 72.98, Dec: Romain Barras 8117, 10000mW: Yohann Diniz 38:44.97, 20kW: Antonin Boyez 1:26:07, 50kW: Hervé Davaux 4:02:08. **Women**: 100m: Veronique Mang 11.11, 200m: Myriam Soumaré 22.86w, 400m: Elea Mariama Diarra 53.01, 800m: Clarisse Moh 2:03.61, 1500m: Hind Dehiba 4:08.17, 5000m: Christine Daunay 16:03.64, HMar: Fatiha Klilech-Fauvel 72:38, Mar: Aline Camboulives 2:38:42, 3000mSt: Sophie Duarte 10:00.70, 100mh: Sandra Gomis 12.93, 400mh: Phara Anacharsis 57.61, HJ: Mélanie Melfort 1.89, PV: Maria-Eleanor Tavares POR 4.50, LJ: Eloyse Lesueur 6.62w, TJ: Nathalie Marie-Nely 14.18w, SP: Jessica Cérival 16.92, DT: Mélina Robert-Michon 57.37, HT: Manuèla Montebrun 69.06, JT: Nadia Vigliano 55.59, Hep: Blandine Maisonnier 5870, 10000mW/20kW: Sylwia Korzeniowska 46:21.67/1:32:15.

Mehdi BAALA b. 17 Aug 1978 Strasbourg 1.83m 65kg. Lille Métropole Athlétisme.
At 1500m (800m): OG: '00- 4, '04- h, '08- 3; WCh: '01- 12, '03- 2, '05- sf (6), '07- dq sf, '09- 7, '11- 9; EC: '02- 1, '06- 1; WJ: '96- h; EU23: '99- 3; EJ: '97- 7; EI: '00- 3; WCp: '02- 3; ECp: '00-01-02-04-07-08: 1 (1)/2/1/1/1/1. Won FRA 800m 2001, 1500m 2002, 2005, 2009.
French records 800m 2002, 1000m (2) 2002-03, 1500m (2) 2003, 2000m 2005.
Progress at 800m, 1500m: 1994- 1:56.5, 4:08.1; 1995- 1:53.76, 3:48.74; 1996- 1:49.62, 3:43.50; 1997- 1:50.08, 3:45.34; 1998- 1:49.57, 3:41.86; 1999- 1:46.41, 3:34.83; 2000- 1:46.24, 3:32.05; 2001- 1:46.94, 3:31.97; 2002- 1:43.15, 3:32.03; 2003- 1:44.17, 3:28.98; 2004- 1:45.52, 3:31.25; 2005- 1:44.74, 3:30.80; 2006- 1:44.04, 3:32.01; 2007- 3:31.01, 2008- 3:32.00, 2009- 3:30.96, 2010- 3:34.59, 2011- 3:33.69. pbs: 1000m 2:13.96 '03, 1M 3:52.51i '09, 2000m 4:53.12 '05, 3000m 8:08.06i/8:23.69 '98.
Married Hanane Sabri (ht WC 1500m '01, FRA champion 2001) in September 2000. His elder brother Samir won French marathon in 2002 and 2008.

Romain BARRAS b. 1 Aug 1980 Calais 1.94m 86kg. SO Calais.
At Dec: OG: '04- 13, '08- 5; WCh: '05- 7, '07- 7, '09- 12; EC: '06- 8, '10- 1; EU23: '01- 4; WUG: '01- 5, 03- 1; ECp: '03-06-08-10: 1/1/2/1; Won French 2005, 2011;, MedG & Franc G 2005. At Hep: EI: '07- 6.
Progress at Dec: 1998- 6505, 1999- 7147, 2000- 7609, 2001- 7876, 2002- 7835, 2003- 8196, 2004- 8067, 2005- 8185, 2006- 8416w/8138, 2007- 8298, 2008- 8253, 2009- 8239, 2010- 8453, 2011- 8134. pbs: 60m 7.21i '07, 100m 11.02 '03, 10.94w '06; 400m 48.21 '06, 1000m 2:39.89i '06, 1500m 4:21.79 '06, 50mh 7.09i '04, 6.8i '03; 60mh 8.14i '01, 110mh 14.11 '08, HJ 2.01 '03, PV 5.05 '07, LJ 7.35 '05, SP 16.19 '10, DT 47.21 '04, JT 65.84 '05, Hep 5895i '06.
Won IAAF Combined Events Challenge 2010. Brother Guillaume has Dec pb 7523 '08, younger sister Diane Hep pb 5449 '11.

Jérôme CLAVIER b. 3 May 1983 Chambray-lès-Tours 1.85m 73kg. Athletic Trois Tours.
At PV: OG: '08- 7; WCh: '07/11- dnq 20/18=; WJ: '02- 6; EU23: '03- dnq, '05- 3; WI: '08- 4; EI: '07- 6, '11- 2; French champion 2007.
Progress at PV: 1998- 3.90, 1999- 4.40, 2000- 4.80, 2001- 5.10, 2002- 5.40, 2003- 5.56i/5.50, 2004- 5.65i/5.60, 2005- 5.63, 2006- 5.65i/5.51, 2007- 5.70, 2008- 5.80i/5.75, 2009- 5.62i/5.60, 2010- 5.71i/5.70, 2011- 5.81i/5.63. pb Dec 6307 '01.

Benjamin COMPAORÉ b. 5 Aug 1987 Bar-le-Duc 1.88m 83kg. Strasbourg AA.
At TJ: WCh: '11- 8; EWI: '12- 6; C: '10- 5; WJ: '06- 1; EJ: '05- 9.
Progress at TJ: 2003- 14.50, 2004- 15.48, 2005- 16.00/16.12w, 2006- 16.61, 2007- 16.62, 2008-

17.05, 2009- 16.98, 2010- 17.21/17.28w, 2011- 17.31. pbs: 60m 7.13i '08, 100m 10.96 '07, 110h 15.96 '06, LJ 7.88 '08.

Garfield DARIEN b. 22 Dec 1987 Lyon 1.87m 76kg. EA Chambéry.
At 110mh: WCh: '09- sf; EC: '10- 2; WJ: '04- 7; EJ: '05- 1; CCp: '10- 4; ET: '11- 2. At 60mh: EI: '09- 6, '11- 2.
Progress at 110mh: 2004- 14.03/13.98w, 2005- 13.73, 2006- 13.94/13.92w, 2008- 13.50/13.43w, 2009- 13.36, 2010- 13.34, 2011- 13.37. pbs: 200m 22.05 '06, 60mh 7.56i '11, HJ 1.83 '04.
His father Daniel Darien had 110mh pb 13.76 '87.

Yohann DINIZ b. 1 Jan 1978 Epernay 1.85m 69kg. EFS Reims Athlétisme.
At 20kW: ECp: '07- 1; At 50kW: OG: '08- dnf; WCh: '05-07-09-11: dq/2/12/dq; EC: '06- 1, '10- 1; ECp: '05- 4. Won French 10000mW 2010, 20kW 2007-09, 50kW 2005.
World record 50,000m track walk 2011. French records 5000mW (3) 2006-08, 20kW (3) 2005-12, 50kW 2006 & 2009, 1 Hr 2010.
Progress at 20kW, 50kW: 2001- 1:35:05.0t, 2002- 1:30:40, 2003- 1:26:54.99t, 2004- 1:24:25, 3:52:11.0t; 2005- 1:20:20, 3:45:17; 2006- 1:23:19, 3:41:39; 2007- 1:18:58, 3:44:22; 2008- 1:22:31, 2009- 1:22:50, 3:38:45; 2010- 1:20:23, 3:40:37; 2011- 3:35:27.2t, 2012- 1:17:43. pbs: 3000mW 10:52.44 '08, 5000mW 18:18.01 '08, 10000mW 38:44.97 '11, 1HrW 15,395m '10.

Leslie DJHONE b. 18 Mar 1981 Abidjan, CIV 1.87m 76kg. ES Montgeron.
At 400m/4x400m: OG: '04- 7, '08- 5; WCh: '03- 4/1R, '05- h, '07- 5, '09- 8; EC: '02- 3R, '06- 3/1R, '10- 6; EU23: '03- 1; EI: '11- 1/1R; ECp: '04-06-07-08-10: 3/1R/1/1R/2. At LJ/4x100m: WJ: '98- dnq, '00- 2R; EU23: '01- 4/4R, '03- 2R; EJ: '99- 1/1R. At 200m: ECp: '03- 5. Won FRA 200m 2004, 400m 2006-10.
French 400m records 2004 & 2007, European indoor 300m best (32.47) 2010.
Progress at 400m: 2001- 47.01, 2002- 45.63, 2003- 44.83, 2004- 44.64, 2005- 45.56, 2006- 44.91, 2007- 44.46, 2008- 44.79, 2009- 44.80, 2010- 44.87, 2011- 45.54i. pbs: 100m 10.52 '03, 200m 20.51i '03, 20.67 '04; 300m 32.18 '03, LJ 7.92 '99, 8.06w '01.
Began as a long jumper, winning the European Junior title in 1999, before turning to 400m.

Kafétien GOMIS b. 23 Mar 1980 Saint Quentin 1.85m 70kg.Lille Metropole Athlétisme.
At LJ: OG: '04- dnq 14; WCh: '09- dnq 21; EC: '06- 5, '10- 2; EI: '07-09-11: 4/4/2; CCp: '10- 2; ET: '10- 2. French champion 2007.
Progress at LJ: 2000- 7.35w, 2001- 7.56i/7.53, 2002- 7.77, 2003- 7.85, 2004- 8.21, 2005- 7.98, 2006- 8.03, 2007- 8.09i/7.91, 2008- 8.08, 2009- 8.15, 2010- 8.24, 2011- 8.12/8.22w. pbs: 60 6.91i '06, 100m 10.76 '03, HJ 2.07 '00.

Renaud LAVILLENIE b. 18 Sep 1986 Barbezieux-Saint-Hilaire 1.77m 69kg. Clermont

Athl. Auvergne.
At PV: WCh: '09- 3, '11- 3; WI: '12- 1; EC: '10- 1; EU23: '07- 10; EI: '09- 1, '11- 1; CCp: '10- 1; ET: '09-10: 1/1. Won DL 2010, French 2010.
French record (indoors) 2011.
Progress at 100m: 2002- 3.40, 2003- 4.30, 2004- 4.60, 2005- 4.81i/4.70, 2006- 5.25i/5.22, 2007- 5.58i/5.45, 2008- 5.81i/5.65, 2009- 6.01, 2010- 5.94, 2011- 6.03i/5.90, 2012- 5.95i. pbs: 60m 7.23i '08, 60mh 8.41i '08, 100m 11.20 '11, 110mh 14.51 '10, HJ 1.89i '08, 1.87 '07; LJ 7.31 '10, Hep 5363i '08.

Christophe LEMAITRE b. 11 Jun 1990 Annecy 1.89m 74kg. AS Aix-les-Bains.
At 100m/(200m): WCh: '09- qf, '11- 4/3/2R; EC: '10- 1/1/1R; WJ: '08- (1); WY: '07- 4/5; EJ: '09- 1; CCp: '10- 1; ET: '10- 2, '11- 1/1. At 60m: EI: '11- 3. Won French 100m & 200m 2010-11.
French records 100m (7) 2010-11, 200m (2) 2010-11, European junior 100m 2009. U23 2010-11.
Progress at 100m, 200m: 2005- 11.46, 2006- 10.96, 2007- 10.53, 21.08; 2008- 10.26, 20.83; 2009- 10.04/10.03w, 20.68; 2010- 9.97, 20.16; 2011- 9.92, 19.80. pb 60m 6.55i '10.
First Caucasian sub-10.00 100m runner and first to win sprint treble at European Champs.

Martial MBANDJOCK b. 14 Oct 1985 Roubaix 1.87m 84kg. Lagardère Paris Racing.
At 100m/(200m): OG- '08- sf; WCh: '07- qf, '09- sf/sf; EC: '10- 3/3/1R; WJ: '04- (sf); EU23: '07- 3; ECp: '07-08-09-10: 2/2/(3)/(1). At 60m: EI: '11- 5. Won FRA 100m 2008, 200m 2009, MedG 100m 2009,
Progress at 100m, 200m: 2003- 11.00w, 21.59; 2004- 10.85, 21.06; 2006- 10.45, 21.06; 2007- 10.16, 2008- 10.06, 20.69; 2009- 10.11, 20.43; 2010- 10.08, 20.38; 2011- 10.13, 20.59w. pbs: 60m 6.61i '11, 400m 47.59 '08.

Mahiédine MEKHISSI-BENABBAD b. 15 Mar 1985 Reims 1.90m 75kg. EFS Reims.
At 3000mSt: OG: '08- 2; WCh: '07/09- h, '11- 3; EC: '10- 1; WJ: '04- h; EU23: '05- h, '07- 1; CCp: '10- 3; ECp: '07- 2, '08- 1; French champion 2008.
At 1500m: WI: '10- 8; WCp: '06- 7.
World best 2000m steeplechase 2010.
Progress at 3000mSt: 2003- 9:52.07, 2004- 9:01.01, 2005- 8:34.45, 2006- 8:28.25, 2007- 8:14.22, 2008- 8:08.95, 2009- 8:06.98, 2010- 8:02.52, 2011- 8:02.09.
pbs: 800m 1:53.61 '04, 1000m 2:17.14 '09, 1500m 3:33.86 '11, 2000m 5:00.17 '11, 3000m 7:44.98 '10, 5000m 14:32.9 '05, 2000mSt 5:10.68 '10.

Romain MESNIL b. 13 Jun 1977 Le Plessis Bouchard 1.88m 82kg. AC Paris Joinville. IT Engineer.
At PV: OG: '00/04/08- dnq 31/18/14=; WCh: '99-01-03-07-09-11: nh/5/dnq/2/2/nh; EC: '02- dnq, '06- 2=, '10- 8; EU23: '99-1; WJ: '96- dnq 13=; WI: '99-01-03-04-12: 6=/3/7/7/8; EI: '09- 7; WCp: '06- 4; ECp: '03-04-06-07: 1/1/1/2. French champion 2000-03, 2008-09, 2011.

Progress at PV: 1993- 4.30, 1994- 4.65, 1995- 5.15, 1996- 5.30, 1997- 5.40, 1998- 5.80, 1999- 5.93, 2000- 5.75, 2001- 5.86i/5.85, 2002- 5.75, 2003- 5.95, 2004- 5.80, 2005- 5.75, 2006- 5.81, 2007- 5.86, 2008- 5.71, 2009- 5.85, 2010- 5.80, 2011- 5.80i/5.73. pb Dec 5724 '98.
Former gymnast. Married to Karine Bénézech (PV 3.75i '99).

Salim SDIRI b. 26 Oct 1978 Ajaccio, Corsica 1.85m 80kg. Lagardère Paris Racing.
At LJ: OG: '04- 12, '08- dnq 21; WCh: '03- dnq 13, '05- 5, '09- 6, '11- dnq 28; EC: '02- 7, '06- 10, '10- 4; WI: '03- 7, '10- 4; EI: '07- 3; WCp: '06- 5; ECp: '02-04-05-06: 3/2/2/2; won Med G 2005, 2009; French 2003-06, 2009-10.
French long jump record 2009.
Progress at LJ: 1999- 7.43, 2000- 7.95, 2001- 7.83, 2002- 8.23, 2003- 8.29w, 2004- 8.24, 2005- 8.25, 2006- 8.27i/8.22, 2007- 8.13i/8.01, 2008- 8.21, 2009- 8.42, 2010- 8.24/8.28w, 2011- 8.27. pbs: 60m 6.99i '06, 100m 10.79 '08, 10.6w '01; TJ 16.10 '00.
Seriously injured when speared by a javelin at Rome Golden Gala 2007.

Bouabdellah 'Bob' TAHRI b. 20 Dec 1978 Metz 1.91m 68kg. Athlétisme Metz Métropole.
At 3000mSt: OG: '00- h, '04- 7, '08- 5; WCh: '99-01-03-05-07-09-11: 12/5/4/8/5/3/4; EC: '98-02-06-10: 10/4/3/2; WJ: '96- 7; WCp: '06- 3; ECp: '00-01-02-04: 1/1/1/1. At 5000m: EJ: '97- 1; CCp: '10- 3; ECp: '05- 2. At 3000m: WI: '01- 11; EI: '98-07-09: 8/2/2; ECp: '07- 1. World CC: '97- 22J, '04- 15 4k; Eur CC: '05- 4, '08- 6. Won FRA 1500m 2004, 2006; 3000mSt 1998, 2010-11.
Three European records 3000mSt 2003-09, indoor 5000m (13:11.13) 2010; best 2000mSt 2002 & 2009. World best 2000mSt 2010.
Progress at 3000mSt: 1996- 8:44.65, 1998- 8:19.75, 1999- 8:12.24, 2000- 8:16.14, 2001- 8:09.23, 2002- 8:10.83, 2003- 8:06.91, 2004- 8:14.26, 2005- 8:09.58, 2006- 8:09.53, 2007- 8:09.06, 2008- 8:12.72, 2009- 8:01.18, 2010- 8:03.72, 2011- 8:05.72. pbs: 800m 1:48.96 '01, 1000m 2:20.34 '05, 1500m 3:34.65 '09, 1M 3:52.95 '02, 2000m 4:57.58 '02, 3000m 7:33.18 '09, 5000m 13:12.29 '07, 10000m 27:31.46 '11, HMar 66:12 '03, 2000mSt 5:13.47 '10.

Teddy TAMGHO b. 15 Jun 1989 Paris 1.87m 82kg. CA Montreuil.
At TJ: WCh: '09- 11; EC: '10- 3; WI: '10- 1; WJ: '08- 1; EJ: '07- 4; EI: '11- 1 (4 LJ); ET: '10- 3. Won DL 2010, French 2009-10.
Four World indoor triple jump records 2010 (17.90) & 2011, absolute French record 2009; three French (and Eur U23) records 2010.
Progress at TJ: 2004- 12.56, 2005- 14.89, 2006- 15.58, 2007- 16.53i/16.35/16.42w, 2008- 17.19/17.33w, 2009- 17.58i/17.11, 2010- 17.98, 2011- 17.92i/17.91. pbs: 60m 6.92i '06, 100m 10.60 '09, LJ 8.01i '11, 7.63 '07.
2011 season ended when broke ankle in warm-up for European U23s.

Jimmy VICAUT b. 27 Feb 1992 Bondy 1.84m 75kg. Lagardère Paris Racing.
At 100m/4x100mR: WCh: '11- 6/2R; EC: '10- 1R; WJ: '10- 3; WY: '09- 7; EJ: '11- 1/1R.
Progress at 100m: 2005- 13.0, 2006- 12.50, 2007- 11.0, 2008- 10.75/10.69w, 2009- 10.56, 2010- 10.16, 2011- 10.07. pbs: 60m 6.53i '12, 200m 21.02 '10.

Women

Vanessa BOSLAK b. 11 Jun 1982 Lesquin 1.70m 57kg. Lagardère Paris Racing. Physiotherapist.
At PV: OG: '04- 6=, '08- 9; WCh: '05- 8, '07- 5; EC: '02- 11=, '06- dnq 17=; WJ: '98- 6; '00- 3=; EU23: '03- 2; EJ: '01- 3; WI: '04-06-12: 5=/5/2; EI: '07- 6=; ECp: '01-02-04-06-07: 5/3/5/2/3; won Med G 2005, French 2001, 2003-05, 2007.
13 French pole vault records 2002-07.
Progress at PV: 1995- 3.25, 1996- 3.76, 1997- 3.90, 1998- 4.10, 1999- 4.15i/4.11, 2000- 4.32, 2001- 4.33i/4.30, 2002- 4.46, 2003- 4.50, 2004- 4.51, 2005- 4.60, 2006- 4.70, 2007- 4.70, 2008- 4.60i/4.55, 2011- 4.51i/4.30, 2012- 4.70i. pb JT 44.27 '99.

Hind DEHIBA b. 17 Mar 1979 Khouribga, Morocco 1.62m 44kg. née Chahyd. AS Anzin Athlétisme.
At 1500m: OG: '04- h; WCh: '05- h, 09- sf; EC: '06- 9, '10- 2; WI: '06- 4, '12- 5; EI: '05- 3; CCp: '10- 1. Won French 800m 2009, 1500m 2005-06, 2009, 2011. French 1500m records 2005 & 2010.
Progress at 1500m: 1995- 4:21.0, 1998- 4:11.3, 1999- 4:27.50, 2003- 4:21.52, 2004- 4:03.72, 2005- 4:00.49, 2006- 4:02.74, 2009- 4:03.43, 2010- 3:59.76, 2011- 4:03.02. pbs: 800m 1:58.67 '10, 1000m 2:38.50i '11, 1M 4:29.09 '10, 3000m 8:52.21 '05.
Ex Morocco, married Fodil Dehiba in 2003, naturalised French citizen 2004. Two-year drugs ban 2007-09.

Stéphanie FALZON b. 7 Jan 1983 Bordeaux 1.70m 77kg. B. Sud Médoc Athlé.
At HT: WCh: '07- dnq 16, '09- 9, '11- 12; EC: '06/10- dnq 15/17; WJ: '00- dnq 28, '02- 6; EU23: '03- dnq, '05- 8; EJ: '01- 8; French champion 2006, 2008, 2010.
Progress at HT: 2000- 53.71, 2001- 57.31, 2002- 59.98, 2003- 64.16, 2004- 65.21, 2005- 65.12, 2006- 68.84, 2007- 71.11, 2008- 73.40, 2009- 72.54, 2010- 73.40, 2011- 71.53, 2012- 72.60.

Eloyse LESUEUR b. 15 Jul 1988 Paris 1.79m 65kg. Saint Denis Emotion.
At LJ: WCh: '09- 11: dnq 18/26; WI: '08- 4; WY: '05- 2 (7 100m); EU23: '09- 3; EJ: '07- 2; EI: '11- 3; ET: '10- 1, '11- 3. French champion 2010-11. At Hep: WJ: '06- dnf.
Progress at LJ: 2002- 5.72, 2003- 5.50, 2004- 5.68, 2005- 6.40, 2006- 6.30/6.47w, 2007- 6.47, 2008- 6.84i/6.50, 2009- 6.64/6.72w, 2010- 6.78, 2011- 6.91. pbs: 60m 7.34i '12, 100m 11.57 '06, 200m 24.11 '06, 800m 2:21.67 '06, 100mh 13.89 '06, HJ 1.75 '06, Hep 5370w/5320 '06.

Véronique MANG b. 15 Dec 1984 Douala, Cameroon 1.73m 60kg. Entente Franconville CESAME Val d'Oise. Law student.
At 100m/(200m): OG: '04- qf/3R; WCh: '11- sf; EC: '06- sf, '10- 2/dq/2R; EJ: '03- 2/1R; ECp: '04- 1R, '10- 1/2R, '11- 1. At 60m: EI: '11- 6. Won MedG 2005, FRA 2006, 2010-11.
Progress at 100m: 2000- 11.39, 2001- 11.80, 2003- 11.33/11.29w, 2004- 11.24, 2005- 11.34, 2006- 11.26/11.22w, 2007- 11.46, 2008- 11.96/11.89w, 2010- 11.11/11.06w, 2011- 11.11. pbs: 50m 6.24i '10, 60m 7.19i '11, 200m 22.92 '04, 400m 56.54 '07.
Lived in France from age ten, naturalised French (from Cameroon) 2003.

Mélanie MELFORT b. 8 Nov 1982 Hersbrück, Germany 1.82m 62kg. née Skotnik. Alsace Nord Athlétisme. Secretary.
At HJ: OG: '08- dnq 16=; WCh: '05-07-09-11: dnq 15=/7=/9/dnq 15; WJ: '00- 5; WY: '99- 5; EU23: '03- 5; EI: '07- 5=, '11- 4=; ECp: '05-07- 3/3. German champion 2003, French 2005, 2007-11.
French high jump record 2007.
Progress at HJ: 1995- 1.61, 1996- 1.65, 1997- 1.72, 1998- 1.72, 1999- 1.85, 2000- 1.86, 2001- 1.86, 2002- 1.88, 2003- 1.97i/1.91, 2004- 1.93i/1.90, 2005- 1.95, 2006- 1.93i/1.92, 2007- 1.97i/1.96, 2008- 1.95, 2009- 1.96i/1.93, 2010- 1.92i/1.89, 2011- 1.95. pbs: 200m 25.22i/25.63w '10, 400m 56.34 '10.
French mother. Switched nationality from Germany to France with effect from 6 Mar 2005. Married coach Jimmy Melfort in 2009.

Antoinette NANA DJIMOU Ida b. 2 Aug 1985 Douala, Cameroon 1.74m 69kg. CA Montreuil.
At Hep: OG: '08- 18; WCh: '07- dnf, '09- 7, '11- 7; EC: '06- 21, '10- dnf; WJ: '04- 4; EU23: '05- 5, '07- 7; ECp: '08- 2. At Pen: WI: '10- 5; EI: '09- 3, '11- 1. Won French LJ 2008, Hep 2006-07.
CMR heptathlon record 2003, French indoor pentathlon record 2011.
Progress at Hep: 2003- 5360, 2004- 5649, 2005- 6089w/5792, 2006- 5981, 2007- 5982, 2008- 6204, 2009- 6323, 2010- 5994, 2011- 6409. pbs: 60m 7.51i '11, 100m 11.78 '08, 200m 24.36 '11, 800m 2:13.26 '06, 60mh 8.11i '10, 100mh 13.15 '11, HJ 1.84i '10, 1.83 '11; LJ 6.44i '09, 6.35/6.61w '08; SP 14.81i/14.44 '11, JT 55.79 '11, Pen 4723i '11.
Came to France at age 14, naturalised French citizen in 2004.

Myriam SOUMARÉ b. 29 Oct 1986 Paris 1.67m 57kg. AA Pays de France Athlé 95.
At 100m/(200m): WCh: '09- qf, '11- sf/sf; EC: '10- 3/1/2R; EU23: '07- 3. At 4x400m: EJ: '05- 7. At 60m: WI: '10- 7; EI: '11- 7. Won FRA 100m 2009, 200m, 2011.
Progress at 100m: 2004- 24.66i, 2005- 12.07/11.98w, 24.05; 2006- 11.68, 23.78; 2007- 11.50/11.39w, 23.44; 2008- 11.43, 23.64/23.40w; 2009- 11.34, 23.34; 2010- 11.18/11.13w, 22.32; 2011- 11.17/11.12w, 22.71. pbs: 50m 6.22i '10, 60m 7.18i '11, 400m 53.44'11, LJ 5.72 '07.
Astonishing breakthrough in final of European 200m 2010 when she improved pb from 23.01 to win in 22.32.

GERMANY

Governing body: Deutscher Leichtathletik Verband (DLV), Alsfelder Str. 27, 64289 Darmstadt. Founded 1898.

National Championships first held in 1891. **2011 Champions: Men:** 100m: Tobias Unger 10.40, 200m: Robin Erewa 21.05, 400m: Jonas Plass 46.59, 800m: Sören Ludolph 1:50.42, 1500m: Carsten Schlangen 3:57.94, 5000m: Arne Gabius 13:58.87, 10000m: Musa Roba-Kinkal 29:22.02, HMar: André Pollmächer 64:16, Mar: Stefan Koch 2:20:39, 3000mSt: Steffen Uliczka 8:33.47, 110mh: Matthias Bühler 13.66, 400mh: David Gollnow 49.56, HJ: Raul Spank 2.31, PV: Malte Mohr 5.72, LJ: Sebastian Bayer 8.17, TJ: Andreas Pohle 16.59w, SP: David Storl 20.35, DT: Robert Harting 65.72, HT: Markus Esser 78.44, JT: Mathias de Zordo 81.06, Dec: Andre Niklaus 7536, 10000mW: Christopher Linke 39.52.96, 20kW: André Höhne 1:23:23, 50kW: Carsten Schmidt 3:54:54. **Women:** 100m: Cathleen Tschirch 11.52, 200m: Christina Haack 23.45, 400m: Esther Cremer 52.70, 800m: Jana Hartmann 2:06.67, 1500m: Corrinna Harrer 4:10.47, 5000m/10000m/HMar: Sabrina Mockenhaupt 15:36.89/33:34.99/71:23, Mar: Steffi Volke 2:51:18, 3000mSt: Jana Sussmann 10.05.64, 100mh: Cindy Roleder 13.10, 400mh: Christiane Klopsch 56.97, HJ: Melanie Bauschke 1.86, PV: Martina Strutz 4.65, LJ: Michelle Weitzel 6.52, TJ: Katja Demut 14.22, SP: Christine Schwanitz 18.95, DT: Nadine Müller 63.41, HT: Betty Heidler 76.04, JT: Christina Obergfoll 68.86, Hep: Claudia Rath 5484, 5000mW/20kW: Sabine Krantz 20:56.75/1:31:08.

Ralf BARTELS b. 21 Feb 1978 Malchin 1.86m 128kg. SC Neubrandenburg. Soldier.
At SP: OG: '04- 8; WCh: '01-03-05-07-09-11: dnq 17/5/3/7/3/10; EC: '02- 3, '06- 1, '10- 3; WJ: '96- 1; EU23: '99- 6; EJ: '95- 4, '97- 1; WI: '10- 3; EI: '09- 3, '11- 1; WCp: '02- 3, '06- 1; ECp: '04-05-06-10: 3/1/3/2. German champion 2002-06, 2008-10.
Progress at SP: 1995- 17.63, 1996- 18.71, 1997- 18.35, 1998- 18.50, 1999- 18.95, 2000- 19.34, 2001- 20.30, 2002- 20.85, 2003- 20.67, 2004- 20.88, 2005- 21.36, 2006- 21.43i/21.13, 2007- 20.75, 2008- 20.60, 2009- 21.37, 2010- 21.44i/21.14, 2011- 21.16i/20.58.

Sebastian BAYER b. 11 Jun 1986 Aachen 1.89m 79kg. Hamburger SV.
At LJ: OG: '08- dnq 23; WCh: '09- dnq 19, '11- 8; EC: '06- dnq 20; WJ: '04- dnq 17; EJ: '05- 2; EI: '09- 1, '11- 1. German champion 2006, 2008-09, 2011.
Progress at LJ: 2000- 5.65, 2001- 6.14, 2002- 6.57, 2003- 7.27, 2004- 7.57, 2005- 7.82i/7.73, 2006- 7.95, 2007- 7.88i, 2008- 8.15, 2009- 8.71i/8.49, 2010- 8.06, 2011- 8.17. pbs: 60m 6.80i '09, 100m 10.73 '09, HJ 1.83 '03.
Sensational improvement at 2009 European Indoors – from pb of 8.17 to 8.29 and then European record 8.71 with final jump.

Pascal BEHRENBRUCH b. 19 Jan 1985 Offenbach 1.96m 94kg. LG Eintracht Frankfurt.
At Dec: WCh: '09- 6, '11- 7; EC: '06- 5; EJ: '03- 10; EU23: '07- 2.
Progress at Dec: 2005- 7842, 2006- 8209, 2007- 8239, 2008- 8242, 2009- 8439, 2010- 8202, 2011- 8232. pbs: 60m 7.08i '10, 100m 10.84 '07, 400m 48.48 '06, 1000m 2:53.39i '06, 1500m 4:24.16 '06, 60mh 8.10i '10, 110mh 14.02 '09, HJ 2.03 '08, PV 4.93i '12, 4.90 '11; LJ 7.21 '11, 7.32w '07, SP 16.65 '11, DT 51.31 '09, JT 71.40 '11, Hep 5604i '06.

Matthias de ZORDO b. 21 Feb 1988 Bad Kreuznach 1.90m 97kg. SV Schlau com Saar 05.
At JT: WCh: '11- 1; EC: '10- 2; EU23: '09- 8; EJ: '07- 1, CCp: '10- 3; ET: '10- 1. German champion 2010-11. Left-handed.
Progress at JT: 2006- 71.67, 2007- 78.67, 2008- 82.51, 2009- 80.15, 2010- 87.81, 2011- 88.36.

Markus ESSER b. 3 Feb 1980 Leverkusen 1.80m 105kg. TSV Bayer 04 Leverkusen. Army lieutenant.
At HT: OG: '00-04-08: dnq 35/11/9; WCh: '05-07-09-11: 4/8/6/4; EC: '02- dnq 29, '06- 4, '10- dnq 19; WJ: '98- 12; EJ: '99- 3; EU23: '01- 7; ECp: '04-05-07-08-09-10-11: 2/3/2/3/3/3/1. German champion 2006-08, 2010-11.
Progress at HT: 1997- 64.78, 1998- 73.10, 1999- 70.29, 2000- 76.66, 2001- 75.69, 2002- 76.94, 2003- 78.13, 2004- 79.01, 2005- 80.00, 2006- 81.10, 2007- 80.68, 2008- 79.97, 2009- 79.43, 2010- 78.87, 2011- 79.69.

Mark FRANK b. 21 Jun 1977 Neustrelitz 1.87m 97kg. 1. LAV Rostock. Soldier.
At JT: WCh: '05- 8, '09- 8, '11- 8; EU23: '99- 3; ECp: '05- 07-09: 1/5/1; World Military champion 2002, German 2009.
Progress at JT: 1994- 59.42, 1995- 71.58, 1996- 68.98, 1997- 64.20, 1998- 72.96, 1999- 77.62, 2000- 65.17, 2001- 77.83, 2002- 83.24, 2003- 80.55, 2004- 81.21, 2005- 84.88, 2006- 81.98, 2007- 82.23, 2009- 83.86, 2010- 80.46, 2011- 82.54.
Son-in-law of Anita Weiss (4 OG 1976, 1 EI 1975 at 800m).

Rico FREIMUTH b. 14 Mar 1988 Potsdam 1.96m 91kg. Hallesche LA-Freunde.
At Dec: WCh: '11- dnf; EU23: 09- 10; EJ: '07- 3.
Progress at Dec: 2009- 7689, 2010- 7826, 2011- 8287. pbs: 60m 6.99i '11, 100m 10.79. 10.50w '11, 400m 48.22 '11, 1000m 2:54.95i '11, 1500m 4:35.77 '10, 60mh 8.06i '11, 110mh 13.96 '10, HJ 1.94 '10, PV 4.80 '11, LJ 7.41 '10, 7.42w '11, SP 14.65 '11, DT 48.00 '11, JT 65.04 '11, Hep 5808i '10.
His father Uwe had decathlon best of 8794 (1984), and was 4th at 1983 Worlds and 1986 Europeans and twice winner at Götzis. Uwe and Rico are the highest scoring father-son combination.

Robert HARTING b. 18 Oct 1984 Cottbus 2.01m 129kg. SCC Berlin.

Betty Heidler – set a world hammer record of 79.42

Kirani James – wins World 400m two days before 19th birthday

2009 winner Jessica Ennis is first in the 800m but Tatyana Chernova is World heptathlon champion with 6880 points

Anna Chicherova – world high jump champion

Dwight Phillips won 4th world title at long jump

Abel Kirui retained his World marathon title in brilliant style in Daegu

Ibrahim Jeylan just beats Mo Farah to win the World 10,000m title.

Asbel Kiprop beats Silas Kiplagat in World 1500m.

Finish of the men's 110m hurdles in Daegu. Jason Richardson (right) takes the title after Dayron Robles (second left) disqualified for obstructing Liu Xiang (left)

Pawel Wojciechowski made a great breakthrough in 2011, and won the World pole vault title.

At DT: OG: 08- 4; WCh: '07- 2, '09- 1, '11- 1; ECh: '06- dnq 13, '10- 2; CCp: '10- 1; ECp: '07-08-09-10-11: 2/2/2/1/1; WJ: '02- dnq 13; EU23: '05- 1. German champion 2007-11.
Progress at DT: 2002- 54.25, 2003- 59.54, 2004- 64.05, 2005- 66.02, 2006- 65.22, 2007- 66.93, 2008- 68.65, 2009- 69.43, 2010- 69.69, 2011- 68.99. pb SP 18.63 '07.
Unbeaten in 16 competitions 2011. Brother Christoph (b. 4 Oct 1990) has pb 62.12 '11.

Raphael HOLZDEPPE b. 28 Sep 1989 Kaiserslautern 1.81m 79kg. LAZ Zweibrücken.
At PV: OG: 08- 8; WCh: '11- dnq 20; EC '10- 9; WJ: '06- 5, '08- 1; EU23: '09- 1; EJ: '07- dnq.
World junior pole vault record (=) 2008.
Progress at PV: 2002- 3.45, 2003- 4.25, 2004- 4.50, 2005- 5.00, 2006- 5.42, 2007- 5.50, 2008- 5.80, 2009- 5.65, 2010- 5.80, 2011- 5.72, 2012- 5.82i.

Jan Felix KNOBEL b. 16 Jan 1989 Bad Homburg 1.91m 89kg. LG Eintracht Frankfurt.
At Dec: WCh: '11- 8; EU23: '11- 19; WJ: '06- 1. German champion 2009. At Oct: WY: 05- 5.
Progress at Dec: 2009- 7758, 2010- dnf, 2011- 8288. pbs: 60m 7.18i '10, 100m 11.07 '07, 400m 48.91 '10, 1000m 2:49.22i '10, 1500m 4:43.12 '11, 60mh 8.31i '10, 110mh 14.70 '10, HJ 2.01 '11, PV 5.02 '11, LJ 7.30 '11, 7.32w '10, SP 16.06 '11, DT 49.60 '11, JT 72.99 '11, Hep 5778i '10.

Malte MOHR b. 24 Jul 1986 Bochum 1.92m 78kg. TV Wattenscheid.
At PV: WCh: '09- 14, '11- 5; EC: '10- dnq 17=; WI: '10- 2, '12- 4; EI: '11- 3; ET: '09- 2, '11- 2. German champion 2010-11.
Progress at PV: 2003- 4.81, 2004- 5.11i, 2005- 5.30, 2006- 5.71, 2007- 5.31, 2008- 5.76, 2009- 5.80, 2010- 5.90, 2011- 5.86i/5.85, 2012- 5.87i.
His father (and coach) Wolfgang Mohr had a best of 5.41 in 1976 and his mother Gisela Derksen was a good junior mult-eventer.

Björn OTTO b. 16 Oct 1977 Frechen 1.91m 90kg. TSV Bayer Uerdingen/Dormagen.
At PV: WCh: '07- 5, '09- dnq 18=; WI: '12- 2; EI: '00-05-07: 6/4/3; WUG: '99-01-03-05: 8/7/3=/1.
Progress at PV: 1991- 3.20, 1992- 3.20, 1993- 4.10, 1994- 4.71, 1995- 5.00, 1996- 5.30i/5.20, 1997- 5.40, 1998- 5.52sq/5.40, 1999- 5.55/5.60ex, 2000- 5.65/5.71ex, 2001- 5.51/5.63ex, 2002- 5.63sq/5.60, 2003- 5.72i/5.70, 2004- 5.82i/5.70, 2005- 5.80, 2006- 5.85, 2007- 5.90, 2008- 5.70, 2009- 5.71, 2010- 5.60i/5.41, 2011- 5.75/5.80ex, 2012- 5.92i.

Christian REIF b. 24 Oct 1984 Speyer 1.96m 85kg. ABC Ludwigshafen. Sports student.
At LJ: WCh: '07- 9, '11- 7; EC: '10- 1; WI: '05- 5; CCp: '10- 3. German champion 2010.
Progress at LJ: 2001- 7.15, 2002- 7.55, 2004- 7.83, 2005- 7.64i, 2006- 7.90, 2007- 8.19, 2008- 7.80, 2009- 8.18, 2010- 8.47, 2011- 8.26/8.38w. pbs: 60m 6.86i '06, 100m 10.68 '06, 200m 21.90 '06. Tied pb of 8.27 in qualifying, then 8.47 in final of Europeans 2010.

Raúl SPANK b. 13 Jul 1988 Dresden 1.90m 75kg. Dresdner SC. Economics student.
At HJ: OG: '08- 5; WCh: '09- 3=, '11- 9; WJ: '06- 5; WY: '05- 7; EJ: '07- 2; WI: '12- 9=; EI: '09- 7, '11- 8; ET: '11- 3+; German champion 2008, 2010-11.
Progress at HJ: 2003- 1.88, 2004- 2.02, 2005- 2.12, 2006- 2.23, 2007- 2.24, 2008- 2.32, 2009- 2.33, 2010- 2.30, 2011- 2.32, 2012- 5.92i. pbs: 200m 22.02i '08, 60mh 8.00i '12, LJ 7.36i '11, TJ 15.82i '11.

David STORL b. 21 Jul 1990 Rochlitz 1.99m 115kg. LAC Erdgas Chemnitz.
At SP: WCh: '09- dnq 28. '11- 1; EC: '10- 5; WJ: '08- 1; WY: '07- 1; EU23: '11- 1; EJ: '09- 1; WI: '10- 7, '12- 2; EI: '11- 2; ET: '11- 1. German champion 2011.   World junior shot record and three with 6kg (to 22.73) 2009.
Progress at SP: 2008- 18.46, 2009- 20.43, 2010- 20.77, 2011- 21.78, 2012- 21.88i.

Martin WIERIG b. 10 Jun 1987 Beckendorf-Neindorf 2.02m 108kg. SC Magdeburg.
At DT: WCh: '11- dnq 19; EC: '10- 7; WJ: '04- 8, '06- 3; EU23: '07- 1, '09- 3; EJ: '05- 3 (dnq SP).
Progress at DT: 2005- 57.44, 2006- 57.37, 2007- 61.10, 2008- 63.09, 2009- 63.90, 2010- 64.93, 2011- 67.21. pb SP 17.30 '11.

Till WÖSCHLER b. 9 Jun 1991 Dudweiler 1.96m 110kg. LAZ Zweibrücken.
At JT: WJ: '10- 1; EU23: '11- 1; EJ: '09- 2.
Progress at JT: 2008- 66.21, 2009- 74.71, 2010- 82.52, 2011- 84.38.

Women

Anna BATTKE b. 3 Jan 1985 Düsseldorf 1.73m 58kg. USC Mainz.
At PV: WCh: '09- 7=; EU23: '07- 3; EI: '09- 3; WI: '08- 8.
Progress at PV: 2004- 4.00, 2005- 4.20, 2006- 4.20, 2007- 4.56, 2008- 4.50i/4.40, 2009- 4.68, 2010- 4.60, 2011- 4.51i/4.50.
Twin sister Sara ran 200m pb 23.73 in heats of World Juniors 2004.

Ariane FRIEDRICH b. 10 Jan 1984 Nordhausen/Harz 1.79m 57kg. LG Eintracht Frankfurt.
At HJ: OG: '08- 7=; WCh: '09- 3; EC: '10- 3; EU23: '05- 3; EJ: '03- 1; WI: '08- 8=; EI: '09- 1; ECp: 04-08-09-10: 3/1/1/3; WUG: '05-07-09: 3/2/1. German champion 2008-10.
German high jump record 2009.
Progress at PV: 1998- 1.62, 1999- 1.68, 2000- 1.73, 2001- 1.81, 2002- 1.86, 2003- 1.88, 2004- 1.92, 2005- 1.90, 2006- 1.91, 2007- 1.94, 2008- 2.03, 2009- 2.06, 2010- 2.02.
Missed the 2011 season after surgery to repair a ruptured Achilles tendon.

Kristina GADSCHIEW b. 3 Jul 1984 Vassil-yevka, Russia 1.70m 62kg. LAZ Zweibrücken.
At PV: WCh: '09- 10, '11- 10=; WUG: '07- 2, '09- 3; WI: '10- 7; EI: '09- 5, '11- 3.
Progress at PV: 1999- 3.50, 2000- 3.65, 2001-

3.90i/3.70, 2005- 4.22, 2006- 4.35, 2007- 4.40, 2008-
4.52, 2009- 4.58, 2010- 4.60, 2011- 4.66i/4.60.
Moved to Germany as a child.

Betty HEIDLER b. 14 Oct 1983 Berlin 1.75m
80kg. LG Eintracht Frankfurt. Policewoman.
At HT: OG: '04- 4, '08- 9; WCh: '03-05-07-09-11: 11/
dnq 29/1/2/2; EC: '06- 5, '10- 1; EU23: '03- 4, '05-
2; WJ: '00/02- dnq 19/17; EJ: '01- 9, WUG: '09- 1;
CCp: '10- 4; ECp: '04-07-09-10-11: 3/1/2/1/1.
Won WAF 2006, 2009; German 2005-11.
World hammer record 2011, seven German
records 2004-11.
Progress at HT: 1999- 42.07, 2000- 56.02, 2001-
60.54, 2002- 63.38, 2003- 70.42, 2004- 72.73, 2005-
72.19, 2006- 76.55, 2007- 75.77, 2008- 74.11, 2009-
77.12, 2010- 76.38, 2011- 79.42.

Carolin HINGST b. 18 Sep 1980 Donauwörth
1.74m 60kg. USC Mainz.
At PV: OG: '04- dnq 22=, '08- 6; WCh: '01-03-05-
07: 10/dnq 15=/10/dnq 17=; EC: '02- dnq 13=,
'10- 11; EU23: '01- 3; WI: '04- dnq 9; EI: '05- 4;
ECp: '05- 2; German champion 2004, 2008.
Progress at PV: 1999- 3.60, 2000- 4.01, 2001- 4.50,
2002- 4.50, 2003- 4.51, 2004- 4.66, 2005- 4.65i/4.50,
2006- 4.52, 2007- 4.70i/4.61, 2008- 4.65, 2009-
4.60i/4.53, 2010- 4.72, 2011- 4.65. pbs: 100mh
14.54 '98, HJ 1.75 '98, LJ 5.81 '98.

Kathrin KLAAS b. 6 Feb 1984 Haiger 1.68m
72kg. LG Eintracht Frankfurt.
At HT: OG: '08- dnq 24; WCh: '05- dnq, '07- dnq
27, '09- 4, '11- 7; EC: '06- 6, '10- dnq 15; EJ: '03-8,
EU23: '05- 4; WUG: '09- 3.
Progress at HT: 2000- 44.24, 2001- 50.10, 2002-
57.74, 2003- 63.72, 2004- 68.01, 2005- 70.91, 2006-
71.67, 2007- 73.45, 2008- 70.39, 2009- 74.23, 2010-
74.53, 2011- 75.48.

Nadine KLEINERT b. 20 Oct 1975 Magdeburg
1.90m 90kg. SC Magdeburg. Soldier.
At SP: OG: '00- 8, '04- 2, '08- 7; WCh: '97- 99-01-03-
05-07-09-11: 7/2/2/7/5/3/2/8; EC: '98-02-06-10:
6/6/6/7; WJ: '92- 12, '94- 6; EU23: '94- 3Cp, '97- 1;
EJ: '93- 2; WI: '99-01-04-06-10-12: 5/4/3/2/5/5; EI:
'96-98-00: 5/5/2; ECp: '99-01-04-05-09-11:
2/1/3/2/1/1. Won GP 1999. German champion
1998, 2000-01, 2005, 2008, 2010.
Progress at SP: 1990- 13.85, 1991- 15.08, 1992-
16.32, 1993- 17.07, 1994- 17.44, 1995- 17.13, 1996-
18.37, 1997- 18.91, 1998- 19.22, 1999- 19.61, 2000-
19.81, 2001- 19.86, 2002- 19.24, 2003- 19.33i/19.14,
2004- 19.55, 2005- 20.06, 2006- 19.64i/19.15,
2007- 19.77, 2008- 19.89, 2009- 20.20, 2010- 19.64,
2011- 19.26, 2012- 19.33i. pb DT 50.99 '01.
Made all 23 major World and European finals
she contested 1997-2012.

Irina MIKITENKO b. 23 Aug 1972 Bakanas,
Kazakhstan 1.58m 49kg. née Volynskaya. TV
Wattenscheid 01.
At 5000m: OG: '96- h, '00- 5, '04- 7; WCh: '99- 4,
'01- 5, '03- h; ECp: '99-00: 2/2. At 10000m: EC:
'98- 8, '06- 9; WCp: '98- 5. 3rd GP 3000m 1999.

World 4k CC: '00- 19. Won Central Asian 1500m
1995; German 10000m 1998, 2006, 2008; 5000m
1999-2000, 2006.
W35 marathon best 2008, German records
3000m 2000, 5000m (3) 1999, marathon 2008.
Progress at 5000m, 10000m, Mar: 1995- 15:47.85,
1996- 15:49.59, 1997- 15:48.29, 1998- 15:18.86,
32:10.61; 1999- 14:42.03, 31:38.68; 2000- 14:43.59;
2001- 14:53.00, 31:29.55; 2003- 14:56.64, 31:38.48;
2004- 14:55.43, 32:04.86; 2006- 15:28.00, 31:44.82;
2007- 32:42.95, 2:24:51; 2008- 31:57.71, 2:19:19;
2009- 2:22:11, 2010- 32:48.69, 2:26:40; 2011- 2:22:18.
pbs: 800m 2:09.97 '98, 1500m 4:06.08 '01, 2000m
5:40.6 '01, 3000m 8:30.39 '00, Road: 10km 30:57
'08, HMar 68:51 '08, 25km 1:23:08 '08, 30km
1:39:36 '08.
Made fine marathon debut with 2nd Berlin 2007
and in 2008 won London in pb 2:24:14, improving by 4:55 when she won in Berlin. Won again
in London and 2nd Chicago 2009. She won the
Marathon Majors prize for 2007-08 and 2008-09.
2nd Berlin 2011. German parents; changed
nationality from Kazakhstan to Germany in
March 1998. Her husband Alexander had 5000m
pb of 13:39.95 (1994); son Alexander, and daughter Vanessa (born in July 2005). Her father-in-
law Leonid Mikitenko won the 1966 European
bronze medal at 10,000m with pbs 13.36.4 for
5000m, 28:12.4 at 10,000m.

Katharina MOLITOR b. 8 Nov 1983 Bedurg,
Erft 1.82m 76kg. TSV Bayer 04 Leverkusen.
At JT: OG: '08- 8; WCh: '11- 5; EC: '10- 4; EU23:
'05- 2; WUG: '07- 6, '08- 4. Won GER 2010.
Progress at JT: 2000- 42.94, 2001- 48.53, 2002-
49.01, 2003- 48.03, 2004- 50.04, 2005- 57.01, 2006-
57.58, 2007- 58.87, 2008- 61.74, 2009- 62.69, 2010-
64.53, 2011- 64.67.

Nadine MÜLLER b. 21 Nov 1985 Leipzig 1.92m
95kg. Hallesche LA-Freunde.
At DT: WCh: '07- dnq 23, '09- 6, '11- 2; EC: '10- 8;
WJ: '04- 3; EU23: '05- 10, '07- 8; EJ: '03- 2; ET:
'10- 1. German champion 2010-11.
Progress at DT: 2000- 36.10, 2001- 46,27, 2002-
48.90, 2003- 53.44, 2004- 57.85, 2005- 59.35, 2006-
58.46, 2007- 62.93, 2008- 61.36, 2009- 63.46, 2010-
67.78, 2011- 66.99, 2012- 68.89.

Carolin NYTRA b. 26 Feb 1985 Hamburg 1.75m
62kg. MTG Mannheim. Sports management
student.
At 100mh: OG: '08- sf; WCh: '09- sf; EC: '10- 3;
WJ: '04- 6; EU23: '05- 6, '07- 6; ET: '10- 2. German
champion 2008-10. At 60mh: EI: '11- 1.
Progress at 100mh: 2002- 13.91, 2003- 14.36,
2004- 13.54, 2005- 13.28, 2006- 13.32, 2007- 13.17,
2008- 12.82, 2009- 12.78, 2010- 12.57. pbs: 60m
7.50i '10, 100m 11.96 '07, 60mh 7.80i '11. LJ
6.04i/5.89 '05. Injured in 2011.

Christina OBERGFÖLL b. 22 Aug 1981 Lahr
(Baden) 1.75m 79kg. LG Offenburg. Student.
At JT: OG: '04- dnq 15, '08- 3; WCh: '05-07-09-11:

2/2/5/4; EC: '06- 4, '10- 2; EU23: '01- 9, '03- 8; WJ: '00- 8; ECp: '07-09-10-11: 1/1/1/1. German champion 2007-08, 2011.
European javelin records 2005 & 2007.
Progress at JT: 1997- 49.20, 1998- 48.52, new: 1999- 50.57, 2000- 54.50, 2001- 56.83, 2002- 60.61, 2003- 57.40, 2004- 63.34, 2005- 70.03, 2006- 66.91, 2007- 70.20, 2008- 69.81, 2009- 68.59, 2010- 68.63, 2011- 69.57.
Made a great breakthrough at the 2005 World Champs to take her pb from 64.59 to a European record 70.03 and the silver medal.

Jennifer OESER b. 29 Nov 1983 Brunsbüttel 1.76m 65kg. TSV Bayer 04 Leverkusen. Policewoman.
At Hep: OG: '08- 11; WCh: '07- 7, '09- 2, '11- 3; EC: '06- 4, '10- 3; WJ: '02- 8; EU23: '03- 1. German champion 2006.
Progress at Hep: 2000- 5167, 2001- 5531, 2002- 5595, 2003- 5901, 2004- 5936, 2005- 5637, 2006- 6376, 2007- 6378, 2008- 6436, 2009- 6493, 2010- 6683, 2011- 6663. pbs: 200m 23.95 '11, 800m 2:11.33 '08, 60mh 8.56i '09, 100mh 13.14 '11, HJ 1.86 '06, LJ 6.68 '10, 6.70w '11; SP 14.29 '09, JT 51.30 '11, Pen 4423i '09.
Four pbs in EC Heptathlon bronze 2010.

Elisaveta '**Lisa**' **RYZIH** b. 27 Sep 1988 Omsk, Russia 1.79m 58kg. Formerly Ryshich. ABC Ludwigshafen.
At PV: EC: '10- 3; WJ: '04- 1, '06- nh; WY: '03- 1; EU23: '09- 1; EJ: '07- 4; EI: '11- 7; CCp: '10- 2.
Progress at PV: 2002- 3.92, 2003- 4.10, 2004- 4.30, 2005- 4.15, 2006- 4.35, 2007- 4.35, 2008- 4.52i/4.50, 2009- 4.50, 2010- 4.65, 2011- 4.65i. pb LJ 5.38w '06.
Set world age bests at 13 in 2002 and 15 in 2004. Her sister 'Nastja' was World Indoor champion in 1999 and set four world junior and five European junior PV records in 1996 to 4.15, and three German records in 1999 to 4.50i/4.44 and had a pb of 4.63 in 2006. Their family left Omsk in Siberia in 1992 to live in Ulm; the mother Yekaterina Ryzhikh (née Yefimova b. 20 Jan 1959) had HJ pb 1.91i '85 and 1.89 '81, and father, Vladimir, is a pole vault coach.

Verena SAILER b. 16 Oct 1985 Illertissen 1.66m 57kg. MTG Mannheim
At 100m: OG: '08- 5R; WCh: '07- qf, '09- sf/3R; EC: '06- sf, '10- 1; WJ: '04- 5; EU23: '05- 3, '07- 1; EJ: '03- 6; CCp: '10- 4; ECp: '07- 2. At 60m: EI: '09- 3. German champion 2006-10.
Progress at 100m: 2001- 12.13, 2002- 11.88, 2003- 11.58, 2004- 11.49. 2005- 11.51, 2006- 11.43, 2007- 11.31, 2008- 11.28, 2009- 11.18/11.11w, 2010- 11.10/11.06w, 2011- 11.63/11.46w. pbs: 60m 7.15i '12, 200m 24.01 '06. Former gymnast.

Christina SCHWANITZ b. 24 Dec 1985 Dresden 1.80m 103kg. LV 90 Thum.
At SP: OG: '08- 11; WCh: '05- 9, '09- 12, '11- 12; WJ: '04- 3; EU23: '05- 2; WI: '08- 6; EI: '11- 2; ECp: '08- 1. German champion 2011.
Progress at SP: 2001- 13.57, 2002- 14.26, 2003- 15.25, 2004- 16.98, 2005- 18.84, 2007- 17.06, 2008- 19.68i/19.31, 2009- 19.06, 2010- 18.28, 2011- 19.20. pb DT 47.27 '03.

Lilli SCHWARZKOPF b. 28 Aug 1983 Novo Pokrovka, Kyrgyzhstan 1.74m 65kg. LG Rhein-Wied. Student.
At Hep: OG: '08- 8; WCh: '05-07-09-11: 13/5/dnf/6; EC: '06- 3; WJ: '02- 5; EU23: '05- 2. German champion 2004.
Progress at Hep: 2001- 5079, 2002- 5597, 2003- 5735, 2004- 6161, 2005- 6146, 2006- 6420, 2007- 6439, 2008- 6536, 2009- 6355, 2010- 6386, 2011- 6370. pbs: 100m 12.22 '10, 200m 24.72 '11, 800m 2:09.63 '06, 60mh 8.46i '10, 100mh 13.32 '11, HJ 1.83 '07, LJ 6.35i/6.34 '07, SP 14.89 '11, JT 55.25 '09, Pen 4641i '08.
Has lived in Germany from age 7.

Melanie SEEGER b. 8 Jan 1977 Brandenburg an der Havel 1.69m 55kg. SC Potsdam.
At 20kmW: OG: '04- 5, '08- 22; WCh: '99-01-03-05-07-11: 33/7/8/11/14/dnf; EC: '02-06-10: 14/10/4; EU23: '99- 3. At 5000mW: WJ: '96- 4; EJ: '95- 4. At 10000mW: EC: '98- dnf; EU23: '97- 8. Won GER 5000mW 2001-04, 10000mW 2008, 20kmW 2001-03.
Four German records 20km walk 2001-04.
Progress at 20kmW: 1999- 1:34:17, 2000- 1:32:10, 2001- 1:30:41, 2002- 1:31:08, 2003- 1:29:44, 2004- 1:28:17, 2005- 1:30:21, 2006- 1:29:15, 2007- 1:29:32, 2008- 1:30:08, 2010- 1:29:20, 2011- 1:29:20. pbs: 3000mW 11:50.48i '04, 12:56.0 '00; 5000mW 20:18.87i '04, 20:56.19 '03; 10000mW 46:19.21 '98, 10kmW 42:36 '10.
Daughter Helena born 29 Jun 2009.

Silke SPIEGELBURG b. 17 Mar 1986 Georgsmarienhütte 1.73m 64kg. TSV Bayer 04 Leverkusen. Economics student.
At PV: OG: '04- 13, '08- 7; WCh: '07- nh, '09- 4, '11- 9; EC: '06- 6, '10- 2; WJ: '02- 8; WY: '01- 1; EU23: '07- 4; EJ: '03- 1, '05- 1; WI: '06- 8, '12- 4; EI: '07-09-11: 5/2/2; ECp: '08-09-10-11: 3/3/2/2; Won WAF 2008, German 2005-10.
World junior pole vault record 2005.
Progress at PV: 1998- 2.75, 1999- 3.30, 2000- 3.75, 2001- 4.00, 2002- 4.20, 2003- 4.20i/4.15, 2004- 4.40, 2005- 4.48i/4.42, 2006- 4.56, 2007- 4.60, 2008- 4.70, 2009- 4.75i/4.70, 2010- 4.71, 2011- 4.76i/4.75, 2012- 4.77i.
Brothers: Henrik pb 4.80, Christian (b. 15 Apr 1976) 5.51 '98; **Richard** (b. 12 Aug 1977) has PV pb 5.85 '01; 6= WCh 01, 1 WUG 99;

Linda STAHL b. 2 Oct 1985 Steinheim 1.75m 72kg. TSV Bayer 04 Leverkusen. Medical student.
At JT: WCh: '07- 8, '09- 6, '11- dns; EC: '10- 1; EU23: '07- 1; CCp: '10- 4.
Progress at JT: 2000- 42.94, 2001- 43.96, 2002- 47.23, 2003- 47.32, 2004- 50.11, 2005- 53.94, 2006-

57.17, 2007- 62.80, 2008- 66.06, 2009- 63.86, 2010-
66.81, 2011- 60.78. pb SP 13.91i '06.

Martina STRUTZ b. 4 Nov 1981 Schwerin
1.60m 57kg. SC Neubrandenburg.
At PV: EC: '06- 5; WJ: '00- 5; E23: '01- 4, '03- 9=;
WCp: '06- 4. German champion 2011.
Two German pole vault records 2011.
Progress at PV: 1996- 3.30, 1997- 3.60i/3.50, 1998-
3.80, 1999- 4.10, 2000- 4.20, 2001- 4.42, 2002- 4.30,
2003- 4.20, 2004- 4.31, 2005- 4.40i/4.35, 2006- 4.50,
2007- 4.45, 2008- 4.52, 2009- 4.40, 2010- 4.30, 2011-
4.80.

GHANA

Governing body: Ghana Athletics Association,
National Sports Council, PO Box 1272, Accra.
Founded 1944.

Ignisious GAISAH b. 20 Jun 1983 1.86m 70kg.
Formerly known as Anthony Essuman. Lives in
the Netherlands.
At LJ: OG: '04- 6; WCh: '03- 4, '05- 2, '11- dnq 17;
CG: '06- 1, '10- 3; AfG: '03- 1, '11- 2; AfCh: '06- 1;
WI: '06-10-12: 1/7/7; WCp: '06- 4. Won WAF 2004
Nine Ghana long jump records 2003-06, African
junior record 2002, indoor record 2006.
Progress at LJ: 1998- 7.35, 1999- 7.42, 2000- 7.40,
2002- 8.12, 2003- 8.30, 2004- 8.32, 2005- 8.34,
2006- 8.43/8.51w, 2007- 8.08, 2008- 7.78i, 2009-
7.78, 2010- 8.12, 2011- 8.26. pb 100m 11.04 09.
After injury had to switch his take-off leg.

Women

Margaret Esi **SIMPSON** b. 31 Dec 1981 Kumase
1.62m 53kg.
At Hep: OG: '04- 9; WCh: '01-03-05-07-11: 13/
dnf/3/dnf/14; CG: '02- 3, '10- dnf; WJ: '00- dnf;
AfG: '03-07-11: 1/1/1; AfCh: '00-02-04-10:
5/1/1/1. Won Af-J 1999. At HJ: CCp: '10- 8.
African heptathlon record 2005, Ghana records
at HJ, JT and eight heptathlon 1999-2004.
Progress at Hep: 1999- 5366, 2000- 5543, 2001-
5836, 2002- 6105w/6004, 2003- 6152, 2004- 6306,
2005- 6423, 2007- 6278, 2009- 5872, 2010- 6031A,
2011- 6270w/6183. pbs: 200m 24.38 '07, 800m
2:17.02 '05, 100mh 13.41 '05, HJ 1.85 '05, LJ 6.32
'05, SP 13.33 '05, JT 56.36 '05, Dec 6915 '07.
Child born July 2006.

GREECE

Governing body: Hellenic Amateur Athletic
Association (SEGAS), 137 Siggroú Avenue, 171
21 Nea Smirni, Athens. Founded 1897.
National Championships first held in 1896 (men),
1930 (women). **2011 Champions**: 100m/200m:
Likoúrgos-Stéfanos Tsákonas 10.37/20.89, 400m:
Dimítrios Grávalos 46.77, 800m/1500m: Andréas
Dimitrákis 1:48.60/3:49.99, 5000m/10000m: Dimos
Maggínas 16:38.19/30:35.65, Mar: Dimítrios
Theodorakákos 2:24:10, 3000mSt: Yeóryios Dialektós
9:17.26, 110mh: Konstadínos Douvalídis 13.61,
400mh: Periklís Iakovákis 51.27, HJ: Konstadínos

Baniótis 2.20, PV: Konstadínos Filippídis 5.73, LJ:
Loúis Tsátoumas 8.18, TJ: Nikólaos Lagós 16.31, SP:
Mihaíl Stamatóyiannis 19.90, DT: Yeóryios Trémos
56.75, HT: Aléxandros Papadimitríou 74.01, JT:
Yervásios Filippídis 80.01, Dec: Andréas Tsoúkalis
7501, 20kW: Aléxandros Papamihaiíl 1:27:58, 50kW:
Vasílios Hrisikós 4:17:59. **Women**: 100m: Yeoryía
Koklóni 11.61, 200m/400m: Agní Derveni
24.36/52.47, 800m: Eléni Filándra 2:03.38,
1500m/5000m: Anastasía Karakatsáni 4:20.17/
16:38.19, 10000m: Konstadína Kefalá 33:57.89, Mar:
Sofía Ríga 2:45:43, 3000mSt: Iríni Kokkinaríou
9:55.58, 100mh: Olibía Petsoúdi 13.62, 400mh:
Hristína Hantzí-Neag 59.50, HJ: Adonía Steryíou
1.85, PV: Nikoléta Kiriakopoúlou 4.70, LJ/TJ:
Paraskeví Papahrístou 6.50/14.56, SP: Hrisí
Moisídou 15.45, DT: Hrisoúla Anagnostopoúlou
53.68, HT: Aléxandra Papayeoryíou 70.54, JT: Sávva
Líka 56.96, Hep: Efthimía Kolokithá 5223, 20kW:
Panayióta Tsinopoúlou 1:47:09.

Konstadínos BANIÓTIS b. 6 Nov 1986
Komotini, Rhodope 2.02m 80kg.
At HJ: OG: '08- dnq 37=; WCh: '09/11- dnq
16/15=; EC: '10- 8; WJ: '06- 6; WI: '12- 4=; EU23:
'07- 12; EI: '09- 6, '11- 4.
Progress at HJ: 2005- 2.07, 2006- 2.17, 2007- 2.23,
2008- 2.27, 2009- 2.28, 2010- 2.29i/2.28, 2011-
2.32i/2.28, 2012- 2.31i.

Konstadínos FILIPÍDDIS b. 26 Nov 1986
Athens 1.88m 73kg. Panellínios YS Athens.
Student of Economics at University of Athens.
At PV: WCh: '05- dnq 14=, '09- dnq 17, '11- 6;
EC: '06-10: dnq 26/21=; WJ: '04- 4; WY: '03- 4;
EJ: '05- 2; WI: '10- 4=, '12- 7; WUG: '05- 2; ET:
'09- 4; Won MedG 2005; Greek champion 2005,
2007, 2009-11.
Six Greek pole vault records 2005-11.
Progress at PV: 2001- 3.70, 2002- 4.80, 2003- 5.22,
2004- 5.50, 2005- 5.75, 2006- 5.55, 2007-
5.35i/5.30/5.40dq, 2009- 5.65, 2010- 5.70i/5.55,
2011- 5.75, 2012- 5.75i. Two-year drugs ban
from positive test on 16 June 2007.

Dimiítrios HONDROKOÚKIS b. 26 Jan 1988
Marousi 1.93m 73kg. Student of computer science at Piraeus University.
At HJ: WCh: '11- 5= WJ: '06- 6; WY: '05- 12; EJ:
'07- 4; EU23: '09- 12; WI: '12- 1; EI: '11- 5.
Progress at HJ: 2004- 1.95, 2005- 2.11, 2006- 2.21,
2007- 2.24, 2009- 2.22i/2.18, 2010- 2.23, 2011-
2.32. Father/coach Kiríakos had HJ pb 2.09 '77.

Loúis TSÁTOUMAS b. 12 Feb 1982 Messíni
1.87m 76kg. Olympiakós SF Piraeus.
At LJ: OG: '04- dnq 22, '08- nj; WCh: '03- 12, '09-
11, '11- dnq 14; EC: '06- 8, '10- 6; WJ: '00- dnq 21;
WY: '99- 4; EU23: '03- 1; EJ: '01- 1; WI: '06- 4,
'12- 6; EI: '07- 2; WCp: '06- nj; ECp: '03-07-08-09:
1/1/1/3; Greek champion 2003-08, 2010-11.
Greek long jump record 2007.
Progress at LJ: 1996- 6.56, 1997- 7.07, 1998-
7.41/7.43w, 1999- 7.64, 2000- 7.52, 2001-

7.93/7.98w, 2002- 8.17, 2003- 8.34, 2004-
8.19/8.37w, 2005- 8.15i/8.14, 2006- 8.30, 2007-
8.66 (best outdoors by European at sea-level),
2008- 8.44, 2009- 8.21, 2010- 8.09/8.17w, 2011-
8.26. pb 200m 22.3 '98.

Women

Nikoléta KIRIAKOPOÚLOU b. 21 Mar 1986
Athens 1.67m 56kg.
At PV: OG: '08- dnq 27=; WCh: '09- dnq 19, '11-
8; EC: '10- dnq 13; WJ: '04- 6; EJ: '05- 7. Balkan
champion 2008, Med G 2009, Greek 2009, 2011.
Five Greek pole vault records 2010-11.
Progress at PV: 2003- 3.70, 2004- 4.00, 2005- 4.10,
2006- 3.60, 2007- 4.00i/3.90, 2008- 4.45, 2009-
4.50, 2010- 4.55, 2011- 4.71.

Paraskeví PAPAHRÍSTOU b. 17 Apr 1989
1.70m 53kg.
At TJ: WCh: '09/11- dnq 29/16; WJ: '08- 3;
EU23: '09/11- 1. Won Greek LJ 2011, TJ 2009,
2011.
Progress at LJ: 2005- 12.75, 2006- 12.81/13.13w,
2007- 12.98i/12.92, 2008- 13.86i/13.79/13.94w,
2009- 14.47i/14.35, 2010- 13.94i/13.85, 2011-
14.72. pb LJ 6.55 '11.

GRENADA

Governing body: Grenada Athletic Assocation,
PO Box 419, St George's. Founded 1924.

Rondell BARTHOLOMEW b. 7 Apr 1990 St
Patrick 1.92m 79kg. South Plains College, USA.
At (200m)/400m: WCh: '11- 6; WJ: '08- sf; WI:
'12- 6.
Progress at 400m: 2008- 46.86, 2009- 45.58, 2010-
45.28, 2011- 44.65. pbs: 100m 10.42A '11, 200m
20.95 '10, 20.48w '10; 600y 1:09.45i '10, 600m
1:18.10i '11, 800m 1:51.25 '11.

Kirani JAMES b. 1 Sep 1992 St George's 1.85m
74kg. Student at University of Alabama, USA
At (200m)/400m: WCh: '11- 1; WJ: '08- 2, '10- 1;
WY: '07- 2, '09- 1/1. Won PAm-J 400m 2009,
200m 2011; NCAA 2010-11.
Indoor 400m records: CAC & Commonwealth
2010 (45.24) & 2011, World Junior (44.80) 2011.
GRN 200m record 2011.
Progress at 400m: 2007- 46.96, 2008- 45.70, 2009-
45.24, 2010- 45.01, 2011- 44.61. pb 200m
20.41A/20.53w '11, 20.76 '10.
In 2011 he became the youngest ever World or
Olympic champion at 400m. In January 2012 the
'Kirani James Boulevard' was opened in the
Grenadan capital St.George.

HUNGARY

Governing body: Magyar Atlétikai Szövetség,
1146 Budapest, Istvánmezei út 1-3. Fd. 1897.
National Championships first held in 1896
(men), 1932 (women). **2011 Champions. Men**:
100m: Dániel Karlik 10.71, 200m: Tibor Kása
21.31, 400m: Marcell Deák Nagy 46.41, 800m:
Tamás Kazi 1:48.01; 1500: Péter Szemeti 3:48.08,

5000m/3000mSt: László Tóth 14:25.46/8:36.94,
10000m: Barnabás Bene 29:09.02, HMar: Tamás
Kovács 66:04, Mar: Gábor Józsa 2:27:49, 110mh:
Balázs Baji 14.22, 400mh: Tibor Koroknai 51.27,
HJ: Olivér Harsányi 2.13, PV: Peter Skoumal
5.00, LJ: Bence Bánhidi 7.81, TJ: Stavros Georgiou
15.95, SP: Lajos Kürthy 19.51, DT: Zoltán Kővágó
67.17, HT: Krisztián Pars 80.63, JT: Krisztián
Török 78.51, Dec: Attila Szabó 7362, 20kW: Máté
Helebrandt 1:27:07, 50kW: Róbert Tubak 4:22:32.
Women: 100m/200m: Anasztázia Nguyen
11.83/24.14, 400m: Barbara Petráhn 53.56, 800m:
Zsanett Kenesei 2:18.21, 1500m/5000m: Krisztina
Papp 4:19.55/16:24.98, 10000m: Réka Czebei
35:06.86, HMar: Anikó Kálovics 75:04, Mar:
Judit Földing-Nagy 2:54:47, 3000mSt: Zsófia
Erdélyi 10:27.84, 100mh: Petra Munkácsy 13.95,
400mh: Lilla Loránd 61.59, HJ/TJ: Rita Babos
1.81/13.50, PV: Enikö Erös 3.90, LJ: Xénia
Krizsán 6.25w, SP/DT: Anita Márton
16.70/50.77, HT: Éva Orbán 70.71, JT: Vanda
Juhász 58.03, Hep: Györgyi Farkas 6059, 20kW:
Viktória Madarász 1:36:22.

Róbert FAZEKAS b. 18 Aug 1975 Szombathely
1.93m 110kg. Haladás VSE.
At DT: OG: '00- dnq 16, '04- dq (1), '08- 8; WCh:
'99- 11, '01- dnq 26, '03- 2, '11- dnq; EC: '98- 4,
'02- 1, '10- 3; EU23: '97- 6; WJ: '94- 6 (dnq 18 HT);
WCp: '02- 1; ECp: '00- 2. HUN champion 1998,
2000, 2002-03.
Three Hungarian discus records 2002.
Progress at DT: 1992- 40.08, 1993- 53.48, 1994-
58.00, 1995- 60.34, 1996- 55.08, 1997- 59.32, 1998-
66.61, 1999- 64.92, 2000- 66.11, 2001- 68.09, 2002-
71.70, 2003- 70.78, 2004- 70.83/70.93dq, 2007-
58.32, 2008- 64.56, 2010- 66.43, 2011- 64.30. pbs:
SP 14.07 '02, HT 75.33 '98.
His 71.25 at the 2002 World Cup was the longest
ever discus throw at a major international event.
Two-year drugs ban after attempts to cheat the
test following his Olympic 'win' in 2004.

Zoltán KÖVÁGÓ b. 10 Apr 1979 Szolnok 2.04m
127kg. Budapesti Honvéd SE. Army lieutenant.
At DT: OG: '00- dnq, '04- 2, '08- dnq 21; WCh:
'01-03-05-07-09-11: dnq 20/dnq 19/10/9/6/dnq
15; EC: '02- 7, '10- dnq 21; WJ: '96- 4, '98- 1; EJ:
'97- 3; EU23: '99- 6, '01- 1. HUN champion 2001,
2004-05, 2008-11.
Progress at DT: 1995- 49.78, 1996- 59.70, 1997-
62.16, 1998- 60.27, 1999- 63.23, 2000- 66.76, 2001-
66.93, 2002- 65.98, 2003- 66.03, 2004- 68.93, 2005-
66.00, 2006- 69.95, 2007- 66.42, 2008- 68.17, 2009-
67.64, 2010- 69.69, 2011- 69.50. pb SP 15.93 '01.

Krisztián PARS b. 18 Feb 1982 Körmend 1.88m
113kg. Dobó SE.
At HT: OG: '04- 5, '08- 4; WCh: '05-07-09-11:
7/5/4/2; EC: '06- 6, '10- 3; WY: '99- 1; EJ: '01- 1;
EU23: '03- 1. HUN champion 2005-11.
World junior records with 6kg hammer: 80.64 &
81.34 in 2001.
Progress at HT: 1998- 54.00, 1999- 61.92, 2000-

66.80, 2001- 73.09, 2002- 74.18, 2003- 78.81, 2004-
80.90, 2005- 80.03, 2006- 82.45, 2007- 81.40, 2008-
81.96, 2009- 81.43, 2010- 79.64, 2011- 81.89. pbs:
SP 15.60 '05, DT 53.80 '06.

Women

Éva ORBÁN b. 29 Nov 1984 Pápa 1.73m 75kg.
VEDAC. Was at University of Southern California.
At HT: OG: '04/08- dnq 24/34; WCh: '05/09/11:
dnq 21/14/13; EC: '06 dnq 25, '10- 12; WY: '01-
11; EJ: '03- 6; EU23: '05- 11; WUG: '11- 2. HUN
champion 2005-06, 2008-11; NCAA 2008.
Hungarian hammer record 2011.
Progress at HT: 1999- 47.70, 2000- 53.23, 2001-
58.04, 2002- 62.00, 2003- 65.77, 2004- 67.60, 2005-
68.70, 2006- 69.10, 2007- 66.98, 2008- 70.18, 2009-
70.16, 2010- 69.73, 2011- 71.33. pbs: SP 12.93 '05,
DT 45.40 '05.

ICELAND

2011 National champions: Men: 100m: Óli
Tómas Freysson 10.41w, 200m: Svein Elías
Elíasson 22.20, 400m: Trausti Stafánsson 50.16,
800m: Snorri Sigurdsson 1:58.77, 1500m: Sigur–
björn Árni Arngrímsson 4:16.08, 5000m: Kári
Steinn Karlsson 14:48.07, 3000mSt: Hermann
Sæmundsson 13:13.16, 110mh: Sigurdur Lúdvik
Stefánsson 15.76w, 400mh: Björgvin Vikingsson
53.73, HJ: Orn Davidsson 1.93, PV: Bjarki Gíslason
4.52, LJ/TJ: Kristinn Torfason 7.82w/14.00, SP:
Ódinn Björn Thorsteinsson 15.54, DT: Blake
Thomas Jakobsson 50.89, HT: Bergur Ingi Pétursson
70.14, JT: Gudmundur Sverrison 65.48, **Women**:
100m/200m/LJ: Hafdís   Sigurdóttir
11.96w/25.28/5.99w, 400m: Björg Gunnarsdóttir
61.40,   800m/1500m: Anita   Hinríksdóttir
2:12.35/4:56.69, 3000m: Arndis Yr Hafthorsdóttir
10:32.70,   100mh/400mh/HJ: Fjóla   Signy
Hannesdóttir 14.46w/63.14/1.62, PV: Anna Yr
Jónsdóttir 3.32, TJ: Steinunn Arna Atladóttir
10.96, SP: Sandra Pétursdóttir 10.47, DT:
Ragnheidur Anna Thórsdóttir 41.64, HT: Sandra
Pétursdóttir 52.36, JT: Ásdis Hjálmsdóttir 56.56.

INDIA

Governing body: Athletics Federation of India,
Room No. 44, Second Floor, Palika Place,
Panchkuian Road, New Delhi 110001. Founded
1946.
National Championships first held as Indian
Games in 1924. **2011 Champions: Men**: 100m:
B.G. Nagraj 10.67, 200m M.G.Joseph 21.28, 400m:
Kunhu Muhammed 47.09, 800m/1500m: Sajeesh
Joseph 1:50.28/3:54.59, 5000m: Pritam Kumar
14:23.18, 10000m: Suresh Kumar Patel 30:18.16,
3000mSt: Ramadas Ramchandran 8:45.7, 110mh:
Siddhanth Thingaliya 13.77, 400mh: Satender
Singh & Avin A. Thomas 51.49, HJ: Hari Shankar
Roy & C.Nikhil Chittarasu 2.16, PV: K.P.Bimin
4.95, LJ: Ratish Kumar 7.70, TJ: Arpinder Singh
16.63, SP: Om Prakash Singh 19.45, DT: Vipender
Singh 50.52, HT: Harvinder Singh Dagar 63.37,

JT: Rajendra Singh 75.74, Dec: Vijay Kumar
7106, 20000W: Surinder Singh 1:29:03.90.
Women: 100m/200m: Asha Roy 11.85/24.36,
400m: M.R.Poovamma 53.87, 800m: S.R.Bindu
2:08:40, 1500m: Orchatteri P. Jaisha 4:15.88,
5000m: Kavita Raut 16:46.40, 10000m: Preeja
Sreedharan 35:56.09, 3000mSt: *no entries*, 100mh:
M.M.Anchu 13.90, 400mh: Bhupinder Kaur
60.64, HJ: Sahana Kumari 1.83, PV: K.K.Anoosha
3.40, LJ/TJ: Mayookha Johny 6.54/13.71, SP/JT:
Sundaram Saraswati 13.23/49.05, DT: Harwant
Kaur 53.59, HT: Manju Bala Singh 56.71, Hep:
K.D.Sindhu 4958, 20000mW: Khushbir Kaur
1:45:38.18.

IRAN

Governing body: Amateur Athletic Federation
of Islamic Republic of Iran, Shahid Keshvari
Sports Complex, Razaneh Junibi St Mirdamad
Ave, Tehran. Founded 1936.

Ehsan HADADI b. 21 Jan 1985 Ahvaz 1.98m
115kg.
At DT: OG: '08- dnq 17; WCh: '07- 7, '11- 3; WJ:
'04- 1; AsiG: '06- 1, '10- 1; AsiC: '03-05-07-09-11:
8/1/1/1/1; AsiJ: '04- 1; WCp: '06- 2, '10- 3. West
Asian champion 2005.
Eight Asian discus records 2005-08.
Progress at DT: 2002- 53.66, 2003- 54.40, 2004-
54.96, 2005- 65.25, 2006- 63.79, 2007- 67.95, 2008-
69.32, 2009- 66.19, 2010- 68.45, 2011- 66.08. pb SP
17.82i '08, 16.00 '06.

IRELAND

Governing Body: The Athletic Association of
Ireland (AAI), Unit 19, Northwood Court,
Northwood Business Campus, Santry, Dublin 9.
Founded in 1999. Original Irish AAA founded
in 1885.
National Championships first held in 1873.
2011 Champions: Men: 100m: Jason Smyth
10.52, 200m: Paul Hession 20.51, 400m: Brian
Murphy 46.68, 800m: Mark English 1:50.22,
1500m: Paul Robinson 3:50.41, 5000: Alistair
Cragg 13:48.03, 10000m: Mark Kenneally 28:58.39,
HMar: Sean Hehir 65:24, Mar: Sean Connolly
2:18:54, 3000mSt: Tomas Cotter 9:00.90, 110mh:
Ben Reynolds 14.05, 400mh: Thomas Barr 50.06,
HJ: Simon Phelan 2.05, PV: David Donegan 4.70,
LJ: Adam McMullen 7.26, TJ: Eoin Kelly 14.58,
SP: Sean Breathnach 16.24, DT: Tomas Rauktys
LTU 52.06, HT: Conor McCullough 72.67, JT:
Aaron Crawford 63.27, Dec: Patrick Curran 4772,
10000mW: Robert Heffernan 40:12.64, 20kW:
Michael Doyle 1:26:00, 35kW: Colin Griffin 2:15:17
(held in Feb 2012). **Women**: 100m/200m: Amy
Foster 11.69/23.74, 400m: Joanne Cuddihy
52.15, 800m: Siobhan Eviston 2:06.69, 1500m:
Ciara Mageean 4:16.36, 5000m: Lizzie Lee 17:25.10,
HMar: Ava Hutchinson 74:17, Mar: Linda Bryne
2:36:23, 3000mSt: Kerry Harty 10:23.29, 100mh:
Derval O'Rourke 13.24, 400mh: Jessie Barr

577.38, HJ: Deirdre Ryan 1.90, PV: Tori Pena 4.20, LJ/TJ: Mary McLoone 5.82/12.14, SP/DT: Claire Fitzgerald 14.27/50.07, HT: Cara Kennedy 57.62, JT: Anita Fitzgibbon 47.09, Hep: Leona Bryne 4498, 5000mW: Kate Veale 21:30.18, 20kmW: Olive Loughnane 1:31:55.

Robert HEFFERNAN b. 20 Feb 1978 Cork City 1.73m 55kg. Togher AC.
At 20kW/(50kW): OG: '00- 28, '04- dq, '08- 8; WCh: '01-05-07-09: 14/dq/6/15; EC: '02- 8, '10- 4/4; WCp: '08- 9; ECp: '07- 5, '09- 4. At 10000mW: EJ: '97- 14; EU23: '99- 13. Won Irish 10000mW 2001-02, 2004-5, 2007-11; 20kW 2000-02, 2004, 2009; 30kW 2008.
Four Irish 20kW records 2001-08, two 50kW 2010 (first two races).
Progress at 20kW, 50kW: 1999- 1:26:45, 2000- 1:22:43, 2001- 1:21:11, 2002- 1:20:25, 2003- 1:23:03, 2004- 1:20:55, 2005- 1:24:20, 2006- 1:22:24, 2007- 1:20:15, 2008- 1:19:22, 2009- 1:22:09, 2010- 1:20:45, 3:45:30; 2011- 1:20:54, 3:49:28; 2012- 1:20:39. pbs: 3000mW 11:10.02i '02, 11:27.6 '05; 5000mW 18:51.46i '08, 18:59.37 '07; 10000mW 38:27.57 '08, 30kW 2:07:48 '11, 35kW 2:31:19 '00. Married to Marian Andrews (b. 16 Apr 1982, Irish 400m champion 2008-09).

Women

Fionnuala BRITTON b. 24 Sep 1984 Wicklow 1.58m 45kg. Kilcoole.
At 3000mSt: OG: '08- h; WCh: '07- 12, '11- h; EC: '06- h, '10- 11; EU23: 05- 9. Eur CC: '07-09-10-11: 7/11/4/1.
Progress at 3000mSt: 2004- 10:33.10, 2005- 10:06.26, 2006- 9:49.20, 2007- 9:41.36, 2008- 9:43.57, 2009- 9:54.10, 2010- 9:42.49, 2011- 9:37.60. pbs: 1500m 4:18.03 '11, 3000m 9:00.70i, 9:02.11mx '11; 5000m 15:21.45mx, 15:31.26 '11.

Derval O'ROURKE b. 28 May 1981 Cork 1.68m 57kg. Leevale. Graduate of University College Dublin; sports administrator for Dublin City University.
At 100mh: OG: '04/08- h; WCh: '03- h, '05/07/11- sf, '09- 4; EC: '02- h, '06- 2=, '10- 2; WJ: '00- sf; EU23: '01- 7, '03- 4; EJ: '99- sf; WUG: '05- 3; CCp: '10- 5; Irish champion 2001-02, 2004-08, 2010-11. At 60mh: WI: '06- 1; EI: '09- 3, '11- 4. Seven Irish 100mh records 2003-10.
Progress at 100mh: 1998- 14.29/13.88w, 1999- 13.82, 2000- 13.49, 2001- 13.57, 2002- 13.38, 2003- 12.96, 2004- 13.39, 2005- 13.00/12.95w, 2006- 12.72, 2007- 12.88, 2008- 12.90, 2009- 12.67, 2010- 12.65, 2011- 12.84. pbs: 60m 7.59i '05, 100m 11.54 '05, 11.43w '07; 200m 23.71 '10, 50mh 6.80i '06, 60mh 7.84i '06.
Set six Irish records at 60mh from 8.02 to 7.84 to win World Indoor title in 2006.

ISRAEL

Governing body: Israeli Athletic Association, PO Box 24190, Tel Aviv 61241. Founded as Federation for Amateur Sport in Palestine 1931.
National Championships first held in 1935. **2011 Champions**: **Men**: **Men**: 100m: Asaf Malka 10.59, 200m: Omri Harosh 21.80, 400m: Yuriy Shapsai 48.38, 800m: Yimur Getahun 1:51.45, 1500m/5000m: Indalow Takala 3:51.58/13:49.25, 10000m/HMar: Tasama Moogas 28:46.18/63:20 (130m short), Mar: Ayele Setegne 2:18:57, 3000mSt: Noam Ne'eman 9:09.00, 110mh: Anatoliy Minenko 14.85, 400mh: Ilya Eligulashvili 52.69, HJ: Dmitriy Kroyter 2.16, PV: Yevgeniy Olkhovskiy 5.20, LJ/TJ: Yochai Halevi 7.79/16.79, SP: Itamar Levi 15.56, DT: Felix Gromadskiy 54.36, HT: Viktor Zaginaiko 61.13, JT: Assa'el Arad 59.41, Dec: Anatoliy Minenko 6709. **Women**: 100m/200m: Olga Lenskiy 11.91/24.38, 400m: Annastasia Kyrilov 56.37, 800m: Eli Goldfarb 2:17.08, 1500m: Maor Tyuri 4:37.05, 5000m: Mary Elias 17:25.09, 10000m: Ricki Salem 36:50.28, HMar/Mar: Ya'ara Zanggi 1:22:35 (130m short)/2:51:54. 3000mSt: Meigel Attias 10:52.01, 100mh/Hep: Tal Ben-Artzi 15.02/4476, 400mh: Olga Dogadko-Bronstein (11th title) 61.15, HJ: Daniel Frenkel 1.89, PV: Jillian Schwartz 4.24, LJ: Rotem Battat-Golan 6.24, TJ: Niva Ziv 12.92, SP/DT: Annastasia Metskeyev 15.23/50.25, HT: Yevgeniya Zabolotniy 54.63, JT: Dorit Naor 42.80 (15th title).

ITALY

Governing Body: Federazione Italiana di Atletica Leggera (FIDAL), Via Flaminia Nuova 830, 00191 Roma. Constituted 1926. First governing body formed 1896.
National Championships first held in 1897 (one event)/1906 (men), 1927 (women). **2011 Champions**: **Men**: 100m: Matteo Galvan 10.38, 200m: Andrew Howe 20.52, 400m: Marco Vistalli 45.88, 800m: Giordano Benedetti 1:49.26, 1500m: Merihun Crespi 3:47.53, 5000m: Stefano La Rosa 14:02.29, 10000m: Domenico Ricatt 29:51.84, HMar: Francesco Bona 63:52, Mar: Giovanni Gualdi 2:14:01, 3000mSt: Yuri Floriani 8:37.66, 110mh: Emanuele Abate 13.71, 400mh: José de Leon 50.55, HJ: Silvano Chesani 2.28, PV: Sergio D'Orio 5.30, LJ: Stefano Dacastello 7.82, TJ: Fabrizio Donato 17.17, SP: Paolo Dal Soglio 18.58, DT: Giovanni Faloci 59.05, HT: Nicola Vizzoni 76.29, JT: Leonardo Gottardo 75.15, Dec: Paulo Mottadelli 7250, 10000mW: Jean-Jacques Nkouloukidi 39:44.70, 20kW: Marco De Luca 1:28:54, 50kW: Federico Tontodonati 3:55:04. **Women**: 100m: Ilenia Draisci 11.65, 200m: Marzia Caravelli 23.42, 400m: Marta Milani 52.29, 800m: Elisabetta Artuso 2:07.11, 1500m: Elisa Cusma Piccione 4:13.38, 5000m: Silvia Weissteiner 15:48.94, 10000m/HMar: Nadia Ejjafini 32:28.80/68:27, Mar: Martina Celi 2:36:11, 3000mSt: Valentina Costanza 10:05.52, 100mh: Marzia Caravelli 13.05, 400mh: Manuela Gentili 56.69, HJ: Raffaella Lamera 1.88, PV: Anna

Giordano Bruno 4.40, LJ: Tania Vicenzino 6.26, TJ: Simona La Mantia 14.40, SP: Chiara Rosa 17.64, DT: Laura Bordignon 55.47, HT: Silvia Salis 69.57, JT: Zahra Bani 59.92, Hep: Elisa Trevisan 5649, 10000mW/20kW: Federica Ferraro 46:34.85/1:38:08.

Fabrizio DONATO b. 14 Aug 1976 Latina 1.89m 82kg. Fiamme Gialle.
At TJ: OG: '00/04/08- dnq 25/21/21; WCh: '03/07-09: dnq 13/32/41; EC: '02- 4, '06- dnq 16, '10- 9; EJ: '95- 5; WI: '01-08-10-12: 6/4/5/4; EI: '00-02-09-11: 6/4/1/2; ECp: '00-02-03-04-06: 2/2/1/6/1. Won MedG 2001, Italian 2000, 2004, 2006-08, 2010-11. Italian triple jump record 2000. Progress at TJ: 1992- 12.88, 1993- 14.36, 1994- 15.27, 1995- 15.81, 1996- 16.35, 1997- 16.40A, 1998- 16.73, 1999- 16.66i/16.53w, 2000- 17.60, 2001- 17.05, 2002- 17.17, 2003- 17.16, 2004- 16.90, 2005- 16.65/16.68w, 2006- 17.33i/17.24, 2007- 16.97/17.06w, 2008- 17.27i/16.91/17.29w, 2009- 17.59i/15.81, 2010- 17.39i/17.08, 2011- 17.73i/17.17. pb LJ 8.03i '11, 8.00 '06.
Italian indoor record to win 2009 European Indoor title. Married Patrizia Spuri (400m 51.74 '98, 8 EC 98, 800m 1:59.96 '98) on 27 Sep 2003.

Giuseppe GIBILISCO b. 5 Jan 1979 Siracusa, Sicily 1.83m 78kg. Fiamme Gialle.
At PV: OG: '00- 10=, '04- 3, '08- nh; WCh: '01-03-05-09: dnq/1/5=/7=; EC: '02- 10, '06- 7, '10- 4; WJ: '98- 3=; EU23: '99- 9, '01- 3; EJ: '97- nh; WI: '04- 6; ECp: '00-02-03-05-06: 4/2=/2/1/2. Won World Military 2002. Four Italian records 2003. Progress at PV: 1992- 2.40, 1993- 3.50, 1994- 3.80, 1995- 4.80, 1996- 5.05, 1997- 5.30, 1998- 5.30, 1999- 5.60, 2000- 5.70, 2001- 5.60i/5.50, 2002- 5.70, 2003- 5.90, 2004- 5.85, 2005- 5.83, 2006- 5.80, 2007- 5.70, 2008- 5.65, 2009- 5.70, 2010- 5.75, 2011- 5.55/5.60exh.
Set two Italian vault records in 2003 at both Golden Gala (5.77 & 5.82) and World Champs (5.85 & 5.90). He was accused by the Italian Olympic Committee of "the use or attempted use of a banned substance or of a prohibited practice" but although never testing positive was given a 2-year ban by FIDAL in July 2007. He won an appeal but after the ban was reimposed he took the case to the Court of Arbitration for Sport and itwas overturned on 9 May 2008.

Andrew HOWE b. 12 May 1985 Los Angeles, USA 1.84m 73kg. Aeronautica Militare.
At (200m)/LJ: OG: '04- (h), '08- dnq 20; WCh: '05- (qf), '07- 2; EC: '06- 1, '10- 5; WJ: '02- 5 4x100mR, '04- 1/1; WY: '01- 3; WI: '06- 3; EI: '07- 1; WCp: '06- 2; ECp: '06- 1, '08- (8). Won WAF LJ 2007, Italian 200m 2007, 2011; LJ 2007, 2010.
Italian LJ record 2007. European Junior 200m record 2004.
Progress at 200m, LJ: 1998- 5.88, 1999- 6.51, 2000- 7.52, 2001- 20.99/20.91w, 7.61; 2002- 21.15/21.0, 7.38; 2003- 21.03, 7.63i/7.47; 2004- 20.28, 8.11; 2005- 20.52, 8.02; 2006- 8.41, 2007-

20.53, 8.47; 2008- 20.88, 8.16; 2009- 8.02i/7.85, 2010- 8.16, 2011- 20.31, 7.68. pbs: 60m 6.78i '11, 100m 10.27 '06, 10.24w '04; 150m 15.3 '04, 300m 33.7 '04, 400m 45.70 '11, 110mh 14.65 '02, HJ 2.06 '00, TJ 16.27 '02.
Left the USA with his mother Renée Felton (100mh 13.72 '81) at age five in 1990 – she married an Italian, Ugo Besozzi. Andrew set many Italian age group records. From a previous best of 7.61 he set Italian junior LJ records with 7.93, 8.01, 8.04 and 8.07 in 2004. improving to 8.11 to win World Junior gold. He followed this with pbs of 20.86 ind 20.72 plus an amazing European junior record 20.28 to win the 200m. Achilles surgery in September 2009.

Giorgio RUBINO b. 15 Apr 1986 Roma 1.76m 55kg. Fiamme Gialle.
At 20kW: OG: '08- 18; WCh: '07- 5, '09- 4, '11- dq; EC: '06- 8, '10- 5; EU23: '07- dq; ECp: '09- 1, '11- 5. At 10000mW: WJ: '04- 10; WY: '03- 4; EJ: '05- 3. Won Italian 20kW 2005.
Progress at 20kW: 2005- 1:23:58, 2006- 1:22:05, 2007- 1:21:17, 2008- 1:22:11, 2009- 1:19:37, 2010- 1:22:12, 2011- 1:20:44, 2012- 1:20:10. pbs: 5000mW 19:14.33i '08, 19:38.5 '06; 10000mW 39:43.20 '11, 38:00R '10; 35kW 2:36:50 '09.

Alex SCHWAZER b. 26 Dec 1984 Vipiteno (Bolzano) 1.85m 73kg. Carabinieri Bologna.
At 50kW (20kW): OG: '08- 1; WCh: '05- 3, '07- 3 (10), '09- dnf, '11- (9); EC: '06- dnf, '10- dnf (2); EU23: '05- (dnf); WCp: 08- 2; ECp: '05- 6. Won Italian 10000mW 2007, 2010; 20kW 2007-08, 50kW 2005, 2007-08, 2010.
Italian records 50km walk 2005 and 2007, 20k, 30k and 35k 2010, 20k 2012.
Progress at 20kW, 50kW: 2004- 4:00:51, 2005- 1:25:10, 3:41:54; 2006- 1:21:38, 2007- 1:24:39, 3:36:04; 2008- 1:23:28, 3:37:04; 2009- 1:24:23, 2010- 1:18:24, 3:50:22; 2011- 1:21:50, 2012- 1:17:30, 3:40:58. pbs: 3000mW 11:11.3i '10, 11:38.48 '09; 5000mW 18:46.49i '10, 19:38.09 '08; 10000mW 38:50.28 '11, 30kW: 2:05:24 '10, 35kW 2:26:16 '10.
Rapid improvement in 2005 with 3:56:59 in January, 3:49:42 in May and 3:41:54 to win the World bronze medal at the age of 20 in August. Engaged to ice skating European champion Carolina Kostner.

Nicola VIZZONI b. 4 Nov 1973 Pietrasanta, Lucca 1.93m 126kg. Fiamme Gialle.
At HT: OG: '00- 2, '04- 10, '08- dnq 13; WCh: '97- dnq 22, '99- 7, '01- 4, '03/05/07- dnq 15/25/17, '09- 9, '11- 8; EC: '98-02-06-10: dnq 17/dnq 13/9/2; WJ: '92- 5; EJ: '91- 8; WUG: '97- 5, '99- 5, '01- 1; WCp: '10- 4; ECp: '99-01-02-03-04-05-08-09-10: 4/2/7/5/3/4/2/1/1; E23Cp: '92- 5. Won Med G 2009, ITA 1998, 2000-07, 2009-11.
Progress at HT: 1991- 66.62, 1992- 69.32, 1993- 70.76, 1994- 71.78, 1995- 74.48, 1996- 75.30, 1997- 77.10, 1998- 77.89, 1999- 79.59, 2000- 79.64, 2001- 80.50, 2002- 78.80, 2003- 77.69, 2004- 76.95, 2005-

74.82, 2006- 76.89, 2007- 78.21, 2008- 78.79, 2009-79.74, 2010- 79.12, 2011- 80.29.
Left-handed thrower. Engaged to javelin thrower Claudia Coslovich.

Women

Antonietta DI MARTINO b. 1 Jun 1978 Cava de' Tirreni, Salerno 1.69m 58kg. Fiamme Gialle.
At HJ: OG: '08- 10=; WCh: '01-07-09-11: 12/2=/4/3; EC: '06- 10, '10- dnq 13=; WI: '06- 5, '12- 2=; EI: '07- 2, '11- 1; ECp: '01-02-05-08-09-10: 3=/7=/5/2=/3/1. Won MedG 2009, Italian 2000-01, 2006-08, 2010.
Three Italian high jump records 2007.
Progress at HJ: 1993- 1.63, 1994- 1.71, 1995- 1.69, 1996- 1.66, 1997- 1.78, 1998- 1.73, 1999- 1.63, 2000-1.88, 2001- 1.98, 2002- 1.91, 2003- 1.96i/1.90, 2004-1.86, 2005- 1.90, 2006- 1.96i/1.94, 2007- 2.03, 2008-1.97, 2009- 2.00, 2010- 2.01, 2011- 2.04i/2.00. pbs: 200m 25.93 '00, 800m 2:24.21 '01, 60mh 8.94i '01, 100mh 14.11 '01, LJ 5.60 '01, SP 11.74 '01, JT 46.64 '01, Pen 3980i '01, Hep 5687w/5542 '01.
Has the record for the greatest ever height differential, 35cm, by a woman high jumper. Married Massimilliano Di Matteo Sept. 2009.

Libania GRENOT b. 12 Jul 1983 Santiago de Cuba 1.75m 65kg. Fiamme Galle.
At 400m: OG: '08- sf; WCh: '01- hR, '05- h, '09- sf; EC: '10- 4; WY: '99- 5; PAm: '03- 4; CCp: '10- 6/2R; ET: '10- 1. Won MedG 2009, CUB 2002-05, ITA 2009-10.
Four Italian 400m records 2008-09.
Progress at 400m: 1997- 56.2, 1998- 54.9, 1999-53.87, 2000- 53.79, 2001- 52.91, 2002- 53.34A, 2003- 52.20, 2004- 51.68, 2005- 51.51, 2007- 54.21, 2008- 50.83, 2009- 50.30, 2010- 50.43, 2011- 52.17. pbs: 200m 22.93 '09, 500m 1:08.26 '09.
Switched from Cuba to Italy after she married Silvio Scaffetti in 2006 and gained Italian citizenship in April 2008.

Simone LA MANTIA b. 14 Apr 1983 Palermo 1.77m 65kg. Fiamme Gialle. Studied PE at Palermo University.
At TJ: OG: '04- dnq 17; WCh: '03/05/11- dnq 17/14/15; EC: '10- 2; WJ: '02- 8; EJ: '01- 10; EU23: '03- 2, '05- 1; WI: '04- 11, '06- dnq 16; EI: '05- 8, '11- 1; CCp: '10- 5; ET: '11- 2. Italian champion 2004-06, 2010-11; W.Mil G 2011.
Progress at TJ: 1998- 12.71, 1999- 12.03, 2000-12.50, 2001- 13.51/13.63w, 2002- 13.33, 2003-14.31, 2004- 14.49, 2005- 14.69, 2006- 14.21, 2007-13.89, 2008- 13.79, 2009- 13.79/13.83w, 2010-14.56, 2011- 14.60i/14.43. pb LJ 6.48 '05.
Her father Antonino La Mantia had 3000mSt pb 8:42.2 '74 and mother Monica Mutschlecner 800m 2:08.3 '77.

Elisa RIGAUDO b. 17 Jun 1980 Cuneo 1.68m 56kg. Fiamme Gialle.
At 20kW: OG: '04- 6, '08- 3; WCh: '03-05-07-09-11: 10/7/dnf/9/4; EC: '06- 3; EU23: '03- 1; WCp: '02-04-06: 16/5/10; ECp: '05-07: 3/4. At 5000mW:

WJ: '98- 7; EJ: '99-6. Won MedG 20kW 2005, Italian 5000mW 2004, 2007; 20kW 2004-05, 2008. Progress at 20kW: 1999- 1:42:40. 2000- 1:32:50, 2001- 1:29:54, 2002- 1:30:42, 2003- 1:30:34, 2004-1:27:49, 2005- 1:29:26, 2006- 1:28:37, 2007- 1:29:15, 2008- 1:27:12, 2009- 1:29:04, 2011- 1:30:44, 2012-1:29:25. pbs: 3000mW 11:57.00i '04, 12:28.92 '02; 5000mW 20:56.29 '02, 10kW 42:33 '09, 43:06.4t '04. Won IAAF Walks Challenge 2004.
Daughter Elena born in September 2010.

IVORY COAST

Governing Body: Fédération Ivoirienne d'Athlétisme, Abidjan. Founded 1960.

Muriell AHOURÉ b. 23 Aug 1987 Abidjan 1.67m 57kg. Graduated in criminal law from the University of Miami, USA
At 60m: WI: '12- 2. Won NCAA Indoor 200m 2009. Three CIV 100m records 2009-11.
Progress at 100m: 2005- 11.96, 2006- 11.42, 2007-11.41/11.28w, 2008- 11.45, 2009- 11.09, 2010- 11.41, 2011- 11.06. pbs: 60m 7.04i '12, 200m 22.78 '09, 300m 38.09i '07, 400m 54.77 '08.

JAMAICA

Governing body: Jamaica Athletic Administrative Association, PO Box 272, Kingston 5. Founded 1932.
2011 Champions: **Men**: 100m: Asafa Powell 10.08, 200m: Steve Mullings 20.11, 400m: Riker Hylton 45.30, 800m: Aldwyn Sappleton 1:49.07, 1500m: Rayon Lawrence 3:52.36, 110mh: Andrew Riley 13.36, 400mh: Leford Green 49.19, HJ: Darrel Garwood 2.10, PV: Jabari Ennis 5.00, LJ: Tarik Batcheloe 8.17w, TJ: Nick Thomas 16.12, SP: Dorian Scott 19.50, DT: Travis Smikle 59.83.
Women: 100m/200m: Veronica Campbell-Brown 10.84/22.44, 400m: Novlene Williams-Mills 50.05, 800m/1500m: Kenia Sinclair 2:00.96/4:18.00, 3000mSt: Koreen Hinds 9:41.67, 100mh: Indira Spence 13.08, 400mh: Kaliese Spencer 54.15, HJ: Kimberly Williamson 1.83, LJ: Jovanee Jarrett 6.44, TJ: Sasha-Kay Matthias 13.10, SP: Zara Northover 16.32, DT: Allison Randall 53.28, HT: Natalie Grant 60.33, JT: Olivia McKoy 52.33, Hep: Janieve Russell 5361.

Marvin ANDERSON b. 12 May 1982 Trelawny 1.75m 69kg. Reebok. Was at University of Southern California.
At 200m/4x100mR: OG: '08- qf; WCh: '07- 6/2R, '11- h; PAm: '07- 2; WJ: '00- 6; won CAC-J 100 '00.
Progress at 200m: 2000- 20.84, 2001- 21.01, 2002-21.39, 2003- 21.20, 2004- 20.84, 2005- 20.75/20.36w, 2006- 20.65; 2007- 20.06, 2008- 20.17, 2009- 20.15, 2010- 20.48, 2011- 20.27. pbs: 100m 10.11 '08, 10.07dq '09, 10.03w '07, 400m 48.42 '11.
3-month drugs ban from positive test at Jamaican Champs 25 Jun 2009.

Nickel ASHMEADE b. 7 Apr 1990 1.84m 87kg.
At 200m/4x100mR (100m): WCh: '11- 5; WJ: '08-

2/2R (2 4x400m); WY: '07- 3 (2, 3 MedR); won CAC 200m 2009.
Progress at 100m, 200m: 2006- 10.60, 21.30; 2007- 10.39, 20.76; 2008- 10.34, 20.80/20.16w; 2009- 10.37/10.21w, 20.40; 2010- 10.39, 20.63; 2011- 9.96, 19.91. pbs: 60m 6.92i '09, 400m 47.98 '09.

Yohan BLAKE b. 26 Dec 1989 St. James 1.81m 73kg. Racers TC.
At 100m/4x100mR: WCh: '11- 1/1R; WJ: '06- 3/1R, '08- 4/2R; WY: '05- 7; PAm-J: '07- 2 (3 4x400m); won CAC-J 100m & 200m 2006.
Progress at 100m, 200m: 2005- 10.56, 22.10; 2006- 10.33, 20.92; 2007- 10.11, 20.62; 2008- 10.27/10.20w, 21.06; 2009- 10.07/9.93dq, 20.60; 2010- 9.89, 19.78; 2011- 9.82/9.80w, 19.26. pbs: 60m 6.75i '08, 400m 46.49 '12.
3-month drugs ban from positive test at Jamaican Champs 25 Jun 2009. Cut 200m pb from 20.60 to 19.78 in Monaco 2010 and then to 19.26 in Brussels 2011.

Usain BOLT b. 21 Aug 1986 Sherwood Content, Trelawny 1.96m 88kg. Racers TC.
At (100m)/200m/4x100mR: OG: '04- h, '08- 1/1/1R; WCh: '05- 8, '07- 2/2R, '09- 1/1/1R, '11- dq/1/1R; WJ: 02- 1/2R/2R; WY: '01- sf, '03- 1; PAm-J: '03- 1/2R; WCp: '06- 2; won WAF 200m 2009, CAC 200m 2005, JAM 100m 2008-09, 200m 2005, 2007-09.
World records: 100m (3), 200m (2), 4x100m (3) 2008- 11, best low altitude 300m 2010, CAC records 100m (4) 2008-09, 200m (3) 2007-09, WJR 200m 2003 & 2004, World U18 200m record 2003.
Progress at 100m, 200m, 400m: 2000- 51.7; 2001- 21.73, 48.28; 2002- 20.58, 47.12; 2003- 20.13, 45.35; 2004- 19.93, 2005- 19.99, 2006- 19.88, 2007- 10.03, 19.75, 45.28; 2008- 9.69, 19.30, 46.94; 2009- 9.58, 19.19, 45.54; 2010- 9.82, 19.56, 45.87; 2011- 9.76, 19.40. pbs: 60m 6.31+ '09, 100y 9.14+ '11, 150m 14.35 straight & 14.44+ turn '09 (world bests), 300m 30.97 '10 (world low altitude best).
Bolt was the sensational superstar of the 2008 Olympics when he won triple gold – all in world records – and in the year he won 8 of 9 100m races and all 5 at 200m. In 2009 he smashed both the 100m and 200m WRs at the World Champs. He was then appointed an Ambassador-at-Large for Jamaica. In 2002, after running 20.61 to win the CAC U17 200m title, he became the youngest ever male world junior champion at 15y 332d and set a world age best with 20.58, with further age records for 16 and 17 in 2003-04. Won IAAF 'Rising Star' award for men in 2002 and 2003. He has won 25 of his 27 100m races 2007-11.

Nesta CARTER b. 10 Nov 1985 Banana Ground 1.78m 70kg. MVP TC.
At 100m/4x100mR: OG: '08- 1R; WCh: '07- sf/2R, '11- 7/1R. At 200m: WJ: '04- sf/res (2)R. At 60m: WI: '10- 7, '12- 2.
World record 4x100m 2008 and 2011.
Progress at 100m: 2004- 10.0/10.56/10.52w,
2005- 10.59, 2006- 10.20, 2007- 10.11, 2008- 9.98, 2009- 9.91, 2010- 9.78, 2011- 9.89. pbs: 50m 5.67i '12, 60m 6.49i '12, 200m 20.25 '11, 400m 47.82 '09.

Ricardo CHAMBERS b. 7 Oct 1984 Trelawny 1.77m 73kg. Studied social sciences at Florida State University, USA.
At 400m/4x400mR: OG: '08- sf; WCh: '07/09- sf; CAG: '06- 5/1R; CCp: '10- 2/1R. Won JAM 2006, 2009; NACAC 2006, NCAA 2007.
Progress at 400m: 2003- 46.42, 2004- 46.02, 2005- 44.87, 2006- 44.71, 2007- 44.62, 2008- 44.80, 2009- 45.13, 2010- 44.54, 2011- 46.56. pbs: 100m 10.73 '04, 200m 21.08 '05, 300m 32.49 '10, 800m 1:53.34i '07.

Lerone CLARKE b. 2 Oct 1981 Trelawny Parish 1.74m 66kg. Puma. Graduate of visual arts from Lincoln University, Missouri, USA.
At 100m/4x100mR: WCh: '05- 4R, '09- res1R; CG: '10- 1/2R; PAm: '11- 1; CAG: '06- 4/3R, '10- 3/2R.   CAC 60m indoor record 2012.
Progress at 100m: 2002- 10.50, 2003- 10.43/10.49w, 2004- 10.29/10.12w, 2005- 10.24, 2006- 10.28, 2007- 10.15, 2008- 10.30A, 2009- 9.99, 2010- 10.10/9.98w, 2011- 10.01A/10.05/9.90w. pbs: 50m 5.63i '12, 55m 6.21i '08, 60m 6.47i '12, 100y 9.38+ '10, 200m 20.89 '10.

Michael FRATER b. 6 Oct 1982 Manchester 1.70m 67kg. MVP. Political science graduate of Texas Christian University.
At 100m/4x100mR: OG: '04- sf, '08- 6/1R; WCh: '03- qf, '05- 2, '09- sf/1R, '11- sf/1R; CG: '02- sf, '06- sf/1R; PAm: '03- 1; WJ: '00- 5; PAm-J: '99- 2R. Won NCAA 100m 2004, JAM 100m 2006.
World record 4x100m 2008 and 2011.
Progress at 100m: 1999- 10.73/10.47w, 2000- 10.46, 2001- 10.26, 2002- 10.21/10.05w, 2003- 10.13, 2004- 10.06, 2005- 10.03, 2006- 10.06, 2007- 10.03/9.95w, 2008- 9.97, 2009- 10.02, 2010- 9.98/9.94w, 2011- 9.88/9.86w. pbs: 55m 5.74i '12, 60m 6.62i '12, 200m 20.63, 20.45w '02; 400m 49.13 '07.
Older brother Lindel was former Jamaican champion, pb 100m 10.07 '00, 9.9w '98.

Jermaine GONZALES b. 26 Nov 1984 St. Catherine 1.90m 72kg. Racers TC.
At 400m/4x400mR: OG: '04- hR; WCh: '11- 4/3R; CG: '06- 3/3R; WJ: '02- 3/2R; WY: 01- 3. Jamaican 400m record 2010.
Progress at 400m: 2001- 47.51, 2002- 45.80, 2003- 46.15i/46.81, 2004- 45.41, 2005- 46.51, 2006- 44.85, 2007- 45.78, 2008- 46.32, 2009- 45.81, 2010- 44.40, 2011- 44.69. pbs: 20m 21.12 '09, 300m 32.49 '10.

Leford GREEN b. 14 Nov 1986 St. Catherine 1.86m 79kg.
At 400mh: WCh: '11- sf/3R; CAG: 10- 1; Won CAC 2011, JAM 2009-11. At 400m/4x400m: WCh: '07- 4R, '11- 2R; CAG: '06- sf/1R; PAm: '07- sf.

At 400m: 2004- 48.14, 2005- 46.68, 53.01; 2006- 45.82, 50.81; 2007- 45.71, 52.69; 2008- 45.56, 50.51; 2009- 46.19; 2010- 45.68, 48.47; 2011- 45.46, 49.03. pb 200m 20.61 '11, 20.41w '09; 600m 1:19.41i '12.

Isa PHILLIPS b. 22 Apr 1984 Kingston 1.93m 84kg. Studied political science at Louisiana State University, USA.
At 400mh: OG: '08- sf; WCh: '07/09/11- sf; WY: '01- sf; PAm-J '03- 2/3R. Won NCAA 2007, CAC 2008, JAM 2009.
Progress at 400mh: 2002- 52.96, 2003- 50.95, 2004- 50.39, 2005- 49.96, 2006- 49.36, 2007- 48.51, 2008- 48.78, 2009- 48.05, 2010- 48.68, 2011- 48.64. pbs: 200m 21.05 '09, 400m 46.71 '09, 800m 1:51.45i '06, 1:52.59 '03.

Asafa POWELL b. 23 Nov 1982 St Catherine 1.90m 88kg. MVP. Studied sports medicine at Kingston University of Technology.
At 100m/4x100mR: OG: '04- 5 (dns 200), '08- 5/1R; WCh: '03- qf, '07- 3/2R, '09- 3/1R; CG: '02- sf/2R, '06- 1/1R; PAm-J: '01- 2R. Won JAM 100m 2003-05, 2007, 2011; 200m 2006, 2010; WAF 100m 2004, 2006-08; 200m 2004.
Four world 100m records, five CAC & Commonwealth 2005-07, seven JAM 2004-7; WR 4x100m 2008. Two world bests 100y 2010.
Progress at 100m, 200m: 2001- 10.50, 2002- 10.12, 20.48; 2003- 10.02/9.9, 2004- 9.87, 20.06; 2005- 9.77, 2006- 9.77, 19.90; 2007- 9.74, 20.00; 2008- 9.72, 2009- 9.82, 2010- 9.82/9.72w, 19.97; 2011- 9.78, 20.55. pbs: 50m 5.64i '12, 60m 6.42+ '09, 6.50i '12; 100y 9.07+ '10, 400m 45.94 '09.
Disqualified for false start in World quarters 2003 after fastest time (10.05) in heats. In 2004 he tied the record of nine sub-10 second times in a season and in 2005 he took the world record for 100m at Athens, tying that at Gateshead and Zürich in 2006, when he ran a record 12 sub-10 times and was world athlete of the year. Took record to 9.74 in Rieti 2007 and ran 15 sub-10 times in 2008, including seven sub-9.90 in succession after 5th place at Olympics. Now has record 74 sub-10 times. Withdrew from 2011 Worlds through injury. Elder brother Donovan (b. 31 Oct 1971): at 60m: 6.51i '96 (won US indoors '96, 6 WI '99; 100m 10.07/9.7 '95).

Maurice SMITH b. 28 Sep 1980 St Catherine 1.90m 90kg. Graduated in adult education from Auburn University, USA.
At Dec: OG: '04- 14, '08- 9; WCh: '05/09/11- dnf, '07- 2; CG: '06- 2; PAm: '07- 1, '11- 2; PAm-J: '99- 3; CAG: '10- 1; CAC champion 2001, NACAC 2005, 2011. Won NCAA indoor Hep 2005, JAM SP 2001, DT 2001, 2005, 2007; JT 2000.
Three CAC decathlon records 2006-07, four Jamaican 2005-07.
Progress at Dec: 1999- 6996, 2000- 7090, 2001- 7755, 2003- 7925w/7854, 2004- 8024, 2005- 8232, 2006- 8349, 2007- 8644, 2008- 8434, 2009- 8157, 2010- 8186, 2011- 8214A/8078. pbs: 60m 6.94i

'05, 100m 10.62 '07, 400m 47.48 '07, 1000m 2:39.32i '05, 1500m 4:29.95 '06, 60mh 7.88i '05, 110mh 13.76 '06, HJ 2.03A '01, PV 4.80 '07, LJ 7.51 '06, SP 17.78 '08, DT 55.49 '07, JT 62.07 '02, Hep 6035i '05 (CAC record)

Dwight THOMAS b. 23 Sep 1980 Kingston 1.85m 82kg. adidas.
At 110mh: WCh: '09- 7, '11- dns. At 100m/4x100mR: OG: '04- sf, '08- res 1R; WCh: '03- sf, '05- 5, '07- res 2R, '09- res 1R; CG: '02- 4=/2R; PAm: '99- 3R; WJ: '98- 3/1R. At 200m: OG: '00- qf/4R. At 60m: WI: '03- sf. At 60mh: WI: '04- 8. Won CAC-J 110mh 1998, PAm-J 100m & 200m 1999, Jamaican 100m & 200m 2002.
Jamaican 110mh records 2009 & 2011.
Progress at 100m, 110mh: 1998- 10.38, 14.40/13.86w; 1999- 10.37, 2000- 10.12, 2001- 10.19, 2002- 10.15, 13.74; 2003- 10.19, 2004- 10.12, 13.34; 2005- 10.00, 2006- 10.11, 2007- 10.15/10.07w, 14.25; 2008- 10.20/10.14w; 2009- 10.33, 13.16; 2010- 13.25/13.1w, 2011- 13.15. pbs: 55m 6.27i '01, 60m 6.61i '03, 200m 20.32 '07, 60mh 7.59i '04.

Women

Aleen BAILEY b. 25 Nov 1980 St Mary 1.70m 64g. Student at University of South Carolina.
At 100m/(200m)/4x100mR: OG: '04- 5/4/1R; WCh: '01- (h), '03- 6/qf, '05- sf/2R, '07- (6), '09- 8/1R; WJ: '96- 2R, '98- 3R; PAm: '07- (5)/1R; PAm-J: '97- 2R, '99- 1/1/2R; WCp: '06- 1R. At 60m: WI: '12- 7. Won NCAA 100m & 200m (and indoor 200m) 2003, JAM 100m, 200m 2001, 2003.
Progresion at 100m, 200m: 1995- 12.10, 1996- 11.67, 23.99; 1997- 11.60/11.55w, 23.65; 1998- 11.37, 23.96/23.16w, 1999- 11.41, 23.37; 2000- 11.47/11.38w, 23.45/22.86w; 2001- 11.14, 22.59; 2002- 11.33, 22.54; 2003- 11.07, 22.59; 2004- 11.04, 22.33; 2005- 11.07, 23.00/22.75w; 2006- 11.27, 23.70; 2007- 11.17, 22.60; 2008- 11.20, 22.85/22.82w; 2009- 11.07, 22.83; 2010- 11.19, 23.15; 2011- 11.15, 22.79. pbs: 60m 7.18i '12, 400m 54.43 '07.
Her brother Capleton is a reggae star.

Schillonie CALVERT b. 27 Jul 1988 Saint-James. Racers TC. University of Technology.
At 100m/4x100R: WJ: '04- 7, '06- sf/3/3R; WY: '05- 3.
Progress at 100m: 2004- 11.44/11.33w, 2005- 11.40, 2006- 11.21, 2007- 11.35, 2008- 11.23, 2009- 11.19, 2010- 11.36, 2011- 11.05. pbs: 200m 22.55 '11, 400m 53.50 '12.

Veronica CAMPBELL-BROWN b. 15 May 1982 Clarks Town, Trelawny 1.63m 61kg. Adidas. Was at University of Arkansas, USA.
At (100m)/200m/4x100mR: OG: '00- 2R, '04- 3/1/1R, '08- 1; WCh: '05- 2/4/2R, '07- 1/2/2R, '09- 4/2, '11- 2/1/2R; CG: '02- (2)/2R, '06- 2; WJ: '98- (qf), '00- 1/1/2R; WY: '99- (1)/1R; PAm-J: '99- 2R. At 60m: WI: '10- 1, '12- 1. Won WAF 100m 2004-05, 200m 2004, CAC-J 100m 2000,

JAM 100m 2002, 2004-05, 2007, 2011; 200m 2004-05, 2007-09, 2011.
CAC junior 100m record 2000.
Progress at 100m, 200m: 1999- 11.49, 23.73; 2000- 11.12/11.1, 22.87; 2001- 11.13/22.92; 2002- 11.00, 22.39; 2004- 10.91, 22.05; 2005- 10.85, 22.35/22.29w; 2006- 10.99, 22.51; 2007- 10.89, 22.34; 2008- 10.87/10.85w, 21.74; 2009- 10.89/10.81w, 22.29; 2010- 10.78, 21.98; 2011- 10.76, 22.22. pbs: 50m 6.08i '12, 60m 7.00i '10, 100y 9.91+ '11 (world best), 400m 52.24i '05, 52.25 '11.
In 2000 became the first woman to become World Junior champion at both 100m and 200m. Unbeaten at 200m in 28 finals (42 races in all) from 11 March 2000 to 22 July 2005 (lost to Allyson Felix). Married Omar Brown (1 CG 200m 2006) on 3 Nov 2007.

Vonette DIXON b. 26 Nov 1975 Hanover 1.70m 62kg. Graduate of Auburn University, USA.
At 100mh: OG: '08- sf; WCh: '01-03-05-07-11: 8/9/sf/7/sf; CG: '02- 2; PAm: '07- 4; CAC champion 2011. At 60m: WI: '10- 6.
Progress at 100mh: 1994- 15.13/15.0, 1995- 14.29, 1996- 13.52/13.30w, 1997- 13.26, 1998- 13.52, 1999- 13.40, 2000- 12.90, 2001- 12.83, 2002- 12.83/12.82w, 2003- 12.72, 2004- 12.76, 2005- 12.67, 2006- 12.82/12.80w, 2007- 12.64, 2008- 12.69, 2009- 12.80, 2010- 12.75, 2011- 12.77. pbs: 55m 6.79i '00, 60m 7.33i '00, 100m 11.47/11.40w '00, 200m 23.57/23.48w '00, 50mh 6.85i '02, 55mh 7.55i '00, 60mh 7.92i '02.

Shelly-Ann FRASER-PRYCE b. 27 Dec 1986 Kingston 1.60m 52kg. MVP. Student at University of Technology. née Fraser. Married Jason Pryce on 7 Jan 2011.
At 100m/4x100mR: OG: '08- 1; WCh: '07- res (2) R, '09- 1/1R. '11-4/2R. Won WAF 100m 2008, JAM 100m 2009.
CAC and Commonwealth 100m record 2009.
Progress at 100m, 200m: 2002- 11.8, 2003- 11.57, 2004- 11.72, 24.08; 2005- 11.72; 2006- 11.74, 24.8; 2007- 11.31/11.21w, 23.5; 2008- 10.78, 22.15; 2009- 10.73, 22.58; 2010- 10.82dq, 22.47dq; 2011- 10.95, 22.59/22.10w.
Huge improvement in 2008 and moved to joint third on world all-time list for 100m when winning 2009 world 100m title. 6-month ban for positive test for a non-performance enhancing drug on 23 May 2010.

Anneisha McLAUGHLIN b. 6 Jan 1986 Manch–ester 1.63m 54kg. University of Technology.
At 200m/4x100mR: WCh: '09- 5; WJ: '02- 2/1R, '04- 2/2R; WY: '03- 1 (2 MedR); WUG: '11- 1/3R; PAm-J: '03- 2/2R, '05- 1. At 400m/4x400mR: WJ: '00- 2R; WY: '01- 3 (2 MedR). Won CAC-J 400m 2000, 100m & 200m 2002' JAM 200m 2010.
Progress at 200m: 2000- 24.33w, 2001- 23.11, 2002- 22.94, 2003- 23.19, 2004- 23.21, 2005- 23.00, 2006- 23.47, 2007- 23.28/23.27w, 2008- 23.34, 2009- 22.55, 2010- 22.54, 2011- 22.54. pbs: 100m 11.35 '09, 400m 51.89 '12.

Carrie RUSSELL b. 18 Oct 1990 1.71m 68kg. University of Technology.
At 100m/4x100R: WJ: '06- 3/3R; WUG: '11- 1/3R.
Progress at 100m: 2006- 11.36, 2007- 11.72, 2008- 11.44/11.39w, 2009- 11.27/11.21w, 2010- 11.14, 2011- 11.05. pb 200m 23.87 '06.

Sherone SIMPSON b. 12 Aug 1984 Manchester, Jamaica 1.73m 58kg. MVP. Graduate of Kingston University of Technology.
At 100m/(200m)/4x100mR: OG: '04- 6/1R, '08- 2=/6; WCh: '05- 6/2R, '11- 8/2R; CG: '06- (1)/1R; WJ: '02- 1R; PAm-J: '03- 2/2R; WCp: '06- 1/1R. Won WAF 100m 2006, JAM 100m 2006, 2010; 200m 2006.
Progress at 100m, 200m: 2000- 12.54, 2001- 12.17, 25.01; 2002- 11.60, 24.21; 2003- 11.37/11.1, 23.60; 2004- 11.01, 22.70; 2005- 10.97, 22.54; 2006- 10.82, 22.00; 2007- 11.43, 22.76; 2008- 10.87, 22.11; 2009- 11.15/11.04w; 2010- 11.02, 22.65/22.64w; 2011- 11.00, 22.73. pbs: 400m 51.25 '08, 100mh 14.10 '02.

Kenia SINCLAIR b. 14 July 1980 St Catherine 1.67m 54kg. Was at Seton Hall University, USA.
At 800m: OG: '08- 6; WCh: '05/07/09- sf, '11- 7; CG: '06- 2; WI: '06- 2; CCp: '10- 2. Won JAM 800m 2005-09, 2011; 1500m 2006-07, 2011.
Five Jamaican 800m records 2005-06. CAC indoor 1000m record (2:38.62) 2010.
Progress at 800m: 2002- 2:05.26i/2:07.39, 2003- 2:03.21, 2005- 1:58.88, 2006- 1:57.88, 2007- 1:58.61, 2008- 1:58.24, 2009- 1:59.13, 2010- 1:58.16, 2011- 1-58.21. pbs: 400m 56.84 '03, 600m 1:25.6+ '09, 1000m 2:37.37 '05, 1500m 4:05.56 '07, 1M 4:32.33i '05, 3000m 9:52.71i '02, 10kmRd 34:27 '11.
Based in Gainesville, Florida.

Kaliese SPENCER b. 6 May 1987 Westmoreland 1.73m 59kg. Was at University of Texas.
At 400mh/4x400mR: WCh: '07- sf, '09- 4/res 2R, '11- 4; WJ: '06- 1/3R. Won DL 2010, JAM 400mh 2011.
Progress at 400mh: 2006- 55.11, 2007- 55.62, 2009- 53.56, 2010- 53.33, 2011- 52.79. pbs: 200m 23.84 '08, 400m 50.55 '08, 800m 2:03.01 '11.

Kerron STEWART b. 16 Apr 1984 Kingston 1.75m 61kg. Adult education student at Auburn University, USA.
At 100m/(200m)/4x100mR: OG: '08- 2=/3; WCh: '07- 7/2R, '09- 2/1R, '11- 6/5/2R; WJ: '02- 4/1R; WY: '01- 2/2R. Won NCAA 200m 2007, indoor 60m & 200m 2007; JAM 100m 2008.
Progress at 100m, 200m: 2000- 11.89, 24.09w; 2001- 11.70, 23.90; 2002- 11.46, 24.21; 2003- 11.34, 23.50; 2004- 11.40, 23.63i/23.66; 2005- 11.63, 23.77i/24.22/23.46w; 2006- 11.03, 22.65; 2007- 11.03, 22.41; 2008- 10.80, 21.99; 2009- 10.75, 22.42; 2010- 10.96, 22.57/22.34w; 2011- 10.87, 22.63. pbs: 55m 6.71i '06, 60m 7.14i '07, 400m 52.08 '08.

Melaine WALKER b. 1 Jan 1983 Kingston 1.73m 58kg. MVP. Social work graduate of University of Texas, USA.
At 400mh/4x400mR: OG: '08- 1; WCh: '01-07-

09-11: h/sf/1/2; CG: '02- 4; WJ: '00- 3/2R, '02- 2 (5 100mh); CAG: '06- 3/2R; JAM champion 2006-09, WAF 2008-09. At 200m: WJ: '98- 5/3 4x100R; WY: '99- 2.
Two CAC 400mh records 2008-09.
Progress at 400mh: 1999- 58.99, 2000- 56.96, 2001- 55.62, 2002- 55.84, 2003- 57.24, 2004- 56.62, 2005- 55.09, 2006- 54.87, 2007- 54.14, 2008- 52.64, 2009- 52.42, 2010- 55.33, 2011- 52.73. pbs: 60m 7.40i '05, 100m 11.63 '99, 200m 23.51 '99, 400m 51.61 '08, 800m 2:11.96 '11, 60mh 8.05i '06, 100mh 12.75 '06.

Rosemarie WHYTE b. 8 Sep 1986 1.75m 66kg. Racers TC.
At 400m/4x400mR: OG: '08- 7/3R; WCh: '09- 2R, '11- sf/2R. Won JAM 400m 2008.
Progress at 400m: 2002- 55.51, 2007- 53.47, 2008- 50.05, 2009- 51.55, 2010- 50.67, 2011- 49.84. pbs: 100m 11.60/11.4 '06, 200m 22.74 '09, 100mh 14.27/14.2 '06, 400mh 59.89 '09, HJ 1.65 '06, LJ 6.35 '06, TJ 13.04 '06, JT 31.15 '06, Hep 5262 '06.

Novlene WILLIAMS-MILLS b. 26 Apr 1982 St Ann 1.70m 57kg. Studied recreation at University of Florida, USA.
At 400m/4x400mR: OG: '04- sf/2R, '08- sf/3R; WCh: '05- 2R, '07- 3/2R, '09- 4/2R, '11- 8/2R; CG: '06- 3; PAm: '03- 6/2R; WI: '06- 5; WCp: '06- 3/1R. Won JAM 400m 2006-07, 2009-11.
Progress at 400m: 1999- 55.62, 2000- 53.90, 2001- 54.99, 2002- 52.05, 2003- 51.93, 2004- 50.59, 2005- 51.09, 2006- 49.63, 2007- 49.66, 2008- 50.11, 2009- 49.77, 2010- 50.04, 2011- 50.05. pbs: 200m 23.25 '10, 500m 1:11.83i '03.
Married 2007. Younger sister Clora Williams (b. 26.11.83) joined her on JAM's 3rd place 4x400m team at 2010 WI; she has 400m pb 51.06 and won NCAA 2006.

Shericka WILLIAMS b. 17 Sep 1985 Black River, St. Elizabeth 1.70m 64kg. MVP. Kingston University of Technology.
At 400m/4x400mR: OG: '08- 2/3R; WCh: '05- sf/2R, '07- sf/2R, '09- 2/2R, '11- 6/2R; CG: '06- 5; WCp: '06- 1R, '10- 4/1R; won JAM 400m 2005.
Progress at 200m, 400m: 2001- 24.74, 2003- 23.90, 55.44; 2004- 23.96/23.70w, 53.52; 2005- 23.08, 50.97; 2006- 22.55, 50.24; 2007- 23.32, 50.37; 2008- 22.50, 49.69; 2009- 22.57, 49.32; 2010- 23.25, 50.04; 2011- 23.49/23.16w, 50.45. pb 100m 11.34 '07, 800m 2:9.17 '07.

Nickiesha WILSON b. 28 Jul 1986 Kingston 1.73m 64kg. Racers TC. Was at Louisiana State University, USA.
At 400mh: OG: '08- sf; WCh: '07- 4, '09/11- sf; CG: '10- 3; PAm: '07- 2; PAm-J: '05-1; CAG: '10- 1; CCp: '10- 1/1R; won NCAA 2008, CAC 2009, JAM 2010.
Progress at 100mh, 400mh: 2005- 13.98, 57.38; 2006- 13.64/13.44w, 56.77; 2007- 12.93, 53.97; 2008- 12.85/12.63w, 54.45; 2009- 12.79/12.72w, 54.89; 2010- 13.17, 54.52; 2011- 13.23, 55.57. pbs:

60m 7.55i '10, 200m 23.59i '08, 400m 53.66i '08, 54.88 '06; 60mh 8.01i '07, LJ 6.26 '11.

JAPAN

Governing body: Nippon Rikujo-Kyogi Renmei, 1-1-1 Jinnan, Shibuya-Ku, Tokyo 150-8050. Founded 1911.
National Championships first held in 1914 (men), 1925 (women). **2011 Champions**: **Men**: 100m: Masashi Eriguchi 10.38, 200m: Shinji Takahira 20.49, 400m: Yuzo Kanemaru 45.68, 800m: Masato Yokota 1:47.24, 1500m: Hiroshi Ino 3:48.59, 5000m: Kazuya Watanabe 13:37.41, 10000m: Yuki Sato 28:10.87, 3000mSt: Tsuyoshi Takeda 8:37.14, 110mh: Wataru Yazawa 23.86, 400mh: Takayuki Kishimoto 49.28, HJ: Naoto Tobe 2.22, PV: Daichi Sawano 5.40, LJ: Yohei Sugai 7.94, TJ: Shin-ya Sogame 16.42, SP: Yohei Murakawa 18.35, DT: Shiro Kobayashi 55.42, HT: Koji Murofushi 77.01, JT: Yukifumi Murakami 82.75, Dec: Kesuke Ushiro 8076, 20kW: Yusuke Suzuki 1:21:13, 50kW: Koichiro Morioka 3:44:45.
Women: 100m/200m: Chisato Fukushima 11.39/23.44, 400m: Miho Shingu 54.16, 800m: Akari Kishikawa 2:03.34, 1500m: Mika Kobayashi 4:20.41, 5000m: Megumi Kinukawa 15:09.96, 10000m: Kayo Sugihara 32:18.79, 3000mSt: Minori Hayakari 9:52.98, 100mh: Ayako Kimura 13.32, 400mh: Satomi Kubokura 55.81, HJ: Miyuki Fukumoto 1.79, PV: Tomomi Abiko 4.20, LJ: Kumiko Imura 6.39, TJ: Sayuri Takeda 13.12, SP: Yukino Otani 15.44, DT: Yuka Murofushi 51.85, HT: Masumi Aya 66.32, JT: Risa Miyashita 60.08, Hep: Chie Kiriyama 5445, 20kW: Kumi Otoshi 1:29:11.

Koichiro MORIOKA b. 2 Apr 1985 Isahaya, Nagasaki 1.84m 65kg.
At 20kW: OG: '08- 16; WCh: '05-07-09: 29/11/11; AsiG: '06- 3; AsiC: '07- 2; WUG: '05- 3, '07- 3. At 50kW: WCh: '09- 19, '11- 6; AsiG: '10- 3. At 10,000mW: WJ: '04- 6. Won Asian 20kW 2008, JPN 20kW 2007, 2009-10, 50kW 2011.
Progress at 20kW, 50kW: 2004- 1:28:22, 2005- 1:22:52, 2006- 1:22:46, 2007- 1:21:30, 2008- 1:21:55, 3:55:40; 2009- 1:21:16, 3:49:12; 2010- 1:20:43, 3:47:41; 2011- 1:22:10, 3:44:45. pbs: 5000mW 19:13.77 '09, 10000mW: 39:07.84 '10 (Asian record), 35kW 2:37:43 '11.

Yukifumi MURAKAMI b. 23 Dec 1979 Ueshima, Ehime 1.85m 90kg. Suzuki Motor, Was at Nihon University.
At JT: OG: '04/08- dnq 18/15; WCh: '05-07-11: dnq 27/21/15, '09- 3; WJ: '98- 3; AsiG: 02-06-10: 2/2/1; AsiC: '09- 1, '11- 1; Asi-J: '97- 2; JPN champion 2000-11.
Progress at JT: 19950 56.60, 1996- 68.00, 1997- 76.54, 1998- 73.62, 1999- 71.70, 2000- 78.57, 2001- 80.59, 2002- 78.77, 2003- 78.98, 2004- 81.71, 2005- 79.79, 2006- 78.54, 2007- 79.85, 2008- 79.71, 2009- 83.10, 2010- 83.15, 2011- 83.53.

Koji MUROFUSHI b. 8 Oct 1974 Shizuoka 1.87m 100kg. Graduate of Chukyo University. Mizuno.
At HT: OG: '00- 9, '04- 1, '08- 5; WCh: '95-97-99-01-03-07-11: dnq/10/dnq 14/2/3/6/1; WJ: '92- 8; AsiG: '94- 2, '98- 1, '02- 1; AsiC: '93-5-8-02: 2/2/2/1; WCp: '02- 2 (9 DT), '06- 1. Won GWG 2001, GP 2002 (2nd 2000), WAF 2006. Won E. Asian 1997, 2001; Japanese 1995-2011.
18 Japanese hammer records 1998-2003, Asian records 2001 & 2003.
Progress at HT: 1991- 61.76, 1992- 66.30, 1993- 68.00, 1994- 69.54, 1995- 72.32, 1996- 73.82, 1997- 75.72, 1998- 78.57, 1999- 79.17, 2000- 81.08, 2001- 83.47, 2002- 83.33, 2003- 84.86, 2004- 83.15, 2005- 76.47, 8006- 82.01, 2007- 82.62, 2008- 81.87, 2009- 78.36, 2010- 80.99, 2011- 81.24. pb DT 44.64 '96.
Won IAAF HT Challenge 2010. His father Shigenobu Murofushi won a record five Asian Games gold medals 1970-86 and held the Japanese hammer record with 75.96 (Los Angeles 1984) until Koji broke it for the first time on 26 Apr 1998. His mother was the 1968 European Junior javelin champion, Serafina Moritz (Romania). His sister **Yuka** (b. 11 Feb 77) holds Japanese records: DT 58.62 '07 and HT 67.77 '04; 6th WJ DT 1996.

Daichi SAWANO b. 16 Sep 1980 Nishiyodogawa, Osaka 1.82m 70kg. Nishi Sports. Was at Nihon University.
At PV: OG: '04- 13=, '08- dnq 16=; WCh: '03-05-07-09-11: dns/8/dnq/10=/dnq 14; AsiG: '06- 1; AsiC: '02-05-09-11: 1/1/3/1; WCp: '02- nh, '06- 2. Won Asian indoor 2008, JPN champion 1999-2000, 2003-04, 2006, 2008-09, 2011.
Three Japanese pole vault records 2003-05.
Progress at PV: 1994- 3.80, 1995- 4.30, 1996- 4.80, 1997- 5.25, 1998- 5.40, 1999- 5.50, 2000- 5.45, 2001- 5.52, 2002- 5.51, 2003- 5.75, 2004- 5.80, 2005- 5.83, 2006- 5.75, 2007- 5.75, 2008- 5.70, 2009- 5.70, 2010- 5.70, 2011- 5.65.

Yuki YAMAZAKI b. 16 Jan 1984 Toyama pref. 1.77m 65kg. Was at Juntendo University.
At (20kW)/50kW: OG: '04- 16, '08- 11/7; WCh: '05-07-09: 8/dnf/dq; WCp: '10- 6; AsiG: '02- dq/dq, '06- (4); AsiC: '03- (2), '07- 2. At 10000mW: WJ: '00- 20, '02- 5; WY: '01- 4. Won JPN 20kW 2002, 50kW 2004-10.
Four Japanese 50k walk records 2006-09.
Progress at 50kW: 2004- 3:55:20, 2005- 3:50:40, 2006- 3:43:38, 2007- 3:47:40, 2008- 3:41:29, 2009- 3:40:12, 2010- 3:46:46, 2011- 3:44:03. pbs: 5000mW 19:35.79 '01, 10000mW 39:48.52 '08, 20kW 1:20:38 '03.

Women

Yukiko AKABA b. 18 Oct 1979 Tochigi Prefecture 1.58m 44kg. Hokuren. Was at Jyosai University.
At Mar: WCh: '09- 31, '11- 6. World HMar: '08-10. At (5000m)/10000m: OG: '08- h/20; WUG:'01- 3. Won JPN 10000m 2009.
Progress at Mar: 2009- 2:25:40, 2010- 2:24:55, 2011- 2:24:09. pbs: 3000m 9:20.2 '02, 5000m 15:06.07 '08, 10000m 31:15.34 '08, HMar 68:11 '08. Won Osaka Marathon 2011 (2nd 2009).

Masumi FUCHISE b. 2 Sep 1986 Hyogo pref. 1.60m 45kg.
At 20kW: WCh: '07- 27, '09- 7, '11- dnf; AsiG: '10- 2; AsiC: '08-09-10: 3/1/1; WUG: '09- 2; Japanese champion 2007, 2009; Asian 2009-10.
Two Japanese 20km walk records 2007-09.
Progress at 20kW: 2006- 1:33:59, 2007- 1:29:36, 2008- 1:31:11. 2009- 1:28:03, 2010- 1:29:35, 2011- 1:31:51. pbs: 5000m run 16:59.86 '07, 5000mW 21:37.25 '09, 10kW 43:24.00t '11.

Kayoko FUKUSHI b. 25 Mar 1982 Itayanagi, Aiomori pref. 1.60m 45kg. Wacoal.
At 5000m/(10000m): OG: '04- (26), '08- h/11; WCh: '03- h/11, '05- 12/11, '07- 14/10, '09- (9); WJ: '00- 4; AsiG: '02- 2/2, '06- (1), '10- 5/4; WCp: '06- 3 (5 3000m). World 20km: '06- 6; CC: '02- 15, '06- 6. Won JPN 5000m 2002, 2004-07, 2010; 10000m 2002-07, 2010.
World 15km record & Asian 20km & HMar records 2006, Japanese records: 3000m 2002, 5000m (4) 2002-05.
Progress at 5000m, 10,000m, Mar: 1998- 16:56.35, 1999- 16:38.69, 35:37.54; 2000- 15:29.70, 2001- 15:10.23, 31:42.05; 2002- 14:55.19, 30:51.81; 2003- 15:09.02, 31:10.57; 2004- 14:57.73, 31:05.68; 2005- 14:53.22, 31:03.75; 2006- 15:03.17, 30:57.90; 2007- 15:05.73, 32:13.58; 2008- 15:12.7, 31:01.14, 2:40:54; 2009- 15:23.44mx, 31:23.49; 2010- 15:17.86, 31:29.03; 2011- 30:54.29, 2:24:38. pbs: 3000m 8:44.40 '02, 15km 46:55 '06, 20km 63:41 '06, HMar 67:26 '06, 30km 1:41:25 '08.
Set Japanese junior records at 3000m, 5000m and 10000m in 2001.

Yoshimi OZAKI b. 1 Jul 1981 Yamakita, Kanagawa Pref. 1.54m 41kg. Daiichi Seimei.
At Mar: WCh: '09- 2, '11- 18; JPN champion 2008. At HMar: WCh: '07- 13, '09- 9. World CC: '06- 19.
Progress at 10000m, Mar: 2004- 32:19.30, 2005- 31:47.23, 2006- 31:48.92, 2007- 32:13.95, 2008- 32:01.07, 2:23:30; 2009- 2:25:25, 2011- 2:23:56. pbs: 1500m 4:20.78 '02, 3000m 9:13.09 '04, 5000m 15:28.55 '04, 15km 49:13 '08, 20km 65:57 '08, HMar 69:26 '07.
Second in 2:26:19 on marathon debut in Nagoya 2008, then won at Tokyo in 2:23:30. Won Yokohama Marathon 2011. Her older sister Akemi Ozaki has a marathon best of 2:27:23 '09.

Yoko SHIBUI b. 14 Mar 1979 Kuroiso, Tochigi pref. 1.65m 50kg. Mitsui-Sumitomo.
At Mar: WCh: '01- 4. At 10000m: OG: '08- 17; WCh: '03- 14. Won JPN 10000m 2008, Mar 2009.
Japanese records 10000m 2002, Marathon 2004.
Progress at 10000m, Mar: 1997- 33:53.20, 1999-

32:43.02, 2000- 31:48.89, 2001- 31:48.73, 2:23:11; 2002- 30:48.89, 2:21:22; 2003- 31:42.01, 2004- 32:17.72, 2:19:41; 2005- 32:34.11, 2:27:40; 2006- 32:39.42, 2:23:58; 2007- 31:48.87, 2:34:15; 2008- 31:15.07, 2:25:51; 2009- 2:23:42, 2011- 2:29:03. pbs: 3000m 9:11.37 '96, 5000m 15:18.92 '02, 15km 49:07 '02, HMar 69:20+ '02, 30km 1:40:21 '08.
Ran the fastest ever debut marathon by a woman with 2:23:11 to win at Osaka in January 2001. Her breakthrough came with a 31:59 ekiden road relay leg in January 2000 and she had shown brilliant form with 10km legs of 31:09 and 31:11 in November 2000. She was third in the 2002 Chicago Marathon and returned from injuries to win the Berlin Marathon in 2004 in 2:19:41. 2nd Nagoya 2006, won Osaka 2009.

KAZAKHSTAN

Governing body: Athletic Federation of the Republic of Kazakhstan, Abai Street 48, 480072 Almaty. Founded 1959.
2011 National Champions: Men: 100m/200m: Vyacheslav Muravyev 10.53/21.49, 400m: Vlad–islav Leshin 47.86, 800m: Ivan Obeyzchik 1:49.94, 1500m: Sergey Yershov 3:49.95, 5000m/3000mSt: Artem Kosinov 14:26.2/9:00.73, 10000m: Mikhail Krassilov 30:48.92, HMar: Takhir Mamashayev 66:08, 110mh: Nazar Mukhamedzhan 14.26, 400mh: Dmitriy Komkov 52.11, HJ: Sergey Zassimovich 2.20, PV: Baurzhan Serikbayev 4.80, LJ: Konstantin Safronov 7.82, TJ: Yevgeniy Ektov 16.88, SP: Ivan Ivanov 16.80, DT: Yevgeniy Labutov 52.02, HT: Alexandr Yenchu 54.79, JT: Vladislav Podtsuk 56.91, Dec: Iliya Kuznetsov 6839, 20000mW: Vitaliy Anichkin 1:28:45.2, 20kW: Abdinur Alibek 1:26:58. **Women**: 100m/200m: Viktoriya Zyabkina 11.42/23.26, 400m: Margarita Kudinova 54.66, 800m: Viktoriya Yalovtseva 2:03.13, 1500m/5000m: Anna Pyatkina 4:24.00/17:34.6, HMar: Irina Smolnikova 81:14, 3000mSt: Yelena Gofman 10:57.00, 100mh: Natalya Ivoninskaya 12.95, 400mh: Alexandra Kuzina 58.41, HJ: Marina Aitova 1.92, PV: Olga Lapina 3.00, LJ/TJ: Olga Rypakova 6.56/14.96, SP: Alexandra Fisher 14.23, DT: Mariya Telushkina 39.02, JT: Gulsada Khabiyeva 41.30, Hep: Irina Karpova 4964.

Women

Marina AITOVA b. 13 Sep 1982 Karaganda 1.80m 60kg. née Korzhova.
At HJ: OG: '04- dnq 31=, '08- 10=; WCh: '03-09-11: dnq 22=/13=/19=, '07- 7=; AsiG: '02- 2, '06- 1; AsiC: '00- 2, '02- 3, '11- 3; WJ: '00- 9=; WY: '99- 4; WI: '08- 5, '10- 7=; WUG: '07- 1; WCp: '06- 3. Won Asi-J 2001, Af-AsG & C.Asian G 2003, Asian indoor 2006, 2010; KAZ 2002-04, 2011. Two Asian high jump records 2008-09.
Progress at HJ: 1999- 1.86, 2000- 1.90, 2001- 1.86i/1.85, 2002- 1.94, 2003- 1.89, 2004- 1.91i/1.89, 2005- 1.75, 2006- 1.95, 2007- 1.96, 2008- 1.97, 2009- 1.99, 2010- 1.94i, 2011- 1.94. pb LJ 6.00 '01.

Olga RYPAKOVA b. 30 Nov 1984 Kamenogorsk 1.83m 62kg. née Alekseyeva.
At TJ/(LJ): OG: '08- 4 (dnq 29); WCh: '07- 11, '09- 10, '11- 2; WJ: '00- (dnq 23); AsiG: '06- (3), '10- 1/2; AsiC: '07- 1/1, '09- 1; WI: '08-10-12: 4/1/2; WUG: '07- (1); WCp: '06- (8), '10: 1/3; won Asian Indoor LJ & TJ 2009. At Hep: WJ: '02- 2; WY: '01- 4; AsiG: '06- 1; won C.Asian 2003. Won KAZ LJ 2005, 2008, 2011; TJ 2008, 2011; Hep 2006.
Four Asian TJ records 2008-10, five indoors 2008-10, seven KAZ records 2007-10.
Progress at LJ, TJ: 2000- 6.23, 2001- 6.00, 2002- 6.26, 2003- 6.34i/6.14, 2004- 6.53i, 2005- 6.60, 2006- 6.63, 2007- 6.85, 14.69; 2008- 6.52/6.58w, 15.11; 2009- 6.58i/6.42, 14.53/14.69w; 2010- 6.60, 15.25; 2011- 6.56, 14.96. pbs: 200m 24.83 '02, 800m 2:20.12 '02, 60mh 8.67i '06, 100mh 14.02 '06, HJ 1.92 '06, SP 13.04 '06, JT 41.60 '03, Hep 6122 '06, Pen 4582i '06 (Asian rec).
Former heptathlete, concentrated on long jump after birth of daughter. Four KAZ and three Asian TJ records with successive jumps in Olympic final 2008, three Asian indoor records when won World Indoor gold in 2010.

KENYA

Governing body: Kenya Amateur Athletic Association, PO Box 46722, 00100 Nairobi. Founded 1951.
2011 National Champions: Men: 100m: Ibrahim Muiya 10.63, 200m/400m: Anderson Mutegi 21.07/45.70, 800m: David Rudisha 1:43.76, 1500m: Silas Kiplagat 3:31.39, 5000m: Isiah Koech 13:21.91, 10000m: Peter Kirui 27:32.1, 3000mSt: Brimin Kipruo 8:20.19, 110mh: Amon Chepsongol 14.7, 400mh: Vincent Kosgei 50.09, HJ: Mathew Sawe 2.14, LJ: Elijah Kimitei 7.67, TJ: Tera Langat 16.27, JT: Julius Yego 73.65, 20kW: David Kimutai 1:18:20sh. **Women**: 100m: Deborah Nyasugata 12.03, 200m: Maryline Chelangat 24.33, 400m: Joyce Zakari 51.73, 800m: Janeth Jepkosgei 1:59.34, 1500m: Hellen Obiri 4:08.68, 5000m: Sylvia Kibet 15:38.5, 10000m: Vivian Cheruiyot 31:55.8, 3000mSt: Milka Chemos 9:32.0, 100mh: Ednah Kwamboka 15.02, 400mh: Maureen Maiyo 56.65, PV: Caroline Cherotich 3.10, LJ: Regina Mulatya 5.97, TJ: Gladys Musyoka 12.65, HT: Linda Oseso 56.17, JT: Zeddy Cherotich 47.93, 20kmW: Grace Wanjiru 1:28:15sh.

David Tumo **BARMASAI** b. 1 Jan 1989 1.72m 54kg.   At Mar: WCh: '11- 5.
Progress at Mar: 2010- 2:10:31A, 2011- 2:07:18.
Won $250,000 to win in Dubai 2011 on his first trip outside Kenya.

Josphat Kipkoech **BETT** b. 12 Jun 1990 Kericho 1.73m 60kg.
At 10000m: WJ: '10- 1.
Progress at 5000m, 10000m: 2008- 13:44.51, 27:30.85; 2009- 12:57.43, 28:21.51; 2010- 13:11.60, 28:05.46A; 2011- 13:11.29, 26:48.99. pb 3000m 7:42.38 '09, HMar 61:01 '12.

Wilson Kwambai **CHEBET** b. 12 Jul 1985 Marakwet 1.74m 59kg.
World HMar: '09- 6.
Progress at HMar, Mar: 2005- 62:19, 2006- 62:38, 2007- 60:13, 2008- 59:33, 2009- 59:15, 2010- 60:31. 2:06:12; 2011- 2:05:27. pbs: 5000m 13:38.4A '11, Road: 10km 27:33 '09, 15km 41:44 '09, 20km 57:33 '09.
Second fastest debut marathon for 2nd Amsterdam 2010; won Rotterdam 2011 and Amsterdam 2012. His elder brother Joseph Biwott has marathon pb 2:09:40 '11.

Abrahim Kosgei **CHEBII** b. 23 Dec 1979 Kaptabuk, near Kapsowar 1.72m 63kg. Keiyo.
At 5000m: OG: '04- dnf; WCh: '03- 5; Won GP 3000m 2002. World 4k CC: '00-04-05: 5/19/2.
Progress at 5000m, 10000m: 1999- 13:30.41, 2000- 13:01.9, 2001- 13:12.53, 27:04.20; 2002- 12:58.98, 2003- 12:52.99, 2004- 13:08.01, 2005- 13:22.53, 2006- 13:04.54, 2007- 12:59.63, 2008- 13:07.88, 2009- 13:01.08, 2010- 13:03.11. pbs: 1500m 3:38.5A '04, 1M 3:55.31 '00, 2000m 5:00.5e '06, 3000m 7:33.42 '06, 2M 8:13.28i '08, 8:18.06 '06, HMar 60:07 '10.
Won 2002 GP 3000m final with 50.68 last lap and outsprinted Gebrselassie in Paris and both Geb and Bekele in Rome in 2003 5000m races.

Elijah CHELIMO Kipterege b. 10 Mar 1984.
At 3000mSt: AfG: '07- 4.
Progress at 3000mSt: 2005- 8:28.62, 2006- 8:34.1A, 2007- 8:16.28, 2008- 8:22.1, 2009- 8:10.63, 2010- 8:12.93, 2011- 8:14.22. pbs: 1500m 3:43.96 '07, 3000m 8:02.00 '05, 5000m 14:00.45 '07, 2000mSt 5:23.68 '07, Rd 10km 28:59 '07.

Vincent Kiprop **CHEPKOK** b. 5 Jul 1988 Kapkitony, Keiyo district 1.74m 60kg.
At 5000m: WCh: '09- 9. World CC: '07- 2J, '11- 3.
Progress at 5000m: 2006- 13:17.57, 2008- 13:06.41, 2009- 12:55.98, 2010- 12:51.45, 2011- 12:55.29. pbs: 1500m 3:40.47 '08, 3000m 7:30.15 '11, 10000m 28:23.46 '06.

Nixon Kiplimo **CHEPSEBA** b. 12 Dec 1990 1.84m 73kg.
At 1500m: Af-J: '09- 2.
Progress at 1500m: 2009- 3:37.2A, 2010- 3:32.42, 2011- 3:30.94. pbs: 800m 1:46.82 '11, 1000m 2:18.61 '09, 1M 3:53.36 '11, 3000m 7:37.64i '11.

Robert Kiprono CHERUIYOT b. 10 Aug 1988 Bomet, Rift Valley.
Progress at Mar: 2008- 2:07:21, 2009- 2:06:23, 2010- 2:05:52dh, 2011- 2:06:29. pb HMar 61:22 '09. Won Frankurt marathon 2008 (2nd 2009), Boston 2010.

Augustine Kiprono **CHOGE** b. 21 Jan 1987 Kipsigat, Nandi 1.62m 53kg.
At 5000m: CG: '06- 1; WJ: '04- 1. At 3000m: WY: '03- 1; WI: '10- 11, '12- 2. At 1500m: OG: '08- 9; WCh: '05- h, '09- 5. World CC: '03-05-06-08: 4J/1J/7 (4k)/12. Won E.African Youth 800m/1500m/3000m 2003, Junior 1500m 2004.

Records: World 4x1500m 2009, world youth 5000m 2004, world junior 3000m 2005.
Progress at 1500m, 5000m: 2003- 3:37.48, 13:20.08; 2004- 3:36.64, 12:57.01; 2005- 3:33.99, 12:53.66; 2006- 3:32.48, 12:56.41; 2007- 3:31.73, 2008- 3:31.57, 13:09.75; 2009- 3:29.47, 2010- 3:30.22, 13:04.64; 2011- 3:31.14, 13:21.24. pbs: 800m 1:44.86 '09, 1000m 2:17.79i '09, 1M 3:50.14 '10, 2000m 4:56.30i '07, 3000m 7:28.00i/7:28.76 '11, 10000m 29:06.5A '02.
At 17 in 2004 he become youngest to break 13 minutes for 5000m.

Joseph EBUYA Nawawona b. 20 Jun 1987 Nyan–darua district 1.76m 60kg. South Rift. Turkana.
At 5000m: WCh: '07- h, '09- 13; CG: '06- 4; WJ: '06- 3 (2 10000m). World CC: '06-08-10: 4J/4/1. World junior indoor 2M best 2006.
Progress at 5000m: 2005- 13:03.79, 2006- 12:58.03, 2007- 12:51.00, 2008- 13:06.61, 2009- 12:58.16, 2010- 13:11.09. pbs: 1500m 3:43.0A '07, 3000m 7:34.62 '08, 2M 8:18.33 '07, 10000m 28:53.46 '06, Rd: 10k 27:22+ '10, 15k: 42:11 '10, 10M: 45:16 '10.

Gideon GATHIMBA b. 9 Mar 1980 1.79m 64kg.
At 1500m: CG: '10- 5; AfG: '07- 4; AfCh: '08- 2; KEN champion 2008-09, World Military 2007. World 4x1500m record 2009.
Progress at 1500m: 2003- 3:44.3A, 2006- 3:38.2A, 2007- 3:38.7A, 2008- 3:33.63, 2009- 3:33.97, 2010- 3:34.75, 2011- 3:33.53. pbs: 1M 3:50.53 '10, 2000m 5:00.51i, 5:01.69 '10; 3000m 7:39.70i '12, 7:40.10 '11.

Haron KEITANY b. 17 Dec 1983 Moi's Bridge, Eldoret 1.83m 70kg.
At 1500m: WCh: '09- sf (dns); WI: '10- 3; AfCh: '08- 1, won WAF 2008.
Progress at 1500m: 2005- 3:47.0A, 2006- 3:41.5A, 2007- 3:37.75, 2008- 3:32.06, 2009- 3:30.20, 2010- 3:35.69i/3:37.87, 2011- 3:31.86. pbs: 800m 1:49.86 '10, 1000m 2:16.76i '09, 1M 3:48.78 '09.
His father Paul Keitany was a Kenyan Armed Forces CC champion in the 1960s.

Ezekiel KEMBOI Cheboi b. 25 May 1982 Matira, near Kapsowar, Marakwet District 1.75m 62kg.
At 3000mSt: OG: '04- 1, '08- 7; WCh: '03-05-07-09-11: 2/2/2/1/1; CG: '02-06-10: 2/1/2; AfG: '03- 1, '07- 2; AfCh: '02- 4, '06- dq, '10- 2; Af-J: '01- 1. Won WAF 2009, Kenyan 2003, 2006-07.
Progress at 3000mSt: 2001- 8:23.66, 2002- 8:06.65, 2003- 8:02.49, 2004- 8:02.98, 2005- 8:09.04, 2006- 8:09.29, 2007- 8:05.50, 2008- 8:09.25, 2009- 7:58.85, 2010- 8:01.74, 2011- 7:55.76. pbs: 1500m 3:40.8A '04, 3000m 7:49.95 '11, 5000m 13:50.61 '11, 10km Rd 28:38 '11.

Nicholas KEMBOI b. 18 Dec 1989 Kericho, Rift Valley 1.78m 59kg.
At 1500m: OG: '08- h; AfCh: '10- 5.
Progress at 1500m: 2006- 3:33.72, 2007- 3:36.13, 2008- 3:35.05, 2009- 3:35.47, 2010- 3:31.52, 2011- 3:37.25. pbs: 800m 1:46.65 '06, 1M 3:50.83 '08.

Mike Kipruto **KIGEN** b. 15 Jan 1986 Keiyo district 1.70m 54kg.

At 5000m/(10000m): AfCh: '06- 2/2; WCp: '06-2. World CC: '06- 5. Won Kenyan 5000m 2006. Progress at 5000m: 2005- 13:22.48, 2006- 12:58.58, 2008- 13:09.84, 2009- 13:04.38, 2011- 13:11.65. pbs: 3000m 7:35.87 '06, 2M 8:20.09 '05, 10000m 27:30.53 '11, HMar 60:49 '11.

Eliud KIPCHOGE b. 5 Nov 1984 Kapsisiywa, Nandi 1.67m 52kg.
At 5000m: OG: '04- 3, '08- 2; WCh: '03-05-07-09-11: 1/4/2/5/8; CG: '10- 2. At 3000m: WI: '06- 3. World CC: '02-03-04-05: 5J/1J/4/5. Won WAF 5000m 2003, 3000m 2004, Kenyan CC 2005. World junior 5000m record 2003. World road best 4M 17:10 '05.
Progress at 1500m, 5000m, 10000m: 2002- 13:13.03, 2003- 3:36.17, 12:52.61; 2004- 3:33.20, 12:46.53; 2005- 3:33.80, 12:50.22; 2006- 3:36.25i, 12:54.94; 2007- 3:39.98, 12:50.38, 26:49.02; 2008- 13:02.06, 26:54.32; 2009- 12:56.46, 2010- 3:38.36, 12:51.21; 2011- 12:55.72i/12:59.01, 26:53.27. pbs: 1M 3:50.40 '04, 2000m 4:59.?+ '04, 3000m 7:27.66 '11, 2M 8:07.39i '12, 8:07.68 '05; 10km Rd 26:55dh '06, 27:34 '05.
Kenyan Junior CC champion 2002-03, followed World Junior CC win by winning the World 5000m title, becoming at 18 years 298 days the second youngest world champion. Age 19 bests for 3000m & 5000m 2004. Ran 26:49.02 in 10,000m debut at Hengelo in 2007.

Silas KIPLAGAT b. 20 Aug 1989 Siboh village, Marakwet 1.70m 57kg.
At 1500m: WCh: '11- 2; CG: '10- 1; AfCh: '10- 4; WI: '12- 6. Kenyan champion 2011.
Progress at 1500m: 2009- 3:39.1A, 2010- 3:29.27, 2011- 3:30.47. pbs: 1M 3:49.39 '11, 3000m 7:39.94 '10, 10km Rd 28:00 '09.

Asbel Kipruto **KIPROP** b. 30 Jun 1989 Uasin Gishu, Eldoret. North Rift 1.86m 70kg.
At (800m)/1500m: OG: '08- 1; WCh: '07- 4, '09-sf/4, '11- 1; AfG: '07- 1; AfCh: '10- 1; CCp: '10- 6; Won DL 2010, Kenyan 2007, 2010. At 800m: AfCh: '08- 3. World CC: '07- 1J.
Progress at 800m, 1500m: 2007- 3:35.24, 2008- 1:44.71, 3:31.64; 2009- 1:43.17, 3:31.20; 2010- 1:43.45, 3:31.78; 2011- 1:43.15, 3:30.46. pbs: 1M 3:48.50 '09, 3000m 7:42.32 '07, 5000m 13:59.7A '10. Father David Kebenei was a 1500m runner.

Wilson KIPROP b. 14 Jul 1987 Soi, Uasin Gishu.
At 10000m: AfCh: '10- 1. World HMar: '10- 1. Won KEN 10000m 2010.
Progress at 10000m, Mar: 2010- 27:26.93A, 2:09:09; 2011- 27:32.9A. pbs: 5000m 13:30.13i '09, 13:45.38 '08; 1Hr 20756m '09; 15km Rd 43:50 '08, HMar 59:39 '10.

Brimin KIPRUTO b. 31 Jul 1985 Korkitony, Marakwet District 1.76m 54kg.
At 3000mSt: OG: '04- 2, '08- 1; WCh: '05-07-09-11: 3/1/7.2; CG: '10- 3; Af-J: '03- 2; KEN champion 2011. At 1500m: WJ: '04- 3. At 2000St: WY: '01- 2. World 4k CC: '06- 18.

Commonwealth & African 3000mSt record 2011. Progress at 3000mSt: 2002- 8:33.0A, 2003-8:34.5A, 2004- 8:05.52, 2005- 8:04.22, 2006-8:08.32, 2007- 8:02.89, 2008- 8:10.26, 2009-8:03.17, 2010- 8:00.90, 2011- 7:53.64. pbs: 1500m 3:35.23 '06, 2000m 4:58.76i '07, 3000m 7:42.99i '10, 7:47.33 '06; 5000m 13:58.82 '04, 2000mSt 5:36.81 '01.
First name is actually Firmin, but he has stayed with the clerical error of Brimin written when he applied for a birth certificate in 2001.

Vincent KIPRUTO Limo b. 13 Sep 1987 Keiyo district.
At Mar: WCh: '11- 2.
Progress at Mar: 2008- 2:08:16, 2009- 2:05:47, 2010- 2:05:13, 2011- 2:05:33. Road pbs: 10km 28:45 '11, 15km 43:15 '11, HMar 61:43 '10.
3rd Reims marathon 2008, won Paris & 3rd Chicago 2009, 3rd/2nd Rotterdam 2010/2011.

Wilson KIPSANG Kiprotich b. 15 Mar 1982 Keiyo district 1.78m 59kg.
At HMar: WCh: '09- 4.
Progress at HMar, Mar: 2008- 59:16, 2009- 58:59, 2010- 60:04, 2:04:57; 2011- 2:03:42. pbs: 5000m 13:55.7A '09, 10000m 28:37.0A '07; Road: 10km 27:42 '09, 15km 41:35 '09, 10M 46:04 '08, 20km 56:52 '09, 30km 1:29:12 '10.
At marathon: third in Paris in 2:07:13 on debut, and won Frankfurt for eighth all-time in 2010; won Lake Biwa and Frankfurt 2011.

Eliud KIPTANUI b. 6 Jun 1989 Kaplelach, Uasin Gishu.
At Mar: WCh: '11- 6.
Progress at Mar: 2009- 2:12:17, 2010- 2:05:59, 2011- 2:09:08, 2012- 2:06:44. pbs: 3000m 8:04.57 '09, 30km Rd 1:29:26 '10; HMar 61:24 '11.
Won Safaricom Marathon in Kisimu in December 2009, then made a stunning improvement to win Prague Marathon in 2010; 2nd Seoul 2012.

Mark Kosgei **KIPTOO** b. 21 Jun 1976 Lugafri 1.75m 64kg. Kenyan Air Force.
At 5000m: CG: '10- 3; AfG: '07- 9; AfCh: '10-3. World CC: '08- 14, '09- 7. Won World Military 5000m & 2nd 10000m 2007, KEN 5000m 2008.
Progress at 5000m, 10000m: 2007- 13:12.60, 28:22.62; 2008- 13:06.60, 27:14.67; 2009- 12:57.62, 2010- 12:53.46, 28:37.4A; 2011- 12:59.91, 26:54.64. pbs: 1500m 3:48.0A '05, 3000m 7:32.97 '09, HMar 60:29 '11.

Bernard KIPYEGO Kiprop b. 16 Jul 1986 Kapkitony, Keiyo district 1.60m 50kg.
At 10000m: WCh: '09- 5; Af-J: '03- 3. World CC: '05-07-08: 2J/3/10; HMar: '09- 2.
Progress at 10000m, Mar: 2003- 29:29.09, 2004- 28:18.94, 2005- 27:04.45, 2006- 27:19.45, 2007- 26:59.51, 2008- 27:08.06, 2009- 27:18.47, 2010- 2:07:01, 2011- 2:06:29. pbs: 3000m 7:54.91 '05, 5000m 13:09.96 '05, Road: 15km 42:34 '11, 10M 45:44 '11, HMar 59:10 '09.

Won in Berlin on half marathon debut in 59:34 in 2009, 5th Rotterdam on marathon debut 2010, 2nd Paris and 3rd Chicago 2011.

Abel KIRUI b. 4 Jun 1982 Rift Valley 1.77m 62kg.
At Mar: WCh: '09- 1, '11- 1.
Progress at Mar: 2006- 2:15:22, 2007- 2:06:51, 2008- 2:07:38, 2009- 2:05:04, 2010- 2:08:04, 2011- 2:07:38. pbs: 1500m 3:46.10 '05, 3000m 7:55.90 '06, 5000m 13:52.71 '05, 10000m 28:16.86A '08; Road: 10km 27:59 '09, 15km 42:22 '07, 10M 46:40 '11, HMar 60:11 '07, 25km: 1:13:41 '08, 30km 1:28:25 '08.
Brilliantly retained World marathon title with halves of 65:07 and 62:31 and a fastest 5k split of 14:18. Won Vienna Marathon 2008, 2nd Berlin 2007, 3rd Rotterdam 2009. Uncle Mike Rotich has marathon pb 2:06:33 '03.

Peter Cheruiyot **KIRUI** b. 2 Jan 1988 Mt Elgon 1.82m 66kg.
At 10000m: WCh: '11- 6; KEN champion 2011.
Progress at 10000m: 2011- 27:25.63. pbs: 1500m 3:44.20 '08, 3000m 7:45.79 '09, 5000m 13:15.90 '09, 15km Rd 42:48 '10, HMar 59:39 '12, 30km 1:27:37 '11.
Was pacemaker in Berlin Marathon 2101 and led at 30km at 1:27:37 but ineligible for world record as he did not finish race.

Alfred KIRWA YEGO b. 28 Nov 1986 Eldoret 1.75m 56kg. Cento Torri Pavia, Italy.
At 800m: OG: '08- 3; WCh: '05- h, '07- 1, '09- 2, '11- 7; WJ: '04- 2; AfCh: '06- 3, '10- 2. Won WAF 2008.
Progress at 800m, 1500m: 2004- 1:47.39, 3:37.95; 2005- 1:44.45, 3:50.14; 2006- 1:43.89, 3:38.55; 2007- 1:44.50, 2008- 1:44.01, 3:33.69; 2009- 1:42.67, 3:33.68; 2010- 1:43.97, 2011- 1:44.07. pbs: 1000m 2:17.60 '10, 1M 3:55.18 '11.
Ran 24.6 last 200m to win 2007 World 800m.

Mathew Kipkoech **KISORIO** b. 16 May 1989 Kapchumba, Nandi North District 1.78m 62kg.
At 5000m/(10000m): WJ: '08- 2; AfCh: '10- (4); Af-J: '07- 1/1. World CC: '07-08-09-11: 3J/6J/6/4.
Progress at 5000m, 10000m: 2006- 28:50.1A, 2007- 13:28.43, 2008- 13:11.57, 29:34.96; 2009- 13:02.40, 27:15.44; 2010- 12:57.83, 27:28.13A; 2011- 26:54.25. pbs: 3000m 7:34.29 '09, road: 15km 42:11+ '10, 10M 44:54+ '11, 20km 55:44+ '11, 25km 1:12:13 '11, HMar 58:46 '11, Mar 2:10:58 '11.
His father Some Muge (1959-97) was 3rd at 1983 World Cross (Kenya's first medallist). His younger brother Peter Some was 7th in 2008 World Junior Cross.

Sammy Kiprop **KITWARA** b. 26 Nov 1986 Sagat village, Marakwet district 1.77m 54kg.
At 10000m: Kenyan champion 2009. World HMar: '09- 10, '10- 3.
Progress at 10,000m, HMar: 2007- 28:11.6A, 2008- 28:12.26A, 60:54; 2009- 27:44.46A, 58:58; 2010- 28:32.77A, 59:34; 2011- 58:47. pbs: 5000m

13:34.0A '08, Road: 10km 27:11 '10, 15km 41:54 '09, 10M 45:17 '08, 20km 57:42 '08.

Jackson Mumbwa **KIVUVA** b. 11 Aug 1988 1.70m 59kg.
At 800m: WCh: '09- 9, '11- sf; WJ: '06- 2; WY: '05- 2; AfCh: '08- 4, '10- 3.
Progress at 800m: 2005- 31:48.57, 2006- 1:45.8A, 2008- 1:45.29, 2009- 1:44.86, 2010- 1:43.72, 2011- 1:44.40A. pbs: 600m 1:15.69i '11, 1000m 2:17.47 '08, 1500m 3:42.6 '06.

Isiah Kiplangat **KOECH** b. 19 Oct 1993 Kericho.
At 5000m: WCh: '11- 4; KEN champion 2011. At 3000m: WY: '09- 1. World CC: '10- 4J, '11- 10J. World junior records indoors: 5000m 2011, 3000m 2011 & 2012.
Progress at 5000m: 2010- 13:07.70, 2011- 12:53.29i/12:54.18. 2012- 13:02.36i. pb 3000m 7:32.89i '12, 7:51.51 '09; 2M 8:14.16 '11.

Paul Kipsiele **KOECH** b. 10 Nov 1981 Cheplanget, Buret District 1.68m 57kg.
At 3000mSt: OG: '04- 3; WCh: '05- 7, '09- 4; AfG: '03- 2; AfCh: '06- 1; WCp: '06- 2; won DL 2010, WAF 2005-08. At 3000m: WI: 08- 2.
Progress at 3000mSt: 2001- 8:15.92, 2002- 8:05.44, 2003- 7:57.42, 2004- 7:59.65, 2005- 7:56.37, 2006- 7:59.94, 2007- 7:58.80, 2008- 8:00.57, 2009- 8:01.26, 2010- 8:02.07, 2011- 7:57.32. pbs: 1500m 3:37.92 '07, 2000m 5:00.9+i '08, 3000m 7:32.78i '10, 7:33.93 '05; 2M 8:06.48i/8:13.31 '08, 5000m 13:02.69i 12, 13:05.18 '10.

Micah Kemboi **KOGO** b. 3 Jun 1986 Burnt Forest, Uasin Gishu 1.70m 60kg.
At 10000m: OG: '08- 3; WCh: '09- 7.
World 10k road record (27:01) 2009.
Progress at 5000m, 10000m: 2004- 14:02.99, 2005- 13:16.31, 2006- 13:00.07, 26:35.63; 2007- 13:10.68, 26:58.42; 2008- 13:03.71, 27:04.11; 2009- 13:01.30, 27:26.33; 2010- 13:07.62, 2011- 13:46.01, 27:50.50. pbs: 2000m 5:03.05 '06, 3000m 7:38.67 '07, 2M 8:20.88 '05; Road: 15km 43:05 '08, 10M 46:13 '08, HMar 61:30 '10.
Won Van Damme 10,000m in Brussels in 2006 for 6th world all-time.

Daniel Kipchirchir **KOMEN** b. 27 Nov 1984 Chemorgong, Kolbatek district 1.75m 60kg.
At 1500m: WCh: '05- h, '07/11- sf; WI: '06- 2, '08- 2; won WAF 2007. At 5000m: Af-J: '03- 2.
Progress at 1500m, 5000m: 2003- 13:49.20, 2004- 3:34.66, 13:16.26; 2005- 3:29.72, 2006- 3:29.02, 2007- 3:31.75, 2008- 3:31.49, 13:24.39; 2009- 3:34.86i, 2010- 3:32.16, 13:04.02; 2011- 3:32.47A, 13:20.80. pbs: 800m 1:47.3A '05, 1000m 2:16.9+ '06, 1M 3:48.28 '07, 3000m 7:31.41 '11.

Leonard Patrick **KOMON** b. 10 Jan 1988 Korun–gotuny Village, Mt. Eldon District 1.75m 52kg.
World CC: '06-07-08-09-10: 2J/4J/2/4/4.
World road records 10km and 15km 2010.
Progress at 5000m, 10000m: 2006- 13:04.12, 2007- 13:04.79, 2008- 13:17.48, 26:57.08; 2009- 12:58.24, 28:02.24A; 2010- 12:59.15, 2011- 26:55.29. pbs:

2000m 5:04.0+ '07, 3000m 7:33.27 '09, 2M 8:22.56 '07, road 10km 26:44 '10, 15km 41:13 '10, 10M 44:27 '11.

Leonard Kirwa **KOSENCHA** b. 21 Aug 1994.
At 800m: WY: 11- 1.
World youth 800m record 2011.
Progress at 800m: 2011- 1:44.08.

James Kipsang **KWAMBAI** b. 28 Feb 1983 Marakwet East district 1.62m 52kg
Commonwealth marathon record 2009.
Progress at Mar: 2006- 2:10:20, 2007- 2:12:25, 2008- 2:05:36, 2009- 2:04:27, 2010- 2:11:31, 2011- 2:08:50, 2012- 2:06:03. pbs: Road: 10km 28:17 '02, 20km 58:51 '08, HMar 59:09 '09, 30km 1:28:27 '08. Won Brescia and Beijing marathons 2006, took 4:44 off pb when 2nd in Berlin 2008 and went to joint second all-time when 2nd in Rotterdam 2009. Won Seoul Marathon 2011 (2bd 2012).

Boaz Kiplagat **LALANG** b. 8 Feb 1989 Marakwet 1.74m 62kg. Rend Lake College, USA.
At 800m: OG: '08- sf, CG: '10- 1; AfG: '11- 2; WI: '10- 2.
Progress at 800m: 2008- 1:44.68, 2009- 1:45.36, 2010- 1:42.95, 2011- 1:44.13. pbs: 400m 47.60 '08, 1000m 2:14.83 '10, 1500m 3:35.80 '10, 1M 3:52.18 '10.
His younger brother **Lawi Lalang** (b. 15 Sep 1991) set pbs in 2012: 1M 3:55.09i, 5000m 13:08.28i US collegiate indoor record.

Martin LEL b. 29 Oct 1978 Kapsabet 1.71m 54kg.
At Mar: OG: '08- 5. World HMar: '03- 1.
African record 30km 2008.
Progress at Mar: 2002- 2:10:02, 2003- 2:10:30, 2004- 2:13:38, 2005- 2:07:26, 2006- 2:06:41, 2007- 2:07:41, 2008- 2:05:15, 2011- 2:05:45. pbs: 10km 27:25 '06, 15km 42:41 '07, 10M 45:40 '07, HMar 59:30 '06, 30km 1:28:30 '08.
Exclusively a road runner. Marathons: dnf Prague and 2nd in Venice 2002, 3rd Boston 2003-04, 1st New York 2003 and 2007 and London 2005, 2007 and 2008 (2nd 2006 and 2011). He won the Marathon Majors prize for 2007-08. Won Great North Run 2007, 2009.

Thomas Pkemei **LONGOSIWA** b. 14 Jan 1982 West Pokot 1.75m 57kg. North Rift.
At 5000m: OG: '08- 12; WCh: '11- 6; AfG: '07- 6.
World CC: '06- 13J (but dq after birthdate found to be 1982). Won Kenyan 5000m 2007.
Progress at 5000m: 2006- 13:35.3A, 2007- 12:51.95, 2008- 13:14.36, 2009- 13:03.43, 2010- 13:05.60, 2011- 12:56.08, 2012- 12:58.67i. pbs: 2000m 5:01.6+ '10, 3000m 7:30.09 '09, 10000m 28:11.3A '06.

Patrick MAKAU Musyoki b. 2 Mar 1985 Manyanzwani, Tala Kangundo district.
World HMar: '07- 2, '08- 2.
World 30km and marathon records 2011.
Progress at HMar, Mar: 2005- 62:00, 2006- 62:42, 2007- 58:56, 2008- 59:29, 2009- 58:52, 2:06:14; 2010- 59:51, 2:04:48; 2011- 2:03:38. pbs: 3000m 7:54.50 '07, 5000m 13:42.84 '06. Road: 10km 27:27

'07, 15km 41:30 '09, 20km 55:53 '07, 30km 1:27:38 '11.
Second fastest ever debut marathon when 4th Rotterdam 2009 and won there a year later in 2:04:48 for fourth world all-time. Won Berlin 2010 and 2011.

Moses Ndiema **MASAI** b. 1 Jun 1986 Kapsogom 1.72m 57kg.
At 10000m: OG: '08- 4; WCh: '09- 3; WJ: '04- 10.
World CC: '04-05-08: 16J/7J/5. Won Afr-J 5000 & 10000m 2005, Kenyan CC 2006.
World junior marathon record 2005.
Progress at 5000m, 10000m: 2004- 13:25.5+e, 27:07.29; 2005- 13:24.36, 28:08.6A; 2006- 13:13.28, 27:03.20; 2007- 13:08.81, 26:49.20; 2008- 12:50.55, 27:04.11; 2009- 13:06.16, 26:57.39; 2010- 13:02.45, 2011- 13:13.03, 27:10.05. pbs: 1500m 3:37.3A '08, 3000m 7:44.75 '09; Road: 15km 45:18 '09, 10M 45:16 '09, Mar 2:10:13 '05.
Marathon wins (while a junior) at Hannover 2004 and Essen 2005. His sister is **Linet Masai** (qv) and their younger brother **Dennis** won the World Junior 10000m in pb 27:53.88 in 2010. His partner **Doris Changeiywo** was 4th in the 2008 World CC, 2nd CG 10000m 2010.

Richard Kipkemboi **MATELONG** b. 14 Oct 1983 Lenape, Narok District 1.79m 65g. Police.
At 3000mSt: OG: '08- 3; WCh: '07- 3, '09- 2, '11- 7; CG: '10- 1; AfCh: '04-08-10: 2/1/1; CCp: '10- 1.
World CC: '10- 7. Won Kenyan CC 2007, 3000mSt 2009.
Progress at 3000mSt: 2004- 8:05.96, 2005- 8:10.97, 2006- 8:07.50, 2007- 8:06.66, 2008- 8:07.64, 2009- 8:00.89, 2010- 8:06.44, 2011- 8:07.41. pbs: 1500m 3:41.79 '05, 3000m 7:48.71 '05, 5000m 13:30.4A '06, 10000m 28:18.4A '07.

Martin Irungu MATHATHI b. 25 Dec 1985 Nyahururu 1.67m 52kg. Suzuki, Japan.
At 10000m: OG: '08- 7; WCh: '05- 5, '07- 3, '11- 5.
World CC: '06- 3.
Progress at 5000m, 10000m: 2003- 14:09.3A, 27:43.16; 2004- 13:03.84, 27:22.46; 2005- 13:05.99, 27:08.42; 2006- 13:05.55, 27:10.51; 2007- 13:22.13, 27:09.90; 2008- 13:46.87, 27:08.25; 2009- 13:11.46, 26:59.88; 2010- 13:10.94, 2011- 13:15.93, 27:23.85. pbs: 1500m 3:38.57 '06, Road: 10M 44:51 '04 (world junior best), 15km 42:14 '10, 20km 56:44 '10, HMar 58:56 '11. Won Great North Run 2011.

Titus MBISHEI b. 28 Oct 1990 Mt Elgon 1.78m 59kg.
At 10000m: CG: '10- 4; WJ: '08- 2. World CC: '08-09: 5J/2J.
Progress at 5000m, 10000m: 2008- 13:27.54, 27:31.65; 2009- 13:29.09, 28:14.0A; 2010- 13:00.04, 27:29.13A; 2011- 13:11.76, 26:59.81. pb 3000m 7:44.9+ '10.

Josphat Kiprono MENJO b. 20 Aug 1979 Kapsabet 1.68m 50kg.
At 5000m: AfG: '07- 2; AfCh: '06- 5, '08- 5. At 10000m: WCh: '07- 8; won W.Mil G 2011.

Progress at 5000m, 10000m: 2004- 13:48.7A, 2005- 13:14.38, 2006- 13:09.24, 27:29.45; 2007- 13:06.69, 27:04.61; 2008- 13:06.17, 27:09.37; 2010- 12:55.95, 26:56.74; 2011- 13:21.10, 27:55.81. pbs: 1500m 3:38.40 '10, 1M 3:53.62 '10. 3000m 7:42.6+ '10, 2M 8:18.96 '07, HMar 61:42 '10.

Moses Cheruiyot **MOSOP** b. 17 Jul 1985 Kamasia, Marakwet 1.72m 57kg. Police officer.
At 10000m: OG: '04- 7; WCh: '05- 3. World CC: '02-03-05-07-09: 10J/7J/18/2/11; HMar: '10- 10. Won KEN 10000m 2006, CC 2009.
World records 25,000m and 30,000m 2011.
Progress at 5000m, 10000m: 2002- 29:38.6A, 2003- 13:11.75, 27:13.66; 2004- 13:09.68, 27:30.66; 2005- 13:06.83, 27:08.96; 2006- 12:54.46, 27:17.00; 2007- 13:07.89,26:49.55.AtMar:2011-2:03:06wdh/2:05:37. pbs: 3000m 7:36.88 '06, 15km Rd 42:25+ '10, HMar 59:20 '10, 20000m 58:02.2 '11, 25000m 1:12:25.4 '11, 30000m 1:26:47.4 '11.
Second with fastest ever marathon debut at Boston and won Chiacgo 2011. Married to Florence Kiplagat (qv).

Josphat MUCHIRI Ndambiri b. 12 Feb 1985 1.71m 52kg. Komori, Japan.
At 10000m: WCh: '07- 5.
Progress at 5000m, 10000m, Mar: 2001- 13:54.65, 29:06.30; 2002- 13:36.77, 28:45.05; 2003- 13:36.14, 28:02.09; 2004- 13:27.53, 27:46.10; 2005- 13:05.33, 27:19.19; 2006- 13:09.39, 27:04.79; 2007- 13:18.49, 27:28.38; 2008- 13:23.11, 27:14.03; 2009- 13:11.46, 26:57.36; 2010- 13:09.19, 27:16.51; 2011- 13:12.77, 27:39.21, 2:07:36. pbs: 1500m 3:38.72 '04, 3000m 7:42.98 '06, HMar 61:07 '10.
Won Fukuoka on marathon debut 2011.

Sammy Alex **MUTAHI** b. 1 Jun 1989 1.77m 58kg.
At 3000m: WI: '10- 3.
Progress at 5000m, 10000m: 2007- 13:13.18, 27:12.42; 2008- 13:12.18, 28:26.0A; 2009- 13:10.17, 2010- 13:00.12, 2011- 13:34.32i/13:38.10. pbs: 3000m 7:31.41 '09.
Younger brother of Faith Macharia (800m 4 WCh & 1:58.34 '01).

Emmanuel Kipchirchir **MUTAI** b. 12 Oct 1984 Tulwet, Rift Valley 1.68m 54kg.
At Mar: WCh: '09- 2.
Progress at Mar: 2007- 2:06:29, 2008- 2:06:15, 2009- 2:06:53, 2010- 2:06:23, 2011- 2:04:40. pbs: 10000m 28:21.14 '06, Road: 10km 27:51 '06, 15km 42:11 '10, 20km 56:44 '10, HMar 59:52 '11, 30km 1:28:30 '08.
Made marathon debut with 7th in Rotterdam in 2:13:06 in 2007, then won in Amsterdam. London: 4th 2008 & 2009, 2nd 2010, 1st 2011. 2nd New York 2010-11.

Geoffrey Kiprono **MUTAI** b. 7 Oct 1981 Kolbatek District 1.83m 56kg. Policeman.
At 10000m: AfCh: '10- 3. World CC: '11- 5. Won Kenyan CC 2011.
Progress at 10000m, Mar: 2008- 28:01.74, 2:07:50; 2009- 2:07:01, 2010- 27:27.79A, 2:04:55; 2011-

2:03:02wdh/2:05:06. pbs: 15km 42:25+ '10, HMar 59:38 '10, 30km 1:28:52+ '10.
Marathons: Won Monte Carlo 2008, Eindhoven 2008 & 2009, Boston & New York 2011; 2nd Rotterdam and Berlin 2010.

Jonathan NDIKU Muia b. 18 Sep 1991 1.70m 55kg.
At 3000mSt: WJ: '08- 1, '10- 1; Af-J: '09- 1. At 2000mSt: WY: '07- 4.
Progress at 3000mSt: 2008- 8:17.28, 2009- 8:28.1A, 2010- 8:19.25A. 2011- 8:07.75. pbs: 1500m 3:39.27 '10, 3000m 7:52.89 '09, 5000m 13:11.99 '09, 10000m 27:37.72 '09, 2000mSt 5:37.30 '07.

Gideon NGATUNY b. 10 Oct 1986 Kilgoris 1.73m 55kg. Nissin Foods Corporation, Japan.
At World CC: '07- 4, '08- 7.
Progress at 5000m, 10000m: 2006- 13:15.9, 27:28.42; 2007- 13:12.62, 27:11.36; 2008- 13:11.81, 27:17.91; 2009- 13:12.02, 27:01.83; 2010- 13:26.43, 27:22.46; 2011- 13:21.25, 27:41.32. pbs: 3000m 7:56.48 '06, Road: 15km 42:25 '09, 10M: 45:15 '08, 20km 56:52 '09, HMar 59:50 '09.
Dropped from 2009 Kenyan World Champs team due to competing in road races without permission of Athletics Kenya.

Lucas Kimeli **ROTICH** b. 16 Apr 1990 1.71m 57kg.
At 3000mSt: WY: '07- 2. World CC: '08- 3J, '10- 18
Progress at 5000m, 10000m: 2007- 29:12.5A, 2008- 13:15.54, 2009- 12:58.70, 28:15.0A; 2010- 12:55.06, 27:33.59; 2011- 13:00.02, 26:43.98. pbs: 1500m 3:43.64 '08, 3000m 7:35.57 '11, HMar 59:44 '11.

David Lekuta **RUDISHA** b. 17 Dec 1988 Kilgoris 1.89m 73kg. Masai.
At 800m: WCh: '09- sf; WJ: '06- 1/4R; AfCh: '08- 1, '10- 1; Af-J: '07- 1; CCp: '10- 1. Won DL 2010, WAF 2009, Kenyan 2009-11.
Two world 800m records 2010, four African records 2009-10.
Progress at 800m: 2006- 1:46.3A, 2007- 1:44.15, 2008- 1:43.72, 2009- 1:42.01, 2010- 1:41.01, 2011- 1:41.33. pbs: 400m 45.50 '10, 600m 1:14.28+ '11.
IAAF Male Athlete of the Year 2010, won 26 successive 800m finals 2009-11. His father Daniel won 4x400m silver medal at 1968 Olympics with 440y pb 45.5A '67.

Daniel Lemashon **SALEL** b. 11 Dec 1990 1.73m 57kg.
At 10000m: CG: '10- 2. At 3000m: WY: '07- 1.
Progress at 5000m, 10000m: 2010- 13:08.23, 27:07.85; 2011- 13:19.51, 28:04.63. pbs: 1500m 3:38.79+ '09, 1M 3:54.72 '09, 3000m 7:38.91 '10.

Edwin Cheruiyot **SOI** b. 3 Mar 1986 Kericho 1.68m 53kg.
At 5000m: OG: '08- 3; AfCh: '10- 1; CCp: '10- 4. At 3000m: WI: '08- 4, '12- 3; won WAF 3000m 2007, 5000m 2007-08. World CC: '06- 8 4k, '07- 9.
Progress at 5000m, 10000m: 2002- 29:06.5A, 2004- 13:22.57, 2005- 13:10.78, 2006- 12:52.40,

27:14.83; 2007- 13:10.21, 2008- 13:06.22, 2009- 12:55.03, 2010- 12:58.91, 2011- 12:59.15. pbs: 1500m 3:44.76 '05, 2000m 5:01.4+ '10, 3000m 7:27.55 '11, 2M 8:14.10 '11, 10km Rd 28:13 '08.

Paul Kipngetich **TANUI** b. 22 Dec 1990 Chesubeno village, Moio district 1.68m 49kg. Kyudenko Corporation, Japan.
At 10000m: WCh: '11- 9. World CC: '09-10-11: 4J/8/2. Won Kenyan CC 2010.
Progress at 10000m: 2009- 27:25.24, 2010- 27:17.61, 2011- 26:50.63. pbs: 1500m 3:43.97 '10, 3000m 7:50.88 '11, 5000m 13:04.65 '11.

John Kimondo **THUO** b. 27 Nov 1985 Mailo Inya, Nyahururu 1.68m 53kg. Toyota, Japan. World CC: '08- 18.
Progress at 10000m: 2005- 29:47.6A, 2008- 27:31.61, 2009- 27:11.88, 2010- 27:15.73, 2011- 27:23.99. pbs: 1500m 3:35.27 '07, 3000m 7:46.01 '11, 5000m 13:15.53 '11, 10M Rd 45:23 '09.

Hillary Kipsang **YEGO** b. 2 Apr 1992.
At 2000mSt: WY: '09- 1.
Progress at 3000mSt: 2009- 8:46.8A, 2010- 8:19.50, 2011- 8:07.71. pbs: 1500m 3:43.3 '10, 3000m 7:53.18 '10, 2000mSt 5:25.33 '09, 10km Rd 29:10 '11.

Women

Peninah ARUSEI Jerop b. 23 Feb 1979 Uasin Gishu 1.65m 51kg.
At 10000m: OG: '08- 18. World HMar: '08-09-10: 5/19/3.
Progress at 10000m, HMar: 2001- 34:27.7A, 2005- 71:20, 2006- 70:54, 2007- 69:23, 2008- 30:57.7, 68:20, 2009- 33:01.5A, 68:30; 2010- 32:48.67A, 67:48; 2011- 68:30. pbs: 5000m 15:12.5+ '08, Road: 15km 47:48 '10, 20km: 64:07 '10, 10M 51:26 '09, 25km 1:22:31 '09, Mar 2:27:17 '11.

Emily CHEBET Muge b. 18 Feb 1986 Bornet 1.57m 45kg.
At 10000m: WCh: '07- 9; AfCh: '06- 3. World CC: '03- 5J, '10- 1.
Progress at 10000m: 2006- 31:33.39, 2007- 32:31.21, 2010- 32:49.43A. 2011- 31:30.22. pbs: 1500m 4:18.75 '05, 3000m 8:53.46 '05; Road 10km 31:12 '10, HMar 72:00 '11.
Has daughter Emily.

Milcah CHEMOS Cheywa b. 24 Feb 1986 Bugaa Village, Mt. Elgon district 1.63m 48kg. Police.
At 3000mSt: WCh: '09- 3, '11- 3; CG: '10- 1; AfCh: '10- 1; CCp: '10- 2. Won DL 2010, KEN 2010-11.
Two world junior (four African junior) 3000mSt records 2007.
Progress at 3000mSt: 2009- 9:08.57, 2010- 9:11.71, 2011- 9:12.89. pbs: 800m 2:04.35A '11, 1500m 4:12.3A '09, 2000m 5:41.64 '09, 3000m 8:43.92 '09.
Married to Alex Sang (pb 800m 1:46.84 '08). Started athletics seriously after birth of daughter Lavine Jemutai and in first season, 2008, was 4th in Kenyan 800m. Rapid progress from first steeplechase in April 2009.

Ines Chepkesis **CHENONGE** b. 1 Feb 1982 Trans Zoia 1.68m 54kg.
At 5000m: CG: '02-06-10: 3/6/3; WCh: '09- 6; AfCh: '10- 4. At 3000m: CCp: '10- 5. World CC: '09- 10; HMar: '02- 20.
Progress at 5000m: 2001- 15:45.63, 2002- 15:06.06, 2003- 15:35.04, 2004- 15:00.76, 2005- 14:54.43, 2006- 14:47.98, 2008- 15:20.10, 2009- 14:41.62, 2010- 14:39.19. pbs: 1500m 4:08.61A '09, 2000m 5:44.51 '09, 3000m 8:37.17 '09, 10000m 33:52.3A '10, Road: 10km 32:30 '01, 15km 48:13 '09, HMar 68:54 '02.
Brother Hillary Chenonge won WJ 5000m 2002, pbs: 5000m 13:04.70 '05, 10000m 27:51.92 '07.

Joyce CHEPKIRUI b. 10 Aug 1988.
At 1500m: AfG: '11- 2; AfCh: '07- 5. At HMar: WCh: '10- 5. African CC: '12- 3.
Progress at 10000m, HMar: 2007- 75:11 2009- 71:47, 2010- 69:25, 2011- 31:26.10, 69:04; 2012- 67:03. pbs: 1500m 4:08.80A '11, 3000mSt 10:26.7A '08; Road: 10km 30:38 '11.

Lineth CHEPKURUI b. 23 Feb 1988 Bukacha, Bornet 1.57m 43kg. Kenya Air Force.
World CC: '08-09-10-11: 12/4/5/8.
Progress at HMar: 2005- 73:33A, 2006- 70:09, 2010- 67:47. pbs: 3000m 9:30.24 '06, 5000m 15:15.15 '11, 10000m 31:24.20 '11, 3000mSt 10:07.4A '09; Road: 10km 30:45 '10, 10M 51:38 '10, 25km 1:22:31 '09.

Lydia CHEROMEI b. 11 May 1977 Baringo district 1.62m 47kg. Married Hosea Kogo (5000m 13:24.22 '97) in December 1996.
At 5000m: OG: '96- h, '00- 6; WCh: '97- 5; AfG: '95- 3; 2nd GP 1997. At 10000m: OG: '92- h; WJ: '90- 3, '92- 4; AfG: '91- 2; AfCh: '92- 2, '93- 2 (8 3000m). At HMar: WCh: '04- 2. World CC: '91-2: 1J/3J, '97-00-01: 11/4/3. Won Kenyan 10000m 1991-2, 5000m 1997, 2000.
Records: World junior 5000m 1995, African junior 3000m 1992, Kenyan 5000m 1995, 3000m 1997 and 2000.
Progress at 5000m, 10000m: 1990- 16:56.7, 33:20.83; 1991- 33:07.7, 1992- 15:17.31, 31:41.09; 1993- 32:54.55, 1994- 36:29.0, 1995- 14:53.44, 1996- 15:18.34, 1997- 14:46.72, 2000- 14:47.35. At Mar: 2008- 2:25:57; 2009- 2:28:09, 2011- 2:22:34, 2012- 2:21:30. pbs: 1500m 4:09.32 '97, 2000m 5:38.9 '97, 3000m 8:29.14 '00, road 10km 31:57 '08, 15km 47:50 '11, HMar 67:26 '12, 30km 1:42:47 '08.
Youngest ever world junior cross-country champion at 13 in 1991. World age bests for 3000m, 5000m and 10000m at 13, 5000m at 15. Daughter Faith born 2005. Won at Amsterdam on marathon debut 2008, 2nd Dubai and won Prague 2011. Two year drugs ban 2005-07.

Mercy CHERONO b. 7 May 1991 Kericho 1.78m 59kg.
At 3000m/(5000m): WCh: '11- (5); WJ: '08- 1, '10- 1/2; WY: '07- 1; Af-J: '09- 1/2. World CC: '07-09-10: 23J/2J/1J. Won Afr CC 2011.

Progress at 5000m: 2007- 16:49.13A, 2009- 15:46.74A, 2010- 14:47.13, 2011- 14:35.13. pbs: 1500m 4:02.31 '11, 2000m 5:35.65 '10, 3000m 8:42.09 '10, 10000m 34:33.4A '06.

Priscah Jepleting **CHERONO** b. 27 Jun 1980 Nandi 1.60m 47kg. née Ngetich.
At 5000m: OG: '08- 11; WCh: '05- 7, '07- 3; WJ: '96- 8, '98- 7; AfCh: '04- 2. Kenyan champion 2004. At 10000m: WCh: '11- 4. World CC J/4k: '97-8-02-03-04-0: 2J/11J/18/11/4/2; 8k: '07-08-11: 7/7/5.
Progress at 5000m, 10000m: 1996- 15:39.1A, 1998- 16:07.12, 1999- 16:24.4A, 2001- 16:42.4A, 2002- 15:41.13A, 2003- 15:35.7A, 2004- 14:54.24, 2005- 14:44.00, 2006- 14:35.30, 2007- 14:42.00, 2008- 14:45.12, 2011- 14:40.86, 30:56.43. pbs: 800m 2:07.8A '99, 1500m 4:15.7A '00, 3000m 8:29.06 '07, 2M 9:14.09 '07 (Kenyan best); Road: 15km 48:24 '11. 10M 51:57 '11.
Married Charles Cherono in December 2006; child in 2010.

Sharon Jemutai **CHEROP** b. 16 Mar 1984 Marakwet district 40kg.
At Mar: WCh: '11- 3. At 10000m: AfG: '99- 5. At 5000m: WJ: '00- 3. World CC: '02- 10J.
Progress at Mar: 2007- 2:38:45, 2008- 2:39:52, 2009- 2:33:53, 2010- 2:22:43, 2011- 2:22:42wdh/2:29:14, 2012- 2:22:39. pbs: 3000m 9:09.23 '04, 5000m 15:40.7A '00, 10000m 32:03.0A '11, HMar 67:08 '11. Won Toronto and Hamburg marathon 2010, 3rd Boston 2011.

Vivian CHERUIYOT b. 11 Sep 1983 Keiyo 1.55m 38kg.
At 5000m (/10000m): OG: '00- 14, '08- 5; WCh: '07- 2, '09- 1, '11- 1/1; CG: '10- 1; WJ: '02- 3; AfG '99- 3; AfCh: '10- 1; CCp: '10- 1; won DL 2010. At 3000m: WY: '99- 3; WI: '10- 2. World CC: '98-9-00-01-02-04-06-07-11: 5J/2J/1J/4J/3J/8 4k/8 4k/8/1. Won KEN 1500m 2009, 5000m 2010-11, 10000m 2011.
African 2000m record 2009, Commonwealth 5000m 2009 & 2011, indoor 3000m (8:30.53) 2009; Kenyan 5000m 2007 & 2011.
Progress at 5000m, 10000m: 1999- 15:42.79A, 2000- 15:11.11, 2001- 15:59.4A, 2002- 15:49.7A, 2003- 15:44.8A, 2004- 15:13.26, 2006- 14:47.43, 2007- 14:22.51, 2008- 14:25.43, 2009- 14:37.01, 2010- 14:27.41, 2011- 14:20.87, 30:48.98. pbs: 1500m 4:06.65 '07, 2000m 5:31.52 '09, 3000m 8:28.66 '07, 2M 9:12.35i '10, 10km Rd 30:47 '12.
Laureus Sportswomen of the Year for 2011.

Irene JELAGAT b. 10 Dec 1988 Samutet, Nyanza 1.62m 45kg.
At 1500m: OG: '08- h; WCh: '09- h; CG: '10- 6; AfG: '11- 1; AfCh: '08- 5, '10- 4; WJ: '06- 1; WY: '05- dns; WI: '10- 5.
Progress at 1500m: 2005- 4:21.3A, 2006- 4:08.88, 2007- 4:10.27, 2008- 4:04.59, 2009- 4:03.62, 2010- 4:03.76, 2011- 4:02.59. pb 800m 2:02.99 '06.

Pamela JELIMO b. 5 Dec 1989 Kapsabet 1.75m 60kg.

At 800m: OG: '08- 1; WCh: '09- sf; WI: '12- 1; AfCh: '08- 1/2R. At 400m: Af-J: '07- 1 (7 200m). Won WAF 800m 2008, Kenyan 400m 2008.
Five world junior and four African & Commonwealth 800m records 2008.
Progress at 800m: 2007- c.2:14, 2008- 1:54.01, 2009- 1:59.49A, 2010- 2:01.52, 2011- 2:09.12, 2012- 1:58.83i. pbs: 200m 24.68 '07, 400m 52.78A '08, 600m 1:24.03 '08, 1500m (4:07.11idq '12).
Set world junior records in just third and fourth major 800m finals. Won Golden League jackpot 2008, when in her first season of 800m running she won all 13 finals and three heats. Married Peter Kiprotich Murrey in November 2007. Suffered from a knee injury in 2009.

Janeth JEPKOSGEI b. 13 Dec 1983 Kabirirsang, near Kapsabet 1.67m 47kg. North Rift.
At 800m: OG: '08- 2; WCh: '07- 1, '09- 2, '11- 3; CG: '06- 1; AfCh: '06- 1, '10- 2; WJ: '02- 1; WY: '99- h; WCp: '06- 2, '10- 1; won DL 2010, WAF 2007, KEN 2011.
Five Kenyan 800m records 2005-07.
Progress at 800m, 1500m: 1999- 2:11.0A, 2001- 2:06.21, 2002- 2:00.80, 2003- 2:03.05, 2004- 2:00.52, 4:11.91; 2005- 1:57.82, 4:15.77; 2006- 1:56.66, 4:15.43; 2007- 1:56.04, 4:14.70; 2008- 1:56.07, 4:08.48; 2009- 1:57.90, 4:13.87; 2010- 1:57.84, 4:04.17; 2011- 1:57.42, 4:02.32. pbs: 400m 54.06A '10, 600m 1:25.0+ '08, 1000m 2:37.98 '02, 1M 4:28.72 '08.
Brilliant front-running victory at 2007 Worlds.

Priscah JEPTOO b. 24 Jun 1984.
At Mar: WCh: '11- 2. At 10000m: AfG: '99- 5. At 5000m: WJ: '00- 3. World CC: '02- 10J.
Progress at Mar: 2009- 2:30:40, 2010- 2:27:02, 2011- 2:22:55. Road pbs: 15km 48:48 '11, HMar 70:08u/70:26 '11. Marathon wins: Porto 2009, Turin 2010, Paris 2011.

Mary Jepkosgei **KEITANY** b. 18 Jan 1982 Kisok, Kabarnet 1.68m 53kg.
World HMar: '07- 2, '09- 1.
World records 25km 2010, 10M, 20km, half marathon 2011. African and two Kenyan half marathon records 2009.
Progress at HMar, Mar: 2000- 72:53, 2002- 73:01, 2003- 73:25, 2004- 71:32, 2005- 70:18, 2006- 69:06, 2007- 66:48, 2009- 66:36, 2010- 67:14, 2:29:01; 2011- 65:50, 2:19:19; 2012- 66:49. pbs: 1500m 4:24.33 '99, 10000m 32:18.07 '07; Road: 5km 15:25 '11, 10km 30:45 '11, 15km 46:40 '11, 10M 50:05 '11, 20km: 62:36 '11, 25km 1:19:53 '10.
11 wins in 12 half marathons 2006-12. Marathons: 3rd New York 2010-11, won London 2011. Married to Charles Koech (pbs 10km 27:56 & HMar 61:27 '07), son Jared born in June 2008.

Sylvia Chibiwott **KIBET** b. 28 Mar 1984 Kapchorwa, Keiyo district 1.57m 44kg. Kenya Police.
At 5000m: OG: '08- 4; WCh: '07- 4, '09- 2, '11- 2; CG: '10- 2; AfG: '07- 3; AfCh: '06- 3. At 3000m:

WI: '08-10-12: 4/4/4, won Afr-Y 1998. At 1500m: WY: '99- 2. World CC: '11- 13. Won KEN 5000m 2011.
Progress at 5000m, 10000m: 2006- 15:02.54, 31:39.34; 2007- 14:57.37, 2008- 15:00.03, 2009- 14:37.77, 30:47.20; 2010- 14:31.91, 2011- 14:35.43. pbs: 1500m 4:05.33i/4:07.87 '10, 3000m 8:37.48 '10, 2M 9:16.62 '07, 15km 49:54 '08, HMar 69:51 '09. Did not compete in 2001-02. Married Erastus Limo in 2003, daughter Britney Jepkosgei born in 2004. Older sister is Hilda Kibet NED (qv) and cousin of Lornah Kiplagat NED (qv).

Viola KIBIWOTT b. 22 Dec 1983 Keiyo 1.57m 45kg.
At 1500m: OG: '08- h; WCh: '07- 5, '09/11- sf; CG: '06- 7, '10- 7; WJ: '02- 1. World CC: '00-01-02: 3J/1J/1J.
Progress at 1500m, 5000m: 2003- 15:32.87, 2004- 4:06.64, 2006- 4:08.74, 2007- 4:02.10, 2008- 4:04.17, 14:51.59; 2009- 4:02.70, 2010- 4:03.39, 14:48.57; 2011- 4:05.51, 14:34.86. pbs: 800m 2:04.99 '07, 2000m 5:42.57 '09, 3000m 8:40.14 '03, 2M 9:18.26 '07.

Gladys KIPKEMBOI b. 15 Oct 1986 1.56m 45kg.
At 3000mSt: WCh: '09- 8; CG: '10- 3; WJ: '04- 1. Kenyan champion 2009.
African junior 3000m steeplechase record 2004.
Progress at 3000mSt: 2004- 9:47.26, 2006- 9:32.68, 2007- 9:46.46, 2009- 9:14.62, 2010- 9:13.22. pb 3000m 9:08.22 '06.

Edna Ngeringwony **KIPLAGAT** b. 15 Sep 1979 Eldoret 1.71m 54kg. Corporal in Kenyan Police.
At Mar: WCh: '11- 1. At 3000m: WJ: '96- 2, '98- 3. World CC: '96-97-06: 5J/4J/13.
African record 30km 2008.
Progress at Mar: 2005- 2:50:20, 2010- 2:25:38, 2011- 2:20:46. pbs: 3000m 8:53.06 '96, 5000m 15:57.3A '06, 10000m 33:27.0A '07; Road: 5km 15:20 '10, 10km 31:18 '10, 15km 47:57 '10, 10M 54:56 '09, HMar 69:00 '11.
Won Los Angeles and New York Marathons 2010, 3rd London 2011. Married to Gilbert Koech (10000m 27:55.30 '01, 10km 27:32 '01, Mar 2:13:45 dh '05, 2:14:39 '09).

Florence Jebet **KIPLAGAT** b. 27 Feb 1987 Kapkitony, Keiyo district 1.55m 42kg.
At 5000m: WJ: '06- 2. At 10000m: WCh: '09- 12. World CC: '07- 5, '09- 1; HMar: '10- 1. Won Kenyan 1500m 2007, CC 2007 & 2009.
Kenyan 10000m record 2009.
Progress at 5000m, 10000m, Mar: 2006- 15:32.34, 2007- 14:40.74, 31:06.20; 2009- 14:40.14, 30:11.53; 2010- 14:52.64, 32:46.99A; 2011- 2:19:44. pb 1500m 4:09.0A '07, 3000m 8:40.72 '10, Road: 15km 47:43 '102 20km 64:02 '10, HMar 66:38 '12, 30km 1:40:00 '11.
Successful half marathon debut in Lille in 2010, followed a month later by World title. Did not finish in Boston on marathon debut in 2011, but then won in Berlin. Partner of Moses Mosop,

daughter Aisha Chelagat born April 2008. Niece of William Kiplagat (Mar 2:06:50 '99, 8 WCh '07).

Sally KIPYEGO b. 19 Dec 1985 Kapsowar, Marakwet district 1.68m 52kg. Was at Texas Tech University, USA.
At 10000m: WCh: '11- 2. World CC: '01- 8J. Won record equalling nine NCAA titles 5000m 2008, 10000m 2007, CC 2006-08, indoor 3000m 2007, 5000m 2007-09.
Progress at 5000m, 10000m: 2005- 16:34.90, 2006- 16:13.39, 2007- 15:19.72, 31:56.72; 2008- 15:11.88, 31:25.48; 2009- 15:09.03, 33:44.7A; 2010- 14:38.64, 2011- 14:30.42, 30:38.35. pbs: 800m 2:08.26 '08, 1500m 4:06.23 '11, 1M 4:27.19i/4:29.64 '09, 2000m 5:35.20 '09, 3000m 8:48.77i '09, 8:51.07 '11.
One of her eight brothers is Mike Kipyego (3000mSt 8:08.48).

Pauline Chemning **KORIKWIANG** b. 1 Mar 1988 Kaptabuk Village, West Pokot District 1.63m 39kg.
At 3000m: WJ: '06- 2; WY: '05- 2. At 5000m: Af-J: '03- 4, '07- 3. At 10000m: AfCh: '10- 6. World CC: '05-06-09-11: 7J/1J/11/7.
Progress at 5000m, 10000m: 2003- 16:58.26, 2004- 15:55.5A, 2005- 16:15.8A, 2006- 14:45.98, 2007- 15:59.61, 2008- 16:07.78, 2009- 14:50.08, 2010- 14:46.80, 31:06.29; 2011- 14:41.28, 31:59.5A. pbs: 1500m 4:12.93+ '09, 2000m 5:36.11 '09, 3000m 8:41.11 '10.

Nancy Chebet **LANGAT** (or LAGAT) b. 22 Aug 1981 Eldoret 1.53m 49kg.
At (800m)/1500m: OG: '04- sf, '08- 1; WCh: '05- h, '09/1- sf; CG: '10- 1/1; AfCh: '04-08-10: 1/4/1; CCp: '10- 8; won DL 2010, WAF 2009, KEN 2010. At 800m: WJ: '96- 3, '98- 2, '00- 1; Af-J: '95/97- 1. World 4k CC: '05- 8.
Progress at 800m, 1500m: 1996- 2:03.10A, 4:22.93; 1997- 2:01.6A, 1998- 2:03.88A, 1999- 2:04.7A, 2000- 2:01.26, 4:23.78; 2001- 4:23.78, 2004- 2:05.63, 4:04.76; 2005- 2:02.51, 4:02.31; 2008- 2:05.84, 4:00.23; 2009- 1:59.17, 4:01.64; 2010- 1:57.75, 4:00.13; 2011- 2:02.8A, 4:03.66. pbs: 1000m 2:45.5+ '08, 5000m 16:33.9A '08.
Married to Kenneth Cheruiyot (Mar 2:07:18 '01, 3 WCh HMar 1997 in pb 60:00). Sons Keith (b. 2002) and Klein (b. 2006).

Linet Chepkwemoi **MASAI** b. 5 Dec 1989 Kapsokwony, Mount Elgon district 1.70m 55kg.
At (5000m)/10000m: OG: '08- 4; WCh: '09- 1, '11- 6/3; AfCh: '10- 3. World CC: '07-08-09-10-11: 1J/3/2/2/2. Won Kenyan 10000m 2010, CC 2010-11.
World junior record and Kenyan record at 10000m 2008, World 10 miles road record 2009.
Progress at 5000m, 10000m: 2007- 14:55.50, 2008- 14:47.14, 30:26.50; 2009- 14:34.36, 30:51.24; 2010- 14:31.14, 31:59.36A; 2011- 14:32.95, 30:53.59. pbs: 1500m 4:12.26 '09, 2000m 5:33.43 '09, 3000m 8:38.97 '07. Road: 15km 47:21 '09, 10M 50:39 '09.
Younger sister of Moses (qv) and Dennis Masai.

Grace Kwamboka **MOMANYI** b. 3 Mar 1982 Masimba Village, Kisii 1.70m 48kg.
At 10000m: WCh: '09- 4; CG: '10- 1. At 5000m: AfCh: '08- 3. World CC: '08- 10. Won Kenyan CC 2008.
Progress at 5000m. 10000m: 2004- 16:01.3A, 2005- 16:32.7A, 2008- 15:02.10, 31:08.24; 2009- 14:50.77, 30:52.25; 2010- 32:34.11, 2011- 15:07.49, 32:15.06. pbs: 3000m 8:56.37 '09, road: 15km 48:26+ '10, 10M 52:03 '10, HMar 68:41 '11.
Married to Timothy Momanyi. Son Billy born in 2003.

Mercy Wanjiru **NJOROGE** b. 10 Jun 1986 Njabini, Nyandarua District 1.58m 46kg.
At 3000mSt: WCh: '11- 4; CG: '10- 2; AfG: '07- 5; AfCh: '08- 5, '10- 4; WJ: '04- 4. Won Afr-J 3000m & 3000mSt 2005. World CC: '05- 4J, '06- 12.
Progress at 3000mSt: 2004- 9:52.25, 2005- 9:50.63, 2007- 9:43.02, 2008- 9:42.99, 2010- 9:26.64, 2011- 9:16.94. pbs: 1500m 4:19.08 '11, 3000m 8:39.70i '11, 8:48.16 '06; 5000m 15:17.03 '11, 10kmRd 33:52 '06.

Hellen Onsando **OBIRI** b. 13 Dec 1989 Nyangusu, Kisii.
At 3000m: WI: '12- 1; At 1500m: WCh: '11- 11 (fell). Won Kenyan 1500m 2011.
Progress at 1500m: 2011- 4:02.42. pbs: 800m 2:00.54 '11, 1000m 2:46.00i '12, 2000m 5:44.8+i '12, 3000m 8:35.35i '12.

Philes ONGORI b. 19 Jul 1986 Chironge, Kisii district 1.58m 47kg. Based in Sapporo, Japan.
At 10000m: WCh: '07- 8. World HMar: '09- 2.
Progress at 5000m, 10000m, Mar: 2003- 16:11.32m 2004- 15:08.3mx/15:25.50, 2005- 15:09.49, 32:30.83; 2006- 15:19.90, 31:18.85; 2007- 14:50.15, 31:39.11; 2008- 14:46.20mx/14:46.06, 30:29.21mx/31:19.73; 2009- 15:12.15, 31:53.46; 2011- 2:24:20 pbs: 800m 2:05.56 '04, 1500m 4:11.90 '04, 3000m 8:47.88 '07, Road: 15km 47:38 '08, HMar 67:38 '09.
Won Japanese High School 3000m 2004. Won Rotterdam Marathon 2011 on debut.

Lydia Chebet **ROTICH** b. 8 Aug 1988 Kipkilot, Keiyo District 1.63m 42kg. Kenya Police traffic officer.
At 3000mSt: WCh: '11- 5; AfCh: 10- 3.
Progress at 3000mSt: 2007- 10:44.3A, 2008- 9:55.62, 2009- 9:26.51, 2010- 9:18.03, 2011- 9:19.20. pb 5000m 16:22.1A '09.

Lucy WANGUI KABUU b. 24 Mar 1984 Uasin Gishu 1.55m 41kg. Suzuki, Japan.
At (5000m)/10000m: OG: '04- 9, '08- 7; CG: '06- 3/1; AfCh: '08- 4. World 4k CC: '05- 5.
Progress at 5000m, 10000m: 2001- 15:45.04, 2002- 15:33.03, 32:54.70; 2003- 15:10.23, 31:06.20; 2004- 14:47.09, 31:05.90; 2005- 15:00.20, 31:22.37; 2006- 14:56.09, 31:29.66; 2007- 14:57.55, 31:32.52; 2008- 14:33.49, 30:39.96; 2009- 16:50.3A. At Mar: 2012- 2:19:34. pbs: 1500m 4:09.60 '02, 3000m 8:46.15 '08, HMar 67:04 '11.
At the marathon did not finish in Osaka 2007, but at her next try was 2nd in 2:19:34 at Dubai 2012.

KOREA

Governing body: Korea Athletics Federation, 10 Chamshil Dong, Songpa-Gu, Seoul. Founded 1945. **National Champions 2011**: **Men**: 100m/200m: Kim Duk-young 10.46/21.42, 400m: Park Bong-ko 46.89, 800m: Cho Jae-deuk 1:52.27, 1500m: Shin Sang-min 3:43.54, 5000m: Kim Byong-hyun 14:27.13, 10000m: Baek Seung-ho 30:22.58, HMar: Lee Heon-kang 67:23, 3000mSt: Kwon Jae-woo 9:06.69, 110mh: Park Tae-kyong 14.12, 400mh: Lee Seung-yan 51.54, HJ: Yun Ye-hwang 2.16, PV: Kim Yoo-suk 5.30, LJ: Kim Sang-soo 7.68, TJ: Kim Dong-hyun 16.00, SP: Hwang In-sung 18.33, DT: Choi Jong-bum 54.13, HT: Lee Yun-chul 68.97, JT: Park Jae-myong 77.91, Dec: Kim Kun-woo 7755, 20kW: Park Chil-sung 1:25:27. **Women:** 100m: Jung Hye-lim 11.77, 200m: Park So-yeon 24.94, 400m: Woo Yu-jin 55.17, 800m: Wang Yea-eun 2:12.79, 1500m: Noh Yeo-yeon 4:30.51, 5000m: Kim Do-youn 16:26.66, 10000m: Chung Hye-jung 36:46.65, HMar: Jang Jin-sook 77:20, 3000mSt: Lee Eun-hye 10:44.79, 100mh: Chung Hye-rim 13.41, 400mh: Shon Kyong-mi 59.02, HJ: Noh Joo-hye 1.76, PV: Choi Yun-hee 4.40, LJ: Jung Soon-ok 6.07, TJ: Jung Hye-kyung 13.30, SP: Lee Mi-young 16.76, DT: Kim Ran-hee 50.02, HT: Kang Na-ru 58.58, JT: Kim Kyong-ae 58.24, Hep: Kim Myung-hee 4389, 20kW: Kim Sun-young 1:37:41.

KIM Hyun-sub b. 31 May 1985 1.76m 56kg.
At 20kW: OG: '08- 23; WCh: '07- 20, '09- 34, '11- 6; AsiG: '06- 2, '10- 3; WUG: '05-07-09: 2/6/5. Asian champion 2011, KOR 2005-06, 2008-11.
Three Korean 20km road walk records 2008-11.
Progress at 20kW: 2004- 1:24:58, 2005- 1:22:15, 2006- 1:21:45, 2007- 1:20:54, 2008- 1:19:41, 2009- 1:22:00, 2010- 1:19:36, 2011- 1:19:31. Pb 10000mW 39:30.56 '09, 38:13R '10.

KUWAIT

Governing body: Kuwait Association of Athletic Federation, PO Box 5499, 13055 Safat, Kuwait. Founded 1957.

Ali Mohammed AL-ZANKAWI b. 27 Feb 1984 1.86m 97kg.
At HT: OG: '04/08- dnq 30/18; WCh: '05/09/11- dnq 21/13/13, '07- 12; WJ: '02- 2; AsiG: '06- 2; AsiC: '03-05-07-11: 1/1/1/1; CCp: '10- 3. Pan-Arab champion 2004-05, 2007, 2009, 2011; West Asian 2005, 2010.
13 Kuwait hammer records 2004-09, Asian junior record 2003.
Progress at HT: 2001- 64.66, 2002- 66.88, 2003- 72.70, 2004- 76.54, 2005- 76.25, 2006- 76.97, 2007- 77.14, 2008- 77.25, 2009- 79.74, 2010- 78.40, 2011- 79.27.

LATVIA

Governing body: Latvian Athletic Association, 1 Augsiela Str, Riga LV-1009. Founded 1921.

National Championships first held in 1920 (men), 1922 (women). **2011 Champions: Men:** 100m: Janis Mezitis 10.90, 200m/400m: Janis Baltuss 21.87/47.55, 800m: Valters Kristaps 1:52.84, 1500m/3000m: Janis Razgalis 3:58.90/8:38.96, 5000m/HMar: Valerijs Zolnerovics 14:40.99/66:17, Mar: Raivis Zakis 2:30:55, 3000mSt: Kaspars Gulbis 9:45.80, 110mh: Stanislav Olijar 13.73, 400mh: Andrejs Romanivs 53.05, HJ: Normunds Pupols 2.20, PV: Mereks Arents 5.46, LJ: Janis Leitis 7.98, TJ: Elvijs Misans 15.91, SP/DT: Maris Urtans 19.73/51.00, HT: Ainars Vaiculens 64.22, JT: Vadims Vasilevskis 85.68, Dec: Edgars Erins 8312, 20kW: Artur Rumbanieks 1:29:35, 50kW: Vjaceslavs Grigorjevs 4:29:50. **Women:** 100m: Jekaterina Cekele 12.00, 200m: Marlena Reimane 24.56w, 400m: Ieva Vitola 57.44, 800m: Gunita Sale 2:19.20, 1500m/3000m: Polina Jelizarova 4:20.93/9:30.84, 5000m: Linda Batna 17:31.96, HMar: Dace Lina 1:20:32, Mar/3000mSt: Irina Stula-Pankoka 3:08:28/10:57.06, 100mh/LJ/SP/Hep: Aiga Grabuste 13.73/6.52/14.13/6172, 400mh: Inese Nagle 62.81, HJ: Natalija Cakova 1.84, PV: none (Krista Obizajeva 3.80 too young (15) to take title!), TJ: Santa Matule 12.83, DT: Diana Ozolina 44.97, HT: Karina Orlova 43.28, JT: Madara Palameika 58.10, 10000mW/20kW: Agnese Pastare 45:31.0/1:42:11.

Zigismunds SIRMAIS b. 6 May 1992 Riga 1.91m 90kg.
At JT: WCh: '11: dnq 32; WJ: '10- 7; EJ: '11- 1.
Two world junior javelin records 2011.
Progress at JT: 2009- 65.03, 2010- 82.27, 2011- 84.69

Igors SOKOLOVS b. 17 Aug 1974 Riga 1.87m 107kg. Salaspils.
At HT: OG: '08- dnq 19; WCh: '07/09/11- dnq 14/17/20; EC: '10- dnq 14. LAT champion 1992, 2001-08, 2010.
12 Latvian hammer records 2004-09.
Progress at HT: 1989- 41.08, 1990- 51.96, 1991- 60.82, 1992- 64.80, 1997- 62.54, 2001- 63.65, 2002- 65.96, 2003- 68.56, 2004- 71.49, 2005- 72.46, 2006- 74.32, 2007- 76.22, 2008- 78.23, 2009- 80.14, 2010- 79.09, 2011- 76.60.

Maris URTANS b. 9 Feb 1981 Riga 1.88m 123kg. LSPA.
At SP: OG: '08: dnq 25; WCh: '07-09- dnq 25/16; EC: '06- dnq 25, '10- 4; WJ: '00- dnq; WUG: '07- 2; EU23: '01- 11; EJ: '99- 10. Latvian champion SP 2004-11, DT 2000-02, 2011.
Progress at SP: 1998- 14.14, 1999- 14.97i, 2000- 15.35i, 2001- 16.77i, 2002- 17.90, 2003- 18.48, 2004- 18.60, 2005- 18.73, 2006- 19.40, 2007- 20.18i/20.14, 2008- 20.27, 2009- 20.64, 2010- 21.63, 2011- 20.82. pb DT 53.72 '07.

Vadims VASILEVSKIS b. 5 Jan 1982 Riga 1.88m 101kg. Jekabpils.
At JT: OG: '04- 2, '08- 9; WCh: '05- dnq 16, '07- 4, '09- 4, '11- dnq 25; EC: '02- dnq 16, '06- 4, '10-

dnq 23; WJ: '00- 8; EU23: '03- 7; EJ: '01- 7; WUG: '07- 1. Latvian champion 2008, 2011; WAF 2008.
Three Latvian javelin records 2006-07.
Progress at JT: 1998- 59.17, 1999- 63.82, 2000- 73.07, 2001- 73.25, 2002- 81.92, 2003- 77.81, 2004- 84.95, 2005- 81.30, 2006- 90.43, 2007- 90.73, 2008- 86.65, 2009- 90.71, 2010- 84.08, 2011- 88.22.
Set personal bests in qualifying (84.43) and final at 2004 Olympics.

Women

Aiga GRABUSTE b. 24 Mar 1988 Rezekne 1.78m 67kg. Rezeknes BJSS.
At Hep: OG: '04- 19; WCh: '07- 17, '09- 13, '11- 12; WJ: '06- 9; WY: '05- 27; EJ: '07- 1; EU23: '09- 1.
At Pen: WI: '10- 8; EI: '11- 10. Won LAT 100mh 2007-08, 2011; LJ 2011, SP 2010-11, Hep 2009, 2011.
LAT records: pentathlon 2009, heptathlon 2011.
Progress at Hep: 2006- 5443, 2007- 6019, 2008- 6050, 2009- 6396, 2011- 6507w/6414. Pbs: 60m 7.82i '08, 100m 12.21 '09, 200m 24.42/24.35w '11, 400m 55.43 '11, 800m 2:13.60 '11, 60mh 8.50i '09, 100mh 13.46 '11, HJ 1.79i '11, 1.77 '07; LJ 6.65 '11, SP 14.56 '09, JT 48.67 '11, Hep 4463i '09.

Madara PALAMEIKA b. 18 Jun 1987 Talsi 1.85m 76kg. Ventspils.
At JT: WCh: '09: dnq 27, '11- 11; EC: '10: 8; WJ: '06- dnq 16; EU23: '07- 3, '09- 1; EJ: '05- dnq 17.
LAT champion 2009-11.; LAT javelin record 2009
Progress at JT: 2002- 42.31, 2003- 49.11, 2004- 51.50, 2005- 51.75, 2006- 54.19, 2007- 57.98, 2008- 53.45, 2009- 64.51, 2010- 62.02, 2011- 63.46.

Ineta RADEVICA b. 13 Jul 1981 Kraslava 1.73m 56kg. Was at University of Nebraska.
At LJ/(TJ): OG: '04- dnq 13/20; WCh: '05- dnq 23, '11- 3; EC: '10- 1; WJ: '00- dnq 14; EU23: '03- 3/3; EJ: '99- dnq 19; WI: '06- 5, '08- 6; EI: '05- 5, '07- 8; CCp: '10- 4; won NCAA TJ 2003-04, LAT LJ 2000, 2005-06; TJ 2001.
Latvian long jump record 2010.
Progress at LJ, TJ: 1996- 5.39, 1997- 5.36, 10.85; 1998- 5.59, 11.78/11.86w; 1999- 5.90, 12.64; 2000- 6.33, 12.80; 2001- 6.12/6.14w, 13.14; 2002- 6.32i/6.26, 13.75; 2003- 6.70, 14.04; 2004- 6.53/6.60w, 14.12; 2005- 6.80, 2006- 6.59i/6.46/6.64w, 13.43; 2007- 6.67i/6.35, 13.30i; 2008- 6.66i/6.65/6.75w, 13.71; 2010- 6.92, 13.89/14.40w; 2011- 6.76, 13.89i. pbs: 100m 12.23 '02, 100mh 15.00 '98, HJ 1.70 '99, Hep 4262 '98.
Improved LJ pb from 6.80 to 6.92 to win 2010 European title. Married to Russian ice hockey player Pyotr Schastlivy, their son Mark was born in 2009.

LITHUANIA

Governing body: Athletic Federation of Lithuania, Kareiviu 6, LT-09117 Vilnius. Founded 1921.
National Championships first held in 1921 (women 1922). **2011 Champions: Men:** 100m: Rytis Sakalauskas 10.18, 200m: Egidijus Dilys

21.40, 400m: Zilvinas Adomavicius 48.63, 800m: Vitalij Kozlov 1:49.91, 1500m: Petras Gliebus 3:52.13, 5000m: Martunas Stanys 15:11.60, 10000m/HMar: Mindaugas Virsilas 31:05.54/69:15, Mar: Saulius Vaalis 2:35:09, 3000mSt: Justinas Berzanskis 9:03.24, 110mh: Mantas Silkauskas 14.35, 400mh: Silvestras Guogis 52.17, HJ: Raivydas Stanys 2.26, PV: Irmantas Lianzbergas 4.25, LJ: Povilas Mykolaitis 8.11, TJ: Mantas Dilys 16.03, SP: Rimantas Martisauskas 17.96, DT: Virgilijus Alekna 67.90, HT: Tomas Juknevicius 61.85, JT: Nerijus Luckauskas 70.31, Dec: Benas Kentra 6792, 20kW: Marius Ziukas 1:21:40 (short course), 50kW: Tadas Suskevicius 4:00:54.
Women: 100m/200m: Lina Grincikaite 11.42/23.65, 400m: Agne Orlauskaite 53.92, 800m: Egle Balciunaite 2:04.00, 1500m: Banga Balnaite 4:28.34, 5000m: Gyte Norgiliene 16:54.49, 10000m: Diana Lobacevske 33:36.23, HMar: Gyte Norgiliene 1:19:51, Mar: Modesta Kaminskiene 3:07:29, 3000mSt: Evelina Usevaite 10:45.44, 100m: Sonata Tamosaityte 13.11, 400mh: Irma Maciukaite 61.90, HJ: Viktorija Zemaityte 1.80, PV: Vitalija Dejeva 3.60, LJ: Lina Andrijauskaite 6.17, TJ: Jolanta Verseckaite 13.66w, SP: Austra Skujyte 17.09, DT: Zinaida Sendriute 61.40, HT: Natalija Venckute 48.25, JT: Viktorija Barviciute 53.77, Hep: Diana Pranckute 5072, 10kW: Kristina Saltanovic 45:24, 20kW: Britita Virbalyte 1:30:15 (short course),

Virgilijus ALEKNA b. 13 Feb 1972 Terpeikiai, Kupiskis 2.00m 130kg. Graduate of Lithuanian Academy of Physical Culture. Guard of the Lithuanian president 1995-2010, advisor to the Lithuanian Ministry of the Interior from 2011..
At DT: OG: '96- 5, '00- 1, '04- 1, '08- 3; WCh: '95-97-99-01-03-05-07-09-11: dnq 19/2/4/2/1/1/4/4/6; EC: '98-02-06-10: 3/2/1/5; WCp: '98- 1, '06- 1. Won WAF 2003, 2005-06, 2009; GP 2001 (2nd 1999). LTU champion 1998, 2000-05, 2008-09, 2011.
Four Lithuanian discus records 2000.
Progress at DT: 1990- 52.84, 1991- 57.16, 1992- 60.86, 1993- 62.84, 1994- 64.20, 1995- 62.78, 1996- 67.82, 1997- 67.70, 1998- 69.66A, 1999- 68.25, 2000- 73.88, 2001- 70.99, 2002- 66.90, 2003- 69.69, 2004- 70.97, 2005- 70.67, 2006- 71.08, 2007- 71.56, 2008- 71.25, 2009- 69.59, 2010- 65.33, 2011- 67.90. pb SP: 19.99 '97.
His 72.35 and 73.88 at the 2000 LTU Championships were the second and third longest ever discus throws. His 70.17 to win the 2005 World title (coming from 2nd at 68.10 with the last throw) was the first ever 70m throw at a global championships. He has 19 competitions and 30 throws over 70m. 37 successive wins from August 2005 to 4th at Worlds August 2007. Married on 4 Mar 2000 Kristina Sablovskyte (pb LJ 6.14 '96, TJ 12.90 '97, sister of Remigija Nazaroviene).

Women

Austra SKUJYTE b. 12 Aug 1979 Birzai 1.88m 80kg. Graduated in kinesiology from Kansas State University, USA. Masters degree from the Lithuanian Academy of Physical Culture.
At Hep: OG: '00- 12, '04- 2, '08- dnf; WCh: '01-03-05-07-11: 6/10/4/6/8; EC: '02- 4; WJ: '98- 6; EU23: '99- 6, '01- 3. At Pen: WI: '04-08-12: 3/5/3; EI: '07- 4, '11- 2. At SP: WCh: '09- dnq 17; EC: '10- 12. Won NCAA 2001-02; LTU 100mh 2000, 2005; HJ 2005, LJ 2005, 2007; SP 2001-02, 2004-05, 2007, 2009-11; DT 2009; Hep 1997.
World decathlon record 2005.
Progress at Hep: 1997- 4930, 1998- 5606, 1999- 5724, 2000- 6104, 2001- 6150w, 2002- 6275, 2003- 6213, 2004- 6435, 2005- 6386, 2007- 6380, 2008- 6235, 2011- 6338. pbs: 100m 12.49 '05, 200m 24.82 '04, 24.79w '07; 400m 57.19 '05, 800m 2:15.92 '04, 1500m 5:15.86 '05, 60mh 8.57i '12, 100mh 13.96 '11, 13.83w '04; HJ 1.90i '12, 1.87 '11; PV 3.20 '06, LJ 6.39i '05, 6.32 '04, 6.40w '01; SP 17.86 '09, DT 53.89 '10, JT 52.63 '07, Pen 4802i '12, Dec 8358 '05.
Set three pbs in 2004 Olympics, including two seconds off 800m best to secure silver. Returned to multi-events in 2011 after two years concentrating on shot.

LUXEMBOURG

Governing body: Fédération Luxembourgeoise d'Athlétisme, 3 Route d'Arlon, L-8009 Strassen, Luxembourg. Founded 1928.
2011 National Champions: **Men**:100m: Tom Hutmacher 11.03, 200m: Tom Hutmacher & Wesley Charlet 22.27, 400m: Sven Fischer 49.22, 800m: Christophe Bettgen 1:54.75, 1500m: David Karonei 3:56.58, 5000m/10000m: Pol Mellina 14:58.25/31:08.11, HMar: Pascal Groben 71:44, Mar: Christian Krombach 2:35:25, 3000mSt: Yannick Frantz 11:49.84, 110mh/400mh: Claude Godart 14.60/53.23, HJ: Kevin Rutare 1.95, PV: Steve Thill 4.30, LJ/TJ: Asmir Mirascic 6.54/13.83, SP: Bob Bertemes 15.95, DT: Marc Meyer 35.28, HT: Steve Tonizzo 50.60, JT: Tun Wagner 62.49, Dec: Wesley Charlet 5946.
Women: 100m/200m: Tiffany Tshilumba 12.26/25.03, 400m: Frédérique Hansen 57.06, 800m: Carole Kill 2:15.22, 1500m: Martine Mellina 4:46.80, 3000m/10000m: Pascale Schmoetten 10:11.84/37:15.51, HMar: Liz May 82:42. Mar: Tania Arensdorf 3:10:51, 3000mSt: Liz Weiler 12:21.53, 100mh/Hep: Mandy Charlet 15.58/45.92, 400mh: Nadine Lanners 74.15, HJ: Noémie Pleimling 1.68, PV: Stephanie Vieillevoye 3.50, LJ/TJ: Laurence Kipgen 5.60/11.26, SP/DT/JT: Noémie Pleimling 11.47/34.50/40.73, HT: Daniella Thyssens 42.44.

MEXICO

Governing body: Federación Mexicana de Atletismo, Anillo Periférico y Av. del Conscripto,

11200 México D.F. Founded 1933.
National Champions 2011: Men: 100m: Jorge Alonso 10.63, 200m: José Herrera 20.98, 400m: Orlando García 47.32, 800m: José Juan Esparza 1:49.68, 1500m: Diego Borrego 3:51.03, 5000m: Juan Luis Barrios 14:12.67, 3000mSt: José Rafael Bañales 9:17.21, 110mh: César Rodríguez 14.45, 400mh: José Luis Ceballos 51.66, HJ: Jorge Rouco 2.20, PV: Giovanni Lanaro 5.30, LJ: Vicente Ríos 7.97, TJ: Alberto Álvarez 16.07, SP: Stephen Sáenz 18.04, DT: Mario Cota 56.82, HT: Diego del Real 62.98, JT: José Lagunez 74.45, Dec: Rodrigo Sagaon 7084, 20kmW: Omar Segura 1:24:55. **Women**: 100m: Jessica Sánchez 11.83, 200m: Nayelí Vela 24.08, 400m/800m: Gabriela Medina 52.58/2:07.36, 1500m/3000mSt: Sandra López 4:31.11/10:56.94, 5000m: Marisol Romero 16:52.38, 100mh: Gabriela Santos 13.69, 400mh: Anisia Castro 57.92, HJ: Romary Rifka 1.90, PV: Cecilia Villar 3.75, LJ: Ivonne Treviño 6.22w, TJ: Aída Villarreal 13.58, SP: Laura Pulido 15.25, DT: Iraís Estrada 48.34, HT: Reyna Campoy 58.25, JT: Abigail Gómez 50.67, Hep: Karla Schleske 5256, 20kW: Mónica Equixua 1"37:25.

Jorge **Horacio NAVA** b. 20 Jan 1982 Chihuahua 1.75m 62kg.
At 50kW: OG: '08- 6; WCh: '05- 9, '07- 9, '09- 19; PAm: '07- 2, '11- 1; CAG: '10- 1; WCp: '06-08-10: 7/5/2. At 20kW: WCh: '11- 20. At 10000mW: WY: '99- 5; PAm-J: '01- 2.
Progress at 50kW: 2005- 3:53:57, 2006- 3:48:22, 2007- 3:52:35, 2008- 3:45:21, 2009- 3:56:26, 2010- 3:54:16, 2011- 3:45:29. pbs: 5000m 18:40.11 '09, 10000mW 40:33.52 '04, 20kW 1:22:15 '11.

Éder SÁNCHEZ b. 21 May 1986 Toluca 1.76m 67kg.
At 20kW: OG: '08- 15; WCh: '05-07-09-11: 8/4/3/15; WCp: '08- 3, '10- 7; CAG: '06- 2, '10- 1; won MEX 2006. At 10000mW: WJ: '02- 4; PAm-J: '03- 2; WCp: '04- 2J.
CAC 5000mW record 2009, junior 20kW 2005.
Progress at 20kW: 2005- 1:19:02, 2006- 1:23:24A, 2007- 1:20:08, 2008- 1:18:34, 2009- 1:19:22, 2010- 1:21:16, 2011- 1:19:36. pbs: 3000mW 11:13.45 '09, 5000mW 18:40.11 '09, 10,000mW 40:46.29 '04, 10km Rd 38:31 '09, 50kW 3:53:19 '11.
Won IAAF Race Walking Challenge 2009.

MOLDOVA
Governing Body: Federatia de Atletism din Republica Moldova. Founded 1991.

Zalina MARGHIEVA b. 5 Feb 1988 Osetia-Alaniya, Russia 1.74m 90kg. AS-CSPLN.
At HT: OG: '08- dnq 37; WCh: '09- dnq 26, '11- 8; EC: '10- 5; WJ: '06- 4; WY: '05- 7; EU23: '09- 1; EJ: '07- 5; WUG: '11- 1.
Ten Moldovan hammer records 2005-12.
Progress at HT: 2005- 61.80, 2006- 65.50, 2007- 65.40, 2008- 70.22, 2009- 71.56, 2010- 71.50, 2011- 72.93, 2012- 73.60.

Sister **Marina** (b. 28 Jun 1986) HT: 72.53 '09, five MDA records 2007-09, WCh: '11- dnq 17; EC: '10- 6.

MOROCCO
Governing Body: Fédération Royale Marocaine d'Athlétisme, Complex Sportif Prince Moulay Abdellah, PO Box 1778 R/P, Rabat. Fd. 1957.
2011 National Champions: Men: 100m/200m: Khalid Idrissi Zougari 10.86/21.82, 400m: Abdelkrim Khoudri 46.89, 800m: Sadik Mikhou 1:47.49, 1500m: Mohammed Hajjaj 3:45.65, 5000m: Jamal Hitrane 13:49.33, 3000mSt: Hamid Ezzine 8:20.49, 110mh: El Mehdi El Mellouki 14.51, 400mh: Hassan Akabbou 52.15, HJ: Othmane Khouyahanna 2.00, LJ/TJ: Tarik Bougtaïb 7.41/15.45, SP: Mohammed Gharrous 17.46, DT: Kamal El Idrissi 58.00; HT: Idriss Barid 62.00, JT: Mohammed Driouchi 66.28. **Women**: 100m/LJ: Jamaa Chnaik 12.03/6.10, 200m: Ghita El Kafy 25.79, 400m: Manal El Bahraoui 55.45, 800m: Malika Abakil 2:04.50, 1500m: Kaltoum Bouaa-sayriya 4:20.50, 5000m: Hajiba Hasnaoui 16:58.58, 3000mSt: Salima El Ouali Alami 10:14.05, 100mh/400mh: Lamia Lhabz 14.61/57.13, HJ: Nour Elhouda Dehhaoui 1.50, PV: Nisrin Dinar 3.80, TJ: Fatima Zahra Dkouk 12.83, SP: Rachida Lakhal 12.86, DT/HT: Fatine Oubourogaa 47.45/52.48, JT: Hanane Daoudi 42.74.

Yahya BERRABAH b. 13 Oct 1981 Oujda 1.86m 75kg.
At LJ: OG: '04/08- dnq 30/17=; WCh: '03-05-07- dnq 26/20/24, '09- 10, '11- 4; AfCh: '02-06-08- 7/8/1 (7 TJ '06); WJ: '00- dnq 30; won Pan-Arab 2011.
Two Moroccan long jump records 2009.
Progress at LJ: 2000- 6.91, 2001- 7.81, 2002- 8.18, 2003- 8.33, 2004- 8.12, 2005- 8.18, 2006- 8.13, 2007- 8.04, 2008- 8.23, 2009- 8.40, 2010- 8.02i/7.98, 2011- 8.37/8.40w. pbs: 100m 10.48 '09, 10.2 '04; 200m 21.08 '06, TJ 16.44 '05.

Abderrahim BOURAMDANE b. 1 Jan 1978 1.67m 55kg.
At Mar: OG: '08- 26; WCh: '07- 45, '11- 4.
Progress at Mar: 2004- 2:15:38, 2005- 2:15:16, 2006- 2:10:41, 2007- 2:08:20, 2008- 2:09:04, 2009- 2:12:14, 2010- 2:07:33, 2011- 2:08:42. pbs: 10000m 29:53.21 '04, Rd 10km 29:15 '11, HMar 62:40 '10.

Jaouad GHARIB b. 22 May 1972 Khénifra 1.76m 60kg.
At Mar: OG: '04- 11, '08- 2; WCh: '03- 1, '05- 1. At 10000m: WCh: '01- 11; AfCh: '02- 8. At 3000m: WI: '03- 11. World HMar: '01- 9, '02- 2; CC: '02- 10. Won MedG 10000m 2001.
Moroccan marathon record 2009.
Progress at 5000m, 10000m, Mar: 2001- 13:19.69, 27:29.51; 2002- 13:20.59, 28:02.09i/28:57.12; 2003- 2:08:31, 2004- 2:07:12, 2005- 2:07:49, 2006- 2:07:19, 2007- 2:07:54, 2008- 2:07:16, 2009- 2:05:27, 2010- 2:06:55. pbs: 3000m 7:39.22 '01, 2M 8:29.23i '02, 15km 43:08 '01, HMar 59:56 '04.

Began running at 22, made sudden emergence into top class in 2001. Sixth in 2:09:15 at Rotterdam 2003 on marathon debut and won world title in next marathon; London: 3rd 2004 & 2009-10, 2nd 2005, 4th 2007, 6th 2011, 8th 2006. Won Fukuoka 2010 (3rd 2006), 2nd Chicago 2007, 3rd New York 2009.

Abderrahim GOUMRI b. 21 May 1976 Safi 1.67m 60kg.
At 5000m: OG: '04- 13; WCh: '03- 10. At 10000m: WCh: '01- 16, '05- 8; AfCh: '02- 4. At 3000m: WI: '03- 9. At Mar: OG: '08- 20; WCh: '07/09/11- dnf. World CC: '95-02-03-04-06-07:25J/7/15/14/11/21; 4k: '03- 10, '05- 18; HMar: '03- 12.
Moroccan marathon record 2008.
Progress at 5000m, 10000m, Mar: 1999- 13:20.70, 2001- 13:03.60, 27:26.01; 2002- 13:00.76, 27:52.62i/28:45.92; 2003- 13:05.81, 2004- 12:59.04, 2005- 12:50.25, 27:02.62; 2006- 12:57.89; 2007- 2:07:44, 2008- 2:05:30, 2009- 2:06:04, 2010- 2:10:51, 2011- 2:09:11. pbs: 1500m 3:39.80 '98, 1M 4:02.46 '99, 2000m 5:02.2 '06, 3000m 7:32.36 '01, HMar 61:19 '01, 30km 1:28:30 '08.
Second London 2007 on marathon debut, 2nd New York 2007 & 2008 (4th 2010), 2nd Chicago 2009, 3rd London 2008. Won Seoul 2011.

Abdelaati IGUIDER b. 25 Mar 1987 Errachidia 1.70m 52kg.
At 1500m: OG: '08- 5; WCh: '07- h, '09- 11, '11- 5; WJ: '04- 1, '06- 2; WI: '10- 2, '12- 1.
Progress at 1500m: 2004- 3:35.53, 2005- 3:35.63, 2006- 3:32.68, 2007- 3:32.75, 2008- 3:31.88, 2009- 3:31.47, 2010- 3:34:25, 2011- 3:31.60, 2012- 3:34.10i. pbs: 800m 1:47.14 '07, 1000m 2:19.14 '07, 1M 3:59.79 '07, 3000m 7:41.95 '07.

Amine LAÂLOU b. 13 May 1982 Salé 1.78m 57kg
At 800m(/1500m): OG: '04/08- sf; WCh: '03-05-07: h/sf/6, '09- 5/10, '11- (sf); WJ: '00- sf; WY: '99-h; WI: '04- 10-12: 4/(5)/(9); AfCh: '02- h, '10- (2); AfJ: '01- 2; CCp: '10- (1); Won MAR 800m 2003, MedG 800m 2009, FrancG 800m & 1500m 2009, Arab 1500m 2009.
Moroccan 800m record 2006.
Progress at 800m, 1500m: 2000- 1:51.55, 2001- 1:49.94, 2002- 1:46.5, 2003- 1:45.20, 2004- 1:43.68, 2005- 1:44.22, 2006- 1:43.25, 2007- 1:43.94, 2008- 1:44.27, 2009- 1:43.36, 3:31.56; 2010- 1:43.71, 3:29.53; 2011- 1:45.11, 3:31.92. pbs: 400m 47.21 '04, 47.0 '03; 1000m 2:15.31 '11, 1M 3:50.22 '10.

Mohamed MOUSTAOUI b. 2 Apr 1985 Khouribga 1.74m 60kg.
At 1500m: OG: '08- sf; WCh: '07- sf, '09- 6, '11- 6; AfCh: '06- 5; WJ: '04- 4; AfJ: '03- 2; Arab champion 2007. World CC: '04- 14J, '05- 14 4k.
Progress at 1500m: 2003- 3:42.9, 2004- 3:37.44, 2005- 3:36.20, 2006- 3:32.51, 2007- 3:32.67, 2008- 3:32.06, 2009- 3:32.60, 2010- 3:36.92+, 2011- 3:31.84. pbs: 800m 1:45.44 '09, 1000m 2:20.00i '08, 1M 3:50.08 '08, 2000m 5:00.98i '07, 3000m 7:43.08i '09, 7:43.99 '11; 2M 8:26.49i '05, 5000m 13:22.61 '05.

Women

Btissam Boucif **LAKHOUAD** b. 7 Dec 1980 Khouribga 1.70m 52kg.
At 1500m: OG: '08- 12; WCh: '09- sf, '11- 4; AfCh: '10- 3 (4 800m); CCp: '10- dnf.
Moroccan 1500m record 2010.
Progress at 1500m: 2004- 4:11.26, 2005- 4:18.01, 2006- 4:08.22, 2007- 4:03.4, 2008- 4:06.37, 2009- 4:03.23, 2010- 3:59.35, 2011- 4:01.09. pbs: 800m 2:01.66 '07, 1M 4:25.35 '07, 3000m 9:08.02 '07, 10km Rd 33:22 '06.

Mariem Alaoui SELSOULI b. 8 Apr 1984 Marrakech 1.65m 49kg. Atletismo Santutxu ESP
At 1500m: WCh: '07- 4, '09- dns; WJ: '02- 5; WI: '12- 2. At 3000m: WJ: '02- 2; WY: '01- 5; WI: '06- 6, '08- 3; Af-J: '03- 1. At 5000m: OG: '08- h; WCh: '07- h; AfC: '06- 5; WUG: '05- 5. World CC: '03- 13J, '06- 15 4k, '07- 17. Won W.Students CC 2004.
Progress at 1500m, 5000m: 2002- 4:13.9, 2003- 4:18.37, 2004- 4:19.59, 2005- 4:08.30, 16:07.99; 2006- 4:07.13, 15:04.46; 2007- 4:01.52, 14:36.52; 2008- 15:21.47, 2009- 4:00.95, 2011- 4:00.77, 2012- 4:03.67i. pbs: 800m 2:13.81 '05, 2000m 5:40.0+i '08, 3000m 8:29.52 '07.
Two-year drugs ban for positive test on 3 Aug 2009.

NETHERLANDS

Governing body: Koninklijke Nederlandse Atletiek Unie (KNAU), Postbus 60100, NL-6800 JC Arnhem. Founded 1901.
National Championships first held in 1910 (men), 1921 (women). **2011 Champions: Men**: 100m/200m: Churandy Martina 10.27/20.38, 400m: Joeri Moerman 46.83, 800m: Robert Lathouwers 1:48.58, 1500m: Bram Som 3:48.73, 5000m: Dennis Licht 14:17.70, 10000m: Khalid Choukoud 29:42.95, HMar: Khalid Choukad 64:28, Mar: Michael Butter 2:12:59, 3000mSt: Simon Vroemen 8:56.92, 110mh: Marcel van der Westen 13.77, 400mh: Daniel Franken 51.62, HJ: Douwe Amels 2.16, PV: Robbert Jan Jansen 5.40, LJ/TJ: Fabian Florant 7.41w/15.94, SP: Erik van Vreumingen 18.39, DT: Rutger Smith 63.52, HT: Vincent Onos 63.73, JT: Bjorn Blommerde 75.74, Dec: Adriaan Saman 7410. **Women**: 100m: Dafne Schippers 11.41, 200m: Jamile Samuel 23.43, 400m: Marit Dopheide 53.28, 800m: Yvonne Hak 2:05.54, 1500m: Marija te Raa 4:41.39, 5000m: Ilse Pol 16:03.98, 10000m: Ruth van der Meijden 35:56.15, HMar: Heleen Plaatzer 74:39, Mar: Lornah Kiplagat 2:25:52, 100mh: Rosina Hodde 13.53, 400mh: Sanne Verstegen 59.13. HJ: Nadien Broersen 1.83, PV: Denise Groot 4.26, LJ/TJ: Brenda Baar 6.19/13.53w, SP: Melissa Boekelman 17.73, DT: Monique Jansen 60.75, HT: Eva Reinders 58.03, JT: Bregje Crolla 52.67, Hep: Myrte Goor 5634.

Churandy MARTINA b. 3 Jul 1984 Willemstad, Curaçao 1.80m 68kg. Nike. Studied civil engineering at University of Texas at El Paso, USA.

At 100m/(200m): OG: '04- qf, '08- 4/dq; WCh: '03- h, '05- qf, '07- 5/5, '09- qf, '11- sf/sf; WJ: '00- h/h, '02- qf; WY: '99- sf; PAm: '03- sf, '07- 1; CAG: '06- 1/1R, '10- 1/1/3R; CCp: '10- (2)/1R. Won PAm-J 2003; NED 100m & 200m 2011.
Records: AHO 100m (8) 2004-08, 200m (6) 2005-10, 400m 2007; NED 100m 2011.
Progress at 100m, 200m: 2000- 10.73, 21.73; 2001- 10.64A, 21.55; 2002- 10.30, 20.81; 2003- 10.29/10.26w, 20.71; 2004- 10.13, 20.75; 2005- 10.13/9.93Aw,   20.32/20.31w;   2006- 10.04A/10.06/9.76Aw/9.99w, 20.27A; 2007- 10.06, 20.20; 2008- 9.93, 20.11; 2009- 9.97, 20.76; 2010- 10.03A/10.07/9.92w, 20.08; 2011- 10.10, 20.38. pbs: 60m 6.58i '10, 400m 46.13A '07.
At 2008 Olympics set three national records at 100m and one at 200m before crossing line in second place in final in 19.82 only to be disqualified for running out of his lane. Competed for Netherlands Antilles until 2010.

Eelco SINTNICOLAAS b. 7 Apr 1987 Dordrecht 1.86m 80kg. AV '34 (Apeldoorn). Economics student.
At Dec: WCh: '09- dnf, '11- 5; EC: '10- 2; WJ: '06- 8; EU23: '09- 1; EJ: '05- 14. At Hep: EI: '11- 4.
Progress at Dec: 2007- 7466, 2008- 7507w, 2009- 8112, 2010- 8436, 2011- 8304. pbs: 60m 6.89i '09, 100m 10.71 '10, 10.69w '08; 200m 21.62 '10, 400m 47.88 '10, 1000m 2:37.42i '06, 1500m 4:22.29 '11, 60mh 7.93i '09, 110mh 14.21 '11, 400mh 51.59 '10, HJ 2.00i '11, 1.97 '10; PV 5.52i '11, 5.45 '10; LJ 7.65i, 7.59, 7.76w '09, SP 14.46i/14.31 '11, DT 42.43 '10, JT 62.57 '10, Hep 6175i '11.
Set six pbs in improving pb by 277 points for European silver 2010.

Rutger SMITH b. 9 Jul 1981 Groningen 1.97m 130kg. Groningen Atletiek.
At SP (/DT): OG: '04- dnq 14/16, '08- 9/7; WCh: '03- dnq 25/15, '05- 2, '07- 4/3, '11- (dnq 16); EC: '02- 8. '06- 4/7; WJ: '00- 1/3; EU23: '03- 3/1; EJ: '99- 1/1; WI: '03-08-12: dnq 10/5/7; EI: '05- 2; ECp: '04- 2/2. Won NED SP 2000, 2002-08; DT 2002-08, 2011.
Three Dutch shot records 2005-06.
Progress at SP, DT: 1998- 15.23, 51.18; 1999- 18.27,53.81;2000- 19.48,58.74;2001- 18.92i/18.21, 59.96; 2002- 20.39, 64.69; 2003- 20.52, 62.70; 2004- 20.94, 63.79; 2005- 21.41, 65.51; 2006- 21.62, 64.60; 2007- 21.19, 67.63; 2008- 20.89i/20.80, 66.85, 2011- 19.95i, 67.77; 2012- 20.56i.
First athlete to win World Championships medals in shot and discus.

Bram SOM b. 20 Feb 1980 Terborg 1.79m 66kg. Atletico '73 (Gendringen). Sergeant in Dutch army.
At 800m: OG: '00- h, '04- sf; WCh: '01-03-07-09-11: sfsf/h/7/sf; EC: '02- 6, '06- 1; WJ: '98- 5; EJ: '99- 3; EU23: '01- 5; WI: '03- 5; WCp: '06- 2. Won Dutch 800m 2000-01, 2003-04, 2006, 2010; 1500m 2009, 2011.
Dutch 800m record 2006.

Progress at 800m: 1995- 2:01.27, 1996- 1:53.31, 1997- 1:49.55, 1998- 1:47.99, 1999- 1:46.58, 2000- 1:44.01, 2001- 1:43.98, 2002- 1:45.86, 2003- 1:44.22, 2004- 1:44.37, 2006- 1:43.45, 2007- 1:45.61, 2008- 1:45.55, 2009- 1:43.59, 2010- 1:44.58, 2011- 1:45.69. pbs: 100m 10.97, 200m 21.56 '01, 400m 46.55 '09, 600m 1:15.26 '00, 1000m 2:17.01 '10, 1500m 3:42.75 '11.

Women

Hilda KIBET b. 27 Mar 1981 Kapchorwa, Kenya 1.67m 46kg. AV Castricum. Physiotherapist.
At 10000m: OG: '08- 15; EC: '10- 4; ECp: '08- 3. World CC: '08-09-10: 5/6/10; Eur CC: '08- 1. Won NED Mar 2009.
Dutch martahon record 2011.
Progress at 10000m, Mar: 2003- 34:12.20, 2007- 2:32:10, 2008- 30:58.48, 2009- 30:51.92, 2:30:33; 2010- 31:36.90, 2:26:23; 2011- 2:24:27. pbs: 3000m 9:35.79mx '03, 5000m 15:32.07 '04, Road: 15km 48:03 '10, 10M 51:30 '10, 20km 65:12 '10, HMar 68:39 '10.
2nd Rotterdam Marathon 2011. A cousin of Lornah Kiplagat and sister of Sylvia Kibet KEN, she gained Dutch citizenship on 14 Oct 2007. Engaged to Hugo van den Broek (Mar 2:12:08 '04, 14 EC '10).

Lornah KIPLAGAT b. 1 May 1974 Kabiemit, Kenya 1.67m 49kg. AV Hylas (Alkmaar). Married to Pieter Langerhorst NED.
At 10000m: OG: '04- 5, '08- 8; WCh: '03- 4; EC: '06- 5. World 20k: '06- 1; HMar: '05-07-08: 2/1/1; CC: '04-06-07: 6/5 (4k) & 2/1; Eur CC: '05- 1. Won Dutch 10000m 2006, Mar 2005, 2011.
World road bests 10 miles 2002 & 2006, 20km (3) and HMar (3) 2003-07, European record 15km 2007, Dutch 5000m, 10000m & Marathon 2003.
Progress at 10000m, Mar: 1997- 2:33:50, 1998- 2:34:03, 1999- 2:25:29, 2000- 2:22:36, 2001- 2:27:56, 2002- 2:23:55, 2003- 30:12.53, 2:22:22; 2004- 30:31.92, 2:28:21; 2005- 2:27:36, 2006- 30:37.26, 2:32:31; 2007- 2:24:46, 2008- 30:40.27, 2011- 2:25:52. pbs: 3000m 8:52.82 '00, 5000m 14:51.95mx '02, 14:56.43 '03; Road: 5M 25:09 '97 (former world best), 10km 30:32 '02, 15km 46:59 '07, 10M 50:50 '06, 20km 62:57 '07, HMar 66:25 '07 (all Dutch records).
Five major marathon wins: Los Angeles 1997 and 1998, Amsterdam 1999, Osaka 2002, Rotterdam 2005. Capped a series of fine road runs with second in Chicago marathon 2000. 4th Boston 2001, 4th Osaka and 3rd New York 2003, 5th London 2007. Switched from Kenyan to Dutch (citizen from 23 July 2003).

NEW ZEALAND

Governing body: Athletics New Zealand, PO Box 741, 6001 Wellington 6140.
National Championships first held in 1887 (men), 1926 (women). **2011 Champions: Men**: 100m: Carl van der Speck 11.07, 200m/400m:

Alex Jordan 21.33w/46.40, 800m: Michael Whitehead 1:52.33, 1500m/3000m: Hamish Carson 3:53.59/8:06.70, 5000m: Nick Willis 14:34.32, 10000m: Stephen Lett 30:25.76, HMar: Stephen Lett 67:38, Mar: Dale Warrander 2:23:01, 3000mSt: Ben Tingay 9:21.10, 110mh/PV/LJ/ Dec: Brent Newdick 14.71/4.25/7.36w/7296, 400mh: James Mortimer 50.83, HJ: William Crayford 2.01, TJ: Todd Swanson 14.67, SP: Tom Walsh 18.26, DT: Marshall Hall 53.23, HT: Philip Jensen (16th title) 59.04, JT: Stuart Farquhar 75.47, 3000mW/20kW: Quentin Rew 11:51.59/1:27:47, 50kW: Graeme Jones 4:46:37. **Women**: 100m/200m: Andrea Koenen 12.37/23.87w, 400m: Louise Jones 54.36, 800m/1500m/3000m: Nikki Hamblin 2:05.49/4:29.75/9:32.44, 5000m: Kellie Palmer 16:32.70, 10000m/HMar: Danielle Trevis 33:18.36/78:36, Mar: Johanna Ottosson 2:48:28, 3000mSt: Fiona Crombie 10:25.09, 100mh: Fiona Morrison 13.60, 400mh: Tracey Hale 61.46, HJ/ LJ/Hep: Sarah Cowley 1.84/6.08w/5752, PV: Kerry Charlesworth 3.90, TJ: Nneka Okpala 12.68, SP: Valerie Adams 20.54, DT: Leesa Lealisalanoa 51.53, HT: Julia Ratcliffe 60.58, JT: Hannah Blair 45.01, 3000mW/20kW: Roseanne Robinson 14:36.87/1:51:39.

Jacko GILL b. 20 Dec 1994 Auckland 1.91m 105kg. Takapuna.
At SP: WJ: '10- 1; WY: '11- 1.
Five World youth shot records 5kg 23.86 '10, 24.35 and 24.45 '11; 6kg (4) 21.34 to 22.31, 7.26kg (3) in 2011. Three NZL records 2011.
Progress at SP: 2010- 18.57, 2011- 20.38.
World age 15 and 16 bests for 5kg, 6kg and 7.26kg shot. His father Walter was a NZ shot champion, pb 16.57 '86.

Nick WILLIS b. 25 Apr 1983 Lower Hutt 1.83m 68kg. Economics graduate of University of Michigan, USA.
At 1500m: OG: '04- sf, '08- 2, WCh: '05- sf, '07- 10, '11- 12; CG: '06-1, '10- 3; WJ: '02- 4; WI: '08- dq; WCp: '06- 3. Won NCAA indoor 2005, NZ 1500m 2006, 5000m 2011.
Three NZ 1500m records 2005-11. Oceania indoor 1500m record (3:35.80) 2010.
Progress at 1500m: 2001- 3:43.54, 2002- 3:42.69, 2003- 3:36.58, 2004- 3:32.64, 2005- 3:32.38, 2006- 3:32.17, 2007- 3:35.85, 2008- 3:33.51, 2009- 3:38.85i, 2010- 3:35.17, 2011- 3:31.79. pbs: 800m 1:45.54 '04, 1000m 2:16.93 '08, 1M 3:50.66 '08, 3000m 7:44.90i '04, 7:45.97 '05; 5000m 13:27.54 '05.
His brother Steve (b. 25 Apr 1975) had pbs: 1500m 3:40.29 '99, 1M 3:59.04 '00.

Women

Valerie ADAMS b. 6 Oct 1984 Rotorua 1.93m 123kg. Auckland City.
At SP: OG: '04- 8, '08- 1; WCh: '03-05-07-09-11: 5/3/1/1/1; CG: '02-06-10: 2/1/1; WJ: '02- 1; WY: '99- 10, '01- 1; WI: '04-08-10-12: dnq 10/1/2/1; WCp: '02- 6, '06- 1, '10- 1. Won WAF 2008-09, NZL SP 2001-11, DT 2004, HT 2003.
Nine Oceania & Commonwealth shot records 2005-11, 22 NZ 2002-11, 7 OCE indoor 2004-12.
Progress at SP: 1999- 14.83, 2000- 15.72, 2001- 17.08, 2002- 18.40, 2003- 18.93, 2004- 19.29, 2005- 19.87, 2006- 20.20, 2007- 20.54, 2008- 20.56, 2009- 21.07, 2010- 20.86, 2011- 21.24, 2012- 20.67. pbs: DT 58.12 '04, HT 58.75 '02.
Matched her age with metres at the shot from 14 to 18 and missed that at 19 by only two months. 28 successive shot wins from September 2007 to World Indoor silver in March 2010. Her father came from England and her mother from Tonga. Married New Caledonia thrower Bertrand Vili (SP 17.81 '02, DT 63.66 '09, 4 ECp '07 for France) in November 2004 (now separated).

Kimberley **SMITH** b. 19 Nov 1981 Papakura 1.66m 49kg. Social science graduate of Providence College.
At 5000m: OG: '04- h; WUG: '05- 1; WCp: '06- 4. At 10000m: OG: '08- 9; WCh: '05- 15, '07- 5. '09- 8. At 3000m: WI: '08- 6. World CC: '05- 12, '09- 13; HMar: '09- 7. Won NCAA 5000m and indoor 3000m & 5000m 2004; NZ 5000m 2002, 2006, 2008; CC 2002.
Oceania records: 3000m 2007, 5000m & 10000m 2008; indoor 1M 2008, 3000m 2007, 5000m 2005 & 2009. NZ records 5000m (3) 2005-07, 10000m (3) 2005-08, HMar (4) 2009-11, Mar 2010.
Progress at 5000m, 10000m, Mar: 2002- 16:30.10, 2003- 15:47.92, 2004- 15:09.72, 33:45.81; 2005- 14:50.46i/15:05.68, 31:21.00, 2006- 14:56.58, 2007- 14:49.41, 31:20.63; 2008- 14:45.93, 30:35.54; 2009- 14:39.89i/14:52.49, 31:21.42; 2010- 2:25:21, 2011- 15:14.02, 2:25:46. pbs: 1500m 4:11.25 '04, 1M 4:24.14i '04, 3000m 8:35.31 '07, 2M 9:13.94i '08, Rd: 15km 47:37 '11, 10M 53:10 '10, 20km 63:38+ '11, HMar 67:11 '11.
Did not finish on marathon debut in New York 2008.

NIGERIA

Governing body: The Athletic Federation of Nigeria, P.O.Box 18793, Garki, Abuja. F'd 1944.
2011 National Champions: Men: 100m: Ogho-Oghene Egwero 10.34, 200m: Obinna Metu 20.84, 400m: Godday James 45.93, 800m: Justine Agu 1:51.34, 1500m: Joshua Gowok 3:54.56, 5000m/3000mSt: Sanji Isimael 14:30.83/9:22.61, 10000m: Sanmgo Ismael 30:30.10, HMar: Christopher Tokbe 66:29, 110mh: Samuel Okon 13.92, 400mh: Lucky Iyoha 51.99, HJ: Adio Bayo 2.10, PV: Inah Dennis 3.80, LJ: Stanley Ggagbeke 7.90, TJ: Tosin Oke 17.14, SP/DT: Kenechukwu Ezeofor 15.90/50.80, HT: Ibrahim Baba 53.14, JT: Friday Osayande 66.23, Dec: Lee Okoroafor 6285, 20000mW: Kazeem Adeyemi 1:35:15.76. **Women**: 100m/LJ: Blessing Okagbare 11.22/6.78, 200m: Damola Osayemi 23.33, 400m: Bukola Abogunloko 52.35, 800m: Brittany Ogunmokun 2:10.58, 1500m: Agber Shimenege

4:32.65, 5000m/10000m: Pam Deborah 17:18.87/37:02.85, HMar: Bukola Pereira 87:32, 100mh: Seun Adigun 13.47, 400mh: Ajoke Odumosu 56.24, HJ: Doreen Amata 1.80, PV: Maureen Williams 2.80, TJ: Otonye Iworima 13.70, SP: Chinwe Okoro 16.79, DT: Okwukwe Okolie 49.08, HT: Queen Obisesan 58.39, JT: Patience Okoro 42.74, Hep: Naomi Osazuwa 5668, 20000mW: Joy Davis 1:46:35.83.

Tosin OKE b. 1 Oct 1980 London, UK 1.78m 77kg. Woodford Green, UK. Chemistry graduate of Manchester University.
At TJ: WCh: '09/11- dnq 16/16; EC: '02- nj; CG: '02- 5, '10- 1; AfG: '11- 1; AfCh: '10- 1; EJ: '99- 1; CCp: '10- 6. ECp: '03- 4. Won UK 2007, NGR 2009-10.
Progress at TJ: 1997- 14.07, 1998- 15.16/15.62w, 1999- 16.57, 2000- 16.04/16.37w, 2001- 16.08i/15.72, 2002- 16.65, 2003- 16.61i/16.59, 2004- 16.49/16.75w, 2005- 16.12/16.30w, 2006- 16.33/16.50w, 2007- 16.86, 2008- 16.47/16.63w, 2009- 16.87, 2010- 17.22A/17.16, 2011- 17.21. pb LJ 7.31 '05.
Switched allegiance from Britain to Nigeria (parents) from 10 Feb 2009.

Women

Doreen AMATA b. 6 May 1988. Lagos 1.85m 55kg. Was at Lagos State University.
At HJ: OG: '08- dnq 16=; WCh: '09- dnq 27, '11= 8-; AfG: '07- 1, '11- 1. Won Nigerian 2007-09, 2011. 3 Nigerian high jump records 2009-11.
Progress at HJ: 2005- 1.70, 2006- 1.70, 2007- 1.89, 2008- 1.95, 2009- 1.90, 2011- 1.95.

Ajoke ODUMOSU b. 27 Oct 1987 Lagos 1.68m 59kg. Was at University of South Alabama, USA.
At 400mh: WCh: '07-09-11: h/sf/sf; CG: '10- 1; AfG: '07- 3, '11- 1; AfCh: '08- 1,'10- 2 ; WJ: '06- 5/2R; CCp: '10- 2. Won Af-J 2003, Nigerian 2009-11. At 400m: OG: '08- sf.
Three Nigerian 400mh records 2009-10.
Progress at 400mh: 2003- 60.03, 2004- 57.33, 2006- 56.09, 2007- 55.37, 2008- 55.92A, 2009- 54.80, 2010- 54.59, 2011- 56.23. pbs: 100m 11.71 '09, 200m 23.42 '10, 400m 51.39 '08.

Blessing OKAGBARE b. 9 Oct 1988 Sapele 1.80m 60kg. Student at University of Texas at El Paso, USA.
At LJ/100m: OG: '08- 3; WCh: '11- dnq 18/5; AfG: '07- 2 (4 TJ), '11- 1; AfCh: '10- 1/1/1R; WJ: '06- 16 (dnq 17 TJ); CCp: '10- 6/3/3R; Won Nigerian 100m 2009-11, LJ 2008-09, 2011; TJ 2008; NCAA 100m & LJ 2010.
Nigerian & African junior TJ record 2007.
Progress at 100m, LJ: 2004- 5.85 irreg, 2006- 6.16, 2007- 6.51, 2008- 6.91, 2009- 11.16, 6.73/6.90w; 2010- 11.00/10.98w/10.7Aw, 6.88; 2011- 11.08/11.01w, 6.78/6.84w. pbs: 60m 7.18i '10, 200m 22.71 '10, TJ 14.13 '07.

OluDamola OSAYOMI b. 26 Jun 1986 Ilesha, Osun 1.63m 63kg. Nike.
At 100m(/200m): OG: '04- 7R, '08- sf/qf/3R

WCh: '07- 8, '09- qf/h, '11= sf; CG: '10- sf/sf; WY: '03- sf; AfG: '07- 1/1, '11- 1/1; AfCh: '04-4, '08- 1/3/1R. At 60m: WI:'08- 6. Won NGR 100m & 200m 2008.
Progress at 100m: 2003- 11.69, 2004- 11.34, 2005- 11.51, 2006- 11.31A/11.13Aw/11.16w, 2007- 11.15, 2008- 11.08/10.8, 2009- 11.31, 2010- 11.22A/11.23, 2011- 10.99/10.90w. pbs: 60m 7.19i '08, 200m 22.74 '08

NORWAY

Governing body: Norges Friidrettsforbund, Serviceboks 1, Ullevaal Stadium, 0840 Oslo. Founded 1896.
National Championships first held in 1896 (men), 1947 (women, walks 1937). **2011 Champions**: **Men**: 100m: Jaysuma Saidy Ndure 10.29, 200m: Christian Mogstad 21.30, 400m: Jonas Grønnhaug 48.99, 800m: Håkon Mushom 1:54.98, 1500m: Hans Kristian Fløystad 3:59.36, 5000m: Sondre Nordstad Moen 13:51.83, 10000m: Urige Arado Buta 29:21.62, HMar: Alem Adhanon 67:46, Mar: Andreas Myhre Sjurseth 2:27:28, 3000mSt: Bjørnar Ustad Kristensen 8:46.21, 110mh: Vladimir Vukicevic 14.23, 400mh: Øyvind Kjerpeset 52.78, HJ: Brede Raa Ellingsen 2.11, PV: Hans Olav Uldal 4.70, LJ: Jonas Mögenburg 7.60, TJ: Sindre Almsengen 15.96, SP: Stian Andersen 16.51, DT: Magnus Berntsen 56.75, HT: Eivind Henriksen 71.83, JT: Andreas Thorkildsen 90.61, Dec: Hans Olav Uldal 7348, 5000mW: Joakim Sælen 22:46.08, 10kW/20kW: Trond Nymark 41:44.3/1:25:44, 50kW: *no entries*.
Women: 100m: Ezinne Okparaebo 11.57, 200m: Astrid Cederkvist 34.37, 400m: Martine Borge 54.87, 800m: Ingvill Måkestad Bovim 2:02.93, 1500m: Frida Berge 4:33.26, 5000m/HMar: Christina Bus Holth 16:36.33/75:06, 10000m: Tone Hjalmarsen 33:44.18, Mar: Marthe Katrine Myhre 2:52:30, 100mh: Isabelle Pedersen 13.21, 400mh: Vilde Svortevik 61.00, HJ: Tonje Angelsen 1.86, PV: Cathrine Larsåsen 4.31, LJ: Ida Marcussen 6.09, TJ: Inger Anne Frøysedal 13.30, SP: Kristin Sundsteigen 13.56, DT: Grete Etholm 55.22, HT: Mona Holm 70.43, JT: Tove Dahle 54.23, Hep: Ingvild Kåshagen 3739, 3000mW/5kW: Kjersti Tysse Plätzer 14:00.41/23:44, 10kW: Merete Helgheim 50:33, 20kW: *no entries*.

Trond NYMARK b. 28 Dec 1976 Bergen 1.80m 64kg. TIF Viking, Bergen.
At 50kW: OG: '04- 13, '08- dnf; WCh: '99-01-03-05-07-09-11: dnf/dnf/8/4/8/2/17; EC: '02- 5, '06- 4, '10- dnf; WCp: '06- 2, '08- 3; ECp: '07- 2. At 20kW: EC: '98- 19; EU23: '97- 14. Won NOR 5000mW 2010, 10000mW 1997-8, 10kW 2010-11, 20kW 1997, 2000, 2004, 2010-11; 50kW 1998-9, 2004-05, 2010. NOR records: 30km walk 2000, 50km walk (3) 2005-09.
Progress at 50kW: 1998- 3:57:52, 1999- 3:54:36, 2000- 3:53:10, 2002- 3:49:27, 2003- 3:46:14, 2004-

3:44:55, 2005- 3:44:04, 2006- 3:41:30, 2007- 3:41:31, 2008- 3:44:59, 2009- 3:41:16, 2010- 3:54:22, 2011- 3:54:26. pbs: 3000mW 11:46.09 '11, 5000mW 19:40.1 '08, 10000mW 41:02.69 '11, 20kW 1:22:52.4t '04, 30kW 2:12:27 '09, 35kW 2:33:59 '09.

Jaysuma SAIDY NDURE b. 1 Jan 1984 Bakau, The Gambia 1.92m 72kg. IL i BUL, Oslo.
At (100m)/200m: OG: '04- qf/qf, '08- qf/sf; WCh: '03- h, '05- sf, '09- (sf), '11- sf/4; EC: '10- 6/5; CG: '02- qf, '06- sf; WJ: '02- h; AfG: '03- h/ sf; AfCh: '04- 3/6; CCp: '10- dnf. Won WAF 200m 2007, Norwegian 100m 2007-08, 2011; 200m 2007, 2010.
Records: Gambian 100m & 200m 2001-06, Norwegian 100m (6) 2007-11, 200m 2007.
Progress at 100m, 200m: 2001- 10.66, 21.27; 2002- 10.73/10.59w, 21.20; 2003- 10.52/10.51w, 21.18; 2004- 10.26, 20.69; 2005- 10.31/10.18w, 20.51/20.14w, 2006- 10.27, 20.47; 2007- 10.06, 19.89; 2008- 10.01, 20.45; 2009- 10.10/10.07w, 20.55; 2010- 10.00/9.98w, 20.29; 2011- 9.99, 19.95. pbs: 60m 6.55i '08, 300m 33.76 '09, 400m 48.71 '09.
Having lived in Oslo from 2001, became a Norwegian citizen in November 2006.

Andreas THORKILDSEN b. 1 Apr 1982 Kristiansand 1.88m 90kg. Kristiansands IF.
At JT: OG: '04- 1, '08- 1; WCh: '01-03-05-07-09- 11: dnq 26/11/2/2/1/2; EC: '02- dnq 15, '06- 1, '10- 1; WJ: '00- 2; EU23: '03- 4; EJ: '99- 7, '01- 2; EY: '97- 1; CCp: '10- 1; ET: '10- 1. Won DL 2010, WAF 2006, 2009; NOR 2001-06, 2009-11.
World junior javelin record 2001, seven Norwegian records 2005-06.
Progress at JT: 1996- 53.82, 1998- 61.57, 1999- 72.11, 2000- 77.48, 2001- 83.87, 2002- 83.43, 2003- 85.72, 2004- 86.50, 2005- 89.60, 2006- 91.59, 2007- 89.51, 2008- 90.57, 2009- 91.28, 2010- 90.37, 2011- 90.61. pbs: SP 9.96 '01, DT 38.02 '01.
His mother Bente Amundsen was a Norwegian champion at 100mh (pb 14.6), father Tomm was a junior international with bests of 100m 10.9 and javelin 71.64.

Women

Christina VUKICEVIC b. 18 Jun 1987 Lørenskog, Akershus 1.78m 60kg. Ski IL
At 100mh: OG: '08- h; WCh: '07- h, '09- sf; EC: '10- 4; WJ: '04- 5, '06- 2; EU23: '07- 2, '09- 1; EJ: '05- 2; ET: '10- 3. Won NOR 2005-10. At 60mh: EI: '09- 4, '11- 3.
Two Norwegian 100mh records 2009.
Progress at 100mh: 2004- 13.51, 2005- 13.56, 2006- 13.34, 2007- 13.07, 2008- 13.05/13.04w, 2009- 12.74, 2010- 12.78, 2011- 12.79. pbs: 60m 7.56i '08, 100m 12.26 '04, 200m 24.90 '04, 50mh 6.81i '10, 60mh 7.83i '11, HJ 1.61 '02.
Younger brother Vladimir won World Junior 110mh silver 2010. Father Petar competed for Yugoslavia at 110mh at the 1980 Olympics, pb 13.87 '84.

PANAMA

Governing body: Federación Panameña de Atletismo, Apartado 0860-00684, Villa Lucre, Ciudad de Panamá. Founded 1945.

Alonso EDWARD b. 8 Dec 1989 Ciudad de Panamá 1.83m 73kg. Was at Barton County CC.
At (100m)/200m: WCh: '09- 2, '11- dnf; WJ: '08- (h); SACh: '09- 1/1, SAm-J: '07- (1), SAm-Y: '06- 1/1.
Records: S.American 200m 2009, Panama 100m 2009, 200m (5) 2007-09; South American Junior 100m 2007.
Progress at 100m, 200m: 2006- 10.60, 21.18; 2007- 10.28/10.25w, 20.62; 2008- 10.63, 20.96; 2009- 10.09/9.97w, 19.81; 2010- 10.24/10.08w, 2011- 20.28. pb 400m 47.40i '10.
World age-19 best 19.81 in World final 2009. Injured in April 2010; did not compete for the rest of the season, and then suffered a 10cm career-threatening hamstring tear in the 2011 World 200m final. Younger brother Mateo (b. 1 May 1993): 100m 10.47A (3rd South American Junior Champs), 200m 21.64 in 2011.

Irving SALADINO b. 23 Jan 1983 Ciudad de Colón 1.83m 70kg
At LJ: OG: '04- dnq 36, '08- 1; WCh: '05-07-09-11: 6/1/nj/dnq 22; WJ: '02- dnq; PAm: '07- 1; CAG: '06- 1; SACh: '03- 3; WI: '06- 2; WCp: '06- 1; won WAF & IbAm 2006, SAm U23 2004.
Three South American LJ records 2006-08, indoors (7) 2006-08, 12 Panama 2002-08.
Progress at LJ: 2001- 7.11, 2002- 7.51A/7.39, 2003- 7.46, 2004- 8.12A/7.79, 2005- 8.29/8.51w, 2006- 8.56/8.65w, 2007- 8.57, 2008- 8.73, 2009- 8.63, 2010- 8.30/8.46w, 2011- 8.40. pbs: 100m 10.4 '04, TJ 14.47 '04.
Set South American indoor record in qualifying and four more in final of WI 2006 for the first medal ever for Panama at World Championships. Clear world number one in 2006, winning 15/16 outdoors and in 2007 when he won all nine competitions, 21 successive wins to June 2008.

POLAND

Governing body: Polski Zwiazek Lekkiej Atletyki (PZLA), ul. Myslowicka 4, 01-612 Warszawa. Founded 1919.
National Championships first held in 1920 (men), 1922 (women). **2011 Champions: Men**: 100m: Pawel Stempel 10.48, 200m: Kamil Krynski 20.89, 400m: Marcin Marciniszyn 45.27, 800m: Marcin Lewandowski 1:46.28, 1500m: Bartosz Nowicki 3:41.43, 5000m: Lukasz Kujawski 14:06.96, 10000m: Tomasz Szymkowiak 28:38.42, HMar: Marcin Chabowski 62:26, Mar: Blazej Brzezinski 2:14:16,, 3000mSt: Lukasz Kujawski 8:40.22, 110mh: Dominik Bochenek 13.44, 400mh: Marek Plawgo 50.11, HJ: Piotr Sleboda 2.22, PV: Mateusz Didenkow, Lukasz Michalski 5.72, LJ:

Michal Rosiak 7.68, TJ: Karol Hoffmann 16.21, SP: Tomasz Majewski 20.94, DT: Przemyslaw Czajkowski 63.81, HT: Szymon Ziólkowski 78.79, JT: Lukasz Grzeszczuk 79.73, Dec: Marcin Drózdz 7598, 20kW: Rafal Augustyn 1:22:01, 50kW: Rafal Fedaczynski 3:46:05. **Women:** 100m/200m: Marika Popowicz 11.55/23.49, 400m: Agata Bednarek 53.32, 800m/1500m: Angelika Cichocka 2:01.09/4:15.84, 5000m: Lidia Chojecka 15:46.88; 10000m: Iwona Lewan–dowska 33:34.49, HMar: Agnieszka Gortel 74:43, Mar: Arleta Meloch 2:46:43, 3000mSt: Katarzyna Kowalska 9:44.21, 100mh/Hep: Karolina Tyminska 13.37/6206, 400mh: Tina Polak 55.90, HJ: Karolina Gronau & Magdalena Ogrodnik 1.88, PV: Anna Rogowska 4.60, LJ/TJ: Malgorzata Trybanska 6.65/14.08, SP: Paulina Guba 16.94, DT: Joanna Wisniewska 59.85, HT: Anna Wlodarczyk 73.05, JT: Magdalena Czenska 55.53, 20kW: Agnieszka Dygacz 1:30:56.

Mateusz DIDENKOW b. 28 Jul 1983 Gdynia 1.87m 74kg. SKLA Sopot.
At PV: WCh: '11- 7; EC: '10- 11; WJ: '06- 4; EU23: '07- 9; WUG: '11- 2. Polish champion (tie) 2011.
Progress at PV: 2002- 4.21, 2003- 4.50, 2004- 4.90, 2005- 5.15, 2006- 5.31, 2007- 5.40, 2008- 5.45i/5.41, 2009- 5.62, 2010- 5.70, 2011- 5.75.

Pawel FAJDEK b. 4 Jun 1989 Swiebodzice 1.86m 118kg. KS Agros Zamosc.
At HT: WCh: '11- 11; WJ: '08- 4; EU23: '09- 8, '11- 1; WUG: '11- 1; ET: '11- 2.
Progress at HT: 2008- 64.58, 2009- 72.36, 2010- 76.07, 2011- 78.54.

Igor JANIK b. 18 Jan 1983 Gdansk 2.00m 112kg. AZS AWFIS Gdansk.
At JT: OG: 08- dnq 16; WCh: '07- 7, '09/11- dnq 31/13; WJ: '02- 1; EU23: '03- 2, '05- 1; EJ: '01- 6; WUG: '03-05-07-09-11: 1/2/5/4/3; ECp: '06-07-08-09: 3/3/3/3. Polish champion 2007-08, 2010.
Progress at JT: 2001- 72.08, 2002- 78.90, 2003- 82.54, 2004- 74.49, 2005- 77.25, 2006- 82.86, 2007- 83.38, 2008- 84.76, 2009- 83.52, 2010- 80.83, 2011- 82.81.

Adam KSZCZOT b. 2 Sep 1989 Opoczno 1.78m 64kg. RKS Lódz.
At 800m: WCh: '09- sf, '11- 6; EC: '10- 3; WJ: '08- 4; EU23: '09/11- 1; EJ: '07- 3; WI: '10- 3, '11- 4; EI: '09- 4, '11- 1; ET: '11- 1. Polish champion 2009-10. Polish 1000m record 2011.
Progress at 800m: 2005- 1:59.57, 2006- 1:51.09, 2007- 1:48.10, 2008- 1:47.16, 2009- 1:45.72, 2010- 1:45.07, 2011- 1:43.30, 2012- 1:44.57i. pbs: 400m 46.51 '11, 600m 1:14.55 '10, 1000m 2:16.99 '11, 1500m 3:46.53 '10.

Marcin LEWANDOWSKI b. 13 Jun 1987 Szczecin 1.80m 64kg. Zawisza Bydgoszcz.
At 800m: OG: '08- sf; WCh: '09- 8, '11- 4; EC: '10- 1; WJ: '06- 4; EU23: '07- 1, '09- 2; EI: '09- 6, '11- 2; CCp: '10- 2; ECp: '08- 2, '10- 3. At 1500m: EJ: '05- 7. Won Polish 800m 2011, 1500m 2008,

2010. Polish 1000m record 2011.
Progress at 800m: 2004- 1:51.73, 2005- 1:48.86, 2006- 1:46.69, 2007- 1:45.52, 2008- 1:45.84, 2009- 1:43.84, 2010- 1:44.10, 2011- 1:44.53. pbs: 400m 47.76 '09, 600m 1:15.77 '10, 1000m 2:15.76 '11, 1500m 3:37.76i '12, 3:40.38 '10.

Tomasz MAJEWSKI b. 30 Aug 1981 Nasielsk 2.04m 136kg. AZS-AWF Warszawa. Graduated in politics from Cardinal Wyszynski University.
At SP: OG: '04- dnq 18, '08- 1; WCh: '05-07-09-11: 9/5/2/9; EC: '06- 8, '10- 2; EU23: '03- 4; WI: '04-06-08-10-12: 4/7/3/5/3; EI: '09- 1; WUG: '03- 5, '05- 1; CCp: '10- 2; ECp: '07-08-09-10-11: 3/2/1/1/2. Won WAF 2008, Polish 2002-05, 2007-11. Polish shot record 2009.
Progress at SP: 1998- 12.91, 1999- 15.77, 2000- 17.77, 2001- 18.34, 2002- 19.33, 2003- 20.09, 2004- 20.83i/20.52, 2005- 20.64, 2006- 20.66, 2007- 20.87, 2008- 21.51, 2009- 21.95, 2010- 21.44, 2011- 21.60, 2012- 21.72i. pb DT 51.79 '07.
Improved pb every year of his career to 2009. Went from 20.97 to 21.04 in qualifying and 21.21 and 21.51 in final to win Olympic gold in 2008.

Piotr MALACHOWSKI b. 7 Jun 1983 Zuromin 1.94m 135kg. Slask Wroclaw. Army corporal.
At DT: OG: '08- 2; WCh: '07- 12, '09- 2, '11- 9; EC: '06- 6, '10- 1; WJ: '02- 6; EU23: '03- 9, '05- 2; EJ: '01- 5; CCp: '10- 4; ECp: '06-07-08-09-10-11: 1/1/3/1/2/3. Won DL 2010, POL 2005-10.
Eight Polish discus records 2006-10.
Progress at DT: 2000- 52.04, 2001- 54.19, 2002- 56.84, 2003- 57.83, 2004- 62.04, 2005- 64.74, 2006- 66.21, 2007- 66.61, 2008- 68.65, 2009- 69.15, 2010- 69.83, 2011- 68.49.

Lukasz MICHALSKI b. 2 Aug 1988 Bydgoszcz 1.90m 78kg. SL WKS Zawisza Bydgoszcz.
At PV: WCh: '09- dnq 22=, '11- 4; EC: '10- 7; WJ: '06- 8; WY: '05- 4; EU23: '09- 5; EJ: '07- 3; WUG: '11- 1; WI: '10- 9; EI: '09- 6; ET: '09- 3; Polish champion 2010, 2011 (tie).
Progress at PV: 2004- 4.80, 2005- 5.25, 2006- 5.30, 2007- 5.50, 2008- 5.51, 2009- 5.71, 2010- 5.80, 2011- 5.85. pb LJ 6.95 '08.

Grzegorz SUDOL b. 28 Aug 1978 Nowa Deba 1.76m 63kg. AZS-AWF Kraków.
At 50kW: OG: '04- 7, '08- 9; WCh: '03-05-07-09-11: dq/dq/21/4/dnf; EC: '02- 10, '06- 10, '10- 2. At 10000mW: WJ: '96- 7, EJ: '97- 10. Won POL 20kW 2008-09, 50kW 2002, 2007-08.
Unratified Polish 30,000m record 2011.
Progress at 50kW: 2002- 3:50:37, 2003- 3:55:40, 2004- 3:49:09, 2006- 3:50:24, 2007- 3:55:22, 2008- 3:45:47, 2009- 3:42:34, 2010- 3:42:24. pbs: 3000mW 11:25.93i/11:29.20 '05, 5000mW 18:55.01i '05, 19:09.02 '11; 10kW 39:01 '05, 20kW 1:20:50 '10, 30kW 2:11:12.0t '11, 35kW 2:35:34 '10.
Three times Polish 50k champion – each event held in different countries (CZE, AUT, SVK).

Pawel WOJCIECHOWSKI b. 6 Jun 1989 Byd–goszcz 1.90m 81kg. SL WKS Zawisza Bydgoszcz.

At PV: WCh: '11- 1; WJ: '08- 2; EU23: '11- 1; EJ: '07- dnq 16; EI: '11- 4. Won W.Military 2011. Polish pole vault record 2011.
Progress at PV: 2001- 2.50, 2002- 2.70, 2003- 3.10, 2004- 3.50, 2005- 4.10, 2006- 4.70, 2007- 5.00, 2008- 5.51, 2009- 5.40i/5.22, 2010- 5.60, 2011- 5.91.

Szymon ZIÓLKOWSKI b. 1 Jul 1976 Poznan 1.92m 120kg. AZS Poznan.
At HT: OG: '96- 10, '00- 1, '04- dnq 13, '08- 7; WCh: '95-99-01-05-07-09-11: dnq 22/dnq 23/1/3/7/2/7; EC: '98-02-06-10: 5/dnq 15/5/5; WJ: '94- 1; EJ: '93- 7, '95- 1; EU23: '97- 2; ECp: '96-9-01-04-05-06-07-08-09: 2/2/1/1/1/1/1/1/2. Polish champion 1996-7, 1999-2002, 2004-09, 2011. Six   Polish hammer records 2000-01.
Progress at HT: 1991- 55.96, 1992- 63.84, 1993- 67.34, 1994- 72.48, 1995- 75.42, 1996- 79.52, 1997- 79.14, 1998- 79.58, 1999- 79.01, 2000- 81.42, 2001- 83.38, 2002- 79.78, 2003- 76.97, 2004- 79.41, 2005- 79.35, 2006- 82.31, 2007- 80.70, 2008- 79.55, 2009- 79.30, 2010- 77.99, 2011- 79.02. pbs: SP 15.25 '95, DT 49.58 '00.
Sister Michalina (b. 1983) had HT pb 58.33 '04. Married javelin thrower (50.90 '98 (old), 50.64 '99) Joanna Domagala in December 2000 and and after divorce Iwona Dorobisz (100m 11.47 '09) in 2008.

Women

Zaneta GLANC b. 11 Mar 1983 Poznan 1.87m 86kg. AZS Poznan.
At DT: OG: '08- dnq; WCh: '09- 4, '11- 4; EC: '10- dnq 13; EJ: '05- dnq; WUG: '09- 2, '11- 1; ET: '11- 3. Won POL 2009.
Progress at DT: 2003- 47.03, 2004- 51.30, 2005- 56.15, 2006- 56.00, 2007- 59.36, 2008- 61.42, 2009- 63.96, 2010- 62.16, 2011- 63.99.

Monika PYREK b. 11 Aug 1980 Gdynia 1.70m 58kg. MKL Szczecin. Law graduate of University of Gdansk.
At PV: OG: '00- 7, '04- 4, '08- 5; WCh: '01-03-05-07-09-11: 3/4=/2/4/2=/10=; EC: '98- 7, '02- dnq 13=, '06- 2; WJ: '98- 2=; EU23: '01- 1; EJ: '97- 10, '99- 4; WI: '03-04-06-08: 3/5=/4/3=; EI: '02- 3, '05- 3; WCp: '06- 5; ECp: '04-06-07-09: 2/1/1/1. Polish champion 1999-2002, 2004-08, 2010 and indoors 1998-2006.
41 Polish pole vault records 1996-2004 (and 28 indoors 1996-2006), European record 2001.
Progress at PV: 1995- 2.30, 1996- 3.60, 1997- 3.83, 1998- 4.15, 1999- 4.21i/4.16, 2000- 4.40, 2001- 4.61, 2002- 4.62, 2003- 4.60, 2004- 4.72, 2005- 4.70, 2006- 4.76i/4.75, 2007- 4.82, 2008- 4.78, 2009- 4.78, 2010- 4.60i/4.40, 2011- 4.60. pb HJ 1.72 '03. Won "Dancing with the Stars" TV programme in Poland.

Anna ROGOWSKA b. 21 May 1981 Gdynia 1.71m 55kg. SKLA Sopot. PE student.
At PV: OG: '04- 3, '08- 10=; WCh: '03-05-07-09-11: 7/6=/8/1/10=; EC: '02- 7=; EU23: '03- 3; WI: '03-04-06-08-10: 6=/7/2/6/3; EI: '05-07-11:

2/3/1; ECp: '05-08-10-11: 1/2/3/1. Polish champion 2009, 2011. Nine Polish pole vault records 2004-05, indoors (2) 2010-11.
Progress at PV: 1997- 2.60, 1998- 2.90, 1999- 3.40, 2000- 3.60, 2001- 3.90, 2002- 4.40, 2003- 4.47i/4.45, 2004- 4.71, 2005- 4.83, 2006- 4.80i/4.70, 2007- 4.72i/4.60, 2008- 4.66, 2009- 4.80, 2010- 4.81i/4.71, 2011- 4.85i/4.75. Coached by husband Jacek Torlinski (PV 4.85 '97).

Karolina TYMINSKA b. 4 Oct 1984 Swiebodzin 1.76m 64kg. SKLA Sopot.
At Hep: OG: '08- 7; WCh: '07- 15, '09- dnf, '11- 4; EC: '06- dnf (dnq LJ), '10- 5; EU23: '05- dnf (LJ dnq 17); ECp: '06-'09: 2/3. At Pen: WI: '08-10-12: 6/6/4; EI: '05-07-09-11: 8/7/5/4. Won POL 100mh 2011, Hep 2006-07, 2011.
Progress at Hep: 2002- 5147, 2004- 5787, 2005- 6026, 2006- 6402, 2007- 6200, 2008- 6428, 2009- 6191, 2010- 6230, 2011- 6544. pbs: 60m 7.61i '09, 100m 12.15 '05, 200m 23.32 '06, 800m 2:05.21 '11, 60mh 8.34i '10, 100mh 13.12 '11, HJ 1.78 '11, LJ 6.63 '08, SP 15.11i/14.82 '08, JT 41.32 '11, Pen 4769i '08.

Anita WLODARCZYK b. 8 Aug 1985 Rawicz 1.78m 94kg. RKS Skra Warszawa.
At HT: OG: '08- 6; WCh: '09- 1, '11- 5; EC: '10- 3; EU23: '07- 9; ET: '09- 1. Polish champion 2009, 2011. Two world hammer records, three Polish records 2009-10.
Progress at HT: 2003- 43.24, 2004- 54.74, 2005- 60.51, 2006- 65.53, 2007- 69.07, 2008- 72.80, 2009- 77.96, 2010- 78.30, 2011- 75.33. pbs: SP 13.25 '06, DT 52.26 '08.

PORTUGAL

Governing body: Federação Portuguesa de Atletismo, Largo da Lagoa, 1799-538 Linda-a-Velha. Founded in 1921.

National Championships first held in 1910 (men), 1937 (women). **2011 Champions: Men**: 100m/ 200m: Yazaldes Nascimento 10.15w/20.87, 400m: João Ferreira 46.69, 800m: António Rodrigues 1:51.19, 1500m: Hélio Gomes 3:42.80, 5000m: Rui Silva 13:48.59, 10000m: Manuel Ferraz 30:33.28, Mar: Vasco Azevedo 2:22:03, 3000mSt: Alberto Paulo 8:28.20, 110mh: João Almeida 13.49w, 400mh: Jorge Paula 49.88, HJ: Paulo Gonçalves 2.14, PV: Edi Maia 5.44, LJ: Marcos Chuva 7.79, TJ: Nelson Évora 16.99, SP/DT: Marco Fortes 20.21/56.37, HT: Dário Manso 69.45, JT: Tiago Aperta 65.66, Dec: Tiago Marto 7291, 10,000mW/20kW: João Vieira 39:44.91/1:27:19, 50kW: Jorge Costa 4:07:17. **Women**: 100m/200m: Sónia Tavares 11.46w/23.84w, 400m: Patricia Lopes 54.85, 800m: Joceline Monteiro 2:10.58, 1500m: Jéssica Augusto 4:16.42, 5000m: Dulce Félix 16:15.75, 10000m: Anabela Tavares 37:14.41, Mar: Anabela Tavares 2:50:19, 3000mSt: Sara Moreira 9:41.20, 100mh: Mónica Lopes 13.62, 400mh: Vera Barbosa 56.77, HJ: Liliana

Viana 1.82, PV: Maria Eleonor Tavares 4.20, LJ: Naide Gomes 6.58, TJ: Patricia Mamona 14.42, SP: Diana Hernandez 12.20, DT: Irina Rodrigues 55.83, HT: Vânia Silva 65.55, JT: Sílvia Cruz 49.89, Hep: Cláudia Rodrigues 4791, 10000mW/20kW: Inês Henriques 43:59.08/1:30:38.

Nelson ÉVORA b. 20 Apr 1984 Abidjan, Côte d'Ivoire 1.81m 64kg. Sport Lisboa e Benfica.
At (LJ/)TJ: OG: '04- dnq 40, '08- 1; WCh: '05-07-09-11: dnq 14/1/2/5; EC: '06- 6/4; WJ: '02- dnq 18/6; EU23: '05- 3; EJ: '03- 1/1; WUG: '09- 1, '11- 1; WI: '06- 6, '08- 3; EI: '07- 5; ECp: '09- 2/1; Won WAF TJ 2008, POR LJ 2006-07, TJ 2003-04, 2006-07, 2009-11.
Six Portuguese triple jump records 2006-07, Cape Verde LJ & TJ records 2001-02.
Progress at TJ: 1999- 14.35, 2000- 14.93i, 2001- 16.15, 2002- 15.87, 2003- 16.43, 2004- 16.85i/16.04, 2005- 16.89, 2006- 17.23, 2007- 17.74, 2008- 17.67, 2009- 17.66/17.82w, 2010- 16.36, 2011- 17.35. pbs: HJ 2.07i '05, 1.98 '99; LJ 8.10 '07.
He suffered a serious injury in right tibia (in same place where he had an operation in February 2010) in January 2012 and will miss summer season. Father from Cape Verde, mother from Côte d'Ivoire, relocating to Portugal when he was five. He switched nationality in 2002. Became Portugal's first male world champion in 2007. Sister Dorothé (b. 28 May 1991) has 400m pb 55.57 '11.

Marco FORTES b. 26 Sep 1982 Lisboa 1.89m 139kg. Sport Lisboa e Benfica.
At SP: OG: '08- dnq 38; WCh: '09- dnq 18, '11- 6; EC: '10- dnq 13; WJ: '00- dnq 18 (dnq DT); EU23: '03- 12; EJ: '01- 3; Won IbAm 2010, POR SP 2002-11 (& 10 indoor), DT 2009, 2011
Five Portuguese shot records 2008-12.
Progress at SP: 2000- 17.31, 2001- 18.02, 2002- 18.76, 2003- 18.57, 2004- 18.19, 2005- 17.89, 2006- 18.74, 2007- 19.18, 2008- 20.13, 2009- 20.52, 2010- 20.69, 2011- 20.89, 2012- 21.02. pb DT 58.32 '09.

Women

Jéssica AUGUSTO b. 8 Nov 1981 Paris, France 1.65m 46kg. Nike.
At 3000mSt: OG: '08- h (h 5000); WCh: '09- 11. At 5000m/(10000m): WCh: '05- h, '07- 15, '11- (10); EC: '10- 4/3; EU23: '03- dnf; WUG: '07- 1; CCp: '10- 7. At 3000m (1500m): WJ: '00- 8; EU23: '01- (10); EJ: '99- 6 (12); WI: '08- 8, '10- 8; EI: '09- 10. World CC: '07- 12, '10- 21; Eur CC: '98-99-00-02-04-05-06-07-08-09-10: 12J/8J/1J/16/18/30/9/11/2/4/1. Won POR 1500m 2007, 2011; 5000m 2006, IbAm 3000m 2004, 2006, 2010.
Two Portuguese 3000m steeplechase records 2008-10, European indoor 2M best 2010.
Progress at 5000m, 10000m, 3000mSt: 2003- 15:51.63, 2004- 15:15.76, 2005- 15:20.45, 2006- 15:37.55, 2007- 14:56.39, 2008- 15:19.67, 9:22.50; 2009- 9:25.25, 2010- 14:37.07, 31:19.15, 9:18.54; 2011- 15:19.60, 32:06.68. pbs: 800m 2:07.97i '02, 1500m 4:07.89i/4:08.32 '10, 1M 4:32.58i '09, 4:42.15 '99, 2000m 5:45.6i '09, 3000m 8:41.53 '07, 2M 9:19.39i '10, 9:22.89 '07; road 15km 48:40 '08, 10M 53:15 '08, HMar 69:08 '09, Mar 2:24:33 '11. Won Great North Run 2009.

Ana CABECINHA b. 29 Apr 1984 Beja 1.68m 52kg. CO Pechão.
At 20kW: OG: '08- 8; WCh: '11- 7; EC: '10- 8; EU23: '05- 4; WCp '08- 11, '10- 8. At 5000mW: WY: '01- 10. At 10000mW: WJ: '02- 12; EJ: '03- 3; won IbAm 2010, POR 2005, 2008, 2010, 2012. POR records 10,000m and 20km walk 2008.
Progress at 20kW: 2004- 1:37:39, 2005- 1:34:13, 2006- 1:31:02, 2007- 1:32:46, 2008- 1:27:46, 2009- 1:33:05, 2010- 1:31:14, 2011- 1:31:08, 2012- 1:29:53. pbs: 3000mW 12:42.80 '05, 5000mW 21:46.34 '11, 10000mW 43:08.17 '08; running 1500m 4:31.73 '07.

Susana FEITOR b. 28 Jan 1975 Alcobertas 1.60m 52kg. Clube de Natação de Rio Maior.
At 20kW: OG: '00- 14, '04- 20, '08- dnf; WCh: '99-01-03-05-07-09-11: 4/dq/9/3/5/10/6; EC: '02- dnf, '06- 14; WCp: '99-02-08: 9/14/10; ECp: '03- 5, '05- 2. At 10kW: OG: '92- dq, '96- 13; WCh: '91-93-95-97: 17/11/17/h; EC: '94- 8, '98- 3; EU23: '97- 3; WUG: '95- 4, '97- 4, '01- 2; WCp: '93- 8, '95- 15; ECp: '96- 3. At 5000mW: WJ: '90- 1, '92- dq, 94- 2; EJ: '89- 6, '91- 2, '93- 1. Won POR 10kW 1992, 1994-2000, 2002-04, 2007; 20kW 1998-9, 2001-04, 2007-08.
POR walks records 1989-2001: 3000m (10), 5000m (9), 10km (9), 20km (3), 20,000m track (1:29:36.4 WR '01). World junior 5000m best (21:01.8) '93.
Progress at 10kW, 20kW: 1991- 45:37, 1992- 45:24, 1993- 43:44, 1994- 43:30, 1995- 44:05, 1996- 43:37, 1997- 44:26, 1998- 42:55, 1:31:03, 1999- 44:36, 1:30:13; 2000: 43:55, 1:28:19; 2001- 42:39, 1:27:55; 2002- 44:24, 1:31:12; 2003- 44:07.80t, 1:29:08; 2004- 44:31.21t, 1:29:13; 2005- 44:25+, 1:28:44; 2006- 44:57, 1:31:43; 2007- 44:13.87, 1:31:15; 2008- 44:08.10, 1:29:31; 2009- 44:08, 1:31:37; 2010- 43:41, 1:30:47; 2011- 43:40, 1:30:44. Track pbs: 3000mW 12:08.30 '01, 5000mW 20:40.24 '01, 10000mW 44:07.80 '03.
Had a hugely successful junior career to her world silver medal in front of her home crowd in 1994, four years after she had won this title. Has competed in a record eleven World Championships 1991-2011.

Naide GOMES b. 20 Nov 1979 São Tomé, São Tomé e Principe 1.81m 70kg. Sporting Clube de Portugal.
At LJ/(Hep): OG: '04- (13), '08- dnq 31; WCh: '05- dnq 17/7, '07- 4, '09- 4, '11- 10; EC: '02- 10/18, '06- 2, '10- 2; AfrG: '99- (5); WUG: '05- 2; WI: '06-08-10: 3/1/2; EI: '05-07-11: 1/1/2; WCp: '06- 2, '10- 5; ECp: '09- 1. At Pen: WI: '03- 5, '04- 1; EI: '02- 2. At 100mh: OG: '00- h. Won WAF LJ 2008, POR Hep 2001, 100mh 2004-05, HJ 2002, LJ 2002, 2004, 2006-11.
Portuguese records LJ (9) 2002-08 Heptathlon

(3) 2002-05, indoor HJ & Pen 2004, LJ 2005-08. Progress at LJ, Hep: 1996- 5.60, 1997- 5.63, 4578; 1998- 5.80, 1999- 5.81, 4964; 2000- 6.15, 5671; 2001- 6.36, 5606w; 2002- 6.57, 6160; 2003- 6.53, 6120; 2004- 6.51, 6151; 2005- 6.72, 6230; 2006- 6.82/6.84w, 2007- 7.01, 2008- 7.12, 2009- 6.99, 2010- 6.92, 2011- 6.79i/6.76/6.78w. pbs: 60m 7.84i '04, 200m 24.87 '05, 400m 57.91i '05, 800m 2:16.31 '05, 60mh 8.39i '05, 100mh 13.50 '05, HJ 1.88i '04, 1.86 '02; TJ 11.73 '99, SP 15.08i/14.71 '04, JT 42.86 '00, Pen 4759i '04.
Changed nationality from São Tome e Principe (for whom she set 30 national records – at 100mh, HJ, LJ, TJ. SP, JT & Hep) to Portugal in 2001. Set pbs at HJ (Portuguese record) and SP en route to WI gold in 2004. Full name is Enezenaide do Rosario da Vera Cruz Gomes.

Inês HENRIQUES b 1 May 1980 Santarém 1.56m 48kg. CN Rio Maior.
At 20kW: OG: '04- 25; WCh: '01-05-07-09-11: dq/27/7/11/10; EC: '02-06-10: 15/12/9; EU23: '01- 10; WCp: '10- 3; ECp: '07- 7; Won POR 10000mW & 20kmW 2011. At 5000mW: EJ: '99- 12.
Progress at 20kW: 2000- 1:41:09, 2001- 1:34:49, 2002- 1:34:46.5t, 2003- 1:36:03, 2004- 1:31:23.7t, 2005- 1:33:24, 2006- 1:30:28, 2007- 1:30:24, 2008- 1:31:06, 2009- 1:30:34, 2010- 1:29:36, 2011- 1:30:29, 2012- 1:30:55. pbs: 3000mW 12:28.70i '11, 12:38.75 '07; 5000mW 21:38.05 '10, 10000mW 43:22.05 '08, 43:09R '10.

Vera SANTOS b. 3 Dec 1981 Santarém 1.64m 57kg. Sporting Clube de Portugal.
At 20kW: OG: '08- 9; WCh: '03-05-07-09: 15/15/11/5; EC: '02- 17, '06- 8, '10- 6; EU23: '01- 12, '03- 2; WUG: '05- 2; WCp '08- 3, '10- 2; ECp: '05- 7. At 10000mW: WJ: '00- 5. Won POR 20kW 2005, 2010.
Progress at 20kW: 2000- 1:39:20.5t, 2001- 1:35:51, 2002- 1:34:46.6t, 2003- 1:32:43, 2004- 1:33:00, 2005- 1:31:30, 2006- 1:30:41, 2007- 1:32:53, 2008- 1:28:14, 2009- 1:29:27, 2010- 1:28:29, 2011- 1:29:55. pbs: 3000mW 12:17.59 '10, 5000mW 21:01.43 '10, 10000mW 43:52.73 '10.

PUERTO RICO

Governing body: Federación de Atletismo Amateur de Puerto Rico, 90, Ave. Río Hondo, Bayamón, PR 00961-3113. Founded 1947.
Nation Champions 2011: Men: 100m/200m: Hector de Leon 10.88/21.44, 400m: José Cruz 47.77, 800m: José Serra 1:52.13, 1500m: Jean Otero 3:56.80, 110mh: Héctor Cotto 13.78, 400mh: Eric Alejando 50.80, HJ: Joel Castro 2.10, PV: Yeisel Cintron 4.95, LJ: Marcos Amalbert 7.26, TJ: Michael McAdney 15.46, SP: Steven Marrero 14.25, DT: Alfredo Romero 52.13, HT: Wilfredo de Jesus 61.21, JT: Juan Ayala 65.23.
Women: 100m/200m: Beatriz Cruz 12.03/24.49, 400m: Ginoska Cancel 55.95, 1500m: Belissa del Vale 4:36.02, 3000mSt: Alexandria Oliveras 11:21.74, 100mh: Litzy Vázquez 13.84, HJ: Yozually Ortíz 1.55, PV: Carmen Diaz 3.60, LJ/TJ: Noelis Morales 5.21/11.54, SP: Kim Barrett 15.40, DT: Brittni Borreo 55.19, HT: Taiara Negron 46.79, JT: Coralys Ortiz 51.56.

Javier CULSON b. 25 Jul 1984 Ponce 1.98m 79kg.
At 400mh: OG: '08- sf; WCh: '07- sf, '09- 2, '11- 2; PAm: '07- 6; CAG: '06- 5, '10- 2; PAm-J: '03- 3; WUG: '07- 3; CCp: '10- 2; won IbAm 2006, CAC 2009. 7 Puerto Rican 400mh records 2007-10.
Progress at 400mh: 2003- 51.10, 2004- 50.77, 2005- 50.62, 2006- 49.48, 2007- 49.07, 2008- 48.87, 2009- 48.09, 2010- 47.72. 2011- 48.32. pbs: 200m 21.64w '07, 400m 46.15 '11, 800m 1:49.97 '11, 110mh 13.84 '07.

QATAR

Governing body: Qatar Association of Athletics Federation, PO Box 8139, Doha. Founded 1963.

Mutaz Essa BARSHIM Ahmed b. 24 Jun 1991 1.92m 70kg. Team Aspire.
At HJ: WCh: '11- 7; WJ: '10- 1; AsiG: '10- 1; AsiC: '11- 1; WI: '12- 9=; won Asian indoors 2012; Asi-J 2010, W.Mil G & Pan-Arab 2011.
Nine Qatar high jump records 2010-11.
Progress at HJ: 2008- 2.07, 2009- 2.14, 2010- 2.31, 2011- 2.35, 2012- 2.37i.

Ali Abubaker KAMAL b. 8 Nov 1983 Sudan 1.69m 58kg.
At 3000mSt: OG: '08- 8; WCh: '07- 11, '09- 12; WJ: '02- 3; AsiG: '02- 2; AsiC: '02- 3, '09- 3; AsiJ: '02- 1. At 1500m: WJ: '00- 7; WY: '99- 4; AsiG: '06- 4; AsiC: '07- 3 (5 3000m). Won Gulf 1500m & 3000mSt; Pan-Arab and ArabG 5000m 2011.
Progression at 3000mSt: 2001- 8:41.53, 2002- 8:31.75, 2003- 8:49.74; 2006- 8:23.06, 2007- 8:21.20, 2008- 8:15.80, 2009- 8:18.95, 2010- 8:41.75, 2011- 8:30.23. pbs: 800m 1:46.38 '06, 1500m 3:36.15 '10, 3000m 7:55.95 '06, 5000m 13:45.60 '11, 2000mSt 5:33.76 '07.

Saïf Saeed SHAHEEN b. 15 Oct 1982 Keiyo, Kenya 1.77m 64kg. Formerly Stephen Cherono.
At 3000mSt (5000m): WCh: '03- 1, '05- 1, '09- (h); CG: '02- 1; AfCh: '02- 3; WCp: '06- 1 (1) won KEN 2002, WAF 2003-04, 3rd GP 2001. At 2000mSt: WY: '99- 1. At 1500m/5000m: AsiC: '03- 2/2. At 3000m: WI: '06- 2. World CC: 4k: '04-05-06: 5/4/9; 12k: '05-09: 8/13.
World record 3000m steeplechase 2004, world junior record 2001; Asian records: 3000m 2004, 5000m 2006, 3000mSt (4) 2003-04, indoor 3000m (7:39.77) 2006.
Progress at 5000m, 3000mSt: 1997- 8:43.0A, 1999- 8:19.12, 2000- 8:16.27, 2001- 7:58.66, 2002- 13:11.55, 7:58.10, 2003- 12:48.81, 7:57.38; 2004- 13:14.65, 7:53.63; 2005- 7:55.51, 2006- 12:51.98, 7:56.32; 2008- 13:29.83, 2009- 13:22.70, 2010- 13:00.31, 8:09.63. pbs: 1500m 3:33.51 '06, 2000m 5:03.06 '01, 3000m 7:32.46 '09, 2M 8:18.80 '99, 2000mSt 5:14.53 '05 (Asian best); Road: 10k

28:05+ '10, 15k 43:22+ '10, 10M 46:37 '10.
World age 17-18-19 records for 3000mSt 2000-02.
28 succcessive steeplechase wins (inc. 2 heats) from 16 Aug 2002 to 2006. Controversially transferred allegiance from Kenya to Qatar and set first Asian record (3000mSt 8:02.48) nine days after citizenship granted (9 Aug 2003) and also won the first global gold medal for Qatar. Brother of **Abraham Cherono** (b. 21 Jul 1980): 3 CG 02, 5 WCh 03, pb 8:10.33 '03, and **Christopher Kosgei** (b. 14 Aug 1974): WCh: 95- 2, 99- 1; pb 8:05.43 '99.

ROMANIA

Governing body: Federatia Romana de Atletism, 2 Primo Nebiolo Str, 011349 Bucuresti. Founded 1912.

National Championships first held in 1914 (men), 1925 (women). **2011 Champions**: **Men**: 100m/200m/400m: Marian Câmpeanu 10.39/21.13/47.04, 800m/1500m: Cristian Vorovenci 1:51.42/3:46.55, 5000m: Nicolae Soare 14:22.70, 10000m: Marius Ionescu 30:13.24, HMar: Constanti Ifrim 68:33, Mar: Gheorghe Surlea 2:26:34, 3000mSt: Alexandru Ghinea 8:56.04, 110mh: Cornel Bananau 14.32, 400mh: Csongor Nagy 51.74, HJ: Mihai Donisan 2.28, LJ: Adrian Vasile 7.75, TJ: Marius Anghel 16.09, SP: Laurentiu Popa 19.26, DT: Sergiu Ursu 62.02, HT: Cosmin Sorescu 64.37, JT: Alexandru Craescu 68.45, Dec: Bogdan Popa 7046, 20kW/50kW: Marius Cocioran 1:33:41/4:44:22. **Women**: 100m/200m: Andreea Ograzeanu 11.38/23.65, 400m/800m: Elena Lavric 52.56/2:6.53, 1500m/5000m: Ancuta Bobocel 4:15.51/15:57.84, 10000m/HMar: Paula Todoran 34:47.83/74:43, Mar: Elena Cîrlan 2:42:26, 3000mSt: Cristina Casandra 9:38.42, 100mh/LJ: Viorica Tigau 13.29/6.71, 400mh: Sanda Belgyan 58.91, HJ: Daniela Stanciu 1.85, PV: Lavinia Scurtu 3.40, TJ: Adelina Gavrila 14.23, SP: Simona Neata 15.02, DT: Nicoleta Grasu 62.58, HT: Bianca Perie 70.72, JT: Maria Negoita 50.51, Hep: Judit Nagy 5310, 20kW: Claudia Stef 1:36:05.

Marian OPREA b. 6 Jun 1982 Pitesti 1.90m 80kg. Rapid Bucuresti & Dinamo Bucuresti. Sports teacher.
At TJ: OG: '04- 2, '08- 5; WCh: '01- dnq 13, '03- dnq 17, '05- 3, '11- dnq 15; EC: '02- dnq 14, '06- 3, '10- 2; WJ: '00- 1; WY: '99- 4; EU23: '03- 2; EJ: '99- 3, '01- 1; WI: '03-04-06: 8/5/4; EI: '02- 2, '11- 3; WUG: '01- 2; WCp: '06- 3, '10- 1. ROU champion 2001, 2003-08; Balkan 2001-03.
Romanian TJ records 2003 and 2005.
Progress at TJ: 1997- 14.37, 1998- 14.78, 1999- 15.98, 2000- 16.49, 2001- 17.11/17.13w, 2002- 17.29i/17.11/17.39w, 2003- 17.63, 2004- 17.55, 2005- 17.81, 2006- 17.74i/17.56, 2007- 17.32, 2008- 17.28, 2010- 17.51, 2011- 17.62i/17.19. pb LJ 7.73 '05, 8.06w '11.
Silver medal in 2004 was best ever Olympic placing by a Romanian male.

Women

Cristina BUJIN b. 12 Apr 1988 Constanta 1.71m 52kg. Farul Constanta. Student
At (LJ)/TJ: WCh: '09- 7; WJ: '04- dnq/10, '06- 6; WY: '03- (5), '05- 3; EU23: '09- 2; EJ: '05- dnq/2, '07- 3; WUG: '11- 3; EI: '11- 5. Won ROU 2009.
Progress at TJ: 2004- 13.46, 2005- 13.72, 2006- 14.06i/13.68, 2007- 13.99i/13.57, 2008- 14.07i/13.94, 2009- 14.42, 2010- 13.62, 2011- 14.30. pb LJ 6.38 '09.

Adelina GAVRILA b. 26 Nov 1978 Brãila 1.74m 59kg. Steaua Bucuresti. Sports teacher.
At TJ: OG: '04- 15, '08- dnq 19; WCh: '99- 11, '01- dnq 15, '03- 9, '07- dnq 15; EC: '98- 11, '06- 7; WJ: '96- 3; EJ: '97- 1; EU23: '99- 3; WUG: '99- 3; WI: '99-01-03-04: 12/8/8/7; EI: '05- 5, '07- 5; ECp: '03- 3, '06- 3. Won Balkan 1999, 2001, ROU 2000, 2003-04, 2006-08, 2010-11.
Progress at TJ: 1995- 13.69: 1996- 13.50, 1997- 13.62, 1998- 14.53, 1999- 14.71, 2000- 14.44, 2001- 14.18, 2002- 14.29i/14.13w, 2003- 14.76i/14.75, 2004- 14.71, 2005- 14.58i/14.23, 2006- 14.41, 2007- 14.29i/14.20/14.21w, 2008- 14.78i/14.36, 2009- 13.99, 2010- 14.48, 2011- 14.27. pb LJ 6.24 '01.

Nicoleta GRASU b. 11 Sep 1971 Secuieni 1.76m 88kg. née Gradinaru. Administration officer. Dinamo Bucuresti.
At DT: OG: '92- dnq 13, '96- 7, '00- dnq 19, '04- 6, '08- 12; WCh: '93-95-97-99-01-05-07-09-11: 7/dnq 18/10/3/2/5/3/3/8; EC: '94-98-06-10: 4/3/3/2; WJ: '90- 6; WUG: '97- 3, '99- 1; WCp: '98- 2, '10- 6; ECp: '97-9-00-01-02-05-06: 4/2/1/3/2/4/3; E23Cp: '92- 1. Won Balkan 1992, 1997-9; ROU 1992-3, 1995-7, 1999-2002, 2004-06, 2008-11. 3rd GP 1996.
Progress at DT: 1985- 36.02, 1986- 43.56, 1987- 50.82, 1988- 51.06, 1989- 52.54, 1990- 56.02, 1991- 59.90, 1992- 65.66, 1993- 65.16, 1994- 64.40, 1995- 64.62, 1996- 65.26, 1997- 64.68, 1998- 67.80, 1999- 68.80, 2000- 68.70, 2001- 68.31, 2002- 64.90, 2004- 64.92, 2005- 64.89, 2006- 65.21, 2007- 65.60, 2008- 66.51, 2009- 65.20, 2010- 63.78, 2011- 62.62. pb SP 15.00i '92, 14.56 '91.
Married her coach Costel Grasu (b. 5 Jul 1967) DT pb 67.08 '92; 4 OG 1992.

Bianca PERIE b. 1 Jun 1990 Roman, Neamt district 1.70m 70kg. S.C.M. Bacau. Student.
At HT: OG: '08- dnq 18; WCh: '07/09- dnq 26/19, '11- 6; WJ: '06/08- 1; WY: '05/07- 1; EU23: '11- 1; EJ: '07/09- 1; WUG: '11- 3; ROU champion 2009-11.
Progress at HT: 2003- 47.14, 2004- 57.67, 2005- 65.13, 2006- 67.38, 2007- 67.24, 2008- 69.59, 2009- 69.63, 2010- 73.52, 2011- 72.04. pb SP 13.04i '07.
World age 14 best of 65.13 in 2005. Her younger sister Roxana won the bronze medal in the 2011 World Youth hammer.

Esthera PETRE b. 13 May 1990 Bucuresti 1.75m 60kg.

At HJ: WCh: '11: dnq 14; WJ: '06- dnq 14, '08- 6; WY: '07- 5; WI: '12- 7; EU23: '11- 1; EJ: '07- 9, '09- 5.
Progress at HJ: 2000- 1.80, 2001- 1.81, 2002- 1.83, 2003- 1.86, 2004- 1.88, 2005- 1.94, 2006- 1.90, 2007- 1.94, 2008- 1.93, 2009- 1.88, 2010- 1.85, 2011- 1.98.
Improved from 1.92 to 1.98 to win 2011 European U23 title.

RUSSIA

Governing body: All-Russia Athletic Federation, Luzhnetskaya Nab. 8, Moscow 119992. Founded 1911.
National Championships first held 1908, USSR women from 1922. **2011 Champions**: **Men**: 100m: Aleksandr Brednev 10.42, 200m: Aleksandr Khuytte 21.14, 400m: Pavel Trenikhin 45.60, 800m: Yuriy Borzakovskiy 1:45.76, 1500m: Valentin Smirnov 3:36.14, 5000m: Andrey Safronov 13:42.06, 10000m: Sergey Rybin 28:15.79, HMar: Gleb Sharikov 64:19, Mar: Yuriy Abramov 2:14:53, 3000mSt: Ildar Minshin 8:17.74, 110mh: Aleksey Dryomin 13.79, 400mh: Aleksandr Derevyagin 49.48, HJ: Aleksey Dmitrik 2.36, PV: Yevgemiy Lukyanenko 5.72, LJ: Sergey Mikhailovskiy 8.05, TJ: Aleksey Fyodorov 16.88, SP: Maksim Sidorov 21.45, DT: Bogdan Pishchalnikov 61.33, HT: Igor Vinichenko 79.04, JT: Sergey Makarov 81.21, Dec: Aleksey Drozdov 8334, 20kW: Sergey Morozov 1:19:18, 50k: Sergey Bakulin 3:38:46.
Women: 100m: Yuliya Gushchina 11.38, 200m: Yelizaveta Savlinis 23.02, 400m: Anastasiya Kapachinskaya 49.35, 800m: Mariya Savinova 1:56.95, 1500m: Yekaterina Martynova 4:01.68, 5000m: Yelizaveta Grechishnikova 15:02.38, 10000m: Yelena Nagovitsina 32:08.00, HMar: Yelena Samokhvalova 73:19, Mar: Lyubov Morgunova 2:30:27, 3000mSt: Yuliya Zaripova 9:23.82, 100mh: Tatyana Dektyareva 13.04, 400mh: Natalya Antyukh 53.75, HJ: Anna Chicherova 2.07, PV: Svetlana Feofanova 4.55, LJ: Olga Zaytseva 7.01, TJ: Alsu Murtazina 14.55, SP: Yevgeniya Kolodko 19.33, DT: Darya Pishchal–nikova 62.09, HT: Tatyana Lysenko 73.26, JT: Mariya Abakumova 66.05, Hep: Olga Kurban 6102, 20kW: Tatyana Mineyeva 1:28:09.
Note: Clubs abbreviations: Dyn – Dynamo, TU – Trade Union sports society, VS – Army, YR – Yunest Rossii.

Yuriy ANDRONOV b. 6 Nov 1971 Samara 1.80m 68kg. Samara VS.
At 50kW: OG: '04- 9; WCh: '09- dnf; EC: '02-06-10: dq/3/10; WCp: '04- 3, '06- 3; ECp: '05-09: 3/3; RUS champion 2010
Progress at 50kW: 1991- 4:06:49, 1993- 3:59:28, 1994- 3:52:30, 1995- 3:57:54, 1996- 3:47:04, 1997- 3:54:52, 1999- 3:50:34, 2001- 3:52:57, 2002- 3:42:06, 2003- 3:48:26, 2004- 3:46:49, 2005- 3:42:34, 2006- 3:42:38, 2007- 3:42:55, 2009- 3:49:09, 2010- 3:54:22, 2011- 3:42:25. pbs: 5000mW 19:09.7i '02, 20kW: 1:22:42.0t '02, 30kW 2:07:23 '04, 35kW 2:28:01 '03.

Sergey BAKULIN b. 13 Nov 1986 Insar, Mordoviya. 1.75m 62kg. Mordoviya VS.
At 20kW: EC: '06- 5; EU23: '07- 3; WCp: '06- 6, '10- 8; WUG: '09- 1. At 50kW: WCh: '11- 1; EC: '10- 3; ECp: '09- 4; Russian champion 2011..
Progress at 20kW, 50kW: 2006- 1:19:54, 2007- 1:19:14, 2008- 1:18:18, 3:52:38; 2010- 1:24:05, 3:43:26; 2011- 3:38:46. pbs: 5000mW 18:26.82i '12, 10kW: 39:03 '06, 35kW 2:24:25 '09.

Valeriy BORCHIN b. 11 Sep 1986 Povodimovo, Mordoviya 1.78m 63kg. Saransk VS.
At 20kW: OG: '08- 1; WCh: '07- dnf, '09- 1, '11- 1; EC: '06- 2; EU23: '07- 1; WCp: '08- 2; Russian champion 2006.
Progress at 20kW: 2006- 1:20:00, 2007- 1:18:56, 2008- 1:17:55, 2009- 1:17:38, 2011- 1:18:55. pbs: 3000mW 18:11.8i '10, 5000mW 18:16.54 '12, 10kW: 38:42 '11. One year drugs ban 2005-06.

Yuriy BORZAKOVSKIY b. 12 Apr 1981 Kratovo, Moskva reg. 1.82m 72kg. Moskva Dyn.
At 800m/4x400mR: OG: '00- 6, '04- 1, '08- sf; WCh: '03-05-07-09-11: 2/2/3/4/3; EC: '02- 2R; EJ: '99- 1; WI: '01- 1, '06- 3; EI: '00- 1, '09- 1; ECp: '99-02-10: 1/1/1; 2nd GP 2001. At 400m: EC: '02- sf; EU23: '01- 1; At 1500m: ECp: '03- 3. Won RUS 800m 2004, 2009-11; 1500m 2005, 2007-08.
Records: Two world junior indoor 800m 2000, European Junior 800m (2) & 1000m 2000; Russian: 800m (4) 2001, 1000m 2008.
Progress at 800m: 1997- 1:52.8i/1:53.69, 1998- 1:47.71, 1999- 1:46.13, 2000- 1:44.33, 2001- 1:42.47, 2002- 1:44.20, 2003- 1:43.68, 2004- 1:43.92, 2005- 1:44.18, 2006- 1:43.42, 2007- 1:44.38, 2008- 1:42.79, 2009- 1:43.58, 2010- 1:44.65, 2011- 1:43.99. pbs: 200m 22.56 '99, 400m 45.84 '00, 600m 1:16.02i '10, 1000m 2:15.50 '08, 1500m 3:40.28 '05, 3000m 8:32 '99.
He typically leaves himself a tremendous amount to do on the second lap of his 800m races but Olympic success in 2004 came from a remarkably even-paced race.

Aleksey DMITRIK b. 12 Apr 1984 Slantsy. Leningrad reg, 1.91m 69kg. St Petersburg YR.
At HJ: WCh: '11- 2; EC: '10- 7; WJ: '02- 14; WY: '01- 1; EJ: '03- 2; EU23: '05- 6; EI: '09- 2=; ECp: '05- 1, '11- 2. Russian champion 2011.
Progress at HJ: 2000- 2.08, 2001- 2.23, 2002- 2.26, 2003- 2.28, 2004- 2.30, 2005- 2.34i/2.30, 2006- 2.28, 2007- 2.30, 2008- 2.33i/2.27, 2009- 2.33, 2010- 2.32i/2.31, 2011- 2.36.
Mother Yelana was a 1.75m high jumper.

Aleksey DROZDOV b. 3 Dec 1983 Klintsy, Bryansk Reg. 1.91m 95kg. Bryansk VS.
At Dec: OG: '08- 12; WCh: '05- 10, '07- 4, '11- 4; EC: '06- 3, '10- 7; EU23: '03- 8, '05- 1; Russian champion 2005, 2008, 2011. At Hep: WI: '06- 5, '10- 3; EI: '05- 6, '09- 4.
Progress at Dec: 2002- 7037, 2003- 7536, 2004- 7805, 2005- 8196, 2006- 8350, 2007- 8475, 2008-

8208, 2009- 8081, 2010- 8246, 2011- 8334. pbs: 60m 6.7i '05, 6.94i '06; 100m 11.02 '08, 400m 50.21 '08, 1000m 2:43.17i '05, 1500m 4:32.93 '06, 60mh 8.0i '05, 8.19i '06; 110mh 14.74 '06, HJ 2.15i '10, 2.14 '11; PV 5.20i '10, 5.10 '08; LJ 7.78 '08, SP 17.17i '10, 16.98 '11; DT 51.76 '06, JT 68.97 '07, Hep 6300i '10.

Aleksandr GRIPICH b. 21 Sep 1986 Slavyabsk-n-Kubani 1.90m 80kg. Krasnodar VS.
At PV: WCh: '09- 5; EC: '10- dnq; WUG: '09- 1, '11- 2=.
Progress at PV: 2003- 4.95, 2004- 5.30, 2005- 5.40, 2006- 5.45i/5.20, 2007- 5.65i/5.50, 2008- 5.55, 2009- 5.75, 2010- 5.70i/5.60, 2011- 5.75.

Kirill IKONNIKOV b. 5 Mar 1984 Leningrad 1.85m 100kg.
At HT: OG: '08- dnq 19; WCh: '11- 6; WJ: '02- 5; WY: '03- 4. Russian champion 2011.
Progress at HT: 2003- 68.09, 2004- 71.32, 2005- 70.30, 2006- 70.26, 2007- 78.03, 2008- 79.20, 2009- 75.40, 2010- 77.73, 2011- 79.04.

Vladimir KANAYKIN b. 21 Mar 1985 Atyur–yevo, Mordoviya 1.70m 60kg. Saransk VS.
At 20kW: WCh: '11- 2; ECp: '11- 6. At 50kW: WCh: '05- dq, '07- dnf; EC: '06- 9; WCp: '08-dq(2); ECp: '07- 1; Won RWC 30kW 2007, RUS 20km 2007, 50km 2005-06. At 10000mW: WJ: '02- 1, '04- 2; WY: '01- 1.
World record 20km walk 2007, three world bests 30km & 35km walk 2004-06 (each to win Russian winter 35k).
Progress at 20kW, 50kW: 2003- 1:21:23, 2004-1:22:00, 3:40:40; 2005- 1:21:11, 3:40:40; 2006- 1:21:20, 3:45:57; 2007- 1:17:16, 3:40:57; 2008- 1:16:53dq, 3:36:55dq; 2010- 1:22:23. 2011- 1:19:14. pbs: 5000mW 18:17.13i '12, 20:20.26 '03; 10000mW: 40:58.48 '04, 10kW: 38:16 '04, 30kW 2:01:13 '06, 35kW 2:21:31 '06.
Disqualified when well clear of field in 2004 at World Cup junior 10km. 2-year drugs ban after positive EPO test 20 Apr 2008.

Sergey KIRDYAPKIN b. 16 Jan 1980 Insar, Mordoviya Rep. 1.78m 67kg. Saransk VS.
At 50kW: OG: '08- dnf; WCh: '05-07-09-11: 1/dnf/1/dnf; EC: '10- dnf; WCp: '08- 6; ECp: '05-2. Won RUS 50kW 2009.
Progress at 50kW: 2001- 4:08:16, 2002- 3:52:19, 2004- 3:43:20, 2005- 3:38:08, 2006- 4:23:27, 2008-3:48:29, 2009- 3:38:35. pbs: 10kW 40:23 '10, 20kW 1:23:07 '05, 30kW 2:05:06 '03, 35kW 2:25:42 '12.
Married to Anisya Kirdyapkina (qv).

Andrey KRIVOV b. 14 Nov 1985 1.78m 67kg. Mordoviya.
At 20kW: WCh: '09- 17; EC: '10- 6; EU23: '07- 2; WCp: '08- 5, '10- 3; ECp: '11- 8; WUG: '11- 1. Russian champion 2009.
Progress at 20kW: 2005- 1:22:21, 2007- 1:20:12, 2008- 1:19:06, 2009- 1:19:55, 2010- 1:22:20, 2011-1:20:16, 2012- 1:18:25. pbs: 10000mW: 40:35.2 '05, 35kW 2:29:44 '06.

Sergey LITVINOV b. 27 Jan 1986 Rostov-on-Don, Russia 1.85m 105kg.
At HT: WCh: '09- 5, '11- dnq 15; WJ: '04- 9; EU23: '07- 11; EJ: '05- 9. German champion 2009.
Progress at HT: 2004- 60.00, 2005- 73.98, 2006-66.46, 2007- 74.80, 2008- 75.35, 2009- 77.88, 2010-78.98, 2011- 78.90.
Switched from Belarus to Germany 15 Jul 2008, but for 2011 had moved to Russia. His father Sergey Litvinov (USSR) set three world records at hammer 1980-3 with a pb of 86.04 '86; he was Olympic champion 1988 (2nd 1980) and World champion 1983 and 1987. His mother was born in Germany.

Yevgeniy LUKYANENKO b. 23 Jan 1985 Slavyansk-na-Kubani 1.90m 80kg. Krasnodar VS.
At PV: OG: '08- 2; WCh: '07- 6, '11- dnq 18=; WI: '08- 1; ECp: '07- nh. RUS champion 2008, 2011.
Progress at PV: 2002- 4.90, 2003- 5.10, 2004-5.30i/5.00, 2005- 5.40, 2006- 5.60, 2007- 5.81, 2008-6.01, 2009- 5.82i/5.60, 2010- injured, 2011- 5.72.

Sergey MAKAROV b. 19 Mar 1973 Lyubertsy 1.92m 100kg. Moskva Dyn.
At JT: OG: '96- 6, '00- 3, '04- 3, '08- dnq 26; WCh: '97-99-01-03-05-07-09-11: 5/9/7/1/3/dnq 18/dnq 13/12; EC: '98- 4, '02- 2, '10- 7; WCp: '98- 2, '02- 1; ECp: '96-7-8-9-00-01-02-03-06-11: 2/4/2/2/2/2/1/1/2/1; E23Cp: '94- 2. Won GWG 1998, WAF 2003, RUS 1996-7, 2000-01, 2003, 2005-11.
Six Russian records 1996-2002.
Progress at JT: 1991- 73.48, 1992- 76.08, 1993-75.78, 1994- 82.54, 1995- 84.42, 1996- 88.86, 1997-88.54, 1998- 86.96, 1999- 89.93, 2000- 89.92, 2001-88.42, 2002- 92.61, 2003- 90.11, 2004- 86.19, 2005- 90.33, 2006- 88.49, 2007- 87.46, 2008- 86.88, 2009- 84.24, 2010- 83.59, 2011- 87.12.
Married to Oksana Ovchinnikova (b. 21 Jul 1971, Russian 'old' javelin record 68.72 '96. 2 WJ 1990). His father Aleksandr Makarov (b. 11 Feb 1951) was 2nd in the 1980 Olympic JT with a pb 89.64 (old javelin).

Aleksandr MENKOV b. 7 Dec 1990 Krasnoyarsk 1.73m 68kg. Krasnoyarsk VS.
At LJ: WCh: '09- dnq 32, '11- 6; WI: '12- 3; EU23: '11- 1; EJ: '09- 1; ET: '11- 1.
Progress at LJ: 2008- 6.98, 2009- 8.16, 2010- 8.10, 2011- 8.28, 2012- 8.24i. pbs: HJ 2.15 '10, TJ 15.20 '09.

Sergey MOROZOV b. 21 Mar 1988 Saransk 1.80m 67kg. Russian Army.
At 20kW: WCh: '11- 12; Russian champion 2008, 2011. At 10000mW/10kW: WY: '05- 1; EJ: '07- 1; WCp: '06- 1J; ECp: '07- 1J.
World 20km walk record 2008.
Progress at 20kW: 2008- 1:16:43, 2010- 1:22:45, 2011- 1:19:18, 2012- 1:17:52. pbs: 10000mW 40:02.88 '07, 10kW 39:32 '11, 35kW 2:25:57 '05.
2-year drugs ban for EPO test from 29 Jul 2008.

Denis NIZHEGORODOV b. 26 Jul 1980 Saransk 1.80m 61kg. Saransk VS.
At 50kW: OG: '04- 2, '08- 3; WCh: '03-07-09-11: 5/4/dnf/2; EC: '06- dq; WCp: '06- 1, '08- 1; ECp: '09- 1, '11- 1; RUS champion 2003-04, 2007. At 20kW: EU23: '01- 5; WUG: '01- 4; ECp: '00- 17, '01- 7. World record 50km walk 2008, best (no drugs test) 2004.
Progress at 20kW, 50kW: 2000- 1:21:47, 2001- 1:18:20; 2003- 1:23:23, 3:38:23; 2004- 3:35:29, 2005- dnf, 2006- 1:22:45, 3:38:02; 2007- 3:40:53, 2008- 3:34:14, 2009- 3:42:47, 2011- 3:42:45. pbs: 5000mW 18:58.81i '12, 30kW 2:05:08 '06, 35kW 2:24:50 '06.

Bogdan PISHCHALNIKOV b. 26 Aug 1982 Krasnodar 1.97m 107kg. Moskva Dyn.
At DT: OG: '08- 6; WCh: '05/07- dnq 18/18, '09- 7; EC: '06/10: dnq 16/16; E23: '03- 3; WCp: '06- 7; ET: '10- 3. Russian champion 2005, 2007-11.
Progress at DT: 1999- 42.71, 2000- 50.36, 2001- 52.86, 2002- 56.97, 2003- 57.08, 2004- 60.89, 2005- 64.08, 2006- 64.19, 2007- 64.95, 2008- 65.88, 2009- 65.58, 2010- 67.23, 2011- 62.40. pb SP 16.58 '03.
Brother of Darya Pishchalnikova (qv), married to Olga Ivanova (qv).

Andrey RUZAVIN b. 28 Mar 1986 1.75m 70kg. Mordoviya
At 20kW: WUG: '09- 2; Russian champion 2008, 2011. At 10000m/10kW: WJ: '04- 1; EJ: '05- 1; WCp: '04- 6J; ECp: '05- 1J.
Progress at 20kW: 2004- 1:25:48, 2005- 1:21:51, 2006- 1:24:24, 2007- 1:20:07, 2009- 1:21:08, 2010- 1:21:01, 2011- 1:21:09, 2012- 1:17:47. pbs: 10000mW 38:48.03 '08, 10kW 38:17 '09, 35kW 2:25:19 '09.

Yaroslav RYBAKOV b. 22 Nov 1980 Mogilyev, Belarus 1.98m 82kg. Moskva VS.
At HJ: OG: '04- 6, '08- 3; WCh: '01-03-05-07-09: 2=/9/2=/2/1; EC: '02- 1, '06- 5; WJ: '98- 5; EJ: '99- 3; WI: '01-03-04-06-08-10: 7/2/2/1/2/2; EI: '02- 3, '05- 2; WCp: '02- 1; ECp: '01-02-03: 1/2/1; Won WAF 2003, 2009; 2nd GP 2002. Russian champion 2002-04, 2007-08.
Progress at HJ: 1997- 2.10i/2.09, 1998- 2.20, 1999- 2.19i/2.18, 2000- 2.28, 2001- 2.33, 2002- 2.31, 2003- 2.34, 2004- 2.32, 2005- 2.38i/2.33, 2006- 2.37i/2.33, 2007- 2.38i/2.35, 2008- 2.38i/2.34, 2009- 2.35, 2010- 2.33, 2011- 2.30. pbs: LJ 7.44i '98, Hep 5570i '98.

Aleksandr SHUSTOV b. 29 Jun 1984 Karaganda, Kazakhstan 1.88m 80kg. Moskva VS.
At HJ: WCh: '11- 8; EC: '10- 1; EU23: '05- 12; WUG: '07- 1; EI: '09- 4=, '11- 3; ET: '09-10: 3/1. Russian champion 2010.
Progress at HJ: 2002- 2.10, 2003- 2.11, 2004- 2.15, 2005- 2.23, 2006- 2.28, 2007- 2.31, 2008- 2.30, 2009- 2.32i, 2010- 2.33, 2011- 2.36. pbs: LJ 7.18i '12, Hep 4564i '12.
Married to Yekaterina Kondratyeva (200m 22.64 '04, 2 WUG '03, 6 EC '06).

Maksim SIDOROV b. 11 May 1986 Moskva 1.95m 115kg. Moskva Reg. Dyn.
At SP: WCh: '09/11- dnq 31/15; EU23: '07- 8; EJ: '05- 3; WUG: '07- 1; WI: '12- 5; EI: '11- 3. Russian champion 2009, 2011.
Progress at SP: 2006- 18.52, 2007- 20.01, 2008- 19.98, 2009- 20.92, 2010- 20.50, 2011- 21.45, 2012- 20.98i. pb DT 50.71 '06.

Andrey SILNOV b. 9 Sep 1984 Shakhty, Rostov Reg. 1.98m 83kg. Moskva Reg. VS.
At HJ: OG: '08- 1; WCh: '07- 11=; EC: '06- 1; EU23: '05- 9; WI: '12- 2; WCp: '06- 2; ECp: '06- 1, '08- 1. Won WAF 2008, Russian 2006.
Progress at HJ: 2002- 2.10, 2003- 2.10, 2004- 2.15, 2005- 2.28, 2006- 2.37, 2007- 2.36i/2.30, 2008- 2.38, 2009- 2.21, 2010- 2.33, 2011- 2.36, 2012- 2.36i.

Dmitriy STARODUBTSEV b. 3 Jan 1986 Chelyabinsk 1.85m 80kg. Moskva TU.
At PV: OG: '08- 5; WCh: '11- 12=; EC: '06- dnq 21=, '10- nh; WJ: '04- 1; WY: '03- 2; EU23: '07- 4; EJ: '05- 1; WI: '10- 6=, '12- 9; EI: '07- 6; WUG: '07- 3; WCp: '06- 9. Russian champion 2010.
Progress at PV: 2003- 5.10, 2004- 5.50, 2005- 5.50, 2006- 5.65i/5.61, 2007- 5.70, 2008- 5.75, 2009- 5.70, 2010- 5.70i/5.65, 2011- 5.90i/5.72, 2012- 5.80i. pb Dec 7412 '07.

Dmitriy TARABIN b. 29 Oct 1991 Berlin, Germany 1.76m 85kg.
At JT: WCh: '11- 10; WJ: '09- 3; EU23: '11- 3; EJ: '09- dnq 13.
Progress at JT: 2007- 55.18, 2008- 67.39, 2009- 69.63, 2010- 77.65, 2011- 85.10.
Switched from Moldova to Russia 9 June 2010.

Ivan UKHOV b. 29 Mar 1986 Chelyabinsk 1.92m 83kg. Sverdlovsk TU.
At HJ: WCh: '09- 10, '11- 5=; EC: '06- 12=, '10- 2; WJ: '04- dnq 13; EJ: '05- 1; WUG: '05- 4; WI: '10- 1, '12- 3; EI: '09- 1, '11- 1. Won DL 2010, RUS 2009.
Progress at HJ: 2004- 2.15, 2005- 2.30, 2006- 2.37i/2.33, 2007- 2.39i/2.20, 2008- 2.36i/2.30, 2009- 2.40i/2.35, 2010- 2.38i/2.36, 2011- 2.38i/2.34.
Former discus thrower.

Stanislav YEMELYANOV b. 23 Oct 1990 Pavlovo, Nizhni Novgorod Reg. 1.75m 62kg. Mordoviya VS. Law student.
At 20kmW: WCh: '11- 5; EC: '10- 1; ECp: '11- 1; RUS champion 2010. At 10000mW: WJ: '08- 1; WY: '07- 1; EJ: '09- 1; ECp: '09- 1J.
World junior 10k walk record 2009.
Progress at 20kW: 2010- 1:19:43, 2011- 1:19:33, 2012- 1:18:29. pbs: 10kW 38:28 '09, 39:35.01t '08; 30kW 2:24:25 '09.

Igor YEROKHIN b. 4 Sep 1985 1.68m 56kg.
At 20kmW: WCh: '07- dq; EU23: '05- 1; ECp: '07- 3, At 50kW: WCh: '11- dq; ECp: '11- 2.
Progress at 20kW, 50kW: 2005- 1:20:16, 2006- 1:19:32, 2007- 1:19:21, 2008- 3:38.08, 2011- 3:49:05. pbs: 10000mW: 38:54.07 '06, 30kW 2:05:50 '07, 35kW 2:26:36 '11. Two-year drugs ban 2008-09

Aleksey ZAGORNYI b. 31 May 1978 Yaroslavl 1.97m 130kg. Luch Moskva.
At HT: OG: '00- dnq 22; WCh: '03/07- dnq 22/25, '09- 3; EC: '02- 11; EJ: '97- 5; EU23: '99- 7; WUG: '01- 4. Russian champion 2007, 2009.
Progress at HT: 1994- 59.90, 1995- 71.00, 1996- 71.94, 1997- 71.30, 1998- 77.03, 1999- 77.20, 2000- 79.68, 2001- 80.80, 2002- 83.43, 2003- 80.13, 2004- 78.79, 2005- 80.81, 2006- 78.18, 2007- 79.12, 2008- 81.39, 2009- 80.10, 2010- 78.22, 2011- 81.73.

Women

Mariya ABAKUMOVA b. 15 Jan 1986 Stavropol 1.80m 80kg. Krasnodar VS.
At JT: OG: '08- 2; WCh: '07- 7, '09- 3; EC: '10- 5; WJ: '04- dnq 25; WY: '03- 4; EU23: '07- 6; EJ: '05- 1; CCp: '10- 1; ECp: '08-09-10: 2/3/3. Won WAF 2009, Russian 2008, 2011.
European javelin record 2008, four RUS 2008-11.
Progress at JT: 2002- 51.81, 2003- 51.41, 2004- 58.26, 2005- 59.53, 2006- 60.12, 2007- 64.28, 2008- 70.78, 2009- 68.92, 2010- 68.89, 2011- 71.99.

Inga ABITOVA b. 6 Mar 1982 Novokuibyshevsk 1.53m 47kg. Novokuibyshevsk Dyn
At 10000m: OG: '08- 6; WCh: '07- 12; EC: '06- 1, '10- 2. World HMar: '09- 9. Eur CC: '01- 4J, '05- 7. Won RUS 10000m 2007-08.
Progress at 10000m, Mar: 2004- 2:43:48, 2005- 32:25.83, 2:38:20; 2006- 30:31.42, 2:33:55; 2007- 31:26.08, 2:34:25; 2008- 30:37.33, 2009- 31:40.00, 2:25:55; 2010- 31:22.83, 2:22:19; 2011- 2:26:31.
pbs: 1500m 4:20.10 '00, 3000m 9:02.88 '06, 5000m 15:11.6 '08, HMar 69:53 '09, 30km 1:41:09 '10.
Son Yegor born 2003. Won Belgrade Marathon 2005, Yokohama 2009, 2nd London 2010.

Nadezhda ALEKHINA b. 22 Sep 1978 Vladimir 1.76m 63kg. née Bazhenova. Vladimir TU.
At TJ: WCh: '03/05/09- dnq 23/20/28; EC: '10- 4; WUG: '05- 3; EI: '02- 4. Won RUS 2003, 2005, 2009-10.
Progress at TJ: 1997- 13.21, 1998- 13.04, 1999- 14.25, 2000- 14.13, 2001- 14.60, 2002- 14.65i/14.31, 2003- 14.35, 2004- 14.23, 2005- 14.31, 2007- 14.31, 2008- 14.43, 2009- 15.14, 2010- 14.77/15.00w, 2011- 13.94. pb LJ 6.58 '01.

Elmira ALEMBEKOVA b. 30 Jun 1990. Mordoviya.
At 10000m/10kmW: WJ: '08- 2; WCp: '08- 3J, At 5000mW: WY: '05- 2.
Progress at 20kW: 2010- 1:35:53, 2011- 1:27:35, 2012- 1:25:27. pbs: 10000mW: 43:45.26 '08.

Natalya ANTYUKH b. 26 Jun 1981 Leningrad 1.82m 73kg. Moskva VS.
At 400m/4x400mR: OG: '04- 3/1R; WCh: '05- sf/1R, '07- 6; EC: '02- 2R; WI: '03-04-06: 1R/GR/1R; EI: '02- 1, '07- 2R, '09- 4/1R; WCp: '02- 3R; ECp: '01- 3/1R, '05- 1/1R, '06- 1R. At 200m: ECp: '04- 2. At 400mh: WCh: '09- 6/res 3R, '11- 3/3R; EC: '10- 1; CCp: '10- 4; ET: '10- 1&1R, '11- 2. Won Russian 400m 2007, 400mh 2010-11.
Progress at 400m: 2000- 54.79, 2001- 51.19, 2002-

51.17i/51.24, 2003- 51.73i/52.28, 2004- 49.85, 2005- 50.67, 2006- 50.37i/50.47, 2007- 49.93, 2008- 51.19, 2009- 50.90, 2011- 50.73. At 400mh: 1996- 60.11, 1997- 59.75, 1998- 59.94, 2000- 58.30, 2009- 54.11, 2010- 52.92, 2011- 53.75. pbs: 200m 22.75 '04, 300m 36.0+ '04.

Yelena ARZHAKOVA b. 8 Sep 1989 1.70m 56kg. Moskva SC.
At (800m)/1500m: EU23: '11- 1/1; EI: '11- 1; WUG: '11- 2. At 3000mSt: WJ: '06- h.
Progress at 800m, 1500m: 2006- 4:23.79, 2009- 4:26.17, 2010- 4:08.05; 2011- 1:58.77, 4:07.69 pbs: 1000m 2:35.21i '11, 2000m 5:51.12i '11, 3000m 9:21.71 '10, 3000mSt 9:49.05 '11.

Anna AVDEYEVA b. 6 Apr 1985 Orenburg 1.70m 90kg. Mordovia VS.
At SP: WCh: '07- dnq 14, '09- 5, '11- 7; EC: '10- 3; WJ: 02- 8, '04- 2; EJ: '03- 1; EU23: '03- 6, '05- 3; WI: '10- 4; EI: '09- 6, '11- 1; ET: '10- 1, '11- 2; Russian champion 2009-10.
Progress at SP: 2001- 13.58, 2002- 15.83, 2003- 16.91, 2004- 17.13, 2005- 17.39, 2006- 18.45, 2007- 19.11, 2008- 19.10, 2009- 20.07, 2010- 19.47i/19.39, 2011- 19.54.

Anna BOGDANOVA b. 21 Oct 1984 Leningrad 1.78m 66kg. St. Peterburg.
At Hep: OG: '08- 6; WCh: '07- 10, '11- 11; ECp: '11- 1; Russian champion 2007. At Pen: WI: '08- 3; EI: '09- 1.
Progress at Hep: 2004- 5250, 2006- 5785, 2007- 6289, 2008- 6465. 2011- 6242. pbs: 200m 24.24 '08, 400m 56.96i '09, 800m 2:09.45 '08, 60mh 8.19i '09, 100mh 13.09 '08, HJ 1.88 '08, LJ 6.54i '09, 6.49 '08, 6.59w '07; SP 14.83i '09, 14.64 '08; JT 43.62 '11, Pen 4784i '09.
Her father Andrey Bogdanov won a silver medal at 4x200m freestyle swimming at the 1996 Olympics. Baby born 2010.

Tatyana CHERNOVA b. 29 Jan 1988 Krasnodar 1.89m 63kg. Krasnodar VS.
At Hep: OG: '08- 3; WCh: '07- dnf, '09- 8, '11- 1; EC: '10- 4; WJ: '06- 1; WY: '05- 1. At Pen: WI: '08- 10-12: 7/3/5.
Progress at Hep: 2006- 6227, 2007- 6768w, 2008- 6618, 2009- 6386, 2010- 6572, 2011- 6880. pbs: 200m 23.50 '07, 23.32w '11; 800m 2:06.50 '08, 60mh 8.02i '12, 100mh 13.32 '11, 13.07w '07, 400mh 56.14 '07, HJ 1.87 '07, LJ 6.82 '11, SP 14.54i '10, 14.17 '11, JT 54.49 '06, Pen 4855i '10.
Won at Talence and IAAF Combined Events Challenge 2010 and 2011. Her mother Lyudmila (née Zenina) won a 4x400m Olympic gold medal (ran in heats) for 4x400m in 1980, pbs: 200m 22.9 '82, 400m 50.91 '83.

Anna CHICHEROVA b. 22 Jul 1982 Yerevan, Armenia 1.80m 57kg. Moskva VS. Physical culture graduate.
At HJ: OG: '04- 6, '08- 3; WCh: '03-05-07-09-11: 6/4/2=/2/1; EC: '06- 7=; WJ: '00- 4; WY: '99- 1; EJ: '01- 2; WUG: '05- 1; WI: '03-04-12: 3/2/2=;

EI: '05- 1, '07- 5=; ECp: '06- 3. Russian champion 2004, 2007-09, 2011.
Progress at HJ: 1998- 1.80, 1999- 1.89, 2000- 1.90, 2001- 1.92, 2002- 2.00i/1.89, 2003- 2.04i/2.00, 2004- 2.04i/1.98, 2005- 2.01i/1.99, 2006- 1.96i/1.95, 2007- 2.03, 2008- 2.04, 2009- 2.02, 2011- 2.07, 2012- 2.06i.
Moved with family to Russia at the beginning of the 1990s. Married to Gennadiy Chernoval KAZ, pbs 100m 10.18, 200m 20.44 (both 2002), 2 WUG 100m & 200m 2001, 2 AsiG 2002 2002; their daughter Nika born on 7 Sep 2010.

Tatyana DEKTYAREVA b. 5 Aug 1981 1.74m 60kg. Finpromko.
At 100mh: OG: '08- h; WCh: '09- h, '11- 5; EC: '10- 6; ET: '10- 1, '11- 1; Russian champion 2011. At 60mh: WI: '10- 8.
Progress at 100mh: 2004- 13.98, 2005- 13.36/13.30w, 2006- 13.04, 2007- 13.30/13.10w, 2008- 12.84/12.81w, 2009- 12.96, 2010- 12.68, 2011- 12.76. pbs: 60m 7.42i '08, 100m 11.76 '08, 200m 23.59 '06, 300m 37.93i '06, 800m 2:05.87 '04. 60mh 7.94i '10.

Aleksandra FEDORIVA b. 13 Sep 1988 Moskva 1.72m 61kg. SC Luch Moskva. Student of advertising at Moscow University of Humanitarian Studies.
At 400m/4x400m: WI: '12- 2/3R. At 200m/4x100mR: OG: '08- sf/1R; EC: '10- 3; EU23: '09- 1; CCp: '10- 1; ECp: '10- 1R, '11- 3/2R. At 100m: WCh: '11- sf. At 100mh: WJ: '06- 4; WY: '05- sf; EJ: '07- 1.
Progress at 200m: 2007- 23.29, 2008- 22.56, 2009- 22.97, 2010- 22.41, 2011- 23.17. pbs: 60m 7.24i '10, 100m 11.28, 11.09w '11; 300m 36.54i '12, 400m 51.18i '12, 60mh 7.91i '10, 100mh 12.90 '08.
Her mother Lyudmila Belova/Fedoriva had 400m best 50.63 '84, father Andrey Fedoriv 200m 3rd EC and best 20.53 '86; ran at five Worlds and two Olympics

Svetlana FEOFANOVA b. 16 Jul 1980 Moskva 1.64m 53kg. Moskva TU.
At PV: OG: '00- dnq, '04- 2, '08- 3; WCh: '01-03-07-11: 2/1/3/3; EC: '02- 1, '06- 4, '10- 1; WI: '01-03-04-06-08-10: 2=/1/3/3/5/2; EI: '02- 1, '07- 1; WCp: '02- 2, '10- 1; ECp: '00-01-02-10: 1/1/1/1; 2nd GP 2001. Won RUS 2001, 2006, 2008, 2011. Pole vault records: World 2004, 9 European 2001-04, 11 Russian 2000-04, 9 world indoor 2002-04 (4.71-4.85), 13 European indoor 2001-04.
Progress at PV: 1998- 3.90, 1999- 4.10, 2000- 4.50, 2001- 4.75, 2002- 4.78, 2003- 4.80i/4.75, 2004- 4.88, 2005- 4.70i, 2006- 4.70, 2007- 4.82, 2008- 4.75, 2009- 4.70, 2010- 4.80i/4.75, 2011- 4.75.
Was a top gymnast, winning Russian titles at youth, junior and U23 level at asymmetric bars and floor exercises. Set five indoor world records in a month in 2002.

Tatyana FIROVA b. 10 Oct 1982 Sarov, Nizhegorodskaya region 1.80m 68kg. Moskva Reg. Dyn.
At 400m/4x400m: OG: '04- res 1R, 08- 6/2R; WCh: '05- res 1R, '09- 3R; EC: '06- res 1R, '10- 1/1R; EU23: '03- 3/1R; EJ: '01- 1; WI: '10- 2/2R; WUG: '03- 1; CCp: '10- 3/2R; ECp: '03- 1R.
Progress at 400m: 2000- 53.69, 2001- 52.94, 2002- 53.72, 2003- 51.43, 2004- 50.44, 2005- 50.41, 2006- 50.08, 2007- 50.98, 2008- 50.11, 2009- 50.59, 2010- 49.89, 2011- 50.84. pbs: 200m 23.27 '11, 500m 1:09.41i '08, 600m 1:25.23i '08.

Gulnara GALKINA b. 9 Jul 1978 Naberezhnye Chelny, Tatarstan 1.74m 56kg. née Samitova. Naberezhnye Chelny Dyn.
At 3000mSt (5000m): OG: '04- (6), '08- 1 (12); WCh: '03- (7), '07- 7, '09- 4; ECp: '03-08-11: 1/1/1. At 1500m: WI: '04- 3. At 3000m: ECp: '04-07-09: 1/1/1. Eur CC: '08- 12. Won WAF 3000mSt 2008, RUS 1500m 2004, 5000m 2003-04, 3000mSt 2003, 2008; indoor 1500m & 3000m 2004.
Three world and five Russian records 3000m steeplechase 2003-08.
Progress at 5000m, 3000mSt: 2003- 14:54.38, 9:08.33; 2004- 14:53.70, 9:01.59; 2006- 9:53.83, 2007- 9:11.68, 2008- 14:33.13, 8:58.81; 2009- 9:11.09, 2011- 16:06.09, 9:29.75. pbs: 800m 2:00.29 '09, 1000m 2:35.91i '04, 1500m 4:01.29 '04, 1M 4:20.23 '07, 2000m 5:31.03 '07, 3000m 8:41.72i '04, 8:42.96 '08.
Great breakthrough in 2003, starting with world indoor 3000mSt best of 9:29.54. Married Anton Galkin (400m 44.83 '04) in 2004. Daughter Alina born 24 Jun 2010.

Yuliya GOLUBCHIKOVA b. 27 Mar 1983 Moskva 1.75m 57kg. Moskva City Sport Society.
At PV: OG: '08- 4; WCh: '07- 6=, '09- dns; EC: '10- 7'WJ: '02- 2; EI: '07- 2, '09- 1; ECp: '08-09: 1/2. Russian champion 2009-10.
Progress at PV: 1997- 2.80, 1998- 3.60, 1999- 3.70i/3.60, 2000- 3.60i, 2002- 4.35, 2003- 4.30, 2004- 4.30, 2005- 4.40, 2006- 4.60, 2007- 4.71i/4.70, 2008- 4.75, 2009- 4.75i/4.70, 2010- 4.70i/4.65, 2011- 4.60/4.10.

Irina GORDEYEVA b. 9 Oct 1986 Leningrad 1.83m 52kg. Yunost Rossii.
At HJ: EC: '10- dnq 13=; WJ: '04- 9; WY: '03- 7=; EJ: '05- 4; EI: '09- 5=.
Progress at HJ: 2001- 1.75, 2002- 1.82, 2003- 1.84, 2004- 1.88, 2005- 1.88, 2006- 1.88, 2007- 1.87i/1.83, 2008- 1.95, 2009- 2.02, 2010- 1.97, 2011- 1.94, 2012- 1.97i.

Yuliya GUSHCHINA b. 4 Mar 1983 Novocherkask 1.75m 63kg. Moskva reg. VS.
At 200m(/100m)/4x100mR: OG: '08- 1R; WCh: '05- 6, '07- 5R, '09/11- sf; EC: '06- 2/5/1R, '10- 4R; EU23: '03- 5; WCp: '06- 4/5/1R; ECp: '05-06-07-10-11: 1R/(1)&1R/1R/1R/2R. At 400m/4x400mR: OG: '08- 4/2R; WI: '06-08-12: GR/1R/3R; ECp: '05/07/08- 1R. Won Russian 100m 2011, 200m 2005, 2009; 400m 2008.
WIR 4x200m 2005, 4x400m 2006.

Progress at 200m, 400m: 1997- 25.96, 1998- 25.32, 1999- 58.18, 2000- 25.01, 55.85; 2001- 24.24, 55.91; 2002- 23.92/23.88w, 53.26; 2003- 23.58, 51.94; 2004- 23.06, 2005- 22.53, 53.81i; 2006- 22.69/22.52w, 51.26i; 2007- 22.75, 2008- 22.58, 50.01; 2009- 22.63, 51.06; 2010- 22.80/22.79w, 52.04i; 2011- 22.88/22.69w, 52.18. pbs: 60m 7.24i '07, 7.2i '03; 100m 11.13 '06, 300m 36.93i '10. Married Ivan Buzolin (400m 46.24 '08, 2R EI '07) on 12 Sep 2010.

Yelena ISINBAYEVA b. 3 Jun 1982 Volgograd 1.74m 66kg. Volgograd Dyn.
At PV: OG: '00- dnq, '04- 1, '08- 1; WCh: '03-05-07-09-11: 3/1/1/nh/6; EC: '02- 2, '06- 1; WJ: '98- 9, '00- 1, WY: '99- 1; EU23: '03- 1; EJ: '99- 5, '01- 1; WI: '01-03-04-06-08-10-12: 7/2/1/1/1/4/1; EI: '05- 1; WCp: '06- 1. Won WAF 2004-07, 2009; Russian 2002.
15 outdoor world pole vault records 2003-09, 13 indoor 2004-12 (inc. 3 absolute WR), world junior indoor records 2000 and 2001.
Progress at PV: 1997- 3.30, 1998- 4.00, 1999- 4.20, 2000- 4.45i/4.40, 2001- 4.47i/4.46, 2002- 4.60/4.65ex, 2003- 4.82, 2004- 4.92, 2005- 5.01, 2006- 4.91, 2007- 4.93i/4.91, 2008- 5.05, 2009- 5.06, 2010- 4.85i, 2011- 4.85i/4.76, 2012- 5.01i.
Former gymnast. World age bests at 17-18-19 in 2000-02, world titles as Youth, junior and senior. World indoor records in all four competitions 2005 and a further five outdoors in 2005. These included the first 5m vault by a woman (at the London GP) followed by 5.01 to win the World title by 41 cm. Shared Golden League jackpot in 2007 and 2009. Passed 2010 summer season.

Olga KANISKINA b. 19 Jan 1985 Napolnaya Tavla, Mordoviya 1.60m 43kg. Saransk VS. Mathematics student at University of Mordovia.
At 20kW: OG: '08- 1; WCh: '07- 1, '09- 1, '11 -1; EC: '06- 2, '10- 1; WCp: '06- 5, '08- 1; EU23: '05- 2; ECp: '07- 2; won RWC 2011.
Progress at 20kW: 2005- 1:29:25, 2006- 1:26:02, 2007- 1:26:47, 2008- 1:25:11, 2009- 1:24:56, 2010- 1:27:44, 2011- 1:28:35. pbs: 3000mW 12:23.5 '05, 5000mW 20:38.2 '05, 10kW 41:42R '09.
Eight successive 20km walk wins 2007-09 and 11 wins in 12 races 2008-11.

Anastasiya KAPACHINSKAYA b. 21 Nov 1979 Moskva 1.76m 65kg. Luch Moskva.
At 200m/4x400mR: WCh: '03- 1, '11- 3/3R; EC: '10- 4/1R; WI: '03- 2, '04- dq (1); ECp: '03- 1. At 400m: OG: '08- 5/2R; WCh: '01- sf/3R, '03- 2R, '09- 7/3R; EC: '02- 5/2R. Won Russian 200m 2008, 400m 2011.
Progress at 200m, 400m: 1999- 23.85, 2000- 23.66, 53.32; 2001- 23.24i/22.6, 50.97; 2002- 23.41, 51.39; 2003- 22.38, 50.59; 2004- 22.71i, 2006- 22.80, 51.16; 2007- 23.73, 52.14; 2008- 22.48, 50.02; 2009- 22.92, 49.97; 2010- 22.47, 50.16; 2011- 22.55, 49.35. pbs: 100m 11.79 '99, 300m 36.61 '02, 800m 2:09.75i '07. Served a 2-year drugs ban after finishing first in the World Indoor 200m in 2004.

Lyubov KHARLAMOVA b. 2 Mar 1981, née Ivanova, 1.69m 57kg. Moskva VS.
At 3000mSt: WCh: '11- 11; EC: '06- 4, '10- 3; EU23: '03- 1; ECp: '04- 2, '05- 2. RUS champion 2004, 2006, 2010.
World best 3000m steeple indoors 9:21.37 '04.
Progress at 3000mSt: 2002- 10:14.60, 2003- 9:24.78, 2004- 9:28.02, 2005- 9:46.63, 2006- 9:21.94, 2009- 9:33.20, 2010- 9:29.82, 2011- 9:29.39. pbs: 800m 2:03.30i '04, 2:05.52 '03; 1000m 2:39.27i '04, 1500m 4:11.49 '03, 3000m 8:53.58i/9:11.34 '04, 2000mSt 6:23.04 '05. Failed drugs test at 2006 WAF and received two-year ban.

Anisya KIRDYAPKINA b. 23 Oct 1989 Saransk, Mordoviya 1.65m 51kg. née Kornikova. Mordovia TU.
At 20kmW: WCh: '09- 4. '11- 3; EC: '10- 2; WCp: '10- 6; ECp: '09- 2, '11- 2; RUS champion 2010. At 10000mW: EJ: '07- 1; ECp: '07- 1J.
World junior 20km walk best 2008.
Progress at 20kW: 2007- 1:28:00, 2008- 1:25:30, 2009- 1:25:26, 2010- 1:25:11, 2011- 1:25:09. pbs: 3000mW 11:44.10i '12, 5000mW 21:06.3 '06, 10000mW 43:27.30 '06, 42:04R '11.
Married to Sergey Kirdyapkin (qv)

Aleksandra KIRYASHOVA b. 21 Aug 1985 Leningrad 1.66m 53kg. Luch Moskva.
At PV: WCh: '09- 9; WJ: '04- nh; WY: '01- 2; EU23: '07- 1; EJ: '03- 3; WUG: '07- 1, '11- 1; EI: '09- 4, '11- 6.
Progress at PV: 2000- 3.70, 2001- 4.00, 2002- 4.21, 2003- 4.21i/4.15, 2004- 4.25i/4.20, 2005- 4.30, 2006- 4.30i/4.20, 2007- 4.50, 2008- 4.50, 2009- 4.65, 2010- 4.65i/4.54, 2011- 4.65.

Darya KLISHINA b. 15 Jan 1991 Tver 1.80m 57kg. Moskva. Model.
At LJ: WCh: '11- 7; WY: '07- 1; EU23: '11- 1; EJ: '09- 1; WI: '10- 5, '12- 4; EI: '11- 1, ET: '11- 1.
Progress at LJ: 2005- 5.83, 2006- 6.33/6.47w, 2007- 6.49, 2008- 6.52i/6.20, 2009- 6.80, 2010- 7.03, 2011- 7.05.

Svetlana KLYUKA b. 27 Dec 1978 Belogorsk, Khabarovsk reg. 1.70m 62kg. Moskva VS.
At 800m: OG: '08- 4; WCh: '03/09- sf, '07- 7; EC: '06- 2, '10- 8; WUG: '05- 1; ECp: '05-06-10: 3/1/2.
Progress at 800m: 2002- 2:00.97, 2003- 1:58.47, 2004- 1:59.55, 2005- 1:57.35, 2006- 1:57.21, 2007- 1:58.63, 2008- 1:56.64, 2009- 1:58.23, 2010- 1:58.89, 2011- 1:58.03. pbs: 2000m 24.69 '01, 400m 52.14 '06, 600m 1:26.4+ '09, 1000m 2:38.02 '08.

Yelena KOFANOVA b. 8 Aug 1988 1.74m 61kg. Moskva.
At 800m: WCh: '09- sf; WI: '12- 5; EU23: '09- 1; EJ: '07- h; WUG: '11- 2.
World indoor 4x800m record 2010 & 2011.
Progress at 800m: 2003- 2:13.11, 2005- 2:08.61, 2006- 2:05.82i, 2007- 2:02.66, 2008- 2:01.80, 2009- 1:58.60, 2010- 1:58.50, 2011- 1:58.04. pbs: 400m 53.19 '09, 500m 1:13.23i '06, 600m 1:26.38i '11, 1000m 2:41.19i '11, 1500m 4:15.49 '09.

Lyudmila KOLCHANOVA b. 1 Oct 1979 Sharya, Kostroma. 1.75m 60kg. Kostroma TU.
At LJ: WCh: '07- 2; EC: '06- 1, '10- 5; WUG: '05- 1; EI: '05- 5; WCp: '06- 1; ECp: '08- 1. Russian champion 2007, 2010.
Progress at LJ: 2000- 6.20, 2001- 6.12i/6.07, 2002- 6.32, 2003- 6.09i/6.07, 2004- 6.54, 2005- 6.79, 2006- 7.11, 2007- 7.21, 2008- 7.04, 2009- 6.72, 2010- 7.01, 2011- 6.84/7.06w. pbs: HJ 1.82 ?, TJ 13.88 '04.
Having been a high jumper, she played basketball before returning to athletics in 2000.

Yevgeniya KOLODKO b. 2 Jul 1990 Moskva, 1.88m 85kg.
At SP: WCh: '11- 5; WI: '12- 7; EU23: '11- 1; EJ: '09- 9.
Progress at SP: 2007- 14.26, 2008- 15.04i/14.87, 2009- 15.38, 2010- 16.73, 2011- 19.78, 2012- 19.47i.

Mariya KONOVALOVA b. 14 Aug 1974 Angarsk 1.78m 62kg. née Pantyukhova. Moskva VS.
At 10000m: OG: '08- 5; WCh: '09- 11. At 5000m: WCh: '95- 6, '99- 7, '07- 11; EC: '10- 5. At 3000m: WI: '95- 12; EI: '96- 5. Eur CC: '05-06-08: 10/2/4. Won RUS 5000m 2009-10.
Progress at 5000m, 10000m, Mar: 1995- 15:01.23, 1997- 16:10.4/32:53.69; 1998- 15:13.22, 1999- 14:58.60, 2000- 15:49.04, 2007- 15:02.96, 2008- 14:38.09, 30:35.84; 2009- 14:42.06, 30:31.03; 2010- 14:49.68, 2:23:50; 2011- 2:25:18. pbs: 1500m 4:05.10 '98, 2000m 5:38.98i '10, 3000m 8:30.18 '99, 15km 49:58+ '10, HMar 70:30 '11, 30km 1:41:18+ '10.

Yekaterina KOSTETSKAYA b. 31 Dec 1986 Leningrad 1.68m 59kg. Yunost Rossli. Was at Texas State University, USA.
At 800m: OG: '08- sf; WCh: '11- 5; WUG: '07- 2; ET: '09- 2. At 400mh: WJ: '04- 1; WY: '03- 2; EJ: '03- 1, '05- 2/1R.
Progress at 400mh, 800m, 1500m: 2000- 50.48, 2001- 55.26, 2002- 2:10.36, 59.68; 2003- 2:05.95, 57.52; 2004- 2:11.8i, 55.55; 2005- 55.89, 2006- 56.75, 2007- 1:59.52, 2008- 1:56.67, 2009- 1:59.31, 2010- 2:01.19, 2011- 1:57.19, 4:01.77. pbs: 200m 24.51i '05, 400m 53.72i '05, 53.75 '07; 60mh 8.71i '05, 100mh 13.67 '05, TJ 12.18 '05.
Mother Olga Dvirna was European 1500m champion 1982 (pb 3:54.23 '82), father Aleksandr Kostetskiy 800m pb 1:45.17 '84.

Tatyana KOTOVA b. 11 Dec 1976 Kokand, Uzbekistan 1.82m 60kg. Moskva TU.
At LJ: OG: '00- 3, '04- 3, '08- dnq 13; WCh: '99-01-03-05-07: dnq 13/2/2/2/3; EC: '02- 1, '10- dnq 18; WI: '99-01-03-04-06: 1/2/1/2/1; EU23: '97- 1; WCp: '02- 1; ECp: '02-06-07: 1/1/2; 2nd GP 2002. Won WAF 2005, RUS 1999-2001, 2005, 2008.
Progress at LJ: 1994- 6.32, 1995- 6.32, 1996- 6.65, 1997- 6.76, 1998- 6.82/6.97w, 1999- 6.99/7.01w, 2000- 7.04 (7.05iu), 2001- 7.12, 2002- 7.42, 2003- 6.94, 2004- 7.05, 2005- 6.96/7.20w, 2006- 7.12, 2007- 6.90/7.10w, 2008- 6.86, 2010- 6.90, 2011- 6.74. pbs: HJ 1.75 '95, TJ 13.69i/13.64 '98.
Born in Uzbekistan, she moved to Taboshari

(Tajikistan) and now lives in Central Siberia. Her father came from Cherkassy in the Ukraine. Shared Golden League jackpot 2000. Achieved the world's best long jump for eight years in 2002. Married her coach Vladimir Kudyavtsev in 2007, their son born 19 Apr 2008.

Olesya KRASNOMOVETS b. 8 Jul 1979 Nizhniy Tagil, Sverdlovsk 1.71m 60kg. Moskva reg. Dyn.
At 400m/4x400mR: OG: '04- 1R; WCh: '05- 1R; WI: '04- 2/1R, '06- 1/1R; EI: '11- 2/1R.
World indoor 4x400m record 2004 and 2006.
Progress at 400m: 2001- 53.31, 2003- 53.77, 2004- 50.19, 2005- 50.77, 2006- 50.04i, 2008- 51.63i, 2009- 52.47, 2010- 52.41, 2011- 51.22i/51.86. pbs: 200m 23.09 '05, 300m 36.62i '04, 500m 1:08.84i '04.
Breakthrough in 2004 indoor season to win EI Cup and take silver and gold at World Indoors. Married to **Dmitriy Forshev** (b. 30 May 1976) – 400m 45.62 '03, Russian champion 2005.

Antonina KRIVOSHAPKA b. 21 Jul 1987 Volgograd 1.68m 60kg. Rostov-na-Donu VS.
At 400m/4x400m: WCh: '09- 3/3R, '11- 5/3R; EC: '10- 3/1R; WJ: '04- h; WY: '03- 2; EI: '09- 1/1R; CCp: '10- 2R. Won RUS 2009.
Progress at 400m: 2002- 54.35, 2003- 53.09, 2004- 53.67, 2005- 55.03i/55.63, 2006- 55.40i, 2007- 52.32, 2008- 51.24, 2009- 49.29, 2010- 50.10, 2011- 49.92. pbs: 200m 24.28 '07, 300m 36.38i '09.

Anna KRYLOVA b. 3 Oct 1985. née Kuropatkina. Luch Moskva.
At TJ: WCh: '11- 7; WI: '12- 6; EU23: '07- 4.
Progress at TJ: 2001- 12.85, 2002- 12.75, 2003- 12.86, 2004- 13.34/13.62w, 2005- 13.25, 2006- 14.13, 2007- 14.20, 2008- 13.84i/13.32, 2009- 14.14i/13.27, 2010- 14.02i/13.69/13.77w, 2011- 14.35, 2012- 14.39i. pb LJ 6.45 '06.
Cousin of Denis Kapustin, TJ 1 EC 94, 3 OG 00.

Olga KUCHERENKO b. 5 Nov 1985 Sidory, Volgograd region 1.72m 59kg. Lokomotiv Penza.
At LJ: WCh: '09- 5, '11- 2; EC: '10- 3; EU23: '07- 12; EI: '09-3., ET: '09-10: 2/2.
Progress at LJ: 2002- 6.08, 2004- 6.30, 2005- 6.34, 2006- 6.72/6.80w, 2007- 6.41/6.70w, 2008- 6.87i/6.70, 2009- 6.91, 2010- 7.13, 2011- 6.86.

Mariya KUCHINA b. 14 Jan 1993 Prokhladny, Kabradino-Balkar 1.82m 60kg. Moskovskaya.
At HJ: WY: '09- 2; EJ: '11- 1.
World junior indoor high jump record 2011.
Progress at HJ: 2009- 1.87, 2010- 1.91, 2011- 1.97i/1.95.

Tatyana LEBEDEVA b. 21 Jul 1976 Sterlitamsk, Bashkortostan 1.71m 61kg. Volgograd VS. Studying foreign diplomacy.
At TJ (/LJ): OG: '00- 2, '04- 3/1, '08- 2/2; WCh: '99- 4, '01- 1, '03- 1, '05- dns, '07- 2/1, '09- 6/2; EC: '98- 5, '06- 1; WJ: '94- 3/10; EJ: '95- 2/6; WI: '01- 2, '04- 1/1, '06- 1; EI: '00- 1; WUG: '01- 1; WCp: '98- 2, '06- 1; ECp: '00-01: 1/1. GP: 3rd

1999, 2nd 2001. Won WAF LJ 2006-07, TJ 2003, 2006; GWG TJ 2001, Russian TJ 1998-2001, 2008; LJ 2004.
Three world indoor triple jump records 2004, three Russian records 2000-04.
Progress at LJ, TJ: 1991- 12.91, 1992- 13.03, 1993- 6.17, 13.13i/12.94; 1994- 6.65, 13.69; 1995- 13.88, 1996- 13.62, 1997- 13.89i/13.56, 1998- 14.45/14.58w, 1999- 14.89, 2000- 15.32, 2001- 6.71i, 15.25; 2003- 6.82, 15.18; 2004- 7.33, 15.36i/15.34; 2005- 6.70, 15.11; 2006- 6.97/7.09w, 15.23; 2007- 7.15, 15.14; 2008- 7.03, 15.32; 2009- 6.97, 14.72/15.01w; 2010- 6.64.
Won 2001 World gold by massive margin of 65cm. Married to Nikolay Medveyev (400mh), daughters Anastasiya born in August 2002 and Aleksandra in April 2011. Set three world indoor records (15.16, 15.25, 15.36) at WI 2004, and next day completed unique double with LJ gold. Sole winner of the Golden League Jackpot for 6/6 wins at TJ in 2005. She is a vice-president of the Russian federation.

Lyudmila LITVINOVA b. 8 Jun 1985 Lipetsk 1.77m 60kg. Moskva VS.
At 400m/4x400m: OG: 08- 2R; WCh: '07- 4R, '09- sf/3R, '11- 3R; EU23: '07- 1/1R; ECp: '08- 1R, '09- 2/1R.
Progress at 400m: 2001- 55.59, 2004- 53.84, 2005- 54.36, 2006- 51.99, 2007- 51.25, 2008- 50.62, 2009- 50.27, 2011- 50.92. pb 200m 22.82 '09.
Married Russian team physio Aleksey Kosenkov in August 2009.

Anna LUKYANOVA b. 23 Apr 1991 Mordoviya VS
At 10000mW: WJ: '10- 2; At 10kmW: WCp: '10- 3J.
Progress at 20kW: 2011- 1:27:49. pbs: 5000mW 20:44.25i '10, 10kW 42:55 '09, 44:17.98t '10.

Tatyana LYSENKO b. 9 Oct 1983 Bataisk, Rostov region 1.86m 81kg. Bataisk VS.
At HT: OG: '04- dnq 19; WCh: '05- 3, '09- 6, '11- 1; EC: '06- 1, '10- 2; EU23: '03- 5; WUG: '03- 5; WCp: '06- 2, '10- 1; ECp: '06-07-10-11: 1/ dq1/2/2. Won RUS 2005, 2009-11.
Three world hammer records, seven Russian records 2005-07.
Progress at HT: 2000- 49.08, 2001- 55.73, 2002- 61.85, 2003- 67.19, 2004- 71.54, 2005- 77.06, 2006- 77.80, 2007- 77.30/78.61dq, 2009- 76.41, 2010- 76.03, 2011- 77.13. Two-year drugs ban after positive test on 9 May 2007.

Yekaterina MARTYNOVA b. 6 Aug 1986 Chelyabinsk 1.69m 55kg. Sverdlovsk Dyn.
At 1500m: WCh: '11- sf; EJ: '05- 2; EI: '11- 3; ET: '11- 2. At 800m: WJ: '04- sf; WY: '03- 4; EU23: '07- 7. Won Russian 1500m 2011.
Progress at 1500m: 2004- 4:24.71i, 2005- 4:15.46, 2006- 4:15.09, 2007- 4:15.81, 2008- 4:03.68i/4:05.06, 2009- 4:05.40, 2010- 4:09.46, 2011- 4:01.68. pbs: 400m 55.97i '08, 56.59 '06; 800m 1:59.17 '11, 1000m 2:37.63i '08.

Anna OMAROVA b. 3 Oct 1981 Pyatigorsk 1.80m 108kg. née Tolokina. Moskva VS. Economics student.
At SP: OG: '08- 6; WCh: '07- 9, '11- 10; WJ: 00- 5; WI: '08- 8; EI: '07- 6, '09- 4; ECp: '07- 1, '08- 2. Russian champion 2007.
Progress at SP: 1997- 12.98, 1998- 15.88i/14.18, 1999- 13.45, 2000- 16.12, 2001- 17.13, 2003- 17.28, 2004- 17.12, 2005- 17.04i/16.70, 2006- 18.40, 2007- 19.69, 2008- 19.29, 2009- 18.53, 2010- 19.00i/18.72, 2011- 19.23. pb DT 51.62 '07.
Daughter Aminat born in 2002.

Darya PISHCHALNIKOVA b. 19 Jul 1985 Astrakhan 1.90m 103kg. Saransk VS
At DT: WCh: '07- dq(2), '11- 11; EC: '06- 1; WJ: '02- 8, '04- 2; W23; 2, Muhar SLO 75.94 jnnr rec; Y: '01- 2; E23: '05- 2, '07- dq(2); EJ: '03- 3; EY: '01- 1; WCp: '06- 4; ECp: '06- 2, '07- dq (2), '11- 2. Russian champion 2011.
Progress at DT: 2000- 50.48, 2001- 55.26,) 2002- 56.24, 2003- 54.80, 2004- 58.26, 2005- 60.62, 2006- 65.55, 2007- 63.13/65.78dq, 2008- 67.28dq, 2011- 63.91, 2012- 63.86. pb SP 14.02i '02.
2-year drugs bans from 10 Apr 2007. Sister of Bogdan Pishchalnikov (qv). Their father Vitaliy had DT pb 67.76 '84 and mother Tatyana DT pb 61.62 '84.

Tatyana POLNOVA b. 20 Apr 1979 Slavyansk-na-Kubani 1.73m 64kg. née Zaykova. Krasnodar TU.
At PV: WCh: '05- 4, '07- 9, '09- 7=; EC: '06- 3; WJ: '98- 10; WUG: '03- 1; EI: '05- 5; ECp: '03-04: 2/3. Won WAF 2003.
Progress at PV: 1995- 3.00, 1996- 3.75, 1997- 3.85, 1998- 4.10i/3.90, 2000- 4.20, 2001- 4.20, 2002- 4.60, 2003- 4.70, 2004- 4.78, 2005- 4.60i/4.52, 2006- 4.65, 2007- 4.72, 2008- 4.71, 2009- 4.56, 2010- 4.70i/4.55, 2011- 4.50.
Former gymnast, coached by her husband Sergey Polnov. She competed for Turkey 1998-2000 (setting NRs at 4.20) as Tuna Köstem, but reverted to Russia.

Anastasiya POTAPOVA b. 6 Sep 1985 Volgograd 1.78m 61kg. née Taranova. Volgograd VS.
At TJ: WJ: '04- 1; EJ: '03- 1, EU23: '05- 5, '07- 3; WI: '10- 4; EI: '09- 1.
Progress at TJ: 2002- 13.18, 2003- 13.93, 2004- 14.11, 2005- 14.20, 2006- 14.04i/13.90, 2007- 14.24, 2008- 14.36, 2009- 14.68i/14.40, 2010- 14.44i, 2011- 14.00/14.13w. pb LJ 6.71i '09, 6.52 '08.

Anna PYATYKH b. 4 Apr 1981 Moskva 1.76m 64kg. Moskva VS.
At TJ: OG: '04- 8, '08- 8; WCh: '03-05-07-09: 4/3/4/3; EC: '02- 8, '06- 3; WJ: '00- 2; EJ: '99- 3; WI: '03-06-10: 4/2/3; ECp: '02-03-04-05-09: 1/1/1/1/2. Won WAF 2008, Russian 2004, 2006.
Progress at TJ: 1998- 12.98, 1999- 13.59, 2000- 14.19, 2001- 14.21/14.22w, 2002- 14.67, 2003- 14.79, 2004- 14.85, 2005- 14.88, 2006- 15.02/15.17w, 2007- 14.88, 2008- 14.91, 2009-

14.67/14.84w, 2010- 14.68, 2011- 14.24. pb LJ 6.72 '07.

Yuliya RUSANOVA b3 Jul 1986. Kirskaya Obl.
At 800m: WCh: '11- 8; WI: '12- 6; EI: '11- 3.
Progress at 800m: 2007- 2:03.74, 2008- 2:01.2, 2009- 1:58.99, 2010- 1:59.85, 2011- 1:56.99. pbs: 400m 55.58 '11, 600m 1:24.02i '11, 1000m 2:39.81i '09, 1500m 4:05.14 '11.

Mariya SAVINOVA b. 13 Aug 1985 Chelyabinsk 1.69m 55kg. Sverdlovsk Dyn.
At 800m: WCh: '09- 5, '11- 1; WI: '10- 1; EI: '09- 1; CCp: '10- 3; ET: '11- 1. Won Russian 800m 2009, 2011.   World indoor 4x800m record 2008.
Progress at 800m: 2002- 2:09.68, 2003- 2:08.38, 2004- 2:07.43, 2005- 2:07.03, 2006- 2:05.91, 2007- 2:00.78, 2008- 2:01.07, 2009- 1:57.90, 2010- 1:57.56, 2011- 1:55.87. pbs: 400m 52.05i '10, 52.71 '11; 600m 1:26.11i '09, 1000m 2:34.56i '09, 1500m 4:08.2i, 4:10.25 '10.
Married Aleksey Farnosov (1500m 3:41.69i '1a) on 10 Sep 2010.

Tatyana SHEMYAKINA b. 3 Sep 1987 Mak–arovka, Mordoviya 1.61m 51kg. Saransk VS.
At 20kW: WCh: '07- 2; EU23: '07- 1, '09- 3; WUG: '11- 2. At 10000mW: WJ: '06- 2.
Progress at 20kW: 2007- 1:28:48. 2008- 1:25:46, 2009- 1:29:23, 2011- 1:28:55. pbs: 10000mW 44:26.5 '06, 10kW 42:04+ '11.

Svetlana SHKOLINA b. 9 Mar 1986 Yartsevo, Smolensk reg. 1.87m 66kg. Luch Moskva.
At HJ: OG: '08- 14; WCh: '09- 6. '11- 5; EC: '10- 4; WJ: '04- 2; WY: '03- 2=; E23: '07- 1; EJ: '05- 1; WI: '10- 4; EI: '09- 4=, '11- 4=; WUG: '05-4, '07- 4; ECp: '10: 2. Russian champion 2010.
Progress at HJ: 2001- 1.75, 2002- 1.84, 2003- 1.88, 2004- 1.91, 2005- 1.92, 2006- 1.92, 2007- 1.96, 2008- 1.98, 2009- 1.98, 2010- 2.00i/1.98, 2011- 2.00i/1.99.

Liliya SHOBUKHOVA b. 13 Nov 1977 Beloretsk, Bashkortostan 1.69m 50kg. née Volkova. Beloretsk VS.
At 5000m: OG: '04- 13, '08- 6; WCh: '05- 9; EC: '02- 17, '06- 2; WCp: '06- 2; ECp: '04-05-06: 2/1/1. At 10000m: WCh: '09- 19; EC: '10- dnf. At 3000m: WI: '06- 2; EI: '02- 5, '05- 5. World 4km CC: '02- 23. Eur CC: '02- 17, '04- 11. Won Russian 5000m 2002, 2005, 2008; 10,000m 2009.
Records: European 5000m 2008, World indoor 3000m 2006, world 30km road 2011; 3 Russian marathon records 2010-11.
Progress at 5000m, 10000m, Mar: 1998- 16:50.64, 2001- 15:42.0, 2002- 15:25.00, 2004- 14:52.19, 2005- 14:47.07, 2006- 14:56.57, 2007- 15:51.53, 2008- 14:23.75, 2009- 30:29.36, 2:24:24; 2010- 2:20:25, 2011- 2:18:20. pbs: 800m 2:03.18 '06, 1000m 2:39.81i '06, 1500m 4:03.78 '04, 1M 4:22.14 '04, 2000m 5:35.80 '07, 3000m 8:27.86i '06, 8:34.85 '04; Road: 10km 33:11 '01, HMar 69:25 '11, 30k 1:38:23+ '11.
Marathons: London 3rd on marathon debut 2009, 1st 2010, 2nd 2011; won Chicago, 2009-11 and the World Marathon Majors Series 2009/10

and 2010/11. Daughter Anna born in 2003.

Tatyana SIBILEVA b. 17 May 1980 Chelyabinsk 1.59m 42kg. Chelyabinsk VS.
At 20kW: OG: '08- 11; WCh: '07- 9; EU23: '01- 4; WUG: '03- 1, '05- 3; WCp: '08- 2; ECp: '07- 6.
Progress at 20kW: 1998- 1:29:53, 2000- 1:30:51, 2001- 1:27:33, 2002- 1:32:17, 2003- 1:27:54, 2004- 1:29:12, 2005- 1:31:18, 2006- 1:28:58, 2007- 1:28:51, 2008- 1:26:16, 2009- 1:31:59, 2010- 1:25:52, 2011- 1:30:37, 2012- 1:28:03. pbs: 10kW 42:15+ '08, 45:09.3t '06; 30000mW 2:24:56 '04 (world best).

Yelena SLESARENKO b. 28 Feb 1982 Volgograd 1.78m 57kg. née Sivushenko. Volgograd VS.
At HJ: OG: '04- 1, '08- 4; WCh: '07- 4, '09- 10, '11- 4; EC: '06- 5; EU23: '03- 2; EJ: '01- 4; WUG: '03- 3; WI: '04-06-08: 1/1/2; EI: '02- 5=; WCp: '06- 1; ECp: '04- 1, '07- 1. Won WAF 2004, RUS 2005.
Progress at HJ: 1999- 1.82, 2000- 1.88, 2001- 1.94i/1.88, 2002- 1.97, 2003- 1.98i/1.96, 2004- 2.06, 2005- 2.00, 2006- 2.02i/2.00, 2007- 2.02, 2008- 2.03, 2009- 1.96, 2010- 1.88i, 2011- 1.97.
Tied Russian indoor record to win gold at 2004 World Indoors and set Russian record of 2.06 to win Olympic gold. Expecting a baby in July 2012.

Vera SOKOLOVA b. 8 Jun 1987 Solianoy, Chuvashiya 1.51m 51kg. Mordovia VS.
At 20kmW: WCh: '09- 14, '11- 13; EC: '10- 3; WCp: '10- 4; ECp: '09- 10; Russian champion 2009. At 10000mW: WJ: '02-04-06: 9/3/4; EJ: '05- 1; WCp: '04/06- 1J; ECp: '03- 2J, '05- 1J. At 5000mW: WY: '03- 1.
Walks records: World 20km 2011, world junior 10,000m and 5000m indoors 2005.
Progress at 20kW: 2006- 1:40:03, 2007- 1:32:56, 2008- 1:30:11, 2009- 1:25:26, 2010- 1:25:35, 2011- 1:25:08. pbs: 3000m 12:51.96 '04, 5000mW 20:10.3i '10, 10000mW 43:11.34 '05, 10kW 42:04+ '11

Yelena SOKOLOVA b. 23 Jul 1986 Staryi Oskol, Belgorod reg. 1.73m 76kg. née Kremneva. Krasnodarsk krai.
At LJ: WCh: '09- dnq 13; EU23: '07- 3; EI: '09- 2; WUG: '07- 2. Russian champion 2009.
Progress at LJ: 2002- 6.33, 2003- 6.39i?/6.31, 2006- 6.53, 2007- 6.71, 2008- 6.74, 2009- 6.92, 2010- 6.72/6.90w, 2011- 6.76, 2012- 6.88i. pb 100m 11.97 '10.

Kseniya USTALOVA b. 14 Jan 1988 Sverdlovsk 1.77m 65kg. Sverdlovsk.
At 400m/4x400m: EC: '10- 2/1R; EU23: '09- 1/1R; EJ: '07- 2/1R; WUG: '11- 1R; CCp: '10- 2R; ET: '10- 1/1R. Russian champion 2010.
Progress at 400m: 2005- 55.51, 2006- 54.00i. 2007- 52.90, 2008- 54.57, 2009- 51.45, 2010- 49.92, 2011- 52.03. pbs: 200m 24.09 '10, 300m 36.94i '12.

Natalya YEVDOKIMOVA b. 17 Mar 1978 Leningrad 1.78m 65kg. St Petersburg YR.
At 1500m: OG: '04- 4; WCh: '09- 8, '11- sf; EC: '10- h; EJ: '97- 1; EI: '09- 6. At 800m: WCh: '03- sf; WJ: '96- 8; EJ: '95- 5, '97- 6.

Progress at 800m, 1500m: 1993- 2:07.60, 4:29.2; 1995- 2:04.61, 4:20.29; 1996- 4:24.86, 1997- 2:06.18, 4:20.28; 2000- 2:01.51, 4:09.19; 2002- 2:03.15, 4:09.50i/4:09.65; 2003- 1:58.75, 4:04.61; 2004- 2:03.00, 3:59.05; 2005- 2:00.34, 3:57.73; 2008- 4:04.19, 2009- 2:01.35, 3:59.66; 2010- 4:04.56, 2011- 2:02.8, 4:03.33. pbs: 1000m 2:37.98i '09, 1M 4:24.40 '03, 2000m 5:47.34 '09.
Formerly competed for UKR; RUS from 2000.

Olesya ZABARA b. 6 Oct 1982 Makhoshevskaya, Adygeya 1.65m 56kg. née Bufalova. Maikop TU.
At TJ: WCh: '07- 10; EC: '06- 5; WI: 08- 7; EI: '07- 2, '11- 2. At 400mh: WY: '99- 5.
Progress at TJ: 2001- 13.09, 2005- 13.67, 2006- 14.50, 2007- 14.50i/14.49, 2008- 14.54i/14.48, 2011- 14.45i/14.19/14.36w. pbs: 100mh 14.07 '99, 400mh 59.96 '99. Child born in 2009.

Kseniya ZADORINA b. 2 Mar 1987 Moskva 1.73m 59kg. Moskva Dyn.
At 400m/4x400m: WCh: '11- res (2)R; EC: '10- 1R; WJ: '06- 4; EU23: '07- 3/1R, 09- 2/1R; EJ: '05- 2/1R; WUG: '07- 3/2R; EI: '11- 3/1R; ET: '10- 1R.
Progress at 400m: 2005- 52.64, 2006- 51.81, 2007- 51.06, 2008- 51.48, 2009- 51.41, 2010- 50.87, 2011- 50.92. pbs: 200m 23.66i '11, 24.15 '08; 500m 1:08.94i '06 (WJR).

Yuliya ZARIPOVA b. 26 Apr 1986 Sbetlyi Yar, Volgograd reg. née Zarudneva. 1.72m 54kg. Volgograd Dyn.
At 3000mSt: WCh: '09- 2, '11- 1; EC: '10- 1; CCp: '10- 1; ET: '10- 1. At 800m: EJ: '05- h. At 3000m: EI: '09- 7. Eur CC: '05- 8J, '08- 3 U23. Won Russian 3000mSt 2009, 2011.
Progress at 3000mSt: 2008- 9:54.9, 2009- 9:08.39, 2010- 9:17.57, 2011- 9:07.03. pbs: 800m 2:05.44 '05, 1500m 4:04.59 '09, 3000m 8:54.50i '09, 5000m 16:02.81i '10.
Daughter Lenichke born 2007. Married Ildar Zaripov TJK in 2010.

Olga ZAYTSEVA b. 10 Nov 1984 Kaliningrad 1.76m 67kg. St Peterburg YR.
At 400m/4x400mR: EC: '06- 3/1R; EU23: '05- 1/1R. At 200m: WCh: '09- sf; ECp: '06- 1/1R. At LJ: WCh: '11- dnq 13. Won Russian 200m 2006, LJ 2011. World indoor 4x400m record 2006.
Progress at 400m. LJ: 2003- 6.36, 2004- 51.09, 2005- 50.06, 2006- 49.49, 2007- 52.93i, 2008- 51.42i/51.61; 2011- 7.01. pbs: 100m 11.65 '08, 11.56w '09; 200m 22.67 '06, 600m 1:06.76i '06.
Switched from 400m back to long jump in 2011.

Yevgeniya ZINUROVA b. 16 Nov 1982 Zlatoust, Chelyabinsk. Moskva Youth.
At 800m: WI: '10- 6; EJ: '11- 1.
World indoor 4x800m record 2010.
Progress at 800m: 2006- 2:02.2, 2007- 2:00.93, 2008- 1:58.04, 2009- 1:59.82, 2010- 1:58.65i/2:01.95, 2011- 1:58.49. pbs: 400m 53.92 '10, 1000m 2:36.32i '11, 1500m 4:10.26 '09.

SAINT KITTS & NEVIS

Governing body: Saint Kitts Amateur Athletic Association, PO Box 932, Basseterre, St Kitts. Founded 1961.

Kim COLLINS b. 5 Apr 1976 St Kitts 1.75m 64kg. Studied sociology at Texas Christian University, USA.
At 100m (/200m): OG: '96- qf, 00- 7/sf, '04- 6, '08- sf/6; WCh: '97- h, 99- h/h, '01- 5/3=, '03- 1, '05- 3, '07- sf, '09- qf/qf, '11- 3/sf/3R; CG: '02- 1; PAm: '07- 5, '11- 2; PAm-J: '95- 2; CAC: '99- 2, '01- 1/1, '03- 1; WCp: '02- 2/2R. At 60m: WI: '03- 2, '08- 2=. Won NCAA indoor 60m & 200m 2001. SKN records: 100m from 1996, 200m from 1998, 400m 2000.
Progress at 100m, 200m: 1995- 10.63, 21.85; 1996- 10.27, 21.06; 1998- 10.18/10.16w, 20.88/20.78w; 1999- 10.21, 20.43, 2000- 10.13A/10.15/10.02w, 20.31A/20.18w; 2001- 10.04A/10.00?/9.99w, 20.20/20.08w; 2002- 9.98, 20.49; 2003- 9.99/9.92w, 20.40w; 2004- 10.00, 20.98; 2005- 10.00, 2006- 10.33, 21.53; 2007- 10.14, 2008- 10.05, 20.25; 2009- 10.15/10.08w, 20.45; 2010- 10.20, 21.35/20.76w; 2011- 10.00A/10.01, 20.52. pbs: 60m 6.50i '11, 400m 46.93 '00.
The first athlete from his country to make Olympic and World finals and in 2003 the first to win a World Indoor medal and a World title; won a further medal in his 8th World Champs. There is a 'Kim Collins Highway' in St Kitts.

ST. LUCIA

Governing body: Saint Lucia Athletics Association, Olympic House, Barnard Hill P.O.GM 697 Gable Woods Mall, Castries.

Levern SPENCER b. 23 Jun 1984 Port of Spain, Trinidad 1.80m 54kg. Was at University of Georgia.
At HJ: OG: '08- dnq 27; WCh: '05-07-09-11: dnq 22/15=/dnq 24=/dnq 13; CG: '02-06-10: 12=/5/3; WJ: '02- 8; WY: '01- 3; PAm: '03- 5, '07- 3; CAG: '06- 3, '10- 1; CCp: '10- 3=. CAC champion 2005, 2008-09, 2011.
Nine St. Lucia high jump records 2004-10.
Progress at HJ: 2000- 1.80, 2001- 1.81, 2002- 1.83, 2003- 1.86, 2004- 1.88, 2005- 1.94, 2006- 1.90, 2007- 1.94, 2008- 1.93, 2009- 1.95, 2010- 1.98, 2011- 1.94. pbs: 200m 24.22 '05, LJ 5.95 '05.

SENEGAL

Governing body: Fédération Sénégalaise d'Athlétisme, BP 1737, Stade Iba Mar DIOP, Dakar. Founded 1960.

Ndiss Kaba BADJI b. 21 Sep 1983 1.92m 79kg.
At LJ/(TJ): OG: '04- dnq 27, '08- 6/dnq nj; WCh: '07- 7, '09- dnq 18; WJ: '02- dnq/9; AfG: '03- 2/4, '07- 5/1, '11- 3; AfCh: '02-04-08-10: 5/2/(1)/2; WI: '10- 6, '12- 5; WUG: '03- 5, '07- 2.; CCp: '10- 6
Senégal triple jump records 2007 & 2008.
Progress at LJ: 2001- 7.28, 2002- 7.83/7.90w,

2003- 7.92, 2004- 8.20A/8.03/8.30Aw, 2005- 7.88i/ (8.06/8.30w dq), 2007- 8.11, 2008- 8.16, 2009- 8.32, 2010- 8.27, 2011- 8.08. pb TJ 17.07A '08, 16.80 '07, 17.15dq '05. Drugs disqualification 2005-07.

SERBIA

Governing body: Athletic Federation of Serbia, Strahinjica Bana 73a, 11000 Beograd. Founded in 1921 (as Yugoslav Athletic Federation).
National Championships (Yugoslav) first held in 1920 (men) and 1923 (women). **2011 Champions**: **Men**: 100m: Milos Savic 10.84, 200m: Darko Sarovic 21.94, 400m: Milos Raovic 48.60, 800m: PredragRandjelovic1:52.50,1500m/5000m/10000m: Mirko Petrovic 3:55.62/14:50.77/32:28.04, HMar: Milos Mitric 68:38, Mar: Zivan Milosevic 2:54:36, 3000mSt: Goran Milicic 9:41.75, 110mh: Milan Ristic 14.32, 400mh: Marko Milovanovic 54.03, HJ: Dragutin Topic 2.24, PV: Igor Sarcevic 4.60, LJ/ Dec: Mihail Dudas 7.29/6321, TJ: Aleksandar Bundalo 15.10, SP: Asmir Kolasinac 20.21, DT: Milos Markovic 51.62, HT: Zoran Loncar 57.70, JT: Nikola Prvulovic 69.68, 10000mW: Vladimir Savanovic 44:45.27, 20kW: Predrag Filipovic 1:24:51. **Women**: 100m/200m: Tanja Mitic 11.86/24.81, 400m/100mh/400mh: Mila Andric 55.83/14.07/62.44, 800m/1500m: Amela Terzic 2:05.16/ 4:25.29, 5000m/10000m/3000mSt: Ana Subotic 17:22.53/35:47.30/10:37.86, HMar: Olivera Jevtic 73:12, Mar: *not held*, HJ: Zorana Bukvic 1.76, PV: Jelena Radinovic-Vasic 4.10, LJ: Ivana Spanovic 6.39, TJ: Biljana Topic 14.19, SP: Milena Draguljevic 11.47, DT: Dragana Savanovic 37.65, HT: Sara Savatovic 52.61, JT: Tatjana Jelaca 53.65, Hep: *not held*, 10000mW: Emilija Pesic 58:01.96.

Mihail DUDAS b. 1 Nov 1989 Novi Sad 1.83m 79kg. AV Crvena Zvezda.
At Dec: WCh: '11- 6; EC: '10- dnf; WJ: '08- 3; Eur23: '09- 3, '11- 3; EJ: '07- 15.
Two Serbian decathlon records 2011.
Progress at Dec: 2009- 7855, 2010- 7966, 2011- 8256. pbs: 60m 6.94i '11, 100m 10.71 '11, 400m 47.47 '11, 1000m 2:44.88i '10, 1500m 4:24.30 '09, 60mh 8.24i '11, 110mh 14.80 '09, HJ 2.04 '09, PV 4.90 '11, LJ 7.63 '10, SP 13.92i, 13.85 '11, DT 43.97 '11, JT 58.93 '11, Hep 5873i '12.

Women

Dragana TOMASEVIC b. 4 Jun 1982 Sremska Mitrovica 1.75m 80kg. AK Sirmijum, Sremska Mitrovica.
at DT: OG: '04/08- dnq 26/13; WCh: '05- 7, '07/09- dnq 19/19, '11- 7; EC: '06- 8, '10- 6; EU23: '03- 11; EJ: '01- 10; WUG: '05- 3, '07- 3; Won Balkan 2005, 2007, 2011; MedG 2005, SCG 2001-03, SRB 2006-07.
Four SCG/SRB discus records 2005-06.
Progress at DT: 1999- 34.93, 2000- 45.87/47.04dh, 2001- 52.80/53.00dh, 2002- 54.41/55.33dh, 2003- 56.24/56.74dh, 2004- 59.52, 2005- 62.43, 2006- 63.63, 2007- 61.52, 2008- 62.70, 2009- 61.89, 2010- 62.55, 2011- 62.48. pb SP 14.81 '04.

SLOVAKIA

Governing body: Slovak Athletic Federation, Junácka 6, 832 80 Bratislava. Founded 1939.
National Championships first held in 1939.
2011 Champions: **Men**: **Men**: 100m: Adam Zavacky 10.72, 200m: Roman Turcáni 21.74, 400m/800m: Dusan Páleník 48.64/1:56.32, 1500m: Jozef Pelikán 3:57.74, 5000m: Jaroslav Szabo 15:05.79, 10000m/HMar/Mar: Imrich Magyar 31:23.17/70:24/2:39:42, 3000mSt: Jakub Valachovic 9:28.82, 110mh: Viliam Papso 14.16, 400mh: Sergyi Borodin 52.33, HJ: Peter Horák 2.17, PV: Tomás Krajnák 4.50, LJ: Lukás Lupták 6.83, TJ: Jaroslav Dobrovodsky 15.97w, SP: Daniel Vanek 18.77, DT: Matej Gasaj 56.90, HT: Libor Charfreitag 75.36, JT: Marián Bokor 63.93, 20kW/50kW: Matej Tóth 1:22:47/3:39:46. **Women**: 100m: Erika Brselová 11.87, 200m: Lenka Krsáková 24.92, 400m: Alexandra Stuková 54.96, 800m/1500m: Lucia Klocová 2:12.56/4:30.95, 5000m: Janka Zatlúkalová 17:15.04, 10000m/ Mar: Katarina Beresová 35:09.47/2:43:42, HMar: Sylvia Sebestian 1:27:37, 3000mSt: Lubomíra Maníková 11:34.44, 100mh: Merita Bytyqiová 13.86, 400mh: Monika Ivanková 62.27, HJ: Iveta Srnková 1.71, PV: Slovomíra Slúková 3.60, LJ: Renata Medgyesová 6.51w, TJ: Dana Veldáková 13.59, SP: Ivana Kristofícová 15.35, DT: Ivona Tomanová 48.61, HT: Martina Hrasnová 65.33, JT: Eva Hanuliaková 42.66.

Libor CHARFREITAG b. 11 Sep 1977 Trnava 1.91m 117kg. Studied at Southern Methodist University, USA. ASK Slavia Trnava.
At HT: OG: '00- dnq 30, '04- 7, '08- 8; WCh: '99-01-03-11: dnq 32/18/13/22, '05-07-09: 9/3/10; EC: '02- 7, '06- dnq 14, '10- 1; WJ: '96- dnq 13; EU23: '99- 5; CCp: '10- 1. Won NCAA 1998, 2000; SVK 1998-9, 2002-11.
12 SVK hammer records 1996-2003, six European indoor bests 35lb weight 2003-05.
Progress at HT: 1993- 49.42, 1994- 54.32, 1995- 56.90, 1996- 66.82, 1997- 66.44, 1998- 72.30, 1999- 75.18, 2000- 77.22, 2001- 77.65, 2002- 79.20, 2003- 81.81, 2004- 79.84, 2005- 80.85, 2006- 78.04, 2007- 81.60, 2008- 80.45, 2009- 78.81, 2010- 80.59, 2011- 77.69. pbs: SP 17.27i/16.69 '00, DT 52.63 '02, 35lb Wt 25.68i '05.
In Barcelona he won the first medal for Slovakia at the European Champs since independence. His sister Eva had HT best of 57.46 '01.

Matej TÓTH b. 10 Feb 1983 Nitra 1.85m 72kg. Dukla Banská Bystrica.
At 20kW/(50kW): OG: '04- 32, '08- 26; WCh: '05- 21, 07- 14, '09- 9/10, '11- 14/dnf; EC: '06- 6, '10- 7, EU23: '03- 6; WCp: '10- (1); ECp: '09- 9, '11- 2. At 10000mW: WJ: '02- 16, WY: '99- 8; EJ: '01- 6. Won SVK 20kW 2005-08, 2010-11; 50kW 2011.
SVK 50k walk records 2009 & 2011.
Progress at 20kW, 50kW: 1999- 1:34:29, 2000-

1:30:28, 2001- 1:29:33, 2003- 1:13:17, 2004- 1:23:18, 2005- 1:21:38, 2006- 1:21:39, 2007- 1:25:10, 2008- 1:21:24, 2009- 1:20:53, 3:41:32; 2010- 1:22:04, 3:53:30; 2011- 1:20:16, 3:39:46. pbs: 3000mW 10:57.32i '11, 11:17.35 '03; 5000mW 18:34.56i '12, 18:54.39 '11; 10000W 39:45.03 '06, 39:07R '10; 30kW 2:12:46 '06.

Women

Martina HRASNOVÁ b. 21 Mar 1983 Bratislava 1.80m 100kg. née Danisová. Dukla Banská Bystrica.
At HT: OG: '08- 8; WCh: '01/07: dnq 23/12, '09- 3; EC: '02 & '06- dnq 26; WJ: '00- 5, '02- 2; EJ: '99- 4, '01- 2; WUG: '07- 5, '09- 2. Won SVK SP 2003, 2006; HT 2000-01, 2006, 2008-09, 2011.
14 Slovakian hammer records 2001-09.
Progress at HT: 1999- 58.61, 2000- 61.62, 2001- 68.50, 2002- 68.22, 2003- 66.36, 2005- 69.24, 2006- 73.84, 2007- 69.22, 2008- 76.82, 2009- 76.90, 2011- 72.47. pbs: 60m 7.96i '12, SP 15.02 '06, DT 43.15 '06, Wt 21.74i '11.
Two-year drugs ban (nandrolone) from July 2003. Daughter Rebeka born on 4 July 2010.

Lucia KLOCOVÁ b. 20 Nov 1983 Martin, Zilina 1.76m 53kg. AK ZTS Martin.
At 800m: OG: '04/08- sf; WCh: '03/05/07/09/11- sf; EC: '06- sf, '10- 4; WJ: '00- 3, '02- 2; EU23: '03- 2, '05- 5; EJ: '01- 1. Won SVK 400m 2007, 800m 2004, 2006, 2010-11; 1500m 2010-11.
SVK 1500m record 2010.
Progress at 800m: 1998- 2:11.63, 2000- 2:04.00, 2001- 2:03.06, 2002- 2:01.59, 2003- 2:00.60, 2004- 2:00.79, 2005- 2:00.64, 2006- 2:00.28, 2007- 1:58.62, 2008- 1:58.51, 2009- 1:59.79, 2010- 1:59.31, 2011- 1:59.48. pbs: 400m 52.98 '07, 600m 1:26.96 '08, 1000m 2:39.74i '03, 1500m 4:08.86 '10.

Dana VELDÁKOVÁ b. 3 Jun 1981 Roznava 1.78m 59kg. AK Spartak Dubnica.
At (LJ/)TJ: OG: '08- dnq; WCh: '05- dnq 17, '07- 09-11: 12/8/11; EC: '02/06- dnq 15/24. '10- 7; WJ: '98- 6, '00- 4/3; EU23: '01- 5, '03- 4; EJ: '99- 8; WI: '06-10-12: 8/6/8; EI: '07-09-11: 6/3/3; WUG: '03- 5, '07- 2. Won SVK 100mh 2003, TJ 2002-05, 2007-11, Hep 2001, 2004.
Two SVK triple jump records 2007-08.
Progress at TJ: 1998- 13.12, 1999- 13.13/13.19w, 2000- 13.92, 2001- 13.73, 2002- 13.99, 2003- 14.02, 2004- 13.96A, 2005- 14.16, 2006- 14.19, 2007- 14.41, 2008- 14.51, 2009- 14.43, 2010- 14.32/14.59w, 2011- 14.48. pbs: 60m 7.73i '06, 60mh 8.82i '03, 100mh 14.38 '01, HJ 1.75 '01, LJ 6.56 '08, SP 11.56i '04, Hep 5191 '01, Pen 3746i '03.
Twin **Jana** LJ 6.72 '08, 6.88w '10; TJ 13.40 '04.

SLOVENIA

Governing body: Atletska Zveza Slovenije, Letaliska cesta 33c, 1122 Ljubljana. Current organisation founded 1948.
2011 National Champions: **Men**: 100m: Matic Osovnikar 10.30, 200m: Gregor Kokalovic 21.36, 400m/400mh: Brent LaRue 47.42/49.88, 800m/1500m: Tomaz Rozmaric 1:51.62/3:52.66, 3000m: Bostjan Buc 8:25.82, 5000m: Peter Kastelic 15:09.70, 10000m: Primoz Kobe 30:11.16, HMar: Anton Kosmac 70:59, Mar: Mario Vracic 2:31:48, 3000mSt: Blaz Grad 9:27.51, 110mh: Dragmar Zlatnar 14.73, HJ: Rozle Prezelj 2.22, PV: Andrej Poljanec 5.25, LJ: Lenart Grkman 7.33, TJ: Andrej Batagelj 15.53, SP: Miroslav Vodovnik 18.52, DT: Tadej Hribar 51.48, HT: Primoz Kozmus 76.38, JT: Matija Kranjc 78.55. **Women**: 100m/200m: Sabina Veit 11.65/23.79, 400m: Liona Rebernik 54.85, 800m/1500m: Marusa Mismas 2:15.63/4:39.71, 3000m: Maja Mohorovic 10:35.60, 5000m: Helena Javornik 18:14.81, 10000m: Mateja Simic 36:45.64, HMar: Daneja Grandovec 1:23:17, Mar: Neza Mravlje 2:42:00, 3000mSt: Klara Ljubi 12:36.12, 100mh: Marina Tomic 13.36, 400mh: Eva Ivansek 70.88, HJ: Marusa Cernjul 1.77, PV: Tina Sutej 4.50, LJ: Nina Kolaric 6.43, TJ: Marija Sestak 14.18w, SP: Spela Hus 13.17, DT: Tamara Stojkovic 43.10, HT: Ana Susec 61.40, JT: Martina Ratej 62.33, Hep: Simona Kapl 3785.

Primoz KOZMUS b. 30 Sep 1979 Novo Mesto 1.88m 106kg. Brezice.
At HT: OG: '00- dnq 38, '04- 6, '08- 1; WCh: '03- 07-09-11: 5/2/1/3; EC: '02- dnq 25, '06- 7; EU23: '99- 12, '01- 14; WJ: '98- dnq. SLO champion 1999-2004, 2006, 2008-09, 2011; WAF 2008-09.
Ten SLO hammer records 2000-09.
Progress at HT: 1995- 45.82, 1996- 54.10, 1997- 61.08, 1998- 66.28, 1999- 70.11, 2000- 76.84, 2001- 71.17, 2002- 75.87, 2003- 81.21, 2004- 79.34, 2006- 80.38, 2007- 82.30, 2008- 82.02, 2009- 82.58, 2011- 80.28.
First Slovenian Olympic champion. Older sister Simona set Slovenian women's hammer record (58.60 '01).

Women

Martina RATEJ b. 2 Nov 1981 Loce 1.78m 69kg. AK Sentjur.
At JT: OG: '08- dnq 37; WCh: '09- 11, '11- 7; EC: '06- dnq 21, '10- 7; WJ: '00- dnq 15. SLO champion 2005-11.
Five SLO javelin records 2008-10.
Progress at JT: 1999- 48.74, 2000- 46.83, 2005- 50.86, 2006- 57.49, 2007- 58.49, 2008- 63.44, 2009- 63.42, 2010- 67.16, 2011- 65.89, 2012- 65.24.

Snezana RODIC b. 19 Aug 1982 Koper 1.80m 66kg. née Vukmirovic. AD MASS Ljubljana.
At TJ: WCh: '05/09- dnq 16/19; EC: '10- 6; EU23: '03- 11 (dq LJ); EI: '09- 6, '11- 4. SLO champion LJ 2004, TJ 2003-04, 2008, 2010.
Progress at TJ: 2003- 13.47, 2004- 13.97, 2005- 14.18, 2007- 14.03, 2008- 14.06/14.29w, 2009- 14.18i/14.10, 2010- 14.47/14.52w, 2011- 14.35i/14.23. pbs: 60m 7.92i '03, 60mh 8.27i '05, 100mh 14.27 '03, LJ 6.51 '08, Hep 4897 '00.

SOUTH AFRICA

Governing body: Athletics South Africa, PO Box 2712, Houghton 2041. Original body founded 1894.

National Championships first held in 1894 (men), 1929 (women). **2011 Champions: Men**: 100m: Simon Magakwe 10.31, 200m: Wade van Niekerk 20.57, 400m: Lebogang Moeng 45.57, 800m: Samson Ngoepe 1:45.69, 1500m: Juan van Deventer 3:40.16, 5000m: Tshamano Setone 13:31.87, 10000m/HMar Stephen Mokoka 28:06.65/62:07, Mar: Lusapho April 2:13:21, 3000mSt: Ruben Ramolefi 8:14.06, 110mh: Lehann Fourie 13.65w, 400mh: L.J. van Zyl 47.73, HJ: Hubert de Beer 2.15, PV: Cheyne Rahme 5.10, LJ: Khotso Mokoena 8.29w, TJ: Tumelo Thagane 16.95w, SP: Roelie Potgieter 19.42, DT: Victor Hogan 59.86, HT: Chris Harmse 71.70 (17th successive title), JT: Robert Oosthuizen 81.18, Dec: Willem Coertzen 8014, 20kW: Pierre-Louis de Villiers 1:29:26. **Women**: 100m/200m: Carina Horn 11.68/23.47w, 400m: Rorisang Ramonnye 53.28 (Tjipekapora Herunga NAM 52.70), 800m/1500m: Caster Semenya 2:02.10/4:12.93, 5000m: René Kalmer 15:42.21, 10000m: Portia Ngwenya 36:24.95, HMar: René Kalmer 72:59, Mar: Charné Bosman 2:44:44, 3000mSt: Tebogo Masehla 10:00.01, 100mh: Claudia Viljoen 13.64, 400mh: Wenda Theron 56.74, HJ: Anika Smit 1.85, PV: Honorata Saar 3.60 (Ikuko Nishikori JPN 3.80), LJ: Janice Josephs 6.38w, TJ: Charlene Potgieter 13.45, SP: Veronica Abrahamse 15.19, DT: Elizna Naude 58.69, HT: Annemie Smith 55.85, JT: Sunette Viljoen 58.70, Hep: Bianca Erasmus 4872, 20kW: Susan Swanepoel 1:49:48.

Cornel FREDERICKS b. 3 Mar 1990 Caledon 1.78m 70kg.
At 400mh/4x400mR: WCh: '11- 5; WJ: '08- 4; WY: '07- 5; AfG: '07- 1; AfCh: '10- 2; Won RSA 2010, Af-J 110mh & 400mh 2009.
Progress at 400mh: 2008- 50.39, 2009- 49.92, 2010- 48.79A/48.99, 2011- 48.14. pbs: 400m 46.95 '10, 300mh 35.15 '10.

Luvo MANIYONGA b. 18 Nov 1991 Mbekweni 1.85m 65kg. MATI.
At LJ: WCh: '11- 5; WJ: '10- 1; AfG: '11- 1, Af-J: '09- 3.
African junior long jump record 2010.
Progress at LJ: 2009- 7.65, 2010- 8.19, 2011- 8.26. pb TJ 15.71A '10.

Godfrey Khotso MOKOENA b. 6 Mar 1985 Heidelberg, Gauteng 1.90m 73kg. Tuks AC, Pretoria.
At LJ/(TJ): OG: '04- (dnq 29), '08- 2; WCh: '05-07-09-11: 7/5/2/dnq 15=; CG: '06- 4/2; WJ: '02- 12, '04- 2/1; AfG: '03- 3/2, '07- 3; AfCh: '06- 2/2, '10- 1; WI: '06-08-10: 5/1/2. At HJ: WY: '01- 5. Won RSA LJ 2005-07, 2009-11; TJ 2004-06.
Records: Three African LJ 2009, RSA LJ (5) 2005-

09, TJ (2) 2004-05, African junior TJ 2004.
Progress at LJ, TJ: 2001- 7.17A, 2002- 7.82A, 16.03A; 2003- 7.84A/7.83, 16.28; 2004- 8.09, 16.96A/16.77; 2005- 8.37A/8.22, 17.25; 2006- 8.39/8.45w, 16.95; 2007- 8.34A/8.28/8.32w, 16.75; 2008- 8.25/8.35w, 2009- 8.50, 2010- 8.23A/8.15/8.22w, 2011- 8.25/8.31w. pbs: 100m 10.7A '09, HJ 2.10 '01.

Mbulaeni MULAUDZI b. 8 Sep 1980 Muduluni Village, Limpopo Province 1.71m 62kg. University of Johannesburg AC.
At 800m: OG: '04- 2, '08- sf; WCh: '01-03-05-07-09: 6/3/sf/7/1; CG: '02- 1; AfG: '03- 2, '07- 2; AfCh: '00-02-06: 2/3/6; WI: '04-06-08: 1/2/2; WCp: '06- 3; Won WAF 2006, AfrJ 1999, RSA 2001-03, 2005-09.   RSA 1000m record 2007.
Progress at 800m: 1998- 1:50.33A, 1999- 1:48.33A; 2000- 1:45.55, 2001- 1:44.01, 2002- 1:43.81, 2003- 1:42.89, 2004- 1:44.56, 2005- 1:44.08, 2006- 1:43.09, 2007- 1:43.74, 2008- 1:43.26, 2009- 1:42.86, 2010- 1:43.29, 2011- 1:45.50. pbs: 400m 46.3 '07, 600m 1:17.25i '05, 1000m 2:15.86 '07, 1500m 3:38.55 '09.
Ten successive seasons, 2001-10. under 1:45.

John Robert OOSTHUIZEN b. 23 Jan 1987 Bloemfontein 1.88m 101kg. Maties AC, Stellenbosch
At JT: OG: '08- dnq 19; WCh: '07- 6, '09/11- dnq 44/33; CG: '06- 5; AfG: '07- 1; WJ: '06- 1; WY: '03- 2; RSA champion 2007-09, 2011.
African junior javelin record 2006.
Progress at JT: 2005- 75.94, 2006- 83.07, 2007- 84.52, 2008- 86.80, 2009- 81.18. 2010- 82.96, 2011- 84.38. Father and coach Johan had JT pb 80.92 '90.

Louis J. van ZYL b. 20 Jul 1985 Bloemfontein 1.86m 75kg. Tuks AC, Pretoria.
At 400mh/4x400mR: OG: '08- 5; WCh: '05- 6, '07- h, '09- sf, '11- 3/2R; CG: '06- 1/2R, '10- 2; AfG: '07- 1; AfCh: '06- 1, '08- 1/1R, '10- 1; WJ: '02- 1, '04- 4/2R; WY: '01- 3; WCp: '06- 2, '10- 5; RSA champion 2003, 2005-06, 2008, 2011.
Two RSA 400m hurdles records 2011.
Progress at 400mh: 2001- 51.14A, 2002- 48.89, 2003- 49.22, 2004- 49.06, 2005- 48.11, 2006- 48.05, 2007- 48.24, 2008- 48.22, 2009- 47.94, 2010- 48.51A/48.63, 2011- 47.66. pbs: 100m 10.62 '07, 10.3Aw '03, 10.5A '01; 200m 21.02A '09, 21.0A '03; 300m 32.32 '09, 400m 44.86A '11, 46.02 '08; 300mh 35.76 '04.
Ran world U18 record of 48.89 to win World Junior title in 2002 after world age record at 15 in 2001. Commonwealth Games record to win 400mh gold and ran brilliant final leg in 4x400m to take RSA from fifth to second in 2006. Engaged to Irvette van Blerk (pb HMar 70:56 '11).

Women

Caster SEMENYA b. 7 Jan 1991 Polokwane, Limpopo Province 1.70m 64kg. Tuks AC, Pretoria. Student of sports science at University of Pretoria.
At 800m: WCh: ' 09- 1, '11- 2; WJ: '08- h; Afr-J:

'09- 1 (1 1500m), won RSA 800m & 1500m 2011, Southern Africa 800m 2009.
Two RSA 800m records 2009.
Progress at 800m: 2007- 2:09.35, 2008- 2:04.23, 2009- 1:55.45, 2010- 1:58.16, 2011- 1:56.35. pbs: 400m 52.54A, 53.16 '11, 1500m 4:08.01 '09.
Questions over her gender arose at the African Junior and World Champs in 2009, and she was barred from competing by Athletics South Africa until the IAAF determined whether she was free to compete again. They did so in July 2010 but saying that the medical details of her case remained confidential.

Sunette VILJOEN b. 6 Oct 1983 Johannesburg 1.68m 63kg. Univ. of North West, Potchefstroom.
At JT: OG: '04/08- dnq 35/33; WCh: '03/09- dnq 16/18, '11- 3; CG: '06- 1, '10- 1; AfG: '03- 3, '07- 3; AfCh: '04-06-08-10: 1/2/1/1; WUG: '07- 5, '09- 1, '11- 1; CCp: '10- 2. Won Afro-Asian Games 2003, RSA 2003-04, 2006, 2009-11.
Three African javelin records 2009-11, Commonwealth record 2011.
Progress at JT: 1999- 43.89A, 2000- 45.50A, 2001- 50.70A, 2002- 58.33A, 2003- 61.59, 2004- 61.15A, 2005- 57.31, 2006- 60.72, 2007- 58.39, 2008- 62.24A, 2009- 65.43, 2010- 66.38, 2011- 68.38.
Son Hervé born in 2005.

SPAIN

Governing body: Real Federación Española de Atletismo, Avda. Valladolid, 81 - 1°, 28008 Madrid, Spain. Founded 1918.
National Championships first held in 1917 (men), 1931 (women). **2011 Champions: Men**: 100m/200m: Ángel David Rodríguez 10.40/20.34w, 400m: Roberto Briones 47.07, 800m: Kevin López 1:47.87, 1500m: Manuel Olmedo 3:53.86, 5000m: Jesús España 14:06.37, 10000m: Ricardo Serrano 28:42.91, HMar: Rafael Iglesias 62:40, Mar: Pablo Villalobos 2:12:21, 3000mSt: Tomás Tajadura 8:28.70, 110mh: Jackson Quiñónez 13.70, 400mh: Diego Cabello 50.91, HJ: Miguel Ángel Sancho 2.26, PV: Igor Bychkov 5.35, LJ: Jean Marie Okutu 7.84, TJ: Lisvanys Pérez 16.82, SP: Borja Vivas 19.26, DT: Mario Pestano 67.97 (11th successive title), HT: Isaac Vicente 70.41, JT: Rafael Baraza 72.34, Dec: David Gómez 7298, 10000mW/20kW: Francisco Javier Fernández 40:55.62/1:22:17, 50kW: Mikel Odriozola 3:49:33. **Women**: 100m: Digna Luz Murillo 11.55, 200m: Belén Recio 23.52, 400m: Aauri Lorena Bokesa 54.25, 800m: Nuria Fernández 2:04.18, 1500m: Isabel Macías 4:22.49, 5000m: Dolores Checa 15:46.77, 10000m: Isabel Checa 32:48.76, HMar: Vanessa Veiga 73:04, Mar: Tamara Sanfabio 2:37:24, 3000mSt: Zulema Fuentes-Pila 10:08.62, 100mh: Caridad Jerez 13.72, 400mh: Olga Ortega 58.46, HJ: Ruth Beitia 1.92, PV: Anna María Pinero 4.41, LJ: Concepción Montaner 6.53, TJ: Patricia Sarrapio 14.01, SP: Úrsula Ruiz 16.80, DT: Sabina Asenjo 54.02, HT: Berta Castells 69.53, JT: Mercedes Chilla 60.91, Hep: Laura Ginés 5583, 10000mW: Julia Takacs 44:05.41, 20kW: Beatriz Pascual 1:30:46.

Arturo CASADO b. 26 Jan 1983 Madrid 1.87m 71kg. C.A.Adidas.
At 1500m: OG: '08- sf; WCh: '05- 5, '07- 7, '09- h; EC: '06- 4, '10- 1; WJ: '02- 6, EU23: '03- 7, '05- 1; EJ: '01- 3; WI: '08- 4; EI: '05-07-09: 4/3/5; CCp: '10- 4; ECp: '08- 2; Won Med G 2005, Spanish 2005, 2008.
Progress at 1500m: 2000- 3:57.76, 2001- 3:46.15, 2002- 3:43.66, 2003- 3:41.52, 2004- 3:38.04, 2005- 3:35.64, 2006- 3:35.45, 2007- 3:34.09, 2008- 3:33.14, 2009- 3:34.05, 2010- 3:32.70, 2011- 3:41.86. pbs: 800m 1:44.74 '10, 1000m 2:20.50 '06, 1M 3:52.38 '07, 3000m 7:49.86i '10, 7:58.43 '08; 5000m 14:21.0 '03, 10kmRd 29:18 '05. Missed 2011 outdoor season through injury.

Frank Yennifer **CASAÑAS** b. 18 Oct 1978 La Habana, Cuba 1.87m 115kg. Playas de Castellón.
At DT: OG: '00/04- dnq 24/17, '08- 5; WCh: '03-05-09: dnq 21/21/16; EC: '10- 11; WJ: '96- 3; PAm: '99- 4, '03- 2; CAG: '98- 2; PAm-J: '97- 1; ET: '11- 2; won IbAm 2000, Cuban 2003-05, MedG 2009.
Progress at DT: 1995- 50.08, 1996- 54.86, 1997- 57.36, 1998- 60.52, 1999- 63.90, 2000- 63.32, 2002- 64.04, 2003- 65.08, 2004- 64.20, 2005- 65.32, 2006- 67.14, 2007- 64.68, 2008- 67.91, 2009- 67.17, 2010- 66.95, 2010- 66.62, 2011- 67.18. pb SP 17.68 '07.
Spanish citizen from 27 May 2008. Married to Dolores Pedrares (HT pb 67.14 '04).

Jesús ESPAÑA b. 21 Aug 1978 Madrid 1.73m 56kg. C.A. Valdemoro.
At 1500m: EJ '97- 9. At 3000m: WCp: '06- 6; ECp: '05-08-09-10: 1/2/1/1; WI: '03- 4, '10- 6; EI: '02-07-09-11: 3=/3/3/5. At 5000m: OG: '08- 14; WCh: '05-07-09-11: h/7/10/12; EC: '02- 11, '06- 1, '10- 2; ECp: '03- 2, '11- 1. Eur CC: '07- 6, '10- 9. Won Spanish 5000m 2003, 2005-11; indoor 3000m 2003, 2007, 2009-11.
Progress at 5000m: 1998- 14:33.34, 1999- 14:22.1, 2000- 14:28.24, 2002- 13:22.66, 2003- 13:29.24, 2004- 13:18.31, 2005- 13:15.44, 2006- 13:16.74, 2007- 13:30.24, 2008- 13:13.32, 2009- 13:10.73, 2010- 13:18.46, 2011- 13:04.73. pbs: 800m 1:51.18 '00, 1500m 3:36.53 '02, 2000m 5:05.34 '02, 3000m 7:38.26 '06, 10000m 29:03.20 '00, 10km Rd 28:33 '01.
Younger brother Francisco (b. 27 Oct 1984) was 3rd in EU23 1500m 2005, pb 3:38.68 '08.

Jesús Ángel GARCÍA b. 17 Oct 1969 Madrid 1.72m 64kg. Canal de Isabel II.
At 50kW: OG: '92- 10, '96- dnf, '00- 12, '04- 5, '08- 4; WCh: '93-5-7-9-01-03-05-07-09-11: 1/5/2/ dnf/2/6/dq/dq/3/dq; EC: '94-98-02-06-10: 4/ dq/3/2/5; WCp: '93-5-7-9-02-04-06-08-10: 2/2/1/4/dq/6/6/14/5; ECp: '96-8-00-01-09: 1/2/1/1/2. At 20kW: WUG: '91- 5. Won Spanish 50kW 1997, 2000, 2007.

World M40 50km walk record 2010.
Progress at 50kW: 1991- 4:05:10, 1992- 3:48:24, 1993- 3:41:41, 1994- 3:41:28, 1995- 3:41:54, 1996- 3:46:59, 1997- 3:39.54, 1998- 3:43:17, 1999- 3:40:40, 2000- 3:42:51, 2001- 3:43:07, 2002- 3:44:33, 2003- 3:43:56, 2004- 3:44:42, 2005- 3:48:19, 2006- 3:42:48, 2007- 3:46:08, 2008- 3:44:08, 2009- 3:41:37, 2010- 3:47:56, 2011- 3:48:11. pbs: 5000mW 19:33.3 '01, 10000mW 40:38.86 '09, road: 5kW 20:07 '04, 10kW 40:25 '99, 20kW 1:23:00 '09, 30kW 2:08:47 '01, 35km 2:31:06 '94; running Mar 2:47:43 '09. Competed in all major champs 1992-2011, has 50 races under 4 hours and 38 sub 3:50 for 50km and 20 years walking sub 3:50. In 1997 he married Carmen Acedo, who won a rhythmic gymnastics world title in 1993.

Manuel OLMEDO b. 17 May 1983 Sevilla 1.79m 60kg. FC Barcelona.
At 1500m: WCh: '11- 4; EC: '10- 3; EI: '11- 1; ET: '11- 1. At 800m: OG: '04- h, '08- sf; WCh: '03-05-07-09: h/h/sf/h; EC: '06- sf; WJ: '00-h, '02- 8; EJ: '01-8: ECp: '08- 1, '11- 1; EU23: '03- 3, '05- 2; EI: '09- 5. Won ESP 800m 2007-08, 1500m 2010-11.
Progress at 800m, 1500m: 1999- 1:52.63, 2000- 1:49.73, 2001- 1:49.01, 2002- 1:47.64/1:47.27i, 2003- 1:45.57, 2004- 1:45.30, 2005- 1:45.48, 2006- 1:45.74, 2007- 1:45.13, 3:42.29; 2008- 1:45.20, 2009- 1:45.91, 2010- 1:45.4, 3:36.98; 2011- 1:44.56, 3:34.44. pbs: 200m 22.70 '00, 300m 35.68 '99, 400m 48.49 '00, 600m 1:18.60 '06, 1000m 2:25.92 '01, 3000m 8:21.48 '09.
Successfully changed from 800 to 1500m in 2010.

Mario PESTANO b. 8 Apr 1978 Santa Cruz de Tenerife 1.95m 120kg. Tenerife Cajacanarias.
At DT: OG: '04- dnq 12, '08- 9; WCh: '99-01-03-05-07-09-11: dnq 30/dnq 22/8/11/10/10/11; EC: '02- 4, '06- 4, '10- 6; EU23: '99- 3; EJ: '97- 11; WCp: '02- 3; ECp: '01-05-06-08-09: 2/1/3/1/3. Won WAF 2004, IbAm 2004, 2010; MedG 2005, Spanish 2001-11.
Eight Spanish discus records 2001-08.
Progress at DT: 1995- 49.36, 1996- 50.56, 1997- 53.68, 1998- 54.96, 1999- 61.73, 2000- 61.63, 2001- 67.92, 2002- 67.46, 2003- 64.99, 2004- 68.00, 2005- 66.57, 2006- 66.31, 2007- 68.26, 2008- 69.50, 2009- 66.63, 2010- 66.90, 2011- 67.97. pb SP 18.75i '00, 18.64 '02.

Women

Ruth BEITIA b. 1 Apr 1979 Santander 1.92m 71kg. Piélagos Inelecma. Student of physical therapy at University of Santander.
At HJ: OG: '04- dnq 16=, '08- 7=; WCh: '03-05-07-09-11: 11=/dnq 19=/6/5/dnq 16; EC: '02- 11, '06- 9, '10- 6=; WJ: '96- dnq, '98- 8, EU23: '01- 1; EJ: '97- 9; WI: '01-03-06-08-10-12: 7/5=/3/4/2/6; EI: '05-07-09-11: 2/3/2/2; WCp: '02- 6=; ECp: '03-06-07-09-11: 2/2/2/2/3; Won IbAm 2010, Med G 2005, Spanish 2003, 2006-11 (and 10 indoors).
Nine Spanish HJ records 1998-2007 (and eight indoors 2001-07).

Progress at HJ: 1989- 1.29, 1990- 1.39, 1991- 1.50, 1992- 1.55, 1993- 1.66, 1994- 1.74, 1995- 1.80, 1996- 1.85, 1997- 1.87i/1.86, 1998- 1.89, 1999- 1.83, 2000- 1.86i/1.85, 2001- 1.94i/1.91, 2002- 1.94, 2003- 2.00, 2004- 2.00i/1.96, 2005- 1.99i/1.97, 2006- 1.98i/1.97; 2007- 2.02, 2008- 2.01, 2009- 2.01, 2010- 2.00, 2011- 1.96i/1.95. pbs: 200m 25.26 '02, 100mh 14.95 '97, 14.93w '00; LJ 6.04 '03, TJ 12.43/12.73w '11.
Her sister Inmaculada (b. 8 Sep 1975) had TJ pb 13.43 '00.

Dolores 'Loli' **CHECA** b. 27 Dec 1982 Silla (Valencia) 1.68m 52kg. Playas de Castellón.
At 1500m: WCh: '07- sf. At 5000m: OG: '08- h, ET: '09- 1, '11- 1. At 3000m: EI: '11- 5, ECp: '07- 3. Won Spanish 5000m 2008, 2011.
Progress at 1500m, 5000m: 1998- 4:43.0, 1999- 4:39.73, 2000- 4:33.41, 2001- 4:39.70, 2002- 4:31.47, 17:50.9; 2003- 4:22.47, 2004- 4:16.37, 2005- 4:30.00, 2006- 4:45.70, 2007- 4:06.49, 2008- 4:02.77, 14:55.71; 2009- 4:15.09, 15:08.27; 2011- 4:13.37, 14:46.30. pbs: 800m 2:07.11 '07, 3000m 8:37.78 '08, 10km Rd 32:45 '07.
Gave birth a daughter in March 2010. Twin sister Isabel has pbs 3000m 9:02.26, 5000m: 15:26.57, 10000m 32:07.78 all '08; Spanish champion 10000m 2008, 2011; at 10000m: OG: '08- 29.

Mercedes CHILLA b.19 Jan 1980 Jerez de la Frontera 1.70m 62kg. Valencia Terra i Mar.
At JT: OG: '04- dnq 22, '08- 9; WCh: '05/07/09/11: dnq 15/27/19/17; EC: '06- 3, '10- 6; WJ: '98- dnq 23; EU23: '01- 2; EJ: '99- 10; WUG: '01- 6, '03- 3; ECp: '06- 3; Won Spanish 2003-11, Ib-Am 2010. Four Spanish JT records 2000-10.
Progress at JT: 1996- 39.16, 1997- 50.08, 1998- 53.45, 1999- 55.32; new: 1999- 54.41, 2000- 57.91, 2001- 57.78, 2002- 57.78, 2003- 59.22, 2004- 62.32, 2005- 60.22, 2006- 63.20, 2007- 62.19, 2008- 61.81, 2009- 61.76, 2010- 64.07, 2011- 63.77. pbs: SP 13.66i '08, 13.30 '07; DT 34.69 '04.

Marta DOMÍNGUEZ b. 3 Nov 1975 Palencia 1.63m 52kg. Nike Running.
At 3000mSt: OG: '08- dnf; WCh: '09- 1; EC: '10- 2. At 5000m: OG: '00- h; WCh: '99- 9, '01- 2, '03- 2, '05- 14; EC: '98- 3, '02- 1, '06- 1 (7 10000m); EU23: '97- 3 (1500m 5); WCp: '02- 2; ECp: '06- 2. At 3000m: WI: '95-7-01-03-04: 6/5/4/2/4; EI: '96-8-00-02-07: 3/3/3/1/2; ECp: '96- 3. At 1500m: OG: '96- h; WCh: '95- sf; WJ: '94- 2; EJ: '93- 1. World 4k CC: '00- 14; Eur CC: '07- 1. Won Spanish 1500m 1996, 5000m 1998-2003, 10000m 2006; CC 2006.
Spanish records 3000m 2000, 10000m 2006, 3000mSt (4) 2008-09.
Progress at 3000m, 5000m, 10000m: 1990- 10:15.0, 1991- 9:47.03, 1993- 9:35.16, 1994- 9:24.10, 1995- 9:01.79i, 1996- 8:53.34i/9:06.27, 1997- 8:52.74i/9:01.96, 15:41.91; 1998- 8:44.10, 14:59.49; 1999- 8:46.14, 15:16.93; 2000- 8:28.80, 15:26.00; 2001- 8:36.33, 14:58.12; 2002- 8:47.93, 15:10.67; 2003- 8:41.14i/8:50.6+, 14:48.33; 2004- 8:51.05i,

2005- 9:05.56, 14:54.98; 2006- 8:43.45, 14:56.18, 30:51.69; 2007- 8:44.40i, 2009- 8:36.53. At 3000mSt: 2008- 9:21.76, 2009- 9:07.32, 2010- 9:17.07. pbs: 800m 2:06.1 '95, 1000m 2:50.1 '91, 1500m 4:04.27 '10, 2000m 5:46.64+i '03, HMar 70:54 '09.

Debut at 3000m steeplechase in 2008, set Spanish record in second race, but fell on last lap when in fourth place in Olympic final. Won all three steeplechases in 2009. Son Javier born in May 2011.

Nuria FERNÁNDEZ b. 16 Aug 1976 Luzern, Switzerland 1.70m 57kg. Nike Running.
At 1500m: OG: '00/04- sf; WCh: '99-01-03-05-09-11: h/12/sf/h/4/sf; EC: '02- 8, '06- h, '10- 1; WI: '01- 7; EI: '05- 7, '11- 2; WCp: '02- 7; ECp: '09- 2. At 800m: EC: '98- h; WJ: '94- h; EJ: '93/95- h. At 3000m: EI: '09- 4. Won Spanish 800m 1996, 1999, 2011; 1500m 2006, CC 2011; IbAm 1500m 2000, 2010.   Spanish 1 mile record 2008.
Progress at 1500m: 1993- 4:25.63, 1994- 4:28.78, 1996- 4:17.35, 1997- 4:25.12i/4:27.06, 1998- 4:14.05, 1999- 4:07.46, 2000- 4:06.37, 2001- 4:06.96, 2002- 4:03.99, 2003- 4:03.57, 2004- 4:03.98, 2005- 4:07.57, 2006-   4:03.37,   2008-   4:03.63+,   2009- 4:01.77i/4:02.43, 2010- 4:00.20, 2011- 4:04.64. pbs: 400m 55.79 '98, 800m 2:00.35 '08, 1000m 2:42.31i '01, 2:44.22 '05; 1M 4:21.13 '08, 2000m 5:49.63 '04, 3000m 8:38.05 '10, 10km Rd 33:01 '09, 32:54dh '10.   Daughter Candela born 17 Oct 2007.

María Teresa '**Mayte' MARTÍNEZ** b. 17 May 1976 Valladolid 1.68m 56kg. At. Mayte Martínez.
At 800m: OG: '00/04- sf; WCh: '01-05-07-09: 7/5/3/7, EC: '02- 2, '06- 7, '10- 7, WJ: '94- h; EJ: '95- 6; WI: '03- 3, '08- 4; EI: '02- 4, '05- 2; WCp: '02- 2; ECp: '03-06: 3/3. At 1500m: EI: '07- 5. Won Spanish 800m 2000-02, 2004-07, 2009; 400m 2010.   Spanish 1000m record 2007.
Progress at 800m: 1991- 2:14.48, 1992- 2:13.09, 1993- 2:07.99, 1994- 2:05.68, 1995- 2:05.00, 1996- 2:08.81i, 1997- 2:06.84, 1998- 2:05.49i, 2000- 1:59.60, 2001- 1:59.76, 2002- 1:58.29, 2003- 1:59.53i/1:59.62, 2004- 1:58.58, 2005- 1:59.40, 2006- 1:59.60, 2007- 1:57.62, 2008- 2:00.68i, 2009- 1:58.81, 2010- 1:59.12. pbs: 400m 53.67 '03, 1000m 2:33.06 '07, 1500m 4:05.05 '05.
Married her coach Juan Carlos Granado on 20 Sep 2003. Missed 2011 season through injury.

Beatriz PASCUAL b. 9 May 1982 Barcelona 1.63m 64kg. Valencia Terra i Mar.
At 20kW: OG: '08- 6; WCh: '07- 13, '09- 6, '11- 9; EC: '02- 12, '06- 20, '10- 5; EU23: '03- 4; WCp: '10- 11; ECp: '09- 6. At 10kW: WJ: '00- 6; EJ: '01- 3. Won Spanish 10000mW 2008, 2010; 20kW 2006, 2008-09, 2011.
Spanish walk records 5000m 2008 & 2009, 10000m 2010.
Progress at 20kW: 2002- 1:32:38, 2003- 1:31:31, 2004- 1:30:22, 2005- 1:32:49, 2006- 1:33:55, 2007- 1:30:37, 2008- 1:27:44, 2009- 1:29:54, 2010- 1:28:05,

2011- 1:28:51. pbs: 3000mW 13:06.48 '04, 5000mW 20:48.06 '09, 10000mW 42:40.33 '10; HMar (run) 82:43 '08.

Natalia RODRÍGUEZ b. 2 Jun 1979 Tarragona 1.64m 49kg. C.G.Tarragona.
At 1500m: OG: '00- h, '04- 10, '08- 6; WCh: '01-03-05-09-11: 6/sf/6/dq/3, EC: '02- 6, '10- 3; EU23: '99- 4, '01- 2, WJ: '98- 6, EJ: '97- 5; WI: '10- 2; EI: '09- 2; ECp: '03- 1. At 800m: WJ: '96- h. At 3000m: ET: '11- 3. Won Spanish 1500m 2000-05, 2009-10.
Spanish 1500m record 2005.
Progress at 1500m: 1995- 4:42.4, 1996- 4:38.40, 1997- 4:17.28, 1998- 4:16.20, 1999- 4:10.65, 2000- 4:04.24, 2001- 4:06.32, 2002- 4:02.84, 2003- 4:01.30, 2004- 4:03.01, 2005- 3:59.51, 2008- 4:03.19, 2009- 4:03.73/4:03.36 dq, 2010- 4:01.30, 2011- 4:01.50. pbs: 800m 2:01.35 '01, 1M 4:21.92 '08, 3000m 8:35.86 '09, 5000m 16:15.21 '11, 10km Rd 34:12 '09.
Finished first but disqualified for pushing through on inside and knocking Gelete Burka over in World 1500m 2009. Daughter Guadalupe born in November 2007.

María VASCO b. 26 Dec 1975 Barcelona 1.56m 45kg. AC.A.María Vasco.
At 20kW: OG: '00- 3, '04- 7, '08- 5; WCh: '99-01-03-05-07-09-11: 10/5/dnf/4/3/dnf/13; EC: '02- dnf, '06- 15, '10- dnf; WCp: '99-02-04-08-10: 23/8/3/5/1; ECp: '03-09-11: 3/1/4. At 10kW: OG: '96- 28; WCh: '95- 26; EC: '98- 5; EU23: '97- 2; WCp '95- 26, '97- 22. At 5000mW: WJ: '90- 15, '92- 6, '94- 4; EJ: '93- 4. Won Spanish 10kW 1996 10000mW (t) 1997-9, 2001-05; 20kW 1998, 2001-04. Spanish records 5000m (3) 1997-2007, 10,000m track (5) 1996-2001, 10km 1998, 20km (7) 1998-2008.
Progress at 10kW, 20kW: 1993- 47:11, 1994- 47:05, 1995- 44:53, 1996- 44:51.60t, 1997- 43:54, 1998- 43:02, 1:34:11; 1999- 43:35, 1:32:38; 2000- 43:33.92t, 1:30:20; 2001- 43:02.04t, 1:30:09; 2002- 43:51, 1:28:47; 2003- 44:22, 1:28:10; 2004- 44:07+, 1:27:36; 2005- 43:59, 1:28:51; 2006- 44:43+, 1:32:50; 2007- 45:28+, 1:29:17; 2008- 43:21, 1:27:25; 2009- 43:27, 1:32:53; 2010- 44:43, 1:31:55A; 2011- 44:45.18t, 1:31:41. pbs: 3000mW 12:20.44 '04, 5000mW 20:57.11 '07, HMar (running) 85:48 '07.
Only Spanish female Olympic medallist.

SRI LANKA

Governing body: Athletic Association of Sri Lanka, n°33 Torrington Avenue, Colombo 7. Founded 1922.
National Champions 2011: Men: 100m: Ashan Hasaranga 10.75, 200m: Shehan Abeypitiya 21.20, 400m: K.K.K.Senewirathne 47.25, 800m: K.P.G.P. Amarasiri 1:52.62, 1500m: Chaminda Wijekoon 3:45.01, 5000m/3000mSt: R.M.S.Pushpakumara 15:01.29/9:05.45, 10000m: Saman Kumara 30:54.80, 110mh: K.P.H.Nirmal 14.85, 400mh: H.P. Ajith Yasasiri 52.87, HJ: Manjula Kumara

Wijesekara 2.24, PV: Ruwan Pradeep Perera 4.50, LJ: W.D.M.M.S.Dissanayake 7.72, TJ: Eranda Fernando 15.97, SP: T.S.Wanniarachchi 14.74, DT: Talavou Alaileema 45.42, HT: K.Nilantha 39.62, JT: Sachith Maduranga 77.29. **Women:** 100: Jani C.Silva 12.12, 200m/400m: Chandrika Subashini 24.12/52.94, 800m: Geethani Rajasekara 2:09.73, 1500m/3000mSt: W.K.L.A.Nimali 4:26.25/10:44.92, 5000m: D.P.A.Abeyrathne 17:48.51, 10000m: Lakmini Bogahawatta 36:18.68, 100mh: Harshani Wijesinghe 14.66, 400mh: Christine Merrill 57.90, HJ: Priyangika Madumanthi 1.74, PV: K.A.K.L.Perera 3.20, LJ: N.C.D.Priyadharshani 6.15, TJ: W.M.G.Weerakoon 12.05, SP: Nadeeka Muthunayake 13.83, DT: Sonali Weerasekara 41.96, HT: Janaki Galhena 40.25, JT: Nadeeka Lakmali 55.03.

SUDAN

Governing body: Sudan Athletic Association, PO Box 13274, 11 111 Khartoum. Fd 1959.

Ismail Ahmed **ISMAIL** b. 10 Sep 1984 Khartoum 1.91m 71kg. Nike Oregon.
At 800m: OG: '04- 8, '08- 2; WCh: '03/07/11- h, '09- sf; WJ: '00- h (& h 1500m), '02- 5; AfG: '03- 5; AfCh: '04-06-08: 3/2/2 & 2 4x400m; WI: '10- 4. Sudan 800m record 2006.
Progress at 800m: 2000- 1:53.14, 2001- 1:48.2, 2002- 1:46.36, 2003- 1:46.15, 2004- 1:45.17, 2005- 1:45.32, 2006- 1:44.70, 2007- 1:47.29, 2008- 1:44.34, 2009- 1:43.82, 2011- 1:45.14. pbs: 400m 47.00 '08, 600m 1:16.16i '11, 1000m 2:18.15 '11, 1500m 3:41.97 '05.
First Olympic medallist for Sudan.

Abubaker KAKI Khamis b. 21 Jun 1989 Elmuglad 1.71m 60kg.
At 800m: OG: '08- sf; WCh: '07- h, '09- sf, '11- 2; WJ: '06- 6, '08- 1; WI: '08- 1, '10- 1; AfG: '07- 1. At 1500m: WY: '05- 3. At 4x400m: AfCh: '08- 2R. Won Pan Arab G 800m & 1500m 2007.
World junior records 800m & 1000m (& indoor 1000m) 2008. SUD records 800m (3), 1000m (2) 2008-10, 1500m 2011.
Progress at 800m, 1500m: 2005- 1:48.43, 3:45.06; 2006- 1:45.78, 3:47.58; 2007- 1:43.90, 3:47.92; 2008- 1:42.69, 3:39.71; 2009- 1:43.09, 3:39.89; 2010- 1:42.23, 2011- 1:43.13, 3:31.76. pbs: 1000m 2:13.62 '10, 10km Rd 30:18 '07.
Ran world's fastest 800m (WJR) for five years at Oslo 2008.

SWEDEN

Governing body: Svenska Friidrottsförbundet, Heliosgaten 3, 120 30 Stockholm. Founded 1895.
National Championships first held in 1896 (men), 1927 (women). **2011 Champions: Men:** 100m: Nil de Oliveira 10.65, 200m/400m: Johan Wissman 20.57w/45.82, 800m: Joni Jaako 1:53.07, 1500m: Johan Rogestedt 3:59.95, 5000m/3000mSt: Eric Senorski 14:21.57/8:39.75, 10000m/HMar: Adil Bouafif 29:50.27/64:41, Mar: Daniel Woldu 2:19:34, 110mh: Robert Kronberg 13.87, 400mh: Niclas Åkerström 52.18, HJ: Emil Svensson 2.16, PV: Alhaji Jeng 5.33, LJ: Andreas Otterling 7.97w, TJ: Christian Olsson 17.19, SP/DT: Niklas Arrhenius 18.85/63.09, HT: Mattias Jons 73.37, JT: Kim Amb 80.09, Dec: Petter Olson 7387, 10,000mW/20kW: Andreas Gustafsson 41:31.6/1:32:50, 50kW: Fredrik Svensson 4:32:30. **Women:** 100m/LJ: Carolina Klüft 11.81/6.74w, 200m/400m: Moa Hjelmer 23.16w/51.58, 800m/1500m: Viktoria Tegenfeldt 2:08.33/4:28.36, 5000m: Meraf Bahta 16:37.96, 10000m: Louise Wiker 35:27.76, HMar/Mar: Isabellah Andersson 71:07/2:37:28, 3000mSt: Charlotta Fougberg 10:13.13, 100mh: Ellinore Hallin 13.78w, 400mh: Isabelle Eriksson 60.32, HJ: Emma Tregaro Green 1.93, PV: Malin Dahlström 4.29, TJ: Khaddi Sagnia 13.49, SP: Helena Engman 15.62, DT: Anna Söderberg 50.05, HT: Tracey Andersson 68.61, JT: Anna Wessman 53.74, Hep: Ellinor Rosenquist 5316, 5000mW/10kW: Mari Olsson 23:22.8/48:53, 20kW: Siw Karlsson 1:49:14.

Christian OLSSON b. 25 Jan 1980 Göteborg 1.92m 79kg. Örgryte IS.
At TJ (/HJ): OG: '00- dnq 17, '04- 1; WCh: '01- 2, '03- 1, '11- 6; EC: '02- 1, '06- 1; EU23: '01- 1; EJ: '99- 2/1; WI: '03-04-10: 1/1/4; EI: '02- 1, '11- 5; WCp: '02- 3; ECp: '00-04: 4/1. Won WAF 2003-04, GP 2002, Swedish LJ 2006, TJ 2000-01, 2003, 2009, 2011.
Six Swedish triple jump records 2001-04. WIR 2004.
Progress at TJ: 1995- 12.20w, 1996- 12.44, 1998- 14.48, 1999- 16.30/16.59w, 2000- 16.97, 2001- 17.49, 2002- 17.80i/17.64, 2003- 17.77/17.92w, 2004- 17.83i/17.79, 2006- 17.67, 2007- 17.56, 2008- 17.00, 2009- 17.24, 2010- 17.41/17.62w, 2011- 17.29. pbs: 100m 10.9 '06, 110mh 16.21 '98, HJ 2.28i '02, 2.28 '03; PV 4.04 '99, LJ 7.71 '02, 7.84w '03.
Considered himself a high jumper, but took his TJ best from 14.48 to 16.27w in his first competition of 1999. He was easily the world number one in 2003, when unbeaten outdoors. First jumped 17m on 14 June 2001, and from then surpassed that in 108 of 117 meets to August 2010. Including qualifying he now has 110 17m plus meetings. Shared Golden League jackpot 2004. Missed 2005 season and major champs from 2007 to 2010 through injury; four operations in nine months in 2005. Competed only once in 2008 and three times in 2009. Had surgery again in September and December 2011.

Linus THÖRNBLAD b. 6 Mar 1985 Lund 1.80m 79kg. Malmö AI.
At HJ: OG: '04/08- dnq 24/26=; WCh: '07- 15, '09- 5=; EC: '06- 4, '10- 4; WJ: '02- dnq, '04- 4; WY: '01- dnq; EU23: '05- 10, '07- 1; EJ: '03- 3; WI: '06- 3; EI: '07- 2; ET: '09- 4.
Progress at HJ: 2000- 1.90i, 2001- 2.06, 2002- 2.19, 2003- 2.30, 2004- 2.27, 2005- 2.31i/2.26, 2006-

2.34, 2007- 2.38i/2.31, 2008- 2.35i/2.31, 2009-
2.36i/2.31, 2010- 2.30, 2011- 2.25. pbs: 60m 7.06i
'07, 200m 22.42 '07.

Women

Isabellah ANDERSSON b. 12 Nov 1980
Manga, Kenya 1.67m 50kg. née Isabellah Moraa
Amoro. Hässelby SK.
At Marathon: WCh: '11- 7; EC: '10- 4. Eur CC:
'09- 18. Won Swedish 5000m 2009-10, 10,000m
2008-10, HMar 2009-11, Mar 2008-12.
Swedish records: 10km road 2009, HMar 2008
and 2011, marathon (3) 2010-11.
Progression at marathon: 2006- 2:51:40, 2008-
2:34:14, 2009- 2:33:52, 2010- 2:25:10, 2011- 2:23:41,
2012- 2:25:41. Pbs: 1500m 4:30.27 '09, 3000m
9:21.8m+ '09, 5000m 15:45.08 '09, 10000m 33:32.72
'09; Road: 10km 32:24 '09, HMar 70:02 '10.
Did not seriously pursue running at home in
Kenya and first came to Sweden to learn about
orienteering, met husband-to-be Lars Andersson
(orienteering coach) and together they realised
that her best option was to focus on running.
Daughter Beyoncé was born on 25 Jan 2009. She
became a Swedish citizen on 11 May 2009.

Angelica BENGTSSON b. 8 July 1993
Väckelsång 1.64m 53kg. Hässelby SK
At PV: WJ: '10- 1; WY: '09- 1; EJ: '11- 1; YthOG: '10- 1.
Pole vault records: Two world youth 2010; four
world junior indoors 2011, two world junior
outdoor bests, Swedish 2011.
Progress at PV: 2006- 3.40, 2007- 3.90, 2008- 4.12,
2009- 4.37, 2010- 4.47, 2011- 4.63i/4.57.
IAAF Rising Star award 2010.

Emma GREEN TREGARO b. 8 Dec 1984
Bergsjön Göteborg 1.80m 62kg. Örgryte IS.
At HJ: OG: '08- 9; WCh: '05-07-09-11:
3/7=/7=/11; EC: '06- 11, '10- 2; WJ: '02- 9; EU23:
'05- 2; EJ: '03- 3; WI: '10- 5=; EI: '05- 8; CCp: '10-
2; ECp: '09- 5, '11- 1. At 200m: ECp: '06- 5. Won
Swedish HJ 2005, 2007-11 (& 5 indoors); LJ 2005.
Progress at HJ: 1998- 1.66i, 1999- 1.71, 2000-
1.75i/1.73, 2001- 1.82, 2002- 1.82, 2003- 1.86,
2004- 1.90, 2005- 1.97, 2006- 1.96i/1.92, 2007- 1.95,
2008- 1.98i/1.96, 2009- 1.96, 2010- 2.01, 2011-
1.95, 2012- 1.95i. pbs: 60m 7.42i '06, 100m 11.58
'06, 200m 23.02 '06, 400m 54.95 '06, LJ 6.41 '05,
TJ 13.69i '06, 13.39 '07.
Her uncle Göte Green ran 47.9 for 400m in 1977.
Married coach Yannick Tregaro in March 2011.

Ebba JUNGMARK b. 10 Mar 1987 Onsala
1.79m 57 kg. Mölndals AIK. Was at Washington
State University, USA.
At HJ: WCh: '07/11- dnq 23/17; EC: '10- dnq 17;
WJ: '06- 5; EU23: '07- 3; EJ: '05- 12; WI: '12- 2=;
EI: '11- 3. Wonm NCAA indoors 2008.
Progress at HJ: 2002- 1.73, 2003- 1.78, 2004-
1.77i/1.75, 2005- 1.80, 2006- 1.85i/1.84, 2007-
1.92, 2008- 1.89i/1.84, 2009- 1.86, 2010- 1.90,
2011- 1.96i/1.94, 2012- 1.95i. pbs: LJ 5.59i '09, TJ
12.15i/12.15w '04, 12.03 '03; Pen 3642 '09.

Susanna KALLUR b. 16 Feb 1981 Huntington,
New York, USA 1.70m 62kg. Falu IK. Was at
University of Illinois, USA.
At 100mh: OG: '04/08- sf; WCh: '01/03/05- sf,
'07- 4; WJ: '98- 3, '00- 1/3R; EC: '02- 7, '06- 1;
EU23: '01- 1, '03- 1; EJ: '99- 5; WCp: '06- 2; ECp:
'06- 1. At 60mh: WI: '03-04-06: 7/5/3; EI: '00-05-
07: 6/1/1 (60m: '07- 7). Won Swedish 100m
2005, 100mh 1998, 2000, 2002-05, 2007.
World indoor 60mh record 2008.
Progress at 100mh: 1997- 14.11, 1998- 13.48,
1999- 13.41, 2000- 13.02, 2001- 12.74, 2002- 12.94,
2003- 12.88, 2004- 12.67, 2005- 12.65, 2006- 12.52,
2007- 12.49, 2008- 12.54, 2010- 12.78. pbs: 50m
6.56i '00, 60m 7.24i '07, 100m 11.30 '06, 200m
23.32 '05, 50mh 6.67i '08, 60mh 7.68i '08, HJ 1.72
'98, PV 3.00i '98, LJ 6.11 '01, TJ 11.67i '97, 11.22
'98; SP 10.80i '02, Pen 3917i '02, Hep 5282 '98.
Missed 2009 season after left leg operation in
November 2008 and only three races in 2010
and none in 2011. Twin sister (a few minutes
younger) **Jenny**, who reired in Aoril 2011, had
pbs: 60mh 7.92i '05 (2 EI 05, 8 WI 06); 100mh
12.85 '05 (2 EU23 01, 6 WCh 05, 7 EC 06). Their
father Anders won four Stanley Cups at ice
hockey with the New York Islanders.

Carolina KLÜFT b. 2 Feb 1983 Sandhult, Borås
1.78m 65kg. IFK Växjö.
At Hep (LJ): OG: '04- 1 (10), '08- (9, dnq 20 TJ);
WCh: '03- 1, '05- 1, '07- 1, '11- (5); EC: '02- 1, '06-
1 (6), '10- (11); WJ: '00- 1, '02- 1; EJ: '01- 1; ECp:
'06- 1. At Pen: WI: '03- 1; EI: '02-05-07: 3/1/1. At
LJ: EU23: '03- 1, '05- 1; WI: '04- 3; ET: '11- 2. Won
SWE 100m 2003-04, 2011; 200m 2005, HJ 2004, LJ
2001-02, 2006, 2008, 2010-11; Hep 2001.
At heptathlon: two world junior records 2002,
European record 2007. SWE records: Hep (7)
2002-07, TJ (2) 2008.
Progress at LJ, Hep: 1998- 5.75, 1999- 6.13, 5162;
2000- 6.23, 6056; 2001- 6.26/6.33w, 6022; 2002-
6.48/6.59w, 6542; 2003- 6.86, 7001; 2004- 6.97,
6952; 2005- 6.87/6.92w, 6887; 2006- 6.67, 6740;
2007- 6.85, 7032; 2008- 6.87, 2009- 6.53, 2010- 6.62,
2011- 6.73/6.74w. pbs: 60m 7.40i '05, 100m 11.48
'04, 200m 22.98 '03, 400m 52.98i '08, 53.17 '02;
800m 2:08.89 '05, 60mh 8.19i '03, 100mh 13.15 '05,
HJ 1.95 '07, PV 3.16 '01, TJ 14.29 '08, SP 15.05 '06,
DT 39.92 '11, JT 50.96 '06, Pen 4948i '05.
Thirteen gold medals and two bronze in 16
major championships and won 19 successive
heptathlons 2001-07 and three successive indoor
pentathlon 2003-07. Won IAAF 'Rising Star'
award for women in 2002, when she was the
world's top heptathlete while still a junior.
Added 398 points to her Swedish indoor record
when she won 2003 World Indoor title with
4933, setting pbs at first four events. Set five pbs
en route to winning World title (for third on
world all-time list) in 2003. Her winning margin
at the Athens Olympics was the widest ever, 517
points. Set Swedish LJ record at 6.92 twice at

World indoors 2004. Won at Götzis each year 2003-07 and won the IAAF Combined Events Challenge each year 2003-06. Switched from heptathlon to LJ/TJ in 2008. Missed the 2009 Worlds through leg injury.
Her mother Ingalill had long jump pb 6.09/6.20w (1979). Married (2007) to Patrik Kristiansson (b. 3 Jun 1977, PV 5.85 '02 SWE record, 3 WCh '03, 4 EC '02, 2 EI '02).

SWITZERLAND

Governing body: Schweizerischer Leichtathletikverband (SLV), Haus des Sports, Postfach 606, 3000 Bern 22. Formed 1905 as Athletischer Ausschuss des Schweizerischen Fussball-Verbandes.
National Championships first held in 1906 (men), 1934 (women). **2011 Champions: Men**: 100m: Rolf Malcolm Fongué 10.54, 200m: Alex Wilson 20.79, 400m: Philipp Weissenberger 47.49, 800m: Mario Bächtiger 1:51.35, 1500m: Stefan Briet 3:56.42, 5000m/10000m: Rolf Rüfenacht 14:11.11/29:37.39, HMar: Lukas Ebneter 68:33, Mar: Tarcis Ançay 2:20:02, 3000mSt: Johannes Morgenthaler 9:08.07, 110mh: Andreas Kundert 13.82, 400mh: Kariem Hussein 51.09, HJ: Michael Isler 2.09, PV: Olivier Frey 5.10, LJ: Julien Fivaz 7.40, TJ: Alexandre Hochuli 15.93, SP/DT: Kukas Jost 15.80/51.90, HT: Martim Bingisser 67.90, JT: Stefan Müller 70.89, Dec: Jonas Fringeli 7489, 10000W: Paulo Ghirlanda 54:23.1, 20kW: Bernard Cossy 1:54:20. **Women**: 100m: Mujinga Kambundji 11.80, 200m: Jacqueline Gasser 23.99, 400m: Jessica Martins 54.18, 800m: Selina Büchel 2:06.47, 1500m: Monika Vogel 4:21.34, 5000m: Martina Strägl 16:36.71, 10000m: Susanne Rüegger 36:10.79. HMar/Mar: Patricia Morceli 73:01/2:37:28, 3000mSt: *Not held*; 100mh: Lisa Urech 12.89, 400mh: Valentine Arrieta 58.59, HJ: Beatrice Lundmark 1.82, PV: Anna Katharina Schmid 4.45, LJ: Irène Pusterla 6.55, TJ: Stéphanie Vaucher 13.03w, SP: Ana Zogiovic 14.48, DT: Elisabeth Graf 47.24, HT: Nicole Zihlmann 58.70, JT: Christa Wittwer 45.32. Hep: Valérie Reggel 5513, 5000W: Marie Polli 22:55.9, 10kW: Corinne Henchoz 56:58, 20kW: Laura Polli 1:40:20.

Lisa URECH b. 27 Jul 1989 Langnau im Emmenthal 1.68m 53kg. SK Langnau
At 100mh: WCh: '09- h, '11- sf; WJ: '08- sf; EC: '10- 7; EU23: '09- sf, '11- 2; EJ: '07- h. Swiss champion 2008-11.
Swiss 100mh record 2011.
Progress at 100mh: 2006- 14.51, 2007- 13.82, 2008- 13.45, 2009- 13.01, 2010- 12.81, 2011- 12.62. pbs: 60m 7.77i '08, 100m 12.28 '08, 60mh 8.00i '10

TADJIKISTAN

Governing body: Athletics Federation of Tadjikistan, Rudski Avenue 62, Dushanbe 734025. Founded 1932.

Dilshod NAZAROV b. 6 May 1982 Dushanbe 1.87m 115kg.
At HT: OG: '08- 11; WCh: '05-07-09-11: dnq 16/dnq 21/11/10; WJ: '98- dnq 15, '00- 5, AsiG: '98-02-06-10: 7/9/1/1; AsiC: '03-05-07-09: 3/2/2/1; CCp: '10- 2. Won Asi-J 1999, 2001, C.Asian 2003.
Progress at HT: 1998- 63.91, 1999- 63,56, 2000- 66.50, 2001- 68.08, 2002- 69.86, 2003- 75.56, 2004- 76.58, 2005- 77.63, 2006- 74.43, 2007- 78.89, 2008- 79.05, 2009- 79.28, 2010- 80.11, 2011- 80.30.
President of national federation.

TRINIDAD & TOBAGO

Governing body: National Association of Athletic Admistration of Trinidad & Tobago, PO Box 605, Port of Spain, Trinidad. Fd. 1945, reformed 1971.
National Champions 2011: Men: 100m: Richard Thompson 9.85, 200m: Rondel Sorrillo 20.16, 400m: Rennie Quow 45.89, 800m: Mark London 1:54.23, 1500m: Jules La Rode 4:07.70, 5000m: Denzil Ramirez 15:19.97, 110mh: Carnegie Tirado 14.63, 400mh: Jehue Gordon 48.75, HJ: Rodney Liverpool 1.85, LJ: Dwayne Herbert 7.28, TJ: Chris Hercules 15.75, SP/DT: Quincy Wilson 16.10/59.60, JT: Precious George 41.61. **Women**: 100/200m: Kai Selvon 11.19w/23.27 (drugs dq Semoy Hackett 11.00w), 200m, 400m: Afiya Walker 54.48, 800m: Dawnel Collymore 2:17.37, 1500m: Pilar McShine 4:29.29, 400mh: Janeil Bellille 59.25, LJ: Essence Mayers 5.96w, TJ: Ayanna Alexander 13.64, SP/DT: Annie Alexander 16.53/54.29, JT: Gwendolyn Smith 40.75.

Jehue GORDON b. 15 Dec 1991 Port of Spain 1.90m 77kg. adidas. Sports management student at University of West Indies, Trinidad.
At 400mh: WCh: '09- 4, '11- sf; WJ: '08- sf, '10- 1; PAm-J: '09- 2. TRI champion 2008-10.
Two TRI 400mh records 2009.
Progress at 400mh: 2008- 51.39, 2009- 48.26, 2010- 48.47, 2011- 48.66. pbs: 400m 46.43 '10, 800m 1:53.32 '10, 110mh 13.88 '10.
After 49.45 for 3rd at CAC in 2009, ran world U17 bests of 48.66 and 48.26 at World Champs.

Renny QUOW b. 25 Aug 1987 Morvant 1.70m 66kg. Zenith. Was at Florida State University and South Plains College (Texas).
At 400m/4x400mR: OG: '08- 7; WCh: '05-07-09-11: hR/h/3/sf; WJ: '04- sf, '06- 1; PAm: '07- sf; CAG: '06- sf/2R; WI: '12- 3R. Won CAC 2008, 2011; CAC-J 2004, 2006; TRI 2007-09, 2011.
Progress at 400m: 2004- 46.60, 2005- 45.82, 2006- 45.74, 2007- 45.35, 2008- 44.82, 2009- 44.53, 2010- 45.10, 2011- 44.84. pbs: 200m 20.61 '09, 300m 32.55 '09.
One of triplets with Ronald and Ryan.

Rondell SORRILLO b. 21 Jan 1986 La Brea, Kentucky, USA 1.78m 62kg. Zenith. Was at University of Kentuckuy, USA.

At 200m: OG: '08- qf; WCh: '09- sf, '11- 7. Won NCAA 2010, TRI 2009; 2nd CAC 2008-09, 2011. Progress at 200m: 2006- 20.97, 2007- 21.20, 2008- 20.43, 2009- 20.45, 2010- 20.29, 2011- 20.16. pbs: 60m 6.60i '09, 100m 10.17 '11, 10.05w '10; 400m 48.06 '10.

Richard THOMPSON b. 7 Jun 1985 Cascade 1.87m 79kg. Memphis. Was at Louisiana State University.
At 100m: OG: '08- 2/2R; WCh: '07- qf, '09- 5/2R, '11- sf; PAm: '07- h. Won TRI 100m 2009-11, 200m 2010; NCAC 100m 2007, NCAA 100m & 60m indoor 2008.
Progress at 100m, 200m: 2004- 10.65, 2005- 10.47, 21.73; 2006- 10.27/10.26w, 21.24; 2007- 10.09/9.95w, 20.90; 2008- 9.89, 20.18; 2009- 9.93, 20.65; 2010- 10.01/9.89w, 20.37; 2011- 9.85. pbs: 60m 6.45+ '09, 6.51i '08.

Women

Kelly-Ann BAPTISTE b. 14 Oct 1986 Plymouth, Tobago 1.60m 54kg. Studied psychology at Louisiana State University.
At 100m/(200m): OG: '08- qf; WCh: '05- qf, '09: sf/sf, '11- 3; WJ: '02- sf, '04- (4); WY: '03- 3; PAm: '03- h; CCp: '10- 1/1R. Won NCAA 100m & indoor 60m 2008, TRI 100m 2005-06, 2008-10; 200m 2005.
TRI records: 100m (5) 2005-10, 200m (5) 2005-09.
Progress at 100m, 200m: 2002- 11.71, 24.03; 2003- 11.48, 23.22; 2004- 11.40, 23.41/22.99w; 2005- 11.17/11.04w, 22.93; 2006- 11.08, 22.73; 2007- 11.22, 22.90i/22.95; 2008- 11.06/10.97w, 22.67; 2009- 10.94/10.91w, 22.60; 2010- 10.84, 22.78/22.58w; 2011- 10.90. pbs: 55m 6.73i '06, 60m 7.13i '08.

Cleopatra BOREL-BROWN b. 3 Oct 1979 Port of Spain 1.68m 93kg. Was at University of Maryland; assistant coach at Virginia Tech University.
At SP: OG: '04- 10, '08- dnq 17; WCh: '05/07/09/11- dnq 19/18/13/1; CG: '02- 4, '06- 3, '10- 2; PAm: '03- 6, '07- 3, '11- 2; CAG: '06- 3, '10- 1; WI: '04-06-08: dnq 11/8/7. Won CAC 2008, 2011; TRI 2002, 2004, 2006-10.
Eight TRI records at shot 2004-11.
Progress at SP: 2000- 14.64i, 2001- 16.44, 2002- 17.50i/16.90, 2003- 17.95i/17.79, 2004- 19.48i/18.90, 2005- 18.44, 2006- 18.81, 2007- 18.91, 2008- 18.87, 2009- 18.52, 2010- 19.30, 2011- 19.42. pb HT 51.28 '01.

Josanne LUCAS b. 14 May 1984 Scarborough, Tobago 1.70m 55kg. Graduate of mechanical sciences from Auburn University.
At 400mh: OG: '08- h; WCh: '05- h, '09- 3; PAm-J: '03- 2. Won CAC 400mh 2008, TRI 400m 2005, 100mh 2006, 2009; 400mh 2004, 2008-09.
TRI records 100mh (5) 2006, 400mh (10) 2003-09.
Progress at 400mh: 2002- 62.21, 2003- 57.81, 2004- 56.96, 2005- 55.59, 2006- 55.29, 2007- 56.19, 2008- 55.46, 2009- 53.20, 2010- 54.84, 2011- 56.86.

pbs: 200m 23.65 '09, 23.64w '10; 400m 53.59 '05, 55mh 7.64i '06, 60mh 8.20i '06, 100mh 12.99 '09, 12.98w '06. First TRI woman to win a medal at World Champs or Olympic Games.

TUNISIA

Governing body: Fédération Tunisienne d'Athlétisme, B.P. 264, Cité Mahrajane 1082, Tunis. Founded 1957.

Women

Habiba GHRIBI–Boudraa b. 9 Apr 1984 Kairouan 1.70m 57kg.
At 3000mSt: OG: '08- 13; WCh: '05- h, '09- 6, '11- 2; AfCh: '06- 2. At 5000m: AfCh: '02- 11.
Tunisian records: 3000m (2) 2008-11, 3000mSt (8) 2005-11.
Progress at 3000mSt: 2005- 9:51.49, 2006- 10:14.36, 2007- 9:50.04, 2008- 9:25.50, 2009- 9:12.52, 2011- 9:11.97. pbs: 1500m: 4:12.37 '09, 3000m 8:56.22 '11, 5000m 16:12.9 '03, 10000m 35:03.83 '05, 10kmRd 33:30 '04.
Missed 2010 season after toe surgery.

TURKEY

Governing body: Türkiye Atletizm Federasyonu, 19 Mayis Spor Kompleksi, Ulus-Ankara. Founded 1922.
National Champions 2011: Men: 100m: Yigitcan Hekimoglu 10.66, 200m: Ali Ekber Kayas 21.43, 400m: Serder Tamaç 46.46, 800m: Emrah Çoban 1:52.72, 1500m/3000m: Erdinç Ekin 3:50.47/8:27.39, 5000m: Ugur Koçlardan 14:55.14, 10000m: Ramazan Ismel 33:11.86, Mar: Bekir Karayel 2:15:48, 3000mSt: M.Emin Tan 8:46.43, 110mh: Oktay Gunes 14.54 13.9, 400mh: Tuncay Örs 52.06, HJ: Serhat Birinci 2.10, PV: Mustafa Kivanç 4.40, LJ: Alper Kulaksiz 7.49, TJ: Ferhat Çiçek 14.81, SP: Mehmet Ali Çalidan 17.55, DT: Ercüment Olgundeniz 61.68, HT: Esref Apak 78.04, JT: Muhammet Mavis 59.24, Dec: Hikmet Tugsuz 6535, 20kW: Kemal Gelecek 1:36:01. **Women**: 100m/200m: Nimet Karakus 11.68/23.84, 400m: Birsen Engin 52.4, 800m: Yeliz Kurt 2:01.25, 1500m: Gamze Bulut 4:18.23, 3000m: Duda Karakaya 9:23.12, 5000m: Esma Aydemir 16:28.22, 10000m: Nilay Esen 35:55.40, Mar: Sultan Haydar 2:35:06, 100mh: Nevin Yanit 13.25, 400mh: Nagehan Karadere 55.67, HJ: Candeger Oguz 1.78, PV: Buse Arikazan 3.40, LJ: Pinar Aday 5.91, TJ: Mukadder Yilmaz-Ulusoy 12.82, SP: Nilgün Öztürk 15.54, DT: Gökçe Çelenk 50.02, HT: Zeliha Uzunbilek 61.87, JT: Gülistan Aslan 39.48, Hep: Pinar Aday 5325, 20kW: Semiha Mutlu 1:40:45.

Tarik Langat AKDAG (ex Patrick LANGAT) b. 16 Jun 1988 1.72m 54kg.
Progress at 3000mSt: 2004- 8:53.6A, 2005- 8:40.3A, 2006- 8:37.4A, 2007- 8:46.8A, 2008- 8:19.13, 2009- 8:21.38, 2010- 8:09.12, 2011- 8:08.59. pbs: 3000m 7:47.68 '10, 2M 8:26.96 '10, 5000m

13:45.21A '06, 10000m 29:03.1 '06.
Switched from Kenya to Turkey 22 Jun 2011 with 2-year wait for international eligibility.

Fatih AVAN b. 1 Jan 1989 Kahraman Maras 1.80m 87kg. Sport Kulubu Fenerbahce.
At JT: WCh: '09: dnq 19, '11- 5; EU23: '09- 7, '11- 2; WUG: '11- 1. Won Med G 2009.
Seven Turkish javelin records 2009-11.
Progress at JT: 2006- 61.40, 2007- 66.28, 2008- 71.73, 2009- 79.78, 2010- 79.13, 2011- 84.79.

Ramil GULIYEV b. 29 May 1990 Baku 1.87m 73kg. Baku
At (100m/)200m: OG: '08- qf; WCh: '09- 7; WJ: '06- (h), '08- 5; WY: '07- 2; EJ: '09- 2/1; WUG: '09- 1. At 60m: EI: '09- 7.
Records: European Junior 200m 2009; AZE 100m (2) 2009, 200m (4) 2007-09; TUR 100m (2) & 200m 2011.
Progress at 200m: 2006- 21.74, 2007- 20.72, 2008- 20.66, 2009- 20.04, 2010- 20.73, 2011- 20.32. pbs: 60m 6.58i '12, 100m 10.08 '09, 300m 33.62i '09.
Switched from Azerbaijan to Turkey on 26 Apr 2011, but not eligible to compete for Turkey until 1 Mar 2014.

Ilham Tanui ÖZBILEN (formerly William Biwott Tanui KEN) b. 5 Mar 1990 Keiyo, Kenya 1.77m 60kg.
At 1500m: WI: '12- 2; won WAF 2009.
Records: World 4x1500m & world junior 1M 2009; Turkish 800m (3), 1500m 2011.
Progress at 800m, 1500m: 2008- 3:42.5A, 2009- 3:31.70, 2010- 3:33.67, 2011- 1:44.25, 3:31.37. pbs: 1000m 2:17.08 '11, 1M 3:49.29 '09, 3000m 7:50.61i '12.

Women

Elvan ABEYLEGESSE b. 11 Sep 1982 Addis Ababa, Ethiopia 1.59m 40kg. Enka.
At 5000m/(10000m): OG: '04- 12 (8 1500m), '08- 2/2; WCh: '01- h, '03- 5, '07- 5/2, '09- (dnf); EC: '02- 7, '06- 3/dnf, '10- 2/1; WJ: '00- 6 (6 1500m); WY: '99- (5 3000m); EU23: '03- 1; EJ: '99- 2, '01- 1 (1 3000m); CCp: '10- 4; ECp: '06-07-08: (1/1/1).
Won WAF 5000m 2003-04, Med G 10000m 2009.
World CC: '99- 9J; Eur CC: '00-01-02-03: 3J/1J/3/2.
Records: World 5000m 2004, European 10000m 2008. Turkish 2000m 2003, 3000m 2002, 5000m 2004, 10000m 2006 & 2008, HMar 2010.
Progress at 1500m, 5000m, 10000m: 1999- 4:24.1, 16:06.40; 2000- 4:18.7, 16:33.77; 2001- 4:11.31, 15:21.12, 33:29.20; 2002- 4:11.00, 15:00.49; 2003- 4:07.25, 14:53.56; 2004- 3:58.28, 14:24.68; 2005- 15:08.59; 2006- 4:11.61, 14:59.29, 30:21.67; 2007- 15:00.88, 31:25.15; 2008- 14:58.79, 29:56.34; 2009- 15:30.47, 31:51.98; 2010- 4:15.23, 14:31.52, 31:10.23. pbs: 800m 2:07.10 '04, 2000m 5:33.83 '03, 3000m 8:31.94 '02, Rs: 15km 49:41 '10, HMar 67:07 '10.
Known as Hewan Abeye ETH, then Elvan Can on move to Turkey. She became the first Turkish athlete to set a world record in 2004 and the first Turkish woman to win an Olympic medal in 2008. Married Semeneh Debelie ETH on 25 Feb 2011, their daughter Arsema was born on 28 July 2011.

Alemitu BEKELE Degfa b. 17 Sep 1977 Shoa, Ethiopia 1.65m 48kg. Üsküdar Belediyesi – Istanbul.
At 5000m: OG: '08- 7; WCh: '09- 13 (h 1500m), '11- h; EC: '10- 1; EU23: '99- 14; At 3000m: WI: '10- 5; EI: '09- 1; CCp: '10- 2. World CC: '95- 7J, '99- 6 4k. Won Balkan 5000m 2007, TUR 1500m 2010, 5000m 2008.
European indoor 5000m record 2010.
Progress at 1500m, 5000m: 1999- 4:17.92, 16:26.54; 2000- 4:11.28, 2007- 4:12.68, 16:47.08; 2008- 4:06.32, 15:05.85; 2009- 4:13.69, 15:18.18; 2010- 4:02.2, 14:36.79; 2011- 15:08.86. pbs: 800m 2:05.66 '00, 1M 4:33.46 '08, 3000m 8:35.19 '10, 20km Rd 71:42 '10.
Competed six times for Ethiopia (winning team medals each time) in World CC from 1991-9, but then transferred to Turkey and ran briefly under married name of Almitu Colakoglu. Returned to competition and to Turkey in 2007 after birth of children.

Binnaz USLU b. 12 Mar 1985 Ankara 1.65m 55kg. ENKA Istanbul.
At 3000mSt: WCh: '11- 7; EC: '10- h (h 1500m); WUG: '11- 1 (1 5000m). At 800m: OG: '04- h; WCh: '05- h; WJ: '04- dns; WUG: '05- 2. At 3000m: EJ: '03- 2. At 5000m: EU23: '05- 1. Eur CC: '03- 10J, '04- 1J, '06- 1 U23, '10- 2.
Turkish 3000m steeplechase 2011.
Progress at 3000mSt: 2006- 10:17.48, 2007- 9:48.46, 2008- 9:31.58, 2009- 10:08.64, 2010- 10:00.88, 2011- 9:24.06. pbs: 400m 56.14 '05, 800m 2:00.94 '04, 1000m 2:41.79 '06, 1500m 4:11.36 '10, 1M 4:40.70 '06, 3000m 9:06.82 '10, 5000m 15:41.15 '11, 10000m 34:34.79 '06.
Two-year drugs ban 2007-09.

Nevin YANIT b. 16 Feb 1986 Mersin 1.68m 60kg. Fenerbahce SK.
At 100mh: OG: '08- sf; WCh: '07/09/11- sf; EC: '06- h, '10- 1; WJ: '04- h; EU23: '07- 1; EJ: '05- sf; WUG: '07- 2, '09- 1; CCp: '10- 4. Won Med G 2009, TUR 2008-09.
Six Turkish 100mh records 2006-10.
Progress at 100mh: 2003- 15.25, 2004- 13.75A/13.66w, 2005- 13.45A, 2006- 12.88, 2007- 12.76, 2008- 12.76/12.72w, 2009- 12.89, 2010- 12.63, 2011- 13.07. pbs: 100m 11.71 '08, 200m 23.74 '08, 60mh 8.00i '07.

UGANDA

Governing body: Uganda Athletics Federation, PO Box 22726, Kampala. Founded 1925.

Jacob ARAPTANY b. 11 Feb 1992 1.86m 61kg.
At 3000mSt: WCh: '11- 6; WJ: '10- 3; AfG: '11- 5; Af-J: '11- 5. World CC: '11- 9J.
Progress at 3000mSt: 2009- 8:26.4A, 2010- 8:28.14,

2011- 8:15.72A. pbs: 800m 1:49.95A '11, 1500m 3:36.16A '11, 2000mSt 5:28.48 '11.

Benjamin KIPLAGAT b. 4 Mar 1989 Magoro 1.86m 61kg.
At 3000mSt: OG: '08- 9; WCh: '07- h, '09- 11, '11- 10; CG: '10- 4; WJ: '06- 6, '08- 2; AfG: '07- 7; AfCh: '10- 5; CCp: '10- 4. World CC: '07- 5J, '08- 4J.   Six Ugandan 3000mSt records 2007-10.
Progress at 3000mSt: 2005- 8:39.1A, 2006- 8:34.14, 2007- 8:21.73, 2008- 8:14.29, 2009- 8:12.98, 2010- 8:03.81, 2011- 8:08.43. pbs: 1500m 3:38.86 '09, 3000m 7:46.50 '10, 5000m 13:22.67 '07, 10000m 29:03.1 '06.

Moses KIPSIRO b. 2 Sep 1986 Chesimat 1.74m 59kg.
At 5000m(/10000m): OG: '08- 4; WCh: '05- h, '07- 3, '09- 4; CG: '06- 7, '10- 1/1; AfG: '07- 1, '11- 1; Af Ch: '06- 3/1, '10- 4/2; CCp: '10- 2 (2 3000m). At 3000m: WI: "12- 7. World CC: '03-05-08-09-10-11: 18J/20J/13/2/3/11.
Ugandan records: 3000m (4) 2005-09, 5000m 2007.
Progress at 5000m: 2005- 13:13.81, 2006- 13:01.88, 28:03.46; 2007- 12:50.72, 2008- 12:54.70, 2009- 12:59.27, 2010- 13:00.15, 27:33.37A; 2011- 13:09.17. pbs: 1500m 3:37.6 '08, 2000m 5:00.66+ '11, 3000m 7:30.95 '09, 2M 8:08.16i '12.
Sealed brilliant 5k/10k double at 2010 CG with last laps of 53.01 and 53.96.

UKRAINE

Governing body: Ukrainian Athletic Federation, P.O. Box 607, Kiev 01019. Founded 1991.
National Champions 2011: **Men**: 100m/200m: Igor Bodrov 10.32/20.81, 400m: Volodymyr Burakov 46.70, 800m: Oleksandr Osmolovych 1:47.64, 1500m: Oleksandr Borysyuk 3:40.58, 5000m: Sergiy Lebid 13:34.42, Mar: Oleksandr Sitkovskyy 2:09:26, 3000mSt: Ilya Sukharyev 8:34.50, 110mh: Sergiy Kopanayko 14.05, 400mh: Stanislav Melnykov 49.68, HJ: Bohdan Bondar– enko, PV: Denys Yurchenko 5.42, LJ: Andriy Makarchev 7.81, TJ: Yevgen Semenenko 16.76, SP: Andriy Semenov 20.63, DT: Ivan Hryshyn 64.96, HT: Oleksiy Sokryskyy 75.32, JT: Oleksandr Pyatnytsya 78.64, Dec: Yevhen Nikitin 7795, 20kW: Ruslan Dmyrenko 1:24:52, 35kW: Oleksiy Kazanin 2:35:27, 50kW: Sergiy Budza 4:00:02. **Women**: 100m: Darya Pizhankova 11.57, 200m: Hrystyna Stuy 22.93, 400m: Daryna Prystupa 52.28, 800m: Yuliya Krevsun 2:00.11, 1500m: Anzhelika Shevchenko 4:07.29, 5000m: Olga Skrypak 16:03.96, Mar: Kateryna Karmanenko 2:43:15, 3000mSt: Svitlana Shmidt 9:46.91, 100mh: Yevgeniya Snigur 13.32, 400mh: Anastasiya Lebid 59.01, HJ: Oksana Okunyeva 1.93, PV: Kseniya Chertkoshvili 4.20, LJ: Viktoriya Rybalko 6.87, TJ: Ruslana Tsyhotska 13.97, SP: Halyna Obleshchuk 16.89, DT: Natalya Semenova 59.50, HT: Nataliya Zolotuhina 68.17, JT: Vira Rebryk 58.97, Hep: Lyudmyla Yosypenko 6318, 20kW: Nadiya Borovska 1:33:22.

Roman AVRAMENKO b. 23 Mar 1988 Kirovske 1.85m 90kg. Dynamo Krym.
At JT: OG: '08- dnq 29; WCh: '09- dnq 22, '11- 6; EC: '10- 8; WJ: '04 dnq, 06- 3; WY: '03- 5, '05- 2; EU23: '09- 4; EJ: '07- 2; WUG: '11- 2; ET: '09- 4. Won UKR 2008.   UKR javelin record 2011.
Progress at JT: 2003- 61.95, 2004- 72.68, 2005- 70.27, 2006- 76.01, 2007- 77.88, 2008- 80.08, 2009- 79.50, 2010- 81.12, 2011- 84.30.

Dmytro DEMYANYUK b. 2 Sep 1984 Lviv 1.95m 70kg.
At HJ: OG: '08- dnq 26=; WCh: '07- dnq 25, '11- 12=; EC: '10- dnq 21=; ET: '11- 1. Won UKR 2010.
Progress at HJ: 2002- 2.15, 2003- 2.15i, 2004- 2.26, 2005- 2.26, 2006- 2.15, 2007- 2.32, 2008- 2.30i/2.25, 2009- 2.31, 2010- 2.31i/2.28, 2011- 2.35.
Father Oleksiy had HJ best of 2.33 '81 (11th OG 1980, USSR champion 1982); mother Tetyana Markenyuk pb 1.85.

Sheryf EL-SHERYF b. 2 Jan 1989 Simpheropol 1.83m 73kg. Dnipropetrovskaya. Student.
At TJ: WCh: '11- 12; WJ: '06- 5, '08- 9; WY: '05- 5; EU23: '11- 1; EJ: '07- 6.
Progress at TJ: 2004- 15.53, 2005- 16.18, 2006- 16.30, 2007- 16.10, 2008- 16.60i/16.35, 2009- 15.90i/15.52, 2010- 16.56i/16.42, 2011- 17.72. pb LJ 7.99 '11.
Huge breakthrough at 2011 European U23s, improving pb from 16.92 to 16.99, 17.04 and then 17.72. His father, a gynaecologist, comes from Sudan.

Oleksiy KASYANOV b. 26 Aug 1985 Stakhanov, Lugansk 1.91m 84kg. Spartak Zaporozhye.
At Dec: OG: '08- 7; WCh: '09- 4, '11- 12; EC: '10- dnf; EU23: '07- 4; WUG: '07- 4; ECp: '09- 3. UKR champion 2008. At Hep: WI: '10- 6, '12- 2; EI: '09- 2.
Progress at Dec: 2006- 7599, 2007- 7964, 2008- 8238, 2009- 8479, 2010- 8381, 2011- 8251. pbs: 60m 6.83i '09, 100m 10.51 '09, 400m 47.46 '08, 1000m 2:42.41i '12, 1500m 4:22.27 '08, 60mh 7.99i '09, 110mh 14.24 '10, HJ 2.06i/2.05 '09, PV 4.82 '09, LJ 8.04i '10, 7.88 '10, SP 15.72 '09, DT 51.95 '10, JT 55.84 '07, Hep 6254i '10.
Won Talence decathlon 2009.

Viktor KUZNETSOV b. 14 Jul 1986 Zaporozhye 1.90m 67kg. Kiev Dynamo.
At TJ (LJ): OG: '08- 8; WCh: '09- (dnq 17); EC: '06- (4), '10- 4; WJ: '04- 3; EI: '07- 7; WUG: '07- 2, '11- 2; ET: '10- 1, '11- 3.
World junior long jump best (indoors) 2005.
Progress at LJ, TJ: 2002- 6.89, 2003- 8.12i, 15.17; 2004- 16.84i/16.58, 2005- 8.22i, 16.51i; 2006- 7.96/8.25w, 16.35i/16.17; 2007- 7.74, 16.94; 2008- 17.16, 2009- 8.09, 2010- 8.11i, 17.29; 2011- 17.01.

Maksym MAZURYK b. 2 Apr 1983 Donetsk 1.90m 85kg.
At PV: OG: '08- dnq 16=; WCh: '07- 11, '09- 4; EC: '06- 8, '10- 2; WJ: '02- 1; EU23: '03- 3, '05- 6; WI: '08-6; CCp: '10- 4; ET: '11- 1; won WAF 2009, UKR 2010.

Progress at PV: 1999- 4.49i, 2000- 4.90, 2001- 5.00, 2002- 5.55, 2003- 5.50i/5.45, 2004- 5.75, 2005- 5.65, 2006- 5.70, 2007- 5.76, 2008- 5.82, 2009- 5.80, 2010- 5.80, 2011- 5.88i/5.72.
In 2011 he married Nataliya Kushch (b. 5 Mar 1983) – PV pb 4.52 '08, 2 EJ '01, 1 EU23 '05.

Women

Yelizaveta BRYZGINA b. 28 Nov 1989 Lugansk 1.72m 56kg. Student at Lugansk National teachers' training institute.
At (100m)/200m/4x100mR: WCh: '11- sf; EC: '10- 2/1R; WJ: '08- h/h; EJ: '07- 2/2R; WUG: '11- 1R; CCp: '10- 2/2R; ET: '10- 1. Won BLR 2006-10.
Progress at 200m: 2004- 24.13, 2005- 24.32, 2006- 24.24, 2007- 23.47, 2008- 23.37, 2009- 22.99, 2010- 22.44, 2011- 23.02. pbs: 60m 7.37i '09, 100m 11.44 '07, 400m 54.29i '11.
Parents were Viktor Bryzgin (1 4x100m OG '80, EC '86, 2 WCh '07; 100m 10.03w?/10.11 '86) and Olga Vladykina (400m/400mR: OG '80: 1/1R, '92- 2/1R; WCh: '87- 1/2R, '91- 4/1R; EC: '86- 2, 48.27 '85, 200m 22.44 '85).

Nataliya DOBRYNSKA b. 29 May 1982 Khmelnitsky 1.80m 77kg. Vinnitsa K.
At Hep: OG: '04- 8, '08- 1; WCh: '05- 9, '07- 8, '09- 4 (LJ dnq 20). '11- 5; EC: '06- 6, '10- 2; EU23: '03- 5; EJ: '01- 10. At Pen: WI: '04-08-10-12: 2/4/2/1; EI: '05- 3, '07- 5.
World indoor pentathlon record 2012.
Progress at Hep: 1999- 5226, 2000- 5322, 2001- 5742, 2002- 5936, 2003- 5877, 2004- 6387, 2005- 6299, 2006- 6356, 2007- 6327, 2008- 6733, 2009- 6558, 2010- 6778, 2011- 6539. pbs: 100m 11.60/11.2 '95, 200m 24.23 '10, 800m 2:11.15i '12, 2:11.34 '11; 60mh 8.33i '10, 100mh 13.43 '11, HJ 1.86 '06, LJ 6.63 '08, 6.73w '09; SP 17.29 '08, JT 49.25 '10, Pen 5013i '12.
Four pbs en route to UKR pentathlon record 4727 and WI silver medal 2004. Five pbs in Olympic gold performance 2008 including world heptathlon shot best and four pbs in EC 2nd 2010. Won Götzis and Talence and IAAF Combined Events Challenge 2009. Older sister Viktoriya (b. 18 Jan 1980) has pb 5787 '08.

Kateryna KARSAK b. 26 Dec 1985 Odessa 1.83m 88kg. Dynamo Odessa.
At DT: OG: '08- dnq 21; WCh: '07/09/11- dnq 15/27/20; EC: '06- 4, '10- dnq 15; EU23: '07- 1; WJ: '04- dnq; WUG: '09- 3; ET: '11- 1. Won UKR 2006-07, 2009-10.
Progress at DT: 2001- 47.29, 2003- 52.28, 2004- 56.04, 2005- 58.65, 2006- 62.75, 2007- 64.40, 2008- 62.56, 2009- 61.77, 2010- 60.82, 2011- 63.52. pb SP 13.59 '06.
Her father Yevgeniy Karsak had HT best 74.14 (1979) and mother Valentyna DT 63.92 (1984),

Yuliya KREVSUN b. 8 Dec 1980 Vinnytsya 1.78m 66kg. née Gurtovenko. Fenerbahce Spor Kulübü, Turkey.
At 800m: OG: '08- 7; WCh: '03/07- h, '09- 4, '11-

sf; EC: '02- h, '10- h; EJ: '99- 2; EU23: '01- h; WUG: '07- 1; ECp: '07-09: 2/1; UKR champion 2002, 2007, 2010-11.
Progress at 800m: 1997- 2:10.30, 1998- 2:07.67, 1999- 2:03.81, 2000- 2:02.18, 2001- 2:01.07, 2002- 2:00.49, 2003- 2:01.08, 2004- 2:00.83, 2006- 2:03.25, 2007- 1:57.83, 2008- 1:57.32, 2009- 1:58.00, 2010- 1:58.97, 2011- 1:59.32. pbs: 400m 52.45 '07, 600m 1:26.8+ '09, 1000m 2:39.53i '11, 2:41.65 '06; 1500m 4:13.43i '07.
Son Danil born 21 Apr 2005.

Anna MELNYCHENKO b. 24 Apr 1983 Tbilisi, Georgia 1.78m 59kg.
At Hep: OG: '08- 14; WCh: '07- dnf, '09- 6; EC: '06- 16, '10- dnf; EU23: '05- 13; WUG: '07- 3; ECp: '07-08-09-10: 3/1/1/1. Won UKR 2003.
Progress at Hep: 2001- 4907, 2002- 5083, 2003- 5523, 2004- 5720, 2005- 5809, 2006- 6055w, 2007- 6143, 2008- 6306/6349u, 2009- 6445, 2010- 6098. pbs: 200m 24.11 '09, 24.08w '06; 800m 2:12.85 '09, 60mh 8.33i '07, 100mh 13.28 '08, HJ 1.86 '07, LJ 6.43 '09, 6.51w '06; TJ 13.21/13.40w '03, SP 13.99 '08, JT 45.11 '09, Pen 4748i '12.
Married to William Frullani ITA (Dec 7984 '02, Hep 5972 rec 6th EI '09).

Anna MISHCHENKO b. 25 Aug 1983 1.66m 51kg. Kharkov Dyn.
At 1500m: OG: '08- 9; WCh: '09/11- sf; EC: '10- 11; WUG: '11- 2; ET: '11- 3; won UKR 2010.
Progress at 1500m: 2003- 4:21.41, 2004- 4:14.09, 2005- 4:19.74, 2006- 4:12.17, 2007- 4:14.57, 2008- 4:05.13, 2009- 4:06.45, 2010- 4:03.14, 2011- 4:01.73. pbs: 800m 2:02.44 '11, 1000m 2:39.00 '08, 2000m 5:46.36 '09, 3000m 9:11.09i '11, 9:17.99 '07.

Anastasiya RABCHENYUK b. 14 Sep 1983 Ternovka 1.77m 64kg.
At 400mh: OG: '08- 4; WCh: '07- h, '09- 7, '11- 5; EC: '06- 8, '10- h; WY: '99- h; EJ: '01- 7; EU23: '06- 6; WUG: '03- 3. '07- 2; ECp: '08-09-10: 1/2/3&2R. UKR champion 2003-08.
Progress at 400mh: 1999- 60.88, 2000- 58.01, 2001- 59.31, 2002- 58.38, 2003- 56.30, 2004- 56.39, 2005- 56.14, 2006- 54.73, 2007- 55.48, 2008- 53.96, 2009- 54.49, 2010- 55.29, 2011- 54.18. pbs: 400m 52.64 '06, 800m 2:10.5i '09, 60mh 8.56i '07, 100mh 14.21 '07.
Married Sergiy Basenko (110mh 14.42 '04) in October 2008.

Vira REBRYK b. 25 Feb 1989 Yalta 1.76m 65kg.
At JT: OG: '08- dnq 16; WCh: '09- 9, '11- dnq 16; EC: '10- dnq 17; WJ: '06- 2, '08- 1; WY: '05- 2; EU23: '09- 2; EJ: '07- 1; WUG: '09- 2. '11- 4. Won UKR 2010-11.
World junior javelin record 2008.
Progress at JT: 2003- 44.94, 2004- 52.47, 2005- 57.48, 2006- 59.64, 2007- 58.48, 2008- 63.01, 2009- 62.26, 2010- 63.36, 2011- 61.60.

Viktoriya 'Vita' RYBALKO b. 26 Oct 1982 Dnepropetrovsk 1.77m 60kg. Zaporiziya. Was at Universities of Maine and Rochester, USA.

At LJ: OG: '08- dnq 23; WCh: '07- 11, '09/11-dnq 17/15; EC: '06- 4, '10- 4; WI: '10- 8; EI: '07- 7. UKR champion 2011
Progress at LJ: 1999- 6.43, 2000- 6.17, 2002- 6.08, 2004- 6.30, 2005- 6.34, 2006- 6.82/6.87w, 2007- 6.41/6.70w, 2008- 6.87i/6.70, 2009- 6.70, 2010- 6.74/6.78w, 2011- 6.87. pb TJ 13.95 '11.

Olga SALADUHA b. 4 Jun 1983 Donetsk 1.75m 55kg.
At TJ: OG: '08- 9; WCh: '07- 7, '11- 1; EC: '06- 4, '10- 1; WJ: '02- 5; EU23: '05- 4; EJ: '01- 9; WI: '08- 6; WUG: '05- 2, '07- 1; WCp: '06- 6, '10- 2; ECp: '06-08-10-11: 1/1/1/1. UKR champion 2007-08.
Progress at TJ: 1998- 13.32, 1999- 12.86, 2000- 13.26, 2001- 13.48, 2002- 13.66i/13.63, 2003- 13.26i/13.03, 2004- 13.22, 2005- 14.04, 2006- 14.41/14.50w, 2007- 14.79, 2008- 14.84, 2010- 14.81, 2011- 14.98/15.06w. pb LJ 6.37 '06.

Irina SEKACHYOVA b. 21 Jul 1976 Vasil'kov 1.65m 72kg. Vasil'kov Dyn.
At HT: OG: '00- dnq 16, '04- 8, '08- dnq 25; WCh: '03/09- dnq 23/27, '05- 6; EC: '98- dnq, 02- dnq 14, '06- 8; ECp: '02-04-06: 3/1/3. UKR champion 1996, 2000-06, 2008-09.
Eight Ukraine hammer records 1998-2006.
Progress at HT: 1995- 53.64, 1996- 55.42, 1997- 56.46, 1998- 62.83, 1999- 65.93, 2000- 69.53, 2001- 67.00, 2002- 68.70, 2003- 72.96, 2004- 74.16, 2005- 70.30, 2006- 74.31, 2007- 71.83, 2008- 74.52, 2009- 73.07, 2010- 70.25, 2011- 70.31.

Vita STYOPINA b. 21 Feb 1976 Zaporozhye 1.78m 58kg. Nikolayev U.
At HJ: OG: '96- dnq 19=, '04- 3, '08- 12=; WCh: '99-03-05-11: 7/9=/7/dnq 18; EC: '98- 7, '10- 6=; WJ: '94- 6; EJ: '95- 1; WI: '04- 8, '06- 7; ECp: '08- 2=, '11- 2. Won UKR 1996, 1999, 2004, 2008-09.
Progress at HJ: 1992- 1.83, 1993- 1.89, 1994- 1.86, 1995- 1.92, 1996- 1.92, 1997- 1.93, 1998- 1.94, 1999- 1.96, 2000- 1.96, 2001- 1.94, 2002- 1.92, 2003- 2.00, 2004- 2.02, 2005- 1.95i/1.93, 2006- 1.99i/1.90, 2007- 1.94, 2008- 1.95, 2009- 1.92i/1.90, 2010- 1.95, 2011- 1.95.

Anna YAROSHCHUK b. 24 Nov 1989 1.76m 67kg.
At 400mh/4x400mR: WCh: '11- sf; EC: '10- sf; WJ: '08- 6/2R; EU23: '09- 8, '11- 1/2R; WUG: '11- 1. At 200m: EJ: '07- h/2 4x100m.
Progress at 400mh: 2006- 57.52, 2007- 56.46, 2008- 56.09, 2009- 57.23, 2010- 55.60, 2011- 54.77. pbs: 60m 7.74i '06, 200m 23.49 '10, 400m 53.31 '11, LJ 5.98 '10.

Antonina YEFREMOVA b. 19 Jul 1981 Dnepropetrovsk 1.76m 61kg. Donetsk Dyn. Business student at Donetsk Academy.
At 400m: OG: '04- sf, '08- h; WCh: '03- sf, '05- h, '09- hR, '11- sf; EC: '02- 6, '10- 6; WJ: '00- sf; EU23: '01- 1 (2 4x100mR); WI: '09- 4; WCp: '02- 5R; ECp: '02-04-05-10-11: 1/2&2R/2&3R/ 2&2R/1&3R; WUG: '05- 3R. UKR champion 2002-05, 2009.

Progress at 400m- 1999- 54.85, 2000- 51.95, 2001- 52.29, 2002- 50.70, 2003- 51.36, 2004- 50.74, 2005- 51.40, 2007- 52.09, 2008- 51.17, 2009- 52.85, 2010- 50.81, 2011- 50.69. pbs: 200m 23.4 '03, 24.27 '10; 400mh 57.48 '11.

Lyudmyla YOSYPENKO b. 24 Sep 1984 Jahotyn, Kiev region 1.75m 63kg.
At Hep: WCh: '09- 5, '11- 10; EC: '10- 6. UKR champion 2007-09, 2011.
Progress at Hep: 2002- 5026, 2003- 5327, 2004- 5563, 2005- 5782, 2006- 5708, 2007- 6025, 2008- 6262, 2009- 6423, 2010- 6260, 2011- 6318. pbs: 200m 23.68 '09, 800m 2:12.51 '11, 60mh 8.40i '08, 100mh 13.49 '11, HJ 1.88 '09, LJ 6.40 '09, SP 13.16 '11, JT 51.30 '09, Pen 4298i '07.

UNITED KINGDOM

Governing body: UK Athletics, Alexander Stadium, Walsall, Perry Barr, Birmingham B42 2LR. Founded 1999 (replacing British Athletics, founded 1991, which succeeded BAAB, founded 1932). The Amateur Athletic Association was founded in 1880 and the Women's Amateur Athletic Association in 1922.
National Championships (first were English Championships 1866-79, then AAA 1880-2006, WAAA from 1922). **2011 UK Champions: Men**: 100m: Dwain Chambers 10.09, 200m: Christian Malcolm 20.85, 400m: Martyn Rooney 45.44, 800m: Andrew Osagie 1:46.84, 1500m: James Shane 3:36.22, 5000m: Mohamed Farah 14:00.72, 10000m: James Walsh 28:37.30, Mar: Lee Merrien 2:14:27, 3000mSt: Luke Gunn 8:40.16, 110mh: Lawrence Clarke 13.58, 400mh: Nathan Woodward 49.66, HJ: Tom Parsons 2.28, PV: Steve Lewis 5.50, LJ: Julian Reid 8.08, TJ: Larry Achike 16.83, SP: Carl Myerscough 18.57, DT: Abdul Buhari 63.32, HT: Alex Smith 73.26, JT: Lee Doran 78.63, Dec: Daniel Awde 7869, 5000mW/10kW/20kW: Tom Bosworth 19:29.87/42:44/1:30:13, 50kW: Scott Davis 4:45:22. **Women**: 100m: Jeanette Kwakye 11.23, 200m: Anyika Onuora 23.26, 400m/400mh: Perri Shakes-Drayton 51.52/55.52, 800m: Jennifer Meadows 2:00.55, 1500m: Hannah England 4:07.05, 5000m: Julia Bleasdale 15:49.02, 10000m: Sonia Samuels 33:50.72, Mar: Jo Pavey 2:28:24, 3000mSt: Lennie Waite 10:03.18, 100mh: Tiffany Porter 12.76, HJ: Jessica Ennis 1.89, PV: Holly Bleasdale 4.56, LJ: Shara Proctor 6.65, TJ: Laura Samuel 13.67, SP: Eden Francis 16.73, DT: Jade Nicholls 56.19, HT: Sophie Hitchon 67.69, JT: Goldie Sayers 60.57, Hep: Gemma Weetman 5379, 5000mW/10kW: Johanna Jackson 21:42.32/44:59, 20kW: Joanne Hesketh 1:53:37.

Dwain CHAMBERS b. 5 Apr 1978 London 1.80m 83kg. Belgrave H.
At 100m/(200m)/4x100mR: OG: '00- 4; WCh: '97- res (3)R, '99- 3/2R, '01- 4/qf, '03- dq4/2R, '09- 6, '11- sf; EC: '98- 2/res 1R, '02- dq1/1R. '06- 7/1R, '10- 5; CG: '98- sf/1R, '02- 8; WJ: '96-

5; EJ: '95 & '97- 1/1R; WCp: '98- 3/1R, '02- dq 5, '06- 2R; ECp: '99-00-02-06-09-10-11: 1/1R/1R/2/ 1&1/1/2. Won AAA 2000-1, dq 2003; UK 2008, 2010-11; GWG 2001. At 60m: WI: '08-01-12- 2=/1/3; EI: '09- 1, '11- 2.
Records: World junior 100m 1997, European 100m 2002 (but later ruled out), indoor 60m 2009.
Progression at 100m: 1994- 10.75/10.56w, 1995- 10.41, 1996- 10.42, 1997- 10.06, 1998- 10.03rA/10.10, 1999- 9.97, 2000- 10.08, 2001- 9.99/9.97w?, 2002- 9.87 dq, 2003- 10.03/10.0 dq, 2006- 10.07, 2008- 10.00, 2009- 10.00, 2010- 9.99, 2011- 10.01. pbs: 50m 5.57+ '99, 60m 6.41+ '99, 6.42i '09; 200m 20.31 '01, 20.27dq '02.
Positive test for tetrahydrogestrinome (THG) 1 Aug 2003 which resulted in a two-year ban. He also admitted to drug taking in 2002 and as a result all his results from 1 Jan 2002 were annulled, including his European title and record for 100m.
Older sister Christine Chambers (b. 4 Mar 1969) was 8th at 100m at 1987 European Juniors. pbs: 60m 7.46i '92, 100m 11.84 '87, 11.68w '92.

Mohamed FARAH b. 23 March 1983 Mogadishu, Somalia 1.71m 65kg. Newham & Essex Beagles.
At 5000m (/10000m): OG: '08- h; WCh: '07- 6, '09- 7, '11- 1/2; EC: '06- 2, '10- 1/1; CG: '06- 9; WJ: '00- 10; WY: '99- 6; EJ: '01- 1; EU23: '03 & '05- 2; ECp: '08-09-10: 1/1/1 &(1). At 3000m: WI: '08- 6, '12- 4; EI: '05-07-09-11: 6/5/1/1; ECp: '05-06: 2/2. World CC: '07- 11, '10- 20; Eur CC: '99-00-01-04-05-06-08-09: 5J/7J/2J/15/21/1/2/2. Won UK 5000m 2007, 2011.
Records: European 10000m & indoor 5000m 2011, indoor 2M 2012; UK 5000m 2010 & 2011, half marathon 2011.
Progress at 5000m, 10000m: 2000- 14:05.72, 2001- 13:56.31, 2002- 14:00.5, 2003- 13:38.41, 2004- c.14:25, 2005- 13:30.53, 2006- 13:09.40, 2007- 13:07.00, 2008- 13:08.11, 27:44.54; 2009- 13:09.14, 2010- 12:57.94, 27:28.86; 2011- 12:53.11, 26:46.57. pbs: 800m 1:48.69 '03, 1500m 3:33.98 '09, 1M 3:56.49 '05, 2000m 5:06.34 '06, 3000m 7:34.47i '09, 7:38.15 '06; 2M 8:08.07i '12, 8:20.47 '07: 2000mSt 5:55.72 '00; Rd 15km 43:13 '09, 10M 46:25 '09, HMar 60:23 '11.
Joined his father in England in 1993. Won in New York on half marathon debut 2011.

David GREENE b. 11 Apr 1986 Llanelli 1.83m 75kg. Swansea Harriers.
At 400mh: WCh: '09- 7 (res (2)R), '11- 1; EC: '06- h, '10- 1; CG: '10- 1; EU23: '07- 1; EJ: '05- 2; CCp: '10- 1; ET: '09-10-11: 1/1/1. UK champion 2009-10.
Progress at 400mh: 2003- 55.0/55.06, 2004- 53.42, 2005- 51.14, 2006- 49.91, 2007- 49.58, 2008- 49.53, 2009- 48.27, 2010- 47.88, 2011- 48.20. pbs: 100m 11.1 '06, 200m 22.1 '05, 21.73w '08, 400m 45.82 '11, 600m 1:18.8i '06.

Phillips IDOWU b. 30 Dec 1978 Hackney, London 1.92m 86kg. Belgrave H.
At TJ: OG: '00- 6, '04- nj, '08- 2; WCh: '01-07-09-

11: 9/6/1/2; EC: '02- 5, '06- 5, '10- 1; CG: '02- 2, '06- 1; EU23: '99-5; EJ: '97- 4; WI: '08- 1; EI: '07- 1; CCp: '10- 3; ECp: '04-07-08-09-10: 3/2/1/2/2. Won AAA 2000, 2002, 2006; UK 2008-10.
Progress at TJ: 1995- 13.90, 1996- 15.12/15.53w, 1997- 15.86/16.34w, 1998- 16.35, 1999- 16.41, 2000- 17.12, 2001- 17.33/17.38w, 2002- 17.68, 2004- 17.47, 2005- 17.30i/16.96; 2006- 17.50, 2007- 17.56i/17.35, 2008- 17.75i/17.62, 2009- 17.73, 2010- 17.81, 2011- 17.77. pbs: 60m 6.81i '04, 100m 10.60 '06, LJ 7.83 '00.

Martyn ROONEY b. 3 Apr 1987 Croydon 1.98m 78kg. Croydon H. Student at Loughborough University.
At 400m/4x400mR: OG: '08- 6; WCh: '07- h, '09- sf/2R, '11- sf; EC: '10- 3/2R; CG: '06- 5; WJ: '06- 3/3R; EJ: '05- 2/1R; ECp: '07-08-10: 3/1&2R/1. Won UK 2008, 2010-11.
Progress at 400m: 2003- 49.4, 2004- 47.46, 2005- 46.44, 2006- 45.35, 2007- 45.47, 2008- 44.60, 2009- 45.35, 2010- 44.99, 2011- 45.30. spbs: 60m 7.12i '09, 200m 21.33 '07, 20.87w '11; 600m 1:16.9 '05, 800m 1:50.55 '05.
Ran anchor leg in 43.73 on 4x400m at 2008 Olympics.

Greg RUTHERFORD b. 17 Nov 1986 Milton Keynes 1.88m 84kg. Marshall Milton Keynes.
At LJ: OG: '08- 10; WCh: '07- dnq 21, '09- 5, '11- dnq 15=; EC: '06- 2; CG: '06- 8, '10- 2; EJ: '05- 1; EI: '09- 6. Won AAA 2005-06, UK 2008.
UK record 2009.
Progress at LJ: 1999- 5.04, 2001- 6.16, 2003- 7.04, 2004- 7.28, 2005- 8.14, 2006- 8.26, 2007- 7.96, 2008- 8.20, 2009- 8.30, 2010- 8.22, 2011- 8.27/8.32w. pbs: 60m 6.68i '09, 100m 10.26 '10.
Great-grandfather Jock Rutherford played 11 internationals for England at football in 1904-08.

William SHARMAN b. 12 Sep 1984 Lagos, Nigeria 1.88m 82kg. Belgrave Harriers. Economics graduate of University of Leicester.
At 110mh: WCh: '09- 4, '11- 5=; EC: '06- h, '10- sf; CG: '10- 2; EU23: '05- 4; EJ: '03- 5. Won UK 2010.
Progress at 110mh: 2003- 14.31, 2004- 13.94/ 13.86w, 2005- 13.88/13.72w, 2006- 13.49/13.45w, 2007- 13.68, 2008- 13.67/13.6/13.59w, 2009- 13.30, 2010- 13.39/13.35w/12.9w, 2011- 13.47. pbs: 60m 6.89i '07, 100m 10.86/10.74w '05, 200m 21.59 '06, 400m 48.53 '05, 1500m 4:45.25 '05, 60mh 7.69i '09, HJ 2.08 '05, PV 4.00 '05, LJ 7.14 '04, 7.15w '05; SP 12.99 '05, DT 33.99 '03, JT 43.45 '05, Dec 7384 '05, Hep 5278i '05.
National junior decathlon champion 2003. Improved pb from 13.44 to 13.38 and 13.30 at 2009 Worlds.

Chris TOMLINSON b. 15 Sep 1981 Middles–brough 1.97m 81kg. Newham & Essex Beagles.
At LJ: OG: '04- 5, '08- dnq 27; WCh: '03- 9, '05/07- dnq 14/16, '09- 8, '11- 11; EC: '02- 6, '06- 9, '10- 3; CG: '02-06-10: 6/6/nj; WJ: '00- 12; WI: '04- 6, '08- 2; EI: '07- 5; WCp: '02- 6; ECp: '01-02-

04-10-11: 2/1/1/3/3; AAA champion 2004, UK 2009-10.
Three British long jump records 2002-2011.
Progress at LJ: 1996- 5.91/6.09w, 1997- 6.82w/6.44, 1998- 7.23i, 1999- 7.44i/7.40, 2000- 7.62, 2001- 7.75, 2002- 8.27, 2003- 8.16, 2004- 8.25/8.28w, 2005- 7.95i/7.82/7.83w, 2006- 8.09, 2007- 8.29, 2008- 8.18i/7.95/8.09w, 2009- 8.23. 2010- 8.23, 2011- 8.35. pbs: 60m 6.84i '09, 100m 10.69 '02, 10.61w/10.6 '01; 200m 21.73 '02, 21.43w '10; TJ 15.35 '01.
Jumped 8.27 at Tallahassee in April 2002, from a previous best of 7.87 (and 8.19w), to break the 34-year-old British record set by Lynn Davies.

Andrew TURNER b. 19 Sep 1980 Sutton, Surrey 1.84m 77kg. Sale Harriers Manchester. Was at Loughborough and Brunel Universities.
At 110mh: OG: '04- h, '08- qf; WCh: '07- sf, '09- h. '11- 3; EC: '06- 3, '10- 1; CG: '06- 3, '10- 1; CCp: '10- 2; ECp: '04-06-07-09-10-11: 3/2/2/1/1/1. AAA/UK champion 2006-09. At 60mh: EI: '07- 4, '09- 4.
Progress at 110mh: 1999- 15.2/15.08w/14.9w, 2000- 14.77, 2001- 14.29/14.22w, 2002- 13.90, 2003- 13.66, 2004- 13.47, 2005- 13.63/13.6w, 2006- 13.38/13.24w, 2007- 13.27, 2008- 13.41, 2009- 13.30/13.2u/13.29w, 2010- 13.28, 2011- 13.22. pbs: 60m 6.79i '09, 100m 10.32 '09, 200m 20.90i '11, 20.93 '06, 20.71w '07; 400m 49.17i '01, 60mh 7.55i '07, 200mh straight 22.10 '11, LJ 7.16 00, 7.23w '97.

Women

Yamilé ALDAMA b. 14 Aug 1972 La Habana, Cuba 1.73m 62kg. married name Dodds. Shaftesbury Barnet Harriers, GBR.
At TJ: OG: '00- 4, '04- 5, '08- dnq; WCh: '97-99-05-07-9-11: dnq 13/2/4/dnq 25/dnq 13/5; PAm: '99- 1; AfG: '07- 1; AfCh: '04-06-08: 1/1/2; CAG: '98- 1; WI: '97-9-04-06-08: 6/7/2/3/5; WCp: '98- 3, '06- 3. Won IbAm 1996, 1998; Cuban 1997-2000, AAA 2003; Arab HJ, 2005, LJ & TJ 2005, 2007, 2009.
Nine CAC triple jump records 1999-2003 (if still eligible), CAC indoor (14.65 and 14.88) 2003, three African and Sudan records 2004. SUD records HJ (1.85) 2004, LJ 2005 & 2007; World W35 2008 and 2012 (indoors).
Progress at TJ: 1994- 13.92, 1995- 13.84, 1996- 14.43, 1997- 14.46, 1998- 14.55, 1999- 14.77, 2000- 14.47, 2001- 13.85i, 2002- 14.40/14.54w, 2003- 15.29, 2004- 15.28, 2005- 14.82, 2006- 14.86i/14.78, 2007- 14.58, 2008- 14.51, 2009- 14.48/14.68w, 2010- 12.41i, 2011- 14.50, 2012- 14.82i. pbs: 100mh 14.97/14.8 '92, HJ 1.88 '92, LJ 6.34 '07, Hep 5246 '93.
Aldama, who last competed for Cuba in 2000, competed for Sudan from 2004 before gaining British eligibility on 4 Aug 2011; uniquely she has competed and won medals at World Champs for three nations. She had moved to London with Scottish husband Andrew Dodds in 2001, in which year her son Amil was born, and hoped to be eligible for Britain but a three-year waiting period meant that she was unable to gain a passport in sufficient time to compete at the 2003 Worlds (or 2004 Olympics).

Holly BLEASDALE b. 2 Nov 1991 1.75m 68kg. Blackburn Harriers.
At PV: WCh: '11- dnq; WI: '12- 3; WJ: '10- 3; EU23: '11- 1. UK champion 2011.
Three UK pole vault records 2011, five indoors 2011-12.
Progress at PV: 2007- 2.30, 2008- 3.10i, 2009- 4.05, 2010- 4.35, 2011- 4.71i/4.70, 2012- 4.87i. pbs: SP 11.32 '11, JT 37.60 '11.
World age-19 best 2011, age-20 best 2012.

Kate DENNISON b. 7 May 1984 Durban, South Africa 1.71m 59kg. Sale Harriers Manchester. Psychology graduate of University of Staffordshire.
At PV: OG: '08- dnq 15; WCh: '07- dnq 29, '09- 6; EC: '06- dnq 15, '10- 6; CG: '06- 7, '10- 3=; WJ: '02- 7; EJ: '03- 11=; EI: '09- 6. UK champion 2007, 2009-10.
Six UK pole vault records 2009, five indoors 2009-10.
Progress at PV: 2000- 3.20, 2001- 3.80, 2002- 4.00, 2003- 3.90, 2004- 4.00, 2005- 4.12i/4.11, 2006- 4.35, 2007- 4.40i/4.31, 2008- 4.40, 2009- 4.60, 2010- 4.60i/4.55, 2011- 4.61.
Has lived in England from age four.

Lisa DOBRISKEY b. 23 Dec 1983 New Romney, Kent 1.71m 56kg. Ashford. Graduate of Loughborough University.
At 1500m: OG: '08- 4; WCh: '07- sf, '09- 2, '11- h; EC: '06- h, '10- 4; CG: '06- 1; WJ: '02- 4; EU23: '03- 2; WUG: '05- 5. At 3000m: WI: '08- 10; EI: '07- 5. Won UK 1500m 2008, 4km CC 2005.
Progress at 1500m: 1999- 4:31.7, 2000- 4:28.10, 2001- 4:25.25, 2002- 4:14.58, 2003- 4:12.95, 2004- 4:08.14, 2005- 4:05.42mx/4:07.47, 2006- 4:06.21, 2007- 4:06.22, 2008- 4:00.64mx/4:02.10, 2009- 3:59.50, 2010- 3:59.79, 2011- 4:04.76. pbs: 400m 56.0 '02, 800m 2:00.14 '10, 1000m 2:44.13i '05, 1M 4:20.35 '08, 3000m 8:47.25i/8:54.12 '07, 2M 9:33.78i '07.
Married Ricky Soos (b. 28 Jun 1983, 800m 1:45.70 '04) on 12 Dec 2009.

Hannah ENGLAND b. 6 Mar 1987 Oxford 1.77m 54kg. Oxford City, Graduate of Birmingham and Florida State Universities.
At 1500m (800m): WCh: '11- 2; EC: '10- 10; CG: '10- 4 (5); WJ: '06- h; EU23: '07- 5; ECp: '09- 4 (4), '10- 2. Won UK 2010-11, NCAA 2008.
Progress at 1500m: 2000- 4:46.81, 2001- 4:39.37, 2002- 4:33.05, 2003- 4:28.22, 2004- 4:25.86, 2005- 4:26.16, 2006- 4:17.31, 2007- 4:12.44, 2008- 4:06.19, 2009- 4:04.29, 2010- 4:04.33, 2011- 4:01.89. pbs: 800m 1:59.94 '09, 1M 4:30.29i '09, 4:40.22 '08; 3000m 8:56.72i '10.

Jessica ENNIS b. 28 Jan 1986 Sheffield 1.64m 57kg. Sheffield. Studied psychology at University of Sheffield.
At Hep: WCh: '07- 4, '09- 1, '11- 2; EC: '06- 8, '10- 1; CG: '06- 3; WJ: '04- 8; WY: '03- 5; EJ: '05- 1; WUG: '05- 3; ECp: '07- 1. At Pen: WI: '10- 1, '12- 2; EI: '07- 6. At 100mh: EU23: '07- 3. Won UK 100mh 2007, 2009; HJ 2007, 2009, 2011.
Commonwealth indoor pentathlon records 2010 & 2012, UK high jump record 2007, indoor 60mh 2010.
Progress at Hep: 2001- 4801, 2002- 5194, 2003- 5116, 2004- 5542, 2005- 5910, 2006- 6287, 2007- 6469, 2009- 6731, 2010- 6823, 2011- 6790. pbs: 60m 7.36i '10, 100m 11.39+ '10, 150mStr 16.99 '10, 200m 23.11 '11, 800m 2:07.81 '11, 60mh 7.87i '12, 100mh 12.81 '09, HJ 1.95 '07, LJ 6.51 '10, 6.54w '07; SP 14.79i '12, 14.67 '11; JT 46.71 '10, Pen 4965i '12.
Set four pbs in adding 359 points to best score for third at 2006 Commonwealth Games. Stress fracture ended 2008 season in May. Set SP pb when winning 2009 World title and three indoor bests when winning 2010 World Indoor gold. Won Götzis heptathlon 2010-11.

Jennifer MEADOWS b. 17 Apr 1981 Billinge, Wigan 1.56m 48kg. Wigan.
At 800m/4x400mR: OG: '08- sf; WCh: '03- 6R, '07- sf, '09- 3, '11- sf; EC: '10- 3; CG: '02- SR; WI: '08- 5, '10- 2; EI: '07-09-11: 5/4/2&2R; CCp: '10- 4; ECp: '07-08-09-11: 1R/1/3R/2. At 400m: WJ: '00- sf/1R; EU23: '01- 6/1R, '03- 7/2R; WUG: '01- 2R. Won UK 800m 2011.
Progress at 800m: 1994- 2:16.80, 1995- 2:14.88, 1996- 2:16.4, 1997- 2:16.03, 1999- 2:11.5, 2000- 2:10.7, 2001- 2:05.8, 2002- 2:04.46/2:03.35i, 2003- 2:06.82mx/2:08.0, 2004- 2:06.84i, 2005- 2:02.05, 2006- 2:00.16, 2007- 1:59.39, 2008- 1:59.11, 2009- 1:57.93, 2010- 1:58.43i/1:58.88, 2011- 1:58.60. pbs: 100m 11.94/11.8w '01, 11.9 '02; 200m 24.32 '00, 24.0 '02, 23.90w '01; 400m 52.50mx '05, 52.67 '03; 600m 1:25.81i '07, 1000m 2:39.84 '07, 1500m 4:19.36 '06.

Christine OHURUOGU b. 17 May 1984 Forest Gate, London 1.75m 70kg. Newham & Essex Beagles. Studied linguistics at University College, London.
At 400m: OG: '04- sf/3R, '08- 1; WCh: '05- sf/3R, '07- 1/3R, '09- 5, '11- h; CG: '06- 1; EU23: '05- 2/2R; EJ: '03- 3; WI: '12- 1R. At 200m: ECp: '08- 2, '09- 3. Won AAA 400m 2004, UK 2009.
Progress at 400m: 2000- 59.0, 2001- 55.29, 2003- 54.21, 2004- 50.50, 2005- 50.73, 2006- 50.28, 2007- 49.61, 2008- 49.62, 2009- 50.21, 2010- 50.88, 2011- 50.85. pbs: 60m 7.39i '06, 100m 11.35 '08, 150m Str 16.94 '09, 200m 22.85 '09, 300m 36.76+ '09.
Played for England U17 and U19 at netball. Withdrawn from GB European Champs team in 2006 after missing three drugs tests, receiving a one-year ban.

Tiffany PORTER b. 13 Nov 1987 Ypsilanti, USA 1.72m 62kg. née Ofili. Was at University of Michigan.
At 100mh: WCh: '11- 4; WJ: '06- 3 (for USA). At 60mh: WI: '12- 2; EI: '11- 2. Won UK 100mh 2011, NCAA 100mh & 60mh indoors 2009.
Three British 100mh records 2011.
Progress at 100mh: 2005- 14.19, 2006- 13.37/13.15w, 2007- 12.80, 2008- 12.73, 2009- 12.77/12.57w, 2010- 12.85, 2011- 12.56. pbs: 60m 7.41i '11, 100m 11.70 '09, 11.63w '08; 200m 23.90 '08, 50mh 6.83i '12 (UK record), 60mh 7.80i '11 (UK record), 400mh 61.96 '06, LJ 6.48 '09.
Opted for British nationality in September 2010 through her mother being born in London (father born in Nigeria). Married hurdler Jeff Porter (b. 27 Nov 1985, pb 110mh 13.26 '11) in May 2011.

Shara PROCTOR b. 16 Sep 1988 Anguilla 1.74m 56kg. Birchfield H. Was at University of Florida, USA.
At LJ: WCh: '07-09-11: dnq 29/6/dnq 20; WI: '12- 3; CG: '06- dnq 13; WJ: '06- dnq 16; WY: '05- 6. Won CAC 2009, UK 2011.
Angilla records: LJ 2005-09, TJ 2007-09
Progress at LJ: 2003- 5.64, 2004- 5.99A. 2005- 6.24, 2006- 6.17, 2007- 6.17, 2008- 6.54A/6.52/6.61w, 2009- 6.71, 2010- 6.69, 2011- 6.81, 2012- 6.89i. pbs: 100m 12.27 '08, 12.10w '10; TJ 13.88i '10, 13.74 '09.
Switched from Anguilla (a British Dependent Territory without an National Olympic Committee) to Britain from 16 Nov 2010. Younger sister Shinelle (b. 27 Jun 91) set Anguillan high jump records at 1.70 in 2009 and 2010

Paula RADCLIFFE b. 17 Dec 1973 Northwich 1.73m 54kg. Bedford & County. Degree in European languages from Loughborough University.
At 10000m (Mar): OG: '00- 4, '04- dnf (dnf), '08- (23); WCh: '99- 2, '01- 4, '05- 9 (1); EC: '98- 5, '02- 1; At 5000m: OG: '96- 5; WCh: '95- 5, '97- 4; CG: '02- 1; ECp: '98-9-01-04: 1/1/2/1 (2 1500m '98); 3rd GP 1997. At 3000m: WCh: '93- 7; WJ: '92- 4; EJ: '91- 4; ECp: '97- 3. World HMar: '00-01-03: 1/1/1; CC: '91- 15J, '92- 1J, '93-5-6-7-8-9-00-01-02: 18/18/19/2/2/3/5 (4 4k)/1 (2 4k)/1. Eur CC: '98- 1, '03- 1. Won AAA 5000m 1996, 2000; Mar 2002-03; UK 5000m 1997, CC 1994-5.
Records: World marathon 2002 & 2003; half marathon 2003; Commonwealth & UK 1998-2004: 3000m (3), 5000m (4), 10000m (5); UK 5000m (6) 1996-2004. European 10000m 2002, HMar 2000 & 2001, Marathon 2002.
Progress at 5000m, 10000m, Mar: 1992- 16:16.77i, 1995- 14:49.27, 1996- 14:46.76. 1997- 14:45.51, 1998- 14:51.27, 30:48.58; 1999- 14:43.54, 30:27.13; 2000- 14:44.36, 30:26.97; 2001- 14:32.44, 30:55.80; 2002- 14:31.42, 30:01.09, 2:17:18; 2003- 2:15:25, 2004- 14:29.11, 30:17.15, 2:23:10; 2005- 15:16.29+, 30:42.75, 2:17:42; 2007- 2:23:09, 2008- 2:23:56, 2009- 2:29:27,

2011- 2:23:46. pbs: 400m 58.9 '92, 800m 2:05.22 '95, 1000m 2:47.17 '93, 1500m 4:05.37 '01, 1M 4:24.94 '96, 2000m 5:37.1 '02, 3000m 8:22.20 '02, 2M 9:17.4e '04; Road: 15km 46:41 '03, 10M 50:01 '03, HMar 65:40 '03, 30km 1:36:36 '03, 20M 1:43:33 '03. Has 8 wins in 12 marathons: London 2002-03, 2005, Chicago 2002, New York 2004, 2007-08; World 2005. Her 2:18:56 at London in 2002 the fastest women's debut by over four minutes and beating the women's only world record by over three minutes. She then improved the world record by 1:29 with 2:17:18 in Chicago. In 2003 she ran a world 10km road best of 30:21 in San Juan and a world record 2:15:25 at the London Marathon. After illness and injury, returned with the fastest ever half marathon, 65:40 to win the Great North Run. Improved women's only world best to win London marathon 2005 with fourth sub-2:20 time, 2:17:42 and won World gold. Set European half marathon record to win Great North Run in 2000 and won the World Half marathon by 33 secs. Won 5th Avenue Mile 1996 & 1997. Married Gary Lough (1500m 3:34.76 '95) on 15 April 2000; their daughter Isla born on 17 Jan 2007 and son Raphael on 29 Sep 2010. Her great aunt Charlotte Radcliffe won an Olympic swimming silver medal at 4x100m freestyle relay in 1920.

Goldie SAYERS b. 16 Jul 1982 Newmarket 1.71m 70kg. Belgrave H.
At OG: '04- dnq 20, '08- 4; WCh: '05- 12, '07/09- dnq 18/13, '11- 10; EC: '06- 12; CG: '02- 6, '06- 5; WJ: '00- 6; WY: '99- 5; EJ: '01- 2; EU23: '03- 11; WUG: '03- 5, '05- 4; ECp: '10- 2, '11- 2. AAA champion 2003-06, UK 2007-11.
UK javelin records 2007 & 2008.
Progress at JT: 1996- 41.56, 1997- 45.10, 1998- 51.92, new: 1999- 51.06, 2000- 54.48, 2001- 55.40, 2002- 58.20, 2003- 56.29, 2004- 60.85, 2005- 61.45, 2006- 60.41, 2007- 65.05, 2008- 65.75, 2009- 59.82, 2010- 63.15, 2011- 64.46.

Perri SHAKES-DRAYTON b. 21 Dec 1988 London 1.70m 67kg. Victoria Park & Tower Hamlets, Brunel University.
At 400mh/4x400mR: WCh: '09- sf, '11- sf; EC: '10- 3/3R; ; WI: '12- 1R; WJ: '06- 8; EU23: '09-1; EJ: '07- 2/2R; ET: '11- 3. Won UK 400m 2011, 400mh 2008, 2010-11.
Progress at 400mh: 2006- 57.52, 2007- 56.46, 2008- 56.09, 2009- 55.26, 2010- 54.18, 2011- 54.62. pbs: 60m 7.44i '09, 100m 11.78 '09, 11.7w '07; 200m 23.71mx '10, 400m 51.47 '11, 800m 2:08.35mx/2:08.6 '11, 100mh 14.07 '08.

Jemma SIMPSON b. 17 Feb 1984 Plymouth 1.78m 58kg. Newquay and Par. Was at St Mary's University College.
At 800m: OG: '08- h; WCh: '07/09- sf; EC: '06- sf, '10- 5; CG: '06- 6; WJ: '02- 4; WY: '01- 8; EU23: '05- 2; EJ: '03- 3. UK champion 2007, 2009-10.
Progress at 800m: 1996- 2:22.9, 1997- 2:18.44, 1998- 2:14.4, 1999- 2:13.2, 2000- 2:06.72, 2001-

2:06.62, 2002- 2:04.11, 2003- 2:03.42, 2005- 2:01.90, 2006- 1:59.99. 2007- 2:00.18, 2008- 1:59.17, 2009- 1:59.07, 2010- 1:58.74, 2011- 1:59.59. pbs: 300m 40.2 '00, 400m 55.8 '01, 1000m 2:39.70 '10, 1500m 4:06.39 '10.

Stephanie TWELL b. 17 Aug 1989 Colchester 1.68m 54kg. Student at St Mary's College.
At 1500m(/5000m): OG: '08- h; WCh: '09- h; EC: '10- 7; CG: '10- 3/4; WJ: '06- 8, '08- 1; EJ: '07- 2. Eur CC: '05-06-07-08-11: 7J/1J/1J/1J/4 U23. Won UK CC 2009.
Progress at 1500m, 5000m: 2003- 4:45.98, 2004- 4:26.74, 2005- 4:25.05, 2006- 4:12.76, 2007- 4:06.70, 15:47.53; 2008- 4:05.83, 2009- 4:03.48, 15:18.47; 2010- 4:02.54, 14:54.08. pbs: 400m 58.19 '06, 800m 2:02.59 '10, 1M 4:28.16 '07, 3000m 8:42.75mx '10, 8:50.89 '08; road: 10km 32:26+ '10, 10M 53:52 '10, HMar 71:56 '10.
Uniquely won three European Junior CC titles plus team gold each year 2005-08.

USA

Governing body: USA Track and Field, One RCA Dome, Suite #140, Indianapolis, IN 46225. Founded 1979 as The Athletics Congress, when it replaced the AAU (founded 1888) as the governing body.
National Championships first held in 1876 (men), 1923 (women). **2011 Champions: Men**: 100m/200m: Walter Dix 9.94/19.95w, 400m: Greg Nixon 44.61, 800m: Nick Symmonds 1:44.17, 1500m: Matthew Centrowitz 3:47.63, 5000m: Bernard Lagat 13:23.06, 10000m: Galen Rupp 28:38.17, HMar: Mohamed Trafeh 62:17, Mar; *not held*, 3000mSt: Billy Nelson 8:28.46, 110mh: David Oliver 13.04, 400mh: Jeshua Anderson 47.93, HJ: Jesse Williams 2.37, PV: Derek Miles 5.66, LJ: Marquise Goodwin 8.33w, TJ: Christian Taylor 17.49w, SP: Adam Nelson 22.09, DT: Jarred Rome 63.99, HT: Kibwé Johnson 80.31, JT: Mike Hazle 78.22, Dec: Ashley Eaton 8729, 20kW: Trevor Barron 1:23:26, 50kW: Ben Shorey 4:16:01. **Women**: 100m: Carmelita Jeter 10.74w, 200m: Shalonda Solomon 22.15, 400m: Debbie Dunn 49.64, 800m: Alysia Montano 1:58.33, 1500m: Morgan Uceny 4:03.91, 5000m: Molly Huddle 15:10.01, 10000m: Shalane Flanagan 30:59.97, HMar: Jen Rhines 71:14, Mar; *not held*, 3000mSt: Emma Coburn 9:44.11, 100mh: Kellie Wells 12.50, 400mh: Tierra Brown 54.85, HJ: Brigetta Barrett 1.95, PV: Kylie Hutson 4.65, LJ: Brittney Reese 7.19, TJ: Amanda Smock 14.07, SP: Michelle Carter 19.86, DT: Stephanie Brown Trafton 63.35, HT: Jessica Cosby 71.33, JT: Kara Patterson 59.34, Hep: Sharon Day 6058, 20kW: Maria Michta 1:34:52.
NCAA Championships first held in 1921 (men), 1982 (women). **2011 Champions: Men**: 100m/ LJ: Ngonidzashe Makusha ZIM 9.89/8.40, 200m: Maurice Mitchell 19.99w, 400m: Kirani James GRN 45.10, 800m: Robby Andrews 1:44.71,

1500m: Matthew Centrowitz 3:42.54, 5000m: Samuel Chelanga KEN 13:29.30, 10000m: Leonard Korir KEN 28:07.63, 3000mSt: Matt Hughes CAN 8:24.87, 110mh: Barrett Nugent 13.28w, 400mh: Jeshua Anderson 48.56, HJ: Eric Kynard 2.29, PV: Scott Roth 5.40, TJ: Christian Taylor 17.80w, SP: Jordan Clarke 19.75, DT: Julian Wruck AUS 61.81, HT: Alexander Ziegler GER 72.69. JT: Tim Glover 80.33, Dec: Mike Morrison 8118. **Women**: 100m: Candyce McGrone 11.08, 200m: Kimberlyn Duncan 22.24, 400m: Jessica Beard 51.10, 800m: Anne Kesselring GER 2:02.15, 1500m/5000m: Sheila Reid CAN 4:14.57/15:37.57, 10000m: Juliet Bottorff 34:25.86, 3000mSt: Emma Coburn 9:41.14, 100mh: Nia Ali 12.63w, 400mh: Tierra Brown 55.65, HJ: Brigetta Barrett 1.86, PV: Melissa Gergel 4.45, LJ: Tori Bowie 6.64, TJ: Patricia Mamona POR 14.05, SP: Julie Labonté CAN 18.31, DT: Trecey Rew 58.64, HT: Dorotea Habazin CRO 68.15, JT: Brittany Borman 54.32, Hep: Ryann Krais 5961.

Jeshua ANDERSON b. 22 Jun 1989 Mission Hills, California 1.88m 84kg. Student at Washington State University.
At 400mh/4x400mR: WCh: sf; WJ: '08- 1/1R; WUG: '11- 1. Won US 2011; NCAA 2008-09, 2011.
Progress at 400mh: 2008- 48.68, 2009- 48.47, 2010- 48.63, 2011- 47.93. pbs: 400m 46.08 '09, 500m 1:10.86i '12, 60mh 7.98i '11, 110mh 13.78 '11.
Broke 22 year-old US high school 300mh record with 35.28 in 2007. Plays as wide receiver at American Football.

Ronnie ASH b. 2 Jul 1988 Raleigh NC 1.88m 86kg. Mike. Was at University of Oklahoma.
At 110mh: won NACAC 2010, NCAA 2009.
Progress at 110mh: 2008- 13.44, 2009- 13.27, 2010- 13.19/12.98w, 2011- 13.25/13.24w. pbs: 200m 22.08 '08, 60mh 7.55i '10.

Joel BROWN b. 31 Jan 1980 Baltimore 1.80m 75kg. adidas. Studied financial planning at Ohio State University.
At 110mh: WCh: '05- 6; won US indoor 60mh 2005.
Progress at 110mh: 2000- 14.49, 2001- 14.04, 2003- 13.74/13.58w, 2004- 13.35, 2005- 13.22, 2006- 13.30, 2007- 13.31, 2008- 13.33/13.2w, 2009- 13.27/13.18w, 2010- 13.24/13.1w, 2011- 13.20. pbs: 55m 6.24i '06, 60m 6.74i '05, 100m 10.33 '04, 10.32w '05; 200m 20.54 '09, 20.36w '08; 50mh 6.48i '12, 55mh 7.18i '03, 60mh 7.48i '09, 400mh 51.94 '99.

Christian CANTWELL b. 30 Sep 1980 Jefferson City, Missouri 1.96m 145kg. Nike. Studied hotel and restaurant management at University of Missouri.
At SP: OG: '08- 2; WCh: '05- 5, '09- 1, '11- 4; WI: '04-08-10: 1/1/1; CCp: '10- 1; won DL 2010, WAF 2003, 2009; US 2005, 2009-10. At DT: PAm-J: '99- 2.
Progress at SP: 1999- 15.85, 2000- 19.67, 2001-

19.71, 2002- 21.45, 2003- 21.62, 2004- 22.54, 2005- 21.67, 2006- 22.45, 2007- 21.96, 2008- 22.18i/21.76, 2009- 22.16, 2010- 22.41, 2011- 22.07. pbs: DT 59.32 '01, HT 57.18 '01, Wt 22.04i '03.
After three competitions over 22m in 2004, was 4th in the US Olympic Trials. Married Teri Steer (b. 3 Oct 1975, SP pb 19.21 '01, 3 WI 1999) on 29 Oct 2005.

Xavier CARTER b. 8 Dec 1985 Palm Bay, Florida 1.91m 89kg. Nike. Student at Louisiana State University.
Won NCAA 100m & 400m 2006.
Progress at 200m, 400m: 1999- 22.20, 49.71; 2001- 46.95, 2002- 21.02, 46.90; 2003- 20.69, 45.88; 2004- 20.69i/20.72/20.5, 45.44/45.3; 2005- 20.02, 45.65; 2006- 19.63, 44.53; 2007- 19.92, 45.26; 2008- 20.25, 44.70; 2009- 20.27/20.09w, 45.55; 2010- 20.14, 46.79; 2011- 20.53/20.51w, 48.47. pbs: 60m 6.74i '05, 100m 10.09, 10.08w '06; 300m 31.93 '09.
Played for LSU as wide receiver at American football. Youngest ever to break 50 secs for 400m (49.71 at age 13) with world age record also for 200m.

Matthew CENTROWITZ b. 18 Nov 1989 Arnold, Maryland 1.75m 61kg. Sociology student at the University of Oregon.
At 1500m: WCh: '11- 3; WI: '12- 7. At 5000m WJ: '08- 11. Won US 2011, NCAA 2011, PAm-J 2007.
Progress at 1500m: 2007- 3:49.54, 2008- 3:44.98, 2009- 3:36.92, 2010- 3:40.14, 2011- 3:34.46. pbs: 800m 1:47.77 '11, 1M 3:57.92i '09, 3:59.33 '10; 3000m 7:50.59i '11, 2M 8:40.55 '07, 5000m 13:47.73 '10.
Father Matt pbs: 1500m 3:36.60 '76, 1M 3:53.92i '12, 3:54.94 '82; 5000m 13:12.91 '82, 10000m 28:32.7 '83; h OG 1500m 1976; 1 PAm 5000m 1979.
Sister Lauren (b. 25 Sep 1986) has 1500m pb 4:10.23 '09. Their father Matt was 1979 Pan-American 5000m champion with pbs 1500m 3:36.70 '76, 1M 3:54.94 '82, 5000m 13:12.91 .82.

Bryan CLAY b. 3 Jan 1980 Austin, Texas 1.80m 83kg. Nike. Was at Azusa Pacific University.
At Dec: OG: '04- 2, '08- 1; WCh: '01/03/07- dnf, '05- 1; PAm-J: '99- 1. US champion 2004-05, 2008.
At Hep: WI: '04-06-08-10: 2/2/1/1.
Progress at Dec: 1999- 7312, 2000- 7373, 2001- 8169, 2002- 8230, 2003- 8482, 2004- 8820, 2005- 8732, 2006- 8677, 2007- 8493, 2008- 8832, 2010- 8483, 2011- dnf. pbs: 60m 6.65i '04, 100m 10.35 '10, 200m 21.39 '08, 400m 47.78 '05, 1000m 2:49.41i '04, 1500m 4:38.93 '01, 60mh 7.71Ai '10, 7.74i '08; 110mh 13.64 '10, HJ 2.10i '06, 2.09 '07; PV 5.10 '04, LJ 7.96/8.06w '04, SP 16.27 '08, DT 55.87 '05, JT 72.00 '05, Hep 6371i '08.
Moved from Texas to Hawaii at age five. Brilliant breakthrough with four pbs in 2004 World Indoor heptathlon. Set decathlon discus WR with 55.87 during 2005 US Champs. Set pbs at SP, 400m and JT when winning World gold in 2005. Won Götzis 2006 and 2010.

Will CLAYE b. 13 Jun 1991 Phoenix 1.80m 68kg. Student at University of Florida.
At LJ/TJ: WCh: '11- 9/3; WI: '12- 4/1; won PAm-J and NCAA 2009.
Progress at LJ, TJ: 2007- 14.91/15.19w, 2008- 7.39/7.48w, 15.97; 2009- 7.89/8.00w, 17.19/17.24w; 2010- 7.30w, 16.30; 2011- 8.29, 17.50/17.62w; 2012- 8.24i, 17.70i.
Possibly youngest ever NCAA champion – he won 2009 title on his 18th birthday with 17.24w (and US junior record 17.19).

Kerron CLEMENT b. 31 Oct 1985 Port of Spain, Trinidad 1.88m 84kg. Nike. Was at University of Florida.
At 400mh/4x400mR: OG: '08- 2; WCh: '05- 4, '07- 1/res 1R, '09- 1/1R, '11- sf; WJ: '04- 1/1R; WI: '10- res 1R; WCp: '06- 1. Won WAF 2008-09, US 2005-06, NCAA 2004-05.
World junior 4x400m record 2004, world indoor records: 400m 2005, 4x400m 2006.
Progress at 400m, 400mh: 2002- 49.77H, 2003- 50.13H, 2004- 45.90, 48.51; 2005- 44.57i, 47.24; 2006- 44.71, 47.39; 2007- 44.48, 47.61; 2008- 45.10, 47.79; 2009- 45.08, 47.91; 2010- 46.01, 47.86; 2011- 45.42, 48.74. pbs: 60m 6.89i '10, 100m 10.23 '07, 200m 20.40i '05, 20.49 '07; 300m 31.94i '06, 55mh 7.28i '05, 60mh 7.80i '04, 110mh 13.78 '04.
Born in Trinidad, moved to Texas in 1998, US citizenship confirmed in 2005. Ran world-leading 47.24, the world's fastest time since 1998, to win 2005 US 400mh title.

Shawn CRAWFORD b. 14 Jan 1978 Van Wyck, SC 1.81m 86kg. Nike. Was at Clemson University.
At 200m/4x100mR (100m): OG: '04- 1/2R (4), '08- 2; WCh: '01- 3=, '05- (sf), '09- 4; WI: '01- 1; Won US 2001, 2004, 2009; GWG & GP 2001, NCAA 2000. At 60m: WI: '04- 2.
Progress at 100m, 200m: 1996- 10.62, 21.57; 1997- 10.51w, 20.83; 1998- 10.34/10.15w, 20.44A/20.12w; 1999- 10.41, 20.39; 2000- 10.16, 20.09; 2001- 10.09, 20.17; 2002- 9.94, 19.85A/20.29; 2003- 10.07, 20.02; 2004- 9.88/9.86w, 19.79; 2005- 9.99/9.98w, 20.12; 2006- 10.01, 2007- 10.13/9.96w, 20.21; 2008- 10.09, 19.86; 2009- 10.15/10.06w, 19.89/19.73w; 2010- 10.24, 20.50; 2011- 10.33, 20.45/20.24w. pbs: 60m 6.47i '04, 300m 32.47 '09.
US indoor record 20.26 to win NCAA indoor 200m in 2000. Disqualified in 2003 WI semis. Calls himself 'The Cheetah Man' after racing against a zebra and a cheetah on Fox TV in 2003, made his TV acting debut in October 2004. Married Virginia Powell (qv) on 16 Apr 2010.

Jeffery DEMPS b. 8 Jan 1990 Winter Garden, Florida 1.75m 77kg. University of Florida.
Won NCAA 100m 2010, indoor 60m 2010-12. Tied world junior 100m record in 2008.
Progress at 100m: 2006- 10.43w, 2007- 10.25, 2008- 10.01, 2009- 10.30, 2010- 10.06/9.96w, 2011- 10.04/9.96w. pbs: 60m 6.52i '12, 200m 21.04 '07.
Starred as a running back at American Football at university.

Walter DIX b. 31 Jan 1986 Coral Springs, Florida 1.78m 84kg. Nike. Studied social science at Florida State University.
At 100m/200m: OG: '08- 3/3; WCh: '11- 2/2; won US 100m 2010-11, 200m 2008, 2011; NCAA 100m 2005, 2007; 200m 2006-08.
World junior 200m indoor record (20.37) 2005.
Progress at 100m, 200m: 2002- 10.72/10.67w, 2003- 10.41/10.29w, 21.04/20.94w; 2004- 10.28, 20.62/20.54w; 2005- 10.06/9.96w, 20.18; 2006- 10.12, 20.25; 2007- 9.93, 19.69; 2008- 9.91/9.80w, 19.86; 2009- 10.00, 2010- 9.88, 19.72; 2011- 9.94, 19.53. pbs: 55m 6.19i '07, 60m 6.59i '06, 150mSt 14.65 '11, 400m 46.75 '10, LJ 7.39 '04.

Johnny DUTCH b. 20 Jan 1989 Clayton NC 1.80m 82kg. Nike. Was at University of South Carolina.
At 400mh: WCh: '09- sf; WJ: '08- 2; PAm-J: '07- 1/2R. Won NCAA 2010.
Progress at 400mh: 2005- 52.06, 2006- 52.37, 2007- 50.07, 2008- 48.52, 2009- 48.18, 2010- 47.63, 2011- 48.47 pbs: 400m 47.92 '11, 47.57i '09; 55mh 7.31i '10, 60mh 7.71i '09, 110mh 13.50/13.30w '10.

Ashton EATON b. 21 Jan 1988 Portland, Oregon 1.86m 86kg. Oregon TC. Graduate of University of Oregon.
At Dec: WCh: '09- 18, '11- 2; won NCAA 2008-10. At Hep: WI: '12- 1.
World indoor heptathlon records 2010 (6499), 2011 (6568) and 2012.
Progress at Dec: 2007- 7123, 2008- 8122, 2009- 8241w/8091. 2010- 8457, 2011- 8729. pbs: 60m 6.66i '11, 100m 10.26 '11, 10.19w '10; 200m 21.03 '10, 400m 45.68 '12, 800m 1:55.90i '10, 1000m 2:32.67i '10, 1500m 4:18.94 '11, 60mh 7.60i '11, 110mh 13.35 '11, HJ 2.11i '10, 2.10 '11; PV 5.26i/5.15 '10, LJ 8.16i '12, 8.04 '10; SP 14.74 '11, DT 46.17 '11, JT 57.23 '11, Hep 6645i '12.

Dexter FAULK b. 14 Apr 1984 1.87m 75kg. Nike. Was at Barton County CC.
At 110mh: PAm-J: '03- 2; WY: '01- 6; won NACAC 2007.
Progress at 110mh: 2001- 14.23w, 2002- 13.97, 2003- 13.73/13.58w, 2004- 13.60/13.53w, 2005- 13.63, 2006- 13.68/13.58w, 2007- 13.34, 2008- 13.40, 2009- 13.13, 2010- 13.47, 2011- 13.35. pbs: 60m 6.72i '08, 100m 10.49 '09, 200m 21.34/21.18w '04, 50mh 6.50i '09, 60mh 7.40Ai '12, 7.50 '09; LJ 7.44 '00.

Justin GATLIN b. 10 Feb 1982 Brooklyn, NY 1.85m 79kg. Was at University of Tennessee.
At 100m/200m/4x100mR: OG: '04- 1/3/2R; WCh: '05- 1/1, '11- sf. At 60m: WI: '03- 1, '12- 1. Won US 100m 2005-06, 200m 2005 (indoor 60m 2003), NCAA 100m & 200m 2001-02 (& indoor 60m/200m 2002).
Progress at 100m, 200m: 2000- 10.36, 2001- 10.08, 20.29/19.86w; 2002: under international suspension 10.05/10.00w, 19.86; 2003- 9.97, 20.04; 2004- 9.85, 20.01; 2005- 9.88/9.84w, 20.00; 2006-

9.77dq, 2010- 10.09, 20.63; 2011- 9.95, 20.20. pbs: 60m 6.45i '03, 55mh 7.39i '02, 60mh 7.86i '01, 110mh 13.41dq '02, 13.78/13.74w '01; LJ 7.34i '01, 7.21 '00.

Top hurdler in high school (110mh 13.66 and 300mh 36.74 on junior hurdles). Retained NCAA sprint titles while ineligible for international competition in 2002 after failing a drugs test in 2001 (when he won 100m, 200m and 110mh at the US Juniors) for a prescribed medication to treat Attention Deficit Disorder. Reinstated by IAAF in July 2002. Won 2005 World 100m title by biggest ever winning margin of 0.17. He won all five 100m competitions in 2006, including tying the world record with 9.77 in Doha and taking the US title, but then came news that he had tested positive for testosterone before these performances. He received a four-year drugs ban but returned to competition in August 2010.

Tyson GAY b. 9 Aug 1982 Lexington 1.83m 73kg. adidas. Studied marketing at University of Arkansas.
At 100m/(200m)/4x100mR: OG: '08- sf; WCh: '05- (4), '07- 1/1/1R, '09- 2; WCp: '06- 1/1R, '10- 1R. Won DL 2010, WAF 100m 2009, 200m 2005-06, US 100m 2007-08, 200m 2007; NCAA 100m 2004.
Four N.American 100m records 2008-09.
Progress at 100m, 200m: 2000- 10.56, 21.27; 2001- 10.28, 21.23; 2002- 10.27/10.08w, 20.88/20.21w; 2003- 10.01w, 21.15/20.31w; 2004- 10.06/10.10w, 20.07; 2005- 10.08, 19.93; 2006- 9.84, 19.68; 2007- 9.84/9.76w, 19.62; 2008- 9.77/9.68w, 20.00; 2009- 9.69, 19.58; 2010- 9.78, 19.76; 2011- 9.79. pbs: 60m 6.39+ '09, 6.55i '05; 150mSt 14.51 '11, 200m/220ySt 19.41/19.54 '10, 400m 44.89 '10.
Ran four 200m races in under 19.85 in 2006 and now the all-time best for 100m/200m combined. Greatest ever sprint double (9.84 and 19.62) at 2007 US Champs and ran fastest ever 100m 9.68w/+4.1 (after US record in qf) to win US Olympic Trials in 2008 but then pulled hamstring in 200m qf and unable to compete again until Olympics, where he showed that he was not back to top form.

Justin GAYMON b. 13 Dec 1986 Stewartsville, New Jersey 1.75m 70kg. Nike, Was at University of Georgia.
At 400mh: won NACAC 2008.
Progress at 400mh: 2004- 52.87, 2005- 50.84, 2006- 50.20, 2007- 49.25, 2008- 48.46, 2009- 48.86, 2010- 48.65, 2011- 48.58. pbs: 200m 21.28 '08, 400m 45.94i/46.17 '08, 55mh 7.47i '07, 60mh 7.86i '09, 110mh 13.90 '06, 13.85w '07.

Ryan HALL b. 14 Oct 1982 Big Bear Lake, California 1.80m 64kg. Asics. Graduate of Stanford University.
At 5000m: WCh: '05- h. At Mar: OG: '08- 10. World 4k CC: '06- 19; 20k: '06- 11. Won US HMar & Mar 2007, CC 2006; NCAA 5000m 2005.

US records: 20km 2006, HMar 2007.
Progress at 5000m, Mar: 2004- 13:45.00, 2005- 13:16.03, 2006- 13:28.89, 2007- 2:08:24, 2008- 2:06:17, 2009- 2:09:40, 2010- 2:08:41dh, 2011- 2:04:58wdh/2:08:04, 2012- 2:09:30. pbs: 800m 1:51.07 '01, 1500m 3:42.70 '01, 1M 4:05.50 '05, 3000m 7:53.8+ '06, 2M 8:26.26 '06, 10000m 28:07.93 '07, Road: 15km 42:21 '07, 10M 45:33 '07, 20km 57:06e '07, HMar 59:43 '07, 30km 1:28:38 '08.
Made marathon debut in 2007: 7th London 2:08:24, 1st US Trial 2:09:02; 5th London 2008, 3rd Boston 2009, 4th Boston 2010-11. Married to **Sara Bei-Hall** (b. 15 Apr 1983) pbs: 1500m 4:08.55 '08, 5000m 15:20.88 '06, WI 3000m: '06-12, '12- 8.

James Edward 'Trey' HARDEE b. 7 Feb 1984 Birmingham, Alabama 1.96m 95kg. Nike. Was at Mississippi State University.
At Dec: OG: '08- dnf; WCh: '09- 1, '11- 1; won NCAA 2005, US 2009. At Hep: WI: '10- 2.
Progress at Dec: 2003- 7544, 2004- 8041, 2005- 7881, 2006- 8465, 2008- 8534, 2009- 8790, 2011- 8689. pbs: 55m 6.30i '06, 60m 6.71i '06, 100m 10.39 '10, 10.28w '06; 200m 20.98 '06, 400m 47.51 '06, 1000m 2:47.76i '10, 1500m 4:42.23 '06, 60mh 7.70i '10, 110mh 13.61 '12; HJ 2.06i '10, 2.05 '08; PV 5.30Ai '06, 5.25 '08; LJ 7.88 '11, SP 15.94i '09, 15.63 '11; DT 52.68 '08, JT 68.99 '11, Hep 6208Ai '06.
Won IAAF Combined Events Challenge 2009.

Antwon HICKS b. 12 Mar 1983 1.87m 73kg. adidas. Sociology graduate of the University of Mississippi.
At 110mh: WJ: '02- 1; won NCAA indoor 60mh 2004-05.
Progress at 110mh: 2002- 13.59/13.42w, 2003- 13.49/13.46w, 2004- 13.45, 2005- 13.35, 2006- 13.49/13.37w, 2007- 13.36, 2008- 13.09, 2009- 13.24, 2010- 13.29, 2011- 13.35. pbs: 60m 6.80i '08, 100m 10.94 '07, 200m 21.39 '05, 55mh 7.15i '04, 60mh 7.53i '08, HJ 2.08/2.16i '01.

Reese HOFFA b. 8 Oct 1977 Evans, Georgia 1.82m 133kg. New York AC. Was at University of Georgia.
At SP: OG: '04- dnq 22, '08- 7; WCh: '03-07-09-11: dnq/1/4/5; PAm: '03- 1; WI: '04-06-08-12: 2/1/2/4; WUG: '01- 9; WCp: '06- 2; won WAF 2006-07, USA 2007-08.
Progress at SP: 1998- 19.08, 1999- 19.35, 2000- 19.79, 2001- 20.22, 2002- 20.47, 2003- 20.95, 2004- 21.67, 2005- 21.74i/21.29, 2006- 22.11i/21.96, 2007- 22.43, 2008- 22.10, 2009- 21.89, 2010- 22.16, 2011- 22.09. pbs: DT 58.46 '99, HT 60.05 '02.
Added 37cm to his best to win World Indoor gold 2006.

Bershawn JACKSON b. 8 May 1983 Miami 1.73m 69kg. Nike. Studied accountancy at St Augustine's University, Raleigh.
At 400mh/4x400mR: OG: '08- 3; WCh: '03- h (dq), '05- 1, '07- sf/res 1R, '09- 3/res 1R, '11- 6/1R; WJ: '02- 3/1R; CCp: '10- 3/1R; won DL 2010, WAF 2004-05, US 2003, 2008-10. At 400m:

WI: '10- 5/1R; won US indoor 2005, 2010.
Progress at 400mh: 2000- 52.17, 2001- 50.86, 2002- 50.00, 2003- 48.23, 2004- 47.86, 2005- 47.30, 2006- 47.48, 2007- 48.13, 2008- 48.02, 2009- 47.98, 2010- 47.32, 2011- 47.93. pbs: 200m 21.03/20.46w '04, 400m 45.06 '07, 600m 1:18.65i '06, 800m 1:53.40 '11, 200mhSt 22.26 '11.

Kibwe JOHNSON b. 17 Jul 1981 San Francisco 1.89m 108kg. New York AC. Was at Ashland University.
At HT: WCh: '07- nt, '11- dnq 14; PAm: '07- 2, '11- 1; US champion 2011.
Progress at HT: 2002- 64.26, 2003- 69.11, 2004- 69.49, 2005- 78.25, 2006- 75.32, 2007- 75.95, 2008- 75.53, 2009- 67.80, 2010- 77.07, 2011- 80.31. pbs: SP 16.30i '05, DT 65.11 '05, Wt 25.12i '08.
Married to Crystal Smith (pb 68.60 '07).

Dustin 'Dusty' JONAS b. 19 Apr 1986 Floresville, Texas 1.98m 84kg. Nike. Was at University of Nebraska.
At HJ: OG: '08- dnq 26=; WCh: '11- dnq 30; WI: '10- 3; PAm-J: '05- 1; CCp: '10- 6. Won NCAA indoor 2008.
Progress at HJ: 2002- 2.16, 2003- 2.22, 2004- 2.13, 2005- 2.24, 2006- 2.28, 2007- 2.25i/2.24, 2008- 2.36A, 2009- 2.26i/2.24, 2010- 2.33, 2011- 2.31. pb LJ 7.47/7.76w '07; TJ 15.15i '12, 15.07 '07.

Trell KIMMONS b. 13 Jul 1985 Coldwater, Mississippi 1.78m 77kg. Was at Mississippi State University.
At 100m/4x100mR: WCh: '11- sf; WJ: '04- 1R. At 60m: WI: '10- 4, '12- 4.
Progress at 100m: 2003- 10.3w, 2004- 10.39/10.34w/10.0w, 2005- 10.22/10.16w, 2006- 10.17, 2007- 10.31/10.25w, 2008- 10.30, 2009- 10.16, 2010- 9.95/9.92w, 2011- 10.04/9.97w. pbs: 50m 5.68i '12, 60m 6.45Ai '12, 6.53i '06; 100y 9.37+ '10, 200m 20.37 '10, 20.3 '06, 20.32w '05; 400m 47.53 '10.

Bernard LAGAT b. 12 Dec 1974 Kapsabet, Kenya 1.75m 61kg. Nike. Studied business management at Washington State University, USA.
At 1500m (/5000m): OG: '00- 3, '04- 2, 08- sf/9; WCh: '01- 2, '05- sf, '07- 1/1, '09- 3/2, '11- (2); WI: '03- 2; AfCh: '02- 1; WUG: '99- 1; WCp: '02- 1; 2nd GP 1999-2000-02, WAF 2005-06. At 3000m: WI: '01-04-10-12: 6/1/1/1; CCp: '10- 1/ (1). Won WAF 3000m 2005, 2008; KEN 1500m 2002, US 1500m 2006, 2008; 5000m 2006-08, 2010- 11; NCAA 5000m 1999 (& indoor 1M/3000m).
Records: Commonwealth and KEN 1500m 2001, N.American 1500m 2005, 3000m 2010, 5000m 2010 & 2011, indoor 3000m 2007, 2M 2011, 5000m 2010, 2012. World M35 3000m & 5000m 2010, 1M and 5000m 2011.
Progress at 1500m, 5000m: 1996- 3:37.7A, 1997- 3:41.19, 13:50.33; 1998- 3:34.48, 13:42.73; 1999- 3:30.56, 13:36.12; 2000- 3:28.51, 13:23.46; 2001- 3:26.34, 13:30.54; 2002- 3:27.91, 13:19.14; 2003- 3:30.55, 2004- 3:27.40, 2005- 3:29.30, 12:59.29; 2006- 3:29.68, 12:59.22; 2007- 3:33.85, 13:30.73;

2008- 3:32.75, 13:16.29; 2009- 3:32.56, 13:03.06; 2010- 3:32.51, 12:54.12; 2011- 3:33.11, 12:53.60. pbs: 800m 1:46.00 '03, 1000m 2:16.18 '08, 1M 3:47.28 '01, 2000m 4:55.49 '99, 3000m 7:29.00 '10, 2M 8:10.07i '11, 8:12.45 '08.
Gave up his final year of scholastic eligibility (as under NCAA rules no payments can be received) at his university in order to compete (for money) in the 1999 GP Final, in which he was 2nd. He was 2nd to Hicham El Guerrouj six times in 2001, including his 3:26.34 at Brussels for 2nd on the world all-time list, and six times in 2002. Withdrew from 2003 Worlds after testing positive for EPO, but this was later repudiated. Lives in Tucson, Arizona gained US citizenship 2005. He became the first man ever to win 1500m/5000m double at the US Champs in 2006 and at the World Champs in 2007. Oldest ever male World Indoor champion and medallist at 37y 89d in 2012.
From a large family: a sister **Mary Chepkemboi** competed at the 1982 Commonwealth Games and won African 3000m in 1984, and another **Evelyne Jerotich Langat** has a 71:35 half marathon pb. Of his brothers **William Cheseret** has a marathon pb of 2:12:09 '04 and **Robert Cheseret** won the NCAA 5000m in 2004 and 10000m in 2005, pbs 5000m 13:13.23 & 10000m 28:20.11 '05.

Tony McQUAY b. 16 Apr 1990 1.78m 64kg. Student at University of Florida.
At 400m: WCh: '11- h; US champion 2011.
Progress at 400m: 2008- 48.09, 2009- 46.84, 2010- 45.37, 2011- 44.68. pbs: 100m 10.57 '10, 200m 20.61i '11, 20.64 '10.

Andra MANSON b. 30 Apr 1984 Brenham, Texas 1.96m 75kg. Nike. Kinesociology graduate of University of Texas.
At HJ: OG: '08- dnq 13; WCh: '09- 9; WJ: '02- 1; WI: '08- 3=; won NCAA 2004.
Progress at HJ: 2001- 2.13, 2002- 2.31, 2003- 2.22, 2004- 2.32, 2005- 2.26i/2.23, 2006- 2.28i/2.26, 2007- 2.33i/2.30, 2008- 2.33, 2009- 2.35, 2010- 2.23i/2.31, 2011- 2.25. pbs: 100m 10.81 '07, 10.73w '08; 200m 21.73 '08.
Won 2002 World Junior title with US junior record 2.31.

Leonel MANZANO b. 12 Sep 1984 Dolores Hidalgo, Guanajuato, Mexico 1.65m 57kg. Nike. Was at the University of Texas.
At 1500m: OG: '08- sf; WCh: '07- h, '09- 12, '11- sf; CCp: '10- 3. NCAA champion 2005, 2008.
Progress at 1500m: 2003- 4:07.83M, 2005- 3:37.13, 2006- 3:39.49, 2007- 3:35.29, 2008- 3:36.67, 2009- 3:33.33, 2010- 3:32.37, 2011- 3:33.66. pbs: 800m 1:44.56 '10, 1000m 2:19.73 '09, 1M 3:50.64 '10, 3000m 8:14.59i '06.
Has lived in the USA from the age of 4.

Cory MARTIN b. 22 May 1985 Bloomington, Indiana 1.96m 125kg. Nike. Was at Auburn University.

At SP: WJ: '04-11 (dnq 15 HT); Won NCAA SP & HT 2008.
Progress at SP: 2004- 17.95i/17.60, 2005- 18.85, 2006- 18.42i, 2007- 19.63, 2008- 20.35, 2009- 20.43, 2010- 22.10, 2011- 20.72. pbs: DT 58.59 '08, HT 75.06 '09, 35lbWt 24.38i '10.

Aries MERRITT b. 24 Jul 1985 Marietta, Georgia 1.88m 75kg. Reebok. Studied sports management at University of Tennessee.
At 110mh: WCh: '09- h, '11- 5=; WJ: '04- 1. At 60mh: WI: '12-1, Won NCAA 60mh indoors & 110mh 2006, US indoor 60mh 2012.
Progress at 110mh: 2004- 13.47, 2005- 13.38/13.34w, 2006- 13.12, 2007- 13.09, 2008- 13.24, 2009- 13.15, 2010- 13.61, 2011- 13.12. pbs: 55m 6.43i '05, 60m 6.90i '10, 200m 21.31 '05, 50mh 6.54i '12, 55mh 7.10i '06, 60mh 7.43Ai/7.44i '12, 400mh 51.94 '04.

LaShawn MERRITT b. 27 Jun 1986 Portsmouth, Virginia 1.88m 82kg. Nike. Studying sports management at Old Dominion University, Norfolk, Virginia.
At 400m/4x400mR: OG: '08- 1/1R; WCh: '05- res(1)R, '07- 2/1R, '09- 1/1R, '11- 1/1R; WJ: '04- 1/1R (1 at 4x100); WI: '06- 1R; WCp: '06- 1/1R; won WAF 2007-09, US 2008-09.
World junior records 4x100m and 4x400m 2004, World indoor 400m junior best (44.93) 2005.
Progress at 200m, 400m: 2002- 21.46, 2003- 21.33, 47.9?; 2004- 20.72/20.69w, 45.25; 2005- 20.38, 44.66; 2006- 20.10, 44.14; 2007- 19.98, 43.96; 2008- 20.08/19.80w, 43.75; 2009- 20.07, 44.06; 2011- 20.13, 44.63. pbs: 55m 6.33i '04, 60m 6.68i '06, 100m 10.47/10.38w '04, 300m 31.30 '09, 500m 1:01.39i '12.
World age-18 400m record with 44.66 in 2005 and world low-altitude 300m best 2006 and 2009. Spent a year at East Carolina University before signing for Nike and returning home to Portsmouth. Two-year drugs ban for three positive tests from October 2009, but ban reduced by three months after a US arbitration panel declared that he had taken the steroid accidentally in buying a product intended for sexual enhancement.

Derek MILES b. 28 Sep 1972 Sacramento 1.90m 88kg. Mike. History graduate of University of South Dakota. Academic advisor at Arkansas State University.
At PV: OG: '04- 7, '08- 4; WCh: '03- 6=, '09- nh, '11- 13; WI: '03-08-10: 5/8/4=; CCp: '10- 3. Won WAF 2008, US 2008, 2011.
World M35 pole vault record 2008.
Progress at PV: 1997- 5.50, 1998- 5.35, 1999- 5.40Ai/5.35, 2000- 5.65, 2001- 5.82i/5.74, 2002- 5.82i/5.74, 2003- 5.81, 2004- 5.81, 2005- 5.85i/5.81, 2006- 5.65i/5.50, 2007- 5.75, 2008- 5.85sq, 2009- 5.82i/5.75, 2010- 5.81, 2011- 5.72.

Maurice MITCHELL b. 11 Mar 1989 1.78m 73kg. Social sciences student at Florida State University.

At 200m: NCAA 2011. At 4x100m: WCh: '11- h. Progress at 200m: 2007- 20.77, 2008- 21.40/21.23w/20.5w, 2009- 20.64, 2010- 20.24, 2011- 20.19/19.99w. pbs: 60m 6.55i '11, 100m 10.00 '11, 400m 47.60.

Adam NELSON b. 7 Jul 1975 Atlanta 1.83m 115kg. Saucony. Graduate of Dartmouth University. Training as a financial consultant.
At SP: OG: '00- 2, '04- 2, '08- nt; WCh: '01-03-05-07-09-11: 2/2/1/2/5/8; WI: '01- 2; WJ: '94- 1; WUG: '99- 2; WCp: '02- 1. GP 2002 (2nd 2000 and 3rd overall). Won WAF 2005, PAm-J 1993, GWG 2001, NCAA 1997, US 2000, 2002, 2004, 2006, 2011.
Progress at SP: 1993- 16.56, 1994- 18.34, 1995- 18.27, 1996- 19.14, 1997- 19.62, 1998- 20.61, 1999- 20.64, 2000- 22.12, 2001- 21.53, 2002- 22.51, 2003- 21.29, 2004- 21.68, 2005- 21.92, 2006- 22.04, 2007- 21.61, 2008- 22.40i/22.12, 2009- 21.11, 2010- 21.29i/21.16, 2011- 22.09. pb DT 56.18 '96.
Had a great season in 2000, when he improved his best from 20.64 to 21.70 and then the world's longest throw for four years, 22.12 (to take the US title) in July. Further improvement as world number one in 2002. Small for a shot putter, but very fast and dynamic in the circle. Played American Football at high school and college.

Greg NIXON b. 12 Sep 1981 New Orleans 1.83m 75kg. Asics. Was at Howard Payne University.
At 400m/4x400mR: WCh: '11- sf/1R; PAm: '07- 2R; WI: '08 & '10- 1R; CCp: '10- 1R. US champion 2010.
Progress at 400m: 2007- 45.31, 2008- 45.20, 2009- 45.67, 2010- 44.61, 2011- 44.98. pbs: 100m 10.43 '09, 10.37w '05; 200m 20.39 '09, 300m 32.35 '07. Was a wide receiver at Grambling State University.

David OLIVER b. 24 Apr 1982 Orlando 1.88m 93kg. Nike. Marketing graduate of Howard University.
At 110mh: OG: '08- 3; WCh: '07- sf, '11- 4; CCp: '10- 1. Won DL 2010, WAF 2008, US 2008, 2010-11. At 60mh: WI: '10- 3.
Two North American 110mh records 2010/
Progress at 110mh: 2001- 14.04, 2002- 13.92/13.88w, 2003- 13.60, 2004- 13.55, 2005- 13.29/13.23w, 2006- 13.20, 2007- 13.14, 2008- 12.95/12.89w, 2009- 13.09, 2010- 12.89, 2011- 12.94. pbs: 60m 6.88i '04, 50mh 6.50i '12, 55mh 7.04i '07, 60mh 7.37i '11.
Mother, Brenda Chambers, 400mh pb 58.54 '80.

Travis PADGETT b. 13 Dec 1986 Shelby, North Carolina 1.74m 80kg. adidas. Student of sociology at Clemson University.
At 100m/4x100mR: OG: '08- dnf hR. Won NCAA indoor 60m 2007.
Progress at 100m: 2003- 10.54, 2004- 10.46, 2005- 10.62/10.55w, 2006- 10.00, 2007- 10.09/10.05w, 2008- 9.89/9.85w, 2009- 10.00/9.93w, 2010-

10.10/9.92w, 2011- 9.99/9.96w. pbs: 55m 6.17i '07, 60m 6.55i '10, 200m 20.32 '08.

Darvis PATTON b. 4 Dec 1977 Dallas 1.83m 75kg. Nike. Was at Texas Christian University. At 200m/4x100m: OG: '04- res 2R; WCh: '03- 2/1R, '07- 1R, '11- sf. At 100m: OG: '08- 8; WCh: '09- 8; PAm: '07- 2/3R. Won US 200m 2002-03.
Progress at 100m, 200m: 1998- 10.3, 20.49w; 2000- 10.22w/10.09w, 20.29; 2001- 10.16/10.14w, 20.31; 2002- 10.14, 20.12; 2003- 10.00/9.97w, 20.03, 2004- 10.12/9.89w, 20.17/20.07w; 2005- 10.27; 2006- 10.19, 20.50; 2007- 10.11, 20.49; 2008- 9.89/9.84w; 2009- 9.89, 20.32; 2010- 10.19, 2011- 9.94, 20.25. pbs: 60m 6.58i '03, LJ 8.12 '01, TJ 16.17i '98.
Concentrated on 100m from 2008. Turned to athletics after dislocating his hip playing American football as a teenager.

David PAYNE b. 24 Jul 1982 Cincinnati 1.85m 81kg. Was at University of Cincinnati.
At 110mh: OG: '08- 2; WCh: '07- 3, '09- 3; PAm: '07- 2. US champion 2009.
Progress at 110mh: 2002- 13.92, 2003- 13.53, 2004- 13.48/13.42w, 2005- 13.33, 2006- 13.31, 2007- 13.02, 2008- 13.17/13.06w, 2009- 13.12, 2010- 13.22, 2011- 13.63. pbs: 100m 10.56 '07, 200m 21.15 '07, 60mh 7.51i '07, 400mh 51.16 '04.

Dwight PHILLIPS b. 1 Oct 1977 Decatur, Georgia 1.81m 78kg. Nike. Was at University of Kentucky, then Arizona State University.
At LJ: OG: '00- 8, '04- 1; WCh: '01-03-05-07-09- 11: 8/1/1/3/1/1; WI: '03- 1; PAm: '99- 7; CCp: '10- 1. Won DL 2010, WAF 2003, 2005; US 2003- 04, 2007, 2009-10.
Progress at LJ: 1996- 7.14, 1997- 7.26, 1999- 8.18, 2000- 8.21/8.30w, 2001- 8.13/8.23w, 2002- 8.38, 2003- 8.44, 2004- 8.60, 2005- 8.60, 2006- 8.32, 2007- 8.31/8.37w, 2008- 8.25/8.47w, 2009- 8.74, 2010- 8.46, 2011- 8.45. pbs: 50m 5.70i '05, 60m 6.47i '05, 100m 10.06 '09, 200m 20.68 '02, 400m 46.80 '97, TJ 16.41 '99.
World number one 2003-05, winning 34 of 42 competitions in those three years, and in 2009- 10. Twelve consecutive years over 8m.

Jason RICHARDSON b. 4 Apr 1986 Houston 1.86m 73kg. Nike. Was at University of South Carolina.
At 110mh: WCh: '11- 1; WY: '03- 1 (1 400mh); won NCAA 2008.
Progress at 110mh: 2004- 13.76, 2005- 13.50, 2006- 13.43/13.36w, 2008- 13.21, 2009- 13.29, 2010- 13.34, 2011- 13.04. pbs: 100m 10.90 '03, 200m 21.13 '03, 400m 47.75i '04, 60mh 7.53i '08, 400mh 49.79 '04.

Khadevis ROBINSON b. 19 Jul 1976 Dallas 1.83m 74kg. Nike. Degree in social work from Texas Christian University.
At 800m: OG: '04- h; WCh: '99/01- h, '03/05/07/09/11- sf; WCp: '06- 6. At 400mR: WI: '99- res (1)R. Won US 800m 1999, 2005-07, indoors 1999, 2006, 2008-09; NCAA 1998.

US record 4x800m 2006.
Progress at 800m: 1994- 1:53+, 1995- 1:48.61, 1996- 1:47.85, 1997- 1:47.46, 1998- 1:45.72, 1999- 1:45.23, 2000- 1:45.40, 2001- 1:45.15, 2002- 1:44.41, 2003- 1:45.03, 2004- 1:44.89, 2005- 1:44.62, 2006- 1:43.68, 2007- 1:44.27, 2008- 1:44.55, 2009- 1:44.47, 2010- 1:45.53, 2011- 1:44.03. pbs: 400m 46.55 '98, 600m 1:15.23 '05, 1500m 3:46.74 '08.

Michael RODGERS b. 24 Apr 1985 Brenham, Texas 1.78m 73kg. Nike. Studied kinesiology at Oklahoma Baptist University.
At 100m: WCh: '09- sf; At 60m: WI: '08- 4, '10- 2. Won US 100m 2009, indoor 60m 2008.
Progress at 100m: 2004- 10.55/10.31w, 2005- 10.30/10.25w, 2006- 10.29/10.18w, 2007- 10.10, 10.07w, 2008- 10.06/10.01w, 2009- 9.94/9.9/9.85w, 2010- 10.00/9.99w, 2011- 9.85. pbs: 60m 6.48Ai/6.50i '11, 200m 20.24 '09.
Dropped out of US World Champs team after positive test for stimulant on 19 July 2011, for which he subsequently received a 9-month suspension. Younger sister Alishea Usery won US junior 400m 2009. pb 53.27 '09.

Jarred ROME b. 21 Dec 1976 Seattle 1.94m 140kg. Nike. Studied business education at Boise State University.
At DT: OG: '04- dnq 13; WCh: '05-07-09-11: 7/ dnq 15/11/dnq 14; WUG: '01- 8. US champion 2004, 2011.
Progress at DT: 1996- 53.14, 1997- 59.46, 1998- 59.78, 1999- 56.86, 2000- 64.00, 2001- 65.53, 2002- 65.92, 2003- 62.24, 2004- 67.51, 2005- 67.39, 2006- 67.25, 2007- 68.37, 2008- 68.44, 2009- 65.56, 2010- 66.71, 2011- 68.76. pb SP 20.40 '06.
Was a quarterback in high school.

Galen RUPP b. 8 May 1986 Portland 1.80m 62kg. Nike. Studied business at University of Oregon.
At (5000/)10000m: OG: '08- 13; WCh: '07- 11, '09- 8, '11- 9/7. At 5000m: WJ: '04- 9; PAm-J: '03- 1. At 3000m: WI: '09- 5; WY: '03- 7. Won US 10000m 2009-11, NCAA 5000m & 10000m (& indoor 3000m & 5000m) 2009, CC 2008.
North American records: 10000m 2011, junior 5000m 2004, 10000m 2005; indoor 5000m (13:11.44) 2011, 2M 2012.
Progress at 5000m, 10000m: 2002- 14:34.05, 2003- 14:20.29, 2004- 13:37.91, 29:09.56; 2005- 13:44.72. 28:15.52; 2006- 13:47.04, 30:42.10; 2007- 13:30.49, 27:33.48; 2008- 13:59.14, 27:36.99; 2009- 13:18.12i/13:42.59+, 27:37.99; 2010- 13:07.35, 27:10.74; 2011- 13:06.86, 26:48.00. pbs: 800m 1:49.87i/1:50.00 '09, 1500m 3:39.14 '09, 1M 3:56.22i '10, 4:01.8 '04; 3000m 7:42.40i/7:43.24 '10, 2M 8:09.72i '12, HMar 60:30 '11.

Jeremy SCOTT b. 21 May 1981 Norfolk. Nebraska 2.06m 91kg. Nike. Was at University of Arkansas.
At PV: WCh: '09- dnq 15, '11- 9; PAm: '07- nh, '11- 2; won US indoors 2009.

Progress at PV: 2001- 5.05, 2002- 5.55, 2003- 5.70i, 2004- 5.56, 2005- 5.60i, 2006- 5.62i/5.35, 2007- 5.66, 2008- 5.75i/5.65, 2009- 5.82i/5.75, 2010- 5.82i/5.71/5.76sq, 2011- 5.80i. 5.72.

Chris SOLINSKY b. 5 Dec 1984 Stevens Point, Wisconsin 1.85m 73kg. Nike. Was at University of Wisconsin.
At 5000m: WCh: '09- 12. Won NCAA 5000m 2006-07.
North American record on 10000m debut 2010.
Progress at 5000m, 10000m: 2004- 13:42.44, 2005- 13:37.55, 2006- 13:27.94, 2007- 13:12.24, 2008- 13:18.51, 2009- 13:18.41, 2010- 12:55.53, 26:59.60; 2011- 13:10.22. pbs: 1500m 3:35.89 '11, 1M 3:54.52i '11, 3:57.80 '06; 3000m 7:34.32 '10, 2M 8:15.77 '08.
First athlete not born in Africa to break 27 mins for 10,000m,

Wallace SPEARMON b. 24 Dec 1984 Chicago 1.90m 80kg. Saucony. Was at University of Arkansas.
At 200m/4x100mR: OG: '08- dq; WCh: '05- 2, '07- 3/1R, '09- 3; WCp: '06- 1/1R, '10- 1/1R. Won DL 2010, US 2006, 2010; NCAA 2004-05. At 4x400m: WI: '06- 1R.
WIR 4x400m and world indoor best 300m 2006. Two US indoor 200m records 2005.
Progress at 100m, 200m: 2003- 21.05, 2004- 10.38, 20.25/20.12w; 2005- 10.35/10.21w, 19.89; 2006- 10.11, 19.65; 2007- 9.96, 19.82; 2008- 10.07, 19.90; 2009- 10.18, 19.85; 2010- 10.15, 19.79/19.77w; 2011- 20.18; 2012- 10.06w. pbs: 60m 6.66i '12, 300m 31.88i '06, 32.14 '09; 400m 45.22.
Disqualified for running out of his lane after crossing the line in 3rd place at the 2008 Olympics. His father (also Wallace, b. 3 Sep 1962) had pbs: of 100m 10.19 '87, 10.05w '86, 10.0w '81; 200m 20.27/20.20w '87; 1 WUG 200/ 4x100m, 3 PAm 200m 1987.

Nick SYMMONDS b. 30 Dec 1983 Blytheville, Arkansas 1.78m 73kg. Oregon TC. Biochemistry graduate of Willamette University.
At 800m: OG: '08- sf; WCh: '07- sf, '09- 6, '11- 5; WI: '08- 6; CCp: '10- 5. US champion 2008-11.
Progress at 800m: 2003- 1:49.51, 2004- 1:50.87, 2005- 1:48.82, 2006- 1:45.83, 2007- 1:44.54, 2008- 1:44.10, 2009- 1:43.83, 2010- 1:43.76, 2011- 1:43.83. pbs: 400m 48.84 '04, 600m 1:14.47 '08, 1000m 2:16.35 '10, 1000m 2:20.52 '09, 1500m 3:38.18 '11, 1M 3:56.72i '07, 4:03.85 '03.

Angelo TAYLOR b. 29 Dec 1978 Albany, Georgia 1.88m 84kg. Nike. Was at Georgia Tech University. Electrician.
At 400mh/4x400mR: OG: '00- 1/dq (res 1)R, '04- sf, '08- 1/1R; WCh: '99- h/dq(1)R, '01- sf/ dq(1)R, '07- (3 400m)/1R, '09- h/1R, '11- 7/1R; WJ: '96- 3; PAm-J: '97- 1/1R; won GP 2000 (and overall), NCAA 1998, US 400mh 1999-2001, 400m 2007, indoor 400m 1999
Progress at 400m, 400mh: 1995- -, 52.76, 1996-

46.7, 50.18; 1997- 46.19i/46.81, 48.72; 1998- 45.14, 47.90; 1999- 45.50i, 48.15; 2000- 44.89, 47.50; 2001- 44.68, 47.95; 2002- 44.85, 48.87; 2003- 46.32, 48.94; 2004- 45.85, 48.03; 2006- 45.24, 49.44; 2007- 44.05, 48.45; 2008- 44.38, 47.25; 2009- 45.15, 48.30; 2010- 44.72, 47.79; 2011- 44.82, 47.94. pbs: 100m 10.58 '08, 200m 20.23 '10, 300m 32.67 '02, TJ 14.76 '96.
Brilliant year in 1998, with fastest ever time by a 19 year-old and losing just twice (to Bryan Bronson) at 400mh. Went out in his heat (misjudging the finish) when favourite for 1999 World 400mh, but made amends with relay gold, and, after winning Olympic gold in 2000, stumbled off the last hurdle in 2001 World 400mh semi. Regained Olympic title in 2008.

Christian TAYLOR b. 18 Jun 1990 Fayetteville 1.90m 75kg. Student at University of Florida.
At (LJ/)TJ: WCh: '11- 1; WI: '12- 2; WJ: '08- 7/8 (res 1 4x400m); WY: '07- 3/1. Won NACAC 2010-11, US 2011, NCAA indoor 2009-10.
Progress at TJ: 2007- 15.98, 2008- 16.05, 2009- 16.98i/16.65/16.91w, 2010- 17.18i/17.02/17.09w, 2011- 17.96, 2012- 17.63i. pbs: 60m 6.79i '11, 200m 20.76 '11, 400m 45.34 '09, LJ 8.19 '10.

Dan TAYLOR b. 12 May 1982 Cleveland 1.98m 145kg. Nike. Construction management graduate of Ohio State University.
At SP: WCh: '07/09- dnq 34/26; PAm: '03- 4. Won NCAA indoor 2003-04.
Progress at SP: 2001- 18.31, 2002- 20.01i/19.15, 2003- 21.33i/20.44, 2004- 20.62, 2005- 20.75, 2006- 21.59, 2007- 21.57i/21.18, 2008- 20.85, 2009- 21.78, 2010- 20.89i/20.68, 2011- 20.90. pbs: DT 59.00 '03, HT 69.35 '04, Wt 24.01i '04.
Achieved unique NCAA SP/Wt double 2004.

Matt TEGENKAMP b. 19 Jan 1982 Lee's Summit, Missouri 1.86m 66kg. Nike. Studied human ecology at University of Wisconsin.
At 5000m: OG: '08- 13; WCh: '07- 4, '09- 8; WCp: '06- 3. At 10000m: WCh: '11- 10. World CC: '01- 5J. Won US 5000m 2009.
North American 2M record 2007.
Progress at 5000m, 10000m: 2001- 13:49.64, 2002- 13:44.77, 29:29.35; 2004- 13:30.90, 2005- 13:25.36, 2006- 13:04.90, 2007- 13:07.41, 2008- 13:25.71, 2009- 12:58.56, 2010- 13:25.09, 2011- 13:14.75, 27:28.22. pbs: 1500m 3:34.25 '07, 1M 3:56.38 '06, 2000m 5:01.3 '06, 3000m 7:34.98 '06, 2M 8:07.07 '07.

Michael TINSLEY b. 21 Apr 1984 1.83m 80kg. adidas. Studied criminal justice at Jackson State University.
At 400mh: NCAA champion 2008.
Progress at 400mh: 2002- 52.5, 2004- 50.87, 2005- 48.55, 2006- 48.25, 2007- 48.02, 2008- 48.84, 2009- 48.53, 2010- 48.46, 2011- 48.45. pbs: 60m 6.92i '05, 200m 20.66 '09, 400m 46.02i '06, 46.05 '07; 55mh 7.39i '04, 60mh 7.84i '06, 110mh 13.86 '04.

Terrence TRAMMELL b. 23 Nov 1978 Atlanta 1.88m 84kg. Trackstar Apparel. Studied retail management at University of South Carolina.
At 110mh/4x100m: OG: '00- 2, '04- 2, '08- h; WCh: '01-03-05-07-09: sf/2/5/2/2; WUG: '99- 1/1R; Won US 2004, 2007; NCAA 1999-2000. At 60mh: WI: '01- 1, '06- 1 (60m 3), '10- 2; won US 60mh 2000-01, 2006, 2009-10.
North American indoor 60mh record 2010.
Progress at 110mh: 1997- 13.87, 1998- 13.32, 1999- 13.28, 2000- 13.16, 2001- 13.23, 2002- 13.17, 2003- 13.17, 2004- 13.09, 2005- 13.02, 2006- 13.02, 2007- 12.95, 2008- 13.08/13.00w, 2009- 13.12, 2010- 13.39, 2011- 13.16. pbs: 55m 6.12i '99, 60m 6.45Ai '00, 6.46i '03; 100m 10.04 '00, 200m 20.74 '98, 20.45w '99; 50mh 6.45i '12, 55mh 6.94i '99, 60mh 7.36i '10.
Twice world indoor champion at 60mh and joint fifth all-time at both flat and hurdles at 60m indoors. After 13.02 for 110mh in 2005 and 2006 broke 13 seconds for first time at New York in 2007. Injured in heats of World Indoor 60m 2003 and Olympic 110mh 2008.

Brad WALKER b. 21 Jun 1981 Aberdeen, South Dakota 1.88m 86kg. Nike. Graduated in business administration from University of Washington
At PV: OG: '08- dnq nh; WCh: '05- 2, '07- 1; WI: '06-08-12: 1/2/3; Won WAF 2005, 2007; US 2005, 2007, 2009; indoors 2005-06, NCAA indoor 2003-04. N. American pole vault record 2008.
Progress at PV: 1999- 4.80, 2000- 5.12, 2001- 5.48i/5.36, 2002- 5.64, 2003- 5.80i/5.65, 2004- 5.82, 2005- 5.96, 2006- 6.00, 2007- 5.95, 2008- 6.04, 2009- 5.80, 2010- 5.61, 2011- 5.84. 2012- 5.86Ai.

Jeremy WARINER b. 31 Jan 1984 Irving, Texas 1.83m 70kg. adidas. Student of outdoor recreation at Baylor University.
At 400m/4x400mR: OG: '04- 1/1R, '08- 2/1R; WCh: '05- 1/1R, '07- 1/1R, '09- 2/1R; PAm-J: '03- 2/1R; CCp: '10- 1. Won DL 2010, US 2004- 05, NCAA 2004, WAF 2006.
WIR 4x400m 2006.
Progress at 200m, 400m: 2001- 21.33/21.23w, 46.68; 2002- 21.17/20.8/20.41w, 45.57; 2003- 20.78, 45.13; 2004- 20.59, 44.00; 2005- 20.52w, 43.93; 2006- 20.19, 43.62; 2007- 20.35, 43.45; 2008- 20.37, 43.82; 2009- 20.30, 44.60; 2010- 44.13. 2011- 20.71, 44.88. pbs: 100m 10.52w '02, 300m 31.58+ '07.
His 43.93 to win 2005 World title was world's fastest 400m time for five years, his 43.62 to win Rome GP in 2006 the fastest for seven years and his 43.45 to win the 2007 World title took him to third on the world all-time list. He shared the Golden League jackpot and won all eleven 400m races in 2006 with three sub-44 times (a record seven sub-44.25s and 10 sub 44.50s) until he dropped out in Shanghai. Won all 10 races in 2007 apart from failure to start in Sheffield.

Andrew WHEATING b. 21 Nov 1987 Norwich, Vermont 1.96m 77kg. Oregon TC. Sociology graduate of University of Oregon.
At 800m: OG: '08- h. At 1500m: WCh: '11- h. Won NCAA 800m 2009-10, 1500m 2010.
Progress at 800m, 1500m: 2006- 3:54.28. 2007- 1:50.17, 3:45.17; 2008- 1:45.03, 3:38.60; 2009- 1:46.21, 3:40.92; 2010- 1:44.56, 3:30.90; 2011- 1:45.95, 3:34.59. pb 1M 3:51.74 '10.

Ryan WHITING b. 24 Nov 1986 Harrisburg PA 1.90m 116kg. Nike. Studied civil engineering at Arizona State University.
At SP: WCh: '11- 7; WI: '12- 1; PAm-J: '05- 1 (1 DT); Won NACAC 2009, NCAA 2009-10, indoor 2008-10, DT 2010.
Progress at SP: 2006- 19.75, 2007- 20.35, 2008- 21.73i/20.60, 2009- 20.99, 2010- 21.97, 2011- 21.76, 2012- 22.00i. pb DT 61.11 '08, Wt 18.94i '10.

Ivory WILLIAMS 2 May 1985 Jefferson County, Texas 1.74m 77kg. Nike. Was at Butler County CC.
At 100m/4x10mR: WJ: '02- 1R, '04- 1/1R.
Progress at 100m: 2002- 10.27/10.12w, 2003- 10.16w, 2004- 10.29/10.25w, 2005- 10.39/10.08w, 2006- 10.44/10.21w, 2007- 10.13/10.11w, 2008- 9.94, 2009- 9.93, 2010- 9.95/9.88w, 2011- 10.02/9.95w. pbs: 60m 6.51i (6.49Adq) '10, 200m 20.62 '06, 20.05w '09, 400m 46.25 '05.
'Won' US indoor 60m 2010 but tested positive for marijuana and lost title and time of 6.49A..

Jesse WILLIAMS b. 27 Dec 1983 Modesto 1.84m 75kg. Oregon TC. Graduate of University of Southern California, formerly at North Carolina State.
At HJ: OG: '08- dnq 19=; WCh: '05/07- dnq 15/26, '11- 1; WJ: '02- 4=; WI: '08-10-12: 6=/5/6=; Won US 2008, 2010-11; NCAA indoors and out 2005-06.
Progress at HJ: 2001- 2.16, 2002- 2.21, 2003- 2.24, 2004- 2.24, 2005- 2.30, 2006- 2.32, 2007- 2.33, 2008- 2.32i/2.30, 2009- 2.36i/2.34, 2010- 2.34Ai/2.30, 2011- 2.37. pb LJ 7.53 '06.
Also a wrestler in high school.

Ryan WILSON b. 19 Dec 1980 Columbus, Ohio 1.88m 81kg. Nike. Graduate (art) of University of Southern California.
At 110mh: won NCAA 2003.
Progress at 110mh: 2000- 14.00/13.79w, 2001- 13.69, 2002- 13.55, 2003- 13.35, 2004- 13.65/13.58w, 2005- 13.99, 2006- 13.22, 2007- 13.02, 2008- 13.28, 2009- 13.21, 2010- 13.12, 2011- 13.36/13.35w. pbs: 400m 48.52 '01, 50mh 6.78i '02, 55mh 7.25i '06, 60mh 7.83i '04, 400mh 49.33 '03, LJ 7.29 '02.

Jason YOUNG b. 27 May 1981 Dallas 1.85m 127kg. Nike. Was at Texas Tech University.
At DT: WCh: '11- 10; CCp: '10- 5.
Progress at DT: 1999- 52.06, 2000- 58.80A, 2001- 59.96A, 2002- 61.00, 2003- 61.56, 2004- 62.91, 2006- 67.86, 2008- 65.84, 2009- 61.76, 2010- 69.90, 2011- 65.30. pb Wt 19.23i '02.

Women

Nia ALI b. 23 Oct 1988 Philadelphia 1.70m 40kg. University of Southern California.
At 100mh: WUG: '11- 1. Won NCAA 2011.
Progress at 100mh: 2005- 14.20, 2006- 13.63/13.55w, 2007- 13.25, 2008- 13.14, 2009- 13.17, 2011- 12.73/12.63w. pbs: 200m 23.90 '09, 800m 2:24.55 '07, 60mh 8.06i '11, HJ 1.86 '11, LJ 5.89 '09, SP 13.61 '09, JT 39.24 '09, Hep 5824 '09.

Alexandria ANDERSON b. 28 Jan 1987 Chicago 1.75m 60kg. Nike. Was at University of Texas.
At 100m/4x100mR: WCh: '11- res (1)R; WJ: '04- 1R, '06- 5/1R. At 200m: PAm-J: '05- 2. Won NCAA 100m 2009.
Progress at 100m, 200m: 2002- 11.81, 24.10w; 2003- 11.62, 23.48; 2004- 11.41, 23.45; 2005- 11.39/11.38w, 22.96; 2006- 11.12/11.10w, 23.16/23.14w; 2007- 11.21/11.11w, 22.67; 2008- 11.07/10.98w, 22.75; 2009- 11.02/10.92w, 22.60; 2010- 11.04, 22.83; 2011- 11.01/10.91w, 22.87. pbs: 50m 6.28i '12, 55m 6.88i '06, 60m 7.12Ai '11, 7.17i '08; 400m 52.63 '05, 60mh 8.83Ai '06, LJ 6.32 '05, TJ 11.68 '07.

Brigetta BARRETT b. 24 Dec 1990 Avondale, Arizona 1.83m 64kg. Student at University of Arizona.
At HJ: WCh: '11- 10; WUG: '11- 1. Won US & NCAA 2011.
Progress at HJ: 2007- 1.72, 2008- 1.83A, 2009- 1.83, 2010- 1.91, 2011- 1.96.

Jessica BEARD b. 8 Jan 1989 Euclid, Ohio 1.68m 57kg. adidas. Psychology student at Texas A&M University.
At 400m/4x400mR: WCh: '09- sf/res (1)R, '11- sf/1R; WJ: '06- 5/1R, '08- 2/1R; PAm-J: '07- 3; won NCAA 2011.
Progress at 400m: 2004- 55.22, 2005- 52.39, 2006- 51.89, 2007- 51.63, 2008- 51.09A/51.47, 2009- 50.56, 2010- 51.02, 2011- 51.06. pbs: 60m 7.52i '11, 100m 11.86 '09, 11.49w '11; 200m 22.95i, 23.02 '11.

Becky BREISCH b. 10 Oct 1982 Edwardsburg, Michigan 1.80m 104kg. Nike. Was at University of Nebraska.
At DT: WCh: '05-07-09: dnq 18/18/22; CCp: '10- 5; Won US DT 2010; NCAA SP 2003, DT 2004, NACAC DT 2004.
Progress at DT: 1999- 46.16, 2000- 47.83, 2001- 48.23, 2002- 55.67, 2003- 58.69, 2004- 63.12, 2005- 63.53, 2006- 62.75, 2007- 67.37, 2008- 64.10, 2009- 62.08, 2010- 66.52, 2011- 64.30. pbs: SP 18.46 '06, 20lbWt 19.87i '04.

Stephanie BROWN TRAFTON b. 1 Dec 1979 San Luis Obispo, California 1.93m 102kg. née Brown. Nike. Engineering graduate of Cal Poly San Luis Obispo.
At DT: OG: '04- dnq 24, '08- 1; WCh: '09- 12, '11- 5. US champion 2009, 2011.
Progress at DT: 1997- 45.78, 1998- 55.24, 1999- 52.79, 2001- 51.46, 2002- 54.11, 2003- 57.78, 2004- 61.90, 2005- 55.35, 2006- 59.03, 2007- 61.40, 2008-

66.17, 2009- 66.21, 2010- 61.51, 2011- 64.13. pbs: 400m 57.44 '08, SP 17.86 '04.
Former basketball player.

Jillian CAMARENA-WILLIAMS b. 2 Aug 1982 Woodland, CA 1.80m 91kg. New York AC. Was at Stanford University.
At SP: OG: '08- 12; WCh: '07/09: dnq 21/23, '11- 3; PAm: '07- 4; WI: '06-10-12: 7/6/4; WCp: '06- 6, '10- 5. Won PAm-J 2001, USA 2006 (indoor 2005-12). North American shot record 2011, indoors 2012.
Progress at SP: 1999- 15.53, 2000- 15.23, 2001- 16.38, 2002- 16.82i/16.79, 2003- 17.49, 2004- 18.15, 2005- 17.94, 2006- 19.26i/19.02, 2007- 18.92, 2008- 18.51, 2009- 18.59i/18.08, 2010- 19.50, 2011- 20.18, 2012- 19.89i. pb DT 52.52 '03.
Married to physiotherapist Dustin Williams.

Amber CAMPBELL b. 5 Jun 1981 Indianapolis 1.70m 91kg. Nike. Was at Coastal Carolina University.
At HT: OG: '08- dnq 21; WCh: '05: dnq 18, '09-11, '11- dnq 14; PAm: '11- 3. Won US indoor Wt 2007-11.
Progress at HT: 2000- 49.16, 2001- 62.08, 2002- 63.76, 2003- 64.58, 2004- 67.23, 2005- 69.52, 2006- 67.52, 2007- 70.33, 2008- 70.19, 2009- 70.61, 2010- 71.94, 2011- 72.59. pbs: SP 14.81i '02, 14.42 '04; 20lb Wt 24.70i '10.

Danielle CARRUTHERS b. 22 Dec 1979 Paducah, Kentucky 1.73m 62kg. Nike. Was at University of Indiana.
At 100mh: WCh: '11- 2; WUG: '01- 8. At 60mh: WI: '06- 4. Won US indoor 60mh 2005-06.
Progress at 100mh: 1998- 13.88/13.77w, 2000- 13.33, 2001- 12.96/12.79w, 2002- 12.68, 2003- 12.79, 2004- 12.56, 2005- 12.72/12.63w, 2006- 12.74, 2007- 12.89, 2008- 12.84, 2009- 12.73, 2010- 12.68, 2011- 12.47/12.37w. pbs: 55m 6.79i '00, 60m 7.26i '02, 100m 11.43/11.42w '01, 200m 23.24 '01, 50mh 6.90i '09, 55mh 7.50i '09, 60mh 7.88i '06.

Michelle CARTER b. 12 Oct 1985 San Jose 1.75m 104kg. Nike. Liberal arts graduate from University of Texas.
At SP: OG: '08- 15; WCh: '09- 6, '11- 9; WI: '12- 3; WJ: '04- 1; WY: '01- 2; PAm: '11- 3; PAm-J: '03- 1. US champion 2008-09, 2011; NCAA indoor 2006.
Progress at SP: 2000- 14.76, 2001- 15.23, 2002- 16.25, 2003- 16.73, 2004- 17.55, 2005- 18.26, 2006- 17.98, 2007- 17.57, 2008- 18.85, 2009- 19.13, 2010- 18.80, 2011- 19.86, 2012- 19.58i. pbs: DT 54.06 '07.
Her father Mike set a world junior shot record in 1970 and won the Olympic silver in 1984, seven NCAA titles (4 in, 3 out) (for a unique father-daughter double) and WUG gold in 1981 and 1983, pb 21.76 '84. Her younger sister D'Andra (b. 17 Jun 1987) won the NCAA discus in 2009, pb 57.73 '08.

Kristi CASTLIN b. 7 Jul 1988 Douglasville, Georgia 1.70m 79kg. adidas. Graduate of political science from Virginia Tech University.

At 100mh: Won PAm-J 2007. At 60mh: WI: '12-dq/false start ht; won US indoors 2012.
Progress at 100mh: 2005- 13.85, 2006- 13.73, 2007- 12.91/12.82w, 2008- 12.81, 2009- 12.89, 2010- 12.83/12.59w, 2011- 12.83/12.68w. pbs: 55m 7.04i '08, 60m 7.47i '08, 100m 11.67/11.49w '11, 200m 23.50 '11, 50mh 6.81+i '12, 55mh 7.37i '12, 60mh 7.84Ai/7.91i '12. 400mh 60.44 '07.

Jessica COSBY b. 31 May 1982 1.73m 77kg. Nike. Was at UCLA (now strength coach there). At HT: OG: '08- dnq; WCh: '07: dnq 14, '09- 7, '11- 11; won NACAC 2007, US 2006, 2008-09, 2011. At SP: WJ: '00- 9, won NCAA 2002.
Progress at HT: 2001- 55.73, 2002- 59.54, 2003- 61.15, 2005- 66.88, 2006- 70.78, 2007- 68.34, 2008- 70.72, 2009- 72.21, 2010- 71.24, 2011- 72.65. pbs: SP 17.63 '05, 20lb Wt 20.40i '04.
4 months drugs ban from August 2009. Left-handed thrower.

Virginia CRAWFORD b. 7 Sep 1983 Seattle 1.78m 63kg. née Powell. Nike. Was at University of Southern California.
At 100mh: WCh: '05- sf, '07- 5, '09- 6; WY: '99- 8/2R; WCp: '06- 3. At 60mh: WI: '10- 5. Won US 100mh 2006-07, NCAA 100mh & indoor 60mh 2005-06.
Progress at 100mh: 2000- 14.07, 2001- 13.39, 2002- 13.62, 2003- 13.07, 2004- 13.07, 2005- 12.61, 2006- 12.48, 2007- 12.45, 2008- 12.75/12.74w, 2009- 12.64/12.47w, 2010- 12.63, 2011- 12.73/12.65w. pbs: 60m 7.21i '06, 100m 11.10/10.93Aw '06, 200m 23.29 '06, 50mh 6.90i '12, 60mh 7.84i '06.
Married Shawn Crawford (qv) on 16 Apr 2010.

Janay DeLOACH b. 12 Oct 1985 1.65m 59kg. Psychology graduate of Colorado State Univ. At LJ: WCh: '11- 6; WI: '12- 2; PAm: '07- 10. US indoor champion 2011-12.
Progress at LJ: 2004- 6.14Ai/6.05/6.14w, 2005- 6.27A/6.43w, 2006- 6.21Ai, 2007- 6.42Ai/6.41/6.45w, 2008- 6.48/6.51w, 2009- 6.33i/6.04, 2010- 6.61, 2011- 6.99Ai/6.97, 2012- 6.98i. pb 55m 6.85Ai '05, 60m 7.31Ai '06, 100m 11.45 '08, 200m 24.60 '07, 24.26Aw '08; 60mh 7.98Ai '12, 100mh 13.33/13.23w '10, HJ 1.73i '11, SP 12.67i '11, Pen 4289i '11.

Lashinda DEMUS b. 10 Mar 1983 Palmdale, California 1.70m 62kg. Nike. Student at University of South Carolina.
At 400mh/4x400mR: OG: '04- sf; WCh: '05- 2, '09- 2/1R, '11- 1; WJ: '02- 1/1R; WCp: '06- 2/2R. Won WAF 2005-06, PAm-J 1999, US 2005-06, 2009, 2011; NCAA 2002.
Two world junior records 400mh 2002.
Progress at 400mh: 1998- 64.61, 1999- 57.04, 2001- 55.76, 2002- 54.70, 2003- 55.65, 2004- 53.43, 2005- 53.27, 2006- 53.02, 2008- 53.99, 2009- 52.63, 2010- 52.82, 2011- 52.47. pbs: 50m 6.64i '01, 60m 7.73i '01, 100m 11.5 '01, 200m 24.0 '01, 23.50w '05; 400m 51.09 '10, 500y 1:05.8i '01, 800m 2:08.91i '06, 2:09.16 '04; 55mh 7.65i '04, 60mh

8.11i '04, 100mh 12.96 '11, 12.93w '05.
Twin sons Duane and Donte born 5 Jun 2007. Her mother, Yolanda Rich, had a 400m best of 52.19 in 1980.

Kimberlyn DUNCAN b. 2 Aug 1991 1.73m. Student at Louisiana State University.
At 200m: won NCAA 2011.
Progress at 200m: 2007- 24.54, 2008- 24.33, 2009- 23.46, 2010- 23.08/22.96w, 2011- 22.24/22.18w. pbs: 60m 7.30i '11, 100m 11.09 '11, 10.94w '12.

Debbie DUNN b. 26 Mar 1978 Jamaica 1.68m 57kg. Nike. Graduate of child education from Norfolk State University.
At 400m/4x400mR: WCh: '09- 6/1R; PAm: '07- 8/3R; WI: '06- 2R, '10- 1/1R; CCp: '10- 2/1R; US champion 2010, NACAC 2007.
Progress at 400m: 1998- 53.62, 1999- 54.34, 2000- 52.31, 2001- 54.09, 2002- 52.72, 2003- 51.94, 2004- 51.12, 2005- 52.33, 2006- 52.25, 2007- 51.66, 2008- 51.11/50.9, 2009- 49.95, 2010- 49.64, 2011- 50.70. pbs: 60m 7.46i '05, 100m 11.82 '04, 200m 22.73 '09, 500m 1:09.56i '07.
Switched from Jamaica to USA in 2004.

Allyson FELIX b. 18 Nov 1985 Los Angeles 1.68m 57kg. Nike. Elementary education graduate of University of Southern California.
At 200m/4x400mR: OG: '04- 2, '08- 2/1R; WCh: '03- qf, '05- 1, '07- 1/1 4x100mR/1R, '09- 1/1R, '11- 3/1R (2 400m, 1 4x400m); WJ: '02- 5; PAm: '03- 3; WI: '10- 1R. At 100m: WY: '01- 1 (1 Medley R). Won DL 200m & 400m 2010, WAF 200m 2005-06, 2009; US 100m 2010, 200m 2004- 05, 2007-09; 400m 2011.
World junior record 200m 2004 after unratified (no doping test) at age 17 in 2003.
Progress at 100m, 200m, 400m: 2000- 12.19/11.99w, 23.90; 2001- 11.53, 23.31/23.27w; 2002- 11.40, 22.83/22.69w, 55.01; 2003- 11.29/11.12w, 22.11A/22.51, 52.26; 2004- 11.16, 22.18, 51.83A; 2005- 11.05, 22.13, 51.12; 2006- 11.04, 22.11; 2007- 11.01, 21.81, 49.70; 2008- 10.93, 21.93/21.82w, 49.83; 2009- 11.08, 21.88, 49.83; 2010- 11.27, 22.03, 50.15; 2011- 11.26+, 22.32, 49.59. pbs: 50m 6.43i '02, 60m 7.32i '04, 300m 36.33i '07.
First teenager to won a World sprint title. Unbeaten in ten 200m competitions 2005 and in five 2007. Has women's record eight World gold medals including three in 2007 when she had a record 0.53 winning margin at 200m and ran a 48.0 400m relay leg. Older brother Wes Felix won World Junior bronze at 200m and gold in WJR at 4x100m in 2002, pbs: 100m 10.23 '05, 200m 20.43 '04.

Shalane FLANAGAN b. 8 Jul 1981 Boulder 1.65m 50kg. Nike. Was at University of North Carolina.
At 5000m/(10000m): OG: '04- h, '08- 10/3; WCh: '05- h, '07- 8, '09- (14), '11- (7). World CC: '10- 12, '11-3; 4k: '04- 14, 05- 20. Won US 5000m 2005, 10000m 2008, 2011; HMar 2010, Mar 2012,

CC 2008, 2010-11; 4km CC 2004-05, indoor 3000m 2007, NCAA CC 2002-03, indoor 3000m 2003.
North American records: 5000m and indoor 3000m 2007, 10000m (2) 2008.
Progress at 5000m, 10000m, Mar: 2001- 16:29.68, 2003- 15:20.54, 2004- 15:05.08, 2005- 15:10.96, 2007- 14:44.80, 2008- 14:59.69, 30:22.22; 2009- 14:47.62i/15:10.86, 31:23.43; 2010- 14:49.08, 2:28:40; 2011- 14:45.20, 30:39.57; 2012- 2:25:38. pbs: 800m 2:09.28 '02, 1500m 4:05.86 '07, 1M 4:33.81i '11, 4:48.47 '00; 3000m 8:33.25i/8:35.34 '07, Road: 10M 51:45 '10, HMar 68:37 '10.
2nd New York 2010 on marathon debut and won Olympic Trials 2012. Married to Steve Edwards. Mother, Cheryl Bridges, set marathon world best with 2:49:40 in 1971 and was 4th in 1969 International CC, father Steve ran in World Cross 1976-7, 1979.

Hyleas FOUNTAIN b. 14 Jan 1981 Columbus, Georgia 1.70m 65kg. Nike. University of Georgia.
At Hep: OG: '08- 2; WCh: '05- 12, '07/11- dnf; US champion 2005, 2008. At Pen: WI: '06- 8, '10- 4. Won NCAA Hep 2003, LJ 2004; US Hep 2007, 2010.
North American indoor pentathlon record 2010.
Progress at Hep: 2001- 4905, 2002- 5673w, 2003- 5999, 2004- 6035, 2005- 6502, 2006- 6148, 2007- 6090, 2008- 6667, 2010- 6735w. pbs: 60m 7.47i '11, 200m 23.21 '08, 800m 2:15.32 '08, 55mh 7.61i '05, 60mh 7.98i '09, 100mh 12.78/12.65w '08; HJ 1.90 '10, LJ 6.89/6.95w '09; TJ 13.40 '04, SP 14.26i '10, 13.81 '09; JT 48.15 '08, Pen 4753i '10.
Won Talence and IAAF Combined Events Challenge 2008.

Kara GOUCHER b. 9 Jul 1978 Queens, New York 1.70m 58kg. née Grgas-Wheeler. Nike. Studied psychology at Colorado State Univ.
At (5000m)/10000m: OG: '08- 9/10; WCh: '07- 3, '11- 13. At Mar: WCh: '09- 10. At 3000m: WCp: '06- 3. World 4k CC: '06- 21. Won US 5000m 2008-09, NCAA 3000m, 5000m & CC 2000.
Progress at 5000m, 10000m: 1999- 16:57.31, 2000- 15:28.78, 2001- 15:31.77, 2003- 15:42.97, 33:44.86; 2004- 16:30.35, 2005- 15:17.55, 2006- 15:08.13, 31:17.12; 2007- 14:55.02, 32:02.05; 2008- 14:58.10, 30:55.16; 2009- 15:20.94, 2:27:48; 2011- 15:11.47, 31:16.65, 2:24:52wdh; 2012- 2:26:06. pbs: 800m 2:06.79 '09, 1500m 4:05.14 '06, 1M 4:33.19i/4:37.58 '09, 2000m 5:41.28 '09, 3000m 8:34.99 '07, 2M 9:41.32 '07, Road: 15km 47:36 '07, 10M 50:59 '07, HMar 66:57 '07, 30km 1:43:33 '08, Mar 2:25:53 '08
After surprise World 10000m bronze, made brilliant half marathon debut to win Great North Run 2007 with American best. Third New York Marathon 2008, with fastest ever US women's debut, and Boston 2009.
Married (2001) **Adam Goucher** (18 Feb 1975) (pbs: 1500m 3:36.64 '01, 1M 3:54.17 '99, 2000m 4:58.92 '99, 3000m 7:34.96 '01, 2M 8:12.73 '06,

5000m 13:10.00 '06, 10000m 27:59.41 '06). Their son Colton Mirko born on 24 Sep 2010.

Dawn HARPER b. 13 May 1984 Norman, Oklahoma 1.68m 61kg. Nike. Studied psychology at UCLA.
At 100mh: OG: '08- 1; WCh: '09- 7, '11- 3; won PAm-J 2003, US 2009.
Progress at 100mh: 2002- 13.63, 2003- 13.33/13.21w, 2004- 13.16/12.91w, 2005- 12.91, 2006- 12.80A/12.86, 2007- 12.67, 2008- 12.54, 2009- 12.48/12.36w, 2010- 12.77w, 2011- 12.47.
pbs: 60m 7.70i '05, 100m 11.66 '07, 200m 23.97 '06, 50mh 6.96i '12, 60mh 7.98i '06.
Married to Craig Everhart (b. 13 Sep 1983) 400m 44.89 '04.

Queen HARRISON b. 10 Sep 1988 Loch Sheldrake, New York 1.70m 60kg. Saucony. Student of business marketing at Virginia Tech.
At 400mh: OG: '08- sf; WCh: '11- sf; PAm-J: '07- 1 (2 100mh); won NCAA 100mh, 400mh & 60mh indoors 2010.
Progress at 100mh, 400mh: 2007- 12.98, 55.81; 2008- 12.70, 54.60; 2009- 13.14/12.98w, 56.03; 2010- 12.61/12.44w, 54.55; 2011- 12.88, 54.78.
pbs: 400m 52.88 '08, 60mh 7.94i '10, LJ 5.82i '06.

Natasha HASTINGS b. 23 Jul 1986 Brooklyn, NY 1.73m 63kg. Nike. Student of exercise science at University of South Carolina.
At 400m/4x400m: OG: '08- res 1R; WCh: '07- sf/res 1R, '09/11- res 1R; WJ: '04- 1/1R; WY: '03- 1; WI: '10- 1R, '12- 3/2R; PAm-J: '03- 1R, '05- 1/1R.
Won NCAA indoors and out 2007.
World junior 500m best 2005.
Progress at 400m: 2000- 54.21, 2001- 55.06, 2002- 53.42, 2003- 52.09, 2004- 52.04, 2005- 51.34, 2006- 51.45, 2007- 49.84, 2008- 50.80, 2009- 50.89, 2010- 50.53, 2011- 50.83Ai/50.97. pbs: 55m 7.08i '02, 60m 7.28i '11, 100m 11.40/11.39w '10, 200m 22.61 '07, 300m 35.9+ '07, 500m 1:10.05i '05.
Father from Jamaica, mother Joanne Gardner was British (ran 11.89 to win WAAA U15 100m at 14 in 1977).

Marshevet HOOKER b. 25 Sep 1984 Dallas 1.75m 67kg. Former married name Myers. adidas. Studied Liberal Arts at the University of Texas.
At 100m/4x100m: WCh: '11- 8/1R; WJ: '02- 3/2R. At 200m: OG: '08- 5; WCh: '09- sf. Won NCAA 100m, indoor 60m & LJ 2005.
Progress at 100m, 200m: 2000- 11.94, 24.26; 2001- 11.51, 23.59; 2002- 11.43/11.28w/11.1w, 23.25w; 2004- 11.14, 24.04w; 2005- 11.12/11.03w, 22.80/22.73w; 2006- 11.09, 22.75/22.70w; 2007- 11.06, 23.25/22.95w; 2008- 10.93/10.76w, 22.34/22.20w; 2009- 11.14/10.94w, 22.51/22.35w; 2010- 10.97, 22.90; 2011- 10.86/10.83w, 22.59. pbs: 55m 6.78i '06, 60m 7.18i '06, 400m 54.18 '10, LJ 6.83i '11, 6.65/6.89w '05.
Married Marcus Myers on 3 Oct 2009, but divorced in 2011. Younger sister Destinee

Hooker (b. 7 Sep 1987) won NCAA HJ 2006 & 2009, pb 1.98i/1.95 '09.

Molly HUDDLE b. 31 Aug 1984 Elmira, New York 1.63m 48kg. Saucony. Was at University of Notre Dame.
At 5000m: WCh: '10- h; CCp: '10- 3; won US 2011. World CC: '10- 19, '11- 17.
North American 5000m record 2010.
Progress at 5000m, 10000m: 2003- 15:36.95, 2004- 15:32.55, 2005- 16:12.17i, 2006- 15:40.41, 32:37.87l 2007- 15:17.13, 33:09.27; 2008- 15:25.47, 33:17.73; 2009- 15:53.91, 32:42.11; 2010- 14:44.76, 31:27.12; 2011- 15:10.01, 31:28.66. pbs: 1500m 4:09.22 '10, 1M 4:41.91i '04, 4:46.70 '07; 3000m 8:53.6+ '10, 10M Rd 54:01 '09.

Kylie HUTSON b. 27 Nov 1987 Terre Haute 1.65m xxkg. Nike. Was at Indiana State University.
At PV: WCh: '11- dnq 15; won US 2011, NCAA 2009, 2011.
Progress at PV: 2006- 3.58, 2007- 4.10i/3.96, 2008- 4.30, 2009- 4.40, 2010- 4.51, 2011- 4.70i/4.65.

Lacy JANSON b. 20 Feb 1983 Norfolk, Virginia 1.78m 68kg. Nike. Was at Florida State University.
At PV: WCh: '11- dnq 20; WI: '12- 5; WJ: '02- nh; Won PAm-J 2001, NCAA 2006, US indoor 2010.
Progress at PV: 2001- 4.01, 2002- 4.27, 2003- 4.45i/4.37, 2004- 4.25, 2005- 4.30i/4.11, 2006- 4.58, 2007- 4.60Ai/4.50, 2008- 4.64i/4.55, 2009- 4.50i/4.46, 2010- 4.66i/4.60A, 2011- 4.60i/4.50, 2012- 4.65i.

Carmelita JETER b. 24 Nov 1979 Los Angeles 1.63m 53kg. Nike. Was at California State University, Dominguez Hills.
At 100m/4x100mR: WCh: '07- 3/res 1R, '09- 3, '11- 1/2/1R; won DL 2010, WAF 2007, 2009; US 2009, 2011. At 60m: WI: '10- 2.
Progress at 100m, 200m: 2000- 11.69, 23.65/23.99w; 2001- 11.82, 24.20; 2002- 11.77/11.46w, 24.10; 2003- 11.61/11.43w, 23.67; 2004- 11.56, 23.98; 2005- 12.00/11.72w, 2006- 11.48, 23.54; 2007- 11.02, 22.82; 2008- 10.97, 22.47/22.35w; 2009- 10.64, 22.59; 2010- 10.82, 22.54; 2011- 10.70, 22.20. pbs: 60m 7.02Ai/7.05i '10, 400m 53.08 '09.
Second fastest woman of all-time at 100m.

Oluwafunmilayo 'Funmi' **JIMOH** b. 29 May 1984 Seattle 1.73m 64kg. Was at Rice University.
At LJ: OG: '08- 12; WCh: '09- dnq 21, '11- nj; won US 2008-09, NCAA 2008.
Progress at LJ: 2004- 6.14, 2005- 6.31, 2006- 6.44, 2007- 6.46/6.62w, 2008- 6.91, 2009- 6.96, 2010- 6.81/6.87w, 2011- 6.88, 2012- 6.81Ai. pbs: 60m 7.67i '04, 100m 12.03 '08, 11.65w '11; 200m 23.91A '11, 24.28 '08, 23.65w '06; 400m 59.57i '09, 60mh 8.32i '07, 100mh 13.51 '05, 13.39w '07; HJ 1.75i '05, 1.66 '07; SP 10.68i '06, Pen 3937i '06, Hep 5335 '07.

Lori '**Lolo**' **JONES** b. 5 Aug 1982 Des Moines 1.75m 60kg. Nike. Spanish & economic gradu-ate of Louisiana State University.
At 100mh: OG: '08- 7; WCh: '07- 6; CCp: '10- 2; Won US 2008, 2010; NACAC 2004. At 60mh: WI: '08- 1, '10- 1; won NCAA indoor 2003, US indoor 2007-09.
North American indoor 60m hurdles record 2010.
Progress at 100mh: 2000- 14.04, 2001- 13.31/13.17w/12.7w, 2002- 12.84, 2003- 12.90, 2004- 12.77, 2005- 12.76, 2006- 12.56, 2007- 12.57, 2008- 12.43/12.29w, 2009- 12.47, 2010- 12.55, 2011- 12.67. pbs: 55m 6.87i '03, 60m 7.27i '03, 100m 11.24 '06, 200m 23.76 '04, 23.50w '03; 50mh 6.78i '12, 55mh 7.57i '03, 60mh 7.72i '10, 400mh 59.95 '00.
Crashed into 9th hurdle when leading Olympic final after pb 12.43 in semi in 2008.

Bianca KNIGHT b. 2 Jan 1989 Ridgeland, Mississippi 1.63m 60kg. adidas. Psychology student at University of Texas.
At (100m)/200m: WCh: '11- 1R; WY: '05- 1/2/1 Med R; PAm-J: '07- 1. Won NCAA indoor 2008.
World junior indoor 200m record 2008.
Progress at 100m, 200m: 2002- 12.07, 24.37; 2003- 11.80, 23.81; 2004- 11.56, 23.06; 2005- 11.38, 23.33; 2006- 11.26, 22.94; 2007- 11.36/11.28w, 22.97Ai/23.17A/22.93w; 2008- 11.07, 22.40i/22.43/22.25w; 2009- 11.17/11.12w, 22.50; 2010- 11.40, 22.59; 2011-11.22, 22.35. pbs: 50m 6.28i '12, 55m 6.79i '06, 60m 7.16i '08, 300m 36.41i '11, 400m 52.55 '11.

Yvette LEWIS b. 16 Mar 1985 Germany 1.73m 62kg. Norfolk Read Deal. Was at Hampton.
At 100mh(/TJ): PAm: '07- 8/6, '11- 1/7; WJ: '04- (dnq); won NCAA TJ 2007.
Progress at 100mh: 2005- 13.53, 2006- 13.14, 2007- 13.06, 2008- 12.85, 2009- 12.85, 2010- 13.19, 2011- 12.76. pbs: 55m 6.96i '07, 60m 7.40i '06, 100m 11.56 '07, 200m 23.50 '06, 400m 56.63i '09, 50mh 7.06+i '09, 60mh 7.90i '10, HJ 1.78i '05, 1.78 '07; LJ 6.29i '09, 6.24 '07; TJ 13.84 '08, Pen 3852i '07.

Chaunté LOWE b. 12 Jan 1984 Templeton, California 1.75m 59kg. née Howard. Nike. Economics gradate of Georgia Tech University.
At HJ: OG: '04- dnq 26=, '08- 6; WCh: '05- 2, '09- 7=; PAm-J: '03- 3; WI: '06-01-12: 8/3/1; Won US 2006, 2008-10; NCAA 2004, indoors 2004-05.
Three North American HJ records 2010, indoors 2012.
Progress at HJ: 2000- 1.75, 2001- 1.84, 2002- 1.87, 2003- 1.89, 2004- 1.98A, 2005- 2.00, 2006- 2.01, 2008- 2.00, 2009- 1.98, 2010- 2.05, 2011- 1.78, 2012- 2.02Ai. pbs: 100m 11.83 '05, 100mh 13.78 '04, LJ 6.90 '10, TJ 12.93 '04, 12.98w '05.
Married Mario Lowe (b. 20 Apr 1980, TJ pb 16.15 '02) in 2005, daughters Jasmine born 30 Jul 2007 and Aurora in 4 Apr 2011.

Francena McCORORY b. 20 Oct 1988 Hampton, VA 1.70m. adidas. Psychology graduate of Hampton University.

At 400m/4x400mR: WCh: '11- 4/1R; won NCAA indoors 2009-10, out 2010.
World junior indoor 300m best 2007.
Progress at 400m: 2004- 54.54, 2006- 51.93i, 2008- 51.54, 2009- 50.58, 2010- 50.52, 2011- 50.24. pbs: 55m 6.86i '06, 60m 7.43i '07, 100m 11.68 '05, 11.56w '10; 200m 22.92 '10, 300m 36.67i '07, 500m 1:09.01i '12, 800m 2:20.25i '07.

Tianna MADISON b. 30 Aug 1985 Elyria, Ohio 1.68m 60kg. Studied biology at University of Central Florida, formerly at Un. of Tennessee.
At LJ: WCh: '05- 1, '07- 10; WI: '06- 2; PAm-J: '03- 4, NCAA champion indoors and out 2005.
At 60m: WI: '12- 3; won US indoor 2012.
Progress at 100m, LJ: 2000- 5.73, 2001- 6.07, 2002- 11.98/11.91w, 6.20; 2003- 11.68, 6.28; 2004- 11.50/11.35w, 6.60; 2005- 11.41, 6.89/6.92w; 2006- 11.52/11.50w, 6.80i/6.60; 2007- 6.60/6.61w; 2008- 11.54, 6.53/6.58w; 2009- 11.05, 6.48; 2010- 11.20, 6.44; 2011- 11.29, 6.21/6.58w. pbs: 55m 6.69i '09, 60m 7.02i '12, 200m 23.27 '10.
Set long jump pbs in qualifying and final of 2005 Worlds.

Alysia MONTAÑO b. 26 Apr 1986 Queens, New York 1.70m 61kg. née Johnson. Nike. Was at University of California.
At 800m: WCh: '07- h, '11- 4; PAm: '07- 6; WI: '10- 3; CCp: '10- 8; won US 2007, 2010-11; NCAA 2007.
Progress at 800m: 2004- 2:08.97, 2005- 2:05.49, 2006- 2:01.80, 2007- 1:59.29, 2008- 2:00.57, 2009- 2:01.09, 2010- 1:57.34, 2011- 1:57.48. pbs: 400m 52.09 '10, 600m 1:27.4+ '10, 1500m 4:28.43 '09.

LaShaunte'a MOORE b. 31 Jul 1983 Akron, Ohio 1.70m 56kg. adidas. Was at University of Arkansas. Training to be a nurse.
At 200m: OG: '04- sf, WCh: '07- 7; WY: '99- 4/1 MedR; won NCAA 2004.
Progress at 100m, 200m: 1997- 11.93, 1998- 11.67w, 23.86w; 1999- 11.66, 23.26; 2001- 11.64/11.57w, 23.59/23.40w; 2002- 11.47, 23.13/22.89w; 2003- 11.33/11.27w, 23.09/22.81w; 2004- 11.26, 22.63/22.37w; 2005- 11.39/11.25w, 22.93; 2006- 11.40, 22.89/22.64w; 2007- 11.26/11.10w, 22.46; 2008- 11.03, 22.70; 2009- 11.21, 22.57; 2010- 10.97, 22.46; 2011- 11.17/11.04w, 22.58. pbs: 60m 7.36i '03, 400m 54.92 '07.

Kara PATTERSON b. 10 Apr 1986 Seattle 1.75m 76kg. Asics. Studied interior design at Purdue University.
At JT: OG: '08- dnq 41; WCh: '09/11- dnq 29/21; PAm-J: '05- 2; CCp: '10- 6; Won US 2008-10.
North American javelin record 2010.
Progress at 1500m: 2004- 48.51, 2005- 52.09, 2006- 56.19, 2008- 61.56, 2009- 63.95, 2010- 66.67, 2011- 62.76. pb DT 35.17 '11.

Brittney REESE b. 9 Sep 1986 Gulfport, Mississippi 1.73m 64kg. Nike. English graduate of University of Mississippi.

At LJ: OG: '08- 5; WCh: '07- 8, '09- 1, '11- 1; WI: '10- 1, '12- 1; won DL 2010, WAF 2009, US 2008- 11, NCAA 2008.
North American indoor long jump record 2012.
Progress at LJ: 2004- 6.31, 2007- 6.83, 2008- 6.95, 2009- 7.10, 2010- 6.94/7.05w, 2011- 7.19, 2012- 7.23i. pbs: 50m 6.23i '12, 60m 7.24i '05, 100m 11.63 '09, 11.20w '11; HJ 1.88i/1.84 '08, TJ 13.16 '08.
Played basketball at Gulf Coast Community College in 2005-06 and no athletics.

Sanya RICHARDS-ROSS b. 26 Feb 1985 Kingston, Jamaica 1.73m 61kg. Nike. University of Texas.
At (200m)/400m/4x400m: OG: '04- 6/dq1R, '08- 3/1R; WCh: '03- sf/1R, '05- 2, '07- (5)/1R, '09- 1/1R, '11- 7/1R; WJ: '02- 3/2; WCp: '06- 1/1; WI: '12- 1/2R. Won WAF 200m 2008, 400m 2005- 09, US 2003, 2005-06, 2008-09; NCAA 2003.
US & N.American 400m record 2006, world junior indoor bests 200m, 400m (2) 2004.
Progress at 200m, 400m: 1999- 23.84, 2000- 23.57, 54.34; 2001- 23.09, 53.49; 2002- 23.01, 50.69; 2003- 22.80i/22.86, 50.58; 2004- 22.49i/22.73, 49.89; 2005- 22.53, 48.92; 2006- 22.17, 48.70; 2007- 22.31, 49.27; 2008- 22.49. 49.74; 2009- 22.29, 48.83; 2010- 51.82, 2011- 22.63, 49.66. pbs: 60m 7.21i '04, 100m 10.97 '07, 10.89w '12; 300m 35.6 '05, 800m 2:10.74 '10, LJ 6.08 '01.
Left Jamaica at the age of 12 and gained US citizenship on 20 May 2002. Her 48.92 at Zürich in 2005 and then 48.70 at the World Cup in 2006 (to beat 22 year-old US record) were the world's fastest 400m times since 1996. Unbeaten in 13 finals outdoors at 400m in 2006 and after WAF win scored 200m/400m double at World Cup. Record 41 times sub-50 secs for 400m. Shared Golden League jackpot 2006, 2007 and 2009. Married New York Giants cornerback Aaron Ross on 26 Feb 2010.

Shannon ROWBURY b. 19 Sep 1984 San Francisco 1.65m 52kg. Nike. Was at Duke University.
At 1500m: OG: '08- 7; WCh: '09- 3, '11- sf; Won US 2008-09, NCAA indoor mile 2007. At 3000m: CCp: '10- 3,
Progress at 1500m: 2004- 4:17.41, 2005- 4:14.81, 2006- 4:12.31, 2008- 4:00.33, 2009- 4:00.81, 2010- 4:01.30, 2011- 4:05.73. pbs: 800m 2:00.47 '10, 1M 4:20.34 '08, 3000m 8:31.38 '10, 5000m 15:00.51 '10, 3000mSt 9:59.4 '06.
Former ballet and Irish dancer.

Jennifer SIMPSON b. 23 Aug 1986 Webster City, Iowa 1.65m 50kg. née Barringer. New Balance/ Studied political science at University of Colorado.
At 1500m: WCh: '11- 1. At 3000mSt: OG: '08- 9; WCh: '07- h, '09- 5; won NCAA 2006, 2008-09; US 2009. Three North American 3000m steeplechase records 2008-09.
Progress at 1500m, 3000mSt: 2006- 9:53.04, 2007- 4:21.53, 9:33.95; 2008- 4:11.36, 9:22.26; 2009-

3:59.90, 9:12.50; 2010- 4:03.63, 2011- 4:03.54. pbs: 800m 2:01.20 '11, 1M 4:25.91i '09, 3000m 8:42.03i '09, 5000m 15:01.70i/15:05.25 '09.
Married Jason Simpson on 8 Oct 2010. on 5th Avenue Mile 2011.

Shalonda SOLOMON b. 19 Dec 1985 Inglewood, California 1.69m 56kg. Reebok. Student at University of South Carolina.
At (100m)/200m/4x100m: WCh: '11- 4/res (1)R; WJ: '04- 1/1R; PAm-J: '03- 1/1/1R; CCp: '10- 2/1R. Won NCAA 200m 2006, NCAAC 100m & 200m 2006.
Progress at 100m, 200m: 2001- 11.57/11.37w, 23.65/23.22w; 2002- 11.51/11.46w, 23.31; 2003- 11.35/11.25w, 22.93; 2004- 11.41/11.32w, 22.82; 2005- 11.29, 22.74/22.72w; 2006- 11.09/11.07w, 22.36/22.30w; 2007- 11.33, 22.77; 2008- 11.16, 22.48/22.36w; 2009- 11.04/11.00w, 22.41; 2010- 10.90, 22.47; 2011- 11.08/10.90w, 22.15. pbs: 55m 6.72i '09, 60m 7.15Ai '11, 7.21i '06; 300m 36.45i '09, 400m 53.47 '08.

Jennifer SUHR b. 6 Feb 1982 Fredonia, New York 1.80m 64kg. adidas. née Stuczynski. Graduate of Roberts Wesleyan University, now studying child psychology.
At PV: OG: '08- 2; WCh: '07- 10, '11- 4; WI: '08- 2; WCp: '06- nh; US champion 2006-10, indoors 2005, 2007-09, 2011.
Four North American pole vault records 2007-08, two indoors 2009.
Progress at PV: 2002- 2.75, 2004- 3.49, 2005- 4.57i/4.26, 2006- 4.68i/4.66, 2007- 4.88, 2008- 4.92, 2009- 4.83i/4.81, 2010- 4.89, 2011- 4.91. pbs: 55mh 8.07i '05, JT 46.82 '05.
All-time top scorer at basketball at her university, then very rapid progress at vaulting.

Jeneba TARMOH b. 27 Sep 1989 San Jose CA 1.67m 59kg. Student at Texas A&M University.
At (100m)/200m/4x100m: WCh: '11- h; WJ: '06- 7/1R, '08- (1)/1R. Won NCAAC 100m 2010.
Progress at 100m, 200m: 2004- 12.07w, 2005- 11.81/11.61w, 24.04/23.56w; 2006- 11.24, 23.14; 2007- 11.27, 23.34/23.20w; 2008- 11.21, 22.94; 2009- 11.31, 23.31i/23.43/23.16w; 2010- 11.19/11.00w, 22.65; 2011- 11.23/10.94w, 22.28. pbs: 55m 6.86Ai '06, 60m 7.24i '11.

Aretha THURMOND b. 14 Aug 1976 Seattle 1.81m 98kg. née Hill. Nike. Was at University of Washington.
At DT: OG: '96/04- dnq 34/19, '08- 10; WCh: '99/03/05/11: dnq 24/20/21/13; '09- 10; PAm: '99-03-07: 1/1/2; WUG: '97- 6; WCp: '06- 2. US champion 2003-04, 2006, 2008.
Progress at DT: 1992- 43.38, 1993- 47.48, 1994- 50.52, 1995- 54.84, 1996- 60.50, 1997- 59.92, 1998- 65.62dh/63.68, 1999- 62.15, 2000- 62.91, 2001- 61.64, 2002- 65.21, 2003- 65.10/66.23dh, 2004- 65.86, 2005- 64.56, 2006- 64.41, 2008- 65.20, 2009- 62.51, 2010- 62.47, 2011- 63.85. pb SP 15.91i/15.67 '98.

Married Reedus Thurmond (DT pb 62.06 '00) in May 2005, their son Theo born 4 Jun 2007 (she competed at US Champs 16 days later).

Sheena TOSTA b. 1 Oct 1982 Camden, New Jersey 1.65m 58kg. née Johnson. Nike. Student at UCLA.
At 400mh: OG: '04- 4, '08- 2; WCh: '07/09- sf; WJ: '98- h; PAm: '07- 1. Won US 2004, NCAA 2003-04.
Progress at 400mh: 1998- 58.61, 1999- 59.12, 2000- 56.82, 2001- 56.02, 2002- 55.71, 2003- 54.24, 2004- 52.95, 2005- 54.72, 2006- 53.90, 2007- 53.29, 2008- 53.58, 2009- 54.19, 2010- 54.52, 2011- 55.65. pbs: 60m 7.40i '07, 100m 11.68 '06, 200m 23.42 '07, 23.38w '10; 400m 52.14 '09, 600m 1:30.33i '10, 60mh 8.04 '07, 100mh 12.75 '04, LJ 6.10/6.16w '00, TJ 12.67 '00.

Morgan UCENY b. 10 Mar 1985 Plymouth, Indiana 1.68m 57kg. adidas. Was at Cornell University.
At 800m: PAm: '07- h. At 1500m: WCh: '11- 10 (fell). Won US 1500m 2011.
Progress at 800m, 1500m: 2002- 2:13.04, 2004- 2:19.73, 2005- 2:06.26, 2006- 2:04.32, 2007- 2:01.75, 4:17.18; 2008- 2:00.01, 4:06.93; 2009- 2:00.06, 4:09.95; 2010- 1:58.67, 4:02.40; 2011- 1:58.37, 4:00.06. pbs: 400m 55.50 '06, 600m 1:27.70i '07, 1000m 2:40.07i '10, 1M 4:38.87i '08.

Maggie VESSEY b. 23 Dec 1981 Santa Cruz, California 1.70m 58kg. New Balance. Was at Cal Poly-San Luis Obispo.
At 800m: WCh: '09- sf, '11- 6.
Progress at 800m: 2002- 2:06.53, 2003- 2:05.78, 2005- 2:03.10, 2007- 2:11.57, 2008- 2:02.01, 2009- 1:57.84, 2010- 1:59.00, 2011- 1:58.50. pbs: 400m 53.74 '10, 1500m 4:17.87 '11.

Kellie WELLS b. 16 Jul 1982 Richmond, Virginia 1.63m. Nike. Was at Hampton University.
At 100mh: WCh: '11- dnf. US champion 2011.
Progress at 100mh: 2003- 13.96, 2004- 13.25, 2005- 13.57/13.29w, 2006- 13.25/13.17w, 2007- 12.93, 2008- 12.58, 2009- 13.01, 2010- 12.68, 2011- 12.50/12.35w. pbs: 60m 7.33i '06, 100m 11.50 '08, 200m 23.53 '06, 50mh 6.84i '12, 55mh 7.37i '11, 60mh 7.79Ai/7.82i '11.
Suffered a serious hamstring injury after finishing the 2008 Olympic Trials semi in a pb 12.58 and struggled for two years until brilliant indoor season in 2011.

Lauryn WILLIAMS b. 11 Sep 1983 Pittsburgh 1.57m 57kg. Saucony. Finance graduate of University of Miami.
At 100m/4x100mR: OG: '04- 2, '08- 4; WCh: '03- res (1)R, '05- 1/1R, '07- 2/1R, '09- 5; WJ: '02- 1/2R; PAm: '03- 1/1R. Won NCAA 2004. At 60m: WI: '06- 2.
Progress at 100m, 200m: 1999- 12.00/11.6, 24.2; 2000- 11.70, 24.31; 2001- 11.65/11.60w, 23.85; 2002- 11.33, 23.64/23.63w; 2003- 11.12, 23.25; 2004- 10.96/10.94w, 22.46; 2005- 10.88, 22.27; 2006-

11.09, 22.87; 2007- 11.01, 22.70; 2008- 10.90/ 10.86w, 22.59/22.21w; 2009- 11.01/10.94w, 22.34; 2010- 11.41, 2011- 11.15, 22.65. pbs: 55m 6.70i '04, 60m 7.01i '06.

Christin WURTH-THOMAS b. 11 Jul 1980 Bloomington, Illinois 1.65m 52kg. Nike. Graduate of University of Arkansas.
At 1500m: OG: '08- h; WCh: '07- h, '09- 5; CCp: '10- 3.
Progress at 1500m: 2000- 4:24.21, 2001- 4:24.66, 2002- 4:16.80, 2003- 4:10.49, 2004- 4:15.99, 2005- 4:08.76, 2006- 4:05.05, 2007- 4:07.86, 2008- 4:04.88, 2009- 3:59.88, 2010- 3:59.59, 2011- 4:03.72. pbs: 800m 1:59.35 '09, 1000m 2:34.23 '09, 1M 4:27.18i '08, 3000m 8:43.79i '11, 5000m 15:21.75 '11.

US VIRGIN ISLANDS

Tabarie HENRY b. 1 Dec 1987 Saint-Thomas 1.87m 79kg. Student at Texas A&M University (formerly Barton CC).
At 400m: OG: '08- sf; WCh: '09- 4, '11- 7; CAG: '10- 2; WI: '12- 4.
UVI records: 200m 2009, 400m (5) 2008-09.
Progress at 400m: 2005- 48.82, 2006- 46.51, 2007- 47.04, 2008- 45.19, 2009- 44.77, 2010- 45.07, 2011- 44.83. pbs: 100m 11.05 '07, 200m 20.71 '09, 500m 1:01.28i '11, 600y 1:08.71i '09.
Moved to Miami at age 4.

Women

Laverne JONES-FERRETTE b. 16 Sep 1981 St Croix 1.73m 65kg. née Jones. Was at University of Oklahoma, USA.
At (100m)/200m: OG: '04/08- qf/qf; WCh: '05- qf/sf, '07/09- sf; PAm: '07- (7) (7 400m), '11- 8; CAG: '06- 2/4. At 60m: WI: '10- dq2.
UVI records 60m (8), 100m (5), 200m (5), 400m 2004-10.
Progress at 100m, 200m: 2001- 11.77, 2002- 24.30, 2003- 11.37, 23.16i/23.26/22.93w; 2004- 11.25/ 11.23w, 22.81; 2005- 11.43/11.22w, 23.14; 2006- 11.30/11.29w, 22.92; 2007- 11.32/11.23w, 22.52; 2008- 11.24, 22.62; 2009- 11.13/11.03w, 22.46; 2011- 11.45A/11.45w. pbs: 50m 6.14i '12, 60m 6.97i '10, 400m 51.47 '07.
Married to 400m runner Stephen Ferrette. After a positive test on 16 Feb 2010 she received a six-month ban and lost the 60m World Indoor silver medal. Daughter Asana born February 2011.

UZBEKISTAN

Governing body: Athletic Federation of Uzbekistan, Navoi str. 30, 100129 Tashkent.

Yuliya TARASOVA b. 13 Mar 1986 Tashkent 1.77m 68kg.
At Hep/(LJ): OG: '08- 26; WCh: '09/11: dnq 21/26; WJ: '04- 14; WY: '03- 7; AsiG: '10- 1/3; AsiC: '03-09-11: 9/1/4; WI: '10- (7); CCp: '10- (1). won Asi-J 2004

UZB long jump record 2010.
Progress at LJ: 2003- 5.96, 2004- 5.76, 2005- 6.28, 2006- 6.12, 2007- 5.72, 2008- 5.92, 2009- 6.49, 2010- 6.81, 2011- 6.72. pbs: 100m 11.77 '09, 200m 24.12 '10, 800m 2:22.61 '09, 60mh 8.81i '05, 100mh 13.81 '09, HJ 1.76 '04, SP 13.65 '09, JT 43.31 '08, Pen 4004i '06, Hep 5989 '09.

VENEZUELA

Governing body: Federación Venezolana de Atletismo, Apartado Postal 29059, Caracas. Founded 1948.
National Champions 2011: **Men**: 100m/200m: Diego Rivas 10.49/21.10, 400m: Said Bone 47.83, 800m: Nico Herrera 1:51.06, 1500m: Alexis Peña 3:47.87, 5000m: Nolbert Gutiérrez 14:47.89, 10000m: Lervis Arias 29:59.76, 3000mSt: José Gregorio Peña 9:11.79, 110mh: Albert Bravo 14.60, 400mh: Víctor Solarte 51.12, HJ: Pablo Sánchez 2.09, PV: César González 4.80, LJ: Víctor Castillo 7.70, TJ: Ángel Delgado 15.45, SP/DT: Jesús Parejo 17.13/53.70, HT 6.75kg: Aldo Bello 68.50, JT: Manuel Fuenmayor 63.53, Dec: Georni Jaramillo 7371, 20kW: Omar Bustamante 1:29:37. **Women**: 100m: Lexabeth Hidalgo 12.09, 200m/400m: Nancy Garcés 23.97/54.16, 800m/1500m: María Osorio 2:14.10/4:31.44, 5000m Nubia Arteaga 17:41.32, 10000m: Zuleima Amaya 36:12.94, 3000mSt: Gabriela Contreras 12:59.67, 100mh: Genesis Romero 15.25, 400mh: Magdalena Mendoza 62.32, HJ: ?, PV: Dayan Morales 3.50, LJ: Munich Tovar 6.14, TJ: Yudelsi González 12.99, SP: Ahymara Espinosa 14.35, DT: Eliza–beth Álvarez 44.20, HT: Rosa Rodríguez 65.64, JT: Yusbelys Parra 54.53, Hep: Gillercy González 4834, 20kW: Milánggela Rosales 1:35:10.

ZIMBABWE

Governing body: Amateur Athletic Association of Zimbabwe, PO Box MP 187, Mount Pleasant, Harare. Founded in 1912.

Ngonidzashe MAKUSHA b. 11 Mar 1987 Chitungwiza, Harare 1.78m 73kg. Student at Florida State University, USA.
At LJ (100m): OG: '08- 4; WCh: '11- 3 (sf); WJ: '06- 12 (sf); AfG: '07- 3R (sf). Won NCAA 100m 2011, LJ 2008-09, 2011; ZIM LJ 2006-07.
Zimbabwe records 100 (2) 2011, long jump (5) 2006-11.
Progress at 100m. LJ: 2005- 7.34?, 2006- 10.64Aw, 7.87A; 2007- 10.52, 7.69; 2008- 8.30, 2009- 8.21i/ 7.73/8.11w, 2010- 7.71i/7.54, 2011- 9.89, 8.40. pbs: 55m 6.30i '08, 60m 6.60i '09, 200m 21.38A '06, TJ 14.90A '06.
Superb unique treble at 2011 NCAAs with 100m 9.89 and LJ 8.40 plus 4x100m leg.

INTRODUCTION TO WORLD LISTS AND INDEX

Records

World, World U20 and U18, Olympic, Area and Continental records are listed for standard events. In running events up to and including 400 metres, only fully automatic times are shown. Marks listed are those which are considered statistically acceptable by the ATFS, and thus may differ from official records. These are followed by road bests and bests by over 35/40 masters.

World All-time and Year Lists

Lists are presented in the following format: Mark, Wind reading (where appropriate), Name, Nationality (abbreviated), Date of birth, Position in competition, Meeting name (if significant), Venue, Date of performance.

In standard events the best 30 or so performances are listed followed by the best marks for other athletes. Position, meet and venue details have been omitted beyond 100th in year lists.

In the all-time lists performances which have been world records (or world bests, thus including some unratified marks) are shown with WR against them (or WIR for world indoor records).

Juniors (U20) are shown with-J after date of birth, and Youths (U18) with -Y.

Indexes

These contain the names of all athletes ranked with full details in the world year lists for standard events (and others such as half marathon). The format of the index is as follows:

Family name, First name, Nationality, Birthdate, Height (cm) and Weight (kg), 2011 best mark, Lifetime best (with year) as at the end of 2010.

* indicates an athlete who is profiled in the Biographies section, and ^ one who has been profiled in previous editions.

General Notes

Altitude aid

Marks set at an altitude of 1,000m or higher have been suffixed by the letter "A" in events where altitude may be of significance.

Although there are no separate world records for altitude assisted events, it is understood by experts that in all events up to 400m in length (with the possible exclusion of the 110m hurdles), and in the horizontal jumps, altitude gives a material benefit to performances. For events beyond 800m, however, the thinner air of high altitude has a detrimental effect.

Supplementary lists are included in relevant events for athletes with seasonal bests at altitude who have low altitude marks qualifying for the main list.

Some leading venues over 1000m

Addis Ababa ETH	2365m
Air Force Academy USA	2194
Albuquerque USA	1555
Antananarivo MAD	1350
Ávila ESP	1128
Bloemfontein RSA	1392
Bogotá COL	2644
Boulder USA	1655
Bozeman USA	1467
Calgary CAN	1045
Cali COL	1046
Ciudad de Guatemala GUA	1402
Ciudad de México MEX	2247
Cochabamba BOL	2558
Colorado Springs USA	1823
Cuenca ECU	2561
Denver USA	1609
El Paso USA	1187
Flagstaff USA	2107
Fort Collins USA	1521
Gabarone BOT	1006
Germiston RSA	1661
Guadalajara MEX	1567
Harare ZIM	1473
Johannesburg RSA	1748
Kampala UGA	1189
Krugersdorp RSA	1740
La Paz BOL	3630
Logan USA	1372
Medellín COL	1541
Monachil ESP	2302
Nairobi KEN	1675
Pietersburg RSA	1230
Pocatello USA	1361
Potchefstroom RSA	1351
Pretoria RSA	1400
Provo USA	1380
Reno USA	1369
Roodepoort RSA	1720
Rustenburg RSA	1157
Salt Lake City USA	1321
Secunda RSA	1628
Sestriere ITA	2050
Soría ESP	1056
South Lake Tahoe USA	1909
Sucre BOL	2750
Toluca MEX	2680
Tunja COL	2810
Windhoek NAM	1725
Xalapa MEX	1420

Some others over 500m

Albertville FRA	550
Almaty KZK	847
Ankara TUR	902
Bangalore IND	949
Bern SUI	555
Blacksburg USA	634
Boise USA	818
Canberra AUS	581
La Chaux de Fonds SUI	997

Caracas VEN	922
Edmonton CAN	652
Jablonec CZE	598
Las Vegas USA	619
Lausanne SUI	597
Lubbock USA	988
Madrid ESP	640
Magglingen SUI	751
Malles ITA	980
Moscow, Idaho USA	787
München GER	520
Nampa, Idaho USA	760
Salamanca ESP	806
Santiago de Chile CHI	520
São Paulo BRA	725
Sofia BUL	564
Spokane USA	576
Trípoli GRE	655
Tucson USA	728
Uberlândia BRA	852

350m-500m

Annecy FRA	448
Banská Bystrica SVK	362
Fayetteville USA	407
Genève SUI	385
Götzis AUS	448
Johnson City USA	499
Rieti ITA	402
Sindelfingen GER	440
Stuttgart GER	415
Tashkent UZB	477
Zürich SUI	410

Automatic timing

In the main lists for sprints and hurdles, only times recorded by fully automatic timing devices are included.

Hand timing

In the sprints and hurdles supplementary lists are included for races which are hand timed. Any athlete with a hand timed best 0.01 seconds or more better than his or her automatically timed best has been included, but hand timed lists have been terminated close to the differential levels considered by the IAAF to be equivalent to automatic times, i.e. 0.24 sec. for 100m, 200m, 100mh, 110mh, and 0.14 sec. for 400m and 400mh. It should be noted that this effectively recognises bad hand timekeeping, for there should be no material difference between hand and auto times, but what happens is that badly trained timekeepers anticipate the finish, having reacted to the flash at the start.

In events beyond 400m, auto times are integrated with hand timed marks, the latter identifiable by times being shown to tenths. All-time lists also include some auto times in tenths of a second, identified with '.

Indoor marks

Indoor marks are included in the main lists for field events and straightway track events, but not for other track events. This is because track sizes vary in circumference (200m is the international standard) and banking, while outdoor tracks are standardised at 400m. Outdoor marks for athletes whose seasonal bests were set indoors are shown in a supplemental list.

Mixed races

For record purposes athletes may not, except in road races, compete in mixed sex races. Statistically there would not appear to be any particular logic in this, and women's marks set in such races are shown in our lists – annotated with mx. In such cases the athlete's best mark in single sex competition is appended.

Field event series

Field event series are given (where known) for marks in the top 30 performances lists.

Tracks and Courses

As well as climatic conditions, the type and composition of tracks and runways will affect standards of performance, as will the variations in road race courses.

Wind assistance

Anemometer readings have been shown where available in the lists for sprints and horizontal jumps in metres per second to one decimal place. If the figure was given to two decimal places, it has been rounded to the next tenth upwards, e.g. a wind reading of +2.01m/s, beyond the IAAF legal limit of 2.0, is rounded to +2.1; or -1.22m/s is rounded up to -1.2.

For multi-events a wind-assisted mark in one in which an event is aided by a wind over 4.0m/s and the average of the three wind-measured events is > 2m/s.

Drugs bans

The IAAF Council may decertify an athlete's records, titles and results if he or she is found to have used a banned substance before those performances. Performances at or after such a positive finding are shown in footnotes. Such athletes are shown with ¶ after their name in year lists, and in all-time lists if at any stage of their career they have served a drugs suspension of a year or more (thus not including athletes receiving public warnings or 3 month bans for stimulants etc., which for that year only are indicated with a #). This should not be taken as implying that the athlete was using drugs at that time. Nor have those athletes who have subsequently unofficially admitted to using banned substances been indicated; the ¶ is used only for those who have been caught.

Venues

Place names occasionally change. Our policy is to use names in force at the time that the performance was set. Thus Leningrad prior to 1991, Sankt-Peterburg from its re-naming.

Amendments

Keen observers may spot errors in the lists. They are invited to send corrections as well as news and results for 2012.

Peter Matthews, p.jmatthews@btinternet.com

WORLD & CONTINENTAL RECORDS

As at 1 April 2012. **Key**: W = World, Afr = Africa, Asi = Asia, CAC = Central America & Caribbean, Eur = Europe, NAm = North America, Oce = Oceania, SAm = South America, Com = Commonwealth, W20 = World Junior (U20), W18 = World Youth (U18, not officially ratified by IAAF).
Successive columns show: World or Continent, performance, name, nationality, venue, date.
A altitude over 1000m, + timing by photo-electric-cell, # awaiting ratification, § not officially ratified

100 METRES

W,CAC,Com	9.58	Usain BOLT	JAM	Berlin	16 Aug 2009
NAm	9.69	Tyson GAY	USA	Shanghai	20 Sep 2009
Afr	9.85	Olusoji FASUBA	NGR	Doha	12 May 2006
Eur	9.86	Francis OBIKWELU	POR	Athína	22 Aug 2004
Oce	9.93	Patrick JOHNSON	AUS	Mito	5 May 2003
Asi	9.99	Samuel FRANCIS	QAT	Amman	26 Jul 2007
SAm	10.00A	Róbson da SILVA	BRA	Ciudad de México	22 Jul 1988
W20	10.01	Darrel BROWN	TRI	Saint-Denis	24 Aug 2003
	10.01 §	Jeffery DEMPS	USA	Eugene	28 Jun 2008
W18	10.23	Rynell PARSON	USA	Indianapolis	21 Jun 2007
	10.23 ?	Tamunoski ATORUDIBO	NGR	Enugu	23 Mar 2002

200 METRES

W,CAC,Com	19.19	Usain BOLT	JAM	Berlin	20 Aug 2009
NAm	19.32	Michael JOHNSON	USA	Atlanta	1 Aug 1996
Afr	19.68	Frank FREDERICKS	NAM	Atlanta	1 Aug 1996
Eur	19.72A	Pietro MENNEA	ITA	Ciudad de México	12 Sep 1979
SAm	19.81	Alonso EDWARD	PAN	Berlin	20 Aug 2009
Asi	20.03	Shingo SUETSUGU	JPN	Yokohama	7 Jun 2003
Oce	20.06A	Peter NORMAN	AUS	Ciudad de México	16 Oct 1968
W20	19.93	Usain BOLT	JAM	Hamilton, BER	11 Apr 2004
W18	20.13	Usain BOLT	JAM	Bridgetown	20 Jul 2003

400 METRES

W, NAm	43.18	Michael JOHNSON	USA	Sevilla	26 Aug 1999
Afr	44.10	Gary KIKAYA	COD	Stuttgart	9 Sep 2006
CAC	44.14	Roberto HERNÁNDEZ	CUB	Sevilla	30 May 1990
Com	44.17	Innocent EGBUNIKE	NGR	Zürich	19 Aug 1987
SAm	44.29	Sanderlei PARRELA	BRA	Sevilla	26 Aug 1999
Eur	44.33	Thomas SCHÖNLEBE	GER	Roma	3 Sep 1987
Oce	44.38	Darren CLARK	AUS	Seoul	26 Sep 1988
Asi	44.56	Mohamed AL-MALKY	OMN	Budapest	12 Aug 1988
W20	43.87	Steve LEWIS	USA	Seoul	28 Sep 1988
W18	45.14	Obea MOORE	USA	Santiago de Chile	2 Sep 1995

800 METRES

W, Afr	1:41.01	David RUDISHA	KEN	Rieti	22 Aug 2010
Eur	1:41.11	Wilson KIPKETER	DEN	Köln	24 Aug 1997
Com	1:41.73	Sebastian COE	GBR	Firenze	10 Jun 1981
SAm	1:41.77	Joaquim CRUZ	BRA	Köln	26 Aug 1984
NAm	1:42.60	Johnny GRAY	USA	Koblenz	28 Aug 1985
Asi	1:42.79	Youssef Saad KAMEL	BRN	Monaco	29 Jul 2008
CAC	1:42.85	Norberto TELLEZ	CUB	Atlanta	31 Jul 1996
Oce	1:44.3 m	Peter SNELL	NZL	Christchurch	3 Feb 1962
W20	1:42.69	Abubaker KAKI	SUD	Oslo	6 Jun 2008
W18	1:43.37	Mohamed AMAN	ETH	Rieti	10 Sep 2011

1000 METRES

W, Afr, Com	2:11.96	Noah NGENY	KEN	Rieti	5 Sep 1999
Eur	2:12.18	Sebastian COE	GBR	Oslo	11 Jul 1981
NAm	2:13.9	Rick WOHLHUTER	USA	Oslo	30 Jul 1974
SAm	2:14.09	Joaquim CRUZ	BRA	Nice	20 Aug 1984
Asi	2:14.72	Youssef Saad KAMEL	BRN	Stockholm	22 Jul 2008
Oce	2:16.57	John WALKER	NZL	Oslo	1 Jul 1980
CAC	2:17.0	Byron DYCE	JAM	København	15 Aug 1973
W20	2:13.93 §	Abubaker KAKI	SUD	Stockholm	22 Jul 2008
W18	2:17.44	Hamza DRIOUCH	QAT	Sollentuna	9 Aug 2011

1500 METRES

W, Afr	3:26.00	Hicham EL GUERROUJ	MAR	Roma	14 Jul 1998
Com	3:26.34	Bernard LAGAT	KEN	Bruxelles	24 Aug 2001

Eur	3:28.95	Fermin CACHO	ESP	Zürich	13 Aug 1997
Asi	3:29.14	Rashid RAMZI	BRN	Roma	14 Jul 2006
NAm	3:29.30	Bernard LAGAT	USA	Rieti	28 Aug 2005
Oce	3:31.06	Ryan GREGSON	AUS	Monaco	22 Jul 2010
SAm	3:33.25	Hudson Santos de SOUZA	BRA	Rieti	28 Aug 2005
CAC	3:36.60	Stephen AGAR (later CAN)	DMN	Abbotsford	2 Jun 1996
W20	3:30.24	Cornelius CHIRCHIR	KEN	Monaco	19 Jul 2002
W18	3:33.72	Nicholas KEMBOI	KEN	Zürich	18 Aug 2006

1 MILE

W, Afr	3:43.13	Hicham El GUERROUJ	MAR	Roma	7 Jul 1999
Com	3:43.40	Noah NGENY	KEN	Roma	7 Jul 1999
Eur	3:46.32	Steve CRAM	GBR	Oslo	27 Jul 1985
NAm	3:46.91	Alan WEBB	USA	Brasschaat	21 Jul 2007
Asi	3:47.97	Daham Najim BASHIR	QAT	Oslo	29 Jul 2005
Oce	3:48.98	Craig MOTTRAM	AUS	Oslo	29 Jul 2005
SAm	3:51.05	Hudson de SOUZA	BRA	Oslo	29 Jul 2005
CAC	3:57.34	Byron DYCE	JAM	Stockholm	1 Jul 1974
W20	3:49.29	William BIWOTT	KEN	Oslo	3 Jul 2009
W18	3:54.56	Isaac SONGOK	KEN	Linz	20 Aug 2001

2000 METRES

W, Afr	4:44.79	Hicham EL GUERROUJ	MAR	Berlin	7 Sep 1999
Com	4:48.74	John KIBOWEN	KEN	Hechtel	1 Aug 1998
Oce	4:50.76	Craig MOTTRAM	AUS	Melbourne	9 Mar 2006
Eur	4:51.39	Steve CRAM	GBR	Budapest	4 Aug 1985
NAm	4:52.44	Jim SPIVEY	USA	Lausanne	15 Sep 1987
Asi	4:55.57	Mohammed SULEIMAN	QAT	Roma	8 Jun 1995
W20	4:56.25	Tesfaye CHERU	ETH	Reims	5 Jul 2011
W18	4:56.86	Isaac SONGOK	KEN	Berlin	31 Aug 2001
SAm	5:03.34	Hudson Santos de SOUZA	BRA	Manaus	6 Apr 2002
CAC	5:03.4	Arturo BARRIOS	MEX	Nice	10 Jul 1989

3000 METRES

W, Afr, Com	7:20.67	Daniel KOMEN	KEN	Rieti	1 Sep 1996
Eur	7:26.62	Mohammed MOURHIT	BEL	Monaco	18 Aug 2000
NAm	7:29.00	Bernard LAGAT	USA	Rieti	29 Aug 2010
Asi	7:30.76	Jamal Bilal SALEM	QAT	Doha	13 May 2005
Oce	7:32.19	Craig MOTTRAM	AUS	Athína	17 Sep 2006
CAC	7:35.71	Arturo BARRIOS	MEX	Nice	10 Jul 1989
SAm	7:39.70	Hudson Santos de SOUZA	BRA	Lausanne	2 Jul 2002
W20	7:28.78	Augustine CHOGE	KEN	Doha	13 May 2005
W18	7:32.37	Abreham CHERKOS Feleke	ETH	Lausanne	11 Jul 2006

5000 METRES

W, Afr	12:37.35	Kenenisa BEKELE	ETH	Hengelo	31 May 2004
Com	12:39.74	Daniel KOMEN	KEN	Bruxelles	22 Aug 1997
Eur	12:49.71	Mohammed MOURHIT	BEL	Bruxelles	25 Aug 2000
Asi	12:51.98	Saif Saaeed SHAHEEN	QAT	Roma	14 Jul 2006
NAm	12:53.60	Bernard LAGAT	USA	Monaco	22 Jul 2011
Oce	12:55.76	Craig MOTTRAM	AUS	London	30 Jul 2004
CAC	13:07.79	Arturo BARRIOS	MEX	London (CP)	14 Jul 1989
SAm	13:19.43	Marilson DOS SANTOS	BRA	Kassel	8 Jun 2006
W20	12:52.61	Eliud KIPCHOGE	KEN	Oslo	27 Jun 2003
W18	12:54.19	Abreham CHERKOS Feleke	ETH	Roma	14 Jul 2006

10,000 METRES

W, Afr	26:17.53	Kenenisa BEKELE	ETH	Bruxelles	26 Aug 2005
Com	26:27.85	Paul TERGAT	KEN	Bruxelles	22 Aug 1997
Asi	26:38.76	Abdullah Ahmad HASSAN	QAT	Bruxelles	5 Sep 2003
Eur	26:46.57	Mohamed FARAH	GBR	Eugene	3 Jun 2011
NAm	26:48.00	Galen RUPP	USA	Bruxelles	16 Sep 2011
CAC	27:08.23	Arturo BARRIOS	MEX	Berlin	18 Aug 1989
Oce	27:24.95	Ben ST LAWRENCE	AUS	Stanford	1 May 2011
SAm	27:28.12	Marilson DOS SANTOS	BRA	Neerpelt	2 Jun 2007
W20	26:41.75	Samuel WANJIRU	KEN	Bruxelles	26 Aug 2005
W18	27:02.81	Ibrahim JAYLAN Gashu	ETH	Bruxelles	25 Aug 2006

HALF MARATHON

W, Afr	58:23	Zersenay TADESE	ERI	Lisboa	21 Mar 2010
Com	58:33	Samuel WANJIRU	KEN	Den Haag	17 Mar 2007

SAm	59:33	Marilson DOS SANTOS	BRA	Udine	14 Oct 2007
NAm	59:43	Ryan HALL	USA	Houston	14 Jan 2007
Eur	59:52	Fabian RONCERO	ESP	Berlin	1 Apr 2001
Oce	60:02	Darren WILSON	AUS	Tokyo	19 Jan 1997
Asi	60:25	Atsushi SATO	JPN	Udine	14 Oct 2007
CAC	60:14	Armando QUINTANILLA	MEX	Tokyo	21 Jan 1996
W20	59:14	Dennis KOECH	KEN	Berlin	1 Apr 2012
W18	60:38	Faustin BAHA Sulle	TAN	Lille	4 Sep 1999

MARATHON

W, Afr, Com	2:03:38	Patrick MAKAU	KEN	Berlin	25 Sep 2011
NAm	2:05:38	Khalid KHANNOUCHI (ex MAR)	USA	London	14 Apr 2002
SAm	2:06:05	Ronaldo da COSTA	BRA	Berlin	20 Sep 1998
Asi	2:06:16	Toshinari TAKAOKA	JPN	Chicago	13 Oct 2002
Eur	2:06:36 §	António PINTO	POR	London	16 Apr 2000
	2:06:36	Benoît ZWIERZCHIEWSKI	FRA	Paris	6 Apr 2003
Oce	2:08:16	Steve MONEGHETTI	AUS	Berlin	21 Apr 1986
CAC	2:08:30	Dionicio CERÓN	MEX	London	2 Apr 1995
W20	2:06:07	Edic NDIEMA	KEN	Amsterdam	16 Oct 2011
W18	2:11:43	LI He	CHN	Beijing	14 Oct 2001

3000 METRES STEEPLECHASE

W, Asi	7:53.63	Saïf Saaeed SHAHEEN	QAT	Bruxelles	3 Sep 2004
Afr	7:53.64	Brimin KIPRUTO	KEN	Monaco	22 Jul 2011
Com	7:55.72	Bernard BARMASAI	KEN	Köln	24 Aug 1997
Eur	8:01.18	Bouabdellah TAHRI	FRA	Berlin	18 Aug 2009
NAm	8:08.82	Daniel LINCOLN	USA	Roma	14 Jul 2006
Oce	8:14.05	Peter RENNER	NZL	Koblenz	29 Aug 1984
SAm	8:14.41	Wander MOURA	BRA	Mar del Plata	22 Mar 1995
CAC	8:25.69	Salvador MIRANDA	MEX	Barakaldo	9 Jul 2000
W20	7:58.66	Stephen CHERONO (now Shaheen)	KEN	Bruxelles	24 Aug 2001
W18	8:17.28 §	Jonathan NDIKU	KEN	Bydgoszcz	13 Jul 2008

110 METRES HURDLES

W, CAC	12.87	Dayron ROBLES	CUB	Ostrava	12 Jun 2008
Asi	12.88	LIU Xiang	CHN	Lausanne	11 Jul 2006
NAm	12.89	David OLIVER	USA	Saint-Denis	16 Jul 2010
Eur, Com	12.91	Colin JACKSON	GBR/Wal	Stuttgart	20 Aug 1993
Afr	13.26	Shaun BOWNES	RSA	Heusden	14 Jul 2001
Oce	13.29	Kyle VANDER-KUYP	AUS	Göteborg	11 Aug 1995
SAm	13.27A	Paulo César VILLAR	COL	Guadalajara	28 Oct 2011
W20	13.12	LIU Xiang (with 3'6" hurdles)	CHN	Lausanne	2 Jul 2002
99cm h	13.08 §	Wayne DAVIS	USA	Port of Spain	31 Jul 2009
W18	13.43	SHI Dongpeng	CHN	Shanghai	6 May 2001
W18 (91cm)	13.18	Wayne DAVIS	USA	Ostrava	12 Jul 2007

400 METRES HURDLES

W, NAm	46.78	Kevin YOUNG	USA	Barcelona	6 Aug 1992
Afr, Com	47.10	Samuel MATETE	ZAM	Zürich	7 Aug 1991
CAC	47.25	Felix SÁNCHEZ	DOM	Saint-Denis	29 Aug 2003
Eur	47.37	Stéphane DIAGANA	FRA	Lausanne	5 Jul 1995
Asi	47.53	Hadi Sou'an AL-SOMAILY	KSA	Sydney	27 Sep 2000
SAm	47.84	Bayano KAMANI	PAN	Helsinki	7 Aug 2005
Oce	48.28	Rohan ROBINSON	AUS	Atlanta	31 Jul 1996
W20	48.02	Danny HARRIS	USA	Los Angeles	17 Jun 1984
W18 (84mc)	49.01	William WYNNE	USA	Ostrava	15 Jul 2007

HIGH JUMP

W, CAC	2.45	Javier SOTOMAYOR	CUB	Salamanca	27 Jul 1993
Eur	2.42	Patrik SJÖBERG	SWE	Stockholm	30 Jun 1987
	2.42 i§	Carlo THRÄNHARDT	FRG	Berlin	26 Feb 1988
NAm	2.40 i§	Hollis CONWAY	USA	Sevilla	10 Mar 1991
		Charles AUSTIN	USA	Zürich	7 Aug 1991
Asi	2.39	ZHU Jianhua	CHN	Eberstadt	10 Jun 1984
Com	2.38i	Steve SMITH	GBR/Eng	Wuppertal	4 Feb 1994
	2.38	Troy KEMP	BAH	Nice	12 Jul 1995
Afr, Com	2.38	Jacques FREITAG	RSA	Oudtshoorn	5 Mar 2005
Oce	2.36	Tim FORSYTH	AUS	Melbourne	2 Mar 1997
SAm	2.33	Gilmar MAYO	COL	Pereira	17 Oct 1994
W20	2.37	Dragutin TOPIC	YUG	Plovdiv	12 Aug 1990
		Steve SMITH	GBR	Seoul	20 Sep 1992

W18	2.33	Javier SOTOMAYOR	CUB	La Habana	19 May 1984

POLE VAULT

W, Eur	6.15 i§	Sergey BUBKA	UKR	Donetsk	21 Feb 1993
	6.14 A	Sergey BUBKA	UKR	Sestriere	31 Jul 1994
Oce, Com	6.05	Dmitriy MARKOV	AUS	Edmonton	9 Aug 2001
NAm	6.04	Brad WALKER	USA	Eugene	8 Jun 2008
Afr	6.03	Okkert BRITS	RSA	Köln	18 Aug 1995
Asi	5.92i	Igor POTAPOVICH	KAZ	Stockholm	19 Feb 1998
	5.90	Grigoriy YEGOROV	KAZ	Stuttgart 19 Aug 1993 & London (CP)	10 Sep 1993
	5.90	Igor POTAPOVICH	KAZ	Nice	10 Jul 1996
CAC	5.90	Lázaro BORGES	CUB	Daegu	29 Aug 2011
SAm	5.80	Fábio Gomes da SILVA	BRA	São Caetano do Sul	26 Feb 2011
W20	5.80	Maksim TARASOV	RUS	Bryansk	14 Jul 1989
	5.80	Raphael HOLZDEPPE	GER	Biberach	28 Jun 2008
W18	5.51	Germán CHIARAVIGLIO	ARG	Pôrto Alegre	1 May 2004

LONG JUMP

W, NAm	8.95	Mike POWELL	USA	Tokyo	30 Aug 1991
Eur	8.86 A	Robert EMMIYAN	ARM	Tsakhkadzor	22 May 1987
SAm	8.73	Irving SALADINO	PAN	Hengelo	24 May 2008
CAC	8.71	Iván PEDROSO	CUB	Salamanca	18 Jul 1995
Com	8.62	James BECKFORD	JAM	Orlando	5 Apr 1997
Oce	8.54	Mitchell WATT	AUS	Stockholm	29 Jul 2011
Afr	8.50	Khotso MOKOENA	RSA	Madrid	4 Jul 2009
Asi	8.48	Mohamed Salim AL-KHUWALIDI	KSA	Sotteville	2 Jul 2006
W20	8.34	Randy WILLIAMS	USA	München	8 Sep 1972
W18	8.25	Luis Alberto BUENO	CUB	La Habana	28 Sep 1986

TRIPLE JUMP

W, Eur, Com	18.29	Jonathan EDWARDS	GBR/Eng	Göteborg	7 Aug 1995
NAm	18.09	Kenny HARRISON	USA	Atlanta	27 Jul 1996
CAC	17.92	James BECKFORD	JAM	Odessa, Texas	20 May 1995
SAm	17.90	Jadel GREGÓRIO	BRA	Belém	20 May 2007
Asi	17.59	LI Yanxi	CHN	Jinan	26 Oct 2009
Oce	17.46	Ken LORRAWAY	AUS	London (CP)	7 Aug 1982
Afr	17.37	Ndabezinhle MDHLONGWA	ZIM	Lafayette	28 Mar 1998
	17.37	Tareq BOUGTAÏB	MAR	Khémisset	14 Jul 2007
W20	17.50	Volker MAI	GDR	Erfurt	23 Jun 1985
W18	16.89	GU Junjie	CHN	Dalian	25 Aug 2000

SHOT

W, NAm	23.12	Randy BARNES	USA	Westwood	20 May 1990
Eur	23.06	Ulf TIMMERMANN	GER	Haniá	22 May 1988
Com	22.21	Dylan ARMSTRONG	CAN	Calgary	25 Jun 2011
Afr	21.97	Janus ROBBERTS	RSA	Eugene	2 Jun 2001
CAC	21.45	Dorian SCOTT	JAM	Tallahassee	28 Mar 2008
Oce	21.26	Scott MARTIN	AUS	Melbourne	21 Feb 2008
SAm	21.14	Marco Antonio VERNI	CHI	Santiago de Chile	29 Jul 2004
Asi	21.13	Sultan Abdulmajeed AL-HEBSHI	KSA	Doha	8 May 2009
W20	21.05 i§	Terry ALBRITTON	USA	New York	22 Feb 1974
	20.65 §	Mike CARTER	USA	Boston	4 Jul 1979
	20.43	David STORL	GER	Gerlingen	6 Jul 2009
W18	20.38	Jacko GILL	NZL	Auckland (North Shore)	5 Dec 2011
W20 6kg	22.73	David STORL	GER	Osterode	14 Jul 2009
W18 5kg	24.45	Jacko GILL	NZL	Auckland (North Shore)	19 Dec 2011

DISCUS

W, Eur	74.08	Jürgen SCHULT	GDR	Neubrandenburg	6 Jun 1986
NAm	72.34 ¶	Ben PLUCKNETT	USA	Stockholm	7 Jul 1981
	71.32 §	Ben PLUCKNETT	USA	Eugene	4 Jun 1983
CAC	71.06	Luis DELIS	CUB	La Habana	21 May 1983
Afr, Com	70.32	Frantz KRUGER	RSA	Salon-de-Provence	26 May 2002
Asi	69.32	Ehsan HADADI	IRI	Tallinn	3 Jun 2008
Oce	66.45	Benn HARRADINE	AUS	Salinas	22 May 2008
SAm	66.32	Jorge BALLIENGO	ARG	Rosario	15 Apr 2006
W20	65.62 §	Werner REITERER	AUS	Split	5 Sep 2010
	63.64	Werner HARTMANN	FRG	Strasbourg	25 Jun 1978
W18	58.62	Michal HODUN	POL	Santiago de C hile	21 Oct 2000
W20 1.75kg	70.13	Mykyta NESTERNKO	UKR	Halle	24 May 2008

W18 1.5kg	77.50	Mykyta NESTERNKO	UKR	Koncha Zaspa	19 May 2008

¶ Disallowed by the IAAF following retrospective disqualification for drug abuse, but ratified by the AAU/TAC

HAMMER

W, Eur	86.74	Yuriy SEDYKH	UKR/RUS	Stuttgart	30 Aug 1986
Asi	84.86	Koji MUROFUSHI	JPN	Praha	29 Jun 2003
NAm	82.52	Lance DEAL	USA	Milano	7 Sep 1996
Afr, Com	80.63	Chris HARMSE	RSA	Durban	15 Apr 2005
Oce	79.29	Stuart RENDELL	AUS	Varazdin	6 Jul 2002
CAC	77.78	Alberto SANCHEZ	CUB	La Habana	15 May 1998
SAm	76.42	Juan CERRA	ARG	Trieste	25 Jul 2001
W20	78.33	Olli-Pekka KARJALAINEN	FIN	Seinäjoki	5 Aug 1999
W18	73.66	Vladislav PISKUNOV	UKR	Live	11 Jun 1994
W20 6kg	82.97	Javier CIENFUEGOS	ESP	Madrid	17 Jun 2009
W18 5kg	85.26	Amjad Mohamed ASHRAF	QAT	Rhede	20 Jul 2011

JAVELIN

W, Eur	98.48	Jan ZELEZNY	CZE	Jena	25 May 1996
Com	91.46	Steve BACKLEY	GBR/Eng	Auckland (NS)	25 Jan 1992
NAm	91.29	Breaux GREER	USA	Indianapolis	21 Jun 2007
Oce	89.02	Jarrod BANNISTER	AUS	Brisbane	29 Feb 2008
Afr	88.75	Marius CORBETT	RSA	Kuala Lumpur	21 Sep 1998
Asi	87.60	Kazuhiro MIZOGUCHI	JPN	San José	27 May 1989
CAC	87.20A	Guillermo MARTÍNEZ	CUB	Guadalajara	28 Oct 2011
SAm	84.70	Edgar BAUMANN	PAR	San Marcos	17 Oct 1999
W20	84.69	Zigismunds SIRMAIS	LAT	Bauska	22 Jun 2011
W18 700g	89.34	Braian Ezequiel TOLEDO	ARG	Mar del Plata	6 Mar 2010

DECATHLON

W,Eur	9026	Roman SEBRLE	CZE	Götzis	27 May 2001
NAm	8891	Dan O'BRIEN	USA	Talence	5 Sep 1992
Com	8847	Daley THOMPSON	GBR/Eng	Los Angeles	9 Aug 1984
Asi	8725	Dmitriy KARPOV	KAZ	Athína	24 Aug 2004
CAC	8654	Leonel SUÁREZ	CUB	La Habana	4 Jul 2009
Oce	8490	Jagan HAMES	AUS	Kuala Lumpur	18 Sep 1998
Afr	8302	Larbi BOURAADA	ALG	Ratingen	17 Jul 2011
SAm	8291A m	Tito STEINER	ARG	Provo	23 Jun 1983
	8266	Pedro da SILVA	BRA	Walnut	24 Apr 1987
W20	8397	Torsten VOSS (with 3'6" hurdles)	GDR	Erfurt	7 Jul 1982
W18	8104h	Valter KÜLVET	EST	Viimsi	23 Aug 1981
	7829	Valter KÜLVET	EST	Stockholm	13 Sep 1981

4 X 100 METRES RELAY

W, CAC, Com	37.04	JAM (Carter, Frater, Blake, Bolt)	Daegu	4 Sep 2011
NAm	37.40	USA (Marsh, Burrell, Mitchell, C.Lewis)	Barcelona	8 Aug 1992
	37.40	USA (Drummond, Cason, Mitchell, Burrell)	Stuttgart	21 Aug 1993
Eur	37.73	GBR (Gardener, Campbell, Devonish, Chambers)	Sevilla	29 Aug 1999
SAm	37.90	BRA (V Lima, Ribeiro, A da Silva, Cl da Silva)	Sydney	30 Sep 2000
Afr	37.94	NGR (O Ezinwa, Adeniken, Obikwelu, D Ezinwa)	Athína	9 Aug 1997
Asi	38.03	JPN (Tsukahara, Suetsugu, Takahira, Asahara)	Osaka	1 Sep 2007
Oce	38.17	AUS (Henderson, Jackson, Brimacombe, Marsh)	Göteborg	12 Aug 1995
W20	38.66	USA (Kimmons, Omole, Williams, Merritt)	Grosseto	18 Jul 2004
W18	40.03	JAM (W Smith, M Frater, Spence, O Brown)	Bydgoszcz	18 Jul 1999

4 X 400 METRES RELAY

W, NAm	2:54.29	USA (Valmon, Watts, Reynolds, Johnson)	Stuttgart	22 Aug1993
Eur	2:56.60	GBR (Thomas, Baulch, Richardson, Black)	Atlanta	3 Aug 1996
CAC, Com	2:56.75	JAM (McDonald, Haughton, McFarlane, Clarke)	Athína	10 Aug 1997
SAm	2:58.56	BRA (C da Silva, A J dosSantos, de Araújo, Parrela)	Winnipeg	30 Jul 1999
Afr	2:58.68	NGR (Chukwu, Monye, Nada, Udo-Obong)	Sydney	30 Sep 2000
Oce	2:59.70	AUS (Frayne, Clark, Minihan, Mitchell)	Los Angeles	11 Aug 1984
Asi	3:00.76	JPN (Karube, K Ito, Osakada, Omori)	Atlanta	3 Aug 1996
W20	3:01.09	USA (Johnson, Merritt, Craig, Clement)	Grosseto	18 Jul 2004
W18	3:12.05	POL (Zrada, Kedzia, Grzegorczyk, Kowalski)	Kaunas	5 Aug 2001

20 KILOMETRES WALK

W, Eur	1:17:16		Vladimir KANAYKIN	RUS	Saransk	29 Sep 2007
	1:16:43 §	Sergey MOROZOV	RUS	Saransk	8 Jun 2008
SAm	1:17:21	Jefferson PÉREZ	ECU	Saint-Denis	23 Aug 2003
CAC	1:17:25.6 t	Bernardo SEGURA	MEX	Bergen (Fana)	7 May 1994
Oce, Com	1:17:33	Nathan DEAKES	AUS	Cixi	23 Apr 2005

Asi	1:17:36	WANG Zhen	CHN	Taicang	30 Mar 2012
Afr	1:19:02	Hatem GHOULA	TUN	Eisenhüttenstadt	10 May 1997
NAm	1:21:03	Arturo HUERTA	CAN	Etobicoke	7 Jul 2000
W20	1:18:06 §	Viktor BURAYEV	RUS	Adler	4 Mar 2001
W18	1:18:07	LI Gaobo	CHN	Cixi	23 Apr 2005

20,000 METRES TRACK WALK

W, CAC	1:17:25.6	Bernardo SEGURA	MEX	Bergen (Fana)	7 May 1994
Asi	1:18:03.3	BU Lingtang	CHN	Beijing	7 Apr 1994
Eur	1:18:35.2	Stefan JOHANSSON	SWE	Bergen (Fana)	15 May 1992
Oce, Com	1:19:48.1	Nathan DEAKES	AUS	Brisbane	4 Sep 2001
SAm	1:20:23.8	Andrés CHOCHO	ECU	Buenos Aires	5 Jun 2011
NAm	1:22:27.0	Tim BERRETT	CAN	Edmonds, WA	9 Jun 1996
Afr	1:22:51.84	Hatem GHOULA	TUN	Leutkirch	8 Sep 1994
W20	1:20:11.72	LI Gaobo	CHN	Wuhan	2 Nov 2007
W18	1:24:28.3	ZHU Hongjun	CHN	Xian	15 Sep 1999

50 KILOMETRES WALK

W, Eur	3:34:14	Denis NIZHEGORODOV	RUS	Cheboksary	11 May 2008
Oce, Com	3:35:47	Nathan DEAKES	AUS	Geelong	2 Dec 2006
Asi	3:36:06	YU Chaohong	CHN	Nanjing	22 Oct 2005
CAC	3:41:20	Raúl GONZÁLEZ	MEX	Praha-Podebrady	11 Jun 1978
NAm	3:47:48	Marcel JOBIN	CAN	Québec	20 Jun 1981
SAm	3:49:32	Andrés CHOCHO	ECU	Deagu	3 Sep 2011
Afr	3:58:44	Hatem GHOULA	TUN	Santa Eularia des Riu	4 Mar 2007
W20	3:41:10	ZHAO Jianguo	CHN	Wajima	16 Apr 2006
W18	3:45:46	YU Guoping	CHN	Guangzhou	23 Nov 2001

50,000 METRES TRACK WALK

W, Eur	3:35:27.2	Yoahnn DINIZ	FRA	Reims	12 Mar 2011
CAC	3:41:38.4	Raúl GONZÁLEZ	MEX	Bergen (Fana)	25 May 1979
Oce, Com	3:43:50.0	Simon BAKER	AUS	Melbourne	9 Sep 1990
Asi	3:48:13.7	ZHAO Yongshen	CHN	Bergen (Fana)	7 May 1994
NAm	3:56:13.0	Tim BERRETT	CAN	Saskatoon	21 Jul 1991
SAm	3:57:58.0	Claudio dos SANTOS	BRA	Blumenau	20 Sep 2008
Afr	4:21:44.5	Abdelwahab FERGUÈNE	ALG	Toulouse	25 Mar 1984

World Records at other men's events recognised by the IAAF

20,000m	56:25.98+	Haile GEBRSELASSIE	ETH	Ostrava	27 Jun 2007
1 Hour	21,285 m	Haile GEBRSELASSIE	ETH	Ostrava	27 Jun 2007
25,000m	1:12:25.4	Moses MOSOP	KEN	Eugene	3 Jun 2011
30,000m	1:26:47.4	Moses MOSOP	KEN	Eugene	3 Jun 2011
U18 Octathlon	6491	Jake STEIN	AUS	Villeneuve d'Ascq	7 Jul 2011
4 x 200m	1:18.68	Santa Monica Track Club	USA	Walnut	17 Apr 1994
		(Michael Marsh, Leroy Burrell, Floyd Heard, Carl Lewis)			
4 x 800m	7:02.43	Kenya Team	KEN	Bruxelles	25 Aug 2006
		(Joseph Mutua, William Yiampoy, Ismael Kombich, Wilfred Bungei)			
4 x l500m	14:36.23	W Biwott, Gathimba, G Rono, Choge	KEN	Bruxelles	4 Sep 2009

Walking

2 Hours track	29,572m+	Maurizio DAMILANO	ITA	Cuneo	3 Oct 1992
30km track	2:01:44.1	Maurizio DAMILANO	ITA	Cuneo	3 Oct 1992
U20 10,000m track:	38:46.4	Viktor BURAYEV	RUS	Moskva	20 May 2000
U20 10km road	37:44	Stanislav YEMELYANOV	RUS	Saransk	19 Sep 2009
W18 10km road	38:57	LI Tianlei	CHN	Beijing	18 Sep 2010

WOMEN

100 METRES

W, NAm	10.49	Florence GRIFFITH JOYNER	USA	Indianapolis	16 Jul 1988
Eur	10.73	Christine ARRON	FRA	Budapest	19 Aug 1998
CAC, Com	10.73	Shelly-Ann FRASER	JAM	Berlin	17 Aug 2009
Asi	10.79	LI Xuemei	CHN	Shanghai	18 Oct 1997
Afr	10.90	Glory ALOZIE	NGR	La Laguna	5 Jun 1999
	10.84 §	Chioma AJUNWA	NGR	Lagos	11 Apr 1992
Oce	11.12A	Melinda GAINSFORD/TAYLOR	AUS	Sestriere	31 Jul 1994
SAm	11.15	Ana Claudia SILVA	BRA	São Paulo	4 Sep 2010
W20	10.88	Marlies OELSNER/GÖHR	GDR	Dresden	1 Jul 1977
W18	11.13	Chandra CHEESEBOROUGH	USA	Eugene	21 Jun 1976

200 METRES

W, NAm	21.34	Florence GRIFFITH JOYNER	USA	Seoul	29 Sep 1988

CAC, Com	21.64	Merlene OTTEY	JAM	Bruxelles	13 Sep 1991
Eur	21.71	Marita KOCH	GDR	Chemnitz	10 Jun 1979
	21.71 §	Marita KOCH	GDR	Potsdam	21 Jul 1984
	21.71	Heike DRECHSLER	GDR	Jena	29 Jun 1986
	21.71 §	Heike DRECHSLER	GDR	Stuttgart	29 Aug 1986
Asi	22.01	LI Xuemei	CHN	Shanghai	22 Oct 1997
Afr	22.06 A§	Evette DE KLERK	RSA	Pietersburg	8 Apr 1989
	22.07	Mary ONYALI	NGR	Zürich	14 Aug 1996
Oce	22.23	Melinda GAINSFORD-TAYLOR	AUS	Stuttgart	13 Jul 1997
SAm	22.48	Ana Cláudia da SILVA	BRA	São Paulo	6 Aug 2011
W20	22.18	Allyson FELIX	USA	Athína	25 Aug 2004
	22.11A §	Allyson FELIX (no doping control)	USA	Ciudad de México	3 May 2003
W18	22.58	Marion JONES	USA	New Orleans	28 Jun 1992

400 METRES

W, Eur	47.60	Marita KOCH	GDR	Canberra	6 Oct 1985
Oce, Com	48.63	Cathy FREEMAN	AUS	Atlanta	29 Jul 1996
NAm	48.70	Sanya RICHARDS	USA	Athína	16 Sep 2006
Afr	49.10	Falilat OGUNKOYA	NGR	Atlanta	29 Jul 1996
CAC	48.89	Ana GUEVARA	MEX	Saint-Denis	27 Aug 2003
SAm	49.64	Ximena RESTREPO	COL	Barcelona	5 Aug 1992
Asi	49.81	MA Yuqin	CHN	Beijing	11 Sep 1993
W20	49.42	Grit BREUER	GER	Tokyo	27 Aug 1991
W18	50.01	LI Jing	CHN	Shanghai	18 Oct 1997

800 METRES

W, Eur	1:53.28	Jarmila KRATOCHVÍLOVÁ	CZE	München	26 Jul 1983
Afr,W20,Com	1:54.01	Pamela JELIMO	KEN	Zürich	29 Aug 2008
CAC	1:54.44	Ana Fidelia QUIROT	CUB	Barcelona	9 Sep 1989
Asi	1:55.54	LIU Dong	CHN	Beijing	9 Sep 1993
NAm	1:56.40	Jearl MILES CLARK	USA	Zürich	11 Aug 1999
SAm	1:56.68	Letitia VRIESDE	SUR	Göteborg	13 Aug 1995
Oce	1:58.25	Toni HODGKINSON	NZL	Atlanta	27 Jul 1996
W18	1:57.18	WANG Yuan	CHN	Beijing	8 Sep 1993

1000 METRES

W, Eur	2:28.98	Svetlana MASTERKOVA	RUS	Bruxelles	23 Aug 1996
Afr	2:29.34	Maria Lurdes MUTOLA	MOZ	Bruxelles	25 Aug 1995
Com	2:29.66	Maria Lurdes MUTOLA	MOZ	Bruxelles	23 Aug 1996
NAm	2:31.80	Regina JACOBS	USA	Brunswick	3 Jul 1999
SAm	2:32.25	Letitia VRIESDE	SUR	Berlin	10 Sep 1991
CAC	2:33.21	Ana Fidelia QUIROT	CUB	Jerez de la Frontera	13 Sep 1989
Asi	2:33.6 §	Svetlana ULMASOVA	UZB	Podolsk	5 Aug 1979
Oce	2:38.54	Alison WRIGHT	NZL	Berlin	17 Aug 1979
W20	2:35.4a	Irina NIKITINA	RUS	Podolsk	5 Aug 1979
	2:35.4	Katrin WÜHN	GDR	Potsdam	12 Jul 1984
W18	2:38.58	Jo WHITE	GBR	London (CP)	9 Sep 1977

1500 METRES

W, Asi	3:50.46	QU Yunxia	CHN	Beijing	11 Sep 1993
Eur	3:52.47	Tatyana KAZANKINA	RUS	Zürich	13 Aug 1980
Afr	3:55.30	Hassiba BOULMERKA	ALG	Barcelona	8 Aug 1992
NAm	3:57.12	Mary DECKER/SLANEY	USA	Stockholm	26 Jul 1983
Com	3:57.41	Jackline MARANGA	KEN	Monaco	8 Aug 1998
Oce	4:00.93	Sarah JAMIESON	AUS	Stockholm	25 Jul 2006
CAC	4:01.84	Yvonne GRAHAM	JAM	Monaco	25 Jul 1995
SAm	4:05.67	Letitia VRIESDE	SUR	Tokyo	31 Aug 1991
W20	3:51.34	LANG Yinglai	CHN	Shanghai	18 Oct 1997
W18	3:54.52	ZHANG Ling	CHN	Shanghai	18 Oct 1997

1 MILE

W, Eur	4:12.56	Svetlana MASTERKOVA	RUS	Zürich	14 Aug 1996
NAm	4:16.71	Mary SLANEY	USA	Zürich	21 Aug 1985
Com	4:17.57	Zola BUDD	GBR/Eng	Zürich	21 Aug 1985
Asi	4:17.75	Maryam Yusuf JAMAL	BRN	Bruxelles	14 Sep 2007
Afr	4:18.23	Gelete BURKA	ETH	Rieti	7 Sep 2008
Oce	4:22.66	Lisa CORRIGAN	AUS	Melbourne	2 Mar 2007
CAC	4:24.64	Yvonne GRAHAM	JAM	Zürich	17 Aug 1994
SAm	4:30.05	Soraya TELLES	BRA	Praha	9 Jun 1988
W20	4:17.57	Zola BUDD	GBR	Zürich	21 Aug 1985
W18	4:30.81	Gelete BURKA	ETH	Heusden	2 Aug 2003

2000 METRES

W, Eur	5:25.36	Sonia O'SULLIVAN	IRL	Edinburgh	8 Jul 1994
Com	5:26.93	Yvonne MURRAY	GBR/Sco	Edinburgh	8 Jul 1994
Asi	5:29.43+§	WANG Junxia	CHN	Beijing	12 Sep 1993
NAm	5:32.7	Mary SLANEY	USA	Eugene	3 Aug 1984
Afr	5:30.19	Gelete BURKA	ETH	Bruxelles	4 Sep 2009
Oce	5:37.71	Benita JOHNSON	AUS	Ostrava	12 Jun 2003
W20	5:33.15	Zola BUDD	GBR	London (CP)	13 Jul 1984
W18	5:46.5+	Sally BARSOSIO	KEN	Zürich	16 Aug 1995

3000 METRES

W, Asi	8:06.11	WANG Junxia	CHN	Beijing	13 Sep 1993
Eur	8:21.42	Gabriela SZABO	ROM	Monaco	19 Jul 2002
Com	8:22.20	Paula RADCLIFFE	Eng	Monaco	19 Jul 2002
Afr	8:23.23	Edith MASAI	KEN	Monaco	19 Jul 2002
NAm	8:25.83	Mary SLANEY	USA	Roma	7 Sep 1985
Oce	8:35.31	Kimberley SMITH	NZL	Monaco	25 Jul 2007
CAC	8:37.07	Yvonne GRAHAM	JAM	Zürich	16 Aug 1995
SAm	9:02.37	Delirde BERNARDI	BRA	Linz	4 Jul 1994
W20	8:28.83	Zola BUDD	GBR	Roma	7 Sep 1985
W18	8:36.45	MA Ningning	CHN	Jinan	6 Jun 1993

5000 METRES

W, Afr	14:11.15	Tirunesh DIBABA	ETH	Oslo	6 Jun 2008
Com	14:20.87	Vivian CHERUIYOT	KEN	Stockho;lm	29 Jul 2011
Eur	14:23.75	Liliya SHOBUKHOVA	RUS	Kazan	19 Jul 2008
Asi	14:28.09	JIANG Bo	CHN	Shanghai	23 Oct 1997
NAm	14:44.76	Molly HUDDLE	USA	Bruxelles	27 Aug 2010
Oce	14:45.93	Kimberley SMITH	NZL	Roma	11 Jul 2008
CAC	15:04.32	Adriana FERNÁNDEZ	MEX	Gresham	17 May 2003
SAm	15:18.85	Simone Alves da SILVA	BRA	São Paulo	20 May 2011
W20	14:30.88	Tirunesh DIBABA	ETH	Bergen (Fana)	11 Jun 2004
W18	14:45.71	SONG Liqing	CHN	Shanghai	21 Oct 1997

10,000 METRES

W, Asi	29:31.78	WANG Junxia	CHN	Beijing	8 Sep 1993
Afr	29:53.80	Meselech MELKAMU	ETH	Utrecht	14 Jun 2009
Eur	29:56.34	Elvan ABEYLEGESSE	TUR	Beijing	15 Aug 2008
Com	30:01.09	Paula RADCLIFFE	GBR/Eng	München	6 Aug 2002
NAm	30:22.22	Shalane FLANAGAN	USA	Beijing	15 Aug 2008
Oce	30:35.54	Kimberley SMITH	NZL	Stanford	4 May 2008
CAC	31:10.12	Adriana FERNANDEZ	MEX	Brunswick	1 Jul 2000
SAm	31:47.76	Carmen de OLIVEIRA	BRA	Stuttgart	21 Aug 1993
W20	30:26.50	Linet MASAI	KEN	Beijing	15 Aug 2008
W18	31:11.26	SONG Liqing	CHN	Shanghai	19 Oct 1997

HALF MARATHON

W, Afr, Com	65:50	Mary KEITANY	KEN	Ra's Al Khaymah	18 Feb 2011
Eur	66:25	Lornah KIPLAGAT	NED	Udine	14 Oct 2007
Oce	67:11	Kimberley SMITH	NZL	Philadelphia	18 Sep 2011
Asi	67:26	Kayoko FUKUSHI	JPN	Marugame	5 Feb 2006
NAm	67:34	Deena KASTOR	USA	Berrlin	2 Apr 2006
CAC	68:34 dh	Olga APPELL	MEX	Tokyo	24 Jan 1993
	69:28	Adrian FERNÁNDEZ	MEX	Kyoto	9 Mar 2003
SAm	71:15	Silvana PEREIRA	BRA	Florianópolis	13 Jul 1991
W20	67:57	Abebu GELAN	ETH	Ra's Al Khaymah	20 Feb 2009
W18	72:31	LIU Zhuang	CHN	Yangzhou	24 Apr 2011

MARATHON

W, Eur, Com	2:15:25	Paula RADCLIFFE	GBR/Eng	London	13 Apr 2003
Afr	2:18:47	Catherine NDEREBA	KEN	Chicago	7 Oct 2001
Asi	2:19:12	Mizuki NOGUCHI	JPN	Berlin	25 Sep 2005
NAm	2:19:36	Deena KASTOR	USA	London	23 Apr 2006
Oce	2:22:36	Benita JOHNSON	AUS	Chicago	22 Oct 2006
CAC	2:22:59	Madai PÉREZ	MEX	Chicago	22 Oct 2006
SAm	2:29:17	Adriana da SILVA	BRA	Tokyo	26 Feb 2012
W20	2:22:38	ZHANG Yingying	CHN	Xiamen	5 Jan 008

3000 METRES STEEPLECHASE

W, Eur	8:58.81	Gulnara GALKINA	RUS	Beijing	17 Aug 2008

Afr,Com	9:07.41	Eunice JEPKORIR	KEN	Beijing	17 Aug 2008
NAm	9:12.50	Jennifer BARRINGER	USA	Berlin	17 Aug 2009
Oce	9:18.35	Donna MacFARLANE	AUS	Oslo	6 Jun 2008
Asi	9:26.25	LIU Nian	CHN	Wuhan	2 Nov 2007
CAC	9:27.21	Mardrea HYMAN	JAM	Monaco	9 Sep 2005
SAm	9:41.22	Sabine HEITLING	BRA	London	25 Jul 2009
W20	9:22.51	Almaz AYANA	ETH	Bruxelles	27 Aug 2010
W18	9:29.52	Korahubish ITA'A	ETH	Huelva	10 Jun 2009

100 METRES HURDLES

W, Eur	12.21	Yordanka DONKOVA	BUL	Stara Zagora	20 Aug 1988
Oce, Com	12.28	Sally PEARSON	AUS	Daegu	3 Sep 2011
NAm	12.33	Gail DEVERS	USA	Sacramento	23 Jul 2000
Asi	12.44	Olga SHISHIGINA	KAZ	Luzern	27 Jun 1995
Afr	12.44	Glory ALOZIE	NGR	Monaco	8 Aug 1998
	12.44	Glory ALOZIE	NGR	Bruxelles	28 Aug 1998
	12.44	Glory ALOZIE	NGR	Sevilla	28 Aug 1999
CAC	12.45	Brigitte FOSTER	JAM	Eugene	24 May 2003
SAm	12.71	Maurren MAGGI	BRA	Manaus	19 May 2001
W20	12.84	Aliuska LÓPEZ	CUB	Zagreb	16 Jul 1987
W18	12.95	Candy YOUNG	USA	Walnut	16 Jun 1979

400 METRES HURDLES

Eur, W	52.34	Yuliya PECHONKINA	RUS	Tula	8 Aug 2003
CAC, Com	52.42	Melaine WALKER	JAM	Berlin	20 Aug 2009
NAm	52.47	Lashinda DEMUS	USA	Daegu	1 Sep 2011
Afr	52.90	Nezha BIDOUANE	MAR	Sevilla	25 Aug 1999
Oce	53.17	Debbie FLINTOFF-KING	AUS	Seoul	28 Sep 1988
Asi	53.96	HAN Qing	CHN	Beijing	9 Sep 1993
	53.96	SONG Yinglan	CHN	Guangzhou	22 Nov 2001
SAm	55.84	Lucimar TEODORO	BRA	Belém	24 May 2009
W20	54.40	WANG Xing	CHN	Nanjing	21 Oct 2005
W18	55.20	Leslie MAXIE	USA	San Jose	9 Jun 1984

HIGH JUMP

W, Eur	2.09	Stefka KOSTADINOVA	BUL	Roma	30 Aug 1987
Afr, Com	2.06	Hestrie CLOETE	RSA	Saint-Denis	31 Aug 2003
NAm	2.05	Chaunté HOWARD-LOWE	USA	Des Moines	26 Jun 2010
CAC	2.04	Silvia COSTA	CUB	Barcelona	9 Sep 1989
Oce	1 98	Vanessa WARD	AUS	Perth	12 Feb 1989
	1.98	Alison INVERARITY	AUS	Ingolstadt	17 Jul 1994
Asi	1.99	Marina AITOVA	KAZ	Athína	13 Jul 2009
SAm	1.96	Solange WITTEVEEN	ARG	Oristano	8 Sep 1997
W20	2.01	Olga TURCHAK	KAZ	Moskva	7 Jul 1986
	2.01	Heike BALCK	GDR	Chemnitz	18 Jun 1989
W18	1.96A	Charmaine GALE	RSA	Bloemfontein	4 Apr 1981
	1.96	Olga TURCHAK	UKR	Donetsk	7 Sep 1984

POLE VAULT

W, Eur	5.06	Yelena ISINBAYEVA	RUS	Zürich	28 Aug 2009
NAm	4.92	Jennifer STUCZYNSKI	USA	Eugene	6 Jul 2008
Com	4.87i	Holly BLEASDALE	GBR	Villeurbanne	20 Jan 2012
SAm	4.85	Fabiana MURER	BRA	San Fernando	4 Jun 2010
	4.85	Fabiana MURER	BRA	Daegu	30 Aug 2011
Oce, Com	4.76	Alana BOYD	AUS	Perth	24 Feb 2012
Asi	4.64	GAO Shuying	CHN	New York	2 Jun 2007
CAC	4.75A	Yarisley SLVA	CUB	Guadalajara	24 Oct 2011
Afr	4.42	Elmarie GERRYTS	RSA	Wesel	12 Jun 2000
W20	4.50 §	Valeriya VOLIK	RUS	Krasnodar	4 Jun 2008
W18	4.47	Angelica BENGTSSON	SWE	Moskva	22 May 2010

LONG JUMP

W, Eur	7.52	Galina CHISTYAKOVA	RUS	Sankt-Peterburg	11 Jun 1988
NAm	7.49	Jackie JOYNER-KERSEE	USA	New York	22 May 1994
	7.49A #	Jackie JOYNER-KERSEE	USA	Sestriere	31 Jul 1994
SAm	7.26A	Maurren MAGGI	BRA	Bogotá	26 Jun 1999
CAC,Com	7.16A	Elva GOULBOURNE	JAM	Ciudad de México	22 May 2004
Afr	7.12	Chioma AJUNWA	NGR	Atlanta	1 Aug 1996
Asi	7.01	YAO Weili	CHN	Jinan	5 Jun 1993
Oce	7.00	Bronwyn THOMPSON	AUS	Melbourne	7 Mar 2002

W20	7.14	Heike DAUTE/Drechsler	GDR	Bratislava	4 Jun 1983
W18	6.91	Heike DAUTE/Drechsler	GDR	Jena	9 Aug 1981

TRIPLE JUMP

W, Eur	15.50	Inessa KRAVETS	UKR	Göteborg	10 Aug 1995
Afr, Com	15.39	Françoise MBANGO ETONE	CMR	Beijing	17 Aug 2008
CAC	15.29	Yamilé ALDAMA	CUB	Roma	11 Jul 2003
Asi	15.25	Olga RYPAKOVA	KAZ	Split	4 Sep 2010
SAm	14.99A	Caterine IBARGÜEN	COL	Bogotá	13 Aug 2011
NAm	14.45	Tiombé HURD	USA	Sacramento	11 Jul 2004
Oce	14.04	Nicole MLADENIS	AUS	Hobart	9 Mar 2002
	14.04	Nicole MLADENIS	AUS	Perth	7 Dec 2003
W20	14.62	Tereza MARINOVA	BUL	Sydney	25 Aug 1996
W18	14.57	HUANG Qiuyan	CHN	Shanghai	19 Oct 1997

SHOT

W, Eur	22.63	Natalya LISOVSKAYA	RUS	Moskva	7 Jun 1987
Asi	21.76	LI Meisu	CHN	Shijiazhuang	23 Apr 1988
Oce, Com	21.24	Valerie ADAMS	NZL	Daegu	29 Aug 2011
CAC	20.96	Belsy LAZA	CUB	Ciudad de México	2 May 1992
NAm	20.18	Ramona PAGEL	USA	San Diego	25 Jun 1988
	20.18	Jill CAMARENA-WILLIAMS	USA	Saint-Denis	8 Jul 2011
SAm	19.30	Elisângela ADRIANO	BRA	Tunja	14 Jul 2001
Afr	18.35	Vivian CHUKWUEMEKA	NGR	Ijebu Ode	17 Apr 2006
	18.43 §	Vivian CHUKWUEMEKA	NGR	Walnut	19 Apr 2003
W20	20.54	Astrid KUMBERNUSS	GDR	Orimattila	1 Jul 1989
W18	19.13	GONG Lijiao	CHN	Shijiazhuang	4 Aug 2007

DISCUS

W, Eur	76.80	Gabriele REINSCH	GDR	Neubrandenburg	9 Jul 1988
Asi	71.68	XIAO Yanling	CHN	Beijing	14 Mar 1992
CAC	70.88	Hilda RAMOS	CUB	La Habana	8 May 1992
Oce, Com	68.72	Daniela COSTIAN	AUS	Auckland	22 Jan 1994
NAm	67.67	Suzy POWELL	USA	Wailuku	14 Apr 2007
Afr	64.87	Elizna NAUDE	RSA	Stellenbosch	2 Mar 2007
SAm	62.00	Elisângela ADRIANO	BRA	São Caetano do Sul	22 Jul 2011
W20	74.40	Ilke WYLUDDA	GDR	Berlin	13 Sep 1988
W18	65.86	Ilke WYLUDDA	GDR	Neubrandenburg	1 Aug 1986

HAMMER

W, Eur	79.42	Betty HEIDLER	GER	Halle	21 May 2011
CAC	76.62	Yipsi MORENO	CUB	Zagreb	9 Sep 2008
Asi	75.72	ZHANG Wenxiu	CHN	Chengdu	12 Mar 2012
NAm, Com	75.04	Sultana FRIZELL	CAN	Tucson	16 May 2012
SAm	73.74	Jennifer DAHLGREN	ARG	Buenos Aires	10 Apr 2010
Oce	71.12	Bronwyn EAGLES	AUS	Adelaide	6 Feb 2003
Afr	68.48	Marwa Ahmed HUSSEIN	EGY	Cairo	18 Feb 2005
W20	73.24	ZHANG Wenxiu	CHN	Changsha	24 Jun 2005
W18	70.60	ZHANG Wenxiu	CHN	Nanning	5 Apr 2003

JAVELIN

W, Eur	72.28	Barbora SPOTÁKOVÁ	CZE	Stuttgart	13 Sep 2008
CAC	71.70	Osleidys MENÉNDEZ	CUB	Helsinki	14 Aug 2005
Afr	68.38	Sunette VILJOEN	RSA	Daegu	2 Sep 2011
Oce, Com	66.80	Louise CURREY	AUS	Gold Coast	5 Aug 2000
NAm	66.67	Kara PATTERSON	USA	Des Moines	25 Jun 2010
Asi	63.92	WEI Jianhua	CHN	Beijing	18 Aug 2000
SAm	62.62A	Sabina MOYA	COL	Ciudad de Guatemala	12 May 2002
W20	63.01	Vira REBRYK	UKR	Bydgoszcz	10 Jul 2008
W18	62.93	XUE Juan	CHN	Changsha	27 Oct 2003

HEPTATHLON

W, NAm	7291	Jackie JOYNER-KERSEE	USA	Seoul	24 Sep 1988
Eur	7032	Carolina KLÜFT	RUS	Osaka	26 Aug 2007
Asi	6942	Ghada SHOUAA	SYR	Götzis	26 May 1996
Com	6831	Denise LEWIS	GBR/Eng	Talence	30 Jul 2000
Oce	6695	Jane FLEMMING	AUS	Auckland	28 Jan 1990
CAC	6527	Diane GUTHRIE-GRESHAM	JAM	Knoxville	3 Jun 1995
Afr	6423	Margaret SIMPSON	GHA	Götzis	29 May 2005
SAm	6133A	Lucimara DA SILVA	BRA	Guadalajara	26 Oct 2011
W20	6542	Carolina KLÜFT	SWE	München	10 Aug 2002

W18	6185	SHEN Shengfei	CHN	Shanghai	18 Oct 1997

DECATHLON

W, Eur	8358	Austra SKUJYTE	LTU	Columbia, MO	15 Apr 2005
Asi	7798 §	Irina NAUMENKO	KAZ	Talence	26 Sep 2004
NAm	7577 #	Tiffany LOTT-HOGAN	USA	Lage	10 Sep 2000
CAC	7245 #	Magalys GARCÍA	CUB	Wien	29 Jun 2002
Afr, Com	6915	Margaret SIMPSON	GHA	Réduit	19 Apr 2007
SAm	6570	Andrea BORDALEJO	ARG	Rosario	28 Nov 2004
Oce	5740	Preya CAREY	AUS	Brisbane	6 Sep 2001

4 X 100 METRES RELAY

W, Eur	41.37	GDR (Gladisch, Rieger, Auerswald, Göhr)	Canberra	6 Oct 1985
NAm	41.47	USA (Gaines, Jones, Miller, Devers)	Athína	9 Aug 1997
CAC, Com	41.70	JAM Fraser-Pryce, Stewart, Simpson, Campbell-Brown)	Daegu	4 Sep 2011
Asi	42.23	Sichuan CHN (Xiao Lin, Li Yali, Liu Xiaomei, Li Xuemei)	Shanghai	23 Oct 1997
Afr	42.39	NGR (Utondu, Idehen, Opara-Thompson, Onyali)	Barcelona	7 Aug 1992
SAm	42.85A	BRA (A C Silva, Gomes, Krasucki, R Santos)	Guadalajara	26 Oct 2011
Oce	42.99A	AUS (Massey, Broadrick, Lambert, Gainsford-Taylor)	Pietersburg	18 Mar 2000
W20	43.29	USA (Knight, Tarmoh, Olear, Mayo)	Eugene	8 Aug 2006
W18	44.05	GDR (Koppetsch, Oelsner, Sinzel, Brehmer)	Athína	24 Aug 1975

4 X 400 METRES RELAY

W, Eur	3:15.17	URS (Ledovskaya, Nazarova, Pinigina, Bryzgina)	Seoul	1 Oct 1988
NAm	3:15.51	USA (D.Howard, Dixon, Brisco, Griffith Joyner)	Seoul	1 Oct 1988
CAC, Com	3:18.71	JAM (Whyte, Prendergast, N Williams-Mills, S Williams)	Daegu	3 Sep 2011
Afr	3:21.04	NGR (Bisi Afolabi, Yusuf, Opara, Ogunkoya)	Atlanta	3 Aug 1996
Oce	3:23.81	AUS (Peris, Lewis, Gainsford-Taylor, Freeman)	Sydney	30 Sep 2000
Asi	3:24.28	CHN / Hebei (An X, Bai X, Cao C, Ma Y)	Beijing	13 Sep 1993
SAm	3:26.68	BRA (Coutinho, de Oliveira, Souza, de Lima)	Helsinki	13 Aug 2005
W20	3:27.60	USA (Anderson, Kidd, Smith, Hastings)	Grosseto	18 Jul 2004
W18	3:36.98	GBR (Ravenscroft, E McMeekin, Kennedy, Pettett)	Duisburg	26 Aug 1973

10 KILOMETRES WALK

W, Eur	41:04	Yelena NIKOLAYEVA	RUS	Sochi	20 Apr 1996
Asi	41:16	WANG Yan	CHN	Eisenhüttenstadt	8 May 1999
Oce, Com	41:30	Kerry SAXBY-JUNNA	AUS	Canberra	27 Aug 1988
CAC	42:42	Graciela MENDOZA	MEX	Naumburg	25 May 1997
NAm	44:17	Michelle ROHL	USA	Göteborg	7 Aug 1995
SAm	45:03	Geovanna IRUSTA	BOL	Podebrady	19 Apr 1997
Afr	45:06A	Susan VERMEULEN	RSA	Bloemfontein	17 Apr 1999
W20	41:52 §	Tatyana MINEYEVA	RUS	Penza	5 Sep 2009
	41:57 §	GAO Hongmiao	CHN	Beijing	8 Sep 1993
W18	43:28	Aleksandra KUDRYASHOVA	RUS	Adler	19 Feb 2006

10,000 METRES TRACK WALK

W, Asi	41:37.9 §	GAO Hongmiao	CHN	Beijing	7 Apr 1994
W, Eur	41:56.23	Nadyezhda RYASHKINA	RUS	Seattle	24 Jul 1990
Oce, Com	41:57.22	Kerry SAXBY-JUNNA	AUS	Seattle	24 Jul 1990
NAm	44:30.1 m	Alison BAKER	CAN	Bergen (Fana)	15 May 1992
	44:06 no kerb	Michelle ROHL	USA	Kenosha	2 Jun 1996
CAC	44:16.21	Cristina LÓPEZ	ESA	San Salvador	13 Jul 2007
SAm	45:59.95	Geovanna IRUSTA	BOL	Rio de Janeiro	20 May 2000
Afr	47:32.54A	Nicolene CRONJE	RSA	Pretoria	19 Mar 2005
W20	42:49.7 §	GAO Hongmiao	CHN	Jinan	15 Mar 1992
	42:59.48	Yelena LASHMANOVA	RUS	Tallinn	21 Jul 2011
W18	42:56.09	GAO Hongmiao	CHN	Tangshan	27 Sep 1991

20,000 METRES TRACK WALK

W, Eur	1:26:52.3	Olimpiada IVANOVA	RUS	Brisbane	6 Sep 2001
Asi, W20	1:29:32.4 #	SONG Hongjuan	CHN	Changsha	24 Oct 2003
SAm	1:32:09.4	Ingrid HERNÁNDEZ	COL	Buenos Aires	5 Jun 2011
NAm	1:33:28.2	Teresa VAILL	USA	Carson	25 Jun 2005
Oce,Com	1:33:40.2	Kerry SAXBY-JUNNA	AUS	Brisbane	6 Sep 2001
CAC	1:34:56.7A	Maria del Rosario SÁNCHEZ	MEX	Xalapa	16 Jul 2000
Afr	1:36:43.43A	Nicolene CRONJE	RSA	Germiston	20 Mar 2004
W18	1:37:33.9	GAO Kelian	CHN	Xian	18 Sep 1999

20 KILOMETRES WALK

W, Eur	1:24:50 §	Olimpiada IVANOVA	RUS	Adler	4 Mar 2001
	1:25:08	Vera SOKOLOVA	RUS	Sochi	26 Feb 2011

Asi	1:25:46	LIU Hong	CHN	Taicang	30 Mar 2012
Oce, Com	1:27:44	Jane SAVILLE	AUS	Naumburg	2 May 2004
CAC	1:28:54	Mima ORTIZ	GUA	Lugano	18 Mar 2012
SAm	1:31:25	Miriam RAMÓN	ECU	Lima	7 May 2005
NAm	1:31:51	Michelle ROHL	USA	Kenosha	13 May 2000
Afr	1:34:19 §	Grace WANJIRU-NJUE	KEN	Nairobi	1 Aug 2010
W20	1:25:30	Anisya KIRDYAPKINA	RUS	Adler	23 Feb 2008
W18	1:30:52	JIANG Kun	CHN	Dandong	13 Apr 2001

World Records at other track & field events recognised by the IAAF

1 Hour	18,517 m	Dire TUNE	ETH	Ostrava	12 Jun 2008
20,000m	1:05:26.6	Tegla LOROUPE	KEN	Borgholzhausen	3 Sep 2000
25,000m	1:27:05.84	Tegla LOROUPE	KEN	Mengerskirchen	21 Sep 2002
30,000m	1:45:50.0	Tegla LOROUPE	KEN	Warstein	6 Jun 2003
4x200m	1:27.46	USA (L Jenkins, L Colander, N Perry, M Jones)		Philadelphia	29 Apr 2000
4x800m	7:50.17	USSR (Olizarenko, Gurina, Borisova, Podyalovskaya)		Moskva	5 Aug 1984

WORLD BESTS AT NON-STANDARD EVENTS

50m	5.47+e	Usain Bolt	JAM	Berlin (in 100m)	16 Aug 2009
60m	6.31+	Usain Bolt	JAM	Berlin (in 100m)	16 Aug 2009
100 yards	9.07	Asafa Powell	JAM	Ostrava	27 May 2010
150m turn	14.44+	Usain Bolt	JAM	Berlin (in 200m)	20 Aug 2009
150m straight	14.35	Usain Bolt	JAM	Manchester	17 May 2009
300m	30.85A	Michael Johnson	USA	Pretoria	24 Mar 2000
	30.97	Usain Bolt	JAM	Ostrava	27 May 2010
500m	1:00.08	Donato Sabia	ITA	Busto Arsizio	26 May 1984
600m	1:12.81	Johnny Gray	USA	Santa Monica	24 May 1986
2 miles	7:58.61	Daniel Komen	KEN	Hechtel	19 Jul 1997
2000m Steeple	5:10.68	Mahiedine Mekhissi	FRA	Reims	30 Jun 2010
200mh	22.55	Laurent Ottoz	ITA	Milano	31 May 1995
(hand time)	22.5	Martin Lauer	FRG	Zürich	7 Jul 1959
200mh straight	22.10	Andrew Turner	GBR	Manchester	15 May 2011
220yh straight	21.9	Don Styron	USA	Baton Rouge	2 Apr 1960
300mh	34.48	Chris Rawlinson	GBR	Sheffield	30 Jun 2002
35lb weight	25.41	Lance Deal	USA	Azusa	20 Feb 1993
Pentathlon	4282 points	Bill Toomey	USA	London (CP)	16 Aug 1969
(1985 tables)		(7.58, 66.18, 21.3, 44.52, 4:20.3)			
Double decathlon	14,571 points	Joe Detmer	USA	Lynchburg	24/25 Sep 2010

10.93w, 7.30, 200mh 24.25w, 12.27, 5k 18:25.32, 2:02.23, 1.98, 400m 50.43, HT 31.82, 3kSt 11:22.47
15.01, DT 40.73, 200m 22.58, 4.85, 3k 10:25.99, 400mh 53.83, 51.95, 4:26.66, TJ 13.67, 10k 40:27.26

3000m track walk	10:47.11	Giovanni De Benedictis	ITA	San Giovanni Valdarno	19 May 1990
5000m track walk	18:05.49	Hatem Ghoula	TUN	Tunis	1 May 1997
10,000m track walk	37:53.09	Francisco Javier Fernández	ESP	Santa Cruz de Tenerife	27 Jul 2008
10 km road walk	37:11	Roman Rasskazov	RUS	Saransk	28 May 2000
30 km road walk	2:01:13+	Vladimir Kanaykin	RUS	Adler	19 Feb 2006
35 km road walk	2:21:31	Vladimir Kanaykin	RUS	Adler	19 Feb 2006
100 km road walk	8:38:07	Viktor Ginko	BLR	Scanzorosciate	27 Oct 2002

Women

50m	5.93+	Marion Jones	USA	Sevilla (in 100m)	22 Aug 1999
60m	6.85+	Marion Jones	USA	Sevilla (in 100m)	22 Aug 1999
100 yards	9.91	Veronica-Campbell-Brown	JAM	Ostrava	31 May 2011
150m	16.10+	Florence Griffith-Joyner	USA	Seoul (in 200m)	29 Sep 1988
300m	34.1+	Marita Koch	GDR	Canberra (in 400m)	6 Oct 1985
500m	1:05.9	Tatána Kocembová	CZE	Ostrava	2 Aug 1984
600m	1:22.63	Ana Fidelia Quirot	CUB	Guadalajara, ESP	25 Jul 1997
2 miles	8:58.58	Meseret Defar	ETH	Bruxelles	14 Sep 2007
2000m Steeple	6:03.38	Wioletta Janowska	POL	Gdansk	15 Jul 2006
200mh	25.6	Patricia Girard	FRA	Nantes	23 Aug 2001
	25.82	Patricia Girard	FRA	Nantes	22 Sep 1999
300mh	38.91	Zuzana Hejnová	CZE	Pardubice	13 Aug 2011
	38.6	Mame Tacko Diouf	SEN	Dakar	21 Feb 1999
4 x 1500m	17:08.34	Tennesse University	USA	Philadelphia	24 Apr 2009
		(Price, Wright, Bell, Bowman)			
Double heptathlon	10,798 pts	Milla Kelo	FIN	Turku	7/8 Sep 2002

100mh 14.89, HJ 1.51, 1500m 5:03.74, 400mh 62.18, SP 12.73, 200m 25.16, 100m 12.59
LJ 5.73w, 400m 56.10, JT 32.69, 800m 2:23.94, 200mh 28.72, DT 47.86, 3000m 11:48.68

3000m track walk	11:48.24	Ileana Salvador	ITA	Padova	29 Aug 1993
5000m track walk	20:02.60	Gillian O'Sullivan	IRL	Dublin	13 Jul 2002
50 km road walk	4:10:59	Monica Svensson	SWE	Scanzorosciate	21 Oct 2007
100km road walk	10:04:50	Jolanta Dukure	LAT	Scanzorosciate	21 Oct 2007

LONG DISTANCE WORLD BESTS – MEN TRACK

	hr:min:sec	Name	Nat	Venue	Date
15,000m	0:42:18.7+	Haile Gebrselassie	ETH	Ostrava	27 Jun 2007
10 miles	0:45:23.8+	Haile Gebrselassie	ETH	Ostrava	27 Jun 2007
15 miles	1:11:43.1	Bill Rodgers	USA	Saratoga, Cal.	21 Feb 1979
20 miles	1:39:14.4	Jack Foster	NZL	Hamilton, NZ	15 Aug 1971
30 miles	2:42:00+	Jeff Norman	GBR	Timperley, Cheshire	7 Jun 1980
50 km	2:48:06	Jeff Norman	GBR	Timperley, Cheshire	7 Jun 1980
40 miles	3:48:35	Don Ritchie	GBR	London (Hendon)	16 Oct 1982
50 miles	4:51:49	Don Ritchie	GBR	London (Hendon)	12 Mar 1983
100 km	6:10:20	Don Ritchie	GBR	London (CP)	28 Oct 1978
150 km	10:34:30	Denis Zhalybin	RUS	London (CP)	20 Oct 2002
100 miles	11:28:03	Oleg Kharitonov	RUS	London (CP)	20 Oct 2002
200 km	15:10:27+	Yiannis Kouros	AUS	Adelaide	4-5 Oct 1997
200 miles	27:48:35	Yiannis Kouros	GRE	Montauban	15-16 Mar 1985
500 km	60:23.00+ ??	Yiannis Kouros	GRE	Colac, Aus	26-29 Nov 1984
500 miles	105:42:09+	Yiannis Kouros	GRE	Colac, Aus	26-30 Nov 1984
1000 km	136:17:00	Yiannis Kouros	GRE	Colac, Aus	26-31 Nov 1984
1500 km	10d 17:28:26	Petrus Silkinas	LTU	Nanango, Qld	11-21 Mar 1998
1000 mile	11d 13:54:58+	Petrus Silkinas	LTU	Nanango, Qld	11-22 Mar 1998
2 hrs	37.994 km	Jim Alder	GBR	Walton-on-Thames	17 Oct 1964
12 hrs	162.400 km +	Yiannis Kouros	GRE	Montauban	15 Mar 1985
24 hrs	303.506 km #	Yiannis Kouros	AUS	Adelaide	4-5 Oct 1997
48 hrs	473.797 km	Yiannis Kouros	AUS	Surgères	3-5 May 1996
6 days	1036.8 km	Yiannis Kouros	GRE	Colac, Aus	20-26 Nov 2005

LONG DISTANCE ROAD RECORDS & BESTS – MEN

Where superior to track bests (over 10km) and run on properly measured road courses. (I) IAAF recognition.

		Name	Nat	Venue	Date
10 km (I)	0:26:44	Leonard Patrick Komon	KEN	Utrecht	26 Sep 2010
15 km (I)	0:41:13	Leonard Patrick Komon	KEN	Nijmegen	21 Nov 2010
10 miles	0:44:24 §	Haile Gebrselassie	ETH	Tilburg	4 Sep 2005
	0:44:45	Paul Koech	KEN	Amsterdam-Zaandam	21 Sep 1997
20 km (I)	0:55:21+	Zersenay Tadese	ERI	Lisboa	21 Mar 2010
25 km (I)	1:11:50	Samuel Kosgei	KEN	Berlin	9 May 2010
	1:11:37 §	Haile Gebrselassie	ETH	Alphen aan den Rijn	12 Mar 2006
30 km (I)	1:27:38	Patrick Makau	KEN	Berlin	25 Sep 2011
	1:27:37 §	Peter Kirui	KEN	Berlin (dnf Mar)	25 Sep 2011
20 miles	1:35:22+	Steve Jones	GBR	Chicago	10 Oct 1985
30 miles	2:37:31+	Thompson Magawana	RSA	Claremont-Kirstenbosch	12 Apr 1988
50km	2:43:38+	Thompson Magawana	RSA	Claremont-Kirstenbosch	12 Apr 1988
40 miles	3:45:39	Andy Jones	CAN	Houston	23 Feb 1991
50 miles	4:50:21	Bruce Fordyce	RSA	London-Brighton	25 Sep 1983
100 km (I)	6:13:33	Takahiro Sunada	JPN	Yubetsu	21 Jun 1998
1000 miles	10d:10:30:35	Yiannis Kouros	GRE	New York	21-30 May 1988
Ekiden (6) (I)	1:57:06 #	Kenya	KEN	Chiba	23 Nov 2005
5 stages	1:55:59	Ethiopia	ETH	Chiba	24 Nov 2003

10k Dejene Birhanu, 5k Hailu Mekonnen, 10k Gebr. Gebremariam, 5k Markos Geneti, 12.195k Sileshi Sihine

12 hrs	162.543 km	Yiannis Kouros	GRE	Queen's, New York	7 Nov 1984

LONG DISTANCE WORLD BESTS – WOMEN TRACK

		Name	Nat	Venue	Date
15 km	0:48:54.91+	Dire Tune	ETH	Ostrava	12 Jun 2008
10 miles	0:54:21.8	Lorraine Moller	NZL	Auckland	9 Jan 1993
20 miles	1:59:09 !	Chantal Langlacé	FRA	Amiens	3 Sep 1983
30 miles	3:12:25+	Carolyn Hunter-Rowe	GBR	Barry, Wales	3 Mar 1996
50 km	3:18:52+	Carolyn Hunter-Rowe	GBR	Barry, Wales	3 Mar 1996
40 miles	4:26:43	Carolyn Hunter-Rowe	GBR	Barry, Wales	7 Mar 1993
50 miles	5:48:12.0+	Norimi Sakurai	JPN	San Giovanni Lupatoto	27 Sep 2003
100 km	7:14:05.8	Norimi Sakurai	JPN	San Giovanni Lupatoto	27 Sep 2003
150 km	13:45:54	Hilary Walker	GBR	Blackpool	5-6 Nov 1988
100 miles	14:25:45+	Edit Bérces	HUN	San Giovanni Lupatoto	22 Sep 2002
200 km	18:31:43+	Edit Bérces	HUN	San Giovanni Lupatoto	22 Sep 2002
200 miles	39:09:03	Hilary Walker	GBR	Blackpool	5-7 Nov 1988
500 km	77:53:46	Eleanor Adams	GBR	Colac, Aus.	13-16 Nov 1989
500 miles	130:59:58+	Sandra Barwick	NZL	Campbelltown, AUS	18-23 Nov 1990
1000 km	8d 00:27:06+	Eleanor Robinson	GBR	Nanango, Qld	11-19 Mar 1998
1500 km	12d 06:52:12+	Eleanor Robinson	GBR	Nanango, Qld	11-23 Mar 1998
1000 miles	13d 02:16:49	Eleanor Robinson	GBR	Nanango, Qld	11-24 Mar 1998
2 hrs	32.652 km	Chantal Langlacé	FRA	Amiens	3 Sep 1983
12 hrs	147.600 km	Ann Trason	USA	Hayward, Cal	3-4 Aug 1991
24 hours	255.303 km	Mami Kudo	JPN	Soochow	10-11 Dec 2011

48 hrs	385.130 km	Mami Kudo	JPN	Surgères	22-24 May 2010
6 days	883.631 km	Sandra Barwick	NZL	Campbelltown, AUS	18-24 Nov 1990

! Timed on one running watch only, # lap recorded by computer

LONG DISTANCE ROAD RECORDS & BESTS - WOMEN

	hr:min:sec	Name	Nat	Venue	Date
10 km (l)	0:30:21	Paula Radcliffe	GBR	San Juan	23 Feb 2003
15 km (l)	46:28	Tirunesh Dibaba	ETH	Nijmegen	15 Nov 2009
10 miles	0:50:05+	Mary Keitany	KEN	Ra's Al-Khaymah	18 Feb 2011
	0:50:01+ dh	Paula Radcliffe	GBR	Newcastle	21 Sep 2003
20 km (l)	1:02:36+	Mary Keitany	KEN	Ra's Al-Khaymah	18 Feb 2011
	1:02:21+ dh	Paula Radcliffe	GBR	Newcastle	21 Sep 2003
Half mar (l) qv +	1:05:50	Mary Keitany	KEN	Ra's Al-Khaymah	18 Feb 2011
	1:05:40 dh	Paula Radcliffe	GBR	South Shields	21 Sep 2003
25 km (l)	1:19:53	Mary Keitany	KEN	Berlin	9 May 2010
30 km (l)	1:38:23+ §	Liliya Shobukhova	RUS	Chicago	9 Oct 2011
	1:36:36+ dh	Paula Radcliffe	GBR	London	13 Apr 2003
20 miles	1:43:33+	Paula Radcliffe	GBR	London	13 Apr 2003
30 miles	3:01:16+	Frith van der Merwe	RSA	Claremont-Kirstenbosch	25 Mar 1989
50 km	3:08:39	Frith van der Merwe	RSA	Claremont-Kirstenbosch	25 Mar 1989
40 miles	4:26:13+	Ann Trason	USA	Houston	23 Feb 1991
50 miles	5:40:18	Ann Trason	USA	Houston	23 Feb 1991
100 km (l)	6:33:11	Tomoe Abe	JPN	Yubetsu	25 Jun 2000
100 miles	13:47:41	Ann Trason	USA	Queen's, New York	4 May 1991
200 km	19:00:31	Eleanor Adams	GBR	Milton Keynes (indoor)	3-4 Feb 1990
1000 km	7d 01:11:00+	Sandra Barwick	NZL	New York	16-23 Sep 1991
1000 miles	12d 14:38:40	Sandra Barwick	NZL	New York	16-29 Sep 1991
Ekiden (6 stages)	2:11:22	(l)	ETH	Chiba	24 Nov 2003

   Berhane Adere, Tirunesh Dibaba, Eyerusalem Kuma, Ejegayou Dibaba, Meseret Defar, Werknesh Kidane

12 hours	144.840 km	Ann Trason	USA	Queen's, New York	4 May 1991
24 hours	247.076 km	Lizzie Hawker	GBR	Llandudno	23-24 Sep 2011

100 KILOMETRES CONTINENTAL RECORDS

W, Asi	6:13:33	Takahiro SUNADA	JPN	Yubetsu	21 Jun 1998
Eur	6:16:41	Jean-Paul PRAET	BEL	Torhout	24 Jun 1989
SAm	6:18:09	Valmir NUNES	BRA	Winschoten	16 Sep 1995
Afr	6:25:07	Bruce FORDYCE	RSA	Stellenbosch	4 Feb 1989
Oce	6:29:23	Tim SLOAN	AUS	Ross-Richmond	23 Apr 1995
NAm	6:30:11	Tom JOHNSON	USA	Winschoten	16 Sep 1995

WOMEN

W, Asi	6:33:11	Tomoe ABE	JPN	Yubetsu	25 Jun 2000
NAm	7:00:48	Ann TRASON	USA	Winschoten	16 Sep 1995
Eur	7:10:32	Tatyana ZHYRKOVA	RUS	Winschoten	11 Sep 2004
SAm	7:20:22	Maria VENÂNCIO	BRA	Cubatão	8 Aug 1998
Afr	7:31:47	Helena JOUBERT	RSA	Winschoten	16 Sep 1995
Oce	7:40:58	Linda MEADOWS	AUS	North Otago	18 Nov 1995

WORLD INDOOR RECORDS

Men   to March 2012

50 metres	5.56A	Donovan Bailey	CAN	Reno	9 Feb 1996
60 metres	6.39	Maurice Greene	USA	Madrid	3 Feb 1998
	6.39	Maurice Greene	USA	Atlanta	3 Mar 2001
200 metres	19.92	Frank Fredericks	NAM	Liévin	18 Feb 1996
400 metres	44.57	Kerron Clement	USA	Fayetteville	12 Mar 2005
800 metres	1:42.67	Wilson Kipketer	KEN	Paris (Bercy)	9 Mar 1997
1000 metres	2:14.96	Wilson Kipketer	KEN	Birmingham	20 Feb 2000
1500 metres	3:31.18	Hicham El Guerrouj	MAR	Stuttgart	2 Feb 1997
1 mile	3:48.45	Hicham El Guerrouj	MAR	Gent	12 Feb 1997
2000 metres #	4:49.99	Kenenisa Bekele	ETH	Birmingham	16 Feb 2007
3000 metres	7:24.90	Daniel Komen	KEN	Budapest	6 Feb 1998
2 miles #	8:04.34	Kenenisa Bekele	ETH	Birmingham	16 Feb 2008
5000 metres	12:49.60	Kenenisa Bekele	ETH	Birmingham	20 Feb 2004
10000 metres #	27:50.29	Mark Bett	KEN	Gent	10 Feb 2002
50 m hurdles	6.25	Mark McKoy	CAN	Kobe	5 Mar 1986
60 m hurdles	7.30	Colin Jackson	GBR	Sindelfingen	6 Mar 1994
High jump	2.43	Javier Sotomayor	CUB	Budapest	4 Mar 1989
Pole vault	6.15	Sergey Bubka	UKR	Donetsk	21 Feb 1993
Long jump	8.79	Carl Lewis	USA	New York	27 Jan 1984
Triple jump	17.92	Teddy Tamgho	FRA	Paris (Bercy)	6 Mar 2011

Shot	22.66	Randy Barnes	USA	Los Angeles	20 Jan 1989
Javelin #	85.78	Matti Närhi	FIN	Kajaani	3 Mar 1996
35 lb weight #	25.86	Lance Deal	USA	Atlanta	4 Mar 1995
3000m walk #	10:31.42	Andreas Erm	GER	Halle	4 Feb 2001
5000m walk	18:07.08	Mikhail Shchennikov	RUS	Moskva	14 Feb 1995
10000m walk #	38:31.4	Werner Heyer	GDR	Berlin	12 Jan 1980
4 x 200m	1:22.11	United Kingdom		Glasgow	3 Mar 1991

(Linford Christie, Darren Braithwaite, Ade Mafe, John Regis)

4 x 400m	3:01.96	USA (not ratified – no EPO analysis)		Fayetteville	11 Feb 2006

(Kerron Clement, Wallace Spearmon, Darold Williamson, Jeremy Wariner)

4 x 800m	7:13.94	USA/Global Athletics & Marketing		Boston (Roxbury)	6 Feb 2000

(Joey Woody, Karl Paranya, Rich Kenah, David Krummenacker)

Heptathlon	6645 points	Ashton Eaton	USA	Istanbul	9/10 Mar 2012

(6.79 60m, 8.16 LJ, 14.56 SP, 2.03 HJ, 7.68 60mh, 5.20 PV, 2:32.77 1000m)

Women

50 metres	5.96+	Irina Privalova	RUS	Madrid	9 Feb 1995
60 metres	6.92	Irina Privalova	RUS	Madrid 11 Feb 1993 & 9 Feb 1995	
200 metres	21.87	Merlene Ottey	JAM	Liévin	13 Feb 1993
400 metres	49.59	Jarmila Kratochvílová	CZE	Milano	7 Mar 1982
800 metres	1:55.82	Jolanda Ceplak	SLO	Wien	3 Mar 2002
1000 metres	2:30.94	Maria Lurdes Mutola	MOZ	Stockholm	25 Feb 1999
1500 metres	3:58.28	Yelena Soboleva	RUS	Moskva	18 Feb 2006
1 mile	4:17.14	Doina Melinte	ROM	East Rutherford	9 Feb 1990
2000 metres #	5:30.53	Gabriela Szabo	ROM	Sindelfingen	8 Mar 1998
3000 metres	8:23.72	Meseret Defar	ETH	Stuttgart	3 Feb 2007
2 miles #	9:06.26	Meseret Defar	ETH	Praha	26 Feb 2009
5000 metres	14:24.37	Meseret Defar	ETH	Stockholm	18 Feb 2009
50 m hurdles	6.58	Cornelia Oschkenat	GDR	Berlin	20 Feb 1988
60 m hurdles	7.68	Susanna Kallur	SWE	Karlsruhe	10 Feb 2008
High jump	2.08	Kajsa Bergqvist	SWE	Arnstadt	4 Feb 2006
Pole vault	5.01	Yelena Isinbayeva	RUS	Stockholm	23 Feb 2012
Long jump	7.37	Heike Drechsler	GDR	Wien	13 Feb 1988
Triple jump	15.36	Tatyana Lebedeva	RUS	Budapest	5 Mar 2004
Shot	22.50	Helena Fibingerová	CZE	Jablonec	19 Feb 1977
Javelin #	61.29	Taina Uppa/Kolkkala	FIN	Mustasaari	28 Feb 1999
20 lb weight #	25.56	Brittany Riley	USA	Fayetteville	10 Mar 2007
3000m walk	11:35.34 #	Gillian O'Sullivan	IRL	Belfast	15 Feb 2003
	11:40.33	Claudia Iovan/Stef	ROM	Bucuresti	30 Jan 1999
5000m walk #	20:37.77	Margarita Turova	BLR	Minsk	13 Feb 2005
10000m walk	43:54.63	Yelena Ginko	BLR	Mogilyov	22 Feb 2008
4 x 200m	1:32.41	Russia		Glasgow	29 Jan 2005

(Yekaterina Kondratyeva, Irina Khabarova, Yuliya Pechonkina, Yuliya Gushchina)

4 x 400m	3:23.37	Russia		Glasgow	28 Jan 2006

(Yuliya Gushchina, Olga Kotlyarova, Olga Zaytseva, Olesya Krasnomovets)

4 x 800m	8:06.24	Moskva	RUS	Moskva	18 Feb 2011

(Aleksandra Bulanova, Yekaterina Martynova, Yelena Kofanova , Anna Balakshina)

Pentathlon	5013 points	Nataliya Dobrynska	UKR	Istanbul	9 Mar 2012

(8.38 60mh, 1.84 HJ, 16.51 SP, 6.57 LJ, 2:11.15 800m)

events not officially recognised by the IAAF

WORLD INDOOR JUNIOR (U20) RECORDS

As approved by IAAF Council in 2011 and updated with 2012 marks. **Men**

60 metres	6.51	Mark Lewis-Francis	GBR	Lisboa	11 Mar 2001
200 metres	20.37	Walter Dix	USA	Fayetteville	11 Mar 2005
400 metres	44.80	Kirani James	GRN	Fayetteville	27 Feb 2011
800 metres	1:44.35	Yuriy Borzakovskiy	RUS	Dortmund	30 Jan 2000
1000 metres	2:15.77	Abubaker Kaki	SUD	Stockholm	21 Feb 2008
1500 metres	3:36.28	Belal Mansoor Ali (overage!)	BRN	Stockholm	20 Feb 2007
One mile	3:55.02	German Fernandez	USA	College Station	28 Feb 2009
3000 metres	7:32.89	Isiah Koech	KEN	Liévin	14 Feb 2012
5000 metres	12:53.29	Isiah Koech	KEN	Düsseldorf	11 Feb 2011
60mh (99cm)	7.50	Konstadínos Douvalídis	GRE	Athína	11 Feb 2006
High jump	2.35	Volodymyr Yashchenko	URS	Milano	12 Mar 1978
Pole vault	5.68	Raphael Holzdeppe	GER	Halle	1 Mar 2008
Long jump	8.22	Viktor Kuznetsov	UKR	Brovary	22 Jan 2005
Triple jump	17.14	Volker Mai	GDR	Piréas	2 Mar 1985
Shot (6kg)	22.35	David Storl	GER	Rochlitz	20 Dec 2009
Heptathlon	6022	Gunnar Nixon	USA	Fayetteville	27/28 Jan 2012
(jnr imps)		(6.94, 7.96, 13.19, 1.96, 7.90, 4.60, 2:51.42)			

Women

60 metres	7.09	Joan Uduak Ekah	NGR	Maebashi	7 Mar 1999
200 metres	22.40	Bianca Knight	USA	Fayetteville	14 Mar 2008
400 metres	50.82	Sanya Richards	USA	Fayetteville	13 Mar 2004
800 metres	2:01.03	Meskerem Legesse	ETH	Fayetteville	14 Feb 2004
1000 metres	2:40.1m	Diana Richburg	USA	New London	7 Dec 1982
1500 metres	4:03.28	Kalkidan Gezahegne	ETH	Stockholm	10 Feb 2010
One mile	4:24.10	Kalkidan Gezahegne	ETH	Birmingham	20 Feb 2010
3000 metres	8:33.56	Tirunesh Dibaba	ETH	Birmingham	20 Feb 2004
5000 metres	14:53.99	Tirunesh Dibaba	ETH	Boston	31 Jan 2004
60m hurdles	8.06	Ulrike Denk	FRG	Dortmund	19 Feb 1983
	8.06	Monique Ewanje Épée	FRA	Madrid	22 Feb 1986
High jump	1.97	Mariya Kuchina	RUS	Trinec	26 Jan 2011
Pole vault	4.63	Angelica Bengtsson	SWE	Stockholm	22 Feb 2011
Long jump	6.88	Heike Daute	GDR	Berlin	1 Feb 1983
Triple jump	14.37	Ren Ruiping	CHN	Barcelona	11 Mar 1995
Shot	20.51	Heidi Krieger	GDR	Budapest	8 Feb 1984
Pentathlon	4535	Carolina Klüft	SWE	Wien	1 Mar 2002
		(8.49, 1.81, 12.71, 6.24, 2:14.95)			

WORLD VETERANS/MASTERS RECORDS

MEN – aged 35 or over

100 metres	9.97A	Linford Christie (2.4.60)	GBR	Johannesburg	23 Sep 1995
200 metres	20.11	Linford Christie (2.4.60)	GBR	Villeneuve d'Ascq	25 Jun 1995
400 metres	45.68	Alvin Harrison (20.1.74)	DOM	San Juan	5 Apr 2009
800 metres	1:43.36	Johnny Gray (19.6.60)	USA	Zürich	16 Aug 1995
1000 metres	2:18.8+	William Tanui (22.2.64)	KEN	Rome	7 Jul 1999
1500 metres	3:32.45	William Tanui (22.2.64)	KEN	Athína	16 Jun 1999
1 mile	3:51.38	Bernard Lagat (12.12.74)	USA	London (CP)	6 Aug 2011
2000 metres	4:58.3+ e	William Tanui (22.2.64	KEN	Monaco	4 Aug 1999
	4:57.31i	William Tanui		Sindelfingen	28 Feb 1999
3000 metres	7:29.00	Bernard Lagat (12.12.74)	USA	Rieti	29 Aug 2010
5000 metres	12:53.60	Bernard Lagat (12.12.74)	USA	Monaco	22 Jul 2011
10000 metres	26:51.20	Haile Gebrselassie (18.4.73)	ETH	Hengelo	24 May 2008
20000 metres	57:44.4+	Gaston Roelants (5.2.37)	BEL	Bruxelles	20 Sep 1972
1 Hour	20,822m	Haile Gebrselassie (18.4.73)	ETH	Hengelo	1 Jun 2009
Half Marathon	59:10 dh	Paul Tergat (17.6.69)	KEN	Lisboa	13 Mar 2005
	59:50	Haile Gebrselassie (18.4.73)	ETH	Den Haag	14 Mar 2009
Marathon	2:03:59	Haile Gebrselassie (18.4.73)	ETH	Berlin	28 Sep 2008
3000m steeple	8:04.95	Simon Vroemen (11.5.69)	NED	Bruxelles	26 Aug 2005
110m hurdles	12.96	Allen Johnson (1.3.71)	USA	Athína	17 Sep 2006
400m hurdles	48.13	Danny McFarlane (24.2.72)	JAM	Monaco	28 Jul 2009
High jump	2.31	Dragutin Topic (12.3.71)	SRB	Kragujevac	28 Jul 2009
Pole vault	5.88i	Jeff Hartwig (25.9.67)	USA	Jonesboro	22 Feb 2004
	5.85 sq	Derek miles (28.9.72)	USA	Berlin	7 Sep 2008
Long jump	8.50	Larry Myricks (10.3.56)	USA	New York	15 Jun 1991
	8.50	Carl Lewis (1.7.61)	USA	Atlanta	29 Jul 1996
Triple jump	17.92	Jonathan Edwards (10.5.66)	GBR	Edmonton	6 Aug 2001
Shot	22.67	Kevin Toth ¶ (29.12.67)	USA	Lawrence	19 Apr 2003
Discus	71.56	Virgilijus Alekna (13.2.72)	LTU	Kaunas	25 Jul 2007
Hammer	83.62	Igor Astapkovich (4.1.63)	BLR	Staiki	20 Jun 1998
Javelin	92.80	Jan Zelezny (16.6.66)	CZE	Edmonton	12 Aug 2001
Decathlon	8241	Kip Janvrin (8.7.65)	USA	Eugene	22 Jun 2001
		(10.98, 7.01, 14.21, 1.89, 48.41, 14.72, 45.59, 5.20, 60.41, 4:14.96)			
20 km walk	1:18:44	Vladimir Andreyev (7.9.66)	RUS	Cheboksary	12 Jun 2004
20000m t walk	1:20:55.4+	Maurizio Damilano (6.4.57)	ITA	Cuneo	3 Oct 1992
50 km walk	3:36:03	Robert Korzeniowski (30.7.68)	POL	Saint-Denis	27 Aug 2003
50000m t walk	3:49:29.7	Alain Lemercier (11.1.57)	FRA	Franconville	3 Apr 1994

MEN – aged 40 or over

100 metres	10.29	Troy Douglas (30.11.62)	NED	Leiden	7 Jun 2003
200 metres	20.64	Troy Douglas (30.11.62)	NED	Utrecht	9 Aug 2003
400 metres	47.82	Enrico Saraceni (19.5.64)	ITA	Århus	25 Jul 2004
	47.5u	Lee Evans (25.2.47)	USA		Apr 1989
800 metres	1:50.34	Jim Sorensen (10.5.67)	USA	Bloomington	30 Jun 2007
	1:48.81i	Johnny Gray (19.6.60)	USA	Atlanta	3 Mar 2001
1000 metres	2:24.93i	Vyacheslav Shabunin (27.9.69)	RUS	Moskva	10 Jan 2010
1500 metres	3:42.65	Vyacheslav Shabunin (27.9.69)	RUS	Moskva	27 May 2010
1 mile	4:01.62	Vyacheslav Shabunin (27.9.69)	RUS	Joensuu	21 Aug 2010
	3:58.15i	Eamonn Coghlan (21.11.52)	IRL	Boston	20 Feb 1994
3000 metres	8:02.54	Vyacheslav Shabunin (27.9.69)	RUS	Moskva	7 Jun 2010

	8:01.44i	Vyacheslav Shabunin (27.9.69)	RUS	Moskva	7 Feb 2010
5000 metres	13:43.15	Mohamed Ezzher (26.4.60)	FRA	Sotteville	3 Jul 2000
10000 metres	28:30.88	Martti Vainio (30.12.50)	FIN	Hengelo	25 Jun 1991
1 Hour	19.710k	Steve Moneghetti (26.9.62)	AUS	Geelong	17 Dec 2005
Half marathon	62:28	John Campbell (6.2.49)	NZL	Philadelphia	16 Sep 1990
Marathon	2:08:46	Andrés Espinosa (4.2.63)	MEX	Berlin	28 Sep 2003
3000m steeple	8:38.40	Angelo Carosi (20.1.64)	ITA	Firenze	11 Jul 2004
110m hurdles	13.97	David Ashford (24.1.63)	USA	Indianapolis	3 Jul 2004
	13.79 ?	Roger Kingdom (26.8.62)	USA	Slippery Rock	23 Jun 2004
400m hurdles	52.62	Antônio Dias Ferreira (2.3.60)	BRA	Rio de Janeiro	23 Jul 2000
High jump	2.24	Dragutin Topic (12.3.71)	SRB	Kragujevac	6 Aug 2011
Pole vault	5.71i	Jeff Hartwig (25.9.67)	USA	Jonesboro	31 May 2008
	5.70	Jeff Hartwig		Eugene	29 Jun 2008
Long jump	7.68A	Aaron Sampson (20.9.61)	USA	Cedar City, UT	21 Jun 2002
	7.57	Hans Schicker (3.10.47)	FRG	Kitzingen	16 Jul 1989
Triple jump	16.58	Ray Kimble (19.4.53)	USA	Edinburgh	2 Jul 1993
Shot	21.41	Brian Oldfield (1.6.45)	USA	Innsbruch	22 Aug 1985
Discus	69.46	Al Oerter (19.9.36)	USA	Wichita	31 May 1980
Hammer	82.23	Igor Astapkovich (4.1.63)	BLR	Minsk	10 Jul 2004
Javelin	85.92	Jan Zelezny (16.6.66)	CZE	Göteborg	9 Aug 2006
Pentathlon	3510 pts	Werner Schallau (8.9.38)	FRG	Gelsenkirchen	24 Sep 1978
		6.74, 59.20, 23.0, 43.76, 5:05.7			
Decathlon	7525 pts	Kip Janvrin (8.7.65)	USA	San Sebastián	24 Aug 2005
		11.56, 6.78, 14.01, 1.80, 49.46, 15.40, 42.70, 4.70, 58.43, 4:25.87			
20 km walk	1:21:36	Willi Sawall (7.11.41)	AUS	Melbourne	4 Jul 1982
20000m t walk	1:24:58.8	Marcel Jobin (3.1.42)	CAN	Sept Isles	12 May 1984
50 km walk	3:47:56	Jesús Ángel García (17.10.69)	ESP	Barcelona	30 Jul 2010
50000m t walk	3:51:54.5	José Marín (21.1.50)	ESP	Manresa	7 Apr 1990
4x100m	42.20	SpeedWest TC	USA	Irvine	2 May 2004
		(Frank Strong, Cornell Stephenson, Kettrell Berry, Willie Gault)			
4x400m	3:20.83	S Allah, K Morning, E Gonera, R Blackwell	USA	Philadelphia	27 Apr 2001

WOMEN – aged 35 or over

100 metres	10.74	Merlene Ottey (10.5.60)	JAM	Milano	7 Sep 1996
200 metres	21.93	Merlene Ottey (10.5.60)	JAM	Bruxelles	25 Aug 1995
400 metres	50.27	Jearl miles Clark (4.9.66)	USA	Madrid	20 Sep 2002
800 metres	1:56.53	Lyubov Gurina (6.8.57)	RUS	Hechtel	30 Jul 1994
1000 metres	2:31.5	Maricica Puica (29.7.50)	ROM	Poiana Brasov	1 Jun 1986
1500 metres	3:57.73	Maricica Puica (29.7.50)	ROM	Bruxelles	30 Aug 1985
1 mile	4:17.33	Maricica Puica (29.7.50)	ROM	Zürich	21 Aug 1985
2000 metres	5:28.69	Maricica Puica (29.7.50)	ROM	London (CP)	11 Jul 1986
3000 metres	8:23.23	Edith Masai (4.4.67)	KEN	Monaco	19 Jul 2002
5000 metres	14:33.84	Edith Masai (4.4.67)	KEN	Oslo	2 Jun 2006
10000 metres	30:30.26	Edith Masai (4.4.67)	KEN	Helsinki	6 Aug 2005
Half Marathon	67:16	Edith Masai (4.4.67)	KEN	Berlin	2 Apr 2006
Marathon	2:19:19	Irina Mikitenko (23.8.72)	GER	Berlin	28 Sep 2008
3000m steeple	9:33.93	Minori Hayakari (29.11.72)	JPN	Heusden	20 Jul 2008
100m hurdles	12.40	Gail Devers (19.11.66)	USA	Lausanne	2 Jul 2002
400m hurdles	52.94	Marina Styepanova (1.5.50)	RUS	Tashkent	17 Sep 1986
High jump	2.01	Inga Babakova (27.6.67)	UKR	Oslo	27 Jun 2003
Pole vault	4.70	Stacy Dragila (25.3.71)	USA	Chula Vista	22 Jun 2008
Long jump	6.99	Heike Drechsler (16.12.64)	GER	Sydney	29 Sep 2000
Triple jump	14.51	Yamilé Aldama (14.8.72)	SUD	Réthimno	14 Jul 2008
	14.82i	Yamilé Aldama (14.8.72)	GBR	Istanbul	19 Mar 2012
Shot	21.46	Larisa Peleshenko (29.2.64)	RUS	Moskva	26 Aug 2000
	21.47i	Helena Fibingerová (13.7.49)	CZE	Jablonec	9 Feb 1985
Discus	69.60	Faina Melnik (9.7.45)	RUS	Donetsk	9 Sep 1980
Hammer	72.36	Olga Kuzenkova (4.10.70)	RUS	Tula	2 Aug 2007
Javelin	68.34	Steffi Nerius (1.7.72)	GER	Berlin (Elstal)	31 Aug 2008
Heptathlon	6533 pts	Jane Frederick (7.4.52)	USA	Talence	27 Sep 1987
		13.60, 1.82, 15.50, 24.73; 6.29, 49.70, 2:14.88			
5000m walk	20:12.41	Elisabetta Perrone (9.7.68)	ITA	Rieti	2 Aug 2003
10km walk	41:41	Kjersti Tysse Plätzer (18.1.72)	NOR	Kraków	30 May 2009
10000m t walk	43:26.5	Elisabetta Perrone (9.7.68)	ITA	Saluzzo	4 Aug 2004
20km walk	1:25:59	Tamara Kovalenko (5.6.64)	RUS	Moskva	19 May 2000
20000m t walk	1:27:49.3	Yelena Nikolayeva (1.2.66)	RUS	Brisbane	6 Sep 2001
4x100m	48.63	Desmier, Sulter, Andreas, Apavou	FRA	Eugene	8 Jun 1989
4x400m	3:50.80	Mitchell, Mathews, Beadnall, Gabriel	GBR	Gateshead	8 Aug 1999

WOMEN – aged 40 or over

100 metres	10.99	Merlene Ottey (10.5.60)	JAM	Thessaloniki	30 Aug 2000
200 metres	22.72	Merlene Ottey (10.5.60)	SLO	Athína	23 Aug 2004

Event	Mark	Athlete		Nat	Venue	Date
400 metres	53.05A	María Figueirêdo (11.11.63)		BRA	Bogotá	10 Jul 2004
	53.14	María Figueirêdo (11.11.63)		BRA	San Carlos, VEN	19 Jun 2004
800 metres	1:59.25	Yekaterina Podkopayeva (11.6.52)		RUS	Luxembourg	30 Jun 1994
1000 metres	2:36.16	Yekaterina Podkopayeva (11.6.52)		RUS	Nancy	14 Sep 1994
	2:36.08i	Yekaterina Podkopayeva		RUS	Liévin	13 Feb 1993
1500 metres	3:59.78	Yekaterina Podkopayeva (11.6.52)		RUS	Nice	18 Jul 1994
1 mile	4:23.78	Yekaterina Podkopayeva (11.6.52)		RUS	Roma	9 Jun 1993
3000 metres	9:11.2	Joyce Smith (26.10.37)		GBR	London	30 Apr 1978
	9:02.83i	Lyubov Kremlyova (21.12.61)		RUS	Moskva	22 Jan 2002
5000 metres	15:20.59	Elena Fidatov (24.7.60)		ROM	Bucuresti	7 Aug 2000
10000 metres	31:31.18	Edith Masai (4.4.67)		KEN	Alger	21 Jul 2007
1 hour	16.056k	Jackie Fairweather (10.11.67)		AUS	Canberra	24 Jan 2008
Half Marathon	69:56	Irina Permitina (3.2.68)		RUS	Novosibirsk	13 Sep 2008
Marathon	2:25:43	Lyudmila Petrova (7.10.68)		RUS	New York	2 Nov 2008
3000m steeple	10:38.98	Soraya Telles (15.9.58)		BRA	Rio de Janeiro	5 Jun 1999
100 m hurdles	13.20	Patricia Girard (8.4.68)		FRA	Paris	14 Jul 2008
400 m hurdles	58.35	Barbara Gähling (20.3.65)		GER	Erfurt	21 Jul 2007
	58.3 h	Gowry Retchakan (21.6.60)		GBR	Hoo	3 Sep 2000
High jump	1.78i	Julia Machin (26.3.70)		GBR	London (LV)	27 Mar 2010
	1.78	Julia Machin (26.3.70)		GBR	Milton Keynes	22 May 2010
Pole vault	4.10	Doris Auer (10.5.71)		AUT	Innsbruck	6 Aug 2011
	4.11 §	Doris Auer (10.5.71)		AUT	Wien	5 Jul 2011
Long jump	6.64	Tatyana Ter-Mesrobian (12.5.68)		RUS	Sankt-Peterburg	31 May 2008
	6.64i	Tatyana Ter-Mesrobian		RUS	Sankt-Peterburg	5 Jan 2010
Triple jump	13.05	Katalin Deák (4.3.68)		HUN	Budapest	14 Jun 2009
Shot	19.05	Antonina Ivanova (25.12.32)		RUS	Oryol	28 Aug 1973
	19.16i	Antonina Ivanova		RUS	Moskva	24 Feb 1974
Discus	67.89	Iryna Yatchenko (31.10.65)		BLR	Staiki	29 Jun 2008
Hammer	59.29	Oneithea Lewis (11.6.60)		USA	Princeton	10 May 2003
Javelin	61.96	Laverne Eve (16.6.65)		BAH	Monaco	9 Sep 2005
Heptathlon	5449 pts	Tatyana Alisevich (22.1.69)		BLR	Staiki	3 Jun 2010
	14.80, 1.62, 13.92, 26.18, 5.55, 45.44, 2:24.39					
5000m walk	22:19.91	Joanne Dow (19.3.64)		USA	Philadelphia	24 Apr 2010
10km walk	45:09+	Kerry Saxby-Junna (2.6.61)		AUS	Edmonton	9 Aug 2001
10000m t walk	46:43.94	Graciela Mendoza (23.3.63)		MEX	Iquique	14 Jun 2008
20km walk	1:33:04	Graciela Mendoza (23.3.63)		MEX	Lima	7 May 2005
20000m t walk	1:33:28.15t	Teresa Vaill (20.11.62)		USA	Carson	25 Jun 2005
4x100m	48.22	Cadinot, Barilly, Valouvin, Lapierre		FRA	Le Touquet	24 Jun 2006
4x400m	3:57.28	Loizou, Kay, Smithe, Cearns		AUS	Brisbane	14 Jul 2001

WORLD AND CONTINENTAL RECORDS SET IN 2011

OUTDOORS – MEN

Event	Area	Mark	Athlete	Nat	Venue	Date
800	W18	1:44.08	Leonard KOSENCHA	KEN	Villeneuve d'Ascq	9 Jul 11
	W18	1:43.37	Mohamed AMAN	ETH	Rieti	10 Sep 11
1000	W18	2:17.44	Hamza DRIOUCH	QAT	Sollentuna	9 Aug 11
Mile	W35	3:51.38	Bernard LAGAT	USA	London (CP)	6 Aug 11
2000	W20	4:56.25	Tesfaye CHERU	ETH	Reims	5 Jul 11
5000	W35, NAm	12:53.60	Bernard LAGAT	USA	Monaco	22 Jul 11
10000	Oce	27:24.95	Ben ST.LAWRENCE	AUS	Stanford	1 May 11
	Eur	26:46.57	Mohamed FARAH	GBR	Eugene	03 Jun 11
	NAm	26:48.00	Galen RUPP	USA	Bruxelles	16 Sep 11
10k	Asi=	27:57	Nicholas KEMBOI	QAT	Utrecht	25 Sep 11
25000	W,Afr,Com	1:12:25.4t+	Moses MOSOP	KEN	Eugene	03 Jun 11
25k	SAm	?1:14:17+	Marilson DOS SANTOS	BRA	London	17 Apr 11
		1:14:31+	Marilson DOS SANTOS	BRA	Chicago	9 Oct 11
30k	SAm	1:29:21+	Marilson DOS SANTOS	BRA	London	17 Apr 11
	W,Afr,Com	1:27:37+ §	Peter KIRUI	KEN	Berlin	25 Sep 11
	W,Afr,Com	1:27:38+	Patrick MAKAU	KEN	Berlin	25 Sep 11
30000	W,Afr,Com	1:26:47.4t	Moses MOSOP	KEN	Eugene	03 Jun 11
Mar	W,Afr,Com	2:03:02 § dh	Geoffrey MUTAI	KEN	Boston	18 Apr 11
	NAm	2:04:58 § dh	Ryan HALL	USA	Boston	18 Apr 11
	W,Afr,Com	2:03:38	Patrick MAKAU	KEN	Berlin	25 Sep 11
	W20	2:06:07	Eric NDIEMA	KEN	Amsterdam	16 Oct 11
3000SC	Afr, Com	7:53.64	Brimin KIPRUTO	KEN	Monaco	22 Jul 11
110H	SAm	13.27A	Paulo VILLAR	COL	Guadalajara	28 Oct 11
200H St	W	22.10	Andy TURNER	GBR	Manchester	15 May 11
HJ	W40	2.18, 2.21	Dragutin TOPIC	SRB	Kragujevac	25 Jun 11
	W40	2.22	Dragutin TOPIC	SRB	Kragujevac	14 Jul 11
	W40	2.23	Dragutin TOPIC	SRB	Beograd	2 Aug 11
	W40	2.24	Dragutin TOPIC	SRB	Kragujevac	6 Aug 11

PV	SAm	5.80	Fábio GOMES da SILVA	BRA	São Caetano do Sul	26 Feb 11
	CAC	5.85, 5.90	Lázaro BORGES	CUB	Daegu	29 Aug 11
LJ	Oce	8.54	Mitchell WATT	AUS	Stockholm	29 Jul 11
SP/5kg	W18	24.35	Jacko GILL	NZL	Villeneuve d'Ascq	7 Jul 11
	W18	24.45	Jacko GILL	NZL	Auckland (North Shore)	19 Dec 11
SP/6kg	W18	21.34	Jacko GILL	NZL	Dunedin	26 Mar 11
	W18	22.09, 22.29, 22.31 Jacko GILL		NZL	Auckland (North Shore)	5 Dec 11
SP	W18	19.98, 20.01 Jacko GILL		NZL	Auckland (North Shore)	23 Apr 11
	Com	22.21	Dylan ARMSTRONG	CAN	Calgary	25 Jun 11
	W18	20.38	Jacko GILL	NZL	North Shore	5 Dec 11
HT/5kg	W18	83.36, 83.92 Bence PÁSZTOR		HUN	Veszprém	11 Jun 11
	W18	85.26	Amjad Mohamed ASHRAF	QAT	Rhede	20 Jul 11
JT	W20	84.47	Zigismunds SIRMAIS	LAT	Sofia	20 Mar 11
	W20	84.69	Zigismunds SIRMAIS	LAT	Bauska	22 Jun 11
	CAC	87.20A	Guillermo MARTINEZ	CUB	Guadalajara	28 Oct 11
Oct	W18	6491	Jake STEIN	AUS	Villeneuve d'Ascq	7 Jul 11
		(11.52, 7.22, 17.22, 51.32 / 14.25, 1.98, 59.65, 2:52.93)				
Dec	Afr	8302	Larbi BOURAADA	ALG	Ratingen	17 Jul 11
		(10.61w, 7.94w, 12.82, 2.06, 48.19 / 14.65, 40.34, 4.70, 58.05, 4:21.42)				
Medley R	W18	1:49.47	Darby, Bailey, Glass, Hall	USA	Villeneuve d'Ascq	10 Jul 11
4x100 R	W,CAC.Com	37.04	Carter, Frater, Blake, Bolt	JAM	Daegu	4 Sep 11
20000W	SAm	1:20:23.8t	Andrés CHOCHO	ECU	Buenos Aires	5 Jun 11
50000W	W, Eur	3:35:27.2	Yohann DINIZ	FRA	Reims	12 Mar 11
50kW	SAm	3:49:32	Andrés CHOCHO	ECU	Daegu	3 Sep 11

OUTDOORS – WOMEN

100y	W,Afr,Com	9.91+	Veronica CAMPBELL-BROWN	JAM	Ostrava	31 May 11
200	SAm	22.48	Ana Cláudia da SILVA	BRA	São Paulo	6 Aug 11
5000	SAm	15:18.85	Simone Alves da SILVA	BRA	São Paulo	20 May 11
	Com	14:20.87	Vivian CHERUIYOT	KEN	Stockholm	29 Jul 11
10M	W,Afr,Com	50:05+	Mary KEITANY	KEN	Ra's Al-Khaymah	18 Feb 11
20k	W,Afr,Com	62:36+	Mary KEITANY	KEN	Ra's Al-Khaymah	18 Feb 11
25k	Eur	1:22:34+	Liliya SHOBUKHOVA	RUS	Chicago	9 Oct 11
30k	W, Eur	1:38:23+	Liliya SHOBUKHOVA	RUS	Chicago	9 Oct 11
	Afr	1:38:33+	Mare DIBABA	ETH	Toronto	16 Oct 11
	Afr	1:38:33+	Karen JELELA	ETH	Toronto	16 Oct 11
HMar	Oce	67:36	Kim SMITH	NZL	New Orleans	13 Feb 11
	W,Afr,Com	65:50	Mary KEITANY	KEN	Ra's Al-Khaymah	18 Feb 11
	W18	72:31	Liu Zhuang	CHN	Yangzhou	24 Apr 11
	Oce	67:11	Kim SMITH	NZL	Philadelphia	18 Sep 11
24Hr	W	247.076k	Lizzie HAWKER	GBR	Llandudno	24 Sep 11
	W	255.303k t	Mami KUDO	JPN	Soochow	11 Dec 11
3000SC	W20	9:20.37	Birtukan ADAMU	ETH	Roma	26 May 11
100H	Oce	12.48	Sally PEARSON	AUS	Birmingham	10 Jul 11
	Oce, Com	12.36	Sally PEARSON	AUS	Daegu	3 Sep 11
	Oce, Com	12.28	Sally PEARSON	AUS	Daegu	3 Sep 11
300H	W	38.91	Zuzana HEJNOVÁ	CZE	Pardubice	13 Aug 11
400H	NAm	52.47	Lashinda DEMUS	USA	Daegu	1 Sep 11
PV	CAC	4.50=, 4.55	Yarisley SILVA	CUB	La Habana	17 Feb 11
	W40	3.87, 4.00	Doris AUER	AUT	Wien	12 May 11
	CAC	4.60	Yarisley SILVA	CUB	Rio de Janeiro	26 May 11
	W40	4.01	Doris AUER	AUT	Sankt Pölten	2 Jun 11
	W40	4.03	Doris AUER	AUT	Wien	13 Jun 11
	W40	4.04	Doris AUER	AUT	Wels	18 Jun 11
	CAC=	4.60	Yarisley SILVA	CUB	Velenje	28 Jun 11
	W40	4.06	Doris AUER	AUT	Wien	1 Jul 11
	Com	4.65=, 4.70	Holly BLEASDALE	GBR	Mannheim	2 Jul 11
	W40	4.11 §	Doris AUER	AUT	Wien	5 Jul 11
	CAC	4.61, 4.66	Yarisley SILVA	CUB	Barcelona	22 Jul 11
	W20	4.52, 4.57	Angelica BENGTSSON	SWE	Tallinn	23 Jul 11
	W40	4.10	Doris AUER	AUT	Innsbruck	6 Aug 11
	CAC	4.70	Yarisley SILVA	CUB	Daegu	30 Aug 11
	SAm=	4.85	Fabiana MURER	BRA	Daegu	30 Aug 11
	CAC	4.70A=, 4.75A Yarisley SILVA		CUB	Guadalajara	24 Oct 11
TJ	SAm	14.58, 14.59 Katerina IBARGÜEN		COL	São Paulo	22 May 11
		14.66	Katerina IBARGÜEN	COL	Castres	19 Jul 11
		14.70, 14.83 Katerina IBARGÜEN		COL	Stockholm	29 Jul 11
		14.99A	Katerina IBARGÜEN	COL	Bogotá	13 Aug 11
SP	NAm=	20.18	Jill CAMARENA-WILLIAMS	USA	Saint-Denis	8 Jul 11
	Oce, Com	21.24	Valerie ADAMS	NZL	Daegu	29 Aug 11
DT	SAm	62.00	Elisângela Maria ADRIANO	BRA	São Caetano do Sul	22 Jul 11

HT	W, Eur	79.42	Betty HEIDLER		GER	Halle	21 May 11
	Asi	75.65	ZHANG Wenxiu		CHN	Fränkisch-Crumbach	12 Jun 11
JT	Afr	66.47	Sunette VILJOEN		RSA	Shenzhen	18 Aug 11
	Afr, Com	68.38	Sunette VILJOEN		RSA	Daegu	2 Sep 11
Hep	SAm	6133A	Lucimara DA SILVA		BRA	Guadalajara	26 Oct 11
		(13.50, 1.80, 12.93, 24.76 / 6.36, 42.03, 2:21.39)					
Medley R	W18	2:03.42	Williams, Jackson, Gordon, James		JAM	Villeneuve d'Ascq	10 Jul 11
4x100 R	SAm	42.92	A C Silva, Gomes, Krasucki, R Santos		BRA	Daegu	4 Sep 11
	CAC, Com	41.70	Fraser-Pryce, Stewart, Simpson, Campbell-Brown				
					JAM	Daegu	4 Sep 11
	SAm	42.85A	A C Silva, Gomes, Krasucki, R Santos		BRA	Guadalajara	28 Oct 11
4x400 R	SAm	3:26.68	Coutinho, de Oliveira, Sousa, Lima		BRA	São Paulo	7 Aug 11
	CAC, Com	3:18.71	Whyte, Prendergast, N.Williams-Mills, S.Williams				
					JAM	Daegu	3 Sep 11
3000W	W18	12:18.86t	Kate VEALE		IRL	Tullamore	23 Jul 11
5000W	SAm	21:53.8t	Yuli Magali CAPCHA		PER	Lima	14 May 11
	Afr	22:59.19At	Aynalem ESHETU		ETH	Gaborone	15 May 11
10000W	W20	42:43t §	Svetlana VASILYEVA		RUS	Sochi	27 Feb 11
	W20	42:59.48t	Yelena LASHMANOVA		RUS	Tallinn	21 Jul 11
20000W	SAm	1:32:09.4t	Ingrid HERNÁNDEZ		COL	Buenos Aires	5 Jun 11
20kW	W, Eur	1:25:08	Vera SOKOLOVA		RUS	Sochi	26 Feb 11
Indoor SP	Oce, Com	20.51	Valerie ADAMS		NZL	Zürich	7 Sep 11

See ATHLETICS 2011 for Indoor Records set in January - March 2011

WORLD AND CONTINENTAL RECORDS SET IN JAN – MAR 2012

INDOORS – MEN

60	W40	6.76	Jeff LAYNES		USA	Seattle	14 Jan 12
	CAC	6.47	Lerone CLARKE		JAM	Birmingham	18 Feb 12
1500	W40	3:44.12	Anthony WHITEMAN		GBR	London (LV)	3 Mar 12
3000	W20	7:32.89	Isiah KOECH		KEN	Liévin	14 Feb 12
2M	NAm	8:09.72	Galen RUPP		USA	Fayetteville	11 Feb 12
	Eur	8:08.07	Mohamed FARAH		GBR	Birmingham	18 Feb 12
5000	W35, NAm	13:07.15	Bernard LAGAT		USA	New York (Armory)	11 Feb 12
	CAC	13:23.61	Juan Luis BARRIOS		MEX	New York (Armory)	11 Feb 12
60H	Asi	7.41	LIU Xiang		CHN	Birmingham	18 Feb 12
400H	W	49.25	Felix SÁNCHEZ		DOM	Mondeville	4 Feb 12
(8 hurdles)	W	48.78	Felix SÁNCHEZ		DOM	Val-de-Reuil	18 Feb 12
HJ	Asi	2.33	Moataz Essa BARSHIM		QAT	Spala	11 Feb 12
	Asi	2.34, 2.37	Moataz Essa BARSHIM		QAT	Hangzhou	19 Feb 12
PV	CAC	5.72	Lázaro BORGES		CUB	Donetsk	11 Feb 12
LJ	Oce	8.23	Henry FRAYNE		AUS	Istanbul	10 Mar 12
SP	Asi	20.16	ZHANG Jun		CHN	Nanjing	13 Feb 12
	SAm	20.35, 20.40	Germán LAURO		ARG	Istanbul	9 Mar 12
Hep/1000	W	2:23.63	Curtis BEACH (In 6138 Hep)		USA	Nampa	10 Mar 12
Hep/LJ	W	8.16	Ashton EATON (in 6645 Hep)		USA	Istanbul	9 Mar 12
Hep	W20	6022	Gunnar NIXON		USA	Fayetteville	28 Jan 12
		(7.10, 7.53, 13.97, 2.15 / 8.21, 4.50, 2:40.15)					
	Oce	5758	Brent NEWDICK		NZL	Tallinn	4 Feb 12
		(7.08, 7.14, 14.39, 1.95 / 8.25, 4.73, 2:46.86)					
	W18	5483	WANG Jianan		CHN	Nanjing	14 Feb 12
		(6.89, 7.64, 9.27, 1.94 / 8.46, 4.80, 2:58.17)					
	W, NAm	6645	Ashton EATON		USA	Istanbul	10 Mar 12
		(6.79, 8.16, 14.56, 2.03 / 7.68, 5.20, 2:32.77)					
5000W	W40	19:42.5	Yuriy ANDROPOV		RUS	Chelyabinsk	6 Jan 12

INDOORS – WOMEN

300	CAC, Com	35.69	Patricia HALL		JAM	Liévin	14 Feb 12
1500	Oce	4:11.78	Lucy VAN DALEN		NZL	New York (Armory)	11 Feb 12
3000	W18	8:46.01	Gotytom GEBRESLASE		ETH	Boston (Roxbury)	4 Feb 12
5000	W35	15:43.60	Mariya KONOVALOVA		RUS	Moskva	24 Feb 12
2000SC	W, Eur	6:06.11	Yelena ORLOVA		RUS	Moskva	12 Feb 12
60H	Oce	7.85	Sally PEARSON		AUS	Istanbul	9 Mar 12
	Oce	7.73	Sally PEARSON		AUS	Istanbul	10 Mar 12
	W18	8.19	Dior HALL		USA	New York (Armory)	11 Mar 12
400H	Eur	56.66	Sara PETERSEN		DEN	Val-de-Reuil	18 Feb 12
HJ	NAm	2.02A	Chaunté LOWE		USA	Albuquerque	26 Feb 12
PV	W40	4.05	Doris AUER		AUT	Wien	21 Jan 12
	Com	4.70=, 4.80, 4.87	Holly BLEASDALE		GBR	Villeurbanne	21 Jan 12
	NAm	4.88	Jenn Suhr		USA	Boston (Roxbury)	4 Feb 12

	CAC	4.40, 4.52, 4.60	Yarisley SILVA	CUB	Bydgoszcz	8 Feb 12
	CAC=	4.60	Yarisley SILVA	CUB	Donetsk	11 Feb 12
	CAC	4.60=, 4.71	Yarisley SILVA	CUB	Liévin	14 Feb 12
	Asi	4.50	LI Ling	CHN	Hangzhou	19 Feb 12
	W,Eur	5.01	Yelena ISINBAYEVA	RUS	Stockholm	23 Feb 12
	CAC	4.72	Yarisley SILVA	CUB	Stockholm	23 Feb 12
LJ	NAm	7.23	Brittney REESE	USA	Istanbul	11 Mar 12
TJ	W35	14.62	Yamilé ALDAMA	GBR	Istanbul	9 Mar 12
	W35	14.82	Yamilé ALDAMA	GBR	Istanbul	10 Mar 12
SP	NAm	19.89	Jill CAMARENA-WILLIAMS	USA	Fayetteville	11 Feb 12
	Oce, Com	20.54	Valerie ADAMS	NZL	Istanbul	10 Mar 12
Pen/60H	W	7.91	Jessica ENNIS (in 4965 Pen)	GBR	Istanbul	9 Mar 12
Pen	W,Eur	5013	Nataliya DOBRYNSKA (8.38, 1.84, 16.51, 6.57, 2:11.15)	UKR	Istanbul	9 Mar 12
	Com	4965	Jessica ENNIS (7.91, 1.87, 14.79, 6.19, 2:08.09)	GBR	Istanbul	9 Mar 12

OUTDOORS – MEN

HMar	W20	59:14	Dennis KOECH	KEN	Berlin	1 Apr 12
20kW	Asi	1:17:36	WANG Zhen	CHN	Taicang	30 Mar 12

OUTDOORS – WOMEN

Mar	SAm	2:29:17	Adriana DA SILVA	BRA	Tokyo	26 Feb 12
PV	Oce	4.66	Alana BOYD	AUS	Perth	11 Feb 12
	Oce	4.71, 4.76	Alana BOYD	AUS	Perth	24 Feb 12
HT	Asi	75.72	ZHANG Wenxiu	CHN	Chengdu	12 Mar 12
	Com	75.04	Sultana FRIZELL	CAN	Tucson	16 Mar 12
20kW	CAC	1:28:54	Mirna ORTIZ	GUA	Lugano	18 Mar 12
	Asi	1:25:46	LIU Hong	CHN	Taicang	30 Mar 12
50kW	NAm	4:33:23	Erin TAYLOR-TALCOTT	USA	Santee	22 Jan 12

Transfer of Nationality/Allegiance

Name	From	To	Noted	Eligible
Men				
Tim Abeyie	GBR	GHA	23.6.11	
Ashhad Agyapong	USA	GHA	16.8.11	16.11.11
Mohamed Khaled Belabbas	FRA	ALG	12.9.11	14.6.12
Gregory Bianchi	SUI	ITA	6.7.11	
Urige Buta	ETH	NOR	27.7.11	
Robert Cheseret	KEN	USA	31.12.10	
Wayne Davis	USA	TRI	4.8.11	
Mensah Elliott	GBR	GAM	11.7.11	
Diego Estrada	MEX	USA	18.11.11	
Tesfaye Eticha	ETH	SUI	.11.11	
Hassane Fofana	CIV	ITA	31.12.10	
Mumim Gala	SOM	DJI	22.3.11	
Ramil Guliyev	AZE	TUR	26.4.11	1.3.14
Jeffrey Julmis	USA	HAI	.7.11	
Abraham Kiprotich	KEN	FRA	15.3.11	22.6.12
Nikita Kirillov	KGZ	USA	2.4.11	14.4.11
Brent LaRue	USA	SLO	13.7.11	13.7.13
Michael McCadney	USA	PUR	20.5.11	
Lysvanys Pérez	CUB	ESP	25.3.11	
Julian Reid	JAM	GBR	1.1.11	16.8.11
Ben Reynolds	GBR	IRL	12.12.11	
Justin Rodhe	USA	CAN	1.11.11	31.10.13?
Maciej Rosiewicz	POL	GEO	8.11.11	1.9.12
Stephen Saenz	USA	MEX	.12.10	
Donald Sanford	USA	ISR	18.7.11	12.3.13
Patrick Tambwe	COD	FRA	13.4.11	
Caludio Villanueva	ECU	ESP	18.6.11	
Women				
Yamilé Aldama	SUD	GBR	5.8.11	
Atalelech Asfaw	ETH	USA	13.8.11	
Gloria Asumnu	USA	NGR	2.8.11	30.8.11
Sarah Bensaad	FRA	TUN	23.6.11	
Nora Bicet	CUB	ESP		immediate
Jessica Branker Sánchez	USA	MEX	29.8.11	
Nusrat Ceesay	GBR	GAM	10.6.11	
Janet Cherobon-Bawcom (was Janet Kogo)	KEN	USA	10.11.10	28.8.11
Shana Cox	USA	GBR	10.4.11	29.11.11
Cariya Derkach	UKR	ITA	.11	
Blessing Mayungbe	USA	NGR	4.8.11	23.6.13
Christine Merrill	USA	SRI	4.8.11	
Chinwe Okoro	USA	NGR	4.8.11	23.6.12
Nuta Olaru	ROU	USA	22.11.11	
Allison Randall	USA	JAM	16.6.11	
Chrystal Ruiz	USA	MEX	12.10.11	
Claire Tarplee	GBR	IRL	17.10.11	

Dates in final column indicate that athlete is not eligible to compete in international championships for new nation until later date

Change of name and nationality

Men	William Tanui Biwott KEN	Ilham Tanui Özbilen TUR	20.6.11	8.6.13
	Paul Kipkosgei Kemboi KEN	Polat Kemboi Arikan TUR	9.6.11	8.6.13
	Adam Ismail Khamis BRN	Isaiah Kiplagat Kosgei KEN	23.2.11	return
	Patrick Langat KEN	Tarik Langat Akdag TUR	22.6.11	21.6.13
Women	Bethlem Desalegn ETH	Mariam Abdallah Mubarak UAE		
	Teyba Naser ETH/BRN	Misiker Mekonnin Demissie ETH		
	Adriana Pârtea ROM	Adriana Fisher USA	4.1.11	4.4.12

See also lists on page 278 of ATHLETICS 2011 (and earlier Annuals)

Mark	Wind	Name		Nat	Born	Pos	Meet	Venue	Date

WORLD MEN'S ALL-TIME LISTS

100 METRES

Mark	Wind	Name		Nat	Born	Pos	Meet	Venue	Date
9.58 WR	0.9	Usain	Bolt	JAM	21.8.86	1	WCh	Berlin	16 Aug 09
9.69 WR	0.0		Bolt			1	OG	Beijing	16 Aug 08
9.69	2.0	Tyson	Gay	USA	9.8.82	1		Shanghai	20 Sep 09
9.71	0.9		Gay			2	WCh	Berlin	16 Aug 09
9.72 WR	1.7		Bolt			1	Reebok	New York (RI)	31 May 08
9.72	0.2	Asafa	Powell	JAM	23.11.82	1rA	Athl	Lausanne	2 Sep 08
9.74 WR	1.7		Powell			1h2	GP	Rieti	9 Sep 07
9.76	1.8		Bolt			1		Kingston	3 May 08
9.76	1.3		Bolt			1	VD	Bruxelles	16 Sep 11
9.77 WR	1.6		Powell			1	Tsik	Athína	14 Jun 05
9.77 WR	1.5		Powell			1	BrGP	Gateshead	11 Jun 06
9.77 WR	1.0		Powell			1rA	WK	Zürich	18 Aug 06
9.77	1.6		Gay			1q1	NC/OT	Eugene	28 Jun 08
9.77	-1.3		Bolt			1	VD	Bruxelles	5 Sep 08
9.77	0.9		Powell			1h1	GP	Rieti	7 Sep 08
9.77	0.4		Gay			1	GGala	Roma	10 Jul 09
9.78	0.0		Powell			1	GP	Rieti	9 Sep 07
9.78	-0.4		Gay			1	LGP	London (CP)	13 Aug 10
9.78	0.9	Nesta	Carter	JAM	10.11.85	1		Rieti	29 Aug 10
9.78	1.0		Powell			1	Athl	Lausanne	30 Jun 11
9.79 WR	0.1	Maurice	Greene	USA	23.7.74	1rA	Tsik	Athína	16 Jun 99
9.79	-0.2		Bolt			1	GL	Saint-Denis	17 Jul 09
9.79	0.1		Gay			1	VD	Bruxelles	27 Aug 10
9.79	1.1		Gay			1h1		Clermont	4 Jun 11
9.80	0.2		Greene			1	WCh	Sevilla	22 Aug 99
9.80	0.4	Steve	Mullings ¶	JAM	29.11.82	1	Pre	Eugene	4 Jun 11
9.81	0.0		Bolt			1	WK	Zürich	28 Aug 09
9.82	-0.2		Greene			1	WCh	Edmonton	5 Aug 01
9.82	0.0		Powell			1	Herc	Monaco	29 Jul 08
9.82	1.4		Powell			1	GP	Rieti	7 Sep 08
9.82	1.4		Powell			1	Pedros	Szczecin	15 Sep 09
9.82	0.6		Powell			1	GGala	Roma	10 Jun 10
9.82	0.5		Bolt			1	Athl	Lausanne	8 Jul 10
9.82	0.0	Yohan	Blake	JAM	26.12.89	2	WK	Zürich	8 Sep 11
9.82	0.1		Blake			1	ISTAF	Berlin	11 Sep 11

(35 performances by 7 athletes)

Mark	Wind	Name		Nat	Born	Pos	Meet	Venue	Date
9.84 WR	0.7	Donovan	Bailey	CAN	16.12.67	1	OG	Atlanta	27 Jul 96
9.84	0.2	Bruny	Surin	CAN	12.7.67	2	WCh	Sevilla	22 Aug 99
9.85 WR	1.2	Leroy	Burrell	USA	21.2.67	1rA	Athl	Lausanne	6 Jul 94

(10)

Mark	Wind	Name		Nat	Born	Pos	Meet	Venue	Date
9.85	0.6	Justin	Gatlin ¶	USA	10.2.82	1	OG	Athína	22 Aug 04
9.85	1.7	Olusoji	Fasuba	NGR	9.7.84	2	SGP	Doha	12 May 06
9.85	1.3	Michael	Rodgers	USA	24.4.85	2	Pre	Eugene	4 Jun 11
9.85	1.0	Richard	Thompson	TRI	7.6.85	1	NC	Port of Spain	13 Aug 11
9.86 WR	1.2	Carl	Lewis	USA	1.7.61	1	WCh	Tokyo	25 Aug 91
9.86	-0.4	Frank	Fredericks	NAM	2.10.67	1rA	Athl	Lausanne	3 Jul 96
9.86	1.8	Ato	Boldon	TRI	30.12.73	1rA	MSR	Walnut	19 Apr 98
9.86	0.6	Francis	Obikwelu	NGR/POR	22.11.78	2	OG	Athína	22 Aug 04
9.87	0.3	Linford	Christie ¶	GBR	2.4.60	1	WCh	Stuttgart	15 Aug 93
9.87A	-0.2	Obadele	Thompson	BAR	30.3.76	1	WCp	Johannesburg	11 Sep 98

(20)

Mark	Wind	Name		Nat	Born	Pos	Meet	Venue	Date
9.88	1.8	Shawn	Crawford	USA	14.1.78	1	Pre	Eugene	19 Jun 04
9.88	0.6	Walter	Dix	USA	31.1.86	2		Nottwil	8 Aug 10
9.88	0.9	Ryan	Bailey	USA	13.4.89	2		Rieti	29 Aug 10
9.88	1.0	Michael	Frater	JAM	6.10.82	2	Athl	Lausanne	30 Jun 11
9.89	1.6	Travis	Padgett	USA	13.12.86	1q2	NC/OT	Eugene	28 Jun 08
9.89	1.6	Darvis	Patton	USA	4.12.77	1q3	NC/OT	Eugene	28 Jun 08
9.89	1.3	Ngonidzashe	Makusha	ZIM	11.3.87	1	NCAA	Des Moines	10 Jun 11
9.91	1.2	Dennis	Mitchell ¶	USA	20.2.66	3	WCh	Tokyo	25 Aug 91
9.91	0.9	Leonard	Scott	USA	19.1.80	2	WAF	Stuttgart	9 Sep 06
9.91	-0.5	Derrick	Atkins	BAH	5.1.84	2	WCh	Osaka	26 Aug 07

(30)

Mark	Wind	Name		Nat	Born	Pos	Meet	Venue	Date
9.91	-0.2	Daniel	Bailey	ANT	9.9.86	2	GL	Saint-Denis	17 Jul 09
9.92	0.3	Andre	Cason	USA	20.1.69	2	WCh	Stuttgart	15 Aug 93
9.92	0.8	Jon	Drummond	USA	9.9.68	1h3	NC	Indianapolis	12 Jun 97
9.92	0.2	Tim	Montgomery ¶	USA	28.1.75	2	NC	Indianapolis	13 Jun 97

Mark	Wind	Name		Nat	Born	Pos	Meet	Venue	Date
9.92A	-0.2	Seun	Ogunkoya	NGR	28.12.77	2	WCp	Johannesburg	11 Sep 98
9.92	1.0	Tim	Harden	USA	27.1.74	1		Luzern	5 Jul 99
9.92	2.0	Christophe	Lemaitre	FRA	11.6.90	1	NC	Albi	29 Jul 11
9.93A WR	1.4	Calvin	Smith	USA	8.1.61	1	USOF	USAF Academy	3 Jul 83
9.93	-0.6	Michael	Marsh	USA	4.8.67	1	MSR	Walnut	18 Apr 92
9.93	1.8	Patrick	Johnson	AUS	26.9.72	1		Mito	5 May 03
		(40)							
9.93	0.0	Churandy	Martina	AHO	3.7.84	4	OG	Beijing	16 Aug 08
9.93	1.1	Ivory	Williams #	USA	2.5.85	1rA		Réthimno	20 Jul 09
9.93	1.0	Keston	Bledman	TRI	8.3.88	1		Clermont	4 Jun 11
9.94	0.2	Davidson	Ezinwa ¶	NGR	22.11.71	1	Gugl	Linz	4 Jul 94
9.94	-0.2	Bernard	Williams	USA	19.1.78	2	WCh	Edmonton	5 Aug 01
9.95A WR	0.3	Jim	Hines	USA	10.9.46	1	OG	Ciudad de México	14 Oct 68
9.95A	1.9	Olapade	Adeniken	NGR	19.8.69	1A		El Paso	16 Apr 94
9.95	0.8	Vincent	Henderson	USA	20.10.72	1		Leverkusen	9 Aug 98
9.95	1.8	Joshua 'J.J.'	Johnson	USA	10.5.76	1r6	MSR	Walnut	21 Apr 02
9.95	0.6	Deji	Aliu	NGR	22.11.75	1	Afr G	Abuja	12 Oct 03
		(50)							
9.95	1.8	John	Capel ¶	USA	27.10.78	3	Pre	Eugene	19 Jun 04
9.95	1.6	Rodney	Martin	USA	22.12.82	2q2	NC/OT	Eugene	28 Jun 08
9.95	-0.8	Trell	Kimmons	USA	13.7.85	1	WK	Zürich	19 Aug 10
9.95	0.9	Mario	Forsythe	JAM	30.10.85	3		Rieti	29 Aug 10
		(54)	100th man 10.02, 200th 10.09, 300th 10.13, 400th 10.17, 500th 10.19						

Doubtful wind reading

Mark	Wind	Name		Nat	Born	Pos	Meet	Venue	Date
9.91	-2.3	Davidson	Ezinwa ¶	NGR	22.11.71	1		Azusa	11 Apr 92

Low altitude best: 9.94   0.1   Ogunkoya   1   AfCh   Dakar   19 Aug 98

Wind-assisted – 15 performances to 9.79, performers listed to 9.92

Mark	Wind	Name		Nat	Born	Pos	Meet	Venue	Date
9.68	4.1	Tyson	Gay	USA	9.8.82	1	NC/OT	Eugene	29 Jun 08
9.69A	5+	Obadele	Thompson	BAR	30.3.76	1		El Paso	13 Apr 96
9.72	2.1		Powell			1	Bisl	Oslo	4 Jun 10
9.75	3.4		Gay			1h1	NC	Eugene	25 Jun 09
9.75	2.6		Powell			1h2	DL	Doha	14 May 10
9.76A	6.1	Churandy	Martina	AHO	3.7.84	1		El Paso	13 May 06
		9.92w	2.1			3	Bisl	Oslo	4 Jun 10
9.76	2.2		Gay			1	GP	New York	2 Jun 07
9.77	2.1		Bolt			1	GS	Ostrava	17 Jun 09
9.78	5.2	Carl	Lewis	USA	1.7.61	1	NC/OT	Indianpolis	16 Jul 88
9.78	3.7	Maurice	Greene	USA	23.7.74	1	GP II	Stanford	31 May 04
9.79	5.3	Andre	Cason	USA	20.1.69	1h4	NC	Eugene	16 Jun 93
9.79	4.5		Cason			1s1	NC	Eugene	16 Jun 93
9.79	2.9		Greene			1	Pre	Eugene	31 May 98
9.79	2.5		Gay			1	adidas	Carson	20 May 07
9.79	2.6		Gay			1	DNG	Stockholm	31 Jul 09
9.80	4.1	Walter	Dix	USA	31.1.86	2	NC/OT	Eugene	29 Jun 08
9.80	2.2	Yohan	Blake	JAM	26.12.89	1		Kingston	7 May 11
9.83	7.1	Leonard	Scott	USA	19.1.80	1r1	Sea Ray	Knoxville	9 Apr 99
9.83	2.2	Derrick	Atkins	BAH	5.1.84	2	GP	New York	2 Jun 07
9.84	3.4	Justin	Gatlin ¶	USA	10.2.82	1	Pre	Eugene	4 Jun 05
9.84	5.4	Francis	Obikwelu	NGR/POR	22.11.78	1		Zaragoza	3 Jun 06
9.84	4.1	Darvis	Patton	USA	4.12.77	3	NC/OT	Eugene	29 Jun 08
9.85	4.8	Dennis	Mitchell ¶	USA	20.2.66	2	NC	Eugene	17 Jun 93
9.85A	3.0	Frank	Fredericks	NAM	2.10.67	1		Nairobi	18 May 02
9.85	4.1	Travis	Padgett	USA	13.12.86	4	NC/OT	Eugene	29 Jun 08
9.86	2.6	Shawn	Crawford	USA	14.1.78	1	GP	Doha	14 May 04
9.86	3.6	Michael	Frater	JAM	6.10.82	2h4	NC	Kingston	23 Jun 11
9.87	11.2	William	Snoddy	USA	6.12.57	1		Dallas	1 Apr 78
9.87	4.9	Calvin	Smith	USA	8.1.61	1s2	NC/OT	Indianpolis	16 Jul 88
9.87	2.4	Michael	Marsh	USA	4.8.67	1rA	MSR	Walnut	20 Apr 97
9.88	2.3	James	Sanford	USA	27.12.57	1		Los Angeles (Ww)	3 May 80
9.88	5.2	Albert	Robinson	USA	28.11.64	4	NC/OT	Indianpolis	16 Jul 88
9.88	4.9	Tim	Harden	USA	27.1.74	1	NC	New Orleans	20 Jun 98
9.88	4.5	Coby	Miller	USA	19.10.76	1		Auburn	1 Apr 00
9.88	3.6	Patrick	Johnson	AUS	26.9.72	1		Perth	8 Feb 03
9.88	3.0	Darrel	Brown	TRI	11.10.84	1	NC	Port of Spain	23 Jun 07
9.88	3.7	Ivory	Williams #	USA	2.5.85	1	TexR	Austin	3 Apr 10
9.89	4.2	Ray	Stewart	JAM	18.3.65	1s1	PAm	Indianapolis	9 Aug 87
9.90	5.2	Joe	DeLoach	USA	5.6.67	5	NC/OT	Indianpolis	16 Jul 88
9.90	7.1	Kenny	Brokenburr	USA	29.10.68	2r1	Sea Ray	Knoxville	9 Apr 99
9.90A	7.8	Teddy	Williams	USA	3.7.88	1		El Paso	11 Apr 09
9.90	2.8	Lerone	Clarke	JAM	2.10.81	1		Clermont	11 Jun 11

Mark	Wind	Name		Nat	Born	Pos	Meet	Venue	Date
9.91	5.3	Bob	Hayes	USA	20.12.42	1s1	OG	Tokyo	15 Oct 64
9.91	4.2	Mark	Witherspoon	USA	3.9.63	2s1	PAm	Indianapolis	9 Aug 87
9.91	3.7	Nicolas	Macrozonaris	CAN	22.8.80	1	NC	Edmonton	22 Jun 02
9.92A	4.4	Chidi	Imo ¶	NGR	27.8.63	1s1	AfG	Nairobi	8 Aug 87
9.92A	2.8	Olapade	Adeniken	NGR	19.8.69	1rA		Sestriere	29 Jul 95
9.92	2.8	Kim	Collins	SKN	5.4.76	1rA	Tex R	Austin	5 Apr 03
9.92	3.7	Joshua 'J.J.'	Johnson	USA	10.5.76	2	Aragón	Zaragoza	28 Jul 07
9.92	3.7	Clement	Campbell	JAM	19.2.75	3	Aragón	Zaragoza	28 Jul 07
9.92	2.4	Trell	Kimmons	USA	13.7.85	4	DL	New York	12 Jun 10

Rolling start: 9.89w 3.7 Patrick Jarrett ¶   JAM   2.10.77   1   Pre   Eugene   27 May 01
Hand timing and three men at 9.7w

9.7	1.9	Donovan	Powell ¶	JAM	31.10.71	1rA		Houston	19 May 95
9.7	1.9	Carl	Lewis	USA	1.7.61	2rA		Houston	19 May 95
9.7	1.9	Olapade	Adeniken	NGR	19.8.69	3rA		Houston	19 May 95

Drugs disqualification

9.77	1.7	Justin	Gatlin ¶	USA	10.2.82	(1)	SGP	Doha	12 May 06
9.78	2.0	Tim	Montgomery ¶	USA	28.1.75	(1)	GPF	Paris (C)	14 Sep 02
9.79	1.1	Ben	Johnson ¶	CAN	30.12.61	(1)	OG	Seoul	24 Sep 88
9.87	2.0	Dwain	Chambers ¶	GBR	5.4.78	(2)	GPF	Paris (C)	14 Sep 02
9.7w ht	3.5		Johnson	CAN	30.12.61	(1)		Perth	24 Jan 87

200 METRES

Mark	Wind	Name		Nat	Born	Pos	Meet	Venue	Date
19.19	WR-0.3	Usain	Bolt	JAM	21.8.86	1	WCh	Berlin	20 Aug 09
19.26	0.7	Yohan	Blake	JAM	26.12.89	1	VD	Bruxelles	16 Sep 11
19.30	WR-0.9		Bolt			1	OG	Beijing	20 Aug 08
19.32	WR0.4	Michael	Johnson	USA	13.9.67	1	OG	Atlanta	1 Aug 96
19.40	0.8		Bolt			1	WCh	Daegu	3 Sep 11
19.53	0.7	Walter	Dix	USA	31.1.86	2	VD	Bruxelles	16 Sep 11
19.56	-0.8		Bolt			1		Kingston	1 May 10
19.57	0.0		Bolt			1	VD	Bruxelles	4 Sep 09
19.58	1.3	Tyson	Gay	USA	9.8.82	1	Reebok	New York	30 May 09
19.59	-0.9		Bolt			1	Athl	Lausanne	7 Jul 09
19.62	-0.3		Gay			1	NC	Indianapolis	24 Jun 07
19.63	0.4	Xavier	Carter	USA	8.12.85	1	Athl	Lausanne	11 Jul 06
19.63	-0.9		Bolt			1	Athl	Lausanne	2 Sep 08
19.65	0.0	Wallace	Spearmon	USA	24.12.84	1		Daegu	28 Sep 06
19.66	WR1.7		M Johnson			1	NC	Atlanta	23 Jun 96
19.67	-0.5		Bolt			1	GP	Athína	13 Jul 08
19.68	0.4	Frank	Fredericks	NAM	2.10.67	2	OG	Atlanta	1 Aug 96
19.68	-0.1		Gay			1	WAF	Stuttgart	10 Sep 06
19.68	-0.1		Bolt			1	WAF	Thessaloníki	13 Sep 09
19.69	0.9		Dix			1	NCAA-r	Gainesville	26 May 07
19.70	0.4		Gay			2	Athl	Lausanne	11 Jul 06
19.70	0.8		Dix			2	WCh	Daegu	3 Sep 11
19.71A	1.8		M Johnson			1rA		Pietersburg	18 Mar 00
19.72A	WR 1.8	Pietro	Mennea	ITA	28.6.52	1	WUG	Ciudad de México	12 Sep 79
19.72	1.8		Dix			1	Pre	Eugene	3 Jul 10
19.72	0.1		Gay			1	Herc	Monaco	22 Jul 10
19.73	-0.2	Michael	Marsh (10)	USA	4.8.67	1s1	OG	Barcelona	5 Aug 92
19.75	1.5	Carl	Lewis	USA	1.7.61	1	NC	Indianapolis	19 Jun 83
19.75	1.7	Joe	DeLoach	USA	5.6.67	1	OG	Seoul	28 Sep 88
19.75	0.2		Bolt			1	NC	Kingston	24 Jun 07
		(30/12)							
19.77	0.7	Ato	Boldon	TRI	30.12.73	1rA		Stuttgart	13 Jul 97
19.79	1.2	Shawn	Crawford	USA	14.1.78	1	OG	Athína	26 Aug 04
19.80	0.8	Christophe	Lemaitre	FRA	11.6.90	1	WCh	Daegu	3 Sep 11
19.81	-0.3	Alonso	Edward	PAN	8.12.89	2	WCh	Berlin	20 Aug 09
19.83A	WR 0.9	Tommie	Smith	USA	6.6.44	1	OG	Ciudad de México	16 Oct 68
19.84	1.7	Francis	Obikwelu	NGR/POR	22.11.78	1s2	WCh	Sevilla	25 Aug 99
19.85	-0.3	John	Capel ¶	USA	27.10.78	1	NC	Sacramento	23 Jul 00
19.85	-0.5	Konstadínos	Kedéris ¶	GRE	11.7.73	1	EC	München	9 Aug 02
		(20)							
19.86A	1.0	Don	Quarrie	JAM	25.2.51	1	PAm	Cali	3 Aug 71
19.86	1.6	Maurice	Greene	USA	23.7.74	2rA	DNG	Stockholm	7 Jul 97
19.87	0.8	Lorenzo	Daniel	USA	23.3.66	1	NCAA	Eugene	3 Jun 88
19.87A	1.8	John	Regis	GBR	13.10.66	1		Sestriere	31 Jul 94
19.87	1.2	Jeff	Williams	USA	31.12.65	1		Fresno	13 Apr 96
19.88	-0.3	Floyd	Heard	USA	24.3.66	2	NC	Sacramento	23 Jul 00
19.88	0.1	Joshua 'J.J'	Johnson	USA	10.5.76	1	VD	Bruxelles	24 Aug 01

Mark	Wind	Name		Nat	Born	Pos	Meet	Venue	Date
19.89	-0.8	Claudinei	da Silva	BRA	19.11.70	1	GPF	München	11 Sep 99
19.89	1.3	Jaysuma	Saidy Ndure	NOR	1.1.84	1	WAF	Stuttgart	23 Sep 07
19.90	1.3	Asafa	Powell	JAM	23.11.82	1	NC	Kingston	25 Jun 06
		(30)							
19.91	0.7	Nickel	Ashmeade	JAM	4.7.90	3	VD	Bruxelles	16 Sep 11
19.92A	WR1.9	John	Carlos	USA	5.6.45	1	FOT	Echo Summit	12 Sep 68
19.96	-0.9	Kirk	Baptiste	USA	20.6.63	2	OG	Los Angeles	8 Aug 84
19.96	0.4	Robson	da Silva	BRA	4.9.64	1	VD	Bruxelles	25 Aug 89
19.96	-0.3	Coby	Miller	USA	19.10.76	3	NC	Sacramento	23 Jul 00
19.97	-0.9	Obadele	Thompson	BAR	30.3.76	1	Super	Yokohama	9 Sep 00
19.98	1.7	Marcin	Urbas	POL	17.9.76	2s2	WCh	Sevilla	25 Aug 99
19.98	0.3	Jordan	Vaden ¶	USA	15.9.78	2	NC	Indianapolis	25 Jun 06
19.98	1.4	LaShawn	Merritt ¶	USA	27.6.86	2	adidas	Carson	20 May 07
19.98	-0.3	Steve	Mullings ¶	JAM	29.11.82	5	WCh	Berlin	20 Aug 09
		(40)							
19.99	0.6	Calvin	Smith	USA	8.1.61	1	WK	Zürich	24 Aug 83
19.99	1.7	Rodney	Martin	USA	22.12.82	4	NC/OT	Eugene	6 Jul 08
19.99	2.0	Curtis	Mitchell	USA	11.3.89	1h1	NACAC	Miramar	10 Jul 10
20.00	0.0	Valeriy	Borzov	UKR	20.10.49	1	OG	München	4 Sep 72
20.00	0.0	Justin	Gatlin ¶	USA	10.2.82	1		Monterrey	11 Jun 05
20.01	-1.0	Michael	Bates	USA	19.12.69	3rA	WK	Zürich	19 Aug 92
20.01	0.1	Bernard	Williams	USA	19.1.78	2	VD	Bruxelles	24 Aug 01
20.02	1.7	Christopher	Williams ¶	JAM	15.3.72	1r5	MSR	Walnut	16 Apr 00
20.03	1.6	Clancy	Edwards	USA	9.8.55	1		Los Angeles (Ww)	29 Apr 78
20.03	1.5	Larry	Myricks ¶	USA	10.3.56	2	NC	Indianapolis	19 Jun 83
		(50)							
20.03	1.2	Jon	Drummond	USA	9.9.68	1	VD	Bruxelles	22 Aug 97
20.03	0.6	Shingo	Suetsugu	JPN	2.6.80	1	NC	Yokohama	7 Jun 03
20.03	0.6	Darvis	Patton	USA	4.12.77	1s1	WCh	Saint-Denis	28 Aug 03
		(53)	100th man 20.16, 200th 20.30, 300th 20.37, 400th 20.43, 500th 20.49						

Wind-assisted 3 performances to 19.75, performers listed to 19.99

Mark	Wind	Name		Nat	Born	Pos	Meet	Venue	Date
19.61	>4.0	Leroy	Burrell	USA	21.2.67	1	SWC	College Station	19 May 90
19.70	2.7		Johnson			1s1	NC	Atlanta	22 Jun 96
19.73	3.3	Shawn	Crawford	USA	14.1.78	1	NC	Eugene	28 Jun 09
19.80	3.2	LaShawn	Merritt ¶	USA	27.6.86	1		Greensboro	19 Apr 08
19.83	9.2	Bobby	Cruse	USA	20.3.78	1r2	Sea Ray	Knoxville	9 Apr 99
19.86	4.6	Roy	Martin	USA	25.12.66	1	SWC	Houston	18 May 86
19.86	4.0	Justin	Gatlin ¶	USA	10.2.82	1h2	NCAA	Eugene	30 May 01
19.90	3.8	Steve	Mullings ¶	JAM	29.11.82	1		Fort Worth	17 Apr 04
19.91		James	Jett	USA	28.12.70	1		Morgantown	18 Apr 92
19.93	2.4	Sebastián	Keitel	CHI	14.2.73	1		São Leopoldo	26 Apr 98
19.94	4.0	James	Sanford	USA	27.12.57	1s1	NCAA	Austin	7 Jun 80
19.94	3.7	Chris	Nelloms	USA	14.8.71	1	Big 10	Minneapolis	23 May 92
19.94	2.3	Kevin	Little	USA	3.4.68	1s3	NC	Sacramento	17 Jun 95
19.95	3.4	Mike	Roberson	USA	25.3.56	1h3	NCAA	Austin	5 Jun 80
19.96	2.2	Rohsaan	Griffin	USA	21.2.74	1s1	NC	Eugene	26 Jun 99
19.98	2.1	Aaron	Armstrong	TRI	14.10.77	1	NC	Port of Spain	26 Jun 05
19.98	2.1	Brendan	Christian	ANT	11.12.83	1		Austin	2 May 09
19.98	2.4	Darvis	Patton	USA	4.12.77	2	NC	Eugene	26 Jun 11
19.99	2.7	Ramon	Clay ¶	USA	29.6.75	2s1	NC	Atlanta	22 Jun 96
19.99	2.6	Maurice	Mitchell	USA	22.12.89	1	NCAA	Des Moines	11 Jun 11

Low altitude marks for athletes with lifetime bests at high altitude

19.94 0.3 Regis   2   WCh Stuttgart 20 Aug 93 | 19.96 0.0 Mennea   1   Barletta   17 Aug 80

Suspended under IAAF rules

Mark	Wind	Name		Nat	Born	Pos	Meet	Venue	Date
19.86	1.5	Justin	Gatlin ¶	USA	10.2.82	1	SEC	Starkville	12 May 02

Hand timing   " during 220 yards race, * 220 yards less 0.1 seconds

Mark	Wind	Name		Nat	Born	Pos	Meet	Venue	Date
19.7A		James	Sanford	USA	27.12.57	1		El Paso	19 Apr 80
19.7A	0.2	Robson C.	da Silva	BRA	4.9.64	1	AmCp	Bogotá	13 Aug 89

300 METRES

In 300m races only, not including intermediate times in 400m races

Mark		Name		Nat	Born	Pos	Meet	Venue	Date
30.85A		Michael	Johnson	USA	13.9.67	1		Pretoria	24 Mar 00
30.97		Usain	Bolt	JAM	21.8.86	1	GS	Ostrava	27 May 10
31.30		LaShawn	Merritt	USA	27.6.86	1	Pre	Eugene	7 Jun 09
31.31			Merritt			1		Eugene	8 Aug 06
31.48		Danny	Everett	USA	1.11.66	1		Jerez de la Frontera	3 Sep 90
31.48		Roberto	Hernández	CUB	6.3.67	2		Jerez de la Frontera	3 Sep 90
31.56		Doug	Walker ¶	GBR	28.7.73	1		Gateshead	19 Jul 98
31.61		Anthuan	Maybank	USA	30.12.69	1		Durham	13 Jul 96
31.67		John	Regis	GBR	13.10.66	1	Vaux	Gateshead	17 Jul 92
31.70		Kirk	Baptiste	USA	20.6.63	1	Nike	London (CP)	18 Aug 84
31.72		Jeremy	Wariner (10)	USA	31.1.84	1	GS	Ostrava	12 Jun 08

Mark	Wind	Name		Nat	Born	Pos	Meet	Venue	Date
400 METRES									
43.18 wr		Michael	Johnson	USA	13.9.67	1	WCh	Sevilla	26 Aug 99
43.29 wr		Butch	Reynolds ¶	USA	8.6.64	1	WK	Zürich	17 Aug 88
43.39			Johnson			1	WCh	Göteborg	9 Aug 95
43.44			Johnson			1	NC	Atlanta	19 Jun 96
43.45		Jeremy	Wariner	USA	31.1.84	1	WCh	Osaka	31 Aug 07
43.49			Johnson			1	OG	Atlanta	29 Jul 96
43.50		Quincy	Watts	USA	19.6.70	1	OG	Barcelona	5 Aug 92
43.50			Wariner			1	DNG	Stockholm	7 Aug 07
43.62			Wariner			1rA	GGala	Roma	14 Jul 06
43.65			Johnson			1	WCh	Stuttgart	17 Aug 93
43.66			Johnson			1	NC	Sacramento	16 Jun 95
43.66			Johnson			1rA	Athl	Lausanne	3 Jul 96
43.68			Johnson			1	WK	Zürich	12 Aug 98
43.68			Johnson			1	NC	Sacramento	16 Jul 00
43.71			Watts			1s2	OG	Barcelona	3 Aug 92
43.74			Johnson			1	NC	Eugene	19 Jun 93
43.75			Johnson			1		Waco	19 Apr 97
43.75		LaShawn	Merritt	USA	27.6.86	1	OG	Beijing	21 Aug 08
43.76			Johnson			1	GWG	Uniondale, NY	22 Jul 98
43.81		Danny	Everett	USA	1.11.66	1	NC/OT	New Orleans	26 Jun 92
43.82			Wariner			1	WK	Zürich	29 Aug 08
43.83			Watts			1	WK	Zürich	19 Aug 92
43.84			Johnson			1	OG	Sydney	25 Sep 00
43.86A wr		Lee	Evans	USA	25.2.47	1	OG	Ciudad de México	18 Oct 68
43.86			Johnson			1	Bisl	Oslo	21 Jul 95
43.86			Wariner			1	Gaz	Saint-Denis	18 Jul 08
43.87		Steve	Lewis	USA	16.5.69	1	OG	Seoul	28 Sep 88
43.88			Johnson			1	WK	Zürich	16 Aug 95
43.90			Johnson			1		Madrid	6 Sep 94
43.91			Reynolds			2	NC	Atlanta	19 Jun 96
43.91			Wariner			1	Gaz	Saint-Denis	8 Jul 06
		(31/8)							
43.97A		Larry	James	USA	6.11.47	2	OG	Ciudad de México	18 Oct 68
44.05		Angelo	Taylor	USA	29.12.78	1	NC	Indianapolis	23 Jun 07
		(10)							
44.09		Alvin	Harrison ¶	USA/DOM	20.1.74	3	NC	Atlanta	19 Jun 96
44.09		Jerome	Young ¶	USA	14.8.76	1	NC	New Orleans	21 Jun 98
44.10		Gary	Kikaya	COD	4.2.78	2	WAF	Stuttgart	9 Sep 06
44.13		Derek	Mills	USA	9.7.72	1	Pre	Eugene	4 Jun 95
44.14		Roberto	Hernández	CUB	6.3.67	2		Sevilla	30 May 90
44.15		Anthuan	Maybank	USA	30.12.69	1rB	Athl	Lausanne	3 Jul 96
44.16		Otis	Harris	USA	30.6.82	2	OG	Athína	23 Aug 04
44.17		Innocent	Egbunike	NGR	30.11.61	1rA	WK	Zürich	19 Aug 87
44.18		Samson	Kitur	KEN	25.2.66	2s2	OG	Barcelona	3 Aug 92
44.20A		Charles	Gitonga	KEN	5.10.71	1	NC	Nairobi	29 Jun 96
		(20)							
44.21		Ian	Morris	TRI	30.11.61	3s2	OG	Barcelona	3 Aug 92
44.26		Alberto	Juantorena	CUB	21.11.50	1	OG	Montreal	29 Jul 76
44.27		Alonzo	Babers	USA	31.10.61	1	OG	Los Angeles	8 Aug 84
44.27		Antonio	Pettigrew ¶	USA	3.11.67	1	NC	Houston	17 Jun 89
44.27		Darold	Williamson	USA	19.2.83	1s1	NCAA	Sacramento	10 Jun 05
44.28		Andrew	Valmon	USA	1.1.65	4	NC	Eugene	19 Jun 93
44.28		Tyree	Washington	USA	28.8.76	1		Los Angeles (ER)	12 May 01
44.29		Derrick	Brew	USA	28.12.77	1	SEC	Athens, GA	16 May 99
44.29		Sanderlei	Parrela	BRA	7.10.74	2	WCh	Sevilla	26 Aug 99
44.30		Gabriel	Tiacoh	CIV	10.9.63	1	NCAA	Indianapolis	7 Jun 86
		(30)							
44.30		Lamont	Smith	USA	11.12.72	4	NC	Atlanta	19 Jun 96
44.31		Alejandro	Cárdenas	MEX	4.10.74	3	WCh	Sevilla	26 Aug 99
44.33		Thomas	Schönlebe	GDR	6.8.65	1	WCh	Roma	3 Sep 87
44.34		Darnell	Hall	USA	26.9.71	1	Athl	Lausanne	5 Jul 95
44.35		Andrew	Rock	USA	23.1.82	2	WCh	Helsinki	12 Aug 05
44.36		Iwan	Thomas	GBR	5.1.74	1	NC	Birmingham	13 Jul 97
44.36		Kirani	James	GRN	1.9.92	1	WK	Zürich	8 Sep 11
44.37		Roger	Black	GBR	31.3.66	2rA	Athl	Lausanne	3 Jul 96
44.37		Davis	Kamoga	UGA	17.7.68	2	WCh	Athína	5 Aug 97
44.37		Mark	Richardson	GBR	26.7.72	1	Bisl	Oslo	9 Jul 98
		(40)							
44.38		Darren	Clark	AUS	6.9.65	3s1	OG	Seoul	26 Sep 88

Mark	Wind	Name		Nat	Born	Pos	Meet	Venue	Date
44.40		Fred	Newhouse	USA	8.11.48	2	OG	Montreal	29 Jul 76
44.40		Chris	Brown	BAH	15.10.78	2	Bisl	Oslo	6 Jun 08
44.40		Jermaine	Gonzales	JAM	26.11.84	1	Herc	Monaco	22 Jul 10
44.41A		Ron	Freeman	USA	12.6.47	3	OG	Ciudad de México	18 Oct 68
44.43A		Ezra	Sambu	KEN	4.9.78	1	WCT	Nairobi	26 Jul 03
44.44		Tyler	Christopher	CAN	3.10.83	3	WCh	Helsinki	12 Aug 05
44.45A		Ronnie	Ray	USA	2.1.54	1	PAm	Ciudad de México	18 Oct 75
44.45		Darrell	Robinson	USA	23.12.63	2	Pepsi	Los Angeles (Ww)	17 May 86
44.45		Avard	Moncur	BAH	2.11.78	1		Madrid	7 Jul 01
44.45		Leonard	Byrd	USA	17.3.75	1	GP	Belém	5 May 02
(51)			100th man 44.66, 200th 44.91, 300th 45.15, 400th 45.31, 500th 45.45						
Drugs dq: 44.21 Antonio			Pettigrew ¶	USA	3.11.67	1		Nassau	26 May 99
Hand timing									
44.1		Wayne	Collett	USA	20.10.49	1	OT	Eugene	9 Jul 72
44.2*		John	Smith	USA	5.8.50	1	AAU	Eugene	26 Jun 71
44.2		Fred	Newhouse	USA	8.11.48	1s1	OT	Eugene	7 Jul 72

600 METRES

Mark	Wind	Name		Nat	Born	Pos	Meet	Venue	Date
1:12.81		Johnny	Gray	USA	19.6.60	1		Santa Monica	24 May 86
1:13.2 + ?		John	Kipkurgat	KEN	16.3.44	1		Pointe-à-Pierre	23 Mar 74
1:13.49		Joseph	Mutua	KEN	10.12.78	1		Liège (NX)	27 Aug 02
1:13.80		Earl	Jones	USA	17.7.64	2		Santa Monica	24 May 86

800 METRES

Mark	Wind	Name		Nat	Born	Pos	Meet	Venue	Date
1:41.01 WR		David	Rudisha	KEN	17.12.88	1rA		Rieti	29 Aug 10
1:41.09 WR			Rudisha			1	ISTAF	Berlin	22 Aug 10
1:41.11 WR		Wilson	Kipketer	DEN	12.12.70	1	ASV	Köln	24 Aug 97
1:41.24 WR			Kipketer			1rA	WK	Zürich	13 Aug 97
1:41.33			Rudisha			1		Rieti	10 Sep 11
1:41.51			Rudisha			1	NA	Heusden-Zolder	10 Jul 10
1:41.73!WR		Sebastian	Coe	GBR	29.9.56	1		Firenze	10 Jun 81
1:41.73 WR			Kipketer			1rA	DNG	Stockholm	7 Jul 97
1:41.77		Joaquim	Cruz	BRA	12.3.63	1	ASV	Köln	26 Aug 84
1:41.83			Kipketer			1	GP II	Rieti	1 Sep 96
1:42.01			Rudisha			1	GP	Rieti	6 Sep 09
1:42.04			Rudisha			1	Bisl	Oslo	4 Jun 10
1:42.17			Kipketer			1	TOTO	Tokyo	16 Sep 96
1:42.20			Kipketer			1	VD	Bruxelles	22 Aug 97
1:42.23		Abubaker	Kaki	SUD	21.6.89	2	Bisl	Oslo	4 Jun 10
1:42.27			Kipketer			1	VD	Bruxelles	3 Sep 99
1:42.28		Sammy	Koskei	KEN	14.5.61	2	ASV	Köln	26 Aug 84
1:42.32			Kipketer			1	GP II	Rieti	8 Sep 02
1:42.33 WR			Coe			1	Bisl	Oslo	5 Jul 79
1:42.34			Cruz			1r1	WK	Zürich	22 Aug 84
1:42.34		Wilfred	Bungei	KEN	24.7.80	2	GP II	Rieti	8 Sep 02
1:42.41			Cruz			1	VD	Bruxelles	24 Aug 84
1:42.47		Yuriy	Borzakovskiy	RUS	12.4.81	1	VD	Bruxelles	24 Aug 01
1:42.49			Cruz			1		Koblenz	28 Aug 85
1:42.51			Kipketer			1	Nik	Nice	10 Jul 96
1:42.52			Bungei			1	VD	Bruxelles	5 Sep 03
1:42.54			Cruz			1	ASV	Köln	25 Aug 85
1:42.55		André	Bucher	SUI	19.10.76	1rA	WK	Zürich	17 Aug 01
1:42.57			Kipketer			1	Herc	Monaco	4 Aug 99
1:42.58		Vebjørn	Rodal (10)	NOR	16.9.72	1	OG	Atlanta	31 Jul 96
(30/10)					! photo-electric cell time				
1:42.60		Johnny	Gray	USA	19.6.60	2r1		Koblenz	28 Aug 85
1:42.62		Patrick	Ndururi	KEN	12.1.69	2rA	WK	Zürich	13 Aug 97
1:42.67		Alfred	Kirwa Yego	KEN	28.11.86	2	GP	Rieti	6 Sep 09
1:42.69		Hezekiél	Sepeng ¶	RSA	30.6.74	2	VD	Bruxelles	3 Sep 99
1:42.69		Japheth	Kimutai	KEN	20.12.78	3	VD	Bruxelles	3 Sep 99
1:42.79		Fred	Onyancha	KEN	25.12.69	3	OG	Atlanta	31 Jul 96
1:42.79		Youssef Saad	Kamel	KEN/BRN	29.3.83	2	Herc	Monaco	29 Jul 08
1:42.81		Jean-Patrick	Nduwimana	BDI	9.5.78	2rA	WK	Zürich	17 Aug 01
1:42.85		Norberto	Téllez	CUB	22.1.72	4	OG	Atlanta	31 Jul 96
1:42.86		Mbulaeni	Mulaudzi	RSA	8.9.80	3	GP	Rieti	6 Sep 09
(20)									
1:42.88		Steve	Cram	GBR	14.10.60	1rA	WK	Zürich	21 Aug 85
1:42.91		William	Yiampoy	KEN	17.5.74	3	GP II	Rieti	8 Sep 02
1:42.95		Boaz	Lalang	KEN	8.2.89	2rA		Rieti	29 Aug 10
1:42.97		Peter	Elliott	GBR	9.10.62	1		Sevilla	30 May 90

1:42.98	Patrick	Konchellah	KEN	20.4.68	2	ASV	Köln	24 Aug 97
1:43.03	Kennedy/Kenneth	Kimwetich	KEN	1.1.73	2		Stuttgart	19 Jul 98
1:43.06	Billy	Konchellah	KEN	20.10.62	1	WCh	Roma	1 Sep 87
1:43.07	Yeimer	López	CUB	20.8.82	1		Jerez de la Frontera	24 Jun 08
1:43.08	José Luiz	Barbosa	BRA	27.5.61	1		Rieti	6 Sep 91
1:43.09	Djabir	Saïd Guerni	ALG	29.3.77	5	VD	Bruxelles	3 Sep 99
(30)								
1:43.15	Mehdi	Baala	FRA	17.8.78	5	GP II	Rieti	8 Sep 02
1:43.15	Asbel	Kiprop	KEN	30.6.89	2	Herc	Monaco	22 Jul 11
1:43.16	Paul	Ereng	KEN	22.8.67	1	WK	Zürich	16 Aug 89
1:43.17	Benson	Koech	KEN	10.11.74	1		Rieti	28 Aug 94
1:43.20	Mark	Everett	USA	2.9.68	1rA	Gugl	Linz	9 Jul 97
1:43.22	Pawel	Czapiewski	POL	30.3.78	5rA	WK	Zürich	17 Aug 01
1:43.25	Amine	Laâlou	MAR	13.5.82	1	GGala	Roma	14 Jul 06
1:43.26	Sammy	Langat (Kibet)	KEN	24.1.70	1rB	WK	Zürich	14 Aug 96
1:43.30	William	Tanui	KEN	22.2.64	2		Rieti	6 Sep 91
1:43.30	Adam	Kszczot	POL	2.9.89	2		Rieti	10 Sep 11
(40)								
1:43.31	Nixon	Kiprotich	KEN	4.12.62	1		Rieti	6 Sep 92
1:43.33	Robert	Chirchir	KEN	26.11.72	3		Stuttgart	19 Jul 98
1:43.33	William	Chirchir	KEN	6.2.79	6	VD	Bruxelles	3 Sep 99
1:43.33	Joseph Mwengi	Mutua	KEN	10.12.78	1rA	WK	Zürich	16 Aug 02
1:43.35	David	Mack	USA	30.5.61	3r1		Koblenz	28 Aug 85
1:43.37	Mohammed	Aman	ETH	10.1.94	3		Rieti	10 Sep 11
1:43.38	David (Singoei)	Kiptoo	KEN	26.6.65	2	Herc	Monaco	10 Aug 96
1:43.38	Rich	Kenah	USA	4.8.70	3rA	WK	Zürich	13 Aug 97
1:43.38	Arthémon	Hatungimana	BDI	21.1.74	3	VD	Bruxelles	24 Aug 01
1:43.44 WR	Alberto	Juantorena	CUB	21.11.50	1	WUG	Sofia	21 Aug 77
(50)		100th man 1:43.97, 200th 1:44.76, 300th 1:45.20, 400th 1:45.55, 500th 1:45.81						

1000 METRES

2:11.96 WR	Noah	Ngeny	KEN	2.11.78	1	GP II	Rieti	5 Sep 99
2:12.18 WR	Sebastian	Coe	GBR	29.9.56	1	OsloG	Oslo	11 Jul 81
2:12.66		Ngeny			1	Nik	Nice	17 Jul 99
2:12.88	Steve	Cram	GBR	14.10.60	1		Gateshead	9 Aug 85
2:13.40 WR		Coe			1	Bisl	Oslo	1 Jul 80
2:13.56	Kennedy/Kenneth	Kimwetich	KEN	1.1.73	2	Nik	Nice	17 Jul 99
2:13.62	Abubaker	Kaki	SUD	21.6.89	1	Pre	Eugene	3 Jul 10
2:13.73	Noureddine	Morceli	ALG	28.2.70	1	BNP	Villeneuve d'Ascq	2 Jul 93
2:13.9 WR	Rick	Wohlhuter	USA	23.12.48	1	King	Oslo	30 Jul 74
2:13.96	Mehdi	Baala	FRA	17.8.78	1		Strasbourg	26 Jun 03
2:14.09	Joaquim	Cruz	BRA	12.3.63	1	Nik	Nice	20 Aug 84
2:14.28	Japheth	Kimutai (10)	KEN	20.12.78	1	DNG	Stockholm	1 Aug 00

1500 METRES

3:26.00 WR	Hicham	El Guerrouj	MAR	14.9.74	1	GGala	Roma	14 Jul 98
3:26.12		El Guerrouj			1	VD	Bruxelles	24 Aug 01
3:26.34	Bernard	Lagat	KEN/USA	12.12.74	2	VD	Bruxelles	24 Aug 01
3:26.45		El Guerrouj			1 rA	WK	Zürich	12 Aug 98
3:26.89		El Guerrouj			1	WK	Zürich	16 Aug 02
3:26.96		El Guerrouj			1	GP II	Rieti	8 Sep 02
3:27.21		El Guerrouj			1	WK	Zürich	11 Aug 00
3:27.34		El Guerrouj			1	Herc	Monaco	19 Jul 02
3:27.37 WR	Noureddine	Morceli	ALG	28.2.70	1	Nik	Nice	12 Jul 95
3:27.40		Lagat			1rA	WK	Zürich	6 Aug 04
3.27.52		Morceli			1	Herc	Monaco	25 Jul 95
3:27.64		El Guerrouj			2rA	WK	Zürich	6 Aug 04
3:27.65		El Guerrouj			1	WCh	Sevilla	24 Aug 99
3:27.91		Lagat			2	Herc	Monaco	19 Jul 02
3:28.12	Noah	Ngeny	KEN	2.11.78	2	WK	Zürich	11 Aug 00
3:28.21+		El Guerrouj			1	in 1M	Roma	7 Jul 99
3.28.37		Morceli			1	GPF	Monaco	9 Sep 95
3.28.37		El Guerrouj			1	Herc	Monaco	8 Aug 98
3:28.38		El Guerrouj			1	GP	Saint-Denis	6 Jul 01
3:28.40		El Guerrouj			1	VD	Bruxelles	5 Sep 03
3:28.51		Lagat			3	WK	Zürich	11 Aug 00
3:28.57		El Guerrouj			1rA	WK	Zürich	11 Aug 99
3:28.6+		Ngeny			2	in 1M	Roma	7 Jul 99
3:28.73		Ngeny			2	WCh	Sevilla	24 Aug 99
3:28.84		Ngeny			1	GP	Paris (C)	21 Jul 99
3:28.86 WR		Morceli			1		Rieti	6 Sep 92
3:28.91		El Guerrouj			1rA	WK	Zürich	13 Aug 97

Mark	Wind	Name		Nat	Born	Pos	Meet	Venue	Date
3:28.92			El Guerrouj			1	VD	Bruxelles	22 Aug 97
3:28.93			Ngeny			1	GPF	München	11 Sep 99
3:28.95		Fermín	Cacho	ESP	16.2.69	2rA	WK	Zürich	13 Aug 97
		(30/5))							
3:28.98		Mehdi	Baala	FRA	17.8.78	2	VD	Bruxelles	5 Sep 03
3:29.02		Daniel Kipchirchir	Komen	KEN	27.11.84	1	GGala	Roma	14 Jul 06
3:29.14		Rashid	Ramzi ¶	MAR/BRN	17.7.80	2	GGala	Roma	14 Jul 06
3:29.18		Vénuste	Niyongabo	BDI	9.12.73	2	VD	Bruxelles	22 Aug 97
3:29.27		Silas	Kiplagat	KEN	20.8.89	1	Herc	Monaco	22 Jul 10
		(10)							
3:29.29		William	Chirchir	KEN	6.2.79	3	VD	Bruxelles	24 Aug 01
3:29.46 WR		Saïd	Aouita	MAR	2.11.59	1	ISTAF	Berlin	23 Aug 85
3:29.46		Daniel	Komen	KEN	17.5.76	1	Herc	Monaco	16 Aug 97
3:29.47		Augustine	Choge	KEN	21.1.87	1	ISTAF	Berlin	14 Jun 09
3:29.51		Ali	Saïdi-Sief ¶	ALG	15.3.78	1	Athl	Lausanne	4 Jul 01
3:29.53		Amine	Laâlou	MAR	13.5.82	2	Herc	Monaco	22 Jul 10
3:29.67 WR		Steve	Cram	GBR	14.10.60	1	Nik	Nice	16 Jul 85
3:29.77		Sydney	Maree	USA	9.9.56	1	ASV	Köln	25 Aug 85
3:29.77		Sebastian	Coe	GBR	29.9.56	1		Rieti	7 Sep 86
3:29.91		Laban	Rotich	KEN	20.1.69	2rA	WK	Zürich	12 Aug 98
		(20)							
3:30.04		Timothy	Kiptanui	KEN	5.1.80	2	GP	Saint-Denis	23 Jul 04
3:30.07		Rui	Silva	POR	3.8.77	3	Herc	Monaco	19 Jul 02
3:30.18		John	Kibowen	KEN	21.4.69	3rA	WK	Zürich	12 Aug 98
3:30.20		Haron	Keitany	KEN	17.12.83	2	ISTAF	Berlin	14 Jun 09
3:30.24		Cornelius	Chirchir	KEN	5.6.83	4	Herc	Monaco	19 Jul 02
3:30.33		Ivan	Heshko	UKR	19.8.79	2	VD	Bruxelles	3 Sep 04
3:30.46		Alex	Kipchirchir	KEN	26.11.84	3	VD	Bruxelles	3 Sep 04
3:30.46		Asbel	Kiprop	KEN	30.6.89	1		Rieti	10 Sep 11
3:30.54		Alan	Webb	USA	13.1.83	1	Gaz	Saint-Denis	6 Jul 07
3:30.55		Abdi	Bile	SOM	28.12.62	1		Rieti	3 Sep 89
		(30)							
3:30.57		Reyes	Estévez	ESP	2.8.76	3	WCh	Sevilla	24 Aug 99
3:30.58		William	Tanui	KEN	22.2.64	3	Herc	Monaco	16 Aug 97
3:30.67		Benjamin	Kipkurui	KEN	28.12.80	2	Herc	Monaco	20 Jul 01
3:30.72		Paul	Korir	KEN	15.7.77	3	VD	Bruxelles	5 Sep 03
3:30.77 WR		Steve	Ovett	GBR	9.10.55	1		Rieti	4 Sep 83
3:30.83		Fouad	Chouki ¶	FRA	15.10.78	3	WK	Zürich	15 Aug 03
3:30.90		Andrew	Wheating	USA	21.11.87	4	Herc	Monaco	22 Jul 10
3:30.92		José Luis	González	ESP	8.12.57	3	Nik	Nice	16 Jul 85
3:30.92		Tarek	Boukensa	ALG	19.11.81	1	GGala	Roma	13 Jul 07
3:30.94		Isaac	Viciosa	ESP	26.12.69	5	Herc	Monaco	8 Aug 98
		(40)							
3:30.94		Nixon	Chepseba	KEN	12.12.90	1	Hanz	Zagreb	13 Sep 11
3:30.99		Robert	Rono	KEN	11.10.74	3	VD	Bruxelles	30 Aug 02
3:30.99		Isaac	Songok	KEN	25.4.84	3rA	WK	Zürich	6 Aug 04
3:31.01		Jim	Spivey	USA	7.3.60	1	R-W	Koblenz	28 Aug 88
3:31.04		Daham Najim	Bashir	KEN/QAT	8.11.78	2	SGP	Doha	13 May 05
3:31.06		Ryan	Gregson	AUS	26.4.90	5	Herc	Monaco	22 Jul 10
3:31.10		Adil	Kaouch ¶	MAR	1.1.79	3	GGala	Roma	14 Jul 06
3:31.13		José Manuel	Abascal	ESP	17.3.58	1		Barcelona	16 Aug 86
3:31.13		Mulugeta	Wondimu	ETH	28.2.85	2rA	NA	Heusden-Zolder	31 Jul 04
3:31.17		Robert K.	Andersen	DEN	12.12.72	5rA	WK	Zürich	13 Aug 97
		(50)							

100th man 3:32.37, 200th 3:34.12, 300th 3:35.33, 400th 3:36.11, 500th 3:36.74

Drugs disqualification: 3:30.77 Adil Kaouch ¶   MAR   1.1.79   1   GGala   Roma   13 Jul 07

1 MILE

Mark	Wind	Name		Nat	Born	Pos	Meet	Venue	Date
3:43.13 WR		Hicham	El Guerrouj	MAR	14.9.74	1	GGala	Roma	7 Jul 99
3:43.40		Noah	Ngeny	KEN	2.11.78	2	GGala	Roma	7 Jul 99
3:44.39 WR		Noureddine	Morceli	ALG	28.2.70	1		Rieti	5 Sep 93
3:44.60			El Guerrouj			1	Nik	Nice	16 Jul 98
3:44.90			El Guerrouj			1	Bisl	Oslo	4 Jul 97
3:44.95			El Guerrouj			1	GGala	Roma	29 Jun 01
3:45.19			Morceli			1	WK	Zürich	16 Aug 95
3:45.64			El Guerrouj			1	ISTAF	Berlin	26 Aug 97
3:45.96			El Guerrouj			1	BrGP	London (CP)	5 Aug 00
3:46.24			El Guerrouj			1	Bisl	Oslo	28 Jul 00
3:46.32 WR		Steve	Cram	GBR	14.10.60	1	Bisl	Oslo	27 Jul 85
3:46.38		Daniel	Komen	KEN	17.5.76	2	ISTAF	Berlin	26 Aug 97
3:46.70		Vénuste	Niyongabo	BUR	9.12.73	3	ISTAF	Berlin	26 Aug 97

Mark	Wind	Name		Nat	Born	Pos	Meet	Venue	Date
3:46.76		Saïd	Aouita	MAR	2.11.59	1	WG	Helsinki	2 Jul 87
3:46.78			Morceli			1	ISTAF	Berlin	27 Aug 93
3:46.91		Alan	Webb	USA	13.1.83	1		Brasschaat	21 Jul 07
3:46.92			Aouita			1	WK	Zürich	21 Aug 85
3:47.10			El Guerrouj			1	BrGP	London (CP)	7 Aug 99
3:47.28		Bernard	Lagat	KEN/USA	12.12.74	2	GGala	Roma	29 Jun 01
3:47.30			Morceli			1	VD	Bruxelles	3 Sep 93
3:47.33 WR		Sebastian	Coe	GBR	29.9.56	1	VD	Bruxelles	28 Aug 81
		(21/10)							
3:47.65		Laban	Rotich	KEN	20.1.69	2	Bisl	Oslo	4 Jul 97
3:47.69		Steve	Scott	USA	5.5.56	1	OsloG	Oslo	7 Jul 82
3:47.79		José Luis	González	ESP	8.12.57	2	Bisl	Oslo	27 Jul 85
3:47.88		John	Kibowen	KEN	21.4.69	3	Bisl	Oslo	4 Jul 97
3:47.94		William	Chirchir	KEN	6.2.79	2	Bisl	Oslo	28 Jul 00
3:47.97		Daham Najim	Bashir	KEN/QAT	8.11.78	1	Bisl	Oslo	29 Jul 05
3:48.17		Paul	Korir	KEN	15.7.77	1	GP	London (CP)	8 Aug 03
3:48.23		Ali	Saïdi-Sief ¶	ALG	15.3.78	1	Bisl	Oslo	13 Jul 01
3:48.28		Daniel Kipchirchir	Komen	KEN	27.11.84	1	Pre	Eugene	10 Jun 07
3:48.38		Andrés Manuel	Díaz	ESP	12.7.69	3	GGala	Roma	29 Jun 01
		(20)							
3:48.40 WR		Steve	Ovett	GBR	9.10.55	1	R-W	Koblenz	26 Aug 81
3:48.50		Asbel	Kiprop	KEN	30.6.89	1	Pre	Eugene	7 Jun 09
3:48.78		Haron	Keitany	KEN	17.12.83	2	Pre	Eugene	7 Jun 09
3:48.80		William	Kemei	KEN	22.2.69	1	ISTAF	Berlin	21 Aug 92
3:48.83		Sydney	Maree	USA	9.9.56	1		Rieti	9 Sep 81
3:48.95		Deresse	Mekonnen	ETH	20.10.87	1	Bisl	Oslo	3 Jul 09
3:48.98		Craig	Mottram	AUS	18.6.80	5	Bisl	Oslo	29 Jul 05
3:49.08		John	Walker	NZL	12.1.52	2	OsloG	Oslo	7 Jul 82
3:49.20		Peter	Elliott	GBR	9.10.62	2	Bisl	Oslo	2 Jul 88
3:49.22		Jens-Peter	Herold	GDR	2.6.65	3	Bisl	Oslo	2 Jul 88
		(30)							
3:49.29		William	Biwott/Özbilen	KEN/TUR	5.3.90	2	Bisl	Oslo	3 Jul 09
3:49.31		Joe	Falcon	USA	23.6.66	1	Bisl	Oslo	14 Jul 90
3:49.34		David	Moorcroft	GBR	10.4.53	3	Bisl	Oslo	26 Jun 82
3:49.34		Benjamin	Kipkurui	KEN	28.12.80	3	VD	Bruxelles	25 Aug 00
3:49.38		Andrew	Baddeley	GBR	20.6.82	1	Bisl	Oslo	6 Jun 08
3:49.39		Silas	Kiplagat	KEN	20.8.89	2	Pre	Eugene	4 Jun 11
3:49.40		Abdi	Bile	SOM	28.12.62	4	Bisl	Oslo	2 Jul 88
3:49.45		Mike	Boit	KEN	6.1.49	2	VD	Bruxelles	28 Aug 81
3:49.50		Rui	Silva	POR	3.8.77	3	GGala	Roma	12 Jul 02
3:49.56		Fermín	Cacho	ESP	16.2.69	2	Bisl	Oslo	5 Jul 96
		(40)							
3:49.60		José Antonio	Redolat	ESP	17.2.76	4	GGala	Roma	29 Jun 01
3:49.70		Mekonnen	Gebremedhin	ETH	11.10.88	4	Pre	Eugene	4 Jun 11
3:49.75		Leonard	Mucheru	KEN/BRN	13.6.78	5	GGala	Roma	29 Jun 01
3:49.77		Ray	Flynn	IRL	22.1.57	3	OsloG	Oslo	7 Jul 82
3:49.77		Wilfred	Kirochi	KEN	12.12.69	2	Bisl	Oslo	6 Jul 91
3:49.77		Caleb	Ndiku	KEN	9.10.92	5	Pre	Eugene	4 Jun 11
3:49.80		Jim	Spivey	USA	7.3.60	3	Bisl	Oslo	5 Jul 86
3:49.83		Vyacheslav	Shabunin	RUS	27.9.69	6	GGala	Roma	29 Jun 01
3:49.91		Simon	Doyle	AUS	9.11.66	4	Bisl	Oslo	6 Jul 91
3:49.95		Tarek	Boukensa	ALG	19.11.81	6	Bisl	Oslo	29 Jul 05
3:49.98		Thomas	Wessinghage	FRG	22.2.52	3	ISTAF	Berlin	17 Aug 83
		(51)	100th 3:51.39, 200th 3:53.8, 300th 3:55.31						
Indoors: 3:49.78		Eamonn	Coghlan	IRL	24.11.52	1		East Rutherford	27 Feb 83

2000 METRES

Mark	Wind	Name		Nat	Born	Pos	Meet	Venue	Date
4:44.79 WR		Hicham	El Guerrouj	MAR	14.9.74	1	ISTAF	Berlin	7 Sep 99
4:46.88		Ali	Saïdi-Sief ¶	ALG	15.3.78	1		Strasbourg	19 Jun 01
4:47.88 WR		Noureddine	Morceli	ALG	28.2.70	1		Paris	3 Jul 95
4:48.36			El Guerrouj			1		Gateshead	19 Jul 98
4:48.69		Vénuste	Niyongabo	BUR	9.12.73	1	Nik	Nice	12 Jul 95
4:48.74		John	Kibowen	KEN	21.4.69	1		Hechtel	1 Aug 98
4:49.00			Niyongabo			1		Rieti	3 Sep 97
4:49.55			Morceli			1	Nik	Nice	10 Jul 96
4:50.08		Noah	Ngeny	KEN	2.11.78	1	DNG	Stockholm	30 Jul 99
4:50.76		Craig	Mottram	AUS	18.6.80	1		Melbourne (OP)	9 Mar 06
4:50.81 WR		Saïd	Aouita	MAR	2.11.59	1	BNP	Paris	16 Jul 87
4:51.30		Daniel	Komen	KEN	17.5.76	1		Milano	5 Jun 98
4:51.39 WR		Steve	Cram (10)	GBR	14.10.60	1	BGP	Budapest	4 Aug 85
4:49.99 ind		Kenenisa	Bekele	ETH	13.6.82	1		Birmingham	17 Feb 07

3000 METRES

Mark	Wind	Name		Nat	Born	Pos	Meet	Venue	Date
7:20.67	WR	Daniel	Komen	KEN	17.5.76	1		Rieti	1 Sep 96
7:23.09		Hicham	El Guerrouj	MAR	14.9.74	1	VD	Bruxelles	3 Sep 99
7:25.02		Ali	Saïdi-Sief ¶	ALG	15.3.78	1	Herc	Monaco	18 Aug 00
7:25.09		Haile	Gebrselassie	ETH	18.4.73	1	VD	Bruxelles	28 Aug 98
7:25.11	WR	Noureddine	Morceli	ALG	28.2.70	1	Herc	Monaco	2 Aug 94
7:25.16			Komen			1	Herc	Monaco	10 Aug 96
7:25.54			Gebrselassie			1	Herc	Monaco	8 Aug 98
7:25.79		Kenenisa	Bekele	ETH	13.6.82	1	DNG	Stockholm	7 Aug 07
7:25.87			Komen			1	VD	Bruxelles	23 Aug 96
7:26.02			Gebrselassie			1	VD	Bruxelles	22 Aug 97
7:26.03			Gebrselassie			1	GP II	Helsinki	10 Jun 99
7:26.5 e			Komen			1	in 2M	Sydney	28 Feb 98
7:26.62		Mohammed	Mourhit ¶	BEL	10.10.70	2	Herc	Monaco	18 Aug 00
7:26.69			K Bekele			1	BrGP	Sheffield	15 Jul 07
7:27.18		Moses	Kiptanui	KEN	1.10.70	1	Herc	Monaco	25 Jul 95
7:27.26		Yenew	Alamirew	ETH	27.5.90	1	DL	Doha	6 May 11
7:27.3+			Komen			1	in 2M	Hechtel	19 Jul 97
7:27.42			Gebrselassie			1	Bisl	Oslo	9 Jul 98
7:27.50			Morceli			1	VD	Bruxelles	25 Aug 95
7:27.55		Edwin	Soi (10)	KEN	3.3.86	2	DL	Doha	6 May 11
7:27.59		Luke	Kipkosgei	KEN	27.11.75	2	Herc	Monaco	8 Aug 98
7:27.66		Eliud	Kipchoge	KEN	5.11.84	3	DL	Doha	6 May 11
7:27.67			Saïdi-Sief			1	Gaz	Saint-Denis	23 Jun 00
7:27.72			Kipchoge	KEN	5.11.84	1	VD	Bruxelles	3 Sep 04
7:27.75		Thomas	Nyariki	KEN	27.9.71	2	Herc	Monaco	10 Aug 96
7.28.04			Kiptanui			1	ASV	Köln	18 Aug 95
7:28.28			Kipkosgei			2	Bisl	Oslo	9 Jul 98
7:28.28		James	Kwalia	KEN/QAT	12.6.84	2	VD	Bruxelles	3 Sep 04
7:28.37			Kipchoge			1	SGP	Doha	8 May 09
7:28.41		Paul	Bitok	KEN	26.6.70	3	Herc	Monaco	10 Aug 96
		(30/14)							
7:28.45		Assefa	Mezegebu	ETH	19.6.78	3	Herc	Monaco	8 Aug 98
7:28.67		Benjamin	Limo	KEN	23.8.74	1	Herc	Monaco	4 Aug 99
7:28.70		Paul	Tergat	KEN	17.6.69	4	Herc	Monaco	10 Aug 96
7:28.70		Tariku	Bekele	ETH	21.1.87	1		Rieti	29 Aug 10
7:28.72		Isaac K.	Songok	KEN	25.4.84	1	GP	Rieti	27 Aug 06
		(20)							
7:28.76		Augustine	Choge	KEN	21.1.87	4	DL	Doha	6 May 11
7:28.93		Salah	Hissou	MAR	16.1.72	2	Herc	Monaco	4 Aug 99
7:28.94		Brahim	Lahlafi	FRA/MAR	15.4.68	3	Herc	Monaco	4 Aug 99
7:29.00		Bernard	Lagat	USA	12.12.74	2		Rieti	29 Aug 10
7:29.09		John	Kibowen	KEN	21.4.69	3	Bisl	Oslo	9 Jul 98
7:29.34		Isaac	Viciosa	ESP	26.12.69	4	Bisl	Oslo	9 Jul 98
7:29.45	WR	Saïd	Aouita	MAR	2.11.59	1	ASV	Köln	20 Aug 89
7:29.92		Sileshi	Sihine	ETH	29.1.83	1	GP	Rieti	28 Aug 05
7:30.09		Ismaïl	Sghyr	MAR/FRA	16.3.72	2	Herc	Monaco	25 Jul 95
7:30.09		Thomas	Longosiwa	KEN	14.1.82	2	SGP	Doha	8 May 09
		(30)							
7:30.15		Vincent	Chepkok	KEN	5.7.88	5	DL	Doha	6 May 11
7:30.36		Mark	Carroll	IRL	15.1.72	5	Herc	Monaco	4 Aug 99
7:30.50		Dieter	Baumann ¶	GER	9.2.65	6	Herc	Monaco	8 Aug 98
7:30.53		El Hassan	Lahssini	MAR/FRA	1.1.75	6	Herc	Monaco	10 Aug 96
7:30.53		Hailu	Mekonnen	ETH	4.4.80	1	VD	Bruxelles	24 Aug 01
7:30.62		Boniface	Songok	KEN	25.12.80	3	VD	Bruxelles	3 Sep 04
7:30.76		Jamal Bilal	Salem	KEN/QAT	12.9.78	4	SGP	Doha	13 May 05
7:30.78		Mustapha	Essaïd	FRA	20.1.70	7	Herc	Monaco	8 Aug 98
7:30.84		Bob	Kennedy	USA	18.8.70	8	Herc	Monaco	8 Aug 98
7:30.95		Moses	Kipsiro	UGA	2.9.86	1	Herc	Monaco	28 Jul 09
		(40)							
7:30.99		Khalid	Boulami	MAR	7.8.69	1	Nik	Nice	16 Jul 97
7:31.13		Julius	Gitahi	KEN	29.4.78	6	Bisl	Oslo	9 Jul 98
7:31.14		William	Kalya	KEN	4.8.74	3	Herc	Monaco	16 Aug 97
7:31.20		Joseph	Kiplimo	KEN	20.7.88	1	GP	Rieti	6 Sep 09
7:31.41		Sammy Alex	Mutahi	KEN	1.6.89	2	GP	Rieti	6 Sep 09
7:31.41		Daniel Kipchirchir	Komen	KEN	27.11.84	6	DL	Doha	6 May 11
7:31.59		Manuel	Pancorbo	ESP	7.7.66	7	Bisl	Oslo	9 Jul 98
7:31.68		Yusuf	Biwott	KEN	12.11.86	1	GS	Ostrava	27 May 10
7:31.81		Abreham	Cherkos	ETH	23.9.89	4	GP	Rieti	6 Sep 09

Mark	Wind	Name		Nat	Born	Pos	Meet	Venue	Date
7:32.1	WR	Henry	Rono	KEN	12.2.52	1	Bisl	Oslo	27 Jun 78
		(50)	100th man 7:35.44, 200th man 7:39.82, 300th 7:42.53, 400th 7:44.4, 500th 7:46.16						

Indoors

Mark	Wind	Name		Nat	Born	Pos	Meet	Venue	Date
7:24.90			Komen			1		Budapest	6 Feb 98
7:26.15			Gebrselassie			1		Karlsruhe	25 Jan 98
7:26.80			Gebrselassie			1		Karlsruhe	24 Jan 99
7:27.80			Alamirew			1	Spark	Stuttgart	5 Feb 11
7:27.93			Komen			1	Spark	Stuttgart	1 Feb 98
7:28.00		Augustine	Choge	KEN	21.1.87	2	Spark	Stuttgart	5 Feb 11

2 MILES

Mark	Wind	Name		Nat	Born	Pos	Meet	Venue	Date
7:58.61	WR	Daniel	Komen	KEN	17.5.76	1		Hechtel	19 Jul 97
7:58.91			Komen			1		Sydney	28 Feb 98
8:01.08	WR	Haile	Gebrselassie	ETH	18.4.73	1	APM	Hengelo	31 May 97
8:01.72			Gebrselassie			1	BrGP	London (CP)	7 Aug 99
8:01.86			Gebrselassie			1	APM	Hengelo	30 May 99
8:03.50		Craig	Mottram	AUS	18.6.80	1	Pre	Eugene	10 Jun 07
8:04.83		Tariku	Bekele	ETH	21.1.87	2	Pre	Eugene	10 Jun 07

Indoors

Mark	Wind	Name		Nat	Born	Pos	Meet	Venue	Date
8:04.35		Kenenisa	Bekele	ETH	13.6.82	1	GP	Birmingham	16 Feb 08
8:06.48		Paul Kipsiele	Koech	KEN	10.11.81	2	GP	Birmingham	16 Feb 08

5000 METRES

Mark	Wind	Name		Nat	Born	Pos	Meet	Venue	Date
12:37.35	WR	Kenenisa	Bekele	ETH	13.6.82	1	FBK	Hengelo	31 May 04
12:39.36	WR	Haile	Gebrselassie	ETH	18.4.73	1	GP II	Helsinki	13 Jun 98
12:39.74	WR	Daniel	Komen	KEN	17.5.76	1	VD	Bruxelles	22 Aug 97
12:40.18			K Bekele			1	Gaz	Saint-Denis	1 Jul 05
12:41.86	WR		Gebrselassie			1	WK	Zürich	13 Aug 97
12:44.39	WR		Gebrselassie			1	WK	Zürich	16 Aug 95
12:44.90			Komen			2	WK	Zürich	13 Aug 97
12:45.09			Komen			1	WK	Zürich	14 Aug 96
12:46.53		Eliud	Kipchoge	KEN	5.11.84	1	GGala	Roma	2 Jul 04
12:47.04		Sileshi	Sihine	ETH	29.9.83	2	GGala	Roma	2 Jul 04
12:48.09			K Bekele			1	VD	Bruxelles	25 Aug 06
12:48.25			K Bekele			1	WK	Zürich	18 Aug 06
12:48.66		Isaac K.	Songok	KEN	25.4.84	2	WK	Zürich	18 Aug 06
12:48.81		Stephen	Cherono/Shaheen	KEN/QAT	15.10.82	1	GS	Ostrava	12 Jun 03
12:48.98			Komen			1	GGala	Roma	5 Jun 97
12:49.28		Brahim	Lahlafi	MAR	15.4.68	1	VD	Bruxelles	25 Aug 00
12:49.53			K Bekele			1	Aragón	Zaragoza	28 Jul 07
12:49.64			Gebrselassie			1	WK	Zürich	11 Aug 99
12:49.71		Mohammed	Mourhit ¶	BEL	10.10.70	2	VD	Bruxelles	25 Aug 00
12:49.87		Paul	Tergat (10)	KEN	17.6.69	3	WK	Zürich	13 Aug 97
12:50.16			Sihine			1	VD	Bruxelles	14 Sep 07
12:50.18			K Bekele			1	WK	Zürich	29 Aug 08
12:50.22			Kipchoge			1	VD	Bruxelles	26 Aug 05
12:50.24		Hicham	El Guerrouj	MAR	14.9.74	2	GS	Ostrava	12 Jun 03
12:50.25		Abderrahim	Goumri	MAR	21.5.76	2	VD	Bruxelles	26 Aug 05
12:50.38			Kipchoge			2	VD	Bruxelles	14 Sep 07
12:50.55		Moses	Masai	KEN	1.6.86	1	ISTAF	Berlin	1 Jun 08
12:50.72		Moses	Kipsiro	UGA	2.9.86	3	VD	Bruxelles	14 Sep 07
12:50.80		Salah	Hissou	MAR	16.1.72	1	GGala	Roma	5 Jun 96
12:50.86		Ali	Saïdi-Sief ¶	ALG	15.3.78	1	GGala	Roma	30 Jun 00
		(30/16)							
12:51.00		Joseph	Ebuya	KEN	20.6.87	4	VD	Bruxelles	14 Sep 07
12:51.45		Vincent	Chepkok	KEN	5.7.88	2	DL	Doha	14 May 10
12:51.95		Thomas	Longosiwa	KEN	14.1.82	5	VD	Bruxelles	14 Sep 07
12:52.33		Sammy	Kipketer	KEN	29.9.81	2	Bisl	Oslo	27 Jun 03
		(20)							
12:52.40		Edwin	Soi	KEN	3.3.86	2	Gaz	Saint-Denis	8 Jul 06
12:52.45		Tariku	Bekele	ETH	21.1.87	2	ISTAF	Berlin	1 Jun 08
12:52.80		Gebre-egziabher	Gebremariam	ETH	10.9.84	3	GGala	Roma	8 Jul 05
12:52.99		Abraham	Chebii	KEN	23.12.79	4	Bisl	Oslo	27 Jun 03
12:53.11		Mohamed	Farah	GBR	23.3.83	1	Herc	Monaco	22 Jul 11
12:53.41		Khalid	Boulami	MAR	7.8.69	4	WK	Zürich	13 Aug 97
12:53.46		Mark	Kiptoo	KEN	21.6.76	1	DNG	Stockholm	6 Aug 10
12:53.56		Dejene	Gebremeskel	ETH	24.11.89	2	DNG	Stockholm	6 Aug 10
12:53.58		Imane	Merga	ETH	15.10.88	3	DNG	Stockholm	6 Aug 10
12:53.60		Bernard	Lagat	USA	12.12.74	2	Herc	Monaco	22 Jul 11
		(30)							

Mark	Wind	Name		Nat	Born	Pos	Meet	Venue	Date
12:53.66		Augustine	Choge	KEN	21.1.87	4	GGala	Roma	8 Jul 05
12:53.72		Philip	Mosima	KEN	2.1.77	2	GGala	Roma	5 Jun 96
12:53.84		Assefa	Mezegebu	ETH	19.6.78	1	VD	Bruxelles	28 Aug 98
12:54.07		John	Kibowen	KEN	21.4.69	4	WCh	Saint-Denis	31 Aug 03
12:54.15		Dejene	Berhanu	ETH	12.12.80	3	GGala	Roma	2 Jul 04
12:54.18		Isiah	Koech	KEN	19.12.93	3	Herc	Monaco	22 Jul 11
12:54.19		Abreham	Cherkos	ETH	23.9.89	5	GGala	Roma	14 Jul 06
12:54.46		Moses	Mosop	KEN	17.7.85	3	Gaz	Saint-Denis	8 Jul 06
12:54.58		James	Kwalia	KEN/QAT	12.6.84	5	Bisl	Oslo	27 Jun 03
12:54.70		Dieter	Baumann ¶	GER	9.2.65	5	WK	Zürich	13 Aug 97
		(40)							
12:54.85		Moses	Kiptanui	KEN	1.10.70	3	GGala	Roma	5 Jun 96
12:54.99		Benjamin	Limo	KEN	23.8.74	3	Gaz	Saint-Denis	4 Jul 03
12:55.06		Lucas	Rotich	KEN	16.4.90	4	Bisl	Oslo	4 Jun 10
12:55.52		Hicham	Bellani	MAR	15.9.79	7	GGala	Roma	14 Jul 06
12:55.53		Chris	Solinsky	USA	5.12.84	5	DNG	Stockholm	6 Aug 10
12:55.58		Abebe	Dinkesa	ETH	6.3.84	2	Gaz	Saint-Denis	1 Jul 05
12:55.63		Mark	Bett	KEN	22.12.76	2	Bisl	Oslo	28 Jul 00
12:55.76		Craig	Mottram	AUS	18.6.80	2	GP	London (CP)	30 Jul 04
12:55.85		Boniface	Songok	KEN	25.12.80	4	VD	Bruxelles	26 Aug 05
12:55.94		Thomas	Nyariki	KEN	27.9.71	1	DNG	Stockholm	7 Jul 97
		(50)	100th man 13:02.51, 200th 13:10.40, 300th 13:14.60, 400th 13:18.29, 500th 13:20.6						

Indoors

Mark	Wind	Name		Nat	Born	Pos	Meet	Venue	Date
12:49.60			Bekele			1		Birmingham	20 Feb 04
12:50.38			Gebrselassie			1		Birmingham	14 Feb 99

10,000 METRES

Mark		Name		Nat	Born	Pos	Meet	Venue	Date
26:17.53	WR	Kenenisa	Bekele	ETH	13.6.82	1	VD	Bruxelles	26 Aug 05
26:20.31	WR		K Bekele			1	GS	Ostrava	8 Jun 04
26:22.75	WR	Haile	Gebrselassie	ETH	18.4.73	1	APM	Hengelo	1 Jun 98
26:25.97			K Bekele			1	Pre	Eugene	8 Jun 08
26:27.85	WR	Paul	Tergat	KEN	17.6.69	1	VD	Bruxelles	22 Aug 97
26:28.72			K Bekele			1	FBK	Hengelo	29 May 05
26:29.22			Gebrselassie			1	VD	Bruxelles	5 Sep 03
26:30.03		Nicholas	Kemboi	KEN/QAT	25.11.83	2	VD	Bruxelles	5 Sep 03
26:30.74		Abebe	Dinkesa	ETH	6.3.84	2	FBK	Hengelo	29 May 05
26:31.32	WR		Gebrselassie			1	Bisl	Oslo	4 Jul 97
26:35.63		Micah	Kogo	KEN	3.6.86	1	VD	Bruxelles	25 Aug 06
26:36.26		Paul	Koech	KEN	25.6.69	2	VD	Bruxelles	22 Aug 97
26:37.25		Zersenay	Tadese	ERI	8.2.82	2	VD	Bruxelles	25 Aug 06
26:38.08	WR	Salah	Hissou	MAR	16.1.72	1	VD	Bruxelles	23 Aug 96
26:38.76		Abdullah Ahmad	Hassan (10)	QAT	4.4.81	3	VD	Bruxelles	5 Sep 03
		(Formerly Albert Chepkurui KEN)							
26:39.69		Sileshi	Sihine	ETH	29.9.83	1	FBK	Hengelo	31 May 04
26:39.77		Boniface	Kiprop	UGA	12.10.85	2	VD	Bruxelles	26 Aug 05
26:41.58			Gebrselassie			2	FBK	Hengelo	31 May 04
26:41.75		Samuel	Wanjiru	KEN	10.11.86	3	VD	Bruxelles	26 Aug 05
26:41.95			Kiprop			3	VD	Bruxelles	25 Aug 06
26:43.16			K Bekele			1	VD	Bruxelles	16 Sep 11
26:43.53	WR		Gebrselassie			1	APM	Hengelo	5 Jun 95
26:43.98		Lucas	Rotich	KEN	16.4.90	2	VD	Bruxelles	16 Sep 11
26:46.19			K Bekele			1	VD	Bruxelles	14 Sep 07
26:46.31			K Bekele			1	WCh	Berlin	17 Aug 09
26:46.44			Tergat			1	VD	Bruxelles	28 Aug 98
26:46.57		Mohamed	Farah	GBR	23.3.83	1	Pre	Eugene	3 Jun 11
26:47.89			Koech			2	VD	Bruxelles	28 Aug 98
26:48.00		Galen	Rupp	USA	8.5.86	3	VD	Bruxelles	16 Sep 11
26:48.35		Imane	Merga	ETH	15.10.88	2	Pre	Eugene	3 Jun 11
		(30/17)							
26:48.99		Josphat	Bett	KEN	12.6.90	3	Pre	Eugene	3 Jun 11
26:49.02		Eliud	Kipchoge	KEN	5.11.84	2	FBK	Hengelo	26 May 07
26:49.20		Moses	Masai	KEN	1.6.86	2	VD	Bruxelles	14 Sep 07
		(20)							
26:49.38		Sammy	Kipketer	KEN	29.9.81	1	VD	Bruxelles	30 Aug 02
26:49.55		Moses	Mosop	KEN	17.7.85	3	FBK	Hengelo	26 May 07
26:49.90		Assefa	Mezegebu	ETH	19.6.78	2	VD	Bruxelles	30 Aug 02
26:50.20		Richard	Limo	KEN	18.11.80	3	VD	Bruxelles	30 Aug 02
26:50.63		Paul	Tanui	KEN	22.12.90	4	Pre	Eugene	3 Jun 11
26:51.49		Charles	Kamathi	KEN	18.5.78	1	VD	Bruxelles	3 Sep 99
26:51.95		Emmanuel	Bett	KEN	29.3.85	4	VD	Bruxelles	16 Sep 11

Mark	Wind	Name		Nat	Born	Pos	Meet	Venue	Date
26:52.23	WR	William	Sigei	KEN	14.10.69	1	Bisl	Oslo	22 Jul 94
26:52.30		Mohammed	Mourhit ¶	BEL	10.10.70	2	VD	Bruxelles	3 Sep 99
26:52.33		Gebre-egziabher	Gebremariam	ETH	10.9.84	4	FBK	Hengelo	26 May 07
		(30)							
26:52.87		John Cheruiyot	Korir	KEN	13.12.81	5	VD	Bruxelles	30 Aug 02
26:52.93		Mark	Bett	KEN	22.12.76	6	VD	Bruxelles	26 Aug 05
26:54.25		Mathew	Kisorio	KEN	16.5.89	7	Pre	Eugene	3 Jun 11
26:54.64		Mark	Kiptoo	KEN	21.6.76	8	Pre	Eugene	3 Jun 11
26:55.29		Leonard Patrick	Komon	KEN	10.1.88	9	Pre	Eugene	3 Jun 11
26:55.73		Geoffrey	Kirui	KEN	16.2.93	6	VD	Bruxelles	16 Sep 11
26:56.74		Josphat	Menjo	KEN	20.8.79	1		Turku	29 Aug 10
26:57.36		Josphat	Muchiri Ndambiri	KEN	12.2.85	1		Fukuroi	3 May 09
26:58.38	WR	Yobes	Ondieki	KEN	21.2.61	1	Bisl	Oslo	10 Jul 93
26:59.51		Bernard	Kipyego	KEN	16.7.86	4	VD	Bruxelles	14 Sep 07
		(40)							
26:59.60		Chris	Solinsky	USA	5.12.84	1		Stanford	1 May 10
26:59.81		Titus	Mbishei	KEN	28.10.90	7	VD	Bruxelles	16 Sep 11
26:59.88		Martin Irungu	Mathathi	KEN	25.12.85	2		Fukuroi	3 May 09
27:01.83		Gideon	Ngatuny	KEN	10.10.86	2		Tendo	16 May 09
27:02.62		Abderrahim	Goumri	MAR	21.5.76	3	FBK	Hengelo	29 May 05
27:02.62		Deriba	Merga	ETH	26.10.80	6	FBK	Hengelo	26 May 07
27:02.81		Ibrahim	Jeylan	ETH	12.6.89	4	VD	Bruxelles	25 Aug 06
27:04.18		Robert Kipngetich	Sigei	KEN	3.1.82	1		Neerpelt	2 Jun 07
27:04.20		Abraham	Chebii	KEN	23.12.79	1		Stanford	4 May 01
27:04.54		Felix	Limo	KEN	22.8.80	2	VD	Bruxelles	25 Aug 00
		(50)							

100th man 27:19.72, 200th 27:32.97, 300th 27:42.09, 400th 27:48.07, 500th 27:54.28

20,000 METRES & 1 HOUR

Mark		Name		Nat	Born	Pos	Meet	Venue	Date
56:25.98+	21 285m	Haile	Gebrselassie	ETH	18.4.73	1	GS	Ostrava	27 Jun 07
56:55.6+	21 101	Arturo	Barrios	MEX	12.12.63	1		La Flèche	30 Mar 91
57:24.19+	20 944	Jos	Hermens	NED	8.1.50	1		Papendal	1 May 76
57:18.4+	20 943	Dionísio	Castro	POR	22.11.63	1		La Flèche	31 Mar 90

HALF MARATHON

Included are the slightly downhill courses: Newcastle to South Shields 30.5m, Tokyo 33m, Lisboa (Spring to 2008) 69m

Mark	Wind	Name		Nat	Born	Pos	Meet	Venue	Date
58:23	WR	Zersenay	Tadese	ERI	8.2.82	1		Lisboa	21 Mar 10
58:30			Z Tadese			1		Lisboa	20 Mar 11
58:33	WR	Samuel	Wanjiru	KEN	10.11.86	1		Den Haag	17 Mar 07
58:46		Mathew	Kisorio	KEN	16.5.89	1		Philadelphia	18 Sep 11
58:48		Sammy	Kitwara	KEN	26.11.86	2		Philadelphia	18 Sep 11
58:52		Patrick	Makau	KEN	2.3.85	1		Ra's Al Kháymah	20 Feb 09
58:53	WR		Wanjiru			1		Ra's Al Khaymah	9 Feb 07
58:55	WR	Haile	Gebrselassie	ETH	18.4.73	1		Tempe	15 Jan 06
58:56			Makau			1		Berlin	1 Apr 07
58:56	dh	Martin	Mathathi	KEN	25.12.85	1	GNR	South Shields	18 Sep 11
58:58			Kitwara			1		Rotterdam	13 Sep 09
58:59			Z Tadese			1	WCh	Udine	14 Oct 07
58:59		Wilson	Kipsang	KEN	15.3.82	2		Ra's Al Khaymah	20 Feb 09
59:02			Makau			2	WCh	Udine	14 Oct 07
59:05	dh		Tadese			1	GNR	South Shields	18 Sep 05
59:05		Evans	Cheruiyot	KEN	10.5.82	3	WCh	Udine	14 Oct 07
59:06	dh	Paul	Tergat (10)	KEN	17.6.69	1		Lisboa	26 Mar 00
59:07		Paul	Kosgei	KEN	22.4.78	1		Berlin	2 Apr 06
59:08		Jonathan	Maiyo	KEN	.88	2		Rotterdam	13 Sep 09
59:09		James Kipsang	Kwambai	KEN	28.2.83	3		Rotterdam	13 Sep 09
59:10	dh		Tergat			1		Lisboa	13 Mar 05
59:10		Bernard	Kipyego	KEN	16.7.86	4		Rotterdam	13 Sep 09
59:12			E Cheruiyot			1		Rotterdam	9 Sep 07
59:13			Makau			2		Ra's Al Khaymah	9 Feb 07
59:15			Gebrselassie			1		Lisboa	16 Mar 08
59:15		Deriba	Merga	ETH	26.10.80	1		New Delhi	9 Nov 08
59:15		Wilson	Chebet	KEN	12.7.85	5		Rotterdam	13 Sep 09
59:16	WR		Wanjiru			1		Rotterdam	11 Sep 05
59:16			Tadese			1		Rotterdam	10 Sep 06
59:16			D Merga			4	WCh	Udine	14 Oct 07
59:16			W Kipsang			2		New Delhi	9 Nov 08
		(31/16)							
59:19		Tilahun	Regassa	ETH	18.1.90	1		Abu Dhabi	7 Jan 10

Mark	Wind	Name		Nat	Born	Pos	Meet	Venue	Date
59:20	dh	Hendrick	Ramaala	RSA	2.2.72	2		Lisboa	26 Mar 00
59:20		Moses	Mosop	KEN	17.7.85	1	Stra	Milano	21 Mar 10
59:21	dh	Robert Kipkoech	Cheruiyot	KEN	26.9.78	2		Lisboa	13 Mar 05
		(20)							
59:23		John	Kiprotich	KEN	.89	6		Rotterdam	13 Sep 09
59:26		Francis	Kibiwott	KEN	15.9.78	2		Berlin	1 Apr 07
59:27	dh	Wilson	Kiprotich Kebenei	KEN	20.7.80	3		Lisboa	13 Mar 05
59:27		Patrick	Ivuti	KEN	30.6.78	4		Rotterdam	9 Sep 07
59:28		Robert	Kipchumba	KEN	24.2.84	2		Rotterdam	10 Sep 06
59:30	dh	Martin	Lel	KEN	29.10.78	1		Lisboa	26 Mar 06
59:30		Yonas	Kifle	ERI	24.3.77	5	WCh	Udine	14 Oct 07
59:30		Geoffrey	Mutai	KEN	7.10.81	1		Valencia	22 Nov 09
59:30		Philemon	Limo	KEN	2.8.85	1		Praha	2 Apr 11
59:30		Lelisa	Desisa	ETH	14.1.90	1		New Delhi	27 Nov 11
		(30)							
59:31		Geoffrey	Kipsang	KEN	28.11.92	2		New Delhi	27 Nov 11
59:32		Dieudonné	Disi	RWA	24.4.78	6	WCh	Udine	14 Oct 07
59:33		Marílson	dos Santos	BRA	6.8.77	7	WCh	Udine	14 Oct 07
59:35		Tsegaye	Kebede	ETH	15.1.87	2		Ra's Al Khaymah	8 Feb 08
59:36		Sammy	Kosgei	KEN	20.1.86	2		Berlin	5 Apr 09
59:37	dh	Dejene	Berhanu	ETH	12.12.80	1	GNR	South Shields	26 Sep 04
59:37		Stephen	Kibiwott	KEN	3.4.80	1		Lille	5 Sep 09
59:38	dh	Faustin	Baha	TAN	30.5.82	4		Lisboa	26 Mar 00
59:39		Silas	Kipruto	KEN	26.9.84	2		Milano	21 Mar 10
59:39		Wilson	Kiprop	KEN	14.4.87	1		Lille	4 Sep 10
		(40)							
59:39		Azmeraw	Bekele	ETH	22.1.86	2		Den Haag	13 Mar 11
59:40		Peter	Kirui	KEN	2.1.88	3		Den Haag	13 Mar 11
59:41		Benson	Barus	KEN	4.7.80	1		Udine	28 Sep 08
59:42		Ayele	Abshero	ETH	28.12.90	4		Den Haag	13 Mar 11
59:42		Dino	Sefer	ETH	28.5.88	1		Ivry-sur-Seine	3 Apr 11
59:43	dh	António	Pinto	POR	22.3.66	1		Lisboa	15 Mar 98
59:43		Ryan	Hall	USA	14.10.82	1	NC	Houston	14 Jan 07
59:43		Jairus	Chanchaima	KEN	5.12.84	2		Lille	5 Sep 09
59:43		Tujuba	Beyu Megersa	ETH	15.10.87	2		Ivry-sur-Seine	3 Apr 11
59:44		Charles	Munyeki	KEN	2.11.86	5		Rotterdam	14 Sep 08
59:44	dh	Kenneth	Kimutai	KEN	10.12.81	2	GNR	South Shields	20 Sep 09
59:44		Lucas	Rotich	KEN	16.4.90	5		Den Haag	13 Mar 11
		(52)							

100th man 60:07, 200th man 60:42, 300th 61:03, 400th 61:17, 500th 61:27

Short course: 58:51 Paul Tergat KEN 17.6.69 1 Stra Milano 49m sh 30 Mar 96

MARATHON

In second column: L = loop course or start and finish within 30%, P = point-to-point or start and finish more than 30% apart, D = point-to-point and downhill over 1/1000

Mark		Name		Nat	Born	Pos	Meet	Venue	Date
2:03:59	wRL	Haile	Gebrselassie	ETH	18.4.73	1		Berlin	28 Sep 08
2:03:38	wRL	Patrick	Makau	KEN	2.3.85	1		Berlin	25 Sep 11
2:03:42	L	Wilson	Kipsang Kiprotich	KEN	15.3.82	1		Frankfurt	30 Oct 11
2:03:59	wRL	Haile	Gebrselassie	ETH	18.4.73	1		Berlin	28 Sep 08
2:04:26	wRL		Gebrselassie			1		Berlin	30 Sep 07
2:04:27	L	Duncan	Kibet	KEN	25.4.78	1		Rotterdam	5 Apr 09
2:04:27	L	James Kipsang	Kwambai	KEN	28.2.83	2		Rotterdam	5 Apr 09
2:04:40	L	Emmanuel	Mutai	KEN	12.10.84	1		London	17 Apr 11
2:04:48	L		Makau			1		Rotterdam	11 Apr 10
2:04:53	L		Gebrselassie			1		Dubai	18 Jan 08
2:04:55	wRL	Paul	Tergat	KEN	17.6.69	1		Berlin	28 Sep 03
2:04:55	L	Geoffrey	Mutai	KEN	7.10.81	2		Rotterdam	11 Apr 10
2:04:56	L	Sammy	Korir	KEN	12.12.71	2		Berlin	28 Sep 03
2:04:57	L		Kipsang			1		Frankfurt	31 Oct 10
2:05:04	L	Abel	Kirui (10)	KEN	4.6.82	3		Rotterdam	5 Apr 09
2:05:06	P		G Mutai			1		New York	6 Nov 11
2:05:08	L		Makau			1		Berlin	26 Sep 10
2:05:10	L	Samuel	Wanjiru	KEN	10.11.86	1		London	26 Apr 09
2:05:10	L		Mutai			2		Berlin	26 Sep 10
2:05:13	L	Vincent	Kipruto	KEN	13.9.87	3		Rotterdam	11 Apr 10
2:05:15	L	Martin	Lel	KEN	29.10.78	1		London	13 Apr 08
2:05:16	L	Levi	Matebo Omari	KEN	3.11.89	2		Frankfurt	30 Oct 11
2:05:18	L	Tsegaye	Kebede	ETH	15.1.87	1		Fukuoka	6 Dec 09
2:05:19	L		Kebede			1		London	25 Apr 10
2:05:20	L		Kebede			2		London	26 Apr 09
2:05:23	L	Feyisa	Lilesa	ETH	1.2.90	4		Rotterdam	11 Apr 10

Mark	Wind	Name		Nat	Born	Pos	Meet	Venue	Date
2:05:24	L		Wanjiru			2		London	13 Apr 08
2:05:25	L	Bazu	Worku	ETH	15.9.90	3		Berlin	26 Sep 10
2:05:25	L	Albert	Matebor	KEN	20.12.80	3		Frankfurt	30 Oct 11
2:05:27	L	Jaouad	Gharib	MAR	22.5.72	3		London	26 Apr 09
2:05:27	L	Wilson	Chebet	KEN	12.7.85	1		Rotterdam	10 Apr 11
(30/20)									
2:05:30	L	Abderrahim	Goumri	MAR	21.5.76	3		London	13 Apr 08
2:05:37	L	Moses	Mosop	KEN	17.7.85	1		Chicago	9 Oct 11
2:05:38	wrL	Khalid	Khannouchi	MAR/USA	22.12.71	1		London	14 Apr 02
2:05:39	L	Eliud	Kiptanui	KEN	6.6.89	1		Praha	9 May 10
2:05:44	L	Getu	Feleke	ETH	28.11.86	1		Amsterdam	17 Oct 10
2:05:48	L	Jafred	Kipchumba	KEN	8.8.83	1		Eindhoven	9 Oct 11
2:05:49	L	William	Kipsang	KEN	26.6.77	1		Rotterdam	13 Apr 08
2:05:50	L	Evans	Rutto	KEN	8.4.78	1		Chicago	12 Oct 03
2:06:05	wrL	Ronaldo da	Costa	BRA	7.6.70	1		Berlin	20 Sep 98
2:06:05	L	Laban	Korir	KEN	30.12.85	2		Amsterdam	16 Oct 11
(30)									
2:06:07	L	Eric	Ndiema	KEN	28.12.92	3		Amsterdam	16 Oct 11
2:06:07	L	Philip Sanga	Kimutai	KEN	10.9.83	4		Frankfurt	30 Oct 11
2:06:14	L	Felix	Limo	KEN	22.8.80	1		Rotterdam	4 Apr 04
2:06:14	L	Gilbert	Kirwa Too	KEN	20.12.85	1		Frankfurt	25 Oct 09
2:06:15	L	Titus	Munji	KEN	20.12.79	3		Berlin	28 Sep 03
2:06:15	L	Wesley	Korir	KEN	15.11.82	2		Chicago	9 Oct 11
2:06:16	L	Moses	Tanui	KEN	20.8.65	2		Chicago	24 Oct 99
2:06:16	L	Daniel	Njenga	KEN	7.5.76	2		Chicago	13 Oct 02
2:06:16	L	Toshinari	Takaoka	JPN	24.9.70	3		Chicago	13 Oct 02
2:06:17	L	Ryan	Hall	USA	14.10.82	5		London	13 Apr 08
(40)									
2:06:18	L	Gilbert	Yegon	KEN	16.1.88	1		Amsterdam	18 Oct 09
2:06:23	L	Robert	Cheboror	KEN	9.9.78	1		Amsterdam	17 Oct 04
2:06:23	L	Robert Kiprono	Cheruiyot	KEN	10.8.88	2		Frankfurt	25 Oct 09
2:06:25	L	Evans	Cheruiyot	KEN	10.5.82	1		Chicago	12 Oct 08
2:06:26	L	David	Kemboi Kiyeng	KEN	.83	3		Paris	5 Apr 09
2:06:28	L	Nathaniel	Kipkosgei	KEN	1.9.84	2		Eindhoven	9 Oct 11
2:06:29	L	Bernard	Kipyego	KEN	16.7.86	3		Chicago	9 Oct 11
2:06:30	L	Yemane	Tsegay	ETH	8.4.85	4		Paris	5 Apr 09
2:06:31	L	Tadesse	Tola	ETH	31.10.87	2		Frankfurt	31 Oct 10
2:06:31	L	Benjamin	Kiptoo Kolum	KEN	.79	1		Paris	10 Apr 11
(50)									

100th man 2:07:07, 200th 2:08:03, 300th 2:08:43, 400th 2:09:10, 500th 2:09:40

Downhill point-to-point course – Boston marathon is downhill overall (139m) and sometimes strongly wind-aided.

Mark	Wind	Name		Nat	Born	Pos	Meet	Venue	Date
2:03:02		Geoffrey	Mutai	KEN	7.10.81	1		Boston	18 Apr 11
2:03:06		Moses	Mosop	KEN	17.7.85	2		Boston	18 Apr 11
2:04:53		Gebre-egziabher	Gebremariam	ETH	10.9.84	3		Boston	18 Apr 11
2:04:58		Ryan	Hall	USA	14.10.82	4		Boston	18 Apr 11
2:05:52		Robert Kiprono	Cheruiyot	KEN	10.8.88	1		Boston	19 Apr 10
2:06:13		Abreham	Cherkos	ETH	23.9.89	5		Boston	18 Apr 11

2000 METRES STEEPLECHASE

Mark	Name		Nat	Born	Pos	Meet	Venue	Date
5:10.68	Mahiedine	Mekhissi	FRA	15.3.85	1		Reims	30 Jun 10
5:13.47	Bouabdellah	Tahri	FRA	20.12.78	1		Tomblaine	25 Jun 10
5:14.43	Julius	Kariuki	KEN	12.6.61	1		Rovereto	21 Aug 90
5:14.53	Saïf Saaeed	Shaheen	QAT	15.10.82	1	SGP	Doha	13 May 05
5:16.22	Phillip	Barkutwo	KEN	6.10.66	2		Rovereto	21 Aug 90
5:16.46	Wesley	Kiprotich	KEN	31.7.79	2	SGP	Doha	13 May 05
5:16.85	Eliud	Barngetuny	KEN	20.5.73	1		Parma	13 Jun 95

3000 METRES STEEPLECHASE

Mark		Name		Nat	Born	Pos	Meet	Venue	Date
7:53.63	wr	Saïf Saaeed	Shaheen	KEN/QAT	15.10.82	1	VD	Bruxelles	3 Sep 04
7:53.64		Brimin	Kipruto	KEN	31.7.85	1	Herc	Monaco	22 Jul 11
7:55.28	wr	Brahim	Boulami ¶	MAR	20.4.72	1	VD	Bruxelles	24 Aug 01
7:55.51			Shaheen			1	VD	Bruxelles	26 Aug 05
7:55.72	wr	Bernard	Barmasai	KEN	6.5.74	1	ASV	Köln	24 Aug 97
7:55.76		Ezekiel	Kemboi	KEN	25.5.82	2	Herc	Monaco	22 Jul 11
7:56.16		Moses	Kiptanui	KEN	1.10.70	2	ASV	Köln	24 Aug 97
7:56.32			Shaheen			1	Tsik	Athína	3 Jul 06
7:56.34			Shaheen			1	GGala	Roma	8 Jul 05
7:56.37		Paul Kipsiele	Koech	KEN	10.11.81	2	GGala	Roma	8 Jul 05
7:56.54			Shaheen			1	WK	Zürich	18 Aug 06
7:56.94			Shaheen			1	WAF	Monaco	19 Sep 04
7:57.28			Shaheen			1	Tsik	Athína	14 Jun 05

Mark	Wind	Name		Nat	Born	Pos	Meet	Venue	Date
7:57.29		Reuben	Kosgei	KEN	2.8.79	2	VD	Bruxelles	24 Aug 01
7:57.32			P K Koech			3	Herc	Monaco	22 Jul 11
7:57.38			Shaheen			1	WAF	Monaco	14 Sep 03
7:57.42			P K Koech			2	WAF	Monaco	14 Sep 03
7:58.09			Boulami			1	Herc	Monaco	19 Jul 02
7:58.10			S Cherono			2	Herc	Monaco	19 Jul 02
7:58.50			Boulami			1	WK	Zürich	17 Aug 01
7:58.66			S Cherono			3	VD	Bruxelles	24 Aug 01
7:58.80			P K Koech			1	VD	Bruxelles	14 Sep 07
7:58.85			Kemboi			1	SGP	Doha	8 May 09
7:58.98			Barmasai			1	Herc	Monaco	4 Aug 99
7:59.08 WR		Wilson	Boit Kipketer	KEN	6.10.73	1	WK	Zürich	13 Aug 97
7:59.18 WR			Kiptanui			1	WK	Zürich	16 Aug 95
7:59.42			P K Koech			1	DNG	Stockholm	7 Aug 07
7.59.52			Kiptanui			1	VD	Bruxelles	25 Aug 95
7:59.65			P K Koech			1	GGala	Roma	2 Jul 04
7:59.94			P K Koech			1	GGala	Roma	14 Jul 06
		(30/9)							
8:00.89		Richard	Matelong (10)	KEN	14.10.83	2	WCh	Berlin	18 Aug 09
8:01.18		Bouabdellah	Tahri	FRA	20.12.78	3	WCh	Berlin	18 Aug 09
8:01.69		Kipkirui	Misoi	KEN	23.12.78	4	VD	Bruxelles	24 Aug 01
8:02.09		Mahiédine	Mekhissi	FRA	15.3.85	1	DL	Saint-Denis	8 Jul 11
8:03.41		Patrick	Sang	KEN	11.4.64	3	ASV	Köln	24 Aug 97
8:03.57		Ali	Ezzine	MAR	3.9.78	1	Gaz	Saint-Denis	23 Jun 00
8:03.74		Raymond	Yator	KEN	7.4.81	3	Herc	Monaco	18 Aug 00
8:03.81		Benjamin	Kiplagat	UGA	4.3.89	2	Athl	Lausanne	8 Jul 10
8:03.89		John	Kosgei	KEN	13.7.73	3	Herc	Monaco	16 Aug 97
8:04.95		Simon	Vroemen ¶	NED	11.5.69	2	VD	Bruxelles	26 Aug 05
8:05.01		Eliud	Barngetuny	KEN	20.5.73	1	Herc	Monaco	25 Jul 95
		(20)							
8:05.35 WR		Peter	Koech	KEN	18.2.58	1	DNG	Stockholm	3 Jul 89
8:05.37		Philip	Barkutwo	KEN	6.10.66	2		Rieti	6 Sep 92
8:05.4 WR		Henry	Rono	KEN	12.2.52	1		Seattle	13 May 78
8:05.43		Christopher	Kosgei	KEN	14.8.74	2	WK	Zürich	11 Aug 99
8:05.51		Julius	Kariuki	KEN	12.6.61	1	OG	Seoul	30 Sep 88
8:05.68		Wesley	Kiprotich	KEN	1.8.79	4	VD	Bruxelles	3 Sep 04
8:05.75		Mustafa	Mohamed	SWE	1.3.79	1	NA	Heusden-Zolder	28 Jul 07
8:05.88		Bernard	Nganga (Mbugua)	KEN	.85	2	ISTAF	Berlin	11 Sep 11
8:05.99		Joseph	Keter	KEN	13.6.69	1	Herc	Monaco	10 Aug 96
8:06.13		Tareq Mubarak	Taher	BRN	24.3.84	3	Tsik	Athína	13 Jul 09
		(30)							
8:06.77		Gideon	Chirchir	KEN	24.2.66	2	WK	Zürich	16 Aug 95
8:06.88		Richard	Kosgei	KEN	29.12.70	2	GPF	Monaco	9 Sep 95
8:07.02		Brahim	Taleb	MAR	16.2.85	2	NA	Heusden-Zolder	28 Jul 07
8:07.13		Paul	Kosgei	KEN	22.4.78	2	GP II	Saint-Denis	3 Jul 99
8:07.18		Obaid Moussa	Amer ¶	KEN/QAT	18.4.85	4	OG	Athína	24 Aug 04
8:07.44		Luis Miguel	Martín	ESP	11.1.72	2	VD	Bruxelles	30 Aug 02
8:07.59		Julius	Nyamu	KEN	1.12.77	5	VD	Bruxelles	24 Aug 01
8:07.62		Joseph	Mahmoud	FRA	13.12.55	1	VD	Bruxelles	24 Aug 84
8:07.71		Hillary	Yego	KEN	2.4.92	3	DL	Shanghai	15 May 11
8:07.75		Jonathan	Ndiku Muia	KEN	18.9.91	6	Herc	Monaco	22 Jul 11
		(40)							
8:07.96		Mark	Rowland	GBR	7.3.63	3	OG	Seoul	30 Sep 88
8:08.02 WR		Anders	Gärderud	SWE	28.8.46	1	OG	Montreal	28 Jul 76
8:08.12		Matthew	Birir	KEN	5.7.72	3	GGala	Roma	8 Jun 95
8:08.14		Sa'ad Shaddad	Al-Asmari	KSA	24.9.68	4	DNG	Stockholm	16 Jul 02
8:08.48		Michael	Kipyego	KEN	2.10.83	2	Herc	Monaco	28 Jul 09
8:08.57		Francesco	Panetta	ITA	10.1.63	1	WCh	Roma	5 Sep 87
8:08.59		Patrick	Langat	KEN/TUR	16.6.88	4	DL	Shanghai	15 May 11
8:08.78		Alessandro	Lambruschini	ITA	7.1.65	3	WCh	Stuttgart	21 Aug 93
8:08.78		Abdelkader	Hachlaf ¶	MAR	3.7.79	4	GGala	Roma	14 Jul 06
8:08.82		Dan	Lincoln	USA	22.10.80	5	GGala	Roma	14 Jul 06
		(50)							

100th man 8:12.58, 200th 8:18.91, 300th 8:22.41, 400th 8:25.03, 500th 8:26.91

Drugs disqualification: 7:53.17 Brahim Boulami ¶ MAR 20.4.72 1 WK Zürich 16 Aug 02

110 METRES HURDLES

Mark	Wind	Name		Nat	Born	Pos	Meet	Venue	Date
12.87 WR	0.9	Dayron	Robles	CUB	19.11.86	1	GS	Ostrava	12 Jun 08
12.88 WR	1.1		Liu Xiang	CHN	13.7.83	1rA	Athl	Lausanne	11 Jul 06
12.88	0.5		Robles			1	Gaz	Saint-Denis	18 Jul 08
12.89	0.5	David	Oliver	USA	24.4.82	1	DL	Saint-Denis	16 Jul 10

Mark	Wind	Name		Nat	Born	Pos	Meet	Venue	Date
12.90	1.1	Dominique	Arnold	USA	14.9.73	2rA	Athl	Lausanne	11 Jul 06
12.90	1.6		Oliver			1	Pre	Eugene	3 Jul 10
12.91	wr0.5	Colin	Jackson	GBR	18.2.67	1	WCh	Stuttgart	20 Aug 93
12.91	wr0.3		Liu Xiang			1	OG	Athína	27 Aug 04
12.91	0.2		Robles			1	DNG	Stockholm	22 Jul 08
12.92	wr-0.1	Roger	Kingdom	USA	26.8.62	1	WK	Zürich	16 Aug 89
12.92	0.9	Allen	Johnson	USA	1.3.71	1	NC	Atlanta	23 Jun 96
12.92	0.2		Johnson			1	VD	Bruxelles	23 Aug 96
12.92	1.5		Liu Xiang			1	GP	New York	2 Jun 07
12.92	0.0		Robles			1	WAF	Stuttgart	23 Sep 07
12.93	wr-0.2	Renaldo	Nehemiah	USA	24.3.59	1	WK	Zürich	19 Aug 81
12.93	0.0		Johnson			1	WCh	Athína	7 Aug 97
12.93	-0.6		Liu Xiang			1	WAF	Stuttgart	9 Sep 06
12.93	0.1		Robles			1	OG	Beijing	21 Aug 08
12.93	1.7		Oliver			1	NC	Des Moines	27 Jun 10
12.93	-0.3		Oliver			1	WK	Zürich	19 Aug 10
12.94	1.6	Jack	Pierce	USA	23.9.62	1s2	NC	Atlanta	22 Jun 96
12.94	1.8		Oliver			1	Pre	Eugene	4 Jun 11
12.95	0.6		Johnson			1	OG	Atlanta	29 Jul 96
12.95	1.5	Terrence	Trammell (10)	USA	23.11.78	2	GP	New York	2 Jun 07
12.95	1.7		Liu Xiang			1	WCh	Osaka	31 Aug 07
12.95	2.0		Oliver			1	SGP	Doha	9 May 08
12.95	-1.7		Robles			1		Dubnica nad Váhom	7 Sep 08
12.96	0.4		Johnson			1	WCp	Athína	17 Sep 06
12.96	-0.6		Robles			1		Villeneuve d'Ascq	27 Jun 08
12.97	1.0	Ladji	Doucouré	FRA	28.3.83	1	NC	Angers	15 Jul 05
12.97		six more performances: Johnson 3, Kingdom, Jackson, Robles 1 each						(36/11)	
12.98	0.6	Mark	Crear	USA	2.10.68	1		Zagreb	5 Jul 99
13.00	0.5	Anthony	Jarrett	GBR	13.8.68	2	WCh	Stuttgart	20 Aug 93
13.00	0.6	Anier	García	CUB	9.3.76	1	OG	Sydney	25 Sep 00
13.01	0.3	Larry	Wade ¶	USA	22.11.74	1rA	Athl	Lausanne	2 Jul 99
13.02	1.5	Ryan	Wilson	USA	19.12.80	3	GP	New York	2 Jun 07
13.02	1.7	David	Payne	USA	24.7.82	3	WCh	Osaka	31 Aug 07
13.03	-0.2	Greg	Foster	USA	4.8.58	2	WK	Zürich	19 Aug 81
13.03	1.0	Reggie	Torian	USA	22.4.75	1	NC	New Orleans	21 Jun 98
13.04	-0.2	Jason	Richardson	USA	4.4.86	2	Hanz	Zagreb	13 Sep 11
		(20)							
13.05	1.4	Tony	Dees ¶	USA	6.8.63	1		Vigo	23 Jul 91
13.05	-0.8	Florian	Schwarthoff	GER	7.5.68	1	NC	Bremen	2 Jul 95
13.08	1.2	Mark	McKoy	CAN	10.12.61	1	BNP	Villeneuve-d'Ascq	2 Jul 93
13.08	0.0	Stanislav	Olijar	LAT	22.3.79	2	Athl	Lausanne	1 Jul 03
13.09	0.1	Aries	Merritt	USA	24.7.85	1	DNG	Stockholm	7 Aug 07
13.09	2.0	Antwon	Hicks	USA	12.3.83	2s2	NC/OT	Eugene	6 Jul 08
13.12	1.5	Falk	Balzer ¶	GER	14.12.73	2	EC	Budapest	22 Aug 98
13.12	1.0	Duane	Ross ¶	USA	5.12.72	3	WCh	Sevilla	25 Aug 99
13.12	1.9	Anwar	Moore	USA	5.3.79	1	ModR	Modesto	5 May 07
13.13	1.6	Igor	Kovác	SVK	12.5.69	1	DNG	Stockholm	7 Jul 97
		(30)							
13.13	2.0	Dexter	Faulk	USA	14.4.84	2	GS	Ostrava	17 Jun 09
13.14	0.1	Ryan	Brathwaite	BAR	6.6.88	1	WCh	Berlin	20 Aug 09
13.15	0.3	Robin	Korving	NED	29.7.74	5rA	Athl	Lausanne	2 Jul 99
13.15	0.1	Dwight	Thomas	JAM	23.9.80	2	Bisl	Oslo	9 Jun 11
13.17	-0.4	Sam	Turner	USA	17.6.57	2	Pepsi	Los Angeles (Ww)	15 May 83
13.17	0.0	Tonie	Campbell	USA	14.6.60	3	WK	Zürich	17 Aug 88
13.17	0.5	Courtney	Hawkins	USA	11.7.67	1		Ingolstadt	26 Jul 98
13.17	0.4	Mike	Fenner	GER	24.4.71	1		Leverkusen	9 Aug 98
13.17	-0.1	Maurice	Wignall	JAM	17.4.76	1s1	OG	Athína	26 Aug 04
13.18	0.5	Emilio	Valle	CUB	21.4.67	3s1	OG	Atlanta	29 Jul 96
		(40)							
13.19	1.9	Steve	Brown	USA/TRI	6.1.69	1h4	NC	Atlanta	21 Jun 96
13.19	1.7		Shi Dongpeng	CHN	6.1.84	5	WCh	Osaka	31 Aug 07
13.19	1.7	Ronnie	Ash	USA	2.7.88	3	NC	Des Moines	27 Jun 10
13.20	2.0	Stéphane	Caristan	FRA	31.5.64	1	EC	Stuttgart	30 Aug 86
13.20	1.8	Aleksandr	Markin ¶	RUS	8.9.62	1	Znam	Leningrad	11 Jun 88
13.20	1.7	Larry	Harrington	USA	24.11.70	2s1	NC	Atlanta	22 Jun 96
13.20	0.1	Joel	Brown	USA	31.1.80	3	Bisl	Oslo	9 Jun 11
13.21	wr0.6	Alejandro	Casañas	CUB	29.1.54	1	WUG	Sofia	21 Aug 77
13.21	1.8	Vladimir	Shishkin	RUS	12.1.64	2	Znam	Leningrad	11 Jun 88
13.21	0.9	Eugene	Swift	USA	14.9.64	3	NC	Atlanta	23 Jun 96
		(50)	100th man 13.32, 200th 13.44, 300th 13.53, 400th 13.59, 500th 13.64						

Mark	Wind	Name		Nat	Born	Pos	Meet	Venue	Date

Rolling start but accepted by race officials

Mark	Wind	Name		Nat	Born	Pos	Meet	Venue	Date
13.10A	2.0	Falk	Balzer ¶	GER	14.12.73	1	WCp	Johannesburg	13 Sep 98

Doubtful timing: Scheessel 4 Jun 95 +1.3 1. Mike Fenner GER 24.4.71 13.06, 2. Eric Kaiser ¶ GER 7.3.71 13.08

Wind-assisted marks *Performances to 12.95, performers to 13.20*

12.87	2.6	Roger	Kingdom	USA	26.8.62	1	WCp	Barcelona	10 Sep 89
12.89	3.2	David	Oliver	USA	24.4.82	1s1	NC/OT	Eugene	6 Jul 08
12.91	3.5	Renaldo	Nehemiah	USA	24.3.59	1	NCAA	Champaign	1 Jun 79
12.94A	2.8		Jackson			1rA		Sestriere	31 Jul 94
12.95	2.6		Jackson			2	WCp	Barcelona	10 Sep 89
12.95	3.5		Oliver			1	NC/OT	Eugene	6 Jul 08
12.98	3.1	Ronnie	Ash	USA	2.7.88	1	NACAC	Miramar	9 Jul 10
13.00	2.6	Anwar	Moore	USA	5.3.79	1	DrakeR	Des Moines	28 Apr 07
13.05	3.6	Ryan	Brathwaite	BAR	6.6.88	1		Austin	2 May 09
13.06	2.1	Mark	McKoy	CAN	10.12.61	1	Gugl	Linz	13 Aug 92
13.14	2.9	Igor	Kazanov	LAT	24.9.63	1r1	Znam	Leningrad	8 Jun 86
13.15	2.1	Courtney	Hawkins	USA	11.7.67	1		Salamanca	10 Jul 98
13.18	4.7	Robert	Reading	USA	9.6.67	1		Azusa	23 Apr 94
13.18	2.3	Joel	Brown	USA	31.1.80	1	Tsik	Athína	13 Jul 09
13.18	3.8	Omo	Osaghae	USA	18.5.88	1		Lubbock	22 Apr 11
13.19	3.5	Barrett	Nugent	USA	29.1.90	1	TexR	Austin	9 Apr 11
13.20	2.4	Arthur	Blake	USA	19.8.66	2	IAC	Edinburgh	6 Jul 90
13.20	3.1	Yoel	Hernández	CUB	12.12.77	2		Camagüey	10 Mar 00
13.20	3.1	Dániel	Kiss	HUN	12.2.82	1=		Moskva	29 Jun 10
13.20	3.1	Artur	Noga	POL	2.5.88	1=		Moskva	29 Jun 10

Hand timing

| 12.8 | 1.0 | Renaldo | Nehemiah | USA | 24.3.59 | 1 | | Kingston | 11 May 79 |

Wind-assisted

12.8	2.4	Colin	Jackson	GBR	18.2.67	1		Sydney	10 Jan 90
12.9	4.1	Mark	Crear	USA	2.10.68	1rA	S&W	Modesto	8 May 93
12.9	3.1	William	Sharman	GBR	12.9.84	1r2		Madrid	2 Jul 10

400 METRES HURDLES

Mark		Name		Nat	Born	Pos	Meet	Venue	Date
46.78 WR		Kevin	Young	USA	16.9.66	1	OG	Barcelona	6 Aug 92
47.02 WR		Edwin	Moses	USA	31.8.55	1		Koblenz	31 Aug 83
47.03		Bryan	Bronson	USA	9.9.72	1	NC	New Orleans	21 Jun 98
47.10		Samuel	Matete	ZAM	27.7.68	1rA	WK	Zürich	7 Aug 91
47.13 WR			Moses			1		Milano	3 Jul 80
47.14			Moses			1	Athl	Lausanne	14 Jul 81
47.17			Moses			1	ISTAF	Berlin	8 Aug 80
47.18			Young			1	WCh	Stuttgart	19 Aug 93
47.19		Andre	Phillips	USA	5.9.59	1	OG	Seoul	25 Sep 88
47.23		Amadou	Dia Bâ	SEN	22.9.58	2	OG	Seoul	25 Sep 88
47.24		Kerron	Clement	USA	31.10.85	1	NC	Carson	26 Jun 05
47.25		Félix	Sánchez	DOM	30.8.77	1	WCh	Saint-Denis	29 Aug 03
47.25		Angelo	Taylor	USA	29.12.78	1	OG	Beijing	18 Aug 08
47.27			Moses			1	ISTAF	Berlin	21 Aug 81
47.30		Bershawn	Jackson (10)	USA	8.5.83	1	WCh	Helsinki	9 Aug 05
47.32			Moses			1		Koblenz	29 Aug 84
47.32			Jackson			1	NC	Des Moines	26 Jun 10
47.35			Sánchez			1rA	WK	Zürich	16 Aug 02
47.37			Moses			1	WCp	Roma	4 Sep 81
47.37			Moses			1	WK	Zürich	24 Aug 83
47.37			Moses			1	NC/OT	Indianpolis	17 Jul 88
47.37			Young			1	Athl	Lausanne	7 Jul 93
47.37		Stéphane	Diagana	FRA	23.7.69	1	Athl	Lausanne	5 Jul 95
47.38			Moses			1	Athl	Lausanne	2 Sep 86
47.38		Danny	Harris ¶	USA	7.9.65	1	Athl	Lausanne	10 Jul 91
47.38			Sánchez			1rA	WK	Zürich	17 Aug 01
47.39			Clement			1	NC	Indianapolis	24 Jun 06
47.40			Young			1	WK	Zürich	19 Aug 92
47.42			Young			1	ASV	Köln	16 Aug 92
47.43			Moses			1	ASV	Köln	28 Aug 83
47.43		James	Carter	USA	7.5.78	2	WCh	Helsinki	9 Aug 05
		(31/13)							
47.48		Harald	Schmid	FRG	29.9.57	1	EC	Athína	8 Sep 82
47.53		Hadi Soua'an	Al-Somaily	KSA	21.8.76	2	OG	Sydney	27 Sep 00
47.54		Derrick	Adkins	USA	2.7.70	2	Athl	Lausanne	5 Jul 95
47.54		Fabrizio	Mori	ITA	28.6.69	2	WCh	Edmonton	10 Aug 01
47.60		Winthrop	Graham	JAM	17.11.65	1	WK	Zürich	4 Aug 93

Mark	Wind	Name		Nat	Born	Pos	Meet	Venue	Date
47.63		Johnny	Dutch	USA	20.1.89	2	NC	Des Moines	26 Jun 10
47.66A		L.J. 'Louis'	van Zyl	RSA	20.7.85	1		Pretoria	25 Feb 11
	(20)								
47.67		Bennie	Brazell	USA	2.6.82	2	NCAA	Sacramento	11 Jun 05
47.72		Javier	Culson	PUR	25.7.84	1		Ponce	8 May 10
47.75		David	Patrick	USA	12.6.60	4	NC/OT	Indianpolis	17 Jul 88
47.81		Llewellyn	Herbert	RSA	21.7.77	3	OG	Sydney	27 Sep 00
47.82 WR		John	Akii-Bua	UGA	3.12.49	1	OG	München	2 Sep 72
47.82		Kriss	Akabusi	GBR	28.11.58	3	OG	Barcelona	6 Aug 92
47.82		Periklis	Iakovákis	GRE	24.3.79	2	GP	Osaka	6 May 06
47.84		Bayano	Kamani	PAN	17.4.80	2s1	WCh	Helsinki	7 Aug 05
47.88		David	Greene	GBR	11.4.86	1	C.Cup	Split	4 Sep 10
47.89		Dai	Tamesue	JPN	3.5.78	3	WCh	Edmonton	10 Aug 01
	(30)								
47.91		Calvin	Davis	USA	2.4.72	1s2	OG	Atlanta	31 Jul 96
47.92		Aleksandr	Vasilyev	BLR	26.7.61	2	ECp	Moskva	17 Aug 85
47.93		Kenji	Narisako	JPN	25.7.84	3	GP	Osaka	6 May 06
47.93		Jeshua	Anderson	USA	22.6.89	1	NC	Eugene	26 Jun 11
47.94		Eric	Thomas	USA	1.12.73	1	GGala	Roma	30 Jun 00
47.97		Maurice	Mitchell	USA	14.5.71	2rA	WK	Zürich	14 Aug 96
47.97		Joey	Woody	USA	22.5.73	3	NC	New Orleans	21 Jun 98
47.98		Sven	Nylander	SWE	1.1.62	4	OG	Atlanta	1 Aug 96
47.99A		Omar	Cisneros	CUB	19.11.89	1	PAm	Guadalajara, MEX	25 Oct 11
48.00		Danny	McFarlane	JAM	14.2.72	1s2	OG	Athína	24 Aug 04
	(40)								
48.02A		Ockert	Cilliers	RSA	21.4.81	1		Pretoria	20 Feb 04
48.02		Michael	Tinsley	USA	21.4.84	1s2	NC	Indianapolis	22 Jun 07
48.04		Eronilde	de Araújo	BRA	31.12.70	2	Nik	Nice	12 Jul 95
48.05		Ken	Harnden	ZIM	31.3.73	1	GP	Paris (C)	29 Jul 98
48.05		Kemel	Thompson	JAM	25.9.74	1	GP	London (CP)	8 Aug 03
48.05		Isa	Phillips	JAM	22.4.84	1	NC	Kingston	27 Jun 09
48.06		Oleg	Tverdokhleb	UKR	3.11.69	1	EC	Helsinki	10 Aug 94
48.06		Ruslan	Mashchenko	RUS	11.11.71	1	GP II	Helsinki	13 Jun 98
48.09		Alwyn	Myburgh	RSA	13.10.80	1	WUG	Beijing	31 Aug 01
48.12A WR		David	Hemery	GBR	18.7.44	1	OG	Ciudad de México	15 Oct 68
48.12		Marek	Plawgo	POL	25.2.81	3	WCh	Osaka	28 Aug 07
	(51)	100th man 48.52, 200th man 49.05, 300th man 49.33, 400th 49.54, 500th 49.72							

Best at low altitude: 47.66 van Zyl   1   GS   Ostrava   31 May 11
Drugs Disqualification   47.15 Bronson ¶ 1   GWG   Uniondale, NY 19 Jul 98

HIGH JUMP

Mark		Name		Nat	Born	Pos	Meet	Venue	Date
2.45 WR		Javier	Sotomayor ¶	CUB	13.10.67	1		Salamanca	27 Jul 93
2.44 WR			Sotomayor			1	CAC	San Juan	29 Jul 89
2.43 WR			Sotomayor			1		Salamanca	8 Sep 88
2.43i			Sotomayor			1	WI	Budapest	4 Mar 89
2.42 WR		Patrik	Sjöberg	SWE	5.1.65	1	DNG	Stockholm	30 Jun 87
2.42i WR		Carlo	Thränhardt	FRG	5.7.57	1		Berlin	26 Feb 88
2.42			Sotomayor			1		Sevilla	5 Jun 94
2.41 WR		Igor	Paklin	KGZ	15.6.63	1	WUG	Kobe	4 Sep 85
2.41i			Sjöberg			1		Pireás	1 Feb 87
2.41i			Sotomayor			1	WI	Toronto	14 Mar 93
2.41			Sotomayor			1	NC	La Habana	25 Jun 94
2.41			Sotomayor			1	TSB	London (CP)	15 Jul 94
2.40 WR		Rudolf	Povarnitsyn	UKR	13.6.62	1		Donetsk	11 Aug 85
2.40i			Thränhardt			1		Simmerath	16 Jan 87
2.40i			Sjöberg			1		Berlin	27 Feb 87
2.40			Sotomayor			1	NC	La Habana	12 Mar 89
2.40			Sjöberg			1	ECp-B	Bruxelles	5 Aug 89
2.40			Sotomayor			1	AmCp	Bogota	13 Aug 89
2.40		Sorin	Matei	ROU	6.7.63	1	PTS	Bratislava	20 Jun 90
2.40i		Hollis	Conway	USA	8.1.67	1	WI	Sevilla	10 Mar 91
2.40			Sotomayor			1		Saint Denis	19 Jul 91
2.40		Charles	Austin	USA	19.12.67	1	WK	Zürich	7 Aug 91
2.40			Sotomayor			1	Barr	La Habana	22 May 93
2.40			Sotomayor			1	TSB	London (CP)	23 Jul 93
2.40			Sotomayor			1	WCh	Stuttgart	22 Aug 93
2.40i			Sotomayor			1		Wuppertal	4 Feb 94
2.40i			Sotomayor			1	TSB	Birmingham	26 Feb 94
2.40			Sotomayor			1		Eberstadt	10 Jul 94

Mark	Wind	Name		Nat	Born	Pos	Meet	Venue	Date
2.40			Sotomayor			1	Nik	Nice	18 Jul 94
2.40			Sotomayor			1	GWG	Sankt-Peterburg	29 Jul 94
2.40			Sotomayor			1	WCp	London (CP)	11 Sep 94
2.40			Sotomayor			1	PAm	Mar del Plata	25 Mar 95
2.40		Vyacheslav	Voronin	RUS	5.4.74	1	BrGP	London (CP)	5 Aug 00
2.40i		Stefan	Holm	SWE	25.5.76	1	EI	Madrid	6 Mar 05
2.40i		Ivan	Ukhov	RUS	29.3.86	1		Pireás	25 Feb 09
		(35/11)							
2.39 WR			Zhu Jianhua	CHN	29.5.63	1		Eberstadt	10 Jun 84
2.39i		Dietmar	Mögenburg	FRG	15.8.61	1		Köln	24 Feb 85
2.39i		Ralf	Sonn	GER	17.1.67	1		Berlin	1 Mar 91
2.38i		Gennadiy	Avdeyenko	UKR	4.11.63	2	WI	Indianapolis	7 Mar 87
2.38		Sergey	Malchenko	RUS	2.11.63	1		Banská Bystrica	4 Sep 88
2.38		Dragutin	Topic ¶	YUG	12.3.71	1		Beograd	1 Aug 93
2.38i		Steve	Smith	GBR	29.3.73	2		Wuppertal	4 Feb 94
2.38i		Wolf-Hendrik	Beyer	GER	14.2.72	1		Weinheim	18 Mar 94
2.38		Troy	Kemp	BAH	18.6.66	1	Nik	Nice	12 Jul 95
		(20)							
2.38		Artur	Partyka	POL	25.7.69	1		Eberstadt	18 Aug 96
2.38i		Matt	Hemingway	USA	24.10.72	1	NC	Atlanta	4 Mar 00
2.38i		Yaroslav	Rybakov	RUS	22.11.80	1		Stockholm	15 Feb 05
2.38		Jacques	Freitag	RSA	11.6.82	1		Oudtshoorn	5 Mar 05
2.38		Andriy	Sokolovskyy	UKR	16.7.78	1	GGala	Roma	8 Jul 05
2.38i		Linus	Thörnblad	SWE	6.3.85	2	NC	Göteborg	25 Feb 07
2.38		Andrey	Silnov	RUS	9.9.84	1	LGP	London (CP)	25 Jul 08
2.37		Valeriy	Sereda	RUS	30.6.59	1		Rieti	2 Sep 84
2.37		Tom	McCants	USA	27.11.62	1	Owens	Columbus	8 May 88
2.37		Jerome	Carter	USA	25.3.63	2	Owens	Columbus	8 May 88
		(30)							
2.37		Sergey	Dymchenko	UKR	23.8.67	1		Kiyev	16 Sep 90
2.37i		Dalton	Grant	GBR	8.4.66	1	EI	Paris	13 Mar 94
2.37i		Jaroslav	Bába	CZE	2.9.84	2		Arnstadt	5 Feb 05
2.37		Jesse	Williams	USA	27.12.83	1	NC	Eugene	26 Jun 11
2.36 WR		Gerd	Wessig	GDR	16.7.59	1	OG	Moskva	1 Aug 80
2.36		Sergey	Zasimovich	KZK	6.9.62	1		Tashkent	5 May 84
2.36		Eddy	Annys	BEL	15.12.58	1		Gent	26 May 85
2.36i		Jim	Howard	USA	11.9.59	1		Albuquerque	25 Jan 86
2.36i		Jan	Zvara	CZE	12.2.63	1	vGDR	Jablonec	14 Feb 87
2.36i		Gerd	Nagel	FRG	22.10.57	1		Sulingen	17 Mar 89
		(40)							
2.36		Nick	Saunders	BER	14.9.63	1	CG	Auckland	1 Feb 90
2.36		Doug	Nordquist	USA	20.12.58	2	NC	Norwalk	15 Jun 90
2.36		Georgi	Dakov	BUL	21.10.67	2	VD	Bruxelles	10 Aug 90
2.36		Lábros	Papakóstas	GRE	20.10.69	1	NC	Athína	21 Jun 92
2.36i		Steinar	Hoen	NOR	8.2.71	1		Balingen	12 Feb 94
2.36		Tim	Forsyth	AUS	17.8.73	1	NC	Melbourne	2 Mar 97
2.36		Sergey	Klyugin	RUS	24.3.74	1	WK	Zürich	12 Aug 98
2.36		Konstantin	Matusevich	ISR	25.2.71	1		Perth	5 Feb 00
2.36		Martin	Buss	GER	7.4.76	1	WCh	Edmonton	8 Aug 01
2.36		Aleksander	Walerianczyk	POL	1.9.82	1	EU23	Bydgoszcz	20 Jul 03
		(50)							
2.36		Michal	Bieniek	POL	17.5.84	1		Biala Podlaska	28 May 05
2.36i		Andrey	Tereshin	RUS	15.12.82	1	NC	Moskva	17 Feb 06
2.36A		Dusty	Jonas	USA	19.4.86	1	Big 12	Boulder	18 May 08
2.36		Aleksey	Dmitrik	RUS	12.4.84	1	NC	Cheboksary	23 Jul 11
2.36		Aleksandr	Shustov	RUS	29.6.84	2	NC	Cheboksary	23 Jul 11
		(55)	100th man 2.33, 200th 2.31, 300th 2.28, 400th 2.28, 500th 2.26						

Best outdoor marks for athletes with indoor bests

Mark	Name	Pos	Meet	Venue	Date		Mark	Name	Pos	Meet	Venue	Date
2.39	Conway	1	USOF	Norman	30 Jul 89		2.36	Howard	1		Rehlingen	8 Jun 87
2.38	Avdeyenko	2=	WCh	Roma	6 Sep 87		2.36	Zvara	1		Praha	23 Aug 87
2.37	Thränhardt	2		Rieti	2 Sep 84		2.36	Grant	4	WCh	Tokyo	1 Sep 91
2.37	Smith	1	WJ	Seoul	20 Sep 92		2.36	Hoen	1		Oslo	1 Jul 97
2.37	Holm	1		Athína	13 Jul 08		2.36	Bába	2=	GGala	Roma	8 Jul 05
2.36	Mögenburg	3		Eberstadt	10 Jun 84		2.36	Ukhov	1		Opole	11 Sep 10

Ancillary jumps – en route to final marks

Mark	Name	Date		Mark	Name	Date		Mark	Name	Date
2.40	Sotomayor	8 Sep 88		2.40	Sotomayor	29 Jul 89		2.40	Sotomayor	5 Jun 94

POLE VAULT

Mark	Wind	Name		Nat	Born	Pos	Meet	Venue	Date
6.15i		Sergey	Bubka	UKR	4.12.63	1		Donetsk	21 Feb 93
6.14i			Bubka			1		Liévin	13 Feb 93
6.14A WR			Bubka			1		Sestriere	31 Jul 94

Mark	Wind		Name	Nat	Born	Pos	Meet	Venue	Date
6.13i			Bubka			1		Berlin	21 Feb 92
6.13	WR		Bubka			1	TOTO	Tokyo	19 Sep 92
6.12i			Bubka			1	Mast	Grenoble	23 Mar 91
6.12	WR		Bubka			1		Padova	30 Aug 92
6.11i			Bubka			1		Donetsk	19 Mar 91
6.11	WR		Bubka			1		Dijon	13 Jun 92
6.10i			Bubka			1		San Sebastián	15 Mar 91
6.10	WR		Bubka			1	MAI	Malmö	5 Aug 91
6.09	WR		Bubka			1		Formia	8 Jul 91
6.08i			Bubka			1	NC	Volgograd	9 Feb 91
6.08	WR		Bubka			1	Znam	Moskva	9 Jun 91
6.07	WR		Bubka			1	Super	Shizuoka	6 May 91
6.06	WR		Bubka			1	Nik	Nice	10 Jul 88
6.06i		Steve	Hooker	AUS	16.7.82	1		Boston (R)	7 Feb 09
6.05	WR		Bubka			1	PTS	Bratislava	9 Jun 88
6.05i			Bubka			1		Donetsk	17 Mar 90
6.05i			Bubka			1		Berlin	5 Mar 93
6.05			Bubka			1	GPF	London (CP)	10 Sep 93
6.05i			Bubka			1	Mast	Grenoble	6 Feb 94
6.05			Bubka			1	ISTAF	Berlin	30 Aug 94
6.05			Bubka			1	GPF	Fukuoka	13 Sep 97
6.05		Maksim	Tarasov	RUS	2.12.70	1	GP II	Athína	16 Jun 99
6.05		Dmitriy	Markov	BLR/AUS	14.3.75	1	WCh	Edmonton	9 Aug 01
6.04		Brad	Walker	USA	21.6.81	1	Pre	Eugene	8 Jun 08
6.03	WR		Bubka			1	Ros	Praha	23 Jun 87
6.03i			Bubka			1		Osaka	11 Feb 89
6.03		Okkert	Brits	RSA	22.8.73	1	ASV	Köln	18 Aug 95
6.03		Jeff	Hartwig	USA	25.9.67	1		Jonesboro	14 Jun 00
6.03i		Renaud	Lavillenie	FRA	18.9.86	1	EI	Paris (Bercy)	5 Mar 11
		(32/8)							
6.02i		Rodion	Gataullin	RUS	23.11.65	1	NC	Gomel	4 Feb 89
6.01		Igor	Trandenkov (10)	RUS	17.8.66	1	NC	Sankt Peterburg	4 Jul 96
		Trandenkov hit bar hard, but kept it on with his had illegally. His next best							
5.95						1		Dijon	26 May 96
6.01		Tim	Mack	USA	15.9.72	1	WAF	Monaco	18 Sep 04
6.01		Yevgeniy	Lukyanenko	RUS	23.1.85	1		Bydgoszcz	1 Jul 08
6.00		Tim	Lobinger	GER	3.9.72	1	ASV	Köln	24 Aug 97
6.00i		Jean	Galfione	FRA	9.6.71	1	WI	Maebashi	6 Mar 99
6.00i		Danny	Ecker	GER	21.7.77	1		Dortmund	11 Feb 01
6.00		Toby	Stevenson	USA	19.11.76	1eA	CalR	Modesto	8 May 04
6.00		Paul	Burgess	AUS	14.8.79	1		Perth	25 Feb 05
Most competitions at 6 metres or more: S Bubka 44, Hartwig 8, Gataullin & Tarasov 7, Hooker 4, Brits & Walker 3									
5.98		Lawrence	Johnson	USA	7.5.74	1		Knoxville	25 May 96
5.97		Scott	Huffman	USA	30.11.64	1	NC	Knoxville	18 Jun 94
5.96		Joe	Dial	USA	26.10.62	1		Norman	18 Jun 87
		(20)							
5.95		Andrei	Tivontchik	GER	13.7.70	1	ASV	Köln	16 Aug 96
5.95		Michael	Stolle	GER	17.12.74	1	Herc	Monaco	18 Aug 00
5.95		Romain	Mesnil	FRA	13.6.77	1		Castres	6 Aug 03
5.94i		Philippe	Collet	FRA	13.12.63	1	Mast	Grenoble	10 Mar 90
5.93i	WIR	Billy	Olson	USA	19.7.58	1		East Rutherford	8 Feb 86
5.93i		Tye	Harvey	USA	25.9.74	2	NC	Atlanta	3 Mar 01
5.93		Alex	Averbukh	ISR	1.10.74	1	GP	Madrid (C)	19 Jul 03
5.92		István	Bagyula	HUN	2.1.69	1	Gugl	Linz	5 Jul 91
5.92		Igor	Potapovich	KAZ	6.9.67	2		Dijon	13 Jun 92
5.92		Dean	Starkey	USA	27.3.67	1	Banes	São Paulo	21 May 94
		(30)							
5.91	WR	Thierry	Vigneron	FRA	9.3.60	2	GGala	Roma	31 Aug 84
5.91i		Viktor	Ryzhenkov	UZB	25.8.66	2		San Sebastián	15 Mar 91
5.91A		Riaan	Botha	RSA	8.11.70	1		Pretoria	2 Apr 97
5.91		Pawel	Wojciechowski	POL	6.6.89	1		Szczecin	15 Aug 11
5.90		Pierre	Quinon	FRA	20.2.62	2	Nik	Nice	16 Jul 85
5.90i		Ferenc	Salbert	HUN/FRA	5.8.60	1	Mast	Grenoble	14 Mar 87
5.90		Miroslaw	Chmara	POL	9.5.64	1	BNP	Villeneuve d'Ascq	27 Jun 88
5.90i		Grigoriy	Yegorov	KAZ	12.1.67	1		Yokohama	11 Mar 90
5.90		Denis	Petushinskiy ¶	RUS	28.6.67	1	Znam	Moskva	13 Jun 93
5.90i		Pyotr	Bochkaryov	RUS	3.11.67	1	EI	Paris (B)	12 Mar 94
		(40)							
5.90		Jacob	Davis	USA	29.4.78	1	TexR	Austin	4 Apr 98
5.90		Viktor	Chistyakov	RUS/AUS	9.2.75	1		Salamanca	15 Jul 99

Mark	Wind	Name		Nat	Born	Pos	Meet	Venue	Date
5.90		Pavel	Gerasimov	RUS	29.5.79	1		Rüdlingen	12 Aug 00
5.90		Nick	Hysong	USA	9.12.71	1	OG	Sydney	29 Sep 00
5.90		Giuseppe	Gibilisco	ITA	5.1.79	1	WCh	Saint-Denis	28 Aug 03
5.90i		Igor	Pavlov	RUS	18.7.79	1	EI	Madrid	5 Mar 05
5.90i		Björn	Otto	GER	16.10.77	1	NC	Leipzig	17 Feb 07
5.90	sq	Malte	Mohr	GER	24.7.86	1		Aachen	1 Sep 10
5.90		Lázaro	Borges	CUB	19.6.86	2	WCh	Daegu	29 Aug 11
5.90i		Dmitriy	Starodubtsev	RUS	3.1.86	1		Chelyabinsk	18 Dec 11
		(50)							

100th man 5.80, 200th 5.70, 300th 5.65, 400th 5.60, 500th 5.52

Best outdoor marks for athletes with lifetime bests indoors

6.01	Lavillenie	1	ET	Leiria	21 Jun 09	5.98	Galfione	1		Amiens	23 Jul 99
6.00	Gataullin	1		Tokyo	16 Sep 89	5.93	Ecker	1		Ingolstadt	26 Jul 98
6.00	Hooker	1		Perth	27 Jan 08	5.90	Yegorov	2	WCh	Stuttgart	19 Aug 93

Ancillary jump: 6.05i Bubka   13 Feb 93

Outdoors on built-up runway: 5.90 Pyotr Bochkaryov RUS 3.11.67 1   Karlskrona   28 Jun 96

Exhibition or Market Square competitions

Mark		Name		Nat	Born	Pos		Venue	Date
6.00		Jean	Galfione	FRA	9.6.71	1		Besançon	23 May 97
5.95		Viktor	Chistiakov	RUS/AUS	9.2.75	1		Chiari	8 Sep 99

LONG JUMP

Mark	Wind	Name		Nat	Born	Pos	Meet	Venue	Date
8.95 WR	0.3	Mike	Powell	USA	10.11.63	1	WCh	Tokyo	30 Aug 91
8.90A WR	2.0	Bob	Beamon	USA	29.8.46	1	OG	Ciudad de México	18 Oct 68
8.87	-0.2	Carl	Lewis	USA	1.7.61	*	WCh	Tokyo	30 Aug 91
8.86A	1.9	Robert	Emmiyan	ARM	16.2.65	1		Tsakhkadzor	22 May 87
8.79	1.9		Lewis			1	TAC	Indianapolis	19 Jun 83
8.79i	-		Lewis			1		New York	27 Jan 84
8.76	1.0		Lewis			1	USOF	Indianapolis	24 Jul 82
8.76	0.8		Lewis			1	NC/OT	Indianapolis	18 Jul 88
8.75	1.7		Lewis			1	PAm	Indianapolis	16 Aug 87
8.74	1.4	Larry	Myricks ¶	USA	10.3.56	2	NC/OT	Indianapolis	18 Jul 88
8.74A	2.0	Erick	Walder	USA	5.11.71	1		El Paso	2 Apr 94
8.74	1.2	Dwight	Phillips	USA	1.10.77	1	Pre	Eugene	7 Jun 09
8.73	1.2	Irving	Saladino	PAN	23.1.83	1	FBK	Hengelo	24 May 08
8.72	-0.2		Lewis			1	OG	Seoul	26 Sep 88
8.71	-0.4		Lewis			1	Pepsi	Los Angeles (Ww)	13 May 84
8.71	0.1		Lewis			1	OT	Los Angeles	19 Jun 84
8.71	1.9	Iván	Pedroso	CUB	17.12.72	1		Salamanca	18 Jul 95
8.71i		Sebastian	Bayer (10)	GER	11.6.86	1	EI	Torino	8 Mar 09
8.70	0.8		Myricks			1	NC	Houston	17 Jun 89
8.70	0.7		Powell			1		Salamanca	27 Jul 93
8.70	1.6		Pedroso			1	WCh	Göteborg	12 Aug 95
8.68	1.0		Lewis			Q	OG	Barcelona	5 Aug 92
8.68	1.6		Pedroso			1		Lisboa	17 Jun 95
8.67	0.4		Lewis			1	WCh	Roma	5 Sep 87
8.67	-0.7		Lewis			1	OG	Barcelona	6 Aug 92
8.66	0.8		Lewis			*	MSR	Walnut	26 Apr 87
8.66	1.0		Myricks			1		Tokyo	23 Sep 87
8.66	0.9		Powell			1	BNP	Villeneuve d'Ascq	29 Jun 90
8.66A	1.4		Lewis			*		Sestriere	31 Jul 94
8.66	0.3		Pedroso			1		Linz	22 Aug 95
8.66	1.6	Loúis	Tsátoumas	GRE	12.2.82	1		Kalamáta	2 Jun 07
		(31/11)							
8.63	0.5	Kareem	Streete-Thompson	CAY/USA	30.3.73	1	GP II	Linz	4 Jul 94
8.62	0.7	James	Beckford	JAM	9.1.75	1		Orlando	5 Apr 97
8.59i		Miguel	Pate	USA	13.6.79	1	NC	New York	1 Mar 02
8.56i	-	Yago	Lamela	ESP	24.7.77	2	WI	Maebashi	7 Mar 99
8.54	0.9	Lutz	Dombrowski	GDR	25.6.59	1	OG	Moskva	28 Jul 80
8.54	1.7	Mitchell	Watt	AUS	25.3.88	1	DNG	Stockholm	29 Jul 11
8.53	1.2	Jaime	Jefferson	CUB	17.1.62	1	Barr	La Habana	12 May 90
8.52	0.7	Savanté	Stringfellow	USA	6.11.78	1	NC	Stanford	21 Jun 02
8.51	1.7	Roland	McGhee	USA	15.10.71	2		São Paulo	14 May 95
		(20)							
8.50	0.2	Llewellyn	Starks	USA	10.2.67	2		Rhede	7 Jul 91
8.50	1.3	Godfrey Khotso	Mokoena	RSA	6.3.85	2	GP	Madrid	4 Jul 09
8.49	2.0	Melvin	Lister	USA	29.8.77	1	SEC	Baton Rouge	13 May 00
8.49	0.6	Jai	Taurima	AUS	26.6.72	2	OG	Sydney	28 Sep 00
8.48	0.8	Joe	Greene	USA	17.2.67	3		São Paulo	14 May 95
8.48	0.6	Mohamed Salim	Al-Khuwalidi	KSA	19.6.81	1		Sotteville-lès-Rouen	2 Jul 06
8.47	1.9	Kevin	Dilworth	USA	14.2.74	1		Abilene	9 May 96

Mark	Wind	Name		Nat	Born	Pos	Meet	Venue	Date
8.47	0.9	John	Moffitt	USA	12.12.80	2	OG	Athína	26 Aug 04
8.47	-0.2	Andrew	Howe	ITA	12.5.85	2	WCh	Osaka	30 Aug 07
8.47	1.6	Christian	Reif	GER	24.10.84	1	EC	Barcelona	1 Aug 10
		(30)							
8.46	1.2	Leonid	Voloshin	RUS	30.3.66	1	NC	Tallinn	5 Jul 88
8.46	1.6	Mike	Conley	USA	5.10.62	2		Springfield	4 May 96
8.46	1.8	Cheikh Tidiane	Touré	SEN/FRA	25.1.70	1		Bad Langensalza	15 Jun 97
8.46	0.3	Ibrahin	Camejo	CUB	28.6.82	1		Bilbao	21 Jun 08
8.45	2.0	Nenad	Stekic	YUG	7.3.51	1	PO	Montreal	25 Jul 75
8.44	1.7	Eric	Metcalf	USA	23.1.68	1	NC	Tampa	17 Jun 88
8.43	0.8	Jason	Grimes	USA	10.9.59	*	NC	Indianapolis	16 Jun 85
8.43	1.8	Giovanni	Evangelisti	ITA	11.9.61	1		San Giovanni Valdarno	16 May 87
8.43i	-	Stanislav	Tarasenko	RUS	23.7.66	1		Moskva	26 Jan 94
8.43	0.1	Luis Felipe	Méliz	CUB/ESP	11.8.79	2	OD	Jena	3 Jun 00
		(40)							
8.43	-0.2	Ignisious	Gaisah	GHA	20.6.83	2	GGala	Roma	14 Jul 06
8.42	0.4	Salim	Sdiri	FRA	26.10.78	1		Pierre-Bénite	12 Jun 09
8.41	1.5	Craig	Hepburn	BAH	10.12.69	1	NC	Nassau	17 Jun 93
8.41i	-	Kirill	Sosunov	RUS	1.11.75	2	WI	Paris (B)	8 Mar 97
8.40	1.4	Douglas de	Souza	BRA	6.8.72	1		São Paulo	15 Feb 95
8.40	0.4	Robert	Howard	USA	26.11.75	1	SEC	Auburn	17 May 97
8.40	2.0	Gregor	Cankar	SLO	25.1.75	1		Celje	18 May 97
8.40	0.0		Lao Jianfeng	CHN	24.5.75	1	NC	Zhaoqing	28 May 97
8.40	1.0	Yahya	Berrabah	MAR	13.10.81	1	Franc	Beirut	2 Oct 09
8.40	0.5	Fabrice	Lapierre	AUS	17.10.83	1		Nuoro	14 Jul 10
8.40	0.0	Ngonidzashe	Makusha	ZIM	11.3.87	1	NCAA	Des Moines	9 Jun 11
		(51)	100th man 8.31, 200th 8.22, 300th 8.16, 400th 8.11, 500th 8.08						

Best at low altitude: 8.61 1.3 Emmiyan 1 GWG Moskva 6 Jul 86   8.58 1.8 Walder 1 Springfield 4 May 86

Wind-assisted marks performances to 8.70, performers to 8.42

Mark	Wind	Name		Nat	Born	Pos	Meet	Venue	Date
8.99A	4.4	Mike	Powell	USA	10.11.63	1		Sestriere	21 Jul 92
8.96A	1.2+	Iván	Pedroso	CUB	17.12.72	1		Sestriere	29 Jul 95
8.95A	3.9		Powell			1		Sestriere	31 Jul 94
8.91	2.9	Carl	Lewis	USA	1.7.61	2	WCh	Tokyo	30 Aug 91
8.90	3.7		Powell			1	S&W	Modesto	16 May 92
8.79	3.0		Pedroso			1	Barr	La Habana	21 May 92
8.78	3.1	Fabrice	Lapierre	AUS	17.10.83	1	NC	Perth	18 Apr 10
8.77	3.9		Lewis			1	Pepsi	Los Angeles (Ww)	18 May 85
8.77	3.4		Lewis			1	MSR	Walnut	26 Apr 87
8.73	4.6		Lewis			Q	NC	Sacramento	19 Jun 81
8.73	3.2		Lewis			Q	NC	Indianapolis	17 Jun 83
8.73A	2.6		Powell			1		Sestriere	31 Jul 91
8.73	4.8		Pedroso			1		Madrid	20 Jun 95
8.72	2.2		Lewis			1	NYG	New York	24 May 92
8.72A	3.9		Lewis			2		Sestriere	31 Jul 94
8.70	2.5		Pedroso			1		Padova	16 Jul 95
8.68	4.9	James	Beckford	JAM	9.1.75	1	JUCO	Odessa, Tx	19 May 95
8.66A	4.0	Joe	Greene	USA	17.2.67	2		Sestriere	21 Jul 92
8.64	3.5	Kareem	Streete-Thompson	CAY/USA	30.3.73	2	NC	Knoxville	18 Jun 94
8.63	3.9	Mike	Conley	USA	5.10.62	2	NC	Eugene	20 Jun 86
8.57	5.2	Jason	Grimes	USA	10.9.59	1	vFRG,AFR	Durham	27 Jun 82
8.53	4.9	Kevin	Dilworth	USA	14.2.74	1		Fort-de-France	27 Apr 02
8.51	3.7	Ignisious	Gaisah	GHA	20.6.83	1	AfCh	Bambous	9 Aug 06
8.49	2.6	Ralph	Boston	USA	9.5.39	1	FOT	Los Angeles	12 Sep 64
8.49	4.5	Stanislav	Tarasenko	RUS	23.7.66	2		Madrid	20 Jun 95
8.48	2.8	Kirill	Sosunov	RUS	1.11.75	1		Oristano	18 Sep 95
8.48	3.4	Peter	Burge	AUS	3.7.74	1		Gold Coast (RB)	10 Sep 00
8.48	2.1	Brian	Johnson	USA	25.3.80	1	Conseil	Fort-de-France	8 May 08
8.46	3.4	Randy	Williams	USA	23.8.53	1		Eugene	18 May 73
8.46		Vernon	George	USA	6.10.64	1		Houston	21 May 89
8.44		Keith	Talley	USA	28.1.64	Q		Odessa, Tx	16 May 85
8.42		Anthony	Bailous	USA	6.4.65	Q		Odessa, Tx	16 May 85
8.42A	4.5	Milan	Gombala	CZE	29.1.68	3		Sestriere	21 Jul 92

Exhibition: 8.46 Yuriy Naumkin RUS 4.11.68 1 Iglesias 6 Sep 96

Best outdoors
8.56 1.3 Lamela 1 Torino 24 Jun 99   8.49 1.6 Bayer 1 NC Ulm 4 Jul 09
8.46A 0.0 Pate 1 Cd. de México 3 May 03 and 8.45 1.5 2 NC Stanford 21 Jun 02, 8.48w 5.6 1 Fort Worth 21 Apr 01

Ancillary marks – other marks during series (to 8.67/8.70)

8.84	1.7	Lewis	30 Aug 91	8.68	0.0	Lewis	30 Aug 91	8.84Aw	3.8	Powell	21 Jul 92
8.71	0.6	Lewis	19 Jun 83	8.67	-0.2	Lewis	5 Sep 87	8.83w	2.3	Lewis	30 Aug 91
8.68	0.3	Lewis	18 Jul 88	8.89Aw	2.4	Pedroso	29 Jul 95	8.80Aw	4.0	Powell	21 Jul 92

Mark	Wind	Name		Nat	Born	Pos	Meet	Venue	Date
8.78Aw		Powell	21 Jul 92				8.75Aw 3.4	Powell	21 Jul 92
8.75w	2.1	Lewis	16 Aug 87				8.73w 2.4	Lewis	18 May 85

Mark		Powell	Date
8.73w		Powell	16 May 92
8.71Aw		Powell	31 Jul 91

TRIPLE JUMP

Mark	Wind	Name		Nat	Born	Pos	Meet	Venue	Date
18.29 WR	1.3	Jonathan	Edwards	GBR	10.5.66	1	WCh	Göteborg	7 Aug 95
18.09	-0.4	Kenny	Harrison	USA	13.2.65	1	OG	Atlanta	27 Jul 96
18.01	0.4		Edwards			1	Bisl	Oslo	9 Jul 98
18.00	1.3		Edwards			1	McD	London (CP)	27 Aug 95
17.99	0.5		Edwards			1	EC	Budapest	23 Aug 98
17.98 WR	1.8		Edwards			1		Salamanca	18 Jul 95
17.98	1.2	Teddy	Tamgho	FRA	15.6.89	1	DL	New York	12 Jun 10
17.97 WR	1.5	Willie	Banks	USA	11.3.56	1	TAC	Indianapolis	16 Jun 85
17.96	0.1	Christian	Taylor	USA	18.6.90	1	WCh	Daegu	4 Sep 11
17.93	1.6		Harrison			1	DNG	Stockholm	2 Jul 90
17.92	1.6	Khristo	Markov	BUL	27.1.65	1	WCh	Roma	31 Aug 87
17.92	1.9	James	Beckford	JAM	9.1.75	1	JUCO	Odessa, TX	20 May 95
17.92i WIR	-		Tamgho			1	EI	Paris (Bercy)	6 Mar 11
17.92	0.7		Edwards			1	WCh	Edmonton	6 Aug 01
17.91i WIR	-		Tamgho			1	NC	Aubière	20 Feb 11
17.91	1.4		Tamgho			1	Athl	Lausanne	30 Jun 11
17.90	1.0	Vladimir	Inozemtsev	UKR	25.5.64	1	PTS	Bratislava	20 Jun 90
17.90	0.4	Jadel	Gregório	BRA	16.9.80	1	GP	Belém	20 May 07
17.90i			Tamgho			1	WI	Doha	14 Mar 10
17.89A WR	0.0	João Carlos	de Oliveira (10)	BRA	28.5.54	1	PAm	Ciudad de México	15 Oct 75
17.88	0.9		Edwards			2	OG	Atlanta	27 Jul 96
17.87	1.7	Mike	Conley	USA	5.10.62	1	NC	San José	27 Jun 87
17.86	1.3	Charles	Simpkins	USA	19.10.63	1	WUG	Kobe	2 Sep 85
17.86	0.3		Conley			1	WCh	Stuttgart	16 Aug 93
17.86	0.7		Edwards			1	CG	Manchester	28 Jul 02
17.85	0.9	Yoelbi	Quesada	CUB	4.8.73	1	WCh	Athína	8 Aug 97
17.84	0.7		Conley			1		Bad Cannstatt	4 Jul 93
17.83i WIR	-	Aliecer	Urrutia	CUB	22.9.74	1		Sindelfingen	1 Mar 97
17.83i WIR	-	Christian	Olsson	SWE	25.1.80	1	WI	Budapest	7 Mar 04
17.82	1.6		Edwards			1	WG	Helsinki	25 Jun 96
		(30/15)							
17.81	1.0	Marian	Oprea	ROU	6.6.82	1	Athl	Lausanne	5 Jul 05
17.81	0.1	Phillips	Idowu	GBR	30.12.78	1	EC	Barcelona	29 Jul 10
17.78	1.0	Nikolay	Musiyenko	UKR	16.12.59	1	Znam	Leningrad	7 Jun 86
17.78	0.6	Lázaro	Betancourt ¶	CUB	18.3.63	1	Barr	La Habana	15 Jun 86
17.78	0.8	Melvin	Lister	USA	29.8.77	1	NC/OT	Sacramento	17 Jul 04
		(20)							
17.77	1.0	Aleksandr	Kovalenko	RUS	8.5.63	1	NC	Bryansk	18 Jul 87
17.77i	-	Leonid	Voloshin	RUS	30.3.66	1		Grenoble	6 Feb 94
17.75	0.3	Oleg	Protsenko	RUS	11.8.63	1	Znam	Moskva	10 Jun 90
17.74	1.4	Nelson	Évora	POR	20.4.84	1	WCh	Osaka	27 Aug 07
17.73i		Walter	Davis	USA	2.7.79	1	WI	Moskva	12 Mar 06
17.73i	-	Fabrizio	Donato	ITA	14.8.76	2	EI	Paris (Bercy)	6 Mar 11
17.72i		Brian	Wellman	BER	8.9.67	1	WI	Barcelona	12 Mar 95
17.72	1.3	Sheryf	El-Sheryf	UKR	2.1.89	1	EU23	Ostrava	17 Jul 11
17.69	1.5	Igor	Lapshin	BLR	8.8.63	1		Stayki	31 Jul 88
17.69i		Yoandri	Betanzos	CUB	15.2.82	2	WI	Doha	14 Mar 10
		(30)							
17.68	0.4	Danil	Burkenya	RUS	20.7.78	1	NC	Tula	31 Jul 04
17.68A	1.6	Alexis	Copello	CUB	12.8.85	1		Ávila	17 Jul 11
17.66	1.7	Ralf	Jaros	GER	13.12.65	1	ECp	Frankfurt-am-Main	30 Jun 91
17.65	1.0	Aleksandr	Yakovlev	UKR	8.9.57	1	Znam	Moskva	6 Jun 87
17.65	0.8	Denis	Kapustin	RUS	5.10.70	2	Bisl	Oslo	9 Jul 98
17.65	0.1	Alexis	Copello	CUB	12.8.85	1	Barr/NC	La Habana	30 May 09
17.64	1.4	Nathan	Douglas	GBR	4.12.82	1	NC	Manchester (SC)	10 Jul 05
17.63	0.9	Kenta	Bell	USA	16.3.77	1c2	MSR	Walnut	21 Apr 02
17.62i	-	Yoel	García	CUB	25.11.73	2		Sindelfingen	1 Mar 97
17.62	-0.2	Arne David	Girat	CUB	26.8.84	3	ALBA	La Habana	25 Apr 09
17.60	0.6	Vladimir	Plekhanov	RUS	11.4.58	2	NC	Leningrad	4 Aug 85
		(40)							
17.59i	-	Pierre	Camara	FRA	10.9.65	1	WI	Toronto	13 Mar 93
17.59	0.3	Vasiliy	Sokov	RUS	7.4.68	1	NC	Moskva	19 Jun 93
17.59	0.8	Charles	Friedek	GER	26.8.71	1		Hamburg	23 Jul 97
17.59	0.9	Leevan	Sands	BAH	16.8.81	3	OG	Beijing	21 Aug 08
17.59	0.0		Li Yanxi	CHN	26.6.84	1	NG	Jinan	26 Oct 09
17.58	1.5	Oleg	Sakirkin	KZK	23.1.66	2	NC	Gorkiy	23 Jul 89

Mark	Wind	Name		Nat	Born	Pos	Meet	Venue	Date
17.58	1.6	Aarik	Wilson	USA	25.10.82	1	LGP	London (CP)	3 Aug 07
17.57A	0.0	Keith	Connor	GBR	16.9.57	1	NCAA	Provo	5 Jun 82
17.57	0.2	Dmitriy	Valyukevich/Valukevic	BLR/SVK	31.5.81	1	EU23	Bydgoszcz	19 Jul 03
17.56	1.9	Maris	Bruziks	LAT	25.8.62	1		Riga	3 Sep 88
	(50)		100th man 17.35, 200th 17.14, 300th 17.00, 400th 16.86, 500th 16.75						

Wind-assisted marks – performances to 17.86, performers to 17.58

Mark	Wind	Name		Nat	Born	Pos	Meet	Venue	Date
18.43	2.4	Jonathan	Edwards	GBR	10.5.66	1	ECp	Villeneuve d'Ascq	25 Jun 95
18.20	5.2	Willie	Banks	USA	11.3.56	1	NC/OT	Indianpolis	16 Jul 88
18.17	2.1	Mike	Conley	USA	5.10.62	1	OG	Barcelona	3 Aug 92
18.08	2.5		Edwards			1	BrGP	Sheffield	23 Jul 95
18.03	2.9		Edwards			1	GhG	Gateshead	2 Jul 95
18.01	3.7		Harrison			1	NC	Atlanta	15 Jun 96
17.97	7.5	Yoelbi	Quesada	CUB	4.8.73	1		Madrid	20 Jun 95
17.93	5.2	Charles	Simpkins	USA	19.10.63	2	NC/OT	Indianpolis	16 Jul 88
17.92	3.4	Christian	Olsson	SWE	25.1.80	1	GP	Gateshead	13 Jul 03
17.91	3.2		Simpkins			1	NC	Eugene	21 Jun 86
17.86	3.9		Simpkins			1	NC/OT	New Orleans	21 Jun 92
17.86	5.7	Denis	Kapustin	RUS	5.10.70	1		Sevilla	5 Jun 94
17.82	2.5	Nelson	Évora	POR	20.4.84	1	NC	Seixal	26 Jul 09
17.81	4.6	Keith	Connor	GBR	16.9.57	1	CG	Brisbane	9 Oct 82
17.76A	2.2	Kenta	Bell	USA	16.3.77	1		El Paso	10 Apr 04
17.75		Gennadiy	Valyukevich	BLR	1.6.58	1		Uzhgorod	27 Apr 86
17.75	7.1	Brian	Wellman	BER	8.9.67	2		Madrid	20 Jun 95
17.73	4.1	Vasiliy	Sokov	RUS	7.4.68	1		Riga	3 Jun 89
17.69	3.9	Alexis	Copello	CUB	12.8.85	1	ALBA	La Habana	25 Apr 09
17.63	4.3	Robert	Cannon	USA	9.7.58	3	NC/OT	Indianpolis	16 Jul 88
17.62	2.9	Will	Claye	USA	13.6.91	2	NCAA	Des Moines	11 Jun 11
17.59	2.1	Jerome	Romain	DMA/FRA	12.6.71	3	WCh	Göteborg	7 Aug 95
17.58	5.2	Al	Joyner	USA	19.1.60	5	NC/OT	Indianpolis	16 Jul 88

Best outdoor marks for athletes with indoor bests

17.79	1.4	Olsson	1	OG	Athína	22 Aug 04		17.65	1.4	Betanzos	2	ALBA	La Habana	25 Apr 09
17.75	1.0	Voloshin	2	WCh	Tokyo	26 Aug 91		17.67w	5.4		1		Bilbao	1 Jul 06
17.71	-0.7	Davis	1	NC	Indianapolis	25 Jun 06		17.62A	0.1	Wellman	1		El Paso	15 Apr 95
17.70	1.7	Urrutia	1	GP II	Sevilla	6 Jun 96		17.60	1.9	Donato	1		Milano	7 Jun 00

:ow altitude best: 17.65 0.1 Copello 1 Barr La Habana 30 May 09

Ancillary marks – other marks during series (to 17.78/17.84w)

18.16 WR	1.3	Edwards	7 Aug 95		17.84	1.7	Tamgho	12 Jun 10		18.06w	4.9	Banks	16 Jul 88
										17.90w	2.5	Edwards	25 Jun 95
17.99	0.1	Harrison	27 Jul 96		18.39w	3.7	Edwards	25 Jun 95		17.84w	2.1	Edwards	23 Aug 98

SHOT

Mark	Wind	Name		Nat	Born	Pos	Meet	Venue	Date
23.12 WR		Randy	Barnes ¶	USA	16.6.66	1		Los Angeles (Ww)	20 May 90
23.10			Barnes			1	Jenner	San José	26 May 90
23.06 WR		Ulf	Timmermann	GDR	1.11.62	1	Veniz	Haniá	22 May 88
22.91 WR		Alessandro	Andrei	ITA	3.1.59	1		Viareggio	12 Aug 87
22.86		Brian	Oldfield	USA	1.6.45	1	ITA	El Paso	10 May 75
22.75		Werner	Günthör	SUI	1.6.61	1		Bern	23 Aug 88
22.67		Kevin	Toth ¶	USA	29.12.67	1	KansR	Lawrence	19 Apr 03
22.66i			Barnes			1	Sunkist	Los Angeles	20 Jan 89
22.64 WR		Udo	Beyer	GDR	9.8.55	1		Berlin	20 Aug 86
22.62 WR			Timmermann			1		Berlin	22 Sep 85
22.61			Timmermann			1		Potsdam	8 Sep 88
22.60			Timmermann			1	vURS	Tallinn	21 Jun 86
22.56			Timmermann			1		Berlin	13 Sep 88
22.55i			Timmermann			1	NC	Senftenberg	11 Feb 89
22.54		Christian	Cantwell	USA	30.9.80	1	GP II	Gresham	5 Jun 04
22.52		John	Brenner	USA	4.1.61	1	MSR	Walnut	26 Apr 87
22.51			Timmermann			1		Erfurt	1 Jun 86
22.51		Adam	Nelson (10)	USA	7.7.75	1		Gresham	18 May 02
22.47			Timmermann			1		Dresden	17 Aug 86
22.47			Günthör			1	WG	Helsinki	2 Jul 87
22.47			Timmermann			1	OG	Seoul	23 Sep 88
22.45			Oldfield			1	ITA	El Paso	22 May 76
22.45			Cantwell			1	GP	Gateshead	11 Jun 06
22.43			Günthör			1	v3-N	Lüdenscheid	18 Jun 87
22.43		Reese	Hoffa	USA	8.10.77	1	LGP	London (CP)	3 Aug 07
22.42			Barnes			1	WK	Zürich	17 Aug 88
22.41			Cantwell			1	Pre	Eugene	3 Jul 10
22.40			Barnes			1		Rüdlingen	13 Jul 96
22.40i			Nelson			1		Fayetteville	15 Feb 08

Mark	Wind	Name		Nat	Born	Pos	Meet	Venue	Date
22.39			Barnes			2	OG	Seoul	23 Sep 88
	(30/11)								
22.24		Sergey	Smirnov	RUS	17.9.60	2	vGDR	Tallinn	21 Jun 86
22.21		Dylan	Armstrong	CAN	15.1.81	1	NC	Calgary	25 Jun 11
22.20		John	Godina	USA	31.5.72	1		Carson	22 May 05
22.10		Sergey	Gavryushin	RUS	27.6.59	1		Tbilisi	31 Aug 86
22.10		Cory	Martin	USA	22.5.85	1		Tucson	22 May 10
22.10		Andrey	Mikhnevich ¶	BLR	12.7.76	1		Minsk	11 Aug 11
22.09		Sergey	Kasnauskas	BLR	20.4.61	1		Stayki	23 Aug 84
22.09i		Mika	Halvari	FIN	13.2.70	1		Tampere	7 Feb 00
22.02i		George	Woods	USA	11.2.43	1	LAT	Inglewood	8 Feb 74
	(20)								
22.02		Dave	Laut	USA	21.12.56	1		Koblenz	25 Aug 82
22.00 WR		Aleksandr	Baryshnikov	RUS	11.11.48	1	vFRA	Colombes	10 Jul 76
21.98		Gregg	Tafralis ¶	USA	9.4.58	1		Los Gatos	13 Jun 92
21.97		Janus	Robberts	RSA	10.3.79	1	NCAA	Eugene	2 Jun 01
21.97		Ryan	Whiting	USA	24.11.86	1	NCAA	Eugene	12 Jun 10
21.96		Mikhail	Kostin	RUS	10.5.59	1		Vitebsk	20 Jul 86
21.95		Tomasz	Majewski	POL	30.8.81	1	DNG	Stockholm	30 Jul 09
21.93		Remigius	Machura ¶	CZE	3.7.60	1		Praha	23 Aug 87
21.92		Carl	Myerscough ¶	GBR	21.10.79	1	NCAA	Sacramento	13 Jun 03
21.87		C.J.	Hunter ¶	USA	14.12.68	2	NC	Sacramento	15 Jul 00
	(30)								
21.85 WR		Terry	Albritton	USA	14.1.55	1		Honolulu	21 Feb 76
21.83i		Aleksandr	Bagach ¶	UKR	21.11.66	1		Brovary	21 Feb 99
21.82 WR		Al	Feuerbach	USA	14.1.48	1		San José	5 May 73
21.82		Andy	Bloom	USA	11.8.73	1	GPF	Doha	5 Oct 00
21.81		Yuriy	Belonog	UKR	9.3.74	1	NC	Kiev	3 Jul 03
21.78 WR		Randy	Matson	USA	5.3.45	1		College Station	22 Apr 67
21.78		Dan	Taylor	USA	12.5.82	1		Tucson	23 May 09
21.78		David	Storl	GER	27.7.90	1	WCh	Daegu	2 Sep 11
21.77i		Mike	Stulce ¶	USA	21.7.69	1	v GBR	Birmingham	13 Feb 93
21.77		Dragan	Peric	YUG	8.5.64	1		Bar	25 Apr 98
	(40)								
21.76		Michael	Carter	USA	29.10.60	2	NCAA	Eugene	2 Jun 84
21.74		Janis	Bojars	LAT	12.5.56	1		Riga	14 Jul 84
21.73		Augie	Wolf ¶	USA	3.9.61	1		Leverkusen	12 Apr 84
21.69		Reijo	Ståhlberg	FIN	21.9.52	1	WCR	Fresno	5 May 79
21.68		Geoff	Capes	GBR	23.8.49	1	4-N	Cwmbrân	18 May 80
21.68		Edward	Sarul	POL	16.11.58	1		Sopot	31 Jul 83
21.67		Hartmut	Briesenick	GDR	17.3.49	1		Potsdam	1 Sep 73
21.63i		Joachim	Olsen	DEN	31.5.77	1		Tallinn	25 Feb 04
21.63		Maris	Urtans	LAT	9.2.81	1	ET-2	Beograd	19 Jun 10
21.62		Rutger	Smith	NED	9.7.81	1		Leiden	10 Jun 06

(50) 100th man 21.09, 200th 20.63, 300th 20.26, 400th 19.99, 500th 19.77

Not recognised by GDR authorities

Mark	Wind	Name		Nat	Born	Pos	Meet	Venue	Date
22.11		Rolf	Oesterreich	GDR	24.8.49	1		Zschopau	12 Sep 76

Drugs disqualification

Mark	Wind	Name		Nat	Born	Pos	Meet	Venue	Date
22.84			Barnes			1		Malmö	7 Aug 90
21.82		Mike	Stulce ¶	USA	21.7.69	1		Brenham	9 May 90

Best outdoor marks for athletes with lifetime bests indoors

21.70	Stulce ¶	1	OG	Barcelona	31 Jul 92		21.61	Olsen		1		Köbenhavn	13 Jun 07
21.63	Woods	2	CalR	Modesto	22 May 76								

Ancillary marks – other marks during series (to 22.45)

22.84 WR	Andrei	12 Aug 87	22.72 WR	Andrei	12 Aug 87	22.55	Barnes	20 May 90
22.76	Barnes	20 May 90	22.70	Günthör	23 Aug 88	22.49	Nelson	18 May 02
22.74	Andrei	12 Aug 87	22.58	Beyer	20 Aug 86	22.45	Timmermann	22 May 88

DISCUS

Mark	Wind	Name		Nat	Born	Pos	Meet	Venue	Date
74.08 WR		Jürgen	Schult	GDR	11.5.60	1		Neubrandenburg	6 Jun 86
73.88		Virgilijus	Alekna	LTU	13.2.72	1	NC	Kaunas	3 Aug 00
73.38		Gerd	Kanter	EST	6.5.79	1		Helsingborg	4 Sep 06
72.02			Kanter			1eA		Salinas	3 May 07
71.88			Kanter			1eA		Salinas	8 May 08
71.86 WR		Yuriy	Dumchev	RUS	5.8.58	1		Moskva	29 May 83
71.70		Róbert	Fazekas ¶	HUN	18.8.75	1		Szombathely	14 Jul 02
71.64			Kanter			1		Kohila	25 Jun 09
71.56			Alekna			1		Kaunas	25 Jul 07
71.50		Lars	Riedel	GER	28.6.67	1		Wiesbaden	3 May 97
71.45			Kanter			1		Chula Vista	29 Apr 10

Mark	Wind	Name		Nat	Born	Pos	Meet	Venue	Date
71.32		Ben	Plucknett ¶	USA	13.4.54	1	Pre	Eugene	4 Jun 83
71.26		John	Powell	USA	25.6.47	1	NC	San José	9 Jun 84
71.26		Rickard	Bruch	SWE	2.7.46	1		Malmö	15 Nov 84
71.26		Imrich	Bugár (10)	CZE	14.4.55	1	Jenner	San José	25 May 85
71.25			Fazekas			1	WCp	Madrid (C)	21 Sep 02
71.25			Alekna			1	Danek	Turnov	20 May 08
71.18		Art	Burns	USA	19.7.54	1		San José	19 Jul 83
71.16 WR		Wolfgang	Schmidt	GDR	16.1.54	1		Berlin	9 Aug 78
71.14			Plucknett			1		Berkeley	12 Jun 83
71.14		Anthony	Washington	USA	16.1.66	1eA		Salinas	22 May 96
71.12			Alekna			1	WK	Zürich	11 Aug 00
71.08			Alekna			1		Réthimno	21 Jul 06
71.06		Luis Mariano	Delís ¶	CUB	12.12.57	1	Barr	La Habana	21 May 83
71.06			Riedel			1	WK	Zürich	14 Aug 96
71.00			Bruch			1		Malmö	14 Oct 84
70.99			Alekna			1		Stellenbosch	30 Mar 01
70.98		Mac	Wilkins	USA	15.11.50	1	WG	Helsinki	9 Jul 80
70.98			Burns			1	Pre	Eugene	21 Jul 84
70.97			Alekna			1		Réthimno	23 Jun 04
		(30/15)							
70.82		Aleksander	Tammert	EST	2.2.73	1		Denton	15 Apr 06
70.54		Dmitriy	Shevchenko ¶	RUS	13.5.68	1		Krasnodar	7 May 02
70.38 WRu		Jay	Silvester	USA	27.8.37	1		Lancaster	16 May 71
70.32		Frantz	Kruger	RSA/FIN	22.5.75	1		Salon-de-Provence	26 May 02
70.06		Romas	Ubartas ¶	LTU	26.5.60	1		Smalininkay	8 May 88
		(20)							
70.00		Juan	Martínez ¶	CUB	17.5.58	2	Barr	La Habana	21 May 83
69.95		Zoltán	Kövágó	HUN	10.4.79	1		Salon-de-Provence	25 May 06
69.91		John	Godina	USA	31.5.72	1		Salinas	19 May 98
69.90		Jason	Young	USA	27.5.81	1		Lubbock	26 Mar 10
69.83		Piotr	Malachowski	POL	7.6.83	1		Gateshead	10 Jul 10
69.70		Géjza	Valent	CZE	3.10.53	2		Nitra	26 Aug 84
69.69		Robert	Harting	GER	18.10.84	1		Neubrandenburg	28 Aug 10
69.62		Knut	Hjeltnes ¶	NOR	8.12.51	2	Jen	San José	25 May 85
69.62		Timo	Tompuri	FIN	9.6.69	1		Helsingborg	8 Jul 01
69.50		Mario	Pestano	ESP	8.4.78	1	NC	Santa Cruz de Tenerife	27 Jul 08
		(30)							
69.46		Al	Oerter	USA	19.9.36	1	TFA	Wichita	31 May 80
69.44		Georgiy	Kolnootchenko	BLR	7.5.59	1	vUSA	Indianapolis	3 Jul 82
69.40		Art	Swarts ¶	USA	14.2.45	1		Scotch Plains	8 Dec 79
69.36		Mike	Buncic	USA	25.7.62	1		Fresno	6 Apr 91
69.32		Ehsan	Hadadi	IRI	21.1.85	1		Tallinn	3 Jun 08
69.28		Vladimir	Dubrovshchik	BLR	7.1.72	1	NC	Stayki	3 Jun 00
69.26		Ken	Stadel	USA	19.2.52	2	AAU	Walnut	16 Jun 79
68.94		Adam	Setliff	USA	15.12.69	1		Atascadero	25 Jul 01
68.91		Ian	Waltz	USA	15.4.77	1		Salinas	24 May 06
68.90		Jean-Claude	Retel	FRA	11.2.68	1		Salon-de-Provence	17 Jul 02
		(40)							
68.88		Vladimir	Zinchenko	UKR	25.7.59	1		Dnepropetrovsk	16 Jul 88
68.76		Jarred	Rome	USA	21.12.76	2cA		Chula Vista	6 Aug 11
68.64		Dmitriy	Kovtsun ¶	UKR	29.9.55	1		Riga	6 Jul 84
68.58		Attila	Horváth	HUN	28.7.67	1		Budapest	24 Jun 94
68.52		Igor	Duginyets	UKR	20.5.56	1	NC	Kyiv	21 Aug 82
68.50		Armin	Lemme	GDR	28.10.55	1	vUSA	Karl-Marx-Stadt	10 Jul 82
68.49A		Casey	Malone	USA	6.4.77	1		Fort Collins	20 Jun 09
68.48 WR		John	van Reenen	RSA	26.3.47	1		Stellenbosch	14 Mar 75
68.44		Vaclovas	Kidykas	LTU	17.10.61	1		Sochi	1 Jun 88
68.30		Stefan	Fernholm	SWE	2.7.59	1		Västerås	15 Jul 87
		(50)	100th man 66.89, 200th 65.10, 300th 64.04, 400th 62.76, 500th 61.79						

Subsequent to or at drugs disqualification   ! recognised as US record

Mark	Wind	Name		Nat	Born	Pos	Meet	Venue	Date
72.34!		Ben	Plucknett ¶	USA	13.4.54	(1)	DNG	Stockholm	7 Jul 81
71.20			Plucknett			(1)	CalR	Modesto	16 May 81
70.84		Kamy	Keshmiri ¶	USA	23.1.69	(1)		Salinas	27 May 92

Sloping ground

Mark	Wind	Name		Nat	Born	Pos	Meet	Venue	Date
72.08		John	Powell	USA	25.6.47	1		Klagshamn	11 Sep 87
69.80		Stefan	Fernholm	SWE	2.7.59	1		Klagshamn	13 Aug 87
69.44		Adam	Setliff	USA	15.12.69	1		La Jolla	21 Jul 01
68.46		Andy	Bloom	USA	11.8.73	2cA		La Jolla	25 Mar 00

Ancillary marks – other marks during series (to 70.96)
72.35 Alekna 3 Aug 00   72.30 Kanter 4 Sep 06   71.08 Plucknett 4 Jun 83

Mark	Wind		Name	Nat	Born	Pos	Meet	Venue	Date
									HAMMER
86.74	WR	Yuriy	Sedykh	RUS	11.6.55	1	EC	Stuttgart	30 Aug 86
86.73		Ivan	Tikhon ¶	BLR	24.7.76	1	NC	Brest	3 Jul 05
86.66	WR		Sedykh			1	vGDR	Tallinn	22 Jun 86
86.34	WR		Sedykh			1		Cork	3 Jul 84
86.04		Sergey	Litvinov	RUS	23.1.58	1	OD	Dresden	3 Jul 86
85.74			Litvinov			2	EC	Stuttgart	30 Aug 86
85.68			Sedykh			1	BGP	Budapest	11 Aug 86
85.60			Sedykh			1	PTG	London (CP)	13 Jul 84
85.60			Sedykh			1	Drz	Moskva	17 Aug 84
85.20			Litvinov			2		Cork	3 Jul 84
85.14			Litvinov			1	PTG	London	11 Jul 86
85.14			Sedykh			1	Kuts	Moskva	4 Sep 88
85.02			Sedykh			1	BGP	Budapest	20 Aug 84
84.92			Sedykh			2	OD	Dresden	3 Jul 86
84.90		Vadim	Devyatovskiy ¶	BLR	20.3.77	1		Staiki	21 Jul 05
84.88			Litvinov			1	GP-GG	Roma	10 Sep 86
84.86		Koji	Murofushi	JPN	8.10.74	1	Odlozil	Praha	29 Jun 03
84.80			Litvinov			1	OG	Seoul	26 Sep 88
84.72			Sedykh			1	GWG	Moskva	9 Jul 86
84.64			Litvinov			2	GWG	Moskva	9 Jul 86
84.62		Igor	Astapkovich	BLR	4.1.63	1	Expo	Sevilla	6 Jun 92
84.60			Sedykh			1	8-N	Tokyo	14 Sep 84
84.58			Sedykh			1	Znam	Leningrad	8 Jun 86
84.51			Tikhon	BLR	24.7.76	1	NC	Grodno	9 Jul 08
84.48		Igor	Nikulin	RUS	14.8.60	1	Athl	Lausanne	12 Jul 90
84.46			Sedykh			1		Vladivostok	14 Sep 88
84.46			Tikhon			1		Minsk	7 May 04
84.40		Jüri	Tamm	EST	5.2.57	1		Banská Bystrica	9 Sep 84
84.36			Litvinov			2	vGDR	Tallinn	22 Jun 86
84.32			Tikhon			1		Staiki	8 Aug 03
		(30/8)							
84.19		Adrián	Annus ¶	HUN	28.6.73	1		Szombathely	10 Aug 03
83.68		Tibor	Gécsek ¶	HUN	22.9.64	1		Zalaegerszeg	19 Sep 98
		(10)							
83.46		Andrey	Abduvaliyev	TJK/UZB	30.6.66	1		Adler	26 May 90
83.43		Aleksey	Zagornyi	RUS	31.5.78	1		Adler	10 Feb 02
83.40	@	Ralf	Haber	GDR	18.8.62	1		Athína	16 May 88
82.54						1		Potsdam	9 Sep 88
83.38		Szymon	Ziółkowski	POL	1.7.76	1	WCh	Edmonton	5 Aug 01
83.30		Olli-Pekka	Karjalainen	FIN	7.3.80	1		Lahti	14 Jul 04
83.04		Heinz	Weis	GER	14.7.63	1	NC	Frankfurt	29 Jun 97
83.00		Balázs	Kiss	HUN	21.3.72	1	GP II	Saint-Denis	4 Jun 98
82.78		Karsten	Kobs	GER	16.9.71	1		Dortmund	26 Jun 99
82.64		Günther	Rodehau	GDR	6.7.59	1		Dresden	3 Aug 85
82.62		Sergey	Kirmasov ¶	RUS	25.3.70	1		Bryansk	30 May 98
		(20)		@ competitive meeting but unsanctioned by GDR federation					
82.62		Andrey	Skvaruk	UKR	9.3.67	1		Koncha-Zaspa	27 Apr 02
82.58		Primoz	Kozmus	SLO	30.9.79	1		Celje	2 Sep 09
82.54		Vasiliy	Sidorenko	RUS	1.5.61	1		Krasnodar	13 May 92
82.52		Lance	Deal	USA	21.8.61	1	GPF	Milano	7 Sep 96
82.45		Krisztián	Pars	HUN	18.2.82	1		Celje	13 Sep 06
82.40		Plamen	Minev	BUL	28.4.65	1	NM	Plovdiv	1 Jun 91
82.38		Gilles	Dupray	FRA	2.1.70	1		Chelles	21 Jun 00
82.28		Ilya	Konovalov ¶	RUS	4.3.71	1	NC	Tula	10 Aug 03
82.24		Benjaminas	Viluckis	LIT	20.3.61	1		Klaipeda	24 Aug 86
82.24		Vyacheslav	Korovin	RUS	8.9.62	1		Chelyabinsk	20 Jun 87
		(30)							
82.23		Vladislav	Piskunov ¶	UKR	7.6.78	2		Koncha-Zaspa	27 Apr 02
82.22		Holger	Klose	GER	5.12.72	1		Dortmund	2 May 98
82.16		Vitaliy	Alisevich	BLR	15.6.67	1		Parnu	13 Jul 88
82.08		Ivan	Tanev	BUL	1.5.57	1	NC	Sofia	3 Sep 88
82.00		Sergey	Alay	BLR	11.6.65	1		Stayki	12 May 92
81.88		Jud	Logan ¶	USA	19.7.59	1		State College	22 Apr 88
81.81		Libor	Charfreitag	SVK	11.9.77	3	Odlozil	Praha	29 Jun 03
81.79		Christophe	Épalle	FRA	23.1.69	1		Clermont-Ferrand	30 Jun 00
81.78		Christoph	Sahner	FRG	23.9.63	1		Wemmetsweiler	11 Sep 88
81.70		Aleksandr	Seleznyov	RUS	25.1.63	2		Sochi	22 May 93
		(40)							

Mark	Wind	Name		Nat	Born	Pos	Meet	Venue	Date
81.66		Aleksandr	Krykun	UKR	1.3.68	1		Kiev	29 May 04
81.64		Enrico	Sgrulletti	ITA	24.4.65	1		Ostia	9 Mar 97
81.56		Sergey	Gavrilov	RUS	22.5.70	1	Army	Rostov	16 Jun 96
81.56		Zsolt	Németh	HUN	9.11.71	1		Veszprém	14 Aug 99
81.52		Juha	Tiainen	FIN	5.12.55	1		Tampere	11 Jun 84
81.49		Valeriy	Svyatokho	BLR	20.7.81	1	NCp	Brest	27 May 06
81.45		Esref	Apak	TUR	3.1.82	1	Cezmi	Istanbul	4 Jun 05
81.44		Yuriy	Tarasyuk	BLR	11.4.57	1		Minsk	10 Aug 84
81.35		Wojciech	Kondratowicz	POL	18.4.80	1		Bydgosc999	13 Jul 03
81.33		Miloslav	Konopka	SVK	23.1.79	1		Banská Bystrica	29 May 04
	(50)		100th man 79.90, 200th 77.33, 300th 75.31, 400th 74.08, 500th 72.80						

Ancillary marks – other marks during series (to 84.85)

86.68	Sedykh	30 Aug 86	85.82	Sedykh	22 Jun 86	85.42	Litvinov	3 Jul 86	85.20	Sedykh	3 Jul 84
86.62	Sedykh	30 Aug 86	85.52	Sedykh	13 Jul 84	85.28	Sedykh	30 Aug 86	85.04	Sedykh	13 Jul 84
86.00	Sedykh	3 Jul 84	85.46	Sedykh	30 Aug 86	85.26	Sedykh	11 Aug 86	84.98	Sedykh	4 Sep 88
86.00	Sedykh	22 Jun 86	85.42	Sedykh	11 Aug 86	85.24	Sedykh	11 Aug 86	84.92	Litvinov	3 Jul 86

JAVELIN

Mark	Wind	Name		Nat	Born	Pos	Meet	Venue	Date
98.48 WR		Jan	Zelezny	CZE	16.6.66	1		Jena	25 May 96
95.66 WR			Zelezny			1	McD	Sheffield	29 Aug 93
95.54A WR			Zelezny			1		Pietersburg	6 Apr 93
94.64			Zelezny			1	GS	Ostrava	31 May 96
94.02			Zelezny			1		Stellenbosch	26 Mar 97
93.09		Aki	Parviainen	FIN	26.10.74	1		Kuortane	26 Jun 99
92.80			Zelezny			1	WCh	Edmonton	12 Aug 01
92.61		Sergey	Makarov	RUS	19.3.73	1		Sheffield	30 Jun 02
92.60		Raymond	Hecht	GER	11.11.68	1	Bisl	Oslo	21 Jul 95
92.42			Zelezny			1	GS	Ostrava	28 May 97
92.41			Parviainen			1	ECp-1A	Vaasa	24 Jun 01
92.28			Zelezny			1	GPF	Monaco	9 Sep 95
92.28			Hecht			1	WK	Zürich	14 Aug 96
92.12			Zelezny			1	McD	London (CP)	27 Aug 95
92.12			Zelezny			1	TOTO	Tokyo	15 Sep 95
91.82			Zelezny			1	McD	Sheffield	4 Sep 94
91.69		Kostadínos	Gatsioúdis	GRE	17.12.73	1		Kuortane	24 Jun 00
91.68			Zelezny			1	GP	Gateshead	1 Jul 94
91.59		Andreas	Thorkildsen	NOR	1.4.82	1	Bisl	Oslo	2 Jun 06
91.53		Tero	Pitkämäki	FIN	19.12.82	1		Kuortane	26 Jun 05
91.50			Zelezny			1	Kuso	Lublin	4 Jun 94
91.50A			Zelezny			1		Pretoria	8 Apr 96
91.50			Hecht			1		Gengenbach	1 Sep 96
91.46 WR		Steve	Backley	GBR	12.2.69	1		Auckland (NS)	25 Jan 92
91.40			Zelezny			1	BNP	Villeneuve d'Ascq	2 Jul 93
91.34			Zelezny			1		Cape Town	8 Apr 97
91.33			Pitkämäki			1	WAF	Monaco	10 Sep 05
91.31			Parviainen			2	WCh	Edmonton	12 Aug 01
91.30			Zelezny			1	ISTAF	Berlin	1 Sep 95
91.29		Breaux	Greer	USA	19.10.76	1	NC	Indianapolis	21 Jun 07
	(30/9)		71 over 90m (most: Zelezny 35, Parviainen 8, Hecht, Pitkämäki & Thorkildsen 6, Makarov 5)						
90.73		Vadims	Vasilevskis	LAT	5.1.82	1		Tallinn	22 Jul 07
	(10)								
90.60		Seppo	Räty	FIN	27.4.62	1		Nurmijärvi	20 Jul 92
90.44		Boris	Henry	GER	14.12.73	1	Gugl	Linz	9 Jul 97
89.16A		Tom	Petranoff	USA	8.4.58	1		Potchefstroom	1 Mar 91
89.10 WR		Patrik	Bodén	SWE	30.6.67	1		Austin	24 Mar 90
89.02		Jarrod	Bannister	AUS	3.10.84	1	NC	Brisbane	29 Feb 08
88.90		Aleksandr	Ivanov	RUS	25.5.82	1	Znam	Tula	7 Jun 03
88.75		Marius	Corbett	RSA	26.9.75	1	CG	Kuala Lumpur	21 Sep 98
88.70		Peter	Blank	GER	10.4.62	1	NC	Stuttgart	30 Jun 01
88.36		Matthias	de Zordo	GER	21.2.88	1	VD	Bruxelles	16 Sep 11
88.24		Matti	Närhi	FIN	17.8.75	1		Soini	27 Jul 97
	(20)								
88.23		Petr	Frydrych	CZE	13.1.88	1	GS	Ostrava	27 May 10
88.22		Juha	Laukkanen	FIN	6.1.69	1		Kuortane	20 Jun 92
88.20		Gavin	Lovegrove	NZL	21.10.67	1	Bisl	Oslo	5 Jul 96
88.00		Vladimir	Ovchinnikov	RUS	2.8.70	1		Tolyatti	14 May 95
87.83		Andrus	Värnik	EST	27.9.77	1		Valga	19 Aug 03
87.82		Harri	Hakkarainen	FIN	16.10.69	1		Kuortane	24 Jun 95
87.60		Kazuhiro	Mizoguchi	JPN	18.3.62	1	Jenner	San José	27 May 89
87.40		Vladimir	Sasimovich ¶	BLR	14.9.68	2		Kuortane	24 Jun 95

Mark	Wind	Name		Nat	Born	Pos	Meet	Venue	Date
87.34		Andrey	Moruyev	RUS	6.5.70	1	ECp	Birmingham	25 Jun 94
87.33		Antti	Ruuskanen	FIN	21.2.84	1		Kuortane	25 May 08
	(30)								
87.23		Teemu	Wirkkala	FIN	14.1.84	1		Joensuu	22 Jul 09
87.20		Viktor	Zaytsev	UZB	6.6.66	1	OT	Moskva	23 Jun 92
87.20		Peter	Esenwein	GER	7.12.67	1		Rehlingen	31 May 04
87.20A		Guillermo	Martínez	CUB	28.6.81	1	PAm	Guadalajara	28 Oct 11
87.17		Dariusz	Trafas	POL	16.5.72	1		Gold Coast (RB)	17 Sep 00
87.12		Tom	Pukstys	USA	28.5.68	2	OD	Jena	25 May 97
87.12		Emeterio	González	CUB	11.4.73	1	OD	Jena	3 Jun 00
86.98		Yuriy	Rybin	RUS	5.3.63	1		Nitra	26 Aug 95
86.94		Mick	Hill	GBR	22.10.64	1	NC	London (CP)	13 Jun 93
86.80		Einar	Vihljálmsson	ISL	1.6.60	·1		Reykjavik	29 Aug 92
	(40)								
86.80		Robert	Oosthuizen	RSA	23.1.87	1		Oudtshoorn	1 Mar 08
86.74		Pål Arne	Fagernes	NOR	8.6.74	Q	OG	Sydney	22 Sep 00
86.68		Tero	Järvenpää	FIN	2.10.84	1	NC	Tampere	27 Jul 08
86.67		Andrew	Currey	AUS	7.2.71	1		Wollongong	22 Jul 01
86.64		Klaus	Tafelmeier	FRG	12.4.58	1	NC	Gelsenkirchen	12 Jul 87
86.64		Ainars	Kovals	LAT	21.11.81	2	OG	Beijing	23 Aug 08
86.63		Harri	Haatainen	FIN	5.1.78	2	GP II	Gateshead	19 Aug 01
86.50		Tapio	Korjus	FIN	10.2.61	1		Lahti	25 Aug 88
86.47		Eriks	Rags	LAT	1.6.75	2	BrGP	London (CP)	22 Jul 01
86.45		Vitezslav	Vesely	CZE	27.2.83	1		Olomouc	8 May 10

(50)   100th man 84.11, 200th 81.16, 300th 79.63, 400th 78.54   new javelin introduced in 1986

Ancillary marks – other marks during series (to 91.40)

95.34	Zelezny	29 Aug 93	92.26	Zelezny	26 Mar 97	91.44	Zelezny	25 May 96
92.88	Zelezny	25 May 96	91.88	Zelezny	27 Aug 95	91.44	Zelezny	26 Mar 97
92.30	Zelezny	26 Mar 97	91.48	Zelezny	15 Sep 95			

Javelins with roughened tails, now banned by the IAAF

96.96	WR	Seppo	Räty	FIN	27.4.62	1		Punkalaidun	2 Jun 91
94.74	Irreg		Zelezny			1	Bisl	Oslo	4 Jul 92
91.98	WR		Räty			1	Super	Shizuoka	6 May 91
90.82		Kimmo	Kinnunen	FIN	31.3.68	1	WCh	Tokyo	26 Aug 91
87.00		Peter	Borglund	SWE	29.1.64	1	vFIN	Stockholm	13 Aug 91
Downhill:	87.88	Antti	Ruuskanen	FIN	21.2.84	1		Savonlinna	16 Sep 07

DECATHLON

9026 WR	Roman	Sebrle	CZE	26.11.74	1		Götzis	27 May 01
	10.64/0.0	8.11/1.9	15.33	2.12	47.79	13.92/-0.2	47.92	4.80	70.16	4:21.98

8994 WR Tomás Dvorák CZE 11.5.72 1 ECp Praha 4 Jul 99
10.54/-0.1 7.90/1.1 16.78 2.04 48.08 13.73/0.0 48.33 4.90 72.32 4:37.20

8902 Dvorák 1 WCh Edmonton 7 Aug 01
10.62/1.5 8.07/0.9 16.57 2.00 47.74 13.80/-0.4 45.51 5.00 68.53 4:35.13

8900 Dvorák 1 Götzis 4 Jun 00
10.54/1.3 8.03/0.0 16.68 2.09 48.36 13.89/-1.0 47.89 4.85 67.21 4:42.33

8893 Sebrle 1 OG Athína 24 Aug 04
10.85/1.5 7.84/0.3 16.36 2.12 48.36 14.05/1.5 48.72 5.00 70.52 4:40.01

8891 WR Dan O'Brien USA 18.7.66 1 Talence 5 Sep 92
10.43w/2.1 8.08/1.8 16.69 2.07 48.51 13.98/-0.5 48.56 5.00 62.58 4:42.10

8847 WR Daley Thompson GBR 30.7.58 1 OG Los Angeles 9 Aug 84
10.44/-1.0 8.01/0.4 15.72 2.03 46.97 14.33/-1.1 46.56 5.00 65.24 4:35.00

8844w O'Brien 1 TAC New York 13 Jun 91
10.23 7.96 16.06 2.08 47.70 13.95W/4.2 48.08 5.10 57.40 4:45.54

8842 Sebrle 1 Götzis 30 May 04
10.92/0.5 7.86w/3.3 16.22 2.09 48.59 14.15/0.3 47.44 5.00 71.10 4:34.09

8837 Dvorák 1 WCh Athína 6 Aug 97
10.60/0.8 7.64/-0.7 16.32 2.00 47.56 13.61/0.8 45.16 5.00 70.34 4:35.40

8832 WR Jürgen Hingsen FRG 25.1.58 1 OT Mannheim 9 Jun 84
10.70w/2.9 7.76/-1.6 16.42 2.07 48.05 14.07/0.2 49.36 4.90 59.86 4:19.75

8832 Bryan Clay USA 3.1.80 1 NC/OT Eugene 30 Jun 08
10.39/-0.4 7.39/-1.6 15.17 2.08 48.41 13.75/1.9 52.74 5.00 70.55 4:50.97

8825 WR Hingsen 1 Bernhausen 5 Jun 83
10.92/0.0 7.74 15.94 2.15 47.89 14.10 46.80 4.70 67.26 4:19.74

8824 O'Brien 1 OG Atlanta 1 Aug 96
10.50/0.7 7.57/1.4 15.66 2.07 46.82 13.87/0.3 48.78 5.00 66.90 4:45.89

8820 Clay 2 OG Athína 24 Aug 04
10.44w/2.2 7.96/0.2 15.23 2.06 49.19 14.13/1.5 50.11 4.90 69.71 4:41.65

8817 O'Brien 1 WCh Stuttgart 20 Aug 93
10.57/0.9 7.99/0.4 15.41 2.03 47.46 14.08/0.0 47.92 5.20 62.56 4:40.08

Mark	Wind	Name	Nat	Born	Pos	Meet	Venue	Date
8815		Erki Nool	EST	25.6.70	2	WCh	Edmonton	7 Aug 01
	10.60/1.5	7.63/2.0 14.90	2.03	46.23	14.40/0.0	43.40 5.40	67.01	4:29.58
8812		O'Brien			1	WCh	Tokyo	30 Aug 91
	10.41/-1.6	7.90/0.8 16.24	1.91	46.53	13.94/-1.2	47.20 5.20	60.66	4:37.50
8811		Thompson			1	EC	Stuttgart	28 Aug 86
	10.26/2.0	7.72/1.0 15.73	2.00	47.02	14.04/-0.3	43.38 5.10	62.78	4:26.16
8807		Sebrle			1		Götzis	1 Jun 03
	10.78/-0.2	7.86/1.2 15.41	2.12	47.83	13.96/0.0	43.42 4.90	69.22	4:28.63
8800		Sebrle			1		Götzis	2 Jun 02
	10.95/0.5	7.79/1.8 15.50	2.12	48.35	13.89/1.6	48.02 5.00	68.97	4:38.16
8800		Sebrle			1	EC	München	8 Aug 02
	10.83/1.3	7.92/0.8 15.41	2.12	48.48	14.04/0.0	46.88 5.10	68.51	4:42.94
8792		Uwe Freimuth	GDR	10.9.61	1	OD	Potsdam	21 Jul 84
	11.06/	7.79/ 16.30	2.03	48.43	14.66/	46.58 5.15	72.42	4:25.19
8791		Clay			1	OG	Beijing	22 Aug 08
	10.44/0.3	7.78/0.0 16.27	1.99	48.92	13.93/-0.5	53.79 5.00	70.97	5:06.59
8790		Trey Hardee	USA	7.2.84	1	WCh	Berlin	20 Aug 09
	10.45/0.2	7.83/1.9 15.33	1.99	48.13	13.86/0.3	48.08 5.20	68.00	4:48.91
8784		Tom Pappas (10)	USA	6.9.76	1	NC	Stanford	22 Jun 03
	10.78/0.2	7.96/1.4 16.28	2.17	48.22	14.13/1.7	45.84 5.20	60.77	4:48.12
8774 WR		Thompson			1	EC	Athína	8 Sep 82
	10.51/0.3	7.80/0.8 15.44	2.03	47.11	14.39/0.9	45.48 5.00	63.56	4:23.71
8762		Siegfried Wentz	FRG	7.3.60	2		Bernhausen	5 Jun 83
	10.89	7.49/ 15.35	2.09	47.38	14.00	46.90 4.80	70.68	4:24.90
8757		Sebrle			2		Götzis	4 Jun 00
	10.64/1.3	7.88/1.6 15.19	2.15	49.05	13.99/-1.0	47.21 4.75	67.23	4:35.06
8755		O'Brien			1	GWG	Uniondale, NY	20 Jul 98
	10.71/-2.3	7.78w/2.2 15.67	2.11	48.04	13.67/0.4	48.87 5.20	66.31	5:08.77
(30/11)								
8735		Eduard Hämäläinen	FIN/BLR	21.1.69	1		Götzis	29 May 94
	10.50w/2.1	7.26/1.0 16.05	2.11	47.63	13.82/-3.0	49.70 4.90	60.32	4:35.09
8729		Ashton Eaton	USA	21.1.88	1	NC	Eugene	24 Jun 11
	10.33/0.6	7.80w/3.1 14.14	2.05	46.35	13.52/1.6	41.58 5.05	56.19	4:24.10
8727		Dave Johnson	USA	7.4.63	1		Azusa	24 Apr 92
	10.96/0.4	7.52w/4.5 14.61	2.04	48.19	14.17/0.3	49.88 5.28	66.96	4:29.38
8725		Dmitriy Karpov	KAZ	23.7.81	3	OG	Athína	24 Aug 04
	10.50w/2.2	7.81/-0.9 15.93	2.09	46.81	13.97/1.5	51.65 4.60	55.54	4:38.11
8709		Aleksandr Apaychev	UKR	6.5.61	1	vGDR	Neubrandenburg	3 Jun 84
	10.96/	7.57/ 16.00	1.97	48.72	13.93/	48.00 4.90	72.24	4:26.51
8706		Frank Busemann	GER	26.2.75	2	OG	Atlanta	1 Aug 96
	10.60/0.7	8.07/0.8 13.60	2.04	48.34	13.47/0.3	45.04 4.80	66.86	4:31.41
8698		Grigoriy Degtyaryov	RUS	16.8.58	1	NC	Kiyev	22 Jun 84
	10.87/0.7	7.42/0.1 16.03	2.10	49.75	14.53/0.3	51.20 4.90	67.08	4:23.09
8694		Chris Huffins	USA	15.4.70	1	NC	New Orleans	20 Jun 98
	10.31w/3.5	7.76w/2.5 15.43	2.18	49.02	14.02/1.0	53.22 4.60	61.59	4:59.43
8680		Torsten Voss	GDR	24.3.63	1	WCh	Roma	4 Sep 87
	10.69/-0.3	7.88/1.2 14.98	2.10	47.96	14.13/0.1	43.96 5.10	58.02	4:25.93
(20)								
8667 WR		Guido Kratschmer	FRG	10.1.53	1		Bernhausen	14 Jun 80
	10.58w/2.4	7.80/ 15.47	2.00	48.04	13.92/	45.52 4.60	66.50	4:24.15
8654		Leonel Suárez	CUB	1.9.87	1	CAC	La Habana	4 Jul 09
	11.07/0.7	7.42/0.8 14.39	2.09	47.65	14.15/-0.6	46.07 4.70	77.47	4:27.29
8644		Steve Fritz	USA	1.11.67	4	OG	Atlanta	1 Aug 96
	10.90/0.8	7.77/0.9 15.31	2.04	50.13	13.97/0.3	49.84 5.10	65.70	4:38.26
8644		Maurice Smith	JAM	28.9.80	2	WCh	Osaka	1 Sep 07
	10.62/0.7	7.50/0.0 17.32	1.97	47.48	13.91/-0.2	52.36 4.80	53.61	4:33.52
8634 WR		Bruce Jenner	USA	28.10.49	1	OG	Montreal	30 Jul 76
	10.94/0.0	7.22/0.0 15.35	2.03	47.51	14.84/0.0	50.04 4.80	68.52	4:12.61
8627		Robert Zmelík	CZE	18.4.69	1		Götzis	31 May 92
	10.62w/2.1	8.02/0.2 13.93	2.05	48.73	13.84/1.2	44.44 4.90	61.26	4:24.83
8626		Michael Smith	CAN	16.9.67	1		Götzis	26 May 96
	11.23/-0.6	7.72/0.6 16.94	1.97	48.69	14.77/-2.4	52.90 4.90	71.22	4:41.95
8617		Andrey Kravchenko	BLR	4.1.86	1		Götzis	27 May 07
	10.86/0.2	7.90/0.9 13.89	2.15	47.46	14.05/-0.1	39.63 5.00	64.35	4:29.10
8603		Dean Macey	GBR	12.12.77	3	WCh	Edmonton	7 Aug 01
	10.72/-0.7	7.59/0.4 15.41	2.15	46.21	14.34/0.0	46.96 4.70	54.61	4:29.05
8583w		Jón Arnar Magnússon (30)	ISL	28.7.69	1	ECp-2	Reykjavik	5 Jul 98
	10.68/2.0	7.63/2.0 15.57	2.07	47.78	14.33W/5.2	44.53 5.00	64.16	4:41.60
8573					3		Götzis	31 May 98
	10.74/0.5	7.60/-0.2 16.03	2.03	47.66	14.24/0.7	47.82 5.10	59.77	4:46.43

Mark	Wind	Name		Nat	Born	Pos	Meet	Venue			Date
8574		Christian	Plaziat	FRA	28.10.63	1	EC	Split			29 Aug 90
	10.72/-0.6	7.77/1.1	14.19	2.10	47.10		13.98/0.7	44.36	5.00	54.72	4:27.83
8574		Aleksandr	Yurkov	UKR	21.7.75	4		Götzis			4 Jun 00
	10.69/0.9	7.93/1.8	15.26	2.03	49.74		14.56/-0.9	47.85	5.15	58.92	4:32.49
8571		Lev	Lobodin	RUS	1.4.69	3	EC	Budapest			20 Aug 98
	10.66w/2.2	7.42/0.2	15.67	2.03	48.65		13.97/0.9	46.55	5.20	56.55	4:30.27
8566		Sebastian	Chmara	POL	21.11.71	1		Alhama de Murcia			17 May 98
	10.97w/2.9	7.56/1.2	16.03	2.10	48.27		14.32/1.8	44.39	5.20	57.25	4:29.66
8554		Attila	Zsivoczky	HUN	29.4.77	5		Götzis			4 Jun 00
	10.64w/2.1	7.24/-1.0	15.72	2.18	48.13		14.87/-0.9	45.64	4.65	63.57	4:23.13
8548		Paul	Meier	GER	27.7.71	3	WCh	Stuttgart			20 Aug 93
	10.57/0.9	7.57/1.1	15.45	2.15	47.73		14.63/0.0	45.72	4.60	61.22	4:32.05
8547		Igor	Sobolevskiy	UKR	4.5.62	2	NC	Kiyev			22 Jun 84
	10.64/0.7	7.71/0.2	15.93	2.01	48.24		14.82/0.3	50.54	4.40	67.40	4:32.84
8534		Siegfried	Stark	GDR	12.6.55	1	OT	Halle			4 May 80
	11.10w	7.64	15.81	2.03	49.53		14.86w	47.20	5.00	68.70	4:27.7
8534w/8478		Antonio	Peñalver	ESP	1.12.68	1		Alhama de Murcia			24 May 92
	10.76w/3.9	7.42W/6.2	16.50	2.12	49.50		14.32/0.8	47.38	5.00	59.32	4:39.94
		(7.19w/4.0)									
8528		Aleksandr	Pogorelov	RUS	10.1.80	3	WCh	Berlin			20 Aug 09
	10.95/-0.3	7.49/-0.4	16.65	2.08	50.27		14.19/0.3	48.46	5.10	63.95	4:48.70
	(40)										
8526		Francisco Javier	Benet	ESP	25.3.68	2		Alhama de Murcia			17 May 98
	10.72w/2.9	7.45/-1.2	14.57	1.92	48.10		13.83/1.8	46.12	5.00	65.37	4:26.81
8526		Kristjan	Rahnu	EST	29.8.79	1		Arles			5 Jun 05
	10.52w/2.2	7.58/1.6	15.51	1.99	48.60		14.04w/3.1	50.81	4.95	60.71	4:52.18
8524		Sébastien	Levicq	FRA	25.6.71	4	WCh	Sevilla			25 Aug 99
	11.05/0.2	7.52/-0.4	14.22	2.00	50.13		14.48/0.6	44.65	5.50	69.01	4:26.81
8522		Michael	Schrader	GER	1.7.87	1		Götzis			31 May 09
	10.64/0.8	8.05/1.9	14.33	1.94	49.71		14.21/1.6	43.09	5.00	64.04	4:22.26
8519		Yuriy	Kutsenko	RUS	5.3.52	3	NC	Kiyev			22 Jun 84
	11.07/0.5	7.54/-0.1	15.11	2.13	49.07		14.94/0.3	50.38	4.60	61.70	4:12.68
8506		Valter	Külvet	EST	19.2.64	1		Stayki			3 Jul 88
	11.05/-1.4	7.35/0.4	15.78	2.00	48.08		14.55/-0.8	52.04	4.60	61.72	4:15.93
8500		Christian	Schenk	GER	9.2.65	4	WCh	Stuttgart			20 Aug 93
	11.22/-0.9	7.63/0.0	15.72	2.15	48.78		15.29/0.0	46.94	4.80	65.32	4:24.44
8497		Aleksey	Sysoyev	RUS	8.3.85	2		Götzis			1 Jun 08
	10.86/-0.7	7.01/0.5	15.49	2.03	49.10		14.64/1.3	54.08	5.10	64.22	4:38.82
8496		Yordani	García	CUB	21.11.88	1		La Habana			30 May 09
	10.88/0.1	7.36/0.2	16.50	2.10	48.77		14.07/-0.5	43.97	4.80	68.10	4:46.80
8491		Aleksandr	Nevskiy	UKR	21.2.58	2		Götzis			20 May 84
	10.97/-1.6	7.24/1.2	15.04	2.08	48.44		14.67/1.0	46.06	4.70	69.56	4:19.62
	(50)	100th man 8312, 200th 8148, 300th 8045, 400th 7948, 500th 7877									

4 x 100 METRES RELAY

37.04	WR	JAM	N Carter, Frater, Blake, Bolt	1	WCh	Daegu	4 Sep 11
37.10	WR	JAM	N Carter, Frater, Bolt, Powell	1	OG	Beijing	22 Aug 08
37.31		JAM	Mullings, Frater, Bolt, Powell	1	WCh	Berlin	22 Aug 09
37.40	WR	USA	Marsh, Burrell, Mitchell, C Lewis	1	OG	Barcelona	8 Aug 92
37.40	WR	USA	Drummond, Cason, D Mitchell, L Burrell	1s1	WCh	Stuttgart	21 Aug 93
37.45		USA	Kimmons, Spearmon, Gay, Rodgers	1	WK	Zürich	19 Aug 10
37.48		USA	Drummond, Cason, D Mitchell, L Burrell	1	WCh	Stuttgart	22 Aug 93
37.50	WR	USA	Cason, Burrell, Mitchell, C Lewis	1	WCh	Tokyo	1 Sep 91
37.59		USA	Drummond, Montgomery, B Lewis, Greene	1	WCh	Sevilla	29 Aug 99
37.59		USA	Conwright, Spearmon, Gay, Smoots	1	WCp	Athína	16 Sep 06
37.61		USA	Drummond, Williams, B Lewis, Greene	1	OG	Sydney	30 Sep 00
37.62		TRI	Brown, Burns, Callander, Thompson	2	WCh	Berlin	22 Aug 09
37.65		USA	Drummond, Williams, C Johnson, Greene	1	ISTAF	Berlin	1 Sep 00
37.67	WR	USA	Marsh, Burrell, Mitchell, C Lewis	1	WK	Zürich	7 Aug 91
37.69		CAN	Esmie 10.47, Gilbert 9.02, Surin 9.25, Bailey 8.95	1	OG	Atlanta	3 Aug 96
37.70		JAM	Clarke, Frater, Mullins, Bolt	1	WK	Zürich	28 Aug 09
37.73		GBR	Gardener, Campbell, Devonish, Chambers	2	WCh	Sevilla	29 Aug 99
37.73		USA	Trammell, Rodgers, Patton, Spearmon	2	WK	Zürich	28 Aug 09
37.75		USA	Cason, Burrell, Mitchell, Marsh	1h2	WCh	Tokyo	31 Aug 91
37.76		JAM	Forsythe, Frater, S Mullings, Blake	2	WK	Zürich	19 Aug 10
37.77		GBR	Jackson, Jarrett, Regis, Christie	2	WCh	Stuttgart	22 Aug 93
37.77		USA	A Drummond, B Williams, Patton, Greene	1	ISTAF	Berlin (P)	10 Aug 03
37.78		USA	Patton 10.28, Spearmon 9.22, Gay 9.05, Dixon 9.23	1	WCh	Osaka	1 Sep 07
37.79	WR	FRA	Morinière, Sangouma, Trouabal, Marie-Rose	1	EC	Split	1 Sep 90

Mark	Wind	Name	Nat	Born	Pos	Meet	Venue	Date
37.79	WR	Santa Monica TC/USA Marsh, Burrell, Heard, C Lewis			1	Herc	Monaco	3 Aug 91
37.79		USA - Santa Monica TC Marsh, Burrell, Heard, C Lewis			1	MSR	Walnut	17 Apr 94
37.79		USA Kimmons, Gatlin, M.Mitchell, Padgett			1h1	WCh	Daegu	4 Sep 11
37.80		USA Martin, Padgett, Crawford, Patton			1	LGP	London (CP)	26 Jul 08
37.82		USA Drummond, Williams, B.Lewis, Greene			1s1	OG	Sydney	29 Sep 00
37.83	WR	USA Graddy, R Brown, C Smith, C Lewis			1	OG	Los Angeles	11 Aug 84
37.83		CAN Esmie, Gilbert, Surin, Mahorn			3	WCh	Stuttgart	22 Aug 93

(31 performances by teams from 6 nations)   Further bests by nations:

Mark	Wind	Name	Nat	Born	Pos	Meet	Venue	Date
37.90		BRA de Lima, Ribeiro, A da Silva, Cl da Silva			2	OG	Sydney	30 Sep 00
37.94		NGR O Ezinwa, Adeniken, Obikwelu, D Ezinwa			1s2	WCh	Athína	9 Aug 97
38.00		CUB Simón, Lamela, Isasi, Aguilera			3	OG	Barcelona	8 Aug 92
38.02		URS Yevgenyev, Bryzgin, Muravyov, Krylov			2	WCh	Roma	6 Sep 87

(10)

Mark	Wind	Name	Nat	Born	Pos	Meet	Venue	Date
38.03		JPN Tsukahara, Suetsugu 9.08, Takahira, Asahara			5	WCh	Osaka	1 Sep 07
38.12		GHA Duah, Nkansah, Zakari, Tuffour			1s1	WCh	Athína	9 Aug 97
38.17		AUS Henderson, Jackson, Brimacombe, Marsh			1s2	WCh	Göteborg	12 Aug 95
38.17		ITA Donati, Collio, Di Gregorio, Checcucci			2	EC	Barcelona	1 Aug 10
38.29		GDR Schröder, Kübeck, Prenzler, Emmelmann			2	vUSA	Karl-Marx-Stadt	9 Jul 82
38.33		POL Zwolinski, Licznerski, Dunecki, Woronin			2	OG	Moskva	1 Aug 80
38.45		AHO Goeloe, Raffaela, Duzant, Martina			6	WCh	Helsinki	13 Aug 05
38.46		URS/RUS Zharov, Krylov, Fatun, Goremykin			4	EC	Split	1 Sep 90
38.47		RSA Nagel, du Plessis, Newton, Quinn			1	WCh	Edmonton	12 Aug 01
38.47		SKN Rogers, Collins, Adams, Lawrence			3h2	WCh	Daegu	4 Sep 11

(20, with RUS and UKR for USSR)

Mark	Wind	Name	Nat	Born	Pos	Meet	Venue	Date
38.53		UKR Rurak, Osovich, Kramarenko, Dologodin			1	ECp	Madrid	1 Jun 96
38.54		FRG Heer, Haas, Klein, Schweisfurth			1	R-W	Koblenz	28 Aug 88
38.60		ESP Feo, José, Mayoral, Berlanga			3s1	WCh	Athína	9 Aug 97
38.60		CIV Meité, Douhou, Sonan, N'Dri			3s1	WCh	Edmonton	12 Aug 01
38.61		GRE Séggos, Alexópoulos, Panayiotópoulos, Hoídis			2	ECp	Paris (C)	19 Jun 99
38.62		SUI Mancini, Schenkel, Wilson, Schneeberger			3	WK	Zürich	8 Sep 11
38.63		SWE Karlsson, Mårtensson, Hedner, Strenius			3s2	OG	Atlanta	2 Aug 96
38.63		NED Beck, T Douglas, van Balkom, C Douglas			5s1	WCh	Saint-Denis	30 Aug 03
38.67		HUN Karaffa, Nagy, Tatár, Kovács			1	BGP	Budapest	11 Aug 86
38.78		CHN Lu Bin, Liang Jiahong, Su Bingtian, Lao Yi			1	AsiG	Guangzhou	26 Nov 10

Multi-nation team

Mark	Wind	Name	Nat	Born	Pos	Meet	Venue	Date
37.46		Racers TC Bailey/ANT, Blake JAM, Forsythe JAM, Bolt JAM			1	LGP	London (CP)	25 Jul 09
37.82		Drummond/USA, Jarrett/GBR, Regis/GBR, Mitchell/USA			2	MSR	Walnut	17 Apr 94

One man disqualified for drugs

Mark	Wind	Name	Nat	Born	Pos	Meet	Venue	Date
37.91		NGR Asonze ¶, Obikwelu, Effiong, Aliu			(3)	WCh	Sevilla	29 Aug 99

4 x 200 METRES RELAY

Mark	Wind	Name		Pos	Meet	Venue	Date
1:18.68	WR	USA - Santa Monica Track Cluc					
		Marsh 20.0, Burrell 19.6, Heard 19.7, C Lewis 19.4		1	MSR	Walnut	17 Apr 94
1:19.10		World All-Stars		2	MSR	Walnut	17 Apr 94
		Drummond USA 20.4, Mitchell USA 19.3, Bridgewater USA 20.3, Regis GBR 19.1					
1:19.11	WR	Santa Monica TC/USA M.Marsh, L Burrell, Heard, C Lewis		1	Penn	Philadelphia	25 Apr 92
1:19.16		USA Red Team Crawford, Clay, Patton, Gatlin		1	PennR	Philadelphia	26 Apr 03
1:19.38	WR	Santa Monica TC/USA Everett, Burrell, Heard, C Lewis		1	R-W	Koblenz	23 Aug 89
1:19.39		USA Blue Drummond, Crawford, B Williams, Greene		1	PennR	Philadelphia	28 Apr 01
1:19.45		Santa Monica TC/USA DeLoach, Burrell, C.Lewis, Heard		1	Penn	Philadelphia	27 Apr 91
1:19.47		Nike Int./USA Brokenburr, A Harrison, Greene, M Johnson		1	Penn	Philadelphia	24 Apr 99

Best non-US nations

Mark	Wind	Name		Pos	Meet	Venue	Date
1:20.79		Central Arizona DC/Jamaica		1	MSR	Walnut	24 Apr 88
		Bucknor, Campbell, O'Connor, Davis)					
1:21.10		ITA Tilli, Simionato, Bongiorno, Mennea		1		Cagliari	29 Sep 83
1:21.22		POL Tulin, Balcerzak, Pilarczyk, Urbas		2		Gdansk	14 Jul 01
1:21.29		GBR Adam, Mafe, Christie, Regis		1	vURS	Birmingham	23 Jun 89

4 x 400 METRES RELAY

Mark	Wind	Name	Pos	Meet	Venue	Date
2:54.29	WR	USA Valmon 44.5, Watts 43.6, Reynolds 43.23, Johnson 42.94	1	WCh	Stuttgart	22 Aug 93
2:55.39		USA Merritt 44.4, Taylor 43.7, Neville 44.16, Wariner 43.18	1	OG	Beijing	23 Aug 08
2:55.56		USA Merritt 44.4, Taylor 43.7, Williamson 44.32, Wariner 43.10	1	WCh	Osaka	2 Sep 07
2:55.74	WR	USA Valmon 44.6, Watts 43.00, M.Johnson 44.73, S Lewis 43.41	1	OG	Barcelona	8 Aug 92
2:55.91		USA O Harris 44.5, Brew 43.6, Wariner 43.98, Williamson 43.83	1	OG	Athína	28 Aug 04
2:55.99		USA L Smith 44.62, A Harrison 43.84, Mills 43.66, Maybank 43.87	1	OG	Atlanta	3 Aug 96
2:56.16A	WR	USA Matthews 45.0, Freeman 43.2, James 43.9, Evans 44.1	1	OG	Ciu. México	20 Oct 68
2:56.16	WR	USA Everett 43.79, S Lewis 43.69, Robinzine 44.74, Reynolds 43.94	1	OG	Seoul	1 Oct 88
2:56.60		GBR I Thomas 44.92, Baulch 44.19, Richardson 43.62, Black 43.87	2	OG	Atlanta	3 Aug 96
2:56.65		GBR Thomas 44.8, Black 44.2, Baulch 44.08, Richardson 43.57	2	WCh	Athína	10 Aug 97
2:56.75		JAM McDonald 44.5, Haughton 44.4, McFarlane 44.37, Clarke 43.51	3	WCh	Athína	10 Aug 97

Mark	Wind	Name	Nat	Born	Pos	Meet	Venue	Date
2:56.91		USA Rock 44.7, Brew 44.3, Williamson 44.40, Wariner 43.49			1	WCh	Helsinki	14 Aug 05
2:57.29		USA Everett 45.1, Haley 44.0, McKay 44.20, Reynolds 44.00			1	WCh	Roma	6 Sep 87
2:57.32		USA Ramsey 44.9, Mills 44.6, Reynolds 43.74, Johnson 44.11			1	WCh	Göteborg	13 Aug 95
2:57.32		BAH McKinney 44.9, Moncur 44.6, A.Williams 44.43, Brown 43.42			2	WCh	Helsinki	14 Aug 05
2:57.53		GBR Black 44.7, Redmond 44.0, Regis 44.22, Akabusi 44.59			1	WCh	Tokyo	1 Sep 91
2:57.57		USA Valmon 44.9, Watts 43.4, D.Everett 44.31, Pettigrew 44.93			2	WCh	Tokyo	1 Sep 91
2:57.86		USA Taylor 45.4, Wariner 43.6, Clement 44.72, Merritt 44.16			1	WCh	Berlin	23 Aug 09
2:57.87		USA L Smith 44.59, Rouser 44.33, Mills 44.32, Maybank 44.63			1s2	OG	Atlanta	2 Aug 96
2:57.91		USA Nix 45.59, Armstead 43.97, Babers 43.75, McKay 44.60			1	OG	Los Angeles	11 Aug 84
2:57.97		JAM McDonald , Haughton , McFarlane, D Clarke			1	PAm	Winnipeg	30 Jul 99
2:58.00		POL Rysiukiewicz 45.6, Czubak 44.2, Haczek 44.0, Mackowiak 44.2			2	GWG	Uniondale, NY	22 Jul 98
2:58.03		BAH Bain 45.9, Mathieu 44.1, A Williams 44.02, Brown 44.05			2	OG	Beijing	23 Aug 08
2:58.06		RUS Dyldin 45.5, Frolov 44.6, Kokorin 44.34, Alekseyev 43.56			3	OG	Beijing	23 Aug 08
2:58.07		JAM Ayre 44.9, Simpson 44.9, Spence 44.48, Clarke 43.81			3	WCh	Helsinki	14 Aug 05
2:58.19		BAH Moncur 45.1, C Brown 44.5, McIntosh 44.42, Munnings 44.13			2	WCh	Edmonton	12 Aug 01

(26/6) plus six times for teams that contained an athlete who was subsequently banned for drugs abuse

Mark	Wind	Name	Nat	Born	Pos	Meet	Venue	Date
2:58.56		BRA Cl. da Silva 44.6, A dos Santos 45.1, de Araújo 45.0, Parrela 43.9			2	PAm	Winnipeg	30 Jul 99
2:58.68		NGR Chukwu 45.18, Monye 44.49, Bada 44.70, Udo-Obong 44.31			1	OG	Sydney	30 Sep 00
2:58.96		FRA Djhone 45.4, Keita 44.7, Diagana 44.69, Raquil 44.15			2	WCh	Saint-Denis	31 Aug 03
2:59.13		CUB Martínez 45.6, Herrera 44.38, Tellez 44.81, Hernández 44.34			1h2	OG	Barcelona	7 Aug 92

(10)

Mark	Wind	Name	Nat	Born	Pos	Meet	Venue	Date
2:59.21		RSA Pistorius 45.58, Mogawane 43.97, de Beer 44.46, Victor 45.20			3h1	WCh	Daegu	1 Sep 11
2:59.37		BEL K Borlée 45.4, J Borlée 43.6, Van Branteghem 44.44, Ghislain 45.88			5	OG	Beijing	23 Aug 08
2:59.63		KEN D Kitur 45.4, S Kitur 45.13, Kipkemboi 44.76, Kemboi 44.34			3h2	OG	Barcelona	7 Aug 92
2:59.70		AUS Frayne 45.38, Clark 43.86, Minihan 45.07, Mitchell 45.39			4	OG	Los Angeles	11 Aug 84
2:59.86		GDR Möller 45.8, Schersing 44.8, Carlowitz 45.3, Schönlebe 44.1			1	vURS	Erfurt	23 Jun 85
2:59.95		YUG Jovkovic, Djurovic, Macev, Brankovic 44.3			2h3	WCh	Tokyo	31 Aug 91
2:59.96		FRG Dobeleit 45.7, Henrich 44.3, Itt 45.12, Schmid 44.93			4	WCh	Roma	6 Sep 87
3:00.44A		DOM Cuesta 46.2, Peguero 44.6, Tapia 45.2, L Santos 44.5			2	PAm	Guadalajara	28 Oct 11
3:02.02		Peguero, Santa, Vidal, Sánchez			3	PAm	Santo Domingo	9 Aug 03
3:00.64		SEN Diarra 46.53, Dia 44.94, Ndiaye 44.70, Faye 44.47			4	OG	Atlanta	3 Aug 96
3:00.76		JPN Karube 45.88, Ito 44.86, Osakada 45.08, Omori 44.94			5	OG	Atlanta	3 Aug 96

(20)

Mark	Wind	Name	Nat	Born	Pos	Meet	Venue	Date
3:00.79		ZIM Chiwira 46.2, Mukomana 44.6, Ngidhi 45.79, Harnden 44.20			2h3	WCh	Athína	9 Aug 97
3:00.82A		VEN A Ramírez 45.7, Aguilar 45.3, Acevedo 44.7, Longart 45.2			3	PAm	Guadalajara	28 Oct 11
3:01.05		TRI Delice, A Daniel, De Silva, Morris			1h1	OG	Barcelona	7 Aug 92
3:01.12		FIN Lönnqvist 46.7, Salin 45.1, Karttunen 44.8, Kukkoaho 44.5			6	OG	München	10 Sep 72
3:01.37		ITA Bongiorni 46.2, Zuliani 45.0, Petrella 45.3, Ribaud 44.9			4	EC	Stuttgart	31 Aug 86
3:01.42		ESP I Rodríguez 46.0, Canal 44.1, Andrés 45.88, Reina 45.48			4h1	WCh	Edmonton	11 Aug 01
3:01.60		BAR Louis 46.67, Peltier 44.97, Edwards 45.04, Forde 44.92			6	OG	Los Angeles	11 Aug 84
3:01.61		BUL Georgiev 45.9, Stankulov 46.0, Raykov 45.07, Ivanov 44.66			2h1	WCh	Stuttgart	21 Aug 93
3:02.09		UGA Govile 46.72, Kyeswa 44.60, Rwamuhanda 46.40, Okot 44.37			7	OG	Los Angeles	11 Aug 84
3:02.11		MAR Kasbane, Dahane, Belcaid, Lahlou 44.5			1h2	WCh	Tokyo	31 Aug 91

Including subsequently banned athlete

Mark	Wind	Name	Nat	Born	Pos	Meet	Venue	Date
2:54.20(WR)		USA Young 44.3, Pettigrew ¶ 43.2, Washington 43.5, Johnson 43.2			(1)	GWG	Uniondale, NY	22 Jul 98
2:56.35		USA A Harrison 44.36, Pettigrew 44.17, C Harrison 43.53, Johnson 44.29			(1)	OG	Sydney	30 Sep 00
2:56.45		USA J Davis 45.2, Pettigrew 43.9, Taylor 43.92, M Johnson 43.49			(1)	WCh	Sevilla	29 Aug 99
2:56.47		USA Young 44.6, Pettigrew 43.1, Jones 44.80, Washington 44.80			(1)	WCh	Athína	10 Aug 97
2:56.60		USA Red Taylor 45.0, Pettigrew 44.2, Washington 43.7, Johnson 43.7			(1)	PennR	Philadelphia	29 Apr 00
2:57.54		USA Byrd 45.9, Pettigrew 43.9, Brew 44.03, Taylor 43.71			1	WCh	Edmonton	12 Aug 01

4 x 800 METRES RELAY

Mark		Nat	Name			Pos	Meet	Venue	Date
7:02.43		KEN	Mutua 1:46.73, Yiampoy 1:44.38, Kombich 1:45.92, Bungei 1:45.40			1	VD	Bruxelles	25 Aug 06
7:02.82		USA				2	VD	Bruxelles	25 Aug 06
			J Harris 1:47.05, Robinson 1:44.03, Burley 1:46.05, Krummenacker 1:45.69						
7:03.89 WR		GBR	Elliott 1:49.14, Cook 1:46.20, Cram 1:44.54, Coe 1:44.01			1		London (CP)	30 Aug 82
7:04.70		RSA	van Oudtshoorn 1:46.9, Sepeng 1:45.2, Kotze 1:48.3, J Botha 1:44.3			1		Stuttgart	6 Jun 99
7:06.66		QAT	Sultan 1:45.81, Al-Badri 1:46.71, Suleiman 1:45.89, Ali Kamal 1:48.25			4	VD	Bruxelles	25 Aug 06

4 x 1500 METRES RELAY

Mark		Nat	Name			Pos	Meet	Venue	Date
14:36.23 WR		KEN	W Biwott 3:38.5, Gathimba 3:39.5, G Rono 3:41.4, Choge 3:36.9			1	VD	Bruxelles	4 Sep 09
14:38.8 WR		FRG	Wessinghage 3:38.8, Hudak 3:39.1, Lederer 3:44.6, Fleschen 3:36.3			1		Köln	16 Aug 77
14:40.4 WR		NZL	Polhill 3:42.9, Walker 3:40.4, Dixon 3:41.2, Quax 3:35.9			1		Oslo	22 Aug 73
14:45.63		URS	Kalutskiy, Yakovlev, Legeda, Lotarev			1		Leningrad	4 Aug 85
14:46.16		Larios, ESP	Jiménez 3:40.9, Pancorbo 3:41.2, A García 3:43.9, Viciosa 3:40.2			1		Madrid	5 Sep 97
14:46.3		USA	Aldridge, Clifford, Harbour, Duits			1		Bourges	23 Jun 79
14:46.92		AUS	Birmingham 3:39.2, Gregson 3:44.2, Kealey 3:43.3, Bromlet 3:40.3			3	VD	Bruxelles	4 Sep 09
14:48.2		FRA	Bégouin 3:44.5, Lequement 3:44.3, Philippe 3:42.2, Dien 3:37.2			2		Bourges	23 Jun 79

Mixed Team

Mark		Name				Pos	Meet	Venue	Date
14:44.31		Ali BRN 3:38.1, Birgen KEN 3:43.3, N Kemboi KEN 3:40.0, Campbell IRL 3:43.0				2	VD	Bruxelles	4 Sep 09

Mark	Wind	Name		Nat	Born	Pos	Meet	Venue	Date

4 x 1 MILE RELAY

Mark		Name					Venue	Date
15:49.08	IRL	Coghlan 4:00.2, O'Sullivan 3:55.3, O'Mara 3:56.6, Flynn 3:56.98				1	Dublin	17 Aug 85
15:59.57	NZL	Rogers 3:57.2, Bowden 4:02.5, Gilchrist 4:02.8, Walker 3:57.07				1	Auckland	2 Mar 83

3000 METRES TRACK WALK

Mark	Name		Nat	Born	Pos	Meet	Venue	Date
10:47.11	Giovanni	De Benedictis	ITA	8.1.68	1		S.Giovanni Valdarno	19 May 90
10:52.44+	Yohann	Diniz	FRA	1.1.78	1	in 5k	Villeneuve d'Ascq	27 Jun 08
10:56.22	Andrew	Jachno	AUS	13.4.62	1		Melbourne	7 Feb 91
10:56.34+	Roman	Mrázek	SVK	21.1.62	1k	PTS	Bratislava	14 Jun 89
10:59.04	Luke	Adams	AUS	22.10.76	1		Cork	3 Jul 10
11:00.2+	Jozef	Pribilinec	SVK	6.7.60	1k		Banská Bystrica	30 Aug 85
11:00.50+	Francisco Javier	Fernández ¶	ESP	6.3.77	1	in 5k	Villeneuve d'Ascq	8 Jun 07
11:00.56	David	Smith	AUS	24.7.55	1		Perth	24 Jan 87
11:03.01	Vladimir	Andreyev	RUS	7.9.66	2		Formia	13 Jul 97
Indoors								
10:31.42	Andreas	Erm	GER	12.3.76	1		Halle	4 Feb 01
10:54.61	Carlo	Mattioli	ITA	23.10.54	1		Milano	6 Feb 80
10:56.77+	Ivano	Brugnetti	ITA	1.9.76	1	in 5k	Torino	21 Feb 09
10:56.88	Reima	Salonen	FIN	19.11.55	1		Turku	5 Feb 84
10:57.32	Matej	Tóth	SVK	10.2.83	1		Wien	12 Feb 11
11:00.86+	Frants	Kostyukevich	BLR	4.4.63	1k	EI	Genova	28 Feb 92

5000 METRES TRACK WALK

Mark	Name		Nat	Born	Pos	Meet	Venue	Date
18:05.49	Hatem	Ghoula	TUN	7.6.73	1		Tunis	1 May 97
18:17.22	Robert	Korzeniowski	POL	30.7.68	1		Reims	3 Jul 92
18:18.01	Yohann	Diniz	FRA	1.1.78	1		Villeneuve d'Ascq	27 Jun 08
18:27.34	Francisco Javier	Fernández ¶	ESP	6.3.77	1		Villeneuve d'Ascq	8 Jun 07
18:28.80	Roman	Mrázek	SVK	21.1.62	1	PTS	Bratislava	14 Jun 89
18:30.43	Maurizio	Damilano	ITA	6.4.57	1		Caserta	11 Jun 92
ndoors								
18:07.08	Mikhail	Shchennikov	RUS	24.12.67	1		Moskva	14 Feb 95
18:08.86	Ivano	Brugnetti	ITA	1.9.76	1	NC	Ancona	17 Feb 07
18:11.41	Ronald	Weigel	GDR	8.8.59	1mx		Wien	13 Feb 88
18:15.25	Grigoriy	Kornev	RUS	14.3.61	1		Moskva	7 Feb 92
18:16.54 ?	Frants	Kostyukevich	BLR	4.4.63	2	NC	Gomel	4 Feb 89
18:19.97	Giovanni	De Benedictis	ITA	8.1.68	1	EI	Genova	28 Feb 92
18:22.25	Andreas	Erm	GER	12.3.76	1	NC	Dortmund	25 Feb 01
18:23.18	Rishat	Shafikov	RUS	23.1.70	1		Samara	1 Mar 97
18:24.13	Francisco Javier	Fernández ¶	ESP	6.3.77	1		Belfast	17 Feb 07
18:27.15	Alessandro	Gandellini	ITA	30.4.73	1	NC	Genova	12 Feb 00
18:27.80	Jozef	Pribilinec	SVK	6.7.60	2	WI	Indianapolis	7 Mar 87
18:27.95	Stefan	Johansson	SWE	11.4.67	3	EI	Genova	28 Feb 92
18:30.91	Aleksandr	Yargunkin	RUS	6.1.81	1		Yekaterinburg	7 Jan 07
18:31.63	Vladimir	Andreyev	RUS	7.9.66	2		Moskva	7 Feb 92

10,000 METRES TRACK WALK

Mark	Name		Nat	Born	Pos	Meet	Venue	Date
37:53.09	Francisco Javier	Fernández ¶	ESP	6.3.77	1	NC	Santa Cruz de Tenerife	27 Jul 08
37:58.6	Ivano	Brugnetti	ITA	1.9.76	1		Sesto San Gioavnni	23 Jul 05
38:02.60	Jozef	Pribilinec	SVK	6.7.60	1		Banská Bystrica	30 Aug 85
38:06.6	David	Smith	AUS	24.7.55	1		Sydney	25 Sep 86
38:12.13	Ronald	Weigel	GDR	8.8.59	1		Potsdam	10 May 86
38:18.0+	Valdas	Kazlauskas	LTU	23.2.58	1		Moskva	18 Sep 83
38:20.0	Moacir	Zimmermann	BRA	30.12.83	1		Blumenau	7 Jun 08
38:24 0+	Bernardo	Segura	MEX	11.2.70	1	SGP	Fana	7 May 94
38:24.31	Hatem	Ghoula	TUN	7.6.73	1		Tunis	30 May 98
38:26.4	Daniel	García	MEX	28.10.71	1		Sdr Omme	17 May 97
38:26.53	Robert	Korzeniowski	POL	30.7.68	1		Riga	31 May 02
38:27.57	Robert	Heffernan	IRL	20.2.78	1	NC	Dublin	20 Jul 08
38:32.0	Erik	Tysse	NOR	4.12.80	1	NC	Bergen (Fana)	13 Jun 08
38:37.6+	Jefferson	Pérez	ECU	1.7.74	1	in 20k	Fana	9 May 98
38:38.0	Walter	Arena	ITA	30.5.64	1		Catania	13 Apr 90
Indoors								
38:31.4	Werner	Heyer	GDR	14.11.56	1		Berlin	12 Jan 80

20 KILOMETRES WALK

Mark	Name		Nat	Born	Pos	Meet	Venue	Date
1:16:43	Sergey	Morozov ¶	RUS	21.3.88	1	NC	Saransk	8 Jun 08
1:17:16	Vladimir	Kanaykin ¶	RUS	21.3.85	1	RWC	Saransk	29 Sep 07
1:17:21 WR	Jefferson	Pérez	ECU	1.7.74	1	WCh	Saint-Denis	23 Aug 03
1:17:22 WR	Francisco Javier	Fernández ¶	ESP	6.3.77	1		Turku	28 Apr 02
1:17:23	Vladimir	Stankin	RUS	2.1.74	1	NC-w	Adler	8 Feb 04

A – mark made at an altitude of 1000m or higher, i – indoors, Q – in qualifying competition, WR - world record

Mark	Wind	Name		Nat	Born	Pos	Meet	Venue	Date
1:17:25.6t		Bernardo	Segura	MEX	11.2.70	1	SGP	Bergen (Fana)	7 May 94
1:17:33		Nathan	Deakes	AUS	17.8.77	1		Cixi	23 Apr 05
1:17:36			Kanaykin			1	NC	Cheboksary	17 Jun 07
1:17:38		Valeriy	Borchin	RUS	11.9.86	1	NC-w	Adler	28 Feb 09
1:17:41			Zhu Hongjun	CHN	18.8.83	2		Cixi	23 Apr 05
1:17:46		Julio	Martínez (10)	GUA	27.9.73	1		Eisenhüttenstadt	8 May 99
1:17:46		Roman	Rasskazov	RUS	28.4.79	1	NC	Moskva	19 May 00
1:17:52			Fernández			1		La Coruña	4 Jun 05
1:17:53			Cui Zhide	CHN	11.1.83	3		Cixi	23 Apr 05
1:17:55			Borchin			1	NC-w	Adler	23 Feb 08
1:17:56		Alejandro	López	MEX	9.2.75	2		Eisenhüttenstadt	8 May 99
1:18:00			Fernández			2	WCh	Saint-Denis	23 Aug 03
1:18:03.3twR			Bo Lingtang	CHN	12.8.70	1	NC	Beijing	7 Apr 94
1:18:05		Dmitriy	Yesipchuk	RUS	17.11.74	1	NC-w	Adler	4 Mar 01
1:18:06		Viktor	Burayev ¶	RUS	23.8.82	2	NC-w	Adler	4 Mar 01
1:18:06		Vladimir	Parvatkin	RUS	10.10.84	1	NC-w	Adler	12 Mar 05
1:18:07			Rasskazov			1	NC-w	Adler	20 Feb 00
1:18:07			Rasskazov			3	WCh	Saint-Denis	23 Aug 03
1:18:07			Li Gaobo	CHN	4.5.89	4		Cixi	23 Apr 05
1:18:12		Artur	Meleshkevich	BLR	11.4.75	1		Brest	10 Mar 01
1:18:13 wR		Pavol	Blazek (20)	SVK	9.7.58	1		Hildesheim	16 Sep 90
1:18:13			Wang Hao	CHN	16.8.89	1	NG	Jinan	22 Oct 09
1:18:14		Mikhail	Khmelnitskiy	BLR	24.7.69	1	NC	Soligorsk	13 May 00
1:18:14			Deakes			1		Dublin	16 Jun 01
1:18:14		Noé	Hernández	MEX	15.3.78	4	WCh	Saint-Denis	23 Aug 03
		(30/23)							
1:18:16		Vladimir	Andreyev	RUS	7.9.66	2	NC	Moskva	19 May 00
1:18:17		Ilya	Markov	RUS	19.6.72	2	NC-w	Adler	12 Mar 05
1:18:18		Yevgeniy	Misyulya	BLR	13.3.64	1		Eisenhüttenstadt	11 May 96
1:18:18		Sergey	Bakulin	RUS	13.11.86	2	NC-w	Adler	23 Feb 08
1:18:20 wR		Andrey	Perlov	RUS	12.12.61	1	NC	Moskva	26 May 90
1:18:20		Denis	Nizhegorodov	RUS	26.7.80	3	NC-w	Adler	4 Mar 01
1:18:22		Robert	Korzeniowski	POL	30.7.68	1		Hildesheim	9 Jul 00
		(30)							
1:18:23		Andrey	Makarov	BLR	2.1.71	2	NC	Soligorsk	13 May 00
1:18:24		Alex	Schwazer	ITA	26.12.84	1		Lugano	14 Mar 10
1:18:27		Daniel	García	MEX	28.10.71	2	WCp	Podebrady	19 Apr 97
1:18:27			Xing Shucai	CHN	4.8.84	5		Cixi	23 Apr 05
1:18:30			Yu Chaohong	CHN	12.12.76	6		Cixi	23 Apr 05
1:18:30			Wang Zhen	CHN	24.8.91	1		Taicang	22 Apr 11
1:18:31			Han Yucheng	CHN	16.12.78	7		Cixi	23 Apr 05
1:18:32			Li Zewen	CHN	5.12.73	4	WCp	Podebrady	19 Apr 97
1:18:33			Liu Yunfeng ¶	CHN	3.8.79	8		Cixi	23 Apr 05
1:18:34		Eder	Sánchez	MEX	21.5.86	3	WCp	Cheboksary	10 May 08
		(40)							
1:18:35.2t		Stefan	Johansson	SWE	11.4.67	1	SGP	Bergen (Fana)	15 May 92
1:18:36		Mikhail	Shchennikov	RUS	24.12.67	1	NC	Sochi	20 Apr 96
1:18:37		Aleksandr	Pershin	RUS	4.9.68	2	NC	Moskva	26 May 90
1:18:37		Ruslan	Shafikov	RUS	27.6.75	1	NC-w23	Adler	11 Feb 95
1:18:38			Chu Yafei	CHN	5.9.88	2		Lugano	20 Mar 11
1:18:39			Lu Ronghua	CHN	21.2.83	9		Cixi	23 Apr 05
1:18:40.0t wR		Ernesto	Canto	MEX	18.10.59	1	SGP	Fana	5 May 84
1:18:41		Igor	Kollár	SVK	26.6.65	3		Eisenhüttenstadt	11 May 96
1:18:42		Andreas	Erm	GER	12.3.76	2	ECp	Eisenhüttenstadt	17 Jun 00
1:18:45		Stepan	Yudin	RUS	3.4.80	4	NC-w	Adler	12 Mar 05
1:18:45			Dong Jimin	CHN	10.10.83	6		Yangzhou	22 Apr 06
		(51)	100th man 1:19:36, 200th 1:20:47, 300th 1:21:36, 400th 1:22:08, 500th 1:22:45						

Probable short course

Mark	Wind	Name		Nat	Born	Pos	Meet	Venue	Date
1:18:33		Mikhail	Shchennikov	RUS	24.12.67	1	4-N	Livorno	10 Jul 93

Drugs disqualification

Mark	Wind	Name		Nat	Born	Pos	Meet	Venue	Date
1:16:53dq		Vladimir	Kanaykin ¶	RUS	21.3.85	2	NC	Saransk	8 Jun 08

30 KILOMETRES WALK

Mark	Wind	Name		Nat	Born	Pos	Meet	Venue	Date
2:01:13+		Vladimir	Kanaykin ¶	RUS	21.3.85	1	in 35k	Adler	19 Feb 06
2:01:44.1t		Maurizio	Damilano	ITA	6.4.57	1		Cuneo	3 Oct 92
2:01:47+			Kanaykin			1	in 35k	Adler	13 Mar 05
2:02:27+			Kanaykin			1	in 35k	Adler	8 Feb 04
2:02:41		Andrey	Perlov	RUS	12.12.61	1	NC-w	Sochi	19 Feb 89
2:02:45		Yevgeniy	Misyulya	BLR	13.3.64	1		Mogilyov	28 Apr 91

Mark	Wind	Name		Nat	Born	Pos	Meet	Venue	Date
2:03:06		Daniel	Bautista	MEX	4.8.52	1		Cherkassy	27 Apr 80
2:03:50+		Vladimir	Parvatkin	RUS	10.10.84	2	in 35k	Adler	19 Feb 06
2:03:56.5t		Thierry	Toutain	FRA	14.2.62	1		Héricourt	24 Mar 91
2:04:00		Aleksandr	Potashov	BLR	12.3.62	1		Adler	14 Feb 93
2:04:24		Valeriy	Spitsyn	RUS	5.12.65	1	NC-w	Sochi	22 Feb 92
2:04:30		Vitaliy	Matsko (10)	RUS	8.6.60	2	NC-w	Sochi	19 Feb 89
2:04:49+		Semyon	Lovkin	RUS	14.7.77	1=	in 35k	Adler	1 Mar 03
2:04:49+		Stepan	Yudin	RUS	3.4.80	1=	in 35k	Adler	1 Mar 03
2:04:50+		Sergey	Kirdyapkin	RUS	16.1.80	2	in 35k	Adler	13 Mar 05
2:04:55.5t		Guillaume	Leblanc	CAN	14.4.62	1		Sept-Iles	16 Jun 90

35 KILOMETRES WALK

Mark	Wind	Name		Nat	Born	Pos	Meet	Venue	Date
2:21:31		Vladimir	Kanaykin ¶	RUS	21.3.85	1	NC-w	Adler	19 Feb 06
2:23:17			Kanaykin			1	NC-w	Adler	8 Feb 04
2:23:17			Kanaykin			1	NC-w	Adler	13 Mar 05
2:24:25		Semyon	Lovkin	RUS	14.7.77	1	NC-w	Adler	1 Mar 03
2:24:25		Sergey	Bakulin	RUS	13.11.86	1	NC-w	Adler	1 Mar 09
2:24:50		Denis	Nizhegorodov	RUS	26.7.80	2	NC-w	Adler	19 Feb 06
2:24:56			Nizhegorodov			2	NC-w	Adler	1 Mar 09
2:25:19		Andrey	Ruzavin	RUS	28.3.86	3	NC-w	Adler	1 Mar 09
2:25:38		Stepan	Yudin	RUS	3.4.80	2	NC-w	Adler	1 Mar 03
2:25:57		Sergey	Kirdyapkin	RUS	16.1.80	2	NC-w	Adler	13 Mar 05
2:25:58		German	Skurygin ¶	RUS	15.9.63	1	NC-w	Adler	20 Feb 98
2:25:59			Kanaykin ¶			1	NC-w	Adler	23 Feb 08
		(12/8)							
2:26:16		Alex	Schwazer	ITA	26.12.84	1		Montalto Di Castro	24 Jan 10
2:26:25		Aleksey	Voyevodin ¶ (10)	RUS	9.8.70	2	NC-w	Adler	8 Feb 04
2:26:29		Yuriy	Andronov	RUS	6.11.71	4	NC-w	Adler	1 Mar 09
2:26:36		Igor	Yerokhin ¶	RUS	4.9.85	1	NC-w	Sochi	26 Feb 11
2:26:46		Oleg	Ishutkin	RUS	22.7.75	1	NC-w	Adler	9 Feb 97
2:27:02		Yevgeniy	Shmalyuk	RUS	14.1.76	1	NC-w	Adler	20 Feb 00
2:27:07		Dmitriy	Dolnikov	RUS	19.11.72	2	NC-w	Adler	20 Feb 98
2:27:21		Pavel	Nikolayev	RUS	18.12.77	3	NC-w	Adler	20 Feb 98
2:27:29		Nikolay	Matyukhin	RUS	13.12.68	2	NC-w	Adler	9 Feb 97

50 KILOMETRES WALK

Mark	Wind	Name		Nat	Born	Pos	Meet	Venue	Date
3:34:14	WR	Denis	Nizhegorodov	RUS	26.7.80	1	WCp	Cheboksary	11 May 08
3:35:27.2t	WR	Yohann	Diniz	FRA	1.1.78	1		Reims	12 Mar 11
3:35:29			Nizhegorodov			1	NC	Cheboksary	13 Jun 04
3:35:47		Nathan	Deakes	AUS	17.8.77	1	NC	Geelong	2 Dec 06
3:36:03	WR	Robert	Korzeniowski	POL	30.7.68	1	WCh	Saint-Denis	27 Aug 03
3:36:04		Alex	Schwazer	ITA	26.12.84	1	NC	Rosignano Solvay	11 Feb 07
3:36:06			Yu Chaohong	CHN	12.12.76	1	NG	Nanjing	22 Oct 05
3:36:13			Zhao Chengliang	CHN	1.6.84	2	NG	Nanjing	22 Oct 05
3:36:20			Han Yucheng	CHN	16.12.78	1	NC	Nanning	27 Feb 05
3:36:39	WR		Korzeniowski			1	EC	München	8 Aug 02
3:36:42		German	Skurygin ¶	RUS	15.9.63	2	WCh	Saint-Denis	27 Aug 03
3:37:04			Schwazer			2	WCp	Cheboksary	11 May 08
3:37:09			Schwazer			1	OG	Beijing	22 Aug 08
3:37:26	WR	Valeriy	Spitsyn (10)	RUS	5.12.65	1	NC	Moskva	21 May 00
3:37:41	WR	Andrey	Perlov	RUS	12.12.61	1	NC	Leningrad	5 Aug 89
3:37:46		Andreas	Erm	GER	12.3.76	3	WCh	Saint-Denis	27 Aug 03
3:37:58			Xing Shucai	CHN	4.8.84	2	NC	Nanning	27 Feb 05
3:38:01		Aleksey	Voyevodin ¶	RUS	9.8.70	4	WCh	Saint-Denis	27 Aug 03
3:38:02			Nizhegorodov			1	WCp	La Coruña	14 May 06
3:38:08		Sergey	Kirdyapkin	RUS	16.1.80	1	WCh	Helsinki	12 Aug 05
3:38:08		Igor	Yerokhin ¶	RUS	4.9.85	1	NC	Saransk	8 Jun 08
3:38:17	WR	Ronald	Weigel	GDR	8.8.59	1	IM	Potsdam	25 May 86
3:38:23			Nizhegorodov			5	WCh	Saint-Denis	27 Aug 03
3:38:29		Vyacheslav	Ivanenko	RUS	3.3.61	1	OG	Seoul	30 Sep 88
3:38:31	WR		Weigel			1		Berlin	20 Jul 84
3:38:35			Kirdyapkin			1	WCh	Berlin	21 Aug 09
3:38:43		Valentí	Massana	ESP	5.7.70	1	NC	Orense	20 Mar 94
3:38:45			Diniz			1		Dudince	28 Mar 09
3:38:46			Korzeniowski			1	OG	Athína	27 Aug 04
3:38:46		Sergey	Bakulin (20)	RUS	13.11.86	1	NC	Saransk	12 Jun 11
3:38:48			Si Tianfeng	CHN	17.6.84	1		Taicang	24 Apr 11
		(31/21)							
3:38:56		Jared	Tallent	AUS	17.10.84	1	NC	Melbourne	22 Nov 09

Mark	Wind	Name		Nat	Born	Pos	Meet	Venue	Date
3:39:17			Dong Jimin	CHN	10.10.83	4	NC	Nanning	27 Feb 05
3:39:21		Vladimir	Potemin	RUS	15.1.80	2	NC	Moskva	21 May 00
3:39:22		Sergey	Korepanov	KAZ	9.5.64	1	WCp	Mézidon-Canon	2 May 99
3:39:34		Valentin	Kononen	FIN	7.3.69	1		Dudince	25 Mar 00
3:39:45		Hartwig	Gauder	GDR	10.11.54	3	OG	Seoul	30 Sep 88
3:39:46		Matej	Tóth	SVK	10.2.83	1	NC	Dudince	26 Mar 11
3:39:54		Jesús Angel	García	ESP	17.10.69	1	WCp	Podebrady	20 Apr 97
3:40:02		Aleksandr	Potashov	BLR	12.3.62	1	NC	Moskva	27 May 90
		(30)							
3:40:07		Andrey	Plotnikov	RUS	12.8.67	2	NC	Moskva	27 May 90
3:40:08		Tomasz	Lipiec ¶	POL	10.5.71	2	WCp	Mézidon-Canon	2 May 99
3:40:12		Oleg	Ishutkin	RUS	22.7.75	2	WCp	Podebrady	20 Apr 97
3:40:12		Yuki	Yamazaki	JPN	16.1.84	1		Wajima	12 Apr 09
3:40:13		Nikolay	Matyukhin	RUS	13.12.68	3	WCp	Mézidon-Canon	2 May 99
3:40:23			Gadasu Alatan	CHN	27.1.84	3	NG	Nanjing	22 Oct 05
3:40:40		Vladimir	Kanaykin ¶	RUS	21.3.85	1	NC	Saransk	12 Jun 05
3:40:46	WR	José	Marin	ESP	21.1.50	1	NC	Valencia	13 Mar 83
3:40:57.9t		Thierry	Toutain	FRA	14.2.62	1		Héricourt	29 Sep 96
3:41:02		Francisco Javier	Fernández ¶	ESP	6.3.77	1	NC	San Pedro del Pinatar	1 Mar 09
		(40)							
3:41:10			Zhao Jianguo	CHN	19.1.88	1	AsiC	Wajima	16 Apr 06
3:41:16		Trond	Nymark	NOR	28.12.76	2	WCh	Berlin	21 Aug 09
3:41:20	WR	Raúl	González	MEX	29.2.52	1		Podebrady	11 Jun 78
3:41:20			Zhao Yongsheng	CHN	16.4.70	1	WCp	Beijing	30 Apr 95
3:41:28.2t		René	Piller	FRA	23.4.65	1	SGP	Fana	7 May 94
3:41:30			Ni Liang	CHN	26.7.86	4	NG	Nanjing	22 Oct 05
3:41:47		Mikel	Odriozola	ESP	25.5.73	1	NC	El Prat de Llobregat	27 Feb 05
3:41:51		Venyamin	Nikolayev	RUS	7.10.58	2	NC	Leningrad	3 Aug 85
3:41:51		Oleg	Kistkin	RUS	13.5.83	3	ECp	Leamington	20 May 07
3:41:55			Wang Hao	CHN	16.8.89	2	NG	Jinan	26 Oct 09
		(50)	100th man 3:45:46, 200th 3:50:24, 300th 3:53:03, 400th 3:56:00. 500th 3:58:21						

Drugs disqualification

Mark	Wind	Name		Nat	Born	Pos	Meet	Venue	Date
3:36:55		Vladimir	Kanaykin ¶	RUS	21.3.85	(2)	WCp	Cheboksary	11 May 08

100 KILOMETRES WALK

Mark	Wind	Name		Nat	Born	Pos	Meet	Venue	Date
8:38.07		Viktor	Ginko	BLR	7.12.65	1		Scanzorosciate	27 Oct 02
8:43:30			Ginko			1		Scanzorosciate	29 Oct 00
8:44:28			Ginko			1		Scanzorosciate	19 Oct 03
8:48:28		Modris	Liepins	LAT	30.8.66	1		Scanzorosciate	28 Oct 01
8:54:35		Aleksey	Rodionov	RUS	5.3.57	1		Scanzorosciate	15 Nov 98
8:55:12		Pascal	Kieffer	FRA	6.5.61	1		Besançon	18 Oct 92
8:55:40		Vitaliy	Popovich	UKR	22.10.62	1		Scanzorosciate	31 Oct 99
8:58:12		Gérard	Lelièvre	FRA	13.11.49	1		Laval	7 Oct 84
8:58:47		Zóltan	Czukor	HUN	18.12.62	2		Scanzorosciate	27 Oct 02

Some notes on all-time lists at end of 2011

Deep all-time lists (generally 100 performances and 500 perfromers for all standard men's and women's events) have been compiled by Richard Hymans and Peter Matthews to be published next year by Jonas Hedman in a book that also includes the author's selections of the all-time top ten greats for each event.

Oldest mark in World Lists: Men: in wind assisted sections: LJ 8.49w Ralph Boston USA 2 Sep 1964, 100m 9.91w Bob Hayes USA 15 Oct 1964; in main lists: SP: 32nd 21.78 Randy Matson USA 22 Apr 1967. Women: by an individual 100mh 42nd= 12.59 Anneliese Ehrhardt GDR 8 Sep 1972; by team: 4x100m 43.44A NED 20 Oct 1968

Mark	Wind	Name		Nat	Born	Pos	Meet	Venue	Date
			WOMEN'S ALL-TIME WORLD LISTS						

100 METRES

Mark	Wind	Name		Nat	Born	Pos	Meet	Venue	Date
10.49wr	0.0	Florence	Griffith-Joyner	USA	21.12.59	1q1	NC/OT	Indianpolis	16 Jul 88
		@ Probably strongly wind-assisted, but recognised as a US and world record							
10.61	1.2		Griffith-Joyner			1	NC/OT	Indianpolis	17 Jul 88
10.62	1.0		Griffith-Joyner			1q3	OG	Seoul	24 Sep 88
10.64	1.2	Carmelita	Jeter	USA	24.11.79	1		Shanghai	20 Sep 09
10.65A	1.1	Marion	Jones ¶	USA	12.10.75	1	WCp	Johannesburg	12 Sep 98
10.67	-0.1		Jeter			1	WAF	Thessaloníki	13 Sep 09
10.70 (WR)	1.6		Griffith-Joyner			1s1	NC/OT	Indianapolis	17 Jul 88
10.70	-0.1		Jones			1	WCh	Sevilla	22 Aug 99
10.70	2.0		Jeter			1	Pre	Eugene	4 Jun 11
10.71	0.1		Jones			1		Chengdu	12 May 98
10.71	2.0		Jones			1s2	NC	New Orleans	19 Jun 98
10.72	2.0		Jones			1	NC	New Orleans	20 Jun 98
10.72	0.0		Jones			1	Herc	Monaco	8 Aug 98
10.72	0.0		Jones			1	Athl	Lausanne	25 Aug 98
10.73	2.0	Christine	Arron	FRA	13.9.73	1	EC	Budapest	19 Aug 98
10.73	0.1	Shelly-Ann	Fraser-Pryce	JAM	27.12.86	1	WCh	Berlin	17 Aug 09
10.74	1.3	Merlene	Ottey	JAM/SLO	10.5.60	1	GPF	Milano	7 Sep 96
10.75	0.6		Jones			1	GGala	Roma	14 Jul 98
10.75	0.4	Kerron	Stewart	JAM	16.4.84	1	GGala	Roma	10 Jul 09
10.75	0.1		Stewart			2	WCh	Berlin	17 Aug 09
10.76 wr	1.7	Evelyn	Ashford	USA	15.4.57	1	WK	Zürich	22 Aug 84
10.76	0.9		Jones			1	VD	Bruxelles	22 Aug 97
10.76	0.3		Jones			1q4	WCh	Sevilla	21 Aug 99
10.76	1.1	Veronica	Campbell-Brown	JAM	15.5.82	1	GS	Ostrava	31 May 11
10.77	0.9	Irina	Privalova (10)	RUS	22.11.68	1rA	Athl	Lausanne	6 Jul 94
10.77	-0.9		Jones			1rA	WK	Zürich	12 Aug 98
10.77	0.7	Ivet	Lalova	BUL	18.5.84	1	ECp-1A	Plovdiv	19 Jun 04
10.78A	1.0	Dawn	Sowell	USA	27.3.66	1	NCAA	Provo	3 Jun 89
10.78	1.7		Ottey			1	Expo	Sevilla	30 May 90
10.78	0.4		Ottey			1	GPF	Paris	3 Sep 94
10.78	1.1		Jones			1	BrGP	London (CP)	5 Aug 00
10.78	1.8	Torri	Edwards ¶	USA	31.1.77	1s2	OT	Eugene	28 Jun 08
10.78	0.0		Fraser			1	OG	Beijing	17 Aug 08
10.78	0.8		Campbell-Brown			1	Pre	Eugene	3 Jul 10
10.78	0.4		Jeter			1	VD	Bruxelles	16 Sep 11
		(35 performances by 13 athletes)							
10.79	0.0		Li Xuemei	CHN	5.1.77	1	NG	Shanghai	18 Oct 97
10.79	-0.1	Inger	Miller	USA	12.6.72	2	WCh	Sevilla	22 Aug 99
10.81 wr	1.7	Marlies	Göhr'	GDR	21.3.58	1	OD	Berlin	8 Jun 83
10.82	-1.0	Gail	Devers	USA	19.11.66	1	OG	Barcelona	1 Aug 92
10.82	0.4	Gwen	Torrence	USA	12.6.65	2	GPF	Paris	3 Sep 94
10.82	-0.3	Zhanna	Pintusevich-Block ¶	UKR	6.7.72	1	WCh	Edmonton	6 Aug 01
10.82	-0.7	Sherone	Simpson	JAM	12.8.84	1	NC	Kingston	24 Jun 06
		(20)							
10.83	1.7	Marita	Koch	GDR	18.2.57	2	OD	Berlin	8 Jun 83
10.83	-1.0	Juliet	Cuthbert	JAM	9.4.64	2	OG	Barcelona	1 Aug 92
10.83	0.1	Ekateríni	Thánou ¶	GRE	1.2.75	2s1	WCh	Sevilla	22 Aug 99
10.84	1.3	Chioma	Ajunwa ¶	NGR	25.12.70	1		Lagos	11 Apr 92
10.84	1.9	Chandra	Sturrup	BAH	12.9.71	1	Athl	Lausanne	5 Jul 05
10.84	1.8	Kelly-Ann	Baptiste	TRI	14.10.86	1		Clermont	5 Jun 10
10.85	2.0	Anelia	Nuneva	BUL	30.6.62	1h1	NC	Sofia	2 Sep 88
10.85	1.0	Muna	Lee	USA	30.10.81	1	OT	Eugene	28 Jun 08
10.86	0.6	Silke	Gladisch'	GDR	20.6.64	1	NC	Potsdam	20 Aug 87
10.86	1.2	Chryste	Gaines ¶	USA	14.9.70	1	WAF	Monaco	14 Sep 03
		(30)							
10.86	2.0	Marshevet	Myers	USA	25.9.84	2	Pre	Eugene	4 Jun 11
10.88	0.4	Lauryn	Williams	USA	11.9.83	2	WK	Zürich	19 Aug 05
10.89	1.8	Katrin	Krabbe ¶	GDR	22.11.69	1		Berlin	20 Jul 88
10.89	0.0		Liu Xiaomei	CHN	11.1.72	2	NG	Shanghai	18 Oct 97
10.90	1.4	Glory	Alozie	NGR/ESP	30.12.77	1		La Laguna	5 Jun 99
10.90	1.8	Shalonda	Solomon	USA	19.12.85	2		Clermont	5 Jun 10
10.91	0.2	Heike	Drechsler'	GDR/GER	16.12.64	2	GWG	Moskva	6 Jul 86
10.91	1.1	Savatheda	Fynes	BAH	17.10.74	2	Athl	Lausanne	2 Jul 99
10.91	1.5	Debbie	Ferguson McKenzie	BAH	16.1.76	1	CG	Manchester	27 Jul 02

Mark	Wind	Name		Nat	Born	Pos	Meet	Venue	Date
10.92	0.0	Alice	Brown	USA	20.9.60	2q2	NC/OT	Indianapolis	16 Jul 88
		(40)							
10.92	1.1	D'Andre	Hill	USA	19.4.73	3	NC	Atlanta	15 Jun 96
10.92	0.1	Yuliya	Nesterenko	BLR	15.6.79	1s1	OG	Athína	21 Aug 04
10.93	1.8	Ewa	Kasprzyk	POL	7.9.57	1	NC	Grudziadz	27 Jun 86
10.93	1.0	Tayna	Lawrence	JAM	17.9.75	3	VD	Bruxelles	30 Aug 02
10.93	1.5	Allyson	Felix	USA	18.11.85	1	SGP	Doha	9 May 08
10.94A	0.6	Diane	Williams	USA	14.12.60	2	USOF	USAF Academy	3 Jul 83
10.94	1.0	Carlette	Guidry	USA	4.9.68	1	NC	New York	14 Jun 91
10.95	1.0	Bärbel	Wöckel'	GDR	21.3.55	2	NC	Dresden	1 Jul 82
10.95	2.0	Me'Lisa	Barber	USA	4.10.80	2	adidas	Carson	20 May 07
10.95A	1.8	Simone	Facey	JAM	7.5.85	1	Big 12	Boulder	18 May 08
		(50)	100th women 11.05, 200th 11.14, 300th 11.21, 400th 11.27, 500th 11.30						

Doubtful wind reading

Mark	Wind	Name		Nat	Born	Pos	Meet	Venue	Date
10.83	0.0	Sheila	Echols	USA	2.10.64	1q2	NC/OT	Indianapolis	16 Jul 88
10.86	0.0	Diane	Williams	USA	14.12.60	2q1	NC/OT	Indianapolis	16 Jul 88

Probably semi-automatic timing

10.87	1.9	Lyudmila	Kondratyeva	RUS	11.4.58	1		Leningrad	3 Jun 80

Low altitude best: 10.91 1.6 Sowell 1 NC Houston 16 Jun 89

Wind-assisted to 10.76 performances and 10.91 performers

Mark	Wind	Name		Nat	Born	Pos	Meet	Venue	Date
10.54	3.0		Griffith-Joyner			1	OG	Seoul	25 Sep 88
10.60	3.2		Griffith-Joyner			1h1	NC/OT	Indianpolis	16 Jul 88
10.68	2.2		Jones			1	DNG	Stockholm	1 Aug 00
10.70	2.6		Griffith-Joyner			1s2	OG	Seoul	25 Sep 88
10.72	3.0		Jeter			1s1	NC	Eugene	26 Jun 09
10.74	2.7		Jeter			1	NC	Eugene	24 Jun 11
10.75	4.1		Jones			1h3	NC	New Orleans	19 Jun 98
10.76	3.4	Marshevet	Hooker/Myers	USA	25.9.84	1q1	NC/OT	Eugene	27 Jun 08
10.77	2.3	Gail	Devers	USA	19.11.66	1	Jen	San José	28 May 94
10.77	2.3	Ekateríni	Thánou ¶	GRE	1.2.75	1		Rethymno	28 May 99
10.78	5.0	Gwen	Torrence	USA	12.6.65	1q3	NC/OT	Indianpolis	16 Jul 88
10.78	3.3	Muna	Lee	USA	30.10.81	2	NC	Eugene	26 Jun 09
10.79	3.3	Marlies	Göhr'	GDR	21.3.58	1	NC	Cottbus	16 Jul 80
10.80	2.9	Pam	Marshall	USA	16.8.60	1	NC	Eugene	20 Jun 86
10.80	2.8	Heike	Drechsler'	GDR	16.12.64	1	Bisl	Oslo	5 Jul 86
10.82	2.2	Silke	Gladisch/Möller	GDR	20.6.64	1s1	WCh	Roma	30 Aug 87
10.84	2.9	Alice	Brown	USA	20.9.60	2	NC	Eugene	20 Jun 86
10.86	3.4	Lauryn	Williams	USA	11.9.83	2q1	NC/OT	Eugene	27 Jun 08
10.86	2.9	Murielle	Ahouré	CIV	23.8.87	1		Clermont	4 Jun 11
10.87	3.0	Me'Lisa	Barber	USA	4.10.80	1s1	NC	Carson	25 Jun 05
10.89	3.1	Kerstin	Behrendt	GDR	2.9.67	2		Berlin	13 Sep 88
10.89	4.6	Tahesia	Harrigan #	IVB	15.2.82	1h1		Clermont	4 Jun 11
10.90	2.5	Damola	Osayomi ¶	NGR	26.6.86	1	AfrG	Maputo	12 Sep 11
10.91	4.6	Carlette	Guidry	USA	4.9.68	1s1	NCAA	Eugene	31 May 91
10.91	3.2	Alexandria	Anderson	USA	28.1.87	2A	TexR	Austin	9 Apr 11

Hand timing

Mark	Wind	Name		Nat	Born	Pos	Meet	Venue	Date
10.6	0.1	Zhanna	Pintusevich	UKR	6.7.72	1		Kiev	12 Jun 97
10.7		Merlene	Ottey	JAM	10.5.60	1h	NC	Kingston	15 Jul 88
10.7	1.1	Juliet	Cuthbert	JAM	9.4.64	1	NC	Kingston	4 Jul 92
10.7		Mary	Onyali	NGR	3.2.68	1	NC	Lagos	22 Jun 96
10.7	-0.2	Svetlana	Goncharenko	RUS	28.5.71	1		Rostov-na-Donu	30 May 98
10.7A	1.3	Blessing	Okagbare	NGR	9.10.86	1		El Paso	10 Apr 10
10.7w	2.6	Savatheda	Fynes	BAH	17.10.74	1	NC	Nassau	22 Jun 95

Drugs disqualification

Mark	Wind	Name		Nat	Born	Pos	Meet	Venue	Date
10.75	-0.4		Jones			1	OG	Sydney	23 Sep 00
10.78	0.1		Jones			1	ISTAF	Berlin	1 Sep 00
10.85	0.9	Kelli	White ¶	USA	1.4.77	1	WCh	Saint-Denis	24 Aug 03
10.79w	2.3	Kelli	White ¶	USA	1.4.77	1		Carson	1 Jun 03

200 METRES

Mark	Wind	Name		Nat	Born	Pos	Meet	Venue	Date
21.34WR	1.3	Florence	Griffith-Joyner	USA	21.12.59	1	OG	Seoul	29 Sep 88
21.56WR	1.7		Griffith-Joyner			1s1	OG	Seoul	29 Sep 88
21.62A	-0.6	Marion	Jones ¶	USA	12.10.75	1	WCp	Johannesburg	11 Sep 98
21.64	0.8	Merlene	Ottey	JAM	10.5.60	1	VD	Bruxelles	13 Sep 91
21.66	-1.0		Ottey			1	WK	Zürich	15 Aug 90
21.71WR	0.7	Marita	Koch	GDR	18.2.57	1	v CAN	Karl-Marx-Stadt	10 Jun 79
21.71WR	0.3		Koch			1	OD	Potsdam	21 Jul 84
21.71WR	1.2	Heike	Drechsler'	GDR	16.12.64	1	NC	Jena	29 Jun 86
21.71WR	-0.8		Drechsler			1	EC	Stuttgart	29 Aug 86
21.72	1.3	Grace	Jackson	JAM	14.6.61	2	OG	Seoul	29 Sep 88

Mark	Wind	Name		Nat	Born	Pos	Meet	Venue	Date
21.72	-0.1	Gwen	Torrence	USA	12.6.65	1s2	OG	Barcelona	5 Aug 92
21.74	0.4	Marlies	Göhr'	GDR	21.3.58	1	NC	Erfurt	3 Jun 84
21.74	1.2	Silke	Gladisch'	GDR	20.6.64	1	WCh	Roma	3 Sep 87
21.74	0.6	Veronica (10)	Campbell-Brown	JAM	15.5.82	1	OG	Beijing	21 Aug 08
21.75	-0.1	Juliet	Cuthbert	JAM	9.4.64	2s2	OG	Barcelona	5 Aug 92
21.76	0.3		Koch			1	NC	Dresden	3 Jul 82
21.76	0.7		Griffith-Joyner			1q1	OG	Seoul	28 Sep 88
21.76	-0.8		Jones			1	WK	Zürich	13 Aug 97
21.77	-0.1		Griffith-Joyner			1q2	NC/OT	Indianapolis	22 Jul 88
21.77	1.0		Ottey			1	Herc	Monaco	7 Aug 93
21.77	-0.3		Torrence			1	ASV	Köln	18 Aug 95
21.77	0.6	Inger	Miller	USA	12.6.72	1	WCh	Sevilla	27 Aug 99
21.78	-1.3		Koch			1	NC	Leipzig	11 Aug 85
21.79	1.7		Gladisch			1	NC	Potsdam	22 Aug 87
21.80	-1.1		Ottey			1	Nik	Nice	10 Jul 90
21.80	0.4		Jones			1	GWG	Uniondale, NY	20 Jul 98
21.81	-0.1	Valerie	Brisco	USA	6.7.60	1	OG	Los Angeles	9 Aug 84
21.81	0.4		Ottey			1	ASV	Köln	19 Aug 90
21.81	-0.6		Torrence			1	OG	Barcelona	6 Aug 92
21.81	0.0		Torrence			1	Herc	Monaco	25 Jul 95
21.81	1.6		Jones			1	Pre	Eugene	30 May 99
21.81	1.7	Allyson (32/14)	Felix	USA	18.11.85	1	WCh	Osaka	31 Aug 07
21.83	-0.2	Evelyn	Ashford	USA	15.4.57	1	WCp	Montreal	24 Aug 79
21.85	0.3	Bärbel	Wöckel'	GDR	21.3.55	2	OD	Potsdam	21 Jul 84
21.87	0.0	Irina	Privalova	RUS	22.11.68	2	Herc	Monaco	25 Jul 95
21.93	1.3	Pam	Marshall	USA	16.8.60	2	NC/OT	Indianapolis	23 Jul 88
21.95	0.3	Katrin	Krabbe ¶	GDR	22.11.69	1	EC	Split	30 Aug 90
21.97	1.9	Jarmila (20)	Kratochvílová	CZE	26.1.51	1	PTS	Bratislava	6 Jun 81
21.99	0.9	Chandra	Cheeseborough	USA	10.1.59	2	NC	Indianapolis	19 Jun 83
21.99	1.1	Marie-José	Pérec	FRA	9.5.68	1	BNP	Villeneuve d'Ascq	2 Jul 93
21.99	1.1	Kerron	Stewart	JAM	16.4.84	2	NC	Kingston	29 Jun 08
22.00	1.3	Sherone	Simpson	JAM	12.8.84	1	NC	Kingston	25 Jun 06
22.01	-0.5	Anelia	Nuneva'	BUL	30.6.62	1	NC	Sofiya	16 Aug 87
22.01	0.0		Li Xuemei	CHN	5.1.77	1	NG	Shanghai	22 Oct 97
22.01	0.6	Muna	Lee	USA	30.10.81	4	OG	Beijing	21 Aug 08
22.04A	0.7	Dawn	Sowell	USA	27.3.66	1	NCAA	Provo	2 Jun 89
22.06A	0.7	Evette	de Klerk'	RSA	21.8.65	1		Pietersburg	8 Apr 89
22.07	-0.1	Mary (30)	Onyali	NGR	3.2.68	1	WK	Zürich	14 Aug 96
22.10	-0.1	Kathy	Cook'	GBR	3.5.60	4	OG	Los Angeles	9 Aug 84
22.13	1.2	Ewa	Kasprzyk	POL	7.9.57	2	GWG	Moskva	8 Jul 86
22.14	-0.6	Carlette	Guidry	USA	4.9.68	1	NC	Atlanta	23 Jun 96
22.15	1.1	Shelly-Ann	Fraser-Pryce	JAM	27.12.86	4	NC	Kingston	29 Jun 08
22.15	1.0	Shalonda	Solomon	USA	19.12.85	1	NC	Eugene	26 Jun 11
22.17A	-2.3	Zhanna	Pintusevich-Block ¶	UKR	6.7.72	1		Monachil	9 Jul 97
22.24	-0.3					2	VD	Bruxelles	30 Aug 02
22.17	0.6	Sanya	Richards	USA	26.2.85	2	WAF	Stuttgart	9 Sep 06
22.18	-0.6	Dannette	Young-Stone	USA	6.10.64	2	NC	Atlanta	23 Jun 96
22.18	0.9	Galina	Malchugina	RUS	17.12.62	1s2	NC	Sankt Peterburg	4 Jul 96
22.18	0.5	Merlene (40)	Frazer	JAM	27.12.73	1s2	WCh	Sevilla	25 Aug 99
22.19	1.5	Natalya	Bochina	RUS	4.1.62	2	OG	Moskva	30 Jul 80
22.19	0.0	Debbie	Ferguson McKenzie	BAH	16.1.76	1	GP II	Saint-Denis	3 Jul 99
22.20	2.0	Kim	Gevaert	BEL	5.8.78	1	NC	Bruxelles	9 Jul 06
22.20	-0.4	Carmelita	Jeter	USA	24.11.79	1	Herc	Monaco	22 Jul 11
22.21 WR	1.9	Irena	Szewinska'	POL	24.5.46	1		Potsdam	13 Jun 74
22.22	-0.9	Falilat	Ogunkoya	NGR	12.5.68	1	AfCh	Dakar	22 Aug 98
22.22	0.6	Beverly	McDonald	JAM	15.2.70	2	WCh	Sevilla	27 Aug 99
22.22	0.3	Rachelle	Smith (Boone)	USA	30.6.81	2	NC	Carson	26 Jun 05
22.23	0.8	Melinda	Gainsford-Taylor	AUS	1.10.71	1		Stuttgart	13 Jul 97
22.23A	1.8	Carol (50)	Rodríguez	PUR	16.12.85	1h1	NCAA-r	Provo	26 May 06

100th woman 22.39, 200th 22.65, 300th 22.80, 4th 22.89, 500th 22.99

Wind-assisted   *Performers listed to 22.21*

Mark	Wind	Name		Nat	Born	Pos	Meet	Venue	Date
21.82	3.1	Irina	Privalova	RUS	22.11.68	1	Athl	Lausanne	6 Jul 94
21.91	2.8	Muna	Lee	USA	30.10.81	1		Fort-de-France	10 May 08
22.10	2.4	Shelly-Ann	Fraser-Pryce	JAM	27.12.86	1		Kingston	7 May 11
22.16	3.1	Dannette	Young-Stone	USA	6.10.64	2	Athl	Lausanne	6 Jul 94
22.16	3.2	Nanceen	Perry	USA	19.4.77	1		Austin	6 May 00

Mark	Wind	Name		Nat	Born	Pos	Meet	Venue	Date
22.18A	2.8	Melinda	Gainsford-Taylor	AUS	1.10.71	1		Pietersburg	18 Mar 00
22.18	3.2	Kimberlyn	Duncan	USA	2.8.91	1		Baton Rouge	23 Apr 11
22.19A	3.1	Angella	Taylor'	CAN	28.9.58	1		Colorado Springs	21 Jul 82
22.20	5.6	Marshevet	Hooker/Myers	USA	25.9.84	3	NC/OT	Eugene	6 Jul 08
22.21	5.6	Lauryn	Williams	USA	11.9.83	4	NC/OT	Eugene	6 Jul 08

Hand timing

21.9	-0.1	Svetlana	Goncharenko	RUS	28.5.71	1		Rostov-na-Donu	31 May 98
21.6w	2.5	Pam	Marshall	USA	16.8.60	1	NC	San José	26 Jun 87

Drugs disqualification

22.05	-0.3	Kelli	White ¶	USA	1.4.77	1	WCh	Saint-Denis	28 Aug 03
22.18i		Michelle	Collins ¶	USA	12.2.71	1	WI	Birmingham	15 Mar 03

300 METRES

Times in 300m races only

Mark		Name		Nat	Born	Pos	Meet	Venue	Date
35.30A		Ana Gabriela	Guevara	MEX	4.3.77	1		Ciudad de México	3 May 03
35.46		Kathy	Cook'	GBR	3.5.60	1	Nike	London (CP)	18 Aug 84
35.46		Chandra	Cheeseborough	USA	10.1.59	2	Nike	London (CP)	18 Aug 84

Indoors

35.45		Irina	Privalova	RUS	22.11.68	1		Moskva	17 Jan 93
35.48	#	Svetlana	Goncharenko	RUS	28.5.71	1		Tampere	4 Feb 98

400 METRES

Mark		Name		Nat	Born	Pos	Meet	Venue	Date
47.60 WR		Marita	Koch	GDR	18.2.57	1	WCp	Canberra	6 Oct 85
47.99 WR		Jarmila	Kratochvílová	CZE	26.1.51	1	WCh	Helsinki	10 Aug 83
48.16 WR			Koch			1	EC	Athína	8 Sep 82
48.16			Koch			1	Drz	Praha	16 Aug 84
48.22			Koch			1	EC	Stuttgart	28 Aug 86
48.25		Marie-José	Pérec	FRA	9.5.68	1	OG	Atlanta	29 Jul 96
48.26			Koch			1	GO	Dresden	27 Jul 84
48.27		Olga	Vladykina'	UKR	30.6.63	2	WCp	Canberra	6 Oct 85
48.45			Kratochvílová			1	NC	Praha	23 Jul 83
48.59		Tatána	Kocembová'	CZE	2.5.62	2	WCh	Helsinki	10 Aug 83
48.60 WR			Koch			1	ECp	Torino	4 Aug 79
48.60			Vladykina			1	ECp	Moskva	17 Aug 85
48.61			Kratochvílová			1	WCp	Roma	6 Sep 81
48.63		Cathy	Freeman	AUS	16.2.73	2	OG	Atlanta	29 Jul 96
48.65			Bryzgina'			1	OG	Seoul	26 Sep 88
48.70		Sanya	Richards	USA	26.2.85	1	WCp	Athína	16 Sep 06
48.73			Kocembová			2	Drz	Praha	16 Aug 84
48.77			Koch			1	v USA	Karl-Marx-Stadt	9 Jul 82
48.82			Kratochvílová			1	Ros	Praha	23 Jun 83
48.83		Valerie	Brisco	USA	6.7.60	1	OG	Los Angeles	6 Aug 84
48.83			Pérec			1	OG	Barcelona	5 Aug 92
48.83			Richards			1	VD	Bruxelles	4 Sep 09
48.85			Kratochvílová			2	EC	Athína	8 Sep 82
48.86			Kratochvílová			1	WK	Zürich	18 Aug 82
48.86			Koch			1	NC	Erfurt	2 Jun 84
48.87			Koch			1	VD	Bruxelles	27 Aug 82
48.88			Koch			1	OG	Moskva	28 Jul 80
48.89 WR			Koch			1		Potsdam	29 Jul 79
48.89			Koch			1		Berlin	15 Jul 84
48.89		Ana Gabriela	Guevara	MEX	4.3.77	1	WCh	Saint-Denis	27 Aug 03
		(30/9)							
49.05		Chandra (10)	Cheeseborough	USA	10.1.59	2	OG	Los Angeles	6 Aug 84
49.07		Tonique	Williams-Darling	BAH	17.1.76	1	ISTAF	Berlin	12 Sep 04
49.10		Falilat	Ogunkoya	NGR	12.5.68	3	OG	Atlanta	29 Jul 96
49.11		Olga	Nazarova ¶	RUS	1.6.65	1s1	OG	Seoul	25 Sep 88
49.19		Mariya	Pinigina'	UKR	9.2.58	3	WCh	Helsinki	10 Aug 83
49.24		Sabine	Busch	GDR	21.11.62	2	NC	Erfurt	2 Jun 84
49.28 WR		Irena	Szewinska'	POL	24.5.46	1	OG	Montreal	29 Jul 76
49.28		Pauline	Davis-Thompson	BAH	9.7.66	4	OG	Atlanta	29 Jul 96
49.29		Charity	Opara ¶	NGR	20.5.72	1	GGala	Roma	14 Jul 98
49.29		Antonina	Krivoshapka	RUS	21.7.87	1s1	NC	Cheboksary	23 Jul 09
49.30		Petra	Müller'	GDR	18.7.65	1		Jena	3 Jun 88
		(20)							
49.30		Lorraine	Fenton'	JAM	8.9.73	2	Herc	Monaco	19 Jul 02
49.32		Shericka	Williams	JAM	17.9.85	2	WCh	Berlin	18 Aug 09
49.35		Anastasiya	Kapachinskaya ¶	RUS	21.11.79	1	NC	Cheboksary	22 Jul 11
49.40		Jearl	Miles-Clark	USA	4.9.66	1	NC	Indianapolis	14 Jun 97
49.42		Grit	Breuer ¶	GER	16.2.72	2	WCh	Tokyo	27 Aug 91
49.43		Kathy	Cook'	GBR	3.5.60	3	OG	Los Angeles	6 Aug 84

Mark	Wind	Name		Nat	Born	Pos	Meet	Venue	Date
49.43A		Fatima	Yusuf	NGR	2.5.71	1	AfG	Harare	15 Sep 95
49.47		Aelita	Yurchenko	UKR	1.1.65	2	Kuts	Moskva	4 Sep 88
49.49		Olga	Zaytseva	RUS	10.11.84	1	NCp	Tula	16 Jul 06
49.53		Vanya	Stambolova ¶	BUL	28.11.83	1	GP	Rieti	27 Aug 06
		(30)							
49.56		Bärbel	Wöckel'	GDR	21.3.55	1		Erfurt	30 May 82
49.56		Monique	Hennagan	USA	26.5.76	1	NC/OT	Sacramento	17 Jul 04
49.56		Amantle	Montsho	BOT	4.7.83	1	WCh	Daegu	29 Aug 11
49.57		Grace	Jackson	JAM	14.6.61	1	Nik	Nice	10 Jul 88
49.58		Dagmar	Rübsam'	GDR	3.6.62	3	NC	Erfurt	2 Jun 84
49.59		Marion	Jones ¶	USA	12.10.75	1r6	MSR	Walnut	16 Apr 00
49.59		Katharine	Merry	GBR	21.9.74	1	GP	Athína	11 Jun 01
49.59		Allyson	Felix	USA	18.11.85	2	WCh	Daegu	29 Aug 11
49.61		Ana Fidelia	Quirot	CUB	23.3.63	1	PAm	La Habana	5 Aug 91
49.61		Christine	Ohuruogu ¶	GBR	17.5.84	1	WCh	Osaka	29 Aug 07
		(40)							
49.63		Novlene	Williams-Mills	JAM	26.4.82	1		Shanghai	23 Sep 06
49.64		Gwen	Torrence	USA	12.6.65	2	Nik	Nice	15 Jul 92
49.64		Ximena	Restrepo	COL	10.3.69	3	OG	Barcelona	5 Aug 92
49.64		Deedee	Trotter	USA	8.12.82	1	NC	Indianapolis	23 Jun 07
49.64		Debbie	Dunn	USA	26.3.78	1	NC	Des Moines	26 Jun 10
49.65		Natalya	Nazarova	RUS	26.5.79	1	NC	Tula	31 Jul 04
49.65		Nicola	Sanders	GBR	23.6.82	2	WCh	Osaka	29 Aug 07
49.66		Christina	Brehmer/Lathan	GDR	28.2.58	3	OG	Moskva	28 Jul 80
49.66		Lillie	Leatherwood	USA	6.7.64	1	NC	New York	15 Jun 91
49.67		Sandra	Myers	USA/ESP	9.1.61	1	Bisl	Oslo	6 Jul 91
		(50)	100th woman 50.25, 200th 50.87, 300th 51.23, 400th 51.48, 500th 51.72						

Hand timing

Mark	Wind	Name		Nat	Born	Pos	Meet	Venue	Date
48.9		Olga	Nazarova ¶	RUS	1.6.65	1	NP	Vladivostok	13 Sep 88
49.2A		Ana Fidelia	Quirot	CUB	23.3.63	1	AmCp	Bogotá	13 Aug 89

600 METRES

Mark	Name		Nat	Born	Pos	Meet	Venue	Date
1:22.63	Ana Fidelia	Quirot	CUB	23.3.63	1		Guadalajara, ESP	25 Jul 97
1:22.87	Maria Lurdes	Mutola	MOZ	27.10.72	1		Liège (NX)	27 Aug 02
1:23.5	Doina	Melinte	ROU	27.12.56	1		Poiana Brasov	27 Jul 86
1:23.78	Natalya	Khrushchelyova	RUS	30.5.73	2		Liège (NX)	2 Sep 03

800 METRES

Mark		Name		Nat	Born	Pos	Meet	Venue	Date
1:53.28	WR	Jarmila	Kratochvílová	CZE	26.1.51	1		München	26 Jul 83
1:53.43	WR	Nadezhda	Olizarenko'	UKR	28.11.53	1	OG	Moskva	27 Jul 80
1:54.01		Pamela	Jelimo	KEN	5.12.89	1	WK	Zürich	29 Aug 08
1:54.44		Ana Fidelia	Quirot	CUB	23.3.63	1	WCp	Barcelona	9 Sep 89
1:54.68			Kratochvílová			1	WCh	Helsinki	9 Aug 83
1:54.81		Olga	Mineyeva	RUS	1.9.52	2	OG	Moskva	27 Jul 80
1:54.82			Quirot			1	ASV	Köln	24 Aug 97
1:54.85	WR		Olizarenko			1	Prav	Moskva	12 Jun 80
1:54.87			Jelimo			1	OG	Beijing	18 Aug 08
1:54.94	WR	Tatyana	Kazankina ¶	RUS	17.12.51	1	OG	Montreal	26 Jul 76
1:54.97			Jelimo			1	Gaz	Saint-Denis	18 Jul 08
1:54.99			Jelimo			1	ISTAF	Berlin	1 Jun 08
1:55.04			Kratochvílová			1	OsloG	Oslo	23 Aug 83
1:55.05		Doina	Melinte	ROU	27.12.56	1	NC	Bucuresti	1 Aug 82
1:55.1			Mineyeva			1	Znam	Moskva	6 Jul 80
1:55.16			Jelimo			1	VD	Bruxelles	5 Sep 08
1:55.19		Maria Lurdes	Mutola	MOZ	27.10.72	1	WK	Zürich	17 Aug 94
1:55.19		Jolanda	Ceplak ¶	SLO	12.9.76	1rA	NA	Heusden	20 Jul 02
1:55.26		Sigrun	Wodars/Grau (10)	GDR	7.11.65	1	WCh	Roma	31 Aug 87
1:55.29			Mutola			2	ASV	Köln	24 Aug 97
1:55.32		Christine	Wachtel	GDR	6.1.65	2	WCh	Roma	31 Aug 87
1:55.41			Mineyeva			1	EC	Athína	8 Sep 82
1:55.41			Jelimo			1	Bisl	Oslo	6 Jun 08
1:55.42		Nikolina	Shtereva	BUL	25.1.55	2	OG	Montreal	26 Jul 76
1:55.43			Mutola			1	WCh	Stuttgart	17 Aug 93
1:55.45		Caster	Semenya	RSA	7.1.91	1	WCh	Berlin	19 Aug 09
1:55.46		Tatyana	Providokhina	RUS	26.3.53	3	OG	Moskva	27 Jul 80
1:55.5			Mineyeva			1	Kuts	Podolsk	21 Aug 82
1:55.54		Ellen	van Langen	NED	9.2.66	1	OG	Barcelona	3 Aug 92
1:55.54			Liu Dong	CHN	24.12.73	1	NG	Beijing	9 Sep 93
		(30/16)							
1:55.56		Lyubov	Gurina	RUS	6.8.57	3	WCh	Roma	31 Aug 87

Mark	Wind	Name		Nat	Born	Pos	Meet	Venue	Date
1:55.60		Elfi	Zinn	GDR	24.8.53	3	OG	Montreal	26 Jul 76
1:55.68		Ella	Kovacs	ROU	11.12.64	1	RomIC	Bucuresti	2 Jun 85
1:55.69		Irina	Podyalovskaya	RUS	19.10.59	1	Izv	Kyiv	22 Jun 84
(20)									
1:55.74		Anita	Weiss'	GDR	16.7.55	4	OG	Montreal	26 Jul 76
1:55.87		Svetlana	Masterkova	RUS	17.1.68	1	Kuts	Moskva	18 Jun 99
1:55.87		Mariya	Savinova	RUS	13.8.85	1	WCh	Daegu	4 Sep 11
1:55.96		Lyudmila	Veselkova	RUS	25.10.50	2	EC	Athína	8 Sep 82
1:55.96		Yekaterina	Podkopayeva'	KⁱʸᵉᵛRUS	11.6.52	1		Leningrad	27 Jul 83
1:55.99		Liliya	Nurutdinova ¶	RUS	15.12.63	2	OG	Barcelona	3 Aug 92
1:56.00		Tatyana	Andrianova	RUS	10.12.79	1	NC	Kazan	18 Jul 08
1:56.0	WR	Valentina	Gerasimova	KAZ	15.5.48	1	NC	Kyiv	12 Jun 76
1:56.0		Inna	Yevseyeva	UKR	14.8.64	1		Kyiv	25 Jun 88
1:56.04		Janeth	Jepkosgei	KEN	13.12.83	1	WCh	Osaka	28 Aug 07
(30)									
1:56.09		Zulia	Calatayud	CUB	9.11.79	1	Herc	Monaco	19 Jul 02
1:56.1		Ravilya	Agletdinova'	BLR	10.2.60	2	Kuts	Podolsk	21 Aug 82
1:56.2 '		Totka	Petrova ¶	BUL	17.12.56	1		Paris	6 Jul 79
1:56.2		Tatyana	Mishkel	UKR	10.6.52	3	Kuts	Podolsk	21 Aug 82
1:56.21		Martina	Kämpfert'	GDR	11.11.59	4	OG	Moskva	27 Jul 80
1:56.21		Zamira	Zaytseva	UZB	16.2.53	2		Leningrad	27 Jul 83
1:56.21		Kelly	Holmes	GBR	19.4.70	2	GPF	Monaco	9 Sep 95
1:56.24			Qu Yunxia	CHN	8.12.72	2	NG	Beijing	9 Sep 93
1:56.40		Jearl	Miles-Clark	USA	4.9.66	3	WK	Zürich	11 Aug 99
1:56.42		Paula	Ivan	ROU	20.7.63	1	Balk	Ankara	16 Jul 88
(40)									
1:56.43		Hasna	Benhassi	MAR	1.6.78	2	OG	Athína	23 Aug 04
1:56.44		Svetlana	Styrkina	RUS	1.1.49	5	OG	Montreal	26 Jul 76
1:56.51		Slobodanka	Colovic	YUG	10.1.65	1		Beograd	17 Jun 87
1:56.53		Patricia	Djaté	FRA	3.1.71	3	GPF	Monaco	9 Sep 95
1:56.56		Ludmila	Formanová	CZE	2.1.74	4	WK	Zürich	11 Aug 99
1:56.57		Zoya	Rigel	RUS	15.10.52	3	EC	Praha	31 Aug 78
1:56.59		Natalya	Khrushchelyova	RUS	30.5.73	2	NC	Tula	31 Jul 04
1:56.60		Natalya	Tsyganova	RUS	7.2.71	1	NC	Tula	25 Jul 00
1:56.6		Tamara	Sorokina'	RUS	15.8.50	5	Kuts	Podolsk	21 Aug 82
1:56.61		Yelena	Afanasyeva	RUS	1.3.67	3	WK	Zürich	13 Aug 97
(50)		100th woman 1:57.57, 200th 1:58.65, 300th 1:59.43, 400th 1:59.94, 500th 2:00.45							
Indoors: 1:55.85		Stephanie	Graf	AUT	26.4.73	2	EI	Wien	3 Mar 02
Drugs disqualification									
1:54.85		Yelena	Soboleva ¶	RUS	3.10.82	(1)	NC	Kazan	18 Jul 08

1000 METRES

Mark	Wind	Name		Nat	Born	Pos	Meet	Venue	Date
2:28.98	WR	Svetlana	Masterkova	RUS	17.1.68	1	VD	Bruxelles	23 Aug 96
2:29.34	WR	Maria Lurdes	Mutola	MOZ	27.10.72	1	VD	Bruxelles	25 Aug 95
2:30.6	WR	Tatyana	Providokhina	RUS	26.3.53	1		Podolsk	20 Aug 78
2:30.67	WR	Christine	Wachtel	GDR	6.1.65	1	ISTAF	Berlin	17 Aug 90
2:30.85		Martina	Kämpfert'	GDR	11.11.59	1		Berlin	9 Jul 80
2:31.50		Natalya	Artyomova ¶	RUS	5.1.63	1	ISTAF	Berlin	10 Sep 91
2:31.5		Maricica	Puica	ROU	29.7.50	1		Poiana Brasov	1 Jun 86
2:31.51		Sandra	Gasser ¶	SUI	27.7.62	1		Jerez de la Frontera	13 Sep 89

1500 METRES

Mark	Wind	Name		Nat	Born	Pos	Meet	Venue	Date
3:50.46	WR		Qu Yunxia	CHN	8.12.72	1	NG	Beijing	11 Sep 93
3:50.98			Jiang Bo	CHN	13.3.77	1	NG	Shanghai	18 Oct 97
3:51.34			Lang Yinglai	CHN	22.8.79	2	NG	Shanghai	18 Oct 97
3:51.92			Wang Junxia	CHN	9.1.73	2	NG	Beijing	11 Sep 93
3:52.47	WR	Tatyana	Kazankina ¶	RUS	17.12.51	1	WK	Zürich	13 Aug 80
3:53.91			Yin Lili ¶	CHN	11.11.79	3	NG	Shanghai	18 Oct 97
3:53.96		Paula	Ivan'	ROU	20.7.63	1	OG	Seoul	1 Oct 88
3:53.97			Lan Lixin	CHN	14.2.79	4	NG	Shanghai	18 Oct 97
3:54.23		Olga	Dvirna	RUS	11.2.53	1	NC	Kyiv	27 Jul 82
3:54.52			Zhang Ling (10)	CHN	13.4.80	5	NG	Shanghai	18 Oct 97
3:55.0 '	WR		Kazankina ¶			1	Znam	Moskva	6 Jul 80
3:55.01			Lan Lixin			1h2	NG	Shanghai	17 Oct 97
3:55.07			Dong Yanmei	CHN	16.2.77	6	NG	Shanghai	18 Oct 97
3:55.30		Hassiba	Boulmerka	ALG	10.7.68	1	OG	Barcelona	8 Aug 92
3:55.33		Süreyya	Ayhan ¶	TUR	6.9.78	1	VD	Bruxelles	5 Sep 03
3:55.38			Qu Yunxia			2h2	NG	Shanghai	17 Oct 97
3:55.47			Zhang Ling			3h2	NG	Shanghai	17 Oct 97
3:55.60			Ayhan			1	WK	Zürich	15 Aug 03
3:55.68		Yuliya	Chizhenko ¶	RUS	30.8.79	1	Gaz	Saint-Denis	8 Jul 06

Mark	Wind	Name		Nat	Born	Pos	Meet	Venue	Date
3:55.82			Dong Yanmei			4h2	NG	Shanghai	17 Oct 97
3:56.0	WR		Kazankina ¶			1		Podolsk	28 Jun 76
3:56.14		Zamira	Zaytseva	UZB	16.2.53	2	NC	Kyiv	27 Jul 82
3:56.18		Maryam	Jamal	BRN	16.9.84	1	GP	Rieti	27 Aug 06
3:56.22			Ivan			1	WK	Zürich	17 Aug 88
3:56.31			Liu Dong	CHN	24.12.73	5h2	NG	Shanghai	17 Oct 97
3:56.43		Yelena	Soboleva ¶	RUS	3.10.82	2	Gaz	Saint-Denis	8 Jul 06
3:56.50		Tatyana	Pozdnyakova	RUS	4.3.56	3	NC	Kyiv	27 Jul 82
3:56.55			Jamal			1	GGala	Roma	10 Jul 09
3:56.56			Kazankina ¶			1	OG	Moskva	1 Aug 80
3:56.63		Nadezhda	Ralldugina	UKR	15.11.57	1	Drz	Praha	18 Aug 84
(30/20)									
3:56.65		Yekaterina	Podkopayeva'	RUS	11.6.52	1		Rieti	2 Sep 84
3:56.7 '		Lyubov	Smolka	UKR	29.11.52	2	Znam	Moskva	6 Jul 80
3:56.7		Doina	Melinte	ROU	27.12.56	1		Bucuresti	12 Jul 86
3:56.77+		Svetlana	Masterkova	RUS	17.1.68	1	WK	Zürich	14 Aug 96
3:56.8 '		Nadezhda	Olizarenko'	UKR	28.11.53	3	Znam	Moskva	6 Jul 80
3:56.91		Lyudmila	Rogachova	RUS	30.10.66	2	OG	Barcelona	8 Aug 92
3:56.91		Tatyana	Tomashova ¶	RUS	1.7.75	1	EC	Göteborg	13 Aug 06
3:56.97		Gabriela	Szabo	ROU	14.11.75	1	Herc	Monaco	8 Aug 98
3:57.03			Liu Jing	CHN	3.2.71	6h2	NG	Shanghai	17 Oct 97
3:57.05		Svetlana	Guskova	MDA	19.8.59	4	NC	Kyiv	27 Jul 82
(30)									
3:57.12		Mary	Decker/Slaney	USA	4.8.58	1	vNord	Stockholm	26 Jul 83
3:57.22		Maricica	Puica	ROU	29.7.50	1		Bucuresti	1 Jul 84
3:57.40		Suzy	Favor Hamilton	USA	8.8.68	1	Bisl	Oslo	28 Jul 00
3:57.4 '		Totka	Petrova ¶	BUL	17.12.56	1	Balk	Athína	11 Aug 79
3:57.41		Jackline	Maranga	KEN	16.12.77	3	Herc	Monaco	8 Aug 98
3:57.46			Zhang Linli	CHN	6.3.73	3	NG	Beijing	11 Sep 93
3:57.65		Anna	Alminova #	RUS	17.1.85	1	DL	Saint-Denis	16 Jul 10
3:57.71		Christiane	Wartenberg'	GDR	27.10.56	2	OG	Moskva	1 Aug 80
3:57.71		Carla	Sacramento	POR	10.12.71	4	Herc	Monaco	8 Aug 98
3:57.72		Galina	Zakharova	RUS	7.9.56	1	NP	Baku	14 Sep 84
(40)									
3:57.73		Natalya	Yevdokimova	RUS	17.3.78	2	GP	Rieti	28 Aug 05
3:57.90		Kelly	Holmes	GBR	19.4.70	1	OG	Athína	28 Aug 04
3:57.92		Tatyana	Samolenko/Dorovskikh	UKR	12.8.61	4	OG	Barcelona	8 Aug 92
3:58.12		Naomi	Mugo	KEN	2.1.77	5	Herc	Monaco	8 Aug 98
3:58.20		Anita	Weyermann	SUI	8.12.77	6	Herc	Monaco	8 Aug 98
3:58.2 '		Natalia	Marasescu' ¶	ROU	3.10.52	1	NC	Bucuresti	13 Jul 79
3:58.28		Elvan	Abeylegesse	TUR	11.9.82	1	ECCp-A	Moskva	30 May 04
3:58.29		Violeta	Szekely' ¶	ROU	26.3.65	1	Herc	Monaco	18 Aug 00
3:58.37		Tatyana	Providokhina	RUS	26.3.53	1	Kuts	Podolsk	22 Aug 82
3:58.38		Kutre	Dulecha	ETH	22.8.78	7	Herc	Monaco	8 Aug 98
(50)		100th woman 4:00.15, 200th 4:02.61, 300th 4:04.82, 400th 4:06.20, 500th 4:07.27							

1 MILE

Mark	Wind	Name		Nat	Born	Pos	Meet	Venue	Date
4:12.56	WR	Svetlana	Masterkova	RUS	17.1.68	1	WK	Zürich	14 Aug 96
4:15.61	WR	Paula	Ivan'	ROU	20.7.63	1	Nik	Nice	10 Jul 89
4:15.8		Natalya	Artyomova ¶	RUS	5.1.63	1		Leningrad	5 Aug 84
4:16.71	WR	Mary	Slaney (Decker)	USA	4.8.58	1	WK	Zürich	21 Aug 85
4:17.25		Sonia	O'Sullivan	IRL	28.11.69	1	Bisl	Oslo	22 Jul 94
4:17.33		Maricica	Puica	ROU	29.7.50	2	WK	Zürich	21 Aug 85
4:17.57		Zola	Budd'	GBR	26.5.66	3	WK	Zürich	21 Aug 85
4:17.75		Maryam	Jamal	BRN	16.9.84	1	VD	Bruxelles	14 Sep 07
4:17.14	indoor	Doina	Melinte	ROU	27.12.56	1		East Rutherford	9 Feb 90
Drugs dq: 4:15.63		Yelena	Soboleva ¶	RUS	3.10.82	1		Moskva	29 Jun 07

2000 METRES

Mark	Wind	Name		Nat	Born	Pos	Meet	Venue	Date
5:25.36	WR	Sonia	O'Sullivan	IRL	28.11.69	1	TSB	Edinburgh	8 Jul 94
5:26.93		Yvonne	Murray	GBR	4.10.64	2	TSB	Edinburgh	8 Jul 94
5:28.69	WR	Maricica	Puica	ROU	29.7.50	1	PTG	London (CP)	11 Jul 86
5:28.72	WR	Tatyana	Kazankina ¶	RUS	17.12.51	1		Moskva	4 Aug 84
5:29.43+			Wang Junxia	CHN	9.1.73	1h2	NG	Beijing	12 Sep 93
5:29.64		Tatyana	Pozdnyakova	UKR	4.3.56	2		Moskva	4 Aug 84
5:30.19		Zola	Budd'	GBR	26.5.66	3	PTG	London (CP)	11 Jul 86
5:30.19		Gelete	Burka	ETH	15.2.86	1	VD	Bruxelles	4 Sep 09
5:30.92		Galina	Zakharova	RUS	7.9.56	3		Moskva	4 Aug 84
5:31.03		Gulnara	Samitova/Galkina	RUS	9.7.78	1		Sochi	27 May 07
Indoors: 5:30.53		Gabriela	Szabo	ROU	14.11.75	1		Sindelfingen	8 Mar 98

Mark	Wind	Name		Nat	Born	Pos	Meet	Venue	Date

3000 METRES

Mark	Wind		Name	Nat	Born	Pos	Meet	Venue	Date
8:06.11	WR		Wang Junxia	CHN	9.1.73	1	NG	Beijing	13 Sep 93
8:12.18			Qu Yunxia	CHN	8.12.72	2	NG	Beijing	13 Sep 93
8:12.19	WR		Wang Junxia	CHN		1h2	NG	Beijing	12 Sep 93
8:12.27			Qu Yunxia			2h2	NG	Beijing	12 Sep 93
8:16.50			Zhang Linli	CHN	6.3.73	3	NG	Beijing	13 Sep 93
8:19.78			Ma Liyan	CHN	6.9.68	3h2	NG	Beijing	12 Sep 93
8:21.26			Ma Liyan			4	NG	Beijing	13 Sep 93
8:21.42		Gabriela	Szabo	ROU	14.11.75	1	Herc	Monaco	19 Jul 02
8:21.64		Sonia	O'Sullivan	IRL	28.11.69	1	TSB	London (CP)	15 Jul 94
8:21.84			Zhang Lirong	CHN	3.3.73	5	NG	Beijing	13 Sep 93
8:22.06	WR		Zhang Linli			1h1	NG	Beijing	12 Sep 93
8:22.20		Paula	Radcliffe	GBR	17.12.73	2	Herc	Monaco	19 Jul 02
8:22.44			Zhang Lirong			2h1	NG	Beijing	12 Sep 93
8:22.62	WR	Tatyana	Kazankina ¶	RUS	17.12.51	1		Leningrad	26 Aug 84
8:23.23		Edith	Masai (10)	KEN	4.4.67	3	Herc	Monaco	19 Jul 02
8:23.26		Olga	Yegorova	RUS	28.3.72	1	WK	Zürich	17 Aug 01
8:23.75			Yegorova			1	GP	Saint-Denis	6 Jul 01
8:23.96			Yegorova			1	GGala	Roma	29 Jun 01
8:24.19			Szabo			2	WK	Zürich	17 Aug 01
8:24.31			Szabo			1	GP	Paris	29 Jul 98
8:24.51+		Meseret	Defar	ETH	19.11.83	1	in 2M	Bruxelles	14 Sep 07
8:24.66			Defar			1	DNG	Stockholm	25 Jul 06
8:25.03			Szabo			1	WK	Zürich	11 Aug 99
8:25.40		Yelena	Zadorozhnaya	RUS	3.12.77	2	GGala	Roma	29 Jun 01
8:25.56		Tatyana	Tomashova ¶	RUS	1.7.75	3	GGala	Roma	29 Jun 01
8:25.59			Szabo			1	GP	Paris (C)	21 Jul 99
8:25.62		Berhane	Adere	ETH	21.7.73	3	WK	Zürich	17 Aug 01
8:25.82			Szabo			1	VD	Bruxelles	3 Sep 99
8:25.83		Mary	Slaney	USA	4.8.58	1	GGala	Roma	7 Sep 85
8:25.92		Gelete	Burka	ETH	15.2.86	2	DNG	Stockholm	25 Jul 06
		(30/17)							
8:26.48		Zahra	Ouaziz	MAR	20.12.69	2	WK	Zürich	11 Aug 99
8:26.53		Tatyana	Samolenko' ¶	UKR	12.8.61	1	OG	Seoul	25 Sep 88
8:26.78	WR	Svetlana	Ulmasova	UZB	4.2.53	1	NC	Kyiv	25 Jul 82
		(20)							
8:27.12	WR	Lyudmila	Bragina	RUS	24.7.43	1	v USA	College Park	7 Aug 76
8:27.15		Paula	Ivan'	ROU	20.7.63	2	OG	Seoul	25 Sep 88
8:27.62		Getenesh	Wami	ETH	11.12.74	4	WK	Zürich	17 Aug 01
8:27.83		Maricica	Puica	ROU	29.7.50	2	GGala	Roma	7 Sep 85
8:28.41		Sentayehu	Ejigu	ETH	21.6.85	1	Herc	Monaco	22 Jul 10
8:28.66		Vivian	Cheruiyot	KEN	11.9.83	2	WAF	Stuttgart	23 Sep 07
8:28.80		Marta	Domínguez	ESP	3.11.75	3	WK	Zürich	11 Aug 00
8:28.83		Zola	Budd'	GBR	26.5.66	3	GGala	Roma	7 Sep 85
8:28.87		Maryam	Jamal	BRN	16.9.84	1	Bisl	Oslo	29 Jul 05
8:29.02		Yvonne	Murray	GBR	4.10.64	3	OG	Seoul	25 Sep 88
		(30)							
8:29.06		Priscah	Cherono	KEN	27.6.80	3	WAF	Stuttgart	23 Sep 07
8:29.14		Lydia	Cheromei	KEN	11.5.77	5	WK	Zürich	11 Aug 00
8:29.36		Svetlana	Guskova	MDA	19.8.59	2	NC	Kyiv	25 Jul 82
8:29.52		Mariem Alaoui	Selsouli ¶	MAR	8.4.84	1	Herc	Monaco	25 Jul 07
8:29.55		Tirunesh	Dibaba	ETH	1.10.85	1	LGP	London (CP)	28 Jul 06
8:30.18		Mariya	Pantyukhova	RUS	14.8.74	4	WK	Zürich	11 Aug 99
8:30.22		Carla	Sacramento	POR	10.12.71	2	Herc	Monaco	4 Aug 99
8:30.39		Irina	Mikitenko	GER	23.8.72	6	WK	Zürich	11 Aug 00
8:30.45		Yelena	Romanova	RUS	20.3.63	4	OG	Seoul	25 Sep 88
8:30.59		Daniela	Yordanova ¶	BUL	8.3.76	5	GP	Saint-Denis	6 Jul 01
		(40)							
8:30.66		Fernanda	Ribeiro	POR	23.6.69	3	Herc	Monaco	4 Aug 99
8:30.93		Wude	Ayalew	ETH	4.7.87	3	WAF	Thessaloníki	13 Sep 09
8:30.95		Tegla	Loroupe	KEN	9.5.73	2	Herc	Monaco	18 Aug 00
8:31.27		Joanne	Pavey	GBR	20.9.73	4	VD	Bruxelles	30 Aug 02
8:31.32		Isabella	Ochichi	KEN	28.10.79	1	Gaz	Saint-Denis	23 Jul 04
8:31.38		Shannon	Rowbury	USA	19.9.84	3	Herc	Monaco	22 Jul 10
8:31.67		Natalya	Artyomova ¶	RUS	5.1.63	5	OG	Seoul	25 Sep 88
8:31.69		Lidia	Chojecka	POL	25.1.77	5	VD	Bruxelles	30 Aug 02
8:31.75		Grete	Waitz'	NOR	1.10.53	1	OsloG	Oslo	17 Jul 79
8:31.94		Elvan	Abeylegesse	TUR	11.9.82	6	VD	Bruxelles	30 Aug 02
		(50)							

100th woman 8:37.30, 200th 8:44.14, 300th 8:48.54

Mark	Wind	Name		Nat	Born	Pos	Meet	Venue	Date
Indoors:									
8:23.72		Meseret	Defar	ETH	19.11.83	1	Spark	Stuttgart	3 Feb 07
8:23.74		Meselech	Melkamu	ETH	27.4.85	2	Spark	Stuttgart	3 Feb 07
8:25.27		Sentayehu	Ejigu	ETH	21.6.85	2	Spark	Stuttgart	6 Feb 10
8:27.86		Liliya	Shobukhova	RUS	13.11.77	1	NC	Moskva	17 Feb 06
8:28.49		Anna	Alminova	RUS	17.1.85	2	Spark	Stuttgart	7 Feb 09
8:29.00		Olesya	Syreva	RUS	25.11.83	2	NC	Moskva	17 Feb 06

5000 METRES

Mark	Wind	Name		Nat	Born	Pos	Meet	Venue	Date
14:11.15 WR		Tirunesh	Dibaba	ETH	1.10.85	1	Bisl	Oslo	6 Jun 08
14:12.88		Meseret	Defar	ETH	19.11.83	1	DNG	Stockholm	22 Jul 08
14:16.63 WR			Defar			1	Bisl	Oslo	15 Jun 07
14:20.87		Vivian	Cheruiyot	KEN	11.9.83	1	DNG	Stockholm	29 Jul 11
14:22.51			Cheruiyot			2	Bisl	Oslo	15 Jun 07
14:23.46			T Dibaba			1	GP	Rieti	7 Sep 08
14:23.75		Liliya	Shobukhova	RUS	13.11.77	1	NC	Kazan	19 Jul 08
14:24.53 WR			Defar			1		New York (RI)	3 Jun 06
14:24.68 WR		Elvan	Abeylegesse	TUR	11.9.82	1	Bisl	Bergen (Fana)	11 Jun 04
14:25.43			Cheruiyot			1	VD	Bruxelles	5 Sep 08
14:25.52			Defar			2	VD	Bruxelles	5 Sep 08
14:27.41			Cheruiyot			1	DL	Saint-Denis	16 Jul 10
14:28.09 WR			Jiang Bo	CHN	13.3.77	1	NG	Shanghai	23 Oct 97
14:28.39		Sentayehu	Ejigu	ETH	21.6.85	2	DL	Saint-Denis	16 Jul 10
14:28.98			Defar			1	VD	Bruxelles	26 Aug 05
14:29.11		Paula	Radcliffe	GBR	17.12.73	1	ECpS	Bydgoszcz	20 Jun 04
14:29.32		Olga	Yegorova	RUS	28.3.72	1	ISTAF	Berlin	31 Aug 01
14:29.32		Berhane	Adere (10)	ETH	21.7.73	1	Bisl	Oslo	27 Jun 03
14:29.52			Defar			1	DL	Saint-Denis	8 Jul 11
14:29.82			Dong Yanmei	CHN	16.2.77	2	NG	Shanghai	23 Oct 97
14:30.10			Cheruiyot			1	WK	Zürich	8 Sep 11
14:30.18			Defar			1	GS	Ostrava	27 Jun 07
14:30.40			T Dibaba			1	Bisl	Oslo	2 Jun 06
14:30.42		Sally	Kipyego	KEN	19.12.85	2	WK	Zürich	8 Sep 11
14:30.63			T Dibaba			1	VD	Bruxelles	25 Aug 06
14:30.88		Getenesh	Wami	ETH	11.12.74	1	NA	Heusden-Zolder	5 Aug 00
14:30.88			T Dibaba			2	Bisl	Bergen (Fana)	11 Jun 04
14:30.96			Ejigu			1	DL	Shanghai	23 May 10
14:31.09			Adere			2	VD	Bruxelles	26 Aug 05
14:31.14		Linet	Masai	KEN	5.12.89	2	DL	Shanghai	23 May 10
		(30/14)							
14:31.20		Gelete	Burka	ETH	15.2.86	2	GS	Ostrava	27 Jun 07
14:31.48		Gabriela	Szabo	ROU	14.11.75	1	ISTAF	Berlin	1 Sep 98
14:31.91		Meselech	Melkamu	ETH	27.4.85	3	DL	Shanghai	23 May 10
14:31.91		Sylvia	Kibet	KEN	28.3.84	4	DL	Shanghai	23 May 10
14:32.08		Zahra	Ouaziz	MAR	20.12.69	2	ISTAF	Berlin	1 Sep 98
14:32.33			Liu Shixiang ¶	CHN	13.1.71	3h1	NG	Shanghai	21 Oct 97
		(20)							
14:32.74		Ejagayehu	Dibaba	ETH	25.6.82	3	Bisl	Bergen (Fana)	11 Jun 04
14:33.04		Werknesh	Kidane	ETH	21.11.81	2	Bisl	Oslo	27 Jun 03
14:33.13		Gulnara	Galkina	RUS	9.7.78	2	NC	Kazan	19 Jul 08
14:33.49		Lucy	Wangui Kabuu	KEN	24.3.84	2	Bisl	Oslo	6 Jun 08
14:33.84		Edith	Masai	KEN	4.4.67	3	Bisl	Oslo	2 Jun 06
14:34.86		Viola	Kibiwott	KEN	22.12.83	4	DL	Shanghai	15 May 11
14:35.13		Mercy	Cherono	KEN	7.5.91	3	DL	Saint-Denis	8 Jul 11
14:35.30		Priscah	Jepleting/Cherono	KEN	27.6.80	4	Bisl	Oslo	2 Jun 06
14:36.45 WR		Fernanda	Ribeiro	POR	23.6.69	1		Hechtel	22 Jul 95
14:36.52		Mariem Alaoui	Selsouli ¶	MAR	8.4.84	1	G Gala	Roma	13 Jul 07
		(30)							
14:36.79		Alemitu	Bekele	TUR	17.9.77	4	VD	Bruxelles	27 Aug 10
14:37.07		Jéssica	Augusto	POR	8.11.81	5	DL	Saint-Denis	16 Jul 10
14:37.33 WR		Ingrid	Kristiansen'	NOR	21.3.56	1		Stockholm	5 Aug 86
14:37.56		Genzebe	Dibaba	ETH	8.2.91	3	Bisl	Oslo	9 Jun 11
14:38.09		Mariya	Konovalova	RUS	14.8.74	3	NC	Kazan	19 Jul 08
14:38.21		Isabella	Ochichi	KEN	28.10.79	4	VD	Bruxelles	26 Aug 05
14:38.44		Wude	Ayalew	ETH	4.7.87	5	Bisl	Oslo	3 Jul 09
14:39.19		Ines	Chenonge	KEN	1.2.82	6	DL	Saint-Denis	16 Jul 10
14:39.22		Tatyana	Tomashova ¶	RUS	1.7.75	4	ISTAF	Berlin	31 Aug 01
14:39.83		Leah	Malot	KEN	7.6.72	1	ISTAF	Berlin	1 Sep 00
		(40)							
14:39.96			Yin Lili ¶	CHN	11.11.79	4	NG	Shanghai	23 Oct 97

Mark	Wind	Name		Nat	Born	Pos	Meet	Venue	Date
14:39.96		Jo	Pavey	GBR	20.9.73	3	VD	Bruxelles	25 Aug 06
14:40.14		Florence	Kiplagat	KEN	27.2.87	6	Bisl	Oslo	3 Jul 09
14:40.41			Sun Yingjie ¶	CHN	3.10.77	1	AsiG	Busan	12 Oct 02
14:40.47		Yelena	Zadorozhnaya	RUS	3.12.77	1	ECp-S	Bremen	24 Jun 01
14:41.02		Sonia	O'Sullivan	IRL	28.11.69	2	OG	Sydney	25 Sep 00
14:41.23		Ayelech	Worku	ETH	12.6.79	1	BrGP	London (CP)	5 Aug 00
14:41.28		Pauline	Korikwiang	KEN	1.3.88	7	DL	Shanghai	15 May 11
14:42.03		Irina	Mikitenko	GER	23.8.72	3	ISTAF	Berlin	7 Sep 99
14:42.53		Zhor	El Kamch	MAR	15.3.73	5	GGala	Roma	11 Jul 03
(50)									

100th woman 14:54.08, 200th 15:06.75, 300th 15:15.15, 400th 15:20.53, 500th 15:25.13

Mark	Wind	Name		Nat	Born	Pos	Meet	Venue	Date
Indoors: 14:24.37			Defar			1		Stockholm	18 Feb 09
14:24.79			Defar			1	GE Galan	Stockholm	10 Feb 10
14:27.42			T Dibaba			1	BIG	Boston (R)	27 Jan 07
14:39.89		Kimberley	Smith	NZL	19.11.73	1		New York (Arm)	27 Feb 09

10,000 METRES

Mark	Wind	Name		Nat	Born	Pos	Meet	Venue	Date
29:31.78 WR			Wang Junxia	CHN	9.1.73	1	NG	Beijing	8 Sep 93
29:53.80		Meselech	Melkamu	ETH	27.4.85	1		Utrecht	14 Jun 09
29:54.66		Tirunesh	Dibaba	ETH	1.10.85	1	OG	Beijing	15 Aug 08
29:56.34		Elvan	Abeylegesse	TUR	11.9.82	2	OG	Beijing	15 Aug 08
29:59.20		Meseret	Defar	ETH	19.11.83	1	NC	Birmingham	11 Jul 09
30:01.09		Paula	Radcliffe	GBR	17.12.73	1	EC	München	6 Aug 02
30:04.18		Berhane	Adere	ETH	21.7.73	1	WCh	Saint-Denis	23 Aug 03
30:07.15		Werknesh	Kidane	ETH	21.11.81	2	WCh	Saint-Denis	23 Aug 03
30:07.20			Sun Yingjie ¶	CHN	3.10.77	3	WCh	Saint-Denis	23 Aug 03
30:11.53		Florence	Kiplagat (10)	KEN	27.2.87	2		Utrecht	14 Jun 09
30:11.87		Wude	Ayalew	ETH	4.7.87	3		Utrecht	14 Jun 09
30:12.53		Lornah	Kiplagat (KEN)	NED	1.5.74	4	WCh	Saint-Denis	23 Aug 03
30:13.37			Zhong Huandi	CHN	28.6.67	2	NG	Beijing	8 Sep 93
30:13.74 WR		Ingrid	Kristiansen'	NOR	21.3.56	1	Bisl	Oslo	5 Jul 86
30:15.67			T Dibaba			1		Sollentuna	28 Jun 05
30:17.15			Radcliffe			1	GP	Gateshead	27 Jun 04
30:17.49		Derartu	Tulu	ETH	21.3.72	1	OG	Sydney	30 Sep 00
30:18.39		Ejegayehu	Dibaba	ETH	25.6.82	2		Sollentuna	28 Jun 05
30:19.39			Kidane			1	GP II	Stanford	29 May 05
30:21.67			Abeylegesse			1	ECp	Antalya	15 Apr 06
30:22.22		Shalane	Flanagan	USA	8.7.81	3	OG	Beijing	15 Aug 08
30:22.48		Getenesh	Wami	ETH	11.12.74	2	OG	Sydney	30 Sep 00
30:22.88		Fernanda	Ribeiro	POR	23.6.69	3	OG	Sydney	30 Sep 00
30:23.07		Alla	Zhilyayeva (20)	RUS	5.2.69	5	WCh	Saint-Denis	23 Aug 03
30:23.25			Kristiansen			1	EC	Stuttgart	30 Aug 86
30:24.02			T Dibaba			1	WCh	Helsinki	6 Aug 05
30:24.36			Xing Huina	CHN	25.2.84	1	OG	Athína	27 Aug 04
30:24.56			Wami			1	WCh	Sevilla	26 Aug 99
30:24.98			E Dibaba			2	OG	Athína	27 Aug 04
30:25.41			Adere			2	WCh	Helsinki	6 Aug 05
(30/21)									
30:26.20		Galina	Bogomolova	RUS	15.10.77	6	WCh	Saint-Denis	23 Aug 03
30:26.50		Linet	Masai	KEN	5.12.89	4	OG	Beijing	15 Aug 08
30:29.21mx		Philes	Ongori	KEN	19.7.86	1mx		Yokohama	23 Nov 08
30:29.36		Liliya	Shobukhova	RUS	13.11.77	1	NC	Cheboksary	23 Jul 09
30:30.26		Edith	Masai	KEN	4.4.67	5	WCh	Helsinki	6 Aug 05
30:31.03		Mariya	Konovalova	RUS	14.8.74	2	NC	Cheboksary	23 Jul 09
30:31.42		Inga	Abitova	RUS	6.3.82	1	EC	Göteborg	7 Aug 06
30:32.03		Tegla	Loroupe	KEN	9.5.73	3	WCh	Sevilla	26 Aug 99
30:32.36		Susanne	Wigene	NOR	12.2.78	2	EC	Göteborg	7 Aug 06
(30)									
30:32.72		Lidiya	Grigoryeva	RUS	21.1.74	3	EC	Göteborg	7 Aug 06
30:35.54		Kim	Smith	NZL	19.11.81	2		Stanford	4 May 08
30:37.68		Benita	Johnson	AUS	6.5.79	8	WCh	Saint-Denis	23 Aug 03
30:38.09			Dong Yanmei	CHN	16.2.77	1	NG	Shanghai	19 Oct 97
30:38.33		Mestawat	Tufa	ETH	14.9.83	1		Nijmegen	25 Jun 08
30:38.35		Sally	Kipyego	KEN	19.12.85	1		Stanford	1 May 11
30:38.78		Jelena	Prokopcuka	LAT	21.9.76	6	EC	Göteborg	7 Aug 06
30:39.41			Lan Lixin	CHN	14.2.79	2	NG	Shanghai	19 Oct 97
30:39.96		Lucy	Wangui Kabuu	KEN	24.3.84	7	OG	Beijing	15 Aug 08
30:39.98			Yin Lili ¶	CHN	11.11.79	3	NG	Shanghai	19 Oct 97
(40)									
30:47.20		Sylvia	Kibet	KEN	28.3.84	4		Utrecht	14 Jun 09
30:47.22			Dong Zhaoxia	CHN	13.11.74	4	NG	Shanghai	19 Oct 97

Mark	Wind	Name		Nat	Born	Pos	Meet	Venue	Date
30:47.59		Sonia	O'Sullivan	IRL	28.11.69	2	EC	München	6 Aug 02
30:47.72			Wang Dongmei	CHN	3.12.72	5	NG	Shanghai	19 Oct 97
30:48.26		Aberu	Kebede	ETH	12.9.89	5		Utrecht	14 Jun 09
30:48.89		Yoko	Shibui	JPN	14.3.79	1		Stanford	3 May 02
30:48.98		Vivian	Cheruiyot	KEN	11.9.83	1	WCh	Daegu	27 Aug 11
30:50.32		Deena	Drossin/Kastor	USA	14.2.73	2		Stanford	3 May 02
30:51.69		Marta	Domínguez	ESP	3.11.75	7	EC	Göteborg	7 Aug 06
30:51.81		Kayoko	Fukushi	JPN	25.3.82	2	AsiG	Busan	8 Oct 02

(50)   100th woman 31:14.51, 200th 31:36.88, 300th 31:53.38, 400th 32:05.76, 500th 32:16.50

HALF MARATHON

Slightly downhill courses included: Newcastle-South Shields 30.5m, Tokyo 33m (to 1998), Lisboa (Spring to 2008) 69m

Mark	Wind	Name		Nat	Born	Pos	Meet	Venue	Date
65:40	dh	Paula	Radcliffe	GBR	17.12.73	1	GNR	South Shields	21 Sep 03
65:44	dh	Susan	Chepkemei	KEN	25.6.75	1		Lisboa	1 Apr 01
65:50	WR	Mary	Keitany	KEN	18.1.82	1		Ra's Al Khaymah	18 Feb 11
66:25		Lornah	Kiplagat	NED	1.5.74	1	WCh	Udine	14 Oct 07
66:34	dh		Kiplagat			2		Lisboa	1 Apr 01
66:36		Mary	Keitany	KEN	18.1.82	1	WCh	Birmingham	11 Oct 09
66:40*		Ingrid	Kristiansen	NOR	21.3.56	1	NC	Sandnes	5 Apr 87
66:43	dh	Masako	Chiba	JPN	18.7.76	1		Tokyo	19 Jan 97
66:44		Elana	Meyer	RSA	10.10.66	1		Tokyo	15 Jan 99
66:47			Radcliffe			1	WCh	Bristol	7 Oct 01
66:48			Keitany			2	WCh	Udine	14 Oct 07
66:49		Esther	Wanjiru	KEN	27.3.77	2		Tokyo	15 Jan 99
66:54			Keitany			1		New Delhi	1 Nov 09
66:56			L Kiplagat			1	City-Pier	Den Haag	25 Mar 00
66:57	dh	Kara	Goucher	USA	9.7.78	1	GNR	South Shields	30 Sep 07
67:00			Keitany			1		Lille	5 Sep 09
67:03	dh	Derartu	Tulu (10)	ETH	21.3.72	3		Lisboa	1 Apr 01
67:04		Lucy	Wangui Kabuu	KEN	24.3.84	1		New Delhi	27 Nov 11
67:06	dh		Wangui			1	GNR	South Shields	18 Sep 11
67:07	dh		Radcliffe			1	GNR	South Shields	22 Oct 00
67:07		Elvan	Abeylegesse	TUR	11.9.82	1		Ra's Al Khaymah	19 Feb 10
67:08	dh	Rita	Jeptoo	KEN	15.2.81	1		Lisboa	18 Mar 07
67:08		Sharon	Cherop	KEN	16.3.84	2		New Delhi	21 Nov 11
67:11	dh	Liz	McColgan	GBR	24.5.64	1		Tokyo	26 Jan 92
67:11		Kim	Smith	NZL	19.11.81	1		Philadelphia	18 Sep 11
67:12	dh	Tegla	Loroupe	KEN	9.5.73	1		Lisboa	10 Mar 96
67:13		Mare	Dibaba	ETH	20.10.89	2		Ra's Al Khaymah	19 Feb 10
67:14			Keitany			1		Abu Dhabi	7 Jan 10
67:16		Edith	Masai	KEN	4.4.67	1		Berlin	2 Apr 06
67:18		Dire	Tune	ETH	19.6.85	1		R'as Al Khaymah	20 Feb 09

(30/20)   * uncertain course measurement

Mark	Wind	Name		Nat	Born	Pos	Meet	Venue	Date
67:19	dh	Sonia	O'Sullivan	IRL	28.11.69	1	GNR	South Shields	6 Oct 02
67:21		Aselefech	Mergia	ETH	23.1.85	3		New Delhi	21 Nov 11
67:23		Margaret	Okayo	KEN	30.5.76	1		Udine	28 Sep 03
67:26		Kayoko	Fukushi	JPN	25.3.82	1		Marugame	5 Feb 06
67:27		Belaynesh	Oljira	ETH	26.6.90	4		New Delhi	27 Nov 11
67:28		Worknesh	Kidane	ETH	21.11.81	2		Philadelphia	18 Sep 11
67:32	dh	Berhane	Adere	ETH	21.7.73	2	GNR	South Shields	21 Sep 03
67:33		Lydia	Cheromei ¶	KEN	11.5.77	1		Praha	2 Apr 11
67:34		Deena	Kastor	USA	14.2.73	2		Berlin	2 Apr 06
67:38		Philes	Ongori	KEN	19.7.86	2	WCh	Birmingham	11 Oct 09

(30)

Mark	Wind	Name		Nat	Born	Pos	Meet	Venue	Date
67:39		Aberu	Kebede	ETH	12.9.89	3	WCh	Birmingham	11 Oct 09
67:40		Florence	Kiplagat	KEN	27.2.87	1		Lille	4 Sep 10
67:41		Teyiba	Erkesso	ETH	30.10.82	4		Ra's Al Khaymah	19 Feb 10
67:43		Mizuki	Noguchi	JPN	3.7.78	2		Marugame	5 Feb 06
67:45		Meseret	Defar	ETH	19.11.83	1		Philadelphia	19 Sep 10
67:47		Lineth	Chepkurui	KEN	23.2.88	2		Philadelphia	19 Sep 10
67:48		Kerryn	McCann	AUS	2.5.67	3		Tokyo	10 Jan 00
67:48		Peninah	Arusei	KEN	23.2.79	2		Lille	4 Sep 10
67:50	dh	Catherina	McKiernan	IRL	30.11.69	1		Lisboa	15 Mar 98
67:52	dh	Salina	Kosgei	KEN	16.11.76	1		Lisboa (dh 69m)	26 Mar 06

(40)

Mark	Wind	Name		Nat	Born	Pos	Meet	Venue	Date
67:54		Catherine	Ndereba	KEN	21.7.72	1		Den Haag	24 Mar 01
67:55		Benita	Willis/Johnson	AUS	6.5.79	1	GNR	South Shields	26 Sep 04
67:56		Susie	Power	AUS	26.3.75	2	GNR	South Shields	6 Oct 02
67:57		Gelana	Abebe	ETH	18.1.90	4		R'as Al Khaymah	20 Feb 09

Mark	Wind	Name		Nat	Born	Pos	Meet	Venue	Date
67:58	WR	Uta	Pippig ¶	GER	7.9.65	1		Kyoto	19 Mar 95
67:58		Wude	Ayalew	ETH	4.7.87	2		New Delhi	1 Nov 09
67:59	w	Restituta	Joseph	TAN	30.7.71	1		Malmö	12 Jun 00
68:06		Pamela	Chepchumba ¶	KEN	8.3.79	3	WCh	Udine	14 Oct 07
68:07+		Constantina	Dita	ROU	23.1.70	1	in Mar	Chicago	22 Oct 06
68:07		Bezunesh	Bekele	ETH	18.9.83	4	WCh	Udine	14 Oct 07
68:07		Mamitu	Daska	ETH	16.10.83	4		New Delhi	1 Nov 09
68:07		Sarah	Chepchirchir	KEN	27.7.84	1		Vitry-sur-Seine	3 Apr 11

(52) 100th woman 68:49, 200th 69:35, 300th 70:05, 400th 70:33, 500th 70:57

MARATHON

L = loop course or start and finish within 30%, P = point-to-point or start and finish more than 30% apart, D + point-to-point and downhil over 1/1000. 2nd column: M mixed marathon (men and women), W women only race

Mark		Name		Nat	Born	Pos	Meet	Venue	Date
2:15:25	LM	Paula	Radcliffe	GBR	17.12.73	1		London	13 Apr 03
2:17:18	LM		Radcliffe			1		Chicago	13 Oct 02
2:17:42	LW		Radcliffe			1		London	17 Apr 05
2:18:20	LM	Liliya	Shobukhova	RUS	13.11.77	1		Chicago	9 Oct 11
2:18:47	LM	Catherine	Ndereba	KEN	21.7.72	1		Chicago	7 Oct 01
2:18:56	LW		Radcliffe			1		London	14 Apr 02
2:19:12	LM	Mizuki	Noguchi	JPN	3.7.78	1		Berlin	25 Sep 05
2:19:19	LM	Irina	Mikitenko	GER	23.8.72	1		Berlin	28 Sep 08
2:19:19	LW	Mary	Keitany	KEN	18.1.82	1		London	17 Apr 11
2:19:26	LM		Ndereba			2		Chicago	13 Oct 02
2:19:36	LW	Deena	Kastor	USA	14.2.73	1		London	23 Apr 06
2:19:39	LM		Sun Yingjie ¶	CHN	3.10.77	1		Beijing	19 Oct 03
2:19:41	LM	Yoko	Shibui	JPN	14.3.79	1		Berlin	26 Sep 04
2:19:44	LM	Florence	Kiplagat (10)	KEN	27.2.87	1		Berlin	25 Sep 11
2:19:46	LM	Naoko	Takahashi	JPN	6.5.72	1		Berlin	30 Sep 01
2:19:51	PM		Zhou Chunxiu	CHN	15.11.78	1	Dong-A	Seoul	12 Mar 06
2:19:55	LM		Ndereba			2		London	13 Apr 03
2:20:15	LW	Liliya	Shobukhova			2		London	17 Apr 11
2:20:25	LM		Shobukhova			1		Chicago	10 Oct 10
2:20:38	LW		Zhou Chunxiu			1		London	22 Apr 07
2:20:42	LM	Berhane	Adere	ETH	21.7.73	1		Chicago	22 Oct 06
2:20:43	LM	Tegla	Loroupe	KEN	9.5.73	1		Berlin	26 Sep 99
2:20:46	LW	Edna	Kiplagat	KEN	15.9.79	3		London	17 Apr 11
2:20:47	LM		Loroupe			1		Rotterdam	19 Apr 98
2:20:47	LM	Galina	Bogomolova	RUS	15.10.77	2		Chicago	22 Oct 06
2:20:57	LW		Radcliffe			1	WCh	Helsinki	14 Aug 05
2:21:01	LM		Sun Yingjie ¶			1	NG	Beijing	16 Oct 05
2:21:06	LM	Ingrid	Kristiansen	NOR	21.3.56	1		London	21 Apr 85
2:21:11	LM		Zhou Chunxiu			2	NG	Beijing	16 Oct 05
2:21:16	LM		Drossin/Kastor			3		London	13 Apr 03
		(30/17)							
2:21:21	LM	Joan	Benoit'	USA	16.5.57	1		Chicago	20 Oct 85
2:21:29	LW	Lyudmila	Petrova	RUS	7.10.68	2		London	23 Apr 06
2:21:30	LM	Constantina	Dita	ROU	23.1.70	2		Chicago	9 Oct 05
		(20)							
2:21:31	LM	Svetlana	Zakharova	RUS	15.9.70	4		Chicago	13 Oct 02
2:21:31	LM	Askale	Tafa	ETH	27.9.84	2		Berlin	28 Sep 08
2:21:34	LM	Getenesh	Wami	ETH	11.12.74	1		Berlin	25 Sep 06
2:21:45	LW	Masako	Chiba	JPN	18.7.76	2		Osaka	26 Jan 03
2:21:46	LW	Susan	Chepkemei ¶	KEN	25.6.75	3		London	23 Apr 06
2:21:51	LW	Naoko	Sakamoto	JPN	14.11.80	3		Osaka	26 Jan 03
2:21:59	LM	Mamitu	Daska	ETH	16.10.83	1		Frankfurt	30 Oct 11
2:22:04	LM	Atsede	Bayisa	ETH	16.4.87	1		Paris	11 Apr 10
2:22:08	LM	Tiki	Gelana	ETH	22.10.87	1		Amsterdam	16 Oct 11
2:22:09	LM	Ejegayehu	Dibaba	ETH	25.6.82	2		Chicago	9 Oct 11
		(30)							
2:22:12	LW	Eri	Yamaguchi	JPN	14.1.73	1		Tokyo	21 Nov 99
2:22:19	LW	Inga	Abitova	RUS	6.3.82	2		London	25 Apr 10
2:22:22	LW	Lornah	Kiplagat	KEN/NED	1.5.74	4		Osaka	26 Jan 03
2:22:23	LM	Catherina	McKiernan	IRL	30.11.69	1		Amsterdam	1 Nov 98
2:22:34	LM	Lydia	Cheromei ¶	KEN	11.5.77	1		Praha	8 May 11
2:22:35	LW	Margaret	Okayo	KEN	30.5.76	1		London	18 Apr 04
2:22:36	LM	Benita	Willis/Johnson	AUS	6.5.79	3		Chicago	22 Oct 06
2:22:38	LM		Zhang Yingying	CHN	4.1.90	1	NC	Xiamen	5 Jan 08
2:22:38	LW	Aselefech	Mergia	ETH	23.1.85	3		London	25 Apr 10
2:22:43	LM	Sharon	Cherop	KEN	16.3.84	1		Toronto	26 Sep 10
		(40)							

Mark	Wind	Name		Nat	Born	Pos	Meet	Venue	Date
2:22:43	LM	Korene	Jelila	ETH	18.1.87	4		Toronto	16 Oct 11
2:22:44	LM	Tirfe	Tsegaye	ETH	25.11.84	2		Toronto	26 Sep 10
2:22:46	LW	Reiko	Tosa	JPN	11.6.76	4		London	14 Apr 02
2:22:54	LW	Lidia	Simon	ROU	4.9.73	1		Osaka	30 Jan 00
2:22:55	LM	Priscah	Jeptoo	KEN	26.6.84	1		Paris	10 Apr 11
2:22:56	LW	Harumi	Hiroyama	JPN	2.9.68	2		Osaka	30 Jan 00
2:22:56	LW	Jelena	Prokopcuka	LAT	21.9.76	1		Osaka	30 Jan 05
2:22:59	LM	Madaí	Pérez	MEX	2.2.80	4		Chicago	22 Oct 06
2:23:05	LM	Marleen	Renders	BEL	24.12.68	1		Paris	7 Apr 02
2:23:06	LM	Merima	Mohamed	ETH	10.6.92	3		Toronto	26 Sep 10
	(50)		100th woman 2:24:33, 200th 2:26:21, 300th 2:27:38, 400th 2:28:42, 500th 2:29:37						

Drugs dq: 2:20:23 LM Wei Yanan ¶   CHN   6.12.81   1   Beijing   20 Oct 02

Downhill point-to-point course – Boston marathon is downhill overall (139m) and sometimes strongly wind-aided.

Mark	Wind	Name		Nat	Born	Pos	Meet	Venue	Date
2:20:43	DM	Margaret	Okayo	KEN	30.5.76	1		Boston	15 Apr 02
2:21:45	DM	Uta	Pippig ¶	GER	7.9.65	1		Boston	18 Apr 94
2:22:36	DM	Caroline	Cheptonui Kilel	KEN	21.3.81	1		Boston	18 Apr 11
2:22:38	DM	Desiree	Davila	USA	26.7.83	2		Boston	18 Apr 11
2:22:42	DM	Sharon	Cherop	KEN	16.3.84	3		Boston	18 Apr 11

2000 METRES STEEPLECHASE

Mark	Name		Nat	Born	Pos	Meet	Venue	Date
6:03.38	Wioletta	Janowska	POL	9.6.77	1		Gdansk	15 Jul 06
6:04.46	Dorcus	Inzikuru	UGA	2.2.82	1	GP II	Milano	1 Jun 05
6:11.63	Livia	Tóth	HUN	7.1.80	2		Gdansk	15 Jul 06
6:11.83	Korahubish	Itaa	KEN	28.2.92	1	WY	Bressanone	10 Jul 09
6:11.84	Marina	Pluzhnikova	RUS	25.2.63	1	GWG	Sankt-Peterburg	25 Jul 94

3000 METRES STEEPLECHASE

Mark		Name		Nat	Born	Pos	Meet	Venue	Date
8:58.81	WR	Gulnara	Samitova/Galkina	RUS	9.7.78	1	OG	Beijing	17 Aug 08
9:01.59	WR		Samitova/Galkina			1		Iráklio	4 Jul 04
9:06.57		Yekaterina	Volkova	RUS	16.2.78	1	WCh	Osaka	27 Aug 07
9:07.03		Yuliya	Zaripova (Zarudneva)	RUS	26.4.86	1	WCh	Daegu	30 Aug 11
9:07.32		Marta	Dominguez	ESP	3.11.75	1	WCh	Berlin	17 Aug 09
9:07.41		Eunice	Jepkorir	KEN	17.2.82	2	OG	Beijing	17 Aug 08
9:07.64			Volkova			3	OG	Beijing	17 Aug 08
9:08.21			Galkina			1	NC	Kazan	18 Jul 08
9:08.33	WR		Samitova			1	NC	Tula	10 Aug 03
9:08.39			Zarudneva			2	WCh	Berlin	17 Aug 09
9:08.57		Milcah	Chemos	KEN	24.2.86	3	WCh	Berlin	17 Aug 09
9:09.19		Tatyana	Petrova	RUS	8.4.83	2	WCh	Osaka	27 Aug 07
9:09.39			Domínguez			1		Barcelona	25 Jul 09
9:09.84			Samitova			1		Réthimno	23 Jun 04
9:11.09			Galkina			4	WCh	Berlin	17 Aug 09
9:11.18			Jepkorir			1		Huelva	13 Jun 08
9:11.58			Galkina			1	GGala	Roma	10 Jul 09
9:11.68			Galkina			1	GP	Athína	2 Jul 07
9:11.71			Chemos			1	GGala	Roma	10 Jun 10
9:11.97		Habiba	Ghribi	TUN	9.4.84	2	WCh	Daegu	30 Aug 11
9:12.33			Petrova			4	OG	Beijing	17 Aug 08
9:12.50		Jennifer	Barringer/Simpson	USA	23.8.86	5	WCh	Berlin	17 Aug 09
9:12.52			Ghribi			6	WCh	Berlin	17 Aug 09
9:12.66			Chemos			1	Bisl	Oslo	4 Jun 10
9:12.89			Chemos			1	GGala	Roma	26 May 11
9:13.16		Ruth	Bisibori (10)	KEN	2.1.88	7	WCh	Berlin	17 Aug 09
9:13.18			Zarudneva			1	NC	Cheboksary	23 Jul 09
9:13.22		Gladys	Kipkemboi	KEN	15.10.86	2	GGala	Roma	10 Jun 10
9:13.35			Volkova			1	NC	Tula	31 Jul 07
9:13.43			Bisibori			1	WAF	Thessaloníki	12 Sep 09
		(30/11)							
9:15.04		Dorcus	Inzikuru	UGA	2.2.82	1	SGP	Athína	14 Jun 05
9:15.04		Sofia	Assefa	ETH	14.11.87	2	GGala	Roma	26 May 11
9:16.51	WR	Alesya	Turova	BLR	6.12.79	1		Gdansk	27 Jul 02
9:16.85		Cristina	Casandra	ROU	21.10.77	5	OG	Beijing	17 Aug 08
9:16.94		Mercy	Njoroge	KEN	10.6.86	2	DL	Doha	6 May 11
9:17.15		Wioletta	Frankiewicz/Janowska	POL	9.6.77	1	SGP	Athína	3 Jul 06
9:17.85		Zemzem	Ahmed	ETH	27.12.84	7	OG	Beijing	17 Aug 08
9:18.03		Lydia	Rotich	KEN	8.8.88	3	Bisl	Oslo	4 Jun 10
9:18.35		Donna	MacFarlane	AUS	18.6.77	3	Bisl	Oslo	6 Jun 08
		(20)							
9:18.54		Antje	Möldner	GER	13.6.84	9	WCh	Berlin	17 Aug 09
9:18.54		Jéssica	Augusto	POR	8.11.81	2		Huelva	9 Jun 10

Mark	Wind		Name	Nat	Born	Pos	Meet	Venue	Date
9:20.23		Mekdes	Bekele	ETH	20.1.87	2		Huelva	13 Jun 08
9:20.37		Birtukan	Adamu	ETH	29.4.92	4	GGala	Roma	26 May 11
9:21.94		Lyubov	Ivanova' ¶	RUS	2.3.81	2	Tsik	Athína	3 Jul 06
9:22.12		Hanane	Ouhaddou	MAR	.82	1	NA	Heusden-Zolder	18 Jul 09
9:22.15		Yelena	Sidorchenkova	RUS	30.5.80	2	NC	Cheboksary	23 Jul 09
9:22.29	WR	Justyna	Bak	POL	1.8.74	1		Milano	5 Jun 02
9:22.51		Almaz	Ayana	ETH	21.11.91	3	VD	Bruxelles	27 Aug 10
9:22.76		Anna	Willard/Pierce	USA	31.3.84	2	NA	Heusden-Zolder	20 Jul 08
		(30)							
9:23.35		Jeruto	Kiptum	KEN	12.12.81	2	GP	Rieti	27 Aug 06
9:23.88		Hiwot	Ayalew	ETH	6.3.90	2	LGP	London (CP)	6 Aug 11
9:24.06		Binnaz	Uslu ¶	TUR	12.3.85	1h1	WCh	Daegu	27 Aug 11
9:24.29		Melissa	Rollison	AUS	13.4.83	2	CG	Melbourne	22 Mar 06
9:24.84		Lisa	Aguilera	USA	30.11.79	5	VD	Bruxelles	27 Aug 10
9:25.14		Eva	Arias	ESP	8.10.80	5h1	WCh	Berlin	15 Aug 09
9:25.62		Sophie	Duarte	FRA	31.7.81	6	GGala	Roma	10 Jul 09
9:26.03		Lyudmila	Kuzmina	RUS	13.8.87	2	NC	Cheboksary	23 Jul 11
9:26.07		Salome	Chepchumba	KEN	29.9.82	3	GP	Rieti	27 Aug 06
9:26.23		Rosa María	Morató	ESP	19.6.79	2	NA	Heusden-Zolder	28 Jul 07
		(40)							
9:26.25			Liu Nian	CHN	26.4.88	1		Wuhan	2 Nov 07
9:26.93		Katarzyna	Kowalska	POL	7.4.85	4h2	WCh	Berlin	15 Aug 09
9:27.21		Mardrea	Hyman	JAM	22.12.72	3	WAF	Monaco	9 Sep 05
9:27.26		Valentyna	Horpynych	UKR	12.3.83	1	NCp	Yalta	7 Jun 08
9:27.48		Elena	Romagnolo	ITA	5.10.82	5h3	OG	Beijing	15 Aug 08
9:28.03		Netsanet	Achano	ETH	14.12.87	2		Neerpelt	2 Jun 07
9:28.27		Birtukan	Fente	ETH	18.6.89	6	Athl	Lausanne	30 Jun 11
9:28.29		Roisin	McGettigan	IRL	23.8.80	3	NA	Heusden-Zolder	28 Jul 07
9:28.47		Veerle	Dejaeghere	BEL	1.8.73	3		Neerpelt	2 Jun 07
9:28.64		Sara	Moreira	POR	17.10.85	6h2	WCh	Berlin	15 Aug 09
		(50)	100th woman 9:40.96, 200th 9:55.49						

100 METRES HURDLES

Mark	Wind		Name	Nat	Born	Pos	Meet	Venue	Date
12.21	WR 0.7	Yordanka	Donkova	BUL	28.9.61	1		Stara Zagora	20 Aug 88
12.24	0.9		Donkova			1h		Stara Zagora	28 Aug 88
12.25	WR 1.4	Ginka	Zagorcheva	BUL	12.4.58	1	v TCH,GRE	Drama	8 Aug 87
12.26	WR 1.5		Donkova			1	Balk	Ljubljana	7 Sep 86
12.26	1.7	Lyudmila	Narozhilenko ¶	RUS	21.4.64	1rB		Sevilla	6 Jun 92
		(now Ludmila Engquist SWE)							
12.27	-1.2		Donkova			1		Stara Zagora	28 Aug 88
12.28	1.8		Narozhilenko			1	NC	Kyiv	11 Jul 91
12.28	0.9		Narozhilenko			1rA		Sevilla	6 Jun 92
12.28	1.1	Sally	Pearson'	AUS	19.9.86	1	WCh	Daegu	3 Sep 11
12.29	WR -0.4		Donkova			1	ASV	Köln	17 Aug 86
12.32	1.6		Narozhilenko			1		Saint-Denis	4 Jun 92
12.33	1.4		Donkova			1		Fürth	14 Jun 87
12.33	-0.3	Gail	Devers	USA	19.11.66	1	NC	Sacramento	23 Jul 00
12.34	-0.5		Zagorcheva			1	WCh	Roma	4 Sep 87
12.35	WR 0.1		Donkova			1h2	ASV	Köln	17 Aug 86
12.36	WR 1.9	Grazyna	Rabsztyn	POL	20.9.52	1	Kuso	Warszawa	13 Jun 80
12.36	WR -0.6		Donkova			1	NC	Sofiya	13 Aug 86
12.36	1.1		Donkova			1		Schwechat	15 Jun 88
12.36	0.3		Pearson			1s2	WCh	Daegu	3 Sep 11
12.37	1.4		Donkova			1	ISTAF	Berlin	15 Aug 86
12.37	0.7		Devers			1	WCh	Sevilla	28 Aug 99
12.37	1.5	Joanna	Hayes	USA	23.12.76	1	OG	Athína	24 Aug 04
12.38	0.0		Donkova			1	BGP	Budapest	11 Aug 86
12.38	-0.7		Donkova			1	EC	Stuttgart	29 Aug 86
12.38	0.2		Donkova			1	OG	Seoul	30 Sep 88
12.39	1.5	Vera	Komisova'	RUS	11.6.53	1	GGala	Roma	5 Aug 80
12.39	1.5		Zagorcheva			2	Balk	Ljubljana	7 Sep 86
12.39	1.8	Natalya	Grigoryeva ¶	UKR	3.12.62	2	NC	Kyiv	11 Jul 91
12.39	-0.7		Devers			1	WK	Zürich	11 Aug 00
12.40	0.4		Donkova			1	GWG	Moskva	8 Jul 86
12.40	1.2		Devers			1rA	Athl	Lausanne	2 Jul 02
		(31/9)							
12.42	1.8	Bettine	Jahn (10)	GDR	3.8.58	1	OD	Berlin	8 Jun 83
12.42	2.0	Anjanette	Kirkland	USA	24.2.74	1	WCh	Edmonton	11 Aug 01
12.43	-0.9	Lucyna	Kalek (Langer)	POL	9.1.56	1		Hannover	19 Aug 84

Mark	Wind	Name		Nat	Born	Pos	Meet	Venue	Date
12.43	-0.3	Michelle	Perry	USA	1.5.79	1s1	NC	Carson	26 Jun 05
12.43	0.2	Lolo	Jones	USA	5.8.82	1s1	OG	Beijing	18 Aug 08
12.44	-0.5	Gloria	Uibel (-Siebert)	GDR	13.1.64	2	WCh	Roma	4 Sep 87
12.44	-0.8	Olga	Shishigina ¶	KAZ	23.12.68	1		Luzern	27 Jun 95
12.44	0.4	Glory	Alozie	NGR/ESP	30.12.77	1	Herc	Monaco	8 Aug 98
12.44	0.6	Damu	Cherry ¶	USA	29.11.77	2rA	Athl	Lausanne	11 Jul 06
12.45	1.3	Cornelia	Oschkenat'	GDR	29.10.61	1		Neubrandenburg	11 Jun 87
12.45	1.4	Brigitte	Foster-Hylton	JAM	7.11.74	1	Pre	Eugene	24 May 03
		(20)							
12.45	1.5	Olena	Krasovska	UKR	17.8.76	2	OG	Athína	24 Aug 04
12.45	1.4	Virginia	Powell/Crawford	USA	7.9.83	1	GP	New York	2 Jun 07
12.46	0.7	Perdita	Felicien	CAN	29.8.80	1	Pre	Eugene	19 Jun 04
12.47	1.1	Marina	Azyabina	RUS	15.6.63	1s2	NC	Moskva	19 Jun 93
12.47	1.1	Danielle	Carruthers	USA	22.12.79	2	WCh	Daegu	3 Sep 11
12.47	1.1	Dawn	Harper	USA	13.5.84	3	WCh	Daegu	3 Sep 11
12.49	0.9	Susanna	Kallur	SWE	16.2.81	1	ISTAF	Berlin	16 Sep 07
12.49	1.0	Priscilla	Lopes-Schliep	CAN	26.8.82	2	VD	Bruxelles	4 Sep 09
12.50	0.0	Vera	Akimova'	RUS	5.6.59	1		Sochi	19 May 84
12.50	-0.1	Delloreen	Ennis-London	JAM	5.3.75	3	WCh	Osaka	29 Aug 07
		(30)							
12.50	0.8	Josephine	Onyia ¶	NGR/ESP	15.7.86	1	ISTAF	Berlin	1 Jun 08
12.50	1.8	Kellie	Wells	USA	16.7.82	1	NC	Eugene	26 Jun 11
12.51	1.4	Miesha	McKelvy	USA	26.7.76	2	Pre	Eugene	24 May 03
12.52	-0.4	Michelle	Freeman	JAM	5.5.69	1s1	WCh	Athína	10 Aug 97
12.53	0.2	Tatyana	Reshetnikova	RUS	14.10.66	1rA	GP II	Linz	4 Jul 94
12.53	-0.4	Svetla	Dimitrova ¶	BUL	27.1.70	1	Herc	Stara Zagora	16 Jul 94
12.53	1.0	Melissa	Morrison	USA	9.7.71	1	DNG	Stockholm	5 Aug 98
12.54	0.4	Kerstin	Knabe	GDR	7.7.59	3	EC	Athína	9 Sep 82
12.54	0.9	Sabine	Paetz/John'	GDR	16.10.57	1		Berlin	15 Jul 84
12.54	1.7	Nichole	Denby	USA	10.10.82	2s2	OT	Eugene	6 Jul 08
		(40)							
12.56	1.2	Johanna	Klier'	GDR	13.9.52	1r2		Cottbus	17 Jul 80
12.56	1.2	Monique	Ewanje-Epée	FRA	11.7.67	1	BNP	Villeneuve d'Ascq	29 Jun 90
12.56	0.7	Tiffany	Ofili/Porter	USA/GBR	13.11.87	1s3	WCh	Daegu	3 Sep 11
12.57	0.3	Carolin	Nytra	GER	26.2.85	2	Athl	Lausanne	8 Jul 10
12.59 WR	-0.6	Anneliese	Ehrhardt	GDR	18.6.50	1	OG	München	8 Sep 72
12.59	0.0	Natalya	Shekhodanova ¶	RUS	29.12.71	1	NC	Sankt Peterburg	3 Jul 96
12.59	1.0	Patricia	Girard ¶	FRA	8.4.68	2s2	OG	Atlanta	31 Jul 96
12.59	0.2	Brigita	Bukovec	SLO	21.5.70	2	OG	Atlanta	31 Jul 96
12.59	0.4	Kirsten	Bolm	GER	4.3.75	1	LGP	London (CP)	22 Jul 05
12.60	1.7	Mariya	Koroteyeva	RUS	10.11.81	4s1	OG	Athína	23 Aug 04
		(50)	100th woman 12.73, 200th 12.87, 300th 12.99, 400th 13.08, 599th 13.15						

Wind assisted performances to 12.38, performers to 12.59

Mark	Wind	Name		Nat	Born	Pos	Meet	Venue	Date
12.28	2.7	Cornelia	Oschkenat'	GDR	29.10.61	1		Berlin	25 Aug 87
12.29	3.5		Donkova			1	Athl	Lausanne	24 Jun 88
12.29	2.7	Gail	Devers	USA	19.11.66	1	Pre	Eugene	26 May 02
12.29	3.8	Lolo	Jones	USA	5.8.82	1	NC/OT	Eugene	6 Jul 08
12.35	2.4	Bettine	Jahn	GDR	3.8.58	1	WCh	Helsinki	13 Aug 83
12.35	3.7	Kellie	Wells	USA	16.7.82	1		Gainesville	16 Apr 11
12.36	2.2	Dawn	Harper	USA	13.5.84	1	NC	Eugene	28 Jun 09
12.37	2.7	Gloria	Uibel/Siebert'	GDR	13.1.64	2		Berlin	25 Aug 87
12.37	3.4	Danielle	Carruthers	USA	22.12.79	1s1	NC	Eugene	26 Jun 11
12.40	2.1	Michelle	Freeman	JAM	5.5.69	1	GPF	Fukuoka	13 Sep 97
12.41	2.2	Olga	Shishigina ¶	KAZ	23.12.68	1rA	Athl	Lausanne	5 Jul 95
12.42	2.4	Kerstin	Knabe	GDR	7.7.59	2	WCh	Helsinki	13 Aug 83
12.44	2.6	Melissa	Morrison	USA	9.7.71	1		Carson	22 May 04
12.44	5.3	Queen	Harrison	USA	10.9.88	1		Clemson	17 Apr 10
12.45	2.1	Perdita	Felicien	CAN	29.8.80	1	NC	Victoria	10 Jul 04
12.50	2.7	Svetla	Dimitrova ¶	BUL	27.1.70	1		Saint-Denis	10 Jun 94
12.51	3.2	Johanna	Klier'	GDR	13.9.52	1	NC	Cottbus	17 Jul 80
12.51	3.6	Sabine	Paetz/John'	GDR	16.10.57	1		Dresden	27 Jul 84
12.51A	3.3	Yuliya	Graudyn	RUS	13.11.70	1		Sestriere	31 Jul 94
12.53	2.2	Mihaela	Pogacian	ROU	27.1.58	1	IAC	Edinburgh	6 Jul 90
12.55	4.3	Angela	Whyte	CAN	22.5.80	2	NC	Windsor	14 Jul 07
12.59	5.3	Kristi	Castlin	USA	7.7.88	2		Clemson	17 Apr 10

Probably hand timed Officially 12.36, but subsequent investigations showed this unlikely to have been auto-timed

Mark	Wind	Name		Nat	Born	Pos	Meet	Venue	Date
12.4	0.7	Svetla	Dimitrova ¶	BUL	27.1.70	1		Stara Zagora	9 Jul 97

Hand timed

Mark	Wind	Name		Nat	Born	Pos	Meet	Venue	Date
12.3 WR	1.5	Anneliese	Ehrhardt	GDR	18.6.50	1	NC	Dresden	22 Jul 73
12.3		Marina	Azyabina	RUS	15.6.63	1		Yekaterinburg	30 May 93

Mark	Wind	Name		Nat	Born	Pos	Meet	Venue	Date
12.0w	2.1	Yordanka	Donkova	BUL	28.9.61	1		Sofiya	3 Aug 86
12.1w	2.1	Ginka	Zagorcheva	BUL	12.4.58	2		Sofiya	3 Aug 86

400 METRES HURDLES

Mark	Wind	Name		Nat	Born	Pos	Meet	Venue	Date
52.34 WR		Yuliya	Nosova-Pechonkina'	RUS	21.4.78	1	NC	Tula	8 Aug 03
52.42		Melaine	Walker	JAM	1.1.83	1	WCh	Berlin	20 Aug 09
52.47		Lashinda	Demus	USA	10.3.83	1	WCh	Daegu	1 Sep 11
52.61 WR		Kim	Batten	USA	29.3.69	1	WCh	Göteborg	11 Aug 95
52.62		Tonja	Buford-Bailey	USA	13.12.70	2	WCh	Göteborg	11 Aug 95
52.63			Demus			1	Herc	Monaco	28 Jul 09
52.64			Walker			1	OG	Beijing	20 Aug 08
52.73			Walker			2	WCh	Daegu	1 Sep 11
52.74 WR		Sally	Gunnell	GBR	29.7.66	1	WCh	Stuttgart	19 Aug 93
52.74			Batten			1	Herc	Monaco	8 Aug 98
52.77		Faní	Halkiá	GRE	2.2.79	1s2	OG	Athína	22 Aug 04
52.79		Sandra	Farmer-Patrick	USA	18.8.62	2	WCh	Stuttgart	19 Aug 93
52.79		Kaliese	Spencer	JAM	6.5.87	1	LGP	London (CP)	5 Aug 11
52.82		Deon	Hemmings (10)	JAM	9.10.68	1	OG	Atlanta	31 Jul 96
52.82			Halkiá			1	OG	Athína	25 Aug 04
52.82			Demus			1	GGala	Roma	10 Jun 10
52.84			Batten			1	WK	Zürich	12 Aug 98
52.89		Daimí	Pernía	CUB	27.12.76	1	WCh	Sevilla	25 Aug 99
52.90			Buford			1	WK	Zürich	16 Aug 95
52.90		Nezha	Bidouane	MAR	18.9.69	2	WCh	Sevilla	25 Aug 99
52.90			Pechonkina			1	WCh	Helsinki	13 Aug 05
52.92		Natalya	Antyukh	RUS	26.6.81	1	EC	Barcelona	30 Jul 10
52.94 WR		Marina	Styepanova'	RUS	1.5.50	1s	Spart	Tashkent	17 Sep 86
52.95		Sheena	Johnson/Tosta	USA	1.10.82	1	NC/OT	Sacramento	11 Jul 04
52.96A			Bidouane			1	WCp	Johannesburg	11 Sep 98
52.96			Demus			2	WCh	Berlin	20 Aug 09
52.97			Batten			1	NC	Indianapolis	14 Jun 97
52.97			Bidouane			1	WCh	Athína	8 Aug 97
52.98			Hemmings			1rA	WK	Zürich	13 Aug 97
52.99			Hemmings			1s1	OG	Atlanta	29 Jul 96
		(30/14)							
53.02		Irina	Privalova	RUS	22.11.68	1	OG	Sydney	27 Sep 00
53.11		Tatyana	Ledovskaya	BLR	21.5.66	1	WCh	Tokyo	29 Aug 91
53.17		Debbie	Flintoff-King	AUS	20.4.60	1	OG	Seoul	28 Sep 88
53.20		Josanne	Lucas	TRI	14.5.84	3	WCh	Berlin	20 Aug 09
53.21		Marie-José	Pérec	FRA	9.5.68	2	WK	Zürich	16 Aug 95
		(20)							
53.22		Jana	Pittman/Rawlinson	AUS	9.11.82	1	WCh	Saint-Denis	28 Aug 03
53.24		Sabine	Busch	GDR	21.11.62	1	NC	Potsdam	21 Aug 87
53.25		Ionela	Târlea-Manolache	ROU	9.2.76	2	GGala	Roma	7 Jul 99
53.28		Tiffany	Ross-Williams	USA	5.2.83	1	NC	Indianapolis	24 Jun 07
53.29		Zuzana	Hejnová	CZE	19.12.86	1	DL	Saint-Denis	8 Jul 11
53.32		Sandra	Glover	USA	30.12.68	3	WCh	Helsinki	13 Aug 05
53.36		Andrea	Blackett	BAR	24.1.76	4	WCh	Sevilla	25 Aug 99
53.36		Brenda	Taylor	USA	9.2.79	2	NC/OT	Sacramento	11 Jul 04
53.37		Tetyana	Tereshchuk	UKR	11.10.69	3s2	OG	Athína	22 Aug 04
53.47		Janeene	Vickers	USA	3.10.68	3	WCh	Tokyo	29 Aug 91
		(30)							
53.48		Margarita	Ponomaryova'	RUS	19.6.63	3	WCh	Stuttgart	19 Aug 93
53.58		Cornelia	Ullrich'	GDR	26.4.63	2	NC	Potsdam	21 Aug 87
53.63		Ellen	Fiedler'	GDR	26.11.58	3	OG	Seoul	28 Sep 88
53.65A mx		Myrtle	Bothma'	RSA	18.2.64	mx		Pretoria	12 Mar 90
53.74A						1		Johannesburg	18 Apr 86
53.68		Vania	Stambolova ¶	BUL	28.11.83	1		Rabat	5 Jun 11
53.72		Yekaterina	Bikert	RUS	13.5.80	2	NC	Tula	30 Jul 04
53.84		Natasha	Danvers	GBR	19.9.77	3	OG	Beijing	20 Aug 08
53.86		Anna	Jesien	POL	10.12.78	1s3	WCh	Osaka	28 Aug 07
53.88		Debbie-Ann	Parris	JAM	24.3.73	3s1	WCh	Edmonton	6 Aug 01
53.93		Yevgeniya	Isakova	RUS	27.11.78	1	EC	Göteborg	9 Aug 06
		(40)							
53.95		Angela	Morosanu	ROU	26.7.86	1	NC	Bucuresti	2 Aug 09
53.96			Han Qing ¶	CHN	4.3.70	1	NG	Beijing	9 Sep 93
53.96			Song Yinglan	CHN	14.9.75	1	NG	Guangzhou	22 Nov 01
53.96		Anastasiya	Rabchenyuk	UKR	14.9.83	4	OG	Beijing	20 Aug 08
53.97		Nickiesha	Wilson	JAM	28.7.86	2s3	WCh	Osaka	28 Aug 07
54.00			Huang Xiaoxiao	CHN	3.3.83	2s2	WCh	Osaka	28 Aug 07

Mark	Wind		Name	Nat	Born	Pos	Meet	Venue	Date
54.02	WR	Anna	Ambraziené'	LTU	14.4.55	1	Znam	Moskva	11 Jun 83
54.02A		Judit	Szekeres ¶	HUN	18.11.66	1		Roodepoort	23 Jan 98
54.03		Heike	Meissner	GER	29.1.70	5	OG	Atlanta	31 Jul 96
54.04		Gudrun	Abt	FRG	3.8.62	6	OG	Seoul	28 Sep 88

(50) 100th woman 54.74, 200th 55.53, 300th 55.97, 400th 56.38, 500th 56.68

Mark	Wind		Name	Nat	Born	Pos	Meet	Venue	Date
Drugs disqualification: 53.38			Jiang Limei ¶	CHN	.3.70	(1)	NG	Shanghai	22 Oct 97

HIGH JUMP

Mark	Wind		Name	Nat	Born	Pos	Meet	Venue	Date
2.09	WR	Stefka	Kostadinova	BUL	25.3.65	1	WCh	Roma	30 Aug 87
2.08	WR		Kostadinova			1	NM	Sofiya	31 May 86
2.08i		Kajsa	Bergqvist	SWE	12.10.76	1		Arnstadt	4 Feb 06
2.08		Blanka	Vlasic	CRO	8.11.83	1	Hanz	Zagreb	31 Aug 09
2.07	WR	Lyudmila	Andonova ¶	BUL	6.5.60	1	OD	Berlin	20 Jul 84
2.07	WR		Kostadinova			1		Sofiya	25 May 86
2.07			Kostadinova			1		Cagliari	16 Sep 87
2.07			Kostadinova			1	NC	Sofiya	3 Sep 88
2.07i		Heike	Henkel'	GER	5.5.64	1	NC	Karlsruhe	8 Feb 92
2.07			Vlasic			1	DNG	Stockholm	7 Aug 07
2.07		Anna	Chicherova	RUS	22.7.82	1	NC	Cheboksary	22 Jul 11
2.06			Kostadinova			1	ECp	Moskva	18 Aug 85
2.06			Kostadinova			1		Fürth	15 Jun 86
2.06			Kostadinova			1		Cagliari	14 Sep 86
2.06			Kostadinova			1		Wörrstadt	6 Jun 87
2.06			Kostadinova			1		Rieti	8 Sep 87
2.06i			Kostadinova			1		Pireás	20 Feb 88
2.06			Bergqvist			1		Eberstadt	26 Jul 03
2.06		Hestrie	Cloete	RSA	26.8.78	1	WCh	Saint-Denis	31 Aug 03
2.06		Yelena	Slesarenko	RUS	28.2.82	1	OG	Athína	28 Aug 04
2.06			Vlasic			1		Thessaloníki	30 Jul 07
2.06			Vlasic			1	ECp-1B	Istanbul	22 Jun 08
2.06			Vlasic			1	GP	Madrid	5 Jul 08
2.06		Ariane	Friedrich	GER	10.1.84	1	ISTAF	Berlin	14 Jun 09
2.06i			Vlasic			1		Arnstadt	6 Feb 10
2.05	WR	Tamara	Bykova (10)	RUS	21.12.58	1	Izv	Kyiv	22 Jun 84
2.05		Inga	Babakova	UKR	27.6.67	1		Tokyo	15 Sep 95
2.05i		Tia	Hellebaut	BEL	16.2.78	1	EI	Birmingham	3 Mar 07
2.05			Hellebaut			1	OG	Beijing	23 Aug 08
2.05		Chaunté	Lowe'	USA	12.1.84	1	NC	Des Moines	26 Jun 10

Further 2.05 performances: Kostadinova 10, Vlasic 10, Bergqvist 2, Henkel, Cloete, Freidrich & Chicherova 1

Mark	Wind		Name	Nat	Born	Pos	Meet	Venue	Date
(56/13)									
2.04		Silvia	Costa	CUB	4.5.64	1	WCp	Barcelona	9 Sep 89
2.04i		Alina	Astafei	GER	7.6.69	1		Berlin	3 Mar 95
2.04		Venelina	Veneva ¶	BUL	13.6.74	1		Kalamáta	2 Jun 01
2.04i		Antonietta	Di Martino	ITA	1.6.78	1		Banská Bystrica	9 Feb 11
2.03	WR	Ulrike	Meyfarth	FRG	4.5.56	1	ECp	London (CP)	21 Aug 83
2.03		Louise	Ritter	USA	18.2.58	1		Austin	8 Jul 88
2.03		Tatyana	Motkova	RUS	23.11.68	2		Bratislava	30 May 95
(20)									
2.03		Níki	Bakoyiánni	GRE	9.6.68	2	OG	Atlanta	3 Aug 96
2.03i		Monica	Iagar/Dinescu	ROU	2.4.73	1		Bucuresti	23 Jan 99
2.03i		Marina	Kuptsova	RUS	22.12.81	1	EI	Wien	2 Mar 02
2.02i		Susanne	Beyer'	GDR	24.6.61	2	WI	Indianapolis	8 Mar 87
2.02		Yelena	Yelesina	RUS	4.4.70	1	GWG	Seattle	23 Jul 90
2.02		Viktoriya	Styopina	UKR	21.2.76	3	OG	Athína	28 Aug 04
2.02		Ruth	Beitia	ESP	1.4.79	1	NC	San Sebastián	4 Aug 07
2.02		Irina	Gordeyeva	RUS	9.10.86	1		Eberstadt	30 Aug 09
2.01	WR	Sara	Simeoni	ITA	19.4.53	1	v Pol	Brescia	4 Aug 78
2.01		Olga	Turchak	UKR	5.3.67	2	GWG	Moskva	7 Jul 86
(30)									
2.01		Desiré	du Plessis	RSA	20.5.65	1		Johannesburg	16 Sep 86
2.01i		Gabriele	Günz	GDR	8.9.61	2		Stuttgart	31 Jan 88
2.01		Heike	Balck	GDR	19.8.70	1	vUSSR-j	Karl-Marx-Stadt	18 Jun 89
2.01i		Ioamnet	Quintero	CUB	8.9.72	1		Berlin	5 Mar 93
2.01		Hanne	Haugland	NOR	14.12.67	1	WK	Zürich	13 Aug 97
2.01i		Tisha	Waller	USA	1.12.70	1	NC	Atlanta	28 Feb 98
2.01		Yelena	Gulyayeva	RUS	14.8.67	2		Kalamata	23 May 98
2.01		Vita	Palamar	UKR	12.10.77	2=	WK	Zürich	15 Aug 03
2.01		Amy	Acuff	USA	14.7.75	4	WK	Zürich	15 Aug 03
2.01		Iryna	Myhalchenko	UKR	20.1.72	1		Eberstadt	18 Jul 04
(40)									

Mark	Wind	Name		Nat	Born	Pos	Meet	Venue	Date
2.01		Emma	Green Tregaro	SWE	8.12.84	2	EC	Barcelona	1 Aug 10
2.00	WR	Rosemarie	Ackermann'	GDR	4.4.52	1	ISTAF	Berlin	26 Aug 77
2.00i		Coleen	Sommer'	USA	6.6.60	1		Ottawa	14 Feb 82
2.00		Charmaine	Gale/Weavers	RSA	27.2.64	1		Pretoria	25 Mar 85
2.00i		Emilia	Dragieva'	BUL	11.1.65	3	WI	Indianapolis	8 Mar 87
2.00		Lyudmila	Avdyeyenko'	UKR	14.12.63	1	NC	Bryansk	17 Jul 87
2.00		Svetlana	Isaeva/Leseva	BUL	18.3.67	2	v TCH,GRE	Drama	8 Aug 87
2.00i		Larisa	Kositsyna	RUS	14.12.63	2	NC	Volgograd	11 Feb 88
2.00		Jan	Wohlschlag'	USA	14.7.58	1	Bisl	Oslo	1 Jul 89
2.00		Yolanda	Henry	USA	2.12.64	1	Expo	Sevilla	30 May 90
		(50)							
2.00		Biljana	Petrovic ¶	CRO	28.2.61	1		Saint-Denis	22 Jun 90
2.00		Tatyana	Shevchik ¶	BLR	11.6.69	1		Gomel	14 May 93
2.00i		Britta	Vörös/Bilac	GDR/SLO	4.12.68	1		Frankfurt	9 Feb 94
2.00i		Yuliya	Lyakhova	RUS	8.7.77	1		Wuppertal	5 Feb 99
2.00		Zuzana	Hlavonová	CZE	16.4.73	1	Odlozil	Praha	5 Jun 00
2.00		Dóra	Györffy	HUN	23.2.78	1	NC	Nyíregyháza	26 Jul 01
2.00		Viktoriya	Seryogina	RUS	22.5.73	1	Univ Ch	Bryansk	11 Jun 02
2.00i		Svetlana	Lapina	RUS/AZE	12.4.78	3=	NC	Moskva	26 Feb 03
2.00		Daniela	Rath	GER	6.5.77	1	ECp-S	Firenze	22 Jun 03
2.00		Yekaterina	Savchenko'	RUS	3.6.77	1		Dudelange	1 Jul 07
2.00i		Viktoriya	Klyugina	RUS	28.9.80	2		Arnstadt	7 Feb 09
2.00i		Svetlana	Shkolina	RUS	9.3.86	2		Arnstadt	6 Feb 10
2.00i		Meike	Kröger	GER	21.7.86	2	NC	Karlsruhe	28 Feb 10
		(63)	100th woman 1.97, 200th 1.94, 300th 1.92, 400th 1.91, 500th 1.90						

Best outdoor marks

2.03	Di Martino	1	ECp-1B	Milano	24 Jun 07	2.00	Quintero	1	Herc	Monaco	7 Aug 93
2.02	Iagar/Dinescu	1		Budapest	6 Jun 98	2.00	Kositsyna	1		Chelyabinsk	16 Jul 88
2.02	Kuptsova	1	FBK	Hengelo	1 Jun 03	2.00	Bilac	1	EC	Helsinki	14 Aug 94
2.01	Astafei	2		Wörrstadt	27 May 95	2.00	Waller	1	MSR	Walnut	18 Apr 99

Ancillary jumps: 2.06 Kostadinova 30 Aug 87, 2.05i Henkel 8 Feb 92, 2.05i Bergqvist 4 Feb 06, 2.05 Vlasic 31 Aug 09

POLE VAULT

Mark	Wind	Name		Nat	Born	Pos	Meet	Venue	Date
5.06	WR	Yelena	Isinbayeva	RUS	3.6.82	1	WK	Zürich	28 Aug 09
5.05	WR		Isinbayeva			1	OG	Beijing	18 Aug 08
5.04	WR		Isinbayeva			1	Herc	Monaco	29 Jul 08
5.03	WR		Isinbayeva			1	GGala	Roma	11 Jul 08
5.01	WR		Isinbayeva			2 1	WCh	Helsinki	12 Aug 05
5.00	WR		Isinbayeva			1	LGP	London (CP)	22 Jul 05
5.00i			Isinbayeva			1		Donetsk	15 Feb 09
4.95	WR		Isinbayeva			1	GP	Madrid	16 Jul 05
4.95i			Isinbayeva			1		Donetsk	16 Feb 08
4.93	WR		Isinbayeva			1	Athl	Lausanne	5 Jul 05
4.93			Isinbayeva			1	VD	Bruxelles	26 Aug 05
4.93i			Isinbayeva			1		Donetsk	10 Feb 07
4.93			Isinbayeva			1	LGP	London (CP)	25 Jul 08
4.92	WR		Isinbayeva			1	VD	Bruxelles	3 Sep 04
4.92		Jennifer	Stuczynski/Suhr	USA	5.2.82	1	NC/OT	Eugene	6 Jul 08
4.91	WR		Isinbayeva (this jump on 25 Aug)			1	OG	Athína	25 Aug 04
4.91i			Isinbayeva			1		Donetsk	12 Feb 06
4.91			Isinbayeva			1	LGP	London (CP)	28 Jul 06
4.91			Isinbayeva			1	Gaz	Saint-Denis	6 Jul 07
4.91			Suhr			1		Rochester, NY	26 Jul 11
4.90	WR		Isinbayeva			1	GP	London (CP)	30 Jul 04
4.90i			Isinbayeva			1	EI	Madrid	6 Mar 05
4.90			Isinbayeva			1	Athl	Lausanne	11 Jul 06
4.90			Isinbayeva			1	GGala	Roma	13 Jul 07
4.90			Stuczynski			1	adidas	Carson	18 May 08
4.90i			Isinbayeva			1		Praha (O2)	26 Feb 09
4.89	WR		Isinbayeva			1		Birmingham	25 Jul 04
4.89i			Isinbayeva			1		Liévin	26 Feb 05
4.89			Suhr			1	NC	Des Moines	27 Jun 10
4.88	WR	Svetlana	Feofanova	RUS	16.7.80	1		Iráklio	4 Jul 04

4.88u Isinbayeva 1 GP Birmingham 18 Feb 05 & 4.88 1 WK Zürich 29 Aug 98; Suhr 1 GP New York 2 Jun 07

		(33/3)							
4.85		Fabiana	Murer	BRA	16.3.81	1	IbAm	San Fernando	4 Jun 10
4.85i		Anna	Rogowska	POL	21.5.81	1	EI	Paris (Bercy)	6 Mar 11
4.83		Stacy	Dragila	USA	25.3.71	1	GS	Ostrava	8 Jun 04
4.82		Monika	Pyrek	POL	11.8.80	2	WAF	Stuttgart	22 Sep 07
4.80		Martina	Strutz	GER	4.11.81	2	WCh	Daegu	30 Aug 11

Mark	Wind	Name		Nat	Born	Pos	Meet	Venue	Date
4.78		Tatyana	Polnova	RUS	20.4.79	2	WAF	Monaco	19 Sep 04
4.77		Annika	Becker	GER	12.11.81	1	NC	Wattenscheid	7 Jul 02
(10)									
4.76i		Silke	Spiegelburg	GER	17.3.86	1		Karlsruhe	13 Feb 11
4.75		Katerina	Badurová	CZE	18.12.82	2	WCh	Osaka	28 Aug 07
4.75i		Yuliya	Golubchikova	RUS	27.3.83	1		Athína (P)	13 Feb 08
4.75A		Yarisley	Silva	CUB	1.6.87	1	PAm	Guadalajara, MEX	24 Oct 11
4.73		Chelsea	Johnson	USA	20.12.83	1		Los Gatos	26 Jun 08
4.72i		Kym	Howe	AUS	12.6.80	2		Donetsk	10 Feb 07
4.72i		Jillian	Schwartz	USA/ISR	19.9.79	1		Jonesboro	15 Jun 08
4.72		Carolin	Hingst	GER	18.9.80	1		Biberach	9 Jul 10
4.71		Nikolía	Kiriakopoúlou	GRE	21.3.86	4	LGP	London (CP)	5 Aug 11
4.71i		Holly	Bleasdale	GBR	2.11.91	1		Orleans	10 Dec 11
(20)									
4.70		Yvonne	Buschbaum	GER	14.7.80	1	NC	Ulm	29 Jun 03
4.70		Vanessa	Boslak	FRA	11.6.82	2	ECp-S	Málaga	28 Jun 06
4.70i		Kylie	Hutson	USA	27.11.87	1	DrakeR	Des Moines	27 Apr 11
4.68		Anna	Battke	GER	3.1.85	5	ISTAF	Berlin	14 Jun 09
4.67i		Kellie	Suttle	USA	9.5.73	1		Jonesboro	16 Jun 04
4.66i		Christine	Adams	GER	28.2.74	1	IHS	Sindelfingen	10 Mar 02
4.66i		Lacy	Janson	USA	20.2.83	1		Fayetteville	12 Feb 10
4.66		Jirina	Ptácníková	CZE	20.5.86	1	NC	Trinec	17 Jul 10
4.66i		Kristina	Gadschiew	GER	3.7.84	1		Potsdam	18 Feb 11
4.65		Mary	Sauer/Vincent	USA	31.10.75	2		Madrid (C)	3 Jul 02
(30)									
4.65		Anastasiya	Ivanova/Shvedova	RUS/BLR	3.5.79	1	Odlozil	Praha	13 Jun 07
4.65		Aleksandra	Kiryashova	RUS	21.8.85	1	NCp	Tula	1 Aug 09
4.65		Lisa	Ryzih	GER	27.9.88	3	EC	Barcelona	30 Jul 10
4.64i		Pavla	Hamácková/Rybová	CZE	20.5.78	4		Bydgoszcz	14 Feb 07
4.64			Gao Shuying	CHN	28.10.79	2	GP	New York	2 Jun 07
4.63		Nastja	Ryshich	GER	19.9.77	1		Nürnberg	29 Jul 06
4.63		April	Steiner-Bennett	USA	22.4.80	1		Norman	12 Apr 08
4.63i		Angelica	Bengtsson	SWE	8.7.93	2		Stockholm	22 Feb 11
4.62b		Melissa	Mueller	USA	16.11.72	1		Clovis	4 Aug 01
4.60Ai						1		Flagstaff	9 Feb 02
4.61		Tina	Sutej	SLO	7.11.88	1	SEC	Athens, GA	14 May 11
(40)									
4.61		Kate	Dennison	GBR	7.5.84	2		Barcelona	22 Jul 11
4.60 WR		Emma	George	AUS	1.11.74	1		Sydney	20 Feb 99
4.60		Yelena	Belyakova	RUS	7.4.76	1	NC	Tula	10 Aug 03
4.60A		Andrea	DuToit	USA	28.2.78	1		Albuquerque	1 May 04
4.60		Thórey Edda	Elisdóttír	ISL	30.6.77	2	SGP	Madrid	17 Jul 04
4.60		Tracy	O'Hara	USA	20.7.80	1	GP II	Stanford	30 May 05
4.60i		Julia	Hütter	GER	26.7.83	1	NC	Sindelfingen	24 Feb 08
4.60		Erin	Asay	USA	17.3.83	1		La Jolla	25 Apr 08
4.60		Anna	Giordano Bruno	ITA	13.12.80	1		Milano	2 Aug 09
4.60		Becky	Holliday	USA	12.3.80	2	NC	Des Moines	27 Jun 10
(50)									
4.60		Alana	Boyd	AUS	10.5.84	1		Perth	4 Mar 11
4.60i		Minna	Nikkanen	FIN	9.4.88	4=	EI	Paris (Bercy)	6 Mar 11
4.60		Mary	Saxer	USA	21.6.87	1		Seattle	9 Jul 11
(53)		100th woman 4.45, 200th 4.31, 300th 4.23, 400th 4.16, 500th 4.10							

Outdoor bests

Mark	Name	Pos		Venue	Date		Mark	Name	Pos	Meet	Venue	Date
4.75	Golubchikova	4	OG	Beijing	18 Aug 08		4.60	Suttle	1	ModR	Modesto	12 May 01
4.75	Speigelburg	2	ET	Stockholm	18 Jun 11		4.60	Hamácková	1	ECp-1B	Velenje	21 Jun 03
4.70	Bleasdale	2		Mannheim	2 Jul 11		4.60	Mueller	1		Atascadero	9 Jul 03
4.65	Howe	1		Saulheim	30 Jun 07		4.60	Schwartz	1		Phoenix	14 May 04
4.65	Hutson	1	NC	Eugene	26 Jun 11		4.60A	Janson	1		Missoula	5 Jun 10
							4.60	Gadschiew	1		Reims	30 Jun 10

Ancillary jumps: Isinbayeva: 4.97 15 Feb 09, 4.96 WR 22 Jul 05, 4.95 18 Aug 08, 4.93 29 Jul 08

Exhibition: 4.72 Anastasiya   Shvedova   RUS   3.5.79   1   Aosta   5 Jul 08

LONG JUMP

Mark	Wind	Name		Nat	Born	Pos	Meet	Venue	Date
7.52 WR	1.4	Galina	Chistyakova	RUS	26.7.62	1	Znam	Leningrad	11 Jun 88
7.49	1.3	Jackie	Joyner-Kersee	USA	3.3.62	1	NYG	New York	22 May 94
7.49A	1.7		Joyner-Kersee			1		Sestriere	31 Jul 94
7.48	1.2	Heike	Drechsler	GER	16.12.64	1	v ITA	Neubrandenburg	9 Jul 88
7.48	0.4		Drechsler			1	Athl	Lausanne	8 Jul 92
7.45 WR	0.9		Drechsler'			1	v USSR	Tallinn	21 Jun 86
7.45 WR	1.1		Drechsler			1	OD	Dresden	3 Jul 86
7.45 WR	0.6		Joyner-Kersee			1	PAm	Indianapolis	13 Aug 87

Mark	Wind	Name		Nat	Born	Pos	Meet	Venue	Date
7.45	1.6		Chistyakova			1	BGP	Budapest	12 Aug 88
7.44 WR	2.0		Drechsler			1		Berlin	22 Sep 85
7.43 WR	1.4	Anisoara	Cusmir/Stanciu	ROU	28.6.62	1	RomIC	Bucuresti	4 Jun 83
7.42	2.0	Tatyana	Kotova	RUS	11.12.76	1	ECp-S	Annecy	23 Jun 02
7.40	1.8		Daute' (Drechsler)			1		Dresden	26 Jul 84
7.40	0.7		Drechsler			1	NC	Potsdam	21 Aug 87
7.40	0.9		Joyner-Kersee			1	OG	Seoul	29 Sep 88
7.39	0.3		Drechsler			1	WK	Zürich	21 Aug 85
7.39	0.5	Yelena	Byelevskaya'	BLR	11.10.63	1	NC	Bryansk	18 Jul 87
7.39			Joyner-Kersee			1		San Diego	25 Jun 88
7.37i	-		Drechsler			1	v2N	Wien	13 Feb 88
7.37A	1.8		Drechsler			1		Sestriere	31 Jul 91
7.37		Inessa	Kravets ¶	UKR	5.10.66	1		Kyiv	13 Jun 92
7.36	0.4		Joyner			1	WCh	Roma	4 Sep 87
7.36	1.8		Byelevskaya			2	Znam	Leningrad	11 Jun 88
7.36	1.8		Drechsler			1		Jena	28 May 92
7.35	1.9		Chistyakova			1	GPB	Bratislava	20 Jun 90
7.34	1.6		Daute'			1		Dresden	19 May 84
7.34	1.4		Chistyakova			2	v GDR	Tallinn	21 Jun 86
7.34			Byelevskaya			1		Sukhumi	17 May 87
7.34	0.7		Drechsler			1	v USSR	Karl-Marx-Stadt	20 Jun 87
7.33	0.4		Drechsler			1	v USSR	Erfurt	22 Jun 85
7.33	2.0		Drechsler			1		Dresden	2 Aug 85
7.33	-0.3		Drechsler			1	Herc	Monaco	11 Aug 92
7.33	0.4	Tatyana	Lebedeva	RUS	21.7.76	1	NC	Tula	31 Jul 04
		(33/8)							
7.31	1.5	Yelena	Kokonova'	UKR	4.8.63	1	NP	Alma-Ata	12 Sep 85
7.31	1.9	Marion	Jones ¶	USA	12.10.75	1	Pre	Eugene	31 May 98
		(10)							
7.27	-0.4	Irina	Simagina/Meleshina	RUS	25.5.82	2	NC	Tula	31 Jul 04
7.26A	1.8	Maurren	Maggi ¶	BRA	25.6.76	1	SACh	Bogotá	26 Jun 99
7.24	1.0	Larisa	Berezhnaya	UKR	28.2.61	1		Granada	25 May 91
7.21	1.6	Helga	Radtke	GDR	16.5.62	2		Dresden	26 Jul 84
7.21	1.9	Lyudmila	Kolchanova	RUS	1.10.79	1		Sochi	27 May 07
7.20 WR	-0.5	Valy	Ionescu	ROU	31.8.60	1	NC	Bucuresti	1 Aug 82
7.20	2.0	Irena	Ozhenko'	LTU	13.11.62	1		Budapest	12 Sep 86
7.20	0.8	Yelena	Sinchukova'	RUS	23.1.61	1	BGP	Budapest	20 Jun 91
7.20	0.7	Irina	Mushayilova	RUS	6.1.67	1	NC	Sankt-Peterburg	14 Jul 94
7.19	1.8	Brittney	Reese	USA	9.9.86	1	NC	Eugene	26 Jun 11
		(20)							
7.17	1.8	Irina	Valyukevich	BLR	19.11.59	2	NC	Bryansk	18 Jul 87
7.16		Iolanda	Chen	RUS	26.7.61	1		Moskva	30 Jul 88
7.16A	-0.1	Elva	Goulbourne	JAM	21.1.80	1		Ciudad de México	22 May 04
7.14	1.8	Nijole	Medvedeva ¶	LTU	20.10.60	1		Riga	4 Jun 88
7.14	1.2	Mirela	Dulgheru	ROU	5.10.66	1	Balk G	Sofia	5 Jul 92
7.13	2.0	Olga	Kucherenko	RUS	5.11.85	1		Sochi	27 May 10
7.12	1.6	Sabine	Paetz/John'	GDR	16.10.57	2		Dresden	19 May 84
7.12	0.9	Chioma	Ajunwa ¶	NGR	25.12.70	1	OG	Atlanta	2 Aug 96
7.12	1.3	Naide	Gomes	CPV/POR	10.11.79	1	Herc	Monaco	29 Jul 08
7.11	0.8	Fiona	May	GBR/ITA	12.12.69	2	EC	Budapest	22 Aug 98
		(30)							
7.09 WR	0.0	Vilhelmina	Bardauskiené	LTU	15.6.53	Q	EC	Praha	29 Aug 78
7.09	1.5	Ljudmila	Ninova	AUT	25.6.60	1	GP II	Sevilla	5 Jun 94
7.08	0.5	Marieta	Ilcu ¶	ROU	16.10.62	1	RumIC	Pitesti	25 Jun 89
7.07	0.0	Svetlana	Zorina	RUS	2.2.60	1		Krasnodar	15 Aug 87
7.06	0.4	Tatyana	Kolpakova	KGZ	18.10.59	1	OG	Moskva	31 Jul 80
7.06	-0.1	Niurka	Montalvo	CUB/ESP	4.6.68	1	WCh	Sevilla	23 Aug 99
7.06		Tatyana	Ter-Mesrobyan	RUS	12.5.68	1		Sankt Peterburg	22 May 02
7.05	0.6	Lyudmila	Galkina	RUS	20.1.72	1	WCh	Athína	9 Aug 97
7.05	-0.4	Eunice	Barber	FRA	17.11.74	1	WAF	Monaco	14 Sep 03
7.05	1.1	Darya	Klishina	RUS	15.1.91	1	EU23	Ostrava	17 Jul 11
		(40)							
7.04	0.5	Brigitte	Wujak'	GDR	6.3.55	2	OG	Moskva	31 Jul 80
7.04	0.9	Tatyana	Proskuryakova'	RUS	13.1.56	1		Kyiv	25 Aug 83
7.04	2.0	Yelena	Yatsuk	UKR	16.3.61	1	Znam	Moskva	8 Jun 85
7.04	0.3	Carol	Lewis	USA	8.8.63	5	WK	Zürich	21 Aug 85
7.03	0.6	Níki	Xánthou	GRE	11.10.73	1		Bellinzona	18 Aug 97
7.03i	-	Dawn	Burrell	USA	1.11.73	1	WI	Lisboa	10 Mar 01
7.02	1.5	Oksana	Udmurtova	RUS	1.2.82	2	SGP	Doha	12 May 06
7.01	-0.4	Tatyana	Skachko	UKR	18.8.54	3	OG	Moskva	31 Jul 80

Mark	Wind	Name		Nat	Born	Pos	Meet	Venue	Date
7.01	-0.3	Eva	Murková	SVK	29.5.62	1	PTS	Bratislava	26 May 84
7.01	-1.0	Marina	Kibakina'	RUS	2.8.60	1		Krasnoyarsk	10 Aug 85
7.01	1.4		Yao Weili	CHN	6.5.68	1	NC	Jinan	5 Jun 93
7.01	1.1	Shana	Williams	USA	7.4.72	Q	NC	Atlanta	21 Jun 96
7.01	0.3	Olga	Zaytseva	RUS	10.11.84	1	NC	Cheboksary	22 Jul 11
	(53)		100th woman 6.90, 200th 6.80, 300th 6.73, 400th 6.67, 500th 6.63						
Drugs dq: 7.03	0.1		Xiong Qiying ¶	CHN	14.10.67	Q	NG	Shanghai	21 Oct 97

Wind assisted   *Performances to 7.35, performers to 7.02*

Mark	Wind	Name		Nat	Born	Pos	Meet	Venue	Date
7.63A	2.1	Heike	Drechsler	GER	16.12.64	1		Sestriere	21 Jul 92
7.45	2.6		Joyner-Kersee			1	NC/OT	Indianpolis	23 Jul 88
7.39	2.6		Drechsler			1		Padova	15 Sep 91
7.39	2.9		Drechsler			1	Expo	Sevilla	6 Jun 92
7.39A	3.3		Drechsler			2		Sestriere	31 Jul 94
7.36	2.2		Chistyakova			1	Znam	Volgograd	11 Jun 89
7.35	3.4		Drechsler			1	NC	Jena	29 Jun 86
7.23A	4.3	Fiona	May	ITA	12.12.69	1		Sestriere	29 Jul 95
7.19A	3.7	Susen	Tiedtke ¶	GER	23.1.69	1		Sestriere	28 Jul 93
7.17	3.6	Eva	Murková	SVK	29.5.62	1		Nitra	26 Aug 84
7.14A	4.5	Marieke	Veltman	USA	18.9.71	2		Sestriere	29 Jul 95
7.12A	5.8	Níki	Xánthou	GRE	11.10.73	3		Sestriere	29 Jul 95
7.12A	4.3	Nicole	Boegman	AUS	5.3.67	4		Sestriere	29 Jul 95
7.09	2.9	Renata	Nielsen	DEN	18.5.66	2		Sevilla	5 Jun 94
7.08	2.2	Lyudmila	Galkina	RUS	20.1.72	1		Thessaloniki	23 Jun 99
7.07A	5.6	Valentina	Uccheddu	ITA	26.10.66	5		Sestriere	29 Jul 95
7.07A	2.7	Sharon	Couch	USA	13.9.67	1		El Paso	12 Apr 97
7.07A	w	Erica	Johansson	SWE	5.2.74	1		Vygieskraal	15 Jan 00
7.06	3.4		Ma Miaolan	CHN	18.1.70	1	NG	Beijing	10 Sep 93

Best at low altitude:

7.06	0.8	Maggi ¶	1	Milano	3 Jun 03	7.12w	3.4	May	1	NC	Bologna	25 May 96
		7.17w	2.6	1	São Paulo	13 Apr 02						

Ancillary marks – other marks during series (to 7.34/7.36w)

7.45	1.0	Chistyakova	11 Jun 88	7.47Aw	3.1	Drechsler	21 Jul 92	7.38w	2.2	Chistyakova 11 Jun 88
7.37		Drechsler	9 Jul 88	7.39Aw	3.1	Drechsler	21 Jul 92	7.36w		Joyner-Kersee 31 Jul 94

TRIPLE JUMP

Mark	Wind	Name		Nat	Born	Pos	Meet	Venue	Date
15.50 WR	0.9	Inessa	Kravets ¶	UKR	5.10.66	1	WCh	Göteborg	10 Aug 95
15.39	0.5	Françoise	Mbango	CMR	14.4.76	1	OG	Beijing	17 Aug 08
15.36i		Tatyana	Lebedeva	RUS	21.7.76	1	WI	Budapest	6 Mar 04
15.34	-0.5		Lebedeva			1		Iráklio	4 Jul 04
15.33	-0.1		Kravets			1	OG	Atlanta	31 Jul 96
15.33	1.2		Lebedeva			1	Athl	Lausanne	6 Jul 04
15.32	0.5		Lebedeva			1	Super	Yokohama	9 Sep 00
15.32	0.9	Hrisopiyi	Devetzí ¶	GRE	2.1.76	Q	OG	Athína	21 Aug 04
15.32	0.5		Lebedeva			2	OG	Beijing	17 Aug 08
15.30	0.6		Mbango			1	OG	Athína	23 Aug 04
15.29	0.3	Yamilé	Aldama	CUB/SUD/GBR	14.8.72	1		GGala Roma	11 Jul 03
15.28	0.3		Aldama			1	GP	Linz	2 Aug 04
15.28	0.9	Yargelis	Savigne	CUB	13.11.84	1	WCh	Osaka	31 Aug 07
15.27	1.3		Aldama			1	GP	London (CP)	8 Aug 03
15.25	-0.8		Lebedeva			1	WCh	Edmonton	10 Aug 01
15.25	-0.1		Devetzí			2	OG	Athína	23 Aug 04
15.25	1.7	Olga	Rypakova	KAZ	30.11.84	1	C.Cup	Split	4 Sep 10
15.23	0.8		Lebedeva			1		Réthimno	23 Jun 04
15.23	0.6		Lebedeva			1	Tsik	Athína	3 Jul 06
15.23	1.6		Devetzí			3	OG	Beijing	17 Aug 08
15.22	1.5		Devetzí			1		Thessaloníki	9 Jul 08
15.21	1.2		Aldama			2		Réthimno	23 Jun 04
15.20	0.0	Sarka	Kaspárková	CZE	20.5.71	1	WCh	Athína	4 Aug 97
15.20	-0.3	Tereza	Marinova	BUL	5.9.77	1	OG	Sydney	24 Sep 00
15.20	1.3		Savigne			1	Vard	Réthimno	14 Jul 08
15.19	0.5		Lebedeva			1	Athl	Lausanne	11 Jul 06
15.18	0.3	Iva	Prandzheva ¶ (10)	BUL	15.2.72	2	WCh	Göteborg	10 Aug 95
15.18	-0.2		Lebedeva			1	WCh	Saint-Denis	26 Aug 03
15.16	0.1	Rodica	Mateescu ¶	ROU	13.3.71	2	WCh	Athína	4 Aug 97
15.16i WIR	-	Ashia	Hansen	GBR	5.12.71	1	EI	Valencia	28 Feb 98
15.16	0.7	Trecia	Smith	JAM	5.11.75	2	GP	Linz	2 Aug 04
		(31/12)							
15.14	1.9	Nadezhda	Alekhina	RUS	22.9.78	1	NC	Cheboksary	26 Jul 09

Mark	Wind	Name		Nat	Born	Pos	Meet	Venue	Date
15.09 WR	0.5	Anna	Biryukova	RUS	27.9.67	1	WCh	Stuttgart	21 Aug 93
15.09	-0.5	Inna	Lasovskaya	RUS	17.12.69	1	ECCp-A	Valencia	31 May 97
15.08i		Marija	Sestak	SLO	17.4.79	1		Athína (P)	13 Feb 08
15.07	-0.6	Paraskeví	Tsiamíta	GRE	10.3.72	Q	WCh	Sevilla	22 Aug 99
15.03i		Iolanda	Chen	RUS	26.7.61	1	WI	Barcelona	11 Mar 95
15.03	1.9	Magdelin	Martinez	ITA	10.2.76	1		Roma	26 Jun 04
(20)									
15.02	0.9	Anna	Pyatykh	RUS	4.4.81	3	EC	Göteborg	8 Sep 06
15.00	1.2	Kène	Ndoye	SEN	20.11.78	2		Iráklio	4 Jul 04
14.99A	1.7	Caterine	Ibargüen	COL	12.2.84	1		Bogotá	13 Aug 11
14.98	1.8	Sofia	Bozhanova ¶	BUL	4.10.67	1		Stara Zagora	16 Jul 94
14.98	0.2	Baya	Rahouli	ALG	27.7.79	1	MedG	Almeria	1 Jul 05
14.98	0.6	Olga	Saladuha	UKR	4.6.83	1	Pre	Eugene	4 Jun 11
14.96	0.7	Yelena	Govorova	UKR	18.9.73	4	OG	Sydney	24 Sep 00
14.94i	–	Cristina	Nicolau	ROU	9.8.77	1	NC	Bucuresti	5 Feb 00
14.94i		Oksana	Udmurtova	RUS	1.2.82	1		Tartu	20 Feb 08
14.90	1.0		Xie Limei	CHN	27.6.86	1		Urumqi	20 Sep 07
(30)									
14.85	1.2	Viktoriya	Gurova	RUS	22.5.82	3	NC	Kazan	19 Jul 08
14.83i	-	Yelena	Lebedenko	RUS	16.1.71	1		Samara	1 Feb 01
14.83	0.5	Yelena	Oleynikova	RUS	9.12.76	1	Odlozil	Praha	17 Jun 02
14.79	1.7	Irina	Mushayilova	RUS	6.1.67	1	DNG	Stockholm	5 Jul 93
14.78i		Adelina	Gavrila	ROU	26.11.78	1		Bucuresti	3 Feb 08
14.76	0.9	Galina	Chistyakova	RUS	26.7.62	1		Luzern	27 Jun 95
14.76	1.1	Gundega	Sproge ¶	LAT	12.12.72	3		Sheffield	29 Jun 97
14.72	1.8		Huang Qiuyan	CHN	25.1.80	1	NG	Guangzhou	22 Nov 01
14.72		Paraskeví	Papahrístou	GRE	17.4.89	1	Veniz	Haniá	11 Jun 11
14.70i		Oksana	Rogova	RUS	7.10.78	1		Volgograd	6 Feb 02
(40)									
14.69	1.2	Anja	Valant	SLO	8.9.77	3		Kalamáta	4 Jun 00
14.69	1.2	Simona	La Mantia	ITA	14.4.83	1		Palermo	22 May 05
14.69	2.0	Teresa	N'zola Meso	ANG/FRA	30.11.83	1	ECp-S	München	23 Jun 07
14.68i		Anastasiya	Taranova-Potapova	RUS	6.9.85	1	EI	Torino	8 Mar 09
14.67	1.2	Ólga	Vasdéki	GRE	26.9.73	1	Veniz	Haniá	28 Jul 99
14.67	1.5	Natalya	Kutyakova	RUS	28.11.86	1		Huelva	2 Jun 11
14.67	0.4	Mabel	Gay	CUB	5.5.83	4	WCh	Daegu	1 Sep 11
14.66	1.9		Ren Ruiping	CHN	1.2.76	1	Oda	Hiroshima	29 Apr 97
14.65	0.3	Fiona	May	GBR/ITA	12.12.69	1	ECp	Sankt-Peterburg	27 Jun 98
14.65	2.0	Natalya	Safronova	BLR	11.4.74	1	NCp	Stayki	3 Jun 00
(50)									

100th woman 14.39, 200th 14.09, 300th 13.90, 400th 13.73, 500th 13.60

Wind assisted   *Performances to 15.14, performers to 14.67*

Mark	Wind	Name		Nat	Born	Pos	Meet	Venue	Date
15.24A	4.2	Magdelin	Martinez	ITA	10.2.76	1		Sestriere	1 Aug 04
15.17	2.4	Anna	Pyatykh	RUS	4.4.81	2	SGP	Athína	3 Jul 06
15.10	2.7	Keila	Costa	BRA	6.2.83	1		Uberlandia	6 May 07
15.06	2.6	Olga	Saladuha	UKR	4.6.83	1	DNG	Stockholm	29 Jul 11
14.99	6.8	Yelena	Govorova	UKR	18.9.73	1	WUG	Palma de Mallorca	11 Jul 99
14.84	4.1	Galina	Chistyakova	RUS	26.7.62	1		Innsbruck	28 Jun 95
14.83	8.3		Ren Ruiping	CHN	1.2.76	1	NC	Taiyuan	21 May 95
14.83	2.2	Heli	Koivula-Kruger	FIN	27.6.75	2	EC	München	10 Aug 02
14.75	4.2	Jelena	Blazevica	LAT	11.5.70	1	v2N	Kaunas	23 Aug 97
14.71	2.5	Simona	La Mantia	ITA	14.4.83	1		Roma	25 Jun 04
14.67	3.0	Yusmay	Bicet	CUB	8.12.83	2		Zaragoza	8 Jun 04

Best outdoor mark for athlete with all-time best indoors

15.15	1.7	Hansen	1	GPF	Fukuoka	13 Sep 97	14.85	1.4	Udmurtova	1		Padova	31 Aug 08
15.03	1.1	Sestak	6	OG	Beijing	17 Aug 08	14.75	1.1	Gavrila	3	GP II	Rieti	7 Sep 03
14.97 WR	0.9	Chen	1	NC	Moskva	18 Jun 93	14.70	1.3	Nicolau	1	EU23	Göteborg	1 Aug 99

Ancillary marks – other marks during series (to 15.19)

15.30	0.5	Mbango	23 Aug 04	15.28	-0.3	Ledebeva	4 Jul 04	15.25i		Ledebeva	6 Mar 04
15.21	-0.2	Mbango	23 Aug 04	15.19	1.0	Lebedeva	3 Jul 06	15.19	1.3	Mbango	17 Aug 08

SHOT

Mark		Name		Nat	Born	Pos	Meet	Venue	Date
22.63 WR		Natalya	Lisovskaya	RUS	16.7.62	1	Znam	Moskva	7 Jun 87
22.55			Lisovskaya			1	NC	Tallinn	5 Jul 88
22.53 WR			Lisovskaya			1		Sochi	27 May 84
22.53			Lisovskaya			1		Kyiv	14 Aug 88
22.50i		Helena	Fibingerová	CZE	13.7.49	1		Jablonec	19 Feb 77
22.45 WR		Ilona	Slupianek' ¶	GDR	24.9.56	1		Potsdam	11 May 80
22.41			Slupianek			1	OG	Moskva	24 Jul 80
22.40			Slupianek			1		Berlin	3 Jun 83
22.38			Slupianek			1		Karl-Marx-Stadt	25 May 80
22.36 WR			Slupianek			1		Celje	2 May 80

Mark	Wind	Name		Nat	Born	Pos	Meet	Venue	Date
22.34			Slupianek			1		Berlin	7 May 80
22.34			Slupianek			1	NC	Cottbus	18 Jul 80
22.32 WR			Fibingerová			1		Nitra	20 Aug 77
22.24			Lisovskaya			1	OG	Seoul	1 Oct 88
22.22			Slupianek			1		Potsdam	13 Jul 80
22.19		Claudia	Losch	FRG	10.1.60	1		Hainfeld	23 Aug 87
22.14i			Lisovskaya			1	NC	Penza	7 Feb 87
22.13			Slupianek			1		Split	29 Apr 80
22.06			Slupianek			1		Berlin	15 Aug 78
22.06			Lisovskaya			1		Moskva	6 Aug 88
22.05			Slupianek			1	OD	Berlin	28 May 80
22.05			Slupianek			1		Potsdam	31 May 80
22.04			Slupianek			1		Potsdam	4 Jul 79
22.04			Slupianek			1		Potsdam	29 Jul 79
21.99 WR			Fibingerová			1		Opava	26 Sep 76
21.98			Slupianek			1		Berlin	17 Jul 79
21.96			Fibingerová			1	GS	Ostrava	8 Jun 77
21.96			Lisovskaya			1	Drz	Praha	16 Aug 84
21.96			Lisovskaya			1		Vilnius	28 Aug 88
21.95			Lisovskaya			1	IAC	Edinburgh	29 Jul 88
		(30/4)							
21.89 WR		Ivanka	Khristova	BUL	19.11.41	1		Belmeken	4 Jul 76
21.86		Marianne	Adam	GDR	19.9.51	1	v URS	Leipzig	23 Jun 79
21.76			Li Meisu	CHN	17.4.59	1		Shijiazhuang	23 Apr 88
21.73		Natalya	Akhrimenko	RUS	12.5.55	1		Leselidze	21 May 88
21.70i		Nadezhda	Ostapchuk	BLR	12.10.80	1	NC	Mogilyov	12 Feb 10
21.69		Viktoriya	Pavlysh ¶	UKR	15.1.69	1	EC	Budapest	20 Aug 98
		(10)							
21.66			Sui Xinmei ¶	CHN	29.1.65	1		Beijing	9 Jun 90
21.61		Verzhinia	Veselinova	BUL	18.11.57	1		Sofiya	21 Aug 82
21.60i		Valentina	Fedyushina	UKR	18.2.65	1		Simferopol	28 Dec 91
21.58		Margitta	Droese/Pufe	GDR	10.9.52	1		Erfurt	28 May 78
21.57 @		Ines	Müller'	GDR	2.1.59	1		Athína	16 May 88
21.45						1		Schwerin	4 Jun 86
21.53		Nunu	Abashidze ¶	UKR	27.3.55	2	Izv	Kyiv	20 Jun 84
21.52			Huang Zhihong	CHN	7.5.65	1	NC	Beijing	27 Jun 90
21.46		Larisa	Peleshenko ¶	RUS	29.2.64	1	Kuts	Moskva	26 Aug 00
21.45 WR		Nadezhda	Chizhova	RUS	29.9.45	1		Varna	29 Sep 73
21.43		Eva	Wilms	FRG	28.7.52	2	HB	München	17 Jun 77
		(20)	@ competitive meeting, but unsanctioned by GDR federation						
21.42		Svetlana	Krachevskaya'	RUS	23.11.44	2	OG	Moskva	24 Jul 80
21.31 @		Heike	Hartwig'	GDR	30.12.62	2		Athína	16 May 88
21.27						1		Haniá	22 May 88
21.27		Liane	Schmuhl	GDR	29.6.61	1		Cottbus	26 Jun 82
21.24		Valerie	Adams	NZL	6.10.84	1	WCh	Daegu	29 Aug 11
21.22		Astrid	Kumbernuss	GDR/GER	5.2.70	1	WCh	Göteborg	5 Aug 95
21.21		Kathrin	Neimke	GDR	18.7.66	2	WCh	Roma	5 Sep 87
21.19		Helma	Knorscheidt	GDR	31.12.56	1		Berlin	24 May 84
21.15i		Irina	Korzhanenko ¶	RUS	16.5.74	1	NC	Moskva	18 Feb 99
21.10		Heidi	Krieger	GDR	20.7.65	1	EC	Stuttgart	26 Aug 86
21.06		Svetlana	Krivelyova	RUS	13.6.69	1	OG	Barcelona	7 Aug 92
		(30)							
21.05		Zdenka	Silhavá' ¶	CZE	15.6.54	2	NC	Praha	23 Jul 83
21.01		Ivanka	Petrova-Stoycheva	BUL	3.2.51	1	NC	Sofiya	28 Jul 79
21.00		Mihaela	Loghin	ROU	1.6.52	1		Formia	30 Jun 84
21.00		Cordula	Schulze	GDR	11.9.59	4	OD	Potsdam	21 Jul 84
20.96		Belsy	Laza	CUB	5.6.67	1		Ciudad de México	2 May 92
20.95		Elena	Stoyanova ¶	BUL	23.1.52	2	Balk	Sofiya	14 Jun 80
20.91		Svetla	Mitkova	BUL	17.6.64	1		Sofiya	24 May 87
20.80		Sona	Vasícková	CZE	14.3.62	1		Praha	2 Jun 88
20.72		Grit	Haupt/Hammer	GDR	4.6.66	3		Neubrandenburg	11 Jun 87
20.70		Natalya	Mikhnevich	BLR	25.5.82	2	NC	Grodno	8 Jul 08
		(40)							
20.61		María Elena	Sarría	CUB	14.9.54	1		La Habana	22 Jul 82
20.61		Yanina	Korolchik ¶	BLR	26.12.76	1	WCh	Edmonton	5 Aug 01
20.60		Marina	Antonyuk	RUS	12.5.62	1		Chelyabinsk	10 Aug 86
20.54			Zhang Liuhong	CHN	16.1.69	1	NC	Beijing	5 Jun 94
20.53		Iris	Plotzitzka	FRG	7.1.66	1	ASV	Köln	21 Aug 88
20.50i		Christa	Wiese	GDR	25.12.67	2	NC	Senftenberg	12 Feb 89
20.47		Nina	Isayeva	RUS	6.7.50	1		Bryansk	28 Aug 82

Mark	Wind	Name		Nat	Born	Pos	Meet	Venue	Date
20.47		Cong Yuzhen		CHN	22.1.63	2	IntC	Tianjin	3 Sep 88
20.44		Tatyana	Orlova	BLR	19.7.55	1		Staiki	28 May 83
20.40			Zhou Tianhua ¶	CHN	10.4.66	1		Beijing	5 Sep 91
	(50)		100th woman 19.65, 200th 18.74, 300th 18.05						

Best outdoor marks

21.09	Ostapchuk	1	Staiki	21 Jul 05		20.82	Korzhanenko ¶	1 Rostov na Donu	30 May 98
21.08	Fedyushina	1	Leselidze	15 May 88			21.06 drugs dq (1) OG Athína		18 Aug 04

Ancillary marks – other marks during series (to 22.09)

22.60	Lisovskaya (WR)	7 Jun 87	22.20	Slupianek	13 Jul 80	22.12	Slupianek	13 Jul 80
22.40	Lisovskaya	14 Aug 88	22.19	Lisovskaya	5 Jul 88	22.11	Slupianek	7 May 80
22.34	Slupianek	11 May 80	22.14	Slupianek	25 May 80	22.10	Slupianek	25 May 80
22.33	Slupianek	2 May 80	22.14	Slupianek	13 Jul 80	22.09	Slupianek	7 May 80

DISCUS

Mark	Name		Nat	Born	Pos	Meet	Venue	Date
76.80 WR	Gabriele	Reinsch	GDR	23.9.63	1	v ITA	Neubrandenburg	9 Jul 88
74.56 WR	Zdenka	Silhavá' ¶	CZE	15.6.54	1		Nitra	26 Aug 84
74.56	Ilke	Wyludda	GDR	28.3.69	1	NC	Neubrandenburg	23 Jul 89
74.44		Reinsch			1		Berlin	13 Sep 88
74.40		Wyludda			2		Berlin	13 Sep 88
74.08	Diana	Gansky'	GDR	14.12.63	1	v USSR	Karl-Marx-Stadt	20 Jun 87
73.90		Gansky			1	ECp	Praha	27 Jun 87
73.84	Daniela	Costian ¶	ROU	30.4.65	1		Bucuresti	30 Apr 88
73.78		Costian			1		Bucuresti	24 Apr 88
73.42		Reinsch			1		Karl-Marx-Stadt	12 Jun 88
73.36 WR	Irina	Meszynski	GDR	24.3.62	1	Drz	Praha	17 Aug 84
73.32		Gansky			1		Neubrandenburg	11 Jun 87
73.28	Galina	Savinkova'	RUS	15.7.53	1	NC	Donetsk	8 Sep 84
73.26 WR		Savinkova			1		Leselidze	21 May 83
73.26		Sachse/Gansky			1		Neubrandenburg	6 Jun 86
73.24		Gansky			1		Leipzig	29 May 87
73.22	Tsvetanka	Khristova ¶	BUL	14.3.62	1		Kazanlak	19 Apr 87
73.10	Gisela	Beyer	GDR	16.7.60	1	OD	Berlin	20 Jul 84
73.04		Gansky			1		Potsdam	6 Jun 87
73.04		Wyludda			1	ECp	Gateshead	5 Aug 89
72.96		Savinkova			1	v GDR	Erfurt	23 Jun 85
72.94		Gansky			2	v ITA	Neubrandenburg	9 Jul 88
72.92	Martina	Opitz/Hellmann	GDR	12.12.60	1	NC	Potsdam	20 Aug 87
72.90		Costian			1		Bucuresti	14 May 88
72.78		Hellmann			2		Neubrandenburg	11 Jun 87
72.78		Reinsch			1	OD	Berlin	29 Jun 88
72.72		Wyludda			1		Neubrandenburg	23 Jun 89
72.70		Wyludda			1	NC-j	Karl-Marx-Stadt	15 Jul 88
72.54		Gansky			1	NC	Rostock	25 Jun 88
72.52		Hellmann			1		Frohburg	15 Jun 86
72.52		Khristova			1	BGP	Budapest	11 Aug 86
	(31/10)							
72.14	Galina	Murashova	LTU	22.12.55	2	Drz	Praha	17 Aug 84
71.80 WR	Maria	Vergova/Petkova	BUL	3.11.50	1	NC	Sofiya	13 Jul 80
71.68		Xiao Yanling ¶	CHN	27.3.68	1		Beijing	14 Mar 92
71.58	Ellina	Zvereva' ¶	BLR	16.11.60	1	Znam	Leningrad	12 Jun 88
71.50 WR	Evelin	Schlaak/Jahl	GDR	28.3.56	1		Potsdam	10 May 80
71.30	Larisa	Korotkevich	RUS	3.1.67	1	RusCp	Sochi	29 May 92
71.22	Ria	Stalman	NED	11.12.51	1		Walnut	15 Jul 84
70.88	Hilda Elia	Ramos ¶	CUB	1.9.64	1		La Habana	8 May 92
70.80	Larisa	Mikhalchenko	UKR	16.5.63	1		Kharkov	18 Jun 88
70.68	Maritza	Martén	CUB	16.8.63	1	Ib Am	Sevilla	18 Jul 92
	(20)							
70.50 WR	Faina	Melnik	RUS	9.6.45	1	Znam	Sochi	24 Apr 76
70.34 @	Silvia	Madetzky	GDR	24.6.62	3		Athína	16 May 88
69.34					1		Halle	26 Jun 87
70.02	Natalya	Sadova ¶	RUS	15.7.72	1		Thessaloniki	23 Jun 99
69.86	Valentina	Kharchenko	RUS	.49	1		Feodosiya	16 May 81
69.72	Svetla	Mitkova	BUL	17.6.64	2	NC	Sofiya	15 Aug 87
69.68	Mette	Bergmann	NOR	9.11.62	1		Florø	27 May 95
69.51	Franka	Dietzsch	GER	22.1.68	1		Wiesbaden	8 May 99
69.50	Florenta	Craciunescu'	ROU	7.5.55	1	Balk	Stara Zagora	2 Aug 85
69.14	Irina	Yatchenko	BLR	31.10.65	1		Staiki	31 Jul 04
69.08	Carmen	Romero	CUB	6.10.50	1	NC	La Habana	17 Apr 76
	(30)							
69.08	Mariana	Ionescu/Lengyel	ROU	14.4.53	1		Constanta	19 Apr 86

Mark	Wind	Name		Nat	Born	Pos	Meet	Venue	Date
68.92		Sabine	Engel	GDR	21.4.54	1	v URS,POL	Karl-Marx-Stadt	25 Jun 77
68.80		Nicoleta	Grasu	ROU	11.9.71	1		Poiana Brasov	7 Aug 99
68.64		Margitta	Pufe'	GDR	10.9.52	1	ISTAF	Berlin	17 Aug 79
68.62			Yu Hourun	CHN	9.7.64	1		Beijing	6 May 88
68.62			Hou Xuemei	CHN	27.2.62	1	IntC	Tianjin	4 Sep 88
68.60		Nadezhda	Kugayevskikh	RUS	19.4.60	1		Oryol	30 Aug 83
68.58		Lyubov	Zverkova	RUS	14.6.55	1	Izv	Kyiv	22 Jun 84
68.52		Beatrice	Faumuiná	NZL	23.10.74	1	Bisl	Oslo	4 Jul 97
68.38		Olga	Burova'	RUS	17.9.63	2	RusCp	Sochi	29 May 92
(40)									
68.18		Tatyana	Lesovaya	KAZ	24.4.56	1		Alma-Ata	23 Sep 82
68.18		Irina	Khval	RUS	17.5.62	1		Moskva	8 Jul 88
68.18		Barbara	Hechevarría	CUB	6.8.66	2		La Habana	17 Feb 89
67.98			Li Yanfeng	CHN	15.5.79	1		Schönebeck	5 Jun 11
67.96		Argentina	Menis	ROU	19.7.48	1	RomIC	Bucuresti	15 May 76
67.96		Sandra	Perkovic ¶	CRO	21.6.90	1	NC-w	Bruxelles	26 Feb 11
67.90		Petra	Sziegaud	GDR	17.10.58	1		Berlin	19 May 82
67.82		Tatyana	Belova	RUS	12.2.62	1		Irkutsk	10 Aug 87
67.80		Stefenia	Simova ¶	BUL	5.6.63	1		Stara Zagora	27 Jun 92
67.78		Nadine	Müller	GER	21.11.85	1		Wiesbaden	8 May 10
(50)		100th woman 6564, 200th 63.43, 300th 61.26							

Unofficial meeting: Berlin 6 Sep 88: 1. Martina Hellmann 78.14, 2. Ilke Wyludda 75.36
Downhill: 69.44 Suzy   Powell   USA   3.9.76   1   La Jolla   27 Apr 02
Drugs disqualification: 69.99   Sandra Perkovic ¶ CRO   21.6.90   (1)   Varazdin   4 Jun 11
Ancillary marks – other marks during series (to 72.92)

73.32	Reinsch	13 Sep 88	73.28	Gansky	27 Jun 87	73.10	Reinsch	9 Jul 88
73.28	Gansky	11 Jun 87	73.16	Wyludda	13 Sep 88	73.06	Gansky	27 Jun 87
						72.92	Hellmann	20 Aug 87

HAMMER

Mark	Wind	Name		Nat	Born	Pos	Meet	Venue	Date
79.42 WR		Betty	Heidler	GER	14.10.83	1		Halle	21 May 11
78.30 WR		Anita	Wlodarczyk	POL	8.8.85	1	EAF	Bydgoszcz	6 Jun 10
77.96 WR			Wlodarczyk			1	WCh	Berlin	22 Aug 09
77.80 WR		Tatyana	Lysenko	RUS	9.10.83	1		Tallinn	15 Aug 06
77.53			Heidler			1		Fränkisch-Crumbach	12 Jun 11
77.53			Heidler			1		Elstal	9 Sep 11
77.41 WR			Lysenko			1	Znam	Zhukovskiy	24 Jun 06
77.40			Heidler			1	ISTAF	Berlin	11 Sep 11
77.32		Oksana	Menkova	BLR	28.3.82	1		Staiki	29 Jun 08
77.30			Lysenko			1		Adler	22 Apr 07
77.26 WR		Gulfiya	Khanafeyeva ¶	RUS	4.6.82	1	NC	Tula	12 Jun 06
77.22			Heidler			1	GS	Ostrava	30 May 11
77.20			Wlodarczyk			1		Cottbus	8 Aug 09
77.13			Lysenko			1	WCh	Daegu	4 Sep 11
77.12			Heidler			2	WCh	Berlin	22 Aug 09
77.06 WR			Lysenko			1	Kuts	Moskva	15 Jul 05
76.94			Khanafeyeva			1		Moskva	31 May 06
76.93			Khanafeyeva			1	RUSCp	Tula	15 Jul 06
76.90		Martina	Hrasnová' ¶	SVK	21.3.83	1		Trnava	16 May 09
76.86			Menkova			1	Klim	Minsk	23 Jun 06
76.83		Kamila	Skolimowska	POL	4.11.82	1	SGP	Doha	11 May 07
76.82			Hrasnová'			1		Reims	8 Jul 08
76.67			Lysenko			1	EC	Göteborg	8 Aug 06
76.66		Olga	Tsander	BLR	18.5.76	1		Staiki	21 Jul 05
76.63		Yekaterina	Khoroshikh ¶	RUS	21.1.83	2	Znam	Moskva	24 Jun 06
76.62		Yipsi	Moreno	CUB	19.11.80	1	GP	Zagreb	9 Sep 08
76.59			Wlodarczyk			1	GS	Ostrava	16 Jun 09
76.55			Heidler			1		Leverkusen	28 Jul 06
76.54			Lysenko			1	GP	Zagreb	31 Aug 06
76.50			Lysenko			1	ECp-S	Málaga	29 Jun 06
(30/10)									
76.33		Darya	Pchelnik	BLR	20.12.81	2		Staiki	29 Jun 08
76.21		Yelena	Konevtsova	RUS	11.3.81	3		Sochi	26 May 07
76.07 WR		Mihaela	Melinte ¶	ROU	27.3.75	1		Rüdlingen	29 Aug 99
75.68		Olga	Kuzenkova	RUS	4.10.70	1	NCp	Tula	4 Jun 00
75.65			Zhang Wenxiu	CHN	22.3.86	2		Fränkisch-Crumbach	12 Jun 11
75.48		Kathrin	Klaas	GER	6.2.84	2	GS	Ostrava	30 May 11
75.08		Ivana	Brkljacic	CRO	25.1.83	2	Kuso	Waszawa	17 Jun 07
74.66		Manuèla	Montebrun	FRA	13.11.79	1	GP II	Zagreb	11 Jul 05
74.65		Mariya	Smolyachkova	BLR	10.2.85	2		Staiki	19 Jul 08
74.52		Iryna	Sekachova	UKR	21.7.76	1	NC	Kyiv	2 Jul 08
(20)									

Mark	Wind	Name		Nat	Born	Pos	Meet	Venue	Date
73.90		Arasay	Thondike	CUB	28.5.86	1		La Habana	18 Jun 09
73.87		Erin	Gilreath	USA	11.10.80	1	NC	Carson	25 Jun 05
73.83		Yelena	Matoshko	BLR	23.6.82	3		Staiki	19 Jul 08
73.79		Anna	Bulgakova	RUS	17.1.88	1		Krasnodar	5 Jun 08
73.74		Jennifer	Dahlgren	ARG	21.4.84	1		Buenos Aires	10 Apr 10
73.59		Ester	Balassini	ITA	20.10.77	1	NC	Bressanone	25 Jun 05
73.52		Bianca	Perie	ROU	1.6.90	1	NC	Bucuresti	16 Jul 10
73.40		Stéphanie	Falzon	FRA	7.1.83	1	NC	Albi	26 Jul 08
73.21		Eileen	O'Keeffe	IRL	31.5.81	1	NC	Dublin	21 Jul 07
73.16		Yunaika	Crawford	CUB	2.11.82	3	OG	Athína	25 Aug 04
(30)									
72.93		Zalina	Marghieva	MDA	5.2.88	1	WUG	Shenzhen	19 Aug 11
72.74		Susanne	Keil	GER	18.5.78	1		Nikiti	15 Jul 05
72.65		Jessica	Cosby	USA	31.5.82	1		Los Angeles (ER)	7 May 11
72.59		Amber	Campbell	USA	5.6.81	1	MSR	Walnut	16 Apr 11
72.53		Marina	Marghieva	MDA	28.6.86	1		Chisinau	5 May 09
72.51			Liu Yinghui	CHN	29.6.79	2	WUG	Izmir	16 Aug 05
72.51		Brittany	Riley	USA	26.8.86	1	DrakeR	Des Moines	28 Apr 07
72.46		Clarissa	Claretti	ITA	7.10.80	1	NC	Cagliari	19 Jul 08
72.36			Gu Yuan	CHN	9.5.82	2		Padova	3 Jul 04
72.24		Sultana	Frizell	CAN	24.10.84	3		Fränkisch-Crumbach	23 May 10
(40)									
72.22		Nataliya	Zolotuhina	UKR	4.1.85	1		Uman	21 May 11
72.10		Stilianí	Papadopoúlou	GRE	15.3.82	1		Nikíti	19 Jul 08
72.09		Tatyana	Konstantinova	RUS	18.11.70	2	Znam	Moskva	4 Jun 99
72.01		Anna	Norgren-Mahon	USA	19.12.74	1		Walnut	27 Jul 02
71.93		Silvia	Salis	ITA	17.9.85	1		Savona	18 May 11
71.93		Mariya	Bespalova	RUS	21.5.86	2		Zhukovskiy	6 Jul 11
71.92		Yelena	Priyma/Rigert	RUS	2.12.83	2		Tula	5 Jul 08
71.90		Oksana	Kondratyeva	RUS	22.11.85	2	NCp	Yerino	11 Jun 10
71.82		Iryna	Novozhylova	UKR	7.1.86	2	NC	Kyiv	2 Jul 08
71.56		Inna	Sayenko	UKR	8.3.82	1		Kyiv	17 Jun 08
(50)									

100th woman 69.02, 200th 65.36, 300th 63.20, 400th 61.76, 500th 60.66

Downhill: 75.20 Manuéla   Montebrun   FRA 13.11.79 1   Vineuil   18 May 03

Ancillary marks – other marks during series to 76.80

77.67	Wlodarczyk	6 Jun 10	77.06	Lysenko	24 Jun 06	76.98	Heidler	21 May 11
77.19	Heidler	21 May 11	77.03	Heidler	12 Jun 11	76.80	Lysenko	22 Apr 07
77.09	Lysenko	4 Sep 11	76.99	Heidler	11 Sep 11	76.80	Lysenko	4 Sep 11

Drugs disqualification

78.61		Tatyana	Lysenko	RUS	9.10.83	(1)		Sochi	26 May 07
77.71			Lysenko			(1)	GS	Ostrava	27 Jun 07
77.36		Gulfiya	Khanafeyeva	RUS	4.6.82	(2)		Sochi	26 May 07
77.01			Lysenko			(1)	Znam	Zhukovskiy	9 Jun 07

Ancillary marks: Lysenko: 77.32 27 Jun 07, 77.05 26 May 07

JAVELIN

Mark	Wind	Name		Nat	Born	Pos	Meet	Venue	Date
72.28	WR	Barbora	Spotáková	CZE	30.6.81	1	WAF	Stuttgart	13 Sep 08
71.99		Mariya	Abakumova	RUS	15.1.86	1	WCh	Daegu	2 Sep 11
71.70	WR	Osleidys	Menéndez	CUB	14.11.79	1	WCh	Helsinki	14 Aug 05
71.58			Spotáková			2	WCh	Daegu	2 Sep 11
71.54	WR		Menéndez			1		Réthimno	1 Jul 01
71.53			Menéndez			1	OG	Athína	27 Aug 04
71.42			Spotáková			1	OG	Beijing	21 Aug 08
70.78		Mariya	Abakumova	RUS	15.1.86	2	OG	Beijing	21 Aug 08
70.20		Christina	Obergföll	GER	22.8.81	1	ECp-S	München	23 Jun 07
70.03			Obergföll			2	WCh	Helsinki	14 Aug 05
69.82			Menéndez			1	WUG	Beijing	29 Aug 01
69.81			Obergföll			1		Berlin (Elstal)	31 Aug 08
69.57			Obergföll			1	WK	Zürich	8 Sep 11
69.53			Menéndez			1	WCh	Edmonton	7 Aug 01
69.48	WR	Trine	Hattestad	NOR	18.4.66	1	Bisl	Oslo	28 Jul 00
69.45			Spotáková			1	Herc	Monaco	22 Jul 11
69.15			Spotáková			1		Zaragoza	31 May 08
68.92			Abakumova			Q	WCh	Berlin	16 Aug 09
68.91			Hattestad			1	OG	Sydney	30 Sep 00
68.89			Abakumova			1	DL	Doha	14 May 10
68.86			Obergföll			1	NC	Kassel	24 Jul 11
68.81			Spotáková			1	Odlozil	Praha	16 Jun 08
68.76			Obergföll			Q	WCh	Daegu	1 Sep 11

Mark	Wind	Name		Nat	Born	Pos	Meet	Venue	Date
68.66			Spotáková			1	GGala	Roma	10 Jun 10
68.63			Obergföll			1		Elstal	12 Sep 10
68.59			Obergföll			1	ET	Leiria	20 Jun 09
68.47			Menéndez			1	GP	Helsinki	25 Jul 05
68.40			Menéndez			1		Tartu	19 Jun 01
68.40			Obergföll			1		Halle	23 May 09
68.38		Sunette	Viljoen	RSA	6.1.83	3	WCh	Daegu	2 Sep 11
		(30/6)							
68.34		Steffi	Nerius	GER	1.7.72	2		Berlin (Elstal)	31 Aug 08
67.67		Sonia	Bisset	CUB	1.4.71	1		Salamanca	6 Jul 05
67.51		Miréla	Manjani/Tzelíli	GRE	21.12.76	2	OG	Sydney	30 Sep 00
67.20		Tatyana	Shikolenko	RUS	10.5.68	1	Herc	Monaco	18 Aug 00
		(10)							
67.16		Martina	Ratej	SLO	2.11.81	3	DL	Doha	14 May 10
66.91		Tanja	Damaske	GER	16.11.71	1	NC	Erfurt	4 Jul 99
66.81		Linda	Stahl	GER	2.10.85	1	EC	Barcelona	29 Jul 10
66.80		Louise	McPaul/Currey	AUS	24.1.69	1		Gold Coast (RB)	5 Aug 00
66.67		Kara	Patterson	USA	10.4.86	1	NC	Des Moines	25 Jun 10
65.91		Nikola	Brejchová'	CZE	25.6.74	1	GP	Linz	2 Aug 04
65.75		Goldie	Sayers	GBR	16.7.82	4	OG	Beijing	21 Aug 08
65.30		Claudia	Coslovich	ITA	26.4.72	1		Ljubljana	10 Jun 00
65.29		Xiomara	Rivero	CUB	22.11.68	1		Santiago de Cuba	17 Mar 01
65.17		Karen	Forkel	GER	24.9.70	2	NC	Erfurt	4 Jul 99
		(20)							
65.08		Ana Mirela	Termure ¶	ROU	13.1.75	1	NC	Bucuresti	10 Jun 01
64.90		Paula	Huhtaniemi'	FIN	17.2.73	1	NC	Helsinki	10 Aug 03
64.89		Yekaterina	Ivakina	RUS	4.12.64	4	Bisl	Oslo	28 Jul 00
64.87		Kelly	Morgan	GBR	17.6.80	1	NC	Birmingham	14 Jul 02
64.83		Christina	Scherwin	DEN	11.7.76	3	WAF	Stuttgart	9 Sep 06
64.67		Katharina	Molitor	GER	8.11.83	2	NC	Kassel	24 Jul 11
64.62		Joanna	Stone	AUS	4.10.72	2		Gold Coast (RB)	5 Aug 00
64.62		Nikolett	Szabó	HUN	3.3.80	1		Pátra	22 Jul 01
64.61		Oksana	Makarova	RUS	21.7.71	2	ECp	Paris (C)	19 Jun 99
64.51		Madara	Palameika	LAT	18.6.87	1	EU23	Kaunas	19 Jul 09
		(30)							
64.51		Monica	Stoian	ROU	25.8.82	4	WCh	Berlin	18 Aug 09
64.49		Valeriya	Zabruskova	RUS	29.7.75	1	Znam	Tula	7 Jun 03
64.46		Dörthe	Friedrich	GER	21.6.73	1	NC	Wattenscheid	7 Jul 02
64.19		Kim	Kreiner	USA	26.7.77	1		Fortaleza	16 May 07
64.08		Barbara	Madejczyk	POL	30.9.76	1	ECp-S	Málaga	28 Jun 06
64.07		Mercedes	Chilla	ESP	19.1.80	1		Valencia	12 Jun 10
64.06		Taina	Uppa/Kolkkala	FIN	24.10.76	1		Pihtipudas	23 Jul 00
64.03		Mikaela	Ingberg	FIN	29.7.74	6	ISTAF	Berlin	1 Sep 00
63.92			Wei Jianhua	CHN	23.3.79	1		Beijing	18 Aug 00
63.89		Felicia	Tilea-Moldovan ¶	ROU	29.9.67	2	WK	Zürich	16 Aug 02
		(40)							
63.82		Kimberley	Mickle	AUS	28.12.84	1		Sydney	19 Mar 11
63.73		Laverne	Eve	BAH	16.6.65	1		Nashville	22 Apr 00
63.69			Li Lei	CHN	4.5.74	1	OT	Jinzhou	8 Jun 00
63.65		Indre	Jakubaityté	LTU	24.1.76	1		Kaunas	14 Sep 07
63.53		Urszula	Piwnicka	POL	6.12.83	1		Kalamáta	30 May 09
63.50		Yanet	Cruz	CUB	8.2.88	1	NC	La Habana	19 Mar 11
63.49A		Justine	Robbeson	RSA	15.5.85	1		Potchefstroom	16 Feb 08
63.36		Vira	Rebryk	UKR	25.2.89	1		Istanbul	12 Jun 10
63.35		Lada	Chernova ¶	RUS	1.1.70	1	NC	Tula	1 Aug 07
63.32		Khristina	Georgieva	BUL	3.1.72	3	GP	Athína	28 Jun 00
63.32		Nora Aïda	Bicet	CUB	29.10.77	2		Tallinn	21 Jul 04
		(51)	100th woman 60.76, 200th 57.42						

Ancillary marks – other marks during series (to 68.80)

71.25	Abakumova	2 Sep 11	69.32	Abakumova	21 Aug 08	69.08	Abakumova		21 Aug 08
69.42	Menéndez	7 Aug 01	69.22	Spotáková	21 Aug 08	68.95	Obergföll		8 Sep 11
						68.80	Spotáková		2 Sep 11

Specification changed from 1 May 1999. See ATHLETICS 2000 for Old specification all-time list.

80.00 WR	Petra	Felke	GDR	30.7.59	1		Potsdam	9 Sep 88

HEPTATHLON

7291 WR	Jackie	Joyner-Kersee	USA	3.3.62	1	OG	Seoul	24 Sep 88
	12.69/0.5	1.86	15.80	22.56/1.6	7.27/0.7	45.66	2:08.51	
7215 WR		Joyner-Kersee			1	NC/OT	Indianpolis	16 Jul 88
	12.71/-0.9	1.93	15.65	22.30/ 0.0	7.00/-1.3	50.08	2:20.70	
7158 WR		Joyner-Kersee			1	USOF	Houston	2 Aug 86
	13.18/-0.5	1.88	15.20	22.85/1.2	7.03w/2.9	50.12	2:09.69	

Mark	Wind	Name	Nat	Born	Pos	Meet	Venue	Date
7148 WR		Joyner-Kersee			1	GWG	Moskva	7 Jul 86
	12.85/0.2	1.88 14.76		23.00/0.3	7.01/-0.5		49.86 2:10.02	
7128		Joyner-Kersee			1	WCh	Roma	1 Sep 87
	12.91/0.2	1.90 16.00		22.95/1.2	7.14/0.9		45.68 2:16.29	
7044		Joyner-Kersee			1	OG	Barcelona	2 Aug 92
	12.85/-0.9	1.91 14.13		23.12/0.7	7.10/1.3		44.98 2:11.78	
7032		Carolina Klüft	SWE	2.2.83	1	WCh	Osaka	26 Aug 07
	13.15/0.1	1.95 14.81		23.38/0.3	6.85/1.0		47.98 2:12.56	
7007		Larisa Nikitina ¶	RUS	29.4.65	1	NC	Bryansk	11 Jun 89
	13.40/1.4	1.89 16.45		23.97/1.1	6.73w/4.0		53.94 2:15.31	
7001		Klüft			1	WCh	Saint-Denis	24 Aug 03
	13.18/-0.4	1.94 14.19		22.98/1.1	6.68/1.0		49.90 2:12.12	
6985		Sabine Braun	GER	19.6.65	1		Götzis	31 May 92
	13.11/-0.4	1.93 14.84		23.65/2.0	6.63w/2.9		51.62 2:12.67	
6979		Joyner-Kersee			1	NC	San José	24 Jun 87
	12.90/2.0	1.85 15.17		23.02/0.4	7.25/2.3		40.24 2:13.07	
6952		Klüft			1	OG	Athína	21 Aug 04
	13.21/0.2	1.91 14.77		23.27/-0.1	6.78/0.4		48.89 2:14.15	
6946 WR		Sabine Paetz'	GDR	16.10.57	1	NC	Potsdam	6 May 84
	12.64/0.3	1.80 15.37		23.37/0.7	6.86/-0.2		44.62 2:08.93	
6942		Ghada Shouaa	SYR	10.9.72	1		Götzis	26 May 96
	13.78/0.3	1.87 15.64		23.78/0.6	6.77/0.6		54.74 2:13.61	
6935 WR		Ramona Neubert	GDR	26.7.58	1	v USSR	Moskva	19 Jun 83
	13.42/1.7	1.82 15.25		23.49/0.5	6.79/0.7		49.94 2:07.51	
6910		Joyner			1	MSR	Walnut	25 Apr 86
	12.9/0.0	1.86 14.75		23.24w/2.8	6.85/2.1		48.30 2:14.11	
6897		John'			2	wOG	Seoul	24 Sep 88
	12.85/0.5	1.80 16.23		23.65/1.6	6.71/ 0.0		42.56 2:06.14	
6889		Eunice Barber	FRA	17.11.74	1		Arles	5 Jun 05
	12.62w/2.9	1.91 12.61		24.12/1.2	6.78w/3.4		53.07 2:14.66	
6887		Klüft			1	WCh	Helsinki	7 Aug 05
	13.19/-0.4	1.82 15.02		23.70/-2.5	6.87/0.2		47.20 2:08.89	
6880		Tatyana Chernova	RUS	29.1.88	1	WCh	Daegu	30 Aug 11
	13.32/0.9	1.83 14.17		23.50/-1.5	6.61/-0.7		52.95 2:08.04	
6878		Joyner-Kersee			1	NC	New York	13 Jun 91
	12.77	1.89 15.62		23.42	6.97/0.4		43.28 2:22.12	
6875		Nikitina			1	ECp-A	Helmond	16 Jul 89
	13.55/-2.1	1.84 15.99		24.29/-2.1	6.75/-2.5		56.78 2:18.67	
6861		Barber			1	WCh	Sevilla	22 Aug 99
	12.89/-0.5	1.93 12.37		23.57/0.5	6.86/-0.3		49.88 2:15.65	
6859		Natalya Shubenkova (10)	RUS	25.9.57	1	NC	Kyiv	21 Jun 84
	12.93/1.0	1.83 13.66		23.57/-0.3	6.73/0.4		46.26 2:04.60	
6858		Anke Vater/Behmer	GDR	5.6.61	3	OG	Seoul	24 Sep 88
	13.20/0.5	1.83 14.20		23.10/1.6	6.68/0.1		44.54 2:04.20	
6847		Nikitina			1	WUG	Duisburg	29 Aug 89
	13.47	1.81 16.12		24.12	6.66		59.28 2:22.07	
6845 WR		Neubert			1	v URS	Halle	20 Jun 82
	13.58/1.8	1.83 15.10		23.14/1.4	6.84w/2.3		42.54 2:06.16	
6845		Irina Belova ¶	RUS	27.3.68	2	OG	Barcelona	2 Aug 92
	13.25/-0.1	1.88 13.77		23.34/0.2	6.82/0.0		41.90 2:05.08	
6842		Barber			1		Götzis	4 Jun 00
	12.97/0.2	1.88 12.23		23.84/0.5	6.85/-0.1		51.91 2:11.55	
6841		Joyner			1		Götzis	25 May 86
	13.09/-1.3	1.87 14.34		23.63/-0.8	6.76/-0.3		48.88 2:14.58	
(30/12)								
6832		Lyudmila Blonska ¶	UKR	9.11.77	2	WCh	Osaka	26 Aug 07
	13.25/0.1	1.92 14.44		24.09/0.3	6.88/1.0		47.77 2:16.68	
6831		Denise Lewis	GBR	27.8.72	1		Talence	30 Jul 00
	13.13/1.0	1.84 15.07		24.01w/3.6	6.69/-0.4		49.42 2:12.20	
6823		Jessica Ennis	GBR	28.1.86	1	EC	Barcelona	31 Jul 10
	12.95/-1.0	1.89 14.05		23.21/-0.3	6.43/1.1		46.71 2:10.18	
6803		Jane Frederick	USA	7.4.52	1		Talence	16 Sep 84
	13.27/1.2	1.87 15.49		24.15/1.6	6.43/0.2		51.74 2:13.55	
6778		Nataliya Dobrynska	UKR	29.5.82	2	EC	Barcelona	31 Jul 10
	13.59/-1.6	1.86 15.88		24.23/-0.2	6.56/0.3		49.25 2:12.06	
6765		Yelena Prokhorova	RUS	16.4.78	1	NC	Tula	23 Jul 00
	13.54/-2.8	1.82 14.30		23.37/-0.2	6.72/1.0		43.40 2:04.27	
6750		Ma Miaolan	CHN	18.1.70	1	NG	Beijing	12 Sep 93
	13.28/1.5	1.89 14.98		23.86/	6.64/		45.82 2:15.33	

Mark	Wind	Name	Nat	Born	Pos	Meet	Venue	Date

6741   Heike Drechsler   GER 16.12.64   1   Talence   11 Sep 94
  13.34/-0.3   1.84   13.58   22.84/-1.1   6.95/1.0   40.64   2:11.53
(20)
6735(w)   Hyleas Fountain   USA 14.1.81   1   NC   Des Moines   26 Jun 10
  12.93w/2.6   1.90   13.73   23.28w/3.3   6.79w/2.7   42.26   2:17.80
6703   Tatyana Blokhina   RUS 12.3.70   1   Talence   11 Sep 93
  13.69/-0.6   1.91   14.94   23.95/-0.4   5.99/-0.3   52.16   2:09.65
6702   Chantal Beaugeant ¶   FRA 16.2.61   2   Götzis   19 Jun 88
  13.10/1.6   1.78   13.74   23.96w/3.5   6.45/0.2   50.96   2:07.09
6695   Jane Flemming   AUS 14.4.65   1   CG   Auckland   28 Jan 90
  13.21/1.4   1.82   13.76   23.62w/2.4   6.57/1.6   49.28   2:12.53
6683   Jennifer Oeser   GER 29.11.83   3   EC   Barcelona   31 Jul 10
  13.37/-1.0   1.83   13.82   24.07/-0.3   6.68/-0.3   49.17   2:12.28
6660   Ines Schulz   GDR 10.7.65   3   Götzis   19 Jun 88
  13.56/0.4   1.84   13.95   23.93w/2.8   6.70/0.7   42.82   2:06.31
6658   Svetla Dimitrova ¶   BUL 27.1.70   2   Götzis   31 May 92
  13.41/-0.7   1.75   14.72   23.06w/2.4   6.64/1.9   43.84   2:09.60
6646   Natalya Grachova   UKR 21.2.52   1   NC   Moskva   2 Aug 82
  13.80   1.80   16.18   23.86   6.65w/3.5   39.42   2:06.59
6635   Sibylle Thiele   GDR 6.3.65   2   GWG   Moskva   7 Jul 86
  13.14/0.6   1.76   16.00   24.18   6.62/1.0   45.74   2:15.30
6635   Svetlana Buraga   BLR 4.9.65   3   WCh   Stuttgart   17 Aug 93
  12.95/0.1   1.84   14.55   23.69/0.0   6.58/-0.2   41.04   2:13.65
(30)
6633   Natalya Roshchupkina   RUS 13.1.78   2   NC   Tula   23 Jul 00
  14.05/-2.8   1.88   14.28   23.47/-0.2   6.45/0.4   44.34   2:07.93
6623   Judy Simpson'   GBR 14.11.60   3   EC   Stuttgart   30 Aug 86
  13.05/0.8   1.92   14.73   25.09/0.0   6.56w/2.5   40.92   2:11.70
6619   Liliana Nastase   ROU 1.8.62   4   OG   Barcelona   2 Aug 92
  12.86/-0.9   1.82   14.34   23.70/0.2   6.49/-0.3   41.30   2:11.22
6616   Malgorzata Nowak'   POL 9.2.59   1   WUG   Kobe   31 Aug 85
  13.27w/4.0   1.95   15.35   24.20/0.0   6.37w/3.9   43.36   2:20.39
6604   Remigija Nazaroviene'   LTU 2.6.67   2   URSCh   Bryansk   11 Jun 89
  13.26/1.4   1.86   14.27   24.12/0.7   6.58/0.9   40.94   2:09.98
6604   Irina Tyukhay   RUS 14.1.67   3   Götzis   28 May 95
  13.20/-0.7   1.84   14.97   24.33/1.7   6.71/0.5   43.84   2:17.64
6598   Svetlana Moskalets   RUS 22.1.69   1   NC   Vladimir   17 Jun 94
  13.20/0.8   1.82   13.78   23.56/0.1   6.74/0.8   42.48   2:14.54
6591   Svetlana Sokolova   RUS 9.1.81   1   NC   Tula   23 Jun 04
  13.56/1.1   1.82   15.09   24.02/0.6   6.26/0.3   45.07   2:07.23
6577   DeDee Nathan   USA 20.4.68   1   Götzis   30 May 99
  13.28/-0.1   1.76   14.74   24.23/0.2   6.59/1.6   50.08   2:16.92
6573   Rita Ináncsi   HUN 6.1.71   3   Götzis   29 May 94
  13.66/2.0   1.84   13.94   24.20w/2.5   6.78/1.4   46.28   2:16.02
(40)
6572   Heike Tischler   GDR 4.2.64   2   EC   Split   31 Aug 90
  14.08/-0.9   1.82   13.73   24.29/0.9   6.22/-0.7   53.24   2:05.50
6563   Natalya Sazanovich   BLR 15.8.73   2   OG   Atlanta   28 Jul 96
  13.56/-1.6   1.80   14.52   23.72/-0.3   6.70/1.1   46.00   2:17.92
6559   Olga Kurban   RUS 16.12.87   1   NC   Chelyabinsk   16 Jun 08
  13.29/0.6   1.77   13.71   24.04/0.5   6.51/0.1   49.23   2:12.42
6552   Nadezhda Vinogradova'   RUS 1.5.58   2   NC   Kyiv   21 Jun 84
  13.92/1.0   1.80   15.19   23.84/0.2   6.67/0.1   38.60   2:06.80
6551   Yelena Martsenyuk   RUS 21.2.61   2   Staiki   2 Jul 88
  13.54/-0.4   1.82   15.32   24.25/0.3   6.25/0.7   47.56   2:12.72
6547   Kelly Sotherton   GBR 13.11.76   2   Götzis   29 May 05
  13.27/1.1   1.85   13.84   23.77/1.7   6.67/-0.6   37.21   2:10.29
6546   Mona Steigauf   GER 17.1.70   1   WUG   Catania   27 Aug 97
  13.13/1.6   1.85   12.83   24.14/1.7   6.56/1.3   43.86   2:11.15
6542   Urszula Wlodarczyk   POL 22.12.65   4   WCh   Athína   4 Aug 97
  13.55/0.3   1.81   14.16   24.48/0.1   6.63/0.6   44.18   2:09.59
6541   Mila Kolyadina   RUS 31.12.60   4   v GDR   Moskva   19 Jun 83
  14.05   1.82   16.28   24.81   6.48/0.8   48.26   2:15.26
6539   Tatyana Shpak   UKR 17.11.60   3   Staiki   2 Jul 88
  13.57/-0.4   1.76   15.30   23.61/0.5   6.52/-0.6   39.28   2:07.25
(50)   100th woman 6371, 200th 6182, 300th 6048, 400th 5952, 500th 5859

DECATHLON

8358 WR   Austra Skujyte   LTU 12.8.79   1   Columbia, MO   15 Apr 05
  12.49/1.6   46.19   3.10   48.78   57.19   14.22w/2.4   6.12/1.6   16.42   1.78   5:15.86
8150 WR   Marie Collonvillé   FRA 23.11.73   1   Talence   26 Sep 04
  12.48/0.4   34.69   3.50   47.19   56.15   13.96/0.4   6.18/1.0   11.90   1.80   5:06.09

Mark	Wind	Name	Nat	Born	Pos	Meet	Venue	Date
7885		Mona Steigauf	GER	17.1.70	1		Ahlen	21 Sep 97
	12.15/1.2	5.93 12.49	1.73	55.34	13.75/0.2	34.68	3.10 42.24	5:07.95
7798		Irina Naumenko	KAZ	13.2.80	2		Talence	26 Sep 04
	12.58/0.4	34.63 3.30	37.57	55.91	14.42/0.4	5.98/1.0	12.51 1.77	4:59.03

IAAF approved order: 100m, DT, PV, JT, 400m / 100mh, LJ, SP, HJ, 1500m, 1997/2000 events used men's order

4 x 100 METRES RELAY

Mark	Nat	Name	Pos	Meet	Venue	Date
41.37 wr	GDR	Gladisch, Rieger, Auerswald, Göhr	1	WCp	Canberra	6 Oct 85
41.47	USA	Gaines, Jones, Miller, Devers	1	WCh	Athína	9 Aug 97
41.49	RUS	Bogoslovskaya, Malchugina, Voronova, Privalova	1	WCh	Stuttgart	22 Aug 93
41.49	USA	Finn, Torrence, Vereen, Devers	2	WCh	Stuttgart	22 Aug 93
41.52	USA	Gaines, Jones, Miller, Devers	1h1	WCh	Athína	8 Aug 97
41.53 wr	GDR	Gladisch, Koch, Auerswald, Göhr	1		Berlin	31 Jul 83
41.55	USA	Brown, Williams, Griffith, Marshall	1	ISTAF	Berlin	21 Aug 87
41.56	USA	B Knight, Felix, Myers, Jeter	1	WCh	Daegu	4 Sep 11
41.58	USA	Brown, Williams, Griffith, Marshall	1	WCh	Roma	6 Sep 87
41.58	USA	L.Williams, Felix, Lee, Jeter	1		Cottbus	8 Aug 09
41.60 wr	GDR	Müller, Wöckel, Auerswald, Göhr	1	OG	Moskva	1 Aug 80
41.61A	USA	Brown, Williams, Cheeseborough, Ashford	1	USOF	USAF Academy	3 Jul 83
41.63	USA	Brown, Williams, Cheeseborough, Ashford	1	v GDR	Los Angeles	25 Jun 83
41.65	USA	Brown, Bolden, Cheeseborough, Ashford	1	OG	Los Angeles	11 Aug 84
41.65	GDR	Gladisch, Koch, Auerswald, Göhr	1	ECp	Moskva	17 Aug 85
41.68	GDR	Möller, Krabbe, Behrendt, Günther	1	EC	Split	1 Sep 90
41.69	GDR	Gladisch, Koch, Auerswald, Göhr	1	OD	Potsdam	21 Jul 84
41.70	JAM	Fraser, Stewart, Simpson, Campbell-Brown	2	WCh	Daegu	4 Sep 11
41.73	GDR	Möller, Behrendt, Lange, Göhr	1		Berlin	13 Sep 88
41.73	JAM	Lawrence, Simpson, Bailey, Campbell	1	OG	Athína	27 Aug 04
41.76	GDR	Gladisch, Koch, Auerswald, Göhr	1	WCh	Helsinki	10 Aug 83
41.78	FRA	Girard, Hurtis, Félix, Arron	1	WCh	Saint-Denis	30 Aug 03
41.78	USA	Daigle, Lee, Barber, L.Williams	1	WCh	Helsinki	13 Aug 05

(23 performances by 5 nations) from here just best by nation

Mark	Nat	Name	Pos	Meet	Venue	Date
41.92	BAH	Fynes, Sturrup, Davis-Thompson, Ferguson	1	WCh	Sevilla	29 Aug 99
42.08mx	BUL	Pavlova, Nuneva, Georgieva, Ivanova	mx		Sofiya	8 Aug 84
		42.29 Pencheva, Nuneva, Georgieva, Donkova	1		Sofiya	26 Jun 88
42.23	CHN	(Sichuan) Xiao Lin, Li Yali, Liu Xiaomei, Li Xuemei	1	NG	Shanghai	23 Oct 97
42.29	UKR	Povh, Pogrebnyak, Ryemyen, Bryzgina	1	EC	Barcelona	1 Aug 10
42.39	NGR	Utondu, Idehen, Opara-Thompson, Onyali (10)	2h2	OG	Barcelona	7 Aug 92
42.43	GBR	Hunte, Smallwood, Goddard, Lannaman	3	OG	Moskva	1 Aug 80
42.50	TRI	Selvon, Baptiste, Hackett, Ahyee	1h2	WCh	Daegu	4 Sep 11
42.54	BEL	Borlée, Mariën, Ouédraogo, Gevaert	2	OG	Beijing	22 Aug 08
42.56	BLR	Nesterenko, Sologub, Nevmerzhitskaya, Dragun	3	WCh	Helsinki	13 Aug 05
42.59	FRG	Possekel, Helten, Richter, Kroniger	2	OG	Montreal	31 Jul 76
42.68	POL	Popowicz, Korczynska, Jeschke, Wedler	3	EC	Barcelona	1 Aug 10
42.77	CAN	Bailey, Payne, Taylor, Gareau	2	OG	Los Angeles	11 Aug 84
42.85A	BRA	A da Silva, Gomes, Krasucki, R Santos	1	PAm	Guadalajara	28 Oct 11
42.89	CUB	Ferrer, López, Duporty, Allen	6	WCh	Stuttgart	22 Aug 93
42.98	CZE/TCH	Sokolová, Soborová, Kocembová, Kratochvilová	1	WK	Zürich	18 Aug 82
		(20)				
42.99A	AUS	Massey, Broadrick, Lambert, Gainsford-Taylor	1		Pietersburg	18 Mar 00
43.03A	COL	M.Murillo, Palacios, Obregón, D Murillo	2	SAm-r	Bogotá	10 Jul 04
43.04	ITA	Pistone, Calí, Arcioni, Alloh	3	ECp-S	Annecy	21 Jun 08
43.07	GRE	Tsóni, Kóffa, Vasarmídou, Thánou	2	MedG	Bari	18 Jun 97
43.19	GHA	Akoto, Twum, Anim, Nsiah	5s1	OG	Sydney	29 Sep 00
43.25A	RSA	Hartman, Moropane, Holtshausen, Seyerling	2		Pietersburg	18 Mar 00
43.35	KAZ	Aleksandrova, Kvast, Miljauskiene, Sevalnikova	2	SPART	Taskent	16 Sep 86
43.37	FIN	Pirtimaa, Hanhijoki, Hernesniemi, Salmela	7	WCh	Stuttgart	22 Aug 93
43.38	THA	Jaksunin, Saenrat, Klomdee, Thavoncharoen	2		Nakhon R'sima	26 Jun 08
43.39	JPN	Kitakaze, Takahashi, Fukushima, Ichikawa	1		Kawasaki	8 May 11

Best at low altitude

Mark	Nat	Name	Pos	Meet	Venue	Date
42.92	BRA	A da Silva, Gomes, Krasucki, R Santos	3h1	WCh	Daegu	4 Sep 11
43.03	COL	M.Murillo, Palacios, Obregón, N.González	3h2	WCh	Helsinki	12 Aug 05
43.18	AUS	Wilson, Wells, Robertson, Boyle	5	OG	Montreal	31 Jul 76

One or more athlete susbsequently drugs dq

Mark	Nat	Name	Pos	Meet	Venue	Date
41.67	USA	A Williams, Jones ¶, L Williams, Colander	(1)	3-N	München	8 Aug 04
41.67	USA	A Williams, Jones ¶, L Williams, Colander	(1h1)	OG	Athína	26 Aug 04
41.71	USA	White ¶, Gaines, Miller, Jones ¶	(1)	WCh	Edmonton	11 Aug 01

4 x 200 METRES RELAY

Mark	Nat	Name	Pos	Meet	Venue	Date
1:27.46 wr	USA Blue	Jenkins, Colander-Richardson, Perry, M Jones	1	PennR	Philadelphia	29 Apr 00
1:28.15 wr	GDR	Göhr, R.Müller, Wöckel, Koch	1		Jena	9 Aug 80

Mark	Wind	Name	Nat	Born	Pos	Meet	Venue	Date
1:29.42		Texas A & M (USA) Tarmoh, Mayo, Beard, Lucas			1	Penn R	Philadelphia	24 Apr 10
Drugs dq:	1:29.40	USA Red Colander, Gaines, Miller, M Jones ¶			1	Penn	Philadelphia	24 Apr 04

4 x 400 METRES RELAY

Mark	Wind	Name	Nat	Born	Pos	Meet	Venue	Date
3:15.17	WR	URS			1	OG	Seoul	1 Oct 88
		Ledovskaya 50.12, O.Nazarova 47.82, Pinigina 49.43, Bryzgina 47.80						
3:15.51		USA			2	OG	Seoul	1 Oct 88
		D.Howard 49.82, Dixon 49.17, Brisco 48.44, Griffith-Joyner 48.08						
3:15.92	WR	GDR G.Walther 49.8, Busch 48.9, Rübsam 49.4, Koch 47.8			1	NC	Erfurt	3 Jun 84
3:16.71		USA Torrence 49.0, Malone 49.4, Kaiser-Brown 49.48, Miles 48.78			1	WCh	Stuttgart	22 Aug 93
3:16.87		GDR Emmelmann 50.9, Busch 48.8, Müller 48.9, Koch 48.21			1	EC	Stuttgart	31 Aug 86
3:17.83		USA Dunn 50.5, Felix 48.8, Demus 50.14, Richards 48.44			1	WCh	Berlin	23 Aug 09
3:18.09		USA Richards-Ross 49.3, Felix 49.4, Beard 49.84, McCorory 49.52			1	WCh	Daegu	3 Sep 11
3:18.29		USA			1	OG	Los Angeles	11 Aug 84
		Leatherwood 50.50, S.Howard 48.83, Brisco-Hooks 49.23, Cheeseborough 49.73						
3:18.29		GDR Neubauer 50.58, Emmelmann 49.89, Busch 48.81, Müller 48.99			3	OG	Seoul	1 Oct 88
3:18.38		RUS			2	WCh	Stuttgart	22 Aug 93
		Ruzina 50.8, Alekseyeva 49.3, Ponomaryova 49.78, Privalova 48.47						
3:18.43		URS			1	WCh	Tokyo	1 Sep 91
		Ledovskaya 51.7, Dzhigalova 49.2, Nazarova 48.87, Bryzgina 48.67						
3:18.54		USA Wineberg 51.0, Felix 48.6, Henderson 50.06, Richards 48.93			1	OG	Beijing	23 Aug 08
3:18.55		USA Trotter 51.2, Felix 48.0, Wineberg 50.24, Richards 49.07			1	WCh	Osaka	2 Sep 07
3:18.58		URS I.Nazarova, Olizarenko, Pinigina, Vladykina			1	ECp	Moskva	18 Aug 85
3:18.63		GDR Neubauer 51.4, Emmelmann 49.1, Müller 48.64, Busch 49.48			1	WCh	Roma	6 Sep 87
3:18.71		JAM Whyte 50.0, Prendergast 49.6, Williams-Mills 49.84, Williams 49.22			2	WCh	Daegu	3 Sep 11
3:18.82		RUS Gushchina 50.6, Litvinova 49.2, Firova 49.20, Kapachinskaya 49.82			2	OG	Beijing	23 Aug 08
3:19.01		USA Trotter 49.8, Henderson 49.7, Richards 49.81, Hennagan 49.73			(1)	OG	Athína	28 Aug 04
		Note team was disqualified as Crystal Cox (subject of retrospective drugs ban) ran for them in the heat						
3:19.04	WR	GDR Siemon' 51.0, Busch 50.0, Rübsam 50.2, Koch 47.9			1	EC	Athína	11 Sep 82
3:19.12		URS Baskakova, I.Nazarova, Pinigina, Vladykina			1	Drz	Praha	18 Aug 84
3:19.23	WR	GDR Maletzki 50.05, Rohde 49.00, Streidt 49.51, Brehmer 49.79			1	OG	Montreal	31 Jul 76
3:19.36		RUS			3	WCh	Daegu	3 Sep 11
		Krivoshapka 50.3, Antyukh 50.0, Litvinova 49.96, Kapachinskaya 49.22						
3:19.49		GDR Emmelmann, Busch, Neubauer, Koch 47.9			1	WCp	Canberra	4 Oct 85
3:19.50		URS Yurchenko 51.2, O.Nazarova 50.2, Pinigina 49.09, Bryzgina 49.03			2	WCh	Roma	6 Sep 87
3:19.60		USA Leatherwood, S.Howard, Brisco-Hooks, Cheeseborough			1		Walnut	25 Jul 84
3:19.62		GDR Kotte, Brehmer, Köhn, Koch 48.3			1	ECp	Torino	5 Aug 79
		(26/4 with USSR and Russia counted separately)						
3:19.73		JAM S Williams 50.5, Lloyd 50.1, Prendergast 50.18, NWilliams 48.93			2	WCh	Osaka	2 Sep 07
3:20.04		GBR Ohuruogu 50.6, Okoro 50.9, McConnell 49.79, Sanders 48.76			3	WCh	Osaka	2 Sep 07
3:20.32		CZE/TCH			2	WCh	Helsinki	14 Aug 83
		Kocembová 48.93, Matejkovicová 52.13, Moravcíková 51.51, Kratochvílová 47.75						
3:21.04		NGR Afolabi 51.13, Yusuf 49.72, Opara 51.29, Ogunkoya 48.90			2	OG	Atlanta	3 Aug 96
3:21.21		CAN Crooks 50.30, Richardson 50.22, Killingbeck ¶ 50.62, Payne 50.07			2	OG	Los Angeles	11 Aug 84
3:21.85		BLR Kozak 52.0, Khlyustova 50.3, I Usovich 49.85, S Usovich 49.69			4	OG	Beijing	23 Aug 08
		(10)						
3:21.94		UKR Dzhigalova, Olizarenko, Pinigina, Vladykina			1	URSCh	Kyiv	17 Jul 86
3:22.34		FRA Landre 51.3, Dorsile 51.1, Elien 50.54, Pérec 49.36			1	EC	Helsinki	14 Aug 94
3:22.49		FRG Thimm 50.81, Arendt 49.95, Thomas 51.50, Abt 50.23			4	OG	Seoul	1 Oct 88
3:23.21		CUB Díaz 51.1, Calatayud 51.2, Clement 50.47, Terrero 50.46			6	OG	Beijing	23 Aug 08
3:23.81		AUS Peris-K 51.71, Lewis 51.69, Gainsford-T 51.06, Freeman 49.35			4	OG	Sydney	30 Sep 00
3:24.28		CHN (Hebei) An X, Bai X, Cao C, Ma Y			1	NG	Beijing	13 Sep 93
3:24.49		POL Guzowska 52.2, Bejnar 50.2, Prokopek 50.47, Jesien 51.59			4	WCh	Helsinki	14 Aug 05
3:25.68		ROU Ruicu 52.69, Rîpanu 51.09, Barbu 52.64, Tîrlea 49.26			2	ECp	Paris (C)	20 Jun 99
3:25.7a		FIN Eklund 53.6, Pursiainen 50.6, Wilmi 51.6, Salin 49.9			2	EC	Roma	8 Sep 74
3:25.71		ITA Bazzoni 53.7, Milani 50.8, Spacca 51.64, Grenot 49.61			4	EC	Barcelona	1 Aug 10
		(20)						
3:25.81		BUL Ilieva, Stamenova, Penkova, Damyanova			1	v Hun,Pol	Sofiya	24 Jul 83
3:26.33		GRE Kaidantzi 53.2, Goudenoúdi 51.6, Boudá 51.76, Halkiá 49.75			3	ECpS	Bydgoszcz	20 Jun 04
3:26.68		BRA (Bovespa) Coutinho, de Oliveira, Sousa, de Lima			1	NC	São Paulo	7 Aug 11
3:26.89		IND R Kaur 53.1, Beenamol 51.4, Soman 52.51, M Kaur 49.85			3h2	OG	Athína	27 Aug 04
3:27.08		CMR Nguimgo 51.7, Kaboud 52.1, Atangana 51.98, Béwouda 51.35			7	WCh	Saint-Denis	31 Aug 03
3:27.14		MEX Rodríguez 53.3, Medina 51.2, Vela 52.94, Guevara 49.70			4h2	WCh	Osaka	1 Sep 07
3:27.48		IRL Andrews 53.4, Cuddihy 49.9, Bergin 52.60, Carey 51.54			4h3	WCh	Daegu	2 Sep 11
3:27.54		LTU Navickaite, Valiuliene, Mendzoryte, Ambraziene			3	SPART	Moskva	22 Jun 83
3:27.57		ESP Merino 52.2, Lacambra 52.0, Myers 50.85, Ferrer 52.56			7	WCh	Tokyo	1 Sep 91
3:27.86		HUN Orosz, Forgács, Tóth, Pál			5	OG	Moskva	1 Aug 80

5000 METRES WALK (TRACK)

Mark	Wind	Name		Nat	Born	Pos	Meet	Venue	Date
20:02.60	WR	Gillian	O'Sullivan	IRL	21.8.76	1	NC	Dublin (S)	13 Jul 02

Mark	Wind	Name		Nat	Born	Pos	Meet	Venue	Date
20:03.0	WR	Kerry	Saxby-Junna	AUS	2.6.61	1		Sydney	11 Feb 96
20:07.52	WR	Beate	Anders/Gummelt	GDR	4.2.68	1	vURS	Rostock	23 Jun 90
20:11.45		Sabine	Zimmer	GER	6.2.81	1	NC	Wattenscheid	2 Jul 05
20:12.41		Elisabetta	Perrone	ITA	9.7.68	1	NC	Rieti	2 Aug 03
20:18.87		Melanie	Seeger	GER	8.1.77	1	NC	Braunschweig	10 Jul 04
20:21.69		Annarita	Sidoti	ITA	25.7.69	1	NC	Cesenatico	1 Jul 95
20:27.59	WR	Ileana	Salvador	ITA	16.1.62	1		Trento	3 Jun 89
20:28.05		Tatyana	Kalmykova	RUS	10.1.90	1	WY	Ostrava	12 Jul 07

10 KILOMETRES WALK

Mark	Wind	Name		Nat	Born	Pos	Meet	Venue	Date
41:04	WR	Yelena	Nikolayeva	RUS	1.2.66	1	NC	Sochi	20 Apr 96
41:16			Wang Yan	CHN	3.5.71	1		Eisenhüttenstadt	8 May 99
41:16		Kjersti	Plätzer (Tysse)	NOR	18.1.72	1	NC	Os	11 May 02
41:17		Irina	Stankina	RUS	25.3.77	1	NC-w	Adler	9 Feb 97
41:24		Olimpiada	Ivanova ¶	RUS	26.8.70	2	NC-w	Adler	9 Feb 97
41:29	WR	Larisa	Ramazanova	RUS	23.9.71	1	NC	Izhevsk	4 Jun 95
41:30	WR	Kerry	Saxby-Junna	AUS	2.6.61	1	NC	Canberra	27 Aug 88
41:30			O Ivanova			2	NC	Izhevsk	4 Jun 95
41:31		Yelena	Gruzinova	RUS	24.12.67	2	NC	Sochi	20 Apr 96
41:37.9t			Gao Hongmiao	CHN	17.3.74	1	NC	Beijing	7 Apr 94
41:38		Rossella	Giordano (10)	ITA	1.12.72	1		Naumburg	25 May 97
41:41			Nikolayeva			2		Naumburg	25 May 97
41:41			Tysse Plätzer			1		Kraków	30 May 09
41:42		Olga	Kaniskina	RUS	19.1.85	2		Kraków	30 May 09
41:45			Liu Hongyu	CHN	11.1.75	2		Eisenhüttenstadt	8 May 99
41:46		Annarita	Sidoti	ITA	25.7.69	1		Livorno	12 Jun 94
41:46			O Ivanova			1	NC/w	Adler	11 Feb 96
41:47			Saxby-Junna			1		Eisenhüttenstadt	11 May 96
41:48			Li Chunxiu	CHN	13.8.69	1	NG	Beijing	8 Sep 93
41:49			Ramazanova			3	NC	Sochi	20 Apr 96
41:49			Nikolayeva			1	OG	Atlanta	29 Jul 96
41:50		Yelena	Arshintseva	RUS	5.4.71	1	NC-w	Adler	11 Feb 95
		(22/15)							
41:51		Beate	Anders/Gummelt	GER	4.2.68	2		Eisenhüttenstadt	11 May 96
41:52		Tatyana	Mineyeva	RUS	10.8.90	1	NCp-j	Penza	5 Sep 09
41:52		Tatyana	Korotkova	RUS	24.4.80	1		Buy	19 Sep 10
41:53		Tatyana	Sibileva	RUS	17.5.80	1	RWC-F	Beijing	18 Sep 10
41:56		Yelena	Sayko	RUS	24.12.67	2	NC/w	Adler	11 Feb 96
		(20)							
41:56.23t		Nadezhda	Ryashkina	RUS	22.1.67	1	GWG	Seattle	24 Jul 90
42:01		Tamara	Kovalenko	RUS	5.6.64	3	NC-w	Adler	11 Feb 95
42:01		Olga	Panfyorova	RUS	21.8.77	1	NC-23	Izhevsk	16 May 98
42:04+		Vera	Sokolova	RUS	8.6.87	1=	in 20k	Sochi	26 Feb 11
42:04+		Anisya	Kirdyapkina	RUS	23.10.89	1=	in 20k	Sochi	26 Feb 11
42:04+		Tatyana	Shemyakina	RUS	3.9.87	1=	in 20k	Sochi	26 Feb 11
42:05+		Margarita	Turova	BLR	28.12.80	1+	in 20k	Adler	12 Mar 05
42:06		Valentina	Tsybulskaya	BLR	19.2.68	4		Eisenhüttenstadt	8 May 99
42:07		Ileana	Salvador	ITA	16.1.62	1		Sesto San Giovanni	1 May 92
42:09		Elisabetta	Perrone	ITA	9.7.68	4		Eisenhüttenstadt	11 May 96
		(30)							
42:11		Nina	Alyushenko	RUS	29.5.68	3	NC	Izhevsk	4 Jun 95
42:13		Natalya	Misyulya	BLR	16.4.66	5		Eisenhüttenstadt	8 May 99
42:13.7t		Madelein	Svensson	SWE	20.7.69	2	SGP	Fana	15 May 92
42:15			Gu Yan	CHN	17.3.74	3	WCp	Podebrady	19 Apr 97
42:15		Erica	Alfridi	ITA	22.2.68	5		Naumburg	25 May 97
42:15		Jane	Saville	AUS	5.11.74	6		Eisenhüttenstadt	8 May 99
42:16		Alina	Ivanova	RUS	16.3.69	1		Novopolotsk	27 May 89
42:16		Norica	Cîmpean	ROU	22.3.72	1		Calella	9 May 99
42:17		Katarzyna	Radtke	POL	31.8.69	5		Eisenhüttenstadt	11 May 96
42:19+		Iraida	Pudovkina	RUS	2.11.80	2	in 20k	Adler	12 Mar 05
		(40)							

50th woman 42:35, 100th 43:13, 200th 44:12, 300th 44:52

Probable short course: Livorno 10 Jul 93: 1. Ileana Salvador ITA 16.1.62 41:30, 2. Elisabeta Perrone 9.7.68 41:56

Best track times

Mark	Wind	Name		Nat	Born	Pos	Meet	Venue	Date
41:57.22		Kerry	Saxby-Junna	AUS	2.6.61	2	GWG	Seattle	24 Jul 90
42:11.5		Beate	Anders/Gummelt	GER	4.2.68	1	SGP	Fana	15 May 92

20 KILOMETRES WALK

Mark	Wind	Name		Nat	Born	Pos	Meet	Venue	Date
1:24:50		Olimpiada	Ivanova ¶	RUS	26.8.70	1	NC-w	Adler	4 Mar 01
1:24:56		Olga	Kaniskina	RUS	19.1.85	1	NC-w	Adler	28 Feb 09
1:25:08	WR	Vera	Sokolova	RUS	8.6.87	1	NC-w	Sochi	26 Feb 11

Mark	Wind	Name		Nat	Born	Pos	Meet	Venue	Date
1:25:09		Anisya	Kirdyapkina	RUS	23.10.89	2	NC-w	Sochi	26 Feb 11
1:25:11			Kaniskina			1	NC-w	Adler	23 Feb 08
1:25:11			Kirdyapkina			1	NC-w	Sochi	20 Feb 10
1:25:18		Tatyana	Gudkova	RUS	23.1.78	1	NC	Moskva	19 May 00
1:25:20		Olga	Polyakova	RUS	23.9.80	2	NC	Moskva	19 May 00
1:25:26			Sokolova			2	NC-w	Adler	28 Feb 09
1:25:26			Kirdyapkina			3	NC-w	Adler	28 Feb 09
1:25:29		Irina	Stankina	RUS	25.3.77	3	NC	Moskva	19 May 00
1:25:30			Kirdyapkina			2	NC-w	Adler	23 Feb 08
1:25:32		Yelena	Shumkina	RUS	24.1.88	4	NC-w	Adler	28 Feb 09
1:25:35			Sokolova			2	NC-w	Sochi	20 Feb 10
1:25:41	WR		O Ivanova			1	WCh	Helsinki	7 Aug 05
1:25:42			Kaniskina			1	WCp	Cheboksary	11 May 08
1:25:46		Tatyana	Shemyakina	RUS	3.9.87	3	NC-w	Adler	23 Feb 08
1:25:52		Larisa	Yemelyanova (10)	RUS	6.1.80	5	NC-w	Adler	28 Feb 09
1:25:52		Tatyana	Sibileva	RUS	17.5.80	3	NC-w	Sochi	20 Feb 10
1:25:59		Tamara	Kovalenko	RUS	5.6.64	4	NC	Moskva	19 May 00
1:26:02			Kaniskina			1	NC-w	Adler	19 Feb 06
1:26:08			Ivanova			5	NC	Moskva	19 May 00
1:26:11		Margarita	Turova	BLR	28.12.80	1	NC	Nesvizh	15 Apr 06
1:26:14		Irina	Petrova	RUS	26.5.85	2	NC-w	Adler	19 Feb 06
1:26:16			Sibileva			4	NC-w	Adler	23 Feb 08
1:26:16		Lyudmila	Arkhipova	RUS	25.11.78	5	NC-w	Adler	23 Feb 08
1:26:22	WR		Wang Yan	CHN	3.5.71	1	NG	Guangzhou	19 Nov 01
1:26:22	WR	Yelena	Nikolayeva	RUS	1.2.66	1	ECp	Cheboksary	18 May 03
1:26:23			Wang Liping	CHN	8.7.76	2	NG	Guangzhou	19 Nov 01
1:26:27			Turova			1	WCp	La Coruña	13 May 06
		(30/18)							
1:26:28		Iraida	Pudovkina	RUS	2.11.80	1	NC-w	Adler	12 Mar 05
1:26:34		Tatyana	Kalmykova	RUS	10.1.90	1	NC	Saransk	8 Jun 08
		(20)							
1:26:35			Liu Hongyu	CHN	11.1.75	3	NG	Guangzhou	19 Nov 01
1:26:46			Song Hongjuan	CHN	4.7.84	1	NC	Guangzhou	20 Mar 04
1:26:50		Natalya	Fedoskina	RUS	25.6.80	2	ECp	Dudince	19 May 01
1:26:57		Lyudmila	Yefimkina	RUS	22.8.81	3	NC-w	Adler	19 Feb 06
1:27:07		Kjersti	Tysse Plätzer	NOR	18.1.72	2	OG	Beijing	21 Aug 08
1:27:09		Elisabetta	Perrone	ITA	9.7.68	3	ECp	Dudince	19 May 01
1:27:12		Elisa	Rigaudo	ITA	17.6.80	3	OG	Beijing	21 Aug 08
1:27:14		Antonina	Petrova	RUS	1.5.77	1	NC-w	Adler	1 Mar 03
1:27:17			Liu Hong	CHN	12.5.87	4	OG	Beijing	21 Aug 08
1:27:18		Alena	Nartova	RUS	1.1.82	6	NC-w	Adler	23 Feb 08
		(30)							
1:27:19			Jiang Jing	CHN	23.10.85	1	NC	Nanning	25 Feb 05
1:27:22		Gillian	O'Sullivan	IRL	21.8.76	1		Sesto San Giovanni	1 May 03
1:27:25		María	Vasco	ESP	26.12.75	5	OG	Beijing	21 Aug 08
1:27:27		Vira	Zozulya	UKR	31.8.70	1	NC	Sumy	7 Jun 08
1:27:29		Erica	Alfridi	ITA	22.2.68	4	ECp	Dudince	19 May 01
1:27:30	WB	Nadezhda	Ryashkina	RUS	22.1.67	1	NC-w	Adler	7 Feb 99
1:27:30		Tatyana	Kozlova	RUS	2.9.83	2	NC-w	Adler	12 Mar 05
1:27:35		Tatyana	Korotkova	RUS	24.4.80	2	NC	Cheboksary	12 Jun 04
1:27:35		Elmira	Alembekova	RUS	30.6.90	1		Voronovo	17 Sep 11
1:27:37			Bo Yanmin	CHN	29.6.87	1	NG	Nanjing	20 Oct 05
		(40)							
1:27:41		Claudia	Iovan/Stef ¶	ROU	25.2.78	1		La Coruña	5 Jun 04
1:27:43		Yekaterina	Yezhova	RUS	3.7.82	7	NC-w	Adler	23 Feb 08
1:27:44		Jane	Saville	AUS	5.11.74	4	WCp	Naumburg	2 May 04
1:27:44		Beatriz	Pascual	ESP	9.5.82	6	OG	Beijing	21 Aug 08
1:27:45		Olive	Loughnane	IRL	14.1.76	7	OG	Beijing	21 Aug 08
1:27:46		Norica	Cîmpean	ROU	22.3.72	1		Békéscsaba	28 Mar 99
1:27:46		Ana	Cabecinha	POR	29.4.84	8	OG	Beijing	21 Aug 08
1:27:49		Anna	Lukyanova	RUS	23.4.91	3	NC-w	Sochi	26 Feb 11
1:27:53		Yuliya	Voyevodina	RUS	17.10.71	7	WCp	Naumburg	2 May 04
1:27:54			Song Lijuan	CHN	9.2.75	2		Beijing	1 May 95
		(50)	100th best woman 1:29:36, 200th 1:31:59, 300th 1:33:46						

50 KILOMETRES WALK

Mark	Wind	Name		Nat	Born	Pos	Meet	Venue	Date
4:10:59		Monica	Svensson	SWE	26.12.78	1		Scanzorosciate	21 Oct 07
4:12:16		Yelena	Ginko	BLR	30.7.76	1		Scanzorosciate	17 Oct 04
4:16:27		Jolanta	Dukure	LAT	20.9.79	1		Paralepa	9 Sep 06
4:25:22		Brigita	Virbalyte	LTU	1.2.85	1		Villa di Serio	17 Oct 10

Mark	Wind	Name		Nat	Born	Pos	Meet	Venue	Date

JUNIOR MEN'S ALL-TIME LISTS

100 METRES

Mark	Wind	Name		Nat	Born	Pos	Meet	Venue	Date
10.01	0.0	Darrel	Brown	TRI	11.10.84	1q3	WCh	Saint-Denis	24 Aug 03
10.01	1.6	Jeffery	Demps	USA	8.1.90	2q1	NC/OT	Eugene	28 Jun 08
10.03	0.7	Marcus	Rowland	USA	11.3.90	1	PAm-J	Port of Spain	31 Jul 09
10.04	1.7	DeAngelo	Cherry	USA	1.8.90	1h4	NCAA	Fayetteville	10 Jun 09
10.04	0.2	Christoph	Lemaître	FRA	11.6.90	1	EJ	Novi Sad	24 Jul 09
10.05		Davidson	Ezinwa	NGR	22.11.71	1		Bauchi	4 Jan 90
10.06	2.0	Dwain	Chambers	GBR	5.4.78	1	EJ	Ljubljana	25 Jul 97
10.06	1.5	Walter	Dix	USA	31.1.86	1h1	NCAA-r	New York	27 May 05
10.07	2.0	Stanley	Floyd	USA	23.6.61	1		Austin	24 May 80
10.07	1.1	DaBryan	Blanton	USA	3.7.84	1h2	NCAA-r	Lincoln, NE	30 May 03
10.07	0.2	Tamunosiki	Atorudibo	NGR	21.3.85	1s2	NC	Abuja	9 Jul 04
10.07	0.3	Jimmy	Vicaut	FRA	27.2.92	1	EJ	Tallinn	22 Jul 11

Wind assisted to 10.05

Mark	Wind	Name		Nat	Born	Pos	Meet	Venue	Date
9.83	7.1	Leonard	Scott	USA	19.1.80	1		Knoxville	9 Apr 99
9.96	4.5	Walter	Dix	USA	31.1.86	1rA	TexR	Austin	9 Apr 05
9.97	??	Mark	Lewis-Francis	GBR	4.9.82	1q3	WCh	Edmonton	4 Aug 01
10.02	2.8	DeAngelo	Cherry	USA	1.8.90	1h2	NC-j	Eugene	26 Jun 09
10.02	2.4	Marcus	Rowland	USA	11.3.90	1	NC-j	Eugene	26 Jun 09
10.03	4.9	Christoph	Lemaître	FRA-	11.6.90	1		Forbach	31 May 09
10.05	2.1	J-Mee	Samuels	USA	20.5.87	1s2		Greensboro	23 Jul 05
10.05	3.0	Keston	Bledman	TRI	8.3.88	3	NC	Port of Spain	23 Jun 07
10.05	2.2	Marvin	Bracy	USA	15.12.93	1	NC-j	Eugene	24 Jun 11

200 METRES

Mark	Wind	Name		Nat	Born	Pos	Meet	Venue	Date
19.93	1.4	Usain	Bolt	JAM	21.8.86	1		Hamilton, BER	11 Apr 04
20.04	0.1	Ramil	Guliyev	AZE	29.5.90	1	WUG	Beograd	10 Jul 09
20.07	1.5	Lorenzo	Daniel	USA	23.3.66	1	SEC	Starkville	18 May 85
20.13	1.7	Roy	Martin	USA	25.12.66	1		Austin	11 May 85
20.16A	-0.2	Riaan	Dempers	RSA	4.3.77	1	NC-j	Germiston	7 Apr 95
20.18	1.0	Walter	Dix	USA	31.1.86	1s2	NCAA	Sacramento	9 Jun 05
20.22	1.7	Dwayne	Evans	USA	13.10.58	2	OT	Eugene	22 Jun 76
20.23	0.5	Michael	Timpson	USA	6.6.67	1		State College	16 May 86
20.24	0.2	Joe	DeLoach	USA	5.6.67	3		Los Angeles	8 Jun 85
20.24	0.2	Francis	Obikwelu	NGR	22.11.78	2rB		Granada	29 May 96
20.24	1.4	Roberto	Skyers	CUB	12.11.91	1h5		Camagüey	14 Mar 09

Wind assisted

Mark	Wind	Name		Nat	Born	Pos	Meet	Venue	Date
19.86	4.0	Justin	Gatlin	USA	10.2.82	1h2	NCAA	Eugene	30 May 01
20.01	2.5	Derald	Harris	USA	5.4.58	1		San José	9 Apr 77
20.08	9.2	Leonard	Scott	USA	19.1.80	2r2		Knoxville	9 Apr 99
20.10	4.6	Stanley	Kerr	USA	19.6.67	2r2	SWC	Houston	18 May 86
20.16	5.2	Nickel	Ashmeade	JAM	4.7.90	1	Carifta	Basseterre	24 Mar 08

Hand timing: 19.9 Davidson Ezinwa NGR 22.11.71 1 Bauchi 18 Mar 89

400 METRES

Mark	Wind	Name		Nat	Born	Pos	Meet	Venue	Date
43.87		Steve	Lewis	USA	16.5.69	1	OG	Seoul	28 Sep 88
44.36		Kirani	James	GRN	1.9.92	1	WK	Zürich	8 Sep 11
44.66		Hamdam Odha	Al-Bishi	KSA	5.5.81	1	WJ	Santiago de Chile	20 Oct 00
44.66		LaShawn	Merritt	USA	27.6.86	1		Kingston	7 May 05
44.69		Darrell	Robinson	USA	23.12.63	2	USOF	Indianapolis	24 Jul 82
44.71A		Luguelin	Santos	DOM	12.11.93	2	PAm	Guadalajara, MEX	26 Oct 11
44.73A		James	Rolle	USA	2.2.64	1	USOF	USAF Academy	2 Jul 83
44.75		Darren	Clark	AUS	6.9.65	4	OG	Los Angeles	8 Aug 84
44.75		Deon	Minor	USA	22.1.73	1s1	NCAA	Austin	5 Jun 92
44.93		Nagmeldin	El Abubakr	SUD	22.2.86	1	Is.Sol	Makkah	14 Apr 05

800 METRES

Mark	Wind	Name		Nat	Born	Pos	Meet	Venue	Date
1:42.69		Abubaker	Kaki	SUD	21.6.89	1	Bisl	Oslo	6 Jun 08
1:43.37		Mohammed	Aman	ETH	10.1.94	3		Rieti	10 Sep 11
1:43.64		Japheth	Kimutai	KEN	20.12.78	3rB	WK	Zürich	13 Aug 97
1:43.99		David	Mutua	KEN	20.4.92	4	Herc	Monaco	22 Jul 11
1:44.08		Leonard	Kosencha	KEN	21.8.94	1	WY	Villeneuve d'Ascq	9 Jul 11
1:44.15		David	Rudisha	KEN	17.12.88	1	VD	Bruxelles	14 Sep 07
1:44.27		Majid Saeed	Sultan	QAT	3.11.86	1	AsiC	Inchon	4 Sep 05
1:44.3*		Jim	Ryun	USA	29.4.47	1	USTFF	Terre Haute	10 Jun 66
1:44.3		Joaquim	Cruz	BRA	12.3.63	1		Rio de Janeiro	27 Jun 81
1:44.33		Yuriy	Borzakovskiy	RUS	12.4.81	2s2	OG	Sydney	25 Sep 00
1:44.39		Mohammed	Al-Salhi	KSA	11.5.86	1		Lapinlahti	3 Jul 05
1:44.45		Alfred	Kirwa Yego	KEN	28.11.86	3rA	Bisl	Oslo	29 Jul 05

Mark Wind	Name		Nat	Born	Pos	Meet	Venue	Date

1000 METRES

Mark Wind	Name		Nat	Born	Pos	Meet	Venue	Date
2:13.93	Abubaker	Kaki	SUD	21.6.89	1	DNG	Stockholm	22 Jul 08
2:15.00	Benjamin	Kipkurui	KEN	28.12.80	5	Nik	Nice	17 Jul 99
2:16.84	Ali	Hakimi	TUN	24.4.76	1		Lindau	28 Jul 95

1500 METRES

Mark Wind	Name		Nat	Born	Pos	Meet	Venue	Date
3:30.24	Cornelius	Chirchir	KEN	5.6.83	4	Herc	Monaco	19 Jul 02
3:31.13	Mulugueta	Wondimu	ETH	28.2.85	2rA	NA	Heusden	31 Jul 04
3:31.42	Alex	Kipchirchir	KEN	26.11.84	5	VD	Bruxelles	5 Sep 03
3:31.54	Isaac	Songok	KEN	25.4.84	1	NA	Heusden	2 Aug 03
3:31.64	Asbel	Kiprop	KEN	30.6.89	1	GGala	Roma	11 Jul 08
3:31.70	William	Biwott	KEN	5.3.90	3	GGala	Roma	10 Jul 09
3:32.02	Caleb	Ndiku	KEN	9.10.92	4	FBK	Hengelo	29 May 11
3:32.48	Augustine	Choge	KEN	21.1.87	1	ISTAF	Berlin	3 Sep 06
3:32.68	Abdelaati	Iguider	MAR	25.3.87	5	VD	Bruxelles	25 Aug 06
3:32.91	Noah	Ngeny	KEN	2.11.78	9	Herc	Monaco	16 Aug 97
3:33.16	Benjamin	Kipkurui	KEN	28.12.80	1rB	WK	Zürich	11 Aug 99

1 MILE

Mark Wind	Name		Nat	Born	Pos	Meet	Venue	Date
3:49.29	William	Biwott	KEN	5.3.90	2	Bisl	Oslo	3 Jul 09
3:49.77	Caleb	Ndiku	KEN	9.10.92	5	Pre	Eugene	4 Jun 11
3:50.25	Alex	Kipchirchir	KEN	26.11.84	2	GP II	Rieti	7 Sep 03
3:50.39	James	Kwalia	KEN	12.6.84	1	FBK	Hengelo	1 Jun 03
3:50.41	Noah	Ngeny	KEN	2.11.78	2	Nik	Nice	16 Jul 97
3:50.69	Cornelius	Chirchir	KEN	5.6.83	5	GGala	Roma	12 Jul 02
3:50.83	Nicholas	Kemboi	KEN	18.12.89	6	Bisl	Oslo	6 Jun 08

2000 METRES

Mark Wind	Name		Nat	Born	Pos	Meet	Venue	Date
4:56.25	Tesfaye	Cheru	ETH	2.3.93	1		Reims	5 Jul 11
4:56.86	Isaac	Songok	KEN	25.4.84	6	ISTAF	Berlin	31 Aug 01
4:58.18	Soresa	Fida	ETH	27.5.93	4		Reims	5 Jul 11
4:58.76	Jairus	Kipchoge	KEN	15.12.92	7		Reims	5 Jul 11
4:59.02 i	Remmy	Ndiwa	KEN	3.2.88	4	GP	Birmingham	17 Feb 07

3000 METRES

Mark Wind	Name		Nat	Born	Pos	Meet	Venue	Date
7:28.78	Augustine	Choge	KEN	21.1.87	2	SGP	Doha	13 May 05
7:29.11	Tariku	Bekele	ETH	21.1.87	2	GP	Rieti	27 Aug 06
7:30.67	Kenenisa	Bekele	ETH	13.6.82	2	VD	Bruxelles	24 Aug 01
7:30.91	Eliud	Kipchoge	KEN	5.11.84	2	VD	Bruxelles	5 Sep 03
7:32.37	Abreham	Cherkos	ETH	23.9.89	2	Athl	Lausanne	11 Jul 06
7:32.72	John	Kipkoech	KEN	29.12.91	4		Rieti	29 Aug 10
7:33.00	Hailu	Mekonnen	ETH	4.4.80	2		Stuttgart	6 Jun 99
7:33.01	Levy	Matebo	KEN	3.11.89	2	GP	Rieti	7 Sep 08
7:34.32	Richard	Limo	KEN	18.11.80	4	VD	Bruxelles	3 Sep 99
7:34.58	Sammy	Kipketer	KEN	29.9.81	5	VD	Bruxelles	3 Sep 99

5000 METRES

Mark Wind	Name		Nat	Born	Pos	Meet	Venue	Date
12:52.61	Eliud	Kipchoge	KEN	5.11.84	3	Bisl	Oslo	27 Jun 03
12:53.66	Augustine	Choge	KEN	21.1.87	4	GGala	Roma	8 Jul 05
12:53.72	Philip	Mosima	KEN	2.1.77	2	GGala	Roma	5 Jun 96
12:53.81	Tariku	Bekele	ETH	21.1.87	4	GGala	Roma	14 Jul 06
12:54.07	Sammy	Kipketer	KEN	29.9.81	2	GGala	Roma	30 Jun 00
12:54.18	Isiah	Koech	KEN	19.12.93	3	Herc	Monaco	22 Jul 11
12:53.29i					1		Düsseldorf	11 Feb 11
12:54.19	Abreham	Cherkos	ETH	23.9.89	5	GGala	Roma	14 Jul 06
12:54.58	James	Kwalia	KEN	12.6.84	5	Bisl	Oslo	27 Jun 03
12:56.15	Daniel	Komen	KEN	17.5.76	2	GG	Roma	8 Jun 95
12:57.05	Mulugueta	Wondimu	ETH	28.2.85	2	ISTAF	Berlin	12 Sep 04

10,000 METRES

Mark Wind	Name		Nat	Born	Pos	Meet	Venue	Date
26:41.75	Samuel	Wanjiru	KEN	10.11.86	3	VD	Bruxelles	26 Aug 05
26:55.73	Geoffrey	Kirui	KEN	16.2.93	6	VD	Bruxelles	16 Sep 11
27:02.81	Ibrahim	Jeylan	ETH	12.6.89	4	VD	Bruxelles	25 Aug 06
27:04.00	Boniface	Kiprop	UGA	12.10.85	5	VD	Bruxelles	3 Sep 04
27:04.45	Bernard Kipyego	Kiprop	KEN	16.7.86	4	FBK	Hengelo	29 May 05
27:06.35	Geoffrey	Kipsang	KEN	28.11.92	10	Pre	Eugene	3 Jun 11
27:06.47	Habtanu	Fikadu	ETH	13.3.88	8	FBK	Hengelo	26 May 07
27:07.29	Moses	Masai	KEN	1.6.86	7	VD	Bruxelles	3 Sep 04
27:11.18	Richard	Chelimo	KEN	21.4.72	1	APM	Hengelo	25 Jun 91
27:12.42	Sammy Alex	Mutahi	KEN	1.6.89	1		Tokamchi	29 Sep 07
27:13.66	Moses	Mosop	KEN	17.7.85	7	VD	Bruxelles	5 Sep 03

Mark	Wind	Name		Nat	Born	Pos	Meet	Venue	Date

3000 METRES STEEPLECHASE

Mark	Wind	Name		Nat	Born	Pos	Meet	Venue	Date
7:58.66		Stephen	Cherono	KEN	15.10.82	3	VD	Bruxelles	24 Aug 01
8:03.74		Raymond	Yator	KEN	7.4.81	3	Herc	Monaco	18 Aug 00
8:05.52		Brimin	Kipruto	KEN	31.7.85	1	FBK	Hengelo	31 May 04
8:07.18		Moussa	Omar Obaid	QAT	18.4.85	4	OG	Athína	24 Aug 04
8:07.69		Paul	Kosgei	KEN	22.4.78	5	DNG	Stockholm	7 Jul 97
8:07.71		Hillary	Yego	KEN	2.4.92	3	DL	Shanghai	15 May 11
8:09.37		Abel	Cheruiyot/Yugut	KEN	26.12.84	2	NA	Heusden	2 Aug 03
8:11.31		Jairus	Kipchoge	KEN	15.12.92	5	DL	Saint Denis	8 Jul 11
8:12.91		Thomas	Kiplitan	KEN	15.6.83	7	GP	Doha	15 May 02
8:14.00		Williy	Komen	KEN	22.12.87	1	WJ	Beijing	19 Aug 06
8:14.29		Benjamin	Kiplagat	UGA	4.3.89	2	FBK	Hengelo	24 May 08

110 METRES HURDLES (106cm)

Mark	Wind	Name		Nat	Born	Pos	Meet	Venue	Date
13.12	1.6		Liu Xiang	CHN	13.7.83	1rB	Athl	Lausanne	2 Jul 02
13.23	0.0	Renaldo	Nehemiah	USA	24.3.59	1r2	WK	Zürich	16 Aug 78
13.40	-1.0		Shi Dongpeng	CHN	6.1.84	1	NC	Shanghai	14 Sep 03
13.44	-0.8	Colin	Jackson	GBR	18.2.67	1	WJ	Athína	19 Jul 86
13.46	1.8	Jon	Ridgeon	GBR	14.2.67	1	EJ	Cottbus	23 Aug 85
13.46	-1.6	Dayron	Robles	CUB	19.11.86	1	PAm-J	Windsor	29 Jul 05
13.47	1.9	Holger	Pohland	GDR	5.4.63	2	vUSA	Karl-Marx-Stadt	10 Jul 82
13.47	1.2	Aries	Merritt	USA	24.7.85	4	NCAA	Austin	12 Jun 04
13.47	0.2		Xie Wenjun	CHN	11.7.90	2	GP	Shanghai	20 Sep 08
13.49	0.6	Stanislav	Olijar	LAT	22.3.79	1		Valmiera	11 Jul 98
13.49	1.2	Booker	Nunley	USA	2.7.90	2	SEC	Gainesville	17 May 09

Wind assisted

Mark	Wind	Name		Nat	Born	Pos	Meet	Venue	Date
13.41	2.6	Dayron	Robles	CUB	19.11.86	2	CAC	Nassau	10 Jul 05
13.42	4.5	Colin	Jackson	GBR	18.2.67	2	CG	Edinburgh	27 Jul 86
13.42	2.6	Antwon	Hicks	USA	12.3.83	1	WJ	Kingston	21 Jul 02
13.47	2.1	Frank	Busemann	GER	26.2.75	1	WJ	Lisboa	22 Jul 94

99 cm Hurdles

Mark	Wind	Name		Nat	Born	Pos	Meet	Venue	Date
13.08	2.0	Wayne	Davis	USA	2.7.90	1	PAm-J	Port of Spain	31 Jul 09
13.14	1.6	Eddie	Lovett	USA	25.6.92	1	PAm-J	Miramar	23 Jul 11
13.23	1.5	Artur	Noga	POL	2.5.88	1	WJ	Beijing	20 Aug 06
13.24	1.6	Roy	Smith	USA	12.4.92	2	PAm-J	Miramar	23 Jul 11
13.25*		Arthur	Blake	USA	19.8.66	1		Winter Park	11 May 84

Wind assisted   *120 yards time plus 0.03

Mark	Wind	Name		Nat	Born	Pos	Meet	Venue	Date
13.03	2.9	Eddie	Lovett	USA	25.6.92	1h1	PAm-J	Miramar	23 Jul 11
13.15	2.7	Brendan	Ames	USA	6.10.88	1	NC-j	Indianapolis	21 Jun 07
13.18		Arthur	Blake	USA	19.8.66	1	GWest	Sacramento	9 Jun 84
13.23	2.3	William	Wynne	USA	30.1.90	1h1	NC-j	Eugene	26 Jun 09
Hand timed: 12.9y		Renaldo	Nehemiah	USA	24.3.59	1		Jamaica, NY	30 May 77

400 METRES HURDLES

Mark	Wind	Name		Nat	Born	Pos	Meet	Venue	Date
48.02		Danny	Harris	USA	7.9.65	2s1	OT	Los Angeles	17 Jun 84
48.26		Jehue	Gordon	TRI	15.12.91	4	WCh	Berlin	18 Aug 09
48.51		Kerron	Clement	USA	31.10.85	1	WJ	Grosseto	16 Jul 04
48.52		Johnny	Dutch	USA	20.1.89	5	NC/OT	Eugene	29 Jun 08
48.62		Brandon	Johnson	USA	6.3.85	2	WJ	Grosseto	16 Jul 04
48.68		Bayano	Kamani	USA	17.4.80	1	NCAA	Boise	4 Jun 99
48.68		Jeshua	Anderson	USA	22.6.89	1	WJ	Bydgoszcz	11 Jul 08
48.72		Angelo	Taylor	USA	29.12.78	2	NCAA	Bloomington	6 Jun 97
48.74		Vladimir	Budko	BLR	4.2.65	2	DRZ	Moskva	18 Aug 84
48.76A		Llewellyn	Herbert	RSA	21.7.77	1		Pretoria	7 Apr 96

HIGH JUMP

Mark	Wind	Name		Nat	Born	Pos	Meet	Venue	Date
2.37		Dragutin	Topic	YUG	12.3.71	1	WJ	Plovdiv	12 Aug 90
2.37		Steve	Smith	GBR	29.3.73	1	WJ	Seoul	20 Sep 92
2.36		Javier	Sotomayor	CUB	13.10.67	1		Santiago de Cuba	23 Feb 86
2.35i		Vladimir	Yashchenko	UKR	12.1.59	1	EI	Milano	12 Mar 78
2.34						1	Prv	Tbilisi	16 Jun 78
2.35		Dietmar	Mögenburg	FRG	15.8.61	1		Rehlingen	26 May 80
2.34		Tim	Forsyth	AUS	17.8.73	1	Bisl	Oslo	4 Jul 92
2.33			Zhu Jianhua	CHN	29.5.63	1	AsiG	New Delhi	1 Dec 82
2.33		Patrik	Sjöberg	SWE	5.1.65	1	OsloG	Oslo	9 Jul 83
2.32i		Jaroslav	Bába	CZE	2.9.84	3		Arnstadt	8 Feb 03
2.32			Huang Haiqiang	CHN	8.2.88	1	WJ	Beijing	17 Aug 06

POLE VAULT

Mark	Wind	Name		Nat	Born	Pos	Meet	Venue	Date
5.80		Maksim	Tarasov	RUS	2.12.70	1	vGDR-j	Bryansk	14 Jul 89

Mark	Wind	Name		Nat	Born	Pos	Meet	Venue	Date
5.80		Raphael	Holzdeppe	GER	28.9.89	2		Biberach	28 Jun 08
5.75		Konstadínos	Filippídis	GRE	26.11.86	2	WUG	Izmir	18 Aug 05
5.71		Lawrence	Johnson	USA	7.5.74	1		Knoxville	12 Jun 93
5.71		Germán	Chiaraviglio	ARG	16.4.87	1	WJ	Beijing	19 Aug 06
5.70		Viktor	Chistyakov	RUS	9.2.75	1		Leppävirta	7 Jun 94
5.70		Artyom	Kuptsov	RUS	22.4.84	1	Znam	Tula	7 Jun 03
5.67i		Leonid	Kivalov	RUS	1.4.88	1	NC-j	Penza	1 Feb 07
5.65		Rodion	Gataullin	UZB	23.11.65	2	NC	Donetsk	8 Sep 84
5.65		István	Bagyula	HUN	2.1.69	1	WJ	Sudbury	28 Jul 88
5.65i		Jacob	Davis	USA	29.4.78	1	Big 12	Lincoln	21 Feb 97

LONG JUMP

Mark	Wind	Name		Nat	Born	Pos	Meet	Venue	Date
8.34	0.0	Randy	Williams	USA	23.8.53	Q	OG	München	8 Sep 72
8.28	0.8	Luis Alberto	Bueno	CUB	22.5.69	1		La Habana	16 Jul 88
8.27	1.7	Eusebio	Cáceres	ESP	10.9.91	Q	EC	Barcelona	30 Jul 10
8.24	0.2	Eric	Metcalf	USA	23.1.68	1	NCAA	Indianapolis	6 Jun 86
8.24	1.8	Vladimir	Ochkan	UKR	13.1.68	1	vGDR-j	Leningrad	21 Jun 87
8.22		Larry	Doubley	USA	15.3.58	1	NCAA	Champaign	3 Jun 77
8.22		Iván	Pedroso	CUB	17.12.72	1		Santiago de Cuba	3 May 91
8.22i		Viktor	Kuznetsov	UKR	14.7.86	1		Brovary	22 Jan 05
8.21A	2.0	Vance	Johnson	USA	13.3.63	1	NCAA	Provo	4 Jun 82
8.20	1.5	James	Stallworth	USA	29.4.71	Q	WJ	Plovdiv	9 Aug 90
8.19	1.5	Luvo	Maniyonga	RSA	18.11.91	1		Bottrop	9 Jul 10
Wind assisted									
8.40	3.2	Kareem	Streete-Thompson	CAY	30.3.73	1		Houston	5 May 91
8.35	2.2	Carl	Lewis	USA	1.7.61	1	NCAA	Austin	6 Jun 80
8.29	2.3	James	Beckford	JAM	9.1.75	1		Tempe	2 Apr 94
8.23	4.4	Peller	Phillips	USA	23.6.70	1		Sacramento	11 Jun 88
8.21	2.8	Masaki	Morinaga	JPN	27.3.72	1		Hamamatsu	7 Sep 91

TRIPLE JUMP

Mark	Wind	Name		Nat	Born	Pos	Meet	Venue	Date
17.50	0.4	Volker	Mai	GDR	3.5.66	1	vURS	Erfurt	23 Jun 85
17.42	1.3	Khristo	Markov	BUL	27.1.65	1	Nar	Sofiya	19 May 84
17.40A	0.4	Pedro	Pérez	CUB	23.2.52	1	PAm	Cali	5 Aug 71
17.40	0.8	Ernesto	Revé	CUB	26.2.92	1		La Habana	10 Jun 11
17.31	-0.2	David	Girat Jr.	CUB	26.8.84	Q	WCh	Saint-Denis	23 Aug 03
17.29	1.3	James	Beckford	JAM	9.1.75	1		Tempe	2 Apr 94
17.27		Aliecer	Urrutia	CUB	22.9.74	1		Artemisa	23 Apr 93
17.23	0.2	Yoelbi	Quesada	CUB	4.8.73	1	NC	La Habana	13 May 92
17.19	-0.4	Teddy	Tamgho	FRA	15.6.89	4	Herc	Monaco	29 Jul 08
17.19	2.0	Will	Claye	USA	13.6.91	*	NCAA	Fayetteville	13 Jun 09
Wind assisted to 17.15									
17.33	2.1	Teddy	Tamgho	FRA	15.6.89	1	WJ	Bydgoszcz	11 Jul 08
17.24	2.5	Will	Claye	USA	13.6.91	1	NCAA	Fayetteville	13 Jun 09

SHOT

Mark	Wind	Name		Nat	Born	Pos	Meet	Venue	Date
21.05i		Terry	Albritton	USA	14.1.55	1	AAU	New York	22 Feb 74
		20.38				2	MSR	Walnut	27 Apr 74
20.65		Mike	Carter	USA	29.10.60	1	vSU-j	Boston	4 Jul 79
20.43		David	Storl	GER	27.7.90	2		Gerlingen	6 Jul 09
20.39		Janus	Robberts	RSA	10.3.79	1	NC	Germiston	7 Mar 98
20.38		Jacko	Gill	NZL	10.12.94	1		Auckland (NS)	5 Dec 11
20.20		Randy	Matson	USA	5.3.45	2	OG	Tokyo	17 Oct 64
20.20		Udo	Beyer	GDR	9.8.55	2	NC	Leipzig	6 Jul 74
20.13		Jeff	Chakouian	USA	20.4.82	2		Atlanta	18 May 01
19.99		Karl	Salb	USA	19.5.49	4	OT	Echo Summit	10 Sep 68
19.95		Edis	Elkasevic	CRO	18.2.83	1		Velenje	15 Jun 02
6 kg Shot	(* 6.25kg shot)								
22.73		David	Storl	GER	27.7.90	1		Osterode	14 Jul 09
22.31		Jacko	Gill	NZL	10.12.94	1		Auckland (NS)	5 Dec 11
21.96		Edis	Elkasevic	CRO	18.2.83	1	NC-j	Zagreb	29 Jun 02
21.68		Marin	Premeru	CRO	29.8.90	1		Rijeka	19 May 09
21.25			Gao Yong	CHN	12.10.89	1		Jinzhou	1 Sep 06
21.24		Georgi	Ivanov	BUL	13.3.85	1	NC-j	Sofia	12 Jun 04
21.11		Magnus	Lohse	SWE	28.7.84	1		Lerum	19 Jun 03
21.11			Wang Like	CHN	2.4.89	1	SDG	Yantai	15 Oct 06

DISCUS

Mark	Wind	Name		Nat	Born	Pos	Meet	Venue	Date
65.62		Werner	Reiterer	AUS	27.1.68	1		Melbourne	15 Dec 87
65.31		Mykyta	Nesterenko	UKR	15.4.91	3		Tallinn	3 Jun 08
63.64		Werner	Hartmann	FRG	20.4.59	1	vFRA	Strasbourg	25 Jun 78

Mark	Wind	Name		Nat	Born	Pos	Meet	Venue	Date
63.26		Sergey	Pachin	UKR	24.5.68	2		Moskva	25 Jul 87
63.22		Brian	Milne	USA	7.1.73	1		State College	28 Mar 92
62.52		John	Nichols	USA	23.8.69	1		Baton Rouge	23 Apr 88
62.36		Nuermaimaiti	Tulake	CHN	8.3.82	2	NG	Guangzhou	21 Nov 01
62.16		Zoltán	Kövágó	HUN	10.4.79	1		Budapest	9 May 97
62.04		Kenth	Gardenkrans	SWE	2.10.55	2		Helsingborg	11 Aug 74
62.04			Wu Tao	CHN	3.10.83	1	NGP	Shanghai	18 May 02

1.75kg Discus

Mark	Wind	Name		Nat	Born	Pos	Meet	Venue	Date
70.13		Mykyta	Nesterenko	UKR	15.4.91	1		Halle	24 May 08
67.32		Margus	Hunt	EST	14.7.87	1	WJ	Beijing	16 Aug 06
66.88		Traves	Smikle	JAM	7.5.92	1		Kingston	31 Mar 11
66.45		Gordon	Wolf	GER	17.1.90	1		Halle	23 May 09
65.88		Omar	El-Ghazaly	EGY	9.2.84	1		Cairo	7 Nov 03
65.55		Mihai	Grasu	ROM	21.4.87	1	NC	Bucuresti	23 Jul 06
65.52A		Victor	Hogan	RSA	25.7.89	1		Potchefstroom	3 Jul 08
65.71		Marin	Premeru	CRO	29.8.90	1		Split	31 May 09
65.51		Andrius	Gudzius	LTU	14.2.91	1		Siauliai	30 Jun 10

HAMMER

Mark	Wind	Name		Nat	Born	Pos	Meet	Venue	Date
78.33		Olli-Pekka	Karjalainen	FIN	7.3.80	1	NC	Seinäjoki	5 Aug 99
78.14		Roland	Steuk	GDR	5.3.59	1	NC	Leipzig	30 Jun 78
78.00		Sergey	Dorozhon	UKR	17.2.64	1		Moskva	7 Aug 83
76.54		Valeriy	Gubkin	BLR	3.9.67	2		Minsk	27 Jun 86
76.42		Ruslan	Dikiy	TJK	18.1.72	1		Togliatti	7 Sep 91
75.52		Sergey	Kirmasov	RUS	25.3.70	1		Kharkov	4 Jun 89
75.42		Szymon	Ziolkowski	POL	1.7.76	1	EJ	Nyíregyháza	30 Jul 95
75.24		Christoph	Sahner	FRG	23.9.63	1	vPOL-j	Göttingen	26 Jun 82

6kg Hammer (* 6.25kg hammer)

Mark	Wind	Name		Nat	Born	Pos	Meet	Venue	Date
82.97		Javier	Cienfuegos	ESP	15.7.90	1		Madrid	17 Jun 09
82.84		Quentin	Bigot	FRA	1.12.92	1		Bondoufle	16 Oct 11
82.62		Yevgeniy	Aydamirov	RUS	11.5.87	1	NC-j	Tula	22 Jul 06
81.34		Krisztián	Pars	HUN	18.2.82	1		Szombathely	2 Sep 01
81.15		Ákos	Hudi	HUN	10.8.91	1		Veszprém	7 Jul 10
81.04		Werner	Smit	RSA	14.9.84	1		Bellville	29 Mar 03
80.79		Conor	McCullough	USA	31.1.91	1	WJ	Moncton	25 Jul 10
80.51		Andrey	Azarenkov	RUS	26.9.85	1		Adler	7 Feb 04

JAVELIN

Mark	Wind	Name		Nat	Born	Pos	Meet	Venue	Date
84.69		Zigismunds	Sirmais	LAT	6.5.92	2		Bauska	22 Jun 11
83.87		Andreas	Thorkildsen	NOR	1.4.82	1		Fana	7 Jun 01
83.55		Aleksandr	Ivanov	RUS	25.5.82	2	NC	Tula	14 Jul 01
83.07		Robert	Oosthuizen	RSA	23.1.87	1	WJ	Beijing	19 Aug 06
82.52		Harri	Haatainen	FIN	5.1.78	4		Leppävirta	25 May 96
82.52		Till	Wöschler	GER	9.6.91	1	WJ	Moncton	23 Jul 10
81.95		Jakub	Vadlejch	CZE	10.10.90	1		Domazlice	26 Sep 09
81.80		Sergey	Voynov	UZB	26.2.77	1		Tashkent	6 Jun 96
80.94		Aki	Parviainen	FIN	26.10.74	4	NC	Jyväskylä	5 Jul 92
80.57		Teemu	Wirkkala	FIN	14.1.84	1		Espoo	14 Sep 03
80.43		Tero	Järvenpää	FIN	2.10.84	3	NC	Helsinki	11 Aug 03

DECATHLON

Mark	Name		Nat	Born	Pos	Meet	Venue	Date
8397	Torsten	Voss	GDR	24.3.63	1	NC	Erfurt	7 Jul 82
	10.76 7.66 14.41	2.09 48.37	14.37	41.76 4.80 62.90	4:34.04			
8257	Yordani	Garcia	CUB	21.11.88	8	WCh	Osaka	1 Sep 07
	10.73/0.7 7.15/0.2 14.94	2.09 49.25	14.08/-0.2	42.91 4.70 68.74	4:55.42			
8114	Michael	Kohnle	FRG	3.5.70	1	EJ	Varazdin	26 Aug 89
	10.95 7.09/0.1 15.27	2.02 49.91	14.40	45.82 4.90 60.82	4:49.43			
8104	Valter	Külvet	EST	19.2.64	1		Viimsi	23 Aug 81
	10.7 7.26 13.86	2.09 48.5	14.8	47.92 4.50 60.34	4:37.8			
8082	Daley	Thompson	GBR	30.7.58	1	ECp/s	Sittard	31 Jul 77
	10.70/0.8 7.54/0.7 13.84	2.01 47.31	15.26/2.0	41.70 4.70 54.48	4:30.4			
8041		Qi Haifeng	CHN	7.8.83	1	AsiG	Busan	10 Oct 02
	11.09/0.2 7.22/0.0 13.05	2.06 49.09	14.54/0.0	43.16 4.80 61.04	4:35.17			
8036	Christian	Schenk	GDR	9.2.65	5		Potsdam	21 Jul 84
	11.54 7.18 14.26	2.16 49.23	15.06	44.74 4.20 65.98	4:24.11			
7992	Kevin	Mayer	FRA	10.2.92	8		Kladno	16 Jun 11
	11.23/0.1 7.34/0.2 12.44	2.01 48.66	14.74/-2.0	38.64 4.90 60.96	4:19.79			
7938	Frank	Busemann	GER	26.2.75	1		Zeven	2 Oct 94
	10.68/1.6 7.37/1.1 13.08	2.03 50.41	14.34/-1.1	39.84 4.40 63.00	4:37.31)			
7913	Raul	Duany	CUB	4.1.75	2		La Habana	26 May 94
	11.50 7.13 13.99	2.10 49.70	14.77	37.76 4.50 65.58	4:24.03			

Mark	Wind	Name		Nat	Born	Pos	Meet	Venue			Date

IAAF Junior specifiaction with 99cm 110mh, 6kg shot, 1.75kg Discus

Mark	Wind	Name		Nat	Born	Pos	Meet	Venue			Date
8131		Arkadiy	Vasilyev	RUS	19.1.87	1		Sochi			27 May 06
	11.28/-0.8	7.70/2.0	14.59	2.00	49.17		14.67/0.6	46.30	4.70	56.96	4:32.10
8126		Andrey	Kravchenko	BLR	4.1.86	1	WJ	Grosseto			15 Jul 04
	11.09/-0.5	7.46-0.2	14.51	2.16	48.98		14.55*/0.4	43.41	4.50	52.84	4:28.46
8124		Kévin	Mayer	FRA	10.2.92	1	EJ	Tallin			24 Jul 11
	11.40/-1.7	7.52/1.5	14.65	2.04	49.41		14.09/0.7	41.00	4.80	56.60	4:25.23

10,000 METRES WALK

Mark	Name		Nat	Born	Pos	Meet	Venue	Date
38:46.4	Viktor	Burayev	RUS	23.8.82	1	NC-j	Moskva	20 May 00
38:54.75	Ralf	Kowalsky	GDR	22.3.62	1		Cottbus	24 Jun 81
39:28.45	Andrey	Ruzavin	RUS	28.3.86	1	EJ	Kaunas	23 Jul 05
39:35.01	Stanislav	Yemelyanov	RUS	23.10.90	1	WJ	Bydgoszcz	11 Jul 08
39:44.71	Giovanni	De Benedictis	ITA	8.1.68	1	EJ	Birmingham	7 Aug 87
39:47.20		Chen Ding	CHN	5.8.92	2	WJ	Bydgoszcz	11 Jul 08
39:49.22		Pei Chuang	CHN	5.12.81	2	NSG	Chengdu	8 Sep 00
39:50.32		Cui Jin	CHN	1.12.87	2		Jinzhou	30 Aug 06
39:50.73	Jefferson	Pérez	ECU	1.7.74	1	PAmJ	Winnipeg	15 Jul 93
39:55.52	Ilya	Markov	RUS	19.6.72	1	WJ	Plovdiv	10 Aug 90

20 KILOMETRES WALK

Mark	Name		Nat	Born	Pos	Meet	Venue	Date
1:18:06	Viktor	Burayev	RUS	23.8.82	2	NC-w	Adler	4 Mar 01
1:18:07		Li Gaobo	CHN	23.7.89	4		Cixi	23 Apr 05
1:18:44		Chu Yafei	CHN	5.9.88	5		Yangzhou	22 Apr 06
1:18:52		Chen Ding	CHN	5.8.92	3		Taicang	22 Apr 11
1:18:57		Bai Xuejin	CHN	6.6.87	7		Yangzhou	22 Apr 06
1:19:02	Éder	Sánchez	MEX	21.5.86	11		Cixi	23 Apr 05
1:19:14		Xu Xingde	CHN	12.6.84	3	NC	Yangzhou	12 Apr 03
1:19:34		Li Jianbo	CHN	14.11.86	16		Cixi	23 Apr 05
1:19:38		Yu Guohui	CHN	30.4.77	2	NC	Zhuhai	10 Mar 96
1:19:47		Wang Hao	CHN	16.8.89	4	OG	Beijing	16 Aug 08

4 x 100 METRES RELAY

Mark	Nat	Name	Pos	Meet	Venue	Date
38.66	USA	Kimmons, Omole, I Williams, L Merritt	1	WJ	Grosseto	18 Jun 04
39.05	GBR	Edgar, Grant, Benjamin, Lewis-Francis	1	WJ	Santiago de Chile	22 Oct 00
39.05	JAM	Barnes, Rose, Jervis, Blake	1	WJ	Beijing	20 Aug 06
39.17	TRI	Simpson, Burns, Holder, Brown	3	WJ	Kingston	21 Jul 02
39.25	FRG	Dobeleit, Klameth, Evers, Lübke	1	EJ	Schwechat	28 Aug 83
39.30	JPN	Matsumaga, Noda, Takahira, Aikawa	1	AsiC-j	Bangkok	28 Oct 02
39.33	FRA	Pognon, Calligny, Doucoure, Djhone	2	WJ	Santiago de Chile	22 Oct 00
39.51	CIV	Y.Sonan, Ahmed Douhou, A.Byo, Ibrahim Meité	1	Afr-J	Bouaké	22 Jul 95

4 x 400 METRES RELAY

Mark	Nat	Name	Pos	Meet	Venue	Date
3:01.09	USA	B Johnson, L Merritt, Craig, Clement	1	WJ	Grosseto	18 Jul 04
3:03.80	GBR	Grindley, Patrick, Winrow, Richardson	2	WJ	Plovdiv	12 Aug 90
3:04.06	JAM	S Clarke, Bolt, Myers, Gonzales	2	WJ	Kingston	21 Jul 02
3:04.22	CUB	Cadogan, Mordoche, González, Hernández	2	WJ	Athína	20 Jul 86
3:04.50	RSA	le Roux, Gebhardt, Julius, van Zyl	2	WJ	Grosseto	18 Jul 04
3:04.58	GDR	Preusche, Löper, Trylus, Carlowitz	1	EJ	Utrecht	23 Aug 81
3:04.74	AUS	McFarlane, Batman, Thom, Vincent	1	WJ	Annecy	2 Aug 98
3:05.33	JPN	Ota, Noda, Suzuki, Sasaki	3	WJ	Grosseto	18 Jul 04

JUNIOR WOMEN'S ALL-TIME LISTS

100 METRES

Mark	Wind	Name		Nat	Born	Pos	Meet	Venue	Date
10.88	2.0	Marlies	Oelsner	GDR	21.3.58	1	NC	Dresden	1 Jul 77
10.89	1.8	Katrin	Krabbe	GDR	22.11.69	1rB		Berlin	20 Jul 88
11.03	1.7	Silke	Gladisch	GDR	20.6.64	3	OD	Berlin	8 Jun 83
11.03	0.6	English	Gardner	USA	22.4.92	1	Pac10	Tucson	14 May 11
11.04	1.4	Angela	Williams	USA	30.1.80	1	NCAA	Boise	5 Jun 99
11.07	0.7	Bianca	Knight	USA	2.1.89	4q2	NC/OT	Eugene	27 Jun 08
11.08	2.0	Brenda	Morehead	USA	5.10.57	1	OT	Eugene	21 Jun 76
11.11	0.2	Shakedia	Jones	USA	15.3.79	1		Los Angeles (Ww)	2 May 98
11.11	1.1	Joan Uduak	Ekah	NGR	16.12.80	5	Athl	Lausanne	2 Jul 99
11.12	2.0	Veronica	Campbell	JAM	15.5.82	1	WJ	Santiago de Chile	18 Oct 00
11.12	1.2	Alexandria	Anderson	USA	28.1.87	1	NC-j	Indianapolis	22 Jun 06
11.12	1.1	Aurieyall	Scott	USA	18.5.92	1	NC-j	Eugene	24 Jun 11

Uncertain timing: 10.99 1.9 Natalya Bochina RUS 4.1.62 2 Leningrad 3 Jun 80

Wind assisted to 11.11

Mark	Wind	Name		Nat	Born	Pos	Meet	Venue	Date
10.96	3.7	Angela	Williams	USA	30.1.80	1		Las Vegas	3 Apr 99
10.97	3.3	Gesine	Walther	GDR	6.10.62	4	NC	Cottbus	16 Jul 80

Mark	Wind	Name		Nat	Born	Pos	Meet	Venue	Date
11.02	2.1	Nikole	Mitchell	JAM	5.6.74	1	Mutual	Kingston	1 May 93
11.04	5.6	Kelly-Ann	Baptiste	TRI	14.10.86	1rB	TexR	Austin	9 Apr 05
11.06	2.2	Brenda	Morehead	USA	5.10.57	1s2	OT	Eugene	21 Jun 76
11.09		Angela	Williams	TRI	15.5.65	1		Nashville	14 Apr 84

200 METRES

Mark	Wind	Name		Nat	Born	Pos	Meet	Venue	Date
22.11A	-0.5	Allyson	Felix	USA	18.11.85	1		Ciudad de México	3 May 03
22.18		0.8				2	OG	Athína	25 Aug 04
22.19	1.5	Natalya	Bochina	RUS	4.1.62	2	OG	Moskva	30 Jul 80
22.37	1.3	Sabine	Rieger	GDR	6.11.63	2	vURS	Cottbus	26 Jun 82
22.42	0.4	Gesine	Walther	GDR	6.10.62	1		Potsdam	29 Aug 81
22.43	0.8	Bianca	Knight	USA	2.1.89	1	Reebok	New York (RI)	31 May 08
22.45	0.5	Grit	Breuer	GER	16.2.72	2	ASV	Köln	8 Sep 91
22.51	2.0	Katrin	Krabbe	GDR	22.11.69	3		Berlin	13 Sep 88
22.52	1.2	Mary	Onyali	NGR	3.2.68	6	WCh	Roma	3 Sep 87
22.58	0.8	Marion	Jones	USA	12.10.75	4	TAC	New Orleans	28 Jun 92
22.69	-0.3	Dafne	Schippers	NED	15.6.92	1h3	WCh	Daegu	1 Sep 11

Indoors

Mark	Wind	Name		Nat	Born	Pos	Meet	Venue	Date
22.40		Bianca	Knight	USA	2.1.89	1r2	NCAA	Fayetteville	15 Mar 08
22.49		Sanya	Richards	USA	26.2.85	2rA	NCAA	Fayetteville	12 Mar 04

Wind assisted to 22.65

Mark	Wind	Name		Nat	Born	Pos	Meet	Venue	Date
22.25	5.6	Bianca	Knight	USA	2.1.89	5	NC/OT	Eugene	6 Jul 08
22.34	2.3	Katrin	Krabbe	GDR	22.11.69	1	WJ	Sudbury	30 Jul 88
22.49	2.3	Brenda	Morehead	USA	5.10.57	1	OT	Eugene	24 Jun 76
22.53	2.5	Valerie	Brisco	USA	6.7.60	2	AAU	Walnut	17 Jun 79
22.64	2.3	Chandra	Cheeseborough	USA	10.1.59	2	OT	Eugene	24 Jun 76
22.65	3.5	Shakedia	Jones	USA	15.3.79	1	NC-j	Edwardsville IL	27 Jun 98

400 METRES

Mark	Wind	Name		Nat	Born	Pos	Meet	Venue	Date
49.42		Grit	Breuer	GER	16.2.72	2	WCh	Tokyo	27 Aug 91
49.77		Christina	Brehmer	GDR	28.2.58	1		Dresden	9 May 76
49.89		Sanya	Richards	USA	26.2.85	2	NC/OT	Sacramento	17 Jul 04
50.01			Li Jing	CHN	14.2.80	1	NG	Shanghai	18 Oct 97
50.19		Marita	Koch	GDR	18.2.57	3	OD	Berlin	10 Jul 76
50.59		Fatima	Yusuf	NGR	2.5.71	1	HGP	Budapest	5 Aug 90
50.5 hand						1	NC	Lagos	25 Aug 90
50.74		Monique	Henderson	USA	18.2.83	1		Norwalk	3 Jun 00
50.78		Danijela	Grgic	CRO	28.9.88	1	WJ	Beijing	17 Aug 06
50.86		Charity	Opara	NGR	20.5.72	2		Bologna	7 Sep 91
50.87		Denean	Howard	USA	5.10.64	1	TAC	Knoxville	20 Jun 82
50.87		Magdalena	Nedelcu	ROM	12.5.74	1	NC-j	Bucuresti	31 Jul 92

800 METRES

Mark	Wind	Name		Nat	Born	Pos	Meet	Venue	Date
1:54.01		Pamela	Jelimo	KEN	5.12.89	1	WK	Zürich	29 Aug 08
1:55.45		Caster	Semenya	RSA	7.1.91	1	WCh	Berlin	19 Aug 09
1:57.18			Wang Yuan	CHN	8.4.76	2h2	NG	Beijing	8 Sep 93
1:57.45		Hildegard	Ullrich	GDR	20.12.59	5	EC	Praha	31 Aug 78
1:57.62			Lang Yinglai	CHN	22.8.79	1	NG	Shanghai	22 Oct 97
1:57.63		Maria	Mutola	MOZ	27.10.72	4	WCh	Tokyo	26 Aug 91
1:57.77			Lu Yi	CHN	10.4.74	4	NG	Beijing	9 Sep 93
1:57.86		Katrin	Wühn	GDR	19.11.65	1		Celje	5 May 84
1:58.16			Lin Nuo	CHN	18.1.80	3	NG	Shanghai	22 Oct 97
1:58.18		Marion	Hübner	GDR	29.9.62	2		Erfurt	2 Aug 81
1:58.24		Christine	Wachtel	GDR	6.1.65	3		Potsdam	25 May 84

1500 METRES

Mark	Wind	Name		Nat	Born	Pos	Meet	Venue	Date
3:51.34			Lang Yinglai	CHN	22.8.79	2	NG	Shanghai	18 Oct 97
3:53.91			Yin Lili	CHN	11.11.79	3	NG	Shanghai	18 Oct 97
3:53.97			Lan Lixin	CHN	14.2.79	4	NG	Shanghai	18 Oct 97
3:54.52			Zhang Ling	CHN	13.4.80	5	NG	Shanghai	18 Oct 97
3:59.60		Gelete	Burka	ETH	15.2.86	5	GP	Rieti	28 Aug 05
3:59.81			Wang Yuan	CHN	8.4.76	7	NG	Beijing	11 Sep 93
3:59.96		Zola	Budd	GBR	26.5.66	3	VD	Bruxelles	30 Aug 85
4:00.05			Lu Yi	CHN	10.4.74	8	NG	Beijing	11 Sep 93
4:01.71			Li Ying	CHN	24.6.75	4h2	NG	Beijing	10 Sep 93
4:02.98		Kalkedan	Gezahegn	ETH	8.5.91	3	Tsik	Athína	13 Jul 09
4:03.45		Anita	Weyermann	SUI	8.12.77	1	Athl	Lausanne	3 Jul 96

1 MILE: 4:17.57 Zola Budd GBR 26.5.66 3 WK Zürich 21 Aug 85

2000 METRES: 5:33.15 Zola Budd GBR 26.5.66 1 London 13 Jul 84

Mark	Wind	Name		Nat	Born	Pos	Meet	Venue	Date

3000 METRES

Mark	Wind	Name		Nat	Born	Pos	Meet	Venue	Date
8:28.83		Zola	Budd	GBR	26.5.66	3	GG	Roma	7 Sep 85
8:35.89		Sally	Barsosio	KEN	21.3.78	2	Herc	Monaco	16 Aug 97
8:36.45			Ma Ningning	CHN	1.6.76	4	NC	Jinan	6 Jun 93
8:38.61		Kalkedan	Gezahegn	ETH	8.5.91	5	WAF	Thessaloníki	13 Sep 09
8:38.97		Linet	Masai	KEN	5.12.89	5	GP	Rieti	9 Sep 07
8:39.90		Gelete	Burka	ETH	15.2.86	3	SGP	Doha	13 May 05
8:40.08		Gabriela	Szabo	ROM	14.11.75	3	EC	Helsinki	10 Aug 94
8:40.28		Meseret	Defar	ETH	19.11.83	10	VD	Bruxelles	30 Aug 02
8:41.86		Tirunesh	Dibaba	ETH	2.6.85	11	VD	Bruxelles	30 Aug 02
8:42.09		Mercy	Cherono	KEN	7.5.91	2		Rieti	29 Aug 10

5000 METRES

Mark	Wind	Name		Nat	Born	Pos	Meet	Venue	Date
14:30.88		Tirunesh	Dibaba	ETH	1.10.85	2	Bisl	Bergen (Fana)	11 Jun 04
14:35.18		Sentayehu	Ejigu	ETH	21.6.85	4	Bisl	Bergen (Fana)	11 Jun 04
14:39.96			Yin Lili	CHN	11.11.79	4	NG	Shanghai	23 Oct 97
14:43.29		Emebet	Anteneh	ETH	13.1.92	5	Bisl	Oslo	9 Jun 11
14:45.33			Lan Lixin	CHN	14.2.79	2h2	NG	Shanghai	21 Oct 97
14:45.71			Song Liqing	CHN	20.1.80	3h2	NG	Shanghai	21 Oct 97
14:45.90			Jiang Bo	CHN	13.3.77	1		Nanjing	24 Oct 95
14:45.98		Pauline	Korikwiang	KEN	1.3.88	7	Bisl	Oslo	2 Jun 06
14:46.71		Sally	Barsosio	KEN	21.3.78	3	VD	Bruxelles	22 Aug 97
14:47.13		Mercy	Cherono	KEN	7.5.91	7	DL	Shanghai	23 May 10
14:47.14		Linet	Masai	KEN	5.12.89	4	FBK	Hengelo	24 May 08

10,000 METRES

Mark	Wind	Name		Nat	Born	Pos	Meet	Venue	Date
30:26.50		Linet	Masai	KEN	5.12.89	4	OG	Beijing	15 Aug 08
30:31.55			Xing Huina	CHN	25.2.84	7	WCh	Saint-Denis	23 Aug 03
30:39.41			Lan Lixin	CHN	14.2.79	2	NG	Shanghai	19 Oct 97
30:39.98			Yin Lili	CHN	11.11.79	3	NG	Shanghai	19 Oct 97
30:59.92		Merima	Hashim	ETH	.81	3	NA	Heusden-Zolder	5 Aug 00
31:06.20		Lucy	Wangui	KEN	24.3.84	1rA		Okayama	27 Sep 03
31:11.26			Song Liqing	CHN	20.1.80	7	NG	Shanghai	19 Oct 97
31:15.38		Sally	Barsosio	KEN	21.3.78	3	WCh	Stuttgart	21 Aug 93
31:16.50		Evelyne	Kimwei	KEN	25.8.87	1		Kobe	21 Oct 06
31:17.30			Zhang Yingying	CHN	4.1.90	1		Wuhan	2 Nov 07
31:20.38		Tigist	Kiros	ETH	8.6.92	4	GS	Ostrava	31 May 11

MARATHON

Mark	Wind	Name		Nat	Born	Pos	Meet	Venue	Date
2:22:38			Zhang Yingying	CHN	4.1.90	1	NC	Xiamen	5 Jan 08
2:23:06		Merima	Mohamed	ETH	10.6.92	3		Toronto	26 Sep 10
2:23:37			Liu Min	CHN	29.11.83	1		Beijing	14 Oct 01
2:23:57			Zhu Xiaolin	CHN	20.4.84	4		Beijing	20 Oct 02
2:25:48			Jin Li	CHN	29.5.83	6		Beijing	14 Oct 01
2:26:34			Wei Yanan	CHN	6.12.81	1		Beijing	15 Oct 00
2:27:05			Chen Rong	CHN	18.5.88	1		Beijing	21 Oct 07
2:27:30			Ai Dongmei	CHN	15.10.79	3	NG	Beijing	4 Oct 97

3000 METRES STEEPLECHASE

Mark	Wind	Name		Nat	Born	Pos	Meet	Venue	Date
9:20.37		Birtukan	Adamu	ETH	29.4.92	4	GGala	Roma	26 May 11
9:22.51		Almaz	Ayana	ETH	21.11.91	3	VD	Bruxelles	27 Aug 10
9:24.51		Ruth	Bisibori	KEN	2.1.88	1		Daegu	3 Oct 07
9:26.25			Liu Nian	CHN	26.4.88	1		Wuhan	2 Nov 07
9:29.52		Korahubish	Itaa	ETH	28.2.92	1		Huelva	10 Jun 09
9:30.70		Melissa	Rollison	AUS	13.4.83	1	GWG	Brisbane	4 Sep 01
9:31.35		Christine	Muyanga	KEN	21.3.91	1	WJ	Bydgoszcz	10 Jul 08
9:32.74		Gesa-Felicitas	Krause	GER	3.8.92	9	WCh	Daegu	30 Aug 11
9:33.19		Karoline Bjerkeli	Grøvdal	NOR	14.6.90	4		Neerpelt	2 Jun 07
9:33.49		Elizabeth	Mueni	KEN	28.12.91	5	Bisl	Oslo	3 Jul 09

100 METRES HURDLES

Mark	Wind	Name		Nat	Born	Pos	Meet	Venue	Date
12.84	1.5	Aliuska	López	CUB	29.8.69	2	WUG	Zagreb	16 Jul 87
12.88	1.5	Yelena	Ovcharova	UKR	17.6.76	2	ECp	Villeneuve d'Ascq	25 Jun 95
12.89	1.3	Anay	Tejeda	CUB	3.4.83	1		Padova	1 Sep 02
12.91	1.8	Kristina	Castlin	USA	7.7.88	1	NCAA-r	Gainesville	26 May 07
12.92	0.0		Sun Hongwei	CHN	24.11.79	6	NG	Shanghai	18 Oct 97
12.95	1.5	Candy	Young	USA	21.5.62	2	AAU	Walnut	16 Jun 79
12.95A	1.5	Cinnamon	Sheffield	USA	8.3.70	2	NCAA	Provo	3 Jun 89
12.98	1.8	Queen	Harrison	USA	10.9.88	5	NCAA	Sacramento	8 Jun 07
13.00	0.7	Gloria	Kovarik	GDR	13.1.64	3h2	NC	Karl-Marx-Stadt	16 Jun 83
13.00	2.0	Lyudmila	Khristosenko	UKR	14.10.66	1	NC-j	Krasnodar	16 Jul 85

Mark	Wind	Name		Nat	Born	Pos	Meet	Venue	Date
13.01	0.4	Sally	McLellan	AUS	19.9.86	1		Brisbane	27 Nov 05

Wind assisted to 12.99

Mark	Wind	Name		Nat	Born	Pos	Meet	Venue	Date
12.81	3.4	Anay	Tejeda	CUB	3.4.83	1	WJ	Kingston	21 Jul 02
12.82	2.1	Kristina	Castlin	USA	7.7.88	1		College Park	21 Apr 07
12.90	3.0	Adrianna	Lamalle	FRA	27.9.82	1		Fort-de-France	28 Apr 01
12.95	2.4	Shermaine	Williams	JAM	4.2.90	1	NCAA II	San Angelo	23 May 09

400 METRES HURDLES

Mark	Wind	Name		Nat	Born	Pos	Meet	Venue	Date
54.40			Wang Xing	CHN	30.11.86	2	NG	Nanjing	21 Oct 05
54.58		Ristananna	Tracey	JAM	5.9.92	2	NC	Kingston	24 Jun 11
54.70		Lashinda	Demus	USA	10.3.83	1	WJ	Kingston	19 Jul 02
54.93			Li Rui	CHN	22.11.79	1	NG	Shanghai	22 Oct 97
55.11		Kaliese	Spencer	JAM	6.4.87	1	WJ	Beijing	17 Aug 06
55.15			Huang Xiaoxiao	CHN	3.3.83	2	NG	Guangzhou	22 Nov 01
55.20		Lesley	Maxie	USA	4.1.67	2	TAC	San Jose	9 Jun 84
55.20A		Jana	Pittman	AUS	9.11.82	1		Pietersburg	18 Mar 00
55.22		Tiffany	Ross	USA	5.2.83	2	NCAA	Baton Rouge	31 May 02
55.26		Ionela	Tîrlea	ROM	9.2.76	1	Nik	Nice	12 Jul 95

Drugs disqualification: 54.54 Peng Yinghua ¶ CHN 21.2.79 (2) NG Shanghai 22 Oct 97

HIGH JUMP

Mark	Wind	Name		Nat	Born	Pos	Meet	Venue	Date
2.01		Olga	Turchak	UKR	5.3.67	2	GWG	Moskva	7 Jul 86
2.01		Heike	Balck	GDR	19.8.70	1	vURS-j	Karl-Marx-Stadt	18 Jun 89
2.00		Stefka	Kostadinova	BUL	25.3.65	1		Sofiya	25 Aug 84
2.00		Alina	Astafei	ROM	7.6.69	1	WJ	Sudbury	29 Jul 88
1.98		Silvia	Costa	CUB	4.5.64	2	WUG	Edmonton	11 Jul 83
1.98		Yelena	Yelesina	RUS	5.4.70	1	Druzh	Nyiregyháza	13 Aug 88
1.97		Svetlana	Isaeva	BUL	18.3.67	2		Sofiya	25 May 86
1.97i		Mariya	Kuchina	RUS	14.1.93	1		Trinec	26 Jan 11
1.96A		Charmaine	Gale	RSA	27.2.64	1	NC-j	Bloemfontein	4 Apr 81
1.96i		Desislava	Aleksandrova	BUL	27.10.75	2	EI	Paris	12 Mar 94
1.96		Marina	Kuptsova	RUS	22.12.81	1	NC	Tula	26 Jul 00
1.96		Blanka	Vlasic	CRO	8.11.83	1	WJ	Kingston	20 Jul 02
1.96		Airine	Palsyte	LTU	13.7.92	2	WUG	Shenzhen	21 Aug 11

POLE VAULT

Mark	Wind	Name		Nat	Born	Pos	Meet	Venue	Date
4.63i		Angelica	Bengtsson	SWE	8.7.93	2		Stockholm	22 Feb 11
4.57						1	EJ	Tallinn	23 Jul 11
4.50		Valeriya	Volik	RUS	11.5.89	1		Krasnodar	4 Jun 08
4.48i		Silke	Spiegelburg	GER	17.3.86	2		Münster	25 Aug 05
4.42						3		Beckum	21 Aug 05
4.47i		Yelena	Isinbayeva	RUS	3.6.82	1		Budapest	10 Feb 01
4.46						2	ISTAF	Berlin	31 Aug 01
4.46i			Zhang Yingning	CHN	6.1.90	1		Shanghai	15 Mar 07
4.45						1		Changsha	29 Oct 06
4.45i			Zhao Yingying	CHN	15.2.86	3		Madrid	24 Feb 05
4.40						1		Nanjing	1 May 04
4.45i			Li Ling	CHN	6.7.89	1		Beijing	26 Feb 08
4.45						1		Hangzhou	12 Apr 08
4.45		Marianna	Zachariadi	CYP	25.2.90	2	MedG	Pescara	30 Jun 09
4.42		Yvonne	Buschbaum	GER	14.7.80	1		Rheinau-Freistett	27 Jun 99
4.41		Floé	Kühnert	GER	6.3.84	1		Mannheim	15 Jun 02
4.40		Vicky Parnov AUS 30 Jun 07, Zhou Yang CHN 2 Nov 07, Yekaterina Kolesova RUS 17 Jun 08							

Exhibition: 4.45 Yvonne Buschbaum GER 14.7.80 1 Zeiskam 17 Jul 99

LONG JUMP

Mark	Wind	Name		Nat	Born	Pos	Meet	Venue	Date
7.14	1.1	Heike	Daute	GDR	16.12.64	1	PTS	Bratislava	4 Jun 83
7.03	1.3	Darya	Klishina	RUS	15.1.91	1	Znam	Zhukovskiy	26 Jun 10
7.00	-0.2	Birgit	Grosshennig	GDR	21.2.65	2		Berlin	9 Jun 84
6.94	-0.5	Magdalena	Khristova	BUL	25.2.77	2		Kalamáta	22 Jun 96
6.91	0.0	Anisoara	Cusmir	ROM	28.6.62	1		Bucuresti	23 May 81
6.90	1.4	Beverly	Kinch	GBR	14.1.64	*	WCh	Helsinki	14 Aug 83
6.88	0.6	Natalya	Shevchenko	RUS	28.12.66	2		Sochi	26 May 84
6.84		Larisa	Baluta	UKR	13.8.65	2		Krasnodar	6 Aug 83
6.82	1.8	Fiona	May	GBR	12.12.69	*	WJ	Sudbury	30 Jul 88
6.81	1.6	Carol	Lewis	USA	8.8.63	1	TAC	Knoxville	20 Jun 82
6.81	1.4	Yelena	Davydova	KZK	16.11.67	1	NC-j	Krasnodar	17 Jul 85

Wind assisted

Mark	Wind	Name		Nat	Born	Pos	Meet	Venue	Date
7.27	2.2	Heike	Daute	GDR	16.12.64	1	WCh	Helsinki	14 Aug 83
6.93	4.6	Beverly	Kinch	GBR	14.1.64	5	WCh	Helsinki	14 Aug 83
6.88	2.1	Fiona	May	GBR	12.12.69	1	WJ	Sudbury	30 Jul 88

Mark	Wind	Name		Nat	Born	Pos	Meet	Venue	Date
6.84	2.8	Anu	Kaljurand	EST	16.4.69	2		Riga	4 Jun 88

TRIPLE JUMP

Mark	Wind	Name		Nat	Born	Pos	Meet	Venue	Date
14.62	1.0	Tereza	Marinova	BUL	5.9.77	1	WC	Sydney	25 Aug 96
14.57	0.2		Huang Qiuyan	CHN	25.1.80	1	NG	Shanghai	19 Oct 97
14.52	0.6	Anastasiya	Ilyina	RUS	16.1.82	q	WJ	Santiago de Chile	20 Oct 00
14.46	1.0		Peng Fengmei	CHN	2.7.79	1		Chengdu	18 Apr 98
14.43	0.6	Kaire	Leibak	EST	21.5.88	1	WJ	Beijing	17 Aug 06
14.38	-0.7		Xie Limei	CHN	27.6.86	1	AsiC	Inchon	1 Sep 05
14.37i	-		Ren Ruiping	CHN	1.2.76	3	WI	Barcelona	11 Mar 95
	14.36		0.0			1	NC	Beijing	1 Jun 94
14.36	0.0	Dailenys	Alcántara	CUB	10.8.91	3	Barr/NC	La Habana	29 May 09
14.35		Yana	Borodina	RUS	21.4.92	1J	Mosc Ch	Moskva	15 Jun 11
14.32	-0.1	Yelena	Lysak ¶	RUS	19.10.75	1		Voronezh	18 Jun 94
14.29	1.2	Mabel	Gay	CUB	5.5.83	1		La Habana	5 Apr 02
Wind assisted									
14.83	8.3		Ren Ruiping	CHN	1.2.76	1	NC	Taiyuan	21 May 95
14.43	2.7	Yelena	Lysak ¶	RUS	19.10.75	1	WJ	Lisboa	21 Jul 94

SHOT

Mark	Wind	Name		Nat	Born	Pos	Meet	Venue	Date
20.54		Astrid	Kumbernuss	GDR	5.2.70	1	vFIN-j	Orimattila	1 Jul 89
20.51i		Heidi	Krieger	GDR	20.7.65	2		Budapest	8 Feb 84
	20.24					5		Split	30 Apr 84
20.23		Ilke	Wyludda	GDR	28.3.69	1	NC-j	Karl-Marx-Stadt	16 Jul 88
20.12		Ilona	Schoknecht	GDR	24.9.56	2	NC	Erfurt	23 Aug 75
20.02			Cheng Xiaoyan	CHN	30.11.75	3	NC	Beijing	5 Jun 94
19.90		Stephanie	Storp	FRG	28.11.68	1		Hamburg	16 Aug 87
19.63			Wang Yawen	CHN	23.8.73	1		Shijiazhuang	25 Apr 92
19.57		Grit	Haupt	GDR	4.6.66	1		Gera	7 Jul 84
19.48		Ines	Wittich	GDR	14.11.69	5		Leipzig	29 Jul 87
19.46			Gong Lijiao	CHN	24.1.89	Q	OG	Beijing	16 Aug 08
19.42		Simone	Michel	GDR	18.12.60	3	vSU	Leipzig	23 Jun 79

DISCUS

Mark	Wind	Name		Nat	Born	Pos	Meet	Venue	Date
74.40		Ilke	Wyludda	GDR	28.3.69	2		Berlin	13 Sep 88
	75.36 unofficial meeting					2		Berlin	6 Sep 88
67.38		Irina	Meszynski	GDR	24.3.62	1		Berlin	14 Aug 81
67.00		Jana	Günther	GDR	7.1.68	6	NC	Potsdam	20 Aug 87
66.80		Svetla	Mitkova	BUL	17.6.64	1		Sofiya	2 Aug 83
66.60		Astrid	Kumbernuss	GDR	5.2.70	1		Berlin	20 Jul 88
66.34		Franka	Dietzsch	GDR	22.1.68	2		Saint-Denis	11 Jun 87
66.30		Jana	Lauren	GDR	28.6.70	1	vURS-j	Karl-Marx-Stadt	18 Jun 89
66.08			Cao Qi	CHN	15.1.74	1	NG	Beijing	12 Sep 93
65.96		Grit	Haupt	GDR	4.6.66	3		Leipzig	13 Jul 84
65.22		Daniela	Costian	ROM	30.4.65	3		Nitra	26 Aug 84

HAMMER

Mark	Wind	Name		Nat	Born	Pos	Meet	Venue	Date
73.24			Zhang Wenxiu	CHN	22.3.86	1	NC	Changsha	24 Jun 05
71.71		Kamila	Skolimowska	POL	4.11.82	1	GPF	Melbourne	9 Sep 01
70.39		Mariya	Smolyachkova	BLR	10.2.85	1		Staiki	26 Jun 04
69.73		Natalya	Zolotukhina	UKR	4.1.85	1		Kiev	24 Jul 04
69.63		Bianca	Perie	ROU	1.6.90	1	NC-j	Bucuresti	14 Aug 09
68.74		Arasay	Thondike	CUB	28.5.86	2	Barr	La Habana	2 May 05
68.50		Martina	Danisová	SVK	21.3.83	1		Kladno	16 Jun 01
68.49		Anna	Bulgakova	RUS	17.1.88	6		Sochi	26 May 07
68.40		Bianca	Achilles	GER	17.4.81	1		Dortmund	25 Sep 99
68.26		Katerina	Safránková	CZE	8.6.89	1		Pardubice	7 May 08

JAVELIN

Mark	Wind	Name		Nat	Born	Pos	Meet	Venue	Date
63.01		Vira	Rebryk	UKR	25.2.89	1	WJ	Bydgoszcz	10 Jul 08
62.93			Xue Juan	CHN	10.2.86	1	NG	Changsha	27 Oct 03
62.09			Zhang Li	CHN	17.1.89	1		Beijing	25 May 08
61.99			Wang Yaning	CHN	4.1.80	1	NC	Huizhou	14 Oct 99
61.79		Nikolett	Szabó	HUN	3.3.80	1		Schwechat	23 May 99
61.61			Chang Chunfeng	CHN	4.5.88	1	NC-j	Chengdu	4 Jun 07
61.49			Liang Lili	CHN	16.11.83	1	NC	Benxi	1 Jun 02
61.38		Annika	Suthe	GER	15.10.85	1-j		Halle	23 May 04
Pre 1999 specification									
71.88		Antoaneta	Todorova	BUL	8.6.63	1	ECp	Zagreb	15 Aug 81
71.82		Ivonne	Leal	CUB	27.2.66	1	WUG	Kobe	30 Aug 85

Mark	Wind	Name		Nat	Born	Pos	Meet	Venue		Date
70.12		Karen	Forkel	GDR	24.9.70	1	EJ	Varazdin		26 Aug 89
68.94		Trine	Solberg	NOR	18.4.66	1	vURS	Oslo		16 Jul 85

HEPTATHLON

Mark	Wind	Name		Nat	Born	Pos	Meet	Venue		Date
6768w		Tatyana	Chernova	RUS	29.1.88	1		Arles		3 Jun 07
	13.04w/6.1	1.82	13.57	23.59w/5.2	6.61/1.2	53.43	2:15.05			
	6227				1	WJ	Beijing			19 Aug 06
	13.70/1.6	1.80	12.18	24.05/0.3	6.35/-0.4	50.51	2:25.49			
6542		Carolina	Klüft	SWE	2.2.83	1	EC	München		10 Aug 02
	13.33/-0.3	1.89	13.16	23.71/-0.3	6.36/1.1	47.61	2:17.99			
6465		Sibylle	Thiele	GDR	6.3.65	1	EJ	Schwechat		28 Aug 83
	13.49	1.90	14.63	24.07	6.65	36.22	2:18.36			
6436		Sabine	Braun	FRG	19.6.65	1	vBUL	Mannheim		9 Jun 84
	13.68	1.78	13.09	23.88	6.03	52.14	2:09.41			
6428		Svetla	Dimitrova ¶	BUL	27.1.70	1	NC	Sofiya		18 Jun 89
	13.49/-0.7	1.77	13.98	23.59/-0.2	6.49/0.7	40.10	2:11.10			
6403		Emilia	Dimitrova	BUL	13.11.67	6	GWG	Moskva		7 Jul 86
	13.73	1.76	13.46	23.17	6.29	43.30	2:09.85			
6276		Larisa	Nikitina	RUS	29.4.65	8	URS Ch	Kiyev		21 Jun 84
	13.87/1.6	1.86	14.04	25.26/-0.7	6.31/0.1	48.62	2:22.76			
6218		Jana	Sobotka	GDR	3.10.65	6	OD	Potsdam		21 Jul 84
	14.40	1.74	13.28	24.19	6.27	43.64	2:06.83			
6198		Anke	Schmidt	GDR	5.2.68	7		Götzis		24 May 87
	13.80/0.9	1.72	13.32	23.82/0.3	6.63/2.0	35.78	2:12.44			
6194		Camelia	Cornateanu	ROM	23.1.67	2	NC	Pitesti		8 Aug 86
	14.35	1.86	14.70	24.97	6.15	38.94	2:11.93			
Drugs disqualification: 6534	Svetla Dimitrova			BUL	27.1.70	(3)	ECp	Helmond		16 Jul 89
	13.30/1.0	1.84	14.35	23.33/-2.2	6.47/-1.4	39.20	2:13.56			

10 KILOMETRES WALK

Mark	Wind	Name		Nat	Born	Pos	Meet	Venue	Date
41:52		Tatyana	Mineyeva	RUS	10.8.90	1	NCp-j	Penza	5 Sep 09
41:55		Irina	Stankina	RUS	25.3.77	1	NC-wj	Adler	11 Feb 95
41:57			Gao Hongmiao	CHN	17.3.74	2	NG	Beijing	8 Sep 93
42:15+		Anisya	Kirdyapkina	RUS	23.10.89	1=	in 20k	Adler	23 Feb 08
42:29		Tatyana	Kalmykova	RUS	10.1.90	1	NC-wj	Adler	23 Feb 08
42:31		Irina	Yumanova	RUS	17.6.90	2	NC-wj	Adler	23 Feb 08
42:43.0	t	Svetlana	Vasilyeva	RUS	24.7.92	1	NC-wj	Sochi	27 Feb 11
42:44			Long Yuwen	CHN	1.8.75	3	NC	Shenzen	18 Feb 93
42:45			Li Yuxin	CHN	4.12.74	4		Shenzhen	18 Feb 93
42:45		Kseniya	Trifonova	RUS	7.5.90	2	NC-wj	Adler	28 Feb 09

20 KILOMETRES WALK

Mark	Wind	Name		Nat	Born	Pos	Meet	Venue	Date
1:25:30		Anisya	Kirdyapkina	RUS	23.10.89	2	NC-w	Adler	23 Feb 08
1:26:36		Tatyana	Kalmykova	RUS	10.1.90	1	NC	Saransk	8 Jun 08
1:27:16			Song Hongjuan	CHN	4.7.84	1	NC	Yangzhou	14 Apr 03
1:27:34			Jiang Jing	CHN	23.10.85	2	WCp	Naumburg	2 May 04
1:27:35		Natalya	Fedoskina	RUS	25.6.80	2	WCp	Mézidon-Canon	2 May 99
1:27:37			Bai Yanmin	CHN	29.6.87	1	NG	Nanjing	20 Oct 05

4 X 100 METRES RELAY

Mark	Nat	Name	Pos	Meet	Venue	Date
43.29	USA (Blue)	Knight, Tarmoh, Olear, Mayo	1		Eugene	8 Aug 06
43.40	JAM	Simpson, Stewart, McLaughlin, Facey	1	WJ	Kingston	20 Jul 02
43.42	GER	Burghardt, Grompe, Pinto, Frese	1	EJ	Tallinn	24 Jul 11
43.44A	NGR	Utondu, Iheagwam, Onyali, Ogunkoya	1	AfrG	Nairobi	9 Aug 87
43.48	GDR	Breuer, Krabbe, Dietz, Henke	1	WJ	Sudbury	31 Jul 88
		Unsanctioned race 43.33 Breuer, Krabbe, Dietz, Henke	1		Berlin	20 Jul 88
43.68	FRA	Vouaux, Jacques-Sebastien, Kamga, Banco	3	WJ	Grosseto	18 Jul 04
43.87	URS	Lapshina, Doronina, Bulatova, Kovalyova	1	vGDR-j	Leningrad	20 Jun 87
43.98	BRA	Silva, Leoncio, Krasucki, Santos	2	PAm-J	São Paulo	7 Jul 07
44.04	CUB	Riquelme, Allen, López, Valdivia	2	WJ	Sudbury	31 Jul 88
44.09	NED	Schippers, Kuhurima, Lubbers, Samuel	3	WJ	Moncton	24 Jul 10

4 X 400 METRES RELAY

Mark	Nat	Name	Pos	Meet	Venue	Date
3:27.60	USA	Anderson, Kidd, Smith, Hastings	1	WJ	Grosseto	18 Jul 04
3:28.39	GDR	Derr, Fabert, Wöhlk, Breuer	1	WJ	Sudbury	31 Jul 88
3:29.66	JAM	Stewart, Morgan, Walker, Hall	1	PennR	Philadelphia	28 Apr 01
3:30.03	RUS	Talko, Shapayeva, Soldatova, Kostetskaya	2	WJ	Grosseto	18 Jul 04
3:30.38	AUS	Scamps, R Poetschka, Hanigan, Andrews	1	WJ	Plovdiv	12 Aug 90
3:30.46	GBR	Wall, Spencer, James,. Miller	2	WJ	Kingston	21 Jul 02
3:30.72	BUL	Kireva, Angelova, Rashova, Dimitrova	3	v2N	Sofiya	24 Jul 83
3:30.84	NGR	Abugan, Odumosu, Eze, Adesanya	2	WJ	Beijing	20 Aug 06

Mark	Name		Nat	Born	Pos	Meet	Venue	Date

MEN'S WORLD LISTS 2011

60 METRES INDOORS

Mark	Name		Nat	Born	Pos	Meet	Venue	Date
6.48A	Michael	Rodgers #	USA	24.4.85	1	NC	Albuquerque	27 Feb
6.49A		Rodgers			1h3	NC	Albuquerque	27 Feb
6.50	Kim	Collins	SKN	5.4.76	1h2		Karlsruhe	13 Feb
6.50		Rodgers			1	GP	Birmingham	19 Feb
6.52	Nesta	Carter	JAM	10.11.85	1	Mill	New York	28 Jan
6.52		Collins			1		Düseldorf	11 Feb
6.52	Lerone	Clarke	JAM	12.6.81	1		Karlsruhe	13 Feb
6.53		Rodgers			2		Düseldorf	11 Feb
6.53		Collins			2	GP	Birmingham	19 Feb
6.53	Francis	Obikwelu	POR	22.11.78	1	EI	Paris (Bercy)	6 Mar
6.53	Jeffery	Demps	USA	8.1.90	1	NCAA	College Station	12 Mar
(11/6)								
6.54	Rakieem	Salaam	USA	5.4.90	1s2	Tyson	Fayetteville	11 Feb
6.54A	D'Angelo	Cherry	USA	1.8.90	2	NC	Albuquerque	27 Feb
6.54	Dwain	Chambers	GBR	5.4.78	2	EI	Paris (Bercy)	6 Mar
6.55	Marc	Burns	TRI	7.1.83	4	GP	Birmingham	19 Feb
(10)								
6.55	Christophe	Lemaitre	FRA	11.6.90	1s2	EI	Paris (Bercy)	5 Mar
6.55	Maurice	Mitchell	USA	22.12.89	2h2	NCAA	College Station	11 Mar
6.55	Mike	Granger	USA	17.3.91	2	NCAA	College Station	12 Mar
6.56		Su Bingtian	CHN	29.8.89	1h5	NGP	Chengdu	19 Mar
6.57	Trell	Kimmons	USA	13.7.85	3	Mill	New York	28 Jan
6.58	Josh	Norman	USA	26.7.80	1		Seattle	15 Jan
6.58	Reggie	Dixon	USA	7.6.88	1		University Park	28 Jan
6.59	Gerald	Phiri	ZAM	6.10.88	2		College Station	29 Jan
6.59	Sam	Effah	CAN	29.12.88	1		Winnipeg	26 Feb
6.59	Terrell	Wilks	USA	30.12.89	1		Blacksburg	5 Mar
(20)								
6.59	Emanuele	Di Gregorio	ITA	13.12.80	4	EI	Paris (Bercy)	6 Mar
6.60	Egwero	Ogho-Oghene	NGR	26.11.88	5		Düsseldorf	11 Feb
6.60	Brian	Mariano	NED	22.1.85	2s2	EI	Paris (Bercy)	5 Mar
6.60	Woodrow	Randall	USA	9.11.89	1h3	NCAA	College Station	11 Mar
6.61	Horatio	Williams	USA	28.8.89	1		Baton Rouge	15 Jan
6.61	Christopher	Davis	USA	1.3.86	1s2		University Park	28 Jan
6.61	Prezel	Hardy	USA-J	1.6.92	3		College Station	29 Jan
6.61A	Rubin	Williams	USA	9.7.83	3	NC	Albuquerque	27 Feb
6.61	Pascal	Mancini	SUI	18.4.89	1h1	EI	Paris (Bercy)	5 Mar
6.61	Martial	Mbandjock	FRA	14.10.85	2s1	EI	Paris (Bercy)	5 Mar
(30)								
6.61	Ben Youssef	Meité	CIV	11.11.86	1		Sherbrooke	10 Mar
6.62	Peter	Emelieze	NGR	19.4.88	6		Düsseldorf	11 Feb
6.62	Trevor J.	Graham	USA	27.7.89	2		Blacksburg	26 Feb
6.62A	Leroy	Dixon	USA	20.6.83	4	NC	Albuquerque	27 Feb
6.62	Cédric	Nabe #	SUI	16.6.83	4s2	EI	Paris (Bercy)	5 Mar
6.62A	Kimour	Bruce	JAM	6.9.86	1	NCAA-II	Albuquerque	12 Mar
6.63A	Joe	Morris	USA		1		Boulder	22 Jan
6.63	Joel	Fearon	GBR	11.10.88	1	BirmG	Birmingham	5 Feb
6.63	Mark	Lewis-Francis	GBR	4.9.82	1h3	NC	Sheffield	12 Feb
6.63	Aleksandr	Shpayer	RUS	1.8.89	1	NC	Moskva	16 Feb
(40)								
6.63	Christian	Blum	GER	10.3.87	1	NC	Leipzig	26 Feb
6.63	Harry	Adams	USA	27.11.89	2	SEC	Fayetteville	27 Feb
6.63A	Michael Ray	Garvin	USA	29.9.86	5	NC	Albuquerque	27 Feb
6.64A	Jeremy	Dodson	USA	30.8.87	1		Air Force Academy	14 Jan
6.64	Carey	LaCour	USA	17.2.85	1		Houston	29 Jan
6.64	Harry	Akines-Aryeetey	GBR	29.8.88	2	NC	Sheffield	12 Feb
6.64	Tobias	Unger	GER	10.7.79	5		Karlsruhe	13 Feb
6.64	B.J.	Lawrence	SKN	27.12.89	1		Lincoln NE	19 Feb
6.64	Dentarius	Locke	USA	12.12.89	2		Blacksburg	5 Mar
6.64A	Desmond	Jackson	USA	27.4.89	2	NCAA-II	Albuquerque	12 Mar
(50)								

JUNIORS

Mark	Name		Nat	Born	Pos	Meet	Venue	Date
6.61	Prezel	Hardy	USA-J	1.6.92	3		College Station	29 Jan
6.66	Jimmy	Vicaut	FRA	27.2.92	2		Chemnitz	27 Jan
6.66	Keenan	Brock	USA	6.1.92	1h1		Blacksburg	5 Mar

Mark	Wind	Name		Nat	Born	Pos	Meet	Venue	Date

100 YARDS

In 100m race at Ostrava 31 May: (-0.2) Usain Bolt JAM 9.14, Steve Mullings & JAM 9.19, Kim Collins SKN 9.29, Daniel Bailey ANT 9.30, Lerone Clarke JAM 9.37, Ivory Williams 9.40, Craig Pickering 9.49: B (1.0) Mark Lewis –Francis 9.40.

100 METRES

Mark	Wind	Name		Nat	Born	Pos	Meet	Venue	Date
9.76	1.3	Usain	Bolt	JAM	21.8.86	1	VD	Bruxelles	16 Sep
9.78	1.0	Asafa	Powell	JAM	23.11.82	1	Athl	Lausanne	30 Jun
9.79	1.1	Tyson	Gay	USA	9.8.82	1h1		Clermont	4 Jun
9.80	1.3	Steve	Mullings ¶	JAM	29.11.82	1	Pre	Eugene	4 Jun
9.82	0.0	Yohan	Blake	JAM	26.12.89	1	WK	Zürich	8 Sep
9.82	0.1		Blake			1	ISTAF	Berlin	11 Sep
9.85	1.3	Michael	Rodgers #	USA	24.4.85	2	Pre	Eugene	4 Jun
9.85	1.0	Richard	Thompson	TRI	7.6.85	1	NC	Port of Spain	13 Aug
9.85	0.1		Bolt			1	Hanz	Zagreb	13 Sep
9.86	2.0		Powell			1	Gyulai	Budapest	30 Jul
9.88	1.0	Michael	Frater	JAM	6.10.82	2	Athl	Lausanne	30 Jun
9.88	1.0		Bolt			1	Herc	Monaco	22 Jul
9.89	2.0		Mullings			1		Clermont	21 May
9.89	1.3	Ngonidzashe	Makusha	ZIM	11.3.87	1	NCAA	Des Moines	10 Jun
9.89	1.3	Nesta	Carter (10)	JAM	10.11.85	2	VD	Bruxelles	16 Sep
9.90	2.0		Mullings			1		Starkville	16 Apr
9.90	0.6		Powell			1s2	NC	Kingston	24 Jun
9.90	1.0		Carter			2	Herc	Monaco	22 Jul
9.90	1.8		Powell			1h1	Gyulai	Budapest	30 Jul
9.91	0.6		Bolt			1	GGala	Roma	26 May
9.91+	1.5		Gay			1	in 150m	Manchester	15 May
9.91	-0.2		Bolt			1	GS	Ostrava	31 May
9.91	0.4		Powell			1	DL	Birmingham	10 Jul
9.92	1.3		Carter			3	Pre	Eugene	4 Jun
9.92	2.0	Christophe	Lemaitre	FRA	11.6.90	1	NC	Albi	29 Jul
9.92	-1.4		Blake			1	WCh	Daegu	28 Aug
9.93	0.6		Powell			2	GGala	Roma	26 May
9.93	1.0	Keston	Bledman	TRI	8.3.88	1		Clermont	4 Jun
9.93	0.4		Carter			2	DL	Birmingham	10 Jul
9.94	1.3	Darvis	Patton	USA	4.12.77	4	Pre	Eugene	4 Jun
9.94	1.3		Frater			5	Pre	Eugene	4 Jun
9.94	1.3	Walter	Dix	USA	31.1.86	1	NC	Eugene	24 Jun
		(33/14)							
9.95	1.3	Justin	Gatlin	USA	10.2.82	2	NC	Eugene	24 Jun
9.96	1.1	Nickel	Ashmeade	JAM	4.7.90	2h1		Clermont	4 Jun
9.97	1.3	Rakieem 'Mookie'	Salaam	USA	5.4.90	2	NCAA	Des Moines	10 Jun
9.97	0.5	Daniel	Bailey	ANT	9.9.86	1		Strasbourg	12 Jun
9.99	2.0	Travis	Padgett	USA	13.12.86	2		Clermont	21 May
9.99	1.0	Jaysuma	Saidy Ndure	NOR	1.7.84	5	Athl	Lausanne	30 Jun
		(20)							
10.00	1.3	Maurice	Mitchell	USA	22.12.89	3	NCAA	Des Moines	10 Jun
10.00A	0.4	Kim	Collins	SKN	5.4.76	1s2	PAm	Guadalajara, MEX	24 Oct
10.01	2.0	Dwain	Chambers	GBR	5.4.78	1		São Paulo	22 May
10.01A	1.3	Lerone	Clarke	JAM	2.10.81	1	PAm	Guadalajara, MEX	25 Oct
10.02	1.3	Ivory	Williams	USA	2.5.85	8	Pre	Eugene	4 Jun
10.04	0.7	Jeffrey	Demps	USA	8.1.90	1h4	NC	Eugene	23 Jun
10.04	1.3	Trell	Kimmons	USA	13.7.85	4	NC	Eugene	24 Jun
10.06	1.3	Gerald	Phiri	ZAM	6.10.88	1rA	TexR	Asutin	9 Apr
10.06	2.0	Dexter	Lee	JAM	18.1.91	2		São Paulo	22 May
10.06	2.0	Egweru	Ogho-Oghene	NGR	26.11.88	1s2	AfrG	Maputo	12 Sep
		(30)							
10.07	0.2	Femi Seun	Ogunode	QAT	15.5.91	1	WMilG	Rio de Janeiro	21 Jul
10.07	0.3	Jimmy	Vicaut	FRA-J	27.2.92	1	EJ	Tallinn	22 Jul
10.07	1.0	Aaron	Armstrong	TRI	14.10.77	3	NC	Port of Spain	13 Aug
10.09	1.4	Jacques	Harvey	JAM	5.4.89	1		Kingston	7 May
10.09	0.8	Aziz	Ouhadi	MAR	24.7.84	1		Dakar	28 May
10.09	1.0	Marc	Burns	TRI	7.1.83	4	NC	Port of Spain	13 Aug
10.10	0.3	Churandy	Martina	NED	3.7.84	2	FBK	Hengelo	29 May
10.11	1.1	James	Dasaolu	GBR	5.9.87	1h1		Genève	28 May
10.11	1.1	Mario	Forsythe	JAM	30.10.85	1h1	FBK	Hengelo	29 May
10.11	0.5	Ainsley	Waugh	JAM	17.9.81	2		Lappeenranta	13 Aug
		(40)							
10.12	1.0	Emmanuel	Callander	TRI	10.5.84	5	NC	Port of Spain	13 Aug
10.13	1.7	Prezel	Hardy	USA-J	1.6.92	1		Waco	23 Apr

Mark	Wind	Name		Nat	Born	Pos	Meet	Venue	Date
10.13	2.0	Martial	Mbandjock	FRA	14.10.85	2	KansR	Lawrence	23 Apr
10.13	1.8	Justin	Murdock	USA	21.4.89	1h1		Clemson	13 May
10.13	1.1	Harry	Aikines-Aryeetey	GBR	29.8.88	2h1		Genève	28 May
10.13	1.1	Rae	Edwards	USA	7.5.81	3h1	FBK	Hengelo	29 May
10.13	1.0	Darrel	Brown	TRI	11.10.84	6	NC	Port of Spain	13 Aug
10.13	1.8	Amr Ibrahim	Seoud	EGY	10.6.86	1s1	AfrG	Maputo	12 Sep
10.14	1.8	Calesio	Newman	USA	20.8.86	1		Greensboro	15 May
10.14	0.6	Kimmari	Roach	JAM	21.9.90	5s1	NC	Kingston	24 Jun
		(50)							
10.14	0.0	Andrew	Hinds	BAR	25.4.84	1	NC	Bridgetown	25 Jun
10.14	1.2	Marlon	Devonish	GBR	1.6.76	3	NC	Birmingham	30 Jul
10.14	0.5	Ramil	Guliyev	TUR	29.5.90	3		Lappeenranta	13 Aug
10.14	-0.2	Rytis	Sakalauskas	LTU	27.6.87	2	WUG	Shenzhen	17 Aug
10.14	1.8	Idrissa	Adam	CMR	28.12.84	2s1	AfrG	Maputo	12 Sep
10.14	1.8	Masashi	Eriguchi	JPN	17.12.88	1		Yamaguchi	8 Oct
10.15	1.0	Oshane	Bailey	JAM	9.8.89	3		Clermont	4 Jun
10.15	1.2	Dariusz	Kuc	POL	24.4.86	1		Kraków	12 Jun
10.15	0.9	Justyn	Warner	CAN	28.6.87	1		Toronto	12 Jun
10.16	1.4	Thuso	Mpuang	RSA	1.3.84	1		Donnas	3 Jul
		(60)							
10.16	0.7		Su Bingtian	CHN	29.8.89	1	NC	Hefei	8 Sep
10.17	0.9	Winston	Barnes	JAM	7.11.88	1		Kingston	12 Mar
10.17	0.7	Leroy	Dixon	USA	20.6.83	3	MSR	Walnut	16 Apr
10.17	0.9	Christian	Malcolm	GBR	3.6.79	2s3	NC	Birmingham	30 Jul
10.17	1.0	Rondell	Sorrillo	TRI	21.1.86	7	NC	Port of Spain	13 Aug
10.17	1.8	Barakat	Al-Harthi	OMA	15.6.88	1	Gulf CG	Madinat Isa	17 Oct
10.18	0.8	Kenroy	Anderson	JAM	27.6.87	1		Kingston	12 Mar
10.18	1.6	Simon	Magakwe	RSA	25.5.85	1s3	NC	Durban	9 Apr
10.18	1.3	Shane	Crawford	USA	4.6.88	1	Big 10	Iowa City	15 May
10.18	2.0	Nilson	André	BRA	30.1.86	3		São Paulo	22 May
		(70)							
10.18	1.0	Peter	Emelieze	NGR	19.4.88	1		Weinheim	28 May
10.18	1.2	Francis	Obikwelu	POR	22.11.78	2		Kraków	12 Jun
10.18	1.4	Ronalds	Arajs	LAT	29.11.87	2		Donnas	3 Jul
10.19	1.6	Roscoe	Engel	RSA	6.3.89	2s3	NC	Durban	9 Apr
10.19	1.0	Harry	Adams	USA	27.11.89	1h1	SEC	Athens, GA	14 May
10.19	1.3	Terrell	Wilks	USA	30.12.89	5	NCAA	Des Moines	10 Jun
10.19	0.3	Johnathan	Hancock	USA	31.3.87	1		Charlotte	17 Jun
10.19	1.9	Craig	Pickering	GBR	16.10.86	1s1	ENG Ch	Bedford	16 Jul
10.19	1.4	Amaru Reto	Schenkel	SUI	28.4.88	1		Fribourg	30 Jul
10.19	1.3	Mark	Lewis-Francis	GBR	4.9.82	6	VD	Bruxelles	16 Sep
		(80)							
10.20	1.3	Woodrow	Randall	USA	9.11.89	2rA	TexR	Austin	9 Apr
10.20	1.4	Remaldo	Rose	JAM	18.11.87	2		Kingston	7 May
10.20A	0.7	Charles	Silmon	USA	4.7.91	1h2		Fort Collins, CO	13 May
10.20	1.3	Stanley	Azie	USA/NGR	13.3.89	2	Big 10	Iowa City	15 May
10.20	0.7	Cordero	Gray	USA	9.5.89	3h4	NC	Eugene	23 Jun
10.20	0.9	Gavin	Smellie	CAN	26.6.86	1		Ottawa	17 Jul
10.20	1.9	Alex	Schaf	GER	28.4.87	1r2		Mannheim	13 Aug
10.21	1.9	Marek	Niit	EST	9.8.87	1		Austin	25 Mar
10.21	0.8	Keenan	Brock	USA-J	1.6.92	1		Auburn	2 Apr
10.21	1.2	Daniel	Grueso	COL	30.7.85	1=h2		Ponce	15 Apr
		(90)							
10.21	1.2	Carlos	Jorge	DOM	24.9.86	1=h2		Ponce	15 Apr
10.21	1.4	Chris	Davis	USA	1.3.86	1		Charlotte	23 Apr
10.21	0.5	Ahmad	Rashad	USA	12.12.87	1		Los Angeles (ER)	7 May
10.21	0.8	J-Mee	Samuels	USA	20.5.87	3		Baie Mahault	7 May
10.21	1.3	Justin	Austin	USA	8.10.89	5	Big 10	Iowa City	15 May
10.21	1.8	Danny	Talbot	GBR	1.5.91	1rA	LI	Loughborough	22 May
10.21	0.8	Ben Youssef	Meité	CIV	11.11.86	2		Dakar	28 May
10.21	1.8	Jared	Connaughton	CAN	20.7.85	1h2		Clermont	11 Jun
10.21	0.7		Zhang Peimeng	CHN	13.3.87	2	NC	Hefei	8 Sep
10.21	0.8	Luke	Fagan	GBR	31.7.88	5		Dubnica nad Váhon	15 Sep
		(100)							

Mark	Wind	Name		Nat	Born	Date
10.22	0.9	Sheldon	Mitchell	JAM	.90	12 Mar
10.22	1.7	Desmond	Jackson	USA	27.4.89	23 Apr
10.22	2.0	Jason	Smyth	IRL	4.7.87	21 May
10.22	1.1	Emanuele	Di Gregorio	ITA	13.12.80	29 May
10.22	0.8	Fabio	Cerutti	ITA	26.9.85	3 Jul
10.22	1.8	Sota	Kawatsura	JPN	19.6.89	8 Oct
10.23	0.9	Gabriel	Mvumvure	ZIM	23.4.88	2 Apr
10.23	1.3	D'Angelo	Cherry	USA	1.8.90	9 Apr
10.23	-0.1	Ryan	Milus	USA	19.9.90	13 May
10.23	1.3	Kind	Butler	USA	8.4.88	15 May
10.23	1.3	Nicholas	Watson	JAM	.90	21 May
10.23	0.8	Josh	Norman	USA	26.7.80	28 May
10.23A	1.9	Sam	Effah	CAN	29.12.88	24 Jun
10.23	0.9	James	Alaka	GBR	8.9.89	25 Jun
10.23	0.4	James	Ellington	GBR	6.9.85	27 Jun
10.23	1.9	Sven	Knipphals	GER	20.9.85	13 Aug

Mark	Wind	Name	Nat	Born	Pos	Meet	Venue	Date
10.23	1.8	Ryota Yamagata	JPN-J	10.6.92				8 Oct
10.24	1.5	Álvaro Gómez	COL	21.2.89				15 Apr
10.24	0.3	Deun White	USA	13.7.85				16 Apr
10.24	1.8	Mike Granger	USA	17.3.91				30 Apr
10.24	1.3	Devin Pipkin	USA	7.4.89				15 May
10.24	1.2	Ramon Gittens	BAR	20.7.87				11 Jun
10.24	0.8	Abdul Aziz Zakari	GHA	2.9.76				13 Jun
10.24	0.3	Jacques Riparelli	ITA	27.3.83				13 Jul
10.24	0.8	Tobias Unger	GER	10.7.79				13 Aug
10.25	0.9	Horatio Williams	USA	28.8.89				2 Apr
10.25		Jeffrey Henderson	USA	19.2.89				18 Apr
10.25	1.5	Dentarius Locke	USA	12.12.89				14 May
10.25A	0.0	Ángel David Rodríguez	ESP	25.4.80				17 Jul
10.25	1.4	Su'Waibou Sanneh	GAM	30.10.90				30 Jul
10.25	0.0	Sandro Viana	BRA	26.3.77				4 Aug
10.25	0.5	Bruno de Barros	BRA	7.1.87				4 Aug
10.26A	1.4	Kael Becerra	CHI	4.11.85				6 May
10.26	1.4	Jamial Rolle	BAH	16.4.80				7 May
10.26	2.0	Jonathan Åstrand	FIN	9.9.85				12 Jun
10.26	1.5	Ashton Eaton	USA	21.1.88				13 Aug
10.27	-3.3	Michael Herrera	CUB	5.6.85				17 Mar
10.27	1.9	Hannes Dreyer	RSA	13.1.85				9 Apr
10.27A	1.0	Jeremy Dodson	USA	30.8.87				9 Apr
10.27	1.3	Philip Redrick	USA	2.8.88				9 Apr
10.27	-0.2	Jazeel Murphy	JAM-Y	27.2.94				23 Apr
10.27	2.0	Kemar Hyman	CAY	11.10.89				23 Apr
10.27	0.0	Ryan Shields	JAM	12.5.83				6 May
10.27		Everett Walker	USA	3.10.90				6 May
10.27	1.0	Jon Juin	HAI	17.12.89				14 May
10.27	1.1	Willie Perry	USA	16.5.87				4 Jun
10.27	-0.6	Obinna Metu	NGR	12.7.88				4 Jun
10.27	1.8	Shintaro Kimura	JPN	30.6.87				8 Oct
10.28	1.7	Marvin Bracy	USA-J	15.12.93				26 Mar
10.28	-0.2	Kemar Bailey Cole	JAM-J	10.1.92				23 Apr
10.28	1.2	Yusuke Kotani	JPN	23.9.89				29 Apr
10.28	1.4	Warren Fraser	BAH	8.7.91				7 May
10.28	0.7	Rynell Parson	USA	11.7.90				14 May
10.28	2.0	Rodney Green	BAH	8.12.85				21 May
10.28	2.0	Adam Harris	GUY	21.7.87				22 May
10.28	1.2	Brijesh BJ Lawrence	SKN	27.12.89				26 May
10.28	-0.8	Adrian Griffith	BAH	11.11.84				2 Jun
10.28	0.3	Evander Wells	USA	7.12.87				17 Jun
10.28	0.9	David Lescay	CUB	19.2.89				27 Jul
10.29	1.5	David Bolarinwa	GBR-J	20.10.93				29 May
10.29	1.1	Patrick van Luljk	NED	17.9.84				29 May
10.29	0.9	Andrew Robertson	GBR	17.12.90				25 Jun
10.29	2.0	Yannick Lesourd	FRA	3.4.88				29 Jul
10.29	2.0	Emmanuel Biron	FRA	29.7.88				29 Jul
10.29	1.9	Christian Blum	GER	10.3.87				13 Aug
10.29	2.0	Gerard Kobéané	BUR	24.4.88				12 Sep
10.30	1.1	Cédric Nabe #	SUI	16.6.83				28 May
10.30	-1.4	Yunier Pérez	CUB	16.2.85				8 Jun
10.30	0.8	Simone Collio	ITA	27.12.79				3 Jul
10.30	1.9	Rion Pierre	GBR	24.11.87				16 Jul
10.30	1.3	Martynas Jurgilas	LTU	5.9.88				23 Jul
10.30	0.9	Carey LaCour	USA	17.2.85				23 Jul
10.30	2.0	Teddy Tinmar	FRA	30.3.87				29 Jul
10.30	1.5	Matic Osovnikar	SLO	19.1.80				6 Aug
10.30	2.0	Tim Abeyie	GHA	7.11.82				12 Sep
10.31		Darrion Bent	JAM	17.9.90				5 Mar
10.31	1.1	Isiah Young	USA	5.1.90				23 Apr
10.31	1.5	Remontay McClain	USA-J	21.9.92				21 May
10.31	0.0	Levonte Whitfield	USA-J	8.10.93				28 May
10.31	-1.3	Serhiy Smelyk	UKR	19.4.87				30 May
10.31	1.0	Rubin Williams	USA	9.7.83				4 Jun
10.31	-0.6	Sean McLean	USA-J	23.3.92				17 Jun
10.31	1.1	Matt Davies	AUS	18.4.85				18 Jun
10.31	1.1	Mitchell Watt	AUS	25.3.88				18 Jun
10.31	-0.7	Marlon Robinson	JAM	5.6.85				23 Jun
10.31	0.7	Jason Livermore	JAM	25.4.88				23 Jun
10.31	1.8	Yasser Al-Nashiri	KSA	10.2.87				8 Jul
10.31	1.2	Rikki Fifton	GBR	17.6.85				30 Jul
10.32		Ali Akbar Rabiei	IRI	11.1.88				16 May
10.32	1.0	Ryan Moseley	AUT	8.10.82				31 May
10.32	1.8	Aleksandr Khyutte	RUS	29.9.88				4 Jun
10.32	1.2	Mandela Clifford	LCA	.86				11 Jun
10.32	2.0	Diego Henrique Cavalcanti	BRA	18.3.91				17 Jun
10.32	0.9	Brendan Christian	ANT	11.12.83				24 Jul
10.32	2.0	Ronald Pognon	FRA	16.11.82				29 Jul
10.32	-0.1	Igor Bodrov	UKR	9.7.87				2 Aug
10.32	1.9	Gregor Kokalovic	SLO	1.1.86				6 Aug
10.32	0.5	Dontae Richards-Kwok	CAN	1.3.89				16 Aug
10.32	0.9	Richard Kilty	GBR	2.9.89				27 Aug
10.32	-0.4	Mamadou Lamine Niang	SEN	19.10.84				12 Sep

(200)

Wind assisted to 10.30

Mark	Wind	Name	Nat	Born	Pos	Meet	Venue	Date
9.80	2.2	Yohan Blake	JAM	26.12.89	1		Kingston	7 May
9.83	3.6	Blake			1h4	NC	Kingston	24 Jun
9.86	3.6	Michael Frater	JAM	6.10.82	2h4	NC	Kingston	23 Jun
9.90	2.8	Lerone Clarke	JAM	2.10.81	1		Clermont	11 Jun
9.91	5.1	Thompson			1		Baton Rpuge	23 Apr
9.91	2.7	Mullings			1h2		Clermont	21 May
9.94	2.2	Daniel Bailey	ANT	9.9.86	2		Kingston	7 May
9.95	2.3	Ivory Williams	USA	2.5.85	1h5	NC	Eugene	23 Jun
9.96	2.4	Jeffrey Demps	USA	8.1.90	1		Gainesville	16 Apr
9.96	3.3	Travis Padgett	USA	13.12.86	1h1		Clermont	21 May
9.97	3.5	Trell Kimmons	USA	13.7.85	1		Dorgali	13 Jul
10.03A		Jeremy Dodson	USA	30.8.87	1		Parker, CO	11 Jun
10.03	2.8	Jacques Harvey	JAM	5.4.89	1		Sundsvall	31 Jul
10.04	3.8	Jared Connaughton	CAN	20.7.85	1rB	TexR	Austin	9 Apr
10.04	2.9	Darrel Brown	TRI	11.10.84	1		Port of Spain	31 Jul
10.05	2.2	Marvin Bracy	USA-J	15.12.93	1	NC-j	Eugene	24 Jun
10.06	2.8	Brendan Christian	ANT	11.12.83	3		Clermont	11 Jun
10.07	3.9	Ryan Milus	USA	19.9.90	1		Tempe	23 Apr
10.09	3.5	Harry Aikines-Aryeetey	GBR	29.8.88	1	ENG Ch	Bedford	16 Jul
10.10	4.9	Rae Edwards	USA	7.5.81	1rC	TexR	Austin	9 Apr
10.10	5.1	Gabriel Mvumvure	ZIM	23.4.88	3rA		Baton Rouge	23 Apr
10.10	3.9	Desmond Jackson	USA	27.4.89	1		Stephenville	8 May
10.10	2.8	Rytis Sakalauskas	LTU	27.6.87	1	Vard	Réthimno	13 Jul
10.11	4.7	Gavin Smellie	CAN	26.6.86	1rB		Baton Rouge	23 Apr
10.11A	1.5	Álvaro Gómez	COL	21.2.89	1	NC	Bogotá	6 May
10.11	3.0	Terrell Wilks	USA	30.12.89	1	SEC	Athens, GA	15 May
10.11	3.2	Ramil Guliyev	TUR	29.5.90	1		Bilbao	18 Jun
10.11	3.6	Oshane Bailey	JAM	9.8.89	4h4	NC	Kingston	23 Jun
10.12	3.9	Cordero Gray	USA	9.5.89	1		Natchitoches	15 May
10.12	3.0	Dentarius Locke	USA	12.12.89	2	SEC	Athens, GA	15 May
10.12	3.5	James Ellington	GBR	6.9.85	2	LI	Loughborough	22 May

Mark	Wind	Name		Nat	Born	Pos	Meet	Venue	Date
10.12	2.4	Keenan	Brock	USA-J	1.6.92	2	PAm-J	Miramar	22 Jul
10.12	3.2	Obinna	Metu	NGR	12.7.88	1s3	AfrG	Maputo	12 Sep
10.13	3.3	Woodrow	Randall	USA	9.11.89	1h2	TexR	Austin	8 Apr
10.13	3.9	Deun	White	USA	13.7.85	2		Tempe	23 Apr
10.13	3.0	Jonathan	Juin	HAI	17.12.89	3	SEC	Athens, GA	15 May
10.14	5.1	Isaac	Ntiamoah	AUS	27.10.82	1		Sydney	19 Feb
10.14A	3.3	Ángel David	Rodríguez	ESP	25.4.80	1h1		Avila	17 Jul
10.14	2.9	Omar	Douglas	JAM	30.10.83	2		Mucurapo	31 Jul
10.14	3.2	Ben Youssef	Meité	CIV	11.11.86	2s3	AfrG	Maputo	12 Sep
10.15	4.0	Zye	Boey	USA	8.5.89	1		Charleston	2 Apr
10.15	3.3	D'Angelo	Cherry	USA	1.8.90	2h2	TexR	Austin	8 Apr
10.15	2.4	Jaylon	Hicks	USA-J	13.4.93	1		Austin	14 May
10.15	3.5	Craig	Pickering	GBR	16.10.86	3	LI	Loughborough	22 May
10.15	3.1	Kemour	Bruce	JAM	6.9.86	1	NCAA-2	Turlock, CA	28 May
10.15	2.8	Rodney	Green	BAH	8.12.85	4		Clermont	11 Jun
10.15	2.7	Kenroy	Anderson	JAM	27.6.87	3q3	NC	Kingston	23 Jun
10.15	4.0	Yazaldes	Nascimento	POR	17.4.86	1	NC	Lisboa (U)	30 Jul
10.16	4.9	Carey	LaCour	USA	17.2.85	2rC	TexR	Austin	9 Apr
10.16	5.1	Adrian	Griffith	BAH	11.11.84	4		Baton Rouge	23 Apr
10.16	3.0	Mike	Granger	USA	17.3.91	4	SEC	Athens, GA	15 May
10.16	3.2	Abdul Aziz	Zakari	GHA	2.9.76	2		Bilbao	18 Jun
10.16	4.0	Arnaldo	Abrantes	POR	27.11.86	2	NC	Lisboa (U)	30 Jul
10.16	2.8	Simone	Collio	ITA	27.12.79	2		Sundsvall	31 Jul
10.17A	2.1	Hannes	Dreyer	RSA	13.1.85	1		Germiston	26 Mar
10.17	2.4	Aaron	Ernest	USA-J	8.11.93	1		Mobile	2 Apr
10.17	2.4	Willie	Perry	USA	16.5.87	3		Gainesville	16 Apr
10.17	4.7	Jerel	Hill	USA	13.9.87	2rB		Baton Rouge	23 Apr
10.17	3.2	Shintaro	Kimura	JPN	30.6.87	1h3	Oda	Hiroshima	29 Apr
10.17	3.0	Marek	Niit	EST	9.8.87	5	SEC	Athens, GA	15 May
10.18	3.9	Bradley	Sylve	USA-J	29.1.93	1h4	TexR	Austin	8 Apr
10.18	4.9	Rubin	Williams	USA	9.7.83	3rC	TexR	Austin	9 Apr
10.18	2.8	Yusuke	Kotani	JPN	23.9.89	1h2	Oda	Hiroshima	29 Apr
10.18	3.9	Justin	Walker	USA	30.11.90	2		Natchitoches	15 May
10.19	4.8	Carlin	Isles	USA	21.11.89	1		Arlington	2 Apr
10.19	4.8	Keyth	Talley	USA	3.3.90	2h1	TexR	Austin	8 Apr
10.19	2.4	Charles	Silmon	USA	4.7.91	5		Gainesville	16 Apr
10.19	4.2	Josh	Norman	USA	26.7.80	1		Fresno	30 Apr
10.19	4.3	Konstantin	Petryashov	RUS	16.12.84	1	NCp	Yerino	4 Jun
10.19	4.8	Antoine	Adams	SKN	31.8.88	2		Austin	25 Sep
10.20	4.8	Miles	Smith	USA	24.9.84	2		Arlington	2 Apr
10.20A	2.6	Kael	Becerra	CHI	4.11.85	1h3	NC	Bogota	6 May
10.20	2.8	Javon	Young	USA	21.8.90	1h4		Jacksonville	13 May
10.20	2.2	Everett	Walker	USA	3.10.90	1h1	JUCO	Hutchinson	20 May
10.20	2.8	Rasheed	Dwyer	JAM	29.1.89	5		Clermont	11 Jun
10.20	2.8	Aaron	Rouge-Serret	AUS	21.1.88	2	Vard	Réthimno	13 Jul
10.20	3.5	Luke	Fagan	GBR	31.7.88	3	ENG Ch	Bedford	16 Jul

Mark	Wind	Name		Nat	Born	Date
10.21	3.5	Jacques	Riparelli	ITA	27.3.83	13 Jul
10.22	4.0	Seiya	Hane	JPN	31.1.90	23 Apr
10.22	3.7	Ruslan	Abbyasov	AZE	24.6.86	18 Jun
10.22	3.7	Pavel	Maslák	CZE	21.2.91	2 Jul
10.23	4.8	Philip	Redrick	USA	2.8.88	8 Apr
10.23	5.6	Kawayne	Fisher	JAM	25.10.86	22 Apr
10.23	2.8	David	Bolarinwa	GBR-J	20.10.93	25 Jun
10.23	2.8	Adam	Gemili	GBR-J	6.10.93	25 Jun
10.24	5.1	Patrick	Fakiye	AUS	1.2.91	19 Feb
10.24	3.1	Otis	McDaniel	USA	30.6.86	18 Mar
10.24	4.5	Rynell	Parson	USA	11.7.90	26 Mar
10.24	3.0	Yasser	Al-Nashiri	KSA	10.2.87	12 May
10.24	2.9	Oliver	Bradwell	USA	21.8.92	31 Jul
10.25	3.8	Jarid	Vaughan	CAN	5.2.85	9 Apr
10.25	2.4	Aaron	Brown	CAN-J	27.5.92	22 Jul
10.25	3.2	Mahamadou	Niang	SEN	19.10.84	12 Sep
10.25	2.7		Liu Yuan-Kai	TPE	2.12.81	24 Oct
10.26	3.2	Tatsuya	Hattori	JPN	22.2.88	29 Apr
10.26	5.1	Marvin	Bonde	ZIM	23.7.84	14 May
10.26	3.1	Josh	Schuler	USA	3.5.89	28 May
10.26	4.3	Vyacheslav	Kolesnichenko	RUS	1.2.90	4 Jun
10.26	2.4	Hannu	Hämäläinen	FIN	30.4.85	12 Jun
10.26	3.5	Rion	Pierre	GBR	24.11.87	16 Jul
10.27	5.9	Tim	Price	USA	26.12.87	16 Apr
10.27	2.2	Evander	Wells	USA	7.12.87	11 Jun
10.27	2.8	Naoki	Tsukahara	JPN	10.5.85	25 Sep
10.28	2.8	Jefferson	Lucindo	BRA	17.10.90	25 Mar
10.28	4.8	Chris	Lawson	USA	12.3.83	16 Apr
10.28	3.9	Jusstin	Sims	USA	6.5.91	30 Apr
10.28	2.6	Devery	Bell	USA	.89	6 May
10.28	3.7	Remontay	McClain	USA-J	21.9.92	
10.28	3.7	Deji	Tobais	GBR	31.10.91	25 Jun
10.29	2.5	John	Thomas	JAM-J	4.2.92	2 Apr
10.29	3.7	Mandela	Clifford	LCA	.86	2 Apr
10.29	2.1	Leigh	Julius	RSA	25.3.85	9 Apr
10.29	5.6	Kenneth	Turner	USA	28.8.91	22 Apr
10.29	5.1	Ravyn	Hayward	USA	23.9.85	23 Apr
10.29	5.9	Brandon	McBride	CAN-Y	15.6.94	6 May
10.29	5.9	Deandre	Smith	USA	.90	6 May
10.29	2.2	Markquis	Frazier	USA	2.10.90	20 May
10.29	3.5	Chris	Burrows	USA	15.3.90	26 May
10.29	4.3	Mikhail	Idrisov	RUS	21.6.88	4 Jun
10.29	2.2	Oliver	Bradwell	USA-J	21.8.92	24 Jun
10.30w		eight men				

Unknown irregularity- Wind assisted: At Arkansas City, KS 2 Apr: 1. Everett Walker USA 3.10.90 10.05, 2. Jeremy Hardy USA 10.8.89 10.08, 3, Oliver Bradwell USA-J 21.8.92 10.12

Best at low altitude

Mark	Wind	Name	Pos	Meet	Venue	Date
10.01	0.1	Collins	2	ISTAF	Berlin	11 Sep
10.05	1.3	L Clarke	3	VD	Bruxelles	16 Sep
10.24	0.7	Silmon				23 Jun
10.29	-0.3	A D Rodríguez				16 Jul

Mark	Wind	Name		Nat	Born	Pos	Meet	Venue	Date
Drugs disqualification 9.93 1.4		S Mullings				1		Arzana	30 Jul
Hand timing – doubtful timing									
9.8		Mosito	Lehata	LES	8.4.89	1		Maputo	2 Jul
9.9		Ali Akbar	Rabiei	IRI	11.1.88	1		Ashghabat	20 May

JUNIORS

See main list for top 3 juniors. 11 performances by 4 men to 10.23. Additional marks and further juniors:

```
Vicaut   10.07  2.0 2   NC   Albi          29 Jul    10.13  1.3 5   VD     Bruxelles   16 Sep
         10.10  -0.4 3s1 WCh  Daegu         28 Aug    10.20  1.3 1h1        Antony      25 Jun
         10.12  -1.8 1h1 EJ   Tallinn       21 Jul    10.21  0.3 1h5        Mannheim     2 Jul
Hardy    10.21  0.9 1        Baton Rouge     2 Apr
```

Mark	Wind	Name		Nat	Born	Pos	Meet	Venue	Date
10.23	1.8	Ryota	Yamagata	JPN	10.6.92	3		Yamaguchi	8 Oct
10.27	-0.2	Jazeel	Murphy	JAM-Y	27.2.94	1	Carifta	Montego Bay	23 Apr
10.28	1.7	Marvin	Bracy	USA	15.12.93	1		Tallahassee	26 Mar
10.28	-0.2	Kemar	Bailey Cole	JAM	10.1.92	2	Carifta	Montego Bay	23 Apr
10.29	1.5	David	Bolarinwa	GBR	20.10.93	1	CAU	Bedford	29 May
10.31	1.5	Remontay	McClain	USA	21.9.92	1h1		Norwalk	21 May
10.31	0.0	Levonte	Whitfield (10)	USA	8.10.93	1		Orlando	28 May
10.31	-0.6	Sean	McLean	USA	23.3.92	1		Greensboro	17 Jun
10.33	1.6	Aaron	Ernest	USA	8.11.93	1		Gulf Shores	6 May
10.33	2.0	Jaylon	Hicks	USA	.93	1h7		Wichita	29 Jul
10.34	1.9	Dallas	Burroughs	USA		1		Boise	20 May
10.35		Thomas	Tyner	USA-Y	.94	1		Beaverton	12 May
10.35	1.8	Joe	Craig	USA	6.5.92	2h1		Clemson	13 May
10.35	1.4	Adam	Gemili	GBR	6.10.93	1h2	NC-j	Bedford	25 Jun
10.35	0.6		Zheng Dongsheng	CHN	23.1.92	1	City G	Nanchang	21 Oct
10.36A	1.6	Gideon	Trotter	RSA	3.3.92	1h4	NC-j	Germiston	2 Apr
10.36	1.5		Xie Zhenye (20)	CHN	17.8.93	1h7		Jiaxing	21 May
10.36	-1.0	Clayton	Vaughn	USA	15.5.92	4h1	NCAA	Des Moines	8 Jun
10.36	0.6	Moriba	Morain	TRI-J	8.10.92	1		Couva	11 Jun
10.36A	0.0	Aldemir Gomes	da Silva	BRA	8.5.92	1	SAm-J	Medellín	23 Sep

Wind assisted to 10.33. See main list for top 5 juniors. 10 performances by 4 men to 10.17w.

```
Vicaut   10.11  3.2 1          Reims      22 May    10.16  3.0 2h2 NC   Albi     29 Jul
         10.14  2.2 1          Antony     25 Jun
Bracy    10.09  2.4 1    PAm-J Miramar    22 Jul    10.16  2.6 1h2 NC-j Eugene   24 Jun
Brock    10.17  2.7 1h1  PAm-J Miramar    22 Jul
```

Mark	Wind	Name		Nat	Born	Pos	Meet	Venue	Date
10.23w	2.8	David	Bolarinwa	GBR	20.10.93	1	NC-j	Bedford	25 Jun
10.23w	2.8	Adam	Gemili	GBR	6.10.93	2	NC-j	Bedford	25 Jun
10.25w	2.4	Aaron	Brown	CAN	27.5.92	3	PAm-J	Miramar	22 Jul
10.28	3.7	Remontay	McClain	USA	21.9.92				
10.29w	2.5	John	Thomas	JAM	4.2.92	1		Lubbock	2 Apr
10.29w	5.9	Brandon	McBride	CAN-Y	15.6.94	1h2		Coffeyville	6 May
10.29	2.2	Oliver	Bradwell	USA	21.8.92	3	NC-j	Eugene	24 Jun
10.30	5.9	Akeem	Haynes	CAN	.92	3h2		Coffeyville	6 May
10.30	3.6	D'Andre	Jacobs	USA	25.5.93	1		Baton Rouge	7 May
10.30	2.9	Robin	Edwards	USA	12.11.83	1rB		Clermont	4 Jun
10.30	2.2	Sean	McLean	USA	23.3.92	4	NC-j	Eugene	24 Jun
10.32	2.3		Ng Ka Fung	HKG	27.10.92	1		Hong Kong	30 Oct

150 METRES STRAIGHT

Mark	Wind	Name		Nat	Born	Pos	Meet	Venue	Date
14.51	1.5	Tyson	Gay	USA	9.8.82	1		Manchester	15 May
14.65	1.4	Walter	Dix	USA	31.1.86	1		Gateshead (Q)	17 Sep
14.87	1.4	Marlon	Devonish	GBR	1.6.76	2		Gateshead (Q)	17 Sep

200 METRES

Mark	Wind	Name		Nat	Born	Pos	Meet	Venue	Date
19.26	0.7	Yohan	Blake	JAM	26.12.89	1	VD	Bruxelles	16 Sep
19.40	0.8	Usain	Bolt	JAM	21.8.86	1	WCh	Daegu	3 Sep
19.53	0.7	Walter	Dix	USA	31.1.86	2	VD	Bruxelles	16 Sep
19.70	0.8		Dix			2		Daegu	3 Sep
19.80	0.8	Christophe	Lemaitre	FRA	11.6.90	3	WCh	Daegu	3 Sep
19.86	0.7		Bolt			1	Bisl	Oslo	9 Jun
19.91	0.7	Nickel	Ashmeade	JAM	4.7.90	3	VD	Bruxelles	16 Sep
19.95	1.6		Ashmeade			1		Kingston	7 May
19.95	0.8	Jaysuma	Saidy Ndure	NOR	1.7.84	4	WCh	Daegu	3 Sep
19.97	0.7		Saidy Ndure			4	VD	Bruxelles	16 Sep
20.02	0.0		Dix			1		Luzern	21 Jul
20.03	-0.6		Bolt			1	DL	Saint Denis	8 Jul
20.03	-1.2		Bolt			1	DNG	Stockholm	29 Jul
20.05	0.0	Rakieem Mookie	Salaam	USA	5.4.90	1	Big 12	Norman	15 May
20.06	0.5		Dix			1	DL	Doha	6 May
20.13	0.2	LaShawn	Merritt	USA	27.6.86	1		Rieti	10 Sep

Mark	Wind	Name		Nat	Born	Pos	Meet	Venue	Date
20.15	1.5	Steve	Mullings ¶	JAM	29.11.82	2		Kingston	7 May
20.16	-2.0		Dix			1	LGP	London (CP)	6 Aug
20.16	1.1	Bruno	de Barros (10)	BRA	7.1.87	1h1	NC	São Paulo	6 Aug
20.16	1.6	Rondell	Sorrillo	TRI	21.1.86	1	NC	Port of Spain	14 Aug
20.17	-1.0		Lemaitre			1s1	WCh	Daegu	2 Sep
20.18	1.6	Wallace	Spearmon	USA	24.12.84	3		Kingston	7 May
20.19	1.1	Maurice	Mitchell	USA	22.12.89	1	ACC	Durham	23 Apr
20.19	1.1		Dix			1	Pre	Eugene	4 Jun
20.20	1.9	Justin	Gatlin	USA	10.2.82	1		Clermont	21 May
20.20	-0.3	Rasheed	Dwyer	JAM	29.1.89	1	WUG	Shenzhen	19 Aug
20.21	-0.6		Lemaitre			2	DL	Saint Denis	8 Jul
20.21	0.5		de Barros			1	NC	São Paulo	7 Aug
20.25	1.6	Nesta	Carter	JAM	10.11.85	4		Kingston	7 May
20.25	0.9	Darvis	Patton	USA	4.12.77	1s1	NC	Eugene	26 Jun
		(30/17)							
20.27	-0.3	Marvin	Anderson	JAM	12.5.82	1	GS	Ostrava	31 May
20.28	-0.8	Alonso	Edward	PAN	8.12.89	1		Reims	5 Jul
20.29	-0.8	Mario	Forsythe	JAM	30.10.85	2		Reims	5 Jul
		(20)							
20.30	0.5	Femi Seun	Ogunode	QAT	15.5.91	2	DL	Doha	6 May
20.31	1.1	Andrew	Howe	ITA	12.5.85	1	GGala	Roma	26 May
20.31A	0.2	Roberto	Skyers	CUB	12.11.91	1s1	PAm	Guadalajara, MEX	26 Oct
20.32	0.8	Ramil	Guliyev	TUR	29.5.90	1	Cezmi	Istanbul	11 Jun
20.33	0.9	Jeremy	Dodson	USA	30.8.87	2s1	NC	Eugene	26 Jun
20.33A	0.5	Lansford	Spence	JAM	15.12.82	1s3	PAm	Guadalajara, MEX	26 Oct
20.38	1.4	Michael	Mathieu	BAH	24.6.83	1		Nassau	14 May
20.38	0.0	Churandy	Martina	NED	3.7.84	1	NC	Amsterdam	31 Jul
20.39	0.0	Tran	Howell	USA	27.3.88	2	Big 12	Norman	15 May
20.39A	0.2	Sandro	Viana	BRA	26.3.77	2s1	PAm	Guadalajara, MEX	26 Oct
		(30)							
20.41A	1.1	Kirani	James	GRN-J	1.9.92	1		El Paso	16 Apr
20.42	0.7	Jonathan	Borlée	BEL	22.2.88	1		Rabat	5 Jun
20.43	1.9	Greg	Nixon	USA	12.9.81	1		Walnut	4 Jun
20.43	1.1	Marek	Niit	EST	9.8.87	2s2	NCAA	Des Moines	9 Jun
20.43	-1.0	Warren	Weir	JAM	31.10.89	3		Barcelona	22 Jul
20.44	0.6	Horatio	Williams	USA	28.8.89	1s1	NCAA	Des Moines	9 Jun
20.44	0.3	Amr Ibrahim	Seoud	EGY	10.6.86	2h1	WCh	Daegu	2 Sep
20.45	1.9	Jared	Connaughton	CAN	20.7.85	1		Clermont	11 Jun
20.45	0.9	Shawn	Crawford	USA	14.1.78	2s3	NC	Eugene	26 Jun
20.46	2.0	Justin	Austin	USA	8.10.89	1	Big 10	Iowa City	15 May
		(40)							
20.46	0.8	Harry	Aikines-Aryeetey	GBR	29.8.88	1r2		La Chaux-de-Fonds	3 Jul
20.49	1.9	Ameer	Webb	USA	19.3.91	2		Walnut	4 Jun
20.49	0.0	Shinji	Takahira	JPN	18.7.84	1	NC	Kumagaya	11 Jun
20.49A	0.2	Alex	Quiñónez	ECU	11.8.89	3s1	PAm	Guadalajara, MEX	26 Oct
20.50	1.8	Jonathan	Åstrand	FIN	9.9.85	1	ET-1	Izmir	19 Jun
20.51	1.9	Terrell	Wilks	USA	30.12.89	1		Gainesville	16 Apr
20.51	0.5	Daniel	Bailey	ANT	9.9.86	2		Kingston	16 Apr
20.51	-0.8	Alex	Wilson	SUI	19.9.90	1		Genève	28 May
20.51	0.7	Amaru Reto	Schenkel	SUI	28.4.88	1rA		La Chaux-de-Fonds	3 Jul
20.51	0.7	Leon	Baptiste	GBR	23.5.85	2rA		La Chaux-de-Fonds	3 Jul
		(50)							
20.51	-0.9	Ainsley	Waugh	JAM	17.9.81	1		Bottrop	15 Jul
20.51	0.6	Paul	Hession	IRL	27.1.83	1	NC	Dublin (S)	6 Aug
20.51	1.0	Sebastian	Ernst	GER	11.10.84	1rA		Mannheim	13 Aug
20.52	0.7	Jordan	Boase	USA	10.10.85	3		Rabat	5 Jun
20.52	0.3	Michael	Herrera	CUB	5.6.85	1		La Habana	24 Jun
20.52	0.6	James	Ellington	GBR	6.9.85	1		Metz	27 Jun
20.52	0.7	Marc	Schneeberger	SUI	5.7.81	3rA		La Chaux-de-Fonds	3 Jul
20.52	0.3	Kim	Collins	SKN	5.4.76	3h1	WCh	Daegu	2 Sep
20.53	0.9	Kei	Takase	JPN	25.11.88	1		Kumagaya	22 May
20.53	0.5	Jason	Young	JAM	21.3.91	3s1	NC	Kingston	25 Jun
		(60)							
20.53	0.9	Xavier	Carter	USA	8.12.85	4s1	NC	Eugene	26 Jun
20.53	0.9	Calesio	Newman	USA	20.8.86	4s3	NC	Eugene	26 Jun
20.53	0.7	Richard	Kilty	GBR	2.9.89	4rA		La Chaux-de-Fonds	3 Jul
20.54	1.8	Demetrius	Pinder	BAH	13.2.89	1		San Diego	19 Mar
20.54	-0.8	Danny	Talbot	GBR	1.5.91	2		Genève	28 May
20.54	0.6	LaShawn	Butler	USA	3.2.87	2s1	NCAA	Des Moines	9 Jun
20.54	1.5	Brian	Barnett	CAN	10.2.87	1		Victoria	3 Jul

Mark	Wind	Name		Nat	Born	Pos	Meet	Venue	Date
20.54	-0.8	Christian	Malcolm	GBR	3.6.79	5		Reims	5 Jul
20.55	0.7	Torrin	Lawrence	USA	11.4.89	1		Auburn	16 Apr
20.55	0.5	Asafa	Powell	JAM	23.11.82	3		Kingston	16 Apr
		(70)							
20.55	-0.6	Thuso	Mpuang	RSA	1.3.84	1		Stellenbosch	30 Apr
20.55	1.9	Deun	White	USA	13.7.85	3		Walnut	4 Jun
20.55	0.8	Hitoshi	Saito	JPN	9.10.86	1h1	NC	Kumagaya	10 Jun
20.55	0.4	Kenroy	Anderson	JAM	27.6.87	5	NC	Kingston	26 Jun
20.56A	1.2	Charles	Silmon	USA	4.7.91	1		Fort Collins	14 May
20.56	0.0	Sota	Kawatsura	JPN	19.6.89	1		Tokyo	22 May
20.56	-1.4	Likoúrgos-Stéfanos	Tsákonas	GRE	8.3.90	1	EU23	Ostrava	16 Jul
20.56	0.5	Nilson	André	BRA	30.1.86	3	NC	São Paulo	7 Aug
20.57	1.4	Wayde	van Niekerk	RSA-J	23.3.92	1	NC	Durban	10 Apr
20.57	1.1	Brandon	Byram	USA	11.9.88	2		Durham	23 Apr
		(80)							
20.57	1.9	Joel	Redhead	GRN	3.7.86	2		Clermont	21 May
20.57	0.9	Diego Henrique	Cavalcanti	BRA	18.3.91	1h3	NC	São Paulo	6 Aug
20.58A	0.5	Lebogang	Moeng	RSA	10.10.89	1		Germiston	3 Apr
20.58	1.1	Akheem	Gauntlett	USA	26.8.90	2		Fayetteville	6 May
20.59	0.8	Clement	Campbell	JAM	19.2.75	1		Durham	8 May
20.59	2.0	Dentarius	Locke	USA	12.12.89	3	SEC	Athens, GA	15 May
20.59	0.0	Yuichi	Kobayashi	JPN	25.8.89	2		Tokyo	22 May
20.59	-0.6	Brijesh BJ	Lawrence	SKN	27.12.89	1		Marion, IN	28 May
20.59	0.8	James	Alaka	GBR	8.9.89	1s1	EU23	Ostrava	16 Jul
20.60	2.0	Ben Youssef	Meité	CIV	11.11.86	2		Dakar	28 May
		(90)							
20.60	1.9	Brendan	Christian	ANT	11.12.83	3		Clermont	11 Jun
20.60	-0.9	Marlon	Devonish	GBR	1.6.76	2		Bottrop	15 Jul
20.60	1.5	Luke	Fagan	GBR	31.7.88	1		Manchester (SC)	13 Aug
20.61	0.6	Leford	Green	JAM	14.11.86	1h3		Charlotte	18 Mar
20.61	0.8	Arnaldo	Abrantes	POR	27.11.86	2rB		La Chaux-de-Fonds	3 Jul
20.62	0.0	Ryota	Yamagata	JPN-J	10.6.92	3		Tokyo	22 May
20.62	-0.3	Patrick	van Luijk	NED	17.9.84	5	GS	Ostrava	31 May
20.62	-0.4	Sean	McLean	USA-J	23.3.92	1		Raleigh	18 Jun
20.62	1.2	Aziz	Ouhadi	MAR	24.7.84	2	WMilG	Rio de Janeiro	23 Jul
20.63	1.8	Desmond	Jackson	USA	27.4.89	1	NCAA-2	Turlock, CA	28 May
		(100)							
20.63	-0.3	Pavel	Maslák	CZE	21.2.91	3h3	WCh	Daegu	2 Sep

Mark	Wind	Name		Nat	Born	Date
20.64	0.9	Willie	Perry	USA	16.5.87	4 Jun
20.64	0.0	Shota	Iizuka	JPN	25.6.91	11 Jun
20.64	1.9	Gavin	Smellie	CAN	26.6.86	11 Jun
20.64	0.8	Aleksandr	Linnik	BLR	28.1.91	16 Jul
20.64	-0.3		Zhang Peimeng	CHN	13.3.87	10 Sep
20.65	1.9	Gil	Roberts	USA	15.3.89	2 Apr
20.65	1.5	Prezel	Hardy	USA-J	1.6.92	25 Jun
20.65	1.2	Ofentse	Mogawane	RSA	20.2.82	19 Jul
20.65A	0.2	Cristián	Reyes	CHI	5.8.86	26 Oct
20.66	0.6	Calvin	Dascent	ISV	5.4.89	7 May
20.66	0.8	Kevin	Thompson	USA	5.8.86	9 Jul
20.66	0.5	António César	Rodrigues	BRA-J	12.1.93	7 Aug
20.66	1.7	Idrissa	Adam	CMR	28.12.84	15 Sep
20.67	1.7	Zye	Boey	USA	8.5.89	2 Apr
20.67	1.8	Gabriel	Mvumvure	ZIM	23.4.88	16 Apr
20.67	2.0	Philip	Redrick	USA	2.8.88	1 May
20.67	1.1	Emmanuel	Callander	TRI	10.5.84	4 Jun
20.67	-0.1	Lalonde	Gordon	TRI	25.11.88	9 Jul
20.68	0.2	Michael	Rodgers #	USA	24.4.85	23 Apr
20.68		David	Lescay	CUB	19.2.89	13 May
20.68	2.0	Remontay	McClain	USA-J	21.9.92	21 May
20.69	1.1	Eric	de Jesus	BRA	29.1.90	6 Aug
20.70	0.5	Whitney	Prevost	USA	18.9.88	23 Apr
20.70	2.0	Stanley	Azie	NGR	13.3.89	15 May
20.70	-0.9	Noel	Ruíz	CUB	18.1.87	27 May
20.70	1.7	Konstantin	Petryashov	RUS	16.12.84	2 Aug
20.70A	0.1	Rolando	Palacios	HON	3.5.87	26 Oct
20.71	1.0	Edino	Steele	JAM	6.1.87	5 Mar
20.71	0.1	Jeremy	Wariner	USA	31.1.84	18 Mar
20.71	-0.1	Angelo	Taylor	USA	29.12.78	19 Mar
20.71	0.2	Trell	Kimmons	USA	13.7.85	23 Apr
20.71	1.9	Rubin	Williams	USA	9.7.83	4 Jun
20.71	0.9	Leroy	Dixon	USA	20.6.83	26 Jun
20.72A	1.6	Roscoe	Engel	RSA	6.3.89	2 Apr
20.72	0.7	Brian	Dzingai	ZIM	29.4.81	5 Jun
20.72	0.8	Kévin	Borlée	BEL	22.2.88	23 Jul
20.72	-1.0	Oluwasegun	Makinde	CAN	6.7.91	18 Aug
20.73		Delano	Williams	TKS-J	23.12.93	5 Mar
20.73	0.7	Antonio	Sales	USA	26.1.89	16 Apr
20.73	0.6	Sean	Holston	PUR	10.7.89	7 May
20.73	1.3	Tristan	Walker	USA	24.10.87	13 May
20.73A	0.2	Jason	Livermore	JAM	25.4.88	26 Oct
20.74	-2.5	Harry	Adams	USA	27.11.89	26 Mar
20.74	1.0	David	Dickens	USA	19.3.85	26 Mar
20.74	1.4		Huang Xiang	CHN-J	15.5.92	22 May
20.74	0.6	Simon	Magakwe	RSA	25.5.85	27 Jun
20.74	0.7	Rytis	Sakalauskas	LTU	27.6.87	16 Sep
20.75	1.8	Calvin	Smith	USA	10.12.87	26 Mar
20.75	0.2	Maxwell	Dyce	USA	25.4.91	13 May
20.75A	1.2	Mark	Barnes	USA	27.6.89	14 May
20.75	1.8	Josh	Schuler	USA	3.5.89	28 May
20.75	1.2	Akeem	Williams	USA	7.11.90	9 Jun
20.76	1.9	Christian	Taylor	USA	18.6.90	16 Apr
20.76	2.0	Kind	Butler	USA	8.4.88	15 May
20.76	0.8	Steven	Colvert	IRL	24.8.90	16 Jul
20.76A	0.2	Antoine	Adams	SKN	31.8.88	26 Oct
20.76A	0.8	Daniel	Grueso	COL	30.7.85	26 Oct
20.77	0.7	Keenan	Brock	USA-J	1.6.92	16 Apr
20.77A	1.2	Kael	Becerra	CHI	4.11.85	7 May
20.77	0.7	Hugo	Sousa	BRA	5.3.87	11 Jun
20.77	1.3	Barakat	Al-Harthi	OMA	15.6.88	19 Oct
20.78	1.9	Gerald	Phiri	ZAM	6.10.88	16 Apr
20.78	1.1	Charles	Clark	USA	10.8.87	23 Apr
20.78	-0.4	Ryan	Shields	USA	12.5.83	6 May
20.78	0.0	Seiya	Hane	JPN	31.1.90	22 May
20.78	1.5	Manteo	Mitchell	USA	6.7.87	3 Jul
20.78	0.8	Chris	Lawson	USA	12.3.83	9 Jul
20.78	0.4	Roman	Smirnov	RUS	2.9.84	6 Aug
20.78	0.0	David	Alerte	FRA	18.9.84	31 Aug
20.79	0.4	Everett	Walker	USA	3.10.90	16 Apr
20.79	1.4		Xie Zhenye	CHN-J	17.8.93	22 May
20.79	0.9	Matt	Davies	AUS	18.4.85	18 Jun
20.79	-0.5	Sheldon	Mitchell	JAM	.90	25 Jun
20.79	-0.1	Tobias	Unger	GER	10.7.79	28 Jun

Mark	Wind	Name		Nat	Born	Pos	Meet	Venue	Date
20.79	-0.2	Petar	Kremenski	BUL	14.1.91	3		Jul	3 Jul
20.79	0.9	Iván Jesús	Ramos	ESP	31.7.90	3			3 Jul
20.79	-0.5	Mosito	Lehata	LES	8.4.89	16			16 Jul
20.80	1.0	Darrion	Bent	JAM	17.9.90	5			5 Mar
20.80	1.9	Nicholas	Deshong	BAR-J	24.4.92	18			18 Mar
20.80	0.1	Keith	Ricks	USA	9.10.90	1			1 Apr
20.80	0.5	Woodrow	Randall	USA	9.11.89	23			23 Apr
20.80	1.6	Antoine	Thomas	USA	12.3.86	14			14 May
20.80	1.5	Trey	Hadnot	USA-J	8.10.92	25			25 Jun
20.80	1.6	Moriba	Morain	TRI-J	8.10.92	14			14 Aug
20.80	0.2	Matteo	Galvan	ITA	24.8.88	10			10 Sep
20.81	0.6	Bryshon	Nellum	USA	1.5.89				5 Mar
20.81	-2.5	Jon	Juin	HAI	27.12.89				26 Mar
20.81	0.1	Leonardo	Seymore	USA	.90				1 Apr
20.81	0.5	Aílson	Feitosa	BRA	13,8,88				6 Apr
20.81	0.1	Isiah	Young	USA	5.1.90				30 Apr
20.81	1.9	Jamiel	Rolle	BAH	16.4.80				11 Jun
20.81	-0.8	Igor	Bodrov	UKR	9.7.87				4 Aug
			(190)						

Hand timing

Mark	Wind	Name		Nat	Born	Date
20.4	-1.5	José Eduardo	Acevedo	VEN	30.3.86	14 Dec
20.5		Idrissa	Adam	CMR	28.12.84	14 Aug

Wind assisted to 20.80

Mark	Wind	Name		Nat	Born	Pos	Meet	Venue	Date
19.95	2.4		Dix			1	NC	Eugene	26 Jun
19.98	2.4	Darvis	Patton	USA	4.12.77	2	NC	Eugene	26 Jun
19.99	2.6	Maurice	Mitchell	USA	22.12.89	1	NCAA	Des Moines	11 Jun
20.07	2.4	Jeremy	Dodson	USA	30.8.87	3	NC	Eugene	26 Jun
20.08	2.3		Lemaitre			1	NC	Albi	30 Jul
20.11	3.3	Deun	White	USA	13.7.85	1		Norwalk	16 Apr
20.24	3.5	Shawn	Crawford	USA	14.1.78	1h4	NC	Eugene	25 Jun
20.31	2.4	Justin	Austin	USA	8.10.89	5	NC	Eugene	26 Jun
20.32	4.1	Horatio	Williams	USA	28.8.89	1		Baton Rouge	23 Apr
20.34	4.1	Jared	Connaughton	CAN	20.7.85	2		Baton Rouge	23 Apr
20.34	2.5	Ángel David	Rodríguez	ESP	25.4.80	1	NC	Málaga	7 Aug
20.36	3.4	Willie	Perry	USA	16.5.87	1		Gainesville	16 Apr
20.38	2.7	Markquis	Frazier	USA	2.10.90	1	JUCO	Hutchinson, KS	21 May
20.38	2.6	Marek	Niit	EST	9.8.87	2	NCAA	Des Moines	11 Jun
20.40	2.5	Thuso	Mpuang	RSA	1.3.84	1		Donnas	3 Jul
20.41	2.6	Brandon	Byram	USA	11.9.88	4	NCAA	Des Moines	11 Jun
20.47	4.9	Marcus	Boyd	USA	3.3.89	1		Arlington	2 Apr
20.47	2.7	Everett	Walker	USA	3.10.90	2	JUCO	Hutchinson, KS	21 May
20.48	2.8	Philip	Redrick	USA	2.8.88	1		Jacksonville	14 May
20.48	2.7	Rondell	Bartholomew	GRN	7.4.90	3	JUCO	Hutchinson, KS	21 May
20.51	3.4	Xavier	Carter	USA	8.12.85	4		Gainesville	16 Apr
20.52	3.3	LaShawn	Butler	USA	3.2.87	1h2	NC	Eugene	25 Jun
20.53	2.9	Riker	Hylton	JAM	13.12.88	1rB		Baton Rouge	23 Apr
20.54	4.2	Gavin	Smellie	CAN	26.6.86	1		Ottawa	17 Jul
20.55	4.1	Tristan	Walker	USA	24.10.87	3		Baton Rouge	23 Apr
20.55	3.3	Evander	Wells	USA	7.12.87	3h2	NC	Eugene	25 Jun
20.56	4.1	Cordero	Gray	USA	9.5.89	1		Natchitoches	15 May
20.57	2.2	Johan	Wissman	SWE	2.11.82	1		Gävle	14 Aug
20.58	3.9	Desmond	Jackson	USA	27.4.89	1		Stephenville	8 May
20.59	4.3	Roman	Smirnov	RUS	2.9.84	1	NCp	Yerino	5 Jun
20.59	2.3	Martial	Mbandjock	FRA	14.10.85	2	NC	Albi	30 Jul
20.60	3.9	Jamial	Rolle	BAH	16.4.80	1		Troy, AL	23 Apr
20.60	4.4	Shintaro	Matsuo	JPN-J	16.7.93	1		Ise	30 May
20.60	3.3	Leroy	Dixon	USA	20.6.83	4h2	NC	Eugene	25 Jun
20.60	2.5	Iván Jesús	Ramos	ESP	31.7.90	2	NC	Málaga	7 Aug
20.61	2.2	Gabriel	Mvumvure	ZIM	23.4.88				13 May
20.61	4.4	Tatsuro	Suwa	JPN-Y	17.8.94				30 May
20.62	2.3	Teddy	Tinmar	FRA	30.5.87				30 Jul
20.63	2.9	Roscoe	Engel	RSA	6.3.89				19 Mar
20.64	4.1	Justin	Walker	USA	30.11.90				15 May
20.65	5.3	Marvin	Bonde	ZIM	23.7.84				14 May
20.65	2.6	Pierre-Alexis	Pessonneaux	FRA	25.11.87				3 Jul
20.67	2.6	Jon	Juin	HAI	17.12.89				9 Apr
20.67	2.5	Aleksandr	Khyutte	RUS	29.9.88				4 Jun
20.68	4.1	Errol	Nolan	USA	18.8.91				23 Apr
20.69	4.3	Konstantin	Petryashov	RUS	16.12.84				5 Jun
20.72	2.8	Leonardo	Seymore	USA	.90				16 Apr
20.72		Aaron	Ernest	USA-J	11.8.93				4 Jun
20.72	2.4		Huang Xiang	CHN-J	15.5.92				17 Jul
20.73	2.2	Rodney	Martin	USA	22.12.82				16 Apr
20.73	3.1	Darius	Law	USA	24.7.89				8 May
20.73	2.8	Dennis	Moore	USA	.82				14 May
20.73	?w	Steven	Colvert	IRL	24.8.90				26 Jun
20.73	2.4	Rouven	Christ	GER	12.4.88				13 Aug
20.76	4.4	Shotaro	Aikyo	JPN-Y	8.11.94				30 May
20.76	3.9	Elijah	Hall-Thompson	USA-Y	22.8.94				30 Jul
20.77	3.9	Trevante	Rhodes	USA	10.2.90				25 Mar
20.77	2.7	Niko	Williams-Richey	USA	6.7.91				21 May
20.77	3.5	Mark	Lewis-Francis	GBR	4.9.82				22 May
20.78	2.7	Darius	White	USA	27.8.91				21 May
20.79	2.8	Tabarie	Henry	ISV	1.12.87				16 Apr
20.79	2.5	Edgar	Pérez	ESP	18.9.88				7 Aug
20.80	3.2	Lewis	Banda	ZIM	16.9.82				2 Apr
20.80	4.2	Dontae	Richards-Kwok	CAN	1.3.89				17 Jul

Best at low altitude

Mark	Wind	Name	Pos	Venue	Date
20.41	0.8	Spence	1	Kingston	21 May
20.42	1.1	Viana	2s1 NC	São Paulo	6 Aug

20.60 1.9 Silmon 16 Apr, 20.78 0.4 Reyes 6 Aug
20.75 0.0 Skyers 17 Jun, 20.53w 2.2 K James 23 Jul

Indoors

Mark	Wind	Name		Nat	Born	Pos	Meet	Venue	Date
20.42		Sebastian	Ernst	GER	11.10.84	1	NC	Leipzig	27 Feb
20.61		Tony	McQuay	USA	16.4.90	1	SEC	Fayetteville	27 Feb
20.65		Alexander	Kosenkow	GER	14.3.77				27 Feb
20.79		Trevor J.	Graham	USA	27.7.89				26 Feb

Drugs disqualification

20.11   0.4 Steve   Mullings ¶   JAM   29.11.82   (1)   NC   Kingston   26 Jun
20.17 -1.0 (1) Barcelona 22 Jul, 20.22 0.2 (1) Arzana 30 Jul, 20.25 0.5 (1s1) NC Kingston 25 Jun

---

+ intermediate time in longer race, A made at an altitude of 1000m or higher, D made in a decathlon, h made in a heat, qf quarter-final, sf semi-final, i indoors, Q qualifying round, r race number, -J juniors, -Y youths (b. 1994 or later)

Mark		Name	Nat	Born	Pos	Meet	Venue	Date

JUNIORS

See main list for top 4 juniors. 11 performances by 7 men to 20.68. Additional marks and further juniors:

Mark		Name		Nat	Born	Pos	Meet	Venue	Date
James	20.58Ai		1		Albuquerque	21 Jan			
van Niekerk	20.67A	0.9	1	NC-j	Germiston	3 Apr			
McLean	20.64	1.5	1	NC-j	Eugene	25 Jun			
Rodrigues	20.67	0.9	2h3	NC	São Paulo	7 Aug			
20.65	1.5	Prezel	Hardy	USA	1.6.92	2	NC-j	Eugene	25 Jun
20.66	0.5	António César	Rodrigues	BRA	12.1.93	5	NC	São Paulo	7 Aug
20.68	2.0	Remontay	McClain	USA	21.9.92	1		Norwalk	21 May
20.73		Delano	Williams	TKS	23.12.93	1		Montego Bay	5 Mar
20.74	1.4		Huang Xiang	CHN	15.5.92	1		Jiaxing	22 May
20.77	0.7	Keenan	Brock (10)	USA	1.6.92	2		Auburn	16 Apr
20.79	1.4		Xie Zhenye	CHN	17.8.93	2		Jiaxing	22 May
20.80	1.9	Nicholas	Deshong	BAR-	24.4.92	1J		Bridgetown	18 Mar
20.80	1.5	Trey	Hadnot	USA-	8.10.92	3	NC-j	Eugene	25 Jun
20.80	1.6	Moriba	Morain	TRI	8.10.92	2	NC	Port of Spain	14 Aug
20.82	1.7	Arman	Hall	USA-Y	14.2.94	1		Miami	5 Mar
20.82	0.0	Akiyuki	Hashimoto	JPN-Y	18.11.94	1		Nagoya	23 Oct
20.83A	1.0	Gideon	Trotter	RSA	3.3.92	1s1	NC-j	Germiston	3 Apr
20.86	0.2	Aaron	Ernest	USA	8.11.93	1		Mobile	2 Apr
20.87	1.2	Waymon	Storey	USA	10.5.92	3		Athens, GA	9 Apr
20.89A	0.8	Siphelo	Ngqubaza (20)	RSA	4.2.93	2	NC-j	Germiston	3 Apr
20.89	-0.8	Davonte	Stewart	USA	.93	1		Norwalk	21 May
20.89A	0.2	Trae	Armstrong	USA-Y	.94+	1		Albuquerque	4 May
20.89	1.1	Stephen	Newbold	BAH	5.8.94	1	WY	Villeneuve d'Ascq	10 Jul

Wind assisted

Mark		Name		Nat	Born	Pos	Meet	Venue	Date
James	20.53	3.3	1	PAm-J	Miramar	23 Jul	20.62	3.6 1h3 PAm-J Miramar	23 Jul
20.60	4.4	Shintaro	Matsuo	JPN	16.7.93	1		Ise	30 May
20.61	4.4	Tatsuro	Suwa	JPN-Y	17.8.94	2		Ise	30 May
20.72		Aaron	Ernest	USA-J	11.8.93	1		Montgomery	4 Jun
20.72	2.4		Huang Xiang	CHN-J	15.5.92	1		Nanchang	17 Jul
20.76	4.4	Shotaro	Aikyo	JPN-Y	8.11.94	3		Ise	30 May
20.76	3.9	Elijah	Hall-Thompson	USA-Y	22.8.94	1		Wichita	30 Jul
20.88	2.3	Dedric	Dukes	USA	4.2.92	2		Jacksonville	19 Mar

200 METRES STRAIGHT

At Manchester 15 May: (+2.3) 1. Martial Mbandjock FRA 14.10.85 20.35w, 2. Kim Collins SKN 5.4.76 20.43w

300 METRES

Mark	Name		Nat	Born	Pos	Meet	Venue	Date
32.10	Jonathan	Borlée	BEL	22.2.88	1		Kessel-Lo	13 Aug
32.41	Pavel	Maslák	CZE	21.2.91	1		Pardubice	13 Aug
32.78	Erison	Hurtault	DMA	29.12.84	2		Kessel-Lo	13 Aug

During 400m race: WCh Daegu 30 Aug: LaShawn Merritt 32.5, Kirani James 32.6, Kevin Borlée 32.7, Jermaine Gonzales 32.7, Rondell Bartholomew 32.7.　Eugene 25 Jun: all USA: Jeremy Wariner 32.8, Tony McQuay 32.9
Indoors:　At Liévin 8 Feb: 1. Leslie Djhone FRA 18.3.81 32.68, 2. Roman Smirnov RUS 2.9.84 32.75

400 METRES

Mark	Name		Nat	Born	Pos	Meet	Venue	Date
44.35	LaShawn	Merritt	USA	27.6.86	1h3	WCh	Daegu	28 Aug
44.36	Kirani	James	GRN-J	1.9.92	1	WK	Zürich	8 Sep
44.60		James			1	WCh	Daegu	30 Aug
44.61		James			1	LGP	London (CP)	5 Aug
44.63		Merritt			2	WCh	Daegu	30 Aug
44.65	Rondell	Bartholomew	GRN	7.4.90	1		Lubbock	2 Apr
44.65A	Nery	Brenes	CRC	25.9.85	1	PAm	Guadalajara, MEX	26 Oct
44.67		Merritt			2	WK	Zürich	8 Sep
44.68	Tony	McQuay	USA	16.4.90	1	NC	Eugene	25 Jun
44.69	Jermaine	Gonzales	JAM	26.11.84	1	DNG	Stockholm	29 Jul
44.71A	Luguelin	Santos	DOM-J	12.11.93	2	PAm	Guadalajara, MEX	26 Oct
44.74	Kévin	Borlée	BEL	22.2.88	1		Madrid	9 Jul
44.74		Merritt			2	DNG	Stockholm	29 Jul
44.76		Merritt			1s1	WCh	Daegu	29 Aug
44.77		K Borlée			2h3	WCh	Daegu	28 Aug
44.78	Demetrius	Pinder	BAH	13.2.89	1	NC	Freeport	25 Jun
44.78	Jonathan	Borlée (10)	BEL	22.2.88	1	VD	Bruxelles	16 Sep
44.79		McQuay			1s1	NC	Eugene	24 Jun
44.79	Chris	Brown	BAH	15.10.78	3	DNG	Stockholm	29 Jul
44.82	Angelo	Taylor	USA	29.12.78	4	DNG	Stockholm	29 Jul
44.82		Bartholomew			1h1	WCh	Daegu	28 Aug
44.83	Tabarie	Henry	ISV	1.12.87	1		Baton Rouge	2 Apr
44.84	Renny	Quow	TRI	25.8.87	2h1	WCh	Daegu	28 Aug

Mark	Name		Nat	Born	Pos	Meet	Venue	Date	
44.85		Gonzales			2	LGP	London (CP)	5	Aug
44.86A	Louis 'L.J.'	van Zyl	RSA	20.7.85	1		Germiston	26	Mar
44.86		James			1	SEC	Athens, GA	15	May
44.87		Pinder			1	Big 12	Norman	15	May
44.87		McQuay			1s1	NCAA	Des Moines	8	Jun
44.88	Jeremy	Wariner	USA	31.1.84	1		Baie Mahault	7	May
44.90		K Borlée			3	WCh	Daegu	30	Aug
	(30/16)								
44.91	Michael	Berry	USA	10.12.91	1	Pac-10	Tucson	14	May
44.95	Williams	Collazo	CUB	31.8.86	2		Madrid	9	Jul
44.98	Greg	Nixon	USA	12.9.81	3	NC	Eugene	25	Jun
45.01A	Ramon	Miller	BAH	17.2.87	3	PAm	Guadalajara, MEX	26	Oct
	(20)								
45.05	Joey	Hughes	USA	26.10.90	2	Pac-10	Tucson	14	May
45.11	Jamaal	Torrance	USA	20.7.83	4	NC	Eugene	25	Jun
45.13	Rabah	Yousif	SUD	11.12.86	1		Lapinlahti	24	Jul
45.19	Miles	Smith	USA	24.9.84	1		Luzern	21	Jul
45.22	Gil	Roberts	USA	15.3.89	2s1	NCAA	Des Moines	8	Jun
45.23	Yuzo	Kanemaru	JPN	18.9.87	1		Daegu	12	May
45.24	David	Neville	USA	1.6.84	2		Daegu	12	May
45.26	Calvin	Smith	USA	10.12.87	2s1	NC	Eugene	24	Jun
45.27	Marcin	Marciniszyn	POL	7.9.82	1	NC	Bydgoszcz	12	Aug
45.29	Josh	Mance	USA-J	21.3.92	3s1	NCAA	Des Moines	8	Jun
	(30)								
45.29	Bryan	Miller	USA	31.5.89	3s2	NCAA	Des Moines	8	Jun
45.30	Errol	Nolan	USA	18.8.91	4s2	NCAA	Des Moines	8	Jun
45.30	Riker	Hylton	JAM	13.12.88	1	NC	Kingston	26	Jun
45.30	Martyn	Rooney	GBR	3.4.87	2h5	WCh	Daegu	28	Aug
45.34	Jordan	Boase	USA	10.10.85	3	GS	Ostrava	31	May
45.41	Femi Seun	Ogunode	QAT	15.5.91	4s3	WCh	Daegu	29	Aug
45.42	Marcus	Boyd	USA	3.3.89	3	Big 12	Norman	15	May
45.42	Michael	Bingham	GBR	13.4.86	1rB	adidas	New York	11	Jun
45.42	Kerron	Clement	USA	31.10.85	4s2	NC	Eugene	24	Jun
45.42	Marcell	Deák Nagy	HUN-J	28.1.92	1	EJ	Tallinn	22	Jul
	(40)								
45.42	Oral	Thompson	JAM	11.12.82	1		Mucurapo	31	Jul
45.44	Youssef Ahmed	Al-Masrahi	KSA	31.12.87	1	ArabG	Doha	16	Dec
45.46	Christian	Taylor	USA	18.6.90	1	Fla R	Gainesville	1	Apr
45.46	Leford	Green	JAM	14.11.86	2	NC	Kingston	26	Jun
45.46	Lansford	Spence	JAM	15.12.82	3	NC	Kingston	26	Jun
45.47	Lebogang	Moeng	RSA	10.10.89	1s1	NC	Durban	9	Apr
45.51	Lalonde	Gordon	TRI	25.11.88	1		Rabat	5	Jun
45.51	Brandon	O'Connor	USA	2.9.89	4s1	NCAA	Des Moines	8	Jun
45.51	Zwede	Hewitt	TRI	10.6.89	5s1	NCAA	Des Moines	8	Jun
45.51	Allodin	Fothergill	JAM	2.7.87	4	VD	Bruxelles	16	Sep
	(50)								
45.53	Noel	Ruíz	CUB	18.1.87	1	Alba	Barquisimeto	27	Jul
45.54	Michael	Mathieu	BAH	24.6.83	2		Strasbourg	12	Jun
45.55	Pavel	Trenikhin	RUS	24.3.86	5h3	WCh	Daegu	28	Aug
45.56	Bryshon	Nellum	USA	1.5.89	3	Pac-10	Tucson	14	May
45.56	Thomas	Schneider	GER	7.11.88	4	GS	Ostrava	31	May
45.56	Luke	Lennon-Ford	GBR	5.5.89	1		La Chaux-de-Fonds	3	Jul
45.58	Steven	Solomon	AUS-J	16.5.93	1	NC	Melbourne	17	Apr
45.59	Ofentse	Mogawane	RSA	20.2.82	1		Zeulenroda	29	May
45.60	Maurice	McNeal	USA	4.1.91	1h2	Pac-10	Tucson	13	May
45.60A	Arizmendi	Peguero	DOM	7.8.80	1		Bogotá	13	Aug
	(60)								
45.61	Caleb	Williams	USA	14.12.90	4		Baton Rouge	2	Apr
45.61	Torrin	Lawrence	USA	11.4.89	1		Athens, GA	9	Apr
45.61	Chris	Clarke	GBR	25.1.90	2	NC	Birminggham	31	Jul
45.62	Peter	Matthews	JAM	13.11.89	2	WUG	Shenzhen	18	Aug
45.63	DeWayne	Barrett	JAM	26.9.81	2s1	NC	Kingston	25	Jun
45.63	Conrad	Williams	GBR	20.3.82	1		Amsterdam	6	Aug
45.64	Mychal	Dungey	USA	13.10.88	1		Waco	23	Apr
45.68A	Willie	de Beer	RSA	14.3.88	2		Germiston	26	Mar
45.69	Teddy	Venel	FRA	16.3.85	1		Kessel-Lo	13	Aug
45.70	Andrew	Howe	ITA	12.5.85	1		Pavia	8	May
	(70)								
45.70	Richard	Strachan	GBR	18.11.86	2		Velenje	28	Jun
45.70A	Anderson	Mutegi	KEN	1.5.87	1	NC	Nairobi	16	Jul
45.70	Erison	Hurtault	DMA	29.12.84	1		Ninove	6	Aug

Mark	Name		Nat	Born	Pos	Meet	Venue	Date
45.71	Josh	Scott	USA	9.3.85	6s1	NC	Eugene	24 Jun
45.71A	Ânderson	Henriques	BRA-J	3.3.92	2h1	PAm	Guadalajara, MEX	26 Oct
45.72	Robert	Tobin	GBR	20.12.83	1		Szczecin	25 Jun
45.73	Denis	Alekseyev	RUS	26.12.87	1		Moskva	12 Jun
45.75	Brent	LaRue	USA/SLO	26.4.87	4		Velenje	28 Jun
45.76	Marco	Vistali	ITA	3.10.87	2		Pergine Valsugana	23 Jul
45.77	Omar	Cisneros	CUB	19.11.89	1		Sotteville-les-Rouen	2 Jul
(80)								
45.78	Antoine	Drakeford	USA	15.5.87	1		Louisville	13 May
45.78	Clayton	Parros	USA	11.12.90	1s1	NCAA-E	Bloomington	27 May
45.78	Piotr	Wiaderek	POL	5.2.84	2	NC	Bydgoszcz	12 Aug
45.81	Thomas	Murdaugh	USA	25.9.89	1		Tucson	2 Apr
45.81	Sajjad	Hashemi	IRI	22.8.91	1	WMilG	Rio de Janeiro	21 Jul
45.82	Maksim	Dyldin	RUS	19.5.87	1	ET	Stockholm	18 Jun
45.82	David	Greene	GBR	11.4.86	3	NC	Birmingham	31 Jul
45.82	Johan	Wissman	SWE	2.11.82	1	NC	Gävle	13 Aug
45.82	Tobi	Ogunmola	NGR-J	20.6.92	2	AfrG	Maputo	13 Sep
45.84	Hideyuki	Hirose	JPN	20.7.89	2	NC	Kumagaya	12 Jun
(90)								
45.84	Ahmed Mohamed	Al-Merjabi	OMA	9.9.90	2	ArabG	Doha	16 Dec
45.85	Ben	Offereins	AUS	3.12.86	1		Perth	1 Apr
45.85	Nigel	Levine	GBR	30.4.89	1	NC-23	Bedford	26 Jun
45.86	Winston	George	GUY	19.5.87	2	Alba	Barquisimeto	27 Jul
45.87	Armanti	Hayes	USA	23.9.87	2		Baton Rouge	23 Apr
45.87	Dwight	Mullings	JAM	10.12.86	4s1	NC	Kingston	25 Jun
45.88	Godday	James	NGR	9.1.84	1	NC	Calabar	23 Jun
45.89	Abiola	Onakoya	NGR	10.10.90	1		Abuja	21 May
45.89	Konstantin	Svechkar	RUS	17.7.84	3	NC	Cheboksary	22 Jul
45.91	Segun	Ogunkole	NGR	11.6.84	2		Abuja	21 May
(100)								
45.91	Michael	Mason	JAM	26.4.87	1		Spanish Town	29 May
45.91	Bershawn	Jackson	USA	8.5.83	6	Pre	Eugene	4 Jun
45.91	Mark	Mutai	KEN	23.3.78	2	WMilG	Rio de Janeiro	21 Jul

Mark	Name		Nat	Born	Date
45.93	Sean	Wroe	AUS	18.3.85	18 Aug
45.94	Andrew	Steele	GBR	19.9.84	9 Jul
45.94	Valentin	Kruglyakov	RUS	22.8.85	18 Aug
45.95	Manteo	Mitchell	USA	6.7.87	15 May
45.95	Noah	Akwu	NGR	23.9.90	15 Jun
45.96	Brian	Gregan	IRL	31.12.89	18 Aug
45.97	Hiroyuki	Nakano	JPN	9.12.88	24 Jul
45.99	Richard	Buck	GBR	14.11.86	3 Jul
46.00	Darius	Law	USA	24.7.89	16 Apr
46.00	Sean	Holston	PUR	10.7.89	7 May
46.00	Yannick	Fonsat	FRA	16.6.88	30 Jul
46.01	Arman	Hall	USA-Y	14.2.94	8 Jul
46.01	Nikita	Uglov	RUS-J	11.10.93	22 Jul
46.02	Akino	Ming	JAM	29.11.90	15 May
46.02	Kacper	Kozlowski	POL	7.12.86	21 Jul
46.03	Edino	Steele	JAM	6.1.87	7 May
46.04	Chris	Troode	AUS	10.2.83	4 Jun
46.04	Daniel	Awde	GBR	22.6.88	31 Jul
46.04	Yoan	Décimus	FRA	30.11.87	10 Aug
46.04	Albert	Bravo	VEN	29.8.87	12 Dec
46.06A	Vincent	Mumo	KEN	3.8.82	16 Jul
46.07A	Drew	Morano	USA	28.3.85	6 May
46.07	Kavahra	Holmes	USA-Y	25.2.94	6 Aug
46.07	Alberto	Aguilar	VEN	9.3.85	12 Dec
46.09	David	Verburg	USA	14.5.91	15 May
46.09	Krasimir	Braykov	BUL	17.4.85	2 Jul
46.09	Michele	Tricca	ITA-J	26.4.93	22 Jul
46.10	John	Steffensen	AUS	30.8.82	4 Jun
46.10	Fernando	de Almeida	BRA	3.8.85	26 Aug
46.11	Kyle	Clemons	USA	27.8.90	8 Jun
46.11	Marek	Niit	EST	9.8.87	9 Aug
46.12	Isaac	Makwala	BOT	29.9.86	11 Jun
46.12	Tavaris	Tate	USA	21.12.90	23 Jun
46.13	Shane	Victor	RSA	29.12.89	10 Apr
46.14A	Jacques	de Swardt	RSA-J	12.8.92	26 Mar
46.15	Javier	Culson	PUR	25.7.84	2 Apr
46.15	Jeremy	Davis	USA	16.6.85	12 May
46.16	Nicholas	Fillon	FRA	14.1.86	30 Jul
46.17	Kevin	Moore	AUS	29.7.90	26 Mar
46.17A	James	Davis	USA	28.3.85	6 May
46.17	Mateusz	Fórmanski	POL	22.2.91	2 Jul
46.17	Antoine	Gillet	BEL	22.3.88	3 Jul
46.18	Andrae	Williams	BAH	11.7.83	25 Jun
46.18	Jonas	Plass	GER	1.8.86	28 Jun
46.18	Mehmet	Güzel	TUR	20.8.91	9 Aug
46.19	Lorenzo	Jiménez	DOM	27.4.90	16 Apr
46.19	James	Harris	USA	18.9.91	15 May
46.19	LaToy	Williams	BAH	28.5.88	25 Jun
46.20	Joel	Redhead	GRN	3.7.86	11 Jun
46.20	Yusuke	Ishitsuka	JPN	19.6.87	12 Jun
46.21	Avard	Moncur	BAH	2.11.78	11 Jun
46.22	Nicholas	Maitland	JAM	89	29 May
46.22	Tremaine	Harris	CAN-J	10.2.92	3 Jul
46.22	Mathieu	Lahaye	FRA	25.12.83	7 Aug
46.24	Yuriy	Trambovetskiy	RUS	27.6.87	22 Jul
46.24	Shaun	de Jager	RSA	28.6.91	12 Dec
46.25	Vladimir	Krasnov	RUS	10.8.90	14 Jul
46.27	James	Howell	USA	26.8.86	30 Apr
46.27	William	Henry	USA-J	5.5.92	14 May
46.27	Jarrin	Solomon	TRI	11.1.86	24 Jul
46.28	Charles	Cox	USA	25.1.89	25 Mar
46.28	Satoshi	Kaneko	JPN	29.1.90	24 Jun
46.28	Akihiro	Urano	JPN	17.8.90	9 Sep
46.29	Kelvin	Furlough	USA	27.8.89	16 Apr
46.29	Kelsey	Caesar	USA	16.9.88	30 Apr
46.29	Tewado	Latty	JAM	13.6.90	8 May
46.29A	Jonathan	Kibet	KEN	5.1.82	16 Jul
(170)					

Drugs disqualification

46.16A	Héctor	Carrasquillo ¶	PUR	30.9.87	30 Apr

With prosthetic limbs

45.07	Oscar	Pistorius	RSA	22.11.86	1		Lignano	19 Jul

Best at low altitude

45.29	Brenes	1rB		Madrid	9 Jul
45.31	R Miller	3h4	WCh	Daegu	28 Aug
45.81	Henriques	1	NC	São Paulo	3 Aug
45.87	de Beer	2	NC	Durban	10 Apr
45.95	Mutegi	2		Houston	15 May
45.95	Peguero	3	WMilG	Rio de Janeiro	21 Jul

Mark	Name	Nat	Born	Pos	Meet	Venue	Date

Indoors

Mark	Name	Nat	Born	Pos	Meet	Venue	Date
44.80	James			1	SEC	Fayetteville	27 Feb
45.54	Leslie Djhone	FRA	18.3.81	1	EI	Paris (B)	5 Mar

Mark	Name	Nat	Born	Date		Mark	Name	Nat	Born	Date
45.99	Marek Niit	EST	9.8.87	11 Feb		46.11A	Michael Courtney	USA	12.6.86	27 Feb
46.03	Neal Braddy	USA	18.10.91	26 Feb		46.22	Brady Gehret	USA-J	9.5.92	12 Mar
46.04	Ben Skidmore	USA	26.5.90	27 Feb		46.23	Amaechi Morton	NGR	30.10.89	29 Jan

Hand timing

Mark	Name	Nat	Born	Pos	Meet	Venue	Date
45.5A	Pako Seribe	BOT	7.4.91	1	NC	Orapa	6 Aug

Mark	Name	Nat	Born	Date		Mark	Name	Nat	Born	Date
45.7	Chris Troode	AUS	10.2.83	29 May		45.7A	Zacharia Kamberuka	BOT	27.12.87	6 Aug
45.7A	Isaac Makwala	BOT	29.9.86	6 Aug		45.8A	Bekeret Desta	ETH	23.5.90	6 May

JUNIORS

See main list for top 7 juniors. 14 performances by 4 men to 45.47. Additional marks and further juniors:

Name	Mark	Pos	Meet	Venue	Date		Mark	Pos	Meet	Venue	Date
James 4+	45.10	1	NCAA	Des Moines	10 Jun		45.20	1s2	WCh	Daegu	28 Aug
	45.12	1		Oxford, MS	23 Apr		45.32	1	ISTAF	Berlin	11 Sep
	45.12	1h4	WCh	Daegu	27 Aug		45.47i	1		Notre Dame	5 Feb
Mance	45.47	1q2	NCAAr	Eugene	27 May						

Mark	Name	Nat	Born	Pos	Meet	Venue	Date
46.01	Arman Hall	USA-Y	14.2.94	1	WY	Villeneuve d'Ascq	8 Jul
46.01	Nikita Uglov	RUS	11.10.93	2	EJ	Tallinn	22 Jul
46.07	Kavahra Holmes (10)	USA-Y	25.2.94	1		New Orleans	6 Aug
46.09	Michele Tricca	ITA	26.4.93	3	EJ	Tallinn	22 Jul
46.14A	Jacques de Swardt	RSA-	12.8.92	3		Germiston	26 Mar
46.22i	Brady Gehret	USA	9.5.92	3	NCAA	College Station	12 Mar
46.22	Tremaine Harris	CAN	10.2.92	2		Victoria	3 Jul
46.27	William Henry	USA	5.5.92	6	Pac10	Tucson	14 May
46.33	Pedro de Oliveira	BRA	17.2.92	1	NC-j	São Paulo	8 Oct
46.34A	Alphas Kishoyian	KEN-Y	.94	6		Nairobi	8 Jun
46.37A	Sadam S. Koumi El Nour	SUD	6.4.94	1	Af-J	Gaborone	13 May
46.39	Wang Weihai	CHN	10.5.92	1h9		Fuzhou	25 Jun
46.39	Marco Lorenzi (20)	ITA	20.6.93	1	NC-j	Bressanone	18 Jun

600 METRES

Mark	Name	Nat	Born	Pos	Meet	Venue	Date
1:14.28+	David Rudisha	KEN	17.12.88	1	in 800	Rieti	10 Sep

Mark	Name	Nat	Born	Date		Mark	Name	Nat	Born	Date
1:16:19+	Abubaker Kaki	SUD	21.6.89	4 Jun		1:15.69	Jackson Kivuva	KEN	11.8.88	6 Feb
1:16.46	Marcin Lewandowski	POL	13.6.87	22 May		1:15.92	Richard Kiplagat	KEN	3.7.84	6 Feb
Indoors						1:16.16	Ismail Ahmad Ismail	SUD	10.9.84	6 Feb
1:15.65	Kevin Borlée	BEL	22.2.88	13 Feb		1:16.32	Marcin Lewandowski	POL	13.6.87	13 Feb

800 METRES

Mark	Name	Nat	Born	Pos	Meet	Venue	Date
1:41.33	David Rudisha	KEN	17.12.88	1		Rieti	10 Sep
1:42.61	Rudisha			1	Herc	Monaco	22 Jul
1:42.91	Rudisha			1	LGP	London (CP)	5 Aug
1:43.13	Abubaker Kaki	SUD	21.6.89	2	LGP	London (CP)	5 Aug
1:43.15	Asbel Kiprop	KEN	30.6.89	2	Herc	Monaco	22 Jul
1:43.30	Adam Kszczot	POL	2.9.89	2		Rieti	10 Sep
1:43.37	Mohammed Aman	ETH-Y	10.1.94	3		Rieti	10 Sep
1:43.46	Rudisha			1		Tomblaine	24 Jun
1:43.50	Aman			1		Milano	18 Sep
1:43.57	Rudisha			2		Milano	18 Sep
1:43.68	Kaki			1	Pre	Eugene	4 Jun
1:43.76A	Rudisha			1	NC	Nairobi	16 Jul
1:43.83	Nick Symmonds	USA	30.12.83	3	Herc	Monaco	22 Jul
1:43.88	Rudisha			1		Melbourne	3 Mar
1:43.91	Rudisha			1	WCh	Daegu	30 Aug
1:43.96	Rudisha			1	VD	Bruxelles	16 Sep
1:43.99	Yuriy Borzakovskiy	RUS	12.4.81	1	Znam	Zhukovskiy	3 Jul
1:43.99	David Mutua	KEN-J	20.4.92	4	Herc	Monaco	22 Jul
1:44.03	Khadevis Robinson	USA	19.7.76	5	Herc	Monaco	22 Jul
1:44.06	Mutua			1		Belém	15 May
1:44.07	Alfred Kirwa Yego (10)	KEN	28.11.86	4		Rieti	10 Sep
1:44.08	Leonard Kosencha	KEN-Y	21.8.94	1	WY	Villeneuve d'Ascq	9 Jul
1:44.13	Boaz Lalang	KEN	8.2.89	3	LGP	London (CP)	5 Aug
1:44.15	Rudisha			1	Athl	Lausanne	30 Jun
1:44.17	Symmonds			1	NC	Eugene	26 Jun
1:44.20	Lalang			2	Znam	Zhukovskiy	3 Jul
1:44.20	Rudisha			1s3	WCh	Daegu	28 Aug
1:44.21	Kléberson Davide	BRA	20.7.85	1	NC	São Paulo	7 Aug
1:44.22	Lalang			6	Herc	Monaco	22 Jul
1:44.25	Ilham Tanui Özbilen (30/14)	TUR	5.3.90	1		Ninove	6 Aug
1:44.31	Rafith Rodríguez	COL	1.6.89	3		Belém	15 May

Mark	Name		Nat	Born	Pos	Meet	Venue	Date	
1:44.40A	Jackson	Kivuva	KEN	11.8.88	2	NC	Nairobi	16	Jul
1:44.49	Kevin	López	ESP	12.6.90	1		Barcelona	22	Jul
1:44.53	Marcin	Lewandowski	POL	13.6.87	5		Rieti	10	Sep
1:44.56	Manuel	Olmedo	ESP	17.5.83	2		Barcelona	22	Jul
1:44.64	Jeff	Riseley	AUS	11.11.86	7		Rieti	10	Sep
	(20)								
1:44.67	Charles	Jock	USA	23.11.89	3	NC	Eugene	26	Jun
1:44.71	Cory	Primm	USA	1.12.88	1rA		Los Angeles (ER)	21	May
1:44.71	Robby	Andrews	USA	29.3.91	1	NCAA	Des Moines	10	Jun
1:44.82	Artur	Ostrowski	POL	10.7.88	1		Königs Wusterhausen	9	Sep
1:44.83	Tyler	Mulder	USA	15.2.87	2rA		Los Angeles (ER)	21	May
1:44.98	Timothy	Kitum	KEN-Y	20.11.94	3	WY	Villeneuve d'Ascq	9	Jul
1:45.04	Andrew	Ellerton	CAN	18.11.83	1	Jerome	Burnaby	1	Jul
1:45.04	Sören	Ludolph	GER	25.2.88	2		Königs Wusterhausen	9	Sep
1:45.04	Andreas	Bube	DEN	13.7.87	6	VD	Bruxelles	16	Sep
1:45.06	Elijah	Greer	USA	24.10.90	3	NCAA	Des Moines	10	Jun
	(30)								
1:45.07A	Job	Kinyor	KEN	2.9.90	4	NC	Nairobi	16	Jul
1:45.11	Amine	Laâlou	MAR	13.5.82	3	Athl	Lausanne	30	Jun
1:45.11	Mauris Surel	Castillo	CUB	19.10.84	1		Sevilla	11	Aug
1:45.12	Michael	Rimmer	GBR	3.2.86	2	DL	Doha	6	May
1:45.14	Ismail Ahmed	Ismail	SUD	10.9.84	4		Belém	15	May
1:45.28	Casimir	Loxsom	USA	17.3.91	2	Jerome	Burnaby	1	Jul
1:45.32	Lutimar	Paes	BRA	14.12.88	5		Belém	15	May
1:45.34	Ryan	Martin	USA	23.3.89	1		Irvine	14	May
1:45.35	Mohamed	Al-Azimi	KUW	16.6.82	3	FBK	Hengelo	29	May
1:45.36	Andrew	Osagie	GBR	19.2.88	5	LGP	London (CP)	5	Aug
	(40)								
1:45.38	Antonio Manuel	Reina	ESP	13.6.81	2		Sevilla	11	Aug
1:45.43	David	Torrence	USA	26.11.85	3rA		Los Angeles (ER)	21	May
1:45.46	Amine	El Manaoui	MAR	20.11.91	4		Milano	18	Sep
1:45.47	Ivan	Tukhtachev	RUS	12.7.89	3	Znam	Zhukovskiy	3	Jul
1:45.47	Nicholas	Kiplagat	KEN-J	20.12.92	5		Milano	18	Sep
1:45.48	Richard	Kiplagat	KEN	3.7.84	4	DL	Doha	6	May
1:45.49	Reuben	Bett	KEN	6.11.84	6		Belém	15	May
1:45.50	Mbulaeni	Mulaudzi	RSA	8.9.80	2	GGala	Roma	26	May
1:45.52	Fred	Samoei	KEN	12.1.86	2	MSR	Walnut	16	Apr
1:45.52	Leonel	Manzano	USA	12.9.84	5		Barcelona	22	Jul
	(50)								
1:45.56	Jeff	Lastennet	FRA	26.8.87	2		Tomblaine	24	Jun
1:45.56	Richard	Jones	USA	15.7.88	3	Jerome	Burnaby	1	Jul
1:45.58A	Andy	González	CUB	17.10.87	1	PAm	Guadalajara, MEX	28	Oct
1:45.59	Anis	Ananenko	BLR	29.11.85	4	Znam	Zhukovskiy	3	Jul
1:45.62	Raidel	Acea	CUB	31.10.90	1	Barr	La Habana	28	May
1:45.62	Mouhcine	El Amine	MAR	8.1.82	3		Reims	5	Jul
1:45.66	Lachlan	Renshaw	AUS	4.2.87	3		Melbourne	3	Mar
1:45.66	Fernando	da Silva	BRA	10.10.86	3	NC	São Paulo	7	Aug
1:45.69	Samson	Ngoepe	RSA	28.1.85	1	NC	Durban	10	Apr
1:45.69	Vyacheslav	Sokolov	RUS	15.12.84	5	Znam	Zhukovskiy	3	Jul
	(60)								
1:45.69	Bram	Som	NED	20.2.80	6	LGP	London (CP)	5	Aug
1:45.74	Anthony	Chemut	KEN-J	17.12.92	1	NA	Heusden	16	Jul
1:45.79	Benson	Seurei	KEN	27.3.88	1		Forbach	29	May
1:45.83	Russell	Brown	USA	6.3.85	4rA		Los Angeles (ER)	21	May
1:45.84	Mahfoud	Brahimi	ALG	24.2.85	1		Bottrop	15	Jul
1:45.86	Duane	Solomon	USA	28.12.84	5rA		Los Angeles (ER)	21	May
1:45.90	Yeimer	López	CUB	20.8.82	5		Reims	5	Jul
1:45.90	Mukhtar	Mohammed	GBR	1.12.90	1		Karlstad	2	Aug
1:45.91	Willie	Brown	USA	20.12.90	2s2	NCAA	Des Moines	8	Jun
1:45.92	Abdulrahman Musaab	Balla	QAT	19.3.89	1	ArabG	Doha	17	Dec
	(70)								
1:45.94	Geoffrey	Matum	KEN	22.11.87	3	WMilG	Rio de Janeiro	22	Jul
1:45.95	Andrew	Wheating	USA	21.11.87	5	Pre	Eugene	4	Jun
1:45.95	Luis Alberto	Marco	ESP	20.8.86	3		Sevilla	11	Aug
1:46.00	Mark	Wieczorek	USA	25.12.84	5	NC	Eugene	26	Jun
1:46.01	Fabiano	Peçanha	BRA	5.6.82	7		Belém	15	May
1:46.01	Robert	Novak	USA	20.3.86	6rA		Los Angeles (ER)	21	May
1:46.02	Diego	Gomes	BRA	19.4.85	4	NC	São Paulo	7	Aug
1:46.06	Edward	Kemboi	KEN	12.12.91	3s2	NCAA	Des Moines	8	Jun
1:46.09	Timothy	Limo	KEN	8.2.87	4		Königs Wusterhausen	9	Sep
1:46.11A	Geoffrey	Rono	KEN	21.4.87	7	NC	Nairobi	16	Jul
	(80)								

Mark	Name		Nat	Born	Pos	Meet	Venue	Date
1:46.14	Prince	Mumba	ZAM	28.8.84	4	Jerome	Burnaby	1 Jul
1:46.17	Sadjad	Moradi	IRI	30.3.83	7s1	WCh	Daegu	28 Aug
1:46.18	Pierre-Ambroise	Bossé	FRA-J	11.5.92	6		Reims	5 Jul
1:46.2A	Ismael	Kombich	KEN	16.10.85	4s2	NC	Nairobi	15 Jul
1:46.21	Miguel	Quesada	ESP	18.9.79	8		Barcelona	22 Jul
1:46.26	Jakub	Holusa	CZE	20.2.88	2		Göteborg	11 Jun
1:46.28	Alex	Rowe	AUS-J	8.7.92	5		Melbourne	3 Mar
1:46.29	Kevin	Hautcoeur	FRA	17.1.85	6		Tomblaine	24 Jun
1:46.29	Tamás	Kazi	HUN	16.5.85	1		Budapest	12 Aug
1:46.30	Julius	Mutekanga	UGA	1.12.87	2		Ninove	6 Aug
(90)								
1:46.32	Taoufik	Makhloufi	ALG	29.4.88	1	AfrG	Maputo	13 Sep
1:46.32	Giordano	Benedetti	ITA	22.5.89	7		Milano	18 Sep
1:46.36	Robin	Schembera	GER	1.10.88	1		Rehlingen	13 Jun
1:46.38	Moussa	Camara	MLI	12.2.88	5h3	WCh	Daegu	27 Aug
1:46.39	Hamza	Driouch	QAT-Y	16.11.94	4	WY	Villeneuve d'Ascq	9 Jul
1:46.4A	Abraham	Kipchirchir	KEN-J	.92	2		Nairobi	8 Jun
1:46.44	Mohamed Ahmed	Hamada	EGY-J	22.10.92	1		Huddinge	12 Jul
1:46.46	Arnoud	Okken	NED	20.4.82	6	FBK	Hengelo	29 May
1:46.46	Ghamanda	Ram	IND	1.7.84	3	AsiC	Kobe	10 Jul
1:46.50	Robert	Lathouwers	NED	8.7.83	8		Reims	5 Jul
(100)								

Mark	Name		Nat	Born	Date
1:46.5A	Isaac	Kipketer	KEN	29.9.83	14 Jul
1:46.5A	Eliud	Rutto	KEN	25.11.85	15 Jul
1:46.52	James	Gurr	AUS	20.12.83	3 Mar
1:46.52	Gareth	Warburton	GBR	23.4.83	5 Aug
1:46.53	Hamid	Oualich	FRA	26.4.88	7 Jun
1:46.59	Stepan	Poistogov	RUS	14.12.86	3 Jul
1:46.62	Daniel	Nghipandulwa	NAM	8.6.89	10 Apr
1:46.62	Nabil	Madi	ALG	9.6.81	24 Jun
1:46.62	David	McCarthy	IRL	16.7.83	19 Jul
1:46.62		Teng Haining	CHN-J	25.6.93	21 Aug
1:46.63	Tetlo	Emmen	USA	24.1.84	16 Apr
1:46.63	Abdelslam	Kénouche	FRA	7.10.80	5 Jul
1:46.65	Kevin	Hicks	USA	7.11.84	21 May
1:46.66	Mor	Seck	SEN	24.9.85	19 Jul
1:46.70	James	Shane	GBR	18.12.89	10 Jul
1:46.7A	Yilma	Gurara	ETH	11.9.90	12 Mar
1:46.7A	Shiferaw	Wole	ETH	23.2.89	12 Mar
1:46.73	Mattias	Claesson	SWE	26.7.86	28 Jun
1:46.74	James	Kaan	AUS	17.9.90	19 Mar
1:46.77	Tevan	Everett	USA	27.7.87	24 Jun
1:46.77	Joe	Thomas	GBR	29.1.88	9 Jul
1:46.8	Edwin	Kemboi	KEN	22.8.86	15 Jul
1:46.81	Harun	Abda	USA	1.1.90	27 May
1:46.82	Nixon	Chepseba	KEN	12.12.90	13 Jun
1:46.83	Dustin	Emrani	ISR	6.1.85	15 Jun
1:46.84	André	Olivier	RSA	29.12.89	10 Apr
1:46.84	Joe	Abbott	USA	3.3.90	27 May
1:46.85	Masato	Yokota	JPN	19.11.87	3 May
1:46.85	Kyle	Smith	CAN	25.1.85	21 May
1:46.85	Sam	Borchers	USA	25.5.88	18 Jun
1:46.89	Joey	Roberts	USA	17.4.90	27 May
1:46.89	Nathan	Brannen	CAN	8.9.82	3 Jul
1:46.89	Nick	Willis	NZL	25.4.83	10 Jul
1:46.89	Youssef Saad	Kamel	BRN	29.3.83	22 Jul
1:46.90	Rachid	Khouia	FRA	9.11.79	12 May
1:46.93	Ignacio	Laguna	ESP	18.5.87	9 Jul
1:46.99	Paul	Renaudie	FRA	2.4.90	11 Jun
1:46.99	Nickson	Tuwei	KEN-J	31.10.92	13 Jun
1:47.00	William	Mathosola	RSA	31.3.90	10 Apr
1:47.00	Ivan	Nesterov	RUS	10.2.85	22 Jul
1:47.0A	Isaac	Rogony	KEN	.87	15 Jul
1:47.01	Jan	Van Den Broeck	BEL	11.3.89	30 Apr
1:47.01	Sadik	Mikhou	MAR	25.7.90	14 May
1:47.01	Joni	Jaako	SWE	24.2.86	28 Jun
1:47.06	Szymon	Krawczyk	POL	29.12.88	12 Aug
1:47.09	Michael	Rutt	USA	28.10.87	10 Jul
1:47.09	Mark	English	IRL-J	18.3.93	13 Aug
1:47.10	Abraham	Chepkirwok	UGA	18.11.88	3 Mar
1:47.10	Karjuan	Williams	USA	5.7.87	4 Jun
1:47.10	Zan	Rudolf	SLO-J	9.5.93	13 Sep
1:47.1A	Isaiah	Kibet	KEN		18 Jun
1:47.11	Quin	Ferguson	CAN	15.7.88	21 May
1:47.11	Silas	Kisorio	KEN	8.1.85	10 Jul
1:47.11	Lukas	Rifesser	ITA	17.7.86	19 Jul
1:47.18	Ismaël	Koné	FRA	30.6.87	29 May
1:47.18	Johan	Rogestedt	SWE-J	27.1.93	28 Jun
1:47.18	Péter	Szemeti	HUN	4.1.88	12 Aug
1:47.18	Adnan Taees	Akkar	IRQ	24.3.80	17 Dec
1:47.19	Sharif	Webb	USA	9.6.89	1 Apr
1:47.20	Mario	Scapini	ITA	2.2.89	19 Jun
1:47.20	Girmay	Hadgu	ERI	5.10.84	20 Jul
1:47.2A	Amon Kibet	Cheruiyot	KEN-Y	20.12.94	8 Jun
1:47.22	Bilal Mansour	Ali	BRN	17.10.83	12 May
1:47.22	Yuriy	Koldin	RUS	1.11.83	3 Jul
1:47.22	Jeroen	D'Hoedt	BEL	10.1.90	6 Aug
1:47.24	Thobias	Ekhamre	SWE	17.9.88	28 Jun
1:47.27	Kyle	Miller	USA	15.5.85	11 Jun
1:47.28	Anthony	Kostelac	USA	4.7.91	4 Jun
1:47.28	Azzine	Boudjémaa	ALG/FRA	17.9.82	27 Jun
1:47.28	Nijel	Amos	BOT-Y	15.3.94	9 Jul
1:47.28	El Nazir	Abdelkader	SUD-Y	.94	17 Dec
1:47.29	Martin	Bischoff	GER	18.7.90	26 Jun
1:47.30	Lance	Roller	USA	24.5.90	24 Jun
1:47.3A	Esrael	Awoke	ETH-Y	5.4.94	5 May
1:47.3	Moise	Joseph	HAI	27.12.81	6 Aug
1:47.31	Kipkurui	Mutai	KEN		4 Jun
1:47.31	Paul	Robinson	IRL	24.5.91	24 Jul
1:47.34	Sajeesh	Joseph	IND	14.1.87	14 Jun
1:47.34	Jordan	Williamsz	AUS-J	21.8.92	24 Jul
1:47.35	Oleg	Kayafa	UKR	4.4.89	31 May
1:47.38	Wesley	Vázquez	PUR-Y	27.3.94	14 May
1:47.42	Martijn	Scheepers	BEL-J	9.2.93	25 May
1:47.43	Bartosz	Nowicki	POL	26.2.84	3 Jun
1:47.43	Brice	Leroy	FRA	26.6.89	2 Jul
1:47.47	Christian	Smith	USA	31.10.83	3 Jul
1:47.47	Girmay	Yohannes	ERI	15.5.81	13 Sep
1:47.49	Mohammed	Al-Salhi	KSA	11.5.86	23 Jul
1:47.50	Igor	Davydov	UKR	12.11.88	3 Aug
1:47.5A	Solomon	Teshome	ETH		5 May
1:47.51	Sebastian	Keiner	GER	22.8.89	9 Sep
1:47.52	Dmitrijs	Jurkevics	LAT	7.1.87	4 Jun
1:47.52A	Geoffrey	Kibet	KEN	.90	4 Jun
1:47.52	Nadim	Mansour	ALG	8.6.88	28 Jul
1:47.54	Ahmed	Mainy	MAR	28.8.86	20 Aug
1:47.55	Golden	Coachman	USA	24.7.84	4 Jun
1:47.55	Jaden	Ostapowich	CAN	19.8.89	15 Jun
1:47.58	Samir	Dahmani	FRA	3.4.91	8 May
1:47.59A	Francis	Kalonzi	KEN	.77	4 Jun
1:47.6A	Linus	Kiplagat	KEN-Y	23.12.94	8 Jun
1:47.62	Marouane	Habti	MAR	13.10.87	14 May
1:47.62	Taylor	Milne (201)	CAN	14.9.81	3 Jul

Indoors

Mark	Name		Nat	Born	Pos	Venue	Date
1:46.35	Robin	Schembera	GER	1.10.88	4	Stuttgart	5 Feb
1:46.72	Sebastian	Keiner	GER	22.8.89			5 Feb
1:47.27	Michael	Preble	USA	15.4.90			5 Mar
1:47.30	Chris	Carrington	USA	29.6.90			12 Feb

Mark	Name		Nat	Born	Pos	Meet	Venue	Date

JUNIORS

See main list for top 11 juniors. 12 performances by 5 men to 1:45.6. Additional marks and further juniors:

Mark	Name		Nat	Born	Pos	Meet	Venue	Date
Aman 2+	1:44.29	2	VD	Bruxelles	16 Sep		1:44.68 2 WY Villeneuve d'Ascq 9 Jul	
	1:44.57	1s1	WCh	Daegu	28 Aug		1:45.17 2h3 WCh Daegu 27 Aug	
Mutua 2+	1:45.55A	5	NC	Nairobi	16 Jul			
1:46.62		Teng Haining	CHN	25.6.93	2	WUG	Shenzhen	21 Aug
1:46.99	Nickson	Tuwei	KEN	31.10.92	5		Rehlingen	13 Jun
1:47.09	Mark	English	IRL	18.3.93	1		Kessel-Lo	13 Aug
1:47.10	Zan	Rudolf	SLO	9.5.93	3		Rovereto	13 Sep
1:47.18	Johan	Rogestedt	SWE	27.1.93	6		Sollentuna	28 Jun
1:47.2A	Amon Kibet	Cheruiyot	KEN-Y	20.12.94	4		Nairobi	8 Jun
1:47.28	Nijel	Amos	BOT-Y	15.3.94	5	WY	Villeneuve d'Ascq	9 Jul
1:47.28	El Nazir	Abdelkader	SUD-Y	.94	4	ArabG	Doha	17 Dec
1:47.3A	Esrael	Awoke (20)	ETH-Y	5.4.94	1	NC	Addis Ababa	5 May

1000 METRES

Mark	Name		Nat	Born	Pos	Meet	Venue	Date
2:15.31	Amine	Laâlou	MAR	13.5.82	1		Rabat	5 Jun
2:15.76	Marcin	Lewandowski	POL	13.6.87	2		Rabat	5 Jun
2:15.84	Mohamed	Al-Azimi	KUW	16.6.82	3		Rabat	5 Jun
2:16.75	Jeff	Riseley	AUS	11.11.86	1	GS	Ostrava	31 May
2:16.99	Adam	Kszczot	POL	2.9.89	2	GS	Ostrava	31 May
2:17.08	Ilham Tanui	Özbilen	TUR	5.3.90	3	GS	Ostrava	31 May
2:17.08	Jakub	Holusa	CZE	20.2.88	4	GS	Ostrava	31 May
2:17.44	Hamza	Driouch	QAT-Y	16.11.94	1		Sollentuna	9 Aug

Mark	Name		Nat	Born	Date		Mark	Name		Nat	Born	Date
2:17.89	Geoffrey	Rono	KEN	21.4.87	31 May		2:18.87	Job	Kinyor	KEN	2.9.90	5 Jun
2:18.15	Ismail Ahmed	Ismail	SUD	10.9.84	5 Jun		2:19.18	Benson	Seurei	KEN	27.3.88	22 May
2:18.50	Arnoud	Okken	NED	20.4.82	14 May		2:19.39	David	Mutua	KEN-J	20.4.92	31 May
2:18.53	Pierre-Ambroise Bossé		FRA-J	11.5.92	10 Jul		2:19.4e	Valentin	Smirnov	RUS	13.2.86	4 Jun

Indoors

Mark	Name		Nat	Born	Pos	Meet	Venue	Date
2:17.55	Abubaker	Kaki	SUD	21.6.89	1	XL-Galan	Stockholm	22 Feb

Mark	Name		Nat	Born	Date		Mark	Name		Nat	Born	Date
2:17.81	Boaz	Lalang	KEN	8.2.89	19 Feb		2:18.91	Augustine	Choge	KEN	21.1.87	22 Feb
2:18.46	Jackson	Kivuva	KEN	11.8.88	19 Feb		2:19.03	Bethwel	Birgen	KEN	6.8.88	22 Feb
2:18.56	Andrew	Osagie	GBR	19.2.88	19 Feb		2:19.12	Deresse	Mekonnen	ETH	20.10.87	22 Feb

More JUNIORS

Mark	Name		Nat	Born	Pos	Meet	Venue	Date
2:18.53	Pierre-Ambroise	Bossé	FRA	11.5.92	1		Paris	10 Jul
2:19.39	David	Mutua	KEN	20.4.92	6	GS	Ostrava	31 May

1500 METRES

Mark	Name		Nat	Born	Pos	Meet	Venue	Date
3:30.46	Asbel	Kiprop	KEN	30.6.89	1		Rieti	10 Sep
3:30.47	Silas	Kiplagat	KEN	20.8.89	1	Herc	Monaco	22 Jul
3:30.94	Nixon	Chepseba	KEN	12.12.90	1	Hanz	Zagreb	13 Sep
3:31.14	Augustine	Choge	KEN	21.1.87	1	ISTAF	Berlin	11 Sep
3:31.37	Ilham Tanui	Özbilen	TUR	5.3.90	2	Hanz	Zagreb	13 Sep
3:31.39A		Kiplagat			1	NC	Nairobi	16 Jul
3:31.42		Chepseba			1	DL	Shanghai	15 May
3:31.60	Abdelati	Iguider	MAR	25.3.87	2	ISTAF	Berlin	11 Sep
3:31.66		Chepseba			3	ISTAF	Berlin	11 Sep
3:31.74		Chepseba			2	Herc	Monaco	22 Jul
3:31.76		Kiprop			2	DL	Shanghai	15 May
3:31.76	Abubaker	Kaki	SUD	21.6.89	3	Herc	Monaco	22 Jul
3:31.79	Nick	Willis	NZL	25.4.83	4	Herc	Monaco	22 Jul
3:31.82	Mohamed Othman	Shahween	KSA	15.2.86	1	FBK	Hengelo	29 May
3:31.84		Chepseba			3	DL	Doha	6 May
3:31.84	Mohammed	Moustaoui (10)	MAR	2.4.85	4	ISTAF	Berlin	11 Sep
3:31.86	Haron	Keitany	KEN	17.12.83	2	FBK	Hengelo	29 May
3:31.90	Mekonnen	Gebremedhin	ETH	11.10.88	3	FBK	Hengelo	29 May
3:31.92	Amine	Laâlou	MAR	13.5.82	1	Nebiolo	Torino	10 Jun
3:32.02	Caleb	Ndiku	KEN-J	9.10.92	4	FBK	Hengelo	29 May
3:32.15		Kiplagat			2	DL	Doha	6 May
3:32.15		Laâlou			1	DL	Saint Denis	8 Jul
3:32.23		Özbilen			5	ISTAF	Berlin	11 Sep
3:32.26A		Kiprop			2	NC	Nairobi	16 Jul
3:32.28		Gebremedhin			3	DL	Doha	6 May
3:32.36		Gebremedhin			3	DL	Shanghai	15 May
3:32.45	Collins	Cheboi	KEN	25.9.87	5	Herc	Monaco	22 Jul
3:32.47A	Daniel Kipchirchir	Komen	KEN	27.11.84	3	NC	Nairobi	16 Jul
3:32.70		Kiplagat			4	DL	Shanghai	15 May
3:32.71		Gebremedhin			6	ISTAF	Berlin	11 Sep
	(30/16)							

Mark	Name		Nat	Born	Pos	Meet	Venue	Date	
3:32.90	Deresse	Mekonnen	ETH	20.10.87	6	Herc	Monaco	22	Jul
3:33.11	Bernard	Lagat	USA	12.12.74	3	DL	Saint Denis	8	Jul
3:33.18	Diego	Ruíz	ESP	5.2.82	3		Barcelona	22	Jul
3:33.42	Jeff	Riseley	AUS	11.11.86	7	Herc	Monaco	22	Jul
	(20)								
3:33.53	Gideon	Gathimba	KEN	9.3.80	3	Hanz	Zagreb	13	Sep
3:33.59	Lopez	Lomong	USA	1.1.85	4		Barcelona	22	Jul
3:33.60	Florian	Carvalho	FRA	9.3.89	8	Herc	Monaco	22	Jul
3:33.65	Remmy Ndiwa	Limo	KEN	3.2.88	7	DL	Doha	6	May
3:33.66	Leonel	Manzano	USA	12.9.84	5	DL	Saint Denis	8	Jul
3:33.69	Mehdi	Baala	FRA	17.8.78	9	Herc	Monaco	22	Jul
3:33.75	Yoann	Kowal	FRA	28.5.87	7	DL	Saint Denis	8	Jul
3:33.86	Mahiedine	Mekhissi-Benabbad	FRA	15.3.85	2		Rabat	5	Jun
3:34.01	Fouad	El Kaam #	MAR	27.5.88	3		Rabat	5	Jun
3:34.13	Dawit	Wolde	ETH	19.5.91	1		Oordegem	2	Aug
	(30)								
3:34.32	Ayanleh	Souleiman	DJI-J	3.12.92	1	ArabG	Doha	20	Dec
3:34.38	Ismael	Kombich	KEN	16.10.85	8	DL	Doha	6	May
3:34.39	Andrew	Wheating	USA	21.11.87	9	DL	Saint Denis	8	Jul
3:34.4	Taoufik	Makhloufi	ALG	29.4.88	1		Alger	8	Jul
3:34.43	Hamza	Driouch	QAT-Y	16.11.94	2	ArabG	Doha	20	Dec
3:34.44	Manuel	Olmedo	ESP	17.5.83	10	DL	Saint Denis	8	Jul
3:34.45	Artur	Ostrowski	POL	10.7.88	6	Hanz	Zagreb	13	Sep
3:34.46	Matt	Centrowitz	USA	18.10.89	10	Herc	Monaco	22	Jul
3:34.46	Ciarán	O'Lionáird	IRL	11.4.88	2		Oordegem	2	Aug
3:34.59	Bethwel	Birgen	KEN	6.8.88	7	DL	Shanghai	15	May
	(40)								
3:34.59	Zebene	Alemayehu	ETH-J	4.9.92	2		Cottbus	25	Jun
3:34.61	Mohamed	Al-Garni	QAT-J	2.7.92	3	ArabG	Doha	20	Dec
3:34.67	Benson	Seurei	KEN	27.3.88	2		Rehlingen	13	Jun
3:34.7	Tarek	Boukensa	ALG	19.11.81	2		Alger	8	Jul
3:34.72	Soresa	Fida	ETH-J	27.5.93	3		Cottbus	25	Jun
3:35.07	Geoffrey	Rono	KEN	21.4.87	8	DL	Shanghai	15	May
3:35.09+	Yenew	Alamirew	ETH	27.5.90	5	Pre	Eugene	4	Jun
3:35.2	Abderrahmane	Anou	ALG	29.1.91	3		Alger	8	Jul
3:35.43A	Hillary	Maiyo	KEN-J	2.10.93	1	Af-J	Gaborone	13	May
3:35.52	Brimin	Kipruto	KEN	31.7.85	6	FBK	Hengelo	29	May
	(50)								
3:35.54	Geoffrey	Barusei	KEN-Y	.94	2		Gaborone	13	May
3:35.55	Francisco Javier	Abad	ESP	18.8.81	7	Hanz	Zagreb	13	Sep
3:35.61	Aman	Wote (Wetiye)	ETH	18.4.84	1		Sotteville	2	Jul
3:35.70	Russell	Brown	USA	3.3.85	1	MSR	Walnut	15	Apr
3:35.71	Tesfaye	Cheru	ETH-J	2.3.93	3		Rieti	10	Sep
3:35.74	Carsten	Schlangen	GER	31.12.80	14	DL	Saint Denis	8	Jul
3:35.80	Juan Carlos	Higuero	ESP	3.8.78	7		Barcelona	22	Jul
3:35.80	Nathan	Brannen	CAN	8.9.82	3		Oordegem	2	Aug
3:35.89	Chris	Solinsky	USA	5.12.84	2	MSR	Walnut	15	Apr
3:35.95	David	Torrence	USA	26.11.85	3rB	DNG	Stockholm	29	Jul
	(60)								
3:36.05	Imad	Touil	ALG	11.2.89	4		Rehlingen	13	Jun
3:36.07	Jeroen	D'Hoedt	BEL	10.1.90	4		Oordegem	2	Aug
3:36.09	Otmane	Belharbazi	FRA	3.11.88	12	Herc	Monaco	22	Jul
3:36.14	Valentin	Smirnov	RUS	13.2.86	1	NC	Cheboksary	24	Jul
3:36.15A	Jacob	Araptany	UGA-J	11.2.92	1h2	NC	Kampala	22	Jul
3:36.22	James	Shane	GBR	18.12.89	1	NC	Birmingham	31	Jul
3:36.25	Miles	Batty	USA	1.6.87	3	MSR	Walnut	15	Apr
3:36.25	Yassine	Bensghir	MAR	3.1.83	9		Rabat	5	Jun
3:36.33	Will	Leer	USA	15.4.85	4rB	DNG	Stockholm	29	Jul
3:36.45	Henok	Legesse	ETH	19.9.88	1		Lignano	19	Jul
	(70)								
3:36.47	Andrew	Baddeley	GBR	20.6.82	15	DL	Saint Denis	8	Jul
3:36.51	Cornelius	Ndiwa	KEN	17.12.88	5		Rieti	10	Sep
3:36.60	Mohamed	Bensghir	MAR	16.11.91	5		Cottbus	25	Jun
3:36.64	Ryan	Gregson	AUS	26.4.90	2		Sollentuna	28	Jun
3:36.68	Bartosz	Nowicki	POL	26.2.84	5		Rehlingen	13	Jun
3:36.71	Taylor	Milne	CAN	14.6.81	5		Oordegem	2	Aug
3:36.71	Grégory	Beugnet	FRA	14.9.87	6		Oordegem	2	Aug
3:36.79	Vyacheslav	Sokolov	RUS	20.5.84	2	NC	Cheboksary	24	Jul
3:36.82	Kyle	Miller	USA	15.5.85	2		Los Angeles (ER)	21	May
3:36.87	Collis	Birmingham	AUS	27.12.84	7		Rieti	10	Sep
	(80)								

Mark	Name		Nat	Born	Pos	Meet	Venue	Date
3:36.90	Stephan	Eberhardt	GER	12.1.85	6		Rehlingen	13 Jun
3:36.96	Eduard	Villanueva	VEN	29.12.84	5s2	WCh	Daegu	1 Sep
3:37.00	Nick	McCormick	GBR	11.9.81	3		Sollentuna	28 Jun
3:37.15	Andrew	Bumbalough	USA	14.3.87	6		Los Angeles (ER)	21 May
3:37.19	Jordan	McNamara	USA	7.3.87	2		Lignano	19 Jul
3:37.21	Lander	Tijtgat	BEL	6.4.83	7		Oordegem	2 Aug
3:37.23	Mulugeta	Wondimu	ETH	28.2.85	3	Kuso	Szczecin	25 Jun
3:37.23	Ben	Blankenship	USA	15.12.88	1		Kortrijk	9 Jul
3:37.24	Álvaro	Fernández	ESP	7.4.81	9		Barcelona	22 Jul
3:37.25	Nicholas	Kemboi	KEN	18.12.89	1	Bisl	Oslo	9 Jun
(90)								
3:37.35	Dmitrijs	Jurkevics	LAT	7.1.87	4		Sollentuna	28 Jun
3:37.38	Ali Abubaker	Kamal	QAT	8.11.83	1	Gulf CG	Madinat Isa	19 Oct
3:37.40	Bader	Rassioui	MAR	8.6.85	8		Rehlingen	13 Jun
3:37.53	Craig	Mottram	AUS	18.6.80	1		Uden	2 Jul
3:37.56	Craig	Miller	USA	3.8.87	1		Nijmegen	25 May
3:37.56	Geoffrey	Martinson	CAN	26.3.86	2	Jerome	Burnaby	1 Jul
3:37.67	Merihun	Crespi	ITA	15.12.88	1		Milano	28 Sep
3:37.68	Dorian	Ulrey	USA	11.7.87	3		Lignano	19 Jul
3:37.74	Vickson	Polonet	KEN	2.7.85	3	Odlozil	Praha	13 Jun
3:37.77	Jamel	Aarrass	FRA	15.11.81	2		Kortrijk	9 Jul
(100)								

Mark	Name		Nat	Born	Date
3:37.82	Alan	Webb	USA	13.1.83	3 Mar
3:37.82	Andreas	Vojta	AUT	9.6.89	2 Jul
3:37.84	Yegor	Nikolayev	RUS	12.2.88	24 Jul
3:37.95	Juan	van Deventer	RSA	26.3.83	9 Apr
3:38.09	Szymon	Krawczyk	POL	29.12.88	25 Jun
3:38.09	Kemal	Koyuncu	TUR	25.1.85	29 Jul
3:38.10	Jakub	Holusa	CZE	20.2.88	13 Jun
3:38.11	Kazuya	Watanabe	JPN	7.7.87	29 Jun
3:38.12	Yohan	Durand	FRA	14.5.85	2 Jul
3:38.12	Andrew J	Acosta	USA	13.4.88	22 Jul
3:38.13	Jeremy	Roff	AUS	22.11.83	2 Jul
3:38.16	Mohamed Ahmed Hamada		EGY-J	22.10.92	29 Jul
3:38.18	Nick	Symmonds	USA	30.12.83	21 May
3:38.19	Raymond	Choge	KEN	.83	13 Jun
3:38.22	Mohamed	Hajjaj	MAR	22.3.83	14 May
3:38.24	Nabil	Madi	ALG	9.6.81	15 Jul
3:38.26	Abdelslam	Kénouche	FRA	7.10.80	13 Jun
3:38.34	Matt	Gibney	AUS	16.6.88	1 Jul
3:38.39	John	Bolas	USA	1.11.87	9 Jun
3:38.40	Abdelkader	Bakhtache	FRA	30.1.82	2 Jul
3:38.48	Demma	Daba	ETH	18.7.89	12 Jun
3:38.48	Adrian	Blincoe	NZL	4.11.79	25 Jun
3:38.61	Bilal MansourAli		BRN	17.10.83	20 Dec
3:38.67	Esrael	Awoke	ETH-Y	5.4.94	10 Jun
3:38.68	Álvaro	Rodríguez	ESP	25.5.87	2 Jun
3:38.70	Simon	Denissel	FRA	22.5.90	27 Jun
3:38.71	Richard	Kiplagat	KEN	5.1.81	25 Apr
3:38.76	Teshome	Dirisa	ETH-Y	25.4.94	6 Aug
3:38.80	Evan	Jager	USA	8.3.89	21 May
3:38.90	Edward	Waweru	KEN	3.10.90	19 Jun
3:38.91	Michael	Rimmer	GBR	3.2.86	25 Apr
3:38.94	Maury Surel	Castillo	CUB	19.10.84	2 Jun
3:38.98	Hicham	Siguéni	MAR-J	30.1.93	27 Apr
3:39.03	Garrett	Heath	USA	3.11.85	19 Jul
3:39.04	Benjamin	Kiplagat	UGA	4.3.89	4 Jun
3:39.05	Youssef Saad Kamel		BRN	29.3.83	18 Sep
3:39.09	David	Bustos	ESP	25.8.90	2 Jun
3:39.10	Oleksandr	Borysyuk	UKR	9.12.85	25 Jun
3:39.11	Youcef	Abdi	AUS	7.12.77	15 Jul
3:39.17	Vincent	Mutai	KEN-Y	3.11.94	10 Jul
3:39.20	Kyle	Boorsma	CAN	18.4.88	1 Jul
3:39.28	Suleiman	Simotwo	KEN	21.4.80	13 Jun
3:39.32	Silas	Kisorio	KEN	8.1.83	13 Jul
3:39.36	Luis Alberto	Marco	ESP	20.8.86	2 Jun
3:39.39	David	Vuste	FRA	20.4.88	27 Jun
3:39.39	John	Jefferson	USA	30.12.82	16 Jul
3:39.4A	Degefa	Deribe	ETH	9.6.87	8 May
3:39.4	Mounir	Miout	ALG	14.9.84	8 Jul
3:39.50	Henrik	Ingebrigtsen	NOR	24.2.91	25 May
3:39.5A	Jonathan	Sawe	KEN-Y	22.5.95	8 Jun
3:39.57	Ryan	Foster	AUS	26.8.88	1 Jul
3:39.61	Chaminda Indika Wijekoon		SRI	15.9.81	30 Aug

Mark	Name		Nat	Born	Date
3:39.62	Elkana	Yego	KEN-J	7.12.94	6 Aug
3:39.65	Pharson	Magagane	RSA	6.4.86	9 Apr
3:39.67	Andrew	Bayer	USA	3.2.90	1 May
3:39.69	Kevin	López	ESP	12.6.90	2 Jun
3:39.73	Morten Tuft	Munkholm	DEN	22.9.85	9 Jun
3:39.79	Bryan	Cantero	FRA	28.4.91	27 Jun
3:39.80	Ivan	Tukhtachev	RUS	12.7.89	24 May
3:39.81	Shiferaw	Wole	ETH	23.2.89	4 Jun
3:39.86	Abiyot	Abinet	ETH	1.1.87	22 May
3:39.87	James	Kaan	AUS	17.9.90	3 Mar
3:39.87	Nick	Toohey	AUS	9.4.88	19 Mar
3:39.87	Duncan	Phillips	USA	7.6.89	15 Apr
3:39.90	Tommy	Schmitz	USA	16.7.83	15 Apr
3:39.9	Mustapha	Ferrane	ALG	22.3.84	8 Jul
3:39.9A	John	Mwangangi	KEN	1.11.90	15 Jul
3:39.92	Lukasz	Kujawski	POL	2.3.88	25 Jun
3:39.92	Mateusz	Demczyszak	POL	18.1.86	5 Aug
3:39.94	Emad Hamed Moh. Nour		KSA	21.4.90	20 Dec
3:40.0A	Fredrick Ndunge Musyoki		KEN	14.9.90	18 Jun
3:40.02	Colin	McCourt	GBR	11.12.84	28 Jun
3:40.06	Matt	Tegenkamp	USA	19.1.82	15 Apr
3:40.07	Adam	Czerwinski	POL	2.10.88	25 May
3:40.07	Goran	Nava	SRB	15.4.81	28 Sep
3:40.08	Kim	Ruell	BEL	27.4.87	2 Aug
3:40.10	Haïs	Welday	ERI	24.10.89	22 Jul
3:40.1A	Emmanuel	Sasia	UGA	.92	2 Apr
3:40.1A	Dominic	Mutuku	KEN-Y	.94	18 Jun
3:40.14	Víctor	Riobó	ESP	6.4.80	2 Jun
3:40.15	Hayden	McLaren	NZL	11.8.87	19 Mar
3:40.20	Omar Awadh Al-Rashidi		KUW	10.11.84	13 Jun
3:40.22	Thomas	Solberg Eide	NOR-J	20.11.92	28 Jun
3:40.23	Yuriy	Koldin	RUS	1.11.83	9 Jul
3:40.26	Abdelhakim	Zilali	FRA	20.6.83	2 Jul
3:40.30	Brandon	Rooney	USA	6.8.86	15 Apr
3:40.3A	Nicholas	Kipchumba	KEN	.89	15 Jul
3:40.32	Brandon	Bethke	USA	19.1.87	11 Jun
3:40.36	Timo	Benitz	GER	24.12.91	13 Jun
3:40.37	Abdelhadi	Labäli	MAR	26.4.93	2 Jul
3:40.41	Brett	Robinson	AUS	8.5.91	19 Mar
3:40.43	Michael	Hammond	USA	7.11.89	23 Jun
3:40.44	Geoffrey	Matum	KEN	22.11.87	24 May
3:40.49	Leandro	Oliveira	BRA	2.2.82	6 Apr
3:40.49	Łukasz	Parszczynski	POL	4.5.85	3 Jul
3:40.50	Yusuf	Biwott	KEN	12.11.86	4 Jun
3:40.51	Abdelmadjed Touil		ALG	11.2.89	4 Jun
3:40.52	Hamish	Carson	NZL	1.11.88	9 Mar
3:40.52	Matt	Elliott	USA	8.9.85	13 Jul
3:40.54	Linus	Kiplagat	KEN-Y	23.12.94	6 Jul
3:40.59	Kris	Gauson	GBR	29.1.88	15 Apr
3:40.60	Fekadu	Dejene	ETH-J	29.12.92	9 Jun
3:40.60	Fayidu	Murad	ETH-Y	18.5.95	10 Jul
(200)					

Indoors

Mark	Name		Nat	Born	Pos	Meet	Venue	Date
3:34.13	Ismael	Kombich	KEN	16.10.85	1		Gent	13 Feb

Mark	Name		Nat	Born	Pos	Meet	Venue		Date
3:38.71	Colin	McCourt	GBR	11.12.84	19 Feb				
3:39.03	Kristof	Van Malderen	BEL	30.5.83	8 Feb				
3:39.79	Shadrack	Korir	KEN	14.12.78	25 Feb				
3:39.96	Christoph	Lohse	GER	26.11.83	11 Feb				
3:40.24	Marcin	Lewandowski	POL	13.6.87	11 Feb				

JUNIORS

See main list for top 10 juniors. 13 performances by 9 men to 3:35.71. Additional marks and further juniors:

Mark	Name		Nat	Born	Pos	Meet	Venue	Date
C Ndiku	3:33.05	4	DL			Doha		6 May
	3:34.17	5				Barcelona		22 Jul
	3:34.80+	4	in 1M			Eugene		4 Jun
	3:35.50A	6	NC			Nairobi		16 Jul
3:38.16	Mohamed Ahmed Hamada		EGY	22.10.92	8rB	DNG	Stockholm	29 Jul
3:38.67	Esrael	Awoke	ETH-Y	5.4.94	4	Nebiolo	Torino	10 Jun
3:38.76	Teshome	Dirisa	ETH-Y	25.4.94	3		Ninove	6 Aug
3:38.98	Hicham	Siguéni	MAR	30.1.93	2		Rabat	27 Apr
3:39.17	Vincent	Mutai	KEN-Y	3.11.94	2	WY	Villeneuve d'Ascq	10 Jul
3:39.5A	Jonathan	Sawe	KEN-Y	22.5.95	1		Nairobi	8 Jun
3:39.54					3	WY	Villeneuve d'Ascq	10 Jul
3:39.62	Elkana	Yego	KEN	7.12.94	5		Ninove	6 Aug
3:40.1A	Dominic	Mutuku	KEN-Y	.94	3		Nairobi	18 Jun
3:40.22	Thomas	Solberg Eide	NOR	20.11.92	8		Sollentuna	28 Jun
3:40.54	Linus	Kiplagat (20)	KEN-Y	23.12.94	7	NA	Heusden	6 Jul

1 MILE

Mark	Name		Nat	Born	Pos	Meet	Venue		Date
3:49.09	Haron	Keitany	KEN	17.12.83	1	Pre	Eugene		4 Jun
3:49.39	Silas	Kiplagat	KEN	20.8.89	2	Pre	Eugene		4 Jun
3:49.55	Asbel	Kiprop	KEN	30.6.89	3	Pre	Eugene		4 Jun
3:49.70	Mekonnen	Gebremedhin	ETH	11.10.88	4	Pre	Eugene		4 Jun
3:49.77	Caleb	Ndiku	KEN-J	9.10.92	5	Pre	Eugene		4 Jun
3:50.29	Daniel Kipchirchir	Komen	KEN	27.11.84	6	Pre	Eugene		4 Jun
3:50.43	Yenew	Alamirew	ETH	27.5.90	7	Pre	Eugene		4 Jun
3:50.67	Mohammed	Moustaoui	MAR	2.4.85	8	Pre	Eugene		4 Jun
3:50.86		Kiprop			1	Bisl	Oslo		9 Jun
3:51.02		Keitany			2	Bisl	Oslo		9 Jun
3:51.24	Leonel	Manzano	USA	12.9.84	1	LGP	London (CP)		6 Aug
3:51.30		Mekonnen			3	Bisl	Oslo		9 Jun
3:51.38	Bernard	Lagat (10)	USA	12.12.74	2	LGP	London (CP)		6 Aug
3:51.45	Russell	Brown	USA	3.3.85	9	Pre	Eugene		4 Jun
3:51.50	Augustine	Choge	KEN	21.1.87	3	LGP	London (CP)		6 Aug
3:51.95	Nick	Willis	NZL	25.4.83	10	Pre	Eugene		4 Jun
3:52.00	Mohamed Othman	Shahween	KSA	15.2.86	4	Bisl	Oslo		9 Jun
3:52.53	Jeff	Riseley	AUS	11.11.86	5	Bisl	Oslo		9 Jun
3:53.36	Nixon	Chepseba	KEN	12.12.90	6	Bisl	Oslo		9 Jun
3:53.76	Gideon	Gathimba	KEN	9.3.80	11	Pre	Eugene		4 Jun
	(20/17)								
3:53.85	Lopez	Lomong	USA	1.1.85	12	Pre	Eugene		4 Jun
3:53.86	Ryan	Gregson	AUS	26.4.90	1rB	Pre	Eugene		4 Jun
3:54.01	David	Torrence	USA	26.11.85	2rB	Pre	Eugene		4 Jun
	(20)								
3:54.10	Ben	Blankenship	USA	15.12.88	3rB	Pre	Eugene		4 Jun
3:54.29	Andrew	Baddeley	GBR	20.6.82	8	Bisl	Oslo		9 Jun
3:54.89	Jordan	McNamara	USA	7.3.87	1		Falmouth		13 Aug
3:55.18	Alfred	Kirwa Yego	KEN	28.11.86	4rB	Pre	Eugene		4 Jun
3:55.24	Jeff	See	USA	6.6.86	2		Falmouth		13 Aug

Mark	Name		Nat	Born	Date		Mark	Name		Nat	Born	Date
3:55.30	Andrew J	Acosta	USA	13.4.88	13 Aug		3:57.34	Brandon	Bethke	USA	19.1.87	8 Jul
3:55.38	Kyle	Miller	USA	15.5.85	4 Jun		3:57.70	James	Kaan	AUS	17.9.90	6 Aug
3:55.47	Adrian	Blincoe	NZL	4.11.79	13 Aug		3:57.74	Benson	Seurei	KEN	27.3.88	2 Jun
3:56.19	Nicholas	Kemboi	KEN	18.12.89	4 Jun		3:57.99	Ciarán	O'Lionáird	IRL	11.4.88	8 Jul
3:56.21	Evan	Jager	USA	8.3.89	4 Jun		3:58.06	Matt	Elliott	USA	8.9.85	13 Aug
3:56.22	Bethwel	Birgen	KEN	6.8.88	6 Aug		3:58.15	Álvaro	Rodríguez	ESP	25.5.87	9 Jun
3:56.90	Craig	Miller	USA	3.8.87	13 Aug		3:58.19	Liam	Boylan-Pett	USA	11.9.85	13 Aug
3:57.14	Mohammed	Aman	ETH-J	10.1.92	4 Jun		3:58.26	Boaz	Lalang	KEN	8.2.89	30 Apr
3:57.19	Bartosz	Nowicki	POL	26.2.84	6 Aug		3:58.33	Peter	van der Westhuizen	RSA	21.12.84	30 Apr
3:57.21	Diego	Ruíz	ESP	5.2.82	9 Jun		3:58.41	Will	Leer	USA	15.4.85	13 Aug

Indoors

Mark	Name		Nat	Born	Pos	Meet	Venue		Date
3:54.52	Chris	Solinsky	USA	5.12.84	1		Seattle		12 Feb

Mark	Name		Nat	Born	Date		Mark	Name		Nat	Born	Date
3:55.79	Miles	Batty	USA	1.6.87	12 Feb		3:57.97	Cory	Leslie	USA	24.10.89	29 Jan
3:55.87	Garrett	Heath	USA	3.11.85	5 Feb		3:58.06	Henok	Legesse	ETH	19.8.88	5 Feb
3:56.48	Chris	O'Hare	GBR	23.11.90	11 Feb		3:58.12	Matt	Gibney	AUS	16.6.88	12 Feb
3:56.64	Silas	Kisorio	KEN	8.1.83	11 Feb		3:58.17	Riley	Masters	USA	5.4.90	12 Feb
3:56.84	Dumisani	Hlaselo	RSA	8.6.89	12 Feb		3:58.26	Richard	Peters	GBR	18.2.90	12 Feb
3:57.11	Erik	van Ingen	USA	25.8.89	12 Feb		3:58.41	Michael	Hammond	USA	7.11.89	5 Mar
3:57.75	Andrew	Bayer	USA	3.2.90	28 Jan		3:58.49	Ryan	Foster	AUS	26.8.88	29 Jan

JUNIORS

Mark	Name		Nat	Born	Pos	Meet	Venue		Date
3:57.14	Mohammed	Aman	ETH-J	10.1.92	8rB	Pre	Eugene		4 Jun
3:59.71	Lukas	Verzbicas	LTU	6.1.93	1		New York		11 Jun

Mark	Name		Nat	Born	Pos	Meet	Venue	Date

2000 METRES

Mark	Name		Nat	Born	Pos	Meet	Venue	Date
4:56.25	Tesfaye	Cheru	ETH-J	2.3.93	1		Reims	5 Jul
4:58.01	Abayneh	Ayele	ETH	11.4.87	2		Reims	5 Jul
4:58.03	Juan Carlos	Higuero	ESP	3.8.78	3		Reims	5 Jul
4:58.18	Soresa	Fida	ETH-J	27.5.93	4		Reims	5 Jul
4:58.20	Yusuf	Biwott	KEN	12.11.86	5		Reims	5 Jul
4:58.38	Ismael	Kombich	KEN	16.10.85	6		Reims	5 Jul
4:58.76	Jairus	Kipchoge	KEN-J	15.12.92	7		Reims	5 Jul
4:59.18	Zebene	Alemayehu	ETH-J	4.9.92	8		Reims	5 Jul
5:00.17	Mahiedine	Mekhissi-Benabbad	FRA	15.3.85	9		Reims	5 Jul
5:00.66+	Moses	Kipsiro	UGA	2.9.86	1	DL	Doha	6 May

5:01.?+	Yenew	Alamirew	ETH	27.5.90	6 May	5:01.?+	Thomas	Longosiwa	KEN	14.1.82	6 May
5:01.?+	Eliud	Kipchoge	KEN	5.11.84	6 May	5:01.57	Taylor	Milne	CAN	14.6.81	29 May
						5:01.65+	Joseph	Kiplimo	KEN	20.7.88	10 Sep

Indoors

Mark	Name		Nat	Born	Pos	Meet	Venue	Date
4:59.03	Bethwel	Birgen	KEN	6.8.88	1	in 3000	Stuttgart	5 Feb

3000 METRES

Mark	Name		Nat	Born	Pos	Meet	Venue	Date
7:27.26	Yenew	Alamirew	ETH	27.5.90	1	DL	Doha	6 May
7:27.55	Edwin	Soi	KEN	3.3.86	2	DL	Doha	6 May
7:27.66	Eliud	Kipchoge	KEN	5.11.84	3	DL	Doha	6 May
7:28.76	Augustine	Choge	KEN	21.1.87	4	DL	Doha	6 May
7:30.15	Vincent	Chepkok	KEN	5.7.88	5	DL	Doha	6 May
7:31.41	Daniel Kipchirchir	Komen	KEN	27.11.84	6	DL	Doha	6 May
7:31.83	Moses	Kipsiro	UGA	2.9.86	7	DL	Doha	6 May
7:32.13	Bernard	Lagat	USA	12.12.74	1		Rieti	10 Sep
7:32.38		Chepkok			2		Rieti	10 Sep
7:32.71	Thomas	Longosiwa	KEN	14.1.82	3		Rieti	10 Sep
7:33.50	Tariku	Bekele (10)	ETH	21.1.87	8	DL	Doha	6 May
7:33.93		Longosiwa			9	DL	Doha	6 May
7:34.70	Essa Ismail	Rasheed	QAT	14.12.86	10	DL	Doha	6 May
7:34.71		T Bekele			4		Rieti	10 Sep
7:34.82	John	Kipkoech	KEN	29.12.91	12	DL	Doha	6 May
7:34.82	Mark	Kiptoo	KEN	21.6.76	11	DL	Doha	6 May
7:35.57	Lucas	Rotich	KEN	16.4.90	13	DL	Doha	6 May
7:35.66	Albert	Rop	KEN-Y	20.12.94	5		Rieti	10 Sep
7:36.84	Yusuf	Biwott	KEN	12.11.86	14	DL	Doha	6 May
7:37.23	Haïs	Welday	ERI	24.10.89	15	DL	Doha	6 May
	(20/17)							
7:37.52	James	Kwalia	QAT	12.6.84	16	DL	Doha	6 May
7:39.72	Paul	Lonyangat	KEN-J	12.12.92	1		Strasbourg	12 Jun
7:40.10	William	Sitonik	KEN-Y	1.3.94	1	WY	Villeneuve d'Ascq	10 Jul
	(20)							
7:40.10	Gideon	Gathimba	KEN	9.3.80	6		Rieti	10 Sep
7:40.15	Mohamed	Farah	GBR	23.3.83	1	LGP	London (CP)	5 Aug
7:40.47	Patrick	Mwikya Mutunga	KEN-Y	20.11.94	2	WY	Villeneuve d'Ascq	10 Jul
7:40.89	Abrar	Osman	ERI-Y	1.1.94	3	WY	Villeneuve d'Ascq	10 Jul
7:40.93	Japheth	Korir	KEN-J	30.6.93	4		Strasbourg	12 Jun
7:41.36	Geoffrey	Kusuro	UGA	12.2.89	5		Strasbourg	12 Jun
7:41.42	Mekonnen	Gebremedhin	ETH	11.10.88	2		Milano	18 Sep
7:41.59	Elroy	Gelant	RSA	25.8.86	1		Metz	27 Jun
7:42.10	Solomon	Deksisa	ETH-Y	11.3.94	4	WY	Villeneuve d'Ascq	10 Jul
7:42.11	Collis	Birmingham	AUS	27.12.84	6		Strasbourg	12 Jun
	(30)							
7:42.65	Dawit	Wolde	ETH	19.5.91	2		Metz	27 Jun
7:42.71	Bilisuma	Shugi	BRN	19.7.89	4		Milano	18 Sep
7:42.82	Juan Luis	Barrios	MEX	24.6.83	1		Luzern	21 Jul
7:43.99	Mohammed	Moustaoui	MAR	2.4.85	1		Dakar	28 May
7:44.12	Joseph	Kiplimo	KEN	20.7.88	2		Dakar	28 May
7:44.16	Patrick	Ereng	KEN	.87	3		Dakar	28 May
7:45.11	Hagos	Gebrehiwott	ETH-Y	11.5.94	5	WY	Villeneuve d'Ascq	10 Jul
7:45.38	Isaac	Songok	KEN	25.4.84	4		Metz	27 Jun
7:45.75+	Vincent	Rono	KEN	22.12.90	1	GGala	Roma	26 May
7:46.01	John	Thuo	KEN	27.11.85	1		Tajimi	10 Oct
	(40)							
7:46.29	Alistair	Cragg	IRL	13.6.80	4	LGP	London (CP)	5 Aug
7:46.46	Yohan	Durand	FRA	14.5.85	5		Metz	27 Jun

7:47.17+	Vincent	Yator	KEN	11.7.89	22 Jul	7:47.9+	Abera	Kuma	ETH	31.8.90	22 Jul
7:47.38	Josephat Kiprono Menjo		KEN	20.8.79	2 Jun	7:48.1+	Imane	Merga	ETH	15.10.88	22 Jul
7:47.6+	Isiah	Koech	KEN-J	19.12.93	22 Jul	7:48.2+	Zersenay	Tadese	ERI	8.2.82	22 Jul
7:47.78	Million	Yehualashet	ETH	.89	13 Jun	7:48.6+	Teklemariam	Medhin	ERI	24.6.89	22 Jul

Mark	Name		Nat	Born	Pos	Meet	Venue		Date
7:48.7+	Josphat	Bett	KEN	12.6.90					22 Jul
7:49.0+??	Francisco	España	ESP	27.10.84					22 Jul
7:49.11	Valentin	Smirnov	RUS	13.2.86					25 Jun
7:49.24	Hamish	Carson	NZL	1.11.88					8 Jul
7:49.25	Abayneh	Ayele	ETH	11.4.87					2 Jul
7:49.4+	Matt	Tegenkamp	USA	19.1.82					22 Jul
7:49.45	Sergio	Sánchez	ESP	1.10.82					9 Jul
7:49.53	Ryan	Gregson	AUS	26.4.90					12 Jun
7:49.63	Bitan	Karoki	KEN	21.8.90					10 Apr
7:49.70	Ben	Blankenship	USA	15.12.88					21 Jul
7:49.95	Ezekiel	Kemboi	KEN	25.5.82					30 Jul
7:50.0+	Craig	Mottram	AUS	18.6.80					22 Jul
7:50.18	Arne	Gabius	GER	22.3.81					8 Jul
7:50.21	David	Bett	KEN-J	18.10.92					28 May
7:50.36	Lopez	Lomong	USA	1.1.85					13 Jul
7:50.48	Jordan	McNamara	USA	7.3.87					13 Jul
7:50.54	Will	Leer	USA	15.4.85					21 Jul
7:50.71	Ciarán	O'Lionáird	IRL	11.4.88					13 Jul
7:50.82	Dame	Tasama	ETH	12.10.87					13 Jul
7:50.84	Tonny	Wamulwa	ZAM	6.8.89					27 Jun
7:50.88	Paul	Tanui	KEN	22.12.90					30 Jul
7:50.90	Gladwin	Mzazi	RSA	28.8.88					27 Jun
7:51.33	Hicham	Siguéni	MAR-J	30.1.93					13 Jun
7:51.37	Brandon	Bethke	USA	19.1.87					21 Jul
7:51.46	Abraham	Kasongor	KEN-J	.93					25 Jun
7:51.46	Sergey	Chaberok	BLR	7.11.87					25 Jun
7:51.63	Tiidrek	Nurme	EST	18.11.85					9 Aug
7:51.64	Adrian	Blincoe	NZL	4.11.79					2 Jul
7:51.8A	F. Kipkemboi	Langat	KEN-J						8 Jun
7:51.83	Javier	Carriqueo	ARG	29.5.79					9 Jul
7:51.88	Mumin	Gala	DJI	6.4.86					5 Aug
7:52.25	Sergiy	Lebid	UKR	15.7.75					31 May
7:52.40	Hassan	Hirt	FRA	16.1.80					2 Jul
7:52.56	Fikadu	Haftu	ETH-J	21.2.94					12 Jun
7:52.57	Charles	Ndirangu	KEN-J	8.2.93					2 Jul
7:52.64	Chris	Thompson	GBR	17.4.81					19 Mar
7:52.91	Garrett	Heath	USA	3.11.85					13 Jul
7:52.94	Sammy	Mutahi	KEN	1.6.89					5 Aug
7:52.96	Ben	St. Lawrence	AUS	7.11.81					5 Aug
7:53.06	Nassir	Dawud	ERI	.91					12 Jun
7:53.14	Youcif	Abdi	AUS	7.12.77					18 Sep
7:53.15	Francisco Javier Abad		ESP	18.8.81					12 Jun
7:53.28	Hussein Jamaan Al-Hamdah		KSA	4.8.83					18 Sep

Indoors

Mark	Name		Nat	Born	Pos	Meet	Venue	Date
7:27.80		Alamirew			1		Stuttgart	5 Feb
7:28.00	Augustine	Choge	KEN	21.1.87	2		Stuttgart	5 Feb
7:29.37		Kipchoge			3		Stuttgart	5 Feb
7:35.37	Dejen	Gebremeskel	ETH	24.11.89	1		Boston (R)	5 Feb
7:35.81	Mohamed	Farah	GBR	23.3.83	2		Boston (R)	5 Feb
7:37.50	Isiah	Koech	KEN-J	19.12.93	1		Gent	13 Feb
7:37.64	Nixon	Chepseba	KEN	12.12.90	3		Boston (R)	5 Feb
7:37.87	Vincent	Rono	KEN	22.12.90	2		Gent	13 Feb
7:42.54	Hayle	Ibrahimov	AZE	18.1.90	2		Karlsruhe	13 Feb
7:44.27	Sammy	Mutahi	KEN	1.6.89	4		Stuttgart	5 Feb
7:46.19	Yoann	Kowal	FRA	28.5.87	4		Karlsruhe	13 Feb
7:47.94	Abiyot	Abinet	ETH	1.1.87				13 Feb
7:48.24	Samuel	Chelanga	KEN	23.2.85				5 Feb
7:48.35	Andrew	Bayer	USA	3.2.90				21 Jan
7:48.41	Halil	Akkas	TUR	1.7.83				13 Feb
7:49.93	Dan	Huling	USA	16.7.83				5 Feb
7:49.95	Tim	Nelson	USA	27.2.84				12 Feb
7:50.11	Aaron	Braun	USA	28.5.87				5 Feb
7:50.23	Jeff	See	USA	6.6.86				12 Feb
7:50.28	Garrett	Heath	USA	3.11.85				12 Feb
7:50.59	Matt	Centrowitz	USA	18.10.89				12 Feb
7:50.70	Jesús	España	ESP	21.8.78				19 Feb
7:50.78	Ryan	Hill	USA	31.1.90				12 Feb
7:51.30	Sergey	Ivanov	RUS	3.3.79				16 Feb
7:51.40	Leonard	Korir	KEN	10.12.86				29 Jan
7:51.60	Rui	Silva	POR	3.8.77				27 Feb
7:51.85	Alan	Webb	USA	13.1.83				12 Feb
7:51.95	Víctor	García	ESP	13.3.85				19 Feb
7:52.11	Yegor	Nikolayev	RUS	10.4.88				16 Feb
7:52.12	Andrey	Safronov	RUS	16.12.85				16 Feb
7:52.18	Diego	Estrada	USA	12.12.89				12 Feb
7:52.21	Nour-eddine	Gezzar	FRA	17.2.80				5 Feb
7:52.27	Elliott	Heath	USA	4.2.89				29 Jan
7:52.31	Maverick	Darling	USA	9.6.89				5 Feb
7:52.40	Francisco Javier Alves		ESP	3.9.80				19 Feb
7:52.52	Shadrack	Korir	KEN	14.12.78				13 Feb
7:53.11	Riley	Masters	USA	5.4.90				29 Jan
7:53.11	Florian	Carvalho	FRA	9.3.89				12 Feb
7:53.12	Sebastián	Martos	ESP	20.6.89				19 Feb
7:53.13	Colton	Tully-Doyle	USA					12 Feb

Drugs disqualification

Mark	Name		Nat	Born	Pos	Meet	Venue	Date
7:45.16	Aziz	Lahbabi #	MAR	3.2.91	7		Strasbourg	12 Jun

JUNIORS

See main list for top 7 juniors. 10 & 1 indoors performances by 10 men to 7:50.50. Further juniors:

Mark	Name		Nat	Born	Pos	Meet	Venue	Date
7:47.6+	Isiah	Koech	KEN	19.12.93	3	Herc	Monaco	22 Jul
7:50.21	David	Bett	KEN	18.10.92	4		Dakar	28 May
7:51.33	Hicham	Siguéni (10)	MAR	30.1.93	3		Rehlingen	13 Jun
7:51.46	Abraham	Kasongor	KEN	.93	2		Szczecin	25 Jun
7:51.8A	F. Kipkemboi	Langat	KEN		3		Nairobi	8 Jun
7:52.56	Fikadu	Haftu	ETH	21.2.94	9		Strasbourg	12 Jun
7:52.57	Charles	Ndirangu	KEN	8.2.93	1		Miyoshi	2 Jul
7:57.45	Mohammed	Abid	MAR-Y	18.3.95	6	WY	Villeneuve d'Ascq	10 Jul
8:02.33	Philip	Kipyego	UGA-Y	10.1.95	3	CommY	Douglas	11 Sep

2 MILES

Mark	Name		Nat	Born	Pos	Meet	Venue	Date
8:13.62	Bernard	Lagat	USA	12.12.74	1	Pre	Eugene	4 Jun
8:14.10	Edwin	Soi	KEN	3.3.86	2	Pre	Eugene	4 Jun
8:14.16	Isiah	Koech	KEN-J	19.12.93	3	Pre	Eugene	4 Jun
8:15.40	Tariku	Bekele	ETH	21.1.87	4	Pre	Eugene	4 Jun

Further at Eugene 4 June: 5. Matt Tegenkamp USA 8:15.88, 6. Eliud Kipchoge KEN 8:16.74, 7. Collis Birmingham AUS 8:17.91, 8. David Bett KEN-J 18.72, 9. Will Leer USA 8:19.11, 10. Andrew Bumbalough USA 8:21.65

Indoors

Mark	Name		Nat	Born	Pos	Meet	Venue	Date
8:10.07	Bernard	Lagat	USA	12.12.74	1		New York (Armory)	12 Feb

JUNIORS

Mark	Name		Nat	Born	Pos	Meet	Venue	Date
8:29.46	Lukas	Verzbicas	LTU	6.1.93	11	Pre	Eugene	4 Jun

Mark	Name		Nat	Born	Pos	Meet	Venue	Date	

5000 METRES

Mark	Name		Nat	Born	Pos	Meet	Venue	Date	
12:53.11	Mohamed	Farah	GBR	23.3.83	1	Herc	Monaco	22	Jul
12:53.60	Bernard	Lagat	USA	12.12.74	2	Herc	Monaco	22	Jul
12:54.18	Isiah	Koech	KEN-J	19.12.93	3	Herc	Monaco	22	Jul
12:54.21	Imane	Merga	ETH	15.10.88	1	GGala	Roma	26	May
12:54.59		Koech			2	GGala	Roma	26	May
12:55.29	Vincent	Chepkok	KEN	5.7.88	3	GGala	Roma	26	May
12:55.47		Merga			4	Herc	Monaco	22	Jul
12:55.89	Dejen	Gebremeskel	ETH	24.11.89	4	GGala	Roma	26	May
12:56.08	Thomas	Longosiwa	KEN	14.1.82	5	Herc	Monaco	22	Jul
12:57.86	Sileshi	Sihine	ETH	29.1.83	5	GGala	Roma	26	May
12:58.32		Merga			1	VD	Bruxelles	16	Sep
12:58.70		Longosiwa			2	VD	Bruxelles	16	Sep
12:59.01	Eliud	Kipchoge	KEN	5.11.84	6	Herc	Monaco	22	Jul
12:59.13		Chepkok			1	Athl	Lausanne	30	Jun
12:59.15	Edwin	Soi (10)	KEN	3.3.86	1	FBK	Hengelo	29	May
12:59.25	Tariku	Bekele	ETH	21.1.87	7	Herc	Monaco	22	Jul
12:59.28		Chepkok			2	FBK	Hengelo	29	May
12:59.32	Zersenay	Tadese	ERI	8.2.82	1		Barcelona	22	Jul
12:59.47		Merga			2	Athl	Lausanne	30	Jun
12:59.50		Chepkok			3	VD	Bruxelles	16	Sep
12:59.71		Kipchoge			3	Athl	Lausanne	30	Jun
12:59.91	Mark	Kiptoo	KEN	21.6.76	6	GGala	Roma	26	May
13:00.02	Lucas	Rotich	KEN	16.4.90	7	GGala	Roma	26	May
13:00.15	Abera	Kuma	ETH	31.8.90	8	GGala	Roma	26	May
13:00.46	Yenew	Alamirew	ETH	7.5.90	8	Herc	Monaco	22	Jul
13:01.03	Jacob	Chesari Korir	KEN	6.4.84	3	FBK	Hengelo	29	May
13:01.85		T Bekele			4	VD	Bruxelles	16	Sep
13:02.71		Alamirew			4	FBK	Hengelo	29	May
13:03.53	Alistair	Cragg	IRL	13.6.80	5	VD	Bruxelles	16	Sep
13:03.70	Albert	Rop	KEN-Y	20.12.94	6	VD	Bruxelles	16	Sep
13:03.73		Chesari			4	Athl	Lausanne	30	Jun
13:04.65	Paul	Tanui	KEN	22.12.90	2		Barcelona	22	Jul
	(32/20)								
13:04.73	Jesús	España	ESP	21.8.78	9	Herc	Monaco	22	Jul
13:05.98	Polat (Paul) Kemboi Arikan		KEN/TUR	12.12.90	7	VD	Bruxelles	16	Sep
13:06.73	Bilisuma	Shugi	BRN	19.7.89	3	WMilG	Rio de Janeiro	23	Jul
13:06.86	Galen	Rupp	USA	8.5.86	2	DL	Birmingham	10	Jul
13:08.01	Paul	Lonyangat	KEN-J	12.12.92	3		Barcelona	22	Jul
13:09.17	Moses	Kipsiro	UGA	2.9.86	10	GGala	Roma	26	May
13:09.81	Juan Luis	Barrios	MEX	24.6.83	5	adidas	New York	11	Jun
13:09.95	Ibrahim	Jeylan	ETH	12.6.89	1		Fukuroi	3	May
13:10.08	Ben	St. Lawrence	AUS	7.11.81	2		Melbourne	3	Mar
13:10.22	Chris	Solinsky	USA	5.12.84	3		Melbourne	3	Mar
	(30)								
13:10.40	Abraham	Kiplimo	UGA	14.4.89	4		Barcelona	22	Jul
13:11.01	Abayneh	Ayele	ETH	11.4.87	1		Montreuil-sous-Bois	7	Jun
13:11.19	Yusuf	Biwott	KEN	12.11.86	6	FBK	Hengelo	29	May
13:11.29	Josphat	Bett	KEN	12.6.90	10	Herc	Monaco	22	Jul
13:11.51	Craig	Mottram	AUS	18.6.80	6	DL	Birmingham	10	Jul
13:11.65	Mike	Kigen	KEN	15.1.86	11	GGala	Roma	26	May
13:11.69	Vincent	Yator	KEN	11.7.89	12	GGala	Roma	26	May
13:11.76	Titus	Mbishei	KEN	28.10.90	5		Barcelona	22	Jul
13:12.17	Hussein Jamaan	Al-Hamdah	KSA	4.8.83	4	WMilG	Rio de Janeiro	23	Jul
13:12.23	Geoffrey	Kipsang	KEN-J	28.11.92	9	adidas	New York	11	Jun
	(40)								
13:12.32	Geoffrey	Kusuro	UGA	12.2.89	6		Barcelona	22	Jul
13:12.76	Alex	Oleitiptip	KEN	22.9.82	7		Barcelona	22	Jul
13:12.77	Josphat	Muchiri Ndambiri	KEN	12.2.85	3		Fukuroi	3	May
13:13.03	Moses	Masai	KEN	1.6.86	7	FBK	Hengelo	29	May
13:13.66	David	Bett	KEN-J	18.10.92	2	NA	Heusden	16	Jul
13:13.68	Aziz	Lahbabi #	MAR	3.2.91	2		Rabat	5	Jun
13:13.77	Joseph	Kiplimo	KEN	20.7.88	4		Montreuil-sous-Bois	7	Jun
13:13.80	Edward	Waweru	KEN	3.10.90	4		Fukuroi	3	May
13:14.75	Matt	Tegenkamp	USA	19.1.82	12	Herc	Monaco	22	Jul
13:15.18	Moses	Kibet	UGA	23.3.91	4	NA	Heusden	16	Jul
	(50)								
13:15.44	Charles	Ndirangu	KEN-J	8.2.93	1		Oita	22	Oct

Mark	Name		Nat	Born	Pos	Meet	Venue	Date
13:15.53	John	Thuo	KEN	27.11.85	1		Abashiri	22 Jun
13:15.70	Collis	Birmingham	AUS	27.12.84	8	DL	Birmingham	10 Jul
13:15.76	Bitan	Karoki	KEN	21.8.90	1	JPN Ch	Kumagaya	12 Jun
13:15.93	Martin	Mathathi	KEN	25.12.85	5		Fukuroi	3 May
13:16.25	Amanuel	Mesel	ERI	29.12.90	8		Barcelona	22 Jul
13:16.30	Yitayal	Atnafu Zerihun	ETH-J	20.1.93	1		Nijmegen	25 May
13:16.53	Teklemariam	Medhin	ERI	24.6.89	9		Barcelona	22 Jul
13:16.77	Andrew	Bumbalough	USA	14.3.87	5		Melbourne	3 Mar
13:17.18	Japheth	Korir	KEN-J	30.6.93	3		Nijmegen	25 May
(60)								
13:17.77	Mumin	Gala	DJI	6.4.82	10	DL	Birmingham	10 Jul
13:18.27	Adrian	Blincoe	NZL	4.11.79	10		Barcelona	22 Jul
13:18.35	Philemon	Yator	KEN-J	2.4.92	4		Nijmegen	25 May
13:19.00	Rabah	Aboud	ALG	1.1.81	5	WMilG	Rio de Janeiro	23 Jul
13:19.04	Jonathan	Ndiku	KEN	18.9.91	3		Yokohama	4 Dec
13:19.13	Patrick	Mwikya Mutunga	KEN-Y	20.11.94	8	VD	Bruxelles	16 Sep
13:19.51	Daniel	Salel	KEN	11.12.90	11	adidas	New York	11 Jun
13:19.73	Mounir	Miout	ALG	14.9.84	6	WMilG	Rio de Janeiro	23 Jul
13:19.93	Francisco Javier	Alves	ESP	3.9.80	11		Barcelona	22 Jul
13:20.09	Clement	Langat	KEN	18.12.91	4		Yokohama	4 Dec
(70)								
13:20.54	Geoffrey	Kirui	KEN-J	16.2.93	8	FBK	Hengelo	29 May
13:20.80	Daniel Kipchirchir	Komen	KEN	27.11.84	13	adidas	New York	11 Jun
13:21.10	Josephat Kiprono	Menjo	KEN	20.8.79	1		Lappeenranta	13 Aug
13:21.24	Augustine	Choge	KEN	21.1.87	10	Athl	Lausanne	30 Jun
13:21.25	Gideon	Ngatuny	KEN	10.10.86	6		Fukuroi	3 May
13:21.79	Bisluke	Kiplagat	KEN	8.8.88	1		Belém	15 May
13:22.28	Soyekwo	Kibet	UGA-J	6.6.92	6		Nijmegen	25 May
13:22.38	Jake	Robertson	NZL	14.11.89	7		Nijmegen	25 May
13:22.86	Vincent	Rono	KEN	22.12.90	3		Rabat	5 Jun
13:23.07	Goltom	Kifle	ERI-J	3.12.93	11		Barcelona	22 Jul
(80)								
13:23.15	Kazuya	Watanabe	JPN	7.7.87	1		Nobeoka	28 May
13:23.53	Dennis	Masai	KEN	1.12.91	14	adidas	New York	11 Jun
13:24.11	Ben	True	USA	29.12.85	15	adidas	New York	11 Jun
13:24.23	Alemu	Desta	ETH-J	18.2.92	3		Nobeoka	28 May
13:24.27	Dejene	Regassa	BRN	18.4.89	7	WMilG	Rio de Janeiro	23 Jul
13:24.51	Michael	Tiony	KEN	27.8.85	1	Gyulai	Budapest	30 Jul
13:24.54	Abdullah Abdulaziz	Al-Joud	KSA	10.7.75	5		Rabat	5 Jun
13:24.59	Sergio	Sánchez	ESP	1.10.82	13		Barcelona	22 Jul
13:24.94	Daniele	Meucci	ITA	8.4.85	14		Barcelona	22 Jul
13:25.09	Elroy	Gelant	RSA	25.8.86	1		Uden	2 Jul
(90)								
13:25.13	Moukhled	Al Outaibi	KSA	20.6.76	2	Gyulai	Budapest	30 Jul
13:25.17	Javier	Carriqueo	ARG	29.5.79	15		Barcelona	22 Jul
13:25.17	Hosea	Macharinyang	KEN	12.6.86	4	Gyulai	Budapest	30 Jul
13:25.42	Hassan	Hirt	FRA	16.1.80	8	WMilG	Rio de Janeiro	23 Jul
13:25.53	Yuki	Sato	JPN	26.11.86	5		Nobeoka	28 May
13:25.55	Illias	Fifa	MAR	16.5.89	16		Barcelona	22 Jul
13:25.82	Brandon	Bethke	USA	19.1.87	1	Jordan	Stanford	1 May
13:25.94	Rui	Silva	POR	3.8.77	4		Huelva	2 Jun
13:26.14	Elliott	Heath	USA	4.2.89	2	Jordan	Stanford	1 May
13:26.29	Patrick	Mwaka	KEN-J	2.11.92	3		Kumamoto	9 Apr
(100)								

Mark	Name		Nat	Born	Date		Mark	Name		Nat	Born	Date
13:26.32	Hicham	Sigueni	MAR-J	30.1.93	5 Jun		13:29.30	Samuel	Chelanga	KEN	23.2.85	11 Jun
13:26.59	Thomas	Farrell	GBR	23.3.91	1 May		13:29.37	David	McNeill	AUS	6.10.86	22 Jul
13:26.94	Diego	Estrada	USA	12.12.89	1 May		13:29.40	Juan Carlos	Romero	MEX	15.12.77	15 Apr
13:27.01	Aaron	Braun	USA	28.5.87	15 Apr		13:29.73	Yetwale	Kende	ETH	10.1.91	25 May
13:27.20	Paul	Kuira	KEN	25.1.90	28 May		13:29.74	Chris	Derrick	USA	17.10.90	1 May
13:27.58	Jorge	Torres	USA	22.8.80	15 Apr		13:29.85	Ezekiel	Meli	KEN	21.4.84	10 Jun
13:27.66	Yuichiro	Ueno	JPN	29.7.85	13 Sep		13:30.12	Gladwin	Mzazi	RSA	28.8.88	10 Mar
13:27.85	Andrew	Vernon	GBR	7.1.86	15 Apr		13:30.18	Scott	Bauhs	USA	11.5.86	15 Apr
13:27e+	Kenenisa	Bekele	ETH	13.6.82	16 Sep		13:30.22	Sondre Nordstad Moen		NOR	12.1.91	10 Jul
13:27e+	Emmanuel	Bett	KEN	29.3.85	16 Sep		13:30.26	Nicholas	Togom	KEN-J	17.2.92	30 Jul
13:27.91	Lewis	Korir	KEN	11.6.86	13 Aug		13:30.30	Hamid	Ezzine	MAR	5.10.83	16 Apr
13:28.07	Sindre	Buraas	NOR	8.5.89	25 May		13:30.30	Tsuyoshi	Ugachi	JPN	27.4.87	28 May
13:28.09	Tim	Nelson	USA	27.2.84	3 Mar		13:30.34A	Silas	Kipruto	KEN	26.9.84	16 Jul
13:28.21	Mark	Christie	IRL	12.1.85	1 May		13:30.58	Aron	Rono	KEN	1.11.82	15 Apr
13:28.60	Stephen	Mokoka	RSA	31.1.85	10 Mar		13:30.59	Haron	Lagat	KEN	15.8.83	15 Apr
13:28.80	Olivier	Irabaruta	BDI	25.8.90	23 Jul		13:30.64	Lawi	Lalang	KEN	15.6.91	28 May
13:29.05	Stephen	Furst	USA	16.8.85	1 May		13:30.75	Fikadu	Haftu	ETH-Y	21.2.94	7 Jun
13:29.11	Tetsuya	Yoroizaka	JPN	20.3.90	13 Sep		13:30.77	Tshamano	Setone	RSA	7.5.87	30 Apr
13:29.19	Abraham	Kasongor	KEN-J	.93	18 Jun		13:30.88	Kgosi	Tsosane	RSA	15.4.86	10 Mar

Mark	Name		Nat	Born	Pos	Meet	Venue	Date
13:31.07	Dame	Tasama	ETH	12.10.87				16 Jul
13:31.27	Suguru	Osako	JPN	23.5.91				28 May
13:31.32	Thomas	Ayeko	UGA-J	10.2.92				29 May
13:31.48	Yuta	Takahashi	JPN	13.4.87				20 Nov
13:31.67	Ryan	Hill	USA	31.1.90				1 May
13:31.79	Joílson	da Silva	BRA	29.8.87				25 May
13:31.93	Bolota	Asmerom	USA	12.10.78				15 Apr
13:32.08	Arne	Gabius	GER	22.3.81				13 Sep
13:32.21	Ayele	Abshero	ETH	28.12.90				29 May
13:32.25	Daniel	Gitau	KEN	1.10.87				24 Sep
13:32.74	Andrew	Bayer	USA	3.2.90				25 Mar
13:32.74	Brian	Olinger	USA	2.6.83				30 Jul
13:32.76	Wiilliam	Kibor	KEN	.80				23 Jul
13:32.96	Gemechu	Edeo	ETH	18.1.80				10 Jun
13:32.98	Kensuke	Takezawa	JPN	11.10.86				13 Sep
13:33.06	Justine Kiprop	Cheruiyot	KEN-J	11.11.93				11 May
13:33.35	Jacob	Wanjuki	KEN	16.1.86				20 Nov
13:33.42	Stefano	La Rosa	ITA	22.9.85				10 Jun
13:33.64	Ciarán	O'Lionáird	IRL	11.4.88				16 Jul
13:33.9	Samuel	Tsegay	ERI	24.2.88				29 May
13:34.19	Stephen	Sambu	KEN	7.7.88				15 Apr
13:34.20	Ahmed	El Mazoury	ITA	15.3.90				10 Jun
13:34.23	Mohammed	Ahmed	CAN	5.1.91				28 May
13:34.25	Abraham	Niyonkuru	BDI	26.12.89				11 Jun
13:34.31	Chris	Thompson	GBR	17.4.81				5 Aug
13:34.38	Yusuke	Takabayashi	JPN	19.7.87				6 Aug
13:34.42	Sergey	Lebid	UKR	15.7.75				4 Aug
13:34.44	Joe	Bosshard	USA	30.10.89				28 May
13:34.53	Aleksandr	Orlov	RUS	23.2.81				9 Jul
13:34.54	Hayle	Ibrahimov	AZE	18.1.90				9 Oct
13:34.63	Mark	Draper	GBR	28.6.84				15 Apr
13:34.70	Yusuke	Hasegawa	JPN	8.6.88				24 Sep
13:34.85	Akinobu	Murasawa	JPN	28.3.91				13 Sep
13:34.89	Titus	Waruru	KEN-Y	29.3.94				9 Apr
13:35.38	Takuya	Ishikawa	JPN	29.10.87				9 Apr
13:35.50	Essa Ismail	Rasheed	QAT	14.12.86				5 Jun
13:35.71	Leonard	Korir	KEN	10.12.86				11 Jun
13:35.74	Chihiro	Miyawaki	JPN	28.8.91				28 May
13:35.88	Tonny	Wamulwa	ZAM	6.8.89				10 Jun
13:35.93	Jawad	Laariss	MAR	6.12.83				16 Apr
13:36.01	Suleiman	Simotwo	KEN	21.4.80				11 Jun
13:36.26	Gert	Manora	RSA	29.10.84				16 Apr
13:36.39	Ross	Millington	GBR	19.9.89				28 May
13:36.40	Jonathon	Mellor	GBR	27.12.86				5 Aug
13:36.48	Maksym	Obrubanskyy	UKR	21.6.88				13 Sep
13:36.69	Diego Alberto	Borrego	MEX	9.1.88				1 May
13:36.68	Joseph	Onsarigo	KEN-J	.93				17 Apr
13:36.89	Philipp	Bandi	SUI	28.9.77				30 Jul
13:36.92	Mohamed	Marhoum	ESP	26.11.87				22 Jul
13:37.08	Tiidrek	Nurme	EST	18.11.85				11 Jun
13:37.09	John	Maina	KEN-J	14.7.93?				9 Apr
13:37.21	Sibusiso	Nzima	RSA	23.11.86				16 Apr
13:37.43	Robert Kipngeno	Sigei	KEN	3.1.82				18 Jun
13:37.48	Jeremy	Roff	AUS	22.11.83				3 Mar
13:37.52	Yuki	Matsuoka	JPN	14.1.86				24 Sep
13:37.75	Denis Kipkurui	Mayaud	FRA	22.4.86				11 Jun
								(200)

Indoors

Mark	Name		Nat	Born	Pos	Meet	Venue	Date
12:53.29i	Isiah	Koech	KEN-J	19.12.93	1		Düsseldorf	11 Feb
12:55.72	Eliud	Kipchoge	KEN	5.11.84	2		Düsseldorf	11 Feb
13:15.64	Paul Kipsiele	Koech	KEN	10.11.81	3		Düsseldorf	11 Feb
13:26.01	Leonard	Korir	KEN	10.12.86	1	NCAA	College Station	11 Mar
13:27.34	Samuel	Chelanga	KEN	23.2.85				11 Mar
13:28.48	Stephen	Sambu	KEN	7.7.88				11 Mar
13:30.35	Birhan	Getahun	ETH	5.9.91				11 Feb
13:34.32	Sammy	Mutahi	KEN	1.6.89				11 Feb
13:36.14	Kevin	Schwab	USA	15.4.89				11 Mar
13:36.65	Maverick	Darling	USA	9.6.89				11 Mar
13:37.03	Andrew	Poore	USA	3.12.88				11 Mar

JUNIORS

See main list for top 15 juniors. 16 + 1 indoor performances by 12 men to 13:23.0. Additional marks and further juniors:

Name	Mark	Pos	Meet	Venue	Date			
I Koech 2+	13:07.22	4	DL	New York	11 Jun	13:21.31A	1 NC Nairobi	16 Jul
Rop	13:10.37	1		Heusden-Zolder	16 Jul			
Lonyongat	13:11.22	3		Montreuil-sous-Bois	7 Jun			

Mark	Name		Nat	Born	Pos	Meet	Venue	Date
13:26.32	Hicham	Sigueni	MAR	30.1.93	8		Rabat	5 Jun
13:29.19	Abraham	Kasongor	KEN	.93	1		Bilbao	18 Jun
13:30.26	Nicholas	Togom	KEN	17.2.92	6	Gyulai	Budapest	30 Jul
13:30.75	Fikadu	Haftu	ETH-Y	21.2.94	7		Montreuil-sous-Bois	7 Jun
13:31.32	Thomas	Ayeko	UGA	10.2.92	11	FBK	Hengelo	29 May

Best non-African: 13:47.19 Kenta Murayama JPN 23.2.93 8 Abashiri 22 Jun
Best European: 13:57.16 Jonathan Hay GBR 12.2.92 5 Manchester 28 May

10,000 METRES

Mark	Name		Nat	Born	Pos	Meet	Venue	Date
26:43.16	Kenenisa	Bekele	ETH	13.6.82	1	VD	Bruxelles	16 Sep
26:43.98	Lucas	Rotich	KEN	16.4.90	2	VD	Bruxelles	16 Sep
26:46.57	Mohamed	Farah	GBR	23.3.83	1	Pre	Eugene	3 Jun
26:48.00	Galen	Rupp	USA	8.5.86	3	VD	Bruxelles	16 Sep
26:48.35	Imane	Merga	ETH	15.10.88	2	Pre	Eugene	3 Jun
26:48.99	Josphat	Bett	KEN	12.6.90	3	Pre	Eugene	3 Jun
26:50.63	Paul	Tanui	KEN	22.12.90	4	Pre	Eugene	3 Jun
26:51.09	Zersenay	Tadese	ERI	8.2.82	5	Pre	Eugene	3 Jun
26:51.95	Emmanuel	Bett	KEN	29.3.85	4	VD	Bruxelles	16 Sep
26:52.84	Sileshi	Sihine (10)	ETH	29.1.83	6	Pre	Eugene	3 Jun
26:53.27	Eliud	Kipchoge	KEN	5.11.84	5	VD	Bruxelles	16 Sep
26:54.25	Mathew	Kisorio	KEN	16.5.89	7	Pre	Eugene	3 Jun
26:54.64	Mark	Kiptoo	KEN	21.6.76	8	Pre	Eugene	3 Jun
26:55.29	Leonard Patrick	Komon	KEN	10.1.88	9	Pre	Eugene	3 Jun
26:55.73	Geoffrey	Kirui	KEN-J	16.2.93	6	VD	Bruxelles	16 Sep
26:59.81	Titus	Mbishei	KEN	28.10.90	7	VD	Bruxelles	16 Sep
27:06.35	Geoffrey	Kipsang	KEN-J	28.11.92	10	Pre	Eugene	3 Jun
27:09.02	Ibrahim	Jeylan	ETH	12.6.89	1		Kitami	19 Jun
27:10.05	Moses	Masai	KEN	1.6.86	11	Pre	Eugene	3 Jun
27:12.24		Rotich			11	Pre	Eugene	3 Jun
27:13.67	Bitan	Karoki (20)	KEN	21.8.90	1rA	Jordan	Stanford	1 May
27:13.81		Jeylan			1	WCh	Daegu	28 Aug

Mark	Name		Nat	Born	Pos	Meet	Venue	Date
27:14.07		Farah			2	WCh	Daegu	28 Aug
27:18.58		Tanui			1		Kita-Kyushu	14 May
27:19.14		Merga			3	WCh	Daegu	28 Aug
27:21.62	Paul	Lonyangat	KEN-J	12.12.92	8	VD	Bruxelles	16 Sep
27:22.09	John	Cheruiyot	KEN	5.7.90	13	Pre	Eugene	3 Jun
27:22.53	James	Rungaru	KEN-J	14.1.93	1		Nittai	24 Sep
27:22.54	Abera	Kuma	ETH	31.8.90	14	Pre	Eugene	3 Jun
27:22.57		Tadese			4	WCh	Daegu	28 Aug
(30/24)								
27:23.82	Edward	Waweru	KEN	3.10.90	1		Fukuroi	15 Oct
27:23.85	Martin	Mathathi	KEN	25.12.85	1		Kobe	24 Apr
27:23.99	John	Thuo	KEN	27.11.85	2		Kobe	24 Apr
27:24.67	Bobby	Curtis	USA	28.11.84	2rA	Jordan	Stanford	1 May
27:24.95	Ben	St. Lawrence	AUS	7.11.81	3rA	Jordan	Stanford	1 May
27:25.63	Peter Cheruiyot	Kirui	KEN	2.1.88	6	WCh	Daegu	28 Aug
(30)								
27:27.36	Chris	Thompson	GBR	17.4.81	4rA	Jordan	Stanford	1 May
27:28.19	Tim	Nelson	USA	27.2.84	5rA	Jordan	Stanford	1 May
27:28.22	Matt	Tegenkamp	USA	19.1.82	6rA	Jordan	Stanford	1 May
27:28.64	Stephen	Sambu	KEN	7.7.88	7rA	Jordan	Stanford	1 May
27:29.40	Leonard	Korir	KEN	10.12.86	8rA	Jordan	Stanford	1 May
27:30.50	Kevin	Chelimo	KEN	14.2.83	9rA	Jordan	Stanford	1 May
27:30.53	Mike	Kigen	KEN	15.1.86	9	VD	Bruxelles	16 Sep
27:30.68	Juan Luis	Barrios	MEX	24.6.83	10rA	Jordan	Stanford	1 May
27:31.15	Aron	Rono	KEN	1.11.82	11rA	Jordan	Stanford	1 May
27:31.46	Bouabdellah	Tahri	FRA	20.12.78	12rA	Jordan	Stanford	1 May
(40)								
27:32.59	Bayron	Piedra	ECU	19.8.82	13rA	Jordan	Stanford	1 May
27:32.9A	Wilson	Kiprop	KEN	14.4.87	2	NC	Nairobi	16 Jul
27:32.97	Dennis	Masai	KEN	1.12.91	10	VD	Bruxelles	16 Sep
27:33.14	Patrick	Mwaka	KEN-J	2.11.92	3		Fukuroi	15 Oct
27:37.21	Teklemariam	Medhin	ERI	24.6.89	16	Pre	Eugene	3 Jun
27:38.9A	Geoffrey	Mutai	KEN	7.10.81	4	NC	Nairobi	16 Jul
27:39.21	Josphat	Muchiri Ndambiri	KEN	12.2.85	1		Kumagaya	21 May
27:40.60	Paul	Kuira	KEN	25.1.90	1		Kawasaki	26 Nov
27:40.69	Tsuyoshi	Ugachi	JPN	27.4.87	2		Kawasaki	26 Nov
27:41.32	Gideon	Ngatuny	KEN	10.10.86	2		Kumagaya	21 May
(50)								
27:41.33	Lewis	Korir	KEN	11.6.86	1		Helsinki	31 May
27:41.57	Chihiro	Miyawaki	JPN	28.8.91	3		Kawasaki	26 Nov
27:44.30	Tetsuya	Yoroizaka	JPN	20.3.90	2	UK Ch	Birmingham	29 Jul
27:44.50	Daniele	Meucci	ITA	8.4.85	3	UK Ch	Birmingham	29 Jul
27:47.51	Alex	Mwangi	KEN	14.6.90	3		Fukagawa	25 Jun
27:47.79	Kazuya	Watanabe	JPN	7.7.87	4		Fukagawa	25 Jun
27:48.5A	Kenneth	Kipkemoi	KEN	2.8.84	6	NC	Nairobi	16 Jul
27:48.74	Jacob	Wanjuki	KEN	16.1.86	1		Kobe	23 Apr
27:48.84	Ayele	Abshero	ETH	28.12.90	17	Pre	Eugene	3 Jun
27:50.50	Micah	Kogo	KEN	3.6.86	1	Zat	Melbourne	10 Dec
(60)								
27:51.17	Alemu	Desta	ETH-J	18.2.92	2		Kitakyushu	14 May
27:51.49	Juan Carlos	Romero	MEX	15.12.77	15rA	Jordan	Stanford	1 May
27:51.78	Scott	Bauhs	USA	11.5.86	16rA	Jordan	Stanford	1 May
27:52.19	Vincent	Rono	KEN	22.12.90	1		Pontevedra	2 Apr
27:53.50	Najim	El Qady	MAR	31.12.80	1		Rabat	10 Jul
27:53.55	Rui	Silva	POR	3.8.77	2		Pontevedra	2 Apr
27:55.81	Josephat	Menjo	KEN	20.8.79	1		Turku	11 Sep
27:56.18	Stephen	Mokoka	RSA	31.1.85	1		Stellenbosch	29 Apr
27:57.42	Ryan	Vail	USA	19.3.86	17rA	Jordan	Stanford	1 May
27:57.63	Daniel	Gitau	KEN	1.10.87	7		Kobe	24 Apr
(70)								
27:57.88	Aaron	Braun	USA	28.5.87	18rA	Jordan	Stanford	1 May
27:58.17	Hicham	Bellani	MAR	15.9.79	2		Rabat	10 Jul
27:58.26	Duncan Kipkemboi Muti		KEN	8.3.91	2		Yokohama	29 Oct
27:59.60	Yuki	Sato	JPN	26.11.86	19rA	Jordan	Stanford	1 May
28:00.78	Akinobu	Murasawa	JPN	28.3.91	8		Kobe	24 Apr
28:01.31	Takuya	Fukatsu	JPN	10.11.87	8		Naruto	23 Sep
28:02.46	Ikuto	Yufu	JPN	7.7.91	5		Fukagawa	25 Jun
28:03.27	Hiromitsu	Kakuage	JPN	14.9.90	6		Fukagawa	25 Jun
28:03.43	Benjamin	Gandu	KEN	21.5.90	7		Fukagawa	25 Jun
28:03.46	Yuki	Matsuoka	JPN	14.1.86	1		Niigata	10 Oct
(80)								

Mark	Name		Nat	Born	Pos	Meet	Venue	Date
28:03.48	Micah	Njeru	KEN	5.8.88	8		Fukagawa	25 Jun
28:04.63	Daniel	Salel	KEN	11.12.90	19	Pre	Eugene	3 Jun
28:05.84	Naoki	Okamoto	JPN	26.5.84	9		Kobe	24 Apr
28:06.35	Hiroyuki	Ono	JPN	3.10.86	9		Fukagawa	25 Jun
28:07.52	Brian	Olinger	USA	2.6.83	20rA	Jordan	Stanford	1 May
28:08.53	Hisanori	Kitajima	JPN	16.10.84	10		Naruto	23 Sep
28:09.24	Marílson	dos Santos	BRA	6.8.77	1		São Paulo	20 May
28:09.33	Gladwin	Mzazi	RSA	28.8.88	2		Stellenbosch	29 Apr
28:10.5A	Philemon Kimeli	Limo	KEN	2.8.85	12	NC	Nairobi	16 Jul
28:11.0A	Henry	Chirchir	KEN	14.5.85	13	NC	Nairobi	16 Jul
(90)								
28:11.00	Bobby	Mack	USA	30.12.84	21rA	Jordan	Stanford	1 May
28:12.18	Samuel	Chelanga	KEN	23.2.85	2	NCAA	Des Moines	10 Jun
28:12.25	Jorge	Torres	USA	22.8.80	22rA	Jordan	Stanford	1 May
28:12.66	David	McNeill	AUS	6.10.86	5	2 NC	Melbourne	10 Dec
28:12.82	Dylan	Wykes	CAN	6.6.83	23rA	Jordan	Stanford	1 May
28:13.97A	Soyekwo	Kibet	UGA-J	6.6.92	1	NC	Kampala	22 Jul
28:14.43	Takayuki	Matsumiya	JPN	21.2.80	24rA	Jordan	Stanford	1 May
28:14.44	Takuya	Ishikawa	JPN	29.10.87	10		Kobe	24 Apr
28:15.5A	Michael	Mutai	KEN		1		Amalo	25 Jun
28:15.79	Sergey	Rybin	RUS	30.9.85	1	Znam	Zhukovskiy	3 Jul
(100)								

Mark	Name		Nat	Born	Date		Mark	Name		Nat	Born	Date
28:16.49	Ken-ichi	Jiromaru	JPN	1.10.84	25 Jun		28:28.65	Kazuhiro	Maeda	JPN	19.4.81	14 May
28:16.65	Ben	True	USA	29.12.85	1 May		28:29.16	Tatsunori	Hamasaki	JPN	4.7.88	26 Nov
28:17.57	Kenta	Murayama	JPN-J	23.2.93	15 Oct		28:29.69	Robert	Cheseret	USA	8.10.83	25 Mar
28:17.99	Kenta	Matsumoto	JPN	1.6.91	25 Jun		28:29.71	Nick	Arciniaga	USA	30.6.83	1 May
28:18.13	Hiroki	Mitsuoka	JPN	28.2.89	25 Jun		28:30.0A	Dennis	Kipruto	KEN-Y	.94	16 Jul
28:18.52	Ryo	Kiname	JPN	22.1.91	25 Jun		28:30.07	Christopher	Landry	USA	29.4.86	1 May
28:19.1A	Peter Chesang Kurui		KEN	2.1.90	16 Jul		28:30.32	Hiroyuki	Horibata	JPN	28.10.86	3 May
28:20.03	Youssef	El Kalai	POR	1.3.81	4 Jun		28:30.51	Yuta	Takahashi	JPN	13.4.87	3 Dec
28:20.35	Amos	Sang	KEN	10.1.88	1 May		28:31.15	James	Strang	USA	7.12.84	1 May
28:20.61	Azmeraw	Bekele	ETH	22.1.86	12 Sep		28:31.17	Josphat	Koech	KEN	.82	23 Apr
28:20.66	Kazuya	Deguchi	JPN	14.8.88	3 May		28:31.19	Charles	Kibet	KEN	16.5.91	26 Nov
28:20.98	Daisuke	Shimizu	JPN	2.8.82	1 May		28:31.44	Matthew	Rugut	KEN	24.5.82	23 Apr
28:21.79	Yevgeniy	Rybakov	RUS	27.2.85	3 Jul		28:31.49	Eric	Sebahire	RWA	6.1.85	23 Apr
28:21.86	Yusuke	Hasegawa	JPN	8.6.88	10 Oct		28:31.51	Sibusiso	Nzima	RSA	23.11.86	9 Apr
28:22.55	Samuel	Ndungu	KEN	4.4.88	23 Apr		28:32.18	Michael	Githinji	KEN-J	18.11.92	19 Nov
28:22.84	Ryo	Yamamoto	JPN	18.5.84	19 Nov		28:32.30	Ciarán	O'Lionáird	IRL	11.4.88	25 Mar
28:23.22A	Nicholas	Togom	KEN-J	.92	13 May		28:32.32	Kazuya	Kuga	JPN	7.3.91	25 Jun
28:23.33	Mekubo	Mogusu	KEN	25.12.86	21 May		28:32.38	Hillary	Kiprono	KEN	21.7.85	23 Apr
28:23.40	Dino	Sefer	ETH	28.5.88	12 Sep		28:32.73	Eric	Chirchir	KEN	20.11.83	20 Sep
28:23.61	Shinobu	Kubota	JPN	12.12.91	25 Jun		28:32.86	Fikre	Assefa	ETH	18.1.89	19 Jun
28:23.89	Tony	Okello	UGA	26.12.83	1 May		28:33.04	Hussain	Al-Hamdah	KSA	4.8.83	2 Apr
28:24.16	José Manuel	Martínez	ESP	22.10.71	4 Jun		28:33.32	Maina	Karukawa	KEN	19.6.91	23 Apr
28:24.26	Jacob	Korir	KEN	15.8.80	1 May		28:33.34	Abdennacir	Fathi	MAR	25.1.87	10 Jul
28:24.33	Charlie	Serrano	USA	21.8.84	1 May		28:33.47	Luke	Puskedra	USA	8.2.90	10 Jun
28:24.53	Stephen	Haas	USA	18.4.83	1 May		28:34.21	Yoshikazu	Kawazoe	JPN	26.9.87	14 May
28:24.59	Yoshinori	Oda	JPN	5.12.80	1 May		28:34.22	Patrick	Stitzinger	NED	25.8.81	15 Jun
28:24.59	Yusuke	Takabayashi	JPN	19.7.87	10 Jun		28:34.50	Mike	Fout	USA	7.5.90	1 May
28:24.61	Kazuharu	Takai	JPN	10.5.84	3 May		28:34.66	Minato	Oishi	JPN	19.5.88	26 Nov
28:24.63A	Peter	Kibet	UGA-J	18.6.92	22 Jul		28:35.1A	Bernard	Kipyego	KEN	16.7.86	3 Jun
28:24.82	Yusei	Nakao	JPN	28.2.84	25 Jun		28:35.4A	Philemon	Rono	KEN	.91	3 Jun
28:25.10	Nicholas	Makau	KEN	15.10.90	23 Apr		28:35.49	Hassan	Mahboob Ali	BRN	31.12.81	7 Jul
28:25.17	Ryuji	Kashiwabara	JPN	13.7.89	24 Apr		28:35.63	Kazuyoshi	Shimozato	JPN	9.4.81	25 Jun
28:25.29	Matti	Räsänen	FIN	15.2.83	1 May		28:35.9	Wissam	Hosni	TUN	8.3.85	19 Jun
28:25.29	Julio César	Pérez	MEX	22.5.82	1 May		28:36.17	Sean	Connolly	IRL	3.8.82	29 Jul
28:25.46	Pavel	Shapovalov	RUS	10.10.75	3 Jul		28:36.2A	Wilson	Kipsang	KEN	15.3.82	3 Jun
28:26.59	Jason	Hartmann	USA	21.3.81	1 May		28:36.23	Joseph	Gitau	KEN	3.1.88	14 May
28:26.65	Chris	Derrick	USA	17.10.90	10 Jun		28:36.30	Bilisuma	Shugi	BRN	19.7.89	7 Jul
28:27.03	Keith	Gerrard	GBR	24.3.86	1 May		28:36.4A	Joseph	Kiptum	KEN	25.9.87	3 Jun
28:27.31	Jake	Riley	USA	2.11.88	10 Jun		28:36.49	Tomomi	Itakura	JPN	20.6.84	8 Oct
28:27.54A	Thomas	Ayeko	UGA-J	10.2.92	13 May		28:36.82	Atsushi	Yamazaki	JPN	7.10.86	26 Nov
28:27.63	Fumihiro	Maruyama	JPN	1.7.90	3 May		28:37.12	Takamasa	Uchida	JPN	17.10.81	25 Jun
28:27.86	Muryo	Takase	JPN	31.1.89	25 Jun		28:37.20	Timothy	Ritchie	USA	7.8.87	1 May
28:28.23	Tomoya	Adachi	JPN	18.12.85	3 May		28:37.30	James	Walsh	GBR	22.9.81	29 Jul
28:28.64	Masaki	Ito	JPN	19.5.89	26 Nov		28:37.41	Ryo	Matsumoto (188)	JPN	19.10.90	25 Jun)

JUNIORS

See main list for top 8 juniors. 14 performances by 10 men to 28:24.0. Additional marks and further juniors:

G Kirui	27:55.74A	1	Af-J	Gaborone	13 May				
Rungaru	27:44.86	2		Fukagawa	25 Jun				
Mwaka	27:49.93	3		Kobe	23 Apr	28:02.87	2	Gifu	7 May
28:17.57	Kenta	Murayama	JPN	23.2.93	6		Fukuroi		15 Oct
28:23.22A	Nicholas	Togom (10)	KEN	.92	2	Af-J	Gaborone		13 May
28:24.63A	Peter	Kibet	UGA	18.6.92	2	NC	Kampala		22 Jul
28:27.54A	Thomas	Ayeko	UGA	10.2.92	3	Af-J	Gaborone		13 May

Mark	Name	Nat	Born	Pos	Meet	Venue	Date
28:30.0A	Dennis Kipruto	KEN-Y	.94	2rB	NC	Nairobi	16 Jul
28:32.18	Michael Githinji	KEN	18.11.92	3		Yokohama	19 Nov
28:40.02	Mohamed Karim Tahiri	MAR	1,6.92	4		Rabat	11 Jul
28:44.00	Shota Shinjo	JPN	11.10.92	7r2		Kawasaki	26 Nov
28:44.95A	Mukter Edris	ETH	14.1.94	4	Af-J	Gaborone	13 May
28:50.70	Joseph Onsarigo	KEN	.93	1r5		Yokohama	30 Apr
28:52.22	Yuya Ito	JPN	9.1.92	1r3		Kawasaki	26 Nov
28:52.34	Stephen Njeri (20)	KEN		1		Kagoshima	10 Apr

Best European: 30:01.04 Szymon Kulka POL 22.6.93 1 Lidzbark Warm. 3 May

10 KILOMETRES ROAD

Mark	Name	Nat	Born	Pos	Meet	Venue	Date
27:15	Micah Kogo	KEN	2.6.86	1		Brunssum	3 Apr
27:15	Leonard Patrick Komon	KEN	10.1.88	1		Berlin	9 Oct
27:17+	Komon			1	in 10M	Zaandam	18 Sep
27:19	Geoffrey Mutai	KEN	7.10.81	1		Boston	26 Jun
27:22+	Samuel Tsegay	ERI	24.2.88	2	in 10M	Zaandam	18 Sep
27:26	Mike Kigen	KEN	15.1.86	2		Brunssum	3 Apr
27:28	Philip Langat	KEN	23.4.90	1		Utrecht	25 Sep
(7/6)							
27:31+	Deriba Merga	ETH	26.10.82	1	in HMar	Ra's Al-Khaymah	18 Feb
27:32	Titus Mbishei	KEN	29.10.90	1		Marseille	1 May
27:34	Philemon Limo	KEN	2.8.85	1		Praha	10 Sep
27:35	Sammy Kitwara	KEN	26.11.86	1		San Juan	27 Feb

Where superior to track best

Mark	Name	Nat	Born	Pos	Meet	Venue	Date
27:43+	John Mwangangi	KEN	1.11.90	3	in 10M	Zaandam	18 Sep
27:43+	Kennedy Kimutai	KEN	18.1.90	4	in 10M	Zaandam	18 Sep
27:45	Dejen Gebremeskel	ETH	24.11.89	2		San Juan	27 Feb
27:45	Timothy Kiptoo	KEN	2.8.84	2		Utrecht	25 Sep
27:46	Atsedu Tsegay	ETH	17.12.91	1		Langueux	25 Jun
27:46	Milton Rotich	KRN	.84	1		Cardiff	11 Sep
27:50+	Jonathan Maiyo	KEN	.88	2	in HMar	Newcastle	18 Sep
27:50	Tilahun Regassa	ETH	18.1.90	3		Luanda	31 Dec
27:52	Henry Kiplagat	KEN	.90	3		Berlin	9 Oct
27:53	Azmeraw Bekele	ETH	22.1.86	4		Luanda	31 Dec
27:55+	Levi Matebo Omari	KEN	3.11.89	1=	in HMar	Nice	17 Apr
27:55+	Silas Kipruto	KEN	26.9.84	1=	in HMar	Nice	17 Apr
27:56	Joseph Ebuya	KEN	20.6.87	3		New York	14 May
27:57	Jacob Chesari	KEN	6.4.84	2		Würzburg	17 Apr
27:57	Nicholas Kemboi	QAT	25.11.83	3		Utrecht	25 Sep
27:59	Marílson dos Santos	BRA	6.8.77	1		Santos	15 May
28:00	Edward Muge	KEN	26.6.83	3		Cape Elizabeth	6 Aug
28:01	Hosea Macharinyang	KEN	12.6.86	4		Cape Elizabeth	6 Aug
28:02	Lelisa Desisa	ETH	14.1.90	3		San Juan	27 Feb
28:02	Thomas Ayeko	UGA-J	10.2.92	3		Würzburg	17 Apr
28:02	Boniface Kirui	KEN	27.10.87	1		Appingedam	25 Jun
28:03	Daniel Chebii	KEN	.85	4		Würzburg	17 Apr
28:04+	Bernard Kipyego	KEN	16.7.86		in HMar	Ra's Al-Khaymah	18 Feb
28:04+	Titus Masai	KEN	9.10.89		in HMar	Ra's Al-Khaymah	18 Feb
28:04+	John Kiprotich	KEN	.88		in HMar	Ra's Al-Khaymah	18 Feb
28:04	Leonard Langat	KEN	7.8.90	5		Würzburg	17 Apr
28:05	Ezekiel Meli	KEN	21.4.84	1		Cuneo	13 Nov
28:07	Titus Waruru	KEN-Y	29.3.94	1		Tamana	6 Mar
28:07+	Pius Maiyo Kirop	KEN	6.1.90		in HMar	Verbania	6 Mar
28:07+	Shumi Dechasa	ETH	28.5.89		in HMar	Verbania	6 Mar
28:07	Wilfred Murgor	KEN	12.12.88	1		Hilversum	17 Apr
28:07	Hicham El Abbassi	MAR	15.7.79	2		Cuneo	13 Nov
28:08+	Dereje Hailegiorgis	ETH	27.9.84		in HMar	Verbania	6 Mar
28:08+	Robert Wambua Mbithi	KEN	26.6.89		in HMar	Verbania	6 Mar
28:08+	Henry Chirchir	KEN	14.5.85		in HMar	Praha	2 Apr
28:08+	Jairus Chanchima	KEN	5.12.84		in HMar	Praha	2 Apr
28:08	Haile Gebrselassie	ETH	18.4.73	5		Luanda	31 Dec
28:10	Alex Oleitiptip	KEN	22.9.82	3		Marseille	1 May

Mark	Name	Nat	Born	Date
28:11	Gebregziabher Gebremariam	ETH	10.9.84	26 Jun
28:12+	Mekubo Meguso	JPN	25.12.86	6 Feb
28:12+	Edwin Kipyego	KEN	.91	17 Apr
28:13	Philemon Yator	KEN-J	2.4.92	23 Jul
28:13	Allan Kiprono	KEN	15.2.90	6 Aug
28:14	Belete Assefa	ETH	3.3.91	23 Apr
28:16+	Yrsaw Tegene	ETH	.90	27 Mar
28:16+	Peter Chesang Kurui	KEN	2.1.90	27 Mar
28:16	Richard Sigei	KEN	11.5.84	10 Jun
28:17+	Patrick Makau	KEN	2.3.85	18 Feb
28:17	Edwin Soi	KEN	3.3.86	18 Dec
28:18	Hafid Chani	MAR	12.2.86	2 Oct
28:19	Simon Ndirangu	KEN	1.11.85	14 May
28:20+	Tujuba Megersa	ETH	15.10.87	27 Feb
28:20+	Joel Kimurer Kemboi	KEN	21.1.88	27 Feb
28:20+	Abraham Chebii	KEN	23.12.79	27 Feb
28:20+	Nickson Kurgat	KEN		27 Feb
28:20	Emmanuel Kipkemei	KEN		5 Jun

Mark	Name	Nat	Born	Pos Meet	Venue	Date
28:21+	Elisha Tarus	KEN	.88			6 Mar
28:21	Nicholas Keter	KEN				15 May
28:21+	Paul Kimugul	KEN	4.3.80			21 May
28:21	Solomon Deksisa	ETH-Y	11.3.94			9 Oct
28:22	Charles Maina	KEN	11.10.82			13 Mar
28:22+	Kenneth Kiplimo Kimutai	KEN	10.12.81			21 May
28:22+	Albert Matebor	KEN	20.12.80			21 May
28:22	Isaac Mwangi	KEN	.87			18 Dec
28:24	Stanley Salil	KEN	2.4.86			3 Apr
28:24+	Adugna Tekele	ETH	26.2.89			21 May
28:24	Charlie Serrano	USA	21.8.84			24 Nov
28:25	Tesfaye Girma	ETH	25.9.82			14 May
28:25	Sergiy Lebid	UKR	15.7.75			15 May
28:25	Abraham Niyonkuru	BDI	26.12.89			25 Jun
28:26	Mustapha Riyad	BRN	5.8.75			3 Apr
28:26+	Sentayehu Mergia	ETH	18.3.85			21 May
28:26	Wilson Kipsang	KEN	15.3.82			25 Jun
28:27	Patrick Kimeli	KEN	22.4.89			3 Apr
28:27	Paul Kipkorir	KEN	.82			10 Jun
28:27	Alfred Cherop	KEN	2.3.86			26 Jun
28:27+	Abel Kirui	KEN	4.6.82			30 Oct
28:27dh 34m	Ridouane Harroufi	MAR	30.7.81			4 Jul
28:28	Essa Ismail Rasheed	QAT	14.12.86			3 Apr
28:28	Peter Wanjiru	KEN	.82			3 Apr
28:28dh 34m	Peter Kamais	KEN	7.11.76			4 Jul
28:28+	Abdellatif Meftah	FRA	3.1.82			18 Sep
28:28+	Feyisa Lilesa	ETH	1.2.90			27 Nov
28:29	Moses Mosop	KEN	17.7.85			26 Jun
28:29dh 34m	Ed Moran	USA	27.5.81			4 Jul
28:30+	Joseph Kiptoo Birech	KEN	4.1.84			13 Mar
28:30+	Philemon Rono	KEN	.91			18 Sep
28:30+	Joseph Kiptum	KEN	25.9.87			25 Sep

Downhill

Mark	Name	Nat	Born	Pos	Venue	Date
27:57	Hagos Gebrehiwot	ETH-Y	11.5.94	1	Madrid 50m)	31 Dec
28:06	Julius Kogo	KEN	12.8.85	1	Rockville (60m)	17 Apr
28:08	Reid Coolsaet	CAN	29.7.79	1	Toronto (87m)	1 May
28:09	Eric Gillis	CAN	8.3.80	2	Toronto	1 May
28:10	Kip Kangogo	KEN	20.7.79	3	Toronto	1 May
28:10	Ayad Lamdassem	ESP	11.10.81	3	Madrid	31 Dec
28:12A	Patrick Smyth	USA	6.8.86			25 Jul
28:14	Nicholas Kurgat	KEN				17 Apr
28:18	Mohamed Trafeh	USA	1.5.85			17 Sep
28:18	Abraham Niyonkuru	BDI	26.12.89			30 Oct
28:19	Abiyote Endale	ETH	3.5.86			17 Apr
28:23	Adugna Kumsa	ETH	17.7.86			17 Apr
28:28	Derese Deniboba	ETH	15.5.82			17 Apr

Uncertain measurement: Jan 16, Kapsabet (A): 10k: 1, J Kogo 27:54; 2, N Sirma 28:19; 3, G Kipkosgei 28:25
Short course: Nov 27, Hyderabad: 1, D Yegon KEN 27:30; 2, P Yego KEN 27:35; 3, M Muiamukule KEN 27:38; 4, John Kosgei KEN 27:39; 5, H Kosgei KEN 28:31

15 KILOMETRES ROAD

15k	20k	Name	Nat	Born	Pos	Meet	Venue	Date
		See also intermediate times in 10 Miles and Half Marathon lists						
41:55A		Deriba Merga	ETH	26.10.80	1		Bahir Dar	13 Feb
42:25+	56:56	Sammy Kitwara	KEN	26.11.86		in HMar	New Delhi	27 Nov
42:30+		Dereje Hailegiorgis	ETH	27.9.84		in HMar	Milano	27 Mar
42:33+		Titus Masai Ndiwa	KEN	9.10.89		in HMar	Praha	2 Apr
42:34+		Azmeraw Bekele	ETH	22.1.86		in HMar	Praha	2 Apr
42:34		Philip Langat	KEN	16.2.83	1		s'Heerenberg	4 Dec
42:35+	57:05	John Kiprotich Chemisto	KEN	5.6.83		in HMar	Ra's Al-Khaymah	18 Feb
42:41A		Yakob Jarso	ETH	5.2.88	2		Bahir Dar	13 Feb
42:43A		Feyisa Lilesa	ETH	1.2.90	3		Bahir Dar	13 Feb
42:44		Haile Gebrselassie	ETH	18.4.73	1		Nijmegen	20 Nov
42:52+	57:56	Kenneth Kiplimo Kimutai	KEN	10.12.81		in HMar	Göteborg	21 May
42:55		Hailu Mekonnen	ETH	4.4.80	2		s'Heerenberg	4 Dec
42:56+		Francis Kosgei	KEN	.813		in HMar	Den Haag	13 Mar
42:58		Mohamed Trafeh	USA	1.5.85	1	NC	Jacksonville	12 Mar
42:59+	57:40	Martin Mathathi	KEN	25.12.85		in HMar	Gifu	15 May
43:00+		Emmanuel Bett	KEN	30.3.83		in HMar	New Delhi	27 Sep
43:02+	58:41	Sentayehu Mergia	ETH	18.3.85		in HMar	Göteborg	21 May
43:03+	57:31	Dino Sefer	ETH	28.5.88		in HMar	New Delhi	27 Nov
43:05+		Eliud Kiptanui	KEN	6.6.89		in HMar	Olomouc	19 Jun
43:15		Vincent Kipruto	KEN	13.9.87	2		Nijmegen	20 Nov
43:21+		Abel Kirui	KEN	4.6.82			30 Oct
43:25		Ben True	USA	29.12.85			12 Mar
43:26		Aaron Braun	USA	28.5.87			12 Mar
43:28+		Patrick Makau	KEN	2.3.85			18 Feb
43:29+		Wilson Kiprotich	KEN	20.7.80			21 May
43:30		Ridouane Harroufi	MAR	30.7.81			10 Jul

10 MILES ROAD

10M	15k	Name	Nat	Born	Pos	Meet	Venue	Date
44:27	41:26	Leonard Patrick Komon	KEN	10.1.88	1		Zaandam	18 Sep
44:38	41:31	Samuel Tsegay	ERI	24.2.88	2		Zaandam	18 Sep
44:42+		Martin Mathathi	KEN	25.12.85	1	in HMar	South Shields	18 Sep
44:53+	41:45	Deriba Merga	ETH	26.10.80	1	in HMar	Ra's Al-Khaymah	18 Feb
44:53+		Sammy Kitwara	KEN	26.11.86		in HMar	Philadelphia	18 Sep
44:54+		Mathew Kisorio	KEN	16.5.89		in HMar	Philadelphia	18 Sep
45:13	42:08	John Mwangangi	KEN	1.11.90	3		Zaandam	18 Sep
45:15	42:08	Kennedy Kimutai	KEN	18.1.90	4		Zaandam	18 Sep
45:36		Lelisa Desisa	ETH	14.1.90	1		Washington	3 Apr
45:41		Allan Kiprono	KEN	15.2.90	2		Washington	3 Apr
45:44+		Leonard Langat	KEN	7.8.90		in HMar	Ra's Al-Khaymah	18 Feb
45:44+		Titus Masai Ndiwa	KEN	9.10.89		in HMar	Ra's Al-Khaymah	18 Feb
45:44+		John Kiprotich	KEN	.88		in HMar	Ra's Al-Khaymah	18 Feb

Mark		Name		Nat	Born	Pos	Meet	Venue	Date
45:45+		Bernard	Kipyego	KEN	16.7.86		in HMar	Ra's Al-Khaymah	18 Feb
46:19	43:11	Henry	Kiplagat	KEN	.90	5		Zaandam	18 Sep
46:20	42:52	Joseph Kiptoo	Birech	KEN	4.1.84		in HMar	Den Haag	13 Mar
46:21+		James	Mwangi	KEN	23.6.84		in HMar	Philadelphia	18 Sep
46:21+		Peter	Kamais	KEN	7.11.76		in HMar	Philadelphia	18 Sep
46:22+		Julius	Koskei	KEN	6.4.82		in HMar	Philadelphia	18 Sep
46:26	43:13	Philemon	Rono	KEN	.91	6		Zaandam	18 Sep
46:27		Ridouane	Harroufi	MAR	30.7.81	3		Washington	3 Apr
46:30		Lani	Kiplagat	KEN		4		Washington	3 Apr

20 KILOMETRES ROAD

See Half Marsthon list for intermediate times at 20km and:

58:13+	42:52	Paul	Kimugul	KEN	4.3.80	3	in HMar	Göteborg	21 May

At Paris 9 Oct: 1. John Mwangangi KEN 58:15, 2. Bekele Feyisa ETH 58:23. 3, Mustapha El Aziz MAR 58:26

HALF MARATHON

HMar	20k	15k			Nat	Born	Pos	Meet	Venue	Date
58:30			Zersenay	Tadese	ERI	8.2.82	1		Lisboa	20 Mar
58:46	55:44	41:53	Mathew	Kisorio	KEN	16.5.89	1		Philadelphia	18 Sep
58:48		41:53	Sammy	Kitwara	KEN	26.11.86	2		Philadelphia	18 Sep
58:56dh		41:48	Martin	Mathathi	KEN	25.12.85	1	GNR	South Shields	18 Sep
59:25	56:16	41:44	Deriba	Merga	ETH	26.10.80	1		Ra's Al-Khaymah	18 Feb
59:27dh			Jonathan	Maiyo	KEN	.88	2	GNR	South Shields	18 Sep
59:30		41:56	Philemon	Limo	KEN	2.8.85	1		Praha	2 Apr
59:30				Tadese			1		Porto	18 Sep
59:30	56:38	42:26	Lelisa	Desisa	ETH	14.1.90	1		New Delhi	27 Nov
59:31	56:37	42:25	Geoffrey	Kipsang	KEN-J	28.11.92	2		New Delhi	27 Nov
59:37	56:45	42:36		Desisa			1		Den Haag	13 Mar
59:39	56:45	42:36	Azmeraw	Bekele (10)	ETH	22.1.86	2		Den Haag	13 Mar
59:40	56:45	42:36	Peter Cheruiyot	Kirui	KEN	2.1.88	3		Den Haag	13 Mar
59:42	56:45	42:36	Ayele	Abshero	ETH	28.12.90	4		Den Haag	13 Mar
59:42			Dino	Sefer	ETH	28.5.88	1		Ivry-sur-Seine	3 Apr
59:43			Tujuba	Megersa	ETH	15.10.87	2		Ivry-sur-Seine	3 Apr
59:44	56:46	42:37	Lucas	Rotich	KEN	16.4.90	5		Den Haag	13 Mar
59:45	56:47	42:34	Bernard	Kipyego	KEN	16.7.86	2		Ra's Al-Khaymah	18 Feb
59:45			John	Mwangangi	KEN	1.11.90	1		Valencia	23 Oct
59:47			Kenneth Kiplimo	Kipkemoi	KEN	2.8.84	2		Valencia	23 Oct
59:52	56:49	42:35	Leonard	Langat	KEN	7.8.90	3		Ra's Al-Khaymah	18 Feb
59:52dh			Emmanuel	Mutai (20)	KEN	12.10,84	3	GNR	South Shields	18 Sep
59:58		42:40		Megersa			1		Ostia	27 Feb
59:58	56:51	42:26	Mike	Kigen	KEN	15.1.86	3		New Delhi	27 Nov
60:00			Dereje	Hailegiorgis	ETH	27.9.84	1		Verbania	6 Mar
60:01	56:52	42:37	James	Kwambai	KEN	28.2.83	6		Den Haag	13 Mar
60:02				G Kipsang			1		Lille	3 Sep
60:03		42:35	Shumi	Dechasa	ETH	28,5,89	2		Verbania	6 Mar
60:03		42:24		Kisorio			1		Milano	27 Mar
60:03dh			Micah	Kogo	KEN	3.6.86	4	GNR	South Shields	18 Sep
60:04		42:35	Pius Maiyo	Kirop	KEN	6.1.90	3		Verbania	6 Mar
			(30/26)							
60:05		42:40	Joel	Kimurer Kemboi	KEN	21.1.88	2		Ostia	27 Feb
60:07		42:40	Abraham	Chebii	KEN	23.12.79	3		Ostia	27 Feb
60:07		42:25	Levi	Matebo Omari	KEN	3.11.89	1		Nice	17 Apr
60:10		42:35	John Kiprotich	Chemisto	KEN	5.6.83	4		Ra's Al-Khaymah	18 Feb
			(30)							
60:18			Haile	Gebrselassie	ETH	18.4.73	1		Wien	18 Apr
60:20		42:30	Eric	Ndiema	KEN-J	28.12.92	2		Milano	27 Mar
60:20			Stephen Kipkosgei Kibet		KEN	9.11.86	1		Udine	25 Sep
60:23	57:30	43:37	Mohamed	Farah	GBR	23.3.83	1		New York	20 Mar
60:23			Stanley	Biwott	KEN	21.4.86	1		Azkoitia	26 Mar
60:23			Stephen	Kibiwott	KEN	3.4.80	3		Lille	3 Sep
60:25	57:29	43:38	Gebre-egziabher	Gebremariam	ETH	10.9.84	2		New York	20 Mar
60:29			Mark	Kiptoo	KEN	21.6.76	2		Azkoitia	26 Mar
60:30	57:29	43:37	Galen	Rupp	USA	8.5.86	3		New York	20 Mar
60:35	57:30	43:37	Tesfaye	Girma	ETH	25.9.82	4		New York	20 Mar
			(40)							
60:38			Silas	Sang	KEN	21.8.78	3		Lisboa	20 Mar
60:40			Joseph Kiptoo	Birech	KEN	4.1.84	2		Alicante	23 Jan
60:40	57:27	42:35	Titus	Masai Ndiwa	KEN	9.10.89	5		Ra's Al-Khaymah	18 Feb
60:40		42:35	Peter Chesang	Kurui	KEN	2.1.90	4	Stra	Milano	27 Mar

Mark			Name	Nat	Born	Pos	Meet	Venue	Date
60:43			Robert Kipchumba	KEN	24.2.84	4		Lisboa	20 Mar
60:43			James Mwangi	KEN	23.6.84	3		Philadelphia	18 Sep
60:44		43:05	Abdullah Dawit Shami (Yatich)	ETH	16.7.74	1		Olomouc	19 Jun
60:46	57:42	43:38	Peter Kamais	KEN	7.11.76	5		New York	20 Mar
60:49	57:45	43:38	Alistair Cragg	IRL	13.6.80	6		New York	20 Mar
60:49			Wilson Kipsang	KEN	15.3.82	1		Zwolle	18 Jun
(50)									
60:50	57:41		Feyisa Lilesa	ETH	1.2.90	7		New Delhi	27 Nov
60:52			Eliud Kiplagat	KEN	.85	2		Berlin	3 Apr
60:52	57:38	42:52	Albert Matebor	KEN	20.12.80	1		Göteborg	21 May
60:55	57:47	43:12	Samuel Ndungu	KEN	4.4.88	1		Marugame	6 Feb
60:55			Peter Muriuki	KEN	.83	3		Ivry-sur-Seine	3 Apr
60:56			Daniel Chebii	KEN	.85	3		Berlin	3 Apr
60:58	57:48	43:12	Tsuyoshi Ugachi	JPN	27.4.87	2		Marugame	6 Feb
60:59		42:34	Yrsaw Tegene	ETH	.90	5		Milano	27 Mar
60:59			Nicholas Manza Kamakya	KEN	2.3.85	4		Lille	3 Sep
60:59	57:42	42:41	Tilahun Regassa	ETH	18.1.90	8		New Delhi	27 Nov
(60)									
61:02	57:46	42:44	Shadrack Kemboi	KEN	19.2.86	8		Den Haag	13 Mar
61:02dh			Abdellatif Meftah	FRA	3.1.82	5	GNR	South Shields	18 Sep
61:07		42:43	Boniface Kirui	KEN	27.10.87	4		Verbania	6 Mar
61:07			Nicholas Kemboi	QAT/KEN	25.11.83	3		Valencia	23 Oct
61:08		42:52	Robert Wambua Mbithi	KEN	26.6.89	5		Verbania	6 Mar
61:08			Joseph Kiptum Busienei	KEN	25.9.87	2		Remich	25 Sep
61:08	57:52	43:01	Ezekiel Cherop	KEN	.85	9		New Delhi	27 Nov
61:09			Evans Kosgei	KEN	.89	4		Ivry-sur-Seine	3 Apr
61:09			Philip Sanga Kimutai	KEN	10.9.83	2		Porto	18 Sep
61:10			William Chebor	KEN	22.12.82	2		Udine	25 Sep
(70)									
61:11			Paul Kipkorir	KEN	.82	4		Berlin	3 Apr
61:11+			Eliud Kiptanui	KEN	6.6.89		in 25k	Berlin	8 May
61:11			Stephen Tum	KEN	.86	1		Laayoune	25 Dec
61:12			Atsedu Tsegay	ETH	17.12.91	2		Rabat	3 Apr
61:12			Silas Kipruto	KEN	26.9.84	2		Nice	17 Apr
61:12	58:13	43:05	Milton Rotich	KRN	.84	10		New Delhi	27 Nov
61:13			Marílson dos Santos	BRA	6.8.77	1	SACh	Buenos Aires	11 Sep
61:13			El Hassan El Abassi	MAR	15.7.79	3		Remich	25 Sep
61:14			Richard Sigei	KEN	11.5.84	5		Lille	3 Sep
61:16			Kenneth Kiplimo Kimutai	KEN	10.12.81	5		Berlin	3 Apr
(80)									
61:18			Sammy Kigen Korir	KEN	29.9.85	1		Warszawa	27 Mar
61:18			Geoffrey Ngugi	KEN	11.9.84	1		Krems	18 Sep
61:19	57:52	42:37	Jairus Chanchima	KEN	5.12.84	10		Den Haag	13 Mar
61:19	57:59	43:38	Moses Kigen	KEN	10.1.83	7		New York	20 Mar
61:20			Amanuel Mesel	ERI	29.12.90	4		Porto	18 Sep
61:21	58:04	43:00	Victor Kipchirchir	KRN	.86	11		New Delhi	27 Nov
61:22			Julius Koskei	KEN	6.4.82	5		Philadelphia	18 Sep
61:22			Abdellah Tagharrafet	MAR	.85	2		Laayoune	25 Dec
61:23			Edwin Kipyego	KEN	.91	1		Ribarroja	20 Feb
61:24			Nathaniel Kipkosgei	KEN	1.9.84	3		Rabat	3 Apr
(90)									
61:25	58:13	43:39	Shawn Forrest	AUS	10.7.83	9		New York	20 Mar
61:25		42:54	Henry Chirchir	KEN	14.5.85	4		Praha	2 Apr
61:26			Lawrence Rotich	KEN	20.8.86	5		Ivry-sur-Seine	3 Apr
61:26			Lukas Kanda	KEN	.87	6		Ivry-sur-Seine	3 Apr
61:28	58:22	43:32	Getu Feleke	ETH	28.11.86	6		Ra's Al-Khaymah	18 Feb
61:28			Bernard Rotich	KEN	11.8.86	2		Glasgow	4 Sep
61:29	57:46	42:38	Mekubo Mogusu	KEN	25.12.86	3		Marugame	6 Feb
61:30			Kennedy Kimutai	KEN	18.1.90	1		Leiden	15 May
61:30A			Dennis Koech	KEN-Y	22.1.94	1		Nairobi	30 Oct
61:31dh			Jaouad Gharib	MAR	22.5.72	6	GNR	South Shields	18 Sep
(100)									

Mark	Name	Nat	Born	Date		Mark	Name	Nat	Born	Date
61:33	Mergesa Bacha	ETH	.85	3 Apr		61:40+	Dickson Chumba	KEN	27.10.86	30 Oct
61:33	Mark Korir	KEN	10.1.85	21 Aug		61:41	Mike Mutai	KEN	.87	25 Sep
61:34	Paul Kimugul	KEN	4.3.80	21 May		61:42	Abreham Cherkos	ETH	23.9.89	27 Feb
61:38	Mourad El Bannouri	MAR	27.12.79	3 Apr		61:42	Stephen Mokoka	RSA	31.1.85	24 Apr
61:38	Sentayehu Mergia	ETH	18.3.85	20 Nov		61:42	Abderrahim Goumri	MAR	21.5.76	18 Sep
61:39	Edward Muge (42:46)	KEN	26.6.83	2 Apr		61:43	Nickson Kurgat	KEN	.88	27 Feb
61:39	Adugna Tekele (43:06)	ETH	26.2.89	19 Jun		61:43+	Isaac Macharia	KEN	25.11.80	25 Sep
61:39	Tewelde Estifanos	ERI	2.10.87	20 Nov		61:43+	Henry Sugut	KEN	4.5.85	25 Sep
61:39	Mohamed Trafeh	USA	1.5.85	18 Dec		61:44	Hosea Macharinyang	KEN	12.6.86	18 Sep
61:40	Ezekiel Chebii	KEN	3.1.91	17 Apr		61:44+	Patrick Makau	KEN	2.3.85	25 Sep

Mark	Name	Nat	Born	Pos Meet	Venue	Date
61:44+	Edwin Kimaiyo	KEN	.86			25 Sep
61:44+	Emmanuel Samal	KEN	.89			25 Sep
61:44+	Deresse Chimsa	ETH	21.11.76			30 Oct
61:45+	Onesmus Serem	KEN				8 May
61:45	Barnabas Sigei	KEN				4 Sep
61:45	Charles Kimeli	KEN				25 Sep
61:46+	Robert Kiprono Cheruiyot	KEN	10.8.88			30 Oct
61:47	Moses Mosop	KEN	17.7.85			6 Mar
61:47	Tola Lema	ETH				3 Apr
61:47	Juwawo Wirimai	ZIM	7.11.80			24 Apr
61:47	Cyrus Njui	KEN	11.2.86			3 Jul
61:47	Julius Kogo	KEN	12.8.85			20 Aug
61:47	Philemon Yator	KEN-J	2.4.92			16 Oct
61:47	Robert Kwambai	KEN				18 Dec
61:48	Alfred Cherop	KEN	2.3.86			2 Oct
61:50	Evans Cheruiyot	KEN	10.5.82			20 Mar
61:51	Isaiah Ondieki	KEN	.88			3 Apr
61:52	Rachid Kisri	MAR	1.3.75			6 Feb
61:53	Bobby Curtis	USA	28.11.84			18 Sep
61:54	Habtamu Fikadu	ETH	13.3.88			6 Mar
61:54	Ezekiel Jafari Ngimba	TAN	17.8.85			18 Jun
61:54	Kiflom Sium	ERI	,87			18 Sep
61:54+	Allan Kiprono	KEN	15.2.90			30 Oct
61:55	Gebremedhin Gebre	ETH				25 Dec
61:55	Girma Berhanu	ETH				25 Dec
61:56	Sisay Ezkyas	ETH	5.12.88			20 Mar
61:56	Philip Langat	KEN	16.2.83			18 Jun
61:59	Simon Cherop	KEN				26 Mar
62:00	Mulugeta Wondimu	ETH	28.2.85			30 Jan
62:00	Francis Kosgei	KEN	.81			13 Mar
62:00	Benson Olenakeri	KEN	82			4 Sep
62:00	Humegaw Mesfin	ETH	31.1.89			25 Sep
62:01	Simon Kirwa	KEN				3 Apr
62:01	Eric Kibet	KEN	.80			18 Sep
62:02	Markos Geneti	ETH	30.5.84			18 Sep
62:03	Maregu Zewdie	ETH	23.10.82			18 Feb
62:04	Dickson Marwa	TAN	6.3.82			18 Feb
62:04	Ahmed Baday	MAR	12.1.79			3 Apr
62:04	Bernard Kitur	KEN	.90			9 Oct
62:05	Evans Ruto	KEN	14.1.84			25 Sep
62:06	Mustapha El Aziz	MAR	.85			3 Apr
62:07	Wissam Hosni	TUN	8.3.85			3 Apr
62:07+	Vincent Kipruto	KEN	13.9.87			10 Apr
62:07+	Wilson Chebet	KEN	12.7.85			10 Apr
62:08	Abel Kirui	KEN	4.6.82			6 Mar
62:08+	Chala Dechase	ETH	13.6.84			10 Apr
62:08	Michael Kipyego	KEN	2.10.83			3 Sep
62:08	Samuel Ndereba	KEN	2.2.77			18 Sep
62:09	Koen Raymaekers	NED	31.1.80			13 Mar
62:10	Essa Ismail Rasheed	QAT	14.12.86			4 Sep
62:10	Emmanuel Bett	KEN	30.3.83			27 Sep
62:13	Chris Thompson	GBR	17.4.81			25 Sep
62:13	John Lotiang	KEN				2 Oct
62:13	Eric Chirchir	KEN	20.11.83			18 Dec
62:14	Dylan Wykes	CAN	6.6.83			20 Mar
62:14+	Gilbert Kirwa	KEN	20.12.85			10 Apr
62:16	Alejandro Suárez	MEX	30.11.80			20 Mar
62:16	Michael Tiony	KEN	27.8.85			18 Sep
62:16	Alemayehu Shumye	ETH	6.4.88			25 Sep
62:16	Abderrahime El Asri	MAR	10.7.82			25 Dec
62:17	Charles Maina	KEN	11.10.82			6 Mar
62:17	Maurice Musyoki	KEN	4.11.80			6 Mar
62:17	Peter Wanjiru	KEN	.82			27 Mar
62:17	Meb Keflezighi	USA	5.5.75			2 Oct
62:19u	Peter Kosgei	KEN	3.2.83			30 Jan
62:19	Elisha Meli Tarus	KEN	.88			6 Mar
62:19	Urige Buta	ETH	28.11.78			21 May
62:19	Derese Deniboba	ETH	15.5.82			17 Jun
62:19	Salim Saiti	KEN	28.12.85			2 Oct
62:19	Alexander Tidony	KEN	.83			2 Oct
62:20	Ryan Hall	USA	14.10.82			29 Jan
62:20	Maina Karukawa	KEN	19.6.91			6 Mar
62:20	Tigabu Gebremariam	ETH	.90			3 Apr
62:20A	Geoffrey Mutai	KEN	7.10.81			31 Jul
62:20	Geoffrey Kenesi	KEN	.87			2 Oct

(195)

Excessively downhill: 61:22 Brighton Chipere ZIM 13.11.72 1 Lydenberg (dh 721m!) 26 Mar
Short Course: 61:02 Bamtebe Kew ETH 1 Vadodara 23 Jan
In Boston Marathon: 61:57 Ryan Hall & Gilbert Yegon; 61:58 Geoffrey Mutai & Bekana Daba

JUNIORS

See main list for top 3 juniors. Additional performance and further juniors:

Mark		Name		Nat	Born	Pos	Venue	Date
Kipsang	60:38					1	Berlin	3 Apr
61:47		Philemon	Yator	KEN	2.4.92	1	Reims	16 Oc
63:35		Daniel	Wanjiru	KEN	.92	5	Olomouc	18 Jun
63:37		John	Maina	KEN	14.7.93	8	Ageo	20 Nov
63:45		Justine	Cheruiyot	KEN	11.11.93	7	Valencia	23 Oct
63:45		Daichi	Motomura	JPN	16.1.92	11	Ageo	20 Nov

25 – 30 KILOMETRES ROAD

25k	30k	Name		Nat	Born	Pos		Venue	Date
				See also as intermediate times in Marathon lists					
1:12:13		Mathew	Kisorio	KEN	16.5.89	1		Berlin	8 May
1:12:46		Levi Matebo	Omari	KEN	3.11.89	2		Berlin	8 May
1:12:59		Eliud	Kiptanui	KEN	6.6.89	3		Berlin	8 May
1:13:18+	1:27:37	Peter Cheruiyot	Kirui	KEN	2.1.88		in Mar	Berlin	25 Sep
1:13:09+	1:28:02	Deresse	Chimsa	ETH	21.11.76		in Mar	Frankfurt	30 Oct
1:13:08+	1:28:07	Deriba	Merga	ETH	26.10.80		in Mar	Frankfurt	30 Oct
1:13:17+	1:28:47	Geoffrey	Kipsang	KEN-J	28.11.92		in Mar	Berlin	25 Sep
1:13:17+		Henry	Sugut	KEN	4.5.85		in Mar	Berlin	25 Sep
1:13:18+		Boniface	Kirui	KEN	27.10.87		in Mar	Berlin	25 Sep
1:13:19+	1:28:48	Haile	Gebrselassie	ETH	18.4.73		in Mar	Berlin	25 Sep
1:13:20+	1:28:38	Edwin	Kimaiyo	KEN	.86		in Mar	Berlin	25 Sep
1:13:20+		Isaac	Macharia	KEN	25.11.80		in Mar	Berlin	25 Sep
1:13:38+		Daniel	Chebii	KEN	.85		in Mar	Berlin	25 Sep
1:14:15+	1:28:49+	Bekana	Daba	ETH	29.7.88		in Mar	Chicago	9 Oct
1:14:15+	1:28:51+	Evans	Cheruiyot	KEN	5.10.82		in Mar	Chicago	9 Oct
1:13:44+	1:28:55	Feyisa	Lilesa	ETH	1.2.90		in Mar	Rotterdam	10 Apr
	1:29:00+	Julius	Arile	KEN	.83		in Mar	Eindhoven	9 Oct
1:14:00		Nathaniel	Kipkosgei	KEN	1.9.84	4		Berlin	8 May
1:14:05		Onesmus	Serem	KEN		5		Berlin	8 May
1:14:11	1:29:06+	Joseph	Biwott	KEN	.77		in Mar	Amsterdam	16 Oct
1:14:11	1:29:16+	Evans	Kiplagat	KEN	5.3.88		in Mar	Amsterdam	16 Oct
1:14:16+	1:29:20	Tsegaye	Kebede	ETH	15.1.87		in Mar	London	17 Apr

Mark		Name		Nat	Born	Pos	Meet	Venue	Date
1:14:16+	1:29:21	James Kipsang	Kwambai	KEN	3.11.76		in Mar	London	17 Apr
1:14:16+	1:29:21	Abel	Kirui	KEN	4.6.82		in Mar	London	17 Apr
1:14:14+	1:29:25	Tilahun	Regassa	ETH	18.1.90		in Mar	Chicago	9 Oct
1:13:25+	1:29:36	Emmanuel	Samal	KEN	.89		in Mar	Berlin	25 Sep
1:14:18+		Jackson	Kipkoech Kotut	KEN	12.2.88		in Mar	Paris	10 Apr

Track

Mark		Name		Nat	Born	Pos	Meet	Venue	Date
1:12:25.4	1:26:47.4	Moses	Mosop	KEN	17.7.85	1		Eugene	3 Jun
1:13:52.8	1:30:00.1	Abel	Kirui	KEN	4.6.82	2		Eugene	3 Jun

dh- downhill over 1/1000

MARATHON

Mark	25k	30k	Name		Nat	Born	Pos	Meet	Venue	Date
2:03:38	1:13:18	1:27:38	Patrick	Makau	KEN	2.3.85	1		Berlin	25 Sep
2:03:42	1:13:08	1:27:49	Wilson	Kipsang	KEN	15.3.82	1		Frankfurt	30 Oct
2:04:40	1:14:16	1:29:21	Emmanuel	Mutai	KEN	12.10.84	1		London	17 Apr
2:05:06		1:29:47	Geoffrey	Mutai	KEN	7.10.81	1		New York	6 Nov
2:05:16	1:13:08	1:27:49	Levi Matebo	Omari	KEN	3.11.89	2		Frankfurt	30 Oct
2:05:25	1:13:08	1:27:50	Albert	Matebor	KEN	20.12.80	3		Frankfurt	30 Oct
2:05:27	1:13:43	1:28:44	Wilson	Chebet	KEN	12.7.85	1		Rotterdam	10 Apr
2:05:33	1:13:43	1:28:44	Vincent	Kipruto	KEN	13.9.87	2		Rotterdam	10 Apr
2:05:37	1:14:15	1:28:47	Moses	Mosop	KEN	17.7.85	1		Chicago	9 Oct
2:05:45	1:14:16	1:29:21	Martin	Lel (10)	KEN	29.10.78	2		London	17 Apr
2:05:45	1:14:16	1:29:22		Makau			3		London	17 Apr
2:05:48	1:14:29	1:29:02	Jafred Chirchir	Kipchumba	KEN	8.8.83	1		Eindhoven	9 Oct
2:05:53	1:14:10	1:29:04		Chebet			1		Amsterdam	16 Oct
2:06:05	1:14:11	1:29:06	Laban	Korir	KEN	30.12.85	2		Amsterdam	16 Oct
2:06:07	1:14:10	1:29:04	Eric	Ndiema	KEN-J	28.12.92	3		Amsterdam	16 Oct
2:06:07	1:13:08	1:27:49	Philip Sanga	Kimutai	KEN	10.9.83	4		Frankfurt	30 Oct
2:06:13		1:29:51		W Kipsang			1		Otsu	6 Mar
2:06:15	1:14:15	1:28:46	Wesley	Korir	KEN	15.11.82	2		Chicago	9 Oct
2:06:28	1:14:30	1:29:01	Nathaniel	Kipkosgei	KEN	1.9.84	2		Eindhoven	9 Oct
2:06:28		1:29:46		E Mutai			2		New York	6 Nov
2:06:29	1:14:15	1:28:50	Bernard	Kipyego	KEN	16.7.86	3		Chicago	9 Oct
2:06:29	1:13:25	1:28:41	Robert Kiprono	Cheruiyot	KEN	10.8.88	5		Frankfurt	30 Oct
2:06:31	1:14:17	1:29:41	Benjamin	Kiptoo Kolum	KEN	.79	1		Paris	10 Apr
2:06:31	1:13:08	1:27:49	Peter Cheruiyot	Kirui (20)	KEN	2.1.88	6		Frankfurt	30 Oct
2:06:34	1:14:17	1:29:21	Marílson	dos Santos	BRA	6.8.77	4		London	17 Apr
2:06:34	1:14:11	1:29:05	Nicholas	Manza Kamakya	KEN	2.3.85	4		Amsterdam	16 Oct
2:06:48	1:14:29	1:29:01	Mike	Kipyego	KEN	2.10.83	3		Eindhoven	9 Oct
2:06:53	1:14:10	1:29:05	Elijah	Keitany	KEN	.83	5		Amsterdam	16 Oct
2:06:54	1:14:11	1:29:05	Paul	Biwott	KEN	18.4.78	6		Amsterdam	16 Oct
2:07:03			Stanley (30/26)	Biwott	KEN	21.4.86	1		Chuncheon	23 Oct
2:07:04			Bekana	Daba	ETH	29.7.88	1		Houston	30 Jan
2:07:07			Benson	Barus	KEN	4.7.80	1		Praha	8 May
2:07:08	1:14:11	1:29:05	John Kiprotich	Chemisto	KEN	5.6.83	7		Amsterdam	16 Oct
2:07:13	1:14:32	1:29:02	Tadesse (30)	Tola	ETH	31.10.87	4		Eindhoven	9 Oct
2:07:13			John Kipkorir	Komen	KEN	28.8.77	1		La Rochelle	27 Nov
2:07:14		1:29:46	Tsegaye	Kebede	ETH	15.1.87	3		New York	6 Nov
2:07:18			David	Barmasai	KEN	1.1.89	1		Dubai	21 Jan
2:07:20			Stephen	Kiprotich	UGA	18.4.89	1		Enschede	17 Apr
2:07:23	1:13:25	1:28:41	Dickson	Chumba	KEN	27.10.86	7		Frankfurt	30 Oct
2:07:27			Yared	Asmerom	ERI	3.2.79	2		Chuncheon	23 Oct
2:07:28	1:14:10	1:29:05	Samuel	Tsegay	ERI	24.2.88	8		Amsterdam	16 Oct
2:07:33	1:14:18	1:29:40	Eshetu	Wondimu	ETH	26.1.82	3		Paris	10 Apr
2:07:35	1:15:00	1:29:56	Hailu	Mekonnen	ETH	4.4.80	1		Tokyo	27 Feb
2:07:36			Kenneth (40)	Mungara	KEN	7.9.73	2		Praha	8 May
2:07:36	1:15:10	1:29:42	Josphat	Muchiri Ndambiri	KEN	12.2.85	1		Fukuoka	4 Dec
2:07:38			Abel	Kirui	KEN	4.6.82	1	WCh	Daegu	4 Sep
2:07:41	1:14:36	1:29:57	Alfred	Kering	KEN	.80	4		Paris	10 Apr
2:07:43	1:14:17	1:29:40	Girma	Assefa	ETH	20.2.86	5		Paris	10 Apr
2:07:47			Samuel	Kosgei	KEN	20.1.86	3		Praha	8 May
2:07:55			Stephen	Chemlany	KEN	9.8.82	2		Berlin	25 Sep
2:07:59			Isaiah	Kosgei	KEN	12.2.89	1		Valencia	27 Nov

also Adam Ismail Khamis BRN

Mark	25k	30k	Name		Nat	Born	Pos	Meet	Venue	Date
2:08:00		1:29:47	Gebre-egziabher	Gebremariam	ETH	10.9.84	4		New York	6 Nov
2:08:01			Nicholas	Kemboi	KEN/QAT	25.11.83	2		Valencia	27 Nov
2:08:01			Francis (50)	Kipkoech	KEN	12.10.73	3		Valencia	27 Nov

Mark			Name		Nat	Born	Pos	Venue	Date
2:08:02	1:14:16	1:29:40	Stephen	Chebogut	KEN	84	6	Paris	10 Apr
2:08:04			Ryan	Hall	USA	14.10.82	5	Chicago	5 Oct
2:08:04	1:14:31	1:29:07	Charles	Munyeki Kiama	KEN	2.11.86	5	Eindhoven	9 Oct
2:08:05	1:14:45	1:29:49	Augustine	Rono	KEN	.81	6	Eindhoven	9 Oct
2:08:07			Robert	Kipchumba	KEN	24.2.84	1	Xiamen	2 Jan
2:08:08			Yusuf	Songoka	KEN	5.2.79	1	Daegu	10 Apr
2:08:13			Ennaji	El Idrissi	MAR	8.12.86	1	Torino	13 Nov
2:08:17			Evans	Cheruiyot	KEN	5.10.82	2	Dubai	21 Jan
2:08:17A			Hillary	Kipchirchir	KEN	30.4.81	1	Torreón	6 Mar
2:08:17			Sammy	Kibet	KEN	2.2.82	1	Warszawa	25 Sep
(60)									
2:08:18			Abdellah	Falil	MAR	.76	2	Daegu	10 Apr
2:08:21			Abdellah	Tagharrafet	MAR	.85	1	Bilbao	22 Oct
2:08:21			William	Chebor	KEN	22.12.82	2	Torino	13 Nov
2:08:22		1:29:40	Henry	Sugut	KEN	4.5.85	7	Paris	10 Apr
2:08:25			Daniel Kiprugut	Too	KEN	21.11.76	1	Ljubljana	23 Oct
2:08:26	1:14:16	1:29:22	Jaouad	Gharib	MAR	22.5.72	6	London	17 Apr
2:08:31			Siraj Amda Bene	Gena	ETH	12.11.84	8	Frankfurt	30 Oct
2:08:35			Geoffrey	Ndungu	KEN	11,3.84	1	Dublin	31 Oct
2:08:36dh			Nicolas	Kurgat	KEN	7.11.87	1	Carpi dh 82.7m	9 Oct
2:08:37	1:15:02	1:30:07	Yuki	Kawauchi	JPN	5.3.87	3	Tokyo	27 Feb
(70)									
2:08:38			Duncan	Koech	KEN	28.12.81	9	Frankfurt	30 Oct
2:08:38	1:15:10	1:29:56	James	Mwangi	KEN	23.6.84	2	Fukuoka	4 Dec
2:08:39			Daniel	Limo	KEN	10.12.83	2	La Rochelle	27 Nov
2:08:40	1:14:31	1:29:17	Deribe	Robi	ETH	,86	7	Eindhoven	9 Oct
2:08:40			Lukas	Kanda	KEN	.87	1	Cannes	20 Nov
2:08:41			Patrick	Ivuti	KEN	30.6.78	2	Wien	17 Apr
2:08:42	1:14:16	1:29:21	Abderrahim	Bouramdane	MAR	1.1.78	7	London	17 Apr
2:08:47	1:13:43	1:28:45	Chala	Dechase	ETH	13.6.84	3	Rotterdam	10 Apr
2:08:47			Hassane	Ahouchar	MAR	.75	4	Valencia	27 Nov
2:08:50			Joseph Kimeli	Lagat	KEN	.86	2	Ljubljana	23 Oct
(80)									
2:08:50			James	Kwambai	KEN	28.2.83	1	Seoul	6 Nov
2:08:53			Leonard	Mucheru	KEN	13.6.78	3	Daegu	10 Apr
2:08:55			Megersa	Bacha	ETH	.87	3	Torino	13 Nov
2:08:56			Samson	Barmao	KEN	17.4.82	1	Köln	2 Oct
2:08:56			Peter Chesang	Kurui	KEN	2.1.90	4	Torino	13 Nov
2:08:57	1:14:31	1:29:50	Edwin	Kutto	KEN	8.1.84	8	Eindhoven	9 Oct
2:09:00			Francis	Kiprop	KEN	4.6.82	1	Beijing	16 Oct
2:09:02			Tadesse	Tolesa	ETH	.88	1	Padova	17 Apr
2:09:03	1:15:01	1:30:06	Yoshinori	Oda	JPN	5.12.80	4	Tokyo	27 Feb
2:09:07			Shume	Hailu	ETH	27.10.87	2	Cannes	20 Nov
(90)									
2:09:08			Deresse	Chimsa	ETH	21.11.76	4	Dubai	21 Jan
2:09:08			Eliud	Kiptanui	KEN	6.6.89	4	Rotterdam	10 Apr
2:09:10	1:15:01	1:30:06	Cyrus	Njui	KEN	11.2.86	5	Tokyo	27 Feb
2:09:11			Abderrahim	Goumri	MAR	21.5.76	1	Seoul	20 Mar
2:09:12			Michael	Chege	KEN	.83	3	Ljubljana	23 Oct
2:09:13		1:29:51	Deriba	Merga	ETH	26.10.80	2	Otsu	6 Mar
2:09:13		1:29:47	Mebrahtom	Keflezighi	USA	5.5.75	6	New York	6 Nov
2:09:16			Girma	Gezahegn	ETH	28.11.83	5	Valencia	27 Nov
2:09:19			Simon	Mukun	KEN	5.8.84	2	Venezia	23 Oct
2:09:19			Berhanu	Shiferaw	ETH-J	31.5.93	4	Ljubljana	23 Oct
(100)									

Mark	Name		Nat	Born	Date
2:09:20	Haile Haja	Gemeda	ETH	.88	10 Apr
2:09:21	David	Kemboi Kiyeng	KEN	.83	6 Nov
2:09:22	Evans	Kiplagat	KEN	5.3.88	17 Apr
2:09:23	Wilson	Loyanae	KEN	.86	16 Oct
2:09:25	Hiroyuki	Horibata	JPN	28.10.86	6 Mar
2:09:25	Felix	Keny	KEN	25.12.85	10 Apr
2:09:25	Lusapho	April	RSA	24.5.82	8 May
2:09:26	Benjamin Chebet	Kipruto	KEN	22.2.82	17 Apr
2:09:26	Oleksandr	Sitkovskyy	UKR	9.6.78	2 Oct
2:09:27	Stephen	Kibet	KEN	9.11.86	21 Jan
2:09:27dh	Bertram	Keter	KEN		9 Oct
2:09:28		Jung Jin-hyung	KOR	1.6.90	20 Mar
2:09:30	Raymond	Kandie	KEN	7.9.86	30 Oct
2:09:31	Kentaro	Nakamoto	JPN	7.12.82	6 Mar
2:09:31	Moses	Kurgat	KEN	.77	20 Nov
2:09:35	Dmitriy	Safronov	RUS	9.10.81	17 Apr
2:09:35	Amos	Matui	KEN	27.5.76	2 Oct
2:09:36	Alemayehu	Shumye	ETH	6.4.88	10 Apr
2:09:37	Nixon	Machichim	KEN	.83	10 Apr
2:09:39	Henryk	Szost	POL	20.1.82	30 Oct
2:09:40	Joseph	Biwott	KEN	.77	16 Oct
2:09:42	Abdullah Dawit	Shami	ETH	16.7.84	20 Mar
2:09:42	Rachid	Kisri	MAR	1.3.75	8 May
2:09:43	Isaac Wanhoji	Macharia	KEN	25.11.80	17 Apr
2:09:43	Cosmas	Kigen	KEN	.90	2 Oct
2:09:43	Samuel	Muturi	KEN	2.5.86	16 Oct
2:09:44	Demesse	Tsega	ETH	13.3.88	17 Oct
2:09:46	Juius Kiplagat	Korir	KEN	.82	17 Apr
2:09:46	Abdellatif	Meftah	FRA	3.1.82	30 Oct
2:09:48	Moses	Kangogo	KEN	10.11.79	6 Mar
2:09:48	Anthony	Wairuri	KEN	.85	13 Nov
2:09:50	Hailu	Mesfin	ETH	21.6.82	2 Jan
2:09:50	Edwin	Kimaiyo	KEN	.86	25 Sep
2:09:51	Philemon	Baaru	KEN	20.5.81	6 Nov

Mark	Name	Nat	Born	Date
2:09:52	Haile Abebe	ETH	.85	17 Oct
2:09:52	Berga Bekele	ETH	20.4.81	27 Nov
2:09:52	Gilbert Chepkwony	KEN	.85	31 Oct
2:09:53	Daniel Abera	ETH	15.9.88	13 Feb
2:09:53	Elias Chelimo Kemboi	KEN	10.3.84	10 Apr
2:09:54	Aleksey Reunkov	RUS	28.1.84	30 Oct
2:09:54	Kennedy Kwemoi	KEN		6 Nov
2:09:54	Lema Feyisa	ETH	.85	20 Nov
2:09:57	Botoru Tsegay	ETH	25.10.85	16 Jan
2:09:57	Debebe Tolossa	ETH	7.7.91	23 Oct
2:10:00	Patrick Muriuki	KEN	.89	16 Jan
2:10:00	John Kyui	KEN	20.10.84	17 Apr
2:10:02	Richard Limo	KEN	18.11.80	16 Oct
2:10:02	Johnstone Maiyo	KEN	6.10.88	30 Oct
2:10:04	Robert Mwangi	KEN	.87	8 May
2:10:05	Gosa Megersa	ETH	.82	13 Feb
2:10:08	Tariku Jifar	ETH	18.7.84	16 Jan
2:10:08	Michael Kimani	KEN	16.12.78	4 Sep
2:10:09	Patrick Tambwé	FRA	5.5.75	6 Jan
2:10:10	Carles Castillejo	ESP	18.8.78	11 Dec
2:10:11	Julius Muriuki	KEN	3.7.85	6 Jan
2:10:11	Daniel Rono	KEN	13.7.78	23 Oct
2:10:12	Sahle Warga	ETH	30.1.84	10 Apr
2:10:13	Oleg Kulkov	RUS	6.3.78	20 Mar
2:10:14	Ahmed Ibrahim Baday	MAR	12.1.79	6 Feb
2:10:14	Tola Bane	ETH	21.3.88	30 Oct
2:10:15	Gidena Gebremedhin	ETH	.82	6 Jan
2:10:15	Abraham Chelanga	KEN	9.9.84	16 Oct
2:10:16	Peter Some	KEN	5.6.90	17 Apr
2:10:17	Tekeste Nurelign	ETH	.80	20 Mar
2:10:17	Wilfred Kibet Kigen	KEN	23.2.75	30 Oct
2:10:17	Hailu Gela	ETH	.87	27 Nov
2:10:18	Laban Moiben	KEN	.84	29 May
2:10:18	Bernard Rotich	KEN	11.8.86	30 Oct
2:10:19	Dereje Abera	ETH		29 May
2:10:19	Victor Yator	KEN	.85	16 Oct
2:10:21	Eliud Cheptei	KEN		27 Mar
2:10:21	William Kibor	KEN	.80	4 Dec
2:10:23	Aleksey Sokolov	RUS	14.11.79	17 Apr
2:10:23	Jacob Kitur	KEN	.73	16 Oct
2:10:24	Daniel Njenga	KEN	7.5.76	6 Feb
2:10:24	Simon Njoroge	KEN	10.10.80	9 Oct
2:10:24	Yemane Tsegay Adhane	ETH	8.4.85	18 Dec
2:10:25	Julius Nderitu	KEN	.76	27 Mar
2:10:25	Grigoriy Andreyev	RUS	7.1.76	30 Oct
2:10:25	Jacob Yator	KEN	5.8.82	31 Oct
2:10:26	Samson Bungei	KEN	.82	6 Jan
2:10:26	Abdisa Sorri	ETH	.81	16 Oct
2:10:27	Emmanuel Samal	KEN	.89	21 Jan
2:10:29	Kazuhiro Maeda	JPN	19.4.81	6 Feb
2:10:29	Joseph Maregu	KEN	22.11.77	17 Apr
2:10:29	Stephen Mokoka	RSA	31.1.85	4 Dec
2:10:31	Zenbaba Yegezu	ETH	26.9.83	4 Sep
2:10:32	Feyisa Lilesa	ETH	1.2.90	4 Sep
2:10:32	Masato Imai	JPN	2.4.84	3 Dec
2:10:33	Dino Sefer	ETH	28.5.88	29 May
2:10:34dh	Gezu Belete	ETH		9 Oct
2:10:35	Mehari Baraki	ETH	.89	20 Nov
2:10:38	Solomon Busendich	KEN	10.1.84	10 Apr
2:10:38	Evans Rutto	KEN	8.4.78	10 Apr
2:10:38	Felix Limo	KEN	22.8.80	25 Sep
2:10:41	Yared Dagnaw	ERI	.78	20 Mar
2:10:42	Dereje Tadesse	ETH	24.1.87	10 Apr
2:10:43	Coolboy Ngamole	RSA	27.6.79	27 Nov
2:10:44	Josephat Yego	KEN	1.4.74	6 Mar
2:10:44	Nahashon Kimaiyo	KEN	4.5.83	27 Nov
2:10:45	Satoshi Yoshii	JPN	27.10.83	6 Mar
2:10:46	Dereje Yadete	ETH	5.2.83	20 Mar
2:10:46	Nelson Rotich	KEN	.81	23 Oct
2:10:48	Nicholas Chelimo	KEN	8.1.83	17 Apr
2:10:49	Samuel Woldemanuel	ETH	.81	8 May
2:10:50	Japhet Kipchirchir Kipkorir	KEN	.81	3 Jul
2:10:55	Scott Overall	GBR	9.2.83	25 Sep
2:10:55	Reid Coolsaet	CAN	29.7.79	16 Oct
2:10:55A	Ernest Kebenei	KEN	20.11.84	30 Oct
2:10:55	Mohamed El Hachimi	MAR	5.9.80	4 Dec
2:10:56	Vincent Kiplagat	KEN	8.10.84	8 May
2:10:58	Moses Arusei	KEN	.84	17 Apr
2:10:58	Silas Sang	KEN	21.8.78	29 May
2:10:58	Mathew Kisorio	KEN	16.5.89	6 Nov
2:10:59	Jonathan Chesoo (215)	KEN	.88	31 Oct

Further 56 men 2:11:00 to 2:11:45

Downhill point-to-point courses

Boston marathon is downhill overall (139m) and, as a point-to-point course, in some years, such as 2011, has been strongly wind-aided. Los Angeles is 131m downhill.

Mark			Name		Nat	Born	Pos	Venue	Date
2:03:02	1:13:16	1:28:24	Geoffrey	Mutai	KEN	7.10.81	1	Boston	18 Apr
2:03:06	1:13:16	1:28:23	Moses	Mosop	KEN	17.7.85	2	Boston	18 Apr
2:04:53		1:28:24	Gebre-egziabher	Gebremariam	ETH	10.9.84	3	Boston	18 Apr
2:04:58		1:28:23	Ryan	Hall	USA	14.10.82	4	Boston	18 Apr
2:06:13		1:28:24	Abreham	Cherkos	ETH	23.9.89	5	Boston	18 Apr
2:06:35			Markos	Geneti	ETH	30.5.84	1	Los Angeles	20 Mar
2:06:43		1:28:42	R Kiprono	Cheruiyot			6	Boston	18 Apr
2:07:39			Deressa	Chimsa	ETH	21.11.76	8	Boston	18 Apr
2:09:50			Peter	Kamais	KEN	7.11.76	11	Boston	18 Apr

Also at 30k in Boston: 1:28:23 Philip Sanga, Bekana Daba, Robert Kipchumba

Short course: At Alger 1 Nov: 1. Slimane Mpoulay ALG .80 2:09:11, 2. El Houari Smara ALG 19.6.77 2:10:45

<h2 style="text-align:center">JUNIORS</h2>

Mark	Name	Nat	Born	Pos	Venue	Date
2:09:19	Berhanu Shiferaw	ETH-J	31.5.93	4	Ljubljana	23 Oct
2:12:12	6 Marrakech					30 Jan
2:14:49	Victor Chelokoi	KEN	.92	1	Salzburg	15 May

50 KILOMETRES

In 56k at Cape Town 23 Apr: Motlhokoa Nkhabutlane LES 2:48:06, Mike Fokoroni ZIM 2:48:33, Tsotang Maine LES 2:48:55

100 KILOMETRES

Mark	Name		Nat	Born	Pos	Meet	Venue	Date
6:27:32	Giorgio	Calcaterra	ITA	11.2.72	1	WCh	Winschoten	10 Sep
6:31:06	Kiyokatsu	Hasegawa	JPN	2.4.83	1	L.Saroma	Yubetsu	26 Jun
6:36:29	Hideo	Nojo	JPN	24.12.76	2	L.Saroma	Yubetsu	26 Jun
6:38:40	Erick	Wainaina	KEN	19.12.73	3	L.Saroma	Yubetsu	26 Jun
6:38:56	Asier	Cuevas	ESP	16.1.73	1	NC	S.C.de Bezana	24 Sep
6:41:17	Yoshikazu	Hara	JPN	13.8.72	4	L.Saroma	Yubetsu	26 Jun
6:42:49	Michael	Wardian	USA	12.4.74	2	WCh	Winschoten	10 Sep
6:44:35	Andrew	Henshaw	USA	17.12.85	3	WCh	Winschoten	10 Sep
6:47:01	Pieter	Vermeesch	BEL	6.7.76	4	WCh	Winschoten	10 Sep
6:48:32	Shinji	Nakadai	JPN	19.5.78	5	WCh	Winschoten	10 Sep

Mark	Name		Nat	Born	Pos	Meet	Venue	Date
6:50:23	Matthew	Woods	USA	1.10.79	6	WCh	Winschoten	10 Sep
6:52:19	Jonas	Buud	SWE	28.3.74	7	WCh	Winschoten	10 Sep
6:53:01	Yevgeniy	Glyva	UKR	10.11.83	18 Jun	6:56:49 Masakazu	Takahashi	JPN 23.12.73	26 Jun
6:53:26	Antonio	Armuzzi	ITA	14.8.69	3 Apr	6:57:00 Yoshiki	Takada	JPN 18.7.83	26 Jun
6:54:50	Daniel	Orálek	CZE	29.3.70	26 Mar	6:59:12 David	Riddle	USA 25.9.81	9 Apr

Course alteration not checked by IAAF measurer

Mark	Name		Nat	Born	Pos	Meet	Venue	Date
6:25:47	Giorgio	Calcaterra	ITA	11.2.72	1		Faenza	29 May
6:28:48	Alberico	Di Cecco	ITA	19.4.74	2		Faenza	29 May

24 HOURS

Mark	Name		Nat	Born	Pos	Meet	Venue	Date
261,257k t	Ryoichi	Sekiya	JPN	12.2.67	1		Soochow	11 Dec
259.496	Jean-Marc	Bordus	FRA	11.11.60	1		Séné	25 Apr
254.762 t	Emmanuel	Fontaine	FRA	6.12.68	2		Soochow	11 Dec
253.613	Masahiko	Honda	JPN	15.5.63	1	Shinjuku	Tokyo	15 Oct
252.177	Takahisa	Kokita	JPN	28.6.80	2	Shinjuku	Tokyo	15 Oct
252.014	Ludovic	Dilmi	FRA	11.4.65	2		Séné	25 Apr
250.459		Fontaine			3		Séné	25 Apr
249.152	Denis	Morel	FRA	24.2.73	25 Apr	245.933 Yasutoshi	Oshima	JPN 23.4.76	15 Oct
248.297	Geert	Stynen	BEL	23.12.69	15 May	244.802 Béla	Mazur	HUN 13.4.78	17 Apr
246.825	Philip	McCarthy	USA	23.5.68	18 Sep	244.334 John	Pares	GBR 27.1.66	24 Sep
246.349	Florian	Reus	GER	2.3.84	24 Jul	242.330 Bruno	Olivier	FRA 13.10.60	2 Oct
246.119	Marcin Marek	Sieja	POL	11.11.62	18 Sep	**Indoors**			
246.116	Jean-François	Harruis	FRA	3.5.59	25 Apr	247.944 Jari	Soikkeli	FIN 11.2.70	30 Jan

2000 METRES STEEPLECHASE

Mark		Name		Nat	Born	Pos	Meet	Venue	Date
5:26.4		Ángel	Mullera	ESP	20.4.84	1		Lloret de Mar	28 Jun
5:28.48		Jacob	Araptany	UGA-J	11.2.92	1		Pliezhausen	22 May
5:28.65		Conseslus	Kipruto	KEN-Y	8.12.94	1	WY	Villeneuve d'Ascq	8 Jul
5:30.0A		Gilbert	Kirui	KEN-Y	22.1.94	2		Nairobi	8 Jun
	5:30.49					2	WY	Villeneuve d'Ascq	8 Jul
5:32.3A		Weynay	Gebreselassie	ERI-Y	24.3.94	1		Asmara	20 Feb

JUNIORS

Mark		Name		Nat	Born	Pos	Meet	Venue	Date
5:34.35		Abdellah	Dacha	MAR	26.1.92	1		Rabat	27 Apr
5:35.05		Jaouad	Chemlal	MAR-Y	11.4.94	2		Rabat	27 Apr
5.36.0	A	Peter	Mutheka	KEN	1.12.94	3		Nairobi	7 Jun
5.37.1A		Medhanie	Abraha	ERI		2		Asmara	20 Feb
5.37.98		Zacharia	Kiprotich	UGA		3	WY	Villeneuve d'Ascq	8 Jul
5.40.0A		Michiel	Gebretinsae	ERI		3		Asmara	20 Feb
5.40.0	A	Nicholas	Kiptanui	KEN	4.2.94	4		Nairobi	7 Jun
5.40.51		Martin	Grau	GER	26.3.92	1	NC-j	Jena	6 Aug

3000 METRES STEEPLECHASE

Mark	Name		Nat	Born	Pos	Meet	Venue	Date
7:53.64	Brimin	Kipruto	KEN	31.7.85	1	Herc	Monaco	22 Jul
7:55.76	Ezekiel	Kemboi	KEN	25.5.82	2	Herc	Monaco	22 Jul
7:57.32	Paul Kipsiele	Koech	KEN	10.11.81	3	Herc	Monaco	22 Jul
8:01.83		Koech			1	Bisl	Oslo	9 Jun
8:02.09	Mahiedine	Mekhissi-Benabbad	FRA	15.3.85	1	DL	Saint Denis	8 Jul
8:02.28		Kipruto			1	DL	Shanghai	15 May
8:02.42		Koech			2	DL	Shanghai	15 May
8:02.55		Koech			1	GS	Ostrava	31 May
8:04.48		Koech			1	ISTAF	Berlin	11 Sep
8:05.40		Kipruto			2	Bisl	Oslo	9 Jun
8:05.72	Bouabdellah	Tahri	FRA	20.12.78	4	Herc	Monaco	22 Jul
8:05.88	Bernard Nganga	Mbugua	KEN	.85	2	ISTAF	Berlin	11 Sep
8:05.92		Koech			1	DNG	Stockholm	29 Jul
8:07.14		Kemboi			2	DL	Saint Denis	8 Jul
8:07.41	Richard	Matelong	KEN	14.10.83	5	Herc	Monaco	22 Jul
8:07.71	Hillary	Yego	KEN-J	2.4.92	3	DL	Shanghai	15 May
8:07.72		Kemboi			1	WK	Zürich	8 Sep
8:07.75	Jonathan	Ndiku	KEN	18.9.91	6	Herc	Monaco	22 Jul
8:07.89		Koech			2	WK	Zürich	8 Sep
8:08.22		Yego			7	Herc	Monaco	22 Jul
8:08.34		Kemboi			1	Pre	Eugene	4 Jun
8:08.43	Benjamin	Kiplagat (10)	UGA	4.3.89	3	DL	Saint Denis	8 Jul
8:08.59	Tarik (Patrick)	Langat Akdag	KEN/TUR	22.4.89	4	DL	Shanghai	15 May
8:10.03	Roba	Gari	ETH	12.4.82	4	DL	Saint Denis	8 Jul
8:10.13		Koech			2	Pre	Eugene	4 Jun
8:10.41		Gari			3	Bisl	Oslo	9 Jun
8:10.93		Kemboi			1h2	WCh	Daegu	29 Aug

Mark	Name		Nat	Born	Pos	Meet	Venue	Date
8:11.07		Matelong			5	DL	Shanghai	15 May
8:11.31	Jairus	Kipchoge	KEN-J	15.12.92	5	DL	Saint Denis	8 Jul
8:11.34		Gari			3	Pre	Eugene	4 Jun
(30/13)								
8:11.50	Ruben	Ramolefi	RSA	17.7.78	2h2	WCh	Daegu	29 Aug
8:11.81	Hamid	Ezzine	MAR	5.10.83	3h2	WCh	Daegu	29 Aug
8:12.04	Nahom	Mesfin	ETH	3.6.89	4h2	WCh	Daegu	29 Aug
8:12.17	Silas	Kitum	KEN	25.5.90	3		Daegu	12 May
8:12.25	Nour-eddine	Gezzar	FRA	17.2.80	9	Herc	Monaco	22 Jul
8:13.04	Abdelkader	Hachlaf	MAR	3.7.79	1		Rabat	5 Jun
8:14.22	Elijah	Chelimo	KEN	10.3.84	2	Hanz	Zagreb	13 Sep
(20)								
8:15.47	Lukasz	Parszczynski	POL	4.5.85	8	DL	Saint Denis	8 Jul
8:15.72A	Jacob	Araptany	UGA-J	11.2.92	1	NC	Kampala	24 Jul
8:15.80	Haron	Lagat	KEN	15.8.83	3	Hanz	Zagreb	13 Sep
8:16.41	Youcef	Abdi	AUS	7.12.77	1		Lapinlahti	24 Jul
8:16.47	Ángel	Mullera	ESP	20.4.84	2		Barcelona	22 Jul
8:17.27	Billy	Nelson	USA	11.9.84	11	Herc	Monaco	22 Jul
8:17.36	Birhan	Getahun	ETH	5.9.91	1	AfrG	Maputo	11 Sep
8:17.74	Ildar	Minshin	RUS	5.2.85	1	NC	Cheboksary	21 Jul
8:17.84	Vincent	Zouaoui Dandrieux	FRA	12.10.80	12	Herc	Monaco	22 Jul
8:17.87	Mohamed-Khaled	Belabbas	FRA	4.7.81	3		Barcelona	22 Jul
(30)								
8:19.00	Tomás	Tajadura	ESP	25.6.85	4		Barcelona	22 Jul
8:19.10	Benjamin	Bruce	USA	10.9.82	5		Barcelona	22 Jul
8:19.31	Patrick	Terer	KEN	6.7.89	6		Barcelona	22 Jul
8:19.33	Alexandre	Genest	CAN	30.6.86	7		Barcelona	22 Jul
8:19.69	Ion	Luchianov	MDA	31.1.81	8	WCh	Daegu	1 Sep
8:20.72	Sisay	Korme	ETH	9.1.85	3	AfrG	Maputo	11 Sep
8:21.02	Abel	Mutai	KEN	2.10.88	1		Cottbus	25 Jun
8:21.40	Willy	Komen	KEN	22.12.87	1	LGP	London (CP)	5 Aug
8:21.77	Antonio David	Jiménez	ESP	18.2.77	8	ISTAF	Berlin	11 Sep
8:21.95	Andrey	Farnosov	RUS	9.7.80	5	Znam	Zhukovskiy	3 Jul
(40)								
8:22.00	Abdelaziz	Merzougui	ESP	30.8.91	1		Huelva	2 Jun
8:22.34A	Abraham	Chirchir	KEN	1.8.80	3	NC	Nairobi	16 Jul
8:22.41	Alberto	Paulo	POR	3.10.85	4h3	WCh	Daegu	29 Aug
8:22.61	Víctor	García	ESP	13.3.85	2		Huelva	2 Jun
8:23.02	Sebastián	Martos	ESP	20.6.89	3		Huelva	2 Jun
8:23.19	Bjørnar Ustad	Kristensen	NOR	26.1.82	8	Bisl	Oslo	9 Jun
8:23.27	Kyle	Alcorn	USA	18.3.85	2	Jordan	Stanford	1 May
8:23.28	Rubén	Palomeque	ESP	14.8.80	8		Barcelona	22 Jul
8:23.36	Brian	Olinger	USA	2.6.83	2	LGP	London (CP)	5 Aug
8:23.43	Eliseo	Martín	ESP	5.11.73	9		Barcelona	22 Jul
(50)								
8:24.10	Linus	Chumba	KEN	9.2.80	10	DL	Shanghai	15 May
8:24.87	Matt	Hughes	CAN	3.8.89	1	NCAA	Des Moines	10 Jun
8:25.03A	Gilbert	Kirui	KEN-Y	22.1.94	1	Af-J	Gaborone	12 May
8:25.52	Tomasz	Szymkowiak	POL	5.7.83	2		Bydgoszcz	3 Jun
8:25.82	Abdelhakim	Zilali	FRA	20.6.83	13	DL	Saint Denis	8 Jul
8:25.95	Dan	Huling	USA	16.7.83	5	Pre	Eugene	4 Jun
8:26.03	Nikolay	Chavkin	RUS	22.4.84	1	Déca	Nice	18 Sep
8:26.21	Vadym	Slobodenyuk	UKR	17.3.81	1	NCp	Yalta	31 May
8:26.38	Donnie	Cowart	USA	24.10.85	4		Lapinlahti	24 Jul
8:26.43	Steffen	Uliczka	GER	17.7.84	3		Cottbus	25 Jun
(60)								
8:26.45	Jukka	Keskisalo	FIN	27.3.81	5		Lapinlahti	24 Jul
8:26.75	Ali Ahmed	Al-Amri	KSA	28.12.87	6h2	WCh	Daegu	29 Aug
8:26.82	Edwin	Molepo	RSA	31.5.87	1		Metz	27 Jun
8:27.08	Janne	Ukonmaanaho	FIN	13.3.84	6		Lapinlahti	24 Jul
8:27.12	Lukasz	Kujawski	POL	2.3.88	4		Strasbourg	12 Jun
8:27.30	Consesius	Kipruto	KEN-Y	8.12.94	1		Königs Wusterhausen	9 Sep
8:27.49	Albert	Minczér	HUN	1.10.86	5		Strasbourg	12 Jun
8:27.49	Hassan Ali	Oubassour	FRA	20.7.80	2		Metz	27 Jun
8:27.55	Krystian	Zalewski	POL	11.4.89	3		Bydgoszcz	3 Jun
8:28.13	Clement	Kemboi	KEN-J	1.2.93	2		Königs Wusterhausen	9 Sep
(70)								
8:28.52	Steve	Slattery	USA	14.8.80	14	DL	Shanghai	15 May
8:28.64	Adil	Alilech	MAR	26.6.86	1		Casablanca	21 May
8:28.64	Yuri	Floriani	ITA	25.12.81	2	NA	Heusden	16 Jul
8:29.02	Simon	Ayeko	UGA	10.5.87	7h2	WCh	Daegu	29 Aug

Mark	Name		Nat	Born	Pos	Meet	Venue	Date
8:29.18	Mario	Bazán	PER	1.9.87	4	Jordan	Stanford	1 May
8:29.75	Bostjan	Buc	SLO	13.4.80	7	GS	Ostrava	31 May
8:30.02	Amor	Benyahia	TUN	1.7.85	6h1	WCh	Daegu	29 Aug
8:30.23	Ali Abubaker	Kamal	QAT	8.11.83	1	AsiC	Kobe	8 Jul
8:30.24	Thumelo	Motlagale	RSA	26.11.86	2		Bellville	16 Apr
8:30.49	Yegor	Nikolayev	RUS	12.2.88	1	NCp	Yerino	4 Jun
(80)								
8:30.78	Josh	McAdams	USA	26.3.80	4	NC	Eugene	25 Jun
8:31.06	Habtamu	Jaleta	ETH-J	19.4.93	7		Strasbourg	12 Jun
8:31.09	Halil	Akkas	TUR	1.7.83	6		Dubnica nad Váhon	15 Sep
8:31.52	Derek	Scott	USA	7.11.85	1	MSR	Walnut	14 Apr
8:31.56	Luke	Gunn	GBR	22.3.85	6	LGP	London (CP)	5 Aug
8:31.65	Kaleab	Kishaba	ETH		1		Dar es Salaam	4 Jun
8:32.07	Hubert	Pokrop	POL	2.11.85	8	GS	Ostrava	31 May
8:32.14	Donn	Cabral	USA	12.12.89	2	NCAA	Des Moines	10 Jun
8:32.61	Aleksandr	Pavelyev	RUS	30.7.87	3	NC	Cheboksary	21 Jul
8:32.70	Bisluke	Kiplagat	KEN	8.8.88	11		Barcelona	22 Jul
(90)								
8:33.58	Abdelatif	Hadjam	FRA	8.8.90	3		Metz	27 Jun
8:33.59	Weynay	Gebrselassie	ERI-Y	24.3.94	7	AfrG	Maputo	11 Sep
8:34.15	Enrique	Sánchez	ESP	14.10.83	12		Barcelona	22 Jul
8:34.25A	Ben	Siwa	UGA	27.5.89	2	NC	Kampala	24 Jul
8:34.50	Ilya	Sukharyev	UKR	17.6.86	1	NC	Donetsk	4 Aug
8:34.75	Antonio David	Abadía	ESP	2.7.90	11	GS	Ostrava	31 May
8:34.90	José Gregorio	Peña	VEN	12.1.87	5h2	WMilG	Rio de Janeiro	21 Jul
8:35.03	Vitaliy	Nevsyantsev	RUS	8.9.83	10	Znam	Zhukovskiy	3 Jul
8:35.11	Artom	Kosinov	KAZ	31.7.86	2	AsiC	Kobe	8 Jul
8:35.45	Abdellah	Dacha	MAR-J	26.1.92	9		Rabat	5 Jun
(100)								

Mark	Name		Nat	Born		Date
8:35.73	Diego	Tamayo	ESP	6.12.83	2	Jun
8:35.73	Ilya	Slavenskiy	BLR	2.8.84	4	Aug
8:35.75	Abdelgafour	Lasri	MAR	20.6.79	5	Jun
8:35.86	Dean	Brummer	RSA	15.9.88	10	Apr
8:36.02	Berhanu	Shiferaw	ETH-J	31.5.93	28	Jun
8:36.09	Paul	Kipkorir	KEN	.82	28	Jun
8:36.10	Travis	Mahoney	USA	25.7.90	27	May
8:36.36	Jaiveer	Singh	IND	20.4.86	21	Jul
8:36.40	Andrew	Poore	USA	3.12.88	10	Jun
8:36.50	James	Wilkinson	GBR	13.7.90	5	Aug
8:36.53	Hudson	de Souza	BRA	25.2.77	4	Jun
8:36.68	Jaouad	Chemlal	MAR-Y	11.4.94	5	Jun
8:36.69	John	Ricardi	USA	19.8.86	1	May
8:36.70	Abderraouf	Boubaker	TUN	21.10.88	26	Jun
8:36.81	Hichem	Bouchicha	ALG	19.5.89	28	Jul
8:36.87	Stuart	Stokes	GBR	5.12.76	20	Aug
8:36.94	László	Tóth	HUN	15.9.87	6	Aug
8:36.98	Steve	Finley	USA	11.1.88	1	May
8:37.02	Marvin	Blanco	VEN	16.5.88	4	Jun
8:37.14	Tsuyoshi	Takeda	JPN	22.1.87	11	Jun
8:37.21	Hakan	Duvar	TUR	21.8.90	2	Jul
8:37.48	Alexandru	Ghinea	ROU	11.11.89	2	Jul
8:37.54	Justin	Tyner	USA	20.7.89	1	May
8:37.69	Hiroyoshi	Umegae	JPN	5.1.84	11	Jun
8:37.74	John	Sullivan	USA	17.9.88	10	Jun
8:37.94	Ilgizar	Safiulin	RUS-J	9.12.92	24	Jul
8:37.96	Brett	Hales	USA	18.11.86	10	Jun
8:38.00	Abdelhamid	Zerrifi	ALG	20.6.86	27	Jun
8:38.03	Lahcen	Amguil	ESP	3.3.80	28	May
8:38.28	Lukasz	Oslizlo	POL	14.5.89	15	Jul
8:38.44	Artur	Olejarz	POL	19.8.88	3	Jun
8:38.48	Adu	Dentamo	USA	13.10.86	1	May
8:38.73	Moussa Youssef	Idriss	SUD	17.6.88	12	Jun
8:38.76	Sergey	Litovchuk	BLR	18.2.88	7	Jul
8:38.8A	Paul	Kimugul	KEN	4.3.80	4	Aug
8:38.91	Mariano	Mastromarino	ARG	15.9.82	4	Jun
8:39.05	Gervais	Halkizimana	RWA	5.9.87	28	May
8:39.12	De'Sean	Turner	USA	16.9.88	10	Jun
8:39.24	Tanguy	Pepiot	FRA	6.7.91	28	May
8:39.25	Tareq Mubarak	Taher	BRN	24.3.84	15	Dec
8:39.38	Reuben	Kosgei	KEN	2.8.79	10	Dec
8:39.53	Dejene	Regassa	BRN	18.4.89	15	Dec
8:39.63	Rabia	Makhloufi	ALG	11.11.86	28	Jul
8:39.71	Andrew	Benford	USA	19.12.87	27	May
8:39.75	Eric	Senorski	SWE	25.7.89	13	Aug
8:39.83	Jesús Manuel	Cardo	ESP	16.6.87	22	Jul
8:39.9A	Philip	Yego (147)	KEN		4	Aug

JUNIORS

See main list for top 8 juniors. 13 performances by 3 men to 8:19.0. Additional marks and further juniors:

Name	Mark	Pos	Meet	Venue	Date
Yego 2+	8:12.08	1		Daegu	12 May
	8:12.63	2	GS	Ostrava	31 May
Kipchoge	8:13.06	2		Brazzaville	12 Jun
	8:13.52	1		Barcelona	22 Jul
Araptany	8:18.57	1h1	WCh	Daegu	29 Aug
	8:12.81	1	Hanz	Zagreb	13 Sep
	8:17.23	5	ISTAF	Berlin	11 Sep
	8:16.74	1		Velenje	28 Jun
	8:18.67	6	WCh	Daegu	1 Sep

Mark	Name		Nat	Born	Pos	Meet	Venue	Date
8:36.02	Berhanu	Shiferaw	ETH	31.5.93	2		Biberach	28 Jun
8:36.68	Jaouad	Chemlal (10)	MAR-Y	11.4.94	11		Rabat	5 Jun
8:37.94	Ilgizar	Safiulin	RUS	9.12.92	1	EJ	Tallinn	24 Jul
8:40.3A	Anamute	Minalu	ETH-Y	.95	2	NC	Addis Ababa	8 May
8:46.43	M. Emin	Tan	TUR	20.7.92	1	NC	Izmir	9 Jul
8:47.8A	Afework	Mesfin	ETH	.92	7	NC	Addis Ababa	8 May
8:48.19	Yosvani	Rodríguez	CUB	8.2.92	2		La Habana	17 Jun
8:48.79	Martin	Grau	GER	26.3.92	3	EJ	Tallinn	24 Jul
8:48.9A	Michiel	Gebretinsae	ERI		2		Asmara	3 Apr
8:49.43	Hamtabu	Faisa	ETH	.93	6		Velenje	28 Jun
8:49.99	Romain	Collenot-Spiret	FRA	9.1.92	9		Metz	27 Jun
8:51.60A	Tumisang	Mamatlake (20)	RSA-Y	.95	1		Germiston	2 Apr

Mark	Name		Nat	Born	Pos	Meet	Venue	Date

60 METRES HURDLES INDOORS

Mark	Name		Nat	Born	Pos	Meet	Venue	Date
7.37	David	Oliver	USA	24.4.82	1	Spark	Stuttgart	5 Feb
7.40		Oliver			1h1	Spark	Stuttgart	5 Feb
7.40		Oliver			1		Karlsruhe	13 Feb
7.46	Aries	Merritt	USA	24.7.85	1		Houston	29 Jan
7.48		Oliver			1h2		Karlsruhe	13 Feb
7.48	Petr	Svoboda	CZE	10.10.84	1	NC	Praha	19 Feb
7.49		Merritt			1	GP	Birmingham	19 Feb
7.49		Svoboda			1	EI	Paris (Bercy)	4 Mar
7.50		Merritt			1h1	GP	Birmingham	19 Feb
7.51		Oliver			1	v4N	Glasgow	29 Jan
7.51	Dayron	Robles	CUB	19.11.86	1h2	Spark	Stuttgart	5 Feb
7.51		Svoboda			1h1	NC	Praha	19 Feb
(12/4)								
7.52	Dimitri	Bascou	FRA	20.7.87	1	NC	Aubière	20 Feb
7.52A	Omo	Osaghae	USA	18.5.88	1	NC	Albuquerque	27 Feb
7.55		Liu Xiang	CHN	13.7.83	3		Karlsruhe	13 Feb
7.56	Garfield	Darien	FRA	22.12.87	4		Karlsruhe	13 Feb
7.56	Jarret	Eaton	USA	24.6.89	1		Ithaca	19 Feb
7.56	Felipe	Vivancos	ESP	16.6.80	1h2	EI	Paris (Bercy)	4 Mar
(10)								
7.57	Jeff	Porter	USA	27.11.85	2		Liévin	8 Feb
7.57	Kevin	Craddock	USA	25.6.87	2		Düsseldorf	11 Feb
7.57	Andrew	Turner	GBR	19.9.80	1h2	GP	Birmingham	19 Feb
7.57	Adrien	Deghelt	BEL	10.5.85	3	EI	Paris (Bercy)	4 Mar
7.58	David	Payne	USA	24.7.82	2	XL-Galan	Stockholm	22 Feb
7.58	Andrew	Riley	JAM	6.9.88	1	NCAA	College Station	12 Mar
7.60	Ashton	Eaton	USA	21.1.88	1H		Tallinn	5 Feb
7.60A	Jason	Richardson	USA	4.4.86	3	NC	Albuquerque	27 Feb
7.61A	Esteban	Guzman	USA	2.5.84	1h1	NC	Albuquerque	27 Feb
7.61	Konstantin	Shabanov	RUS	17.11.89	5	EI	Paris (Bercy)	4 Mar
(20)								
7.61	Barrett	Nugent	USA	29.1.90	2	NCAA	College Station	12 Mar
7.62	Joel	Brown	USA	31.1.80	4	GP	Birmingham	19 Feb
7.63	Yevgeniy	Borisov	RUS	7.3.84	2	NC	Moskva	16 Feb
7.63A	Terence	Somerville	USA	5.11.89	6	NC	Albuquerque	27 Feb
7.64	Dexter	Faulk	USA	14.4.84	1		Lawrence	2 Dec
7.66	Antwon	Hicks	USA	12.3.83	1		Saskatoon	4 Feb
7.66	Gregory	Sedoc #	NED	16.10.81	3	Spark	Stuttgart	5 Feb
7.66	Samuel	Coco-Viloin	FRA	19.10.87	4		Liévin	8 Feb
7.66	Ronnie	Ash	USA	2.7.88	1s1		Clemson	11 Feb
7.66	Keiron	Stewart	JAM	21.11.89	1	Big 12	Lincoln NE	26 Feb
(30)								
7.67	Maksim	Lynsha	BLR	6.4.85	1	NC	Mogilyov	11 Jan
7.67	Dayron	Capetillo	CUB	11.9.87	5		Liévin	8 Feb
7.67	Ryan	Fontenot	USA	4.5.86	1		Baton Rouge	18 Feb
7.67	Chris	Thomas	USA	9.2.81	1		Norman	19 Feb
7.67	Devon	Hill	USA	26.10.89	3	NCAA	College Station	12 Mar
7.68	Ty	Akins	USA	6.1.86	6		Liévin	8 Feb
7.68	Dwight	Thomas	JAM	23.9.80	3h1		Karlsruhe	13 Feb
7.68	Brendan	Ames	USA	6.10.88	1h2	NCAA	College Station	11 Mar
7.69	Aleksey	Dryomin	RUS	10.5.89	3	Winter	Moskva	6 Feb
7.69	Lawrence	Clarke	GBR	12.3.90	8	GP	Birmingham	19 Feb
(40)								
7.69A	Dominic	Berger	USA	19.5.86	7	NC	Albuquerque	27 Feb
7.70	Damien	Broothaerts ¶	BEL	12.11.84	2	NC	Gent	20 Feb
7.70	Jackson	Quiñónez	ESP	12.6.80	4h3	EI	Paris (Bercy)	4 Mar
7.71	Pascal	Martinot Lagarde	FRA	22.9.91	1h6		Eaubonne	23 Jan
7.71	Oscar	Spurlock	USA	1.8.89	2		New York (Armory)	4 Feb
7.72	Anwar	Moore	USA	5.3.79	1		Fairfax	8 Jan
7.72	Emanuele	Abate	ITA	8.7.85	1h1		Magglingen	6 Feb
7.72	Othman Hadj	Lazib	ALG	10.5.83	1		Metz	25 Feb
7.72	Jeffery	Julmis	HAI	6.1.87	1		Fayetteville	4 Mar
7.73	Helge	Schwarzer	GER	26.11.85	1h1		Sindelfingen	15 Jan
(50)								
7.73	Stanislav	Olijar	LAT	22.3.79	1		Riga	21 Jan
7.73	Spencer	Adams	USA	10.9.89	1		Clemson	11 Feb
7.73	Nick	McCloud	USA	7.12.89	2		Norman	19 Feb
7.73	Eddie	Lovett	USA-J	25.6.92	1	SEC	Fayetteville	27 Feb

Mark		Name		Nat	Born	Pos	Meet	Venue	Date	

110 METRES HURDLES

Mark		Name		Nat	Born	Pos	Meet	Venue	Date	
12.94	1.8	David	Oliver	USA	24.4.82	1	Pre	Eugene	4	Jun
13.00	1.8		Liu Xiang	CHN	13.7.83	2	Pre	Eugene	4	Jun
13.00	-0.2	Dayron	Robles	CUB	19.11.86	1	Hanz	Zagreb	13	Sep
13.01	0.1		Robles			1	WK	Zürich	8	Sep
13.04	1.4		Oliver			1	NC	Eugene	25	Jun
13.04	-0.4		Robles			1	LGP	London (CP)	5	Aug
13.04	-0.2	Jason	Richardson	USA	4.4.86	2	Hanz	Zagreb	13	Sep
13.07	0.2		Liu Xiang			1	DL	Shanghai	15	May
13.07	0.7		Robles			1	FBK	Hengelo	29	May
13.08	1.0		Oliver			1h2	NC	Eugene	24	Jun
13.09	1.3		Oliver			2	DL	Saint Denis	8	Jul
13.08	-0.4		Richardson			2	LGP	London (CP)	5	Aug
13.08	-0.1		Richardson			1		Dubnica nad Váhon	15	Sep
13.09	1.3		Robles			1	DL	Saint Denis	8	Jul
13.10	0.1		Richardson			2	WK	Zürich	8	Sep
13.10A	1.6		Robles			1	PAm	Guadalajara, MEX	28	Oct
13.11	-1.6		Richardson			1s2	WCh	Daegu	29	Aug
13.12	0.1	Aries	Merritt	USA	24.7.85	1	Bisl	Oalo	9	Jun
13.12	1.4		Merritt			2	NC	Eugene	25	Jun
13.12	2.0		Oliver			1s3	NC	Eugene	25	Jun
13.12	1.0		Robles			1	Athl	Lausanne	30	Jun
13.14	0.0		Oliver			1		Daegu	12	May
13.14	0.3		Robles			1	GS	Ostrava	31	May
13.15	0.1	Dwight	Thomas	JAM	23.9.80	2	Bisl	Oslo	9	Jun
13.15	1.0		Richardson			2h2	NC	Eugene	24	Jun
13.15	1.4		Richardson			3	NC	Eugene	25	Jun
13.16	1.2		Oliver			1		Basseterre	9	Apr
13.16	1.4	Terrence	Trammell	USA	23.11.78	4	NC	Eugene	25	Jun
13.16	1.0		Thomas			2	Athl	Lausanne	30	Jun
13.16	-2.0		Robles			1		Reims	5	Jul
13.16	-0.9		Robles			1	LGP	London (CP)	5	Aug
13.16	-1.1		Richardson			1	WCh	Daegu	29	Aug
13.16	0.7		Richardson			1		Gateshead (Q)	17	Sep
		(33/7)								
13.20	0.1	Joel	Brown	USA	31.1.80	3	Bisl	Oslo	9	Jun
13.22	1.0	Andrew	Turner	GBR	19.9.80	4	Athl	Lausanne	30	Jun
13.23	0.8	Omo	Osaghae	USA	18.5.88	1	Big 12	Norman	15	May
		(10)								
13.24	-0.3	Hansle	Parchment	JAM	17.6.90	1	WUG	Shenzhen	20	Aug
13.25	1.5	Ronnie	Ash	USA	2.7.88	1h1	NC	Eugene	24	Jun
13.26	1.4	Jeff	Porter	USA	27.11.85	5	NC	Eugene	25	Jun
13.27A	1.6	Paulo César	Villar	COL	28.7.78	2	PAm	Guadalajara, MEX	28	Oct
13.29	0.2	Orlando	Ortega	CUB	29.7.91	1		La Habana	24	Sep
13.30	-0.5	Tyrone	Akins	USA	6.1.86	2		Padova	17	Jul
13.32	0.5	Andrew	Riley	JAM	9.6.88	1q1	NCAA-W	Eugene	28	May
13.32	1.5	Dominic	Berger	USA	19.5.86	2h1	NC	Eugene	24	Jun
13.33	1.7	Oscar	Spurlock	USA	1.8.89	1	MSR	Walnut	16	Apr
13.35	1.9	Antwon	Hicks	USA	12.3.83	1	KansR	Lawrence	23	Apr
		(20)								
13.35	1.8	Ashton	Eaton	USA	21.1.88	5	Pre	Eugene	4	Jun
13.35	0.8	Konstandin	Shabanov	RUS	17.11.89	1	NC-23	Yerino	24	Jun
13.35	-0.5	Dexter	Faulk	USA	14.4.84	4		Padova	17	Jul
13.36	0.1	Ryan	Wilson	USA	19.12.80	6	Bisl	Oslo	9	Jun
13.37	1.0	Garfield	Darien	FRA	22.12.87	5	Athl	Lausanne	30	Jun
13.37	1.5	Dimitri	Bascou	FRA	20.7.87	1		La Chaux-de-Fonds	3	Jul
13.39	0.1	Brendan	Ames	USA	6.10.88	1h2	Pac-10	Tucson	13	May
13.39	1.1	Gregory	Sedoc #	NED	16.10.81	1		Leiden	11	Jun
13.40	0.3	Richard	Phillips	JAM	26.1.83	3	NC	Kingston	26	Jun
13.41	0.3	John	Yarbrough	USA	16.8.85	2		Clermont	21	May
		(30)								
13.41	-0.1		Shi Dongpeng	CHN	6.1.84	7	NC	Hefei	11	Sep
13.42	0.6	Fred	Townsend	USA	19.2.82	1h2		Greensboro	15	Apr
13.42	1.7	Ronald	Brookins	USA	5.7.89	2	MSR	Walnut	16	Apr
13.44	1.8	Keiron	Stewart	JAM	21.11.89	1		Austin	25	Mar
13.44	1.5	Terrence	Somerville	USA	5.11.89	1		Villanova	8	May
13.44	0.0	Dominik	Bochenek	POL	14.5.87	1	NC	Bydgoszcz	13	Aug
13.45	1.4	Alexander	John	GER	3.5.86	1rC		Mannheim	13	Aug
13.45	0.7		Xie Wenjun	CHN	11.7.90	1		Saznya	25	Sep

Mark	Wind	Name		Nat	Born	Pos	Meet	Venue	Date	
13.46	-1.2	Dániel	Kiss	HUN	12.2.82	2	ET-1	Izmir	19	Jun
13.46	0.8	Sergey	Shubenkov	RUS	4.10.90	2	NC-23	Yerino	24	Jun
		(40)								
13.46	1.5	Othman Hadj	Lazib	ALG	10.5.83	1rB		Mannheim	13	Aug
13.47	1.5	William	Sharman	GBR	12.9.84	1	LEAP	Loughborough	11	Aug
13.47	1.4		Jiang Fan	CHN	16.9.89	2h3	WCh	Daegu	28	Aug
13.48	1.6	Ray	Stewart	USA	5.4.89	1	Pac-10	Tucson	14	May
13.48	0.9	Barrett	Nugent	USA	29.1.90	3s1	NCAA	Des Moines	9	Jun
13.48	1.9	Ryan	Fontenot	USA	4.5.86	5s2	NC	Eugene	25	Jun
13.48	1.2	Willi	Mathiszik	GER	17.6.84	1h1		Fribourg	30	Jul
13.49	2.0	Kevin	Craddock	USA	25.6.87	5s3	NC	Eugene	25	Jun
13.49	0.7	Eric	Keddo	JAM	1.7.84	1	CAC	Mayagüez	17	Jul
13.49	0.7	Erik	Balnuweit	GER	21.9.88	1		Malles	31	Jul
		(50)								
13.49A	1.6	Héctor	Cotto	PUR	8.8.84	5	PAm	Guadalajara, MEX	28	Oct
13.50	1.8	Ronald	Forbes	CAY	5.4.85	1h1		Clermont	4	Jun
13.50	0.3	Jeffrey	Julmis	USA/HAI	6.1.87	2s3	NCAA	Des Moines	9	Jun
13.51	1.1	Ronnie	McGirt	USA	19.2.88	1		Albany, GA	14	May
13.51	-1.2	Konstadínos	Douvalídis	GRE	10.3.87	3	ET-1	Izmir	19	Jun
13.51	0.8	Aleksey	Dryomin	RUS	10.5.89	3	NC-23	Yerino	24	Jun
13.52	0.3	Ladji	Doucouré	FRA	28.3.83	6	GS	Ostrava	31	May
13.52A	1.6	Enrique	Llanos	PUR	7.5.80	6	PAm	Guadalajara, MEX	28	Oct
13.54	0.7	Devon	Hill	USA	26.10.89	1q1	NCAA-E	Bloomington	28	May
13.54	1.0	Ryan	Brathwaite	BAH	6.6.88	3		Bydgoszcz	3	Jun
		(60)								
13.54	0.9	Wayne	Davis II	USA	22.8.91	4s1	NCAA	Des Moines	9	Jun
13.54	-0.1	Emanuele	Abate	ITA	8.7.85	1		Rieti	10	Sep
13.55	1.7	Spencer	Adams	USA	10.9.89	1q3	NCAA-E	Bloomington	28	May
13.55	-1.0	Gregor	Traber	GER-J	2.12.92	1		Biberach	28	Jun
13.55	0.0	Jackson	Quiñónez	ESP	12.6.80	3		Rovereto	13	Sep
13.56	0.7	Lehann	Fourie	RSA	16.2.87	6	FBK	Hengelo	29	May
13.57	0.0	Artur	Noga	POL	2.5.88	1	Kuso	Szczecin	25	Jun
13.57	0.0	Marlon	Odom	GER	4.12.82	1		Mannheim	3	Jul
13.57	1.5	Gianni	Frankis	GBR	16.4.88	2		La Chaux-de-Fonds	3	Jul
13.57	1.5	Andreas	Kundert	SUI	1.10.84	3		La Chaux-de-Fonds	3	Jul
		(70)								
13.58	1.8	Michael	Hancock	USA	20.2.90	1		Waverly, IA	2	Apr
13.58	1.2	Ignacio	Morales	CUB	28.1.87	1		La Habana	21	May
13.58	0.3	Shane	Brathwaite	BAH	8.2.90	3s3	NCAA	Des Moines	9	Jun
13.58	-0.4	Balázs	Baji	HUN	9.6.89	2	EU23	Ostrava	16	Jul
13.58	1.3	Yuniel	Hernández	CUB	28.3.81	2		Barquisimeto	28	Jul
13.58	-0.7	Lawrence	Clarke	GBR	12.3.90	1h3	NC	Birmingham	31	Jul
13.58	-0.5	Bano	Traoré	FRA	25.4.85	2		La Roche-sur-Yon	10	Aug
13.59	1.8		Yin Jing	CHN	23.5.88	1		Jiaxing	22	May
13.60	0.2	Samuel	Coco-Viloin	FRA	19.10.87	3		Strasbourg	12	Jun
13.60	0.4	Ahmad	Al-Moualed	KSA	16.2.88	1	ArabG	Doha	20	Dec
		(80)								
13.61	2.0	Selim	Nurudeen	NGR	1.2.83	2	AfrG	Maputo	12	Sep
13.62	1.4	Chris	Thomas	USA	9.2.81	1		San Marcos	15	Apr
13.62	0.9	Domonick	Sylve	USA	28.11.88	3s2	NCAA	Des Moines	9	Jun
13.62	1.3	Jhoanis C.	Portilla	CUB	24.7.90	1		La Habana	17	Jun
13.62	-0.4	Thomas	Delmestre	FRA	31.3.91	4	EU23	Ostrava	16	Jul
13.63	0.2	David	Payne	USA	24.7.82	3	Fla R	Gainesville	1	Apr
13.63	-0.7	Mikel	Thomas	TRI	23.11.87	2		Knoxville	15	Apr
13.63	1.4	Jarret	Eaton	USA	24.6.89	1rB	PennR	Philadelphia	30	Apr
13.64	1.7	Eddie	Lovett	USA-J	25.6.92	2q3	NCAA-E	Bloomington	28	May
13.64	1.0	Johnny	Dutch	USA	20.1.89	1rB	GS	Ostrava	31	May
		(90)								
13.64	2.0	Andrew	Brunson	USA	4.4.86	2		Atlanta	5	Jun
13.64	0.4	Matheus	Inocêncio	BRA	17.5.81	1		São Paulo	17	Jun
13.64	0.7	Matthias	Bühler	GER	2.9.86	3=		Malles	31	Jul
13.65	1.8	Aleec	Harris	USA	31.10.90	2		Norman	16	Apr
13.65	0.9	Keith	Hayes	USA	16.2.90	4s2	NCAA	Des Moines	9	Jun
13.66	0.3	Thiago	Castelo Branco	BRA	6.11.79	1h1		Piracicaba	10	Apr
13.66	0.3	Adams	Abdulrazaaq	USA	27.4.88	4s3	NCAA	Des Moines	9	Jun
13.66	-0.8		Park Tae-kyong	KOR	30.7.80	3	AsiC	Kobe	10	Jul
13.67	1.6	Damien	Broothaerts ¶	BEL	12.11.84	2		Heusden-Zolder	16	Jul
13.67	1.4	Marcel	van der Westen	NED	1.8.76	2rD		Mannheim	13	Aug
		(100)								
13.67	0.6	Paolo	Dal Molin	ITA	31.7.87	2		Bellinzona	15	Sep
13.67	-1.3	Hiroyuki	Sato	JPN	6.8.90	1		Mito	3	Nov

Mark	Wind	Name		Nat	Born	Pos	Meet	Venue	Date
13.68	1.6	Brandon	Tucker	USA	20.3.90				18 Mar
13.68	1.6	Martin	Mazác	CZE	6.5.90				28 Jun
13.68	1.8	Yuji	Ohashi	JPN	5.9.83				2 Jul
13.68	0.7		Zhang Jianxin	CHN	29.10.87				17 Jul
13.69	1.0	Cédric	Lavanne	FRA	13.11.80				15 May
13.69	1.7	Wataru	Yazawa	JPN	2.7.91				17 Jun
13.69	0.6	Trey	Hardee	USA	7.2.84				24 Jun
13.70	1.9	Tasuku	Tanonaka	JPN	23.9.78				10 Oct
13.70	0.6	Yoichi	Iwafune	JPN	12.6.85				15 Oct
13.71		Rohallah	Ashgari	IRI	8.1.82				17 May
13.71	1.7	Aramis	Massenberg	USA	6.8.89				28 May
13.71	0.6	Philip	Nossmy	SWE	6.12.82				11 Jun
13.72	1.9	Deuce	Carter	JAM	28.9.90				30 Apr
13.72	1.5	Esteban	Guzman	USA	2.5.84				15 May
13.72	1.5		Ji Wei	CHN	5.2.84				20 Jul
13.72A	1.8	Jorge	McFarlane	PER	20.2.88				27 Oct
13.73	0.4	Yoisel	Pumariega	CUB	4.2.88				24 Feb
13.73	1.3	Ethan	Holmes	USA	16.3.91				15 May
13.73	0.4	Carrington	Queen	USA	21.9.87				18 Jun
13.73	1.5	Tatsuya	Wado	JPN	4.10.90				18 Jun
13.73	-0.4	Stanislav	Olijar	LAT	22.3.79				30 Jul
13.73	1.5	Andrew	Pozzi	GBR-J	15.5.92				11 Aug
13.73	1.9	Masayuki	Ida	JPN	11.8.87				10 Oct
13.74	0.0	Dayron	Capetillo	CUB	11.9.87				26 May
13.74	0.2	Helge	Schwarzer	GER	26.11.85				2 Jul
13.74	1.5	Julian	Adeniran	GBR	28.9.88				11 Aug
13.75	0.9	Chris	Kinney	USA	9.11.88				9 Jun
13.75	-0.5	Felipe	Vivancos	ESP	16.6.80				10 Jun
13.75	1.8	Ben	Reynolds	GBR	26.9.90				29 Jun
13.75	0.0	Maksim	Lynsha	BLR	6.4.85				7 Jul
13.75	0.0	Éder Antônio	Souza	BRA	15.10.86				7 Aug
13.75	2.0	Samuel	Okon	NGR	6.6.86				12 Sep
13.75	0.0	Fawaz Dahesh	Al-Shammari	KUW	3.4.77				27 Oct
13.75	-1.3	Hideki	Omuro	JPN	25.7.90				3 Nov
13.76	1.8	Logan	Taylor	USA	3.4.86				23 Apr
13.76	1.5	Kandrick	Cooper	USA	28.3.86				15 May
13.76	0.7		Hong Xiaofeng	CHN	5.2.88				17 Jul
13.76	0.7	Carlos	Jorge	DOM	24.9.86				17 Jul
13.77A	0.1	Ruan	de Vries	RSA	1.2.86				26 Mar
13.77	1.3	Nick	McCloud	USA	7.12.89				15 May
13.77	0.0	Mariusz	Kubaszewski	POL	11.7.82				25 Jun
13.77	0.2	Kenji	Yahata	JPN	4.11.80				26 Jun
13.77	-0.3	Thingalaya	Siddhanth	IND	1.3.91				13 Sep
13.77	0.7	Jumrut	Rittidet	THA	1.2.89				13 Nov
13.78	0.2	Jeshua	Anderson	USA	22.6.89				13 May
13.78	1.1	Kemar	Clarke	USA	20.5.88				14 May
13.78	1.0	Igor	Peremota	RUS	14.1.81				3 Jun
13.78	1.5	Ali Hussein	Al-Zaki	KSA	11.5.85				20 Jul
13.78	1.0	João	Almeida	POR	5.4.88				7 Aug
13.78	-0.4	Abdulaziz	Al-Mandeel	KUW	22.5.89				19 Dec
13.79	0.1	Jordan	Mullen	USA	6.4.90				16 Apr
13.79	-1.8	Mantas	Silkauskas	LTU	10.4.88				7 May
13.79	0.5	Paul	Dittmer	GER	1.1.87				2 Jul
13.80	0.7	Yume	Moses	JPN	1.2.88				29 Apr
13.80	1.0	Stefano	Tedesco	ITA	4.7.88				15 May
13.80	1.3	Malcolm	Anderson	USA	.89/90				27 May
13.80	1.9	Masanori	Nishizawa	JPN	16.7.87				10 Oct
13.80	0.0	Lyès	Mokdel	ALG	20.6.90				27 Oct
13.81	-0.1	Michele	Calvi	ITA	7.6.90				25 Jun
13.81	2.0	Jordan	Nicolas	FRA	13.12.90				23 Jul
13.81	1.5	Nick	Gayle	GBR	4.1.85				11 Aug
13.81	0.4	Yuta	Kawauchi	JPN	19.8.89				16 Oct
13.82	1.7	David	Klech	USA	29.4.88				14 Apr
13.82	0.2	Yutaro	Furukawa	JPN	3.6.85				26 Jun
13.83	-0.4	Jurica	Grabusic	CRO	28.3.83				5 Jun
13.83	1.3	David	Arzola	CUB	24.2.89				17 Jun
13.83	1.5	Michael	Page	SUI	24.5.88				3 Jul
13.83	1.0	Alexander	Al-Ameen	GBR	2.3.89				17 Jul
13.84	0.6	Jason	Boyd	USA	16.9.88				16 Apr
13.84	2.0	Virgil	Mitchell	USA	28.8.86				27 May
13.84	0.7	Greggmar	Swift	BAR	16.2.91				17 Jul
13.84	-1.5	Andres	Raja	EST	2.6.82				9 Aug
13.85	1.5	Jerome	Miller	USA	13.9.83				23 Apr
13.85	0.5	Sheldon	Wilkinson	USA	21.12.86				1 May
13.85	1.3	Kendall	Parks	USA	.89				7 May
13.85	0.0	Sergiy	Kopanayko	UKR	5.11.88				31 May
13.85	1.9	Kazuyuki	Yoshinaga	JPN	6.6.84				10 Oct
13.86	0.8	Jamele	Mason	PUR	19.10.89				15 May
13.86	0.5	Rasul	Dabo	POR	14.2.89				12 Jun
13.86	0.7	Rayzamshah	Wan Sofian	MAS	11.1.88				13 Nov
13.87		Keyunta	Hayes	USA-J	15.2.92				2 Apr
13.87	0.6	Jacoby	DuBose	USA	11.12.82				16 Apr
13.87A	-1.0	Damian	Warner	CAN	4.10.89				24 Jun
13.87	1.4	Robert	Kronberg	SWE	15.8.76				14 Aug

(186)

Disqualified for obstruction: 13.14 -1.1 Robles — WCh Daegu 29 Aug

Wind assisted

Mark	Wind	Name		Nat	Born	Pos	Meet	Venue	Date
13.09	4.6		Oliver			1r2		Gainseville	16 Apr
13.12	5.7		Oliver			1r1		Gainseville	16 Apr
13.14	2.3		Richardson			1s1	NC	Eugene	25 Jun
13.16	4.6		Merritt			1r3	TexR	Austin	9 Apr
13.18	3.8	Omo	Osaghae	USA	18.5.88	1		Lubbock	22 Apr
13.19	3.5	Barrett	Nugent	USA	29.1.90	1	TexR	Austin	9 Apr
13.24	2.8	Ronald	Forbes	CAY	5.4.85	1		Clermont	4 Jun
13.24	2.3	Ronnie	Ash	USA	2.7.88	3s1	NC	Eugene	25 Jun
13.26	4.1	Dimitri	Bascou	FRA	20.7.87	1	NC	Albi	30 Jul
13.34	2.8	Richard	Phillips	JAM	26.1.83	2		Clermont	4 Jun
13.34	3.6	Brendan	Ames	USA	6.10.88	3	NCAA	Des Moines	11 Jun
13.35	3.4	Ryan	Wilson	USA	19.12.80	2	MSR	Walnut	16 Apr
13.38	3.6	Jeffrey	Julmis	USA/HAI	6.1.87	4	NCAA	Des Moines	11 Jun
13.38	3.6	Keiron	Stewart	JAM	21.11.89	5	NCAA	Des Moines	11 Jun
13.40	3.3	Fred	Townsend	USA	19.2.82	1		Castres	19 Jul
13.40	2.2	Alexander	John	GER	3.5.86	1rA		Mannheim	13 Aug
13.45	3.4	Héctor	Cotto	PUR	8.8.84	3	MSR	Walnut	16 Apr
13.48	2.3	Spencer	Adams	USA	10.9.89	5s1	NC	Eugene	25 Jun
13.49	3.3	João	Almeida	POR	5.4.88	1	NC	Lisboa (U)	31 Jul
13.51	2.1	Bano	Traoré	FRA	25.4.85	1h2	NC	Albi	30 Jul
13.52	2.1	Devon	Hill	USA	26.10.89	5h4	NC	Eugene	24 Jun
13.53	3.1	Damien	Broothaerts ¶	BEL	12.11.84	2h1	FRA Ch	Albi	30 Jul
13.54	2.2	Matheus	Inocêncio	BRA	17.5.81	1		São Paulo	30 Apr
13.54	2.8	Kandrick	Cooper	USA	28.3.86	2h1		Clemson	13 May
13.54	3.5	Michael	Hancock	USA	20.2.90	1	JUCO	Hutchinson, KS	21 May
13.55	2.5	Aleec	Harris	USA	31.10.90	1rB	TexR	Austin	9 Apr
13.58	3.8	Brandon	Tucker	USA	20.3.90	2		Lubbock	22 Apr
13.60	3.9	Chris	Thomas	USA	9.2.81	1rC	TexR	Austin	9 Apr
13.60	3.3	Rasul	Dabo	POR	14.2.89	2	NC	Lisboa (U)	31 Jul
13.61	3.9	Trey	Hardee	USA	7.2.84	2rC	TexR	Austin	9 Apr

Mark	Wind	Name		Nat	Born	Pos	Meet	Venue	Date
13.61	3.9	Nick	McCloud	USA	7.12.89	3rC	TexR	Austin	9 Apr
13.61	2.4	Dayron	Capetillo	CUB	11.9.87	2		La Habana	10 Jun
13.61	3.0	Helge	Schwarzer	GER	26.11.85	1r1		Garbsen	30 Jul
13.62	2.9	Martin	Mazác	CZE	6.5.90	1	NC	Brno	2 Jul
13.63	2.4	Tasuku	Tanonaka	JPN	23.9.78	1	Oda	Hiroshima	29 Apr
13.63	2.3	Aramis	Massenberg	USA	6.8.89	1h1		Greensboro	6 May
13.65	2.2	Jamele	Mason	PUR	19.10.89	3		Lubbock	2 Apr
13.65	3.0	Yoichi	Iwafune	JPN	12.6.85	1		Tajimi	10 Oct
13.66	2.4	Hideki	Omuro	JPN	25.7.90	2	Oda	Hiroshima	29 Apr
13.66	2.3	Andrew	Pozzi	GBR-J	15.5.92	1h2	LEAP	Loughborough	11 Aug

Mark	Wind	Name		Nat	Born	Date
13.67	4.3	Mantas	Silkauskas	LTU	10.4.88	8 Apr
13.70	3.4	Lawson	Montgomery	USA	9.7.90	6 May
13.71w	2.1	Andres	Raja	EST	2.6.82	19 Jul
13.72w	2.5	Ruan	de Vries	RSA	1.2.86	10 Apr
13.72w	2.4	Yume	Moses	JPN	1.2.88	29 Apr
13.72w	2.3	Keith	Nkrumah	USA	28.11.90	6 May
13.72w	4.0	Julian	Adeniran	GBR	28.9.88	22 May
13.76w	3.3	Kendall	Parks	USA	.89	16 Apr
13.76w	2.6	Todd	McKown	USA	19.1.90	6 May
13.77w	2.6	Jordan	Nicolas	FRA	13.12.90	24 Jul
13.77w	2.2	Ko Wen-Ting		TPE	17.4.89	25 Oct
13.78w	3.4	Caleb	Cross	USA	31.5.91	6 May
13.78w	3.4	Stefano	Tedesco	ITA	4.7.88	15 May
13.79	4.8	Andrew	McDowell	USA	11.4.88	2 Apr
13.80	3.8	Harold	Lathan	USA-J	15.7.92	2 Apr
13.81	2.3	Miller	Moss	USA	14.3.88	13 May
13.84	3.5	Moussa	Dembélé	SEN	30.10.88	21 May
13.84	3.7	Matthew	Hudson	GBR	29.2.88	4 Jun
13.84	3.7	Daniel	Davis	GBR	12.12.87	4 Jun
13.86	2.1	Tremaine	Grant	CAN	23.11.91	14 May

Best at low altitude

Mark	Wind	Name	Pos	Meet	Venue	Date
13.54	0.7	Cotto	2	CAC	Mayagüez	17 Jul
13.55	0.1	Villar	1s1	BRA Ch	São Paulo	6 Aug
13.77	0.3	Jorge McFarlane				2 Jun
13.79	-1.6	Ruan de Vries				16 Apr

Hand timing

Mark	Wind	Name		Nat	Born	Pos	Venue	Date
13.4	-1.0	Ignacio	Morales	CUB	28.1.87	2h2	La Habana	17 Mar
13.5	-1.0	Yidiel Islay	Contreras	CUB-J	27.11.92	3h2	La Habana	17 Mar

Wind assisted

Mark	Wind	Name		Nat	Born	Pos	Venue	Date
13.1	3.4	Jhoanis	Portilla	CUB	24.7.90	1r1	La Habana	24 Feb
13.1	3.4	Orlando	Ortega	CUB	29.7.91	2r1	La Habana	24 Feb
13.3	3.4	Yoisel	Pumariega	CUB	4.2.88	3r1	La Habana	24 Feb
13.4	3.4	David	Arzola	CUB	24.2.89	4r1	La Habana	24 Feb

JUNIORS

See main list for top 2 juniors. 9 performances by 3 men to 13.79. Additional marks and further juniors:

Name	Mark	Wind	Pos	Meet	Venue	Date	Mark	Wind	Pos	Meet	Venue	Date
Traber	13.56	0.2	1		Mannheim	2 Jul	13.71	0.9	2		Weinheim	28 May
	13.67	-0.4	1		Biberach	28 Jun	13.73	-1.4	1h2		Mannheim	2 Jul
Lovett	13.77	0.3	6h3	NCAA	Des Moines	9 Jun	13.79	0.7	2h2	PennR	Philadelphia	29 Apr

Mark	Wind	Name		Nat	Born	Pos	Meet	Venue	Date
13.73	1.5	Andrew	Pozzi	GBR	15.5.92	3	LEAP	Loughborough	11 Aug
13.87		Keyunta	Hayes	USA	15.2.92	1h1		San Antonio	2 Apr
13.90	1.8	Harold	Lathan	USA	.92	4		Norman	16 Apr
13.99	1.6	Jordan	Pitts	USA-Y	.94+	4		Fort Worth	18 Mar
14.04	1.9	Dario	Seghers	BEL	20.3.92	1		Tielt	15 May
14.06	0.0		Chu Pengfei	CHN	28.12.93	3h2		Fuzhou	26 Jun
14.07	2.0	DeAnthony	Henderson	USA		2h1		Fayetteville	6 May
14.07	-1.6	João Vitor	de Oliveira (10)	BRA	15.5.92	1	NC-j	São Paulo	8 Oct
14.08	1.2	Sebastian	Barth	GER	1.2.93	1		München	11 Jun
14.09	-1.0	Tyrell	Forde	BAR	.92	4	NC	Bridgetown	25 Jun

Wind assisted. See main list for 1 junior. Additional mark and further juniors:

Name	Mark	Wind	Pos	Meet	Venue	Date
Lovett	13.64	2.1	2	SEC	Athens, GA	15 May

Mark	Wind	Name		Nat	Born	Pos	Meet	Venue	Date
13.80	3.8	Harold	Lathan	USA-J	15.7.92	1		Hutchinson	2 Apr
14.01	2.4	Genta	Masuno	JPN	.93	1		Kitakami	6 Aug
14.05	4.0	Jack	Meredith	GBR	14.8.92	3	LI	Loughborough	22 May

110 Metres Hurdles – 99 cm hurdles

Mark	Wind	Name		Nat	Born	Pos	Meet	Venue	Date
13.14	1.6	Eddie	Lovett	USA	25.6.92	1	PAm-J	Miramar	23 Jul
13.23	1.8					1h2	NC-j	Eugene	24 Jun
13.33	1.9					1	NC-j	Eugene	24 Jun
13.24	1.6	Roy	Smith	USA	12.4.92	2	PAm-J	Miramar	23 Jul
13.29	0.0	Andrew	Pozzi	GBR	15.5.92	1r1		Mannheim	3 Jul
13.31	1.1	Gregor	Traber	GER	2.12.92	1		Oberkirch	19 Jun
13.37	0.5					1h1		Oberkirch	19 Jun
13.40	-0.1					1	NC-j	Jena	6 Aug
13.32	0.7		Lu Jialeng	CHN	18.6.93	1h2	CityG	Nanchang	22 Oct
13.36	1.9	Johnathan	Cabral	USA	31.12.92	1h1		Eugene	24 Jun
13.38	1.2		Wang Dongqiang	CHN	13.1.93	1	CityG	Nanchang	23 Oct
13.47	0.6	Dario	Seghers	BEL	20.3.92	2		Mannheim	2 Jul
13.48	0.6	Jack	Meredith	GBR	14.8.92	3		Mannheim	2 Jul
13.56	0.6		Chu Pengfei (10)	CHN	29.12.93	1	NC-j	Jinan	4 Jun
13.57	1.2		Lei Ywen	CHN	11.12.93	3	CityG	Nanchang	23 Oct
13.58	-1.0	Demetrius	Lindo	USA	28.3.92	1		Greensboro	17 Jun
13.61	1.7	Filip	Drozdowski	POL	28.4.93	1	NC-j	Torun	26 Jun
13.63	0.7	Artie	Burns	USA	1.5.95	1		Winter Park	7 May
13.63	-0.1	Martin	Vogel	GER	16.3.92	2	NC-j	Jena	6 Aug
13.64	-0.1	Yordan L.	O'Farrill	CUB	9.2.93	1		La Habana	24 Feb
13.64	1.1	Lorenzo	Johnson	USA		1		Austin	14 May

Mark	Wind	Name		Nat	Born	Pos	Meet	Venue	Date	
13.64	0.0	Cherif	Banda	FRA	29.1.92	1r2		Mannheim	3	Jul
13.66	2.0	Stefan	Fennell	JAM	5.11.93	1		Kingston	5	Feb
13.66	-0.4		Chen Shuyan (20)	CHN	26.1.93	1h1	NC-j	Jinan	3	Jun

Wind assisted

Mark	Wind	Name		Nat	Born	Pos	Meet	Venue	Date	
13.03	2.9	Eddie	Lovett	USA	25.6.92	1h1	PAm-J	Miramar	23	Jul
Smith		13.33w 2.8 1h2 PAm-JMiramar			23	Jul				
13.65	4.4	Jonathan	Jones	USA		1	TexR	Austin	9	Apr
13.65	2.9	Gregory	MacNeill	CAN	15.4.92	2h1	PAm-J	Miramar	23	Jul

200 METRES HURDLES STRAIGHT

At Manchester 15 May: (2.0) 1. Andrew Turner GBR 22.10, 2. Bershawn Jackson USA 22.26, 3. Angelo Taylor USA 22.84

300 METRES HURDLES

Mark		Name		Nat	Born	Pos	Meet	Venue	Date	
35.3		Silvio	Schirrmeister	GER	7.12.88	1		Pliezhausen	22	May
36.20		Jonathan	Cabral	USA-J	31.12.92	1		Clovis	4	Jun
36.25		Josef	Prorok	CZE	16.11.87	1		Praha	6	May
36.34		Gregory	Coleman	USA	24.7.93	1		Austin	14	May

400 METRES HURDLES

Mark		Name		Nat	Born	Pos	Meet	Venue	Date	
47.66A		Louis 'L.J.'	van Zyl	RSA	20.7.85	1		Pretoria	25	Feb
47.66			van Zyl			1	GS	Ostrava	31	May
47.73			van Zyl			1	NC	Durban	10	Apr
47.91			van Zyl			1	GGala	Roma	26	May
47.93		Jeshua	Anderson	USA	22.6.89	1	NC	Eugene	26	Jun
47.93		Bershawn	Jackson	USA	8.5.83	2	NC	Eugene	26	Jun
47.94		Angelo	Taylor	USA	29.12.78	3	NC	Eugene	26	Jun
47.97			Taylor			1	Herc	Monaco	22	Jul
47.99A		Omar	Cisneros	CUB	19.11.89	1	PAm	Guadalajara, MEX	27	Oct
48.11			van Zyl			1	DL	Doha	6	May
48.13			Anderson			1	Pac-10	Tucson	14	May
48.14		Cornel	Fredericks	RSA	3.3.90	2	NC	Durban	10	Apr
48.20		David	Greene	GBR	11.4.86	1	DL	Birmingham	10	Jul
48.22			Jackson			2	DL	Birmingham	10	Jul
48.22			Jackson			2	Herc	Monaco	22	Jul
48.24			Greene			2	GGala	Roma	26	May
48.26			Greene			1	WCh	Daegu	1	Sep
48.32		Javier	Culson	PUR	25.7.84	1	VD	Bruxelles	16	Sep
48.33			Culson			1	LGP	London (CP)	6	Aug
48.34			Culson			3	DL	Birmingham	10	Jul
48.41			Greene			1	Athl	Lausanne	30	Jun
48.43			Fredericks			2	DL	Doha	6	May
48.43			Greene			3	Herc	Monaco	22	Jul
48.44			Jackson			3	DL	Doha	6	May
48.44			Culson			2	WCh	Daegu	1	Sep
48.45		Michael	Tinsley	USA	21.4.84	4	NC	Eugene	26	Jun
48.47			Greene			2	GS	Ostrava	31	May
48.47		Johnny	Dutch	USA	20.1.89	5	NC	Eugene	26	Jun
48.50			Culson			1	adidas	New York	11	Jun
48.52			Greene			1h1	WCh	Daegu	29	Aug
48.52			Fredericks			2h1	WCh	Daegu	29	Aug
48.52			Culson			1s1	WCh	Daegu	30	Aug
		(32/10)								
48.58		Justin	Gaymon	USA	13.12.86	1		Kingston	7	May
48.64		Isa	Phillips	JAM	22.4.84	2h2	WCh	Daegu	29	Aug
48.66		Jehue	Gordon	TRI	15.12.91	1	ISTAF	Berlin	11	Sep
48.71		Nathan	Woodward	GBR	17.10.89	1		La Chaux-de-Fonds	3	Jul
48.72		Georg	Fleischauer	GER	21.10.88	3h1	WCh	Daegu	29	Aug
48.74		Kerron	Clement	USA	31.10.85	2		Kingston	7	May
48.74		Félix	Sánchez	DOM	30.8.77	3h2	WCh	Daegu	29	Aug
48.98		Jack	Green	GBR	6.10.91	4	DL	Birmingham	10	Jul
49.03		Leford	Green	JAM	14.11.86	1	CAC	Mayagüez	16	Jul
49.04		Danny	McFarlane	JAM	14.2.72	3		Kingston	7	May
		(20)								
49.04		Bryce	Brown	USA	17.9.88	1	Big 12	Norman	15	May
49.07		Aleksandr	Derevyagin	RUS	24.3.79	3s3	WCh	Daegu	30	Aug
49.08		Amaechi	Morton	NGR	30.10.89	2	NCAA	Des Moines	10	Jun
49.16		Andrés	Silva	URU	27.3.86	1		Rio de Janeiro	26	May
49.17		Mahau	Suguimati	BRA	13.11.84	1		Fukuroi	3	May
49.20A		Winder	Cuevas	DOM	1.8.88	4	PAm	Guadalajara, MEX	27	Oct

Mark	Wind	Name		Nat	Born	Pos	Meet	Venue	Date
49.24		Stanislav	Melnykov	UKR	26.2.87	3h5	WCh	Daegu	29 Aug
49.27		Takayuki	Kishimoto	JPN	6.5.90	2		Fukuroi	3 May
49.27		Yuta	Imazeki	JPN	6.11.87	1		Osaka	26 Jun
49.28			Cheng Wen	CHN-J	18.3.92	1		Fuzhou	26 Jun
		(30)							
49.30		Jamele	Mason	PUR	19.10.89	1		Lubbock	2 Apr
49.37		Josef	Robertson	JAM	14.5.87	5	GS	Ostrava	31 May
49.41		Reggie	Wyatt	USA	17.9.90	2	Pac-10	Tucson	14 May
49.41		Yuta	Konishi	JPN	31.7.90	2		Osaka	26 Jun
49.43		Kurt	Couto	MOZ	14.5.85	1		Biberach	28 Jun
49.47			Li Zhilong	CHN	9.3.88	1	NC	Hefei	9 Sep
49.49		Vincent	Kosgei	KEN	11.11.85	5h2	WCh	Daegu	29 Aug
49.55		Emir	Bekric	SRB	14.3.91	2s1	WUG	Shenzhen	18 Aug
49.56		David	Gollnow	GER	8.4.89	1	NC	Kassel	24 Jul
49.59		Rhys	Williams	GBR	27.2.84	1		Sollentuna	28 Jun
		(40)							
49.60		Brendan	Cole	AUS	29.5.81	1		Kawasaki	8 May
49.62		Nikita	Andriyanov	RUS	7.2.90	4	EU23	Ostrava	16 Jul
49.63		João	Ferreira	POR	20.10.86	4	WUG	Shenzhen	19 Aug
49.64		Takatoshi	Abe	JPN	12.11.91	1	AsiC	Kobe	9 Jul
49.66		Roxroy	Cato	JAM	1.5.88	3	NC	Kingston	24 Jun
49.70		Varg	Königsmark	GER-J	28.4.92	1	EJ	Talinn	24 Jul
49.71		Michael	Bultheel	BEL	30.6.86	1		Lebbeke	31 Jul
49.72		Jorge	Paula	POR	8.10.84	1		Albertville	1 Jul
49.72		Adrien	Clémenceau	FRA	25.5.88	2		Chambéry	10 Jul
49.76		Niall	Flannery	GBR	26.4.91	3	NC-23	Bedford	26 Jun
		(50)							
49.76		Hugo	Grillas	FRA	28.2.89	5	EU23	Ostrava	16 Jul
49.76		Yasmany	Copello	CUB	15.4.87	1		Pátra	20 Jul
49.76		Richard	Davenport	GBR	12.9.85	2	NC	Birmingham	30 Jul
49.77		Brent	LaRue	USA/SLO	26.4.87	1		Celje	12 Jun
49.78		Thomas	Phillips	GBR	23.4.89	4	NC-23	Bedford	26 Jun
49.79		Vyacheslav	Sakayev	RUS	12.1.88	2	NC	Cheboksary	23 Jul
49.81		David	Hughes	GBR	31.5.84	2		La Chaux-de-Fonds	3 Jul
49.81		Tobias	Giehl	GER	25.7.91	2	NC	Kassel	24 Jul
49.82		Lee	Moore	USA	20.12.88	1		Oxford, MS	23 Apr
49.86A		Emanuel	Mayers	TRI	9.3.89	2h1	PAm	Guadalajara, MEX	26 Oct
		(60)							
49.87		Noriuki	Ideura	JPN	29.10.87	4	NC	Kumagaya	11 Jun
49.87			Xu Xiangchao	CHN-J	26.10.93	1	CityG	Nanchang	22 Oct
49.89		Dai	Tamesue	JPN	3.5.78	1rB		Fukuroi	3 May
49.91		Minas	Alozidis	CYP	7.7.84	2		Pátra	20 Jul
49.94		David	Aristil	USA	12.12.88	4	NCAA	Des Moines	10 Jun
49.94		José	Bencosme de Leon	ITA-J	16.5.92	1		Marano	20 Sep
49.95		Leslie	Murray	ISV	24.1.91	1h1	CAC	Mayagüez	15 Jul
49.96		Aleksey	Pogorelov	RUS	26.3.83	1		Irkutsk	5 Aug
49.97		Reuben	McCoy	USA	16.3.86	5		Kingston	7 May
50.00		LaRon	Bennett	USA	25.11.82	1		Auburn	16 Apr
		(70)							
50.00		Silvio	Schirrmeister	GER	7.12.88	1		Zeven	12 Jun
50.01		Josef	Prorok	CZE	16.11.87	3	Odlozil	Praha	13 Jun
50.01		Stef	Vanhaeren	BEL-J	15.1.92	2	EJ	Tallinn	24 Jul
50.01		Richard	Yates	GBR	26.1.86	3	NC	Birmingham	30 Jul
50.01		Kenta	Takeda	JPN	27.4.86	2h1		Yamaguchi	7 Oct
50.03		Ludovic	Dubois	FRA	13.4.86	5		Ninove	6 Aug
50.04		Eric	Bailey	USA	23.5.89	3	Big 12	Norman	15 May
50.04		Akihiko	Nakamura	JPN	23.10.90	5	NC	Kumagaya	11 Jun
50.05		Markino	Buckley	JAM	16.4.86	6		Kingston	7 May
50.06		Thomas	Barr	IRL-J	24.7.92	1	NC	Dublin (S)	7 Aug
		(80)							
50.06		Tetsuya	Tateno	JPN	5.8.91	3		Kumamoto	11 Sep
50.10		Denis	Teslenko	UKR	18.4.89	1		Vinnytsa	15 Aug
50.11		Adam	Dailey	USA	19.3.89	4	Big 12	Norman	15 May
50.11		Hiroaki	Masuoka	JPN	18.2.86	2h1	NC	Kumagaya	10 Jun
50.11		Marek	Plawgo	POL	25.2.81	1	NC	Bydgoszcz	12 Aug
50.12		Yeison	Rivas	COL	24.9.87	1		Ponce	16 Apr
50.12		Naohiro	Kawakita	JPN	10.7.80	4		Osaka	26 Jun
50.14			Chen Chieh	TPE-J	8.5.92	3		Fuzhou	26 Jun
50.14		Rasmus	Mägi	EST-J	4.5.92	4s1	WUG	Shenzhen	18 Aug
50.15		Richard	Lowe	USA	21.2.89	2s2	NCAA	Des Moines	8 Jun
		(90)							

Mark	Name		Nat	Born	Pos	Meet	Venue	Date
50.16	Eric	Alejandro	PUR	15.4.86	2		Clermont	4 Jun
50.19	Heni	Kéchi	FRA	31.8.80	2	NC	Albi	30 Jul
50.20	Raphael	Fernandes	BRA	8.11.84	3	NC	São Paulo	7 Aug
50.22	Abderahmane	Hamadi	ALG	24.3.84	6		Cottbus	25 Jun
50.23	Thomas	Kortbeek	NED	2.4.81	2		Genève	28 May
50.24	Naman	Keïta	FRA	9.4.78	3		Chambéry	10 Jul
50.26	Periklís	Iakovákis	GRE	24.3.79	1	ET-1	Izmir	18 Jun
50.26	Kazuaki	Yoshida	JPN	31.8.87	1r2		Inba	22 Oct
50.27	Nathan	Arnett	BAH	15.12.90	1	JUCO	Hutchinson, KS	21 May
50.28	Tibor	Koroknai	HUN	24.1.90	7	EU23	Ostrava	16 Jul
	(100)							

Mark	Name		Nat	Born	Date
50.29	Ben	Sumner	GBR	16.8.83	25 Jun
50.32	Isaiah	Gill	USA	20.6.90	2 Apr
50.32	Adrian	Findlay	JAM	1.10.82	24 Jun
50.32	Keisuke	Nozawa	JPN	7.6.91	8 Oct
50.33	Jun-ya	Imai	JPN	23.6.87	2 Jul
50.34	Cody	Wisslead	USA	22.9.88	8 Jun
50.35A	Boniface	Mucheru	KEN-J	.92	11 Jun
50.35A	Julius	Oletygor	KEN	12.12.90	16 Jul
50.36	Tatsuhiko	Mizuno	JPN	25.10.90	22 May
50.36		Chen Ke	CHN	14.9.89	9 Sep
50.37	Ivan	Shablyuev	RUS	17.4.88	22 Jul
50.37	Vladimir	Antmanis	RUS	12.3.84	23 Jul
50.37	Shuji	Miyake	JPN	4.8.89	10 Sep
50.38	Joseph G.	Abraham	IND	11.9.81	20 Feb
50.38	Andre	Walsh	JAM	14.9.89	6 May
50.38	Mamadou	Kasse Hann	SEN	10.10.86	14 Jun
50.38	Kenneth	Medwood	BIZ	14.12.87	6 Aug
50.39	Satinder	Singh	IND	7.2.87	20 Feb
50.39A	Nicholas	Bett	KEN-J	.92	16 Jul
50.41	James	Forman	GBR	12.12.91	27 Jun
50.42	P C	Beneke	RSA	18.7.90	10 Apr
50.42	Tasuhiro	Fueki	JPN	20.12.85	24 Sep
50.45	Shingo	Akimoto	JPN	7.4.82	3 May
50.45	Reggie	Rucker	USA	7.10.83	17 Jun
50.46	Sergiy	Borodin	UKR	14.10.81	30 May
50.46	Masahira	Yoshikata	JPN	23.8.82	10 Jun
50.46	Eusebio	Haliti	ALB	.91	12 Jun
50.47	Alex	Wilright	USA	12.6.88	27 May
50.47	Atsushi	Yamada	JPN	3.7.91	24 Jul
50.48	Miloud	Rahmani	ALG	13.12.83	18 Jun
50.49	Leonardo	Capotosti	ITA	24.7.88	10 Jul
50.50	Carson	Blanks	USA	19.9.89	16 Apr
50.51	Joe	Greene	USA	20.11.87	9 Apr
50.52	Loïc	Miath	FRA	7.2.84	10 Jul
50.53	Rafal	Ostrowski	POL	28.2.85	10 Sep
50.54	Trey	Charles	USA	15.6.89	15 May
50.56	Radoslaw	Czyz	POL	7.1.88	23 Jul
50.57	Kenji	Narisako	JPN	25.7.84	26 Jun
50.57	Yuta	Amano	JPN	29.5.90	11 Sep
50.59	Fawaz Dahesh	Al-Shammari	KUW	3.4.77	3 Apr
50.59	Eric	Lund	USA	1.4.88	30 Apr
50.59	Jon	DeGrave	USA	12.5.90	27 May
50.59		Chen Dayu	CHN	11.1.88	9 Sep
50.60	Giacomo	Panizza	ITA	30.7.89	18 Jun
50.60	Víctor	Solarte	VEN	6.1.86	20 Jul
50.60	Tim	Rummens	BEL	16.12.87	13 Aug
50.61	Mickaël	François	FRA	12.3.88	29 May
50.62	Mike	Cochrane	NZL	13.8.91	29 Jan
50.62	Aramís	Díaz	CUB	22.11.74	25 Sep
50.63	Bandar Yahya	Sharahili	KSA	6.3.87	17 Dec
50.65	Ethan	Holmes	USA	16.3.91	15 May
50.65	Jason	Harvey	IRL	9.8.91	7 Aug
50.66	Jermaine	Lowery	USA	13.1.90	27 May
50.67	Yoan	Décimus	FRA	30.11.87	26 Jun
50.68	Naoki	Ihara	JPN	22.4.82	3 May
50.68	Adam	Kunkel	CAN	24.2.81	10 Jul
50.69	João	Eufrázio Neto	BRA	5.1.83	12 May
50.69	Takyuki	Koike	JPN	12.10.84	30 Oct
50.70	Miles	Ukaoma	USA-J	21.7.92	27 May
50.72	Nils	Duerinck	BEL	20.3.84	13 Jun
50.73	James	Mortimer	NZL	1.3.83	3 Mar
50.74A	Kiprono	Kosgei	KEN	.88	16 Jul
50.75A	Julius	Bungei	KEN	16.6.84	11 Jun
50.75	Sébastien	Maillard	FRA	2.5.81	10 Jul
50.75	Stéphan	Yato	FRA-J	11.9.92	24 Jul
50.76	Aaron	Younger	USA	11.2.89	8 May
50.76	Tom	Burton	GBR	29.10.88	2 Jul
50.76	Takehiro	Matsumoto	JPN-Y	19.9.94	8 Oct
50.77	Gabriel	El-Hanbli	CAN	12.4.90	30 Apr
50.78	Robert	Brylinski	POL	2.4.91	3 Jul
50.79	Tsuyoshi	Miyadera	JPN-J	.92	23 Oct
50.80	Amaurys	Valle	CUB	18.1.90	7 May
50.80	Diego	Venâncio	BRA	10.5.85	12 May
50.80	Hideki	Yano	JPN	13.12.85	10 Jun
50.80	Oskari	Mörö	FIN-J	31.1.93	23 Jul
50.82	Jeffrey	Gibson	BAH	15.8.90	25 Jun
50.83	Adam	Durham	USA	30.8.85	9 Jul
50.84	Nick	Dodson	USA	24.3.88	28 May
50.84	Diego	Cabello	ESP	14.1.88	18 Jun
50.85	Chance	Casey	USA	11.3.91	14 May
50.85	Kotaro	Miyao	JPN	.91	26 Jun
50.85	Michal	Pietrzak	POL	3.4.89	3 Aug
50.85	Tomoharu	Kino (183)	JPN	4.8.89	10 Sep

Drugs disqualification

Mark	Name		Nat	Born	Date
50.31	Kuldev	Singh ¶	IND	4.4.81	20 Feb

Best at low altitude

Mark	Name	Pos	Venue	Date				
49.26	Cisneros	1	Cottbus	25 Jun	50.43	Mayers	14 Aug	50.81 Cuevas 16 Jul

JUNIORS

See main list for top 8 juniors. 10 performances by 8 men to 50.14. Additional marks and further juniors:

Mark	Name		Nat	Born	Pos	Meet	Venue	Date
Cheng Wen	49.60	1h2	Fuzhou	25 Jun	50.11	1	Jiaxing	22 May
50.35A	Boniface	Mucheru	KEN	.92	1		Nairobi	11 Jun
50.39A	Nicholas	Bett (10)	KEN	.92	3	NC	Nairobi	16 Jul
50.70	Miles	Ukaoma	USA	21.7.92	4h3	NCAA-W	Eugene	27 May
50.75	Stéphan	Yato	FRA	11.9.92	5	EJ	Tallinn	24 Jul
50.76	Takehiro	Matsumoto	JPN-Y	19.9.94	1		Yamaguchi	8 Oct
50.79	Tsuyoshi	Miyadera	JPN	.92	1		Nagoya	23 Oct
50.80	Oskari	Mörö	FIN	31.1.93	3s2	EJ	Tallinn	23 Jul
50.86	Durgesh	Kumar	IND-Y	20.4.94	1		Ranchi	3 Nov
50.87	Juan	Stenner	MEX	26.1.92	4h1	PAm	Guadalajara	26 Oct
50.90	Ali	Arastu	USA	18.6.92	2r2		Bloomington	27 May
50.96	Seiya	Kato	JPN	22.11.92	1		Kumagaya	24 Jun
51.04	Kyle	Dunn (20)	USA	.92	1r3		Des Moines	21 May

Mark	Name			Nat	Born	Pos	Meet	Venue	Date
2.38i	Ivan		Ukhov	RUS	29.3.86	1		Hustopece	29 Jan
	2.20/1 2.24/1 2.30/1 2.34/1 2.38/2 2.44/xxx								
	2.38i	1	Banská Bystrica		9 Feb	2.20/1 2.26/1 2.30/1 2.34/1 2.38/1 2.44/xxx			
	2.38i	1 EI	Paris (Bercy)		5 Mar	2.20/1 2.25/1 2.29/2 2.32/1 2.34/1 2.36/1 2.38/1 2.44/xxx			
	2.36i	1	Bydgoszcz		16 Feb	2.20/1 2.27/2 2.32/x 2.34/1 2.36/3 2.41/xxx			
	2.34i	1 Winter	Moskva		6 Feb	2.15/1 2.24/1 2.31/1 2.34/1 2.41/xxx			
	2.34i	1	Arnstadt		19 Feb	2.20/1 2.25/1 2.31/1 2.34/1 2.39/xxx			
	2.34	3 NC	Cheboksary		23 Jul	2.15/1 2.23/1 2.30/1 2.34/1 2.36/xxx			
	2.34	1 DNG	Stockholm		29 Jul	2.15/1 2.22/1 2.27/1 2.30/1 2.32/2 2.34/2 2.38/x			
2.37	Jesse		Williams	USA	27.12.83	1	NC	Eugene	26 Jun
	2.20/1 2.24/1 2.28/1 2.31/1 2.34/1 2.37/3 2.41/xxx								
	2.35	1 WCh	Daegu		1 Sep	2.20/1 2.25/1 2.29/1 2.32/1 2.35/1 2.37/xxx			
	2.34i	2	Banská Bystrica		9 Feb	2.20/1 2.26/1 2.30/1 2.34/1 2.38/xxx			
	2.34	1 MSR	Walnut		16 Apr	2.15/1 2.20/1 2.24/2 2.28/1 2.31/3 2.34/1 2.37/x			
	2.34	2 LGP	London (CP)		6 Aug	2.22/1 2.25/1 2.28/1 2.31/1 2.34/1 2.36/x 2.38/xx			
	2.33	1 DL	Doha		6 May	2.20/2 2.23/1 2.26/1 2.29/2 2.31/1 2.33/3 2.37/x			
	2.33	1 ISTAF	Berlin		11 Sep	2.18/1 2.22/1 2.26/1 2.30/1 2.33/3 2.38/x			
2.36	Aleksey		Dmitrik	RUS	12.4.84	1	NC	Cheboksary	23 Jul
2.36	Aleksandr		Shustov	RUS	13.8.84	2	NC	Cheboksary	23 Jul
	2.19/1 2.23/1 2.27/1 2.30/1 2.32/1 2.34/2 2.36/2 2.38/xxx								
	2.34i	3 EI	Paris (Bercy)		5 Mar	2.20/1 2.25/2 2.29/2 2.32/2 2.34/3 2.36/xxx			
2.36	Andrey		Silnov	RUS	9.9.84	1	LGP	London (CP)	6 Aug
	2.18/1 2.22/2 2.25/1 2.28/2 2.31/3 2.34/3 2.36/1 2.38/xx 2.40/x								
	2.34	4 NC	Cheboksary		23 Jul	2.19/1 2.23/1 2.27/1 2.30/1 2.32/1 2.34/2 2.36/xxx			
2.35	Dmytro		Demyanyuk	UKR	30.6.83	1	ET	Stockholm	18 Jun
	2.15/1 2.20/2 2.24/1 2.28/1 2.31/1 2.33/1 2.35/1 2.39/xx								
2.35	Mutaz Essa		Barshim	QAT	24.6.91	1	AsiC	Kobe	9 Jul
	2.10/2 2.15/1 2.18/1 2.21/1 2.24/1 2.26/1 2.28/1 2.33/1 2.35/2 2.38/xx								
2.34i	Jaroslav		Bába	CZE	2.9.84	2	EI	Paris (Bercy)	5 Mar
	2.15/1 2.20/1 2.25/1 2.29/1 2.32/1 2.34/1 2.36/x 2.38/x 2.40/x								
2.33i	Osku		Torro	FIN	21.8.79	1		Tampere	5 Feb
	2.14/1 2.20/1 2.24/1 2.28/1 2.30/3 2.33/1 2.35/xxx								
2.33i	Eric		Kynard (10)	USA	3.2.91	1		Fayetteville	12 Feb
	2.15/1 2.18/1 2.21/1 2.24/2 2.27/1 2.30/1 2.33/1								
2.33i	Derek		Drouin	CAN	6.3.90	1	NCAA	College Station	12 Mar
	2.10/1 2.15/1 2.20/1 2.23/1 2.26/1 2.30/1 2.33/2 2.37/xxx								
2.33	Kyriakos		Ioannou	CYP	26.7.84	2	DL	Doha	6 May
	(29/12)	2.15/1 2.20/1 2.26/2 2.29/1 2.31/3 2.33/3 2.35/xxx							
2.32i	Donald		Thomas	BAH	1.7.84	2		Bydgoszcz	16 Feb
2.32i	Konstadínos		Baniótis	GRE	6.11.86	4	EI	Paris (Bercy)	5 Mar
2.32	Raúl		Spank	GER	13.7.88	2	GS	Ostrava	31 May
2.32	Dimítrios		Hondrokoúkis	GRE	26.1.88	1	ET-1	Izmir	18 Jun
2.32	Trevor		Barry	BAH	14.6.83	3	WCh	Daegu	1 Sep
2.31i	Tom		Parsons	GBR	5.5.84	1	NC	Sheffield	13 Feb
2.31	Tora		Harris	USA	21.9.78	2	MSR	Walnut	16 Apr
2.31	Dusty		Jonas	USA	19.4.86	1	DrakeR	Des Moines	30 Apr
	(20)								
2.31	Eike		Onnen	GER	3.8.82	1		Hannover	28 May
2.31	Andriy		Protsenko	UKR	20.5.88	1		Kyiv	9 Jul
2.31	Darwin		Edwards	LCA	11.9.86	Q	WCh	Daegu	30 Aug
2.31			Zhang Guowei	CHN	4.6.91	Q	WCh	Daegu	30 Aug
2.30i	Mikhail		Tsvetkov	RUS	4.5.80	2		Yekaterinburg	7 Jan
2.30i	Sergey		Mudrov	RUS	8.9.90	3		Yekaterinburg	7 Jan
2.30	Nikita		Anishchenkov	RUS-J	25.7.92	1	NC-j	Cheboksary	3 Jul
2.30	Bogdan		Bondarenko	UKR	30.8.89	1	EU23	Ostrava	17 Jul
2.30	Yaroslav		Rybakov	RUS	22.11.80	5	NC	Cheboksary	23 Jul
2.30	Mihai		Donisan	ROU	24.7.88	1		New York	29 Aug
	(30)								
2.30A	Diego		Ferrín	ECU	21.3.88	2	PAm	Guadalajara, MEX	27 Oct
2.29i	Marco		Fassinotti	ITA	29.4.89	6	EI	Paris (Bercy)	5 Mar
2.29	Ricky		Robertson	USA	19.9.90	1	SEC	Athens, GA	15 May
2.29	Viktor		Ninov	BUL	19.6.88	1		Plovdiv	9 Jul
2.28i	Nicola		Ciotti	ITA	5.10.76	6		Banská Bystrica	9 Feb
2.28	Dmitriy		Kroyter	ISR-J	18.2.93	1		Tel Aviv	12 Feb
2.28i	Aleksandr		Nartov	UKR	21.5.88	1	NC	Sumy	16 Feb
2.28i	Eduard		Malchenko	RUS	24.10.86	1		Tallinn	19 Feb
2.28	Edgar		Rivera	MEX	13.2.91	4	MSR	Walnut	16 Apr
2.28	James		Nieto	USA	2.11.76	3	DrakeR	Des Moines	30 Apr
	(40)								

Mark	Name		Nat	Born	Pos	Meet	Venue	Date
2.28	Maalik	Reynolds	USA-J	26.4.92	1		New Haven	8 May
2.28	Silvano	Chesani	ITA	17.7.88	1		Orvieto	22 May
2.28	Rozle	Prezelj	SLO	26.9.79	1		Postojna	5 Jun
2.28	Raivydas	Stanys	LTU	3.2.87	1		Besancon	14 Jun
2.28	Jim	Dilling	USA	23.4.85	6	NC	Eugene	26 Jun
2.28	Majed El Dein	Ghazal	SYR	21.4.87	2	AsiC	Kobe	9 Jul
2.28		Wang Yu	CHN	18.8.91	1		Nanchang	16 Jul
2.28	Matthias	Haverney	GER	21.7.85	2	NC	Kassel	24 Jul
2.28	Victor	Moya	CUB	24.10.82	1		Barquisimeto	29 Jul
2.28	Martyn	Bernard	GBR	15.12.84	2	NC	Birmingham	31 Jul
	(50)							
2.28	Robbie	Grabarz	GBR	3.10.87	3	NC	Birmingham	31 Jul
2.27i	Keith	Moffatt	USA	20.6.84	3		Praha	10 Feb
2.27i	Janick	Klausen	DEN-J	3.4.93	Q	EI	Paris (Bercy)	4 Mar
2.27	Samson	Oni	GBR	25.6.81	1		London (He)	10 Jul
2.27	Piotr	Sleboda	POL	22.1.87	1		Ilawa	19 Aug
2.26i	Wojciech	Theiner	POL	25.6.86	7		Banská Bystrica	9 Feb
2.26i	Peter	Horák	SVK	7.12.83	8		Banská Bystrica	9 Feb
2.26	Josh	Hall	AUS	3.4.90	1		Melbourne	5 Mar
2.26	Zach	Riley	USA-J	20.5.92	1	JUCO	Manhattan, KS	21 May
2.26	Mathias	Cianci	FRA	25.10.82	1		La Chaux-de-Fonds	3 Jul
	(60)							
2.26	Daniyil	Tsyplakov	RUS-J	29.7.92	2	NC-j	Cheboksary	3 Jul
2.26		Wang Chen	CHN	27.2.90	3	AsiC	Kobe	9 Jul
2.26	Mickaël	Hanany	FRA	25.3.83	1	NC	Albi	30 Jul
2.26	Miguel Ángel	Sancho	ESP	24.4.90	1	NC	Málaga	6 Aug
2.25i	Anton	Sayevych	UKR	15.6.88	1		Kyiv	11 Jan
2.25i	Nick	Ross	USA	8.8.91	1		Nampa	15 Jan
2.25i	Andrey	Tereshin	RUS	15.12.82	1		Dresden	28 Jan
2.25i	Sergey	Milokumov	RUS	13.11.87	1		Volgograd	3 Feb
2.25i	Major	Clay	USA	24.12.88	1		Allendale	11 Feb
2.25i	Yuriy	Krymarenko	UKR	11.8.83	2	NC	Sumy	16 Feb
	(70)							
2.25Ai	James	Harris	USA	15.9.91	3	NC	Albuquerque	26 Feb
2.25	Andra	Manson	USA	30.4.84	2	TexR	Austin	9 Apr
2.25	Amin	Hosseinzadeh	IRI	23.3.87	1	NC	Shiraz	15 Apr
2.25	Ivan	Ilyichev	RUS	14.10.86	4	NCp	Yerino	5 Jun
2.25	Gianmarco	Tamberi	ITA-J	1.6.92	1	NC-j	Bressanone	17 Jun
2.25	Fabrice	Saint-Jean	FRA	21.11.80	1		Antony	26 Jun
2.25	Andrea	Bettinelli	ITA	6.10.78	3	NC	Torino	26 Jun
2.25	Viktor	Shapoval	UKR	17.10.79	2		Kyiv	9 Jul
2.25	James	Grayman	ANT	11.10.85	2	CAC	Mayagüez	17 Jul
2.25	Linus	Thörnblad	SWE	6.3.85	1		Nerja	23 Jul
	(80)							
2.25	Kabelo Mmono	Kgosiemang	BOT	7.1.86	1		Buhl	29 Jul
2.25	Stefan	Vasilache	ROU	9.5.79	2	NC	Bucuresti	9 Aug
2.25	Ali Mohamed Younes Idriss		SUD	15.9.89	1	AfrG	Maputo	15 Sep
2.25i	Andrey	Patrakov	RUS	7.11.89	1		Moskva	24 Dec
2.24i	Yevgeniy	Shishakov	RUS	10.6.88	5		Yekaterinburg	7 Jan
2.24i	Artyom	Zaytsev	BLR	7.12.84	1		Mogilyov	29 Jan
2.24i	Normunds	Pupols	LAT	5.10.84	1		Tallinn	3 Feb
2.24Ai	Clint	Silcock	USA	15.11.86	1		Albuquerque	4 Feb
2.24i	Jussi	Viita	FIN	26.9.85	2		Tampere	5 Feb
2.24Ai	Jamal	Wilson	BAH	1.9.88	1		Albuquerque	11 Feb
	(90)							
2.24i	Robert	Wolski	POL	8.12.82	4		Bydgoszcz	16 Feb
2.24i		Jin Qichao	CHN	24.11.91	2		Shanghai	27 Feb
2.24	Randal	Carter	USA	7.4.89	1		Sioux Falls	7 May
2.24	Tanner	Anderson	USA-J	4.5.92	1	IC4A	Princeton	15 May
2.24	Abdoulaye	Diarra	FRA	27.5.88	1		Rehlingen	13 Jun
2.24	Javier	Bermejo	ESP	23.12.78	7	ET	Stockholm	18 Jun
2.24	Geoffrey	Davis	USA	8.8.90	9	NC	Eugene	26 Jun
2.24	Takashi	Eto	JPN	5.2.91	4	AsiC	Kobe	9 Jul
2.24		Yi Shisuo	CHN	20.2.90	2		Nanchang	16 Jul
2.24	Dragutin	Topic	SRB	12.3.71	1	NC	Kragujevac	6 Aug
	(100)							
2.24	Manjula Kuma	Wijesekara	SRI	30.1.84	1	NC	Diyagama	8 Aug
2.24		Zhao Kuansong	CHN	11.2.86	1		Sanya	28 Sep

Mark	Name		Nat	Born	Date	Mark	Name		Nat	Born	Date
2.23i	Filippo	Campioli	ITA	21.2.82	20 Feb	2.23	Ed	Wright	USA	3.3.86	1 May
2.23	Dwight	Barbiasz	USA	16.7.90	26 Mar	2.23	Alessandro	Talotti	ITA	7.10.80	6 May
2.23	Jeron	Robinson	USA	30.4.91	23 Apr	2.23	Donte	Nall	USA	27.1.88	7 May

Mark	Name		Nat	Born	Pos Meet	Date
2.23	Sergey	Goleshov	BLR	30.6.84		3 Jun
2.23	Stanislav	Malyarenko	RUS	19.5.85		5 Jun
2.23	Jaroslaw	Rutkowski	POL	11.8.91		12 Jun
2.23	Ryan	Ingraham	BAH-J	2.11.93		25 Jun
2.23	Justin	Frick	USA	3.8.88		7 Jul
2.23i	Semen	Pozdnyakov	RUS-J	28.11.92		24 Dec
2.22i	Darrell	Roddick	USA	6.4.88		29 Jan
2.22i	Ray	Bobrownicki	USA	3.3.84		20 Feb
2.22i	Tim	Riedel	GER	22.2.84		27 Feb
2.22i	Tomislav	Popek	CRO	2.1.86		4 Mar
2.22	Edward	Dudley	USA-J	21.6.92		17 Apr
2.22	David	Smith	USA-J	2.5.92		30 Apr
2.22	Konrad	Owczarek	POL	11.12.87		22 May
2.22	Naoto	Tobe	JPN-J	31.3.92		12 Jun
2.22	David	Smith	GBR	14.7.91		25 Jun
2.22	Wanner	Miller	COL	22.7.87		17 Jul
2.22	Guillherme	Cobbo	BRA	1.10.87		25 Sep
2.22i	Montez	Blaire	USA	23.10.90		3 Dec
2.21i	Andrey	Chubsa	BLR	29.11.82		21 Jan
2.21i	Benjamin	Lauckner	GER	3.4.87		27 Jan
2.21Ai	Jules	Sharpe	USA	11.10.91		11 Feb
2.21i	Michael	Salomon	FRA	1.6.89		11 Feb
2.21i	James	White	USA-J	22.1.92		12 Feb
2.21i	Martin	Günther	GER	8.10.86		19 Feb
2.21i	Adónios	Mástoras	GRE	6.1.91		19 Feb
2.21i	Andrea	Lemmi	ITA	12.5.84		20 Feb
2.21i	Paul	Hamilton	USA	3.8.88		5 Mar
2.21	Jorge Ignacio	Rouco	MEX	15.11.87		28 Apr
2.21	Anthony	May	USA	19.9.90		7 May
2.21	Mehdi	Alkhatib	SWE	13.11.87		28 May
2.21A	Carlos	Hernandez	USA-J	27.9.92		11 Jun
2.21	Cedric	Norman	USA	5.10.81		16 Jun
2.21	Fedor	Getov	RUS	14.3.84		18 Jun
2.21	Simón	Siverio	ESP	2.8.88		25 Jun
2.21A	Gerardo	Martínez	MEX	9.3.79		26 Jun
2.21	Szymon	Kiecana	POL	26.3.89		17 Jul
2.21	Rafael	dos Santos	BRA	10.10.91		26 Aug
2.21		Li Peng	CHN	1.6.90		28 Sep
2.21A	Branden	Wilhelm	CAN-J	10.1.92		27 Oct
2.21	Rashid Ahmad	Al-Mannai	QAT	18.6.88		16 Dec
2.20i	Roman	Yevgenyev	RUS	4.2.88		7 Jan
2.20i	Martin	Heindl	CZE-J	2.6.92		8 Jan

Mark	Name		Nat	Born	Pos Meet	Date
2.20i	Leonid	Biryukov	RUS	16.11.91		9 Jan
2.20i	Andriy	Rubel	UKR	24.5.89		11 Jan
2.20i	Radu	Tucan	MDA	13.5.86		20 Jan
2.20i	Mark	Dillon	CAN	6.10.84		22 Jan
2.20i	Vitaliy	Samoylenko	UKR	22.5.84		28 Jan
2.20i	Roman	Stupachenko	UKR	8.9.88		28 Jan
2.20i	Nikita	Palli	ISR	28.5.87		3 Feb
2.20i	Sven	Tarnowski	GER	4.3.90		6 Feb
2.20i	Michal	Durkác	SVK	14.8.88		9 Feb
2.20i	Viktor	Brumel	RUS-J	8.10.92		11 Feb
2.20i	Giulio	Ciotti	ITA	5.10.76		16 Feb
2.20i	Serhat	Birinci	TUR	13.5.90		19 Feb
2.20i	Abdelaziz	Namaoui	FRA	22.4.87		19 Feb
2.20	Hugo César	Ramírez	MEX	12.6.90		20 Feb
2.20i		Chen Ji	CHN	27.1.90		23 Feb
2.20	Raudelys	Rodriguez	CUB-J	27.9.92		24 Feb
2.20i	Andriy	Kovalyov	UKR-J	11.6.92		25 Feb
2.20	Sergio	Mestre	CUB	30.8.91		10 Mar
2.20i	Jonathon	Christensen	USA-J	30.12.92		19 Mar
2.20	Joshua	Lodge	AUS	14.9.81		31 Mar
2.20	Talles	Silva	BRA	20.8.91		7 Apr
2.20	Frankie	Hammond	USA	17.2.90		16 Apr
2.20	Olivér	Harsányi	HUN	20.3.87		16 Apr
2.20	Matt	Fisher	USA	3.3.88		17 Apr
2.20	Gaël	Rotardier	FRA-Y	5.9.94		8 May
2.20	Mateusz	Przybylko	GER-J	9.3.92		14 May
2.20	Dmitriy	Semyonov	RUS-J	2.8.92		28 May
2.20	Carlos	Layoy	ARG	26.2.91		3 Jun
2.20	Hikaru	Tsuchiya	JPN	1.2.86		5 Jun
2.20	Matús	Bubeník	SVK	14.11.89		11 Jun
2.20		Zhang Xiuyuan	CHN	15.8.91		11 Jun
2.20	Keyvan	Ghanbarzadeh	IRI	26.5.90		17 Jun
2.20		Chen Cheng	CHN	10.10.89		25 Jun
2.20	Angel	Kararadev	BUL	18.4.79		28 Jun
2.20	Kourosh	Foroughi	IRL	14.8.90		2 Jul
2.20	Ilya	Ivanyuk	RUS-J	9.3.93		3 Jul
2.20	Sergey	Zasimovich	KAZ	11.3.86		28 Jul
2.20	Anton	Bodnar	KAZ-J	12.4.92		28 Jul
2.20	Hiromi	Takahari	JPN	13.11.87		12 Aug
2.20		Lee Sung	KOR	6.5.88		8 Sep
2.20	Hsiang	Chun-Hsieng	TPE-J	4.9.93		9 Oct
2.20	Brandon	Starc	AUS-J	24.11.93		16 Oct
	(192)					

Best outdoors

Mark	Name	Pos	Meet	Venue	Date
2.32	Thomas	1	NC	Freeport	25 Jun
2.32	Bába	1=	DL	Saint Denis	8 Jul
2.31	Kynard	2	DrakeR	Des Moines	30 Apr
2.30	Mudrov	2	EU23	Ostrava	17 Jul
2.28	Baniótis	3	Odlozil	Praha	13 Jun
2.28	Parsons	1		London (He)	2 Jul
2.26	Theiner	1		Sosnowiec	16 Jul

Mark	Name	Date		Mark	Name	Date
2.23	Drouin	26 Mar		2.23	Malchenko	23 Jul
2.23	J Harris	26 Mar		2.22	M Clay	23 Apr
2.23	Zaytsev	21 May		2.22	Campioli	22 May
2.23	Viita	2 Jun		2.22	Wolski	29 Jul
2.23	Shishakov	5 Jun		2.21	Ross	30 Apr
2.23	Tereshin	25 Jun		2.21	Wilson	14 May
2.23	Krymarenko	20 Jul				

Mark	Name	Pos	Meet	Venue	Date
2.25	Fassinotti	2	NC	Torino	26 Jun
2.25	Klausen	1	EJ	Tallinn	23 Jul
2.25	Nartov	2	NC	Donetsk	4 Aug
2.24	Moffatt	5	DrakeR	Des Moines	30 Apr
2.24	N Ciotti	2		Orvieto	22 May
2.24	Jin Qichao	2		Kunshan	26 May
2.24	Torro	5=	Bisl	Oslo	9 Jun

Mark	Name	Date		Mark	Name	Date
2.21	J White	21 May		2.20	Pupols	28 May
2.21	Patrakov	26 Jun		2.20	Palli	9 Jun
2.21	Pozdnyakov	23 Jul		2.20	Samoylenko	11 Jun
2.20	Lemmi	22 May		2.20	Namaoui	5 Jul
2.20	Salomon	22 May		2.20	Dillon	8 Jul
2.20	Milokumov	25 May		2.20	Sayevych	9 Jul
				2.20	Lauckner	14 Aug

JUNIORS

See main list for top 8 juniors. 9 performances by 6 men to 2.26 (8 perfs at 2.25). Additional marks and further juniors:

Mark	Name		Nat	Born	Pos	Meet	Venue	Date
Anishchenkov	2.27				1	EJ	Tallinn	23 Jul
	2.26				1	AsiG	Viljandi	9 Aug
Klausen	2.26i				1		Malmö	30 Jan
2.23	Ryan	Ingraham	BAH	2.11.93	1	NC-j	Freeport	25 Jun
2.23i	Semen	Pozdnyakov (10)	RUS	28.11.92	1		Bryansk	24 Dec
2.21					5	EJ	Tallinn	23 Jul
2.22	Edward	Dudley	USA	21.6.92	1		High Point, OH	17 Apr
2.22	David	Smith	USA	2.5.92	1eB	DrakeR	Des Moines	30 Apr
2.22	Naoto	Tobe	JPN	31.3.92	1	NC	Kumagaya	12 Jun
2.21i	James	White	USA	22.1.92	1		Ames	12 Feb
2.21					2	JUCO	Hutchinson, KS	21 May
2.21A	Carlos	Hernandez	USA	27.9.92	1		El Paso	11 Jun
2.21A	Branden	Wilhelm	CAN	10.1.92	5	PAm	Guadalajara, MEX	27 Oct
2.20i	Martin	Heindl	CZE	2.6.92	1		Brno	8 Jan
2.20i	Viktor	Brumel	RUS	8.10.92	1		Moskva	11 Feb
2.20	Raudelys	Rodriguez	CUB	27.9.92	2		La Habana	24 Feb
2.20i	Andriy	Kovalyov (20)	UKR	11.6.92	1		Mogilyov	25 Feb

Mark	Name		Nat	Born	Pos	Meet	Venue	Date
2.20i	Jonathon	Christensen	USA	30.12.92	1		Crawfordsville	19 Mar
2.20	Gaël	Rotardier	FRA-Y	5.9.94	1		Franconville	8 May
2.20	Mateusz	Przybylko	GER	9.3.92	1		Leverkusen	14 May
2.20	Dmitriy	Semyonov	RUS	2.8.92	1J		Bryansk	28 May
2.20	Ilya	Ivanyuk	RUS	9.3.93	4	NC-j	Cheboksary	3 Jul
2.20	Anton	Bodnar	KAZ	12.4.92	2	NC	Almaty	28 Jul
2.20		Hsiang Chun-Hsieng	TPE	4.9.93	1		Nantou	9 Oct
2.20	Brandon	Starc	AUS	24.11.93	1		Sydney	16 Oct

POLE VAULT

Mark	Name		Nat	Born	Pos	Meet	Venue	Date
6.03i	Renaud	Lavillenie	FRA	18.9.86	1	EI	Paris (Bercy)	5 Mar

5.61/2 5.71/1 5.81/1 5.91/3 6.03/1 6.16/xxx

5.93i 1 Donetsk 12 Feb — 5.60/1 5.70/1 5.82/2 5.93/xxx　　5.88/1 5.93/1
5.92i 1 Aubière 15 Jan — 5.47/1 5.72/1 5.82/1 5.92/1 6.02/xxx
5.90i 1 Liévin 8 Feb — 5.50/2 5.60/1 5.70/1 5.80/2 5.90/3 6.01/xxx
5.90 1 Herc Monaco 22 Jul — 5.60/1 5.75/2 5.85/1 5.90/3 6.05/xxx
5.85i 1 Cottbus 26 Jan — 5.50/1 5.75/2 5.85/2 6.02/xxx
5.85i 1 NC Aubière 19 Feb — 5.55/1 5.70/2 5.85/2 6.02/xxx
5.85 3 WCh Daegu 29 Aug — 5.65/1 5.75/1 5.85/1 5.90/xxx
5.83 1 Montreuil-sous-Bois 7 Jun — 5.43/3 5.63/1 5.73/1 5.83/1 5.88/xxx
5.83 1 Athl Lausanne 30 Jun — 5.63/1 5.73/1 5.83/1 5.88/xxx
5.82 1 GGala Roma 26 May — 5.41/1 5.62/2 5.72/2 5.82/1 5.87/x 5.92/xx
5.82 1 Paris 18 Sep — 5.30/1 5.50/3 5.67/1 5.82/1 5.92/xxx
5.80i 1 Chemnitz 27 Jan — 5.60/2 5.80/2 6.03/xxx

Mark	Name		Nat	Born	Pos	Meet	Venue	Date
5.91	sq Pawel	Wojciechowski	POL	6.6.89	1		Szczecin	15 Aug

5.40/1 5.60/1 5.75/1 5.91/2 6.01/xx

5.90 1 WCh Daegu 29 Aug — 5.50/1 5.65/1 5.75/1 5.85/x 5.90/2 5.95/xxx
5.86i 1 Gent 12 Feb — 5.20/1 5.35/1 5.50/1 5.65/2 5.75/3 5.86/1 5.90/x
5.81 1 WMilG Rio de Jaaneiro 23 Jul — 5.20/1 5.40/1 5.50/1 5.60/1 5.70/3 5.81/2 5.91/xxx

Mark	Name		Nat	Born	Pos	Meet	Venue	Date
5.90	Lázaro	Borges	CUB	19.6.86	2	WCh	Daegu	29 Aug

5.50/1 5.65/1 5.75/3 5.85/1 5.90/3 5.95/xxx

5.81 1 Rieti 10 Sep — 5.51/1 5.61/1 5.66/1 5.71/1 5.83/3
5.80A 1 PAm Guadalajara, MEX 28 Oct — 5.40/1 5.50/1 5.60/1 5.70/1 5.76/3 5.88/1 5.90/x

Mark	Name		Nat	Born	Pos	Meet	Venue	Date
5.90i	Dmitriy	Starodubtsev	RUS	3.1.86	1		Chelyabinsk	17 Dec

raised floor　　　5.40/1 5.60/1 5.80/1 5.90/1 6.00/xxx

5.90i 1 Chelyabinsk 29 Dec — 5.40/1 5.60/1 5.70/1 5.80/1 5.90/1

Mark	Name		Nat	Born	Pos	Meet	Venue	Date
5.88i	Maksym	Mazuryk	UKR	2.4.83	2		Donetsk	12 Feb

5.45/1 5.60/1 5.82/2 5.93/xxx　　5.88/1 5.93/xxx

5.86i 2 Potsdam 19 Feb — 5.41/1 5.61/3 5.71/2 5.86/3 5.91/xxx

Mark	Name		Nat	Born	Pos	Meet	Venue	Date
5.86i	Malte	Mohr	GER	24.7.86	1		Potsdam	19 Feb

5.51/2 5.71/3 5.86/3 5.91/xxx

5.85i 1 Düsseldorf 11 Feb — 5.50/1 5.70/1 5.85/3 5.95/xxx
5.85 5 WCh Daegu 29 Aug — 5.50/1 5.65/2 5.75/1 5.85/3 5.90/xxx
5.84i 1 Stuttgart 5 Feb — 5.40/1 5.60/1 5.70/2 5.84/1 5.93/xxx
5.83i 1 Dessau 2 Feb — 5.50 5.60 5.83/3 6.01/xxx
5.81 1 DL Doha 6 May — 5.40/2 5.60/2 5.70/1 5.81/2 5.91/xxx
5.80i 1 Sindelfingen 23 Jan — 5.40/2 5.60/3 5.70/1 5.80/1 5.93/xxx

Mark	Name		Nat	Born	Pos	Meet	Venue	Date
5.85	Lukasz	Michalski	POL	2.8.88	4	WCh	Daegu	29 Aug

5.50/1 5.65/1 5.75/2 5.85/1 5.90/xxx

Mark	Name		Nat	Born	Pos	Meet	Venue	Date
5.84	Brad	Walker	USA	21.6.81	1		Chula Vista	16 Jun

5.50/1 5.65/xx　　5.72/1 5.84/1 5.94/xxx

Mark	Name		Nat	Born	Pos	Meet	Venue	Date
5.81i	Jérôme	Clavier	FRA	3.5.83	1		Villeurbanne	22 Jan

5.33/1 5.53/3 5.63/2 5.70/1 5.75/2 5.81/1 5.86/xxx

Mark	Name		Nat	Born	Pos	Meet	Venue	Date
5.80i	Romain	Mesnil (10)	FRA	13.6.77	2	NC	Aubière	19 Feb

5.65/1 5.80/1 5.90/xxx

Mark	Name		Nat	Born	Pos	Meet	Venue	Date
5.80	Fábio	Gomes da Silva	BRA	4.8.83	1		São Caetano do Sul	26 Feb

5.40/1 5.60/3 5.70/3 5.80/2 5.90/xxx

Mark	Name		Nat	Born	Pos	Meet	Venue	Date
5.80i	Jeremy (37/12)	Scott	USA	21.5.81	1		Jonesboro	10 Aug
5.75	Björn	Otto	GER	16.10.77	1		Berlin	18 Aug
5.75	Mateusz	Didenkow	POL	22.4.87	2=	WUG	Shenzhen	20 Aug
5.75	Aleksandr	Gripich	RUS	21.9.86	2=	WUG	Shenzhen	20 Aug
5.75	Konstadínos	Filippídis	GRE	26.11.86	6	WCh	Daegu	29 Aug
5.72	Scott	Roth	USA	25.6.88	1	MSR	Walnut	16 Apr
5.72i	Derek	Miles	USA	28.9.72	1		Jonesboro	22 May
5.72	Aleksey	Kovalchuk	RUS	22.7.88	1		Kyiv	18 Jun
5.72	Raphael (20)	Holzdeppe	GER	28.9.89	1	NC-23	Bremen	26 Jun
5.72	Yevgeniy	Lukyanenko	RUS	23.1.85	1		Madrid	9 Jul
5.72	Karsten	Dilla	GER	17.7.89	1		Jockgrim	27 Jul

Mark	Name		Nat	Born	Pos	Meet	Venue	Date
5.70i	Fabian	Schulze	GER	7.3.84	2		Sindelfingen	23 Jan
5.70i	Igor	Pavlov	RUS	18.7.79	1		Moskva	29 Jan
5.70i	Michal	Balner	CZE	12.9.82	3		Donetsk	12 Feb
5.66	Viktor	Kozlitin	RUS	12.6.88	3	NC	Cheboksary	23 Jul
5.65i	Tim	Lobinger	GER	3.9.72	Q	EI	Paris (Bercy)	4 Mar
5.65i	Sergey	Kucheranyu	RUS	30.6.85	1		Tsaotun	24 Mar
5.65	Jack	Whitt	USA	12.4.90	1		Putnam City	18 Jun
5.65	Daichi	Sawano	JPN	16.9.80	14	WCh	Daegu	29 Aug
(30)								
5.65	Jan	Kudlicka	CZE	29.4.88	9=	WCh	Daegu	29 Aug
5.65	Steve	Lewis	GBR	20.5.86	9=	WCh	Daegu	29 Aug
5.63i	Mark	Hollis	USA	1.12.84	1		Notre Dame	4 Mar
5.63	Emile	Denecker	FRA-J	28.3.92	1	NC-j	Dreux	17 Jul
5.62	Giovanni	Lanaro	MEX	27.9.81	2	MSR	Walnut	16 Apr
5.62	Oleksandr	Korchmid	UKR	22.1.82	2		Kyiv	18 Jun
5.62	Denys	Yurchenko	UKR	27.1.78	3		Kyiv	18 Jun
5.61i	Damiel	Dossévi	FRA	3.2.83	1		Mondeville	5 Feb
5.61i	Max	Eaves	GBR	31.5.88	1	NC	Sheffield	12 Feb
5.60i	Luke	Cutts	GBR	13.2.88	2		Birmingham	19 Feb
(40)								
5.60	Jere	Bergius	FIN	4.4.87	1		Espoo	5 Jun
5.60	Edi	Maia	POR	10.11.87	1		Lisboa (U)	10 Jun
5.60	Vincent	Favretto	FRA	5.4.84	1		Aix-les-Bains	19 Jun
5.60	Eemeli	Salomäki	FIN	11.10.87	1		Somero	24 Jun
5.60	Alexander	Straub	GER	14.10.83	2		Rottach-Egern	2 Jul
5.60	Igor	Bychkov	ESP	7.3.87	1		Zaragoza	20 Jul
5.60	Steve	Hooker	AUS	16.7.82	2		Leverkusen	30 Jul
5.60	Alhaji	Jeng	SWE	13.12.81	1		Karlstad	2 Aug
5.60		Yang Yansheng	CHN	5.1.88	1	NC	Hefei	10 Sep
5.55i	Viktor	Chistyakov	RUS	9.2.75	1		Moskva	9 Jan
(50)								
5.55i	Giorgio	Piantella	ITA	6.7.81	1	NC	Ancona	19 Feb
5.55	Nick	Mossberg	USA	5.4.86	1		Phoenix	2 Apr
5.55	Giuseppe	Gibilisco	ITA	5.1.79	1		Firenze	4 Jun
5.55	Vladislav	Revenko	UKR	15.11.84	1		Kalamáta	4 Jun
5.55	Dmitry	Zhelyabin	RUS	20.5.90	3	EU23	Ostrava	16 Jul
5.55	Claudio Michel	Stecchi	ITA	23.11.91	4	EU23	Ostrava	16 Jul
5.55	Hendrik	Gruber	GER	28.9.86	3		Leverkusen	30 Jul
5.53	Robbert Jan	Jansen	NED	22.7.83	3		Tomblaine	24 Jun
5.53 ex?	Michel	Frauen	GER	19.1.86	2=		Silandro	12 Aug
5.51					2		Rottach-Egern	2 Jul
5.53	Matteo	Rubbiani	ITA	31.8.78	2=		Silandro	12 Aug
(60)								
5.52i	Eelco	Sintnicolaas	NED	7.4.87	2	NC	Apeldoorn	13 Feb
5.52	Brandon	Estrada	PUR	28.10.87	4	MSR	Walnut	16 Apr
5.52i	Jacob	Pauli	USA	15.6.79	5	DrakeR	Des Moines	30 Apr
5.52	Anton	Ivakin	RUS	3.2.91	1	Gyulai	Budapest	30 Jul
5.52	Danny	Ecker	GER	21.7.77	3=		Mannheim	13 Aug
5.51i	Jason	Colwick	USA	25.1.88	1		Seattle	12 Feb
5.51i	Paul	Litchfield	USA	27.11.80	1		Burnsville	8 Jun
5.51	Germán	Chiaraviglio	ARG	16.4.87	5		Rieti	10 Sep
5.51	Ivan	Horvat	CRO-J	17.8.93	1		Split	11 Sep
5.50i	Ivan	Gertleyn	RUS	25.9.87	1		Chelyabinsk	9 Jan
(70)								
5.50i	Anatoliy	Bednyuk	RUS	30.1.89	2		Chelyabinsk	9 Jan
5.50Ai	Victor	Weirich	USA	25.10.87	1		Albuquerque	22 Jan
5.50i	Denis	Goossens	BEL	12.12.87	3		Cottbus	26 Jan
5.50Ai	Jordan	Scott	USA	22.2.88	2		Reno	28 Jan
5.50i	Artem	Burya	RUS	11.4.86	2		Krasnodar	29 Jan
5.50i	Leonid	Kivalov	RUS	1.4.88	3		Bordeaux	29 Jan
5.50i	Nikita	Filippov	KAZ	7.10.91	1	NC	Karaganda	5 Feb
5.50i	Pavel	Burlachenko	RUS	7.4.76	1		Moskva	11 Feb
5.50Ai	Rory	Quiller	USA	17.4.84	1		Golden, CO	18 Feb
5.50i	Carlo	Paech	GER-J	18.11.92	1		Hamburg	5 Mar
(80)								
5.50i	Ben	Peterson	USA	9.1.88	2	NCAA	College Statiion	11 Mar
5.50	Nicolas	Guigon	FRA	10.10.80	1		Saint-Etienne	8 May
5.50		Kim Yoo-suk	KOR	19.1.82	1		Chula Vista	12 May
5.50	Tyler	Wallace	USA	31.7.90	1		Irvine	14 May
5.50	Albert	Vélez	ESP	26.10.88	1		Zaragoza	25 Jun
5.50	Daniel	Clemens	GER-J	28.4.92	1		Mannheim	3 Jul

Mark	Name		Nat	Born	Pos	Meet	Venue	Date
5.50	Jeff	Coover	USA	1.12.87	2		Eindhoven	10 Jul
5.50	Kevin	Ménaldo	FRA-J	12.7.92	2	EJ	Tallinn	24 Jul
5.50	Nick	Frawley	USA	21.6.88	1		Clovis	12 Aug
5.50	Mitch	Greeley	USA	5.5.86	1		Lausanne	13 Aug
(90)								
5.50	Mikael	Westö	FIN	3.4.82	2	v SWE	Helsinki	9 Sep
5.50	Hiroki	Ogita	JPN	30.12.87	1		Yamaguchi	9 Oct
5.47i	Yevgeniy	Olkhovskiy	ISR	22.12.83	1		Blacksburg	19 Feb
5.46	Mareks	Arents	LAT	6.8.86	1	NC	Liepaja	30 Jul
5.45i	Melker	Svärd Jacobsson	SWE-Y	8.1.94	1		Tampere	5 Feb
5.45i	Adam	Ptácek	CZE	8.10.80	1		Praha	16 Feb
5.45i	Nate	Polacek	USA	22.6.90	4	NCAA	College Station	11 Mar
5.45	Stéphane	Díaz	FRA	24.12.78	3		Bonneuil-sur-Marne	2 Jun
5.45	Xavier	Tromp	FRA	3.3.84	2		Vénissieux	3 Jul
5.45	Wout	van Wengerden	NED	16.2.87	1		Bruxelles	10 Jul
(100)								

Mark	Name		Nat	Born	Date
5.43i	Luis Fernando	Moro	ESP	12.4.87	22 Jan
5.43A	Cheyne	Rahme	RSA	23.1.91	26 Mar
5.43	Sébastien	Homo	FRA	27.4.82	24 Jun
5.43	Flavien	Basson	FRA	15.5.88	9 Jul
5.42Ai	Chris	Little	USA	26.6.86	12 Feb
5.42	Denys	Fedas	UKR	24.8.85	18 Jun
5.42	Joe	Berry	USA	17.2.89	24 Jun
5.42	Nick	Cruchley	GBR	1.1.90	3 Jul
5.42	Manel	Concepción	ESP	27.3.90	11 Aug
5.42	Dídac	Salas	ESP-J	19.5.93	11 Aug
5.41i	Jeremy	Klas	USA	5.9.89	19 Feb
5.41i	Stephan	Munz	GER	19.10.88	26 Feb
5.41	Jason	Wurster	CAN	23.9.84	14 Jun
5.41i	Andrew	Irwin	USA-J	23.1.93	14 Jun
5.40i	Nikolay	Lavrinenko	RUS	16.5.84	9 Jan
5.40i	Oleksandr	Bubka	UKR	9.9.86	14 Jan
5.40i	Lukás	Bechyne	CZE	4.10.83	12 Feb
5.40i	Dimitrios	Patsoukákis	GRE	18.3.87	20 Feb
5.40	Chris	Swanson	USA	6.6.82	15 Apr
5.40	Hunter	Hall	USA	3.11.88	16 Apr
5.40	Jun-ya	Nagata	JPN	15.4.88	29 Apr
5.40	Naoya	Kawaguchi	JPN	18.6.87	21 May
5.40	Gayk	Kazaryan	RUS	19.5.90	24 May
5.40	Yankier	Lara	CUB	1.1.89	28 May
5.40	Sergey	Horovyy	UKR	11.7.87	11 Jun
5.40	Ivan	Yeryomin	UKR	30.5.89	11 Jun
5.40i	Stanislav	Tivonchik	BLR	5.3.85	19 Jun
5.40	Florian	Gaul	GER	21.9.91	26 Jun
5.40	Robert	Sobera	POL	19.1.91	2 Jul
5.40	Spas	Bukhalov	BUL	14.11.80	9 Jul
5.40	Cyriel	Verberne	NED	4.12.84	10 Jul
5.40	Akira	Onodera	JPN	2.4.80	18 Jul
5.40	Ryo	Onodera	JPN	8.10.84	18 Jul
5.40	Rasmus	Jørgensen	DEN	23.1.89	26 Jul
5.40	Panayiótis	Láskaris	GRE-J	10.3.92	30 Jul
5.40		Xie Xing	CHN	3.2.88	10 Sep
5.40	Hiroki	Sasase	JPN	17.8.89	11 Sep
5.40	Takafumi	Suzuki	JPN	25.5.87	25 Sep
5.40Ai	Rob	Simmons	USA	5.2.91	9 Dec
5.38i	Brian	Hancock	USA	25.9.87	18 Feb
5.38i	Joe	Samaniuk	USA	26.8.84	5 Mar
5.38	Michael	Viken	USA	21.9.90	9 Apr
5.38A	Cale	Simmons	USA	5.2.91	23 Apr
5.38	Marcus	McGehee	USA	30.7.89	23 Apr
5.37i	Kolby	Shephard	USA	9.4.89	22 Jan
5.37i	Nikandros	Stylianou	CYP	22.8.89	29 Jan
5.37i	David	Slovenski	USA	15.3.90	10 Dec
5.36i	Karlis	Pujats	LAT	10.9.88	29 Jan
5.36i	Ryan	Vu	CAN	16.5.88	12 Feb
5.36i	Parker	Smith	USA	25.7.88	26 Feb
5.36	Sean	Young	USA	27.12.85	13 May
5.36	Jason	Scott	USA	10.4.85	20 May
5.36 sq	Chip	Heuser	USA	9.2.85	18 Jun
5.36 sq	Stéfanos	Koufídis	GRE	14.5.88	22 Jun
5.36	Vesa	Rantanen	FIN	2.12.75	6 Aug
5.35Ai	Whitney	Neves	USA	.4.84	8 Jan
5.35Ai	Sam	Pierson	USA	7.4.88	11 Feb
5.35Ai	Michael	Arnold	USA	7.4.88	11 Feb
5.35i	Matt	Shuler	USA	25.3.89	12 Feb
5.35i		Zhou Bo	CHN	10.1.89	22 Feb
5.35i	Pierrick	Mille	FRA	20.5.84	20 Mar
5.35	Kyal	Meyers	USA	5.9.91	9 Apr
5.35	Gregory	Woepse	USA	16.11.87	17 Apr
5.35	Alexandre	Feger	FRA	22.1.90	20 Apr
5.35	Cory	Altenberg	USA	26.9.87	22 Apr
5.35	Mickey	DeFilippo	USA	9.12.88	7 May
5.35	Robbie	Haynie	USA	.85	28 May
5.35	Sergio	D'Orio	ITA	25.10.78	2 Jun
5.35	Heorgiy	Bykov	UKR-Y	31.1.94	18 Jun
5.35	Darren	Niedermeyer	USA	2.4.82	25 Jun
5.35	Brad	Holtz	USA	11.11.86	2 Jul
5.35	Paul	Walker	GBR	15.8.85	9 Jul
5.35	Alexandre	Marchand	FRA	23.2.90	23 Jul
5.35	Andrej	Poljanec	SLO	10.11.84	27 Jul
5.35		Jin Min-sup	KOR-J	2.9.92	20 Aug
5.35	Seito	Yamamoto (176)	JPN-J	11.3.92	24 Sep

Best outdoors

Mark	Name	Pos	Meet	Venue	Date
5.73	Mesnil	2		Montreuil-sous-Bois	7 Jun
5.72	Mazuryk	1	NCp	Yalta	30 May
5.72	Starodubtsev	2	NC	Cheboksary	23 Jul
5.72	Jeremy Scott	3		Jockgrim	27 Jul
5.72	Miles	6		Jockgrim	27 Jul
5.64	Pavlov	1		Sochi	24 May
5.63	Clavier	1		Tomblaine	24 Jun
5.62	Hollis	2		Des Moines	27 Apr
5.62	Lobinger	1	FBK	Hengelo	29 May
5.62	Kucheranyu	1		Karlsruhe	12 Jul
5.62	Schulze	2	NC	Kassel	24 Jul
5.60	Dossévi	5	Herc	Monaco	22 Jul
5.55	Chistyakov	2		Moskva	9 Jul
5.50	Jordan Scott	2	TexR	Austin	9 Apr
5.46	Burlachenko	2		Praha	22 Jun

Mark	Name	Date		Mark	Name	Date
5.41	Goossens	20 Aug		5.40	Gertleyn	24 May
5.40	Quiller	19 Mar		5.40	Burya	24 May
5.40	Sintnicolaas	8 May		5.40	Eaves	4 Jun
5.40	Tivonchik	21 May		5.40	Filippov	10 Jun
5.40	Balner	24 Jun		5.35	Little	9 Apr
5.38	Peterson	23 Apr		5.35	Weirich	9 Apr
5.36	Hancock	9 Apr		5.35	Paech	26 Jun
5.35	Shephard	9 Apr		5.35	Stylianou	20 Aug

Downhill runway

Mark	Name		Nat	Born	Pos	Venue	Date
5.70	Jordan	Scott	USA	22.2.88	2=	Champaign	2 Jul
5.70	Mark	Hollis	USA	1.12.84	2=	Champaign	2 Jul

Exhibition

Mark	Name		Nat	Born	Pos	Venue	Date
5.81	Jan	Kudlicka	CZE	29.4.88	1	Plzen	13 Jul
5.80	Björn	Otto	GER	16.10.77	1	Landau	2 Aug
5.60	Giuseppe	Gibilisco	ITA	5.1.79	4	Landau	2 Aug
5.55	Matteo	Rubbiani	ITA	31.8.78	1	Bisceglie	20 Aug
5.41	Lukás	Bechyne	CZE	4.10.83			13 Jul
5.40	Marco	Boni	ITA	21.5.84			3 Sep

Mark	Name		Nat	Born	Pos	Meet	Venue	Date

JUNIORS

11 performances by 6 men to 5.41. Additional marks and further juniors:

Mark	Name		Nat	Born	Pos	Meet	Venue	Date
Denecker	5.50	1 EJ				Tallinn	24 Jul	5.42 1 Halluin 29 Jun
Clemens	5.45	2 NC-23				Bremen	26 Jun	
5.42	Dídac	Salas	ESP	19.5.93	3		Zaragoza	11 Aug
5.41i	Andrew	Irwin	USA	23.1.93	1		Black Springs	14 Jun
	5.34				1		Pearcy	4 Mar
5.40	Panayiótis	Láskaris	GRE	10.3.92	2	NC	Athína (Peanía)	30 Jul
5.35	Heorgiy	Bykov (10)	UKR-Y	31.1.94	6		Kyiv	18 Jun
5.35		Jin Min-sup	KOR	2.9.92	7	WUG	Shenzhen	20 Aug
5.35	Seito	Yamamoto	JPN	11.3.92	1		Toyota	24 Sep
Best o ut:	5.35 Carlo	Paech	GER-J	18.11.92	4	NC-23	Bremen	26 Jun
5.33i	Reese	Watson	USA	8.10.93	1		Belton	31 Dec
5.31	Jonas	Efferoth	GER	3.2.93	1		Leverkusen	7 Jun
5.31	Thiago	da Silva	BRA	16.12.93	1		São Caetano do Sul	16 Jul
5.31	Robert	Renner	SLO-Y	8.3.94	1	EYOF	Trabzon	29 Jul
5.30	Vitaliy	Podgorbunskikh	RUS	21.5.92	7		Moskva	9 Jul
5.30		Zhang Wei	CHN-Y	22.3.94	4	NC	Hefei	10 Sep
5.30	Arnaud	Art	BEL	28.1.93	1	NC-j	Vilvoorde	11 Sep
5.28	Matthew	Bane (20)	USA	3.2.92	1	Big10	Champaign	27 Feb

LONG JUMP

Mark		Name		Nat	Born	Pos	Meet	Venue			Date
8.54	1.7	Mitchell	Watt	AUS	25.3.88	1	DNG	Stockholm			29 Jul
					8.34/1.5	8.54	p	7.96	p	p	
	8.45	1.4 1 LGP	London (CP)		5 Aug	x	8.45	p	8.22	p	p
	8.44	1.7 1	Melbourne		17 Apr	8.17	6.72w	x	8.03	8.23	8.44
	8.44	0.8 1 DL	Shanghai		15 May	8.14	8.34/0.7	x	x	x	8.44
	8.38	1.5 1	Sydney		19 Mar	x	x	x	8.08	x	8.38
	8.33	0.4 2 WCh	Daegu		2 Sep	x	8.33	4.90	7.79	x	8.06
	8.28	0.8 1	Perth		26 Mar	8.28	8.12	x	p	p	p
8.45	0.0	Dwight	Phillips	USA	1.10.77	1	WCh	Daegu			2 Sep
					8.31/0.4	8.45	x	p	x	x	
	8.32	-0.2 Q WCh	Daegu		1 Sep	8.32	p	p			
8.40	0.9	Ngonidzashe	Makusha	ZIM	11.3.87	1	NCAA	Des Moines			9 Jun
					7.79	7.97	7.93	8.40	8.36/0.9	p	
	8.29	0.3 3 WCh	Daegu		2 Sep	8.29	8.15	8.14	8.00	8.07	x
8.40	0.2	Irving	Saladino	PAN	23.1.83	1	DL	Saint Denis			8 Jul
					x	8.19	x	7.78	8.40	7.81
	8.30	0.1 * FBK	Hengelo		29 May	8.05	x	x	x	8.38w/3.1	8.30
8.37	0.0	Yahya	Berrabah	MAR	13.10.81	1		Barcelona			22 Jul
					x	8.07	x	8.37	p	p
	8.25	1.5 1	Rabat		16 Apr						
	8.23	0.4 4 WCh	Daegu		2 Sep	8.03	8.23	x	x	x	x
8.35	0.9	Chris	Tomlinson	GBR	15.9.81	2	DL	Saint Denis			8 Jul
					8.10	8.21	8.35	p	7.96	7.99
	8.25	1.1 * LGP	London (CP)		5 Aug	8.14	8.25	8.13	8.30w	6.43	8.02
8.34	1.8	Marcos	Chuva	POR	8.8.89	1		Viljandi			9 Aug
					7.96w	x	8.11	x	x	8.34
8.29	1.9	Will	Claye	USA	13.6.91	1	SEC	Athens, GA			14 May
					7.84	7.95	8.29	x	p	8.04
8.28	1.9	Aleksandr	Menkov	RUS	7.12.90	1		Kalamáta			4 Jun
					7.78	7.86	8.13	8.05	8.09	8.28
8.27	0.3	Greg	Rutherford (10)	GBR	17.11.86	3	DL	Saint Denis			8 Jul
					8.02	x	8.11	8.06	8.27	8.01
8.27	0.0	Salim	Sdiri	FRA	26.10.78	1		Lausanne			13 Aug
					7.89	x	x	x	x	8.27
8.27	1.1	Mauro Vinícius	da Silva	BRA	26.12.86	1		São Paulo			24 Sep
					8.13	7.98w	7.92w	x	8.02	8.27
8.26	1.6	Ignisious	Gaisah	GHA	20.6.83	2	FBK	Hengelo			29 May
					8.04	7.80	x	8.03	8.26	x
8.26	0.6	Christian	Reif	GER	24.10.84	1		Wesel			13 Jun
					x	x	8.20	p	8.26	x
8.26	0.9	Luvo	Maniyonga	RSA	18.11.91	1		Jämsä			2 Jul
					7.86	8.02	x	x	8.26	7.12w
8.26	1.4	Loúis	Tsátoumas	GRE	12.2.82	1	Vard	Réthimno			13 Jul
					8.26	8.22	x	x	8.20	x
8.25	0.7	Khotso	Mokoena	RSA	6.3.85	4	DL	Saint Denis			8 Jul
					7.91	7.94	6.65	7.93	8.25	8.15
8.23	0.6	Damar	Forbes	JAM	18.9.90	2	NCAA	Des Moines			9 Jun
					7.49	7.65w	8.15	8.23	x	p

Mark	Wind	Name		Nat	Born	Pos	Meet	Venue	Date
8.23	2.0	Eusebio	Cáceres	ESP	10.9.91	1		Zaragoza	25 Jun
		(31/19)			7.87	8.23	p	p	
8.21	0.1	Trevell	Quinley	USA	16.1.83	1		Clermont	11 Jun
		(20)							
8.20	1.5	Aleksandr	Petrov	RUS	19.8.86	1		Moskva	9 Jul
8.19	1.8	Mohamed Fathallah	Difallah	EGY	26.8.87	1		El Maadi	5 May
8.19	-0.1		Su Xiongfeng	CHN	21.3.87	2	DL	Shanghai	15 May
8.19	1.4	Michel	Tornéus	SWE	26.5.86	2	ET	Stockholm	18 Jun
8.18	1.1	Luis Felipe	Méliz	ESP	11.8.79	3		Barcelona	22 Jul
8.17	0.5	Marquise	Goodwin	USA	19.11.90	1	Big 12	Norman	14 May
8.17	0.1	Sebastian	Bayer	GER	11.6.86	1	NC	Kassel	23 Jul
8.16	1.8	Tyrone	Smith	BER	7.8.86	1		Houston	30 Jun
8.15	1.2	Stanley	Gbabeke	NGR	24.7.89	1		Nashville	9 Apr
8.15	0.6	Raymond	Higgs	BAH	24.1.91	3	SEC	Athens, GA	14 May
		(30)							
8.15	0.5	Povilas	Mykolaitis	LTU	23.2.83	1	NCp	Kaunas	4 Jun
8.15	0.9	Bryce	Lamb	USA	9.11.90	5	NCAA	Des Moines	9 Jun
8.12	1.1	Kafétien	Gomis	FRA	23.3.80	1		Pierre-Bénite	10 Jun
8.12	2.0	Robert	Crowther	AUS	2.8.87	4	DNG	Stockholm	29 Jul
8.12	1.9	Frédéric	Erin	FRA	23.4.80	1		Nouméa	7 Sep
8.12	-1.0		Jiang Zhaodan	CHN	19.2.89	1		Sanya	25 Sep
8.11	1.6		Lin Ching-Hsuan	TPE-J	14.5.92	1		Taichung	10 May
8.11	0.4	Leonard	Hunt	ISV	17.5.87	1		Tallahassee	18 Jun
8.11	1.0	Tomasz	Jaszczuk	POL-J	9.3.92	2	EJ	Tallinn	22 Jul
8.11	0.0	Wilfredo	Martínez	CUB	9.1.85	4		Barcelona	22 Jul
		(40)							
8.10	0.5	Norris	Frederick	USA	17.2.86	1	Jerome	Burnaby	1 Jul
8.10	0.2	Sergey	Morgunov	RUS-J	9.2.93	*	EJ	Tallinn	22 Jul
8.09	1.2	Andrly	Makarchev	UKR	15.11.85	1		Yalta	18 May
8.09	0.2	Ndiss Kaba	Badji	SEN	21.9.83	1		Dakar	13 Aug
8.08i		Zedric	Thomas	USA	21.4.88	1		Fayetteville	11 Feb
8.08	1.2	Alyn	Camara	GER	31.3.89	2		Wesel	13 Jun
8.08	0.7	Julian	Reid	JAM/GBR	23.9.88	2	JAM Ch	Kingston	25 Jun
8.08	0.6	Pavel	Karavayev	RUS	27.8.88	2		Moskva	9 Jul
8.08	1.4	Tommy	Evilä	FIN	6.4.80	1	NC	Turku	6 Aug
8.07i		Tarik	Batchelor	JAM	22.3.90	1	SEC	Fayetteville	26 Feb
		(50)							
8.07	1.4	Oliver	Koenig	GER	31.1.81	3		Wesel	13 Jun
8.05	0.9	Rikiya	Saruyama	JPN	15.2.84	2	MSR	Walnut	16 Apr
8.05	-0.1		Yun Zhiming	CHN	9.10.88	1		Kunshan	26 May
8.05	1.8	Ahmed Nezar	Al-Shourafa	KSA	9.7.87	4		Wesel	13 Jun
8.05	1.3	Suphanara S.	Ayudhaya	THA-J	11.6.92	2	AsiC	Kobe	10 Jul
8.05	1.3		Yu Zhenwei	CHN	18.3.86	1	WMilG	Rio de Janeiro	22 Jul
8.05	0.0	Sergey	Mikhailovskiy	RUS	20.5.87	1	NC	Cheboksary	23 Jul
8.04	0.4		Zhang Xiaoyi	CHN	25.5.89	5	DL	Shanghai	15 May
8.04	2.0	J.J.	Jegede	GBR	3.10.85	2	NC	Birmingham	30 Jul
8.04	1.9	Rogério	Bispo	BRA	16.11.85	1	NC	São Paulo	4 Aug
		(60)							
8.04	1.7	Ronni	Ollikainen	FIN	27.8.90	2	NC	Turku	6 Aug
8.03i		Fabrizio	Donato	ITA	14.8.76	1	NCAA	Ancona	19 Feb
8.03	1.9	Yeóryios	Tsákonas	GRE	22.1.88	3		Kalamáta	4 Jun
8.03	1.8	Yohei	Sugai	JPN	30.8.85	1		Maebashi	26 Jun
8.03	2.0	Víctor	Castillo ¶	VEN	8.6.81	1	Alba	Barquisimeto	27 Jul
8.02	0.3	Rafael	Mello	BRA	22.9.85	2		Rio de Janeiro	26 May
8.02	-0.4		Li Jinzhe	CHN	1.9.89	3		Fuzhou	25 Jun
8.02	0.7	Fabrice	Lapierre	AUS	17.10.83	3		Sotteville	2 Jul
8.02	0.4		Kim Duk-hyun	KOR	8.12.85	Q	WCh	Daegu	1 Sep
8.01i		Teddy	Tamgho	FRA	15.6.89	1		Eaubonne	13 Feb
		(70)							
8.01i		Roman	Novotny	CZE	5.1.86	1	NC	Praha	19 Feb
8.01	0.9	Morten	Jensen	DEN	2.12.82	2	Bisl	Oslo	9 Jun
8.01	1.1	Jarod	Tobler	USA	30.9.82	3		Kumasi	6 Aug
8.00i		Elvijs	Misans	LAT	8.4.89	1		Riga	25 Feb
8.00A	1.4	Mpho	Maphutha	RSA-J	21.1.93	1	NC-j	Germiston	3 Apr
8.00A	1.3	Daniel	Pineda	CHI	19.9.85	1	NC	Bogotá	7 May
8.00	0.0	Christian	Taylor	USA	18.6.90	4	SEC	Athens, GA	14 May
8.00	0.7	Sergey	Polyanskiy	RUS	29.10.89	1		Sochi	24 May
8.00A	0.8	Vardan	Pahlevanyan	ARM	27.2.88	1		Artashat	19 Aug
7.99	2.0	Sherif	El-Sheryf	UKR	2.1.89	2		Yalta	18 May
		(80)							

Mark	Wind	Name		Nat	Born	Pos	Meet	Venue	Date
7.98	0.5	Henry	Frayne	AUS	14.4.90	1		Brisbane	11 Feb
7.98	0.6	Abdelhakim	Mlaab	MAR	22.9.88	1		Ifrane	28 May
7.98	0.0	Janis	Leitis	LAT	13.4.89	1	NC	Liepaja	30 Jul
7.97i		Alexandr	Cuharenco	MDA	7.3.87	1	NC	Chisinau	5 Feb
7.97	1.7	Randall	Flimmons	USA	31.12.84	*	NC	Eugene	25 Jun
7.97	-0.5	Jeremy	Hicks	USA	19.9.86	6		Barcelona	22 Jul
7.97A	1.4	Vicente	Ríos	MEX	5.4.83	1	NC	Ciudad de México	5 Aug
7.96i		Justin	Hunter	USA	20.5.91	1		State College, PA	28 Jan
7.96i		Pavel	Shalin	RUS	15.3.87	2	Winter	Moskva	6 Feb
7.96	1.2	Nikolay	Atanasov	BUL	11.12.74	1		Sofia	26 May
		(90)							
7.96	-0.1		Zhuang Haitao	CHN	6.1.89	4		Fuzhou	25 Jun
7.95	1.9	Vadym	Adamchuk	UKR-Y	30.5.94	3		Yalta	18 May
7.95	1.2	Jorge	McFarlane	PER	20.2.88	1	SACh	Buenos Aires	5 Jun
7.95	0.8	Dino	Pervan	CRO	12.1.91	1		Zagreb	11 Jun
7.95	1.7	Johnta	Griffin	USA	16.10.83	2		Tallahassee	18 Jun
7.95	1.1	Yasumichi	Konishi	JPN	13.4.90	1		Tokyo	17 Jul
7.95	0.0		Lin Qing	CHN-Y	5.4.95	1	CityG	Nanchang	20 Oct
7.94i		Stepán	Wagner	CZE	5.10.81	1		Praha	6 Feb
7.94i		Nick	Gordon	JAM	17.9.88	2	Big 12	Lincoln	25 Feb
7.94	1.9	Tyron	Stewart	USA	8.7.89	2		Waco	23 Apr
		(100)							
7.94		El Mehdi	Kabachi	MAR-J	4.10.92	1		Rabat	10 Jul

Mark	Wind	Name		Nat	Born	Date
7.93i			Li Runrun	CHN	24.2.83	22 Feb
7.93	1.1	Clayton	Latham	VIN	18.4.80	8 May
7.93	0.0	Dmitriy	Plotnikov	RUS	30.1.87	23 Jul
7.93	-0.5	Dimítrios	Diamadáras	GRE	18.7.84	30 Jul
7.93	1.5	Mario	Kral	GER	15.2.89	31 Jul
7.93	1.5	Masaya	Tsuji	JPN	21.5.89	10 Sep
7.92i		Nils	Winter	GER	27.3.77	26 Feb
7.92A	1.5	Marcos	Amalbert	PUR	9.4.88	7 May
7.92	1.8	Kaan	Sencan	TUR-J	9.2.93	21 May
7.92	0.2	Robert	Martey	GHA	27.12.84	8 Jul
7.92	1.0	Darius	Aucyna	LTU	7.5.89	23 Jul
7.92	-0.1		Zhang Yu	CHN-J	17.7.92	20 Oct
7.91	0.8	Mike	Hartfield	USA	29.3.90	2 Apr
7.91	1.9	Collister	Fahie	USA/ISV	31.8.89	8 Apr
7.90i		Stefano	Tremigliozzi	ITA	7.5.85	6 Feb
7.90	0.4	Nicolas	Gomont	FRA	15.9.86	24 Jun
7.90	-0.1	Samson	Idiata	NGR	28.2.82	22 Jul
7.89i		Adrian	Vasile	ROU	9.4.86	29 Jan
7.89i		Andreas	Otterling	SWE	25.5.86	5 Feb
7.89	0.0	David	Registe	USA/DMA	2.5.88	5 Mar
7.89	1.1	Yves	Renaux	FRA	12.6.86	10 Jun
7.89	0.7		Gu Junjie	CHN	5.5.83	11 Jun
7.89	0.0	Sergey	Nikolayev	RUS	1.9.87	23 Jul
7.89	1.8	Mikko	Kivinen	FIN	16.1.88	6 Aug
7.89	0.3		Fu Haitao	CHN-J	1.11.93	20 Oct
7.88	1.0	Ryan	Grinnell	USA	4.2.87	13 May
7.88	1.2	Julian	Howard	GER	3.4.89	15 May
7.88	0.6	Trey	Hardee	USA	7.2.84	28 May
7.88	0.2	Benoit	Maxwell	FRA	2.5.88	8 Jul
7.88	0.8	Adrian	Strzalkowski	POL	28.3.90	27 Aug
7.88	0.6	Krzysztof	Lewandowski	POL	8.11.86	27 Aug
7.87i		Christoph	Stolz	GER	17.1.80	13 Feb
7.87A	1.7	Roelf	Pienaar	RSA-J	23.12.93	3 Apr
7.87	1.8	Joabson	do Nascimento	BRA	20.1.88	14 May
7.87	2.0	Olivier	Huet	FRA	26.5.90	26 Jun
7.86i		Marquis	Dendy	USA-J	17.11.92	5 Mar
7.86	0.2	Naohiro	Shinada	JPN	10.2.86	16 Apr
7.86	-0.2		He Tian	CHN	26.11.89	28 Apr
7.86	1.9	Bence	Bánhidi	HUN	20.11.89	28 May
7.86	0.9	Stephan	Louw	NAM	26.2.75	13 Jun
7.86	1.8	Guillaume	Victorin	FRA	26.5.90	15 Jul
7.86	0.7		Chen Changhang	CHN-J	3.10.93	20 Oct
7.85i		Yegor	Archibasov	RUS	20.8.84	15 Jan
7.85	2.0	Zark	Visser	RSA	15.9.89	29 Apr
7.85	0.7	Bracin	Walker	USA	31.5.90	20 May
7.85	1.5	Emanuele	Catania	ITA	3.10.88	22 May
7.85	0.0	Konrad	Podgórski	POL	1.6.89	29 May
7.85A	1.0	Miguel	Hernández	MEX	1.9.89	5 Aug
7.85i		Muhammad	Halim	ISV	26.10.86	3 Dec
7.84i		Emanuele	Formichetti	ITA	28.5.83	6 Feb
7.84	0.0	Mohamed S.	Al-Khuwalidi	KSA	19.6.81	16 Feb
7.84		Shamsher Pratap	Singh	IND	19.9.86	3 Mar
7.84	-0.2	Konstantin	Safronov	KAZ	2.9.87	18 Jun
7.84	1.3		Kim Sang-su	KOR	5.6.84	21 Jun
7.84	1.8	Aleksey	Zolotoglavyi	RUS	22.10.89	9 Jul
7.84	-0.1	Jean Marie	Okutu	ESP	4.8.88	6 Aug
7.84A	1.2	Dmitriy	Ilin	KGZ	24.5.89	17 Sep
7.83i		Christopher	Phipps	USA	14.9.90	4 Feb
7.83		Oslay	Vilches	CUB	13.7.88	18 Feb
7.83i			Qi Zhen	CHN	9.11.89	22 Feb
7.83	1.7	Clive	Chafausipo	ZIM	2.6.88	2 Apr
7.83	0.8		Zhang Yaoguang	CHN-J	21.6.93	23 Apr
7.83	0.0	Shola	Anota	NGR	14.8.85	21 May
7.83	1.2	Ivan	Pucelj	CRO	11.7.81	11 Jun
7.83	0.1	James	Beckford	JAM	9.1.75	12 Jun
7.83	1.9	Petteri	Lax	FIN	12.10.85	5 Aug
7.83	0.2	Saleh Abdelaziz	Al-Haddad	KUW	7.4.86	17 Dec
7.82	0.7	Caio	dos Santos	BRA-J	24.3.93	23 Feb
7.82	1.3	Ivan	Lihachov	UKR	27.4.89	31 May
7.82	-0.2	Stefano	Dacastello	ITA	17.2.80	25 Jun
7.82	1.3	Denis	Bogdanov	RUS	2.4.91	25 Jun
7.82	2.0	Herbert	McGregor	JAM	13.9.81	25 Jun
7.82		Julien	Fivaz	SUI	9.1.79	9 Jul
7.82	1.0	Michal	Rosiak	POL	9.5.86	3 Sep
7.81A		Luis	Rivera	MEX	21.6.87	27 Apr
7.81	0.0	Ashton	Eaton	USA	21.1.88	6 May
7.81	-0.3	Jaroslav	Dobrovodsky	SVK	13.12.84	8 May
7.81	-0.5	Amrit	Pal Singh	IND	6.10.83	14 Jun
7.81	0.7	Karl	Taillepierre	FRA	13.8.76	30 Jul
7.81	1.6	Taras	Neledva	UKR-J	7.6.92	3 Aug
7.81A	0.4	Emiliano	Lasa	URU	25.1.90	24 Oct
7.80	1.0	Tyrone	Harris	USA	21.3.79	13 May
7.80	-0.9		Zhao Xiaoxi	CHN	19.3.89	25 May
7.80	1.0	Marius	Vadeikis	LTU	2.8.89	23 Jul
7.80	-0.1	Benjamin	Compaoré	FRA	5.8.87	18 Sep
		(186)				

Wind assisted   # for series see in main list

Mark	Wind	Name		Nat	Born	Pos	Meet	Venue	Date
8.40	4.0		Makusha			1	TexR	Austin	8 Apr

7.93 7.93 8.18w 8.00w 8.40w 8.17w

8.35w 2.6 1 Tallahassee 7 May — 7.62 7.97 8.14w 8.35w 8.22w p

| 8.40 | 2.5 | Yahya | Berrabah | MAR | 13.10.81 | 2 | DNG | Stockholm | 29 Jul |

8.07 x 8.40w 7.97 x p

8.28w 5.6 1 Bilbao 18 Jun — 7.94w 8.28w 8.26w/4.6 x p p

| 8.38 # | 3.1 | | Saladino | | | 1 | FBK | Hengelo | 29 May |
| 8.38 | 2.2 | Christian | Reif | GER | 24.10.84 | 1 | | Bad Langensalza | 2 Jul |

x 8.20 8.26w 8.27w 8.38w 8.18

Mark	Wind	Name	Nat	Born	Pos	Meet	Venue	Date
8.33	3.6	Pavel Shalin	RUS	15.3.87	1	NCp	Yerino	5 Jun
		7.94w 8.13w 8.05w 8.33w x 8.23w						
8.33	2.1	Marquise Goodwin	USA	19.11.90	1	NC	Eugene	25 Jun
		8.13w 8.15 7.99 8.33w x 8.16						
8.32	2.1	Greg Rutherford	GBR	17.11.86	1	Pre	Eugene	4 Jun
		7.82 x x 8.01w 8.32w 8.03						
8.31	2.6	Khotso Mokoena	RSA	6.3.85	2	Pre	Eugene	4 Jun
		8.11w 8.19 8.19w 8.16w 8.31w 8.14						
8.29w	3.2	(Mokoena)			1	NC	Durban	8 Apr
		8.13 x 8.13w p p 8.29w						
8.30 #	2.2	Tomlinson			2	LGP	London (CP)	5 Aug
8.22	3.9	Jarod Tobler	USA	30.9.82	1		Chula Vista	16 Jun
8.22	4.0	Kafétien Gomis	FRA	23.3.80	1	NC	Albi	30 Jul
8.20	3.3	Luis Felipe Méliz	ESP	11.8.79	2		V.R. de Sto. Antônio	28 May
8.20	6.6	Sergey Nikolayev	RUS	1.9.87	2	NCp	Yerino	5 Jun
8.19	3.3	Tarik Batchelor	JAM	22.3.90	2	SEC	Athens, GA	14 May
8.18	3.7	Sergey Polyanskiy	RUS	29.10.89	3	NCp	Yerino	5 Jun
8.18	3.6	Sergey Morgunov	RUS-J	9.2.93	1	EJ	Tallinn	22 Jul
8.14	3.3	Nick Gordon	JAM	17.9.88	2	Big 12	Norman	14 May
8.12	4.6	Artis Edwards	USA	20.11.88	1		Waco	23 Apr
8.10	3.1	Jeremy Hicks	USA	19.9.86	3	NC	Eugene	25 Jun
8.09	2.3	Melvin Echard	USA	29.8.89	2	TexR	Austin	8 Apr
8.09	4.3	Clive Chafausipo	ZIM	2.6.88	1		Joplin, MO	29 Apr
8.09	2.6	Yohei Sugai	JPN	30.8.85	1		Naruto	24 Sep
8.07	2.6	Jadel Gregório	BRA	16.9.80	1		São Paulo	17 Jun
8.07	2.5	Nicolas Gomont	FRA	15.9.86	1		Tomblaine	24 Jun
8.07	4.0	Christian Taylor	USA	18.6.90	4	NC	Eugene	25 Jun
8.06		Marian Oprea	ROU	6.6.82	1		Izmir	21 May
8.06	3.8	Benoit Maxwell	FRA	2.5.88	3	NC	Albi	30 Jul
8.04	3.0	Abdelhakim Mlaab	MAR	22.9.88	1		Khouribga	26 Mar
8.04	3.2	Emanuele Formichetti	ITA	28.5.83	1		Latina	29 May
8.03	2.5	Mamoru Niimura	JPN	18.4.86	1		Fukui	27 Aug
8.02	2.5	Randall Flimmons	USA	31.12.84	5	NC	Eugene	25 Jun
8.02	3.0	Collister Fahie	ISV	31.8.89	6	NC	Eugene	25 Jun
8.00	2.3	Kaan Sencan	TUR-J	9.2.93	1		Samsun	15 Aug
7.99	5.5	Chris Phipps	USA	14.9.90	1	DrakeR	Des Moines	29 Apr
7.99	2.1	Jaroslav Dobrovodsky	SVK	13.12.84	1		Pergine Valsugana	23 Jul
7.98	2.6	Marcos Amalbert	PUR	9.4.88	1		Ponce	2 Apr
7.97	2.3	Andreas Otterling	SWE	25.5.86	1	NC	Gävle	13 Aug
7.96	2.2	Joabson do Nascimento	BRA	20.1.88	3		Rio de Janeiro	26 May
7.96	3.6	Giorgio Bryant	USA	4.7.89	1	NCAA-2	Turlock, CA	26 May
7.96	2.1	Darius Aucyna	LTU	7.5.89	2	NC	Kaunas	23 Jul
7.95	2.7	Mike Hartfield	USA	29.3.90	2	DrakeR	Des Moines	29 Apr
7.95	3.2	Samson Idiata	NGR	28.2.82	1		Huelva	2 Jun

Mark	Wind	Name	Nat	Born	Date
7.94	2.5	Paul Madzivire	ZIM	28.5.91	7 May
7.94	2.7	Larbi Bouraada	ALG	10.5.88	16 May
7.93	2.2	Ashton Eaton	USA	21.1.88	4 Jun
7.93	4.6	Vladimir Golovin	RUS	22.6.91	5 Jun
7.93	2.9	Julien Fivaz	SUI	9.1.79	3 Jul
7.92	2.7	Vasiliy Kopeykin	RUS	9.3.88	7 Jun
7.91	3.9	Hussein Al-Sabee	KSA	14.11.79	29 Jun
7.91	2.3	Lin Hung-Min	TPE	7.9.90	25 Oct
7.87	2.6	George Kitchens	USA	16.1.83	7 May
7.87	5.7	Nafee Harris	USA	29.5.86	26 May
7.86	3.5	Arnaud Assoumani	FRA	4.9.85	24 Jun
7.85	3.2	Karl Taillepierre	FRA	13.8.76	30 Jul
7.84	2.4	Oslay Vilches	CUB	13.7.88	18 Mar
7.84	2.2	Jeff Billing	USA		8 Apr
7.84	2.8	Tareq Bougtaïb	MAR	30.4.81	16 Apr
7.84	5.4	Denis Bogdanov	RUS	2.4.91	5 Jun
7.84	2.1	Ala Eddine Ben Hassine	TUN	16.5.90	27 Jul
7.83	4.7	Matthew Burton	GBR	18.12.87	9 Jul
7.83	2.9	Yevgeniy Antonov	RUS-J	26.4.92	22 Jul
7.82	2.9	Shin-ichiro Shimono	JPN	10.10.90	21 May
7.82	5.0	Kristinn Torfason	ISL	31.8.84	23 Jul
7.82	3.4	Ramon Cooper	JAM	10.8.88	25 Jun
7.82	5.1	Tsai Yi-Da	TPE	20.5.84	25 Oct
7.81	2.2	Jaanus Uudmäe	EST	24.12.80	7 Jun
7.81	2.2	Nils Winter	GER	27.3.77	13 Jun
7.80	3.5	Rushwal Samaai	RSA	.91	9 Apr
7.80	5.9	Rainer Maria Groh	GER	1.6.80	2 May

Best outdoors

8.05 0.3 Batchelor * NC Kingston 25 Jun	7.94 1.3 Novotny 1 Ostrava 21 May	
7.92 1.7 Gordon 29 Apr	7.91 1.7 Shalin 9 Aug	7.88 1.9 Misans 9 Aug
7.92 0.0 Z Thomas 14 May	7.89 1.7 Wagner 31 Jul	7.83 1.4 Formichetti 29 May
7.93w 3.0 25 Jun	7.88 1.6 Hunter 29 Apr	

Best at low altitude: 7.82 1.0 Pineda 5 Jun . 7.90w 2.4 Pahlevanyan 18 Jun

Drugs disqualification

Mark	Wind	Name	Nat	Born	Pos	Meet	Venue	Date
8.05A	-0.8	Víctor Castillo ¶	VEN	8.6.81	1	PAm	Guadalajara, MEX	25 Oct

JUNIORS

See main list for top 8 juniors (+ 1w). 12 (+2w) performances by 10 men to 7.89. Additional marks and further juniors:

Suksawat 7.90 0.0 Q WUG Shenzhen 20 Aug 7.89 0.4 6 WUG Shenzhen 21 Aug

Mark	Wind	Name	Nat	Born	Pos	Meet	Venue	Date
7.92	1.8	Kaan Sencan	TUR	9.2.93				21 May
7.92	-0.1	Zhang Yu (10)	CHN	17.7.92	2	CityG	Nanchang	20 Oct
7.89	0.3	Fu Haitao	CHN	1.11.93	3	CityG	Nanchang	20 Oct
7.87A	1.7	Roelf Pienaar	RSA	23.12.93	2	NC-j	Germiston	3 Apr

Mark	Wind	Name	Nat	Born	Pos	Meet	Venue	Date
7.86i		Marquis Dendy	USA	17.11.92	1		Landover	5 Mar
7.86	0.7	Chen Changhang	CHN	3.10.93	4		Nanchang	20 Oct
7.83	0.8	Zhang Yaoguang	CHN	21.6.93	3		Zhaoqing	23 Apr
7.82	0.7	Caio dos Santos	BRA	24.3.93	2		São Paulo	23 Feb
7.81	1.6	Taras Neledva	UKR	7.6.92	2	NC	Donetsk	3 Aug
7.79	+0.8	Artem Shpytko	UKR	26.4.92	3	NC	Donetsk	3 Aug
7.77	+1.1	Carlton Lavong	USA	18.6.92	1		Pueblo	16 Apr
7.77	+1.5	Hashim Nizar Al Sharfa (20)	KSA	.93	6		Kobe	10 Jul

Wind assisted see main list for two juniors

Mark	Wind	Name	Nat	Born	Pos	Meet	Venue	Date
7.83	2.9	Yevgeniy Antonov	RUS-J	26.4.92	3	EJ	Tallinn	22 Jul

TRIPLE JUMP

Mark	Wind	Name	Nat	Born	Pos	Meet	Venue	Date
17.96	0.1	Christian Taylor	USA	18.6.90	1	WCh	Daegu	4 Sep
							x 17.04 17.40/0.3 17.96 x 15.64	
17.68	1.3				1	LGP	London (CP)	6 Aug
							16.95 17.21 17.68 x p x	
17.40	2.0 *					NCAA	Des Moines	11 Jun
							17.28 16.76w 16.90 17.40/2.0 17.16 17.80w	
17.36i	1						Fayetteville	27 Feb
							15.53 16.83 16.74 16.58 16.81 17.36	
17.92i		Teddy Tamgho	FRA	15.6.89	1	EI	Paris (Bercy)	6 Mar
							17.46 17.92 17.65 17.92 x x	
17.91i	1					NC	Aubière	20 Feb
							x x 17.36 17.91 17.58 17.08	
17.91	1.4	1				Athl	Lausanne	30 Jun
							x x 17.91 x x x	
17.67	0.6	1					Montreuil-sous-Bois	7 Jun
							17.01 17.67 17.28 x 17.47/0.3 x	
17.64i	1						Liévin	8 Feb
							17.64 17.22 x 17.47 x 16.53	
17.59i	1						Eaubonne	28 Jan
							17.33 17.59 17.56 17.13	
17.49	1.0	1				DL	Doha	6 May
							x 17.49 17.44/1.3 x	
17.46i	1						Liévin	22 Jan
							17.46 x 16.37 x 16.05 x	
17.59w	1						Bondoufle	22 May
							17.15 17.59w 15.68 17.16w 17.45w/3.9 17.41w/3.1	
17.77	0.0	Phillips Idowu	GBR	30.12.78	2	WCh	Daegu	4 Sep
							17.56/0.0 17.38 17.70/0.2 17.77 17.48/0.1 17.49/-0.6	
17.59	-0.6	1				GGala	Roma	26 May
							17.25 x 17.29 17.59 x x	
17.57i	1						Birmingham	19 Feb
							16.93 x 17.16 17.26 p 17.57	
17.54	-0.2	1				DL	Birmingham	10 Jul
							17.06 17.13 17.54 17.03 x 17.29	
17.52	1.0	2				Athl	Lausanne	30 Jun
							17.26w 17.21 17.22 17.52 x 17.14	
17.48i	1						Stockholm	22 Feb
							17.21 x x 17.48 17.38 x	
17.36	-0.6	2				Herc	Monaco	22 Jul
							17.00 17.36 16.90 17.11 16.76 x	
17.32	1.7 *						Bydgoszcz	3 Jun
							x 17.52w 16.92 17.32 17.18w x	
17.73i		Fabrizio Donato	ITA	14.8.76	2	EI	Paris (Bercy)	6 Mar
							x 17.70 15.50 17.73 17.49 x	
17.72	1.3	Sherif El-Sheryf	UKR	2.1.89	1	EU23	Ostrava	17 Jul
							16.99 17.04 16.88 x x 17.72	
17.68A	1.6	Alexis Copello	CUB	12.8.85	1		Ávila	17 Jul
							17.68 16.55 x p p p	
17.47	0.1	4				WCh	Daegu	4 Sep
							x 17.19 x 17.36 17.47 16.11	
17.62i		Marian Oprea	ROU	6.6.82	3	EI	Paris (Bercy)	6 Mar
							17.62 17.43 x x p 15.41	
17.37i	2						Stockholm	22 Feb
							16.71 17.37 17.08 p p x	
17.50	0.1	Will Claye	USA	13.6.91	3	WCh	Daegu	4 Sep
							x x 17.50 17.30 p 17.14	
17.35	1.5 *					NCAA	Des Moines	11 Jun
							16.84 17.07 17.35 17.41w x 17.62w	
17.40	0.8	Ernesto Revé	CUB-J	26.2.92	1		La Habana	10 Jun
							17.06 x 17.40 16.96 x p	
17.35	0.0	Nelson Évora (10)	POR	20.4.84	5	WCh	Daegu	4 Sep
							17.35 16.80 16.63 16.18 16.57 16.95	
17.32i		Lyukman Adams (31/11)	RUS	24.9.88	1		Moskva	30 Jan
17.31	-0.6	Benjamin Compaoré	FRA	5.8.87	1	VD	Bruxelles	16 Sep
17.29	-0.2	Christian Olsson	SWE	25.1.80	2	GGala	Roma	26 May
17.29	0.0	Arnie David Girat	CUB	26.8.84	3	Herc	Monaco	22 Jul
17.23i		Yoann Rapinier	FRA	29.9.89	4	EI	Paris (Bercy)	6 Mar
17.23A	0.3	Yoandris Betanzos	CUB	15.2.82	2		Ávila	17 Jul
17.22	0.3	Osniel Tosca	CUB	30.6.84	1		La Habana	11 Feb
17.21	0.7	Tosin Oke	NGR	1.10.80	2	LGP	London (CP)	6 Aug
17.21	-0.2	Leevan Sands	BAH	16.8.81	7	WCh	Daegu	4 Sep
17.16	1.9	Yevgen Semenenko (20)	UKR	17.7.84	1		Kyiv	6 Jun
17.09	-0.5	Samyr Laine	HAI	17.7.84	1	CAC	Mayagüez	17 Jul
17.08	-0.2	Fabrizio Schembri	ITA	27.1.81	5	GGala	Roma	26 May
17.08	1.6	Karl Taillepierre	FRA	13.8.76	1		Forbach	29 May
17.07	0.4	Jefferson Dias Sabino	BRA	4.11.82	1	NC	São Paulo	7 Aug
17.06i		Dimítrios Tsiámis	GRE	12.1.82	1	NC	Athína (Peanía)	20 Feb

Mark	Wind	Name		Nat	Born	Pos	Meet	Venue	Date	
17.06	1.8	Yuriy	Kovalyov	RUS	18.6.91	1	NC-23	Yerino	26	Jun
17.05i		Aleksey	Fyodorov	RUS	25.5.91	1		Orel	23	Jan
17.04	0.3	Henry	Frayne	AUS	14.4.90	2		Barcelona	22	Jul
17.02	1.1	Dmitriy	Detsuk	BLR	9.4.85	1		Minsk	4	Jun
17.02	1.4	Walter	Davis	USA	2.7.79	3	NC	Eugene	23	Jun
		(30)								
17.01i			Dong Bin	CHN	22.11.88	1		Nanjing	23	Feb
17.01	1.5	Viktor	Kuznetsov	UKR	14.7.86	1	NCp	Yalta	1	Jun
16.99	1.3		Kim Duk-hyun	KOR	8.12.85	1		Daegu	12	May
16.97A	1.3	Tumelo	Thagane	RSA	3.7.84	1		Germiston	26	Mar
16.97	1.1	Kane	Brigg	AUS	14.1.88	1		Perth	31	Mar
16.95	0.2	Daniele	Greco	ITA	1.3.89	1		Lecce	27	May
16.93	0.1	Hílton	da Silva	BRA	13.4.87	2	NC	São Paulo	7	Aug
16.91	0.0	Yevgeniy	Ektov	KAZ	1.9.86	1	AsiC	Kobe	8	Jul
16.90	0.5	Ruslan	Samitov	RUS	11.2.91	1	Znam	Zhukovskiy	3	Jul
16.89		Dmitriy	Kolosov	RUS	19.5.86	1		Moskva	22	May
		(40)								
16.88Ai		Rafeeq	Curry	USA	19.8.83	1	NC	Albuquerque	26	Feb
16.88	2.0	Sief el Islem	Temacini	ALG	5.3.88	1		Alger	23	Apr
16.88	0.6	Anders	Møller	DEN	5.9.77	1	NC	Østerbro	7	Aug
16.87i		Randy	Lewis	GRN	14.10.80	6		Stockholm	22	Feb
16.87	-0.3	Jadel	Gregório	BRA	16.9.80	1		São Paulo	26	Jun
16.87i		Muhammad	Halim	ISV	26.10.86	1		Ithaca	3	Dec
16.86	0.3		Cao Shuo	CHN	8.10.91	1		Wujiang	29	May
16.86	1.5	Chris	Carter	USA	11.3.89	4	NC	Eugene	23	Jun
16.85i		Igor	Spasovkhodskiy	RUS	1.8.79	1	NC	Moskva	17	Feb
16.83	0.7	Dmitriy	Platnitskiy	BLR	26.8.88	1		Brest	21	May
		(50)								
16.83	0.6	Larry	Achike	GBR	31.1.75	1	NC	Birmingham	31	Jul
16.82	0.3	Osviel	Hernández	CUB	31.5.89	2		La Habana	11	Feb
16.82	2.0	Gaetan	Saku Bafuanga	FRA	22.7.91	2	NC	Albi	29	Jul
16.82	-0.2	Lysvanys	Pérez	ESP	24.1.82	1	NC	Málaga	7	Aug
16.80	1.3	Issam	Nima	ALG	8.4.79	1		Alger	28	Jul
16.79	0.8		Wu Bo	CHN	17.6.84	2		Nanchang	16	Jul
16.78	1.9	Aleksandr	Petrenko	RUS	8.2.83	3		Sochi	25	May
16.78	0.4		Gu Junjie	CHN	5.5.83	1	NC	Hefei	11	Sep
16.77	1.3	Julian	Reid	JAM/GBR	23.9.88	3	NCAA	Des Moines	11	Jun
16.77	0.3	Yochai	Halevi	ISR	10.5.82	1	NC	Tel Aviv	6	Jul
		(60)								
16.76	1.0	Colomba	Fofana	FRA	11.4.77	3	NC	Albi	29	Jul
16.75i		Taras	Moiseyenko	RUS	5.5.86	3	NC	Moskva	17	Feb
16.75	1.6	Momchil	Karailiev	BUL	21.5.82	1		Sofia	25	Jun
16.74	1.4	Alphonso	Jordan	USA	1.11.87	1	MSR	Walnut	16	Apr
16.74	0.6		Li Yanxi	CHN	26.6.84	*		Nanchang	16	Jul
16.74	1.2	Julien	Kapek	FRA	12.1.79	4	NC	Albi	29	Jul
16.73i		Brandon	Roulhac	USA	13.12.83	1		Kenosha, WI	28	Jan
16.72	0.2	Mykola	Savolaynen	UKR	25.3.80	2	NC	Donetsk	5	Aug
16.71i		Vladimir	Letnicov	MDA	7.10.81	1	NC-23	Chisinau	6	Feb
16.70	1.1	Jonathan	Silva	BRA	21.7.91	1		São Paulo	12	May
		(70)								
16.68	1.3	Yevgeniy	Zhukov	RUS	3.1.89	2	NC-23	Yerino	26	Jun
16.66i		Adrian	Swiderski	POL	27.9.86	1		Lodz	5	Feb
16.66	1.2	Josh	Como	USA	25.5.88	1		Los Angeles (Ww)	9	Apr
16.66	1.9	Viktor	Yastrebov	UKR	13.1.82	3	NCp	Yalta	1	Jun
16.64	0.9	Aarik	Wilson	USA	25.10.82	8	NC	Eugene	23	Jun
16.63	1.2	Sergey	Laptyev	RUS	7.2.91	3	Znam	Zhukovskiy	3	Jul
16.63		Arpinder	Singh	IND-J	30.12.92	1	NC	Kolkata	11	Sep
16.62	2.0	Roman	Valiyev	KAZ	27.3.84	3	AsiC	Kobe	8	Jul
16.61i		Vicente	Docavo	ESP-J	13.2.92	1	NC	Valencia	20	Feb
16.60i		Aleksandr	Sergeyev	RUS	29.7.83	1		Moskva	9	Jan
		(80)								
16.60i		Dmytro	Tyden	UKR	17.1.85	1		Zaporozhye	28	Jan
16.60i		Sergey	Ivanov	BLR	28.3.84	2	NC	Mogilyov	12	Feb
16.60i		Alin	Anghel	ROU	13.5.86	2	NC	Bucuresti	18	Feb
16.60	1.5	Zedric	Thomas	USA	21.4.88	*	NC	Eugene	23	Jun
16.59i		Tydree	Lewis	USA	26.11.85	3		Fayetteville	12	Feb
16.59	0.5	Shin-ya	Sogame	JPN	8.3.87	1		Naruto	25	Sep
16.58	1.7	Ryan	Grinnell	USA	4.2.87	1		Athens, GA	8	Apr
16.58	0.3	Elvijs	Misans	LAT	8.4.89	6	WUG	Shenzhen	18	Aug
16.58	0.2	Fabien	Florant	NED	1.2.83	1		Mölndal	3	Sep

Mark	Wind	Name		Nat	Born	Pos	Meet	Venue	Date
16.57i		Omar	Craddock	USA	26.4.91	3	SEC	Fayetteville	27 Feb
		(90)							
16.56	0.2	Yevgeniy	Plotnir	RUS	26.6.77	5	NC	Cheboksary	24 Jul
16.56	1.1	Hugo	Mamba-Schlick	CMR	1.2.82	1		La Roche-sur-Yon	10 Aug
16.56	0.8		Fu Haitao	CHN-J	1.11.93	1		Nanchang	23 Oct
16.55i		Jaroslav	Dobrovodsky	SVK	13.12.84	Q	EI	Paris (Bercy)	4 Mar
16.55	-0.2	Latario	Minns	BAH-Y	10.3.94	1		Nassau	26 Mar
16.55	1.0	José Emilio	Bellido	ESP	25.5.87	1		Mataró	5 Jun
16.54i		Harold	Correa	FRA	26.6.88	6	NC	Aubière	20 Feb
16.54	1.7	Kazuyoshi	Ishikawa	JPN	16.11.82	1		Yamaguchi	13 Nov
16.53	0.9		Hou Yue	CHN	12.2.91	4		Nanchang	16 Jul
16.53	-0.5	Andreas	Pohle	GER	6.4.81	*	NC	Kassel	23 Jul
		(100)							
16.53	-0.6	Igor	Syunin	EST	4.12.90	1		Rakvere	10 Sep

Mark	Wind	Name		Nat	Born	Date
16.52i		Tarik	Batchelor	JAM	22.3.90	7 Jan
16.51	1.2	Maximiliano	Díaz	ARG	15.11.88	4 Jun
16.50	-0.3	Nkosinza	Balumbu	USA	16.3.87	1 May
16.50	1.6	Karol	Hoffmann	POL	1.6.89	3 Jul
16.50	1.2	Matthias	Uhrig	GER	6.9.88	23 Jul
16.49	0.7	Peder	Nielsen	DEN	13.9.88	7 Aug
16.48i		Aleksandr	Lebedzko	BLR	24.5.87	22 Jan
16.48	-0.5	Allen	Simms	USA	26.7.82	1 Jun
16.46i		Troy	Doris	USA	12.4.89	29 Jan
16.45	0.2	Maksim	Shakko	RUS	14.5.84	24 Jul
16.44	1.6	Alexandru	Baciu	ROM	25.2.91	17 Jul
16.43	2.0	Luis F.	Gutiérez	CUB	1.9.88	4 Apr
16.43	1.5	Teymur	Abbyasov	AZE	12.3.85	3 Jul
16.43	1.3	Elton	Walcott	TRI-J	23.2.92	23 Jul
16.43	-0.5	Theerayot	Philakong	THA	27.2.84	15 Nov
16.41i		Sergey	Sutygin	RUS	2.5.87	21 Jan
16.41	0.2	Mohammed Abbas Darwish		UAE	28.3.86	20 Dec
16.40		Tareq	Bougtaïb	MAR	30.4.81	18 Jun
16.40	0.1	Sergey	Yarmak	RUS	21.3.86	19 Jun
16.39i		Jules	Lechanga	FRA	19.11.86	20 Feb
16.39	1.6	Zlatozar	Atanasov	BUL	12.12.89	17 Jul
16.39	0.3	Rodrigo de Souza Silva		BRA	21.6.91	7 Aug
16.39	-0.1		Nguyen Van Hung	VIE	4.3.89	15 Nov
16.37i		Oleg	Danysh	UKR	17.5.86	17 Feb
16.37	-0.1	Michele	Boni	ITA	2.4.81	26 Jun
16.37	1.7	Adrian	Daianu	ROU	27.11.87	29 Jun
16.36i		Kyron	Blaise	TRI	3.10.89	27 Feb
16.36	0.0	Yevgeniy	Chetykbayev	KAZ	29.3.88	25 Apr
16.35	0.5		Kong Guanyong	CHN	18.3.88	29 Apr
16.35	2.0	Aleksandr	Yurchenko	RUS-J	30.7.92	3 Jul
16.35	-0.2	Fernando	dos Santos	BRA	23.9.83	7 Aug
16.34	0.4	Jean	Cassimiro Rosa	BRA	1.2.90	17 Apr
16.34	0.1	Mantas	Dilys	LTU	30.3.84	12 Jun
16.34	0.0	Michael	McCadney	USA/PUR	27.11.84	18 Jun
16.33		Mamadou	Guèye	SEN	1.4.86	5 Apr
16.32	0.2		Xia Zhongwei ¶	CHN-J	14.9.92	23 Apr
16.32	1.9	Aleksey	Tsapik	BLR	4.8.88	21 May
16.31i		Nikólaos	Lágos	GRE	20.2.82	20 Feb
16.30	1.2	Aboubacar	Bamba	FRA	20.6.91	25 Jun
16.30	0.4		Jia Lingli	CHN	16.2.84	25 Jun
16.30	1.5	Yuma	Okabe	JPN	13.7.90	9 Sep
16.29	1.3	Nick	Thomas	JAM	4.4.79	22 May
16.28	1.8	Myhaylo	Vlasov	UKR	13.6.90	19 May
16.27	1.5		Ma Le	CHN	26.4.88	29 Apr
16.27	1.9	Oleksandr	Ryzhykov	UKR	21.6.89	19 May
16.27	1.1	José Ernesto Martinez		CUB	1.1.91	10 Jun
16.27A		Tera	Langat	KEN	26.12.85	16 Jul
16.26	0.6	Panayiótis	Baltadoúros	GRE	24.9.84	29 Jul
16.25	0.8	Alwyn	Jones	AUS	28.2.85	20 Feb
16.25	0.0	Lavell	Handy	USA	17.8.90	15 May
16.25		Vladimir	Chicherov	RUS	2.4.85	22 May
16.25	0.5	Hasheem	Halim	ISV	12.2.90	11 Jun
16.25	1.3	Murad	Ibadullayev	AZE-J	6.4.92	24 Jul
		(154)				

Drugs disqualification

Mark	Wind	Name		Nat	Born	Date
16.38	1.2	Dmitriy	Sorokin ¶	RUS-J	27.9.92	18 May

for series see in main list

Wind assisted

Mark	Wind	Name		Nat	Born	Pos	Meet	Venue	Date
17.80 #	2.3		Taylor			1	NCAA	Des Moines	11 Jun
	17.49w 3.5 1 NC Eugene 23 Jun	17.19w	17.49w	17.39w/2.2	p	p		p	
17.62 #	2.9	Will	Claye	USA	13.6.91	2	NCAA	Des Moines	11 Jun
17.52 #	3.3		Idowu			1		Bydgoszcz	3 Jun
17.42	3.4	Arne David	Girat	CUB	26.8.84	1		Bilbao	18 Jun
	17.42w 16.64w 17.10				p	p		p	
17.39	2.2	Leevan	Sands	BAH	16.8.81	1		Auburn	16 Apr
	17.39w 17.02 17.00				p	p		p	
17.05	3.1	Zedric	Thomas	USA	21.4.88	1		Baton Rouge	23 Apr
17.05	2.1		Dong Bin	CHN	22.11.88	1		Nanchang	16 Jul
17.00	6.0	Igor	Spasovkhodskiy	RUS	1.8.79	1	NCp	Yerino	4 Jun
16.93	3.3	Momchil	Karailiev	BUL	21.5.82	1	Balk C	Sliven	3 Jul
16.87	2.2	Karol	Hoffmann	POL	1.6.89	3		Bydgoszcz	3 Jun
16.86	2.3	Nkosinza	Balumbu	USA	16.3.87	1		Walnut	4 Jun
16.77	2.5	Maximiliano	Díaz	ARG	15.11.88	1		Buenos Aires	26 Mar
16.76	2.2		Li Yanxi	CHN	26.6.84	3		Nanchang	16 Jul
16.72	2.7	Adrian	Swiderski	POL	27.9.86	4		Bydgoszcz	3 Jun
16.69	2.3	Aleksey	Tsapik	BLR	4.8.88	1		Minsk	28 Jul
16.68	5.4	Vladimir	Chicherov	RUS	2.4.85	3	NCp	Yerino	4 Jun
16.67	6.6	Fredrick	Brown	USA	.89	1		Joplin, MO	29 Apr
16.65	2.5	Aarik	Wilson	USA	25.10.82	2		Walnut	4 Jun
16.61	2.2	Igor	Syunin	EST	4.12.90	1	NC-23	Rakvere	6 Jul
16.59	2.8	Andreas	Pohle	GER	6.4.81	1	NC	Kassel	23 Jul

Mark	Wind	Name		Nat	Born	Date
16.51	2.3	Elton	Walcott	TRI-J	23.2.92	23 Jul
16.49	2.2	Tyron	Stewart	USA	8.7.89	15 May
16.46	3.2	Yoann	Rapinier	FRA	29.9.89	22 May
16.45	4.0	Jonathon	Allen	USA	18.12.86	23 Apr
16.44	2.1	J'Vente	Deveaux	BAH	11.7.90	9 Apr
16.44	2.4		Li Pangshuai	CHN-J		21 Jul
16.43	2.6	Michal	Lewandowski	POL	28.8.88	3 Jun
16.42	2.3	Kenta	Bell	USA	16.3.77	23 Jun
16.41	2.3	Mantas	Dilys	LTU	30.3.84	2 Jul
16.38	3.1	Chamara Nuwan Gamage		SRI	18.6.85	9 Apr
16.38	2.1		Yoo Jae-hyuk	KOR	13.5.89	10 Oct
16.37	3.7		Li Li	CHN	6.8.87	16 Jul
16.35A	3.7	Boipelo	Mothlahlego	RSA	27.11.90	3 Apr
16.30	2.3	Nick	Thomas	JAM	4.4.79	10 Jul
16.27	4.0	Daigo	Hasegawa	JPN	27.2.90	15 Oct
16.25	2.9	Darius	Aucyna	LTU	7.5.89	17 Jul
16.25	2.9	Daniel	Kohle	GER	8.10.83	23 Jul

Mark	Wind	Name		Nat	Born	Pos	Meet	Venue	Date

Best outdoors

17.19 1.2 Oprea 1 Izmir 22 May
17.17 0.2 Donato 1 NC Torino 26 Jun
17.01 1.6 Fyodorov 1 Sochi 25 May
16.86 1.0 Dong Bin 1 Zhaoqing 23 Apr
16.82 1.9 Spasovkhodskiy 2 Sochi 25 May
16.62 -0.3 Lewis 6 Daegu 12 May

16.61 Halim 1 Baltimore 23 Apr
16.61 1.3 Roulhac 1 Clermont 4 Jun
16.57 1.0 Ivanov 1 Minsk 22 Jun
16.54 0.1 Tyden 3 NC Donetsk 5 Aug
16.51 1.4 Letnicov * BalkC Sliven 3 Jul
16.67w 2.8 2 BalkC Sliven 3 Jul

16.49 0.5 Moiseyenko 24 Jul | 16.46 1.0 Craddock 30 Apr | 16.31 1.0 Lágos 29 Jul
16.48 0.4 Curry 6 May | 16.46 1.1 Doris 23 Jun | 16.29 1.1 Sutygin 24 Jul
16.48 0.7 Swiderski 19 Jun | 16.40 1.0 Correa 29 Jul | 16.21 0.0 Docavo 6 Aug
16.48 1.4 Lebedzko 28 Jul | 16.39 1.6 Rapinier 10 Aug | 16.39w 3.1 10 Jul
| | 16.48w 3.7 T Lewis 30 Apr

Best at low altitude

17.18 0.2 Yoandris Betanzos CUB 15.2.82 2 NC La Habana 19 Mar
16.78 0.6 Tumelo Thagane RSA 3.7.84 * NC Durban 10 Apr
       16.95w 2.5 1 NC Durban 10 Apr

<h2 align="center">JUNIORS</h2>

See main list for top 5 juniors. 10 performances by 6 men to 16.40 (& 3 wa by 2 men). Additional marks and further juniors:

Revé 17.05 0.6 1 La Habana 17 Feb | 16.85 0.0 1 La Habana 16 Jun
      16.93 0.0 1 La Habana 1 Jul
Singh 16.62 0.1 1 NG Ranchi 20 Feb
16.43 1.3 Elton Walcott TRI-J 23.2.92 * PAm-J Miramar, FL 23 Jul
16.35 2.0 Aleksandr Yurchenko RUS-J 30.7.92 1 NC-j Cheboksary 3 Jul
16.32 0.2 Xia Zhongwei ¶ CHN-J 14.9.92 4 Zhaoqing 23 Apr
16.25 1.3 Murad Ibadullayev AZE-J 6.4.92 2 EJ Tallinn 24 Jul
16.16i Pablo Torrijos (10) ESP 12.5.92 3 Valencia 20 Feb
16.12i Georgi Tsonov BUL 2.5.93 1 Sofia 12 Feb
16.11i Dmitriy Sorokin ¶ RUS-J 27.9.92 1 NC-j Saransk 6 Feb
16.11 0.1 Ruslan Kurbanov UZB 10.2.93 2 NC Tashkent 1 Oct
16.10 Martin Elsey GHA-Y .94 1 NC-j Kumasi 27 Apr
16.09 1.0 Pedro Pablo Pichardo CUB 30.6.93 1 Barr La Habana 28 May
16.07 -0.5 Xiao Yangbao CHN 5.3.92 7 Fuzhou 25 Jun
16.04 0.3 He Guang CHN .92 1 Zhaqing 27 Aug
16.01 -0.4 Sergiu Caciuriac ROU 22.4.93 1 Bucureşti 28 May
16.01 1.0 Pávlos Bóftsis GRE 17.8.92 1 NC-j Lárisa 9 Jul
16.01 -0.6 Xu Xiaolong (20) CHN 20.12.92 4 Baotou 21 Jul

Wind assisted

Fu Haitao 16.46 2.9 1 Baotou 21 Jul
16.51 2.3 Elton Walcott TRI 23.2.92 1 PAm-J Miramar, FL 23 Jul
16.44 2.4 Li Pangshuai CHN-J 2 Baotou 21 Jul
16.15 4.4 Daniel Pacheco ESP 15.3.93 2 NC-j Xátiva 10 Jul
16.10 2.3 He Guang CHN .92 3 Baotou 21 Jul
16.01 2.7 Phillip Young USA 9.10.92 2 PAm-J Miramar 23 Jul

SHOT

22.21 Dylan Armstrong CAN 15.1.81 1 NC Calgary 25 Jun
       21.75 21.89 x x 21.78 22.21
  21.75 1 Tanger 18 Sep
  21.72 1 La Jolla 23 Apr 21.01 21.02 21.72 20.71 21.09 20.97
  21.64 2 WCh Daegu 2 Sep 20.79 20.58 20.82 21.64 21.40 x
  21.63i 1 WK Zürich 8 Sep 20.85 20.73 21.35 20.59 20.79 21.63
  21.60 1 GGala Roma 26 May 20.81 21.11 21.02 21.10 21.60 21.40
  21.60 2 Pre Eugene 4 Jun 21.10 21.60 21.28 x 21.13 21.19
  21.55 1 DL Birmingham 10 Jul 20.70 20.45 21.34 21.55
22.10 Andrey Mikhnevich BLR 12.7.76 1 Minsk 11 Aug
       21.90 22.10 21.57 22.01 x 21.84
  21.63 1 Brest 29 Apr 21.53 21.35 x 21.27 21.37 21.63
  21.56 3 VD Bruxelles 16 Sep 21.15 x 21.56 20.77 20.84 21.10
22.09 Adam Nelson USA 7.7.75 1 NC Eugene 26 Jun
       20.05 22.09 x x x x
22.09 Reese Hoffa USA 8.10.77 1 VD Bruxelles 16 Sep
       21.10 x 20.99 21.67 21.51 22.09
  21.87 1 FBK Hengelo 28 May 21.87 21.34 x 21.19 21.60 x
  21.86 3 NC Eugene 26 Jun 21.86 x 21.53 x 21.59 21.31
  21.73 1 Hanz Zagreb 13 Sep 20.73 x 21.01 21.73 21.49 21.10
  21.65 1 Pre Eugene 4 Jun 21.05 21.65 x x 21.27 x
  21.63 1 Athens, GA 19 Aug 20.89 x 21.63 x x x
  21.56 1 Athens, GA 9 Apr 21.56 21.17 21.51 x x 21.47
22.07 Christian Cantwell USA 30.9.80 2 VD Bruxelles 16 Sep
       21.46 21.11 21.27 21.50 22.07 21.91
  21.87 2 NC Eugene 26 Jun 21.87 x 21.77 x 21.69 x

Mark	Name		Nat	Born	Pos	Meet	Venue		Date
	21.83 1 Athl	Lausanne		30 Jun	21.48	21.81 21.83	x	21.62	x
	21.70 1 DNG	Stockholm		28 Jul	21.44	21.21 21.10	21.70	x	x
	21.59 3 Pre	Eugene		4 Jun	21.23	x 21.55	21.59	21.22	21.26
	21.55 2 Hanz	Zagreb		13 Sep	20.80 20.62 21.55 21.08		x	x	
21.78	David	Storl	GER	27.7.90	1	WCh	Daegu		2 Sep
				x	21.60 20.82	x	x	21.78	
21.76	Ryan	Whiting	USA	24.11.86	2	Athl	Lausanne		30 Jun
				21.76	x x	x	x	x	
	21.61 1 ISTAF	Berlin		11 Sep	20.18	x 20.44	20.54	21.61	21.37
21.60	Tomasz	Majewski	POL	30.8.81	2	DNG	Stockholm		28 Jul
				20.79	20.57 x	x	21.16	21.60	
	21.55 3 Athl	Lausanne		30 Jun	x	20.71 21.07	20.50	20.84	21.55
21.45	Maksim	Sidorov	RUS	13.5.86	1	NC	Cheboksary		22 Jul
	(31/9)			20.95	20.89 21.45	20.72	x	20.08	
21.16i	Ralf	Bartels (10)	GER	21.2.78	1	EI	Paris (Bercy)		4 Mar
21.00	Aleksandr	Lobynya	RUS	31.5.84	1		Sochi		25 May
20.94	Russ	Winger	USA	2.8.84	1		Chula Vista		9 Jun
20.90	Dan	Taylor	USA	12.5.82	5	NC	Eugene		26 Jun
20.89	Marco	Fortes	POR	26.9.82	1		København		11 Aug
20.85	Pavel	Lyzhin	BLR	24.3.81	2		Brest		29 Apr
20.82	Maris	Urtans	LAT	9.2.81	4	DL	Doha		6 May
20.80	Noah	Bryant	USA	11.5.84	6	NC	Eugene		26 Jun
20.77i	Justin	Rodhe	USA/CAN	17.10.84	1		Kent		10 Dec
20.76	Jan	Marcell	CZE	4.6.85	1		Olomouc		8 May
20.76	Soslan	Tsirikhov	RUS	24.11.84	2	NC	Cheboksary		22 Jul
	(20)								
20.76	Carlos	Véliz	CUB	12.8.87	2	PAm	Guadalajara, MEX		25 Oct
20.72	Cory	Martin	USA	22.5.85	4	KansR	Lawrence		20 Apr
20.71i	Mason	Finley	USA	7.10.90	1		Lawrence		14 Jan
20.64	Ivan	Emelianov ¶	MDA	19.2.77	1	NC	Chisinau		29 May
20.63	Andriy	Semenov	UKR	4.7.84	1	NC	Donetsk		3 Aug
20.61	Ivan	Yushkov	RUS	15.1.81	1	NCp	Yerino		5 Jun
20.58		Chang Ming-Huang	TPE	7.8.82	3		Athens, GA		19 Aug
20.51	Marco	Schmidt	GER	5.9.83	1		Neubrandenburg		28 May
20.50	Asmir	Kolasinac	SRB	15.10.84	1	NCp	Novi Sad		4 Jun
20.43i	Nedzad	Mulabegovic	CRO	4.2.81	4	EI	Paris (Bercy)		4 Mar
	(30)								
20.42i	Valeriy	Kokoyev	RUS	25.7.88	Q	NC	Moskva		17 Feb
20.42	Germán	Lauro	ARG	2.4.84	1		Santa Fe		2 Oct
20.39i	Gaëtan	Bucki	FRA	9.5.80	Q	EI	Paris (Bercy)		4 Mar
20.39i	Kim	Christensen	DEN	1.4.84	1		Växjö		12 Mar
20.38	Hamza	Alic	BIH	20.1.79	1		Slovenska Bistrica		29 May
20.38	Jacko	Gill	NZL-Y	10.12.94	1		Auckland (NS)		5 Dec
20.34	Andriy	Borodkin	UKR	18.4.78	2		Uman		21 May
20.31i	Zack	Lloyd	USA	10.10.84	1		Ogden		18 Feb
20.31	Anton	Lyuboslavskiy	RUS	26.6.84	4	NCp	Yerino		5 Jun
20.27	Antonin	Zalsky	CZE	7.8.80	2		Olomouc		8 May
	(40)								
20.20	Lajos	Kürthy	HUN	22.10.86	1		Celje		8 Jun
20.18i	Borja	Vivas	ESP	26.5.84	1	NC	Valencia		19 Feb
20.17	Milan	Jotanovic	SRB	11.1.84	3		Senta		14 May
20.17	Mihaíl	Stamatóyiannis	GRE	20.5.82	1		Pátra		20 Jul
20.13	Dorian	Scott	JAM	1.2.82	6	KansR	Lawrence		20 Apr
20.13	Kevin	Bookout	USA	12.2.83	1		Mesa		5 Jun
20.10	Damian	Kusiak	POL	14.4.88	1		Lublin		14 May
20.07i	Luke	Pinkelman	USA	5.5.88	1	Big 12	Lincoln		26 Feb
20.07	Om Prakash	Singh	IND	11.1.87	1		Szombathely		7 Sep
20.05	Dale	Stevenson	AUS	1.1.88	2		Hobart		20 Feb
	(50)								
20.05	Amin	Nikfar	IRI	2.1.81	2		Toronto		13 Jul
19.98	Candy	Bauer	GER	31.7.86	2		Biberach		27 Jun
19.95i	Rutger	Smith	NED	9.7.81	1	NC	Gent		20 Feb
19.93	O'Dayne	Richards	JAM	14.12.88	1	WUG	Shenzhen		16 Aug
19.92i	Leif	Arrhenius	SWE	15.7.86	1	NCAA	College Station		11 Mar
19.85		Zhang Jun	CHN	11.4.83	1		Beijing		29 Apr
19.84i	Joe	Kovacs	USA	28.6.89	1	Big 10	Champaign		26 Feb
19.84	Andrey	Sinyakov	BLR	6.1.82	3		Brest		29 Apr
19.83	Odinn Björn	Thorsteinsson	ISL	3.12.81	3		Göteborg		11 Jun
19.83	Eric	Werskey	USA	17.7.87	1		Marietta		12 Jun
	(60)								
19.82i	Matt	DeChant	USA	27.3.89	1		State College		29 Jan

Mark	Name		Nat	Born	Pos	Meet	Venue	Date
19.82	Stephen	Saenz	MEX	23.8.90	1	NCAA-E	Bloomington	26 May
19.79	Niklas	Arrhenius	SWE	10.9.82	4		Göteborg	11 Jun
19.75	Jordan	Clarke	USA	10.7.90	1	NCAA	Des Moines	10 Jun
19.73	Yasser Fathi	Ibrahim	EGY	2.5.84	1	AfrG	Maputo	12 Sep
19.67	Kamil	Zbroszczyk	POL	24.1.87	1		Czestochowa	6 Aug
19.65	Pavel	Sofyin	RUS	4.9.81	2		Moskva	12 May
19.65	Kemal	Mecic	BIH	4.8.85	1	NC	Banka Luka	4 Jun
19.62	Jakub	Giza	POL	26.4.85	1		Torun	17 Jun
19.61		Wang Like	CHN	2.4.89	1	NC	Hefei	9 Sep
	(70)							
19.60	Aleksandr	Lesnoy	RUS	28.7.88	6	NC	Cheboksary	22 Jul
19.55	Kurt	Roberts	USA	20.2.88	1		Ashland, OH	22 Apr
19.51	Hayden	Baillio	USA	22.7.91	1	PennR	Philadelphia	29 Apr
19.51i	Tim	Nedow	CAN	16.10.90	1		Notre Dame	2 Dec
19.49i	Sergey	Bakhar	BLR	27.6.89	1		Minsk	14 Jan
19.48i	Ryan	Crouser	USA-J	18.12.92	1		Nampa, ID	29 Jan
19.48	Andy	Dittmar	GER	5.7.74	2		Rodenbach	24 Jun
19.48	Edder	Moreno	COL	4.2.89	5	PAm	Guadalajara, MEX	25 Oct
19.47	Aleksandr	Bulanov	RUS	26.12.89	3	Kuts	Moskva	6 Aug
19.44	Robert	Golabek	USA	27.4.89	12	NC	Eugene	26 Jun
	(80)							
19.42	Roelie	Potgieter	RSA	20.3.80	1	NC	Durban	9 Apr
19.42	Jaco	Engelbrecht	RSA	8.3.87	1		Stellenbosch	30 Apr
19.40	Emanuele	Fuamatu	SAM	27.10.89	1		Sydney	30 Dec
19.39i	Derrick	Vicars	USA	8.5.89	1		Findlay	3 Dec
19.37	Marin	Premeru	CRO	29.8.90	3		Zenica	1 Jun
19.33i	Nick	Petersen	DEN	25.4.87	1		Helsingør	26 Feb
19.32	Artur	Hoppe	GER	3.5.88	3		Rodenbach	24 Jun
19.31	Carl	Myerscough	GBR	21.10.79	1		Portland	9 Jul
19.30	Rafal	Kownatke	POL	24.3.85	1		Salamanca	1 May
19.29	Yoisel	Toledo	CUB	24.4.83	1		Alcobendas	11 Jun
	(90)							
19.26	Daniel	Vanek	SVK	18.1.83	1		West Lafayette	16 Apr
19.26	Justin	Clickett	USA	12.4.85	1		Arlington	15 May
19.26	Laurentiu	Popa	ROU	19.1.84	1	NC	Bucuresti	10 Aug
19.23i	Yegor	Malinkin	RUS	18.4.84	1		Sankt Peterburg	21 Jan
19.23i	Georgi	Ivanov	BUL	13.3.85	1	NC	Sofia	19 Feb
19.21i	Yevgeniy	Plakhin	RUS	28.1.85	2		Moskva	9 Jan
19.19	Tumatai	Dauphin	FRA	12.1.88	2	NC	Albi	29 Jul
19.19	Reinaldo	Proenza	CUB	20.11.84	7	PAm	Guadalajara, MEX	25 Oct
19.18	Dmytro	Savytskyy	UKR	14.12.90	2	EU23	Ostrava	14 Jul
19.18	Krzysztof	Brzozowski	POL-J	15.7.93	3	NC	Bydgoszcz	11 Aug
	(100)							

Mark	Name		Nat	Born	Date		Mark	Name		Nat	Born	Date
19.16	Jacob	Thormaehlen	USA	13.2.90	14 May		18.86i	Dubravko	Brdovcak	CRO	25.3.78	22 Jan
19.16	Martin	Stasek	CZE	8.4.89	21 May		18.86	Bozidar	Antunovic	SRB	24.7.91	10 Jun
19.15	Meshari Suroor Saad		KUW	2.7.87	26 Oct		18.83	Tomasz	Walsh	NZL-J	1.3.92	5 Dec
19.12	Blake	Eaton	USA	2.5.89	26 Jun		18.81i	Richard	Garrett	USA	.90	26 Feb
19.11	Kyle	Scofield	USA		20 May		18.79i	Nick	Robinson	USA	26.1.88	5 Mar
19.10	Rhuben	Williams	USA	14.2.82	22 May		18.78	Ronald	Julião	BRA	16.6.85	16 Aug
19.07		Wang Guangfu	CHN	15.11.87	9 Sep		18.77	Scott	Rider	GBR	22.9.77	12 Jun
19.06	Robert	Dippl	GER	21.10.83	20 Mar		18.76	Georgios	Arestis	CYP	27.12.81	25 Mar
19.05i	Miroslav	Vodovnik	SLO	11.9.77	20 Feb		18.75i	Viktor	Samolyuk	UKR	5.9.86	15 Feb
19.04i	Scott	Barnas	USA	9.10.86	14 Jan		18.74	Marco	Di Maggio	ITA	22.5.83	1 Jul
19.04	Germán	Millán	ESP	21.5.79	6 Jul		18.74	Ahmed Hassan Gholoum		KUW	31.5.80	19 Dec
19.02	Mateusz	Mikos	POL	10.4.87	3 May		18.73	Robert	Gire	USA	.88	15 Apr
19.02	Denis	Kurtsev	RUS	20.8.88	12 May		18.71i	Andrew	Smith	CAN	19.11.88	26 Feb
19.01	Markus	Bandekow	GER	22.5.87	19 Jun		18.69		Hwang In-sung	KOR	15.8.84	24 Apr
19.00	Ross	Jordaan	RSA	29.3.85	30 Apr		18.68	Vladislav	Tulácek	CZE	9.7.88	10 Sep
19.00		Guo Yanxiang	CHN	29.1.87	16 Jul		18.67	Adam	Kuehl	USA	19.1.84	3 Jul
18.99	Saurabh	Vij	IND	14.6.87	13 Jun		18.66	Yeóryios	Yeromarkákis	GRE	17.3.88	29 Jul
18.98	Hendrik	Müller	GER	28.8.90	21 May		18.65	Erik	van Vreumingen	NED	15.6.78	14 Aug
18.98	Jacob	Domingue	USA	6.1.89	9 Jun		18.62i	Cody	Hunt	USA	8.2.88	29 Jan
18.98	Timothy	Hendry	CAN	3.2.90	17 Jul		18.62	Tobias	Dahm	GER	23.5.87	24 Jun
18.97	Dmitriy	Lobynya	RUS	14.11.80	20 Mar		18.61i		Zuo Shihao	CHN	7.2.91	26 Feb
18.96	Hüseyin	Atici	TUR	3.5.86	16 Aug		18.60	Max	Bedewitz	GER	18.10.90	14 Jul
18.95	Brandon	Fugett	USA	.88	5 Mar		18.59i	Martin	Gratzer	AUT	23.1.82	15 Jan
18.94	Orazio	Cremona	RSA	1.7.89	25 Feb		18.59	Paolo	Dal Soglio	ITA	29.7.70	25 Aug
18.93i	Konstantin	Lyadusov	RUS	2.3.88	16 Jan		18.57i	Zack	Hill	USA	3.3.91	26 Feb
18.92i	Manuel	Martínez	ESP	7.12.74	19 Feb		18.57	Mehmet Ali	Calidan	TUR	5.11.88	9 May
18.92	Seued Mehdi Shahrokhi		IRI	23.5.85	20 Oct		18.56		Liu Yang	CHN	29.10.86	25 Mar
18.90	Nick	Jones	USA	22.6.89	27 May		18.55	Daniele	Secci	ITA-J	9.3.92	18 Sep
18.90	Michael	Putman	PER	7.3.89	10 Jun		18.55		Li Meng	CHN-J	22.7.93	11 Sep
18.88	Sylwester	Zielinski	POL	13.8.89	7 May		18.53	Tyler	Hitchler	USA	16.11.88	14 May
18.87i	Mihai-Liviu	Grasu	ROU	21.4.87	18 Feb		18.52	Kristo	Galeta	EST	9.4.83	1 Oct

Mark	Name	Nat	Born	Pos	Meet	Venue	Date
18.50	Milos Markovic	SRB	22.11.89				14 May
18.48	Arsi Harju	FIN	18.3.74				21 May
18.48	Henri Pakisjärvi	FIN	6.1.89				13 Jun
18.47i	Matt Armstrong	USA	24.5.90				12 Mar
18.47	Raigo Toompuu	EST	17.7.81				25 Jul
18.46	Dane Tobey	USA	3.8.86				9 May
18.46	Darlan Romani	BRA	9.4.91				12 Nov
18.43	Eugenio Mannucci	ITA	13.9.86				12 May
18.43	Nicolás Martina	ARG	18.8.89				28 Aug
18.43	Željko Milovanovic	SRB	3.5.80				27 Sep
18.42	Raymond Brown	JAM	15.1.88				5 Mar
18.41	Michał Bosko	POL	25.7.88				22 May
18.41	Ladislav Prásil	CZE	17.5.90				14 Jul
18.40	Cody Riffle	USA	14.4.91				9 Apr
18.40	Maximiliano Alonso	CHI	10.10.86				27 May
18.40	Tomas Söderlund	FIN	14.5.89				13 Jun
18.39i	Billy Hardcastle	USA	6.10.87				19 Feb
18.39	Morteza Nazemi	IRI					12 May
18.39	Ding Weiye	CHN	13.4.90				9 Sep
18.38i	Mitchell Pope	USA	21.1.84				22 Jan
18.38	Patrick Cronie	NED	5.11.89				14 Jul
18.37	Oshane Harris	JAM	11.1.90				27 Feb
18.36i	António Vital e Silva	POR	23.1.88				20 Feb
18.36	Jon Arthur	USA					9 Apr
18.35	Jeff Chakouian	USA	20.4.82				26 Mar
18.35	Yohei Murakawa	JPN	1.5.81				12 Jun
18.34i	Stéphane Szuster	FRA	4.2.74				8 Jan
18.33i	John Ybarra	USA	5.6.84				27 Feb
18.33	Vadim Fomin	RUS-J	30.5.92				12 May
18.33	Tobias Hepperle	GER	8.5.87				23 Jul
18.32i	Ben Glauser	USA-J	12.8.93				5 Feb
18.32	Sotaro Yamada	JPN	7.8.85				24 Apr
18.31i	Vincent Elardo	USA	18.12.88				21 Jan
18.31i	Tyler Blatchley	USA	12.3.86				3 Dec
18.30i	Lukas Weisshaidinger	AUT-J	20.2.92				19 Feb
18.30	Jake Deaton (198)	USA	26.6.90				26 May

Best outdoors

Mark	Name	Pos	Meet	Venue	Date
20.58	Bartels	2		Halle	21 May
20.21	Lloyd	1		Orem, UT	1 Apr
20.10	Mulabegovic	6	Hanz	Zagreb	13 Sep
20.06	Rodhe	3		Tucson	21 May
20.06	Kokoyev	3		Moskva	10 Jul
20.06	Christensen	2		København	11 Aug
20.01	Vivas	1		Pergine Valsugana	23 Jul
19.87	Bucki	1		Halluin	29 Jun
19.84	Finley	1	KansR	Lawrence	22 Apr
19.37	Arrhenius	2	NCAA	Des Moines	10 Jun
19.25	Bakhar	1		Minsk	4 Jun

Mark	Name	Date
19.17	Pinkelman	14 May
19.15	Kovacs	26 Jun
18.97	Vodovnik	11 Jun
18.90	Ivanov	20 Mar
18.89	Lyadusov	5 Jun
18.84	Nedow	13 May
18.84	Plakhin	21 May
18.68	Samolyuk	11 Jun
18.61	Smith	3 Jul
18.57	Barnas	2 Apr
18.47	Martinez	26 Feb
18.46	Zuo Shihao	21 May
18.39	Brdovcak	11 Jun
18.35	Vicars	7 May
18.31	Grasu	10 Aug

Underweight implement at Brazzaville 12 Jun
1. Carlos Véliz CUB 21.40, 2. Damian Kusiak POL 14.4.88 20.65, 3. Marco Dodoni ITA 519.25, 4. Paolo Capponi ITA 18.30

Drugs disqualification

Mark	Name	Nat	Born	Pos	Meet	Venue	Date
19.26	Benik Abramyan	GEO	31.7.85	1		Artashat	18 Aug

JUNIORS

See main list for top 3 juniors. 11 performances by 6 men to 18.55. Additional marks and further juniors:

Mark	Name	Nat	Born	Pos	Meet	Venue	Date
Gill 20.07				1		Auckland (NS)	19 Dec
20.01				1		Auckland (NS)	23 Apr
Brzozowski 19.00				3		Kielce	21 Aug
18.83	Tomasz Walsh	NZL	1.3.92	2		Auckland (NS)	5 Dec
18.55	Daniele Secci	ITA	9.3.92	5		Tanger	18 Sep
18.55	Li Meng	CHN	22.7.93	3	NC	Hefei	11 Sep
18.33	Vadim Fomin	RUS	30.5.92	4		Moskva	12 May
18.32i	Ben Glauser	USA	12.8.93	1		Johnson City	5 Feb
18.30i	Lukas Weisshaidinger	AUT	20.2.92	1	NC	Wien	19 Feb
18.13	Tian Zhizhong (10)	CHN	15.12.92	7		Hefei	9 Sep
17.98	Stephen Boals	USA		7		Sacramento	30 Apr
17.92	Frédéric Dagee	FRA	11.12.92	3	NC	Albi	29 Jul
17.88	Damien Birkinhead	AUS	8.4.93	2		Melbourne	5 Mar
17.74	Caleb Whitener	USA	29.5.92	2		Athens, GA	23 Apr
17.72	Jasdeep Singh	IND	6.10.92	4	IS	Bangalore	13 Jun
17.61	Lukas Weisshaidinger	AUT	20.2.92	3	NC	Innsbruck	7 Aug
17.60	Ivan Ivanov	KAZ	3.1.92	1	NCp	Almaty	15 Sep
17.58	Jaromír Mazgal	CZE	20.1.93	1		Trebíc	17 Sep
17.57	Li Jun	CHN	2.1.93	12		Kunshan	25 May
17.57	Christian Jagusch (20)	GER	13.7.92	2		Neubrandenburg	18 Jun

6 KG SHOT

Mark	Name	Nat	Born	Pos	Meet	Venue	Date
22.31	Jacko Gill	NZL-Y	10.12.94	1		Auckland (NS)	5 Dec
21.71				1		Auckland (NS)	22 Dec
21.40				1		Nouméa	6 May
21.34				1	NC-j	Dunedin	26 Mar
20.98				1		Nouméa	4 May
20.92	Krzysztof Brzozowski	POL-Y	15.7.93	1	EJ	Tallinn	21 Jul
20.61				1	NC-j	Torun	24 Jun
20.63	Li Meng	CHN	22.7.93	1	CityG	Nanchang	24 Oct
20.61	Danielle Secci	ITA	9.3.92	1	NC-j	Bressanone	19 Jun
20.56	Tomasz Walsh	NZL	1.3.92	1		Mannheim	2 Jul
20.21i	Frédéric Dagee	FRA	11.12.92	1		Orleans	17 Dec
19.90				1	NC-j	Dreux	16 Jul
20.10	Denis Lewke	GER	23.7.93	2		Mannheim	2 Jul
20.10	Damien Birkinhead	AUS	8.4.93	3		Mannheim	2 Jul
20.05	Tian Zhizhong	CHN	15.12.92	2	City G	Nanchang	24 Oct
20.00	Gregori Ott (10)	SUI-Y	4.5.94	1		Zürich	8 Sep
19.97	Ashinia Miller	JAM	6.6.93	1	PAm-J	Miramar	24 Jul
19.96	Martin Novák	CZE	5.10.92	1		Ostrava	1 Oct
19.92	Christian Jagusch	GER	13.7.92			Rostock	25 Jun

Mark	Name		Nat	Born	Pos	Meet	Venue			Date
19.90	Lukas	Weisshaidinger	AUT	20.2.92	4		Mannheim			2 Jul
19.70	Pawel	Regin	POL	27.2.92	2	MC-j	Torun			24 Jun
19.65	Vadim	Fomin	RUS	30.5.92	1		Moskva			14 Jun
19.53	Maksim	Afonin	RUS	6.1,92	1		Krasnodar			18 May
19.38	Danijel	Furtula	MNE	31.7.92	1		Bar			1 May
19.33	Luka	Mustafi⊠	CRO	3.3.92	1	NC-j	Zagreb			25 Jun
19.32	Joaquín José	Ballivián (20)	CHI	22.4.93	1		Santiago de Chile			27 Aug

12 LB (5.44 KG) SHOT

Mark	Name		Nat	Born	Pos	Meet	Venue			Date
22.38	Ryan	Crouser	USA-J	18.12.92	1		Portland			9 Jul
	22.27i	1	Nampa	29 Jan	22.14	1	Eugene			15 Jun
	22.13	1	Gresham	23 Apr						

DISCUS

Mark	Name		Nat	Born	Pos	Meet	Venue			Date
69.50	Zoltán	Kövágó	HUN	10.4.79	1	Gyulai	Budapest			30 Jul
				x	x	65.47	x	69.50	x	
	67.17	1 NC	Szekszard	7 Aug	61.50	x	63.09	x	66.05	67.17
68.99	Robert	Harting	GER	18.10.84	1		Halle			21 May
				67.38	67.49	68.66	68.02	68.99	67.17	
	68.97	1 WCh	Daegu	30 Aug	68.49	x	68.10	68.97	66.33	x
	68.51	1	Cottbus	25 Jun	64.59	68.51	65.50	x	65.54	x
	68.40	1 Pre	Eugene	4 Jun	66.06	x	67.59	68.40	x	x
	68.23	1 FBK	Hengelo	29 May	63.32	x	68.23	66.13	x	x
	67.32	1 DL	Saint Denis	8 Jul	67.32	x	x	x	x	x
	67.22	1 ISTAF	Berlin	11 Sep	67.22	x	66.03	x	66.41	65.66
	67.02	1 WK	Zürich	8 Sep	62.28	67.02	65.99	65.30	x	x
68.76	Jarred	Rome	USA	21.12.76	1		Chula Vista			6 Aug
				63.71	65.78	x	x	65.86	68.76	
68.49	Piotr	Malachowski	POL	7.6.83	1	Kuso	Szczecin			25 Jun
				65.25	68.49	x	67.13	x	66.52	
	67.97	1	Kraków	12 Jun	65.95	66.68	67.97	x	x	66.86
	67.26	2 DL	Saint Denis	8 Jul	62.86	66.45	x	67.26	x	64.31
67.99	Gerd	Kanter	EST	6.5.79	1	Skol M	Warszawa			20 Sep
				64.66	66.74	67.34	66.15	67.99	64.63	
	67.49	1 DL	Doha	6 May	65.56	x	x	67.49		
	67.30	1	Kohila	30 Jun	x	66.44	64.45	66.63	65.07	67.30
	67.27	1 NC	Tallinn	31 Jul	x	66.08	67.27	65.30	x	63.26
	67.24	3 DL	Saint Denis	8 Jul	66.52	x	66.81	x	67.24	x
67.97	Mario	Pestano	ESP	8.4.78	1	NC	Málaga			7 Aug
				60.97	66.21	67.09	67.76	x	67.97	
67.90	Virgilijus	Alekna	LTU	13.2.72	1	NC	Kaunas			24 Jul
				64.00	67.90	66.17	64.10	66.58	65.73	
	67.88	1	Rethimno	13 Jul	67.88	x	x	x	66.03	x
	67.19	2 Pre	Eugene	4 Jun	x	64.17	66.28	63.67	67.19	x
	67.05	1	Padova	17 Jul	65.07	66.88	x	67.05	66.86	66.82
67.77	Rutger	Smith	NED	9.7.81	1		Weert			6 Sep
				65.13	67.77	62.86	x	60.51	x	
	67.15	1	Groningen	12 Sep						
67.63	Lawrence	Okoye	GBR	6.10.91	1		London (He)			9 Jul
				59.58	58.46	62.59	54.83	67.63	63.96	
67.21	Martin	Wierig (10)	GER	10.6.87	2		Halle			21 May
				67.21	63.65	66.92	66.15	65.53	64.04	
67.18	Frank	Casañas	ESP	18.10.78	1		Castellón			28 Jun
				67.18	66.12	65.20	p	p	p	
66.98	Märt	Israel	EST	23.9.83	1		Chula Vista			12 May
	(30/12)									
66.95	Erik	Cadée	NED	15.2.84	1		Chula Vista			28 Apr
66.89	Ercüment	Olgundeniz	TUR	7.7.76	1		Ankara			31 Jul
66.87	Markus	Münch	GER	13.6.86	2		Cottbus			25 Jun
66.22	Niklas	Arrhenius	SWE	10.9.82	1		Helsingborg			8 Aug
66.08	Ehsan	Hadadi	IRI	21.1.85	3	WCh	Daegu			30 Aug
66.07	Benn	Harradine	AUS	14.10.82	3		Halle			21 May
66.06	Brett	Morse	GBR	11.2.89	1		Helsingborg			27 Jul
66.04	Russ	Winger	USA	2.8.84	1		Chula Vista			2 Jun
	(20)									
66.00	Jan	Marcell	CZE	4.6.85	1		Brno			23 Apr
65.95	Roland	Varga	CRO	22.10.77	3	Gyulai	Budapest			30 Jul
65.89	Jorge	Fernández	CUB	2.10.87	3		Cottbus			25 Jun
65.81	Martin	Maric	CRO	19.4.84	1		Chula Vista			19 May
65.74	Julian	Wruck	AUS	6.7.91	1		Geelong			18 Dec
65.44	Abdul	Buhari	GBR	26.6.82	2		London (He)			9 Jul

Mark	Name		Nat	Born	Pos	Meet	Venue	Date
65.43	Ian	Waltz	USA	15.4.77	1		Chula Vista	16 Jun
65.30	Jason	Young	USA	27.5.81	2		Chula Vista	6 Aug
65.04	Carl	Myerscough	GBR	21.10.79	2		Chula Vista	16 Jun
65.03	Lois Maikel	Martínez	CUB	3.6.81	1		Donnas	3 Jul
	(30)							
64.96	Ivan	Hyrshyn	UKR	26.7.88	1	NC	Donetsk	2 Aug
64.91	Vikas	Gowda	IND	5.7.83	1		Chula Vista	9 Jun
64.76	Omar	El-Ghazaly	EGY	9.2.84	1		El Maadi	6 May
64.49	Stanislav	Nesterovskyy	UKR	31.7.80	1		Kyiv	16 Aug
64.47	John	Bowman	USA	29.8.86	1		Marion, IN	8 Jun
64.46	Leif	Arrhenius	SWE	15.7.86	1		Växjö	3 Aug
64.38	Lance	Brooks	USA	1.1.84	1		Wailuku, HI	29 Apr
64.38	Wesley	Stockbarger	USA	5.6.85	1		Irvine	30 Apr
64.37	Robert	Urbanek	POL	29.4.87	1		Warszawa	20 Sep
64.30	Róbert	Fazekas	HUN	18.8.75	2		Zagreb	11 Jun
	(40)							
64.21	Przemyslaw	Czajkowski	POL	26.10.88	1	Sidlo	Sopt	5 Aug
64.11	Jason	Morgan	JAM	6.10.82	1		Monroe, LA	28 May
64.10	Mohammed	Samimi	IRI	29.3.87	1		Shahrekord	12 May
63.98	Mahmoud	Samimi	IRI	18.9.88	2		Shahrekord	12 May
63.89	Giovanni	Faloci	ITA	13.10.85	1		Tarquinia	9 Jun
63.82	Adam	Kuehl	USA	19.1.84	3		Chula Vista	26 May
63.58	Hannes	Kirchler	ITA	22.12.78	2		Tarquinia	9 Jun
63.54		Wu Jian	CHN	25.5.86	1		Zhaoqing	23 Apr
63.54	Vadim	Hranovschi	MDA	14.2.83	1	NC	Chisinau	28 May
63.35	Gerhard	Mayer	AUT	20.5.80	2		Helsingborg	27 Jul
	(50)							
63.30	Ronald	Julião	BRA	16.6.85	3	WUG	Shenzhen	21 Aug
63.30	Yasser Fathi	Ibrahim	EGY	2.5.84	1	AfrG	Maputo	11 Sep
63.00	Chris	Scott	GBR	21.3.88	3		London (He)	9 Jul
62.82	Yunio	Lastre	CUB	26.10.81	1		La Habana	17 Jun
62.77	Germán	Lauro	ARG	2.4.84	1		Buenos Aires	4 May
62.74	Mikko	Kyyrö	FIN	12.7.80	1		Ikaalinen	7 Jun
62.66	Sergiu	Ursu	ROU	26.4.80	3		Kraków	12 Jun
62.60	Mykyta	Nesterenko	UKR	15.4.91	4	WUG	Shenzhen	21 Aug
62.60	Victor	Hogan	RSA	25.7.89	2	AfrG	Maputo	11 Sep
62.40	Bogdan	Pishchalnikov	RUS	26.8.82	6	Kuso	Szczecin	25 Jun
	(60)							
62.39A	Casey	Malone	USA	6.4.77	1		Boulder	16 Jun
62.29	Rashid	Al-Dosari	QAT	8.5.81	1	ArabG	Doha	17 Dec
62.20	Oleksiy	Semenov	UKR	27.6.82	1	NC-w	Yalta	25 Feb
62.20	Mihai-Liviu	Grasu	ROU	21.4.87	1		Bucuresti	20 May
62.20	Brian	Trainor	USA	14.3.80	5		Chula Vista	9 Jun
62.12	Christoph	Harting	GER	4.10.90	5		Wiesbaden	14 May
62.11	Nikolay	Sedyuk	RUS	29.4.88	1	Kuts	Moskva	6 Aug
61.95	Pedro José	Cuesta	ESP	22.8.83	1		León	23 Jul
61.86	Libor	Malina	CZE	14.6.73	1		Kladno	2 Jun
61.70	Sergiy	Pruglo	UKR	18.11.83	2	NC-w	Yalta	25 Feb
	(70)							
61.66	Pavlo	Karsak	UKR	11.11.87	2		Kyiv	6 Jun
61.55	Miroslav	Pudivítr	CZE	8.5.78	1		Chodov	7 May
61.49	Gordon	Wolf	GER	17.1.90	1		Schönebeck	5 Jun
61.44	Apostolos	Parellis	CYP	24.7.85	6	WUG	Shenzhen	21 Aug
61.38	Aleksas	Abromavicius	LTU	6.12.84	1		Palanga	30 Apr
61.38	Konrad	Szuster	POL	21.1.84	3	Sidlo	Sopot	5 Aug
61.34	Greg	Garza	USA	6.1.85	5		Chula Vista	26 May
61.28	Maarten	Persoon	NED	15.3.87	1		Vught	2 Jun
61.28	Daniel	Jasinski	GER	5.8.89	4		Osterode	15 Jun
61.26	Dan	Hytinen	USA	18.10.85	1		Lisle	12 Jun
	(80)							
61.14	Axel	Härstedt	SWE	28.2.87	1		Helsingborg	3 Jul
61.12	Will	Conwell	USA	12.9.82	1		Marietta, GA	12 Jun
61.10	Aleksander	Tammert	EST	2.2.73	5		Viljandi	9 Aug
60.97	Musaeb	Al-Momani	JOR	28.8.86	3	WMilG	Rio de Janeiro	23 Jul
60.79	Drew	Ulrick	USA	13.1.85	7		Chula Vista	9 Jun
60.75	Nick	Jones	USA	22.6.89	1	NCAA-2	Turlock, CA	28 May
60.69	Priidu	Niit	EST	27.1.90	1	NC-23	Rakvere	5 Jul
60.65	Mason	Finley	USA	7.10.90	1		Monroe, LA	30 Apr
60.64	Chase	Madison	USA	13.9.85	1		Pella, IA	2 Apr
60.53	Jason	Tunks	CAN	7.5.75	1		London, ON	5 Jun
	(90)							

Mark	Name		Nat	Born	Pos	Meet	Venue	Date
60.45	Jorge	Balliengo	ARG	5.1.78	1		Rosario	28 May
60.43	James	Plummer	USA	.90	1		Princeton, NJ	23 Apr
60.37	Jon	Tipton	USA	10.5.86	1		Houston	16 Jun
60.34	Volodomyr	Kostyuchenko	UKR	20.9.88	4		Yalta	30 May
60.33	Yeóryios	Trémos	GRE	21.3.89	1		Thessaloníki	28 May
60.19	Jared	Schuurmans	USA	20.8.87	5		Chula Vista	14 Apr
60.19	Danijel	Furtula	MNE-J	31.7.92	1		Sremska Mitrovica	10 Sep
60.18	Martin	Kupper	EST	31.5.89	1		Kärdla	22 Jun
60.07	Péter	Savanyú	HUN	26.6.87	4		Zenica	1 Jun
59.98	Tom	Norman	GBR	15.9.82	2	South	Ashford	18 Jun
	(100)							

Mark	Name		Nat	Born	Date
59.83	Traves	Smikle	JAM-J	7.5.92	25 Jun
59.75	Federico	Apolloni	ITA	14.3.87	9 Jun
59.74	Colin	Boevers	USA	17.5.89	15 May
59.74	Gábor	Máté	HUN	9.2.79	18 Jun
59.65	Nazzareno	Di Marco	ITA	30.4.85	4 Jun
59.60	Quincy	Wilson	TRI	3.4.91	14 Aug
59.52	Robert	Sammler	GER	5.12.87	12 Apr
59.50	Jason	Schutz	USA	24.9.84	8 Apr
59.43	Jouni	Waldén	FIN	9.1.82	24 Jun
59.42	Fredrik	Amundgård	NOR	12.1.89	17 Jul
59.41	Carter	Comito	USA	26.10.90	16 Apr
59.37	Jorge	Grave	POR	1.9.82	9 Jun
59.35	Marin	Premeru	CRO	29.8.90	11 Jun
59.35	Brian	Bishop	USA	16.4.89	12 Jun
59.34	Jean-François	Aurokiom	FRA	14.4.81	25 Jun
59.30	Mario	Cota	MEX	11.9.90	25 Mar
59.30	Leonid	Artyukhov	UKR	19.7.84	25 Sep
59.27	Gleb	Sidorchenko	RUS	15.5.86	23 Jul
59.26	Reza	Shirian	IRI	17.11.88	12 May
59.25	Igor	Gondor	CZE	10.3.79	17 Sep
59.21	Ulf	Ankarling	SWE	12.4.88	13 Aug
59.17	Mikhail	Dvornikov	RUS	15.8.89	26 Jun
59.14	Tomás	Vonavka	CZE	4.6.90	13 Aug
59.09	András	Seres	HUN	31.1.89	16 Jul
59.00	Marco	Zitelli	ITA	5.2.82	4 Jun
58.90	Rosen	Karamfilov	BUL	4.1.89	26 May
58.81	Sultan M.	Al-Dawoodi	KSA	16.6.77	2 Jul
58.77	Kevin	Bookout	USA	12.2.83	12 May
58.71	Diego	Fortuna	ITA	14.2.68	3 Jul
58.70	Alex	Rose	USA	7.11.91	9 Apr
58.70	Eduardo	Albertazzi	ITA	14.9.91	23 Oct
58.68	Dan	Block	USA	8.1.91	6 May
58.52	Shigeo	Hatakeyama	JPN	9.3.77	4 Jun
58.51	Petr	Vuklisevic	CZE	25.2.82	11 Jun
58.50	Andrius	Gudzius	LTU	14.2.91	24 Jul
58.44	Bo	Taylor	USA	5.1.88	19 May
58.43	Tyler	Hitchler	USA	16.11.88	9 Apr
58.35	Luke	Bryant	USA	5.12.88	16 Apr
58.35	Magnus Røsholm	Berntsen	NOR	19.10.89	8 Aug
58.31	Orestis	Antoniades	CYP	10.7.85	6 Jul
58.28	Haidar Nasser	Abdul Jabreen	IRQ	13.1.81	26 May
58.21	Nathaniel	Moses	USA	1.4.90	9 Apr
58.15	Sergey	Roganov	BLR	18.4.86	25 Jun
58.09	Michael	Lischka	GER	23.12.73	17 Apr
58.09	Juan	Infamte	DOM	10.11.81	9 Jul
58.03	Adonson	Shallow	VIN	17.8.86	13 May
58.02	Olgierd	Stanski	POL	4.4.73	11 Aug
58.01	Stéphane	Marthély	FRA	9.9.79	30 Jul
58.01	Gaute	Myklebust	NOR	29.4.79	17 Sep
58.00	Maximiliano	Alonso	CHI	10.10.86	12 May
58.00	Kamal El Omrani	El Idrissi	MAR	5.6.87	25 Jun
57.96	Michael	Putman	PER	7.3.89	18 Mar
57.91	Dmitriy	Chebotaryov	RUS	9.10.88	24 May
57.88	Chad	Wright	JAM	25.3.91	16 Apr
57.80	Andrés	Rossini	ARG	12.4.88	13 May
57.76	Geoffrey	Tabor	USA	8.3.89	14 May
57.70	Kamal El Amri	Idrissi	MAR		18 Jun
57.66	Lolassonn	Djouhan	FRA	18.5.91	30 Jul
57.60	Essa	Al-Zankawi	KUW-J	17.10.92	18 Oct
57.59	Jake	Deiters	USA	21.7.89	2 Apr
57.58	Johnny	Karlsson	SWE	22.8.89	22 Jun
57.54	Mika	Loikkanen	FIN	20.2.74	10 Sep
57.53	Joni	Mattila	FIN	30.11.88	22 Jun
57.52	Stéfanos	Kónstas	GRE	16.5.77	26 Jun
57.51A	Dean	Wattrus	RSA	10.5.89	25 Jun
57.50A	Russel	Tucker (166)	RSA	4.11.90	3 Apr

JUNIORS

Mark	Name		Nat	Born	Pos	Meet	Venue	Date
60.19	Danijel	Furtula	MNE	31.7.92	1		Sremska Mitrovica	11 Sep
59.83	Traves	Smikle	JAM	7.5.92	1	NC	Kingston	25 Jun
	57.55		1			Kingston	4 Jun	4 performances by 3 men to 57.00
57.60	Essa Mohamed	Al-Zankawi	KUW	17.10.92	1	Gulf CG	Madinat Isa	18 Oct
56.43	Marek	Bárta	CZE	8.12.92	2	NC-j	Písek	10 Sep
55.60	Daniel	Ståhl	SWE	27.8.92	5	NC	Gävle	13 Aug
55.46	Benedikt	Stienen	GER	12.1.92	5	NC-23	Bremen	26 Jun
55.31	Amine	Atik	MAR	19.5.92	1		Ifrane	28 May
55.18	János	Huszák	HUN	5.2.92	3	NC-w	Szombathely	6 Mar
54.85	Lukas	Weisshaidinger	AUT	20.2.92	1		Wels	10 Jul
54.58	Colin	Burton	USA	.93	1		Baton Rouge	25 Mar
54.25	Hamid	Mansour (10)	SYR	29.4.92	1		Damascus	17 Sep
54.10	Wojciech	Praczyk	POL	10.1.93	1		Szprotawa	7 May
54.06	Tavis	Bailey	USA	1.6.92	1		Charlotte	17 Jun

1.75KG DISCUS

Mark	Name		Nat	Born	Pos	Meet	Venue	Date
66.88	Traves	Smikle	JAM	7.5.92	1		Kingston	31 Mar
	66.58		1	PAmJ	Miramar	22 Jul	63.96 1 Kingston	5 Feb
64.03	Essa Mohamed	Al-Zankawi	KUW	17.10.92	1		Szeged	27 Aug
	63.06		1		Veszprém	8 Sep	9 performances by 6 men to 62.90	
63.83	Lukas	Weisshaidinger	AUT	20.2.92	1	EJ	Tallinn	24 Jul
63.54	Danijel	Furtula	MNE	31.7.92	2	RJ	Tallinn	24 Jul
63.52	Benedikt	Stienen	GER	12.1.92	1		Mannheim	2 Jul
62.90	Philippe	Grewe	GER	30.12.92	1		Wiesbaden	14 May
62.68	Marek	Bárta	CZE	8.12.92	1		Ostrava	1 Oct
62.26	Wojciech	Praczyk	POL	10.1.93	1	NC-j	Torun	26 Jun
61.22	Michael	Klatsias	CYP	12.11.92	4	EJ	Tallinn	24 Jul
61.16	Amine	Atik (10)	MAR	19.5.92	1		Meknès	27 Feb
60.85	Daniel	Ståhl	SWE	27.8.92	1		Bålsta	14 May

Mark	Name		Nat	Born	Pos	Meet	Venue	Date
60.59	Damian	Kaminski	POL	15.12.93	1		Warszawa	12 Jun
59.34	Gabe	Hull	USA	1.12.93	1	NC-j	Eugene	25 Jun
59.03	Martin	Novák	CZE	5.10.92	2		Opava	24 Sep
58.76	Viktor	Butenko	RUS	10.3.93	1	NC-j	Cheboksary	3 Jul
58.69	János	Huszák	HUN	5.2.92	3		Mannheim	2 Jul
58.48A	Mauricio	Ortega	COL-Y	4.8.94	1	SAm-J	Medellín	25 Sep
58.44	Jordan	Young	CAN	21.6.93	1		Tempe	19 Mar
57.92	Behnam	Shiri	IRI		1	NC-j	Shiraz	26 Oct
57.87	Jaromír	Mazgal (20)	CZE	20.1.93	1		Liberec	22 May

HAMMER

Mark	Name		Nat	Born	Pos	Meet	Venue	Date
81.89	Krisztián	Pars	HUN	18.2.82	1		Szombathely	23 Sep

76.95 79.87 80.06 81.89 79.99 x

81.18	2	WCh	Daegu	29 Aug	77.26	78.84	79.14	79.97	60.34	81.18
81.12	Q		Rieti	9 Sep	77.58	81.12	p			
80.63	1	NC	Szekszárd	7 Aug	78.82	x	80.27	79.50	79.31	80.63
80.17	1		Szombathely	18 May	only best throw measured					
80.14	1	ET-1	Izmir	18 Jun	75.48	x	x	80.14		
79.95	1		Dubnica nad Váhon	15 Sep	77.20	76.75	78.81	78.75	79.95	79.24
79.86	3	Hanz	Zagreb	13 Sep		x	79.86	79.63	x	
79.84	1	EC-w	Sofia	19 Mar	79.66	79.47	79.19	79.29	79.84	78.27
79.77	1		Tapolca	13 Aug	78.32	78.93	x	78.56	79.77	x
79.70	1	Znam	Zhukovskiy	3 Jul		x	79.70	x	x	
79.61	1		Szekesfehervar	11 Jun	x	79.61	77.77	x	77.21	79.54
79.47	1		Kawasaki	8 May	79.47	x	x	78.86	x	79.43
79.37	1	Gyulai	Budapest	30 Jul	75.34	79.04	x	x	79.37	78.81

81.73	Aleksey	Zagornyi	RUS	31.5.78	1	NCp	Yerino	4 Jun

x 79.74 81.73 x p p

81.54	1		Adler	22 Apr	80.21	x	81.54	x	x	p
81.49	1	Nebiolo	Torino	10 Jun	77.33	x	79.92	81.49	p	p
80.96	1		Adler	24 May	79.29	80.96	79.10	x		
80.02	1	GS	Ostrava	30 May	73.91	77.52	78.91	x	79.55	80.02
79.99	1		Adler	12 Feb	x	73.25	77.12	79.99	77.20	x
79.80	1	ECCp	V.R. de Sto. Antônio	28 May	78.99	77.99	79.80	x		

81.24	Koji	Murofushi	JPN	8.10.74	1	WCh	Daegu	29 Aug

79.72 81.03 81.24 79.42 81.24 80.83

80.67	Pavel	Krivitskiy	BLR	17.4.84	1		Minsk	11 Aug

77.05 78.72 80.67 79.71 77.57 76.33

80.31	Kibwé	Johnson	USA	17.7.81	1	NC	Eugene	23 Jun

75.21 78.91 78.66 75.10 74.27 80.31

80.09	1		Uberlândia	18 May	x	73.89	x	76.50	80.09	76.03
79.63	1	PAm	Guadalajara, MEX	26 Oct	73.87	77.24	76.56	76.82	79.63	77.19

80.30	Dilshod	Nazarov	TJK	6.5.82	1	Hanz	Zagreb	13 Sep

x 77.93 x 80.30

80.29	Nicola	Vizzoni	ITA	4.11.73	1		Firenze	5 Jun

77.97 76.48 80.29 x 75.20 75.66

80.28	Primoz	Kozmus	SLO	30.9.79	2	Hanz	Zagreb	13 Sep

77.13 79.43 80.28 x

79.39	3	WCh	Daegu	29 Aug	77.50	79.39	78.93	x	76.01	78.19

79.69	Markus	Esser	GER	3.2.80	1		Leichlingen	9 Apr

(31/9)

Mark	Name		Nat	Born	Pos	Meet	Venue	Date
79.27	Ali Mohamed	Al-Zankawi (10)	KUW	27.2.84	1	PArab	Al Ain	27 Oct
79.04	Kirill	Ikonnikov	RUS	5.3.84	1	NC	Cheboksary	24 Jul
79.02	Szymon	Ziólkowski	POL	1.7.76	1		Castres	19 Jul
78.90	Sergey	Litvinov	RUS	27.1.86	2	NC-w	Adler	23 Feb
78.70	Yuriy	Shayunov	BLR	22.10.87	1		Minsk	28 Jul
78.54	Pawel	Fajdek	POL	4.6.89	1	EU23	Ostrava	17 Jul
78.33	Oleksey	Sokyrskyy	UKR	16.3.85	1		Kyiv	20 Jul
78.04	Esref	Apak	TUR	3.1.82	1	NC	Izmir	9 Jul
78.02	Valeriy	Svyatokho	BLR	20.7.81	2		Minsk	28 Jul
77.69	Libor	Charfreitag	SVK	11.9.77	1	ET-2	Novi Sad	18 Jun
77.52	Sergey	Kolomoyets (20)	BLR	11.8.89	2		Minsk	4 Jun
77.34	David	Söderberg	FIN	11.8.79	1		Kaustinen	2 Jul
77.01	Igor	Vinichenko	RUS	11.4.84	2		Moskva	10 Jul
76.96	Lorenzo	Povegliano	ITA	11.11.84	1		Pordenone	18 Sep
76.60	Matt	DiBuono ¶	USA	14.12.86	1		West Point	1 Jun
76.60	Igors	Sokolovs	LAT	17.8.74	4		Bydgoszcz	3 Jun
76.60	Olli-Pekka	Karjalainen	FIN	7.3.80	Q	WCh	Daegu	27 Aug
76.59	Aleksandr	Pozdnyakov	RUS	1.2.87	4		Madrid	9 Jul

Mark	Name		Nat	Born	Pos	Meet	Venue	Date	
76.53	A.G.	Kruger	USA	18.2.79	1		Ashland	17	Jun
76.47	Frédéric	Pouzy	FRA	18.2.83	1		Schönebeck	5	Jun
76.40	Roberto	Janet	CUB	29.8.86	1		La Habana	10	Jun
	(30)								
76.31	Dmitriy	Velikopolskiy	RUS	27.11.84	3		Sochi	24	May
76.29	Kristóf	Németh	HUN	17.9.87	1		Maribor	6	Jul
76.27	Jim	Steacy	CAN	29.5.84	1	NC-w	Calgary	25	Jun
76.12	Marco	Lingua	ITA	4.6.78	2	NC	Torino	26	Jun
76.09	Andrey	Vorontsov	BLR	24.7.75	1		Minsk	22	Jun
75.84	Marcel	Lomnicky	SVK	6.7.87	1		Durham	23	Apr
75.78	Nicolas	Figère	FRA	19.5.79	2		Schönebeck	5	Jun
75.77	András	Haklits	CRO	23.9.77	2		Tapolca	13	Aug
75.76	Artyom	Rubanko	UKR	21.3.74	1		Uman	21	May
75.49	Fatih	Eryildirim	TUR	1.3.79	2	NC	Izmir	9	Jul
	(40)								
75.48	Aleksandr	Drygol	UKR	25.4.66	2		Kyiv	20	Jul
75.40	Lukás	Melich	CZE	16.9.80	1		Lovosice	14	May
75.40	Noleysis	Vicet	CUB	6.2.81	1		La Habana	20	May
75.31	Javier	Cienfuegos	ESP	15.7.90	1		Madrid	21	May
75.31	Tuomas	Seppänen	FIN	16.5.86	1		Kuortane	25	Jun
75.26	Kaveh	Mousavi	IRI	27.5.85	1		Shahrekord	12	May
75.24	Dmytro	Mykolaychuk	UKR	30.1.87	3		Uman	21	May
74.90	Chris	Harmse	RSA	31.5.73	1		Pretoria	22	Oct
74.78	Sergey	Aydamirov	RUS	11.5.87	7	NC-w	Adler	23	Feb
74.76	Mostafa Hicham	El-Gamal	EGY	1.10.88	1	AfrG	Maputo	14	Sep
	(50)								
74.69	Michael	Mai	USA	27.7.77	2	NC	Eugene	23	Jun
74.67	Drew	Loftin	USA	15.9.80	1		Boulder	2	Jun
74.62	Alex	Smith	GBR	6.3.88	1		Hull	3	Aug
74.59	Eivind	Henriksen	NOR	14.9.90	1eB		Halle	22	May
74.40	Chris	Rohr	USA	28.12.85	3		Ashland, OH	29	Apr
74.38	Konstadínos	Stathelákos	GRE	30.12.87	1		Athína (Ellinikó)	9	Jun
74.30	Hassan Mohamed	Mahmoud	EGY	10.2.84	1		Cairo	29	Mar
74.24	Denis	Lukyanov	RUS	11.7.89	1	NC-w/23	Adler	23	Feb
74.23	Mattias	Jons	SWE	19.11.82	3	v FIN	Helsinki	9	Sep
74.04	Dmitriy	Marshin	AZE	24.2.72	3		Minsk	22	Jun
	(60)								
74.01	Alexándros	Papadimitríou	GRE	18.6.73	1	NC	Athína	30	Jul
73.91	Aleksey	Kochnev	RUS	6.4.90	2	NC-w/23	Adler	23	Feb
73.70	Jens	Rautenkrantz	GER	11.4.82	2	NC	Kassel	24	Jul
73.63	Jérôme	Bortoluzzi	FRA	20.5.82	2	NC	Albi	28	Jul
73.60	Oleg	Dubitskiy	BLR	14.10.90	5		Minsk	28	Jul
73.53	Mirko	Micuda	CRO	22.12.89	1		Varazdin	22	May
73.39	Reinier	Mejías	CUB	22.9.90	3		La Habana	13	May
73.10	Andriy	Martynyuk	UKR	25.9.90	1		Yalta	18	May
72.99	Garland	Porter	USA	10.2.82	4		Ashland, OH	29	Apr
72.79	Andy	Frost	GBR	17.4.81	1	LI	Loughborough	22	May
	(70)								
72.72	Wojciech	Nowicki	POL	22.2.89	1		Bialystok	19	Jun
72.71	Juha	Kauppinen	FIN	16.8.86	2		Mänttä-Vilppula	11	Jul
72.71	Quentin	Bigot	FRA-J	1.12.92	1		Ettelbruck	8	Oct
72.69	Alexander	Ziegler	GER	7.7.87	1	NCAA	Des Moines	9	Jun
72.67	Conor	McCullough	USA	31.1.91	1	IRL Ch	Dublin	7	Aug
72.63	Markus	Kahlmeyer	GER	20.1.82	1		Braunschweig	1	Jun
72.49	Mark	Dry	GBR	11.10.87	2	LI	Loughborough	22	May
72.45	Mike	Floyd	GBR	26.9.76	1		Birmingham	20	Aug
72.40	Markus	Johansson	SWE	8.5.90	1		Karlstad	13	Jun
72.37	Arno	Laitinen	FIN	9.3.88	5		Kuortane	25	Jun
	(80)								
72.12	Juan Ignacio	Cerra	ARG	16.10.76	1	SACh	Buenos Aires	3	Jun
72.12	Sven	Möhsner	GER	30.1.86	3		Fränkisch-Crumbach	12	Jun
72.06	Mohsen	Anani	EGY	25.5.85	1	TUN Ch	Radès	26	Jun
72.05	Stamátios	Papadoníou	GRE	3.5.84	2	NC	Athína	30	Jul
72.00	Andy	Fryman	USA	3.2.85	2		Clemson	14	May
71.82	Ákos	Hudi	HUN	10.8.91	1		Veszprém	30	Apr
71.82	Reza	Moghaddam	IRI	17.11.88	1		Tehran	16	Jun
71.73	Benjamin	Boruschewski	GER	23.4.80	4		Fränkisch-Crumbach	12	Jun
71.60	Wágner	Domingos	BRA	23.6.83	1		São Caetano do Sul	14	May
71.25	Dário	Manso	POR	1.7.82	1		Lovelhe	10	Jun
	(90)								
71.22	Joachim	Koivu	FIN	5.9.88	4		Kaustinen	2	Jul

Mark	Name	Nat	Born	Pos	Meet	Venue	Date
71.00	Alaa El-Din M. El-Ashry	EGY	6.1.91	1		Cairo	9 May
70.99	Ainars Vaiculens	LAT	21.1.83	2	ET-2	Novi Sad	18 Jun
70.89	Hiroshi Noguchi	JPN	3.5.83	2	AsiC	Kobe	9 Jul
70.86	Dániel Szabó	HUN	28.6.91	2		Szombathely	15 Jun
70.69	Hiroaki Doi	JPN	2.12.78	3	AsiC	Kobe	9 Jul
70.65	Giovanni Sanguin	ITA	14.5.69	1		Savona	18 May
70.51	Michal Fiala	CZE	22.6.85	1		Jablonec	30 Apr
70.45	Mats Granö	FIN	6.9.81	1		Oulu	10 Aug
70.44	Norbert Rauhut	POL	17.1.90	11	EU23	Ostrava	17 Jul
	(100)						
70.41	Isaac Vicente	ESP	30.4.87				7 Aug
70.40	Andreas Sahner	GER	27.1.85				24 Jul
70.38	Lorenzo Rocchi	ITA	24.3.87				22 May
70.22	Adonson Shallow	VIN	17.8.86				19 Mar
70.18	Roman Rozna	MDA	25.3.76				18 Jun
70.15	Ryan Loughney	USA	21.8.89				26 May
70.14	Bergur Ingi Pétursson	ISL	5.10.85				23 Jul
70.04	Richard Olbrich	GER	7.4.90				14 May
69.88	Tibor Petrovszki	HUN	8.11.89				21 May
69.87	Wan Yong	CHN	22.7.87				23 Apr
69.64	Eric Flores	USA	30.12.86				14 Apr
69.62	Pavel Bareysho	BLR	16.2.91				4 Jun
69.59	Wang Shizhu	CHN	20.2.89				29 Mar
69.56	Brian Richotte	USA	17.4.84				8 Jun
69.48	Kai Räsänen	FIN	29.6.90				29 May
69.45	Trey Henderson	CAN	10.10.89				1 Apr
69.45	Oleksandr Myagkyh	UKR	7.5.86				15 Aug
69.37	Lee Yun-chul	KOR	28.3.82				28 Jul
69.29	Johannes Bichler	GER	3.7.90				13 Jun
69.24	James Bedford	GBR	29.12.88				17 Jul
69.20	Zech Whittington	USA	10.8.79				12 Mar
69.15	Amanmurad Hommadov	TKM	28.1.89				21 May
69.13	Chris Cralle	USA	13.6.88				18 Mar
69.09	Walter Henning	USA	24.1.89				27 May
69.06	Allan Wolski	BRA	18.1.90				30 Jun
69.05	Dan Zhangcheng	CHN	14.12.88				23 Apr
68.84	Chris Bennett	GBR	17.12.89				2 Jul
68.80	Simone Falloni	ITA	26.9.91				29 Sep
68.74	Vinny Tortorella	USA	2.2.80				6 Aug
68.63	Tim Driesen	AUS	27.3.84				15 Apr
68.63	Justin Welch	USA	29.9.91				30 Apr
68.59	Simon Wardhaugh	AUS	14.1.86				29 Jan
68.51	Sergey Chekomasov	RUS	5.8.89				4 Jun
68.49	Kevin Becker	USA	5.1.84				12 May
68.43	Pedro José Martin	ESP-J	12.8.92				7 Aug
68.40	Artem Vynnyk	UKR	1.1.88				24 Feb
68.39	Mergen Mamedov	TKM	24.12.90				19 Jun
68.34	Aldo Bello	VEN	23.5.75				27 Aug
68.32	John Freeman	USA	21.8.87				22 May
68.30	Nick Welihozkiy	USA	12.2.81				22 Apr
68.28	Pellegrino Delli Carri	ITA	4.8.76				5 Jun
68.28	Anton Krykun	UKR	22.1.90				15 Aug
68.24	Zhao Yihai	CHN	29.3.85				8 Sep
68.24	Bruno Boccalatte	FRA	10.11.88				16 Oct
68.20	Alec Faldermeyer	USA-J	9.7.92				14 May
68.18	Marco Felice	ITA	20.10.79				30 Jul
68.12	Colin Dunbar	USA	27.6.88				13 May
68.11	Zoltán Fabián	HUN	22.4.69				4 Jun
68.10	Zakhar Makhrosenko (149)	BLR	10.10.91				4 Jun

JUNIORS

Mark	Name	Nat	Born	Pos	Meet	Venue	Date
72.71	Quentin Bigot	FRA	1.12.92	1		Ettelbruck	8 Oct
71.79				3	NC	Albi	28 Jul
69.49				1		Sarreguemines	8 May
69.62				1		Antony	22 May
69.15				2		Polignu	5 Jun
68.43	Pedro José Martín	ESP	12.8.92	2	NC	Málaga	7 Aug
68.20	Alec Faldermeyer	USA	9.7.92	1	Pac10	Tucson	14 May
67.54	Sergiu Marghiev	MDA	7.11.92	1		Chisinau	4 May
66.44	Ilmari Lahtinen	FIN	12.10.93	3cB		Kaustinen	3 Jul
66.35	Huw Peacock	AUS	12.5.92	1		Hobart	14 Aug
66.27	Sukhrob Khodyayev	UZB	21.5.93	1	NC	Tashkent	1 Oct
65.90	Peyman Ghalehnoei	IRI	29.1.92	3	NC	Shiraz	15 Apr
65.69	Elias Håkansson	SWE	29.2.92	5	NC	Gävle	12 Aug
64.94	Juho Saarikoski (10)	FIN	19.5.93	4cB		Kaustinen	3 Jul
64.92	Bence Pásztor	HUN-Y	5.2.95	4	NC	Szekszárd	7 Aug
64.61	Chen Hongqiu	CHN	11.8.92	4		Fuzhou	25 Jun

6 KG HAMMER

Mark	Name	Nat	Born	Pos	Meet	Venue	Date
82.84	Quentin Bigot	FRA-J	1.12.92	1		Bondoufle	16 Oct
79.76				1		Luxemboiurg	8 Jul
77.98				1		Veszprém	11 May
78.45				1	EJ	Tallinn	22 Jul
77.98				1	NC-j	Dreux	17 Jul
78.00				1		Metz	27 Jun
77.73				1		Mannheim	2 Jul
76.60	Sergiu Marghiev	MDA	7.11.92	2	EJ	Tallinn	22 Jul
74.99	Elias Håkansson	SWE	29.2.92	3	EJ	Tallinn	22 Jul
74.58	Pedro José Martín	ESP	12.8.92	1		Manresa	13 Jul
74.56	Ilmari Lahtinen	FIN	12.10.93	4	EJ	Tallinn	22 Jul
73.79	Bence Pásztor	HUN	5.2.95	1		Budapest	29 May
73.76	Juho Saarikoski	FIN	19.5.93	1	NC-j	Valkeakoski	20 Aug
73.52	Alec Faldermeyer	USA	9.7.92	1	NC-j	Eugene	24 Jun
72.82	Yevgeniy Korotovskiy	RUS	1.6.92	1	NC-j	Cheboksary	2 Jul
72.70	Tristan Schwandke (10)	GER	23.5.92	1	NC-j	Jena	6 Aug
72.60	Jesse Lehto	FIN	12.2.93	3		Pori	9 Jun
72.57	Edgars Timermanis	LAT	26.8.92	1	NC-j	Jekabpils	10 Jul
72.43	Krisztián Árvai	HUN	27.4.93	1		Tapolca	13 Aug
72.25	Nikolay Bashan	RUS	18.11.92	2	NC-j	Cheboksary	2 Jul
71.94	Yebgeniy Ivanov	BLR	11.6.92	2		Brest	29 Apr
71.75	Tomás Kruzliak	SVK	9.2.92	1		Trnava	9 Jul
71.54	Daniel A. Cruz	CUB	17.4.93	1	NC	La Habana	19 Mar
71.26	Nils Lindner	GER	25.5.93	2		Mannheim	2 Jul
71.06	Serhiy Reheda	UKR	6.2.94	1	NC-wj	Yalta	30 Mar
70.99	Nejc Plesko (20)	SLO	9.10.92	1		Novo Mesto	20 Jun

JAVELIN

Mark	Name	Nat	Born	Pos	Meet	Venue	Date	Series
90.61	Andreas Thorkildsen	NOR	1.4.82	1	NC	Byrkjelo	14 Aug	x x 90.61 85.55 84.85 p
88.43				1	DNG	Stockholm	29 Jul	85.35 88.43 84.63 x 81.97 p
88.30				1	DL	Birmingham	10 Jul	86.99 83.23 88.30 85.99 87.43 p
88.19				1	Athl	Lausanne	30 Jun	88.19 84.20 p p p p
85.12				2	DL	Shanghai	15 May	82.18 79.63 85.12 85.11 x p
84.78				3	WCh	Daegu	3 Sep	80.75 80.46 80.60 84.78 x 80.28
88.36	Matthias de Zordo	GER	21.2.88	1	VD	Bruxelles	16 Sep	84.79 82.18 88.36 80.56 p x
86.27				1	WCh	Daegu	3 Sep	86.27 85.51 p p 82.88 81.40
85.78				1	GS	Ostrava	31 May	79.48 81.62 79.78 77.49 76.72 85.78
88.22	Vadims Vasilevskis	LAT	5.1.82	1		Tartu	28 May	78.48 79.76 80.73 x 81.25 88.22
87.11				1		Bauska	22 Jun	78.73 79.78 82.67 x 87.11 x
85.68				1	NC	Liepaja	30 Ju	x 76.52 85.68 p p p
85.33				1		Ventspils	4 Jun	
85.12				1		Riga	2 Jun	79.98 x 80.07 85.12 84.80 81.88
85.06				2	VD	Bruxelles	16 Sep	85.06 82.44 84.94 x 74.26 x
87.20A	Guillermo Martínez	CUB	28.6.81	1	PAm	Guadalajara, MEX	28 Oct	87.20 x p p p p
84.68				1	NC	La Habana	18 Mar	75.42 84.68 82.34 p p p
87.12	Sergey Makarov	RUS	19.3.73	2	Athl	Lausanne	30 Jun	84.89 82.23 x 83.33 87.12 80.01
86.14				1	Znam	Zhukovskiy	3 Jul	81.82 82.48 82.54 86.14
85.19				1	NCp	Yerino	4 Jun	85.19 81.92 81.93 83.73 p p
85.33				1		Adler	22 Apr	85.33 81.13 82.30 84.29 78.27 77.60
85.33	Tero Pitkämaki	FIN	19.12.82	1	DL	Shanghai	15 May	x 80.56 85.33 x 77.59 x
85.32	Petr Frydrych	CZE	13.1.88	1	DL	Doha	6 May	x 85.32 x x
85.12	Ari Mannio	FIN	23.7.87	1	NC	Turku	7 Aug	80.21 x 82.29 x 85.12 79.15
85.10	Dmitriy Tarabin	RUS	29.10.91	1	NC-23	Yerino	25 Jun	80.16 78.92 85.10 x 78.03 83.59
84.81	Scott Russell (10)	CAN	16.1.79	1		Toronto	13 Jul	77.72 75.21 84.81 p p p
84.79	Fatih Avan	TUR	1.1.89	3	VD	Bruxelles	16 Sep	x 82.46 83.14 81.15 84.79 x
84.69				2		Riga	2 Jun	75.52 84.69 x x 77.45 83.30
84.69	Zigismunds Sirmais	LAT-J	6.5.92	2		Bauska	22 Jun	84.69 75.52 78.34 78.29 x 78.97
84.47				1	EC-w	Sofia	20 Mar	84.47 76.65 81.09 p p 81.47
(30/12)								
84.41	Lassi Etelätalo	FIN	30.4.88	1		Leppävirta	28 May	
84.38	Robert Oosthuizen	RSA	23.1.87	2	DL	Doha	6 May	
84.38	Till Wöschler	GER	9.6.91	1	EU23	Ostrava	16 Jul	
84.30	Roman Avramenko	UKR	23.3.88	1		Yalta	18 May	
84.21	Stuart Farquhar	NZL	15.3.82	4	DNG	Stockholm	29 Jul	
84.11	Vitezslav Vesely	CZE	27.2.83	4	WCh	Daegu	3 Sep	
84.08	Jakub Vadlejch	CZE	10.10.90	2		Domazlice	24 Sep	
83.77	Sampo Lehtola	FIN	10.5.89	1		Lappeenranta	13 Aug	
(20)								
83.53	Yukifumi Murakami	JPN	23.12.79	1		Matsuyama	14 Aug	
83.52	Mervyn Luckwell	GBR	27.11.84	1		Wrexham	25 Sep	
83.39	Dmytro Kosynskyy ¶	UKR	31.3.89	1	NCp	Yalta	31 May	
82.81	Igor Janik	POL	18.1.83	2	Znam	Zhukovskiy	3 Jul	
82.61	Oleksandr Pyatnytsya	UKR	14.7.85	2	NCp	Yalta	31 May	
82.54	Mark Frank	GER	21.6.77	1		Schönebeck	5 Jun	
82.53	Pawel Rakoczy	POL	15.5.87	1		Bialystok	1 Oct	
82.39	Teemu Wirkkala	FIN	14.1.84	4	DL	Shanghai	15 May	
82.38	Yervásios Filippídis	GRE	24.7.87	1		Kalamáta	4 Jun	
82.29	Antti Ruuskanen	FIN	21.2.84	1		Lapinlahti	24 Jul	
(30)								
82.25	Jarrod Bannister	AUS	3.10.84	7	WCh	Daegu	3 Sep	
82.24A	Cyrus Hostetler	USA	8.8.86	2	PAm	Guadalajara, MEX	28 Oct	
82.17	Aleksandr Ivanov	RUS	25.5.82	2	NCp	Yerino	4 Jun	
81.70	Corey White	USA	31.1.86	1		Tucson	21 May	
81.62	Sean Furey	USA	31.8.82	1	MSR	Walnut	15 Apr	
81.56	Risto Mätas	EST	30.4.84	1		Viljandi	9 Aug	

Mark	Name		Nat	Born	Pos	Meet	Venue	Date	
81.53	Jarko	Koski-Vähälä	FIN	21.11.78	1		Pihtipudas	3	Jul
81.12	Spirídon	Lebésis	GRE	30.5.87	2		Kalamáta	4	Jun
81.09	Mike	Hazle	USA	22.3.79	2		Tucson	21	May
81.01	Harri	Haatainen	FIN	5.1.78	2		Lapinlahti	24	Jul
	(40)								
80.88	Gabriel	Wallin	SWE	14.10.81	2	ET	Stockholm	18	Jun
80.87	Eriks	Rags	LAT	1.6.75	1	LTU Ch	Kaunas	23	Jul
80.76		Chen Qi	CHN	10.3.82	1	NC	Hefei	10	Sep
80.58	Lukasz	Grzeszczuk	POL	3.3.90	1		Warszawa	14	May
80.45	Leslie	Copeland	FIJ	23.4.88	Q	WUG	Shenzhen	17	Aug
80.40	Ansis	Bruns	LAT	30.3.89	1		Riga	9	Aug
80.38		Jung Sang-jin	KOR	16.4.84	1		Goyang	23	Jul
80.34	Viktor	Goncharov	RUS	9.5.91	2	NC-23	Yerino	25	Jun
80.33	Tim	Glover	USA	1.11.90	1	NCAA	Des Moines	8	Jun
80.33	Marko	Jänes	EST	29.8.76	2		Viljandi	9	Aug
	(50)								
80.19		Park Jae-myong	KOR	15.12.81	2	AsiC	Kobe	10	Jul
80.18	James	Campbell	GBR	1.4.88	Q	Univ Ch	Bedford	1	May
80.15	Valeriy	Iordan	RUS-J	14.2.92	3		Adler	22	Apr
80.10	Tero	Järvenpää	FIN	2.10.84	2	NC	Turku	7	Aug
80.09	Kim	Amb	SWE	31.7.90	1	NC	Gävle	13	Aug
80.07	Mihkel	Kukk	EST	8.10.83	3		Viljandi	9	Aug
79.89	Ryan	Young	USA	3.1.87	1		Amsterdam	6	Aug
79.81	Tino	Häber	GER	6.10.82	3		Dessau	1	Jun
79.72	Matija	Kranjc	SLO	12.6.84	1		Postojna	5	Jun
79.55		Jiang Xingyu	CHN	16.3.87	1		Nanchang	17	Jul
	(60)								
79.53A	Braian	Toledo	ARG-J	8.9.93	3	PAm	Guadalajara, MEX	28	Oct
79.41	Martin	Benák	SVK	27.5.88	1		Trnava	14	May
79.39	Ivan	Zaytsev	UZB	7.11.88	1		Tashkent	12	Jun
79.35A	Dayron	Márquez	COL	19.11.83	1		Bogotá	13	Aug
79.22		Qin Qiang	CHN	18.4.83	7	DL	Shanghai	15	May
79.20	Genki	Dyene	JPN	30.12.91	2	NC	Kumagaya	12	Jun
79.19	Marcin	Krukowski	POL-J	14.6.92	2	EJ	Tallinn	23	Jul
79.15	Chris	Hill	USA	26.2.88	4		Tucson	21	May
79.07	Igor	Sukhomlinov	RUS	13.2.77	4	NC-23	Cheboksary	22	Jul
78.99	Björn	Lange	GER	15.6.79	1		Magdeburg	30	Apr
	(70)								
78.87	Ken	Arai	JPN	22.12.81	3	NC	Kumagaya	12	Jun
78.83	Pawel	Rozinski	POL	11.7.87	4	NC	Bydgoszcz	12	Aug
78.83	Ihab Abdelrahman	Sayed	EGY	1.5.89	1	PArab	Al Ain	28	Oct
78.69	Ignacio	Guerra	CHI	15.9.87	1	FlaR	Gainesville	1	Apr
78.69	Mika	Aalto	FIN	11.3.82	1		Virrat	6	Jul
78.63	Lee	Doran	GBR	5.3.85	1	NC	Birmingham	30	Jul
78.55	Bernhard	Seifert	GER-J	15.2.93	1	NC-j	Jena	7	Aug
78.51	Krisztián	Török	HUN	4.5.87	1	NC	Szekszárd	6	Aug
78.40		Zhao Qinggang	CHN	24.7.85	4		Kawasaki	8	May
78.39	Nick	Lyons	USA	8.2.89	1		Waco	23	Apr
	(80)								
78.39	Bobur	Shokirjanov	UZB	5.12.90	2		Kaohsiung	28	May
78.39	Ainars	Kovals	LAT	21.11.81	4		Riga	2	Jun
78.34	Julius	Yego	KEN	4.1.89	1	Afr G	Maputo	15	Sep
78.23	Juan José	Méndez	MEX	27.4.88	Q	WUG	Shenzhen	17	Aug
78.21	Ryohei	Arai	JPN	23.6.91	4	NC	Kumagaya	12	Jun
78.20	Thomas	Röhler	GER	30.9.91	7	EU23	Ostrava	16	Jul
78.18	Tanel	Laanmäe	EST	29.9.89	1		Viljandi	11	Aug
78.17	Bjorn	Blommerde	NED	6.7.87	1		Zwolle	26	Jun
78.10	Leonardo	Gottardo	ITA	21.3.88	1		Nembro	1	Jul
78.08	Pavel	Meleshko	BLR-J	24.11.92	1		Savonlinna	24	Aug
	(90)								
77.88	Matthias	Treff	GER	27.2.88	2	NCAA	Des Moines	8	Jun
77.83A	Arley	Ibargüen	COL	4.12.82	1		Cali	18	Jun
77.80	Bernard	Crous	RSA	13.4.89	1		Stellenbosch	30	Apr
77.72	Vedran	Samac	SRB	22.1.90	1	NC-w	Sremska Mitrovica	27	Mar
77.70	Júlio César	de Oliveira	BRA	4.2.86	1		São Paulo	17	May
77.68	Nobuhiro	Sato	JPN	28.4.88	2		Wakayana	24	Apr
77.65	Hardus	Pienaar	RSA	10.8.81	1		Bellville	10	Mar
77.58	Hamish	Peacock	AUS	15.10.90	1		Hobart	8	Oct
77.52	Anatoliy	Adakhovskiy	BLR	18.12.87	1		Brest	14	May
77.38	Rinat	Tarzumanov	UZB	26.3.84	1	NC	Almaty	29	Jul
	(100)								

Mark	Name		Nat	Born	Pos	Meet	Venue	Date
77.29	Sachith	Maduranga	SRI	15.6.90	8 Aug			
77.27	Aleksey	Tovarnov	RUS	21.1.85	24 Feb			
77.24	Kyle	Nielsen	CAN	22.4.89	26 May			
77.15	Ioánnis-Yeóryios Smaliós		GRE	17.2.87	3 Sep			
77.07		Cheng Chao-Tsun	TPE-J	17.10.93	25 Oct			
77.03	Hubert	Chmielak	POL	19.6.89	11 Jun			
76.99	Erkki	Leppik	EST	18.3.88	14 Sep			
76.94	Stefan	Müller	SUI	20.9.79	27 May			
76.92A	Víctor	Fatecha	PAR	10.3.88	28 Oct			
76.77	Matthew	Hunt	GBR	1.10.90	1 May			
76.73	Sam	Humphreys	USA	12.9.90	8 Apr			
76.64A	Ruan	Erasmus	RSA-J	9.3.93	11 Nov			
76.63	Barry	Krammes	USA	1.9.81	21 May			
76.63	Tom	Goyvaerts	BEL	20.3.84	14 Sep			
76.62	Krzysztof	Szalecki	POL	3.2.91	28 May			
76.46	Timo	Moorast	EST	26.3.86	18 May			
76.38	Laurent	Dorique	FRA	10.7.76	13 Aug			
76.33	Craig	Kinsley	USA	19.1.89	16 Apr			
76.25	Thomas	Smet	BEL	12.7.88	27 Aug			
76.23	Daan	Meijer	NED	17.2.83	8 May			
76.23	Aleksandr	Kharitonov	RUS	19.7.90	25 Jun			
76.20	Andrus	Värnik	EST	27.9.77	18 May			
76.18	Gerbrand	Grobler	RSA	26.1.83	3 Jul			
76.15		Wang Qingbo	CHN	24.5.88	10 Sep			
76.11	Mikko	Löppönen	FIN	29.9.83	14 Jul			
76.02	Karol	Jakimowicz	POL	15.6.87	11 Jun			
75.89	Daniel	Pembroke	GBR	16.7.91	12 Jun			
75.86	Yasuo	Ikeda	JPN	28.7.77	10 Oct			
75.81	Alexander	Vieweg	GER	28.6.86	1 Jun			
75.77A	Keshorn	Walcott	TRI-J	2.4.93	28 Oct			
75.74	Rajender	Singh Dalvir	IND	5.4.89	13 Sep			
75.72A	Rocco	van Rooyen	RSA-J	23.12.92	14 May			
75.71	Rolands	Strobinders	LAT-J	14.4.92	23 Jul			
75.66	Brian	Moore	USA	5.9.88	14 May			
75.63	Lars	Timmerman	NED	19.4.91	31 Jul			
75.63	Naoyo	Imada	JPN	21.5.90	9 Sep			
75.58	Ranno	Koorep	EST	24.1.90	14 Jun			
75.53	Curtis	Moss	CAN	12.4.87	3 Jul			
75.52	Norbert	Bonvecchio	ITA	14.8.85	8 May			
75.49	Leonel	Suárez	CUB	1.9.87	29 May			
75.41	Waruna Lakshanb Dayarathna		SRI	14.5.88	25 May			
75.39	Janis	Kiiskilä	FIN	28.12.89	23 Jun			
75.38	Manuel	Nau	GER	2.7.77	16 Sep			
75.33	Ahti	Peder	EST	29.8.76	9 Aug			
75.28	Oleksandr	Nychyporchuk	UKR-J	14.4.92	23 Jul			
75.13	Michel	Miranda	CUB	26.7.89	29 Jul			
75.03	Rohit	Kumar	IND-Y	15.7.94	19 Feb			
75.01	Stipe	Zunic	CRO	13.12.90	8 Jun			
75.00	Aris	Borjas	USA	28.9.84	30 Apr			
74.89	Matt	Byers	USA	12.11.90	2 Apr			
74.85		Ku Yun-hoi	KOR	30.7.78	22 Jun			
74.85	Lars	Hamann	GER	4.4.89	25 Jun			
74.79A	José	Lagunes	MEX	30.6.85	28 Apr			
74.77	Bence	Papp	HUN	5.9.85	6 Aug			
74.73	Roald	Bradstock	GBR	24.4.62	19 May			
74.68A	Melik	Janoyan	ARM	24.3.85	22 May			
74.66	Ilya	Korotkov	RUS	6.12.83	22 Jul			
74.65	Philmar Janse	van Rensburg	RSA	23.6.89	10 Apr			
74.64	Trent	Mazanec	USA	9.5.87	21 May			
74.54		Park Won-kil	KOR	24.2.90	12 Apr			
74.50	Sergiy	Dyachok	UKR	12.6.90	18 May			
74.46	Kazuki	Yamamoto	JPN	8.10.83	10 Apr			
74.44	Alexandru	Craescu	ROU	10.2.89	14 May			
74.44	Roberto	Bertolini	ITA	9.10.85	18 Sep			
74.29A	Tobie	Holtzhausen	RSA	25.5.87	19 Feb			
74.26	Marcin	Plener	POL	22.8.90	2 Jul			
74.20	Tun	Wagner	LUX	20.10.88	1 May			
74.20	Daniel	Ragnvaldsson	SWE	3.1.76	4 Jun			
74.17	Kashinath	Naik	IND	12.5.83	20 Jul			
74.13	Aleksandr	Ashomko	BLR	18.2.84	29 Apr			
74.11	Rafael	Baraza	ESP	29.8.81	18 Jun			
74.09		Kang Byong-hoon	KOR	4.3.87	9 Jun			
74.07	Jens	Merseburg	GER	1.1.88	23 Jul			
(173)								

Drugs disqualification

Mark	Name		Nat	Born	Pos	Meet	Venue	Date
77.22	Vipin	Kasana	IND	4.8.84	1	NG	Ranchi	19 Feb

JUNIORS

See main list for top 6 juniors. 13 performances by 5 men to 78.50. Additional marks and further juniors:

Mark	Name		Nat	Born	Pos	Meet	Venue	Date
Sirmais 2+	82.50			1		Liepaja	7 May	
	81.53			1	EJ	Tallinn	23 Jul	
	81.00			1		Ventspils	4 Jun	
Iordan	79.40			3	EC-w	Sofia	20 Mar	
	80.59			3		Tartu	28 May	
	80.28			1J		Bauska	22 Jun	
	79.36			2		Kohila	30 Jun	
77.07		Cheng Chao-Tsun	TPE	17.10.93	1	NG	Changhua	25 Oct
76.64A	Ruan	Erasmus	RSA	9.3.93	1		Potchefstroom	11 Nov
75.77A	Keshorn	Walcott	TRI	2.4.93	7	PAm	Guadalajara, MEX	28 Oct
75.72A	Rocco	van Rooyen (10)	RSA	23.12.92	1	Af-J	Gaborone	14 May
75.71	Rolands	Strobinders	LAT	14.4.92	4	EJ	Tallinn	23 Jul
75.28	Oleksandr	Nychyporchuk	UKR	14.4.92	7	EJ	Tallinn	23 Jul
75.03	Rohit	Kumar	IND-Y	15.7.94	2	NG	Ranchi	19 Feb
73.94	Tiago	Aperta	POR	15.1.92	1	NC-j	Lisboa	10 Jul
73.82	Andrej	Benák	SVK	8.8.93	2		Bratislava	28 Aug
73.63		Huang Shih-Feng	TPE	2.3.92	2	NG	Changhua	25 Oct
73.62	Luanga	Andria	AUS	1.1.92	2		Launceston	25 Nov
73.59	Intars	Isejevs	LAT	15.2.93	2		Valmiera	10 Jun
73.58	Igor	Derevyanko	UKR	26.2.92	1	NC-j	Donetsk	16 Jun
73.50	Cody	Parker (20)	CAN	.92	2	PAm-J	Miramar	23 Jul

PENTATHLON

Points						Name		Nat	Born	Pos	Venue	Date
3644	6.89	59.49	23.38	39.24	4:32.77	Matthias	Laube	GER	24.5.83	1	Pliezhausen	16 Jul

DECATHLON

Points	Name		Nat	Born	Pos	Meet	Venue	Date
8729	Ashton	Eaton	USA	21.1.88	1	NC	Eugene	24 Jun
	10.33/0.6 7.80w/3.1 14.14 2.05 46.35 13.52/1.6 41.58 5.05 56.19 4:24.10							
8689	Trey	Hardee	USA	7.2.84	1		Götzis	29 May
	10.44/-0.7 7.88/0.6 15.63 2.00 48.12 13.73/0.0 45.20 5.06 63.33 4:46.88							
8607		Hardee			1	WCh	Daegu	28 Aug
	10.55/-0.5 7.45/0.1 15.09 2.02 48.37 13.97/-0.8 49.89 4.80 68.99 4:45.68							
8505		Eaton			2	WCh	Daegu	28 Aug
	10.46/-0.5 7.46/0.0 14.44 2.02 46.99 13.85/-0.8 46.17 4.60 55.17 4:18.94							
8501	Leonel	Suárez	CUB	1.9.87	3	WCh	Daegu	28 Aug
	11.07/-0.2 7.33 14.54 2.05 49.17 14.29/-0.7 46.25 5.00 69.12 4:24.16							

Mark	Name	Nat	Born	Pos	Meet	Venue	Date
8440	Suárez			2		Götzis	29 May
	11.06/0.6 7.21/-0.4 13.48		2.06 48.85			14.35/-0.9 44.57 4.86 75.49	4:25.33
8398	Mikk Pahapill	EST	18.7.83	3		Götzis	29 May
	11.08/0.9 7.39/-1.3 15.48		2.03 50.95			14.70/-0.9 48.79 5.06 69.53	4:39.41
8397	Yordani García	CUB	21.11.88	1		La Habana	6 May
	10.86/0.0 7.00/0.0 15.90		2.07 49.15			14.47/1.6 45.22 4.80 67.70	4:31.40
8373A	Suárez			1	PAm	Guadalajara, MEX	25 Oct
	11.01/1.6 7.39/0.1 14.64		2.08 49.76			14.26/1.4 45.54 4.80 72.19	4:45.78
8334	Aleksey Drozdov	RUS	3.12.83	1	NC	Cheboksary	10 Jun
	11.28/-0.8 7.27/0.0 16.31		2.12 51.67			14.98/0.0 51.24 5.10 63.82	4:45.00
8313	Drozdov			4	WCh	Daegu	28 Aug
	11.34/0.0 7.45/0.3 16.17		2.14 51.35			15.49/-0.1 50.29 5.00 64.80	4:41.73
8312	Edgars Erins	LAT	18.6.86	1	NC	Valmiera	4 Jun
	10.79w/2.1 7.67/0.2 14.19		1.90 48.65			14.56/1.2 49.94 4.50 58.30	4:14.25
8304	Eelco Sintnicolaas	NED	7.4.87	4		Götzis	29 May
	10.84/0.4 7.40/-0.9 14.31		1.91 48.69			14.57/-0.9 41.74 5.36 59.48	4:22.29
8302	Larbi Bouraada	ALG	10.5.88	1		Ratingen	17 Jul
	10.61w/3.4 7.94w/2.7 12.82		2.06 48.19			14.65/-0.3 40.34 4.70 58.05	4:21.42
8298	Sintnicolaas			5	WCh	Daegu	28 Aug
	10.76/0.5 7.29/0.3 14.13		1.93 48.35			14.42/-0.7 42.23 5.20 61.07	4:25.40
8288	Jan-Felix Knobel (10)	GER	16.1.89	5		Götzis	29 May
	11.14/-0.8 7.23/1.2 15.47		1.94 49.23			14.77/-0.4 46.68 4.96 72.99	4:43.39
8287	Rico Freimuth	GER	14.3.88	2		Ratingen	17 Jul
	10.50w/3.4 7.42w/2.2 14.44		1.88 48.46			14.14/-0.3 47.42 4.80 65.04	4:49.44
8256	Mihail Dudas	SRB	1.11.89	6	WCh	Daegu	28 Aug
	10.81/-0.5 7.41/0.5 13.76		2.02 47.73			14.89/-0.1 43.97 4.90 58.93	4:26.06
8251	Oleksiy Kasyanov	UKR	26.8.85	6		Götzis	29 May
	10.75/-0.7 7.38/0.8 14.08		2.03 48.11			14.26/-0.9 46.94 4.76 51.62	4:27.14
8232	Pascal Behrenbruch	GER	19.1.85	3		Ratingen	17 Jul
	10.86w/3.4 7.21/1.9 16.02		1.94 49.83			14.49/-0.3 46.33 4.40 71.40	4:36.17
8231	Suárez			1		Kladno	16 Jun
	11.17/-2.4 7.02/0.5 13.59		2.07 49.55			14.67/-2.6 45.66 5.00 67.18	4:27.98
8214A	Maurice Smith	JAM	28.9.80	2	PAm	Guadalajara, MEX	25 Oct
	10.86/1.6 7.36/-2.3 17.35		1.99 49.26			14.20/1.4 48.79 4.40 59.57	4:55.18
8211	Behrenbruch			7	WCh	Daegu	28 Aug
	11.08/-0.2 6.80/0.5 16.01		1.93 49.90			14.33/-0.5 48.56 4.90 66.50	4:36.64
8200	Knobel			8	WCh	Daegu	28 Aug
	11.18/0.0 7.30/0.4 16.06		1.96 49.46			14.92/-0.1 47.93 4.70 68.42	4:43.12
8200	Hans Van Alphen	BEL	12.1.82	1		Talence	18 Sep
	11.33/-08 7.24/-0.2 15.30		1.97 49.63			14.88/0.1 46.11 4.90 63.22	4:21.10
8184	Pahapill			2		Talence	18 Sep
	11.27/-0.2 7.23/0.7 15.51		1.97 50.32			14.38/0.1 46.58 5.10 61.53	4:38.43
8166	Vasiliy Kharlamov	RUS	8.10.86	1	WUG	Shenzhen	18 Aug
	11.25/0.7 7.37/0.0 15.01		1.95 49.76			14.95/-0.5 46.03 5.20 62.82	4:38.88
8170	Sintnicolaas			3		Talence	18 Sep
	10.88/0.0 7.30/0.1 13.92		1.94 48.66			14.40/0.1 36.51 5.40 60.40	4:29.11
8164	Pahapill			9	WCh	Daegu	28 Aug
	11.28/-0.2 7.12/0.3 14.76		2.02 50.65			14.54/-0.5 47.16 4.90 66.40	4:35.41
8158	Freimuth			7		Götzis	29 May
	10.79/0.4 7.11/-0.3 14.65		1.94 48.22			14.05/0.0 46.25 4.76 60.33	4:44.39
8158	Bouraada			10	WCh	Daegu	28 Aug
	10.88/0.0 7.42/0.2 13.11		1.96 47.34			14.56/-0.5 37.84 4.90 59.00	4:14.97
	(31/17)						
8157	Thomas Van Der Plaetsen	BEL	24.12.90	1	EU23	Ostrava	15 Jul
	11.29/-1.9 7.68/1.3 13.31		2.07 48.64			14.68/-0.9 37.73 5.10 63.57	4:35.84
8152	Eduard Mikhan	BLR	7.6.89	2	EU23	Ostrava	15 Jul
	10.77/1.6 7.54/0.6 13.98		1.95 48.02			14.80/-0.5 44.54 4.60 57.10	4:23.67
8134	Romain Barras	FRA	1.8.80	11	WCh	Daegu	28 Aug
	11.20/-0.2 7.06/0.0 14.92		1.99 49.50			14.37/-0.7 41.65 5.00 63.25	4:29.19
	(20)						
8118	Michael Morrison	USA	18.3.88	1	NCAA	Des Moines	9 Jun
	10.66w/2.8 7.52/0.8 13.00		1.87 48.06			14.48/1.8 41.82 5.00 60.47	4:35.35
8115	Luiz Alberto de Araújo	BRA	27.9.87	1	NC	São Paulo	6 Aug
	10.77/1.7 7.26/1.8 15.64		1.90 49.24			14.48/0.1 47.41 4.70 54.63	4:32.59
8114	Brent Newdick	NZL	31.1.85	8		Götzis	29 May
	10.95/0.6 7.45/0.4 14.17		1.94 49.61			14.76/-0.9 46.65 4.66 63.03	4:32.50
8114	Andres Raja	EST	2.6.82	1	ECp	Torun	3 Jul
	10.91/0.2 7.37/0.5 14.75		2.04 49.10			14.01/0.7 43.80 4.60 59.93	4:50.22
8109	Roman Sebrle	CZE	26.11.74	2	FRA Ch	Albi	29 Jul
	11.22/-0.5 7.45/2.5 15.56		2.02 51.61			14.77/0.4 47.06 4.70 68.90	4:51.70

Mark	Name			Nat	Born	Pos	Meet	Venue			Date
8105	Ingmar	Vos		NED	28.5.86	9		Götzis			29 May
	10.85/0.4	7.45/-0.4	13.94	2.00	51.12		14.45/-0.8	41.51	4.66	65.28	4:27.73
8102A	Damian	Warner		CAN	4.10.89	1	NC	Calgary			23 Jun
	10.41/0.4	7.36w/2.3	13.60	2.03	48.94		13.87/-1.0	45.67	4.30	56.30	4:44.64
8095	Willem	Coertzen		RSA	30.12.82	4		Ratingen			17 Jul
	10.97w/3.4	7.64w/2.6	13.52	2.03	49.78		14.49/-0.3	42.73	4.30	64.16	4:26.51
8089	Dmitriy	Karpov		KAZ	23.7.81	4		Kladno			16 Jun
	11.02/0.3	6.87/1.2	16.69	1.98	49.77		14.65/-1.8	51.18	5.10	51.82	4:52.73
8083	Curtis	Beach		USA	22.7.90	2	NCAA	Des Moines			9 Jun
	10.78/1.6	7.36/-1.1	12.08	2.02	46.90		14.76/0.4	38.07	4.80	48.42	3:59.13
	(30)										
8076w/8073	Keisuke	Ushiro		JPN	24.7.86	1	NC	Kawasaki			5 Jun
	11.39/-1.1	6.97W/7.3	13.71	2.06	50.28		14.93/0.5	43.67	4.90	73.06	4:35.83
	8073 with 6.96/0.9 LJ										
8068	Carlos Eduardo	Chinin		BRA	3.5.85	5		Kladno			16 Jun
	11.08/-2.4	7.39/1.0	13.57	2.07	49.38		14.33/-1.5	44.99	4.70	55.47	4:34.42
8058	Simon	Hechler		GER	15.6.88	1	vUSA	Chula Vista			14 Aug
	10.62w/1.5	7.67w/2.9	13.85	1.92	49.89		14.56/1.5	44.09	4.61	58.18	4:35.39
8053	Junior	Díaz		CUB	28.4.87	2		La Habana			6 May
	11.01/0.0	7.39/1.3	14.99	1.92	48.14		14.84/1.6	45.00	4.40	62.14	4:32.56
8023	Andrey	Kravchenko		BLR	4.1.86	5		Talence			18 Sep
	11.35/-0.8	7.26/1.0	14.16	2.06	50.16		14.44/-0.3	43.22	5.00	60.56	4:43.98
8011	Ryan	Harlan		USA	25.4.81	2	NC	Eugene			24 Jun
	11.17/0.2	6.66/0.4	16.51	2.05	52.04		14.48/1.5	46.37	4.95	65.10	4:56.44
8004	Mikhail	Logvinenko		RUS	19.4.84	3	NC	Cheboksary			10 Jun
	11.26/-0.8	7.25/0.3	13.77	1.97	48.72		14.32/0.8	46.26	5.10	46.75	4:28.95
7997	Norman	Müller		GER	7.8.85	12		Götzis			29 May
	11.07/0.6	7.30/0.7	14.82	2.00	49.43		14.98/-0.8	38.79	4.76	58.64	4:22.09
7996	Miller	Moss		USA	14.3.88	3	NCAA	Des Moines			9 Jun
	10.58w/2.8	7.24/1.6	13.59	1.99	47.23		14.10/-0.4	39.08	4.90	49.81	4:44.71
7993	Jangy	Addy		LBR	2.3.85	1	AfrG	Maputo			12 Sep
	10.61	7.76/-0.5	15.38	1.912	48.75		14.15	48.14	4.40	50.71	5:08.88
	(40)										
7992	Kevin	Mayer		FRA-J	10.2.92	8		Kladno			16 Jun
	11.23/0.1	7.34/0.2	12.44	2.01	48.66		14.74/-2.0	38.64	4.90	60.96	4:19.79
7986A	Gonzalo	Barroilhet		CHI	19.8.86	4	PAm	Guadalajara, MEX			25 Oct
	11.06/0.5	7.05/-0.2	14.21	2.05	51.08		14.23/1.4	43.40	5.30	56.24	4:54.34
7975	Rifat	Artikov		UZB	24.1.83	1		Tashkent			12 Jun
	10.97/2.0	6.76/-1.4	15.65	2.07	49.60		14.61/1.4	45.82	4.80	63.27	5:10.15
7973	Simon	Walter		SUI	13.3.85	1	ECp-1	Bressanone			3 Jul
	11.02w/2.1	7.25/0.7	13.80	2.04	48.97		14.96/1.4	42.94	4.90	55.40	4:37.58
7969	Adam Sebastian	Helcelet		CZE	27.10.91	1	NC	Praha			29 May
	11.04/0.5	7.21/-0.7	14.56	2.05	48.66		14.60/-1.5	39.99	4.60	59.36	4:39.75
7954	Aleksandr	Tabala		RUS	23.5.86	4	NC	Cheboksary			10 Jun
	11.75/-0.8	7.02/0.0	14.04	2.06	51.85		14.86/0.8	48.00	5.00	63.24	4:33.65
7942	Lars	Rise		NOR	23.11.88	4	NCAA	Des Moines			9 Jun
	11.16/1.8	7.06/0.1	15.65	1.93	49.77		15.23/0.0	40.95	4.60	68.12	4:31.23
7939	Gaël	Quérin		FRA	26.6.87	9		Kladno			16 Jun
	11.25/0.1	7.36/0.8	13.37	1.98	48.65		14.57/-2.6	40.46	4.60	55.11	4:14.52
7932	Florian	Geffrouais		FRA	5,12.88	3	NC	Albi			29 Jul
	11.07/2.1	7.18/1.0	15.43	1.90	49.18		14.94/0.4	40.90	4.60	60.12	4:25.18
7923(w)	Mathias	Prey		GER	9.8.88	6		Ratingen			17 Jul
	11.10w/3.8	7.52w/2.8	15.49	1.88	50.70		14.79/0.5	47.78	4.50	56.58	4:36.83
	(50)										
7914	Gray	Horn		USA	18.2.90	5	NCAA	Des Moines			9 Jun
	10.71w/2.8	7.43/1.4	12.61	1.99	49.42		14.32/1.8	37.13	4.90	52.32	4:29.45
7903	Michael	Ayers		USA	7.11.88	6	NCAA	Des Moines			9 Jun
	10.66w/2.8	7.54/-0.8	13.29	1.96	49.58		15.57/0.0	41.04	5.10	57.05	4:48.04
7894	Ilya	Shkurenov		RUS	11.1.91	5	EU23	Ostrava			15 Jul
	11.09/0.3	7.27/1.4	12.88	2.01	49.84		14.97/0.0	42.55	5.00	59.01	4:40.56
7889	Daniel	Awde		GBR	22.6.88	2	ECp-1	Bressanone			3 Jul
	10.67w/2.1	7.34/1.4	12.64	1.86	46.70		14.56/-1.3	40.44	5.10	43.65	4:29.52
7874	André	Niklaus		GER	30.8.81	8		Ratingen			17 Jul
	11.19w/3.8	7.12/1.2	14.85	1.94	51.12		14.35/0.5	46.74	4.70	62.08	4:53.22
7873	Pelle	Rietveld		NED	4.2.85	1		Woerden			28 Aug
	10.95/0.9	7.17/2.7	14.76	1.84	49.05		14.51/0.4	40.65	4.43	67.23	4.40.45
7870	Mateo	Sossah		FRA	28.4.88	7	NCAA	Des Moines			9 Jun
	11.38/1.8	7.20/1.5	13.00	2.05	49.40		14.66/0.4	40.24	4.70	56.05	4:19.72
7869	Artem	Lukyanenko		RUS	30.1.90	5	NC	Cheboksary			10 Jun
	10.92/-0.8	7.21/1.0	14.45	1.94	49.23		14.30/0.8	41.20	4.50	57.56	4:39.02

Mark	Name		Nat	Born	Pos	Meet	Venue				Date
7867(w)	Romain	Martin	FRA	12.7.88	2	TexR	Austin				7 Apr
	10.86w/3.6	7.10w/3.9 13.02	2.05	49.94		14.51/1.2	38.10	4.80	58.72		4:37.22
7860		Kim Kun-woo	KOR	29.2.80	17	WCh	Daegu				28 Aug
	11.11/-0.2	7.24/0.2 12.96	1.96	49.24		14.95/-0.1	39.53	4.90	53.33		4:15.63
(60)											
7846(w)	Joe	Detmer	USA	3.9.83	2	vGER	Chula Vista				14 Aug
	10.95/1.5	7.38w/2.4 12.11	1.92	49.35		15.07w/3.1	40.28	4.81	57.20		4:18.69
7845(w)	Steffen	Fricke	GER	25.3.83	3	vUSA	Chula Vista				14 Aug
	11.24/2.1	7.32w/2.4 14.22	2.07	49.26		14.79w/3.1	42.08	4.01	58.33		4:25.91
7845		Yu Bin	CHN	26.11.85	1	NC	Hefei				11 Sep
	10.99/1.2	7.27/-0.5 14.42	1.97	49.61		14.45/-1.1	42.03	4.60	56.64		4:46.25
7840	Dominik	Distelberger	AUT	16.3.90	14		Götzis				29 May
	10.79/-0.7	7.62/0.5 11.66	1.94	48.16		14.28/-0.8	39.69	4.76	50.26		4:36.05
7838	Moritz	Cleve	GER	18.2.87	8	NCAA	Des Moines				9 Jun
	10.94/1.8	6.78/0.6 14.41	1.90	48.41		14.55/-0.4	41.78	4.70	56.09		4:30.46
7826A	Román	Gastaldi	ARG	25.9.89	5	PAm	Guadalajara, MEX				25 Oct
	10.65/1.6	7.37/-0.7 14.01	1.99	49.54		14.71/1.7	43.08	4.20	55.97		4:42.95
7822	Yevgeniy	Sarantsev	RUS	5.8.88	2		Sochi				18 Sep
	11.32/1.5	7.16/0.6 14.19	1.94	50.99		15.08/-0.2	43.96	4.80	64.40		4:39.74
7818	Patrick	Spinner	GER	28.11.85	1		Bernhausen				5 Jun
	10.98/0.3	7.47/0.3 14.37	1.92	49.69		15.32/-0.1	38.86	4.50	63.93		4:35.96
7818	Cedric	Nolf	BEL	18.6.89	4	WUG	Shenzhen				18 Aug
	11.09/0.7	7.35/0.2 13.70	1.95	51.30		14.90/-0.4	39.76	4.90	66.89		4:59.66
7814(w)	Chris	Randolph	USA	25.4.84	1		Claremont				13 May
	11.25/1.2	6.99w/3.3 13.32	1.94	50.48		14.88w/3.3	46.06	4.73	61.54		4:32.79
(70)											
7813	Aleksandr	Parkhomenko	BLR	22.3.81	1		Minsk				8 Jun
	11.54/0.2	6.90/0.2 15.05	1.91	50.69		15.28/0.2	45.33	4.80	65.21		4:33.14
7806	Isaac	Murphy	USA	5.10.90	9	NCAA	Des Moines				9 Jun
	10.57w/2.8	7.22/1.0 12.54	1.84	48.28		14.65/1.0	42.18	4.60	52.53		4:26.49
7806	Tarmo	Riitmuru	EST	31.1.86	1	NC	Tartu				5 Aug
	11.40/-0.9	6.91/1.5 13.49	1.98	51.78		14.61/1.2	44.63	5.07	58.98		4:34.90
7802	Kai	Kazmirek	GER	28.1.91	1U23		Bernhausen				5 Jun
	10.97/0.6	7.27/0.8 12.56	2.10	48.16		14.86/-0.3	39.29	4.70	48.80		4:34.86
7802	Kevin	Lazas	USA-J	25.1.92	10	NCAA	Des Moines				9 Jun
	10.96/1.6	7.39/1.7 13.15	1.96	50.58		15.29/0.0	40.46	4.90	58.78		4:36.34
7800(w)	Ânderson	Venâncio	BRA	6.1.87	2	NC	São Paulo				6 Aug
	10.80/1.7	7.09w/3.1 13.96	1.93	49.36		14.65/0.1	39.99	5.00	59.39		5:01.01
7795	Yevgen	Nikitin	UKR	9.1.85	1	NC	Donetsk				3 Aug
	11.09/1.1	6.97/0.0 14.43	1.97	49.68		15.22/1.1	42.18	4.70	59.87		4:36.96
7789	Ashley	Bryant	GBR	17.5.91	5	WUG	Shenzhen				18 Aug
	11.08/0.1	7.48/0.3 13.52	1.89	48.59		14.71/-0.5	40.46	4.30	64.08		4:39.51
7770	Andrey	Demyanov	RUS	22.8.86	6	NC	Cheboksary				10 Jun
	11.70/-0.8	7.19 13.39	2.00	50.49		14.82/0.8	44.06	4.80	60.44		4:36.65
7760	Frédéric	Xhonneux	BEL	11.5.83	1	NC	Dilbeek				7 Aug
	11.70/04	7.07/0.1 13.79	1.99	49.79		15.26/-0.1	41.92	4.80	57.11		4:18.59
(80)											
7742	Jeremy	Taiwo	USA	15.1.90	1	Pac-10	Tucson				7 May
	10.98/0.7	7.30/1.0 13.08	2.11	48.49		14.41w/3.9	36.22	4.82	32.85		4:18.69
7736	Chris	Helwick	USA	18.3.85	4	NC	Eugene				24 Jun
	11.42/0.2	6.88/-0.1 13.32	1.96	51.19		15.36/2.0	44.89	4.85	62.70		4:29.00
7734	Darius	Draudvila	LTU	29.3.83	10		Kladno				16 Jun
	10.84/0.3	7.27w/2.2 15.61	1.98	49.49		14.31/-2.6	41.52	4.50	55.20		5:19.70
7734	Stephen	Cain	AUS	23.7.84	11		Kladno				16 Jun
	11.42/-1.6	6.90/1.8 14.22	1.95	50.39		15.00/-2.0	42.50	4.80	59.88		4:32.75
7731	Hamdhi	Dhouibi	TUN	24.1.82	3		Desenzano del Garda				8 May
	11.18/-2.1	6.78/-2.7 14.54	1.89	48.87		14.75w/3.3	42.98	4.55	57.91		4:32.37
7731	Sami	Itani	FIN	24.3.87	1	NC	Turku				7 Aug
	11.32/-0.2	6.93/0.2 14.61	2.04	50.78		14.62/1.4	45.70	4.53	55.25		4:45.60
7724	Petter	Olson	SWE	14.2.91	8	EU23	Ostrava				15 Jul
	10.99/1.6	7.09/0.6 12.90	1.95	48.36		14.73/-0.9	40.54	4.60	50.66		4:26.29
7719	Aleksey	Sysoyev	RUS	8.3.85	10		Ratingen				17 Jul
	11.20w/3.4	6.68w/2.1 15.72	1.94	52.72		15.76/0.5	50.21	4.80	60.11		4:42.75
7717	Maximilian	Gilde	GER	5.1.90	2U23		Bernhausen				5 Jun
	11.20/0.5	7.50/1.0 12.93	1.98	49.58		15.07/-0.3	41.36	4.40	59.85		4:39.51
7712	Lars	Albert	GER	9.2.82	1		Hannover				26 Jun
	11.44	6.99 15.59	1.88	51.79		15.14	46.40	4.80	59.41		4:41.17
(90)											
7710	Quentin	Jammier	FRA	24.7.88	5		Desenzano del Garda				8 May
	11.61/-0.4	6.77/-1.5 14.47	1.95	50.03		15.10w/4.0	41.20	4.75	59.22		4:20.81

Mark	Name			Nat	Born	Pos	Meet	Venue			Date
7707	Thorsten	Margis		GER	14.8.89	11		Ratingen			17 Jul
	10.75w/3.8	7.32w/2.4	14.75	1.88	49.51	16.12/-0.7	44.12	4.50	57.06		4:41.70
7686w	Matt	Johnson		USA	4.10.89	3	TexR	Austin			7 Apr
	10.58W/4.4	7.41W/5.4	12.32	1.87	51.14	15.10/1.9	45.77	4.80	59.68		5:03.55
7685	Ali	Kamé		MAD	21.5.84	1		Bambous			17 Apr
	11.03w/2.9	7.33/0.7	13.65	2.02	50.00	15.20/-3.0	36.66	4.40	58.78		4:33.60
7683	Bastien	Auzeil		FRA	22.10.89	1		Aubagne			12 Jun
	11.20/1.5	7.03/1.9	15.28	2.01	51.55	15.00/-1.8	42.72	5.00	55.54		5:05.43
7682	José Ángel	Mandieta		CUB	16.10.91	1		La Habana			27 May
	11.08/-1.28	7.12/-1.1	15.35	1.88	49.63	14.70/-1.0	37.80	4.30	55.54		5:05.43
7681	William	Valor		VEN	11.11.84	1	NG	Barquisimeto			13 Dec
	11.04/0.0	7.13w/2.5	13.96	2.02	49.86	15.06/-0.5	40.51	4.40	61.95		4:53.19
7679	Nick	Adcock		USA	2.4.88	5	vGER	Chula Vista			14 Aug
	11.23/1.1	7.28/0.8	13.52	1.98	48.85	14.41/1.5	38.32	4.61	51.32		4:39.58
7679A	Georni	Jaramillo		VEN	6.3.89	6	PAm	Guadalajara, MEX			25 Oct
	10.85/1.6	7.41/-1.4	14.96	1.84	48.30	14.22/1.4	41.99	3.90	56.35		4:52.26
7678	Nikolay	Shubyanok		BLR	4.5.85	6	ECp	Torun			3 Jul
	11.55/0.1	7.09/-0.1	14.90	2.01	50.89	14.73/0.8	40.01	4.40	58.76		4:31.80

(100)

Mark		Name	Nat	Born	Date
7677	Mohamed Jassem	Al-Qaree	KSA	11.5.88	20 Dec
7675	Akihiko	Nakamura	JPN	23.10.90	15 May
7661	Aleksandr	Korzun	BLR	17.3.85	3 Jul
7658	Bhartender	Singh	IND	23.10.88	12 Jun
7654	Thomas	Barrineau	FIN	28.8.88	13 May
7651	Björn	Barrefors	SWE	27.10.87	10 Jun
7627		Zhu Hengjun	CHN	5.2.87	11 Sep
7625	Philipp	Britner	RUS	11.9.86	10 Jun
7616	Aleksandr	Kislov	RUS	4.11.84	10 Jun
7607w	Tom	Fitzsimons	USA	8.3.89	7 Apr
7601	Sergey	Sviridov	RUS	20.10.90	10 Jun
7600	Takumi	Otobe	JPN	22.4.89	10 Sep
7599	Anatoliy	Koshar	BLR	11.6.89	8 Jun
7598	Marcin	Drózdz	POL	21.3.83	29 May
7593	Lars Niklas	Heinke	GER	7.11.89	5 Jun
7593	Nick	Huber	USA	7.6.89	9 Apr
7592	Aleksandr	Frolov	RUS	5.3.87	10 Jun
7587	Einar Dadi	Lárusson	ISL	10.5.90	16 Jun
7583	Kenny	Greaves	USA	13.10.88	14 May
7581	David	Klech	USA	29.4.88	7 May
7577w/7524	Gunnar	Nixon	USA-J	13.1.93	9 Apr
7576	Mark	Jellison	USA	25.4.80	24 Jun
7571(w)	Wesley	Bray	USA	11.4.88	7 Apr
7558	Eric	Broadbent	USA	5.8.85	11 May
7558	Hiromasa	Tanaka	JPN	28.9.81	5 Jun
7554	Ivan	Grigoryev	RUS	27.10.89	10 Jun
7546	Mattias	Cerlati	FRA	25.10.83	12 Jun
7541	François	Gourmet	BEL	28.12.82	7 Aug
7539	William	Frullani	ITA	21.9.79	3 Jul
7528	Jérémy	Solot	BEL	2.3.87	3 Jul
7528	Tom	Bechert	GER	2.7.87	12 Jun
7525	Frantisek	Stanek	CZE	11.1.87	3 Jul
7514	Phil	Adam	USA	21.5.87	13 May
7514	Ryota	Tsujii	JPN	6.7.86	19 Nov
7510	Ben	Hazell	GBR	1.10.84	7 Aug
7506	Hadi	Sepehrzad	IRI	19.1.83	8 Jul
7504	Marcin	Przybyl	POL	16.3.89	29 May
7502		Qi Haifeng	CHN	7.8.83	11 Sep
7501	Andréas	Tsoúkalis	GRE	9.8.82	5 Jun
7500	Jarrod	Sims	AUS	11,6,84	1 Apr
7500	Matthew	Clark	USA	31.5.87	28 Apr
7493	David	Sazima	CZE	8.12.87	29 May
7489	Daisuke	Ikeda	JPN	15.4.86	5 Jun
7489	Jonas	Fringeli	SUI	12.1.88	28 Aug
7488	Martin	Brockman	GBR	13.11.87	7 Aug
7479	Guillaume	Thierry	MRI	15.9.86	12 Sep
7478	Nick	Armstrong	USA	15.12.87	14 Apr
7472	Szymon	Czapiewski	POL	19.5.89	29 May
7468	Ryu	Murata	JPN	15.3.88	5 Jun
7468	Jérémy	Lelièvre	FRA	8.2.91	12 Jun
7465w	Bruno	Carton-Delcourt	BEL	15.2.88	28 Aug
7462(w)	Brent	Vogel	USA	2.5.90	27 May
7456	Steffen	Kahlert	GER	30.5.87	26 Jun
7449	Björn	Johansson	SWE	31.3.88	10 Jun
7441	Agustín	Félix	ESP	14.3.79	5 Jun
7436	Renato	da Cámara	BRA	16.9.85	6 Aug
7435	Adam	Nejedly	CZE	3.2.88	16 Jun
7435	Tiago	Marto	POR	5.4.86	18 Aug
7431	Sors	Joubert	RSA	24.5.84	17 Apr
7423	Keith	Baker	USA	2.6.83	5 Jun
7420	Patrick	Scherfose	GER	28.11.91	5 Jun
7417	David	Kallebäck	SWE	14.4.89	30 Jun
7410	Adriaan	Saman	NED	12.10.83	22 May
7409	Julian	Ade	GER	30.5.87	22 May
7400	Marcus	Nilsson	SWE	3.5.91	3 Jul

Best at low altitude

Mark	Name			Nat	Born	Pos	Meet	Venue			Date
8078	Maurice	Smith		JAM	28.9.80	1	NACAC	Kingston			28 May
	10.94/-1.8	7.16w/2.2	16.88	1.91	49.80	14.01/0.6	47.61	4.60	56.60		4:48.13
7845	Gonzalo	Barroilhet		CHI	19.8.86	2	BRA Ch	São Paulo			6 Aug
	11.17/2.0	7.28w/3.5	10.44	2.02	50.91	14.05/0.1	42.99	5.30	57.83		4:47.89
7832	Damian	Warner		CAN	4.10.89	18	WCh	Daegu			28 Aug
	10.56/-0.5	7.35/1.1	13.26	2.02	50.12	14.19/-0.8	41.71	4.50	54.61		4:54.37

Best without wind assistance

Mark	Name			Nat	Born	Pos	Meet	Venue			Date
7827	Mathias	Prey		GER	9.8.88	4	vUSA	Chula Vista			14 Aug
	11.28/1.1	7.38/2.0	16.20	1.86	51.00	15.05/1.5	50.88	4.21	58.87		4:39.78
7727	Romain	Martin		FRA	12.7.88	11	NCAA	Des Moines			9 Jun
	10.91w/2.8	7.17/0.1	13.25	1.99	49.48	14.94/0.5	38.58	4.70	58.96		4:46.00

Mark		Name	Nat	Born	Date
7675	Matt	Johnson	USA	4.10.89	14 Aug
7664	Chris	Randolph	USA	25.4.84	14 Apr
7610	Steffen	Fricke	GER	25.3.83	17 Jul
7430	Ânderson	Venâncio	BRA	6.1.87	28 Aug

Note that the NCAA event at Des Moines was held over three days (8-10 June) due to bad weather

JUNIORS

See main list for top 2 juniors. 13 performances by 5 men to 78.50. Additional marks and further juniors:

Lazas   7702   2   SEC   Athens, GA   13 May   Nixon (below) 7524 with LJ 7.14/1.4

Mark	Name			Nat	Born	Pos	Meet	Venue			Date
7577w/7524	Gunnar	Nixon		USA-J	13.1.93	1		Arcadia			9 Apr
	11.06/0.6	7.36w/4.4	12.14	2.02	48.37	14.60/2.0	35,38	4.40	52.00		4:39.64
7115	Liam	Ramsay		GBR	18.11.92	1	GBR	Stoke-on-Trent			4 Sep
	11.11/-1.7	6.81/0.4	12.36	1.92	49.17	14.96/1.9	34.78	4.04	45.99		4:32.58

Mark	Name		Nat	Born	Pos	Meet	Venue	Date
7085	Juuso	Hassi	FIN	4.4.93	4	NC	Turku	7 Aug
	11.41/-0.2 6.59/0.7 11.70		1.83 49.93		15.20/1.4 39.75 4.43 56.75			4:49.17
7078	Danilo Rey	Batista	CUB	5.4.92	3	NC	La Habana	18 Mar
	11.37/-1.8 6.97/0.0 11.32		1.86 50.06		14.92/-1.3 38.41 3.60 59.72			4:36.76
7032	William	Markert	USA	.92	10	YexR	Austin	7 Apr
	11.23w/3.6 6.53w/5.0 13.97		1.93 53.56		15.44/2.0 41.90 4.60 46.06			4:57.80
7025	Auston	Chen	USA	7.3.92	5		Fayetteville	23 Apr
	10.70w/4.9 7.30w/3.1 13.36		1.64 50.75		15.46/0.1 42.93 4.10 44.00			4:56.39
7015		Li Mingyang	CHN	15.3.93	9	NC	Hefei	11 Sep
	11.17/0.6 7.03/-0.5 11.28		1.88 49.13		15.81/-0.5 37.65 4.00 48.80			4:37.20

IAAF JUNIOR SPECIFICATION – WITH 99CM 110MH, 6KG SP, 1.75KG DT

Mark	Name		Nat	Born	Pos	Meet	Venue	Date
8124	Kévin	Mayer	FRA	10.2.92	1	EJ	Tallin	24 Jul
	11.40/-1.7 7.52/1.5 14.65		2.04 49.41		14.09/0.7 41.00 4.80 56.60			4:25.23
8016	Kevin	Lazas	USA	25.1.92	1	NC-j	Eugene	25 Jun
	11.11/0.4 7.35/1.1 15.24		1.99 50.95		14.80/0.3 45.08 5.05 59.38			4:50.52
	7979(w) 1 PAm-J Miramar		23 Jul					
7853	Mathias	Brugger	GER	6.8.92	2	EJ	Tallinn	24 Jul
	11.37/-1.7 7.35/1.3 14.71		2.01 50.25		14.56/-0.4 44.91 4.60 51.52			4:34.10
	7730 1 NC Vaterstetten		28 Aug	7702	1		Büdelsdorf	15 May
7846	Johannes	Hock	GER	24.3.92	1		Bernhausen	5 Jun
	10.94/0.7 6.88/0.4 15.71		1.89 49.96		14.59/-0.3 46.84 4.70 57.28			4:51.06
	7806 1 EJ Tallinn		24 Jul					
7749	Steffen	Klink	GER	3.2.92	2		Bernhausen	5 Jun
	11.14/0.7 7.01/0.9 14.67		2.04 51.57		14.41/-0.3 44.09 4.50 53.95			4:41.22
7748	Gunnar	Nixon	USA	13.1.93	2	NC-j	Eugene	24 Jun
	11.03/0.4 7.30/0.3 13.09		2.14 49.35		14.39/0.3 41.75 4.15 51.81			4:43.68
7725	Mark	Jacobs	NED	20.4.92	4	EJ	Tallinn	24 Jul
	10.98/-1.3 7.40w/3.0 12.79		1.95 49.27		14.66/0.7 43.81 4.50 53.36			4:43.49
7668	Pavel	Rudnev	RUS	26.10.92	1	NC-j	Cheboksary	10 Jun
	11.15/0.0 7.47/0.0 13.28		2.06 50.02		14.42/1.6 38.06 4.70 45.80			4:42.52
7639	Reinis	Kregers	LAT	22.1.92	5	EJ	Tallinn	24 Jul
	11.31/-0.1 6.90/0.0 15.05		2.04 51.70		15.70/-0.1 45.41 4.60 59.54			4:49.50
7618	Martin	Røe (10)	NOR	1.4.92	7	EJ	Tallinn	24 Jul
	11.11/-1.3 7.10/1.8 14.91		1.86 49.69		15.48/-0.1 46.91 4.10 62.46			4:47.55
7575	Aleksey	Spirin	BLR	3.6.92	1	NC-j	Brest	15 Jun
	11.54/0.8 6.81/2.2 15.28		2.03 50.36		14.92/1.2 43.46 4.20 54.50			4:36.28
7526	Aleksandr	Kopeykin	RUS	4.1.92	2	NC-j	Cheboksary	10 Jun
	11.14/0.0 7.42/0.0 14.22		1.94 51.33		14.55/1.6 43.25 4.50 52.09			5:06.99
7501w	Dominik	Alberto	SUI	28.4.92	1		Landquart	22 May
	10.92w/4.3 6.70/1.9 14.33		1.86 48.82		14.26w/2.2 39.73 4.80 48.85			4:54.52
7474	Pieter	Braun	NED	21.1.93	1	NC-j	Emmeloord	22 May
	11.63/0.0 7.09w/2.7 14.16		2.02 50.15		14.80/0.0 42.34 4.00 51.59			4:32.15
7453	Karl-Robert	Saluri	EST	6.8.93	8	EJ	Tallinn	24 Jul
	11.10/-1.3 7.25/1.8 14.21		1.83 49.75		15.57/-0.1 36.65 4.50 53.32			4:30.12
7408	Maicel	Uibo	EST	27.12.92	1		Rakvere	24 Sep
	11.38w/2.8 7.10w/2.3 14.00		1.90 53.23		15.19/0.9 41.59 4.60 54.07			4.34.55
7400	Juuso	Hassi	FIN	4.4.93	9	EJ	Tallinn	24 Jul
	11.45/-1.7 6.66/2.6 13.56		1.83 49.60		14.86/0.7 45.95 4.40 57.95			4:48.97
7369	Niels	Pittomvils	NED	18.7.92	11	EJ	Tallinn	24 Jul
	11.62/-0.1 6.81/2.4 13.18		1.86 51.52		15.05/-0.1 44.09 4.60 58.35			4:40.82
7330	Christian	Loosli	SUI	12.6.92	1		Götzis	12 Jun
	11.48/-0.2 6.82/0.0 13.38		1.96 50.70		15.12/0.5 38.46 4.10 63.33			4:43.08
7308w	Liam	Ramsay	GBR	18.11.92	1	N.Sch	Exeter	18 Sep
	11.00w/4.6 6.94w/2.6 12.78		1.96 49.26		14.46/1.2 37.66 4.03 43.75			4:33.44

4 X 100 METRES RELAY

Mark	Nat	Team	Pos	Meet	Venue	Date
37.04	JAM	N.Carter, Frtaer, Blake, Bolt	1	WCh	Daegu	4 Sep
37.79	USA	Kimmons, Gatlin, M.Mitchell, Padgett	1h1	WCh	Daegu	4 Sep
37.91	TRI	Bledman, Burns, Armstrong, Thompson	1h2	WCh	Daegu	4 Sep
38.07	JAM	N.Carter, Frater, Blake, Lee	2h2	WCh	Daegu	4 Sep
38.18A	BRA	Feitosa, Viana, André, de Barros	1	PAm	Guadalajara	28 Oct
38.20	FRA	Tinmar, Lemaitre, Lesourd, Vicaut	2	WCh	Daegu	4 Sep
38.29	GBR	Malcolm, Pickering, Devonish, Aikines-Aryeetey	1h3	WCh	Daegu	4 Sep
38.31	USA	Merritt, Padgett, I.Williams, J. Brown	1	WK	Zürich	8 Sep
38.33	JAM	Powell, Frater, N.Carter, Mullings	1	PennR	Philadelphia	30 Apr
38.35	GBR	Ellington, Pickering, Devonish, Lewis-Francis	2	WK	Zürich	8 Sep
38.37	POL	Stempel, Kuc, Kubaczyk, Krynski	2h3	WCh	Daegu	4 Sep
38.38	FRA	Tinmar, Lemaitre, Lesourd, Vicaut	2h1	WCh	Daegu	4 Sep
38.41	USA	Team Speed Unlimited Kimmons, Rodgers, Patton, Spearmon	1	TexR	Austin	9 Apr

Mark	Name	Nat	Born	Pos	Meet	Venue	Date
38.41	ITA	Tumi, Collio, Di Gregorio, Cerutti		3h3	WCh	Daegu	4 Sep
38.43	USA Red	Dix, Spearmon, Kimmons, Rodgers		2	PennR	Philadelphia	30 Apr
38.47	SKN	Rogers, Collins, Adams, Lawrence		3	WCh	Daegu	4 Sep
38.49	University of Florida USA	Lovett, CTaylor, Wilks, Demps		1h2	NCAA	Des Moines	8 Jun
38.49	SKN	Rogers, Collins, Adams, Lawrence		3h2	WCh	Daegu	4 Sep

(20 performances by teams from 9 nations)

Mark	Name	Nat	Born	Pos	Meet	Venue	Date
38.62	SUI	Mancini, Schenkel, Wilson, Schneeberger (10)		3	WK	Zürich	8 Sep
38.65	CAN	Smellie, S.Smith, Connaughton, Barnett		1	G Gala	Roma	26 May
38.66	GER	Unger, Broening, Ernst, Keller		1		Regensburg	4 Jun
38.66	JPN	Kobayashi, Eriguchi, Takahira, Saito		4h2	WCh	Daegu	4 Sep
38.69	AUS	Alozie, M.Davies, Rouge-Serret, Ntiamoah		4h3	WCh	Daegu	4 Sep
38.72	RSA	Dreyer, Mogawane, Engel, Mpuang		5h2	WCh	Daegu	4 Sep
38.87	CHN	Chen, Liang, Su, Lao		6h2	WCh	Daegu	4 Sep
38.93	GHA	Appiah, Agyapong, Abeyie, Zakari		1		Kumasi	6 Aug
38.93	NGR	Adukwu, Emelieze, Metu, Egweru		1	AfrG	Maputo	13 Sep
39.04	KOR	Yeo, Jeon, Kim, Lim		1r2	As GP	Jiaxing	22 May
39.04	PUR	Amalbert, Rodríoguez, Holston, M López		7h2	WCh	Daegu	4 Sep

(20)

Mark	Name	Nat	Born	Pos	Meet	Venue	Date
39.09	RUS	Brednyev, Petryashkov, Smirnov, Khuytte		4r2	ET	Stockhom	18 Jun
39.09	NED	van Kruchten, van Luijk, Mariano, Martina		4		Lignano	19 Jul
39.09	POR	Monteiro, Ferreira, Abrantes, Nascimento		3h1	WCh	Daegu	4 Sep
39.09	BOT	Seribe, Kenosi, Ketlogetswe, Ngwigwa		3	AfrG	Maputo	13 Sep
39.24	HKG	Tang, Lai, Ng, Tsui		3	As GP	Jiaxing	22 May
39.27	CZE	Veleba, Vojtik, Sulc, Milo		1	Odlozil	Praha	13 Jun
39.29	BAH	Rolle, Griffith, Pinder, Mathieu		2h1	CAC	Mayagüez	16 Jul
39.30	TPE	Liang, Liu, Tsai, Yi		3	AsiC	Kobe	10 Jul
39.34	CUB	Lescay, Skyers, Herrera, Hernández		1	Alba	Barquisimeto	29 Jul
39.35A	COL	Montoya, Gómez, Mosquera, Grueso		1		Cali	18 Jun

(30)

39.48	FIN	24 Jul	39.67	KSA	20 Dec	39.83	LTU	30 Jul	39.91	INA	15 Nov	39.96	NOR	18 Jun
39.49	OMA	18 Oct	39.68A	CHI	28 Oct	39.85	ESP	18 Jun	39.91	SIN	15 Nov	39.98A	KEN	14 Jul
39.50	CIV	13 Sep	39.71	DEN	18 Jun	39.85	MRI	13 Sep	39.93	DOM	16 Jul	**Hand timed**		
39.54	THA	4 Sep	39.76A	ECU	28 Oct	39.85	UAE	28 Oct	39.94	IND	19 Feb	39.9A	KEN (Pr16	Jul
39.61	IRL	18 Jun	39.81	TUR	2 Jul	39.89	HUN	18 Jun	39.94	SWE	18 Jun			

Best at low altitude: 38.77 BRA Feotosa, de Morães, André, Viana — 1 São Paulo 22 May

Mixed nationality teams

Mark	Name	Nat	Pos	Meet	Venue	Date
38.20	All Stars Saidy Ndure/NOR, M.Mitchell/USA, Dodson/USA, Thompson/TRI	2		Lignano	19 Jul
38.38	Texas A&M Un. Howell, Phiri/ZIM, Pinder/BAH, Hardy	1s3	NCAA	Des Moines	8 Jun
38.43	Racers TC Bailey/ANT, Rose, K.Anderson, Blake all JAM	1		Kingston	12 Mar

Drugs disqualification

Mark	Name	Nat	Pos	Meet	Venue	Date
37.90	USA Kimmons, Rodgers #, Gatlin, Dix	(1)		Lignano	19 Jul
38.23	USA Stars & Stripes Kimmons, Rodgers #, Tinsley, J Brown	(1)	LGP	London (CP)	6 Aug
38.94	KOR Yeo, Cho, Kim, Lim ¶	(5h3)	WCh	Daegu	4 Sep

JUNIORS

Mark	Name	Nat	Pos	Meet	Venue	Date
39.35	FRA	V Michalet, Vicaut, John, Romain	1	EJ	Tallinn	24 Jul
39.43	USA	McLean, Bracy, Brock, Bradwell	1	PAm-J	Miramar	24 Jul
39.48	JPN		4		Kawasaki	8 May
39.48	GBR	Walker-Khan, Watts, Gemili, Bolarinwa	2		Tallinn	24 Jul
39.63A	BRA	da Silva Barbosa, da Silva Jr, César da Silva, Rocha	1	SAm-J	Medellín	25 Sep
39.75	JAM	Todd, Bailey, Brown, Murphy	1	Carifta	Montego Bay	24 Apr
39.86	CHN	(Guangzhou)	1	NC-j	Jinan	5 Jun
39.91	TRI	Holder, Morain, Taffe, James	2	Carifta	Montego Bay	24 Apr
39.97	CAN	Laidlaw-Allen, Brown, Haynes, Harris	2	PAm-J	Miramar	24 Jul
40.08A	COL	Valois, Palomeque, Valoyes, Cuero	2	SAm-J	Medellín	25 Sep
40.26	BAH	Barlett, Hart, Davis, Mackey	3	PAm-J	Miramar	24 Jul
40.40	POL		1		Warszawa	18 Jun

4 X 200 METRES RELAY

Mark	Name	Pos	Meet	Venue	Date
1:20.45	Louisiana State Un. USA Talley, C Williams, Walker, Mvumvure ZIM	1	TexR	Austin	9 Apr
	Talley, C Williams, Walker, Mvumvure ZIM				
1:20.62	LSU USA Hylton JAM, C Williams, Walker, Mvumvure ZIM	1	PennR	Philadelphia	30 Apr
1:20.72	Texas A&M University Howell, Phiri ZAM, Henry ISV, Pinder BAH	2	PennR	Philadelphia	30 Apr

4 X 400 METRES RELAY

Mark	Name	Pos	Meet	Venue	Date
2:58.82	USA Nixon 45.1, Torrance 43.9, Berry 43.95, Merritt 45.87	1h1	WCh	Daegu	1 Sep
2:59.13	JAM Fothergill 45.3, Hylton 44.4, Spence 44.79, L.Green 44.66	2h1	WCh	Daegu	1 Sep
2:59.21	RSA Pistorius 45.58, Mogawane 43.97, de Beer 44.46, Victor 45.20	3h1	WCh	Daegu	1 Sep
2:59.31	USA Nixon 44.8, Jackson 45.4, Taylor 45.00, Merritt 44.17	1	WCh	Daegu	2 Sep
2:59.43A	CUB Ruíz 44.9, Acea 44.9, Cisneros 44.6, Collazo 45.1	1	PAm	Guadalajara	28 Oct
2:59.87	RSA Victor 46.0, Mogawane 43.9, de Beer 44.88, van Zyl 45.03	2	WCh	Daegu	2 Sep
3:00.10	JAM Fothergill 45.5, Gonzales 44.2, Hylton 44.94, L.Green 45.53	3	WCh	Daegu	2 Sep

Mark	Name	Nat	Born	Pos	Meet	Venue	Date
3:00.22	RUS	Dyldin 45.5, Svechkar 45.6, Trenikhin 44.80, Alekseyev 44.41		4	WCh	Daegu	2 Sep
3:00.38	GBR	Strachan 46.0, Levine 45.1, Clarke 44.99, Rooney 44.56		4h1	WCh	Daegu	1 Sep
3:00.41	BEL	J.Borlée 45.0, Gillet 45.6, Duerinck 45.76, K.Borlée 44.11		5	WCh	Daegu	2 Sep
3:00.44A	DOM	Guesta 46.2, Peguero 44.6, Tapia 45.2, L Santos 44.5		2	PAm	Guadalajara	28 Oct
3:00.68	GER	Plass 45.8, Gaba 44.8, Krüger 45.18, Schneider 44.90		5h1	WCh	Daegu	1 Sep
3:00.71	BEL	Gillet 46.45, J.Borlée 44.24, Duerinck 45.42, K.Borlée 44.19		1h2	WCh	Daegu	1 Sep
3:00.80	USA	GW Express J.Scott, C.Smith, Torrance, B.Jackson		1	Fla R	Gainesville	2 Apr
3:00.81	RUS	Dyldin 46.1, Svechkar 45.4, Trenikhin 44.52, Alekseyev 44.77		2h2	WCh	Daegu	1 Sep
3:00.82A	VEN	Ramírez 45.7, Aguilar 45.3, Acevedo 44.7, Longart 45.2		3	PAm	Guadalajara	28 Oct
3:00.97	KEN	Kosgei 45.8, Mutegi 45.4, Mumo 45.0, Mutai 44.8		3h2	WCh	Daegu	1 Sep
3:01.15	KEN	V Kosgei 45.9, Kiilu 45.5, Mutegi 45,34, Mutai 44.48		6	WCh	Daegu	2 Sep
3:01.16	GBR	Strachan 46.25, Levine 45.32, Clarke 45.47, Rooney 44.12		7	WCh	Daegu	2 Sep
3:01.33	BAH	L.Wiliiams, Moncur, Mathieu, Miller		1	CAC	Mayagüez	17 Jul
3:01.37	GER	Plass 45.6, Gaba 45.6, Rigau 45.61, Schneider 44.61		8	WCh	Daegu	2 Sep

(21 performances by teams from 12 nations)

Mark	Name	Nat	Born	Pos	Meet	Venue	Date
3:01.56	AUS	Offereins 46.6, Thomas 44.8, Solomon 45.40, Wroe 44.75		5h2	WCh	Daegu	1 Sep
3:01.65	TRI	L.Gordon, Solomon, Lendore, Quow		2	CAC	Mayagüez	17 Jul
3:01.84	POL	Kozlowski 46.5, Wiaderek 44.8, Krzewina 45.68, Marciniszyn 44.90		6h2	WCh	Daegu	1 Sep
3:02.64	JPN	Takase 46.0, Kanemaru 44.6, Ishitsuka 47.02, Hirose 44.98		7h1	WCh	Daegu	1 Sep
3:03.33	FRA	Fillon 46.2, Venel 45.4, Hanne 45.68, Anne 45.94		2r2	ET	Stockholm	19 Jun
3:03.92	TUR	Kayas, Kilic, Can, Tamaç		1		Ankara	9 Aug
3:04.05	KOR	Park 46.7, Lim 44.8, Lee 46.71, Sung 44.89		8h1	WCh	Daegu	1 Sep
3:04.27	GRN	Redhead, James, Charles, Bartholomew		5	CAC	Mayagüez	17 Jul

(20)

Mark	Name	Nat	Born	Pos	Meet	Venue	Date
3:04.39	BOT	Ketlogetswe, Ngwigwa, Kamberuka, Makwala		3	NA	Heusden	16 Jul
3:04.99	NGR	Ogunkole, Godday, Ogunmola, Welgopwa		1	NC	Calabar	25 Jun
3:05.65	KSA	Al-Sabyani 47.4, Al-Masrahi 46.1, Al-Bishi 47.22, Al-Salhi 44.93		8h2	WCh	Daegu	1 Sep
3:05.66	ITA	Juarez, Galletti, Galvan, Vistalli		1r1	ET	Stockholm	19 Jun
3:05.69	BRA	A da Silva, de Almeida, Neto, Kléberson		1	NC	São Paulo	7 Aug
3:05.76	PUR	Holston, Mason, Alejandro, Cruz		7	CAC	Mayagüez	17 Jul
3:05.80	CHN	Liaoning Su Pengfei, Sun Yi, Zhang Yunpeng, Wang Xiaolong		1	NC	Hefei	11 Sep
3:05.93	UKR	Hutsol, Melnykov, Knysh, Burakov		5r2	ET	Stockholm	19 Jun
3:06.30	GRE	Grávalos, Dardaneliótis, S Iakovákis, P Iakovákis		2r2	ET-1	Izmir	19 Jun
3:06.42	HUN	Z Kovács, Kolossváry, Lukács, Deák Nagy		3r2	ET-1	Izmir	19 Jun

(30)

Mark	Nat	Date		Mark	Nat	Date		Mark	Nat	Date		Mark	Nat	Date
3:06.76	IRL	19 Jun		3:06.97	SUD	29 Oct		3:07.12A	CAN	28 Oct		3:07.37	ESP	19 Jun		3:07.88	SWE	19 Jun
3:06.76	CZE	19 Jun		3:07.08	DEN	2 Jul		3:07.22	KSA	20 Dec		3:07.79	OMA	19 Oct		3:07.96	COL	7 Aug
								3:07.30	NED	19 Jun		3:07.80	QAT	19 Oct		3:08.16	EST	19 Jun

Mixed nationality teams

Mark	Name		Pos	Meet	Venue	Date
3:00.45	Texas A&M U. B.Miller 45.2, Henry/ISV 45.0, Preble 45.3, Pinder/BAH 45.0		1	TexR	Austin	9 Apr
3:00.62	Texas A&M U. B.Miller 45.5, Pinder/BAH 44.6, Preble 45.60 ,Henry/ISV 44.86		1	NCAA	Des Moines	11 Jun
3:01.07	Louisiana State University USA		2	NCAA	Des Moines	11 Jun

Simmons 46.7, Alleyne-Forte/TRI 45.0, C.Williams 44.54, Hylton/JAM 44.88

JUNIORS

Mark	Nat	Name		Pos	Meet	Venue	Date
3:06.46	ITA	Tricca, Danesini, Rontini, Lorenzi		1	EJ	Tallinn	24 Jul
3:07.47	RUS	Khokhlov, Kashefrazov, Nesmashniy, Uglov		2	EJ	Tallinn	24 Jul
3.08.20	USA	Gravesande, Henry, Sanders, Mance		1	PAm-J	Miramar	24 Jul
3:08.24	CHN	(Guangzhou)		1	NC-j	Jinan	5 Jun
3:08.35A	BRA	de Araújo, dos Santos, de Oliveira, Henriques		1	SAm-J	Medellín	25 Sep
3:08.56	GER	Königsmark, Schmitz, Hamich, Trefz		3	EJ	Tallinn	24 Jul
3:08.71	GBR	Caddick, Louden, Lagerberg, Dunn		4	EJ	Tallinn	24 Jul
3:08.71A	COL	Valoyes, Ardila, Palomeque, Solís		2	SAM-J	Medellín	25 Sep
3:08.96	TRI	Richards, Foncette, Lendore, Sandy		1	Carifta	Montego Bay	25 Apr
3:08.96	JPN			3h3		Kumamoto	10 Sep
3:09.41	JAM	Bell, McDonald, McCleod, Smith		2	Carifta	Montego Bay	25 Apr
3:09.77A	SUD			1	Af-J	Gaborone	15 May
3:10.20	CZE	Vinš, Šorm, Brož, Pavlíŵek		5	EJ	Tallinn	24 Jul
3:10.74	NZL	Burch, Collings, Jordan, Whyte		1		Sydney	19 Mar
3:10.89	BEL	Thys, Vanhaeren, Lins, Borlee		6	EJ	Tallinn	24 Jul

4 X 800 METRES RELAY

Mark	Name		Pos	Meet	Venue	Date
7:12.15	University of Virginia USA		1	PennR	Philadelphia	30 Apr
	Johnson 1:50.97, Roller 1:48.13. Kostelac 1:47.05, Andrews 1:45.00					
7:12.90	Penn State University USA		2	PennR	Philadelphia	30 Apr
	Williams 1:50.69, Borchers 1:47.56, Foster AUS 1:47.95, Loxsom 1:46.70					
7:14.02	Texas A&M University USA		3	PennR	Philadelphia	30 Apr

Mark	Name		Nat	Born	Pos	Meet	Venue	Date	

3000 METRES WALK

Mark	Name		Nat	Born	Pos	Meet	Venue	Date	
11:10.79	David	Tomala	POL	27.8.89	1		Sosnowiec	21	Sep
11:14.63	Francisco Javier	Fernández	ESP	6.3.77	1		Cork	2	Jul
11:17.82	Rafal	Augustyn	POL	14.5.84	2		Sosnowiec	21	Sep
11:26.34	Hatem	Ghoula	TUN	7.6.73	2		Cork	2	Jul
11:28.76	Rafal	Fedaczynski	POL	3.12.80	3		Sosnowiec	21	Sep
11:29.71	Wojciech	Halman	POL	10.1.90	1		Gdansk	11	Jun
11:33.63	Pierre-Louis	de Villiers	RSA	18.8.85	3		Cork	2	Jul
11:34.39	Artur	Brzozowski	POL	29.3.85	4		Sosnowiec	21	Sep
11:37.5	Chris	Erickson	AUS	1.12.81	1		Canberra	21	Oct

Indoors

Mark	Name		Nat	Born	Pos	Meet	Venue	Date	
10:57.32	Matej	Tóth	SVK	10.2.83	1		Wien	12	Feb
11:31.77+	Grzegorz	Sudol	POL	28.8.78	1	in 5000	Spala	20	Feb
11:38.46+	Christopher	Linke	GER	24.10.88	1	in 5000	Leipzig	26	Feb
11:39.80	Marius	Ziukas	LTU	29.6.85	1		Vilnius	13	Jan

5000 METRES WALK

Mark	Name		Nat	Born	Pos	Meet	Venue	Date	
18:35.96	Yohann	Diniz	FRA	1.1.78	1		Reims	5	Jul
18:38.42		Diniz			1		Compiègne	8	May
18:45.98		Diniz			1		Tomblaine	24	Jun
18:54.39	Matej	Tóth	SVK	10.2.83	1		Banská Bystrica	11	Jun
19:01.00	Jared	Tallent	AUS	17.10.84	1		Sydney	19	Mar
19:07.59	Luke	Adams	AUS	22.10.76	2		Sydney	19	Mar
19:07.91		Adams			2		Reims	5	Jul
19:09.02	Grzegorz	Sudol	POL	28.8.78	1		Katowice	27	May
19:19.02	Rafal	Fedaczynski	POL	3.12.80	1		Kraków	18	Sep
19:19.44	Inaki	Gomez	CAN	16.1.88	1		Vancouver	26	Mar
19:20.34	Anton	Kucmin	SVK	7.6.84	2		Banská Bystrica	11	Jun
19:20.70	Sérgio	Vieira	POR	20.2.76	1		Rio Maior	10	Jun
19:22.93	Isamu	Fujisawa (10)	JPN	12.10.87	1		Kumagaya	21	May
19:23.03	Bertrand	Moulinet	FRA	6.1.87	2		Compiègne	8	May
19:23.77	Evan	Dunfee	CAN	28.9.90	1		Coquitlam	11	Jun
19:24.57	Lukasz	Nowak	POL	18.12.88	2		Katowice	27	May
19:24.85	Chris	Erickson	AUS	1.12.81	1		Canberra	18	Nov
19:26.55	Rafal	Augustyn	POL	14.5.84	2		Kraków	18	Sep

Mark	Name		Nat	Born	Date	
19:28.4+	Alex	Schwazer	ITA	26.12.84	23	Jul
19:28.86	Jakub	Jelonek	POL	7.7.85	27	May
19:29.87	Tom	Bosworth	GBR	17.1.90	31	Jul
19:33.91	David	Tomala	POL	27.8.89	27	May
19:34.58	Cédric	Houssaye	FRA	13.12.79	5	Jul
19:35.29	Yusuke	Suzuki	JPN	2.1.88	19	Jun
19:35.75	Adam	Rutter	AUS	24.12.86	19	Mar
19:38.03	Rafal	Sikora	POL	17.2.87	27	May
19:38.13	Hiroki	Arai	JPN	18.5.88	14	May
19:39.16	Koichiro	Morioka	JPN	2.4.85	19	Jun

Indoors

Mark	Name		Nat	Born	Pos	Meet	Venue	Date	
19:09.56	Robert	Heffernan	IRL	20.2.78	1	NC	Belfast	19	Feb
19:19.45	Christopher	Linke	GER	24.10.88	1	NC	Leipzig	26	Feb
19:29.6	Yuriy	Andronov	RUS	6.11.71	6	Jan			
19:31.35	Carsten	Schmidt	GER	29.5.86	26	Feb			
19:32.8	Pyotr	Trofimov	RUS	18.12.83	25	Dec			
19:33.98	Oleksandr	Venglovskyy	UKR	5.8.85	27	Jan			
19:37.0	Dmitriy	Shorin	RUS	26.3.88	6	Jan			
19:38.15	Máté	Helebrandt	HUN	12.1.89	19	Feb			
19:38.69	João	Vieira	POR	20.2.76	12	Feb			

JUNIORS

Mark	Name		Nat	Born	Pos	Meet	Venue	Date	
19:44.4	Dane	Bird-Smith	AUS	15.7.92	1		Brisbane	5	Feb
19:49.62	Benjamin	Thorne	CAN	.93	1		Coquitlam	17	Jul
19:56.74i	Igor	Lyashenko	UKR	24.8.93	1		Sumy	8	Feb

10,000 METRES WALK

Mark	Name		Nat	Born	Pos	Meet	Venue	Date	
38:44.97	Yohann	Diniz	FRA	1.1.78	1	NC	Albi	29	Jul
38:50.28	Alex	Schwazer	ITA	26.12.84	1		Pergine Valsugana	23	Jul
39:24.8	Matej	Tóth	SVK	10.2.83	1		Banská Bystrica	29	Apr
39:43.20	Giorgio	Rubino	ITA	15.4.86	1		Firenze	4	Jun
39:44.70	Jean-Jacques	Nkouloukidi	ITA	15.4.82	1	NC	Torino	25	Jun
39:44.91	João	Vieira	POR	20.2.76	1	NC	Lisboa	30	Jul
39:46.83A	Eder	Sánchez	MEX	21.5.86	1		Ciudad de México	26	Jun
39:47.0	Anton	Kucmin	SVK	7.6.84	2		Banská Bystrica	29	Apr
39:51.44	Yusuke	Suzuki	JPN	2.1.88	1		Abashiri	22	Jun
39:52.96	Christopher	Linke (10)	GER	24.10.88	1	NC	Kassel	24	Jul
39:55.2	Jarkko	Kinnunen	FIN	19.1.84	1	vSWE	Helsinki	9	Sep
39:55.21	Isamu	Fujisawa	JPN	12.10.87	1		Naruto	24	Sep
39:56.01A	Eider	Arévalo	COL-J	9.3.93	1	SAm-J	Medellin	24	Sep
39:56.5	Heiki	Kukkonen	FIN	18.3.87	2	vSWE	Helsinki	9	Sep
40:01.58	Inaki	Gomez	CAN	16.1.88	1		Coquitlam	17	Jul
40:08.54	Koichiro	Morioka	JPN	2.4.85	2		Abashiri	22	Jun
40:10.99	André	Höhne	GER	10.3.78	2	NC	Kassel	24	Jul

Mark	Name		Nat	Born	Pos	Meet	Venue	Date
40:12.64	Robert	Heffernan	IRL	20.2.78	1	NC	Dublin (S)	7 Aug
40:13.33	Hagen	Pohle	GER-J	5.3.92	1	NC-j	Jena	7 Aug

Mark	Name		Nat	Born	Date		Mark	Name		Nat	Born	Date
40:14.14	Kevin	Campion	FRA	23.5.88	29 Jul		40:22.6	Aku	Partanen	FIN	28.10.91	9 Sep
40:15.98	Moacir	Zimmerman	BRA	30.12.83	8 Oct		40:27.9	Matteo	Giupponi	ITA	8.10.88	17 Apr
40:21.6	Miguel Ángel	López	ESP	3.7.88	7 May		40:28.14	Carsten	Schmidt	GER	29.5.86	24 Jul
40:22.09	Hiroki	Arai	JPN	18.5.88	22 Jun		40:34.3	Andreas	Gustafsson	SWE	10.8.81	9 Sep

Indoors

Mark	Name		Nat	Born	Pos	Meet	Venue	Date
40:03.08	Ruslan	Dmytrenko	UKR	22.3.86	1	NC	Sumy	15 Feb
40:08.89	Ivan	Losyev	UKR	26.1.86	2	NC	Sumy	15 Feb
40:11.13	Oleksandr	Venglovskyy	UKR	5.8.85	3	NC	Sumy	15 Feb
40:12.2	Sergiy	Budza	UKR	6.12.84	1		Sumy	24 Dec

JUNIORS

Mark	Name		Nat	Born	Pos	Meet	Venue	Date
39:56.01A	Eider	Arévalo	COL	9.3.93	1	SAm-J	Medellin	24 Sep
40:13.33	Hagen	Pohle	GER	5.3.92	1	NC-j	Jena	7 Aug
	40:38.21 1 NC-23 Bremen	26 Jun		40:43.73 1 EJ			Tallinn	23 Jul
40:44.70	Takumi	Saito	JPN	23.3.93	4		Yamaguchi	9 Oct
40:51.31	Pavel	Parshin	RUS-Y	2.1.94	1	WY	Villeneuve d'Ascq	9 Jul
40:59.25	Kenny Martín	Pérez	COL-Y	10.8.94	2		Villeneuve d'Ascq	9 Jul
41:02.18	Dane	Bird-Smith	AUS	15.7.92	1	NC-j	Sydney	12 Mar
41:09.60	Erwin	González	MEX-Y	7.2.94	3	WY	Villeneuve d'Ascq	9 Jul
41:09.61	Jesús	Vega	MEX-Y	23.5.94	4	WY	Villeneuve d'Ascq	9 Jul
41:10.43	Igor	Lyashchenko	UKR	24.8.93	2	EJ	Tallinn	23 Jul
41:23.14	Tyler	Sorensen (10)	USA-Y	18.2.94	5	WJ	Villeneuve d'Ascq	9 Jul
41:34.0	Benjamin	Thorne	CAN	.93	1		Calgary	25 Jun
41:34.13	Luis Alberto	Amezcua	ESP	1.5.92	3	EJ	Tallinn	23 Jul
41:37.65A	José Leonardo	Montaña	COL	21.3.92	2	SAm-J	Medellín	28 Aug
41:39.16	Trevor	Barron	USA	30.9.92	1	PAm-J	Miramar	24 Jul
41:39.30	Oleksandr	Verbytskyy	UKR	28.7.92	1	NC-j	Donetsk	15 Jun
41:47.98	Yosuke	Kimura	JPN	.93	4		Hiratsuka	18 Jun
41:50.75		Wang Kaihua	CHN-Y	.94	6	WY	Villeneuve d'Ascq	9 Jul

10 KILOMETRES ROAD WALK

Mark	Name		Nat	Born	Pos	Meet	Venue	Date
38:43	Valeriy	Borchin	RUS	11.9.86	1	RWC-F	La Coruña	17 Sep
38:50		Wang Zhen	CHN	24.8.91	2	RWC-F	La Coruña	17 Sep
39:07		Chu Yafei	CHN	5.9.88	3	RWC-F	La Coruña	17 Sep
39:10	João	Vieira	POR	20.2.76	4	RWC-F	La Coruña	17 Sep
39:14	Eder	Sánchez	MEX	21.5.86	5	RWC-F	La Coruña	17 Sep
39:15	Robert	Heffernan	IRL	20.2.78	6	RWC-F	La Coruña	17 Sep
39:19	Isamu	Fujisawa	JPN	12.10.87	7	RWC-F	La Coruña	17 Sep
39:34+	Jared	Tallent	AUS	17.10.84	1	in 10k	Hobart	19 Feb
39:36	Moacir	Zimmerman	BRA	30.12.83	1		Blumenau	7 May
39:46	Luke	Adams	AUS	22.10.76	8	RWC-F	La Coruña	17 Sep
39:47	Ever	Palma	MEX-J	18.3.92	9	RWC-F	La Coruña	17 Sep
39:47	Andriy	Kovenko	UKR	25.11.73	1	NCp	Mukachevo	29 Oct

Where faster than track best

Mark	Name		Nat	Born	Pos	Meet	Venue	Date
39:52	Matteo	Giupponi	ITA	8.10.88	2		Genova	27 Feb
40:02	Pedro	Gómez	MEX	31.12.90	11	RWC-F	La Coruña	17 Sep
40:12+	Hassanine	Sbaï	TUN	21.4.84		in 20k	Rio Maior	9 Apr

Mark	Name		Nat	Born	Date		Mark	Name		Nat	Born	Date
40:15	Sergiy	Budza	UKR	6.12.84	29 Oct		40:23+	Adam	Rutter	AUS	24.12.86	9 Apr
40:18+	Pyotr	Trofimov	RUS	18.12.83	20 Mar		40:23	Oleksandr	Romanenko	UKR	26.6.81	29 Oct
40:18	Oleksiy	Kazanin	UKR	22.5.82	26 Jun		40:25	Oleksandr	Venhlovskyy	UKR	5.8.85	26 Jun

JUNIORS

Where inferior to track best

Mark	Name		Nat	Born	Pos	Meet	Venue	Date
39:47	Ever	Palma	MEX	18.3.92	9	RWC-F	La Coruña	17 Sep
39:57+		Chen Ding	CHN	5.8.92	1=	in 20k	Taicang	22 Apr
40:29	Igor	Lyashchenko	UKR	24.8.93	1	NCp	Mukachevo	30 Oct
40:30	Oleksandr	Verbitskiy	UKR	28.7.92	2	NCp	Mukachevo	30 Oct
40:56	Dane	Bird-Smith	AUS	15.7.92	1	NC-j	Hobart	19 Feb
41:18	Pavel	Parshin	RUS-Y	2.1.94	1	NC-wj	Sochi	27 Feb
41:23	Yevgeniy	Zaleskiy	BLR	18.7.93	1	NCp	Nesvizh	9 Apr
41:52		Yin Jiaxing	CHN-Y	16.3.94	1	NC-y	Baoji	16 Sep
41:55		Wang Kaihua	CHN-Y	16.2.94	2	NC-y	Baoji	16 Sep
41:58	Dementiy	Cheparev	RUS	28.10.92	3	ECp-J	Olhão	21 May

20 KILOMETRES WALK

Mark	at 10k	Name	Nat	Born	Pos	Venue	Date
1:18:30	39:57	Wang Zhen	CHN	24.8.91	1	Taicang	22 Apr
1:18:37	39:46	Wang Zhen			1	Lugano	20 Mar
1:18:38	39:46	Chu Yafei	CHN	5.9.88	2	Lugano	20 Mar
1:18:45	39:57	Chu Yafei			2	Taicang	22 Apr
1:18:52	39:57	Chen Ding	CHN-J	5.8.92	3	Taicang	22 Apr

Mark		Name		Nat	Born	Pos	Meet	Venue	Date	
1:18:55	40:08	Valeriy	Borchin	RUS	11.9.86	1		Rio Maior	9	Apr
1:19:14		Vladimir	Kanaykin	RUS	21.3.85	1	NC-w	Sochi	26	Feb
1:19:18	39:32	Sergey	Morozov	RUS	21.3.88	1	NC	Saransk	1	Jun
1:19:31	39:48		Kim Hyun-sub	KOR	31.5.85	1	AsiC	Nomi	13	Mar
1:19:33	40:11	Stanislav	Yemelyanov	RUS	23.10.90	2		Rio Maior	9	Apr
1:19:36	40:14	Eder	Sánchez	MEX	21.5.86	3		Rio Maior	9	Apr
1:19:39	40:02		Chen Ding			3		Lugano	20	Mar
1:19:43	40:14		Borchin			1		Sesto San Giovanni	1	May
1:19:46			Wang Zhen			1		Dublin	26	Jun
1:19:56			Borchin			1	WCh	Daegu	28	Aug
1:19:57	39:57	Jared	Tallent (10)	AUS	17.10.84	4		Taicang	22	Apr
1:20:08			Morozov			2	NC-w	Sochi	26	Feb
1:20:10	40:18		Kum Hyun-sub			5		Taicang	22	Apr
1:20:16		Andrey	Krivov	RUS	14.11.85	3	NC-w	Sochi	26	Feb
1:20:16	40:12	Matej	Tóth	SVK	10.2.83	4		Rio Maior	9	Apr
1:20:18		Pyotr	Bogatyrev	RUS	11.3.91	4	NC-w	Sochi	26	Feb
1:20:19			Tallent			1	NC	Hobart	19	Feb
1:20:19	40:02	Hassanine	Sbaï	TUN	21.4.84	4		Lugano	20	Mar
1:20:19	40:03		Sanchez			6		Taicang	22	Apr
1:20:23			Sbaï			2		Dublin	26	Jun
1:20:23.8t		Andrés	Chocho	ECU	4.11.83	1	SACh	Buenos Aires	5	Jun
1:20:27			Kanaykin			2	WCh	Daegu	28	Aug
1:20:31		Pyotr	Trofimov	RUS	28.11.83	5	NC-w	Sochi	26	Feb
1:20:35		Gurmeet	Singh	IND	1.7.85	1		Patiala	3	Ma
1:20:36.6t		Gustavo	Restrepo	COL	27.7.82	2	SACh	Buenos Aires	5	Jun
1:20:38		Luis Fernando	López	COL	3.6.79	3	WCh	Daegu	28	Aug
1:20:43			Yu Wei	CHN	11.9.87	1		Xintai	11	Mar
		(32/20)								
1:20:44		Giorgio	Rubino	ITA	15.4.86	3		Dublin	26	Jun
1:20:47.2t		Yerko	Araya	CHI	14.2.86	3	SACh	Buenos Aires	5	Jun
1:20:48		Ivan	Trotskiy	BLR	27.5.76	1	NC	Grodno	7	Jul
1:20:51		Grzegorz	Sudol	POL	28.8.78	1		Zaniemysl	16	Apr
1:20:51		Christopher	Linke	GER	24.10.88	7		Taicang	22	Apr
1:20:54	40:02	Robert	Heffernan	IRL	20.2.78	5		Lugano	20	Mar
1:20:57		Rafal	Augustyn	POL	14.5.84	2		Zaniemysl	16	Apr
1:20:58		Erick	Barrondo	GUA	14.6.91	4		Dublin	26	Jun
1:20:58.5t		Caio	Bonfim	BRA	19.3.91	4	SACh	Buenos Aires	5	Jun
1:21:00	40:15	Luke	Adams	AUS	22.10.76	2	NC	Hobart	19	Feb
		(30)								
1:21:01		Denis	Simanovich	BLR	20.4.87	2	NC	Grodno	7	Jul
1:21:02		Ever	Palma	MEX-J	18.3.92	1		Naumburg	24	Sep
1:21:02.5t		Moacir	Zimmerman	BRA	30.12.83	1	NC	São Paulo	5	Aug
1:21:03			Wang Hao	CHN	16.8.89	5		Dublin	26	Jun
1:21:04		Rafal	Sikora	POL	17.2.87	3		Zaniemysl	16	Apr
1:21:07	40:04		Cai Zelin	CHN	11.4.91	8		Taicang	22	Apr
1:21:09	40:30	Andrey	Ruzavin	RUS	28.3.86	3	NC	Saransk	12	Jun
1:21:13	39:48	Yusuke	Suzuki	JPN	2.1.88	1	NC	Kobe	20	Feb
1:21:13.6t		James	Rendón	COL	7.4.85	5	SACh	Buenos Aires	5	Jun
1:21:19		Anatoliy	Kukushkin	RUS	12.2.86	6	NC-w	Sochi	26	Feb
		(40)								
1:21:31		Ruslan	Dmytrenko	UKR	22.3.86	7	WCh	Daegu	28	Aug
1:21:34	40:19	Nazar	Kovalenko	UKR	9.2.89	6		Lugano	20	Mar
1:21:41		Miguel Ángel	López	ESP	3.7.88	6		Dublin	26	Jun
1:21:44		Andriy	Kovenko	UKR	25.11.73	1		Dudince	26	Mar
1:21:46	40:30	Valeriy	Filipchuk	RUS	30.6.91	6	NC	Saransk	12	Jun
1:21:49		Mikhail	Ryzhov	RUS	17.12.91	7	NC-w	Sochi	26	Feb
1:21:50		Bertrand	Moulinet	FRA	6.1.87	8		Lugano	20	Mar
1:21:50		Alex	Schwazer	ITA	26.12.84	9	WCh	Daegu	28	Aug
1:21:52			Cui Zhide	CHN	11.1.83	1r2		Taicang	22	Apr
1:21:57			Xu Dexing	CHN	20.8.88	2		Xintai	11	Mar
		(50)								
1:22:01		Isamu	Fujisawa	JPN	12.10.87	1		Takahata	30	Oct
1:22:04			Xu Faguang	CHN	17.5.87	9		Lugano	20	Mar
1:22:05			Cong Fudong	CHN-J	28.5.92	2j		Xintai	11	Mar
1:22:05			Zhao Qi	CHN-J	14.1.93	3j		Xintai	11	Mar
1:22:06		Inaki	Gomez	CAN	16.1.88	4		Naumburg	24	Sep
1:22:07		Rafal	Fedaczynski	POL	3.12.80	2	NC	Warszawa	17	Sep
1:22:10	40:09	Koichiro	Morioka	JPN	2.4.85	2	NC	Kobe	20	Feb
1:22:15		Horacio	Nava	MEX	20.1.82	7		Rio Maior	9	Apr

Mark		Name		Nat	Born	Pos	Meet	Venue	Date
1:22:17		Francisco Javier	Fernández	ESP	6.3.77	1	NC	Benicàssim	6 Mar
1:22:18			Wang Gang	CHN	2.4.91	2	AsiC	Nomi	13 Mar
(60)									
1:22:23	40:39	Takayuki	Tanii	JPN	14.2.83	3	NC	Kobe	20 Feb
1:22:23			Li Tianlei	CHN-Y	13.1.95	10		Taicang	22 Apr
1:22:25	40:33	Adam	Rutter	AUS	24.12.86	3	NC	Hobart	19 Feb
1:22:27	40:33	Yusuke	Yachi	JPN	2.1.80	3	AsiC	Nomi	13 Mar
1:22:28	40:40		Park Chil-sung	KOR	8.7.82	4	AsiC	Nomi	13 Mar
1:22:30		José	Leyver	MEX	12.11.85	9		Rio Maior	9 Apr
1:22:31		Recep	Celik	TUR	10.8.83	1	BalkC	Bucuresti	9 Apr
1:22:31		Marius	Ziukas	LTU	29.6.85	4		Naumburg	24 Sep
1:22:32		Jakub	Jelonek	POL	7.7.85	4		Zaniemysl	16 Apr
1:22:36A		David	Mejía	MEX	7.12.86	3		Chihuahua	5 Mar
(70)									
1:22:36		Matteo	Giupponi	ITA	8.10.88	1		Podébrady	9 Apr
1:22:38		Ivan	Losyev	UKR	26.1.86	4		Warszawa	17 Sep
1:22:42			Bian Fongda	CHN	1.4.91	3		Xintai	11 Mar
1:22:44		João	Vieira	POR	20.2.76	10		Rio Maior	9 Apr
1:22:47		Carsten	Schmidt	GER	29.5.86	2		Podebrabdy	9 Apr
1:22:47		Hiroki	Arai	JPN	18.5.88	2		Takahata	30 Oct
1:22:48		Kevin	Campion	FRA	23.5.88	10		Dublin	26 Jun
1:22:57		Sergey	Kirdyapkin	RUS	16.1.80	11		Rio Maior	9 Apr
1:22:57A		Rolando	Saquipay	ECU	21.7.79	4	PAm	Guadalajara, MEX	23 Oct
1:22:58		André	Höhne	GER	10.3.78	7		Sesto San Giovanni	1 May
(80)									
1:23:01		Andrey	Stepanchuk	BLR	12.6.79	3		Grodno	1 Oct
1:23.09.0t		Juan Manuel	Cano	ARG	12.12.87	6	SACh	Buenos Aires	5 Jun
1:23:04			Du Yunpeng	CHN	6.9.88	4		Xintai	11 Mar
1:23:04		Babubhai	Panocha	IND	10.8.78	11		Dublin	26 Jun
1:23:06			Liu Jianmin	CHN	9.3.88	5		Xintai	11 Mar
1:23:12			He Yongqiang	CHN-J	27.11.93	4j		Xintai	11 Mar
1:23:15		Sérgio	Vieira	POR	20.2.76	12		Rio Maior	9 Apr
1:23:17		Aleksandr	Yargunkin	RUS	6.1.81	14		Lugano	20 Mar
1:23:20		Hiroki	Nagaiwa	JPN	25.5.89	5	NC	Kobe	20 Feb
1:23:20		Edgar	Hernández	MEX	8.6.77	13		Rio Maior	9 Apr
(90)									
1:23:20		Dawid	Wolski	POL	15.6.89	5		Zaniemysl	16 Apr
1:23:21		Antón	Kucmin	SVK	7.6.84	6		Zaniemysl	16 Apr
1:23:21		Aléxandros	Papamihaíl	GRE	18.9.88	1		Villa di Serri	23 Oct
1:23:25		Andrey	Talashko	BLR	31.5.82	1		Nesvizh	9 Apr
1:23:26			Bo Xiangdong	CHN	1.10.87	4		Taicang	22 Apr
1:23:26		Trevor	Barron	USA-J	30.9.92	1	NC	Eugene	26 Jun
1:23:32		Yuriy	Andronov	RUS	6.11.71	2		Voronovo	17 Sep
1:23:34			Ji Chunlong	CHN	25.2.88	5		Taicang	22 Apr
1:23:35			Chen Xinrong	CHN	17.6.90	6		Xintai	11 Mar
1:23:40		Jarkko	Kinnunen	FIN	19.1.84	1	NC	Turku	4 Aug
(100)									

Mark	Name		Nat	Born	Date
1:23:41	Lukasz	Nowak	POL	18.12.88	26 Jun
1:23:43.0	Andreas	Gustafsson	SWE	10.8.81	1 May
1:23:45		Su Guanyu	CHN-Y	26.6.94	16 Sep
1:23:45	Evans	Dunfee	CAN	28.9.90	24 Sep
1:23:45	Takumi	Saito	JPN-J	23.3.93	30 Oct
1:23:46		Hu Wanli	CHN-J	27.5.92	22 Apr
1:23:46.5t	Mauricio	Arteaga	ECU	8.8.88	5 Jun
1:23:47	Predrag	Filipovic	SRB	5.10.78	9 Apr
1:23:49	Ivan	Noskov	RUS	16.7.88	17 Sep
1:23:49	Takeshi	Okuma	JPN	14.12.83	20 Feb
1:23:50	Vitaliy	Talankov	BLR	29.4.82	9 Apr
1:23:51	José Ignacio	Díaz	ESP	22.11.79	9 Apr
1:23:52	John	Nunn	USA	3.2.78	26 Jun
1:23:53A	Diego	Flores	MEX	23.3.87	5 Mar
1:23:56	Aleksandr	Lyakhovich	BLR	4.7.89	1 Oct
1:23:57	Hayato	Katsuki	JPN	28.11.90	20 Feb
1:23:59	Dmitriy	Shorin	RUS	26.3.88	26 Feb
1:24:00		Chen Zongliang	CHN-J	9.1.92	11 Mar
1:24:04A	Isaac	Palma	MEX	26.10.90	5 Mar
1:24:06A	Aníbal	Paau	GUA	12.1.87	23 Oct
1:24:07		Wang Leilei	CHN	14.2.89	16 Sep
1:24:07.52t	Heikki	Kukkonen	FIN	18.3.87	17 Sep
1:24:12	Benjamín	Sánchez	ESP	10.3.85	21 May
1:24:13	Cristian D.	Berdeja	MEX	21.6.81	9 Apr
1:24:17	Artur	Brzozowski	POL	29.3.85	16 Apr
1:24:20		Lin Dexin	CHN-J	21.10.92	16 Sep
1:24:20	Andrey	Ryabushev	RUS	29.11.88	26 Feb
1:24:21	Dawid	Tomala	POL	27.8.89	17 Jul
1:24:25		Men Fuqiang	CHN-J	22.6.92	11 Mar
1:24:25	Oleksiy	Kazanin	UKR	22.5.82	18 Jun
1:24:25	Denis	Strelkov	RUS	26.10.90	17 Jul
1:24:25	Ian	Rayson	AUS	4.2.88	13 Nov
1:24:26	Mikel	Odriozola	ESP	25.5.73	6 Feb
1:24:27	Wojciech	Halman	POL	10.1.90	16 Apr
1:24:29		Si Tianfeng	CHN	17.6.84	20 Mar
1:24:30	Daichi	Aono	JPN	12.5.89	20 Feb
1:24:32		Byun Young-jun	KOR	20.3.84	13 Mar
1:24:32	Sergiy	Budza	UKR	6.12.84	18 Jun
1:24:33	Viktor	Burayev	RUS	23.2.82	12 Jun
1:24:35	Jesús Ángel	García	ESP	17.10.69	20 Mar
1:24:35		Sun Chengang	CHN	11.3.91	22 Apr
1:24:47	Basant Bahadur Rana		IND	18.1.84	3 May
1:24:49		Bai Xuejin	CHN	6.6.87	11 Mar
1:24:49	Kostyantyn	Puzanov	UKR	19.5.91	18 Jun
1:24:50	Chandan	Singh	IND	8.6.87	3 May
1:24:51	Brendon	Reading	AUS	26.1.89	22 Apr
1:24:51	Baljinder	Singh	IND	18.9.86	3 May
1:24:51.0t	Mani Ram	Patel	IND	16.9.91	17 Feb
1:24:54	Ken	Akashi	JPN	6.11.76	20 Feb
1:24:55	Anatole	Ibáñez	SWE	14.11.85	19 Feb
1:24:55A	Omar	Segura	MEX	24.3.81	5 Aug
1:24:56	Dementiy	Cheparyev	RUS-J	28.10.92	17 Sep
1:24:57	Mikhail	Orlov	RUS	25.6.67	26 Feb
1:24:58	Takafumi	Higuma (154)	JPN	3.9.82	10 Feb

Mark		Name		Nat	Born	Pos	Meet	Venue	Date
Best track times									
1:23:05.9		Gurmeet	Singh	IND	1.7.85	1		Chennai	10 Feb
1:23:19.9		Rolando	Saquipay	ECU	21.7.79	2	BRA Ch	São Paulo	5 Aug
1:23:46.9		Recep	Celik	TUR	10.8.83	1		Faro	8 May
Short course									
1:18:20Asc		David	Kimutai	KEN	19.8.69	1	NC	Nairobi	16 Jul
1:21:30		Lukasz	Nowak	POL	18.12.88	3		Alytus	17 Jun
1:21:40		Marius	Ziukas	LTU	29.6.85	4		Alytus	17 Jun
1:21:50Asc		Josphat	Sirma	KEN	6.9.73	2	NC	Nairobi	16 Jul
1:22:27		Diego	Flores	MEX	23.3.87	6		Alytus	17 Jun

Also at Alytus 17 Jun: 1:23:28 Dawid Tomala, 1:23:47 Trond Nymark, 1:24:14 Wojciech Halman, 1:24:35 Patryk Rogowski

JUNIORS

See main list for top 7 juniors. 10 performances by 7 men to 1:23:30. Additional marks and further juniors:

Mark		Name		Nat	Born	Pos	Meet	Venue	Date
Chen Ding 2+	1:21:40 1J	Xintai	11 Mar	1:21:48	1		NC-j	Baoji	16 Sep
1:23:45		Su Guanyu		CHN-Y	26.6.94	3	NC-j	Baoji	16 Sep
1:23:45	Takumi	Saito		JPN	23.3.93	3		Takahata	30 Oct
1:23:46		Hu Wanli (10)		CHN	27.5.92	1j		Taicang	22 Apr
1:24:00		Chen Zongliang		CHN	9.1.92	5j		Xinati	11 Mar
1:24:20		Lin Dexin		CHN	21.10.92	4	NC-j	Baoji	16 Sep
1:24:25		Men Fuqiang		CHN	22.6.92	6j		Xintai	11 Mar
1:24:56	Dementiy	Cheparyev		RUS	28.10.92	4		Voronovo	17 Sep
1:25:02	Takaki	Matsuzaki		JPN	.92	5		Takahata	30 Oct
1:25:23		Wei Xubao		CHN	1.2.93	6	NC-j	Baoji	16 Sep
1:25:28		Yu Jiandong		CHN	6.12.93	9		Xintai	11 Mar
1:25:33	Hagen	Pohle		GER	5.3.92	6		Naumburg	24 Sep
1:25:52		Yang Yang		CHN	6.6.92	12		Xintai	11 Mar
1:25:53		Luo Yadong (20)		CHN	92	7	NC-j	Baoji	16 Sep

30-35 KILOMETRES WALK

Mark		Name		Nat	Born	Pos	Meet	Venue	Date
	2:26:36	Igor	Yerokhin	RUS	4.9.85	1	NC-w	Sochi	26 Feb
	2:27:08	Denis	Nizhegorodov	RUS	26.7.80	2	NC-w	Sochi	26 Feb
	2:27:52	Denis	Strelkov	RUS	26.10.90	3	NC-w	Sochi	26 Feb
2:07:48		Robert	Heffernan	IRL	20.2.78	1	NC 2010	Cork	30 Jan
	2:28:17	Andrey	Ruzavin	RUS	28.3.86	4	NC-w	Sochi	26 Feb
	2:28:24	Koichiro	Morioka	JPN	2.4.85	1	in 50k	Wajima	17 Apr
2:10:49		Chen Zongliang		CHN-J	9.1.92	1		Taicang	24 Apr
	2:32:29	Sergey	Sergachev	RUS	10.7.87	5	NC-w	Sochi	26 Feb
	2:32:49	Yuriy	Andronov	RUS	6.11.71	6	NC-w	Sochi	26 Feb
	2:32:52	Marco	De Luca	ITA	12.5.81	1	NC	Binaco	30 Jan
2:11:12.0t+		Grzegorz	Sudol	POL	28.8.78	(1)	in 50k	Reims	12 Mar
2:11:13	2:32:56t+	Yohann	Diniz	FRA	1.1.78	2	in 50k	Reims	12 Mar
	2:33:00	Aleksandr	Yargunkin	RUS	6.1.81	7	NC-w	Sochi	26 Feb
2:11:31		Zhao Qi		CHN-J	14.1.93	1		Xintai	13 Mar
2:11:31		He Yongqiang		CHN-J	27.11.93	2		Xintai	13 Mar
2:11:55+	2:33:44e	Si Tianfeng		CHN	17.6.84		in 50k	Taicang	24 Apr
2:11:55+	2:33:44e	Li Jianbo		CHN	14.11.86		in 50k	Taicang	24 Apr
2:11:55+		Li Lei		CHN	29.11.87	2=	in 50k	Taicang	24 Apr
2:11:56+	2:33:45e	Xu Faguang		CHN	17.5.87		in 50k	Taicang	24 Apr
2:11:51	2:33:48+	Sergey	Bakulin	RUS	13.11.86		in 50k	Daegu	3 Sep
2:12:05+	2:34:04e	Niu Wenbin		CHN	20.1.91	5	in 50k	Taicang	24 Apr
	2:34:36	Aleksey	Bartsaykin	RUS	22.3.89	8	NC-w	Sochi	26 Feb
2:12:38+	2:34:50e	Li Gaobo		CHN		6	in 50k	Taicang	24 Apr
	2:35:27	Oleksiy	Kazanin	UKR	22.5.82	1	NC-w	Yevpatoriya	26 Feb
	2:35:49	Ivan	Trotskiy	BLR	27.5.76	1		Nesvizh	9 Apr
	2:36:00	Ivan	Losyev	UKR	26.1.86	2	NC-w	Yevpatoriya	26 Feb
2:11:33	2:36:02+	Nathan	Deakes	AUS	17.8.77		in 50k	Daegu	3 Sep
2:12:06		Jarkko	Kinnunen	FIN	19.1.84	1	NC	Kauhava	12 Jun
2:12:21		Zhao Fujie		CHN-J	11.11.93	2		Taicang	24 Apr
2:13:30		Hu Wanlie		CHN-J	27.5.92	3		Taicang	24 Apr
2:13:51	2:36:02+	Jared	Tallent	AUS	17.10.84		in 50k	Daegu	3 Sep
2:13:50	2:36:03+	Si Tianfeng					in 50k	Daegu	3 Sep
2:13:54	2:36:28+	Andrés	Chocho	ECU	4.11.83		in 50k	Daegu	3 Sep
2:13:59		Jamie	Costin	IRL	1.6.77	2	NC 10	Cork	30 Jan
2:14:14	2:36:33+	Luke	Adams	AUS	22.10.76		in 50k	Daegu	3 Sep
2:14:30	2:36:50+	Yuki	Yamazaki	JPN	16.1.84	1	in 50k	Takahata	30 Oct
2:14:17	2:37:08+	Park Chil-sung		KOR	8.7.82		in 50k	Daegu	3 Sep
2:14:37	2:37:08+	Xu Faguang					in 50k	Daegu	3 Sep
	2:37:28	Sergiy	Budza	UKR	6.12.84	3	NC-w	Yevpatoriya	26 Feb
2:15:19	2:37:43+	Koichiro	Morioka	JPN	2.4.85		in 50k	Daegu	3 Sep

Mark	Name		Nat	Born	Pos	Meet	Venue	Date
							50 KILOMETRES WALK	
3:35:27.2 t	Yohann	Diniz	FRA	1.1.78	1		Reims	12 Mar
3:38:46	Sergey	Bakulin	RUS	13.11.86	1	NC	Saransk	12 Jun
3:38:48		Si Tianfeng	CHN	17.6.84	1		Taicang	24 Apr
3:39:46	Matej	Tóth	SVK	10.2.83	1	NC	Dudince	26 Mar
3:41:24		Bakulin			1	WCh	Daegu	3 Sep
3:42:20		Xu Faguang	CHN	17.5.87	2		Taicang	24 Apr
3:42:25	Yuriy	Andronov	RUS	6.11.71	2	NC	Saransk	12 Jun
3:42:45	Denis	Nizhegorodov	RUS	26.7.80	2	WCh	Daegu	3 Sep
3:43:36	Jared	Tallent	AUS	17.10.84	3	WCh	Daegu	3 Sep
3:43:38		Li Jianbo	CHN	14.11.86	3		Taicang	24 Apr
3:44:03	Yuki	Yamazaki (10)	JPN	16.1.84	1		Takahata	30 Oct
3:44:40		Si Tianfeng			4	WCh	Daegu	3 Sep
3:44:45	Koichiro	Morioka	JPN	2.4.85	1	NC	Wajima	17 Apr
3:45:29	Horacio	Nava	MEX	20.1.82	3	RUS Ch	Saransk	12 Jun
3:45:31	Luke	Adams	AUS	22.10.76	5	WCh	Daegu	3 Sep
3:45:58		Nizhegorodov			1	ECp	Olhão	21 May
3:46:05	Rafal	Fedaczynski	POL	3.12.80	2	1 NC	Dudince	26 Mar
3:46:16	Rafal	Sikora	POL	17.2.87	3	2 NC	Dudince	26 Mar
3:46:21		Morioka			6	WCh	Daegu	3 Sep
3:46:40	Lukasz	Nowak	POL	18.12.88	4	3 NC	Dudince	26 Mar
3:46:56	Rafal	Augustyn	POL	14.5.84	5	4 NC	Dudince	26 Mar
3:47:13		Park Chil-sung	KOR	8.7.82	7	WCh	Daegu	3 Sep
3:47:19		Xu Faguang			8	WCh	Daegu	3 Sep
3:48:02	Nathan	Deakes	AUS	17.8.77	6		Dudince	26 Mar
3:48:03	Takayuki	Tanii (20)	JPN	14.2.83	9	WCh	Daegu	3 Sep
3:48:11	Jesús Ángel	García	ESP	17.10.69	1		Naumburg	24 Sep
3:48:19		Cui Zhide	CHN	11.1.83	1e2		Taicang	24 Apr
3:48:21		Tanii			2	NC	Wajima	17 Apr
3:48:40	Hiroki	Arai	JPN	18.5.88	10	WCh	Daegu	3 Sep
3:48:46		Arai			3	NC	Wajima	17 Apr
3:48:58A		Nava			1	PAm	Guadalajara, MEX	29 Oct
	(31/23)							
3:49:05	Igor	Yerokhin	RUS	4.9.85	2	ECp	Olhão	21 May
3:49.16A	José	Leyver	MEX	12.11.85	2	PAm	Guadalajara, MEX	29 Oct
3:49:28	Robert	Heffernan	IRL	20.2.78	2		Naumburg	24 Sep
3:49:32	Andrés	Chocho	ECU	4.11.83	11	WCh	Daegu	3 Sep
3:49:33	Mikel	Odriozola	ESP	25.5.73	1	NC	Benicássim	6 Mar
3:49:40	Marco	De Luca	ITA	12.5.81	12	WCh	Daegu	3 Sep
3:50:18		Zhao Jianguo	CHN	19.1.88	1	NC	Baoji	18 Sep
	(30)							
3:50:26	Omar	Zepeda	MEX	8.6.77	7		Dudince	26 Mar
3:50:33A	Jaime	Quiyuch	GUA	24.4.88	3	PAm	Guadalajara, MEX	29 Oct
3:50:49	Bertrand	Moulinet	FRA	6.1.87	8		Dudince	26 Mar
3:51:12		Kim Dong-young	KOR	6.3.80	14	WCh	Daegu	3 Sep
3:51:46		Yu Wei	CHN	11.9.87	2e2		Taicang	24 Apr
3:51:57	Chris	Erickson	AUS	1.12.81	3	NC	Melbourne	11 Dec
3:52:32	Jarkko	Kinnunen	FIN	19.1.84	15	WCh	Daegu	3 Sep
3:52:35	Jean-Jacques	Nkouloukidi	ITA	15.4.82	16	WCh	Daegu	3 Sep
3:52:56	Christopher	Linke	GER	24.10.88	4	ECp	Olhão	21 May
3:53:05		Lim Jung-hyun	KOR	8.9.87	5		Taicang	24 Apr
	(40)							
3:53:19	Eder	Sánchez	MEX	21.5.86	9		Dudince	26 Mar
3:53:24	Cédric	Houssaye	FRA	13.12.79	10		Dudince	26 Mar
3:53:26		Geng Zhiyao	CHN	15.8.87	6		Taicang	24 Apr
3:53:49		Byun Young-joon	KOR	20.3.84	7		Taicang	24 Apr
3:53:51	Artur	Brzozowski	POL	29.3.85	5	ECp	Olhão	21 May
3:53:55	José Ignacio	Díaz	ESP	22.11.79	2	NC	Benicàssim	6 Mar
3:54:08	Andreas	Gustafsson	SWE	10.8.81	1		Valley Cottage	30 Oct
3:54:19		Niu Wenbin	CHN	20.1.91	9		Taicang	24 Apr
3:54:20		Oh Se-hyun	KOR	17.11.88	10		Taicang	24 Apr
3:54:26	Trond	Nymark	NOR	28.12.76	17	WCh	Daegu	3 Sep
	(50)							
3:54:46	Edgar	Hernández	MEX	8.6.77	18	WCh	Daegu	3 Sep
3:54:54	Carsten	Schmidt	GER	29.5.86	3		Naumburg	24 Sep
3:55:04	Federico	Tontodonati	ITA	30.10.89	1	NC	Villa Di Serio	23 Oct
3:55:32		Du Yunpeng	CHN	6.9.88	3	NC	Baoji	18 Sep
3:56:09	Emerson	Hernández	ESA	20.1.89	11		Taicang	24 Apr
3:56:18	Oleksiy	Kazanin	UKR	22.5.82	20	WCh	Daegu	3 Sep

Mark	Name		Nat	Born	Pos	Meet	Venue	Date
3:56:35	Takafumi	Higuma	JPN	3.9.82	4	NC	Wajima	17 Apr
3:56:46	Milos	Bátovsky	SVK	26.5.79	4		Naumburg	24 Sep
3:56:51	Antti	Kempas	FIN	3.10.80	5		Naumburg	24 Sep
3:57:32	Lorenzo	Dessi	ITA	4.5.89	2	NC	Villa Di Serio	23 Oct
(60)								
3:57:48	Ken	Akashi	JPN	6.11.76	5	NC	Wajima	17 Apr
3:57:55	Ian	Rayson	AUS	4.2.88	4	NC	Melbourne	11 Dec
3:57:58	Brendan	Boyce	IRL	15.10.86	6		Naumburg	24 Sep
3:59:14A	Cristian D.	Berdeja	MEX	21.6.81	1	PAm Cp	Envigado	27 Mar
3:59:17	Nenad	Filipovic	SRB	5.10.78	12		Dudince	26 Mar
3:59:21		Bai Xuejin	CHN	6.6.87	4	NC	Baoji	18 Sep
3:59:22	Aleksandr	Yargunkin	RUS	6.1.81	4	NC	Saransk	12 Jun
3:59:39		Wu Qianlong	CHN	30.1.90	5	NC	Baoji	18 Sep
3:59:40A	Fredy	Hernández	COL	25.4.78	2	PAm Cp	Envigado	27 Mar
3:59:43	Igors	Kazakevics	LAT	19.4.80	13		Dudince	26 Mar
(70)								
4:00:02	Sergiy	Budza	UKR	6.12.84	1		Ivano-Frankivsk	9 Oct
4:00:52	Claudio	Villanueva	ESP	3.8.88	3	NC	Benicàssim	6 Mar
4:00:54	Tadas	Suskevicius	LTU	22.5.85	14		Dudince	26 Mar
4:01:00	Clemente	García	MEX	21.8.89	5	Rus Ch	Saransk	12 Jun
4:01:00	Teodorico	Caporaso	ITA	14.9.87	3	NC	Villa Di Serio	23 Oct
4:01:05	Oleksandr	Romanenko	UKR	26.6.81	15		Dudince	26 Mar
4:01:13	Semyon	Lovkin	RUS	14.7.77	6	NC	Saransk	12 Jun
4:01:14	Denis	Kravchuk	BLR	17.4.87	7		Naumburg	24 Sep
4:01:20	Rolando	Saquipay	ECU	21.7.79	3	PAm Cp	Envigado	27 Mar
4:01:29	Diego	Cafagna	ITA	9.7.75	8		Naunburg	24 Sep
(80)								
4:02:07	Vladimir	Savanovic	SRB	5.10.78	17		Dudince	26 Mar
4:02:08	Hervé	Davaux	FRA	22.8.78	1	NC	Fameck	9 Oct
4:02:51	Michal	Stasiewicz	POL	28.9.88	8	ECp	Olhão	21 May
4:03:02	Edwar	Araya	CHI	14.2.86	1	NC	Arica	26 Feb
4:03:18	Igor	Hlavan	UKR	25.9.90	2		Ivano-Frankivsk	9 Oct
4:03:35	Miguel Ángel	Prieto	ESP	20.9.64	4	NC	Benicàssim	6 Mar
4:03:35	Yusuke	Yachi	JPN	2.1.80	6	NC	Wajima	17 Apr
4:03:41	Sergey	Korepanov	RUS	15.7.84	7	NC	Saransk	12 Jun
4:03:50	Andrey	Stepanchuk	BLR	12.6.79	3		Ivano-Frankivsk	9 Oct
4:04:07A	Jonathan	Rieckmann	BRA	20.8.87	5	PAm	Guadalajara, MEX	29 Oct
(90)								
4:04:33		Li Gaobo	CHN	4.5.89	3		Xintai	13 Mar
4:04:36	Denis	Strelkov	RUS	26.10.90	12	ECp	Olhão	21 May
4:04:48	Håvard	Haukenes	NOR	22.4.90	18		Dudince	26 Mar
4:05:16		Sun Chengang	CHN	11.3.91	8	NC	Baoji	18 Sep
4:05:25	Luis Manuel	Corchete	ESP	14.5.84	13	ECp	Olhão	21 May
4:05:32	Hidehito	Kusaka	JPN	22.6.86	7	NC	Wajima	17 Apr
4:05:52	Pavel	Yarokhov	BLR	21.7.82	19		Dudince	26 Mar
4:06:14	Yuriy	Burban	UKR	18.4.80	20		Dudince	26 Mar
4:06:15	Xavier	Le Coz	FRA	30.12.79	21		Dudince	26 Mar
4:06:52	Ivan	Banzeruk	UKR	9.2.90	4		Ivano-Frankivsk	9 Oct
(100)								

Mark	Name		Nat	Born	Date		Mark	Name		Nat	Born	Date
4:06:57	Quentin	Rew	NZL	16.7.84	24 Apr		4:08:20	Yuriy	Chesnokov	RUS	29.12.79	12 Jun
4:06:57	Ferrán	Collados	ESP	27.10.85	21 May		4:08:26	Vladislav	Hafizov	RUS	1.8.88	12 Jun
4:07:17	Jorge	Costa	POR	20.3.61	19 Feb		4:08:53		Xu Dexing	CHN	20.8.88	13 Mar
4:07:21	Konstandinós	Stefanópoulos	GRE	11.7.84	26 Mar		4:09:50		Liu Rusi	CHN	6.8.91	24 Apr
4:07:27	Aleksey	Khimin	RUS	26.2.89	12 Jun		4:09:58	Eddy	Rozé (10)	FRA	13.11.70	9 Oct
4:07:54	Predrag	Filipovic	SRB	5.10.78	21 May							

WOMEN'S WORLD LISTS 2011

60 METRES INDOORS

Mark	Name		Nat	Born	Pos	Meet	Venue	Date
7.09	LaKya	Brookins	USA	28.7.89	1	NCAA	College Station	12 Mar
7.11	Veronica	Campbell-Brown	JAM	15.5.82	1	Mill	New York	28 Jan
7.12A	Alexandria	Anderson	USA	28.1.87	1	NC	Albuquerque	27 Feb
7.13	Olesya	Povh	UKR	18.10.87	1		Düsseldorf	11 Feb
7.13A	Carmelita	Jeter	USA	24.11.79	2	NC	Albuquerque	27 Feb
7.14	Gloria	Asumnu	USA/NGR	22.5.85	2		Düsseldorf	11 Feb
7.15	Ruddy	Zang Milama	GAB	6.6.87	1	Winter	Moskva	6 Feb
7.15	Mariya	Ryemyen	UKR	2.8.87	1h2		Karlsruhe	13 Feb
7.15A	Shalonda	Solomon	USA	19.12.85	3	NC	Albuquerque	27 Feb
7.21					1B	Tyson	Fayetteville	11 Feb
7.17	Lauryn	Williams	USA	11.9.83	1		Boston (Roxbury)	5 Feb
(10)								

Mark		Name	Nat	Born	Pos	Meet	Venue	Date
7.17	Ezinne	Okparaebo	NOR	3.3.88	2h2		Karlsruhe	13 Feb
7.17A	Jessica	Young	USA	6.4.87	1	MWC	Albuquerque	26 Feb
7.17					2	NCAA	College Station	12 Mar
7.18	Marshevet	Hooker/Myers	USA	25.9.84	2		Boston (Roxbury)	5 Feb
7.18	Myriam	Soumaré	FRA	29.10.86	2s2	EI	Paris (B)	5 Mar
7.18	Kenyanna	Wilson	USA	27.10.88	3	NCAA	College Station	12 Mar
7.19	Véronique	Mang	FRA	15.12.84	1h1		Metz	25 Feb
7.19	Aurieyall	Scott	USA-J	18.5.92	1h3	NCAA	College Station	11 Mar
7.20	Amber	Purvis	USA	23.1.90	2h3	NCAA	College Station	11 Mar
7.20	Scottesha	Miller	USA	14.1.88	4	NCAA	College Station	12 Mar
7.21	Jodie	Williams	GBR-J	28.9.93	4s2	EI	Paris (B)	5 Mar
(20)								
7.21	Hrystyna	Stuy	UKR	3.2.88	5	EI	Paris (B)	6 Mar
7.22	Stormy	Kendrick	USA	6.1.91	1		Blacksburg	21 Jan
7.22	Mikele	Barber	USA	4.10.80	2	Winter	Moskva	6 Feb
7.22	Semoy	Hackett #	TRI	27.11.88	1h2	NCAA	College Station	11 Mar
7.23	Me'Lisa	Barber	USA	4.10.80	3	Mill	New York	28 Jan
7.23	Yevgeniya	Polyakova	RUS	29.5.83	1	Mosc Ch	Moskva	29 Jan
7.23	Yeoryía	Koklóni	GRE	7.5.81	5s2	EI	Paris (B)	5 Mar
7.23	Tiffany	Townsend	USA	14.6.89	2h1	NCAA	College Station	11 Mar
7.24	Brittney	Reese	USA	9.9.86	1		Saskatoon	4 Feb
7.24	Jeneba	Tarmoh	USA	27.9.89	2		New York (Armory)	4 Feb
(30)								
7.24	Dominique	Booker	USA-J	10.2.92	3s1	Tyson	Fayetteville	11 Feb
7.25	Olga	Belkina	RUS	23.8.90	1		Sankt Peterburg	22 Jan
7.25	Bernice	Wilson ¶	GBR	21.4.84	2	NC	Sheffield	12 Feb
7.25	Miana	Griffiths	CAN	17.1.90	1		Toronto	20 Feb
7.25	Verena	Sailer	GER	16.10.85	1s1	NC	Leipzig	26 Feb
7.26	Trisha-Ann	Hawthorne	JAM	8.11.89	1	Big East	Akron	20 Feb
7.26	Dezerea	Bryant	USA-J	27.4.93	1		Seattle	27 Feb
7.26	Marecia	Pemberton	SKN	7.1.90	1		Ames	5 Mar
7.26	Funmi	Alabi	USA	25.4.91	1s2		Blacksburg	5 Mar
7.26	Chastity	Riggien	USA	5.7.89	4h3	NCAA	College Station	11 Mar
(40)								
7.27	Madison	McNary	USA	1.3.90	1	Big 10	West Lafayette	27 Feb
7.27	Lina	Grincikaite	LTU	3.5.87	4s1	EI	Paris (B)	5 Mar
7.28	Jeanette	Kwakye	GBR	20.3.83	1	South	London (LV)	16 Jan
7.28	Natasha	Hastings	USA	23.7.86	1		New York (Armory)	21 Jan
7.28	Dafne	Schippers	NED-J	15.6.92	1		Kirchberg	29 Jan
7.28	Candyce	McGrone	USA	24.3.89	5h1	NCAA	College Station	11 Mar
7.29	English	Gardner	USA-J	22.4.92	1		Seattle	15 Jan
7.29	Svetlana	Nabokina	RUS	5.6.82	1		Volgograd	22 Jan
7.29	Bianca	Knight	USA	2.1.89	1h6	Tyson	Fayetteville	11 Feb
7.29	Sheniqua	Ferguson	BAH	24.11.89	1h1	SEC	Fayetteville	26 Feb
(50)								
7.29	Christina	Manning	USA	29.5.90	2	Big 10	West Lafayette	27 Feb

Outdoors

7.16	0.7	Sally	Pearson	AUS	19.9.86	1		Gold Coast	25 Jun

100 YARDS

In 100m race at Ostrava 31 May: (1.1) Veronica Campbell-Brown 9.91, Debbie Ferguson-McKenzie 10.21, Shillonie Calvert 10.22, Ruddy Zang-Milama 10.30, Barbara Pierre 10.38, LaShauntea Moore 10.46, Katerina Cechová 10.49.

100 METRES

Mark		Name		Nat	Born	Pos	Meet	Venue	Date
10.70	2.0	Carmelita	Jeter	USA	24.11.79	1	Pre	Eugene	4 Jun
10.76	1.1	Veronica	Campbell-Brown	JAM	15.5.82	1	GS	Ostrava	31 May
10.78	0.4		Jeter			1	VD	Bruxelles	16 Sep
10.84	0.3		Campbell-Brown			1	NC	Kingston	24 Jun
10.85	0.4		Campbell-Brown			2	VD	Bruxelles	16 Sep
10.86	1.9		Jeter			1		Kingston	7 May
10.86	2.0	Marshevet	Hooker/Myers	USA	25.9.84	2	Pre	Eugene	4 Jun
10.87	2.0	Kerron	Stewart	JAM	16.4.84	3	Pre	Eugene	4 Jun
10.87	1.6		Hooker			1h1	NC	Eugene	23 Jun
10.88	1.7		Jeter			1h3	NC	Eugene	23 Jun
10.90	-1.4		Jeter			1	WCh	Daegu	29 Aug
10.90	0.4	Kelly-Ann	Baptiste	TRI	14.10.86	3	VD	Bruxelles	16 Sep
10.91	0.6		Baptiste			1	DL	Saint-Denis	8 Jul
10.92	1.2		Campbell-Brown			1	DL	Shanghai	15 May
10.93	-0.4		Jeter			1	LGP	London (CP)	6 Aug

Mark	Wind	Name		Nat	Born	Pos	Meet	Venue	Date
10.94	1.9		Baptiste			2		Kingston	7 May
10.95	1.2		Jeter			2	DL	Shanghai	15 May
10.95	2.0	Shelly-Ann	Fraser-Pryce	JAM	27.12.86	4	Pre	Eugene	4 Jun
10.95	1.8		Campbell-Brown			1h1	NC	Kingston	24 Jun
10.95	0.6		Campbell-Brown			2	DL	Saint-Denis	8 Jul
10.96	0.8	Ivet	Lalova	BUL	18.5.84	1	Balk C	Sliven	2 Jul
10.97	0.3		Stewart			2	NC	Kingston	24 Jun
10.97	-0.4		Baptiste			2	LGP	London (CP)	6 Aug
10.97	-1.4		Campbell-Brown			2	WCh	Daegu	29 Aug
10.98	-1.4		Baptiste			3	WCh	Daegu	29 Aug
10.99	-0.1		Jeter			1	MSR	Walnut	16 Apr
10.99	1.8	Damola	Osayomi	NGR	26.6.86	1		São Paulo	22 May
10.99	-1.4		Fraser-Pryce			4	WCh	Daegu	29 Aug
11.00	2.0	Sherone	Simpson	JAM	12.8.84	5	Pre	Eugene	4 Jun
11.00	-1.0		Jeter			1h2	LGP	London (CP)	6 Aug
11.00	-0.5		Jeter			1	Hanz	Zagreb	13 Sep
11.01	1.8	Alexandria	Anderson	USA	28.1.87	2		São Paulo	22 May
		(32/10)							
11.03	0.6	English	Gardner	USA-J	22.4.92	1	Pac10	Tucson	14 May
11.05	1.7	Schillonie	Calvert	JAM	27.7.88	1	FBK	Hengelo	29 May
11.05	0.5	Carrie	Russell	JAM	18.10.90	1s1	WUG	Shenzhen	17 Aug
11.06	1.9	Murielle	Ahouré	CIV	23.8.87	1		Greensboro	15 May
11.08	2.0	Blessing	Okagbare	NGR	9.10.88	7	Pre	Eugene	4 Jun
11.08	1.5	Candyce	McGrone	USA	24.3.89	1	NCAA	Des Moines	10 Jun
11.08	0.4	Shalonda	Solomon	USA	19.12.85	4	VD	Bruxelles	16 Sep
11.09	1.1	Debbie	Ferguson McKenzie	BAH	16.1.76	2	GS	Ostrava	31 May
11.09	1.5	Kimberlyn	Duncan	USA	2.8.91	2	NCAA	Des Moines	10 Jun
11.09	1.6	Mikele	Barber	USA	4.10.80	2h1	NC	Eugene	23 Jun
		(20)							
11.09	1.4	Ruddy	Zang Milama	GAB	6.6.87	1	FRA Ch	Albi	29 Jul
11.10	0.1	LaKya	Brookins	USA	28.7.89	1		Auburn	16 Apr
11.10	0.3	Jura	Levy	JAM	4.11.90	3	NC	Kingston	24 Jun
11.11	1.4	Véronique	Mang	FRA	15.12.84	2	NC	Albi	29 Jul
11.12	1.1	Aurieyall	Scott	USA-J	18.5.92	1	NC-j	Eugene	24 Jun
11.14	1.5	Jessica	Young	USA	6.4.87	3	NCAA	Des Moines	10 Jun
11.14	2.0	Barbara	Pierre	USA	28.4.87	1		Clermont	11 Jun
11.15	2.0	Lauryn	Williams	USA	11.9.83	8	Pre	Eugene	4 Jun
11.15	1.8	Aleen	Bailey	JAM	25.11.80	2h1	NC	Kingston	24 Jun
11.15	1.6	Jeanette	Kwakye	GBR	20.3.83	1		La Chaux-de-Fonds	3 Jul
		(30)							
11.17	0.1	Sheniqua	Ferguson	BAH	24.11.89	2		Auburn	16 Apr
11.17	-0.1	Semoy	Hackett #	TRI	27.11.88	1h2	SEC	Athens GA	14 May
11.17	-1.2	Nataliya	Pogrebnyak	UKR	19.2.88	1h3	NCp	Yalta	30 May
11.17	1.6	LaShaunte'a	Moore	USA	31.7.83	3s1	NC	Eugene	24 Jun
11.17	1.4	Myriam	Soumaré	FRA	29.10.86	3	NC	Albi	29 Jul
11.18	1.6	Anyika	Onuora	GBR	28.10.84	1		Zeulenroda	29 May
11.18	0.5	Jodie	Williams	GBR-J	28.9.93	1	EJ	Tallinn	22 Jul
11.19	1.0	Ana Cláudia	Silva	BRA	6.11.88	1h1		São Paulo	26 Mar
11.19		Tiffany	Townsend	USA	14.6.89	2	DrakeR	Des Moines	30 Apr
11.19	0.6	Jessica	Davis	USA-J	31.10.92	2	Pac10	Tucson	14 May
		(40)							
11.19	0.5	Gloria	Asumnu	USA/NGR	22.5.85	3		Río de Janeiro	26 May
11.19	1.6	Kenyanna	Wilson	USA	27.10.88	4s1	NC	Eugene	24 Jun
11.19	1.2	Dafne	Schippers	NED-J	15.6.92	1		Mannheim	13 Aug
11.20	1.5	Shayla	Mahan	USA	18.1.89	1rB		Columbia SC	26 Mar
11.20	0.5	Sally	Pearson	AUS	19.9.86	1		Perth	31 Mar
11.20	-1.2	Inna	Eftimova	BUL	19.6.88	1		Plovdiv	9 Jul
11.20	1.0	Michelle Lee	Ahyee	TRI-J	10.4.92	3h3	WCh	Daegu	28 Aug
11.21	0.6	Amber	Purvis	USA	23.1.90	3	Pac10	Tucson	14 May
11.21	1.9	Rachelle	Smith	USA	30.6.81	2		Greensboro	15 May
11.21	0.3	Octavious	Freeman	USA-J	20.4.92	1		Orlando	28 May
		(50)							
11.21	2.0	Scottesha	Miller	USA	14.1.88	2		Clermont	11 Jun
11.21	0.4	Mariya	Ryemyen	UKR	2.8.87	1		Strasbourg	12 Jun
11.21	1.4	Ezinne	Okparaebo	NOR	3.3.88	3h2	WCh	Daegu	28 Aug
11.22	0.2	Bianca	Knight	USA	2.1.89	3	GP	Ponce	14 May
11.22A	-0.2	Rosângela	Santos	BRA	20.12.90	1	PAm	Guadalajara, MEX	25 Oct
11.23	1.6	Jeneba	Tarmoh	USA	27.9.89	4h1	NC	Eugene	23 Jun
11.23	0.1	Laura	Turner	GBR	12.8.82	1		Bedford	16 Jul
11.24	0.4	Olesya	Povh	UKR	18.10.87	2		Strasbourg	12 Jun

Mark	Wind	Name		Nat	Born	Pos	Meet	Venue	Date
11.24	-0.3	Chisato	Fukushima	JPN	27.6.88	1r1		Tottori	26 Jun
11.26	1.8	Tahesia	Harrigan #	IVB	15.2.82	4	Caioxa	São Paulo	22 May
(60)									
11.26A	-0.2	Shakera	Reece	BAR	31.8.88	3	PAm	Guadalajara, MEX	25 Oct
11.27	1.0	Cydonie	Mothersill	CAY	19.3.78	1		Atlanta	5 Jun
11.28	1.4	Carima	Louami	FRA	12.5.79	4	NC	Albi	29 Jul
11.28	0.5	Aleksandra	Fedoriva	RUS	13.9.88	3h7	WCh	Daegu	28 Aug
11.29	0.6	Jasmine	Baldwin-Foss	USA	27.9.86	1		Los Angeles (ER)	7 May
11.29	1.8	Christina	Manning	USA	29.5.90	1	Big 10	Iowa City	15 May
11.29	0.6	Tianna	Madison	USA	30.8.85	1h2		Clermont	21 May
11.29	1.0	Yasmin	Kwadwo	GER	9.11.90	1		Weinheim	28 May
11.30	1.9	Simone	Facey	JAM	7.5.85	8		Kingston	7 May
11.30	1.3	Yelizaveta	Savlinis	RUS	14.8.87	1h2	Mosc Ch	Moskva	9 Jul
(70)									
11.30	2.0	Joanna	Atkins	USA	31.1.89	2	Vard	Réthimno	13 Jul
11.30	0.0	Yuliya	Gushchina	RUS	4.3.83	1h3	NC	Cheboksary	21 Jul
11.31	0.9	Trisha-Ann	Hawthorne	JAM	8.11.89	1		Storrs	9 Apr
11.31	-0.1	Connie	Moore	USA	29.8.81	2	MSR	Walnut	16 Apr
11.31		Nelkys Teresa	Casabona	CUB	12.5.84	1		La Habana	12 May
11.31	1.7	Stephanie	Durst	USA	11.4.82	5	FBK	Hengelo	29 May
11.31	2.0	Toyin	Olupona	CAN	29.1.83	3=		Clermont	11 Jun
11.31	2.0	Nickesha	Williams	USA	2.4.87	3=		Clermont	11 Jun
11.32A	0.9	Endurance	Abinuwa	NGR	31.7.87	2		El Paso	16 Apr
11.32	0.6	Dominique	Duncan	USA	7.5.90	1h3	Big 12	Norman OK	14 May
(80)									
11.32	1.4	Céline	Distel	FRA	25.7.87	5	NC	Albi	29 Jul
11.33	1.9	Marta	Jeschke	POL	2.6.86	1		Kraków	12 Jun
11.33	1.6	Leena	Günther	GER	16.4.91	1r5		Mannheim	13 Aug
11.34	0.6	Marecia	Pemberton	SKN	7.1.90	1		Tallahassee	8 Apr
11.34	1.9	Chelsea	Hayes	USA	2.2.88	1h1	WAC	Honolulu	14 May
11.34	1.3	Chastity	Riggien	USA	5.7.89	3h4	NC	Eugene	23 Jun
11.34	1.8	Andreea	Ograzeanu	ROU	24.3.90	1	NC	Bucuresti	29 Jun
11.34	1.4	Ayodelé	Ikuesan	FRA	15.5.85	6	NC	Albi	29 Jul
11.34	-0.7	Hrystyna	Stuy	UKR	3.2.88	2	WUG	Shenzhen	17 Aug
11.35	2.0	Dominique	Holmes	USA	25.6.86	1		Nashville	9 Apr
(90)									
11.35	1.1	Sheila	Paul	USA	30.9.89	2	Conf USA	Houston	15 May
11.35	1.7	Samantha	Henry-Robinson	JAM	25.9.88	2h1		Clermont	21 May
11.35	1.2	Grecia	Bolton	USA	2.10.89	1h4	NCAA-W	Eugene	26 May
11.35	1.0	Marion	Wagner	GER	1.2.78	2		Weinheim	28 May
11.35	0.0	Darya	Pizhankova ¶	UKR	9.1.90	2	NCp	Yalta	30 May
11.35	2.0	Weronika	Wedler	POL	17.7.89	1h3		Sosnowiec	11 Jun
11.35	-2.1	Yuna	Mekhti-Zade	RUS	25.4.86	2	Mosc Ch	Moskva	9 Jul
11.36	-0.1	Virginia	Crawford	USA	7.9.83	3	MSR	Walnut	16 Apr
11.36		Ayanna	Hutchinson	TRI	18.2.78	2		Couva	10 Jul
11.36	1.6		Wei Yongli	CHN	11.10.91	1	NGPF	Nanchang	16 Jul
(100)									
11.36	1.2	Charonda	Williams	USA	27.3.87	1		Lapinlahti	24 Jul
11.36	0.1	Guzel	Khubbieva	UZB	2.5.76	1	NC	Tashkent	30 Sep

Mark	Wind	Name		Nat	Born	Date
11.37	1.4	Judith	Riley	JAM	4.11.88	2 Apr
11.37		Gayon	Evans	JAM	15.1.90	7 May
11.37	1.8	Olga	Bludova	KAZ	5.11.91	18 Jun
11.37	1.6		Tao Yujia	CHN	16.2.87	16 Jul
11.37	0.7	Agnes	Osazuwa	NGR	21.6.90	24 Sep
11.38	-0.8	Antonique	Strachan	BAH-J	22.8.93	23 Apr
11.38A	2.0	Yomara	Hinestroza	COL	20.5.88	6 May
11.38	0.3	Dezerea	Bryant	USA-J	27.4.93	4 Jun
11.38	1.4	Émilie	Gaydu	FRA	5.2.89	25 Jun
11.38	-1.4	Phylicia	George	CAN	16.11.87	3 Jul
11.38	1.6	Ashlee	Nelson	GBR	20.2.91	3 Jul
11.38	0.9	Anna	Babicheva	RUS	10.7.87	8 Jul
11.38	1.6	Anne	Möllinger	GER	27.9.85	13 Aug
11.39	1.3	Christiania	Williams	JAM-Y	17.10.94	19 Mar
11.39	1.5	Keilah	Tyson	USA-J	6.11.92	4 Jun
11.39	0.7	Franciela	Krasucki	BRA	26.4.88	25 Jun
11.39	0.1	Montell	Douglas	GBR	24.1.86	16 Jul
11.39		Yevgeniya	Polyakova	RUS	29.5.83	30 Jul
11.40	2.0	Melissa	Breen	AUS	17.9.90	29 Apr
11.40	0.7	Crystal	Emmanuel	CAN	27.11.91	28 May
11.40	1.1	Katerina	Cechová	CZE	21.3.88	31 May
11.40	0.8	Me'Lisa	Barber	USA	4.10.80	11 Jun
11.40	1.8	Yeoryía	Koklóni	GRE	7.5.81	24 Jun
11.40	1.5	Yekaterina	Filatova	RUS	11.8.89	24 Jun

Mark	Wind	Name		Nat	Born	Date
11.41	1.0	Brianna	Glenn	USA	18.4.80	15 Apr
11.41	0.0	Tynia	Gaither	BAH-J	16.3.93	7 May
11.41	1.9	Kerri Ann	Mitchell	CAN	29.3.83	21 May
11.41	1.6	Anne Christina	Haack	GER	15.4.87	13 Aug
11.42	0.6	Lauretta	Ozoh	NGR	5.9.90	7 May
11.42	0.6	Ashley	Collier	USA-J	4.2.92	14 May
11.42	1.4	Yuliya	Balykina	BLR	12.4.84	21 May
11.42	-0.4	Santana	Lowery	USA	15.1.87	27 May
11.42	1.1	Tezdzhan	Naimova	BUL	1.5.87	11 Jun
11.42A	-0.1	Eliecet	Palacios	COL	15.8.87	18 Jun
11.42	1.6	Natasha	Morrison	JAM-J	17.11.92	24 Jun
11.42	1.4	Lina	Grincikaite	LTU	3.5.87	23 Jul
11.42	0.7	Viktoriya	Zyabkina	KAZ-J	4.9.92	27 Jul
11.42	1.2	Morolake	Akinosun	USA-Y	17.5.94	3 Aug
11.43	1.2	Georgina	Nembhard	JAM	24.11.88	9 Apr
11.43	1.0	Leslie	Cole	USA	16.2.87	15 Apr
11.43	0.1	Tawanna	Meadows	USA	4.8.86	16 Apr
11.43	2.0	Kana	Ichikawa	JPN	14.1.91	29 Apr
11.43		Shawna	Anderson	JAM	3.5.89	30 Apr
11.43	1.1	Whitney	Harris	USA	11.6.89	15 May
11.43	0.5	Porscha	Lucas	USA	18.6.88	26 May
11.43	0.1	Yekaterina	Voronenkova	RUS	8.2.88	12 Jun
11.43	1.9	Marika	Popowicz	POL	28.4.88	12 Jun
11.43	1.9	Yekaterina	Hanchar	BLR	30.8.88	22 Jun

Mark	Wind	Name		Nat	Born	Pos	Meet	Venue	Date
11.43	-0.7	Delphine	Atangana	CMR	16.8.84				10 Jul
11.43	0.5	Jamile	Samuel	NED-J	24.4.92				22 Jul
11.43	-0.1	Kai	Selvon	TRI-J	13.4.92				13 Aug
11.43A	0.4	Alejandra	Idrobo	COL	8.4.88				13 Aug
11.43A	0.0	Tamiris	de Líz	BRA-Y	18.11.95				23 Sep
11.44	1.8	Aaliyah	Brown	USA-Y	6.1.95				20 May
11.44	0.3	Cathleen	Tschirch	GER	23.7.79				28 May
11.44	0.9	Olga	Belkina	RUS	23.8.90				24 Jun
11.44	1.7	Mayumi	Watanabe	JPN	6.6.83				15 Jul
11.45	1.5	Gabrielle	Glenn	USA	28.1.89				26 Mar
11.45A	1.5	Terra	Evans	USA	7.10.89				26 Mar
11.45	1.4	Shayla	Sanders	USA-Y	6.1.94				28 Apr
11.45	0.5	Aareon	Payne	USA	3.9.90				1 May
11.45	1.1	Dominique	Booker	USA-J	10.2.92				15 May
11.45	4.0	Anna	Gurova ¶	RUS	29.4.81				4 Jun
11.45	0.5	Marina	Panteleyeva	RUS	16.5.89				24 Jun
11.45A	0.5	Laverne	Jones-Ferrette	ISV	16.9.81				24 Oct
11.46	1.8	Madison	McNary	USA	1.3.90				15 May
11.46	1.4	Yelena	Nevmerzhitskaya	BLR	27.7.80				21 May
11.46	0.0	Deborah	Odeyemi	NGR-Y	21.11.95				21 May
11.46	1.8	Rosemar	Coelho Neto	BRA	2.1.77				22 May
11.47	1.1	Sónia	Tavares	POR	21.3.86				8 Jun
11.47	-0.4	Myasia	Jacobs	USA-Y	8.1.94				9 Jun
11.47	2.0	Courtney	Patterson	ISV	10.2.85				11 Jun
11.47	0.7	Asha	Philip	GBR	25.10.90				3 Jul
11.48A	2.0	Merlin	Palacios	COL-Y	13.6.94				6 May
11.48	0.4	Jasmine	Edgerson	USA	6.6.91				14 May
11.48	1.4	Alina	Talay	BLR	14.5.89				21 May
11.48	1.6	Margaret	Adeoye	GBR	27.4.85				3 Jul
11.48	-2.1	Anna	Kaygorodova	RUS	10.3.83				9 Jul
11.48	0.5	Tatjana	Pinto	GER-J	2.7.92				22 Jul
11.48	0.0	Yuliya	Kashina	RUS	26.2.87				22 Jul
11.48	0.5		Ha Xianping	CHN	15.10.90				8 Sep
11.48+	1.5	Abi	Oyepitan	GBR	30.12.79				17 Sep
11.49	1.5	Shataya	Hendricks	USA	15.8.89				16 Apr
11.49	1.1	Digna Luz	Murillo	ESP	22.5.81				8 Jun
11.49	1.4	Jessie	Saint-Marc	FRA	16.7.91				25 Jun
11.49	0.6	Amy	Foster	IRL	2.10.88				8 Jul
11.49A	-0.2	Mariely	Sánchez (189)	DOM	30.12.88				25 Oct

Hand timing

Mark		Name		Nat	Born	Pos	Meet	Venue	Date
11.1		Yekaterina	Voronenkova	RUS	8.2.88				21 May
11.2		Yelena	Aksyonova	RUS	1.3.88				8 Jul

Wind assisted perfomances to 10.99

Mark	Wind	Name		Nat	Born	Pos	Meet	Venue	Date
10.74	2.7		Jeter			1	NC	Eugene	24 Jun
10.83	2.7	Marshevet	Hooker/Myers	USA	25.9.84	2	NC	Eugene	24 Jun
10.86	2.9	Murielle	Ahouré	CIV	23.8.87	1		Clermont	4 Jun
10.90	3.2		Myers			1r2	TexR	Austin	9 Apr
10.90	2.9	Shalonda	Solomon	USA	19.12.85	2		Clermont	4 Jun
10.90	4.6		Solomon			2h1		Clermont	4 Jun
10.90	2.3		Hooker			1s2	NC	Eugene	24 Jun
10.90	2.5	Damola	Osayomi	NGR	26.6.86	1	AfG	Maputo	12 Sep
10.91	3.2	Alexandria	Anderson	USA	28.1.87	2r2	TexR	Austin	9 Apr
10.94	2.9	Jeneba	Tarmoh	USA	27.9.89	1r1	TexR	Austin	9 Apr
10.96	2.7	Mikele	Barber	USA	4.10.80	3	NC	Eugene	24 Jun
10.98	2.9	Semoy	Hackett #	TRI	27.11.88	2r1	TexR	Austin	9 Apr
11.01	2.4		Hackett			1	SEC	Athens GA	15 May
11.01	2.2		Lalova			1	Bisl	Oslo	9 Jun
11.01	2.5	Blessing	Okagbare	NGR	9.10.88	2	AfG	Maputo	12 Sep
11.02	2.4	LaKya	Brookins	USA	28.7.89	2	SEC	Athens GA	15 May
11.02	2.4	Kimberlyn	Duncan	USA	2.8.91	3	SEC	Athens GA	15 May
11.04	2.7	LaShaunte'a	Moore	USA	31.7.83	4	NC	Eugene	24 Jun
11.05	3.1	Dominique	Duncan	USA	7.5.90	1h3	TexR	Austin	8 Apr
11.07	3.6	Jura	Levy	JAM	4.11.90	1	JUCO	Hutchinson	21 May
11.07	2.7	Candyce	McGrone	USA	24.3.89	6	NC	Eugene	24 Jun
11.08	3.4	Jasmine	Baldwin-Foss	USA	27.9.86	1		Walnut	4 Jun
11.08	2.7	Jessica	Young	USA	6.4.87	7	NC	Eugene	24 Jun
11.09	3.1	Tiffany	Townsend	USA	14.6.89	2h3	TexR	Austin	8 Apr
11.09	4.2	Aleksandra	Fedoriva	RUS	13.9.88	1	NCp	Yerino	4 Jun
11.10	4.1	Lauryn	Williams	USA	11.9.83	1	KansR	Lawrence	23 Apr
11.11	2.4	Kenyanna	Wilson	USA	27.10.88	4	SEC	Athens GA	15 May
11.12	2.2	Myriam	Soumaré	FRA	29.10.86	1h6	WCh	Daegu	28 Aug
11.13	2.9	Chastity	Riggien	USA	5.7.89	6r1	TexR	Austin	9 Apr
11.13	4.6	Samantha	Henry-Robinson	JAM	25.9.88	3h1		Clermont	4 Jun
11.13	2.8	Dafne	Schippers	NED-J	15.6.92	1	NC-j	Alphen aan der Rijn	9 Jul
11.14	3.2	Porscha	Lucas	USA	18.6.88	4r2	TexR	Austin	9 Apr
11.14	2.2	Olesya	Povh	UKR	18.10.87	2	Bisl	Oslo	9 Jun
11.15	2.6	Michelle Lee	Ahyee	TRI-J	10.4.92	1h1	PAm-J	Miramar	22 Jul
11.16	3.4	Chisato	Fukushima	JPN	27.6.88	1r2		Tottori	26 Jun
11.17	4.2	Yelizaveta	Savlinis	RUS	14.8.87	2	NCp	Yerino	4 Jun
11.17	2.2	Ezinne	Okparaebo	NOR	3.3.88	3	Bisl	Oslo	9 Jun
11.17	2.8	Cathleen	Tschirch	GER	23.7.79	1h2		Mannheim	13 Aug
11.18	2.5	Chelsea	Hayes	USA	2.2.88	3		Baton Rouge	23 Apr
11.18	2.9	Simone	Facey	JAM	7.5.85	4		Clermont	4 Jun
11.18	2.2	Mariya	Ryemyen	UKR	2.8.87	4	Bisl	Oslo	9 Jun
11.19	4.0	Tawanna	Meadows	USA	4.8.86	1		Troy	23 Apr
11.19	2.2	Kai	Selvon	TRI-J	13.4.92	1	NC	Port of Spain	13 Aug
11.20	2.6	Brittney	Reese	USA	9.9.86	1		Oxford MS	9 Apr
11.21	3.4	Connie	Moore	USA	29.8.81	2		Walnut	4 Jun
11.22	3.4	Ashley	Collier	USA-J	4.2.92	2		Gainesville	16 Apr
11.22	2.8	Yasmin	Kwadwo	GER	9.11.90	2rB		Mannheim	13 Aug
11.23	3.1	Stormy	Kendrick	USA	6.1.91	4h3	TexR	Austin	8 Apr
11.25	5.4	Judith	Riley	JAM	4.11.88	1	MIAA	Emporia	8 May
11.25	3.3	Carima	Louami	FRA	12.5.79	1		Castres	19 Jul

Mark	Wind	Name		Nat	Born	Pos	Meet	Venue	Date
11.26+	2.6	Allyson	Felix	USA	18.11.85	1	CityG	Manchester	15 May
11.26	4.2	Yuliya	Kashina	RUS	26.2.87	3	NCp	Yerino	4 Jun
11.27	2.6	Melissa	Breen	AUS	17.9.90	1	Oda	Hiroshima	29 Apr
11.27	2.4	Nivea	Smith	BAH	18.2.90	5	SEC	Athens GA	15 May
11.27	5.4	Yuna	Mekhti-Zade	RUS	25.4.86	1h2	NCp	Yerino	4 Jun
11.28	2.6	Kana	Ichikawa	JPN	14.1.91	2	Oda	Hiroshima	29 Apr
11.29	6.0	Toshika	Sylvester	USA	3.12.91	1		Baton Rouge	26 Mar
11.29	2.4	Endurance	Abinuwa	NGR	31.7.87	2r3	TexR	Austin	9 Apr
11.29	2.2	Andreea	Ograzeanu	ROU	24.3.90	2h1	NC	Bucuresti	29 Jun
11.30	3.1	Grecia	Bolton	USA	2.10.89	5h3	TexR	Austin	8 Apr
11.30	2.3	Yuliya	Nesterenko	BLR	15.6.79	1rB	NCp	Brest	21 May
11.30	3.2	Céline	Distel	FRA	25.7.87	1r3		Bonneuil-sur-Marne	2 Jun
11.30	2.2	Ayanna	Hutchinson	TRI	18.2.78	3	NC	Port of Spain	13 Aug
11.31	2.4	Terra	Evans	USA	7.10.89	4r3	TexR	Austin	9 Apr
11.31	2.8	Shawna	Anderson	JAM	3.5.89	3	Johnson	Waco	23 Apr
11.31	3.2	Delphine	Atangana	CMR	16.8.84	2r3		Bonneuil-sur-Marne	2 Jun
11.32	2.4	Darshay	Davis	USA	23.9.91	6	SEC	Athens GA	15 May
11.33	6.0	Kasey	Rodgers	USA	3.4.90	2		Baton Rouge	26 Mar
11.33	2.1	Tameka	Williams	SKN	31.8.89	1		Basseterre	19 Jun

Mark	Wind	Name		Nat	Born	Date
11.34	3.6	Erica	Alexander	USA	24.6.90	2 Apr
11.34	5.4	Natalya	Murinovich	RUS	27.5.85	4 Jun
11.35	2.9	Patricia	Hall	JAM	16.10.82	15 Apr
11.35	4.2	Yekaterina	Voronenkova	RUS	8.2.88	4 Jun
11.35	3.3	Katerina	Cechová	CZE	21.3.88	2 Jul
11.35	2.6	Charonda	Williams	USA	27.3.87	24 Jul
11.36	2.4	Jasmine	Edgerson	USA	6.6.91	23 Apr
11.36	3.6	Reyare	Thomas	TRI	23.11.87	21 May
11.37	2.8	Tiffani	McReynolds	USA	4.12.91	23 Apr
11.37	4.2	Anna	Babicheva	RUS	10.7.87	4 Jun
11.37	2.5	Vida	Anim	GHA	7.12.83	12 Sep
11.38	3.7	Indira	Spence	JAM	8.9.86	26 May
11.38	2.6	Karoline	Köhler	GER	20.2.84	25 Jun
11.39	2.1	Mandy	White	USA	23.10.88	13 May
11.39	7.1	Ashlee	Abraham	USA	24.9.91	14 May
11.39	2.4	Georgina	Nembhard	JAM	24.11.88	15 May
11.39	2.1	Virgil	Hodge	SKN	17.11.83	19 Jun
11.40	2.6	Saori	Kitakaze	JPN	3.4.85	29 Apr
11.40	3.5	Christelle	Monne	FRA	30.6.87	2 Jun
11.40	4.0	Nelly	Banco	FRA	17.2.86	2 Jun
11.40	2.4	Chalonda	Goodman	USA	29.9.90	23 Jun
11.41	2.6	Momoko	Takahashi	JPN	16.11.88	29 Apr
11.41	2.4	Gabby	Glenn	USA	28.1.89	15 May
11.41	2.4	Bernice	Wilson ¶	GBR	21.4.84	22 May
11.41	2.1	Sónia	Tavares	POR	21.3.86	1 Jul
11.42	4.5	Annie	Tagoe	GBR-J	4.6.93	25 Jun
11.43	3.9	Francesca	Okwaro	USA		1 May
11.43	2.9	Shanneka	Claiborne	USA	20.1.88	6 May
11.43	7.1	Diona	Graves	USA	.89	14 May
11.44	2.6	Jenna	Prandini	USA-J	20.11.92	22 Jul
11.45	3.4	Shayla	Sanders	USA-Y	6.1.94	20 Apr
11.46A	2.3	Carina	Horn	RSA	9.3.89	26 Mar
11.46	4.0	Allison	Peter	ISV-J	14.7.92	8 Apr
11.46	2.6	Nao	Okabe	JPN	28.8.88	29 Apr
11.46	2.8		Ha Xianping	CHN	15.10.90	21 May
11.46	3.7	Danielle	Williams	USA	10.10.89	26 May
11.46	2.2	Verena	Sailer	GER	16.10.85	9 Jun
11.47	3.1	Loudia	Laarman	CAN	4.10.91	8 Apr
11.47	3.5	Tiffany	George	USA-J	13.8.92	23 Apr
11.47	3.6	Tasha	Allen	USA	8.5.90	21 May
11.47	3.3	Iveta	Mazácová	CZE	15.12.86	2 Jul
11.48	3.4	Lynne	Layne	USA	1.4.88	16 Apr
11.48	3.1	Serene	Williams	USA	21.10.90	20 May
11.48A	2.5	Tiana	Valentine	USA-Y	15.5.94	4 Jun
11.49	3.2	Allison	George	GRN	3.1.88	9 Apr
11.49	3.8	Jessica	Beard	USA	8.1.89	16 Apr
11.49	7.1	Jeanette	Pettigrew	USA	6.11.89	14 May
11.49	2.1	Kristi	Castlin	USA	7.7.88	14 May
11.49	2.4	Daria	Korczynska	POL	30.7.81	3 Jun
11.49	3.3	Denisa	Rosolová	CZE	21.8.86	2 Jul

Best at low altitude

11.36 1.7 R Santos 2 NC São Paulo 4 Aug	11.37	0.9 Abinuwa	23 Jun	11.46	0.5 Hinestroza	15 Jul
	11.46	-0.1 T Evans	16 Apr	11.39w	4.6 S Reece	3 Jul
				11.45w	5.4 Jones-Ferrette	25 Sep

Drugs disqualification

Mark	Wind	Name	Nat	Born	Pos	Meet	Venue	Date
11.00	2.2	Hackett #			1	NC	Port of Spain	13 Aug
11.14	0.5	Tahesia Harrigan #	IVB	15.2.82	1		Río de Janeiro	26 May
		10.89w 4.6 1h1 and 10.97w 2.9 at Clermont 4 Jun						
11.41	0.0	Anna Gurova ¶	RUS	29.4.81	(2s2)	NC	Cheboksary	22 Jul

JUNIORS

See main list for top 7 juniors (& 5 wa). 11 performances by 7 women to 11.22. Additional marks and further juniors:

Mark	Wind	Name		Nat	Born	Pos	Meet	Venue	Date
Gardner	11.17	-0.4 1h3 NCAA Des Moines				8 Jun			
	11.18	1.1 2 NC-j Eugene							24 Jun
Scott	11.19	1.5 4 NCAA Des Moines				10 Jun			
	11.22	1.9 1h1 NC-j Eugene							24 Jun
11.38	-0.8	Antonique	Strachan	BAH	22.8.93	1	Carifta	Montego Bay	23 Apr
11.38	0.3	Dezerea	Bryant	USA	27.4.93	1		La Crosse	4 Jun
11.39	1.3	Christiania	Williams (10)	JAM-Y	17.10.94	1J		Kingston	19 Mar
11.39	1.5	Keilah	Tyson	USA	6.11.92	1		Richmond	4 Jun
11.41	0.0	Tynia	Gaither	BAH	16.3.93	1		Winter Park	7 May
11.42	0.6	Ashley	Collier	USA	4.2.92	2h3	Big 12	Norman OK	14 May
11.42	1.6	Natasha	Morrison	JAM	17.11.92	4h2	NC	Kingston	24 Jun
11.42	0.7	Viktoriya	Zyabkina	KAZ	4.9.92	1	NC	Almaty	27 Jul
11.42	1.2	Morolake	Akinosun	USA-Y	17.5.94	1s3	Jnr Oly	New Orleans	3 Aug
11.43	0.5	Jamile	Samuel	NED	24.4.92	2	EJ	Tallinn	22 Jul
11.43	-0.1	Kai	Selvon	TRI	13.4.92	2h2	NC	Port of Spain	13 Aug
11.43A	0.0	Tamiris	de Líz	BRA-Y	18.11.95	1	SAm-J	Medellín	23 Sep
11.44	1.8	Aaliyah	Brown (20)	USA-Y	6.1.95	1h3		Charleston	20 May

Wind assisted: See main list for top 4 juniors. 6 performances by 4 women to 11.20w.

Mark	Wind		Venue	Date
Schippers	11.16	2.1 1B1	Mannheim	12 Aug
Scott	11.17	3.4 1	Gainesville	16 Apr
Ahyee	11.20	2.2 3 NC	Port of Spain	13 Aug

Mark	Wind	Name		Nat	Born	Pos	Meet	Venue	Date
11.42	4.5	Annie	Tagoe	GBR	4.6.93	1h2	NC-j	Bedford	25 Jun

Mark	Wind	Name		Nat	Born	Pos	Meet	Venue	Date

150 METRES STRAIGHT

At Gateshead (Q) 17 Sep: (1.5) 1, Carmelita Jeter USA 16.50, 2. Anyika Onuora GBR 16.90, 3, Abi Oyepitan GBR 16.98
Turn: At Lisse 14 May: (1.6) Dafne Schippers NED-J 16.96

200 METRES

Mark	Wind	Name		Nat	Born	Pos	Meet	Venue	Date
22.15	1.0	Shalonda	Solomon	USA	19.12.85	1	NC	Eugene	26 Jun
22.20	-0.4	Carmelita	Jeter	USA	24.11.79	1	Herc	Monaco	22 Jul
22.22	-1.0	Veronica	Campbell-Brown	JAM	15.5.82	1	WCh	Daegu	2 Sep
22.23	1.0		Jeter			2	NC	Eugene	26 Jun
22.24	1.5	Kimberlyn	Duncan	USA	2.8.91	1	NCAA	Des Moines	11 Jun
22.24	1.8		Jeter			1s3	NC	Eugene	26 Jun
22.26	1.2		Campbell-Brown			1	Gyulai	Budapest	30 Jul
22.27	-0.1		Jeter			1	WK	Zürich	8 Sep
22.28	1.0	Jeneba	Tarmoh	USA	27.9.89	3	NC	Eugene	26 Jun
22.32	-0.4	Allyson	Felix	USA	18.11.85	2	Herc	Monaco	22 Jul
22.34	1.5		Tarmoh			2	NCAA	Des Moines	11 Jun
22.35	1.0	Bianca	Knight	USA	2.1.89	4	NC	Eugene	26 Jun
22.35	1.0		Duncan			5	NC	Eugene	26 Jun
22.37	1.2		Knight			1s2	NC	Eugene	26 Jun
22.37	-1.0		Jeter			2	WCh	Daegu	2 Sep
22.38	0.4		Felix			1	Colorful	Daegu	12 May
22.39	1.2		Duncan			1h1	NCAA	Des Moines	9 Jun
22.39	1.6		Knight			1h4	NC	Eugene	25 Jun
22.40	-0.1		Felix			2	WK	Zürich	8 Sep
22.42	-1.0		Felix			3	WCh	Daegu	2 Sep
22.44	0.1		Campbell-Brown			1	NC	Kingston	26 Jun
22.44	1.2		Solomon			2s2	NC	Eugene	26 Jun
22.46	-0.3		Tarmoh			1	Big 12	Norman OK	15 May
22.46	-0.2		Campbell-Brown			1h5	WCh	Daegu	1 Sep
22.46	-0.1		Solomon			1s2	WCh	Daegu	1 Sep
22.47	-0.7		Jeter			1s1	WCh	Daegu	1 Sep
22.48	1.0	Ana Cláudia	Silva	BRA	6.11.88	1h1	NC	São Paulo	7 Aug
22.53	-1.8		Campbell-Brown			1s3	WCh	Daegu	1 Sep
22.54	1.1		Duncan			1h1	NC	Eugene	25 Jun
22.54	0.7	Anneisha	McLaughlin	JAM	6.1.86	1	WUG	Shenzhen	19 Aug
22.55	-0.4	Anastasiya	Kapachinskaya	RUS	21.11.79	1		Yerino	25 Jun
22.55	-0.2	Schillonie	Calvert	JAM	27.7.88	1	Hanz	Zagreb	13 Sep
		(31/11)							
22.58	0.0	Olesya	Povh	UKR	18.10.87	1	NCp	Yalta	31 May
22.58	1.5	Tiffany	Townsend	USA	14.6.89	3	NCAA	Des Moines	11 Jun
22.58	1.0	LaShaunte'a	Moore	USA	31.7.83	6	NC	Eugene	26 Jun
22.59	1.0	Marshevet	Hooker/Myers	USA	25.9.84	2	BrGP	Birmingham	10 Jul
22.59	-0.1	Shelly-Ann	Fraser-Pryce	JAM	27.12.86	3	WK	Zürich	8 Sep
22.62	1.9	Yelizaveta	Savlinis	RUS	14.8.87	1h2	Mosc Ch	Moskva	10 Jul
22.62	-0.2	Ivet	Lalova	BUL	18.5.84	2h5	WCh	Daegu	1 Sep
22.63	0.1	Kerron	Stewart	JAM	16.4.84	2	NC	Kingston	26 Jun
22.63	1.2	Sanya	Richards-Ross	USA	26.2.85	2	Gyulai	Budapest	30 Jul
		(20)							
22.65	1.7	Lauryn	Williams	USA	11.9.83	1		Coral Gables	16 Apr
22.68	0.7	Mariya	Ryemyen	UKR	2.8.87	1		Strasbourg	12 Jun
22.68	1.6	Joanna	Atkins	USA	31.1.89	1	Vard	Réthimno	13 Jul
22.69	-0.3	Dafne	Schippers	NED-J	15.6.92	1h3	WCh	Daegu	1 Sep
22.70	2.0	Antonique	Strachan	BAH-J	22.8.93	1	PAm-J	Miramar	23 Jul
22.71	-0.1	Myriam	Soumaré	FRA	29.10.86	1h1	WCh	Daegu	1 Sep
22.73	0.1	Sherone	Simpson	JAM	12.8.84	3	NC	Kingston	26 Jun
22.76	1.8	Jura	Levy	JAM	4.11.90	1	JUCO	Hutchinson	21 May
22.76	0.9	Debbie	Ferguson McKenzie	BAH	16.1.76	3	GGala	Roma	26 May
22.77	1.7	Natasha	Hastings	USA	23.7.86	1	FlaR	Gainesville	1 A3r
		(30)							
22.79	0.1	Aleen	Bailey	JAM	25.11.80	4	NC	Kingston	26 Jun
22.79	-0.1	Hrystyna	Stuy	UKR	3.2.88	3s2	WCh	Daegu	1 Sep
22.80	1.2	Nivea	Smith	BAH	18.2.90	3h1	NCAA	Des Moines	9 Jun
22.81	-0.5	Yuliya	Chermoshanskaya	RUS	6.1.86	1		Sochi	25 May
22.81	1.2	Candyce	McGrone	USA	24.3.89	1q2	NCAA-W	Eugene	28 May
22.81	1.1	Stephanie	Durst	USA	11.4.82	2h1	NC	Eugene	25 Jun
22.82	1.5	Cydonie	Mothersill	CAY	19.3.78	1		Atlanta	5 Jun
22.83	1.3	Aareon	Payne	USA	3.9.90	1	MSR	Walnut	16 Apr
22.83	0.9	Aurieyall	Scott	USA-J	18.5.92	1	NC-j	Eugene	25 Jun
22.84	1.1	Jessica	Davis	USA-J	31.10.92	1	Pac10	Tucson	14 May
		(40)							

Mark	Wind	Name		Nat	Born	Pos	Meet	Venue	Date
22.85	1.3	Charonda	Williams	USA	27.3.87	2	MSR	Walnut	16 Apr
22.86	1.9	Damola	Osayomi	NGR	26.6.86	1	AfG	Maputo	15 Sep
22.86A	0.5	Simone	Facey	JAM	7.5.85	2	PAm	Guadalajara, MEX	27 Oct
22.87	1.5	Semoy	Hackett #	TRI	27.11.88	6	NCAA	Des Moines	11 Jun
22.87	1.0	Alex	Anderson	USA	28.1.87	4	BrGP	Birmingham	10 Jul
22.88	-0.1	Yuliya	Gushchina	RUS	4.3.83	3h1	WCh	Daegu	1 Sep
22.89	1.7	Rachelle	Smith	USA	30.6.81	3h2	NC	Eugene	25 Jun
22.89	0.3	Kai	Selvon	TRI-J	13.4.92	3h4	WCh	Daegu	1 Sep
22.90	0.9	Crystal	Emmanuel	CAN	27.11.91	1		Toronto	12 Jun
22.91A	1.0	Janelle	Redhead	GRN	27.12.89	1		El Paso	16 Apr
		(50)							
22.91	0.1	Darya	Pizhankova ¶	UKR	9.1.90	1h1	NCp	Yalta	31 May
22.91	0.9	Leslie	Cole	USA	16.2.87	1		Walnut	4 Jun
22.92	-0.4	Sheniqua	Ferguson	BAH	24.11.89	1		Tallahassee	8 Apr
22.93	-0.2	Anyika	Onuora	GBR	28.10.84	5h5	WCh	Daegu	1 Sep
22.94	-0.6	Amantle	Montsho	BOT	4.7.83	1		Bambous	17 Apr
22.94	-1.5	Jodie	Williams	GBR-J	28.9.93	1	EJ	Tallinn	23 Jul
22.94	1.2	Blessing	Okagbare	NGR	9.10.88	3	Gyulai	Budapest	30 Jul
22.96	0.1	Octavious	Freeman	USA-J	20.4.92	1		Orlando	28 May
22.97	1.1	Amber	Purvis	USA	23.1.90	2	Pac10	Tucson	14 May
22.97	2.0	Nelkys Teresa	Casabona	CUB	12.5.84	1	Alba	Barquisimeto	29 Jul
		(60)							
22.99	-0.2	Debbie	Dunn	USA	26.3.78	2rB	GP	Ponce	14 May
22.99	1.6	Jessica	Young	USA	6.4.87	3h4	NC	Eugene	25 Jun
23.01	-0.4	Dezerea	Bryant	USA-J	27.4.93	1		La Crosse	4 Jun
23.01	0.2	Samantha	Henry-Robinson	JAM	25.9.88	2h1	NC	Kingston	25 Jun
23.02	1.1	English	Gardner	USA-J	22.4.92	3	Pac10	Tucson	14 May
23.02	-1.7	Jessica	Beard	USA	8.1.89	1h3	Big 12	Norman OK	14 May
23.02	0.1	Yelizaveta	Bryzgina	UKR	28.11.89	2h1	NCp	Yalta	31 May
23.02A	0.5	Mariely	Sánchez	DOM	30.12.88	3	PAm	Guadalajara, MEX	27 Oct
23.03	-0.3	Dominique	Duncan	USA	7.5.90	4	Big 12	Norman OK	15 May
23.03	1.7	Christy	Udoh	USA	30.9.91	4h2	NC	Eugene	25 Jun
		(70)							
23.05	0.4	Sally	Pearson	AUS	19.9.86	1		Brisbane	11 Feb
23.06	2.0	Porscha	Lucas	USA	18.6.88	2	KansR	Lawrence	23 Apr
23.06A	1.0	Norma	González	COL	11.8.82	1	NC	Bogotá	7 May
23.06	1.4	Ndèye Fato	Soumah	SEN	6.4.86	1		Donnas	3 Jul
23.06	0.2	Lina	Jacques-Sébastien	FRA	10.4.85	1		Paris (C)	10 Jul
23.06	1.9	Vida	Anim	GHA	7.12.83	2	AfG	Maputo	15 Sep
23.06A	0.5	Tameka	Williams	SKN	31.8.89	4	PAm	Guadalajara, MEX	27 Oct
23.07	2.0	Patricia	Hall	JAM	16.10.82	2		Clermont	4 Jun
23.07	1.1	Shareese	Woods	USA	20.2.85	4h1	NC	Eugene	25 Jun
23.07	0.7	Geisa	Coutinho	BRA	1.6.80	1h2	NC	São Paulo	7 Aug
		(80)							
23.08	0.2	Denisa	Rosolová	CZE	21.8.86	3	Odložil	Praha	13 Jun
23.09	1.2	Stormy	Kendrick	USA	6.1.91	1	ACC	Durham NC	23 Apr
23.10	1.2	Allison	Peter	ISV-J	14.7.92	5h1	NCAA	Des Moines	9 Jun
23.10	0.9	Phylicia	George	CAN	16.11.87	2		Toronto	12 Jun
23.10	0.1	Gloria	Asumnu	USA/NGR	22.5.85	2		Sotteville-lès-Rouen	2 Jul
23.11A	1.0	Endurance	Abinuwa	NGR	31.7.87	3		El Paso	16 Apr
23.11	1.8	Jessica	Ennis	GBR	28.1.86	2H4		Götzis	28 May
23.12	0.9	Connie	Moore	USA	29.8.81	2		Walnut	4 Jun
23.13	-0.7	Chisato	Fukushima	JPN	27.6.88	1		Fukuroi	3 May
23.13	1.4	Anastacia	Le-Roy	JAM	11.9.87	3	CAC	Mayagüez	17 Jul
		(90)							
23.14	1.2	Chalonda	Goodman	USA	29.9.90	6h1	NCAA	Des Moines	9 Jun
23.15	0.0	Ashley	Collier	USA-J	4.2.92	2h4	Big 12	Norman OK	14 May
23.15	2.0	Kseniya	Vdovina	RUS	19.4.87	1h3	Mosc Ch	Moskva	10 Jul
23.16	0.7	Anna	Kaygorodova	RUS	10.3.83	3	WUG	Shenzhen	19 Aug
23.17		Tynia	Gaither	BAH-J	16.3.93	1		Tampa	19 Mar
23.17	0.4	Aleksandra	Fedoriva	RUS	13.9.88	3	Colorful	Daegu	12 May
23.20	0.6	Moa	Hjelmer	SWE	19.6.90	1s1	EU23	Ostrava	16 Jul
23.21	2.0	Abi	Oyepitan	GBR	30.12.79	1		Norwalk	16 Apr
23.21		Gayon	Evans	JAM	15.1.90	1		Shawnee OK	7 May
23.21	1.4	Dominique	Holmes	USA	25.6.86	1		Louisville KY	13 May
		(100)							

Mark	Wind	Name		Nat	Born	Date		Mark	Wind	Name		Nat	Born	Date
23.22	-0.7	Trisha-Ann	Hawthorne	JAM	8.11.89	8 May		23.23	-0.6	Cathleen	Tschirch	GER	23.7.79	13 Sep
23.22	1.9	Madison	McNary	USA	1.3.90	15 May		23.24	0.9	Kimberley	Hyacinthe	CAN	28.3.89	12 Jun
23.23	0.7	Joice	Maduaka	GBR	30.9.73	12 Jun		23.25	0.1	Desiree	Henry	GBR-Y	26.8.95	10 Jul
23.23	-1.0	Anna	Kielbasinska	POL	26.6.90	16 Jul		23.26	1.2	Marlena	Wesh	HAI	16.2.91	23 Apr
23.23	-0.3	Vanda	Gomes	BRA	7.11.88	7 Aug		23.26	0.2	Viktoriya	Zyabkina	KAZ-J	4.9.92	28 Jul

Mark	Wind	Name	Nat	Born	Pos	Meet	Venue	Date
23.27	1.3	Stacey-Ann Smith	USA	8.1.91				19 Mar
23.27	0.0	Grecia Bolton	USA	2.10.89				9 Jun
23.27	0.9	Tatyana Firova	RUS	10.10.82				6 Aug
23.27	0.5	Johanna Danois	FRA	4.4.87				10 Aug
23.28	-0.7	Jamile Samuel	NED-J	24.4.92				19 Jun
23.29	1.7	Ciara Short	USA	11.3.89				30 Apr
23.29	0.0	Natalya Rusakova	RUS	12.12.79				23 Jul
23.30	1.2	Shericka Ward	USA	30.3.90				7 May
23.30	1.7	Margaret Adeoye	GBR	22.4.85				4 Jun
23.31	0.9	Monica Hargrove	USA	30.12.82				16 Apr
23.32	1.1	Shericka Jackson	JAM-Y	15.7.94				24 Apr
23.32	-1.0	Marit Dopheide	NED	28.12.90				16 Jul
23.33	0.6	Sharay Hale	USA	21.4.89				14 May
23.33	-0.9	Esther Akinsulie	CAN	22.4.84				28 May
23.34	1.3	Carol Rodriguez	PUR	16.12.85				16 Apr
23.35	0.9	Candace Jackson	USA	13.2.91				16 Apr
23.35	1.5	Olga Bludova	KAZ	5.11.91				6 May
23.35	1.5	Taylor Houston	USA-J	17.2.92				14 May
23.35	1.8	Tasha Allen	USA	8.5.90				21 May
23.35	0.9	Akawkaw Ndipagbor	USA-J	30.4.93				25 Jun
23.35	-1.5	Jennifer Galais	FRA-J	7.3.92				23 Jul
23.35	-0.6	Yuliya Katsura	RUS	28.5.83				23 Jul
23.35	-2.9	Olivia Ekpone	USA-J	5.1.91				2 Aug
23.35A	0.1	Yenifer Padilla	COL	1.1.90				13 Aug
23.35A	0.0	Tamiris de Liz	BRA-Y	18.11.95				24 Sep
23.36	0.5	Lauretta Ozoh	NGR	5.9.90				7 May
23.36	0.8	Anne Christina Haack	GER	15.4.87				3 Jul
23.36	1.0	Franciela Krasucki	BRA	26.4.88				7 Aug
23.37	0.1	Chantel Malone	IVB	2.12.91				26 Mar
23.37	0.2	Nelly Banco	FRA	17.2.86				29 May
23.37	1.7	Natalie Knight	USA	24.10.86				25 Jun
23.38A	1.0	Yomara Hinestroza	COL	20.5.88				7 May
23.38	1.8	Reyare Thomas	TRI	23.11.87				21 May
23.38	0.0	Valentina Karnaukhova	RUS	2.2.88				5 Aug
23.39	0.0	Jade Bailey	BAR	10.6.83				26 Jun
23.39	0.6	Anouk Hagen	NED	30.4.90				16 Jul
23.40	1.4	Georgina Nembhard	JAM	24.11.88				16 Apr
23.40A	1.4	Erika Chávez	ECU	4.6.90				30 Apr
23.40	0.4	Sheila Paul	USA	30.9.89				14 May
23.41	-0.2	Mikele Barber	USA	4.10.80				19 Mar
23.41	1.7	Shana Cox	GBR	22.1.85				1 Apr
23.41	2.0	Nyoka Cole	JAM	7.10.85				2 Apr
23.41	1.4	Quina Fortune	USA	17.10.89				6 May
23.41	-0.5	Nina Argunova	RUS	15.9.89				25 May
23.41	0.2	Emily Diamond	GBR	11.6.91				28 May
23.41	0.7	Céline Distel	FRA	25.7.87				12 Jun
23.41	-0.7	Sabina Veit	SLO	2.12.85				19 Jun
23.42	2.0	Dulaini Débora Odelín	CUB-J	21.8.92				18 Mar
23.42	-0.1	Marzia Caravelli	ITA	23.10.81				26 Jun
23.42	0.0	Yekaterina Voronenkova	RUS	8.2.88				23 Jul
23.43	-0.1	Tawanna Meadows	USA	4.8.86				16 Apr
23.43	-0.6	Carina Horn	RSA	9.3.89				17 Apr
23.43	1.7	Shannon Gagne	USA	3.9.87				28 May
23.43	0.1	Muriel Hurtis	FRA	25.3.79				2 Jul
23.43	1.8	Christian Brennan	CAN-Y	27.3.95				7 Aug
23.43	-0.9	Ezinne Okparaebo	NOR	3.3.88				19 Jun
23.44	-0.6	Whitney Harris	USA	11.6.89				15 May
23.45A	1.4	Alejandra Idrobo	COL	8.4.88				30 Apr
23.45	-0.5	Lyudmila Litvinova	RUS	8.6.85				25 May
23.45	0.1	Shayla Sanders	USA-Y	6.1.94				28 May
23.45	0.0	Oksana Shcherbak	UKR	24.2.82				31 May
23.45A	0.5	Roxana Díaz	CUB	16.5.81				27 Oct
23.46	1.3	Keshia Baker	USA	30.1.88				16 Apr
23.46	0.7	Dominique Booker	USA-J	10.2.92				14 May
23.46	0.5	Sónia Tavares	POR	21.3.86				26 Jun
23.46	1.2	Shereefa Lloyd	JAM	2.9.82				30 Jul
23.46	1.8	Khamica Bingham	CAN-Y	15.6.94				7 Aug
23.47	1.7	Indira Spence	JAM	8.9.86				28 May
23.47	1.7	Toyin Olupona	CAN	29.1.83				21 May
23.48	1.3	Lee McConnell	GBR	9.10.78				17 Jul
23.49	0.3	Shericka Williams	JAM	17.9.85				16 Apr
23.49	1.0	Kelsey McCorkle	USA	15.8.90				13 May
23.49	1.9	Ashley Kelly	IVB	25.3.91				15 May
23.49	1.1	Marika Popowicz	POL	28.4.88				29 May
23.49	-0.4	Andreea Ogrăzeanu	ROU	24.3.90				30 Jun
23.49	-1.8	Morolake Akinosun	USA-Y	17.5.94				4 Aug
23.49	0.5	Delphine Atangana (187)	CMR	16.8.84				10 Aug

Wind assisted

Mark	Wind	Name		Nat	Born	Pos	Meet	Venue	Date
22.10	2.4	Shelly-Ann	Fraser-Pryce	JAM	27.12.86	1		Kingston	7 May
22.18	3.2	Kimberlyn	Duncan	USA	2.8.91	1		Baton Rouge	23 Apr
22.27	3.4		Duncan			1	SEC	Athens GA	15 May
22.31	3.2	Murielle	Ahouré	CIV	23.8.87	2		Baton Rouge	23 Apr
22.37	2.4		Campbell-Brown			2		Kingston	7 Ma
22.37	2.7		Jeter			1h3	NC	Eugene	25 Jun
22.41	3.4	Semoy	Hackett #	TRI	27.11.88	2	SEC	Athens GA	15 May
22.44	3.4	Nivea	Smith	BAH	18.2.90	3	SEC	Athens GA	15 May
22.48	2.7		Solomon			2h3	NC	Eugene	25 Jun
22.50	2.7	Debbie	Ferguson McKenzie	BAH	16.1.76	1		Clermont	21 May
22.69	5.7	Yuliya	Gushchina	RUS	4.3.83	2	NCp	Yerino	5 Jun
22.78	2.7	Charonda	Williams	USA	27.3.87	4h3	NC	Eugene	25 Jun
22.79	2.7	Dominique	Duncan	USA	7.5.90	1		Gainesville	16 Apr
22.82	3.7	Aurieyall	Scott	USA-J	18.5.92	1h2	NC-j	Eugene	25 Jun
22.84	3.2	Patricia	Hall	JAM	16.10.82	3		Baton Rouge	23 Apr
22.85	2.4	Abi	Oyepitan	GBR	30.12.79	1		Los Angeles	23 Apr
22.85	2.7	Porscha	Lucas	USA	18.6.88	5h3	NC	Eugene	25 Jun
22.87	2.8	Cathleen	Tschirch	GER	23.7.79	1		Mannheim	13 Aug
22.88	2.8	Amantle	Montsho	BOT	4.7.83	1		Dakar	28 May
22.89	2.3	Candace	Jackson	USA	13.2.91	1		Lubbock	2 Apr
22.89	2.8	Tameka	Williams	SKN	31.8.89	1		Basseterre	19 Jun
22.97	2.7	Samantha	Henry-Robinson	JAM	25.9.88	3		Clermont	21 May
22.98	3.2	Adrienne	Power	CAN	11.12.81	4		Baton Rouge	23 Apr
22.99	5.0	Lina	Jacques-Sébastien	FRA	10.4.85	2	NC	Albi	30 Jul
23.00	5.0	Johanna	Danois	FRA	4.4.87	3	NC	Albi	30 Jul
23.02	2.3	Terra	Evans	USA	7.10.89	2		Lubbock	2 Apr
23.06	5.5	Judith	Riley	JAM	4.11.88	1	MIAA	Emporia	8 May
23.07	2.3	Endurance	Abinuwa	NGR	31.7.87	3		Lubbock	2 Apr
23.09	2.8	Hanna	Mariën	BEL	16.5.82	1	NC	Bruxelles	24 Jul
23.10	5.7	Yekaterina	Voronenkova	RUS	8.2.88	3	NCp	Yerino	5 Jun
23.12	3.4	Darshay	Davis	USA	23.9.91	4	SEC	Athens GA	15 May
23.13	2.8	Esther	Cremer	GER	29.3.88	2		Mannheim	13 Aug
23.14	2.4	Margaret	Adeoye	GBR	27.4.85	2r1		La Chaux-de-Fonds	3 Jul
23.15	2.1	Grecia	Bolton	USA	2.10.89	4q1	NCAA-W	Eugene	28 May
23.16	2.4	Shericka	Williams	JAM	17.9.85	7		Kingston	7 May

Mark	Wind	Name		Nat	Born	Pos	Meet	Venue	Date
23.16	2.6	Moa	Hjelmer	SWE	19.6.90	1	NC	Gävle	14 Aug
23.17	2.4	Carol	Rodriguez	PUR	16.12.85	2		Los Angeles	23 Apr
23.18	3.5	Richesa	McCaleb	USA	.88	3		Oxford MS	23 Apr
23.18	2.4	Oksana	Shcherbak	UKR	24.2.82	1		Florø	4 Jun
23.21	3.0	Teona	Rodgers	USA	26.6.89				14 May
23.21	5.0	Céline	Distel	FRA	25.7.87				30 Jul
23.25	2.3	Unique	Singleton	USA	.89				16 Apr
23.27	3.4	Regina	George	USA	17.2.91				15 May
23.28	2.3	Weronika	Wedler	POL	17.7.89				3 Jun
23.29	5.3	Chastity	Riggien	USA	5.7.89				23 Apr
23.30A	2.9	Taylor	Evans	USA	7.10.89				26 Mar
23.31	3.0	Mujinga	Kambundji	SUI-J	17.6.92				3 Jul
23.31	2.8	Esther	Akinsulie	CAN	22.4.84				17 Jul
23.31	2.6	Shayla	Mahan	USA	18.1.89				31 Jul
23.32	2.5	Tatyana	Chernova	RUS	29.1.88				15 Jun
23.34	5.7	Yuliya	Katsura	RUS	28.5.83				5 Jun
23.34	2.3	Telena	Migunova	RUS	4.1.84				10 Jul
23.34	2.8	Kerri-Ann	Mitchell	CAN	29.3.83				17 Jul
23.35	3.5	Francesca	Okwaro	USA	.89				1 May
23.38	3.5	Quina	Fortune	USA	17.10.89				23 Apr
23.38	3.9	Lyudmila	Litvinova	RUS	8.6.85				5 Jun
23.40	2.3	Tawanna	Meadows	USA	4.8.86				23 Apr
23.40	3.0	Amy	Foster	IRL	2.10.88				3 Jul
23.41	3.2	Rebecca	Alexander	USA	2.5.90				23 Apr
23.41A	3.6	Indira	Spence	JAM	8.9.86				10 May
23.41	5.0	Carima	Louami	FRA	12.5.79				30 Jul
23.44	2.7	Tianna	Madison	USA	30.8.85				21 May
23.44	w?	Morolake	Akinosun	USA-Y	17.5.94				3 Jul
23.45	3.1	Jernail	Hayes	USA	8.7.88				5 May
23.45	3.2	Véronique	Mang	FRA	15.12.84				22 May
23.46	3.3	Jessica	Cousins	USA	10.4.85				16 Apr
23.46	2.5	Lynne	Layne	USA	1.4.88				16 Apr
23.46	3.6	Karene	King	IVB	24.10.87				13 May
23.46	2.4	Jeanette	Kwakye	GBR	20.3.83				22 May
23.46	2.3	Marika	Popowicz	POL	28.4.88				3 Jun
23.47	2.5	Laura	Turner	GBR	12.8.82				17 Jul
23.49	2.4	Christine	Ohuruogu	GBR	17.5.84				23 Apr
23.49	2.6	Émilie	Gaydu	FRA	5.2.89				15 May

Hand timing

Mark	Wind	Name		Nat	Born	Pos	Meet	Venue	Date
22.8	-1.4	Nercely	Soto	VEN	26.8.90	1	NG	Barquisimeto	14 Dec
23.1	0.9	Marzia	Caravelli	ITA	23.10.81				29 May
23.2	1.1	Inna	Eftimova	BUL	19.6.88				12 Jun

Indoors

Mark	Name		Nat	Born	Pos	Meet	Venue	Date
22.84	Semoy	Hackett #	TRI	27.11.88	1	SEC	Fayetteville	27 Feb
22.95	Jessica	Beard	USA	8.1.89	1		College Station	22 Jan
22.96	Rebecca	Alexander	USA	2.5.90	2h1	SEC	Fayetteville	26 Feb
23.16	Jasmine	Chaney	USA	25.8.88	3		College Station	12 Feb
23.18	Shavon	Greaves	USA	20.12.88	2		State College	29 Jan
23.26	Dominique	Booker	USA-J	10.2.92				29 Jan
23.27	Tarika	Williams	JAM	26.9.89				26 Feb
23.35	Yuliya	Katsura	RUS	28.5.83				19 Jan
23.37	Yekaterina	Voronenkova	RUS	8.2.88				17 Feb
23.39	Émilie	Gaydu	FRA	5.2.89				19 Feb
23.43	Regina	George	USA	17.2.91				26 Feb
23.45A	Shanae	Roach	USA					26 Feb
23.47	Marlena	Wesh	HAI	16.2.91				26 Feb

Best at low altitude

Mark	Wind	Name	Pos	Meet	Venue	Date
23.07	1.7	Facey	1		Orlando	26 Mar
23.11	-0.3	Redhead	4h3	WCh	Daegu	1 Sep
23.22	0.4	González				4 Jun
23.45	1.9	Abinuwa				14 May

JUNIORS

See main list for top 12 juniors (& 2 wa). 13 perfs by 7 women to 22.96 (& 2 wa). Additional marks and further juniors:

Name	Mark	Wind	Pos	Meet	Venue	Date	Mark	Wind	Pos	Meet	Venue	Date
Schippers	22.90	1.8	1H		Götzis	28 May	22.92	-0.1	5s2	WCh	Daegu	1 Sep
	22.91	-0.4	1H	EJ	Tallinn	21 Jul						
Strachan	22.90	1.4	2	CAC	Mayagüez	17 Jul	22.93	1.1	1h1	Carifta	Montego Bay	24 Apr
Davis	22.93	0.9	2	NC-j	Eugene	25 Jun	22.91w	2.1	1	NCAA-r	Eugene	27 May

Mark	Wind	Name		Nat	Born	Pos	Meet	Venue	Date
23.25	0.1	Desiree	Henry	GBR-Y	26.8.95	1	WY	Villeneuve d'Ascq	10 Jul
23.26	0.2	Viktoriya	Zyabkina	KAZ	4.9.92	1	NC	Almaty	28 Jul
23.28	-0.7	Jamile	Samuel	NED	24.4.92	1r2	ET-1	Izmir	19 Jun
23.32	1.1	Shericka	Jackson	JAM-Y	15.7.94	2h1	Carifta	Montego Bay	24 Apr
23.35	1.5	Taylor	Houston	USA	17.2.92	1		Austin	14 May
23.35	0.9	Akawkaw	Ndipagbor	USA	30.4.93	3	NC-j	Eugene	25 Jun
23.35	-1.5	Jennifer	Galais (20)	FRA	7.3.92	2h3	EJ	Tallinn	23 Jul
23.35	-2.9	Olivia	Ekpone	USA	5.1.91	1h2	Jnr Oly	New Orleans	2 Aug
23.35A	0.0	Tamiris	de Liz	BRA-Y	18.11.95	1	SAm-J	Medellín	24 Sep
23.26 indoors		Dominique	Booker	USA	10.2.92	1rB		State College	29 Jan

Wind assisted   See main list for top junior

Mark	Wind	Name		Nat	Born	Pos	Meet	Venue	Date
23.31	3.0	Mujinga	Kambundji	SUI-J	17.6.92	1B		La Chaux-de-Fonds	3 Jul

200 METRES STRAIGHT

Mark	Wind	Name		Nat	Born	Pos	Meet	Venue	Date
22.12w	2.6	Allyson	Felix	USA	18.11.85	1		Manchester	15 May

300 METRES

Mark	Name		Nat	Born	Pos	Venue	Date
36.92	Bukola	Abogunloko	NGR-Y	18.8.94	1	Sagamu	19 Feb
37.24	Denisa	Rosolová	CZE	21.8.86			17 May
37.25	Janin	Lindenberg	GER	20.1.87			22 May

During 400m race: WCh Daegu 29 Aug: Amantle Montsho 35.7, Allyson Felix 35.9, Francena McCorory 36.1, Anastasiya Kapachinskaya & Novlene Williams-Mills 36.3, Antonina Krivoshapka 36.6, Shericka Williams 36.7, Sanya Richards-Ross 36.8;   Eugene 25 Jun: Debbie Dunn 37.0, Jessica Beard 37.1, Natasha Hastings 37.2

Indoors

Mark	Name		Nat	Born	Pos	Venue	Date
36.41	Bianca	Knight	USA	2.1.89	1	Fayetteville	12 Feb
37.04	Charonda	Williams	USA	27.3.87			12 Feb
37.09	Francena	McCorory	USA	20.10.88			12 Feb
37.14	Denisa	Rosolová	CZE	21.8.86			21 Jan
37.50	Vania	Stambolova	BUL	28.11.83			13 Feb

WOMEN 2011

Mark	Name		Nat	Born	Pos	Meet	Venue	Date	
400 METRES									
49.35	Anastasiya	Kapachinskaya	RUS	21.11.79	1	NC	Cheboksary	22	Jul
49.56	Amantle	Montsho	BOT	4.7.83	1	WCh	Daegu	29	Aug
49.59	Allyson	Felix	USA	18.11.85	2	WCh	Daegu	29	Aug
49.66	Sanya	Richards-Ross	USA	26.2.85	1	LGP	London (CP)	6	Aug
49.71		Montsho			1	Herc	Monaco	22	Jul
49.81		Felix			1	GGala	Roma	26	May
49.84	Rosemarie	Whyte	JAM	8.9.86	2	LGP	London (CP)	6	Aug
49.92	Antonina	Krivoshapka	RUS	21.7.87	2	NC	Cheboksary	22	Jul
50.05	Novlene	Williams-Mills	JAM	26.4.82	1	NC	Kingston	26	Jun
50.10		Montsho			1	Bisl	Oslo	9	Jun
50.13		Montsho			1s3	WCh	Daegu	28	Aug
50.16		Montsho			1	VD	Bruxelles	16	Sep
50.19		Krivoshapka			1s3	NC	Cheboksary	21	Jul
50.20		Montsho			1	BrGP	Birmingham	10	Jul
50.23		Montsho			1	Athl	Lausanne	30	Jun
50.24		Kapachinskaya			3	WCh	Daegu	29	Aug
50.24	Francena	McCorory	USA	20.10.88	1s2	WCh	Daegu	28	Aug
50.29		McCorory			2	Herc	Monaco	22	Jul
50.31		Williams-Mills			1	Hanz	Zagreb	13	Sep
50.33		Felix			1	DL	Doha	6	May
50.36		Felix			1s1	WCh	Daegu	28	Aug
50.38		Williams-Mills			1		Reims	5	Jul
50.40		Felix			1	NC	Eugene	25	Jun
50.40		Whyte			2	NC	Kingston	26	Jun
50.40		Kapachinskaya			2	Hanz	Zagreb	13	Sep
50.41		Montsho			2	DL	Doha	6	May
50.41		Kapachinskaya			2s3	WCh	Daegu	28	Aug
50.45	Shericka	Williams	JAM	17.9.85	3	Hanz	Zagreb	13	Sep
50.45		McCorory			4	WCh	Daegu	29	Aug
50.46		Williams-Mills			3	LGP	London (CP)	6	Aug
50.46		S Williams			2s2	WCh	Daegu	28	Aug
	(30/9)								
50.67	Kseniya	Vdovina (10)	RUS	19.4.87	3	NC	Cheboksary	22	Jul
50.69	Antonina	Yefremova	UKR	19.7.81	1	NCp	Yalta	31	May
50.70	Debbie	Dunn	USA	26.3.78	3	NC	Eugene	25	Jun
50.71	Kaliese	Spencer	JAM	6.5.87	1s1	NC	Kingston	25	Jun
50.73	Natalya	Antyukh	RUS	26.6.81	1	Kuts	Moskva	6	Aug
50.84	Denisa	Rosolová	CZE	21.8.86	2	GS	Ostrava	31	May
50.84	Tatyana	Firova	RUS	10.10.82	3	VD	Bruxelles	16	Sep
50.85	Christine	Ohuruogu	GBR	17.5.84	4	Hanz	Zagreb	13	Sep
50.86	Davita	Prendergast	JAM	16.12.84	4	NC	Kingston	26	Jun
50.92	Lyudmila	Litvinova	RUS	8.6.85	4	NC	Cheboksary	22	Jul
50.92	Kseniya	Zadorina	RUS	2.3.87	5	NC	Cheboksary	22	Jul
	(20)								
50.97	Natasha	Hastings	USA	23.7.86	1	GP	Ponce	14	May
50.98	Vania	Stambolova	BUL	28.11.83	1	ET-2	Novi Sad	18	Jun
51.01	Lee	McConnell	GBR	9.10.78	5	LGP	London (CP)	6	Aug
51.06	Jessica	Beard	USA	8.1.89	4	NC	Eugene	25	Jun
51.08	Geisa	Coutinho	BRA	1.6.80	1	WMilG	Río de Janeiro	22	Jul
51.10	Olga	Topilskaya	RUS	4.10.90	1	NC-23	Yerino	25	Jun
51.17	Deedee	Trotter	USA	8.12.82	6	NC	Eugene	25	Jun
51.20	Svetlana	Usovich	BLR	14.10.80	1		Minsk	4	Jun
51.24	Shana	Cox	GBR	22.1.85	2	GP	Ponce	14	May
51.26	Yelena	Migunova	RUS	4.1.84	2s1	NC	Cheboksary	21	Jul
	(30)								
51.40	Patricia	Hall	JAM	16.10.82	5	NC	Kingston	26	Jun
51.42	Leslie	Cole	USA	16.2.87	1		Los Angeles (ER)	7	May
51.43	Nataliya	Pygyda	UKR	30.1.81	1	NCp	Vinnytsa	15	Aug
51.47	Perri	Shakes-Drayton	GBR	21.12.88	6	GGala	Roma	26	May
51.49	Marina	Karnaushchenko	RUS	2.10.88	3s3	NC	Cheboksary	21	Jul
51.50	Joanna	Atkins	USA	31.1.89	2	NCAA	Des Moines	10	Jun
51.52A	Natoya	Goule	JAM	30.3.91	1		El Paso	16	Apr
51.53	Pinar	Saka	TUR	5.11.85	1		Ankara	30	Jul
51.53A	Yenifer	Padilla	COL	1.1.90	1	PAm	Guadalajara, MEX	26	Oct
51.55	Diamond	Dixon	USA-J	29.6.92	1	Big 12	Norman OK	15	May
	(40)								
51.58	Norma	González	COL	11.8.82	2		São Paulo	22	May
51.58	Moa	Hjelmer	SWE	19.6.90	1	NC	Gävle	13	Aug

Mark	Name		Nat	Born	Pos	Meet	Venue	Date
51.61	Keshia	Baker	USA	30.1.88	1		Los Angeles	23 Apr
51.62	Chris-Ann	Gordon	JAM-Y	18.9.94	1		Kingston	2 Apr
51.62	Muriel	Hurtis	FRA	25.3.79	2		Strasbourg	12 Jun
51.66	Jaílma	de Lima	BRA	31.12.86	3		São Paulo	22 May
51.66	Aliann	Pompey	GUY	9.3.78	1		New York	9 Jul
51.67	Ndèye Fato	Soumah	SEN	6.4.86	1		Celle Ligure	5 Jul
51.69	Shereefa	Lloyd	JAM	2.9.82	1	CAC	Mayagüez	15 Jul
51.69A	Daysiurami	Bonne	CUB	9.3.88	2	PAm	Guadalajara, MEX	26 Oct
	(50)							
51.71	Mary	Wineberg	USA	3.1.80	1		Genève	28 May
51.73A	Joyce	Zakari	KEN	6.6.86	1	NC	Nairobi	16 Jul
51.76	Monica	Hargrove	USA	30.12.82	2		Uberlândia	18 May
51.77	Ami Mbacké	Thiam	SEN	10.11.76	2	AfG	Maputo	13 Sep
51.79	Hanna	Tashpulatova	BLR	21.10.87	2		Minsk	4 Jun
51.82	Joanne	Cuddihy	IRL	11.5.84	3h1	WCh	Daegu	27 Aug
51.84	Shelise	Williams	USA	15.8.89	2h3	NCAA	Des Moines	8 Jun
51.84	Shaunae	Miller	BAH-Y	15.4.94	1	WY	Villeneuve d'Ascq	8 Jul
51.84	Nicola	Sanders	GBR	23.6.82	1		Ninove	7 Aug
51.84	Tjipekapora	Herunga	NAM	1.1.88	3	AfG	Maputo	13 Sep
	(60)							
51.85	Ciara	Short	USA	11.3.89	2h1	NCAA	Des Moines	8 Jun
51.86	Olesya	Krasnomovets	RUS	8.7.79	4s3	NC	Cheboksary	21 Jul
51.86	Marta	Milani	ITA	9.3.87	5s2	WCh	Daegu	28 Aug
51.93	Aymée	Martínez	CUB	17.11.88	1	Barr	La Habana	26 May
51.94	Aiesha	Goggins	USA	13.9.91	1	Conf USA	Houston	15 May
51.95	Ristananna	Tracey	JAM-J	5.9.92	1		Mona	21 May
51.95A	Jenna	Martin	CAN	31.3.88	1	NC	Calgary	25 Jun
51.96	Bianca	Râzor	ROU-Y	8.8.94	1	EJ	Tallinn	22 Jul
51.97	Janin	Lindenberg	GER	20.1.87	1		Regensburg	4 Jun
52.03	Alycia	Williams	USA	8.1.85	2		Clermont	4 Jun
	(70)							
52.03	Kseniya	Ustalova	RUS	14.1.88	4s2	NC	Cheboksary	21 Jul
52.08	Esther	Cremer	GER	29.3.88	1		Gladbeck	10 Jul
52.08	Christine	Day	JAM	23.8.86	2		Kingston	16 Apr
52.09	Marilyn	Okoro	GBR	23.9.84	1		La Chaux-de-Fonds	3 Jul
52.09A	Fantu	Magiso	ETH-J	9.6.92	1	Af-J	Gaborone	13 May
52.12	Brooklyn	Morris	USA	27.3.86	1		San Antonio	12 May
52.12	Christian	Brennan	CAN-Y	27.3.95	2	WY	Villeneuve d'Ascq	8 Jul
52.14	Olivia	James	JAM-Y	1.6.94	3	WY	Villeneuve d'Ascq	8 Jul
52.15	Tamsyn	Manou	AUS	20.7.78	1		Glendale	29 Jan
52.15	Birsen	Engin	TUR	18.10.80	2		Ankara	30 Jul
	(80)							
52.15	Claudia	Hoffmann	GER	10.12.82	2		Mannheim	13 Aug
52.17	Libania	Grenot	ITA	12.7.83	5	GP	Rieti	10 Sep
52.18	Yuliya	Gushchina	RUS	4.3.83	1		Yerino	30 Jul
52.19	Yulyana	Yushchenko	BLR	14.8.84	2		Minsk	11 Aug
52.21	Maris	Mägi	EST	11.8.87	1		Sydney	19 Mar
52.22	Indira	Terrero	CUB	29.11.85	7		Barcelona	22 Jul
52.23	Jasmine	Chaney	USA	25.8.88	1	Pac10	Tucson	14 May
52.23	Joelma	Souza	BRA	13.7.84	5		São Paulo	22 May
52.24	Kseniya	Karandyuk	UKR	21.6.86	2	NCp	Yalta	31 May
52.25	Veronica	Campbell-Brown	JAM	15.5.82	2		Orlando	26 Mar
	(90)							
52.26	Nadine	Okyere	GBR	29.11.86	2		Ninove	7 Aug
52.27	Jessica	Young	USA	6.4.87	1		Tempe	26 Mar
52.28	Endurance	Abinuwa	NGR	31.7.87	1		Lubbock	22 Apr
52.28	Marlena	Wesh	HAI	16.2.91	1	ACC	Durham NC	23 Apr
52.28	Eilidh	Child	GBR	20.2.87	1	Scot	Glasgow (S)	17 Jul
52.29	Yuliya	Terekhova	RUS	20.2.90	2	NC-23	Yerino	25 Jun
52.31	Regina	George	USA	17.2.91	1q1	NCAA-W	Eugene	27 May
52.32	Shareese	Woods	USA	20.2.85	3	DrakeR	Des Moines	30 Apr
52.32	Jessica	Cousins	USA	10.4.85	1		Clermont	11 Jun
52.33A	Esther	Akinsulie	CAN	22.4.84	2	NC	Calgary	25 Jun
	(100)							

Mark	Name		Nat	Born	Date		Mark	Name		Nat	Born	Date
52.35	Bukola	Abogunloko	NGR-Y	18.8.94	24 Jun		52.46A	Maureen	Maiyo	KEN	28.5.85	16 Jul
52.39	Bárbara	de Oliveira	BRA	12.3.91	5 Aug		52.47	Agní	Dervéni	GRE	7.11.87	29 Jul
52.40	Sharay	Hale	USA	21.4.89	8 May		52.50A	Gabriela	Medina	MEX	3.3.85	9 Jul
52.41	Whitney	Jones	USA	15.6.86	27 May		52.51	Kelly	Sotherton	GBR	13.11.76	25 Jun
52.42	Yekaterina	Voronenkova	RUS	8.2.88	28 May		52.51A	Amonn	Nelson	CAN	23.12.88	25 Jun
52.42	Anastacia	Le-Roy	JAM	11.9.87	25 Jun		52.52	Darya	Safonova	RUS	21.3.80	24 May
52.43	Adrienne	Power	CAN	11.12.81	3 Jul		52.52	Yevgeniya	Subbotina	RUS	30.10.89	25 Jun
52.45	Yekaterina	Yefimova	RUS	28.6.89	25 Jun		52.52	Chandrika	Subashini	SRI	20.6.87	22 Jul

Mark	Name		Nat	Born	Pos	Meet	Venue	Date
52.54A	Caster	Semenya	RSA	7.1.91				26 Mar
52.55	Bianca	Knight	USA	2.1.89				23 Apr
52.56	Mirela	Lavric	ROU	17.2.91				9 Aug
52.56		Chen Jingwen	CHN	8.2.90				9 Sep
52.57	Tatyana	Veshkurova	RUS	23.9.81				21 Jul
52.58	Valentina	Karnaukhova	RUS	2.2.88				21 Jul
52.59	Olivia	Tauro	AUS	11.6.90				29 Jan
52.59	Susana	Clement	CUB	18.8.89				26 May
52.59	Clora	Williams	JAM	26.11.83				23 Jun
52.59	Joke	Odumosu	NGR	27.10.87				24 Jun
52.60	Candace	Jackson	USA	13.2.91				22 Apr
52.61	Joy	Eaton	USA	9.7.89				14 May
52.61	Maria Enrica	Spacca	ITA	20.3.86				10 Sep
52.62	Ebony	Eutsey	USA-J	3.5.92				15 May
52.62	Yuliya	Baraley	UKR	25.4.90				31 May
52.62	Estie	Wittstock	RSA	15.9.80				13 Jun
52.62	Lena	Schmidt	GER	4.8.89				26 Jun
52.62		Zhao Yanmin	CHN	26.1.91				9 Sep
52.63	Fawn	Dorr	USA	19.4.87				1 Apr
52.63	Blessing	Mayungbe	NGR-J	15.4.92				15 May
52.64	Tiandra	Ponteen	SKN	9.11.84				7 May
52.64	Jody Ann	Muir	JAM	1.1.91				26 May
52.65	Kateryna	Plyashchuk	UKR	8.12.90				31 May
52.65	Kelly	Massey	GBR	11.1.85				4 Jun
52.67	Ilona	Usovich	BLR	14.11.82				11 Aug
52.69	Briana	Nelson	USA-J	18.7.92				15 May
52.70	Aline	dos Santos	BRA	5.5.85				18 May
52.71	Charonda	Williams	USA	27.3.87				25 Mar
52.71	April	Rotilio	USA					8 May
52.71	Chizoba	Okodogbe	NGR-J	3.11.92				14 May
52.71	Ashley	Kelly	IVB	25.3.91				8 Jun
52.71	Mariya	Savinova	RUS	13.8.85				12 Jul
52.72	Chiara	Bazzoni	ITA	5.7.84				28 May
52.72	Marina	Maslenko	KAZ	3.7.82				29 May
52.72	Verone	Chambers	JAM	16.12.88				25 Jun
52.72	Robin	Reynolds	USA-Y	22.2.94				8 Jul
52.73	Hanna	Titimets	UKR	5.3.89				2 Aug
52.74	Omolara	Omotosho	NGR-J	25.5.93				24 Jun
52.74	Miel Blessing	Ayédou	BEN	17.8.91				23 Jul
52.75	Anastasiya	Rabchenyuk	UKR	14.9.83				9 Jul
52.75	Olga	Mykhaylychenko	UKR	15.7.88				2 Aug
52.77	Floria	Guéi	FRA	2.5.90				29 May
52.77	Margaret	Etim	NGR-J	28.11.92				23 Jun
52.77	Adelina	Pastor	ROU-J	5.5.93				21 Jul
52.79	Meghan	Beesley	GBR	15.11.89				3 Jul
52.79	Olga	Tovarnova	RUS	11.4.85				21 Jul
52.80	Amber	Purvis	USA	23.1.90				9 Apr
52.80	Phara	Anacharsis	FRA	17.12.83				12 Jun
52.83	Irina	Khlyustova	BLR	25.8.78				4 Jun
52.85	Olga	Tereshkova ¶	KAZ	26.10.84				18 Jun
52.86	Ashlea	McLaughlin	USA	2.12.89				14 May
52.86	Brianna	Frazier	USA-J	19.2.92				8 Jun
52.86	Olga	Zavgorodnya	UKR	6.1.83				2 Aug
52.86A	Raysa	Sánchez	DOM	6.5.88				26 Oct
52.87	Amber	Evans	USA	31.12.89				15 May
52.87	Kendall	Baisden	USA-Y	5.3.95				18 Jun
52.90	Sherone	Simpson	JAM	12.8.84				5 Mar
52.91	Yuliya	Olishevska	UKR	2.2.89				15 Aug
52.91	Nataliya	Lupu	UKR	4.11.87				15 Aug
52.93A	Meliz	Redif	TUR	26.3.89				9 May
52.93A	Justine	Palframan	RSA-J	4.11.93				13 May
52.93	Diosmely	Peña	CUB	12.6.85				26 May
52.93	Agata	Bednarek	POL	28.6.88				18 Jun
52.93	Phyllis	Francis	USA-J	4.5.92				25 Jun
52.94	Shericka	Jackson	JAM-Y	15.7.94				2 Apr
52.94	Dominique	Blake	JAM	15.2.87				23 Jun
52.96		Cheng Chong	CHN-J	24.12.92				9 Sep
52.97	Jernail	Hayes	USA	8.7.88				8 May
52.98	Oksana	Shcherbak	UKR	24.2.82				4 Jun
52.98	Pirrenee	Stewart	AUS	20.2.85				10 Dec
52.99	Aleksandra	Bulanova	RUS	10.6.89				9 Jun
53.00	Melissa	DeLeon	TRI	9.4.81				16 Apr
53.00	Yelena	Voynova (89)	RUS	10.3.85				12 Jun

Indoors

Mark	Name		Nat	Born	Pos	Meet	Venue	Date
50.79	Jessica	Beard	USA	8.1.89	1rB	NCAA	College Station	12 Mar
50.83A	Natasha	Hastings	USA	23.7.86	1	NC	Albuquerque	27 Feb
51.22	Olesya	Krasnomovets	RUS	8.7.79	1	NC	Moskva	17 Feb
52.18	Briana	Nelson	USA-J	18.7.92	2	Big 12	Lincoln NE	26 Feb
52.30	Regina	George	USA	17.2.91	2rB	NCAA	College Station	12 Mar
52.57	Yekaterina	Shestakova	RUS	3.4.85				16 Feb
52.69	Angele	Cooper	USA	3.11.90				29 Jan
52.83	Aleksandra	Bulanova	RUS	10.6.89				29 Jan
52.85	Erica	Moore	USA	25.3.88				15 Jan
52.86	Zuzana	Hejnová	CZE	19.12.86				13 Feb

Hand times

Mark	Name		Nat	Born	Pos	Meet	Venue	Date
51.7	Christine	Day	JAM	23.8.86	2		Saint-Martn	14 May
51.9	Kseniya	Karandyuk	UKR	21.6.86	1		Yalta	17 May
52.1	Yuliya	Baraley	UKR	25.4.90	2		Yalta	17 May
52.3	Darya	Safonova	RUS	21.3.80				23 Apr
52,9	Kou	Wright	LBR	11.6.84				14 May

Best at low altitude

Mark	Name	Pos Meet	Venue	Date
52.04	J Martin	3h3NCAA	Des Moines	8 Jun
52.04	Bonne	2 Alba	Barquisimeto	27 Jul
52.18	Zakari	5 AfG	Maputo	13 Sep
52.20	Padilla	1h1CAC	Mayagüez	15 Jul
52.23	Goule	2h2NC	Kingston	23 Jun
52.23	Magiso	4h3WCh	Daegu	27 Aug
52.76	Nelson			13 Jul
52.93	Akinsulie			13 Jul

Drugs disqualification

Mark	Name		Nat	Born	Pos	Meet	Venue	Date
51.27	Olga	Tereshkova ¶	KAZ	26.10.84	(2)	WMilG	Río de Janeiro	22 Jul
52.80	Kolestane Mahmoud Ieso ¶ IRQ			1.8.91				8 Jul
52.82	Akkunji	Ashwini ¶	IND	7.10.87				12 Jun

JUNIORS

See main list for top 8 juniors. 12 perfs by 9 women (inc. 1 indoor) to 52.20. Additional marks and further juniors:

Dixon	51.64	1h3 NCAA Des Moines	8 Jun	51.88	3	NCAA	Des Moines	10 Jun
Miller	51.85	1 NC Freeport	25 Jun					

Mark	Name		Nat	Born	Pos	Meet	Venue	Date
52.35	Bukola	Abogunloko	NGR-Y	18.8.94	1	NC	Calabar	24 Jun
52.62	Ebony	Eutsey (10)	USA	3.5.92	5	SEC	Athens GA	15 May
52.63	Blessing	Mayungbe	NGR	15.4.92	3	Big 12	Norman OK	15 May
52.69	Briana	Nelson	USA	18.7.92	4	Big 12	Norman OK	15 May
52.71	Chizoba	Okodogbe	NGR	3.11.92	3	Pac10	Tucson	14 May
52.72	Robin	Reynolds	USA-Y	22.2.94	4	WY	Villeneuve d'Ascq	8 Jul
52.74	Omolara	Omotosho	NGR	25.5.93	3	NC	Calabar	24 Jun
52.77	Margaret	Etim	NGR	28.11.92	1h1	NC	Calabar	23 Jun
52.77	Adelina	Pastor	ROU	5.5.93	1h1	EJ	Tallinn	21 Jul
52.86	Brianna	Frazier	USA	19.2.92	4h3	NCAA	Des Moines	8 Jun
52.87	Kendall	Baisden	USA-Y	5.3.95	1		Greensboro	18 Jun
52.93A	Justine	Palframan (20)	RSA	4.11.93	2	Af-J	Gaborone	13 May
52.93	Phyllis	Francis	USA	4.5.92	2	NC-j	Eugene	25 Jun

Mark	Name		Nat	Born	Pos	Meet	Venue	Date

600 METRES

Mark	Name		Nat	Born	Pos	Meet	Venue	Date
1:26:07+	Janeth	Jepkosgei	KEN	13.12.83	1	in 800	Daegu	4 Sep
1:26.6+	Jennifer	Meadows	GBR	17.4.81	2+	in 800	Oslo	9 Jun

Also WCh Daegu 4 Sep in 800m: Caster Semenya 1:26.2, Kenia Sinclair 1:26.3, Mariya Savinova
 1:26.5, Alysia Montano 1:26.6, Yekaterina Kostetskaya 1:26.8. Maggie Vessey 1:27.2

Indoors

Mark	Name		Nat	Born	Pos	Meet	Venue	Date
1:24.02	Yuliya	Rusanova	RUS	3.7.86	1	Winter	Moskva	6 Feb
1:26.23	Mariya	Savinova	RUS	13.8.85	2	Winter	Moskva	6 Feb
1:26.38	Yelena	Kofanova	RUS	8.8.88	3	Winter	Moskva	6 Feb
1:26.90	Natoya	Goule	JAM	30.3.91	5 Mar			
1:27.38	Phyllis	Francis	USA-J	4.5.92	15 Jan			
1:26.91	Marina	Pospelova	RUS	23.7.90	6 Feb			

800 METRES

Mark	Name		Nat	Born	Pos	Meet	Venue	Date
1:55.87	Mariya	Savinova	RUS	13.8.85	1	WCh	Daegu	4 Sep
1:56.35	Caster	Semenya	RSA	7.1.91	2	WCh	Daegu	4 Sep
1:56.95		Savinova			1	NC	Cheboksary	22 Jul
1:56.99	Yuliya	Rusanova	RUS	3.7.86	2	NC	Cheboksary	22 Jul
1:57.19	Yekaterina	Kostetskaya	RUS	31.12.86	3	NC	Cheboksary	22 Jul
1:57.42	Janeth	Jepkosgei	KEN	13.12.83	3	WCh	Daegu	4 Sep
1:57.48	Alysia	Montaño	USA	26.4.86	4	WCh	Daegu	4 Sep
1:57.82		Kostetskaya			5	WCh	Daegu	4 Sep
1:58.03		Savinova			1h5	NC	Cheboksary	21 Jul
1:58.03	Svetlana	Klyuka	RUS	27.12.78	4	NC	Cheboksary	22 Jul
1:58.04	Yelena	Kofanova	RUS	8.8.88	1	Kuts	Moskva	6 Aug
1:58.07		Semenya			1s3	WCh	Daegu	2 Sep
1:58.12	Svetlana	Usovich	BLR	14.10.80	1	Kuso	Szczecin	25 Jun
1:58.21	Kenia	Sinclair (10)	JAM	14.7.80	1	DNG	Stockholm	29 Jul
1:58.25		Kostetskaya			1	Mosc Ch	Moskva	10 Jul
1:58.25		Kofanova			5	NC	Cheboksary	22 Jul
1:58.26		Jepkosgei			1	ISTAF	Berlin	11 Sep
1:58.27	Halima	Hachlaf	MAR	6.9.88	1	Bisl	Oslo	9 Jun
1:58.27		Savinova			1	WK	Zürich	8 Sep
1:58.29		Sinclair			1	Pre	Eugene	4 Jun
1:58.30	Liliya	Lobanova	UKR	14.10.85	1	NCp	Yalta	31 May
1:58.33		Montaño			1	NC	Eugene	26 Jun
1:58.37	Morgan	Uceny	USA	10.3.85	1		Lignano	19 Jul
1:58.41		Sinclair			1		Kingston	7 May
1:58.41		Montaño			2	WK	Zürich	8 Sep
1:58.44		Savinova			2	Bisl	Oslo	9 Jun
1:58.45		Savinova			1s2	WCh	Daegu	2 Sep
1:58.49	Yevgeniya	Zinurova	RUS	16.11.82	2	Mosc Ch	Moskva	10 Jul
1:58.50		Jepkosgei			2s2	WCh	Daegu	2 Sep
1:58.50	Maggie (30/15)	Vessey	USA	23.12.81	6	WCh	Daegu	4 Sep
1:58.60	Jennifer	Meadows	GBR	17.4.81	1	LGP	London (CP)	5 Aug
1:58.61	Alice	Schmidt	USA	3.10.81	2		Lignano	19 Jul
1:58.70	Yusneisis	Santiusti	CUB	24.12.84	2	Hanz	Zagreb	13 Sep
1:58.71	Irina	Maracheva	RUS	29.9.84	3	Mosc Ch	Moskva	10 Jul
1:58.77	Yelena (20)	Arzhakova	RUS	8.9.89	2	Kuts	Moskva	6 Aug
1:59.12	Nataliya	Lupu	UKR	4.11.87	2	NCp	Yalta	31 May
1:59.12	Molly	Beckwith	USA	4.8.87	3		Lignano	19 Jul
1:59.17	Yekaterina	Martynova	RUS	6.8.86	1		Moskva	12 Jun
1:59.17	Fantu	Magiso	ETH-J	9.6.92	4s3	WCh	Daegu	2 Sep
1:59.21	Zahra	Bouras	ALG	13.1.87	1	Odlozil	Praha	13 Jun
1:59.25	Phoebe	Wright	USA	30.8.88	4	NC	Eugene	26 Jun
1:59.30	Marina	Arzamasova	BLR	17.12.87	1	NCp	Brest	21 May
1:59.32	Yuliya	Krevsun	UKR	8.12.80	3	NCp	Yalta	31 May
1:59.38	Ilona	Usovich	BLR	14.11.82	2	NCp	Brest	21 May
1:59.48	Lucia (30)	Klocová	SVK	20.11.83	2	Odlozil	Praha	13 Jun
1:59.53	Marilyn	Okoro	GBR	23.9.84	1		London	6 Aug
1:59.56	Olga	Zavgorodnya	UKR	6.1.83	1	WUG	Shenzhen	18 Aug
1:59.59	Jemma	Simpson	GBR	10.2.84	5	ISTAF	Berlin	11 Sep
1:59.62	Geena	Gall	USA	18.1.87	5		Lignano	19 Jul
1:59.66A	Eunice	Sum	KEN	2.9.88	2	NC	Nairobi	16 Jul
1:59.67	LaTavia	Thomas	USA	17.12.88	1		Ninove	7 Aug
1:59.68A	Cherono	Koech	KEN-J	8.12.92	3	NC	Nairobi	16 Jul
1:59.75	Malika	Akkaoui	MAR	25.12.87	2	DNG	Stockholm	29 Jul
1:59.76	Tatyana	Paliyenko	RUS	18.11.83	6	NC	Cheboksary	22 Jul

Mark	Name		Nat	Born	Pos	Meet	Venue	Date	
1:59.77	Emma	Jackson	GBR	7.6.88	5s2	WCh	Daegu	2	Sep
	(40)								
1:59.79	Tetyana	Petlyuk	UKR	22.2.82	1h1	NC	Donetsk	3	Aug
1:59.83	Yuliya	Tutayeva	RUS	7.12.88	5	Mosc Ch	Moskva	10	Jul
2:00.14	Aleksandra	Bulanova	RUS	10.6.89	1		Moskva	15	Jun
2:00.17	Erica	Moore	USA	25.3.88	6	NC	Eugene	26	Jun
2:00.19	Anna	Pierce	USA	31.3.84	8	Pre	Eugene	4	Jun
2:00.20	Angelika	Cichocka	POL	15.3.88	6	Hanz	Zagreb	13	Sep
2:00.30	Yvonne	Hak	NED	30.6.86	9	Bisl	Oslo	9	Jun
2:00.32	Anastasiya	Vosmerikova	RUS	15.7.88	2h2	NC	Cheboksary	21	Jul
2:00.37	Anastasiya	Tkachuk	UKR-J	20.4.93	4	NCp	Yalta	31	May
2:00.40	Annet	Negesa	UGA-J	24.4.92	3	FBK	Hengelo	29	May
	(50)								
2:00.41	Heather	Kampf	USA	19.1.87	6		Lignano	19	Jul
2:00.45	Treniere	Moser	USA	27.10.81	8		Lignano	19	Jul
2:00.46	Merve	Aydin	TUR	17.3.90	2	EU23	Ostrava	15	Jul
2:00.54	Hellen	Obiri	KEN	13.12.89	7	LGP	London (CP)	5	Aug
2:00.56	Rose Mary	Almanza	CUB-J	13.7.92	1		La Habana	6	May
2:00.57	Viktoriya	Yalovtseva	KAZ	4.11.77	1		Bishkek	5	Jun
2:00.65	Lynsey	Sharp	GBR	11.7.90	3	EU23	Ostrava	15	Jul
2:00.68	Ingvill	Måkestad Bovim	NOR	7.8.81	8	LGP	London (CP)	5	Aug
2:00.72	Christin	Wurth-Thomas	USA	11.7.80	1	Jordan	Stanford	1	May
2:00.76	Marina	Pospelova	RUS	23.7.90	3h1	NC	Cheboksary	21	Jul
	(60)								
2:00.78	Tamsyn	Manou	AUS	20.7.78	4rB	DNG	Stockholm	29	Jul
2:00.79	Rosibel	García	COL	13.2.81	5s1	WCh	Daegu	2	Sep
2:00.83	Hind	Dehiba	FRA	17.3.79	3		Reims	5	Jul
2:00.84	Danuta	Urbanik	POL	24.12.89	4	Kuso	Szczecin	25	Jun
2:00.85	Lemlem	Ogbasilassie	CAN	10.12.87	2		Ninove	7	Aug
2:00.89	Margarita	Matsko	KAZ	4.1.86	1	AsiGP	Kunshan	26	May
2:00.92	Lenka	Masná	CZE	22.4.85	4	Odlozil	Praha	13	Jun
2:00.92	Tatyana	Markelova	RUS	19.12.88	3h5	NC	Cheboksary	21	Jul
2:00.93	Jana	Hartmann	GER	23.5.81	5	Odlozil	Praha	13	Jun
2:00.95	Tintu	Luka	IND	26.4.89	6s2	WCh	Daegu	2	Sep
	(70)								
2:00.96	Annet	Mwanzi	KEN	21.7.87	5		Rovereto	13	Sep
2:01.04	Elisa	Cusma Piccione	ITA	24.7.81	5	ET	Stockholm	18	Jun
2:01.05	Laura	Januszewski	USA	28.2.86	9		Lignano	19	Jul
2:01.07	Brenda	Martinez	USA	8.9.87	10		Lignano	19	Jul
2:01.17	Christine	Schmaltz	USA	14.4.88	8	NC	Eugene	26	Jun
2:01.20	Jenny	Simpson	USA	23.8.86	6		Los Angeles (ER)	21	May
2:01.26	Yeliz	Kurt	TUR	15.1.84	1	NC	Izmir	10	Jul
2:01.33	Heidi	Dahl	USA	15.2.86	4		Kingston	7	May
2:01.34		Wang Chunyu	CHN-Y	17.1.95	1	City G	Nanchang	23	Oct
2:01.40	Olga	Soldatova	RUS	8.9.85	2rB	Mosc Ch	Moskva	10	Jul
	(80)								
2:01.41		Truong Thanh Hang	VIE	1.5.86	1	AsiC	Kobe	10	Jul
2:01.41	Anzhelika	Shevchenko	UKR	29.10.87	5	NC	Donetsk	4	Aug
2:01.44	Yekaterina	Kupina	RUS	2.2.86	1		Zhukovskiy	6	Jul
2:01.45	Egle	Balciunaite	LTU	31.10.88	6	Odlozil	Praha	13	Jun
2:01.45	Natoya	Goule	JAM	30.3.91	2	NC	Kingston	25	Jun
2:01.47	Nuria	Fernández	ESP	16.8.76	1		Zaragoza	25	Jun
2:01.50	Marta	Milani	ITA	9.3.87	4	Nebiolo	Torino	10	Jun
2:01.50	Gabriela	Medina	MEX	3.3.85	1	CAC	Mayagüez	17	Jul
2:01.54	Jessica	Smith	CAN	11.10.89	2	Jerome	Burnaby	1	Jul
2:01.55	Mariem Alaoui	Selsouli	MAR	8.4.84	4	Notturna	Milano	18	Sep
	(90)								
2:01.61A	Sylvia	Chesebe	KEN	.87	4	NC	Nairobi	16	Jul
2:01.62	Tatyana	Andrianova	RUS	10.12.79	2h3	NC	Cheboksary	21	Jul
2:01.73	Oksana	Dyomina	RUS	4.8.90	2		Yerino	30	Jul
2:01.76	Alena	Fesenko	RUS	4.10.88	3h4	NC	Cheboksary	21	Jul
2:01.77	Neisha	Bernard-Thomas	GRN	21.1.81	5		Kingston	7	May
2:01.78	Yelena	Kobeleva	RUS	12.6.88	4h1	NC	Cheboksary	21	Jul
2:01.78	Tugba	Karakaya	TUR	16.2.91	1		Ankara	31	Jul
2:01.8 mx	Ewelina	Setowska-Dryk	POL	5.3.80	1		Wroclaw	3	Sep
2:01.85mx	Corinna	Harrer	GER	19.1.91	1		Neustadt	8	Jul
	2:02.27				1		Besigheim	27	Jul
2:01.86	(100)	Guan Yue	CHN-J	23.5.92	2	City G	Nanchang	23	Oct

Mark	Name		Nat	Born	Date		Mark	Name		Nat	Born	Date	
2:01.88	Natalya	Koreyvo	BLR	14.11.85	12	Jul	2:01.98	Élodie	Guégan	FRA	19.12.85	20	Jul
2:01.90	Ruriko	Kubo	JPN	23.1.89	7	Aug	2:02.02	Natalya	Peryakova	RUS	4.3.83	21	Jul
2:01.91	Tereza	Capková	CZE	24.7.87	13	Jun	2:02.04	Amy	Weissenbach	USA-Y	16.6.94	4	Jun

Mark	Name	Nat	Born	Pos	Meet	Venue	Date
2:02.04	Siham Hilali	MAR	2.5.86				15 Jul
2:02.05	Mariya Zhuravlyova	RUS	7.11.86				30 Jul
2:02.08	Christiane dos Santos	BRA	6.10.81				20 Jul
2:02.10	Renata Plis	POL	5.2.85				29 Jul
2:02.10	Zhao Jing	CHN	9.7.88				18 Aug
2:02.12	Helen Crofts	CAN	28.5.90				28 May
2:02.15	Anne Maria Kesselring	GER	4.12.89				10 Jun
2:02.15	Lea Wallace	USA	19.12.88				1 Jul
2:02.16	Natalija Piliusina	LTU	22.10.90				10 Jun
2:02.23	Karine Belleau-Béliveau	CAN	29.12.83				18 Sep
2:02.24	Anna Konovalova	RUS	4.7.88				21 Jul
2:02.27	Clarisse Moh	FRA	6.12.86				5 Jul
2:02.29	Annett Horna	GER	4.2.87				3 Jun
2:02.31mx	Ciara Mageean	IRL-J	12.3.92				12 Aug
2:02.32	Anna Luchkina	RUS	13.1.86				10 Jul
2:02.34	Hasna Benhassi	MAR	1.6.78				15 Jul
2:02.38	Anna Sidorova	UZB	9.9.84				22 May
2:02.40	Erin Donohue	USA	8.5.83				30 Jul
2:02.41	Diosmely Peña	CUB	12.6.85				28 May
2:02.44	Anna Mishchenko	UKR	25.8.83				4 Aug
2:02.48A	Nelly Jepkosgei	KEN	14.7.91				16 Jul
2:02.50	Lindsey Schnell	USA	1.8.79				21 May
2:02.50	Eléni Filándra	GRE	12.1.84				18 Jun
2:02.55	Andrea Ferris	PAN	21.9.87				1 May
2:02.55A	Jane Jelagat	KEN	.82				16 Jul
2:02.55	Adriana Muñoz	CUB	16.3.82				29 Jul
2:02.59	Stephanie Brown	USA	29.7.91				27 May
2:02.59	Olga Nitsina	RUS	11.2.89				25 Jun
2:02.60	Katherine Katsanevakis	AUS	11.6.88				3 Mar
2:02.63	Katie Follett	USA	12.11.87				11 Jun
2:02.64	Holly Noack	AUS	30.11.83				3 Mar
2:02.64	Yekaterina Zavyalova	RUS	1.3.91				25 Jun
2:02.64	Ajee' Wilson	USA-Y	8.5.94				10 Jul
2:02.67	Karoline Pilawa	GER	19.9.85				15 Jul
2:02.68	Rachel Aubry	CAN	.90				7 Aug
2:02.69	Melissa Bishop	CAN	5.8.88				1 Jul
2:02.70	Jessica Judd	GBR-Y	7.1.95				15 Jun
2:02.73	Charlotte Best	GBR	7.3.85				11 Jun
2:02.73A	Nancy Langat	KEN	22.8.81				11 Jun
2:02.77	Tara Bird	GBR	22.7.87				20 Aug
2:02.79	Svetlana Cherkasova	RUS	20.5.78				6 Jul
2:02.8	Natalya Yevdokimova	RUS	17.3.78				30 Jun
2:02.94							8 Jul
2:02.81	Nadezhda Viderker	RUS	12.7.89				25 Jun
2:02.84	Chanelle Price	USA	22.8.90				8 Jun
2:02.87	Nikki Hamblin	NZL	20.5.88				1 Sep
2:02.88	Sianne Toemoe	AUS	17.6.89				1 Apr
2:02.88	Karen Harewood	GBR	19.8.75				20 Aug
2:02.89	Kelly Hetherington	AUS	10.3.89				1 Apr
2:02.94	Luiza Gega	ALB	5.11.88				7 Jun
2:03.01	Kaliese Spencer	JAM	6.5.87				5 Mar
2:03.03	Gabriele Anderson	USA	25.6.86				30 Jul
2:03.10	Lydia Wafula	KEN	15.2.88				25 May
2:03.10	Justyna Zembrzuska	POL	3.3.86				12 Aug
2:03.10	Fanjanteino Félix	FRA	26.1.80				18 Sep
2:03.12	Laura Roesler	USA	19.12.91				27 May
2:03.13	Genzeb Shumi Regasa	BRN	29.1.91				27 Oct
2:03.15	Joanna Józwik	POL	30.1.91				3 Jun
2:03.20	Malindi Elmore	CAN	13.3.80				3 Jul
2:03.29	Stacey Smith	GBR	4.2.90				23 Jul
2:03.34	Celia Taylor	GBR	22.1.77				1 May
2:03.34	Akari Kishikawa	JPN	13.9.85				12 Jun
2:03.40	Diana Sujew	GER	2.11.90				13 Aug
2:03.41	Kate Grace	USA	.88				27 May
2:03.43	Karin Storbacka	FIN	27.4.87				24 Jul
2:03.43	Rowena Cole	GBR-J	13.1.92				23 Jul
2:03.45	Yelena Soboleva	RUS	3.10.82				25 May
2:03.45	Devotia Moore	USA	21.8.89				11 Jun
2:03.48	Anna Layman	USA	23.2.88				14 May
2:03.48	Marina Muncan	SRB	6.11.82				13 Jul
2:03.49	Isabel Macías	ESP	11.8.84				18 Jun
2:03.52	Christina Rodgers	USA	4.8.88				14 May
2:03.55	Annie Leblanc	CAN-J	29.4.92				1 Jul
2:03.58	Teodora Kolarova	BUL	29.5.81				18 Jun
2:03.59	Tatyana Gudkova	RUS	26.3.85				21 Jul
2:03.59	Ayvika Malanova	RUS-J	28.11.92				23 Jul
2:03.59	Nicole Sifuentes	CAN	30.6.86				23 Jul
2:03.60	Mirela Lavric	ROU	17.2.91				30 Jun
2:03.61	Mason Cathey	USA	29.4.82				11 Jun
2:03.62A	Sheila Chesang	KEN	.86				4 Jun
2:03.62	Elián Périz	ESP	1.4.84				22 Jul
2:03.63	Jesse Carlin	USA	13.10.86				24 Jul
2:03.67	Charlotte Debroux	BEL	27.9.83				13 Aug
2:03.68	Olga Lvova	RUS	21.9.89				25 May
2:03.69	Denise Krebs	GER	27.6.87				13 Jun
2:03.69	Viktoria Tegenfeldt	SWE	27.9.87				2 Aug
2:03.70	Sara Vaughn	USA	16.5.86				11 Jun
2:03.71	Diane Cummins	CAN	19.1.74				7 Jun
2:03.71	Monika Merl	GER	21.9.79				13 Aug
2:03.72	Zoe Buckman	AUS	21.12.88				13 Jul
2:03.73	Charlene Lipsey	USA	16.7.91				10 Jun
2:03.74	Alena Glazkova	RUS	6.5.88				10 Jul
2:03.74	Elisabetta Artuso	ITA	25.4.74				30 Jul
2:03.74	Bethany Praska	USA	10.6.89				13 Aug
2:03.79	Jennifer Lozano (200)	FRA	16.1.85				29 Jul

Indoors

Mark	Name	Nat	Born	Pos	Meet	Venue	Date
1:58.14	Rusanova			1	NC	Moskva	17 Feb
1:58.83	Zinurova			2	NC	Moskva	17 Feb
2:01.14	Anna Balakshina	RUS	22.11.85	1h1	NC	Moskva	16 Feb
2:01.23	Egle Balciunaite	LTU	31.10.88	1		Düsseldorf	11 Feb
2:01.32	Linda Marguet	FRA	11.9.83	3s2	EI	Paris (B)	5 Mar
2:03.31	Elián Périz	ESP	1.4.84				5 Mar
2:03.63	Alena Glazkova	RUS	6.5.88				19 Jan
2:03.79	Rebecca Addison	USA	28.5.91				11 Feb

JUNIORS

See main list for top 7 juniors. 10 performances by 6 women to 2:01.5. Additional mark and further juniors:

Mark	Name	Nat	Born	Pos	Meet	Venue	Date
Magiso	2:00.44			7		Lignano	17 Jul
Koech	2:00.34			1		Milano	18 Sep
	2:01.03			3h4	WCh	Daegu	1 Sep
	2:01.48			6s3	WCh	Daegu	2 Sep
2:02.04	Amy Weissenbach	USA-Y	16.6.94	1		Clovis	4 Jun
2:02.31mx	Ciara Mageean	IRL	12.3.92	1		Belfast	12 Aug
2:02.64	Ajee' Wilson (10)	USA-Y	8.5.94	1	WY	Villeneuve d'Ascq	10 Jul
2:02.70	Jessica Judd	GBR-Y	7.1.95	1		Watford	15 Jun
2:03.43	Rowena Cole	GBR	13.1.92	2	EJ	Tallinn	23 Jul
2:03.55	Annie Leblanc	CAN	29.4.92	7	Jerome	Burnaby	1 Jul
2:03.59	Ayvika Malanova	RUS	28.11.92	3	EJ	Tallinn	23 Jul
2:03.97	Ristananna Tracey	JAM	5.9.92	1		Kingston	16 Apr
2:04.09	Sahily Diago	CUB-Y	26.8.95	1r2		La Habana	16 Jun
2:04.12	Ioana Doaga	ROU	5,4,92	2	NC	Bucureşti	30 Jun
2:04.42	Gemeda Feyne	ETH	.92	1		Pergine Valsug.	23 Jul
2:04.47	Olga Lyakhova	UKR	18.3.92	6r2		Yalta	31 May
2:04.57	Svetlana Rogozina (20)	RUS	26.12.92	2	NC-j	Cheboksary	2 Jul

Mark	Name		Nat	Born	Pos	Meet	Venue	Date

1000 METRES

Mark	Name		Nat	Born	Pos	Meet	Venue	Date
2:35.3e	Irina	Maracheva	RUS	29.9.84	1		Florø	4 Jun
2:36.0e	Marina	Arzamasova	BLR	17.12.87	2		Florø	4 Jun
2:36.7e	Ingvill	Måkestad Bovim	NOR	7.8.81	3		Florø	4 Jun
2:37.28	Adriana	Muñoz	CUB	16.3.82	1		La Habana	23 Sep
2:37.33	Angelika	Cichocka	POL	15.3.88	1		Warszawa	20 Sep

Mark	Name		Nat	Born	Date		Mark	Name		Nat	Born	Date
2:37.89	Renata	Plis	POL	5.2.85	20 Sep		2:39.3e	Lydia	Wafula	KEN	15.2.88	4 Jun
2:38.18mx	Jennifer	Wenth	AUT	24.7.91	5 Jul		2:39.5	Rose Mary	Almanza	CUB-J	13.7.92	9 Sep
2:38.46	Ewelina	Setowska-Dryk	POL	5.3.80	20 Sep		2:40.03	Diana	Sujew	GER	2.11.90	22 May
2:38.71	Denise	Krebs	GER	27.6.87	22 May		2:40.75	Elina	Sujew	GER	2.11.90	22 May
							2:40.9	Kelly	Hetherington	AUS	10.3.89	20 Dec

Indoors

Mark	Name		Nat	Born	Pos	Meet	Venue	Date
2:35.21	Yelena	Arzhakova	RUS	8.9.89	1rB	Winter	Moskva	6 Feb
2:36.32	Yevgeniya	Zinurova	RUS	16.11.82	1	Winter	Moskva	6 Feb
2:37.07	Olesya	Syreva	RUS	25.11.83	2	Winter	Moskva	6 Feb
2:37.33	Natalya	Koreyvo	BLR	14.11.85	2rB	Winter	Moskva	6 Feb

Mark	Name		Nat	Born	Date		Mark	Name		Nat	Born	Date
2:37.63	Tatyana	Paliyenko	RUS	18.11.83	6 Feb		2:38.50	Hind	Dehiba	FRA	17.3.79	6 Feb
2:37.66	Yekaterina	Martynova	RUS	6.8.86	6 Feb		2:38.83	Yevgeniya	Zolotova	RUS	28.4.83	9 Jan
2:38.25	Aleksandra	Bulanova	RUS	10.6.89	6 Feb		2:39.35	Anna	Luchkina	RUS	13.1.86	6 Feb
2:38.27	Anastasiya	Vosmerikova	RUS	15.7.88	6 Feb		2:39.53	Yuliya	Krevsun	UKR	8.12.80	6 Feb
2:38.50	Anna	Balakshina	RUS	22.11.85	9 Jan		2:40.53	Yuliya	Tutayeva	RUS	7.12.88	6 Feb

JUNIORS

Mark	Name		Nat	Born	Pos	Meet	Venue	Date
2:39.5	Rose Mary	Almanza	CUB-J	13.7.92	2		La Habana	9 Sep
	2:39.85				2		La Habana	23 Sep
2:41.59	Gesa-Felicitas	Krause	GER	3.8.92	1		Wehrheim	31 Jul
2:42.07	Annet	Negesa	UGA	24.4.92	1		Pliezhausen	22 May
2:42.22	Urdileidis	Quiala	CUB	9.1.93	3		La Habana	23 Sep

1500 METRES

Mark	Name		Nat	Born	Pos	Meet	Venue	Date
4:00.06	Morgan	Uceny	USA	10.3.85	1	VD	Bruxelles	16 Sep
4:00.33	Maryam	Jamal	BRN	16.9.84	1	FBK	Hengelo	29 May
4:00.59		Jamal			1	Herc	Monaco	22 Jul
4:00.77	Mariem Alaoui	Selsouli	MAR	8.4.84	2	VD	Bruxelles	16 Sep
4:00.97	Kalkidan	Gezahegne	ETH	8.5.91	2	FBK	Hengelo	29 May
4:01.02	Yekaterina	Gorbunova	RUS	17.1.89	1		Barcelona	22 Jul
4:01.04		Selsouli			1	GP	Rieti	10 Sep
4:01.09	Btissam	Lakhouad	MAR	7.12.80	2	Herc	Monaco	22 Jul
4:01.33	Siham	Hilali	MAR	2.5.86	3	FBK	Hengelo	29 May
4:01.40		Jamal			3	VD	Bruxelles	16 Sep
4:01.50	Natalia	Rodríguez	ESP	2.6.79	2		Barcelona	22 Jul
4:01.51		Uceny			3	Herc	Monaco	22 Jul
4:01.60		Jamal			1	GGala	Roma	26 May
4:01.68	Yekaterina	Martynova	RUS	6.8.86	1	NC	Cheboksary	24 Jul
4:01.73	Anna	Mishchenko (10)	UKR	25.8.83	4	VD	Bruxelles	16 Sep
4:01.77	Yekaterina	Kostetskaya	RUS	31.12.86	2	NC	Cheboksary	24 Jul
4:01.89	Hannah	England	GBR	6.3.87	3		Barcelona	22 Jul
4:02.03		England			5	VD	Bruxelles	16 Sep
4:02.10		Martynova			2	GP	Rieti	10 Sep
4:02.12	Meskerem	Assefa	ETH	20.9.85	2	GGala	Roma	26 May
4:02.31	Mercy	Cherono	KEN	7.5.91	4		Barcelona	22 Jul
4:02.32	Janeth	Jepkosgei	KEN	13.12.83	6	VD	Bruxelles	16 Sep
4:02.42	Helen	Obiri	KEN	13.12.89	7	VD	Bruxelles	16 Sep
4:02.57		Rodríguez			8	VD	Bruxelles	16 Sep
4:02.59	Irene	Jelagat	KEN	10.12.88	4	FBK	Hengelo	29 May
4:02.73	Olesya	Syreva	RUS	25.11.83	3	NC	Cheboksary	24 Jul
4:02.75		Hilali			4	Herc	Monaco	22 Jul
4:02.79		Mishchenko			3	GP	Rieti	10 Sep
4:03.00		Mishchenko			1	DL	Doha	6 May
4:03.02	Hind	Dehiba	FRA	17.3.79	4	GP	Rieti	10 Sep
4:03.13	Mimi	Belete	BRN	9.6.88	9	VD	Bruxelles	16 Sep
	(31/20)							
4:03.28	Gelete	Burka	ETH	15.2.86	3	GGala	Roma	26 May
4:03.33	Natalya	Yevdokimova	RUS	17.3.78	4	NC	Cheboksary	24 Jul
4:03.41	Tugba	Karakaya	TUR	16.2.91	1		Samsun	15 Aug
4:03.50	Renata	Plis	POL	5.2.85	12	VD	Bruxelles	16 Sep
4:03.54	Jenny	Simpson	USA	23.8.86	5	Herc	Monaco	22 Jul
4:03.59	Anastasiya	Vosmerikova	RUS	15.7.88	5	NC	Cheboksary	24 Jul
4:03.66	Nancy	Langat	KEN	22.8.81	5	GGala	Roma	26 May
4:03.69	Tatyana	Tomashova	RUS	1.7.75	5	GP	Rieti	10 Sep
4:03.72	Christin	Wurth-Thomas	USA	11.7.80	6	GGala	Roma	26 May

Mark	Name		Nat	Born	Pos	Meet	Venue	Date
4:03.79	Ingvill (30)	Måkestad Bovim	NOR	7.8.81	14	VD	Bruxelles	16 Sep
4:03.92	Anna	Konovalova	RUS	4.7.88	7	NC	Cheboksary	24 Jul
4:03.94	Tizita	Bogale	ETH-J	13.7.93	6		Barcelona	22 Jul
4:04.64	Nuria	Fernández	ESP	16.8.76	7		Barcelona	22 Jul
4:04.76	Lisa	Dobriskey	GBR	23.12.83	8	Herc	Monaco	22 Jul
4:04.82	Nikki	Hamblin	NZL	20.5.88	8		Barcelona	22 Jul
4:04.85	Bertukan	Feyisa	ETH	4.7.91	1	CAA	Brazzaville	12 Jun
4:04.96	Malika	Akkaoui	MAR	25.12.87	4	Colorful	Daegu	12 May
4:05.06	Zoe	Buckman	AUS	21.12.88	9	GP	Rieti	10 Sep
4:05.14	Yuliya	Rusanova	RUS	3.7.86	8	NC	Cheboksary	24 Jul
4:05.51	Viola (40)	Kibiwott	KEN	22.12.83	5	FBK	Hengelo	29 May
4:05.53	Nataliya	Tobias	UKR	22.11.80	2	NCp	Yalta	30 May
4:05.53	Aslı	Çakir	TUR	20.8.85	2	Gyulai	Budapest	30 Jul
4:05.65	Kaila	McKnight	AUS	5.5.86	5	Colorful	Daegu	12 May
4:05.73	Shannon	Rowbury	USA	19.9.84	3	LGP	London (CP)	6 Aug
4:05.90	Genzebe	Dibaba	ETH	8.2.91	2rB	GP	Rieti	10 Sep
4:06.23	Sally	Kipyego	KEN	19.12.85	1		Eugene	22 Apr
4:06.40	Natalya	Koreyvo	BLR	14.11.85	9		Barcelona	22 Jul
4:06.49	Helen	Clitheroe	GBR	2.1.74	4	BrGP	Birmingham	10 Jul
4:06.50	Kenia	Sinclair	JAM	14.7.80	1		Sydney	19 Mar
4:06.50	Isabel (50)	Macías	ESP	11.8.84	10		Barcelona	22 Jul
4:06.50	Angelika	Cichocka	POL	15.3.88	2	Sidlo	Sopot	5 Aug
4:06.63	Shalane	Flanagan	USA	8.7.81	10	Herc	Monaco	22 Jul
4:06.64	Yelena	Soboleva	RUS	3.10.82	2	Mosc Ch	Moskva	9 Jul
4:06.72	Sylwia	Ejdys	POL	15.7.84	6	FBK	Hengelo	29 May
4:06.75	Olga	Golovkina	RUS	17.12.86	3	Mosc Ch	Moskva	9 Jul
4:06.77	Gabriele	Anderson	USA	25.6.86	4	LGP	London (CP)	6 Aug
4:06.78	Irina	Maracheva	RUS	29.9.84	9	NC	Cheboksary	24 Jul
4:06.81	Stacey	Smith	GBR	4.2.90	5	BrGP	Birmingham	10 Jul
4:06.85	Charlene	Thomas	GBR	6.5.82	1	ET	Stockholm	19 Jun
4:07.01	Yuliya (60)	Zaripova	RUS	26.4.86	1		Sochi	24 May
4:07.04	Erin	Donohue	USA	8.5.83	2		Joensuu	27 Jul
4:07.18	Hilary	Stellingwerff	CAN	7.8.81	3	Sidlo	Sopot	5 Aug
4:07.20	Svetlana	Kireyeva	RUS	12.6.87	5	Mosc Ch	Moskva	9 Jul
4:07.24	Anzhelika	Shevchenko	UKR	29.10.87	3	NCp	Yalta	30 May
4:07.28	Lidia	Chojecka	POL	25.1.77	11		Barcelona	22 Jul
4:07.29	Sara	Moreira #	POR	17.10.85	12		Barcelona	22 Jul
4:07.40	Natalya	Popkova	RUS	21.9.88	6	Mosc Ch	Moskva	9 Jul
4:07.44	Katie	Follett	USA	12.11.87	1		Los Angeles (ER)	21 May
4:07.45	Ciara	Mageean	IRL-J	12.3.92	1		Birmingham	20 Aug
4:07.53	Jemma (70)	Simpson	GBR	10.2.84	2		Birmingham	20 Aug
4:07.57	Treniere	Moser	USA	27.10.81	7	Pre	Eugene	4 Jun
4:07.63	Nancy	Chepkwemoi	KEN-J	8.10.93	1		Kessel-Lo	13 Aug
4:07.69	Yelena	Arzhakova	RUS	8.9.89	4	WUG	Shenzhen	21 Aug
4:07.70	Denise	Krebs	GER	27.6.87	5	WUG	Shenzhen	21 Aug
4:07.74	Ann	Mwangi	KEN	8.12.88	7	Colorful	Daegu	12 May
4:07.86	Alfiya	Khasanova	RUS	3.10.88	3		Sochi	24 May
4:07.86	Malindi	Elmore	CAN	13.3.80	1	Jerome	Burnaby	1 Jul
4:07.90		Liu Fang	CHN	25.2.90	6	WUG	Shenzhen	21 Aug
4:07.94mx	Laura	Weightman	GBR	1.7.91	1mx		Manchester (Str)	6 Sep
4:08.09	Alice (80)	Schmidt	USA	3.10.81	1		Padova	17 Jul
4:08.10	Nelly	Jepkosgei	KEN	14.7.91	4	CAA	Brazzaville	12 Jun
4:08.45	Nicole	Sifuentes	CAN	30.6.86	1		Gent	30 Jul
4:08.56	Tetyana	Petlyuk	UKR	22.2.82	2	NC	Donetsk	2 Aug
4:08.60	Phoebe	Wright	USA	30.8.88	3		Los Angeles (ER)	21 May
4:08.60	Lyubov	Pulyayeva	RUS	26.4.82	3h1	NC	Cheboksary	23 Jul
4:08.63	Corinna	Harrer	GER	19.1.91	2		Gent	30 Jul
4:08.74	Sara	Vaughn	USA	16.5.86	3	Jerome	Burnaby	1 Jul
4:08.80A	Joyce	Chepkirui	KEN	10.8.88	2	NC	Nairobi	16 Jul
4:08.89	Tereza	Capková	CZE	24.7.87	7	WUG	Shenzhen	21 Aug
4:08.96	Emily (90)	Infeld	USA	21.3.90	5	NC	Eugene	25 Jun
4:09.04	Danuta	Urbanik	POL	24.12.89	4h1	EU23	Ostrava	16 Jul
4:09.08A	Mary	Wangare	KEN	29.11.87	1		Nairobi	4 Jun
4:09.13	Diana	Sujew	GER	2.11.90	5h1	EU23	Ostrava	16 Jul

Mark	Name		Nat	Born	Pos	Meet	Venue	Date
4:09.17A	Annet	Negesa	UGA-J	24.4.92	1	Af-J	Gaborone	15 May
4:09.48	Faith	Kipyegon	KEN-Y	10.1.94	1	WY	Villeneuve d'Ascq	9 Jul
4:09.69	Anna	Luchkina	RUS	13.1.86	4h1	NC	Cheboksary	23 Jul
4:09.69	Elizabeth	Maloy	USA	10.8.85	4		Gent	30 Jul
4:09.71	Iris María	Fuentes-Pila	ESP	10.8.80	14		Barcelona	22 Jul
4:09.80	Senbera	Teferi	ETH-Y	3.5.95	2		Kessel-Lo	13 Aug
4:09.88	Alena	Fesenko	RUS	4.10.88	8	Mosc Ch	Moskva	9 Jul
	(100)							

Mark	Name		Nat	Born	Pos	Date
4:09.92	Beverly	Ramos	PUR	24.8.87	1	Jul
4:09.92	Fadime	Suna	TUR	25.10.86	30	Jul
4:09.95	Brie	Felnagle	USA	9.12.86	23	Jun
4:10.01	Kaltoum	Bouaasayriya	MAR	23.8.82	30	Apr
4:10.10	Georgie	Clarke	AUS	17.6.84	19	Mar
4:10.19	Lindsey	De Grande	BEL	26.4.89	1	May
4:10.22	Yuliya	Chizhenko	RUS	30.8.79	7	Jul
4:10.28	Jordan	Hasay	USA	12.9.91	1	May
4:10.30	Abeba	Arigawi	ETH	5.7.90	22	Jul
4:10.32	Bridey	Delaney	AUS	16.7.89	19	Mar
4:10.37	Almensch	Belete	ETH	26.7.89	23	Jul
4:10.38	Anna	Pierce	USA	31.3.84	11	Jun
4:10.49		Xue Fei	CHN	8.8.89	9	Sep
4:10.63	Gemeda	Feyne	ETH-J	28.6.92	12	Jun
4:10.67		Zhao Jing	CHN	9.7.88	9	Sep
4:10.77	Brenda	Martinez	USA	8.9.87	21	May
4:10.77	Lea	Wallace	USA	19.12.88	3	Jul
4:10.80	Elina	Sujew	GER	2.11.90	2	Jul
4:10.99	Olga	Nitsina	RUS	11.2.89	4	Aug
4:11.01	Lauren	Hagans	USA	27.6.86	1	Jul
4:11.07	Jennifer	Wenth	AUT	24.7.91	30	Jul
4:11.25		Guan Yue	CHN-J	23.5.92	21	Oct
4:11.26	Sultan	Haydar	TUR	23.5.87	21	May
4:11.26	Angela	Bizzarri	USA	15.2.88	21	May
4:11.27	Genzeb	Shumi Regasa	BRN	29.1.91	24	Jun
4:11.32	Katarzyna	Broniatowska	POL	22.2.90	1	Jun
4:11.39	Yelena	Korobkina	RUS	25.11.90	30	Jul
4:11.53	Fanjanteino	Félix	FRA	26.1.80	22	Jul
4:11.56	Genet	Tibieso	ETH-Y	23.1.94	9	Jul
4:11.59	Lucy	Van Dalen	NZL	18.11.88	17	Jul
4:11.85	Sheila	Reid	CAN	2.8.89	15	Apr
4:11.88	Kara	Goucher	USA	9.7.78	1	Jul
4:12.01	Ihsan	Gibril	SUD-J	.92	4	Jun
4:12.03	Molly	Huddle	USA	31.8.84	11	Jun
4:12.05	Kim	Conley	USA	14.3.86	21	May
4:12.09	Heather	Kampf	USA	19.1.87	17	Jul
4:12.18	Lauren	Bonds	USA	9.6.88	21	May
4:12.19	Barbara	Parker	GBR	8.11.82	30	Jul
4:12.23	Geena	Gall	USA	18.1.87	1	May
4:12.28	Kate	Van Buskirk	CAN	9.6.87	21	Aug
4:12.36	Mariam Abdallah	Mubarak	UAE	13.11.91	2	Jun
4:12.38	Sanae	El Otmani	MAR	20.12.86	30	Apr
4:12.41	Eunice	Sum	KEN	2.9.88	6	May
4:12.42	Emma	Jackson	GBR	7.6.88	25	May
4:12.45	Nadia	Noujani	MAR	3.9.81	13	Aug
4:12.55	Jackie	Areson	USA	31.3.88	21	May
4:12.75	Barbara	Maveau	BEL	16.2.87	24	Jul
4:12.75		Xu Qiuzi	CHN	8.2.91	9	Sep
4:12.78	Heidi	Dahl	USA	15.2.86	21	May
4:12.93	Caster	Semenya	RSA	7.1.91	10	Apr
4:12.97	Emma	Coburn	USA	19.10.90	30	Jul
4:13.04	Karly	Hamric	USA	13.10.87	3	Jul
4:13.04	Svetlana	Podosenova	RUS	24.5.88	24	May
4:13.15	Renee	Tomlin	USA	21.11.88	15	Apr
4:13.23		Zhang Jie	CHN	2.10.87	9	Sep
4:13.37	Dolores	Checa	ESP	27.12.82	22	Jul
4:13.38	Elisa	Cusma Piccione	ITA	24.7.81	25	Jun
4:13.4A	Nancy	Cherono	KEN		16	Apr
4:13.42	Habiba	Ghribi	TUN	9.4.84	22	May
4:13.47	Olesya	Mikheyeva	RUS	23.7.81	6	Jul
4:13.60	Annett	Horna	GER	4.2.87	1	Jun
4:13.62	Anna	Laman	AUS-Y	25.5.95	19	Mar
4:13.64	Anna	Levchenko	RUS	11.5.85	23	Jul
4:13.66	Karin	Storbacka	FIN	27.4.87	27	Jul
4:13.73	Fabiana Cristine	da Silva	BRA	3.9.78	25	Jun
4:13.73	Kristina	Khaleyeva	RUS	22.10.87	23	Jul
4:13.83	Valérie	Lehmann	SUI	19.9.80	1	Jun
4:13.86	Sultana	Aït Hammou	MAR	10.5.80	21	May
4:13.86	Svetlana	Cherkasova	RUS	20.5.78	23	Jul
4:13.89	Dinahrose Lebogang	Phalula	RSA	9.12.83	10	Apr
4:13.93	Hannah	Newbould	NZL	19.6.91	2	Jul
4:14.02	Lauren	Centrowitz	USA	25.9.86	15	Apr
4:14.07+	Tatyana	Gudkova	RUS	26.3.85	7	Jun
4:14.08	Orla	Drumm	IRL	6.4.84	30	Jul
4:14.10	Korine	Hinds	JAM	18.1.76	15	Apr
4:14.21	Jessica	Judd	GBR-Y	7.1.95	28	May
4:14.21	Stevie	Stockton	GBR	23.8.89	6	Aug
4:14.22	Luiza	Gega	ALB	5.11.88	2	Jul
4:14.28	Sandra	Michalak	POL	1.4.87	5	Aug
4:14.30	Darya	Yachmeneva	RUS	9.9.90	23	Jul
4:14.36	Annick	Lamar	USA	10.12.85	11	Jun
4:14.37	Stephanie	Reilly	IRL	23.2.78	13	Jul
4:14.44	Eilish	McColgan	GBR	25.11.90	11	Jun
4:14.51	Lisa	Corrigan	AUS	2.12.84	19	Mar
4:14.64	Karine	Belleau-Béliveau	CAN	29.12.83	3	Jul
4:14.65	Jillian	Smith	USA	2.7.91	16	Apr
4:14.67	Kelly	Young	AUS	12.5.84	19	Mar
4:14.67mx	Claire	Tarplee	GBR/IRL	22.9.88	27	Jul
4:14.68	Viktoriya	Pogoryelska	UKR	4.8.90	30	May
4:14.70	Dudu	Karakaya	TUR	11.11.85	21	May
4:14.70	Ayako	Jinnouchi	JPN	21.1.87	27	Jul
4:14.72	Morgane	Gay	USA	19.8.90	9	Jun
4:14.75	Lauren	Fleshman	USA	26.9.81	11	Jun
4:14.78	Gete	Dima	ETH-J	10.3.92	4	Jun
4:14.8A	Sheila	Chepngetich	KEN-Y	.95	8	Jun
4:14.87	Heidi	Eriksson	FIN	27.4.86	28	Jun
4:14.89	Larisa	Arcip	ROU	19.2.86	2	Jul
4:14.90		Jin Yuan	CHN	11.2.88	9	Sep
4:14.93	Olga	Soldatova	RUS	8.9.85	23	Jul
4:14.95	Claire	Navez	FRA	6.10.87	2	Jul
4:14.97	Marina	Muncan (201)	SRB	6.11.82	9	Jul

Indoors

Mark	Name		Nat	Born	Pos	Meet	Venue	Date
4:01.47	Abeba	Arigawi	ETH	5.7.90	1	XL-Galan	Stockholm	22 Feb
4:05.38	Sylwia	Ejdys	POL	15.7.84	5	XL-Galan	Stockholm	22 Feb
4:05.47	Yevgeniya	Zolotova	RUS	28.4.83	1	Mosc Ch	Moskva	29 Jan
4:08.13	Ancuta	Bobocel	ROU	3.10.87	1	Spark	Stuttgart	5 Feb
4:08.71	Yelena	Korobkina	RUS	25.11.90	4	Mosc Ch	Moskva	29 Jan
4:08.76	Fanjanteino	Félix	FRA	26.1.80	2	Spark	Stuttgart	5 Feb
4:09.18	Lindsey	De Grande	BEL	26.4.89	4		Gent	13 Feb
4:09.67	Sigrid	Vanden Bempt	BEL	10.2.81	10	XL-Galan	Stockholm	22 Feb

Mark	Name		Nat	Born	Date
4:10.21	Anna	Balakshina	RUS	22.11.85	29 Jan
4:10.39	Charlotte	Schönbeck	SWE	22.12.84	22 Feb
4:12.03	Svetlana	Podosenova	RUS	24.5.88	21 Jan
4:12.26	Ioana	Doagâ	ROU-J	5.4.92	4 Mar
4:12.4+	Carmen	Douma-Hussar	CAN	12.3.77	22 Jan
4:12.6+	Frances	Koons	USA	2.4.86	22 Jan
4:13.35	Olesya	Mikheyeva	RUS	23.7.81	18 Feb
4:13.4+	Megan	Metcalfe Wright	CAN	27.1.82	22 Jan
4:13.7+	Marina	Muncan	SRB	6.11.82	22 Jan
4:13.90	Olga	Soldatova	RUS	8.9.85	29 Jan

JUNIORS

See main list for top 6 juniors. 10 performances by 6 women to 4:10.0. Additional marks and further juniors:

Bogale 4:06.15 6 Daegu 12 May 4:08.25 8 Pre Eugene 4 Jun
4:06.47 3 Madrid 9 Jul

Mark	Name		Nat	Born	Pos	Meet	Venue	Date
Chepkwemoi 4:09.25A		2 Af-J					Gaborone	15 May
4:10.63	Gemeda	Feyne	ETH	28.6.92	5	CAA	Brazzaville	12 Jun
4:11.25		Guan Yue	CHN	23.5.92	1	City G	Nanchang	21 Oct
4:11.56	Genet	Tibieso	ETH-Y	23.1.94	3	WY	Villeneuve d'Ascq	9 Jul
4:12.01	Ihsan	Gibril (10)	SUD	.92	1	E.African	Dar es Salaam	4 Jun
4:13.62	Anna	Laman	AUS-Y	25.5.95	4		Sydney	19 Mar
4:14.21	Jessica	Judd	GBR-Y	7.1.95	1		Manchester (SC)	28 May
4:14.78	Gete	Dima	ETH	10.3.92	2		Dar es Salaam	4 Jun
4:14.8A	Sheila	Chepngetich	KEN-Y	.95	1		Nairobi	8 Jun
4:15.40	Amela	Terzic	SRB	2.4.93	1	EJ	Tallinn	24 Jul
4:15.55		Wu Limin	CHN	19.11.93	7	NC	Hefei	9 Sep
4:15.48	Ioana	Doaga	ROU	5.4.92	1	NC	Bucuresti	29 Jun
4:12.26 i					6h1	EI	Paris (B)	4 Mar
4:16.30	Tomoka	Kimura	JPN-Y	12.11.94	1		Fukuoka	27 May
4:16.36	Georgia	Peel	GBR-Y	26.5.94	4	WY	Villeneuve d'Ascq	9 Jul
4:16.39	Cory Ann	McGee (20)	USA	29.5.92	2		Gainesville	16 Apr

1 MILE

Mark	Name		Nat	Born	Pos		Venue	Date
4:29.59	Hind	Dehiba	FRA	17.3.79	1		Montreuil-sous-Bois	7 Jun
4:30.51	Barbara	Parker	GBR	8.11.82				4 Jun
4:31.04	Bertukan	Feyisa	ETH	4.7.91				7 Jun
4:31.98	Nicole	Sifuentes	CAN	30.6.86				13 Aug
4:32.29	Brenda	Martinez	USA	8.9.87				13 Aug
4:32.52	Erin	Donohue	USA	8.5.83				13 Aug
4:32.89	Tatyana	Gudkova	RUS	26.3.85				7 Jun
4:33.57	Gabriele	Anderson	USA	25.6.86				13 Aug
4:33.95	Maggie	Infeld	USA	10.4.86				13 Aug
4:34.29	Sara	Vaughn	USA	16.5.86				13 Aug

Indoors

Mark	Name		Nat	Born	Pos		Venue	Date
4:28.60	Jenny	Simpson	USA	23.8.86	1		New York (Armory)	22 Jan
4:30.88	Carmen	Douma-Hussar	CAN	12.3.77				22 Jan
4:31.53	Frances	Koons	USA	2.4.86				22 Jan
4:31.72	Hilary	Stellingwerff	CAN	7.8.81				22 Jan
4:31.84	Marina	Muncan	SRB	6.11.82				22 Jan
4:32.51	Megan	Metcalfe Wright	CAN	27.1.82				22 Jan
4:32.95	Lucy	Van Dalen	NZL	18.11.88				4 Mar
4:33.01	Jordan	Hasay	USA	12.9.91				12 Mar
4:33.64	Lauren	Johnson	USA	4.5.87				29 Jan
4:33.71	Kate	Van Buskirk	CAN	9.6.87				12 Mar
4:33.76	Zoe	Buckman	AUS	21.12.88				12 Mar
4:33.81	Shalane	Flanagan	USA	8.7.81				29 Jan
4:34.65	Lauren	Bonds	USA	9.6.88				12 Feb

JUNIORS

Mark	Name		Nat	Born	Pos		Venue	Date
4:34.93	Gemeda	Feyne	ETH	28.6.92	4		Montreuil-sous-Bois	7 Jun
4:37.13	Gemeda	Genet	ETH-Y	23.1.94	6		Montreuil-sous-Bois	7 Jun

2000 METRES

Mark	Name		Nat	Born	Pos	Meet	Venue	Date
5:47.19+	Olga	Golovkina	RUS	17.12.86				29 Jul
5:48.73+	Mary	Wangari	KEN	4.10.86				8 Jul

Indoors

Mark	Name		Nat	Born	Pos	Meet	Venue	Date
5:43.45+	Sentayehu	Ejigu	ETH	21.6.85	1	in 3000	Birmingham	19 Feb
5:44.89	Olesya	Syreva	RUS	25.11.83	1		Yekaterinburg	7 Jan
5:45.40	Yelena	Zadorozhnaya	RUS	3.12.77				7 Jan
5:46.0+	Helen	Clitheroe	GBR	2.1.74				19 Feb
5:45.60	Irina	Maracheva	RUS	29.9.84				7 Jan
5:46.16	Yevgeniya	Zolotova	RUS	28.4.83				7 Jan

3000 METRES

Mark	Name		Nat	Born	Pos	Meet	Venue	Date
8:38.67+	Vivian	Cheruiyot	KEN	11.9.83	1	in 5000	Stockholm	29 Jul
8:45.75+	Sentayehu	Ejigu	ETH	21.6.85	1	in 5000	Saint-Denis	8 Jul
8:46.84	Viola	Kibiwott	KEN	22.12.83	1		Rabat	5 Jun
8:47.15	Priscah	Cherono	KEN	27.6.80	2		Rabat	5 Jun
8:47.42	Sule	Utura	ETH	8.2.90	3		Rabat	5 Jun
8:48.63	Azemra	Gebru	ETH-J	5.5.92	4		Rabat	5 Jun
8:48.89	Ann	Mwangi	KEN	8.12.88	1		Kobe	6 Oct
8:49.99	Olesya	Syreva	RUS	25.11.83	1		Irkutsk	5 Aug
8:50.36+	Meseret	Defar	ETH	19.11.83	1	in 5000	Oslo	9 Jun
8:50.92mx	Nikki	Hamblin (10)	NZL	20.5.88	1		Auckland	16 Mar
8:51.07	Sally	Kipyego	KEN	19.12.85	1		Eugene	19 Mar
8:51.31	Sylvia	Kibet	KEN	28.3.84	5		Rabat	5 Jun
8:51.43	Yelena	Zadorozhnaya	RUS	3.12.77	2		Irkutsk	5 Aug
8:51.76	Waganesh	Mekasha	ETH-J	16.1.92	6		Rabat	5 Jun
8:52.37+	Mercy	Cherono	KEN	7.5.91	1	WK	Zürich	8 Sep
8:53.0	Natalya	Popkova	RUS	21.9.88	1	Mosc Ch	Moskva	10 Jul
8:53.49	Almaz	Ayana	ETH	21.11.91	7		Rabat	5 Jun
8:54.16	Nataliya	Tobias	UKR	22.11.80	2	ET	Stockholm	18 Jun
8:55.07	Erin	Donohue	USA	8.5.83	1		Lapinlahti	24 Jul
8:55.09	Natalia	Rodríguez (20)	ESP	2.6.79	3	ET	Stockholm	18 Jun
8:55.13	Alfiya	Khasanova	RUS	3.10.88	1		Cheboksary	12 Jul
8:55.73	Lidia	Chojecka	POL	25.1.77	4	ET	Stockholm	18 Jun
8:56.22	Habiba	Ghribi	TUN	9.4.84	1		Franconville	8 May
8:56.36	Geytetom	Gebreselassie	ETH-Y	15.1.95	1	WY	Villeneuve d'Ascq	6 Jul
8:56.79+	Wude	Ayalew	ETH	4.7.87	1	Pre	Eugene	3 Jun

Mark	Name		Nat	Born	Pos	Meet	Venue	Date
8:56.79	Roxana	Bârcâ	ROU	22.6.88	1	EAF	Bydgoszcz	3 Jun
8:56.82	Ziporah	Kingori	KEN-Y	12.8.94	2	WY	Villeneuve d'Ascq	6 Jul
8:56.99	Kaltoum	Bouaasayriya	MAR	23.8.82	8		Rabat	5 Jun
8:57.35	Sabrina	Mockenhaupt	GER	6.12.80	1		Siegburg	13 Jun
(30)								

Mark	Name		Nat	Born	Date
8:58.07	Mary	Waithera	KEN-J	.93	24 Sep
8:58.10	Silvia	Weissteiner	ITA	13.7.79	18 Jun
8:58.46	Kaila	McKnight	AUS	5.5.86	29 Jan
8:58.63	Caroline	Kipkirui	KEN-Y	26.5.94	6 Jul
8:59.07	Susan	Wairimu	KEN-J	11.10.92	22 Oct
8:59.20	Rkia	El Moukim	MAR	22.2.88	3 Jun
9:00.06	Svetlana	Kudzelich	BLR	7.5.87	18 Jun
9:00.39	Etenesh	Diro	ETH	10.5.91	8 Jun
9:00.65	Yelena	Korobkina	RUS	25.11.90	6 Aug
9:00.67	Stevie	Stockton	GBR	23.8.89	18 Jun
9:00.87	Genet	Tibeso	ETH-Y	23.1.94	4 Jun
9:01.25	Viktoriya	Pogoryelska	UKR	4.8.90	4 Jun
9:01.27	Georgie	Clarke	AUS	17.6.84	29 Jan
9:01.29	Corinna	Harrer	GER	19.1.91	18 Jun
9:01.51	Alena	Kudashkina	RUS-Y	10.4.94	6 Jul
9:01.91	Olga	Golovkina	RUS	17.12.86	6 Aug
9:02.06	Natalya	Puchkova	RUS	28.1.87	12 Jul
9:02.11mx	Fionnuala	Britton	IRL	24.9.84	15 May
9:02.16	Christelle	Daunay	FRA	5.12.74	18 Jun
9:02.35	Beatrice	Wainaina Murugi	KEN-J	20.11.93	15 Oct
9:02.46	Grace	Kimanzi	KEN-J	1.3.92	24 Sep
9:02.59	Lyudmila	Kuzmina	RUS	13.8.87	12 Jul
9:02.71	Mika	Yoshikawa	JPN	16.9.84	22 Jun
9:02.90	Nelly	Ngeiywo	KEN-J	10.1.92	5 Jun
9:02.97	Svetlana	Kireyeva	RUS	12.6.87	12 Jul
9:03.1	Lyubov	Pulyayeva	RUS	26.4.82	10 Jul
9:03.53	Lisa	Corrigan	AUS	2.12.84	12 Nov
9:04.20	Emma	Rilen	AUS	23.3.83	29 Jan
9:04.47	Tomoka	Kimura	JPN-Y	12.11.94	15 May
9:04.53	Alemitu	Haroye	ETH-Y	9.5.95	6 Jul
9:04.55	Sultan	Haydar	TUR	23.5.87	24 Jun
9:04.85	Asmerawork	Bekele	ETH	11.8.91	30 Jul
9:05.23	Jéssica	Augusto	POR	8.11.81	16 Jul
9:05.28	Wioletta	Frankiewicz	POL	9.6.77	3 Jun
9:05.57+	Grace	Momanyi	KEN	3.3.82	6 Aug
9:05.62	Katsuki	Suga	JPN-Y	1.2.94	6 Jul
9:05.83	Karoline Bjerkeli	Grøvdal (67)	NOR	14.6.90	4 Jun

Indoors

Mark	Name		Nat	Born	Pos	Meet	Venue	Date
8:30.26	Sentayehu	Ejigu	ETH	21.6.85	1	BrGP	Birmingham	19 Feb
8:36.91	Meseret	Defar	ETH	19.11.83	1	XL-Galan	Stockholm	22 Feb
8:37.47	Kalkidan	Gezahegne	ETH	8.5.91	2	BrGP	Birmingham	19 Feb
8:39.18	Shalane	Flanagan	USA	8.7.81	2	XL-Galan	Stockholm	22 Feb
8:39.70	Mercy	Njoroge	KEN	10.6.86	3	BrGP	Birmingham	19 Feb
8:39.81	Helen	Clitheroe	GBR	2.1.74	4	BrGP	Birmingham	19 Feb
8:41.35	Olesya	Syreva	RUS	25.11.83	1	NC	Moskva	16 Feb
8:41.64	Yelena	Zadorozhnaya	RUS	3.12.77	2	NC	Moskva	16 Feb
8:42.75		Njoroge			1		Karlsruhe	13 Feb
8:43.22	Sylwia	Ejdys	POL	15.7.84	2		Karlsruhe	13 Feb
8:43.79	Christin	Wurth-Thomas	USA	11.7.80	1		Fayetteville	12 Feb
8:44.22	Sara	Moreira #	POR	17.10.85	3		Karlsruhe	13 Feb
8:44.25	Lidia	Chojecka	POL	25.1.77	3	XL-Galan	Stockholm	22 Feb
8:44.25	Mekdes	Bekele	ETH	20.1.87	4		Karlsruhe	13 Feb
8:49.74	Sally	Kipyego	KEN	19.12.85	1		Boston (Roxbury)	5 Feb
8:50.78	Jenny	Simpson	USA	23.8.86	2		Boston (Roxbury)	5 Feb
8:51.78	Dolores	Checa	ESP	27.12.82	7	XL-Galan	Stockholm	22 Feb
8:52.01	Megan	Metcalfe Wright	CAN	27.1.82	3		Boston (Roxbury)	5 Feb
8:52.12	Yelena	Korobkina	RUS	25.11.90	3	NC	Moskva	16 Feb
8:53.01	Mary	Cullen	IRL	17.8.82	5	BrGP	Birmingham	19 Feb
8:53.14	Lisa	Uhl	USA	31.8.87	1		Seattle	15 Jan
8:56.77	Lucy	Van Dalen	NZL	18.11.88	1		Boston (Allston)	11 Feb
8:56.92	Sheila	Reid	CAN	2.8.89	1		New York	29 Jan
8:57.24	Gemma	Turtle	GBR	15.5.86	2	NC	Sheffield	12 Feb
8:57.30	Molly	Huddle	USA	31.8.84	1		Notre Dame	5 Mar

Mark	Name		Nat	Born	Date
8:58.34	Yevgeniya	Zolotova	RUS	28.4.83	19 Jan
8:59.41	Renata	Plis	POL	5.2.85	5 Feb
8:59.60	Siham	Hilali	MAR	2.5.86	19 Feb
9:00.37	Layes	Abdullayeva	AZE	29.5.91	6 Mar
9:00.64	Christine	Bardelle	FRA	16.8.74	8 Feb
9:00.70	Fionnuala	Britton	IRL	24.9.84	5 Feb
9:01.25	Ancuta	Bobocel	ROU	3.10.87	19 Feb
9:01.43	Charlene	Thomas	GBR	6.5.82	19 Feb
9:01.46	Frances	Koons	USA	2.4.86	5 Feb
9:01.91	Jackie	Areson	USA	31.3.88	29 Jan
9:02.47	Elizabeth	Maloy	USA	10.8.85	5 Feb
9:02.55	Svetlana	Kireyeva	RUS	12.6.87	16 Feb
9:02.63	Fanjanteino	Félix	FRA	26.1.80	8 Feb
9:03.39	Emily	Pidgeon	GBR	1.6.89	19 Feb
9:03.50	Sultan	Haydar	TUR	23.5.87	5 Mar
9:03.91A	Sara	Hall	USA	15.4.83	26 Feb
9:04.06	Birtukan	Adamu	ETH-J	29.4.92	8 Feb
9:04.70	Malindi	Elmore	CAN	13.3.80	12 Feb
9:05.00	Julie	Culley	USA	10.9.81	5 Feb
9:05.42	Jordan	Hasay	USA	12.9.91	29 Jan

JUNIORS

See main list for top 4 juniors. 7 performances by 7 women under 9:00.0. Further juniors:

Mark	Name		Nat	Born	Pos	Meet	Venue	Date
8:58.07	Mary	Waithera	KEN	.93	1		Yokohama	24 Sep
8:58.63	Caroline	Kipkirui	KEN-Y	26.5.94	3	WY	Villeneuve d'Ascq	6 Jul
8:59.07	Susan	Wairimu	KEN	11.10.92	1		Oita	22 Oct
9:00.87	Genet	Tibeso	ETH-Y	23.1.94	1		Marseille	4 Jun
9:01.51	Alena	Kudashkina	RUS-Y	10.4.94	4	WY	Villeneuve d'Ascq	6 Jul
9:02.35	Beatrice (10)	Wainaina Murugi	KEN	20.11.93	1		Fukuroi	15 Oct
9:02.46	Grace	Kimanzi	KEN	1.3.92	1		Naruto	24 Sep
9:02.90	Nelly	Ngeiywo	KEN	10.1.92	9		Rabat	5 Jun
9:04.47	Tomoka	Kimura	JPN-Y	12.11.94	1		Fukuoka	15 May
9:04.53	Alemitu	Haroye	ETH-Y	9.5.95	5	WY	Villeneuve d'Ascq	6 Jul
9:05.62	Katsuki	Suga	JPN-Y	1.2.94	6	WY	Villeneuve d'Ascq	6 Jul
9:07.19	Shiori	Yano	JPN	.94	2		Nagasaki	19 Jun

Mark	Name		Nat	Born	Pos	Meet	Venue	Date
9:07.20	Tsfereda	Girma	ETH-Y	95	1		Pliezhausen	22 May
9:07.31	Miki	Sakakibara	JPN	5.4..93	2		Yamaguchi	11 Oct
9:07.51	Hyvin	Jepkemoi	KOR	.92	2		Pliezhausen	22 May
9:07.53	Gemeda	Feyne (20)	ETH	.92	2		Arzana	30 Jul
9:04.06 indoors	Birtukan	Adamu	ETH-J	29.4.92	7		Liévin	8 Feb

5000 METRES

Mark	Name		Nat	Born	Pos	Meet	Venue	Date
14:20.87	Vivian	Cheruiyot	KEN	11.9.83	1	DNG	Stockholm	29 Jul
14:29.52	Meseret	Defar	ETH	19.11.83	1	DL	Saint-Denis	8 Jul
14:30.10		Cheruiyot			1	WK	Zürich	8 Sep
14:30.42	Sally	Kipyego	KEN	19.12.85	2	WK	Zürich	8 Sep
14:31.66	Sentayehu	Ejigu	ETH	21.6.85	2	DL	Saint-Denis	8 Jul
14:31.92		Cheruiyot			1	DL	Shanghai	15 May
14:32.87		Ejigu			2	DL	Shanghai	15 May
14:32.95	Linet	Masai	KEN	5.12.89	3	DL	Shanghai	15 May
14:33.96		Cheruiyot			1	Pre	Eugene	3 Jun
14:34.86	Viola	Kibiwott	KEN	22.12.83	4	DL	Shanghai	15 May
14:35.11		Masai			3	WK	Zürich	8 Sep
14:35.13	Mercy	Cherono	KEN	7.5.91	3	DL	Saint-Denis	8 Jul
14:35.43	Sylvia	Kibet	KEN	28.3.84	4	WK	Zürich	8 Sep
14:35.44		Masai			2	Pre	Eugene	3 Jun
14:37.01		M Cherono			3	Pre	Eugene	3 Jun
14:37.17		M Cherono			5	DL	Shanghai	15 May
14:37.32		Defar			1	Bisl	Oslo	9 Jun
14:37.50		Ejigu			2	Bisl	Oslo	9 Jun
14:37.56	Genzebe	Dibaba	ETH	8.2.91	3	Bisl	Oslo	9 Jun
14:39.44	Meselech	Melkamu (10)	ETH	27.4.85	4	Bisl	Oslo	9 Jun
14:39.71		Kipyego			4	Pre	Eugene	3 Jun
14:40.86	Priscah	Cherono	KEN	27.6.80	6	DL	Shanghai	15 May
14:41.28	Pauline	Korikwiang	KEN	1.3.88	7	DL	Shanghai	15 May
14:43.29	Emebet	Anteneh	ETH-J	13.1.92	5	Bisl	Oslo	9 Jun
14:43.30		P Cherono			6	Bisl	Oslo	9 Jun
14:43.87		Kipyego			2	DNG	Stockholm	29 Jul
14:44.82		P Cherono			5	WK	Zürich	8 Sep
14:45.20	Shalane	Flanagan	USA	8.7.81	4	DL	Saint-Denis	8 Jul
14:45.31		Kibet			3	DNG	Stockholm	29 Jul
14:45.48		Defar			1	FBK	Hengelo	29 May
(30/14)								
14:46.30	Dolores	Checa	ESP	27.12.82	7	Bisl	Oslo	9 Jun
14:46.32	Sule	Utura	ETH	8.2.90	8	DL	Shanghai	15 May
14:49.36	Hiwot	Ayalew	ETH	6.3.90	8	Bisl	Oslo	9 Jun
14:58.34	Azemra	Gebru	ETH-J	5.5.92	9	DL	Saint-Denis	8 Jul
14:59.71	Wude	Ayalew	ETH	4.7.87	7	Pre	Eugene	3 Jun
15:00.08	Esther	Chemtai	KEN	4.6.88	8	Pre	Eugene	3 Jun
(20)								
15:00.57	Lauren	Fleshman	USA	26.9.81	1	LGP	London (CP)	6 Aug
15:02.38	Yelizaveta	Grechishnikova	RUS	12.12.83	1	NC	Cheboksary	23 Jul
15:03.63	Almensch	Belete	ETH	26.7.89	1		Kessel-Lo	13 Aug
15:05.24	Yelena	Zadorozhnaya	RUS	3.12.77	2	NC	Cheboksary	23 Jul
15:06.75	Helen	Clitheroe	GBR	2.1.74	2	LGP	London (CP)	6 Aug
15:07.49	Grace	Momanyi	KEN	3.3.82	3	LGP	London (CP)	6 Aug
15:08.64	Desiree	Davila	USA	26.7.83	4	LGP	London (CP)	6 Aug
15:08.86	Alemitu	Bekele	TUR	17.9.77	9	WK	Zürich	8 Sep
15:09.96	Megumi	Kinukawa	JPN	7.8.89	1	NC	Kumagaya	12 Jun
15:10.01	Molly	Huddle	USA	31.8.84	1	NC	Eugene	24 Jun
(30)								
15:10.44	Jen	Rhines	USA	1.7.74	5	LGP	London (CP)	6 Aug
15:10.45	Genet	Ayalew	ETH-J	31.12.92	2	NA	Heusden-Zolder	16 Jul
15:10.53	Sally	Chepyego	KEN	3.10.85	1		Shibetsu	29 Jun
15:11.47	Kara	Goucher	USA	9.7.78	9	Pre	Eugene	3 Jun
15:11.49	Jenny	Simpson	USA	23.8.86	2	MSR	Walnut	15 Apr
15:11.50	Waganesh	Mekasha	ETH-J	16.1.92	3	NA	Heusden-Zolder	16 Jul
15:11.97	Sara	Moreira #	POR	17.10.85	10	Bisl	Oslo	9 Jun
15:12.24	Almaz	Ayana	ETH	21.11.91	1		Belém	15 May
15:13.12	Hitomi	Niiya	JPN	26.2.88	2		Shibetsu	29 Jun
15:14.02	Kim	Smith	NZL	19.11.81	4	NA	Heusden-Zolder	16 Jul
(40)								
15:14.25	Magdalena	Lewy Boulet	USA	1.8.73	10	DNG	Stockholm	29 Jul
15:14.31	Amy	Hastings	USA	21.1.84	2	NC	Eugene	24 Jun
15:14.62	Tejitu	Daba	BRN	20.8.91	9	WCh	Daegu	2 Sep

Mark	Name		Nat	Born	Pos	Meet	Venue	Date
15:15.15	Lineth	Chepkurui	KEN	23.2.88	10	Pre	Eugene	3 Jun
15:15.33	Megan	Metcalfe Wright	CAN	27.1.82	11	Pre	Eugene	3 Jun
15:15.33mx	Mika	Yoshikawa	JPN	16.9.84	1		Yokohama	24 Dec
15:31.78					2		Naruto	24 Sep
15:15.34	Liz	Maloy	USA	10.8.85	1		Lignano	19 Jul
15:15.5 mx	Anna	Incerti	ITA	19.1.80	1		Palermo	1 Jun
15:15.89	Ann	Mwangi	KEN	8.12.88	1rA		Nobeoka	28 May
15:16.04	Angela	Bizzarri	USA	15.2.88	3	NC	Eugene	24 Jun
(50)								
15:17.03	Mercy	Njoroge	KEN	10.6.86	11	DL	Shanghai	15 May
15:17.18	Zakya	Mrisho	TAN	19.2.84	10	WK	Zürich	8 Sep
15:18.85	Simone	da Silva ¶	BRA	12.9.84	1		São Paulo	20 May
15:19.60	Jéssica	Augusto	POR	8.11.81	8	LGP	London (CP)	6 Aug
15:19.89	Margaret	Muriuki	KEN	21.3.86	12	DL	Shanghai	15 May
15:19.94	Yekaterina	Gorbunova	RUS	17.1.89	1	NC-23	Yerino	24 Jun
15:20.29	Natalya	Popkova	RUS	21.9.88	3	NC	Cheboksary	23 Jul
15:20.93	Purity	Rionoripo	KEN-J	10.6.93	11	WK	Zürich	8 Sep
15:21.18	Julie	Culley	USA	10.9.81	5	NC	Eugene	24 Jun
15:21.45 mx	Fionnuala	Britton	IRL	24.9.84	1		Gent	30 Jul
15:31.26					11	FBK	Hengelo	29 May
(60)								
15:21.51	Etenesh	Diro	ETH	10.5.91	1		Bilbao	18 Jun
15:21.75	Christin	Wurth-Thomas	USA	11.7.80	4	MSR	Walnut	15 Apr
15:22.10	Olesya	Syreva	RUS	25.11.83	1		Sochi	25 May
15:22.14	Yelena	Korobkina	RUS	25.11.90	2	NC-23	Yerino	24 Jun
15:22.16	Ana Dulce	Félix	POR	23.10.82	6	NA	Heusden-Zolder	16 Jul
15:22.87mx	Ryoko	Kizaki	JPN	21.6.85	1		Yokohama	25 Sep
15:23.80	Kasumi	Nishihara	JPN	1.3.89	1		Yamaguchi	7 Oct
15:23.9	Susan	Wairimu	KEN-J	11.10.92	2		Hiroshima	26 Nov
15:24.30	Sabrina	Mockenhaupt	GER	6.12.80	10	FBK	Hengelo	29 May
15:24.49 mx	Sabine	Fischer	SUI	29.6.73	1		Oordegem	2 Jul
15:30.25					1		Watford	11 Jun
(70)								
15:24.66A	Caroline	Chepkoech	KEN-Y	26.5.94	1	Af-J	Gaborone	14 May
15:24.75A	Janet	Kisa	KEN-J	5.3.92	2	Af-J	Gaborone	14 May
15:25.58	Jessica	Pixler	USA	8.4.88	1		Stanford	25 Mar
15:26.07mx	Rosemary	Wanjiru	KEN-Y	1.1.94	1mx		Yokohama	4 Dec
15:26.31	Alfiya	Khasanova	RUS	3.10.88	4	NC	Cheboksary	23 Jul
15:27.03	Barbara	Parker	GBR	8.11.82	2		Bilbao	18 Jun
15:27.14	Ferhiwot	Goshu	ETH	28.6.90	1		Mataró	5 Jun
15:27.33	Svetlana	Kireyeva	RUS	12.6.87	5	NC	Cheboksary	23 Jul
15:27.46		Xue Fei	CHN	8.8.89	1	NC	Hefei	11 Sep
15:27.71	Sara	Hall	USA	15.4.83	6	MSR	Walnut	15 Apr
(80)								
15:27.72	Neely	Spence	USA	16.4.90	7	NC	Eugene	24 Jun
15:27.74	Cruz Nonata	da Silva	BRA	18.8.74	1		Fortaleza	11 May
15:27.84	Nicole	Sifuentes	CAN	30.6.86	1	Jordan	Stanford	1 May
15:27.94	Marisol	Romero	MEX	26.11.83	7	MSR	Walnut	15 Apr
15:28.06	Yelena	Nagovitsyna	RUS	7.12.82	3		Sochi	25 May
15:28.25		Hao Xiaofan	CHN	9.12.89	2	NC	Hefei	11 Sep
15:28.30	Alissa	McKaig	USA	21.2.86	8	MSR	Walnut	15 Apr
15:28.70	Nadia	Ejjafini	ITA	8.11.80	7	NA	Heusden-Zolder	16 Jul
15:28.71	Sandra	López	MEX	16.4.84	2	Jordan	Stanford	1 May
15:28.75		Wang Xueqin	CHN	1.1.91	3	NC	Hefei	11 Sep
(90)								
15:29.12	Megan	Hogan	USA	10.2.88	9	MSR	Walnut	15 Apr
15:29.42	Lidia	Chojecka	POL	25.1.77	13	WK	Zürich	8 Sep
15:29.47	Layes	Abdullayeva	AZE	29.5.91	1	EU23	Ostrava	17 Jul
15:29.69	Hiroko	Shoi	JPN	18.6.80	2		Yamaguchi	7 Oct
15:29.79 mx	Doricah	Obare	KEN	10.1.90	1r8		Yokohama	17 Apr
15:29.96	Frances	Koons	USA	2.4.86	5	Jordan	Stanford	1 May
15:30.94	Hikari	Yoshimoto	JPN	14.1.90	3		Yamaguchi	7 Oct
15:31.21	Alia Mohamed	Saeed	UAE	18.5.91	2		Mataró	5 Jun
15:31.47	Fadime	Suna	TUR	25.10.86	1		Izmir	21 May
15:31.67+	Worknesh	Kidane	ETH	21.11.81	1	in 10k	Birmingham	30 Jul
(100)								

Mark	Name		Nat	Born	Date	Mark	Name		Nat	Born	Date
15:31.70	Daniela	Yordanova	BUL	8.3.76	13 Sep	15:33.77	Kaila	McKnight	AUS	5.5.86	13 Sep
15:32.96	Silvia	Weissteiner	ITA	13.7.79	13 Sep	15:33.89	Yuko	Shimizu	JPN	13.7.85	24 Sep
15:33.36	Yuriko	Kobayashi	JPN	12.12.88	24 Sep	15:34.24	Marta	Tigabea	ETH	4.10.90	18 Jun
15:33.47	Ayuko	Suzuki	JPN	8.10.91	2 Oct	15:34.47	Misaki	Onishi	JPN	24.2.85	24 Sep
15:33.54	Risa	Takenaka	JPN	6.1.90	7 Oct	15:34.75	Rkia	El Moukim	MAR	22.2.88	16 Jul

Mark	Name	Nat	Born	Date
15:35.54	Chinami Mori	JPN	5.5.90	7 Oct
15:36.61	Mariam Abdallah Mubarak	UAE	13.11.91	18 Jun
15:36.86mx	Mary Waithera	KEN-J	12.12.94	20 Nov
15:37.29	Jordan Hasay	USA	12.9.91	15 Apr
15:37.56	Mai Ishibashi	JPN	2.7.89	8 Oct
15:37.57	Sheila Reid	CAN	2.8.89	10 Jun
15:37.79mx	Yoshimi Ozaki	JPN	1.7.81	2 Oct
15:37.84	Katie Follett	USA	12.11.87	15 Apr
15:37.96mx	Misaki Katsumata	JPN	26.12.85	24 Dec
15:38.13	Kim Conley	USA	14.3.86	24 Jun
15:38.23	Emily Infeld	USA	21.3.90	10 Jun
15:38.80	Grace Kimanzi	KEN-J	1.3.92	29 Jun
15:39.67	Fabiana Cristine da Silva	BRA	3.9.78	2 Jun
15:39.71	Elena Romagnolo	ITA	5.10.82	16 Jul
15:39.95	Felista Wanjugu	KEN	18.2.90	22 May
15:40.31	Wei Jie	CHN-J	25.1.93	11 Sep
15:40.60	Rei Ohara	JPN	10.8.90	7 Oct
15:40.69	Abbey D'Agostino	USA-J	25.5.92	10 Jun
15:40.72	Chihiro Takato	JPN	20.7.91	24 Sep
15:40.75	Tsgereda Girma	ETH-Y		29 May
15:41.01	Yoshie Kurisu	JPN	21.8.85	24 Sep
15:41.15	Binnaz Uslu	TUR	12.3.85	20 Aug
15:41.38	Yurie Doi	JPN	8.12.88	24 Sep
15:41.49	Eloise Wellings	AUS	9.11.82	3 Jun
15:41.59mx	Tomoni Tanaka	JPN	25.1.88	2 Oct
15:41.68	Regina Kashayeva	RUS	17.5.79	25 May
15:41.68	Holly Van Dalen	NZL	18.11.88	30 Jul
15:41.78	Erin Donohue	USA	8.5.83	1 May
15:41.78	Kayo Sugihara	JPN	24.2.83	30 Aug
15:42.15mx	Mutsumi Ikeda	JPN-J	30.9.92	24 Dec
15:42.18mx	Toshika Tamura	JPN	6.6.90	30 Oct
15:42.21	Renè Kalmer	RSA	3.11.80	9 Apr
15:42.4A	Pauline Njeri	KEN	.85	4 Jun
15:42.60mx	Bethlehem Moges	ETH	3.5.91	20 Nov
15:42.64	Hyvin Jepkemoi	KEN-J	.92	11 Sep
15:43.19	Hitomi Nakamura	JPN	23.6.87	8 Oct
15:43.27mx	Kaho Tanaka	JPN	24.6.91	12 Jun
15:43.36	Rosa Godoy	ARG	19.3.82	2 Jun
15:43.71	Li Jiayi	CHN-J	26.12.93	22 Oct
15:43.77	Katrina Wootton	GBR	2.9.85	11 Jun
15:43.78	Kaoru Nagao	JPN	26.9.89	22 May
15:43.81	Meghan Armstrong	USA	6.1.86	12 Jun
15:43.87	Brie Felnagle	USA	9.12.86	22 Apr
15:43.90mx	Misaki Kato	JPN	15.6.91	4 Dec
15:44.00	Julia Bleasdale	GBR	9.9.81	13 Sep
15:44.11	Katsuki Suga	JPN-Y	1.12.94	4 Dec
15:44.16	Natalya Gorchakova	RUS	17.4.83	23 Jul
15:44.24	Sonia Samuels	GBR	16.5.79	11 Jun
15:44.31	Akane Yabushita	JPN	6.6.91	7 Oct
15:44.43mx	Shiori Yano	JPN-J	.94	4 Dec
15:44.61	Mariko Nakao	JPN	24.8.84	24 Sep
15:44.75	Holly Van Dalen	NZL	18.11.88	28 Apr
15:44.92	Karoline Bjerkeli Grøvdal	NOR	14.6.90	19 Jun
15:45.08mx	Rie Mizutake	JPN	17.10.91	25 Sep
15:45.15mx	Kumiko Ogura	JPN	24.6.85	30 Oct
15:45.17mx	Yume Tanaka	JPN-Y	.94	25 Sep
15:45.38	Risa Kikuchi	JPN	5.2.90	24 Sep
15:45.38	Kellyn Johnson	USA	22.7.86	11 Jun
15:45.43mx	Yuka Kakimi	JPN	4.4.86	12 Jun
15:45.55	Kathy Kroeger	USA	20.6.91	10 Jun
15:45.55	Simret Restle	GER	4.5.84	3 Aug
15:45.60mx	Christine Bardelle	FRA	16.8.74	2 Jul
15:45.60	Xiao Huimin	CHN-J	1.3.92	11 Sep
15:45.61	Isabel Checa	ESP	27.12.82	18 Jun
15:45.63	Sara Slattery	USA	2.10.81	11 Jun
15:45.74mx	Eina Yokozawa	JPN-J	29.10.92	24 Dec
15:45.8A	Jane Wanjiku	KEN		4 Jun
15:45.85mx	Miki Sakakibara	JPN-J	5.4.93	25 Sep
15:45.99	Gabriele Anderson	USA	25.6.86	19 Jul
(180)				

Indoors

Mark	Name	Nat	Born	Date
15:39.40	Natalya Gorchakova	RUS	17.4.83	18 Feb
15:39.40	Natalya Puchkova	RUS	28.1.87	18 Feb
15:39.81	Jackie Areson	USA	31.3.88	11 Feb
15:40.00	Yuliya Vasilyeva	RUS	23.3.87	18 Feb
15:42.58	Megan Brown	CAN	30.4.85	11 Feb
15:44.60	Alex Kosinski	USA	29.3.89	11 Feb

JUNIORS

See main list for top 9 juniors. 10 performances by 5 women to 15:21.0. Additional marks and further juniors:

	Mark	Pos	Meet	Venue	Date	Mark	Pos	Meet	Venue	Date
Anteneh	14:57.66	8	DL	Saint-Denis	8 Jul	15:12.15	7	FBK	Hengelo	29 May
G Ayalew	15:12.42	6	FBK	Hengelo	29 May	15:16.13	12	Bisl	Oslo	9 Jun
	15:15.67	11	DL	Saint-Denis	8 Jul					

Mark	Name	Nat	Born	Pos	Meet	Venue	Date
15:36.86mx	Mary Waithera (10)	KEN	12.12.94	1		Yokohama	20 Nov
15:38.80	Grace Kimanzi	KEN	1.3.92	3		Shibetsu	29 Jun
15:40.31	Wei Jie	CHN	25.1.93	4	NC	Hefei	11 Sep
15:40.69	Abbey D'Agostino	USA	25.5.92	3	NCAA	Des Moines	10 Jun
15:40.75	Tsgereda Girma	ETH-Y		13	FBK	Hengelo	29 May
15:42.15mx	Mutsumi Ikeda	JPN	30.9.92	3		Yokohama	24 Dec
15:42.64	Hyvin Jepkemoi	KEN	.92	4	AfG	Maputo	11 Sep
15:43.71	Li Jiayi	CHN	26.12.93	1	City G	Nanchang	22 Oct
15:44.11	Katsuki Suga	JPN-Y	1.12.94	3		Nagasaki	4 Dec
15:44.43mx	Shiori Yano	JPN	.94	4		Nagasaki	4 Dec
15:45.17mx	Yume Tanaka	JPN-Y	.94	3		Yokohama	25 Sep

10,000 METRES

Mark	Name	Nat	Born	Pos	Meet	Venue	Date
30:38.35	Sally Kipyego	KEN	19.12.85	1	Jordan	Stanford	1 May
30:39.57	Shalane Flanagan	USA	8.7.81	2	Jordan	Stanford	1 May
30:48.98	Vivian Cheruiyot	KEN	11.9.83	1	WCh	Daegu	27 Aug
30:50.04	Kipyego			2	WCh	Daegu	27 Aug
30:53.59	Linet Masai	KEN	5.12.89	3	WCh	Daegu	27 Aug
30:54.29	Kayoko Fukushi	JPN	25.3.82	3	Jordan	Stanford	1 May
30:56.43	Priscah Cherono	KEN	27.6.80	4	WCh	Daegu	27 Aug
30:56.55	Meselech Melkamu	ETH	27.4.85	5	WCh	Daegu	27 Aug
30:59.97	Flanagan			1	NC	Eugene	23 Jun
31:05.05	Meseret Defar	ETH	19.11.83	1		Dorgali	13 Jul
31:07.02	Cheruiyot			1		Pontevedra	2 Apr
31:08.92	Worknesh Kidane	ETH	21.11.81	1		Birmingham	30 Jul
31:10.02mx	Megumi Kinukawa (10)	JPN	7.8.89	1		Abashiri	22 Jun
31:14.83	Melkamu			1	GS	Ostrava	31 May
31:16.65	Cherono			2	GS	Ostrava	31 May
31:16.65	Kara Goucher	USA	9.7.78	2	NC	Eugene	23 Jun
31:17.80	Belaynesh Oljira	ETH	26.6.90	3	GS	Ostrava	31 May

Mark		Name	Nat	Born	Pos	Meet	Venue	Date
31:20.38	Tigist	Kiros	ETH-J	8.6.92	4	GS	Ostrava	31 May
31:21.57	Shitaye	Eshete	BRN	21.5.90	6	WCh	Daegu	27 Aug
31:24.09	Wude	Ayalew	ETH	4.7.87	5	GS	Ostrava	31 May
31:24.20	Lineth	Chepkurui	KEN	23.2.88	4	Jordan	Stanford	1 May
31:25.57		Flanagan			7	WCh	Daegu	27 Aug
31:26.10	Joyce	Chepkirui	KEN	10.8.88	1	Zát	Melbourne	10 Dec
31:27.98	Sally	Chepyego	KEN	3.10.85	1		Fukagawa	25 Jun
31:28.66	Molly	Huddle	USA	31.8.84	5	Jordan	Stanford	1 May
31:30.22	Emily	Chebet (20)	KEN	18.2.86	2	Zát	Melbourne	10 Dec
31:30.37	Jen	Rhines	USA	1.7.74	3	NC	Eugene	23 Jun
31:33.42	Ana Dulce	Félix	POR	23.10.82	2		Pontevedra	2 Apr
31:34.35	Kayo	Sugihara	JPN	24.2.83	6	Jordan	Stanford	1 May
31:37.03		Félix			8	WCh	Daegu	27 Aug
	(30/23)							
31:37.14	Desiree	Davila	USA	26.7.83	4	NC	Eugene	23 Jun
31:38.15		Wang Jiali	CHN	1.2.86	1	NC	Hefei	8 Sep
31:39.11	Sara	Moreira #	POR	17.10.85	1	ECp	Oslo	4 Jun
31:39.77		Chen Rong	CHN	18.5.88	2	NC	Hefei	8 Sep
31:41.31	Eloise	Wellings	AUS	9.11.82	7	Jordan	Stanford	1 May
31:43.25mx	Yuko	Shimizu	JPN	13.7.85	1		Yokohama	24 Dec
31:44.52	Sabrina	Mockenhaupt	GER	6.12.80	1		Bergisch Gladbach	1 Sep
	(30)							
31:44.84	Christelle	Daunay	FRA	5.12.74	2	ECp	Oslo	4 Jun
31:45.82	Hikari	Yoshimoto	JPN	14.1.90	2		Kobe	24 Apr
31:48.58	Magdalena	Lewy Boulet	USA	1.8.73	5	NC	Eugene	23 Jun
31:55.06	Mika	Yoshikawa	JPN	16.9.84	1		Niigata	10 Oct
31:55.31		Wang Xueqin	CHN	1.1.91	3	NC	Hefei	8 Sep
31:59.11	Simone	da Silva ¶	BRA	12.9.84	1	SACh	Buenos Aires	5 Jun
31:59.5A	Pauline	Korikwiang	KEN	1.3.88	4	NC	Nairobi	15 Jul
32:03.0A	Sharon	Cherop	KEN	16.3.84	5	NC	Nairobi	15 Jul
32:05.06	Abebech	Afework	ETH	11.12.90	6	GS	Ostrava	31 May
32:05.90	Genet	Ayalew	ETH-J	31.12.92	7	GS	Ostrava	31 May
	(40)							
32:06.68	Jéssica	Augusto	POR	8.11.81	10	WCh	Daegu	27 Aug
32:06.89	Sule	Utura	ETH	8.2.90	1	Znam	Zhukovskiy	3 Jul
32:07.0A	Pauline	Njeri	KEN	.85	6	NC	Nairobi	15 Jul
32:08.00	Yelena	Nagovitsyna	RUS	7.12.82	3	Znam	Zhukovskiy	3 Jul
32:08.21	Aheza	Kiros	ETH	26.3.82	8	GS	Ostrava	31 May
32:10.46	Kaoru	Nagao	JPN	26.9.89	3		Kobe	24 Apr
32:11.29	Helen	Clitheroe	GBR	2.1.74	4	ECp	Oslo	4 Jun
32:12.64mx	Seika	Nishikawa	JPN	17.7.87	2		Fukagawa	25 Jun
32:14.51	Alissa	McKaig	USA	21.2.86	9	Jordan	Stanford	1 May
32:14.63	Nadia	Ejjafini	ITA	8.11.80	5	ECp	Oslo	4 Jun
	(50)							
32:15.06	Grace	Momanyi	KEN	3.3.82	3		Pontevedra	2 Apr
32:15.09mx	Yoko	Miyauchi	JPN	19.6.83	2		Abashiri	22 Jun
32:16.84mx	Eriko	Kushima	JPN-J	.93	3		Fukagawa	25 Jun
32:17.39mx	Hiroko	Shoi	JPN	18.6.80	3		Abashiri	22 Jun
32:17.59	Kasumi	Nishihara	JPN	1.3.89	1		Naruto	23 Sep
32:18.00mx	Miho	Ihara	JPN	4.2.88	4		Fukagawa	25 Jun
32:18.05	Layes	Abdullayeva	AZE	29.5.91	1	EU23	Ostrava	15 Jul
32:18.88	Tatyana	Petrova	RUS	8.4.83	7	Znam	Zhukovskiy	3 Jul
32:20.81	Remi	Nakazato	JPN	24.6.88	2	NC	Kumagaya	10 Jun
32:21.17	Natalya	Popkova	RUS	21.9.88	8	Znam	Zhukovskiy	3 Jul
	(60)							
32:22.3A	Susan	Tanui	KEN		7	NC	Nairobi	15 Jul
32:22.8A	Doris	Changeiywo	KEN	12.12.84	8	NC	Nairobi	15 Jul
32:23.29mx	Hiroko	Miyauchi	JPN	19.6.83	4		Abashiri	22 Jun
32:23.49		Xiao Huimin	CHN-J	1.3.92	4	NC	Hefei	8 Sep
32:23.49	Hitomi	Nakamura	JPN	23.6.87	2		Naruto	23 Sep
32:26.46	Tomoka	Inadomi	JPN	16.1.86	4		Kobe	24 Apr
32:27.56	Hanae	Tanaka	JPN	12.2.90	5		Kobe	24 Apr
32:27.89mx	Yuko	Watanabe	JPN	3.11.87	5		Fukagawa	25 Jun
32:32.62	Valentina	Galimova	RUS	11.5.86	9	Znam	Zhukovskiy	3 Jul
32:34.45	Kazue	Kojima	JPN	14.10.87	1rB		Naruto	23 Sep
	(70)							
32:34.75	Amy	Begley	USA	11.1.78	6	NC	Eugene	23 Jun
32:35.11	Valeria	Straneo	ITA	5.4.76	2	NC	Torino	25 Jun
32:36.32	Krisztina	Papp	HUN	17.12.82	6	ECp	Oslo	4 Jun
32:37.03	Ayumi	Sakaida	JPN	7.11.85	3		Naruto	23 Sep

Mark	Name		Nat	Born	Pos	Meet	Venue	Date
32:37.25	Mai	Ishibashi	JPN	2.7.89	6		Kobe	24 Apr
32:37.89mx	Korei	Omata	JPN	15.7.87	6		Fukagawa	25 Jun
32:39.99		Fu Tinglian	CHN	5.7.87	5	NC	Hefei	8 Sep
32:40.39	Chinami	Mori	JPN	5.5.90	7		Kobe	24 Apr
32:40.40	Megan	Metcalfe Wright	CAN	27.1.82	11	Jordan	Stanford	1 May
32:40.61	Svetlana	Kudzelich	BLR	7.5.87	7	ECp	Oslo	4 Jun
(80)								
32:43.66	Kumi	Ogura	JPN	24.6.85	1		Marugame	8 Oct
32:44.00mx	Misato	Horie	JPN	10.3.87	7		Fukagawa	25 Jun
32:44.60mx	Yoshiko	Fujinaga	JPN	15.8.81	8		Fukagawa	25 Jun
32:44.86		Ding Changqin	CHN	27.11.91	6	NC	Hefei	8 Sep
32:45.05	Marisol	Romero	MEX	26.11.83	12	Jordan	Stanford	1 May
32:45.65	Sayuri	Oka	JPN	19.9.90	1		Kumamoto	9 Sep
32:46.27	Natalya	Puchkova	RUS	28.1.87	10	Znam	Zhukovskiy	3 Jul
32:47.70	Rosaria	Console	ITA	17.12.79	8	ECp	Oslo	4 Jun
32:48.16	Serena	Burla	USA	29.7.82	1		Bloomington IN	29 Oct
32:48.25	Elena	Romagnolo	ITA	5.10.82	9	ECp	Oslo	4 Jun
(90)								
32:48.76	Isabel	Checa	ESP	27.12.82	4	1 NC	Pontevedra	2 Apr
32:50.22	Yoshie	Kurisu	JPN	21.8.85	2rB		Naruto	23 Sep
32:50.50	Rei	Ohara	JPN	10.8.90	5		Abashiri	22 Jun
32:50.70	Karima Saleh	Jassem	BRN	18.2.88	2	AsiC	Kobe	7 Jul
32:51.07	Asami	Kato	JPN	12.10.90	3rB		Naruto	23 Sep
32:51.10	Rosa	Godoy	ARG	19.3.82	2	SAmC	Buenos Aires	5 Jun
32:51.21	Madoka	Ogi	JPN	26.10.83	8		Naruto	23 Sep
32:51.92	Misaki	Katsumata	JPN	26.12.85	3		Kumagaya	22 May
32:52.95	Chizuru	Ideta	JPN	15.11.86	9		Naruto	23 Sep
32:53.44mx	Akane	Sekino	JPN	28.7.90	10		Fukagawa	25 Jun
(100)								

Mark	Name		Nat	Born	Date
32:53.62		Jiang Xiaoli	CHN	6.4.89	8 Sep
32:53.63		Wei Jie	CHN-J	25.1.93	8 Sep
32:53.72	Cruz Nonata	da Silva	BRA	18.8.74	5 Jun
32:54.08	Annie	Bersagel	USA	30.3.83	23 Jun
32:54.15	Mai	Ito	JPN	23.5.84	24 Apr
32:55.06	Akane	Wakita	JPN	15.12.87	23 Sep
32:55.09 mx	Jeri	Emeru	ETH	.89	23 Aug
32:55.98	Cassie	Slade	USA	22.6.83	23 Jun
32:56.45mx	Mao	Kuroda	JPN	1.11.89	25 Jun
32:57.15	Sarah	Porter	USA	22.8.89	23 Jun
32:57.23	Sonia	Samuels	GBR	16.5.79	1 May
32:57.51	Kathy	Newberry	USA	31.8.78	1 May
32:57.57	Allison	Grace Morgan	USA	1.12.82	23 Jun
32:57.69	Sayo	Nomura	JPN	18.4.89	24 Apr
32:59.11	Meghan	Armstrong	USA	6.1.86	1 May
32:59.31	Tetyana	Holovchenko	UKR	13.2.80	30 May
32:59.31	Christine	Bardelle	FRA	16.8.74	4 Jun
33:00.74	Emily	Brown	USA	6.7.84	23 Jun
33:02.11mx	Yoko	Aizu	JPN	28.4.86	25 Jun
33:02.55	Emily	Brichacek	AUS	7.7.90	10 Dec
33:02.74	Mary	Cullen	IRL	17.8.82	4 Jun
33:02.98mx	Fumiko	Hashimoto	JPN	1.4.89	25 Jun
33:04.17	Dani	Stack	USA	5.3.90	23 Jun
33:04.56	Chika	Horie	JPN	15.2.81	24 Apr
33:04.73		Jia Chaofeng	CHN	16.11.88	22 May
33:04.77	Irina	Sergeyeva	RUS	26.12.87	3 Jul
33:08.02mx	Kyoko	Aizu	JPN	28.4.86	25 Jun
33:08.18	Meriyem	Lamachi	MAR	20.12.87	17 Apr
33:08.39	Addie	Bracy	USA	4.8.86	1 May
33:09.18	Tejitu	Daba	BRN	20.8.91	15 Dec
33:09.40	Michi	Numata	JPN	6.5.89	24 Dec
33:09.50 mx	Hannah	Walker	GBR	9.8.91	13 Aug
33:10.15	Tara	Erdmann	USA	14.6.89	25 Mar
33:10.38mx	Aimi	Horikoshi	JPN	22.11.87	24 Sep
33:10.47	Megan	Brown	CAN	30.4.85	8 May
33:10.68	Estela	Navascués	ESP	3.2.81	2 Apr
33:10.85	Aya	Goto	JPN-J	8.2.93	24 Dec
33:10.98mx	Rika	Shintaku	JPN	19.10.85	25 Jun
33:11.00	Katie	Matthews	USA	19.11.90	23 Jun
33:11.71	Tonya	Nero	TRI	27.11.88	25 Mar
33:11.92	Fadime	Suna	TUR	25.10.86	16 Aug
33:13.40mx	Yuka	Hakoyama	JPN	9.3.90	22 Jun
33:13.87	Betsy	Saina	KEN	30.6.88	25 Mar
33:14.14	Ümmü	Kiraz	TUR	27.9.82	4 Jun
33:14.35mx	Shino	Saito	JPN	7.9.88	25 Jun
33:14.8A	Workitu	Ayanu	ETH	19.4.87	4 May
(146)					

Drugs disqualification

Mark	Name		Nat	Born	Pos	Meet	Venue	Date
31:16.56	Simone	da Silva ¶	BRA	12.9.84	1	NC	São Paulo	3 Aug

JUNIORS

See main list for top 4 juniors. 10 performances by 6 women to 33:15.0. Additional marks and further juniors:

	Mark	Pos	Meet	Venue	Date				
Kiros	32:11.37	11	WCh	Daegu	27 Aug	32:58.9A	2	NC	Addis Ababa	5 May
	32:29.33	2		Dongali	13 Jul				
Kushima	33:09.95	2		Kumamoto	9 Sep				

Mark	Name		Nat	Born	Pos	Meet	Venue	Date
32:53.63		Wei Jie	CHN	25.1.93	8	NC	Hefei	8 Sep
33:10.85	Aya	Goto	JPN	8.2.93	4		Yokohama	24 Dec
33:28.29		Liu Zhuang	CHN-Y	18.1.95	1		Nanchang	24 Oct
33:34.0A	Tsegereda	Girma	ETH-Y	.95	5	NC	Addis Ababa	5 May
33:33.22	Mai	Shinozuka	JPN	.93	4		Kumamoto	9 Sep
33:34.32	Jennifer	Bergman (10)	USA	1.11.92	8h1	NCAA-W	Eugene	26 May
33:34.97	Rina	Yonetsu	JPN	28.4.92	7		Kumamoto	9 Sep
33:38.85		Cao Mojie	CHN	10.4.92	2	City G	Nanchang	24 Oct
33:42.47		Xu Lihong	CHN	1.11.93	9		Jiaxing	22 May
33:45.34	Ai	Kokubo	JPN		10		Kumamoto	9 Sep
33:51.21	Lauren	Sara	USA	31.3.92	7	NCAA-E	Bloomington	26 May
33:51.26		Wu Xufeng	CHN	10.1.93	3	City G	Nanchang	24 Oct
33:51.82		Ma Zhen	CHN	10.11.93	4	City G	Nancheng	24 Oct

Mark	Name		Nat	Born	Pos	Meet	Venue	Date
33:52.2A	Goyetetom	Gebrselassie	ETH-Y	.95	8	NC	Addis Ababa	7 May
34:00.49		Che Xueyan	CHN	19.2.92	11		Jiaxing	22 May
34:00.7mx	Marie	Yamakami (20)	JPN	.92	16		Kure	11 Nov
Best European: 34:13.55 Louise Small			GBR	27.3.92	1	Univ Ch	Bedford	1 May

10 KILOMETRES ROAD

Mark	Name		Nat	Born	Pos	Meet	Venue	Date
30:38	Joyce	Chepkirui	KEN	10.8.88	1		Tilburg	4 Sep
30:43		Chepkirui			1		Appingedam	25 Jun
30:45+	Mary	Keitany	KEN	18.1.82	1	in HMar	Ra's Al-Khaymah	18 Feb
31:18	Emily	Chebet Muge	KEN	18.2.86	2		Tilburg	4 Sep
31:23	Worknesh	Kidane	ETH	21.11.81	1	Peach	Atlanta	4 Jul
31:26	Doris	Changeiywo	KEN	12.12.84	1		Würzburg	17 Apr
31:27	Esther	Chemtai	KEN	4.6.88	2		Würzburg	17 Apr
31:29	Margaret	Muriuki	KEN	21.3.86	1		Houilles	18 Dec
31:30+	Lucy	Wangui Kabuu	KEN	24.3.84	1	in HMar	New Delhi	27 Nov
31:31+	Sharon	Cherop	KEN	16.3.84	2	in HMar	New Delhi	27 Nov
31:32	Winnie	Jepkemoi	KEN-J	9.10.93	1		Utrecht	25 Sep
31:32+	Aselefech	Mergia	ETH	23.1.85	3=	in HMar	New Delhi	27 Nov
31:32+	Belaynesh	Oljira	ETH	26.6.90	3=	in HMar	New Delhi	27 Nov
31:33+	Lydia	Cheromei	KEN	11.5.77	5	in HMar	New Delhi	27 Nov
31:34+	Kim	Smith	NZL	19.11.81	1=	in HMar	Philadelphia	18 Sep
31:36	Wude	Ayalew	ETH	4.7.87	1	Cres C	New Orleans	23 Apr
31:36+		Kidane			1=	in HMar	Philadelphia	18 Sep

Where better than track best   With 15km times in 2nd column

Mark	Name		Nat	Born	Pos	Meet	Venue	Date
31:44	Dire	Tune	ETH	19.5.85	1		Ottawa	28 May
31:45	Helen	Clitheroe	GBR	2.1.74	1		Manchester	15 May
31:48 dh	Alice	Timbilil	KEN	16.6.83	2	Peach	Atlanta	4 Jul
31:50	Sentayehu	Ejigu	ETH	21.6.85	1		San Juan	27 Feb
31:54	Atsede	Habtamu	ETH	26.10.87	3		San Juan	27 Feb
31:55+48:37	Mare	Dibaba	ETH	20.10.89		in HMar	New Delhi	27 Nov
31:58	Belaynesh	Zemedkun	ETH	23.12.87	3	Cres C	New Orleans	23 Apr
31:58	Caroline	Kilel	KEN	21.3.81	1		Boston	26 Jun
32:01+48:38	Valentine	Kipketer	KEN-J	5.1.93		in HMar	New Delhi	27 Nov
32:03+48:42	Aberu	Kebede	ETH	12.9.89		in HMar	New Delhi	27 Nov
32:04+	Peninah	Arusei	KEN	23.2.79	1	in HMar	Paris	6 Mar
32:04	Rose	Chelimo	KEN	.89	1		Montereau	23 Oct
32:04	Cynthia	Jerotich	KEN	.89	2		Montereau	23 Oct
32:05+48:46	Rose	Kosgei	KEN	22.8.81		in HMar	Ra's Al-Khaymah	18 Feb
32:05	Grace	Momanyi	KEN	3.3.82	3		Manchester	15 May
32:06+49:07	Sultan	Haydar	TUR	23.5.87		in HMar	Ra's Al-Khaymah	18 Feb
32:06+48:51	Agnes	Kiprop	KEN	12.12.79		in HMar	Ra's Al-Khaymah	18 Feb
32:06	Irina	Mikitenko	GER	23.8.72	1	Parelloop	Brunssum	3 Apr
32:06	Paula	Radcliffe	GBR	17.12.73	1		Monaco	11 Dec
32:06	Azemra	Gebru	ETH-J	5.5.92	2		Houilles	18 Dec
32:07	Eunice	Jepkirui	KEN	20.5.84	1		Santos	15 May
32:07	Sarah	Chepchirchir	KEN	27.7.84	1		Melun	10 Jun
32:07	Valeria	Straneo	ITA	5.4.76	1	NC	Lucca	11 Sep
32:08	Anna	Incerti	ITA	19.1.80	3		Houilles	18 Dec
32:09	Josephine	Kimuyu	KEN	18.7.87	1		Leiden	15 May
32:13	Flomena	Chepchirchir	KEN	1.12.81	2		Appingedam	25 Jun
32:13	Elizeba	Cherono	KEN	6.6.88	2		Utrecht	25 Sep
32:13	Rkia	El Moukim	MAR	22.2.88	3		Utrecht	25 Sep
32:13	Maila	Asahssah	MAR	24.9.82	1		Valencia	27 Nov
32:17+	Philes	Ongori	KEN	19.7.86	2	in HMar	Paris	6 Mar
32:18+	Firehiwot	Dado	ETH	9.1.84		in HMar	Göteborg	21 May
32:19	Fate	Tola	ETH	22.10.87	1	Spark	Oelde	10 Jun
32:19	Mara	Yamauchi	GBR	13.8.73	1		Berlin	9 Oct
32:20+48:58	Atsede	Baysa	ETH	16.4.87		in HMar	Göteborg	21 May
32:20	Meseret	Mengistu	ETH	6.3.90	1		Luanda	31 Dec
32:22	Jo	Pavey	GBR	20.9.73	1		London	30 May
32:23	Mona Jaber	Salem	BRN	.83	3		Würzburg	17 Apr
32:24	Edna	Kiplagat	KEN	15.9.79	4		New York	11 Jun
32:24	Salomé	Rocha	POR	25.4.90	1		Porto	18 Dec
32:25	Rosaria	Console	ITA	17.12.79	2	NC	Lucca	11 Sep
32:26	Waganesh	Mekasha	ETH-J	16.1.92	1		Wierden	23 Jul
32:27	Lara	Tamsett	AUS	12.10.88	1		Sydney	4 Jun
32:28dh41m	Miriam	Wangari	KEN	22.2.79	1		Clermont	11 Jun
32:29	Edinah	Kwambai	KEN	.86	1		Bristol	15 May
32:29	Feyse	Tadese	ETH	19.11.88	1		Marseille	20 Nov

32:31+	Hilda	Kibet	NED	27.3.81	18 Feb		32:32	Alena	Shewarge	ETH	9.12.86	5 Feb
32:31	Emily	Chebet	UGA	12.12.87	11 Jun		32:32+	Alice	Mogire	KEN	.87	16 Oct

Mark	Name		Nat	Born	Pos	Meet	Venue	Date
32:32+	Koren	Jelela	ETH	18.1.87				16 Oct
32:33A	G	Chepkurui	KEN					16 Jan
32:33	Lauren	Howarth	GBR	21.4.90				22 Apr
32:33+	Diane	Chepkemoi	KEN	.87				18 Sep
32:34	Jelliah	Kerubo	KEN	10.10.85				11 Jun
32:35	Risper	Gesabwa	KEN	1.1..89				27 Feb
32:35A	Mamitu	Daska	ETH	16.10.83				30 May
32:35+	Jane	Kibii	KEN	10.3.85				18 Sep
32:36	Claire	Hallissey	GBR	17.3.83				15 May
32:36	Bizunesh	Deba	ETH	8.9.87				6 Aug
32:37	Cruz Nonata	da Silva	BRA	18.8.74				15 May
32:38	Diane	Nukuri-Johnson	BDI	1.12.84				6 Aug
32:39	Lucy	Macharia	KEN	.91				19 Mar
32:39+	Lornah	Kilpagat	NED	1.5.74				18 Sep
32:40	Susan	Chepkemei	KEN	25.6.75				23 Jul
32:40	Justina	Heslop	GBR	3.3.79				25 Sep
32:42	Charlotte	Purdue	GBR	10.6.91				9 Apr
32:43+	Tsegereda	Girma	ETH-Y	.95				13 Mar
32:44	Pamela	Lisoreng	KEN	5.8.88				17 Apr
32:44+	Netsanet	Achamo	ETH	14.12.87				16 Oct
32:45+48:56	Yukiko	Akaba	JPN	18.10.79				23 Dec
32:46+	Ejegayehu	Dibaba	ETH	25.6.82				9 Oct
32:46+49:01	Mai	Ito	JPN	23.5.84				23 Dec
32:46	Alice	Mogire	KEN	.87				31 Dec
32:47A	Gladys	Chebet	KEN					16 Jan
32:47	Eunice	Chebichii	KEN-J	23.5.93				17 Apr
32:47	Ann	Mwangi	KEN	8.12.88				22 Dec
32:48	Lucy	Murigi	KEN	7.7.85				13 Mar
32:48+	Birhane	Ababel	ETH	10.6.90				27 Mar
32:48	Ferhiwot	Goshu	ETH	28.6.90				17 Apr
32:48	Samira	Raïf	MAR	4.4.74				28 May
32:48	Gemma	Steel	GBR	12.11.85				30 May
32:48	Feysa	Tadesse	ETH	19.11.88				5 Jun
32:48	Edith	Chelimo	KEN	16.7.86				25 Sep
32:49	Yebrgual	Melese	ETH	.90				11 Jun
32:49 dh	Adriana	Nelson	USA	31.1.80				4 Jul
32:49	Caroline	Chepkwony	KEN	18.4.84				11 Sep
32:50	Yelena	Korobkina	RUS	25.11.90				30 Apr
32:50	Abigail	Bayley	GBR	26.11.77				19 Jun
32:50	Irvette	van Blerk	RSA	5.7.87				19 Jun
32:50+	Mizuki	Noguchi	JPN	3.7.78				23 Dec
32:52+	Eunice	Kales	KEN	6.12.84				18 Feb
32:53+49:58	Tabitha	Wambui	KEN	29.12.83				18 Se
32:52		Kibet	KEN					4 Sep
32:54+		Zhu Xiaolin	CHN	20.2.84				6 Mar
32:54+		Jia Chaofeng	CHN	16.11.88				6 Mar
32:54	Karolina	Jarzynska	POL	6.9.81				1 May
32:54	Afera	Godfay	ETH	25.9.91				25 Jun
32:56	Fatima	Ayachi	MAR	31.8.85				17 Apr
32:56	Alessandra	Aguilar	ESP	1.7.78				11 Jun
32:56	Grace	Kimanzi	KEN-J	1.3.92				23 Dec
32:57+	Rei	Ohara	JPN	10.8.90				6 Feb
32:57 dh	Madaí	Pérez	MEX	2.2.80				4 Jul
32:58+49:56	Nan	Kennard	USA	14.8.81				12 Mar
32:58	Yelena	Zadorozhnaya	RUS	3.12.77				30 Apr
32:58	Marisa	Barros	POR	25.2.80				18 Dec
32:59		Hyun Suh-yong	KOR-Y	.94				11 Oct

Excessively downhill: Dec 31. Madrid (50m): 1. Tirunesh Dibaba ETH 1.10.85 31:30, 2. Gelete Burka ETH 31:30, 3. Susan Partridge GBR 4.1.80 32:44, 4, Marta Domínguez ESP 3.11.75 32:49;
Apr 17, Rockville (60m): 1. Risper Gesabwa KEN .89 32:07, 2. Alemtsehay Misganaw ETH 24.8.80 32:08, 3. Aziza Aliyu ETH 1.1.85 32:22, 4. Malika Medjoub MAR 10.5.82 32:42 , 5. Hirut Mandefro ETH 5.8.85 32:48, 6. Hellen Jemutai KEN 32:54

32:27	Janet	Cherobon-Bawcom	USA	22.8.78	1		Northport (dh 41m)	17 Sep

15 KILOMETRES ROAD

See also intermediate times in 10km, 10 miles, 20km and half marathon lists

Mark	Name		Nat	Born	Pos	Meet	Venue	Date
48:16A	Faridah	Chelanga	UGA	8.10.89	1		Eldoret	25 Se5
48:32A	Dire	Tune	ETH	19.5.85	1		Bahir Dar	13 Feb
48:32A	Atsede	Habtamu	ETH	26.10.87	2		Bahir Dar	13 Feb
48:33	Waganesh	Mekasha	ETH-J	16.1.92	1		Nijmegen	20 Nov
48:36A	Koren	Jelela	ETH	18.1.87	3		Bahir Dar	13 Feb
48:41	Alice	Timbilil	KEN	16.6.83	1		Utica	10 Jul
48:48	Priscah	Jeptoo	KEN	24.6.84	1		São Paulo	31 Dec
48:52	Wude	Ayalew	ETH	4.7.87	2		São Paulo	31 Dec
49:14	Winnie	Jepkemoi	KEN-J	9.10.93	1		Massamagrell	14 May
49:24+	Sarah	Chepchirchir	KEN	27.7.84	1	in 20k	Paris	9 Oct
49:31	Jen	Rhines	USA	1.7.74	1	NC	Jacksonville	12 Mar
49:38	Alvetiona	Ivanova	RUS	22.5.75	3		Utica	10 Jul
49:38	Birhane	Ababel	ETH	10.6.90	1	in HMar	Milano	27 Mar
49:42	Aki	Odagiri	JPN	20.8.90	2		Nijmegen	20 Nov
49:44	Ayame	Takagi	JPN-J	.92	3		Nijmegen	20 Nov
49:54+	Pamela	Lisoreng	KEN	5.8.88		in HMar	Göteborg	21 May
49:57	Megan	Hogan	USA	10.2.88	3	NC	Jacksonville	12 Mar
49:58	Janet	Cherobon-Bawcom	USA	22.8.78	1		Pensacola	5 Feb
49:59+	Tabitha	Wambui	KEN	29.12.83		in 10M	Zaandam	18 Sep

10 MILES ROAD

10M	15k	Name		Nat	Born	Pos	Meet	Venue	Date
50:05+		Mary	Keitany	KEN	18.1.82	1	in HMar	Ra's Al-Khaymah	18 Feb
50:58+		Lucy	Wangui Kabuu	KEN	24.3.84	1	in HMar	Newcastle	18 Sep
51:03+		Kim	Smith	NZL	19.11.81	1	in HMar	Philadelphia	18 Sep
51:05+		Worknesh	Kidane	ETH	21.11.81	2	in HMar	Philadelphia	18 Sep
51:57	48:25	Priscah	Cherono	KEN	27.6.80	1		Zaandam	18 Sep
52:28+		Dire	Tune	ETH	19.5.85		in HMar	Ra's Al-Khaymah	18 Feb
52:29+		Mare	Dibaba	ETH	20.10.89		in HMar	Ra's Al-Khaymah	18 Feb
52:29+		Agnes	Kiprop	KEN	12.12.79		in HMar	Ra's Al-Khaymah	18 Feb
52:28+		Rose	Kosgei	KEN	22.8.81		in HMar	Ra's Al-Khaymah	18 Feb
52:46	49:17	Diane	Chepkemoi	KEN	.87	2		Zaandam	18 Sep
52:48	49:15	Abebech	Afework	ETH	11.12.90	3		Zaandam	18 Sep
52:53		Jess	Coulson	GBR	18.4.90	1		Twickenham	16 Oct
52:54+		Bizunesh	Deba	ETH	8.9.87		in HMar	Philadelphia	16 Sep
52:55+		Sultan	Haydar	TUR	23.5.87		in HMar	Ra's Al-Khaymah	18 Feb

Mark		Name		Nat	Born	Pos	Meet	Venue	Date
52:55		Tabitha	Wambui	KEN	29.12.83	1		Schortens	20 Aug
52:55		Aselefech	Mergia	ETH	23.1.85	1		Portsmouth	30 Oct
53:01+		Hilda	Kibet	NED	27.3.81		in HMar	Ra's Al-Khaymah	18 Feb
53:01	49:17	Lornah	Kiplagat	NED	1.5.74	4		Zaandam	18 Sep
53:06+		Caroline	Kilel	KEN	21.3.81		in Mar	New York	6 Nov
53:07+		Firehiwot	Dado	ETH	9.1.84		in Mar	New York	6 Nov
53:15+		Jane	Kibii	KEN	10.3.85		in HMar	Philadelphia	18 Sep
53:34	49:50	Doris	Changeiywo	KEN	12.12.84	2		Portsmouth	30 Oct
53:36+		Eunice	Kales	KEN	6.12.84		in HMar	Ra's Al-Khaymah	18 Feb
53:43		Irene	Kosgei	KEN	8.9.74	3		Portsmouth	30 Oct
53:45	50:00	Charlotte	Purdue	GBR	10.6.91	4		Portsmouth	30 Oct

More 10M at Ra's Al-Khaymah: D Tune ETH & A Kiprop KEN 52:28; M Dibaba ETH & R Kosgei KEN 52:29; S Haydar
TUR 52:54; H Kibet NED 53:01; E Kales KEN 53:36

20 KILOMETRES ROAD

Mark		Name		Nat	Born	Pos	Meet	Venue	Date
65:21+		Mare	Dibaba	ETH	20.10.89		in HMar	New Delhi	27 Nov
65:27+	48:53	Flomena	Chepchirchir	KEN	1.12.81		in HMar	Den Haag	13 Mar
65:33+	48:38	Valentine	Kipketer	KEN-J	5.1.93		in HMar	New Delhi	27 Nov
65:35+	48:42	Aberu	Kebede	ETH	12.9.89		in HMar	New Delhi	27 Nov
65:57+	49:32	Worknesh	Kidane	ETH	21.11.81		in Mar	New York	6 Nov
66:07	49:27	Sarah	Chepchirchir	KEN	27.7.84	1		Paris	9 Oct
66:16	49:34	Miriam	Wangari	KEN	22.2.79	2		Paris	9 Oct
66:21+		Jéssica	Augusto	POR	8.11.81		in Mar	Paris	20 Mar
66:24	49:34	Rose	Chelimo	KEN	.89	3		Paris	9 Oct
66:27+		Atsede	Baysa	ETH	16.4.87		in HMar	Göteborg	21 May
66:28	49:35	Cynthia	Jerotich	KEN	.89	4		Paris	9 Oct
66:28+	49:32	Bizunesh	Deba	ETH	8.9.87		in Mar	New York	6 Nov
66:29+		Caroline	Kilel	KEN	21.3.81		in Mar	New York	6 Nov
66:32+	49:50	Florence	Kiplagat	KEN	27.2.87		in Mar	Berlin	25 Sep
67:08	49:48	Gladys	Chepchirchir	KEN	.86	5		Paris	9 Oct
67:10+		Belaynesh	Zemedkun	ETH	23.12.87		in HMar	Chicago	9 Oct
67:30+		Doris	Changeiywo	KEN	12.12.84		in HMar	New Delhi	27 Nov
67:37		Shitaye	Bedaso	ETH	.80	1		Alphen aan den Rijn	6 Mar

HALF MARATHON

HMar	20k	15k	Name		Nat	Born	Pos	Meet	Venue	Date
65:50	62:36	46:40	Mary	Keitany	KEN	18.1.82	1		Ra's Al-Khaymah	18 Feb
67:04	63:43	47:47	Lucy	Wangui Kabuu	KEN	24.3.84	1		New Delhi	27 Nov
67:06dh		47:27		Wangui			1	GNR	South Shields	18 Sep
67:08	63:44	47:48	Sharon	Cherop	KEN	16.3.84	2		New Delhi	27 Nov
67:11	63:38	47:37	Kim	Smith	NZL	19.11.81	1		Philadelphia	18 Sep
67:21	64:01	47:48	Aselefech	Mergia	ETH	23.1.85	3		New Delhi	27 Nov
67:27	64:01	47:49	Belaynesh	Oljira	ETH	26.6.90	4		New Delhi	27 Nov
67:28		47:37	Worknesh	Kidane	ETH	21.11.81	2		Philadelphia	18 Sep
67:33		47:50	Lydia	Cheromei	KEN	11.5.77	1		Praha	2 Apr
67:36				Smith			1		New Orleans	13 Feb
67:54				Keitany			1		Lisboa	25 Sep
67:56+	64:21	47:59		Keitany			1	in Mar	New York	6 Nov
68:02			Florence	Kiplagat	KEN	27.2.87	1		Klagenfurt	21 Aug
68:07			Sarah	Chepchirchir (10)	KEN	27.7.84	1		Vitry-sur-Seine	3 Apr
68:21			Valentine	Kipketer	KEN-J	5.1.93	1		Lille	3 Sep
68:22			Flomena	Chepchirchir	KEN	1.12.81	1		Zwolle	18 Jun
68:27			Nadia	Ejjafini	ITA	8.11.80	1	NC	Cremona	16 Oct
68:28			Aberu	Kebede	ETH	12.9.89	1		Lisboa	20 Mar
68:30		48:17	Peninah	Arusei	KEN	23.2.79	1		Paris	6 Mar
68:32		48:33	Philes	Ongori	KEN	19.7.86	2		Paris	6 Mar
68:33			Ana Dulce	Félix	POR	23.10.82	2		Lisboa	20 Mar
68:39+			Koren	Jelela	ETH	18.1.87	1	in Mar	Toronto	16 Oct
68:39+			Mare	Dibaba	ETH	20.10.89	1=	in Mar	Toronto	16 Oct
68:41			Grace	Momanyi (20)	KEN	3.3.82	3		Lisboa	20 Mar
68:44			Feysa	Tadesse	ETH	19.11.88	1		Rabat	3 Apr
68:49			Doris	Changeiywo	KEN	12.12.84	2		Rabat	3 Apr
68:50	65:14			Cheromei			5		New Delhi	27 Nov
68:51				Chepchirchir			3		Rabat	3 Apr
68:52	65:41	48:51	Dire	Tune	ETH	19.5.85	2		Ra's Al-Khaymah	18 Feb
68:52	65:26	49:38	Caroline (30/24)	Rotich	KEN	13.5.84	1		New York	20 Mar
68:55			Pauline	Njeri	KEN	.85	4		Lisboa	20 Mar

Mark			Name		Nat	Born	Pos	Meet	Venue	Date
68:57	65:42	48:51		M Dibaba			3		Ra's Al-Khaymah	18 Feb
68:57			Helena	Kirop	KEN	9.9.76	2		Lisboa	25 Sep
69:00			Berhane	Abadel	ETH	10.6.90	1		Vadodara	23 Jan
69:00	65:22	48:46	Kayoko	Fukushi	JPN	25.3.82	1		Marugame	6 Feb
69:00	65:30	49:37	Edna	Kiplagat	KEN	15.9.79	2		New York	20 Mar
69:02			Fatuma	Sado	ETH	11.10.91	2		Vitry-sur-Seine	3 Apr
			(30)							
69:03	65:36	49:37	Kara	Goucher	USA	9.7.78	3		New York	20 Mar
69:04	65:42	48:51	Rose	Kosgei	KEN	22.8.81	4		Ra's Al-Khaymah	18 Feb
69:04	65:25	48:13	Joyce	Chepkirui	KEN	10.8.88	1		Göteborg	21 May
69:06		49:03	Anna	Incerti	ITA	19.1.80	1		Ostia	27 Feb
69:08			Iness	Chenonge	KEN	1.2.82	5		Lisboa	20 Mar
69:08			Georgina	Rono	KEN	19.5.84	4		Rabat	3 Apr
69:08	65:35	48:43	Bezunesh	Bekele	ETH	18.9.83	9		New Delhi	27 Nov
69:10		49:03	Jéssica	Augusto	POR	8.11.81	2		Ostia	27 Feb
69:10		48:33	Aheza	Kiros	ETH	26.3.82	3		Paris	6 Mar
69:11	65:42	48:51	Agnes	Kiprop	KEN	12.12.79	5		Ra's Al-Khaymah	18 Feb
			(40)							
69:16	65:35	48:56	Yukiko	Akaba	JPN	18.10.79	1		Okayama	23 Dec
69:17		48:28	Belaynesh	Gebre Zemedkun	ETH	23.12.87	2		Praha	2 Apr
69:23	65:44	49:01	Yoko	Miyauchi	JPN	19.6.83	2		Okayama	23 Dec
69:25	65:44	49:38	Alene	Amare	ETH	9.12.86	4		New York	20 Mar
69:25+	65:48	49:19	Liliya	Shobukhova	RUS	13.11.77	1=	in Mar	Chicago	9 Oct
69:25+	65:48	49:20	Ejegayehu	Dibaba	ETH	25.6.82	1=	in Mar	Chicago	9 Oct
69:34	65:59?	49:38	Jo	Pavey	GBR	20.9.73	6		New York	20 Mar
69:35	66:01	49:24	Hilda	Kibet	NED	27.3.81	6		Ra's Al-Khaymah	18 Feb
69:42			Valeria	Straneo	ITA	5.4.76	2	NC	Cremona	16 Oct
69:45			Rose	Chelimo	KEN	.89	2		Lille	3 Sep
			(50)							
69:46+	66:09	49:21	Mamitu	Daska	ETH	16.10.83	1=	in Mar	Frankfurt	30 Oct
69:46+	66:09	49:21	Merima	Mohammed	ETH-J	10.6.92	1=	in Mar	Frankfurt	30 Oct
69:50			Merima	Hashim	ETH	.81	2		Vadodara	23 Jan
69:55			Bizunesh	Deba	ETH	8.9.87	3		Philadelphia	16 Sep
69:58			Atsede	Baysa	ETH	16.4.87	1		Reims	16 Oct
69:58			Shalane	Flanagan	USA	8.7.81	1		Miami Beach	11 Dec
69:58	66:09	49:00	Sally	Chepyego	KEN	3.10.85	3		Okayama	23 Dec
70:02	66:28	49:05	Sultan	Haydar	TUR	23.5.87	7		Ra's Al-Khaymah	18 Feb
70:03	66:16	49:01	Mai	Ito	JPN	23.5.84	4		Okayama	23 Dec
70:04			Lucy	Macharia	KEN	.91	3		Vitry-sur-Seine	3 Apr
			(60)							
70:08			Fatna	Maraoui	ITA	10.7.77	3	NC	Cremona	16 Oct
70:13+	66:29	49:32	Firehiwot	Dado	ETH	9.1.84	2=	in Mar	New York	6 Nov
70:13+		49:33	Caroline	Kilel	KEN	21.3.81	2=	in Mar	New York	6 Nov
70:18	66:43	49:48	Olesya	Syreva	RUS	25.11.83	8		New York	20 Mar
70:22			Megumi	Kinukawa	JPN	7.8.89	1		Shanghai	4 Dec
70:25			Jane	Kibii	KEN	10.3.85	4		Philadelphia	18 Sep
70:26			Priscah	Jeptoo	KEN	24.6.84	1		Goyang	6 Mar
			70:08u				1		Barcelona	30 Jan
70:26			Malika	Asahssah	MAR	24.9.82	1		Valencia	23 Oct
70:28		49:45		Zhu Xiaolin	CHN	20.2.84	4		Paris	6 Mar
70:29			Eunice	Jepkirui	KEN	20.5.84	1		Río de Janeiro	21 Aug
			(70)							
70:29	dh		Marisa	Barros	POR	25.2.80	3	GNR	South Shields	18 Sep
70:30	66:43	49:22	Tsegereda	Girma	ETH-Y	.95	2		Den Haag	13 Mar
70:30+			Ashu	Kasim	ETH	20.10.84		in Mar	Paris	10 Apr
70:30			Mariya	Konovalova	RUS	14.8.74	1		Novosibirsk	10 Sep
70:30			Abebech	Afework	ETH	11.12.90	1	RdVin	Remich	25 Sep
70:30+	66:49	49:59	Paula	Radcliffe	GBR	17.12.73	2	in Mar	Berlin	25 Sep
70:34			Desiree	Davila	USA	26.7.83	2		Naples	16 Jan
70:34			Rita	Jeptoo	KEN	15.2.81	4		Lisboa	25 Sep
70:34			Sabrina	Mockenhaupt	GER	6.12.80	1		Köln	2 Oct
70:36	66:54	49:56	Karolina	Jarzynska	POL	6.9.81	2		Marugame	6 Feb
			(80)							
70:38+			Askale	Tafa	ETH	27.9.84		in Mar	London	17 Apr
70:38			Rkia	El Moukim	MAR	22.2.88	2		Valencia	23 Oct
70:39			Cynthia	Jerotich	KEN	.89	2		Reims	16 Oct
70:40			Diane	Chepkemoi	KEN	.87	7		Lisboa	20 Mar
70:40			Benita	Willis	AUS	6.5.79	1		Las Vegas	4 Dec
70:41	67:00	49:52	Eunice	Kales	KEN	6.12.84	8		Ra's Al-Khaymah	18 Feb
70:41		49:45	Netsanet	Achamo	ETH	14.12.87	1		Olomouc	19 Jun

Mark			Name	Nat	Born	Pos	Meet	Venue	Date
70:43			Kejeta Melat	ETH-J	.92	5		Rabat	3 Apr
70:43			Gladys Cherono	KEN	.84	1		Zhuhai	18 Dec
70:45	49:44		Jia Chaofeng	CHN	16.11.88	5		Paris	6 Mar
(90)									
70:47			Asmae Leghzaoui	MAR	30.8.76	1		Marrakech	30 Jan
70:48	67:02	49:43	Mizuki Noguchi	JPN	3.7.78	5		Okayama	23 Dec
70:50	67:10	49:53	Rei Ohara	JPN	10.8.90	3		Marugame	6 Feb
70:56	67:20		Irvette van Blerk	RSA	5.7.87	9		New York	20 Mar
70:57 dh			Helen Clitheroe	GBR	2.1.74	5	GNR	South Shields	18 Sep
70:57			Goitetom Haftu	ETH	.87	1		Boulogne-Billancourt	20 Nov
71:03 dh			Irene Jerotich	KEN	8.9.74	6	GNR	South Shields	18 Sep
71:05			Molly Pritz	USA	1.1.88	2		New Orleans	13 Feb
71:05			Maegan Krifchin	USA	8.4.88	5		Philadelphia	18 Sep
71:06			Karima Saleh Jassem	BRN	18.2.88	2		Marrakech	30 Jan
(100)									

Mark	Name	Nat	Born	Date
71:07	Susan Tanui	KEN	.81	24 Apr
71:07	Isabellah Andersson	SWE	12.11.80	17 Sep
71:09	Adhane Tsegay	ETH	8.4.85	20 Nov
71:10	Samira Raïf	MAR	4.4.74	30 Jan
71:10	Miriam Wangari	KEN	22.2.79	16 Oct
71:11	Alice Timbilil	KEN	16.6.83	6 Mar
71:12+	Atsede Habtamu	ETH	26.10.87	21 Jan
71:12+	Genet Getaneh	ETH	6.1.86	21 Jan
71:12	Helaria Johannes	NAM	13.8.80	15 Sep
71:13 67:32	Mika Yoshikawa	JPN	16.9.84	6 Feb
71:13 67:30	Madaí Pérez	MEX	2.2.80	20 Mar
71:13 dh	Irene Kemunto	KEN	10.1.85	18 Sep
71:14	Jen Rhines	USA	1.7.74	29 Jan
71:14 67:35	Christelle Daunay	FRA	5.12.74	18 Feb
71:18	Genet Adeke	ETH		23 Jan
71:21	Aynalem Woldemichael	ETH	.84	6 Mar
71:21	Jane Muia	KEN	20.12.86	3 Apr
71:22	Edith Chelimo	KEN	16.7.86	20 Mar
71:22	Eri Okubo	JPN	2.6.83	16 Oct
71:22	Amy Hastings	USA	21.1.84	4 Dec
71:24u	Kaori Yoshida	JPN	4.8.81	9 Jan
71:25	Megeretu Geletu	ETH	.91	6 Mar
71:25	Gladys Chepchirchir	KEN	.85	2 Oct
71:25 67:41	Peninah Kigen	KEN	.86	27 Nov
71:26	Elizeba Cherono	KEN	6.6.88	27 Mar
71:26	Alice Mogire	KEN	.87	16 Oct
71:27	Katarzyna Kowalska	POL	7.4.85	27 Mar
71:27+	Inga Abitova	RUS	6.3.82	17 Apr
71:27+67:41	Azusa Nojiri	JPN	6.6.82	17 Apr
71:27+67:42	Madoka Ogi	JPN	26.10.83	17 Apr
71:28+67:41	Yoshiko Fujinaga	JPN	15.8.81	17 Apr
71:28+67:42	Noriko Matsuoka	JPN	2.5.79	17 Apr
71:28+67:42	Mizuho Nasukawa	JPN	22.11.79	17 Apr
71:29	Everlyne Lagat	KEN	2.12.80	7 May
71:32	Fridah Domongole	KEN	15.1.84	26 Mar
71:34+67:50	Irina Mikitenko	GER	23.8.72	25 Sep
71:35+67:50	Tiki Gelana	ETH	22.10.87	16 Oct
71:35+67:50+	Eyerusalem Kuma	ETH	4.11.81	16 Oct
71:37+67:50	Albina Mayorova	RUS	16.5.77	20 Feb
71:37+67:50	Yoshimi Ozaki	JPN	1.7.81	20 Feb
71:37+67:50	Remi Nakazato	JPN	24.6.88	20 Feb
71:37+	Adriana Pârtea/Nelson	ROU/USA	31.1.80	20 Feb
71:37	Monica Wangari	KEN	4.10.86	27 Feb
71:37 67:48	Pamela Lisoreng	KEN	5.8.88	21 May
71:38	Serena Burla	USA	29.7.82	29 Jan
71:38+67:50	Kaoru Nagao	JPN	26.9.89	20 Feb
71:38 67:51	Janet Cherobon-Bawcom	USA	22.8.78	20 Mar
71:40	Fate Tola	ETH	22.10.87	3 Apr
71:40	Yebrgual Melese	ETH	.90	16 Oct
71:40 68:00	Yuko Watanabe	JPN	3.11.87	23 Dec
71:41	Leonida Mosop	KEN	.91	2 Oct
71:43	Hao Xiaofan	CHN	9.12.89	24 Apr
71:44	Tadelech Bekele	ETH	.91	18 Dec
71:45	Katie McGregor	USA	2.9.77	4 Dec
71:45	Ehite Gebireyes	ETH	.91	16 Oct
71:46	Dayna Pidhoresky	CAN	18.11.86	23 Oct
71:46dh	Renè Kalmer	RSA	3.11.80	18 Sep
71:47	Krisztina Papp	HUN	17.12.82	27 Mar
71:48	Deena Kastor	USA	14.2.73	30 Oct
71:49	Aki Otagiri	JPN	20.8.90	6 Feb
71:50	Joyce Kandie	KEN	30.5.79	13 Mar
71:50	Edinah Kwambai	KEN	.86	8 May
71:50	Cruz Nonata da Silva	BRA	18.8.74	21 Aug
71:51	Lucy Murigi	KEN	7.7.85	27 Mar
71:51	Mayumi Fujita	JPN	26.5.83	4 Sep
71:53	Rebby Koech	KEN	30.10.80	27 Mar
71:54	Magdaline Mukunzi	KEN	22.10.83	25 Sep
71:55	Tirfe Tsegaye	ETH	25.11.84	3 Sep
71:55	Josephine Kimuyu	KEN	18.7.87	18 Sep
71:55	Salina Kosgei	KEN	16.11.76	25 Sep
71:57	Sharon Tavengwa	ZIM	9.12.83	27 Mar
71:59	Catherine Ndereba	KEN	21.7.72	18 Dec
72:00	Liz Yelling	GBR	5.12.74	20 Mar
72:00	Emily Chebet	KEN	18.2.86	2 Apr
72:01+	Risa Shigetomo	JPN	29.8.87	17 Apr
72:01	Naoko Sakamoto	JPN	14.11.80	23 Dec
72:03	Nan Kennard	USA	14.8.81	29 Jan
72:03+	Azalech Woldeselassie	ETH	4.5.88	20 Feb
72:04	Megumi Seike	JPN	26.2.87	6 Feb
72:05	Eunice Orwaru	KEN	.82	23 Jan
72:05+	Anikó Kálovics	HUN	13.5.77	30 Jan
72:05	Bahar Dogan	TUR	2.9.74	19 May
72:06+	Chika Horie	JPN	15.2.81	30 Jan
72:06+	Ryoko Kizaki	JPN	21.6.85	30 Jan
72:06+	Hiroko Miyauchi	JPN	19.6.83	30 Jan
72:08	Woynishet Girma	ETH	,86	13 Feb
72:10	Yurika Nakamura	JPN	1.4.86	4 Sep
72:10	Lishan Dula	BRN	17.2.87	28 Oct
72:10A	Elisabet Chelagat	KEN	.80	30 Oct
72:11	Malika Belfakir	MAR	.86	30 Jan
72:11	Diane Nukuri-Johnson	BDI	1.12.84	18 Sep
72:12+	Fantu Eticha	ETH	.91	23 Oct
72:12+	Harun Makda	ETH	.88	23 Oct
72:15+	Melkaw Gizaw	ETH	.90	9 Oct
72:16	Fatima Ayachi	MAR	31.8.85	30 Jan
72:16	Misato Horie	JPN	10.3.87	6 Feb
72:16+	Shetaye Bedaso	ETH	.80	9 Oct
72:17	Kenza Dahmani	ALG	18.11.80	23 Apr
72:17+	Rael Kiyara Kguriatukei	KEN	4.4.84	9 Oct
(199) 72:19 four women				

Excessively downhill: San Diego 5 Jun (in Mar): Misiker Mekonnin 69:20, Bizunesh Deba 69:53

JUNIORS

See main list for top 4 juniors. 7 performances by 5 women to 72:31. Additional marks and further juniors:

Kipketer 70:12 1 Berlin 3 Apr   70:54 2 Zwolle 18 Jun

Mark	Name	Nat	Born	Pos	Venue	Date
72:31	Liu Zhuang	CHN-Y	18.1.95	4	Yangzhou	24 Apr
73:10	Korahubsh Itaa	ETH	28.2.92	7	Praha	2 Apr
73:23	Cao Mojie	CHN	10.4.92	5	Yangzhou	24 Apr
73:57	Karima El Aabbouz	MAR-Y	22.8.96	12	Rabat	3 Apr
74:00	Hua Shaoqing	CHN-Y	12.2.94	7	Yangzhou	24 Apr
74:03A	Helen Jepkurgat	KEN	.92	2	Nairobi	30 Oct
74:06	Xu Kelian	CHN-Y	19.5.94	8	Yangzhou	24 Apr

Mark	Name	Nat	Born	Pos	Meet	Venue	Date

25 – 30 KILOMETRES ROAD

20k	25k	30k	Name		Nat	Born	Pos	Meet	Venue	Date
			See also intermediate times shown in marathon list							
	1:23:22		Flomena	Chepchirchir	KEN	1.12.81	1		Berlin	8 May
	1:23:54+		Koren	Jelela	ETH	18.1.87		in Mar	Paris	10 Apr
	1:23:54	1:41:47	Ashu	Kasim	ETH	20.10.84		in Mar	Paris	10 Apr
	1:23:57	1:40:46	Worknesh	Kidane	ETH	21.11.81		in Mar	New York	6 Nov
		1:41:14	Aselefech	Mergia	ETH	23.1.85		in Mar	London	17 Apr
67:50+	1:24:43	1:41:51	Peninah	Arusei	KEN	23.2.79		in Mar	Amsterdam	16 Oct
67:50+	1:24:58	1:42:05	Albina	Mayorova	RUS	16.5.77		in Mar	Yokohama	20 Feb
67:50+	1:24:58		Adriana	Nelson	ROU/USA	31.1.80		in Mar	Yokohama	20 Feb
		1:42:10	Netsanet	Achamo	ETH	14.12.87		in Mar	Toronto	16 Oct
		1:42:10	Diane	Chepkemoi	KEN	.87		in Mar	Toronto	16 Oct
	1:25:28	1:42:36	Hilda	Kibet	NED	27.3.81		in Mar	Eindhoven	9 Oct
	1:25:38		Molly	Pritz	USA	1.1.88	1	NC	Grand Rapids	14 May
	1:25:43+		Anikó	Kálovics	HUN	13.5.77		in Mar	Osaka	30 Jan
	1:25:44	1:43:12	Ryoko	Kizaki	JPN	21.6.85		in Mar	Osaka	30 Jan
		1:43:13	Mizuho	Nasukawa	JPN	22.11.79		in Mar	London	17 Apr
	1:25:44	1:43:26	Yoko	Miyauchi	JPN	19.6.83		in Mar	Osaka	30 Jan
	1:25:45	1:43:30	Hiroko	Miyauchi	JPN	19.6.83		in Mar	Osaka	30 Jan
	1:26:09	1:43:34	Fate	Tola	ETH	22.10.87		in Mar	Frankfurt	30 Oct

L = loop course, P = point-to-point, D = downhill over 1/1000, W women only, M mixed race

MARATHON

Mark		25k	35k	Name		Nat	Born	Pos	Venue	Date
2:18:20	LM	1:22:34	1:38:23	Liliya	Shobukhova	RUS	13.11.77	1	Chicago	9 Oct
2:19:19	LW	1:23:10	1:39:11	Mary	Keitany	KEN	18.1.82	1	London	17 Apr
2:19:44	LM	1:23:15	1:39:48	Florence	Kiplagat	KEN	27.2.87	1	Berlin	25 Sep
2:20:15	LW	1:23:17	1:39:44		Shobukhova			2	London	17 Apr
2:20:46	LW	1:23:16	1:39:45	Edna	Kiplagat	KEN	15.9.79	3	London	17 Apr
2:21:59	LM	1:22:47	1:39:45	Mamitu	Daska	ETH	16.10.83	1	Frankfurt	30 Oct
2:22:08	LM	1:24:42	1:41:29	Tiki	Gelana	ETH	22.10.87	1	Amsterdam	16 Oct
2:22:09	LM	1:22:14	1:39:19	Ejegayehu	Dibaba	ETH	25.6.82	2	Chicago	9 Oct
2:22:18	LM	1:24:54	1:41:31	Irina	Mikitenko	GER	23.8.72	2	Berlin	25 Sep
2:22:34	LM		1:41:00	Lydia	Cheromei	KEN	11.5.77	1	Praha	8 May
2:22:43	LM		1:38:33	Koren	Jelela (10)	ETH	18.1.87	1	Toronto	16 Oct
2:22:45	LM			Aselefech	Mergia	ETH	23.1.85	1	Dubai	21 Jan
2:22:55	LM	1:23:54	1:42:46	Priscah	Jeptoo	KEN	24.6.84	1	Paris	10 Apr
2:23:01	LM				Cheromei			2	Dubai	21 Jan
2:23:15	PW	1:23:57	1:40:45	Firehiwot	Dado	ETH	9.1.84	1	New York	6 Nov
2:23:19	PW	1:23:57	1:40:45	Bizunesh	Deba	ETH	8.9.87	2	New York	6 Nov
2:23:25	LM		1:38:33	Mare	Dibaba	ETH	20.10.89	2	Toronto	16 Oct
2:23:31	DM				Deba			1	San Diego	5 Jun
2:23:37	PM	1:25:27	1:42:13	Helena	Kirop	KEN	9.9.76	1	Venezia	23 Oct
2:23:38	PW	1:21:38	1:38:57		Keitany			3	New York	6 Nov
2:23:41	LM			Isabellah	Andersson	SWE	12.11.80	3	Dubai	21 Jan
2:23:42	LW		1:40:09	Bezunesh	Bekele	ETH	18.9.83	4	London	17 Apr
2:23:46	LM	1:23:50	1:41:07	Paula	Radcliffe	GBR	17.12.73	3	Berlin	25 Sep
2:23:50	LW		1:41:04	Atsede	Baysa (20)	ETH	16.4.87	5	London	17 Apr
2:23:54	LM	1:23:21	1:40:36	Agnes	Kiprop	KEN	12.12.79	2	Frankfurt	30 Oct
2:23:56	LW	1:24:59	1:42:05	Yoshimi	Ozaki	JPN	1.7.81	1	Yokohama	20 Feb
2:24:09	LW	1:24:33	1:41:36	Yukiko	Akaba	JPN	18.10.79	6	London	17 Apr
2:24:09	LM			Haile	Kebebush	ETH	.86	1	Shanghai	4 Dec
2:24:12	LM			Tirfe	Tsegaye	ETH	25.11.84	2	Shanghai	4 Dec
2:24:13	LM				Dado			1	Roma	20 Mar
2:24:20	LM	1:26:08	1:43:18	Philes	Ongori	KEN	19.7.86	1	Rotterdam	10 Apr
2:24:21	LM	1:24:38	1:41:37	Flomena	Chepchirchir	KEN	1.12.81	3	Frankfurt	30 Oct
2:24:24	LW				Mikitenko			7	London	17 Apr
2:24:25	LM	1:24:54	1:41:31	Atsede	Habtamu	ETH	26.10.87	4	Berlin	25 Sep
2:24:26	LM				Habtamu			4	Dubai	21 Jan
2:24:27	LM			Hilda	Kibet	NED	27.3.81	2	Rotterdam	10 Apr
2:24:29	LW	1:24:59	1:42:05	Remi	Nakazato (30)	JPN	24.6.88	2	Yokohama	20 Feb
2:24:32	LM	1:22:47	1:39:45	Merima	Mohammed	ETH-J	10.6.92	4	Frankfurt	30 Oct
2:24:33	LW		1:41:37	Jéssica	Augusto	POR	8.11.81	8	London	17 Apr
2:24:33	LM	1:25:28	1:42:34	Georgina (40/33)	Rono	KEN	19.5.84	1	Eindhoven	9 Oct
2:24:34	LW		1:39:45	Aberu	Kebede	ETH	12.9.89	9	London	17 Apr
2:24:38	LM	1:22:31	1:40:07	Kayoko	Fukushi	JPN	25.3.82	3	Chicago	9 Oct
2:24:55	LM	1:24:42	1:41:29	Eyerusalem	Kuma	ETH	4.11.81	2	Amsterdam	16 Oct

Mark				Name		Nat	Born	Pos	Meet	Venue	Date	
2:25:01	LM	1:26:01	1:43:22	Tatyana	Petrova	RUS	8.4.83	5		Berlin	25	Sep
2:25:04	LW	1:24:59	1:42:05	Marisa	Barros	POR	25.2.80	3		Yokohama	20	Feb
2:25:09	LM	1:25:29	1:42:37	Shitaye	Bedaso	ETH	.80	2		Eindhoven	9	Oct
2:25:18	LW		1:40:58	Mariya	Konovalova	RUS	14.8.74	10		London	17	Apr
				(40)								
2:25:20	LM	1:25:28	1:42:37	Feysa	Tadesse	ETH	19.11.88	3		Eindhoven	9	Oct
2:25:21	DM			Misiker	Mekonnin	ETH	23.7.86	2		San Diego (86.5mdh)	5	Jun
2:25:23	LM	1:25:29	1:42:38	Rael	Kiyara Kguriatukei	KEN	4.4.84	4		Eindhoven	9	Oct
2:25:24	LW		1:41:38	Askale	Tafa	ETH	27.9.84	11		London	17	Apr
2:25:29	LW	1:24:39	1:42:15	Azusa	Nojiri	JPN	6.6.82	12		London	17	Apr
2:25:32	LM	1:26:12	1:43:23	Anna	Incerti	ITA	19.1.80	6		Berlin	25	Sep
2:25:40	LW	1:24:53	1:42:14	Yoshiko	Fujinaga	JPN	15.8.81	13		London	17	Apr
2:25:40	PW	1:25:26	1:42:19	Ana Dulce	Félix	POR	23.10.82	4		New York	6	Nov
2:25:44	LM	1:26:09	1:43:34	Rita	Jeptoo	KEN	15.2.81	5		Frankfurt	30	Oct
2:25:46	PW	1:25:31	1:42:19	Kim	Smith	NZL	19.11.81	5		New York	6	Nov
				(50)								
2:25:52	LM	1:25:35	1:42:44	Lornah	Kiplagat	NED	1.5.74	3		Amsterdam	16	Oct
2:25:57	LM	1:24:42	1:41:28	Genet	Getaneh	ETH	6.1.86	4		Amsterdam	16	Oct
2:25:57	PW	1:23:57	1:40:25	Caroline	Kilel	KEN	21.3.81	6		New York	6	Nov
2:26:04	L			Yeshi	Esayias	ETH	28.12.85	2		Daegu	10	Apr
2:26:10	LM	1:26:13	1:43:23	Rosaria	Console	ITA	17.12.79	7		Berlin	25	Sep
2:26:12	L				Wang Jiali	CHN	1.2.86	1	NC	Dalian	30	Apr
2:26:15	LM	1:26:08	1:43:34	Nadia	Ejjafini	ITA	8.11.80	6		Frankfurt	30	Oct
2:26:17	LM	1:24:18	1:41:53	Belaynesh	Zemedkun	ETH	23.12.87	4		Chicago	9	Oct
2:26:21	LM	1:26:57	1:43:53	Goitetom	Haftu	ETH	.87	2		Roma	20	Mar
2:26:21	LM			Fate	Tola	ETH	22.10.87	1		Wien	17	Apr
				(60)								
2:26:28	LW		1:41:38		Zhu Xiaolin	CHN	20.2.84	14		London	17	Apr
2:26:31	LW		1:42:21	Inga	Abitova	RUS	6.3.82	15		London	17	Apr
2:26:32	LW	1:26:41	1:43:59	Ryoko	Kizaki	JPN	21.6.85	1		Yokohama	20	Nov
2:26:33	L			Alemitu	Abera	ETH	.86	3		Daegu	10	Apr
2:26:33	LM	1:26:56	1:44:12	Valeria	Straneo	ITA	5.4.76	8		Berlin	25	Sep
2:26:39	LM	1:25:34	1:42:47	Nailya	Yulamanova	RUS	6.9.80	5		Amsterdam	16	Oct
2:26:41					Wei Xiaojie	CHN	.89	1		Zhengzhou	27	Mar
2:26:41	LM	1:25:37	1:43:14	Christelle	Daunay	FRA	5.12.74	5		Chicago	9	Oct
2:26:49					Chen Rong	CHN	18.5.88	2	NC	Dalian	30	Apr
2:26:51				Robe	Guta	ETH	12.10.86	1	Dong-A	Seoul	20	Mar
				(70)								
2:26:52	LM	1:25:28	1:42:36	Melkaw	Gizaw	ETH	.90	6		Eindhoven	9	Oct
2:26:53	LM			Diane	Chepkemoi	KEN	.87	6		Dubai	21	Jan
2:26:54	LW	1:24:42	1:42:22	Noriko	Matsuoka	JPN	2.5.79	16		London	17	Apr
2:26:55	LW	1:25:43	1:43:08	Mai	Ito	JPN	23.5.84	2		Osaka	30	Jan
2:26:56	LM	1:26:07	1:43:18	Lishan	Dula	BRN	17.2.87	3		Rotterdam	10	Apr
2:26:58	LM	1:24:59	1:42:05	Kaoru	Nagao	JPN	26.9.89	4		Yokohama	20	Feb
2:27:00	LM			Alessandra	Aguilar	ESP	1.7.78	4		Rotterdam	10	Apr
2:27:02	LW		1:43:40	Madaí	Pérez	MEX	2.2.80	17		London	17	Apr
2:27:03	DM			Amy	Hastings	USA	21.1.84	2	122mdh	Los Angeles	20	Mar
2:27:06	PW	1:25:01	1:42:05	Caroline	Rotich	KEN	13.5.84	7		New York	6	Nov
				(80)								
2:27:07	LM		1:44:08	Margarita	Plaksina	RUS	1.10.77	5		Paris	10	Apr
2:27:10	LM		1:44:52	Yuliya	Ruban	UKR	6.10.83	1		Torino	13	Nov
2:27:13					Wei Yanan	CHN	6.12.81	2	Dong-A	Seoul	20	Mar
2:27:15	LM			Worknesh	Kidane	ETH	21.11.81	8		Dubai	21	Jan
2:27:16	LW	1:25:59	1:43:36	Karolina	Jarzynska	POL	6.9.81	5		Yokohama	20	Feb
2:27:17	LM	1:25:18		Peninah	Arusei	KEN	23.2.79	3		Wien	17	Apr
2:27:24	LW	1:26:41	1:43:59	Mara	Yamauchi	GBR	13.8.73	3		Yokohama	20	Nov
2:27:26	LW	1:25:45	1:43:09	Chika	Horie	JPN	15.2.81	3		Osaka	30	Jan
2:27:30	PM	1:25:27	1:42:35	Harun	Makda	ETH	.88	2		Venezia	23	Oct
2:27:34	LM	1:26:08	1:43:34	Eshetu	Degefa	ETH	.82	8		Frankfurt	30	Oct
				(90)								
2:27:47	LM			Ashu	Kasim	ETH	20.10.84	2		Houston	30	Jan
2:27:51	LM		1:43:41	Silviya	Skvortsova	RUS	16.11.74	3		Toronto	16	Oct
2:27:55	L				Yin Yuanyuan	CHN	31.5.91	3	NC	Dalian	30	Apr
2:28:01	L		1:44:35	Fatuma	Sado	ETH	11.10.91	2		Istanbul	16	Oct
2:28:08	LM	1:26:08	1:43:34	Sabrina	Mockenhaupt	GER	6.12.80	9		Frankfurt	30	Oct
2:28:14	LM			Tetyana	Hamera-Shmyrko	UKR	1.6.83	1		Kraków	17	Apr
2:28:24	LW		1:44:12	Jo	Pavey	GBR	20.9.73	19		London	17	Apr
2:28:24				Yeshimabet	Tadesse	ETH	.88	1	Twin C	St. Paul	2	Oct
2:28:28	LM	1:26:58		Netsanet	Achamo	ETH	14.12.87	4		Roma	20	Mar
2:28:32	L			Jemima	Jelagat	KEN	.85	1		Castellón	11	Dec
				(100)								

Mark		Name	Nat	Born	Date
2:28:34	DM	Olena Shurhno	UKR	8.1.78	5 Jun
2:28:38		Tsega Gelaw	ETH	9.10.90	16 Oct
2:28:43	LM	Alena Samokhvalova	RUS	21.11.80	30 Oct
2:28:49	LM	Noriko Higuchi	JPN	23.5.85	27 Feb
2:28:49	LM	Eri Okubo	JPN	2.6.83	25 Sep
2:28:49	LM	Susanne Hahn	GER	23.4.78	30 Oct
2:29:00	LW	Alevtina Ivanova	RUS	22.5.75	20 Feb
2:29:03	LM	Yoko Shibui	JPN	14.3.79	27 Feb
2:29:03	PW	Galina Bogomolova	RUS	15.10.77	6 Nov
2:29:04		Elfenesh Alemu	ETH	10.6.75	16 Jan
2:29:09	LM	Meseret Legesse	ETH	.87	10 Apr
2:29:14	LW	Sharon Cherop	KEN	16.3.84	27 Aug
2:29:23	LM	Miranda Boonstra	NED	29.8.72	25 Sep
2:29:23	LM	Lisa Weightman	AUS	16.1.79	30 Oct
2:29:25	PM	Florence Chepsoi	KEN	1.2.84	17 Apr
2:29:27	LM	Claire Hallissey	GBR	17.3.83	9 Oct
2:29:35	LM	Stephanie Rothstein	USA	14.1.84	30 Jan
2:29:36	LM	Julia Mombi	KEN	25.9.85	16 Oct
2:29:37	LM	Workitu Ayanu	ETH	19.4.87	20 Mar
2:29:40	L	Jia Chaofeng	CHN	16.11.88	30 Apr
2:29:41	LM	Elza Kireyeva	RUS	26.3.79	17 Apr
2:29:46	L	Sun Weiwei	CHN	13.1.85	30 Apr
2:29:47	LM	Aberesh Bedasa	ETH	.85	16 Oct
2:29:47	LM	Raza Drasdauskaite	LTU	20.3.81	13 Nov
2:29:50	L	Yue Chao	CHN	5.1.91	30 Apr
2:29:52	LW	Madoka Ogi	JPN	26.10.83	17 Apr
2:29:57		Lyudmila Biktasheva	RUS	25.7.74	15 Oct
2:29:59		Renè Kalmer	RSA	3.11.80	20 Nov
2:30:00	LW	Mizuho Nasukawa	JPN	22.11.79	17 Apr
2:30:00	LW	Louise Damen	GBR	12.10.82	17 Apr
2:30:14		Catherine Ndereba	KEN	21.7.72	16 Oct
2:30:19A		Margaret Toroitich	KEN	29.12.79	30 Oct
2:30:24		Marta Ayele	ETH	.85	27 Mar
2:30:25	PM	Fantu Eticha	ETH	.91	23 Oct
2:30:27		Lyubov Morgunova	RUS	14.1.71	14 May
2:30:27		Jin Lingling	CHN	16.1.87	16 Oct
2:30:30		Valentina Galimova	RUS	11.5.86	14 May
2:30:36		Mika Okunaga	JPN	27.10.82	30 Jan
2:30:37		Helaria Johannes	NAM	13.8.80	31 Oct
2:30:38	LM	Iwona Lewandowska	POL	19.2.85	25 Sep
2:30:39		Delelecha Yihunlish	ETH	.81	17 Jun
2:30:42	LW	Mayumi Fujita	JPN	26.5.83	20 Feb
2:30:46		Lisa Christina Stublic	CRO	18.5.84	10 Apr
2:30:53		Teamo Shumye	ETH	.80	20 Nov
2:30:55	LM	Shiteye Gemechu	ETH	17.6.80	13 Nov
2:31:10		Misaki Katsumata	JPN	26.12.85	27 Feb
2:31:10		Asha Gigi	ETH	15.10.73	8 May
2:31:10		Hellen Kimutai	KEN	28.12.77	15 Oct
2:31:11	LM	Marina Kovaleva	RUS	19.8.84	10 Apr
2:31:16		Albina Mayorova	RUS	16.5.77	16 Oct
2:31:22	LW	Magdalena Lewy Boulet	USA	1.8.73	17 Apr
2:31:28	LW	Risa Shigemoto	JPN	29.8.87	17 Apr
2:31:28		Svitlana Stanko-Klymenko	UKR	13.5.76	25 Sep
2:31:29		Irene Jerotich	KEN	8.9.74	27 Aug
2:31:30		Emmah Muthoni	KEN	4.1.81	4 Sep
2:31:32		Everlyne Lagat	KEN	2.12.80	17 Jun
2:31:38		Seada Kedir	ETH	.88	27 Nov
2:31:41		Woynishet Girma	ETH	.86	4 Dec
2:31:45	LM	Azalech Woldeselassie	ETH	4.5.88	4 Dec
2:31:49		Amane Gobena	ETH	1.9.82	2 Jan
2:31:50		Dorothy McMahan	USA	6.11.76	17 Jun
2:31:52	PW	Molly Pritz	USA	7.4.88	6 Nov
2:31:54A		Winfrida Kwamboka	KEN	4.3.82	30 Oct
2:31:57		Nadezhda Leontyeva	RUS	26.6.84	14 May
2:31:59	LM	Olga Dubovskaya	BLR	2.10.83	30 Oct
2:32:02	LM	Sumiko Suzuki	JPN	10.3.86	27 Feb
2:32:04		Tera Moody	USA	18.12.80	27 Aug
2:32:06		Ro Un-ok	PRK	14.11.89	10 Apr
2:32:06	DM	Salina Kosgei	KEN	16.11.76	5 Jun
2:32:09	LM	Olivera Jevtic	SRB	24.7.77	13 Nov
2:32:10		Desta Girma	ETH	29.3.87	2 Jan
2:32:11		Rehima Kedir	ETH	11.12.85	10 Apr
2:32:11	LM	Nina Podnebesnova	RUS	6.3.80	20 Mar
2:32:12		Esther Wanjiru	KEN	27.3.77	9 Oct
2:32:12	LM	Beata Naigambo	NAM	11.3.80	16 Oct
2:32:12		Emily Rotich	KEN	29.8.79	31 Oct
2:32:13	LM	He Yinli	CHN	1.2.88	4 Dec
2:32:22		Deribe Godana	ETH	.88	9 Oct
2:32:24		Mekuria Aberume	ETH		2 Oct
2:32:24		Radiya Adlo	ETH	22.9.89	31 Oct
2:32:26		Chung Yun-hee	KOR	3.1.83	20 Mar
2:32:26	LM	Ayele Lemma	ETH		16 Oct
2:32:28		Bizunesh Urgesa	ETH	18.6.89	16 Jan
2:32:31		Doreen Kitaka	KEN	.83	17 Jun
2:32:31A		Emily Chepkorir	KEN	.85	30 Oct
2:32:32		Gladys Tejeda	PER	30.9.85	20 Mar
2:32:33	LM	Andrea Mayr	AUT	15.10.79	30 Oct
2:32:39		Yuko Machida	JPN	11.8.80	10 Apr
2:32:42		Halima Hassen	ETH-J	10.11.92	22 May
2:32:44		Adriana Nelson	ROU/USA	31.1.80	30 Jan
2:32:44		Rose Nyangacha	KEN	28.10.76	4 Dec
2:32:47	LM	Olga Ochal	UKR	15.7.85	17 Apr
2:32:48		Lidia Simon	ROU	4.9.73	30 Oct
2:32:51	LM	Rina Yamazaki	JPN	6.5.88	27 Feb
2:32:53		Natalya Sokolova	RUS	12.3.82	15 Oct
2:32:54	L	Zheng Wenrong	CHN	26.11.88	30 Apr
2:32:55	LM	Elizabeth Chemweno	KEN	13.7.78	17 Apr
2:32:55		Leah Malot	KEN	7.6.72	2 Oct
2:32:55		Emily Harrison	USA	13.2.86	2 Oct
2:32:57		Lee Sun-young	KOR	20.8.84	20 Mar
2:32:57		Vanessa Veiga	ESP	20.7.79	4 Dec
2:32:58A		Beatrice Toroitich	KEN	15.12.81	30 Oct

(202)

Excessively Downhill

Boston course is downhill overall (139m) and sometimes, as in 2011, strongly wind-aided, as is Sacramento (104m dh)

Mark			Name	Nat	Born	Pos	Venue	Date
2:22:36	1:25:01	1:41:49	Caroline Kilel	KEN	21.3.81	1	Boston	18 Apr
2:22:38	1:25:03	1:41:54	Desiree Davila	USA	26.7.83	2	Boston	18 Apr
2:22:42		1:41:50	Sharon Cherop	KEN	16.3.84	3	Boston	18 Apr
2:24:26			Caroline Rotich	KEN	13.5.84	4	Boston	18 Apr
2:24:52			Kara Goucher	USA	9.7.78	5	Boston	18 Apr
2:25:08			Dire Tune	ETH	19.5.85	6	Boston	18 Apr
2:26:15			Worknesh Kidane	ETH	21.11.81	7	Boston	18 Apr
2:26:17			Yolanda Caballero	COL	19.3.82	8	Boston	18 Apr
2:26:34			Alice Timbilil	KEN	16.6.83	9	Boston	18 Apr
2:27:00			Yuliya Ruban	UKR	6.10.83	10	Boston	18 Apr

Mark	Name	Nat	Born	Date		Mark	Name	Nat	Born	Date
2:28:48	Woynishet Girma	ETH	.86	18 Apr		2:29:20	Tatyana Pushkareva	RUS	26.9.85	18 Apr
2:29:06	Hellen Mugo	KEN	12.12.85	18 Apr		2:29:54	Clara Grandt	USA	24.3.87	18 Apr

Drugs disqualification

Mark			Name	Nat	Born	Pos	Venue	Date
2:27:29	LM	1:45:02	Tatyana Aryasova #	RUS	2.4.79	(1)	Tokyo	27 Feb
2:31:28			Rose Chesire	KEN		(1)	Macau	4 Dec

JUNIORS

Mark	Name	Nat	Born	Pos	Meet	Venue	Date
2:24:32	Merima Mohammed	ETH	10.6.92	4		Frankfurt	30 Oct
2:26:57[2]						Mumbai	16 Jan
2:28:15[1]						Düsseldorf	8 May
2:32:42	Halima Hassen	ETH-J	10.11.92	2	NC	Hamburg	22 May
2:35:47[2]						Kosice	2 Oct
2:35:47	Abebech Tsegaye	ETH-Y	.96	2		Luxembourg	11 Jun
2:39:32	Shin Sa-hin	KOR	23.4.92	15		Daegu	10 Apr
2:40:51	Anastasiya Zuyeva	RUS	1.2.92	8		Moskva	14 May

Mark	Name		Nat	Born	Pos	Meet	Venue	Date

50 KILOMETRES

In 56k at Cape Town 23 Apr: Olesya Nurgaliyeva RUS 1.9.76 3:10:18, Yelena Nurgaliyeva RUS 1.9.76 3:13:59, Mamor-allo Tjoka LES .85 3:15:07, Nina Podnebesnova RUS 6.3.80 3:16:25, Simona Staicu HUN .5.5.71 3:18:56

Mark	Name		Nat	Born	Pos	Meet	Venue	Date
3:17:30	Emma	Gooderham	GBR	20.2.71	1	WTrophy	Assen	20 Aug

100 KILOMETRES

Mark	Name		Nat	Born	Pos	Meet	Venue	Date
7:27:19	Marina	Bychkova	RUS	18.12.75	1	IAU-WCh	Winschoten	10 Sep
7:37:40	Marija	Vrajic	CRO	22.9.76	1		Torhout	18 Jun
7:41:06	Joanna	Zakrzewski	GBR	19.1.76	2	IAU-WCh	Winschoten	10 Sep
7:42:05	Lindsay	van Aswegen	RSA	29.8.68	3	IAU-WCh	Winschoten	10 Sep
7:45:27	Irina	Vishnevskaya	RUS	2.6.82	4	IAU-WCh	Winschoten	10 Sep
7:46:34	Devon	Crosby-Helms	USA	23.6.82	1		Madison	9 Apr
7:51:10	Meghan	Arbogast	USA	16.4.61	5	IAU-WCh	Winschoten	10 Sep
7:53:18	Pam	Smith	USA	22.9.74	2		Madison	9 Apr
7:54:08	Naomi	Ochiai	JPN	13.5.80	1	L.Saroma	Yubetsu	26 Jun
7:54:20	Shiho	Katayama	JPN	18.12.77	2	L.Saroma	Yubetsu	26 Jun
7:54:59	Annette	Bednosky	USA	27.11.66	6	IAU-WCh	Winschoten	10 Sep
7:55:09	Gloria	Vinstedt	SWE	13.1.83	7	IAU-WCh	Winschoten	10 Sep
7:56:55	Michaela	Dimitriadu	CZE	23.12.73	1	NC	Plzen	26 Mar
7:59:06	Anne-Cécile	Fontaine	FRA	4.11.71	1	NC	Theillay	27 Aug
7:59:15	Yuko	Ito	JPN	3.8.72	3	L.Saroma	Yubetsu	26 Jun
8:00:37	Emily	Gelder	GBR	1.4.75	1	NC	Perth	27 Mar
8:02:15	Wakako	Oyagi	JPN	6.5.78	4	L.Saroma	Yubetsu	26 Jun
8:02:17	Sabine	Hofer	AUT	11.9.61	8	IAU-WCh	Winschoten	10 Sep
8:02:25	Mai	Fujisawa	JPN	21.9.74	5	L.Saroma	Yubetsu	26 Jun
8:04:15	Yukiko	Oda	JPN	31.1.74	6	L.Saroma	Yubetsu	26 Jun
8:06:29	Kerry	Koen	RSA	8.11.75	9	IAU-WCh	Winschoten	10 Sep
8:06:54	Mariya	Aksenova	RUS	25.10.88	10	IAU-WCh	Winschoten	10 Sep
8:08:27	Tressa	Lindenberg	AUS	6.3.69	1		Broadbeach	12 Jun
8:08:42	Brigitte	Bec	FRA	7.4.64	2	NC	Theillay	27 Aug

Mark	Name		Nat		Pos		Mark	Name		Nat		Pos
8:10:11	Amy	Sproston	USA	5.2.74	10 Sep		8:13:01	Francesca	Marin	ITA	23.2.77	3 Apr
8:10:31	Mariya	Aksenova	RUS	25.10.88	14 May		8:13:14	Pamela	Veith	GER	10.7.73	30 Apr
8:10:59	Daniela	Sommer	SUI	.68	18 Jun		8:14:19	Caroline	Dubois	FRA	8.5.83	15 Oct
8:11:53	Monica	Casiraghi	ITA	4.4.69	3 Apr		8:14:22	Mikiko	Ota	JPN	28.4.75	26 Jun
							8:14:39	Tanja	Hooss	GER	25.9.67	10 Sep

Course alteration not checked by IAAF measurer

Mark	Name		Nat	Born	Pos	Meet	Venue	Date
7:45:28	Monica	Carlin	ITA	20.6.71	1		Faenza	29 May

24 HOURS

Mark	Name		Nat	Born	Pos	Meet	Venue	Date
255.503k t	Mami	Kudo	JPN	17.7.64	1		Soochow	11 Dec
247.076	Elizabeth	Hawker	GBR	10.3.76	1	Comm	Llandudno	24 Sep
232.904	Connie	Gardner	USA	6.11.63	1		Cleveland	18 Sep
232.418	Kiyoko	Shirakawa	JPN	22.6.66	1	Shinjuku	Tokyo	15 Oct
230.410	Sumie	Inagaki	JPN	6.4.66	1		Athínai	10 Apr
228.490	Antje	Krause	GER	1.5.72	1		Reichenbach	24 Jul
227.346	Anne-Marie	Vernet	FRA	15.12.67	1		Aulnat	11 Nov
224.714	Cecile	Nissen	FRA	21.3.72	2		Aulnat	11 Nov
223.659	Yuko	Ito	JPN	3.8.72	2	Shinjuku	Tokyo	15 Oct
221.681	Anna	Grundahl	SWE	6.4.76	1		Rønne	19 Jun
220.676	Aleksandra	Niwinska	POL	23.1.86	1		Katowice	18 Sep
220.480	Emily	Gelder	GBR	1.4.75	2	Comm	Llandudno	24 Sep
218.759	Leonie	van den Haak	NED	14.3.81	3		Aulnat	11 Nov
218.227	Denise	Paiva Campos	BRA	12.7.79	1		Rio de Janeiro	18 Sep
217.631	Meredith	Quinlan	AUS	16.4.72	3	Comm	Llandudno	24 Sep

Mark	Name		Nat		Pos		Mark	Name		Nat		Pos
216.246	Pascale	Bouly	FRA	9.1.62	11 Nov		214.368	Sylvie	Peuch	FRA	22.11.61	25 Apr
215.862	Akie	Kuwabara	JPN	2.7.66	15 Oct		212.031	Debra	Horn	USA	11.3.59	18 Sep
214.942	Catherine	Massif	FRA	6.8.64	9 Oct		211.683	Veronika	Görög	HUN	21.9.81	17 Apr

Indoors

Mark	Name		Nat	Born	Pos	Meet	Venue	Date
240.631	Sumie	Inagaki	JPN	6.4.66	1		Espoo	30 Jan
217.809	Valerie	Glavin	IRL	13.2.75	2		Espoo	30 Jan
211.738	Maria	Jansson	SWE	10.7.85	1		Oslo	27 Nov

2000 METRES STEEPLECHASE

Mark	Name		Nat	Born	Pos	Meet	Venue	Date
6:16.41	Norah	Tanui	KEN-Y	2.10.95	1	WY	Villeneuve d'Ascq	10 Jul
6:19.20	Giulia	Martinelli	ITA	16.6.91	1		Rieti	11 Sep
6:20.24mx	Aleksandra	Lisowska	POL	12.12.90	1		Olsztyn	12 Sep
6:20.98	Fadwa Sidi	Madane	MAR-Y	20.11.94	2	WY	Villeneuve d'Ascq	10 Jul
6:21.85	Lilian	Chemweno	KEN-Y	10.5.95	3	WY	Villeneuve d'Ascq	10 Jul
6:22.45	Gesa-Felicitas	Krause	GER-J	3.8.92	1		Pfungstadt	25 May
6:25.31	Bridget	Franek	USA	8.11.87	1		Eugene	19 Mar
6:26.56	Sandra	Michalak	POL	1.4.87	1		Sosnowiec	16 Jul

Mark	Name		Nat	Born	Pos	Meet	Venue	Date	
6:28.21	Motu	Megersa	ETH-Y	22.10.94	4	WY	Villeneuve d'Ascq	10	Jul
6:29.08	Tejinesh	Gebisa	ETH-Y	3.3.95	5	WY	Villeneuve d'Ascq	10	Jul
6:29.20	Madeleine	Meyers	USA-Y	30.7.94	6	WY	Villeneuve d'Ascq	10	Jul
6:29.56	Brianna	Nerud	USA-Y	16.9.94	7	WY	Villeneuve d'Ascq	10	Jul

MORE JUNIORS

Mark	Name		Nat	Born	Pos	Meet	Venue	Date	
6:32.86	Dana Elena	Loghin	ROU-Y	23.10.94	1	Balk C	Bursa	13	Aug
6:33.01	Mary Kate	Anselmini	USA-J	22.4.93	1		Port Jefferson	4	Jun
6:34.38	Nancy	Cheptegei	UGA-Y	12.12.94	8	WY	Villeneuve d'Ascq	10	Jul
6:34.71	Oona	Kettunen	FIN-Y	10.2.94	9	WY	Villeneuve d'Ascq	10	Jul
6:35.40	Belén	Casetta	ARG-Y	26.9.94	4h1	WY	Villeneuve d'Ascq	8	Jul
6:35.74	Gulshat	Fazlitdinova	RUS	28.8.92	1h1	EJ	Tallinn	21	Jul
6:37.27	Amy-Eloise	Neale	GBR	5.8.95	11	WY	Villeneuve d'Ascq	10	Jul
6:39.61	Regina	Neumayer	GER	24.7.92	1	NC-j	Jena	5	Aug

3000 METRES STEEPLECHASE

Mark	Name		Nat	Born	Pos	Meet	Venue	Date	
9:07.03	Yuliya	Zaripova	RUS	26.4.86	1	WCh	Daegu	30	Aug
9:11.97	Habiba	Ghribi	TUN	9.4.84	2	WCh	Daegu	30	Aug
9:12.89	Milcah	Chemos	KEN	24.2.86	1	GGala	Roma	26	May
9:15.04	Sofia	Assefa	ETH	14.11.87	2	GGala	Roma	26	May
9:15.43		Zaripova			1	VD	Bruxelles	16	Sep
9:16.44		Chemos			1	DL	Doha	6	May
9:16.57		Ghribi			2	VD	Bruxelles	16	Sep
9:16.94	Mercy	Njoroge	KEN	10.6.86	2	DL	Doha	6	May
9:17.16		Chemos			3	WCh	Daegu	30	Aug
9:17.88		Njoroge			4	WCh	Daegu	30	Aug
9:19.20	Lydia	Rotich	KEN	8.8.88	3	DL	Doha	6	May
9:19.87		Chemos			1	Athl	Lausanne	30	Jun
9:20.09		Njoroge			3	VD	Bruxelles	16	Sep
9:20.33		Ghribi			3	GGala	Roma	26	May
9:20.37	Birtukan	Adamu	ETH-J	29.4.92	4	GGala	Roma	26	May
9:20.50		Assefa			2	Athl	Lausanne	30	Jun
9:20.51		Njoroge			3	Athl	Lausanne	30	Jun
9:21.02		Ghribi			4	Athl	Lausanne	30	Jun
9:21.20		Assefa			4	VD	Bruxelles	16	Sep
9:21.41		Chemos			5	VD	Bruxelles	16	Sep
9:22.80		Chemos			1	LGP	London (CP)	6	Aug
9:23.82		Zaripova			1	NC	Cheboksary	23	Jul
9:23.88	Hiwot	Ayalew	ETH	6.3.90	2	LGP	London (CP)	6	Aug
9:24.06	Binnaz	Uslu	TUR	12.3.85	1h1	WCh	Daegu	27	Aug
9:24.56		Ghribi			2h1	WCh	Daegu	27	Aug
9:24.95		Njoroge			3h1	WCh	Daegu	27	Aug
9:25.08		Assefa			4	DL	Doha	6	May
9:25.16		Rotich			5	GGala	Roma	26	May
9:25.74		Rotich			5	WCh	Daegu	30	Aug
9:25.87		Assefa			1	BrGP	Birmingham	10	Jul
9:25.96	Hanane	Ouhaddou	MAR	.82	4h1	WCh	Daegu	27	Aug
	(31/10)								
9:26.03	Lyudmila	Kuzmina	RUS	13.8.87	2	NC	Cheboksary	23	Jul
9:26.51	Mekdes	Bekele	ETH	20.1.87	7	VD	Bruxelles	16	Sep
9:28.27	Birtukan	Fente	ETH	18.6.89	6	Athl	Lausanne	30	Jun
9:29.39	Lyubov	Kharlamova	RUS	2.3.81	3	NC	Cheboksary	23	Jul
9:29.75	Gulnara	Galkina	RUS	9.7.78	3	DL	New York	11	Jun
9:30.23	Almaz	Ayana	ETH	21.11.91	1		Bottrop	15	Jul
9:30.73	Lidya	Chepkurui	KEN	23.8.84	2		Barcelona	22	Jul
9:32.74	Gesa-Felicitas	Krause	GER-J	3.8.92	9	WCh	Daegu	30	Aug
9:34.12	Christine	Muyanga	KEN	21.3.91	2	Odlozil	Praha	13	Jun
9:35.11	Sara	Moreira #	POR	17.10.85	2	ET	Stockholm	18	Jun
	(20)								
9:35.46	Barbara	Parker	GBR	8.11.82	1	Spitzen	Luzern	21	Jul
9:37.16	Emma	Coburn	USA	19.10.90	8	LGP	London (CP)	6	Aug
9:37.60	Fionnuala	Britton	IRL	24.9.84	5	DL	New York	11	Jun
9:37.85	Purity	Kirui	KEN	13.8.91	3	Odlozil	Praha	13	Jun
9:37.95	Hatti	Dean	GBR	2.2.82	6	GGala	Roma	26	May
9:38.07	Korine	Hinds	JAM	18.1.76	1		Gent	30	Jul
9:38.42	Cristina Casandra		ROU	21.10.77	1	NC	Bucuresti	9	Aug
9:38.92	Bridget	Franek	USA	8.11.87	6	DL	New York	11	Jun
9:39.21	Giulia	Martinelli	ITA	16.6.91	9	VD	Bruxelles	16	Sep
9:39.48	Sara	Hall	USA	15.4.83	7	GGala	Roma	26	May
	(30)								

Mark	Name		Nat	Born	Pos	Meet	Venue	Date	
9:39.53	Iríni	Kokkinaríou	GRE	14.2.81	2	WMilG	Río de Janeiro	19	Jul
9:39.83	Gülcan	Mingir	TUR	21.5.89	1		Bursa	23	Jun
9:40.12		Li Zhenzhu	CHN	13.12.85	1	Déca	Nice	18	Sep
9:40.28	Diana	Martín	ESP	1.4.81	3		Barcelona	22	Jul
9:40.63	Delilah	DiCrescenzo	USA	28.2.83	5	BrGP	Birmingham	10	Jul
9:41.12	Stephanie	Garcia	USA	3.5.88	2		Gent	30	Jul
9:41.73	Marcela	Lustigová	CZE	11.11.82	5	Odlozil	Praha	13	Jun
9:41.87	Beverly	Ramos	PUR	24.8.87	11	LGP	London (CP)	6	Aug
9:42.51	Salima	El Ouali Alami	MAR	29.12.83	3	WMilG	Río de Janeiro	19	Jul
9:42.91	Stephanie	Reilly	IRL	23.2.78	7	DL	New York	11	Jun
	(40)								
9:43.23	Eunice	Jepkorir	KEN	17.2.82	1		Cáceres	29	Jun
9:43.28	Jana	Sussmann	GER	12.10.90	3	ET	Stockholm	18	Jun
9:43.52	Olga	Dereveva	RUS	5.4.85	5	NC	Cheboksary	23	Jul
9:43.71		Fu Tinglian	CHN	5.7.87	1	NC	Hefei	10	Sep
9:43.95	Lisa	Aguilera	USA	30.11.79	1		Los Angeles (ER)	21	May
9:44.18	Sophie	Duarte	FRA	31.7.81	8	BrGP	Birmingham	10	Jul
9:44.21	Katarzyna	Kowalska	POL	7.4.85	1	NC	Bydgoszcz	13	Aug
9:44.60	Natalya	Tarantinova	RUS	28.11.87	6	NC	Cheboksary	23	Jul
9:44.80	Eilish	McColgan	GBR	25.11.90	12	LGP	London (CP)	6	Aug
9:45.1A	Norah	Tanui	KEN-Y	2.10.95	4	NC	Nairobi	16	Jul
	(50)								
9:45.21		Jin Yuan	CHN	11.2.88	3	WUG	Shenzhen	19	Aug
9:45.24	Justyna	Korytkowska	POL	12.3.86	2	NC	Bydgoszcz	13	Aug
9:45.85	Layes	Abdullayeva	AZE	29.5.91	1		Tbilisi	9	Oct
9:46.07	Karoline Bjerkeli	Grøvdal	NOR	14.6.90	2	ET-1	Izmir	18	Jun
9:46.15	Mardrea	Hyman	JAM	22.12.72	2	NC	Kingston	25	Jun
9:46.91	Svitlana	Shmidt	UKR	20.3.90	1	NC	Donetsk	4	Aug
9:47.03	Lindsey	Allen	USA	30.6.86	3		Gent	30	Jul
9:48.22	Mariya	Shatalova	UKR	3.3.89	3	EU23	Ostrava	16	Jul
9:48.77	Matylda	Szlezak	POL	11.1.89	4	EU23	Ostrava	16	Jul
9:49.18	Etenesh	Diro	ETH	10.5.91	1		Besançon	14	Jun
	(60)								
9:49.46	Sandra	Eriksson	FIN	4.6.89	1		Lappeenranta	13	Aug
9:49.55		Yin Annuo	CHN-J	23.3.92	4	NC	Hefei	10	Sep
9:49.67	Lennie	Waite	GBR	4.5.86	2		Ninove	7	Aug
9:50.04	Sabine	Heitling	BRA	2.7.87	2h2	WUG	Shenzhen	17	Aug
9:50.13	Valeriya	Mara	UKR	22.2.83	2	NC	Donetsk	4	Aug
9:50.35	Veerle	Dejaeghere	BEL	1.8.73	4		Gent	30	Jul
9:50.47	Valentyna	Zhudina	UKR	12.3.83	3	NC	Donetsk	4	Aug
9:51.26	Shayla	Houlihan	USA	26.2.85	5		Gent	30	Jul
9:51.88	Minori	Hayakari	JPN	29.11.72	1		Naruto	24	Sep
9:51.96	Martina	Tresch	SUI	10.6.89	5	EU23	Ostrava	16	Jul
	(70)								
9:53.12	Rebeka	Stowe	USA	9.3.90	5	Jordan	Stanford	1	May
9:53.66	Mason	Cathey	USA	29.4.82	3h1	NC	Eugene	24	Jun
9:54.19	Tebogo	Masehla	RSA	6.1.79	2		Oordegem	4	Jun
9:54.50	Dorcus	Inzikuru	UGA	2.2.82	10	BrGP	Birmingham	10	Jul
9:54.71	Eva	Krchová	CZE	10.9.89	8	EU23	Ostrava	16	Jul
9:54.71	Silje	Fjørtoft	NOR	23.6.87	1	NC	Byrkjelo	13	Aug
9:54.72	Luiza	Gega	ALB	5.11.88	1	NC	Tirana	8	Jun
9:54.8A	Netsanet	Achamo	ETH	14.12.87	1	NC	Addis Ababa	4	May
9:55.01	Geneviève	Lalonde	CAN	5.9.91	7		Los Angeles (ER)	21	May
9:55.05	Natalya	Vlasova	RUS	19.7.88	7	NC	Cheboksary	23	Jul
	(80)								
9:55.17	Nicole	Bush	USA	4.4.86	11	DL	New York	11	Jun
9:56.04	Natalya	Aristarkhova	RUS	31.10.89	1	NC-23	Yerino	25	Jun
9:56.37	Shalaya	Kipp	USA	19.8.90	3	NCAA	Des Moines	11	Jun
9:56.43	Urszula	Necka	POL	28.6.84	3	NC	Bydgoszcz	13	Aug
9:56.68		Li Jiayi	CHN-J	26.12.93	1	City G	Nanchang	20	Oct
9:56.82	Stephanie	Pezzullo	USA	29.5.82	8		Los Angeles (ER)	21	May
9:56.87	Tsehaynesh	Tsale	ETH-J	29.1.93	8	Nebiolo	Torino	10	Jun
9:56.88	Polina	Jelizarova	LAT	1.5.89	9	EU23	Ostrava	16	Jul
9:56.98	Gulshat	Fazlitdinova	RUS-J	28.8.92	2	EJ	Tallinn	23	Jul
9:57.30	Salomé	Rocha	POR	25.4.90	9	Nebiolo	Torino	10	Jun
	(90)								
9:57.51	Alyssa	Kulik	USA	2.2.90	4	NCAA	Des Moines	11	Jun
9:57.79	Clarisse	Cruz	POR	9.7.78	2	ECCp	V.R. de Santo António	28	May
9:57.84	Zulema	Fuentes-Pila	ESP	25.5.77	5		Barcelona	22	Jul
9:58.00	Ángela	Figueroa	COL	28.6.84	1	SAmC	Buenos Aires	4	Jun
9:58.49	Veronicah	Jepkosgei	KEN-J	.93	10	Nebiolo	Torino	10	Jun

Mark	Name		Nat	Born	Pos	Meet	Venue	Date
9:58.61	Helen	Hofstede	NED	31.12.80	1		Birmingham	20 Aug
9:59.16	Lesley	Higgins	USA	10.6.80	9		Gent	30 Jul
9:59.17	Lyudmila	Lebedeva	RUS	23.5.90	1		Sochi	24 May
9:59.40	Selien	De Schrijder	BEL	10.11.86	10		Gent	30 Jul
9:59.44	Genevieve	LaCaze	AUS	4.8.89	5	NCAA	Des Moines	11 Jun
	(100)							
9:59.47	Élodie	Olivarès	FRA	22.5.76				27 Jun
9:59.6A	Jacqueline	Chepkok	KEN					4 Jun
9:59.61	Valentina	Costanza	ITA	27.2.87	15			Jul
9:59.79	Irina	Ananenko	BLR	9.1.86	7			Jul
9:59.89	Nolene	Conrad	RSA	26.7.85	17			Aug
9:59.99	Janica	Mäkelä	FIN	24.6.86	6			Aug
10:00.16	Nanae	Kuwashiro	JPN	16.10.82	14			May
10:00.19	María	Pardaloú	GRE	21.4.84	13			Jul
10:00.50	Hyvin	Jepkemoi	KEN-J	.92	13			Sep
10:00.58	Rini	Budiarti	INA	22.1.83	12			Nov
10:00.78	Ashley	Higginson	USA	17.3.89	27			May
10:01.18	Lucie	Sekanová	CZE	5.8.89	4			Jun
10:01.21	Olga	Gorshkova	RUS	9.3.83	23			Jul
10:01.24	Sudha	Singh	IND	25.6.86	14			Jun
10:01.49	Gezashign	Safarova	AZE	5.2.90	18			Jun
10:01.89	Sanaa	Koubaa	GER	6.1.85	27			Jun
10:01.9A	Zewdnesh	Belachew	ETH-J	.93	26			Mar
10:02.18	Jamie	Cheever	USA	28.2.87	14			Apr
10:02.24	Misato	Horie	JPN	10.3.87	11			Jun
10:02.55	Claire	Michel	USA	13.10.88	27			May
10:02.94	Nicol	Traynor	USA	6.5.89	9			Jun
10:02.94	Lindsay	Sundell	USA	21.4.86	24			Jun
10:03.04	Jekaterina	Patjuk	EST	6.4.83	29			Jul
10:03.32	Juliane	Masciana	USA	10.6.85	21			May
10:03.38	Erin	Bedell	USA	22.5.87	24			Jun
10:03.53		Zhang Xinyan	CHN-Y	9.2.94	10			Sep
10:03.74	Melanie	Thompson	USA	18.4.91	9			Jun
10:03.85	Sandra	López	MEX	16.4.84	14			Apr
10:03.90		Wang Kaiqiu	CHN	9.10.89	10			Sep
10:03.99	Estefanía	Tobal	ESP	9.5.91	22			Jul
10:04.00	Chantelle	Groenewoud	CAN	3.3.89	9			Jun
10:04.42		Nguyen Thi Phuong	VIE	2.9.90	12			Nov
10:04.5A	Regina	Cherotich	KEN		16			Apr
10:04.8A	Consulata	Chemutai	KEN	,83	4			Jun
10:04.85	Kara	June	USA	10.8.82	24			Jun
10:04.9A	Marceline	Ondieki	KEN	1.1.90	16			Jul
10:05.06	Yelena	Petrova	RUS	1.6.87	23			Jul
10:05.30	Janet	Achola	UGA	26.6.88	13			Jun
10:05.40	Azusa	Saito	JPN	9.6.86	11			Jun
10:05.54	Aleksandra	Alekseyenko	RUS	18.5.90	25			Jun
10:05.60	Meredith	McGregor	CAN	10.3.85	4			Jun
10:05.71	Dana	Buchanan	CAN	6.5.84	21			May
10:05.74	Eva	Arias	ESP	5.10.80	16			Sep
10:05.89	Sarah	Pease	USA	9.11.87	9			Jun
10:06.36	Eliane	Saholinirina	MAD	20.3.82	28			Jul
10:06.63	Klara	Bodinson	SWE	11.6.90				14 Apr
10:06.69	Verena	Dreier	GER	15.1.85				27 Jun
10:07.18	Lois	Ricardi Keller	USA	29.9.84				1 May
10:07.79	Megumi	Takayanagi	JPN-J	21.12.92				11 Sep
10:08.26	Oksana	Juravel	MDA	23.2.86				13 Jun
10:08.41	Kanako	Ushirogata	JPN	27.1.91				11 Jun
10:08.44	Katie	Hursey	USA	1.6.89				27 May
10:08.46	Kristen	Hemphill	USA	30.6.87				14 Apr
10:08.67	Claire	Navez	FRA	6.10.87				7 Aug
10:08.83	Mary	Dell	USA	31.7.88				28 Apr
10:08.84	Kerry	Harty	IRL	15.7.81				15 Jul
10:09.05	Charlotta	Fougberg	SWE	19.6.85				4 Jun
10:09.28		Fang Xiaoyu	CHN	6.3.87				10 Sep
10:09.50	Keara	Thomas	USA	15.8.89				9 May
10:09.54	Hannah	Moen	USA	1.11.89				24 Jun
10:09.64	Micaela	Bonessi	ITA	20.7.80				22 Jul
10:09.88	Jane	Rudkin	USA	15.5.80				21 May
10:10.09	Rimma	Antipina	RUS	4.11.87				23 Jul
10:10.14	Yevdokiya	Bukina	RUS-J	10.2.93				2 Jul
10:10.35	Ecaterina	Gheorghiu	ROU	15.10.89				27 May
10:10.55	Anna	Wojna	POL	28.9.86				11 Jun
10:10.58	Susanne	Lutz	GER	26.3.87				4 Jun
10:10.65		Wang Huan	CHN	12.1.89				10 Sep
10:10.66	Victoria	Mitchell	AUS	25.4.82				16 Apr
10:10.78	Mariola	Slusarczyk	POL	4.1.90				13 Aug
10:10.98	Silvia	Danekova	BUL	7.2.83				3 Jul
10:11.44	Kara	DeWalt	USA	27.7.88				1 May
10:11.57	Meghan	Cunningham	USA	2.3.89				27 May
10:11.73	Friederike	Feil	GER	23.5.86				15 Jul
10:11.77	Maggie	Callahan	USA	28.9.88				27 May
10:11.88	Tomoyo	Izumi	JPN	12.7.85				24 Apr
10:12.04	Katy	Andrews	USA					14 Apr
10:12.05	Özlem	Kaya	TUR	20.4.90				16 Jul
10:12.45	Martina	Barinová	CZE	28.1.90				9 Apr
10:12.87	Sarah	Madebach	USA	7.10.85				4 Jun
10:13.40		Pak Kum-hyang	PRK					28 May
10:13.42	Andrea	Parker	USA	10.10.82				11 Jun
10:13.73	Gamze	Bulut	TUR-J	3.8.92				5 Jun
10:14.17	Caroline	Mellsop	NZL	5.9.91				16 Apr
10:14.19		Wang Mei	CHN-J	22.12.93				20 Oct
10:14.40	Raquel	Gómez	ESP	30.9.82				2 Jun
10:14.46	Antonina	Behnke	POL	13.6.89				2 Jul
10:14.72	Miranda	Boonstra	NED	29.8.72				25 May
10:14.94	Rowena	Tam	USA	8.9.88				27 May
	(190)							

JUNIORS

See main list for top 8 juniors. 10 performances by 4 women to 9:50.0. Additional marks and further juniors:

Mark	Name		Nat	Born	Pos	Meet	Venue	Date
Adamu	9:26.31	5 Athl					Lausanne	30 Jun
	9:37.31	4h3 WCh					Daegu	27 Aug
	9:35.72	2					Bottrop	15 Jul
	9:41.95	7 BrGP					Birmingham	10 Jul
Krause	9:35.83	3h3 WCh					Daegu	27 Aug
	9:35.97	6 LGP					London (CP)	6 Aug
10:00.50	Hyvin	Jepkemoi	KEN	.92	1	AfG	Maputo	13 Sep
10:01.9A	Zewdnesh	Belachew (10)	ETH	.93	2		Addis Ababa	26 Mar
10:03.53		Zhang Xinyan	CHN-Y	9.2.94	5	NC	Hefei	10 Sep
10:07.79	Megumi	Takayanagi	JPN	21.12.92	1		Kumamoto	11 Sep
10:10.14	Yevdokiya	Bukina	RUS	10.2.93	2	NC-j	Cheboksary	2 Jul
10:13.73	Gamze	Bulut	TUR	3.8.92	1		Istanbul	5 Jun
10:14.19		Wang Mei	CHN	22.12.93	2	City G	Nanchang	20 Oct
10:15.82	Jannika	John	GER	26.12.92	7		Regensburg	4 Jun
10:17.37	Elena	Panaet	ROU	5.6.93	3	EJ	Tallinn	23 Jul
10:17.79		Wang Jing	CHN-Y	18.9.95	9	NC	Hefei	10 Sep
10:20.18	Eleanor	Wardleworth	AUS	5.8.93	3	NC	Melbourne	16 Apr
10:20.88	Justyna	Jendro	POL	2,2,92	1		Plock	15 Jun

60 METRES HURDLES INDOORS

Mark	Name		Nat	Born	Pos	Meet	Venue	Date
7.79A	Kellie	Wells	USA	16.7.82	1h2	NC	Albuquerque	27 Feb
7.79A		Wells			1	NC	Albuquerque	27 Feb
7.80	Carolin	Nytra	GER	26.2.85	1	EI	Paris (B)	4 Mar
7.80	Tiffany	Porter	GBR	13.11.87	2	EI	Paris (B)	4 Mar
7.82		Wells			1		Karlsruhe	13 Feb

Mark		Name	Nat	Born	Pos	Meet	Venue	Date
7.83	Christina	Vukicevic	NOR	18.6.87	3	EI	Paris (B)	4 Mar
7.84		Wells			1h1		Düsseldorf	11 Feb
7.85		Wells			1		Liévin	8 Feb
7.87		Wells			1h2		Liévin	8 Feb
7.87		Wells			1h2		Karlsruhe	13 Feb
7.87		Wells			1		Birmingham	19 Feb
	(11/4)							
7.89	Danielle	Carruthers	USA	22.12.79	1		Gent	13 Feb
7.93	Aleksandra	Antonova	RUS	24.3.80	2	Spark	Stuttgart	5 Feb
7.94	Lolo	Jones	USA	5.8.82	3	Spark	Stuttgart	5 Feb
7.95	Alina	Talay	BLR	14.5.89	2s1	EI	Paris (B)	4 Mar
7.96	Vonette	Dixon	JAM	26.11.75	3		Düsseldorf	11 Feb
7.96	Derval	O'Rourke	IRL	28.5.81	4	EI	Paris (B)	4 Mar
	(10)							
7.96	Brianna	Rollins	USA	18.8.91	1	NCAA	College Station	12 Mar
7.97	Jessica	Ennis	GBR	28.1.86	1	v4N	Glasgow	29 Jan
7.97	Alice	Decaux	FRA	10.4.85	1	NC	Aubière	19 Feb
7.99A	Queen	Harrison	USA	10.9.88	1h1	NC	Albuquerque	27 Feb
8.00	Lisa	Urech	SUI	27.7.89	1h1		Karlsruhe	13 Feb
8.00	Sandra	Gomis	FRA	21.11.83	2	NC	Aubière	19 Feb
8.00A	Nichole	Denby	USA	10.10.82	2	NC	Albuquerque	27 Feb
8.00	Lucie	Skrobáková	CZE	4.1.82	4s1	EI	Paris (B)	4 Mar
8.01	Yvette	Lewis	USA	16.3.85	4		Karlsruhe	13 Feb
8.01	Christina	Manning	USA	29.5.90	1	Big 10	West Lafayette	27 Feb
	(20)							
8.02	Kristi	Castlin	USA	7.7.88	2		Gent	13 Feb
8.02	Anastasiya	Solovyova	RUS	18.2.85	5s1	EI	Paris (B)	4 Mar
8.02	Elisabeth	Davin	BEL	3.6.81	5s2	EI	Paris (B)	4 Mar
8.03	Perdita	Felicien	CAN	29.8.80	3h1		Düsseldorf	11 Feb
8.03	Letecia	Wright	USA	1.2.89	2	Big 10	West Lafayette	27 Feb
8.03	Cindy	Roleder	GER	21.8.89	2	NC	Leipzig	27 Feb
8.03	Tiffani	McReynolds	USA	4.12.91	2	NCAA	College Station	12 Mar
8.04A	Celriece	Law	USA	2.9.86	4	NC	Albuquerque	27 Feb
8.06	Josephine	Onyia ¶	ESP	15.7.86	1		Zaragoza	29 Jan
8.06	Nia	Ali	USA	23.10.88	1		New York (Armory)	4 Feb
	(30)							
8.06	Jackie	Coward	USA	5.11.89	1		Fayetteville	11 Feb
8.07A	Indira	Spence	JAM	8.9.86	1	NCAA-II	Albuquerque	12 Mar
8.08	Chelsea	Carrier	USA	21.8.89	4	NCAA	College Station	12 Mar
8.09	Nadine	Hildebrand	GER	20.9.87	1h3	NC	Leipzig	27 Feb
8.09	Gabby	Mayo	USA	26.1.89	1h3	NCAA	College Station	11 Mar
8.10A	Tiki	James	USA	21.10.86	3h2	NC	Albuquerque	27 Feb
8.11	Michaylin	Golladay	USA	10.4.88	2		Clemson SC	11 Feb
8.11	Antoinette	Nana Djimou	FRA	2.8.85	1P2	EI	Paris (B)	4 Mar
8.12	Jasmin	Stowers	USA	23.9.91	1	SEC	Fayetteville	27 Feb
8.12	Angela	Whyte	CAN	22.5.80	1		Seattle	5 Mar
	(40)							
8.12	Tamika	Robinson	USA	24.8.89	2h1	NCAA	College Station	11 Mar
8.13	Jenna	Pletsch	GER	11.9.91	2		Karlsruhe	30 Jan
8.13	Yekaterina	Galitskaya	RUS	24.2.87	5	Winter	Moskva	6 Feb
8.13	Giulia	Pennella	ITA	27.10.89	1	NC-23	Ancona	12 Feb
8.14A	Candice	Davis	USA	26.10.85	1		Albuquerque	5 Feb
8.14	Yekaterina	Poplavskaya	BLR	7.5.87	7s2	EI	Paris (B)	4 Mar
8.15	Eline	Berings	BEL	28.5.86	2h2		Chemnitz	27 Jan
8.15	Anne	Zagré	BEL	13.3.90	4		Gent	13 Feb
8.15	Gemma	Bennett	GBR	4.1.84	5	BrGP	Birmingham	19 Feb
8.15A	Hyleas	Fountain	USA	14.1.81	4h2	NC	Albuquerque	27 Feb
	(50)							

100 METRES HURDLES

Mark		Name	Nat	Born	Pos	Meet	Venue	Date
12.28	1.1	Sally	Pearson	AUS	19.9.86	1	WCh	Daegu	3 Sep
12.36	0.3		Pearson			1s2	WCh	Daegu	3 Sep
12.47	1.1	Danielle	Carruthers	USA	22.12.79	2	WCh	Daegu	3 Sep
12.47	1.1	Dawn	Harper	USA	13.5.84	3	WCh	Daegu	3 Sep
12.48	0.7		Pearson			1	BrGP	Birmingham	10 Jul
12.50	1.8	Kellie	Wells	USA	16.7.82	1	NC	Eugene	26 Jun
12.51	0.9		Pearson			1	Herc	Monaco	22 Jul
12.52	0.7		Carruthers			2	BrGP	Birmingham	10 Jul
12.52	0.2		Pearson			1	WK	Zürich	8 Sep
12.53	-0.6		Pearson			1h2	WCh	Daegu	2 Sep

Mark		Name		Nat	Born	Pos	Meet	Venue	Date	
12.55	-0.6		Pearson			1h1	LGP	London (CP)	6	Aug
12.56	0.7	Tiffany	Porter	GBR	13.11.87	1s3	WCh	Daegu	3	Sep
12.57	1.9		Pearson			1h1	BrGP	Birmingham	10	Jul
12.58	1.3		Wells			1	DL	Doha	6	May
12.58	1.2		Harper			1s3	NC	Eugene	26	Jun
12.58	0.9		Wells			2	Herc	Monaco	22	Jul
12.58	-0.4		Pearson			1	LGP	London (CP)	6	Aug
12.59	1.8		Carruthers			2	NC	Eugene	26	Jun
12.60	0.9		Porter			3	Herc	Monaco	22	Jul
12.61	1.0		Carruthers			1h2	BrGP	Birmingham	10	Jul
12.62	0.5	Lisa	Urech	SUI	27.7.89	1		La Chaux-de-Fonds	3	Jul
12.62	1.0		Wells			2h2	BrGP	Birmingham	10	Jul
12.63	1.1		Porter			4	WCh	Daegu	3	Sep
12.64	1.3		Carruthers			2	DL	Doha	6	May
12.64	1.0		Carruthers			1	FBK	Hengelo	29	May
12.65	1.0		Wells			2	FBK	Hengelo	29	May
12.65	1.8		Harper			3	NC	Eugene	26	Jun
12.65	0.7		Carruthers			2s3	WCh	Daegu	3	Sep
12.65	0.4		Carruthers			1	VD	Bruxelles	16	Sep
12.67	1.3	Lolo	Jones	USA	5.8.82	3	DL	Doha	6	May
12.67	-0.4		Carruthers			2	LGP	London (CP)	6	Aug
		(31/7)								
12.73	1.3	Virginia	Crawford	USA	7.9.83	4	DL	Doha	6	May
12.73	1.3	Perdita	Felicien	CAN	29.8.80	1		Montreuil-sous-Bois	7	Jun
12.73	1.5	Nia	Ali	USA	23.10.88	1h4	NC	Eugene	25	Jun
		(10)								
12.73	-0.1	Phylicia	George	CAN	16.11.87	1s1	WCh	Daegu	3	Sep
12.76	0.1	Yvette	Lewis	USA	16.3.85	1	Gyulai	Budapest	30	Jul
12.76	0.3	Tatyana	Dektyareva	RUS	8.5.81	3s2	WCh	Daegu	3	Sep
12.77	0.9	Vonette	Dixon	JAM	26.11.75	1	CAC	Mayagüez	17	Jul
12.79	1.0	Christina	Vukicevic	NOR	18.6.87	1	Bisl	Oslo	9	Jun
12.79	1.5	Jessica	Ennis	GBR	28.1.86	1h1	LEAP	Loughborough	11	Aug
12.81	0.7	Loreal	Smith	USA	12.10.85	2		Baie Mahault	7	May
12.83	-0.3	Kristi	Castlin	USA	7.7.88	1	Odlozil	Praha	13	Jun
12.84	0.5	Derval	O'Rourke	IRL	28.5.81	2		La Chaux-de-Fonds	3	Jul
12.84	0.7	Nikkita	Holder	CAN	7.5.87	3s3	WCh	Daegu	3	Sep
		(20)								
12.86	0.9	Christina	Manning	USA	29.5.90	1	Big 10	Iowa City	15	May
12.87	1.5	Letecia	Wright	USA	1.2.89	1rB	DrakeR	Des Moines	30	Apr
12.87	1.2	Jackie	Coward	USA	5.11.89	4s3	NC	Eugene	26	Jun
12.87	0.7	Brigitte	Foster-Hylton	JAM	7.11.74	4s3	WCh	Daegu	3	Sep
12.88	1.0	Jasmin	Stowers	USA	23.9.91	1	SEC	Athens GA	15	May
12.88	-0.7	Angela	Whyte	CAN	22.5.80	2	Jerome	Burnaby	1	Jul
12.88	1.2	Queen	Harrison	USA	10.9.88	1	Znam	Zhukovskiy	3	Jul
12.89	0.9	Briggite	Merlano	COL	29.4.82	2	CAC	Mayagüez	17	Jul
12.89	0.0	Lucie	Skrobáková	CZE	4.1.82	3h4	WCh	Daegu	2	Sep
12.91	1.9	Tiki	James	USA	21.10.86	1rB		Gainesville	16	Apr
		(30)								
12.91	1.4	Candice	Davis	USA	26.10.85	3		Walnut	4	Jun
12.91	-1.0	Alina	Talay	BLR	14.5.89	1	EU23	Ostrava	16	Jul
12.91	2.0	Cindy	Roleder	GER	21.8.89	1		Fribourg	30	Jul
12.93	0.7	Cindy	Billaud	FRA	11.3.86	1		Paris (C)	10	Jul
12.93	1.0	Sandra	Gomis	FRA	21.11.83	1	NC	Albi	29	Jul
12.93	0.4	Hyleas	Fountain	USA	14.1.81	1H1	WCh	Daegu	29	Aug
12.93	0.3	Indira	Spence	JAM	8.9.86	5s2	WCh	Daegu	3	Sep
12.94	1.9	Tierra	Brown	USA	24.10.89	1	ACC	Durham NC	23	Apr
12.94	1.7		Sun Yawei	CHN	17.10.87	1	NGPF	Nanchang	17	Jul
12.94	0.9	Lina	Florez	COL	1.11.84	3	CAC	Mayagüez	17	Jul
		(40)								
12.95	1.9	Josephine	Onyia ¶	ESP	15.7.86	1		Valencia	11	Jun
12.95	0.7	Alice	Decaux	FRA	10.4.85	2		Paris (C)	10	Jul
12.95	-0.9	Natalya	Ivoninskaya	KAZ	22.2.85	1	NC	Almaty	28	Jul
12.95		Yekaterina	Galitskaya	RUS	24.2.87	1		Yerino	30	Jul
12.95	2.0	Beate	Schrott	AUT	15.4.88	2		Fribourg	30	Jul
12.96	-1.1	Lashinda	Demus	USA	10.3.83	4	MSR	Walnut	16	Apr
12.96	0.9	Lavonne	Idlette	DOM	31.10.85	3		Clermont	11	Jun
12.98	1.3	Nichole	Denby	USA	10.10.82	5	DL	Doha	6	May
12.99	0.0	Natasha	Ruddock	JAM	25.12.89	2		Gainesville	16	Apr
12.99	1.9	Brianna	Rollins	USA	18.8.91	2	ACC	Durham NC	23	Apr
		(50)								

Mark	Wind	Name		Nat	Born	Pos	Meet	Venue	Date
12.99	1.4	Vanneisha	Ivy	USA	26.10.87	1		Greensboro	15 May
12.99	-0.9	Anastasiya	Soprunova	KAZ	14.1.86	2	NC	Almaty	28 Jul
13.01	1.1	Kierre	Beckles	BAR	21.5.90	2q3	NCAA-E	Bloomington IN	28 May
13.01	1.0	Michaylin	Golladay	USA	10.4.88	1s3	NCAA	Des Moines	9 Jun
13.01	0.7	Marzia	Caravelli	ITA	23.10.81	1		Pergine Valsugana	23 Jul
13.01	0.1	Adrianna	Lamalle	FRA	27.9.82	1		La Roche-sur-Yon	10 Aug
13.01	0.4	Jessica	Zelinka	CAN	3.9.81	3H1	WCh	Daegu	29 Aug
13.02	0.4	Nina	Argunova	RUS	15.9.89	1h3	NC-23	Yerino	24 Jun
13.03	0.1	Josanne	Lucas	TRI	14.5.84	2		Auburn	16 Apr
13.03	1.4	Shermaine	Williams	JAM	4.2.90	2		Greensboro	15 May
		(60)							
13.04	1.9	Delloreen	Ennis	JAM	5.3.75	2rB		Gainesville	16 Apr
13.04	0.4	Irina	Shevchenko	RUS	2.9.75	1	Kuts	Moskva	6 Aug
13.05	2.0	Tiffani	McReynolds	USA	4.12.91	2h1	TexR	Austin	8 Apr
13.06	1.1	Irina	Lenskiy	ISR	12.6.71	1		Haifa	17 Feb
13.06	0.1	Lauren	Blackburn	USA	18.11.91	2	Pac10	Tucson	14 May
13.06	1.2	Chelsea	Carrier	USA	21.8.89	5s3	NC	Eugene	26 Jun
13.06	1.7		Zhang Rong	CHN	5.1.83	2	NGPF	Nanchang	17 Jul
13.07	1.0	LaTisha	Holden	USA	29.8.89	2s3	NCAA	Des Moines	9 Jun
13.07	0.7	Aisseta	Diawara	FRA	29.6.89	3		Paris (C)	10 Jul
13.07	1.0	Nevin	Yanıt	TUR	16.2.86	5h1	WCh	Daegu	2 Sep
		(70)							
13.08	0.5	Bridgette	Owens-Mitchell	USA-J	14.3.92	2q1	NCAA-E	Bloomington IN	28 May
13.08	0.5	Gemma	Bennett	GBR	4.1.84	4		La Chaux-de-Fonds	3 Jul
13.08	0.3	Veronica	Borsi	ITA	13.6.87	2	WMilG	Río de Janeiro	22 Jul
13.09	0.0	Anne	Zagré	BEL	13.3.90	1r1		Bruxelles	10 Jul
13.10	0.8	Sonata	Tamosaityte	LTU	26.6.87	1		Tartu	28 May
13.10	1.0	Yekaterina	Poplavskaya	BLR	7.5.87	1		Brest	14 Jun
13.10	-1.3	Marina	Tomic	SLO	9.11.82	3r2	ET-1	Izmir	19 Jun
13.11	1.0	Evonne	Britton	USA	10.10.91	3q2	NCAA-E	Bloomington IN	28 May
13.11	-0.9		Chung Hye-rim	KOR	1.7.87	2	AsiC	Kobe	10 Jul
13.11	-0.2	Aleksandra	Antonova	RUS	24.3.80	2h1	NC	Cheboksary	22 Jul
		(80)							
13.12	1.0	Kori	Carter	USA-J	6.3.92	1	Jordan	Stanford	1 May
13.12	0.6	Yenima	Arencibia	CUB	25.12.84	1		La Habana	10 Jun
13.12	-1.1	Anastasiya	Solovyova	RUS	18.2.85	2	NC	Cheboksary	22 Jul
13.12	2.0	Elisabeth	Davin	BEL	3.6.81	3		Fribourg	30 Jul
13.12	0.9	Karolina	Tyminska	POL	4.10.84	1H2	WCh	Daegu	29 Aug
13.13	1.0	Reina-Flor	Okori	FRA	2.5.80	5	NC	Albi	29 Jul
13.13	0.1	Rosvitha	Okou	FRA	5.9.86	3		La Roche-sur-Yon	10 Aug
13.13	0.0	Seun	Adigun	NGR	3.1.87	6h4	WCh	Daegu	2 Sep
13.14	1.3	Vashti	Thomas	USA	21.4.90	1		Berkeley	22 Apr
13.14	1.2	Jennifer	Oeser	GER	29.11.83	1H		Ratingen	16 Jul
		(90)							
13.14	-1.1	Svetlana	Topylina	RUS	6.1.85	3	NC	Cheboksary	22 Jul
13.14A	-0.1	Maíla	Machado	BRA	22.1.81	5	PAm	Guadalajara, MEX	26 Oct
13.15	0.4	Andrea	Miller	NZL	13.3.82	1		Brisbane	11 Feb
13.15	0.1	Jasmine	Chaney	USA	25.8.88	3	Pac10	Tucson	14 May
13.15	1.3	Antoinette	Nana Djimou	FRA	2.8.85	7		Montreuil-sous-Bois	7 Jun
13.15	1.6	Trinity	Wilson	USA-Y	4.9.94	1	NC-j	Eugene	24 Jun
13.15	1.0	Anne-Kathrin	Elbe	GER	24.2.87	2r3		Mannheim	13 Aug
13.16	1.8	Nadine	Hildebrand	GER	20.9.87	1h3		Weinheim	28 May
13.16	0.6	Shericka	Ward	USA	30.3.90	1	NJ Int	Holmdel	18 Jun
13.16	-1.6	Andrea	Bliss	JAM	5.10.80	4	NC	Kingston	26 Jun
		(100)							

Mark	Wind	Name		Nat	Born	Date		Mark	Wind	Name		Nat	Born	Date
13.18	1.0	Cassandra	Lloyd	USA	27.1.90	28 May		13.24A	1.2	Eliecít	Palacios	COL	15.8.87	6 May
13.18A	1.4	Dior	Hall	USA-Y	2.1.96	4 Jun		13.24	0.4	Louise	Hazel	GBR	6.10.85	29 Aug
13.18	1.8	Angie	Broadbelt-Blake	GBR	12.9.85	11 Jun		13.25	1.0	Kelsey	Lloyd	USA	10.12.88	18 Mar
13.19	1.3	Celriece	Law	USA	2.9.86	6 May		13.25	-0.1	Teona	Rodgers	USA	26.6.89	9 Apr
13.19	1.2		Wu Shujiao	CHN-J	19.6.92	22 May		13.25	0.6		Lee Yeon-kyong	KOR	15.4.81	12 May
13.19	0.4	Ayako	Kimura	JPN	11.6.88	10 Oct		13.25	1.5	Alysha	Adams	USA	29.9.88	25 Jun
13.20	1.4	Ivanique	Kemp	BAH	11.6.91	28 May		13.25	1.6	Yariatou	Touré	FRA	27.12.90	29 Jul
13.20	1.5	Sarah	Claxton	GBR	23.9.79	10 Jun		13.25	1.0	Clémence	Vifquin	FRA	9.6.86	29 Jul
13.20A	1.3	Christie	Gordon	CAN	5.10.86	25 Jun		13.26	2.0	Raven	Clay	USA	5.10.90	27 May
13.21	1.8	Katie	Grimes	USA	22.12.90	22 Apr		13.26	2.0	Victoria	Schreibeis	AUT	9.1.79	3 Jul
13.21	1.0	Tenaya	Jones	USA	22.3.89	15 May		13.27	0.4	Airi	Ito	JPN	5.7.89	12 May
13.21	-0.4	Isabelle	Pedersen	NOR-J	27.1.92	13 Aug		13.27	0.9	Tamika	Robinson	USA	24.8.89	15 May
13.21	1.5	Yuka	Nomura	JPN	18.6.87	15 Oct		13.27	1.9	Serita	Solomon	GBR	1.3.90	3 Jul
13.22	0.8	Karessa	Farley	BAR	8.12.88	5 May		13.27	0.3	Dafne	Schippers	NED-J	15.6.92	21 Jul
13.23	1.9	LaToya	James	USA	18.1.89	23 Apr		13.27	-0.2	Yekaterina	Gubina	RUS	27.11.85	22 Jul
13.23	1.7		Kang Ya	CHN	16.3.90	17 Jul		13.28	0.8	Falesha	Ankton	USA	8.6.87	16 Apr
13.23	0.8	Clélia	Reuse	SUI	1.8.88	30 Jul		13.28	1.1	Takecia	Jameson	USA	11.8.89	28 May

Mark	Wind	Name	Nat	Born	Pos	Meet	Venue	Date
13.28	0.9	April Garner	USA	25.12.83				11 Jun
13.28	-0.3	Micol Cattaneo	ITA	14.5.82				25 Jun
13.28	-0.4	Ashley Helsby	GBR	1.7.90				10 Jul
13.28	0.3	Yevheniya Snigur	UKR	7.3.84				22 Jul
13.29	0.9	Julian Purvis	USA	8.9.90				15 May
13.29	1.1	Gabby Mayo	USA	26.1.89				28 May
13.29	-0.2	Giulia Pennella	ITA	27.10.89				18 Jun
13.29	0.9	Aleesha Barber	TRI	16.5.87				17 Jul
13.29	0.8	Viorica Tigău	ROU	12.8.79				9 Aug
13.30	1.1	Kimberley Laing	JAM	8.1.89				9 Apr
13.30	0.5	Jessie Gaines	USA	12.8.90				28 May
13.30	0.7	Nooralotta Neziri	FIN-J	9.11.92				13 Aug
13.31 nwi		Lauren Smith	USA	27.8.81				19 May
13.31	-1.6	Latoya Greaves	JAM	31.5.86				26 Jun
13.31	1.7	Mónica Lopes	POR	18.1.86				16 Jul
13.32	0.1	Petra McDonald	BAH	17.7.84				21 May
13.32	0.0	Olena Yanovska	UKR	15.2.90				30 May
13.32	-0.5	Tatyana Chernova	RUS	29.1.88				15 Jun
13.32	1.2	Lilli Schwarzkopf	GER	28.8.83				16 Jul
13.32	1.0	Danielle Williams	JAM-J	14.9.92				22 Jul
13.33	0.8	Yvana Hepburn-Bailey	USA	9.11.87				5 May
13.33	-0.3	Mami Ishino	JPN	10.1.83				8 May
13.33	1.5	Keisha Wallace	JAM	25.1.90				12 May
13.33	1.2	Brittany Hyter	USA	24.10.89				14 May
13.33		Irina Reshetnikova	RUS	30.1.89				9 Jun
13.34	0.7	Lindsay Rowe	USA	6.10.89				2 Apr
13.34	1.2	Deng Ru	CHN	21.11.89				22 May
13.34	0.5	Melia Cox	USA-J	23.11.92				27 May
13.34A	0.2	Fabiana Moraes	BRA	5.6.86				13 Aug
13.35	2.0	Marlen Affentranger	SUI	28.3.87				30 Jul
13.36	1.2	Dahlys Marshall	USA	9.3.90				13 May
13.36	-2.1	Landria Buckley	USA	2.7.88				4 Jun
13.36	1.1	Zuzana Hejnová	CZE	19.12.86				28 Jun
13.37	0.5	Jasmine Edgerson	USA	6.6.91				28 May
13.37	1.0	Dimitra Arachoviti	CYP	18.7.87				4 Jun
13.37	1.0	Louise Wood	GBR	13.5.83				10 Jul
13.38	-0.7	Jasmine Anderson	USA	22.5.88				15 May
13.38	-0.9	Alina Antipova	RUS	11.1.91				9 Jul
13.38	1.7	Sara Aerts	BEL	25.1.84				29 Aug
13.39	1.2	Yanique Booth	JAM	3.5.84				16 Apr
13.39	1.7	Tiavanni Thompson	BAH	13.3.83				6 May
13.39	1.4	Demeeka Jones	USA	4.10.88				28 May
13.39	1.6	Solene Hamelin	FRA	9.12.88				29 Jul
13.40	0.2	Giselle de Albuquerque	BRA	11.7.88				15 May
13.40	1.8	Femke van der Meij	NED	20.5.85				2 Jun
13.41	0.0	Micaela Wimberly	USA	26.3.89				16 Apr
13.41	0.4	Danielle Gilchrist	USA	15.7.88				16 Apr
13.41A	0.7	Princesa Oliveros	COL	10.8.75				30 Apr
13.41	0.3	Noelle Montcalm	CAN	3.4.88				21 May
13.41	2.0	Rosemarie Carty	JAM	26.2.90				27 May
13.41	-0.4	Lucile Berliat	FRA	7.12.82				10 Jul
13.41	1.7	Wang Li	CHN	24.8.89				17 Jul
13.41	1.6	Hitomi Shimura	JPN	8.11.90				10 Sep
13.42	1.2	Irina Reshetkina	RUS	30.1.89				24 Jun
13.42	-0.2	Dedeh Erawati	INA	25.5.79				2 Jul
13.43	1.2	Lauren Williams	USA	27.7.89				23 Apr
13.43	1.5	Gnima Faye	SEN	17.11.84				10 Jun
13.43	-0.4	Sharona Bakker	NED	12.4.90				13 Jun
13.43	-0.4	Pamela Spindler	GER	16.3.82				21 Aug
13.43	1.6	Margaret Simpson	GHA	2.8.82				29 Aug
13.43	1.7	Nataliya Dobrynska	UKR	29.5.82				29 Aug
13.43	-0.1	Shameka Marshall	USA	9.9.83				18 Jun
13.43	1.4	Emma Tuvesson (197)	SWE	6.3.91				31 Jul

Wind assisted

Mark	Wind	Name	Nat	Born	Pos	Meet	Venue	Date
12.35	3.7	Kellie Wells	USA	16.7.82	1r1		Gainesville	16 Apr
12.37	3.4	Danielle Carruthers	USA	22.12.79	1s1	NC	Eugene	26 Jun
12.47	3.3	Pearson			1	Athl	Lausanne	30 Jun
12.47	3.4	Virginia Crawford	USA	7.9.83	2s1	NC	Eugene	26 Jun
12.48	3.3	Carruthers			2	Athl	Lausanne	30 Jun
12.51	2.5	Wells			1s2	NC	Eugene	26 Jun
12.53	3.4	Wells			1h3	NC	Eugene	25 Jun
12.63	2.1	Nia Ali	USA	23.10.88	1	NCAA	Des Moines	11 Jun
12.64	3.3	Porter			3	Athl	Lausanne	30 Jun
12.64	2.5	Loreal Smith	USA	12.10.85	2s2	NC	Eugene	26 Jun
12.65	3.3	Crawford			4	Athl	Lausanne	30 Jun
12.68	4.9	Kristi Castlin	USA	7.7.88	1r2	TexR	Austin	9 Apr
12.70	2.4	Tiki James	USA	21.10.86	2h1	NC	Eugene	25 Jun
12.72	2.1	Christina Manning	USA	29.5.90	2	NCAA	Des Moines	11 Jun
12.74	3.6	Tiffani McReynolds	USA	4.12.91	1r1	TexR	Austin	9 Apr
12.74	2.5	Yvette Lewis	USA	16.3.85	3s2	NC	Eugene	26 Jun
12.76	4.9	Angela Whyte	CAN	22.5.80	3r2	TexR	Austin	9 Apr
12.78	2.5	Nichole Denby	USA	10.10.82	2h2	NC	Eugene	25 Jun
12.79	2.1	Jackie Coward	USA	5.11.89	3	NCAA	Des Moines	11 Jun
12.82	3.4	Michaylin Golladay	USA	10.4.88	4s1	NC	Eugene	26 Jun
12.85	3.4	Lucie Skrobáková	CZE	4.1.82	1		Ostrava	21 May
12.86	3.6	Jasmin Stowers	USA	23.9.91	3r1	TexR	Austin	9 Apr
12.88	2.4	Brianna Rollins	USA	18.8.91	3h1	NC	Eugene	25 Jun
12.89	2.1	LaTisha Holden	USA	29.8.89	4	NCAA	Des Moines	11 Jun
12.91	2.2	Nadine Hildebrand	GER	20.9.87	1		Weinheim	28 May
12.95	3.2	Shermaine Williams	JAM	4.2.90	1	NCAA-II	Turlock	28 May
12.95	4.2	Andrea Bliss	JAM	5.10.80	3r2		Clermont	4 Jun
12.96	2.3	Natasha Ruddock	JAM	25.12.89	1	Johnson	Waco	23 Apr
12.96	2.4	Chelsea Carrier	USA	21.8.89	6h1	NC	Eugene	25 Jun
13.04	3.3	Lauren Smith	USA	27.8.81	3		Baton Rouge	23 Apr
13.05	3.6	Bridgette Owens-Mitchell	USA-J	14.3.92	5r1	TexR	Austin	9 Apr
13.05	3.3	Tenaya Jones	USA	22.3.89	4		Baton Rouge	23 Apr
13.06	3.8	Tamika Robinson	USA	24.8.89	2h2	NCAA-W	Eugene	27 May
13.06	2.3	Aïsseta Diawara	FRA	29.6.89	2h1	NC	Albi	29 Jul
13.07	3.7	Angie Broadbelt-Blake	GBR	12.9.85	4r1		Gainesville	16 Apr
13.08	3.0	Alysha Adams	USA	29.9.88	2	Lane	Arlington	2 Apr
13.09	2.3	Reina-Flor Okori	FRA	2.5.80	3h1	NC	Albi	29 Jul
13.12	2.2	Celriece Law	USA	2.9.86	7	DrakeR	Des Moines	30 Apr
13.13	3.2	Danielle Williams	JAM-J	14.9.92	3	NCAA-II	Turlock	28 May
13.13	2.7	Ashley Helsby	GBR	1.7.90	1B		La Chaux-de-Fonds	3 Jul
13.16	3.6	Kelsey Lloyd	USA	10.12.88				9 Apr
13.17	3.0	Ivanique Kemp	BAH	11.6.91				6 May
13.17	2.6	Tiavanni Thompson	BAH	13.3.83				6 May
13.18	4.5	Yekaterina Gubina	RUS	27.11.85				4 Jun

Mark	Wind	Name		Nat	Born	Pos	Meet	Venue			Date
13.19	3.3	Jasmine	Anderson	USA	22.5.88			23 Apr			
13.22	3.4	Zuzana	Hejnová	CZE	19.12.86			21 May			
13.23	2.5	Aleesha	Barber	TRI	16.5.87			23 Apr			
13.23	2.7	Nickiesha	Wilson	JAM	28.7.86			14 May			
13.24	2.4	Keisha	Wallace	JAM	25.1.90			14 May			
13.25	3.8	Demeeka	Jones	USA	4.10.88			19 Mar			
13.25	2.7	Landria	Buckley	USA	2.7.88			14 May			
13.26	2.2	Monique	Gracia	USA	20.4.90			14 May			
13.27	2.6	Latoya	Greaves	JAM	31.5.86			6 May			
13.27	3.6	Irina	Reshetnikova	RUS	30.1.89			29 Jul			
13.28	2.9	Lindsay	Rowe	USA	6.10.89			7 May			
13.29	2.6	Brittany	Hyter	USA	24.10.89			6 May			
13.32	3.0	Francesca	Doveri	ITA	21.12.82			7 May			

Mark	Wind	Name		Nat	Born	Pos	Meet	Venue			Date
13.34	3.0	Louise	Wood	GBR	13.5.83						7 May
13.34	3.4	Jana	Koresová	CZE	8.4.81						21 May
13.34	2.2	Sara	McGreavy	GBR	13.12.82						11 Aug
13.36	2.1		Wang Dou	CHN-J	18.5.93						22 May
13.36	4.2	Jessica	Ohanaja	NGR	6.12.85						13 Sep
13.38	3.9	Racquel	Vassell	USA	24.10.89						7 May
13.39	3.8	Meredith	Hayes	USA	25.6.88						27 May
13.41	2.2	Miriam	Hehl	GER	14.4.91						28 May
13.41	2.2	Kylie	Robilliard	GBR	11.6.88						11 Aug
13.42	2.2	Emma	Tuvesson	SWE	6.3.91						4 Jun
13.43	5.1	Tiana	Davis	USA	12.8.89						16 Apr
13.43	3.6	Stacey	Young	USA							14 May
13.43	2.8	Donique	Flemings	USA	1.11.91						15 May

Hand timing

12.9	1.2	Yenima	Arencibia	CUB	25.12.84	1r1		La Habana	21 May

Best at low altitude

13.20	-0.6	Machado	5 Aug	13.29	0.2	Palacios	14 May	13.33	-0.4	Gordon	19 Aug

JUNIORS

See main list for top 3 juniors. 11 performances by 6 women to 13.21. Additional marks and further juniors:

Owens-M	13.16	1.9 4		Durham	23 Apr	13.17	2.0 3h1	TexR	Austin	8 Apr
	13.16	0.9 2		Clemson	7 May	13.21	1.0 4h3	NCAA	Des Moines	9 Jun
Wilson	13.17	1.0	PAm-J	Miramar	22 Jul					

Mark	Wind	Name		Nat	Born	Pos	Meet	Venue	Date
13.18A	1.4	Dior	Hall	USA-Y	2.1.96	1		Albuquerque	4 Jun
13.19	1.2		Wu Shujiao	CHN	19.6.92	1	NGP	Jiaxing	22 May
13.21	-0.4	Isabelle	Pedersen	NOR	27.1.92	1	NC	Byrkjelo	13 Aug
13.27	0.3	Dafne	Schippers	NED	15.6.92	1H3	EJ	Tallinn	21 Jul
13.30	0.7	Nooralotta	Neziri	FIN	9.11.92	2	LappG	Lappeenranta	13 Aug
13.32	1.0	Danielle	Williams	JAM	14.9.92	2	PAm-J	Miramar	22 Jul
13.34	0.5	Melia	Cox (10)	USA	23.11.92	1		Norwalk	27 May
13.47	-1.0	Yekaterina	Bleskina	RUS	29.1.93	3	EJ	Tallinn	23 Jul
13.48	-1.9		Wang Dou	CHN	18.5.93	1	NC-j	Jinan	2 Jun
13.49	-0.4	Kendra	Harrison	USA	18.9.92	1		Greensboro	17 Jun
13.50	-0.4	Kendell	Williams	USA-Y	14.6.95	2		Greensboro	17 Jun
13.51	1.5	Kim	Francis	USA	6.1.92	4		Baton Rouge	26 Mar
13.51	-0.4	Morgan	Snow	USA	26.7.93	3		Greensboro	17 Jun
13.53	1.7	Breeana	Coleman	USA	19.6.92	2h2		Fayetteville	6 May
13.56	1.3	Dotrine	Jacobs	USA	16.8.92	1r2		Greensboro	15 May
13.57	1.0	Katie	Nelms	USA	25.9.92	4		Stanford	1 May
13.57	0.4	Aya	Ito (20)	JPN	29.12.92	5		Yamaguchi	10 Oct

Wind assisted See main lists for top 2 juniors. 4 performances by 2 women to 13.20

Owens-M	13.10	2.7 2		Clemson	14 May	13.15	3.4 5h3	NC-j	Eugene	25 Jun
13.36	2.1		Wang Dou	CHN-J	18.5.93	1h1	NGP	Jiaxing	22 May
13.45	2.3	Kendell	Williams	USA-Y	14.6.95	1		Knoxville	23 Apr

300 METRES HURDLES

38.91		Zuzana	Hejnová	CZE	19.12.86	1		Pardubice	13 Aug

400 METRES HURDLES

Mark		Name		Nat	Born	Pos	Meet	Venue	Date
52.47		Lashinda	Demus	USA	10.3.83	1	WCh	Daegu	1 Sep
52.73		Melaine	Walker	JAM	1.1.83	2	WCh	Daegu	1 Sep
52.79		Kaliese	Spencer	JAM	6.5.87	1	LGP	London (CP)	5 Aug
53.29		Zuzana	Hejnová	CZE	19.12.86	1	DL	Saint-Denis	8 Jul
53.31			Demus			1	Pre	Eugene	4 Jun
53.36			Spencer			1	WK	Zürich	8 Sep
53.43			Walker			2	WK	Zürich	8 Sep
53.45			Spencer			2	Pre	Eugene	4 Jun
53.45			Spencer			2	DL	Saint-Denis	8 Jul
53.56			Walker			3	Pre	Eugene	4 Jun
53.60			Spencer			1	GP	Rieti	10 Sep
53.68		Vania	Stambolova	BUL	28.11.83	1		Rabat	5 Jun
53.70			Stambolova			1	ET-2	Novi Sad	18 Jun
53.74			Spencer			1	DNG	Stockholm	29 Jul
53.75		Natalya	Antyukh	RUS	26.6.81	1	NC	Cheboksary	23 Jul
53.82			Demus			1s3	WCh	Daegu	30 Aug
53.85			Antyukh			3	WCh	Daegu	1 Sep
53.87			Hejnová			1r2	ET	Stockholm	18 Jun
53.90			Walker			2	LGP	London (CP)	5 Aug
54.01			Spencer			4	WCh	Daegu	1 Sep
54.04			Demus			3	WK	Zürich	8 Sep
54.09			Walker			1		Río de Janeiro	26 May

Mark	Wind	Name		Nat	Born	Pos	Meet	Venue	Date
54.15			Spencer			1	NC	Kingston	24 Jun
54.18			Demus			1	Spitzen	Luzern	21 Jul
54.18		Anastasiya	Rabchenyuk	UKR	14.9.83	5	WCh	Daegu	1 Sep
54.20			Spencer			1	DL	Shanghai	15 May
54.21			Demus			1	NC	Eugene	25 Jun
54.23			Stambolova			1	Balk C	Sliven	2 Jul
54.23			Stambolova			6	WCh	Daegu	1 Sep
54.23			Hejnová			7	WCh	Daegu	1 Sep
		(30/7)							
54.26			Hejnová			4	Pre	Eugene	4 Jun
54.33			Stambolova			1	Cezmi	Istanbul	11 Jun
54.38			Hejnová			1	Bisl	Oslo	9 Jun
54.38			Stambolova			1		Barcelona	22 Jul
54.41			Antyukh			3	DL	Saint-Denis	8 Jul
54.44			Hejnová			1	Odlozil	Praha	13 Jun
54.50			Antyukh			4	WK	Zürich	8 Sep
54.51			Antyukh			1s2	WCh	Daegu	30 Aug
54.52			Antyukh			2r2	ET	Stockholm	18 Jun
54.58			Demus			2	DL	Shanghai	15 May
54.58		Ristananna	Tracey	JAM-J	5.9.92	2	NC	Kingston	24 Jun
54.62		Perri	Shakes-Drayton	GBR	21.12.88	3	LGP	London (CP)	5 Aug
54.69		Hanna	Titimets	UKR	5.3.89	1	NCp	Yalta	31 May
		(10)							
54.77		Anna	Yaroshchuk	UKR	24.11.89	1	EU23	Ostrava	16 Jul
54.78		Queen	Harrison	USA	10.9.88	2	NC	Eugene	25 Jun
54.79		Yelena	Churakova	RUS	16.12.86	2	NC	Cheboksary	23 Jul
55.09		Nagihan	Karadere	TUR	1.1.84	1		Ankara	31 Jul
55.22		Jasmine	Chaney	USA	25.8.88	3	NC	Eugene	25 Jun
55.29		Elodie	Ouédraogo	BEL	27.2.81	5s1	WCh	Daegu	30 Aug
55.34		Satomi	Kubokura	JPN	27.4.82	1		Osaka	26 Jun
55.48		Irina	Davydova	RUS	27.5.88	3	NC	Cheboksary	23 Jul
55.53		Turquoise	Thompson	USA	31.7.91	4	NC	Eugene	25 Jun
55.57		Nickiesha	Wilson	JAM	28.7.86	2		Río de Janeiro	26 May
		(20)							
55.59		Tierra	Brown	USA	24.10.89	1h1	NCAA	Des Moines	8 Jun
55.65		Sheena	Tosta	USA	1.10.82	1	GP	Ponce	14 May
55.67		Eilidh	Child	GBR	20.2.87	3	Spitzen	Luzern	21 Jul
55.68		Ryann	Krais	USA	21.3.90	2h1	NCAA	Des Moines	8 Jun
55.69		Meghan	Beesley	GBR	15.11.89	3	EU23	Ostrava	16 Jul
55.70		Ellen	Wortham	USA	5.1.90	1	SEC	Athens GA	15 May
55.75		Jana	Rawlinson	AUS	9.11.82	1		Perth	1 Apr
55.76		Anastasiya	Ott	RUS	7.9.88	4	NC	Cheboksary	23 Jul
55.77		Tiffany	Williams	USA	5.2.83	1		Clermont	21 May
55.78		Lauren	Boden	AUS	3.8.88	4h1	WCh	Daegu	29 Aug
		(30)							
55.80		Janeil	Bellille	TRI	18.6.89	1		Lubbock	2 Apr
55.81		Vera	Barbosa	POR	13.1.89	4	EU23	Ostrava	16 Jul
55.83		LaToya	James	USA	18.1.89	1	ACC	Durham NC	23 Apr
55.90		Christine	Spence	USA	25.11.81	2	GP	Ponce	14 May
55.90		Tina	Polak	POL	12.7.88	1	NC	Bydgoszcz	12 Aug
55.97		Takecia	Jameson	USA	11.8.89	2s1	NC	Eugene	24 Jun
55.97		Sara	Petersen	DEN	9.4.87	1		Ljubljana	27 Jul
55.99		Cassandra	Tate	USA	11.9.90	1h3	NCAA	Des Moines	8 Jun
55.99		LaTosha	Wallace	USA	25.3.85	1		Clermont	11 Jun
56.00		Jaílma	de Lima	BRA	31.12.86	3		Río de Janeiro	26 May
		(40)							
56.04		Dalilah	Muhammad	USA	7.2.90	2h3	NCAA	Des Moines	8 Jun
56.08		Nicole	Leach	USA	18.7.87	2		Kingston	7 May
56.12		Yadisleidis	Pedroso	CUB	28.1.87	1		Reggio Emilia	3 Sep
56.13		Wanda	Theron	RSA	30.7.88	3h5	WCh	Daegu	29 Aug
56.22		Zuzana	Bergrová	CZE	24.11.84	1		Praha	17 Sep
56.23		Manuela	Gentili	ITA	7.2.78	1		Saint Christophe	17 Jul
56.23		Joke	Odumosu	NGR	27.10.87	4h4	WCh	Daegu	29 Aug
56.26A		Princesa	Oliveros	COL	10.8.75	1	PAm	Guadalajara, MEX	26 Oct
56.38		Stine Meland	Tomb	NOR	27.8.86	2r2	ET-1	Izmir	18 Jun
56.39		Anna	Jesien	POL	10.12.78	2		Barcelona	22 Jul
		(50)							
56.44		Andrea	Sutherland	JAM	26.5.88	4	NC	Kingston	24 Jun
56.46		Brittany	Hyter	USA	24.10.89	1h2	NCAA	Des Moines	8 Jun
56.48		Birsen	Engin	TUR	18.10.80	2		Ankara	31 Jul
56.49		Darya	Korableva	RUS	23.5.88	1	Kuts	Moskva	6 Aug

Mark	Name		Nat	Born	Pos	Meet	Venue	Date	
56.53	Phara	Anacharsis	FRA	17.12.83	8	DL	Saint-Denis	8	Jul
56.54	Ayla	Smith	USA	16.5.88	3h2	NCAA	Des Moines	8	Jun
56.54	Nikolina	Horvat	CRO	18.9.86	2		Ljubljana	27	Jul
56.58	Lamia	Lhabz	MAR	19.5.84	7		Rabat	5	Jun
56.58		Huang Xiaoxiao	CHN	3.3.83	1	NC	Hefei	9	Sep
56.62	Sayaka	Aoki	JPN	15.12.86	2		Osaka	26	Jun
(60)									
56.62	Jessie	Barr	IRL	24.7.89	5	EU23	Ostrava	16	Jul
56.65A	Maureen	Maiyo	KEN	28.5.85	1	NC	Nairobi	16	Jul
56.66	Miel Blessing	Ayédou	BEN	17.8.91	1		Ougadougou	24	Jul
56.69		Yang Qi	CHN	13.4.91	2	AsiC	Kobe	10	Jul
56.70	Miyabi	Tago	JPN	15.7.88	3		Osaka	26	Jun
56.72	Hayat	Lambarki	MAR	18.5.88	1	ArabG	Doha	17	Dec
56.73	Kianna	Elahi	USA	24.8.90	2	DrakeR	Des Moines	30	Apr
56.73	MacKenzie	Hill	USA	5.1.86	5s1	NC	Eugene	24	Jun
56.79	Landria	Buckley	USA	2.7.88	1		Clemson SC	7	May
56.83	Christine	Merrill	SRI	20.8.87	3h1	AsiC	Kobe	8	Jul
(70)									
56.86	Josanne	Lucas	TRI	14.5.84	1		Rehlingen	13	Jun
56.91	Svetlana	Gogoleva	RUS	11.12.86	2h1	NC	Cheboksary	22	Jul
56.92	Shiori	Miki	JPN	25.12.91	3	NC	Kumagaya	12	Jun
56.92	Aleksandra	Kuzina	KAZ	26.12.90	1	Kozanov	Almaty	19	Jun
56.95A	Lucy	Jaramillo	ECU	23.2.83	2	PAm	Guadalajara, MEX	26	Oct
56.97	Christiane	Klopsch	GER	21.8.90	1	NC	Kassel	24	Jul
57.03	Angele	Cooper	USA	3.11.90	2h1	TexR	Austin	7	Apr
57.04	Yuka	Nomura	JPN	18.6.87	4	NC	Kumagaya	12	Jun
57.04	Irina	Grebneva	RUS	5.2.85	6	NC	Cheboksary	23	Jul
57.05	Özge	Gürler	TUR	17.6.85	3	NC	Izmir	10	Jul
(80)									
57.06	Miyuki	Yano	JPN	1.4.90	1		Kumamoto	11	Sep
57.08A	Yolanda	Osana	DOM	11.8.87	3	PAm	Guadalajara, MEX	26	Oct
57.09A	Sema	Apak	TUR	17.8.85	1	Univ Ch	Konya	10	May
57.09	Tina	Kron	GER	3.4.81	1		Rhede	8	Jul
57.10	Kou	Wright	LBR	11.6.84	4		Baie Mahault	7	May
57.10	Kori	Carter	USA-J	6.3.92	3	Pac10	Tucson	14	May
57.10	Tomomi	Yoneda	JPN	11.8.90	1		Tokyo	22	May
57.10	Vera	Rudakova	RUS-J	20.3.92	1	NC-j	Cheboksary	2	Jul
57.14	Leslie	Njoku	NGR	30.5.89	6h1	NCAA	Des Moines	8	Jun
57.18	Shevon	Stoddart	JAM	21.11.82	2		Clermont	11	Jun
(90)									
57.19	Houria	Moussa	ALG	14.5.82	1		Annaba	4	Jul
57.20	Jernail	Hayes	USA	8.7.88	4h3	NC	Eugene	23	Jun
57.20	Marzena	Koscielniak	POL	28.12.89	3h1	EU23	Ostrava	14	Jul
57.20	Marta	Chrust-Rozej	POL	29.9.78	3	NC	Bydgoszcz	12	Aug
57.21	Danielle	Gilchrist	USA	15.7.88	1		Clermont	4	Jun
57.23A	Sharolyn	Scott	CRC	27.10.84	1h2	PAm	Guadalajara, MEX	24	Oct
57.24	Katrina	Seymour	BAH-J	7.1.93	3	CAC	Mayagüez	16	Jul
57.25	Sheryl	Morgan	JAM	6.11.83	4	CAC	Mayagüez	16	Jul
57.25	Olga	Razanamalala	MAD	8.9.88	7h2	WCh	Daegu	29	Aug
57.26	Fawn	Dorr	USA	19.4.87	3	KansR	Lawrence	23	Apr
(100)									

Mark	Name		Nat	Born	Date	
57.31	Sonni	Austin	USA	5.12.90	27	May
57.33	Danielle	Dowie	JAM-J	5.5.92	19	Mar
57.34	Aleksandra	Kurakina	RUS	15.8.87	22	Jul
57.35	Megan	Duncan	USA	28.12.88	15	May
57.35	Aurélie	Chaboudez	FRA-J	9.5.93	24	Jul
57.36	Claudia	Wehrsen	GER	18.10.84	24	Jul
57.36	Jill	Richards	GER	14.1.87	24	Jul
57.37	Valentine	Arrieta	SUI	29.4.90	18	Jun
57.38	Joanna	Linkiewicz	POL	2.5.90	12	Jun
57.41	Georgeanne	Moline	USA	6.3.90	2	Apr
57.41	Evonne	Britton	USA	10.10.91	15	May
57.41	Noraseela Mohd Khalid		MAS	27.9.79	15	Nov
57.42	Natalya	Asanova	UZB	29.11.89	30	Sep
57.48	Chelsea	Carrier	USA	21.8.89	8	May
57.48	Antonina	Yefremova	UKR	19.7.81	22	May
57.49	Marlena	Wesh	HAI	16.2.91	7	Apr
57.50	Elaine	Paixão	BRA	15.6.88	26	May
57.51	Miki	Sawada	JPN	20.6.86	26	Jun
57.52		Wang Jinping	CHN	14.12.88	9	Sep
57.56	Sofie	Persson	SWE	16.1.87	30	Apr
57.56	Mame Fatou	Faye	SEN	19.8.86	16	Aug
57.58	Justine	Kinney	IRL	6.4.88	10	Jul

Mark	Name		Nat	Born	Date	
57.59	Jackie	Coward	USA	5.11.89	15	May
57.59		Deng Xiaoqing	CHN	13.6.89	9	Sep
57.61	Caryl	Granville	GBR	24.9.89	20	Aug
57.62	LaToya	Wright	USA	.88	7	May
57.68	Axelle	Dauwens	BEL	1.12.90	2	Aug
57.70	Kayla	Sanchez	USA	29.1.90	14	May
57.71	Thandi	Stewart	USA	19.12.91	23	Apr
57.71	Janeive	Russell	JAM-J	14.11.93	24	Apr
57.71	Valeriya	Znamenskaya	RUS	25.3.90	25	Jun
57.72	Leah	Nugent	USA-J	23.11.92	18	Jun
57.81		Ruan Zhuofen	CHN	21.1.85	16	Aug
57.82	Christina	Holland	USA	5.8.91	14	May
57.83	Shamier	Little	USA-Y	20.3.95	3	Aug
57.88	Sparkle	McKnight	TRI	21.12.91	23	Apr
57.88	Gnima	Faye	SEN	17.11.84	24	Jul
57.90	Tracey	Duncan	GBR	16.5.79	10	Jul
57.91	Olga	Ortega	ESP	8.3.85	8	Jun
57.92A	Anisia	Castro	MEX	5.3.86	7	Aug
57.93	Anastasiya	Buldakova	BLR	29.4.88	7	Jul
57.93	Nnenya	Hailey	USA-Y	23.2.94	9	Jul
57.94	Lena Anna	Raukuc	GER	7.1.90	23	Jul
57.94	Liliane Cristina	Barbosa	BRA	8.10.87	7	Aug

Mark	Name		Nat	Born	Pos Meet	Venue	Date
57.97	Keia	Pinnick	USA	23.1.91			15 Apr
57.97	Anastasiya	Korshunova	RUS-J	17.5.92			2 Jul
57.97	Iryna	Holovchenko	UKR	21.7.88			15 Aug
58.00	Oksana	Volosyuk	UKR	28.11.81			11 Jun
58.01	Olesya	Tsaranok	RUS	3.7.89			15 May
58.01	Nyjah	Cousar	USA	23.5.91			15 May
58.03	Maeva	Contion	FRA-J	31.5.92			24 Jul
58.04	Emily	Parker	GBR	7.11.84			17 Jul
58.05	Angela	Morosanu	ROU	26.7.86			8 May
58.05	Sarah	Carli	AUS-Y	5.9.94			9 Jul
58.06	Irina	Takuncheva	RUS	14.11.90			25 Jun
58.06	Valeriya	Khramova	RUS-J	13.8.92			2 Jul
58.07	Ebony	Collins	USA	11.3.89			23 Jun
58.09	Oarabile	Babolayi	BOT-J	8.3.92			14 Sep
58.11	Nikita	Tracey	JAM	18.9.90			28 May
58.14	Lyndsay	Pekin	AUS	13.6.86			19 Mar
58.15	Benedetta	Ceccarelli	ITA	23.1.80			15 May
58.15	Cécile	Bernaleau	FRA	29.3.88			10 Jul
58.18	Iris	Campbell	USA	16.7.91			27 May
58.20	Aida	Valente	ITA	25.10.78			26 Jun
58.20	Nusrat	Ceesay	GAM	18.3.81			13 Aug
58.22	Leslie	Farmer	USA	18.4.90			15 May
58.27A	Francisca	Koki	KEN-J	.93			16 Jul
58.29	Gisele	Cruz	BRA	18.6.87			26 Jun
58.29	Sylvaine	Derycke	FRA	4.1.82			9 Jul
58.33	Sonali	Merrill	USA				5 Jun
58.33	Bianca	Baak	NED-J	25.1.92			23 Jul
58.34	Kendra	Harrison	USA-J	18,9,92			3 Jul
58.34	Kristina	Volfová	CZE	16.5.88			7 Jun
58.35	Yekaterina	Brodovaya	RUS	28.6.91			25 Jun
58.37	Zurian	Hechavarría	CUB-Y	10.8.95			9 Jul
58.37	Egle	Staisiunaite	LTU	30.9.88			8 Jun
58.38	Abigayle	Fitzpatrick	GBR-J	10.6.93			23 Jul
58.38	Joanna	Banach	POL-J	28.8.92			23 Jul
58.40	Kaila	Barber	USA-J	4.4.93			18 Jun
58.41	Midori	Chiba	JPN	15.5.89			11 Sep
58.44	Sharyn	Dahl (181)	USA	10.7.88			15 May

Hand timing

Mark	Name		Nat	Born	Pos		Venue	Date
57.0	Houria	Moussa	ALG	14.5.82	1		Alger	8 Jul

Best at low altitude

57.20 Osana 2h1CAC Mayagüez 15 Jul   57.49 Maiyo 15 Sep   58.07 Oliveros 3 Jun
57.22 Apak 1 Izmir 22 May   57.66 S Scott 15 Jul

JUNIORS

See main list for top 4 juniors. 12 performances by 4 women to 57.24. Additional marks and further juniors:

Mark	Name		Nat	Born	Pos	Meet	Venue	Date
Tracey	55.55	4s3 WCh					Daegu	30 Aug
	55.81	1					Kingston	1 Apr
	55.96	2h4 WCh					Daegu	29 Aug
	56.07	7				LGP	London (CP)	5 Aug
	56.17	1				PennR	Philadelphia	28 Apr
	56.32	7				DL	Saint-Denis	8 Jul
Rudakova	57.24	1s2 EJ					Tallinn	23 Jul
	57.24	1				EJ	Tallinn	24 Jul
57.33	Danielle	Dowie	JAM	5.5.92	1r2		Orlando	19 Mar
57.35	Aurélie	Chaboudez	FRA	9.5.93	2	EJ	Tallinn	24 Jul
57.71	Janeive	Russell	JAM	14.11.93	1	Carifta	Montego Bay	24 Apr
57.72	Leah	Nugent	USA	23.11.92	1	N.Sch	Greensboro	18 Jun
57.83	Shamier	Little	USA-Y	20.3.95	1	Jnr Oly	New Oreeans	3 Aug
57.93	Nnenya	Hailey (10)	USA-Y	23.2.94	1	WY	Villeneuve d'Ascq	9 Jul
57.97	Anastasiya	Korshunova	RUS	17.5.92	2	NC-j	Cheboksary	2 Jul
58.03	Maeva	Contion	FRA	31.5.92	3	EJ	Tallinn	24 Jul
58.05	Sarah	Carli	AUS-Y	5.9.94	2	WY	Villeneuve d'Ascq	9 Jul
58.06	Valeriya	Khramova	RUS	13.8.92	3	NC-j	Cheboksary	2 Jul
58.09	Oarabile	Babolayi	BOT	8.3.92	4h1	AfG	Maputo	14 Sep
58.27A	Francisca	Koki	KEN	.93	2	NC	Nairobi	16 Jul
58.33	Bianca	Baak	NED	25.1.92	2s2	EJ	Tallinn	23 Jul
58.34	Kendra	Harrison	USA	18,9,92	1		Myrtle Beach	3 Jul
58.37	Zurian	Hechavarría	CUB-Y	10.8.95	3	WY	Villeneuve d'Ascq	9 Jul
58.38	Abigayle	Fitzpatrick (20)	GBR	10.6.93	3=s2	EJ	Tallinn	23 Jul
58.38	Joanna	Banach	POL	28.8.92	3=s2	EJ	Tallinn	23 Jul

HIGH JUMP

Mark	Name		Nat	Born	Pos	Meet	Venue	Date
2.07	Anna	Chicherova	RUS	22.7.82	1	NC	Cheboksary	22 Jul

1.88/1 1.91/1 1.94/1 1.97/1 2.00/1 2.04/2 2.07/3

	2.05	1	VD	Bruxelles	16 Sep	1.85/1 1.90/1 1.93/1 1.96/1 1.99/1 2.02/3 2.05/2 2.10/xxx
	2.03	1	WCh	Daegu	3 Sep	1.89/1 1.93/1 1.97/1 2.00/1 2.03/1 2.05/xxx
	2.00	1	Hanz	Zagreb	13 Sep	1.85/1 1.90/1 1.94/1 2.00/1 2.04/xxx
	1.99	2	BrGP	Birmingham	10 Jul	1.83/1 1.87/1 1.90/1 1.93/1 1.96/2 1.99/3 2.01/xxx

2.04i	Antonietta	Di Martino	ITA	1.6.78	1		Banská Bystrica	9 Feb

1.82/1 1.86/1 1.89/1 1.92/1 1.94 1.96/1 2.00/1 2.02/1 2.04/3

	2.01i	1	EI	Paris (B)	6 Mar	1.82/1 1.87/1 1.92/1 1.96/1 1.99/1 2.01/2 2.03/xxx
	2.00	1	ESPCh	Málaga	7 Aug	1.80, 1.83, 1.86, 1.89, 1.92/1 1.94/2 1.97/1 2.00/3 2.02/x
	2.00	3	WCh	Daegu	3 Sep	1.89/1 1.93/1 1.97/1 2.00/3 2.03/xxx

2.03	Blanka	Vlasic	CRO	8.11.83	2	WCh	Daegu	3 Sep

1.89/1 1.93/1 1.97/1 2.00/2 2.03/2 2.05/xxx

	2.00	1		Split	24 Jun	1.88/1 1.91/1 1.94/1 1.98/2 2.00/2 2.02/xxx
	2.00	2	Hanz	Zagreb	13 Sep	1.85/1 1.90/1 1.94/1 2.00/2 2.04/xxx
	1.99	1	BrGP	Birmingham	10 Jul	1.83/1 1.87/1 1.90/1 1.93/1 1.96/2 1.99/2 2.01/xxx
	1.97	1		Rabat	5 Jun	1.86/1 1.92/1 1.95/2 1.97/1 2.00/xxx
	1.97	2		Eberstadt	16 Jul	1.84/1 1.90/2 1.93/1 1.95/1 1.97/1 2.01/xxx
	1.97	1	Herc	Monaco	22 Jul	1.85/1 1.89/1 1.95/2 1.97/2 2.01/xxx

2.00i	Svetlana	Shkolina	RUS	9.3.86	2		Banská Bystrica	9 Feb

1.86/1 1.89/1 1.92/1 1.94/1 1.96/x 1.98/2 2.00/3 2.04/xxx

	1.99	1		Eberstadt	16 Jul	1.84/1 1.87/1 1.90/1 1.93/2 1.95/1 1.97/1 1.99/1
	1.97	2	NC	Cheboksary	22 Jul	1.83/1 1.88/1 1/91/1 1.94/1 1.97/1 2.00/xxx
	1.97	5	WCh	Daegu	3 Sep	1.89/1 1.93/1 1.97/3 2.00/xxx

Mark	Name		Nat	Born	Pos	Meet	Venue	Date
1.98	Venelina	Veneva-Mateeva	BUL	13.6.74	2		Split	24 Jun
		1.80/2 1.88/1 1.91/1 1.94/1 1.96/2 1.98/1 2.00/xxx						
	1.97i 1	Bucuresti 18 Feb		1.75/1 1.80/1 1.88/1 1.92/1 1.95/3 1.97/3				
1.98	Esthera	Petre	ROU	13.5.90	1	EU23	Ostrava	16 Jul
		1.80/1 1.84/1 1.87/1 1.90/1 1.92/2 1.94/1 1.96/3 1.98/3 2.00/xxx						
1.97i	Mariya	Kuchina	RUS-J	14.1.93	1		Trinec	26 Jan
		1.76/1 1.81/1 1.85/1 1.88/1 1.90/1 1.92/2 1.94/1 1.97/2						
1.97	Yelena	Slesarenko	RUS	28.2.82	3	NC	Cheboksary	22 Jul
		1.83/1 1.88/1 1/91/1 1.94/1 1.97/2 2.00/xxx						
	1.97 4 WCh	Daegu 3 Sep		1.89/1 1.93/2 1.97/1 2.00/xxx				
	(26/8)							
1.96i	Ruth	Beitia	ESP	1.4.79	2	EI	Paris (B)	6 Mar
1.96i	Ebba	Jungmark	SWE	10.3.87	3	EI	Paris (B)	6 Mar
	(10)							
1.96	Anna	Iljustsenko	EST	12.10.85	1		Viljandi	9 Aug
1.96	Brigetta	Barrett	USA	24.12.90	1	WUG	Shenzhen	21 Aug
1.96	Airine	Palsyte	LTU-J	13.7.92	2	WUG	Shenzhen	21 Aug
1.95	Viktoriya	Styopina	UKR	21.2.76	1	NCp	Yalta	30 May
1.95	Mélanie	Melfort	FRA	8.11.82	2		Rabat	5 Jun
1.95	Tatyana	Mnatsakanova	RUS	25.5.83	2	Mosc Chall	Moskva	12 Jun
1.95	Doreen	Amata	NGR	6.5.88	3		Eberstadt	16 Jul
1.95	Emma	Green Tregaro	SWE	8.12.84	Q	WCh	Daegu	1 Sep
1.95	Deirdre	Ryan	IRL	1.6.82	Q	WCh	Daegu	1 Sep
1.95	Svetlana	Radzivil	UZB	17.1.87	Q	WCh	Daegu	1 Sep
	(20)							
1.95		Zheng Xingjuan	CHN	20.3.89	Q	WCh	Daegu	1 Sep
1.94i	Danielle	Frenkel	ISR	8.9.87	Q	EI	Paris (B)	5 Mar
1.94i	Oksana	Okuneva	UKR	14.3.90	Q	EI	Paris (B)	5 Mar
1.94	Marina	Aitova	KAZ	13.9.82	2	Colorful	Daegu	12 May
1.94	Irina	Gordeyeva	RUS	9.10.86	2		Sochi	25 May
1.94	Anna	Shorstova	RUS	10.4.89	1		Chelyabinsk	28 May
1.94	Levern	Spencer	LCA	23.6.84	1	FBK	Hengelo	29 May
1.94	Burcu	Ayhan	TUR	3.5.90	3	EU23	Ostrava	16 Jul
1.93	Marie-Laurence	Jungfleisch	GER	7.10.90	1		Eppingen	22 May
1.93A	Inika	McPherson	USA	29.9.86	1		El Paso	22 May
	(30)							
1.93	Raffaella	Lamera	ITA	13.4.83	1	Ita Cup	Firenze	4 Jun
1.92i	Grete	Udras	EST	11.3.88	1		Tartu	27 Jan
1.92i	Ana	Simic	CRO	5.5.90	3		Banská Bystrica	9 Feb
1.92i	Viktoriya	Klyugina	RUS	28.9.80	2		Karlsruhe	13 Feb
1.92i	Tonje	Angelsen	NOR	17.1.90	10q	EI	Paris (B)	5 Mar
1.92	Wanida	Boonwan	THA	30.8.86	2	AsiGP	Kunshan	26 May
1.92i	Remona	Fransen	NED	25.11.85	1P	EI	Paris (B)	4 Mar
1.92	Yuliya	Kostrova	RUS	20.8.91	2	NC-23	Yerino	25 Jun
1.92	Magdalena	Ogrodnik	POL	25.7.89	5	EU23	Ostrava	16 Jul
1.92	Ma'ayan	Furman	ISR	9.11.86	1		Neurim	9 Aug
	(40)							
1.91i	Epley	Bullock	USA	12.11.87	1		Fayetteville	12 Feb
1.91	Jessica	Ennis	GBR	28.1.86	1H		Götzis	28 May
1.91	Karolina	Blazej	POL	21.11.86	1		Opole	12 Jun
1.90i	Elena	Vallortigara	ITA	21.9.91	1		Padova	29 Jan
1.90i	Megan	Seidl	USA	4.11.86	1		Ames	12 Feb
1.90	Fabiola Elizabeth	Ayala	MEX	31.12.86	1		Monterrey	11 Mar
1.90	Sheree	Francis	JAM	20.10.83	1	DrakeR	Des Moines	30 Apr
1.90	Nadezhda	Dusanova	UZB	17.11.87	2=	DL	Shanghai	15 May
1.90	Adonía	Steryíou	GRE	7.7.85	1		Pátra	25 Jun
1.90	Yekaterina	Fedotova	RUS-J	3.7.92	2	NC-j	Cheboksary	2 Jul
	(50)							
1.90	Iryna	Myhalchenko	UKR	20.1.72	2	NC	Donetsk	3 Aug
1.90A	Romary	Rifka	MEX	8.4.73	1	NC	Ciudad de México	5 Aug
1.90	Øyunn	Grindem	NOR	11.11.87	1		Oslo	20 Aug
1.90		Duong Thi Viet Anh	VIE	30.12.90	1H	NC	Ho Chi Minh	12 Sep
1.89i	Julia	Wanner	GER	8.12.87	3		Dessau	2 Feb
1.89i	Alessia	Trost	ITA-J	8.3.93	1	NC-j	Ancona	12 Feb
1.89i	Stine	Kufaas	NOR	7.4.86	2	NC	Trondheim	13 Feb
1.89	Oldriska	Maresová	CZE	14.10.86	1		Ostrava	21 May
1.89	Liz	Patterson	USA	9.6.88	2	NC	Eugene	24 Jun
1.89	Raquel	Álvarez	ESP	13.6.83	1		Zaragoza	11 Aug
	(60)							
1.89	Olena	Holosha	UKR	26.1.82	1	NCp	Vinnytsa	15 Aug
1.89	Hyleas	Fountain	USA	14.1.81	1H	WCh	Daegu	29 Aug

Mark	Name	Nat	Born	Pos	Meet	Venue	Date
1.89A	Lesyaní Mayor	CUB	8.7.89	1	PAm	Guadalajara, MEX	26 Oct
1.89A	Marielys Rojas	VEN	30.4.86	2	PAm	Guadalajara, MEX	26 Oct
1.88i	Elena Meuti	ITA	26.6.83	1		Gent	13 Feb
1.88i	Hannelore Desmet	BEL	25.2.89	1	NC	Gent	20 Feb
1.88i	Kamila Stepaniuk	POL	22.3.86	1	NC	Spala	20 Feb
1.88i	Beatrice Lundmark	SUI	26.4.80	1	NC	St. Gallen	20 Feb
1.88	Kimberly Williamson	JAM-J	2.10.93	1		Spanish Town	25 Feb
1.88i	Chen Yanjun	CHN	13.1.88	2	NGP	Chengdu	20 Mar
(70)							
1.88	Valeriya Bogdanovich	BLR-J	1.5.92	1	NCp	Brest	21 May
1.88	Daniela Stanciu	ROU	15.10.87	1		Bucuresti	21 May
1.88	Qiao Yanrui	CHN	29.9.88	1	NGP	Kunshan	25 May
1.88	Yana Maksimova	BLR	9.1.89	2H		Götzis	28 May
1.88	Urszula Domel	POL	21.7.88	3		Opole	12 Jun
1.88	Deirdre Mullen	USA	21.5.82	1	NJ Int	Holmdel	18 Jun
1.88	Shanay Briscoe	USA-J	7.8.92	1	NC-j	Eugene	25 Jun
1.88	Stephanie Pywell	GBR	12.6.87	1		London (He)	10 Jul
1.88	Oksana Starostina	RUS	1.4.88	6	NC	Cheboksary	22 Jul
1.88	Nadja Kampschulte	GER-J	5.9.92	3	EJ	Tallinn	24 Jul
(80)							
1.88	Karolina Gronau	POL	12.7.84	1=	NC	Bydgoszcz	12 Aug
1.88	Monika Gollner	AUT	23.10.74	1		Bratislava	28 Aug
1.88	Anna Bogdanova	RUS	21.10.84	1H	Décastar	Talence	17 Sep
1.87i	Iva Straková	CZE	4.8.80	1		Ostrava	20 Jan
1.87	Rita Babos	HUN	21.10.80	1H	NC	Debrecen	21 May
1.87	Iryna Herashchenko	UKR-Y	10.3.95	1	NC-j	Donetsk	16 Jun
1.87	Austra Skujyte	LTU	12.8.79	1H	ECp-2	Ribeira Brava	2 Jul
1.87	Ligia Damaris Grozav	ROU-Y	26.1.94	1	WY	Villeneuve d'Ascq	8 Jul
1.87	Natalija Cakova	LAT	20.10.80	2		Jogeva	12 Jul
1.87	Hanne Van Hessche	BEL	5.7.91	9	EU23	Ostrava	16 Jul
(90)							
1.87	Nadine Broersen	NED	29.4.90	1H	EU23	Ostrava	16 Jul
1.87	Anastasiya Belyakova	RUS	4.12.90	2H	EU23	Ostrava	16 Jul
1.87	Miyuki Fukumoto	JPN	4.1.77	1		Tokyo	24 Jul
1.87	Vita Palamar	UKR	12.10.77	3	NC	Donetsk	3 Aug
1.87	Viktoriya Dobrynska	UKR	18.1.80	4	NC	Donetsk	3 Aug
1.87	Pham Thi Diem	VIE	24.1.90	3	SEAG	Palembang	13 Nov

Mark	Name	Nat	Born	Date
1.86i	Brittani Carter	USA	29.9.88	5 Feb
1.86i	Becky Christensen	USA	24.2.87	12 Feb
1.86Ai	Ada Robinson	USA	20.10.89	12 Feb
1.86i	Chiara Vitobello (100)	ITA	21.10.91	19 Feb
1.86i	Persefóni Hatzinákou	GRE	6.6.84	20 Feb
1.86	Liz Lamb	NZL	12.5.91	26 Feb
1.86i	Isobel Pooley	GBR-J	21.12.92	27 Feb
1.86i	Desirée Rossit	ITA-J	19.3.94	5 Mar
1.86	Kaitlin Morgan	AUS-Y	5.1.95	11 Mar
1.86	Kristen Meister	USA	28.12.87	1 May
1.86	Nia Ali	USA	23.10.88	14 May
1.86	Anastasiya Andreyeva	RUS-J	11.1.92	18 May
1.86	Alina Fyodorova	UKR	31.7.89	30 May
1.86	Marija Vukovic	MNE-J	21.1.92	1 Jun
1.86	Taylor Burke	USA-J	4.6.93	4 Jun
1.86	Gema Martín-Pozuelo	ESP	21.6.87	11 Jun
1.86	Melanie Bauschke	GER	14.7.88	18 Jun
1.86	Svetlana Linkevich	RUS	26.9.91	25 Jun
1.86	Jayne Nisbet	GBR	17.7.88	10 Jul
1.86	Viktorija Zemaityte	LTU	11.3.85	19 Aug
1.85i	Melina Brenner	GER-J	28.6.93	15 Jan
1.85Ai	Langley Iverson	USA	18.4.90	21 Jan
1.85i	Romana Dubnova	CZE	4.11.78	26 Jan
1.85i	Mirela Demireva	BUL	28.9.89	29 Jan
1.85i	Aleksandra Yaryshkina	RUS-Y	10.6.94	30 Jan
1.85i	Georgiana Zârcan	ROU	30.5.88	5 Feb
1.85i	Erika Schroll	USA	24.4.88	18 Feb
1.85i	Nele Hollmann	GER-J	18.10.92	19 Feb
1.85i	Krystle Schade	USA	2.7.90	26 Feb
1.85	Ellen Pettitt	AUS	13.5.86	6 Mar
1.85	Chanice Porter	JAM-Y	25.5.94	20 Mar
1.85	Viktoria Andonova	USA	19.11.86	1 Apr
1.85	Hollye Parent	CAN	8.1.91	2 Apr
1.85	Anika Smit	RSA	26.5.86	10 Apr
1.85	Lisa Egarter	AUT	1.5.91	15 Apr
1.85	Caterine Ibargüen	COL	12.2.84	15 Apr
1.85	Marjolein Lindemans	BEL-Y	17.2.94	7 May
1.85	Maya Pressley	USA	1.2.91	14 May
1.85	Anna Ustinova	KAZ	8.12.85	15 May
1.85	Peter-Gaye Reid	JAM-J	14.3.93	12 Jun
1.85	Meike Kröger	GER	21.7.86	13 Jun
1.85	Noengrothai Chaipetch	THA	1.12.82	10 Jul
1.85	Claudia García	ESP-J	30.9.92	24 Jul
1.85	Dior Delophont	FRA-Y	19.10.94	26 Jul
1.85	Marina Smolyakova	RUS	20.6.89	5 Aug
1.85	Kristina Poltavets	RUS	6.11.90	5 Aug
1.85	Olga Kurban	RUS	16.12.87	5 Aug
1.85	Lyudmyla Yosypenko	UKR	24.9.84	17 Sep
1.85	Valdiléia Martins	BRA	19.9.89	1 Oct
1.85A	Julia du Plessis	RSA-Y		5 Nov
1.85i	Yevgeniya Kononova	RUS	28.9.89	29 Dec
1.84i	Julia Hartmann	GER	10.4.86	26 Jan
1.84i	Christina Kiffe	GER-J	2.5.92	30 Jan
1.84i	Justyna Kasprzycka	POL	20.8.87	20 Feb
1.84i	Ye Jiaying	CHN-J	7.1.93	23 Feb
1.84i	Magdaléna Nová	CZE-J	27.10.92	26 Feb
1.84i	Wang Yang	CHN	14.2.89	27 Feb
1.84i	Tynita Butts	USA	10.6.90	11 Mar
1.84i	Victoria Lucas	USA	18.9.89	11 Mar
1.84i	Brianne Theisen	CAN	18.12.88	11 Mar
1.84	Amy Pejkovic	AUS-J	1.2.93	14 Mar
1.84	Sarah Cowley	NZL	3.2.84	26 Mar
1.84	Gu Xuan	CHN	19.11.87	21 May
1.84	Liu Xiaoyun	CHN-J	12.6.93	5 Jun
1.84A	Jillian Drouin	CAN	30.9.86	24 Jun
1.84	Giovanna Demo	ITA	29.6.87	25 Jun
1.84	Charlotte Brauch	GER	25.6.91	26 Jun
1.84	Katarina Mögenburg	NOR	16.6.91	26 Jun
1.84	Maiju Mattila	FIN	12.1.89	14 Jul
1.84	Elina Smolander	FIN	11.10.89	16 Jul
1.84	Wu Yin	CHN-J		21 Jul
1.84	Katarina Johnson-Thompson	GBR-J	9.1.93	21 Jul
1.84	Erika Wiklund	SWE	10.3.88	2 Aug
1.84	Lucimara da Silva	BRA	10.7.85	4 Aug
1.84	Bettie Wade	USA	11.9.86	13 Aug
1.84	Victoria Dronsfield (172)	SWE	6.6.91	18 Aug

Mark	Name		Nat	Born	Pos	Meet	Venue	Date

Best outdoor marks

Mark	Name	Pos	Meet	Venue	Date
1.95	Kuchina	1	EJ	Tallinn	24 Jul
1.95	Beitia	1		Los Corrales de Buelna	25 Jul
1.94	Okuneva	2	EU23	Ostrava	16 Jul
1.94	Jungmark	3	Hanz	Zagreb	13 Sep
1.92	Simic	1		Beograd	25 May
1.92	Angelsen	4	EU23	Ostrava	16 Jul
1.90	Frenkel	1		Neurim	26 Jun
1.88	Kufaas	1		Sollentuna	28 Jun
1.87	Trost	1	NC-j	Bressanone	18 Jun

1.86A	Robinson	13 May	1.85	Vitobello	14 May	
1.86	Fransen	14 May	1.85	Brenner	4 Jun	
1.86	Lundmark	21 Jul	1.85	Hollmann	4 Jun	
1.85	Christensen	4 Jun	1.84	Wang Yang	26 May	
1.85	Zârcan	10 Aug	1.84	Desmet	29 May	
1.84	Ye Jiaying	21 May	1.84	Demireva	29 Jun	
			1.84	Dubnova	23 Jul	

JUNIORS

See main list for top 10 juniors. 11 performances by 2 women to 1.91. Additional marks and further juniors:

Kuchina 2+

Mark	Pos	Meet	Venue	Date
1.95	1	EJ	Tallinn	24 Jul
1.94i	2		Hustopece	29 Jan
1.94	1	NC-j	Cheboksary	2 Jul
1.93i	1		Stockholm	22 Feb

Palsyte

Mark	Pos	Meet	Venue	Date
1.92	3		Madrid	9 Jul
1.92i	9q	EI	Paris (B)	4 Mar
1.92	3		Sochi	25 May
1.92	1		ISR Ch Tel Aviv	7 Jul
1.91	2	EJ	Tallinn	24 Jul

Mark	Name		Nat	Born	Pos	Meet	Venue	Date
1.86i	Isobel	Pooley	GBR	21.12.92	1	NC-j	Birmingham	27 Feb
1.86i	Desirée	Rossit	ITA	19.3.94	1	v2N-j	Hamburg	5 Mar
1.86	Kaitlin	Morgan	AUS-Y	5.1.95	1	NC-j	Sydney	11 Mar
1.86	Anastasiya	Andreyeva	RUS	11.1.92	2J		Krasnodar	18 May
1.86	Marija	Vukovic	MNE	21.1.92	1	S.States	Schaan	1 Jun
1.86	Taylor	Burke	USA	4.6.93	1		Columbus	4 Jun
1.85i	Melina	Brenner	GER	28.6.93	1J		Leverkusen	15 Jan
1.85					1		Regensburg	4 Jun
1.85i	Aleksandra	Yaryshkina	RUS-Y	10.6.94	1		Penza	30 Jan
1.85i	Nele	Hollmann	GER	18.10.92	1	NC-j	Leverkusen	19 Feb
1.85					2		Regensburg	4 Jun
1.85	Chanice	Porter (20)	JAM-Y	25.5.94	1J		Kingston	20 Mar
1.85	Marjolein	Lindemans	BEL-Y	17.2.94	1		Heusden-Zolder	7 May
1.85	Peter-Gaye	Reid	JAM	14.3.93	1	NC-j	Kingston	12 Jun
1.85	Claudia	García	ESP	30.9.92	6	EJ	Tallinn	24 Jul
1.85	Dior	Delophont	FRA-Y	19.10.94	1	EYOF	Trabzon	26 Jul
1.85A	Julia	du Plessis	RSA-Y		1		Potchefstroom	5 Nov

POLE VAULT

Mark	Name		Nat	Born	Pos	Meet	Venue	Date
4.91	Jenn	Suhr	USA	5.2.82	1		Rochester, NY	26 Jul

    ?? 4.81 4.91 5.00/xxx

4.86Ai	1	NC	Albuquerque	27 Feb	4.55/1 4.65/1 4.75/3 4.86/3 4.93/xxx
4.79	1	LGP	London (CP)	5 Aug	4.55/1 4.71/3 4.79/2 4.93/xxx
4.72	1	WK	Zürich	8 Sep	4.52/1 4.62/3 4.72/1 4.79/xxx
4.71i	1		Toronto	20 Feb	4.50/1 4.61/2 4.71/3 4.84/xxx
4.70	4	WCh	Daegu	30 Aug	4.55/1 4.70/2 4.75/xxx

4.85i	Yelena	Isinbayeva	RUS	3.6.82	1		Donetsk	12 Feb

    4.60/1 4.70/x 4.75/1 4.85/2 5.01/xxx

4.81i	1	Winter	Moskva	6 Feb	4.61/1 4.81/1 4.91/xxx
4.76	1	DNG	Stockholm	29 Jul	4.64/2 4.76/1 4.86/xxx

4.85i	Anna	Rogowska	POL	21.5.81	1	EI	Paris (B)	6 Mar

    4.35/1 4.60/2 4.70/1 4.75/2 4.80/1 4.85/2 4.91/xxx

4.76i	1	Pedro	Bydgoszcz	16 Feb	4.40/1 4.58/2 4.70/2 4.76/2 4.82/xx 4.84/x
4.75	1	ET	Stockholm	18 Jun	4.40/2 4.55/1 4.65/x 4.70/1 4.75/1 4.86/xxx
4.70i	2		Donetsk	12 Feb	4.40/2 4.60/2 4.70/1 4.80/xx 4.85/x
4.70	1	Slus	Otwock	4 Sep	??

4.85	Fabiana	Murer	BRA	16.3.81	1	WCh	Daegu	30 Aug

    4.55/1 4.65/1 4.75/1 4.80/2 4.85/1 4.90/xx 4.92/x

4.74i	1	Mill	New York	28 Jan	4.54/1 4.64/2 4.74/2 4.84/xxx
4.71	2	LGP	London (CP)	5 Aug	4.55/1 4.71/1 4.79/xxx
4.70	1	SAmC	Buenos Aires	2 Jun	4.50/3 4.70/3 4.90/xx-
4.70A	2	PAm	Guadalajara, MEX	24 Oct	4.50/3 4.60/x 4.65/2 4.70/1 4.75/x 4.80/xx

4.80	Martina	Strutz	GER	4.11.81	2	WCh	Daegu	30 Aug

    4.45/2 4.55/1 4.65/1 4.70/1 4.75/2 4.80/1 4.85/x 4.90/xx

4.78	1		Karlsruhe	12 Jul	4.40/1 4.50/1 4.60/1 4.67/1 4.78/1
4.71	1		Praha	22 Jun	4.36/2 4.46/1 4.56/1 4.66/1 4.71/3
4.70	1		Neubrandenburg	18 Jun	4.40/1 4.50/2 4.62/1 4.70/1
4.70	1		Sopot	29 Jun	4.40/2 4.50/1 4.60/1 4.70/1 4.78/xxx
4.70	1		Mannheim	2 Jul	4.40/2 4.50/1 4.60/1 4.70/2 4.78/xxx
4.70	1		Reims	5 Jul	4.45/1 4.55/1 4.65/2 4.70/1 4.78/xxx
4.70	1		Beckum	31 Jul	4.40/2 4.50/2 4.60/3 4.65/1 4.70/3 4.79/xxx

4.76i	Silke	Spiegelburg	GER	17.3.86	1		Karlsruhe	13 Feb

    4.45/1 4.61/xx 4.66/1 4.76/3

4.75i	2	EI	Paris (B)	6 Mar	4.50/1 4.65/2 4.70/1 4.75/2 4.80/x 4.85/xx
4.75	2	ET	Stockholm	18 Jun	4.35/1 4.45/1 4.55/1 4.65/1 4.70/x 4.75/2 4.80/xx

Mark	Name		Nat	Born	Pos	Meet	Venue	Date
	4.72	2 WK Zürich		8 Sep			4.42/1 4.52/2 4.62/1 4.72/2 4.79/xxx	
	4.71	1 ISTAF Berlin		11 Sep			4.46/1 4.56/3 4.66/1 4.71/2 4.81/xxx	
	4.70i	1 Spark Stuttgart		5 Feb			4.40/2 4.58/1 4.64/1 4.70/1 4.76/xxx	
	4.70	2 DNG Stockholm		29 Jul			4.41/1 4.51/1 4.64/3 4.70/3 4.76/xxx	
4.75	Svetlana	Feofanova	RUS	16.7.80	3	WCh	Daegu	30 Aug
							4.45/1 4.55/1 4.65/1 4.75/1 4.80/xxx	
	4.71	3 LGP London (CP)		5 Aug			4.45/1 4.55/3 4.63/1 4.71/2 4.79/xxx	
	4.70i	2 Pedro Bydgoszcz		16 Feb			4.40/2 4.58/2 4.70/1 4.76/xx 4.82/x	
	4.70	1 Kuso Szczecin		25 Jun			4.40/1 4.60/1. 4.70/1 4.80/xxx	
	4.70	1 Velenje		28 Jun			.40/1 4.60/1 4.70/3 4.81/xx	
4.75A	Yarisley	Silva	CUB	1.6.87	1	PAm	Guadalajara, MEX	24 Oct
							4.30/1 4.40/1 4.50/1 4.60/1 4.70/1 4.75/1 4.80/xxx	
	4.70	5 WCh Daegu		30 Aug			4.45/1 4.55/1 4.65/1 4.70/3 4.80/xxx	
4.71	Nikoléta	Kiriakopoúlou	GRE	21.3.86	4	LGP	London (CP)	5 Aug
							4.30/1 4.45/1 4.55/1 4.63/1 4.71/3 4.79/xxx	
	4.70	1 NC Athína		29 Jul			4.30/1 4.40/1 4.50/2 4.62/1 4.70/1	
4.71i	Holly	Bleasdale (10)	GBR	2.11.91	1		Orleans	10 Dec
							4.21/1 4.36/1 4.51/1 4.61/2 4.71/1 4.81/xxx	
	4.70	2 Mannheim		2 Jul			4.30/1 4.50/1 4.60/1 4.65/2 4.70/2 4.75/x	
4.70i	Kylie	Hutson	USA	27.11.87	1		Des Moines	27 Apr
	(45/11)						4.10/1 4.25/1 4.40/1 4.50/2 4.60/1 4.65/1 4.70/1 4.75/xxx	
4.66i	Kristina	Gadschiew	GER	3.7.84	1		Potsdam	18 Feb
4.65i	Lisa	Ryzih	GER	27.9.88	1	NC	Leipzig	27 Feb
4.65	Aleksandra	Kiryashova	RUS	21.8.85	1	WUG	Shenzhen	19 Aug
4.65	Carolin	Hingst	GER	18.9.80	2		Beckum	31 Jul
4.65	Jirina	Ptácníková	CZE	20.5.86	7	WCh	Daegu	30 Aug
4.63i	Angelica	Bengtsson	SWE-J	8.7.93	2	XL-Galan	Stockholm	22 Feb
4.61	Tina	Sutej	SLO	7.11.88	1	SEC	Athens GA	14 May
4.61	Kate	Dennison	GBR	7.5.84	2		Barcelona	22 Jul
4.60i	Monika	Pyrek	POL	11.8.80	4		Donetsk	12 Feb
	(20)							
4.60i	Yuliya	Golubchikova	RUS	27.3.83	7		Donetsk	12 Feb
4.60	Alana	Boyd	AUS	10.5.84	1		Perth	4 Mar
4.60i	Minna	Nikkanen	FIN	9.4.88	4=	EI	Paris (B)	6 Mar
4.60i	Lacy	Janson	USA	20.2.83	2		Des Moines	27 Apr
4.60	Mary	Saxer	USA	21.6.87	1		Seattle	9 Jul
4.55Ai	Becky	Holliday	USA	12.3.80	2	NC	Albuquerque	27 Febl
4.55Ai	Melinda	Owen	USA	30.10.84	3	NC	Albuquerque	27 Feb
4.55i	Anastasiya	Shvedova	BLR	3.5.79	Q	EI	Paris (B)	5 Mar
4.51i	Anna	Battke	GER	3.1.85	4		Karlsruhe	13 Feb
4.51	Daylis	Caballero	CUB	6.3.88	2		La Habana	25 Feb
	(30)							
4.51i	Vanessa	Boslak	FRA	11.6.82	1		Orleans	10 Dec
4.50i	Malin	Dahlström	SWE	26.8.89	3		Potsdam	18 Feb
4.50	Jillian	Schwartz	ISR	19.9.79	1		Tel Aviv	30 Apr
4.50	Nicole	Büchler	SUI	17.12.83	1		Bern	25 Jun
4.50	Tatyana	Polnova	RUS	20.4.79	4	Kuso	Szczecin	25 Jun
4.50	Anna	Giordano Bruno	ITA	13.12.80	1		Vicenza	10 Jul
4.50	Eleonor	Tavares	POR	24.9.85	1	FRA Ch	Albi	29 Jul
4.50	Marion	Lotout	FRA	19.11.89	2	NC	Albi	29 Jul
4.50	Julia	Hütter	GER	26.7.83	2		Mannheim	13 Aug
4.45	Shade	Weygandt	USA	24.1.91	2	TexR	Austin	9 Apr
	(40)							
4.45	Stélla-Iró	Ledáki	GRE	18.7.88	1		Haniá	4 Jun
4.45	Melissa	Gergel	USA	24.4.89	1	NCAA	Des Moines	10 Jun
4.45	Ekateríni	Stefanídi	GRE	4.2.90	2	EU23	Ostrava	17 Jul
4.45	Anna Katharina	Schmid	SUI	2.12.89	1	NC	Basel	5 Aug
4.45	April	Steiner Bennett	USA	22.4.80	1		Clovis	12 Aug
4.42	Janice	Keppler	USA	22.3.87	1		Seaside Heights	7 Aug
4.41	Telie	Mathiot	FRA	25.5.87	1	Univ Ch	Saran	4 Jun
4.41	Anna María	Pinero	ESP	15.1.86	1		Zaragoza	25 Jun
4.40i	Anastasiya	Savchenko	RUS	15.11.89	1	Mosc Ch	Moskva	30 Jan
4.40i	Anzhelika	Sidorova	RUS	28.6.91	1-22	Mosc Ch	Moskva	10 Feb
	(50)							
4.40i	Caroline Bonde	Holm	DEN	19.7.90	4		Potsdam	18 Feb
4.40		Li Ling	CHN	6.7.89	6=	DL	Shanghai	15 May
4.40	Kelsie	Hendry	CAN	29.6.82	3		Chula Vista	19 May
4.40		Xu Huiqin	CHN-J	4.9.93	1	NC-j	Jinan	3 Jun
4.40		Choi Yun-hee	KOR	28.5.86	1	NC	Daegu	10 Jun
4.40	Natalya	Demidenko	RUS-J	7.3.93	1	NC-j	Cheboksary	1 Jul
4.40	Annika	Roloff	GER	10.3.91	5		Mannheim	2 Jul

Mark	Name		Nat	Born	Pos	Meet	Venue	Date	
4.40	Tori	Pena	IRL	30.7.87	1		Frauenkappelen	1	Aug
4.40	Cathrine	Larsåsen	NOR	5.12.86	1	DEN Ch	København	6	Aug
4.40i	Yekaterina	Kazeka	RUS	7.10.90	1		Chelyabinsk	18	Dec
	(60)								
4.37i	Natalie	Willer	USA	10.2.90	1	Big 12	Lincoln NE	26	Feb
4.36	Vera	Neuenswander	USA	3.12.87	1	Big 10	Iowa City	13	May
4.36i	Marion	Fiack	FRA-J	13.10.92	3		Orleans	10	Dec
4.35i	Giorgia	Benecchi	ITA	9.7.89	1		Aosta	29	Jan
4.35	Karla	da Silva	BRA	12.11.84	1		São Caetano do Sul	26	Feb
4.35i	Anna	Schultze	GER	26.5.85	5	NC	Leipzig	27	Feb
4.35	Rachel	Laurent	USA	21.9.89	3	TexR	Austin	9	Apr
4.35	Sam	Sonnenberg	USA	10.2.88	1		St. Paul	4	May
4.35		Wu Sha	CHN	21.10.87	1	AsiC	Kobe	9	Jul
4.35	Dímitra	Emmanouíl	GRE	13.5.84	2	NC	Athína	29	Jul
	(70)								
4.35	Sally	Peake	GBR	8.2.86	4	WUG	Shenzhen	19	Aug
4.35	Joanna	Piwowarska	POL	4.11.83	5	WUG	Shenzhen	19	Aug
4.34	Morgann	LeLeux	USA-J	14.11.92	1		Lafayette	27	Apr
4.33	Keisa	Monterola	VEN	26.2.88	1		Spokane	23	May
4.32i	Mami	Nakano	JPN	12.3.79	1		Kan-onji	13	Feb
4.32	Desiree	Singh	GER-Y	17.8.94	1	NC-j	Jena	5	Aug
4.31i	Rianna	Galiart	NED	22.11.85	1		Kirchberg	29	Jan
4.31i	Romana	Malácová	CZE	15.5.87	4		Landau	5	Feb
4.31i	Katharina	Bauer	GER	12.6.90	4		Landau	5	Feb
4.31i	Denise	von Eynatten	GER	30.12.87	1	Big East	Akron	20	Feb
	(80)								
4.31	Joanna	Wright	USA	3.5.89	1		Tallahassee	9	Apr
4.31	Katy	Viuf	USA	23.5.87	2		Chula Vista	2	Jun
4.30i	Lyudmila	Yeremina	RUS	8.8.91	2		Moskva	9	Jan
4.30i	Naroa	Agirre	ESP	15.5.79	1		Valencia	22	Jan
4.30i	Kelly	Phillips	USA	12.9.88	1		Blacksburg	5	Feb
4.30i	Anastasiya	Biryukova	RUS-J	12.7.92	5	NC	Moskva	16	Feb
4.30i	Afrodíti	Skafída	GRE	20.3.82	2	NC	Athína (Peanía)	19	Feb
4.30i	Leslie	Brost	USA	28.9.89	1		Fargo	28	Feb
4.30i	Natalya	Bartnovskaya	RUS	7.1.89	1	JUCO	Lubbock	4	Mar
4.30i	Tara	Diebold	USA	28.11.88	6	NCAA	College Station	12	Mar
	(90)								
4.30	Sandi	Morris	USA-J	8.7.92	1		Durham NC	8	Apr
4.30	Alejandra	García	ARG	13.6.73	1	NC	Buenos Aires	16	Apr
4.30	Denise	Groot	NED	26.5.90	1		Hoorn	21	May
4.30	Hanna	Shelekh	UKR-J	14.7.93	1	NCp	Yalta	30	May
4.30i	Katelin	Rains	USA	20.8.87	1		Jonesboro	9	Jun
4.30	Kelsie	Ahbe	USA	6.7.91	6	NCAA	Des Moines	10	Jun
4.30	Victoria	von Eynatten	GER	6.10.91	2	NC-23	Bremen	25	Jun
4.30	Gabriella	Duclos-Lasnier	CAN	1.3.88	2	Jerome	Burnaby	1	Jul
4.30	Carly	Dockendorf	CAN	31.12.83	2		Seattle	9	Jul
4.30	Mélanie	Blouin	CAN	14.7.90	1		Québec City	16	Jul
	(100)								
4.30	Liz	Parnov	AUS-Y	9.5.94	5	NA	Heusden-Zolder	16	Jul
4.30	Elena	Scarpellini	ITA	14.1.87	4		Lignano	19	Jul
4.30	Martina	Schultze	GER	12.9.90	1		Mössingen	3	Aug
4.30	Brysun	Stately	USA	22.11.86	1c2		Clovis	12	Aug
4.30i	Angelina	Zhuk	RUS	7.2.91	2		Omsk	23	Dec

Mark	Name		Nat	Born	Date		Mark	Name		Nat	Born	Date	
4.29	Kat	Majester	USA	22.5.87	11	Jun	4.21i	MacKenzie	Fields	USA	19.1.90	11	Feb
4.27	Katie	Tannehill	USA	9.9.87	9	Jun	4.21i	Emma	Lyons	GBR	14.6.87	26	Feb
4.26i	Rachel	Fisher	USA	9.1.91	5	Mar	4.21	Neal	Tisher	USA	3.7.91	14	May
4.26i	Allison	Stokke	USA	22.3.89	5	Mar	4.21	Anjuli	Knäsche	GER-J	18.10.93	7	Aug
4.26	Michaela	Meijer	SWE-J	30.7.93	3	Sep	4.20i	Alicia	Rue	USA	4.8.88	22	Jan
4.25i	Amy	Fryt	USA	27.3.89	19	Feb	4.20i	Roberta	Bruni	ITA-Y	8.3.94	29	Jan
4.25i	Yekaterina	Kolesova	RUS	4.9.90	22	Feb	4.20Ai	Shaylah	Simpson	USA-J	16.3.92	29	Jan
4.25i	Sonia	Grabowska	POL	15.12.88	25	Feb	4.20i	Karmen	Bunikowska	POL	21.3.88	30	Jan
4.25	Jessica	Hemingway	USA	6.10.88	15	Apr	4.20	Charmaine	Lucock	AUS	8.4.87	27	Feb
4.25	Alixe	Guigon	FRA	24.1.85	12	Jun	4.20	Kat	Schauerhamer	USA	24.9.84	4	May
4.25	Joana	Kraft	GER	27.7.91	23	Jul	4.20	Bethany	Buell	USA	4.12.91	7	May
4.25	Alice	Ost	FRA	25.10.87	29	Jul	4.20		Li Caixia	CHN	23.8.87	15	May
4.25	Jelena	Radinovic-Vasic	SRB	5.7.83	19	Aug	4.20	Heather	Hamilton	CAN	31.3.88	21	May
4.25	Agnieszka	Wrona	POL	5.5.82	21	Aug	4.20	Loréla	Mánou	GRE	20.12.90	25	May
4.24i	Sandra-Hélèna	Tavares/Homo	POR	29.5.82	27	Feb	4.20	Kseniya	Chertkoshvili	UKR-J	18.2.92	30	May
4.23	Laura	Asimakis	USA	26.11.88	15	May	4.20	Megumi	Nakada	JPN	6.12.88	4	Jun
4.23	Alex	Acker	USA	12.9.88	15	May	4.20	Aurélie	De Ryck	BEL-J	17.12.92	13	Jun
4.22i	Tomomi	Abiko	JPN	17.3.88	5	Mar	4.20	Katie	Byres	GBR-J	11.9.93	2	Jul
4.22Ai	Christen	Botteron	USA	14.9.89	25	Feb	4.20	Vicky	Robson	CAN	9.4.85	3	Jul
4.22i	Chloe	Henry	BEL	5.3.87	29	Dec	4.20 sq	Agnieszka	Kolasa	POL-J	20.5.92	7	Jul

Mark	Name	Nat	Born	Date
4.20	Lillian Schnitzerling	GER-J	5.12.93	10 Jul
4.20	Leonie Schilder	NED	15.9.90	10 Jul
4.20	Iben Høgh-Pedersen	DEN	14.8.90	6 Aug
4.20	Alissa Söderberg	SWE-Y	12.4.94	26 Aug
4.20	Valeria Chiaraviglio	ARG	9.4.89	2 Oct
4.20	Roslinda Samsu	MAS	9.6.82	15 Nov
4.20	Le Thi Phuong	VIE	12.11.83	15 Nov
4.18	Sarah Pappas	USA	30.3.87	6 May
4.17i	Abby Schaffer	USA	26.3.90	12 Mar
4.16i	Jordan Roskelley	USA	19.9.89	12 Feb
4.16i	Sally Scott	GBR	12.4.91	13 Feb
4.16	Kaitlin Petrillose	USA-J	10.12.92	14 Apr
4.16	Ellie McCardwell	USA-J	11.6.92	23 Apr
4.16	Bryony Raine	GBR	30.8.86	9 Jul
4.16	Sara Pereira	BRA	3.8.90	13 Aug
4.15i	Brigitte Gross	USA	22.11.90	21 Jan
4.15i	Olga Lapina	KAZ	6.7.90	8 Feb
4.15i	Jenny Soceka	USA	1.3.87	11 Feb
4.15i	Becca Pilkerton	USA	11.6.90	11 Feb
4.15i	Fanny Berglund	SWE	8.2.88	15 Feb
4.15i	Stephanie Foreman	USA	10.3.90	28 Feb
4.15	Tori Anthony	USA	19.4.89	9 Apr
4.15	Kelsey Hintz	USA	21.9.90	23 Apr
4.15	Katherine Lee	USA	3.8.90	23 Apr
4.15	Allison Koressel	USA	2.3.91	23 Apr
4.15	Rita Ciambra	USA	23.3.88	7 May
4.15	Patrícia dos Santos	BRA	13.6.84	17 May
4.15	Camille Simon	FRA	24.4.86	12 Jun
4.15	Daniela Höllwarth	AUT	24.8.87	17 Jul
4.15	Hortense Lecuyot	FRA	4.2.89	29 Jul
4.15	Ren Mengqian	CHN-J	4.10.93	23 Oct
4.14i	Lynda Cooper	USA	29.6.87	5 Feb
4.14	Catherine Street	USA	9.5.90	27 May
4.13Ai	Lauren Stelten	USA		11 Mar
4.13Ai	Lauren Graham	USA	17.10.91	11 Mar
4.13	Jaci Perryman	USA	25.2.88	15 May
4.12i	Marion Buisson	FRA	19.2.88	15 Jan
4.12i	Stephanie Duffy	USA	8.2.89	5 Feb
4.12i	Cami Jiskra	USA	22.2.89	26 Feb
4.12i	Karin Fisher	USA	28.12.88	4 Mar
4.12	Fanny Smets	BEL	21.4.86	4 Jun
4.12	Reena Koll	EST-Y	15.11.96	19 Jun
4.11i	Lembi Vaher	EST	11.2.87	19 Feb
4.11i	Ariana Ince	USA	14.3.89	5 Mar
4.11i	Lizzy Norvell	USA	23.9.88	5 Mar
4.11	Daisy Glasser	USA	10.7.89	14 May
4.11	Anginae Monteverde	USA-J	15.1.93	4 Jun
4.11 sq	Doris Auer	AUT	10.5.71	5 Jul
4.11	Emily Grive	USA-J	22.5.93	15 Jul
4.11	Robin Wingbermühle	NED-J	20.5.92	30 Jul

(195)   27 women at 4.10

Best outdoors

Mark	Name	Pos	Meet	Venue	Date
4.65	Hutson	1	NC	Eugene	26 Jun
4.60	Gadschiew	3	NC	Kassel	23 Jul
4.60	Pyrek	2	NC	Bydgoszcz	12 Aug
4.57	Bengtsson	1	EJ	Tallinn	23 Jul
4.55	Holliday	1		Chula Vista	16 Jun
4.50	Janson	3	NC	Eugene	26 Jun
4.50	Shvedova	1	ISR Ch	Tel Aviv	6 Jul
4.50sq	Battke	2=		Karlsruhe	12 Jul
4.40	Savchenko	6=	DL	Shanghai	15 May
4.36	Dahlström	2		Göteborg	11 Jun
4.33	Willer	1	Big 12	Norman OK	15 May
4.31	Galiart	2		Sittard	9 Sep
4.30	D von Eynatten	4	TexR	Austin	9 Apr
4.30	Holm	6=	Kuso	Szczecin	25 Jun
4.30	Nikkanen	2		Kuortane	25 Jun
4.30	Agirre	1		Majadahonda	8 Jul
4.30	Sidorova	4	NC	Cheboksary	22 Jul
4.30	Skafída	3	NC	Athína	29 Jul
4.30	Yeremina	1		Irkutsk	4 Aug
4.30	Boslak	1		Mortagne-au-Perche	25 Sep

Mark	Name	Date		Mark	Name	Date
4.25	Kazeka	18 Jun		4.20	Brost	6 May
4.25	Zhuk	24 Jun		4.20	Bartnovskaya	20 May
4.25	Bauer	25 Jun		4.20	Bruni	2 Jun
4.25	Malácová	19 Aug		4.20	Abiko	10 Jun
4.20	Diebold	2 Apr		4.20	Kolesova	24 Jun

Mark	Name	Date		Mark	Name	Date
4.20	Rains	26 Jun		4.15	Fiack	29 Jul
4.20	Biryukova	1 Jul		4.15	S-H Tavares	29 Jul
4.20	Nakano	17 Jul		4.14	Schaffer	27 May
4.20	Benecchi	25 Sep		4.12	Duffy	18 Mar
4.16	Fields	22 Apr		4.12	Foreman	23 Apr
				4.11	Henry	9 Sep

Downhill runway: 4.61 Becky Holliday USA 12.3.80 1 Champaign 2 Jul
Exhibition: 4.40 Giorgia Benecchi ITA 9.7.89 1 Bisceglie 20 Aug

JUNIORS

See main list for top 10 juniors. 12 performances by 6 women to 4.32. Additional marks and further juniors:

Bengtsson 2+4.52i 1 NC-j Sätra 20 Feb   4.41 8 DNG Stockholm 29 Jul
       4.42i 1 Örebro 15 Jan   4.35 12=q EI Paris (B) 5 Mar
       4.41i 3 v4N Glasgow 29 Jan

Mark	Name	Nat	Born	Pos	Meet	Venue	Date
4.26	Michaela Meijer	SWE	30.7.93	1	Nordic-J	København	3 Sep
4.21	Anjuli Knäsche	GER	18.10.93	1	NC-j	Jena	7 Aug
4.20i	Roberta Bruni	ITA-Y	8.3.94	1		Fermo	29 Jan
4.20				1		Rieti	2 Jun
4.20	Kseniya Chertkoshvili	UKR	18.2.92	2	NCp	Yalta	30 May
4.20	Aurélie De Ryck	BEL	17.12.92	2		Rehlingen	13 Jun
4.20	Katie Byres	GBR	11.9.93	1J		Mannheim	2 Jul
4.20 sq	Agnieszka Kolasa	POL	20.5.92	1		Ostrava	7 Jul
4.20	Lillian Schnitzerling	GER	5.12.93	1		Gladbeck	10 Jul
4.20	Alissa Söderberg (20)	SWE-Y	12.4.94	1	NC-j	Vellinge	26 Aug

Best out: 4.20 Anastasiya Biryukova RUS 12.7.92 2 NC-j Cheboksary 1 Jul

LONG JUMP

Mark	Wind	Name	Nat	Born	Pos	Meet	Venue	Date
7.19	1.8	Brittney Reese	USA	9.9.86	1	NC	Eugene	26 Jun

7.02/1.7 x p x x 7.19
| 6.94 | -0.4 | 1 | GGala | Roma | | | | 26 May |

6.84/-0.4 x x 6.94/-0.4 x 6.94/-0.2
| 6.86Ai | | 2 | NC | Albuquerque | | | | 27 Feb |

6.86 x x x x x
| 6.85 | 0.1 | 1 | Athl | Lausanne | | | | 30 Jun |

6.27 6.73 6.85 x p x
| 6.83 | 1.5 | 1 | MSR | Walnut | | | | 16 Apr |

6.60 6.58 x 6.82/0.9 x 6.83
| 6.98w | 3.5 | 1 | | Oxford MS | | | | 9 Apr |

??

| 7.05 | 1.1 | Darya Klishina | RUS | 15.1.91 | 1 | EU23 | Ostrava | 17 Jul |

7.05 x 6.53 x p 6.71

| 7.01 | 0.3 | Olga Zaytseva | RUS | 10.11.84 | 1 | NC | Cheboksary | 22 Jul |

6.85/1.0 7.01 6.96/0.1 6.75 x 6.95/-1.5
| 6.84 | 0.2 | 1 | GP | Rieti | | | | 10 Sep |

6.83 6.84 6.62 6.29 4.92 6.21

Mark	Wind	Name		Nat	Born	Pos	Meet	Venue	Date
6.99Ai		Janay	DeLoach	USA	12.10.85	1	NC	Albuquerque	27 Feb
					6.59 6.74 6.99 x 6.69 6.80				
		6.97 2.0 2 NC	Eugene	26 Jun	6.97 6.80/0.1 p 6.79w 6.83w/2.3 x				
6.95	0.2	Veranika	Shutkova	BLR	26.5.86	1	NCp	Brest	21 May
					6.95 p p x 6.59 p				
6.94A	1.1	Maurren	Maggi	BRA	25.6.76	1	PAm	Guadalajara, MEX	26 Oct
					6.58 6.80 6.94 p 6.60 p				
		6.89 -0.2 1	São Paulo	22 May	6.84/1.1 6.84/0.0 6.89/-0.2 p 6.84/1.8 x				
		6.87 1.5 2 DL	Doha	6 May	x 6.87 6.76/1.6 x				
		6.86 Q WCh	Daegu	27 Aug	6.55 6.86				
6.91	0.8	Éloyse	Lesueur	FRA	15.7.88	1	Déca	Nice	18 Sep
					6.83/0.8 6.71 6.91				
6.89i		Anna	Nazarova	RUS	14.3.86	1		Krasnodar	29 Jan
					6.73 6.89 6.80 6.74 6.71 6.84				
		6.88 0.7 Q NC	Cheboksary	21 Jul	6.88 only jump				
6.89	0.7	Olga	Balayeva	RUS	31.7.84	1		Kohila	30 Jun
					x x 6.50 6.52 6.57 6.89				
6.88	1.6	Funmi	Jimoh (10)	USA	29.5.84	1	DL	Doha	6 May
					6.88 6.85w/2.5 6.73w x				
		6.88 1.5 3 NC	Eugene	26 Jun	6.88 x 6.85w/2.9 x 6.78w 6.54				
		6.87 -0.1 2 GGala	Roma	26 May	6.30 6.87 6.58 x x 6.21				
6.87	1.3	Brianna	Glenn	USA	18.4.80	*		Chula Vista	16 Jun
					7.00w 6.96w/3.3 6.85w/2.3 x 6.72 6.87				
6.87	2.0	Viktoriya	Rybalko	UKR	26.10.82	1	NC	Donetsk	3 Aug
					6.70 p p 6.87 p p				
6.86	1.8	Lauma	Griva	LAT	27.10.84	1		Valmiera	10 Jun
					6.46 6.86 p p p p				
6.86	0.0	Olga	Kucherenko	RUS	5.11.85	2	NC	Cheboksary	22 Jul
					6.66 6.65 6.72 6.78 6.86 6.79				
6.85	2.0	Anastasiya	Mironchik-Ivanova	BLR	13.4.89	1		Minsk	3 Jun
					6.83/2.0 6.46w x 6.85 6.77 6.68w				
6.84	1.5	Lyudmila	Kolchanova	RUS	1.10.79	1	Znam	Zhukovskiy	3 Jul
					6.84 6.82 x x 6.47w x				
6.84	1.0	Irène	Pusterla	SUI	21.6.88	1		Chiasso	20 Aug
					6.46 6.77/0.9 5.48 x 6.41 6.81				
6.83i		Marshevet	Hooker/Myers	USA	25.9.84	1		Fayetteville	11 Feb
					x x 6.26 6.33 6.83 p				
6.83	1.7	Inna	Ahkozova	UKR	16.9.84	1		Yalta	18 May
					6.58w x 6.35 6.54 6.59 6.83				
6.83	0.4	Yuliya	Pidluzhnaya (20)	RUS	1.10.88	3	NC	Cheboksary	22 Jul
					6.83 x 6.74 6.75 6.71 6.58				
6.83	0.8	Sosthene	Moguenara	GER	17.10.89	1		Mannheim	13 Aug
		(33/21)			6.68 6.78 6.83 x 6.76 6.62w				
6.82	1.7	Tatyana	Chernova	RUS	29.1.88	1H		Götzis	29 May
6.81	1.4	Shara	Proctor	GBR	16.9.88	1		Clermont	11 Jun
6.81	0.4	Bianca	Kappler	GER	8.8.77	1		Wesel	13 Jun
6.81	0.7	Bianca	Stuart	BAH	17.5.88	1	CAC	Mayagüez	17 Jul
6.79i		Naide	Gomes	POR	20.11.79	2	EI	Paris (B)	6 Mar
6.78	1.5	Blessing	Okagbare	NGR	9.10.88	1	NC	Calabar	25 Jun
6.78	-0.6	Teresa	Dobija	POL	19.10.82	1		Bialogard	3 Aug
6.76	1.2	Yelena	Sokolova	RUS	23.7.86	Q	NC	Cheboksary	21 Jul
6.76	-0.3	Ineta	Radevica	LAT	13.7.81	3	WCh	Daegu	28 Aug
		(30)							
6.76	1.0	Hyleas	Fountain	USA	14.1.81	3	Déca	Nice	18 Sep
6.75	1.8	Tori	Polk	USA	21.9.83	2		Clermont	11 Jun
6.74	2.0	Tatyana	Kotova	RUS	11.12.76	4	DL	Doha	6 May
6.73i		Ksenija	Balta	EST	11.1.86	1		Tallinn	19 Feb
6.73	0.7	Carolina	Klüft	SWE	2.2.83	2	ET	Stockholm	19 Jun
6.72i		Irina	Meleshina	RUS	25.5.82	1	Mosc Ch	Moskva	29 Jan
6.72	1.8	Concepción	Montaner	ESP	14.1.81	1		Valencia	14 May
6.72	1.2	Yuliya	Tarasova	UZB	13.3.86	1	NC	Tashkent	2 Oct
6.71	0.8	Ola	Sesay	SLE	30.5.79	1		Houston	19 May
6.71	1.1	Ivana	Spanovic	SRB	10.5.90	*	EU23	Ostrava	17 Jul
		(40)							
6.71	0.6	Viorica	Tigâu	ROU	12.8.79	1	NC	Bucuresti	10 Aug
6.71	1.1	Marestella	Torres	PHI	20.2.81	1	SEAG	Palembang	12 Nov
6.70	0.5	Lena	Malkus	GER-J	6.8.93	1	NC-23	Bremen	25 Jun
6.70	0.2	Yekaterina	Koneva	RUS	25.9.88	1		Bryansk	18 Jun
6.67	0.4	Keila	Costa	BRA	6.2.83	3		São Paulo	22 May
6.67	1.9	Nina	Kolaric	SLO	12.12.86	1		Ptuj	14 Aug
6.66	1.0	Karen Melis	Mey	TUR	31.5.84	2		Wesel	13 Jun

Mark	Wind	Name		Nat	Born	Pos	Meet	Venue	Date	
6.66	1.4	Melanie	Bauschke	GER	14.7.88	3		Wesel	13	Jun
6.66	1.4	Jana	Veldáková	SVK	3.6.81	1		Ptuj	14	Aug
6.65i		Chantel	Malone	IVB	2.12.91	1		Fayetteville	28	Jan
		(50)								
6.65	0.1	Jovanee	Jarrett	JAM	15.1.83	2		Auburn	16	Apr
6.65	0.0	Aiga	Grabuste	LAT	24.3.88	1H		Kladno	16	Jun
6.65	0.7	Malgorzata	Trybanska	POL	21.6.81	1	NC	Bydgoszcz	12	Aug
6.65	1.5	Nadja	Käther	GER	29.9.88	3		Mannheim	13	Aug
6.64	0.7	Ruky	Abdulai	CAN	8.8.82	2	GP	Ponce	14	May
6.64	0.9	Michelle	Weitzel	GER	18.6.87	3		Weinheim	28	May
6.64	-1.6	Tori	Bowie	USA	27.8.90	1	NCAA	Des Moines	8	Jun
6.64	-0.8	Ti'Anca	Mock	USA	5.6.88	2	NCAA	Des Moines	8	Jun
6.64	1.6	Renata	Medgyesová	SVK	28.1.83	2	Gyulai	Budapest	30	Jul
6.63	0.7	Mayookha	Johny	IND	9.4.88	1	IS	Bangalore	11	Jun
		(60)								
6.63	1.4	Whitney	Gipson	USA	20.9.90	*	NC	Eugene	26	Jun
6.63A	1.6	Caterine	Ibargüen	COL	12.2.84	3	PAm	Guadalajara, MEX	26	Oct
6.62	1.8	Anna	Jagaciak	POL	10.2.90	4	EU23	Ostrava	17	Jul
6.62	0.3	Krysha	Bayley	CAN	21.1.84	1		Edmonton	6	Aug
6.61	0.7	Suslaidy	Girat	CUB	19.8.87	1		La Habana	17	Feb
6.61i		Cornelia	Deiac	ROU	20.3.88	1	NC	Bucuresti	19	Feb
6.60	-1.6	Vanessa	Seles	BRA	26.10.81	1		São Paulo	16	Apr
6.60	1.1	Brooke	Stratton	AUS-J	12.7.93	1		Mannheim	3	Jul
6.60	0.5	Clélia	Reuse	SUI	1.8.88	1		Bulle	9	Jul
6.60	0.0	Oksana	Zhukovskaya	RUS	12.9.84	7	NC	Cheboksary	22	Jul
		(70)								
6.59	1.3	Comfort	Onyali	NGR	25.4.83	1		Valencia	8	Jul
6.59	2.0	Mara	Griva	LAT	4.8.89	5	EU23	Ostrava	17	Jul
6.58i			Lu Minjia	CHN-J	29.12.92	1	NGP	Nanjing	22	Feb
6.58	0.2	Yekaterina	Malysheva	RUS	16.4.88	1		Krasnodar	1	Jun
6.58	1.8	Karolina	Tyminska	POL	4.10.84	3H		Kladno	16	Jun
6.58	1.6	Eliane	Martins	BRA	26.5.86	2	NC	São Paulo	7	Aug
6.56	0.4	April	Sinkler	USA	1.9.89	1		Clemson	7	May
6.56	0.6	Saeko	Okayama	JPN	12.4.82	*		Kawasaki	8	May
6.56	-1.8	Olga	Rypakova	KAZ	30.11.84	1	NC	Almaty	29	Jul
6.55i		Kimberly	Williams	JAM	3.11.88	1	ACC	Blacksburg	25	Feb
		(80)								
6.55	1.9	Tatyana	Voykina	RUS	16.10.81	2		Tartu	28	May
6.55	0.1	Paraskeví	Papahrístou	GRE	17.4.89	1		Athína (Filothéi)	1	Jun
6.55	0.0	Haoua	Kessely	FRA	2.2.88	1		Marseille	4	Jun
6.55	-1.0	Darya	Akhmedova	UZB	3.4.91	1	Kozanov	Almaty	19	Jun
6.55	1.5	Yana	Gubar	RUS	2.7.90	1	NC-23	Yerino	24	Jun
6.55	1.9	Shameka	Marshall	USA	9.9.83	*	NC	Eugene	26	Jun
6.55	1.6	Daria	Derkach	UKR-J	27.3.93	1		Nembro	1	Jul
6.54i		Cristina	Sandu	ROU	4.3.90	3	NC	Bucuresti	19	Feb
6.54	1.7	Rose	Richmond	USA	29.1.81	8	NC	Eugene	26	Jun
6.54	0.7	Lorraine	Ugen	GBR	22.8.91	2	NC	Birmingham	31	Jul
		(90)								
6.54	0.5	Tania	Vicenzino	ITA	1.4.86	1		Brugnera	3	Sep
6.53	0.8	Margrethe	Renstrøm	NOR	21.3.85	2		Warszawa	20	Sep
6.52	-1.2	Janice	Josephs	RSA	31.3.82	1		Stellenbosch	15	Dec
6.51	0.0	Jessica	Ennis	GBR	28.1.86	2H	WCh	Daegu	30	Aug
6.50i		Anika	Leipold	GER	13.4.87	2	NC	Leipzig	27	Feb
6.50	0.8	Sonnisha	Williams	USA	20.4.91	1	Conf USA	Houston	14	May
6.50	0.0	Alice	Falaiye	CAN	24.12.78	2		Houston	19	May
6.50	0.9	Chelsea	Hayes	USA	2.2.88	1q	NCAA-E	Bloomington IN	26	May
6.50	1.1	Yekaterina	Khalyutina	RUS	16.1.91	1		Moskva	10	Jun
6.50	-1.2	Anastasiya	Kudinova	KAZ	27.2.88	1H	UZB Cup	Tashkent	12	Jun
		(100)								

Mark	Wind	Name		Nat	Born	Date	
6.49i		Yelena	Ivanova	RUS	16.3.79	21	Jan
6.49	0.0	Christabel	Nettey	CAN	2.6.91	13	May
6.49	1.4	Natasha	Coleman	USA	9.2.79	19	May
6.49	0.2	Yekaterina	Levitskaya	RUS	2.1.87	21	Jul
6.49	0.0	Olga	Pushkina	UKR	23.3.89	15	Aug
6.48	0.6	Jamesha	Youngblood	USA	24.4.89	13	May
6.48	1.2	Rochelle	Farquharson	JAM-J	16.1.93	14	May
6.48	-1.1	Aleksandra	Berezhnaya	RUS-J	26.7.92	17	May
6.48	1.0	Svetlana	Denyayeva	RUS	12.5.91	24	Jun
6.47i		Darya	Pizhankova ¶	UKR	9.1.90	29	Jan
6.47	0.4	Maliakhal	Prajusha	IND	20.5.87	11	Jun
6.47	1.6	Maryna	Bekh	UKR-Y	18.7.95	16	Jun
6.47	0.8	Arantxa	King	BER	27.11.89	17	Jul
6.47	-0.8	Dafne	Schippers	NED-J	15.6.92	22	Jul
6.47	0.9	Lucimara	da Silva	BRA	10.7.85	7	Aug
6.47	1.9	Daniela	Pávez	CHI	6.3.82	2	Oct
6.47	1.1	Maria Natalia Londa		INA	29.10.90	12	Nov
6.46	0.0	Akiba	McKinney	USA	9.3.79	7	May
6.46	0.7	Alina	Rotaru	ROU-J	5.6.93	21	May
6.46	0.0	Viktoriya	Molchanova	UKR	26.5.82	31	May
6.46	1.9	Sinje	Florczak	GER	28.11.86	13	Jun
6.46	1.7	Romaissa	Belbiod	ALG	28.2.91	14	Sep
6.45i			Liu Xiao	CHN	19.1.86	22	Feb
6.45i		Kelly	Proper	IRL	1.5.88	5	Mar
6.45	0.0	Hanako	Kotake	JPN	13.9.90	21	May
6.44i			Xu Xiaoling	CHN-J	13.5.92	22	Feb

Mark	Wind	Name	Nat	Born	Date
6.44	1.7	Nickevea Wilson	JAM-J	11.5.92	2 Apr
6.44A	1.7	Samantha Pretorius	RSA-J	3.2.92	3 Apr
6.44	0.3	Ksenia Achkinadze	GER	14.1.89	22 May
6.44	-0.6	Ruslana Tsyhotska	UKR	23.3.86	31 May
6.44	1.3	Katarina Johnson-Thompson	GBR-J	9.1.93	26 Jun
6.43i		Nina Kokot	SLO	15.5.88	11 Feb
6.43i		Amy Harris	GBR	14.9.87	25 Feb
6.43	1.8	Sarah Nambawa	UGA	23.9.85	9 Apr
6.43	-0.8	Kristina Damyanova	BUL	13.10.86	4 Jun
6.43	1.7	Aleksandra Kotlyarova	UZB	10.10.88	12 Jun
6.42i		Wang Wupin	CHN	18.1.91	22 Feb
6.42	-0.2	Gisele de Oliveira	BRA	1.8.80	15 Apr
6.42	1.2	Kerrie Perkins	AUS	2.4.79	17 Apr
6.42	0.6	Chelsea Carrier	USA	21.8.89	7 May
6.42	1.0	Jana Koresová	CZE	8.4.81	7 Jun
6.42	0.8	Magdalena Khristova	BUL	25.2.77	9 Jul
6.42	-0.4	Jennifer Oeser	GER	29.11.83	17 Jul
6.42	1.5	Tilia Udelhoven	GER-J	4.9.92	6 Aug
6.42	0.0	Erica Jarder	SWE	2.4.86	7 Aug
6.42	1.1	Jéssica Carolina dos Reis	BRA-J	17.3.93	10 Sep
6.41i		Yuliya Nosova	RUS	2.8.89	29 Jan
6.41	1.1	Anastasiya Mokhnyuk	UKR	1.1.91	11 Jun
6.41	2.0	Viktoriya Dolgacheva	RUS	17.4.91	24 Jun
6.41	-	Anastasiya Kadicheva	RUS-Y	23.2.94	27 Dec
6.40i		Beatrice Marscheck	GER	23.9.85	8 Jan
6.40i		Eléni-María Kafoúrou	GRE	2.9.86	29 Jan
6.40i		La'Taish Brown	USA	3.6.88	26 Feb
6.40	1.0	Malaina Payton	USA	16.10.91	1 May
6.40	1.2	Olga Sudarova	BLR	22.2.84	21 May
6.40	1.3	Anzhelika Rachitskaya	RUS	16.2.89	21 Jul
6.40	0.8	Malaika Mihambo	GER-Y	3.2.94	6 Aug
6.39i		Yao Jiajia	CHN	7.4.88	26 Feb
6.39	-0.1	Brittni Dixon-Smith	USA		13 May
6.39	0.0	Krystyna Hryshutyna	UKR-J	21.3.92	31 May
6.39	1.5	Kumiko Imura	JPN	10.1.81	12 Jun
6.39	0.4	Anna Bogdanova	RUS	21.10.84	3 Jul
6.38		Irina Gumenyuk	RUS	6.1.88	31 May
6.38	1.9	Juliet Itoya	ESP	17.8.86	2 Jul
6.38	0.4	Zhou Xiaoxue	CHN-J	19.6.92	21 Oct
6.37	0.3	Veera Baranova	EST	12.2.84	7 Jun
6.37	0.5	Amy Woodman	GBR	1.11.84	19 Jun
6.37	1.6	Margaryta Tverdohlib	UKR	2.6.91	3 Aug
6.37	0.0	Wang Huiqin	CHN	7.2.90	27 Sep
6.37	1.5	Macarena Reyes	CHI	30.3.84	2 Oct
6.36i		Austra Skujyte	LTU	12.8.79	13 Jan
6.36	1.2	Francine Simpson	JAM	1.11.89	8 Apr
6.36	1.6	Jillisa Grant	JAM	21.10.89	26 May
6.36	1.2	María del Mar Jover	ESP	21.4.88	16 Jul
6.36	-0.4	Louise Hazel	GBR	6.10.85	17 Jul
6.36	1.6	Laura Strati	ITA	3.10.90	17 Jul
6.35i		Malgorzata Reszka	POL	23.8.89	19 Feb
6.35i		Julia Gerter	GER-Y	13.7.94	20 Feb
6.35i		Zhang Lan	CHN	27.2.88	22 Feb
6.35	0.7	Tina Harris	USA	17.11.84	2 Apr
6.35	0.5	Yorsiris Urrutia	COL	26.6.86	14 May
6.35	0.7	Nektaria Panagi	CYP	20.3.90	3 Jun
6.35		Chanice Porter	JAM-Y	25.5.94	12 Jun
6.35	0.7	Yelena Sitnikova	RUS	12.11.89	18 Jun
6.35	0.8	Oksana Reva (185)	RUS	16.3.90	24 Jun

Wind assisted   # see main list for series

Mark	Wind	Name	Nat	Born	Pos	Meet	Venue	Date
7.06	5.9	Lyudmila Kolchanova	RUS	1.10.79	1	NCp	Yerino	5 Jun

6.82w   x   x   6.73w   7.06w   4.03w

| 7.00 # | 4.1 | Brianna Glenn | USA | 18.4.80 | 1 | | Chula Vista | 16 Jun |
| 6.95 | 7.5 | Oksana Zhukovskaya | RUS | 12.9.84 | 2 | NCp | Yerino | 5 Jun |

6.42w   6.76w   6.56w   6.95w   6.72w   6.88w/4.4

| 6.92 | 2.9 | Anastasiya Mironchik-Ivanova | BLR | 13.4.89 | 1 | | Minsk | 28 Jul |

6.63   6.78w   x   6.65   6.81/1.4   6.92w

| 6.91 | 2.7 | Bianca Stuart | BAH | 17.5.88 | 1 | | Clermont | 4 Jun |
| 6.90 | 5.0 | Bianca Kappler | GER | 8.8.77 | 1 | | Bad Langensalza | 2 Jul |

6.42w   6.30   6.34w   6.90w   6.44   6.53w

| 6.85 | 4.4 | Yuliya Pidluzhnaya | RUS | 1.10.88 | 2 | Déca | Nice | 18 Sep |

x   6.85w   6.74w   x

| 6.84 | 2.9 | Blessing Okagbare | NGR | 9.10.88 | 1 | Gyulai | Budapest | 30 Jul |

6.56   6.38   6.05   6.84   x   p

6.80	5.5	Yekaterina Koneva	RUS	25.9.88	3	NCp	Yerino	5 Jun
6.74	3.5	Jovanee Jarrett	JAM	15.1.83	2		Clermont	4 Jun
6.74	3.2	Ivana Spanovic	SRB	10.5.90	2	EU23	Ostrava	17 Jul
6.74	2.6	Carolina Klüft	SWE	2.2.83	1	NC	Gävle	14 Aug
6.73A	2.2	Shameka Marshall	USA	9.9.83	2	PAm	Guadalajara, MEX	26 Oct
6.70	3.6	Mara Griva	LAT	4.8.89	1	Big 12	Norman OK	14 May
6.70	2.8	Jennifer Oeser	GER	29.11.83	1H		Ratingen	17 Jul
6.69	5.6	Whitney Gipson	USA	20.9.90	1	PennR	Philadelphia	28 Apr
6.64	3.3	April Sinkler	USA	1.9.89	1		Clemson SC	13 May
6.61	2.3	Saeko Okayama	JPN	12.4.82	1	Super	Kawasaki	8 May
6.61	2.3	Lu Minjia	CHN-J	29.12.92	2	Super	Kawasaki	8 May
6.59	2.2	Jamesha Youngblood	USA	24.4.89	3	NCAA	Des Moines	8 Jun
6.58	7.3	Tianna Madison	USA	30.8.85	3		Dakar	28 May
6.56	3.2	Rose Richmond	USA	29.1.81	2	KansR	Lawrence	23 Apr
6.55	3.0	Hanako Kotake	JPN	13.9.90	1		Fukuoka	25 Jun
6.54	2.5	Christabel Nettey	CAN	2.6.91	1	Pac10	Tucson	13 May
6.53	2.9	Sinje Florczak	GER	28.11.86	4		Wesel	13 Jun
6.53	2.2	Chelsea Hayes	USA	2.2.88	9	NC	Eugene	26 Jun
6.52	2.7	Elysée Vésanes	FRA	25.1.84	2	NC	Albi	28, Jul
6.51	3.6	Dominique Blaize	GBR	3.10.87	1H		Desenzano del Garda	8 May

Mark	Wind	Name	Nat	Born	Date
6.49	2.5	Whitney Carlson	USA	20.10.87	26 Jun
6.49	2.2	Macarena Reyes	CHI	30.3.84	2 Oct
6.48	3.8	Amy Harris	GBR	14.9.87	3 Jul
6.47	4.3	Francine Simpson	JAM	1.11.89	8 Apr
6.47	3.5	Wang Wupin	CHN	18.1.91	8 May
6.47	2.1	Nina Kokot	SLO	15.5.88	8 Jun
6.47	3.3	Antoinette Nana Djimou	FRA	2.8.85	28 Jul
6.46	3.3	Sarah Ngo Ngoa	CMR	.83	14 Sep
6.44	3.0	Todea-Kay Willis	JAM	23.11.88	23 Apr
6.44	3.7	Andrea Geubelle	USA	21.6.91	14 May
6.43	3.9	Erica Jarder	SWE	2.4.86	7 Aug
6.42A	3.9	Patricia Sylvester	GRN	3.2.83	24 Jun
6.42	3.2	Yevgeniya Frolenkova	RUS	31.12.85	5 Jun
6.41	2.8	Amy Woodman	GBR	1.11.84	12 Jun
6.41	2.3	Louise Hazel	GBR	6.10.85	17 Jul
6.41	2.2	Grit Sadeiko	EST	29.7.89	9 Aug
6.39A	W/	Patience Ntshingila	RSA	26.8.89	25 Jun
6.38	2.4	Kortney Thurman	USA	8.7.89	9 Apr
6.38	2.2	Zhang Lan	CHN	27.2.88	26 Jun
6.38	2.6	Jasmine Simmons	USA	28.2.89	14 May
6.37	4.9	Alesha Walker	USA	9.4.88	8 Apr
6.37	2.6	Francesca Doveri	ITA	21.12.82	8 May

Mark	Wind	Name		Nat	Born	Pos	Meet	Venue	Date
6.37	2.7	Anja	Schulz	GER	6.7.90				13 Jun
6.36	2.7	Amber	Bledsoe	USA					4 Jun
6.36	4.0	Blandine	Maisonnier	FRA	3.1.86				29 Jul
6.35	3.8	Jessica	Samuelsson	SWE	14.3.85				14 Aug
6.35	2.1	Sandrine	Mbumi	CMR	22.5.86				14 Sep

Best outdoors

6.76 0.2 Gomes Q WCh Daegu 27 Aug
    6.78w 2.7 2 Bad Langensalza 2 Jul
6.58 1.1 Deiac 1 Debrecen 23 Jul
6.54 0.5 Lu Minjia 1 NC-j Jinan 2 Jun
6.49 1.8 Malone 8 Jun | 6.46 0.1 Sandu 3 Jun | 6.41 0.3 Liu Xiao 9 Sep
6.48 1.1 Leipold 30 Jul | 6.42 0.3 A Harris 31 Jul | 6.38 1.8 Kokot 8 Jun
6.41 1.9 Wang Wupin 17 Jul | 6.35 3.8 Samuelsson 14 Aug

Best at low altitude: 6.58 0.5 Ibargüen 2 Ponce 14 May
Doubtful measurement: 6.63 nwi Champagne Bell USA 3.1.91 1 Baltimore 23 Apr

JUNIORS

See main list for top 4 juniors. 10 performances (and 1 wa) by 4 women to 6.50. Additional marks and further juniors:

Malkus 6.69 1.1 1 NC-j Jena 6 Aug | 6.52 1.2 1 Garbsen 22 May
    6.65 1.1 2 Weinheim 28 May
Lu Minjia 2+ 6.52 -0.2 2 AsiC Kobe 7 Jul | 6.50 0.1 1 NC Hefei 9 Sep

Mark	Wind	Name		Nat	Born	Pos	Meet	Venue	Date
6.48	1.2	Rochelle	Farquharson	JAM-J	16.1.93	1	SEC	Athens GA	14 May
6.48	-1.1	Aleksandra	Berezhnaya	RUS-J	26.7.92	1J		Krasnodar	17 May
6.47	1.6	Maryna	Bekh	UKR-Y	18.7.95	1	NC-j	Donetsk	16 Jun
6.47	-0.8	Dafne	Schippers	NED-J	15.6.92	1H	EJ	Tallinn	22 Jul
6.46	0.7	Alina	Rotaru	ROU-J	5.6.93	2		Bucuresti	21 May
6.44i			Xu Xiaoling (10)	CHN-J	13.5.92	3	NGP	Nanjing	22 Feb
6.44	1.7	Nickevea	Wilson	JAM-J	11.5.92	1J		Kingston	2 Apr
6.44A	1.7	Samantha	Pretorius	RSA-J	3.2.92	1	NC-j	Germiston	3 Apr
6.44	1.3	Katarina	Johnson-Thompson	GBR-J	9.1.93	1	NC-j	Bedford	26 Jun
6.42	1.5	Tilia	Udelhoven	GER-J	4.9.92	2	NC-j	Jena	6 Aug
6.42	1.1	Jéssica Carolina	dos Reis	BRA-J	17.3.93	1	NC-j	Maringá	10 Sep
6.41	-	Anastasiya	Kadicheva	RUS-Y	23.2.94	1		Sankt-Peterburg	27 Dec
6.40	0.8	Malaika	Mihambo	GER-Y	3.2.94	1	NC-j	Jena	6 Aug
6.39	0.0	Krystyna	Hryshutyna	UKR-J	21.3.92	4	NCp	Yalta	31 May
6.38	0.4		Zhou Xiaoxue	CHN-J	19.6.92	1	City G	Nanchang	21 Oct
6.35i		Julia	Gerter (20)	GER-Y	13.7.94	2	NC-j	Leverkusen	20 Feb
6.35		Chanice	Porter	JAM-Y	25.5.94	1	NC-j	Kingston	12 Jun

TRIPLE JUMP

14.99 -0.1 Yargeris Savigne CUB 13.11.84 1 DL Saint-Denis 8 Jul
    14.36 14.43 14.66/-0.1 14.99 p x
  14.95 -0.2 1 NC La Habana 19 Mar 14.63/1.4 14.95 14.63/-0.1 13.35 14.76/0.5 x
  14.92 0.0 1 La Habana 18 Feb 14.47 14.92 14.69/1.1 14.75/1.9 p p
  14.81 1.4 1 Bisl Oslo 9 Jun 14.71/-0.7 14.57 14.53 14.70/0.2 x 14.81
  14.68 0.5 1 DL Shanghai 15 May 14.05 x 14.41 14.40 14.03 14.68
  14.62 0.4 Q WCh Daegu 30 Aug 14.32 14.40 14.62
  14.87w 2.1 2 DNG Stockholm 29 Jul x 14.87w 14.48 x 14.65w 14.83w/3.3

14.99A 1.7 Caterine Ibargüen COL 12.2.84 1 Bogotá 13 Aug
    14.71w/2.1 x 14.99 p p p
  14.92A 0.1 1 PAm Guadalajara, MEX 28 Oct 14.80/1.2 14.49 14.75 x 14.73 14.92
  14.84 0.4 3 WCh Daegu 1 Sep 14.64/-0.1 14.67/0.0 13.76 14.81/-0.6 14.84 14.80/0.1
  14.83 1.9 3 DNG Stockholm 29 Jul 14.70/1.7 14.69/1.4 14.27 x 14.62/1.1 14.83
  14.66 1.7 1 Castres 19 Jul 14.56 p 14.40 14.20 p 14.66
  14.59 0.4 1 São Paulo 22 May 14.08 14.58/1.1 14.59 p p p
  14.59 1.6 1 Lapinlahti 24 Jul 14.59 14.52 p x x x
  14.63Aw2.2 1 NC Bogotá 8 May 13.90 14.40 14.50 x 14.38w 14.63w
  14.59w 2.2 1 SAmC Buenos Aires 4 Jun 14.15 x 14.41 14.59w 14.48 14.32

14.98 0.6 Olga Saladuha UKR 4.6.83 1 Pre Eugene 4 Jun
    14.81/1.5 14.89/1.4 14.98 p p p
  14.94 0.2 1 WCh Daegu 1 Sep 14.94 13.64 14.68/0.1 14.65/0.0 14.22 14.48
  14.85 1.8 1 ET Stockholm 18 Jun 14.51 14.85 14.44 14.53
  14.81 0.0 2 DL Saint-Denis 8 Jul 14.14 14.58/0.1 14.81 14.61/-0.1 14.52 14.49
  14.80 0.8 1 LGP London (CP) 5 Aug 14.61/1.4 14.80 14.73/1.7 13.43 14.76/1.4 14.60
  14.76 1.8 * DNG Stockholm 29 Jul 15.06w 14.76 13.16 14.48 x 14.89w/2.1
  14.71 0.3 2 Bisl Oslo 9 Jun 13.72 14.69/-0.5 14.71 x 14.57 14.56
  14.67 0.4 1 VD Bruxelles 16 Sep 14.67 14.46 x,14.67/1.2

14.96 1.9 Olga Rypakova KAZ 30.11.84 1 NC Almaty 27 Jul
    14.95/1.6 14.87/1.0 p p 14.96 p
  14.89 0.2 2 WCh Daegu 1 Sep x 14.72/0.2 x x 14.89 14.54
  14.69w 2.8 2 Nott Milano 18 Sep 14.69w x p x p p

14.72 1.0 Paraskeví Papahrístou GRE 17.4.89 1 Veniz Haniá 11 Jun
    x 14.72 14.47 p p p

14.67 1.5 Natalya Kutyakova RUS 28.11.86 1 Huelva 2 Jun
    x 14.67 x x x 13.53

14.67 0.4 Mabel Gay CUB 5.5.83 4 WCh Daegu 1 Sep
    14.45 14.31 x 14.53 14.67 14.18

Mark	Wind	Name		Nat	Born	Pos	Meet	Venue	Date	Series
Gay	14.65	1.6 2 NC	La Habana		19 Mar					14.11 x 14.65 13.30 14.24 13.51
	14.58	1.4 2 VD	Bruxelles		16 Sep					x 14.20 x 14.58
	14.57	-0.5 4 DNG	Stockholm		29 Jul					14.57 x 12.79 14.14 14.01 14.19
14.61	-0.2	Josleidy	Ribalta	CUB	2.5.90	2		La Habana	18 Feb	x 14.61 x 14.31w 13.15 p
14.60i		Simona	La Mantia	ITA	14.4.83	1	EI	Paris (B)	5 Mar	14.17 14.60 14.49. x 14.60 x
14.57	1.2	Katja	Demut	GER	21.12.83	1		Wesel	13 Jun	x x 14.21 14.18 14.57 14.36
(32/10)										
14.56	2.0	Dailenys	Alcántara	CUB	10.8.91	3		La Habana	18 Feb	
14.55	0.5	Alsu	Murtazina	RUS	12.12.87	1	NC	Cheboksary	24 Jul	
14.55	1.2	Níki	Panéta	GRE	21.4.86	2	NC	Athína	30 Jul	
14.54	1.9		Xie Limei	CHN	27.6.86	1	AsiC	Kobe	9 Jul	
14.50	1.7	Nataliya	Yastrebova	UKR	12.10.84	1	NCp	Yalta	1 Jun	
14.50	0.4	Yamilé	Aldama	GBR	14.8.72	5	WCh	Daegu	1 Sep	
14.49	1.9	Baya	Rahouli	ALG	27.7.79	1	NC	Castres	27 Jul	
14.48	1.1	Irina	Ektova	KAZ	8.1.87	2	NC	Almaty	27 Jul	
14.48	0.9	Dana	Veldáková	SVK	3.6.81	3	LGP	London (CP)	5 Aug	
14.46	1.2	Yekaterina	Koneva	RUS	25.9.88	1		Bryansk	19 Jun	
(20)										
14.45i		Olesya	Zabara	RUS	6.10.82	2	EI	Paris (B)	5 Mar	
14.45	1.3	Ruslana	Tsyhotska	UKR	23.3.86	2	NCp	Yalta	1 Jun	
14.42	1.2	Yarianna	Martínez	CUB	20.9.84	4		La Habana	18 Feb	
14.42	1.5	Patrícia	Mamona	POR	21.11.88	1	NC	Lisboa (U)	31 Jul	
14.35i		Snezana	Rodic	SLO	19.8.82	4	EI	Paris (B)	5 Mar	
14.35	0.3		Li Yanmei	CHN	6.2.90	2	DL	Shanghai	15 May	
14.35	2.0	Anna	Kuropatkina	RUS	3.10.85	1		Sochi	24 May	
14.35	1.4	Aleksandra	Kotlyarova	UZB	10.10.88	1	NCp	Tashkent	12 Jun	
14.35		Yana	Borodina	RUS-J	21.4.92	1J	Mosc Ch	Moskva	15 Jun	
14.34	1.3	Andiana	Banova	BUL	1.5.87	1	Balk C	Sliven	2 Jul	
(30)										
14.33	0.9	Trecia	Smith	JAM	5.11.75	1		Montgeron	15 May	
14.32	0.4	Anastasiya	Juravlyeva	UZB	9.10.81	2	NCp	Tashkent	12 Jun	
14.32	1.2	Natalya	Vyatkina	BLR	10.2.87	1		Minsk	22 Jun	
14.31i		Svetlana	Bolshakova	BEL	14.10.84	1		Gent	13 Feb	
14.30	0.9	Yusmay	Bicet	CUB	8.12.83	5		La Habana	18 Feb	
14.30	1.8	Marija	Sestak	SLO	17.4.79	1		Ljubljana	27 Jul	
14.30	0.3	Cristina	Bujin	ROU	12.4.88	Q	WUG	Shenzhen	18 Aug	
14.29	1.9	Anastasiya	Mironchik-Ivanova	BLR	13.4.89	1		Minsk	4 Jun	
14.28	0.9	Valeriya	Kanatova	UZB-J	29.8.92	3	NCp	Tashkent	12 Jun	
14.27	-0.5	Adelina	Gavrila	ROU	26.11.78	1	IntC	Constanta	3 Jun	
(40)										
14.26	1.3	Svitlana	Mamyeyeva	UKR	19.4.82	3	NCp	Yalta	1 Jun	
14.25	-1.2	Kimberly	Williams	JAM	3.11.88	1		Kingston	7 May	
14.25	2.0	Anna	Jagaciak	POL	10.2.90	1	NC-23	Gdansk	3 Jul	
14.24	-0.8	Keila	Costa	BRA	6.2.83	1		São Paulo	23 Feb	
14.24	-0.6	Anna	Pyatykh	RUS	4.4.81	1	Mosc Ch	Moskva	10 Jul	
14.21	1.2	Valeriya	Zavyalova	RUS	16.1.88	1		Krasnodar	1 Jun	
14.21	0.1	Biljana	Topic	SRB	17.10.77	11q	WCh	Daegu	30 Aug	
14.20i		Athanasía	Pérra	GRE	2.2.83	2	NC	Athína (Peanía)	20 Feb	
14.20i		Petia	Dacheva	BUL	10.3.85	Q	EI	Paris (B)	4 Mar	
14.20	1.9	Hanna	Knyazheva	UKR	25.9.89	4	NCp	Yalta	1 Jun	
(50)										
14.18	2.0	Amanda	Smock	USA	27.4.82	1		Chula Vista	6 Aug	
14.16i		Malgorzata	Trybanska	POL	21.6.81	2		Chemnitz	27 Jan	
14.14	0.9	Irina	Gumenyuk	RUS	6.1.88	6	NC	Cheboksary	24 Jul	
14.13i		Yelena	Ivanova	RUS	16.3.79	1		Sankt Peterburg	1 Feb	
14.12	1.4	Gisele	de Oliveira	BRA	1.8.80	*		São Paulo	26 Aug	
14.11	0.9	Mayookha	Johny	IND	9.4.88	3	AsiC	Kobe	9 Jul	
14.10i		Kristin	Gierisch	GER	20.8.90	1		Chemnitz	23 Jan	
14.10	1.7	Patricia	Sarrapio	ESP	16.11.82	3	ET	Stockholm	18 Jun	
14.07	0.7	Carmen	Toma	ROU	28.3.89	2	NC	Bucuresti	9 Aug	
14.06	0.0	Sarah	Nambawa	UGA	23.9.85	1		Nashville	9 Apr	
(60)										
14.06	1.0	Blessing	Ufodiama	USA	28.11.81	2	Pre	Eugene	4 Jun	
14.05	1.5	Kseniya	Detsuk	BLR	23.4.86	2	NC	Grodno	7 Jul	
14.03	0.0	Françoise	Mbango	FRA	14.4.76	1		Forbach	29 May	
14.03	0.0		Wang Huiqin	CHN	7.2.90	1	Univ Ch	Sanya	25 Sep	
14.02i		Yekaterina	Kayukova	RUS	9.10.86	5	NC	Moskva	18 Feb	
14.01	0.1	Nathalie	Marie-Nély	FRA	24.11.86	2		Forbach	29 May	
14.00	0.8	Anastasiya	Potapova	RUS	6.9.85	*	NC	Cheboksary	24 Jul	

Mark	Wind	Name	Nat	Born	Pos	Meet	Venue	Date
13.98	0.8	Ayanna Alexander	TRI	20.7.82	1	Hampton	Port of Spain	24 Jul
13.97	2.0	Martyna Bielawska	POL	15.11.90	2	NC-23	Gdansk	3 Jul
13.96	1.5	Veera Baranova	EST	12.2.84	*		Rakvere	7 Jun
(70)								
13.95	1.4	Viktoriya Rybalko	UKR	26.10.82	5	NCp	Yalta	1 Jun
13.94	0.2	Nadezhda Alekhina	RUS	22.9.78	4	Pre	Eugene	4 Jun
13.94	2.0	Crystal Manning	USA	15.4.86	2	NC	Eugene	24 Jun
13.93	0.3	Haoua Kessely	FRA	2.2.88	1		Paris (C)	10 Jul
13.92i		Jenny Elbe	GER	18.4.90	4		Chemnitz	27 Jan
13.90	0.3	Nelly Tchayem	FRA	4.8.83	2	MSR	Walnut	16 Apr
13.89i		Ineta Radevica	LAT	13.7.81	12q	EI	Paris (B)	4 Mar
13.89	1.7	Toni Smith	USA	13.10.84	1		Jacksonville	14 May
13.89	0.0	Deng Lina	CHN-J	16.3.92	Q	WUG	Shenzhen	18 Aug
13.88i		Hanna Demydova	UKR	8.4.87	1	Conf USA	Houston	26 Feb
(80)								
13.84i		Shakeema Welsch	USA	10.11.76	1		Blacksburg	5 Feb
13.83	1.5	Anja Valant Velepec	SLO	8.9.77	2		Celje	8 Jun
13.82	0.2	Linda Allen	AUS	22.3.87	5	AsiGP	Wujiang	29 May
13.82	0.7	Xu Tingting	CHN	12.7.89	2	NGPF	Nanchang	17 Jul
13.81	2.0	Mara Griva	LAT	4.8.89	1	Big 12	Norman OK	15 May
13.78	1.1	Ruth Marie Ndoumbe	ESP	1.1.87	2	NC	Málaga	6 Aug
13.77	1.7	Nadia Williams	GBR	17.11.81	1	BIG	Bedford	12 Jun
13.76i		Dominike Nkiruka	NGR	28.8.85	2		Fayetteville	12 Feb
13.76	0.0	Yasmine Regis	GBR	12.12.86	6	LGP	London (CP)	5 Aug
13.76	-0.5	Tran Hue Hoa	VIE	8.8.91	1	SEAG	Palembang	14 Nov
(90)								
13.75i		Liu Yanan	CHN	18.1.87	3	NGP	Nanjing	23 Feb
13.75	1.3	Jung Hye-kyung	KOR	13.4.81	1		Andong	12 Apr
13.75	1.0	Ioánna Grammatikopoúlou	GRE	19.10.83	5	Veniz	Haniá	11 Jun
13.73	0.6	Maria Natalia Londa	INA	29.10.90	2	SEAG	Palembang	14 Nov
13.72	1.0	Katarzyna Plonka	POL	28.6.88	1		Lódz	22 May
13.70i		Yao Jiajia	CHN	7.4.88	1	NGP	Shanghai	27 Feb
13.70		Nina Serbezova	BUL/CYP	6.5.81	1		Limassol	25 Mar
13.70	1.9	Anna Kornuta	UKR	10.11.88	2		Yalta	19 May
13.70	0.0	Liuba María Zaldívar	CUB-J	5.4.93	1c2		La Habana	10 Jun
13.70	1.9	Iworima Otonye	NGR	13.4.76	1	NC	Calabar	23 Jun
(100)								
13.70	0.9	Susana Costa	POR	22.9.84	*	NC	Lisboa	31 Jul

Mark	Wind	Name	Nat	Born	Date
13.69	1.6	Yvette Lewis	USA	16.3.85	4 Jun
13.69		Anastasiya Matveyeva	RUS	12.12.88	15 Jun
13.69	1.8	Cagdas Arslan	TUR	10.3.86	2 Jul
13.69	-0.7	Kéne Ndoye	SEN	20.11.78	15 Sep
13.68	1.8	Svetlana Semyonova	RUS	24.8.80	5 Jun
13.68	1.6	Svetlana Denyayeva	RUS	12.5.91	26 Jun
13.68	0.0	Li Jingyu	CHN-Y	4.6.95	22 Oct
13.67	0.5	Elina Torro	FIN	22.7.86	11 Jun
13.67	-0.8	Kristiina Mäkelä	FIN-J	20.11.92	22 Jul
13.67	0.8	Laura Samuel	GBR	19.2.91	29 Jul
13.67	-0.3	Chen Mudan	CHN-J	4.10.93	22 Oct
13.66	1.3	Sun Yan	CHN	30.3.91	26 Jun
13.65	1.1	Yekaterina Malysheva	RUS	16.4.88	1 Jun
13.65	0.9	Khaddi Sagnia	SWE-Y	20.4.94	26 Aug
13.64	0.7	Thitima Muangjan	THA	13.4.83	14 Nov
13.63i		Oksana Udmurtova	RUS	1.2.82	4 Feb
13.63	0.9	Nadezhda Korytkina	RUS	7.2.91	26 Jun
13.63	1.3	Maliakhal Prajusha	IND	20.5.87	9 Jul
13.62	1.1	Ana José Tima	DOM	10.10.89	25 Jun
13.61	1.0	Hu Qian	CHN	14.1.89	16 Jul
13.60	2.0	Jamaa Chnaïk	MAR	28.7.84	30 Apr
13.59	0.4	Maja Bratkic	SLO	14.5.91	28 May
13.59	0.5	Chen Yufei	CHN	26.1.89	10 Sep
13.58	1.7	Sheena Gordon	USA	26.9.83	24 Jun
13.58A	-0.1	Aída Yesenia Villarreal	MEX	12.1.86	6 Aug
13.57i		Inger Anne Frøysedal	NOR	25.4.89	29 Jan
13.57i		Diao Limin	CHN-J	12.6.92	23 Feb
13.57	0.0	Hanna Aleksandrova	UKR-J	11.7.93	1 Jun
13.57	1.2	Eleonora D'Elicio	ITA	28.5.89	15 Jul
13.56i		Daria Derkach	UKR-J	27.3.93	12 Feb
13.55	1.7	Irina Vaskovskaya	BLR	2.4.91	21 May
13.55	1.2	Olesya Tikhonova	RUS	22.1.90	1 Jun
13.55	1.9	Maitane Azpeitia	ESP	1.3.89	30 Jul
13.54	0.0	Ivana Spanovic	SRB	10.5.90	18 Jun
13.51	-0.4	Brenda Baar	NED	19.7.87	18 Jun
13.51	1.9	Blessing Ibrahim	NGR	4.4.90	23 Jun
13.51	0.0	Cristine Spâtaru	ROU	4.2.86	9 Aug
13.50i		Colleen Felix	GRN	30.11.89	27 Feb
13.50	1.8	Rita Babos	HUN	21.10.80	7 Aug
13.49	0.1	Elysée Vésanes	FRA	25.1.84	23 Jul
13.48i		Silvia Cucchi	ITA	1.10.78	20 Feb
13.48	-0.2	Yelena Sidorkina	RUS	27.9.88	23 Jul
13.47	0.5	Alina Elena Popescu	ROU	27.10.85	3 Jun
13.47	0.8	Yan Xianting	CHN	16.5.90	25 Sep
13.46i		Alisa Vlasova	RUS	16.9.90	6 Jan
13.46i		Lelo Patricia Kiala	FRA	22.3.89	20 Feb
13.46i		April Sinkler	USA	1.9.89	12 Mar
13.46	0.8	Lyudmila Grankovskaya	KAZ	13.2.89	18 Jun
13.46	1.1	Jolanta Verseckaite	LTU	9.2.88	24 Jul
13.45	0.0	Charlene Potgieter	RSA	22.9.85	10 Apr
13.45	-0.3	Liu Jiaqi	CHN	3.8.87	24 Apr
13.45	0.6	Tracey Stewart	USA	15.3.88	24 Jun
13.44	1.3	Jessica Ubanyionwu	USA	12.7.90	15 May
13.44	1.5	Whitney Liehr	USA	9.6.88	10 Jun
13.44	-0.9	Hannah Frankson	GBR	11.1.89	26 Jun
13.44	0.1	Lin Yan	CHN-J	26.1.93	22 Oct
13.43	1.3	Maike Nieklauson	GER	13.11.89	13 Jun
13.43	0.8	Vanessa Gladone	FRA	3.6.82	7 Aug
13.42	0.0	Anna Bondarenko	KAZ	20.6.88	25 Apr
13.42	1.2	Irina Beskrovnaja	SVK	28.12.82	8 Jun
13.42	-0.3	Sokhna Gallé	FRA-Y	23.4.94	6 Jul
13.42	0.7	Irène Pusterla	SUI	21.6.88	25 Sep
13.42	0.0	Fu Bingling	CHN-J	15.9.93	22 Oct
13.41	0.5	Teresa Nzola Méso	FRA	30.11.83	5 Jul
13.40	-0.4	Xu Yue	CHN	12.3.90	28 Apr
13.40	1.4	Santa Matule	LAT-J	13.12.92	3 Jun
13.39	0.0	Cindy Peters	RSA	12.2.84	10 Apr
13.39	0.1	Wei Mingchen	CHN	4.1.91	24 Apr
13.39	2.0	Bae Chan-mi	KOR	24.3.91	22 Jun
13.39A	1.2	Giselly Andrea Landázuri	COL-J	8.8.92	24 Sep
13.38	1.7	Sabine Skrodere	LAT	31.10.85	3 Jun
13.38	0.1	Anna Zych	POL	15.5.88	13 Aug
13.38	-0.1	Li Xiaohong	CHN-Y	8.1.95	22 Oct
13.35	1.6	Ti'Ara Walpool	USA	31.1.89	15 May

Mark	Wind	Name	Nat	Born	Pos	Meet	Venue	Date
13.35	1.7	Dovile Dzindzaletaite	LTU-J	14.7.93	5			Jun
13.35		Olga Salomatina	RUS-J	15.8.92	15			Jun
13.35	1.0	Gita Dodova	BUL	2.5.82	23			Jun
13.34	-0.2	Hu Guanlian	CHN	18.7.90	24			Apr
13.34	-0.1	Zhang Guihua	CHN	15.10.85	12			Jun
13.33	0.0	Oleksandra Stadnyuk	UKR	16.4.80	1			Jun
13.33		Noor Amira Mohd Nafiah	MAS	16.7.89	22			Oct
13.32		Viktoriya Bazarbayeva	RUS	23.1.88	12			Jun
13.32	-1.5	Worokia Sanou	BUR	31.12.89	15			Sep
13.32	-0.5	Sandrine Mbumi	CMR	22.5.86	15			Sep
13.31		Violetta Maksimchuk	RUS	1.12.90	22			May
13.31	1.3	Mariya Grigoryeva	RUS	21.9.89	1			Jun
13.31	1.9	Lecabela Quaresma	STP	26.12.89	2			Jun
13.30i		Michaela Egger	AUT	15.2.84	13			Feb
13.30	-0.5	Mukadder Ulusoy	TUR	23.3.82	21			May
13.30	0.0	Cecilia Pacchetti	ITA	18.5.89	18			Jun

Wind assisted   # see main list for series

Mark	Wind	Name	Nat	Born	Pos	Meet	Venue	Date
15.06 #	2.3	Olga Saladuha	UKR	4.6.83	1	DNG	Stockholm	29 Jul
		14.94 2.4 1 Notturna Milano 18 Sep 14.28 14.94w p x p						
14.62	2.4	Xie Limei	CHN	27.6.86	1	NGPF	Nanchang	17 Jul
14.39	4.7	Anna Kuropatkina	RUS	3.10.85	3	NCp	Yerino	4 Jun
14.20	2.9	Gisele de Oliveira	BRA	1.8.80	1		São Paulo	26 Aug
14.18	3.2	Nathalie Marie-Nély	FRA	24.11.86	1	NC	Albi	30 Jul
14.14	3.2	Haoua Kessely	FRA	2.2.88	2		Montgeron	15 May
14.13	2.6	Anastasiya Potapova	RUS	6.9.85	7	NC	Cheboksary	24 Jul
14.00	2.3	Veera Baranova	EST	12.2.84	1		Rakvere	7 Jun
13.96	2.7	Cagdas Arslan	TUR	10.3.86	2		Izmir	21 May
13.94	2.8	Nadia Williams	GBR	17.11.81	1	ENG Ch	Bedford	17 Jul
13.91	4.9	Hanna Demydova	UKR	8.4.87	2	TexR	Austin	9 Apr
13.86	2.2	Khaddi Sagnia	SWE-Y	20.4.94	*		Karlstad	2 Aug
13.77	2.4	Laura Samuel	GBR	19.2.91	2	ENG Ch	Bedford	17 Jul
13.77	4.9	Amy Zongo-Filet	FRA	4.10.80	2	NC	Albi	30 Jul
13.77	2.9	Susana Costa	POR	22.9.84	2	NC	Lisboa	31 Jul
13.74	4.1	Sheena Gordon	USA	26.9.83	2		Jacksonville	14 May
13.73	3.7	Svetlana Semyonova	RUS	24.8.80	4		Montgeron	15 May
13.70	3.3	Vanessa Gladone	FRA	3.6.82	3	NC	Albi	30 Jul
13.68	3.2	Teresa Nzola Méso	FRA	30.11.83				30 Jul
13.66	2.1	Mayra Pachito	ECU	28.10.85				30 Apr
13.66	3.0	Jolanta Verseckaite	LTU	9.2.88				24 Jul
13.62	2.2	Sokhna Gallé	FRA-Y	23.4.94				8 Jul
13.62	2.4	Hu Qian	CHN	14.1.89				17 Jul
13.60	6.0	Violetta Maksimchuk	RUS	1.12.90				4 Jun
13.58	2.1	Colleen Felix	GRN	30.11.89				8 Apr
13.58	3.0	Lyudmila Grankovskaya	KAZ	13.2.89				27 Jul
13.56	2.5	Débora Calveras	ESP	26.12.88				29 Jun
13.54	2.1	Chantel Malone	IVB	2.12.91				15 May
13.53	2.3	Brenda Baar	NED	19.7.87				31 Jul
13.53	4.9	Nneka Okpala	NZL	27.4.88				3 Dec
13.50A	?	Patience Ntshingila	RSA	26.8.89				11 Nov
13.48	3.6	Mathilde Boateng	FRA	24.7.89				30 Jul
13.46	2.4	Teresa Dobija	POL	19.10.82				10 Sep
13.45	2.3	Liliya Kulyk	UKR	27.1.87				19 May
13.44	2.6	Gabriela Petrova	BUL-J	29.6.92				12 Jun
13.43	3.7	Dovile Dzindzaletaite	LTU-J	14.7.93				5 Jun
13.43	3.0	Gita Dodova	BUL	2.5.82				12 Jun
13.43	2.8	Anna Bondarenko	KAZ	20.6.88				27 Jul
13.39	2.4	Tânia da Silva	BRA	17.12.86				12 May
13.36	3.7	Olesya Kabardina	RUS	18.4.90				26 Jun
13.31	3.2	Mukadder Ulusoy	TUR	23.3.82				21 May

Best outdoors

Mark	Wind	Name	Pos	Meet	Venue	Date
14.43	1.5	La Mantia	1		Palermo	14 May
14.23	1.6	Rodic	1	NCp	Celje	11 Jun
14.19	1.8	Zabara	4	NC	Cheboksary	24 Jul
14.36w	2.4		2		Huelva	2 Jun
14.16	-0.5	Trybanska	1		Bialogard	3 Aug
14.05	-0.1	Pérra	5	DL	Shanghai	15 May
13.89	1.5	Elbe	2		Wesel	13 Jun
13.82	0.3	Welsch	3	MSR	Walnut	16 Apr
13.70	-0.3	Bolshakova	5		Rabat	5 Jun

Mark	Wind	Name	Date
13.64	0.2	Demydova	10 Jun
13.59	1.0	Dacheva	22 May
13.56	1.3	Derkach	4 Jun
13.51	0.1	Y Ivanova	23 Jul
13.68w	3.2		2 Jun
13.50	1.9	Felix	8 Apr
13.49	1.7	Nkiruka	23 Jun
13.47	0.9	Gierisch	13 Jun
13.45	0.2	Kayukova	19 Jun
13.41	0.8	Frøysedal	3 Sep
13.38	0.3	Liu Yanan	10 Sep
13.36	0.0	Cucchi	25 Jun

Best at low altitude

Mark	Wind	Name	Date
13.40	-0.8	Villarreal	15 Jul

JUNIORS

See main list for top 4 juniors (& 1w). 10 perfs (& 2 wa) by 3 (4) women to 13.80. Additional marks and further juniors:

Borodina 14.00 0.1 1 Krasnodar 18 May 13.90 0.5 1 NC-j Cheboksary 3 Jul
          14.00 1.0 1 EJ Tallinn 22 Jul
Kanatova 14.05 0.2 • AsiC Kobe 9 Jul 13.87 0.8 1 Kaohsiung 28 May
          14.14w 2 AsiC Kobe 9 Jul 13.86 0.0 22q WCh Daegu 30 Aug
Deng Lina 13.85i 2 Nanjing 23 Mar

Mark	Wind	Name	Nat	Born	Pos	Meet	Venue	Date
13.68	0.0	Li Jingyu	CHN-Y	4.6.95	1	City G	Nanchang	22 Oct
13.67	-0.8	Kristiina Mäkelä	FIN	20.11.92	2	EJ	Tallinn	22 Jul
13.67	-0.3	Chen Mudan	CHN	4.10.93	2	City G	Nanchang	22 Oct
13.65	0.9	Khaddi Sagnia	SWE-Y	20.4.94	*	NC-j	Vellinge	26 Aug
13.57i		Diao Limin	CHN	12.6.92	4	NGP	Nanjing	23 Feb
13.57	0.0	Hanna Aleksandrova (10)	UKR	11.7.93	6	NCp	Yalta	1 Jun
13.56i		Daria Derkach	UKR	27.3.93	1	NC-j	Ancona	12 Feb
13.56	1.3				2		Firenze	4 Jun
13.44	0.1	Lin Yan	CHN	26.1.93	3	City G	Nanchang	22 Oct
13.42	-0.3	Sokhna Gallé	FRA-Y	23.4.94	Q	WY	Villeneuve d'Ascq	6 Jul
13.42	0.0	Fu Bingling	CHN	15.9.93	4	City G	Nanchang	22 Oct
13.40	1.4	Santa Matule	LAT	13.12.92	1		Valmiera	3 Jun
13.39A	1.2	Giselly Andrea Landázuri	COL	8.8.92	1	SAm-J	Medellín	24 Sep
13.38	-0.1	Li Xiaohong	CHN-Y	8.1.95	5	City G	Nanchang	22 Oct
13.35	1.7	Dovile Dzindzaletaite	LTU	14.7.93	*	NCp	Kaunas	5 Jun
13.35		Olga Salomatina	RUS	15.8.92	2J	Mosc Ch	Moskva	15 Jun

Mark	Wind	Name	Surname	Nat	Born	Pos	Meet	Venue	Date	1	2	3	4	5	6
13.29	0.6	Andreea-Maria	Todereanu (20)	ROU	9.5.92	2		Bucuresti	20 May						

Wind assisted see main list for top junior

Mark	Wind	Name	Surname	Nat	Born	Pos	Meet	Venue	Date	1	2	3	4	5	6
13.62	2.2	Sokhna	Gallé	FRA-Y	23.4.94	1	WY	Villeneuve d'Ascq	8 Jul						
13.44	2.6	Gabriela	Petrova	BUL	29.6.92	2	NC	Sliven	12 Jun						
13.43	3.7	Dovile	Dzindzaletaite	LTU	14.7.93	1	NCp	Kaunas	5 Jun						

SHOT

Mark	Name	Surname	Nat	Born	Pos	Meet	Venue	Date	1	2	3	4	5	6
21.24	Valerie	Adams	NZL	6.10.84	1	WCh	Daegu	29 Aug	19.37	x	20.04	20.72	x	21.24
20.83					1		Dubnica nad Váhom	15 Sep	19.26	20.42	20.83	x	20.07	20.50
20.78					1	DL	Saint-Denis	8 Jul	20.48	20.78	20.72	20.34	x	20.26
20.59					1		Bad Köstritz	17 Sep	x	20.05	20.26	19.94	20.33	20.59
20.57					1	DNG	Stockholm	28 Jul	19.59	20.57	19.97	x	x	20.08
20.55					1		Sydney	19 Mar	20.01	20.02	20.04	19.95	20.55	20.22
20.54					1	NC	Dunedin	26 Mar	20.09	x	20.54	20.20	20.27	20.40
20.51i					1	WK	Zürich	7 Sep	19.87	20.09	20.33	20.32	20.51	20.35
20.33					1		Auckland	27 Feb	19.96	20.33	19.89	x	19.38	x
20.26					1	Bisl	Oslo	9 Jun	x	20.14	20.10	20.26	20.17	19.90
20.19					1		Besançon	14 Jun	19.72	x	20.19	20.10	20.18	19.79
20.13					1		Melbourne	3 Mar	20.13	x	x	20.08	x	x
20.07					1	LGP	London (CP)	6 Aug	19.80	19.72	20.07	x	19.79	19.85
20.94	Nadzeya	Ostapchuk	BLR	12.10.80	1	Znam	Zhukovskiy	3 Jul	18.94	x	x	20.94		
20.59					1	Pre	Eugene	4 Jun	19.94	x	20.14	20.13	20.59	19.77
20.49					2	DL	Saint-Denis	8 Jul	x	20.42	20.49	x	20.48	x
20.48i					2	WK	Zürich	7 Sep	18.98	19.02	x	19.91	20.48	19.59
20.37					2	DNG	Stockholm	28 Jul	19.52	20.24	x	20.13	20.37	x
20.05					2	WCh	Daegu	29 Aug	19.58	19.34	19.87	19.87	20.05	19.60
19.92					2	Bisl	Oslo	9 Jun	x	19.66	19.06	x	18.84	19.92
20.18	Jill	Camarena-Williams	USA	2.8.82	3	DL	Saint-Denis	8 Jul	19.28	20.18	x	x	19.80	x
20.02					3	WCh	Daegu	29 Aug	19.63	18.53	19.24	20.02	18.80	19.44
19.87i					1	NC	Albuquerque	27 Feb	18.81	x	19.87	x	19.29	x
19.87					3	DNG	Stockholm	28 Jul	x	19.87	x	19.56	x	x
20.11		Gong Lijiao	CHN	24.1.89	1	NGPF	Nanchang	16 Jul						
20.10					1	NGP	Kunshan	25 May						
19.97					4	WCh	Daegu	29 Aug	19.64	x	x	19.82	19.97	x
19.94					1	DL	Shanghai	15 May	19.82	19.94	19.53	19.74	x	19.69
19.93i					1	NGP	Chengdu	19 Mar						
19.86					1	NGP	Zhaoqing	23 Apr						
19.86					1	NC	Hefei	8 Sep	19.44	19.01	18.72	19.22	19.86	x
19.86	Michelle	Carter	USA	12.10.85	1	NC	Eugene	23 Jun	19.16	19.86	18.57	18.41	18.52	18.73
	(32/5)													
19.78	Yevgeniya	Kolodko	RUS	2.7.90	5	WCh	Daegu	29 Aug						
19.72		Li Ling	CHN	7.2.85	2	NGP	Kunshan	25 May						
19.54	Anna	Avdeyeva	RUS	6.4.85	7	WCh	Daegu	29 Aug						
19.42	Cleopatra	Borel-Brown	TRI	3.10.79	4	DL	Saint-Denis	8 Jul						
19.26	Nadine	Kleinert	GER	20.10.75	8	WCh	Daegu	29 Aug						
	(10)													
19.23	Anna	Omarova	RUS	3.10.81	1	NCp	Yerino	5 Jun						
19.20	Christina	Schwanitz	GER	24.12.85	Q	WCh	Daegu	28 Aug						
19.13	Mailín	Vargas	CUB	24.3.83	1		La Habana	3 Jun						
19.05	Natalya	Mikhnevich	BLR	25.5.82	1	NC	Grodno	7 Jul						
19.04	Misleydis	González	CUB	19.6.78	1		Barcelona	22 Jul						
18.82i	Yelena	Kopets	BLR	14.2.88	1		Minsk	14 Jan						
18.74		Liu Xiangrong	CHN	6.6.88	3	NGPF	Nanchang	16 Jul						
18.72	Irina	Tarasova	RUS	15.4.87	2		Adler	24 May						
18.59	Chiara	Rosa	ITA	28.1.83	1	NCp	Firenze	4 Jun						
18.34	Olesya	Sviridova	RUS	28.10.89	3		Adler	24 May						
	(20)													
18.33	Yanina	Provalinskaya	BLR	26.12.76	1	NCp	Brest	21 May						
18.31	Julie	Labonté	CAN	12.1.90	1	NCAA	Des Moines	11 Jun						
18.31		Meng Qianqian	CHN	6.1.91	1	AsiC	Kobe	10 Jul						
18.29	Josephine	Terlecki	GER	17.2.86	2		Celle	9 Jul						
18.15	Natalia	Ducó	CHI	31.1.89	2		La Habana	10 Mar						
18.15	Anita	Márton	HUN	15.1.89	1		Drazevina	24 Apr						
18.12	Sarah	Stevens-Walker	USA	2.4.86	3	NC	Eugene	23 Jun						
18.00i	Faith	Sherrill	USA	5.4.88	1		Bloomington IN	8 Jan						
18.00	Tia	Brooks	USA	2.8.90	2	NCAA	Des Moines	11 Jun						
17.99i	Jessica	Cérival	FRA	20.1.82	1	NC	Aubière	19 Feb						
	(30)													

Mark	Name		Nat	Born	Pos	Meet	Venue	Date	
17.97i	Karen	Shump	USA	14.8.89	1		Norman OK	19	Feb
17.97	Melissa	Boekelman	NED	11.5.89	1		Hengelo	31	May
17.95i	Vera	Yepimashko	BLR	10.7.76	2	NC	Mogilyov	11	Feb
17.92	Sophie	Kleeberg	GER	30.5.90	2	EU23	Ostrava	15	Jul
17.82	Helena	Engman	SWE	16.6.76	1		Sävedalen	12	Jun
17.81i	Denise	Hinrichs	GER	7.6.87	3		Nordhausen	21	Jan
17.77	Ifeatu	Okafor	USA	20.8.90	1	Big 12	Norman OK	14	May
17.70	Lyudmila	Morunova	RUS	27.1.85	1		Bryansk	19	Jun
17.66	Annie	Alexander	TRI	28.8.87	3	NCAA	Des Moines	11	Jun
17.56	Alyssa	Hasslen	USA	13.5.91	4	NC	Eugene	23	Jun
	(40)								
17.55	Yevgeniya	Solovyova	RUS	28.6.86	5	NC	Cheboksary	22	Jul
17.54i	Radoslava	Mavrodieva	BUL	13.3.87	1	NC	Sofia	20	Feb
17.53i	Austra	Skujyte	LTU	12.8.79	1P	EI	Paris (B)	4	Mar
17.49i	Simoné	du Toit	RSA	27.9.88	1		Houston	29	Jan
17.46	Jessica	Pressley	USA	27.12.84	1		Phoenix	2	Apr
17.45		Ma Qiao	CHN	28.9.89	5	NC	Hefei	8	Sep
17.41	Liana	Osorio	CUB	23.11.88	3		La Habana	10	Mar
17.41		Yang Yanbo	CHN	9.3.90	6	Anhalt	Dessau	1	Jun
17.38	Trecey	Rew	USA	11.1.88	1		Houston	16	Jun
17.38i	Jeneva	McCall	USA	28.10.89	1		Carbondale	3	Dec
	(50)								
17.33i	Oksana	Chibisova	RUS	31.3.77	3		Volgograd	16	Jan
17.33	Kristin	Heaston	USA	23.11.75	1		San Mateo	29	May
17.31	Adriane	Blewitt	USA	24.5.80	1		Marion IN	8	Jun
17.27	Halyna	Obleshchuk	UKR	23.2.89	1		Yalta	19	May
17.26	Keely	Medeiros	BRA	30.4.87	2	DrakeR	Des Moines	29	Apr
17.24	Anna	Jelmini	USA	15.7.90	4	MSR	Walnut	16	Apr
17.22	Rebecca	O'Brien	USA	30.4.90	1	MAC	DeKalb	14	May
17.20	Hanna	Samolyuk	UKR	13.1.88	1		Kyiv	9	Jul
17.19i	Brittany	Smith	USA	25.3.91	3	NCAA	College Station	12	Mar
17.17	Paulina	Guba	POL	14.5.91	4	EU23	Ostrava	15	Jul
	(60)								
17.16	Skylar	White	USA	15.9.91	1		Tempe	26	Mar
17.16	Abby	Ruston	USA	3.4.83	2		Houston	16	Jun
17.12	Anyela	Rivas	COL	13.8.89	2	CAC	Mayagüez	17	Jul
17.10	Nieves	Berroa	CUB	16.3.90	1		La Habana	13	May
17.09	Samira	Burkhardt	GER	9.8.90	5	NCAA	Des Moines	11	Jun
17.07	Baillie	Gibson	USA	18.11.91	6	MSR	Walnut	16	Apr
17.03	Geisa	Arcanjo	BRA	19.9.91	1		São Caetano do Sul	26	Aug
17.02	Úrsula	Ruiz	ESP	11.8.83	6	WUG	Shenzhen	20	Aug
17.00	Zara	Northover	JAM	6.3.84	1		Baton Rouge	23	Apr
16.99i	Sandra	Perkovic ¶	CRO	21.6.90	1	NC	Rijeka	19	Feb
	(70)								
16.99	Gwen	Berry	USA	29.6.89	1	MVC	Cedar Falls	14	May
16.99	Stacey	Wannemacher	USA	22.11.87	3q	NCAA-E	Bloomington IN	27	May
16.99	Vera	Kunova	RUS	2.4.90	6	NCp	Yerino	5	Jun
16.98	Viktoriya	Degtyar	UKR	5.11.83	2	NCp	Yalta	1	Jun
16.98		Guo Tianqian	CHN-Y	1.6.95	1	City G	Nanchang	20	Oct
16.97	D'Ana	McCarty	USA	14.7.89	4q	NCAA-E	Bloomington IN	27	May
16.96		Zhang Guirong	SIN	5.2.78	1	SEAG	Palembang	14	Nov
16.95	Julaika	Nicoletti	ITA	20.3.88	1		Ascoli Piceno	30	Jul
16.85	Denise	Kemkers	NED	11.4.85	1		Hoorn	21	May
16.83	Olga	Holodnaya	UKR	14.11.91	3	NCp	Yalta	1	Jun
	(80)								
16.79	Danielle	Frere	USA	27.4.90	1		Ames	16	Jun
16.79	Chinwe	Okoro	USA/NGR	20.6.89	1	NC	Calabar	23	Jun
16.77	Ashley	Muffet	USA	16.9.86	2	AI	Ashland	30	Apr
16.77i	Leyla	Rajabi	IRI	18.4.83	1		Tehran	11	Nov
16.76		Lee Mi-young	KOR	19.8.79	1	NC	Daegu	10	Jun
16.74	Natalya	Troneva	RUS-J	24.3.93	4	Kuts	Moskva	6	Aug
16.74	Andréa Maria	Brito	BRA	8.12.73	2		São Caetano do Sul	26	Aug
16.73	Eden	Francis	GBR	19.10.88	1	NC	Birmingham	30	Jul
16.71i	Tiffany	Howard	USA	28.12.86	2		Bloomington IN	21	Jan
16.71i	Laurence	Manfrédi	FRA	2.5.74	1		Nice	6	Feb
	(90)								
16.71	Irache	Quintanal	ESP	18.9.78	2	NC	Málaga	7	Aug
16.70i	Khadija	Abdullah	USA	24.7.90	1	Big Esat	Akron	20	Feb
16.70		Dong Yangzi	CHN-J	22.10.92	1	NC-j	Jinan	3	Jun
16.70	Sofia	Burkhanova	UZB	1.12.89	1	NCp	Tashkent	12	Jun
16.68	Anastasiya	Bessoltseva	RUS	18.8.90	1		Moskva	14	Jun

Mark	Name		Nat	Born	Pos	Meet	Venue	Date
16.66i	Monique	Riddick	USA	8.11.89	2		Ames	5 Mar
16.65i	Wilamena	Hopkins	USA	21.10.90	1	SEC	Fayetteville	27 Feb
16.65	Lena	Urbaniak	GER-J	31.10.92	3	NC-23	Bremen	26 Jun
16.65	Elisângela	Adriano	BRA	27.7.72	1		León	13 Jul
16.60	Kelly	Closse	FRA	8.8.88	7	MSR	Walnut	16 Apr
	(100)							

Mark	Name		Nat	Born	Date
16.59		Gu Siyu	CHN-J	11.2.93	20 Oct
16.56	Chandra	Brewer	USA	26.7.81	23 Jun
16.55	Felisha	Johnson	USA	24.7.89	27 May
16.50i	Aleksandra	Fisher	KAZ	3.6.88	5 Feb
16.48	Catarina	Andersson	SWE	17.11.77	3 Jul
16.47	Jana	Kárníková	CZE	14.2.81	21 May
16.44i	Christina	Hillman	USA	6.10.93	9 Dec
16.42i		Li Fengfeng	CHN	9.1.79	22 Feb
16.41	Michelle	Anumba	USA	18.9.91	2 Apr
16.41		Cai Yilin	CHN	27.11.90	25 Jun
16.40	Kim	Barrett	PUR	18.11.81	19 Mar
16.40		Lin Chia-Ying	TPE	5.11.82	26 Oct
16.38		Wang Ping	CHN	28.7.90	8 Sep
16.34i	Elena	Carini	ITA	5.4.87	22 Jan
16.34		Bian Ka	CHN-J	5.1.93	25 Jun
16.31	Sandra	Lemus	COL	1.1.89	6 May
16.31	Mary	Angell	USA	29.8.89	15 May
16.30	Kearsten	Peoples	USA	20.12.91	2 Apr
16.30	Vanessa	Henry	DMA	11.9.90	28 Apr
16.29		Cui Shuang	CHN	9.8.91	16 Jul
16.29	Rebecca	Peake	GBR	22.6.83	20 Aug
16.28i	Victoria	Flowers	USA	17.1.90	26 Feb
16.28	Rachel	Wallader	GBR	1.9.89	17 Jul
16.28	Anna	Wloka	POL-J	14.3.93	11 Aug
16.28	Nataliya	Dobrynska	UKR	29.5.82	17 Sep
16.26		Xu Yang	CHN	22.4.91	8 Sep
16.26i	Emel	Dereli	TUR-Y	25.2.96	17 Dec
16.24	Ana	Po'uhila-Kisina	TGA	12.10.79	9 Apr
16.18i	Irina	Khudoroshkina	RUS	13.10.68	17 Feb
16.14i		Wang Xiaoyun	CHN-J	7.12.93	22 Feb
16.14	Hilenn	James	TRI	16.3.90	2 Apr
16.12i	Irina	Kirichenko	RUS	18.5.87	17 Feb
16.12	Helen	Ubabuike	USA		9 Apr
16.11Ai	Lauren	Buresh	USA		12 Mar
16.10i		Rong Jun	CHN	7.4.89	22 Feb
16.08i		Zhai Zongling	CHN-J	18.9.93	19 Mar
16.07i	Dani	Bunch	USA	16.5.91	19 Feb
16.07	Kristin	Zaumsegel	GER-J	9.6.92	6 Aug
16.03i	Kelsey	Samuels	USA	28.6.91	12 Feb
16.03	Auriel	Dogmo	CMR	3.8.88	15 Sep
16.01i	Amanda	Latsch	USA	7.4.87	12 Feb
16.01	Anna	Rüh	GER-J	17.6.93	23 Jul
16.00	Jane	Swenson	USA	1.1.90	28 Apr
15.99	Betty	Williams	USA		2 Apr
15.98i	Fidela	James	USA	6.1.89	27 Feb
15.98	Yevgeniya	Smirnova	RUS	16.3.91	14 May
15.98	Ahymara	Espinoza	VEN	28.5.85	27 Jul
15.97	Yekaterina	Zyuganova	RUS	18.1.91	5 Jun
15.96	Annie	Jackson	USA	11.3.90	14 May
15.96	Suvi	Helin	FIN	10.5.85	21 Jun
15.95i	Kristy	Woods	USA	24.2.90	15 Jan
15.95i	Nilgün	Öztürk	TUR	30.1.82	17 Jan
15.93	Viktoriya	Korzh	UKR-J	17.7.92	6 May
15.92i	Magdalena	Zebrowska	POL	11.1.91	22 Jan
15.91i	Amanda	Van Dyke	USA	27.2.90	26 Feb
15.91	Tori	Ziegler	USA	14.7.90	14 May
15.90i		Shou Qianwen	CHN	29.5.90	26 Feb
15.90	Agnieszka	Dudzinska	POL	16.3.88	14 May
15.89	Margaret	Satupai	SAM-J	9.7.92	10 Feb
15.89	Hrisí	Moisídou	GRE	5.8.85	29 May
15.88	Chid	Onyewuenyi	USA		23 Apr
15.86i		Sun Yuting	CHN-Y	6.5.94	22 Feb
15.86	Tynisha	McMillian (166)	USA	7.2.88	15 May

Best outdoors

Mark	Name	Pos	Meet	Venue	Date
17.71	Kopets	1	ECp-w	Sofia	19 Mar
17.64	Sherrill	1	PennR	Philadelphia	28 Apr
17.52	Cérival	2	ECp-w	Sofia	19 Mar
17.36	Shump	2	Sun A	Tempe	9 Apr
17.09	Yepimashko	3	NCp	Brest	21 May
17.09	Skujyte	1	NC	Kaunas	23 Jul
16.96	McCall	2	MVC	Cedar Falls	14 May
16.79	Mavrodieva	6	ECp-w	Sofia	19 Mar
16.78	du Toit	8	WUG	Shenzhen	20 Aug
16.75	Rajabi	1		Tehran	27 Oct

16.58 Abdullah 27 May | 16.37 Chibisova 19 Mar | 16.03 Wang Xiaoyun 20 Oct | 15.91 Öztürk 21 May
16.40 Perkovic ¶ 26 Feb | 16.17 Manfrédi 8 May | 16.02 Hinrichs 16 Oct | 15.88 Hopkins 8 Apr
16.39 Riddick 6 May | 16.09 T Howard/White 6 May | 15.95 Dereli 13 Aug

JUNIORS

See main list for top 4 juniors. 11 performances by 5 women to 16.37. Additional marks and further juniors:

Name	Mark	Pos	Meet	Venue	Date	Mark	Pos	Meet	Venue	Date
Guo Tianqian	16.45	2	C-j	Jinan	3 Jan	16.37	1		Chengdu	29 Mar
Dong Yangzi	16.46	3	CityG	Nanchang	20 Oct					
Urbaniak	16.60	1		Neubrandenburg	28 May	16.48	1		Halle	21 May
	16.49i	1		Karlsruhe	29 Jan					

Mark	Name		Nat	Born	Pos	Meet	Venue	Date
16.59		Gu Siyu	CHN	11.2.93	2	City G	Nanchang	20 Oct
16.34		Bian Ka	CHN	5.1.93	6	NGP	Fuzhou	25 Jun
16.28	Anna	Wloka	POL	14.3.93	2	NC	Bydgoszcz	11 Aug
16.26i	Emel	Dereli	TUR-Y	25.2.96	1		Izmir	17 Dec
15.95					1	Balk C	Bursa	13 Aug
16.14i		Wang Xiaoyun	CHN	7.12.93	4	NGP	Nanjing	22 Feb
16.03					4	City G	Nanchang	20 Oct
16.08i		Zhai Zongling (10)	CHN	18.9.93	4	NGP	Chengdu	19 Mar
16.07	Kristin	Zaumsegel	GER	9.6.92	1	NC-j	Jena	6 Aug
16.01	Anna	Rüh	GER	17.6.93	3	EJ	Tallinn	23 Jul
15.93	Viktoriya	Korzh	UKR	17.7.92	1		Kharkov	6 May
15.89	Margaret	Satupai	SAM	9.7.92	1		Melbourne	10 Feb
15.86i		Sun Yuting	CHN-Y	6.5.94	6	NGP	Nanjing	22 Feb
15.74i	Shanice	Craft	GER	15.5.93	3		Leverkusen	19 Feb
15.74	Valentina	Muzaric	CRO	23.7.92	1	NC	Zagreb	31 Jul
15.71	Sophie	McKinna	GBR-Y	31.8.94	1		King's Lynn	15 May
15.62	Omotayo	Talabi	USA	11.8.92	10		Tucson	21 May
15.55	Luise	Weber (20)	GER	6.4.92	2		Halle	21 May

Mark	Name		Nat	Born	Pos	Meet	Venue	Date
67.98		Li Yanfeng	CHN	15.5.79	1		Schönebeck	5 Jun
						67.98	60.81	x	x	64.20	63.71

Mark	Name	Nat	Born	Pos	Meet	Venue	Date	Series
Li 66.52				1	WCh	Daegu	28 Aug	65.28 66.52 65.50 64.32 64.34 63.83
66.27				1	VD	Bruxelles	16 Sep	65.79 x 61.24 61.78 66.27 62.45
66.18				1		Halle	21 May	66.18 x x 60.71 62.40 x
64.58				1	NGPF	Nanchang	17 Jul	
64.48				1		Zhaoqing	24 Apr	
64.44				Q	WCh	Daegu	27 Aug	x 64.44
67.96	Sandra	Perkovic ¶	CRO	21.6.90	1	NC-w	Split	26 Feb
								59.39 59.49 67.96 60.53 65.14 x
66.99	Nadine	Müller	GER	21.11.85	1		Kienbaum	12 Aug
								63.62 65.29 66.99 x x 65.14
66.05					2		Halle	21 May	x 66.05 64.14 65.91 x 64.30
65.97					2	WCh	Daegu	28 Aug	65.06 65.97 64.08 62.55 x x
65.90					1	Herc	Monaco	22 Jul	65.90 61.88 65.16 x x x
65.75					1	BrGP	Birmingham	10 Jul	65.24 59.24 61.83 61.53 65.75 65.19
65.55					1	Anhalt	Dessau	1 Jun	59.42 65.55 60.78 64.69 62.77 62.36
65.54					Q	WCh	Daegu	27 Aug	65.54 only throw
65.38					2		Schönebeck	5 Jun	65.38 62.38 x x 58.36 x
66.40A	Yarelys	Barrios	CUB	12.7.83	1	PAm	Guadalajara, MEX	28 Oct
								66.40 62.88 x 63.13 63.41 61.39
65.73					3	WCh	Daegu	28 Aug	x 61.87 65.73 63.93 x 63.90
65.44					2	Herc	Monaco	22 Jul	64.60 65.44 64.86 61.39 65.01 x
65.33					2	VD	Bruxelles	16 Sep	64.95 64.55 65.33 63.15 63.88 x
64.48					1		Elstal	9 Sep	63.09 63.77 59.27 62.37 x 64.48
64.34					1		Reims	5 Jul	64.34 63.90 x 62.34 x 60.96
64.29					1	Athl	Lausanne	30 Jun	62.55 64.29 61.80 63.99 63.76 x
64.19					1	NC	La Habana	17 Mar	57.21 64.19 63.12 61.92 p x
64.18					1	GGala	Roma	26 May	53.77 64.18 x x 58.26 x
65.77	Yevgeniya	Pecherina ¶	RUS	9.5.89	1		Krasnodar	1 Jun
64.30	Becky	Breisch	USA	16.3.83	1		Chula Vista	16 Jun
								x 62.76 x 60.32 62.26 64.30
64.13	Stephanie	Brown Trafton	USA	1.12.79	1		Wailuku	29 Apr
								62.72 62.20 64.13 62.06 63.50 x
63.99	Zaneta	Glanc	POL	11.3.83	1	WUG	Shenzhen	17 Aug
								58.14 62.16 59.21 x 59.30 63.99
63.93		Ma Xuejun	CHN	26.3.85	2	Anhalt	Dessau	1 Jun
								63.93 62.55 63.08 x x 63.28
63.91	Darya	Pishchalnikova	RUS	19.7.85	1	Pavlov	Sofia	25 Jun
								61.68 60.38 61.48 x 63.91 x
	(31/10)							
63.85	Aretha	Thurmond	USA	14.8.76	2	Athl	Lausanne	30 Jun
63.72		Tan Jian	CHN	20.1.88	2	NGPF	Nanchang	17 Jul
63.61	Vera	Ganeyeva	RUS	6.11.88	1	Mosc Ch	Moskva	9 Jul
63.52	Kateryna	Karsak	UKR	26.12.85	1	EAF	Bydgoszcz	3 Jun
63.40	Vera	Cechlová	CZE	19.11.78	1	NC	Brno	2 Jul
63.28	Suzy	Powell	USA	3.9.76	1		Mesa	8 Apr
62.94	Denia	Caballero	CUB	13.1.90	1	Barr	La Habana	26 May
62.62	Nicoleta	Grasu	ROU	11.9.71	1	IntC	Constanta	3 Jun
62.56		Jiang Fengjing	CHN	28.8.87	1cB		Schönebeck	5 Jun
62.49	Zinaida	Sendriute	LTU	10.6.84	2	WUG	Shenzhen	17 Aug
	(20)							
62.48	Olesya	Korotkova	RUS	21.12.83	1	Lunyev	Adler	11 Feb
62.48	Dragana	Tomasevic	SRB	4.6.82	7	WCh	Daegu	28 Aug
62.33	Dani	Samuels	AUS	26.5.88	3	BrGP	Birmingham	10 Jul
62.26	Gia	Lewis-Smallwood	USA	1.4.79	2		Wailuku	28 Apr
62.26		Yang Yanbo	CHN	9.3.90	2cB		Schönebeck	5 Jun
62.25	Krishna	Poonia	IND	5.5.82	1		Portland	17 Oct
62.22	Monique	Jansen	NED	3.10.78	1		Chula Vista	28 Apr
62.00	Elisângela	Adriano	BRA	27.7.72	1		São Caetano do Sul	23 Jul
61.85	Yanisley	Collado	CUB	30.4.85	1		La Habana	11 Mar
61.47		Sun Taifeng	CHN	26.8.82	7		Halle	21 May
	(30)							
61.27	Svetlana	Saykina	RUS	10.7.85	2	Kuts	Moskva	6 Aug
61.07	Mélina	Robert-Michon	FRA	18.7.79	1	NCp	Bondoufle	15 Oct
60.91	Vera	Begic	CRO	17.3.82	1		Rijeka	20 May
60.91	Fernanda Raquel	Borges	BRA	26.7.88	1		León	13 Jul
60.76	Jade	Nicholls	GBR	30.3.87	1		London (He)	9 Jul
60.67	Sabine	Rumpf	GER	18.3.83	3		Fränkisch-Crumbach	12 Jun
60.54	Anna	Jelmini	USA	15.7.90	2		La Jolla	22 Apr
60.48	Karen	Gallardo	CHI	6.3.84	1		Santiago de Chile	22 Oct
59.97	Anna	Rüh	GER-J	17.6.93	8		Dessau	1 Jun
59.86	Joanna	Wisniewska	POL	24.5.72	1		Bottnaryd	2 Jul
	(40)							

Mark	Name		Nat	Born	Pos	Meet	Venue	Date
59.84	Julia	Bremser	GER	27.4.82	1		Lindschied	2 Jul
59.78	Natalya	Sadova	RUS	15.7.72	2		Adler	24 May
59.78	Eden	Francis	GBR	19.10.88	1		London (LV)	6 Aug
59.61	Yekaterina	Strokova	RUS	17.12.89	2	NC-w	Adler	23 Feb
59.60	Julia	Fischer	GER	1.4.90	1	EU23	Ostrava	15 Jul
59.56	Andressa	de Morais	BRA	21.12.90	1		São Caetano do Sul	26 Feb
59.50	Nataliya	Semenova	UKR	7.7.82	1	NC	Donetsk	2 Aug
59.45		Yang Fei	CHN	20.7.87	1	AsiGP	Wujiang	29 May
59.32	Suzanne	Kragbé	CIV	22.12.81	2		Donnas	3 Jul
59.26	Yaimé	Pérez	CUB	29.5.91	3		La Habana	18 Feb
(50)								
59.04	Rebecca	O'Brien	USA	30.4.90	1		DeKalb	14 May
59.00	Summer	Pierson	USA	3.9.78	5		La Jolla	22 Apr
58.96	Elizna	Naude	RSA	14.9.78	1		Bellville	16 Apr
58.84	Wioletta	Potepa	POL	14.12.80	1		Slubice	17 Jun
58.81	Simoné	du Toit	RSA	27.9.88	1		Arlington	2 Apr
58.78	Harwant	Kaur	IND	5.7.80	1	IS	Bangalore	12 Jun
58.73	Ulrike	Giesa	GER	16.8.84	3		Leipzig	11 Jun
58.65	Shanice	Craft	GER-J	15.5.93	1	EJ	Tallinn	22 Jul
58.64	Trecey	Rew	USA	11.1.88	1	NCAA	Des Moines	8 Jun
58.58	Annie	Alexander	TRI	28.8.87	1q	NCAA-E	Bloomington IN	28 May
(60)								
58.35	Irina	Rodrigues	POR	5.2.91	1		Leiria	7 Aug
58.07		Li Wen-Hua	TPE	3.12.89	1	NG	Changhua	24 Oct
57.99	Heike	Koderisch	GER	27.5.85	2	NC	Kassel	23 Jul
57.98	Kelechi	Anyanwu	USA	27.12.85	1c2		Portland	11 Jun
57.82A	Liz	Podominick	USA	5.12.84	1		Fort Collins	2 Apr
57.82	Eliska	Stanková	CZE	11.11.84	2	NC	Brno	2 Jul
57.80	Oksana	Yesipchuk	RUS	13.12.75	1		Bryansk	28 May
57.62	Laura	Bordignon	ITA	26.3.81	3		Donnas	3 Jul
57.61		Lu Xiaoxin	CHN	22.2.89	2	NGP	Fuzhou	26 Jun
57.57		Su Xinyue	CHN	8.11.91	1	NGP	Kunshan	26 May
(70)								
57.49	Agnieszka	Jarmuzek	POL	3.2.84	1		Warszawa	16 Jul
57.40		Xu Shaoyang	CHN	9.2.83	1	NGP	Shenzhen	12 Jun
57.38	Anastasiya	Kashtonova	BLR	14.1.89	1		Minsk	22 Jun
57.37	Jitka	Kubelová	CZE	2.10.91	3	NC	Brno	2 Jul
57.30	Sanna	Kämäräinen	FIN	8.2.86	1		Orimattila	31 Jul
57.25	Jeré	Summers	USA	21.5.87	2c2		Portland	11 Jun
57.24	Kimberley	Mulhall	AUS	9.1.91	1		Geelong	18 Dec
57.16	Lisandra	Rodríguez	CUB	14.10.86	4		La Habana	11 Feb
57.14	Allison	Randall	USA/JAM	25.5.88	1		Baltimore	23 Apr
57.14		Wang Bin	CHN	7.1.87	2	NGP	Kunshan	26 May
(80)								
57.10	Tanja	Komulainen	FIN	2.3.80	1		Tampere	12 Jun
56.92	Sofia	Larsson	SWE	22.7.88	1		Göteborg	24 May
56.85		Weng Chunxia	CHN-J	29.8.92	1	City G	Nanchang	23 Oct
56.83	Rachel	Longfors	USA	6.6.83	2	DrakeR	Des Moines	29 Apr
56.80		Xi Shangxue	CHN	27.1.89	2	NGP	Shenzhen	12 Jun
56.77	Jessica	Kolotzei	GER	6.4.85	5cB		Halle	21 May
56.69	Alla	Denisenko	RUS	12.10.83	2		Moskva	10 Jun
56.62	Natalia	Artîc	MDA	24.7.87	1	NC-w	Chisinau	6 Feb
56.58	Grete	Etholm	NOR	25.1.76	1		Hafnarfjördur	26 Jun
56.54	Yelena	Panova	RUS	2.3.87	4	NC-w	Adler	23 Feb
(90)								
56.46	Baillie	Gibson	USA	18.11.91	5	NCAA	Des Moines	8 Jun
56.44	Brittany	Borman	USA	1.7.89	3		Mesa	8 Apr
56.39	Rocío	Comba	ARG	14.7.87	1		Buenos Aires	8 Oct
56.38		Chen Dongxia	CHN	12.7.89	3	NGP	Kunshan	26 May
56.26	Mary	Angell	USA	29.8.89	2q	NCAA-E	Bloomington IN	28 May
56.19	Irène	Donzelot	FRA	8.12.88	1	NC	Albi	30 Jul
56.17	Yohana	Rodríguez	CUB	9.1.90	5		La Habana	11 Feb
56.16	Ashley	Hearn	USA		1		Berkeley	23 Apr
56.16		Lin Xiaojing	CHN	8.1.86	2	AsiGP	Wujiang	29 May
56.12	Anita	Márton	HUN	15.1.89	1		Békéscsaba	6 May
(100)								
56.12		Gu Siyu	CHN-J	11.2.93	2	City G	Nanchang	23 Oct

Mark	Name		Nat	Born	Date	Mark	Name		Nat	Born	Date
55.94	Beth	Rohl	USA	7.11.90	15 May	55.78	Pauline	Pousse	FRA	17.9.87	10 Jun
55.94		Feng Bin	CHN-Y	3.4.94	23 Oct	55.68	Hristína	Anagnostopoúlou	GRE	27.8.91	9 Jun
55.86	Adriane	Blewitt	USA	24.5.80	8 Jun	55.56	Liliana	Cá	POR	5.11.86	27 Feb
55.82	Rachel	Talbert	USA	21.4.87	19 Mar	55.48	Jasmine	Burrell	USA-J	27.2.92	5 Jun

Mark	Name		Nat	Born	Pos Meet	Venue	Date
55.35	Emily	Pendleton	USA	16.4.89			16 Apr
55.32	Olga	Olshevskaya	RUS	5.7.82			9 Jul
55.19	Brittnni	Borrero	PUR	10.9.87			21 May
55.18	María Angélica	Cubillán	VEN	22.4.81			23 Apr
55.17	Kirsty	Law	GBR	11.10.86			22 May
55.16	Tamara	Apostolico	ITA	28.4.89			24 Jul
55.13	Svetlana	Siarova	BLR	28.8.86			29 Apr
55.05		Wang Lan	CHN-J	8.7.93			19 Jul
55.02		Li Shanshan	CHN-J	6.1.92			26 May
54.93		Ma Shuli	CHN	20.1.78			24 Apr
54.91	Keely	Medeiros	BRA	30.4.87			29 Apr
54.91	Jeneva	McCall	USA	28.10.89			15 May
54.88	Nicole	Tzanakis	USA	13.8.88			8 Apr
54.75	Whitney	Ashley	USA	18.2.89			8 Jun
54.74	Erin	Pendleton	USA	13.3.91			29 Apr
54.64	Arasay	Morales	CUB-J	22.12.92			18 Feb
54.64	Kateryna	Shyshkina	UKR	27.2.87			25 Feb
54.64	Philippa	Roles	GBR	1.3.78			19 Jun
54.54	Viktoriya	Klochko	UKR-J	2.9.92			21 Jul
54.50		Liu Jing	CHN	1.1.91			26 May
54.42		Liang Yan	CHN-Y	2.1.95			23 Oct
54.38	Marike	Steinacker	GER-J	4.3.92			7 Aug
54.34	Skylar	White	USA	15.9.91			23 Apr
54.30	Sonka	Kielmann	GER-J	17.1.92			7 Aug
54.28	Yuliya	Maltseva	RUS	30.11.90			5 Jun
54.26	Karen	Shump	USA	14.8.89			15 May
54.24	Chinwe	Okoro	USA/NGR	20.6.89			13 May
54.22	Katerina	Klausová	CZE	28.2.89			7 Jun
54.21	Jessica	Maroszek	USA-J	26.2.92			23 Apr
54.15	Kristin	Pudenz	GER-J	9.2.93			14 May
54.13	Rachel	Varner	USA	20.7.83			22 Apr
54.09	Taylor	Freeman	USA	28.1.90			14 May
54.06	Sarah	Thornton	USA	29.8.86			30 Apr
54.05	Samia	Stokes	USA	22.7.89			19 Mar
54.02	Sabina	Asenjo	ESP	3.8.86			6 Aug
54.00	Rosalía	Vázquez	CUB-Y	11.10.95			17 Mar
54.00	Lucie	Catouillart	FRA	21.10.91			24 Jul
53.92	Betty	Williams	USA				26 Mar
53.90	Gökce	Celenk	TUR	22.7.88			24 Jun
53.78	Shelbi	Vaughan	USA-Y	24.8.94			8 Jul
53.77	Ifeatu	Okafor	USA	20.8.90			22 Apr
53.72	Mary	Theisen	USA	3.11.90			14 May
53.72	Anna-Katharina	Weller	GER	5.2.89			26 Jun
53.70	Evaggelía	Sofáni	GRE	28.1.85			9 Jun
53.64	Tai	Battle	USA	4.5.86			9 Apr
53.63	Katri	Hirvonen	FIN	25.6.90			1 Jul
53.58	Coralie	Glatre	FRA	26.9.89			29 May
53.56	Valerie	Wert	USA	4.10.86			14 May
53.54	Sara	Ackman (158)	USA	15.7.87			29 Apr

Drugs disqualification

69.99	Sandra	Perkovic ¶	CRO	21.6.90	(1)		Varazdin	4 Jun
				62.37	x	64.23	x	x	69.99
	65.58	(1) DL	Shanghai		15 May	64.93	65.18	x	65.58	x	59.28
	65.56	(1) GGala	Roma		26 May	64.06	65.56	x	x	63.87	63.72

JUNIORS

See main list for top 4 juniors. 10 performances by 2 women to 57.30. Additional marks and further juniors:

Rüh	59.15	1J		Neubrandenburg	28 May	58.10	2	EJ	Tallinn	22 Jul
	58.80	1J		Halle	21 May	57.65	1	NC-j	Jena	7 Aug
	58.70	2cB		Halle	21 May	57.31	1		Mannheim	3 Jul
Craft	57.89	2J		Halle	21 May	57.86	1		Wiesbaden	14 May
55.94			Feng Bin	CHN-Y	3.4.94	3	City G	Nanchang		23 Oct
55.48	Jasmine		Burrell	USA-J	27.2.92	1		San Diego		5 Jun
55.05			Wang Lan	CHN	8.7.93	1	MSG	Baotou		19 Jul
55.02			Li Shanshan	CHN	6.1.92	6	NGP	Kunshan		26 May
54.64	Arasay		Morales	CUB	22.12.92	6		La Habana		18 Feb
54.54	Viktoriya		Klochko (10)	UKR	2.9.92	Q	EJ	Tallinn		21 Jul
54.42			Liang Yan	CHN-Y	2.1.95	4	City G	Nanchang		23 Oct
54.38	Marike		Steinacker	GER	4.3.92	3	NC-j	Jena		7 Aug
54.30	Sonka		Kielmann	GER	17.1.92	4	NC-j	Jena		7 Aug
54.21	Jessica		Maroszek	USA	26.2.92	1	KansR	Lawrence		23 Apr
54.15	Kristin		Pudenz	GER	9.2.93	3J		Wiesbaden		14 May
54.00	Rosalía		Vázquez	CUB-Y	11.10.95	6	NC	La Habana		17 Mar
53.78	Shelbi		Vaughan	USA-Y	24.8.94	Q	WY	Villeneuve d'Ascq		8 Jul
53.16	Siositina		Hakeai	NZL-Y	1.3.94	1		Wellington		28 Jan
53.10	Taryn		Gollshewsky	AUS	18.5.93	1	NC-j	Sydney		11 Mar
52.96	Estephania		da Costa (20)	BRA	3.1.93	2	PAm-J	Miramar		23 Jul

HAMMER

79.42	Betty	Heidler	GER	14.10.83	1		Halle	21 May
				77.19	76.98	79.42	75.34	75.62	76.00
	77.53	1	Fränkisch-Crumbach	12 Jun	75.80	73.35	73.23	74.16	77.03	77.53
	77.53	1	Elstal	9 Sep	76.15	75.21	76.02	74.14	77.53	75.97
	77.40	1 ISTAF	Berlin	11 Sep	76.99	77.40	72.78	73.48	x	74.88
	77.22	1 GS	Ostrava	30 May	71.29	77.22	73.77	73.89	74.45	75.17
	76.06	2 WCh	Daegu	4 Sep	x	73.96	74.70	x	76.06	x
	76.04	1 NC	Kassel	23 Jul	73.85	x	75.02	73.08	76.04	74.30
	75.83	1	Dubnica nad Váhom	15 Sep	74.63	75.16	75.65	73.93	75.83	75.70
	75.54	1 Znam	Zhukovskiy	3 Jul	75.54	74.67	75.28	72.35		
	75.33	1	Dakar	28 May	70.19	73.95	72.15	75.33	x	70.16
	74.72	2	Potchefstroom	9 Feb	??					
	74.65	1	Kassel	8 Jun	71.19	74.47	x	74.65	73.80	74.53
77.13	Tatyana	Lysenko	RUS	9.10.83	1 WCh	Daegu		4 Sep
				76.80	77.09	77.13	74.51	75.05	x
	75.80	2	Dubnica nad Váhom	15 Sep	73.68	75.80	x	75.16	74.55	74.07
	75.70	1 Kuts	Moskva	6 Aug	72.14	72.36	72.83	75.70	x	x
	75.58	1 GP	Rieti	10 Sep	71.01	72.95	73.67	75.58		
	74.67	2 ISTAF	Berlin	11 Sep	70.89	73.23	74.33	74.67	74.67	x

Mark			Name		Nat	Born	Pos	Meet	Venue		Date
75.65			Zhang Wenxiu		CHN	22.3.86	2		Fränkisch-Crumbach		12 Jun
						74.33	74.12	73.90	x	73.77	75.65
	75.03	3 WCh	Daegu		4 Sep	75.03	74.31	x	73.17	71.86	74.79
	74.29	1 WMilG	Río de Janeiro		22 Jul	73.88	71.11	x	74.29	72.24	x
	74.26	1	Chengdu		29 Mar	??					
75.62			Yipsi	Moreno	CUB	19.11.80	1	PAm	Guadalajara, MEX		24 Oct
						73.67	x	x	x	x	75.62
	74.48	4 WCh	Daegu		4 Sep	73.29	x	74.48	x	x	x
	74.46	1	Leiria		7 Aug	x	74.46	71.41	x	x	x
	74.26	1	Río de Janeiro		26 May	71.91	74.26	70.89	73.29	x	72.42
	74.21	3	Dubnica nad Váhom		15 Sep	73.44	x	x	x	72.78	74.21
75.48			Kathrin	Klaas	GER	6.2.84	2	GS	Ostrava		30 May
						x	71.56	x	75.48	x	72.71
	75.30	1	Potchefstroom		9 Feb	??					
	74.58	3 ISTAF	Berlin		11 Sep	x	74.58	68.59	68.83	74.06	72.35
75.33			Anita	Wlodarczyk	POL	8.8.85	2		Elstal		9 Sep
	(30/6)					73.99	73.50	72.86	x	73.67	75.33
73.44			Jennifer	Dahlgren	ARG	27.8.84	4	ISTAF	Berlin		11 Sep
72.93			Zalina	Marghieva	MDA	5.2.88	1	WUG	Shenzhen		19 Aug
72.86			Yelena	Matoshko	BLR	23.6.82	1		Minsk		11 Aug
72.65			Jessica	Cosby	USA	31.5.82	1		Los Angeles (ER)		7 May
	(10)										
72.59			Amber	Campbell	USA	5.6.81	1	MSR	Walnut		16 Apr
72.47			Martina	Hrasnová	SVK	21.3.83	1	Towns	Athens GA		8 Apr
72.22			Nataliya	Zolotuhina	UKR	4.1.85	1		Uman		21 May
72.04			Bianca	Perie	ROU	1.6.90	6	WCh	Daegu		4 Sep
71.93			Silvia	Salis	ITA	17.9.85	1		Savona		18 May
71.93			Mariya	Bespalova	RUS	21.5.86	2		Zhukovskiy		6 Jul
71.86			Arasay	Thondike	CUB	28.5.86	1		La Habana		3 Jun
71.58			Marina	Marghieva	MDA	28.6.86	1	Univ Ch	Chisinau		4 May
71.53			Stéphanie	Falzon	FRA	7.1.83	1		Forbach		29 May
71.46			Sultana	Frizell	CAN	24.10.84	1c2		Edmonton		23 Jul
	(20)										
71.33			Éva	Orbán	HUN	29.11.84	2	WUG	Shenzhen		19 Aug
71.11			Gulfiya	Khanafeyeva	RUS	4.6.82	3		Zhukovskiy		6 Jul
70.98			Heather	Steacy	CAN	14.4.88	1		Lethbridge		22 May
70.54			Alexándra	Papayeoryíou	GRE	17.12.80	1	NC	Athína		29 Jul
70.52			Gwen	Berry	USA	29.6.89	1	DrakeR	Des Moines		30 Apr
70.43			Mona	Holm	NOR	5.8.83	1	NC	Byrkjelo		13 Aug
70.31			Iryna	Sekachyova	UKR	21.7.76	1	NCp	Yalta		31 May
70.09			Tugçe	Sahutoglu	TUR	1.5.88	1		Mersin		5 Mar
70.06			Joanna	Fiodorow	POL	4.3.89	2	EU23	Ostrava		16 Jul
69.87			Oksana	Kondratyeva	RUS	22.11.85	2	NC	Cheboksary		24 Jul
	(30)										
69.79			Amanda	Bingson	USA	20.2.90	1		Irvine		30 Apr
69.64			Britney	Henry	USA	17.10.84	1		Tucson		19 May
69.59			Sophie	Hitchon	GBR	11.7.91	3	EU23	Ostrava		16 Jul
69.55			Vânia	Silva	POR	8.6.80	1	ECCp	V.R. de Santo António		29 May
69.55			Jeneva	McCall	USA	28.10.89	1		St. Charles MO		9 Jul
69.53			Berta	Castells	ESP	24.1.84	1	NC	Málaga		6 Aug
69.50			Crystal	Smith	CAN	6.3.81	1		Kamloops		6 Aug
69.46				Liu Tingting	CHN	29.10.90	2		Schönebeck		5 Jun
69.39			Katerina	Safránková	CZE	8.6.89	3	ET	Stockholm		18 Jun
69.37				Hao Shuai	CHN	19.7.87	4	WUG	Shenzhen		19 Aug
	(40)										
69.30			Merja	Korpela	FIN	15.5.81	1		Kuortane		25 Jun
69.24			Manuèla	Montebrun	FRA	13.11.79	1		Amnéville		26 Jun
69.10			Anna	Bulgakova	RUS	17.1.88	1		Adler		22 Apr
69.08			Olga	Tsander	BLR	18.5.76	2		Minsk		4 Jun
69.02			Ariannis	Vichy	CUB	18.5.89	3	NC	La Habana		19 Mar
68.93			Jessika	Guéhaseim	FRA	23.8.89	2		Forbach		29 May
68.92			Daryia	Pchelnik	BLR	20.12.81	1		Minsk		28 Jul
68.90			Keelin	Godsey	USA	2.1.84	3	NC	Eugene		25 Jun
68.75				Wang Zheng	CHN	14.12.87	2	NC	Hefei		8 Sep
68.61			Tracey	Andersson	SWE	5.12.84	1	NC	Gävle		14 Aug
	(50)										
68.53			Johana	Moreno	COL	15.4.85	2	SAmC	Buenos Aires		2 Jun
68.53			Laëtitia	Bambara	FRA	30.3.84	2		Amnéville		26 Jun
68.45			Amy	Sène	SEN	6.4.85	4		Tomblaine		24 Jun
68.36			Dorotea	Habazin	CRO	14.6.88	1		Durham NC		23 Apr
68.35			Andrea	Bunjes	GER	5.2.76	4		Fränkisch-Crumbach		12 Jun

Mark	Name		Nat	Born	Pos	Meet	Venue	Date
68.26	Loree	Smith	USA	6.11.82	1		Boulder	2 Jun
68.14	Malgorzata	Zadura	POL	3.10.82	1		Lublin	14 May
68.05	Aleksandra	Lushcheko	RUS	1.3.87	1		Bryansk	28 May
67.90	Rosa	Rodríguez	VEN	2.7.86	1		Barquisimeto	14 May
67.78	Oksana	Menkova	BLR	28.3.82	3		Minsk	4 Jun
(60)								
67.66	Amy	Haapanen	USA	23.3.84	2		Tucson	21 May
67.56	Anna	Skydan	UKR-J	14.5.92	1		Uman	21 May
67.54	Yarisleydi	Ford	CUB	18.8.91	4	NC	La Habana	19 Mar
67.52	Iryna	Novozhylova	UKR	7.1.86	1		Yalta	18 May
67.33	Elisa	Palmieri	ITA	18.9.83	2	NC	Torino	25 Jun
67.30	Yunaika	Crawford	CUB	2.11.82	3		La Habana	3 Jun
67.30	Alina	Kastrova	BLR	2.3.90	1		Minsk	22 Jun
67.30	Yelena	Rigert	RUS	2.12.83	3	Mosc Ch	Moskva	10 Jul
67.19	Masumi	Aya	JPN	1.1.80	1	AsiC	Kobe	7 Jul
67.12	Laura	Redondo	ESP	3.7.88	1		Vitoria	2 Jul
(70)								
67.06	Barbara	Spiler	SLO-J	2.1.92	1	EJ	Tallinn	23 Jul
67.03	Megann	Rodhe	CAN	27.8.85	6	MSR	Walnut	16 Apr
66.87	Kristin	Smith	USA	23.12.87	1		Marietta	12 Jun
66.74	Kivilcim	Kaya	TUR-J	27.3.92	2	EJ	Tallinn	23 Jul
66.70	Lidiya	Provozina	UKR	13.2.86	2		Uman	21 May
66.63	Tereza	Králová	CZE	22.10.89	1		Pardubice	11 Jun
66.63	Odette	Palma	CHI	7.8.82	1		Santiago de Chile	24 Sep
66.46	Sarah	Holt	GBR	17.4.87	2		London (He)	10 Jul
66.36	Zlata	Tarasova	RUS	2.12.86	2		Adler	22 Apr
66.34	Jennifer	Joyce	CAN	25.9.80	4	NC	Calgary	25 Jun
(80)								
65.91	Alena	Krechyk	BLR	20.7.87	1		Baldwin City	30 Apr
65.88	Yuliet	Hernández	CUB	2.4.90	2		La Habana	12 May
65.69	Olivia	Waldet	FRA	23.5.84	7		Tomblaine	24 Jun
65.62		Zhang Li	CHN-J	13.3.93	3		Chengdu	29 Mar
65.62	Ashley	Harbin	USA	15.2.86	1		Glassboro	28 May
65.53	Aubrey	Baxter	USA	7.11.85	1		Manhattan	3 Jun
65.39	Cecilia	Nilsson	SWE	22.6.79	1		Karlstad	3 Sep
65.37	Zoë	Derham	GBR	24.11.80	3		London (He)	10 Jul
65.29	Emma	Johannesson	SWE	16.1.84	2		Leiria	23 Apr
65.18	Lena	Solvin	FIN	4.7.86	2		Kaustinen	2 Jul
(90)								
65.10	Sini	Latvala	FIN	3.2.80	1		Kristiinankaupunki	3 Sep
65.06	Karina	Frolova	RUS	2.3.90	2		Moskva	10 Jun
65.06	Nikola	Lomnická	SVK	16.9.88	1		West Point	16 Jun
65.03	Susan	McKelvie	GBR	15.6.85	2		Birmingham	20 Aug
65.02	Gabi	Wolfarth	GER	6.9.89	5		Kassel	8 Jun
65.02	Alexia	Sedykh	FRA-J	13.9.93	3	EJ	Tallinn	23 Jul
64.97	Natalya	Shayunova	BLR	11.9.89	5		Minsk	4 Jun
64.87	Nina	Volkova	RUS	26.8.84	Q	NC	Cheboksary	23 Jul
64.79	Kristal	Kostiew	USA	8.1.82	1		Baton Rouge	25 Mar
64.79	Yuka	Murofushi	JPN	11.2.77	2	NC	Kumagaya	10 Jun
(100)								

Mark	Name		Nat	Born	Date		Mark	Name		Nat	Born	Date
64.75	Katarzyna	Kita	POL	4.7.84	16 Jul		63.22	Natalya	Polyakova	RUS	9.12.90	28 May
64.70		Wang Yingying	CHN-J	16.5.93	29 Mar		63.16	Chandra	Andrews	USA	4.9.83	3 Jun
64.70	Jenny	Ozorai	HUN	3.12.90	30 Apr		63.08	Sharon	Ayala	MEX	28.9.86	13 May
64.49	Annabelle	Rolnin	FRA	28.12.87	22 May		63.05	Cintia	Gergelics	HUN	16.11.91	6 Aug
64.46	Gabrielle	Neighbour	AUS	22.11.83	10 Feb		62.94	Jenni	Penttilä	FIN	9.3.91	23 Jul
64.44	Laura	Igaune	LAT	10.2.88	6 May		62.92	D'Ana	McCarty	USA	14.7.89	10 Jun
64.44	Caressa	Sims	USA	7.3.86	21 May		62.90	Shant'e	White	USA	1.5.90	12 May
64.35	Shelby	Ashe	USA-J	13.3.93	15 May		62.90	Ana	Susec	SLO	23.11.85	19 Aug
64.28	Carolin	Paesler	GER	16.12.90	23 Jul		62.88	Brittany	Smith	USA	25.3.91	13 May
64.26	Chelsea	Cassulo	USA	10.6.90	25 Jun		62.85	Laura	Gibilisco	ITA	17.1.86	23 Jul
64.21	Mariya	Smolyachkova	BLR	10.2.85	29 Apr		62.78	Magdalena	Szewa	POL	20.9.90	7 May
64.14	Brittany	Hinchcliffe	USA	24.7.82	25 Jun		62.73	Marte Rygg	Årdal	NOR-J	5.7.92	4 Jul
64.11	Sarah	Bensaad	FRA/TUN	27.1.87	6 Feb		62.68		Luo Nuo	CHN-J	8.10.93	8 Sep
64.10	Alena	Lysenko	RUS	3.2.88	9 Jul		62.66	Rachel	Gair	GBR	12.9.86	20 Aug
64.09	Marissa	Minderler	USA	7.5.89	13 May		62.62	Shannon	Popp	USA	23.10.84	15 Apr
64.05	Laura	Douglas	GBR	4.1.83	22 May		62.58	Kelsey	Hanley	USA	23.7.88	13 May
64.04		Yang Youyu	CHN	14.9.85	29 Mar		62.55	Mélanie	Fromentin	FRA	10.10.81	8 Jul
63.86	Carys	Parry	GBR	24.7.81	30 Jul		62.48		Kang Na-ru	KOR	25.4.83	7 Jul
63.82	Johanna	Salmela	FIN	6.11.90	2 Jul		62.46	Nicky	Grant	JAM	25.5.81	15 Jul
63.82		Wang Lu	CHN	22.12.91	8 Sep		62.39	Karolina	Pedersen	SWE	16.4.87	3 Jul
63.72	Ida	Storm	SWE	11.10.91	13 May		62.37		Li Juan	CHN	6.2.88	25 Jun
63.70	Irina	Sarvilova	RUS	11.11.91	13 May		62.35	Agata	Jelonkiewicz	POL-J	10.9.92	11 Aug
63.43	Trude	Raad	NOR	27.4.90	15 Jul		62.28	Julia	Ratcliffe	NZL-J	14.7.93	19 Feb

Mark	Name		Nat	Born	Date
62.26	Mélanie	Viniger	FRA	16.7.84	10 Jul
62.24	Yelena	Navrakhodskaya	BLR-J	11.5.93	22 Jul
62.13	Josiane	Soares	BRA	21.6.76	26 Jul
62.13	Alexandra	Tavernier	FRA-J	13.12.93	23 Oct
62.05	Tatiana	Massamba	FRA	17.8.89	25 Jun
61.97	Zeliha	Uzunbilek	TUR	10.6.91	9 Jul
61.94	Myra	Perkins	GBR-J	21.1.92	1 May
61.86	Juliana	Smith	USA	12.12.89	1 Apr
61.85	Brynn	Smith	USA		7 May
61.78	Breann	Fife	USA	13.9.89	24 Apr
61.74	Bronwyn	Eagles	AUS	23.8.80	19 Mar
61.74		Wang Lamei	CHN	15.1.90	8 Sep
61.70	Ayla	Gill	NZL	9.1.91	18 Mar
61.67	Amy	Thayer	USA	26.7.81	21 May
61.66	Fruzsina	Fertig	HUN-J	2.9.93	15 Oct
61.65	Aysegül	Alniaçik	TUR	15.4.87	5 Jun
61.55	Micaela	Mariani	ITA	11.2.88	16 Jul
61.50	Vanda	Nickl	HUN	4.9.85	6 Mar
61.50	Alicja	Filipkowska	POL	15.4.87	11 Aug
61.49	Galina	Kulkova	RUS	3.4.80	10 Jul
61.49		Liu Jingnan	CHN-J	2.11.92	17 Aug
61.47	Delphine	Ramothe	FRA	17.7.91	26 Jun
61.43	Amélie	Perrin	FRA	30.3.80	2 Jul
61.42	Rana Taha	Ibrahim	EGY-J	9.7,92	30 Sep
61.33	Elisabeth	Dubourt	CAN	.86	12 Jul
61.29		Liu Wei	CHN	9.3.91	29 Mar
61.22	Jean	Marqueling	USA	.89	8 Jun
61.21	Elizabeth	Murphy	USA	23.4.90	9 Apr
61.20	Kristyna	Krouzková	CZE	5.3.90	23 Jul
61.19	Francesca	Massobrio	ITA-J	9.7.93	25 Jun
61.14	Felisha	Johnson	USA	24.7.89	9 Apr
61.14	Suesanna	Williams	JAM	9.11.85	30 Apr
61.14	Hannele	Kuutti	FIN	16.3.84	2 Jul
61.08		Dan Dongxue	CHN-J	23.3.92	2 Jun
61.06	Hanna	Lutska	UKR	6.5.88	31 May
60.95	Holly	Ozanich	USA	8.3.89	27 May
60.92	Kirsten	Münchow	GER	21.1.77	12 Jun
60.88	Terran	Alexander	USA	29.4.89	7 Apr
60.87	Nahal Kamel	Fehmi Ahmed	EGY-J	14.8.92	21 Oct
60.83	Paraskevi	Theodorou	CYP	15.3.86	26 Jun
60.76	Melissa	Kurzdorfer	USA	30.12.91	12 May
60.76	Malin	Johansson	SWE-J	28.4.92	28 May
60.74	Josefin	Berg	SWE	27.12.85	3 Sep
60.72	Jonna	Miettinen	FIN	7.12.90	2 Jul
60.68	Olga	Ciura	USA	27.2.89	13 May
60.68	Diurkina	Freites	VEN	5.11.89	11 Dec
60.66	Kimery	Hern	USA	24.2.87	15 Apr
60.66	Daniela	Manz	GER	19.9.86	29 May
60.60	Daina	Levy	CAN-J	27.5.93	11 Jun
60.56	Darya	Belaya	RUS	13.12.91	1 Jun
60.55	Katja	Vangsnes	NOR	16.11.91	21 May
60.54	Romana	Grómanová	CZE	11.10.84	30 May
60.52	Bianca	Wiecken	GER	17.4.81	8 May
60.50	Dóra	Lévai (200)	HUN	20.6.88	18 May

JUNIORS

See main list for top 5 juniors. 10 performances by 5 women to 64.90. Additional marks and further juniors:

Mark	Name		Nat	Born	Pos	Meet	Venue	Date
Skydan	66.31	2					Yalta	18 May
Spiler	66.55	1					Maribor	6 Jul
	65.48	1					Novo Mesto	13 Jul
Kaya	65.77	Q	EJ				Tallinn	22 Jul
	64.90	1					Bursa	23 Jun
64.70		Wang Yingying	CHN	16.5.93	5		Chengdu	29 Mar
64.35	Shelby	Ashe	USA	13.3.93	1		Marietta	15 May
62.73	Marte Rygg	Årdal	NOR	5.7.92	1J		Helsingborg	4 Jul
62.68		Luo Nuo	CHN	8.10.93	6	NC	Hefei	8 Sep
62.35	Agata	Jelonkiewicz (10)	POL	10.9.92	4	NC	Bydgoszcz	11 Aug
62.28	Julia	Ratcliffe	NZL	14.7.93	1	Porritt	Hamilton	19 Feb
62.24	Yelena	Navrakhodskaya	BLR	11.5.93	Q	EJ	Tallinn	22 Jul
62.13	Alexandra	Tavernier	FRA	13.12.93	1		Viry-Châtillon	23 Oct
61.94	Myra	Perkins	GBR	21.1.92	2	Univ Ch	Bedford	1 May
61.66	Fruzsina	Fertig	HUN	2.9.93	1J		Veszprém	15 Oct
61.49		Liu Jingnan	CHN	2.11.92	17q	WUG	Shenzhen	17 Aug
61.42	Rana Taha	Ibrahim	EGY	9.7,92	1		El Maadi	30 Sep
61.19	Francesca	Massobrio	ITA	9.7.93	4	NC	Torino	25 Jun
61.08		Dan Dongxue	CHN	23.3.92	2	NC-j	Jinan	2 Jun
60.87	Nahal Kamel	Fehmi Ahmed (20)	EGY	14.8.92	1		El Maadi	21 Oct

Mark	Pos	Meet	Venue	Nat/Born	Date	Series					
71.99			Mariya Abakumova	RUS	15.1.86	1 WCh Daegu					2 Sep
					60.38	71.25	p	x	71.99	64.27	
67.98	1		Velenje		28 Jun	62.62	65.95	62.97	61.36	67.98	63.45
66.05	1	NC	Cheboksary		23 Jul	66.05	x	x	x	x	64.02
65.81	1	GS	Ostrava		31 May	65.56	x	62.49	p	62.77	65.81
65.40	1	GGala	Roma		26 May	63.52	51.71	x	65.40	61.08	p
65.30	2	Pre	Eugene		4 Jun	x	56.41	63.46	60.64	65.30	x
65.12	1	NC-w	Adler		24 Feb	??					
65.12	3	DL	Saint-Denis		8 Jul	65.12	x	x	62.18	x	59.11
71.58			Barbora Spotáková	CZE	30.6.81	2 WCh Daegu					2 Sep
					68.80	67.90	68.64	67.12	71.58	66.80	
69.45	1	Herc	Monaco		22 Jul	64.54	64.66	63.18	66.40	64.50	69.45
67.57	2	DL	Saint-Denis		8 Jul	60.73	67.57	x	64.04	62.20	65.82
67.14	1	ISTAF	Berlin		11 Sep	61.93	67.14	x	65.20	63.96	63.33
66.41	2	LGP	London (CP)		5 Aug	63.72	62.81	64.26	x	66.41	x
65.77	1	Odlozil	Praha		13 Jun	60.61	61.49	64.06	62.07	64.07	65.77
64.87	3	Pre	Eugene		4 Jun	64.87	x	x	60.78	x	x
69.57			Christina Obergföll	GER	22.8.81	1 WK Zürich					8 Sep
					x	68.95	x	64.99	69.57	x	
68.86	1	NC	Kassel		24 Jul	64.32	68.86	64.81	64.28	x	65.30
68.76	Q	WCh	Daegu		1 Sep	68.76	only throw				
68.01	1	DL	Saint-Denis		8 Jul	68.01	x	61.28	x	x	x
66.74	1	LGP	London (CP)		5 Aug	60.19	63.63	66.13	65.15	66.74	65.73
66.22	1	ET	Stockholm		18 Jun	66.22	61.07	x	62.32		
65.48	1	Pre	Eugene		4 Jun	62.97	x	x	64.22	65.48	x

Mark	Name			Nat	Born	Pos	Meet	Venue			Date
	65.24	4	WCh	Daegu	2 Sep	61.74	64.39	64.80	65.24	63.51	x
	65.01	1		Elstal	9 Sep	65.01	64.33	62.40	x	58.16	57.58
	64.95	2	ISTAF	Berlin	11 Sep	x	64.40	x	x	64.95	x
68.38	Sunette			Viljoen	RSA	6.1.83	3	WCh	Daegu		2 Sep
						64.36	65.20	63.12	58.48	68.38	62.68
	67.46	2	WK	Zürich	8 Sep	62.30	x	61.16	66.96	67.46	67.22
	66.47	1	WUG	Shenzhen	18 Aug	x	66.47	x	57.46	60.36	58.82
	65.34	Q	WCh	Daegu	1 Sep	65.34			only throw		
65.89	Martina			Ratej	SLO	2.11.81	1		Slovenska Bistrica		29 May
	(30/5)					59.96	x		56.92	65.89 p	p
64.67	Katharina			Molitor	GER	8.11.83	2	NC	Kassel		24 Jul
64.46	Goldie			Sayers	GBR	16.7.82	2	ET	Stockholm		18 Jun
63.82	Kimberley			Mickle	AUS	28.12.84	1		Sydney		19 Mar
63.77	Mercedes			Chilla	ESP	19.1.80	1		Rabat		5 Jun
63.50	Yanet			Cruz	CUB	8.2.88	1	NC	La Habana		19 Mar
	(10)										
63.46	Madara			Palameika	LAT	18.6.87	1	ET-2	Novi Sad		18 Jun
62.76	Kara			Patterson	USA	10.4.86	4	GGala	Roma		26 May
62.30	Yainelis			Ribiaux	CUB	30.12.87	1		La Habana		5 Aug
61.60	Vira			Rebryk	UKR	25.2.89	1	NCp	Yalta		31 May
61.26	Justine			Robbeson	RSA	15.5.85	1		Maputo		2 Jul
61.12	Jarmila			Klimesová	CZE	9.2.81	4	GS	Ostrava		31 May
60.78	Linda			Stahl	GER	2.10.85	2		Velenje		28 Jun
60.73	Marina			Maksimova	RUS	20.5.85	1	NCp	Yerino		4 Jun
60.65				Liu Chunhua	CHN	1.10.86	1	NGP	Zhaoqing		23 Apr
60.64	Lina			Muze	LAT-J	4.12.92	1		Riga		2 Jun
	(20)										
60.40	Rachel			Yurkovich	USA	10.10.86	1	Jerome	Burnaby		1 Jul
60.32	Yuki			Ebihara	JPN	28.10.85	1		Toyama		8 May
60.30	Zahra			Bani	ITA	31.12.79	1		Gorizia		30 Jun
60.26				Du Xiaowei	CHN	11.8.87	1	NC	Hefei		11 Sep
60.25	Maria			Negoita	ROU	6.12.86	1		Onesti		14 May
60.10	Hanna			Hatsko	UKR	3.10.90	1	NC-w	Yalta		24 Feb
60.08	Risa			Miyashita	JPN	26.4.84	1	NC	Kumagaya		11 Jun
60.07	Elisabeth			Eberl	AUT	25.3.88	1		Lappeenranta		13 Aug
60.06	Anastasiya			Svechnikova	UZB-J	20.9.92	1	NC	Tashkent		30 Sep
60.02	Indre			Jakubaityte	LTU	24.1.76	1		Besançon		14 Jun
	(30)										
59.95	Laura			Whittingham	GBR	6.6.86	1		Saarijärvi		26 Jun
59.86	Nora Aída			Bicet	ESP	29.10.77	2	NC	Málaga		6 Aug
59.74	Christin			Hussong	GER-Y	17.4.94	1	WY	Villeneuve d'Ascq		7 Jul
59.52	Sílvia			Cruz	POR	29.12.80	1		Leiria		12 Mar
59.50				Chang Chunfeng	CHN	4.5.88	1	NGPF	Nanchang		16 Jul
59.50	Sinta			Ozolina-Kovale	LAT	26.2.88	1		Riga		9 Aug
59.47	Kathryn			Mitchell	AUS	10.7.82	1		Gold Coast		13 Aug
59.41	Esther			Eisenlauer	GER	29.10.77	3	NC	Kassel		24 Jul
59.29	Sarah			Mayer	GER	20.5.91	1	EU23	Ostrava		16 Jul
59.15	Ásdís			Hjálmsdóttir	ISL	28.10.85	13q	WCh	Daegu		1 Sep
	(40)										
59.00	Sávva			Líka	GRE	27.6.70	1		Kalamáta		4 Jun
58.72				Lu Huihui	CHN	26.6.89	2	NGP	Zhaoqing		23 Apr
58.72	Oona			Sormunen	FIN	2.8.89	Q	EU23	Ostrava		14 Jul
58.64	Krista			Woodward	CAN	22.11.84	1	MSR	Walnut		15 Apr
58.61	Oksana			Gromova	RUS	3.9.80	1		Adler		22 Apr
58.52				Kim Kyung-ae	KOR	5.3.88	1	NG	Goyang		9 Oct
58.46	Viktoriya			Sudarushkina	RUS	2.9.90	1	NC-23-w	Adler		24 Feb
58.42				Wang Ping	CHN	28.7.90	2		Chengdu		29 Mar
58.40	Elizabeth			Gleadle	CAN	5.12.88	1		Lethbridge		20 May
58.25	Melissa			Dupre	BEL	5.11.86	5	WUG	Shenzhen		18 Aug
	(50)										
58.24	Sanni			Utriainen	FIN	5.2.91	1		Lahti		8 Jun
58.24	Mareike			Rittweg	GER	1.6.84	1		Bottrop		15 Jul
58.03	Vanda			Juhász	HUN	6.6.89	1	NC	Szekszárd		6 Aug
58.01A	Alicia			DeShasier	USA	15.4.84	1	PAm	Guadalajara, MEX		27 Oct
57.93	Maryna			Novik	BLR	19.1.84	1		Minsk		3 Jun
57.82	Liina			Laasma	EST-J	13.1.92	1	NC-j	Rakvere		6 Jul
57.81	Laila			Silva	BRA	30.7.82	1	NC	São Paulo		6 Aug
57.74	Laura			Cornford	AUS	11.6.88	2		Sydney		19 Mar
57.58	Yusbelys			Parra	VEN	31.7.86	1	NG	Barquisimeto		12 Dec
57.50	Osleidys			Menéndez	CUB	14.11.79	2		La Habana		13 May
	(60)										

Mark	Name		Nat	Born	Pos	Meet	Venue	Date
57.50	Lisanne	Schol	NED	22.6.91	Q	EU23	Ostrava	14 Jul
57.47		Suh Hae-an	KOR	1.7.85	2	NG	Goyang	9 Oct
57.40	Lada	Chernova	RUS	1.1.70	3	NC-w	Adler	24 Feb
57.40	Aggelikí	Tsiolakoúdi	GRE	10.5.76	2		Kalamáta	4 Jun
57.40	Hanna	Habina	UKR-J	26.10.92	2	NC	Donetsk	4 Aug
57.39		Li Lingwei	CHN	26.1.89	2	NC	Hefei	11 Sep
57.32	Linda	Selui	FRA	15.11.77	1		Nouméa	6 Sep
57.26	Flor Dennis	Ruiz	COL	24.1.91	1		Ponce	2 Apr
57.18	Prescilla	Lecurieux	FRA-J	1.12.92	Q	NC-j	Dreux	16 Jul
57.11	Nadeeka	Lakmali	SRI	18.9.81	1	NSF	Diyagama	9 Sep
(70)								
57.10	Alexia	Kogut-Kubiak	FRA	22.1.88	1		Reims	22 May
57.09	Anna	Wessman	SWE	9.10.89	1	vFIN	Helsinki	10 Sep
56.75		Xue Juan	CHN	10.2.86	1	AsiGP	Jiaxing	22 May
56.68	Tatjana	Jelaca	SRB	10.8.90	24q	WCh	Daegu	1 Sep
56.51	Bernarda	Letnar	SLO	26.12.89	1		Palmanova	1 May
56.46	Xénia	Nagy	HUN	29.3.86	1		Debrecen	21 May
56.42		Chen Ping	CHN	8.9.89	4	NC	Hefei	11 Sep
56.41	Romina	Ugatai	FRA	10.10.86	2		Strasbourg	12 Jun
56.38	Irena	Sedivá	CZE-J	19.1.92	7	Odlozil	Praha	13 Jun
56.31	Kateryna	Derun	UKR-J	24.9.93	Q	EJ	Tallinn	23 Jul
(80)								
56.27		Sui Liping	CHN	1.5.91	4	NGP	Jiaxing	21 May
56.17	Leryn	Franco	PAR	1.3.82	2	Alba	Barquisimeto	29 Jul
56.08		Zhang Li	CHN	17.1.89	3	NGP	Fuzhou	25 Jun
56.04A	Gerlize	de Klerk	RSA	23.3.89	3		Germiston	26 Mar
56.02	Marissa	Tschida	USA	7.7.89	1	Pac10	Tucson	13 May
55.94	Tatyana	Kholadovich	BLR	29.8.91	2	NC	Grodno	7 Jul
55.93	Margaret	Simpson	GHA	2.8.82	1H	AfG	Maputo	14 Sep
55.85	María Lucelly	Murillo	COL	5.5.91	1	SAmC	Buenos Aires	5 Jun
55.82	Lismania	Muñoz	CUB-J	28.2.93	3	NC	La Habana	19 Mar
55.80	Aida	Sellam	TUN	13.9.77	1	NC	Radès	26 Jun
(90)								
55.79	Antoinette	Nana Djimou	FRA	2.8.85	1H	WCh	Daegu	30 Aug
55.71	Susanne	Rosenbauer	GER	2.8.84	1		Turkheim	15 May
55.70	Haruka	Matoba	JPN	24.4.87	3	NC	Kumagaya	11 Jun
55.59	Nadia	Vigliano	FRA	24.6.77	1	NC	Albi	28 Jul
55.53	Magdalena	Czenska	POL	14.6.81	1	NC	Bydgoszcz	13 Aug
55.52	Laura	Henkel	GER-J	29.2.92	1	NC-j	Jena	6 Aug
55.44	Jucilene	de Lima	BRA	14.9.90	1		São Paulo	1 Oct
55.35		Song Xiaodan	CHN-J	23.1.93	1	NC-j	Jinan	5 Jun
55.34	Felicia	Moldovan	ROU	29.9.67	1	CAA	Brazzaville	12 Jun
55.34	Alessandra	Resende	BRA	5.3.75	2	NC	São Paulo	6 Aug
(100)								

Mark		Name	Nat	Born	Date		Mark		Name	Nat	Born	Date
55.25		Zhang Ying	CHN	5.1.88	11 Sep		54.20	Bregje	Crolla	NED	31.1.86	21 May
55.15	Rafaela	Gonçalves	BRA	27.11.91	14 May		54.12	Lyubov	Zhatkina	RUS	30.3.90	12 Feb
55.11		Yao Xia	CHN	3.3.90	16 Jul		54.04	Sofía	Ifadídou	GRE	5.1.85	8 May
55.10		Liu Shiying	CHN-J	24.9.93	5 Jun		54.04	Kseniya	Zybina	RUS	1.2.89	8 Jul
55.09		Wang Beibei	CHN	22.1.89	29 Mar		53.99	Silvia	Carli	ITA	17.9.85	26 Jun
55.09		Song Dan	CHN	5.7.90	25 Jun		53.94		Tian Haixia	CHN	3.6.90	25 Jun
55.00	Séphora	Bissoly	FRA	6.11.81	28 Jul		53.87	Momoko	Matsumoto	JPN	7.12.87	21 May
54.99		Yang Xinli	CHN	7.2.88	11 Sep		53.86	Alina	Gerasimchuk	RUS-Y	11.10.94	29 Jul
54.97A	Erma-Gene	Evans	LCA	25.1.84	16 Apr		53.85	Avione	Allgood	USA-J	14.12.93	25 Jun
54.93		Zhu Dandan	CHN-J		11 Aug		53.82	Eliza	Toader	ROU	12.5.90	3 Jun
54.90	Marion	Bonaudo	FRA	12.9.82	8 May		53.77	Viktorija	Barviciute	LTU	27.1.89	23 Jul
54.88	Alanna	Kovacs	CAN	25.8.90	16 Apr		53.73	Lindy	Leveau-Agricole	SEY	14.11.79	12 Aug
54.83	Aleksandra	Spikina	RUS	16.1.89	24 Feb		53.68	Carmen	Sánchez	ESP-J	29.2.92	6 Aug
54.83	Sofi	Flinck	SWE-Y	8.7.95	24 Jul		53.65	Janice	Waldvogel	GER-J	7.4.93	20 Feb
54.76	Kim	Hamilton	USA	28.11.85	10 Jul		53.65	Kateema	Riettie	JAM	12.5.73	21 May
54.73	Marija	Vucenovic	SRB-J	3.4.93	24 Jul		53.61A	Katie	Coronado	USA	13.9.86	2 Apr
54.71	Alexandra	Tsisiou	CYP	2.7.81	4 Jun		53.60	Abigail	Gómez	MEX	30.6.91	13 Feb
54.68	Anaëlle	Fournier	FRA	20.1.88	27 Feb		53.54	Alexie	Alaïs	FRA-Y	9.10.94	6 Jul
54.60	Mariya	Yakovenko	RUS	6.1.82	24 Feb		53.45	Nathalie	Meier	SUI-J	30.3.93	23 Jul
54.50	Yuka	Sato	JPN-J	21.7.92	17 Jun		53.29		Lee Hye-rim	KOR	6.3.89	25 Apr
54.49	Ismaray	Armentero	CUB-Y	13.10.94	28 May		53.20	Dana	Lyon	USA	5.6.84	6 May
54.47	Niina	Kelo	FIN	26.3.80	5 Jun		53.20	Nikolett	Szabó	HUN	3.3.80	2 Oct
54.47	Annika	Petersson	SWE	10.1.79	12 Jun		53.19	Jenni	Kangas	FIN-J	3.7.92	3 Jul
54.46	Nikol	Ogrodníková	CZE	18.8.90	14 May		53.16	Zaneta	Lenczewska	POL-J	23.2.92	3 May
54.44	Ióli	Panídi	GRE	16.2.83	29 May		53.13	Tiziana	Rocco	ITA	2.12.78	26 Jun
54.40	Marharyta	Dorozhon	UKR	4.9.87	4 Aug		53.12	Kanako	Shiba	JPN	11.5.90	9 Sep
54.32	Brittany	Borman	USA	1.7.89	9 Jun		53.09	Amanda	Peterson	USA	14.3.89	9 Apr
54.29	Freisa Iris	Núñez	DOM	24.7.87	17 Jul		53.04	Urszula	Jakimowicz	POL	11.6.88	28 May
54.24	Mathilde	Andraud	FRA	28.4.89	14 Jul		53.02	Mai	Inaoka	JPN	23.10.89	5 Apr
54.23	Tove Beate	Dahle	NOR	6.4.88	14 Aug		53.00	Karen	Clarke (160)	AUS	23.6.90	16 Apr

Mark	Name		Nat	Born	Pos	Meet	Venue	Date

JUNIOR

See main list for top 11 juniors. 11 performances by 6 women to 56.99. Additional marks and further juniors:

Mark	Name		Nat	Born	Pos	Meet	Venue	Date
Muze	59.65		1	NC-j	Jekabpils	19 Jul	56.99 1 Ääneskoski	10 Jun
	57.34		1		Starsbiurg	12 Jun		
Laasma	57.04		2	EThr-J	Sofia	19 Mar		
Lecurieux	56.99		Q	EJ	Talinn	23 Jul		
55.10		Liu Shiying	CHN	24.9.93	2	NC-j	Jinan	5 Jun
54.93		Zhu Dandan	CHN		1		Ningxiang	11 Aug
54.83	Sofi	Flinck	SWE-Y	8.7.95	1		Gävle	24 Jul
54.73	Marija	Vucenovic	SRB	3.4.93	5	EJ	Tallinn	24 Jul
54.50	Yuka	Sato	JPN	21.7.92	1		Hiratsuka	17 Jun
54.49	Ismaray	Armentero	CUB-Y	13.10.94	3	Barr	La Habana	28 May
53.86	Alina	Gerasimchuk	RUS-Y	11.10.94	1	EYOF	Trabzon	29 Jul
53.85	Avione	Allgood	USA	14.12.93	4	NC	Eugene	25 Jun
53.68	Carmen	Sánchez (20)	ESP	29.2.92	3	NC	Málaga	6 Aug

HEPTATHLON

Score	Name		Nat	Born	Pos	Meet	Venue	Date
6880	Tatyana	Chernova	RUS	29.1.88	1	WCh	Daegu	30 Aug
	13.32/0.9	1.83 14.17 23.50/-1.5			6.61/-0.7	52.95	2:08.04	
6790	Jessica	Ennis	GBR	28.1.86	1		Götzis	29 May
	13.03/0.0	1.91 13.94 23.11/1.8			6.37/0.5	43.83	2:08.46	
6773		Chernova			1		Kladno	16 Jun
	13.32/-0.5	1.83 13.22 23.32w/2.5			6.59/0.6	52.00	2:10.62	
6751		Ennis			2	WCh	Daegu	30 Aug
	12.94/0.4	1.86 14.67 23.27/-1.5			6.51/0.0	39.95	2:07.81	
6679		Chernova			1	Décastar	Talence	18 Sep
	13.37/-0.7	1.82 12.90 23.61/-0.7			6.57/1.8	50.62	2:09.92	
6663	Jennifer	Oeser	GER	29.11.83	1		Ratingen	17 Jul
	13.14/1.2	1.80 13.85 23.95/1.3			6.70w/2.8	47.19	2:12.09	
6572		Oeser			3	WCh	Daegu	30 Aug
	13.33/0.4	1.83 13.70 24.58/-1.5			6.28/0.2	51.30	2:10.39	
6544	Karolina	Tyminska	POL	4.10.84	4	WCh	Daegu	30 Aug
	13.12/0.9	1.74 14.70 23.87/-1.5			6.39/-0.5	41.32	2:05.21	
6539		Chernova			2		Götzis	29 May
	13.79/0.0	1.79 12.67 23.51/1.8			6.82/1.7	47.07	2:13.36	
6539	Nataliya	Dobrynska	UKR	29.5.82	5	WCh	Daegu	30 Aug
	13.43/1.7	1.83 16.14 25.35/-1.1			6.18/-1.0	48.00	2:11.34	
6537		Dobrynska			2	Décastar	Talence	18 Sep
	13.76/-0.5	1.82 16.28 24.81/0.0			6.31/1.8	47.40	2:13.50	
6516		Tyminska			2		Kladno	16 Jun
	13.35/-0.5	1.74 14.41 23.52w/2.5			6.58/1.8	40.17	2:08.33	
6507(w)/6414	Aiga	Grabuste	LAT	24.3.88	2		Ratingen	17 Jul
	13.46/1.2	1.77 14.30 24.35w/2.9			6.62w/3.5	46.40	2:13.60 & LJ 6.33/0.8	
6409	Antoinette	Nana Djimou	FRA	2.8.85	3		Götzis	29 May
	13.48/0.0	1.76 14.44 24.36/1.9			6.29/-0.5	51.11	2:18.99	
6370	Lilli	Schwarzkopf	GER	28.8.83	3		Ratingen	17 Jul
	13.32/1.2	1.74 14.23 24.72/1.3			6.04/-0.3	51.75	2:13.66	
6359		Oeser			4		Götzis	29 May
	13.67/0.0	1.82 13.73 24.57/1.8			6.26/1.1	47.21	2:15.14	
6353	Jessica	Zelinka	CAN	3.9.81	5		Götzis	29 May
	13.21/0.0	1.79 13.03 23.71/1.8			6.09/1.7	41.27	2:08.51	
6338	Austra	Skujyte (10)	LTU	12.8.79	1	ECp-2	Ribeira Brava	3 Jul
	14.43/-2.8	1.87 16.81 25.37/-0.9			6.11/-0.4	47.34	2:19.89	
6332		Dobrynska			6		Götzis	29 May
	14.04/0.3	1.82 15.28 25.20/1.0			6.25/0.6	46.31	2:15.09	
6321		Schwarzkopf			6	WCh	Daegu	30 Aug
	13.65/0.4	1.80 14.89 25.82/-1.1			6.18/-0.5	49.69	2:15.26	
6318	Lyudmyla	Yosypenko	UKR	24.9.84	1	NC	Donetsk	3 Aug
	13.84/-0.1	1.82 12.64 23.98/-0.1			6.12/1.1	47.50	2:12.51	
6309		Nana Djimou Ida			7	WCh	Daegu	30 Aug
	13.48/0.4	1.83 14.07 25.19/-1.2			6.13/0.3	55.79	2:28.74	
6301		Tyminska			3	Décastar	Talence	18 Sep
	13.49/-0.7	1.73 13.92 24.07/-0.7			6.33/0.5	37.85	2:06.51	
6297		Tyminska			1	ECp-1	Bressanone	3 Jul
	13.52/0.4	1.72 14.11 23.79/1.0			6.38/0.5	36.15	2:07.22	
6297		Skujyte			8	WCh	Daegu	30 Aug
	13.96/1.7	1.86 16.71 26.04/-1.3			6.05/-1.6	49.19	2:23.21	
6296		Zelinka			4	Décastar	Talence	18 Sep
	13.07/-0.7	1.70 14.02 23.92/-0.7			6.04/0.5	43.57	2:11.28	

Mark	Name		Nat	Born	Pos	Meet	Venue	Date
6270(w)	Margaret	Simpson	GHA	2.8.82	1		Desenzano del Garda	8 May
	13.60w/3.0	1.78 13.06 25.06/1.6		6.08w/3.3 53.81			2:17.27	
6268		Zelinka			9	WCh	Daegu	30 Aug
	13.01/0.4	1.68 14.91 24.06/-1.5		6.16/0.6 39.59			2:12.62	
6263		Yosypenko			10	WCh	Daegu	30 Aug
	13.49/0.9	1.83 13.16 24.09/-1.5		6.03/-0.7 42.94			2:14.37	
6252		Grabuste			3		Kladno	16 Jun
	13.81/-0.5	1.74 12.73 24.42/0.7		6.65/0.0 43.13			2:13.68	
	(30/12)							
6242	Anna	Bogdanova	RUS	21.10.84	11	WCh	Daegu	30 Aug
	13.44/0.9	1.83 14.52 25.64/-1.3		6.38/0.4 41.38			2:18.34	
6212	Ruky	Abdulai	CAN	8.8.82	13	WCh	Daegu	30 Aug
	13.60/1.6	1.80 11.72 24.50/-1.2		6.30/0.7 46.35			2:15.29	
6198	Remona	Fransen	NED	25.11.85	4		Ratingen	17 Jul
	13.84/1.6	1.86 13.06 24.49w/2.9		6.28/1.0 36.83			2:12.09	
6194	Julia	Mächtig	GER	1.1.86	5		Ratingen	17 Jul
	14.25/1.6	1.74 14.66 25.13w/2.7		6.27/0.0 48.01			2:16.01	
6182	Jessica	Samuelsson	SWE	14.3.85	7	Décastar	Talence	18 Sep
	13.93/-0.4	1.73 13.81 24.03/-0.5		6.11w/2.8 41.26			2:09.62	
6172	Dafne	Schippers	NED-J	15.6.92	8		Götzis	29 May
	13.60/-0.3	1.70 13.89 22.90/1.8		6.13/0.9 38.20			2:15.74	
6166(w)/6150	Louise	Hazel	GBR	6.10.85	7		Ratingen	17 Jul
	13.36/1.2	1.71 11.83 23.90w/2.9		6.41w/2.3 42.87			2:15.36 & LJ 6.36/-0.4	
6151	Olga	Kurban	RUS	16.12.87	1	WUG	Shenzhen	20 Aug
	13.84/-0.3	1.80 13.69 24.19/-1.4		6.02/0.0 41.59			2:15.77	
	(20)							
6134	Grit	Sadeiko	EST	29.7.89	1	EU23	Ostrava	17 Jul
	13.68/0.4	1.78 12.35 24.44/-1.4		6.20w/2.3 47.93			2:21.57	
6133A	Lucimara	da Silva	BRA	10.7.85	1	PAm	Guadalajara, MEX	26 Oct
	13.50/0.5	1.80 12.93 24.76/0.7		6.36/0.2 44.03			2:21.39	
6123	Katerina	Cachová	CZE	26.2.90	2	EU23	Ostrava	17 Jul
	13.87/0.4	1.81 12.90 24.77/0.6		6.21/1.1 41.99			2:15.53	
6108	Sara	Gambetta	GER-J	18.2.93	2	EJ	Tallinn	22 Jul
	14.85/-0.6	1.81 14.74 24.73/-0.4		6.20/-1.9 48.36			2:24.74	
6098	Claudia	Rath	GER	25.4.86	8		Ratingen	17 Jul
	13.98/1.2	1.77 12.72 24.76/1.3		6.28/1.5 40.47			2:11.38	
6094	Yana	Maksimova	BLR	9.1.89	10		Götzis	29 May
	14.19/0.0	1.88 13.50 25.24/1.3		5.87/1.8 42.19			2:13.31	
6068	Györgyi	Farkas	HUN	13.2.85	2	ECp-1	Bressanone	3 Jul
	14.23/0.4	1.78 12.79 25.54/1.0		6.25/1.8 46.36			2:14.41	
6063	Laura	Ikauniece	LAT-J	31.5.92	3	EJ	Tallinn	22 Jul
	13.97/0.3	1.78 12.09 24.93/-1.1		5.90/-1.9 50.70			2:16.31	
6058	Sharon	Day	USA	9.6.85	1	NC	Eugene	26 Jun
	13.85/1.2	1.81 13.51 24.74/1.7		5.92/1.5 41.67			2:16.53	
6052(w)	Bettie	Wade	USA	11.9.86	1	v GER	Chula Vista	14 Aug
	13.77/1.9	1.84 13.74 25.05/1.5		6.18w/3.0 35.51			2:16.85	
	(30)							
6039	Maren	Schwerdtner	GER	3.10.85	11		Götzis	29 May
	13.81/0.0	1.73 13.67 24.44/1.9		6.16/1.6 43.10			2:21.27	
6030	Ryann	Krais	USA	21.3.90	2	NC	Eugene	26 Jun
	13.70/1.6	1.75 12.21 24.69/1.7		5.99/1.9 40.53			2:08.96	
6030	Ida	Marcussen	NOR	1.11.87	9	Décastar	Talence	18 Sep
	14.14/-0.4	1.73 12.96 25.50/0.0		6.09/1.1 48.01			2:13.42	
6017	Gretchen	Quintana	CUB	30.6.84	1		La Habana	6 May
	13.96/1.3	1.70 13.47 24.17/1.9		6.20/0.0 40.09			2:16.34	
6010	Anastasiya	Belyakova	RUS	4.12.90	4	EU23	Ostrava	17 Jul
	14.48/1.3	1.87 12.97 25.32/-0.6		6.01/2.3 43.03			2:16.69	
6008	Alina	Fyodorova	UKR	31.7.89	1	NCp	Yalta	31 May
	14.26/-0.9	1.86 13.91 25.37/0.0		6.20w/2.3 36.75			2:17.81	
6003	Chantae	McMillan	USA	1.5.88	3	NC	Eugene	26 Jun
	13.93/1.2	1.66 14.75 25.25/1.6		6.18/-1.7 47.58			2:22.99	
6000	Tilia	Udelhoven	GER-J	4.9.92	4	EJ	Tallinn	22 Jul
	14.24/0.3	1.75 11.58 24.63/-0.4		6.26/-1.0 46.73			2:17.50	
5995(w)	Marina	Goncharova	RUS	26.4.86	2		Desenzano del Garda	8 May
	14.24w/3.0	1.72 13.65 25.69/1.6		6.03w/2.4 45.68			2:11.68	
5989	Kristina	Savitskaya	RUS	10.6.91	3	NC	Cheboksary	10 Jun
	13.90/-0.9	1.77 14.15 25.07/0.2		6.18/0.5 37.47			2:18.31	
	(40)							
5988(w)	Francesca	Doveri	ITA	21.12.82	3		Desenzano del Garda	8 May
	13.32w/3.0	1.66 12.72 24.40/1.6		6.37w/2.6 33.95			2:11.97	

Mark	Name		Nat	Born	Pos	Meet	Venue	Date
5981	Aleksandra	Butvina	RUS	14.2.86	4	NC	Cheboksary	10 Jun
	14.28/0.3	1.74 13.63 24.61/0.2		6.05/2.0		40.51	2:14.15	
5958	Viktorija	Zemaityte	LTU	11.3.85	2	WUG	Shenzhen	20 Aug
	14.35/1.8	1.86 13.86 25.52/-0.3		6.02/0.9		40.67	2:20.67	
5941	Carolin	Schäfer	GER	5.12.91	5	EU23	Ostrava	17 Jul
	14.13/0.4	1.78 13.11 24.40/0.6		6.03/1.2		44.03	2:25.84	
5932(w)	Nadine	Broersen	NED	29.4.90	4		Desenzano del Garda	8 May
	14.01/3.0	1.84 12.03 26.01/2.0		5.68w/3.7		51.56	2:19.98	
5927w	Chelsea	Carrier	USA	21.8.89	1	TexR	Austin	7 Apr
	13.04w/5.4	1.73 11.75 23.64/4.0		6.22/1.8		31.24	2:18.88	
5927	Abbie	Norton	USA	28.4.85	5	NC	Eugene	26 Jun
	14.25/1.6	1.75 13.82 24.94/1.6		6.09/1.7		40.54	2:18.85	
5905	Inna	Ahkozova	UKR	16.9.84	2	NCp	Yalta	31 May
	14.14/-0.9	1.71 12.44 24.45/0.0		6.38/1.9		35.32	2:14.20	
5877	Yana	Panteleyeva	RUS	16.6.88	6	NC	Cheboksary	10 Jun
	15.74/0.3	1.80 13.55 25.40/0.2		6.08/1.0		45.85	2:15.56	
5870(w)	Blandine	Maisonnier	FRA	3.1.86	1	NC	Albi	29 Jul
	13.92/1.9	1.73 11.66 24.88/1.7		6.36w/4.0		38.14	2:17.51	
	(50)							
5867(w)	Sofía	Ifadídou	GRE	5.1.85	5		Desenzano del Garda	8 May
	13.95w/3.0	1.60 13.33 25.84/2.0		5.77w/3.6		54.04	2:16.82	
5861	Hyleas	Fountain	USA	14.1.81	6	NC	Eugene	26 Jun
	13.17/1.6	1.72 12.97 23.77/1.7		5.96/0.0		37.46	2:29.49	
5857	Liane	Weber	GER	24.2.86	2	NCAA	Des Moines	10 Jun
	13.85/1.4	1.69 13.21 25.55/-1.7		5.83/0.6		45.24	2:16.57	
5856	Helga Margrét	Thorsteinsdóttir	ISL	15.11.91	5		Kladno	16 Jun
	14.95/-0.5	1.77 13.68 26.05/0.8		5.45/0.3		50.84	2:11.76	
5844	Ellen	Sprunger	SUI	5.8.86	14		Götzis	29 May
	13.95/0.3	1.70 12.07 24.07/1.0		5.64/-0.2		42.38	2:13.80	
5813	Anna	Blank	RUS	12.1.90	8	NC	Cheboksary	10 Jun
	14.62/-0.9	1.71 13.45 25.66/0.2		6.10/0.7		41.77	2:15.29	
5812	Yasmiany	Pedroso	CUB	5.8.84	1		La Habana	17 Jun
	14.23/0.2	1.76 13.90 25.89/2.0		5.95/1.1		44.11	2:24.49	
5811(w)	Daphne	Fitzpatrick	USA	6.4.88	2	Big 12	Norman OK	14 May
	14.22w/2.7	1.78 11.94 24.13/0.0		5.82w/3.6		41.16	2:21.70	
5804	Jolanda	Keizer	NED	5.4.85	6		Kladno	16 Jun
	14.38/-0.5	1.71 14.65 25.22/0.7		5.63/1.5		41.79	2:16.80	
5794	Xénia	Krizsán	HUN-J	13.1.93	4	ECp-1	Bressanone	3 Jul
	14.60/1.1	1.78 12.44 25.74/1.0		5.90/0.0		47.54	2:21.41	
	(60)							
5793	Christina	Kiffe	GER-J	2.5.92	5	EJ	Tallinn	22 Jul
	13.88/0.3	1.81 12.62 25.77/-1.1		5.81/-0.8		44.10	2:25.50	
5787	Emily	Pearson	USA	8.8.85	7	NC	Eugene	26 Jun
	13.77/1.6	1.69 11.56 24.46/1.7		5.84w/2.6		44.90	2:21.59	
5787	Katarina	Johnson-Thompson	GBR-J	9.1.93	6	EJ	Tallinn	22 Jul
	14.01/0.3	1.84 10.29 24.25/-0.4		6.05/-0.6		35.11	2:19.03	
5779	Izabela	Mikolajczyk	POL	4.9.90	6	ECp-1	Bressanone	3 Jul
	14.27/1.1	1.81 10.57 24.62/1.0		6.18/0.0		38.33	2:20.43	
5772	Judith	Nagy	ROU	14.9.89	8	EU23	Ostrava	17 Jul
	13.85/0.8	1.66 11.26 25.14/-0.6		6.13/1.9		44.75	2:19.43	
5760 (w)	Annett	Fleming	GER	4.5.84	4	MSR	Azusa	14 Apr
	14.48/1.8	1.76 12.75 26.02w/2.2		5.63w/2.1		46.80	2:16.07	
5759		Mei Yiduo	CHN	27.3.91	1	NC	Hefei	9 Sep
	13.89/0.9	1.78 13.86 26.01/0.8		5.92/0.6		40.75	2:27.53	
5752	Sarah	Cowley	NZL	3.2.84	1	NC	Tauranga	13 Feb
	14.10/1.6	1.75 12.93 25.58/1.2		6.03/0.0		37.15	2:18.58	
5752	Yilían	Durruthy	CUB	30.1.90	2		La Habana	17 Jun
	13.55/0.2	1.76 11.85 24.19/2.0		6.03/0.2		33.52	2:24.36	
5752	Niina	Kelo	FIN	26.3.80	1	NC	Turku	6 Aug
	14.29/1.4	1.62 14.72 26.18/0.7		5.74/1.2		51.84	2:24.38	
	(70)							
5743 (w)	Mari	Klaup	EST	27.2.90	8		Desenzano del Garda	8 May
	14.28/1.8	1.81 11.61 25.87/2.0		5.57w/2.4		47.04	2:18.35	
5733	Barbara	Nwaba	USA	18.1.89	8	NC	Eugene	26 Jun
	14.28/1.2	1.78 12.61 24.69/1.7		5.66/1.8		41.25	2:22.79	
5712	Gabriela	Kouassi	CIV	18.11.79	2	AfG	Maputo	14 Sep
	13.76/1.2	1.62 14.10 26.70/1.0		5.70		49.55	2:22.33	
5710	Wassanee	Winatho	THA	30.6.80	1	AsiC	Kobe	9 Jul
	13.95/-0.4	1.79 11.91 24.97/1.1		6.08/1.8		34.18	2:22.96	
5706	Elisa	Trevisan	ITA	5.3.80	8	ECp-1	Bressanone	3 Jul
	13.78/1.1	1.66 13.22 25.21/1.0		6.04/0.0		42.56	2:29.26	

Mark	Name		Nat	Born	Pos	Meet	Venue	Date
5702	Yekaterina	Netsvetayeva	BLR	26.6.89	1		Brest	15 May
	14.63/0.0 1.65 14.26 25.76/1.4			5.93w/3.8	41.66		2:17.37	
5696	Marisa	De Aniceto	FRA	11.11.86	8	ECp-S	Torun	3 Jul
	14.12/0.2 1.72 11.89 25.90/0.1			5.41/-0.3	50.75		2:18.27	
5685	Jennifer	Cotten	CAN	14.10.87	8	WUG	Shenzhen	20 Aug
	13.97/0.1 1.68 10.98 24.55/-0.2			6.21/0.1	31.62		2:12.57	
5680	Kelsey	Rubeor	USA	1.8.89	1	Big East	Villanova	7 May
	15.15/-3.7 1.70 13.82 25.19w/3.2			5.93/1.0	46.30		2:26.67	
5673	Janet	Lawless	RSA	15.5.85	2		Bambous	17 Apr
	13.84/1.8 1.76 11.49 24.66w/4.2			5.56/-0.8	37.97		2:17.76	
(80)								
5668	Uhunoma	Osazuwa	NGR	23.11.87	1	NC	Calabar	24 Jun
	13.75/-0.2 1.79 11.89 24.74/-1.6			5.89/0.0	33.75		2:24.80	
5663	Jana	Koresová	CZE	8.4.81	1	NC	Praha	29 May
	13.61/-0.7 1.66 10.03 24.86/-0.7			5.93/-0.6	39.25		2:13.69	
5660	Aurélie	Chaboudez	FRA-J	9.5.93	3	NC	Albi	29 Jul
	13.96/1.2 1.70 11.31 24.85/1.7			5.76/1.8	38.27		2:15.01	
5657	Élodie	Jakob	SUI-J	8.10.93	8	EJ	Tallinn	22 Jul
	13.80/0.3 1.66 10.60 25.51/-1.1			5.70/-1.6	46.93		2:16.34	
5651	Léa	Sprunger	SUI	5.3.90	18		Götzis	29 May
	14.31/0.0 1.73 12.30 23.81/1.0			5.91/1.1	38.09		2:30.07	
5646	Makeba	Alcide	LCA	24.2.90	1	SEC	Athens GA	13 May
	14.23/1.5 1.79 12.09 25.08/-0.4			5.65/1.7	35.60		2:17.25	
5644w	Grace	Clements	GBR	2.5.84	9		Desenzano del Garda	8 May
	14.56/1.8 1.69 12.60 25.86/0.6			5.90w/5.3	42.65		2:17.75	
5644A	Francia	Manzanillo	DOM	3.6.80	3	PAm	Guadalajara, MEX	26 Oct
	14.12/0.5 1.59 12.89 24.87/0.7			5.40/-1.6	46.73		2:16.46	
5641	Anastasiya	Sinkevich	RUS	4.3.90	9	NC	Cheboksary	10 Jun
	14.16/-0.9 1.68 12.07 25.06/0.2			5.48/0.0	40.56		2:11.96	
5640	Ellinor	Rosenquist	SWE	14.7.89	2	v2N	Seinäjoki	5 Jun
	15.05w/4.7 1.76 11.78 26.52/-1.5			6.08/-0.1	43.75		2:16.98	
(90)								
5637	Veronica	Torr	NZL	17.5.87	1		Townsville	25 Sep
	13.92/0.3 1.65 13.64 25.05/2.0			5.94/0.6	38.72		2:27.28	
5634	Myrte	Goor	NED	3.4.89	1	NC	Emmeloord	22 May
	14.23/0.5 1.72 13.01 24.56/0.0			5.67w/2.5	32.61		2:16.10	
5632		Wang Qingling	CHN-J	14.1.93	2	NC	Hefei	9 Sep
	13.94/0.9 1.72 11.08 24.46/0.8			6.22/0.1	30.82		2:20.36	
5625	Sushmita	Singha Roy	IND	26.3.84	1	IS	Bangalore	11 Jun
	14.53 1.72 12.09 24.56			5.98	39.74		2:26.20	
5617	Lisandra	Carrión	CUB	18.9.89	2	Barr	La Habana	27 May
	14.87/-1.7 1.73 13.60 25.0/0.1			5.89/-1.6	39.92		2:25.32	
5610w	Lindsay	Lettow	USA	6.6.90	1		San Angelo	25 Mar
	13.98/1.4 1.73 11.18 25.43w/6.5			5.83w/2.7	37.00		2:16.23	
5610	Mariya	Novozhenkova	RUS-J	21.7.92	1	NC-j	Cheboksary	10 Jun
	14.74/0.0 1.79 11.09 25.19/0.0			6.08/0.5	33.28		2:15.57	
5607	Darya	Khramtsova	RUS	7.1.90	10	NC	Cheboksary	10 Jun
	14.77/0.0 1.71 11.35 24.90/0.3			6.19/0.1	36.02		2:17.70	
5594	Yasmina	Omrani	FRA	1.1.88	19		Götzis	29 May
	13.97/-0.3 1.76 12.80 24.35/1.0			5.27/1.2	37.34		2:23.83	
5593	Natasha	Miller	CAN	10.6.89	10	WUG	Shenzhen	20 Aug
	13.64/0.1 1.74 10.18 24.70/-0.2			5.97/0.5	33.12		2:19.70	
(100)								

Mark	Name		Nat	Born	Date		Mark	Name		Nat	Born	Date
5591	Kristina	Poltavets	RUS	6.11.90	10 Jun		5539	Lauren	Foote	AUS	27.4.84	1 Apr
5589	Peaches	Roach	JAM	21.12.84	17 Jul		5538	Jenni	Kivioja	FIN	30.6.87	6 Aug
5588	Selloane	Tsoaeli	LES	10.7.77	14 Sep		5536	Miia	Kurppa	FIN	30.1.88	6 Aug
5585	Estefanía	Fortes	ESP	25.4.87	5 Jun		5534	Salsa	Slack	JAM	10.12.89	28 May
5583	Laura	Ginés	ESP	11.6.86	7 Aug		5523		Wang Yunhan	CHN-J	20.2.93	22 Oct
5572	Sara	Tani	ITA	29.1.83	29 May		5516(w)	Elisa	Bettini	ITA	6.2.82	8 May
5567	Karolina	Kedzia	POL	8.7.90	29 May		5513	Valérie	Reggel	SUI	3.1.87	28 Aug
5566(w)	Dominique	Blaize	GBR	3.10.87	8 May		5507	Kasey	Hill	USA	10.10.85	26 Jun
5564	Lucie	Slanicková	SVK	8.11.88	16 Jun		5500	Yelena	Molodchinina	RUS	16.4.91	10 Jun
5562	Cecilia	Ricali	ITA	20.1.85	3 Jul		5499w	Kaylon	Eppinger	USA	17.9.89	25 Mar
5556w	Louise	Wood	GBR	13.5.83	8 May		5497	Anastasiya	Mokhnyuk	UKR	1.1.91	31 May
5556	Whitney	Carlson	USA	20.10.87	10 Jun		5497	Liz	Roehrig	USA	19.11.85	26 Jun
5554	Dorcas	Akinniyi	USA	23.1.90	10 Jun		5493	Elisabeth	Graf	SUI	9.3.89	22 May
5551	Veera	Baranova	EST	12.2.84	3 Jul		5491	Fumie	Takehara	JPN	14.7.87	9 Jul
5549	Anouk	Vetter	NED-J	4.2.93	22 May		5487w	Aisha	Adams	USA	24.9.87	15 Apr
5546	Meilín	Lanz	CUB-J	14.8.93	19 Mar		5482	Elise-Sophie	Döbel	GER	27.1.90	15 May
5545	Vanessa	Spínola	BRA	5.3.90	5 Aug		5480	Tanja	Mayer	SUI-J	2.7.93	22 Jul
5545A	Tamara	de Souza	BRA-J	8.9.93	25 Sep		5472A	Agustina	Zerboni	ARG	24.8.88	26 Oct
5544	Yusleidys	Mendieta	CUB-Y	17.2.94	19 Mar		5470	Samantha	Henderson	USA	5.4.89	7 May
5540	Bárbara	Hernando	ESP	12.8.88	15 May		5466	Ulyana	Aleksandrova	RUS	1.1.91	18 Sep

Mark	Name		Nat	Born	Pos	Meet	Venue		Date
5463	Chie	Kiriyama	JPN	2.8.91					15 May
5462	Stefanie	Saumweber	GER	5.3.88					14 Aug
5459w	Crystal	Ruiz	MEX	1.1.88					25 Mar
5455	Keia	Pinnick	USA	23.1.91					1 Apr
5455	Ivona	Dadic	AUT-J	29.12.93					22 Jul
5452	Brittany	Harrell	USA	.91					13 May
5447	Lucie	Ondraschková	CZE	12.10.89					14 Apr
5446	Krystyna	Alekseyenko	BLR	2.8.91					8 Jun
5442w	Michelle	Zeltner	SUI	22.12.91					22 May
5440	Jessica	Flax	USA	4.9.90					10 Jun
5438	Lucija	Cvitanovic	CRO	17.9.91					17 Jul
5431	Svetlana	Nedopasova	RUS	31.1.89					10 Jun
5424	Aliona	Rabtsevich	BLR-J	1.3.92					15 Jun
5419	Tatyana	Tarasova	RUS	2.10.90					10 Jun
5408A(w)	Allison	Reaser	USA-J	9.9.92					12 May
5403	Madelaine	Buttinger	CAN	3.11.89					7 May
5403	Emi	Yoshida	JPN	11.5.88					10 Sep

Best without wind assistance

Mark	Name	Pos	Meet	Venue	Date
6183	Simpson	14	WCh	Daegu	30 Aug
	13.43/1.6 1.80 12.48 25.23/-1.1 5.88/-0.9 53.13 2:17.91				
5949	Wade	4	NC	Eugene	26 Jun
	13.68/1.2 1.78 13.56 24.91/1.7 6.16/1.7 34.94 2:18.63				
5947	Goncharova	5	NC	Cheboksary	10 Jun
	14.16/0.3 1.71 14.02 25.55/0.2 6.09/1.0 42.54 2:14.55				
5854	Broersen	2		Woerden	28 Aug
	14.18/0.2 1.82 12.70 25.89/1.1 5.94/1.7 43.68 2:20.62				
5814	Maisonnier	6	ECp-S	Torun	3 Jul
	14.02/0.1 1.75 12.07 24.98/-0.2 6.05/1.3 37.85 2:16.16				
5786	Doveri	23	WCh	Daegu	30 Aug
	13.44/0.9 1.71 11.76 25.45/-1.2 6.09/-0.1 35.09 2:13.14				
5761	Carrier	3	NCAA	Des Moines	10 Jun
	13.31/-2.1 1.69 11.76 23.95/-0.1 5.94/0.5 33.08 2:18.50				
5599	Fitzpatrick	4	NCAA	Des Moines	10 Jun
	14.22/1.3 1.72 11.80 24.89/-0.1 5.56/0.3 40.34 2:19.00				

5547	Lettow	26 Jun	5484 Wood	3 Jul	5479 Eppinger	13 May	5445 Klaup	17 Jul
5541	Ifadídou	3 Jul					5437 Clements	3 Jul

JUNIORS

See main list for top 11 juniors. 11 performances by 7 women to 5780. Additional marks and further juniors:

Schippers	6153	1	EJ	Tallinn			22 Jul
Gambetta	5907	1		Bernhausen			5 Jun
Ikauniece	6879	1		Rakvere			16 Jun
Kifle	5790	2		Bernhausen			5 Jun

Mark	Name		Nat	Born	Pos	Meet	Venue	Date
5549	Anouk	Vetter	NED-J	4.2.93	1	NC-j	Emmeloord	22 May
	14.49/0.1 1.72 12.27 24.76/0.5 5.85w/4.1 41.88 2:32.22							
5546	Meilín	Lanz	CUB-J	14.8.93	3	NC	La Habana	19 Mar
	14.14/-1.0 1.67 13.94 25.01w/2.6 6.05/1.6 38.22 2:38.12							
5545A	Tamara	de Souza	BRA-J	8.9.93	1	SAm-J	Medellín	25 Sep
	14.10/0.4 1.72 13.86 24.44/0.1 5.71/1.5 39.49 2:41.26							
	5477w	best at low altitude			1	PAm-J	Miramar	24 Jul
	14.41/0.1 1.73 13.56 24.39w/4.2 5.94w/2.7 37.08 2:45.30							
5544	Yusleidys	Mendieta	CUB-Y	17.2.94	4	NC	La Habana	19 Mar
	14.69/-1.0 1.76 12.95 24.98w/2.6 5.95/1.6 42.64 2:40.46							
5523	Wang Yunhan		CHN-J	20.2.93	1	City G	Nanchang	22 Oct
	14.26/1.3 1.73 11.29 25.37/1.0 6.06/-0.2 33.58 2:21.01							
5480	Tanja	Mayer	SUI-J	2.7.93	9	EJ	Tallinn	22 Jul
	14.28/-0.7 1.63 12.52 24.36/-0.4 5.57/-1.1 38.28 2:23.70							
5455	Ivona	Dadic	AUT-J	29.12.93	10	EJ	Tallinn	22 Jul
	14.88/-0.6 1.66 10.08 24.20/-0.4 5.71/-3.0 37.22 2:13.22							
5424	Aliona	Rabtsevich	BLR-J	1.3.92	1	NC-j	Brest	15 Jun
	14.29/0.6 1.68 12.41 25.64/2.4 5.80/1.7 32.67 2:20.04							
5408A(w)	Allison	Reaser (20)	USA-J	9.9.92	1	MWC	Fort Collins CO	12 May
	13.87w/2.5 1.56 10.82 24.54w/2.4 6.04w/2.9 37.86 2:27.69							

4 X 100 METRES RELAY

Mark	Nat		Pos	Meet	Venue	Date
41.56	USA	B Knight, Felix, Myers, Jeter	1	WCh	Daegu	4 Sep
41.70	JAM	Fraser, Stewart, Simpson, Campbell-Brown	2	WCh	Daegu	4 Sep
41.94	USA	B Knight, Solomon, Myers, Anderson	1h3	WCh	Daegu	4 Sep
42.23	JAM	Fraser-Pryce, Stewart, Simpson, Levy	1h1	WCh	Daegu	4 Sep
42.28	USA Red	L Williams, Felix, Myers, Jeter	1	PennR	Philadelphia	30 Apr
42.45	USA	Speed Divas	1r2	TexR	Austin	9 Apr
42.45	USA	B Knight, Young, L Williams, Pierre	1		Lignano	19 Jul
42.51	UKR	Povh, Pogrebnyak, Ryemyen, Stuy	3	WCh	Daegu	4 Sep
42.60	FRA	Soumaré, Distel, Jacques-Sébastien, Mang	2h1	WCh	Daegu	4 Sep
42.63	UKR	Povh, Pogrebnyak, Ryemyen, Stuy	1h2	WCh	Daegu	4 Sep
42.64	USA Blue	Asumnu, Miki Barber, B Knight, Anderson	2	PennR	Philadelphia	30 Apr
42.70	FRA	Soumaré, Distel, Jacques-Sébastien, Mang	4	WCh	Daegu	4 Sep
42.74	JAM	Stewart, Simpson, Bailey, Fraser-Pryce	3	PennR	Philadelphia	30 Apr
42.74	NGR	Asumnu, Osayomi, Osazuwa, Okagbare	2h3	WCh	Daegu	4 Sep
42.75	USA Speed Divas	L Williams, Hastings, Knight, Myers	1	FlaR	Gainesville	2 Apr
42.78	RUS	Gushchina, Rusakova, Savlinis, Fedoriva	2h2	WCh	Daegu	4 Sep

Mark	Name	Nat	Born	Pos	Meet	Venue	Date
42.85	UKR Povh, Pogrebnyak, Ryemyen, Stuy			1r2	ET	Stockholm	18 Jun
42.85A	BRA A Silva, Gomes, Krasucki, R Santos			1	PAm	Guadalajara	28 Oct
42.87	USA Texas A&M Univ Collier, Tarmoh, D Duncan, Beard			1r1	TexR	Austin	9 Apr
	(19 performances by teams from 7 nations)						
43.33	GER Kwadwo, Tschirch, Wagner, Gunther			1		Weinheim	28 May
43.39	JPN Kitakaze, Takahashi, Fukushima, Ichikawa			1		Kawasaki	8 May
43.44	NED Vassell, Schippers, Hagen, Samuel			3h3	WCh	Daegu	4 Sep
	(10)						
43.44A	COL Florez, Padilla, Hinestroza, González			3	PAm	Guadalajara	28 Oct
43.47	TRI Howell, Ahyee, Hutchinson, Hackett			1	CAC	Mayagüez	16 Jul
43.50	GBR Kwakye, Onuora, Turner, Oyepitan			4r2	ET	Stockholm	18 Jun
43.62	BAH V Robinson, N Smith, S Ferguson, D Ferguson			2		Freeport	25 Jun
43.67	BLR Nesterenko, Talay, Nevmerzhitskaya, Balykina			1r1	ET	Stockholm	18 Jun
43.69	AUS Pearson, van Veenendaal, Whaler, Breen			2		Kawasaki	8 May
43.77	POL Ptak, Popowicz, Jeschke, Kielbasinska			2r1	ET	Stockholm	18 Jun
43.90	CHN Liang Qiuping, Wei Yongli, Jiang Lan, Tao Yujia			2r1		Wujiang	29 May
43.90	SUI Kambundji, Gasser, Reuse, Sprunger			2	Athl	Lausanne	30 Jun
43.97A	CUB Díaz, Casabona, Guillén, Odelín			4	PAm	Guadalajara	28 Oct
	(20)						
44.00	BEL Borlée, Mariën, Ouédraogo, Vervaet			5	LGP	London (CP)	5 Aug
44.13	THA Seangdee, Jaksuninkorn, Wannakit, Sanrat			5	WUG	Shenzhen	21 Aug
44.28	SWE Berntsson, Klüft, Backman, Hjelmer			3r1	ET	Stockholm	18 Jun
44.33	GHA Amponsah, Owusu-Agyapong, Gyaman, Anim			2	AfG	Maputo	13 Sep
44.33A	CAN Mitchell, Bayley, Brennan, Whyte			5	PAm	Guadalajara	28 Oct
44.40	CZE Mazácová, Humpolíková, Táborská, Cechová			4r1	ET	Stockholm	18 Jun
44.40	SLO Sitar, Veit, Zumer, Ottey			6	LGP	London (CP)	5 Aug
44.41	ITA Balboni, D'Angelo, Amidei, Draisci			4	EU23	Ostrava	17 Jul
44.49	BUL Eftimova, Gachevska, Nikolova, Lalova			1	BalkC	Sliven	2 Jul
44.54	ESP Valencia Terra I Mar Onyia, Murillo, García, Cotán			1	ECCp	VR de St Antônio	28 May
	(30)						

44.67	LTU	18 Jun	44.71	TUR	18 Jun	44.82	GRE	18 Jun	45.00	CMR	13 Sep	45.01	ROU	18 Jun
44.68	DOM	16 Jul	44.72	POR	18 Jun	44.88	SKN	14 Aug	45.00	INA	15 Nov	45.12	VIE	15 Nov
												45.14	CRO	18 Jun

Best at low altitude

42.92	BRA A Silva, Gomes, Krasucki, R Santos			3h1	WCh	Daegu	4 Sep
43.53	COL Hinestroza, Idrobo, Obregón, González			4h1	WCh	Daegu	4 Sep

Mixed nationality teams

42.64	Univ. of Louisiana Wilson, Hackett TRI, Alexander , K Duncan			1	NCAA	Des Moines	11 Jun
42.72	Pure Athletics ?, Solomon USA, Bailey JAM, Ferguson-M BAH			1		Coaral Gables	16 Apr

Drugs disqualification

42.50	TRI Selvon, Baptiste, Hackett #, Ahyee			(1h2)	WCh	Daegu	4 Sep
42.58	TRI Selvon, Baptiste, Hackett , Ahyee			(4)	WCh	Daegu	4 Sep

JUNIORS

43.42	GER Burghardt, Grompe, Pinto, Frese			1	EJ	Tallinn	24 Jul
44.08	JAM Williams, Whitehorne, Walters, Jackson			1	Carifta	Montego Bay	24 Apr
44.52	ITA De Fazio, Siragusa, Bongiorni, Hooper			2	EJ	Tallinn	24 Jul
44.64A	BRA de Moraes, dos Reis, Fidelis, de Liz			1	SAm-J	Medellín	25 Sep
44.79A	USA Valentine, Chaney, Johnson, Ewing			1		Albuquerque	4 Jun
44.97	POL Kisiel, Sokólska, Stepie⊠, Kalinowska			2h2		Tallinn	24 Jul
45.00	GBR Nwawulor, B. Williams, Batten, J. Williams			3	EJ	Tallinn	24 Jul
45.04	BAH Charlton, Cox, Robinson, Strachan			1	PAm-J	Miramar	24 Jul
45.11	SUI Kambundji, Miani, Mayer, Dupasquier			5		La Chaux-de-Fonds	3 Jul
45.15	BEL Bolingo Mbongo, Laus, De Maitre, Rutjens			5	EJ	Tallinn	24 Jul
45.24	HUN Munkácsy, Schmelcz, Kerekes, Nguyen			6	EJ	Tallinn	24 Jul
45.73	CZE Seidlová, Kr⊠oulová, Domská, ⊠ernochová			2	GS	Ostrava	31 May

4 X 200 METRES RELAY

1:29.96	Texas A & M (USA) L Stewart, Collier, Beard, D Duncan)			1	PennR	Philadelphia	30 Apr
1:31.02	Speed Divas (USA)			1	FlaR	Gainseville	2 Apr

Mixed nation team

1:30.88	Louisiana State University USA Alexander, Hackett TRI, Tate, K Duncan			1	TexR	Austin	9 Apr

4 X 400 METRES RELAY

3:18.09	USA Richards-Ross 49.3, Felix 49.4, Beard 49.84, McCorory 49.52			1	WCh	Daegu	3 Sep
3:18.71	JAM Whyte 50.0, Prendergast 49.6, Williams-Mills 49.84, Williams 49.22			2	WCh	Daegu	3 Sep
3:19.36	RUS Krivoshapka 50.3, Antyukh 50.0, Litvinova 49.96, Kapachinskaya 49.22			3	WCh	Daegu	3 Sep
3:20.94	RUS Vdovina 51.4, Zadorina 49.8, Litvinova 49.55, Krivoshapka 50.28			1h2	WCh	Daegu	2 Sep
3:22.01	JAM Whyte 51.4e, Lloyd 49.9e, Hall 50.98, Prendergast 49.75			1h3	WCh	Daegu	2 Sep
3:22.92	USA Red Dunn 51.1, Felix 50.3, Hastings 50.30, Richards-Ross 51.18			1	PennR	Philadelphia	30 Apr
3:23.05	GBR Ohuruogu 51.78, Sanders 51.31, McConnell 50.06, S-Drayton 49.90			2h3	WCh	Daegu	2 Sep
3:23.17	USA Blue Trotter 51.5, McCorory 49.8, Baker 50.51, Hargrove 51.39			2	PennR	Philadelphia	30 Apr

Mark	Name	Nat	Born	Pos	Meet	Venue	Date
3:23.57	USA Hastings 50.8, Beard 49.9, McCorory 51.18, Baker 51.65			1h1	WCh	Daegu	2 Sep
3:23.63	GBR Sh-Drayton 50.5, Sanders 50.7, Ohuruogu 51.98, McConnell 50.43			4	WCh	Daegu	3 Sep
3:23.82	JAM Sher. Williams 51.5, N Williams-Mills 50.4, Day 51.33, Spencer 50.59			3	PennR	Philadelphia	30 Apr
3:23.86	UKR Pygyda 50.8, Rabchenyuk 50.5, Yaroshchuk 52.00, Yefremova 50.50			5	WCh	Daegu	3 Sep
3:24.13	UKR Pygyda 51.1e, Zavgoodnya 51.3e, Yaroshchuk 51.54, Yefremova 50.18			2h1	WCh	Daegu	2 Sep
3:24.28	BLR Tashpulatova 51.8e, Yushchenko 50.6e, I Usovich51.64, S Usovich 50.22			3h1	WCh	Daegu	2 Sep
3:25.59	NGR Omotosho 51.6e, Odumosu 51.2e, Etim 51.36, Abogunloko 51.44			2h2	WCh	Daegu	2 Sep
3:25.64	BLR Tashpulatova 51.68, Yushchenko 51.27, I Usovich 52.56, S Usovich 50.13			6	WCh	Daegu	3 Sep
3:26.01	CZE Rosolová 52.2e, Bergrová 51.1e, Bartoníčková 52.14, Hejnová 50.59			3h2	WCh	Daegu	2 Sep
3:26.48	ITA Bazzoni 52.9e, Spacca 51.3e, Grenot 51.01, Milani 51.28			3h3	WCh	Daegu	2 Sep
3:26.57	CZE Rosolová 52.3, Bergrová 51.5, Bartoníčková 52.16, Hejnová 50.67			7	WCh	Daegu	3 Sep
3:26.68	BRA (BM&F Bovespa) Coutinho, de Oliveira, Souza, de Lima			1	NC	São Paulo	7 Aug
	(20 performances by teams from 10 nations)						
3:26.74	CUB A Martínez 52.88, Peña 50.86, Clement 51.95, Bonne 51.05			4h2	WCh	Daegu	2 Sep
3:27.31	GER Lindenberg 52.7e, Cremer 50.9e, Schmidt 52.66, Hoffmann 51.07			4h1	WCh	Daegu	2 Sep
3:27.48	IRL Andrews 53.4, Cuddihy 49.9, Bergin 52.60, Carey 51.54			4h3	WCh	Daegu	2 Sep
3:27.92	CAN Power 51.9e, Akinsulie 51.6e, Martin 51.35, Ogbasilassie 53.03			5h2	WCh	Daegu	2 Sep
3:28.02	FRA Anacharsis 52.74, Hurtis 50.81, Gayot 52.10, Guéi 52.37			5h1	WCh	Daegu	2 Sep
3:29.40	TUR Engin, Aydin, Redif, Saka			1r2	ET-1	Izmir	19 Jun
3:29.94A	COL Oliveros 54.0, González 51.3, Aguilar 52.8, Padilla 51.9			3	PAm	Guadalajara	28 Oct
3:31.24	CHN Guangdong Chen Yi, Li Xueji, Zhou Yanling, Chen Yanmei			1		Hefei	11 Sep
3:31.49	BEL Den Haeze, Ouédraogo, Borlée, Dauwens			2		Gent	30 Jul
3:32.21	SEN Fatou Faye, Sylla, Soumah, Thiam			2	AfG	Maputo	15 Sep
	(20)						
3:32.27	AUS Sargent 54.1e, Pincott 51.8e, Boden 52.74, Rubie 53.60			6h1	WCh	Daegu	2 Sep
3:33.96	ROU Pastor, Nunu, Blegyan, Razor			2r2	ET-1	Izmir	19 Jun
3:34.59	RSA Theron, van Wyk, van der Merwe, Ramonnye			5	WUG	Shenzhen	21 Aug
3:34.73	DOM R Sánchez, D Taylor, Fabian, Osana			2	CAC	Mayagüez	17 Jul
3:34.84	TRI Brooks, Howell, Lucas, Walker			3	CAC	Mayagüez	17 Jul
3:35.00	JPN Aoki, Tanaka, Kubokura, Shingu			1	AsiC	Kobe	10 Jul
3:35.12	MEX Rodríguez, Dueñas, Vela, Medina			4	CAC	Mayagüez	17 Jul
3:35.35	POL Wyciszkiewicz, Holub, Swiety, Gorzkowska			2	EJ	Tallinn	24 Jul
3:35.44A	KEN Police Nyakawa, Shikanda, Kemunto, Zakari			1	NC	Nairobi	16 Jul
3:36.03	GRN Bernard-Thomas, Bartholomew, Beckles, Redhead			6	PennR	Philadelphia	30 Apr
	(30)						

3:36.25 NOR	19 Jun	3:37.10 BUL	19 Jun	3:37.66 ESP	19 Jun	3:38.54 BOT	15 Sep	3:39.37 PUR	17 Jul
3:36.47 SWE	19 Jun	3:37.28 POR	17 Jul	3:37.82 SUI	21 Aug	3:38.64 MAR	20 Dec	3:39.80 BAH	14 May
3:36.85 ETH	25 Jun	3:37.44 NED	24 Jul	3:37.98 GRE	19 Jun	3:38.92 HUN	19 Jun	3:39.88 TRI	25 Apr
3:37.03 CRO	19 Jun	3:37.47 KAZ	30 Jul	3:38.13 FIN	19 Jun	3:39.14 IND	21 Feb	**Drugs dq**	
								3:36.61 KAZ	10 Jul

Best at low altitude

3:32.84	COL Padilla, González, Olivero, Aguilar			2		São Paulo	22 May

Mixed nationality teams

3:26.31	Texas A&M Univ. Tarmoh, Mayungbe NGR, Sutherland JAM, Beard			1	NCAA	Des Moines	11 Jun
3:26.46	Auburn Univ. C Williams JAM, Atkins, Armbrister, Selvon TRI			2	NCAA	Des Moines	11 Jun

JUNIORS

3:31.47	JAM	James, Russell, Campbell, Gordon			1	Carifta	Montego Bay	25 Apr
3.34.71	USA	Eutsey, Francis, Nelson, Dixon			1	PAm-J	Miramar	24 Jul
3:35.29	GBR	Kirk, James, Clifford, McAslan			1	EJ	Tallinn	24 Jul
3:35.35	POL	Wyciskiewicz, Holub, Swiety, Gorzkowska			2	EJ	Tallinn	24 Jul
3:36.26	GER	Häfele, S. Schmidt, K.C. Schmidt, Zwirner			3	EJ	Tallinn	24 Jul
3:36.74A	COL	Escobar, Aguilar, Largacha, Torres			1	SAm-J	Medellín	25 Sep
3:37.44	NED	De Witte, Wever, Voskamp, Ghafoor			4	EJ	Tallinn	24 Jul
3:37.57	FRA	Raharolahy, Bertheau, Contion, Chaboudez			5	EJ	Tallinn	24 Jul
3:38.11	RUS	(Moskva)			1	NC-j	Cheboksary	3 Jul
3:38.15	BLR	Klimovich, Amialiashchyk, Andrykevich, Yurenya			6	EJ	Tallinn	24 Jul
3:38.16A	RSA	Steyn, vd Merwe, Senekal, Palframan			1	Af-J	Gaborone	15 May
3:38.97A	NGR	Etim, Nwankwe, Adegoke, Isoken			2	Af-J	Gaborone	15 May
3:38.99	CAN	Balkwill, Leblanc, Reid, Francois			2	PAm-J	Miramar	24 Jul
3:39.88	TRI	Spann, Campbell, Gale, Williams			2	Carifta	Montego Bay	25 Apr

4 X 800 METRES RELAY

8:06.24i	Moscow Bulanova 2:01.8, Martynova 2:03.1, Kofanova 2:00.4, Balakshina 2:00.6			1	NC	Moskva	18 Feb

4 X 120 YARDS HURDLES

53.41	Texas A&M Un. USA Mayo, Flemings, Fitzpatrick, Ruddock			1	PennR	Philadelphia	29 Apr
53.83	Central Florida Un. USA Farley, Coward, Wimberly, Bolling			2	PennR	Philadelphia	29 Apr
53.95	Star Athletics			1	FlaR	Gainesville	2 Apr
53.98	Clemson Un. Owens, Golladay, Edgerson, Jackson			3	PennR	Philadelphia	29 Apr

+ intermediate time in longer race, A made at an altitude of 1000m or higher, D made in a decathlon, h made in a heat, qf quarter-final, sf semi-final, i indoors, Q qualifying round, r race number, -J juniors, =Y youths (b. 1994 or later)

Mark		Name	Nat	Born	Pos	Meet	Venue			Date

3000 METRES WALK

Mark		Name	Nat	Born	Pos	Meet	Venue			Date
12:18.86	Kate	Veale	IRL-Y	5.1.94	1		Tullamore			23 Jul
12:36.6+mx	Elisa	Rigaudo	ITA	17.6.80	1	in 10k	Mondovì			12 Jun

Indoors

12:18.12	Sabine	Krantz	GER	6.2.81	1	NC	Leipzig			26 Feb
12:28.70	Ines	Henriques	POR	1.5.80	1	NC	Pombal			26 Feb
12:31.43	Melanie	Seeger	GER	8.1.77	2	NC	Leipzig			26 Feb
12:37.98	Vera	Santos	POR	3.12.81	2	NC	Pombal			29 Jan
12:42.61	Sibilla	Di Vincenzo	ITA	22.1.83	19 Feb	12:43.16 Agnes	Pastare	LAT	27.10.88	29 Jan

5000 METRES WALK

20:56.1+mx	Elisa	Rigaudo	ITA	17.6.80	1	in 10k	Mondovì			12 Jun
20:56.75	Sabine	Krantz	GER	6.2.81	1	NC	Kassel			24 Jul
21:03.8	Beatriz	Pascual	ESP	9.5.82	1		Pamplona			30 Jul
21:11.24	Melanie	Seeger	GER	8.1.77	2	NC	Kassel			24 Jul
21:12.73		Rigaudo			1		Firenze			4 Jun
21:19.6	Julia	Takács	ESP	29.6.89	2		Pamplona			30 Jul
21:21.29	Sibilla	Di Vincenzo	ITA	22.1.83	1		Sulmona			24 Sep
21:22.49	Kumi	Otoshi	JPN	29.7.85	1		Kitami			19 Jun
21:22.80		Otoshi			1		Kumagaya			21 May
21:30.18	Kate	Veale	IRL-Y	5.1.94	1	NC	Dublin (S)			6 Aug
21:33.53	Masumi	Fuchise	JPN	2.9.86	1		Naruto			15 May
21:42.32	Johanna	Jackson	GBR	17.1.85	31 Jul	21:52.12 Lucie	Pelantová	CZE	7.5.86	23 Jul
21:43.97	Agnieszka	Dygacz	POL	18.7.85	10 Sep	21:53.8A Yuli	Magali Capcha	PER-Y	10.8.94	14 May
21:46.34	Ana	Cabecinha	POR	29.4.84	15 Jan	21:54.86 Paulina	Buziak	POL	16.12.86	10 Sep
21:48.36	Agnese	Pastare	LAT	27.10.88	12 Jun	21:55.22 Agnieszka	Szwarnóg	POL	28.12.86	27 May
21:49.11	Mayumi	Kawasaki	JPN	10.5.80	19 Jun	**Indoors**				
21:50.05	Chiaki	Asada	JPN	21.1.91	19 Jun	21:41.3 Natalya	Makarova	RUS	17.4.87	6 Jan
21:50.90	Maria	Vasco	ESP	26.12.75	5 Jun	21:51.51 Olena	Shumkina	UKR	24.1.88	15 Feb

JUNIORS

Veale	21:45.49		1	WY		Villeneuve d'Ascq	8 Jul		
21:53.8A	Yuli	Magali Capcha	PER-Y	10.8.94	1		Lima			14 May
22:00.15		Mao Yanxue	CHN-Y	15.2.94	2	WY	Villeneuve d'Ascq			8 Jul
22:00.84	Nadezhda	Leontyeva	RUS-Y	6.11.94	3	WY	Villeneuve d'Ascq			8 Jul
22:12.47	Alina	Halchenko	UKR-Y	18.9.94	4	WY	Villeneuve d'Ascq			8 Jul
22:17.85	Alejandra	Ortega	MEX-Y	8.7.94	5	WY	Villeneuve d'Ascq			8 Jul
22:20.8 i	Lyudmila	Olyanovska	UKR	20.2.93	1		Sumy			24 Dec

10 KILOMETRES WALK

See also 20km lists for intermediate times at 10km

42:04+	Tatyana	Shemyakina	RUS	3.9.87	1=	in 20k	Sochi	26 Feb
42:16+	Tatyana	Sibileva	RUS	17.5.80	4	in 20k	Sochi	26 Feb
42:39	Olga	Kaniskina	RUS	19.1.85	1	RWC-F	La Coruña	17 Sep
42:43.0 t	Svetlana	Vasilyeva	RUS-J	24.7.92	1	NC-wj	Sochi	27 Feb
42:57		Liu Hong	CHN	12.5.87	2	RWC-F	La Coruña	17 Sep
42:59.48 t	Yelena	Lashmanova	RUS-J	12.11.92	1	EJ	Tallinn	21 Jul
43:09	Melanie	Seeger	GER	8.1.77	3	RWC-F	La Coruña	17 Sep
43:10		Lashmanova			1J	ECp	Olhão	21 May
43:15	Ana	Cabecinha (10)	POR	29.4.84	4	RWC-F	La Coruña	17 Sep
43:15.43 t	Kumi	Otoshi	JPN	29.7.85	1		Naruto	24 Sep
43:24.00 t	Masumi	Fuchise	JPN	2.9.86	2		Naruto	24 Sep
43:30.15 t		Liu Hong			1		Mondovì	12 Jun
(16/14)								
43:32.21 t	Elisa	Rigaudo	ITA	17.6.80	2		Mondovì	12 Jun
43:40	Susana	Feitor	POR	28.1.75	5	RWC-F	La Coruña	17 Sep
43:47	Nadiya	Borovska	UKR	25.2.81	1		Lutsk	26 Jun
43:49	Beatriz	Pascual	ESP	9.5.82	6	RWC-F	La Coruña	17 Sep
43:59+	Yelena	Kruchinkina	RUS	26.10.88	6	in 20k	Sochi	26 Feb
43:59.08 t	Inês	Henriques	POR	1.5.80	1	NC	Lisboa (U)	30 Jul
(20)								
44:00+	Lyudmila	Arkhipova	RUS	25.11.78	7	in 20k	Sochi	26 Feb
44:04.51 t	Julia	Takács	ESP	29.6.89	1	NC	Málaga	6 Aug
44:07	Anastasiya	Yatsevich	BLR	18.1.85	1		Grodno	1 Oct
44:15	María José	Poves	ESP	16.3.78	7	RWC-F	La Coruña	17 Sep
44:17+		Lu Xiuzhi	CHN-J	26.10.93	3	in 20k	Taicang	22 Apr
44:25	Olga	Yakovenko	UKR	1.6.87	2		Lutsk	26 Jun
44:30	Olive	Loughnane	IRL	14.1.76	10	RWC-F	La Coruña	17 Sep
44:33	Brigita	Virbalyte	LTU	1.2.85	11	RWC-F	La Coruña	17 Sep
44:33.98 t	Kristina	Saltanovic	LTU	20.2.75	1		Luso	16 Jul
44:42+	Irina	Yumanova	RUS	6.11.90	3	in 20k	Saransk	12 Jun
44:45.18 t	María	Vasco	ESP	26.12.75	2	NC	Málaga	6 Aug

Mark	Name		Nat	Born	Pos	Meet	Venue	Date
44:53	Elmira	Alembekova	RUS	30.6.90	1		Yerino	9 May
44:55	Agnieszka	Dygacz	POL	18.7.85	1		Bacúch	24 Sep
44:59	Johanna	Jackson	GBR	17.1.85	1		London (VP)	11 Sep
45:25.45	Rei	Inoue	JPN	23.7.91	3		Naruto	24 Sep
45:31.0 t	Agnese	Pastare	LAT	27.10.88	1	NC	Murjani	16 Apr
45:38.02 t	Sibilla	Di Vincenzo	ITA	22.1.83	1		Pordenone	27 Mar
45:40	Olena	Shevchuk	UKR	23.3.86	3	NCp	Mukachevo	29 Oct
45:45.14 t	Eleonora	Giorgi	ITA	14.9.89	1	U23	Pordenone	27 Mar
45:49.26 t	Serena	Pruner	ITA	21.5.86	2		Pordenone	27 Mar
45:51	Rossella	Giordano	ITA	1.12.72	1		Roma	15 Oct
45:53	Claudia	Stef	ROU	25.2.78	12	RWC-F	La Coruña	17 Sep
45:58	Vera	Santos	POR	3.12.81	13	RWC-F	La Coruña	17 Sep
45:59.86 t	Fumika	Kiryu	JPN	12.7.87	2		Abashiri	22 Jun

Mark		Name	Nat	Born	Date
46:01+	Olena	Shumkina	UKR	24.1.88	21 May
46:01.15t	Federica	Ferraro	ITA	18.8.88	27 Mar
46:03+	Claire	Tallent	AUS	7.6.81	19 Feb
46:03		Li Leilei	CHN	18.8.89	29 Apr
46:08+	Lina	Bikulova	RUS	1.10.88	12 Jun
46:11.64t	Yelena	Fatakhetdinova	RUS	.89	28 May
46:14.0 t	Anita	Kazemaka	LAT	30.5.90	16 Apr
46:15A+	Mirna	Flores	GUA	28.2.87	23 Oct
46:18+	Paulina	Buziak	POL	16.12.86	17 Sep
46:19	Cheryl	Webb	AUS	3.10.76	22 May
46:20		Duan Dandan	CHN-Y	23.5.95	23 Apr
46:21.67t	Sylwia	Korzeniowska	POL	25.4.80	28 Jul
46:26.42t	Antonella	Palmisano	ITA	6.8.91	27 Mar
46:27.2 t	Galina	Kireyeva	RUS	11.11.91	1 Jun
46:29	Neringa	Aidietyte	LTU	5.6.83	11 Sep
46:29+	Ingrid	Hernández	COL	29.11.88	23 Oct
46:32	Kate	Veale	IRL-Y	5.1.94	21 May
46:33+	Larisa	Yemelyanova	RUS	6.1.80	1 May
46:34.62t	Kumiko	Okada	JPN	17.10.91	10 Oct
46:35+	Chiaki	Asada	JPN	21.1.91	13 Mar
46:35+	Ana Maria	Groza	ROU	1.6.76	1 May
46:37	Hiroi	Maeda	JPN	1.6.91	16 Apr
46:37+	Érica	de Sena	BRA	3.5.85	23 Oct
46:43+	Guadalupe	Sánchez	MEX	14.2.74	9 Apr
46:44.19t	Ai	Michiguchi	JPN	3.6.88	30 Apr

Other best track times

44:13.33	Feitor	2 NC	Lisboa (U)		30 Jul
46:25.68	Poves				6 Aug
45:42.0	Yatsevich	1	Minsk		3 Jun
45:55.90	Cabecinha	3 NC	Lisboa (U)		30 Jul
46:39.73	Santos				6 Aug
46:43.59	Maeda				10 Oct

Indoors: 45:42.85 Anastasiya Pavlenko RUS 28.9.89 1 Sankt Peterburg 23 Jan
Short course: 45:24 Yaneli Caballero MEX-J 29.5.93 1 Alytus 17 Jun

JUNIORS

See main list for top 3 juniors. 12 performances by 10 women to 45:30. Additional marks and further juniors:

Mark		Name	Nat	Born	Pos	Meet	Venue	Date
Vasilyeva		44:02			2		Olhão	21 May
Lashmanova		43:41.0t			2	NC-wj	Sochi	27 Feb
46:20		Duan Dandan	CHN-Y	23.5.95	1J	NGP	Taicang	23 Apr
46:32	Kate	Veale	IRL-Y	5.1.94	3	ECp-J	Olhão	21 May
46:46	Anezka	Drahotová	CZE-Y	22.7.95	1		Villa Di Serio	23 Oct
46:49.00t	Anna	Yermina	RUS	24.6.93	3	EJ	Tallinn	21 Jul
47:06.20t	Charlyne	Czychy	GER	14.3.92	1		Halle	1 Jun
47:09	Anna	Clemente	ITA-Y	6.1.94	5		Roma	15 Oct

20 KILOMETRES WALK

Mark	at 10k	Name		Nat	Born	Pos	Meet	Venue	Date
1:25:08	42:04	Vera	Sokolova	RUS	8.6.87	1	NC-w	Sochi	26 Feb
1:25:09	42:04	Anisya	Kirdyapkina	RUS	23.10.89	2	NC-w	Sochi	26 Feb
1:27:17	44:16		Liu Hong	CHN	12.5.87	1		Taicang	22 Apr
1:27:35		Elmira	Alembekova	RUS	30.6.90	1	NCp	Voronovo	17 Sep
1:27:49	43:27	Anna	Lukyanova	RUS	23.4.91	3	NC-w	Sochi	26 Feb
1:28:04	44:16		Qieyang Shenjie	CHN	11.11.90	2		Taicang	22 Apr
1:28:09	44:17	Tatyana	Mineyeva	RUS	10.8.90	1	NC	Saransk	12 Jun
1:28:35	43:54	Olga	Kaniskina	RUS	19.1.85	1		Rio Maior	9 Apr
1:28:38	43:27	Tatyana	Korotkova	RUS	24.4.80	4	NC-w	Sochi	26 Feb
1:28:41	44:17	Nina	Ochotnikova (10)	RUS	11.3.91	2	NC	Saransk	12 Jun
1:28:43	44:16		Li Yanfei	CHN	12.1.90	3		Taicang	22 Apr
1:28:51	44:13	Beatriz	Pascual	ESP	9.5.82	2		Rio Maior	9 Apr
1:28:55	44:17	Tatyana	Shemyakina	RUS	3.9.87	3	NC	Saransk	12 Jun
1:29:11		Kumi	Otoshi	JPN	29.7.85	1	NC	Kobe	20 Feb
1:29:12			Korotkova			2	NCp	Voronovo	17 Sep
1:29:19	44:17	Lyudmila	Arkhipova	RUS	25.11.78	4	NC	Saransk	12 Jun
1:29:20		Melanie	Seeger	GER	8.1.77	1	NC	Naumburg	24 Sep
1:29:26		Irina	Yumanova	RUS	6.11.90	5	NC-w	Sochi	26 Feb
1:29:29			Liu Hong			1		Lugano	20 Mar
1:29:30		Anastasiya	Yatsevich	BLR	18.1.85	1	NC	Grodno	7 Jul
1:29:32			Kaniskina			1		Sesto San Giovanni	1 May
1:29:35			Arkhipova			3	NCp	Voronovo	17 Sep
1:29:38	44:16		Gao Ni	CHN	14.9.91	4		Taicang	22 Apr
1:29:42			Kaniskina			1	WCh	Daegu	31 Aug
1:29:44			Liu Hong			1		Dublin	26 Jun

Mark		Name		Nat	Born	Pos	Meet	Venue	Date
1:29:46			Sun Huanhuan (20)	CHN	15.3.90	1	NGP	Taicang	22 Apr
1:29:48		Yelena	Kruchinkina	RUS	26.10.88	4	NCp	Voronovo	17 Sep
1:29:50			Lu Xiuzhi	CHN-J	26.10.93	1	NC-j	Baoji	17 Sep
1:29:55	44:37	Vera	Santos	POR	3.12.81	3		Rio Maior	9 Apr
1:30:00			Liu Hong			2	WCh	Daegu	31 Aug
		(30/23)							
1:30:01			Wang Shanshan	CHN	16.6.87	1	NC	Baoji	17 Sep
1:30:13			He Qin	CHN-J	23.3.92	1J	NGP	Taicang	22 Apr
1:30:25	44:22	Mayumi	Kawasaki	JPN	10.5.80	2	NC	Kobe	20 Feb
1:30:27	44:50	Natalya	Makarova	RUS	17.4.87	7	NC-w	Sochi	26 Feb
1:30:29		Inês	Henriques	POR	1.5.80	3		Sesto San Giovanni	1 May
1:30:37		Tatyana	Sibileva	RUS	17.5.80	2		Lugano	20 Mar
1:30:44	45:14	Susana	Feitor	POR	28.1.75	4		Rio Maior	9 Apr
		(30)							
1:30:44		Elisa	Rigaudo	ITA	17.6.80	4	WCh	Daegu	31 Aug
1:30:56		Agnieszka	Dygacz	POL	18.7.85	1	NC	Warszawa	17 Sep
1:31:00			Yang Mingxia	CHN	13.1.90	2	NC	Baoji	17 Sep
1:31:00			Nie Jingjing	CHN	1.3.88	3	NC	Baoji	17 Sep
1:31:03			Mao Yanxue	CHN-Y	15.2.94	2	NC-j	Baoji	17 Sep
1:31:08		Ana	Cabecinha	POR	29.4.84	4		Lugano	20 Mar
1:31:08		Sabine	Krantz	GER	6.2.81	1	NC	Erfurt	11 Jun
1:31:23			Ding Huiqin	CHN	5.2.90	4	NGP	Taicang	22 Apr
1:31:32		Julia	Takács	ESP	29.6.89	2	NC	Benicàssim	6 Mar
1:31:33			He Dan	CHN	22.7.84	5	NGP	Taicang	22 Apr
		(40)							
1:31:39	45:42	Regan	Lamble	AUS	14.10.91	7		Taicang	22 Apr
1:31:40		Kristina	Saltanovic	LTU	20.2.75	8	WCh	Daegu	31 Aug
1:31:41		María	Vasco	ESP	26.12.75	4	ECp	Olhão	21 May
1:31:50		Johanna	Jackson	GBR	17.1.85	1		London	30 May
1:31:52		Masumi	Fuchise	JPN	2.9.86	2	AsiC	Nomi	13 Mar
1:31:53			Shi Tianshu	CHN	7.6.88	6	NGP	Taicang	22 Apr
1:31:55		Svetlana	Solovyova	RUS	6.11.86	11	NC-w	Sochi	26 Feb
1:31:55		Olive	Loughnane	IRL	14.1.76	2	1 NC	Dublin	26 Jun
1:31:56			Ni Yuanyuan	CHN-Y	6.4.95	3	NC-j	Baoji	17 Sep
1:32:03			Luo Xingcai	CHN-Y	18.7.94	4	NC-j	Baoji	17 Sep
		(50)							
1:32:08		Olga	Yakovenko	UKR	1.6.87	5	ECp	Olhão	21 May
1:32:09.4	45:29.7t	Ingrid	Hernández	COL	29.11.88	1	SACh	Buenos Aires	5 Jun
1:32:10	45:55	Zuzana	Schindlerová	CZE	25.4.87	5		Lugano	20 Mar
1:32:15		Sylwia	Korzeniowska	FRA	25.4.80	1	NC	Saint-Renan	17 Apr
1:32:17		Olena	Shumkina	UKR	24.1.88	12	WCh	Daegu	31 Aug
1:32:17.6	45:29.6t	Milánggela	Rosales	VEN	21.2.87	2	SACh	Buenos Aires	5 Jun
1:32:18	45:01		Yang Yawei	CHN	16.10.83	8		Taicang	22 Apr
1:32:21		María José	Poves	ESP	16.3.78	4	NC	Benicàssim	6 Mar
1:32:30		Nadiya	Borovska	UKR	25.2.81	7	ECp	Olhão	21 May
1:32:30		Mirna	Flores	GUA	28.2.87	2	NC	Warszawa	17 Sep
		(60)							
1:32:38A	46:12	Jamy	Franco	GUA	1.7.91	1	PAm	Guadalajara, MEX	23 Oct
1:32:39	46:03	Claire	Tallent	AUS	7.6.81	9		Taicang	22 Apr
1:32:45			Zhao Jing	CHN-J	18.2.92	3J	NGP	Xintai	12 Mar
1:32:45		Lina	Bikulova	RUS	1.10.88	6	NCp	Voronovo	17 Sep
1:32:47		Déspina	Zapounídou	GRE	5.10.85	1		Villa di Serri	23 Oct
1:32:48.7	45:29.9t	Arabelly	Orjuela	COL	24.7.88	3	SACh	Buenos Aires	5 Jun
1:32:49		Sibilla	Di Vincenzo	ITA	22.1.83	1		Chiasso	2 Oct
1:33:00		Marina	Pandakova	RUS	1.3.89	7	NCp	Voronovo	17 Sep
1:33:03			Song Xiaoling	CHN	21.12.87	2	NGP	Xintai	12 Mar
1:33:07		Claudia	Stef	ROU	25.2.78	5		Sesto San Giovanni	1 May
		(70)							
1:33:09		Beki	Lee	AUS	25.11.86	2		Melbourne	11 Dec
1:33:14	46:26		Tong Lingling	CHN-J	25.1.92	8		Lugano	20 Mar
1:33:18.0 t		Yadira	Guamán	ECU	8.6.86	4	SACh	Buenos Aires	5 Jun
1:33:20			Li Li	CHN	18.6.87	7	NC	Baoji	17 Sep
1:33:24		Brigita	Virbalyte	LTU	1.2.85	9		Lugano	20 Mar
1:33:30		Larisa	Yemelyanova	RUS	6.1.80	7		Sesto San Giovanni	1 May
1:33:33		Rachel	Lavallée Seaman	CAN	14.1.86	3	NC	Naumburg	24 Sep
1:33:36		Federica	Ferraro	ITA	18.8.88	3	NC	Warszawa	17 Sep
1:33:44		Paulina	Buziak	POL	16.12.86	4	NC	Warszawa	17 Sep
1:33:46		Eleonora	Giorgi	ITA	14.9.89	1		Bianco	30 Jan
		(80)							
1:33:50		Agnieszka	Szwarnóg	POL	28.12.86	4		Dublin	26 Jun
1:33:52	46:19	Lucie	Pelantová	CZE	7.5.86	10		Lugano	20 Mar

Mark		Name	Nat	Born	Pos	Meet	Venue	Date
1:33:54		Li Hua	CHN	15.1.91	9	NC	Baoji	17 Sep
1:33:56		Serena Pruner	ITA	21.5.86	3		Chiasso	2 Oct
1:33:57		Huang Jing	CHN	28.2.88	10	NC	Baoji	17 Sep
1:33:59	46:10	Lorena Luaces	ESP	29.2.84	5	NC	Benicàssim	6 Mar
1:34:01		Chiaki Asada	JPN	21.1.91	3	AsiC	Nomi	13 Mar
1:34:01		Neringa Aidietyte	LTU	5.6.83	2		London	30 May
1:34:11		Ana Maria Groza	ROU	1.6.76	9		Sesto San Giovanni	1 May
1:34:21		Bo Yanmin	CHN	29.6.87	11	NC	Baoji	17 Sep
		(90)						
1:34:22		Rei Inoue	JPN	23.7.91	2		Takahata	30 Oct
1:34:23		Ainhoa Pinedo	ESP	17.2.83	6	NC	Benicàssim	6 Mar
1:34:28		Eva María Iglesias	ESP	10.6.85	1		Podébrady	9 Apr
1:34:30		Kumiko Okada	JPN	17.10.91	4	AsiC	Nomi	13 Mar
1:34:31		Antonella Palmisano	ITA	6.8.91	2		Villa di Serri	23 Oct
1:34:37	46:42	Viktória Madarász	HUN	12.5.85	12		Lugano	20 Mar
1:34:39		Mayra Carolina Herrera	GUA	.88	1		Valley Cottage	30 Oct
1:34:42		Zhou Tongmei	CHN	4.4.88	9	NGP	Taicang	22 Apr
1:34:50A		Mónica Equixua	MEX	23.9.82	4	PAm	Guadalajara, MEX	23 Oct
1:34:52		Maria Michta	USA	23.6.86	1	NC	Eugene	26 Jun
		(100)						

Mark	Name	Nat	Born	Date
1:35:02	Jiang Jing	CHN	23.10.85	17 Sep
1:35:05	Agnese Pastare	LAT	27.10.88	20 Mar
1:35:10	Paula Pérez	ECU	21.12.89	30 Oct
1:35:14	Wang Min	CHN	2.12.91	13 Mar
1:35:14	Pei Mowen	CHN-Y	17.9.95	17 Sep
1:35:15	Cisiane Lopes	BRA	17.2.83	9 Apr
1:35:16	Guadalupe Sánchez	MEX	14.2.74	9 Apr
1:35:20	Alina Matveyuk	BLR	29.7.90	7 Jul
1:35:22	Olena Shevchuk	UKR	23.3.86	18 Jun
1:35:23	Lyudmyla Shelest	UKR	4.10.74	18 Jun
1:35:26	Mami Urabe	JPN	18.1.88	20 Feb
1:35:29.6t	Érica de Sena	BRA	3.5.85	5 Aug
1:35:33	Chen Shuangyan	CHN	14.8.91	22 Apr
1:35:34	Laura Reynolds	IRL	20.1.89	20 Mar
1:35:36	Teresa Vaill	USA	20.11.62	26 Jun
1:35:37	Marie Polli	SUI	28.10.80	21 May
1:35:40	Li Maocuo	CHN-J	20.10.92	17 Sep
1:35:44	Sun Xueping	CHN	10.12.88	12 Mar
1:35:45	Fumika Kiryu	JPN	12.7.87	13 Mar
1:35:50	Shi Yang	CHN	24.1.83	17 Sep
1:35:52	Jeon Yong-eun	KOR	24.5.88	31 Aug
1:35:53	Xu Liqin	CHN	6.2.90	22 Apr
1:35:55	Nicole Fagan	AUS	24.7.89	19 Feb
1:36:03	Xie Lijuan	CHN-J	14.5.93	12 Mar
1:36:08	Anna Drabenya	BLR	15.8.87	9 Apr
1:36:10A	Rosalía Ortiz	MEX	3.9.87	23 Oct
1:36:13	Edina Füsti	HUN	24.6.82	17 Sep
1:36:16	Erandi Uribe	MEX	1.3.90	9 Apr
1:36:24	Leisy Rodríguez	CUB	6.5.86	25 Feb
1:36:26	Hiroi Maeda	JPN	1.6.91	20 Feb
1:36:27	Johana Ordóñez	ECU	12.12.87	30 Oct
1:36:28	Natalya Kholodilina	RUS	21.7.89	26 Feb
1:36:31	Ai Michiguchi	JPN	3.6.88	20 Feb
1:36:32	Christine Guinaudeau	FRA	20.6.78	26 Jun
1:36:34	Zhang Ting	CHN-J	8.6.92	12 Mar
1:36:36	Sandra Galvis	COL	28.6.86	9 Oct
1:36:39	Liu Ke	CHN	2.10.90	12 Mar
1:36:40	Nelly Lekareva	RUS	18.8.89	26 Feb
1:36:42A	Grace Wanjiru	KEN	10.1.79	10 Jun
1:36:46	Olena Myroshnychenko	UKR	1.3.77	18 Jun
1:36:50	Kang Jinzi	CHN	25.1.90	22 Apr
1:36:50	Eszter Gerendási	HUN	16.4.85	17 Apr
1:36:52	Mariya Tyureva	RUS	24.7.91	17 Sep
1:36:55	Cheryl Webb	AUS	3.10.76	19 Feb
1:37:04	Zhang Xin	CHN	17.8.89	17 Sep
1:37:06	Semiha Mutlu	TUR	15.3.87	26 Mar
1:37:06	Yevdokiya Korotkova	RUS	28.2.79	17 Sep
1:37:14	Irina Shushkina	RUS	.86	17 Sep
1:37:23	Katarzyna Kwoka	POL	29.6.85	21 May
1:37:23	Cláudia Alejandra Cornejo	BOL	23.7.89	26 Feb
1:37:29	Mari Olsson	SWE	27.4.86	26 Mar
1:37:32A	Claudia Balderrama	BOL	13.11.83	23 Oct
1:37:33	Yang Lixia	CHN	18.9.91	12 Mar
1:37:36	Galina Kireyeva	RUS	11.11.91	17 Sep
1:37:41	Laura Polli	SUI	7.9.83	20 Mar
1:37:41	Lauren Forgues	USA	16.4.88	26 Jun
1:37:42	Christin Elss	GER	4.9.89	16 Apr
1:37:45	Weon Ases-byeol	KOR	8.4.90	10 Oct
1:37:47	Wang Jiaojiao	CHN-J	11.12.93	17 Sep
1:37:48	Yekaterina Yezhova	RUS	18.2.82	26 Feb
1:37:52	Duan Dandan	CHN-Y	23.5.95	17 Sep
1:37:53	Miki Miyamoto	JPN-J	27.3.92	20 Feb
1:37:54	Tanya Holliday	AUS	21.9.88	21 Aug
1:37:56	Mária Czaková	SVK	2.10.88	20 Mar
1:37:56	Ana Veronica Rodean	ROU	23.6.84	24 Jun
1:37:57	Wang Xiaolan	CHN	5.2.90	22 Apr
1:37:59	Mu Juan	CHN	20.6.89	17 Sep
1:38:01	Miranda Melville	USA	20.3.89	26 Jun
1:38:02	Ayman Kozhakhmetova	KAZ	23.4.91	12 Jun
1:38:03	Dan Hongying	CHN-J	17.5.92	17 Sep
1:38:04	María del Rosario Sánchez	MEX	26.10.73	9 Apr
1:38:14	Nadzeya Darazhuk	BLR	23.1.90	7 Jul
1:38:18	Xu Yaozhi	CHN	20.5.90	17 Sep
1:38:19	Anita Kazemaka	LAT	30.5.90	27 Aug
1:38:21	Karoliina Kaasalainen	FIN	1.4.88	21 May
1:38:28	Ikumi Tamakawa	JPN		20 Feb
1:38:28	Zhu Dan	CHN-J	27.1.93	17 Sep
1:38:33	Emilie Menuet	FRA	27.11.91	21 May
1:38:38	Tatyana Stefanenko	BLR	27.10.91	7 Jul
1:38:45	Liu Huan	CHN-J	24.2.93	22 Apr
1:38:48	Liu Shuyu	CHN-J	13.12.93	18 Jun
1:38:52	Anastasiya Pavlenko	RUS	28.9.89	26 Feb
1:38:53	Chaïma Trabelsi	TUN	11.3.82	1 May
1:38:55	Song Meiying	CHN	8.9.89	17 Sep
1:38:59 (185)	Wang Tingting	CHN	18.1.87	22 Apr

Short courses

Mark	Name	Nat	Born	Pos	Meet	Venue	Date
1:28:15A	Grace Wanjiru	KEN	10.1.79	1	NC	Nairobi	15 Jul
1:30:15	Brigita Virbalyte	LTU	1.2.85	1		Alytus	17 Jun
1:30:36	Kristina Saltanovic	LTU	20.2.75	2		Alytus	17 Jun
1:31:54A	Emily Ngii	KEN	13.8.86	2	NC	Nairobi	15 Jul
1:32:10	Agnese Pastare	LAT	27.10.88	3		Alytus	17 Jun
1:34:35A	Grace Thoithi	KEN		3	NC	Nairobi	15 Jul
1:35:52	Anita Kazemaka	LAT	30.5.90				17 Jun
1:36:42A	Rebecca Jeptum	KEN	.80				15 Jul

Other best track times

Mark	Name	Nat	Born	Date
1:35:49.6	Cisiane Lopes	BRA	17.2.83	5 Aug
1:37:45.0	Paola Pérez	ECU	21.12.89	1 May

Insufficient judges

Mark	Name	Nat	Born	Pos	Venue	Date
1:30:23	Inês Henriques	POR	1.5.80	1	Montemor o Velho	8 Jan

Mark	Name	Nat	Born	Pos	Meet	Venue	Date

JUNIORS

See main list for top 7 juniors. 11 performances by 7 women to 1:33:15. Additional marks and further juniors:

Mark	Name	Nat	Born	Pos	Meet	Venue	Date
Lu Xiuzhi 1:30:06 5			Taicang	22 Apr	1:32:31 2J	Xintai	12 Mar
He Qin 1:32:20 1J			Xintai	12 Mar	1:32:59 5	NC-j Baoji	17 Sep
1:35:14	Pei Mowen	CHN-Y	17.9.95	6	NC-j	Baoji	17 Sep
1:35:40	Li Maocuo	CHN	20.10.92	7	NC-j	Baoji	17 Sep
1:36:03	Xie Lijuan (10)	CHN	14.5.93	5J	NGP	Xintai	12 Mar
1:36:34	Zhang Ting	CHN	8.6.92	6J	NGP	Xintai	12 Mar
1:37:47	Wang Jiaojiao	CHN	11.12.93	10	NC-j	Baoji	17 Sep
1:37:52	Duan Dandan	CHN-Y	23.5.95	11	NC-j	Baoji	17 Sep
1:37:53	Miki Miyamoto	JPN	27.3.92	9	NC	Kobe	20 Feb
1:38:03	Dan Hongying	CHN	17.5.92	12	NC-j	Baoji	17 Sep
1:38:28	Zhu Dan	CHN	27.1.93	13	NC-j	Baoji	17 Sep
1:38:45	Liu Huan	CHN	24.2.93	3J	NGP	Taicang	22 Apr
1:38:48	Liu Shuyu	CHN	13.12.93	1J	NGP	Benxi	18 Jun
1:39:03	Yang Liu	CHN	26.2.92	8J	NGP	Xintai	12 Mar
1:39:11	Xiao Junying (20)	CHN	16.6.92	9J	NGP	Xintai	12 Mar
Best European: 1:41:19 Anna Krakhmaleva		RUS	1.5.92	2		Izhevsk	24 Apr

Mark	Name		Nat	Born	Pos	Meet	Venue	Date
4723	Antoinette	Nana Djimou	FRA	2.8.85	1	EI	Paris (B)	4 Mar
4706	Austra	Skujyte	LTU	12.8.79	2	EI	Paris (B)	4 Mar
4665	Remona	Fransen	NED	25.11.85	3	EI	Paris (B)	4 Mar
4612	Karolina	Tyminska	POL	4.10.84	4	EI	Paris (B)	4 Mar
4578		Skujyte			1	NC	Klaipeda	19 Feb
4540		Nana Djimou			1	v4N	Reims	29 Jan
4540	Brianne	Theisen	CAN	18.12.88	1	NCAA	College Station	11 Mar
4513	Anna	Bogdanova	RUS	21.10.84	1	NCp	Belgorod	26 Feb
4500	Aleksandra	Butvina	RUS	14.2.86	1	NC	Penza	5 Feb
4497	Jessica	Samuelsson	SWE	14.3.85	5	EI	Paris (B)	4 Mar
4469	Marina	Goncharova	RUS	26.4.86	6	EI	Paris (B)	4 Mar
4453	Zuzana (10)	Hejnová	CZE	19.12.86	7	EI	Paris (B)	4 Mar
4439	Bettie	Wade	USA	11.9.86	1	NC	Bloomington IN	6 Mar
4436	Yana	Panteleyeva	RUS	16.6.88	3	NC	Penza	5 Feb
4422	Grit	Sadeiko	EST	29.7.89	1		Tallinn	6 Feb
4420	Sofía	Ifadídou	GRE	5.1.85	1		Lárisa	20 Apr
4399	Kaie	Kand	EST	31.3.84	8	EI	Paris (B)	4 Mar
4396	Chantae	McMillan	USA	1.5.88	2=	NCAA	College Station	11 Mar
4396	Kiani	Profit	USA	18.2.90	2=	NCAA	College Station	11 Mar
4381	Bárbara	Hernando	ESP	12.8.88	1	NC	Valencia	19 Feb
4369	Aiga	Grabuste	LAT	24.3.88	1	NC	Riga	29 Jan
4352	Marisa (20)	De Aniceto	FRA	11.11.86	3	v4N	Reims	29 Jan
4349	Yana	Maksimova	BLR	9.1.89	1		Gomel	19 Feb
4339	Claudia	Rath	GER	25.4.86	1	NC	Frankfurt-Kalbach	30 Jan
4338	Yasmina	Omrani	FRA	1.1.88	4	v4N	Reims	29 Jan
4337	Abbie	Norton	USA	28.4.85	2	NC	Bloomington IN	6 Mar
4334	Viktorija	Zemaityte	LTU	11.3.85	2	NC	Klaipeda	19 Feb
4325	Kamila	Chudzik	POL	12.9.86	1	NC	Spala	19 Feb
4323	Inna	Ahkozova	UKR	16.9.84	1	NC	Sumy	15 Feb
4295	Györgyi	Farkas	HUN	13.2.85	1	NC	Budapest (S)	5 Feb
4291	Eliska	Klucinová	CZE	14.4.88	1	NC	Praha	13 Feb
4289	Janay (30)	DeLoach	USA	12.10.85	3	NC	Bloomington IN	6 Mar
4283	Ida	Marcussen	NOR	1.11.87	11	EI	Paris (B)	4 Mar
4282	Sara	Aerts	BEL	25.1.84	12	EI	Paris (B)	4 Mar
4262	Alina	Fyodorova	UKR	31.7.89	2	NCp	Zaporizhzhya	28 Jan
4254	Dorcas	Akinniyi	USA	23.1.90	4	NCAA	College Station	11 Mar
4250	Anastasiya	Belyakova	RUS	4.12.90	5	NC	Penza	5 Feb
4250	Anastasiya	Mokhnyuk	UKR	1.1.91	2	NC	Sumy	15 Feb
4241	Kasey	Hill	USA	10.10.85	4	NC	Bloomington IN	6 Mar
4238	Olga	Kurban	RUS	16.12.87	6	NC	Penza	5 Feb
4235	Olga	Zaynutdinova	RUS	29.10.86	3	NCp	Belgorod	26 Feb
4224	Francesca (40)	Doveri	ITA	21.12.82	1	NC	Ancona	30 Jan
4221	Christina	Kiffe	GER-J	2.5.92	1	NC-j	Frankfurt-Kalbach	30 Jan
4213	Katarina	Johnson-Thompson	GBR	9.1.93	1	v2N-j	Sheffield	5 Mar
4207	Nadine	Broersen	NED	29.4.90	1	NC	Apeldoorn	20 Feb
4206	Laura	Ikauniece	LAT-J	31.5.92	3		Tallinn	6 Feb

WORLD LIST TRENDS – MEN

This table shows the 10th and 100th bests in the year lists for the last eight years and the best prior to 2004.

Men 10th Bests	Pre 2004	2004	2005	2006	2007	2008	2009	2010	2011
100m	9.98- 97	10.01	10.00	10.02	10.02	9.95	9.97	9.95	**9.89**
200m	**20.03**- 00	20.17	20.21	20.19	20.06	20.17	20.17	20.11	20.16
400m	**44.51**- 96	44.72	44.70	44.73	44.62	44.70	44.81	44.81	44.78
800m	**1:43.66**- 96	1:44.09	1:44.34	1:43.93	1:44.27	1:44.10	1:43.82	1:43.89	1:44.07
1500m	3:31.49- 01	**3:31.10**	3:31.95	3:31.85	3:32.13	3:32.16	3:31.90	3:32.20	3:31.84
5000m	**12:54.99**- 03	12:59.04	12:56.13	12:56.41	13:02.89	13:03.04	12:58.16	12:55.95	12:59.15
10000m	27:14.61- 03	27:05.14	27:04.45	27:14.84	**27:00.30**	27:08.06	27:15.94	27:17.61	26:52.84
Half Mar	60:20- 02	60:22	60:20	60:12	59:32	59:37	**59:30**	59:40	59:39
Marathon	2:06:48- 03	2:07:43	2:07:46	2:07:14	2:07:19	2:06:25	2:06:14	2:05:52	**2:05:45**!
3000mSt	**8:08.14**- 02	8:11.44	8:09.43	8:11.36	8:09.72	8:12.72	8:10.63	8:09.87	8:08.43
110mh	13.20- 98	13.22	13.23	13.22	13.19	13.24	13.21	13.28	13.23
400mh	48.25- 02	48.16	48.24	48.57	48.26	48.52	48.30	48.47	48.47
HJ	**2.36**- 88	2.32	2.33	2.33	2.34	2.34	2.33	2.32	2.33
PV	**5.90**- 98	5.81	5.85	5.81	5.83	5.81	5.80	5.80	5.80
LJ	**8.35**- 97	8.28	8.28	8.32	8.26	8.25	8.30	8.25	8.27
TJ	**17.48**- 85	17.41	17.30	17.38	17.39	17.43	17.41	17.29	17.35
SP	**21.63**- 84	21.14	20.94	20.85	20.87	21.19	20.99	21.29	21.16
DT	**68.20**- 82	66.73	66.56	66.50	66.61	67.91	66.19	66.90	67.21
HT	**81.88**- 88	80.90	80.00	80.54	80.00	80.58	79.48	78.73	79.27
JT	**87.12**- 96/97	85.83	84.06	85.30	84.35	85.05	84.24	85.12	84.81
Decathlon	**8526**- 98	8285	8185	8310	8298	8372	8406	8253	8288
20kmW	1:19:05- 97	1:19:30	**1:18:30**	1:19:12	1:19:34	1:19:15	1:19:55	1:20:36	1:19:57
50kmW	3:44:19- 96	3:44:42	**3:41:30**	3:43:58	3:44:26	3:45:21	3:41:55	3:47:54	3:44:03

Peak years shown in bold.

Men 100th Bests

	Pre 2004	2004	2005	2006	2007	2008	2009	2010	2011
100m	10.24- 00	10.26	10.29	10.27	10.25	10.23	10.22	10.26	**10.21**
200m	20.66- 99/00	20.67	20.70	20.70	**20.66**	20.67	20.68	20.71	20.63
400m	**45.78**- 00	45.86	45.98	45.90	45.91	45.89	45.86	45.92	45.91
800m	**1:46.54**- 99	1:46.67	1:46.93	1:46.80	1:46.99	1:46.70	1:46.88	1:46.76	1:46.50
1500m	3:38.42- 97	3:38.50	3:39.05	3:39.26	3:38.66	3:38.57	3:38.60	3:38.47	**3:37.77**
5000m	13:28.62- 00	13:25.52	13:25.68	13:27.46	13:27.48	**13:25.05**	13:26.90	13:25.88	13:26.29
10000m	28:15.98- 00	28:21.4	28:22.85	28:21.98	28:10.73	**28:04.47**	28:18.00	28:21.00	28:15.79
Half Mar	62:00- 00	62:06	62:04	62:07	61:54	61:50	**61:28**	61:38	61:31
Marathon	2:10:38- 03	2:11:13	2:11:20	2:10:54	2:10:43	2:10:22	2:09:53	2:09:31	**2:09:19**!
3000mSt	8:33.58- 03	**8:31.06**	8:33.37	8:34.10	8:32.94	8:32.12	8:35.21	8:35.29	8:35.45
110mh	13.72- 96	13.70	13.73	13.77	13.72	**13.67**	13.71	13.68	**13.67**
400mh	**50.06**- 00	50.14	50.10	50.37	50.28	50.33	50.35	50.41	50.28
HJ	**2.24**- 84/88/89/92/96	2.23	2.22	2.23	2.23	2.23	2.23	2.23	**2.24**
PV	**5.55**- 00	5.50	5.50	5.50	5.50	5.50	5.46	5.42	5.45
LJ	7.94- 96	**7.96**	7.90	7.90	7.90	7.93	7.94	7.91	7.94
TJ	**16.60**- 88	16.55	16.42	16.43	16.44	16.53	16.46	16.46	16.53
SP	**19.48**- 84	19.28	19.08	19.12	19.22	19.21	19.15	19.08	19.18
DT	**60.96**- 84	60.05	59.50	59.63	59.75	60.77	60.00	59.77	59.98
HT	**73.06**- 84	71.12	70.72	70.19	70.58	70.89	70.66	70.78	70.44
JT	77.14- 91	76.31	76.10	75.98	75.66	76.28	77.03	76.71	**77.38**
Decathlon	**7702**- 88	7572	7490	7496	7545	7594	7623	7526	7678
20kmW	1:23:39- 95	1:23:25	**1:22.48**	1:23:47	1:23:55	1:23:32	1:23:57	1:24:24	1:23:40
50kmW	**4:03:49**- 99	4:05:13	4:05:04	4:13:16	4:04:52	4:05:05	4:09:24	4:08:08	4:06:15

! From 2011 main marathon lists no longer include Boston or other such excessively downhill races.

Number of athletes achieving base level standards for world lists:

Men		2006	2007	2008	2009	2010	2011
100m	10.32	151	174	189	202	174	201
200m	20.85	174	187	194	214	189	212
400m	46.29	177	186	183	185	177	170
800m	1:47.70	171	160	188	169	186	207
1500m	3:40.7	164	172	167	166	191	207
5000m	13:40.0	178	197	202	211	203	213
10000m	28:40.0	180	218	247	180	198	196
HMar	62:15	111	133	144	188	176	176
Mar	2:11:30	129	140	163	182	204	254
3000St	8:40.0	156	157	166	140	135	147
110mh	13.95	195	196	210	204	223	224
400mh	50.85	158	159	173	156	165	183

		2006	2007	2008	2009	2010	2011
HJ	2.20	169	197	180	184	194	192
PV	5.35	168	178	179	172	172	176
LJ	7.80	164	179	191	182	173	186
TJ	16.30	125	137	167	123	139	142
SP	18.30	193	188	189	190	199	198
DT	57.80	151	150	172	164	156	155
HT	68.00	135	135	155	149	158	149
JT	74.00	137	145	152	166	168	173
Dec	7400	127	137	155	150	136	165
20kmW	1:25:00	143	144	147	136	124	154
50kmW	4:10:00	87	115	123	105	103	110
TOTAL		3548	3784	4031	4022	3943	4190

The 2011 numbers compared to those of 2010: for 10th best 16-5 (2 ties), 100th best 21-2, base level 16-6 (1 tie)

WORLD LIST TRENDS – WOMEN

This table shows the 10th and 100th bests in the year lists for the last eight years and the best prior to 2004.

10th Bests	Pre 2004	2004	2005	2006	2007	2008	2009	2010	2011
100m	**10.92**- 88	11.04	11.05	11.08	11.04	10.95	11.04	11.08	11.01
200m	**22.24**- 88	22.46	22.46	22.51	22.49	22.43	22.45	22.49	22.55
400m	**49.74**- 84	50.19	50.38	50.14	50.16	50.11	50.27	50.43	50.67
800m	**1:56.91**- 88	1:57.96	1:58.41	1:57.88	1:58.61	1:57.9	1:58.80	1:58.67	1:58.21
1500m	**3:58.07**- 97	4:01.29	4:01.14	4:01.31	4:02.8	4:02.44	4:00.86	4:00.25	4:01.73
5000m	14:45.35- 00	14:44.81	14:43.87	14:46.99	14:45.22	14:43.89	14:41.62	**14:38.64**	14:39.44
10,000m	31:01.07- 03	31:04.34	30:55.67	31:14.80	31:22.80	**30:39.96**	30:51.92	31:29:03	31:10.02
Half Mar	68:23- 00	68:52	69:17	69:17	68:28	68:51	68:14	**67:52**	68:07
Marathon	2:23:33- 02	2:24:27	2:23:59	2:23:22	2:24:23	2:24:14	2:25:06	2:23:44	**2:22:43!**
3000mSt	9:44.95- 03	9:39.84	9:35.51	9:27.35	9:26.63	9:21.76	**9:18.54**	9:24.84	9:25.96
100mh	12.67- 98	12.60	12.66	12.66	12.67	**12.58**	12.67	12.65	12.73
400mh	54.15- 99	**53.99**	54.47	54.47	54.14	54.45	54.49	54.58	54.69
HJ	**2.01**- 03	2.00	1.97	1.98	1.97	1.98	1.98	1.97	1.96
PV	4.60- 02/03	4.60	4.60	4.62	4.70	4.70	4.65	4.66	**4.71**
LJ	**7.07**- 88	6.83	6.79	6.83	6.89	6.89	6.87	6.89	6.88
TJ	14.76- 03	14.78	14.69	14.54	14.69	**14.84**	14.62	14.48	14.57
SP	**20.85**- 87	19.29	19.05	19.10	19.13	19.29	19.38	19.47	19.26
DT	**70.34**- 88	65.25	64.56	64.20	64.87	64.10	63.89	64.04	63.91
HT	71.12- 03	72.57	73.08	74.31	73.94	**74.40**	73.07	73.40	72.65
JT	**64.89**- 00	63.07	62.64	63.20	63.58	63.24	63.89	63.36	63.50
Heptathlon	**6540**- 88	6287	6291	6356	6327	6465	6323	6204	6338
20kmW	1:27:55- 01	1:27:52	1:28:01	1:28:26	1:28:51	**1:27:18**	1:28:50	1:29:20	1:28:41

100th Bests	Pre 2004	2004	2005	2006	2007	2008	2009	2010	2011
100m	**11.36**- 00	11.38	11.42	11.41	11.37	**11.36**	11.41	11.40	**11.36**
200m	**23.21**- 00	23.20	23.29	23.28	23.27	**23.17**	23.26	23.27	23.21
400m	**52.25**- 00	52.14	52.30	52.24	52.14	**52.08**	52.44	52.52	52.33
800m	**2:01.50**- 84	2:01.98	2:02.58	2:02.31	2:02.25	2:02.50	2:02.13	2:02.14	2:01.86
1500m	**4:10.22**- 84	4:10.34	4:12.12	4:11.61	4:11.67	4:11.64	4:11.06	4:10.50	**4:09.88**
5000m	15:29.36- 00	**15:27.20**	15:29.96	15:31.57	15:33.90	15:27.50	15:37.31	15:37.45	15:31.67
10000m	32:32.47- 00	32:37.88	32:34.11	32:42.44	32:46.28	**32:30.10**	32:54.64	32:57.59	32:53.44
Half Mar	71:29- 01	71:44	71:52	71:37	71:15	71:19	**70:57**	70:59	71:06
Marathon	2:31:05- 01	2:31:53	2:31:43	2:31:08	2:31:25	2:29:53	2:30:08	2:29:36	**2:28:32**
3000mSt	10:23.76- 03	10:18.55	10:13.00	10:06.30	10:03.2	**9:56.48**	10:02.94	10:03.50	9:59.44
100mh	13.22- 00	13.26	13.32	13.30	13.25	13.22	13.28	13.23	**13.16**
400mh	57.48- 00	57.33	57.47	57.35	**57.21**	57.46	57.45	57.22	57.26
HJ	**1.88**- 86/87/88/92/93	1.87	1.86	1.86	1.87	1.86	1.86	1.87	1.86
PV	4.15- 03	4.20	4.20	4.20	4.22	4.25	4.21	4.25	**4.30**
LJ	**6.53**- 88	6.50	6.48	6.51	6.49	6.52	6.49	6.51	6.50
TJ	13.68- 00	13.70	13.62	13.66	13.64	**13.75**	13.65	13.67	13.70
SP	**17.19**- 87	16.76	16.55	16.60	16.54	16.49	16.43	16.46	16.60
DT	**58.50**- 92	55.15	56.32	55.93	55.92	55.43	56.06	55.05	56.12
HT	63.23- 03	63.73	63.14	63.72	64.34	**64.81**	63.77	64.12	64.79
JT	**55.55**- 00	55.09	54.91	55.00	55.07	54.81	55.16	54.98	55.34
Heptathlon	**5741**- 88	5631	5650	5633	5674	5687	5586	5568	5591
20kmW	1:34:44- 00	1:34:32	**1:34:11**	1:36:01	1:35:57	1:34:30	1:35:54	1:36:32	1:34:52

All-time record levels indicated in bold.

! From 2011 main marathon lists no longer include Boston or other such excessively downhill races.

Number of athletes achieving base level standards for world lists:

Women		2006	2007	2008	2009	2010	2011
100m	11.50	161	183	202	185	171	195
200m	23.50	175	188	219	165	175	191
400m	53.04	198	198	204	177	176	197
800m	2:04.0	161	174	178	183	182	214
1500m	4:15.5	171	176	175	211	198	219
5000m	15:45.0	173	171	178	136	139	163
10,000m	33:15.0	159	150	160	144	133	146
HMar	72:15	142	165	206	225	200	194
Mar	2:33:00	137	126	205	219	236	203
3000mSt	10:15.0	131	153	195	194	189	189
100mh	13.54	180	196	231	210	223	239

		2006	2007	2008	2009	2010	2011
400mh	58.44	168	178	177	179	169	181
HJ	1.85	140	149	144	136	142	172
PV	4.10	183	189	208	190	196	221
LJ	6.35	199	180	205	181	180	185
TJ	13.30	172	181	189	183	182	191
SP	15.85	154	159	160	159	159	163
DT	53.65	145	146	154	139	144	153
HT	60.00	184	203	206	194	193	219
JT	53.00	141	149	158	154	151	160
Hep	5450	142	157	155	137	126	146
20kmW	1:40:00	162	168	189	163	155	207
TOTAL		3576	3739	4093	3969	3819	4148

The 2011 marks compared to those of 2010: for 10th best 9-13, 100th best 18-4, base level 19-2 (1 tie).

	Name		Nat	Born	Ht/Wt	Event	2011 Mark	Pre-2011 Best

MEN'S INDEX 2011

Athletes included are those ranked in the top 100s at standard (World Championships) events (plus shorter lists for 1000m, 1M, 2000m and 3000m). Those with detailed biographical profiles are indicated in first column by:

	Name	First	Nat	Born	Ht/Wt	Event	2011 Mark	Pre-2011 Best
	Aalto	Mika	FIN	11.3.82	178/88	JT	78.69	78.94- 09
	Aarrass	Jamel	FRA	15.11.81	187/75	1500	3:37.77	3:37.49- 10
	Abad	Francisco Javier	ESP	18.8.81	180/70	1500	3:35.55	3:40.28- 09
	Abadía	Antonio David	ESP	2.7.90	181/70	3kSt	8:34.75	8:47.45- 09
	Abate	Emanuele	ITA	8.7.85	190/78	110h	13.54	13.59- 06
	Abdi	Youcef	AUS	7.12.77	178/66	3kSt	8:16.41	8:16.36- 08
	Abdulrazaaq	Adams	USA	27.4.88	185/80	110h	13.66	13.85- 10
	Abe	Takatoshi	JPN	12.11.91	182/68	400h	49.64	49.46- 10
	Aboud	Rabah	ALG	1.1.81	169/54	5000	13:19.00	13:39.28- 05
	Abramyan	Benik	GEO	31.7.85		SP	19.26dq	17.69- 10
	Abrantes	Arnaldo	POR	27.11.86	176/70	100	10.16w	10.19, 10.13w- 09
						200	20.61	20.48- 07
	Abromavicius	Aleksas	LTU	6.12.84	197/115	DT	61.38	63.32- 10
*	Abshero	Ayele	ETH	28.12.90	167/52	10k	27:48.84	27:54.29- 09
						HMar	59:42	-0-
	Acea	Raidel	CUB	31.10.90	188/77	800	1:45.62	1:46.68- 09
^	Achike	Larry	GBR	31.1.75	188/75	TJ	16.83	17.30, 17.31w- 00
	Acosta	Andrew J	USA	13.4.88	188/73	1M	3:55.30	3:53.76- 10
	Adakhovskiy	Anatoliy	BLR	18.12.87		JT	77.52	79.18- 10
	Adam	Idrissa	CMR	28.12.84	183/77	100	10.14	10.50- 08
	Adamchuk	Vadym	UKR-Y	30.5.94	185/72	LJ	7.95	7.41- 10
	Adams	Antoine	SKN	31.8.88	174/72	100	10.19w	10.49- 10, 10.34w- 07
	Adams	Harry	USA	27.11.89	182/81	100	10.19	10.33- 06, 10.17w- 10
*	Adams	Luke	AUS	22.10.76	189/70	20kW	1:21:00	1:19:15- 08
						50kW	3:45:31	3:43:39- 09
	Adams	Lyukman	RUS	24.9.88	188/75	TJ	17.32i	17.17, 17.21w- 10
	Adams	Spencer	USA	10.9.89	188/84	110h	13.55, 13.48w	13.84, 13.79w- 10
	Adcock	Nick	USA	2.4.88	188/82	Dec	7679	7704- 10
	Addy	Jangy	LBR	2.3.85	190/93	Dec	7993	8025- 08
	Ahouchar	Hassane	MAR	.75		Mar	2:08:47	2:13:20- 10
	Aikines-Aryeetey	Harry	GBR	29.8.88	176/86	100	10.13, 10.09w	10.10- 08
						200	20.46	20.91- 05
	Akashi	Ken	JPN	6.11.76	169/59	50kW	3:57:48	3:50:11- 08
	Akdag	Tarik (Patrick Langat)	KEN/TUR	22.4.89	172/54	3kSt	8:08.59	8:09.12- 10
	Akins	Tyrone	USA	6.1.86	180/79	110h	13.30	13.25- 08, 13.2w- 10
^	Akkas	Halil	TUR	1.7.83	175/60	3kSt	8:31.09	8:18.43- 07
	Al Outaibi	Moukhled	KSA	20.6.76	174/67	5000	13:25.13	12:58.58- 05
	Al-Amri	Ali Ahmed	KSA	28.12.87	186/70	3kSt	8:26.75	8:21.87- 06
^	Al-Azimi	Mohamed	KUW	16.6.82	176/70	800	1:45.35	1:44.13- 06
						1000	2:15.84	
	Al-Dosari	Rashid	QAT	8.5.81	197/123	DT	62.29	64.43- 02
	Al-Garni	Mohamed	QAT-J	2.7.92	178/65	1500	3:34.61	3:36.32- 10
	Al-Hamdah	Hussein Jamaan	KSA	4.8.83	170/55	5000	13:12.17	13:11.64- 09
	Al-Harthi	Barakat	OMA	15.6.88	172/64	100	10.17	10.26- 10
	Al-Joud	Abdullah Abdulaziz	KSA	10.7.75	178/60	5000	13:24.54	13:30.18- 10
	Al-Masrahi	Youssef Ahmed	KSA	31.12.87	176/76	400	45.44	45.48- 10
	Al-Merjabi	Ahmed Mohamed	OMA	9.9.90		400	45.84	-0-
	Al-Momani	Musaeb	JOR	28.8.86	184/110	DT	60.97	62.36- 09
	Al-Moualed	Ahmad	KSA	16.2.88	180/66	110h	13.60	13.64- 08
	Al-Shourafa	Ahmed Nezar	KSA	9.7.87	170/60	LJ	8.05	7.96- 09
*	Al-Zankawi	Ali Mohamed	KUW	27.2.84	186/97	HT	79.27	79.74- 09
	Alaka	James	GBR	8.9.89	180/73	200	20.59	20.71- 10
	Alamirew	Yenew	ETH	27.5.90	175/57	1500	3:35.09+	
	1M	3:50.43				3000	7:27.26	7:28.82- 10
						5000	13:00.46	13:16.53- 10
	Albert	Lars	GER	9.2.82	196/98	Dec	7712	7920- 05
	Alcorn	Kyle	USA	18.3.85	193/80	3kSt	8:23.27	8:21.46- 08
	Alejandro	Eric	PUR	15.4.86	180/70	400h	50.16	50.92- 10
*	Alekna	Virgilijus	LTU	13.2.72	200/130	DT	67.90	73.88- 00
	Alekseyev	Denis	RUS	26.12.87	185/73	400	45.73	45.35- 08
	Alemayehu	Zebene	ETH-J	4.9.92	175/57	1500	3:34.59	3:38.39- 10
						2000	4:59.18	
	Alic	Hamza	BIH	20.1.79	192/108	SP	20.38	20.56- 08
	Alilech	Adil	MAR	26.6.86		3kSt	8:28.64	
	Almeida	João	POR	5.4.88	188/79	110h	13.78, 13.49w	13.94, 13.71w- 09
	Alozidis	Minas	CYP	7.7.84	185/72	400h	49.91	49.16- 07
	Alves	Francisco Javier	ESP	3.9.80	180/66	5000	13:19.93	13:11.01- 06

Name		Nat	Born	Ht/Wt	Event	2011 Mark	Pre-2011 Best
Amalbert	Marcos	PUR	9.4.88	183/68	LJ	7.92A, 7.98w	7.78- 10
Aman	Mohammed	ETH-Y	10.1.94	169/55	800	1:43.37	1:46.34- 09
Amb	Kim	SWE	31.7.90	180/86	JT	80.09	77.81- 10
Ames	Brendan	USA	6.10.88	190/79	110h	13.39, 13.34w	13.80- 10
Ananenko	Anis	BLR	29.11.85	173/60	800	1:45.59	1:47.66- 10
Anani	Mohsen	EGY	25.5.85	187/117	HT	72.06	77.36- 10
* Anderson	Jeshua	USA	22.6.89	187/84	400h	47.93	48.47- 09
Anderson	Kenroy	JAM	27.6.87	172/64	100	10.18, 10.15w	10.29- 10
Anderson	Kenroy	JAM	27.6.87	172/64	200	20.55	
* Anderson	Marvin	JAM	12.5.82	175/69	200	20.27	20.06- 07
Anderson	Tanner	USA-J	4.5.92	186/73	HJ	2.24	2.215- 10
André	Nilson	BRA	30.1.86	173/70	100	10.18	10.21 - 10
					200	20.56	20.41- 10
Andrews	Robby	USA	29.3.91	177/68	800	1:44.71	1:45.54- 10
Andriyanov	Nikita	RUS	7.2.90	183/73	400h	49.62	51.43- 09
* Andronov	Yuriy	RUS	6.11.71	180/68	20kW	1:23:32	1:22:42.0t- 02
					50kW	3:42:25	3:42:06- 02
Anghel	Alin	ROU	13.5.86	186/77	TJ	16.60i	16.69i- 10, 16.65- 09
Anishchenkov	Nikita	RUS-J	25.7.92	188/80	HJ	2.30	2.21- 10
Anou	Abderrahmane	ALG	29.1.91	172/60	1500	3:35.2	3:38.86- 10
^ Apak	Esref	TUR	3.1.82	186/100	HT	78.04	81.45- 05
Arai	Hiroki	JPN	18.5.88	179/61	20kW	1:22:47	1:26:04- 10
					50kW	3:48:40	3:55:56- 10
Arai	Ken	JPN	22.12.81	172/75	JT	78.87	76.66- 10
Arai	Ryohei	JPN	23.6.91		JT	78.21	
Arajs	Ronalds	LAT	29.11.87	179/70	100	10.18	10.31A, 10.30w- 10, 10.21Aw- 09
* Araptany	Jacob	UGA-J	11.2.92	171/57	1500	3:36.15A	3:42.0A- 10
					3kSt	8:15.72A	8:28.14- 10
de Araújo	Luiz Alberto	BRA	27.9.87	190/90	Dec	8115	7816- 10
Araya	Edwar	CHI	14.2.86	177/58	50kW	4:03:02	4:14:10- 10
Araya	Yerko	CHI	14.2.86	177/58	20kW	1:20:47.2t	1:23:08.2t- 09
Arents	Mareks	LAT	6.8.86	188/86	PV	5.46	5.31i- 10, 5.30- 09
Arikan	Polat (Paul) Kemboi	KEN/TUR	12.12.90	170/55	5000	13:05.98	13:18.12- 10
Aristil	David	USA	12.12.88	183/73	400h	49.94	50.13- 10
^ Armstrong	Aaron	TRI	14.10.77	173/70	100	10.07	10.03- 09, 10.00w- 05, 9.8w- 99
* Armstrong	Dylan	CAN	15.1.81	190/125	SP	22.21	21.58- 10
Arnett	Nathan	BAH	15.12.90	191/82	400h	50.27	51.01- 10
Arrhenius	Leif	SWE	15.7.86	192/120	SP	19.92i, 19.37	18.86- 10
					DT	64.46	63.12- 08
Arrhenius	Niklas	SWE	10.9.82	194/120	SP	19.79	19.91i- 04, 19.75- 10
					DT	66.22	65.77- 07
Artikov	Rifat	UZB	24.1.83	194/87	Dec	7975	7568- 10, 7958 irr- 08
Arzola	David	CUB	24.2.89	183/75	110h	13.83, 13.4w	13.76- 09, 13.4- 10
* Ash	Ronnie	USA	2.7.88	188/86	110h	13.25, 13.24w	13.19, 12.98w- 10
* Ashmeade	Nickel	JAM	4.7.90	184/77	100	9.96	10.34- 08, 10.21w- 09
					200	19.91	20.40- 09, 20.16w- 08
Asmerom	Yared	ERI	3.2.79	171/58	Mar	2:07:27	2:08:34- 08
Assefa	Girma	ETH	20.2.86	165/45	Mar	2:07:43	2:09:58- 09
Åstrand	Jonathan	FIN	9.9.85	179/67	200	20.50	20.78, 20.69w- 10
Atanasov	Nikolay	BUL	11.12.74	188/72	LJ	7.96	8.31- 03
Atnafu Zerihun	Yitayal	ETH-J	20.1.93	170/60	5000	13:16.30	13:38.52- 10
Aucyna	Darius	LTU	7.5.89	193/80	LJ	7.92, 7.96w	7.83i- 09, 7.82- 08
Augustyn	Rafal	POL	14.5.84	178/71	20kW	1:20:57	1:21:36- 05
					50kW	3:46:56	3:49:54- 10
Austin	Justin	USA	8.10.89	186/80	100	10.21	10.35- 10
					200	20.46, 20.31w	20.99- 09
Auzeil	Bastien	FRA	22.10.89	195/86	Dec	7683	-0-
* Avan	Fatih	TUR	1.1.89	180/87	JT	84.79	79.78- 09
* Avramenko	Roman	UKR	23.3.88	184/84	JT	84.30	81.12- 10
Awde	Daniel	GBR	22.6.88	182/75	Dec	7889	7751- 08
Aydamirov	Sergey	RUS	11.5.87	183/100	HT	74.78	74.92- 10
Ayeko	Simon	UGA	10.5.87	178/62	3kSt	8:29.02	8:18.04- 09
Ayele	Abayneh	ETH	11.4.87	175/57	2000	4:58.01	
3000	7:49.25				5000	13:11.01	
Ayers	Michael	USA	7.11.88	183/81	Dec	7903	7794- 09
Ayudhaya	Suphanara S.	THA-J	11.6.92	182/65	LJ	8.05	8.04- 10
Azie	Stanley	USA/NGR	13.3.89	170/66	100	10.20	10.63- 10
* Baala	Mehdi	FRA	17.8.78	183/65	1500	3:33.69	3:28.98- 03
* Bába	Jaroslav	CZE	2.9.84	196/82	HJ	2.34i, 2.32	2.37i, 2.36- 05
Bacha	Megersa	ETH	.87		Mar	2:08:55	

Name		Nat	Born	Ht/Wt	Event	2011 Mark	Pre-2011 Best
^ Baddeley	Andrew	GBR	20.6.82	186/70	1500	3:36.47	3:34.36- 08
					1M	3:54.29	3:49.38- 08
* Badji	Ndiss Kaba	SEN	21.9.83	192/79	LJ	8.09	8.32- 09
Bai Xuejin		CHN	6.6.87	176/63	50kW	3:59:21	3:54:41- 05
* Bailey	Daniel	ANT	9.9.86	178/77	100	9.97, 9.94w	9.91- 09
					200	20.51	20.81A- 04, 20.80w- 05
Bailey	Eric	USA	23.5.89	186/75	400h	50.04	50.17- 10
Bailey	Oshane	JAM	9.8.89	168/64	100	10.15, 10.11w	10.11- 10
Baillio	Hayden	USA	22.7.91	186/141	SP	19.51	19.08i, 18.78- 10
Baji	Balázs	HUN	9.6.89	192/84	110h	13.58	13.79- 10
Bakhar	Sergey	BLR	27.6.89	195/130	SP	19.49i, 19.25	19.30- 10
* Bakulin	Sergey	RUS	13.11.86	175/62	50kW	3:38:46	3:43:26- 10
Balla	Abdulrahman Musaab	QAT	19.3.89	175/75	800	1:45.92	1:46.19- 10
Balliengo	Jorge	ARG	5.1.78	194/110	DT	60.45	66.32- 06
Balner	Michal	CZE	12.9.82	193/78	PV	5.70i, 5.40	5.76i, 5.73- 10
Balnuweit	Erik	GER	21.9.88	189/75	110h	13.49	13.59- 09
Balumbu	Nkosinza	USA	16.3.87	175/64	TJ	16.50, 16.86w	16.59- 10, 16.72w- 09
* Baniótis	Konstadínos	GRE	6.11.86	202/80	HJ	2.32i, 2.28	2.29i, 2.28- 09
* Bannister	Jarrod	AUS	3.10.84	190/100	JT	82.25	89.02- 08
Baptiste	Leon	GBR	23.5.85	181/82	200	20.51	20.43- 10
Barmao	Samson	KEN	17.4.82		Mar	2:08:56	2:09:01- 08
* Barmasai	David	KEN	1.1.89	172/54	Mar	2:07:18	2:10:31A- 10
Barnes	Winston	JAM	7.11.88	178/73	100	10.17	10.16- 09
Barnett	Brian	CAN	10.2.87	185/84	200	20.54	20.31- 07
Barr	Thomas	IRL-J	24.7.92	183/73	400h	50.06	56.47- 10
* Barras	Romain	FRA	1.8.80	194/86	Dec	8134	8453- 10
Barrett	DeWayne	JAM	26.9.81	185/75	400	45.63	45.74- 08
Barrios	Juan Luis	MEX	24.6.83	175/63	3000	7:42.82	7:37.64- 06
5000	13:09.81		13:11.37- 07		10k	27:30.68	27:40.10- 09
Barroilhet	Gonzalo	CHI	19.8.86	196/96	Dec	7986A, 7845	7907- 08
Barron	Trevor	USA-J	30.9.92	190/73	20kW	1:23:26	1:23:49.39t- 10
Barrondo	Erick	GUA	14.6.91	172/60	20kW	1:20:58	-0-
de Barros	Bruno	BRA	7.1.87	178/70	200	20.16	20.47- 08
* Barry	Trevor	BAH	14.6.83	190/77	HJ	2.32	2.29- 10
* Barshim	Mutaz Essa	QAT	24.6.91	192/70	HJ	2.35	2.31- 10
* Bartels	Ralf	GER	21.2.78	186/138	SP	21.16i, 20.58	21.44i- 10, 21.37- 09
* Bartholomew	Rondell	GRN	7.4.90	192/79	200	20.48w	20.95- 10
					400	44.65	45.28- 10
Barus	Benson	KEN	4.7.80	167/54	Mar	2:07:07	2:08:34- 06
Barusei	Geoffrey	KEN-Y	.94	164/53	1500	3:35.54	
Bascou	Dimitri	FRA	20.7.87	182/81	110h	13.37, 13.26w	13.41- 10
Batchelor	Tarik	JAM	22.3.90	188/82	LJ	8.07i, 8.05, 8.29w	8.09i- 10, 7.86- 09
Bátovsky	Milos	SVK	26.5.79	178/65	50kW	3:56:46	3:54:08- 04
Batty	Miles	USA	1.6.87	183/68	1500	3:36.25	3:42.42- 10
Bauer	Candy	GER	31.7.86	190/110	SP	19.98	19.46- 10
Bauhs	Scott	USA	11.5.86	176/62	10k	27:51.78	27:48.06- 08
* Bayer	Sebastian	GER	11.6.86	189/79	LJ	8.17	8.71i, 8.49- 09
Bazán	Mario	PER	1.9.87	172/64	3kSt	8:29.18	8:28.67- 09
Beach	Curtis	USA	22.7.90	183/76	Dec	8083	7466- 09
Becerra	Kael	CHI	4.11.85	183/84	100	10.26A, 10.20Aw	10.31- 06
Bednyuk	Anatoliy	RUS	30.1.89		PV	5.50i	5.40i, 5.30- 09
* Behrenbruch	Pascal	GER	19.1.85	196/96	Dec	8232	8439- 09
Bekele	Azmeraw	ETH	22.1.86		HMar	59:39	60:57- 10
* Bekele	Kenenisa	ETH	13.6.82	160/54	10k	26:43.16	26:17.53- 05
* Bekele	Tariku	ETH	21.1.87	168/52	3000	7:33.50	7:28.70- 10
2M	8:15.40		8:04:83- 07		5000	12:59.25	12:52.45- 08
Bekric	Emir	SRB	14.3.91	196/87	400h	49.55	50.67- 10
Belabbas	Mohamed-Khaled	FRA	4.7.81	178/65	3kSt	8:17.87	8:17.37- 08
Belharbazi	Otmane	FRA	3.11.88	174/57	1500	3:36.09	3:39.68- 09
Bellani	Hicham	MAR	15.9.79	180/64	10k	27:58.17	29:33.51- 09
Bellido	José Emilio	ESP	25.5.87	180/68	TJ	16.55	16.18- 07
Benák	Martin	SVK	27.5.88	193/98	JT	79.41	79.90- 10
Bencosme de Leon	José	ITA-J	16.5.92	187/73	400h	49.94	51.04- 10
Benedetti	Giordano	ITA	22.5.89	189/67	800	1:46.32	1:47.18- 10
Bennett	LaRon	USA	25.11.82	183/75	400h	50.00	48.74- 05
Bensghir	Mohamed	MAR	16.11.91	171/60	1500	3:36.60	3:35.76- 10
Bensghir	Yassine	MAR	3.1.83	170/68	1500	3:36.25	3:33.04- 07
Benyahia	Amor	TUN	1.7.85		3kSt	8:30.02	8:37.08- 10
Berdeja	Cristian D.	MEX	21.6.81	169/58	50kW	3:59:14A	3:56:26A- 10
Berger	Dominic	USA	19.5.86	181/79	110h	13.32	13.49- 06
Bergius	Jere	FIN	4.4.87	182/72	PV	5.60	5.50- 10

Name		Nat	Born	Ht/Wt	Event	2011 Mark	Pre-2011 Best
Bermejo	Javier	ESP	23.12.78	190/77	HJ	2.24	2.28- 04
Bernard	Martyn	GBR	15.12.84	196/83	HJ	2.28	2.30i- 07, 2.30- 08
* Berrabah	Yahya	MAR	13.10.81	186/75	LJ	8.37, 8.40w	8.40- 09
Berry	Michael	USA	10.12.91	184/73	400	44.91	46.13- 10
* Betanzos	Yoandris	CUB	15.2.82	179/71	TJ	17.23A,17.18	17.69i- 10,17.65- 09,17.67w- 06
Bethke	Brandon	USA	19.1.87	180/68	5000	13:25.82	13:27.79- 09
Bett	David	KEN-J	18.10.92	169/54	2M	8:18.72	
					5000	13:13.66	13:06.06- 10
Bett	Emmanuel	KEN	29.3.85	165/52	10k	26:51.95	-0-
* Bett	Josphat	KEN	12.6.90	173/60	5000	13:11.29	12:57.43- 09
					10k	26:48.99	27:30.85- 08
Bett	Reuben	KEN	6.11.84	180/70	800	1:45.49	1:44.79- 09
Bettinelli	Andrea	ITA	6.10.78	194/82	HJ	2.25	2.31- 03
Beugnet	Grégory	FRA	14.9.87	173/64	1500	3:36.71	3:39.73- 10
Bian Fongda		CHN	1.4.91		20kW	1:22:42	1:24:45- 10
Bigot	Quentin	FRA-J	1.12.92	179/95	HT	72.71	62.86- 10
^ Bingham	Michael	GBR	13.4.86	183/75	400	45.42	44.74- 09
Birech	Joseph Kiptoo	KEN	4.1.84		HMar	60:40	60:13- 09
Birgen	Bethwel	KEN	6.8.88	178/64	1500	3:34.59	3:35.60- 10
					2000	4:59.03i	
Birmingham	Collis	AUS	27.12.84	189/71	1500	3:36.87	3:35.50- 10
3000	7:42.11		7:38.77- 10		2M	8:17.91	
					5000	13:15.70	13:10.97- 10
Bispo	Rogério	BRA	16.11.85	180/75	LJ	8.04	8.21, 8.32Aw- 06
Biwott	Paul	KEN	18.4.78	167/52	Mar	2:06:54	2:07:02- 09
Biwott	Stanley	KEN	21.4.86		HMar	60:23	61:20- 07
					Mar	2:07:03	2:09:41- 10
Biwott	Yusuf	KEN	12.11.86	175/64	2000	4:58.20	4:59.48i- 07, 5:01.1+- 06
3000	7:36.84		7:31.68- 10		5000	13:11.19	12:58.49- 07
* Blake	Yohan	JAM	26.12.89	181/79	100	9.82, 9.80w	9.89- 10
					200	19.26	19.78- 10
Blankenship	Ben	USA	15.12.88	180/66	1500	3:37.23	3:39.77- 10
					1M	3:54.10	3:57.87i- 10
Bledman	Keston	TRI	8.3.88	183/75	100	9.93	10.01, 9.93w- 10, 10.0- 09
Blincoe	Adrian	NZL	4.11.79	181/61	5000	13:18.27	13:10.19- 08
Blommerde	Bjorn	NED	6.7.87	190/83	JT	78.17	78.22- 10
Bo Xiangdong		CHN	1.10.87	180/66	20kW	1:23:26	1:21:47- 09
Boase	Jordan	USA	10.10.85	181/75	200	20.52	20.37- 08
					400	45.34	44.82- 08
Bochenek	Dominik	POL	14.5.87	182/70	110h	13.44	13.56, 13.3w- 10
Boey	Zye	USA	8.5.89	178/82	100	10.15w	10.20- 09
Bogatyrev	Pyotr	RUS	11.3.91		20kW	1:20:18	-0-
* Bolt	Usain	JAM	21.8.86	196/88	100	9.76	9.58- 09
					200	19.40	19.19- 09
Bondarenko	Bogdan	UKR	30.8.89	195/72	HJ	2.30	2.27- 09
Bonfim	Caio	BRA	19.3.91	170/58	20kW	1:20:58.5t	1:27:21.3t- 10
Bookout	Kevin	USA	12.2.83	203/118	SP	20.13	19.91- 10
* Borchin	Valeriy	RUS	11.9.86	178/63	20kW	1:18:55	1:17:38- 09
* Borges	Lázaro	CUB	19.6.86	173/70	PV	5.90	5.70- 08
* Borlée	Jonathan	BEL	22.2.88	180/70	200	20.42	20.61- 10
					400	44.78	44.71- 10
* Borlée	Kévin	BEL	22.2.88	180/71	400	44.74	44.88- 08
Borodkin	Andriy	UKR	18.4.78	202/135	SP	20.34	20.38- 04
Bortoluzzi	Jérôme	FRA	20.5.82	180/111	HT	73.63	77.33- 08
Boruschewski	Benjamin	GER	23.4.80	190/130	HT	71.73	76.19- 09
* Borzakovskiy	Yuriy	RUS	12.4.81	182/72	800	1:43.99	1:42.47- 01
Bossé	Pierre-Ambroise	FRA-J	11.5.92	185/68	800	1:46.18	1:48.38- 10
^ Boukensa	Tarek	ALG	19.11.81	178/62	1500	3:34.7	3:30.92- 07
* Bouraada	Larbi	ALG	10.5.88	184/82	Dec	8302	8171- 09
* Bouramdane	Abderrahim	MAR	1.1.78	167/55	Mar	2:08:42	2:07:33- 10
Bowman	John	USA	29.8.86	186/107	DT	64.47	60.18- 10
Boyce	Brendan	IRL	15.10.86	183/76	50kW	3:57:58	4:08:07- 10
Boyd	Marcus	USA	3.3.89	185/75	200	20.47w	21.24- 07
					400	45.42	45.53- 08
Bracy	Marvin	USA-J	15.12.93	178/74	100	10.28, 10.05w	10.42, 10.19w- 10
Brahimi	Mahfoud	ALG	24.2.85	178/64	800	1:45.84	1:48.90- 08
Brannen	Nathan	CAN	8.9.82	175/59	1500	3:35.80	3:34.65- 08
* Brathwaite	Ryan	BAH	6.6.88	186/75	110h	13.54	13.14, 13.05w- 09
Brathwaite	Shane	BAH	8.2.90	185/75	110h	13.58	13.71A, 13.80w- 10, 13.83- 09
Braun	Aaron	USA	28.5.87	183/65	10k	27:57.88	
* Brenes	Nery	CRC	25.9.85	174/62	400	44.65A, 45.29	44.84- 10

Name		Nat	Born	Ht/Wt	Event	2011 Mark	Pre-2011 Best
Brigg	Kane	AUS	14.1.88	185/78	TJ	16.97	16.59- 10
Brock	Keenan	USA-J	1.6.92	172/64	100	10.21, 10.12w	10.37- 10
Brookins	Ronald	USA	5.7.89	185/75	110h	13.42	13.61- 10
Brooks	Lance	USA	1.1.84	198/109	DT	64.38	64.79A- 10
Broothaerts ¶	Damien	BEL	12.11.84	179/75	110h	13.67, 13.53w	13.62- 09
Brown	Bryce	USA	17.9.88	180/79	400h	49.04	49.31- 10
* Brown	Chris	BAH	15.10.78	178/68	400	44.79	44.40- 08
Brown	Darrel	TRI	11.10.84	179/85	100	10.13, 10.04w	9.99- 05, 9.88w- 07
Brown	Fredrick	USA	.89	183/79	TJ	16.67w	15.36- 10
* Brown	Joel	USA	31.1.80	180/73	110h	13.20	13.22- 05, 13.18w- 09, 13.1w- 10
Brown	Russell	USA	6.3.85	188/77	800	1:45.83	1:47.96- 07
1500	3:35.70		3:36.89- 10		1M	3:51.45	3:55.79i- 10, 3:56.63- 09
Brown	Willie	USA	20.12.90	186/75	800	1:45.91	1:50.30- 10
Bruce	Benjamin	USA	10.9.82	185/68	3kSt	8:19.10	8:22.88- 10
Bruce	Kemour	JAM	6.9.86	173/66	100	10.15w	10.22- 09
Bruns	Ansis	LAT	30.3.89	182/93	JT	80.40	79.35- 10
Brunson	Andrew	USA	4.4.86	182/75	110h	13.64	13.33- 08
Bryant	Ashley	GBR	17.5.91	178/75	Dec	7789	7194- 10
Bryant	Giorgio	USA	4.7.89	188/77	LJ	7.96w	7.38- 09, 7.56w- 10
Bryant	Noah	USA	11.5.84	185/120	SP	20.80	20.69- 10
Brzozowski	Artur	POL	29.3.85	172/65	50kW	3:53:51	3:50:07- 10
Brzozowski	Krzysztof	POL-J	15.7.93	190/110	SP	19.18	18.07- 10
Bube	Andreas	DEN	13.7.87	180/64	800	1:45.04	1:48.48- 09
Buc	Bostjan	SLO	13.4.80	178/60	3kSt	8:29.75	8:16.96- 03
Bucki	Gaëtan	FRA	9.5.80	195/135	SP	20.39i, 19.87	20.01i- 07, 19.86- 06
Buckley	Markino	JAM	16.4.86	190/80	400h	50.05	48.50- 08
Budza	Sergiy	UKR	6.12.84	180/72	50kW	4:00:02	3:53:33- 09
Buhari	Abdul	GBR	26.6.82	195/130	DT	65.44	61.30- 08
Bühler	Matthias	GER	2.9.86	189/74	110h	13.64	13.36- 09, 13.2w- 10
Bulanov	Aleksandr	RUS	26.12.89		SP	19.47	19.07- 09
Bultheel	Michael	BEL	30.6.86	189/81	400h	49.71	49.38- 10
Bumbalough	Andrew	USA	14.3.87	173/64	1500	3:37.15	3:38.23- 09
					5000	13:16.77	13:30.77- 09
Burlachenko	Pavel	RUS	7.4.76	184/80	PV	5.50i, 5.46	5.86A- 01, 5.81- 98
^ Burns	Marc	TRI	7.1.83	183/84	100	10.09	9.96- 05
Burya	Artem	RUS	11.4.86	183/77	PV	5.50i, 5.40	5.50- 08
Butler	LaShawn	USA	3.2.87	178/77	200	20.54, 20.52w	20.80- 10
Bychkov	Igor	ESP	7.3.87	188/77	PV	5.60	5.50- 10
Byram	Brandon	USA	11.9.88	188/82	200	20.57, 20.41w	20.31- 10
Byun Young-joon		KOR	20.3.84		50kW	3:53:49	3:56:40- 10
Cabral	Donn	USA	12.12.89	175/60	3kSt	8:32.14	8:35.60- 10
^ Cáceres	Eusebio	ESP	10.9.91	176/69	LJ	8.23	8.27- 10
Cadée	Erik	NED	15.2.84	200/110	DT	66.95	66.20- 10
Cafagna	Diego	ITA	9.7.75	173/57	50kW	4:01:29	3:53:46- 08
Cai Zelin		CHN	11.4.91	170/57	20kW	1:21:07	1:22:28- 10
Cain	Stephen	AUS	23.7.84	180/75	Dec	7734	7547- 10
Callander	Emmanuel	TRI	10.5.84	182/73	100	10.12	10.05- 09
Camara	Alyn	GER	31.3.89	195/82	LJ	8.08	7.75- 10
Camara	Moussa	MLI	12.2.88	181/70	800	1:46.38	1:51.25- 09
Campbell	Clement	JAM	19.2.75	184/82	200	20.59	20.29- 07
Campbell	James	GBR	1.4.88	185/91	JT	80.18	80.38- 10
Campion	Kevin	FRA	23.5.88	183/63	20kW	1:22:48	1:24:01- 10
Cano	Juan Manuel	ARG	12.12.87	168/57	20kW	1:23.09.0t	1:24:13t- 08
* Cantwell	Christian	USA	30.9.80	193/145	SP	22.07	22.54- 04
Cao Shuo		CHN	8.10.91	183/70	TJ	16.86	17.13- 09
Capetillo	Dayron	CUB	11.9.87	185/77	110h	13.74, 13.61w	13.48, 13.39w- 09, 13.2- 08
Caporaso	Teodorico	ITA	14.9.87	166/60	50kW	4:01:00	4:07:34- 10
Carriqueo	Javier	ARG	29.5.79	175/60	5000	13:25.17	13:35.30- 09
Carter	Chris	USA	11.3.89	186/80	TJ	16.86	16.34- 09
* Carter	Nesta	JAM	10.11.85	178/70	100	9.89	9.78- 10
					200	20.25	20.31- 08
Carter	Randal	USA	7.4.89	183/84	HJ	2.24	2.23- 07
* Carter	Xavier	USA	8.12.85	190/86	200	20.53, 20.51w	19.63- 06
Carvalho	Florian	FRA	9.3.89	183/70	1500	3:33.60	3:38.53- 10
* Casañas	Frank	ESP	18.10.78	187/115	DT	67.18	67.91- 08
Castelo Branco	Thiago	BRA	6.11.79	183/80	110h	13.66	13.64- 07
Castillo	Mauris Surel	CUB	19.10.84	182/60	800	1:45.11	1:47.04- 05
Castillo ¶	Víctor	VEN	8.6.81	180/74	LJ	8.03, 8.05Adq	8.34A- 04, 7.98, 8.10w- 03
Cato	Roxroy	JAM	1.5.88	175/66	400h	49.66	49.45- 10
Cavalcanti	Diego Henrique	BRA	18.3.91	175/68	200	20.57	20.77- 09
Celik	Recep	TUR	10.8.83	175/65	20kW	1:22:31	1:22:36- 06

Name		Nat	Born	Ht/Wt	Event	2011 Mark	Pre-2011 Best
* Centrowitz	Matt	USA	18.10.89	173/61	1500	3:34.46	3:36.92- 09
Cerra	Juan Ignacio	ARG	16.10.76	180/95	HT	72.12	76.42- 01
Chafausipo	Clive	ZIM	2.6.88	178/75	LJ	7.83, 8.09w	7.61- 10
* Chambers	Dwain	GBR	5.4.78	180/83	100	10.01	9.97- 99, 9.87dq- 02
Chanchima	Jairus	KEN	5.12.84		HMar	61:19	59:43- 09
Chang Ming-Huang		TPE	7.8.82	194/130	SP	20.58	20.37- 10
* Charfreitag	Libor	SVK	11.9.77	191/117	HT	77.69	81.81- 03
Chavkin	Nikolay	RUS	22.4.84	183/70	3kSt	8:26.03	
* Chebet	Wilson	KEN	12.7.85	174/59	Mar	2:05:27	2:06:12- 10
* Chebii	Abraham	KEN	23.12.79	172/63	HMar	60:07	63:35A- 10
Chebii	Daniel	KEN	.85		HMar	60:56	61:55- 10
Chebogut	Stephen	KEN	84		Mar	2:08:02	2:09:38- 10
Cheboi	Collins	KEN	25.9.87	175/64	1500	3:32.45	3:34.17- 10
Chebor	William	KEN	22.12.82		HMar	61:10	60:49- 10
					Mar	2:08:21	2:10:15dh- 10
Chege	Michael	KEN	.83		Mar	2:09:12	
Chelanga	Samuel	KEN	23.2.85	168/57	10k	28:12.18	27:08.39- 10
* Chelimo	Elijah	KEN	10.3.84	175/57	3kSt	8:14.22	8:10.63- 09
Chelimo	Kevin	KEN	14.2.83	170/59	10k	27:30.50	28:21.29- 07
Chemisto	John Kiprotich	KEN	5.6.83		HMar	60:10	59:23- 09
					Mar	2:07:08	2:15:51- 09
Chemlany	Stephen	KEN	9.8.82		Mar	2:07:55	2:13:10- 10
Chemut	Anthony	KEN-J	17.12.92	176/62	800	1:45.74	1:47.58- 10
Chen Chieh		TPE-J	8.5.92	174/55	400h	50.14	50.94- 09
Chen Ding		CHN-J	5.8.92		20kW	1:18:52	1:20:16- 08
Chen Qi		CHN	10.3.82	189/92	JT	80.76	81.38- 04
Chen Xinrong		CHN	17.6.90		20kW	1:23:35	1:25:48- 10
Cheng Wen		CHN-J	18.3.92	187/77	400h	49.28	49.89- 10
* Chepkok	Vincent	KEN	5.7.88	174/60	3000	7:30.15	7:31.41- 10
					5000	12:55.29	12:51.45- 10
* Chepseba	Nixon	KEN	12.12.90	184/73	1500	3:30.94	3:32.42- 10
1M	3:53.36				3000	7:37.64i	
* Cherkos	Abreham	ETH	23.9.89	160/52	Mar	2:06:13dh	2:07:29- 10
Cherop	Ezekiel	KEN	.85		HMar	61:08	
Cherry	D'Angelo	USA	1.8.90	163/64	100	10.23, 10.15w	10.04, 10.02w- 09
Cheru	Tesfaye	ETH-J	2.3.93	171/55	1500	3:35.71	
					2000	4:56.25	
^ Cheruiyot	Evans	KEN	5.10.82	168/52	Mar	2:08:17	2:06:25- 08
Cheruiyot	John	KEN	5.7.90	167/55	10k	27:22.09	27:29.82- 10
* Cheruiyot	Robert Kiprono	KEN	10.8.88	175/60	Mar	2:06:29	2:05:52- 10
Chesani	Silvano	ITA	17.7.88	190/75	HJ	2.28	2.25- 10
Chesari Korir	Jacob	KEN	6.4.84	178/64	5000	13:01.03	12:59.72- 10
Chiaraviglio	Germán	ARG	16.4.87	192/77	PV	5.51	5.71- 06
Chicherov	Vladimir	RUS	2.4.85	188/79	TJ	16.68w, 16.25	16.73- 07
Chimsa	Deressa	ETH	21.11.76	175/60	Mar	2:07:39dh, 2:09:08	2:07:54- 09
Chinin	Carlos Eduardo	BRA	3.5.85	1995/82	Dec	8068	7977- 07
Chirchir	Abraham	KEN	1.8.80	173/59	3kSt	8:22.34A	8:19.81- 08
Chirchir	Henry	KEN	14.5.85		10k	28:11.0A	28:36.02A- 10
					HMar	61:25	63:12- 10
^ Chistyakov	Viktor	RUS	9.2.75	202/92	PV	5.55i, 5.55	5.90, 5.95ex- 99
Chocho	Andrés	ECU	4.11.83	167/57	20kW	1:20:23.8t	1:22:05- 08
					50kW	3:49:32	3:54:42- 10
* Choge	Augustine	KEN	21.1.87	162/53	1500	3:31.14	3:29.47- 09
1M	3:51.50		3:50.14- 10		3000	7:28.76, 7:28.00i	7:28.78- 05
					5000	13:21.24	12:53.66- 05
Christensen	Kim	DEN	1.4.84	187/115	SP	20.39i, 20.06	19.65- 09
Christian	Brendan	ANT	11.12.83	178/70	100	10.32, 10.06w 10.09-09, 10.01w- 07, 9.9- 02	
					200	20.60 20.12- 08, 20.1- 02, 19.98w- 09	
* Chu Yafei		CHN	5.9.88	172/55	20kW	1:18:38	1:18:44- 06
Chumba	Dickson	KEN	27.10.86	167/50	Mar	2:07:23	2:09:20- 10
Chumba	Linus	KEN	9.2.80	171/57	3kSt	8:24.10	8:11.98- 05
Chuva	Marcos	POR	8.8.89	183/73	LJ	8.34	7.96, 8.16w- 10
Cianci	Mathias	FRA	25.10.82	196/73	HJ	2.26	2.24- 09
Cienfuegos	Javier	ESP	15.7.90	188/120	HT	75.31	74.77- 09
Ciotti	Nicola	ITA	5.10.76	188/78	HJ	2.28i, 2.24	2.30i- 02, 2.30- 03
Cisneros	Omar	CUB	19.11.89	186/80	400	45.77	45.76- 09, 45.7- 08, 44.8dt- 07
					400h	47.99A, 49.26	48.21- 10
Clarke	Chris	GBR	25.1.90	176/70	400	45.61	45.59- 09
Clarke	Jordan	USA	10.7.90	193/125	SP	19.75	19.49- 09
Clarke	Lawrence	GBR	12.3.90	186/75	110h	13.58	13.69, 13.51w- 10
* Clarke	Lerone	JAM	2.10.81	174/66	100	10.01A, 10.05, 9.90w	9.99- 09, 9.98w- 10

Name		Nat	Born	Ht/Wt	Event	2011 Mark	Pre-2011 Best
* Clavier	Jérôme	FRA	3.5.83	185/73	PV	5.81i, 5.63	5.80i, 5.75- 08
Clay	Major	USA	24.12.88	181/76	HJ	2.25i, 2.22	2.21- 10
* Claye	Will	USA	13.6.91	180/68	LJ	8.29	7.89, 8.00w- 10
					TJ	17.50, 17.62w	17.19, 17.24w- 09
Clémenceau	Adrien	FRA	25.5.88	186/76	400h	49.72	50.67- 10
Clemens	Daniel	GER-J	28.4.92	181/74	PV	5.50	5.43- 09
* Clement	Kerron	USA	31.10.85	188/84	400	45.42	44.48- 07
					400h	48.74	47.24- 05
Cleve	Moritz	GER	18.2.87	193/75	Dec	7838	8004- 09
Clickett	Justin	USA	12.4.85	191/118	SP	19.26	19.23i- 05, 19.23- 10
Coco-Viloin	Samuel	FRA	19.10.87	186/76	110h	13.60	13.46- 08
Coertzen	Willem	RSA	30.12.82	187/82	Dec	8095	8146- 09
Cole	Brendan	AUS	29.5.81	187/81	400h	49.60	49.35- 09
Collazo	Williams	CUB	31.8.86	174/72	400	44.95	44.93- 09
* Collins	Kim	SKN	5.4.76	175/64	100	10.00A, 10.01	9.98- 02, 9.92w- 03
					200	20.52	20.20, 20.08w- 01
Collio	Simone	ITA	27.12.79	180/74	100	10.30, 10.16w	10.06- 09
Colwick	Jason	USA	25.1.88	182/77	PV	5.51i	5.72- 09
Como	Josh	USA	25.5.88	183/75	TJ	16.66	16.64- 10
* Compaoré	Benjamin	FRA	5.8.87	188/83	TJ	17.31	17.21, 17.28w- 10
Cong Fudong		CHN-J	28.5.92		20kW	1:22:05	1:24:47- 10
Connaughton	Jared	CAN	20.7.85	175/77	100	10.21, 10.04w	10.15- 08
					200	20.45, 20.34w	20.34- 08
Conwell	Will	USA	12.9.82	196/111	DT	61.12	63.61- 07
Cooper	Kandrick	USA	28.3.86	178/75	110h	13.76, 13.54w	13.82- 09
Coover	Jeff	USA	1.12.87	185/77	PV	5.50	5.50i- 10, 5.45- 09
Copeland	Leslie	FIJ	23.4.88	183/93	JT	80.45	76.95- 10
* Copello	Alexis	CUB	12.8.85	185/80	TJ	17.68A, 17.47	17.65, 17.69w- 09
Copello	Yasmany	CUB	15.4.87	196/86	400h	49.76	49.56- 09
Correa	Harold	FRA	26.6.88	190/78	TJ	16.54i, 16.40	16.43- 10
Cotto	Héctor	PUR	8.8.84	190/81	110h	13.49A, 13.54, 13.45w	13.54- 10
Couto	Kurt	MOZ	14.5.85	180/67	400h	49.43	49.12- 07
Cowart	Donnie	USA	24.10.85	168/57	3kSt	8:26.38	8:41.02- 10
Craddock	Kevin	USA	25.6.87	193/84	110h	13.49	13.46, 13.41w- 08
Craddock	Omar	USA	26.4.91	178/79	TJ	16.57i, 16.46	16.56- 10
^ Cragg	Alistair	IRL	13.6.80	183/59	3000	7:46.29	7:32.49- 07
5000	13:03.53		13:07.10- 07		HMar	60:49	61:58- 10
Crawford	Shane	USA	4.6.88	183/79	100	10.18	10.62- 10
* Crawford	Shawn	USA	14.1.78	181/86	200	20.45, 20.24w	19.79- 04, 19.73w- 09
Crespi	Merihun	ITA	15.12.88	172/60	1500	3:37.67	3:47.41- 08
Crous	Bernard	RSA	13.4.89	182/80	JT	77.80	71.41- 10
Crouser	Ryan	USA-J	18.12.92	201/109	SP	19.48i	
Crowther	Robert	AUS	2.8.87	188/77	LJ	8.12	8.02, 8.15w- 07
Cuesta	Pedro José	ESP	22.8.83	187/108	DT	61.95	60.37- 09
Cuevas	Winder	DOM	1.8.88	178/73	400h	49.20A, 50.81	49.71- 10
Cuharenco	Alexandr	MDA	7.3.87	183/77	LJ	7.97i	7.83- 10
Cui Zhide		CHN	11.1.83	182/73	20kW	1:21:52	1:17:53- 05
					50kW	3:48:19	3:44:20- 05
* Culson	Javier	PUR	25.7.84	198/79	400h	48.32	47.72- 10
Curry	Rafeeq	USA	19.8.83	183/68	TJ	16.88Ai, 16.48	17.22- 08
Curtis	Bobby	USA	28.11.84	182/68	10k	27:24.67	27:33.38- 10
Cutts	Luke	GBR	13.2.88	190/82	PV	5.60i	5.62i, 5.60- 09
^ Czajkowski	Przemyslaw	POL	26.10.88	197/108	DT	64.21	64.42- 10
D'Hoedt	Jeroen	BEL	10.1.90	182/59	1500	3:36.07	3:41.44- 10
Daba	Bekana	ETH	29.7.88	170/55	Mar	2:07:04	2:14:40- 10
Dabo	Rasul	POR	14.2.89	183/73	110h	13.86. 13.60w	14.26, 14.21w- 10
Dacha	Abdellah	MAR-J	26.1.92		3kSt	8:35.45	8:34.48- 10
Dailey	Adam	USA	19.3.89	186/77	400h	50.11	50.33- 08
Dal Molin	Paolo	ITA	31.7.87	179/76	110h	13.67	13.78- 08
* Darien	Garfield	FRA	22.12.87	187/76	110h	13.37	13.34- 10
Dasaolu	James	GBR	5.9.87	180/75	100	10.11	10.09- 09, 10.06w- 10
Dauphin	Tumatai	FRA	12.1.88	188/138	SP	19.19	18.88- 10
Davaux	Hervé	FRA	22.8.78	166/55	50kW	4:02:08	3:57:10- 09
Davenport	Richard	GBR	12.9.85	180/78	400h	49.76	50.09- 10
Davide	Kléberson	BRA	20.7.85	175/67	800	1:44.21	1:44.65- 09
Davis	Chris	USA	1.3.86	172/64	100	10.21	10.57- 09, 10.26ui- 07
Davis	Geoffrey	USA	8.8.90	193/79	HJ	2.24	2.22i, 2.20- 10
^ Davis	Walter	USA	2.7.79	188/83	TJ	17.02	17.73i, 17.71- 06
Davis II	Wayne	USA	22.8.91	178/72	110h	13.54	14.36- 09
de Beer	Willie	RSA	14.3.88	187/79	400	45.68A, 45.87	46.31- 07
De Luca	Marco	ITA	12.5.81	189/72	50kW	3:49:40	3:46:31- 09

Name		Nat	Born	Ht/Wt	Event	2011 Mark	Pre-2011 Best
* de Zordo	Matthias	GER	21.2.88	190/97	JT	88.36	87.81- 10
Deák Nagy	Marcell	HUN-J	28.1.92	188/79	400	45.42	46.03- 10
* Deakes	Nathan	AUS	17.8.77	183/66	50kW	3:48:02	3:35:47- 06
DeChant	Matt	USA	27.3.89	195/115	SP	19.82i	18.62- 08
Dechasa	Shumi	ETH	28,5,89		HMar	60:03	61:38- 10
Dechase	Chala	ETH	13.6.84	167/52	Mar	2:08:47	2:06:33- 10
Deksisa	Solomon	ETH-Y	11.3.94	170/55	3000	7:42.10	-0-
Delmestre	Thomas	FRA	31.3.91	188/80	110h	13.62	14.03- 10
* Demps	Jeffrey	USA	8.1.90	175/77	100	10.04, 9.96w	10.01- 08, 9.96w- 10
Demyanov	Andrey	RUS	22.8.86		Dec	7770	7544- 10
* Demyanyuk	Dmytro	UKR	30.6.83	195/75	HJ	2.35	2.32- 07
Denecker	Emile	FRA-J	28.3.92	197/82	PV	5.63	5.05- 10
Derevyagin	Aleksandr	RUS	24.3.79	178/80	400h	49.07	49.00- 08
* Desisa	Lelisa	ETH	14.1.90		HMar	59:30	59:39- 10
Dessi	Lorenzo	ITA	4.5.89		50kW	3:57:32	4:04:46- 10
Desta	Alemu	ETH-J	18.2.92	173/54	5000	13:24.23	13:16.60- 10
Desta	Alemu	ETH-J	18.2.92	173/54	10k	27:51.17	
Detmer	Joe	USA	3.9.83	180/73	Dec	7846(w)	8090- 10
Detsuk	Dmitriy	BLR	9.4.85	196/78	TJ	17.02	16.96i, 16.91- 09
Devonish	Marlon	GBR	1.6.76	183/76	100	10.14	10.06- 07
					200	20.60	20.19, 20.18w- 02
Dhouibi	Hamdhi	TUN	24.1.82	190/85	Dec	7731	8023- 05
Diarra	Abdoulaye	FRA	27.5.88	184/82	HJ	2.24	2.27i- 09, 2.24- 10
Dias Sabino	Jefferson	BRA	4.11.82	192/94	TJ	17.07	17.28- 08
Díaz	José Ignacio	ESP	22.11.79	173/63	50kW	3:53:55	3:51:09- 05
* Díaz	Junior	CUB	28.4.87	193/80	Dec	8053	8357- 09
Díaz	Maximiliano	ARG	15.11.88	186/88	TJ	16.51, 16.77w	16.43- 09
Díaz	Stéphane	FRA	24.12.78	179/68	PV	5.45	5.45- 07
DiBuono ¶	Matt	USA	14.12.86	178/105	HT	76.60	72.40- 10
* Didenkow	Mateusz	POL	22.4.87	187/76	PV	5.75	5.70- 10
Difallah	Mohamed Fathallah	EGY	26.8.87		LJ	8.19	8.12- 10
Dilla	Karsten	GER	17.7.89	188/74	PV	5.72	5.60i, 5.55- 10
Dilling	Jim	USA	23.4.85	198/86	HJ	2.28	2.30- 07
* Diniz	Yohann	FRA	1.1.78	185/69	50kW	3:35:27.2	3:38:45- 09
Distelberger	Dominik	AUT	16.3.90	186/79	Dec	7840	7713- 10
Dittmar	Andy	GER	5.7.74	196/120	SP	19.48	20.55- 06
* Dix	Walter	USA	31.1.86	178/84	100	9.94	9.88- 10, 9.80w- 08
					200	19.53	19.69- 07
Dixon	Leroy	USA	20.6.83	177/72	100	10.17	10.02, 9.99w- 08
					200	20.71, 20.60w	20.44- 06, 20.26w- 10
* Djhone	Leslie	FRA	18.3.81	187/76	400	45.54i	44.46- 07
* Dmitrik	Aleksey	RUS	12.4.84	191/69	HJ	2.36	2.34i- 05, 2.33- 09
Dmytrenko	Ruslan	UKR	22.3.86	180/62	20kW	1:21:31	1:21:21- 09
do Nascimento	Joabson	BRA	20.1.88		LJ	7.96w	7.76, 7.91w- 09
Dobrovodsky	Jaroslav	SVK	13.12.84	181/70	LJ	7.81, 7.99w	8.02- 10
					TJ	16.55i	16.46- 09
Docavo	Vicente	ESP-J	13.2.92	181/69	TJ	16.61i	15.99- 10
Dodson	Jeremy	USA	30.8.87	184/75	100	10.27A, 10.03Aw	10.35, 10.15Aw- 10
					200	20.33, 20.07w 20.37A- 07,	20.63, 20.40w- 10
Doi	Hiroaki	JPN	2.12.78	180/125	HT	70.69	74.08- 07
Domingos	Wágner	BRA	23.6.83	183/126	HT	71.60	71.84- 10
* Donato	Fabrizio	ITA	14.8.76	189/82	LJ	8.03i	8.02i- 07, 8.00- 06
					TJ	17.73i, 17.17	17.60- 00
Dong Bin		CHN	22.11.88	179/67	TJ	17.01i, 16.86, 17.05w	16.89i- 09, 16.86- 10
Donisan	Mihai	ROU	24.7.88	193/74	HJ	2.30	2.25- 10
Doran	Lee	GBR	5.3.85	178/85	JT	78.63	75.12- 10
^ dos Santos	Marílson	BRA	6.8.77	174/58	10k	28:09.24	27:28.12- 07
HMar	61:13		59:33- 07		Mar	2:06:34	2:08:37- 07
^ Dossévi	Damiel	FRA	3.2.83	182/82	PV	5.61i, 5.60	5.75- 05
^ Doucouré	Ladji	FRA	28.3.83	183/75	110h	13.52	12.97- 05
Douglas	Omar	JAM	30.10.83		100	10.14w	10.43- 10
Douvalídis	Konstadínos	GRE	10.3.87	184/78	110h	13.51	13.46- 08
Drakeford	Antoine	USA	15.5.87	182/73	400	45.78	45.83- 09
Draudvila	Darius	LTU	29.3.83	188/87	Dec	7734	8032- 10
Dreyer	Hannes	RSA	13.1.85	178/75	100	10.27, 10.17Aw	10.0A- 06, 10.33A- 10
Driouch	Hamza	QAT-Y	16.11.94	180/67	800	1:46.39	1:46.85- 10
1000	2:17.44		2:19.56- 10		1500	3:34.43	3:42.25- 10
Drouin	Derek	CAN	6.3.90	193/82	HJ	2.33i, 2.23	2.28i- 10, 2.27- 09
* Drozdov	Aleksey	RUS	3.12.83	184/80	Dec	8334	8475- 07
Dry	Mark	GBR	11.10.87	184/110	HT	72.49	71.88- 10
Drygol	Aleksandr	UKR	25.4.66	184/95	HT	75.48	77.96- 90

Name		Nat	Born	Ht/Wt	Event	2011 Mark	Pre-2011 Best
Dryomin	Aleksey	RUS	10.5.89	184/75	110h	13.51	13.77- 10
Du Yunpeng		CHN	6.9.88	186/70	20kW	1:23:04	1:23:54- 08
					50kW	3:55:32	3:51:37- 10
Dubitskiy	Oleg	BLR	14.10.90	184/100	HT	73.60	70.06- 10
Dubois	Ludovic	FRA	13.4.86	186/72	400h	50.03	50.34- 09
* Dudas	Mihail	SRB	1.11.89	183/82	Dec	8256	7966- 10
Dungey	Mychal	USA	13.10.88	178/75	400	45.64	44.73A, 45.19- 00
Durand	Yohan	FRA	14.5.85	174/58	3000	7:46.46	8:03.75- 10
* Dutch	Johnny	USA	20.1.89	180/82	110h	13.64	13.50, 13.30w- 10
					400h	48.47	47.63- 10
Dwyer	Rasheed	JAM	29.1.89	188/80	100	10.20w	10.29- 10, 10.21w- 09
					200	20.20	20.49- 10
Dyene	Genki	JPN	30.12.91	182/85	JT	79.20	78.57- 10
Dyldin	Maksim	RUS	19.5.87	185/78	400	45.82	45.42- 08
* Eaton	Ashton	USA	21.1.88	186/86	110h	13.35	13.54- 10
					Dec	8729	8457- 10
Eaton	Jarret	USA	24.6.89	183/82	110h	13.63	13.83- 10
Eaves	Max	GBR	31.5.88	183/82	PV	5.61i, 5.40	5.40- 10
Eberhardt	Stephan	GER	12.1.85	192/73	1500	3:36.90	3:33.92- 09
Echard	Melvin	USA	29.8.89	183/75	LJ	8.09w	7.93- 10
Ecker	Danny	GER	21.7.77	191/82	PV	5.52	6.00i- 01, 5.93- 98
* Edward	Alonso	PAN	8.12.89	183/73	200	20.28	19.81- 09
Edwards	Artis	USA	20.11.88	185/79	LJ	8.12w	7.46, 7.75w- 10
Edwards	Darwin	LCA	11.9.86	196/84	HJ	2.31	2.23A- 08, 2.22- 09
Edwards	Rae	USA	7.5.81	183/77	100	10.13, 10.10w	10.00- 10, 9.98w- 09
Ektov	Yevgeniy	KAZ	1.9.86	186/72	TJ	16.91	17.07- 08
El Abassi	El Hassan	MAR	15.7.79		HMar	61:13	
El Amine	Mouhcine	MAR	8.1.82	175/64	800	1:45.62	1:45.91- 10
El Idrissi	Ennaji	MAR	8.12.86		Mar	2:08:13	2:11:09- 10
El Kaam #	Fouad	MAR	27.5.88	177/62	1500	3:34.01	3:35.84- 09
El Manaoui	Amine	MAR	20.11.91	180/62	800	1:45.46	1:47.79- 08
El Qady	Najim	MAR	31.12.80	173/57	10k	27:53.50	28:56.66- 10
El-Ashry	Alaa El-Din M.	EGY	6.1.91		HT	71.00	70.34- 10
El-Gamal	Mostafa Hicham	EGY	1.10.88		HT	74.76	73.27- 10
* El-Ghazaly	Omar	EGY	9.2.84	200/130	DT	64.76	66.58- 07
* El-Sheryf	Sherif	UKR	2.1.89	176/64	LJ	7.99	7.82i- 08, 7.59- 10
					TJ	17.72	16.60i- 08, 16.42- 10
Ellerton	Andrew	CAN	18.11.83	181/68	800	1:45.04	1:46.07- 08
Ellington	James	GBR	6.9.85	180/75	100	10.23, 10.12w	10.23, 10.22w- 10
					200	20.52	20.95- 07, 20.86w 10
Emelianov ¶	Ivan	MDA	19.2.77	202/130	SP	20.64	20.26i- 00, 20.08- 03
Emelieze	Peter	NGR	19.4.88	167/68	100	10.18	10.18- 08
Engel	Roscoe	RSA	6.3.89	178/72	100	10.19	10.47- 08
Engelbrecht	Jaco	RSA	8.3.87	200/125	SP	19.42	17.71- 10
Ereng	Patrick	KEN	.87		3000	7:44.16	
Erickson	Chris	AUS	1.12.81	175/62	50kW	3:51:57	3:55:28- 08
Eriguchi	Masashi	JPN	17.12.88	170/58	100	10.14	10.07- 09
Erin	Frédéric	FRA	23.4.80	189/83	LJ	8.12	8.09- 04, 8.10w- 10
Erins	Edgars	LAT	18.6.86	181/84	Dec	8312	7961- 07
Ernest	Aaron	USA-J	8.11.93	183/75	100	10.17w	10.48- 10
Ernst	Sebastian	GER	11.10.84	183/72	200	20.51, 20.42i	20.36- 04
Eryildirim	Fatih	TUR	1.3.79	183/89	HT	75.49	75.90- 08
* España	Jesús	ESP	21.8.78	173/56	5000	13:04.73	13:10.73- 09
* Esser	Markus	GER	3.2.80	178/105	HT	79.69	81.10- 06
Estrada	Brandon	PUR	28.10.87	188/79	PV	5.52	5.50i, 5.40- 10
Etelätalo	Lassi	FIN	30.4.88	193/80	JT	84.41	79.70- 09
Eto	Takashi	JPN	5.2.91	182/67	HJ	2.24	2.19- 09
^ Evilä	Tommy	FIN	6.4.80	194/83	LJ	8.08	8.22- 08, 8.41w- 07
* Évora	Nelson	POR	20.4.84	181/64	TJ	17.35	17.74- 07, 17.82w- 09
Ezzine	Hamid	MAR	5.10.83	174/60	3kSt	8:11.81	8:09.72- 07
Fagan	Luke	GBR	31.7.88	181/75	100	10.21, 10.20w	10.51- 09, 10.39w- 07
					200	20.60	20.86- 07
Fahie	Collister	ISV	31.8.89	175/77	LJ	7.91, 8.02w	7.49- 10
* Fajdek	Pawel	POL	4.6.89	186/118	HT	78.54	76.07- 10
Falil	Abdellah	MAR	.76	172/57	Mar	2:08:18	2:09:24- 10
Faloci	Giovanni	ITA	13.10.85	193/108	DT	63.89	62.56- 09
* Farah	Mohamed	GBR	23.3.83	171/65	3000	7:40.15	7:34.47i- 09, 7:38.15- 06
3000	7:35.81i	7:34.47i- 09, 7:38.15- 06			5000	12:53.11	12:57.94- 10
10k	26:46.57	27:28.86- 10			HMar	60:23	-0-
Farnosov	Andrey	RUS	9.7.80	182/66	3kSt	8:21.95	8:25.28- 08
Farquhar	Stuart	NZL	15.3.82	190/97	JT	84.21	85.35- 10

Name		Nat	Born	Ht/Wt	Event	2011 Mark	Pre-2011 Best
Fassinotti	Marco	ITA	29.4.89	190/75	HJ	2.29i, 2.25	2.28- 10
* Faulk	Dexter	USA	14.4.84	187/75	110h	13.35	13.13- 09
Favretto	Vincent	FRA	5.4.84	188/73	PV	5.60	5.65- 06
* Fazekas	Róbert	HUN	18.8.75	193/110	DT	64.30	71.70- 02
Fedaczynski	Rafal	POL	3.12.80	168/61	20kW	1:22:07	1:22:36- 10
					50kW	3:46:05	3:46:51- 08
Feleke	Getu	ETH	28.11.86		HMar	61:28	59:56- 10
Fernandes	Raphael	BRA	8.11.84	178/67	400h	50.20	49.29- 07
Fernández	Álvaro	ESP	7.4.81	180/67	1500	3:37.24	3:32.88- 04
^ Fernández	Francisco Javier	ESP	6.3.77	175/65	20kW	1:22:17	1:17:22- 02
* Fernández	Jorge	CUB	2.10.87	190/100	DT	65.89	66.00- 10
Ferreira	João	POR	20.10.86	183/76	400h	49.63	50.21- 10
Ferrín	Diego	ECU	21.3.88	180/68	HJ	2.30A	2.21- 09
Fiala	Michal	CZE	22.6.85	191/108	HT	70.51	69.12- 05
Fida	Soresa	ETH-J	27.5.93	168/55	1500	3:34.72	3:46.4A- 10
					2000	4:58.18	5:02.1+- 00
Fifa	Illias	MAR	16.5.89	174/55	5000	13:25.55	13:54.16- 10
^ Figère	Nicolas	FRA	19.5.79	177/91	HT	75.78	80.88- 01
Filipchuk	Valeriy	RUS	30.6.91		20kW	1:21:46	-0-
Filipovic	Nenad	SRB	5.10.78	182/72	50kW	3:59:17	4:02:16- 08
* Filippídis	Konstadínos	GRE	26.11.86	188/73	PV	5.75	5.75- 05
Filippídis	Yervásios	GRE	24.7.87	186/90	JT	82.38	81.01- 07
Filippov	Nikita	KAZ	7.10.91	194/84	PV	5.50i, 5.40	5.20- 10
Finley	Mason	USA	7.10.90	203/150	SP	20.71i, 19.84	19.74- 10
					DT	60.65	60.18- 10
Flannery	Niall	GBR	26.4.91	178/70	400h	49.76	51.07- 09
Fleischauer	Georg	GER	21.10.88	192/82	400h	48.72	49.85- 10
Flimmons	Randall	USA	31.12.84	186/77	LJ	7.97, 8.02w	8.10- 09
Florant	Fabien	NED	1.2.83	176/73	TJ	16.58	16.65- 09
Floriani	Yuri	ITA	25.12.81	180/64	3kSt	8:28.64	8:28.90- 08
Floyd	Mike	GBR	26.9.76	185/118	HT	72.45	70.45- 10
Fofana	Colomba	FRA	11.4.77	187/81	TJ	16.76	17.34- 08
Fontenot	Ryan	USA	4.5.86	188/75	110h	13.48	13.48- 10
Forbes	Damar	JAM	18.9.90	185/77	LJ	8.23	7.93- 10
Forbes	Ronald	CAY	5.4.85	186/79	110h	13.50, 13.24w	13.59- 08
Formichetti	Emanuele	ITA	28.5.83	178/70	LJ	7.84i, 7.83, 8.04w	8.10- 10
Forrest	Shawn	AUS	10.7.83	180/64	HMar	61:25	62:44- 10
Forsythe	Mario	JAM	30.10.85	173/68	100	10.11	9.95- 10
					200	20.29	20.43- 10
* Fortes	Marco	POR	26.9.82	189/139	SP	20.89	20.69- 10
Fothergill	Allodin	JAM	2.7.87	183/75	400	45.51	45.24- 10
Fourie	Lehann	RSA	16.2.87	196/99	110h	13.56	13.44, 13.41w, 13.4w- 10
* Frank	Mark	GER	21.6.77	187/97	JT	82.54	84.88- 05
Frankis	Gianni	GBR	16.4.88	190/77	110h	13.57	13.57- 09
* Frater	Michael	JAM	6.10.82	170/67	100	9.88, 9.86w	9.97- 08, 9.94w- 10
Frauen	Michel	GER	19.1.86	179/70	PV	5.53, 5.51	5.53- 09
Frawley	Nick	USA	21.6.88	178/70	PV	5.50	5.51Ai, 5.35- 09
* Frayne	Henry	AUS	14.4.90	187/72	LJ	7.98	7.99- 09
					TJ	17.04	16.63- 10
Frazier	Markquis	USA	2.10.90	173/70	200	20.38w	
Frederick	Norris	USA	17.2.86	183/79	LJ	8.10	8.12- 08
* Fredericks	Cornel	RSA	3.3.90	178/70	400h	48.14	48.79A, 49.19- 10
* Freimuth	Rico	GER	14.3.88	196/91	Dec	8287	7826- 10
Fricke	Steffen	GER	25.3.83		Dec	7845(w), 7610	7601- 10
Frost	Andy	GBR	17.4.81	189/115	HT	72.79	72.62- 06
* Frydrych	Petr	CZE	13.1.88	198/99	JT	85.32	88.23- 10
Fryman	Andy	USA	3.2.85	188/130	HT	72.00	70.13- 10
Fu Haitao		CHN-J	1.11.93		TJ	16.56	16.33- 10
Fuamatu	Emanuele	SAM	27.10.89	180/138	SP	19.40	18.43- 09
Fujisawa	Isamu	JPN	12.10.87	164/55	20kW	1:22:01	1:20:12- 10
Fukatsu	Takuya	JPN	10.11.87	168/53	10k	28:01.31	27:56.29- 10
Furey	Sean	USA	31.8.82	190/95	JT	81.62	80.45- 08
Furtula	Danijel	MNE-J	31.7.92	195/115	DT	60.19	
Fyodorov	Aleksey	RUS	25.5.91	184/73	TJ	17.05i, 17.01	17.12, 17.18w- 10
* Gaisah	Ignisious	GHA	20.6.83	186/70	LJ	8.26	8.43, 8.51w- 06
Gala	Mumin	DJI	6.4.82	173/55	5000	13:17.77	13:34.66- 09
Gandu	Benjamin	KEN	21.5.90	169/57	10k	28:03.43	28:21.31- 10
García	Clemente	MEX	21.8.89		50kW	4:01:00	4:24:57- 10
* García	Jesús Ángel	ESP	17.10.69	172/64	50kW	3:48:11	3:39:54- 97
García	Víctor	ESP	13.3.85	173/56	3kSt	8:22.61	8:26.45- 10
* García	Yordani	CUB	21.11.88	193/88	Dec	8397	8496- 09

Name		Nat	Born	Ht/Wt	Event	2011 Mark	Pre-2011 Best
* Gari	Roba	ETH	12.4.82	181/60	3kSt	8:10.03	8:09.87- 10
Garza	Greg	USA	6.1.85	193/109	DT	61.34	64.30- 08
Gastaldi	Román	ARG	25.9.89	188/83	Dec	7826A	7423- 10
* Gathimba	Gideon	KEN	9.3.80	179/64	1500	3:33.53	3:33.63- 08
1M	3:53.76		3:50.53- 10		3000	7:40.10	7:49.65i- 09
Gatlin	Justin	USA	10.2.82	185/79	100	9.95	9.85- 04, 9.84w- 05, 9.77dq- 06
					200	20.20	20.00- 05, 19.86w- 01, 19.86dq- 02
Gauntlett	Akheem	USA	26.8.90	184/70	200	20.58	20.84- 09
* Gay	Tyson	USA	9.8.82	183/73	100	9.79	9.69- 09, 9.68w- 08
* Gaymon	Justin	USA	13.12.86	175/70	400h	48.58	48.46- 08
Gbabeke	Stanley	NGR	24.7.89	183/70	LJ	8.15	8.06- 09
Gebrehiwott	Hagos	ETH-Y	11.5.94	174/57	3000	7:45.11	-0-
* Gebremariam	Gebre-egziabher	ETH	10.9.84	178/56	HMar	60:25	60:25- 10
					Mar	2:08:00, 2:04:53h	2:08:14- 10
* Gebremedhin	Mekonnen	ETH	11.10.88	180/64	1500	3:31.90	3:31.57- 10
1M	3:49.70		3:49.83- 10		3000	7:41.42	
* Gebremeskel	Dejen	ETH	24.11.89	178/53	3000	7:35.37i	7:44.26i, 7:45.9- 10
					5000	12:55.89	12:53.56- 10
* Gebrselassie	Haile	ETH	18.4.73	164/53	HMar	60:18	58:55- 06
Gebrselassie	Weynay	ERI-Y	24.3.94		3kSt	8:33.59	8:33.13- 00
Geffrouais	Florian	FRA	5,12.88	186/83	Dec	7932	8057- 10
Gelant	Elroy	RSA	25.8.86	174/55	3000	7:41.59	7:54.36- 09
					5000	13:25.09	13:25.88- 10
Gemeda	Haile Haja	ETH	.88		Mar	2:09:20	2:09:44- 10
Gena	Siraj Amda Bene	ETH	12.11.84	170/52	Mar	2:08:31	2:08:39- 10
Genest	Alexandre	CAN	30.6.86	175/57	3kSt	8:19.33	8:27.53- 09
* Geneti	Markos	ETH	30.5.84	175/55	Mar	2:06:35dh	-0-
Geng Zhiyao		CHN	15.8.87	182/67	50kW	3:53:26	3:55:34- 09
George	Winston	GUY	19.5.87	167/52	400	45.86	
Gertleyn	Ivan	RUS	25.9.87	184/75	PV	5.50i, 5.40	5.55- 10
Getahun	Birhan	ETH	5.9.91	181/64	3kSt	8:17.36	8:21.20- 10
Gezahegn	Girma	ETH	28.11.83	158/48	Mar	2:09:16	2:09:52- 10
Gezzar	Nour-eddine	FRA	17.2.80	184/60	3kSt	8:12.25	8:24.87, 8:15.04dq- 06
* Gharib	Jaouad	MAR	22.5.72	176/66	HMar	61:31dh	59:59- 09, 59:56dh- 04
					Mar	2:08:26	2:05:27- 09
Ghazal	Majed El Dein	SYR	21.4.87	193/70	HJ	2.28	2.22i- 09, 2.22- 10
* Gibilisco	Giuseppe	ITA	5.1.79	183/79	PV	5.55, 5.60ex	5.90- 03
Giehl	Tobias	GER	25.7.91	193/77	400h	49.81	50.85- 09
Gilde	Maximilian	GER	5.1.90		Dec	7717	8036- 01
* Gill	Jacko	NZL-Y	10.12.94	191/105	SP	20.38	18.57- 10
* Girat	Arnie David	CUB	26.8.84	182/72	TJ	17.29, 17.42w	17.62- 09
Girma	Tesfaye	ETH	25.9.82	168/50	HMar	60:35	61:24- 06
Gitau	Daniel	KEN	1.10.87	174/55	10k	27:57.63	27:59.05- 08
Giupponi	Matteo	ITA	8.10.88	190/65	20kW	1:22:36	1:23:00- 09
Giza	Jakub	POL	26.4.85	188/140	SP	19.62	20.06- 10
Glover	Tim	USA	1.11.90	185/86	JT	80.33	71.31- 10
Golabek	Robert	USA	27.4.89	178/116	SP	19.44	18.28- 10
Gollnow	David	GER	8.4.89	180/69	400h	49.56	50.47- 10
Gomes	Diego	BRA	19.4.85	184/73	800	1:46.02	1:46.75- 05
* Gomes da Silva	Fábio	BRA	4.8.83	178/74	PV	5.80	5.77- 07
Gomez	Inaki	CAN	16.1.88	173/61	20kW	1:22:06	1:24:48- 10
Gómez	Álvaro	COL	21.2.89	176/68	100	10.24, 10.11Aw	10.32A- 08, 10.41, 10.26Aw- 10
* Gomis	Kafétien	FRA	23.3.80	85/70	LJ	8.12, 8.22w	8.24- 10
Gomont	Nicolas	FRA	15.9.86	193/89	LJ	7.90, 8.07w	7.92, 7.98w- 10
Goncharov	Viktor	RUS	9.5.91		JT	80.34	77.77- 10
Gonzales	Jermaine	JAM	26.11.84	190/72	400	44.69	44.40- 10
* González	Andy	CUB	17.10.87	177/65	800	1:45.58A	1:45.3- 08, 1:45.41- 09
Goodwin	Marquise	USA	19.11.90	173/70	LJ	8.17, 8.33w	8.18- 09
Goossens	Denis	BEL	12.12.87	190/84	PV	5.50i, 5.41	5.61- 09
* Gordon	Jehue	TRI	15.12.91	190/75	400h	48.66	48.26- 09
Gordon	Lalonde	TRI	25.11.88	188/77	400	45.51	46.33- 10
Gordon	Nick	JAM	17.9.88	174/73	LJ	7.94i, 7.92, 8.14w	8.11- 09
Gottardo	Leonardo	ITA	21.3.88	183/91	JT	78.10	76.18- 10
* Goumri	Abderrahim	MAR	21.5.76	167/60	Mar	2:09:11	2:05:30- 08
Gowda	Vikas	IND	5.7.83	196/115	DT	64.91	64.96- 07
Grabarz	Robbie	GBR	3.10.87	192/75	HJ	2.28	2.28- 10
Granger	Mike	USA	17.3.91	168/68	100	10.24, 10.16w	10.29- 10
Granö	Mats	FIN	6.9.81	190/105	HT	70.45	70.66- 04
Grasu	Mihai-Liviu	ROU	21.4.87	190/110	DT	62.20	62.05- 10
Gray	Cordero	USA	9.5.89	173/68	100	10.20, 10.12w	10.26- 09, 10.16w- 10
					200	20.56w	20.73- 10
Grayman	James	ANT	11.10.85	193/63	HJ	2.25	2.27- 07

Name		Nat	Born	Ht/Wt	Event	2011 Mark	Pre-2011 Best
Greco	Daniele	ITA	1.3.89	184/75	TJ	16.95	17.20- 09
Greeley	Mitch	USA	5.5.86	185/74	PV	5.50	5.56sq- 08, 5.55- 09
Green	Jack	GBR	6.10.91	182/75	400h	48.98	50.49- 10
* Green	Leford	JAM	14.11.86	186/79	200	20.61	20.66, 20.41w- 09
400	45.46			45.56- 08	400h	49.03	48.47- 10
Green	Rodney	BAH	8.12.85	172/68	100	10.28, 10.15w	10.28- 08, 10.25w- 10
* Greene	David	GBR	11.4.86	183/75	400	45.82	46.38- 10
					400h	48.20	47.88- 10
Greer	Elijah	USA	24.10.90	185/66	800	1:45.06	1:46.99- 10
^ Gregório	Jadel	BRA	16.9.80	202/102	LJ	8.07w	8.22- 04, 8.26w- 07
					TJ	16.87	17.90- 07
* Gregson	Ryan	AUS	26.4.90	184/68	1500	3:36.64	3:31.06- 10
					1M	3:53.86	3:52.24- 10
Griffin	Johnta	USA	16.10.83	178/73	LJ	7.95	8.01w- 10. 7.99- 09
Griffith	Adrian	BAH	11.11.84	178/75	100	10.28, 10.16w	10.19- 10
Grillas	Hugo	FRA	28.2.89	180/68	400h	49.76	49.78- 10
Grinnell	Ryan	USA	4.2.87	188/82	TJ	16.58	16.25- 10, 16.55w- 08
* Gripich	Aleksandr	RUS	21.9.86	190/80?	PV	5.75	5.75- 09
Gruber	Hendrik	GER	28.9.86	192/80	PV	5.55	5.70- 10
Grueso	Daniel	COL	30.7.85	180/68	100	10.21	10.17A- 08, 10.22- 09
Grzeszczuk	Lukasz	POL	3.3.90	189/95	JT	80.58	76.65- 10
Gu Junjie		CHN	5.5.83	190/83	TJ	16.78	17.23- 04
Guerra	Ignacio	CHI	15.9.87	180/80	JT	78.69	78.54- 08
Guigon	Nicolas	FRA	10.10.80	181/60	PV	5.50	5.75- 04
* Guliyev	Ramil	TUR	29.5.90	187/73	100	10.14, 10.11w	10.08- 09
					200	20.32	20.04- 09
Gunn	Luke	GBR	22.3.85	182/63	3kSt	8:31.56	8:28.48- 08
Gustafsson	Andreas	SWE	10.8.81	180/67	50kW	3:54:08	3:57:53- 09
Haatainen	Harri	FIN	5.1.78	186/85	JT	81.01	86.63- 01
Häber	Tino	GER	6.10.82	185/76	JT	79.81	83.46- 09
^ Hachlaf	Abdelkader	MAR	3.7.79	182/68	3kSt	8:13.04	8:08.78- 06
* Hadadi	Ehsan	IRI	21.1.85	193/125	DT	66.08	69.32- 08
Hadjam	Abdelatif	FRA	8.8.90	181/63	3kSt	8:33.58	8:42.24- 10
Hailegiorgis	Dereje	ETH	27.9.84		HMar	60:00	62:20- 08
Hailu	Shume	ETH	27.10.87		Mar	2:09:07	2:11:48- 10
Haklits	András	CRO	23.9.77	189/103	HT	75.77	80.41- 05
Halevi	Yochai	ISR	10.5.82	184/78	TJ	16.77	16.76- 10
Halim	Muhammad	ISV	26.10.86	193/84	TJ	16.87i, 16.61 16.70i, 16.53- 10, 16.66w- 08	
Hall	Josh	AUS	3.4.90	197/86	HJ	2.26	2.22- 10
* Hall	Ryan	USA	14.10.82	180/64	Mar	2:08:04, 2:04:58dh	2:06:17- 08
Hamada	Mohamed Ahmed	EGY-J	22.10.92	176/64	800	1:46.44	
Hamadi	Abderahmane	ALG	24.3.84	188/80	400h	50.22	49.84A- 08
Hanany	Mickaël	FRA	25.3.83	198/84	HJ	2.26	2.32- 08
Hancock	Johnathan	USA	31.3.87	188/82	100	10.19	10.31- 09, 10.28w- 08
Hancock	Michael	USA	20.2.90	183/75	110h	13.58, 13.54w	13.87, 13.77w- 10
* Hardee	Trey	USA	7.2.84	196/95	110h	13.69, 13.61w	13.71- 08
					Dec	8689	8790- 09
Hardy	Prezel	USA-J	1.6.92	168/64	100	10.13	10.34, 10.08w- 09
Harlan	Ryan	USA	25.4.81	190/93	Dec	8011	8171- 04
Harmse	Chris	RSA	31.5.73	184/118	HT	74.90	80.63- 05
* Harradine	Benn	AUS	14.10.82	198/115	DT	66.07	66.45- 10
Harris	Aleec	USA	31.10.90	185/77	110h	13.65, 13.55w	14.15, 13.88w- 10
Harris	James	USA	15.9.91	196/88	HJ	2.25Ai, 2.23	2.215- 10
Harris	Tora	USA	21.9.78	190/83	HJ	2.31	2.33- 06
Härstedt	Axel	SWE	28.2.87	196/115	DT	61.14	58.53- 10
Harting	Christoph	GER	4.10.90	205/117	DT	62.12	61.10- 10
* Harting	Robert	GER	18.10.84	201/129	DT	68.99	69.69- 10
Harvey	Jacques	JAM	5.4.89	182/73	100	10.09, 10.03w	10.26- 10
Hashemi	Sajjad	IRI	22.8.91	178/70	400	45.81	46.57- 10
Haukenes	Håvard	NOR	22.4.90	180/68	50kW	4:04:48	-0-
Hautcoeur	Kevin	FRA	17.1.85	180/67	800	1:46.29	1:47.12- 09
Haverney	Matthias	GER	21.7.85	198/78	HJ	2.28	2.25- 05
Hayes	Armanti	USA	23.9.87	180/73	400	45.87	45.65- 10
Hayes	Keith	USA	16.2.90	186/77	110h	13.65	13.85- 10, 13.73w- 09
Hazle	Mike	USA	22.3.79	183/93	JT	81.09	82.21- 08
He Yongqiang		CHN-J	27.11.93		20kW	1:23:12	-0-
Heath	Elliott	USA	4.2.89	174/60	5000	13:26.14	13:29.75- 10
Hechler	Simon	GER	15.6.88	189/79	Dec	8058	7624- 10
* Heffernan	Robert	IRL	20.2.78	173/55	20kW	1:20:54	1:19:22- 08
					50kW	3:49:28	3:45:30- 10
Helcelet	Adam Sebastian	CZE	27.10.91	187/86	Dec	7969	-0-

Name		Nat	Born	Ht/Wt	Event	2011 Mark	Pre-2011 Best
Helwick	Chris	USA	18.3.85	193/89	Dec	7736	8143- 08
Henriksen	Eivind	NOR	14.9.90	191/110	HT	74.59	72.86- 10
Henriques	Ânderson	BRA-J	3.3.92	187/80	400	45.71A, 45.81	46.24- 10
* Henry	Tabarie	ISV	1.12.87	187/79	400	44.83	44.77- 09
Hernández	Edgar	MEX	8.6.77	174/57	20kW	1:23:20	1:21:30- 00
					50kW	3:54:46	3:46:12- 01
Hernández	Emerson	ESA	20.1.89		50kW	3:56:09	4:06:47A- 10
Hernández	Fredy	COL	25.4.78	173/60	50kW	3:59:40A	4:03:10- 07
Hernández	Osviel	CUB	31.5.89	179/76	TJ	16.82	17.08- 09
Hernández	Yuniel	CUB	28.3.81	183/76	110h	13.58	13.26- 01, 13.24w- 04, 13.2- 10
Herrera	Michael	CUB	5.6.85	176/75	200	20.52	20.31- 07
^ Hession	Paul	IRL	27.1.83	184/76	200	20.51	20.30- 07, 20.26w- 08
Hewitt	Zwede	TRI	10.6.89	186/75	400	45.51	45.70- 10
* Hicks	Antwon	USA	12.3.83	187/73	110h	13.35	13.09- 08
Hicks	Jaylon	USA-J	13.4.93	175/70	100	10.15w	10.50- 10
Hicks	Jeremy	USA	19.9.86	178/75	LJ	7.97, 8.10w	8.06, 8.20Aw- 10
Higgs	Raymond	BAH	24.1.91	188/75	LJ	8.15	
^ Higuero	Juan Carlos	ESP	3.8.78	180/60	1500	3:35.80	3:31.57- 06
					2000	4:58.03	5:04.26- 05
Higuma	Takafumi	JPN	3.9.82		50kW	3:56:35	4:01:24- 10
Hill	Chris	USA	26.2.88	183/93	JT	79.15	83.87- 09
Hill	Devon	USA	26.10.89	185/75	110h	13.54, 13.52w	13.88, 13.80w- 10
Hill	Jerel	USA	13.9.87	178/75	100	10.17w	10.22- 10
Hinds	Andrew	BAR	25.4.84	175/72	100	10.14	10.03- 09
Hirose	Hideyuki	JPN	20.7.89	176/62	400	45.84	45.84- 09
Hirt	Hassan	FRA	16.1.80	179/65	5000	13:25.42	
Hlavan	Igor	UKR	25.9.90		50kW	4:03:18	4:08:08- 10
* Hoffa	Reese	USA	8.10.77	182/133	SP	22.09	22.43- 07
Hoffmann	Karol	POL	1.6.89	196/78	TJ	16.50, 16.87w	16.00- 09
Hogan	Victor	RSA	25.7.89	198/108	DT	62.60	59.21- 08
Höhne	André	GER	10.3.78	185/72	20kW	1:22:58	1:20:00- 05
Hollis	Mark	USA	1.12.84	190/84	PV	5.63i, 5.62, 5.70dh	5.75- 08
Holusa	Jakub	CZE	20.2.88	183/72	800	1:46.26	1:45.56- 10
					1000	2:17.08	2:17.82- 10
* Holzdeppe	Raphael	GER	28.9.89	181/79	PV	5.72	5.80- 08
* Hondrokoúkis	Dimítrios	GRE	26.1.88	193/73	HJ	2.32	2.24- 07
* Hooker	Steve	AUS	16.7.82	187/85	PV	5.60	6.06i- 09, 6.00- 08
Hoppe	Artur	GER	3.5.88	188/115	SP	19.32	19.64i- 10
Horák	Peter	SVK	7.12.83	197/83	HJ	2.26i	2.30i- 07, 2.28- 09
Horn	Gray	USA	18.2.90	191/91	Dec	7914	7652- 10
Horvat	Ivan	CRO-J	17.8.93	188/77	PV	5.51	5.26- 10
Hosseinzadeh	Amin	IRI	23.3.87	188/70	HJ	2.25	2.21- 09
Hostetler	Cyrus	USA	8.8.86	190/95	JT	82.24A	83.16- 09
Hou Ye		CHN	12.2.91		TJ	16.53	15.94- 10
Houssaye	Cédric	FRA	13.12.79	178/65	50kW	3:53:24	3:56:43- 08
* Howe	Andrew	ITA	12.5.85	183/71	200	20.31	20.28- 04
					400	45.70	46.03- 06
Howell	Tran	USA	27.3.88	172/68	200	20.39	20.81- 10
Hranovschi	Vadim	MDA	14.2.83	198/110	DT	63.54	64.43- 10
Hudi	Ákos	HUN	10.8.91	185/95	HT	71.82	72.60- 10
Hughes	David	GBR	31.5.84	194/86	400h	49.81	49.58- 10
Hughes	Joey	USA	26.10.90	178/70	400	45.05	45.15- 10
Hughes	Matt	CAN	3.8.89	180/64	3kSt	8:24.87	8:34.18- 10
Huling	Dan	USA	16.7.83	185/70	3kSt	8:25.95	8:13.29- 10
Hunt	Leonard	ISV	17.5.87	186/77	LJ	8.11	7.65- 09
Hunter	Justin	USA	20.5.91	196/82	LJ	7.96i	7.89- 10
Hurtault	Erison	DMA	29.12.84	182/75	400	45.70	45.40- 07
Hylton	Riker	JAM	13.12.88	190/73	200	20.53w	20.98- 09
					400	45.30	45.92- 09
Hyrshyn	Ivan	UKR	26.7.88	202/100	DT	64.96	63.27- 10
Hytinen	Dan	USA	18.10.85	188/101	DT	61.26	60.54- 09
^ Iakovákis	Periklís	GRE	24.3.79	185/76	400h	50.26	47.82- 06
Ibargüen	Arley	COL	4.12.82	183/84	JT	77.83A	81.07- 09
Ibrahim	Yasser Fathi	EGY	2.5.84	185/127	SP	19.73	19.97- 09
					DT	63.30	63.37i, 62.28- 10
Ibrahimov	Hayle	AZE	18.1.90	172/54	3000	7:42.54i	7:51.68- 09
Ideura	Noriuki	JPN	29.10.87	175/63	400h	49.87	50.73- 10
* Idowu	Phillips	GBR	30.12.78	193/89	TJ	17.77	17.81- 10
Idriss	Ali Mohamed Younes	SUD	15.9.89	191/75	HJ	2.25	2.21- 10
* Iguider	Abdelati	MAR	25.3.87	170/52	1500	3:31.60	3:31.47- 09
* Ikonnikov	Kirill	RUS	5.3.84	185/100	HT	79.04	79.20- 08

Name		Nat	Born	Ht/Wt	Event	2011 Mark	Pre-2011 Best
Ilyichev	Ivan	RUS	14.10.86		HJ	2.25	2.28i- 06, 2.26- 08
Imazeki	Yuta	JPN	6.11.87	176/59	400h	49.27	49.66- 09
^ Inocêncio	Matheus	BRA	17.5.81	192/94	110h	13.64, 13.54w	13.33- 04
* Ioannou	Kyriakos	CYP	26.7.84	193/66	HJ	2.33	2.35- 07
Iordan	Valeriy	RUS-J	14.2.92		JT	80.15	74.86- 10
Ishikawa	Kazuyoshi	JPN	16.11.82	179/70	TJ	16.54	16.98- 04
Ishikawa	Takuya	JPN	29.10.87	173/55	10k	28:14.44	28:17.39- 10
Isles	Carlin	USA	21.11.89	175/75	100	10.19w	10.46- 10, 10.42w- 09
* Ismail	Ismail Ahmed	SUD	10.9.84	191/71	800	1:45.14	1:43.82- 09
* Israel	Märt	EST	23.9.83	189/118	DT	66.98	66.56- 07
Itani	Sami	FIN	24.3.87	189/81	Dec	7731	7527- 09
Ivakin	Anton	RUS	3.2.91	178/73	PV	5.52	5.50- 10
^ Ivanov	Aleksandr	RUS	25.5.82	194/100	JT	82.17	88.90- 03
Ivanov	Georgi	BUL	13.3.85	188/108	SP	19.23i, 18.90	20.02- 08
Ivanov	Sergey	BLR	28.3.84		TJ	16.60i, 16.57	16.79- 10
^ Ivuti	Patrick	KEN	30.6.78	165/52	Mar	2:08:41	2:07:46- 05
* Jackson	Bershawn	USA	8.5.83	170/68	400	45.91	45.06- 07
					400h	47.93	47.30- 05
Jackson	Desmond	USA	27.4.89	180/73	100	10.22. 10.10w	10.34, 10.31w- 10
					200	20.63. 20.58w	20.96- 10
Jaleta	Habtamu	ETH-J	19.4.93		3kSt	8:31.06	8:58.6A- 10
James	Godday	NGR	9.1.84	187/80	400	45.88	44.90- 08
* James	Kirani	GRN-J	1.9.92	185/74	200	20.41A, 20.53w	20.76- 10
					400	44.36	45.01- 10
Jammier	Quentin	FRA	24.7.88	191/85	Dec	7710	7685- 09
Jänes	Marko	EST	29.8.76	186/83	JT	80.33	78.50- 06
Janet	Roberto	CUB	29.8.86	187/95	HT	76.40	76.50- 10
* Janik	Igor	POL	18.1.83	200/112	JT	82.81	84.76- 08
Jansen	Robbert Jan	NED	22.7.83	175/67	PV	5.53	5.60- 10
Jaramillo	Georni	VEN	6.3.89	185/80	Dec	7679A	
^ Järvenpää	Tero	FIN	2.10.84	187/95	JT	80.10	86.68- 08
Jasinski	Daniel	GER	5.8.89	207/114	DT	61.28	59.02- 10
Jaszczuk	Tomasz	POL-J	9.3.92	195/83	LJ	8.11	7.52- 09
Jegede	J.J.	GBR	3.10.85	179/73	LJ	8.04	7.85- 07, 7.94w- 09
Jelonek	Jakub	POL	7.7.85	182/60	20kW	1:22:32	1:22:17- 09
^ Jeng	Alhaji	SWE	13.12.81	185/77	PV	5.60	5.81i- 10, 5.80- 06
Jensen	Morten	DEN	2.12.82	189/81	LJ	8.01	8.25- 05
* Jeylan	Ibrahim	ETH	12.6.89	168/57	5000	13:09.95	13:09.38- 06
					10k	27:09.02	27:02.81- 06
Ji Chunlong		CHN	25.2.88	180/62	20kW	1:23:34	1:25:46- 08
Jiang Fan		CHN	16.9.89	188/75	110h	13.47	13.69- 09
Jiang Xingyu		CHN	16.3.87	182/78	JT	79.55	78.52- 10
Jiang Zhaodan		CHN	19.2.89		LJ	8.12	7.87- 10
^ Jiménez	Antonio David	ESP	18.2.77	178/63	3kSt	8:21.77	8:11.52- 01
Jin Qichao		CHN	24.11.91	191/70	HJ	2.24i, 2.24	2.24- 10
Jock	Charles	USA	23.11.89	188/73	800	1:44.67	1:45.65- 10
Johansson	Markus	SWE	8.5.90	183/110	HT	72.40	69.28- 10
John	Alexander	GER	3.5.86	185/77	110h	13.45, 13.40w	13.35- 09
* Johnson	Kibwé	USA	17.7.81	189/108	HT	80.31	78.25- 05
Johnson	Matt	USA	4.10.89	188/84	Dec	7686w, 7675	7266- 10
* Jonas	Dusty	USA	19.4.86	198/84	HJ	2.31	2.36A- 08, 2.33- 10
Jones	Nick	USA	22.6.89	188/109	DT	60.75	60.92- 10
Jones	Richard	USA	15.7.88	180/73	800	1:45.56	1:46.42- 10
Jons	Mattias	SWE	19.11.82	182/108	HT	74.23	74.76- 10
Jordan	Alphonso	USA	1.11.87	190/75	TJ	16.74	16.56, 16.62w- 10
Jorge	Carlos	DOM	24.9.86	183/77	100	10.21	10.26- 09
Jotanovic	Milan	SRB	11.1.84	184/123	SP	20.17	20.14- 09
Juin	Jonathan	HAI	17.12.89	170/68	100	10.27, 10.13w	10.50- 09, 10.28w- 10
Julião	Ronald	BRA	16.6.85	194/110	DT	63.30	63.09- 10
Julmis	Jeffrey	USA/HAI	6.1.87	183/80	110h	13.50, 13.38w	13.59- 10
Jung Sang-jin		KOR	16.4.84	188/95	JT	80.38	80.89- 10
Jurkevics	Dmitrijs	LAT	7.1.87	186/70	1500	3:37.35	3:39.69- 09, 3:39.6- 10
Kabachi	El Mehdi	MAR-J	4.10.92		LJ	7.94	7.87- 10
Kahlmeyer	Markus	GER	20.1.82	189/110	HT	72.63	74.95- 07
* Kaki	Abubaker	SUD	21.6.89	175/60	800	1:43.13	1:42.23- 10
1000	2:17.55i		2:13.62- 10		1500	3:31.76	3:39.71- 08
Kakuage	Hiromitsu	JPN	14.9.90	170/47	10k	28:03.27	28:57.47- 10
Kamais	Peter	KEN	7.11.76		HMar	60:46	59:53- 10
* Kamal	Ali Abubaker	QAT	8.11.83	169/58	1500	3:37.38	3:36.15- 10
					3kSt	8:30.23	8:15.80- 08
Kamé	Ali	MAD	21.5.84	188/82	Dec	7685	7363- 09

	Name		Nat	Born	Ht/Wt	Event	2011 Mark	Pre-2011 Best
*	Kanaykin	Vladimir	RUS	21.3.85	170/60	20kW	1:19:14	1:17:16- 07, 1:16:53dq- 08
	Kanda	Lukas	KEN	.87		HMar	61:26	61:01- 09
						Mar	2:08:40	
	Kanemaru	Yuzo	JPN	18.9.87	177/73	400	45.23	45.16- 09
*	Kanter	Gerd	EST	6.5.79	196/126	DT	67.99	73.38- 06
	Kapek	Julien	FRA	12.1.79	178/70	TJ	16.74	17.38- 06
^	Karailiev	Momchil	BUL	21.5.82	188/75	TJ	16.75, 16.93w	17.41- 09
	Karavayev	Pavel	RUS	27.8.88	185/74	LJ	8.08	7.97, 7.99w- 09
*	Karjalainen	Olli-Pekka	FIN	7.3.80	194/118	HT	76.60	83.30- 04
	Karoki	Bitan	KEN	21.8.90	169/53	5000	13:15.76	13:23.85- 10
						10k	27:13.67	27:23.62- 10
^	Karpov	Dmitriy	KAZ	23.7.81	198/94	Dec	8089	8725- 04
	Karsak	Pavlo	UKR	11.11.87	204/96	DT	61.66	61.13- 07
*	Kasyanov	Oleksiy	UKR	26.8.85	191/82	Dec	8251	8479- 09
	Kauppinen	Juha	FIN	16.8.86	182/103	HT	72.71	74.38- 09
	Kawakita	Naohiro	JPN	10.7.80	182/74	400h	50.12	49.04- 09
	Kawatsura	Sota	JPN	19.6.89	172/58	200	20.56	20.74- 09
	Kawauchi	Yuki	JPN	5.3.87	172/59	Mar	2:08:37	2:12:36- 10
	Kazakevics	Igors	LAT	19.4.80	176/67	50kW	3:59:43	3:52:38- 08
	Kazanin	Oleksiy	UKR	22.5.82	170/58	50kW	3:56:18	3:50:30- 08
	Kazi	Tamás	HUN	16.5.85	179/70	800	1:46.29	1:45.55- 09
	Kazmirek	Kai	GER	28.1.91	189/86	Dec	7802	-0-
*	Kebede	Tsegaye	ETH	15.1.87	158/50	Mar	2:07:14	2:05:18- 09
	Kéchi	Heni	FRA	31.8.80	186/75	400h	50.19	49.34- 10
	Keddo	Eric	JAM	1.7.84	186/77	110h	13.49	13.52, 13.51w, 13.0- 10
^	Keflezighi	Mebrahtom	USA	5.5.75	170/58	Mar	2:09:13	2:09:15- 09
	Keïta	Naman	FRA	9.4.78	196/86	400h	50.24	48.17- 04
	Keitany	Elijah	KEN	.83		Mar	2:06:53	2:06:41- 09
*	Keitany	Haron	KEN	17.12.83	183/70	1500	3:31.86	3:30.20- 09
						1M	3:49.09	3:48.78- 09
	Kemboi	Clement	KEN-J	1.2.93		3kSt	8:28.13	9:03.4A- 10
	Kemboi	Edward	KEN	12.12.91	170/57	800	1:46.06	
*	Kemboi	Ezekiel	KEN	25.5.82	175/62	3kSt	7:55.76	7:58.85- 09
*	Kemboi	Nicholas	KEN	18.12.89	178/59	1500	3:37.25	3:31.52- 10
	Kemboi	Nicholas	QAT/KEN	25.11.83	163/50	HMar	61:07	60:31- 03
						Mar	2:08:01	-0-
	Kemboi	Shadrack	KEN	19.2.86		HMar	61:02	62:07- 10
	Kempas	Antti	FIN	3.10.80	191/70	50kW	3:56:51	3:55:19- 08
	Kering	Alfred	KEN	.8	172/57	Mar	2:07:41	2:07:11- 10
^	Keskisalo	Jukka	FIN	27.3.81	184/66	3kSt	8:26.45	8:10.67- 09
	Kgosiemang	Kabelo Mmono	BOT	7.1.86	184/70	HJ	2.25	2.34A- 08, 2.30- 06
	Kharlamov	Vasiliy	RUS	8.10.86	182/77	Dec	8166	8113- 09
	Kibet	Moses	UGA	23.3.91	165/55	5000	13:15.18	13:21.81- 10
	Kibet	Sammy	KEN	2.2.82		Mar	2:08:17	2:11:08- 09
	Kibet	Soyekwo	UGA-J	6.6.92	167/54	5000	13:22.28	14:20.5A- 09
						10k	28:13.97A	-0-
	Kibet	Stephen Kipkosgei	KEN	9.11.86		HMar	60:20	60:09- 10
	Kibiwott	Stephen	KEN	3.4.80	168/46	HMar	60:23	59:37- 09
	Kifle	Goltom	ERI-J	3.12.93	178/60	5000	13:23.07	
*	Kigen	Mike	KEN	15.1.86	170/54	5000	13:11.65	12:58.58- 06
	10k	27:30.53			28:03.70- 06		HMar	59:58	-0-
	Kigen	Moses	KEN	10.1.83		HMar	61:19	60:38- 10
	Kigen Korir	Sammy	KEN	29.9.85		HMar	61:18	63:08- 10
	Kilty	Richard	GBR	2.9.89	184/75	200	20.53	20.80- 09
	Kim Dong-young		KOR	6.3.80	174/56	50kW	3:51:12	3:53:52- 10
	Kim Duk-hyun		KOR	8.12.85	180/68	LJ	8.02	8.20, 8.41w- 09
						TJ	16.99	17.10- 09
*	Kim Hyun-sub		KOR	31.5.85	176/65	20kW	1:19:31	1:19:41- 08
	Kim Kun-woo		KOR	29.2.80	185/84	Dec	7860	7824- 06
	Kim Yoo-suk		KOR	19.1.82	191/87	PV	5.50	5.66- 07
*	Kimmons	Trell	USA	13.7.85	178/77	100	10.04, 9.97w	9.95, 9.92w- 10
	Kimura	Shintaro	JPN	30.6.87	171/68	100	10.27, 10.17w	10.21- 09
	Kimurer Kemboi	Joel	KEN	21.1.88		HMar	60:05	60:09- 10
	Kimutai	Kennedy	KEN	18.1.90		HMar	61:30	
	Kimutai	Philip Sanga	KEN	10.9.83	170/60	HMar	61:09	
						Mar	2:06:07	2:07:11- 10
	Kinnunen	Jarkko	FIN	19.1.84	187/69	20kW	1:23:40	1:24:43- 10
						50kW	3:52:32	3:47:36- 09
	Kinyor	Job	KEN	2.9.90	176/68	800	1:45.07A	1:45.86- 10
	Kipchirchir	Abraham	KEN-J	.92	181/62	800	1:46.4A	
	Kipchirchir	Hillary	KEN	30.4.81		Mar	2:08:17A	2:09:54- 08

Name		Nat	Born	Ht/Wt	Event	2011 Mark	Pre-2011 Best
Kipchirchir	Victor	KRN	.86		HMar	61:21	63:18- 10
* Kipchoge	Eliud	KEN	5.11.84	167/52	3000	7:27.66	7:27.72- 04
2M	8:16.74		8:07.68- 05		5000	12:59.01, 12:55.72i	12:46.53- 04
					10k	26:53.27	26:49.02- 07
Kipchoge	Jairus	KEN-J	15.12.92	168/54	2000	4:58.76	
					3kSt	8:11.31	
Kipchumba	Jafred Chirchir	KEN	8.8.83	178/60	Mar	2:05:48	2:08:10- 10
^ Kipchumba	Robert	KEN	24.2.84	170/62	HMar	60:43	59:28- 06
					Mar	2:08:07	2:09:56- 09
Kipkemoi	Kenneth Kiplimo	KEN	2.8.84	165/52	10k	27:48.5A	
					HMar	59:47	-0-
Kipkoech	Francis	KEN	12.10.73		Mar	2:08:01	2:10:41- 07
Kipkoech	John	KEN	29.12.91	160/52	3000	7:34.82	7:32.72- 10
Kipkorir	Paul	KEN	.82		HMar	61:11	63:59- 09
Kipkosgei	Nathaniel	KEN	1.9.84	185/64	HMar	61:24	
					Mar	2:06:28	
* Kiplagat	Benjamin	UGA	4.3.89	186/61	3kSt	8:08.43	8:03.81- 10
Kiplagat	Bisluke	KEN	8.8.88	175/59	5000	13:21.79	
					3kSt	8:32.70	8:16.68- 10
Kiplagat	Eliud	KEN	.85		HMar	60:52	61:29- 10
Kiplagat	Nicholas	KEN-J	20.12.92		800	1:45.47	1:47.0A- 10
Kiplagat	Richard	KEN	3.7.84	178/64	800	1:45.48	1:44.77- 10
* Kiplagat	Silas	KEN	20.8.89	170/57	1500	3:30.47	3:29.27- 10
					1M	3:49.39	3:52.32- 10
Kiplimo	Abraham	UGA	14.4.89	164/50	5000	13:10.40	13:17.68- 10
Kiplimo	Joseph	KEN	20.7.88	173/57	3000	7:44.12	7:31.20- 09
					5000	13:13.77	13:09.34- 09
Kiplimo Kimutai	Kenneth	KEN	10.12.81	170/55	HMar	61:16	59:44- 09
* Kiprop	Asbel	KEN	30.6.89	186/70	800	1:43.15	1:43.17- 09
1500	3:30.46		3:31.20- 09		1M	3:49.55	3:48.50- 09
Kiprop	Francis	KEN	4.6.82	172/54	Mar	2:09:00	2:07:04- 09
* Kiprop	Wilson	KEN	14.4.87	179/62	10k	27:32.9A	27:26.93A- 10
Kiprotich	Stephen	UGA	18.4.89	168/54	Mar	2:07:20	-0-
* Kipruto	Brimin	KEN	31.7.85	176/54	1500	3:35.52	3:35.23- 06
					3kSt	7:53.64	8:00.90- 10
Kipruto	Consesius	KEN-Y	8.12.94		3kSt	8:27.30	
Kipruto	Silas	KEN	26.9.84	184/66	HMar	61:12	59:39- 10
* Kipruto	Vincent	KEN	13.9.87	172/57	Mar	2:05:33	2:05:13- 10
Kipsang	Geoffrey	KEN-J	28.11.92	176/60	5000	13:12.23	13:42.01- 10
10k	27:06.35				HMar	59:31	
* Kipsang	Wilson	KEN	15.3.82	178/59	HMar	60:49	58:59- 09
					Mar	2:03:42	2:04:57- 10
* Kipsiro	Moses	UGA	2.9.86	174/59	2000	5:00.66+	5:03.99- 06
3000	7:31.83		7:30.95- 09		5000	13:09.17	12:50.72- 07
* Kiptanui	Eliud	KEN	6.6.89	169/55	HMar	61:11+	63:49A- 09
					Mar	2:09:08	2:05:39- 10
* Kiptoo	Mark	KEN	21.6.76	175/64	3000	7:34.82	7:32.97- 09
5000	12:59.91		12:53.46- 10		10k	26:54.64	27:14.67- 08
					HMar	60:29	60:50- 10
Kiptoo Kolum	Benjamin	KEN	.79	162/50	Mar	2:06:31	2:07:17- 09
Kiptum Busienei	Joseph	KEN	25.9.87		HMar	61:08	61:40- 10
* Kipyego	Bernard	KEN	16.7.86	160/50	HMar	59:45	59:10- 09
					Mar	2:06:29	2:07:01- 10
Kipyego	Edwin	KEN	.91		HMar	61:23	63:03- 10
^ Kipyego	Mike	KEN	2.10.83	162/58	Mar	2:06:48	-0-
Kirchler	Hannes	ITA	22.12.78	191/105	DT	63.58	65.01- 07
^ Kirdyapkin	Sergey	RUS	16.1.80	178/67	20kW	1:22:57	1:23:24+- 03
Kirop	Pius Maiyo	KEN	6.1.90		HMar	60:04	60:39- 10
* Kirui	Abel	KEN	4.6.82	177/62	Mar	2:07:38	2:05:04- 09
Kirui	Boniface	KEN	27.10.87	171/57	HMar	61:07	63:08- 09
Kirui	Geoffrey	KEN-J	16.2.93	158/50	5000	13:20.54	
					10k	26:55.73	
Kirui	Gilbert	KEN-Y	22.1.94	172/55	3kSt	8:25.03A	8:40.1A- 10
^ Kirui	Peter Cheruiyot	KEN	2.1.88	182/66	10k	27:25.63	
HMar	59:40		60:17- 10		Mar	2:06:31	-0-
* Kirwa Yego	Alfred	KEN	28.11.86	171/56	800	1:44.07	1:42.67- 09
					1M	3:55.18	
Kishaba	Kaleab	ETH			3kSt	8:31.65	8:53.70- 10
Kishimoto	Takayuki	JPN	6.5.90	170/62	400h	49.27	49.77- 10
* Kisorio	Mathew	KEN	16.5.89	178/62	10k	26:54.25	27:15.44- 09
					HMar	58:46	60:10- 10

Name		Nat	Born	Ht/Wt	Event	2011 Mark	Pre-2011 Best
^ Kiss	Dániel	HUN	12.2.82	195/73	110h	13.46	13.32, 13.20w- 10
Kitajima	Hisanori	JPN	16.10.84	170/55	10k	28:08.53	28:27.50- 08
Kitum	Silas	KEN	25.5.90	167/52	3kSt	8:12.17	8:12.42- 10
Kitum	Timothy	KEN-Y	20.11.94	177/60	800	1:44.98	
* Kitwara	Sammy	KEN	26.11.86	177/54	HMar	58:48	58:58- 09
Kivalov	Leonid	RUS	1.4.88	183/75	PV	5.50i	5.71i- 08, 5.60- 07
* Kivuva	Jackson	KEN	11.8.88	170/59	800	1:44.40A	1:43.72- 10
Klausen	Janick	DEN-J	3.4.93	175/68	HJ	2.27i, 2.25	2.22i- 10, 2.21- 09
* Knobel	Jan-Felix	GER	16.1.89	191/89	Dec	8288	7758- 09
Kobayashi	Yuichi	JPN	25.8.89	172/59	200	20.59	20.79- 09, 20.52w- 10
Kochnev	Aleksey	RUS	6.4.90	185/110	HT	73.91	73.93- 10
Koech	Dennis	KEN-Y	22.1.94		HMar	61:30A	
Koech	Duncan	KEN	28.12.81		Mar	2:08:38	2:11:53- 10
* Koech	Isiah	KEN	19.12.93	178/60	3000	7:37.50i, 7:47.6+	7:51.51- 09
2M 8:14.16					5000	12:54.18, 12:53.29i	13:07.70- 10
* Koech	Paul Kipsiele	KEN	10.11.81	168/57	5000	13:15.64	13:02.95i, 13:05.18- 10
					3kSt	7:57.32	7:56.37- 05
Koenig	Oliver	GER	31.1.81	180/79	LJ	8.07	8.01- 06, 8.08w- 02
* Kogo	Micah	KEN	3.6.86	170/60	10k	27:50.50	26:35.63- 06
					HMar	60:03dh	61:30- 10
Koivu	Joachim	FIN	5.9.88	195/104	HT	71.22	70.12- 10
Kokoyev	Valeriy	RUS	25.7.88	202/118	SP	20.42i, 20.06	20.20- 09
Kolasinac	Asmir	SRB	15.10.84	185/132	SP	20.50	20.52i, 19.95- 10, 20.41- 09
Kolomoyets	Sergey	BLR	11.8.89	190/102	HT	77.52	72.11- 10
Kolosov	Dmitriy	RUS	19.5.86		TJ	16.89	16.68- 07, 17.00w- 08
^ Kombich	Ismael	KEN	16.10.85	183/73	800	1:46.2A	1:44.24- 06
1500 3:34.38, 3:34.13i		3:33.31- 10			2000	4:58.38	
* Komen	Daniel Kipchirchir	KEN	27.11.84	175/60	1500	3:32.47A	3:29.02- 06
1M 3:50.29		3:48.28- 07			3000	7:31.41	7:31.98- 05
					5000	13:20.80	13:04.02- 10
Komen	John Kipkorir	KEN	28.8.77	173/58	Mar	2:07:13	2:08:12- 09
Komen	Willy	KEN	22.12.87	168/55	3kSt	8:21.40	8:11.18- 07
* Komon	Leonard Patrick	KEN	10.1.88	175/52	10k	26:55.29	26:57.08- 08
Königsmark	Varg	GER-J	28.4.92	193/84	400h	49.70	50.47- 10
Konishi	Yuta	JPN	31.7.90	176/60	400h	49.41	49.83- 10
Korchmid	Oleksandr	UKR	22.1.82	188/89	PV	5.62	5.81- 05
Korepanov	Sergey	RUS	15.7.84		50kW	4:03:41	3:56:16- 08
Korir	Japheth	KEN-J	30.6.93	168/55	3000	7:40.93	7:41.38- 10
					5000	13:17.18	13:19.43- 10
Korir	Laban	KEN	30.12.85		Mar	2:06:05	
Korir	Leonard	KEN	10.12.86	164/49	5000	13:26.01	-
					10k	27:29.40	
Korir	Lewis	KEN	11.6.86	168/52	10k	27:41.33	28:14.54- 10
Korir	Wesley	KEN	15.11.82		Mar	2:06:15	2:08:24- 09
Korme	Sisay	ETH	9.1.85	170/62	3kSt	8:20.72	
Koroknai	Tibor	HUN	24.1.90	190/77	400h	50.28	52.25- 10
Kortbeek	Thomas	NED	2.4.81	191/78	400h	50.23	48.95- 03
* Kosencha	Leonard	KEN-Y	21.8.94	175/64	800	1:44.08	
Kosgei	Evans	KEN	.89		HMar	61:09	63:25- 10
Kosgei	Samuel	KEN	20.1.86	173/55	Mar	2:07:47	-0-
Kosgei	Vincent	KEN	11.11.85	175/68	400h	49.49	49.36- 10
Kosgei	Isaiah	KEN	12.2.89	172/67	Mar	2:07:59 (Adam Ismail Khamis BRN)	2:09:09- 09
Kosinov	Artom	KAZ	31.7.86	182/67	3kSt	8:35.11	9:05.78- 07
Koskei	Julius	KEN	6.4.82		HMar	61:22	
Koski-Vähälä	Jarko	FIN	21.11.78	194/97	JT	81.53	84.12- 05
Kostyuchenko	Volodomyr	UKR	20.9.88		DT	60.34	56.45- 10
Kosynskyy ¶	Dmytro	UKR	31.3.89	191/95	JT	83.39	79.53- 10
Kotani	Yusuke	JPN	23.9.89	177/62	100	10.28, 10.18w	10.34, 10.28w- 10
Kovacs	Joe	USA	28.6.89	188/114	SP	19.84i, 19.15	19.36i, 18.73- 10
* Kövágó	Zoltán	HUN	10.4.79	204/127	DT	69.50	69.95- 06
Kovalchuk	Aleksey	RUS	22.7.88	188/79	PV	5.72	5.50- 10
Kovalenko	Nazar	UKR	9.2.89	177/65	20kW	1:21:34	1:22:23- 10
^ Kovals	Ainars	LAT	21.11.81	192/105	JT	78.39	86.64- 08
Kovalyov	Yuriy	RUS	18.6.91		TJ	17.06	16.35- 10
Kovenko	Andriy	UKR	25.11.73	174/64	20kW	1:21:44	1:21:53- 05
Kowal	Yoann	FRA	28.5.87	172/58	1500	3:33.75	3:35.14- 10
					3000	7:46.19i	8:01.04- 08
Kownatke	Rafal	POL	24.3.85	189/133	SP	19.30	19.51i, 18.92- 10
Kozlitin	Viktor	RUS	12.6.88	190/80	PV	5.66	5.30- 10
* Kozmus	Primoz	SLO	30.9.79	188/106	HT	80.28	82.58- 09
Kranjc	Matija	SLO	12.6.84	181/81	JT	79.72	78.08- 07

Name		Nat	Born	Ht/Wt	Event	2011 Mark	Pre-2011 Best
* Kravchenko	Andrey	BLR	4.1.86	187/84	Dec	8023	8617- 07
Kravchuk	Denis	BLR	17.4.87		50kW	4:01:14	4:02:23- 10
Kristensen	Bjørnar Ustad	NOR	26.1.82	172/57	3kSt	8:23.19	8:16.75- 07
* Krivitskiy	Pavel	BLR	17.4.84	188/100	HT	80.67	80.44- 10
* Krivov	Andrey	RUS	14.11.85	178/67	20kW	1:20:16	1:19:06- 08
Kroyter	Dmitriy	ISR-J	18.2.93	189/71	HJ	2.28	2.24i, 2.22- 10
Kruger	A.G.	USA	18.2.79	193/118	HT	76.53	79.26- 04
Krukowski	Marcin	POL-J	14.6.92	182/92	JT	79.19	72.10- 10
^ Krymarenko	Yuriy	UKR	11.8.83	187/65	HJ	2.25i, 2.23	2.34i- 07, 2.33- 05
* Kszczot	Adam	POL	2.9.89	178/64	800	1:43.30	1:45.07- 10
					1000	2:16.99	2:26.11i- 09
Kuc	Dariusz	POL	24.4.86	178/64	100	10.15	10.17- 06
Kucheranyu	Sergey	RUS	30.6.85	185/75	PV	5.65i, 5.62	5.81- 08
Kucmin	Antón	SVK	7.6.84	180/64	20kW	1:23:21	1:23:37- 10
Kudlicka	Jan	CZE	29.4.88	184/76	PV	5.65, 5.81ex	5.70- 08
Kuehl	Adam	USA	19.1.84	188/116	DT	63.82	64.98- 07
Kuira	Paul	KEN	25.1.90	172/53	10k	27:40.60	27:50.64- 10
Kujawski	Lukasz	POL	2.3.88	184/71	3kSt	8:27.12	-0-
Kukk	Mihkel	EST	8.10.83	187/100	JT	80.07	81.77- 08
Kukushkin	Anatoliy	RUS	12.2.86	179/67	20kW	1:21:19	1:23:38- 07
* Kuma	Abera	ETH	31.8.90	160/50	3000	7:47.9+	7:51.21- 10
5000	13:00.15		13:07.83- 10		10k	27:22.54	
Kundert	Andreas	SUI	1.10.84	184/76	110h	13.57	13.41- 08
Kupper	Martin	EST	31.5.89	195/108	DT	60.18	55.19- 10
Kurgat	Nicolas	KEN	7.11.87		Mar	2:08:36	-0-
Kürthy	Lajos	HUN	22.10.86	190/125	SP	20.20	20.78- 08
Kurui	Peter Chesang	KEN	2.1.90		HMar	60:40	61:07- 09
Kurui	Peter Chesang	KEN	2.1.90		Mar	2:08:56	2:13:06- 10
Kusiak	Damian	POL	14.4.88	190/105	SP	20.10, 20.65lt	18.91- 10
Kusuro	Geoffrey	UGA	12.2.89	169/55	3000	7:41.36	
					5000	13:12.32	13:18.38- 08
Kutto	Edwin	KEN	8.1.84		Mar	2:08:57	2:09:51- 10
* Kuznetsov	Viktor	UKR	14.7.86	190/75	TJ	17.01	17.29- 10
Kwalia	James	QAT	12.6.84	176/68	3000	7:37.52	7:28.28- 04
* Kwambai	James Kipsang	KEN	28.2.83	162/52	HMar	60:01	59:09- 09
					Mar	2:08:50	2:05:36- 08
Kynard	Eric	USA	3.2.91	196/80	HJ	2.33i, 2.31	2.27i, 2.25- 10
Kyyrö	Mikko	FIN	12.7.80	191/106	DT	62.74	64.14- 07
* Laâlou	Amine	MAR	13.5.82	178/57	800	1:45.11	1:43.25- 06
1000	2:15.31				1500	3:31.92	3:29.53- 10
Laanmäe	Tanel	EST	29.9.89	183/82	JT	78.18	81.96- 09
LaCour	Carey	USA	17.2.85	180/73	100	10.30, 10.16w	10.28- 09, 10.22w- 10
* Lagat	Bernard	USA	12.12.74	174/61	1500	3:33.11	3:26.34- 01
1M	3:51.38		3:47.28- 01		3000	7:32.13	7:29.00- 10
2M	8:13.62, 8:10.07i		8:12.45- 08		5000	12:53.60	12:54.12- 10
Lagat	Haron	KEN	15.8.83	174/57	3kSt	8:15.80	8:25.04- 10
Lagat	Joseph Kimeli	KEN	.86		Mar	2:08:50	2:10:24- 10
Lahbabi #	Aziz	MAR	3.2.91	178/62	3000	7:45.16dq	8:09.4- 09
					5000	13:13.68	13:28.92- 10
Laine	Samyr	HAI	17.7.84	188/82	TJ	17.09	17.39A, 17.45w- 09, 17.01- 10
Laitinen	Arno	FIN	9.3.88	187/95	HT	72.37	70.71- 10
* Lalang	Boaz	KEN	8.2.89	174/62	800	1:44.13	1:42.95- 10
					1000	2:17.81i	2:14.83- 10
Lamb	Bryce	USA	9.11.90	183/80	LJ	8.15	8.14i, 8.05w- 10, 7.89- 09
Lanaro	Giovanni	MEX	27.9.81	185/82	PV	5.62	5.82- 07
Langat	Clement	KEN	18.12.91	180/67	5000	13:20.09	13:19.76- 10
Langat	Leonard	KEN	7.8.90		HMar	59:52	59:56- 10
Lange	Björn	GER	15.6.79	194/110	JT	78.99	85.21- 01
* Lapierre	Fabrice	AUS	17.10.83	179/66	LJ	8.02	8.40, 8.78w- 10
Laptyev	Sergey	RUS	7.2.91	176/70	TJ	16.63	16.28- 10
LaRue	Brent	USA/SLO	26.4.87	188/84	400	45.75	46.89- 10
					400h	49.77	50.20- 10
Lastennet	Jeff	FRA	26.8.87	179/64	800	1:45.56	1:46.30- 09
Lastre	Yunio	CUB	26.10.81	189/104	DT	62.82	64.58- 10
Lathouwers	Robert	NED	8.7.83	189/78	800	1:46.50	1:44.75- 08
Lauro	Germán	ARG	2.4.84	190/110	SP	20.42	20.43- 10
					DT	62.77	62.53- 10
* Lavillenie	Renaud	FRA	18.9.86	177/69	PV	6.03i, 5.90	6.01- 09
Lawrence	Brijesh BJ	SKN	27.12.89	181/75	200	20.59	20.99- 10
^ Lawrence	Torrin	USA	11.4.89	186/77	200	20.55	20.77- 08
					400	45.61	46.18i- 09, 46.69- 08

Name		Nat	Born	Ht/Wt	Event	2011 Mark	Pre-2011 Best
Lazas	Kevin	USA-J	25.1.92	178/84	Dec	7802	-0-
Lazib	Othman Hadj	ALG	10.5.83	186/85	110h	13.46	13.51- 10
Lebésis	Spirídon	GRE	30.5.87	192/94	JT	81.12	82.90- 10
Lee	Dexter	JAM	18.1.91	186/77	100	10.06	10.16, 10.15w- 10
Leer	Will	USA	15.4.85	184/70	1500	3:36.33	3:37.26- 10
1M	3:58.41	3:55./56i- 10, 3:56,63- 09			2M	8:19.11	
Legesse	Henok	ETH	19.9.88	174/62	1500	3:36.45	3:34.42- 09
Lehata	Mosito	LES	8.4.89	178/70	100	9.8	10.63- 10
Lehtola	Sampo	FIN	10.5.89	188/82	JT	83.77	77.19- 10
Leitis	Janis	LAT	13.4.89	188/70	LJ	7.98	7.90- 09
* Lel	Martin	KEN	29.10.78	171/54	Mar	2:05:45	2:05:15- 08
* Lemaitre	Christophe	FRA	11.6.90	189/74	100	9.92	9.97- 10
					200	19.80	20.16- 10
Lennon-Ford	Luke	GBR	5.5.89	184/73	400	45.56	46.70- 10
Lesnoy	Aleksandr	RUS	28.7.88	194/116	SP	19.60	19.09- 10
Letnicov	Vladimir	MDA	7.10.81	174/68	TJ	16.71i, 16.51, 16.67w	17.06- 02
Levine	Nigel	GBR	30.4.89	175/68	400	45.85	45.78- 09
Lewandowski	Marcin	POL	13.6.87	180/64	800	1:44.53	1:43.84- 09
					1000	2:15.76	2:17.29- 10
^ Lewis	Randy	GRN	14.10.80	188/79	TJ	16.87i, 16.62	17.49- 08
Lewis	Steve	GBR	20.5.86	191/83	PV	5.65	5.75i, 5.72- 09
Lewis	Tydree	USA	26.11.85	184/79	TJ	16.59i, 16.48w	16.52i- 08, 16.25- 09
Lewis-Francis	Mark	GBR	4.9.82	180/82	100	10.19	10.04- 02, 9.97w?-01
Leyver	José	MEX	12.11.85	178/65	20kW	1:22:30	1:25:22- 09
Leyver	José	MEX	12.11.85	178/65	50kW	3:49.16A	3:57:14- 09
^ Li Gaobo		CHN	4.5.89	176/55	50kW	4:04:33	-0-
Li Jianbo		CHN	14.11.86	172/50	50kW	3:43:38	3:43:02- 06
Li Jinzhe		CHN	1.9.89	188/64	LJ	8.02	8.18- 09, 8.29w- 10
Li Tianlei		CHN-Y	13.1.95		20kW	1:22:23	-0-
* Li Yanxi		CHN	26.6.84	182/72	TJ	16.74, 16.76w	17.59- 09
Li Zhilong		CHN	9.3.88	185/75	400h	49.47	51.11- 10
* Lilesa	Feyisa	ETH	1.2.90		HMar	60:50	60:33- 10
Lim Jung-hyun		KOR	8.9.87	182/66	50kW	3:53:05	3:53:24- 10
Limo	Daniel	KEN	10.12.83	174/53	Mar	2:08:39	2:10:54- 09
Limo	Philemon Kimeli	KEN	2.8.85	183/64	HMar	59:30	61:34- 10
					10k	28:10.5A	27:36.94A- 10
Limo	Remmy Ndiwa	KEN	3.2.88	173/55	1500	3:33.65	3:32.83- 10
Limo	Timothy	KEN	8.2.87		800	1:46.09	1:47.94- 10
Lin Ching-Hsuan		TPE-J	14.5.92	168/60	LJ	8.11	7.71, 7.94w- 10
Lin Qing		CHN-Y	5.4.95		LJ	7.95	
^ Lingua	Marco	ITA	4.6.78	179/112	HT	76.12	79.97- 08
Linke	Christopher	GER	24.10.88	191/64	20kW	1:20:51	1:24:29- 09
					50kW	3:52:56	3:53:24- 10
Litchfield	Paul	USA	27.11.80	185/80	PV	5.51i	5.60Ai-05, 5.50- 08
* Litvinov	Sergey	RUS	27.1.86	185/95	HT	78.90	78.98- 10
Liu Jianmin		CHN	9.3.88		20kW	1:23:06	1:24:36- 10
* Liu Xiang		CHN	13.7.83	189/74	110h	13.00	12.88- 06
Llanos	Enrique	PUR	7.5.80	186/79	110h	13.52A	13.64, 13.57dq- 08
Lloyd	Zack	USA	10.10.84	191/141	SP	20.31i, 20.21	21.03- 08
^ Lobinger	Tim	GER	3.9.72	193/86	PV	5.65i, 5.62	6.00- 97
Lobynya	Aleksandr	RUS	31.5.84	193/115	SP	21.00	19.65- 10
Locke	Dentarius	USA	12.12.89	170/68	100	10.25, 10.12w	10.32- 09
					200	20.59	20.58- 09
Loftin	Drew	USA	15.9.80	190/102	HT	74.67	75.42- 10
Logvinenko	Mikhail	RUS	19.4.84	186/83	Dec	8004	7811- 08
Lomnicky	Marcel	SVK	6.7.87	180/90	HT	75.84	74.83- 10
* Lomong	Lopez	USA	1.1.85	178/67	1500	3:33.59	3:32.20- 10
					1M	3:53.85	3:53.18- 10
* Longosiwa	Thomas	KEN	14.1.82	175/57	3000	7:32.71	7:30.09- 09
					5000	12:56.08	12:51.95- 07
Lonyangat	Paul	KEN-J	12.12.92	173/57	3000	7:39.72	7:53.38- 10
5000	13:08.01		13:19.07- 10		10k	27:21.62	28:14.55- 10
López	Kevin	ESP	12.6.90	182/60	800	1:44.49	1:45.8- 10
* López	Luis Fernando	COL	3.6.79	173/60	20kW	1:20:38	1:20:03- 09
López	Miguel Ángel	ESP	3.7.88	180/69	20kW	1:21:41	1:22:23- 09
* López	Yeimer	CUB	20.8.82	184/73	800	1:45.90	1:43.07- 08
Losyev	Ivan	UKR	26.1.86	176/65	20kW	1:22:38	1:21:31- 10
Lovett	Eddie	USA-J	25.6.92	181/73	110h	13.64	-0-
Lovkin	Semyon	RUS	14.7.77	180/67	50kW	4:01:13	3:51:36- 03
Lowe	Richard	USA	21.2.89	185/80	400h	50.15	50.79- 10
Loxsom	Casimir	USA	17.3.91	183/64	800	1:45.28	1:46.57- 10

Name		Nat	Born	Ht/Wt	Event	2011 Mark	Pre-2011 Best
Luchianov	Ion	MDA	31.1.81	178/67	3kSt	8:19.69	8:18.97- 08
Luckwell	Mervyn	GBR	27.11.84	192/108	JT	83.52	81.05- 09
Ludolph	Sören	GER	25.2.88	180/68	800	1:45.04	1:46.69- 09
Lukyanenko	Artem	RUS	30.1.90		Dec	7869	7542- 10
* Lukyanenko	Yevgeniy	RUS ·	23.1.85	190/80	PV	5.72	6.01- 08
Lukyanov	Denis	RUS	11.7.89	190/115	HT	74.24	71.32- 09
Lyons	Nick	USA	8.2.89	186/93	JT	78.39	73.02- 10
Lyuboslavskiy	Anton	RUS	26.6.84	190/137	SP	20.31	20.77- 07
* Lyzhin	Pavel	BLR	24.3.81	189/110	SP	20.85	21.21- 10
Macharinyang	Hosea	KEN	12.6.86	160/45	5000	13:25.17	13:09.85- 07
Mack	Bobby	USA	30.12.84	170/57	10k	28:11.00	-0-
Madison	Chase	USA	13.9.85	192/130	DT	60.64	62.85- 08
Magakwe	Simon	RSA	25.5.85	177/73	100	10.18	10.14A- 10, 10.21- 09
Mägi	Rasmus	EST-J	4.5.92	186/75	400h	50.14	52.75- 09
Mahmoud	Hassan Mohamed	EGY	10.2.84	186/103	HT	74.30	73.87- 10
Mai	Michael	USA	27.7.77	188/123	HT	74.69	76.28- 08
Maia	Edi	POR	10.11.87	176/75	PV	5.60	5.55- 10
Maiyo	Hillary	KEN-J	2.10.93	174/61	1500	3:35.43A	3:36.42- 10
Maiyo	Jonathan	KEN	.88		HMar	59:27dh	59:08- 09
* Majewski	Tomasz	POL	30.8.81	204/140	SP	21.60	21.95- 09
Makarchev	Andrly	UKR	15.11.85	192/76	LJ	8.09	8.15- 09
* Makarov	Sergey	RUS	19.3.73	192/100	JT	87.12	92.61- 02
* Makau	Patrick	KEN	2.3.85	173/57	Mar	2:03:38	2:04:48- 10
Makhloufi	Taoufik	ALG	29.4.88	181/66	800	1:46.32	1:48.39- 10
					1500	3:34.4	3:32.94- 10
* Makusha	Ngonidzashe	ZIM	11.3.87	175/72	100	9.89	10.52- 07
					LJ	8.40	8.30- 08
* Malachowski	Piotr	POL	7.6.83	194/135	DT	68.49	69.83- 10
Malchenko	Eduard	RUS	24.10.86	192/79	HJ	2.28i, 2.23	2.30- 10
^ Malcolm	Christian	GBR	3.6.79	174/67	100	10.17	10.11, 10.09w?- 01
					200	20.54	20.08- 01
Malina	Libor	CZE	14.6.73	193/115	DT	61.86	67.13- 01
Malinkin	Yegor	RUS	18.4.84	196/123	SP	19.23i	18.50- 10
^ Malone	Casey	USA	6.4.77	203/109	DT	62.39A	68.49A- 09
Mamba-Schlick	Hugo	CMR	1.2.82	195/85	TJ	16.56	17.14- 10
Mance	Josh	USA-J	21.3.92	190/77	400	45.29	45.90- 10
Mandieta	José Ángel	CUB	16.10.91	191/93	Dec	7682	7192- 09
* Maniyonga	Luvo	RSA	18.11.91	185/65	LJ	8.26	8.19- 10
* Mannio	Ari	FIN	23.7.87	185/104	JT	85.12	85.70- 09
Manso	Dário	POR	1.7.82	183/117	HT	71.25	74.98- 07
* Manson	Andra	USA	30.4.84	196/75	HJ	2.25	2.35- 09
Manza Kamakya	Nicholas	KEN	2.3.85		HMar	60:59	60:09- 09
					Mar	2:06:34	2:08:42- 09
* Manzano	Leonel	USA	12.9.84	165/57	800	1:45.52	1:44.56- 10
1500	3:33.66		3:32.37- 10		1M	3:51.24	3:50.64- 10
Maphutha	Mpho	RSA-J	21.1.93	172/65	LJ	8.00A	7.51A- 10
Marcell	Jan	CZE	4.6.85	197/111	SP	20.76	20.20i- 10, 19.07- 09
					DT	66.00	64.83- 09
Marciniszyn	Marcin	POL	7.9.82	185/72	400	45.27	45.54- 06
Marco	Luis Alberto	ESP	20.8.86	183/70	800	1:45.95	1:45.26- 10
Margis	Thorsten	GER	14.8.89	190/90	Dec	7707	7492- 09
Maric	Martin	CRO	19.4.84	196/115	DT	65.81	64.74- 10
Márquez	Dayron	COL	19.11.83	181/93	JT	79.35A	79.32A- 09, 82.20Au- 08
Marshin	Dmitriy	AZE	24.2.72	180/100	HT	74.04	77.01- 10
* Martin	Cory	USA	22.5.85	196/125	SP	20.72	22.10- 10
^ Martín	Eliseo	ESP	5.11.73	172/61	3kSt	8:23.43	8:09.09- 03
Martin	Romain	FRA	12.7.88	198/86	Dec	7867(w), 7727	7294- 10
Martin	Ryan	USA	23.3.89	185/68	800	1:45.34	1:46.71- 10
* Martina	Churandy	NED	3.7.84	180/68	100	10.10	9.93- 08, 9.76Aw- 06
					200	20.38	20.08- 10
* Martínez	Guillermo	CUB	28.6.81	187/107	JT	87.20A	87.17- 06
Martínez	Lois Maikel	CUB	3.6.81	185/90	DT	65.03	67.45- 05
* Martínez	Wilfredo	CUB	9.1.85	180/82	LJ	8.11	8.31A- 08, 8.20- 10
Martinson	Geoffrey	CAN	26.3.86	181/67	1500	3:37.56	3:39.21- 08
Martos	Sebastián	ESP	20.6.89	177/60	3kSt	8:23.02	8:42.37- 10
Martynyuk	Andriy	UKR	25.9.90	179/86	HT	73.10	73.00- 10
Masai	Dennis	KEN	1.12.91	168/52	5000	13:23.53	
					10k	27:32.97	27:53.88- 10
* Masai	Moses	KEN	1.6.86	172/57	5000	13:13.03	12:50.55- 08
					10k	27:10.05	26:49.20- 07

Name		Nat	Born	Ht/Wt	Event	2011 Mark	Pre-2011 Best
Masai Ndiwa	Titus	KEN	9.10.89		HMar	60:40	59:51- 10
Maslák	Pavel	CZE	21.2.91	174/60	200	20.63	21.05- 10
Mason	Jamele	PUR	19.10.89	190/85	400h	49.30	49.97- 10
Mason	Michael	JAM	26.4.87	181/75	400	45.91	46.03- 07
Massenberg	Aramis	USA	6.8.89	186/79	110h	13.71, 13.63w	13.91- 10
Masuoka	Hiroaki	JPN	18.2.86	185/70	400h	50.11	49.76- 08
Mätas	Risto	EST	30.4.84	190/87	JT	81.56	80.53- 06
Matebo Omari	Levi	KEN	3.11.89	173/55	HMar	60:07	62:48A- 10
Matebor	Albert	KEN	20.12.80	174/57	HMar	60:52	61:39- 07
					Mar	2:05:25	2:09:33- 07
* Matelong	Richard	KEN	14.10.83	179/65	3kSt	8:07.41	8:00.89- 09
* Mathathi	Martin	KEN	25.12.85	1167/52	5000	13:15.93	13:03.84- 04
10k	27:23.85		26:59.88- 09		HMar	58:56dh	59:48- 10
Mathieu	Michael	BAH	24.6.83	180/78	200	20.38	20.80- 07, 20.62w- 08
				8	400	45.54	45.17- 08
Mathiszik	Willi	GER	17.6.84	185/70	110h	13.48	13.49- 09
Matsumiya	Takayuki	JPN	21.2.80	163/49	10k	28:14.43	27:41.75- 08
Matsuo	Shintaro	JPN-J	16.7.93		200	20.60w	
Matsuoka	Yuki	JPN	14.1.86	176/59	10k	28:03.46	28:19.06- 10
Matthews	Peter	JAM	13.11.89	189/77	400	45.62	46.63- 10
Matum	Geoffrey	KEN	22.11.87	178/64	800	1:45.94	1:47.01- 10
Maxwell	Benoit	FRA	2.5.88	181/72	LJ	7.88, 8.06w	7.91i- 10, 7.83- 08
Mayer	Gerhard	AUT	20.5.80	191/100	DT	63.35	65.24- 10
Mayer	Kevin	FRA-J	10.2.92	185/75	Dec	7992	-0-
Mayers	Emanuel	TRI	9.3.89	178/70	400h	49.86A, 50.43	49.65- 10
Mazác	Martin	CZE	6.5.90	187/74	110h	13.68, 13.62w	13.64- 10
* Mazuryk	Maksym	UKR	2.4.83	190/85	PV	5.88i, 5.72	5.82- 08
* Mbandjock	Martial	FRA	14.10.85	187/84	100	10.13	10.06- 08
					200	20.59w	20.38- 10
* Mbishei	Titus	KEN	28.10.90	178/59	5000	13:11.76	13:00.04- 10
					10k	26:59.81	27:29.13A- 10
Mbithi	Robert Wambua	KEN	26.6.89		HMar	61:08	61:00- 10
Mbugua	Bernard Nganga	KEN	.85	170/55	3kSt	8:05.88	8:16.22- 10
McAdams	Josh	USA	26.3.80	175/68	3kSt	8:30.78	8:21.36- 07
McCloud	Nick	USA	7.12.89	185/77	110h	13.77, 13.61w	13.67- 10
McCormick	Nick	GBR	11.9.81	188/72	1500	3:37.00	3:35.74- 05
McCoy	Reuben	USA	16.3.86	186/75	400h	49.97	48.37- 08
McCullough	Conor	USA	31.1.91	186/102	HT	72.67	70.78- 10
^ McFarlane	Danny	JAM	14.2.72	185/81	400h	49.04	48.00- 04
McFarlane	Jorge	PER	20.2.88	176/70	LJ	7.95	8.10A- 09, 7.59- 10
McGirt	Ronnie	USA	19.2.88	190/84	110h	13.51	13.96, 13.72w- 10
McLean	Sean	USA-J	23.3.92	185/77	200	20.62	21.28- 09
McNamara	Jordan	USA	7.3.87	178/64	1500	3:37.19	3:41.13- 07
					1M	3:54.89	3:59.87- 09
McNeal	Maurice	USA	4.1.91	187/80	400	45.60	45.58- 02
McNeill	David	AUS	6.10.86	175/59	10k	28:12.66	28:03.02- 08
* McQuay	Tony	USA	16.4.90	178/64	200	20.61i	20.64- 10
					400	44.68	45.37- 10
Mecic	Kemal	BIH	4.8.85	196/110	SP	19.65	19.68- 09
* Medhin	Teklemariam	ERI	24.6.89	178/57	5000	13:16.53	13:04.55- 10
					10k	27:37.21	27:46.50- 08
Meftah	Abdellatif	FRA	3.1.82		HMar	61:02dh	60:46- 10
Megersa	Tujuba	ETH	15.10.87	171/52	HMar	59:43	60:16- 09
Meité	Ben Youssef	CIV	11.11.86	179/70	100	10.21, 10.14w	10.08A- 10, 10.21, 10.15w- 09
					200	20.60	20.37- 09
Mejía	David	MEX	7.12.86	164/54	20kW	1:22:36A	1:22:47- 08
Mejías	Reinier	CUB	22.9.90	180/96	HT	73.39	71.47- 10
Mekhissi-Benabbad	Mahiedine	FRA	15.3.85	190/75	1500	3:33.86	3:35.06- 09
2000	5:00.17				3kSt	8:02.09	8:02.52- 10
* Mekonnen	Deresse	ETH	20.10.87	175/60	1500	3:32.90	3:32.18- 09
^ Mekonnen	Hailu	ETH	4.4.80	172/61	Mar	2:07:35	2:07:37- 10
Meleshko	Pavel	BLR-J	24.11.92		JT	78.08	-0-
Melich	Lukás	CZE	16.9.80	186/105	HT	75.40	79.36- 05
^ Méliz	Luis Felipe	ESP	11.8.79	182/80	LJ	8.18, 8.20w	8.43- 00
Mello	Rafael	BRA	22.9.85		LJ	8.02	7.90A- 08
Melnykov	Stanislav	UKR	26.2.87	184/70	400h	49.24	49.09- 10
Ménaldo	Kevin	FRA-J	12.7.92	176/66	PV	5.50	5.10i- 10, 5.05- 09
Méndez	Juan José	MEX	27.4.88	180/80	JT	78.23	76.50- 10
* Menjo	Josephat Kiprono	KEN	20.8.79	168/50	3000	7:47.38	7:42.6- 10
5000	13:21.10		12:55.95- 10		10k	27:55.81	26:56.74- 10

Name		Nat	Born	Ht/Wt	Event	2011 Mark	Pre-2011 Best
* Menkov	Aleksandr	RUS	7.12.90	173/68	LJ	8.28	8.16- 09
* Merga	Deriba	ETH	26.10.80	168/52	HMar	59:25	59:15- 08
					Mar	2:09:13	2:06:38- 08
* Merga	Imane	ETH	15.10.88	172/55	3000	7:48.1+	7:45.8- 10
5000	12:54.21		12:53.58- 10		10k	26:48.35	27:15.94- 09
* Merritt	Aries	USA	24.7.85	188/75	110h	13.12	13.09- 07
* Merritt	LaShawn	USA	27.6.86	188/82	200	20.13	19.98- 07, 19.80w- 08
					400	44.35	43.75- 08
Merzougui	Abdelaziz	ESP	30.8.91	179/64	3kSt	8:22.00	8:33.29- 10
Mesel	Amanuel	ERI	29.12.90	175/57	5000	13:16.25	13:25.23- 08
					HMar	61:20	61:54A- 10
Mesfin	Nahom	ETH	3.6.89	180/62	3kSt	8:12.04	8:14.68- 08
* Mesnil	Romain	FRA	13.6.77	188/80	PV	5.80i, 5.73	5.95- 03
Metu	Obinna	NGR	12.7.88	185/75	100	10.27, 10.12w	10.16, 10.0- 08
Meucci	Daniele	ITA	8.4.85	178/62	5000	13:24.94	13:24.38- 10
					10k	27:44.50	28:08.4- 08
* Michalski	Lukasz	POL	2.8.88	190/78	PV	5.85	5.80- 10
Micuda	Mirko	CRO	22.12.89	185/110	HT	73.53	74.06- 10
Mikhailovskiy	Sergey	RUS	20.5.87	190/82	LJ	8.05	8.00- 10
Mikhan	Eduard	BLR	7.6.89	194/85	Dec	8152	7999- 10
* Mikhnevich	Andrey	BLR	12.7.76	202/140	SP	22.10	22.09- 10
* Miles	Derek	USA	28.9.72	190/88	PV	5.72i, 5.72	5.85i- 05, 5.85sq- 08
Miller	Bryan	USA	31.5.89	190/79	400	45.29	45.57- 09
Miller	Craig	USA	3.8.87	185/72	1500	3:37.56	3:37.81- 09
Miller	Kyle	USA	15.5.85	188/73	1500	3:36.82	3:41.67- 08
Miller	Ramon	BAH	17.2.87	180/73	400	45.01A, 45.31	44.99- 09
Milne	Taylor	CAN	14.6.81	180/66	1500	3:36.71	3:36.00- 08
Milokumov	Sergey	RUS	13.11.87		HJ	2.25i, 2.20	2.24- 10
Milus	Ryan	USA	19.9.90	178/70	100	10.23, 10.07w	10.33- 09
Minczér	Albert	HUN	1.10.86	180/60	3kSt	8:27.49	8:31.82- 09
Minns	Latario	BAH-Y	10.3.94		TJ	16.55	15.78- 10
Minshin	Ildar	RUS	5.2.85	172/63	3kSt	8:17.74	8:21.16- 08
Miout	Mounir	ALG	14.9.84		5000	13:19.73	14:10.08- 09
Misans	Elvijs	LAT	8.4.89	182/73	LJ	8.00i, 7.88	7.54- 10
					TJ	16.58	16.16- 08
* Mitchell	Maurice	USA	22.12.89	181/73	100	10.00	10.14, 10.04w- 10, 10.0w- 08
					200	20.19, 19.99w	20.24- 10
Miyawaki	Chihiro	JPN	28.8.91	174/55	10k	27:41.57	28:21.00- 10
Mlaab	Abdelhakim	MAR	22.9.88	182/78	LJ	7.98, 8.04w	8.00- 10
Moeng	Lebogang	RSA	10.10.89	173/67	200	20.58A	
					400	45.47	
Moffatt	Keith	USA	20.6.84	203/84	HJ	2.27i, 2.24	2.30- 06
Mogawane	Ofentse	RSA	20.2.82	179/63	400	45.59	45.11- 06
Moghaddam	Reza	IRI	17.11.88		HT	71.82	70.16- 10
Mogusu	Mekubo	KEN	25.12.86	165/52	HMar	61:29	59:48- 07
Mohammed	Mukhtar	GBR	1.12.90	175/59	800	1:45.90	1:46.92- 10
* Mohr	Malte	GER	24.7.86	193/78	PV	5.86i, 5.85	5.90- 10
Möhsner	Sven	GER	30.1.86	190/115	HT	72.12	73.82- 09
Moiseyenko	Taras	RUS	5.5.86		TJ	16.75i, 16.49	16.99- 09
* Mokoena	Khotso	RSA	6.3.85	190/73	LJ	8.25, 8.31w	8.50- 09
Mokoka	Stephen	RSA	31.1.85	153/50	10k	27:56.18	28:18.54- 10
Molepo	Edwin	RSA	31.5.87	175/65	3kSt	8:26.82	8:31.21- 10
Møller	Anders	DEN	5.9.77	185/81	TJ	16.88	17.01i- 06, 16.76- 05
Moore	Lee	USA	20.12.88	192/82	400h	49.82	49.52- 10
Moradi	Sadjad	IRI	30.3.83	182/67	800	1:46.17	1:44.74- 05
Morales	Ignacio	CUB	28.1.87	183/69	110h	13.58, 13.4	13.1- 08, 13.51- 09
Moreno	Edder	COL	4.2.89	185/120	SP	19.48	19.11- 10
Morgan	Jason	JAM	6.10.82	186/114	DT	64.11	62.95- 07
Morgunov	Sergey	RUS-J	9.2.93	173/64	LJ	8.10, 8.18w	7.66- 10
* Morioka	Koichiro	JPN	2.4.85	184/65	20kW	1:22:10	1:20:43- 10
					50kW	3:44:45	3:47:41- 10
* Morozov	Sergey	RUS	21.3.88	170/60	20kW	1:19:18	1:16:43- 08
Morrison	Michael	USA	18.3.88	183/77	Dec	8118	7803- 08
Morse	Brett	GBR	11.2.89	191/117	DT	66.06	63.35- 10
Morton	Amaechi	NGR	30.10.89	181/73	400h	49.08	48.94- 10
* Mosop	Moses	KEN	17.7.85	172/57	Mar	2:05:37, 2:03:06dh	-0-
Moss	Miller	USA	14.3.88	193/86	Dec	7996	7628- 10
Mossberg	Nick	USA	5.4.86	178/77	PV	5.55	5.46- 09
Motlagale	Thumelo	RSA	26.11.86		3kSt	8:30.24	
^ Mottram	Craig	AUS	18.6.80	188/72	1500	3:37.53	3:33.97- 06, 3:32.7?+- 05
3000	7:50.0+		7:32.19-06		5000	13:11.51	12:55.76- 04

Name		Nat	Born	Ht/Wt	Event	2011 Mark	Pre-2011 Best
Moulinet	Bertrand	FRA	6.1.87	178/63	20kW	1:21:50	1:23:23- 10
					50kW	3:50:49	4:04:13- 09
Mousavi	Kaveh	IRI	27.5.85	196/105	HT	75.26	73.00- 09
* Moustaoui	Mohammed	MAR	2.4.85	174/60	1500	3:31.84	3:32.06- 08
1M	3:50.67		3:50.08- 08		3000	7:43.99	7:43.08i- 08, 7:49.57- 05
^ Moya	Victor	CUB	24.10.82	196/80	HJ	2.28	2.35- 05
Mpuang	Thuso	RSA	1.3.84	177/75	100	10.16	10.27- 09
					200	20.55, 20.40w	20.53A- 08, 20.61- 09
Mucheru	Leonard	KEN	13.6.78	182/66	Mar	2:08:53	2:09:37- 09
* Muchiri Ndambiri	Josphat	KEN	12.2.85	171/52	5000	13:12.77	13:05.33- 05
10k	27:39.21		26:57.36- 09		Mar	2:07:36	-0-
Mudrov	Sergey	RUS	8.9.90	188/79	HJ	2.30i, 2.30	2.30i- 09, 2.27- 10
Mukun	Simon	KEN	5.8.84		Mar	2:09:19	2:09:35- 10
Mulabegovic	Nedzad	CRO	4.2.81	189/100	SP	20.43i, 20.10	20.56- 10
* Mulaudzi	Mbulaeni	RSA	8.9.80	171/62	800	1:45.50	1:42.86- 09
Mulder	Tyler	USA	15.2.87	189/77	800	1:44.83	1:46.32- 10
Müller	Norman	GER	7.8.85	195/84	Dec	7997	8295- 09
Mullera	Ángel	ESP	20.4.84	175/62	3kSt	8:16.47	8:22.75- 09
Mullings	Dwight	JAM	10.12.86	178/74	400	45.87	44.98- 09
* Mullings ¶	Steve	JAM	29.11.82	173/68	100	9.80	10.01- 09, 9.91w- 07
					200	20.15, 20.11dq	19.98- 09, 19.90w- 04
Mumba	Prince	ZAM	28.8.84	167/67	800	1:46.14	1:46.3- 09
Münch	Markus	GER	13.6.86	207/130	DT	66.87	65.37- 10
Mungara	Kenneth	KEN	7.9.73	170/52	Mar	2:07:36	2:07:58- 10
Munyeki Kiama	Charles	KEN	2.11.86		Mar	2:08:04	2:07:06- 09
* Murakami	Yukifumi	JPN	23.12.79	185/92	JT	83.53	83.15- 10
Murasawa	Akinobu	JPN	28.3.91	166/53	10k	28:00.78	28:44.23- 09
Murdaugh	Thomas	USA	25.9.89	182/73	400	45.81	45.78- 09
Murdock	Justin	USA	21.4.89	178/73	100	10.13	10.30- 10
Muriuki	Peter	KEN	.83		HMar	60:55	61:22- 08
* Murofushi	Koji	JPN	8.10.74	187/100	HT	81.24	84.86- 03
Murphy	Isaac	USA	5.10.90	188/83	Dec	7806	7010- 10
Murray	Leslie	ISV	24.1.91	188/77	400h	49.95	49.83- 09
* Mutahi	Sammy	KEN	1.6.89	177/58	3000	7:44.27i, 7:52.94	7:31.41- 09
Mutai	Abel	KEN	2.10.88	172/55	3kSt	8:21.02	8:11.40- 09
* Mutai	Emmanuel	KEN	12.10,84	168/54	HMar	59:52dh	60:03- 10
					Mar	2:04:40	2:06:15- 08
* Mutai	Geoffrey	KEN	7.10.81	170/54	10k	27:38.9A	27:27.79A- 10
					Mar	2:05:06, 2:03:02dh	2:04:55- 10
Mutai	Mark	KEN	23.3.78	178/68	400	45.91	45.28A, 45.44- 10
Mutai	Michael	KEN			10k	28:15.5A	
Mutegi	Anderson	KEN	1.5.87	188/75	400	45.70A, 45.95	45.22- 10
Mutekanga	Julius	UGA	1.12.87	175/64	800	1:46.30	1:48.22- 07
Muti	Duncan Kipkemboi	KEN	8.3.91	162/54	10k	27:58.26	27:53.00- 10
Mutua	David	KEN-J	20.4.92	184/68	800	1:43.99	1:45.90- 10
Mvumvure	Gabriel	ZIM	23.4.88	172/75	100	10.10w	
Mwaka	Patrick	KEN-J	2.11.92	165/45	5000	13:26.29	13:21.45- 10
					10k	27:33.14	27:56.39- 10
Mwangangi	John	KEN	1.11.90		HMar	59:45	59:56- 10
Mwangi	Alex	KEN	14.6.90	158/50	10k	27:47.51	27:42.20- 10
Mwangi	James	KEN	23.6.84	176/56	HMar	60:43	60:34- 08
					Mar	2:08:38	2:10:27-- 07
Mwikya Mutunga	Patrick	KEN-Y	20.11.94	175/55	3000	7:40.47	-0-
					5000	13:19.13	
^ Myerscough	Carl	GBR	21.10.79	209/149	SP	19.31	21.92- 03
					DT	65.04	65.10- 04
Mykolaitis	Povilas	LTU	23.2.83	187/79	LJ	8.15	8.13i, 8.09- 05
Mykolaychuk	Dmytro	UKR	30.1.87	192/89	HT	75.24	72.85- 08
Mzazi	Gladwin	RSA	28.8.88	160/48	10k	28:09.33	28:20.40- 10
Nagaiwa	Hiroki	JPN	25.5.89	174/58	20kW	1:23:20	1:24:15- 10
Nakamura	Akihiko	JPN	23.10.90	179/63	400h	50.04	50.66- 10
Nartov	Aleksandr	UKR	21.5.88	182/67	HJ	2.28i, 2.25	2.30i- 07, 2.30- 08
Nascimento	Yazaldes	POR	17.4.86	181/75	100	10.15w	10.42- 07
* Nava	Horacio	MEX	20.1.82	175/62	20kW	1:22:15	1:22:53- 04
					50kW	3:45:29	3:45:21- 08
* Nazarov	Dilshod	TJK	6.5.82	187/115	HT	80.30	80.11- 10
Ndiema	Eric	KEN-J	28.12.92		HMar	60:20	59:57- 09
					Mar	2:06:07	
Ndiku	Caleb	KEN-J	9.10.92	175/62	1500	3:32.02	3:37.30- 10
					1M	3:49.77	
* Ndiku	Jonathan	KEN	18.9.91	173/60	5000	13:19.04	13:11.99- 09
					3kSt	8:07.75	8:17.28- 08

Name		Nat	Born	Ht/Wt	Event	2011 Mark	Pre-2011 Best
Ndirangu	Charles	KEN-J	8.2.93	166/49	5000	13:15.44	
Ndiwa	Cornelius	KEN	17.12.88	183/64	1500	3:36.51	3:36.09- 10
Ndungu	Geoffrey	KEN	11,3.84		Mar	2:08:35	-0-
Ndungu	Samuel	KEN	4.4.88	166/53	HMar	60:55	61:17- 08
Nedow	Tim	CAN	16.10.90	200/120	SP	19.51i, 18.84	17.90- 10
Nellum	Bryshon	USA	1.5.89	183/79	400	45.56	45.38- 07
* Nelson	Adam	USA	7.7.75	183/115	SP	22.09	22.51- 02
Nelson	Billy	USA	11.9.84	167/55	3kSt	8:17.27	8:21.47- 08
Nelson	Tim	USA	27.2.84	173/59	10k	27:28.19	27:31.56- 10
Németh	Kristóf	HUN	17.9.87	190/97	HT	76.29	76.45- 10
Nesterenko	Mykyta	UKR	15.4.91	208/112	DT	62.60	65.31- 08
Nesterovskyy	Stanislav	UKR	31.7.80	198/120	DT	64.49	64.94- 07
^ Neville	David	USA	1.6.84	193/77	400	45.24	44.61- 08
Nevsyantsev	Vitaliy	RUS	8.9.83	177/69	3kSt	8:35.03	8:38.25- 08
Newdick	Brent	NZL	31.1.85	189/89	Dec	8114	8091- 10
Newman	Calesio	USA	20.8.86	172/66	100	10.14	10.27- 10, 10.08w- 08
					200	20.53	20.77, 20.59w- 08
* Ngatuny	Gideon	KEN	10.10.86	173/54	5000	13:21.25	13:11.81- 08
					10k	27:41.32	27:01.83- 09
Ngoepe	Samson	RSA	28.1.85	180/60	800	1:45.69	1:45.17- 09
Ngugi	Geoffrey	KEN	11.9.84		HMar	61:18	60:49- 99
Nieto	James	USA	2.11.76	193/79	HJ	2.28	2.34- 04
Niimura	Mamoru	JPN	18.4.86	180/62	LJ	8.03w	7.89- 08
Niit	Marek	EST	9.8.87	183/75	100	10.21, 10.17w	10.42- 07, 10.34w- 10
					200	20.43, 20.38w	20.69- 07
Niit	Priidu	EST	27.1.90	198/113	DT	60.69	57.60- 10
Nikfar	Amin	IRI	2.1.81	193/130	SP	20.05	19.94- 08
Nikitin	Yevgen	UKR	9.1.85	186/75	Dec	7795	7853- 09
^ Niklaus	André	GER	30.8.81	190/82	Dec	7874	8371- 07
Nikolayev	Sergey	RUS	1.9.87		LJ	7.89, 8.20w	8.07- 10
Nikolayev	Yegor	RUS	12.2.88	182/66	3kSt	8:30.49	8:37.01- 09
Nima	Issam	ALG	8.4.79	186/74	TJ	16.80	16.50- 10
Ninov	Viktor	BUL	19.6.88		HJ	2.29	2.26- 10
Niu Wenbin		CHN	20.1.91	173/60	50kW	3:54:19	-0-
* Nixon	Greg	USA	12.9.81	183/75	200	20.43	20.39- 09
					400	44.98	44.61- 10
* Nizhegorodov	Denis	RUS	26.7.80	180/61	50kW	3:42:45	3:34:14- 08
Njeru	Micah	KEN	5.8.88	166/53	10k	28:03.48	27:48.40- 07
Njui	Cyrus	KEN	11.2.86	171/52	Mar	2:09:10	2:11:22- 10
Nkouloukidi	Jean-Jacques	ITA	15.4.82	172/58	50kW	3:52:35	3:55:40- 10
^ Noga	Artur	POL	2.5.88	195/82	110h	13.57	13.29, 13.20w- 10
Noguchi	Hiroshi	JPN	3.5.83	176/106	HT	70.89	71.58- 10
Nolan	Errol	USA	18.8.91	178/73	400	45.30	45.59- 10
Nolf	Cedric	BEL	18.6.89	182/79	Dec	7818	7370- 10
Norman	Josh	USA	26.7.80	188/75	100	10.23, 10.19w	10.09- 04
Norman	Tom	GBR	15.9.82		DT	59.98	56.12- 08
Novak	Robert	USA	20.3.86	180/78	800	1:46.01	1:46.85- 10
Novotny	Roman	CZE	5.1.86	180/73	LJ	8.01i, 7.94	8.21- 08
Nowak	Lukasz	POL	18.12.88	186/59	50kW	3:46:40	3:50:30- 10
Nowicki	Bartosz	POL	26.2.84	187/70	1500	3:36.68	3:37.90- 08
Nowicki	Wojciech	POL	22.2.89	190/90	HT	72.72	69.59- 10
Ntiamoah	Isaac	AUS	27.10.82	178/74	100	10.14w	10.40- 08, 10.2- 03
Nugent	Barrett	USA	29.1.90	186/77	110h	13.48, 13.19w	13.35- 10
Nurudeen	Selim	NGR	1.2.83	183/75	110h	13.61	13.55- 10
* Nymark	Trond	NOR	28.12.76	180/64	50kW	3:54:26	3:41:16- 09
O'Connor	Brandon	USA	2.9.89	188/75	400	45.51	46.04- 09
O'Lionáird	Ciarán	IRL	11.4.88	180/64	1500	3:34.46	3:48.36- 08
^ Obikwelu	Francis	POR	22.11.78	195/79	100	10.18	9.86- 04, 9.84w- 06
Oda	Yoshinori	JPN	5.12.80	163/49	Mar	2:09:03	-0-
Odom	Marlon	GER	4.12.82	189/75	110h	13.57	13.50- 10, 13.45w- 06
^ Odriozola	Mikel	ESP	25.5.73	180/62	50kW	3:49:33	3:41:47- 05
Offereins	Ben	AUS	3.12.86	182/72	400	45.85	44.86- 10
Ogho-Oghene	Egweru	NGR	26.11.88	171/66	100	10.06	10.10- 10, 10.0- 08
Ogita	Hiroki	JPN	30.12.87	185/78	PV	5.50	5.56- 08
Ogunkole	Segun	NGR	11.6.84	188/73	400	45.91	46.60- 09
Ogunmola	Tobi	NGR-J	20.6.92	182/73	400	45.82	46.77- 10
Ogunode	Femi Seun	QAT	15.5.91	180/75	100	10.07	10.25- 10
200	20.30		20.43- 10		400	45.41	45.12- 10
Oh Se-hyun		KOR	17.11.88		50kW	3:54:20	3:56.43- 10
Okamoto	Naoki	JPN	26.5.84	176/56	10k	28:05.84	28:07.99- 10
* Oke	Tosin	NGR	1.10.80	178/77	TJ	17.21	17.22A, 17.16- 10

	Name		Nat	Born	Ht/Wt	Event	2011 Mark	Pre-2011 Best
	Okken	Arnoud	NED	20.4.82	182/65	800	1:46.46	1:45.64- 01
	Okoye	Lawrence	GBR	6.10.91	198/137	DT	67.63	-0-
	Oleitiptip	Alex	KEN	22.9.82	176/58	5000	13:12.76	13:14.08- 10
	Olgundeniz	Ercüment	TUR	7.7.76	203/120	DT	66.89	64.70- 08
	Olinger	Brian	USA	2.6.83	178/62	10k	28:07.52	28:45.69- 06
						3kSt	8:23.36	8:19.29- 07
	de Oliveira	Júlio César	BRA	4.2.86	185/97	JT	77.70	80.05, 80.29 irreg- 09
*	Oliver	David	USA	24.4.82	188/93	110h	12.94	12.89- 10
	Olkhovskiy	Yevgeniy	ISR	22.12.83	181/73	PV	5.47i	5.55i- 09, 5.50- 10
	Ollikainen	Ronni	FIN	27.8.90	188/76	LJ	8.04	8.00- 10
*	Olmedo	Manuel	ESP	17.5.83	179/60	800	1:44.56	1:45.13- 07
						1500	3:34.44	3:36.98- 10
	Olson	Petter	SWE	14.2.91	183/79	Dec	7724	7470- 10
*	Olsson	Christian	SWE	25.1.80	192/78	TJ	17.29	17.83i, 17.79- 04, 17.92w- 03
	Omari	Levi Matebo	KEN	3.11.89	173/55	Mar	2:05:16	2:12:06- 10
	Onakoya	Abiola	NGR	10.10.90	175/73	400	45.89	46.49- 09
	Oni	Samson	GBR	25.6.81	184/74	HJ	2.27	2.31i- 10, 2.30- 08
	Onnen	Eike	GER	3.8.82	194/83	HJ	2.31	2.34- 07
	Ono	Hiroyuki	JPN	3.10.86	170/56	10k	28:06.35	28:26.61- 07
*	Oosthuizen	Robert	RSA	23.1.87	188/101	JT	84.38	86.80- 08
*	Oprea	Marian	ROU	6.6.82	190/80	LJ	8.06w	7.73- 05
						TJ	17.62i, 17.19	17.81- 05
	Ortega	Orlando	CUB	29.7.91	185/70	110h	13.29, 13.1w	13.99- 10
	Osaghae	Omo	USA	18.5.88	188/82	110h	13.23, 13.18w	13.51, 13.42w- 09
	Osagie	Andrew	GBR	19.2.88	189/72	800	1:45.36	1:46.41- 10
	Osman	Abrar	ERI-Y	1.1.94	173/55	3000	7:40.89	-0-
	Ostrowski	Artur	POL	10.7.88	181/60	800	1:44.82	1:47.52- 09
						1500	3:34.45	3:46.57- 09
	Otterling	Andreas	SWE	25.5.86	183/80	LJ	7.89i, 7.97w	7.67- 10
*	Otto	Björn	GER	16.10.77	188/84	PV	5.75, 5.80ex	5.90- 07
	Oubassour	Hassan Ali	FRA	20.7.80	176/60	3kSt	8:27.49	8:32.46- 10
	Ouhadi	Aziz	MAR	24.7.84	175/73	100	10.09	10.25, 10.17w, 9.9- 09
						200	20.62	20.51A, 20.86- 10
*	Özbilen	Ilham Tanui	TUR	5.3.90	177/60	800	1:44.25	–
	1000	2:17.08			–	1500	3:31.37	3:31.70- 09
*	Padgett	Travis	USA	13.12.86	174/80	100	9.99, 9.96w	9.89, 9.85w- 08
	Paech	Carlo	GER-J	18.11.92	190/84	PV	5.50i, 5.35	5.40i, 5.21- 10
	Paes	Lutimar	BRA	14.12.88	179/70	800	1:45.32	1:46.70- 10
*	Pahapill	Mikk	EST	18.7.83	197/91	Dec	8398	8298- 10
	Pahlevanyan	Vartan	ARM	27.2.88		LJ	8.00A, 7.90w	7.82- 09
	Palma	Ever	MEX-J	18.3.92		20kW	1:21:02	
	Palomeque	Rubén	ESP	14.8.80	175/57	3kSt	8:23.28	8:20.07- 08
	Panocha	Babubhai	IND	10.8.78		20kW	1:23:04	1:23:06- 09
^	Papadimitríou	Alexándros	GRE	18.6.73	185/115	HT	74.01	80.45- 00
	Papadoníou	Stamátios	GRE	3.5.84	191/117	HT	72.05	74.73- 09
	Papamihaíl	Aléxandros	GRE	18.9.88	178/63	20kW	1:23:21	1:25:06- 09
	Parchment	Hansle	JAM	17.6.90	193/82	110h	13.24	13.71- 10
	Parellis	Apostolos	CYP	24.7.85	188/95	DT	61.44	61.92- 10
	Park Chil-sung		KOR	8.7.82	174/64	20kW	1:22:28	1:20:17- 08
						50kW	3:47:13	3:56:45- 09
	Park Jae-myong		KOR	15.12.81	180/95	JT	80.19	83.99- 04
	Park Tae-kyong		KOR	30.7.80	181/75	110h	13.66	13.48- 10
	Parkhomenko	Aleksandr	BLR	22.3.81	182/82	Dec	7813	8136- 06
	Parros	Clayton	USA	11.12.90	178/70	400	45.78	45.71- 09
*	Pars	Krisztián	HUN	18.2.82	188/104	HT	81.89	82.45- 06
	Parsons	Tom	GBR	5.5.84	192/80	HJ	2.31i, 2.28	2.30- 08
	Parszczynski	Lukasz	POL	4.5.85	180/64	3kSt	8:15.47	8:29.46- 08
	Patrakov	Andrey	RUS	7.11.89	188/65	HJ	2.25i, 2.21	2.21i- 09, 2.20- 10
*	Patton	Darvis	USA	4.12.77	183/75	100	9.94	9.89, 9.84w- 08
						200	20.25, 19.98w	20.03- 03
	Paula	Jorge	POR	8.10.84	188/78	400h	49.72	50.49- 08
	Pauli	Jacob	USA	15.6.79	191/86	PV	5.52i	5.82- 07
	Paulo	Alberto	POR	3.10.85	178/62	3kSt	8:22.41	8:24.06- 10
	Pavelyev	Aleksandr	RUS	30.7.87	175/62	3kSt	8:32.61	8:34.12- 09
^	Pavlov	Igor	RUS	18.7.79	187/83	PV	5.70i, 5.64	5.90i- 05, 5.81- 07
*	Payne	David	USA	24.7.82	185/81	110h	13.63	13.02- 07
	Peacock	Hamish	AUS	15.10.90	186/106	JT	77.58	73.66- 10
	Peçanha	Fabiano	BRA	5.6.82	186/73	800	1:46.01	1:44.60- 07
	Peguero	Arizmendi	DOM	7.8.80	173/76	400	45.60A, 45.95	44.92- 07
	Peña	José Gregorio	VEN	12.1.87	163/60	3kSt	8:34.90	8:36.17- 09
	Pérez	Lysvanys	ESP	24.1.82	198/76	TJ	16.82	16.42- 08

Name		Nat	Born	Ht/Wt	Event	2011 Mark	Pre-2011 Best
Perry	Willie	USA	16.5.87	178/73	100	10.27, 10.17w	10.12- 06
					200	20.64, 20.36w	20.42- 06, 20.40w- 08
Persoon	Maarten	NED	15.3.87	190/110	DT	61.28	60.90- 10
Pervan	Dino	CRO	12.1.91	192/75	LJ	7.95	7.65- 10
* Pestano	Mario	ESP	8.4.78	195/120	DT	67.97	69.50- 08
Petersen	Nick	DEN	25.4.87	190/128	SP	19.33i	18.94- 09
Peterson	Ben	USA	9.1.88	183/75	PV	5.50i, 5.38	5.40- 10
^ Petrenko	Aleksandr	RUS	8.2.83	189/81	TJ	16.78	17.43- 08
Petrov	Aleksandr	RUS	19.8.86	184/73	LJ	8.20	8.15- 08
Petryashov	Konstantin	RUS	16.12.84	184/75	100	10.19w	10.40- 09
* Phillips	Dwight	USA	1.10.77	181/82	LJ	8.45	8.74- 09
* Phillips	Isa	JAM	22.4.84	193/84	400h	48.64	48.05- 09
Phillips	Richard	JAM	26.1.83	188/75	110h	13.40, 13.34w	13.39- 04, 13.33w- 08
Phillips	Thomas	GBR	23.4.89	196/91	400h	49.78	50.96- 09
Phipps	Chris	USA	14.9.90	183/73	LJ	7.99w	
Phiri	Gerald	ZAM	6.10.88	184/80	100	10.06	10.13- 09, 10.03Aw- 08
Piantella	Giorgio	ITA	6.7.81	181/75	PV	5.55i	5.60- 10
^ Pickering	Craig	GBR	16.10.86	182/78	100	10.19, 10.15w	10.14- 07, 10.08w- 09
Piedra	Bayron	ECU	19.8.82	174/65	10k	27:32.59	31:10.7A- 09
Pienaar	Hardus	RSA	10.8.81	190/88	JT	77.65	84.50- 03
* Pinder	Demetrius	BAH	13.2.89	178/70	200	20.54	21.18- 10
					400	44.78	44.93- 10
Pineda	Daniel	CHI	19.9.85	178/72	LJ	8.00A	7.98A, 7.97- 10
Pinkelman	Luke	USA	5.5.88	190/114	SP	20.07i, 19.17	19.13- 10
* Pishchalnikov	Bogdan	RUS	26.8.82	197/115	DT	62.40	67.23- 10
Pistorius	Oscar	RSA	22.11.86		400	45.07 prosthetics	46.02- 10
* Pitkämaki	Tero	FIN	19.12.82	195/92	JT	85.33	91.53- 05
Plakhin	Yevgeniy	RUS	28.1.85	188/110	SP	19.21i, 18.84	19.34- 09
Platnitskiy	Dmitriy	BLR	26.8.88	189/80	TJ	16.83	16.91- 10
^ Plawgo	Marek	POL	25.2.81	183/72	400h	50.11	48.12- 07
Plotnir	Yevgeniy	RUS	26.6.77	196/85	TJ	16.56	17.21- 06
Plummer	James	USA	.9	194/125	DT	60.43	59.10- 10
Pogorelov	Aleksey	RUS	26.3.83	178/62	400h	49.96	51.32, 49.42dt- 08
Pohle	Andreas	GER	6.4.81	178/65	TJ	16.53, 16.59w	16.99- 04
Pokrop	Hubert	POL	2.11.85	173/60	3kSt	8:32.07	8:24.04- 10
Polacek	Nate	USA	22.6.90	183/77	PV	5.45i	5.21- 10
Polonet	Vickson	KEN	2.7.85	177/57	1500	3:37.74	3:36.45- 08
Polyanskiy	Sergey	RUS	29.10.89		LJ	8.00, 8.18w	7.70- 10, 7.79w- 09
Popa	Laurentiu	ROU	19.1.84	201/127	SP	19.26	19.45- 10
Porter	Garland	USA	10.2.82	193/118	HT	72.99	72.26- 10
Porter	Jeff	USA	27.11.85	188/84	110h	13.26	13.37- 09
Portilla	Jhoanis C.	CUB	24.7.90	181/70	110h	13.62, 13.1w	13.98- 09, 13.3- 10
Potgieter	Roelie	RSA	20.3.80	197/128	SP	19.42	19.38- 10
Pouzy	Frédéric	FRA	18.2.83	184/88	HT	76.47	76.95- 07
Povegliano	Lorenzo	ITA	11.11.84	187/102	HT	76.96	75.03- 07
* Powell	Asafa	JAM	23.11.82	190/88	100	9.78	9.72- 08
					200	20.55	19.90- 06
Pozdnyakov	Aleksandr	RUS	1.2.87	187/100	HT	76.59	75.50- 10
Premeru	Marin	CRO	29.8.90	186/115	SP	19.37	19.80-09
Prey	Mathias	GER	9.8.88	192/89	Dec	7923(w), 7827	7797- 10
Prezelj	Rozle	SLO	26.9.79	193/73	HJ	2.28	2.31i- 04, 2.30- 06
Prieto	Miguel Ángel	ESP	20.9.64	187/81	50kW	4:03:35	
Primm	Cory	USA	1.12.88	178/64	800	1:44.71	1:45.70- 10
Proenza	Reinaldo	CUB	20.11.84	186/100	SP	19.19	20.30- 08
Prorok	Josef	CZE	16.11.87	190/78	400h	50.01	49.68- 10
Protsenko	Andriy	UKR	20.5.88	190/65	HJ	2.31	2.30- 08
Pruglo	Sergiy	UKR	18.11.83	187/109	DT	61.70	62.74- 04
Ptácek	Adam	CZE	8.10.80	178/65	PV	5.45i	5.81i- 03, 5.80- 02, 5.82ex- 07
Pudivítr	Miroslav	CZE	8.5.78	203/132	DT	61.55	61.92- 09
Pumariega	Yoisel	CUB	4.2.88	182/75	110h	13.73, 13.3w	13.69, 13.5- 10
Pupols	Normunds	LAT	5.10.84	186/73	HJ	2.24i, 2.20	2.28- 06
Pyatnytsya	Oleksandr	UKR	14.7.85	186/84	JT	82.61	84.11- 10
Qin Qiang		CHN	18.4.83	179/94	JT	79.22	81.48- 09
Quérin	Gaël	FRA	26.6.87	182/76	Dec	7939	7814- 09
Quesada	Miguel	ESP	18.9.79	176/60	800	1:46.21	1:45.58- 08
Quiller	Rory	USA	17.4.84	190/82	PV	5.50Ai, 5.40	5.65i- 08, 5.51- 07
Quinley	Trevell	USA	16.1.83	198/86	LJ	8.21	8.36- 08
Quiñónez	Alex	ECU	11.8.89	175/75	200	20.49A	21.29A- 09
^ Quiñónez	Jackson	ESP	12.6.80	190/91	110h	13.55	13.33- 07
Quiyuch	Jaime	GUA	24.4.88	178/57	50kW	3:50:33A	-0-
* Quow	Renny	TRI	25.8.87	170/66	400	44.84	44.53- 09

Name		Nat	Born	Ht/Wt	Event	2011 Mark	Pre-2011 Best
Rabiei	Ali Akbar	IRI	11.1.88	182/73	100	9.9	10.62- 10
^ Rags	Eriks	LAT	1.6.75	184/95	JT	80.87	86.47- 01
Raja	Andres	EST	2.6.82	187/82	Dec	8114	8119- 09
Rakoczy	Pawel	POL	15.5.87	187/90	JT	82.53	79.73- 09
Ram	Ghamanda	IND	1.7.84	178/65	800	1:46.46	1:46.67- 05
Ramolefi	Ruben	RSA	17.7.78	174/56	3kSt	8:11.50	8:11.63- 09
Ramos	Iván Jesús	ESP	31.7.90	180/66	200	20.79, 20.60w	21.32- 10
Randall	Woodrow	USA	9.11.89	173/73	100	10.20. 10.13w	10.30- 09
Randolph	Chris	USA	25.4.84	188/82	Dec	7814(w), 7664	8066- 08
Rapinier	Yoann	FRA	29.9.89	182/70	TJ	17.23i	16.58, 16.73w- 10
Rashad	Ahmad	USA	12.12.87	175/70	100	10.21	10.10- 09, 10.08w- 10
Rasheed	Essa Ismail	QAT	14.12.86	176/63	3000	7:34.70	7:39.61- 10
Rassioui	Bader	MAR	8.6.85	179/66	1500	3:37.40	3:35.00- 10
Rauhut	Norbert	POL	17.1.90	196/103	HT	70.44	68.22- 10
Rautenkrantz	Jens	GER	11.4.82	189/95	HT	73.70	77.35- 08
Rayson	Ian	AUS	4.2.88	185/75	50kW	3:57:55	3:59:43- 10
Redhead	Joel	GRN	3.7.86	183/79	200	20.57	20.49- 09
Redrick	Philip	USA	2.8.88	183/79	200	20.67, 20.48w	21.04- 09
Regassa	Dejene	BRN	18.4.89	176/68	5000	13:24.27	13:50.60- 10
Regassa	Tilahun	ETH	18.1.90	170/54	HMar	60:59	59:19- 10
Reid	Julian	JAM/GBR	23.9.88	186/77	LJ	8.08	8.04, 8.18w- 09
					TJ	16.77	16.98, 17.10w- 09
* Reif	Christian	GER	24.10.84	195/85	LJ	8.26, 8.38w	8.47- 10
^ Reina	Antonio Manuel	ESP	13.6.81	186/71	800	1:45.38	1:43.83- 02
Rendón	James	COL	7.4.85	155/55	20kW	1:21:13.6t	1:21:40- 08
Renshaw	Lachlan	AUS	4.2.87	180/70	800	1:45.66	1:45.73- 09
Restrepo	Gustavo	COL	27.7.82	165/60	20kW	1:20:36.6t	1:22:01- 05
Revé	Ernesto	CUB-J	26.2.92	181/65	TJ	17.40	16.73- 10
Revenko	Vladislav	UKR	15.11.84	181/71	PV	5.55	5.80- 05
Reynolds	Maalik	USA-J	26.4.92	193/73	HJ	2.28	2.20- 10
Richards	O'Dayne	JAM	14.12.88	180/114	SP	19.93	18.74- 10
* Richardson	Jason	USA	4.4.86	186/73	110h	13.04	13.21- 08
Rieckmann	Jonathan	BRA	20.8.87		50kW	4:04:07A	4:17:15- 08
Rietveld	Pelle	NED	4.2.85	184/75	Dec	7873	7955- 07
Riitmuru	Tarmo	EST	31.1.86		Dec	7806	7694(w), 7626- 10
Riley	Andrew	JAM	9.6.88	188/80	110h	13.32	13.45- 10
Riley	Zach	USA-J	20.5.92	178/68	HJ	2.26	2.185- 10
^ Rimmer	Michael	GBR	3.2.86	180/71	800	1:45.12	1:43.89- 10
Ríos	Vicente	MEX	5.4.83	179/75	LJ	7.97A	7.66A- 10
Rise	Lars	NOR	23.11.88	184/86	Dec	7942	7776- 09
Riseley	Jeff	AUS	11.11.86	192/75	800	1:44.64	1:45.48- 09
1000	2:16.75		2:17.35- 09		1500	3:33.42	3:32.93- 09
					1M	3:52.53	3:51.25- 09
Rivas	Yeison	COL	24.9.87		400h	50.12	49.7A- 08
Rivera	Edgar	MEX	13.2.91	191/80	HJ	2.28	2.23i- 10, 2.20- 09
Roach	Kimmari	JAM	21.9.90	175/73	100	10.14	10.13- 10
Roberts	Gil	USA	15.3.89	183/75	400	45.22	44.86- 09
Roberts	Kurt	USA	20.2.88	191/127	SP	19.55	19.80i- 10, 18.78- 09
Robertson	Jake	NZL	14.11.89	180/65	5000	13:22.38	13:32.92- 10
Robertson	Josef	JAM	14.5.87	174/64	400h	49.37	49.22- 09
Robertson	Ricky	USA	19.9.90	178/70	HJ	2.29	2.28- 10
Robi	Deribe	ETH	,86		Mar	2:08:40	-0-
* Robinson	Khadevis	USA	19.7.76	183/74	800	1:44.03	1:43.68-06
* Robles	Dayron	CUB	19.11.86	191/91	110h	13.00	12.87- 08
* Rodgers #	Michael	USA	24.4.85	178/73	100	9.85	9.94, 9.9, 9.85w- 09
Rodhe	Justin	USA/CAN	17.10.84	188/125	SP	20.77i, 20.06	19.44- 09
Rodríguez	Rafith	COL	1.6.89	187/73	800	1:44.31	1:46.71- 10
Rodríguez	Ángel David	ESP	25.4.80	178/66	100	10.29, 10.14Aw	
					200	20.34w	20.61- 08
Röhler	Thomas	GER	30.9.91	195/83	JT	78.20	76.37- 10
Rohr	Chris	USA	28.12.85	193/116	HT	74.40	74.61- 10
Rolle	Jamial	BAH	16.4.80	174/70	200	20.60w	20.62- 08
Romanenko	Oleksandr	UKR	26.6.81	168/60	50kW	4:01:05	4:05:57- 03
* Rome	Jarred	USA	21.12.76	194/140	DT	68.76	68.44- 08
Romero	Juan Carlos	MEX	15.12.77	177/62	10k	27:51.49	27:47.46- 08
Rono	Aron	KEN	1.11.82	173/57	10k	27:31.15	28:13.75- 08
Rono	Augustine	KEN	.81		Mar	2:08:05	2:13:05- 09
Rono	Geoffrey	KEN	21.4.87	175/60	800	1:46.11A	1:45.13- 08
1000	2:17.89		2:15.97- 08		1500	3:35.07	3:32.55- 08
Rono	Vincent	KEN	22.12.90	165/55	3000	7:45.75+, 7:37.87i	7:41.18- 10
5000	13:22.86		13:21.96- 10		10k	27:52.19	

	Name		Nat	Born	Ht/Wt	Event	2011 Mark	Pre-2011 Best
*	Rooney	Martyn	GBR	3.4.87	198/78	400	45.30	44.60- 08
	Rop	Albert	KEN-Y	20.12.94	176/55	3000	7:35.66	
						5000	13:03.70	
	Rose	Remaldo	JAM	18.11.87	178/68	100	10.20	10.29- 06
	Ross	Nick	USA	8.8.91	188/75	HJ	2.25i, 2.21	2.23i- 10, 2.22- 09
	Roth	Scott	USA	25.6.88	180/73	PV	5.72	5.72i- 10, 5.60- 09
	Rotich	Bernard	KEN	11.8.86		HMar	61:28	61:58- 10
	Rotich	Lawrence	KEN	20.8.86		HMar	61:26	62:58- 09
*	Rotich	Lucas	KEN	16.4.90	171/57	3000	7:35.57	7:37.33- 10
		5000 13:00.02			12:55.06- 10	10k	26:43.98	27:33.59- 10
						HMar	59:44	-0-
	Rotich	Milton	KRN	.84		HMar	61:12	
	Rouge-Serret	Aaron	AUS	21.1.88	170/74	100	10.20w	10.17- 10
^	Roulhac	Brandon	USA	13.12.83	188/73	TJ	16.73i, 16.61	17.26, 17.44w- 09
	Rowe	Alex	AUS-J	8.7.92	183/73	800	1:46.28	1:47.56- 10
	Rozinski	Pawel	POL	11.7.87	198/91	JT	78.83	77.88- 10
	Rubanko	Artyom	UKR	21.3.74	191/110	HT	75.76	80.44- 04
	Rubbiani	Matteo	ITA	31.8.78	180/72	PV	5.53, 5.55ex	5.53ex- 08, 5.50- 10
*	Rubino	Giorgio	ITA	15.4.86	174/56	20kW	1:20:44	1:19:37- 09
*	Rudisha	David	KEN	17.12.88	189/73	800	1:41.33	1:41.01- 10
	Ruíz	Diego	ESP	5.2.82	178/68	1500	3:33.18	3:35.04- 10
	Ruíz	Noel	CUB	18.1.87	182/69	400	45.53	45.71- 09
	Rungaru	James	KEN-J	14.1.93	176/61	10k	27:22.53	
*	Rupp	Galen	USA	8.5.86	180/62	5000	13:06.86	13:07.35- 10
		10k 26:48.00			27:10.74- 10	HMar	60:30	
	Russell	Scott	CAN	16.1.79	206/122	JT	84.81	84.41- 05
	Rutherford	Greg	GBR	17.11.86		LJ	8.32w, 8.27	
	Rutter	Adam	AUS	24.12.86	168/54	20kW	1:22:25	1:21:49- 08
*	Ruuskanen	Antti	FIN	21.2.84	189/86	JT	82.29	87.33- 08, 87.88dh- 07
	Ruzavin	Andrey	RUS	28.3.86	175/70	20kW	1:21:09	1:20:07- 07
*	Rybakov	Yaroslav	RUS	22.11.80	198/84	HJ	2.30	2.38i- 05, 2.35- 07
	Rybin	Sergey	RUS	30.9.85	170/60	10k	28:15.79	
	Ryzhov	Mikhail	RUS	17.12.91	176/64	20kW	1:21:49	-0-
	Saenz	Stephen	MEX	23.8.90	190/110	SP	19.82	18.43- 10
*	Saidy Ndure	Jaysuma	NOR	1.7.84	192/72	100	9.99	10.00, 9.98w- 10
						200	19.95	19.89- 07
	Saint-Jean	Fabrice	FRA	21.11.80	190/84	HJ	2.25	2.25- 10
	Saito	Hitoshi	JPN	9.10.86	180/69	200	20.55	20.42- 09
	Sakalauskas	Rytis	LTU	27.6.87	185/83	100	10.14, 10.10w	10.24- 10, 10.0dt- 09
	Sakayev	Vyacheslav	RUS	12.1.88	185/79	400h	49.79	50.19- 09
	Saku Bafuanga	Gaetan	FRA	22.7.91	181/75	TJ	16.82	16.41i, 16.20- 10
	Salaam	Rakieem 'Mookie'	USA	5.4.90	180/73	100	9.97	10.25, 10.21w- 10
						200	20.05	20.41- 10
*	Saladino	Irving	PAN	23.1.83	183/70	LJ	8.40	8.73- 08
*	Salel	Daniel	KEN	11.12.90	173/57	5000	13:19.51	13:08.23- 10
						10k	28:04.63	27:07.85- 10
	Salomäki	Eemeli	FIN	11.10.87	182/71	PV	5.60	5.60- 09
	Samac	Vedran	SRB	22.1.90	183/90	JT	77.72	75.06- 10
	Sambu	Stephen	KEN	7.7.88	169/55	10k	27:28.64	28:37.96- 09
	Samimi	Mahmoud	IRI	18.9.88	190/105	DT	63.98	64.67- 09
	Samimi	Mohammed	IRI	29.3.87	188/104	DT	64.10	65.41- 10
	Samitov	Ruslan	RUS	11.2.91	187/77	TJ	16.90	16.51i, 16.42- 10
	Samoei	Fred	KEN	12.1.86	174/62	800	1:45.52	1:45.94- 10
	Samuels	J-Mee	USA	20.5.87	172/76	100	10.21	10.03- 10
*	Sánchez	Eder	MEX	21.5.86	176/67	20kW	1:19:36	1:18:34- 08
						50kW	3:53:19	-0-
	Sánchez	Enrique	ESP	14.10.83	178/62	3kSt	8:34.15	8:29.12- 09
*	Sánchez	Félix	DOM	30.8.77	178/73	400h	48.74	47.25- 03
^	Sánchez	Sergio	ESP	1.10.82	178/64	5000	13:24.59	13:19.21- 10
	Sancho	Miguel Ángel	ESP	24.4.90	180/67	HJ	2.26	2.27i, 2.25- 09
*	Sands	Leevan	BAH	16.8.81	190/75	TJ	17.21, 17.39w	17.59- 08
	Sang	Silas	KEN	21.8.78		HMar	60:38	60:20- 09
	Sanguin	Giovanni	ITA	14.5.69	185/100	HT	70.65	74.52- 97
	Santos	Luguelin	DOM-J	12.11.93	188/72	400	44.71A	46.19- 10
	Saquipay	Rolando	ECU	21.7.79	166/57	20kW	1:22:57A	1:19:21- 05
						50kW	4:01:20	-0-
	Sarantsev	Yevgeniy	RUS	5.8.88		Dec	7822	7643- 10
	Saruyama	Rikiya	JPN	15.2.84	175/68	LJ	8.05	7.91- 09, 7.94w- 10
	Sato	Hiroyuki	JPN	6.8.90		110h	13.67	13.90- 10
	Sato	Nobuhiro	JPN	28.4.88	172/75	JT	77.68	77.76- 10

Name		Nat	Born	Ht/Wt	Event	2011 Mark	Pre-2011 Best
Sato	Yuki	JPN	26.11.86	178/59	5000	13:25.53	13:23.57- 06
					10k	27:59.60	27:38.25- 09
Savanovic	Vladimir	SRB	5.10.78	179/67	50kW	4:02:07	4:06:47- 10
Savanyú	Péter	HUN	26.6.87		DT	60.07	56.82- 10
Savolaynen	Mykola	UKR	25.3.80	189/76	TJ	16.72	17.17- 07
Savytskyy	Dmytro	UKR	14.12.90		SP	19.18	18.46i- 08, 17.98- 10
* Sawano	Daichi	JPN	16.9.80	183/74	PV	5.65	5.83- 05
Sayed	Ihab Abdelrahman	EGY	1.5.89	195/96	JT	78.83	81.84- 10
Sayevych	Anton	UKR	15.6.88	186/69	HJ	2.25i, 2.20	2.28i- 10, 2.15- 08
Sbaï	Hassanine	TUN	21.4.84	176/60	20kW	1:20:19	1:21:47, 1:20:36sh- 10
Schaf	Alex	GER	28.4.87	177/85	100	10.20	10.36- 10
Schembera	Robin	GER	1.10.88	186/67	800	1:46.36	1:45.63- 09
Schembri	Fabrizio	ITA	27.1.81	183/74	TJ	17.08	17.27- 09
Schenkel	Amaru Reto	SUI	28.4.88	173/66	100	10.19	10.45- 06
					200	20.51	21.06- 08
Schirrmeister	Silvio	GER	7.12.88	195/80	400h	50.00	49.86- 10
Schlangen	Carsten	GER	31.12.80	189/68	1500	3:35.74	3:34.19- 10
Schmidt	Carsten	GER	29.5.86	179/60	20kW	1:22:47	1:23:51- 06
					50kW	3:54:54	4:02:51- 10
Schmidt	Marco	GER	5.9.83	202/106	SP	20.51	20.58i- 10
Schneeberger	Marc	SUI	5.7.81	185/76	200	20.52	20.42- 10
Schneider	Thomas	GER	7.11.88	186/80	400	45.56	46.03- 10
Schulze	Fabian	GER	7.3.84	192/79	PV	5.70i, 5.62	5.83i- 07 , 5.81- 06
Schuurmans	Jared	USA	20.8.87	198/118	DT	60.19	59.20- 09
Schwarzer	Helge	GER	26.11.85	185/76	110h	13.74, 13.61w	13.39- 09
* Schwazer	Alex	ITA	26.12.84	185/73	20kW	1:21:50	1:18:24- 10
Scott	Chris	GBR	21.3.88	198/110	DT	63.00	59.90- 10
Scott	Derek	USA	7.11.85	175/66	3kSt	8:31.52	
^ Scott	Dorian	JAM	1.2.82	185/136	SP	20.13	21.45- 08
* Scott	Jeremy	USA	21.5.81	206/91	PV	5.80i, 5.72	5.82i, 5.75- 09
Scott	Jordan	USA	22.2.88	188/84	PV	5.50Ai, 5.50, 5.70dh	5.71- 10
Scott	Josh	USA	9.3.85	193/84	400	45.71	45.01- 10
* Sdiri	Salim	FRA	26.10.78	185/80	LJ	8.27	8.42- 09
* Sebrle	Roman	CZE	26.11.74	186/88	Dec	8109	9026- 01
Sedoc #	Gregory	NED	16.10.81	179/74	110h	13.39	13.37- 07, 13.1w- 10
Sedyuk	Nikolay	RUS	29.4.88	198/115	DT	62.11	63.20- 08
See	Jeff	USA	6.6.86	186/72	1M	3:55.24	3:58.70- 07
* Sefer	Dino	ETH	28.5.88	171/60	HMar	59:42	-0-
Seifert	Bernhard	GER-J	15.2.93	190/86	JT	78.55	-0-
Semenenko	Yevgen	UKR	17.7.84	178/67	TJ	17.16	17.16- 09
Semenov	Andriy	UKR	4.7.84	204/117	SP	20.63	20.51- 08
Semenov	Oleksiy	UKR	27.6.82	204/115	DT	62.20	65.40- 08
Sencan	Kaan	TUR-J	9.2.93	177/62	LJ	8.00w	7.12- 10
Seoud	Amr Ibrahim	EGY	10.6.86	180/70	100	10.13	10.18A, 10.22- 10
					200	20.44	20.36A- 10, 20.52- 09
Seppänen	Tuomas	FIN	16.5.86	180/107	HT	75.31	74.73- 10
^ Sergeyev	Aleksandr	RUS	29.7.83	191/78	TJ	16.60i	17.23i, 17.11- 04
Seribe	Pako	BOT	7.4.91	185/75	400	45.5A	46.1A- 10
Seurei	Benson	KEN	27.3.88	172/62	800	1:45.79	1:47.20- 10
					1500	3:34.67	
Shabanov	Konstandin	RUS	17.11.89	183/75	110h	13.35	13.66- 09, 13.42w- 10
Shahween	Mohamed Othman	KSA	15.2.86	168/57	1500	3:31.82	3:33.90- 08
					1M	3:52.00	3:52.52- 08
Shalin	Pavel	RUS	15.3.87	175/73	LJ	7.96i, 7.91, 8.33w	8.25, 8.26w- 10
Shami (Yatich)	Abdullah Dawit	ETH	16.7.74		HMar	60:44	
Shane	James	GBR	18.12.89	173/55	1500	3:36.22	3:42.81- 10
Shapoval	Viktor	UKR	17.10.79	198/75	HJ	2.25	2.34- 09
* Sharman	William	GBR	12.9.84	188/82	110h	13.47	13.30- 09, 12.9w- 10
* Shayunov	Yuriy	BLR	22.10.87	193/105	HT	78.70	80.72- 09
^ Shi Dongpeng		CHN	6.1.84	192/85	110h	13.41	13.19- 07
Shiferaw	Berhanu	ETH-J	31.5.93		Mar	2:09:19	-0-
Shishakov	Yevgeniy	RUS	10.6.88		HJ	2.24i, 2.23	2.27i- 08, 2.24- 09
Shkurenov	Ilya	RUS	11.1.91		Dec	7894	-0-
Shokirjanov	Bobur	UZB	5.12.90	190/84	JT	78.39	79.31- 09
Shubenkov	Sergey	RUS	4.10.90	185/75	110h	13.46	13.54- 10
Shubyanok	Nikolay	BLR	4.5.85	190/75	Dec	7678	8028- 07
Shugi	Bilisuma	BRN	19.7.89	178/60	3000	7:42.71	7:51.11- 10
					5000	13:06.73	13:38.26- 10
* Shustov	Aleksandr	RUS	13.8.84	188/80	HJ	2.36	2.33- 10
* Si Tianfeng		CHN	17.6.84	180/75	50kW	3:38:48	3:42:55- 05
* Sidorov	Maksim	RUS	13.5.86	195/115	SP	21.45	20.92- 09

Name		Nat	Born	Ht/Wt	Event	2011 Mark	Pre-2011 Best
Sigei	Richard	KEN	11.5.84		HMar	61:14	
* Sihine	Sileshi	ETH	29.1.83	171/55	5000	12:57.86	12:47.04- 04
					10k	26:52.84	26:39.69- 04
Sikora	Rafal	POL	17.2.87	187/76	20kW	1:21:04	1:23:14- 10
					50kW	3:46:16	3:52:33- 09
Silcock	Clint	USA	15.11.86	198/86	HJ	2.24Ai	2.26A- 10
Silmon	Charles	USA	4.7.91	175/72	100	10.20A, 10.24, 10.19w	10.23- 10
					200	20.56A, 20.60	20.65A. 20.68, 20.58w- 10
* Silnov	Andrey	RUS	9.9.84	198/83	HJ	2.36	2.38- 08
Silva	Andrés	URU	27.3.86	180/76	400h	49.16	49.17- 10
da Silva	Fernando	BRA	10.10.86	177/65	800	1:45.66	1:46.86-09
da Silva	Hílton	BRA	13.4.87		TJ	16.93	16.93- 10
Silva	Jonathan	BRA	21.7.91	185/75	TJ	16.70	16.07, 16.44w- 10
* da Silva	Mauro Vinícius	BRA	26.12.86	183/69	LJ	8.27	8.12- 10, 8.20w- 08
^ Silva	Rui	POR	3.8.77	175/65	5000	13:25.94	13:19.20- 04
					10k	27:53.55	
Simanovich	Denis	BLR	20.4.87	179/58	20kW	1:21:01	1:21:39- 10
Singh	Arpinder	IND-J	30.12.92	186/77	TJ	16.63	16.45- 10
Singh	Gurmeet	IND	1.7.85		20kW	1:20:35	1:25:57- 06
Singh	Om Prakash	IND	11.1.87	196/125	SP	20.07	20.02- 09
* Sintnicolaas	Eelco	NED	7.4.87	186/78	PV	5.52i, 5.40	5.45- 10
					Dec	8304	8436- 10
Sinyakov	Andrey	BLR	6.1.82	189/117	SP	19.84	20.20- 08
* Sirmais	Zigismunds	LAT-J	6.5.92	191/90	JT	84.69	82.27- 10
Sitonik	William	KEN-Y	1.3.94	165/52	3000	7:40.10	-0-
Siwa	Ben	UGA	27.5.89		3kSt	8:34.25A	8:29.1A- 10
Skyers	Roberto	CUB	12.11.91	187/75	200	20.31A, 20.75	20.24- 09
Slattery	Steve	USA	14.8.80	180/73	3kSt	8:28.52	8:15.69- 07
Sleboda	Piotr	POL	22.1.87	185/62	HJ	2.27	2.19- 08
Slobodenyuk	Vadym	UKR	17.3.81	189/74	3kSt	8:26.21	8:24.15- 06
Smellie	Gavin	CAN	26.6.86	180/75	100	10.20, 10.11w	10.29- 09
					200	20.64. 20.54w	
Smirnov	Roman	RUS	2.9.84	184/74	200	20.78, 20.59w	20.57- 08
Smirnov	Valentin	RUS	13.2.86	177/62	1500	3:36.14	3:40.06- 10
Smith	Alex	GBR	6.3.88	184/105	HT	74.62	72.95- 10
Smith	Calvin	USA	10.12.87	180/75	400	45.26	44.81- 10
* Smith	Maurice	JAM	28.9.80	190/90	Dec	8214A, 8078	8644- 07
Smith	Miles	USA	24.9.84	190/77	100	10.20w	10.32, 10.26w- 03
					400	45.19	45.16- 05
* Smith	Rutger	NED	9.7.81	197/129	SP	19.95i	21.62- 06
					DT	67.77	67.63- 07
Smith	Tyrone	BER	7.8.86	183/70	LJ	8.16	8.22- 10
Söderberg	David	FIN	11.8.79	185/100	HT	77.34	78.83- 03
^ Sofyin	Pavel	RUS	4.9.81	200/120	SP	19.65	20.82- 09
Sogame	Shin-ya	JPN	8.3.87	179/68	TJ	16.59	16.22- 08
* Soi	Edwin	KEN	3.3.86	168/53	3000	7:27.55	7:29.75- 10
2M	8:14.10				5000	12:59.15	12:52.40- 06
Sokolov	Vyacheslav	RUS	15.12.84	179/65	800	1:45.69	1:47.52- 10
Sokolov	Vyacheslav	RUS	20.5.84	179/65	1500	3:36.79	3:39.53- 08
* Sokolovs	Igors	LAT	17.8.74	187/107	HT	76.60	80.14- 09
Sokyrskyy	Oleksey	UKR	16.3.85	185/95	HT	78.33	76.62- 10
* Solinsky	Chris	USA	5.12.84	185/73	1500	3:35.89	3:37.27- 07
1M	3:54.52i	3:55.75i- 10, 3:57.80- 06			5000	13:10.22	12:55.53- 10
Solomon	Duane	USA	28.12.84	191/73	800	1:45.86	1:45.23- 10
Solomon	Steven	AUS-J	16.5.93	180/70	400	45.58	46.44- 10
* Som	Bram	NED	20.2.80	178/67	800	1:45.69	1:43.45- 06
Somerville	Terrence	USA	5.11.89	184/75	110h	13.44	14.06- 09
^ Songok	Isaac	KEN	25.4.84	170/54	3000	7:45.38	7:28.72- 06
Songoka	Yusuf	KEN	5.2.79	170/55	Mar	2:08:08	2:08:55- 10
* Sorrillo	Rondell	TRI	21.1.86	178/62	100	10.17	10.19, 10.05w- 10
					200	20.16	20.29- 10
Sossah	Mateo	FRA	28.4.88	194/93	Dec	7870	8044- 09
Souleiman	Ayanleh	DJI-J	3.12.92	172/60	1500	3:34.32	
* Spank	Raúl	GER	13.7.88	190/75	HJ	2.32	2.33- 09
^ Spasovkhodskiy	Igor	RUS	1.8.79	191/91	TJ	16.85i, 16.82, 17.00w	17.44- 01
* Spearmon	Wallace	USA	24.12.84	190/80	200	20.18	19.65- 06
Spence	Lansford	JAM	15.12.82	188/75	200	20.33A, 20.41	20.49- 10
					400	45.46	44.77- 05
Spinner	Patrick	GER	28.11.85		Dec	7818	7589- 10
Spurlock	Oscar	USA	1.8.89	180/75	110h	13.33	13.56, 13.51w- 09

Name		Nat	Born	Ht/Wt	Event	2011 Mark	Pre-2011 Best
St. Lawrence	Ben	AUS	7.11.81	176/62	5000	13:10.08	13:25.88- 09
					10k	27:24.95	28:05.25- 10
Stamatóyiannis	Mihaíl	GRE	20.5.82	188/112	SP	20.17	20.36i- 10, 19.98- 04
Stanys	Raivydas	LTU	3.2.87	184/77	HJ	2.28	2.25- 09
* Starodubtsev	Dmitriy	RUS	3.1.86	188/82	PV	5.90i, 5.72	5.75- 08
Stasiewicz	Michal	POL	28.9.88	181/63	50kW	4:02:51	3:57:52- 10
Stathelákos	Konstadínos	GRE	30.12.87	181/105	HT	74.38	71.35- 08
Steacy	Jim	CAN	29.5.84	191/111	HT	76.27	79.13- 08
Stecchi	Claudio Michel	ITA	23.11.91	187/75	PV	5.55	5.40- 10
Stepanchuk	Andrey	BLR	12.6.79	176/65	20kW	1:23:01	1:21:31- 08
					50kW	4:03:50	3:51:40- 05
Stevenson	Dale	AUS	1.1.88	183/107	SP	20.05	19.99- 10
Stewart	Keiron	JAM	21.11.89	180/73	110h	13.44, 13.38w	13.61, 13.39w- 10
Stewart	Ray	USA	5.4.89	183/79	110h	13.48	13.71- 10
Stewart	Tyron	USA	8.7.89	180/70	LJ	7.94	7.83i, 7.82- 10, 7.83w- 09
Stockbarger	Wesley	USA	5.6.85	190/120	DT	64.38	61.96- 09
* Storl	David	GER	27.7.90	198/122	SP	21.78	20.77- 10
Strachan	Richard	GBR	18.11.86	175/73	400	45.70	45.74- 09
^ Straub	Alexander	GER	14.10.83	180/78	PV	5.60	5.81- 08
Strelkov	Denis	RUS	26.10.90		50kW	4:04:36	-0-
Su Bingtian		CHN	29.8.89	185/65	100	10.16	10.28- 09
Su Xiongfeng		CHN	21.3.87	183/70	LJ	8.19	8.27i, 8.17- 10
* Suárez	Leonel	CUB	1.9.87	197/93	Dec	8501	8654- 09
* Sudol	Grzegorz	POL	28.8.78	174/60	20kW	1:20:51	1:20:50- 10
Sugai	Yohei	JPN	30.8.85	179/74	LJ	8.03, 8.09w	8.10- 10, 8.13w- 08
Suguimati	Mahau	BRA	13.11.84	184/78	400h	49.17	48.67- 09
Sugut	Henry	KEN	4.5.85		Mar	2:08:22	2:08:40- 10
Sukharyev	Ilya	UKR	17.6.86	190/68	3kSt	8:34.50	8:33.22- 09
Sukhomlinov	Igor	RUS	13.2.77	182/100	JT	79.07	83.34- 07
Suskevicius	Tadas	LTU	22.5.85	175/65	50kW	4:00:54	3:52:31- 10
Suzuki	Yusuke	JPN	2.1.88	169/58	20kW	1:21:13	1:20:06- 10
Svärd Jacobsson	Melker	SWE-Y	8.1.94	186/77	PV	5.45i	5.11- 10
Svechkar	Konstantin	RUS	17.7.84	173/68	400	45.89	46.00- 09
* Svyatokho	Valeriy	BLR	20.7.81	186/112	HT	78.02	81.49- 06
Swiderski	Adrian	POL	27.9.86	188/74	TJ	16.66i, 16.48, 16.72w	16.69- 10
Sylve	Bradley	USA-J	29.1.93	180/79	100	10.18w	10.48, 10.35w- 09
Sylve	Domonick	USA	28.11.88	183/77	110h	13.62	13.67- 10
* Symmonds	Nick	USA	30.12.83	178/73	800	1:43.83	1:43.76- 10
Sysoyev	Aleksey	RUS	8.3.85	194/96	Dec	7719	8497- 08
Syunin	Igor	EST	4.12.90	173/70	TJ	16.53, 16.61w	16.86- 10
Szabó	Dániel	HUN	28.6.91	182/95	HT	70.86	68.32- 10
Szuster	Konrad	POL	21.1.84	192/115	DT	61.38	62.70- 10
Szymkowiak	Tomasz	POL	5.7.83	176/58	3kSt	8:25.52	8:18.23- 10
Tabala	Aleksandr	RUS	23.5.86		Dec	7954	7979- 10
* Tadese	Zersenay	ERI	8.2.82	160/56	5000	12:59.32	12:59.27- 06
10k	26:51.09		26:37.25- 06		HMar	58:30	58:23- 10
Tagharrafet	Abdellah	MAR		.85	HMar	61:22	61:36- 10
					Mar	2:08:21	
* Tahri	Bouabdellah	FRA	20.12.78	191/68	10k	27:31.46	-0-
					3kSt	8:05.72	8:01.18- 09
^ Taillepierre	Karl	FRA	13.8.76	176/67	TJ	17.08	17.45- 05
Taiwo	Jeremy	USA	15.1.90	196/85	Dec	7742	7521- 10
Tajadura	Tomás	ESP	25.6.85	183/64	3kSt	8:19.00	8:41.72- 09
Takahira	Shinji	JPN	18.7.84	180/60	200	20.49	20.22- 09
Takase	Kei	JPN	25.11.88	179/61	200	20.53	20.93, 20.74w- 10
Takeda	Kenta	JPN	27.4.86	182/67	400h	50.01	50.01- 09
Talashko	Andrey	BLR	31.5.82	173/65	20kW	1:23:25	1:19:12- 06
Talbot	Danny	GBR	1.5.91	184/73	100	10.21	10.58, 10.48w- 10
					200	20.54	20.97- 10
* Tallent	Jared	AUS	17.10.84	178/60	20kW	1:19:57	1:19:15- 10
					50kW	3:43:36	3:38:56- 09
Talley	Keyth	USA	3.3.90	184/73	100	10.19w	10.35, 10.28w 09
Tamberi	Gianmarco	ITA-J	1.6.92	189/71	HJ	2.25	2.14- 10
Tamesue	Dai	JPN	3.5.78	170/67	400h	49.89	47.89- 01
* Tamgho	Teddy	FRA	15.6.89	187/82	LJ	8.01i	7.72i- 08, 7.63 07
					TJ	17.92i/17.91	17.98- 10
^ Tammert	Aleksander	EST	2.2.73	196/126	DT	61.10	70.82- 06
Tanii	Takayuki	JPN	14.2.83	166/57	20kW	1:22:23	1:20:39- 04
					50kW	3:48:03	3:47:23- 06
Tanonaka	Tasuku	JPN	23.9.78	185/80	110h	13.70, 13.63w	13.55, 13.51w- 06

Name		Nat	Born	Ht/Wt	Event	2011 Mark	Pre-2011 Best
* Tanui	Paul	KEN	22.12.90	172/54	5000	13:04.65	13:14.87- 10
					10k	26:50.63	27:17.61- 10
* Tarabin	Dmitriy	RUS	29.10.91	176/85	JT	85.10	77.65- 10
Tarzumanov	Rinat	UZB	26.3.84	196/100	JT	77.38	79.88- 04
Tateno	Tetsuya	JPN	5.8.91		400h	50.06	50.61- 10
* Taylor	Angelo	USA	29.12.78	188/84	400	44.82	44.05- 07
					400h	47.94	47.25- 08
* Taylor	Christian	USA	18.6.90	190/75	400	45.46	45.34- 09
LJ	8.00, 8.07w		8.19- 10		TJ	17.96	17.18i, 17.02, 17.09w- 10
* Taylor	Dan	USA	12.5.82	198/145	SP	20.90	21.78- 09
Tegene	Yrsaw	ETH	.90		HMar	60:59	
* Tegenkamp	Matt	USA	19.1.82		2M	8:15.88	
5000	13:14.75		12:58.56- 09		10k	27:28.22	29:29.35- 02
Temacini	Sief el Islem	ALG	5.3.88	180/65	TJ	16.88	15.89- 10
Terer	Patrick	KEN	6.7.89	178/60	3kSt	8:19.31	8:13.96- 09
^ Tereshin	Andrey	RUS	15.12.82	195/77	HJ	2.25i, 2.23	2.36i- 06, 2.34- 07
Teslenko	Denis	UKR	18.4.89		400h	50.10	51.67- 10
Thagane	Tumelo	RSA	3.7.84	180/70	TJ	16.97A, 16.78, 16.95w	17.09- 10
Theiner	Wojciech	POL	25.6.86	187/74	HJ	2.26i, 2.26	2.30- 10
Thomas	Chris	USA	9.2.81	178/76	110h	13.62, 13.60w	13.54- 08
* Thomas	Donald	BAH	1.7.84	190/75	HJ	2.32i, 2.32	2.35- 07
* Thomas	Dwight	JAM	23.9.80	185/82	110h	13.15	13.16- 09
Thomas	Mikel	TRI	23.11.87	182/77	110h	13.63	13.62, 13.57w- 08
Thomas	Zedric	USA	21.4.88	180/75	LJ	8.08i, 7.92, 7.93w	8.00i, 7.84- 10
					TJ	16.60, 17.05w	16.30i, 16.12- 10
Thompson	Chris	GBR	17.4.81	176/70	10k	27:27.36	27:29.61- 10
Thompson	Oral	JAM	11.12.82	180/73	400	45.42	45.50- 10
* Thompson	Richard	TRI	7.6.85	187/79	100	9.85	9.89- 08
* Thorkildsen	Andreas	NOR	1.4.82	188/90	JT	90.61	91.59- 06
* Thörnblad	Linus	SWE	6.3.85	180/77	HJ	2.25	2.38i- 07, 2.34- 06
Thorsteinsson	Odinn Björn	ISL	3.12.81	200/128	SP	19.83	19.37- 10
* Thuo	John	KEN	27.11.85	168/55	3000	7:46.01	7:46.65- 07
5000	13:15.53		13:21.02- 10		10k	27:23.99	27:11.88- 09
Tijtgat	Lander	BEL	6.4.83	179/65	1500	3:37.21	3:44.41- 10
* Tinsley	Michael	USA	21.4.84	183/80	400h	48.45	48.02- 07
Tiony	Michael	KEN	27.8.85		5000	13:24.51	13:19.41- 06
Tipton	Jon	USA	10.5.86		DT	60.37	59.90- 09
Tobin	Robert	GBR	20.12.83	190/75	400	45.72	45.01- 05
Tobler	Jarod	USA	30.9.82	180/79	LJ	8.01, 8.22w	8.16- 08
Tola	Tadesse	ETH	31.10.87	178/60	Mar	2:07:13	2:06:31- 10
Toledo	Braian	ARG-J	8.9.93	186/90	JT	79.53A	73.07- 10
Toledo	Yoisel	CUB	24.4.83	196/100	SP	19.29	19.05- 06
Tolesa	Tadesse	ETH	.88	180/64	Mar	2:09:02	2:12:41- 10
* Tomlinson	Chris	GBR	15.9.81	196/84	LJ	8.35	8.29- 07
Tontodonati	Federico	ITA	30.10.89	169/55	50kW	3:55:04	4:11:29A- 10
Too	Daniel Kiprugut	KEN	21.11.76		Mar	2:08:25	2:08:38- 09
^ Topic	Dragutin	SRB	12.3.71	197/77	HJ	2.24	2.38- 93
Tornéus	Michel	SWE	26.5.86	184/70	LJ	8.19	8.12, 8.21w- 10
Török	Krisztián	HUN	4.5.87	187/100	JT	78.51	76.16- 10
Torrance	Jamaal	USA	20.7.83	168/64	400	45.11	44.80- 10
Torrence	David	USA	26.11.85	175/61	800	1:45.43	1:45.14- 10
1500	3:35.95		3:34.25- 10		1M	3:54.01	3:54.47- 10
Torres	Jorge	USA	22.8.80	170/62	10k	28:12.25	27:42.91- 07
Torro	Osku	FIN	21.8.79	183/68	HJ	2.33i, 2.24	2.32i- 10, 2.27- 07
* Tosca	Osniel	CUB	30.6.84	182/78	TJ	17.22	17.52- 07
* Tóth	Matej	SVK	10.2.83	185/72	20kW	1:20:16	1:20:53- 09
					50kW	3:39:46	3:41:32- 09
Touil	Imad	ALG	11.2.89	172/62	1500	3:36.05	3:37.50- 09
Townsend	Fred	USA	19.2.82	188/82	110h	13.42, 13.40w	13.50- 08, 13.47w- 09
Traber	Gregor	GER-J	2.12.92	189/77	110h	13.55	13.90- 10
Trainor	Brian	USA	14.3.80	193/118	DT	62.20	64.58- 08
* Trammell	Terrence	USA	23.11.78	188/84	110h	13.16	12.95- 07
Traoré	Bano	FRA	25.4.85	180/65	110h	13.58, 13.51w	13.49A, 13.54- 08
Treff	Matthias	GER	27.2.88	190/95	JT	77.88	73.09- 09
Trémos	Yeóryios	GRE	21.3.89	196/103	DT	60.33	59.96- 10
Trenikhin	Pavel	RUS	24.3.86	187/77	400	45.55	46.00- 10
Trofimov	Pyotr	RUS	28.11.83	174/63	20kW	1:20:31	1:19:02- 09
Tromp	Xavier	FRA	3.3.84	191/86	PV	5.45	5.55i, 5.50- 06
Trotskiy	Ivan	BLR	27.5.76	167/50	20kW	1:20:48	1:19:40- 03
True	Ben	USA	29.12.85	183/70	5000	13:24.11	13:43.98- 10
Tsákonas	Likoúrgos-Stéfanos	GRE	8.3.90	184/67	200	20.56	20.67- 10

Name		Nat	Born	Ht/Wt	Event	2011 Mark	Pre-2011 Best
Tsákonas	Yeóryios	GRE	22.1.88	190/78	LJ	8.03	7.98i- 09, 7.93, 8.04w- 08
Tsapik	Aleksey	BLR	4.8.88		TJ	16.32, 16.69w	16.46- 10
* Tsátoumas	Loúis	GRE	12.2.82	187/76	LJ	8.26	8.66- 07
Tsegay	Atsedu	ETH	17.12.91		HMar	61:12	
Tsegay	Samuel	ERI	24.2.88	176/55	Mar	2:07:28	-0-
Tsiámis	Dimítrios	GRE	12.1.82	178/67	TJ	17.06i	17.55- 06
Tsirikhov	Soslan	RUS	24.11.84	193/94	SP	20.76	19.77- 08
Tsvetkov	Mikhail	RUS	4.5.80	194/73	HJ	2.30i	2.30i- 02, 2.30- 03
Tsyplakov	Daniyil	RUS-J	29.7.92		HJ	2.26	2.21- 09
Tucker	Brandon	USA	20.3.90	188/84	110h	13.58w	13.82- 10
Tukhtachev	Ivan	RUS	12.7.89	173/61	800	1:45.47	1:47.0- 10
Tum	Stephen	KEN	.86		HMar	61:11	60:58- 09
Tunks	Jason	CAN	7.5.75	200/125	DT	60.53	67.88- 98
* Turner	Andrew	GBR	19.9.80	184/77	110h	13.22	13.27- 07, 13.24w- 06, 13.2u- 09
Tyden	Dmytro	UKR	17.1.85	188/75	TJ	16.60i, 16.54	17.04- 10
Ugachi	Tsuyoshi	JPN	27.4.87	164/49	10k	27:40.69	28:01.54- 10
					HMar	60:58	61:49- 10
* Ukhov	Ivan	RUS	29.3.86	192/83	HJ	2.38i, 2.34	2.40i- 09, 2.36- 10
Ukonmaanaho	Janne	FIN	13.3.84	184/71	3kSt	8:27.08	8:33.48- 10
Uliczka	Steffen	GER	17.7.84	179/65	3kSt	8:26.43	8:25.39- 10
Ulrey	Dorian	USA	11.7.87	175/64	1500	3:37.68	3:35.23- 09
Ulrick	Drew	USA	13.1.85	196/114	DT	60.79	62.79- 09
Urbanek	Robert	POL	29.4.87	196/115	DT	64.37	62.22- 08
Ursu	Sergiu	ROU	26.4.80	202/127	DT	62.66	64.74- 10
* Urtans	Maris	LAT	9.2.81	188/123	SP	20.82	21.63- 10
Ushiro	Keisuke	JPN	24.7.86	196/90	Dec	8076w/8073	7930- 10
Vadlejch	Jakub	CZE	10.10.90	188/83	JT	84.08	84.47- 10
Vaiculens	Ainars	LAT	21.1.83	194/95	HT	70.99	74.76- 09
Vail	Ryan	USA	19.3.86	173/59	10k	27:57.42	30:33.85- 09
Valiyev	Roman	KAZ	27.3.84	190/73	TJ	16.62	16.98- 06
Valor	William	VEN	11.11.84		Dec	7681	
Van Alphen	Hans	BEL	12.1.82	191/92	Dec	8200	8091- 10
Van Der Plaetsen	Thomas	BEL	24.12.90	188/82	Dec	8157	7564- 10
van der Westen	Marcel	NED	1.8.76	191/87	110h	13.67	13.35- 08
van Luijk	Patrick	NED	17.9.84	189/87	200	20.62	20.52- 09
van Niekerk	Wayde	RSA-J	23.3.92	178/68	200	20.57	21.02- 10
van Wengerden	Wout	NED	16.2.87	183/84	PV	5.45	5.55- 08
* van Zyl	Louis 'L.J.'	RSA	20.7.85	186/75	400	44.86A	45.82A- 09, 46.02- 08
					400h	47.66	47.94- 09
Vanek	Daniel	SVK	18.1.83	188/110	SP	19.26	19.75- 08
Vanhaeren	Stef	BEL-J	15.1.92	184/60	400h	50.01	50.71- 10
^ Varga	Roland	CRO	22.10.77	197/102	DT	65.95	67.38- 02
Vasilache	Stefan	ROU	9.5.79	190/79	HJ	2.25	2.30- 03
* Vasilevskis	Vadims	LAT	5.1.82	188/101	JT	88.22	90.73- 07
Vélez	Albert	ESP	26.10.88	180/68	PV	5.50	5.41- 10
Velikopolskiy	Dmitriy	RUS	27.11.84	188/110	HT	76.31	78.76- 08
Véliz	Carlos	CUB	12.8.87	185/120	SP	20.76, 21.40lt	20.72- 08
Venâncio	Ânderson	BRA	6.1.87	177/79	Dec	7800(w)	7765- 10
Venel	Teddy	FRA	16.3.85	184/77	400	45.69	45.54- 08
* Vesely	Vitezslav	CZE	27.2.83	186/92	JT	84.11	86.45- 10
Viana	Sandro	BRA	26.3.77	188/77	200	20.39A, 20.42	20.32- 08
Vicars	Derrick	USA	8.5.89		SP	19.39i, 18.35	17.93- 10
* Vicaut	Jimmy	FRA-J	27.2.92	184/75	100	10.07	10.16- 10
Vicet	Noleysis	CUB	6.2.81	193/103	HT	75.40	74.20- 10
^ Vieira	João	POR	20.2.76	174/58	20kW	1:22:44	1:20:09- 06
Vieira	Sérgio	POR	20.2.76	174/58	20kW	1:23:15	1:20:58- 97
Viita	Jussi	FIN	26.9.85	186/75	HJ	2.24i, 2.23	2.22- 09
Villanueva	Claudio	ESP	3.8.88		50kW	4:00:52	-0-
Villanueva	Eduard	VEN	29.12.84	171/62	1500	3:36.96	3:38.96- 10
Villar	Paulo César	COL	28.7.78	175/64	110h	13.27A, 13.55	13.29- 06
Vinichenko	Igor	RUS	11.4.84	196/119	HT	77.01	80.00- 07
Vistali	Marco	ITA	3.10.87	184/70	400	45.76	45.38- 10
Vivas	Borja	ESP	26.5.84	203/140	SP	20.18i, 20.01	20.01- 09
* Vizzoni	Nicola	ITA	4.11.73	193/122	HT	80.29	80.50- 01
Vorontsov	Andrey	BLR	24.7.75	191/105	HT	76.09	81.31- 08
Vos	Ingmar	NED	28.5.86	185/81	Dec	8105	8009- 09
Wagner	Stepán	CZE	5.10.81	187/74	LJ	7.94i, 7.89	8.15, 8.18w- 09
* Walker	Brad	USA	21.6.81	188/86	PV	5.84	6.04- 08
Walker	Everett	USA	3.10.90	180/75	100	10.27,10.20w,10.05w irr	10.55- 09, 10.35w- 10
					200	20.79, 20.47w	21.43, 21.14w- 09
Walker	Justin	USA	30.11.90	175/70	100	10.18w	10.46, 10.13w- 10

Name		Nat	Born	Ht/Wt	Event	2011 Mark	Pre-2011 Best
Walker	Tristan	USA	24.10.87	190/82	200	20.73, 20.55w	21.15- 07
Wallace	Tyler	USA	31.7.90	190/80	PV	5.50	4.92- 10
Wallin	Gabriel	SWE	14.10.81	193/95	JT	80.88	80.71- 04
Walter	Simon	SUI	13.3.85	192/84	Dec	7973	7820- 10
Waltz	Ian	USA	15.4.77	186/122	DT	65.43	68.91- 06
Wang Chen		CHN	27.2.90	193/65	HJ	2.26	2.26- 09
Wang Gang		CHN	2.4.91		20kW	1:22:18	1:25:41- 10
* Wang Hao		CHN	16.8.89	180/65	20kW	1:21:03	1:18:13- 09
Wang Like		CHN	2.4.89	190/120	SP	19.61	19.18- 10
Wang Yu		CHN	18.8.91	189/64	HJ	2.28	2.24- 10
* Wang Zhen		CHN	24.8.91		20kW	1:18:30	1:20:42- 10
Wanjuki	Jacob	KEN	16.1.86	178/52	10k	27:48.74	27:49.44- 10
* Wariner	Jeremy	USA	31.1.84	183/70	400	44.88	43.45- 07
Warner	Damian	CAN	4.10.89		Dec	8102A, 7832	7449- 10
Warner	Justyn	CAN	28.6.87	174/70	100	10.15	10.23- 08
Watanabe	Kazuya	JPN	7.7.87	172/52	5000	13:23.15	13:39.45- 07
					10k	27:47.79	28:29.34- 10
* Watt	Mitchell	AUS	25.3.88	184/83	LJ	8.54	8.43- 09
Waugh	Ainsley	JAM	17.9.81	186/84	100	10.11	10.14- 08
					200	20.51	20.22- 09
Waweru	Edward	KEN	3.10.90	178/60	5000	13:13.80	13:16.49- 10
					10k	27:23.82	27:13.94- 10
Webb	Ameer	USA	19.3.91	175/75	200	20.49	20.70- 10
Weir	Warren	JAM	31.10.89	179/73	200	20.43	21.52- 10, 21.46w- 09
Weirich	Victor	USA	25.10.87	188/86	PV	5.50Ai, 5.35	5.22- 07
Welday	Haïs	ERI	24.10.89	161/54	3000	7:37.23	7:45.44i- 10
Wells	Evander	USA	7.12.87	173/73	200	20.55w	20.25- 08
Werskey	Eric	USA	17.7.87	188/120	SP	19.83	19.18i- 09, 18.95- 10
Westö	Mikael	FIN	3.4.82	189/85	PV	5.50	5.50- 08
* Wheating	Andrew	USA	21.11.87	195/77	800	1:45.95	1:44.56- 10
					1500	3:34.39	3:30.90- 10
White	Corey	USA	31.1.86	185/91	JT	81.70	78.79- 10
White	Deun	USA	13.7.85	183/77	100	10.24, 10.13w	10.33, 10.23w- 09
					200	20.55, 20.11w	20.61, 20.56w- 09
* Whiting	Ryan	USA	24.11.86	190/122	SP	21.76	21.97- 10
Whitt	Jack	USA	12.4.90	191/82	PV	5.65	5.60i- 10, 5.48- 09
Wiaderek	Piotr	POL	5.2.84	186/76	400	45.78	46.23- 08
Wieczorek	Mark	USA	25.12.84	178/68	800	1:46.00	1:47.11- 09
* Wierig	Martin	GER	10.6.87	202/108	DT	67.21	64.93- 10
Wijesekara	Manjula Kuma	SRI	30.1.84	183/73	HJ	2.24	2.27- 04
Wilks	Terrell	USA	30.12.89	188/82	100	10.19, 10.11w	10.15- 09
					200	20.51	20.53- 10
Williams	Caleb	USA	14.12.90	175/70	400	45.61	46.50- 10
Williams	Conrad	GBR	20.3.82	182/76	400	45.63	45.45- 10
Williams	Horatio	USA	28.8.89	188/79	200	20.44, 20.32w	20.48- 09
* Williams	Ivory	USA	2.5.85	174/77	100	10.02, 9.95w	9.93- 09, 9.88w- 10
* Williams	Jesse	USA	27.12.83	184/75	HJ	2.37	2.36i, 2.34- 09
Williams	Rhys	GBR	27.2.84	183/73	400h	49.59	48.96- 10
Williams	Rubin	USA	9.7.83	175/70	100	10.31, 10.18w	10.12, 9.96w- 08
* Willis	Nick	NZL	25.4.83	183/68	1500	3:31.79	3:32.17- 06
					1M	3:51.95	3:50.66- 08
^ Wilson	Aarik	USA	25.10.82	190/88	TJ	16.64, 16.65w	17.58- 07
Wilson	Alex	SUI	19.9.90	179/77	200	20.51	20.93- 10
Wilson	Jamal	BAH	1.9.88	188/68	HJ	2.24Ai, 2.21	2.23A- 08
* Wilson	Ryan	USA	19.12.80	188/81	110h	13.36, 13.35w	13.02- 07
Winger	Russ	USA	2.8.84	191/120	SP	20.94	21.29i- 08, 21.25- 10
					DT	66.04	62.88- 10
* Wirkkala	Teemu	FIN	14.1.84	187/85	JT	82.39	87.23- 09
^ Wissman	Johan	SWE	2.11.82	180/75	200	20.57w	20.30- 07, 20.26w- 05
					400	45.82	44.56- 07
* Wojciechowski	Pawel	POL	6.6.89	186/77	PV	5.91sq	5.60- 10
Wolde	Dawit	ETH	19.5.91	184/64	1500	3:34.13	3:36.74- 09
					3000	7:42.65	7:49.52- 10
Wolf	Gordon	GER	17.1.90	199/102	DT	61.49	62.16- 10
Wolski	Dawid	POL	15.6.89	175/62	20kW	1:23:20	1:25:49- 10
Wolski	Robert	POL	8.12.82	181/63	HJ	2.24i, 2.22	2.31- 06
Wondimu	Eshetu	ETH	26.1.82	165/52	Mar	2:07:33	2:06:46- 10
Wondimu	Mulugeta	ETH	28.2.85	173/57	1500	3:37.23	3:31.13- 04
Woodward	Nathan	GBR	17.10.89	193/79	400h	48.71	49.70- 10
* Wöschler	Till	GER	9.6.91	196/110	JT	84.38	82.52- 10

Name		Nat	Born	Ht/Wt	Event	2011 Mark	Pre-2011 Best
Wote (Wetiye)	Aman	ETH	18.4.84	178/62	1500	3:35.61	3:38.89- 10
Wruck	Julian	AUS	6.7.91	198/125	DT	65.74	61.02- 10
Wu Bo		CHN	17.6.84	174/60	TJ	16.79	17.10- 08
Wu Jian		CHN	25.5.86	189/95	DT	63.54	60.75- 08
Wu Qianlong		CHN	30.1.90	176/62	50kW	3:59:39	3:57:56- 09
Wyatt	Reggie	USA	17.9.90	188/73	400h	49.41	49.46- 10
Wykes	Dylan	CAN	6.6.83	184/70	10k	28:12.82	28:58.45- 09
Xhonneux	Frédéric	BEL	11.5.83	183/81	Dec	7760	8142- 08
Xie Wenjun		CHN	11.7.90	186/74	110h	13.45	13.47- 08
Xu Dexing		CHN	20.8.88	183/60	20kW	1:21:57	1:23:59- 10
Xu Faguang		CHN	17.5.87	178/69	20kW	1:22:04	1:20:26- 08
					50kW	3:42:20	3:47:54- 10
Xu Xiangchao		CHN-J	26.10.93		400h	49.87	52.75- 10
Yachi	Yusuke	JPN	2.1.80	172/55	20kW	1:22:27	1:22:11- 10
					50kW	4:03:35	3:52:37- 08
Yamagata	Ryota	JPN-J	10.6.92	178/62	200	20.62	20.81- 10
* Yamazaki	Yuki	JPN	16.1.84	177/65	50kW	3:44:03	3:40:12- 09
Yang Yansheng		CHN	5.1.88	189/75	PV	5.60	5.75- 10
Yarbrough	John	USA	16.8.85	193/89	110h	13.41	13.36, 13.2w- 10
Yargunkin	Aleksandr	RUS	6.1.81	182/68	20kW	1:23:17	1:19:57- 09
					50kW	3:59:22	3:56:56- 02
Yastrebov	Viktor	UKR	13.1.82	185/73	TJ	16.66	17.32- 04
Yates	Richard	GBR	26.1.86	185/77	400h	50.01	49.06- 08
Yator	Philemon	KEN-J	2.4.92	174/57	5000	13:18.35	
Yator	Vincent	KEN	11.7.89	170/55	5000	13:11.69	13:04.50- 10
* Yego	Hillary	KEN-J	2.4.92	178/60	3kSt	8:07.71	8:19.50- 10
Yego	Julius	KEN	4.1.89		JT	78.34	75.44A- 10
* Yemelyanov	Stanislav	RUS	23.10.90	175/62	20kW	1:19:33	1:19:43- 10
* Yerokhin	Igor	RUS	4.9.85	176/64	50kW	3:49:05	3:38:08- 08
Yi Shisuo		CHN	20.2.90	188/65	HJ	2.24	2.31- 93
Yin Jing		CHN	23.5.88	184/65	110h	13.59	13.38- 09
Yoroizaka	Tetsuya	JPN	20.3.90	166/52	10k	27:44.30	28:34.12- 10
Yoshida	Kazuaki	JPN	31.8.87	180/73	40h	50.26	49.45- 09
Young	Jason	JAM	21.3.91	180/68	200	20.53	
* Young	Jason	USA	27.5.81	185/116	DT	65.30	69.90- 10
Young	Javon	USA	21.8.90	175/70	100	10.20w	10.23, 10.17w- 10
Young	Ryan	USA	3.1.87	196/100	JT	79.89	76.45- 09
Yousif	Rabah	SUD	11.12.86	183/73	400	45.13	45.15- 09
Yu Bin		CHN	26.11.85	186/80	Dec	7845	7824- 07
Yu Wei		CHN	11.9.87	180/60	20kW	1:20:43	1:20:41- 09
					50kW	3:51:46	3:58:00- 09
Yu Zhenwei		CHN	18.3.86		LJ	8.05	8.12- 10
Yufu	Ikuto	JPN	7.7.91	177/54	10k	28:02.46	28:51.71- 09
Yun Zhiming		CHN	9.10.88	184/60	LJ	8.05	8.04- 10
^ Yurchenko	Denys	UKR	27.1.78	175/76	PV	5.62	5.85i- 05, 5.83-08
Yushkov	Ivan	RUS	15.1.81	193/115	SP	20.61	21.01- 08
* Zagornyi	Aleksey	RUS	31.5.78	197/130	HT	81.73	83.43- 02
^ Zakari	Abdul Aziz	GHA	2.9.76	178/73	100	10.24, 10.16w	9.99- 05, 9.98w- 03
Zalewski	Krystian	POL	11.4.89	185/67	3kSt	8:27.55	8:36.50- 10
Zalsky	Antonin	CZE	7.8.80	200/124	SP	20.27	20.71- 04
Zaytsev	Artyom	BLR	7.12.84	202/75	HJ	2.24i, 2.23	2.28i- 07, 2.28- 09
Zaytsev	Ivan	UZB	7.11.88	190/84	JT	79.39	75.32- 10
Zbroszczyk	Kamil	POL	24.1.87	189/116	SP	19.67	18.51- 10
Zepeda	Omar	MEX	8.6.77		50kW	3:50:26	3:49:01- 05
Zhang Guowei		CHN	4.6.91		HJ	2.31	2.23- 10
Zhang Jun		CHN	11.4.83	186/125	SP	19.85	20.41- 09
Zhang Peimeng		CHN	13.3.87	186/78	100	10.21	10.23- 08
Zhang Xiaoyi		CHN	25.5.89	186/65	LJ	8.04	8.27- 09
Zhao Jianguo		CHN	19.1.88	170/58	50kW	3:50:18	3:41:10- 06
Zhao Kuansong		CHN	11.2.86	189/70	HJ	2.24	2.24- 10
Zhao Qi		CHN-J	14.1.93		20kW	1:22:05	-0-
Zhao Qinggang		CHN	24.7.85	184/75	JT	78.40	79.80- 10
Zhelyabin	Dmitry	RUS	20.5.90	187/75	PV	5.55	5.30- 09
Zhuang Haitao		CHN	6.1.89	170/60	LJ	7.96	8.00- 09
Zhukov	Yevgeniy	RUS	3.1.89		TJ	16.68	16.09, 16.20w- 10
Ziegler	Alexander	GER	7.7.87	180/89	HT	72.69	73.68- 10
Zilali	Abdelhakim	FRA	20.6.83	188/73	3kSt	8:25.82	8:25.42- 07
Zimmerman	Moacir	BRA	30.12.83	170/52	20kW	1:21:02.5t	1:21:35- 09
* Ziólkowski	Szymon	POL	1.7.76	192/120	HT	79.02	83.38- 01
Ziukas	Marius	LTU	29.6.85	185/70	20kW	1:22:31	1:23:55- 08
Zouaoui Dandrieux	Vincent	FRA	12.10.80	188/72	3kSt	8:17.84	8:14.74- 08

WOMEN'S INDEX 2011

old javelin.

Name		Nat	Born	Ht/Wt	Event	2011 Mark	Pre-2011 Best
Abadel	Berhane	ETH	10.6.90		HMar	69:00	
* Abakumova	Mariya	RUS	15.1.86	180/80	JT	71.99	70.78- 08
Abdulai	Ruky	CAN	8.8.82	180/59	LJ	6.64	6.74- 09, 6.79w- 06
					Hep	6212	6086- 10
Abdullah	Khadija	USA	24.7.90		SP	16.70i, 16.58	16.96i, 15.91- 10
Abdullayeva	Layes	AZE	29.5.91	170/54	5000	15:29.47	16:03.60- 10
10k	32:18.05				3kSt	9:45.85	9:34.75- 10
Abera	Alemitu	ETH	.86		Mar	2:26:33	2:27:56- 10
Abinuwa	Endurance	NGR	31.7.87	160/54	100	11.32A, 11.37, 11.29w	
200	23.11A, 23.45, 23.07w		23.73- 10		400	52.28	52.43- 09
* Abitova	Inga	RUS	6.3.82	153/47	Mar	2:26:31	2:22:19- 10
Achamo	Netsanet	ETH	14.12.87	171/57	HMar	70:41	
Mar	2:28:28				3kSt	9:54.8A	9:28.03- 07
Adams	Alysha	USA	29.9.88		100h	13.08w	13.31- 10
* Adams	Valerie	NZL	6.10.84	193/123	SP	21.24	21.07- 09
* Adamu	Birtukan	ETH-J	29.4.92		3kSt	9:20.37	9:31.39- 10
Adeoye	Margaret	GBR	27.4.85	175/64	200	23.30, 23.14w	23.76, 23.41w- 10
Adigun	Seun	NGR	3.1.87		100h	13.13	12.88- 09
^ Adriano	Elisângela	BRA	27.7.72	180/95	SP	16.65	19.30- 01
					DT	62.00	61.96- 98, 62.23dq- 99
Afework	Abebech	ETH	11.12.90		10k	32:05.06	32:52.67- 09
					HMar	70:30	70:49- 10
^ Agirre	Naroa	ESP	15.5.79	177/64	PV	4.30i, 4.30	4.56i, 4.50- 07
Aguilar	Alessandra	ESP	1.7.78	164/50	Mar	2:27:00	2:29:01- 09
Aguilera	Lisa	USA	30.11.79	160/46	3kSt	9:43.95	9:24.84- 10
Ahbe	Kelsie	USA	6.7.91		PV	4.30	4.10- 10
Ahkozova	Inna	UKR	16.9.84	176/65	LJ	6.83	6.58- 10
Ahkozova	Inna	UKR	16.9.84	176/65	Hep	5905	6015- 09
* Ahouré	Murielle	CIV	23.8.87	167/57	100	11.06, 10.86w	11.09- 09
					200	22.31w	22.78- 09
Ahyee	Michelle Lee	TRI-J	10.4.92		100	11.20, 11.15w	11.32- 10
Aidietyte	Neringa	LTU	5.6.83	177/64	20kW	1:34:01	1:33:54- 07
* Aitova	Marina	KAZ	13.9.82	180/60	HJ	1.94	1.99- 09
* Akaba	Yukiko	JPN	18.10.79	158/44	HMar	69:16	68:11- 08
					Mar	2:24:09	2:24:55- 10
Akhmedova	Darya	UZB	3.4.91		LJ	6.55	6.26- 10
Akinsulie	Esther	CAN	22.4.84	175/65	400	52.33A, 52.93	51.70- 09
Akkaoui	Malika	MAR	25.12.87	160/46	800	1:59.75	2:00.6- 10
					1500	4:04.96	4:25.09- 08
Alcántara	Dailenys	CUB	10.8.91	163/56	TJ	14.56	14.36- 09, 14.55w- 10
Alcide	Makeba	LCA	24.2.90		Hep	5646	5172- 10
* Aldama	Yamilé	GBR	14.8.72	173/62	TJ	14.50	15.29- 03
* Alekhina	Nadezhda	RUS	22.9.78	176/62	TJ	13.94	15.14- 09
Alembekova	Elmira	RUS	30.6.90		20kW	1:27:35	1:35:53- 10
Alexander	Annie	TRI	28.8.87	175/91	SP	17.66	17.45- 08
					DT	58.58	57.68- 08
Alexander	Ayanna	TRI	20.7.82	172/65	TJ	13.98	13.96- 09
Alexander	Rebecca	USA	2.5.90		200	22.96i, 23.41w	23.90, 23.78w- 09
* Ali	Nia	USA	23.10.88	170/64	100h	12.73, 12.63w	13.14- 08
Allen	Linda	AUS	22.3.87	178/63	TJ	13.82	13.55- 09
Allen	Lindsey	USA	30.6.86	162/50	3kSt	9:47.03	9:40.83- 09
Almanza	Rose Mary	CUB-J	13.7.92	166/53	800	2:00.56	2:02.04- 10
Álvarez	Raquel	ESP	13.6.83	174/61	HJ	1.89	1.85i- 06. 1.85- 07
Amare	Alene	ETH	9.12.86		HMar	69:25	73:54- 10
* Amata	Doreen	NGR	6.5.88	185/55	HJ	1.95	1.95- 08
Anacharsis	Phara	FRA	17.12.83	177/58	400h	56.53	56.56- 10
Anderson	Alex	USA	28.1.87	175/60	200	22.87	22.60- 09
* Anderson	Alexandria	USA	28.1.87	175/60	100	11.01, 10.91w	11.02, 10.92w- 09
Anderson	Gabriele	USA	25.6.86		1500	4:06.77	4:12.06- 10
Anderson	Shawna	JAM	3.5.89		100	11.43, 11.31w	11.58- 08, 11.49w- 10
* Andersson	Isabellah	SWE	12.11.80	167/51	Mar	2:23:41	2:25:10- 10
Andersson	Tracey	SWE	5.12.84	167/80	HT	68.61	69.28- 10
^ Andrianova	Tatyana	RUS	10.12.79	176/56	800	2:01.62	1:56.00- 08
Angell	Mary	USA	29.8.89		DT	56.26	52.74- 10
Angelsen	Tonje	NOR	17.1.90	179/62	HJ	1.92i, 1.92	1.89- 10
Anim	Vida	GHA	7.12.83	168/58	200	23.06	22.81- 06
Anteneh	Emebet	ETH-J	13.1.92		5000	14:43.29	14:44.90- 10
Antonova	Aleksandra	RUS	24.3.80	162/59	100h	13.11	12.78- 06
* Antyukh	Natalya	RUS	26.6.81	182/73	400	50.73	49.85- 04
					400h	53.75	52.92- 10

Name		Nat	Born	Ht/Wt	Event	2011 Mark	Pre-2011 Best
Anyanwu	Kelechi	USA	27.12.85		DT	57.98	58.01- 08
Aoki	Sayaka	JPN	15.12.86	162/51	400h	56.62	55.94- 08
Apak	Sema	TUR	17.8.85	170/54	400h	57.09A, 57.22	-0-
Arcanjo	Geisa	BRA	19.9.91		SP	17.03	17.11- 10
Arencibia	Yenima	CUB	25.12.84	167/55	100h	13.12, 12.9	12.95A, 12.4- 08, 13.08- 10
Argunova	Nina	RUS	15.9.89		100h	13.02	13.29- 10
* Arigawi	Abeba	ETH	5.7.90		1500	4:01.47i, 4:10.30	4:01.96- 10
Aristarkhova	Natalya	RUS	31.10.89		3kSt	9:56.04	10:30.98- 10
Arkhipova	Lyudmila	RUS	25.11.78	167/55	20kW	1:29:19	1:26:16- 08
Arslan	Cagdas	TUR	10.3.86	170/55	TJ	13.69, 13.96w	13.33, 13.38w- 10
Artîc	Natalia	MDA	24.7.87		DT	56.62	53.25- 10
* Arusei	Peninah	KEN	23.2.79	165/51	HMar	68:30	67:48- 10
					Mar	2:27:17	-0-
Aryasova #	Tatyana	RUS	2.4.79	160/52	Mar	2:27:29dq	2:26:13- 10
Arzamasova	Marina	BLR	17.12.87	170/56	800	1:59.30	2:02.67- 08
					1000	2:36.0e	
* Arzhakova	Yelena	RUS	8.9.89	170/56	800	1:58.77	
1000	2:35.21i				1500	4:07.69	4:08.05- 10
Asada	Chiaki	JPN	21.1.91		20kW	1:34:01	1:32:27- 10
Asahssah	Malika	MAR	24.9.82	173/56	HMar	70:26	69:54- 09
Assefa	Meskerem	ETH	20.9.85	155/43	1500	4:02.12	4:05.62- 10
* Assefa	Sofia	ETH	14.11.87	171/58	3kSt	9:15.04	9:19.91- 09
Asumnu	Gloria	USA/NGR	22.5.85	168/59	100	11.19	11.03- 08
					200	23.10	22.70- 07
Atangana	Delphine	CMR	16.8.84	170/56	100	11.43, 11.31w	11.24- 03
Atkins	Joanna	USA	31.1.89		100	11.30	11.32- 10
200	22.68		22.89- 09		400	51.50	50.39- 09
* Augusto	Jéssica	POR	8.11.81	165/46	5000	15:19.60	14:37.07- 10
10k	32:06.68		31:19.15- 10		HMar	69:10	69:08- 09
					Mar	2:24:33	-0-
* Avdeyeva	Anna	RUS	6.4.85	170/90	SP	19.54	20.07- 09
Aya	Masumi	JPN	1.1.80	165/75	HT	67.19	67.26- 06
Ayala	Fabiola Elizabeth	MEX	31.12.86	175/54	HJ	1.90	1.90A- 10
Ayalew	Genet	ETH-J	31.12.92		5000	15:10.45	15:03.52- 10
					10k	32:05.90	
Ayalew	Hiwot	ETH	6.3.90		5000	14:49.36	16:17.1- 10
					3kSt	9:23.88	
* Ayalew	Wude	ETH	4.7.87	150/44	3000	8:56.79+	8:30.93- 09
5000	14:59.71		14:38.44- 09		10k	31:24.09	30:11.87- 09
Ayana	Almaz	ETH	21.11.91		3000	8:53.49	
5000	15:12.24				3kSt	9:30.23	9:22.51- 10
Aydin	Merve	TUR	17.3.90	170/57	800	2:00.46	2:00.33- 08
Ayédou	Miel Blessing	BEN	17.8.91		400h	56.66	58.44A- 10, 58.53- 09
Ayhan	Burcu	TUR	3.5.90	180/56	HJ	1.94	1.92- 10
Babos	Rita	HUN	21.10.80	175/57	HJ	1.87	1.86- 07
* Bailey	Aleen	JAM	25.11.80	170/64	100	11.15	11.04- 04
					200	22.79	22.33- 04
Baker	Keshia	USA	30.1.88		400	51.61	50.76- 10
Balakshina	Anna	RUS	22.11.85		800	2:01.14i	2:00.19- 10
Balayeva	Olga	RUS	31.7.84		LJ	6.89	6.69- 09
Balciunaite	Egle	LTU	31.10.88	175/60	800	2:01.45, 2:01.23i	1:59.29- 10
Baldwin-Foss	Jasmine	USA	27.9.86		100	11.29, 11.08w	11.33- 04, 11.24w- 10
* Balta	Ksenija	EST	11.1.86	168/53	LJ	6.73i	6.87i- 09, 6.87- 10
Bambara	Laëtitia	FRA	30.3.84	180/75	HT	68.53	66.83- 07
Bani	Zahra	ITA	31.12.79	173/73	JT	60.30	62.75- 05
Banova	Andiana	BUL	1.5.87		TJ	14.34	14.21- 10
* Baptiste	Kelly-Ann	TRI	14.10.86	160/54	100	10.90	10.84- 10
Baraley	Yuliya	UKR	25.4.90	178/60	400	52.1, 52.62	52.40- 08
Baranova	Veera	EST	12.2.84	176/60	TJ	13.96, 14.00w	14.17- 10
^ Barber	Mikele	USA	4.10.80	157/50	100	11.09, 10.96w	11.02- 07
Barbosa	Vera	POR	13.1.89		400h	55.81	58.89- 10
Bârcâ	Roxana	ROU	22.6.88	165/44	3000	8:56.79	9:10.71- 10
Barr	Jessie	IRL	24.7.89	178/59	400h	56.62	58.74- 10
* Barrett	Brigetta	USA	24.12.90	183/84	HJ	1.96	1.91- 10
* Barrios	Yarelys	CUB	12.7.83	172/98	DT	66.40A	66.13- 08, 66.68ex- 07
Barros	Marisa	POR	25.2.80	160/50	HMar	70:29dh	69:09- 10
					Mar	2:25:04	2:25:44- 10
Bartnovskaya	Natalya	RUS	7.1.89		PV	4.30i, 4.20	4.10- 08
* Battke	Anna	GER	3.1.85	173/58	PV	4.51i, 4.50sq	4.68- 09
Bauer	Katharina	GER	12.6.90	178/66	PV	4.31i, 4.25	4.25i- 10, 4.21- 09
Bauschke	Melanie	GER	14.7.88	178/62	LJ	6.66	6.83- 09

Name		Nat	Born	Ht/Wt	Event	2011 Mark	Pre-2011 Best
Baxter	Aubrey	USA	7.11.85		HT	65.53	63.30- 10
Bayley	Krysha	CAN	21.1.84	188/53	LJ	6.62	6.57i- 05. 6.52, 6.55w- 09
* Baysa	Atsede	ETH	16.4.87		HMar	69:58	68:42- 10
					Mar	2:23:50	2:22:04- 10
* Beard	Jessica	USA	8.1.89	168/57	200	23.02, 22.95i	23.05- 10
					400	51.06, 50.79i	50.56- 09
Beckles	Kierre	BAR	21.5.90	169/54	100h	13.01	13.22A, 13.26, 13.14w- 10
Beckwith	Molly	USA	4.8.87	173/	800	1:59.12	1:59.83- 10
Bedaso	Shitaye	ETH	.80		Mar	2:25:09	2:29:48- 10
Beesley	Meghan	GBR	15.11.89	165/63	400h	55.69	56.65- 10
Begic	Vera	CRO	17.3.82	169/69	DT	60.91	61.52- 09
^ Begley	Amy	USA	11.1.78	168/52	10k	32:34.75	31:13.78- 09
* Beitia	Ruth	ESP	1.4.79	192/71	HJ	1.96i, 1,95	2.02- 07
Bekele	Alemitu	TUR	17.9.77	165/48	5000	15:08.86	14:36.79- 10
* Bekele	Bezunesh	ETH	18.9.83	145/38	HMar	69:08	68:07- 07
					Mar	2:23:42	2:23:09- 08
Bekele	Mekdes	ETH	20.1.87	180/58	3000	8:44.25i	9:01.17- 10
					3kSt	9:26.51	9:20.23- 08
Belete	Almensch	ETH	26.7.89		5000	15:03.63	15:17.37- 10
* Belete	Mimi	BRN	9.6.88	164/62	1500	4:03.13	4:00.25- 10
Bellille	Janeil	TRI	18.6.89	172/60	400h	55.80	56.81- 10
Belyakova	Anastasiya	RUS	4.12.90	179/56	HJ	1.87	1.79- 10
					Hep	6010	5435- 10
Benecchi	Giorgia	ITA	9.7.89	164/55	PV	4.35i, 4.40ex	4.36i, 4.20- 10
* Bengtsson	Angelica	SWE-J	8.7.93	164/53	PV	4.63i, 4.57	4.47- 10
Bennett	Gemma	GBR	4.1.84	176/66	100h	13.08	13.02- 08
Bergrová	Zuzana	CZE	24.11.84	174/62	400h	56.22	55.96- 10
Bernard-Thomas	Neisha	GRN	21.1.81	165/56	800	2:01.77	1:59.60- 10
Berroa	Nieves	CUB	16.3.90	175/72	SP	17.10	16.55- 10
Berry	Gwen	USA	29.6.89		SP	16.99	16.30i, 15.99- 10
					HT	70.52	62.55- 10
Bespalova	Mariya	RUS	21.5.86	183/80	HT	71.93	69.02- 09
Bessoltseva	Anastasiya	RUS	18.8.90		SP	16.68	16.46- 10
Bicet	Nora Aída	ESP	29.10.77	178/78	JT	59.86	63.32- 04
Bicet	Yusmay	CUB	8.12.83	188/	TJ	14.30	14.61, 14.67w- 04
Bielawska	Martyna	POL	15.11.90	175/58	TJ	13.97	12.87i, 12.54- 10
Bikulova	Lina	RUS	1.10.88		20kW	1:32:45	1:32:39- 09
Billaud	Cindy	FRA	11.3.86	168/57	100h	12.93	12.97- 09, 12.97w- 08
Bingson	Amanda	USA	20.2.90		HT	69.79	64.07- 10
Biryukova	Anastasiya	RUS-J	12.7.92		PV	4.30i, 4.20	3.90- 10
Bizzarri	Angela	USA	15.2.88		5000	15:16.04	15:33.02- 09
Blackburn	Lauren	USA	18.11.91		100h	13.06	13.39- 10
Blank	Anna	RUS	12.1.90		Hep	5813	5650- 10
Blazej	Karolina	POL	21.11.86	170/53	HJ	1.91	1.87- 09
* Bleasdale	Holly	GBR	2.11.91	175/68	PV	4.71i, 4.70	4.35- 10
Blewitt	Adriane	USA	24.5.80	178/79	SP	17.31	18.29- 05
Bliss	Andrea	JAM	5.10.80	173/63	100h	13.16, 12.95w	12.83- 05
Blouin	Mélanie	CAN	14.7.90		PV	4.30	3.95i- 10, 3.80- 09
Bo Yanmin		CHN	29.6.87	170/51	20kW	1:34:21	1:27:37- 05
Bobocel	Ancuta	ROU	3.10.87	163/52	1500	4:08.13i, 4:15.51	4:12.01i, 4:13.20- 10
Boden	Lauren	AUS	3.8.88	179/64	400h	55.78	55.25- 10
Boekelman	Melissa	NED	11.5.89	177/66	SP	17.97	18.17- 10
Bogale	Tizita	ETH-J	13.7.93		1500	4:03.94	4:08.06- 10
* Bogdanova	Anna	RUS	21.10.84	178/66	HJ	1.88	1.88- 08
					Hep	6242	6465- 08
Bogdanovich	Valeriya	BLR-J	1.5.92		HJ	1.88	1.80- 10
* Bolshakova	Svetlana	BEL	14.10.84	178/68	TJ	14.31i, 13.70	14.55- 10
Bolton	Grecia	USA	2.10.89		100	11.35, 11.30w	11.50- 09
					200	23.27, 23.15w	23.34- 09
Bonne	Daysiurami	CUB	9.3.88	173/56	400	51.69A, 52.04	51.81- 09
Boonwan	Wanida	THA	30.8.86	185/52	HJ	1.92	1.91i, 1.88- 09
Bordignon	Laura	ITA	26.3.81	180/78	DT	57.62	59.21- 08
* Borel-Brown	Cleopatra	TRI	3.10.79	168/93	SP	19.42	19.48i- 04, 19.30- 10
Borges	Fernanda Raquel	BRA	26.7.88	165/65	DT	60.91	57.56- 10
Borman	Brittany	USA	1.7.89		DT	56.44	56.72- 10
Borodina	Yana	RUS-J	21.4.92		TJ	14.35	13.70- 10
Borovska	Nadiya	UKR	25.2.81	165/50	20kW	1:32:30	1:32:44- 07
Borsi	Veronica	ITA	13.6.87	169/48	100h	13.08	13.37- 10
* Boslak	Vanessa	FRA	11.6.82	170/57	PV	4.51i, 4.30	4.70- 06
Bouaasayriya	Kaltoum	MAR	23.8.82		3000	8:56.99	9:15.85- 10
Bouras	Zahra	ALG	13.1.87	170/52	800	1:59.21	1:59.54- 10

	Name		Nat	Born	Ht/Wt	Event	2011 Mark	Pre-2011 Best
	Bowie	Tori	USA	27.8.90		LJ	6.64	6.43, 6.50w- 10
	Boyd	Alana	AUS	10.5.84	171/60	PV	4.60	4.56- 08
	Breen	Melissa	AUS	17.9.90	174/66	100	11.40, 11.27w	11.33- 08, 11.22w- 09
*	Breisch	Becky	USA	16.3.83	180/104	DT	64.30	67.37- 07
	Bremser	Julia	GER	27.4.82	176/78	DT	59.84	58.00- 10
	Brennan	Christian	CAN-Y	27.3.95		400	52.12	54.15- 10
	Briscoe	Shanay	USA-J	7.8.92		HJ	1.88	1.86- 08
	Brito	Andréa Maria	BRA	8.12.73		SP	16.74	16.90- 07
*	Britton	Evonne	USA	10.10.91		100h	13.11	13.37- 10
	Britton	Fionnuala	IRL	24.9.84	158/45	5000	15:21.45, 15:21.26	15:44.76- 10
						3kSt	9:37.60	9:41.36- 07
	Broadbelt-Blake	Angie	GBR	12.9.85		100h	13.18, 13.07w	13.20- 10
	Broersen	Nadine	NED	29.4.90	171/62	HJ	1.87	1.84- 10
						Hep	5932(w), 5854	5842- 10
	Brookins	LaKya	USA	28.7.89	157/53	100	11.10, 11.02w	11.20- 09
	Brooks	Tia	USA	2.8.90		SP	18.00	17.37- 10
	Brost	Leslie	USA	28.9.89	163/	PV	4.30i	4.30- 10
	Brown	Tierra	USA	24.10.89		100h	12.94	12.84, 12.70w- 10
						400h	55.59	54.74- 10
*	Brown Trafton	Stephanie	USA	1.12.79	193/102	DT	64.13	66.21- 09
	Bryant	Dezerea	USA-J	27.4.93		200	23.01	23.51, 23.37w- 10
*	Bryzgina	Yelizaveta	UKR	28.11.89	172/56	200	23.02	22.44- 10
	Büchler	Nicole	SUI	17.12.83	161/56	PV	4.50	4.50- 09
	Buckley	Landria	USA	2.7.88		400h	56.79	57.88- 09
	Buckman	Zoe	AUS	21.12.88	167/50	1500	4:05.06	4:12.80- 10
*	Bujin	Cristina	ROU	12.4.88	171/52	TJ	14.30	14.42- 09
	Bulanova	Aleksandra	RUS	10.6.89		800	2:00.14	2:00.17- 10
	Bulgakova	Anna	RUS	17.1.88	173/90	HT	69.10	73.79- 08
	Bullock	Epley	USA	12.11.87		HJ	1.91i	1.90- 10
^	Bunjes	Andrea	GER	5.2.76	175/80	HT	68.35	70.73- 04
*	Burka	Gelete	ETH	15.2.86	165/45	1500	4:03.28	3:58.79- 09
	Burkhanova	Sofia	UZB	1.12.89	170/60	SP	16.70	17.19- 10
	Burkhardt	Samira	GER	9.8.90	182/82	SP	17.09	17.08- 10
	Burla	Serena	USA	29.7.82		10k	32:48.16	32:47.48- 08
	Bush	Nicole	USA	4.4.86	172/54	3kSt	9:55.17	9:39.38- 09
	Butvina	Aleksandra	RUS	14.2.86	181/71	Hep	5981	6079- 10
	Buziak	Paulina	POL	16.12.86	168/54	20kW	1:33:44	1:32:44- 10
	Caballero	Daylis	CUB	6.3.88	166/59	PV	4.51	4.30- 09
	Caballero	Denia	CUB	13.1.90	175/73	DT	62.94	59.92- 10
	Caballero	Yolanda	COL	19.3.82	153/49	Mar	2:26:17dh	
*	Cabecinha	Ana	POR	29.4.84	168/52	20kW	1:31:08	1:27:46- 08
	Cachová	Katerina	CZE	26.2.90	171/60	Hep	6123	5911- 10
	Çakir	Aslı	TUR	20.8.85	168/50	1500	4:05.53	4:02.17- 10
	Cakova	Natalija	LAT	20.10.80	180/65	HJ	1.87	1.89- 07
*	Calvert	Schillonie	JAM	27.7.88	166/57	100	11.05	11.19- 09
						200	22.55	23.13- 10
*	Camarena-Williams	Jill	USA	2.8.82	180/91	SP	20.18	19.50- 10
*	Campbell	Amber	USA	5.6.81	170/91	HT	72.59	71.94- 10
*	Campbell-Brown	Veronica	JAM	15.5.82	163/61	100	10.76	10.78- 10
	200	22.22			21.74- 08	400	52.25	52.24i- 05, 52.77- 10
	Capková	Tereza	CZE	24.7.87	162/53	1500	4:08.89	4:15.09- 08
	Caravelli	Marzia	ITA	23.10.81	176/64	100h	13.01	13.10- 10
	Carrier	Chelsea	USA	21.8.89		100h	13.06, 12.96w	13.30- 09
						Hep	5927w, 5761	5188- 08
	Carrión	Lisandra	CUB	18.9.89	173/65	Hep	5617	5417- 10
*	Carruthers	Danielle	USA	22.12.79	173/62	100h	12.47, 12.37w	12.56- 04
	Carter	Kori	USA-J	6.3.92		100h	13.12	13.54, 13.33w- 10
						400h	57.10	59.89- 09
*	Carter	Michelle	USA	12.10.85	175/104	SP	19.86	19.13- 09
	Casabona	Nelkys Teresa	CUB	12.5.84	175/62	100	11.31	11.39- 10, 10.9- 09
	Casabona	Nelkys Teresa	CUB	12.5.84	175/62	200	22.97	23.63- 09, 23.2- 10
	Casandra	Cristina	ROU	21.10.77	168/50	3kSt	9:38.42	9:16.85- 08
	Castells	Berta	ESP	24.1.84	174/73	HT	69.53	69.36- 10
*	Castlin	Kristi	USA	7.7.88	170/57	100h	12.83, 12.68w	12.81 -08, 12.59w- 10
	Cathey	Mason	USA	29.4.82		3kSt	9:53.66	10:03.08- 09
*	Cechlová	Vera	CZE	19.11.78	178/78	DT	63.40	67.71- 03
	Cérival	Jessica	FRA	20.1.82	187/120	SP	17.99i, 17.52	17.87- 09
	Chaboudez	Aurélie	FRA-J	9.5.93	173/55	Hep	5660	
	Chaney	Jasmine	USA	25.8.88		200	23.16i	23.55- 10
	400	52.23				100h	13.15	13.26- 10
						400h	55.22	57.67- 10

Name		Nat	Born	Ht/Wt	Event	2011 Mark	Pre-2011 Best
Chang Chunfeng		CHN	4.5.88	179/75	JT	59.50	61.61- 07
Changeiywo	Doris	KEN	12.12.84	160/43	10k	32:22.8A	31:31.01- 08
					HMar	68:49	70:40- 10
* Chebet	Emily	KEN	18.2.86	157/45	10k	31:30.22	31:33.39- 06
* Checa	Dolores	ESP	27.12.82	168/52	1500	4:13.37	4:02.77- 08
3000	8:51.78i		8:37.78- 08		5000	14:46.30	14:55.71- 08
Checa	Isabel	ESP	27.12.82	160/55	10k	32:48.76	32:07.78- 08
Chelimo	Rose	KEN	.89		HMar	69:45	72:48- 10
* Chemos	Milcah	KEN	24.2.86	163/48	3kSt	9:12.89	9:08.57- 09
Chemtai	Esther	KEN	4.6.88		5000	15:00.08	14:57.16- 10
Chen Dongxia		CHN	12.7.89	180/78	DT	56.38	56.13- 10
Chen Ping		CHN	8.9.89	170/67	JT	56.42	55.12- 10
Chen Rong		CHN	18.5.88	160/43	10k	31:39.77	31:41.60- 08
					Mar	2:26:49	2:27:05- 07
Chen Yanjun		CHN	13.1.88	180/58	HJ	1.88i	1.88- 10
* Chenonge	Iness	KEN	1.2.82	168/54	HMar	69:08	68:54- 02
Chepchirchir	Flomena	KEN	1.12.81	165/43	HMar	68:22	70:41- 07
					Mar	2:24:21	
Chepchirchir	Sarah	KEN	27.7.84		HMar	68:07	69:27- 10
Chepkemoi	Diane	KEN	.87		HMar	70:40	
					Mar	2:26:53	
* Chepkirui	Joyce	KEN	10.8.88		1500	4:08.80A	4:19.8- 07
10k	31:26.10		-0-		HMar	69:04	69:25- 10
Chepkoech	Caroline	KEN-Y	26.5.94		5000	15:24.66A	16:09.0- 10
Chepkurui	Lidya	KEN	23.8.84		3kSt	9:30.73	
* Chepkurui	Lineth	KEN	23.2.88	157/43	5000	15:15.15	15:55.3- 08
					10k	31:24.20	31:31.92- 09
Chepkwemoi	Nancy	KEN-J	8.10.93		1500	4:07.63	4:11.04- 10
Chepyego	Sally	KEN	3.10.85	160/42	5000	15:10.53	15:06.26- 06
10k	31:27.98		31:39.84- 07		HMar	69:58	75:27- 09
^ Chermoshanskaya	Yuliya	RUS	6.1.86	176/65	200	22.81	22.57- 08
Chernova	Lada	RUS	1.1.70		JT	57.40	63.35- 07
* Chernova	Tatyana	RUS	29.1.88	189/63	LJ	6.82	6.78- 08, 6.79w- 10
					Hep	6880	6768w- 07, 6618- 08
* Cheromei	Lydia	KEN	11.5.77	162/47	HMar	67:33	68:14- 09
					Mar	2:22:34	2:25:57- 08
Cherono	Gladys	KEN	.84		HMar	70:43	69:26- 09
* Cherono	Mercy	KEN	7.5.91	178/59	1500	4:02.31	4:13.70- 09
3000	8:52.37+		8:42.09- 10		5000	14:35.13	14:47.13- 10
* Cherono	Priscah	KEN	27.6.80	160/47	3000	8:47.15	8:29.06- 07
5000	14:40.86		14:35.30- 06		10k	30:56.43	
* Cherop	Sharon	KEN	16.3.84	/40	10k	32:03.0A	32:52.8- 99
HMar	67:08		68:51- 10		Mar	2:22:42dh	2:22:43- 10
* Cheruiyot	Vivian	KEN	11.9.83	155/38	3000	8:38.67+	8:28.66- 07
5000	14:20.87		14:22.51- 07		10k	30:48.98	-0-
Chesebe	Sylvia	KEN	.87		800	2:01.61A	2:05.64- 10
Chibisova	Oksana	RUS	31.3.77	177/87	SP	17.33i, 16.37	18.62- 05
* Chicherova	Anna	RUS	22.7.82	180/57	HJ	2.07	2.04- 08
Child	Eilidh	GBR	20.2.87	172/59	400	52.28	53.71- 08
					400h	55.67	55.16- 10
* Chilla	Mercedes	ESP	19.1.80	169/62	JT	63.77	64.07- 10
Choi Yun-hee		KOR	28.5.86	172/62	PV	4.40	4.30- 10
^ Chojecka	Lidia	POL	25.1.77	166/46	1500	4:07.28	3:59.22- 00
3000	8:55.73, 8:44.25i		8:31.69- 02		5000	15:29.42	15:04.88- 02
Chrust-Rozej	Marta	POL	29.9.78	161/51	400h	57.20	55.49- 05
Chung Hye-rim		KOR	1.7.87	169/51	100h	13.11	13.13- 10
Churakova	Yelena	RUS	16.12.86		400h	54.79	55.52- 08
Cichocka	Angelika	POL	15.3.88	169/54	800	2:00.20	2:00.86i, 2:01.17- 10
1000	2:37.33		2:37.01- 09		1500	4:06.50	4:10.54i- 10, 4:12.31- 09
Clements	Grace	GBR	2.5.84	170/64	Hep	5644w, 5437	5819- 10
Clitheroe	Helen	GBR	2.1.74	168/57	1500	4:06.49	4:01.10- 02
2000	5:46.0+		5:53.2+i- 08		3000	8:39.81i	8:51.02i- 08, 8:51.82- 10
5000	15:06.75		15:49.98- 08		10k	32:11.29	-0-
					HMar	70:57dh	-0-
Closse	Kelly	FRA	8.8.88	178/83	SP	16.60	16.40- 10
Coburn	Emma	USA	19.10.90		3kSt	9:37.16	9:51.86- 10
Cole	Leslie	USA	16.2.87		200	22.91	22.92A- 08, 22.93- 09
					400	51.42	51.20- 09
^ Collado	Yanisley	CUB	30.4.85	178/74	DT	61.85	64.10- 09
Collier	Ashley	USA-J	4.2.92		100	11.42, 11.22w	11.58- 08, 11.37w- 10
					200	23.15	23.49- 07, 23.43w- 10

Name		Nat	Born	Ht/Wt	Event	2011 Mark	Pre-2011 Best
Comba	Rocío	ARG	14.7.87	175/78	DT	56.39	59.86- 08
Console	Rosaria	ITA	17.12.79	160/42	10k	32:47.70	32:55.42- 00
					Mar	2:26:10	2:26:45- 09
Cooper	Angele	USA	3.11.90		400h	57.03	56.24- 10
Cornford	Laura	AUS	11.6.88	176/74	JT	57.74	57.37- 07
* Cosby	Jessica	USA	31.5.82	173/77	HT	72.65	72.21- 09
* Costa	Keila	BRA	6.2.83	170/62	LJ	6.67	6.88- 07
					TJ	14.24	14.57, 15.10w- 07
Costa	Susana	POR	22.9.84	176/65	TJ	13.70, 13.77w	13.77i, 13.36- 08
Cotten	Jennifer	CAN	14.10.87		Hep	5685	5491- 10
Cousins	Jessica	USA	10.4.85	165/	400	52.32	51.92- 07
Coutinho	Geisa	BRA	1.6.80	160/53	200	23.07	23.10- 03
					400	51.08	51.44- 03
Coward	Jackie	USA	5.11.89	167/55	100h	12.87, 12.79w	13.04, 12.99w- 10
Cowley	Sarah	NZL	3.2.84	176/66	Hep	5752	5710- 06
Cox	Shana	GBR	22.1.85	171/57	400	51.24	50.84- 08
Craft	Shanice	GER-J	15.5.93	185/87	DT	58.65	55.49- 10
* Crawford	Virginia	USA	7.9.83	178/63	100	11.36	11.10, 10.93Aw- 06
					100h	12.73, 12.47w	12.45- 07
^ Crawford	Yunaika	CUB	2.11.82	164/78	HT	67.30	73.16- 04
Cremer	Esther	GER	29.3.88	170/55	200	23.13w	23.10- 10
					400	52.08	52.16- 10
Cruz	Clarisse	POR	9.7.78	170/54	3kSt	9:57.79	9:44.94- 08
Cruz	Sílvia	POR	29.12.80	175/85	JT	59.52	59.76- 08
Cruz	Yanet	CUB	8.2.88	170/70	JT	63.50	62.90- 09
Cuddihy	Joanne	IRL	11.5.84	184/65	400	51.82	50.73- 07
Cullen	Mary	IRL	17.8.82	165/54	3000	8:53.01i	8:43.74i- 09, 8:48.17- 07
Culley	Julie	USA	10.9.81		5000	15:21.18	15:21.87- 09
^ Cusma Piccione	Elisa	ITA	24.7.81	167/49	800	2:01.04	1:58.63- 07
Czenska	Magdalena	POL	14.6.81	164/58	JT	55.53	56.92- 04
Daba	Tejitu	BRN	20.8.91	157/56	5000	15:14.62	15:29.78- 10
Dacheva	Petia	BUL	10.3.85	168/52	TJ	14.20i	14.45- 10
* Dado	Firehiwot	ETH	9.1.84	165/	HMar	70:13+	69:26- 09
					Mar	2:23:15	2:25:28- 10
Dahl	Heidi	USA	15.2.86		800	2:01.33	2:00.88- 09
* Dahlgren	Jennifer	ARG	27.8.84	180/115	HT	73.44	73.74- 10
Dahlström	Malin	SWE	26.8.89	171/59	PV	4.50i, 4.36	4.25i, 4.20- 10
Danois	Johanna	FRA	4.4.87	169/53	200	23.27, 23.00w	23.03- 09
* Daska	Mamitu	ETH	16.10.83	165/	HMar	69:46+	68:07- 09
					Mar	2:21:59	2:24:18- 10
Daunay	Christelle	FRA	5.12.74	163/43	10k	31:44.84	31:47.19- 09
					Mar	2:26:41	2:24:22- 10
Davila	Desiree	USA	26.7.83	157/	5000	15:08.64	15:29.78- 10
10k	31:37.14		32:06.85- 10		HMar	70:34	72:10- 08
					Mar	2:22:38dh	2:26:20- 10
Davin	Elisabeth	BEL	3.6.81	170/56	100h	13.12	12.97- 09
Davis	Candice	USA	26.10.85	170/62	100h	12.91	12.71, 12.66w- 08
Davis	Darshay	USA	23.9.91		100	11.32w	11.61- 10
					200	23.12w	24.04- 10
Davis	Jessica	USA-J	31.10.92		100	11.19	11.53, 11.49w- 10
					200	22.84	23.42- 10
Davydova	Irina	RUS	27.5.88	170/58	400h	55.48	55.74- 10
Day	Christine	JAM	23.8.86		400	52.08, 51.7	51.54- 09
Day	Sharon	USA	9.6.85	175/70	Hep	6058	6177- 09
De Aniceto	Marisa	FRA	11.11.86	162/57	Hep	5696	6080- 09
De Grande	Lindsey	BEL	26.4.89		1500	4:09.18i, 4:10.19	4:09.20- 10
de Klerk	Gerlize	RSA	23.3.89	176/80	JT	56.04A	56.61- 09
De Schrijder	Selien	BEL	10.11.86	169/56	3kSt	9:59.40	9:54.79- 10
Dean	Hatti	GBR	2.2.82	164/52	3kSt	9:37.95	9:30.19- 10
* Deba	Bizunesh	ETH	8.9.87		HMar	69:55, 69:53dh	72:50- 10
					Mar	2:23:19	2:27:24- 10
Decaux	Alice	FRA	10.4.85	165/61	100h	12.95	13.06- 10, 13.05w- 07
* Defar	Meseret	ETH	19.11.83	155/42	3000	8:50.36+, 8:36.91i	8:23.72i, 8:24.51- 05
5000	14:29.52		14:12.88- 08		10k	31:05.05	29:59.20- 09
Degefa	Eshetu	ETH	.82		Mar	2:27:34	
Degtyar	Viktoriya	UKR	5.11.83	186/83	SP	16.98	17.08- 09
* Dehiba	Hind	FRA	17.3.79	162/44	800	2:00.83	1:58.67- 10
1500	4:03.02		3:59.76- 10		1M	4:29.59	4:29.09- 10
Deiac	Cornelia	ROU	20.3.88	171/55	LJ	6.61i, 6.58	6.70- 10
Dejaeghere	Veerle	BEL	1.8.73	159/46	3kSt	9:50.35	9:28.47- 07
Dektyareva	Tatyana	RUS	8.5.81	174/60	100h	12.76	12.68- 10

Name		Nat	Born	Ht/Wt	Event	2011 Mark	Pre-2011 Best
* DeLoach	Janay	USA	12.10.85	165/59	LJ	6.99Ai, 6.97	6.61- 10
Demidenko	Natalya	RUS-J	7.3.93		PV	4.40	4.25- 10
* Demus	Lashinda	USA	10.3.83	170/62	100h	12.96	13.08- 04, 12.93w- 05
					400h	52.47	52.63- 09
Demut	Katja	GER	21.12.83	176/55	TJ	14.57	14.31- 10
Demydova	Hanna	UKR	8.4.87	178/50	TJ	13.88i, 13.64, 13.91w	13.88- 10
^ Denby	Nichole	USA	10.10.82	163/52	100h	12.98, 12.78w	12.54- 08
Deng Lina		CHN-J	16.3.92	165/44	TJ	13.89	13.72- 10
Denisenko	Alla	RUS	12.10.83		DT	56.69	56.78- 07
* Dennison	Kate	GBR	7.5.84	171/59	PV	4.61	4.60- 09
Dereveva	Olga	RUS	5.4.85	158/54	3kSt	9:43.52	10:15.47- 05
Derham	Zoë	GBR	24.11.80	180/118	HT	65.37	68.63- 08
Derkach	Daria	UKR-J	27.3.93		LJ	6.55	6.07- 10
Derun	Kateryna	UKR-J	24.9.93	168/67	JT	56.31	54.59- 10
DeShasier	Alicia	USA	15.4.84		JT	58.01A	55.53- 10
Desmet	Hannelore	BEL	25.2.89	167/48	HJ	1.88i	1.89- 10
Detsuk	Kseniya	BLR	23.4.86	177/56	TJ	14.05	14.39, 14.54w- 10
* Di Martino	Antonietta	ITA	1.6.78	169/57	HJ	2.04i/2.00	2.03- 07
Di Vincenzo	Sibilla	ITA	22.1.83	173/50	20kW	1:32:49	1:32:10- 10
Diawara	Aisseta	FRA	29.6.89	169/54	100h	13.07, 13.06w	13.20, 13.10w- 10
* Dibaba	Ejegayehu	ETH	25.6.82	160/46	HMar	69:25+	-0-
					Mar	2:22:09	-0-
* Dibaba	Genzebe	ETH	8.2.91		1500	4:05.90	4:04.80i, 4:06.10- 10
					5000	14:37.56	14:55.52- 09
* Dibaba	Mare	ETH	20.10.89	160/42	HMar	68:39+	67:13- 10
					Mar	2:23:25	2:25:27- 10
DiCrescenzo	Delilah	USA	28.2.83	168/53	3kSt	9:40.63	9:41.68- 08
Diebold	Tara	USA	28.11.88	167/	PV	4.30i, 4.20	4.17i, 4.12- 09
Ding Changqin		CHN	27.11.91		10k	32:44.86	33:13.42- 10
Ding Huiqin		CHN	5.2.90		20kW	1:31:23	1:40:39- 10
Diro	Etenesh	ETH	10.5.91		5000	15:21.51	
					3kSt	9:49.18	
Distel	Céline	FRA	25.7.87	170/60	100	11.32, 11.30w	11.45- 10
Dixon	Diamond	USA-J	29.6.92		400	51.55	52.92- 10
* Dixon	Vonette	JAM	26.11.75	170/62	100h	12.77	12.64- 07
Dobija	Teresa	POL	19.10.82	175/58	LJ	6.78	6.74- 09, 6.78w- 10
* Dobriskey	Lisa	GBR	23.12.83	171/56	1500	4:04.76	3:59.50- 09
* Dobrynska	Nataliya	UKR	29.5.82	180/77	Hep	6539	6778- 10
Dobrynska	Viktoriya	UKR	18.1.80	176/65	HJ	1.87	1.90- 07
Dockendorf	Carly	CAN	31.12.83	165/59	PV	4.30	4.45- 07
Domel	Urszula	POL	21.7.88	177/55	HJ	1.88	1.86- 09
Dong Yangzi		CHN-J	22.10.92		SP	16.70	15.76- 10
Donohue	Erin	USA	8.5.83	173/66	1500	4:07.04	4:03.49- 10
					3000	8:55.07	9:07.88i- 08
Donzelot	Irène	FRA	8.12.88	170/68	DT	56.19	53.89- 10
Dorr	Fawn	USA	19.4.87		400h	57.26	55.57- 10
Doveri	Francesca	ITA	21.12.82	179/64	Hep	5988(w), 5786	5885- 08
du Toit	Simoné	RSA	27.9.88	184/113	SP	17.49i, 16.78	17.13- 05
					DT	58.81	57.35- 09
Du Xiaowei		CHN	11.8.87	180/72	JT	60.26	58.41- 10
^ Duarte	Sophie	FRA	31.7.81	170/54	3kSt	9:44.18	9:25.62- 09
Duclos-Lasnier	Gabriella	CAN	1.3.88	178/62	PV	4.30	4.36- 09
Ducó	Natalia	CHI	31.1.89	177/95	SP	18.15	18.65- 08
Dula	Lishan	BRN	17.2.87	157/63	Mar	2:26:56	2:33:56- 10
Duncan	Dominique	USA	7.5.90		100	11.32, 11.05w	11.37- 08
					200	23.03, 22.79w	23.24- 10, 23.18w- 09
* Duncan	Kimberlyn	USA	2.8.91	173/	100	11.09, 11.02w	11.84- 10
					200	22.24, 22.18w	23.08, 22.96w- 10
* Dunn	Debbie	USA	26.3.78	168/57	200	22.99	22.73- 09
					400	50.70	49.64- 10
Duong Thi Viet Anh		VIE	30.12.90		HJ	1.90	1.88- 09
Dupre	Melissa	BEL	5.11.86	170/61	JT	58.25	56.62- 09
Durruthy	Yilían	CUB	30.1.90	177/77	Hep	5752	5460- 10
^ Durst	Stephanie	USA	11.4.82	168/58	100	11.31	11.09- 07
					200	22.81	22.48, 22.46w- 02
Dusanova	Nadezhda	UZB	17.11.87	174/56	HJ	1.90	1.96i- 09, 1.95- 10
Dygacz	Agnieszka	POL	18.7.85	160/51	20kW	1:30:56	1:32:17- 10
Dyomina	Oksana	RUS	4.8.90		800	2:01.73	2:04.47- 10
Eberl	Elisabeth	AUT	25.3.88	170/67	JT	60.07	57.04- 10
Ebihara	Yuki	JPN	28.10.85	164/66	JT	60.32	61.56- 10
Eftimova	Inna	BUL	19.6.88	167/57	100	11.20	11.26- 08

Name		Nat	Born	Ht/Wt	Event	2011 Mark	Pre-2011 Best
Eisenlauer	Esther	GER	29.10.77	180/75	JT	59.41	61.04- 10
Ejdys	Sylwia	POL	15.7.84	162/50	1500	4:06.72, 4:05.38i	4:02.30- 09
					3000	8:43.22i	8:54.34i, 8:58.26- 09
* Ejigu	Sentayehu	ETH	21.6.85	160/45	2000	5:43.45+	5:41.6+i- 10
3000	8:45.75+, 8:30.26i8:25.27i, 8:28.41- 10				5000	14:31.66	14:28.39- 10
Ejjafini	Nadia	ITA	8.11.80	172/62	5000	15:28.70	15:22.39- 06
10k	32:14.63		32:29.53- 07		HMar	68:27	70:38- 07
					Mar	2:26:15	2:37:25- 07
Ektova	Irina	KAZ	8.1.87	172/63	TJ	14.48	14.33- 08
El Moukim	Rkia	MAR	22.2.88		HMar	70:38	
El Ouali Alami	Salima	MAR	29.12.83	175/53	3kSt	9:42.51	10:16.62- 10
Elahi	Kianna	USA	24.8.90		400h	56.73	57.12- 10
Elbe	Anne-Kathrin	GER	24.2.87	172/60	100h	13.15	13.08- 10
Elbe	Jenny	GER	18.4.90	180/60	TJ	13.92i, 13.89	13.69- 10
Elmore	Malindi	CAN	13.3.80	168/53	1500	4:07.86	4:02.64- 04
Emmanouíl	Dímitra	GRE	13.5.84	172/63	PV	4.35	4.31- 10
Emmanuel	Crystal	CAN	27.11.91		200	22.90	23.96- 10
Engin	Birsen	TUR	18.10.80	178/56	400	52.15	52.82- 10
					400h	56.48	56.15- 10
* England	Hannah	GBR	6.3.87	177/54	1500	4:01.89	4:04.29- 09
Engman	Helena	SWE	16.6.76	171/94	SP	17.82	18.17- 10
Ennis	Delloreen	JAM	5.3.75	178/70	100h	13.04	12.50- 07
* Ennis	Jessica	GBR	28.1.86	164/57	200	23.11	23.15- 07
100h	12.79		12.81- 09		HJ	1.91	1.95- 07
LJ	6.51		6.51- 10, 6.54w- 07		Hep	6790	6823- 10
Equixua	Mónica	MEX	23.9.82	167/53	20kW	1:34:50A	1:42:12- 10
Eriksson	Sandra	FIN	4.6.89	163/48	3kSt	9:49.46	9:45.50- 09
Esayias	Yeshi	ETH	28.12.85		Mar	2:26:04	2:29:17- 10
* Eshete	Shitaye	BRN	21.5.90	159/56	10k	31:21.57	31:53.27- 10
Etholm	Grete	NOR	25.1.76	183/72	DT	56.58	59.48- 03
Evans	Gayon	JAM	15.1.90		200	23.21	23.86- 09
Evans	Terra	USA	7.10.89		100	11.45A, 11.31w	11.28, 11.19w- 10
					200	23.02w	23.24, 23.18w- 10
^ Facey	Simone	JAM	7.5.85	162/53	100	11.30, 11.18w	10.95A, 11.11- 08, 11.0- 04
					200	22.86A, 23.07	22.25- 08
Falaiye	Alice	CAN	24.12.78	168/55	LJ	6.50	6.72, 6.76w- 09
* Falzon	Stéphanie	FRA	7.1.83	170/77	HT	71.53	73.40- 10
Farkas	Györgyi	HUN	13.2.85	170/58	Hep	6068	5874- 10
Fazlitdinova	Gulshat	RUS-J	28.8.92		3kSt	9:56.98	
* Fedoriva	Aleksandra	RUS	13.9.88	172/61	100	11.28, 11.09w	11.31- 10
					200	23.17	22.41- 10
Fedotova	Yekaterina	RUS-J	3.7.92		HJ	1.90	
* Feitor	Susana	POR	28.1.75	160/52	20kW	1:30:44	1:27:55- 01
* Felicien	Perdita	CAN	29.8.80	165/57	100h	12.73	12.46, 12.45w- 04
* Felix	Allyson	USA	18.11.85	168/57	100	11.26+w	10.93- 08
200	22.32		21.81- 07		400	49.59	49.70- 07
Félix	Ana Dulce	POR	23.10.82	165/53	5000	15:22.16	15:08.02- 09
10k	31:33.42	31:30.90*, 31:40.60- 09			HMar	68:33	69:01- 10
					Mar	2:25:40	
Félix	Fanjanteino	FRA	26.1.80	154/45	1500	4:08.76i	4:01.17- 10
Fente	Birtukan	ETH	18.6.89		3kSt	9:28.27	9:39.67- 10
Feofanova	Svetlana	RUS	16.7.80	164/53	PV	4.75	4.88- 04
Ferguson	Sheniqua	BAH	24.11.89	170/57	100	11.17	11.19- 10
					200	22.92	22.85- 08
* Ferguson McKenzie	Debbie	BAH	16.1.76	170/57	100	11.09	10.91- 02
					200	22.76, 22.50w	22.19- 99
* Fernández	Nuria	ESP	16.8.76	170/58	800	2:01.47	2:00.35- 08
					1500	4:04.64	4:00.20- 10
Ferraro	Federica	ITA	18.8.88	168/51	20kW	1:33:36	1:34:21- 10
Fesenko	Alena	RUS	4.10.88		800	2:01.76	2:00.65- 10
					1500	4:09.88	4:07.63- 09
Feyisa	Bertukan	ETH	4.7.91		1500	4:04.85	4:09.22- 10
Fiack	Marion	FRA-J	13.10.92	170/60	PV	4.36i, 4.15	4.12- 10
Figueroa	Ángela	COL	28.6.84	167/60	3kSt	9:58.00	9:53.44- 10
Fiodorow	Joanna	POL	4.3.89	168/77	HT	70.06	64.66- 10
* Firova	Tatyana	RUS	10.10.82	180/68	400	50.84	49.89- 10
Fischer	Julia	GER	1.4.90	190/84	DT	59.60	57.49- 10
Fischer	Sabine	SUI	29.6.73	174/59	5000	15:24.49, 15:30.25	15:19.80- 10
Fitzpatrick	Daphne	USA	6.4.88		Hep	5811(w), 5599	5395- 10
Fjørtoft	Silje	NOR	23.6.87	170/50	3kSt	9:54.71	9:37.97- 09

Name		Nat	Born	Ht/Wt	Event	2011 Mark	Pre-2011 Best
* Flanagan	Shalane	USA	8.7.81	165/50	1500	4:06.63	4:05.86- 07
3000	8:39.18i	8:33.25i, 8:35.54- 07			5000	14:45.20	14:44.80- 07
10k	30:39.57	30:22.22- 08			HMar	69:58	68:37- 10
Fleming	Annett	GER	4.5.84	178/66	Hep	5760 (w)	5675- 09
Fleshman	Lauren	USA	26.9.81	173/54	5000	15:00.57	14:58.48- 08
Florczak	Sinje	GER	28.11.86		LJ	6.53w	6.27- 10
Flores	Mirna	GUA	28.2.87		20kW	1:32:30	1:44:33- 10
Florez	Lina	COL	1.11.84	170/58	100h	12.94	13.15A- 09, 13.24- 08
Follett	Katie	USA	12.11.87		1500	4:07.44	4:10.66- 10
Ford	Yarisleydi	CUB	18.8.91	168/69	HT	67.54	67.93- 09
Foster-Hylton	Brigitte	JAM	7.11.74	170/62	100h	12.87	12.45- 03
* Fountain	Hyleas	USA	14.1.81	170/65	100h	12.93	12.78, 12.65w- 08
HJ	1.89		1.90- 10		LJ	6.76	6.89, 6.95w- 10
					Hep	5861	6735w- 10, 6667- 08
Francis	Eden	GBR	19.10.88	178/85	SP	16.73	16.53- 09
					DT	59.78	59.27- 09
Francis	Sheree	JAM	20.10.83	177/63	HJ	1.90	1.93- 10
Franco	Jamy	GUA	1.7.91	170/48	20kW	1:32:38A	1:43:20, 1:33:23Adt- 10
Franco	Leryn	PAR	1.3.82	174/54	JT	56.17	55.38- 07
Franek	Bridget	USA	8.11.87	160/50	3kSt	9:38.92	9:32.35- 10
Fransen	Remona	NED	25.11.85	189/71	HJ	1.92i, 1.86	1.87- 10
					Hep	6198	5993- 10
* Fraser-Pryce	Shelly-Ann	JAM	27.12.86	160/62	100	10.95	10.73- 09
					200	22.59, 22.10w	22.15- 08
Freeman	Octavious	USA-J	20.4.92	169/	100	11.21	11.16, 11.11Aw- 10
					200	22.96	23.20- 09, 23.19Aw- 10
Frenkel	Danielle	ISR	8.9.87	173/55	HJ	1.94i, 1.90	1.92- 10
Frere	Danielle	USA	27.4.90		SP	16.79	15.08- 10
* Frizell	Sultana	CAN	24.10.84	183/110	HT	71.46	72.24- 10
Frolova	Karina	RUS	2.3.90		HT	65.06	64.55- 10
Fu Tinglian		CHN	5.7.87		10k	32:39.99	
					3kSt	9:43.71	10:40.06- 10
* Fuchise	Masumi	JPN	2.9.86	160/45	20kW	1:31:52	1:28:03- 09
Fuentes-Pila	Iris María	ESP	10.8.80	162/48	1500	4:09.71	4:04.25- 02
Fuentes-Pila	Zulema	ESP	25.5.77	166/52	3kSt	9:57.84	9:29.40- 08
Fujinaga	Yoshiko	JPN	15.8.81	171/52	10k	32:44.60mx	31:47.82- 01
					Mar	2:25:40	2:28:13- 09
Fukumoto	Miyuki	JPN	4.1.77	172/53	HJ	1.87	1.92- 04
Fukushi	Kayoko	JPN	25.3.82	161/45	10k	30:54.29	30:51.81- 02
HMar	69:00		67:26- 06		Mar	2:24:38	2:40:54- 08
Fukushima	Chisato	JPN	27.6.88	165/50	100	11.24, 11.16w	11.21- 10
					200	23.13	22.89- 10
Furman	Ma'ayan	ISR	9.11.86	184/62	HJ	1.92	1.89- 10
Fyodorova	Alina	UKR	31.7.89		Hep	6008	5760- 10
* Gadschiew	Kristina	GER	3.7.84	170/52	PV	4.66i, 4.60	4.60- 10
Gaither	Tynia	BAH-J	16.3.93		200	23.17	23.68- 10
Galiart	Rianna	NED	22.11.85	168/56	PV	4.31i, 4.31	4.31i- 08, 4.25- 07
Galimova	Valentina	RUS	11.5.86		10k	32:32.62	32:24.47- 09
Galitskaya	Yekaterina	RUS	24.2.87		100h	12.95	13.12- 10
Galkina	Gulnara	RUS	9.7.78	174/56	3kSt	9:29.75	8:58.81- 08
Gall	Geena	USA	18.1.87	172/57	800	1:59.62	2:00.44- 09
Gallardo	Karen	CHI	6.3.84	175/95	DT	60.48	57.48- 09
Gambetta	Sara	GER-J	18.2.93	183/67	Hep	6108	5854- 10
Ganeyeva	Vera	RUS	6.11.88	172/87	DT	63.61	59.38- 10
Gao Ni		CHN	14.9.91	163/51	20kW	1:29:38	1:31:21- 10
Garcia	Stephanie	USA	3.5.88		3kSt	9:41.12	10:05.05- 10
García	Alejandra	ARG	13.6.73	174/60	PV	4.30	4.43- 04
García	Rosibel	COL	13.2.81	171/62	800	2:00.79	1:59.38- 08
Gardner	English	USA-J	22.4.92		100	11.03	11.61- 07
Gardner	English	USA-J	22.4.92		200	23.02	24.01- 07
* Gavrila	Adelina	ROU	26.11.78	174/59	TJ	14.27	14.76i, 14.75- 03
* Gay	Mabel	CUB	5.5.83	185/69	TJ	14.67	14.66- 07
Gebre Zemedkun	Belaynesh	ETH	23.12.87		HMar	69:17	69:43- 10
Gebreselassie	Geytetom	ETH-Y	15.1.95		3000	8:56.36	
Gebru	Azemra	ETH-J	5.5.92		3000	8:48.63	
					5000	14:58.34	
Gega	Luiza	ALB	5.11.88	168/56	3kSt	9:54.72	
Gelana	Tiki	ETH	22.10.87		Mar	2:22:08	2:28:28- 10
Gentili	Manuela	ITA	7.2.78	163/52	400h	56.23	55.78- 10
George	Phylicia	CAN	16.11.87	170/64	200	23.10	23.72- 08
					100h	12.73	13.39- 10

Name		Nat	Born	Ht/Wt	Event	2011 Mark	Pre-2011 Best
George	Regina	USA	17.2.91		400	52.31, 52.30i	52.60- 10
Gergel	Melissa	USA	24.4.89	170/62	PV	4.45	4.45i. 4.35- 10
Getaneh	Genet	ETH	6.1.86		Mar	2:25:57	2:26:37- 09
* Gezahegne	Kalkidan	ETH	8.5.91		1500	4:00.97	4:02.98- 09
					3000	8:37.47i	8:38.61- 09
* Ghribi	Habiba	TUN	9.4.84	173/52	3000	8:56.22	8:58.92- 08
					3kSt	9:11.97	9:12.52- 09
Gibson	Baillie	USA	18.11.91		SP	17.07	14.86- 10
Gibson	Baillie	USA	18.11.91		DT	56.46	48.75- 10
Gierisch	Kristin	GER	20.8.90	177/57	TJ	14.10i, 13.47	14.02- 09
Giesa	Ulrike	GER	16.8.84	183/93	DT	58.73	60.63- 05
Gilchrist	Danielle	USA	15.7.88		400h	57.21	56.84- 08
Giordano Bruno	Anna	ITA	13.12.80	171/63	PV	4.50	4.60- 09
Giorgi	Eleonora	ITA	14.9.89	163/52	20kW	1:33:46	1:34:00- 10
Gipson	Whitney	USA	20.9.90		LJ	6.63, 6.69w	6.60A, 6.43- 10
Girat	Suslaidy	CUB	19.8.87	166/59	LJ	6.61	6.40- 10
Girma	Tsegereda	ETH-Y	.95		HMar	70:30	
Gizaw	Melkaw	ETH	.90		Mar	2:26:52	2:31:55- 09
* Glanc	Zaneta	POL	11.3.83	187/86	DT	63.99	63.96- 09
Gleadle	Elizabeth	CAN	5.12.88	183/75	JT	58.40	58.21- 09
Glenn	Brianna	USA	18.4.80	168/57	LJ	6.87, 7.00w	6.81- 10, 6.82w- 09
Godoy	Rosa	ARG	19.3.82		10k	32:51.10	
Godsey	Keelin	USA	2.1.84		HT	68.90	66.99- 09
Goggins	Aiesha	USA	13.9.91		400	51.94	54.36- 10
Gogoleva	Svetlana	RUS	11.12.86		400h	56.91	56.56- 07
Golladay	Michaylin	USA	10.4.88		100h	13.01, 12.82w	13.07- 10
Gollner	Monika	AUT	23.10.74	180/62	HJ	1.88	1.92- 96
Golovkina	Olga	RUS	17.12.86		1500	4:06.75	4:12.47- 09
* Golubchikova	Yuliya	RUS	27.3.83	175/57	PV	4.60i	4.75- 08
* Gomes	Naide	POR	20.11.79	181/70	LJ	6.79i, 6.76, 6.78w	7.12- 08
Gomis	Sandra	FRA	21.11.83	165/53	100h	12.93	12.96- 09
Goncharova	Marina	RUS	26.4.86	173/64	Hep	5995(w), 5947	6319- 08
* Gong Lijiao		CHN	24.1.89	174/110	SP	20.11	20.35- 09
* González	Misleydis	CUB	19.6.78	178/85	SP	19.04	19.50- 08
González	Norma	COL	11.8.82	172/53	200	23.06A, 23.22	22.90A, 23.02- 05
					400	51.58	51.86- 09
Goodman	Chalonda	USA	29.9.90		200	23.14	22.94- 09
Goor	Myrte	NED	3.4.89		Hep	5634	5119- 07
Gorbunova	Yekaterina	RUS	17.1.89	164/52	1500	4:01.02	4:10.78- 09
					5000	15:19.94	15:41.00- 09
* Gordeyeva	Irina	RUS	9.10.86	183/52	HJ	1.94	2.02- 09
Gordon	Chris-Ann	JAM-Y	18.9.94		400	51.62	52.68- 09
Gordon	Sheena	USA	26.9.83	178/55	TJ	13.58, 13.74w	13.76- 08
Goshu	Ferhiwot	ETH	28.6.90		5000	15:27.14	15:21.44- 09
* Goucher	Kara	USA	9.7.78	170/57	5000	15:11.47	14:55.02- 07
10k	31:16.65		30:55.16- 08		HMar	69:03	66:57- 07
					Mar	2:24:52dh	2:25:53- 08
Goule	Natoya	JAM	30.3.91		400	51.52A, 52.23	54.03- 10
					800	2:01.45	2:03.52- 10
* Grabuste	Aiga	LAT	24.3.88	178/67	LJ	6.65	6.51, 6.62w- 09
					Hep	6507(w)/6414	6396- 09
Grammatikopoúlou	Ioánna	GRE	19.10.83	170/63	TJ	13.75	14.01- 09
* Grasu	Nicoleta	ROU	11.9.71	176/88	DT	62.62	68.80- 99
Greaves	Shavon	USA	20.12.88		200	23.18i	22.98i, 23.07- 10
Grebneva	Irina	RUS	5.2.85		400h	57.04	56.92- 06
Grechishnikova	Yelizaveta	RUS	12.12.83		5000	15:02.38	15:07.15- 08
* Green Tregaro	Emma	SWE	8.12.84	180/62	HJ	1.95	2.01- 10
* Grenot	Libania	ITA	12.7.83	175/65	400	52.17	50.30- 09
Grindem	Øyunn	NOR	11.11.87	180/64	HJ	1.90	1.89- 10
Griva	Lauma	LAT	27.10.84	180/64	LJ	6.86	6.60, 6.65w- 10
Griva	Mara	LAT	4.8.89	170/55	LJ	6.59, 6.70w	6.50A, 6.34- 10
					TJ	13.81	13.28, 13.32w- 10
Gromova	Oksana	RUS	3.9.80	178/75	JT	58.61	61.12- 03
Gronau	Karolina	POL	12.7.84	180/60	HJ	1.88	1.92- 07
Groot	Denise	NED	26.5.90	172/59	PV	4.30	4.35- 10
Grøvdal	Karoline Bjerkeli	NOR	14.6.90	167/52	3kSt	9:46.07	9:33.19- 07
Groza	Ana Maria	ROU	1.6.76	167/53	20kW	1:34:11	1:29:31- 04
Grozav	Ligia Damaris	ROU-Y	26.1.94		HJ	1.87	1.75- 10
Gu Siyu		CHN-J	11.2.93		DT	56.12	53.79- 10
Guamán	Yadira	ECU	8.6.86	165/60	20kW	1:33:18.0t	1:36:22- 06
Guan Yue		CHN-J	23.5.92		800	2:01.86	2:07.30- 10

Name		Nat	Born	Ht/Wt	Event	2011 Mark	Pre-2011 Best
Guba	Paulina	POL	14.5.91	184/90	SP	17.17	15.80i, 15.70- 10
Gubar	Yana	RUS	2.7.90		LJ	6.55	6.42- 10
Guéhaseim	Jessika	FRA	23.8.89	176/79	HT	68.93	66.30- 10
Gumenyuk	Irina	RUS	6.1.88		TJ	14.14	13.65- 08
Günther	Leena	GER	16.4.91	164/50	100	11.33	11.44- 09
Guo Tianqian		CHN-Y	1.6.95		SP	16.98	14.80- 10
Gürler	Özge	TUR	17.6.85	168/58	400h	57.05	56.33- 07
* Gushchina	Yuliya	RUS	4.3.83	174/63	100	11.30	11.13- 06
200	22.88, 22.69w		22.53- 05		400	52.18	50.01- 08
Guta	Robe	ETH	12.10.86		Mar	2:26:51	2:24:35- 06
Haapanen	Amy	USA	23.3.84		HT	67.66	66.25- 10
Habazin	Dorotea	CRO	14.6.88	173/82	HT	68.36	66.74- 10
Habina	Hanna	UKR-J	26.10.92		JT	57.40	53.88- 09
* Habtamu	Atsede	ETH	26.10.87	162/50	Mar	2:24:25	2:24:47- 09
Hachlaf	Halima	MAR	6.9.88	168/564	800	1:58.27	1:58.40- 10
Hackett #	Semoy	TRI	27.11.88	173/70	100	11.17, 10.98w	11.18- 09
					200	22.87, 22.84i, 22.41w	22.75- 10
Haftu	Goitetom	ETH	.87		HMar	70:57	71:16- 10
					Mar	2:26:21	2:28:24- 10
Hak	Yvonne	NED	30.6.86	177/57	800	2:00.30	1:58.85- 10
Hall	Patricia	JAM	16.10.82	165/58	100	11.35w	12.11- 09
200	23.07, 22.84w		23.23- 06		400	51.40	51.45- 06
Hall	Sara	USA	15.4.83	163/48	5000	15:27.71	15:20.88- 06
					3kSt	9:39.48	10:00.20- 10
Hamblin	Nikki	NZL	20.5.88	165/52	1500	4:04.82	4:05.93- 10
					3000	8:50.92mx	9:10.95mx- 08
Hamera-Shmyrko	Tetyana	UKR	1.6.83		Mar	2:28:14	
Hao Shuai		CHN	19.7.87	178/65	HT	69.37	68.77- 07
Hao Xiaofan		CHN	9.12.89	165/55	5000	15:28.25	15:29.68- 09
Harbin	Ashley	USA	15.2.86		HT	65.62	63.71- 08
Hargrove	Monica	USA	30.12.82	173/58	400	51.76	50.39- 09
* Harper	Dawn	USA	13.5.84	168/61	100h	12.47	12.48, 12.36w- 09
Harrer	Corinna	GER	19.1.91	167/55	800	2:01.85, 2:02.27	2:04.14- 09
					1500	4:08.63	4:15.16- 09
^ Harrigan #	Tahesia	IVB	15.2.82	157/54	100	11.26, dq:11.14/10.97/10.89w	11.13,11.02w- 06
* Harrison	Queen	USA	10.9.88	170/60	100h	12.88	12.61, 12.44w- 10
					400h	54.78	54.55- 10
Hartmann	Jana	GER	23.5.81	178/62	800	2:00.93	2:00.71- 09
Hashim	Merima	ETH	.81	162/49	HMar	69:50	71:09- 05
Hasslen	Alyssa	USA	13.5.91		SP	17.56	15.87i, 15.55- 10
Hastings	Amy	USA	21.1.84	163/46	5000	15:14.31	15:43.99- 09
					Mar	2:27:03	
* Hastings	Natasha	USA	23.7.86	173/63	200	22.77	22.61- 07
					400	50.97, 50.83Ai	49.84- 07
Hatsko	Hanna	UKR	3.10.90		JT	60.10	55.47- 10
Hawthorne	Trisha-Ann	JAM	8.11.89		100	11.31	11.31- 10
Hayakari	Minori	JPN	29.11.72	165/47	3kSt	9:51.88	9:33.93- 08
Haydar	Sultan	TUR	23.5.87	163/53	HMar	70:02	-0-
Hayes	Chelsea	USA	2.2.88		100	11.34, 11.81w	11.70- 10
					LJ	6.50, 6.53w	6.17- 10
Hayes	Jernail	USA	8.7.88		400h	57.20	56.53- 10
Hazel	Louise	GBR	6.10.85	167/57	Hep	6166(w), 6150	6156- 10
He Dan		CHN	22.7.84	160/46	20kW	1:31:33	1:28:20- 06
He Qin		CHN-J	23.3.92		20kW	1:30:13	1:33:55- 10
Hearn	Ashley	USA			DT	56.16	52.87- 10
Heaston	Kristin	USA	23.11.75	183/127	SP	17.33	18.74- 07
* Heidler	Betty	GER	14.10.83	174/80	HT	79.42	77.12- 09
Heitling	Sabine	BRA	2.7.87	167/52	3kSt	9:50.04	9:41.22- 09
* Hejnová	Zuzana	CZE	19.12.86	170/54	400h	53.29	54.13- 10
Helsby	Ashley	GBR	1.7.90		100h	13.13w	13.50, 13.39w- 10
Hendry	Kelsie	CAN	29.6.82	170/59	PV	4.40	4.55- 08
Henkel	Laura	GER-J	29.2.92	181/76	JT	55.52	54.22- 10
* Henriques	Inês	POR	1.5.80	158/46	20kW	1:30:29	1:29:36- 10
Henry	Britney	USA	17.10.84	170/82	HT	69.64	71.27- 10
Henry-Robinson	Samantha	JAM	25.9.88	160/52	100	11.35, 11.13w	11.14- 09, 11.04w- 08
					200	23.01, 22.97w	22.80- 09
Herashchenko	Iryna	UKR-Y	10.3.95		HJ	1.87	1.83- 10
Hernández	Ingrid	COL	29.11.88	169/61	20kW	1:32:09.4t	1:37:56- 08
Hernández	Yuliet	CUB	2.4.90	165/53	HT	65.88	66.86- 10
Herrera	Mayra Carolina	GUA	.88		20kW	1:34:39	
Herunga	Tjipekapora	NAM	1.1.88		400	51.84	52.46- 07

Name		Nat	Born	Ht/Wt	Event	2011 Mark	Pre-2011 Best
Higgins	Lesley	USA	10.6.80	163/	3kSt	9:59.16	9:58.63- 08
Hilali	Siham	MAR	2.5.86	161/58	1500	4:01.33	4:03.74- 09
Hildebrand	Nadine	GER	20.9.87	158/51	100h	13.16, 12.91w	12.96- 10
Hill	MacKenzie	USA	5.1.86		400h	56.73	56.89- 10
Hinds	Korine	JAM	18.1.76	163/54	3kSt	9:38.07	9:28.86- 07
* Hingst	Carolin	GER	18.9.80	174/60	PV	4.65	4.72- 10
^ Hinrichs	Denise	GER	7.6.87	181/81	SP	17.81i, 16.02	19.63i, 19.47- 09
Hitchon	Sophie	GBR	11.7.91		HT	69.59	66.01- 10
Hjálmsdóttir	Ásdís	ISL	28.10.85	175/65	JT	59.15	61.37- 09
Hjelmer	Moa	SWE	19.6.90	172/60	200	23.20, 23.16w	23.55- 10
					400	51.58	53.53- 09
Hoffmann	Claudia	GER	10.12.82	171/62	400	52.15	51.65- 10
Hofstede	Helen	NED	31.12.80		3kSt	9:58.61	10:05.84- 05
Hogan	Megan	USA	10.2.88		5000	15:29.12	16:12.10- 10
Holden	LaTisha	USA	29.8.89		100h	13.07, 12.89w	13.34- 10
Holder	Nikkita	CAN	7.5.87	170/57	100h	12.84	13.44- 07
Holliday	Becky	USA	12.3.80	160/52	PV	4.55Ai, 4.55, 4.61dh	4.60- 10
Holm	Caroline Bonde	DEN	19.7.90		PV	4.40i, 4.30	4.33i- 10, 4.20- 09
Holm	Mona	NOR	5.8.83	169/78	HT	70.43	67.96- 10
Holmes	Dominique	USA	25.6.86		100	11.35	11.85- 09
					200	23.21	23.53- 09, 23.49w- 10
Holodnaya	Olga	UKR	14.11.91		SP	16.83	15.70- 10
Holosha	Olena	UKR	26.1.82	182/56	HJ	1.89	1.92- 07
Holt	Sarah	GBR	17.4.87	183/76	HT	66.46	65.51- 10
* Hooker/Myers	Marshevet	USA	25.9.84	175/67	100	10.86, 10.83w	10.93, 10.76w- 08
200	22.59		22.34, 22.20w- 08		LJ	6.83i	6.71i- 06, 6.65, 6.89w- 05
Hopkins	Wilamena	USA	21.10.90		SP	16.65i, 15.88	15.93- 10
Horie	Chika	JPN	15.2.81	161/45	Mar	2:27:26	2:26:11- 02
Horie	Misato	JPN	10.3.87	168/48	10k	32:44.00mx	33:06.72- 10
Horvat	Nikolina	CRO	18.9.86	160/52	400h	56.54	56.28- 08
Houlihan	Shayla	USA	26.2.85		3kSt	9:51.26	9:57.11- 10
Howard/White	Tiffany	USA	28.12.86		SP	16.71i, 16.09	16.87- 09
* Hrasnová	Martina	SVK	21.3.83	180/100	HT	72.47	76.90- 09
Huang Jing		CHN	28.2.88	167/52	20kW	1:33:57	1:35:17- 08
Huang Xiaoxiao		CHN	3.3.83	175/65	400h	56.58	54.00- 07
* Huddle	Molly	USA	31.8.84	163/48	3000	8:57.30i	8:53.6- 10
5000	15:10.01		14:44.76- 10		10k	31:28.66	31:27.12- 08
Hurtis	Muriel	FRA	25.3.79	180/68	400	51.62	51.41- 10
Hussong	Christin	GER-Y	17.4.94	187/82	JT	59.74	55.35- 10
Hutchinson	Ayanna	TRI	18.2.78	165/60	100	11.36, 11.30w	11.26- 00
* Hutson	Kylie	USA	27.11.87	165/	PV	4.70i, 4.65	4.51- 10
Hütter	Julia	GER	26.7.83	169/57	PV	4.50	4.60i- 08. 4.57- 07
Hyman	Mardrea	JAM	22.12.72	170/54	3kSt	9:46.15	9:27.21- 05
Hyter	Brittany	USA	24.10.89		400h	56.46	57.52- 10
Ibargüen	Caterine	COL	12.2.84	181/65	LJ	6.63A, 6.58	6.54A- 05, 6.42- 04
					TJ	14.99A, 14.84	14.29- 10
Ichikawa	Kana	JPN	14.1.91	164/49	100	11.43, 11.28w	11.66- 10
Ideta	Chizuru	JPN	15.11.86	164/48	10k	32:52.95	33:06.33- 10
Idlette	Lavonne	DOM	31.10.85	170/61	100h	12.96	13.30- 09
Ifadídou	Sofía	GRE	5.1.85	164/53	Hep	5867(w), 5541	6004- 10
Iglesias	Eva María	ESP	10.6.85	162/51	20kW	1:34:28	1:39:36- 10
Ihara	Miho	JPN	4.2.88	154/40	10k	32:18.00mx	
Ikauniece	Laura	LAT-J	31.5.92	179/60	Hep	6063	5618- 10
Ikuesan	Ayodelé	FRA	15.5.85	176/60	100	11.34	11.47- 10
* Iljustsenko	Anna	EST	12.10.85	168/49	HJ	1.96	1.95- 10
Inadomi	Tomoka	JPN	16.1.86	160/44	10k	32:26.46	32:41.57- 09
Incerti	Anna	ITA	19.1.80	168/45	5000	15:15.5mx	15:29.06- 09
HMar	69:06		69:24- 09		Mar	2:25:32	2:27:42- 08
Infeld	Emily	USA	21.3.90		1500	4:08.96	4:13.61- 10
Inoue	Rei	JPN	23.7.91	155/41	20kW	1:34:22	
^ Inzikuru	Dorcus	UGA	2.2.82	158/49	3kSt	9:54.50	9:15.04- 05
Ishibashi	Mai	JPN	2.7.89	163/46	10k	32:37.25	
* Isinbayeva	Yelena	RUS	3.6.82	174/66	PV	4.85i, 4.76	5.06- 09
Ito	Mai	JPN	23.5.84	156/41	HMar	70:03	71:11- 06
					Mar	2:26:55	2:29:13- 10
Ivanova	Yelena	RUS	16.3.79	175/64	TJ	14.13i, 13.51, 13.68w	14.39- 04
Ivoninskaya	Natalya	KAZ	22.2.85	175/60	100h	12.95	12.82- 08
Ivy	Vanneisha	USA	26.10.87		100h	12.99	13.08, 13.06w- 10
Jackson	Candace	USA	13.2.91		200	23.35, 22.89w	23.82- 10
Jackson	Emma	GBR	7.6.88	173/63	800	1:59.77	2:00.46- 10
Jackson	Johanna	GBR	17.1.85	168/54	20kW	1:31:50	1:30:41- 10

Name		Nat	Born	Ht/Wt	Event	2011 Mark	Pre-2011 Best
Jacques-Sébastien	Lina	FRA	10.4.85	176/62	200	23.06, 22.99w	22.59- 10
Jagaciak	Anna	POL	10.2.90	177/59	LJ	6.62	6.74- 10
					TJ	14.25	13.93, 14.16w- 10
Jakob	Élodie	SUI-J	8.10.93		Hep	5657	5283- 10
Jakubaityte	Indre	LTU	24.1.76	177/70	JT	60.02	63.65- 07
* Jamal	Maryam	BRN	16.9.84	155/44	1500	4:00.33	3:56.18- 06
James	LaToya	USA	18.1.89		400h	55.83	56.38- 09
James	Olivia	JAM-Y	1.6.94	/66	400	52.14	53.89- 10
James	Tiki	USA	21.10.86		100h	12.91, 12.70w	13.03- 09
Jameson	Takecia	USA	11.8.89		400h	55.97	56.29- 08
Jansen	Monique	NED	3.10.78	186/95	DT	62.22	60.29- 10
* Janson	Lacy	USA	20.2.83	178/68	PV	4.60i, 4.60	4.66i, 4.60A- 10
Januszewski	Laura	USA	28.2.86		800	2:01.05	2:01.19- 10
Jaramillo	Lucy	ECU	23.2.83	168/65	400h	56.95A	57.58- 05
Jarmuzek	Agnieszka	POL	3.2.84	190/97	DT	57.49	59.74- 09
Jarrett	Jovanee	JAM	15.1.83	170/62	LJ	6.65, 6.74w	6.75- 09, 6.85w- 08
Jarzynska	Karolina	POL	6.9.81	165/54	HMar	70:36	71:37- 10
					Mar	2:27:16	2:29:10- 09
Jassem	Karima Saleh	BRN	18.2.88	168/59	10k	32:50.70	32:17.14- 06
Jelaca	Tatjana	SRB	10.8.90	178/76	JT	56.68	60.35- 09
* Jelagat	Irene	KEN	10.12.88	162/45	1500	4:02.59	4:03.62- 09
* Jelela	Koren	ETH	18.1.87		HMar	68:39+	70:52- 10
					Mar	2:22:43	2:24:33- 10
Jelizarova	Polina	LAT	1.5.89	155/47	3kSt	9:56.88	9:54.94- 08
Jelmini	Anna	USA	15.7.90	176/	SP	17.24	17.63- 10
					DT	60.54	60.80- 10
Jepkirui	Eunice	KEN	20.5.84	158/45	HMar	70:29	73:34- 09
^ Jepkorir	Eunice	KEN	17.2.82	164/48	3kSt	9:43.23	9:07.41- 08
* Jepkosgei	Janeth	KEN	13.12.83	167/47	800	1:57.42	1:56.04- 07
					1500	4:02.32	4:04.17- 10
Jepkosgei	Nelly	KEN	14.7.91		1500	4:08.10	4:27.48- 09
Jepkosgei	Veronicah	KEN-J	.93		3kSt	9:58.49	9:59.6A- 10
* Jeptoo	Priscah	KEN	24.6.84		HMar	70:26	71:13- 10
					Mar	2:22:55	2:27:02- 10
^ Jeptoo	Rita	KEN	15.2.81	165/48	HMar	70:34	67:08- 07
					Mar	2:25:44	2:23:38- 06
Jerotich	Cynthia	KEN	.89		HMar	70:39	73:19- 10
Jerotich	Irene	KEN	8.9.74		HMar	71:03dh	71:17- 10
Jeschke	Marta	POL	2.6.86	167/55	100	11.33	11.50- 10, 11.49w- 08
^ Jesien	Anna	POL	10.12.78	168/56	400h	56.39	53.86- 07
* Jeter	Carmelita	USA	24.11.79	163/53	100	10.70	10.64- 09
					200	22.20	22.47, 22.35w- 08
Jia Chaofeng		CHN	16.11.88	164/47	HMar	70:45	72:46- 10
Jiang Fengjing		CHN	28.8.87	180/75	DT	62.56	60.78- 10
* Jimoh	Funmi	USA	29.5.84	173/64	LJ	6.88	6.96- 09
Jin Yuan		CHN	11.2.88	168/49	3kSt	9:45.21	9:41.60- 08
Johannesson	Emma	SWE	16.1.84		HT	65.29	64.54- 09
Johnson-Thompson	Katarina	GBR-J	9.1.93	183/70	Hep	5787	5481- 09
Johny	Mayookha	IND	9.4.88		LJ	6.63	6.64- 10
					TJ	14.11	13.68- 10
* Jones	Lolo	USA	5.8.82	175/59	100h	12.67	12.43, 12.29w- 08
Jones	Tenaya	USA	22.3.89		100h	13.21, 13.05w	13.20- 10
Josephs	Janice	RSA	31.3.82	160/60	LJ	6.52	6.79- 07
Joyce	Jennifer	CAN	25.9.80	178/80	HT	66.34	70.35- 09
Juhász	Vanda	HUN	6.6.89		JT	58.03	52.14- 10
Jung Hye-kyung		KOR	13.4.81	166/53	TJ	13.75	13.77- 06
Jungfleisch	Marie-Laurence	GER	7.10.90	181/68	HJ	1.93	1.90- 10
* Jungmark	Ebba	SWE	10.3.87	179/57	HJ	1.96i, 1.94	1.92- 07
Juravlyeva	Anastasiya	UZB	9.10.81	172/57	TJ	14.32	14.55- 05
Kales	Eunice	KEN	6.12.84		HMar	70:41	69:50- 10
Kämäräinen	Sanna	FIN	8.2.86	182/72	DT	57.30	56.19- 10
Kampf	Heather	USA	19.1.87		800	2:00.41	2:01.05- 07
Kampschulte	Nadja	GER-J	5.9.92	186/66	HJ	1.88	1.85i- 10, 1.83- 09
Kanatova	Valeriya	UZB-J	29.8.92	180/70	TJ	14.28	13.89- 10
* Kaniskina	Olga	RUS	19.1.85	161/45	20kW	1:28:35	1:24:56- 09
* Kapachinskaya	Anastasiya	RUS	21.11.79	176/65	200	22.55	22.38- 03
					400	49.35	49.97- 09
^ Kappler	Bianca	GER	8.8.77	180/62	LJ	6.81, 6.90w	6.90- 07, 6.97w- 08
Karadere	Nagihan	TUR	1.1.84	173/65	400h	55.09	56.42- 07
Karakaya	Tugba	TUR	16.2.91	167/56	800	2:01.78	2:10.04- 09
					1500	4:03.41	4:17.57- 10

Name		Nat	Born	Ht/Wt	Event	2011 Mark	Pre-2011 Best
Karandyuk	Kseniya	UKR	21.6.86	178/60	400	52.24, 51.9	52.19- 06
Karnaushchenko	Marina	RUS	2.10.88	168/56	400	51.49	53.02- 10
* Karsak	Kateryna	UKR	26.12.85	183/88	DT	63.52	64.40- 07
Kashina	Yuliya	RUS	26.2.87	170/56	100	11.48, 11.26w	11.34. 11.16w- 10
Kashtonova	Anastasiya	BLR	14.1.89	163/50	DT	57.38	56.74- 10
Kasim	Ashu	ETH	20.10.84		HMar	70:30+	
					Mar	2:27:47	2:25:49- 09
Kastrova	Alina	BLR	2.3.90		HT	67.30	64.20- 10
Käther	Nadja	GER	29.9.88	178/62	LJ	6.65	6.66- 10
Kato	Asami	JPN	12.10.90	156/38	10k	32:51.07	34:05.96- 10
Katsumata	Misaki	JPN	26.12.85	164/47	10k	32:51.92	32:54.78- 10
Kaur	Harwant	IND	5.7.80	166/72	DT	58.78	63.05- 04
Kawasaki	Mayumi	JPN	10.5.80	167/52	20kW	1:30:25	1:28:49- 09
Kaya	Kivilcim	TUR-J	27.3.92	166/82	HT	66.74	65.10- 10
Kaygorodova	Anna	RUS	10.3.83	170/58	200	23.16	23.95- 10
Kayukova	Yekaterina	RUS	9.10.86		TJ	14.02i, 13.45	14.64- 09
Kazeka	Yekaterina	RUS	7.10.90		PV	4.40i, 4.25	4.20i- 09, 4.20- 10
Kebebush	Haile	ETH	.86		Mar	2:24:09	2:25:31- 10
* Kebede	Aberu	ETH	12.9.89	163/50	HMar	68:28	67:39- 09
					Mar	2:24:34	2:23:58- 10
* Keitany	Mary	KEN	18.1.82	168/53	HMar	65:50	66:36- 09
					Mar	2:19:19	2:29:01- 10
Keizer	Jolanda	NED	5.4.85	183/70	Hep	5804	6370- 08
Kelo	Niina	FIN	26.3.80	178/69	Hep	5752	5956- 06
Kemkers	Denise	NED	11.4.85	182/81	SP	16.85	17.66i, 17.30- 09
Kendrick	Stormy	USA	6.1.91		100	11.23w	11.36, 11.24w- 10
					200	23.09	22.99, 22.83w- 10
Keppler	Janice	USA	22.3.87	178/	PV	4.42	4.21- 10
Kessely	Haoua	FRA	2.2.88	174/66	LJ	6.55	6.36- 09
					TJ	13.93, 14.14w	13.79i- 10, 13.69- 09
Khalyutina	Yekaterina	RUS	16.1.91		LJ	6.50	6.37- 10
^ Khanafeyeva	Gulfiya	RUS	4.6.82	170/84	HT	71.11	77.26- 06, 77.36dq- 07
* Kharlamova	Lyubov	RUS	2.3.81	169/57	3kSt	9:29.39	9:21.94- 06
Khasanova	Alfiya	RUS	3.10.88	158/46	1500	4:07.86	4:13.16- 09
3000	8:55.13		9:16.83i- 10, 9:18.44- 09		5000	15:26.31	15:48.14- 09
Kholadovich	Tatyana	BLR	29.8.91		JT	55.94	53.51- 08
Khramtsova	Darya	RUS	7.1.90		Hep	5607	5308- 10
Khubbieva	Guzel	UZB	2.5.76	173/65	100	11.36	11.20- 07
* Kibet	Hilda	NED	27.3.81	168/46	HMar	69:35	68:39- 10
					Mar	2:24:27	2:26:23- 10
* Kibet	Sylvia	KEN	28.3.84	157/44	3000	8:51.31	8:37.48- 10
					5000	14:35.43	14:31.91- 10
Kibii	Jane	KEN	10.3.85		HMar	70:25	72:26- 09
* Kibiwott	Viola	KEN	22.12.83	157/45	1500	4:05.51	4:02.10- 07
3000	8:46.84		8:40.14- 03		5000	14:34.86	14:48.57- 10
* Kidane	Worknesh	ETH	21.11.81	158/41	5000	15:31.67+	14:33.04- 03
10k	31:08.92		30:07.15- 03		HMar	67:28	68:09- 05
					Mar	2:27:15, 2:26:15dh	-0-
Kiffe	Christina	GER-J	2.5.92	179/64	Hep	5793	5607- 10
Kilel	Caroline	KEN	21.3.81		HMar	70:13+	68:16- 09
					Mar	2:25:57, 2:22:36dh	2:23:25- 10
Kim Kyung-ae		KOR	5.3.88	163/62	JT	58.52	58.76- 08
Kingori	Ziporah	KEN-Y	12.8.94		3000	8:56.82	9:29.66- 10
Kinukawa	Megumi	JPN	7.8.89	153/38	5000	15:09.96	15:27.98- 07
10k	31:10.02mx		31:23.21- 08		HMar	70:22	
Kipketer	Valentine	KEN-J	5.1.93		HMar	68:21	
* Kiplagat	Edna	KEN	15.9.79	171/54	HMar	69:00	69:32- 06
					Mar	2:20:46	2:25:38- 10
* Kiplagat	Florence	KEN	27.2.87	155/42	HMar	68:02	67:40- 10
					Mar	2:19:44	
* Kiplagat	Lornah	NED	1.5.74	167/49	Mar	2:25:52	2:22:22- 03
Kipp	Shalaya	USA	19.8.90		3kSt	9:56.37	9:59.37- 10
Kiprop	Agnes	KEN	12.12.79	171/51	HMar	69:11	68:48- 10
					Mar	2:23:54	2:24:07- 10
* Kipyego	Sally	KEN	19.12.85	168/52	1500	4:06.23	4:06.67- 08
3000	8:51.07, 8:49.74i8:48.77i- 09, 8:53.5+- 10				5000	14:30.42	14:38.64- 10
					10k	30:38.35	31:25.45- 08
Kipyegon	Faith	KEN	10.1.94		1500	4:09.48	4:17.1- 10
* Kirdyapkina	Anisya	RUS	23.10.89	165/51	20kW	1:25:09	1:25:11- 10
Kireyeva	Svetlana	RUS	12.6.87		1500	4:07.20	4:14.19- 09
					5000	15:27.33	15:47.84- 10

Name		Nat	Born	Ht/Wt	Event	2011 Mark	Pre-2011 Best
* Kiriakopoúlou	Nikoléta	GRE	21.3.86	167/56	PV	4.71	4.55- 10
Kirop	Helena	KEN	9.9.76	165/48	HMar	68:57	70:10- 10
					Mar	2:23:37	2:24:54- 10
Kiros	Aheza	ETH	26.3.82	152/42	10k	32:08.21	31:06.93- 08
					HMar	69:10	
Kiros	Tigist	ETH-J	8.6.92	159/56	10k	31:20.38	
Kirui	Purity	KEN	13.8.91		3kSt	9:37.85	9:36.34- 10
* Kiryashova	Aleksandra	RUS	21.8.85	166/53	PV	4.65	4.65- 09
Kisa	Janet	KEN-J	5.3.92		5000	15:24.75A	
Kiyara Kguriatukei	Rael	KEN	4.4.84		Mar	2:25:23	2:30:18- 10
Kizaki	Ryoko	JPN	21.6.85	157/44	5000	15:22.87mx	15:35.12- 09
					Mar	2:26:32	2:27:34- 10
* Klaas	Kathrin	GER	6.2.84	168/72	HT	75.48	74.53- 10
Klaup	Mari	EST	27.2.90	180/58	Hep	5743(w), 5445	5739- 10
Kleeberg	Sophie	GER	30.5.90	182/82	SP	17.92	17.19- 10
* Kleinert	Nadine	GER	20.10.75	190/90	SP	19.26	20.20- 09
Klimesová	Jarmila	CZE	9.2.81	172/78	JT	61.12	62.60- 06
* Klishina	Darya	RUS	15.1.91	180/57	LJ	7.05	7.03- 10
* Klocová	Lucia	SVK	20.11.83	176/53	800	1:59.48	1:58.51- 08
Klopsch	Christiane	GER	21.8.90	175/58	400h	56.97	57.00- 10
* Klüft	Carolina	SWE	2.2.83	178/65	LJ	6.73, 6.74w	6.97- 04
^ Klyugina	Viktoriya	RUS	28.9.80	178/54	HJ	1.92i	2.00i- 09, 1.98- 08
* Klyuka	Svetlana	RUS	27.12.78	170/62	800	1:58.03	1:56.64- 08
* Knight	Bianca	USA	2.1.89	163/50	100	11.22	11.07- 08
					200	22.35	22.40i, 22.43, 22.25w- 08
Knyazheva	Hanna	UKR	25.9.89	178/61	TJ	14.20	13.85- 07
Kobeleva	Yelena	RUS	12.6.88		800	2:01.78	2:06.36- 10
Koderisch	Heike	GER	27.5.85	188/87	DT	57.99	58.62- 10
Koech	Cherono	KEN-J	8.12.92	158/53	800	1:59.68	2:00.40- 10
* Kofanova	Yelena	RUS	8.8.88	174/61	800	1:58.04	1:58.50- 10
Kogut-Kubiak	Alexia	FRA	22.1.88	169/68	JT	57.10	54.91- 10
Kojima	Kazue	JPN	14.10.87	164/49	10k	32:34.45	32:55.43- 09
Kokkinaríou	Iríni	GRE	14.2.81	170/55	3kSt	9:39.53	9:30.72- 08
Kolaric	Nina	SLO	12.12.86	175/60	LJ	6.67	6.78- 08
* Kolchanova	Lyudmila	RUS	1.10.79	175/60	LJ	6.84, 7.06w	7.21- 07
Kolodko	Yevgeniya	RUS	2.7.90	188/85	SP	19.78	16.73- 10
Kolotzei	Jessica	GER	6.4.85	186/86	DT	56.77	60.31- 08
Komulainen	Tanja	FIN	2.3.80	170/74	DT	57.10	57.03- 10
Kondratyeva	Oksana	RUS	22.11.85	180/80	HT	69.87	71.90- 10
Koneva	Yekaterina	RUS	25.9.88	169/55	LJ	6.70, 6.80w	
					TJ	14.46	13.93, 14.00w- 10
Konovalova	Anna	RUS	4.7.88		1500	4:03.92	4:15.50- 10
* Konovalova	Mariya	RUS	14.8.74	179/58	HMar	70:30	70:48- 08
					Mar	2:25:18	2:23:50- 10
Koons	Frances	USA	2.4.86		5000	15:29.96	15:43.78- 10
Kopets	Yelena	BLR	14.2.88	178/72	SP	18.82i, 17.71	17.99- 10
Korableva	Darya	RUS	23.5.88		400h	56.49	56.01- 09
Koresová	Jana	CZE	8.4.81	168/57	Hep	5663	5956- 09
Koreyvo	Natalya	BLR	14.11.85	172/49	1000	2:37.33i	2:38.47- 07
					1500	4:06.40	4:06.52- 10
* Korikwiang	Pauline	KEN	1.3.88	163/39	5000	14:41.28	14:45.98- 06
					10k	31:59.5A	31:06.29- 10
Kornuta	Anna	UKR	10.11.88		TJ	13.70	13.52- 10
Korobkina	Yelena	RUS	25.11.90		1500	4:08.71i, 4:11.39	4:07.82- 10
3000	8:52.12i		8:51.41- 10		5000	15:22.14	
Korotkova	Olesya	RUS	21.12.83		DT	62.48	61.12- 09
Korotkova	Tatyana	RUS	24.4.80	165/58	20kW	1:28:38	1:27:35- 04
Korpela	Merja	FIN	15.5.81	170/75	HT	69.30	69.56- 09
Korytkowska	Justyna	POL	12.3.86	171/50	3kSt	9:45.24	10:15.63- 09
Korzeniowska	Sylwia	FRA	25.4.80	165/52	20kW	1:32:15	1:30:31- 06
Koscielniak	Marzena	POL	28.12.89	180/57	400h	57.20	56.52- 10
Kosgei	Rose	KEN	22.8.81	/53	HMar	69:04	69:03- 09
* Kostetskaya	Yekaterina	RUS	31.12.86	168/59	800	1:57.19	1:56.67- 08
					1500	4:01.77	-0-
Kostiew	Kristal	USA	8.1.82		HT	64.79	69.26- 07
Kostrova	Yuliya	RUS	20.8.91	174/59	HJ	1.92	1.83- 10
Kotlyarova	Aleksandra	UZB	10.10.88	170/64	TJ	14.35	14.09i, 14.08- 10
* Kotova	Tatyana	RUS	11.12.76	182/60	LJ	6.74	7.42- 02
Kouassi	Gabriela	CIV	18.11.79	170/65	Hep	5712	5775- 08
Kowalska	Katarzyna	POL	7.4.85	177/55	3kSt	9:44.21	9:26.93- 09
Kragbé	Suzanne	CIV	22.12.81	179/92	DT	59.32	57.98- 10

Name		Nat	Born	Ht/Wt	Event	2011 Mark	Pre-2011 Best
Krais	Ryann	USA	21.3.90	173/55	400h	55.68	57.20- 07
					Hep	6030	5779- 10
Králová	Tereza	CZE	22.10.89		HT	66.63	65.63- 10
Krantz	Sabine	GER	6.2.81	167/51	20kW	1:31:08	1:27:56- 04
* Krasnomovets	Olesya	RUS	8.7.79	171/60	400	51.86, 51.22i	50.04i- 06, 50.19- 04
Krause	Gesa-Felicitas	GER-J	3.8.92	167/49	3kSt	9:32.74	9:47.78- 10
Krchová	Eva	CZE	10.9.89	187/70	3kSt	9:54.71	10:11.43- 10
Krebs	Denise	GER	27.6.87	157/48	1500	4:07.70	4:11.62- 10
Krechyk	Alena	BLR	20.7.87		HT	65.91	68.61- 09
* Krevsun	Yuliya	UKR	8.12.80	178/66	800	1:59.32	1:57.32- 08
Krifchin	Maegan	USA	8.4.88		HMar	71:05	
Krivoshapka	Antonina	RUS	21.7.87	168/60	400	49.92	49.29- 09
Krizsán	Xénia	HUN-J	13.1.93		Hep	5794	5594- 10
Kron	Tina	GER	3.4.81	173/55	400h	57.09	55.58- 07
Kruchinkina	Yelena	RUS	26.10.88	167/	20kW	1:29:48	1:32:01- 10
Kubelová	Jitka	CZE	2.10.91		DT	57.37	53.55- 10
Kubokura	Satomi	JPN	27.4.82	161/52	400h	55.34	55.46- 08
* Kucherenko	Olga	RUS	5.11.85	172/59	LJ	6.86	7.13- 10
* Kuchina	Mariya	RUS-J	14.1.93	182/60	HJ	1.97i, 1.95	1.91- 10
Kudinova	Anastasiya	KAZ	27.2.88	175/56	LJ	6.50	6.20- 10
Kudzelich	Svetlana	BLR	7.5.87		10k	32:40.61	32:53.64- 10
Kufaas	Stine	NOR	7.4.86	176/62	HJ	1.89i, 1.88	1.93- 10
Kulik	Alyssa	USA	2.2.90		3kSt	9:57.51	10:32.46- 10
Kuma	Eyerusalem	ETH	4.11.81	157/45	Mar	2:24:55	2:26:51- 09
Kunova	Vera	RUS	2.4.90		SP	16.99	15.84- 08
Kupina	Yekaterina	RUS	2.2.86		800	2:01.44	2:02.94- 08
Kurban	Olga	RUS	16.12.87	178/66	Hep	6151	6559- 08
Kurisu	Yoshie	JPN	21.8.85	157/45	10k	32:50.22	34:18.61- 07
* Kuropatkina/Krylova Anna		RUS	3.10.85		TJ	14.35, 14.39w	14.20- 07
Kurt	Yeliz	TUR	15.1.84	165/50	800	2:01.26	2:00.91- 08
Kushima	Eriko	JPN-J	.93		10k	32:16.84mx	
Kutyakova	Natalya	RUS	28.11.86		TJ	14.67	14.55- 10
Kuzina	Aleksandra	KAZ	26.12.90	172/67	400h	56.92	58.15- 10
Kuzmina	Lyudmila	RUS	13.8.87	158/49	3kSt	9:26.03	9:34.88- 10
Kwadwo	Yasmin	GER	9.11.90	171/62	100	11.29, 11.22w	11.33- 10
^ Kwakye	Jeanette	GBR	20.3.83	163/60	100	11.15	11.14- 08
* La Mantia	Simona	ITA	14.4.83	177/65	TJ	14.60i, 14.43	14.69- 05, 14.71w- 04
Laasma	Liina	EST-J	13.1.92		JT	57.82	54.25- 10
Labonté	Julie	CAN	12.1.90	183/91	SP	18.31	16.83- 10
LaCaze	Genevieve	AUS	4.8.89		3kSt	9:59.44	10:26.92- 09
* Lakhouad	Btissam	MAR	7.12.80	170/52	1500	4:01.09	3:59.35- 10
Lakmali	Nadeeka	SRI	18.9.81	165/60	JT	57.11	58.48- 07
Lalonde	Geneviève	CAN	5.9.91	167/47	3kSt	9:55.01	9:57.74- 10
* Lalova	Ivet	BUL	18.5.84	168/56	100	10.96	10.77- 04
					200	22.62	22.51- 04
Lamalle	Adrianna	FRA	27.9.82	170/58	100h	13.01	12.67- 06
Lambarki	Hayat	MAR	18.5.88	168/62	400h	56.72	55.96A, 56.74- 10
Lamble	Regan	AUS	14.10.91	173/55	20kW	1:31:39	1:36:40- 10
Lamera	Raffaella	ITA	13.4.83	175/56	HJ	1.93	1.95- 10
* Langat	Nancy	KEN	22.8.81	153/49	1500	4:03.66	4:00.13- 10
Larsåsen	Cathrine	NOR	5.12.86	172/66	PV	4.40	4.35- 10
Larsson	Sofia	SWE	22.7.88	174/82	DT	56.92	58.65- 09
Latvala	Sini	FIN	3.2.80	182/88	HT	65.10	69.16- 04
Laurent	Rachel	USA	21.9.89	168/	PV	4.35	4.36i- 10, 4.30- 09
Lavallée Seaman	Rachel	CAN	14.1.86	173/60	20kW	1:33:33	1:37:22- 09
Law	Celriece	USA	2.9.86		100h	13.19, 13.12w	13.11- 09
Lawless	Janet	RSA	15.5.85		Hep	5673	5736- 10
Le-Roy	Anastacia	JAM	11.9.87	172/56	200	23.13	23.08- 08
Leach	Nicole	USA	18.7.87	170/60	400h	56.08	54.32- 07
Lebedeva	Lyudmila	RUS	23.5.90		3kSt	9:59.17	9:53.15- 10
Lecurieux	Prescilla	FRA-J	1.12.92	180/85	JT	57.18	48.41- 10
Ledáki	Stélla-Iró	GRE	18.7.88	170/58	PV	4.45	4.20- 10
Lee	Beki	AUS	25.11.86	165/46	20kW	1:33:09	1:42:38- 10
Lee Mi-young		KOR	19.8.79	174/81	SP	16.76	17.62- 05
^ Leghzaoui	Asmae	MAR	30.8.76	158/44	HMar	70:47	68:34- 99
Leipold	Anika	GER	13.4.87	168/63	LJ	6.50i, 6.48	6.67- 09
LeLeux	Morgann	USA-J	14.11.92	167/52	PV	4.34	4.27- 10
Lenskiy	Irina	ISR	12.6.71	176/57	100h	13.06	12.80- 02
* Lesueur	Éloyse	FRA	15.7.88	179/65	LJ	6.91	6.84i- 08. 6.78- 10
Letnar	Bernarda	SLO	26.12.89		JT	56.51	55.69- 10
Lettow	Lindsay	USA	6.6.90		Hep	5610w, 5547	5386- 10

Name		Nat	Born	Ht/Wt	Event	2011 Mark	Pre-2011 Best
Levy	Jura	JAM	4.11.90		100	11.10, 11.07w	11.28, 11.15w- 10
					200	22.76	23.20- 09, 22.95w- 10
* Lewis	Yvette	USA	16.3.85	173/62	100h	12.76, 12.74w	12.85- 09
Lewis-Smallwood	Gia	USA	1.4.79		DT	62.26	65.58- 10
Lewy Boulet	Magdalena	USA	1.8.73	160/50	5000	15:14.25	16:04.86- 97
					10k	31:48.58	32:20.45- 09
Lhabz	Lamia	MAR	19.5.84	178/59	400h	56.58	56.07A- 08, 56.18- 07
Li Hua		CHN	15.1.91	165/50	20kW	1:33:54	1:34:55- 09
Li Jiayi		CHN-J	26.12.93		3kSt	9:56.68	
Li Li		CHN	18.6.87	164/50	20kW	1:33:20	1:31:33- 10
Li Ling		CHN	6.7.89	185/70	PV	4.40	4.45- 08
* Li Ling		CHN	7.2.85	183/84	SP	19.72	19.94- 10
Li Lingwei		CHN	26.1.89	172/75	JT	57.39	60.60- 10
Li Wen-Hua		TPE	3.12.89	180/130	DT	58.07	57.19- 10
Li Yanfei		CHN	12.1.90	168/55	20kW	1:28:43	1:28:57- 09
* Li Yanfeng		CHN	15.5.79	179/90	DT	67.98	66.40- 09
Li Yanmei		CHN	6.2.90	171/56	TJ	14.35	13.93- 07
Li Zhenzhu		CHN	13.12.85	168/45	3kSt	9:40.12	9:32.35- 07
Líka	Sávva	GRE	27.6.70	173/68	JT	59.00	63.13- 07
de Lima	Jaílma	BRA	31.12.86		400	51.66	51.99- 09
					400h	56.00	
de Lima	Jucilene	BRA	14.9.90		JT	55.44	56.75- 09
Lin Xiaojing		CHN	8.1.86	178/82	DT	56.16	57.95- 06
Lindenberg	Janin	GER	20.1.87	175/60	400	51.97	52.20- 10
* Litvinova	Lyudmila	RUS	8.6.85	177/60	400	50.92	50.27- 09
Liu Chunhua		CHN	1.10.86	164/65	JT	60.65	60.65- 09
Liu Fang		CHN	25.2.90	174/52	1500	4:07.90	4:14.54- 08
* Liu Hong		CHN	12.5.87	161/48	20kW	1:27:17	1:27:17- 08
Liu Tingting		CHN	29.10.90		HT	69.46	62.66- 09
Liu Xiangrong		CHN	6.6.88	182/84	SP	18.74	18.69- 08
Liu Yanan		CHN	18.1.87	168/55	TJ	13.75i	14.09- 09
Lloyd	Shereefa	JAM	2.9.82	164/53	400	51.69	50.62- 08
Lobanova	Liliya	UKR	14.10.85	168/54	800	1:58.30	2:01.33- 09
Lomnická	Nikola	SVK	16.9.88	166/70	HT	65.06	66.90- 10
Londa	Maria Natalia	INA	29.10.90		TJ	13.73	13.49- 10
Longfors	Rachel	USA	6.6.83		DT	56.83	57.48- 04
López	Sandra	MEX	16.4.84	155/47	5000	15:28.71	
Lotout	Marion	FRA	19.11.89	165/54	PV	4.50	4.30- 10
Louami	Carima	FRA	12.5.79	165/50	100	11.28, 11.25w	11.31- 08
^ Loughnane	Olive	IRL	14.1.76	160/49	20kW	1:31:55	1:27:45- 08
Lu Huihui		CHN	26.6.89	168/60	JT	58.72	55.35- 10
Lu Minjia		CHN-J	29.12.92	172/58	LJ	6.58i, 6.65, 6.61w	6.74- 09
Lu Xiaoxin		CHN	22.2.89		DT	57.61	56.62- 10
Lu Xiuzhi		CHN-J	26.10.93	167/52	20kW	1:29:50	
Luaces	Lorena	ESP	29.2.84	161/48	20kW	1:33:59	1:32:42- 10
* Lucas	Josanne	TRI	14.5.84	170/55	100h	13.03	12.99- 09, 12.98w- 06
					400h	56.86	53.20- 09
Lucas	Porscha	USA	18.6.88		100	11.43, 11.14w	11.12- 09, 11.07w- 10
					200	23.06, 22.85w	22.29A- 08, 22.38- 09
Luchkina	Anna	RUS	13.1.86		1500	4:09.69	4:11.06- 09
Luka	Tintu	IND	26.4.89		800	2:00.95	1:59.17- 10
* Lukyanova	Anna	RUS	23.4.91		20kW	1:27:49	-0-
Lundmark	Beatrice	SUI	26.4.80	184/63	HJ	1.88i, 1.86	1.92- 10
Luo Xingcai		CHN-Y	18.7.94		20kW	1:32:03	
Lupu	Nataliya	UKR	4.11.87	170/50	800	1:59.12	1:59.59- 10
Lushcheko	Aleksandra	RUS	1.3.87		HT	68.05	66.76- 10
Lustigová	Marcela	CZE	11.11.82	163/50	3kSt	9:41.73	9:41.85- 10
* Lysenko	Tatyana	RUS	9.10.83	180/84	HT	77.13	77.80- 06, 78.61dq- 07
Ma Qiao		CHN	28.9.89	185/150	SP	17.45	17.50- 10
* Ma Xuejun		CHN	26.3.85	185/96	DT	63.93	65.00- 06
Machado	Maíla	BRA	22.1.81	167/62	100h	13.14A, 13.20	12.86- 04
Macharia	Lucy	KEN	.91		HMar	70:04	
Mächtig	Julia	GER	1.1.86	187/80	Hep	6194	6320- 09
Macías	Isabel	ESP	11.8.84	162/49	1500	4:06.50	4:11.73- 06
Madarász	Viktória	HUN	12.5.85	153/46	20kW	1:34:37	1:36:27- 10
* Madison	Tianna	USA	30.8.85	168/60	100	11.29	11.05- 09
					LJ	6.58w	6.89, 6.92w- 05
Mageean	Ciara	IRL-J	12.3.92	168/56	1500	4:07.45	4:09.51- 10
* Maggi	Maurren	BRA	25.6.76	178/66	LJ	6.94A, 6.89 7.26A- 99, 7.06- 03, 7.17w- 02	
Mägi	Maris	EST	11.8.87	168/54	400	52.21	52.68- 10
Magiso	Fantu	ETH-J	9.6.92		400	52.09A, 52.23	
					800	1:59.17	

Name		Nat	Born	Ht/Wt	Event	2011 Mark	Pre-2011 Best
Mahan	Shayla	USA	18.1.89	160/50	100	11.20	11.31- 10
Maisonnier	Blandine	FRA	3.1.86	179/64	Hep	5870(w), 5814	6157- 08
Maiyo	Maureen	KEN	28.5.85	157/58	400h	56.65A, 57.49	56.74A- 10
Makarova	Natalya	RUS	17.4.87		20kW	1:30:27	1:31:45- 08
Makda	Harun	ETH	.88		Mar	2:27:30	2:28:08- 10
Måkestad Bovim	Ingvill	NOR	7.8.81	172/58	800	2:00.68	1:59.82- 10
1000	2:36.7e		2:48.7- 98		1500	4:03.79	4:02.20- 10
Maksimova	Marina	RUS	20.5.85	177/80	JT	60.73	60.04- 10
Maksimova	Yana	BLR	9.1.89	182/70	HJ	1.88	1.88- 10
					Hep	6094	6031- 10
Malácová	Romana	CZE	15.5.87	164/57	PV	4.31i, 4.25	4.41- 10
Malkus	Lena	GER-J	6.8.93	180/74	LJ	6.70	6.44- 10
Malone	Chantel	IVB	2.12.91		LJ	6.65i, 6.49	6.56- 10
Maloy	Elizabeth	USA	10.8.85		1500	4:09.69	4:09.24- 10
3000	9:02.47i		8:56.89- 10		5000	15:15.34	15:39.07- 10
Malysheva	Yekaterina	RUS	16.4.88		LJ	6.58	6.70- 09
Mamona	Patrícia	POR	21.11.88	168/53	TJ	14.42	14.12- 10
Mamyeyeva	Svitlana	UKR	19.4.82	175/65	TJ	14.26	14.38- 09
Manfrédi	Laurence	FRA	2.5.74	174/83	SP	16.71i, 16.17	18.69i, 18.68- 00
* Mang	Véronique	FRA	15.12.84	173/63	100	11.11	11.11, 11.06w- 10
Manning	Christina	USA	29.5.90	163/54	100	11.29	11.54- 10
					100h	12.86, 12.72w	13.10- 10
Manning	Crystal	USA	15.4.86	173/64	TJ	13.94	13.96- 10
^ Manou	Tamsyn	AUS	20.7.78	173/60	400	52.15	51.42- 09
					800	2:00.78	1:59.21- 00
Manzanillo	Francia	DOM	3.6.80	182/85	Hep	5644A	5604- 10
Mao Yanxue		CHN-Y	15.2.94	162/44	20kW	1:31:03	
Mara	Valeriya	UKR	22.2.83	163/50	3kSt	9:50.13	9:38.91- 10
Maracheva	Irina	RUS	29.9.84	165/50	800	1:58.71	1:59.36i- 09, 1:59.70- 08
1000	2:35.3e				1500	4:06.78	4:10.14- 10
					2000	5:45.60i	
Maraoui	Fatna	ITA	10.7.77		HMar	70:08	72:27- 07
Marcussen	Ida	NOR	1.11.87	173/67	Hep	6030	6226- 07
Maresová	Oldriska	CZE	14.10.86	187/67	HJ	1.89	1.90i- 09, 1.89- 10
Marghieva	Marina	MDA	28.6.86	185/85	HT	71.58	72.53- 09
* Marghieva	Zalina	MDA	5.2.88	174/90	HT	72.93	71.56- 09
Marguet	Linda	FRA	11.9.83	164/58	800	2:01.32i	2:01.20- 10
Marie-Nély	Nathalie	FRA	24.11.86	175/66	TJ	14.01, 14.18w	13.56- 07
Mariën	Hanna	BEL	16.5.82	170/65	200	23.09w	22.68- 06
Markelova	Tatyana	RUS	19.12.88		800	2:00.92	2:02.54- 10
Marshall	Shameka	USA	9.9.83	163/54	LJ	6.55, 6.73Aw	6.73, 6.74w- 10
Martin	Jenna	CAN	31.3.88		400	51.95A, 52.04	51.91- 07
Martín	Diana	ESP	1.4.81	162/50	3kSt	9:40.28	9:42.39- 09
Martinelli	Giulia	ITA	16.6.91	165/42	3kSt	9:39.21	10:05.43- 10
Martinez	Brenda	USA	8.9.87		800	2:01.07	2:00.85- 09
Martínez	Aymée	CUB	17.11.88	168/52	400	51.93	51.74- 07
Martínez	Yarianna	CUB	20.9.84	167/56	TJ	14.42	14.40- 09
Martins	Eliane	BRA	26.5.86		LJ	6.58	6.66A- 07, 6.61- 09
Márton	Anita	HUN	15.1.89	171/84	SP	18.15	18.20- 10
					DT	56.12	56.62- 10
* Martynova	Yekaterina	RUS	6.8.86	169/55	800	1:59.17	2:00.85- 06
1000	2:37.66i		2:37.63i- 08		1500	4:01.68	4:03.68i, 4:05.06- 08
* Masai	Linet	KEN	5.12.89	170/55	5000	14:32.95	14:31.14- 10
					10k	30:53.59	30:26.50- 08
Masehla	Tebogo	RSA	6.1.79	165/50	3kSt	9:54.19	9:55.11- 07
Masná	Lenka	CZE	22.4.85		800	2:00.92	1:59.71- 10
Mathiot	Telie	FRA	25.5.87	168/57	PV	4.41	4.35- 10
Matoba	Haruka	JPN	24.4.87	163/54	JT	55.70	55.58- 09
Matoshko	Yelena	BLR	23.6.82	177/	HT	72.86	73.83- 08
Matsko	Margarita	KAZ	4.1.86	166/50	800	2:00.89	2:00.29- 10
Matsuoka	Noriko	JPN	2.5.79	156/44	Mar	2:26:54	
Mavrodieva	Radoslava	BUL	13.3.87		SP	17.54i, 16.79	17.42- 10
Mayer	Sarah	GER	20.5.91	170/60	JT	59.29	55.14- 10
Mayor	Lesyaní	CUB	8.7.89	176/58	HJ	1.89A	1.93- 10
^ Mbango	Françoise	FRA	14.4.76	172/60	TJ	14.03	15.39- 08
McCall	Jeneva	USA	28.10.89		SP	17.38i, 16.96	17.25i, 16.54- 10
					HT	69.55	64.17- 10
McCarty	D'Ana	USA	14.7.89		SP	16.97	15.91- 10
McColgan	Eilish	GBR	25.11.90		3kSt	9:44.80	10:52.13- 08
^ McConnell	Lee	GBR	9.10.78	178/64	400	51.01	50.82- 02
* McCorory	Francena	USA	20.10.88	170/	400	50.24	50.52- 10

Name		Nat	Born	Ht/Wt	Event	2011 Mark	Pre-2011 Best
McGrone	Candyce	USA	24.3.89		100	11.08, 11.07w	11.44- 09, 11.37w- 08
					200	22.81	22.84- 10
McKaig	Alissa	USA	21.2.86		5000	15:28.30	15:55.36- 10
					10k	32:14.51	33:48.17- 09
McKelvie	Susan	GBR	15.6.85		HT	65.03	62.03- 06
McKnight	Kaila	AUS	5.5.86	172/52	1500	4:05.65	4:08.78- 10
* McLaughlin	Anneisha	JAM	6.1.86	163/54	200	22.54	22.54- 10
McMillan	Chantae	USA	1.5.88	170/	Hep	6003	5583- 10
McPherson	Inika	USA	29.9.86		HJ	1.93A	1.88- 05
McReynolds	Tiffani	USA	4.12.91		100h	13.05, 12.74w	13.75- 09
* Meadows	Jennifer	GBR	17.4.81	156/48	800	1:58.60	1:57.93- 09
Meadows	Tawanna	USA	4.8.86		100	11.19w	11.27, 11.13w- 08, 11.1w- 10
Medeiros	Keely	BRA	30.4.87		SP	17.26	16.64- 10
Medgyesová	Renata	SVK	28.1.83	172/53	LJ	6.64	6.79- 10
Medina	Gabriela	MEX	3.3.85	160/55	800	2:01.50	2:03.43- 06
Mei Yiduo		CHN	27.3.91		Hep	5759	5689- 09
Mekasha	Waganesh	ETH-J	16.1.92		3000	8:51.76	9:09.47- 10
					5000	15:11.50	
Mekhti-Zade	Yuna	RUS	25.4.86	170/58	100	11.35, 11.27w	11.28- 10, 11.2- 08
Mekonnin	Misiker	ETH	23.7.86		HMar	69:20+dh	71:35- 10
					Mar	2:25:21	2:37:39- 10
Melat	Kejeta	ETH-J	.92		HMar	70:43	
^ Meleshina	Irina	RUS	25.5.82	171/60	LJ	6.72i	7.27- 04
* Melfort	Mélanie	FRA	8.11.82	182/62	HJ	1.95	1.97i- 03, 1.96- 07
* Melkamu	Meselech	ETH	27.4.85	158/48	5000	14:39.44	14:31.91- 10
					10k	30:56.55	29:53.80- 09
* Menéndez	Osleidys	CUB	14.11.79	174/84	JT	57.50	71.70- 05
Meng Qianqian		CHN	6.1.91	178/85	SP	18.31	17.52- 09
* Menkova	Oksana	BLR	28.3.82	183/91	HT	67.78	77.32- 08
* Mergia	Aselefech	ETH	23.1.85	168/45	HMar	67:21	67:22- 10
					Mar	2:22:45	2:22:38- 10
Merlano	Briggite	COL	29.4.82	174/64	100h	12.89	13.04- 09
Merrill	Christine	SRI	20.8.87		400h	56.83	58.04- 10
Metcalfe Wright	Megan	CAN	27.1.82	157/51	3000	8:52.01i	8:44.29- 10
5000	15:15.33		15:11.23- 08		10k	32:40.40	
Meuti	Elena	ITA	26.6.83	175/56	HJ	1.88i	1.92- 06
^ Mey	Karen Melis	TUR	31.5.84	168/57	LJ	6.66	6.93- 07
Michta	Maria	USA	23.6.86		20kW	1:34:52	1:38:20- 10
* Mickle	Kimberley	AUS	28.12.84	169/69	JT	63.82	63.49- 09
Migunova	Yelena	RUS	4.1.84	173/65	400	51.26	50.59- 08
* Mikhnevich	Natalya	BLR	25.5.82	180/85	SP	19.05	20.70- 08
Miki	Shiori	JPN	25.12.91	164/50	400h	56.92	57.35- 10
* Mikitenko	Irina	GER	23.8.72	158/49	Mar	2:22:18	2:19:19- 08
Mikolajczyk	Izabela	POL	4.9.90	177/60	Hep	5779	5305- 10
Milani	Marta	ITA	9.3.87	174/61	400	51.86	51.87- 10
					800	2:01.50	2:05.98- 10
Miller	Andrea	NZL	13.3.82	170/67	100h	13.15	13.10- 09
Miller	Natasha	CAN	10.6.89	178/59	Hep	5593	5310- 10
Miller	Scottesha	USA	14.1.88		100	11.21	11.21A- 08, 11.30- 10
Miller	Shaunae	BAH-Y	15.4.94		400	51.84	52.45- 10
Mineyeva	Tatyana	RUS	10.8.90		20kW	1:28:09	1:28:33- 10
Mingir	Gülcan	TUR	21.5.89	165/52	3kSt	9:39.83	10:02.19- 10
* Mironchik-Ivanova	Anastasiya	BLR	13.4.89	171/54	LJ	6.85, 6.92w	6.84- 10
					TJ	14.29	13.70i- 10, 13.59- 09
* Mishchenko	Anna	UKR	25.8.83	166/51	1500	4:01.73	4:03.14- 10
Mitchell	Kathryn	AUS	10.7.82	168/75	JT	59.47	59.68- 10
Miyashita	Risa	JPN	26.4.84	171/70	JT	60.08	55.08- 09
Miyauchi	Hiroko	JPN	19.6.83	153/42	10k	32:23.29mx	31:42.86mx – 08, 32:18.57- 07
Miyauchi	Yoko	JPN	19.6.83	154/41	10k	32:15.09mx	31:50.45- 07
					HMar	69:23	69:51- 10
Mnatsakanova	Tatyana	RUS	25.5.83		HJ	1.95	1.94i, 1.89- 07
Mock	Ti'Anca	USA	5.6.88		LJ	6.64	6.64- 09
^ Mockenhaupt	Sabrina	GER	6.12.80	156/45	3000	8:57.35	8:44.65- 03
5000	15:24.30	14:59.88mx- 09, 15:03.47- 04			10k	31:44.52	31:14.21- 08
HMar	70:34		68:45- 09		Mar	2:28:08	2:26:21- 10
Moguenara	Sosthene	GER	17.10.89	182/68	LJ	6.83	6.75i, 6.65- 10, 6.69w- 09
Mohammed	Merima	ETH-J	10.6.92	154/41	HMar	69:46+	68:36- 10
					Mar	2:24:32	2:23:06- 10
^ Moldovan	Felicia	ROU	29.9.67	169/70	JT	55.34	63.89- 02
* Molitor	Katharina	GER	8.11.83	182/76	JT	64.67	64.53- 10
* Momanyi	Grace	KEN	3.3.82	170/48	5000	15:07.49	14:50.77- 09
10k	32:15.06		30:52.25- 09		HMar	68:41	72:55- 05

Name		Nat	Born	Ht/Wt	Event	2011 Mark	Pre-2011 Best
^ Montaner	Concepción	ESP	14.1.81	170/56	LJ	6.72	6.92- 05
* Montaño	Alysia	USA	26.4.86	170/61	800	1:57.48	1:57.34- 10
^ Montebrun	Manuèla	FRA	13.11.79	175/85	HT	69.24	74.66- 05
Monterola	Keisa	VEN	26.2.88	173/60	PV	4.33	4.30- 05
* Montsho	Amantle	BOT	4.7.83	173/64	200	22.94, 22.88w	23.01- 08
					400	49.56	49.83A- 08, 49.89- 09
Moore	Connie	USA	29.8.81	165/63	100	11.31, 11.21w	11.21- 03
					200	23.12	22.40- 10
Moore	Erica	USA	25.3.88	178/64	800	2:00.17	2:08.07- 10
* Moore	LaShaunte'a	USA	31.7.83	170/56	100	11.17, 11.04w	10.97- 10
					200	22.58	22.46- 07, 22.37w- 04
de Morais	Andressa	BRA	21.12.90		DT	59.56	58.06- 10
Moreira #	Sara	POR	17.10.85	168/51	1500	4:07.29	4:07.11- 10
3000	8:44.22i		8:42.69- 10		5000	15:11.97	14:54.71- 10
10k	31:39.11		31:26.55- 10		3kSt	9:35.11	9:28.64- 09
Moreno	Johana	COL	15.4.85	175/78	HT	68.53	69.80- 09
* Moreno	Yipsi	CUB	19.11.80	171/81	HT	75.62	76.62- 08
Morgan	Sheryl	JAM	6.11.83	170/57	400h	57.25	56.81- 02
Mori	Chinami	JPN	5.5.90		10k	32:40.39	
Morris	Brooklyn	USA	27.3.86		400	52.12	52.73- 07
Morris	Sandi	USA-J	8.7.92		PV	4.30	4.05- 10
Morunova	Lyudmila	RUS	27.1.85		SP	17.70	17.89- 08
Moser	Treniere	USA	27.10.81	159/50	800	2:00.45	1:59.15- 07
					1500	4:07.57	4:03.32- 06
* Mothersill	Cydonie	CAY	19.3.78	170/54	100	11.27	11.08, 11.02w- 06
					200	22.82	22.39, 22.26w- 05
Moussa	Houria	ALG	14.5.82	165/52	400h	57.19, 57.0	56.66- 06
Mrisho	Zakya	TAN	19.2.84	166/48	5000	15:17.18	14:43.87- 05
Muffet	Ashley	USA	16.9.86		SP	16.77	17.46i- 10, 16.80- 08
Muhammad	Dalilah	USA	7.2.90	170/52	400h	56.04	56.49- 09
Mulhall	Kimberley	AUS	9.1.91	175/85	DT	57.24	56.85- 10
Mullen	Deirdre	USA	21.5.82		HJ	1.88	1.92- 10
* Müller	Nadine	GER	21.11.85	192/95	DT	66.99	67.78- 10
Muñoz	Adriana	CUB	16.3.82	165/54	1000	2:37.28	2:41.0- 02
Muñoz	Lismania	CUB-J	28.2.93	171/63	JT	55.82	55.68- 10
* Murer	Fabiana	BRA	16.3.81	172/64	PV	4.85	4.85- 10
Murillo	María Lucelly	COL	5.5.91		JT	55.85	57.16- 10
Muriuki	Margaret	KEN	21.3.86		5000	15:19.89	14:48.94- 10
Murofushi	Yuka	JPN	11.2.77	170/67	HT	64.79	67.77- 04
Murtazina	Alsu	RUS	12.12.87		TJ	14.55	14.44- 09, 14.63w- 10
Muyanga	Christine	KEN	21.3.91		3kSt	9:34.12	9:31.35- 08
Muze	Lina	LAT-J	4.12.92	181/75	JT	60.64	56.64- 10
Mwangi	Ann Karindi	KEN	8.12.88	172/51	1500	4:07.74	4:06.58- 10
3000	8:48.89		8:43.54- 09		5000	15:15.89	15:05.34mx- 09, 15:15.19- 10
Mwanzi	Annet	KEN	21.7.87		800	2:00.96	2:06.08- 06
Myhalchenko	Iryna	UKR	20.1.72	179/60	HJ	1.90	2.01- 04
Nagao	Kaoru	JPN	26.9.89	158/46	10k	32:10.46	
					Mar	2:26:58	
Nagovitsyna	Yelena	RUS	7.12.82		5000	15:28.06	16:06.23- 10
					10k	32:08.00	
Nagy	Judith	ROU	14.9.89	171/58	Hep	5772	5394- 09
Nagy	Xénia	HUN	29.3.86		JT	56.46	54.49- 10
Nakamura	Hitomi	JPN	23.6.87	157/43	10k	32:23.49	32:51.61mx- 09, 32:51.63- 10
Nakano	Mami	JPN	12.3.79	167/58	PV	4.32i, 4.20	4.31- 04
Nakazato	Remi	JPN	24.6.88	153/37	10k	32:20.81	31:53.22mx- 10, 32:29.45- 09
					Mar	2:24:29	2:34:29- 10
Nambawa	Sarah	UGA	23.9.85	165/64	TJ	14.06	13.95A- 10, 13.94- 09
* Nana Djimou	Antoinette	FRA	2.8.85	174/69	100h	13.15	13.40- 10
JT	55.79		49.96- 08		Hep	6409	6323- 09
^ Naude	Elizna	RSA	14.9.78	180/105	DT	58.96	64.87- 07
Nazarova	Anna	RUS	14.3.86	175/58	LJ	6.89i, 6.88	6.81- 07
Ndoumbe	Ruth Marie	ESP	1.1.87	173/59	TJ	13.78	13.43- 09
Necka	Urszula	POL	28.6.84	165/42	3kSt	9:56.43	10:11.52- 03
Negesa	Annet	UGA-J	24.4.92	172/58	800	2:00.40	2:02.27- 10
					1500	4:09.17A	4:19.3- 09
Negoita	Maria	ROU	6.12.86	171/74	JT	60.25	62.20- 09
Nelson	Briana	USA-J	18.7.92		400	52.18i	52.38- 09
Nesterenko	Yuliya	BLR	15.6.79	173/61	100	11.30w	10.92- 04
Netsvetayeva	Yekaterina	BLR	26.6.89		Hep	5702	5624- 09
Nettey	Christabel	CAN	2.6.91		LJ	6.49, 6.54w	6.42i, 6.28- 10
Neuenswander	Vera	USA	3.12.87	170/	PV	4.36	4.31- 09

Name		Nat	Born	Ht/Wt	Event	2011 Mark	Pre-2011 Best
Ngii	Emily	KEN	13.8.86	152/48	20kW	1:31:54Ash	1:49:01, 1:44:51sh- 10
Ni Yuanyuan		CHN-Y	6.4.95		20kW	1:31:56	
Nicholls	Jade	GBR	30.3.87	183/81	DT	60.76	58.38- 10
Nicoletti	Julaika	ITA	20.3.88	178/92	SP	16.95	16.35i, 16.25- 10
Nie Jingjing		CHN	1.3.88	168/45	20kW	1:31:00	1:29:50- 06
Niiya	Hitomi	JPN	26.2.88	166/44	5000	15:13.12	15:23.27- 09
Nikkanen	Minna	FIN	9.4.88	169/53	PV	4.60i, 4.30	4.46- 09
Nilsson	Cecilia	SWE	22.6.79	178/88	HT	65.39	69.09- 08
Nishihara	Kasumi	JPN	1.3.89	162/46	5000	15:23.80	15:25.50mx- 10, 15:32.89- 09
					10k	32:17.59	32:29.59- 09
Nishikawa	Seika	JPN	17.7.87	169/50	10k	32:12.64mx	32:38.94- 09
Njeri	Pauline	KEN	.85		10k	32:07.0A	
					HMar	68:55	70:23- 08
Njoku	Leslie	NGR	30.5.89		400h	57.14	58.11- 10
* Njoroge	Mercy	KEN	10.6.86	158/46	3000	8:39.70i	8:48.16- 06
5000	15:17.03		15:25.68- 06		3kSt	9:16.94	9:26.64- 10
Nkiruka	Dominike	NGR	28.8.85	165/60	TJ	13.76i, 13.49	13.95- 09
Noguchi	Mizuki	JPN	3.7.78	150/41	HMar	70:48	67:43- 06
Nojiri	Azusa	JPN	6.6.82	156/43	Mar	2:25:29	2:29:12- 10
Nomura	Yuka	JPN	18.6.87	164/49	400h	57.04	56.96- 10
Northover	Zara	JAM	6.3.84	175/70	SP	17.00	17.56- 08
Norton	Abbie	USA	28.4.85		Hep	5927	5755- 10
Novik	Maryna	BLR	19.1.84		JT	57.93	63.25- 09
Novozhenkova	Mariya	RUS-J	21.7.92		Hep	5610	
Novozhylova	Iryna	UKR	7.1.86	175/71	HT	67.52	71.82- 08
Nwaba	Barbara	USA	18.1.89		Hep	5733	5552- 10
O'Brien	Rebecca	USA	30.4.90		SP	17.22	16.31- 10
					DT	59.04	50.67- 10
* O'Rourke	Derval	IRL	28.5.81	168/57	100h	12.84	12.65- 10
Obare	Doricah	KEN	10.1.90	162/48	5000	15:29.79 mx	15:04.87mx- 09, 15:21.08- 08
* Obergföll	Christina	GER	22.8.81	175/79	JT	69.57	70.20- 07
* Obiri	Hellen	KEN	13.12.89		800	2:00.54	
					1500	4:02.42	
Obleshchuk	Halyna	UKR	23.2.89		SP	17.27	16.32- 10
Ochotnikova	Nina	RUS	11.3.91	162/46	20kW	1:28:41	1:39:17- 10
* Odumosu	Joke	NGR	27.10.87	168/59	400h	56.23	54.59- 10
* Oeser	Jennifer	GER	29.11.83	176/64	100h	13.14	13.37- 10
LJ	6.42, 6.70w		6.68- 10		Hep	6663	6683- 10
Ogbasilassie	Lemlem	CAN	10.12.87		800	2:00.85	2:02.88- 10
Ogi	Madoka	JPN	26.10.83	159/43	10k	32:51.21	32:06.94- 06
Ograzeanu	Andreea	ROU	24.3.90	179/62	100	11.34, 11.29w	11.45- 09
Ogrodnik	Magdalena	POL	25.7.89		HJ	1.92	1.82- 10
Ogura	Kumi	JPN	24.6.85	159/48	10k	32:43.66	32:53.94- 10
Ohara	Rei	JPN	10.8.90	165/48	10k	32:50.50	
					HMar	70:50	
* Ohuruogu	Christine	GBR	17.5.84	173/70	400	50.85	49.61- 07
Oka	Sayuri	JPN	19.9.90	155/45	10k	32:45.65	
Okada	Kumiko	JPN	17.10.91	158/44	20kW	1:34:30	
Okafor	Ifeatu	USA	20.8.90		SP	17.77	15.83- 10
* Okagbare	Blessing	NGR	9.10.88	180/60	100	11.08, 11.01w	11.00, 10.7A, 10.98w- 10
200	22.94		22.71- 10		LJ	6.78, 6.84w	6.91- 08
Okayama	Saeko	JPN	12.4.82	180/64	LJ	6.56, 6.61w	6.39- 08
Okori	Reina-Flor	FRA	2.5.80	165/56	100h	13.13, 13/09w	12.65- 08
Okoro	Chinwe	USA/NGR	20.6.89		SP	16.79	16.16- 08
^ Okoro	Marilyn	GBR	23.9.84	167/60	400	52.09	52.02- 06
					800	1:59.53	1:58.45- 08
Okou	Rosvitha	FRA	5.9.86	165/62	100h	13.13	13.45- 08
Okparaebo	Ezinne	NOR	3.3.88	164/56	100	11.21, 11.17w	11.23- 10, 11.12w- 09
Okuneva	Oksana	UKR	14.3.90	165/55	HJ	1.94i, 1.94	1.92- 10
Okyere	Nadine	GBR	29.11.86	165/63	400	52.26	52.89- 10
de Oliveira	Gisele	BRA	1.8.80	180/57	TJ	14.12, 14.20w	14.28, 14.31w- 08
Oliveros	Princesa	COL	10.8.75	168/53	400h	56.26A	57.19- 01
Oljira	Belaynesh	ETH	26.6.90		10k	31:17.80	
					HMar	67:27	70:22- 10
Olupona	Toyin	CAN	29.1.83	177/63	100	11.31	11.29- 08
* Omarova	Anna	RUS	3.10.81	180/103	SP	19.23	19.69- 07
Omata	Korei	JPN	15.7.87	154/42	10k	32:37.89mx	34:36.93- 09
Omrani	Yasmina	FRA	1.1.88	183/67	Hep	5594	5979- 10
* Ongori	Philes	KEN	19.7.86	158/47	HMar	68:32	67:38- 09
					Mar	2:24:20	-0-
Onuora	Anyika	GBR	28.10.84	175/69	100	11.18	11.31- 06
					200	22.93	23.13- 08

Name		Nat	Born	Ht/Wt	Event	2011 Mark	Pre-2011 Best
Onyali	Comfort	NGR	25.4.83		LJ	6.59	6.62- 10
^ Onyia ¶	Josephine	ESP	15.7.86	166/60	100h	12.95	12.50- 08
* Orbán	Éva	HUN	29.11.84	173/75	HT	71.33	70.18- 08
Orjuela	Arabelly	COL	24.7.88	150/43	20kW	1:32:48.7t	1:39:34A- 10
Osana	Yolanda	DOM	11.8.87	165/56	400h	57.08A, 57.20	57.16- 09
* Osayomi	Damola	NGR	26.6.86	163/63	100	10.99, 10.90w	11.08, 10.8- 08
					200	22.86	22.74- 08
Osazuwa	Uhunoma	NGR	23.11.87	178/65	Hep	5668	5549- 10
Osorio	Liana	CUB	23.11.88	175/91	SP	17.41	17.23- 09
* Ostapchuk	Nadzeya	BLR	12.10.80	180/90	SP	20.94	21.09- 05
Otonye	Iworima	NGR	13.4.76		TJ	13.70	13.87- 06, 14.10w- 07
Otoshi	Kumi	JPN	29.7.85	160/45	20kW	1:29:11	1:30:36- 10
Ott	Anastasiya	RUS	7.9.88	175/61	400h	55.76	54.74- 08
Ouédraogo	Elodie	BEL	27.2.81	175/62	400h	55.29	55.72- 07
Ouhaddou	Hanane	MAR	.82	158/46	3kSt	9:25.96	9:22.12- 09
Owen	Melinda	USA	30.10.84		PV	4.55Ai	4.52- 10
Owens-Mitchell	Bridgette	USA-J	14.3.92		100h	13.08, 13.05w	13.74- 10
^ Oyepitan	Abi	GBR	30.12.79	165/53	200	23.21, 22.85w	22.50- 04
* Ozaki	Yoshimi	JPN	1.7.81	155/41	Mar	2:23:56	2:23:30- 08
Ozolina-Kovale	Sinta	LAT	26.2.88	186/72	JT	59.50	60.13- 08
Padilla	Yenifer	COL	1.1.90	187/63	400	51.53A, 52.2	52.45A- 10, 53.1- 09
^ Palamar	Vita	UKR	12.10.77	187/66	HJ	1.87	2.01- 03
* Palameika	Madara	LAT	18.6.87	185/76	JT	63.46	64.51- 09
Paliyenko	Tatyana	RUS	18.11.83		800	1:59.76	1:59.81- 07
					1000	2:37.63i	2:38.26i- 09
Palma	Odette	CHI	7.8.82	171/68	HT	66.63	64.55- 09
Palmieri	Elisa	ITA	18.9.83	167/82	HT	67.33	66.84- 10
Palmisano	Antonella	ITA	6.8.91	166/46	20kW	1:34:31	1:30:21- 10
Palsyte	Airine	LTU-J	13.7.92	186/62	HJ	1.96	1.92- 10
Pandakova	Marina	RUS	1.3.89		20kW	1:33:00	1:38:19- 08
Panéta	Níki	GRE	21.4.86	171/54	TJ	14.55	14.16- 07
Panova	Yelena	RUS	2.3.87		DT	56.54	56.83- 10
^ Panteleyeva	Yana	RUS	16.6.88		Hep	5877	6430- 08
* Papahrístou	Paraskeví	GRE	17.4.89	170/53	LJ	6.55	6.28- 09
					TJ	14.72	14.47i, 14.35- 09
Papayeoryíou	Alexándra	GRE	17.12.80	176/76	HT	70.54	70.73- 09
Papp	Krisztina	HUN	17.12.82	170/54	10k	32:36.32	31:46.47- 10
Parker	Barbara	GBR	8.11.82	170/54	5000	15:27.03	15:39.76- 10
Parnov	Liz	AUS-Y	9.5.94	176/57	PV	4.30	4.40- 10
Parra	Yusbelys	VEN	31.7.86	170/65	JT	57.58	52.27- 07
* Pascual	Beatriz	ESP	9.5.82	163/64	20kW	1:28:51	1:27:44- 08
Pastare	Agnese	LAT	27.10.88		20kW	1:35:05, 1:32:10sh	1:31:25- 10
* Patterson	Kara	USA	10.4.86	175/76	JT	62.76	66.67- 10
Patterson	Liz	USA	9.6.88	183/	HJ	1.89	1.95i- 09, 1.91- 10
Paul	Sheila	USA	30.9.89		100	11.35	11.51- 09, 11.36w- 10
^ Pavey	Jo	GBR	20.9.73	162/51	HMar	69:34	68:53- 08
					Mar	2:28:24	-0-
Payne	Aareon	USA	3.9.90	168/61	200	22.83	23.47- 09
^ Pchelnik	Daryia	BLR	20.12.81	185/97	HT	68.92	76.33- 08
Peake	Sally	GBR	8.2.86	164/57	PV	4.35	4.10- 10
Pearson	Emily	USA	8.8.85		Hep	5787	5726w, 5640- 10
* Pearson	Sally	AUS	19.9.86	167/60	100	11.20	11.14- 07
	200	23.05		23.02, 22.66w- 09	100h	12.28	12.50- 09
Pecherina ¶	Yevgeniya	RUS	9.5.89		DT	65.77	58.94- 10
Pedroso	Yadisleidis	CUB	28.1.87	167/50	400h	56.12	56.91- 09, 56.1- 10
Pedroso	Yasmiany	CUB	5.8.84	179/75	Hep	5812	5942- 07
Pelantová	Lucie	CZE	7.5.86	168/60	20kW	1:33:52	1:32:57- 10
Pemberton	Marecia	SKN	7.1.90		100	11.34	11.29, 11.12w- 10
Pena	Tori	IRL	30.7.87	168/	PV	4.40	4.35- 10
^ Pérez	Madaí	MEX	2.2.80	158/44	Mar	2:27:02	2:22:59- 06
Pérez	Yaimé	CUB	29.5.91	174/78	DT	59.26	59.30- 10
* Perie	Bianca	ROU	1.6.90	170/70	HT	72.04	73.52- 10
* Perkovic ¶	Sandra	CRO	21.6.90	183/80	SP	16.99i, 16.40	16.23i, 16.02- 10
					DT	67.96, 69.99dq	66.93- 10
Pérra	Athanasía	GRE	2.2.83	167/55	TJ	14.20i, 14.05	14.62- 09
Peter	Allison	ISV-J	14.7.92		200	23.10	23.08- 09
Petersen	Sara	DEN	9.4.87	171/57	400h	55.97	56.40- 09
^ Petlyuk	Tetyana	UKR	22.2.82	174/60	800	1:59.79	1:57.34- 06
					1500	4:08.56	4:06.51- 09
* Petre	Esthera	ROU	13.5.90	175/60	HJ	1.98	1.88- 09
^ Petrova	Tatyana	RUS	8.4.83	160/53	10k	32:18.88	32:17.49- 05
					Mar	2:25:01	2:25:53- 09

Name		Nat	Born	Ht/Wt	Event	2011 Mark	Pre-2011 Best
Pezzullo	Stephanie	USA	29.5.82		3kSt	9:56.82	10:07.13- 10
Pham Thi Diem		VIE	24.1.90		HJ	1.87	1.79- 10
Phillips	Kelly	USA	12.9.88		PV	4.30i	4.13i, 4.10- 08
Pidluzhnaya	Yuliya	RUS	1.10.88	180/63	LJ	6.83, 6.85w	6.84- 10
* Pierce	Anna	USA	31.3.84	163/54	800	2:00.19	1:58.80- 09
Pierre	Barbara	USA	28.4.87		100	11.14	11.18- 09
Pierson	Summer	USA	3.9.78	180/64	DT	59.00	61.19, 61.25dh- 09
Pinedo	Ainhoa	ESP	17.2.83	171/60	20kW	1:34:23	1:34:05- 10
Pinero	Anna María	ESP	15.1.86	168/60	PV	4.41	4.31- 10
* Pishchalnikova	Darya	RUS	19.7.85	190/103	DT	63.91	65.55- 06, 67.28dq- 08
Piwowarska	Joanna	POL	4.11.83	173/60	PV	4.35	4.53- 06
Pixler	Jessica	USA	8.4.88		5000	15:25.58	15:44.07- 10
Pizhankova ¶	Darya	UKR	9.1.90		100	11.35	11.61- 10
					200	22.91	
Plaksina	Margarita	RUS	1.10.77		Mar	2:27:07	2:28:44- 10
Plis	Renata	POL	5.2.85	165/51	1000	2:37.89	2:38.05- 09
					1500	4:03.50	4:06.76- 10
Plonka	Katarzyna	POL	28.6.88	178/67	TJ	13.72	13.42, 13.43w- 10
Podominick	Liz	USA	5.12.84		DT	57.82A	54.30- 08
Pogrebnyak	Nataliya	UKR	19.2.88	171/62	100	11.17	11.28- 08
Polak	Tina	POL	12.7.88	161/52	400h	55.90	56.54- 09
Polk	Tori	USA	21.9.83		LJ	6.75	6.58, 6.62Aw- 09
* Polnova	Tatyana	RUS	20.4.79	173/64	PV	4.50	4.78- 04
^ Pompey	Aliann	GUY	9.3.78	168/55	400	51.66	50.71- 09
Poonia	Krishna	IND	5.5.82	180/86	DT	62.25	63.69- 10
Popkova	Natalya	RUS	21.9.88	165/50	1500	4:07.40	4:05.86- 09
3000	8:53.0		8:45.10- 10		5000	15:20.29	15:05.95- 09
					10k	32:21.17	32:46.94- 09
Poplavskaya	Yekaterina	BLR	7.5.87	172/60	100h	13.10	13.11- 08
* Porter	Tiffany	GBR	13.11.87	172/62	100h	12.56	12.73- 08, 12.57w- 09
Pospelova	Marina	RUS	23.7.90		800	2:00.76	2:05.74- 10
* Potapova	Anastasiya	RUS	6.9.85	178/61	TJ	14.00, 14.13w	14.44i- 10, 14.40- 09
^ Potepa	Wioletta	POL	14.12.80	189/86	DT	58.84	66.01- 06
Poves	María José	ESP	16.3.78	167/52	20kW	1:32:21	1:29:31- 08
Povh	Olesya	UKR	18.10.87	169/58	100	11.24, 11.14w	11.29- 10
					200	22.58	23.92- 08
^ Powell	Suzy	USA	3.9.76	180/80	DT	63.28	67.67- 07, 69.44dh- 02
Power	Adrienne	CAN	11.12.81	163/64	200	22.98w	22.86A, 23.02- 08
Prendergast	Davita	JAM	16.12.84	169/58	400	50.86	51.24- 07
Pressley	Jessica	USA	27.12.84	178/100	SP	17.46	18.79- 08
Pritz	Molly	USA	1.1.88		HMar	71:05	72:14- 10
* Proctor	Shara	GBR	16.9.88	174/56	LJ	6.81	6.71- 09
* Provalinskaya	Yanina	BLR	26.12.76	186/85	SP	18.33	20.61- 01
Provozina	Lidiya	UKR	13.2.86	176/75	HT	66.70	66.07- 10
Pruner	Serena	ITA	21.5.86	154/44	20kW	1:33:56	1:38:33- 10
* Ptácníková	Jirina	CZE	20.5.86	175/69	PV	4.65	4.66- 10
Puchkova	Natalya	RUS	28.1.87		10k	32:46.27	33:52.01- 09
Pulyayeva	Lyubov	RUS	26.4.82		1500	4:08.60	4:10.09- 07
Purvis	Amber	USA	23.1.90		100	11.21	11.38. 11.32w- 09
					200	22.97	22.74- 10
Pusterla	Irène	SUI	21.6.88	176/64	LJ	6.84	6.76- 10
* Pyatykh	Anna	RUS	4.4.81	176/64	TJ	14.24	15.02, 15.17w- 06
Pygyda	Nataliya	UKR	30.1.81	167/54	400	51.43	51.38- 09
* Pyrek	Monika	POL	11.8.80	170/58	PV	4.60i, 460	4.82- 07
Pywell	Stephanie	GBR	12.6.87	181/60	HJ	1.88	1.90- 07
Qiao Yanrui		CHN	29.9.88	178/54	HJ	1.88	1.88- 09
Qieyang Shenjie		CHN	11.11.90		20kW	1:28:04	1:30:33- 10
Quintana	Gretchen	CUB	30.6.84	173/60	Hep	6017	6076- 07
Quintanal	Irache	ESP	18.9.78	174/75	SP	16.71	18.20- 07
Râzor	Bianca	ROU-Y	8.8.94	167/50	400	51.96	52.69- 10
* Rabchenyuk	Anastasiya	UKR	14.9.83	177/64	400h	54.18	53.96- 08
* Radcliffe	Paula	GBR	17.12.73	173/54	HMar	70:30+	65:40- 03
					Mar	2:23:46	2:15:25- 03
* Radevica	Ineta	LAT	13.7.81	176/56	LJ	6.76	6.92- 10
					TJ	13.89i	14.12- 04, 14.40w- 10
Radzivil	Svetlana	UZB	17.1.87	184/61	HJ	1.95	1.95- 10
* Rahouli	Baya	ALG	27.7.79	179/64	TJ	14.49	14.98- 05
Rains	Katelin	USA	20.8.87	168/59	PV	4.30i, 4.20	4.40i, 4.24- 09
Rajabi	Leyla	IRI	18.4.83	185/85	SP	16.77i, 16.85	18.06- 06
Ramos	Beverly	PUR	24.8.87	163/51	3kSt	9:41.87	9:59.03- 10
Randall	Allison	USA/JAM	25.5.88	180/95	DT	57.14	52.65- 10

Name		Nat	Born	Ht/Wt	Event	2011 Mark	Pre-2011 Best
* Ratej	Martina	SLO	2.11.81	178/69	JT	65.89	67.16- 10
Rath	Claudia	GER	25.4.86	175/58	Hep	6098	6107- 10
^ Rawlinson	Jana	AUS	9.11.82	181/68	400h	55.75	53.22- 03
Razanamalala	Olga	MAD	8.9.88		400h	57.25	57.51A- 10
* Rebryk	Vira	UKR	25.2.89	176/65	JT	61.60	63.36- 10
Redhead	Janelle	GRN	27.12.89		200	22.91A, 23.11	23.23A, 23.04w- 10
Redondo	Laura	ESP	3.7.88	165/80	HT	67.12	63.49- 10
Reece	Shakera	BAR	31.8.88	165/64	100	11.26A, 11.39w	11.34- 07, 11.2A- 10
* Reese	Brittney	USA	9.9.86	173/64	100	11.20w	11.63, 11.58w- 09
					LJ	7.19	7.10- 09
Regis	Yasmine	GBR	12.12.86	163/63	TJ	13.76	13.85A- 08, 13.75, 13.82w- 09
Reid	Sheila	CAN	2.8.89	166/52	3000	8:56.92i	9:01.13i- 10
Reilly	Stephanie	IRL	23.2.78		3kSt	9:42.91	9:48.94- 10
Renstrøm	Margrethe	NOR	21.3.85	179/60	LJ	6.53	6.68- 10
Resende	Alessandra	BRA	5.3.75	169/69	JT	55.34	59.58- 07
Reuse	Clélia	SUI	1.8.88	171/58	LJ	6.60	6.44i, 6.48w- 10, 6.35- 09
Rew	Trecey	USA	11.1.88		SP	17.38	16.74- 10
					DT	58.64	54.57- 10
Rhines	Jen	USA	1.7.74	160/48	5000	15:10.44	14:54.29- 08
					10k	31:30.37	31:17.31- 07
Ribalta	Josleidy	CUB	2.5.90	183/74	TJ	14.61	14.14, 14.16w- 10
Ribiaux	Yainelis	CUB	30.12.87	163/57	JT	62.30	63.18- 09
* Richards-Ross	Sanya	USA	26.2.85	173/61	200	22.63	22.17- 06
					400	49.66	48.70- 06
Richmond	Rose	USA	29.1.81	168/61	LJ	6.54, 6.56w	6.84- 06
Riddick	Monique	USA	8.11.89		SP	16.66i, 16.39	16.26- 10
Rifka	Romary	MEX	8.4.73	180/64	HJ	1.90A	1.97- 04
* Rigaudo	Elisa	ITA	17.6.80	168/56	20kW	1:30:44	1:27:12- 08
Rigert	Yelena	RUS	2.12.83	167/73	HT	67.30	71.92- 08
Riggien	Chastity	USA	5.7.89		100	11.34, 11.13w	11.40, 11.31w- 10
Riley	Judith	JAM	4.11.88		100	11.37, 11.25w	11.78- 09
					200	23.06w	24.79- 05
Rionoripo	Purity	KEN-J	10.6.93		5000	15:20.93	
Rittweg	Mareike	GER	1.6.84	173/78	JT	58.24	60.63- 07
Rivas	Anyela	COL	13.8.89	180/82	SP	17.12	16.86- 10
^ Robbeson	Justine	RSA	15.5.85	167/58	JT	61.26	63.49A- 08
^ Robert-Michon	Mélina	FRA	18.7.79	180/85	DT	61.07	65.78- 02
Robinson	Ada	USA	20.10.89		HJ	1.86A	
Robinson	Tamika	USA	24.8.89		100h	13.27. 13.06w	13.18, 13.06w- 10
Rocha	Salomé	POR	25.4.90		3kSt	9:57.30	10:02.02- 10
Rodgers	Kasey	USA	3.4.90		100	11.33w	11.81- 10
Rodhe	Megann	CAN	27.8.85	180/90	HT	67.03	65.93- 10
* Rodic	Snezana	SLO	19.8.82	180/66	TJ	14.35i, 14.23	14.47, 14.52w- 10
Rodrigues	Irina	POR	5.2.91	182/81	DT	58.35	58.21- 10
Rodriguez	Carol	PUR	16.12.85	175/65	200	23.34, 23.17w	22.23A, 22.80- 06
Rodríguez	Lisandra	CUB	14.10.86	179/76	DT	57.16	59.08- 10
* Rodríguez	Natalia	ESP	2.6.79	164/49	1500	4:01.50	3:59.51- 05
					3000	8:55.09	8:35.86- 09
Rodríguez	Rosa	VEN	2.7.86	179/78	HT	67.90	69.46- 09
Rodríguez	Yohana	CUB	9.1.90	175/63	DT	56.17	55.78- 10
* Rogowska	Anna	POL	21.5.81	171/55	PV	4.85i, 4.70	4.83- 05
Rojas	Marielys	VEN	30.4.86	173/54	HJ	1.89A	1.90- 08
Roleder	Cindy	GER	21.8.89	176/62	100h	12.91	12.98- 10
Rollins	Brianna	USA	18.8.91		100h	12.99, 12.88w	13.83- 09
Roloff	Annika	GER	10.3.91	166/54	PV	4.40	4.15- 10
Romagnolo	Elena	ITA	5.10.82	163/47	10k	32:48.25	32:41.26- 10
Romero	Marisol	MEX	26.11.83	155/46	5000	15:27.94	15:40.75- 10
					10k	32:45.05	33:28.18- 10
Rono	Georgina	KEN	19.5.84		HMar	69:08	73:41- 06
					Mar	2:24:33	2:30:55- 10
^ Rosa	Chiara	ITA	28.1.83	176/95	SP	18.59	19.15- 07
Rosales	Milánggela	VEN	21.2.87	165/60	20kW	1:32:17.6t	1:38:20- 10
Rosenbauer	Susanne	GER	2.8.84	173/68	JT	55.71	58.83- 09
Rosenquist	Ellinor	SWE	14.7.89		Hep	5640	5692- 10
* Rosolová	Denisa	CZE	21.8.86	175/63	200	23.08	23.03- 10
					400	50.84	50.85- 10
Rotich	Caroline	KEN	13.5.84		HMar	68:52	70:23- 09
					Mar	2:27:06, 2:24:26dh	2:29:46- 10
* Rotich	Lydia	KEN	8.8.88	163/42	3kSt	9:19.20	9:18.03- 10
* Rowbury	Shannon	USA	19.9.84	165/52	1500	4:05.73	4:00.33- 08
Ruban	Yuliya	UKR	6.10.83	162/50	Mar	2:27:10, 2:27:00dh	2:27:44- 10

Name		Nat	Born	Ht/Wt	Event	2011 Mark	Pre-2011 Best
Rubeor	Kelsey	USA	1.8.89		Hep	5680	
Rudakova	Vera	RUS-J	20.3.92		400h	57.10	57.16- 10
Ruddock	Natasha	JAM	25.12.89		100h	12.99, 12.96w	12.87- 10
Rüh	Anna	GER-J	17.6.93	186/78	DT	59.97	51.67- 10
Ruiz	Flor Dennis	COL	24.1.91		JT	57.26	50.58- 10
Ruiz	Úrsula	ESP	11.8.83	170/84	SP	17.02	16.97- 10
Rumpf	Sabine	GER	18.3.83	176/95	DT	60.67	62.21- 10
* Rusanova	Yuliya	RUS	3.7.86		800	1:56.99	1:58.99- 09
					1500	4:05.14	4:06.08- 09
* Russell	Carrie	JAM	18.10.90	171/68	100	11.05	11.14- 10
Ruston	Abby	USA	3.4.83		SP	17.16	18.13- 08
Ryan	Deirdre	IRL	1.6.82	183/62	HJ	1.95	1.93i- 09, 1.92- 06
* Rybalko	Viktoriya	UKR	26.10.82	177/60	LJ	6.87	6.87i- 08, 6.82, 6.87w- 06
					TJ	13.95	12.47- 03
Ryemyen	Mariya	UKR	2.8.87		100	11.21, 11.18w	11.25- 10
					200	22.68	23.16- 10
* Rypakova	Olga	KAZ	30.11.84	183/62	LJ	6.56	6.85- 07
					TJ	14.96	15.25- 10
* Ryzih	Lisa	GER	27.9.88	179/59	PV	4.65i	4.65- 10
Sadeiko	Grit	EST	29.7.89	174/62	Hep	6134	5813- 09
Sado	Fatuma	ETH	11.10.91		HMar	69:02	72:02- 10
					Mar	2:28:01	
Sadova	Natalya	RUS	15.7.72	180/90	DT	59.78	70.02- 99
Saeed	Alia Mohamed	UAE	18.5.91		5000	15:31.21	-0-
Safránková	Katerina	CZE	8.6.89	191/105	HT	69.39	68.95- 10
Sagnia	Khaddi	SWE-Y	20.4.94	172/60	TJ	13.65, 13.86w	13.56- 10
Sahutoglu	Tugçe	TUR	1.5.88	177/86	HT	70.09	64.15- 10
Saka	Pinar	TUR	5.11.85	165/53	400	51.53	53.04i- 09, 53.49- 10
Sakaida	Ayumi	JPN	7.11.85	157/45	10k	32:37.03	32:59.92- 10
* Saladuha	Olga	UKR	4.6.83	175/55	TJ	14.98, 15.06w	14.84- 08
Salis	Silvia	ITA	17.9.85	179/74	HT	71.93	71.77- 09
Saltanovic	Kristina	LTU	20.2.75	163/54	20kW	1:31:40, 1:30:36sh	1:30:44- 02
Samolyuk	Hanna	UKR	13.1.88	174/80	SP	17.20	16.45- 10
Samuel	Laura	GBR	19.2.91		TJ	13.67, 13.77w	13.75- 10
* Samuels	Dani	AUS	26.5.88	182/82	DT	62.33	65.84- 10
Samuelsson	Jessica	SWE	14.3.85	176/65	Hep	6182	6146- 10
Sánchez	Mariely	DOM	30.12.88	170/57	200	23.02A	23.50- 08
Sanders	Nicola	GBR	23.6.82	171/59	400	51.84	49.65- 07
Sandu	Cristina	ROU	4.3.90	172/58	LJ	6.54i, 6.46	6.53- 09
Santiusti	Yusneisis	CUB	24.12.84	166/60	800	1:58.70	2:00.47- 09
Santos	Rosângela	BRA	20.12.90		100	11.22A, 11.36	11.41- 08
* Santos	Vera	POR	3.12.81	164/57	20kW	1:29:55	1:28:14- 08
Sarrapio	Patricia	ESP	16.11.82	168/58	TJ	14.10	14.10- 10
Savchenko	Anastasiya	RUS	15.11.89	175/65	PV	4.40i, 4.40	4.30i- 09, 4.30- 10
* Savigne	Yargeris	CUB	13.11.84	165/55	TJ	14.99	15.28- 07
* Savinova	Mariya	RUS	13.8.85	169/55	800	1:55.87	1:57.56- 10
Savitskaya	Kristina	RUS	10.6.91		Hep	5989	5642- 09
Savlinis	Yelizaveta	RUS	14.8.87		100	11.30, 11.17w	11.46, 11.32w- 10
					200	22.62	23.20- 09, 23.08w- 10
Saxer	Mary	USA	21.6.87	169/	PV	4.60	4.50- 10
* Sayers	Goldie	GBR	16.7.82	171/70	JT	64.46	65.75- 08
Saykina	Svetlana	RUS	10.7.85	177/82	DT	61.27	63.42- 08
Scarpellini	Elena	ITA	14.1.87	177/60	PV	4.30	4.40i- 10, 4.36- 08
Schäfer	Carolin	GER	5.12.91	176/66	Hep	5941	5833- 08
Schindlerová	Zuzana	CZE	25.4.87	173/59	20kW	1:32:10	1:32:26- 09
Schippers	Dafne	NED-J	15.6.92	179/65	100	11.19, 11.13w	11.56- 10
	200	22.69			23.70, 23.41w- 10		
					Hep	6172	5967- 10
Schmaltz	Christine	USA	14.4.88		800	2:01.17	
Schmid	Anna Katharina	SUI	2.12.89	166/56	PV	4.45	4.35- 10
Schmidt	Alice	USA	3.10.81	178/66	800	1:58.61	1:58.75- 07
					1500	4:08.09	4:08.89- 07
Schol	Lisanne	NED	22.6.91	174/62	JT	57.50	53.07- 10
Schrott	Beate	AUT	15.4.88	177/68	100h	12.95	13.29- 09
Schultze	Anna	GER	26.5.85	173/61	PV	4.35i	4.40i- 06, 4.40- 07
Schultze	Martina	GER	12.9.90	172/59	PV	4.30	4.40- 10
* Schwanitz	Christina	GER	24.12.85	180/103	SP	19.20	19.68i, 19.31- 08
^ Schwartz	Jillian	ISR	19.9.79	173/63	PV	4.50	4.72i- 08, 4.60- 04
* Schwarzkopf	Lilli	GER	28.8.83	174/65	Hep	6370	6536- 08
Schwerdtner	Maren	GER	3.10.85	182/72	Hep	6039	6167- 10
Scott	Aurieyall	USA-J	18.5.92		100	11.12	11.89- 09
					200	22.83, 22.82w	23.75- 09

Name		Nat	Born	Ht/Wt	Event	2011 Mark	Pre-2011 Best
Scott	Sharolyn	CRC	27.10.84		400h	57.23A, 57.66	58.89- 10
Sedivá	Irena	CZE-J	19.1.92		JT	56.38	50.82- 10
Sedykh	Alexia	FRA-J	13.9.93	173/69	HT	65.02	62.17- 10
* Seeger	Melanie	GER	8.1.77	169/55	20kW	1:29:20	1:28:17- 04
Seidl	Megan	USA	4.11.86		HJ	1.90i	1.85i, 1.81- 10
* Sekachyova	Iryna	UKR	21.7.76	165/72	HT	70.31	74.52- 08
Sekino	Akane	JPN	28.7.90	160/42	10k	32:53.44mx	33:16.50- 10
Seles	Vanessa	BRA	26.10.81		LJ	6.60	6.53- 08
Sellam	Aida	TUN	13.9.77	167/74	JT	55.80	60.87- 04
* Selsouli	Mariem Alaoui	MAR	8.4.84	165/49	800	2:01.55	2:13.81- 05
					1500	4:00.77	4:00.95- 09
Selui	Linda	FRA	15.11.77	172/68	JT	57.32	53.50- 06
Selvon	Kai	TRI-J	13.4.92		100	11.43, 11.19w	11.41- 10
					200	22.89	23.33- 10
Semenova	Nataliya	UKR	7.7.82	178/85	DT	59.50	64.70- 08
* Semenya	Caster	RSA	7.1.91	170/64	800	1:56.35	1:55.45- 09
Semyonova	Svetlana	RUS	24.8.80		TJ	13.68. 13.73w	14.02- 05, 14.10w- 10
Sendriute	Zinaida	LTU	10.6.84	188/89	DT	62.49	60.70- 10
Sène	Amy	SEN	6.4.85	174/70	HT	68.45	64.11- 10
Serbezova	Nina	BUL/CYP	6.5.81		TJ	13.70	13.98- 04
Sesay	Ola	SLE	30.5.79	173/64	LJ	6.71	6.73- 09
Sestak	Marija	SLO	17.4.79	178/56	TJ	14.30	15.08i, 15.03- 08
Setowska-Dryk	Ewelina	POL	5.3.80	171/56	800	2:01.8 mx	1:58.96- 06
Seymour	Katrina	BAH-J	7.1.93		400h	57.24	
* Shakes-Drayton	Perri	GBR	21.12.88	170/67	400	51.47	51.48- 10
					400h	54.62	54.18- 10
Sharp	Lynsey	GBR	11.7.90		800	2:00.65	2:04.44- 08
Shatalova	Mariya	UKR	3.3.89		3kSt	9:48.22	9:47.21- 10
Shayunova	Natalya	BLR	11.9.89		HT	64.97	65.60- 09
Shelekh	Hanna	UKR-J	14.7.93	166/54	PV	4.30	4.30- 10
* Shemyakina	Tatyana	RUS	3.9.87	161/51	20kW	1:28:55	1:25:46- 08
Sherrill	Faith	USA	5.4.88		SP	18.00i, 17.64	17.20- 10
Shevchenko	Anzhelika	UKR	29.10.87	177/55	800	2:01.41	2:04.06- 06
					1500	4:07.24	4:14.71- 10
Shevchenko	Irina	RUS	2.9.75	171/64	100h	13.04	12.67- 04
Shi Tianshu		CHN	7.6.88	174/55	20kW	1:31:53	1:32:57- 10
Shimizu	Yuko	JPN	13.7.85	158/48	10k	31:43.25mx	33:12.85mx- 10
* Shkolina	Svetlana	RUS	9.3.86	187/66	HJ	2.00i, 1.99	2.00i- 10, 1.98- 08
Shmidt	Svitlana	UKR	20.3.90		3kSt	9:46.91	
* Shobukhova	Liliya	RUS	13.11.77	169/50	HMar	69:25+	70:00+- 10
					Mar	2:18:20	2:20:25- 10
Shoi	Hiroko	JPN	18.6.80	152/42	5000	15:29.69	15:43.18- 09
					10k	32:17.39mx	32:36.36mx- 10, 33:02.77- 03
Shorstova	Anna	RUS	10.4.89		HJ	1.94	1.90i, 1.87- 10
Short	Ciara	USA	11.3.89		400	51.85	52.36- 10
Shumkina	Olena	UKR	24.1.88	153/47	20kW	1:32:17	1:25:32- 09
Shump	Karen	USA	14.8.89		SP	17.97i, 17.36	17.43- 10
Shutkova	Veranika	BLR	26.5.86	171/51	LJ	6.95	6.69i- 10, 6.68- 10, 6.74w- 07
* Shvedova	Anastasiya	BLR	3.5.79	174/63	PV	4.55i, 4.50	4.65, 4.72ex- 08
* Sibileva	Tatyana	RUS	17.5.80	159/42	20kW	1:30:37	1:25:52- 10
Sidorova	Anzhelika	RUS	28.6.91		PV	4.40i, 4.30	4.30- 10
Sifuentes	Nicole	CAN	30.6.86	173/57	1500	4:08.45	4:06.34- 10
					5000	15:27.84	15:33.51- 10
Silva	Ana Cláudia	BRA	6.11.88		100	11.19	11.15- 10
					200	22.48	23.07- 10
da Silva	Cruz Nonata	BRA	18.8.74		5000	15:27.74	16:08.59- 10
da Silva	Karla	BRA	12.11.84	168/58	PV	4.35	4.30- 07
Silva	Laila	BRA	30.7.82		JT	57.81	56.68- 10
da Silva	Lucimara	BRA	10.7.85	172/63	Hep	6133A	6076- 08
da Silva ¶	Simone	BRA	12.9.84		5000	15:18.85	15:49.79- 10
					10k	31:59.11, 31:16.56dq	33:25.6h- 10
Silva	Vânia	POR	8.6.80	174/78	HT	69.55	68.82- 04
* Silva	Yarisley	CUB	1.6.87	169/68	PV	4.75A	4.50- 08
Simic	Ana	CRO	5.5.90	177/58	HJ	1.92i, 1.92	1.92- 10
* Simpson	Jemma	GBR	10.2.84	168/58	800	1:59.59	1:58.74- 10
					1500	4:07.53	4:06.39- 10
* Simpson	Jenny	USA	23.8.86	165/54	800	2:01.20	2:02.12- 10
	1500	4:03.54		3:59.90- 09	1M	4:28.60i	4:25.91i- 09
	3000	8:50.78i		8:42.03i, 9:12.50- 09	5000	15:11.49	15:01.70i, 15:05.25- 09
* Simpson	Margaret	GHA	2.8.82	162/53	JT	55.93	56.36- 05
					Hep	6270(w), 6183	6423- 05

	Name		Nat	Born	Ht/Wt	Event	2011 Mark	Pre-2011 Best
*	Simpson	Sherone	JAM	12.8.84	163/59	100	11.00	10.82- 06
						200	22.73	22.00- 06
*	Sinclair	Kenia	JAM	14.7.80	167/54	800	1:58.21	1:57.88- 06
						1500	4:06.50	4:05.56- 07
	Singh	Desiree	GER-Y	17.8.94	166/54	PV	4.32	4.20- 10
	Singha Roy	Sushmita	IND	26.3.84	175/66	Hep	5625	6027- 08
	Sinkevich	Anastasiya	RUS	4.3.90		Hep	5641	5568- 10
	Sinkler	April	USA	1.9.89		LJ	6.56, 6.64w	6.55i, 6.51- 10
	Skafída	Afrodíti	GRE	20.3.82	167/63	PV	4.30i, 4.30	4.55- 08
	Skrobáková	Lucie	CZE	4.1.82	170/62	100h	12.89, 12.85w	12.73- 09
*	Skujyte	Austra	LTU	12.8.79	188/80	HJ	1.87	1.89i, 1.86- 06
	SP	17.53i, 17.09		17.86- 09		Hep	6338	6435- 04
	Skvortsova	Silviya	RUS	16.11.74		Mar	2:27:51	2:26:24- 09
	Skydan	Anna	UKR-J	14.5.92		HT	67.56	56.90- 09
*	Slesarenko	Yelena	RUS	28.2.82	178/57	HJ	1.97	2.06- 04
	Smith	Ayla	USA	16.5.88		400h	56.54	58.14- 10
	Smith	Brittany	USA	25.3.91		SP	17.19i	15.98- 10
	Smith	Crystal	CAN	6.3.81	172/86	HT	69.50	68.60- 07
	Smith	Jessica	CAN	11.10.89		800	2:01.54	2:04.72- 10
*	Smith	Kimberley	NZL	19.11.81	166/49	5000	15:14.02	14:45.93- 08
	HMar	67:11		67:55- 10		Mar	2:25:46	2:25:21- 10
	Smith	Kristin	USA	23.12.87		HT	66.87	64.80- 10
	Smith	Lauren	USA	27.8.81		100h	13.31, 13.04w	13.00, 12.94w- 07
	Smith	Loreal	USA	12.10.85		100h	12.81, 12.64w	12.97, 12.90w- 09
	Smith	Loree	USA	6.11.82	168/85	HT	68.26	70.64- 09
	Smith	Nivea	BAH	18.2.90		100	11.27w	11.52, 11.37w- 10
						200	22.80, 22.44w	22.71- 10
^	Smith	Rachelle	USA	30.6.81	163/59	100	11.21	11.13- 07, 11.02w- 05
						200	22.89	22.22- 05
	Smith	Stacey	GBR	4.2.90	168/58	1500	4:06.81	4:10.00- 10
	Smith	Toni	USA	13.10.84		TJ	13.89	13.99- 08, 14.02w- 10
	Smith	Trecia	JAM	5.11.75	185/76	TJ	14.33	15.16- 04
	Smock	Amanda	USA	27.4.82	170/57	TJ	14.18	13.84- 08
^	Soboleva	Yelena	RUS	3.10.82	176/66	1500	4:06.64	3:56.43- 06
*	Sokolova	Vera	RUS	8.6.87	151/51	20kW	1:25:08	1:25:26- 09
*	Sokolova	Yelena	RUS	23.7.86	173/76	LJ	6.76	6.92- 09
	Soldatova	Olga	RUS	8.9.85		800	2:01.40	2:00.53- 10
*	Solomon	Shalonda	USA	19.12.85	169/56	100	11.08, 10.90w	10.90- 10
						200	22.15	22.36, 22.30w- 06
	Solovyova	Anastasiya	RUS	18.2.85	170/60	100h	13.12	13.02- 09
	Solovyova	Svetlana	RUS	6.11.86	169/50	20kW	1:31:55	1:29:37- 10
	Solovyova	Yevgeniya	RUS	28.6.86	185/90	SP	17.55	17.01- 10
	Solvin	Lena	FIN	4.7.86	163/73	HT	65.18	66.26- 08
	Song Xiaodan		CHN-J	23.1.93		JT	55.35	46.47- 10
	Song Xiaoling		CHN	21.12.87	167/49	20kW	1:33:03	1:28:23- 06
	Sonnenberg	Sam	USA	10.2.88		PV	4.35	4.30i, 4.12- 10
	Soprunova	Anastasiya	KAZ	14.1.86	165/60	100h	12.99	13.22- 10
	Sormunen	Oona	FIN	2.8.89		JT	58.72	57.68- 09
	Soto	Nercely	VEN	26.8.90		200	22.8	24.22- 10
	Soumah	Ndèye Fato	SEN	6.4.86	169/59	200	23.06	23.94- 10
						400	51.67	51.93A- 10, 52.79- 09
*	Soumaré	Myriam	FRA	29.10.86	167/57	100	11.17, 1.12w	11.18, 11.13w- 10
						200	22.71	22.32- 10
	Souza	Joelma	BRA	13.7.84		400	52.23	52.57- 10
	Spanovic	Ivana	SRB	10.5.90	176/67	LJ	6.71, 6.74w	6.78- 10
	Spence	Christine	USA	25.11.81		400h	55.90	54.21- 08
	Spence	Indira	JAM	8.9.86	/61	100h	12.93	13.05- 10
	Spence	Neely	USA	16.4.90		5000	15:27.72	16:13.34- 10
*	Spencer	Kaliese	JAM	6.5.87	173/59	400	50.71	50.55- 08
						400h	52.79	53.33- 10
*	Spencer	Levern	LCA	23.6.84	180/54	HJ	1.94	1.98- 10
*	Spiegelburg	Silke	GER	17.3.86	173/64	PV	4.76i, 4.75	4.75i- 09, 4.71- 10
	Spiler	Barbara	SLO-J	2.1.92		HT	67.06	66.18- 09
*	Spotáková	Barbora	CZE	30.6.81	182/80	JT	71.58	72.28- 08
	Sprunger	Ellen	SUI	5.8.86	172/56	Hep	5844	5824- 09
	Sprunger	Léa	SUI	5.3.90		Hep	5651	5603- 08
*	Stahl	Linda	GER	2.10.85	172/72	JT	60.78	66.81- 10
*	Stambolova	Vania	BUL	28.11.83	175/53	400	50.98	49.53- 06
						400h	53.68	53.82- 10
	Stanciu	Daniela	ROU	15.10.87	175/57	HJ	1.88	1.86- 10
	Stanková	Eliska	CZE	11.11.84		DT	57.82	55.50- 10

Name		Nat	Born	Ht/Wt	Event	2011 Mark	Pre-2011 Best
Starostina	Oksana	RUS	1.4.88		HJ	1.88	
Stately	Brysun	USA	22.11.86	165/57	PV	4.30	4.35- 07
Steacy	Heather	CAN	14.4.88	175/73	HT	70.98	67.20- 10
^ Stef	Claudia	ROU	25.2.78	160/48	20kW	1:33:07	1:27:41- 04
Stefanídi	Ekateríni	GRE	4.2.90	172/60	PV	4.45	4.37i, 4.30- 05
Steiner Bennett	April	USA	22.4.80	175/61	PV	4.45	4.63- 08
Stellingwerff	Hilary	CAN	7.8.81	160/48	1500	4:07.18	4:05.69- 07
Stepaniuk	Kamila	POL	22.3.86	184/65	HJ	1.88i	1.93- 09
Steryíou	Adonía	GRE	7.7.85	180/58	HJ	1.90	1.97- 08
Stevens-Walker	Sarah	USA	2.4.86	178/83	SP	18.12	18.40- 07
* Stewart	Kerron	JAM	16.4.84	175/61	100	10.87	10.75- 09
					200	22.63	21.99- 08
Stoddart	Shevon	JAM	21.11.82	165/52	400h	57.18	54.47- 05
Stowe	Rebeka	USA	9.3.90		3kSt	9:53.12	10:03.41- 10
Stowers	Jasmin	USA	23.9.91		100h	12.88, 12.86w	13.59- 09
Strachan	Antonique	BAH-J	22.8.93		200	22.70	23.66- 10
Straková	Iva	CZE	4.8.80	187/65	HJ	1.87i	1.98i- 08, 1.95- 07
Straneo	Valeria	ITA	5.4.76		10k	32:35.11	34:54.80- 04
HMar 69:42			74:07- 09		Mar	2:26:33	2:41:15- 09
Stratton	Brooke	AUS-J	12.7.93		LJ	6.60	6.30- 10
Strokova	Yekaterina	RUS	17.12.89		DT	59.61	58.41- 10
* Strutz	Martina	GER	4.11.81	160/57	PV	4.80	4.52- 08
Stuart	Bianca	BAH	17.5.88		LJ	6.81, 6.91w	6.56i- 09. 6.54A, 6.59w- 08
Stuy	Hrystyna	UKR	3.2.88	168/57	100	11.34	11.32- 10
					200	22.79	23.76- 09
* Styopina	Viktoriya	UKR	21.2.76	175/56	HJ	1.95	2.02- 04
Su Xinyue		CHN	8.11.91	179/70	DT	57.57	56.11- 10
Sudarushkina	Viktoriya	RUS	2.9.90		JT	58.46	54.59- 10
Sugihara	Kayo	JPN	24.2.83	161/44	10k	31:34.35	31:44.93mx- 10, 31:47.60- -06
Suh Hae-an		KOR	1.7.85	3JT		57.47	57.61- 10
* Suhr	Jenn	USA	5.2.82	180/64	PV	4.91	4.92- 08
Sui Liping		CHN	1.5.91	174/65	JT	56.27	55.27- 10
Sujew	Diana	GER	2.11.90	166/52	1500	4:09.13	4:13.69- 10
Sum	Eunice	KEN	2.9.88		800	1:59.66	2:00.28- 10
Summers	Jeré	USA	21.5.87		DT	57.25	57.68- 08
Sun Huanhuan		CHN	15.3.90	161/50	20kW	1:29:46	1:30:35- 10
^ Sun Taifeng		CHN	26.8.82	185/105	DT	61.47	64.98- 07
Sun Yawei		CHN	17.10.87	169/55	100h	12.94	13.12- 09
Suna	Fadime	TUR	25.10.86	166/50	5000	15:31.47	17:18.42- 08
Sussmann	Jana	GER	12.10.90	166/47	3kSt	9:43.28	10:11.15- 10
Sutej	Tina	SLO	7.11.88	173/58	PV	4.61	4.50- 10
Sutherland	Andrea	JAM	26.5.88		400h	56.44	57.12- 10
Svechnikova	Anastasiya	UZB-J	20.9.92	165/60	JT	60.06	58.62- 10
Sviridova	Olesya	RUS	28.10.89		SP	18.34	16.68- 10
Sylvester	Toshika	USA	3.12.91		100	11.29w	11.85- 10
Syreva	Olesya	RUS	25.11.83	164/50	1000	2:37.07i	2:37.06i- 06
1500 4:02.73			4:06.47- 06		2000	5:44.89i	5:54.38- 07
3000 8:49.99, 8:41.35i		8:29.00i- 06, 8:55.09- 08			5000	15:22.10	15:19.96- 08
					HMar	70:18	69:52- 08
Szlezak	Matylda	POL	11.1.89	165/54	3kSt	9:48.77	10:15.99- 10
Szwarnóg	Agnieszka	POL	28.12.86	167/59	20kW	1:33:50	1:37:30- 10
Tadesse	Feysa	ETH	19.11.88		HMar	68:44	68:50- 10
					Mar	2:25:20	2:36:57- 09
Tadesse	Yeshimabet	ETH	.88		Mar	2:28:24	2:27:45- 10
* Tafa Magarsa	Askale	ETH	27.9.84		HMar	70:38+	69:37+- 08
					Mar	2:25:24	2:21:31- 08
Tago	Miyabi	JPN	15.7.88	169/50	400h	56.70	55.99- 10
Takács	Julia	ESP	29.6.89	171/55	20kW	1:31:32	1:30:14- 10
Talay	Alina	BLR	14.5.89		100h	12.91	12.87- 10
Tallent	Claire	AUS	7.6.81	163/50	20kW	1:32:39	1:32:02- 10
Tamosaityte	Sonata	LTU	26.6.87	172/57	100h	13.10	13.10- 09
* Tan Jian		CHN	20.1.88	179/80	DT	63.72	59.65- 10
Tanaka	Hanae	JPN	12.2.90	160/47	10k	32:27.56	32:28.09mx, 33:17.52- 10
Tanui	Norah	KEN-Y	2.10.95		3kSt	9:45.1A	
Tanui	Susan	KEN			10k	32:22.3A	33:50.6- 08
Tarantinova	Natalya	RUS	28.11.87		3kSt	9:44.60	10:08.26- 10
Tarasova	Irina	RUS	15.4.87	183/105	SP	18.72	18.45- 08
* Tarasova	Yuliya	UZB	13.3.86	177/68	LJ	6.72	6.81- 10
Tarasova	Zlata	RUS	2.12.86		HT	66.36	62.95- 07
* Tarmoh	Jeneba	USA	27.9.89	167/59	100	11.23, 10.94w	11.19, 11.00w- 10
					200	22.28	22.65- 10

Name		Nat	Born	Ht/Wt	Event	2011 Mark	Pre-2011 Best
Tashpulatova	Hanna	BLR	21.10.87		400	51.79	52.86- 10
Tate	Cassandra	USA	11.9.90		400h	55.99	56.87- 10
Tavares	Eleonor	POR	24.9.85	164/55	PV	4.50	4.35i- 09, 4.30- 10
Tchayem	Nelly	FRA	4.8.83	173/60	TJ	13.90	13.76, 13.91w- 10
Teferi	Senbera	ETH-Y	3.5.95		1500	4:09.80	
Terekhova	Yuliya	RUS	20.2.90		400	52.29	53.26- 10
Tereshkova ¶	Olga	KAZ	26.10.84	175/55	400	52.85, 51.27dq	51.62- 07
Terlecki	Josephine	GER	17.2.86	182/78	SP	18.29	18.00- 08
Terrero	Indira	CUB	29.11.85	161/52	400	52.22	50.98A, 50.5- 08, 51.00- 07
Theron	Wanda	RSA	30.7.88	165/60	400h	56.13	56.45- 09
Thiam	Ami Mbacké	SEN	10.11.76	183/70	400	51.77	49.86- 01
Thomas	Charlene	GBR	6.5.82	166/52	1500	4:06.85	4:05.06- 09
Thomas	LaTavia	USA	17.12.88	173/	800	1:59.67	2:01.40- 10
Thomas	Vashti	USA	21.4.90		100h	13.14	13.03- 07
Thompson	Turquoise	USA	31.7.91		400h	55.53	56.92- 10
^ Thondike	Arasay	CUB	28.5.86	165/83	HT	71.86	73.90- 09
Thorsteinsdóttir	Helga Margrét	ISL	15.11.91		Hep	5856	5878- 09
* Thurmond	Aretha	USA	14.8.76	178/97	DT	63.85	65.86- 04, 66.23dh- 03
Tigâu	Viorica	ROU	12.8.79	171/60	LJ	6.71	6.85, 6.87w- 00
^ Timbilil	Alice	KEN	16.6.83	155/45	Mar	2:26:34dh	2:25:03- 10
Titimets	Hanna	UKR	5.3.89	173/62	400h	54.69	55.58- 10
Tkachuk	Anastasiya	UKR-J	20.4.93	168/56	800	2:00.37	2:02.11- 10
^ Tobias	Nataliya	UKR	22.11.80	160/48	1500	4:05.53	4:01.78- 08
					3000	8:54.16	8:51.32- 03
Tola	Fate	ETH	22.10.87		Mar	2:26:21	2:28:22- 10
Toma	Carmen	ROU	28.3.89	168/50	TJ	14.07	14.29- 09
* Tomasevic	Dragana	SRB	4.6.82	175/80	DT	62.48	63.63- 06
Tomashova	Tatyana	RUS	1.7.75	164/50	1500	4:03.69	3:56.91- 06
Tomb	Stine Meland	NOR	27.8.86	170/61	400h	56.38	57.10- 10
Tomic	Marina	SLO	9.11.82	167/55	100h	13.10	13.19- 04
Tong Lingling		CHN-J	25.1.92		20kW	1:33:14	1:34:32- 10
Topic	Biljana	SRB	17.10.77	180/60	TJ	14.21	14.56- 09
Topilskaya	Olga	RUS	4.10.90	172/60	400	51.10	56.22- 08
Topylina	Svetlana	RUS	6.1.85	173/62	100h	13.14	13.14- 07
Torr	Veronica	NZL	17.5.87		Hep	5637	5520- 10
Torres	Marestella	PHI	20.2.81	164/53	LJ	6.71	6.68- 09
* Tosta	Sheena	USA	1.10.82	165/57	400h	55.65	52.95- 04
Townsend	Tiffany	USA	14.6.89	163/50	100	11.19, 11.09w	11.13- 09
					200	22.58	22.75A- 08, 22.84- 07
Tracey	Ristananna	JAM-J	5.9.92		400	51.95	53.54- 10
					400h	54.58	57.77- 10
Tran Hue Hoa		VIE	8.8.91		TJ	13.76	13.39- 10
Tresch	Martina	SUI	10.6.89		3kSt	9:51.96	10:04.27- 10
Trevisan	Elisa	ITA	5.3.80	166/55	Hep	5706	5844- 04
Troneva	Natalya	RUS-J	24.3.93	186/63	SP	16.74	15.66- 10
Trost	Alessia	ITA-J	8.3.93	188/66	HJ	1.89i, 1.87	1.90- 10
^ Trotter	Deedee	USA	8.12.82	178/65	400	51.17	49.64- 07
Truong Thanh Hang		VIE	1.5.86	165/50	800	2:01.41	2:00.91- 10
Trybanska	Malgorzata	POL	21.6.81	177/59	LJ	6.65	6.80, 6.81w- 07
					TJ	14.16i, 14.16	14.44- 10
Tsale	Tsehaynesh	ETH-J	29.1.93		3kSt	9:56.87	10:09.00- 09
Tsander	Olga	BLR	18.5.76	174/83	HT	69.08	76.66- 05
Tschida	Marissa	USA	7.7.89		JT	56.02	56.71- 10
Tschirch	Cathleen	GER	23.7.79	167/54	100	11.44, 11.17w	11.35- 09
					200	23.23, 22.87w	22.97- 07
Tsegaye	Tirfe	ETH	25.11.84		Mar	2:24:12	2:22:44- 10
Tsiolakoúdi	Aggelikí	GRE	10.5.76	165/70	JT	57.40	63.14- 02
Tsyhotska	Ruslana	UKR	23.3.86	166/49	TJ	14.45	13.80- 10
* Tune	Dire	ETH	19.5.85	158/42	HMar	68:52	67:18- 09
					Mar	2:25:08dh	2:23:44- 10
Turner	Laura	GBR	12.8.82	168/57	100	11.23	11.11- 10, 11.09w- 07
Turtle	Gemma	GBR	15.5.86		3000	8:57.24i	8:56.23imx- 10, 9:14.80- 09
Tutayeva	Yuliya	RUS	7.12.88		800	1:59.83	2:00.40- 10
* Tyminska	Karolina	POL	4.10.84	178/61	100h	13.12	13.54- 10
LJ 6.58				6.63- 08	Hep	6544	6428- 08
* Uceny	Morgan	USA	10.3.85	168/57	800	1:58.37	1:58.67- 10
					1500	4:00.06	4:02.40- 10
Udelhoven	Tilia	GER-J	4.9.92	183/74	Hep	6000	5683- 10
Udoh	Christy	USA	30.9.91		200	23.03	23.70- 10
Udras	Grete	EST	11.3.88	180/59	HJ	1.92i	1.89- 09
Ufodiama	Blessing	USA	28.11.81		TJ	14.06	13.59- 09, 13.62w- 10

Name		Nat	Born	Ht/Wt	Event	2011 Mark	Pre-2011 Best
Ugatai	Romina	FRA	10.10.86	174/69	JT	56.41	54.24- 10
Ugen	Lorraine	GBR	22.8.91		LJ	6.54	6.35, 6.42w- 10
Uhl	Lisa	USA	31.8.87		3000	8:53.14i	8:56.09i, 9:05.62- 10
Urbaniak	Lena	GER-J	31.10.92	175/	SP	16.65	15.80- 10
Urbanik	Danuta	POL	24.12.89	167/58	800	2:00.84	2:05.02- 08
					1500	4:09.04	4:15.85- 10
Urech	Lisa	SUI	27.7.89	168/53	100h	12.62	12.81- 10
Uslu	Binnaz	TUR	12.3.85	165/55	3kSt	9:24.06	10:00.88- 10
^ Usovich	Ilona	BLR	14.11.82	170/60	800	1:59.38	2:02.75- 08
^ Usovich	Svetlana	BLR	14.10.80	165/52	400	51.20	50.55i- 05, 50.79- 04
					800	1:58.12	1:58.11- 07
* Ustalova	Kseniya	RUS	14.1.88	177/65	400	52.03	49.92- 10
Utriainen	Sanni	FIN	5.2.91	170/64	JT	58.24	57.26- 10
Utura	Sule	ETH	8.2.90	169/50	3000	8:47.42	8:43.72- 10
					5000	14:46.32	14:44.21- 10
					10k	32:06.89	
^ Valant Velepec	Anja	SLO	8.9.77	183/66	TJ	13.83	14.69- 00
Vallortigara	Elena	ITA	21.9.91	179/56	HJ	1.90i	1.91- 10
van Blerk	Irvette	RSA	5.7.87		HMar	70:56	71:09- 10
Van Dalen	Lucy	NZL	18.11.88		3000	8:56.77i	9:17.23- 10
Van Hessche	Hanne	BEL	5.7.91		HJ	1.87	1.87- 09
Vanden Bempt	Sigrid	BEL	10.2.81	173/58	1500	4:09.67i	4:12.36i- 09, 4:13.85- 08
Vargas	Mailín	CUB	24.3.83	175/77	SP	19.13	19.02- 09
* Vasco	María	ESP	26.12.75	156/44	20kW	1:31:41	1:27:25- 08
Vaughn	Sara	USA	16.5.86		1500	4:08.74	4:11.39- 09
Vdovina	Kseniya	RUS	19.4.87		200	23.15	22.91- 10
					400	50.67	51.41- 10
* Veldáková	Dana	SVK	3.6.81	178/59	TJ	14.48	14.51- 08, 14.59w- 10
Veldáková	Jana	SVK	3.6.81	177/59	LJ	6.66	6.72- 08, 6.88w- 10
* Veneva-Mateeva	Venelina	BUL	13.6.74	179/61	HJ	1.98	2.04- 06
Vésanes	Elysée	FRA	25.1.84	171/60	LJ	6.52w	6.53- 07
* Vessey	Maggie	USA	23.12.81	170/58	800	1:58.50	1:57.84- 09
Vicenzino	Tania	ITA	1.4.86	168/56	LJ	6.54	6.54- 09
Vichy	Ariannis	CUB	18.5.89	170/70	HT	69.02	68.61- 10
Vigliano	Nadia	FRA	24.6.77	180/76	JT	55.59	57.31- 08
* Viljoen	Sunette	RSA	6.1.83	168/63	JT	68.38	66.38- 10
Virbalyte	Brigita	LTU	1.2.85	165/50	20kW	1:33:24, 1:30:15sh	1:32:08- 09
Viuf	Katy	USA	23.5.87	175/	PV	4.31	4.32- 10
Vlasic	Blanka	CRO	8.11.83	192/75	HJ	2.03	2.08- 09
Vlasova	Natalya	RUS	19.7.88		3kSt	9:55.05	9:57.27- 10
Volkova	Nina	RUS	26.8.84		HT	64.87	62.02- 10
von Eynatten	Denise	GER	30.12.87	179/61	PV	4.31i, 4.30	4.30- 07
von Eynatten	Victoria	GER	6.10.91	174/54	PV	4.30	4.35i, 4.25- 10
Voronenkova	Yekaterina	RUS	8.2.88		200	23.42, 23.10w	23.59- 09
Vosmerikova	Anastasiya	RUS	15.7.88	172/59	800	2:00.32	2:00.15- 10
					1500	4:03.59	4:06.67- 10
Voykina	Tatyana	RUS	16.10.81		LJ	6.55	6.75- 05
* Vukicevic	Christina	NOR	18.6.87	178/60	100h	12.79	12.74- 09
Vyatkina	Natalya	BLR	10.2.87	176/50	TJ	14.32	14.32- 10
Wade	Bettie	USA	11.9.86	173/71	Hep	6052(w), 5949	6000- 10
Wagner	Marion	GER	1.2.78	178/60	100	11.35	11.24- 09
Wairimu	Susan	KEN-J	11.10.92	160/40	5000	15:23.9	15:52.55- 10
Waite	Lennie	GBR	4.5.86	173/60	3kSt	9:49.67	9:50.48- 09
Waldet	Olivia	FRA	23.5.84	177/85	HT	65.69	67.20- 08
* Walker	Melaine	JAM	1.1.83	173/58	400h	52.73	52.42- 09
Wallace	LaTosha	USA	25.3.85	173/60	400h	55.99	55.85- 08
Wang Bin		CHN	7.1.87	176/70	DT	57.14	57.52- 09
Wang Chunyu		CHN-Y	17.1.95		800	2:01.34	
Wang Huiqin		CHN	7.2.90	168/52	TJ	14.03	13.94- 10
Wang Jiali		CHN	1.2.86	165/47	10k	31:38.15	32:49.23- 09
					Mar	2:26:12	2:26:34- 08
Wang Ping		CHN	28.7.90		JT	58.42	56.75- 10
Wang Qingling		CHN-J	14.1.93		Hep	5632	
Wang Shanshan		CHN	16.6.87	168/50	20kW	1:30:01	1:29:54- 09
Wang Xueqin		CHN	1.1.91		5000	15:28.75	
					10k	31:55.31	
Wang Zheng		CHN	14.12.87	174/87	HT	68.75	71.19- 10
Wangare	Mary	KEN	29.11.87		1500	4:09.08A	
* Wangui Kabuu	Lucy	KEN	24.3.84	155/42	HMar	67:04	69:47- 04
Wanjiru	Grace	KEN	10.1.79	154/45	20kW	1:36:42A, 1:28:15Ash	1:37:49, 1:34:19Ash- 10
Wanjiru	Rosemary	KEN-Y	1.1.94	157/43	5000	15:26.07mx	
Wannemacher	Stacey	USA	22.11.87		SP	16.99	16.53- 09

Name		Nat	Born	Ht/Wt	Event	2011 Mark	Pre-2011 Best
Wanner	Julia	GER	8.12.87	177/61	HJ	1.89i	1.93- 09
Ward	Shericka	USA	30.3.90		100h	13.16	13.12- 10
Watanabe	Yuko	JPN	3.11.87	156/45	10k	32:27.89mx	
Weber	Liane	GER	24.2.86	179/60	Hep	5857	5928- 10
Wedler	Weronika	POL	17.7.89	174/57	100	11.35	11.38- 10
Wei Xiaojie		CHN	.89		Mar	2:26:41	
^ Wei Yanan		CHN	6.12.81	162/49	Mar	2:27:13	2:23:12- 07, 2;20:23dq- 02
Wei Yongli		CHN	11.10.91		100	11.36	11.75- 10
Weightman	Laura	GBR	1.7.91		1500	4:07.94mx	4:09.60mx, 4:12.82- 10
Weitzel	Michelle	GER	18.6.87	181/63	LJ	6.64	6.49- 10
Wellings	Eloise	AUS	9.11.82	167/44	10k	31:41.31	32:08.32- 10
* Wells	Kellie	USA	16.7.82	163/	100h	12.50, 12.35w	12.58- 08
Welsch	Shakeema	USA	10.11.76	182/61	TJ	13.84i, 13.82	14.17- 08, 14.30w- 09
Weng Chunxia		CHN-J	29.8.92		DT	56.85	55.00- 10
Wenth	Jennifer	AUT	24.7.91	166/48	1000	2:38.18mx	
Wesh	Marlena	HAI	16.2.91	167/	400	52.28	53.74- 09
Wessman	Anna	SWE	9.10.89	164/70	JT	57.09	56.20- 10
Weygandt	Shade	USA	24.1.91	168/54	PV	4.45	4.34i, 4.30- 10
White	Skylar	USA	15.9.91		SP	17.16	15.51- 10
Whittingham	Laura	GBR	6.6.86	177/71	JT	59.95	60.68- 10
^ Whyte	Angela	CAN	22.5.80	170/56	100h	12.88, 12.76w	12.63, 12.55w- 07
* Whyte	Rosemarie	JAM	8.9.86	175/66	400	49.84	50.05- 08
Willer	Natalie	USA	10.2.90	169/61	PV	4.37i, 4.33	4.38- 09
Williams	Alycia	USA	8.1.85	173/	400	52.03	52.52- 10
Williams	Charonda	USA	27.3.87	165/54	200	22.85, 22.78w	22.55, 22.39w- 09
Williams	Danielle	JAM-J	14.9.92		100h	13.32, 13.13w	13.46, 13.41w- 10
Williams	Jodie	GBR-J	28.9.93	170/	100	11.18	11.24- 10
					200	22.94	22.79- 10
Williams	Kimberly	JAM	3.11.88	169/66	LJ	6.55i	6.51i- 10, 6.42, 6.66w- 09
					TJ	14.25	14.23- 10, 14.38w- 09
* Williams	Lauryn	USA	11.9.83	157/57	100	11.15, 11.10w	10.88- 05, 10.86w- 08
					200	22.65	22.27- 05
Williams	Nadia	GBR	17.11.81	170/66	TJ	13.77, 13.94w	13.68, 13.75w- 10
Williams	Nickesha	USA	2.4.87		100	11.31	11.84- 08
Williams	Shelise	USA	15.8.89	165/58	400	51.84	51.71- 10
* Williams	Shericka	JAM	17.9.85	170/64	200	23.49, 23.16w	22.50- 08
					400	50.45	49.32- 09
Williams	Shermaine	JAM	4.2.90	173/62	100h	13.03, 12.95w	13.06, 12.95w- 09
Williams	Sonnisha	USA	20.4.91		LJ	6.50	6.25- 10
Williams	Tameka	SKN	31.8.89	165/52	100	11.33w	11.42, 11.39w- 10
					200	23.06A, 22.89w	23.19- 08
Williams	Tiffany	USA	5.2.83	160/57	400h	55.77	53.28- 07
* Williams-Mills	Novlene	JAM	26.4.82	167/55	400	50.05	49.63- 06
Williamson	Kimberly	JAM-J	2.10.93		HJ	1.88	1.80- 09
Willis	Benita	AUS	6.5.79	166/50	HMar	70:40	67:55- 04
Wilson	Kenyanna	USA	27.10.88	168/	100	11.19, 11.11w	11.20- 09
* Wilson	Nickiesha	JAM	28.7.86	173/64	400h	55.57	53.97- 07
Wilson	Trinity	USA-Y	4.9.94		100h	13.15	13.49, 13.35w- 10
Winatho	Wassanee	THA	30.6.80	170/57	Hep	5710	5889- 07
^ Wineberg	Mary	USA	3.1.80	178/62	400	51.71	50.24- 07
^ Wisniewska	Joanna	POL	24.5.72	187/82	DT	59.86	63.97- 99
* Wlodarczyk	Anita	POL	8.8.85	178/94	HT	75.33	78.30- 10
Wolfarth	Gabi	GER	6.9.89	175/67	HT	65.02	62.59- 08
^ Woods	Shareese	USA	20.2.85	165/52	200	23.07	22.71- 10, 22.70w- 06
					400	52.32	51.05- 09
Woodward	Krista	CAN	22.11.84	163/59	JT	58.64	56.06- 07
Wortham	Ellen	USA	5.1.90		400h	55.70	56.83- 10
Wright	Joanna	USA	3.5.89	165/	PV	4.31	4.21i, 4.10- 10
Wright	Kou	LBR	11.6.84		400h	57.10	55.55- 09
Wright	Letecia	USA	1.2.89		100h	12.87	13.07, 13.05w- 10
Wright	Phoebe	USA	30.8.88		800	1:59.25	1:58.22- 10
					1500	4:08.60	4:15.66- 10
Wu Sha		CHN	21.10.87	172/64	PV	4.35	4.40- 09
* Wurth-Thomas	Christin	USA	11.7.80	165/54	800	2:00.72	1:59.35- 09
1500 4:03.72			3:59.59- 10		3000	8:43.79i	8:54.97i- 08
					5000	15:21.75	15:28.04- 08
Xi Shangxue		CHN	27.1.89	179/85	DT	56.80	57.52- 09
Xiao Huimin		CHN-J	1.3.92		10k	32:23.49	36:52.38- 10
* Xie Limei		CHN	27.6.86	173/57	TJ	14.54, 14,62w	14.90- 07
Xu Huiqin		CHN-J	4.9.93		PV	4.40	4.15- 10
Xu Shaoyang		CHN	9.2.83	173/70	DT	57.40	63.29- 08

Name		Nat	Born	Ht/Wt	Event	2011 Mark	Pre-2011 Best
Xu Tingting		CHN	12.7.89	182/65	TJ	13.82	14.15- 08
Xue Fei		CHN	8.8.89	164/45	5000	15:27.46	15:02.73- 07
Xue Juan		CHN	10.2.86	174/65	JT	56.75	62.93- 03
Yakovenko	Olga	UKR	1.6.87	160/45	20kW	1:32:08	1:35:16- 09
Yalovtseva	Viktoriya	KAZ	4.11.77	154/50	800	2:00.57	2:03.19- 06
^ Yamauchi	Mara	GBR	13.8.73	161/52	Mar	2:27:24	2:23:12- 09
Yang Fei		CHN	20.7.87	186/90	DT	59.45	57.14- 07
Yang Mingxia		CHN	13.1.90	163/44	20kW	1:31:00	1:28:56- 08
Yang Qi		CHN	13.4.91	171/58	400h	56.69	56.77- 10
Yang Yanbo		CHN	9.3.90		SP	17.41	17.37- 10
					DT	62.26	60.01- 09
Yang Yawei		CHN	16.10.83	168/51	20kW	1:32:18	1:27:58- 05
* Yanıt	Nevin	TUR	16.2.86	168/60	100h	13.07	12.63- 10
Yano	Miyuki	JPN	1.4.90	162/57	400h	57.06	59.07- 10
Yao Jiajia		CHN	7.4.88	173/50	TJ	13.70i	13.78- 08
* Yaroshchuk	Anna	UKR	24.11.89	176/67	400h	54.77	55.60- 10
Yastrebova	Nataliya	UKR	12.10.84	175/57	TJ	14.50	14.03- 09
Yatsevich	Anastasiya	BLR	18.1.85		20kW	1:29:30	1:32:28- 06
* Yefremova	Antonina	UKR	19.7.81	176/60	400	50.69	50.70- 02
Yemelyanova	Larisa	RUS	6.1.80	164/52	20kW	1:33:30	1:25:52- 09
Yepimashko	Vera	BLR	10.7.76	181/74	SP	17.95i, 17.09	18.95- 10
Yeremina	Lyudmila	RUS	8.8.91		PV	4.30i, 4.30	4.30i- 10, 4.20- 09
Yesipchuk	Oksana	RUS	13.12.75	183/95	DT	57.80	63.68- 00
* Yevdokimova	Natalya	RUS	17.3.78	178/65	1500	4:03.33	3:57.73- 05
Yin Annuo		CHN-J	23.3.92		3kSt	9:49.55	10:10.43- 10
Yin Yuanyuan		CHN	31.5.91		Mar	2:27:55	2:37:10- 09
Yoneda	Tomomi	JPN	11.8.90	167/54	400h	57.10	58.02- 10
Yoshikawa	Mika	JPN	16.9.84	155/39	5000	15:15.33mx, 15:31.78	15:28.44- 10
					10k	31:55.06	
Yoshimoto	Hikari	JPN	14.1.90	157/41	5000	15:30.94	15:26.72- 10
					10k	31:45.82	31:30.92- 10
* Yosypenko	Lyudmyla	UKR	24.9.84	175/63	Hep	6318	6423- 09
Young	Jessica	USA	6.4.87		100	11.14, 11.08w	11.18, 11.06w- 09
200	22.99			23.16- 09	400	52.27	52.25- 08
Youngblood	Jamesha	USA	24.4.89		LJ	6.59w	6.63- 10
Yulamanova	Nailya	RUS	6.9.80		Mar	2:26:39	2:26:05- 10
Yumanova	Irina	RUS	6.11.90		20kW	1:29:26	1:35:29- 10
Yurkovich	Rachel	USA	10.10.86	180/77	JT	60.40	60.11- 10
Yushchenko	Yulyana	BLR	14.8.84	173/56	400	52.19	51.01- 07
* Zabara	Olesya	RUS	6.10.82	165/56	TJ	14.45i, 14.19, 14.36w	14.54i- 08, 14.50- 06
Zadorina	Kseniya	RUS	2.3.87	173/59	400	50.92	50.87- 10
^ Zadorozhnaya	Yelena	RUS	3.12.77	157/42	2000	5:45.40i	5:40.95i- 08, 5:43.38- 03
3000	8:51.43, 8:41.64i		8:25.40- 01		5000	15:05.24	14:40.47- 01
Zadura	Malgorzata	POL	3.10.82	171/85	HT	68.14	70.36- 10
Zagré	Anne	BEL	13.3.90	176/63	100h	13.09	13.18- 09
Zakari	Joyce	KEN	6.6.86		400	51.73A, 52.18	51.56- 09
Zaldívar	Liuba María	CUB-J	5.4.93	163/53	TJ	13.70	13.01- 10
Zang Milama	Ruddy	GAB	6.6.87	156/46	100	11.09	11.15- 10
Zapounídou	Déspina	GRE	5.10.85	166/55	20kW	1:32:47	1:33:23- 08
* Zaripova	Yuliya	RUS	26.4.86	172/54	1500	4:07.01	4:04.59- 09
					3kSt	9:07.03	9:08.39- 09
Zavgorodnya	Olga	UKR	6.1.83	171/57	800	1:59.56	2:00.87- 10
Zavyalova	Valeriya	RUS	16.1.88		TJ	14.21	13.58- 10
* Zaytseva	Olga	RUS	10.11.84	176/67	LJ	7.01	6.36- 03
* Zelinka	Jessica	CAN	3.9.81	172/62	100h	13.01	12.97- 08
					Hep	6353	6490- 08
Zemaityte	Viktorija	LTU	11.3.85	184/65	Hep	5958	6219- 07
Zemedkun	Belaynesh	ETH	23.12.87		Mar	2:26:17	2:32:13- 10
Zhang Guirong		SIN	5.2.78	182/95	SP	16.96	18.57- 05
Zhang Li		CHN-J	13.3.93		HT	65.62	66.26- 10
Zhang Li		CHN	17.1.89	174/65	JT	56.08	62.09- 08
Zhang Rong		CHN	5.1.83	174/65	100h	13.06	13.11- 05
* Zhang Wenxiu		CHN	22.3.86	182/108	HT	75.65	74.86- 07
Zhao Jing		CHN-J	18.2.92		20kW	1:32:45	1:32:59- 10
Zheng Xingjuan		CHN	20.3.89	184/60	HJ	1.95	1.95- 09
Zhou Tongmei		CHN	4.4.88		20kW	1:34:42	1:30:35- 05
* Zhu Xiaolin		CHN	20.2.84	166/50	HMar	70:28	70:07- 10
					Mar	2:26:28	2:23:57- 02
Zhudina	Valentyna	UKR	12.3.83		3kSt	9:50.47	
Zhuk	Angelina	RUS	7.2.91		PV	4.30i, 4.25	4.10- 10
Zhukovskaya	Oksana	RUS	12.9.84		LJ	6.60, 6.95w	6.77- 07

Name		Nat	Born	Ht/Wt	Event	2011 Mark	Pre-2011 Best
* Zinurova	Yevgeniya	RUS	16.11.82	164/49	800	1:58.49	1:58.04- 08
					1000	2:36.32i	2:39.55i- 08
Zolotova	Yevgeniya	RUS	28.4.83		1500	4:05.47i	4:02.49- 09
	2000 5:46.16i		6:00.06i- 10		3000	8:58.34i	
Zolotuhina	Nataliya	UKR	4.1.85	180/76	HT	72.22	70.30- 10
Zongo-Filet	Amy	FRA	4.10.80	165/51	TJ	13.77w	14.03- 08

WORLD INDOOR LISTS 2012 – MEN

60 METRES

! In late 2011, # Oversized track (over 200m)

Mark	First	Surname	Nat	Born	Place/Round	Meet	Venue	Date	
6.45A	Trell	Kimmons	USA	13.7.85	1	NC	Albuquerque	26	Feb
6.46	Justin	Gatlin	USA	10.2.82	1	WI	Istanbul	10	Mar
6.47	Lerone	Clarke	JAM	12.6.81	1	GP	Birmingham	18	Feb
6.49	Nesta	Carter	JAM	10.11.85	2	GP	Birmingham	18	Feb
6.50	Asafa	Powell	JAM	23.11.82	1h1	GP	Birmingham	18	Feb
6.52	Jeffery	Demps	USA	8.1.90	1h1	NCAA	Nampa	9	Mar
6.53	Jimmy	Vicaut	FRA	27.2.92	1		Düsseldorf	10	Feb
6.55	Harry	Adams	USA	27.11.89	1		Birmingham, AL	21	Jan
6.55	Yunier	Pérez	CUB	16.2.85	1		Gent	18	Feb
6.55A	Phil	DeRosier	USA	11.4.84	1s1	NC	Albuquerque	26	Feb
6.56	Kemar	Hyman	CAY	11.10.89	2		Birmingham, AL	21	Jan
6.56	Richard	Thompson	TRI	7.6.85	1h1		Fayetteville	11	Feb
6.56	Kim	Collins	SKN	5.4.76	2h1	GP	Birmingham	18	Feb
6.57	Christophe	Lemaitre	FRA	11.6.90	2		Liévin	14	Feb
6.57	Andrew	Riley	JAM	6.9.88	2	NCAA	Nampa	10	Mar
6.58	Ramil	Guliyev	TUR	29.5.90	1		Sumy	13	Jan
6.58A	Ryan	Milus	USA	19.9.90	2		Albuquerque	10	Feb
6.58	Dwain	Chambers	GBR	5.4.78	1	NC	Sheffield	12	Feb
6.58A	Rakieem	Salaam	USA	5.4.90	1h2	NC	Albuquerque	25	Feb
6.58A	DeAngelo	Cherry	USA	1.8.90	3	NC	Albuquerque	26	Feb
6.59	Julian	Reus	GER	29.4.88	1		Chemnitz	27	Jan
6.59	Justyn	Warner	CAN	28.6.87	1		Toronto	29	Jan
6.59	Gerald	Phiri	ZAM	6.10.88	4		Fayetteville	11	Feb
6.59	Hasan	Heidarpoor	IRI	31.1.88	1s1	AsiC	Hangzhou	18	Feb
6.59	Terrell	Wilks	USA	20.12.89	6	GP	Birmingham	18	Feb
6.59A	Joshua	Norman	USA	26.7.80	3s2	NC	Albuquerque	26	Feb
6.59	Maurice	Mitchell	USA	22.12.89	2h1	NCAA	Nampa	9	Mar

Mark	First	Surname	Nat	Born	Date		Mark	First	Surname	Nat	Born	Date	
6.60	Reggie	Dixon	USA	7.6.88	27	Jan	6.61	Marc	Burns	TRI	7.1.83	3	Mar
6.60	Peter	Emelieze	NGR	19.4.88	18	Feb	6.61	Ángel David	Rodriguez	ESP	25.4.80	3	Mar
6.60	Christian	Blum	GER	10.3.87	25	Feb	6.61	Keenan	Brock	USA	1.6.92	9	Mar
6.60	Emmanuel	Biron	FRA	29.7.88	25	Feb	6.61	Clayton	Vaughn	USA	15.5.92	9	Mar
6.61	Keith	Ricks	USA	9.10.90	3	Feb	6.61	Isiah	Young	USA	5.1.90	9	Mar
6.61	Richard	Kilty	GBR	2.9.89	4	Feb	6.61	Michael	Granger	USA	17.3.91	9	Mar
6.61	Andrew	Robertson	GBR	17.12.90	12	Feb	6.62	Reza	Ghasemi	IRI	24.7.87	19	Jan
6.61	Michael	LeBlanc	CAN	25.2.87	19	Feb	6.62	Simone	Collio	ITA	27.12.79	4	Feb
6.61A	Calesio	Newman	USA	20.8.86	26	Feb	6.62	Keston	Bledman	TRI	8.3.88	11	Feb
6.61A	Cordero	Gray	USA	9.5.89	26	Feb	6.62	Michael	Frater	JAM	6.10.82	14	Feb

200 METRES

Mark	First	Surname	Nat	Born	Place/Round	Meet	Venue	Date	
20.39	Ameer	Webb	USA	19.3.91	1h2	NCAA	Nampa	9	Mar
20.50A	Demetrius	Pinder	BAH	13.2.89	1		Albuquerque	3	Feb
20.58	Lalonde	Gordon	TRI	25.11.88	1		Boston (Allston)	28	Jan
20.58A	Gil	Roberts	USA	15.3.89	1r1		Albuquerque	10	Feb
20.60	Maurice	Mitchell	USA	22.12.89	1h3	NCAA	Nampa	9	Mar
20.62	Akheem	Gauntlett	USA	26.8.90	1r1	NCAA	Nampa	9	Mar

Mark	First	Surname	Nat	Born	Date		Mark	First	Surname	Nat	Born	Date	
20.66	Anaso	Jobodwana	RSA	30.7.92	9	Mar	20.77	Horatio	Williams	USA	28.8.89	9	Mar
20.77	Kind	Butler	USA	8.4.88	9	Mar	20.79	LaShawn	Butler	USA	3.2.87	2	Mar

400 METRES

Mark	First	Surname	Nat	Born	Place/Round	Meet	Venue	Date	
45.11	Nery	Brenes	CRC	25.9.85	1	WI	Istanbul	10	Mar
45.19	Kirani	James	GRN	1.9.92	1		Fayetteville	11	Feb
45.34	Demetrius	Pinder	BAH	13.2.89	2	WI	Istanbul	10	Mar
45.39A	Gil	Roberts	USA	15.3.89	1		Albuquerque	10	Feb
45.71	Nigel	Levine	GBR	30.4.89	1rA	GP	Birmingham	18	Feb
45.72	Frankie	Wright	USA	1.2.85	1r1	Tyson	Fayetteville	10	Feb
45.73	Calvin	Smith	USA	10.12.87	2r1		Fayetteville	11	Feb
45.77	Tony	McQuay	USA	16.4.90	1r2	NCAA	Nampa	10	Mar
45.82	Brycen	Spratling	USA	10.3.92	2r2	NCAA	Nampa	10	Mar
45.88	Richard	Buck	GBR	14.11.86	1rB	GP	Birmingham	18	Feb
45.90	Christopher	Brown	BAH	15.10.78	3	WI	Istanbul	10	Mar
45.93	Michael	Berry	USA	10.12.91	1r1	NCAA	Nampa	10	Mar

Mark	First	Surname	Nat	Born	Date		Mark	First	Surname	Nat	Born	Date	
45.96	Tabarie	Henry	ISV	1.12.87	10	Mar	46.14	Pavel	Maslák	CZE	21.2.91	18	Feb
46.04	Marek	Niit	EST	9.8.87	10	Mar	46.17A	Manteo	Mitchell	USA	6.7.87	26	Feb
46.12	Errol	Nolan	USA	18.8.91	11	Feb	46.19	Torrin	Lawrence	USA	11.4.89	9	Mar

46.19   Caleb   Williams   USA   14.12.90   9 Mar | 46.20   Conrad   Williams   GBR   20.3.82   18 Feb

Oversized track
46.01   Torrin   Lawrence   USA   11.4.89   25 Feb | 46.10   Tavaris   Tate   USA   21.12.90   3 Mar
46.06   Najee   Glass   USA-J   12.6..94   26 Feb | 46.16   Amaechi   Morton   NGR   30.10.89   25 Feb
46.07   Aldrich   Bailey   USA-J   6.2.94   26 Feb | 46.17   Thomas   Murdaugh   USA   25.9.89   3 Mar

500m: 1:00.63   Brycen   Spratling   USA   10.3.92   1   Big East   New York (Armory)   19 Feb
600y: 1:07.66#   Harun   Abda   USA   1.1.90   1   Ames   11 Feb

600 METRES

1:15.26   Adam   Kszczot   POL   2.9.89   1rA   Winter   Moskva   5 Feb
1:15.86   Harun   Abda   USA   1.1.90   1   Big 10   Lincoln   25 Feb

1:16.08 Yuriy   Borzakovskiy   RUS   12.4.81   5 Feb | 1:16.23 Antonio Manuel Reina   ESP   13.6.81   3 Mar

800 METRES

1:44.57   Adam   Kszczot   POL   2..9.89   1   Liévin   14 Feb
1:45.40   Mohammed   Aman   ETH-J   10.1.94   1   GP   Birmingham   18 Feb
1:45.41   Marcin   Lewandowski   POL   13.6.87   2   GP   Birmingham   18 Feb
1:45.71#   Ismail Ahmed   Ismail   SUD   10.9.84   1   Mustasaari   7 Feb
1:45.75   Boaz   Lalang   KEN   8.2.89   3   GP   Birmingham   18 Feb
1:45.96   Timothy   Kitum   KEN-J   20.11.94   2   Liévin   14 Feb
1:46.08   Yuriy   Borzakovskiy   RUS   12.4.81   3   Liévin   14 Feb
1:46.33   Joe   Thomas   GBR   29.1.88   4   Stockholm   23 Feb
1:46.53   Andrew   Osagie   GBR   19.2.88   5   GP   Birmingham   18 Feb
1:46.64#   Edward   Kemboi   KEN   12.12.91   1   Ames   3 Mar
1:46.65   Andreas   Rapatz   AUT   5.9.86   1   Wien   11 Feb

1:46.78 Jackson   Kivuva   KEN   11.8.88   14 Feb | 1:47.34 Selasi   Lumax   USA   1.8.90   26 Feb
1:46.97# Harun   Abda   USA   1.1.90   28 Jan | 1:47.36 Tevan   Everett   USA   27.7.87   11 Feb
1:46.98# David   Pachuta   USA   21.6.89   28 Jan | 1:47.36 Antonio Manuel Reina   ESP   13.6.81   18 Feb
1:47.11 Michael   Rutt   USA   28.10.87   11 Feb | 1:47.37 Mohamed   Al-Azimi   KUW   16.6.82   19 Feb
1:47.14 Joey   Roberts   USA   17.4.90   28 Jan | 1:47.43 Ben   Scheetz   USA   5.6.90   26 Feb
1:47.19 Jan   Van Den Broeck   BEL   11.3.89   7 Jan | 1:47.50 Andreas   Bube   DEN   13.7.87   18 Feb
1:47.22 Sean   Obinwa   USA   4.1.91   28 Jan | 1:47.52 Michael   Preble   USA   15.4.90   11 Feb
1:47.22 Richard   Kiplagat   KEN   3.7.84   18 Feb | 1:47.41 Michael   Rutt   USA   28.10.87   26 Feb
1:47.23 Jakub   Holusa   CZE   20.2.88   10 Mar | 1:47.44 Mario   Scapini   ITA   2.2.89   11 Feb
 | 1:47.54# Joey   Roberts   USA   17.4.90   5 Mar

1000 METRES

2:19.53 Robert   Creese   USA-J   30.8.93   14 Jan | 2:19.78 Tevan   Everett   USA   13.1.87   13 Jan

1500 METRES

3:34.10   Abdelaati   Iguider   MAR   25.3.87   1   Liévin   14 Feb
3:34.65   Bethwell   Birgen   KEN   6.8.88   1   Karlsruhe   12 Feb
3:34.70   Nixon   Chepseba   KEN   12.12.90   1   GP   Birmingham   18 Feb
3:34.76   Ilham   Özbilen   TUR   5.3.90   2   Karlsruhe   12 Feb
3:34.89   Mekonnen   Gebremehdin   ETH   11.10.88   3   GP   Birmingham   18 Feb
3:35.26   Silas   Kiplagat   KEN   20.8.89   3   Liévin   14 Feb
3:35.49   Ismael   Kombich   KEN   16.10.85   4   Liévin   14 Feb
3:36.20   Bernard   Lagat   USA   12.12.74   4   GP   Birmingham   18 Feb
3:36.43   Collins   Cheboi   KEN   25.9.87   4   Karlsruhe   12 Feb
3:36.88   Mohamed   Al-Garni   QAT   2.7.92   4   Düsseldorf   10 Feb
3:36.96   Daniel Kipchirchir Komen   KEN   27.11.84   5   Liévin   14 Feb
3:37.03   Amine   Laâlou   MAR   13.5.82   3   Stockholm   23 Feb
3:37.08   Aman   Wote (Wetiya)   ETH   18.4.84   4   Stockholm   23 Feb
3:37.16   Andrew   Baddeley   GBR   20.6.82   5   GP   Birmingham   18 Feb
3:37.61   Augustine   Choge   KEN   21.1.87   6   GP   Birmingham   18 Feb
3:37.76   Marcin   Lewandowski   POL   13.6.87   7   Liévin   14 Feb
3:37.95   Dawit   Wolde   ETH   19.5.91   5   Düsseldorf   10 Feb
3:38.03   James   Brewer   GBR   18.6.88   7   GP   Birmingham   18 Feb
3:38.22   Gideon   Gathimba   KEN   9.3.80   5   Karlsruhe   12 Feb
3:38.51   Yoann   Kowal   FRA   28.5.87   5   Stockholm   23 Feb
3:38.92+   Matthew   Centrowitz   USA   18.10.89   1   in 1M   New York (Armory)   11 Feb
3:38.99   Andreas   Vojta   AUT   9.6.89   1   Wien   31 Jan

3:39.03 Mo   Farah   GBR   23.3.83   28 Jan | 3:39.90 Francisco Javier Abad   ESP   18.8.81   4 Feb
3:39.06 Grégory   Beugnet   FRA   14.9.87   10 Feb | 3:39.92 Yegor   Nikolayev   RUS   12.2.88   5 Feb
3:39.15+ Miles   Batty   USA   1,6,87   11 Feb | 3:40.20 Aleksey   Popov   RUS   17.6.87   5 Feb
3:39.36 Yohan   Durand   FRA   14.5.85   29 Feb | 3:40.21 Abdellah   Haidane   MAR   28.3.89   29 Feb
3:39.42 Mehdi   Baala   FRA   17.8.78   14 Feb | 3:40.28+ Erik   van Ingen   USA   25.8.89   11 Feb
3:39.51 Ayanleh   Souleiman   DJI   3.12.92   9 Mar | 3:40.31 Manuel   Olmedo   ESP   17.5.83   4 Feb
3:39.54+ Silas   Kisorio   KEN   8.1.85   11 Feb | 3:40.41 Carsten   Schlangen   GER   31.12.80   12 Feb
3:39.68 Zebene   Alemayehu   ETH   4.9.92   29 Feb | 3:40.48+ David   McCarthy   IRL   16.7.83   11 Feb
3:39.71+ Garrett   Heath   USA   3.11.85   11 Feb | 3:40.53 Florian   Carvalho   FRA   9.3.89   29 Feb
3:39.73 Valentin   Smirnov   RUS   13.2.86   5 Feb | 3:40.61 Álvaro   Rodríguez   ESP   25.5.87   12 Feb
3:39.74 Soresa   Fida   ETH-J   27.5..93   27 Jan | 3:40.62+ Chris   O'Hare   GBR   23.11.90   11 Feb
 | 3:40.65+ Ciaran   O'Lionaird   IRL   11.4.88   4 Feb

1 MILE

3:52.63   Silas   Kiplagat   KEN   20.8.89   1   Fayetteville   11 Feb
3:52.66   Caleb   Ndiku   KEN   9.10.92   2   Fayetteville   11 Feb
3:53.92   Matthew   Centrowitz   USA   18.10.89   1   Mill   New York (Armory)   11 Feb

3:53.93	Daniel Kipchirchir Komen		KEN	27.11.84	3		Fayetteville	11 Feb
3:54.08	Russell	Brown	USA	6.3.85	4		Fayetteville	11 Feb
3:54.49	Amine	Laâlou	MAR	13.5.82	5		Fayetteville	11 Feb
3:54.54	Miles	Batty	USA	1.6.87	2	Mill	New York (Armory)	11 Feb
3:54.76	Ciaran	O'Lionaird	IRL	11.4.88	6		Fayetteville	11 Feb
3:55.09	Lawi	Lalang	KEN	15.6.91	1		Fayetteville	28 Jan
3:55.24	Garrett	Heath	USA	3.11.85	3	Mill	New York (Armory)	11 Feb
3:55.47	Jeff	See	USA	6.6.86	7		Fayetteville	11 Feb
3:55.75	David	McCarthy	IRL	16.7.83	1		Boston (Allston)	28 Jan
3:55.84	Silas	Kisorio	KEN	8.1.85	4	Mill	New York (Armory)	11 Feb
3:56.37	Erik	van Ingen	USA	25.8.89	5	Mill	New York (Armory)	11 Feb
3:56.40	Taylor	Milne	CAN	14.9.81	2		Boston (Roxbury)	4 Feb

3:56.63	Chris	O'Hare	GBR	23.11.90	11 Feb		3:57.86	Sam	McEntee	AUS	3.2.92	28 Jan
3:56.85	Cory	Leslie	USA	24.10.89	28 Jan		3:57.91	Brian	Gagnon	USA	8.5.87	11 Feb
3:57.10	Galen	Rupp	USA	8.5.86	4 Feb		3:57.92	James	Brewer	GBR	18.6.88	21 Jan
3:57.16	Cameron	Levins	CAN	28.3.89	11 Feb		3:57.92	Mohammed Farah		GBR	23.3.83	4 Feb
3:57.22	Andrew	Baddeley	GBR	20.6.82	21 Jan		3:57.92	Leonel	Manzano	USA	12.9.84	11 Feb
3:57.59#	John	Mickowski	USA	24.4.86	3 Mar		3:58.14	Robert	Novak	USA	20.3.86	11 Feb
3:57.83	Richard	Peters	GBR	18.2.90	11 Feb		3:58.23	Andrew	Bayer	USA	3.2.90	27 Jan

3000 METRES

7:29.94	Augustine	Choge	KEN	21.1.87	1		Karlsruhe	12 Feb
7:29.94	Edwin	Soi	KEN	3.3.86	2		Karlsruhe	12 Feb
7:31.23	Yenew	Alamirew	ETH	27.5.90	3		Karlsruhe	12 Feb
7:32.03	Eliud	Kipchoge	KEN	5.11.84	4		Karlsruhe	12 Feb
7:32.89	Isiah	Koech	KEN	19.12.93	2		Liévin	14 Feb
7:34.14	Dejene	Gebremeskel	ETH	24.11.89	2		Stockholm	23 Feb
7:34.81	Thomas	Longosiwa	KEN	14.1.82	4		Liévin	14 Feb
7:35.42	Caleb	Ndiku	KEN	9.10.92	4		Stockholm	23 Feb
7:37.0+	Tariku	Bekele	ETH	21.1.87	1+	GP	Birmingham	18 Feb
7:37.4+	Mo	Farah	GBR	23.3.83	3+	GP	Birmingham	18 Feb
7:37.4+	Moses	Kipsiro	UGA	2.9.86	4+	GP	Birmingham	18 Feb
7:38.13	Arne	Gabius	GER	22.3.81	5		Karlsruhe	12 Feb
7:39.07	Brimin	Kipruto	KEN	31.7.85	5		Liévin	14 Feb
7:39.09	Abera	Kuma	ETH	31.8.90	7		Stockholm	23 Feb
7:39.70	Gideon	Gathimba	KEN	9.3.80	8		Stockholm	23 Feb
7:39.78	Yitayal	Atnafu	ETH-J	20.1..93	6		Karlsruhe	12 Feb
7:41.02	Silas	Kiplagat	KEN	20.8.89	3		Boston (Roxbury)	4 Feb
7:41.44	Bernard	Lagat	USA	12.12.74	1	WI	Istanbul	11 Mar
7:41.48	Hayle	Ibrahimov	AZE	18.1.90	8		Karlsruhe	12 Feb
7:42.49	Polat	Arikan	TUR	12.12.90	2	Balk C	Istanbul	18 Feb
7:43.08#	Ryan	Hill	USA	31.1.90	1r1		Seattle	11 Feb
7:43.35	Abiyot	Abinet	ETH	1.1.87	9		Stockholm	23 Feb
7:43.88	Bilisuma	Shugi	BRN	19.7.89	1	AsiC	Hangzhou	19 Feb
7:44.08	Hagos	Gebrehiwot	ETH-J	11.5.94	4		Boston (Roxbury)	4 Feb
7:44.16	Lopez	Lomong	USA	1.1.85	6	WI	Istanbul	11 Mar
7:44.26	Yoann	Kowal	FRA	28.5.87	7		Liévin	14 Feb

7:44.45#	Andrew	Bumbalough	USA	14.3.87	3 Mar		7:46.95	Paul	Koech	KEN	.91	14 Feb
7:44.46	Yohan	Durand	FRA	14.5.85	28 Jan		7:47.09	Andrew	Baddeley	GBR	20.6.82	4 Feb
7:44.48#	Lawi	Lalang	KEN	15.6.91	25 Feb		7:47.88	Mourad	Amdouni	FRA	21.1.88	28 Jan
7:44.63#	Diego	Estrada	USA	12.12.89	11 Feb		7:48.04	Alemu	Bekele	BRN	90	19 Feb
7:45.75	Cameron	Levins	CAN	28.3.89	4 Feb		7:48.23	Craig	Mottram	AUS	18.6.80	11 Mar
7:45.80	Garrett	Heath	USA	3.11.85	4 Feb		7:48.25#	Cameron	Levins	CAN	28.3.89	28 Jan
7:46.17	Mohamed	Al-Garni	QAT	2.7.92	19 Feb		7:48.62	Florian	Carvalho	FRA	9.3.89	14 Feb
7:46.19	Matthew	Centrowitz	USA	18.10.89	4 Feb		7:48.64	Elroy	Gelant	RSA	25.8.86	11 Mar
7:46.42#	Evan	Jager	USA	8.3.89	3 Mar		7:48.96	Benson	Seurei	KEN	27.3.88	2 Feb
7:46.81	Chris	Derrick	USA	17.10.90	10 Mar		7:48.96	Dawit	Wolde	ETH	19.5.91	14 Feb
7:46.89	Mekonnen	Gebremehdin	ETH	11.10.88	23 Feb		7:49.11#	Ross	Millington	GBR	19.9.89	11 Feb

2 MILES

Birmingham 18 Feb: 1. Eliud Kipchoge 8:07.39, 2. Mo Farah 8:08.07, 3. Moses Kipsiro 8:08.16, 4. Tariku Bekele 8:08.27. 5, Arne Gabius 8:10.78.   Fayetteville 11 Feb: 1. Galen Rupp 8:09.72

5000 METRES

12:58.67	Thomas	Longosiwa	KEN	14.1.82	1		Düsseldorf	10 Feb
13:02.36	Isiah	Koech	KEN-J	19.12.93	2		Düsseldorf	10 Feb
13:02.69	Paul Kipsiele	Koech	KEN	10.11.81	3		Düsseldorf	10 Feb
13:04.18	Yitayal	Atnafu	ETH-J	20.1.93	4		Düsseldorf	10 Feb
13:07.15	Bernard	Lagat	USA	12.12.74	1	Mill	New York (Armory)	11 Feb
13:08.28	Lawi	Lalang	KEN	15.6.91	2	Mill	New York (Armory)	11 Feb
13:10.96	Albert	Rop	KEN	20.12.94	5		Düsseldorf	10 Feb
13:11.44	Japhet	Korir	KEN-J	.93	6		Düsseldorf	10 Feb
13:12.55	Polat	Arikan	TUR	12.12.90	7		Düsseldorf	10 Feb
13:13.74	Stephen	Sambu	KEN	7.7.88	3	Mill	New York (Armory)	11 Feb
13:19.54	Leonard	Korir	KEN	10.12.86	4	Mill	New York (Armory)	11 Feb
13:19.58	Chris	Derrick	USA	17.10.90	5	Mill	New York (Armory)	11 Feb

13:22.44	Andrew	Baddeley	GBR	20.6.82	11 Feb
13:23.61	Juan Luis	Barrios	MEX	24.6.83	11 Feb

13:29.94#	Chris	Thompson	GBR	17.4.81	10 Feb
13:30.85#	Kevin	Chelimo	KEN	14.2.83	10 Feb

50 Metres Hurdles: New York 28 Jan: 1. Terrence Trammell 6.45, 2. David Oliver 6.50, 3. Omo Osaghae 6.52

60 METRES HURDLES

Mark	First	Last	Nat	DOB	Pos	Meet	Venue	Date
7.40A	Dexter	Faulk	USA	14.4.84	1h3	NC	Albuquerque	25 Feb
7.41		Liu Xiang	CHN	13.7.83	1	GP	Birmingham	18 Feb
7.43A	Aries	Merritt	USA	24.7.85	1	NC	Albuquerque	26 Feb
7.46A	Kevin	Craddock	USA	25.6.87	2	NC	Albuquerque	26 Feb
7.49	Jarret	Eaton	USA	24.6.89	1		University Park	27 Jan
7.50	Dayron	Robles	CUB	19.11.86	2	GP	Birmingham	18 Feb
7.51	David	Oliver	USA	24.4.82	1	Mill	New York (Armory)	11 Feb
7.51A	Terrence	Trammell	USA	23.11.78	3	NC	Albuquerque	26 Feb
7.52	Konstantin	Shabanov	RUS	17.11.89	1h1		Karlsruhe	12 Feb
7.53	Andrew	Riley	JAM	6.9.88	1		Fayetteville	11 Feb
7.53A	Omo	Osaghae	USA	18.5.88	1h1	NC	Albuquerque	25 Feb
7.53	Pascal	Martinot-Lagarde	FRA	22.9.91	3	WI	Istanbul	11 Mar
7.54	Jeff	Porter	USA	27.11.85	1		Karlsruhe	12 Feb
7.54	Fred	Townsend	USA	19.2.82	1		Val-de-Reuil	18 Feb
7.55	Devon	Hill	USA	26.10.89	2	NCAA	Nampa	10 Mar
7.55	Barrett	Nugent	USA	29.1.90	3	NCAA	Nampa	10 Mar
7.56	Joel	Brown	USA	31.1.80	2		Liévin	14 Feb
7.56	Sergey	Shubenkov	RUS	4.10.90	1	NC-23	Saransk	2 Mar
7.56	Andrew	Pozzi	GBR	15.5.92	2s1	WI	Istanbul	11 Mar
7.57	Emanuele	Abate	ITA	8.7.85	1		Magglingen	4 Feb
7.57	Orlando	Ortega	CUB	29.7.91	1r2		Metz	29 Feb
7.58	Helge	Schwarzer	GER	26.11.85	1		Kirchberg	4 Feb

7.59	Ronald	Ash	USA	2.7.88	21 Jan
7.59	Gregor	Traber	GER	2.12.92	25 Feb
7.60	Spencer	Adams	USA	10.9.89	10 Mar
7.61	Cédric	Lavanne	FRA	13.11.80	29 Feb
7.63	Maksim	Lynsha	BLR	6.4.85	5 Feb
7.63	Konstadínos	Douvalídis	GRE	10.3.87	22 Feb
7.64	Lehann	Fourie	RSA	16.2.87	4 Feb
7.64	Yevgeniy	Borisov	RUS	7.3.84	22 Feb
7.65	Thomas	Delmestre	FRA	31.3.91	18 Feb
7.65	Artur	Noga	POL	2.5.88	26 Feb

7.66A	Ashton	Eaton	USA	21.1.88	25 Feb
7.66	Edward	Lovett	USA	25.6.92	9 Mar
7.67 OUT	David	Payne	USA	24.7.82	28 Jan
7.67	Lawrence	Clarke	GBR	12.3.90	28 Jan
7.67	Balázs	Baji	HUN	9.6.89	4 Feb
7.67A	Drew	Brunson	USA	4.4.86	25 Feb
7.67	Richard	Phillips	JAM	26.1.83	26 Feb
7.67	Caleb	Cross	USA	31.5.91	9 Mar
7.68A	Dominic	Berger	USA	19.5.86	25 Feb
7.68	Dominik	Bochenek	POL	14.5.87	26 Feb

HIGH JUMP

Mark	First	Last	Nat	DOB	Pos	Meet	Venue	Date
2.37	Moataz Essa	Barshim	QAT	24.6.91	1	AsiC	Hangzhou	19 Feb
2.36	Andrey	Silnov	RUS	9.9.84	1	Winter	Moskva	5 Feb
2.35	Aleksey	Dmitrik	RUS	12.4.84	1		Hustopece	28 Jan
2.34	Robert	Grabarz	GBR	3.10.87	1		Wuppertal	21 Jan
2.34	Ivan	Ukhov	RUS	29.3.86	1	NC	Moskva	23 Feb
2.33	Dimítrios	Hondrokoúkis	GRE	26.1.88	1	WI	Istanbul	11 Mar
2.32	Jesse	Williams	USA	27.12.83	1	Mill	New York (Armory)	11 Feb
2.32	Raúl	Spank	GER	13.7.88	1	NC	Karlsruhe	26 Feb
2.31	Eric	Kynard	USA	3.2.91	1		Manhattan KS	10 Dec
2.31	Andriy	Protsenko	UKR	20.5.88	1		Lviv	20 Jan
2.31	Aleksandr	Shustov	RUS	13.8.84	1		Volgograd	21 Jan
2.31	Samson	Oni	GBR	25.6.81	3=		Hustopece	28 Jan
2.31	Jaroslav	Bába	CZE	2.9.84	5		Hustopece	28 Jan
2.31	Konstadinos	Baniotis	GRE	6.11.86	3=		Banská Bystrica	8 Feb
2.31	Michal	Kabelka	CZE	4.2.85	3=		Banská Bystrica	8 Feb
2.31	Silvano	Chesani	ITA	17.7.88	1	NC	Ancona	26 Feb
2.31	Trevor	Barry	BAH	14.6.83	8	WI	Istanbul	11 Mar
2.30	Andrey	Patrakov	RUS	7.11.89	2		Moskva	1 Feb
2.30	Sergey	Mudrov	RUS	8.9.90	1		Moskva	19 Feb
2.28	Peter	Horák	SVK	7.12.83	6		Hustopece	28 Jan

2.27	Viktor	Shapoval	UKR	17.10.79	20 Jan
2.27	Filippo	Campioli	ITA	21.2.82	21 Jan
2.27	James	Harris	USA	15.9.91	4 Feb
2.27	Viktor	Ninov	BUL	19.6.88	16 Feb
2.27	Piotr	Sleboda	POL	22.1.87	16 Feb
2.27	Marius	Dumitrache	ROU	15.6.89	24 Feb
2.26	Mihai	Donisan	ROU	24.7.88	15 Jan
2.26	Andra	Manson	USA	30.4.84	28 Jan
2.26A	Olivér	Harsányi	HUN	20.3.87	10 Feb
2.26A	Bryan	McBride	USA	10.12.91	10 Feb
2.26	Keith	Moffatt	USA	20.6.84	11 Feb
2.26	Abdoulaye	Diarra	FRA	27.5.88	11 Feb
2.26	Major	Clay	USA	24.12.88	17 Feb
2.26	Rozle	Prezelj	SLO	26.9.79	25 Feb

2.26A	James	Nieto	USA	2.11.76	25 Feb
2.26	Mickaël	Hanany	FRA	25.3.83	26 Feb
2.26	Marco	Fassinotti	ITA	29.4.89	26 Feb
2.26	Matthias	Haverney	GER	21.7.85	26 Feb
2.26	James	White	USA	22.1.92	3 Mar
2.26	Majed El Dein Ghazal		SYR	21.4.87	10 Mar
2.25	Nikita	Anishchenkov	RUS	25.7.92	29 Dec
2.25	Sergey	Milokumov	RUS	13.11.87	21 Jan
2.25	Yuriy	Krymarenko	UKR	11.8.83	28 Jan
2.25	Dusty	Jonas	USA	19.4.86	28 Jan
2.25	Janick	Klausen	DEN-J	3.4.93	29 Jan
2.25	Bohdan	Bondarenko	UKR	30.8.89	8 Feb
2.25	Matus	Bubenik	SVK	14.11.89	8 Feb
2.25	Rauvydas	Stanys	LTU	3.2.87	12 Feb
2.25	Richard	Robertson	USA	19.9.90	25 Feb

POLE VAULT

Mark	First	Last	Nat	DOB	Pos	Meet	Venue	Date
5.95	Renaud	Lavillenie	FRA	18.9.86	1	WI	Istanbul	10 Mar

5.92	Björn	Otto	GER	16.10.77	1		Potsdam	18 Feb
5.90	Dmitriy	Starodubtsev	RUS	3.1.86	1		Chelyabinsk	17 Dec
5.87	Malte	Mohr	GER	24.7.86	2	NC	Karlsruhe	26 Feb
5.86A	Brad	Walker	USA	21.6.81	1	NC	Albuquerque	26 Feb
5.82	Raphael	Holzdeppe	GER	28.9.89	3	NC	Karlsruhe	26 Feb
5.77	Steven	Lewis	GBR	20.5.86	2		Dessau	2 Mar
5.75	Konstadinos	Filippídis	GRE	26.11.86	1	Balk C	Istanbul	18 Feb
5.73	Karsten	Dilla	GER	12.5.89	1		Bad Oeynhausen	3 Mar
5.72	Lukasz	Michalski	POL	2.8.88	1		Bordeaux	28 Jan
5.72	Lazaro	Borges	CUB	19.6.86	4	Stars	Donetsk	11 Feb
5.72	Romain	Mesnil	FRA	12.6.77	2		Liévin	14 Feb
5.72	Maksym	Mazuryk	UKR	2.4.83	2		Potsdam	18 Feb
5.70	Hendrik	Gruber	GER	28.9.86	1		Metz	29 Feb
5.64		Yang Yansheng	CHN	5.1.88	3		Villeurbanne	20 Jan
5.64	Edi	Maia	POR	10.11.87	1		Pombal	25 Feb
5.62	Denys	Yurchenko	UKR	27.1.78	5	Stars	Donetsk	11 Feb
5.62	Jan	Kudlicka	CZE	29.4.88	1		Praha (Strahov)	15 Feb

5.60	Sergey	Kucheryanu	RUS	30.6.85	9	Jan	5.56	Igor	Bychkov	ESP	7.3.87	18	Feb
5.60	Yevgeniy	Lukyanenko	RUS	23.1.85	14	Jan	5.55	Jere	Bergius	FIN	4.4.87	4	Feb
5.60	Derek	Miles	USA	28.9.72	2	Feb	5.55	Eemeli	Salomäki	FIN	11.10.87	7	Feb
5.60	Hiroki	Ogita	JPN	30.12.87	4	Feb	5.55	Andrew	Sutcliffe	GBR	10.7.91	11	Feb
5.60	Daichi	Sawano	JPN	16.9.80	11	Feb	5.55	Andrew	Irwin	USA-J	23.1.93	9	Mar
5.60	Claudio Michel Stecchi		ITA	23.11.91	25	Feb	5.54	Damiel	Dossévi	FRA	3.2.83	20	Jan
5.60A	Scott	Roth	USA	25.6.88	26	Feb	5.53	Jason	Colwick	USA	25.1.88	11	Feb
5.60A	Mark	Hollis	USA	1.12.84	26	Feb	5.53	Tim	Lobinger	GER	3.9.72	3	Mar
5.60	Marco	Boni	ITA	21.5.84	4	Mar	5.53	Rasmus	Jørgensen	DEN	23.1.89	3	Mar
							5.53	Michel	Frauen	GER	19.1.86	3	Mar

LONG JUMP

8.28	Mauro Vinicius	da Silva	BRA	26.12.86	Q	WI	Istanbul	9 Mar
8.24	Aleksandr	Menkov	RUS	7.12.90	1	Winter	Moskva	5 Feb
8.24	Will	Claye	USA	13.6.91	1	Tyson	Fayetteville	10 Feb
8.23	Henry	Frayne	AUS	14.4.90	2	WI	Istanbul	10 Mar
8.20		Zhang Xiaoyi	CHN	25.5.89	1		Nanjing	13 Feb
8.17		Yun Zhiming	CHN	9.10.88	2		Nanjing	13 Feb
8.16	Ashton	Eaton	USA	21.1.88	1H	WI	Istanbul	9 Mar
8.12	Damar	Forbes	JAM	18.9.90	1cB	Tyson	Fayetteville	10 Feb
8.12	Sebastian	Bayer	GER	11.6.86	1	NC	Karlsruhe	25 Feb
8.10	Marquise	Goodwin	USA	19.11.90	1		Fayetteville	27 Jan
8.10	Luis Felipe	Méliz	ESP	11.8.79	Q	WI	Istanbul	9 Mar
8.09	Alexandr	Cuharenco	MDA	7.3.87	1	NC	Chisinau	3 Feb
8.06	Marquis	Dendy	USA	17.11.92	1	SEC	Lexington	25 Feb
8.05	Louis	Tsátoumas	GRE	12.2.82	1	NC	Athina (Pireás)	21 Feb
8.05	Nicolas	Gomont	FRA	15.9.86	1	NC	Aubière	26 Feb
8.04	Khotso	Mokoena	RSA	6.3.85	2	Winter	Moskva	5 Feb
8.04	J.J.	Jegede	GBR	3.10.85	1	GP	Birmingham	18 Feb
8.03		Tang Gongchen	CHN	24.4.89	3		Nanjing	13 Feb
8.02	Roman	Novotny	CZE	5.1.86	1		Praha (Strahov)	15 Feb
8.01	Eusebio	Cáceres	ESP	10.9.91	1		Antequera	11 Feb
8.01	Kendall	Spencer	USA	24.7.91	1	NCAA	Nampa	9 Mar

8.00	Norris	Frederick	USA	17.2.86	14	Jan	7.96		Xu Jianping	CHN	1.1.90	10	Mar
8.00	Elvijs	Misans	LAT	4.8.89	3	Feb	7.95	Fabrizio	Donato	ITA	14.8.76	25	Feb
8.00	Marcos	Chuva	POR	8.8.89	18	Feb	7.94	Bryce	Lamb	USA	9.11.90	20	Jan
8.00	Yeóryios	Tsákonas	GRE	22.1.88	21	Feb	7.94	Sergey	Morgunov	RUS-J	9.2.93	12	Feb
8.00	Sergey	Nikolayev	RUS	1.9.87	24	Feb	7.94		Zhuang Haitao	CHN	6.1.89	13	Feb
7.99	Michel	Tornéus	SWE	26.5.86	23	Feb	7.94	Andrey	Khaylov	RUS	3.7.89	24	Feb
7.99		Li Jinzhe	CHN	1.9.89	10	Mar	7.94	Salim	Sdiri	FRA	26.10.78	26	Feb
7.98	Ignisious	Gaisah	GHA	20.6.83	10	Feb	7.93	Pavel	Karavayev	RUS	27.8.88	14	Jan
7.97	Ndiss Kaba	Badji	SEN	21.9.83	26	Feb	7.93	Raymond	Higgs	BAH	24.1.91	10	Feb

TRIPLE JUMP

17.70	Will	Claye	USA	13.6.91	1	WI	Istanbul	11 Mar
17.63	Christian	Taylor	USA	18.6.90	2	WI	Istanbul	11 Mar
17.36	Lyukman	Adams	RUS	24.9.88	3	WI	Istanbul	11 Mar
17.28	Fabrizio	Donato	ITA	14.8.76	4	WI	Istanbul	11 Mar
17.28	Daniele	Greco	ITA	1.3.89	5	WI	Istanbul	11 Mar
17.14	Benjamin	Compaoré	FRA	5.8.87	2		Liévin	14 Feb
17.04	Yuriy	Kovalyov	RUS	18.6.91	1	NC-23	Saransk	2 Mar
17.02	Alexis	Copello	CUB	12.8.85	1	NC	Sabadell	26 Feb
17.01		Dong Bin	CHN	22.11.88	1	AsiC	Hangzhou	19 Feb
17.01		Cao Shuo	CHN	8.10.91	2	AsiC	Hangzhou	19 Feb
16.97	Marian	Oprea	ROU	6.6.82	1	NC	Bucuresti	24 Feb
16.92	Aleksey	Fyodorov	RUS	25.5.91	2	NC-23	Saransk	2 Mar
16.87	Muhammad	Halim	ISV	26.10.86	1		Ithaca	3 Dec
16.86	Aleksey	Tsapik	BLR	4.8.88	1		Mogilyov	26 Feb
16.85	Andrea	Chiari	ITA	12.2.91	1	NC	Ancona	26 Feb

Mark	First	Last	Nat	DOB	Pos	Meet	Venue	Date
16.81	Sheryf	El-Sheryf	UKR	2.1.89	1	NC	Sumy	18 Feb
16.75	Fabian	Florant	NED	1.2.83	1		Kenosha	27 Jan
16.75	Omar	Craddock	USA	26.4.91	1	NCAA	Nampa	10 Mar

Mark	First	Last	Nat	DOB	Date
16.74	Arnie David	Girat	CUB	26.8.84	26 Feb
16.72	Harold	Correa	FRA	26.6.88	25 Feb
16.71		Li Yanxi	CHN	26.6.84	14 Feb
16.71	Fabrizio	Schembri	ITA	27.1.81	26 Feb
16.67	Jefferson	Dias Sabino	BRA	4.11.82	10 Mar
16.66	Igor	Spasovkhodskiy	RUS	1.8.79	23 Feb
16.65	Walter	Davis	USA	2.7.79	17 Feb
16.64	Ruslan	Samitov	RUS	11.2.91	2 Mar
16.63	Marcus	Robinson	USA	18.12.88	11 Feb
16.60	Ryan	Grinell	USA	4.2.87	4 Feb
16.60	Dimítrios	Tsiámis	GRE	12,1,82	24 Feb
16.57	Colomba	Fofana	FRA	11.4.77	25 Feb

SHOT

Mark	First	Last	Nat	DOB	Pos	Meet	Venue	Date
22.00	Ryan	Whiting	USA	24.11.86	1	WI	Istanbul	9 Mar
21.88	David	Storl	GER	27.7.90	2	WI	Istanbul	9 Mar
21.87	Reese	Hoffa	USA	8.10.77	1		Chemnitz	27 Jan
21.72	Tomasz	Majewski	POL	30.8.81	3	WI	Istanbul	9 Mar
21.53	Christian	Cantwell	USA	30.9.80	3	NC	Albuquerque	26 Feb
21.27	Adam	Nelson	USA	7.7.75	1		Boston (Roxbury)	4 Feb
20.98	Maksim	Sidorov	RUS	13.5.86	1	NC	Moskva	23 Feb
20.95	Justin	Rodhe	CAN	17.10.84	2		Fayetteville	11 Feb
20.91	Marco	Fortes	POR	26.9.82	1		Pombal	12 Feb
20.86	Jordan	Clarke	USA	10.7.90	1	NCAA	Nampa	9 Mar
20.64	Asmir	Kolasinac	SRB	15.10.84	1		Linz	2 Feb
20.63	Dylan	Armstrong	CAN	15.1.81	3		Fayetteville	11 Feb
20.61	Ivan	Yushkov	RUS	15.1.81	2	NC	Moskva	23 Feb
20.56	Rutger	Smith	NED	9.7.81	1		Apeldoorn	25 Feb
20.54	Zach	Lloyd	USA	10.10.84	1		Provo	20 Jan
20.51	Tim	Nedow	CAN	16.10.90	1	Big East	New York (Armory)	19 Feb
20.50	Jacob	Thormaehlen	USA	13.2.90	2	NCAA	Nampa	9 Mar
20.44	Cory	Martin	USA	22.5.85	2		Boston (Roxbury)	4 Feb
20.44	Kemal	Mesic	BIH	4.8.85	3	NCAA	Nampa	9 Mar
20.41	Soslan	Tsirikhov	RUS	24,11,84	2		Volgograd	21 Jan
20.40	German	Lauro	ARG	2.4.84	Q	WI	Istanbul	9 Mar
20.30	Kurt	Roberts	USA	20.2.88	1		Findlay	3 Feb
20.29	Ryan	Crouser	USA	18.12.92	1		Fayetteville	27 Jan
20.16		Zhang Jun	CHN	11.4.83	1		Nanjing	13 Feb
20.14	Joe	Kovacs	USA	28.6.89	6	NC	Albuquerque	26 Feb
20.10	Candy	Bauer	GER	31.7.86	2		Rochlitz	5 Feb

Mark	First	Last	Nat	DOB	Date
20.08	Stephen	Saenz	MEX	23.8.90	9 Mar
20.05	Valeriy	Kokoyev	RUS	25.7.88	23 Feb
20.02	Lajos	Kürthy	HUN	22.10.86	26 Feb
19.95	Russell	Winger	USA	2.8.84	26 Feb
19.86	Jakub	Giza	POL	26.4.85	18 Feb
19.83	Martin	Premeru	CRO	29.8.90	25 Feb
19.80	Pavel	Lyzhyn	BLR	24.3.81	10 Feb
19.80	Dale	Stevenson	AUS	1.1.88	9 Mar
19.77	Kim	Christensen	DEN	1.4.84	8 Feb
19.75	Anton	Lyuboslavskiy	RUS	26.6.84	22 Jan
19.75	Konstantin	Lyadusov	RUS	2.3.88	23 Feb
19.74	Niklas	Arrhenius	SWE	10.9.82	20 Jan
19.74	Carlos	Véliz	CUB	12.8.87	25 Feb
19.71!	Luke	Pinkelman	USA	5.5.88	10 Dec
19.70	Denis	Kurtsev	RUS	88	5 Feb
19.70	Borja	Vivas	ESP	26.5.84	19 Feb
19.70	Mihaíl	Stamatóyiannis	GRE	20.5.82	21 Feb
19.67	Ralf	Bartels	GER	21.2.78	20 Jan
19.67	Hayden	Baillio	USA	22.7.91	25 Feb
19.64	Andriy	Semenov	UKR	4.7.84	16 Feb
19.60	Blake	Eaton	USA	2.5.89	4 Feb

35 LB WEIGHT

Mark	First	Last	Nat	DOB	Pos	Meet	Venue	Date
25.18	A.G.	Kruger	USA	18.2.79	1		Findlay	20 Jan
23.91	Michael	Mai	USA	27.7.77	2	NC	Albuquerque	25 Feb
23.37	Garland	Porter	USA	10.2.82	3	NC	Albuquerque	25 Feb
23.19	Conor	McCullough	USA	31.1.91	1		Boston (Allston)	11 Feb
23.05	Marcel	Lomnicky	SVK	6.7.87	1		Blacksburg	3 Feb
23.04	Alexander	Ziegler	GER	7.7.87	2		Blacksburg	3 Feb
22.99	Ryan	Loughney	USA	21.8.89	2		Findlay	3 Feb
22.66	J.C.	Lambert	USA	12.4.90	1		Carbondale	13 Jan

Mark	First	Last	Nat	DOB	Date
22.40	Mattias	Jons	SWE	19.11.82	1 Mar
22.10	Michael	Lauro	USA	1.7.89	2 Mar
22.03	Brian	Tolcser	USA	14.10.82	14 Jan
21.95	Micah	Hegerle	USA	2.10.89	17 Feb

HEPTATHLON

Points	First	Last	Nat	DOB	Pos	Meet	Venue	Date
6645	Ashton	Eaton	USA	21.1.88	1	WI	Istanbul	10 Mar
	6.79	8.16	14.56	2.03	7.68	5.20	2:32.77	
6237	Oleksiy	Kasyanov	UKR	26.8.85	1		Zaporozhye	28 Jan
	6.83	7.62	15.38	2.05	7.92	4.80	2:45.44	
6205	Andrey	Kravchenko	BLR	4.1.86	1	NC	Gomel	27 Jan
	7.24	7.75	14.91	2.10	8.09	5.00	2:41.22	
6138	Curtis	Beach	USA	22.7.90	1	NCAA	Nampa	10 Mar
	7.03	7.52	12.62	1.99	8.15	4.90	2:23.63	
6105	Roman	Sebrle	CZE	26.11.74	1	NC	Praha (Strom)	12 Feb
	7.19	7.67	15.67	2.11	8.22	4.80	2:46.82	
6082	Japheth	Cato	USA	25.12.90	2	NCAA	Nampa	10 Mar
	7.08	7.61	12.54	2.08	7.91	5.20	2:49.34	
6071	Artem	Lukyanenko	RUS	30.1.90	1	NC	Moskva	7 Feb
	6.99	7.26	15.05	2.06	7.97	4.80	2:44.94	

Score	First	Last	Nat	DOB	Pos	Meet	Venue	Date
6043	Vasiliy	Kharlamov	RUS	8.1.86	2	NC	Moskva	7 Feb
7.08	7.30	15.75	1.94	8.25 5.20	2:44.36			
6022	Gunnar	Nixon	USA-J	13.1.93	1		Fayetteville	28 Jan
7.10	7.53	13.97	2.15	8.21 4.50	2:40.15			
5985	Ilya	Shkurenyov	RUS	11.1.91	1		Krasnodar	14 Jan
7.12	7.50	13.28	2.06	8.17 5.20	2:50.89			
5971	Gray	Horn	USA	18.2.90	1		College Station	28 Jan
6.96	7.34	13.78	2.07	8.09 4.66	2:44.09			
5951	Adam Sebastian	Helcelet	CZE	27.10.91	2	NC	Praha (Strom)	12 Feb
7.06	7.35	14.73	2.05	8.08 4.80	2:50.75			
5948	Mikhail	Logvinenko	RUS	19.4.84	1	NCp	Belgorod	28 Feb
7.15	7.16	13.95	2.00	8.08 5.10	2:43.46			
5931	Aleksandr	Frolov	RUS	5.3.87	2		Krasnodar	14 Jan
7.14	7.28	15.15	2.09	8.47 5.00	2:51.15			
5930	Kevin	Lazas	USA	25.1.92	3	NCAA	Nampa	10 Mar
7.03	7.45	14.26	1.96	8.35 5.20	2:50.85			
5928	Dmitriy	Karpov	KAZ	23.7.81	1	AsiC	Hangzhou	19 Feb
7.20	7.10	16.26	2.00	8.09 5.00	2:52.61			
5908	Eric	Broadbent	USA	5.8.85	1	NC	Bloomington	4 Mar
7.05	7.06	13.70	2.18	8.14 4.30	2:39.17			

Score	First	Last	Nat	DOB	Date		Score	First	Last	Nat	DOB	Date
5894	Björn	Barrefors	SWE	27.10.87	10 Mar		5855	Sergey	Sviridov	RUS	20.10.90	28 Feb
5891	Bastien	Auzeil	FRA	22.10.89	26 Feb		5837	Yevgeniy	Sarantsev	RUS	5.8.88	28 Feb
5880	Romain	Martin	FRA	12.7.88	10 Mar		5813	Steffen	Kahlert	GER	30.5.87	29 Jan
5873	Mihail	Dudas	SRB	15.11.89	19 Feb		5809	David	Klech	USA	29.4.88	4 Mar
5873	Cory	Holman	USA	11.288	10 Mar		5803	Dominik	Distelberger	AUT	16.3.90	4 Feb
5868	Petter	Olson	SWE	14.2.91	10 Mar		5799	Gaël	Quérin	FRA	26.6.87	26 Feb
							5796	Nicholas	Adcock	USA	2.4.88	4 Mar

5000 METRES WALK

Time	First	Last	Nat	DOB	Pos	Meet	Venue	Date
18:16.54	Valeriy	Borchin	RUS	11.9.86	1	Winter	Moskva	5 Feb
18:17.13	Vladimir	Kanaykin	RUS	21.3.85	2	Winter	Moskva	5 Feb
18:26.82	Sergey	Bakulin	RUS	13.11.86	3	Winter	Moskva	5 Feb
18:34.56	Matej	Tóth	SVK	10.2.83	1		Wien	11 Feb
18:44.45	Ruslan	Dmytrenko	UKR	22.3.86	4	Winter	Moskva	5 Feb
18:47.80	Yohann	Diniz	FRA	1.1.78	5	Winter	Moskva	5 Feb
18:58.81	Denis	Nizhegorodov	RUS	26.7.80	6	Winter	Moskva	5 Feb
19:06.58	Robert	Heffernan	IRL	20.2.78	1	NC	Belfast	11 Feb

Time	First	Last	Nat	DOB	Date		Time	First	Last	Nat	DOB	Date
19:08.84	João	Vieira	POR	20.2.76	28 Jan		19:21.33	Bertrand	Moulinet	FRA	6.1.87	19 Feb
19:14.86	Anton	Kucmin	SVK	7.6.84	11 Feb		19:22.15	Rafal	Sikora	POL	17.2.87	26 Feb
19:20.12	Dawid	Tomala	POL	27.8.89	26 Feb		19:22.80	Giorgio	Rubino	ITA	15.4.86	25 Feb

WORLD INDOOR LISTS 2012 – WOMEN

60 METRES

Time	First	Last	Nat	DOB	Pos	Meet	Venue	Date
7.01	Veronica	Campbell-Brown	JAM	15.5.82	1	WI	Istanbul	11 Mar
7.02	Tianna	Madison	USA	30.8.85	1		Fayetteville	11 Feb
7.04	Murielle	Ahouré	CIV	23.8.87	2	WI	Istanbul	11 Mar
7.05	Laverne	Jones-Ferrette	ISV	16.9.81	1		Eaubonne	16 Feb
7.06A	Barbara	Pierre	USA	28.4.87	2	NC	Albuquerque	26 Feb
7.07	Gloria	Asumnu	NGR	22.5.85	1		Birmingham, AL	3 Mar
7.10	Allyson	Felix	USA	18.11.85	2h2		Fayetteville	11 Feb
7.12	English	Gardner	USA	22.4.92	1	NCAA	Nampa	10 Mar
7.13	Olesya	Povh	UKR	18.10.87	1		Düsseldorf	10 Feb
7.13A	LaKya	Brookins	USA	28.7.89	1h2	NC	Albuquerque	25 Feb
7.14	Ivet	Lalova	BUL	18.5.84	2	GP	Birmingham	18 Feb
7.15	Verena	Sailer	GER	16.10.85	1	NC	Karlsruhe	25 Feb
7.15	Octavious	Freeman	USA	29.4.92	2	NCAA	Nampa	10 Mar
7.17	Mariya	Ryemyen	UKR	2.8.87	1		Zaporozhye	27 Jan
7.17	Ezinne	Okparaebo	NOR	3.3.88	3	GP	Birmingham	18 Feb
7.18	Aleen	Bailey	JAM	25.11.80	2		Karlsruhe	12 Feb
7.18A	Alexandria	Anderson	USA	28.1.87	2s1	NC	Albuquerque	26 Feb
7.18A	Bianca	Knight	USA	2.1.89	3s1	NC	Albuquerque	26 Feb
7.18	Aurieyall	Scott	USA	18.5.92	2h2	NCAA	Nampa	9 Mar
7.19	Asha	Philip	GBR	25.10.90	4	GP	Birmingham	18 Feb
7.19	Dafne	Schippers	NED	15.6.92	1		Apeldoorn	26 Feb
7.19	Chandra	Sturrup	BAH	12.9.71	5	WI	Istanbul	11 Mar

Time	First	Last	Nat	DOB	Date		Time	First	Last	Nat	DOB	Date
7.20	Jeanette	Kwakye	GBR	20.3.83	12 Feb		7.23	Christina	Manning	USA	29.5.90	25 Feb
7.20	Kai	Selvon	TRI	13.4.92	26 Feb		7.23	Me'Lisa	Barber	USA	4.10.80	28 Jan
7.21	Shayla	Sanders	USA-J	6.1.94	26 Feb		7.23	Yevgeniya	Polyakova	RUS	29.5.83	29 Jan
7.21A	Candyce	McGrone	USA	24.3.89	26 Feb		7.23	Yeoryía	Koklóni	GRE	7.5.81	5 Mar
7.22	Stormy	Kendrick	USA	6.1.91	3 Feb		7.23	Tiffany	Townsend	USA	14.6.89	11 Mar
7.22	Jeneba	Tarmoh	USA	27.9.89	11 Feb		7.24	Brittney	Reese	USA	9.9.86	4 Feb
7.22A	Me'Lisa	Barber	USA	4.10.80	25 Feb		7.24	Jeneba	Tarmoh	USA	27.9.89	4 Feb
7.22A	Leslie	Cole	USA	16.2.87	26 Feb		7.24	Dominique	Booker	USA-J	10.2.92	11 Feb
7.23	Lauryn	Williams	USA	11.9.83	26 Jan		7.25	five women				

200 METRES

22.74	Kimberlyn	Duncan	USA	2.8.91	1r1	NCAA	Nampa	9 Mar
22.86	Kamaria	Brown	USA	21.12,92	1	Big 12	College Station	25 Feb
22.88	Patricia	Hall	JAM	16.10.82	1		Eaubonne	16 Feb
22.95	Allison	Peter	ISV	14.7.92	1r2	NCAA	Nampa	9 Mar

23.11	Myriam	Soumaré	FRA	29.10.86	26 Feb
23.14	Dominique	Duncan	USA	7.5.90	24 Feb
23.15	Lina	Jacques-Sébastien	FRA	10.4.85	26 Feb
23.18	Sanya	Richards-Ross	USA	26.2.85	28 Jan
23.18	Ashley	Collier	USA	4.2.92	25 Feb
23.18	Octavious	Freeman	USA	20.4.92	9 Mar
23.21	Cathleen	Tschirch	GER	23.7.79	26 Feb

23.23	Muriel	Hurtis	FRA	25.3.79	29 Feb
23.24	Ashley	Spencer	USA		25 Feb
23.26	Dezerea	Bryant	USA-J	27.4..93	25 Feb

Oversized track

23.03	Jura	Levy	JAM	4.11.90	3 Mar
23.11	Janelle	Redhead	GRN	27.12.89	3 Mar
23.15	Kai	Selvon	TRI	13.4.92	26 Feb

300 METRES

35.69	Patricia	Hall	JAM	16.10.82	1	Liévin	14 Feb
36.42	Antonina	Krivoshapka	RUS	21.7.87	2	Liévin	14 Feb
36.54	Aleksandra	Fedoriva	RUS	13.9.88	1	Moskva	14 Jan

36.81	Vania	Stambolova	BUL	28.11.83	14 Feb
36.94	Kseniya	Ustalova	RUS	14.1.88	7 Jan

37.07	Deedee	Trotter	USA	8.12.82	4 Feb
37.12	Bianca	Knight	USA	2.1.89	4 Feb

400 METRES

50.71A	Sanya	Richards-Ross	USA	26.2.85	1r1	NC	Albuquerque	26 Feb
51.18	Aleksandra	Fedoriva	RUS	13.9.88	1	NC	Moskva	23 Feb
51.66	Patricia	Hall	JAM	16.10.82	1		Stockholm	23 Feb
51.66A	Natasha	Hastings	USA	23.7.86	2r1	NC	Albuquerque	26 Feb
51.68A	Deedee	Trotter	USA	8.12.82	3h1	NC	Albuquerque	26 Feb
51.81	Antonina	Krivoshapka	RUS	21.7.87	2		Stockholm	23 Feb
51.92	Yuliya	Gushchina	RUS	4.3.83	2	NC	Moskva	23 Feb
51.94	Irina	Davydova	RUS	27.5.88	1h8	NC	Moskva	22 Feb
51.98	Nataliya	Pygyda	UKR	30.1.81	3s1	WI	Istanbul	9 Mar

52.10A	Leslie	Cole	USA	16.2.87	26 Feb
52.13	Shana	Cox	GBR	22.1.85	10 Mar
52.17	Kseniya	Ustalova	RUS	14.1.88	22 Feb
52.21	Marlena	Wesh	HAI	16.2.91	4 Feb
52.28	Tatyana	Firova	RUS	10.10.82	11 Feb
52.29	Moa	Hjelmer	SWE	19.6.90	9 Mar

52.44	Denisa	Rosolová	CZE	21.8.86	18 Feb
52.45	Esther	Cremer	GER	29.3.88	26 Feb
52.46	Marina	Karnaushchenko	RUS	2.10.88	11 Feb
52.48	Hanna	Tashpulatova	BLR	21.10.87	10 Feb
52.48	Nicola	Sanders	GBR	23.6.82	19 Feb
52.54	Regina	George	USA	17.2.91	10 Mar

800 METRES

1:58.83	Pamela	Jelimo	KEN	5.12.89	1	WI	Istanbul	11 Mar
1:59.01	Malika	Akkaoui	MAR	25.12.87	1		Liévin	14 Feb
1:59.45	Marina	Pospelova	RUS	23.7.90	1h6	NC	Moskva	22 Feb
1:59.63	Yelena	Kofanova	RUS	8.8.88	2h6	NC	Moskva	22 Feb
1:59.67	Nataliya	Lupu	UKR	4.11.87	2	WI	Istanbul	11 Mar
1:59.97	Erica	Moore	USA	25.3.88	3	WI	Istanbul	11 Mar
2:00.18	Yuliya	Tutayeva	RUS	7.12.88	3		Liévin	14 Feb
2:00.26	Yuliya	Rusanova	RUS	3.7.86	1h1	WI	Istanbul	9 Mar
2:00.30	Fantu	Magiso	ETH	9.8.92	4	WI	Istanbul	11 Mar
2:00.73	Yekaterina	Poistogova	RUS	1.3.91	1h2	NC	Moskva	22 Feb
2:00.80	Tatyana	Paliyenko	RUS	18.11.83	4		Liévin	14 Feb
2:00.88	Yekaterina	Kupina	RUS	2.2.86	1h1	NC	Moskva	22 Feb
2:01.04	Yelena	Arzhakova	RUS	8.9.89	2h2	NC	Moskva	22 Feb
2:01.13	Maryna	Arzamasova	BLR	17.12.87	1		Mogilyov	26 Feb
2:01.16	Tatyana	Markelova	RUS	19.12.88	3h6	NC	Moskva	22 Feb
2:01.19	Merve	Aydin	TUR	17.3.90	3h3	WI	Istanbul	9 Mar
2:01.29	Carolin	Walter	GER	29.2.88	1	NC	Karlsruhe	26 Feb

2:01.53	Elisa	Cusma Piccione	ITA	24.7.81	14 Feb
2:01.79	Yekaterina	Martynova	RUS	6.8.86	14 Feb
2:01.81	Oksana	Dyomina	RUS	4.8.90	22 Feb
2:01.90	Angelika	Cichocka	POL	15.3.88	18 Feb
2:02.03	Vania	Stambolova	BUL	28.11.83	21 Jan
2:02.06	Anna	Luchkina	RUS	13.1.86	22 Feb

2:02.08	Eléni	Filándra	GRE	12.1.84	4 Feb
2:02.16	Mariya	Savinova	RUS	13.8.85	3 Feb
2:02.26	Irina	Maracheva	RUS	29.9.84	14 Feb
2:02.32	Phoebe	Wright	USA	30.8.88	21 Jan
2:02.37	Maggie	Vessey	USA	23.12.81	4 Feb
2:02.50	Alena	Glazkova	RUS	6.5.88	22 Feb

1000 METRES

2:36.69	Yelena	Arzhakova	RUS	8.9.89	5 Feb
2:37.36	Natalya	Koreyvo	BLR	14.11.85	5 Feb
2:37.58	Yelena	Kofanova	RUS	8.8.88	5 Feb

2:38.14	Ibtissam	Lakhouad	MAR	7.12.80	4 Feb
2:38.16	Yekaterina	Martynova	RUS	6.8.86	5 Feb
2:38.44	Morgan	Uceny	USA	10.3.85	4 Feb

1500 METRES

4:00.13	Genzebe	Dibaba	ETH	8.2.91	3		Karlsruhe	12 Feb
4:03.67	Mariem Alaoui	Selsouli	MAR	8.4.84	1		Liévin	14 Feb
4:04.53	Siham	Hilali	MAR	2.5.86	2		Liévin	14 Feb
4:06.01	Tizita	Bogale	ETH-J	13.7.93	3		Liévin	14 Feb
4:06.25	Hellen	Obiri	KEN	13.12.89	2		Karlsruhe	12 Feb
4:06.78	Anzhela	Shevchenko	RUS	29.10.87	4		Liévin	14 Feb
4:07.27	Jenny	Simpson	USA	23.8.86	1	Mill	New York (Armory)	11 Feb
4:07.65	Meskerem	Assefa	ETH	20.9.85	5		Liévin	14 Feb
4:07.66	Shannon	Rowbury	USA	19.9.84	2	Mill	New York (Armory)	11 Feb

4:07.72 mx	Elina	Sujew	GER	2.11.90	1mx		Potsdam		22 Jan
4:07.83	Angelika	Cichocka	POL	15.3.88	3		Karlsruhe		12 Feb
4:07.86	Ibtissam	Lakhouad	MAR	7.12.80	1		Stockholm		23 Feb
4:07.99 mx	Diana	Sujew	GER	2.11.90	2mx		Potsdam		22 Jan
4:08.06	Morgan	Uceny	USA	10.3.85	3		Stockholm		23 Feb
4:08.55	Hind	Dehiba	FRA	17.3.79	6		Liévin		14 Feb
4:08.60	Natalya	Koreyvo	BLR	14.11.85	1		Gomel		27 Jan
4:08.74	Asli	Cakir	TUR	20.8.85	3	WI	Istanbul		10 Mar
4:08.80	Isabel	Macías	ESP	11.8.84	3	Mill	New York (Armory)		11 Feb
4:08.86	Nataliya	Tobias	UKR	22.11.80	4		Karlsruhe		12 Feb
4:08.93	Svitlana	Shmidt	UKR	20.3.90	2		Zaporozhye		27 Jan

4:09.04	Fanjanteino	Félix	FRA	26.1.80	14 Feb	4:09.79	Hannah	England	GBR	6.3.87	18 Feb
4:09.11	Renata	Plis	POL	5.2.85	14 Feb	4:09.84	Stephanie	Twell	GBR	17.8.89	12 Feb
4:09.15	Yelena	Arzhakova	RUS	8.9.89	9 Mar	4:09.96	Brenda	Martinez	USA	8.9.87	11 Feb
4:09.37	Lidia	Chojecka	POL	25.1.77	12 Feb	4:10.12	Maggie	Infeld	USA	10.4.86	11 Feb
4:09.46	Kristina	Khaleyeva	RUS	22.10.87	11 Feb	4:10.75	Luiza	Gega	ALB	5.11.88	18 Feb
4:09.70	Helen	Clitheroe	GBR	2.1.74	23 Feb	4:10.84	Ioana	Doaga	ROU	5.4.92	18 Feb
4:09.71		Xue Fei	CHN	8.8.89	13 Feb	4:10.92	Nicole	Sifuentes	CAN	30.6.86	11 Feb

1 MILE

4:28.41#	Sally	Kipyego	KEN	19.12.85	1			Seattle			11 Feb
4:28.48#	Katie	Flood	USA	29.2.92	2			Seattle			11 Feb
4:29.37#	Hilary	Stellingwerff	CAN	7.8.81	11 Feb	4:31.38	Nataliya	Tobias	UKR	22.11.80	3 Feb
4:29.73	Kristina	Khaleyeva	RUS	22.10.87	3 Feb	4:31.52	Yuliya	Vasilyeva	RUS	23.3.87	3 Feb
						4:31.98	Oksana	Suntsova	RUS	25.2.81	3 Feb

3000 METRES

8:31.56	Meseret	Defar	ETH	19.11.83	1	GP	Birmingham		18 Feb
8:35.35	Hellen	Obiri	KEN	13.12.89	2	GP	Birmingham		18 Feb
8:36.59	Gelete	Burka	ETH	15.2.86	3	GP	Birmingham		18 Feb
8:36.87	Mariem Alaoui	Selsouli	MAR	8.4.84	1		Karlsruhe		12 Feb
8:40.50	Sylvia	Kibet	KEN	28.3.84	4	WI	Istanbul		11 Mar
8:41.01	Svitlana	Shmidt	UKR	20.3.90	1	NC	Sumy		18 Feb
8:43.93	Meselech	Melkamu	ETH	27.4.85	3		Karlsruhe		12 Feb
8:45.59	Helen	Clitheroe	GBR	2.1.74	2	v4N	Glasgow		28 Jan
8:46.01	Geytetom	Gebreselassie	ETH-Y	15.1.95	2		Boston (Roxbury)		4 Feb
8:46.17	Siham	Hilali	MAR	2.5.86	3		Boston (Roxbury)		4 Feb
8:47.91#	Sally	Kipyego	KEN	19.12.85	1		Seattle		28 Jan
8:49.27	Shitaye	Eshete	BRN	21.5.90	1	AsiC	Hangzhou		19 Feb
8:49.50	Mekdes	Bekele	ETH	20.1.87	4		Karlsruhe		12 Feb

8:53.02	Yuliya	Vasilyeva	RUS	23.3.87	22 Feb	8:55.06	Shannon	Rowbury	USA	19.9.84	4 Feb
8:53.18	Meskerem	Assefa	ETH	20.9.85	16 Feb	8:55.25	Almaz	Ayana	ETH	21.1191	16 Feb
8:53.56	Belayneh	Desalegn	UAE	13.11.91	19 Feb	8:55.31#	Katie	Flood	USA	29.2.92	28 Jan
8:53.75	Tejitu	Daba	BRN	20.8.91	19 Feb	8:56.80#	Nicole	Sifuentes	CAN	30.6.86	3 Mar
8:54.40	Mestawet	Tadesse	ETH	19.7.85	16 Feb	8:57.37	Kristina	Khaleyeva	RUS	22.10.87	22 Feb
8:54.75	Sara	Hall	USA	15.4.83	4 Feb	8:57.52	Olga	Golovkina	RUS	17.12.86	22 Feb
8:55.05	Lidia	Chojecka	POL	25.1.77	16 Feb	8:57.62#	Kim	Conley	USA	14.3.86	11 Feb

2 Miles: 9:21.60 Tirunesh Dibaba ETH 1.10.85 1 Boston (Roxbury) 4 Feb
5000 Metres: 15:15.41# Sally Kipyego KEN 19.12.85 1 Seattle 10 Feb

2000 METRES STEEPLECHASE

6:06.11	Yelena	Orlova	RUS	30.5.80	1		Moskva		12 Feb
6:13.10	Lyubov	Kharlamova	RUS	2.3.81	1		Moskva		24 Jan
6:15.97	Natalya	Aristarkhova	RUS	31.10.89	2	NC	Moskva		23 Feb

50 Metres Hurdles: New York 28 Jan: 1. Lolo Jones 6.78, 2. Tiffany Porter 6.83, 3. Kellie Wells 6.84

60 METRES HURDLES

7.73	Sally	Pearson	AUS	19.9.86	1	WI	Istanbul		10 Mar
7.84A	Kristi	Castlin	USA	7.7.88	1	NC	Albuquerque		26 Feb
7.87	Jessica	Ennis	GBR	28.1.86	1	GP	Birmingham		18 Feb
7.89	Lolo	Jones	USA	5.8.82	1	Winter	Moskva		5 Feb
7.91	Danielle	Carruthers	USA	22.12.79	2	GP	Birmingham		18 Feb
7.91	Christina	Manning	USA	29.5.90	1	NCAA	Nampa		10 Mar
7.93	Tiffany	Porter	GBR	13.11.87	2	Mill	New York (Armory)		11 Feb
7.93A	Vanneisha	Ivy	USA	26.10.87	2	NC	Albuquerque		26 Feb
7.93	Brianna	Rollins	USA	18.8.91	1h2	NCAA	Nampa		9 Mar
7.95A	Yvette	Lewis	USA	16.3.85	1h1	NC	Albuquerque		26 Feb
7.95	Bridgette	Owens	USA	14.3.92	2h2	NCAA	Nampa		9 Mar
7.96	Cindy	Roleder	GER	21.8.89	1	NC	Karlsruhe		25 Feb
7.97	Virginia	Crawford	USA	7.9.83	1r1		Fayetteville		11 Feb
7.97	Carolin	Nytra	GER	26.2.85	1h2		Karlsruhe		12 Feb
7.97	Alina	Talay	BLR	14.5.89	3	WI	Istanbul		10 Mar
7.98A	Janay	DeLoach	USA	12.10.85	2h1	NC	Albuquerque		26 Feb
7.99	Yekaterina	Poplavskaya	BLR	7.5.87	1		Gomel		18 Feb
8.00	Nikita	Holder	CAN	7.5.87	2		Liévin		14 Feb

Mark	First	Last	Nat	DOB	Date
8.02	Angela	Whyte	CAN	22.5.80	3 Feb
8.02	Tatyana	Dektaryeva	RUS	8,5,81	12 Feb
8.02	Beate	Schrott	AUT	15.4.88	19 Feb
8.02	Tatyana	Chernova	RUS	29.1.88	22 Feb
8.02	Jackie	Coward	USA	5.11.89	9 Mar
8.03	Dawn	Harper	USA	13.5.84	11 Feb
8.03	Sharona	Bakker	NED	12.4.90	12 Feb
8.03	Phylicia	George	CAN	16.11.87	14 Feb
8.03	Jasmin	Stowers	USA	23.9.91	26 Feb
8.03A	Michaylin	Golladay	USA	10.4.88	26 Feb
8.03	Eline	Berings	BEL	28.5.86	10 Mar
8.03	Sonata	Tamosaityte	LTU	26.6.87	10 Mar
8.04	Yekaterina	Galitskaya	RUS	24.2.87	22 Feb
8.04	Marzia	Caravelli	ITA	23.10.81	25 Feb
8.04A	Gabby	Mayo	USA	26.1.89	26 Feb
8.04	Tiffany	McReynolds	USA	4.12.91	10 Mar
8.05	Loreal	Smith	USA	12.10.85	2 Feb
8.05	Lucie	Skrobáková	CZE	4.1.82	10 Feb
8.05	Queen	Harrison	USA	10.9.88	3 Mar
8.06	Natasha	Ruddock	JAM	25.12.89	11 Feb
8.07	Reina-Flor	Okori	FRA	2.5.80	25 Feb
8.07	Seun	Adigun	NGR	3.1.87	10 Mar
8.08	Svetlana	Topylina	RUS	6.1.85	22 Feb
8.08	Ann-Kathrin	Elbe	GER	24.2.87	25 Feb
8.09	Adrianna	Lamalle	FRA	27.9.82	25 Feb
8.09A	Korey	Hardiway	USA	21.8.86	26 Feb

HIGH JUMP

Mark	First	Last	Nat	DOB	Pos	Meet	Venue	Date
2.06	Anna	Chicherova	RUS	22.7.82	1		Arnstadt	4 Feb
2.02A	Chaunte	Lowe	USA	12.1.84	1	NC	Albuquerque	26 Feb
1.97	Brigetta	Barrett	USA	24.12.90	1		Fayetteville	27 Jan
1.97	Irina	Gordeyeva	RUS	9.10.86	2		Arnstadt	4 Feb
1.97	Tia	Hellebaut	BEL	16.2.78	3		Arnstadt	4 Feb
1.96	Svetlana	Shkolina	RUS	9.3.86	1		Cottbus	25 Jan
1.96	Mariya	Kuchina	RUS-J	14.1.93	1		Vendryne	30 Jan
1.95	Ebba	Jungmark	SWE	10.3.87	1	NC	Örebro	19 Feb
1.95	Emma	Green Tregaro	SWE	8.12.84	2	NC	Örebro	19 Feb
1.95	Antonietta	Di Martino	ITA	1.6.78	Q	WI	Istanbul	9 Mar
1.95	Svetlana	Radzivil	UZB	17.1.87	Q	WI	Istanbul	9 Mar
1.95	Ruth	Beitia	ESP	1.4.79	6	WI	Istanbul	10 Mar
1.94	Esthera	Petre	ROU	13.5.90	1		Bucuresti	15 Jan
1.94	Venelina	Veneva-Mateeva	BUL	13.6.74	1		Wien	21 Jan
1.93	Tonje	Angelsen	NOR	17.1.90	1		Trondheim	22 Jan
1.93	Viktoriya	Styopina	UKR	21.2.76	1	NC	Sumy	17 Feb
1.93	Oksana	Okuneva	UKR	14.3.90	2	NC	Sumy	17 Feb
1.93	Anja	Iljustsenko	EST	12.10.85	1		Tartu	19 Feb
1.93	Mélanie	Melfort	FRA	8.11.82	1	NC	Aubière	25 Feb
1.92	Yekaterina	Bolshova	RUS	4.2.88	1P	NC	Moskva	7 Feb
1.92		Zheng Xingyuan	CHN	20.3.89	1	AsiC	Hangzhou	18 Feb
1.92	Airine	Palsyte	LTU	13.7.92	9=q	WI	Istanbul	9 Mar

Mark	First	Last	Nat	DOB	Date
1.91	Alessia	Trost	ITA-J	8.3.93	29 Jan
1.91	Nadja	Kampschulte	GER	5.9.92	5 Feb
1.91	Jessica	Ennis	GBR	28.1.86	11 Feb
1.91	Ana	Simic	CRO	5.5.90	18 Feb
1.91	Yevgeniya	Kononova	RUS	28.9.89	25 Feb
1.91	Ariane	Friedrich	GER	10.1.84	26 Feb
1.91	Oldriska	Maresová	CZE	14.10.86	16 Mar
1.90	Olena	Holosha	UKR	26.1.82	28 Jan
1.90	Yuliya	Kostrova	RUS	20.8.91	28 Jan
1.90	Ma'ayan	Furman	ISR	9.11.86	3 Feb
1.90	Mirela	Demireva	BUL	28.9.89	4 Feb
1.90	Austra	Skujyte	LTU	12.8.79	9 Mar
1.90	Yana	Maksimova	BLR	9.1.89	9 Mar
1.90	Eleriin	Haas	EST	4.7.92	9 Mar
1.89	Tamara	Biryuk	UKR-Y	11.4.95	20 Jan
1.89	Oyunn	Grindem	NOR	11.11.87	21 Jan
1.89	Gemma	Martín-Pozuelo	ESP	21.6.87	21 Jan
1.89	Iryna	Kovalenko	UKR	17.6.86	28 Jan
1.89	Emma	Perkins	GBR	4.9.85	11 Feb
1.89	Raffaella	Lamera	ITA	13.4.83	25 Feb
1.89	Monika	Gollner	AUT	23.10.74	25 Feb
1.89	Marie-Laurence	Jungfleisch	GER	7.10.90	26 Feb

POLE VAULT

Mark	First	Last	Nat	DOB	Pos	Meet	Venue	Date
5.01	Yelena	Isinbayeva	RUS	3.6.82	1		Stockholm	23 Feb
4.88	Jennifer	Suhr	USA	5.2.82	1		Boston (Roxbury)	4 Feb
4.87	Holly	Bleasdale	GBR	2.11.91	1		Villeurbanne	20 Jan
4.77	Silke	Spiegelburg	GER	17.3.86	1		Leverkusen	15 Jan
4.72	Yarisley	Silva	CUB	1.6.87	3		Stockholm	23 Feb
4.71	Anna	Rogowska	POL	21.5.81	1	NC	Spala	26 Feb
4.70	Jirina	Ptácnáková	CZE	20.5.86	1	Stars	Donetsk	11 Feb
4.70	Vanessa	Boslak	FRA	11.6.82	2	WI	Istanbul	11 Mar
4.65	Lacy	Janson	USA	20.2.83	5	WI	Istanbul	11 Mar
4.62A	Mary	Saxer	USA	21.6.87	2	NC	Albuquerque	25 Feb
4.60	Hanna	Sheleh	UKR-J	14.7.93	3	Stars	Donetsk	11 Feb
4.60A	Kelsie	Hendry	CAN	29.6.82	1		Flagstaff	16 Feb
4.55	Tina	Sutej	SLO	7.11.88	1	SEC	Lexington	25 Feb
4.55	Nicole	Büchler	SUI	17.12.83	8	WI	Istanbul	11 Mar
4.55	Alana	Boyd	AUS	10.5.84	9	WI	Istanbul	11 Mar
4.52	Anna	Battke	GER	3.1.85	1		Ludwigshafen	21 Jan
4.52	Martina	Strutz	GER	4.11.81	2		Dresden	27 Jan
4.52	Jillian	Schwartz	ISR	19.9.79	1	US Open	New York	28 Jan
4.52	Kristina	Gadschiew	GER	3.7.84	1		Sindelfingen	28 Jan
4.52	Svetlana	Feofanova	RUS	16.7.80	5		Bydgoszcz	8 Feb
4.52	Katherine	Dennison	GBR	7.5.84	1		Nevers	18 Feb
4.52	Katie	Byres	GBR-J	11.9.93	2		Nevers	18 Feb
4.52	Anastasiya	Savchenko	RUS	15.1.89	1	NC	Moskva	22 Feb
4.52	Anastasiya	Shvedova	BLR	3.5.79	1		Tallinn	25 Feb
4.52A	Kylie	Hutson	USA	27.11.87	4	NC	Albuquerque	25 Feb
4.50		Li Ling II	CHN	6.7.89	1	AsiC	Hangzhou	19 Feb

4.47	Lisa	Ryzih	GER	27.9.88	3	NC	Karlsruhe	25 Feb
4.47A	Becky	Holliday	USA	12.3.80	5	NC	Albuquerque	25 Feb
4.45A	Tori	Pena	IRL	30.7.87	2		Reno	20 Jan

4.42	Janice	Keppler	USA	22.3.87	28 Jan		4.41	Monika	Pyrek	POL	11.8.80	18 Feb
4.42	Anna Katharina	Schmid	SUI	2.12.89	4 Feb		4.41	Joanna	Piwowarska	POL	4.11.83	18 Feb
4.42	Annika	Roloff	GER	10.3.91	12 Feb		4.40	Yekaterina	Kazeka	RUS	7.10.90	24 Dec
4.42	Caroline Bonde	Holm	DEN	19.7.90	17 Feb		4.40	Julia	Hütter	GER	26.7.83	15 Jan
4.42	Marion	Fiack	FRA	13.10.92	18 Feb		4.40	Anna	Giordano Bruno	ITA	13.12.80	22 Jan
4.42	Sally	Peake	GBR	8.2.86	18 Feb		4.40	Nataliya	Mazuryk	UKR	5.3.83	11 Feb
4.42	Aleksandra	Kiryashova	RUS	21.8.85	22 Feb		4.40	Lyudmila	Yeremina	RUS	8.8.91	15 Feb
4.42	Dailis	Caballero	CUB	6.3.88	23 Feb		4.40	Anzhelika	Sidorova	RUS	28.6.91	2 Mar
4.42A	Katy	Viuf	USA	23.5.87	25 Feb		4.40	Morgann	LeLeux	USA	14.11.92	10 Mar
4.42	Maria Eleonor	Tavares	POR	24.9.85	26 Feb		4.37	Keisa	Monterola	VEN	26.2.88	28 Jan
4.41	Cathrine	Larsåsen	NOR	5.12.86	11 Feb		4.37	Victoria	von Eynatten	GER	6.10.91	18 Feb
							4.37	Tara	Diebold	USA	28.11.88	25 Feb

LONG JUMP

7.23	Brittney	Reese	USA	9.9.86	1	WI	Istanbul	11 Mar
6.98	Janay	DeLoach	USA	12.10.85	2	WI	Istanbul	11 Mar
6.91	Olga	Kucherenko	RUS	5.11.85	1		Krasnodar	29 Jan
6.91	Whitney	Gipson	USA	20.9.90	1	NCAA	Nampa	9 Mar
6.89	Shara	Proctor	GBR	16.9.88	3	WI	Istanbul	11 Mar
6.88	Yelena	Sokolova	RUS	23.7.86	1	NC	Moskva	23 Feb
6.86	Darya	Klishina	RUS	15.1.91	1	Winter	Moskva	5 Feb
6.82	Anastasiya	Mironchyk-Ivanova	BLR	13.4.89	1		Gomel	27 Jan
6.81A	Funmilayo	Jimoh	USA	29.5.84	3	NC	Albuquerque	26 Feb
6.79	Bianca	Stuart	BAH	17.5.88	2		Fayetteville	11 Feb
6.77	Veronika	Shutkova	BLR	26.5.86	2		Gomel	27 Jan
6.73	Volha	Sudareva	BLR	22.2.84	3		Gomel	27 Jan
6.72	Oksana	Zhukovskaya	RUS	12.9.84	1		Sankt Petersburg	4 Jan
6.70	Katsiaryna	Poplavskaya	BLR	7.5.87	1		Gomel	20 Feb
6.67	Cornelia	Deiac	ROU	20.3.88	1		Bucuresti	28 Jan
6.66	Nadja	Käther	GER	29.9.88	1		Bielefeld	12 Feb
6.66	Karin Melis	Mey	TUR	31.5.84	2	GP	Birmingham	18 Feb
6.64	Viorica	Tigau	ROU	12.8.79	Q	WI	Istanbul	10 Mar
6.61	Tatyana	Chernova	RUS	29.1.88	Q	NC	Moskva	22 Feb
6.61	Chelsea	Hayes	USA	2.2.88	2	NCAA	Nampa	9 Mar
6.60	Yuliya	Pidluzhnaya	RUS	1.10.88	1		Chelyabinsk	13 Jan

6.57	Nataliya	Dobrynska	UKR	29.5.82	9 Mar		6.52	Cristina	Sandu	ROU	4.3.90	25 Feb
6.56	Xenia	Achkinadze	GER	14.1.89	26 Feb		6.52	Yekaterina	Bolshova	RUS	4.2.88	9 Mar
6.55	Concepcion	Montaner	ESP	14.1.81	12 Feb		6.51	Ineta	Radevica	LAT	13.7.81	14 Jan
6.54	Jamesha	Youngblood	USA	24.4.89	11 Feb		6.51A	Lorraine	Ugen	GBR	22.8.91	24 Feb
6.54	Karolina	Tyminska	POL	4.10.84	18 Feb		6.51	Haoua	Kessely	FRA	2.2.88	25 Feb
6.53	Inna	Akhozova	UKR	16.9.84	18 Feb		6.51	Irene	Pusterla	SUI	21.6.88	26 Feb
							6.50	Bianca	Kappler	GER	8.8.77	15 Jan

TRIPLE JUMP

14.84	Olga	Rypakova	KAZ	30.11.84	1	NC	Karaganda	27 Jan
14.82	Yamilé	Aldama	GBR	14.8.72	1	WI	Istanbul	10 Mar
14.79	Olha	Saladuha	UKR	4.6.83	1		Stockholm	23 Feb
14.60	Yekaterina	Koneva	RUS	25.9.88	1		Krasnodar	29 Jan
14.55	Yargeris	Savigne	CUB	13.11.84	1		Metz	29 Feb
14.48	Kseniya	Detsuk	BLR	23.4.86	1		Gomel	27 Jan
14.47	Niki	Panéta	GRE	21.4.86	1	NC	Athina (Pireás)	22 Feb
14.39	Anna	Krylova	RUS	3.10.85	2		Krasnodar	29 Jan
14.34	Mabel	Gay	CUB	5.5.83	1		Madrid	18 Feb
14.31	Hanna	Knyazeva	UKR	25.9.89	1		Kyiv	14 Jan
14.29	Viktoriya	Valyukevich	RUS	22.5.82	2	NC	Moskva	24 Feb
14.28	Kimberly	Williams	JAM	3.11.88	1		Fayetteville	11 Feb
14.24	Adelina	Gavrila	ROU	26.11.78	1	NC	Bucuresti	24 Feb
14.23	Anastasiya	Potapova	RUS	6.9.85	3		Krasnodar	29 Jan
14.23		Li Yanmei	CHN	6.2.90	Q	WI	Istanbul	9 Mar
14.22	Yana	Borodina	RUS	21.4.92	4	NC	Moskva	24 Feb
14.21		Xie Limei	CHN	27.6.86	1		Nanjing	14 Feb
14.21	Dana	Veldáková	SVK	3.6.81	Q	WI	Istanbul	9 Mar
14.19	Marija	Sestak	SLO	17.4.79	1		Bratislava	29 Jan
14.19	Kristin	Gierisch	GER	20.8.90	1	NC	Karlsruhe	25 Feb
14.17	Viktoriya	Dolgacheva	UKR	17.4.91	1	NC-23	Saransk	4 Mar
14.16	Paraskeví	Papahrístou	GRE	17.4.89	3		Düsseldorf	10 Feb
14.14	Cristina	Bujin	ROU	12.4.88	1		Bucuresti	27 Jan
14.14	Andriana	Banova	BUL	1.5.87	1	NC	Dobrich	12 Feb
14.09	Irina	Ektova	KAZ	8.1.87	2	NC	Karaganda	27 Jan

14.05	Snezana	Rodic	SLO	19.8.82	25 Feb		14.01	Nathalie	Marie-Nely	FRA	24.11.86	26 Feb
14.05	Simona	La Mantia	ITA	14.4.83	26 Feb		14.00	Ruslana	Tsyhotska	UKR	23.3.86	14 Jan
14.04	Nadezhda	Alekhina	RUS	22.9.78	24 Feb		14.00	Valeriya	Kanatova	UZB	29.8.92	29 Jan
14.02	Jenny	Elbe	GER	18.4.90	25 Feb		13.98	Athanasia	Pérra	GRE	2.2.83	22 Feb
14.01	Aleksandra	Kotlyarova	UZB	10.10.88	29 Jan		13.97	Valeriya	Zavyalova	RUS	16.1.88	24 Feb

Mark	First	Last	Nat	DOB	Pos	Meet	City	Date
13.95	Mayookha	Johny	IND	9.4.88	9			Mar
13.94	Patricia	Mamona	POR	21.11.88	19			Feb
13.93	Keila	Costa	BRA	6.2.83	23			Feb
13.91	Dailenys	Alcántara	CUB	10.8.91	18			Feb
13.86	Anastasiya	Juravlyeva	UZB	9.10.81	2			Feb
13.85	Biljana	Topic	SRB	17.10.77	27			Jan
13.85	Patricia	Sarrapio	ESP	16.11.82	18			Feb

SHOT

Mark	First	Last	Nat	DOB	Pos	Meet	City	Date
20.70	Nadezhda	Ostapchuk	BLR	12.10.80	1	NC	Mogilyov	10 Feb
20.54	Valerie	Adams	NZL	6.10.84	1	WI	Istanbul	10 Mar
19.89	Jillian	Camarena-Williams	USA	2.8.82	1		Fayetteville	11 Feb
19.58	Michelle	Carter	USA	12.10.85	3	WI	Istanbul	10 Mar
19.47	Yevgeniya	Kolodko	RUS	2.7.90	1		Volgograd	21 Jan
19.33	Nadine	Kleinert	GER	20.10.75	1		Rochlitz	5 Feb
19.15	Natalya	Mikhnevich	BLR	25.5.82	2	NC	Mogilyov	10 Feb
19.15	Christina	Schwanitz	GER	24.12.85	1		Leipzig	12 Feb
19.00	Tia	Brooks	USA	2.8.90	1	NCAA	Nampa	10 Mar
18.90	Alena	Kopets	BLR	14.2.88	3	NC	Mogilyov	10 Feb
18.76	Irina	Tarasova	RUS	15.4.87	2		Volgograd	21 Jan
18.71	Yevgeniya	Solovyova	RUS	28.6.86	2	Winter	Moskva	5 Feb
18.63		Liu Xiangrong	CHN	6.6.88	6	WI	Istanbul	10 Mar
18.48	Anna	Omarova	RUS	3.10.81	3		Volgograd	21 Jan
18.42	Sarah	Walker	USA	2.4.86	2		Flagstaff	4 Feb
18.35	Cleopatra	Borel-Brown	TRI	3.10.79	3		Fayetteville	11 Feb
18.32	Anna	Avdeyeva	RUS	6.4.85	3	NC	Moskva	23 Feb
18.29	Josephine	Terlecki	GER	17.2.86	3		Nordhausen	20 Jan
18.07	Yanina	Provalinskaya	BLR	26.12.76	2		Gomel	27 Jan
18.06	Denise	Hinrichs	GER	7.6.87	3	NC	Karlsruhe	25 Feb
18.02	Halyna	Obleshchuk	UKR	23.2.89	1	NC	Sumy	17 Feb
18.01	Julie	Labonté	CAN	12.1.90	1		Fayetteville	27 Jan

Mark	First	Last	Nat	DOB	Date
17.97	Jeneva	McCall	USA	28.10.89	10 Mar
17.92	Chiara	Rosa	ITA	28.1.83	20 Jan
17.89	Lyudmila	Morunova	RUS	27.1.85	11 Feb
17.79	Paulina	Guba	POL	14.5.91	26 Feb
17.77A	Alyssa	Hasslen	USA	13.5.91	4 Feb
17.70	Annie	Alexander	TRI	28.8.87	21 Jan
17.63	Ursula	Ruiz	ESP	11.8.83	26 Feb
17.60	Leyla	Rajabi	IRI	18.4.83	20 Jan
17.58	Rebecca	O'Brien	USA	30.4.90	11 Feb
17.57	Ashley	Duncan	USA	16.9.86	10 Feb
17.57	Misleydis	González	CUB	19.6.78	26 Feb
17.52	Melissa	Boekelman	NED	11.5.89	22 Jan
17.47	Danielle	Frere	USA	27.4.90	11 Feb
17.43	Sophie	Kleeberg	GER	30.5.90	25 Feb
17.42	Skylar	White	USA	15.9.91	10 Mar
17.36	Olha	Holodnaya	UKR	14.11.91	14 Jan

20 LB WEIGHT

Mark	First	Last	Nat	DOB	Pos	Meet	City	Date
25.12	Brittany	Riley	USA	26.8.86	1		Carbondale	13 Jan
24.78	Amber	Campbell	USA	5.6.81	1	NC	Albuquerque	25 Feb
23.76	Jeneva	McCall	USA	28.10.89	2		Carbondale	13 Jan
23.51	Gwendolyn	Berry	USA	29.6.89	2		Carbondale	3 Feb
21.90	Shelby	Ashe	USA-J	13.3..93	4	NC	Albuquerque	25 Feb

Mark	First	Last	Nat	DOB	Date
21.67	Felisha	Johnson	USA	24.7.89	9 Dec
21.62	Kelly	Closse	FRA	8.8.88	10 Feb
21.48	Ida	Storm	SWE	26.12.91	9 Mar
21.47	Kristin	Smith	USA	23.12.87	10 Feb
21.42	Amanda	Bingson	USA	20.2.90	11 Feb
21.33	Taylor	Smith	USA	20.7.91	17 Feb
21.28	Denise	Hinton	USA	17.12.91	2 Mar

PENTATHLON

Score	First	Last	Nat	DOB	Pos	Meet	City	Date
5013	Nataliya	Dobrysnka	UKR	29.5.82	1	WI	Istanbul	9 Mar
	8.38	1.84	16.51	6.57		2:11.15		
4965	Jessica	Ennis	GBR	28.1.86	2	WI	Istanbul	9 Mar
	7.91	1.87	14.79	6.19		2:08.09		
4896	Yekaterina	Bolshova	RUS	4.2.88	1	NC	Moskva	7 Feb
	8.41	1.92	13.79	6.45		2:10.60		
4802	Austra	Skujyte	LTU	12.8.79	3	WI	Istanbul	9 Mar
	8.57	1.90	16.26	6.24		2:19.99		
4792	Olga	Kurban	RUS	16.12.87	2	NC	Moskva	7 Feb
	8.45	1.86	14.68	6.34		2:13.44		
4748	Anna	Melnychenko	UKR	24.4.83	2	NC	Sumy	16 Feb
	8.34	1.84	13.89	6.41		2:14.35		
4725	Karolina	Tyminska	POL	4.10.84	4	WI	Istanbul	9 Mar
	8.52	1.72	14.68	6.49		2:08.25		
4725	Tatyana	Chernova	RUS	29.1.88	5	WI	Istanbul	9 Mar
	8.29	1.84	13.90	6.25		2:13.23		
4616	Yana	Maksimova	BLR	9.1.89	1		Gomel	20 Feb
	8.65	1.86	15.02	5.95		2.15.77		
4590	Kristina	Savitskaya	RUS	10.6.91	3	NC	Moskva	7 Feb
	8.37	1.86	14.61	6.14		2:24.60		
4567	Sharon	Day	USA	9.6.85	1	NC	Bloomington	4 Mar
	8.46	1.85	13.29	5.89		2:11.89		
4555	Brianne	Theisen	CAN	18.12.88	1		College Station	28 Jan
	8.38	1.88	12.87	5.99		2:16.90		
4553	Remona	Fransen	NED	25.11.85	1	v4N	Praha Strom	29 Jan
	8.53	1.84	14.01	6.02		2:17.10		
4526	Katarina	Johnson-Thompson	GBR-J	9.1.93	1	v2N	Cardiff	25 Mar
	8.48	1.88	11.68	6.24		2:17.24		

Continued on page 84